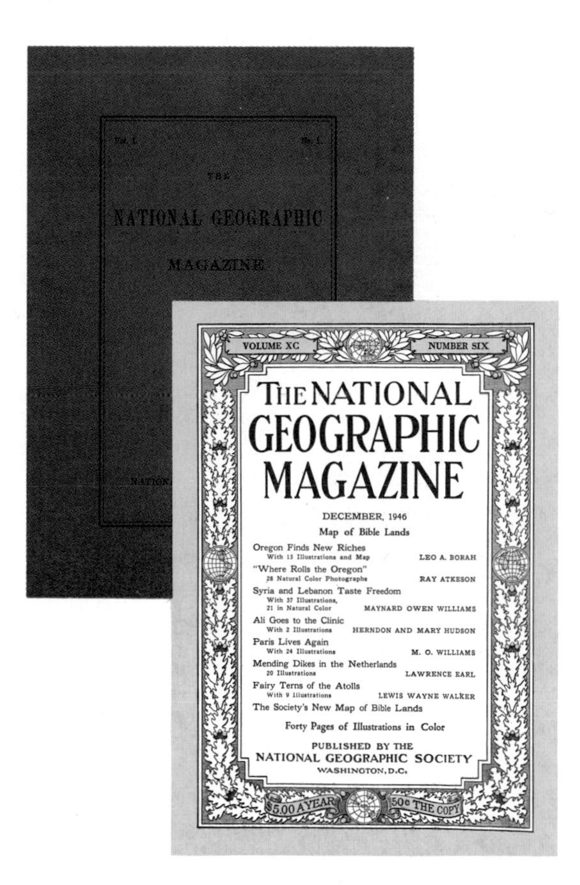

INDEX

1888-1946

NATIONAL GEOGRAPHIC

INDEX

1888-1946

INCLUSIVE

WITH A FOREWORD BY
MELVILLE BELL GROSVENOR
AND AN INTRODUCTION BY
GILBERT HOVEY GROSVENOR

NATIONAL GEOGRAPHIC SOCIETY

WASHINGTON, D. C.

Contents

5 Foreword by Melville Bell Grosvenor

7 The Story of the Geographic by Gilbert Hovey Grosvenor

57 INDEX to the NATIONAL GEOGRAPHIC, 1888-1946
(including separate map index on blue pages)

FRONT ENDLEAF: The Society's first headquarters building:
Gardiner Greene Hubbard Memorial Hall, completed in 1903.
Photograph by John Oliver La Gorce, 1907.

BACK ENDLEAF: By 1932 expansion of the Society's home
had created this stately building on 16th Street.
Photograph by Edwin L. Wisherd.

A publication of the National Geographic Society
MELVIN M. PAYNE *President*

MELVILLE BELL GROSVENOR *Editor-in-Chief*
FREDERICK G. VOSBURGH *Editor*
GILBERT M. GROSVENOR, FRANC SHOR *Associate Editors*
ROBERT L. CONLY, HOWELL WALKER *Assistant Editors*
DOROTHY M. CORSON *Compilation and editing of index*
ROBERT S. PATTON, HOWARD E. PAINE, CHARLES C. UHL,
and SARA L. DANIS *Design and production*
JAMES R. WHITNEY, JOHN R. METCALFE *Engraving and printing*

LIBRARY OF CONGRESS CATALOG CARD NUMBER 14-7038
Reprinted and bound by R. R. Donnelley & Sons Company, Chicago, Illinois

OVERLEAF: BRIDALVEIL FALL IN YOSEMITE NATIONAL PARK, CALIFORNIA, FROM THE NATIONAL GEOGRAPHIC MAGAZINE'S FIRST NATURAL-COLOR SERIES, "THE LAND OF THE BEST," APRIL, 1916. LUMIÈRE AUTOCHROME BY FRANKLIN PRICE KNOTT.

BUST OF GILBERT HOVEY GROSVENOR, FORMER PRESIDENT OF THE SOCIETY AND EDITOR OF ITS MAGAZINE, OVERLOOKS THE DESK OF HIS SON MELVILLE BELL GROSVENOR, PRESIDENT AND EDITOR, 1957-1967, AND CHAIRMAN OF THE BOARD AND EDITOR-IN-CHIEF, 1967-. EKTACHROME BY NATIONAL GEOGRAPHIC PHOTOGRAPHER WINFIELD PARKS; SCULPTURE BY FELIX DE WELDON.

Foreword

AN INVALUABLE TOOL, a guide to a remarkable collection of articles and pictures about the world and the people who live in it: That is the new *National Geographic Index,* 1888-1946. But more than that, the volume stands as a monument to a man and an idea. The man was Gilbert Hovey Grosvenor, who joined the infant GEOGRAPHIC in 1899 and served it successively as Assistant Editor, Managing Editor, Editor, President, and Chairman of the Board until his death in 1966 at age 90.

The idea, when he conceived it, was entirely new: That the story of the world around us—the thousand-and-one stories we call geography—could be made fascinating if told simply, personally, and accurately, and if fully illustrated.

How the idea grew appears on the following pages in Gilbert Grosvenor's own words, written for the GEOGRAPHIC's 75th anniversary issue. Yet he would have been the first to agree that the true drama of the story unfolds in the index itself, a listing of thousands of articles, pictures, and maps—643 magazines equal to a set of encyclopedias 17 feet long.

Fifty-nine years of GEOGRAPHICS! The scope and size of subject matter ranges from insects to elephants, from molecules to the moon. The index can guide you to some of the greatest adventures of this century and the last: Polar exploration by Amundsen, Peary, and Byrd; the building of the Panama Canal; the discovery of Machu Picchu; the battlefields of two World Wars.

In the long list of entries under "Peary, Robert E.," one reads simply, "Peary to Try Again," and the reference is to the April, 1907, GEOGRAPHIC. Page 281 carries a brief announcement that the Society has granted $1,000 to Commander Peary for a new assault on the North Pole—an assault which succeeded in 1909. That was the first cash grant the Society ever made from its own resources for research and exploration. Such grants by the Society in 1966 alone amounted to more than $1,000,000.

The new index, which supersedes the earlier *Cumulative Index,* 1899-1946, lists for the first time the contents of the first 11 years of NATIONAL GEOGRAPHICS—68 issues in all, since the magazine came out only sporadically in the first decade. In 1964 the Society published reprints of these earliest issues.

These first GEOGRAPHICS, though unrelentingly learned and sparsely illustrated, nonetheless have great historical interest. The new index, for instance, contains an entry under "Meteorology": "The Great Storm of March 11-14, 1888"—or, as it is now remembered, the Blizzard of '88. It refers the reader to two articles in the very first issue, October, 1888, which offer a day-by-day account of the famous storm, including barometric pressures, wind velocities, and temperatures. I still shiver when I read that the storm dumped 40 inches of snow on the northeastern United States while freezing winds blew up to 70 miles an hour.

Gilbert Grosvenor started the Society's Cartographic Department in 1915. Since that time hundreds of millions of large 10- and 11-color supplement maps have been distributed free to members. These, as well as the many maps published in the pages of the magazine, are listed separately in the blue-tinted pages at the back of the book.

The index ends with the year 1946, and is designed to be used with a matching volume indexing NATIONAL GEOGRAPHICS from January, 1947, which in turn is brought up to date each year by supplements. Thus libraries and members who use their GEOGRAPHICS as reference works may now span the entire period of the Society's existence. Together, the volumes constitute a unique guide to the world and world events since 1888—and a unique tribute to the life work of a great man.

Melville Bell Grosvenor

EDITOR-IN-CHIEF

GEN. SHERMAN

The Story of the Geographic

An introduction by

GILBERT HOVEY GROSVENOR, Litt.D., LL.D., Sc.D.

President, 1920-1954; Editor, 1899-1954; Chairman of the Board, 1954-1966

FATE DOES NOT often permit a man to engage in a single labor of love for more than half a century, and only rarely does it reward his life's work with fruits beyond the boldest dreams of youth.

Yet I have been greatly blessed in both respects. For 55 eventful, challenging years I served as Editor of the NATIONAL GEOGRAPHIC MAGAZINE and chief executive of the National Geographic Society. At my retirement, May 5, 1954, I had also been President of the National Geographic Society for 34 years. During that long and happy tenure, I witnessed the growth of the Society and its publication from relative anonymity to worldwide strength, influence, and prestige.

Now, in retrospect, those golden years of my editorship bring to mind a fragment from Tennyson's beautiful poem *Ulysses:*

For always roaming with a hungry heart
Much have I seen and known; cities of men
And manners, climates, councils, governments

The key phrase, which suggests a theme for this history of the Geographic, is simply "roaming with a hungry heart." The world teems with people who long to visit faraway places, to travel adventurously, to see strange customs and races, to explore mysteries of the sea and air. Not many persons can do these things in the physical sense, but they can venture far and wide through the pages of the NATIONAL GEOGRAPHIC MAGAZINE.

With my wife at my side, I have roamed this fascinating globe of ours beyond the wanderings of a legendary Ulysses, and always with a heart hungry for the magic of unfamiliar scenes and peoples. Members of the Society, through their publication, have accompanied us on many of our journeys, just as they have traveled afar with hundreds of other GEOGRAPHIC authors and photographers.

"Much have I seen and known," said Tennyson's Ulysses—and the National Geographic Society's millions of members can say the same.

Recently, with the care one reserves for fragile treasures, I examined a personal copy of the first NATIONAL GEOGRAPHIC. Its cover of a terra-cotta shade bore no date, merely the imprint Vol. I, No. 1, and the magazine's now-familiar name. The lead offering was a technical paper entitled "Geographic Methods in Geologic Investigation." Indeed, the entire issue was determinedly technical in its approach to geography. It contained not even one photograph.

The little journal was essentially unchanged

Arms outstretched, 20 men encircle the General Sherman Tree in Sequoia National Park, California, in 1915, demonstrating its extraordinary girth—102 feet. To help save 2,239 acres of giant trees, the National Geographic Society and its members donated $100,000. The Society, under its proud banner, has always fought to preserve natural wonders.

GILBERT H. GROSVENOR, APRIL, 1916, NATIONAL GEOGRAPHIC

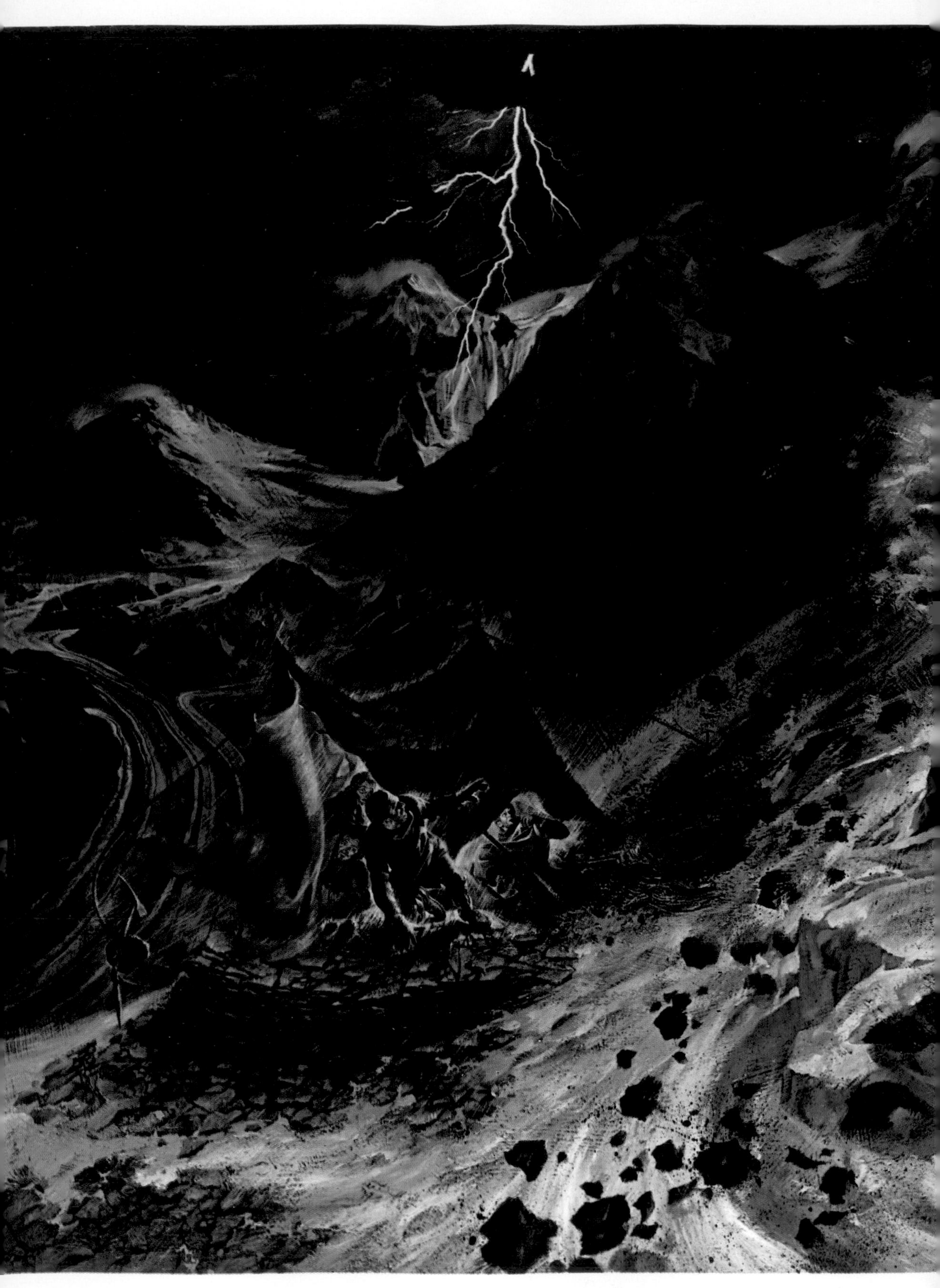

PAINTING BY PAUL CALLE FOR NATIONAL GEOGRAPHIC

GILBERT H. GROSVENOR COLLECTION

First President of the Society, Gardiner Greene Hubbard, with his wife Gertrude McCurdy Hubbard, pioneered in education for the deaf and helped finance the invention of the telephone. In January, 1888, he and 32 other public-spirited men met in Washington, D. C., to create a new organization, the National Geographic Society, for "the increase and diffusion of geographical knowledge." They issued membership invitations to interested laymen as well as to geographers.

In his inaugural address, Mr. Hubbard said, "Through the medium of a national organization, we may hope to promote geographic research in a manner that could not be accomplished by scattered individuals . . . we may also hope . . . to diffuse the results of geographic research over a wider area. . . ."

Late in 1888 the Society began to issue at irregular intervals a scholarly journal, the NATIONAL GEOGRAPHIC MAGAZINE, featuring such articles as "On the Telegraphic Determinations of Longitude by the Bureau of Navigation." After Mr. Hubbard's death, his son-in-law, the distinguished scientist and inventor of the telephone, Alexander Graham Bell, accepted the presidency in January, 1898.

Thundering avalanche, loosed by rain, clips a tent during the first expedition organized by the Society. Led by geologist Israel C. Russell, the party explored and mapped Mount St. Elias along the then unknown borderland of southern Alaska and Canada, and discovered Canada's loftiest peak, 19,850-foot Mount Logan. Russell's first-person account in the May 29, 1891, GEOGRAPHIC set the pattern for reporting explorations.

UNDERWOOD AND UNDERWOOD (BELOW); GILBERT H. GROSVENOR COLLECTION

Early partnership: Alexander Graham Bell, right, second President of the Geographic, sought a full-time editor to put new life into the little technical magazine. He offered the post to a brilliant young graduate of Amherst College, Massachusetts, suggesting it as "a steppingstone to something better." Thus, in 1899, Gilbert Hovey Grosvenor, left, launched his 67-year career with the Society.

To Gilbert, geography was much more than a dry classroom subject. Born in Constantinople, Turkey, he had mingled with many races and creeds, learned history and geography on travels with the family, and helped his father, a professor at Robert College, prepare an illustrated book about the city. He found geography alive and romantic, and determined to convey his fascination to readers. Supported by Dr. Bell, he embarked on a revolutionary path: to make the magazine interest the public and thus win support for the Society's great work.

"He speedily captured the Society," Dr. Bell later recalled, "and incidentally he captured one of my daughters." Elsie May Bell and Gilbert Hovey Grosvenor were wed in King's Weigh House Church, London, on October 23, 1900.

when Alexander Graham Bell, the inventor of the telephone, put me in charge of it on April 1, 1899. That date, so memorable to me, launched my career with the NATIONAL GEOGRAPHIC.

When I came to the magazine, a young man of 23, it had a circulation of only 1,000, and I was the Society's sole employee. I personally addressed all the wrappers for the first issue I edited (April, 1899), and carried the entire mail edition to the post office in one trip. I would not care to undertake a similar task with the millions of copies making up the print order for a current issue!

Minority Group Seeks Control

The magazine's evolution from obscurity to phenomenal prominence makes a fascinating and often dramatic story. I hadn't been employed a year before I became involved in a fight for control of the magazine. A determined minority group wanted to publish it in New York City, sell it on newsstands, and omit all reference to the Society. If these proposals had been accepted, the magazine inevitably would have become a commercial venture. But the NATIONAL GEOGRAPHIC remains today the official journal of a nonprofit educational and scientific association. There is no personal ownership, and there are no stockholders.

Once the fight for control had been won, I faced the task of evolving a magazine unlike any other in the world. It required an entirely new approach to the subject matter of geography. It meant breaking with tradition by using photoengravings, particularly color, in unprecedented number. Above all it demanded the enthusiasm of a romanticist, young in heart, eager and inquiring.

Here, to make the story clear, I must inject a personal note. In 1897, two years before I reported to Alexander Graham Bell in Washington as an aspiring young editor, I had met him when I was a house guest at his estate on Cape Breton, Nova Scotia. More important, I had made friends with his lovely daughter, Elsie May Bell, who was eventually to become my wife.

When Elsie Bell and I first met in that long-ago summer, we had no premonition that a great task awaited us. We swam and sailed, strolled and talked. Three weeks later my visit ended, we parted, and in the autumn of 1897 I accepted a teaching position at the Englewood, New Jersey, Academy for Boys.

At that time Elsie Bell's grandfather, Gardiner Greene Hubbard, was serving as first President of the National Geographic Society. The first issue of its magazine had gone to press in October, 1888; the Society had been formed nine months earlier. But in December, 1897, Mr. Hubbard died, and his son-in-law, Dr. Bell, took the Society's helm.

Dr. Bell had been an original member, though not a founder, and this busy man accepted the post only after considerable persuasion. He said he was not a geographer, and he knew the little organization was moribund.

The distinguished gentlemen who founded your Society had hoped that a magazine would attract members and bring in money for expeditions and research. At first the magazine appeared at irregular intervals. Then the Board of Managers decided to issue it every month, beginning in January, 1896, and to increase circulation by newsstand sales.

But the magazine did not sell. Geography, at that time, was regarded by the public as one of the dullest of subjects, something to inflict upon schoolboys and to avoid in later life. The Society's key to success, a popular approach to geography, was missing.

By the end of Dr. Bell's first year in office, the Society had an indebtedness of $2,000, and its magazine tottered feebly on the brink of bankruptcy. The Board was much discouraged—but not Dr. Bell. He could never resist a challenge, and his extraordinary mind had been at work. Now he acted.

Inventor Suggests a Bold Plan

In effect, this is what he told the Board: Geography is a fascinating subject, and it can be made interesting. Let's hire a promising young man to put some life into the magazine and promote the membership. I will pay his salary. Secondly, let's abandon our unsuccessful campaign to increase circulation by newsstand sales. Our journal should go to *members,* people who believe in our work and want to help. Support of exploration, research, and education is not a prerogative of the rich. Persons from all walks of life will join us if we arouse their interest with a lively journal.

Board members, though not nearly as optimistic as their President, gave their consent. The National Geographic Society had dispatched several notable expeditions, thanks to contributions from President Hubbard, but the magazine never brought in enough money to support itself, let alone field work.

Now it was up to Dr. Bell to find a "promising young man." Elsie knew of the plan, and she decided her father would benefit from a little adroit prompting. With every appearance of casualness, she mentioned the identical twin sons of her father's friend, Dr. Edwin A. Grosvenor, professor of modern governments at Amherst. Surely her father would recall that both young men had been his guests at Cape Breton following their graduation from Amherst, where they had shared academic honors. Perhaps a job in Washington, D. C., would appeal to one of the twins.

Dr. Bell, who greatly admired my father, embraced the idea as his own. Soon he was at his desk, writing to his friend. Would either of the twins, Edwin or Gilbert, be interested in a job that might be "a steppingstone to something better"? To my brother and me Dr. Bell sent a brief personal note with a copy of his letter to our father.

Job Offer Appeals to Gilbert

Edwin was interested in a law career—a fact not unknown to Elsie. He had no desire to be an editor. He recommended that I follow my heart, take the job, and be near the young lady in Washington.

I confess this consideration was the most persuasive one in my mind. Yet the idea of becoming an editor had a strong appeal of its own. It seemed to me that much of my young life had been spent in preparation for just such an opportunity.

I had been born in Constantinople—today's İstanbul—where for 23 years my father served as professor of history at Robert College, and years of living abroad had given me a deep interest in geography. Moreover, ours had always been a household that lived with the excitement of book proofs, manuscripts, and publishers' deadlines. My father was a prolific author as well as a professor, and from my early childhood he taught me the arts of writing and editing.

For example, I helped with the proofs and layout of father's two-volume book, *Constantinople*. He persuaded the publisher to illustrate this erudite work with 230 photographs, and in October, 1895, it became the first scholarly work to be profusely illustrated by photoengravings, made by the then new Levy process. Father personally prepared an attractive brochure describing his book, and I mailed thousands of copies to editors and librarians. As a result, the edition of 3,000 soon sold out at $10 a copy—quite a remarkable record for those days.

My father subscribed to a clipping service that sent him hundreds of reviews and comments about his books—his *Contemporary History* and his translations of French and modern Greek works. We spent many hours

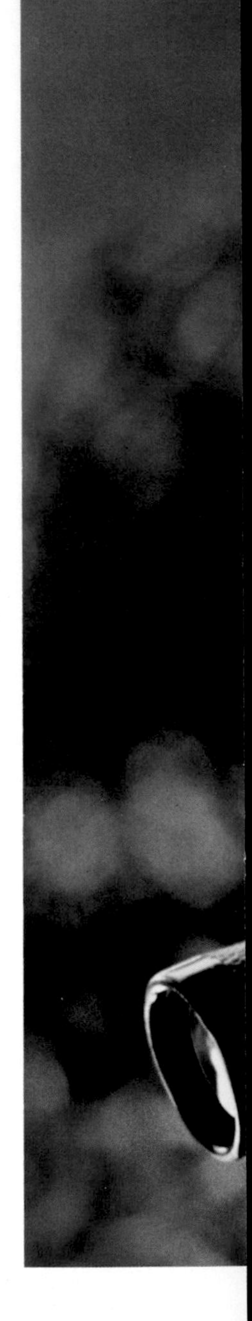

Acclaimed "Mr. Geography," Gilbert Grosvenor discovered the earth anew—for himself and for millions around the globe. In charting the course of the Society, first as Editor, then as President and Editor, and finally as Chairman of the Board, he forged an instrument for world education and understanding unique in this or any age.

As Editor, he made the magazine so interesting, readable, and reliable that it attracted thousands, then millions, to membership in the Society. Modest dues made each member a patron of the sciences. With these funds, Dr. Grosvenor dispatched expeditions to the ends of the earth, the depths of the sea, and the reaches of the stratosphere.

In recognition of his many achievements, honors poured in: landmarks named Grosvenor, academic degrees, medals, and citations. But the greatest tribute to his genius remains the NATIONAL GEOGRAPHIC MAGAZINE.

Here in his 90th year, Gilbert Grosvenor watches for birds—his hobby for decades—in Coconut Grove, Florida.

EKTACHROME BY THOMAS NEBBIA, 1965

discussing these reviews and analyzing the periodicals that came into our home: *Harper's Weekly, The Review of Reviews, McClure's, The Independent, The Century,* and others.

From time to time family friends, among them Lew Wallace, the Civil War general and author of *Ben Hur,* Albert Shaw, editor of *The Review of Reviews,* and William Hayes Ward, editor of *The Independent,* joined our discussions of writing and current topics.

Following such sessions, or after I had given my father an opinion on arranging or cutting a manuscript, my mother would say, "Bert, you really should be an editor." And often she would add, "How can we get a chance for you?"

The chance came with Dr. Bell's offer. I wanted it badly. But, with the loyalty so typical of identical twins, I was unwilling to deprive my brother of an opportunity, even if he did disclaim interest in it. But Edwin, who later became a prominent attorney in New York City, was sincere in his refusal. Again he urged my acceptance.

So I wrote to Dr. Bell, and he invited me to a meeting at his home in Washington. Mrs. Bell and Elsie, but no others, participated in our discussion. It proved a fateful meeting, for during it I made several decisions that affected the course of future events for the Geographic—and for me.

Dr. Bell began by showing me leading magazines of the day: *Harper's, McClure's, Munsey's, The Century.*

"Can you create a geographic magazine as popular as these, one that will support the Society instead of the Society being burdened with the magazine?" he asked.

"Yes, I believe I can," I replied, "but I must proceed slowly and feel my way."

Bell Proposes a Large Investment

Indeed I emphasized that point repeatedly. There would have to be a period of evolution. I felt that the famous inventor did not fully realize the magnitude of the task he offered, and I wanted him to remember that it could not be done overnight. As later events showed, I had gauged my man well. Like most successful men, Dr. Bell expected quick results.

He accepted my point, and then suggested a proposition that immediately made me wary. Some years earlier he and Mr. Hubbard had spent $87,000 in an attempt to establish a magazine called *Science*. The magazine had failed, and he and Mr. Hubbard had sold the name *Science* for $25—although they had paid $5,000 for the right to use it. Despite this editorial tragedy, he offered to invest an equal sum, $87,000, in the NATIONAL GEOGRAPHIC MAGAZINE.

I knew that sheer weight of money would not accomplish what he wanted. I also realized that, despite Dr. Bell's good will, a youth of 23 was not prepared to administer so large a sum. Older men, men unwilling to experiment, inevitably would push me aside, and I would have little opportunity to create and to try new ideas. Yet, without imagination and a new approach, there could be no hope for the magazine.

So, firmly and determinedly, I said I would take the job only if Dr. Bell limited his gift to $100 a month for my salary—considerably less than I received as a teacher. He was reluctant, but Mrs. Bell gave me strong support. "Bert, I am much relieved by your attitude," she said. "You are right to insist that he limit his donation. Money is not the answer. You have a difficult job, and as you said, you must proceed slowly."

Dr. Bell finally accepted my condition, and the meeting ended. Elsie and I had a moment alone before I left, and she whispered, "I told Papa I thought you had the talent he sought and would like to come to Washington!"

Headquarters Crowded Into Half a Room

So, on April 1, 1899, Dr. Bell took me to the Society headquarters in the old Corcoran office building, across the street from the U. S. Treasury. It consisted of half of one small room (the other half occupied by the American Forestry Association), two rickety chairs, a table, a litter of papers and ledgers, and six enormous boxes crammed with GEOGRAPHICS returned by newsstands.

"No desk!" exclaimed Dr. Bell. "I'll send you mine." That afternoon deliverymen brought me a handsome roll-top desk made of Circassian walnut. Many years later, after I had moved into a magnificently equipped new office, Mrs. Bell asked me for her husband's desk, saying she needed an extra one. "I won't part with it for its weight in gold," I replied. I thought she would be offended, but my reply delighted her.

Dr. Bell introduced me to his colleagues in the Society, all much older men than I, and gave advice and encouragement. Then he left for his laboratory at Cape Breton. His

GILBERT H. GROSVENOR COLLECTION

"An eye-opener," Editor Grosvenor called his experience with the 1904 traveling sessions of the Eighth International Geographic Congress, meeting in the United States for the first time. In Chicago, delegates ride a horse-drawn sightseeing coach. The Editor (hat on knee) sits on the top deck, facing his wife. Reports from international congresses appeared in early issues, giving readers a look at geographers' work around the world.

family soon followed, but Mrs. Bell asked her mother, Mrs. Hubbard (page 9), to look out for my welfare, and I spent many pleasant weekends at the Hubbard estate, "Twin Oaks," in northwest Washington.

Meanwhile I dug into a monumental task. It was clear that I must proceed simultaneously on two fronts. First, I had to get new members, lots of them, and quickly. The Society's bank account was exhausted. Secondly, I had to issue the magazine on time (it had been habitually late) and make it more readable and better known. Of the two tasks, the first—increasing the membership—seemed to demand the greater emphasis.

But how to do it? I began by asking prominent men to nominate their friends for membership. Initially that meant seeking nominations from my father and Dr. Bell, and I badgered them unceasingly. I was scarcely less persistent with the officers and Board members of the Society, and they responded generously. As fast as the names came in—all distinguished men and women—the Admissions Committee would approve them, and letters would be sent inviting the nominees to join.

My membership campaign gathered quick momentum. By June 20, 1899, I could write exultantly to my father, "We are going to have a bully number for July. I have obtained 100 new members at $2 apiece and one life member at $50 since June 1. How's that! Going to get more though."

300 Names for "Your Royal Highness"

Throughout the summer and fall I wrote my patient father almost daily, and my letters soon took on the tone of an athletic coach exhorting his star performer. Here are a few excerpts, each from a different letter: "Your men are doing fine.... Your men have done

TSYBIKOFF AND NORZUNOFF

Honeycomb palace of the Dalai Lama rises above Lhasa, and Tibetan women trudge to market in pictures marking a turning point in the GEOGRAPHIC's history. While most editors scorned photographs, Editor Grosvenor sought them to dramatize geography. When he received from Russian explorers an envelope of photographs showing the mysterious capital of Tibet, he filled 11 pages with their pictures and captions in the January, 1905, issue—the magazine's first photograph-story and extraordinary coverage for that time. He expected to be fired. Instead, he recalled, "Society members congratulated me on the street."

the best of any, even better than Mr. Bell's. . . . 14 new members to your credit. . . . Your lists have almost a clean record. . . ."

Meanwhile I was successfully using similar tactics with Dr. Bell. Finally, almost in self-defense, he wrote me that I could nominate in his name 100 of the most prominent men in the National Education Association, 100 in the American Association for the Advancement of Science, and the entire membership of the National Academy of Sciences—a grand total of 300 names. Then, with typical humor, he added this postscript:

"You asked for an inch and I have given you a mile. You asked me to nominate 100 members, and I have given you permission to nominate 300. Is that enough for Your Royal Highness! Or will you have the face to ask me for any more."

Today I smile at the extremes of my youthful zeal, but zeal was precisely the stimulus needed. Other membership promotion methods also proved effective, such as a letter to members inviting them to nominate friends and the first appearance in the magazine of the now-familiar nomination form.

Conservative Officials Resist Change

That letter, I recall, brought about my first difficulty with conservative members of the Board. Shortly after reporting for work, I drafted a message to members stressing the need of their cooperation in building the Society, and Dr. Bell approved it before leaving for Cape Breton. Soon, however, I had to send him a new version.

"The original letter," I wrote, "the one which I submitted to you that last Sunday afternoon, was condemned by the Board of Managers in a most emphatic way; in fact, the different men tore it so to pieces, the idea, language, begging character, and undignified

COURTESY THE BELL FAMILY—J. A. D. McCURDY, JANUARY, 1908, GEOGRAPHIC (ABOVE); J. A. D. McCURDY

Giant network of tetrahedral cells, a man-carrying kite rests on its floating launch pad at Baddeck, Nova Scotia; the kite lifted Lt. Thomas Selfridge, U. S. Army, to a height of 168 feet in a 7-minute flight. Its inventor, Alexander Graham Bell, at right, applied findings from the experiment to his investigations for a flying machine. Gilbert Grosvenor published Dr. Bell's first report on tetrahedral kites in 1903. For several summers he edited such articles in his "private office" (left), a tent pitched in a sylvan glade on the Bell estate at Baddeck. Here his daughter Gertrude, his son Melville, and Dr. Bell pay a call.

method of procedure as they put it, that nothing was left when they finished. . . . A committee was appointed to draw up this letter, but as each wished the others to write it . . . I had to do it myself."

This incident illustrates a recurrent problem of those first few years. The executive structure of the Society then was top-heavy with various committees, all composed of busy men of affairs, and I often had to do the work of these groups and make decisions when they failed to act. It required the greatest tact and diplomacy.

By the end of the first year of my employment, I had more than doubled the Society's membership, raising it from 1,000 to 2,200.

In the meantime I had not been neglecting my "second front"—improvement of the magazine. Funds were so limited that I could not pay authors, let alone publish pictures on a major scale. But I did obtain articles of general rather than academic interest. Sometimes my father and Dr. Bell, both omnivorous readers, suggested timely topics. I also spent long hours polishing sentences.

As the summer of '99 waned, I was able to increase the number of pages in the magazine and to step up the print order from 2,000 to 3,000. But in many ways I had to move slowly and temper my wishes with those of the Board. The GEOGRAPHIC then had a nominal Editor in Chief and no less than 12 Associate Editors, all unpaid and all members of the Board of Managers. Many of them, being technical minded, wanted to insert material unintelligible to the layman.

GEORGE SHIRAS

Hunting with film and flash powder, former Congressman George Shiras, 3d, originated a new sport, photoflashing animals at night. Roaming waterways, he carried two cameras on a revolving table. When a light picked up the glowing eyes of an animal, he triggered a flash.

Doe and twin fawns: This Shiras photograph won awards at two international expositions. The Editor chose it and 73 others for the July, 1906, GEOGRAPHIC. Two shocked Board members resigned, stating that "wandering off into nature is not geography." But many applauded.

GEORGE SHIRAS

Quiet as a tabby cat, a lynx in Ontario eyes the approaching light with undisturbed curiosity—until the flash explodes. Florida raccoon, below, takes its own picture. Pulling at a bait, it trips a string that sets off hidden camera and magnesium flash.

Dr. Bell, remote from the scene, did not always appreciate my situation. I had stressed to him that we would have to feel our way for a time, but he liked quick results. After six months at my tasks, I wrote him:

"If you will give me time, I confidently believe you will have the circulation, the 'ads,' the influence and reputation that such a publication should have. But it takes more than six months to make a *Century.*"

In the latter sentence I was referring pointedly to the inventor's fondness for one of the leading magazines of the day. He sometimes thought of *The Century* as a guide we should follow, but I knew it was imperative that we not copy another publication but evolve something new and fresh.

Reprints Publicize the Magazine

Dr. Bell, however, never posed as an Olympian figure issuing orders. He was both warmhearted and reasonable. No one was more pleased than he when one of my first GEOGRAPHIC articles, "Plans for Reaching the South Pole" (August, 1899), illustrated with the first map I prepared for the magazine, was reprinted in *The Literary Digest.* Also, he gave me unstinting credit for the attention the magazine was receiving in other publications. Each month I mailed out digests or excerpts of the most interesting material in the NATIONAL GEOGRAPHIC, and many were reprinted with appropriate credit. In this way, people all over the Nation learned for the first time that there was a journal called the NATIONAL GEOGRAPHIC MAGAZINE.

Responsibility for both the business and editorial affairs of the Society left me few spare moments, but in September of 1899 I decided I would have to do something about the Society's lecture series in Washington. The committee charged with responsibility for the annual program had failed to make any firm arrangements. So I inquired of Dr. Bell, "Is that included under the Assistant Editorship? If so, I will take it up immediately."

Yes, he replied, and I had a third job.

I at once thought of an old family friend, former Secretary of State John W. Foster. My father helped me enlist him as the opening lecturer of the season, and he spoke as an expert on a major topic of the day, "The Alaskan Boundary." A sellout crowd attended, and I, the nervous impresario, projected Mr. Foster's lantern slides myself.

Mr. Foster's talk, though excellent and

Eyes intent on a long-sought goal, Comdr. Robert E. Peary reached the North Pole over the ice on April 6, 1909 —a feat never accomplished before or since. Living like Eskimos in igloos and trekking through a chaos of ridged sea ice in husky-drawn sledges (right), the indomitable 52-year-old explorer and his men braved 475 miles of white hell to reach their goal. Encouraging Peary, the Society in 1906 had awarded him its Hubbard Medal for Arctic exploration and in 1907 subscribed $1,000 for his successful expedition, the first grant from its own funds.

newsworthy, won only local notice, but when I published it as an article in the November, 1899, issue, long editorials about it appeared in important newspapers throughout the Nation.

McClure Says, "Move to New York"

Thus we entered 1900 with rising prospects—or so Dr. Bell and I thought. However, the Executive Committee, a five-man minority of the Board but a determined one, believed our plans hopelessly optimistic. These men wanted to stop "undignified" membership promotion and sell the magazine on newsstands, although that approach previously had led to a debt-ridden Society.

Dr. Bell himself had invited many prominent editors and publishers to Washington as consultants. The most influential was S. S. McClure, publisher of *McClure's Magazine,* with a circulation of 370,000.

Mr. McClure's success commanded respect. But I was deeply disturbed by his suggestions: (1) publish the NATIONAL GEOGRAPHIC in New York, since it is impossible to establish a popular magazine in Washington; (2) change the magazine's name to something simpler; (3) abandon the plan to build circulation by membership in a geographic society; (4) depend upon newsstand sales and advertising to increase the circulation; (5) never mention the name National Geographic Society in the magazine, since people abhor geography.

Mr. McClure's eloquence entranced the members of the Executive Committee. They knew little of editorial and publishing problems—less than I, despite my youth. To

ROBERT E. PEARY COLLECTION

them the fact that I had more than doubled the GEOGRAPHIC's circulation in less than a year seemed unimpressive compared to the enormous readership Mr. McClure had built.

These men were not interested in the letters from new members, but I was—I read all of them. Each day I opened the membership mail, studied it, listed the enclosed dues, and took the money to the bank. A phenomenal 99 percent of the letters contained some expression of faith and gratification in the Society's altruistic aims. The new members' desire to help promote science and education was as strong as their desire to get a good NATIONAL GEOGRAPHIC MAGAZINE.

I felt that I had made more than a thousand new friends, and the prospect of breaking faith with them—as we would have to do if Mr. McClure's ideas controlled the magazine—rasped painfully on my conscience.

Fortunately the Board of Managers saw the pitfalls. It reaffirmed its belief in Dr. Bell's plan, and on June 30, 1900, the inventor took his family to Europe, believing he was leaving me free to carry out our agreement.

Strident Hurdy-gurdy Brightens the Days

No sooner had the Bells sailed than the difficulty with the Executive Committee resumed. My father and two members of the Board of Managers, Gen. A. W. Greely and Frederick V. Coville, had submitted to me more than 1,100 nominations for membership, yet the five-man Executive Committee ordered me not to accept them. So I pushed the nominations to a corner of my desk and

B. B. FULTON (ABOVE), JANUARY, 1917, GEOGRAPHIC; E. C. KOLB, NATIONAL GEOGRAPHIC SOCIETY KATMAI EXPEDITION, SEPTEMBER, 1921, GEOGRAPHIC

Ash-choked waters of the Katmai River slow Robert F. Griggs, discoverer of the Valley of Ten Thousand Smokes (below). In June of 1912 eruptions rent the Alaska Peninsula, opening fumaroles and spewing debris. Dr. Griggs explored the volcanic wonderland on five Society expeditions. His reports in the GEOGRAPHIC aroused such interest that in 1918 President Woodrow Wilson proclaimed the area Katmai National Monument.

worked doggedly on magazine copy, though often tired and drawn from sweltering heat that persisted week after week.

Occasionally I clambered onto the fire escape outside my window for a breath of air, and one day I heard beneath me the strident tones of a hurdy-gurdy playing Sousa marches. On the curb an organ grinder cranked tinny tunes while a monkey capered, grimaced, and bowed. It was absurd, ridiculous—and delightful. Listening daily to the hurdy-gurdy became my sole diversion from care.

During those trying days my father counseled, "Just be patient, be patient." His advice brought to my mind a line from Longfellow's *A Psalm of Life:* "Learn to labor and to wait." This became my philosophy during the dreadfully hot summer of 1900.

I had been unwilling to burden Dr. Bell with my troubles. But, on August 6, 1900, with the time near for his return to Washington, I wrote him frankly. It was his fight, too, and he would soon have to face it again.

"Naturally I am very much distressed with the committee," my letter said, "but as I firmly believe that they are working not against me personally... but against your plans for the Society and for their individual interests, I do not intend to get out of their way, as they plainly hint they want me to."

In September Dr. Bell convened the Board of Managers in Washington. The Executive Committee had no support in this distinguished group of scientists and men of affairs. Board members pointedly complimented me on my work, unanimously reaffirmed my permanent status with the Society, appointed me Managing Editor, and increased my salary, the increase of $800 to be paid by the Society.

I assumed that our house divided, the Society, was made whole again. It proved a wrong assumption, but at the time my personal happiness permitted no doubts to intrude. Elsie Bell and I had become engaged; in the fall I obtained a long leave, and we were married in London on October 23, 1900 (page 10).

When her father, Dr. Bell, had sent congratulations on our engagement, I had replied, "By persuading Elsie Bell to marry me, I have done more for the National Geographic Society than has happened to it in all of its twelve years of existence."

The Lady With the "Magic Touch"

Mrs. Grosvenor brought a magic touch to the work of the Society. With dedication and unwavering faith, my wife became my partner in transforming the Society and its magazine.

She read hundreds of manuscripts, examined thousands of pages of proof and tens of thousands of photographs, and contributed three notable GEOGRAPHIC articles of her own.* She was at my side during hundreds of thousands of miles of travel across the length and breadth of the globe. And she designed the Society's honored flag. Her interest in geography had been strong long before our marriage, for she had studied in France and Italy and traveled in England, Norway, and Japan with her parents.

Elsie and I had reached Vienna on our honeymoon trip when I began to worry about the magazine. I had an instinctive feeling that something was wrong. We had hoped to go to Constantinople, city of my birth and boyhood, but instead we rushed home, arriving early in December, 1900.

And just in time, too. The Executive Committee had arranged to have the magazine printed in New York by McClure, Phillips & Company. Mr. McClure's eloquence had made a deep impression upon Dr. Bell, as well as on the committee members. The New York editor's success in creating *McClure's Magazine*—one of the first prosperous 10-cent monthly magazines—was proof of his ability, and Dr. Bell had countenanced the agreement.

My father-in-law held aloof from events that followed. I showed him a very costly bill

BRADFORD WASHBURN (OPPOSITE); NATIONAL GEOGRAPHIC SOCIETY YUKON EXPEDITION

Mapping the unknown Yukon, Bradford Washburn sights through a theodolite. Exploring here for the Society in 1938, he discovered one of the world's largest icefields outside the polar regions.

Where ice and storm wage ceaseless war, Mount McKinley shows its pristine beauty. In 1936, Dr. Washburn, then 26, photographed the Alaskan giant from an open airplane door. "A stout rope . . . let me lean just far enough out the opening to take pictures—and no farther," he wrote. His reward: The first comprehensive camera record of the highest peak in North America.

* "Alaska's Warmer Side," June, 1956; "Safari From Congo to Cairo," December, 1954; and "Safari Through Changing Africa," August, 1953. In recognition of Mrs. Grosvenor's services to geography, the University of Alaska made her an honorary alumna by the award of a Doctorate of Laws, May 13, 1957.

LUMIÈRE AUTOCHROME (ABOVE) BY DR. W. H. LONGLEY AND CHARLES MARTIN, JANUARY, 1927, GEOGRAPHIC

First underwater photographs in color opened a new world to the camera in 1926. Assisting scientist Dr. W. H. Longley, Charles Martin of the GEOGRAPHIC staff rigged a raft with a pound of flash powder. When a camera-carrying diver triggered the flash, a reflector bounced it into the water to illuminate this Florida hogfish amid gorgonians.

Eight-foot foldout dramatizes the Canadian Rockies. Editor Grosvenor, who published the huge panorama in June, 1911, said, "The mind must see before it can believe."

First aerial color photograph of the U. S. Capitol appeared in the September, 1930, GEOGRAPHIC. Melville Bell Grosvenor took the view from 1,200 feet, riding in a dirigible to avoid vibration, since Finlay color plates required an exposure of 1/25 of a second at f/4.5, even in sunlight. He made other aerial shots over New York and New Jersey.

Half-clad harvester at work on a rice plantation helped illustrate a 1903 article about American development of the Philippines. From the early days the GEOGRAPHIC has portrayed peoples of the world in their natural attire —or lack of it.

DEAN C. WORCESTER, MAY, 1903, GEOGRAPHIC

from McClure, Phillips & Company for the printing of the January, 1901, issue and told him that the New York firm had failed to get us any new members, subscribers, or advertising. His only comment was, "Well, Bert, the Board made you the Managing Editor. You are responsible now."

So the fight was mine alone. As Managing Editor, I had authority; I went to New York immediately. Two issues, January and February of 1901, were printed there before I could reverse the Executive Committee's action.

Recently I came across the contract I signed with the printing firm of Judd & Detweiler after returning the magazine to Washington. The costs add up to half what we paid for New York publication. But I had saved something more important than dollars: Dr. Bell's original plan to enlist members who would help us create a great educational institution.

I wish to remark here that S. S. McClure and John S. Phillips and their associates were fine gentlemen. They expressed regret that their responsibilities had become so heavy that they had not been able to help the GEOGRAPHIC and Dr. Bell as they had hoped. They wished me well sincerely.

New Geography Embraces the World

In February, 1903, I was made Editor, with full authority to try my own ideas for development of the magazine, and also became the Society's Director, with control of all business and membership affairs.

I thought of geography in terms of its Greek root: *geographia*—a description of the world. It thus becomes the most catholic of subjects, universal in appeal, and embracing nations, people, plants, animals, birds, fish.

We would never lack interesting subjects. I had long considered how that interest could

CHARLES D. WALCOTT

WILLIAM W. CHAPIN

Walking haystack: A Korean farmer dresses for rain. This and other photographs in a 24-page color spread caused a sensation when they appeared in the November, 1910, GEOGRAPHIC. No magazine had ever run so much color at one time. Traveler William W. Chapin recorded "Scenes in Korea and China" in black and white; a Japanese artist tinted them by hand. In response to members' enthusiasm, the Editor determined to insert a color feature every November.

Coiffured and costumed with elaborate care, Manchu women passing along Peking streets proved so timid that Chapin had trouble photographing them. Other scenes from his published collection include heavily laden coolies, shackled prisoners, and Buddhist nuns.

be captured in words. At night I pored over other geographic journals and studied great geographic books that had been widely read —Darwin's *The Voyage of the Beagle,* Dana's *Two Years Before the Mast,* Joshua Slocum's *Sailing Alone Around the World.*

What was there in Herodotus's travels, *The History,* written 2,300 years earlier, that gave the book such life that it was still going strong? What was the secret of the great geographic books that men and women should turn to them through the centuries?

Experiments Test a Popular Style

Finally I was convinced I had the answer, one we would put to good use in NATIONAL GEOGRAPHIC: Each article would be a vivid eyewitness account; each would contain simple, straightforward writing that would make pictures in the readers' minds.

Next I undertook an experiment to determine the kind of articles readers liked. It would have been simple enough to insert my own articles in NATIONAL GEOGRAPHIC, but I decided a sterner test would be to see if other editors would buy my writing. That should be a good gauge of popular appeal.

So for several years I wrote and sold numerous articles. For the yearbook of the Smithsonian Institution, Secretary S. P. Langley accepted a survey of 19th-century exploration and explorers and paid me $100. The New York Herald Syndicate distributed widely an article on James Smithson, founder of the Smithsonian Institution, a story entitled "Reindeer Breeding in Alaska," and one on Dr. Bell's flight experiments with tetrahedral kites. I got a total of only $75 for these, but I felt like Croesus when *Century Magazine,* then the leading quality publication, paid $250 each for three articles.

Outside writing gave me useful experience, but my editorial duties at the GEOGRAPHIC soon required all my time.

In those days many publications scorned photographic illustrations. The famous and successful editor of *The Century* had gone so far as to predict in print that "people will tire of photographic reproduction, and those magazines will find most favor which lead in original art."

I rejected the conservative view, and it was like striking gold in my own backyard when I found Government agencies would lend me plates from their publications. I illustrated numerous articles in this way. For example, plates from the U. S. Bureau of Education illustrated my article on "Reindeer in Alaska" in the April, 1903, issue.

Sometimes, if I had suitable photographs and enough money, I contracted for photoengravings. A popular feature of 1903, Dr. Bell's article on "The Tetrahedral Principle in Kite Structure," was accompanied by many photographs. A later article by him, "Aërial Locomotion" in January, 1907, proved even more popular. These papers marked the beginning of the GEOGRAPHIC's long and authoritative coverage of aviation.

The Society's flag was born in this period. Elsie Grosvenor designed it for the 1903 Ziegler Polar Expedition. We wanted an emblem that could be instantly recognized, and she chose stripes of blue, brown, and green—for sky, earth, and sea (page 7).

Late in 1903 the Society moved into a handsome new headquarters given it by the family of Gardiner Greene Hubbard—an expression of confidence in the future. Today the structure appears modest and small. Then, however, it seemed like the Taj Mahal, and it gave a picture of affluence hardly warranted by the Society's circumstances. By the end of 1904 we had 3,662 members, not enough for good financial health. I resolved to take some calculated risks in the new year 1905.

By sheer chance I received in the mail 50 beautiful photographs of Lhasa, the mysterious capital of Tibet, on the very day that I urgently needed 11 pages of material for the January, 1905, issue. The Russian explorers who took the pictures offered them free. So I filled the entire 11 pages with the photographs, raiding the Society's slim treasury to make the plates (pages 16-17).

Views of Lhasa Set a New Style

I expected to be fired. But when the magazine appeared, people stopped me on the street to congratulate me, and membership applications took a decided upturn.

Soon another windfall came my way. My cousin William Howard Taft told me that in April the U. S. Government would publish a copiously illustrated Census Report of the Philippines. I borrowed 32 full-page plates—138 pictures—and printed them in the April,

WILLIAM W. CHAPIN

1905, magazine. The Philippines number brought so many new members I had to reprint the issue.

Now seemed the time for a determined campaign to build the membership. I hired additional clerical help and began pouring money into an all-out membership drive. It was an audacious gamble, but by the middle of 1905 it was clearly paying off.

"I have never worked so hard in my life as during the past few months," I wrote to my mother-in-law, Mrs. Bell, on June 23. "I have made up my mind that . . . the Society must 'go bust' or become independent this year. It's been awfully hard work and worried me too, for during the past two months I have been spending money like water. I wasn't sure whether I'd get it back. . . . As it is, everything has turned out even better than I had hoped."

By September, 1905, the membership had zoomed to more than 10,000—three times the September, 1904, figure. By the end of 1905 it reached nearly 11,500.

The year 1905 marked the turning point in the Society's fortunes, the "end of the beginning." In September I reported to the Board that we would end the year with a surplus of $3,500. I then offered the following resolution:

"Resolved, That the National Geographic Society, through its Board of Managers, thank Dr. Bell for his generous subscription to the work of the Society from 1899 to 1904, and inform Dr. Bell that the Society is now on such a substantial basis that it can relieve him of his subscription for 1905."

Elsie and I were jubilant. At last her generous father had seen his dream realized: a geographic magazine that would support the Society. His total gift to establish the magazine was $6,900 instead of the $87,000 he had offered in 1899.

"That was in '26. Now here I am again in the spring of '29."

Famous enough for fun, the magazine takes a ribbing from a cartoonist, who lampoons repeated coverage of remote tribes. But members continue to treasure the old issues for their living history of peoples in all parts of the world.

Muscle-straining tug-of-war tests rival tribesmen of northern Luzon, as an American shouts encouragement. When the Secretary of the Interior of the Philippines, Dean Worcester, could find little reliable information about the tribes, he traveled extensively in the hill country. To reduce the "sport" of head-hunting, he introduced athletics and encouraged dancing. Pipe-smoking girls (opposite) pose before a dance contest. Worcester's report appeared in March, 1911.

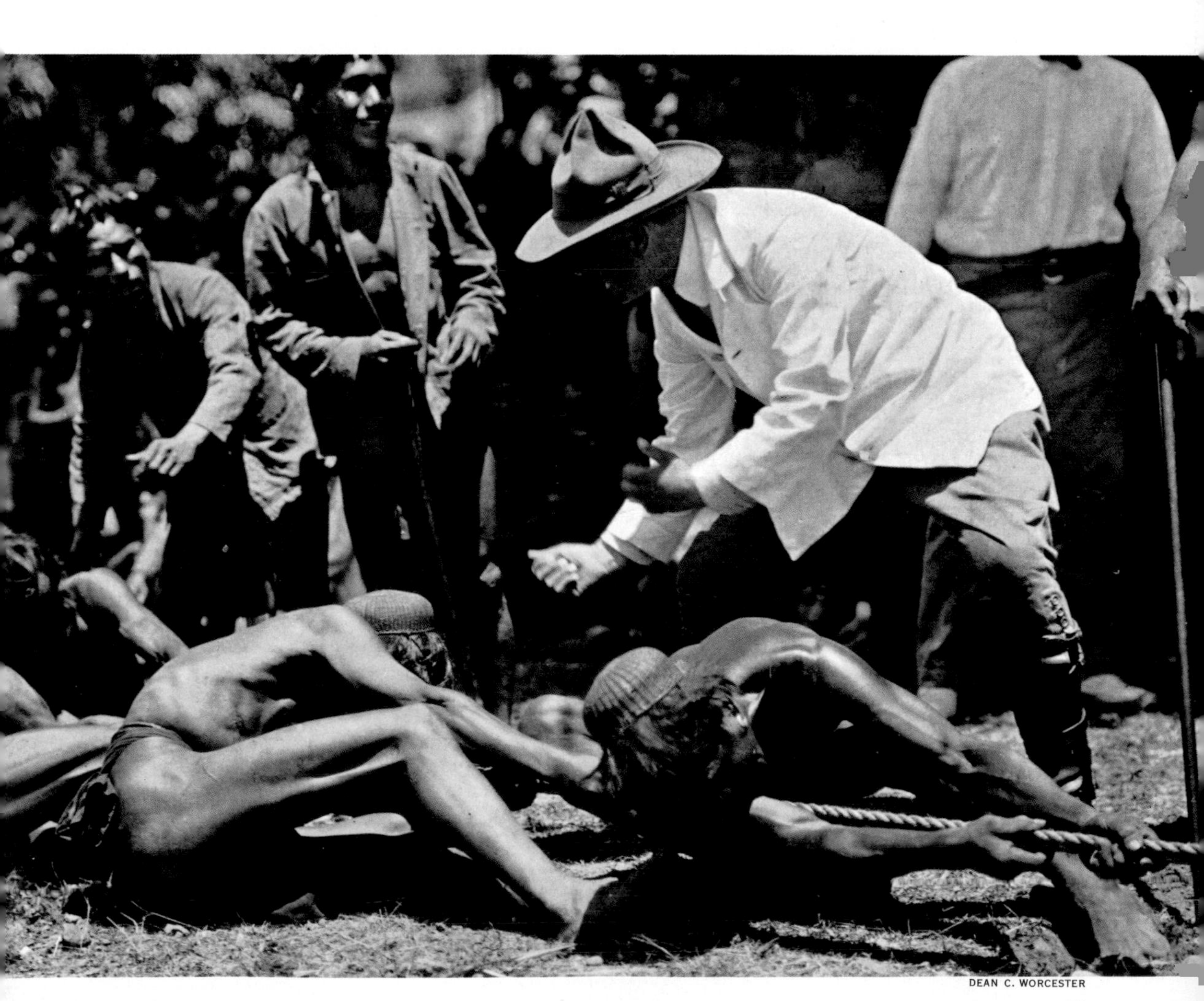

DEAN C. WORCESTER

GILBERT H. GROSVENOR

Close-up of Tsarist Russia: Dr. Grosvenor on a visit just before World War I captured illuminating details, including this peasant woman wearing straw sandals, then considered a luxury. He published the picture in November, 1914, with the first series made up of his own photographs—61 in black and white, 10 tinted by hand, including the scene on the opposite page reproduced from the original plate.

Multicolored onion domes of a revered cathedral, today a museum near the Kremlin walls, rise above Moscow. The Editor's article—still consulted for its view of pre-Communist Russia—revealed the devoutness of the people, their high birth rate, low literacy rate, resources, and problems. He judged the sprawling country a "land of unlimited possibilities."

Meanwhile the GEOGRAPHIC was becoming known as a magazine on the move, with articles that were not only interesting but frequently newsworthy. For example, John W. Foster contributed an article on China in December, 1904, that won wide attention. Mr. Foster had represented China in the settlement of the Sino-Japanese War in 1895.

For the August, 1905, issue, Mr. Taft wrote the first of three reports on our country's altruistic program in the Philippines, a program he had initiated as the islands' Civil Governor. They explain the foundation on which the firm friendship of the Filipinos for the United States has been built.

High Standards Maintained in Ads

By 1906 the magazine's increased circulation warranted a campaign for additional advertising, a task I assigned to John Oliver La Gorce, whom I engaged in September, 1905, to assist me.* I gave him a free hand, except for policy rules that I imposed, among them a firm ban on liquor, beer, wine, and patent medicine advertisements. The magazine even then was widely used in schools. Also, I decided it would benefit both advertisers and readers if ads were printed separately from pictures and text.

Incidentally, these rules still apply. Our advertising philosophy is unchanged.

Ishbel Ross, writing years ago in the old *Scribner's Magazine,* put it this way:

"Dr. Grosvenor once said that he would take his readers around the world and that he would take them first class. He has done it and, most remarkable of all, he has done it without letting his fireside travelers have a drink, a smoke, or a bicarbonate of soda."

In 1907, with the greatest satisfaction, I advised the Board that our receipts permitted the Society to begin annual grants for research, and I recommended $1,000 toward the cost of Comdr. Robert E. Peary's final assault on the North Pole. This was the first grant by the Society from its own resources for the express purpose of exploration. Since then the Society has sponsored several hundred expeditions and research projects.†

Compared to the $1,000,000 in research grants, public service funds, and educational subsidies now authorized each year by our

*See "Colleague of the Golden Years: John Oliver La Gorce," by Gilbert Grosvenor, NATIONAL GEOGRAPHIC, March, 1960.

†See "75 Years Exploring Earth, Sea, and Sky," by Melvin M. Payne, GEOGRAPHIC, January, 1963.

Photo by Gilbert H. Grosvenor

THE CATHEDRAL OF ST. BASIL'S: MOSCOW

St. Basil's is remarkable for its bizarre outlines and the gaudy color of its exterior. The interior is very disappointing, being divided into eleven small and gloomy chapels, which resemble dungeons. In this they are unlike the typical Russian church, which is elaborately adorned in gold and other rich colors.

Picnicking conservationists work to savc the big trees in Sequoia National Park in 1915. Stephen T. Mather, later the first Director of the National Park Service, heads the table. To his left: Gilbert Grosvenor, who made the picture with a delayed-action device. Horace M. Albright, second Park Service Director, sits in front of the cook. To Mather's right: E. O. McCormick, Vice President of Southern Pacific, and Massachusetts Congressman Frederick H. Gillett, later Speaker of the House of Representatives.

Gray Horse Troop of U. S. Cavalry lines up beside and atop a fallen sequoia. The Army patrolled parks before the Park Service was established.

GILBERT H. GROSVENOR (ABOVE) AND A. R. MOORE, JANUARY, 1917, GEOGRAPHIC

Board of Trustees, the aid to Peary may seem insignificant, but it was a vital first step. We had kept faith with the thousands of loyal members who believed in our objectives.

In 1906 a remarkable amateur photographer, George Shiras, 3d, walked into my office with a box full of magnificent flashlight photographs of wild animals. Mr. Shiras, a former Congressman from Pennsylvania, had invented the technique for taking such pictures; his work had won medals and diplomas at expositions in Paris in 1900 and St. Louis in 1904.

With mounting excitement I sorted the photographs into two piles, one towering, the other small. Mr. Shiras had been able to interest a leading New York publication in only three of his pictures, so he was astounded when told I intended to print every photograph in the large pile. And I did—74 of them on 50 pages with only four pages of text, in the July issue.

When these extraordinary pictures of wildlife appeared, letters poured in demanding more natural history. But two distinguished geographers on the Board resigned, stating emphatically that "wandering off into nature is not geography."

All other members of the Board encouraged and supported me. The Society owes much to those men. I recall two with special gratitude: John Joy Edson, our Treasurer, a prominent banker who had been Chairman of President McKinley's 1901 Inaugural Committee, and O. P. Austin, our Secretary. These men, both of whom served the Society without pay for 30 years, became my staunch friends.

My heart bids me pay warm tribute also to 14 able, farsighted men, none now living, who served on the Society's Board of Managers during the critical years 1901 to 1910. Success would have been impossible without the patience, understanding, and loyal support of Alexander Graham Bell; Charles J. Bell,* President, American Security and Trust Company; Henry F. Blount, banker; Rear Adm. Colby M. Chester, U. S. Navy; Frederick V. Coville, botanist; David Fairchild, botanist; Henry Gannett,* Chief Geographer, U. S. Geological Survey; G. K. Gilbert,* Chief Geologist, U. S. Geological Survey; Daniel C. Gilman, President, Johns Hopkins University; Maj. Gen. A. W. Greely,* U. S. Army; Rudolph Kauffmann, Managing Editor, Washington *Evening Star;* C. Hart Merriam,* Chief, U. S. Biological Survey; O. H. Tittmann,*

*Founders of the National Geographic Society.

Superintendent, U. S. Coast and Geodetic Survey; and Brig. Gen. John M. Wilson, U. S. Army.

In April of 1907 I filled 24 pages with another series of photographs, "Women and Children of the East," and it made a great hit. The next issue showed immigrants landing in America. Still in the picturesque costumes of their homelands, they looked surprised and a bit apprehensive at the wonder that was New York even then.

During this period American Consul General to Smyrna Ernest L. Harris persuaded me to run three articles by him on buried cities of Asia Minor, illustrated with his own photographs. I was doubtful concerning the reaction of members, but they expressed overwhelming approval, and archeology remains one of our most popular subjects.

First Photographs in Color Published in 1910

The next striking change came when I introduced color photographs. Frank Luther Mott, in Volume IV of his Pulitzer Prize-winning work, *A History of American Magazines,* says color "transformed the GEOGRAPHIC into a kind of periodical never before known."

Our first series of color illustrations, "Scenes in Korea and China," appeared in the November, 1910, issue. Twenty-four pages long, it was the largest collection of photographs ever published in color in a magazine (pages 30-31).

These pictures were contributed by a much-traveled member of the Society, William Wisner Chapin of Rochester, New York. Color film had not yet been perfected, so he took careful notes on costumes and backgrounds and had a Japanese artist color his photographs.

Other color series by Mr. Chapin followed. Since each color page cost four times as much as a black-and-white page to reproduce, I was tempted to print the pictures a few at a time throughout the year to spread the cost. But I decided this would spoil the effect. I always used Mr. Chapin's beautiful photographs as a full series of 16 to 24 pages.

By 1910 income was sufficient for me to start a photographic laboratory. Soon the NATIONAL GEOGRAPHIC began pioneering in the use of color photographs made by the Lumière Autochrome process and later by other processes—Agfacolor, Finlay, Dufay.

All but the Dufay involved the use of heavy, cumbersome glass plates. W. Robert Moore of the Foreign Staff recalls taking 150 pounds of Finlay plates to China in 1931. Camera and holders added another 50 pounds. Mr. Moore led the staff cheering when color film in rolls—the first 35-millimeter Eastman Kodachrome—was introduced in 1936. This easily portable film, with its faster emulsion, permitted our photographers to make dramatic action pictures in color.

At first our large supplement maps were obtained from commercial cartographers, but by 1915 I was able to organize the Society's own Cartographic Department. Through the years this excellent group has produced and distributed millions of 10- and 11-color maps, while winning world renown for the quality of its work.

During World War II a number of the Society's maps were enlarged and reproduced in great quantity by the Armed Forces. Indeed, the Commander in Chief himself, Franklin D. Roosevelt, followed the course of the war on National Geographic maps mounted on rollers in a cabinet just behind his desk.

Renowned dance team, Ted Shawn and Ruth St. Denis pose for the first natural-color series to appear in the magazine, "The Land of the Best," an appreciation of the United States published in April, 1916.

LUMIÈRE AUTOCHROME BY FRANKLIN PRICE KNOTT

KODACHROMES BY LILIAN GROSVENOR JONES (BELOW) AND GILBERT H. GROSVENOR

Cigar-shaped hydrofoil, the HD-4, designed by Alexander Graham Bell and Frederick W. (Casey) Baldwin, roars across Baddeck Bay, Nova Scotia. It achieved a

"I enjoyed a 'flight' in a new hydrofoil ferry, *Arrow of the Sun,"* wrote Dr. Grosvenor in the April, 1957, GEOGRAPHIC. He drove it too, on one of its first crossings from the Italian mainland to Messina, Sicily (right). The sleek vessel awakened memories of the days when he recorded the historic trials of his father-in-law's experimental hydrofoil (top).

GILBERT H. GROSVENOR

world speedboat record of 71 miles an hour in 1919. Twin Liberty aircraft engines powered the five-ton vessel, riding above the waves on thin steel blades.

Shortly after Pearl Harbor, the President had requested a map showing a town near Singapore, then under Japanese attack. I sent it to him, and the next day dispatched the special cabinet to the White House. Within an hour it was behind his desk, and two days later he wrote me his thanks for "one of the most convenient and complete collections that I have ever seen."

At the President's request, we made a duplicate map cabinet, and Mr. Roosevelt gave it to Winston Churchill as a Christmas gift at their conference in Cairo in 1943.

After the war, when Mr. Churchill visited the United States, I wrote and asked him if he would care to return the cabinet to the Society "because of its association with the greatest Englishman and greatest American of our time." I assured him we would replace it with a newer one filled with later maps.

In his graceful reply, Mr. Churchill said he appreciated the Society's desire to preserve this historic cabinet, but added: "I feel, however, that as this was a gift from my true and devoted friend, I wish to keep it with my family possessions. I hope you will understand my sentiments."

Paintings Enhance the Magazine

Planning the contents of each issue held a special fascination for me. With the whole world to choose from, selection was exciting always, never a bore. But perhaps I derived greatest pleasure from bringing our members interesting subjects that were neglected or overlooked by other magazines.

The June, 1913, issue, for example, contained full-color portraits of 50 common birds from paintings by Louis Agassiz Fuertes. My twin brother Edwin had told me that the U. S. Department of Agriculture's edition of 100,000 copies of a circular, *Fifty Common Birds of Farm and Orchard,* had been exhausted in two weeks and that the department was receiving thousands of applications for more, which it could not supply. So I borrowed the color plates and republished the bulletin as an article, of course with credit.

This turned out to be one of the most enduringly popular features ever published in the magazine. Later I engaged Mr. Fuertes and other artists to paint bird portraits for us.

Many of these paintings were assembled in the Society's two-volume *The Book of Birds.* This work proved extremely popular, but I was somewhat mystified when I received an urgent cablegram request for a set from Gen. Dwight D. Eisenhower during World War II.

Of course I forwarded the books at once to the general in North Africa. But not until after the war did he explain the incident to me.

General Eisenhower liked to be on a first-name basis with the military leaders of our Allies, but he had never penetrated the British reserve of Gen. Sir Alan F. Brooke, Chief of the Imperial General Staff. Sir Alan (later Lord Alanbrooke) was an avid bird-watcher and photographer, and one day he confided to General Eisenhower that he had been trying unsuccessfully to obtain our *Book of Birds*.

The general immediately dispatched his cablegram. By obliging Sir Alan, General Eisenhower hoped to make a friend and cement Anglo-American relations.

World's Peoples Shown in Color

Not only birds but the whole range of nature appeared in the growing magazine's increasingly colorful pages—from the ant to the elephant, and from the tiny reef-building coral polyps to the whales.

The GEOGRAPHIC has also presented many penetrating ethnographic studies. Two early articles that set our high standards in this field were Dean C. Worcester's "Non-Christian Peoples of the Philippine Islands," in the November, 1913, issue, and Dr. Edwin A. Grosvenor's memorable "Races of Europe," which filled the December, 1918, issue.

Often the magazine has published definitive articles which have performed a distinct public service. President Woodrow Wilson so appreciated the first flag issue (October, 1917) that he sent me his congratulations "on the thoroughness and intelligence with which the work has been done. It constitutes," he wrote, "a very valuable document indeed."

The second flag issue, in September, 1934, reproduced 808 of the world's flags and emblems, the most comprehensive collection ever published in color. A truly vast undertaking was the publication during World War II of *Insignia and Decorations of the U.S. Armed Forces.*

Looking back over the years, I recall with pride the Society's part in scores of history-making research expeditions. We have enjoyed close associations with such explorers

Sights no Westerner had ever seen came into camera range when scientist-explorer Joseph F. Rock marched two expeditions into the unmapped borderlands of Tibet and China's Yünnan and Szechwan provinces in 1923-24 and 1927-30. Loyal Nashi (opposite) served as one of his guards, "knowing of the danger we would have to incur," said Rock. The party passed unharmed through territory of fierce Tibetan bandits, below with Dr. Rock. He brought back an unparalleled collection of plants and animals.

LUMIÈRE AUTOCHROME (OPPOSITE) AND PHOTOGRAPH (ABOVE) BY JOSEPH F. ROCK, JULY, 1931, GEOGRAPHIC

CHARLES AND ANNE LINDBERGH (ABOVE); WIDE WORLD PHOTOS (OPPOSITE)

WEST INDIAN AERIAL EXPRESS

"The Lone Eagle," Capt. Charles A. Lindbergh won the world's acclaim by flying solo across the Atlantic in 1927. Later he piloted his famous single-seater airplane (above) on a 9,500-mile good-will journey to 13 Latin American countries, and wrote of it in the May, 1928, issue. During a tour of Mexico City (opposite), Lindbergh rides through the canals of Xochimilco with U. S. Ambassador Dwight Morrow, center. In 1929 he married the ambassador's daughter Anne. As copilot and radio operator (top), she flew the Atlantic with her husband in 1933, pioneering commercial air routes, an adventure reported in the September, 1934, GEOGRAPHIC.

as Robert E. Peary, discoverer of the North Pole, and Richard E. Byrd, first to fly over both Poles. During a stratosphere expedition sponsored by the Society and the U. S. Army Air Corps, Albert W. Stevens and Orvil A. Anderson in 1935 soared to 13.71 miles, at that time the highest altitude ever reached by man. With Society grants William Beebe made his deep-sea descent, in 1934, to 3,028 feet—a record that stood for 15 years. Hiram Bingham in 1912 excavated Machu Picchu, the vanished city of the Incas, atop a Peruvian mountain.

Many other famous and distinguished men have contributed personal narratives. Here are the travel observations of former Presidents, foreign statesmen, men of letters, scientists, aviation pioneers.

Long ago I evolved an editorial policy to govern these many and varied contributions. One principle was absolute accuracy. Others required that each article be of permanent value and avoid partisanship and controversy. I also decided that no derogatory material would be printed about any country or people. The GEOGRAPHIC has always dealt in facts, not bias, rumor, or prejudice.

Photo Technicians Trained Abroad

In photography—and particularly in the use of color—we have led the way from the first. Other magazines maintained a stolid indifference to color illustrations for 20 years after the GEOGRAPHIC pioneered in their use.

Perhaps this was due to the difficulty of early color-photo processes. To master each process, the Society sent its technicians to research laboratories in England, France, Germany, and to the Eastman Kodak headquarters in Rochester, New York. As a result, NATIONAL GEOGRAPHIC men have scored many notable firsts in color photography.

The late Charles Martin made the first successful natural-color photographs beneath the sea in 1926 (page 28). He hypersensitized Autochrome plates, then devised a means of lighting the water for a diver with a camera. There were no flash bulbs in those days, so Mr. Martin rigged a raft containing a pound of flash powder. The undersea camera triggered the powder, and a reflector bounced the blinding flash down into the water.

It was extremely dangerous. Premature ignition of a full pound of flash powder would have been as lethal as a bomb.

Four years later, in 1930, Melville Bell

Half a mile down: Scientist-adventurers William Beebe, right, and Otis Barton entered their tiny bathysphere on August 15, 1934, and plunged 3,028 feet, a depth no man had penetrated before. The Society sponsored the deep-sea investigation off Bermuda, and Dr. Beebe told of his journey to "a world almost as unknown as Mars" in the December, 1934, GEOGRAPHIC. In this issue also appeared color reproductions of paintings based on Dr. Beebe's observations of strange fish in the eerie realm.

JOHN TEE-VAN

RICHARD H. STEWART

Thirteen and a half miles up: Pioneers of the Space Age, Capt. Orvil A. Anderson, left, and Capt. Albert W. Stevens rode the gondola of the stratosphere balloon *Explorer II* to 72,395 feet in 1935, a record that stood for 21 years. The Society and the U. S. Army Air Corps sponsored the expedition (page 56). Wearing football helmets borrowed from a high-school squad, the men sealed themselves in the airtight cabin and manned instruments that trapped secrets of the sun, ozone, and cosmic rays. Today the gondola fascinates visitors to Explorers Hall in Society headquarters, Washington, D. C.

Grosvenor made the first published natural-color photographs from the air. An airplane's vibration and speed would have spoiled the pictures, so he flew in dirigibles over Washington, D. C., New York City, and Asbury Park, New Jersey, to make his historic photographs. At his signal the dirigibles cut their engines.

"Frequently the photographic voyages consisted of shadow-chasing," Melville recalls. "Sometimes, after scurrying over Washington at express-train speed, the ship would arrive at the desired spot just in time to have a wisp of cloud form between the scene and the sun."

Presidents Active in Society Affairs

All funds derived from publication of the NATIONAL GEOGRAPHIC go into its work of increasing and diffusing geographic knowledge and improving its facilities. This policy has contributed greatly to the magazine's loyal support by members.

Indeed, the members own the National Geographic Society—an organization that is directed and supervised in their behalf by a Board of Trustees of eminent Americans.

The Nation's highest officials have honored the Society by participation in its affairs. Presidents Theodore Roosevelt, William Howard Taft, Woodrow Wilson, Calvin Coolidge, and Herbert Hoover, and Vice Presidents Charles W. Fairbanks and Lyndon B. Johnson have presented National Geographic Society medals to prominent explorers at meetings of the Society. Coolidge and Hoover, as well as four other Presidents—Franklin D.

"Admiral of the Ends of the Earth," Richard E. Byrd, here with his pet terrier Igloo, made the first flights over the North and South Poles. President Calvin Coolidge (inset) presents the Society's Hubbard Medal to Byrd for his North Pole flight in 1926. Dr. Grosvenor sits at right. The GEOGRAPHIC's map of 1932 reflects Byrd's accomplishments at the South Pole. True to the resolve written to Gilbert Grosvenor on the map, Byrd did more than any one man to fill in the continent's blank spaces.

BYRD ANTARCTIC EXPEDITION (LEFT), AUGUST, 1930, GEOGRAPHIC; INTERNATIONAL NEWSREEL

Dear Bert,

Here is your mountain Range and the Grosvenor [illegible]. With them go my affectionate regard and appreciation and congratulations for producing this splendid map.

Dick Byrd

P.S. I think I'll try to clean up some of these blank spaces.

R.E.B.

An impossible picture in its day—without Kodachrome: Exuberant Austrian folk dancers swirl, as the new fast color film captures the action. Photographer W. Robert Moore recalls the milestone, "With five rolls of the new 35-mm. Eastman film, I took pot shots of dancers, parades, and water sports at the then unbelievable speed of 1/100 of a second. The Editor published 19 frames in April, 1938."

Roosevelt, Harry S Truman, Dwight D. Eisenhower, and John F. Kennedy—have awarded medals in the Society's behalf at special White House functions.

Several of these men participated in the Society's work after their White House tenures. Mr. Taft, my cousin, and Mr. Coolidge, a worthy opponent at handball in our student days at Amherst, served on the Society's Board of Trustees. Both appeared on the Society's lecture program, as did Theodore Roosevelt.

Mr. Taft addressed the Society in Washington no less than ten times. I recall one occasion when he arose, placed his manuscript on the rostrum, and then began a search through his pockets. Finally he began to chuckle, then laugh, and he had a booming laugh in keeping with his formidable size.

"I've lost my spectacles," he announced, "and I can't read my speech. Perhaps someone in the audience might lend me a pair."

With the audience in a merry, uncontrollable uproar, we passed around hats and collected 50 pairs of spectacles. Mr. Taft, still shaking with laughter, tried them on until he found a pair that suited him. The remaining spectacles were claimed by their owners from a table near the speaker's dais. Mr. Taft then held his audience with one of the best lectures I ever heard him give.

In 1910 Theodore Roosevelt thrilled the

KODACHROME BY W. ROBERT MOORE

Faded color marks a transparency from Kodachrome's infancy. Eastman soon perfected permanent dyes. "Thanks to Kodachrome, we could abandon heavy cameras," said Mr. Moore of the GEOGRAPHIC's Foreign Staff. "We became the first magazine to use this color film in quantity."

MAYNARD OWEN WILLIAMS, MACMILLAN ARCTIC EXPEDITION, MARCH, 1926, GEOGRAPHIC

Posing quietly, a Greenland girl defers to Lumière Autochrome, glass plates requiring at least half-second exposures.

Society with an account of his adventures on an African safari. But when he addressed members in 1914 shortly after returning, tired and sick, from explorations in South America, he could scarcely speak. I sat in the front row and could hear only part of what he said. Yet, with the courage so typical of him, he completed his speech—and not a person in the audience of 5,000 left the hall.

President William McKinley, an honorary member of the Society, was one of the first of many notable men Dr. Bell introduced me to. Later it became a tradition among occupants of the White House to attend annual banquets given by the Society for its Washington membership. Our growing roster eventually made such functions impractical, but they were gala news events in their day.

As Trustees, ex-Presidents Taft and Coolidge were no mere honorary figureheads. The National Geographic Society's Board of Trustees has always been a harmonious working group. It is composed of men distinguished for achievement in Government or military service, science, exploration, banking, or industry. These 24 busy men have many demands upon their time, but the average attendance at our Board meetings is gratifyingly high.

To these men, and to the many who preceded them, I am deeply indebted for sage advice and unswerving support. But my debt

NATIONAL GEOGRAPHIC PHOTOGRAPHER B. ANTHONY STEWART

U. S. NAVY, MAY, 1945, GEOGRAPHIC (ABOVE) AND JUNE, 1946, GEOGRAPHIC (BELOW)

Going to war with thc Nation in 1941, the Society assisted the military by supplying geographic facts and maps indispensable to planning. Chief of Staff Gen. Dwight D. Eisenhower, in his postwar Pentagon office, consults the map of Germany that traveled with him during his 1945 offensive.

GEOGRAPHIC articles showed where our men were fighting . . . and the face of victory. Landing craft, below, disgorge supplies for Americans on Normandy's Omaha Beach in June, 1944, just after D-Day.

Cheering Navy pilots celebrate aboard their carrier near the Marshall Islands after downing 17 Japanese Zeros without losing a man.

In a Paris again free, Britain's Prime Minister Winston Churchill, French Gen. Charles de Gaulle, and British Foreign Secretary Anthony Eden review troops on the Champs Elysées, November 11, 1944.

U. S. ARMY SIGNAL CORPS, APRIL, 1945, GEOGRAPHIC

RICHARD H. STEWART, AUGUST, 1939, GEOGRAPHIC

is equally great to the Society's able staff, which has grown from a single employee to nearly two thousand men and women.

My heartfelt gratitude goes, too, to the thousands of persons who have contributed valuable articles and illustrations to the magazine; and to the millions of members who have believed wholeheartedly and enthusiastically in the National Geographic Society's educational purposes and have strengthened the Society by obtaining many new members.

In my own lifetime I have seen a small educational and scientific society grow into a great world force for knowledge and understanding. In the years since I retired, I have rejoiced at the great and continuing progress of the Society under the able leadership of President and Editor Melville Bell Grosvenor, Vice President and Treasurer Robert V. Fleming, Executive Vice Presidents Thomas W. McKnew and Melvin M. Payne, and Associate Editor and Vice President Frederick G.

RICHARD H. STEWART

Probing the past, eight Geographic-Smithsonian Institution expeditions led by Dr. Matthew W. Stirling, now a member of the Society's Research Committee, uncovered stone relics of the 2,500-year-old Olmec civilization in Mexico. Workers at left pry a carved figure from the mud. Thirty-ton basalt head above, largest of 11 found, gets a facial.

Vosburgh. Members numbered 2,041,000 when I left my editorial desk. Within a decade that figure had better than doubled.

As I look back upon the yesteryears, it hardly seems possible that more than half a century has passed since a young schoolteacher took an editor's job that might be "a steppingstone to something better." Each year seems as fleeting as a summer holiday when one is happy and productive.

But not for youth itself would I trade the treasures stored in my memory: the rich experiences of one who roamed always "with a hungry heart," the friendships I have enjoyed with men and women of courage and destiny, and, above all, the immeasurable satisfaction of seeing the National Geographic Society and its magazine surpass my every dream.

This introduction is based on "The Romance of the Geographic" in the October, 1963, issue, by Gilbert Grosvenor, who died in February, 1966.—THE EDITOR

NATIONAL GEOGRAPHIC INDEX 1888-1946 INCLUSIVE

This index covers issues of October, 1888, through December, 1946. Its companion volume begins with the January, 1947, issue, and is brought up to date each year by supplements.

The National Geographic Society publishes semiannually for each six-issue volume of the Magazine a detailed index, available on request to members who bind their copies as works of reference.

A

AAFTTC (Army Air Forces Technical Training Command). *See* Army Air Forces Training Command

ABAIANG (Atoll), Gilbert Islands:

Gilbert Islands in the Wake of Battle. By W. Robert Moore. LXXXVII, pp. 129-162, 11 ills. in black and white, 19 ills. in color, map, Feb., 1945

ABBE, CLEVELAND. *See* NGS: Board of Managers

ABBOT, C. G.:

Do Volcanic Explosions Affect Our Climate? By C. G. Abbot. XXIV, pp. 181-198, 9 ills., diagr., Feb., 1913

Hunting an Observatory: A Successful Search for a Dry Mountain on Which to Establish the National Geographic Society's Solar Radiation Station. By C. G. Abbot. L, pp. 503-518, 13 ills., map, Oct., 1926

Measuring the Sun's Heat and Forecasting the Weather: The National Geographic Society to Maintain a Solar Station in a Remote Part of the World to Coöperate with Smithsonian Institution Stations in California and Chile. By C. G. Abbot. XLIX, pp. 111-126, 15 ills., chart, Jan., 1926

ABBOT, JOHN M.:

The Buried City of Ceylon. By John M. Abbot. XVII, pp. 613-622, 8 ills., Nov., 1906

ABDUL AZIZ AL SAUD (King of Saudi Arabia). *See* Al Saud

ABEMAMA (Atoll), Gilbert Islands:

Gilbert Islands in the Wake of Battle. By W. Robert Moore. LXXXVII, pp. 129-162, 11 ills. in black and white, 19 ills. in color, map, Feb., 1945

The **ABERRATION** of Sound as Illustrated by the Berkeley Powder Explosion. By Robert H. Chapman. VII, pp. 246-249, 3 diagrs., July, 1896

ABOARD a Blimp Hunting U-boats: A Day above the Atlantic Reveals Navy Talk and Navy Ways, Creeping Convoys, and Torpedoed Wrecks. By Mason Sutherland. LXXXIV, pp. 79-96, 18 ills., July, 1943

ABORIGINES:

Earth's Most Primitive People: A Journey with the Aborigines of Central Australia. By Charles P. Mountford. LXXXIX, pp. 89-112, 10 ills. in black and white, 8 ills. in color, map, Jan., 1946

See also Eskimos; Indians of Central America; Indians of North America; Indians of South America; *and* place names

ABRUZZI, DUKE OF THE:

Duke of the Abruzzi in the Himalayas. (By A. W. G.). XXI, pp. 245-249, Mar., 1910

Honors to Peary (Presentation of Hubbard Medal). XVIII, pp. 49-60, ill., Jan., 1907

The Mt. St. Elias Expedition of Prince Luigi Amadeo of Savoy, 1897. (By E. R. S.). IX, pp. 93-96, Mar., 1898

Nansen's "Farthest North" Eclipsed. XI, pp. 411-413, ills., Oct., 1900

Portrait. XI, pl. 10 (front.), Oct., 1900

ABSD (Advanced Base Sectional Dock). *See* Docks

ABYDOS, Egypt:

Excavations at Abydos. (By W. M. Flinders Petrie). XIV, pp. 358-359, Sept., 1903

Reconstructing Egypt's History. By Wallace N. Stearns. XXIV, pp. 1021-1042, 21 ills., Sept., 1913

On the mark, *Explorer II* poises on the floor of the Stratobowl near Rapid City, South Dakota, five minutes before its ascent to record-breaking heights on November 11, 1935. The stratosphere expedition is one of more than a hundred explorations and research projects listed in this index—all sponsored by the National Geographic Society.

MAJOR H. LEE WELLS, JR., JANUARY, 1936, GEOGRAPHIC

ABYDOS, Egypt—*Continued*

The Resurrection of Ancient Egypt. By James Baikie. XXIV, pp. 957-1020, 46 ills., map, Sept., 1913

The Sacred Ibis Cemetery and Jackal Catacombs at Abydos. By Camden M. Cobern. XXIV, pp. 1042-1056, 10 ills., Sept., 1913

ABYSSINIA. *See* Ethiopia

ABYSSINIA—The Country and People. By Oscar T. Crosby. XII, pp. 89-102, Mar., 1901

ACES Among Aces (Aviators). By Laurence La Tourette Driggs. XXXIII, pp. 568-580, 9 ills., June, 1918

ACES of Aviation (Gulls). 16 photos by A. H. Hall. XLVII, pp. 665-672, June, 1925

ACES of the Air. By Captain Jacques De Sieyes. XXXIII, pp. 5-9, ills., Jan., 1918

The **ACORN,** a Possibly Neglected Source of Food. By C. Hart Merriam. XXXIV, pp. 129-137, 8 ills., Aug., 1918

ACROSS French and Spanish Morocco. By Harriet Chalmers Adams. XLVII, pp. 327-356, 19 ills. in black and white, 16 ills. in color, map, Mar., 1925

ACROSS Madagascar by Boat, Auto, Railroad, and Filanzana. By Charles F. Swingle. LVI, pp. 179-211, 42 ills., maps, Aug., 1929

ACROSS Nicaragua with Transit and Machéte. By R. E. Peary. I, pp. 315-335, 3 ills. (tinted), foldout map, Oct., 1889

ACROSS the Equator with the American Navy. By Herbert Corey. XXXIX, pp. 571-624, 53 ills., June, 1921

ACROSS the Gulf by Rail to Key West (Florida). By Jefferson B. Browne. VII, pp. 203-207, June, 1896

ACROSS the Midi in a Canoe: Two Americans Paddle Along the Canals of Southern France from the Atlantic to the Mediterranean. By Melville Chater. LII, pp. 127-167, 49 ills., map, Aug., 1927

ACROSS Tibet from India to China. By Lt. Col. Ilia Tolstoy, AUS. XC, pp. 169-222, 53 ills., map, Aug., 1946

ACROSS Widest Africa (Ethiopia, French Somaliland, and Nuer Country). By A. Henry Savage Landor. XIX, pp. 694-737, 38 ills., map, Oct., 1908

ACTION Photographs of the Balloon's Perfect Landing. 8 ills. in black and white, special photos I-VIII (bet. pp. 84-85). LXIX, Jan., 1936

ADAK (Island), Aleutian Islands:

A Navy Artist Paints the Aleutians. By Mason Sutherland. Paintings by Lt. William F. Draper. LXXXIV, pp. 157-176, 4 ills. in black and white, 16 ills. in color, Aug., 1943

ADALIA, Turkey:

Historic Islands and Shores of the Ægean Sea. By Ernest Lloyd Harris. XXVIII, pp. 231-261, 28 ills., map, Sept., 1915

ADAM, TASSILO:

Java, Queen of the East Indies. 3 color photos by Tassilo Adam. LVI, pp. 335-358, Sept., 1929

ADAMS, CLIFTON:

Arizona: Adventures in Arizona Color Photography. 14 color photos by Clifton Adams. LV, pp. 29-36, Jan., 1929

California: A Sunshine Land of Fruits, Flowers, Movies, and Sport. 41 color photos by Clifton Adams and Fred Payne Clatworthy. LXVI, pp. 545-592, Nov., 1934

Chicago, Titan of the Middle West. 12 color photos by Clifton Adams. LIX, pp. 585-592, May, 1931

England: Cradles of English History. 14 color photos by Clifton Adams. LIX, pp. 269-276, Mar., 1931

England: From Stratford to the North Sea. 16 color photos by Clifton Adams. LV, pp. 617-624, May, 1929

England: Lakeland, Home of England's Nature Poets. 15 color photos by Clifton Adams. LV, pp. 593-600, May, 1929

England: Nooks and Bays of Storied England. 11 color photos by Clifton Adams. LXI, pp. 183-190, Feb., 1932

Florida: High Lights in the Sunshine State. 38 color photos by Clifton Adams. LVII, pp. 27-82, Jan., 1930

Gettysburg: The Most Famous Battle Field in America. 9 color photos by Clifton Adams. LX, pp. 66-75, July, 1931

Haiti: Gay Colors in the Land of Black Majesty. 13 color photos by Clifton Adams. LXVI, pp. 445-452, Oct., 1934

Illinois: Rambles Through the Prairie State. 15 color photos by Clifton Adams. LIX, pp. 545-552, May, 1931

Ireland: The Hills and Dales of Erin. 11 color photos by Clifton Adams. LI, pp. 317-326, Mar., 1927

London: Highlights of London Town. 15 color photos by Clifton Adams. LV, pp. 569-576, May, 1929

Massachusetts: Coasting Through the Bay State. 12 color photos by Clifton Adams. LX, pp. 287-294, Sept., 1931

Mexico: In the Land of the Montezumas. 16 color photos by Clifton Adams. XLIII, pp. 265-280, Mar., 1923

Minnesota: The State of Sky-Blue Water and Verdure. 11 color photos by Clifton Adams and Edwin L. Wisherd. LXVII, pp. 289-296, Mar., 1935

Mount Vernon: The Home of the First Farmer of America. 17 color photos by Clifton Adams. LIII, pp. 605-620, May, 1928

New England's Wonderland of Mountain, Lake, and Seascape. 14 color photos by Clifton Adams. LX, pp. 263-270, Sept., 1931

New York (City): Tempo and Color of a Great City. 42 color photos by Clifton Adams and Edwin L. Wisherd. LVIII, pp. 539-578, Nov., 1930

ADAMS, CLIFTON—*Continued*

New York (State): Color Highlights of the Empire State. 30 color photos by Clifton Adams. LXIV, pp. 529-576, Nov., 1933

Philadelphia: Colorful Corners of the City of Homes. 13 color photos by Clifton Adams and Edwin L. Wisherd. LXII, pp. 675-682, Dec., 1932

Rhode Island: Sauntering Through the Land of Roger Williams. 14 color photos by Clifton Adams. LX, pp. 311-318, Sept., 1931

Sardinia: Sardinian Smiles. 16 color photos by Clifton Adams. XLIII, pp. 31-46, Jan., 1923

Vermont: The Green Mountain State. 6 color photos by Clifton Adams. LI, pp. 327-332, Mar., 1927

Virginia: Scenes and Shrines of the Cavalier Country. 3 color photos by Clifton Adams. LV, pp. 425-432, Apr., 1929

Washington (State): Sunset Hues in the Pacific Northwest. 8 color photos by Clifton Adams. LXIII, pp. 155-162, Feb., 1933

Washington (State): Where the Last of the West Was Won. 4 color photos by Clifton Adams. LXIII, pp. 179-186, Feb., 1933

Washington, D. C.: Our Colorful City of Magnificent Distances. 17 color photos by Clifton Adams. LX, pp. 531-610, Nov., 1931

Washington, D. C.: Secrets of Washington's Lure. 15 color photos: 2 by Clifton Adams. LVII, pp. 377-384, Mar., 1930

Washington, D. C.: Unique Gifts of Washington to the Nation. 2 color photos by Clifton Adams. LV, pp. 473-480, Apr., 1929

ADAMS, CYRUS C.:

"The United States—Land and Waters." By Cyrus C. Adams. XIV, pp. 171-185, 8 ills., map, May, 1903

ADAMS, HARRIET CHALMERS:

Across French and Spanish Morocco. By Harriet Chalmers Adams. XLVII, pp. 327-356, 19 ills. in black and white, 16 ills. in color, map, Mar., 1925

Adventurous Sons of Cádiz (Spain). By Harriet Chalmers Adams. XLVI, pp. 153-204, 37 ills. in black and white, 26 ills. in color, Aug., 1924

Along the Old Inca Highway (Peru). By Harriet Chalmers Adams. XIX, pp. 231-250, 21 ills., Apr., 1908

An Altitudinal Journey Through Portugal: Rugged Scenic Beauty, Colorful Costumes, and Ancient Castles Abound in Tiny Nation That Once Ruled a Vast Empire. By Harriet Chalmers Adams. LII, pp. 567-610, 44 ills., map, Nov., 1927

Barcelona, Pride of the Catalans. By Harriet Chalmers Adams. LV, pp. 373-402, 32 ills., Mar., 1929

Cirenaica, Eastern Wing of Italian Libia. By Harriet Chalmers Adams. LVII, pp. 689-726, 35 ills. in black and white, 13 ills. in color, map, June, 1930

Cuzco, America's Ancient Mecca. By Harriet Chalmers Adams. XIX, pp. 669-689, 19 ills., Oct., 1908

ADAMS, HARRIET CHALMERS—*Continued*

The East Indians in the New World (Trinidad). By Harriet Chalmers Adams. XVIII, pp. 485-491, 6 ills., July, 1907

European Outpost: The Azores. By Harriet Chalmers Adams. LXVII, pp. 35-66, 25 ills. in black and white, 13 ills. in color, map, Jan., 1935

The First Transandine Railroad from Buenos Aires to Valparaiso. By Harriet Chalmers Adams. XXI, pp. 397-417, 14 ills., diagr., map, May, 1910

The Grand Canyon Bridge. By Harriet Chalmers Adams. XXXIX, pp. 645-650, 6 ills., June, 1921

In French Lorraine: That Part of France Where the First American Soldiers Have Fallen. By Harriet Chalmers Adams. XXXII, pp. 499-518, 16 ills., Nov.-Dec., 1917

Kaleidoscopic La Paz: The City of the Clouds. By Harriet Chalmers Adams. XX, pp. 119-141, 23 ills., Feb., 1909

A Longitudinal Journey Through Chile. By Harriet Chalmers Adams. XLII, pp. 219-273, 60 ills., map, Sept., 1922

Madeira the Florescent. By Harriet Chalmers Adams. LXVI, pp. 81-106, 19 ills. in black and white, 13 ills. in color, map, July, 1934

Madrid Out-of-Doors. By Harriet Chalmers Adams. LX, pp. 225-256, 35 ills., Aug., 1931

Picturesque Paramaribo (Surinam). By Harriet Chalmers Adams. XVIII, pp. 365-373, 7 ills., June, 1907

Rio de Janeiro, in the Land of Lure. By Harriet Chalmers Adams. XXXVIII, pp. 165-210, 39 ills., map, Sept., 1920

River-Encircled Paraguay. By Harriet Chalmers Adams. LXIII, pp. 385-416, 35 ills., map, Apr., 1933

Some Wonderful Sights in the Andean Highlands: The Oldest City in America. Sailing on the Lake of the Clouds: The Yosemite of Peru. By Harriet Chalmers Adams. XIX, pp. 597-618, 19 ills., map, Sept., 1908

Volcano-Girded Salvador: A Prosperous Central American State with the Densest Rural Population in the Western World. By Harriet Chalmers Adams. XLI, pp. 189-200, 10 ills., Feb., 1922

ADAMS, M. P. GREENWOOD:

Australia's Wild Wonderland. By M. P. Greenwood Adams. XLV, pp. 329-356, 36 ills., map, Mar., 1924

ADAMS, Mount, Washington:

The Altitude of Mount Adams, Washington. By Edgar McClure. VII, pp. 151-153, tables, Apr., 1896

ADAMS (Schooner):

Capturing Giant Turtles in the Caribbean. By David D. Duncan. LXXXIV, pp. 177-190, 13 ills., map, Aug., 1943

ADAM'S Second Eden (Ceylon). By Eliza Ruhamah Scidmore. XXIII, pp. 105-173, 206, 61 ills., Feb., 1912

ADDIS ABABA, Ethiopia:

Coronation Days in Addis Ababa. By W. Robert Moore. LIX, pp. 738-746, 8 ills., June, 1931

Present Day Scenes in the World's Oldest Empire. 27 color photos by W. Robert Moore. LIX, pp. 691-722, June, 1931

ADDRESS by Commander Robert E. Peary, U.S.N., On the Assembling of the Congress in Washington, September 8, 1904. XV, pp. 387-392, Oct., 1904

ADDRESS of the President of the Board of Managers, June 1, 1900. (By Alexander Graham Bell). XI, pp. 401-408, chart, Oct., 1900

ADELAIDE, Australia:

Capital Cities of Australia. By W. Robert Moore. LXVIII, pp. 667-722, 32 ills. in black and white, 24 ills. in color, two-page map, Dec., 1935

Lonely Australia: The Unique Continent. By Herbert E. Gregory. XXX, pp. 473-568, 68 ills., 5 maps (1 two-page), Dec., 1916

ADELAIDE UNIVERSITY: Expeditions:

Earth's Most Primitive People: A Journey with the Aborigines of Central Australia. By Charles P. Mountford. LXXXIX, pp. 89-112, 10 ills. in black and white, 8 ills. in color, map, Jan., 1946

ADÉLIE PENGUINS:

Antarctica's Most Interesting Citizen: The Comical Penguin Is Both Romantic and Bellicose. By Worth E. Shoults. LXI, pp. 251-260, 8 ills., Feb., 1932

ADEN, Arabian Peninsula:

"The Flower of Paradise": The Part Which Khat Plays in the Life of the Yemen Arab. By Charles Moser. XXXII, pp. 173-186, 10 ills., map, Aug., 1917

The Rock of Aden: The Volcanic Mountain Fortress, on the Sea Route from Suez to India, Assumes New Importance. By H. G. C. Swayne. LXVIII, pp. 723-742, 24 ills., map, Dec., 1935

ADIRONDACK Idyls. 10 color photos by Harrison Howell Walker. LXXIII, pp. 729-736, June, 1938

ADIRONDACK MOUNTAINS, New York:

New York State's Air-Conditioned Roof. By Frederick G. Vosburgh. LXXIII, pp. 715-748, 23 ills. in black and white, 10 ills. in color, map, June, 1938

ADMIRAL Byrd Receives New Honor From The Society. LVIII, pp. 228-238, 4 ills., Aug., 1930

ADMIRAL R. W. Meade, U. S. N. (Obituary). VIII, p. 142, May, 1897

ADOLPHUS FREDERICK, DUKE OF MECKLENBURG:

A Land of Giants and Pygmies (Ruanda). By the Duke Adolphus Frederick of Mecklenburg. XXIII, pp. 369-388, 16 ills., map, Apr., 1912

ADVANCED BASE SECTIONAL DOCK. *See* Docks

ADVANCES in Geographic Knowledge During the Nineteenth Century. By Brig.-Gen. A. W. Greely. XII, pp. 143-152, maps, Apr., 1901

ADVENTURE (Ship):

The Columbus of the Pacific: Captain James Cook, Foremost British Navigator, Expanded the Great Sea to Correct Proportions and Won for Albion an Insular Empire by Peaceful Exploration and Scientific Study. By J. R. Hildebrand. LI, pp. 85-132, 45 ills., maps, Jan., 1927

ADVENTURES Among the "Lost Tribes of Islam" in Eastern Darfur: A Personal Narrative of Exploring, Mapping, and Setting up a Government in the Anglo-Egyptian Sudan Borderland. By Major Edward Keith-Roach. XLV, pp. 41-73, 32 ills., map, Jan., 1924

ADVENTURES in Arizona Color Photography. 14 color photos by Clifton Adams. LV, pp. 29-36, Jan., 1929

ADVENTURES in Color on Mexico's West Coast. 13 color photos by Fred Payne Clatworthy. LVIII, pp. 61-68, July, 1930

ADVENTURES with a Camera in Many Lands. By Maynard Owen Williams. XL, pp. 87-112, 24 ills., July, 1921

ADVENTURES with Birds of Prey. By Frank and John Craighead. LXXII, pp. 109-134, 25 ills., July, 1937

ADVENTURING Down the West Coast of Mexico. By Herbert Corey. XLII, pp. 449-503, 44 ills., map, Nov., 1922

ADVENTUROUS Sons of Cádiz (Spain). By Harriet Chalmers Adams. XLVI, pp. 153-204, 37 ills. in black and white, 26 ills. in color, Aug., 1924

AEGEAN REGIONS:

Asia Minor in the Time of the Seven Wise Men. By Mary Mills Patrick. XXXVII, pp. 47-67, 19 ills., Jan., 1920

Greece—the Birthplace of Science and Free Speech: Explorations on the Mainland and in Crete and the Aegean Isles Reveal Ancient Life Similar to That of the Present. By Richard Stillwell. Paintings by H. M. Herget. LXXXV, pp. 273-353, 13 ills. in black and white, 32 ills. in color, two-page map, Mar., 1944

Historic Islands and Shores of the Ægean Sea. By Ernest Lloyd Harris. XXVIII, pp. 231-261, 28 ills., map, Sept., 1915

The Isles of Greece. By Lt. Richard Stillwell, USNR. LXXXV, pp. 593-622, 11 ills. in black and white, 20 ills. in color, map, May, 1944

Modern Odyssey in Classic Lands: Troy's Treasures, Athens' Parthenon, and Rome's First "Broad Way" Influence Today's Banks, Costumes, Jewelry, and Railroad Timetables. By Maynard Owen Williams. LXXVII, pp. 291-337, 27 ills. in black and white, 22 ills. in color, Mar., 1940

Rhodes, and Italy's Aegean Islands. By Dorothy Hosmer. LXXIX, pp. 449-480, 32 ills., map, Apr., 1941

Santorin and Mýkonos, Aegean Gems. 8 color photos: 7 by B. Anthony Stewart. LXXVII, pp. 339-346, Mar., 1940

AEGEAN REGIONS—*Continued*

Seeing 3,000 Years of History in Four Hours: A Panorama of Ancient, Medieval, and Modern Events Against a Background of Mythology Unfolds During an Airplane Journey from Constantinople to Athens. By Maynard Owen Williams. LIV, pp. 719-739, 24 ills., map, Dec., 1928

See also Greece

AERIAL Color Photography Becomes a War Weapon. By H. H. Arnold. LXXVII, pp. 757-766, 8 ills. in color, June, 1940

The **AËRIAL** Conquest of Everest: Flying Over the World's Highest Mountain Realizes the Objective of Many Heroic Explorers. By Lieut. Col. L. V. S. Blacker. LXIV, pp. 127-162, 35 ills., map, Aug., 1933

The **AERIAL** Invasion of Burma. By General H. H. Arnold. LXXXVI, pp. 129-148, 20 ills., Aug., 1944

AËRIAL Locomotion: With a Few Notes of Progress in the Construction of an Aërodrome. By Alexander Graham Bell. XVIII, pp. 1-34, 33 ills., Jan., 1907

AEROGRAPHY:

New Frontier in the Sky. By F. Barrows Colton. XC, pp. 379-408, 28 ills., diagr., Sept., 1946

AERONAUTICS:

Aboard a Blimp Hunting U-boats: A Day above the Atlantic Reveals Navy Talk and Navy Ways, Creeping Convoys, and Torpedoed Wrecks. By Mason Sutherland. LXXXIV, pp. 79-96, 18 ills., July, 1943

Aces Among Aces. By Laurence La Tourette Driggs. XXXIII, pp. 568-580, 9 ills., June, 1918

Aces of the Air. By Captain Jacques De Sieyes. XXXIII, pp. 5-9, ills., Jan., 1918

Admiral Byrd Receives New Honor From The Society. LVIII, pp. 228-238, 4 ills., Aug., 1930

The Aërial Conquest of Everest: Flying Over the World's Highest Mountain Realizes the Objective of Many Heroic Explorers. By Lieut. Col. L. V. S. Blacker. LXIV, pp. 127-162, 35 ills., map, Aug., 1933

The Aerial Invasion of Burma. By General H. H. Arnold. LXXXVI, pp. 129-148, 20 ills., Aug., 1944

Aërial Locomotion. By Alexander Graham Bell. XVIII, pp. 1-34, 33 ills., Jan., 1907

Air Adventures in Peru: Cruising Among Andean Peaks, Pilots and Cameramen Discover Wondrous Works of an Ancient People. By Robert Shippee. LXIII, pp. 81-120, 40 ills., map, Jan., 1933

Air Conquest: From the Early Days of Giant Kites and Birdlike Gliders, the National Geographic Society Has Aided and Encouraged the Growth of Aviation. LII, pp. 233-242, 13 ills., Aug., 1927

Air Power for Peace. By General H. H. Arnold. LXXXIX, pp. 137-193, 35 ills. in black and white, 28 ills. in color, map supplement, Feb., 1946

AERONAUTICS—*Continued*

America From the Air: No Such Series of Airplane Views Has Ever Before Been Printed. Photos by Lieutenant A. W. Stevens. XLVI, pp. 85-92, 8 ills., July, 1924

America in the Air: The Future of Airplane and Airship, Economically and as Factors in National Defense. By Brigadier-General William Mitchell. XXXIX, pp. 339-352, 8 ills., map, Mar., 1921

American Bombers Attacking from Australia. By Howell Walker. LXXXIII, pp. 49-70, 19 ills., map, Jan., 1943

American Wings Soar Around the World: Epic Story of the Air Transport Command of the U. S. Army Is a Saga of Yankee Daring and Doing. By Donald H. Agnew and William A. Kinney. LXXXIV, pp. 57-78, 22 ills., July, 1943

America's Part in the Allies' Mastery of the Air. By Major Joseph Tulasne. XXXIII, pp. 1-5, ills., Jan., 1918

The Arctic as an Air Route of the Future. By Vilhjalmur Stefansson. XLII, pp. 205-218, 8 ills., map, Aug., 1922

Aviation in Commerce and Defense. By F. Barrows Colton. LXXVIII, pp. 685-726, 39 ills., Dec., 1940

The Azores: Picturesque and Historic Half-way House of American Transatlantic Aviators. By Arminius T. Haeberle. XXXV, pp. 514-545, 26 ills., map, June, 1919

Ballooning in the Stratosphere: Two Balloon Ascents to Ten-Mile Altitudes Presage New Mode of Aërial Travel. By Auguste Piccard. LXIII, pp. 353-384, 34 ills., Mar., 1933

Building America's Air Army. By Hiram Bingham. XXXIII, pp. 48-86, 43 ills., Jan., 1918

By Seaplane to Six Continents: Cruising 60,000 Miles, Italian Argonauts of the Air See World Geography Unroll, and Break New Sky Trails Over Vast Brazilian Jungles. By Commander Francesco de Pinedo. LIV, pp. 247-301, 60 ills., two-page map, Sept., 1928

Canada from the Air: Flights Aggregating 10,000 Miles Reveal the Marvelous Scenic Beauties and Amazing Natural Resources of the Dominion. By J. A. Wilson. L, pp. 389-466, 76 ills., map, Oct., 1926

The Charm of Cape Breton Island: The Most Picturesque Portion of Canada's Maritime Provinces—A Land Rich in Historic Associations, Natural Resources, and Geographic Appeal. By Catherine Dunlop Mackenzie. XXXVIII, pp. 34-60, 22 ills., map, July, 1920

Included: Alexander Graham Bell's kites

Commander Byrd Receives the Hubbard Gold Medal: The First Explorer to Reach the North Pole by Air Receives Coveted Honor at Brilliant National Geographic Society Reception. L, pp. 377-388, 5 ills., chart, Sept., 1926

The Conquest of Antarctica by Air. By Richard Evelyn Byrd. LVIII, pp. 127-227, 71 ills. in black and white, 16 ills. in gravure, map, Aug., 1930

Cruise on an Escort Carrier. By Melville Bell Grosvenor. LXXXIV, pp. 513-546, 14 ills. in black and white, 20 ills. in color, Nov., 1943

Dr. Bell's Man-Lifting Kite. By Gilbert H. Grosvenor. XIX, pp. 35-52, 27 ills., Jan., 1908

AERONAUTICS—*Continued*

8th Air Force in England. 10 ills. in color from U. S. Army Air Forces official photos. LXXXVII, pp. 297-304, Mar., 1945

Exploring the Earth's Stratosphere: The Holder of the American Altitude Record Describes His Experiences in Reaching the "Ceiling" of His Plane at an Elevation of Nearly Eight Miles. By First Lieutenant John A. Macready. L, pp. 755-776, 18 ills., Dec., 1926

Exploring the Stratosphere. By Captain Albert W. Stevens. LXVI, pp. 397-434, 43 ills., chart, Oct., 1934

Exploring the Valley of the Amazon in a Hydroplane: Twelve Thousand Miles of Flying Over the World's Greatest River and Greatest Forest to Chart the Unknown Parima River from the Sky. By Captain Albert W. Stevens. XLIX, pp. 353-420, 86 ills., map, Apr., 1926

Fighting Insects with Airplanes: An Account of the Successful Use of the Flying-Machine in Dusting Tall Trees Infested with Leaf-Eating Caterpillars. By C. R. Neillie and J. S. Houser. XLI, pp. 333-338, 6 ills., Mar., 1922

The First Airship Flight Around the World: Dr. Hugo Eckener Tells of an Epochal Geographic Achievement upon the Occasion of the Bestowal of the National Geographic Society's Special Gold Medal. LVII, pp. 653-688, 37 ills., June, 1930

The First Alaskan Air Expedition. By Captain St. Clair Streett. XLI, pp. 499-552, 37 ills., map, May, 1922

The First Flight to the North Pole. By Lieutenant Commander Richard Evelyn Byrd. L, pp. 357-376, 14 ills., Sept., 1926

First natural-color photograph taken in the stratosphere. By Major Albert W. Stevens. LXXI, ill. p. 340, Mar., 1937

Flights from Arctic to Equator: Conquering the Alps, the Ice Peaks of Spitsbergen, of Persia, and Africa's Mountains of the Moon. By Walter Mittelholzer. LXI, pp. 445-498, 53 ills., map, Apr., 1932

Flying. By Gilbert Grosvenor. LXIII, pp. 585-630, 33 ills. in black and white, 17 ills. in duotone, May, 1933

Flying Around the North Atlantic. By Anne Morrow Lindbergh. Foreword by Charles A. Lindbergh. LXVI, pp. 259-337, 82 ills., maps (1 two-page), Sept., 1934

Flying in France. By Captain André de Berroeta. XXXIII, pp. 9-26, 12 ills., Jan., 1918

Flying Our Wounded Veterans Home. By Catherine Bell Palmer. LXXXVIII, pp. 363-384, 17 ills., Sept., 1945

Flying Over Egypt, Sinai, and Palestine: Looking Down Upon the Holy Land During an Air Journey of Two and a Half Hours from Cairo to Jerusalem. By Brigadier General P. R. C. Groves and Major J. R. McCrindle. L, pp. 313-355, 26 ills. in black and white, 23 ills. in color, map, Sept., 1926

Flying Over the Arctic. By Lieutenant Commander Richard E. Byrd. XLVIII, pp. 519-532, 10 ills., Nov., 1925

Flying the "Hump" of the Andes. By Capt. Albert W. Stevens. LIX, pp. 595-636, 36 ills., map, May, 1931

AERONAUTICS—*Continued*

Flying the Pacific. By William Burke Miller. LXX, pp. 665-707, 39 ills., Dec., 1936

Flying the World: In a Homemade Airplane the Author and Her Husband Enjoy 16,000 Miles of Adventurous Flight Across Europe, Asia, and America. By Gladys M. Day. LXI, pp. 655-690, 41 ills., map, June, 1932

Flying the World's Longest Air-Mail Route: From Montevideo, Uruguay, Over the Andes, Up the Pacific Coast, Across Central America and the Caribbean to Miami, Florida, in 67 Thrilling Flying Hours. By Junius B. Wood. LVII, pp. 261-325, 65 ills., map, Mar., 1930

Four Thousand Hours Over China. By Capt. Hans Koester. LXXIII, pp. 571-598, 25 ills., map, May, 1938

From London to Australia by Aëroplane: A Personal Narrative of the First Aërial Voyage Half Around the World. By Sir Ross Smith. XXXIX, pp. 229-339, 76 ills. in black and white, 8 ills. in color, map, Mar., 1921

The Future of the Airplane. By Rear Admiral Robert E. Peary. XXXIII, pp. 107-113, 4 ills., Jan., 1918

Gentlemen Adventurers of the Air: Many Regions of Canada's Vast Wilderness, Long Hidden Even from Fur Trappers, Are Now Revealed by Exploring Airmen. By J. A. Wilson. LVI, pp. 597-642, 55 ills., map, Nov., 1929

Germany's Air Program. XXXIII, p. 114, Jan., 1918

Gliders—Silent Weapons of the Sky. By William H. Nicholas. LXXXVI, pp. 149-160, 8 ills., Aug., 1944

Helium, the New Balloon Gas. By G. Sherburne Rogers. XXXV, pp. 441-456, 11 ills., May, 1919

How Latin America Looks from the Air: U. S. Army Airplanes Hurdle the High Andes, Brave Brazil Jungles, and Follow Smoking Volcanoes to Map New Sky Paths Around South America. By Major Herbert A. Dargue. LII, pp. 451-502, 52 ills., map, Oct., 1927

How the United States Grew. By McFall Kerbey. LXIII, pp. 631-649, 17 ills., map, May, 1933

In Honor of the Army and Aviation (National Geographic Society Banquet). XXII, pp. 267-284, 5 ills., Mar., 1911

Into Primeval Papua by Seaplane: Seeking Disease-resisting Sugar Cane, Scientists Find Neolithic Man in Unmapped Nooks of Sorcery and Cannibalism. By E. W. Brandes. LVI, pp. 253-332, 98 ills., map, Sept., 1929

Italy's Eagles of Combat and Defense: Heroic Achievements of Aviators Above the Adriatic, the Apennines and the Alps. By General P. Tozzi. XXXIII, pp. 38-47, 8 ills., Jan., 1918

The Life Story of an American Airman in France: Extracts from the Letters of Stuart Walcott, Who, Between July and December, 1917, Learned to Fly in French Schools of Aviation, Won Fame at the Front, and Fell Near Saint Souplet. XXXIII, pp. 86-106, 9 ills., Jan., 1918

Looking Down on Europe: The Thrills and Advantages of Sight-seeing by Airplane, as Demonstrated on a 6,500-mile Tour Over Commercial Aviation Routes. By Lieutenant J. Parker Van Zandt. XLVII, pp. 261-326, 67 ills., map, Mar., 1925

AERONAUTICS—*Continued*

Looking Down on Europe Again: Crisscrossing Air Tracks Reveal Nature's Scenic Masterpieces and Man's Swift-changing Boundaries and Structures. By J. Parker Van Zandt. LXXV, pp. 791-822, 31 ills., map, June, 1939

The MacMillan Arctic Expedition Returns: U. S. Navy Planes Make First Series of Overland Flights in the Arctic and National Geographic Society Staff Obtains Valuable Data and Specimens for Scientific Study. By Donald B. MacMillan. XLVIII, pp. 477-518, 42 ills., Nov., 1925

Man's Amazing Progress in Conquering the Air. By J. R. Hildebrand. XLVI, pp. 93-122, 28 ills., diagr., July, 1924

Man's Farthest Aloft: Rising to 13.71 Miles, the National Geographic Society–U. S. Army Stratosphere Expedition Gathers Scientific Data at Record Altitude. By Capt. Albert W. Stevens. Action Photographs of the Balloon's Perfect Landing, included. LXIX, pp. 59-94, 39 ills., map, Jan., 1936

Mapping the Antarctic from the Air: The Aërial Camera Earns Its Place as the Eyes and Memory of the Explorer. By Capt. Ashley C. McKinley. LXII, pp. 471-485, 13 ills., map supplement, Oct., 1932

Men-Birds Soar on Boiling Air. By Frederick G. Vosburgh. LXXIV, pp. 123-140, 15 ills., July, 1938

My Flight Across Antarctica. By Lincoln Ellsworth. LXX, pp. 1-35, 37 ills., map, July, 1936

My Flight from Hawaii. By Amelia Earhart. LXVII, pp. 593-609, 4 ills. in black and white, 8 ills. in duotone, May, 1935

My Four Antarctic Expeditions: Explorations of 1933-1939 Have Stricken Vast Areas from the Realm of the Unknown. By Lincoln Ellsworth. LXXVI, pp. 129-138, 9 ills., map, July, 1939

National Geographic Society–U. S. Army Air Corps Stratosphere Flight of 1935 in Balloon *Explorer II* (Contributed Technical Papers, *Stratosphere Series No. 2*). LXXI, p. 340, Mar., 1937; p. 802, June, 1937

Navigating the "Norge" (Airship) from Rome to the North Pole and Beyond: The Designer and Pilot of the First Dirigible to Fly Over the Top of the World Describes a Thrilling Voyage of More Than 8,000 Miles. By General Umberto Nobile. LII, pp. 177-215, 36 ills., map, Aug., 1927

Navy Wings over the Pacific. 12 ills. in color from U. S. Navy official photos. LXXXVI, pp. 241-248, Aug., 1944

New Frontier in the Sky. By F. Barrows Colton. XC, pp. 379-408, 28 ills., diagr., Sept., 1946

The New Queen of the Seas (Aircraft Carrier). By Melville Bell Grosvenor. LXXXII, pp. 1-30, 27 ills., drawing, two-page map, July, 1942

The Non-Stop Flight Across America. By Lieutenant John A. Macready. Photos by Lieutenant Albert W. Stevens. XLVI, pp. 1-83, 68 ills., maps, July, 1924

On the Trail of the Air Mail: A Narrative of the Experiences of the Flying Couriers Who Relay the Mail Across America at a Speed of More than 2,000 Miles a Day. By Lieut. J. Parker Van Zandt. XLIX, pp. 1-61, 67 ills., map, Jan., 1926

AERONAUTICS—*Continued*

On the Wings of the Wind: In Motorless Planes, Pilots Ride in Flying-Fox Fashion, Cruising on Upward Air Streams and Lifted by the Suction of Moving Clouds. By Howard Siepen. LV, pp. 751-780, 40 ills., June, 1929

Our Conquest of the Pacific: The Narrative of the 7,400-Mile Flight from San Francisco to Brisbane in Three Ocean Hops. By Squadron-Leader Charles E. Kingsford-Smith and Flight-Lieut. Charles T. P. Ulm. LIV, pp. 371-402, 27 ills., map, Oct., 1928

Our Search for the Lost Aviators: An Arctic Area Larger Than Montana First Explored in Hunt for Missing Russians. By Sir Hubert Wilkins. LXXIV, pp. 141-172, 29 ills., two-page map, Aug., 1938

Our Transatlantic Flight. By Commander Richard Evelyn Byrd. LII, pp. 347-368, 17 ills., map, Sept., 1927

Over the Roof of Our Continent (Mount McKinley). By Bradford Washburn. LXXIV, pp. 78-98, 17 ills. in duotone, map, July, 1938

Painting History in the Pacific. 19 ills. in color from paintings by Lt. William F. Draper, USNR. LXXXVI, pp. 408-424, Oct., 1944

Photographing the Eclipse of 1932 from the Air: From Five Miles Above the Earth's Surface, the National Geographic Society–Army Air Corps Survey Obtains Successful Photographs of the Moon's Shadow. By Capt. Albert W. Stevens. LXII, pp. 581-596, 18 ills., Nov., 1932

The Polar Airship. By Walter Wellman. XVII, pp. 208-228, 5 diagrs., Apr., 1906

President Coolidge Bestows Lindbergh Award: The National Geographic Society's Hubbard Medal Is Presented to Aviator Before the Most Notable Gathering in the History of Washington. LIII, pp. 132-140, 4 ills., Jan., 1928

Remarkable Photograph of Lilienthal's Gliding Machine. By R. W. Wood. XIX, p. 596, ill., Aug., 1908. XXII, ill. p. 271, Mar., 1911. LII, ill. p. 235, Aug., 1927

A Report of the Second Stratosphere Expedition. LXVIII, pp. 535-536, Oct., 1935

Return to Florence (Italy). By 1st Lt. Benjamin C. McCartney. LXXXVII, pp. 257-296, 18 ills. in black and white, 18 ills. in color, Mar., 1945

Seeing America from the "Shenandoah": An Account of the Record-making 9,000-mile Flight from the Atlantic to the Pacific Coast and Return in the Navy's American-built, American-manned Airship. By Junius B. Wood. XLVII, pp. 1-47, 39 ills., diagr., map, Jan., 1925

Seeing America with Lindbergh: The Record of a Tour of More Than 20,000 Miles by Airplane Through Forty-eight States on Schedule Time. By Lieutenant Donald E. Keyhoe. LIII, pp. 1-46, 46 ills., map, Jan., 1928

Seeing the World from the Air. By Sir Alan J. Cobham. LIII, pp. 349-384, 37 ills., map, Mar., 1928

Seeing 3,000 Years of History in Four Hours: A Panorama of Ancient, Medieval, and Modern Events Against a Background of Mythology Unfolds During an Airplane Journey from Constantinople to Athens. By Maynard Owen Williams. LIV, pp. 719-739, 24 ills., map, Dec., 1928

AERONAUTICS—*Continued*

Skypaths Through Latin America: Flying From Our Nation's Capital Southward Over Jungles, Remote Islands, and Great Cities on an Aërial Survey of the East Coast of South America. By Frederick Simpich. LIX, pp. 1-79, 77 ills., map, Jan., 1931

The Society Announces New Flight into the Stratosphere. By Gilbert Grosvenor. LXVII, pp. 265-272, ills., map, Feb., 1935

The Society Awards Hubbard Medal to Anne Morrow Lindbergh. LXV, pp. 791-794, 4 ills., June, 1934

The Society's Special Medal Awarded to Amelia Earhart: First Woman to Receive Geographic Distinction at Brilliant Ceremony in the National Capital. LXII, pp. 358-367, 7 ills., Sept., 1932

Studies Planned for New Stratosphere Flight with Helium. LXVII, pp. 795-800, 5 ills., June, 1935

Take-off for Japan. 22 ills. in color from U. S. Navy official photos. LXXXVIII, pp. 193-208, Aug., 1945

Tales of the British Air Service. By Major William A. Bishop. XXXIII, pp. 27-37, 12 ills., Jan., 1918

The Tetrahedral Kite. XIV, p. 294, ill., July, 1903

The Tetrahedral Principle in Kite Structure. By Alexander Graham Bell. XIV, pp. 219-251, 79 ills., 15 diagrs., June, 1903

They Sustain the Wings (Ground Crews). By Frederick Simpich. LXXXIV, pp. 333-354, 19 ills., Sept., 1943

Through Pathless Skies to the North Pole (Commander Byrd's Flight). Reproduction in color of the painting by N. C. Wyeth, National Geographic Society, Washington, D. C. LIII, supplement, May, 1928

To Bogotá and Back by Air: The Narrative of a 9,500-Mile Flight from Washington, Over Thirteen Latin-American Countries and Return, in the Single-Seater Airplane "Spirit of St. Louis." By Col. Charles A. Lindbergh. LIII, pp. 529-601, 98 ills., map, May, 1928

To Seek the Unknown in the Arctic: United States Navy Flyers to Aid MacMillan Expedition Under the Auspices of the National Geographic Society in Exploring Vast Area. XLVII, pp. 673-675, ill., map, June, 1925

The Unexplored Philippines from the Air: Mapmaking Over Jungle Lands Never Before Seen By White Men. By Lieut. George W. Goddard. LVIII, pp. 311-343, 38 ills., map, Sept., 1930

Unknown New Guinea: Circumnavigating the World in a Flying Boat, American Scientists Discover a Valley of 60,000 People Never Before Seen by White Men. By Richard Archbold. LXXIX, pp. 315-344, 28 ills., map, Mar., 1941

Walter Wellman's Expedition to the North Pole. XVII, pp. 205-207, chart, Apr., 1906

World's Largest Free Balloon to Explore Stratosphere. LXVI, pp. 107-110, ills., July, 1934

Your Navy as Peace Insurance. By Fleet Admiral Chester W. Nimitz. LXXXIX, pp. 681-736, 32 ills. in black and white, 26 ills. in color, June, 1946

AERONAUTICS—*Continued*

Your New World of Tomorrow. By F. Barrows Colton. LXXXVIII, pp. 385-410, 25 ills., Oct., 1945

Your Society Sponsors an Expedition to Explore the Stratosphere. LXV, pp. 528-530, ill., Apr., 1934

See also Balloons; *and* NGS: Aeronautics

AFGHANISTAN:

The Afghan Borderland. By Ellsworth Huntington. Part I: The Russian Frontier. XX, pp. 788-799, 14 ills., Sept., 1909. Part II: The Persian Frontier. XX, pp. 866-876, 12 ills., Oct., 1909

Afghanistan Makes Haste Slowly. By Maynard Owen Williams. LXIV, pp. 731-769, 33 ills. in black and white, 12 ills. in color, map, Dec., 1933

Back to Afghanistan. By Maynard Owen Williams. XC, pp. 517-544, 27 ills., map, Oct., 1946

Bright Pages from an Asiatic Travel Log. 4 color photos by Maynard Owen Williams. LXII, pp. 545-552, Nov., 1932

The Citroën Trans-Asiatic Expedition Reaches Kashmir: Scientific Party Led by Georges-Marie Haardt Successfully Crosses Syria, Iraq, Persia, and Afghanistan to Arrive at the Pamir. By Maynard Owen Williams. LX, pp. 387-443, 62 ills., map, Oct., 1931

Every-Day Life in Afghanistan. By Frederick Simpich and "Haji Mirza Hussein." XXXIX, pp. 85-110, 26 ills., map, Jan., 1921

AFIELD with the Spiders: Web Hunting in the Marshlands and Woodlands and Along the Lanes. By Henry E. Ewing. Paintings by Hashime Murayama. LXIV, pp. 163-194, 26 ills. in black and white, 64 ills. in color, Aug., 1933

AFRICA:

Across Widest Africa. By A. Henry Savage Landor. XIX, pp. 694-737, 38 ills., map, Oct., 1908

Africa, Its Past and Future. (By Gardiner G. Hubbard). I, pp. 99-124, foldout map, Apr., 1889

Africa First of 1943 Global Warfare Maps. By William H. Nicholas. Text with a map supplement. LXXXIII, pp. 261-276, 13 ills., Feb., 1943

Africa Since 1888, with Special Reference to South Africa and Abyssinia. By Hon. Gardiner G. Hubbard. VII, pp. 157-175, ill., foldout map, May, 1896

Africa the Largest Game Preserve in the World. (By John B. Torbert). XI, pp. 445-448, map, Nov., 1900

African Scenes from the Equator to the Cape. 16 ills. XLII, pp. 431-446, Oct., 1922

Amid the Snow Peaks of the Equator: A Naturalist's Explorations Around Ruwenzori, with an Excursion to the Congo State, and an Account of the Terrible Scourge of Sleeping Sickness. By A. F. R. Wollaston. XX, pp. 256-277, 11 ills., Mar., 1909

The Black Man's Continent. Text with map supplement. XX, p. 312, Mar., 1909

AFRICA—*Continued*

Cairo to Cape Town, Overland: An Adventurous Journey of 135 Days, Made by an American Man and His Wife, Through the Length of the African Continent. By Felix Shay. XLVII, pp. 123-260, 118 ills., map, Feb., 1925

Camera Adventures in the African Wilds (Book Review). Photos by A. Radclyffe Dugmore. XXI, pp. 385-396, 11 ills., May, 1910

Elephant Hunting in Equatorial Africa with Rifle and Camera. By Carl E. Akeley. XXIII, pp. 779-810, 30 ills., Aug., 1912

Explorations in Central East Africa. XII, pp. 42-43, Jan., 1901

The Flags of Europe, Asia, and Africa. By Byron McCandless and Gilbert Grosvenor. XXXII, pp. 372-378, 101 ills. in color, Oct., 1917

Flights from Arctic to Equator: Conquering the Alps, the Ice Peaks of Spitsbergen, of Persia, and Africa's Mountains of the Moon. By Walter Mittelholzer. LXI, pp. 445-498, 53 ills., map, Apr., 1932

Geographic Progress of Civilization. Annual Address by the President, Honorable Gardiner G. Hubbard. VI, pp. 1-22, Feb. 14, 1894

Geography of the Land. Annual Report by Vice-President Herbert G. Ogden. III, pp. 31-40, Apr. 30, 1891

The Gold Coast, Ashanti, and Kumassi. By George K. French. VIII, pp. 1-15, 9 ills., Jan., 1897

The Great Unmapped Areas on the Earth's Surface Awaiting the Explorer and Geographer. By J. Scott Keltie. VIII, pp. 251-266, Sept., 1897

The Heart of Africa. By E. C. Hore. III, pp. 238-247, Feb. 19, 1892

Here and There in Northern Africa. By Frank Edward Johnson. XXV, pp. 1-132, 113 ills., Jan., 1914

In Civilized French Africa. By James F. J. Archibald. XX, pp. 303-311, 14 ills., Mar., 1909

In the Valley of the Niger. XIX, p. 164, ill., Mar., 1908

The Magnetic Survey of Africa. By Dr. L. A. Bauer. XX, pp. 291-297, 6 ills., Mar., 1909

Methods of Exploration in Africa. By Major A. St. H. Gibbons. XV, pp. 408-410, Oct., 1904

Mr. Roosevelt's "African Game Trails." XXI, pp. 953-962, 9 ills., Nov., 1910

The National Geographic Society's New Map of Africa. By Gilbert Grosvenor. Text with map supplement. LXVII, pp. 731-752, 20 ills. in duotone, June, 1935

Nature's Most Amazing Mammal: Elephants, Unique Among Animals, Have Many Human Qualities When Wild That Make Them Foremost Citizens of Zoo and Circus. By Edmund Heller. LXV, pp. 729-759, 37 ills., June, 1934

The Pathfinder of the East: Setting Sail to Find "Christians and Spices," Vasco da Gama Met Amazing Adventures, Founded an Empire, and Changed the History of Western Europe. By J. R. Hildebrand. LII, pp. 503-550, 43 ills., map, Nov., 1927

Peoples and Places of Northern Africa. 16 ills. XLII, pp. 363-378, Oct., 1922

Recent Explorations in Equatorial Africa. (By Ernest de Sasseville). VIII, pp. 88-91, Mar., 1897

AFRICA—*Continued*

Recent French Explorations in Africa. By Dr. Charles Rabot. XIII, pp. 119-132, 20 ills., Apr., 1902

Recent Geographic Advances, Especially in Africa. By Major General A. W. Greely. XXII, pp. 383-398, 5 ills., 5 maps, Apr., 1911

Report—Geography of the Land. By Herbert G. Ogden. II, pp. 31-48, Apr., 1890

Return of the Hourst Niger Expedition. (By Ernest de Sasseville). VIII, pp. 24-25, Jan., 1897

Rubber Forests of Nicaragua and Sierra Leone. By General A. W. Greely. VIII, pp. 83-88, Mar., 1897

Sailing Forbidden Coasts. By Ida Treat. LX, pp. 357-386, 31 ills., map, Sept., 1931

Seeing the World from the Air. By Sir Alan J. Cobham. LIII, pp. 349-384, 37 ills., map, Mar., 1928

The Society's New Map of Africa. Text with map supplement. XLII, pp. 447-448, Oct., 1922

Three-Wheeling Through Africa: Two Adventurers Cross the So-called Dark Continent North of Lake Chad on Motorcycles with Side Cars. By James C. Wilson. LXV, pp. 37-92, 64 ills., two-page map, Jan., 1934

Through the Deserts and Jungles of Africa by Motor: Caterpillar Cars Make 15,000-Mile Trip from Algeria to Madagascar in Nine Months. By Georges-Marie Haardt. XLIX, pp. 651-720, 95 ills., map, June, 1926

Through the Heart of Africa. XI, pp. 408-411, map, Oct., 1900

Trans-Africa Safari: A Motor Caravan Rolls Across Sahara and Jungle Through Realms of Dusky Potentates and the Land of Big-Lipped Women. By Lawrence Copley Thaw and Margaret Stout Thaw. LXXIV, pp. 327-364, 29 ills. in black and white, 14 ills. in color, map, Sept., 1938

Transporting a Navy Through the Jungles of Africa in War Time. By Frank J. Magee. XLII, pp. 331-362, 31 ills., Oct., 1922

Western Front Map Embraces Three Continents (Europe, Africa, Asia). Text with map supplement. LXXXII, pp. 139-140, July, 1942

Where Exploration Is Needed. XI, pp. 163-164, Apr., 1900

Where Roosevelt Will Hunt. By Sir Harry Johnston. XX, pp. 207-256, 43 ills., map supplement, Mar., 1909

Wings Over Nature's Zoo in Africa. 20 photos in duotone by Reginald A. Bourlay. LXXVI, pp. 527-542, Oct., 1939

See also Algeria; Anglo-Egyptian Sudan; Angola; Belgian Congo; Cameroons; Egypt; Eritrea; Ethiopia; French West Africa; Gold Coast; Kenya; Liberia; Libia; Morocco; Mozambique; Nigeria; Rhodesia; South-West Africa; Tanganyika; Tunisia; Uganda; Union of South Africa; *and* islands: Madagascar; Zanzibar

AFRICA on Parade. 14 color photos by Lawrence Thaw. LXXIV, pp. 343-350, Sept., 1938

AFRICAN Rainbow. 10 color photos by W. Robert Moore. LXXXVI, pp. 289-296, Sept., 1944

AFRICAN Scenes from the Equator to the Cape. 16 ills. XLII, pp. 431-446, Oct., 1922

AGAVE. *See* Henequen

AGELESS Luster of Greece and Rhodes. 16 ills. in duotone by Arnold Genthe. LXXIII, pp. 477-492, Apr., 1938

AGETON, ARTHUR A.:

Annapolis, Cradle of the Navy. By Lieutenant Arthur A. Ageton. LXIX, pp. 789-800, 13 ills. in color, June, 1936

AGNEW, DONALD H.:

American Wings Soar Around the World: Epic Story of the Air Transport Command of the U. S. Army Is a Saga of Yankee Daring and Doing. By Donald H. Agnew and William A. Kinney. LXXXIV, pp. 57-78, 22 ills., July, 1943

AGRA, India:

Through the Heart of Hindustan: A Teeming Highway Extending for Fifteen Hundred Miles, from the Khyber Pass to Calcutta. By Maynard Owen Williams. XL, pp. 433-467, 29 ills., Nov., 1921

AGRICULTURAL AND BOTANICAL EXPLORERS:

Aleutians: Riddle of the Aleutians: A Botanist Explores the Origin of Plants on Ever-misty Islands Now Enshrouded in the Fog of War. By Isobel Wylie Hutchison. LXXXII, pp. 769-792, 24 ills., Dec., 1942

Asia: A Hunter of Plants. By David Fairchild. XXXVI, pp. 57-77, 18 ills., July, 1919

Canary Islands: Hunting for Plants in the Canary Islands. By David Fairchild. LVII, pp. 607-652, 37 ills. in black and white, 39 ills. in color, map, May, 1930

Caribbean Regions: Hunting Useful Plants in the Caribbean. By David Fairchild. LXVI, pp. 705-737, 39 ills., Dec., 1934

China: Experiences of a Lone Geographer: An American Agricultural Explorer Makes His Way Through Brigand-infested Central China en Route to the Amne Machin Range, Tibet. By Joseph F. Rock. XLVIII, pp. 331-347, 16 ills., map, Sept., 1925

China: Exploring a Grass Wonderland of Wild West China. By Ray G. Johnson. LXXXV, pp. 713-742, 24 ills., map, June, 1944

China: Peacetime Plant Hunting About Peiping. By P. H. and J. H. Dorsett. LXXII, pp. 509-534, 21 ills., map, Oct., 1937

China: The Road to Wang Ye Fu: An Account of the Work of the National Geographic Society's Central-China Expedition in the Mongol Kingdom of Ala Shan. By Frederick R. Wulsin. XLIX, pp. 195-234, 44 ills., map, Feb., 1926

China: Through the Great River Trenches of Asia: National Geographic Society Explorer Follows the Yangtze, Mekong, and Salwin Through Mighty Gorges, Some of Whose Canyon Walls Tower to a Height of More Than Two Miles. By Joseph F. Rock. L, pp. 133-186, 47 ills., map, Aug., 1926

AGRICULTURAL AND BOTANICAL EXPLORERS—*Continued*

Colombia: Round About Bogotá: A Hunt for New Fruits and Plants Among the Mountain Forests of Colombia's Unique Capital. By Wilson Popenoe. XLIX, pp. 127-160, 34 ills., map, Feb., 1926

Ecuador: Quinine Hunters in Ecuador. By Froelich Rainey. LXXXIX, pp. 341-363, 21 ills., map, Mar., 1946

Ethiopia: A Caravan Journey Through Abyssinia: From Addis Ababa Through Lalibela, the Strange Jerusalem of Ethiopia, in Search of New Grains for American Farms. By Harry V. Harlan. XLVII, pp. 613-663, 46 ills., map, June, 1925

New Guinea: Into Primeval Papua by Seaplane: Seeking Disease-resisting Sugar Cane, Scientists Find Neolithic Man in Unmapped Nooks of Sorcery and Cannibalism. By E. W. Brandes. LVI, pp. 253-332, 98 ills., map, Sept., 1929

Our Plant Immigrants. By David Fairchild. XVII, pp. 179-201, 29 ills., Apr., 1906

U. S. S. R.: Roaming Russia's Caucasus: Rugged Mountains and Hardy Fighters Guard the Soviet Union's Caucasian Treasury of Manganese and Oil. By Rolf Singer. LXXXII, pp. 91-121, 33 ills., July, 1942

AGRICULTURAL Capacity of Alaska: What Population Can the Territory Support? By C. C. Georgeson. XX, pp. 676-679, July, 1909

AGRICULTURAL Possibilities in Tropical Mexico. By Dr. Pehr Olsson-Seffer. XXI, pp. 1021-1040, 19 ills., Dec., 1910

AGRICULTURE:

Alaska: Agricultural Capacity of Alaska: What Population Can the Territory Support? By C. C. Georgeson. XX, pp. 676-679, July, 1909

Alaska: Agriculture in Alaska. (By Henry Gannett). XIII, p. 112, Mar., 1902

Alaska: Agriculture in the Yukon Valley. IX, pp. 189-190, Apr., 1898

Alaska: Gardening in Northern Alaska. By Middleton Smith. XIV, pp. 355-357, Sept., 1903

Alaska: Some of the Conditions and Possibilities of Agriculture in Alaska. By Walter H. Evans. IX, pp. 178-187, Apr., 1898

Argentina: Life on the Argentine Pampa. By Frederick Simpich. LXIV, pp. 449-491, 41 ills. in black and white, 8 ills. in color, Oct., 1933

Ascension Island: Greens Grow for GI's on Soilless Ascension. By W. Robert Moore. LXXXVIII, pp. 219-230, 12 ills., Aug., 1945

Australia: Beyond Australia's Cities. By W. Robert Moore. LXX, pp. 709-747, 27 ills. in black and white, 12 ills. in color, Dec., 1936

Bulgaria, Farm Land Without a Farmhouse: A Nation of Villagers Faces the Challenge of Modern Machinery and Urban Life. By Maynard Owen Williams. LXII, pp. 185-218, 19 ills. in black and white, 27 ills. in color, map, Aug., 1932

California. By the Hon. George C. Perkins. VII, pp. 317-327, Oct., 1896

California: The Man Without the Hoe. XXI, pp. 967-969, ills., Nov., 1910

AGRICULTURE—*Continued*

California: More Water for California's Great Central Valley. By Frederick Simpich. XC, pp. 645-664, 16 ills., map, Nov., 1946

California: Seed Farms in California. By A. J. Wells. XXIII, pp. 515-530, 14 ills., May, 1912

China: Farmers Since the Days of Noah: China's Remarkable System of Agriculture Has Kept Alive the Densest Population in the World. By Adam Warwick. LI, pp. 469-500, 37 ills., Apr., 1927

China: The Geography of China: The Influence of Physical Environment on the History and Character of the Chinese People. By Frank Johnson Goodnow. LI, pp. 651-664, 11 ills., June, 1927

China: How Half the World Works. By Alice Tisdale Hobart and Mary A. Nourse. LXI, pp. 509-524, 22 ills., Apr., 1932

China: A Hunter of Plants. By David Fairchild. XXXVI, pp. 57-77, 18 ills., July, 1919

China Fights Erosion with U. S. Aid. By Walter C. Lowdermilk. LXXXVII, pp. 641-680, 10 ills. in black and white, 26 ills. in color, June, 1945

Cuba. By Robert T. Hill. IX, pp. 193-242, 12 ills., 7 diagrs., tables, 5 maps (1 foldout), May, 1898

Denmark and the Danes. By Maurice Francis Egan. XLII, pp. 115-164, 38 ills., map, Aug., 1922

Egypt: The Land of Egypt: A Narrow Green Strip of Fertility Stretching for a Thousand Miles Through Walls of Desert. By Alfred Pearce Dennis. XLIX, pp. 271-298, 28 ills., map, Mar., 1926

England: Britain Fights in the Fields. By Francis A. Flood. LXXXVI, pp. 31-65, 17 ills. in black and white, 21 ills. in color, July, 1944

Georgia: Marching Through Georgia Sixty Years After: Multifold Industries and Diversified Agriculture Are Restoring the Prosperity of America's Largest State East of the Mississippi. By Ralph A. Graves. L, pp. 259-311, 47 ills., map supplement, Sept., 1926

How the World Is Fed. By William Joseph Showalter. XXIX, pp. 1-110, 101 ills., Jan., 1916

Japan: Agriculture in Japan. By Consul-General Bellows. XV, pp. 323-326, Aug., 1904

Mexico: Agricultural Possibilities in Tropical Mexico. By Dr. Pehr Olsson-Seffer. XXI, pp. 1021-1040, 19 ills., Dec., 1910

Mexico: A Mexican Hacienda. By J. E. Kirkwood. XXV, pp. 563-584, 18 ills., May, 1914

Mexico: Notes on Southern Mexico. By G. N. Collins and C. B. Doyle. XXII, pp. 301-320, 16 ills., map, Mar., 1911

Mexico: Unearthing America's Ancient History: Investigation Suggests That the Maya May Have Designed the First Astronomical Observatory in the New World in Order to Cultivate Corn. By Sylvanus Griswold Morley. LX, pp. 99-126, 28 ills., July, 1931

Montana: The Irrigation Problem in Montana. By H. M. Wilson. II, pp. 212-229, 4 tables, July, 1890

Mount Vernon: The Home of the First Farmer of America. By Worth E. Shoults. LIII, pp. 603-628, 6 ills. in black and white, 26 ills. in color, May, 1928

AGRICULTURE—*Continued*

New Jersey Now! By E. John Long. LXIII, pp. 519-584, 49 ills. in black and white, 24 ills. in color, maps, May, 1933

New Plant Immigrants. By David Fairchild. XXII, pp. 879-907, 34 ills., Oct., 1911

New York: Black Acres: A Thrilling Sketch in the Vast Volume of Who's Who Among the Peoples That Make America. By Dorothea D. and Fred Everett. LXXX, pp. 631-652, 13 ills. in black and white, 12 ills. in color, Nov., 1941

New York: Fruitful Shores of the Finger Lakes. By Harrison Howell Walker. LXXIX, pp. 559-594, 15 ills. in black and white, 22 ills. in color, map, May, 1941

North Carolina: Motor-Coaching Through North Carolina. By Melville Chater. XLIX, pp. 475-523, 43 ills., map, May, 1926

Oregon Finds New Riches. By Leo A. Borah. XC, pp. 681-728, 15 ills. in black and white, 28 ills. in color, two-page map, Dec., 1946

Palestine: Village Life in the Holy Land. By John D. Whiting. XXV, pp. 249-314, 27 ills. in black and white, 21 ills. in color, Mar., 1914

Palestine Today. By Francis Chase, Jr. XC, pp. 501-516, 16 ills., Oct., 1946

Panama: Farming on the Isthmus of Panama. By Dillwyn M. Hazlett. XVII, pp. 229-234, 5 ills., Apr., 1906

Peru: Staircase Farms of the Ancients: Astounding Farming Skill of Ancient Peruvians, Who Were Among the Most Industrious and Highly Organized People in History. By O. F. Cook. XXIX, pp. 474-534, 48 ills., May, 1916

The Philippine Islands. By F. F. Hilder. IX, pp. 257-284, 10 ills., table, maps, June, 1898

Philippine Islands: The Economic Conditions of the Philippines. By Max L. Tornow. X, pp. 33-64, 10 ills., Feb., 1899

The Texas Delta of an American Nile: Orchards and Gardens Replace Thorny Jungle in the Southmost Tip of the Lone Star State. By McFall Kerbey. LXXV, pp. 51-96, 27 ills. in black and white, 24 ills. in color, map, Jan., 1939

United States: America Fights on the Farms. 21 ills. in color. LXXXVI, pp. 33-48, July, 1944

United States: Big Things of the West. By Charles F. Holder. XIV, pp. 279-282, ills., July, 1903

United States: Boys' and Girls' Agricultural Clubs. XXII, pp. 639-641, 4 ills., July, 1911

United States: The Discovery of Cancer in Plants. XXIV, pp. 53-70, 12 ills., Jan., 1913

United States: Farmers Keep Them Eating. By Frederick Simpich. LXXXIII, pp. 435-458, 22 ills., Apr., 1943

United States: The Farmers of the United States. XVI, pp. 39-46, Jan., 1905

United States: Forming New Fashions in Food: The Bearing of Taste on One of Our Great Food Economies, the Dried Vegetable, Which Is Developing into a Big War Industry. By David Fairchild. XXXIII, pp. 356-368, 11 ills., Apr., 1918

United States: Helping the Farmers. XVI, pp. 82-85, ill., Feb., 1905

United States: Helping the Farmers. XVIII, pp. 746-749, 7 ills., Nov., 1907

AGRICULTURE—*Continued*

United States: Helping to Solve Our Allies' Food Problem: America Calls for a Million Young Soldiers of the Commissary to Volunteer for Service in 1918. By Ralph Graves. XXXIII, pp. 170-194, 23 ills., Feb., 1918

United States: Inoculating the Ground. XV, pp. 225-228, ills., May, 1904

The United States; Its Soils and Their Products. By H. W. Wiley. XIV, pp. 263-279, 11 ills., July, 1903

United States: The Modern Alchemist (Work of the Department of Agriculture). By James Wilson. XVIII, pp. 781-795, 6 ills., Dec., 1907

United States: Our Greatest Plant Food (Phosphorus). By Guy Elliott Mitchell. XXI, pp. 783-791, 5 ills., diagrs., Sept., 1910

United States: Our Plant Immigrants. By David Fairchild. XVII, pp. 179-201, 29 ills., Apr., 1906

United States: Pests and Parasites. By Charles Lester Marlatt. XXII, pp. 321-346, 29 ills., maps, Apr., 1911

United States: The Policemen of the Air: An Account of the Biological Survey of the Department of Agriculture. By Henry Wetherbee Henshaw. XIX, pp. 79-118, 38 ills., Feb., 1908
Included: The relation of birds and mammals to agriculture; Life and crop zones

United States: Protecting the United States from Plant Pests. By Charles Lester Marlatt. XL, pp. 205-218, 16 ills., Aug., 1921

United States: Soldiers of the Soil: Our Food Crops Must Be Greatly Increased. By David F. Houston. XXXI, pp. 273-280, 4 ills., Mar., 1917

United States: The Southwest: Its Splendid Natural Resources, Agricultural Wealth, and Scenic Beauty. By N. H. Darton. XXI, pp. 631-665, 21 ills., map, Aug., 1910

United States: The Spirit of the West: The Wonderful Agricultural Development Since the Dawn of Irrigation. By C. J. Blanchard. XXI, pp. 333-360, 15 ills., Apr., 1910

United States: War, Patriotism, and the Food Supply. By Frederick V. Coville. XXXI, pp. 254-256, Mar., 1917

United States: What the United States Government Does to Promote Agriculture. XIV, pp. 35-39, Jan., 1903

See also names of products

AGUALULCOS (Indians):

The Isthmus of Tehuantepec: "The Bridge of the World's Commerce." By Helen Olsson-Seffer. XXI, pp. 991-1002, 7 ills., Dec., 1910

AIKMAN, LONNELLE DAVISON:

Bizarre Battleground—the Lonely Aleutians. By Lonnelle Davison. LXXXII, pp. 316-317, ill., Sept., 1942

Platinum in the World's Work. By Lonnelle Davison. LXXII, pp. 345-360, 17 ills., Sept., 1937

AILINGLAPALAP (Atoll), Marshall Islands:

Our New Military Wards, the Marshalls. By W. Robert Moore. LXXXVIII, pp. 325-360, 14 ills. in black and white, 20 ills. in color, map, Sept., 1945

AIR Adventures in Peru: Cruising Among Andean Peaks, Pilots and Cameramen Discover Wondrous Works of an Ancient People. By Robert Shippee. LXIII, pp. 81-120, 40 ills., map, Jan., 1933

AIR BASES:

Air Power for Peace. By General H. H. Arnold. LXXXIX, pp. 137-193, 35 ills. in black and white, 28 ills. in color, map supplement, Feb., 1946

Americans Stand Guard in Greenland. By Andrew H. Brown. XC, pp. 457-500, 23 ills. in black and white, 19 ills. in color, map, Oct., 1946

China's Hand-built Air Bases. 9 ills. LXXXVIII, pp. 231-236, Aug., 1945

Servicing Arctic Airbases. By Robert A. Bartlett. LXXXIX, pp. 602-616, 3 ills. in black and white, 10 ills. in color, map, May, 1946

See also Airfields

AIR CARRIER CONTRACT PERSONNEL:

Heroes of Wartime Science and Mercy. By Elizabeth W. King. LXXXIV, pp. 715-740, 11 ills. in black and white, 334 ills. in color, Dec., 1943

AIR COMMANDO FORCE. *See* U. S. First Air Commando Force

AIR Conquest: From the Early Days of Giant Kites and Birdlike Gliders, the National Geographic Society Has Aided and Encouraged the Growth of Aviation. LII, pp. 233-242, 13 ills., Aug., 1927

AIR Cruising Through New Brazil: A National Geographic Reporter Spots Vast Resources Which the Republic's War Declaration Adds to Strength of United Nations. By Henry Albert Phillips. LXXXII, pp. 503-536, 32 ills., Oct., 1942

AIR EVACUATION OF WOUNDED:

Flying Our Wounded Veterans Home. By Catherine Bell Palmer. LXXXVIII, pp. 363-384, 17 ills., Sept., 1945

See also Aerial Invasion of Burma

AIR FORCE. *See* U. S. Army Air Forces

AIR MAIL:

Flying. By Gilbert Grosvenor. LXIII, pp. 585-630, 33 ills. in black and white, 17 ills. in duotone, May, 1933

Flying the "Hump" of the Andes. By Capt. Albert W. Stevens. LIX, pp. 595-636, 36 ills., map, May, 1931

Flying the World's Longest Air-Mail Route: From Montevideo, Uruguay, Over the Andes, Up the Pacific Coast, Across Central America and the Caribbean to Miami, Florida, in 67 Thrilling Flying Hours. By Junius B. Wood. LVII, pp. 261-325, 65 ills., map, Mar., 1930

On the Trail of the Air Mail: A Narrative of the Experiences of the Flying Couriers Who Relay the Mail Across America at a Speed of More than 2,000 Miles a Day. By Lieut. J. Parker Van Zandt. XLIX, pp. 1-61, 67 ills., map, Jan., 1926

AIR Power for Peace. By General H. H. Arnold. LXXXIX, pp. 137-193, 35 ills. in black and white, 28 ills. in color, map supplement, Feb., 1946

AIR RAIDS:

Air Power for Peace. By General H. H. Arnold. LXXXIX, pp. 137-193, 35 ills. in black and white, 28 ills. in color, map supplement, Feb., 1946

A City That Refused to Die (Plymouth, England). By Harvey Klemmer. LXXXIX, pp. 211-236, 13 ills. in black and white, 9 ills. in color, map, Feb., 1946

Everyday Life in Wartime England. By Harvey Klemmer. LXXIX, pp. 497-534, 48 ills., Apr., 1941

Front-line Town of Britain's Siege (Dover). By Harvey Klemmer. LXXXV, pp. 105-128, 21 ills., Jan., 1944

Malta Invicta. By Bartimeus (A Captain in the Royal Navy). LXXXIII, pp. 375-400, 27 ills., map, Mar., 1943

Return to Florence (Italy). By 1st Lt. Benjamin C. McCartney. LXXXVII, pp. 257-296, 18 ills. in black and white, 18 ills. in color, Mar., 1945

See also Bombs, Flying

AIR TRANSPORT COMMAND, U. S. Army Air Forces:

American Wings Soar Around the World: Epic Story of the Air Transport Command of the U. S. Army Is a Saga of Yankee Daring and Doing. By Donald H. Agnew and William A. Kinney. LXXXIV, pp. 57-78, 22 ills., July, 1943

Flying Our Wounded Veterans Home. By Catherine Bell Palmer. LXXXVIII, pp. 363-384, 17 ills., Sept., 1945

See also Air Carrier Contract Personnel

AIRCRAFT CARRIERS:

Navy Wings over the Pacific. 12 ills. in color from U. S. Navy official photos. LXXXVI, pp. 241-248, Aug., 1944

The New Queen of the Seas. By Melville Bell Grosvenor. LXXXII, pp. 1-30, 27 ills., drawing, two-page map, July, 1942

Painting History in the Pacific. 19 ills. in color from paintings by Lt. William F. Draper, USNR. LXXXVI, pp. 408-424, Oct., 1944

Saga of the Carrier *Princeton*. By Capt. William H. Buracker, USN. LXXXVIII, pp. 189-218, 8 ills. in black and white, 22 ills. in color, map, Aug., 1945

Victory's Portrait in the Marianas. By Lt. William Franklin Draper, USNR. With 17 ills. in color from paintings by author. LXXXVIII, pp. 599-616, Nov., 1945

Your Navy as Peace Insurance. By Fleet Admiral Chester W. Nimitz. LXXXIX, pp. 681-736, 32 ills. in black and white, 26 ills. in color, June, 1946

See also Escort Carriers

AIRCRAFT INDUSTRY:

American Industries Geared for War. By Thornton Oakley. With 16 ills. in color from paintings by author. LXXXII, pp. 716-734, ill. in black and white, Dec., 1942

Michigan Fights. By Harvey Klemmer. LXXXVI, pp. 677-715, 20 ills. in black and white, 19 ills. in color, Dec., 1944

The Miracle of War Production: For Victory the United States Transforms Its Complex Industry into the Biggest Factory and Mightiest Arsenal the World Has Ever Known. By Albert W. Atwood. With paintings by Thornton Oakley. LXXXII, pp. 693-715, 17 ills. in black and white, 16 ills. in color, Dec., 1942

Women at Work. By La Verne Bradley. LXXXVI, pp. 193-220, 23 ills., Aug., 1944

AIRCRAFT Insignia, Spirit of Youth. By Gerard Hubbard. LXXXIII, pp. 710-722, 3 ills. in black and white, 337 ills. in color, June, 1943

AIRFIELDS:

Ascension Island, an Engineering Victory. By Lt. Col. Frederick J. Clarke. LXXXV, pp. 623-640, 21 ills., May, 1944

See also Air Bases

AIRPLANE CARRIERS. *See* Aircraft Carriers; Escort Carriers

AIRPLANES. *See* Aeronautics; Aircraft Industry; Bombers; Seaplanes

AIRPLANES Come to the Isles of Spice: Once Magnet of World Explorers, the Moluccas Again Stand at Crossroads of History in the Netherlands Indies. By Maynard Owen Williams. LXXIX, pp. 535-558, 26 ills., map, May, 1941

AIRSHIPS:

Aboard a Blimp Hunting U-boats: A Day above the Atlantic Reveals Navy Talk and Navy Ways, Creeping Convoys, and Torpedoed Wrecks. By Mason Sutherland. LXXXIV, pp. 79-96, 18 ills., July, 1943

America in the Air: The Future of Airplane and Airship, Economically and as Factors in National Defense. By Brigadier-General William Mitchell. XXXIX, pp. 339-352, 8 ills., map, Mar., 1921

The Polar Airship. By Walter Wellman. XVII, pp. 208-228, 5 diagrs., Apr., 1906

Walter Wellman's Expedition to the North Pole. XVII, pp. 205-207, chart, Apr., 1906

The Wellman Polar Expedition. XVII, p. 712, Dec., 1906

See also Graf Zeppelin; Norge; Shenandoah

AISAWA (Dance):

Two Great Moorish Religious Dances (Tangier, Morocco). By George Edmund Holt. XXII, pp. 777-785, 6 ills., Aug., 1911

AK BULAK, U. S. S. R.:

Observing an Eclipse in Asiatic Russia. By Irvine C. Gardner. LXXI, pp. 179-197, 19 ills. in black and white, ill. in color, Feb., 1937

AKELEY, CARL E.:

Elephant Hunting in Equatorial Africa with Rifle and Camera. By Carl E. Akeley. XXIII, pp. 779-810, 30 ills., Aug., 1912

ALABAMA:

Smoke Over Alabama. By Frederick Simpich. LX, pp. 703-758, 43 ills. in black and white, 26 ills. in color, map, Dec., 1931

ALAMOGORDO, New Mexico:

The White Sands of Alamogordo: A Dry Ocean of Granular Gypsum Billows Under Desert Winds in a New National Playground. By Carl P. Russell. LXVIII, pp. 250-264, 12 ills., Aug., 1935

ALAND (Islands), Finland:

Flashes from Finland. 19 ills. LXXVII, pp. 239-254, Feb., 1940

Where the Sailing Ship Survives. By A. J. Villiers. LXVII, pp. 101-128, 31 ills., map, Jan., 1935

ALAOUITE (Region), Syria:

A New Alphabet of the Ancients Is Unearthed: An Inconspicuous Mound in Northern Syria Yields Archeological Treasures of Far-reaching Significance. By F. A. Schaeffer. LVIII, pp. 477-516, 47 ills., map, Oct., 1930

Secrets from Syrian Hills: Explorations Reveal World's Earliest Known Alphabet, Deciphered from Schoolboy Slates and Dictionaries of 3,000 Years Ago. By Claude F. A. Schaeffer. LXIV, pp. 97-126, 40 ills., map, July, 1933

ALA SHAN (Mongol Kingdom):

The Road to Wang Ye Fu: An Account of the Work of the National Geographic Society's Central-China Expedition in the Mongol Kingdom of Ala Shan. By Frederick R. Wulsin. XLIX, pp. 197-234, 44 ills., map, Feb., 1926

ALASKA:

Agricultural Capacity of Alaska: What Population Can the Territory Support? By C. C. Georgeson. XX, pp. 676-679, July, 1909

Agriculture in Alaska. (By Henry Gannett). XIII, p. 112, Mar., 1902

Agriculture in the Yukon Valley. IX, pp. 189-190, Apr., 1898

Alaska and Its Mineral Resources. By Samuel Franklin Emmons. IX, pp. 139-172, 3 ills., map supplement, Apr., 1898

The Alaskan Boundary. By John W. Foster. X, pp. 425-456, 10 maps, map supplements, Nov., 1899

Alaskan Boundary Decision. XIV, p. 423, Nov., 1903

Alaskan Boundary Dispute. XIV, p. 79, Feb., 1903

The Alaskan Boundary Survey. I—Introduction. By Dr. T. C. Mendenhall. II—The Boundary South of Fort Yukon. By J. E. McGrath. III—The Boundary North of Fort Yukon. By J. Henry Turner. IV, pp. 177-197, Feb. 8, 1893

The Alaskan Boundary Tribunal. By John W. Foster. XV, pp. 1-12, map, map supplement, Jan., 1904

The Alaskan Brown Bear. (By Wilfred H. Osgood). XX, pp. 332-333, Apr., 1909

Alaskan Highway an Engineering Epic: Mosquitoes, Mud, and Muskeg Minor Obstacles of 1,671-mile Race to Throw the Alcan Life Line Through Thick Forests and Uninhabited Wilderness. By Froelich Rainey. LXXXIII, pp. 143-168, 21 ills., 3 maps, Feb., 1943

Alaska's New Railway. XXVIII, pp. 567-589, 20 ills., Dec., 1915

Anglo-American Polar Expedition. XVIII, p. 796, Dec., 1907

The Arctic Cruise of the U. S. S. Thetis in the Summer and Autumn of 1889. By Charles H. Stockton. II, pp. 171-198, ill., foldout map, July, 1890

The Big Game of Alaska. By Wilfred H. Osgood. XX, pp. 624-636, 10 ills., July, 1909

ALASKA—*Continued*

The "Breaking Up" of the Yukon. By Captain George S. Gibbs. XVII, pp. 268-272, 6 ills., May, 1906

The Brooks Alaskan Expedition. XIII, p. 389, Oct., 1902

Building the Alaskan Telegraph System. By Captain William Mitchell. XV, pp. 357-361, Sept., 1904

The Camel of the Frozen Desert (Reindeer). By Carl J. Lomen. XXXVI, pp. 539-556, 19 ills., Dec., 1919

The Cape Nome Gold District. By F. C. Schrader. XI, pp. 15-23, 3 ills., map, Jan., 1900

Charting a Coast-Line of 26,000 Miles. XX, pp. 608-609, July, 1909

The Civil Government of Alaska. By Hon. George C. Perkins. IX, pp. 172-178, Apr., 1898

Climatic Conditions of Alaska. By General A. W. Greely. IX, pp. 132-137, Apr., 1898

The Coal-Fields of Alaska. XXI, pp. 82-87, 6 ills., Jan., 1910

Coal Resources of Alaska. XIII, pp. 172-174, May, 1902

The Conquest of Mount Crillon. By Bradford Washburn. LXVII, pp. 361-400, 40 ills., maps, Mar., 1935

The Copper River Delta. (By E. D. Preston). XI, pp. 29-31, Jan., 1900

Cryptogams, Collected by Dr. C. Willard Hayes in Alaska, 1891. By Clara E. Cummings. IV, pp. 160-162, May 15, 1892

Decision of the Alaskan Boundary Tribunal. XV, pp. 12-14, Jan., 1904

Discovering Alaska's Oldest Arctic Town (Ipiutak): A Scientist Finds Ivory-eyed Skeletons of a Mysterious People and Joins Modern Eskimos in the Dangerous Spring Whale Hunt. By Froelich G. Rainey. LXXXII, pp. 319-336, 15 ills., Sept., 1942

The Discovery of Glacier Bay, Alaska. By Eliza Ruhamah Scidmore. VII, pp. 140-146, ill., map, Apr., 1896

The Economic Evolution of Alaska. By Major General A. W. Greely. XX, pp. 585-593, 4 ills., July, 1909

Evidence of Recent Volcanic Action in Southeast Alaska. XVII, pp. 173-176, Mar., 1906

An Expedition through the Yukon District. By Charles Willard Hayes. IV, pp. 117-159, 3 maps (2 foldouts), May 15, 1892

An Expedition to Mount St. Elias, Alaska. By Israel C. Russell. III, pp. 53-191, 17 ills., 3 diagrs., tables, 7 maps (1 foldout), May 29, 1891

Appendices: Official Instructions Governing the Expedition, pp. 192-194; Report on Topographic Work, p. 195; Report on Auriferous Sands from Yakutat Bay, pp. 196-198; Report on Fossil Plants, pp. 199-200

Explorations in Alaska. X, pp. 269-271, July, 1899

Exploring Frozen Fragments of American History: On the Trail of Early Eskimo Colonists Who Made a 55-Mile Crossing from the Old World to the New. By Henry B. Collins, Jr. LXXV, pp. 633-656, 24 ills., map, May, 1939

ALASKA—*Continued*

The First Alaskan Air Expedition. By Captain St. Clair Streett. XLI, pp. 499-552, 37 ills., map, May, 1922

A Game Country Without Rival in America: The Proposed Mount McKinley National Park. By Stephen R. Capps. XXXI, pp. 69-84, 14 ills., map, Jan., 1917

Gardening in Northern Alaska. By Middleton Smith. XIV, pp. 355-357, Sept., 1903

The General Geography of Alaska. By Henry Gannett. XII, pp. 180-196, 9 ills., May, 1901

The Geography of Alaska. By Alfred H. Brooks. XV, pp. 213-219, map supplement, May, 1904

The Glaciers of Alaska. (By Grove Karl Gilbert). XV, pp. 449-450, Nov., 1904

Greely's "Handbook of Alaska." By Gilbert H. Grosvenor. XX, pp. 491-492, May, 1909

A Growing Camp in the Tanana Gold Fields, Alaska. By Sidney Paige. XVI, pp. 104-111, 4 ills., Mar., 1905

The Harriman Alaska Expedition. By Henry Gannett. X, pp. 507-512, chart, map, Dec., 1899

The Harriman Alaska Expedition in Cooperation with the Washington Academy of Sciences. (By G. H. G.). X, pp. 225-227, June, 1899

How Much Is Known of Alaska? By Alfred H. Brooks. XVII, pp. 112-114, ill., map, Feb., 1906

Hunting the Great Brown Bear of Alaska. By George Mixter, 2d. XX, pp. 313-333, 35 ills., Apr., 1909

Ice-cliffs on the Kowak River. By Lieut. J. C. Cantwell. VII, pp. 345-346, Oct., 1896

A Jack in the Box: An Account of the Strange Performances of the Most Wonderful Island in the World (Bogoslof Volcano). By Captain F. M. Munger. XX, pp. 194-199, 8 ills., Feb., 1909

Ketchikan. XVI, pp. 508-509, ill., Nov., 1905

Kodiak Not Kadiak. (By M. B.). XII, pp. 397-398, Nov., 1901

Lake Clark, a Little Known Alaskan Lake. By Wilfred H. Osgood. XV, pp. 326-331, ills., map, Aug., 1904

Magnetic Observations in Alaska. By Daniel L. Hazard. XX, pp. 675-676, map, July, 1909

Making the Fur Seal Abundant. By Hugh M. Smith. XXII, pp. 1139-1165, 18 ills., map, Dec., 1911

Map of Alaska. Announcement of map supplement (May, 1904). XV, p. 188, Apr., 1904; p. 236, May, 1904

Mapping the Home of the Great Brown Bear: Adventures of the National Geographic Society's Pavlof Volcano Expedition to Alaska. By Dr. Thomas A. Jaggar. LV, pp. 109-134, 30 ills., map, Jan., 1929

Marking the Alaskan Boundary. XIX, pp. 176-189, 16 ills., Mar., 1908

Marking the Alaskan Boundary. By Thomas Riggs, Jr. XX, pp. 593-607, 17 ills., July, 1909

The Metlakatla Mission in Danger. (By Wm. H. Dall). IX, pp. 187-189, Apr., 1898

A Mind's-Eye Map of America. By Franklin K. Lane. XXXVII, pp. 479-518, 25 ills. in black and white, 8 ills. in color, June, 1920

The Monarchs of Alaska (Mountains). By R. H. Sargent. XX, pp. 610-623, 9 ills., July, 1909

ALASKA—*Continued*

Mount St. Elias expedition, the Society's first scientific exploration, under the leadership of I. C. Russell. III, pp. 39-40, Apr. 30, 1891

The Mt. St. Elias Expedition of Prince Luigi Amadeo of Savoy, 1897. (By E.R.S.). IX, pp. 93-96, Mar., 1898

Mountains on Unimak Island, Alaska. By Ferdinand Westdahl. XIV, pp. 91-99, 4 ills., map, Mar., 1903

Muir Glacier. (By C. L. Andrews). XIV, pp. 441-444, ills., map, Dec., 1903

"Nakwasina" Goes North: A Man, a Woman, and a Pup Cruise from Tacoma to Juneau in a 17-Foot Canoe. By Jack Calvin. LXIV, pp. 1-42, 24 ills., map, July, 1933

National Geographic Society Alaska Expedition. XX, pp. 581-584, June, 1909

The National Geographic Society Researches in Alaska. By Lawrence Martin. XXII, pp. 537-561, 17 ills., 5 maps, June, 1911

The National Geographic Society's Alaskan Expedition. XXI, p. 370, Apr., 1910

The National Geographic Society's Alaskan Expedition of 1909. By Ralph S. Tarr and Lawrence Martin. XXI, pp. 1-54, 42 ills., 12 maps, Jan., 1910

The Nation's Undeveloped Resources. By Franklin K. Lane. XXV, pp. 183-225, 32 ills., Feb., 1914

The Nome Gold Fields. XIX, pp. 384-385, May, 1908

A Northern Crusoe's Island: Life on a Fox Farm Off the Coast of Alaska, Far from Contact with the World Eleven Months a Year. By Margery Pritchard Parker. XLIV, pp. 313-326, 15 ills., map, Sept., 1923

The Northwest Passes to the Yukon. By Eliza Ruhamah Scidmore. IX, pp. 105-112, 3 ills., Apr., 1898

Note on the Activity of Shishaldin Volcano. (By Homer P. Ritter). XVI, p. 249, May, 1905

Notes on the Wild Fowl and Game Animals of Alaska. By E. W. Nelson. IX, pp. 121-132, 6 ills., Apr., 1898

On Eskimo Geographic Names Ending in Miut. (By John Murdoch). IX, p. 190, Apr., 1898

Opening of the Alaskan Territory. By Harrington Emerson. XIV, pp. 99-106, 5 ills., Mar., 1903

Origin of the Name "Cape Nome." (By George Davidson). XII, p. 398, Nov., 1901

Our Air Frontier in Alaska. By Major General H. H. Arnold. LXXVIII, pp. 487-504, 15 ills., map, Oct., 1940

Our Greatest National Monument: The National Geographic Society Completes Its Explorations in the Valley of Ten Thousand Smokes. By Robert F. Griggs. XL, pp. 219-292, 73 ills. in black and white, 16 ills. in color, maps, Sept., 1921

Our Youngest Volcano. By J. S. Diller. V, pp. 93-96, ill., July 10, 1893

Over the Roof of Our Continent. By Bradford Washburn. LXXIV, pp. 78-98, 17 ills. in duotone, map, July, 1938

Photography in Glacial Alaska. By O. D. von Engeln. XXI, pp. 54-62, 4 ills., Jan., 1910

ALASKA—*Continued*

Plan for Climbing Mt. McKinley. By Alfred H. Brooks and D. L. Reaburn. XIV, pp. 30-35, map, Jan., 1903

The Possibilities of Alaska. By C. C. Georgeson. XIII, pp. 81-85, Mar., 1902

Proposed Surveys in Alaska in 1902. By Alfred H. Brooks. XIII, pp. 133-135, map, Apr., 1902

Railway Routes in Alaska. By Alfred H. Brooks. XVIII, pp. 165-190, 9 ills., diagrs., 8 maps, Mar., 1907

The Recent Eruption of Katmai Volcano in Alaska. By George C. Martin. XXIV, pp. 131-181, 45 ills., diagr., map, Feb., 1913

Recent Explorations in Alaska. By Eliza Ruhamah Scidmore. V, pp. 173-179, Jan. 31, 1894

The Recession of the Glaciers of Glacier Bay, Alaska. By Fremont Morse. XIX, pp. 76-78, map, Jan., 1908

Reindeer in Alaska. By Gilbert H. Grosvenor. XIV, pp. 127-149, 19 ills., map, Apr., 1903

Report of Committee on Exploration in Alaska. III, pp. 248-250, Feb. 19, 1892

The Returns from Alaska. XVI, p. 513, map, Nov., 1905

Shishaldin (Mountain) as a Field for Exploration. By Joseph Stanley-Brown. X, pp. 281-288, 3 ills., map, Aug., 1899

Some Notes on the Fox Island Passes, Alaska. By J. J. Gilbert. XVI, pp. 427-429, Sept., 1905

Some of the Conditions and Possibilities of Agriculture in Alaska. By Walter H. Evans. IX, pp. 178-187, Apr., 1898

The Stikine River in 1898. By Eliza Ruhamah Scidmore. X, pp. 1-15, 4 ills., Jan., 1899

Strategic Alaska Looks Ahead: Our Vast Territory, Now Being More Closely Linked to Us by Road and Rail, Embodies the American Epic of Freedom, Adventure, and the Pioneer Spirit. By Ernest H. Gruening. LXXXII, pp. 281-315, 18 ills. in black and white, 16 ills. in color, two-page map, Sept., 1942

Studies of Muir Glacier, Alaska. By Harry Fielding Reid. IV, pp. 19-55, 13 ills., 6 diagrs., table, 2 maps (1 foldout), Mar. 21, 1892

Supplements I-III, drawings, map, pp. 56-78

Appendices I-IV, 3 tables, pp. 79-84

See Muir Glacier, for contents of this article

Summary of Reports on the Mt. St. Elias Expedition. II, pp. 302-304, Apr., 1891

Surveying the 141st Meridian (Boundary Line Between Canada and Alaska). By Thomas Riggs, Jr. XXIII, pp. 685-713, 46 ills., map, July, 1912

The Sushitna River, Alaska. By W. A. Dickey. VIII, pp. 322-327, map, Nov., 1897

The Ten Thousand Smokes Now a National Monument: The President of the United States Sets Aside for the American People the Extraordinary Valley Discovered and Explored by the National Geographic Society. XXXV, pp. 359-366, 5 ills., Apr., 1919

To-day on "The Yukon Trail of 1898." By Amos Burg. LVIII, pp. 85-126, 52 ills., map, July, 1930

Transportation Methods in Alaska. By Captain George S. Gibbs. XVII, pp. 69-82, 19 ills., Feb., 1906

ALASKA—*Continued*

Two Hundred Miles up the Kuskokwim. By Charles Hallock. IX, pp. 85-92, 6 ills., Mar., 1898

An Undiscovered Island off the Northern Coast of Alaska. I—By Marcus Baker. II—By Captain Edward Perry Herendeen. III—By General A. W. Greely. V, pp. 76-83, July 10, 1893

The Valley of Ten Thousand Smokes: An Account of the Discovery and Exploration of the Most Wonderful Volcanic Region in the World. By Robert F. Griggs. XXXIII, pp. 115-169, 46 ills., map, panorama, Feb., 1918

The Awe-Inspiring Spectacle of the Valley of Ten Thousand Smokes, Discovered and Explored by National Geographic Society Expeditions (panorama)

The Valley of Ten Thousand Smokes: National Geographic Society Explorations in the Katmai District of Alaska. By Robert F. Griggs. XXXI, pp. 13-68, 51 ills., map, Jan., 1917

Volcanoes of Alaska (Report by Capt. K. W. Perry). XXIII, pp. 824-832, 11 ills., Aug., 1912

The White Sheep, Giant Moose, and Smaller Game of the Kenai Peninsula, Alaska. By George Shiras, 3d. XXIII, pp. 423-494, 59 ills., maps (1 two-page), May, 1912

A World Inside a Mountain: Aniakchak, the New Volcanic Wonderland of the Alaska Peninsula, Is Explored. By Bernard R. Hubbard. LX, pp. 319-345, 34 ills., map, Sept., 1931

The World's Highest Altitudes and First Ascents. By Charles E. Fay. XX, pp. 493-530, 25 ills., June, 1909

The Wrangell Mountains, Alaska. By Walter C. Mendenhall. XIV, pp. 395-407, 3 ills., panorama, Nov., 1903

The Wrangell Mountains. Panorama taken by author from the ridge east of the Dadina River

A Yukon Pioneer, Mike Lebarge. (By Wm. H. Dall). IX, pp. 137-139, ill., Apr., 1898

See also Aleutian Islands; Kodiak (Island); McKinley, Mount; St. Elias, Mount; Yakutat Bay

ALASKA—Our Northwestern Outpost. 16 color photos by Ernest H. Gruening, Amos Burg, Froelich Rainey. LXXXII, pp. 297-308, Sept., 1942

The **ALASKA** Brown Bear: The Largest Carnivorous Animal Extant. XXX, pictorial supplement, Nov., 1916

ALASKA MILITARY HIGHWAY:

Alaskan Highway an Engineering Epic: Mosquitoes, Mud, and Muskeg Minor Obstacles of 1,671-mile Race to Throw the Alcan Life Line Through Thick Forests and Uninhabited Wilderness. By Froelich Rainey. LXXXIII, pp. 143-168, 21 ills., 3 maps, Feb., 1943

The **ALASKAN** Boundary. By John W. Foster. X, pp. 425-456, 10 maps, map supplements, Nov., 1899

ALASKAN Boundary Decision. XIV, p. 423, Nov., 1903

ALASKAN Boundary Dispute. XIV, p. 79, Feb., 1903

The **ALASKAN** Boundary Survey. I—Introduction. By Dr. T. C. Mendenhall. II—The Boundary South of Fort Yukon. By J. E. McGrath. III—The Boundary North of Fort Yukon. By J. Henry Turner. IV, pp. 177-197, Feb. 8, 1893

The **ALASKAN** Boundary Tribunal. By John W. Foster. XV, pp. 1-12, map, map supplement, Jan., 1904

The **ALASKAN** Brown Bear. (By Wilfred H. Osgood). XX, pp. 332-333, Apr., 1909

ALASKAN-CANADIAN MILITARY HIGHWAY:

Alaskan Highway an Engineering Epic: Mosquitoes, Mud, and Muskeg Minor Obstacles of 1,671-mile Race to Throw the Alcan Life Line Through Thick Forests and Uninhabited Wilderness. By Froelich Rainey. LXXXIII, pp. 143-168, 21 ills., 3 maps, Feb., 1943

ALASKAN Highway an Engineering Epic: Mosquitoes, Mud, and Muskeg Minor Obstacles of 1,671-mile Race to Throw the Alcan Life Line Through Thick Forests and Uninhabited Wilderness. By Froelich Rainey. LXXXIII, pp. 143-168, 21 ills., 3 maps, Feb., 1943

ALASKA'S New Railway. XXVIII, pp. 567-589, 20 ills., Dec., 1915

ALBANIA:

The Albanians. By Theron J. Damon. XXIII, pp. 1090-1103, 14 ills., Nov., 1912

The Changing Map in the Balkans. By Frederick Moore. XXIV, pp. 199-226, 27 ills., map, Feb., 1913

Europe's Newest Kingdom: After Centuries of Struggle, Albania at Last Enjoys an Era of Peace and Stability. By Melville Chater. LIX, pp. 131-190, 37 ills. in black and white, 39 ills. in color, map, Feb., 1931

The Races of Europe. By Edwin A. Grosvenor. XXXIV, pp. 441-534, 62 ills., diagr. and index, maps, map supplement, Dec., 1918

Recent Observations in Albania. By Brig. Gen. George P. Scriven. XXXIV, pp. 90-114, 21 ills., map, Aug., 1918

The Young Turk. By Rear-Admiral Colby M. Chester. XXIII, pp. 43-89, 39 ills., Jan., 1912

The **ALBANIANS**. By Theron J. Damon. XXIII, pp. 1090-1103, 14 ills., Nov., 1912

ALBATROSS (Ship):

Deep-Sea Exploring Expedition of the Steamer "Albatross." By Hugh M. Smith. X, pp. 291-296, ills., diagr., Aug., 1899

ALBATROSSES (Birds):

A Bird City (Laysan Island, Hawaii). XV, pp. 494-498, 6 ills., Dec., 1904

Birds of the High Seas: Albatrosses and Petrels; Gannets, Man-o'-war-birds, and Tropic-birds. By Robert Cushman Murphy. Paintings by Major Allan Brooks. LXXIV, pp. 226-251, 7 ills. in black and white, 36 portraits in color, Aug., 1938

South Georgia, an Outpost of the Antarctic. By Robert Cushman Murphy. XLI, pp. 409-444, 41 ills., maps, Apr., 1922

ALBEE, RUTH:

Family Afoot in Yukon Wilds: Two Young Children and Their Parents Live Off the Country in the Northwest Canada Wilderness Now To Be Traversed by the Alaska Highway. By William Hamilton Albee, with Ruth Albee. LXXXI, pp. 589-616, 18 ills. in black and white, 14 ills. in color, May, 1942

ALBEE, WILLIAM HAMILTON:

Family Afoot in Yukon Wilds: Two Young Children and Their Parents Live Off the Country in the Northwest Canada Wilderness Now To Be Traversed by the Alaska Highway. By William Hamilton Albee, with Ruth Albee. LXXXI, pp. 589-616, 18 ills. in black and white, 14 ills. in color, May, 1942

ALBEMARLE (County), Virginia:

Albemarle in Revolutionary Days. By Dr. G. Brown Goode. VII, pp. 271-281, Aug., 1896

ALBERTA (Province), Canada:

The Columbia (River) Turns on the Power. By Maynard Owen Williams. LXXIX, pp. 749-792, 25 ills. in black and white, 18 ills. in color, June, 1941

Exploration in the Canadian Rockies. X, pp. 135-136, Apr., 1899

Hunting Big Game of Other Days: A Boating Expedition in Search of Fossils in Alberta, Canada. By Barnum Brown. XXXV, pp. 407-429, 24 ills., map, May, 1919

Landslides and Rock Avalanches. By Guy Elliott Mitchell. XXI, pp. 277-287, 6 ills., Apr., 1910

The Monarch of the Canadian Rockies: The Robson Peak District of British Columbia and Alberta. By Charles D. Walcott. XXIV, pp. 626-639, 13 ills., panorama, May, 1913

The Monarch of the Canadian Rockies—Robson Peak (panorama).

The Mother of Rivers: An Account of a Photographic Expedition to the Great Columbia Ice Field of the Canadian Rockies. By Lewis R. Freeman. XLVII, pp. 377-446, 60 ills., maps, Apr., 1925

Peaks and Parks of Western Canada. 11 photos: 5 by W. J. Oliver. LXXX, pp. 516-526, Oct., 1941

Peaks and Trails in the Canadian Alps. 16 photos in duotone by Byron Harmon and Clifford White. LXV, pp. 627-642, May, 1934

Recent Exploration in the Canadian Rockies. By Walter D. Wilcox. XIII, pp. 151-168, 12 ills., map, May, 1902; Part II, pp. 185-200, 9 ills., June, 1902

ALBRECHT, FLORENCE CRAIG:

Austro-Italian Mountain Frontiers. By Florence Craig Albrecht. XXVII, pp. 321-376, 60 ills., map, Apr., 1915

Channel Ports—And Some Others. By Florence Craig Albrecht. XXVIII, pp. 1-55, 45 ills., July, 1915

The City of Jacqueline (Ter Goes, Netherlands). By Florence Craig Albrecht. XXVII, pp. 29-56, 31 ills., Jan., 1915

Frontier Cities of Italy. By Florence Craig Albrecht. XXVII, pp. 533-586, 45 ills., June, 1915

London. By Florence Craig Albrecht. XXVIII, pp. 263-294, 29 ills., Sept., 1915

The Splendor of Rome. By Florence Craig Albrecht. XLI, pp. 593-626, 28 ills., June, 1922

ALBRECHT, FLORENCE CRAIG—*Continued*

The Town of Many Gables (Münster, Germany). By Florence Craig Albrecht. XXVII, pp. 107-140, 28 ills., Feb., 1915

"ALCAN" HIGHWAY. *See* Alaskan-Canadian Military Highway

ALDEN, CARROLL STORRS:

Megaspelæon, the Oldest Monastery in Greece. By Carroll Storrs Alden. XXIV, pp. 310-323, 11 ills., Mar., 1913

ALDERNEY (Island), Channel Islands:

The Channel Islands. By Edith Carey. XXXVIII, pp. 143-164, 24 ills., map, Aug., 1920

ALEPPO, Syria:

From Jerusalem to Aleppo. By John D. Whiting. XXIV, pp. 71-113, 30 ills., map, Jan., 1913

Impressions of Asiatic Turkey. By Stephen van Rensselaer Trowbridge. XXVI, pp. 598-609, 6 ills., Dec., 1914

Syria and Lebanon Taste Freedom. By Maynard Owen Williams. With 21 color photos by author. XC, pp. 729-763, 16 ills. in black and white, Dec., 1946

ALERT Anatolia. 13 ills. LXXXV, pp. 481-492, Apr., 1944

ALEUTIAN ISLANDS, Alaska:

Bizarre Battleground—the Lonely Aleutians. By Lonnelle Davison. LXXXII, pp. 316-317, ill., Sept., 1942

A Jack in the Box: An Account of the Strange Performances of the Most Wonderful Island in the World (Bogoslof Volcano). By Captain F. M. Munger. XX, pp. 194-199, 8 ills., Feb., 1909

A Navy Artist Paints the Aleutians. By Mason Sutherland. Paintings by Lt. William F. Draper. LXXXIV, pp. 157-176, 4 ills. in black and white, 16 ills. in color, Aug., 1943

Riddle of the Aleutians: A Botanist Explores the Origin of Plants on Ever-misty Islands Now Enshrouded in the Fog of War. By Isobel Wylie Hutchison. LXXXII, pp. 769-792, 24 ills., Dec., 1942

See also Unimak

ALEUTS (People):

Indians of Our North Pacific Coast. By Matthew W. Stirling. Paintings by W. Langdon Kihn. LXXXVII, pp. 25-52, 3 ills. in black and white, 16 ills. in color, Jan., 1945

ALGERIA:

The American Eclipse Expedition. By Rear Admiral Colby M. Chester. XVII, pp. 589-612, 23 ills., col. pl., Nov., 1906

Americans on the Barbary Coast. By Willard Price. LXXXIV, pp. 1-31, 13 ills. in black and white, 10 ills. in color, map, July, 1943

Biskra, the Ziban Queen. By Mrs. George C. Bosson, Jr. XIX, pp. 563-593, 29 ills., map, Aug., 1908

The Conquest of the Sahara by the Automobile. XLV, pp. 87-93, 9 ills., map, Jan., 1924

The Country of the Ant Men. By Thomas H. Kearney. XXII, pp. 367-382, 13 ills., map, panorama, Apr., 1911

ALGERIA—*Continued*

The Date Gardens of the Jerid. By Thomas H. Kearney. XXI, pp. 543-567, 20 ills., July, 1910

Eastward from Gibraltar: Overland Route Across North Africa to Tunisia and Libia. By Cyrus French Wicker. LXXXIII, pp. 115-142, 28 ills., Jan., 1943

Here and There in Northern Africa. By Frank Edward Johnson. XXV, pp. 1-132, 113 ills., Jan., 1914

In Civilized French Africa. By James F. J. Archibald. XX, pp. 303-311, 14 ills., Mar., 1909

On the Fringe of the Great Desert. 32 color photos by Gervais Courtellemont. LIII, pp. 207-222, Feb., 1928

Trans-Africa Safari: A Motor Caravan Rolls Across Sahara and Jungle Through Realms of Dusky Potentates and the Land of Big-Lipped Women. By Lawrence Copley Thaw and Margaret Stout Thaw. LXXIV, pp. 327-364, 29 ills. in black and white, 14 ills. in color, map, Sept., 1938

See also Algiers

ALGIERS, Algeria:

Eastward from Gibraltar: Overland Route Across North Africa to Tunisia and Libia. By Cyrus French Wicker. LXXXIII, pp. 115-142, 28 ills., Jan., 1943

The White City of Algiers. By Lieut. Col. Gordon Casserly. LIII, pp. 206-232, 9 ills. in black and white, 32 ills. in color, Feb., 1928

ALGONQUIAN INDIANS:

America's First Settlers, the Indians. By Matthew W. Stirling. Paintings by W. Langdon Kihn. LXXII, pp. 535-596, 34 ills. in black and white, 24 ills. in color, Nov., 1937

ALGUÉ, JOSÉ:

The Manila Observatory. By Rev. Father José Algué. XI, pp. 427-438, ills., Nov., 1900

ALI Goes to the Clinic. By Herndon and Mary Hudson. XC, pp. 764-766, ills., Dec., 1946

ALICE (Yacht):

Southward Ho! In the "Alice." By Henry Howard. LXXIII, pp. 265-312, 38 ills. in black and white, 13 ills. in color, maps, Mar., 1938

ALIKULUF INDIANS:

The Indian Tribes of Southern Patagonia, Tierra del Fuego, and the Adjoining Islands. By J. B. Hatcher. XII, pp. 12-22, 4 ills., Jan., 1901

Inside Cape Horn. By Amos Burg. LXXII, pp. 743-783, 29 ills. in black and white, 10 ills. in color, two-page map, Dec., 1937

ALKMAAR, Netherlands:

A North Holland Cheese Market. By Hugh M. Smith. XXI, pp. 1051-1066, 17 ills., Dec., 1910

ALL Around the Bay of Passamaquoddy. By Albert S. Gatschet. VIII, pp. 16-24, Jan., 1897

ALLAGASH COUNTRY, Maine:

In the Allagash Country. By Kenneth Fuller Lee. LV, pp. 505-520, 19 ills., Apr., 1929

ALLAHABAD, India:

Through the Heart of Hindustan: A Teeming Highway Extending for Fifteen Hundred Miles, from the Khyber Pass to Calcutta. By Maynard Owen Williams. XL, pp. 433-467, 29 ills., Nov., 1921

ALLEMAN, IRVIN E.:

Seals of Our Nation, States, and Territories. 84 ills. in color from paintings by Carlotta Gonzales Lahey, Irvin E. Alleman, Theodora Price. XC, pp. 17-32, July, 1946

ALLEN, ARTHUR A.:

Ambassadors of Good Will (Birds): Annual Messengers from Our Neighbor Republics to the South Bring Cheer and Add Interest to the Out-of-Doors. By Arthur A. Allen. LXXXI, pp. 786-796, 13 ills. in color, June, 1942

Birds of Timberline and Tundra. By Arthur A. Allen. With 24 color photos by author. XC, pp. 313-339, 8 ills. in black and white, Sept., 1946

Birds on the Home Front. By Arthur A. Allen. LXXXIV, pp. 32-56, 7 ills. in black and white, 30 ills. in color, July, 1943

Blackbirds and Orioles. By Arthur A. Allen. Paintings by Major Allan Brooks. LXVI, pp. 111-130, 48 portraits in color, July, 1934

Hunting with a Microphone the Voices of Vanishing Birds. By Arthur A. Allen. LXXI, pp. 697-723, 32 ills., June, 1937

The Shore Birds, Cranes, and Rails: Willets, Plovers, Stilts, Phalaropes, Sandpipers, and Their Relatives Deserve Protection. By Arthur A. Allen. Paintings by Major Allan Brooks. LXXII, pp. 183-222, 4 ills. in black and white, 101 portraits in color, Aug., 1937

Sights and Sounds of the Winged World: Study of Birds to Make National Geographic Color Photographs Yields Rich Scientific Knowledge of Their Habits and Behavior. By Arthur A. Allen. LXXXVII, pp. 721-744, ill. in black and white, drawings, 26 ills. in color, June, 1945

Stalking Birds With a Color Camera: An Expert in Avian Habits Persuades His Subjects to Sit Where He Wants Them, Even in His Hat. By Arthur A. Allen. LXXV, pp. 777-789, 3 ills. in black and white, 14 ills. in color, June, 1939

Color Close-ups of Familiar Birds. 14 color photos by author, pp. 779-786

The Tanagers and Finches: Their Flashes of Color and Lilting Songs Gladden the Hearts of American Bird Lovers East and West. By Arthur A. Allen. Paintings by Maj. Allan Brooks. LXVII, pp. 505-532, 6 ills. in black and white, 55 portraits in color, Apr., 1935

Touring for Birds with Microphone and Color Cameras. By Arthur A. Allen. LXXXV, pp. 689-712, 3 ills. in black and white, 24 ills. in color, June, 1944

A Bag of Bird Portraits. 24 color photos: 23 by author, pp. 697-712

ALLENBY, EDMUND HENRY HYNMAN:

Old Jewel in the Proper Setting: An Eyewitness's Account of the Reconquest of the Holy Land by Twentieth Century Crusaders. By Charles W. Whitehair. XXXIV, pp. 325-344, 17 ills., Oct., 1918

ALLIED MILITARY GOVERNMENT:

Americans Help Liberated Europe Live Again. By Lt. Col. Frederick Simpich, Jr. LXXXVII, pp. 747-768, 17 ills., June, 1945

ALLIED MILITARY GOVERNMENT—*Continued*

Europe's Looted Art. By John Walker. LXXXIX, pp. 39-52, 11 ills., Jan., 1946

See also American Military Government

ALMADA, Lisbon, Portugal:

Lisbon, the City of the Friendly Bay. By Clifford Albion Tinker. XLII, pp. 505-552, 30 ills. in black and white, 16 ills. in color, map, Nov., 1922

ALMASY, PAUL:

Madagascar: Mystery Island: Japan's Push into the Indian Ocean Swings the Searchlight of World Attention to This Huge French Sentinel off the African Coast. By Paul Almasy. LXXXI, pp. 797-830, 37 ills., 3 maps, June, 1942

ALONG London's Coronation Route. By Maynard Owen Williams. LXXI, pp. 609-632, 22 ills., map, May, 1937

ALONG Our Side of the Mexican Border. By Frederick Simpich. XXXVIII, pp. 61-80, 9 ills., map, July, 1920

ALONG the Banks of the Colorful Nile. 23 color photos by Gervais Courtellemont. L, pp. 323-338, Sept., 1926

ALONG the Nile, Through Egypt and the Sudan. By Frederick Simpich. XLII, pp. 379-410, 29 ills., Oct., 1922

ALONG the Old Inca Highway. By Harriet Chalmers Adams. XIX, pp. 231-250, 21 ills., Apr., 1908

ALONG the Old Mandarin Road of Indo-China. By W. Robert Moore. LX, pp. 157-199, 32 ills. in black and white, 28 ills. in color, map, Aug., 1931

ALONG the Old Silk Routes: A Motor Caravan with Air-conditioned Trailer Retraces Ancient Roads from Paris across Europe and Half of Asia to Delhi. By Lawrence Copley Thaw and Margaret S. Thaw. LXXVIII, pp. 453-486, 33 ills., map, Oct., 1940

ALONG the Old Spanish Road in Mexico: Life Among the People of Nayarit and Jalisco, Two of the Richest States of the Southern Republic. By Herbert Corey. XLIII, pp. 225-281, 36 ills. in black and white, 16 ills. in color, map, Mar., 1923

ALONG the Way of the Magi. 14 color photos by American Colony Photographers. LVI, pp. 709-716, Dec., 1929

ALPACAS:

Camels of the Clouds. By W. H. Hodge. LXXXIX, pp. 641-656, 15 ills., map, May, 1946

ALPHABETS:

A New Alphabet of the Ancients Is Unearthed: An Inconspicuous Mound in Northern Syria Yields Archeological Treasures of Far-reaching Significance. By F. A. Schaeffer. LVIII, pp. 477-516, 47 ills., map, Oct., 1930

Secrets from Syrian Hills: Explorations Reveal World's Earliest Known Alphabet, Deciphered from Schoolboy Slates and Dictionaries of 3,000 Years Ago. By Claude F. A. Schaeffer. LXIV, pp. 97-126, 40 ills., map, July, 1933

ALPHABETS—*Continued*
Turkey Goes to School. By Maynard Owen Williams. LV, pp. 95-108, 17 ills., Jan., 1929
See also Languages

ALPINE Peaks and Pastures of South Island (New Zealand). 11 color photos by W. Robert Moore. LXIX, pp. 205-212, Feb., 1936

ALPINE Villagers of Austria. 15 color photos by Hans Hildenbrand and Wilhelm Tobien. LVI, pp. 669-676, Dec., 1929

ALPS (Mountains), Europe:
Alpine Villagers of Austria. 15 color photos by Hans Hildenbrand and Wilhelm Tobien. LVI, pp. 669-676, Dec., 1929
The Ascent of Mont Blanc. By Walter Woodburn Hyde. XXIV, pp. 861-942, 69 ills., Aug., 1913
Austro-Italian Mountain Frontiers. By Florence Craig Albrecht. XXVII, pp. 321-376, 60 ills., map, Apr., 1915
The Beauty of the Bavarian Alps. By Colonel Fitzhugh Lee Minnigerode. XLIX, pp. 632-649, 16 ills. in color, June, 1926
Flights from Arctic to Equator: Conquering the Alps, the Ice Peaks of Spitsbergen, of Persia, and Africa's Mountains of the Moon. By Walter Mittelholzer. LXI, pp. 445-498, 53 ills., map, Apr., 1932
In Valais. By Louise Murray. XXI, pp. 249-256, 6 ills., Mar., 1910
Letters from the Italian Front. By Marchesa Louise de Rosales to Ethel Mather Bagg. XXXII, pp. 47-67, 22 ills., July, 1917
The Majesty of the Matterhorn. XXIII, text p. 514; pictorial supplement, May, 1912
Manless Alpine Climbing: The First Woman to Scale the Grépon, the Matterhorn, and Other Famous Peaks Without Masculine Support Relates Her Adventures. By Miriam O'Brien Underhill. LXVI, pp. 131-170, 30 ills. in black and white, 12 ills. in color, Aug., 1934
Over the Alps to Brenner Pass. 15 photos, two-page map. LXXXIV, pp. 701-714, Dec., 1943
Scenes in Switzerland. 13 ills. XXI, pp. 257-268, Mar., 1910
Skiing in Switzerland's Realm of Winter Sports. 10 photos in duotone by Jean Gaberell, E. Gyger, A. Klopfenstein. LXIII, pp. 345-352, Mar., 1933
Swiss Cherish Their Ancient Liberties. 21 ills. LXXIX, pp. 481-496, Apr., 1941
This Was Austria. 18 ills. LXXXVIII, pp. 71-86, July, 1945
A Woman's Climbs in the High Alps. By Dora Keen. XXII, pp. 643-675, 26 ills., July, 1911
The World's Highest Altitudes and First Ascents. By Charles E. Fay. XX, pp. 493-530, 25 ills., June, 1909

AL QOSH (Monastery), Iraq:
Mountain Tribes of Iran and Iraq. By Harold Lamb. LXXXIX, pp. 385-408, 15 ills., two-page map, Mar., 1946

ALSACE (Region), France:
In French Lorraine: That Part of France Where the First American Soldiers Have Fallen. By Harriet Chalmers Adams. XXXII, pp. 499-518, 16 ills., Nov.-Dec., 1917

ALSACE (Region), France—*Continued*
In Smiling Alsace, Where France Has Resumed Sway. LII, pp. 168-176, 11 ills. in color, Aug., 1927

AL SAUD, ABDUL AZIZ (King of Saudi Arabia):
Guest in Saudi Arabia. By Maynard Owen Williams. LXXXVIII, pp. 463-487, 24 ills., map, Oct., 1945

ALTAI MOUNTAINS, Outer Mongolia-Sinkiang:
Western Siberia and the Altai Mountains: With Some Speculations on the Future of Siberia. By James Bryce. XXXIX, pp. 469-507, 39 ills., May, 1921

ALTAÏR (Ship):
Sailing Forbidden Coasts (Africa). By Ida Treat. LX, pp. 357-386, 31 ills., map, Sept., 1931

The **ALTITUDE** of Mount Adams, Washington. By Edgar McClure. VII, pp. 151-153, tables, Apr., 1896

ALTITUDES:
The Highest Point in Each State. XX, pp. 539-541, ills., June, 1909
The World's Highest Altitudes and First Ascents. By Charles E. Fay. XX, pp. 493-530, 25 ills., June, 1909

An **ALTITUDINAL** Journey Through Portugal: Rugged Scenic Beauty, Colorful Costumes, and Ancient Castles Abound in Tiny Nation That Once Ruled a Vast Empire. By Harriet Chalmers Adams. LII, pp. 567-610, 44 ills., map, Nov., 1927

AMADEO, LUIGI, Prince of Savoy. *See* Abruzzi, Duke of the

AMAMI O SHIMA (Island), Ryukyu Retto:
Peacetime Rambles in the Ryukyus. By William Leonard Schwartz. LXXXVII, pp. 543-561, 12 ills., maps, May, 1945

AMAZON (River), South America:
The Amazon, Father of Waters: The Earth's Mightiest River Drains a Basin of More Than 2,700,000 Square Miles, from Which Came Originally the World's Finest Rubber. By W. L. Schurz. XLIX, pp. 445-463, 15 ills., Apr., 1926
Exploring the Valley of the Amazon in a Hydroplane: Twelve Thousand Miles of Flying Over the World's Greatest River and Greatest Forest to Chart the Unknown Parima River from the Sky. By Captain Albert W. Stevens. XLIX, pp. 353-420, 86 ills., map, Apr., 1926
Fishing and Hunting Tales from Brazil. By Dewey Austin Cobb. XX, pp. 917-920, Oct., 1909
A Journey by Jungle Rivers to the Home of the Cock-of-the-rock: Naturalists Enter the Amazon, Voyage Through the Heart of Tropical South America, and Emerge at the Mouth of the Orinoco. By Ernest G. Holt. LXIV, pp. 585-630, 49 ills., map, Nov., 1933
A New Peruvian Route to the Plain of the Amazon. By Solon I. Bailey. XVII, pp. 432-448, 12 ills., Aug., 1906
South America. Annual Address by the President, Gardiner G. Hubbard. III, pp. 1-29, foldout map, Mar. 28, 1891

AMBASSADORS of Good Will (Birds): Annual Messengers from Our Neighbor Republics to the South Bring Cheer and Add Interest to the Out-of-Doors. By Arthur A. Allen. LXXXI, pp. 786-796, 13 ills. in color, June, 1942

AMBERGRIS:

The Islands of Bermuda: A British Colony with a Unique Record in Popular Government. By William Howard Taft. XLI, pp. 1-26, 15 ills., map, Jan., 1922

AMCHITKA (Island), Aleutian Islands:

A Navy Artist Paints the Aleutians. By Mason Sutherland. Paintings by Lt. William F. Draper. LXXXIV, pp. 157-176, 4 ills. in black and white, 16 ills. in color, Aug., 1943

AMERICA:

Discoverers of America. Annual Address by the President, Hon. Gardiner G. Hubbard. V, pp. 1-20, charts, maps, 3 map supplements, Apr. 7, 1893

Discovery of America: Fourth Centennial Anniversary: International Literary Contest (Madrid, Spain). I, pp. 273-276, July, 1889

See also New World

AMERICA (Airplane):

Our Transatlantic Flight. By Commander Richard Evelyn Byrd. LII, pp. 347-368, 17 ills., map, Sept., 1927

AMERICA Fights on the Farms. 21 ills. in color. LXXXVI, pp. 33-48, July, 1944

AMERICA from the Air: No Such Series of Airplane Views Has Ever Before Been Printed. (Photos by Lieutenant Albert W. Stevens). XLVI, pp. 85-92, 8 ills., July, 1924

AMERICA in the Air: The Future of Airplane and Airship, Economically and as Factors in National Defense. By Brigadier-General William Mitchell. XXXIX, pp. 339-352, 8 ills., map, Mar., 1921

AMERICA on the Move. 26 photos by J. Baylor Roberts, B. Anthony Stewart, and others. XC, pp. 357-378, Sept., 1946

AMERICAN Airmen in the Azores. 10 ills. in color. LXXXIX, pp. 177-184, Feb., 1946

AMERICAN Alma Maters in the Near East. By Maynard Owen Williams. LXXXVIII, pp. 237-256, 16 ills., Aug., 1945

AMERICAN ASSOCIATION FOR THE ADVANCEMENT OF SCIENCE:

The American Association at Buffalo. VII, pp. 315-316, Sept., 1896

The American Association for the Advancement of Science. (By G.H.G.). X, pp. 355-359, Sept., 1899

American Association for the Advancement of Science. (By J.H.). IX, pp. 412-413, Sept., 1898

Frederic W. Putnam. (By J. H.). IX, pp. 429-431, ill. (front.), Oct., 1898

AMERICAN Berries of Hill, Dale, and Wayside. Paintings by Mary E. Eaton. XXXV, pp. 168-184, ill. in black and white, 29 ills. in color, Feb., 1919

AMERICAN Birds of Prey—A Review of Their Value. XXXVIII, pp. 460-467, 6 ills., Dec., 1920

AMERICAN Bombers Attacking from Australia. By Howell Walker. LXXXIII, pp. 49-70, 19 ills., map, Jan., 1943

AMERICAN COLLEGE FOR GIRLS, Turkey. *See* Istanbul Woman's College

AMERICAN COLONY PHOTOGRAPHERS: Jerusalem:

Along the Way of the Magi. 14 color photos by American Colony Photographers. LVI, pp. 709-716, Dec., 1929

Palestine. 21 (col.) photos by the American Colony, Jerusalem. XXV, pp. 265-313, Mar., 1914

AMERICAN Decorations and Insignia of Honor and Service. By Col. Robert E. Wyllie. XXXVI, pp. 502-526, 6 ills. in black and white, 119 ills. in color, Dec., 1919

The **AMERICAN** Deserts. XV, pp. 153-163, 7 ills., map, Apr., 1904

AMERICAN Development of the Philippines. XIV, pp. 197-203, 4 ills., May, 1903

AMERICAN Discoverers of the Antarctic Continent. By Major General A. W. Greely. XXIII, pp. 298-312, 7 ills., map, Mar., 1912

AMERICAN Discoveries in Egypt. XVIII, pp. 801-806, 8 ills., Dec., 1907

The **AMERICAN** Eclipse Expedition. By Rear Admiral Colby M. Chester. XVII, pp. 589-612, 23 ills., col. pl., Nov., 1906

An **AMERICAN** Fable (Conservation of Natural Resources). By Gifford Pinchot. XIX, pp. 345-350, May, 1908

AMERICAN Fighters Visit Bible Lands. By Maynard Owen Williams. With 23 color photos by author. LXXXIX, pp. 311-340, 10 ills. in black and white, Mar., 1946

An **AMERICAN** Floating Exposition. XII, pp. 204-205, May, 1901

AMERICAN FORESTRY ASSOCIATION:

Summer Meeting of the American Forestry Association. XIII, pp. 352-358, Sept., 1902

AMERICAN Game Birds. By Henry Wetherbee Henshaw. Paintings by Louis Agassiz Fuertes. XXVIII, pp. 105-158, 4 ills. in black and white, 72 ills. in color, Aug., 1915

AMERICAN Geographic Education. By W J McGee. IX, pp. 305-307, July, 1898

An **AMERICAN** Gibraltar: Notes on the Danish West Indies. XXX, pp. 89-96, 4 ills., map, July, 1916

An **AMERICAN** Girl Cycles Across Romania: Two-wheel Pilgrim Pedals the Land of Castles and Gypsies, Where Roman Empire Traces Mingle With Remnants of Oriental Migration. By Dorothy Hosmer. LXXIV, pp. 557-588, 31 ills., map, Nov., 1938

AMERICAN Goods in China. XVII, pp. 173-175, 4 ills., Mar., 1906

AMERICAN Industries Geared for War. By Thornton Oakley. With 16 ills. in color from paintings by author. LXXXII, pp. 716-734, ill. in black and white, Dec., 1942

"AMERICAN MEDITERRANEAN." *See* Caribbean Regions

AMERICAN MILITARY GOVERNMENT:

Sunset in the East (Japan). By Blair A. Walliser. LXXXIX, pp. 797-812, 17 ills., June, 1946

AMERICAN MUSEUM OF NATURAL HISTORY: Expeditions:

Fighting Giants of the Humboldt. By David D. Duncan. LXXIX, pp. 373-400, 28 ills., map, Mar., 1941

On the Bottom of a South Sea Pearl Lagoon. By Roy Waldo Miner. LXXIV, pp. 365-390, 17 ills. in black and white, 8 ills. in color, Sept., 1938

Unknown New Guinea: Circumnavigating the World in a Flying Boat, American Scientists Discover a Valley of 60,000 People Never Before Seen by White Men. By Richard Archbold. LXXIX, pp. 315-344, 28 ills., map, Mar., 1941

AMERICAN NATIONAL RED CROSS:

The American Red Cross in Italy. By Mabel Boardman. XX, pp. 396-397, Apr., 1909

America's Duty. By Newton D. Baker. XXXI, pp. 453-457, 5 ills., May, 1917

Bind the Wounds of France. By Herbert C. Hoover. XXXI, pp. 439-444, 5 ills., May, 1917

The Great Mississippi Flood of 1927: Since White Man's Discovery This Mighty River Has Served Him Well, Yet It Has Brought Widespread Devastation Along Its Lower Reaches. By Frederick Simpich. LII, pp. 243-289, 53 ills., map, Sept., 1927

The Healer of Humanity's Wounds. XXXIV, pp. 308-324, 16 ills., Oct., 1918

Help Our Red Cross. By Woodrow Wilson. XXXI, p. 422, May, 1917

Heroes of Wartime Science and Mercy. By Elizabeth W. King. LXXXIV, pp. 715-740, 11 ills. in black and white, 334 ills. in color, Dec., 1943

Honors to the American Navy (National Geographic Society Banquet: Speech by Mabel Boardman). XX, pp. 77-95, Jan., 1909

The National Geographic Society (Speech by Mabel Boardman). XXIII, pp. 272-298, 5 ills., Mar., 1912

Our Armies of Mercy. By Henry P. Davison. XXXI, pp. 423-427, 3 ills., May, 1917

A Poisoned World. By William Howard Taft. XXXI, pp. 459-467, 7 ills., May, 1917

Red Cross Girl Overseas. By Margaret Cotter. LXXXVI, pp. 745-768, 22 ills., Dec., 1944

The Red Cross Spirit. By Eliot Wadsworth. XXXI, pp. 467-474, 8 ills., May, 1917

Stand by the Soldier. By Major General John J. Pershing. XXXI, pp. 457-459, ill., May, 1917

The Symbol of Service to Mankind. By Stockton Axson. XXXIII, pp. 375-390, 11 ills., Apr., 1918

AMERICAN Pathfinders in the Pacific. By William H. Nicholas. LXXXIX, pp. 617-640, 17 ills., two-page map, May, 1946

The **AMERICAN** People Must Become Ship-Minded. By Edward N. Hurley. XXXIV, pp. 201-211, 7 ills., Sept., 1918

AMERICAN Potash for America. By Guy Elliott Mitchell. XXII, pp. 399-405, 4 ills., Apr., 1911

AMERICAN Progress in Cuba. XIII, p. 76, Feb., 1902

AMERICAN Progress in Habana. XIII, pp. 97-108, 10 ills., Mar., 1902

AMERICAN REVOLUTION:

Albemarle in Revolutionary Days. By Dr. G. Brown Goode. VII, pp. 271-281, Aug., 1896

See also Our First Alliance (France)

The **AMERICAN** Scene. 29 winning photos in the Sixth Annual Newspaper National Snapshot Awards, with explanatory note. LXXIX, pp. 220-246, Feb., 1941

AMERICAN Soldier in Reykjavík. By Corporal Luther M. Chovan. LXXXVIII, pp. 536-568, 6 ills. in black and white, 34 ills. in color, Nov., 1945

AMERICAN South Polar Expedition. XIX, pp. 885-888, Dec., 1908

AMERICAN Transportation Vital to Victory. By Thornton Oakley. With 16 ills. in color from paintings by author. LXXXIV, pp. 671-688, Dec., 1943

AMERICAN UNIVERSITY AT CAIRO, Egypt:

American Alma Maters in the Near East. By Maynard Owen Williams. LXXXVIII, pp. 237-256, 16 ills., Aug., 1945

AMERICAN UNIVERSITY OF BEIRUT, Lebanon:

American Alma Maters in the Near East. By Maynard Owen Williams. LXXXVIII, pp. 237-256, 16 ills., Aug., 1945

The **AMERICAN** Virgins (Virgin Islands): After Dark Days, These Adopted Daughters of the United States Are Finding a New Place in the Caribbean Sun. By DuBose Heyward and Daisy Reck. LXXVIII, pp. 273-308, 15 ills. in black and white, 23 ills. in color, map, Sept., 1940

AMERICAN Wild Flowers. 29 ills. in color from paintings by Mary E. Eaton. XXVII, pp. 507-517, May, 1915

AMERICAN Wings Soar Around the World: Epic Story of the Air Transport Command of the U. S. Army Is a Saga of Yankee Daring and Doing. By Donald H. Agnew and William A. Kinney. LXXXIV, pp. 57-78, 22 ills., July, 1943

AMERICANA. 11 winning photos in the Seventh Annual Newspaper National Snapshot Awards. LXXXI, pp. 657-666, May, 1942

AMERICANIZATION:

New York—The Metropolis of Mankind. By William Joseph Showalter. XXXIV, pp. 1-49, 39 ills., July, 1918

What Is It To Be an American? By Franklin K. Lane. XXXIII, pp. 348-354, 4 ills., diagr., Apr., 1918

AMERICANS Help Liberated Europe Live Again. By Lt. Col. Frederick Simpich, Jr. LXXXVII, pp. 747-768, 17 ills., June, 1945

AMERICANS in the Caribbean. By Luis Marden. LXXXI, pp. 723-758, 16 ills. in black and white, 22 ills. in color, map, June, 1942

AMERICANS on the Barbary Coast (Africa). By Willard Price. LXXXIV, pp. 1-31, 13 ills. in black and white, 10 ills. in color, map, July, 1943

AMERICANS Stand Guard in Greenland. By Andrew H. Brown. XC, pp. 457-500, 23 ills. in black and white, 19 ills. in color, map, Oct., 1946

AMERICA'S Amazing Railway Traffic. By William Joseph Showalter. XLIII, pp. 353-404, 46 ills., map, Apr., 1923

AMERICA'S Debt to the Hen. By Harry R. Lewis. LI, pp. 453-467, 15 ills., Apr., 1927

AMERICA'S Duty. By Newton D. Baker. XXXI, pp. 453-457, 5 ills., May, 1917

AMERICA'S First Settlers, the Indians. By Matthew W. Stirling. Paintings by W. Langdon Kihn. LXXII, pp. 535-596, 34 ills. in black and white, 24 ills. in color, Nov., 1937

AMERICA'S Most Valuable Fishes. By Hugh M. Smith. XXIII, pp. 494-514, 17 ills., May, 1912

AMERICA'S New Crescent of Defense (Air and Naval Bases). 8 photos, map. LXXVIII, pp. 621-628, Nov., 1940

AMERICA'S New Soldier Cities: The Geographical and Historical Environment of the National Army Cantonments and National Guard Camps. By William Joseph Showalter. XXXII, pp. 439-476, 18 ills., map, Nov.-Dec., 1917

AMERICA'S Part in the Allies' Mastery of the Air. By Major Joseph Tulasne. XXXIII, pp. 1-5, ills., Jan., 1918

AMERICA'S South Sea Soldiers (American Samoa). By Lorena MacIntyre Quinn. XXXVI, pp. 267-274, 8 ills., Sept., 1919

AMERICA'S Surpassing Fisheries: Their Present Condition and Future Prospects, and How the Federal Government Fosters Them. By Hugh M. Smith. XXIX, pp. 546-583, 35 ills., June, 1916

AMERNATH (Cave), India:

A Pilgrimage to Amernath, Himalayan Shrine of the Hindu Faith. By Louise Ahl Jessop. XL, pp. 513-542, 29 ills., Nov., 1921

AMG. *See* Allied Military Government

AMID the Snow Peaks of the Equator: A Naturalist's Explorations Around Ruwenzori, with an Excursion to the Congo State, and an Account of the Terrible Scourge of Sleeping Sickness. By A. F. R. Wollaston. XX, pp. 256-277, 11 ills., Mar., 1909

AMID the Snows and Swamps of Tropical Africa. 16 photos: 7 by Vittorio Sella. XLVII, pp. 163-178, Feb., 1925

AMID the Snows of Switzerland. 16 ills. in duotone by Albert Steiner. XLI, pp. 277-292, Mar., 1922

AMIDST the Templed Hills of Greece. 13 color photos by Maynard Owen Williams. LVIII, pp. 665-672, Dec., 1930

AMIENS, France:

The Beauties of France. By Arthur Stanley Riggs. XXVIII, pp. 391-491, 73 ills. in black and white, 16 ills. in color, map, Nov., 1915

AMNE MACHIN SHAN (Mountains), China:

Experiences of a Lone Geographer: An American Agricultural Explorer Makes His Way Through Brigand-infested Central China en Route to the Amne Machin Range, Tibet. By Joseph F. Rock. XLVIII, pp. 331-347, 16 ills., map, Sept., 1925

Seeking the Mountains of Mystery: An Expedition on the China-Tibet Frontier to the Unexplored Amnyi Machen Range, One of Whose Peaks Rivals Everest. By Joseph F. Rock. LVII, pp. 131-185, 54 ills., two-page map, Feb., 1930

AMONG the Bethlehem Shepherds: A Visit to the Valley Which David Probably Recalled When He Wrote the Twenty-third Psalm. By John D. Whiting. L, pp. 729-753, 19 ills., Dec., 1926

AMONG the Big Knot Lois of Hainan: Wild Tribesmen With Topknots Roam the Little-known Interior of This Big and Strategically Important Island in the China Sea. By Leonard Clark. LXXIV, pp. 391-418, 28 ills., map, Sept., 1938

AMONG the Big Trees of California. By John R. White. LXVI, pp. 219-232, 14 ills., Aug., 1934

AMONG the Cannibals of Belgian Kongo (Taken from the Notes of E. Torday). XXI, pp. 969-971, 4 ills., Nov., 1910

AMONG the "Craters of the Moon": An Account of the First Expeditions Through the Remarkable Volcanic Lava Beds of Southern Idaho. By R. W. Limbert. XLV, pp. 303-328, 23 ills., map, Mar., 1924

AMONG the Great Himalayan Glaciers. XIII, pp. 405-406, Nov., 1902

AMONG the Highlands of the Equator Republic (Ecuador). 12 color photos by Jacob Gayer. LV, pp. 69-76, Jan., 1929

AMONG the Hill Tribes of Burma—An Ethnological Thicket. By Sir George Scott. XLI, pp. 293-321, 22 ills., Mar., 1922

AMONG the Hill Tribes of Sumatra. By W. Robert Moore. LVII, pp. 187-227, 31 ills. in black and white, 25 ills. in color, map, Feb., 1930

AMONG the Mahogany Forests of Cuba. By Walter D. Wilcox. XIX, pp. 485-498, 6 ills., map, July, 1908

AMONG the Peaks and Parks of the Rockies (Colorado). 12 color photos by Fred Payne Clatworthy and H. L. Standley. LXII, pp. 39-46, July, 1932

AMONG the People of Cathay (China). 16 ills. in duotone. LI, pp. 701-716, June, 1927

AMONG the Plains and Hill People of Siam. 14 color photos by Amos Burg, Gervais Courtellemont, W. Robert Moore. LXV, pp. 563-570, May, 1934

AMONG the Snows and Flowers of Peru. 25 color photos by Jacob Gayer. LVII, pp. 733-764, June, 1930

AMONG the Zapotecs of Mexico: A Visit to the Indians of Oaxaca, Home State of the Republic's Great Liberator, Juárez, and Its Most Famous Ruler, Diaz. By Herbert Corey. LI, pp. 501-553, 59 ills., map, May, 1927

AMPHIBIOUS FORCE, U. S. Navy:
Landing Craft for Invasion. By Melville Bell Grosvenor. LXXXVI, pp. 1-30, 26 ills., July, 1944

AMPHIBIOUS TRAINING BASE, Solomons Island, Maryland:
Landing Craft for Invasion. By Melville Bell Grosvenor. LXXXVI, pp. 1-30, 26 ills., July, 1944

AMRITSAR, India:
Through the Heart of Hindustan: A Teeming Highway Extending for Fifteen Hundred Miles, from the Khyber Pass to Calcutta. By Maynard Owen Williams. XL, pp. 433-467, 29 ills., Nov., 1921

AMSTERDAM, Netherlands:
Behind Netherlands Sea Ramparts: Dikes and Pumps Keep Ocean and Rivers at Bay While a Busy People Carries on Peacetime Work. By McFall Kerbey. LXXVII, pp. 255-290, 26 ills. in black and white, 11 ills. in duotone, map, Feb., 1940
Glimpses of Holland. By William Wisner Chapin. XXVII, pp. 1-29, 26 ills., Jan., 1915
Holland Rises from War and Water. By Thomas R. Henry. LXXXIX, pp. 237-260, 18 ills., map, Feb., 1946

AMU DARYA (Oxus River), U. S. S. R.:
Surveying Through Khoresm: A Journey into Parts of Asiatic Russia Which Have Been Closed to Western Travelers Since the World War. By Lyman D. Wilbur. LXI, pp. 753-780, 31 ills., map, June, 1932

AMUNDSEN, ROALD:
Amundsen's Attainment of the South Pole. XXIII, pp. 205-208, map, Feb., 1912
Election of Roald Amundsen as Honorary Member of the Society. XVIII, p. 51, Jan., 1907
The First Meeting of the Poles (Photograph of the first meeting of Robert E. Peary, discoverer of the North Pole, and Roald Amundsen, discoverer of the South Pole, at the National Geographic Society, January 11, 1913). XXIV, ill. p. 114, Jan., 1913. LXIX, ill. p. 126, Jan., 1936
Honors for Amundsen (Presentation of Hubbard Medal). XIX, pp. 55-76, 13 ills., Jan., 1908
Honors to Amundsen and Peary (Presentation of Special Gold Medal). XXIV, pp. 113-130, 5 ills., Jan., 1913
A Modern Viking. XVII, pp. 38-41, ills., map, Jan., 1906
Navigating the "Norge" from Rome to the North Pole and Beyond: The Designer and Pilot of the First Dirigible to Fly Over the Top of the World Describes a Thrilling Voyage of More Than 8,000 Miles. By General Umberto Nobile. LII, pp. 177-215, 36 ills., map, Aug., 1927
Norwegian Expedition to the Magnetic North Pole by Roald Amundsen. XIV, pp. 293-294, July, 1903

AMUNDSEN, ROALD—*Continued*
See also NGS: Medals: Hubbard Medal; Special Gold Medal

ANATOLIA:
Alert Anatolia. 13 ills. LXXXV, pp. 481-492, Apr., 1944
East of Constantinople: Glimpses of Village Life in Anatolia, the Battleground of East and West, Where the Turks Reorganized Their Forces After the World War. By Melville Chater. XLIII, pp. 509-534, 27 ills., map, May, 1923
Turkey, Where Earthquakes Followed Timur's Trail. 15 photos by Maynard Owen Williams. LXXVII, pp. 395-406, Mar., 1940
The Turkish Republic Comes of Age. By Maynard Owen Williams. LXXXVII, pp. 581-616, 4 ills. in black and white, 29 ills. in color, map, May, 1945
See also Asia Minor; Turkey

ANCESTOR of the British Navy: England's Oldest Known War Vessel Is Unearthed, Laden with Remarkable Treasures of an Anglo-Saxon Ruler. By C. W. Phillips. LXXIX, pp. 247-268, 22 ills., 4 drawings, Feb., 1941

An **ANCIENT** Capital (Boghaz Keoy, Turkey). By Isabel F. Dodd. XXI, pp. 111-124, 11 ills., Feb., 1910

ANCIENT Carthage in the Light of Modern Excavation. By Count Byron Khun de Prorok. XLV, pp. 391-423, 27 ills. in black and white, 16 ills. in color, map, Apr., 1924

ANCIENT Iceland, New Pawn of War. 21 photos, map. LXXX, pp. 75-90, July, 1941

ANCIENT Rome Brought to Life. By Rhys Carpenter. Paintings by H. M. Herget. XC, pp. 567-633, 2 ills. in black and white, 32 ills. in color, map, Nov., 1946

ANCIENT Temples and Modern Guns in Thailand. 10 photos: 6 by Maynard Owen Williams. LXXX, pp. 653-660, Nov., 1941

ANDALUSIA (Region), Spain:
In Andalusia, Home of Song and Sunshine. 14 color photos by Gervais Courtellemont. LV, pp. 301-308, Mar., 1929

ANDERSEN, MAGNUS:
Norway and the Vikings. By Captain Magnus Andersen. V, pp. 132-136, Jan. 31, 1894

ANDERSON, GEORGE E.:
The Wonderful Canals of China. By George E. Anderson. XVI, pp. 68-69, Feb., 1905

ANDERSON, ORVIL A.:
Exploring the Stratosphere. By Captain Albert W. Stevens. LXVI, pp. 397-434, 43 ills., chart, Oct., 1934
Hubbard Medals Awarded to Stratosphere Explorers: Presentation by General Pershing. LXIX, pp. 713-714, ill. p. 712, May, 1936
Man's Farthest Aloft: Rising to 13.71 Miles, the National Geographic Society-U. S. Army Stratosphere Expedition Gathers Scientific Data at Record Altitude. By Capt. Albert W. Stevens. LXIX, pp. 59-94, 39 ills., map, Jan., 1936

ANDES (Mountains), South America:

Air Adventures in Peru: Cruising Among Andean Peaks, Pilots and Cameramen Discover Wondrous Works of an Ancient People. By Robert Shippee. LXIII, pp. 81-120, 40 ills., map, Jan., 1933

Bolivia—Tin Roof of the Andes. By Henry Albert Phillips. LXXXIII, pp. 309-332, 5 ills. in black and white, 20 ills. in color, Mar., 1943

Chile's Land of Fire and Water: Smoking Volcanoes and Ice-hooded Peaks Stand Sentinel Over Limpid Lakes in the Far Southern Andes. By W. Robert Moore. LXXX, pp. 91-110, 9 ills. in black and white, 10 ills. in color, map, July, 1941

The First Transandine Railroad from Buenos Aires to Valparaiso. By Harriet Chalmers Adams. XXI, pp. 397-417, 14 ills., diagr., map, May, 1910

Flying the "Hump" of the Andes. By Capt. Albert W. Stevens. LIX, pp. 595-636, 36 ills., map, May, 1931

Flying the World's Longest Air-Mail Route: From Montevideo, Uruguay, Over the Andes, Up the Pacific Coast, Across Central America and the Caribbean to Miami, Florida, in 67 Thrilling Flying Hours. By Junius B. Wood. LVII, pp. 261-325, 65 ills., map, Mar., 1930

A Forgotten Valley of Peru: Conquered by Incas, Scourged by Famine, Plagues, and Earthquakes, Colca Valley Shelters the Last Fragment of an Ancient Andean Tribe. By Robert Shippee. LXV, pp. 111-132, 22 ills., map, Jan., 1934

The Heart of Aymará Land: A Visit to Tiahuanacu, Perhaps the Oldest City of the New World, Lost Beneath the Drifting Sand of Centuries in the Bolivian Highlands. By Stewart E. McMillin. LI, pp. 213-256, 23 ills. in black and white, 18 ills. in color, map, Feb., 1927

How Latin America Looks from the Air: U. S. Army Airplanes Hurdle the High Andes, Brave Brazil Jungles, and Follow Smoking Volcanoes to Map New Sky Paths Around South America. By Major Herbert A. Dargue. LII, pp. 451-502, 52 ills., map, Oct., 1927

A Longitudinal Journey Through Chile. By Harriet Chalmers Adams. XLII, pp. 219-273, 60 ills., map, Sept., 1922

The Lure of Lima, City of the Kings. By William Joseph Showalter. LVII, pp. 727-784, 41 ills. in black and white, 25 ills. in color, June, 1930

A New Peruvian Route to the Plain of the Amazon. By Solon I. Bailey. XVII, pp. 432-448, 12 ills., Aug., 1906

Over the Andes to Bogotá. By Frank M. Chapman. XL, pp. 353-373, 19 ills., Oct., 1921

Some Wonderful Sights in the Andean Highlands: The Oldest City in America. Sailing on the Lake of the Clouds: The Yosemite of Peru. By Harriet Chalmers Adams. XIX, pp. 597-618, 19 ills., map, Sept., 1908

The Volcanoes of Ecuador, Guideposts in Crossing South America. By G. M. Dyott. LV, pp. 49-93, 42 ills. in black and white, 12 ills. in color, map, Jan., 1929

ANDES (Mountains), South America—*Continued*

The World's Highest Altitudes and First Ascents. By Charles E. Fay. XX, pp. 493-530, 25 ills., June, 1909

The World's Highest International Telephone Cable. LVIII, pp. 722-731, 8 ills., Dec., 1930

See also San Agustín Region

ANDORRA:

Andorra—Mountain Museum of Feudal Europe. By Lawrence A. Fernsworth. LXIV, pp. 493-512, 21 ills., map, Oct., 1933

A Unique Republic, Where Smuggling Is an Industry. By Herbert Corey. XXXIII, pp. 279-299, 16 ills., map, Mar., 1918

ANDORRA LA VELLA, Andorra:

Andorra—Mountain Museum of Feudal Europe. By Lawrence A. Fernsworth. LXIV, pp. 493-512, 21 ills., map, Oct., 1933

ANDREANOF ISLANDS, Aleutians. *See* Adak

ANDRÉE, S. A.:

Geographic Notes (No News of Andrée). XIII, p. 177, May, 1902

An Interesting Rumor Concerning Andrée. (By J. H.). IX, pp. 102-103, Mar., 1898

No Man's Land—Spitzbergen. XVIII, pp. 455-458, July, 1907

Some Recent Geographic Events. (By J. H.). VIII, pp. 359-362, ill., Dec., 1897

ANDREWS, C. L.:

Muir Glacier (Alaska). (By C. L. Andrews). XIV, pp. 441-444, ills., map, Dec., 1903

ANDREWS, ROY CHAPMAN:

Explorations in the Gobi Desert. By Roy Chapman Andrews. LXIII, pp. 653-716, 50 ills. in black and white, 20 ills. in color, map, June, 1933

Exploring Unknown Corners of the "Hermit Kingdom" (Korea). By Roy Chapman Andrews. XXXVI, pp. 25-48, 30 ills., map, July, 1919

Hubbard Medal winner. LXV, p. 792, June, 1934

Shore-Whaling: A World Industry. By Roy Chapman Andrews. XXII, pp. 411-442, 34 ills., May, 1911

ANDROS (Island), West Indies:

Coral Castle Builders of Tropic Seas. By Roy Waldo Miner. Paintings by Else Bostelmann. LXV, pp. 703-728, 15 ills. in black and white, 8 ills. in color, maps, June, 1934

ANGAUR (Island), Palau Islands, Carolines:

South from Saipan. By W. Robert Moore. LXXXVII, pp. 441-474, 11 ills. in black and white, 17 ills. in color, map, Apr., 1945

ANGERS, France:

The Beauties of France. By Arthur Stanley Riggs. XXVIII, pp. 391-491, 73 ills. in black and white, 16 ills. in color, map, Nov., 1915

ANGKOR, Cambodia:

The Forgotten Ruins of Indo-China. By Jacob E. Conner. XXIII, pp. 209-272, 63 ills., maps, Mar., 1912

Four Faces of Siva: The Mystery of Angkor. By Robert J. Casey. LIV, pp. 303-332, 13 ills. in black and white, 6 ills. in color, map, Sept., 1928

ANGLER (Fish):

Fishes That Carry Lanterns. XXI, pp. 453-456, 5 ills., May, 1910

The Purple Veil: A Romance of the Sea. (By H. A. L.). XVI, pp. 337-341, 9 ills., July, 1905

The **ANGLO-AMERICAN** Polar Expedition. (By E. de K. Leffingwell). XVIII, p. 796, Dec., 1907

ANGLO-EGYPTIAN SUDAN:

Adventures Among the "Lost Tribes of Islam" in Eastern Darfur: A Personal Narrative of Exploring, Mapping, and Setting Up a Government in the Anglo-Egyptian Sudan Borderland. By Major Edward Keith-Roach. XLV, pp. 41-73, 32 ills., map, Jan., 1924

Along the Nile, Through Egypt and the Sudan. By Frederick Simpich. XLII, pp. 379-410, 29 ills., Oct., 1922

Crossing the Untraversed Libyan Desert: The Record of a 2,200-Mile Journey of Exploration Which Resulted in the Discovery of Two Oases of Strategic Importance on the Southwestern Frontier of Egypt. By A. M. Hassanein Bey. XLVI, pp. 233-277, 46 ills., map, Sept., 1924

The New British Empire of the Sudan. By Herbert L. Bridgman. XVII, pp. 241-267, 32 ills., map, May, 1906

Two Fighting Tribes of the Sudan. By Merian C. Cooper. Photos by Ernest B. Schoedsack. LVI, pp. 465-486, 27 ills., map, Oct., 1929

An Unbeliever Joins the Hadj: On the Age-Old Pilgrimage to Mecca, Babies Are Born, Elders Die, and Families May Halt a Year to Earn Funds in Distant Lands. By Owen Tweedy. LXV, pp. 761-789, 30 ills., map, June, 1934

ANGLO-JAPANESE ALLIANCE:

The Purpose of the Anglo-Japanese Alliance. By Eki Hioki. XVI, pp. 333-337, July, 1905

The **ANGLO-VENEZUELAN** Boundary Dispute. By Marcus Baker. XI, pp. 129-144, ills., map, Apr., 1900

ANGMAGSSALIK, Greenland:

Desolate Greenland, Now an American Outpost. 17 photos: 12 by Willie Knutsen, 4 by F. Vogel. LXXX, pp. 393-406, Sept., 1941

ANGOLA:

Angola, the Last Foothold of Slavery. XXI, pp. 625-630, 6 ills., July, 1910

ANGRA DO HEROISMO, Terceira (Island), Azores:

American Airmen in the Azores. 10 ills. in color. LXXXIX, pp. 177-184, Feb., 1946

ANIAKCHAK CRATER, Alaska:

A World Inside a Mountain: Aniakchak, the New Volcanic Wonderland of the Alaska Peninsula, Is Explored. By Bernard R. Hubbard. LX, pp. 319-345, 34 ills., map, Sept., 1931

ANIMAL Wealth of the United States. By Francis E. Warren. XVII, pp. 511-524, 6 ills., diagrs., Sept., 1906

ANIMALS:

Laws of Temperature Control of the Geographic Distribution of Terrestrial Animals and Plants. Annual Address by Vice-President, Dr. C. Hart Merriam. VI, pp. 229-238, table, 3 maps, Dec. 29, 1894

See also Mammals

ANIMALS Were Allies, Too. 16 ills. LXXXIX, pp. 75-88, Jan., 1946

ANKARA, Turkey:

Alert Anatolia. 13 ills. LXXXV, pp. 481-492, Apr., 1944

The Transformation of Turkey: New Hats and New Alphabet are the Surface Symbols of the Swiftest National Changes in Modern Times. By Douglas Chandler. LXXV, pp. 1-50, 27 ills. in black and white, 23 ills. in color, map, Jan., 1939

The Turkish Republic Comes of Age. By Maynard Owen Williams. LXXXVII, pp. 581-616, 4 ills. in black and white, 29 ills. in color, map, May, 1945

ANNAM (State), French Indo-China:

Along the Old Mandarin Road of Indo-China. By W. Robert Moore. LX, pp. 157-199, 32 ills. in black and white, 28 ills. in color, Aug., 1931

ANNAPOLIS, Maryland:

Annapolis, Cradle of the Navy. By Lieutenant Arthur A. Ageton. LXIX, pp. 789-800, 13 ills. in color, June, 1936

Old Line State Cyclorama. 22 color photos by W. Robert Moore, B. Anthony Stewart, and others. LXXIX, pp. 409-432, Apr., 1941

ANNETTE ISLAND, Alaska:

The Metlakatla Mission in Danger. (By Wm. H. Dall). IX, pp. 187-189, Apr., 1898

The **ANNEXATION** Fever. (By Henry Gannett). VIII, pp. 354-358, Dec., 1897

ANNOUNCEMENT (Organization of the National Geographic Society and Publication of the Magazine). I, pp. i-ii, Oct., 1888

ANNOUNCEMENT of the Seventh Annual Excursion and Field Meeting (Fredericksburg, Va.), Saturday, May 4, 1895. VI, foldout, Apr. 20, 1895

ANNOUNCEMENTS. *See* NGS: Essay Contests; Excursions and Field Meetings; Publications

ANNUAL Report of the Superintendent of the United States Coast and Geodetic Survey. VII, pp. 186-188, May, 1896

ANNUAL REPORTS. *See* names of NGS Presidents and Vice-Presidents; NGS: Committees; Secretary; Treasurer; *and* names of U. S. Government Bureaus

ANOPHELES MOSQUITOES:

Life Story of the Mosquito. By Graham Fairchild. With 10 ills. in color from paintings. LXXXV, pp. 180-195, 5 ills. in black and white, drawing, Feb., 1944

Saboteur Mosquitoes. By Harry H. Stage. LXXXV, pp. 165-179, 12 ills., Feb., 1944

ANT MEN (Tribespeople):

The Country of the Ant Men (Algeria). By Thomas H. Kearney. XXII, pp. 367-382, 13 ills., map, panorama, Apr., 1911

ANTARCTIC REGIONS:

Admiral Byrd Receives New Honor From The Society. LVIII, pp. 228-238, 4 ills., Aug., 1930

American Claims in the Antarctic. (By Edwin Swift Balch). XIV, pp. 77-78, Feb., 1903

American Discoverers of the Antarctic Continent. By Major General A. W. Greely. XXIII, pp. 298-312, 7 ills., map, Mar., 1912

An American South Polar Expedition. XIX, pp. 885-888, Dec., 1908

Amundsen's Attainment of the South Pole (Roald Amundsen Awarded the Hubbard Medal by the National Geographic Society). XXIII, pp. 205-208, map, Feb., 1912

The Antarctic Climate. X, pp. 520-521, Dec., 1899

Antarctic Continent. XV, pp. 185-186, Apr., 1904

The Antarctic Continent (Geographic Notes. By Cyrus C. Babb). VI, pp. 217-223, map, Dec. 29, 1894

Antarctica's Most Interesting Citizen: The Comical Penguin Is Both Romantic and Bellicose. By Worth E. Shoults. LXI, pp. 251-260, 8 ills., Feb., 1932

The Belgian Antarctic Expedition. X, pp. 229-230, June, 1899

The British Antarctic Expedition. XII, pp. 339-345, Sept., 1901

British Antarctic Expedition under Captain Robert F. Scott. 16 ills. XLV, pp. 255-270, Mar., 1924

The British South Polar Expedition. XIV, pp. 210-212, May, 1903

The Conquest of Antarctica by Air. By Richard Evelyn Byrd. LVIII, pp. 127-227, 71 ills. in black and white, 16 ills. in gravure, map, Aug., 1930

Expeditions in the Arctic and Antarctic. XIII, pp. 179-180, May, 1902

Exploring the Ice Age in Antarctica. By Richard Evelyn Byrd. LXVIII, pp. 399-474, maps (1 two-page), Oct., 1935

Geography. By Rear-Admiral Sir W. J. L. Wharton. XVI, pp. 483-498, Nov., 1905

The German South Polar Expedition. XII, p. 311, Aug., 1901

German South Polar Expedition. XIV, pp. 296-297, July, 1903

The German South Polar Expedition. By Dr. Georg Kollm. XII, pp. 377-379, Oct., 1901

The Great Ice Barrier. By Henry Gannett. XXI, pp. 173-174, ill., Feb., 1910

The Great Unmapped Areas of the Earth's Surface Awaiting the Explorer and Geographer. By J. Scott Keltie. VIII, pp. 251-266, Sept., 1897

The Heart of the Antarctic. By Ernest H. Shackleton. XX, pp. 972-1007, 27 ills., map, Nov., 1909

Honors to the American Navy (Banquet). XX, pp. 77-95, Jan., 1909

An Ice Wrapped Continent. (By G.H.G.). XVIII, pp. 95-117, 20 ills., map, Feb., 1907

ANTARCTIC REGIONS—*Continued*

Mapping the Antarctic from the Air: The Aërial Camera Earns Its Place as the Eyes and Memory of the Explorer. By Capt. Ashley C. McKinley. LXII, pp. 471-485, 13 ills., map supplement, Oct., 1932

Motor Sledges in the Antarctic. XVIII, pp. 214-215, Mar., 1907

My Flight Across Antarctica. By Lincoln Ellsworth. LXX, pp. 1-35, 37 ills., map, July, 1936

My Four Antarctic Expeditions: Explorations of 1933-39 Have Stricken Vast Areas from the Realm of the Unknown. By Lincoln Ellsworth. LXXVI, pp. 129-138, 9 ills., map, July, 1939

National Geographic Society Honors Byrd Antarctic Expedition. LXVIII, pp. 107-114, 6 ills., July, 1935

Plans for Reaching the South Pole. By Gilbert H. Grosvenor. X, pp. 316-319, map supplement, Aug., 1899

The Race for the South Pole (Presentation of Hubbard Medal to Shackleton). XXI, pp. 185-186, Mar., 1910

Sailing the Seven Seas in the Interest of Science: Adventures Through 157,000 Miles of Storm and Calm, from Arctic to Antarctic and Around the World, in the Non-magnetic Yacht "Carnegie." By J. P. Ault. XLII, pp. 631-690, 47 ills., chart, Dec., 1922

Scottish Antarctic Expedition. XIV, p. 162, Apr., 1903

Shackleton's Farthest South. XX, pp. 398-402, map, Apr., 1909

The Society's Map of the Antarctic. Text with map supplement. LXII, pp. 485-486, ill., Oct., 1932

The Society's Special Medal Is Awarded to Dr. Thomas C. Poulter: Admiral Byrd's Second-in-Command and Senior Scientist Is Accorded High Geographic Honor. LXXII, pp. 105-108, ills., July, 1937

Some Recent English Statements About the Antarctic. (By Edwin Swift Balch). XV, p. 266, June, 1904

South Georgia, an Outpost of the Antarctic. By Robert Cushman Murphy. XLI, pp. 409-444, 41 ills., maps, Apr., 1922

The South Polar Expedition (Proposed by Peary for Consideration of the National Geographic Society). XXI, pp. 167-170, map, Feb., 1910

South Polar Explorations. XII, p. 47, Jan., 1901

South Polar Explorations. XXII, pp. 407-409, 4 ills., map, Apr., 1911

Swedish South Polar Expedition. XII, p. 406, Nov., 1901

Swedish South Polar Expedition. XIV, p. 296, July, 1903

Termination Land. (By Edwin Swift Balch). XV, pp. 220-221, May, 1904

Wilkes' and D'Urville's Discoveries in Wilkes Land. By Rear Admiral John E. Pillsbury. XXI, pp. 171-173, Feb., 1910

Work in the Antarctics. XII, pp. 203-204, May, 1901

Work in the Arctic and Antarctic. XI, pp. 164-165, Apr., 1900

Work in the Far South. XIV, p. 109, map, Mar., 1903

ANTARCTICA. *See* Antarctic Regions

ANTARCTICA by Sea, Land and Air. 16 ills. in gravure from photos by the Byrd Antarctic Expedition. LVIII, pp. 159-206, Aug., 1930

ANTARCTICA'S Most Interesting Citizen: The Comical Penguin Is Both Romantic and Bellicose. By Worth E. Shoults. LXI, pp. 251-260, 8 ills., Feb., 1932

ANTELOPE, American. *See* Pronghorns

ANTHONY, A. W.:

A Cruise Among Desert Islands (Baja California). By G. Dallas Hanna and A. W. Anthony. XLIV, pp. 71-99, 32 ills., map, July, 1923

ANTHONY, H. E.:

Over Trail and Through Jungle in Ecuador: Indian Head-Hunters of the Interior, an Interesting Study in the South American Republic. By H. E. Anthony. XL, pp. 327-352, 28 ills., Oct., 1921

ANTHROPOLOGY:

America's First Settlers, the Indians. By Matthew W. Stirling. Paintings by W. Langdon Kihn. LXXII, pp. 535-596, 34 ills. in black and white, 24 ills. in color, Nov., 1937

The Battle-Line of Languages in Western Europe: A Problem in Human Geography More Perplexing Than That of International Boundaries. By A. L. Guerard. XLIII, pp. 145-180, 36 ills., Feb., 1923

Bedouin Life in Bible Lands: The Nomads of the "Houses of Hair" Offer Unstinted Hospitality to an American. By John D. Whiting. LXXI, pp. 59-83, 27 ills., map, Jan., 1937

Burma: Where India and China Meet: In the Massive Mountains of Southeast Asia, Swarming Road Builders Wage the "War of the Highways" for Free China and Her Allies. By John LeRoy Christian. LXXXIV, pp. 489-512, 18 ills., map, Oct., 1943
Contents: Chins, Kachins, Karens, Kaws, Padaungs, Shans

The Cradle of Civilization: The Historic Lands Along the Euphrates and Tigris Rivers Where Briton Is Fighting Turk. By James Baikie. XXIX, pp. 127-162, 25 ills., Feb., 1916

Discovering Alaska's Oldest Arctic Town (Ipiutak): A Scientist Finds Ivory-eyed Skeletons of a Mysterious People and Joins Modern Eskimos in the Dangerous Spring Whale Hunt. By Froelich G. Rainey. LXXXII, pp. 319-336, 15 ills., Sept., 1942

Dusky Tribesmen of French West Africa. 26 color photos by Enzo de Chetelat. LXXIX, pp. 639-662, May, 1941

Earth's Most Primitive People: A Journey with the Aborigines of Central Australia. By Charles P. Mountford. LXXXIX, pp. 89-112, 10 ills. in black and white, 8 ills. in color, map, Jan., 1946

The Effects of Geographic Environment in the Development of Civilization in Primitive Man. By Hon. Gardiner G. Hubbard. VIII, pp. 161-176, June, 1897

The Enchanted Mesa (New Mexico). By F. W. Hodge. VIII, pp. 273-284, 6 ills., map, Oct., 1897

ANTHROPOLOGY—*Continued*

Explorations by the Bureau of American Ethnology in 1895. By W J McGee. VII, pp. 77-80, Feb., 1896

A Few Thoughts Concerning Eugenics. By Alexander Graham Bell. XIX, pp. 119-123, Feb., 1908

How Old Is Man? By Theodore Roosevelt. XXIX, pp. 111-127, 12 ills., 3 maps, Feb., 1916

I Lived on Formosa. By Joseph W. Ballantine. LXXXVII, pp. 1-24, 19 ills., maps, Jan., 1945
Contents: The seven aboriginal tribes, including the Paiwan and Taiyal tribesmen

In the Empire of the Aztecs: Mexico City Is Rich in Relics of a People Who Practiced Human Sacrifice, Yet Loved Flowers, Education, and Art. By Frank H. H. Roberts, Jr. Paintings by H. M. Herget. LXXI, pp. 725-750, 14 ills. in black and white, 10 ills. in color, June, 1937

Indian Tribes of Pueblo Land. By Matthew W. Stirling. Paintings by W. Langdon Kihn. LXXVIII, pp. 549-596, 16 ills. in black and white, 25 ills. in color, Nov., 1940

Indians of Our Western Plains. By Matthew W. Stirling. Paintings by W. Langdon Kihn. LXXXVI, pp. 73-108, 14 ills. in black and white, 16 ills. in color, July, 1944

Mountain Tribes of Iran and Iraq. By Harold Lamb. LXXXIX, pp. 385-408, 15 ills., two-page map, Mar., 1946

National Growth and National Character. By W J McGee. X, pp. 185-206, June, 1899

New Guinea's Mountain and Swampland Dwellers. By Col. Ray T. Elsmore. LXXXVIII, pp. 671-694, 15 ills. in black and white, 7 ills. in color, map, Dec., 1945

Nigeria: From the Bight of Benin to Africa's Desert Sands. By Helen Trybulowski Gilles. LXXXV, pp. 537-568, 17 ills. in black and white, 10 ills. in color, map, May, 1944
Contents: Bororoje, Egbas, Fulani, Hausa, Ibo, Ijebas, Yorubas

Notes on Some Primitive Philippine Tribes. By Dean C. Worcester. IX, pp. 284-301, 11 ills., June, 1898
Included: Aëtas, or Negritos; Battaks; Mangyans; Moros; Tagbanuas

The Origin of Stefansson's Blond Eskimo. By Major General A. W. Greely. XXIII, pp. 1225-1238, 10 ills., map, Dec., 1912

Our Immigration Laws from the Viewpoint of National Eugenics. By Prof. Robert De C. Ward. XXIII, pp. 38-41, Jan., 1912

Parade of Life Through the Ages: Records in Rocks Reveal a Strange Procession of Prehistoric Creatures, from Jellyfish to Dinosaurs, Giant Sloths, Saber-toothed Tigers, and Primitive Man. By Charles R. Knight. With 24 ills. in color from paintings by author. LXXXI, pp. 141-184, 13 ills. in black and white, Feb., 1942

The Races of Europe. By Edwin A. Grosvenor. XXXIV, pp. 441-534, 62 ills., diagr. and index, maps, map supplement, Dec., 1918

The Sex, Nativity, and Color of the People of the United States. (By G.H.G.). XII, pp. 381-389, 17 charts, Nov., 1901

Shan Tribes Make Burma's Hills Flash With Color. 15 color photos by W. Robert Moore. LX, pp. 455-462, Oct., 1931
Contents: Kang, Kaw, Khun, Lahu Na, Lahu Shi, Shan, Wa

ANTHROPOLOGY—*Continued*

Strange Tribes in the Shan States of Burma. 15 color photos by W. Robert Moore. LVIII, pp. 247-254, Aug., 1930
Contents: Kang, Kaw, Khun, Lahu Na, Lahu Shi, Shan

The Supposed Birthplace of Civilizations. XVI, pp. 499-504, 6 ills., Nov., 1905

Unknown New Guinea: Circumnavigating the World in a Flying Boat, American Scientists Discover a Valley of 60,000 People Never Before Seen by White Men. By Richard Archbold. LXXIX, pp. 315-344, 28 ills., map, Mar., 1941

War Finds Its Way to Gilbert Islands: United States Forces Dislodge Japanese from Enchanted Atolls Which Loom Now as Stepping Stones along South Sea Route from Australia to Hawaii. By Sir Arthur Grimble. LXXXIII, pp. 71-92, 19 ills., map, Jan., 1943

Who Shall Inherit Long Life? On the Existence of a Natural Process at Work Among Beings Tending to Improve the Vigor and Vitality of Succeeding Generations. By Alexander Graham Bell. XXXV, pp. 505-514, 13 ills., June, 1919

With the Nomads of Central Asia: A Summer's Sojourn in the Tekes Valley, Plateau Paradise of Mongol and Turkic Tribes. By Edward Murray. Paintings by Alexandre Iacovleff. LXIX, pp. 1-57, 43 ills. in black and white, 26 ills. in color, map, Jan., 1936

A Woman's Experiences among Stone Age Solomon Islanders: Primitive Life Remains Unchanged in Tropical Jungleland Where United States Forces Now Are Fighting. By Eleanor Schirmer Oliver. LXXXII, pp. 813-836, 26 ills., map, Dec., 1942

Work of the Bureau of American Ethnology. By W J McGee. XII, pp. 369-372, Oct., 1901

Yap Meets the Yanks. By David D. Duncan, 1st Lt., USMC. With 11 color photos by author. LXXXIX, pp. 364-372, Mar., 1946

See also Arabs; Cliff Dwellers; Dyaks; Eskimos; Indians of Central America; Indians of Mexico; Indians of North America; Indians of South America; Lapps; Mongols; Moros; Tibetans; Troglodytes and Christian "Troglodytes"; *and* Archeology

ANTICOSTI ISLAND, Canada:

Anticosti Island, Nugget of the North. By Eugene E. Wilson. LXXXI, pp. 121-140, 19 ills., map, Jan., 1942

ANTIGUA, Guatemala:

Guatemala, the Country of the Future. By Edine Frances Tisdel. XXI, pp. 596-624, 33 ills., map, July, 1910

To Market in Guatemala. By Luis Marden. With 19 color photos by Giles Greville Healey and Charles S. Pineo. LXXXVIII, pp. 87-104, July, 1945

ANTIGUA (Island), West Indies:

Americans in the Caribbean. By Luis Marden. LXXXI, pp. 723-758, 16 ills. in black and white, 22 ills. in color, map, June, 1942

British West Indian Interlude. By Anne Rainey Langley. LXXIX, pp. 1-46, 23 ills. in black and white, 21 ills. in color, maps, Jan., 1941

ANTILLES, Greater. *See* Cuba; Dominican Republic; Haiti; Jamaica; Puerto Rico

ANTILLES, Lesser. *See* Antigua; Aruba; Bonaire; Curaçao; Dominica; Guadeloupe; Martinique; Saba; St. Kitts; St. Lucia; St. Vincent; Trinidad; Virgin Islands

ANTIOCH the Glorious. By William H. Hall. XXXVIII, pp. 81-103, 20 ills., map, Aug., 1920

ANTIQUITIES:

The Greek Way. By Edith Hamilton. LXXXV, pp. 257-271, 12 ills., Mar., 1944

The Roman Way. By Edith Hamilton. XC, pp. 545-565, 14 ills., two-page map, Nov., 1946

See also Archeology; *and* names of ancient cities and countries

ANTLERED Majesties of Many Lands (Deer). 23 ills. in color from paintings by Walter A. Weber. LXXVI, pp. 479-510, Oct., 1939

ANTOFAGASTA, Chile:

A Longitudinal Journey Through Chile. By Harriet Chalmers Adams. XLII, pp. 219-273, 60 ills., map, Sept., 1922

ANTS (Insects):

Color Glows in the Guianas, French and Dutch. By Nicol Smith. LXXXIII, pp. 459-480, 8 ills. in black and white, 13 ills. in color, map, Apr., 1943
Included: The Atta Ant

Living Casks of Honey. By Jennie E. Harris. LXVI, pp. 193-199, 4 ills., Aug., 1934

Lonely Australia: The Unique Continent. By Herbert E. Gregory. XXX, pp. 473-568, 68 ills., 5 maps (1 two-page), Dec., 1916

The Monsters of Our Back Yard. By David Fairchild. XXIV, pp. 575-626, 38 ills., May, 1913

Notes About Ants and Their Resemblance to Man. By William Morton Wheeler. XXIII, pp. 731-766, 32 ills., diagrs., Aug., 1912

The Red Ant Versus the Boll Weevil. XV, pp. 262-264, June, 1904

Stalking Ants, Savage and Civilized: A Naturalist Braves Bites and Stings in Many Lands to Learn the Story of an Insect Whose Ways Often Parallel Those of Man. By W. M. Mann. Paintings by Hashime Murayama. LXVI, pp. 171-192, 7 ills. in black and white, 18 ills. in color, Aug., 1934

ANURADHPURA, Ceylon:

Adam's Second Eden. By Eliza Ruhamah Scidmore. XXIII, pp. 105-173, 206, 61 ills., Feb., 1912

The Buried City of Ceylon. By John M. Abbot. XVII, pp. 613-622, 8 ills., Nov., 1906

ANZACS (Australia-New Zealand Army Corps):

The Making of an Anzac. By Howell Walker. LXXXI, pp. 409-456, 31 ills. in black and white, 20 ills. in color, two-page map, Apr., 1942

APACHE INDIANS:

Along Our Side of the Mexican Border. By Frederick Simpich. XXXVIII, pp. 61-80, 9 ills., map, July, 1920

Indian Tribes of Pueblo Land. By Matthew W. Stirling. Paintings by W. Langdon Kihn. LXXVIII, pp. 549-596, 16 ills. in black and white, 25 ills. in color, Nov., 1940

The North American Indian. XIX, pp. 448-454, 5 ills., June, 1908

APES:

Man's Closest Counterparts: Heavyweight of Monkeydom Is the "Old Man" Gorilla, by Far the Largest of the Four Great Apes. By William M. Mann. Paintings by Elie Cheverlange. LXXVIII, pp. 213-236, 10 ills. in black and white, 10 ills. in color, Aug., 1940

APHIDS:

An Insect Community Lives in Flower Heads. By James G. Needham. XC, pp. 340-356, 5 ills. in black and white, 11 ills. in color, Sept., 1946

APHRODISIAS (Ancient City):

The Buried Cities of Asia Minor. By Ernest L. Harris. XX, pp. 1-18, 10 ills., Jan., 1909

APIA, Samoa:

Sailing the Seven Seas in the Interest of Science: Adventures Through 157,000 Miles of Storm and Calm, from Arctic to Antarctic and Around the World, in the Non-magnetic Yacht "Carnegie." By J. P. Ault. XLII, pp. 631-690, 47 ills., chart, Dec., 1922

APPALACHIAN MOUNTAINS, U. S.:

Geomorphology of the Southern Appalachians. By Charles Willard Hayes and Marius R. Campbell. VI, pp. 63-126, diagrs., 4 maps, May 23, 1894

An **APPEAL** to Members of the National Geographic Society (Food Conservation). XXXIII, pp. 347-348, ills., Apr., 1918

APPERCEPTION in Geography. By M. E. Kelton. XI, pp. 192-199, May, 1900

APPLIED Physiography in South Carolina. By L. C. Glenn. VIII, pp. 152-154, diagr., May, 1897

APPROACH to Peiping. By Major John W. Thomason, Jr. LXIX, pp. 275-308, 24 ills., map, Feb., 1936

APPROACHING Washington by Tidewater Potomac. By Paul Wilstach. LVII, pp. 372-392, 7 ills. in black and white, 15 ills. in color, Mar., 1930

'AQABA, Trans-Jordan:

On the Trail of King Solomon's Mines: The Bible, in Addition to Its Spiritual Values, Continues to Prove a Rich Geography and Guide to Exploration of the Holy Land. By Nelson Glueck. LXXXV, pp. 233-256, 20 ills., map, Feb., 1944

AQUARIUMS:

Net Results from Oceania: Collecting Aquarium Specimens in Tropical Pacific Waters. By Walter H. Chute. LXXIX, pp. 347-372, 8 ills. in black and white, 24 ills. in color, Mar., 1941

Treasure-House of the Gulf Stream: The Completion and Opening of the New Aquarium and Biological Laboratory at Miami, Florida. By John Oliver La Gorce. Paintings by Hashime Murayama. XXXIX, pp. 53-68, 5 ills. in black and white, 16 ills. in color, Jan., 1921

AQUARIUMS—*Continued*

Tropical Fish Immigrants Reveal New Nature Wonders. By Walter H. Chute. LXV, pp. 93-109, 8 ills. in black and white, 16 ills. in color, Jan., 1934

Tropical Toy Fishes: More Than 600 Varieties of Aquarium Pygmies Afford a Fascinating Field of Zoölogical Study in the Home. By Ida Mellen. Paintings by Hashime Murayama. LIX, pp. 287-317, 20 ills. in black and white, 8 ills. in color, Mar., 1931

See also Goldfish

AQUEDUCTS:

Carrying Water Through a Desert. By Burt A. Heinly. XXI, pp. 568-596, 19 ills., map, July, 1910

New York—The Metropolis of Mankind. By William Joseph Showalter. XXXIV, pp. 1-49, 39 ills., July, 1918

Staircase Farms of the Ancients: Astounding Farming Skill of Ancient Peruvians, Who Were Among the Most Industrious and Highly Organized People in History. By O. F. Cook. XXIX, pp. 474-534, 48 ills., May, 1916

The Washington Aqueduct and Cabin John Bridge. By D. D. Gaillard. VIII, pp. 337-344, ills., Dec., 1897

ARABIAN PENINSULA:

Arabia, the Desert of the Sea. By Archibald Forder. XX, pp. 1039-1062, 1117, 20 ills., map, Dec., 1909

Damascus and Mecca Railway. XII, p. 408, Nov., 1901

"The Flower of Paradise": The Part Which Khat Plays in the Life of the Yemen Arab. By Charles Moser. XXXII, pp. 173-186, 10 ills., map, Aug., 1917

Geographic Progress of Civilization. Annual Address by the President, Honorable Gardiner G. Hubbard. VI, pp. 1-22, Feb. 14, 1894

Into Burning Hadhramaut: The Arab Land of Frankincense and Myrrh, Ever a Lodestone of Western Exploration. By D. van der Meulen. LXII, pp. 387-429, 44 ills., map, Oct., 1932

Mecca the Mystic: A New Kingdom Within Arabia (Hejaz). By S. M. Zwemer. XXXII, pp. 157-172, 13 ills., Aug., 1917

Notes on Oman. By S. M. Zwemer. XXII, pp. 89-98, 8 ills., map, Jan., 1911

One Thousand Miles of Railway Built for Pilgrims and Not for Dividends (Damascus to Mecca). By Colonel F. R. Maunsell. XX, pp. 156-172, 12 ills., map, Feb., 1909

The Rise of the New Arab Nation. By Frederick Simpich. XXXVI, pp. 369-393, 17 ills., map, Nov., 1919

Sheik Said. (By Ernest de Sasseville). VIII, pp. 155-156, May, 1897

Travels in Arabia and Along the Persian Gulf. By David G. Fairchild. XV, pp. 139-151, 20 ills., Apr., 1904

An Unbeliever Joins the Hadj: On the Age-Old Pilgrimage to Mecca, Babies Are Born, Elders Die, and Families May Halt a Year to Earn Funds in Distant Lands. By Owen Tweedy. LXV, pp. 761-789, 30 ills., map, June, 1934

ARABIAN PENINSULA—*Continued*

A Visit to Three Arab Kingdoms: Transjordania, Iraq, and the Hedjaz Present Many Problems to European Powers. By Junius B. Wood. XLIII, pp. 535-568, 30 ills., map, May, 1923

See also Aden; Mecca; Saudi Arabia

ARABS:

Ali Goes to the Clinic. By Herndon and Mary Hudson. XC, pp. 764-766, ills., Dec., 1946

Along the Nile, Through Egypt and the Sudan. By Frederick Simpich. XLII, pp. 379-410, 29 ills., Oct., 1922

Among the Bethlehem Shepherds: A Visit to the Valley Which David Probably Recalled When He Wrote the Twenty-third Psalm. By John D. Whiting. L, pp. 729-753, 19 ills., Dec., 1926

Archeology, the Mirror of the Ages: Our Debt to the Humble Delvers in the Ruins at Carchemish and at Ur. By C. Leonard Woolley. LIV, pp. 207-226, 19 ills., Aug., 1928

Bedouin Life in Bible Lands: The Nomads of the "Houses of Hair" Offer Unstinted Hospitality to an American. By John D. Whiting. LXXI, pp. 59-83, 27 ills., map, Jan., 1937

Cirenaica, Eastern Wing of Italian Libia. By Harriet Chalmers Adams. LVII, pp. 689-726, 35 ills. in black and white, 13 ills. in color, map, June, 1930

Forty Years Among the Arabs. By John Van Ess. LXXXII, pp. 385-420, 27 ills., two-page map, Sept., 1942

Guest in Saudi Arabia. By Maynard Owen Williams. LXXXVIII, pp. 463-487, 24 ills., map, Oct., 1945

Here and There in Northern Africa. By Frank Edward Johnson. XXV, pp. 1-132, 113 ills., Jan., 1914

The Mole Men: An Account of the Troglodytes of Southern Tunisia. By Frank Edward Johnson. XXII, pp. 787-846, 60 ills., Sept., 1911

New Light on Ancient Ur: Excavations at the Site of the City of Abraham Reveal Geographical Evidence of the Biblical Story of the Flood. By M. E. L. Mallowan. LVII, pp. 95-130, 44 ills., map, Jan., 1930

On the Trail of King Solomon's Mines: The Bible, in Addition to Its Spiritual Values, Continues to Prove a Rich Geography and Guide to Exploration of the Holy Land. By Nelson Glueck. LXXXV, pp. 233-256, 20 ills., map, Feb., 1944

Palestine Today. By Francis Chase, Jr. XC, pp. 501-516, 16 ills., Oct., 1946

Pearl Fishing in the Red Sea. By Henri de Monfreid. LXXII, pp. 597-626, 24 ills., map, Nov., 1937

Pilgrims' Progress to Mecca. 22 ills. in duotone: 18 by Oscar Marcus. LXXII, pp. 627-642, Nov., 1937

Where Adam and Eve Lived. By Frederick and Margaret Simpich. XXVI, pp. 546-588, 35 ills., Dec., 1914

The White City of Algiers. By Lieut. Col. Gordon Casserly. LIII, pp. 206-232, 9 ills. in black and white, 32 ills. in color, Feb., 1928

See also Arabian Peninsula

ARAN ISLANDS, Ireland:

The Timeless Arans: The Workaday World Lies Beyond the Horizon of Three Rocky Islets Off the Irish Coast. By Robert Cushman Murphy. LIX, pp. 747-775, 35 ills., map, June, 1931

ARAUCANIAN INDIANS:

Chile's Land of Fire and Water: Smoking Volcanoes and Ice-hooded Peaks Stand Sentinel Over Limpid Lakes in the Far Southern Andes. By W. Robert Moore. LXXX, pp. 91-110, 9 ills. in black and white, 10 ills. in color, map, July, 1941

A Longitudinal Journey Through Chile. By Harriet Chalmers Adams. XLII, pp. 219-273, 60 ills., map, Sept., 1922

The **ARBITRATION** Treaties. By William Howard Taft. XXII, pp. 1165-1172, Dec., 1911

ARBUTUS (Flower):

American Wild Flowers. 29 ills. in color from paintings by Mary E. Eaton. XXVII, pp. 483-517, May, 1915

The Cultivation of the Mayflower. By Frederick V. Coville. XXVII, pp. 518-519, ill., May, 1915

ARCHÆOLOGY in the Air. By Eliza R. Scidmore. XVIII, pp. 151-163, 11 ills., Mar., 1907

ARCHANGEL, U. S. S. R.:

The Murman Coast: Arctic Gateway for American and Allied Expeditionary Forces in Northern European Russia. XXXV, pp. 331-348, 30 ills., map, Apr., 1919

ARCHBOLD, RICHARD:

Unknown New Guinea: Circumnavigating the World in a Flying Boat, American Scientists Discover a Valley of 60,000 People Never Before Seen by White Men. By Richard Archbold. LXXIX, pp. 315-344, 28 ills., map, Mar., 1941

ARCHEOLOGY:

Adam's Second Eden (Ceylon). By Eliza Ruhamah Scidmore. XXIII, pp. 105-173, 206, 61 ills., Feb., 1912

Air Adventures in Peru: Cruising Among Andean Peaks, Pilots and Cameramen Discover Wondrous Works of an Ancient People. By Robert Shippee. LXIII, pp. 81-120, 40 ills., map, Jan., 1933

American Discoveries in Egypt. XVIII, pp. 801-806, 8 ills., Dec., 1907

Ancestor of the British Navy: England's Oldest Known War Vessel Is Unearthed, Laden with Remarkable Treasures of an Anglo-Saxon Ruler. By C. W. Phillips. LXXIX, pp. 247-268, 22 ills., 4 drawings, Feb., 1941

An Ancient Capital (Boghaz Keoy, Turkey). By Isabel F. Dodd. XXI, pp. 111-124, 11 ills., Feb., 1910

Ancient Carthage in the Light of Modern Excavation. By Count Byron Khun de Prorok. XLV, pp. 391-423, 27 ills. in black and white, 16 ills. in color, map, Apr., 1924

Ancient Rome Brought to Life. By Rhys Carpenter. Paintings by H. M. Herget. XC, pp. 567-633, 2 ills. in black and white, 32 ills. in color, map, Nov., 1946

Archæology in the Air. By Eliza R. Scidmore. XVIII, pp. 151-163, 11 ills., Mar., 1907

ARCHEOLOGY—*Continued*

Archeology, the Mirror of the Ages: Our Debt to the Humble Delvers in the Ruins at Carchemish and at Ur. By C. Leonard Woolley. LIV, pp. 207-226, 19 ills., Aug., 1928

At the Tomb of Tutankhamen: An Account of the Opening of the Royal Egyptian Sepulcher Which Contained the Most Remarkable Funeral Treasures Unearthed in Historic Times. By Maynard Owen Williams. XLIII, pp. 461-508, 53 ills., map, May, 1923

The Buried Cities of Asia Minor. By Ernest L. Harris. XX, pp. 1-18, 10 ills., Jan., 1909

The Buried City of Ceylon. By John M. Abbot. XVII, pp. 613-622, 8 ills., Nov., 1906

The Channel Islands. By Edith Carey. XXXVIII, pp. 143-164, 24 ills., map, Aug., 1920

Chichen Itzá, an Ancient American Mecca: Recent Excavations in Yucatan Are Bringing to Light the Temples, Palaces, and Pyramids of America's Most Holy Native City. By Sylvanus Griswold Morley. XLVII, pp. 63-95, 34 ills., diagr., map, Jan., 1925

China's Treasures. By Frederick McCormick. XXIII, pp. 996-1040, 50 ills., Oct., 1912

The Cone-Dwellers of Asia Minor: A Primitive People Who Live in Nature-Made Apartment Houses, Fashioned by Volcanic Violence and Trickling Streams. By J. R. Sitlington Sterrett. XXXV, pp. 281-331, 52 ills., map, Apr., 1919

The Cradle of Civilization: The Historic Lands Along the Euphrates and Tigris Rivers Where Briton Is Fighting Turk. By James Baikie. XXIX, pp. 127-162, 25 ills., Feb., 1916

Crete, Where Sea-Kings Reigned. By Agnes N. Stillwell. LXXXIV, pp. 547-568, 20 ills., map, Nov., 1943

Daily Life in Ancient Egypt (Part I). Daily Life in Ancient Egypt: *The Later Period* (Part II). By William C. Hayes. Paintings by H. M. Herget. LXXX, pp. 419-515, 34 ills. in black and white, 32 ills. in color, map, Oct., 1941

Discovering Alaska's Oldest Arctic Town (Ipiutak): A Scientist Finds Ivory-eyed Skeletons of a Mysterious People and Joins Modern Eskimos in the Dangerous Spring Whale Hunt. By Froelich G. Rainey. LXXXII, pp. 319-336, 15 ills., Sept., 1942

Discovering the New World's Oldest Dated Work of Man: A Maya Monument Inscribed 291 B. C. is Unearthed Near a Huge Stone Head by a Geographic-Smithsonian Expedition in Mexico. By Matthew W. Stirling. LXXVI, pp. 183-218, 40 ills., map, Aug., 1939

Discovering the Oldest Statues in the World: A Daring Explorer Swims Through a Subterranean River of the Pyrenees and Finds Rock Carvings Made 20,000 Years Ago. By Norbert Casteret. XLVI, pp. 123-152, 24 ills., maps, Aug., 1924

Dwellings of the Saga-Time in Iceland, Greenland, and Vineland. By Cornelia Horsford. IX, pp. 73-84, ill., 9 sketches, Mar., 1898

Everyday Life in Pueblo Bonito: As Disclosed by the National Geographic Society's Archeologic Explorations in the Chaco Canyon National Monument, New Mexico. By Neil M. Judd. XLVIII, pp. 227-262, 37 ills., map, Sept., 1925

ARCHEOLOGY—*Continued*

Excavations at Abydos. (By W. M. Flinders Petrie). XIV, pp. 358-359, Sept., 1903

Excavations at Nippur (Iraq). XI, p. 392, Oct., 1900

Excavations at Quirigua, Guatemala. By Sylvanus Griswold Morley. XXIV, pp. 339-361, 24 ills., diagr., Mar., 1913
  Note. XXIV, p. 1056, Sept., 1913

Excavations of M. de Morgan at Susa. XII, p. 315, Aug., 1901

Expedition Unearths Buried Masterpieces of Carved Jade (Cerro de las Mesas, Mexico). By Matthew W. Stirling. LXXX, pp. 277-302, 14 ills. in black and white, 20 ills. in color, map, Sept., 1941

Explorations in Crete. By Edith H. Hall. XX, pp. 778-787, 15 ills., Sept., 1909

Explorations in Peru. XXIII, pp. 417-422, 7 ills., map, Apr., 1912

Explorations in the Gobi Desert. By Roy Chapman Andrews. LXIII, pp. 653-716, 50 ills. in black and white, 20 ills. in color, map, June, 1933

Exploring Frozen Fragments of American History: On the Trail of Early Eskimo Colonists Who Made a 55-Mile Crossing from the Old World to the New. By Henry B. Collins, Jr. LXXV, pp. 633-656, 24 ills., map, May, 1939

Exploring in the Canyon of Death (Arizona): Remains of a People Who Dwelt in Our Southwest at Least 4,000 Years Ago Are Revealed. By Earl H. Morris. XLVIII, pp. 263-300, 24 ills. in black and white, 22 ills. in color, Sept., 1925

Exploring the Secrets of Persepolis. By Charles Breasted. LXIV, pp. 381-420, 48 ills., plan, map, Oct., 1933

Finding Jewels of Jade in a Mexican Swamp (La Venta). By Matthew W. and Marion Stirling. LXXXII, pp. 635-661, 15 ills. in black and white, 12 ills. in color, map, Nov., 1942

The Foremost Intellectual Achievement of Ancient America: The Hieroglyphic Inscriptions on the Monuments in the Ruined Cities of Mexico, Guatemala, and Honduras Are Yielding the Secrets of the Maya Civilization. By Sylvanus Griswold Morley. XLI, pp. 109-130, 27 ills., 17 diagrs., map supplement, Feb., 1922

The Forgotten Ruins of Indo-China. By Jacob E. Conner. XXIII, pp. 209-272, 63 ills., maps, Mar., 1912

Four Faces of Siva: The Mystery of Angkor (Cambodia). By Robert J. Casey. LIV, pp. 303-332, 13 ills. in black and white, 27 ills. in color, map, Sept., 1928

From Jerusalem to Aleppo. By John D. Whiting. XXIV, pp. 71-113, 30 ills., map, Jan., 1913

Further Explorations in the Land of the Incas: The Peruvian Expedition of 1915 of the National Geographic Society and Yale University. By Hiram Bingham. XXIX, pp. 431-473, 29 ills., maps, panorama, May, 1916
  The Greatest Achievement of Ancient Man in America (Fortress of Sacsahuaman, Peru). Panorama from photo by author

The Geography of the Jordan. By Nelson Glueck. LXXXVI, pp. 719-744, 23 ills., map, Dec., 1944

Great Stone Faces of Easter Island. 11 ills. LXXXV, pp. 225-232, Feb., 1944

ARCHEOLOGY—*Continued*

Great Stone Faces of the Mexican Jungle: Five Colossal Heads and Numerous Other Monuments of Vanished Americans Are Excavated by the Latest National Geographic-Smithsonian Expedition. By Matthew W. Stirling. LXXVIII, pp. 309-334, 26 ills., map, Sept., 1940

Greece—the Birthplace of Science and Free Speech: Explorations on the Mainland and in Crete and the Aegean Isles Reveal Ancient Life Similar to That of the Present. By Richard Stillwell. Paintings by H. M. Herget. LXXXV, pp. 273-353, 13 ills. in black and white, 32 ills. in color, two-page map, Mar., 1944

Greece of Today. By George Higgins Moses. XXVIII, pp. 295-329, 27 ills., Oct., 1915

The Greek Bronzes. Text regarding requests for photographs of bronzes. XXIII, p. 104, Jan., 1912

The Greek Bronzes of Tunisia. By Frank Edward Johnson. XXIII, pp. 89-103, 11 ills., Jan., 1912

Guatemala, the Country of the Future. By Edine Frances Tisdel. XXI, pp. 596-624, 33 ills., map, July, 1910

The Heart of Aymará Land: A Visit to Tiahuanacu, Perhaps the Oldest City of the New World, Lost Beneath the Drifting Sands of Centuries in the Bolivian Highlands. By Stewart E. McMillin. LI, pp. 213-256, 23 ills. in black and white, 18 ills. in color, map, Feb., 1927

Hewers of Stone (Mitla, Mexico). By Jeremiah Zimmerman. XXI, pp. 1002-1020, 9 ills., Dec., 1910

The Home of a Forgotten Race: Mysterious Chichen Itza, in Yucatan, Mexico. By Edward H. Thompson. XXV, pp. 585-648, 59 ills., June, 1914

Homer's Troy Today. By Jacob E. Conner. XXVII, pp. 521-532, 11 ills., map, May, 1915

In the Empire of the Aztecs: Mexico City Is Rich in Relics of a People Who Practiced Human Sacrifice, Yet Loved Flowers, Education, and Art. By Frank H. H. Roberts, Jr. Paintings by H. M. Herget. LXXI, pp. 725-750, 14 ills. in black and white, 10 ills. in color, June, 1937

In the Wonderland of Peru. By Hiram Bingham. XXIV, pp. 387-574, 250 ills., 3 diagrs., map, panorama, Apr., 1913

The Ruins of an Ancient Inca Capital, Machu Picchu. Panorama from photo by author

The Indian Village of Baum (Ohio). (By H. C. Brown). XII, pp. 272-274, July, 1901

An Interesting Visit to the Ancient Pyramids of San Juan Teotihuacan. By A. C. Galloway. XXI, pp. 1041-1050, 8 ills., map, Dec., 1910

La Venta's Green Stone Tigers (Mexico). By Matthew W. Stirling. LXXXIV, pp. 321-332, 4 ills. in black and white, 6 ills. in color, map, Sept., 1943

Little-Known Sardinia. By Helen Dunstan Wright. XXX, pp. 97-120, 23 ills., map, Aug., 1916

The Luster of Ancient Mexico (Aztecs). By William H. Prescott. XXX, pp. 1-32, 22 ills., July, 1916

ARCHEOLOGY—*Continued*

Malta: The Halting Place of Nations: First Account of Remarkable Prehistoric Tombs and Temples Recently Unearthed on the Island. By William Arthur Griffiths. XXXVII, pp. 445-478, 35 ills., map, May, 1920

Mesa Verde. By F. H. Newell. IX, pp. 431-434, Oct., 1898

Modern Odyssey in Classic Lands: Troy's Treasures, Athens' Parthenon, and Rome's First "Broad Way" Influence Today's Banks, Costumes, Jewelry, and Railroad Timetables. By Maynard Owen Williams. LXXVII, pp. 291-337, 27 ills. in black and white, 22 ills. in color, Mar., 1940

The Mole Men: An Account of the Troglodytes of Southern Tunisia. By Frank Edward Johnson. XXII, pp. 787-846, 60 ills., Sept., 1911

Monte Albán, Richest Archeological Find in America: A Tomb in Oaxaca, Mexico, Yields Treasures Which Reveal the Splendid Culture of the Mixtecs. By Dr. Alfonso Caso. LXII, pp. 487-512, 28 ills., Oct., 1932

The Mysterious Prehistoric Monuments of Brittany (France). By Charles Buxton Going. XLIV, pp. 53-69, 16 ills., July, 1923

Mysterious Temples of the Jungle: The Prehistoric Ruins of Guatemala. By W. F. Sands. XXIV, pp. 325-338, 10 ills., Mar., 1913

The Mystery of Easter Island. By Mrs. Scoresby Routledge. XL, pp. 629-646, 13 ills., map, Dec., 1921

A New Alphabet of the Ancients Is Unearthed: An Inconspicuous Mound in Northern Syria Yields Archeological Treasures of Far-reaching Significance. By F. A. Schaeffer. LVIII, pp. 477-516, 47 ills., map, Oct., 1930

New Light on Ancient Ur: Excavations at the Site of the City of Abraham Reveal Geographical Evidence of the Biblical Story of the Flood. By M. E. L. Mallowan. LVII, pp. 95-130, 44 ills., map, Jan., 1930

A New National Geographic Society Expedition: Ruins of Chaco Canyon, New Mexico, Nature-Made Treasure-Chest of Aboriginal American History, To Be Excavated and Studied; Work Begins This Month. XXXIX, pp. 637-643, 7 ills., June, 1921

On the Trail of King Solomon's Mines: The Bible, in Addition to Its Spiritual Values, Continues to Prove a Rich Geography and Guide to Exploration of the Holy Land. By Nelson Glueck. LXXXV, pp. 233-256, 20 ills., map, Feb., 1944

Petra, Ancient Caravan Stronghold: Mysterious Temples and Tombs, Carved in Glowing Cliffs of Eroded Sandstone, Are Remnants of a City David Longed to Storm. By John D. Whiting. LXVII, pp. 129-165, 15 ills. in black and white, 21 ills. in color, maps, Feb., 1935

The Prehistoric Ruin of Tsankawi (New Mexico). By George L. Beam. XX, pp. 807-822, 12 ills., Sept., 1909

Preserving Ancient America's Finest Sculptures (Guatemala). By J. Alden Mason. Paintings by H. M. Herget. LXVIII, pp. 537-570, 24 ills. in black and white, 10 ills. in color, Nov., 1935

Pueblo Bonito, the Ancient: The National Geographic Society's Third Expedition to the Southwest Seeks to Read in the Rings of Trees the Secret of the Age of Ruins. By Neil M. Judd. XLIV, pp. 99-108, 9 ills., diagr., July, 1923

The Pueblo Bonito Expedition of the National Geographic Society. By Neil M. Judd. XLI, pp. 323-331, 10 ills., diagr., Mar., 1922

Pushing Back History's Horizon: How the Pick and Shovel Are Revealing Civilizations That Were Ancient When Israel Was Young. By Albert T. Clay. XXIX, pp. 162-216, 47 ills., map, Feb., 1916

Recent Discoveries in Egypt. XII, pp. 396-397, Nov., 1901

Reconstructing Egypt's History. By Wallace N. Stearns. XXIV, pp. 1021-1042, 21 ills., Sept., 1913

The Resurrection of Ancient Egypt. By James Baikie. XXIV, pp. 957-1020, 46 ills., map, Sept., 1913

The Rock City of Petra. By Franklin E. Hoskins. XVIII, pp. 283-291, 5 ills., May, 1907

The Ruined Cities of Asia Minor. By Ernest L. Harris. XIX, pp. 741-760, 11 ills., Nov., 1908

The Ruins at Selinus (Sicily). (By Marion Crawford). XX, p. 117, Jan., 1909

Ruins of Cuicuilco May Revolutionize Our History of Ancient America: Lofty Mound Sealed and Preserved by Great Lava Flow for Perhaps Seventy Centuries Is Now Being Excavated in Mexico. By Byron Cummings. XLIV, pp. 203-220, 21 ills., map, Aug., 1923

The Sacred Ibis Cemetery and Jackal Catacombs at Abydos. By Camden M. Cobern. XXIV, pp. 1042-1056, 10 ills., Sept., 1913

The Sea-Kings of Crete. By Rev. James Baikie. XXIII, pp. 1-25, 13 ills., Jan., 1912

The Secret of the Southwest Solved by Talkative Tree Rings: Horizons of American History Are Carried Back to A. D. 700 and a Calendar for 1,200 Years Established by National Geographic Society Expeditions. By Andrew Ellicott Douglass. LVI, pp. 737-770, 33 ills., map, Dec., 1929

Secrets from Syrian Hills: Explorations Reveal World's Earliest Known Alphabet, Deciphered from Schoolboy Slates and Dictionaries of 3,000 Years Ago. By Claude F. A. Schaeffer. LXIV, pp. 97-126, 40 ills., map, July, 1933

Sicily: Island of Vivid Beauty and Crumbling Glory. 22 color photos: 21 by Luigi Pellerano. LII, pp. 432-449, Oct., 1927

Sigiriya, "A Fortress in the Sky." By Wilson K. Norton. XC, pp. 665-680, 14 ills., map, Nov., 1946

Some Ruined Cities of Asia Minor. By Ernest L. Harris. XIX, pp. 833-858, 19 ills., Dec., 1908

Some Wonderful Sights in the Andean Highlands: The Oldest City in America. Sailing on the Lake of the Clouds: The Yosemite of Peru. By Harriet Chalmers Adams. XIX, pp. 597-618, 19 ills., map, Sept., 1908

Staircase Farms of the Ancients: Astounding Farming Skill of Ancient Peruvians, Who Were Among the Most Industrious and Highly Organized People in History. By O. F. Cook. XXIX, pp. 474-534, 48 ills., May, 1916

Stone Idols of the Andes Reveal a Vanished People: Remarkable Relics of One of the Oldest Aboriginal Cultures of America are Unearthed in Colombia's San Agustín Region. By Hermann von Walde-Waldegg. LXXVII, pp. 627-647, 22 ills., map, May, 1940

Storied Islands of the South Sea. 20 color photos by Irving Johnson, Malcolm Evans, and others. LXXXI, pp. 9-40, Jan., 1942

The Story of Machu Picchu: The Peruvian Expeditions of the National Geographic Society and Yale University. By Hiram Bingham. XXVII, pp. 172-217, 60 ills., Feb., 1915

The Supposed Birthplace of Civilizations. XVI, pp. 499-504, 6 ills., Nov., 1905

Three Weeks in Hubbard Bay, West Greenland. By Robert Stein. IX, pp. 1-11, 6 ills., maps, Jan., 1898

Unearthing America's Ancient History: Investigation Suggests That the Maya May Have Designed the First Astronomical Observatory in the New World in Order to Cultivate Corn. By Sylvanus Griswold Morley. LX, pp. 99-126, 28 ills., July, 1931

Where Early Christians Lived in Cones of Rock: A Journey to Cappadocia in Turkey Where Strange Volcanic Pinnacles Are Honeycombed With Hermit Cells and Monasteries. By John D. Whiting. LXXVI, pp. 763-802, 20 ills. in black and white, 20 ills. in color, map, Dec., 1939

Yucatán, Home of the Gifted Maya: Two Thousand Years of History Reach Back to Early American Temple Builders, Corn Cultivators, and Pioneers in Mathematics. By Sylvanus Griswold Morley. Paintings by H. M. Herget. LXX, pp. 591-644, 28 ills. in black and white, 35 ills. in color, map, Nov., 1936

See also Antiquities

ARCHIBALD, JAMES F. J.:

In Civilized French Africa. By James F. J. Archibald. XX, pp. 303-311, 14 ills., Mar., 1909

ARCH-ISOLATIONISTS, the San Blas Indians: Coconuts Serve as Cash on Islands Off the Panama Coast Where Tribesmen Cling to Their Ancient Ways and Discourage Visitors. By Corinne B. Feeney. LXXIX, pp. 193-220, 15 ills. in black and white, 12 ills. in color, map, Feb., 1941

ARCHITECTURE:

Cathedrals of England: An Artist's Pilgrimage to These Majestic Monuments of Man's Genius and Faith. By Norman Wilkinson. LXXVI, pp. 741-762, 3 ills. in black and white, 16 ills. in gravure from dry-point engravings by author, Dec., 1939

Cathedrals of the Old and New World. By J. Bernard Walker. XLII, pp. 61-114, 50 ills., July, 1922

Charleston: Where Mellow Past and Present Meet. By DuBose Heyward. LXXV, pp. 273-312, 20 ills. in black and white, 24 ills. in color, map, Mar., 1939

Country-House Life in Sweden: In Castle and Cottage the Landed Gentry Gallantly Keep the Old Traditions. By Amelie Posse-Brázdová. LXVI, pp. 1-64, 51 ills. in black and white, 13 ills. in color, map, July, 1934

The Nation's Capital by Night. By Volkmar Wentzel. With 16 photos in duotone by author. LXXVII, pp. 514-530, Apr., 1940

Nepal: A Little-Known Kingdom. By John Claude White. XXXVIII, pp. 245-283, 32 ills., map, Oct., 1920

ARCHITECTURE—*Continued*

Peking, the City of the Unexpected. By James Arthur Muller. XXXVIII, pp. 335-355, 18 ills., Nov., 1920

The Restoration of Colonial Williamsburg. By W. A. R. Goodwin. LXXI, pp. 402-443, 21 ills. in black and white, 25 ills. in color, Apr., 1937

Sculptured Gates to English Learning (Cambridge University). 19 color photos by B. Anthony Stewart. LXXXIX, pp. 417-440, Apr., 1946

The Smallest State in the World: Vatican City on Its 108 Acres Is a Complete Sovereignty Internationally Recognized. By W. Coleman Nevils. LXXV, pp. 377-412, 37 ills., two-page map, Mar., 1939

Wartime Washington (D.C.). By William H. Nicholas. LXXXIV, pp. 257-290, 12 ills. in black and white, 16 ills. in color, Sept., 1943

Washington, Home City and Show Place: To Residents and Visitors the Nation's Capital Presents Varied Sides as the City Steadily Grows in Beauty and Stature. By Leo A. Borah. LXXI, pp. 663-695, 11 ills. in black and white, 20 ills. in color, June, 1937

Washington—Storehouse of Knowledge. By Albert W. Atwood. LXXXI, pp. 325-359, 20 ills. in black and white, 9 ills. in color, Mar., 1942

Wonders of the New Washington: Efficient Modern Structures Rise in the Biggest Government Building Program Since the Capital City Was Founded in a Wilderness. By Frederick G. Vosburgh. LXVII, pp. 457-488, 20 ills. in black and white, 13 ills. in color, Apr., 1935

See also Archeology; Castles; Cathedrals and Churches; Houses; Mosques; Palaces; Temples; Tombs

ARCTIC BIRDS:

Birds of Timberline and Tundra. By Arthur A. Allen. With 24 color photos by author. XC, pp. 313-339, 8 ills. in black and white, Sept., 1946

The **ARCTIC** Cruise of the United States Revenue Cutter "Bear." By Dr. Sheldon Jackson. VII, pp. 27-31, 3 ills., Jan., 1896

The **ARCTIC** Cruise of the U. S. S. Thetis in the Summer and Autumn of 1889. By Charles H. Stockton. II, pp. 171-198, ill., foldout map, July, 1890

ARCTIC REGIONS:

The Alaskan Boundary Survey. I—Introduction. By Dr. T. C. Mendenhall. II—The Boundary South of Fort Yukon. By J. E. McGrath. III—The Boundary North of Fort Yukon. By J. Henry Turner. IV, pp. 177-197, Feb., 1893

The Anglo-American Polar Expedition. (By E. de K. Leffingwell). XVIII, p. 796, Dec., 1907

The Arctic as an Air Route of the Future. By Vilhjalmur Stefansson. XLII, pp. 205-218, 8 ills., map, Aug., 1922

The Arctic Cruise of the United States Revenue Cutter "Bear." By Dr. Sheldon Jackson. VII, pp. 27-31, 3 ills., Jan., 1896

The Arctic Cruise of the U. S. S. Thetis in the Summer and Autumn of 1889. By Charles H. Stockton. II, pp. 171-198, ill., foldout map, July, 1890

Arctic Expeditions Commanded by Americans. XVIII, pp. 458-468, 10 ills., July, 1907

ARCTIC REGIONS—*Continued*

The Baldwin-Ziegler Arctic Expedition. XIII, pp. 358-359, Sept., 1902

The "Bowdoin" (Ship) in North Greenland: Arctic Explorers Place Tablet to Commemorate Sacrifices of the Lady Franklin Bay Expedition. By Donald B. MacMillan. XLVII, pp. 677-722, 49 ills., June, 1925

Charles Francis Hall and Jones Sound. (By A.W.G.). VII, pp. 308-310, Sept., 1896

Coast Guard Patrol in Greenland. 9 color photos by Lieut. Thomas S. La Farge. LXXXIII, pp. 565-572, May, 1943

Collinson's Arctic Journey. By General A. W. Greely. IV, pp. 198-200, Feb. 8, 1893

Commander Byrd at the North Pole. Reproduction in color of the painting by N. C. Wyeth, National Geographic Society, Washington, D.C. LIII, supplement, May, 1928

Commander Byrd Receives the Hubbard Gold Medal: The First Explorer to Reach the North Pole by Air Receives Coveted Honor at Brilliant National Geographic Society Reception. L, pp. 377-388, 5 ills., chart, Sept., 1926

Desolate Greenland, Now an American Outpost. 17 photos: 12 by Willie Knutsen, 4 by F. Vogel. LXXX, pp. 393-406, Sept., 1941

Discovering Alaska's Oldest Arctic Town: A Scientist Finds Ivory-eyed Skeletons of a Mysterious People and Joins Modern Eskimos in the Dangerous Spring Whale Hunt. By Froelich G. Rainey. LXXXII, pp. 319-336, 15 ills., Sept., 1942

The Discovery of the North Pole. XXI, pp. 63-82, Jan., 1910

The Discovery of the Pole (First Reports by Dr. Frederick A. Cook and Commander Robert E. Peary). XX, pp. 892-916, 11 ills., map, Oct., 1909

Drifting Across the Pole. XVII, pp. 40-42, Jan., 1906

European Tributes to Peary. XXI, pp. 536-540, 4 ills., June, 1910

Farthest North (Peary). XVII, pp. 638-644, 9 ills., Nov., 1906

Fighting the Polar Ice (Book Review). XVIII, pp. 72-77, 7 ills., Jan., 1907

The First Flight to the North Pole. By Lieutenant Commander Richard Evelyn Byrd. L, pp. 357-376, 14 ills., Sept., 1926

Flights from Arctic to Equator: Conquering the Alps, the Ice Peaks of Spitsbergen, of Persia, and Africa's Mountains of the Moon. By Walter Mittelholzer. LXI, pp. 445-498, 53 ills., map, Apr., 1932

Flying Over the Arctic. By Lieutenant Commander Richard E. Byrd. XLVIII, pp. 519-532, 10 ills., Nov., 1925

The Great Unmapped Areas on the Earth's Surface Awaiting the Explorer and Geographer. By J. Scott Keltie. VIII, pp. 251-266, Sept., 1897

Greenland from 1898 to Now: "Captain Bob," Who Went North with Peary, Tells of 42 Years of Exploration in the Orphan Island of New Aerial and Naval Interest. By Robert A. Bartlett. LXXVIII, pp. 111-140, 25 ills., two-page map, July, 1940

Greenland Turns to America. By James K. Penfield. LXXXII, pp. 369-383, 7 ills. in black and white, 5 ills. in color, two-page map, Sept., 1942

Honors for Amundsen. XIX, pp. 55-76, 13 ills., Jan., 1908

Honors to the American Navy. XX, pp. 77-95, Jan., 1909

Ice-cliffs on the Kowak River. By Lieut. J. C. Cantwell. VII, pp. 345-346, Oct., 1896

The Lure of the Frozen Desert. XXIII, panorama, Dec., 1912

The MacMillan Arctic Expedition Returns: U. S. Navy Planes Make First Series of Overland Flights in the Arctic and National Geographic Society Staff Obtains Valuable Data and Specimens for Scientific Study. By Donald B. MacMillan. XLVIII, pp. 477-518, 42 ills., Nov., 1925

The MacMillan Arctic Expedition Sails. XLVIII, pp. 225-226, 3 ills., Aug., 1925

MacMillan in the Field. XLVIII, pp. 473-476, 3 ills., Oct., 1925

Magnetic Observations in Iceland, Jan Mayen and Spitzbergen in 1892 (Geographic Notes. By Cyrus C. Babb). VI, pp. 223-224, table, Dec. 29, 1894

Map of the North Polar Regions. Text with map supplement. XVIII, pp. 454-455, July, 1907

The Meteorological Observations of the Second Wellman Expedition. By Evelyn B. Baldwin. X, pp. 512-516, Dec., 1899

The Midnight Sun in the Klondike. (By Alice Rollins Crane). XII, pp. 66-67, ill., Feb., 1901

The Mission of the "Diana" (Peary Arctic Club). X, p. 273, July, 1899

Mr. Ziegler and the National Geographic Society. XIV, pp. 251-254, June, 1903

A Modern Viking (Amundsen). XVII, pp. 38-41, ills., map, Jan., 1906

The Nansen Polar Expedition. Special Report of the Hon. Ernest A. Man. VII, pp. 339-344, map supplement, Oct., 1896

Nansen's "Farthest North" Eclipsed. XI, pp. 411-413, ills., Oct., 1900

Nansen's Polar Expedition. By General A. W. Greely. VII, pp. 98-101, ill., table, Mar., 1896

National Geographic Society (Records of North Pole Discovery). XXI, p. 276, Mar., 1910

A Naturalist with MacMillan in the Arctic. By Walter N. Koelz. XLIX, pp. 299-318, 22 ills. in color, Mar., 1926

Navigating the "Norge" (Airship) from Rome to the North Pole and Beyond: The Designer and Pilot of the First Dirigible to Fly Over the Top of the World Describes a Thrilling Voyage of More Than 8,000 Miles. By General Umberto Nobile. LII, pp. 177-215, 36 ills., map, Aug., 1927

Nearest the Pole (Commander Robert E. Peary's Address to the Society). XVIII, pp. 446-450, July, 1907

No Man's Land—Spitzbergen. XVIII, pp. 455-458, July, 1907

The Nomads of Arctic Lapland: Mysterious Little People of a Land of the Midnight Sun Live Off the Country Above the Arctic Circle. By Clyde Fisher. LXXVI, pp. 641-676, 28 ills. in black and white, 12 ills. in color, map, Nov., 1939

The North Pole (Peary). XX, pp. 921-922, Nov., 1909

The North Pole (Resolutions of the Society Acknowledging Peary's Discovery). XX, pp. 1008-1009, Nov., 1909

Norwegian Expedition to the Magnetic North Pole by Roald Amundsen. XIV, pp. 293-294, July, 1903

The Origin of Stefansson's Blond Eskimo. By Major General A. W. Greely. XXIII, pp. 1225-1238, 10 ills., map, Dec., 1912

Our Search for the Lost Aviators: An Arctic Area Larger Than Montana First Explored in Hunt for Missing Russians. By Sir Hubert Wilkins. LXXIV, pp. 141-172, 29 ills., two-page map, Aug., 1938

Peary and the North Pole. XIV, pp. 379-381, Oct., 1903

Peary as a Leader: Incidents from the Life of the Discoverer of the North Pole Told by One of His Lieutenants on the Expedition Which Reached the Goal. By Donald B. MacMillan. XXXVII, pp. 293-317, 20 ills., map, Apr., 1920

Peary on the North Pole. XIV, p. 29, map, Jan., 1903

Peary's Explorations in the Far North. By Gilbert Grosvenor. XXXVII, pp. 319-322, 3 ills., Apr., 1920

Peary's Polar Expedition. XIX, p. 447, June, 1908

Peary's Twenty Years' Service in the Arctics. By Maj. Gen. A. W. Greely. XVIII, pp. 451-454, July, 1907

Peary's Work and Prospects. (By H. L. Bridgman). X, pp. 414-415, Oct., 1899

Peary's Work in 1900 and 1901. XII, pp. 357-361, ills., Oct., 1901

Peary's Work in 1901-1902. (By G.H.G.). XIII, pp. 384-386, Oct., 1902

The Polar Airship. By Walter Wellman. XVII, pp. 208-228, 5 diagrs., Apr., 1906

A Polar Map. Announcement of map supplement (July, 1907). XVII, p. 533, Sept., 1906

Polar Photography. By Anthony Fiala. XVIII, pp. 140-142, Feb., 1907

The Return of Dr. Nansen. VII, p. 290, Sept., 1896

The Return of Wellman. By J. Howard Gore. X, pp. 348-351, ills., Sept., 1899

The Russian Expedition to Spitzbergen. XII, p. 404, Nov., 1901

Sailing the Seven Seas in the Interest of Science: Adventures Through 157,000 Miles of Storm and Calm, from Arctic to Antarctic and Around the World, in the Non-magnetic Yacht "Carnegie." By J. P. Ault. XLII, pp. 631-690, 47 ills., chart, Dec., 1922

Scientific Aspects of the MacMillan Arctic Expedition. XLVIII, pp. 349-354, 5 ills., Sept., 1925

The Scope and Value of Arctic Explorations. By General A. W. Greely. VII, pp. 32-39, Jan., 1896

Servicing Arctic Airbases. By Robert A. Bartlett. LXXXIX, pp. 602-616, 3 ills. in black and white, 10 ills. in color, map, May, 1946

Seventy-Five Days in the Arctics. By Max Fleischman. XVIII, pp. 439-446, 5 ills., July, 1907

ARCTIC REGIONS—*Continued*

The So-called "Jeannette Relics." By Professor William H. Dall. VII, pp. 93-98, Mar., 1896

Some Indications of Land in the Vicinity of the North Pole. By R. A. Harris. XV, pp. 255-261, map, June, 1904

A Summer Voyage to the Arctic. By G. R. Putnam. VIII, pp. 97-110, 6 ills., map, Apr., 1897

Sverdrup's Work in the Arctics. XII, p. 461, map, Dec., 1902

Ten Years of the Peary Arctic Club. By Herbert L. Bridgman. XIX, pp. 661-668, 3 ills., Sept., 1908

Three Weeks in Hubbard Bay, West Greenland. By Robert Stein. IX, pp. 1-11, 6 ills., maps, Jan., 1898

Through Franz Josef Land. X, p. 362, Sept., 1899

To Seek the Unknown in the Arctic: United States Navy Fliers to Aid MacMillan Expedition Under the Auspices of the National Geographic Society in Exploring Vast Area. XLVII, pp. 673-675, ill., map, June, 1925

An Undiscovered Island Off the Northern Coast of Alaska. I—By Marcus Baker. II—By Captain Edward Perry Herendeen. III—By General A. W. Greely. V, pp. 76-83, July 10, 1893

The Value of Arctic Exploration. By Commander Robert E. Peary. XIV, pp. 429-436, Dec., 1903

Walter Wellman's Expedition to the North Pole. XVII, pp. 205-207, chart, Apr., 1906

Wellman Polar Expedition. IX, pp. 373-375, Aug., 1898

The Wellman Polar Expedition. X, pp. 361-362, Sept., 1899

The Wellman Polar Expedition. XVII, p. 712, Dec., 1906

The Wellman Polar Expedition. (By J. Howard Gore). X, pp. 267-268, July, 1899

The Wellman Polar Expedition. By Walter Wellman. X, pp. 481-505, 10 ills., diagr., map, Dec., 1899

With an Exile in Arctic Siberia: The Narrative of a Russian Who Was Compelled to Turn Polar Explorer for Two Years. By Vladimir M. Zenzinov. XLVI, pp. 695-718, 30 ills., map, Dec., 1924

A Woman's Winter on Spitsbergen. By Martha Phillips Gilson. LIV, pp. 227-246, 20 ills., map, Aug., 1928

Work in the Arctic and Antarctic. XI, pp. 164-165, Apr., 1900

The Ziegler Polar Expedition. XIV, pp. 414-417, 5 ills., Nov., 1903

Ziegler Polar Expedition. XV, pp. 427-428, Oct., 1904

The Ziegler Polar Expedition. XVI, p. 198, Apr., 1905

The Ziegler Polar Expedition. XVI, pp. 439-440, Sept., 1905

AREA and Drainage Basin of Lake Superior. By Dr. Mark W. Harrington. VIII, pp. 111-120, tables, Apr., 1897

The **AREA** of the Philippines. X, pp. 182-183, May, 1899

ARECUNA INDIANS:

Kaieteur and Roraima: The Great Falls and the Great Mountain of the Guianas. By Henry Edward Crampton. XXXVIII, pp. 227-244, 12 ills., map, Sept., 1920

Through Brazil to the Summit of Mount Roraima. By G. H. H. Tate. LVIII, pp. 585-605, 24 ills., map, Nov., 1930

ARGAEUS, Mount, Turkey:

The Cone-Dwellers of Asia Minor: A Primitive People Who Live in Nature-Made Apartment Houses, Fashioned by Volcanic Violence and Trickling Streams. By J. R. Sitlington Sterrett. XXXV, pp. 281-331, 52 ills., map, Apr., 1919

ARGENTINA:

Argentina-Chile Boundary. XIII, p. 117, Mar., 1902

Argentina-Chile Boundary Award. XIV, pp. 115-116, Mar., 1903

Argentine-Chile Boundary Dispute. XIII, pp. 27-28, Jan., 1902

The Awakening of Argentina and Chile: Progress in the Lands That Lie Below Capricorn. By Bailey Willis. XXX, pp. 121-142, 14 ills., Aug., 1916

Buenos Aires and Its River of Silver: A Journey Up the Paraná and Paraguay to the Chaco Cattle Country. By William R. Barbour. XL, pp. 393-432, 38 ills., Oct., 1921

Buenos Aires to Washington by Horse: A Solitary Journey of Two and a Half Years, Through Eleven American Republics, Covers 9,600 Miles of Mountain and Plain, Desert and Jungle. By A. F. Tschiffely. LV, pp. 135-196, 75 ills., map, Feb., 1929

Chile-Argentina Boundary Dispute. XIII, p. 220, June, 1902

The Falls of Iguazu. By Marie Robinson Wright. XVII, pp. 456-460, 4 ills., Aug., 1906

The Fertile Pampas of Argentine. XVII, pp. 453-456, Aug., 1906

The First Transandine Railroad from Buenos Aires to Valparaiso. By Harriet Chalmers Adams. XXI, pp. 397-417, 14 ills., diagr., map, May, 1910

Flying the World's Longest Air-Mail Route: From Montevideo, Uruguay, Over the Andes, Up the Pacific Coast, Across Central America and the Caribbean to Miami, Florida, in 67 Thrilling Flying Hours. By Junius B. Wood. LVII, pp. 261-325, 65 ills., map, Mar., 1930

Hatcher's Work in Patagonia. (By W J McGee). VIII, pp. 319-322, Nov., 1897

The Indian Tribes of Southern Patagonia, Tierra del Fuego, and the Adjoining Islands. By J. B. Hatcher. XII, pp. 12-22, 4 ills., Jan., 1901

Life on the Argentine Pampa. By Frederick Simpich. Paintings by Cesáreo Bernaldo de Quirós. LXIV, pp. 449-491, 41 ills. in black and white, 8 ills. in color, Oct., 1933

Patagonia. By J. B. Hatcher. VIII, pp. 305-319, 6 ills., map, Nov., 1897

Some Geographic Features of Southern Patagonia, with a Discussion of Their Origin. By J. B. Hatcher. XI, pp. 41-55, 4 ills., Feb., 1900

South America. Annual Address by the President, Gardiner G. Hubbard. III, pp. 1-29, foldout map, Mar. 28, 1891

ARGENTINA—*Continued*

The World's Great Waterfalls: Visits to Mighty Niagara, Wonderful Victoria, and Picturesque Iguazu. By Theodore W. Noyes. L, pp. 29-59, 29 ills., July, 1926

See also Buenos Aires

The **ARGOSY** of Geography (Sailing Ship). XXXIX, pictorial supplement, Jan., 1921

ARICA, Chile-Peru:

Some Personal Experiences with Earthquakes. By Rear Adm. L. G. Billings. XXVII, pp. 57-71, 7 ills., Jan., 1915

The **ARID** Regions of the United States. By F. H. Newell. V, pp. 167-172, Jan. 31, 1894

ARIZA, JOHN FRANCIS:

Dismal Swamp in Legend and History: George Washington Owned Large Tracts in Region Which He Described as a "Glorious Paradise." By John Francis Ariza. LXII, pp. 121-130, 11 ills., July, 1932

ARIZONA:

Along Our Side of the Mexican Border. By Frederick Simpich. XXXVIII, pp. 61-80, 9 ills., map, July, 1920

Arizona and New Mexico. By B. S. Rodey. XVII, pp. 100-102, ills., Feb., 1906

Arizona Comes of Age. By Frederick Simpich. LV, pp. 1-47, 40 ills. in black and white, 14 ills. in color, map, Jan., 1929

The Call of the West. By C. J. Blanchard. XX, pp. 403-437, 20 ills., map, May, 1909

Camp Fires on Desert and Lava (Book Review). XXI, pp. 715-718, 3 ills., Aug., 1910

Encircling Navajo Mountain (Utah) with a Pack-Train: An Expedition to a Hitherto Untraversed Region of Our Southwest Discovers a New Route to Rainbow Natural Bridge. By Charles L. Bernheimer. XLIII, pp. 197-224, 33 ills., map, Feb., 1923

Experiences in the Grand Canyon. By Ellsworth and Emery Kolb. XXVI, pp. 99-184, 70 ills., map, Aug., 1914

Exploring in the Canyon of Death: Remains of a People Who Dwelt in Our Southwest at Least 4,000 Years Ago Are Revealed. By Earl H. Morris. XLVIII, pp. 263-300, 24 ills. in black and white, 22 ills. in color, Sept., 1925

Flaming Cliffs of Monument Valley. By Lt. Jack Breed, USNR. With 9 color photos by author and Warren T. Mithoff. LXXXVIII, pp. 452-461, Oct., 1945

The Forests and Deserts of Arizona. By Bernhard E. Fernow. VIII, pp. 203-226, 5 ills., July-Aug., 1897

The Grand Canyon Bridge. By Harriet Chalmers Adams. XXXIX, pp. 645-650, 6 ills., June, 1921

The Highest Dam in the World (Roosevelt Dam). XVI, pp. 440-441, Sept., 1905

Home-Making by the Government: An Account of the Eleven Immense Irrigating Projects to be Opened in 1908. By C. J. Blanchard. XIX, pp. 250-287, 23 ills., Apr., 1908

The Man Without the Hoe. XXI, pp. 967-969, ills., Nov., 1910

ARIZONA—*Continued*

The Mysterious Tomb of a Giant Meteorite (Meteor Crater, Arizona). By William D. Boutwell. LIII, pp. 721-730, 10 ills., June, 1928

Notes on the Deserts of the United States and Mexico (Extracted from a Publication of Dr. Daniel T. MacDougal). XXI, pp. 691-714, 16 ills., Aug., 1910

The Old Yuma Trail. By W J McGee. XII, pp. 103-107, Mar., 1901; pp. 129-143, 7 ills., map, Apr., 1901

Ostrich Farming in the United States. XVII, pp. 569-574, 6 ills., Oct., 1906

Papagueria. By W J McGee. IX, pp. 345-371, 9 ills., Aug., 1898

Photographing the Marvels of the West in Colors. By Fred Payne Clatworthy. LIII, pp. 694-719, 5 ills. in color, June, 1928

The Saguaro, Cactus Camel of Arizona. By Forrest Shreve. LXXXVIII, pp. 695-704, 9 ills. in color, Dec., 1945

The Saguaro Forest. By H. L. Shantz. LXXI, pp. 515-532, 18 ills., Apr., 1937

The Scenery of North America. By James Bryce. XLI, pp. 339-389, 45 ills., Apr., 1922

Scenes from America's Southwest. 14 ills. XXXIX, pp. 651-664, June, 1921

Scenic Glories of Western United States. 12 color photos by Fred Payne Clatworthy. LVI, pp. 223-230, Aug., 1929

The Secret of the Southwest Solved by Talkative Tree Rings: Horizons of American History Are Carried Back to A. D. 700 and a Calendar for 1,200 Years Established by National Geographic Society Expeditions. By Andrew Ellicott Douglass. LVI, pp. 737-770, 33 ills., map, Dec., 1929

Seeing Our Spanish Southwest. By Frederick Simpich. LXXVII, pp. 711-756, 25 ills. in black and white, 17 ills. in duotone, map supplement, June, 1940

The Snake Dance (Hopi Indians). By Marion L. Oliver. XXII, pp. 107-137, 31 ills., Feb., 1911

The Southwest: Its Splendid Natural Resources, Agricultural Wealth, and Scenic Beauty. By N. H. Darton. XXI, pp. 631-665, 21 ills., map, Aug., 1910

Surveying the Grand Canyon of the Colorado: An Account of the 1923 Boating Expedition of the United States Geological Survey. By Lewis R. Freeman. XLV, pp. 471-548, 62 ills., map, May, 1924

ARIZONA Sands, Home of the Cactus King. 11 ills. LXXI, pp. 521-528, Apr., 1937

ARKANSAS:

Arkansas Rolls Up Its Sleeves. By Frederick Simpich. XC, pp. 273-312, 16 ills. in black and white, 23 ills. in color, map, Sept., 1946

The Great Mississippi Flood of 1927: Since White Man's Discovery This Mighty River Has Served Him Well, Yet It Has Brought Widespread Devastation Along Its Lower Reaches. By Frederick Simpich. LII, pp. 243-289, 53 ills., map, Sept., 1927

Land of a Million Smiles (Ozarks). By Frederick Simpich. LXXXIII, pp. 589-623, 14 ills. in black and white, 20 ills. in color, map, May, 1943

ARKANSAS Traveler of 1946. 23 color photos by Willard R. Culver. XC, pp. 289-312, Sept., 1946

ARLES, France:

Camargue, the Cowboy Country of Southern France. By Dr. André Vialles. XLII, pp. 1-34, 33 ills., map, July, 1922

ARLINGTON COUNTY, Virginia:

Wartime Washington. By William H. Nicholas. LXXXIV, pp. 257-290, 12 ills. in black and white, 16 ills. in color, Sept., 1943

ARLINGTON NATIONAL CEMETERY, Virginia:

Fame's Eternal Camping Ground: Beautiful Arlington, Burial Place of America's Illustrious Dead. By Enoch A. Chase. LIV, pp. 621-638, 19 ills., Nov., 1928

ARMED FORCES, U. S. *See* U. S. Armed Forces

ARMENIA AND ARMENIANS:

Armenia and the Armenians. By Hester Donaldson Jenkins. XXVIII, pp. 329-360, 27 ills., map, Oct., 1915

Between Massacres in Van. By Maynard Owen Williams. XXXVI, pp. 181-184, 3 ills., Aug., 1919

The Cone-Dwellers of Asia Minor: A Primitive People Who Live in Nature-Made Apartment Houses, Fashioned by Volcanic Violence and Trickling Streams. By J. R. Sitlington Sterrett. XXXV, pp. 281-331, 52 ills., map, Apr., 1919

East of Constantinople: Glimpses of Village Life in Anatolia, the Battleground of East and West, Where the Turks Reorganized Their Forces After the World War. By Melville Chater. XLIII, pp. 509-534, 27 ills., map, May, 1923

The Fringe of Verdure Around Asia Minor. By Ellsworth Huntington. XXI, pp. 761-775, 15 ills., Sept., 1910

The Land of the Stalking Death: A Journey Through Starving Armenia on an American Relief Train. By Melville Chater. XXXVI, pp. 393-420, 23 ills., Nov., 1919

The Mountaineers of the Euphrates. By Ellsworth Huntington. XX, pp. 142-156, 13 ills., Feb., 1909

The Old Post-Road from Tiflis to Erivan. By Esther Lancraft Hovey. XII, pp. 300-309, 9 ills., Aug., 1901

The Races of Europe. By Edwin A. Grosvenor. XXXIV, pp. 441-534, 62 ills., diagr. and index, maps, map supplement, Dec., 1918

Under the Heel of the Turk: A Land with a Glorious Past, a Present of Abused Opportunities, and a Future of Golden Possibilities. By William H. Hall. XXXIV, pp. 51-69, 14 ills., July, 1918

ARMIES:

The Citizen Army of Holland. By Henrik Willem Van Loon. XXIX, pp. 609-622, 9 ills., June, 1916

The Citizen Army of Switzerland. XXVIII, pp. 503-510, 7 ills., Nov., 1915

Fiji Patrol on Bougainville. By David D. Duncan. LXXXVII, pp. 87-104, 9 ills. in black and white, 11 ills. in color, Jan., 1945

ARMIES—*Continued*

India Mosaic. By Peter Muir and Frances Muir. LXXXIX, pp. 443-470, 5 ills. in black and white, 22 ills. in color, map, Apr., 1946

See also Soldiers; U. S. Army

ARMISTICE Day and the American Battle Fields. By J. J. Jusserand. LVI, pp. 509-554, 32 ills. in black and white, 23 ills. in color, Nov., 1929

ARMORICA (Region), France. *See* Brittany

ARMY AIR FORCES. *See* U. S. Army Air Forces

ARMY AIR FORCES TECHNICAL TRAINING COMMAND. *See* Army Air Forces Training Command

ARMY AIR FORCES TRAINING COMMAND:

They Sustain the Wings (Ground Crews). By Frederick Simpich. LXXXIV, pp. 333-354, 19 ills., Sept., 1943

ARMY DOGS. *See* War Dogs

An **ARMY** Engineer Explores Nicaragua: Mapping a Route for a New Canal Through the Largest of Central American Republics. By Lieut. Col. Dan I. Sultan. LXI, pp. 593-627, 39 ills., map, May, 1932

ARMY MAP SERVICE. *See* U. S. Army Map Service

ARMY TRANSPORTATION CORPS. *See* U. S. Army Transportation Corps

ARNAUTKÖY, Turkey:

American Alma Maters in the Near East. By Maynard Owen Williams. LXXXVIII, pp. 237-256, 16 ills., Aug., 1945

ARNOLD, FREDERIC K.:

Islands Adrift: St. Pierre and Miquelon: In a Key Position on the North Atlantic Air Route, France's Oldest Colony Rides Out Another Storm. By Frederic K. Arnold. LXXX, pp. 743-768, 23 ills., map, Dec., 1941

ARNOLD, H. H.:

Aerial Color Photography Becomes a War Weapon. By H. H. Arnold. LXXVII, pp. 757-766, 8 ills. in color, June, 1940

The Aerial Invasion of Burma. By General H. H. Arnold. LXXXVI, pp. 129-148, 20 ills., Aug., 1944

Air Power for Peace. By General H. H. Arnold. LXXXIX, pp. 137-193, 35 ills. in black and white, 28 ills. in color, map supplement, Feb., 1946

Note: President Truman presents Hubbard Medal to General Arnold, Nov. 16, 1945, ill. p. 141

Our Air Frontier in Alaska. By Major General H. H. Arnold. LXXVIII, pp. 487-504, 15 ills., map, Oct., 1940

ARNOLD ARBORETUM:

The Kingdom of Flowers: An Account of the Wealth of Trees and Shrubs of China and of What the Arnold Arboretum, with China's Help, Is Doing to Enrich America. By Ernest H. Wilson. XXII, pp. 1003-1035, 24 ills., Nov., 1911

AROUND the Clock with Your Soldier Boy. By Frederick Simpich. LXXX, pp. 1-36, 42 ills., July, 1941

An **AROUND-THE-WORLD** American Exposition. By O. P. Austin. XII, pp. 49-53, chart, Feb., 1901

AROUND the World for Animals. By William M. and Lucile Q. Mann. LXXIII, pp. 665-714, 33 ills. in black and white, 23 ills. in color, map, June, 1938

AROUND the World in the "Islander": A Narrative of the Adventures of a Solitary Voyager on His Four-Year Cruise in a Thirty-Four-Foot Sailing Craft. By Capt. Harry Pidgeon. LIII, pp. 141-205, 75 ills., two-page map, Feb., 1928

AROUND the World with the Salvation Army. By Evangeline Booth. XXXVII, pp. 347-368, 23 ills., Apr., 1920

ART SUPPLEMENTS. *See* Pictorial Supplements: Enlargements and Panoramas

ARTESIAN Water Predictions. XXI, pp. 361-363, ill., Apr., 1910

ARTIST Adventures on the Island of Bali. By Franklin Price Knott. LIII, pp. 326-347, 20 ills. in color, Mar., 1928

ARTS:

Europe's Looted Art. By John Walker. LXXXIX, pp. 39-52, 11 ills., Jan., 1946

Manchuria: Mukden, the Manchu Home, and Its Great Art Museum. By Eliza R. Scidmore. XXI, pp. 289-320, 30 ills., Apr., 1910

Persia: Exploring the Secrets of Persepolis. By Charles Breasted. LXIV, pp. 381-420, 48 ills., plan, map, Oct., 1933

Vatican: The Smallest State in the World: Vatican City on Its 108 Acres Is a Complete Sovereignty Internationally Recognized. By W. Coleman Nevils. LXXV, pp. 377-412, 37 ills., two-page map, Mar., 1939

See also Archeology; Architecture; Paintings; Sculpture

ARTVIN, Turkey:

On the Turks' Russian Frontier: Everyday Life in the Fastnesses between the Black Sea and Ararat, Borderland of Oil and Minerals that Hitler Covets. By Edward Stevenson Murray. LXXX, pp. 367-392, 21 ills., map, Sept., 1941

ARUBA (Island), West Indies:

Curaçao and Aruba on Guard. By W. Robert Moore. LXXXIII, pp. 169-192, 12 ills. in black and white, 10 ills. in color, 4 maps, Feb., 1943

AS London Toils and Spins. By Frederick Simpich. LXXI, pp. 1-57, 38 ills. in black and white, 23 ills. in color, Jan., 1937

AS São Paulo Grows: Half the World's Coffee Beans Flavor the Life and Speed the Growth of an Inland Brazil City. By W. Robert Moore. LXXV, pp. 657-688, 33 ills., map, May, 1939

AS Seen from a Dutch Window. By James Howard Gore. XIX, pp. 619-634, 3 ills., Sept., 1908

"**AS** the Tuan Had Said." By George M. Hanson. LXIV, pp. 631-644, 19 ills., Nov., 1933

AS 2,000 Ships Are Born. By Frederick Simpich. LXXXI, pp. 551-588, 34 ills., May, 1942

ASCENSION ISLAND, Atlantic Ocean:

Ascension Island, an Engineering Victory. By Lt. Col. Frederick J. Clarke. LXXXV, pp. 623-640, 21 ills., May, 1944

Greens Grow for G.I.'s on Soilless Ascension. By W. Robert Moore. LXXXVIII, pp. 219-230, 12 ills., Aug., 1945

The **ASCENT** of Mont Blanc. By Walter Woodburn Hyde. XXIV, pp. 861-942, 69 ills., Aug., 1913

ASHANTI (Division), Gold Coast:

The Gold Coast, Ashanti, and Kumassi. By George K. French. VIII, pp. 1-15, 9 ills., Jan., 1897

The Revolt of the Ashantis. XI, p. 244, map, June, 1900

ASHEVILLE, North Carolina:

Round About Asheville. By Bailey Willis. I, pp. 291-300, map supplement, Oct., 1889

ASHLEY RIVER GARDENS, South Carolina:

The Ashley River and Its Gardens. By E. T. H. Shaffer. XLIX, pp. 525-550, 6 ills. in black and white, 18 ills. in color, May, 1926

ASHOKAN RESERVOIR, New York:

New York—The Metropolis of Mankind. By William Joseph Showalter. XXXIV, pp. 1-49, 39 ills., July, 1918

ASIA:

Adventures with a Camera in Many Lands. By Maynard Owen Williams. XL, pp. 87-112, 24 ills., July, 1921

Along the Old Silk Routes: A Motor Caravan with Air-conditioned Trailer Retraces Ancient Roads from Paris across Europe and Half of Asia to Delhi. By Lawrence Copley Thaw and Margaret S. Thaw. LXXVIII, pp. 453-486, 33 ills., map, Oct., 1940

Asia, the Cradle of Humanity. By W J McGee. XII, pp. 281-290, Aug., 1901

By Coolie and Caravan Across Central Asia: Narrative of a 7,900-Mile Journey of Exploration and Research Over "the Roof of the World," from the Indian Ocean to the Yellow Sea. By William J. Morden. LII, pp. 369-431, 73 ills., map, Oct., 1927

The Citroën Trans-Asiatic Expedition Reaches Kashmir: Scientific Party Led by Georges-Marie Haardt Successfully Crosses Syria, Iraq, Persia, and Afghanistan to Arrive at the Pamir. By Maynard Owen Williams. LX, pp. 387-443, 62 ills., map, Oct., 1931

Commercial Prize of the Orient. By O. P. Austin. XVI, pp. 399-423, 10 ills., 10 charts, map, Sept., 1905

The Desert Road to Turkestan: Twentieth Century Travel Through Innermost Asia, Along Caravan Trails Over Which Oriental Commerce Was Once Borne from China to the Medieval Western World. By Owen Lattimore. LV, pp. 661-702, 45 ills., map, June, 1929

First Over the Roof of the World by Motor: The Trans-Asiatic Expedition Sets New Records for Wheeled Transport in Scaling Passes of the Himalayas. By Maynard Owen Williams. LXI, pp. 321-363, 45 ills., maps, Mar., 1932

ASIA—*Continued*

The Flags of Europe, Asia, and Africa. By Byron McCandless and Gilbert Grosvenor. XXXII, pp. 372-378, 101 ills. in color, Oct., 1917

From England to India by Automobile: An 8,527-mile Trip Through Ten Countries, from London to Quetta, Requires Five and a Half Months. By Major F. A. C. Forbes-Leith. XLVIII, pp. 191-223, 33 ills., map, Aug., 1925

From London to Australia by Aëroplane: A Personal Narrative of the First Aërial Voyage Half Around the World. By Sir Ross Smith. XXXIX, pp. 229-339, 76 ills. in black and white, 8 ills. in color, map, Mar., 1921

From the Mediterranean to the Yellow Sea by Motor: The Citroën-Haardt Expedition Successfully Completes Its Dramatic Journey. By Maynard Owen Williams. LXII, pp. 513-580, 45 ills. in black and white, 25 ills. in color, maps, Nov., 1932

Geographic Progress of Civilization. Annual Address by the President, Honorable Gardiner G. Hubbard. VI, pp. 1-22, Feb. 14, 1894
  Included: Arabia; China; India; Mesopotamia; Persia; Syria

Geographical Pivot of History (Steppes of Central Asia). (By H. J. Mackinder). XV, pp. 331-335, Aug., 1904

The Great Unmapped Areas on the Earth's Surface Awaiting the Explorer and Geographer. By J. Scott Keltie. VIII, pp. 251-266, Sept., 1897

The Link Relations of Southwestern Asia. By Talcott Williams. XII, pp. 249-265, 12 maps, July, 1901; pp. 291-299, maps, Aug., 1901

The New Map of Asia. Text with map supplement. XXXIX, pp. 552-570, 17 ills., May, 1921

New Map Shows Asia's Role in Global Warfare. Text with map supplement. LXXXII, pp. 767-768, Dec., 1942

New Road to Asia (U.S.S.R.). By Owen Lattimore. LXXXVI, pp. 641-676, 15 ills. in black and white, 26 ills. in color, Dec., 1944

On the World's Highest Plateaus: Through an Asiatic No Man's Land to the Desert of Ancient Cathay. By Hellmut de Terra. LIX, pp. 319-367, 39 ills. in black and white, 32 ills. in color, map, Mar., 1931

Place Names in Eastern Asia. XV, p. 136, Mar., 1904

Race Prejudice in the Far East. By Melville E. Stone. XXI, pp. 973-985, 6 ills., Dec., 1910

Seeing the World from the Air. By Sir Alan J. Cobham. LIII, pp. 349-384, 37 ills., map, Mar., 1928

The Society's New Map of Asia. Text with map supplement. LXIV, pp. 770-772, ill., Dec., 1933

The Society's New Map of Southeast Asia. Text with map supplement. LXXXVI, pp. 449-450, ill., Oct., 1944

Sven Hedin's Explorations in Central Asia. XII, pp. 393-395, Nov., 1901

The Trans-Asiatic Expedition Starts. By Georges-Marie Haardt. LIX, pp. 776-782, 6 ills., June, 1931

Western Front Map Embraces Three Continents (Europe, Africa, Asia). Text with map supplement. LXXXII, pp. 139-140, July, 1942

ASIA—*Continued*

With the Nomads of Central Asia: A Summer's Sojourn in the Tekes Valley, Plateau Paradise of Mongol and Turkic Tribes. By Edward Murray. Paintings and drawings by Alexandre Iacovleff. LXIX, pp. 1-57, 43 ills. in black and white, 26 ills. in color, map, Jan., 1936

The World's Greatest Overland Explorer: How Marco Polo Penetrated Farthest Asia, "Discovered" Many Lands Unknown to Europe, and Added Numerous Minerals, Animals, Birds, and Plants to Man's Knowledge. By J. R. Hildebrand. LIV, pp. 505-568, 53 ills., two-page map, Nov., 1928

See also Siberia; *and* names of countries

ASIA MINOR:

Alert Anatolia. 13 ills. LXXXV, pp. 481-492, Apr., 1944

Asia Minor in the Time of the Seven Wise Men. By Mary Mills Patrick. XXXVII, pp. 47-67, 19 ills., Jan., 1920

The Buried Cities of Asia Minor. By Ernest L. Harris. XX, pp. 1-18, 10 ills., Jan., 1909

The Cone-Dwellers of Asia Minor: A Primitive People Who Live in Nature-Made Apartment Houses, Fashioned by Volcanic Violence and Trickling Streams. By J. R. Sitlington Sterrett. XXXV, pp. 281-331, 52 ills., map, Apr., 1919

Crossing Asia Minor, the Country of the New Turkish Republic. By Major Robert Whitney Imbrie. XLVI, pp. 445-472, 31 ills., map, Oct., 1924

East of Constantinople: Glimpses of Village Life in Anatolia, the Battleground of East and West, Where the Turks Reorganized Their Forces After the World War. By Melville Chater. XLIII, pp. 509-534, 27 ills., map, May, 1923

The Fringe of Verdure Around Asia Minor. By Ellsworth Huntington. XXI, pp. 761-775, 15 ills., Sept., 1910

Peculiar Caves of Asia Minor. By Elizabeth H. Brewer. XXII, pp. 870-875, 5 ills., Sept., 1911

The Ruined Cities of Asia Minor. By Ernest L. Harris. XIX, pp. 741-760, 11 ills., Nov., 1908

Scenes in Asia Minor. 35 ills., map. XX, pp. 173-193, Feb., 1909

A Sketch of the Geographical History of Asia Minor. By Sir William Ramsay. XLII, pp. 553-570, 12 ills., Nov., 1922

Some Ruined Cities of Asia Minor. By Ernest L. Harris. XIX, pp. 833-858, 19 ills., Dec., 1908

Turkey, Where Earthquakes Followed Timur's Trail. 15 photos by Maynard Owen Williams. LXXVII, pp. 395-406, Mar., 1940

See also Turkey

ASQUITH, HERBERT HENRY:

A Tribute to America. By Herbert Henry Asquith. XXXI, pp. 295-296, ills., Apr., 1917

ASSAM (Province), India:

Stilwell Road—Land Route to China. By Nelson Grant Tayman. LXXXVII, pp. 681-698, 18 ills., June, 1945

ASSISI, Italy:

Inexhaustible Italy. By Arthur Stanley Riggs. XXX, pp. 273-368, 76 ills., map, Oct., 1916

An **ASSUMED** Inconstancy in the Level of Lake Nicaragua; A Question of Permanency of the Nicaragua Canal. By C. Willard Hayes. XI, pp. 156-161, Apr., 1900

ASSYRIA (Ancient Empire):

The Cradle of Civilization: The Historic Lands Along the Euphrates and Tigris Rivers Where Briton Is Fighting Turk. By James Baikie. XXIX, pp. 127-162, 25 ills., Feb., 1916

Pushing Back History's Horizon: How the Pick and Shovel Are Revealing Civilizations That Were Ancient When Israel Was Young. By Albert T. Clay. XXIX, pp. 162-216, 47 ills., map, Feb., 1916

ASTRONOMY:

The American Eclipse Expedition. By Rear Admiral Colby M. Chester. XVII, pp. 589-612, 23 ills., col. pl., Nov., 1906

Eclipse Adventures on a Desert Isle (Canton). By Capt. J. F. Hellweg. LXXII, pp. 377-394, 14 ills., map, Sept., 1937

Exploring the Glories of the Firmament. By William Joseph Showalter. XXXVI, pp. 153-181, 17 ills., diagr., 3 charts, Aug., 1919

First natural-color photograph of an eclipse ever reproduced, showing the corona. By Irvine C. Gardner. LXXI, ill. p. 178, Feb., 1937

Girdling the Globe. XV, p. 236, May, 1904

The Heavens Above: On Land, Sea, and in the Air the Stars Serve Modern Man as Map, Compass, and Clock. By Donald H. Menzel. With 12 charts, designed by author, showing star positions for each month, and 13 drawings of the constellations by Carlotta Gonzales Lahey. LXXXIV, pp. 97-128, map, July, 1943

Interviewing the Stars: How Twentieth Century Astronomers are Inducing the Heavens to Reveal Their Secrets. By William Joseph Showalter. XLVII, pp. 97-122, 18 ills., diagr., charts, Jan., 1925

The Magic Mountain (Mount Wilson, California). By J. N. Patterson. XIX, pp. 457-468, 9 ills., July, 1908

The Manila Observatory. By Rev. Father José Algué. XI, pp. 427-438, ills., Nov., 1900

The National Geographic Society's Eclipse Expedition to Norfolk, Va. By Marcus Baker. XI, p. 320, Aug., 1900

Nature's Most Dramatic Spectacle (Eclipse). By S. A. Mitchell. LXXII, pp. 361-376, 16 ills., map, Sept., 1937

News of the Universe: Mars Swings Nearer the Earth, Sunspots Wane, and a Giant New Telescopic Eye Soon Will Peer Into Unexplored Depths of Space. By F. Barrows Colton. Paintings by Charles Bittinger. LXXVI, pp. 1-32, 23 ills. in black and white, 10 ills. in color, July, 1939

Observing a Total Eclipse of the Sun: Dimming Solar Light for a Few Seconds Entails Years of Work for Science and Attracts Throngs to "Nature's Most Magnificent Spectacle." By Paul A. McNally. LXII, pp. 597-605, 6 ills., Nov., 1932

Observing an Eclipse in Asiatic Russia. By Irvine C. Gardner. LXXI, pp. 179-197, 19 ills. in black and white, ill. in color, Feb., 1937

ASTRONOMY—*Continued*

Photographing the Eclipse of 1932 from the Air: From Five Miles Above the Earth's Surface, the National Geographic Society-Army Air Corps Survey Obtains Successful Photographs of the Moon's Shadow. By Capt. Albert W. Stevens. LXII, pp. 581-596, 18 ills., Nov., 1932

Scientific Work of the National Geographic Society's Eclipse Expedition to Norfolk, Va. By Simon Newcomb. XI, pp. 321-324, Aug., 1900

Special Telegraphic Time Signal from the Naval Observatory. XV, pp. 411-415, Oct., 1904

To Observe Solar Eclipse. XVI, p. 88, Feb., 1905

The Total Eclipse of the Sun, May 28, 1900. (By F. H. Bigelow). XI, pp. 33-34, Jan., 1900

Unfurling Old Glory on Canton Island. 11 ills. in color: painting by Charles Bittinger and color photo of the eclipse, showing the corona. LXXIII, pp. 753-760, June, 1938

See also Solar Radiation

ASUNCIÓN, Paraguay:

River-Encircled Paraguay. By Harriet Chalmers Adams. LXIII, pp. 385-416, 35 ills., map, Apr., 1933

Through Paraguay and Southern Matto Grosso. By Sir Christopher H. Gibson. LXXXIV, pp. 459-488, 20 ills. in black and white, 11 ills. in color, map, Oct., 1943

AT Ease in the South Seas. By Maj. Frederick Simpich, Jr. LXXXV, pp. 79-104, 32 ills., Jan., 1944

AT Home on the Oceans: Whales and Sharks Make Exciting Neighbors for a Professor's Wife, Turned Able Seaman, On a Three-year Voyage Around the World. By Edith Bauer Strout. LXXVI, pp. 33-86, 54 ills., map, July, 1939

AT the Tomb of Tutankhamen: An Account of the Opening of the Royal Egyptian Sepulcher Which Contained the Most Remarkable Funeral Treasures Unearthed in Historic Times. By Maynard Owen Williams. XLIII, pp. 461-508, 53 ills., map, May, 1923

ATATÜRK, MUSTAPHA KEMAL:

The Turkish Republic Comes of Age. By Maynard Owen Williams. LXXXVII, pp. 581-616, 4 ills. in black and white, 29 ills. in color, map, May, 1945

ATHENS, Greece:

Classic Greece Merges Into 1941 News. 19 photos: 15 by B. Anthony Stewart, 3 by Maynard Owen Williams. LXXIX, pp. 93-108, Jan., 1941

"The Glory That Was Greece." By Alexander Wilbourne Weddell. XLII, pp. 571-630, 51 ills., map, Dec., 1922

Greece of Today. By George Higgins Moses. XXVIII, pp. 295-329, 27 ills., Oct., 1915

Modern Odyssey in Classic Lands: Troy's Treasures, Athens' Parthenon, and Rome's First "Broad Way" Influence Today's Banks, Costumes, Jewelry, and Railroad Timetables. By Maynard Owen Williams. LXXVII, pp. 291-337, 27 ills. in black and white, 22 ills. in color, Mar., 1940

ATHENS, Greece—*Continued*

New Greece, the Centenarian, Forges Ahead. By Maynard Owen Williams. LVIII, pp. 649-721, 51 ills. in black and white, 40 ills. in color, map, Dec., 1930

The Whirlpool of the Balkans. By George Higgins Moses. XXXIX, pp. 179-197, 15 ills., Feb., 1921

ATHOS, Mount, Greece:

The Hoary Monasteries of Mt. Athos. By H. G. Dwight. XXX, pp. 249-272, 24 ills., map, Sept., 1916

ATITLAN, Lake, Guatemala:

Guatemala, the Country of the Future. By Edine Frances Tisdel. XXI, pp. 596-624, 33 ills., map, July, 1910

ATKESON, RAY:

"Where Rolls the Oregon." 28 color photos by Ray Atkeson. XC, pp. 689-728, Dec., 1946

ATKINS, PAUL M.:

French West Africa in Wartime. By Paul M. Atkins. LXXXI, pp. 371-408, 37 ills., maps, Mar., 1942

ATKINSON, AGNES AKIN:

Befriending Nature's Children: An Experiment With Some of California's Wild Folk. By Agnes Akin Atkinson. LXI, pp. 199-215, 26 ills., Feb., 1932

Where Birds and Little Animals Find Haven (Eaton Canyon Bird and Game Sanctuary). By Agnes Akin Atkinson. LXX, pp. 232-241, 14 ills., Aug., 1936

ATKINSON, EDWARD:

Some Lessons in Geography. By Edward Atkinson. XVI, pp. 193-198, Apr., 1905

ATLANTIC CITY, New Jersey:

New Jersey Now! By E. John Long. LXIII, pp. 519-584, 49 ills. in black and white, 24 ills. in color, maps, May, 1933

ATLANTIC OCEAN:

Atlantic Coast Tides. By Mark S. W. Jefferson. IX, pp. 497-509, 3 charts, Dec., 1898

Atlantic Estuarine Tides. By Mark S. W. Jefferson. IX, pp. 400-409, diagrs., 7 tables, maps, Sept., 1898

A Battle-Ground of Nature: The Atlantic Seaboard. By John Oliver La Gorce. XXXIII, pp. 511-546, 23 ills., 4 maps, June, 1918

Flying Around the North Atlantic. By Anne Morrow Lindbergh. Foreword by Charles A. Lindbergh. LXVI, pp. 259-337, 82 ills., maps (1 two-page), Sept., 1934

The Law of Storms, Considered with Special Reference to the North Atlantic. By Everett Hayden. II, pp. 199-211, ill., 3 diagrs., 3 foldout diagrs., foldout charts, July, 1890

New Map of the Atlantic Ocean: Foremost Sea of Commerce Becomes World's Battleground and Its Peaceful Islands Rise to Strategic Importance. By Leo A. Borah and Wellman Chamberlin. Text with map supplement. LXXX, pp. 407-418, 9 ills., Sept., 1941

ATLANTIC OCEAN—*Continued*

Our Global Ocean—Last and Vast Frontier. By F. Barrows Colton. LXXXVII, pp. 105-128, 19 ills., drawing, Jan., 1945

Our Transatlantic Flight. By Commander Richard Evelyn Byrd. LII, pp. 347-368, 17 ills., map, Sept., 1927

Sindbads of Science: Narrative of a Windjammer's Specimen-Collecting Voyage to the Sargasso Sea, to Senegambian Africa and Among Islands of High Adventure in the South Atlantic. By George Finlay Simmons. LII, pp. 1-75, 89 ills., map, July, 1927

Standing Iceberg Guard in the North Atlantic: International Patrol Safeguards the Lives of Thousands of Travelers and Protects Trans-Atlantic Liners from a "Titanic" Fate. By Lieutenant Commander F. A. Zeusler. L, pp. 1-28, 29 ills., map, July, 1926

The Submarine Cables of the World. By Gustave Herrle. With chart compiled by U. S. Hydrographic Office. VII, pp. 102-107, Mar., 1896

What Is the Tide of the Open Atlantic? By Mark S. W. Jefferson. IX, pp. 465-475, 6 charts, Nov., 1898

The World That Rims the Narrowing Atlantic: Latest Ten-color Map Supplement Shows Four Continents and New Transatlantic Air Routes Which Make This Ocean Only One Day Wide. By James M. Darley. Text with map supplement. LXXVI, pp. 139-142, ill., July, 1939

ATLAS MOUNTAINS, Morocco:

Beyond the Grand Atlas: Where the French Tricolor Flies Beside the Flag of the Sultan of Morocco. By V. C. Scott O'Connor. LXI, pp. 261-319, 52 ills. in black and white, 12 ills. in color, map, Mar., 1932

ATLASES:

The Geologic Atlas of the United States. (By W J M.). IX, pp. 339-342, July, 1898

The Topographic Atlas of the United States. (By W J M.). IX, pp. 343-344, July, 1898

See also Map Articles; *and* Index to Maps, *following this index*

ATOMIC BOMB AND ATOMIC POWER:

Air Power for Peace. By General H. H. Arnold. LXXXIX, pp. 137-193, 35 ills. in black and white, 28 ills. in color, map supplement, Feb., 1946

Farewell to Bikini. By Carl Markwith. XC, pp. 97-116, 16 ills., July, 1946

Your New World of Tomorrow. By F. Barrows Colton. LXXXVIII, pp. 385-410, 25 ills., Oct., 1945

ATREVIDA GLACIER, Alaska:

The National Geographic Society's Alaskan Expedition of 1909. By Ralph S. Tarr and Lawrence Martin. XXI, pp. 1-54, 42 ills., 12 maps, Jan., 1910

ATTA ANTS:

Color Glows in the Guianas, French and Dutch. By Nicol Smith. LXXXIII, pp. 459-480, 8 ills. in black and white, 13 ills. in color, map, Apr., 1943

ATTAR OF ROSES:

Bulgaria's Valley of Roses. 13 color photos by Wilhelm Tobien and Georg Paskoff. LXII, pp. 187-194, Aug., 1932

ATWOOD, ALBERT W.:

Coal: Prodigious Worker for Man. By Albert W. Atwood. LXXXV, pp. 569-592, 19 ills., drawing, May, 1944

The Healing Arts in Global War: As Weapons Grow Deadlier, Scientific Medicine Pits Its Ever-rising Skill Against Them. By Albert W. Atwood. LXXXIV, pp. 599-618, 17 ills., Nov., 1943

The Long River of New England: In War and Peace, from Mountain Wilderness to the Sea, Flows the Connecticut River, Through a Valley Abounding in History, Scenery, Inventive Genius, and Industry. By Albert W. Atwood. LXXXIII, pp. 401-434, 12 ills. in black and white, 24 ills. in color, map, Apr., 1943

The Miracle of War Production: For Victory the United States Transforms Its Complex Industry into the Biggest Factory and Mightiest Arsenal the World Has Ever Known. By Albert W. Atwood. With paintings by Thornton Oakley. LXXXII, pp. 693-715, 17 ills. in black and white, 16 ills. in color, Dec., 1942

Northeast of Boston. By Albert W. Atwood. LXXXVIII, pp. 257-292, 12 ills. in black and white, 17 ills. in color, map supplement, Sept., 1945

Potomac, River of Destiny. By Albert W. Atwood. LXXXVIII, pp. 33-70, 15 ills. in black and white, 18 ills. in color, map, July, 1945

Revealing Earth's Mightiest Ocean (Pacific). By Albert W. Atwood. LXXXIV, pp. 291-306, 10 ills., map supplement, Sept., 1943

Tidewater Virginia, Where History Lives. By Albert W. Atwood. LXXXI, pp. 617-656, 18 ills. in black and white, 20 ills. in color, map, May, 1942

Washington—Storehouse of Knowledge. By Albert W. Atwood. LXXXI, pp. 325-359, 20 ills. in black and white, 9 ills. in color, Mar., 1942

ATWOOD, WALLACE W., JR.:

Crater Lake and Yosemite Through the Ages. By Wallace W. Atwood, Jr. Paintings by Eugene Kingman. LXXI, pp. 327-343, 7 ills. in black and white, 13 ills. in color, Mar., 1937

An **AUGUST** First in Gruyères (Switzerland). By Melville Bell Grosvenor. LXX, pp. 137-168, 12 ills. in black and white, 23 ills. in color, Aug., 1936

AUGUSTA NATURAL BRIDGE, Utah:

Colossal Natural Bridges of Utah. XV, pp. 367-369, ills., Sept., 1904

AUGUSTUS—Emperor and Architect: Two Thousand Years Ago Was Born the Physically Frail But Spiritually Great Roman Who Became the Master of His World. By W. Coleman Nevils. LXXIV, pp. 535-556, 17 ills., map, Oct., 1938

AUKLETS (Birds):

Birds of the Northern Seas. By Alexander Wetmore. Paintings by Maj. Allan Brooks. LXIX, pp. 95-122, 12 ills. in black and white, 34 portraits in color, Jan., 1936

AUKS (Birds):

Birds of the Northern Seas. By Alexander Wetmore. Paintings by Maj. Allan Brooks. LXIX, pp. 95-122, 12 ills. in black and white, 34 portraits in color, Jan., 1936

AUKS and Their Northland Neighbors. 34 portraits from paintings by Maj. Allan Brooks. LXIX, pp. 101-116, Jan., 1936

AULT, J. P.:

Sailing the Seven Seas in the Interest of Science: Adventures Through 157,000 Miles of Storm and Calm, from Arctic to Antarctic and Around the World, in the Non-magnetic Yacht "Carnegie." By J. P. Ault. XLII, pp. 631-690, 47 ills., chart, Dec., 1922

AURIFEROUS SANDS:

Report on Auriferous Sands from Yakutat Bay (Alaska). By J. Stanley-Brown. III, pp. 196-198, May 29, 1891

AURORAS:

The Mystery of Auroras: National Geographic Society and Cornell University Study Spectacular Displays in the Heavens. LXXV, pp. 689-690, May, 1939

The Northern Lights. (By Alice Rollins Crane). XII, p. 69, ill., Feb., 1901

See also NGS: Research

AUSTIN, O. P.:

An Around-the-World American Exposition. By O. P. Austin. XII, pp. 49-53, chart, Feb., 1901

Colonial Systems of the World. By O. P. Austin. X, pp. 21-26, Jan., 1899

Commerce of Mexico and the United States. By O. P. Austin. XIII, pp. 25-26, Jan., 1902

The Commercial Development of Japan. By O. P. Austin. X, pp. 329-337, Sept., 1899

The Commercial Importance of Samoa. (By O. P. Austin). X, pp. 218-220, June, 1899

Commercial Prize of the Orient. By O. P. Austin. XVI, pp. 399-423, 10 ills., 10 charts, map, Sept., 1905

National Geographic Society (O. P. Austin Elected Secretary). XIV, p. 425, Nov., 1903

Our New Possessions and the Interest They Are Exciting. (By O. P. Austin). XI, pp. 32-33, Jan., 1900

The Probable Effect of the Panama Canal on the Commercial Geography of the World. By O. P. Austin. XXV, pp. 245-248, Feb., 1914

Problems of the Pacific—The Commerce of the Great Ocean. By O. P. Austin. XIII, pp. 303-318, 7 maps, Aug., 1902

Progress of the National Geographic Society (Report of O. P. Austin). XXIV, pp. 251-256, ill., Feb., 1913

Queer Methods of Travel in Curious Corners of the World. By O. P. Austin. XVIII, pp. 687-715, 29 ills., Nov., 1907

The Remarkable Growth of Europe During 40 Years of Peace. (By O. P. Austin). XXVI, pp. 272-274, Sept., 1914

The United States: Her Industries. By O. P. Austin. XIV, pp. 301-320, 24 diagrs., Aug., 1903

See also NGS: Secretary

AUSTRALASIA:

Treasure Islands of Australasia: New Guinea, New Caledonia, and Fiji Trace across the South Pacific a Fertile Crescent Incredibly Rich in Minerals and Foods. By Douglas L. Oliver. LXXXI, pp. 691-722, 23 ills., two-page map, June, 1942

See also Australia; New Guinea; New Zealand; *and* adjacent islands

AUSTRALIA:

American Bombers Attacking from Australia. By Howell Walker. LXXXIII, pp. 49-70, 19 ills., map, Jan., 1943

At Ease in the South Seas. By Maj. Frederick Simpich, Jr. LXXXV, pp. 79-104, 32 ills., Jan., 1944

Australia's Future. (By Walter J. Ballard). XVI, pp. 570-571, Dec., 1905

Australia's Wild Wonderland. By M. P. Greenwood Adams. XLV, pp. 329-356, 36 ills., map, Mar., 1924

Beyond Australia's Cities. By W. Robert Moore. LXX, pp. 709-747, 27 ills. in black and white, 12 ills. in color, Dec., 1936

The British Commonwealth of Nations: "Organized Freedom" Around the World. By Eric Underwood. LXXXIII, pp. 485-524, 31 ills., Apr., 1943

Capital Cities of Australia. By W. Robert Moore. LXVIII, pp. 667-722, 32 ills. in black and white, 24 ills. in color, two-page map, Dec., 1935

The completion of the cable between Canada and Australia. XIII, p. 410, Nov., 1902

Earth's Most Primitive People: A Journey with the Aborigines of Central Australia. By Charles P. Mountford. LXXXIX, pp. 89-112, 10 ills. in black and white, 8 ills. in color, map, Jan., 1946

The Fairy Wrens of Australia: The Little Longtailed "Blue Birds of Happiness" Rank High Among the Island Continent's Remarkable Birds. By Neville W. Cayley. With 8 ills. in color from paintings by author. LXXXVIII, pp. 488-498, ill. in black and white, Oct., 1945

From London to Australia by Aëroplane: A Personal Narrative of the First Aërial Voyage Half Around the World. By Sir Ross Smith. XXXIX, pp. 229-339, 76 ills. in black and white, 8 ills. in color, map, Mar., 1921

The Great Barrier Reef and Its Isles: The Wonder and Mystery of Australia's World-Famous Geographical Feature. By Charles Barrett. LVIII, pp. 355-384, 38 ills., map, Sept., 1930

Great Britain's Bread Upon the Waters: Canada and Her Other Daughters. By William Howard Taft. XXIX, pp. 217-272, 56 ills., Mar., 1916

The Great Unmapped Areas on the Earth's Surface Awaiting the Explorer and Geographer. By J. Scott Keltie. VIII, pp. 251-266, Sept., 1897

The Koala, or Australian Teddy Bear. By F. Lewis. LX, pp. 346-355, 13 ills., Sept., 1931

Lonely Australia: The Unique Continent. By Herbert E. Gregory. XXX, pp. 473-568, 68 ills., 5 maps (1 two-page), Dec., 1916

The Making of an Anzac. By Howell Walker. LXXXI, pp. 409-456, 31 ills. in black and white, 20 ills. in color, two-page map, Apr., 1942

AUSTRALIA—*Continued*

Sailing the Seven Seas in the Interest of Science: Adventures Through 157,000 Miles of Storm and Calm, from Arctic to Antarctic and Around the World, in the Non-magnetic Yacht "Carnegie." By J. P. Ault. XLII, pp. 631-690, 47 ills., chart, Dec., 1922

Seeing the World from the Air. By Sir Alan J. Cobham. LIII, pp. 349-384, 37 ills., map, Mar., 1928

Shark Fishing—An Australian Industry. By Norman Ellison. LXII, pp. 369-386, 22 ills., Sept., 1932

The Tallest Tree That Grows (Eucalyptus). By Edgerton R. Young. XX, pp. 664-667, 3 ills., July, 1909

What the Fighting Yanks See. By Wanda Burnett. LXXXVI, pp. 451-476, 27 ills., Oct., 1944

Where Nature Runs Riot: On Australia's Great Barrier Reef Marine Animals Grow to Unusual Size, Develop Strange Weapons of Attack and Defense, and Acquire Brilliant Colors. By T. C. Roughley. LXXVII, pp. 823-850, 18 ills. in black and white, 15 ills. in color, map, June, 1940

See also Darwin; Sydney; *and* Lord Howe (Island)

AUSTRALIA-NEW ZEALAND ARMY CORPS. *See* Anzacs

AUSTRALIA'S Future. (By Walter J. Ballard). XVI, pp. 570-571, Dec., 1905

AUSTRALIA'S Patchwork Creature, the Platypus: Man Succeeds in Making Friends with This Duck-billed, Fur-coated Paradox which Lays Eggs and Suckles Its Young. By Charles H. Holmes. LXXVI, pp. 273-282, 13 ills., Aug., 1939

AUSTRALIA'S Stone Age Men. 8 color photos by Charles P. Mountford. LXXXIX, pp. 105-112, Jan., 1946

AUSTRALIA'S Wild Wonderland. By M. P. Greenwood Adams. XLV, pp. 329-356, 36 ills., map, Mar., 1924

AUSTRIA:

Austrian August—and September. By W. Robert Moore. LXXIII, pp. 493-524, 11 ills. in black and white, 19 ills. in color, Apr., 1938

Austro-Italian Mountain Frontiers. By Florence Craig Albrecht. XXVII, pp. 321-376, 60 ills., map, Apr., 1915

The Danube, Highway of Races: From the Black Forest to the Black Sea, Europe's Most Important River Has Borne the Traffic of Centuries. By Melville Chater. LVI, pp. 643-697, 54 ills., Dec., 1929

Entering the Front Doors of Medieval Towns: The Adventures of an American Woman and Her Daughter in a Folding Boat on Eight Rivers of Germany and Austria. By Cornelia Stratton Parker. LXI, pp. 365-394, 23 ills. in black and white, 11 ills. in color, map, Mar., 1932

Flags of Austria-Hungary, Bulgaria, Germany, and Turkey. By Byron McCandless and Gilbert Grosvenor. XXXII, pp. 386-388, 38 ills. in color, Oct., 1917

AUSTRIA—*Continued*

The Land of Contrast: Austria-Hungary. By D. W. and A. S. Iddings. XXIII, pp. 1188-1217, 1284, 33 ills., map, Dec., 1912

Merry Maskers of Imst. 14 photos by Francis C. Fuerst. LXX, pp. 201-208, Aug., 1936

The New Map of Europe: Showing the Boundaries Established by the Peace Conference at Paris and by Subsequent Decisions of the Supreme Council of the Allied and Associated Powers. By Ralph A. Graves. Text with map supplement. XXXIX, pp. 157-177, 18 ills., Feb., 1921

The Salzkammergut, a Playground of Austria. By Florence Polk Holding. LXXI, pp. 445-485, 34 ills. in black and white, 13 ills. in color, map, Apr., 1937

Styria, a Favored Vacation Land of Central Europe. By Melville Bell Grosvenor. LXII, pp. 430-439, 14 ills. in color, Oct., 1932

This Was Austria. 18 ills. LXXXVIII, pp. 71-86, July, 1945

See also Vienna

AUSTRIA-HUNGARY. *See* Austria; Hungary

An **AUSTRIAN** Album. 13 color photos by Hans Hildenbrand and Wilhelm Tobien. LXXI, pp. 457-464, Apr., 1937

AUSTRIAN August—and September. By W. Robert Moore. LXXIII, pp. 493-524, 11 ills. in black and white, 19 ills. in color, Apr., 1938

AUSTRIAN Kodachromes from a Candid Camera. 19 color photos by W. Robert Moore. LXXIII, pp. 501-524, Apr., 1938

An **AUSTRO-HUNGARIAN** floating exposition. XII, p. 164, Apr., 1901

AUSTRO-ITALIAN Mountain Frontiers. By Florence Craig Albrecht. XXVII, pp. 321-376, 60 ills., map, Apr., 1915

The **AUTOMOBILE** Industry: An American Art That Has Revolutionized Methods in Manufacturing and Transformed Transportation. By William Joseph Showalter. XLIV, pp. 337-414, 76 ills., Oct., 1923

AUVERGNE, France:

The Beauties of France. By Arthur Stanley Riggs. XXVIII, pp. 391-491, 73 ills. in black and white, 16 ills. in color, map, Nov., 1915

AVALANCHES:

Landslides and Rock Avalanches. By Guy Elliott Mitchell. XXI, pp. 277-287, 6 ills., Apr., 1910

AVENGERS (Torpedo Bombers):

Cruise on an Escort Carrier. By Melville Bell Grosvenor. LXXXIV, pp. 513-546, 14 ills. in black and white, 20 ills. in color, Nov., 1943

Take-off for Japan. 22 ills. in color from U. S. Navy official photos. LXXXVIII, pp. 193-208, Aug., 1945

AVIATION. *See* Aeronautics

AVIATION CADETS, U. S. Navy:

Pocket Carriers Fight the Submarines. 20 ills. in color from U. S. Navy official photos. LXXXIV, pp. 521-544, Nov., 1943

AVIATION in Commerce and Defense. By F. Barrows Colton. LXXVIII, pp. 685-726, 39 ills., Dec., 1940

AVIATION MEDICINE:

Flying Our Wounded Veterans Home. By Catherine Bell Palmer. LXXXVIII, pp. 363-384, 17 ills., Sept., 1945

The Healing Arts in Global War: As Weapons Grow Deadlier, Scientific Medicine Pits Its Ever-rising Skill Against Them. By Albert W. Atwood. LXXXIV, pp. 599-618, 17 ills., Nov., 1943

New Frontier in the Sky. By F. Barrows Colton. XC, pp. 379-408, 28 ills., diagr., Sept., 1946

AVIATORS. *See* Aeronautics

AVOCET (Ship):

Eclipse Adventures on a Desert Isle (Canton). By Capt. J. F. Hellweg. LXXII, pp. 377-394, 14 ills., map, Sept., 1937

AVON RIVER, England:

Through the Heart of England in a Canadian Canoe. By R. J. Evans. XLI, pp. 473-497, 26 ills., map, May, 1922

An **AWAKENED** Continent to the South of Us. By Elihu Root. XVIII, pp. 61-72, Jan., 1907

The **AWAKENING** of Argentina and Chile: Progress in the Lands That Lie Below Capricorn. By Bailey Willis. XXX, pp. 121-142, 14 ills., Aug., 1916

The **AWE-INSPIRING** Spectacle of the Valley of Ten Thousand Smokes, Discovered and Explored by National Geographic Society Expeditions. XXXIII, panorama, Feb., 1918

AXSON, STOCKTON:

The Symbol of Service to Mankind (American National Red Cross). By Stockton Axson. XXXIII, pp. 375-390, 11 ills., Apr., 1918

AYERS ROCK, Australia:

Earth's Most Primitive People: A Journey with the Aborigines of Central Australia. By Charles P. Mountford. LXXXIX, pp. 89-112, 10 ills. in black and white, 8 ills. in color, map, Jan., 1946

AYMARÁ INDIANS:

The Heart of Aymará Land: A Visit to Tiahuanacu, Perhaps the Oldest City of the New World, Lost Beneath the Drifting Sand of Centuries in the Bolivian Highlands. By Stewart E. McMillin. LI, pp. 213-256, 23 ills. in black and white, 18 ills. in color, map, Feb., 1927

AYMARÁ LAND, Bolivia:

The Heart of Aymará Land: A Visit to Tiahuanacu, Perhaps the Oldest City of the New World, Lost Beneath the Drifting Sand of Centuries in the Bolivian Highlands. By Stewart E. McMillin. LI, pp. 213-256, 23 ills. in black and white, 18 ills. in color, map, Feb., 1927

AZERBAIJAN:

The British Take Baku. XXXIV, pp. 163-164, ill., Aug., 1918

AZERBAIJAN—*Continued*

Russia's Orphan Races: Picturesque Peoples Who Cluster on the Southeastern Borderland of the Vast Slav Dominions. By Maynard Owen Williams. XXXIV, pp. 245-278, 26 ills., map, Oct., 1918

AZON BOMBS:

Air Power for Peace. By General H. H. Arnold. LXXXIX, pp. 137-193, 35 ills. in black and white, 28 ills. in color, map supplement, Feb., 1946

AZORES (Islands), Atlantic Ocean:

American Airmen in the Azores. 10 ills. in color. LXXXIX, pp. 177-184, Feb., 1946

The Azores: Picturesque and Historic Half-way House of American Transatlantic Aviators. By Arminius T. Haeberle. XXXV, pp. 514-545, 26 ills., map, June, 1919

European Outpost: The Azores. By Harriet Chalmers Adams. LXVII, pp. 35-66, 25 ills. in black and white, 13 ills. in color, map, Jan., 1935

New Map of the Atlantic Ocean: Foremost Sea of Commerce Becomes World's Battleground and Its Peaceful Islands Rise to Strategic Importance. By Leo A. Borah and Wellman Chamberlin. Text with map supplement. LXXX, pp. 407-418, 9 ills., Sept., 1941

The **AZORES,** Communications Hub of the Atlantic. 13 color photos by Wilhelm Tobien. LXVII, pp. 41-48, Jan., 1935

AZTECS:

Adventuring Down the West Coast of Mexico. By Herbert Corey. XLII, pp. 449-503, 44 ills., map, Nov., 1922

The Foremost Intellectual Achievement of Ancient America: The Hieroglyphic Inscriptions on the Monuments in the Ruined Cities of Mexico, Guatemala, and Honduras Are Yielding the Secrets of the Maya Civilization. By Sylvanus Griswold Morley. XLI, pp. 109-130, 27 ills., 17 diagrs., map supplement, Feb., 1922

In the Empire of the Aztecs: Mexico City Is Rich in Relics of a People Who Practiced Human Sacrifice, Yet Loved Flowers, Education, and Art. By Frank H. H. Roberts, Jr. Paintings by H. M. Herget. LXXI, pp. 725-750, 14 ills. in black and white, 10 ills. in color, June, 1937

An Interesting Visit to the Ancient Pyramids of San Juan Teotihuacan. By A. C. Galloway. XXI, pp. 1041-1050, 8 ills., map, Dec., 1910

The Isthmus of Tehuantepec: "The Bridge of the World's Commerce." By Helen Olsson-Seffer. XXI, pp. 991-1002, 7 ills., Dec., 1910

The Luster of Ancient Mexico. By William H. Prescott. XXX, pp. 1-32, 22 ills., July, 1916

The Venice of Mexico. By Walter Hough. XXX, pp. 69-88, 18 ills., July, 1916

AZTECS Under the War God's Reign. 10 ills. in color from paintings by H. M. Herget. LXXI, pp. 735-742, June, 1937

B

B-17's. *See* Flying Fortresses

B-24's. *See* Liberators

B-26's. *See* Marauders

BAALBEK, Lebanon:

From Jerusalem to Aleppo. By John D. Whiting. XXIV, pp. 71-113, 30 ills., map, Jan., 1913

BABB, CYRUS C.:

Geographic Notes. By Cyrus C. Babb. VI, pp. 217-228, table, map, Dec. 29, 1894
Included: The Antarctic Continent, pp. 217-223; Magnetic Observations in Iceland, Jan Mayen and Spitzbergen in 1892, pp. 223-224; A New Light on the Discovery of America, pp. 224-225; Monographs of the National Geographic Society, pp. 225-227; Important Announcement Concerning Essays, pp. 227-228

A Relic of the Lewis and Clarke Expedition. (By Cyrus C. Babb). IX, pp. 100-101, ill., Mar., 1898

See also NGS: Secretary

"**BABES** in the Wood" (Bears). XXXII, pictorial supplement, Aug., 1917

BABYLONIA:

The Cradle of Civilization: The Historic Lands Along the Euphrates and Tigris Rivers Where Briton Is Fighting Turk. By James Baikie. XXIX, pp. 127-162, 25 ills., Feb., 1916

Excavations at Nippur. XI, p. 392, Oct., 1900

The Most Historic Lands on Earth. XXVI, p. 615, map, Dec., 1914

New Light on Ancient Ur: Excavations at the Site of the City of Abraham Reveal Geographical Evidence of the Biblical Story of the Flood. By M. E. L. Mallowan. LVII, pp. 95-130, 44 ills., map, Jan., 1930

Pushing Back History's Horizon: How the Pick and Shovel Are Revealing Civilizations That Were Ancient When Israel Was Young. By Albert T. Clay. XXIX, pp. 162-216, 47 ills., map, Feb., 1916

Where Adam and Eve Lived. By Frederick and Margaret Simpich. XXVI, pp. 546-588, 35 ills., Dec., 1914

BACK to Afghanistan. By Maynard Owen Williams. XC, pp. 517-544, 27 ills., map, Oct., 1946

BAD GODESBERG, Germany:

War's Wake in the Rhineland. By Thomas R. Henry. LXXXVIII, pp. 1-32, 29 ills., map, July, 1945

The **BAD** Lands of South Dakota. By N. H. Darton. X, pp. 339-343, 4 ills., Sept., 1899

BADDECK, Nova Scotia:

The Charm of Cape Breton Island: The Most Picturesque Portion of Canada's Maritime Provinces—A Land Rich in Historic Associations, Natural Resources, and Geographic Appeal. By Catherine Dunlop Mackenzie. XXXVIII, pp. 34-60, 22 ills., map, July, 1920

Salty Nova Scotia: In Friendly New Scotland Gaelic Songs Still Answer the Skirling Bagpipes. By Andrew H. Brown. LXXVII, pp. 575-624, 30 ills. in black and white, 21 ills. in color, two-page map, May, 1940

BADEN (State), Germany:

Wandering Through the Black Forest. 13 color photos by Hans Hildenbrand. LIV, pp. 659-666, Dec., 1928

BADGES, Military and Naval:
Decorations, Medals, Service Ribbons, Badges, and Women's Insignia. LXXXIV, pp. 414-444, 6 ills. in black and white, 376 ills. in color, Oct., 1943

BAFFIN ISLAND, N. W. T., Canada:
Servicing Arctic Airbases. By Robert A. Bartlett. LXXXIX, pp. 602-616, 3 ills. in black and white, 10 ills. in color, map, May, 1946

BAFFINLAND (Island), Canada:
Dr. Bell's Survey in Baffinland. (By W J McGee). XIII, p. 113, Mar., 1902

A **BAG** of Bird Portraits. 24 color photos: 23 by Arthur A. Allen. LXXXV, pp. 697-712, June, 1944

BAGG, ETHEL MATHER:
Letters from the Italian Front. By Marchesa Louise de Rosales to Ethel Mather Bagg. XXXII, pp. 47-67, 22 ills., July, 1917

BAGHDAD, Iraq:
Travels in Arabia and Along the Persian Gulf. By David G. Fairchild. XV, pp. 139-151, 20 ills., Apr., 1904
Where Adam and Eve Lived. By Frederick and Margaret Simpich. XXVI, pp. 546-588, 35 ills., Dec., 1914

BAHAMA ISLANDS, West Indies:
Bahama Holiday. By Frederick Simpich. LXIX, pp. 219-245, 29 ills., map, Feb., 1936
Coral Castle Builders of Tropic Seas. By Roy Waldo Miner. Paintings by Else Bostelmann. LXV, pp. 703-728, 15 ills. in black and white, 8 ills. in color, maps, June, 1934
Devil-Fishing in the Gulf Stream. By John Oliver La Gorce. XXXV, pp. 476-488, 7 ills., June, 1919
The First Landfall of Columbus. By Jacques W. Redway, F. R. G. S. VI, pp. 179-192, 4 maps, Dec. 29, 1894
Included: Mariguana (Mayaguana); Samaná; Watling (San Salvador)

BAHIA, Brazil. *See* Salvador

BAHREIN ISLANDS, Persian Gulf:
Bahrein: Port of Pearls and Petroleum. By Maynard Owen Williams. LXXXIX, pp. 195-210, 6 ills. in black and white, 11 ills. in color, map, Feb., 1946
The Rise of the New Arab Nation. By Frederick Simpich. XXXVI, pp. 369-393, 17 ills., map, Nov., 1919

BAIKAL, Lake, U. S. S. R.:
Western Siberia and the Altai Mountains: With Some Speculations on the Future of Siberia. By James Bryce. XXXIX, pp. 469-507, 39 ills., May, 1921

BAIKIE, JAMES:
The Cradle of Civilization: The Historic Lands Along the Euphrates and Tigris Rivers Where Briton Is Fighting Turk. By James Baikie. XXIX, pp. 127-162, 25 ills., Feb., 1916
The Resurrection of Ancient Egypt. By James Baikie. XXIV, pp. 957-1020, 46 ills., map, Sept., 1913

BAIKIE, JAMES—*Continued*
The Sea-Kings of Crete. By Rev. James Baikie. XXIII, pp. 1-25, 13 ills., Jan., 1912

BAILEY, ALFRED M.:
Cruise of the *Kinkajou:* Among Desert Islands of Mexico Voyagers Find Outdoor Laboratories for the Naturalist and Ideal Fishing Grounds for the Sportsman. By Alfred M. Bailey. LXXX, pp. 339-366, 13 ills. in black and white, 12 ills. in color, map, Sept., 1941
Birds and Beasts of Mexico's Desert Islands. 12 color photos: 8 by Ed N. Harrison, 4 by author and Robert J. Niedrach, pp. 353-360
High Country of Colorado. By Alfred M. Bailey. With 23 color photos by author, Robert J. Niedrach, F. G. Brandenburg. XC, pp. 43-72, 9 ills. in black and white, July, 1946
Nature and Man in Ethiopia. By Wilfred H. Osgood. LIV, pp. 121-176, 64 ills., map, Aug., 1928
Note: Photos by author and Alfred M. Bailey, a member of the Abyssinian Expedition of 1926-1927

BAILEY, SOLON I.:
A New Peruvian Route to the Plain of the Amazon. By Solon I. Bailey. XVII, pp. 432-448, 12 ills., Aug., 1906

BAILEY, TRUMAN:
Samoa—South Sea Outpost of the U. S. Navy. 20 photos by Truman Bailey. LXXIX, pp. 615-630, May, 1941

BAILEY, VERNON:
Bats of the Carlsbad Cavern (New Mexico). By Vernon Bailey. XLVIII, pp. 321-330, 11 ills., Sept., 1925

BAINBRIDGE, OLIVER:
The Chinese Jews. By Oliver Bainbridge. XVIII, pp. 621-632, 7 ills., Oct., 1907

BAJA CALIFORNIA (Lower California), Mexico:
Adventuring Down the West Coast of Mexico. By Herbert Corey. XLII, pp. 449-503, 44 ills., map, Nov., 1922
Baja California Wakes Up. By Frederick Simpich. LXXXII, pp. 253-275, 19 ills., map, Aug., 1942
A Cruise Among Desert Islands. By G. Dallas Hanna and A. W. Anthony. XLIV, pp. 71-99, 32 ills., map, July, 1923
Cruise of the *Kinkajou:* Among Desert Islands of Mexico Voyagers Find Outdoor Laboratories for the Naturalist and Ideal Fishing Grounds for the Sportsman. By Alfred M. Bailey. LXXX, pp. 339-366, 13 ills. in black and white, 12 ills. in color, map, Sept., 1941
A Land of Drought and Desert—Lower California: Two Thousand Miles on Horseback Through the Most Extraordinary Cacti Forests in the World. By E. W. Nelson. XXII, pp. 443-474, 25 ills., maps, May, 1911
A Mexican Land of Canaan: Marvelous Riches of The Wonderful West Coast of Our Neighbor Republic. By Frederick Simpich. XXXVI, pp. 307-330, 16 ills., map, Oct., 1919

BAKER, MARCUS:
The Anglo-Venezuelan Boundary Dispute. By Marcus Baker. XI, pp. 129-144, ills., map, Apr., 1900

BAKER, MARCUS—*Continued*

Geographic Literature. VIII, p. 232, July-Aug., 1897

Geographic Nomenclature. Remarks by Herbert G. Ogden, Gustave Herrle, Marcus Baker, and A. H. Thompson. II, pp. 261-278, Aug., 1890

Geographical Research in the United States. By Gardiner G. Hubbard and Marcus Baker. VIII, pp. 285-293, Oct., 1897

The Historical Development of the National Capital. By Marcus Baker. IX, pp. 323-329, July, 1898

Kodiak Not Kadiak. (By M. B.). XII, pp. 397-398, Nov., 1901

The Lost Boundary of Texas. By Marcus Baker. XII, pp. 430-432, map, Dec., 1901

Marcus Baker (Memorial Address by Dr. Wm. H. Dall). XV, pp. 40-43, ill., Jan., 1904

The National Geographic Society's Eclipse Expedition to Norfolk, Va. By Marcus Baker. XI, p. 320, Aug., 1900

On the Alleged Observation of a Lunar Eclipse by Bering in 1728-9. By Marcus Baker. II, pp. 167-169, 4 tables, May, 1890

Portrait. XV, ill. p. 41, Jan., 1904

Sarichef's Atlas, 1826. By Marcus Baker. XIII, pp. 86-92, Mar., 1902

Surveys and Maps of the District of Columbia. By Marcus Baker. VI, pp. 149-178, diagr., tables, map, Nov. 1, 1894
Included: List of Maps of Washington and the District of Columbia

An Undiscovered Island Off the Northern Coast of Alaska. I—By Marcus Baker. V, pp. 76-78, July 10, 1893

The Venezuelan Boundary Commission and Its Work. By Marcus Baker. VIII, pp. 193-201, July-Aug., 1897

See also NGS: Board of Managers; Secretary; Vice-President

BAKER, NEWTON D.:

America's Duty. By Newton D. Baker. XXXI, pp. 453-457, 5 ills., May, 1917

BAKER, ROY W.:

The Balearics, Island Sisters of the Mediterranean. By Roy W. Baker. LIV, pp. 177-206, 11 ills. in black and white, 29 ills. in color, map, Aug., 1928

BAKHTIARI (Tribespeople):

Mountain Tribes of Iran and Iraq. By Harold Lamb. LXXXIX, pp. 385-408, 15 ills., two-page map, Mar., 1946

BAKLUZAN DERE (Tribespeople):

The Cone-Dwellers of Asia Minor: A Primitive People Who Live in Nature-Made Apartment Houses, Fashioned by Volcanic Violence and Trickling Streams. By J. R. Sitlington Sterrett. XXXV, pp. 281-331, 52 ills., map, Apr., 1919

BAKU, U. S. S. R.:

The British Take Baku. XXXIV, pp. 163-164, ill., Aug., 1918

Russia's Orphan Races: Picturesque Peoples Who Cluster on the Southeastern Borderland of the Vast Slav Dominions. By Maynard Owen Williams. XXXIV, pp. 245-278, 26 ills., map, Oct., 1918

BALATON, Lake, Hungary:

Hungary, a Kingdom Without a King: A Tour from Central Europe's Largest Lake to the Fertile Plains of the Danube and the Tisza. By Elizabeth P. Jacobi. LXI, pp. 691-728, 22 ills. in black and white, 27 ills. in color, map, June, 1932

BALCH, EDWIN SWIFT:

American Claims in the Antarctic. (By Edwin Swift Balch). XIV, pp. 77-78, Feb., 1903

Highest Camps and Climbs. By Edwin Swift Balch. XVII, p. 713, Dec., 1906

Some Recent English Statements About the Antarctic. (By Edwin Swift Balch). XV, p. 266, June, 1904

Termination Land (Antarctica). (By Edwin Swift Balch). XV, pp. 220-221, May, 1904

BALDWIN, EVELYN B.:

The Baldwin-Ziegler Arctic Expedition. XIII, pp. 358-359, Sept., 1902

The Meteorological Observations of the Second Wellman Expedition. By Evelyn B. Baldwin. X, pp. 512-516, Dec., 1899

Portrait. XII, ill. p. 118, Mar., 1901

BALEARIC ISLANDS, Spain:

The Balearics, Island Sisters of the Mediterranean. By Roy W. Baker. LIV, pp. 177-206, 11 ills. in black and white, 29 ills. in color, map, Aug., 1928

Keeping House in Majorca. By Phoebe Binney Harnden. XLV, pp. 425-440, 18 ills., map, Apr., 1924

BALFOUR, ARTHUR J.:

The Oldest Free Assemblies: Address of Right Hon. Arthur J. Balfour, in the United States House of Representatives, May 5, 1917. XXXI, pp. 368-371, Apr., 1917

BALI, Gem of the Netherlands Indies. 11 color photos: 10 by Maynard Owen Williams. LXXV, pp. 329-336, Mar., 1939

BALI (Island), Netherlands East Indies:

Artist Adventures on the Island of Bali. By Franklin Price Knott. LIII, pp. 326-347, 20 ills. in color, Mar., 1928

Bali and Points East: Crowded, Happy Isles of the Flores Sea Blend Rice Terraces, Dance Festivals, and Amazing Music in Their Pattern of Living. By Maynard Owen Williams. LXXV, pp. 313-352, 33 ills. in black and white, 11 ills. in color, map, Mar., 1939

BALIM (River), Netherlands New Guinea:

"Shangri-la" in Panorama. 7 color photos by Ray T. Elsmore. LXXXVIII, pp. 681-688, Dec., 1945

BALKAN PENINSULA:

The Changing Map in the Balkans. By Frederick Moore. XXIV, pp. 199-226, 27 ills., map, Feb., 1913

The Danube, Highway of Races: From the Black Forest to the Black Sea, Europe's Most Important River Has Borne the Traffic of Centuries. By Melville Chater. LVI, pp. 643-697, 54 ills., Dec., 1929

The Great Turk and His Lost Provinces. By William E. Curtis. XIV, pp. 45-61, 7 ills., Feb., 1903

BALKAN PENINSULA—*Continued*

Map of Europe Including the New Balkan States. Text with map supplement. XXVI, pp. 191-192, Aug., 1914

The New Map of Europe: Showing the Boundaries Established by the Peace Conference at Paris and by Subsequent Decisions of the Supreme Council of the Allied and Associated Powers. By Ralph A. Graves. Text with map supplement. XXXIX, pp. 157-177, 18 ills., Feb., 1921

The Races of Europe. By Edwin A. Grosvenor. XXXIV, pp. 441-534, 62 ills., diagr. and index, maps, map supplement, Dec., 1918

Two Possible Solutions for the Eastern Problem. By James Bryce. XXIII, pp. 1149-1157, 5 ills., map, Nov., 1912

The Whirlpool of the Balkans. By George Higgins Moses. XXXIX, pp. 179-197, 15 ills., Feb., 1921

See also Albania; Bulgaria; Greece; Turkey; Yugoslavia

BALL, ALBERT:

Tales of the British Air Service. By Major William A. Bishop. XXXIII, pp. 27-37, 12 ills., Jan., 1918

BALL, J. H.:

Surf-Boarders Capture California. 8 photos by J. H. Ball. LXXXVI, pp. 355-362, Sept., 1944

BALL, SIR ROBERT:

The Eruption of Krakatoa. By Sir Robert Ball. XIII, pp. 200-204, June, 1902

BALLANTINE, JOSEPH W.:

I Lived on Formosa. By Joseph W. Ballantine. LXXXVII, pp. 1-24, 19 ills., maps, Jan., 1945

BALLARD, WALTER J.:

Australia's Future. (By Walter J. Ballard). XVI, pp. 570-571, Dec., 1905

European Populations. (By Walter J. Ballard). XVI, p. 432, Sept., 1905

The Population of Japan. (By Walter J. Ballard). XVI, p. 482, Oct., 1905

BALLESTAS (Islands), Peru:

Peru's Wealth-Producing Birds: Vast Riches in the Guano Deposits of Cormorants, Pelicans, and Petrels which Nest on Her Barren, Rainless Coast. By R. E. Coker. XXXVII, pp. 537-566, 28 ills., June, 1920

BALLOONING in the Stratosphere: Two Balloon Ascents to Ten-Mile Altitudes Presage New Mode of Aërial Travel. By Auguste Piccard. LXIII, pp. 353-384, 34 ills., Mar., 1933

BALLOONS:

Helium, the New Balloon Gas. By G. Sherburne Rogers. XXXV, pp. 441-456, 11 ills., May, 1919

No Man's Land—Spitzbergen. XVIII, pp. 455-458, July, 1907

Included: The balloon flight of S. A. Andrée

See also Airships; Stratosphere

BALMAT, JACQUES:

The Ascent of Mont Blanc. By Walter Woodburn Hyde. XXIV, pp. 861-942, 69 ills., Aug., 1913

See also Tribute to American Topographers

BALOGH, RUDOLF:

Rural Hungarian Rhapsody. 20 color photos by Rudolf Balogh and Hans Hildenbrand. LXXIII, pp. 17-48, Jan., 1938

Yugoslavia: Where Oriental Hues Splash Europe. 34 color photos by Konstantin J. Kostich and Rudolf Balogh. LXXV, pp. 699-738, June, 1939

BALSAS, Río, Mexico:

Down Mexico's Río Balsas. By John W. Webber. With 9 color photos by author, Kenneth Segerstrom, Jack Breed. XC, pp. 253-272, 5 ills. in black and white, map, Aug., 1946

BALTIC REGIONS:

Estonia: At Russia's Baltic Gate: War Often Has Ravaged This Little Nation Whose Identity Was Long Submerged in the Vast Sea of Russian Peoples. By Baroness Irina Ungern-Sternberg. LXXVI, pp. 803-834, 33 ills., map, Dec., 1939

Flying Around the Baltic. By Douglas Chandler. LXXIII, pp. 767-806, 31 ills. in black and white, 13 ills. in duotone, map, June, 1938

See also names of countries and cities

BALTIMORE, Maryland:

Colossal Work in Baltimore. By Calvin W. Hendrick. XX, pp. 365-373, 6 ills., Apr., 1909

Maryland Presents—. By W. Robert Moore. LXXIX, pp. 401-448, 17 ills. in black and white, 32 ills. in color, map, Apr., 1941

BALUCHISTAN (Province), India:

Adventures With a Camera in Many Lands. By Maynard Owen Williams. XL, pp. 87-112, 24 ills., July, 1921

BAMBALAS (Tribespeople):

Curious and Characteristic Customs of Central African Tribes (Belgian Congo). By E. Torday. XXXVI, pp. 342-368, 35 ills., Oct., 1919

BAMBOOS (Plants):

Lessons from Japan. XV, pp. 221-225, 3 ills., May, 1904

New Plant Immigrants. By David Fairchild. XXII, pp. 879-907, 34 ills., Oct., 1911

BAMIAN (Region), Afghanistan:

Back to Afghanistan. By Maynard Owen Williams. XC, pp. 517-544, 27 ills., map, Oct., 1946

BAMPTON, England:

England's Wild Moorland Ponies. 10 ills. LXXXIX, pp. 129-136, Jan., 1946

BANANAS:

Costa Rica, Land of the Banana. By Paul B. Popenoe. XLI, pp. 201-220, 17 ills., Feb., 1922

How the World Is Fed. By William Joseph Showalter. XXIX, pp. 1-110, 101 ills., Jan., 1916

Land of the Painted Oxcarts (Costa Rica). By Luis Marden. With 31 color photos by author. XC, pp. 409-456, 30 ills. in black and white, map, Oct., 1946

Where Our Bananas Come From (Costa Rica). By Edwin R. Fraser. XXIII, pp. 713-730, 14 ills., July, 1912

BANDAI-SAN (Mountain), Japan:
Do Volcanic Explosions Affect Our Climate? By C. G. Abbot. XXIV, pp. 181-198, 9 ills., diagr., Feb., 1913

BANGKOK, Thailand:
Ancient Temples and Modern Guns in Thailand. 10 photos: 6 by Maynard Owen Williams. LXXX, pp. 653-660, Nov., 1941
The Coronation of His Majesty King Maha-Vajiravudh of Siam. By Colonel Lea Febiger. XXIII, pp. 389-416, 25 ills., Apr., 1912
Hunting the Chaulmoogra Tree. By Joseph F. Rock. XLI, pp. 243-276, 39 ills., map, Mar., 1922
"Land of the Free" in Asia: Siam Has Blended New With Old in Her Progressive March to Modern Statehood in the Family of Nations. By W. Robert Moore. LXV, pp. 531-576, 28 ills. in black and white, 26 ills. in color, map, May, 1934

BANISHING the Devil of Disease Among the Nashi: Weird Ceremonies Performed by an Aboriginal Tribe in the Heart of Yünnan Province, China. By Joseph F. Rock. XLVI, pp. 473-499, 26 ills., map, Nov., 1924

BANNINGA, JOHN J.:
The Indian Census of 1911. By John J. Banninga. XXII, pp. 633-638, 4 ills., July, 1911
The Marriage of the Gods (Religious Festival). By John J. Banninga. XXIV, pp. 1314-1330, 16 ills., Dec., 1913

BANQUETS. *See* NGS: Banquets

BARBADOS (Island), West Indies:
British West Indian Interlude. By Anne Rainey Langley. LXXIX, pp. 1-46, 23 ills. in black and white, 21 ills. in color, maps, Jan., 1941

BARBOUR, THOMAS:
Further Notes on Dutch New Guinea. By Thomas Barbour. XIX, pp. 527-545, 19 ills., Aug., 1908
Notes on a Zoological Collecting Trip to Dutch New Guinea. By Thomas Barbour. XIX, pp. 469-484, 12 ills., maps, July, 1908
Notes on Burma. By Thomas Barbour. XX, pp. 841-866, 34 ills., Oct., 1909

BARBOUR, WILLIAM R.:
Buenos Aires and Its River of Silver: A Journey Up the Paraná and Paraguay to the Chaco Cattle Country. By William R. Barbour. XL, pp. 393-432, 38 ills., Oct., 1921

BARCELONA, Spain:
Barcelona, Pride of the Catalans. By Harriet Chalmers Adams. LV, pp. 373-402, 32 ills., Mar., 1929
See also Montserrat (Shrine)

BARE Feet and Burros of Haiti. By Oliver P. Newman. LXXXVI, pp. 307-328, 10 ills. in black and white, 10 ills. in color, map, Sept., 1944

BARNES, A. H.:
Beauty Spots in the United States. 4 color photos by A. H. Barnes. XXIX, pp. 406-409, Apr., 1916
The Great White Monarch of the Pacific Northwest (Mount Rainier). By A. H. Barnes. XXIII, pp. 593-626, 31 ills., map, June, 1912
See also Tribute to American Topographers

BARRA, FRANCISCO LEON DE LA:
In Honor of the Army and Aviation (Speech by Senor de la Barra). XXII, pp. 267-284, ill., Mar., 1911

The **BARRAGE** of the Nile. By Day Allen Willey. XXI, pp. 175-184, 14 ills., Feb., 1910

BARRETT, CHARLES:
The Great Barrier Reef and Its Isles: The Wonder and Mystery of Australia's World-Famous Geographical Feature. By Charles Barrett. LVIII, pp. 355-384, 38 ills., map, Sept., 1930

BARRETT, JOHN:
China: Her History and Development. By John Barrett. XII, pp. 209-218, June, 1901; pp. 266-272, July, 1901
The Discovery of the North Pole (Speech by John Barrett). XXI, pp. 63-82, Jan., 1910
Latin America and Colombia. By John Barrett. XVII, pp. 692-709, 10 ills., Dec., 1906
The Philippine Islands and Their Environment. By John Barrett. XI, pp. 1-14, map supplement, Jan., 1900

BARRETT, O. W.:
Impressions and Scenes of Mozambique. By O. W. Barrett. XXI, pp. 807-830, 31 ills., Oct., 1910

BARRO COLORADO ISLAND, Panama Canal Zone:
Who Treads Our Trails? A Camera Trapper Describes His Experiences on an Island in the Canal Zone, a Natural-History Laboratory in the American Tropics. By Frank M. Chapman. LII, pp. 331-345, 18 ills., map, Sept., 1927

BARROWS, DAVID P.:
The Colorado Desert. By David P. Barrows. XI, pp. 337-351, 4 ills., map, Sept., 1900

BARTIMEUS (Pseudonym):
Malta Invicta. By Bartimeus (A Captain in the Royal Navy). LXXXIII, pp. 375-400, 27 ills., map, Mar., 1943

BARTLETT, CHARLES H.:
Untoured Burma. By Charles H. Bartlett. XXIV, pp. 835-853, 17 ills., July, 1913

BARTLETT, JOHN R. *See* NGS: Vice-President

BARTLETT, ROBERT A.:
"Captain Bob" Bartlett awarded the Hubbard Medal. LXXXIX, p. 609, May, 1946
The Discovery of the North Pole (Presentation of Hubbard Gold Medal to Captain Bartlett). XXI, pp. 63-82, Jan., 1910
Greenland from 1898 to Now: "Captain Bob," Who Went North with Peary, Tells of 42 Years of Exploration in the Orphan Island of New Aerial and Naval Interest. By Robert A. Bartlett. LXXVIII, pp. 111-140, 25 ills., two-page map, July, 1940
Resolution awarding medal to Captain Bartlett. XX, p. 1009, Nov., 1909
The Sealing Saga of Newfoundland. By Captain Robert A. Bartlett. LVI, pp. 91-130, 44 ills., July, 1929
Servicing Arctic Airbases. By Robert A. Bartlett. LXXXIX, pp. 602-616, 3 ills. in black and white, 10 ills. in color, map, May, 1946

BARTON, OTIS:

A Half Mile Down: Strange Creatures, Beautiful and Grotesque as Figments of Fancy, Reveal Themselves at Windows of the Bathysphere. By William Beebe. Paintings by Else Bostelmann, Helen D. Tee-Van, E. J. Geske. LXVI, pp. 661-704, 28 ills. in black and white, 16 ills. in color, map, Dec., 1934

BASQUES (People):

The Land of the Basques: Home of a Thrifty, Picturesque People, Who Take Pride in the Sobriquet, "The Yankees of Spain." By Harry A. McBride. XLI, pp. 63-87, 25 ills., map, Jan., 1922

The Races of Europe. By Edwin A. Grosvenor. XXXIV, pp. 441-534, 62 ills., diagr. and index, maps, map supplement, Dec., 1918

BASRA, Iraq:

From London to Australia by Aëroplane: A Personal Narrative of the First Aërial Voyage Half Around the World. By Sir Ross Smith. XXXIX, pp. 229-339, 76 ills. in black and white, 8 ills. in color, map, Mar., 1921

BASSARIS (Tribespeople):

Dusky Tribesmen of French West Africa. 26 color photos by Enzo de Chetelat. LXXIX, pp. 639-662, May, 1941

BATAK HIGHLANDS, Sumatra:

By Motor Through the East Coast and Batak Highlands of Sumatra. By Melvin A. Hall. XXXVII, pp. 69-102, 27 ills., Jan., 1920

BATAVIA, Java:

Java Assignment. By Dee Bredin. LXXXI, pp. 89-119, 32 ills., map, Jan., 1942

A Traveler's Notes on Java. By Henry G. Bryant. XXI, pp. 91-111, 17 ills., Feb., 1910

BATCHELDER, A. G.:

The Immediate Necessity for Military Highways. By A. G. Batchelder. XXXII, pp. 477-499, 22 ills., Nov.-Dec., 1917

BATCHELDER, R. N. *See* NGS: Vice-President

The **BATHING** and Burning Ghats at Benares. By Eliza R. Scidmore. XVIII, pp. 118-128, 7 ills., Feb., 1907

BATHYMETRICAL Survey of the Fresh-water Lakes of England. XII, p. 408, Nov., 1901

BATHYSPHERE:

A Half Mile Down: Strange Creatures, Beautiful and Grotesque as Figments of Fancy, Reveal Themselves at Windows of the Bathysphere. By William Beebe. Paintings by Else Bostelmann, Helen D. Tee-Van, E. J. Geske. LXVI, pp. 661-704, 28 ills. in black and white, 16 ills. in color, map, Dec., 1934

A Round Trip to Davy Jones's Locker: Peering into Mysteries a Quarter Mile Down in the Open Sea, by Means of the Bathysphere. By William Beebe. Paintings by E. Bostelmann. LIX, pp. 653-678, 14 ills. in black and white, 8 ills. in color, map, June, 1931

BATS:

Bats of the Carlsbad Cavern (New Mexico). By Vernon Bailey. XLVIII, pp. 321-330, 11 ills., Sept., 1925

BATS—*Continued*

A Mexican Land of Canaan: Marvelous Riches of the Wonderful West Coast of Our Neighbor Republic. By Frederick Simpich. XXXVI, pp. 307-330, 16 ills., map, Oct., 1919

Mystery Mammals of the Twilight. By Donald R. Griffin. XC, pp. 117-134, 19 ills., July, 1946

Nature's Transformation at Panama: The Remarkable Changes in Faunal and Physical Conditions in the Gatun Lake Region. By George Shiras, 3d. XXVIII, pp. 159-194, 33 ills., maps, Aug., 1915

BATTLE GLACIER, Canada:

Some Tramps Across the Glaciers and Snowfields of British Columbia. By Howard Palmer. XXI, pp. 457-487, 25 ills., June, 1910

The **BATTLE-LINE** of Languages in Western Europe: A Problem in Human Geography More Perplexing Than That of International Boundaries. By A. L. Guerard. XLIII, pp. 145-180, 36 ills., Feb., 1923

The **BATTLE** of the Forest. By B. E. Fernow. VI, pp. 127-148, 5 ills., map, June 22, 1894

BATTLEFIELDS:

Armistice Day and the American Battle Fields. By J. J. Jusserand. LVI, pp. 509-554, 32 ills. in black and white, 23 ills. in color, Nov., 1929

The Most Famous Battle Field in America (Gettysburg). 14 color photos by Clifton Adams and Orren R. Louden. LX, pp. 66-75, July, 1931

Our National War Memorials in Europe. By John J. Pershing. LXV, pp. 1-36, 24 ills. in black and white, 11 ills. in color, map, Jan., 1934

The **BATTLE FIELDS** of France Eleven Years After. 23 color photos by Gervais Courtellemont. LVI, pp. 523-538, Nov., 1929

A **BATTLE-GROUND** of Nature: The Atlantic Seaboard. By John Oliver La Gorce. XXXIII, pp. 511-546, 23 ills., 4 maps, June, 1918

BATTLESHIPS:

Battleship *Missouri* Comes of Age. 11 ills. in color from U. S. Navy official photos. LXXXVII, pp. 353-360, Mar., 1945

Victory's Portrait in the Marianas. By Lt. William Franklin Draper, USNR. With 17 ills. in color from paintings by author. LXXXVIII, pp. 599-616, Nov., 1945

Your Navy as Peace Insurance. By Fleet Admiral Chester W. Nimitz. LXXXIX, pp. 681-736, 32 ills. in black and white, 26 ills. in color, June, 1946

BATTLING with the Panama Slides. By William Joseph Showalter. XXV, pp. 133-153, 15 ills., Feb., 1914

BAUER, L. A.:

The Magnetic Survey of Africa. By Dr. L. A. Bauer. XX, pp. 291-297, 6 ills., Mar., 1909

Magnetic Survey of the Pacific Ocean. (By L. A. Bauer). XVII, p. 237, Apr., 1906

Magnetic Survey of the United States. By Dr. L. A. Bauer. XIII, pp. 92-95, map, Mar., 1902

Magnetic Work of the Coast and Geodetic Survey. By L. A. Bauer. X, pp. 288-289, Aug., 1899

BAUER, L. A.—*Continued*

Most Curious Craft Afloat: The Compass in Navigation and the Work of the Non-Magnetic Yacht "Carnegie." By L. A. Bauer. XXI, pp. 223-245, 31 ills., Mar., 1910

The San Francisco Earthquake of April 18, 1906, as Recorded by the Coast and Geodetic Survey Magnetic Observatories. By L. A. Bauer and J. E. Burbank. XVII, pp. 298-300, tables, May, 1906

The Work in the Pacific Ocean of the Magnetic Survey Yacht "Galilee." By L. A. Bauer. XVIII, pp. 601-611, 15 ills., Sept., 1907

BAUER, SIEGBERT:

Behind the Scenes in the Home of the Passion Play (Oberammergau, Germany). 11 color photos: 4 by Siegbert Bauer. LXVIII, pp. 753-760, Dec., 1935

BAUM, Ohio:

The Indian Village of Baum. (By H. C. Brown). XII, pp. 272-274, July, 1901

BAVARIA (Region), Germany:

The Beauty of the Bavarian Alps. By Colonel Fitzhugh Lee Minnigerode. XLIX, pp. 632-649, 16 ills. in color, June, 1926

From Chalet to Palace in Bavaria. 14 color photos by Hans Hildenbrand. LIV, pp. 683-690, Dec., 1928

The Races of Europe. By Edwin A. Grosvenor. XXXIV, pp. 441-534, 62 ills., diagr. and index, maps, map supplement, Dec., 1918

See also Berchtesgaden; Dinkelsbühl; Nördlingen; Oberammergau; Rothenburg

BAYEUX TAPESTRY:

The Beauties of France. By Arthur Stanley Riggs. XXVIII, pp. 391-491, 73 ills. in black and white, 16 ills. in color, map, Nov., 1915

BAYNES, ERNEST HAROLD:

Mankind's Best Friend (Dog): Companion of His Solitude, Advance Guard in the Hunt, and Ally of the Trenches. By Ernest Harold Baynes. XXXV, pp. 185-201, 11 ills., Mar., 1919

Our Common Dogs. By Louis Agassiz Fuertes and Ernest Harold Baynes. Paintings by Louis Agassiz Fuertes. XXXV, pp. 201-253, 73 ills. in color, index p. 280, Mar., 1919

BAZAARS:

Peiping's Happy New Year: Lunar Celebration Attracts Throngs to Temple Fairs, Motley Bazaars, and Age-old Festivities. By George Kin Leung. LXX, pp. 749-792, 31 ills. in black and white, 16 ills. in color, Dec., 1936

BB (Boat):

Experimental boat of Dr. Alexander Graham Bell, driven by aërial propellers. XVIII, ill. p. 671, Oct., 1907

BEACHES and Bathers of the Jersey Shore. 11 color photos by Edwin L. Wisherd. LXIII, pp. 535-542, May, 1933

BEACONS of the Sea. By George R. Putnam. XXIV, pp. 1-53, 65 ills., diagrs., map, Jan., 1913

BEACONSFIELD, England: Toy Town:

Bekonscot, England's Toy-Size Town. By Andrew H. Brown and B. Anthony Stewart. LXXI, pp. 649-661, 2 ills. in black and white, 15 ills. in color, May, 1937

BEAM, GEORGE L.:

The Prehistoric Ruin of Tsankawi (New Mexico). By George L. Beam. XX, pp. 807-822, 12 ills., Sept., 1909

BEAR (Revenue Cutter):

The Arctic Cruise of the United States Revenue Cutter "Bear." By Dr. Sheldon Jackson. VII, pp. 27-31, 3 ills., Jan., 1896

BEARING of Physiography Upon Suess' Theories. By Wm. M. Davis. XV, p. 430, Oct., 1904

BEARS:

The Alaskan Brown Bear. (By Wilfred H. Osgood). XX, pp. 332-333, Apr., 1909

"Babes in the Wood." XXXII, pictorial supplement, Aug., 1917

The Bear Hunt. XIX, p. 222, Mar., 1908

A Bear Hunt in Montana. By Arthur Alvord Stiles. XIX, pp. 149-154, 5 ills., Feb., 1908

The Big Game of Alaska. By Wilfred H. Osgood. XX, pp. 624-636, 10 ills., July, 1909

Hunting Bears on Horseback (Wyoming). By Alan D. Wilson. XIX, pp. 350-356, 4 ills., May, 1908

Hunting the Great Brown Bear of Alaska. By George Mixter, 2d. XX, pp. 313-333, 35 ills., Apr., 1909

Hunting the Grizzly in British Columbia. By Joseph Wendle. XVIII, pp. 612-615, 3 ills., Sept., 1907

The Larger North American Mammals. By E. W. Nelson. Paintings by Louis Agassiz Fuertes. XXX, pp. 385-472, 24 ills. in black and white, 49 ills. in color, pictorial supplement, Nov., 1916

The Largest Carnivorous Animal Extant: The Alaska Brown Bear (supplement)

Lords of the Rockies: Photographing Big Game Animals in Their Primeval Surroundings, from Arizona to Canada, Brings Adventure to Two Wilderness Wanderers. By Wendell and Lucie Chapman. LXXVI, pp. 87-128, 14 ills. in black and white, 28 ills. in color, July, 1939

Once in a Lifetime: Black Bears Rarely Have Quadruplets, But Goofy Did—and the Camera Caught Her Nursing Her Remarkable Family. By Paul B. Kinney. LXXX, pp. 249-258, 11 ills., Aug., 1941

BEAUMONT, ARTHUR:

Painting the Army on Maneuvers. By Arthur Beaumont. Text with 16 ills. in color from paintings by author. LXXXII, pp. 601-602, Nov., 1942

U. S. Army. 16 ills. in color from paintings by author, pp. 577-600

Ships of Our Navy. 8 ills. in color from paintings by Arthur Beaumont. LXXX, pp. 329-336, Sept., 1941

The **BEAUTIES** of France. By Arthur Stanley Riggs. XXVIII, pp. 391-491, 73 ills. in black and white, 16 ills. in color, map, Nov., 1915

BEAUTIES of Our Common Grasses. 8 ills. in color from paintings by E. J. Geske. XXXIX, pp. 627-634, June, 1921

The **BEAUTIES** of the Severn Valley. By Frank Wakeman. LXIII, pp. 417-452, 24 ills. in black and white, 15 ills. in color, map, Apr., 1933

BEAUTIFUL Belgium, Restored by Peace. 16 color photos by Paul G. Guillumette and A. Buyssens. LVI, pp. 555-562, Nov., 1929

BEAUTIFUL Ecuador. By Joseph Lee. XVIII, pp. 81-91, 9 ills., Feb., 1907

BEAUTY, History, and Romance Enrich the Château Country (France). 10 color photos by Gervais Courtellemont. LVIII, pp. 467-474, Oct., 1930

The **BEAUTY** of the Bavarian Alps. By Colonel Fitzhugh Lee Minnigerode. XLIX, pp. 632-649, 16 ills. in color, June, 1926

BEAVERS:

Mickey the Beaver: An Animal Engineer Performs for the Camera as a Star in the Activities of His Species. By James MacGillivray. LIV, pp. 741-756, 23 ills., Dec., 1928

Wild Animals That Took Their Own Pictures by Day and by Night. By George Shiras, 3d. XXIV, pp. 763-834, 68 ills., map, pictorial supplement, July, 1913

The Wild Life of Lake Superior, Past and Present: The Habits of Deer, Moose, Wolves, Beavers, Muskrats, Trout, and Feathered Wood-Folk Studied with Camera and Flashlight. By George Shiras, 3d. XL, pp. 113-204, 76 ills., map, pictorial supplement, Aug., 1921

BECK, CHARLES W., Jr.:

Rothenburg, the City Time Forgot. By Charles W. Beck, Jr. XLIX, pp. 184-194, 8 ills. in color, Feb., 1926

BECK, FRANCIS:

California Trapdoor Spider Performs Engineering Marvels. By Lee Passmore. LXIV, pp. 195-211, 23 ills., Aug., 1933

BECK, ROLLO H.:

Iridescent Isles of the South Seas. 12 color photos by Rollo H. Beck. XLVIII, pp. 403-418, Oct., 1925

BECKER, GEORGE F.:

The Witwatersrand and the Revolt of the Uitlanders. By George F. Becker. VII, pp. 349-367, 4 ills., Nov., 1896

BEDOUIN (Tribespeople):

Ali Goes to the Clinic. By Herndon and Mary Hudson. XC, pp. 764-766, ills., Dec., 1946

Among the Bethlehem Shepherds: A Visit to the Valley Which David Probably Recalled When He Wrote the Twenty-third Psalm. By John D. Whiting. L, pp. 729-753, 19 ills., Dec., 1926

Bedouin Life in Bible Lands: The Nomads of the "Houses of Hair" Offer Unstinted Hospitality to an American. By John D. Whiting. LXXI, pp. 59-83, 27 ills., map, Jan., 1937

Cirenaica, Eastern Wing of Italian Libia. By Harriet Chalmers Adams. LVII, pp. 689-726, 35 ills. in black and white, 13 ills. in color, map, June, 1930

BEDOUIN (Tribespeople)—*Continued*

Forty Years Among the Arabs. By John Van Ess. LXXXII, pp. 385-420, 27 ills., two-page map, Sept., 1942

On the Trail of King Solomon's Mines: The Bible, in Addition to Its Spiritual Values, Continues to Prove a Rich Geography and Guide to Exploration of the Holy Land. By Nelson Glueck. LXXXV, pp. 233-256, 20 ills., map, Feb., 1944

Where Adam and Eve Lived. By Frederick and Margaret Simpich. XXVI, pp. 546-588, 35 ills., Dec., 1914

BEEBE, WILLIAM:

The Depths of the Sea: Strange Life Forms a Mile Below the Surface. By William Beebe. Paintings by E. Bostelmann. LXI, pp. 65-88, 15 ills. in black and white, 8 ills. in color, map, Jan., 1932

A Half Mile Down: Strange Creatures, Beautiful and Grotesque as Figments of Fancy, Reveal Themselves at Windows of the Bathysphere. By William Beebe. Paintings by Else Bostelmann, Helen D. Tee-Van, E. J. Geske. LXVI, pp. 661-704, 28 ills. in black and white, 16 ills. in color, map, Dec., 1934

A Round Trip to Davy Jones's Locker: Peering into Mysteries a Quarter Mile Down in the Open Sea, by Means of the Bathysphere. By William Beebe. Paintings by E. Bostelmann. LIX, pp. 653-678, 14 ills. in black and white, 8 ills. in color, map, June, 1931

The Society Takes Part in Three Geographic Expeditions. LXV, pp. 625-626, May, 1934

A Wonderer Under Sea. By William Beebe. Paintings by E. Bostelmann. LXII, pp. 741-758, 13 ills. in black and white, 8 ills. in color, Dec., 1932

BEECH, JOSEPH:

The Eden of the Flowery Republic (Sze-chuan, China). By Dr. Joseph Beech. XXXVIII, pp. 355-390, 18 ills. in black and white, 16 ills. in color, Nov., 1920

BEECHEY ISLAND, Arctic Region:

Location of the Sir John Franklin Monument. By James White. XIX, p. 596, Aug., 1908

BEEHIVE HOMES:

The Stone Beehive Homes of the Italian Heel: In Trulli-Land the Native Builds His Dwelling and Makes His Field Arable in the Same Operation. By Paul Wilstach. LVII, pp. 229-260, 25 ills. in black and white, 12 ills. in color, map, Feb., 1930

BEES:

Man's Winged Ally, the Busy Honeybee: Modern Research Adds a New Chapter to Usefulness of the Insect Which Has Symbolized Industry Since Early Bible Times. By James I. Hambleton. Paintings by Hashime Murayama. LXVII, pp. 401-428, 18 ills. in black and white, 16 ills. in color, Apr., 1935

The Monsters of Our Back Yards. By David Fairchild. XXIV, pp. 575-626, 38 ills., May, 1913

Our Friends, the Bees. By A. I. Root and E. R. Root. XXII, pp. 675-694, 21 ills., July, 1911

BEETLES:

Explorers of a New Kind: Successful Introduction of Beetles and Parasites to Check Ravages of the Gipsy-moth and Brown-tail Moth. By L. O. Howard. XXVI, pp. 38-67, 11 ills. in black and white, 5 ills. in color, July, 1914

The Monsters of Our Back Yards. By David Fairchild. XXIV, pp. 575-626, 38 ills., May, 1913

Protecting the United States from Plant Pests. By Charles Lester Marlatt. XL, pp. 205-218, 16 ills., Aug., 1921

BEFRIENDING Nature's Children: An Experiment With Some of California's Wild Folk. By Agnes Akin Atkinson. LXI, pp. 199-215, 26 ills., Feb., 1932

BEGRAM, Afghanistan:

Back to Afghanistan. By Maynard Owen Williams. XC, pp. 517-544, 27 ills., map, Oct., 1946

BEHIND Netherlands Sea Ramparts: Dikes and Pumps Keep Ocean and Rivers at Bay While a Busy People Carries on Peacetime Work. By McFall Kerbey. LXXVII, pp. 255-290, 26 ills. in black and white, 11 ills. in duotone, map, Feb., 1940

BEHIND New Delhi's News (India). 13 color photos by Maynard Owen Williams. LXXXII, pp. 477-484, Oct., 1942

BEHIND the Lines in Italy. By Corporal Macon Reed, Jr. LXXXVI, pp. 109-128, 20 ills., July, 1944

BEHIND the Mask of Modern Japan. By Willard Price. LXXXVIII, pp. 513-535, 14 ills., Nov., 1945

BEHIND the News in Singapore. By Frederick Simpich. LXXVIII, pp. 83-110, 26 ills., map, July, 1940

BEHIND the Scenes in the Home of the Passion Play (Oberammergau, Germany). 11 ills. in color. LXVIII, pp. 753-760, Dec., 1935

BEIRUT, Lebanon:

American Alma Maters in the Near East. By Maynard Owen Williams. LXXXVIII, pp. 237-256, 16 ills., Aug., 1945

Syria: The Land Link of History's Chain. By Maynard Owen Williams. XXXVI, pp. 437-462, 20 ills., map, Nov., 1919

Syria and Lebanon Taste Freedom. By Maynard Owen Williams. With 21 color photos by author. XC, pp. 729-763, 16 ills. in black and white, Dec., 1946

BEKONSCOT (Toy Town), Beaconsfield, England:

Bekonscot, England's Toy-Size Town. By Andrew H. Brown and B. Anthony Stewart. LXXI, pp. 649-661, 2 ills. in black and white, 15 ills. in color, May, 1937

BELAUNSARAN, ISABEL:

Cuernavaca, the Sun Child of the Sierras (Mexico). By Russell Hastings Millward. XXII, pp. 291-301, 9 ills., Mar., 1911

Note: Isabel Belaunsaran, maker of diminutive dolls

BELED EL JERID (Region), Tunisia:

The Date Gardens of the Jerid. By Thomas H. Kearney. XXI, pp. 543-567, 20 ills., July, 1910

BELÉM, Brazil:

Air Cruising Through New Brazil: A National Geographic Reporter Spots Vast Resources Which the Republic's War Declaration Adds to Strength of United Nations. By Henry Albert Phillips. LXXXII, pp. 503-536, 32 ills., Oct., 1942

The **BELGIAN** Antarctic Expedition. X, pp. 229-230, June, 1899

BELGIAN CONGO:

Amid the Snow Peaks of the Equator: A Naturalist's Explorations Around Ruwenzori, with an Excursion to the Congo State, and an Account of the Terrible Scourge of Sleeping Sickness. By A. F. R. Wollaston. XX, pp. 256-277, 11 ills., Mar., 1909

Among the Cannibals of Belgian Kongo (Taken from the Notes of E. Torday). XXI, pp. 969-971, 4 ills., Nov., 1910

Curious and Characteristic Customs of Central African Tribes. By E. Torday. XXXVI, pp. 342-368, 35 ills., Oct., 1919

A Journey Through the Eastern Portion of the Congo State. By Major P. H. G. Powell-Cotton. XIX, pp. 155-163, 9 ills., Mar., 1908

Keeping House on the Congo. By Ruth Q. McBride. LXXII, pp. 643-670, 29 ills., Nov., 1937

A Land of Giants and Pygmies (Ruanda). By the Duke Adolphus Frederick of Mecklenburg. XXIII, pp. 369-388, 16 ills., map, Apr., 1912

Lloyd's Journey Across the Great Pygmy Forest. X, pp. 26-30, Jan., 1899

Recent Geographic Advances, Especially in Africa. By Major General A. W. Greely. XXII, pp. 383-398, 5 ills., 5 maps, Apr., 1911

Some Peculiar Features of Central African Geography. (By Samuel P. Verner). XV, p. 448, Nov., 1904

Trans-Africa Safari: A Motor Caravan Rolls Across Sahara and Jungle Through Realms of Dusky Potentates and the Land of Big-Lipped Women. By Lawrence Copley Thaw and Margaret Stout Thaw. LXXIV, pp. 327-364, 29 ills. in black and white, 14 ills. in color, map, Sept., 1938

Transporting a Navy Through the Jungles of Africa in War Time. By Frank J. Magee. XLII, pp. 331-362, 31 ills., Oct., 1922

The Truth About the Congo. XVIII, pp. 811-813, 6 ills., Dec., 1907

We Keep House on an Active Volcano: After Flying to Study a Spectacular Eruption in Belgian Congo, a Geologist Settles Down on a Newborn Craterless Vent for Eight Months' Study. By Dr. Jean Verhoogen. LXXVI, pp. 511-550, 28 ills., map, Oct., 1939

Where Exploration Is Needed (Africa). XI, pp. 163-164, Apr., 1900

BELGIAN Portraits. 20 color photos by B. Anthony Stewart. LXXIII, pp. 413-444, Apr., 1938

BELGIUM:

Beautiful Belgium, Restored by Peace. 16 color photos by Paul G. Guillumette and A. Buyssens. LVI, pp. 555-562, Nov., 1929

BELGIUM—*Continued*

Belgium—Europe in Miniature. By Douglas Chandler. LXXIII, pp. 397-450, 34 ills. in black and white, 20 ills. in color, Apr., 1938

Belgium: The Innocent Bystander. By William Joseph Showalter. XXVI, pp. 223-264, 35 ills., Sept., 1914

Belgium's Plight. By John H. Gade. XXXI, pp. 433-439, 3 ills., May, 1917

Low Countries Await Liberation. 10 ills. LXXXVI, pp. 221-228, Aug., 1944

The New Map of Europe: Showing the Boundaries Established by the Peace Conference at Paris and by Subsequent Decisions of the Supreme Council of Allied and Associated Powers. By Ralph A. Graves. Text with map supplement. XXXIX, pp. 157-177, 18 ills., Feb., 1921

The Races of Europe. By Edwin A. Grosvenor. XXXIV, pp. 441-534, 62 ills., diagr. and index, maps, map supplement, Dec., 1918

The Singing Towers of Holland and Belgium. By William Gorham Rice. XLVII, pp. 357-376, 22 ills., Mar., 1925

Through the Back Doors of Belgium: Artist and Author Paddle for Three Weeks Along 200 Miles of Low-Countries Canals in a Canadian Canoe. By Melville Chater. XLVII, pp. 499-540, 39 ills., map, May, 1925

BELGIUM'S Plight. By John H. Gade. XXXI, pp. 433-439, 3 ills., May, 1917

BELKNAP, REGINALD R.:

The North Sea Mine Barrage. By Capt. Reginald R. Belknap. XXXV, pp. 85-110, 23 ills., diagr., map, Feb., 1919

BELL, ALEXANDER GRAHAM:

Address of the President to the Board of Managers, June 1, 1900 (Early History of the Society). (By Alexander Graham Bell). XI, pp. 401-408, chart, Oct., 1900

Aërial Locomotion: With a Few Notes of Progress in the Construction of an Aërodrome. By Alexander Graham Bell. XVIII, pp. 1-34, 33 ills., Jan., 1907

Air Conquest: From the Early Days of Giant Kites and Birdlike Gliders, the National Geographic Society Has Aided and Encouraged the Growth of Aviation. LII, pp. 233-242, 13 ills., Aug., 1927

Alexander Graham Bell (Announcement of the Death of Alexander Graham Bell). XLII, p. 302, Sept., 1922

The "B B," experimental boat of Dr. Alexander Graham Bell, driven by aërial propellers. XVIII, ill. p. 671, Oct., 1907

The Charm of Cape Breton Island: The Most Picturesque Portion of Canada's Maritime Provinces—A Land Rich in Historic Associations, Natural Resources, and Geographic Appeal (Dr. Bell's Laboratories and Home). By Catherine Dunlop Mackenzie. XXXVIII, pp. 34-60, 22 ills., map, July, 1920

Daughter of, marries Gilbert Grosvenor. XXIII, p. 274, Mar., 1912

Discovery and Invention. By Alexander Graham Bell. XXV, pp. 649-655, June, 1914

Dr. Bell's Man-Lifting Kite. By Gilbert H. Grosvenor. XIX, pp. 35-52, 27 ills., Jan., 1908

BELL, ALEXANDER GRAHAM—*Continued*

Dr. Bell's Tetrahedral Tower. By Gilbert H. Grosvenor. XVIII, pp. 672-675, 5 ills., Oct., 1907

Elected President of the Society. IX, p. 28, Jan., 1898; p. 416, Sept., 1898

Employs Gilbert Grosvenor, Apr. 1, 1899, for the National Geographic Society. XXIII, p. 274, Mar., 1912

A Few Thoughts Concerning Eugenics. By Alexander Graham Bell. XIX, pp. 119-123, Feb., 1908

Future of the Airplane (Dr. Bell's Support of Aviation). By Rear Admiral Robert E. Peary. XXXIII, pp. 107-113, 4 ills., Jan., 1918

Gardiner Greene Hubbard: Memorial Meeting, Prof. Alexander Graham Bell, LL. D., President of the National Geographic Society, presiding. IX, pp. 39-70, Feb., 1898

Honors to Peary (Address by Alexander Graham Bell). XVIII, pp. 49-60, ill., Jan., 1907

Letter to Captain C. D. Sigsbee, U. S. N., Commander of the *Maine.* IX, p. 251, May, 1898

The National Geographic Society (Address by Alexander Graham Bell Concerning Early History of the Society). XXIII, pp. 272-298, 5 ills., Mar., 1912

National Geographic Society (Resignation of Alexander Graham Bell as President of the Society). XIV, pp. 254-255, June, 1903

Our Heterogeneous System of Weights and Measures. By Alexander Graham Bell. XVII, pp. 158-169, Mar., 1906

Portraits. IX, pl. 3 (front.); text, p. 104, Mar., 1898. XII, ill. p. 353, Oct., 1901. XLII, ill. p. 302, Sept., 1922

Prehistoric Telephone Days. By Alexander Graham Bell. XLI, pp. 223-241, 17 ills., Mar., 1922

President Alexander Graham Bell on Japan (Abstract of Address Delivered Before the International Journalists' Association, Tokyo). (By J.H.). IX, pp. 509-512, Dec., 1898

Prizes for the Inventor: Some of the Problems Awaiting Solution. By Alexander Graham Bell. XXXI, pp. 131-146, 7 ills., Feb., 1917

The Tetrahedral Kite. XIV, p. 294, ill., July, 1903

The Tetrahedral Principle in Kite Structure. By Alexander Graham Bell. XIV, pp. 219-251, 89 ills., 15 diagrs., June, 1903

Voice Voyages by the National Geographic Society: A Tribute to the Geographical Achievements of the Telephone (Address by Alexander Graham Bell). XXIX, pp. 296-326, 15 ills., chart, Mar., 1916

Who Shall Inherit Long Life? On the Existence of a National Process at Work Among Human Beings Tending to Improve the Vigor and Vitality of Succeeding Generations. By Dr. Alexander Graham Bell. XXXV, pp. 505-514, 13 ills., June, 1919

See also Largelamb, H. A. (Pseudonym); NGS: Board of Managers; President

BELL, ALEXANDER MELVILLE:

Prehistoric Telephone Days. By Alexander Graham Bell. XLI, pp. 223-241, 17 ills., Mar., 1922

BELL, CARL S.:

Bolivia—Tin Roof of the Andes. 20 color photos by Carl S. Bell and Fenno Jacobs. LXXXIII, pp. 311-326, Mar., 1943

BELL, CHARLES J. *See* NGS: Board of Managers; Treasurer

BELL, ROBERT J.:

Dr. Bell's Survey in Baffinland. By W J McGee. XIII, p. 113, Mar., 1902

BELL TOWERS:

The Singing Towers of Holland and Belgium. By William Gorham Rice. XLVII, pp. 357-376, 22 ills., Mar., 1925

BELLOWS, U. S. CONSUL-GENERAL:

Agriculture in Japan. By U. S. Consul-General Bellows. XV, pp. 323-326, Aug., 1904

BELO HORIZONTE, Brazil:

Air Cruising Through New Brazil: A National Geographic Reporter Spots Vast Resources Which the Republic's War Declaration Adds to Strength of United Nations. By Henry Albert Phillips. LXXXII, pp. 503-536, 32 ills., Oct., 1942

Bright Facets of Brazil. 18 color photos by W. Robert Moore. LXXXV, pp. 49-72, Jan., 1944

BENARES, India:

The Bathing and Burning Ghats at Benares. By Eliza R. Scidmore. XVIII, pp. 118-128, 7 ills., Feb., 1907

Through the Heart of Hindustan: A Teeming Highway Extending for Fifteen Hundred Miles, from the Khyber Pass to Calcutta. By Maynard Owen Williams. XL, pp. 433-467, 29 ills., Nov., 1921

BENEATH Colombia's Azure Skies. 18 color photos: 17 by Luis Marden. LXXVIII, pp. 513-536, Oct., 1940

BENGASI, Libia:

Red Cross Girl Overseas. By Margaret Cotter. LXXXVI, pp. 745-768, 22 ills., Dec., 1944

BENGUET—The Garden of the Philippines. XIV, pp. 203-210, 6 ills., May, 1903

BENJAMIN, MARCUS:

Gardiner Greene Hubbard: Memorial Meeting. Address by Dr. Marcus Benjamin. IX, pp. 53-57, Feb., 1898

BENNETT, FLOYD:

Awarded Gold Medal. LII, p. 238, Aug., 1927

Commander Byrd Receives the Hubbard Gold Medal: The First Explorer to Reach the North Pole by Air Receives Coveted Honor at Brilliant National Geographic Society Reception (Also Presentation of Gold Medal to Floyd Bennett). L, pp. 377-388, 5 ills., chart, Sept., 1926

BENTLEY, WILSON A.:

The Magic Beauty of Snow and Dew. By Wilson A. Bentley. XLIII, pp. 103-112, 9 ills., Jan., 1923

Snow Crystals. 31 photos by Wilson A. Bentley. XV, pp. 30-37, Jan., 1904

BEQUESTS. *See* NGS: Bequests

BERBERS (Tribespeople):

Morocco, "The Land of the Extreme West" and the Story of My Captivity. By Ion Perdicaris. XVII, pp. 117-157, 24 ills., Mar., 1906

BERCHTESGADEN, Germany:

This Was Austria. 18 ills. LXXXVIII, pp. 71-86, July, 1945
Included: Illustrations of Berchtesgaden, on the Austrian border

BERGEN, Norway:

The White War in Norway. By Thomas R. Henry. LXXXVIII, pp. 617-640, 23 ills., map, Nov., 1945

BERING, VITUS:

The Cartography and Observations of Bering's First Voyage. By General A. W. Greely. III, pp. 205-230, map supplement, Jan. 28, 1892; Feb. 19, 1892

A Critical Review of Bering's First Expedition, 1725-30, Together with a Translation of His Original Report Upon It. With a Map. By Wm. H. Dall. II, pp. 111-169, 8 tables, foldout map, May, 1890
Included: Supplementary Note by Marcus Baker, On the Alleged Observation of a Lunar Eclipse by Bering in 1728-9, pp. 167-169

BERING SEA AND BERING STRAIT:

The Arctic Cruise of the U. S. S. Thetis in the Summer and Autumn of 1889. By Charles H. Stockton. II, pp. 171-198, ill., foldout map, July, 1890

BERKELEY, California:

The Aberration of Sound as Illustrated by the Berkeley Powder Explosion. By Robert H. Chapman. VII, pp. 246-249, 3 diagrs., July, 1896

BERLIN, Germany:

Changing Berlin. By Douglas Chandler. LXXI, pp. 131-177, 30 ills. in black and white, 24 ills. in color, Feb., 1937

Renascent Germany. By Lincoln Eyre. LIV, pp. 639-717, 59 ills. in black and white, 39 ills. in color, Dec., 1928

BERMUDA (Islands), Atlantic Ocean:

Americans in the Caribbean. By Luis Marden. LXXXI, pp. 723-758, 16 ills. in black and white, 22 ills. in color, map, June, 1942

The Depths of the Sea: Strange Life Forms a Mile Below the Surface. By William Beebe. Paintings by E. Bostelmann. LXI, pp. 65-88, 15 ills. in black and white, 8 ills. in color, map, Jan., 1932

A Half Mile Down: Strange Creatures, Beautiful and Grotesque as Figments of Fancy, Reveal Themselves at Windows of the Bathysphere. By William Beebe. Paintings by Else Bostelmann, Helen D. Tee-Van, E. J. Geske. LXVI, pp. 661-704, 28 ills. in black and white, 16 ills. in color, map, Dec., 1934

Happy Landing in Bermuda. By E. John Long. LXXV, pp. 213-238, 14 ills. in black and white, 12 ills. in color, Feb., 1939

BERMUDA (Islands), Atlantic Ocean—*Continued*

The Islands of Bermuda: A British Colony with a Unique Record in Popular Government. By William Howard Taft. XLI, pp. 1-26, 15 ills., map, Jan., 1922

A Round Trip to Davy Jones's Locker: Peering into Mysteries a Quarter Mile Down in the Open Sea, by Means of the Bathysphere. By William Beebe. Paintings by E. Bostelmann. LIX, pp. 653-678, 14 ills. in black and white, 8 ills. in color, map, June, 1931

BERNADOU, J. B.:

Korea and the Koreans. By J. B. Bernadou. II, pp. 231-242, map, foldout map, Aug., 1890

BERNHEIMER, CHARLES L.:

Encircling Navajo Mountain (Utah) with a Pack-Train: An Expedition to a Hitherto Untraversed Region of Our Southwest Discovers a New Route to Rainbow Natural Bridge. By Charles L. Bernheimer. XLIII, pp. 197-224, 33 ills., map, Feb., 1923

BERNSTORFF, JOHANN HEINRICH, COUNT VON:

Honors to Colonel Goethals: The Presentation, by President Woodrow Wilson, of the National Geographic Society Special Gold Medal, and Addresses by Secretary of State Bryan, the French Ambassador, the German Ambassador, and Congressman James R. Mann. XXV, pp. 677-690, 6 ills., June, 1914

In Honor of the Army and Aviation (Address by Count von Bernstorff). XXII, pp. 267-284, ill., Mar., 1911

BERRIES:

American Berries of Hill, Dale, and Wayside. Paintings by Mary E. Eaton. XXXV, pp. 168-184, ill. in black and white, 29 ills. in color, Feb., 1919

Contents: American Bittersweet, American Cranberry, American Holly, American Mountain Ash, Bayberry, Black Alder, Black Gum, Blue Cohosh, Blueleaf Greenbriar, Bunchberry, Chokeberries, Coral Berry, Early Highbush Blueberry, Highbush Blueberry, Highbush Cranberry, Longspine Thorn, Mapleleaf Arrowwood, Roundleaf Greenbriar, Shadbush, Silky Cornel, Smooth Sumac, Snowberry, Spicebush, Sweet Cherry, Sweet Elder, Wild Black Cherry, Wintergreen

Taming the Wild Blueberry. By Frederick V. Coville. XXII, pp. 137-147, 5 ills., Feb., 1911

The Wild Blueberry Tamed: The New Industry of the Pine Barrens of New Jersey. By Frederick V. Coville. XXIX, pp. 535-546, 10 ills., June, 1916

BERROETA, ANDRÉ DE:

Flying in France. By Captain André de Berroeta. XXXIII, pp. 9-26, 12 ills., Jan., 1918

BERTHOUD, EDWARD L.:

Sir Francis Drake's Anchorage. By Edward L. Berthoud. VI, pp. 208-214, Dec. 29, 1894

BERYL:

India's Treasures Helped the Allies. By John Fischer. LXXXIX, pp. 501-522, 18 ills., Apr., 1946

BESIDE the Bosporus, Divider of Continents. 11 color photos by Maynard Owen Williams. LVI, pp. 493-500, Oct., 1929

BESSARABIA (Division), Romania:

Roumania and Its Rubicon. By John Oliver La Gorce. XXX, pp. 185-202, 11 ills., Sept., 1916

BEST, EMORY F.:

The Utilization of the Vacant Public Lands. By Emory F. Best. VIII, pp. 49-57, Feb., 1897

BETHELL, UNION NOBLE:

Voice Voyages by the National Geographic Society: A Tribute to the Geographic Achievements of the Telephone (Address by Union Noble Bethell). XXIX, pp. 296-326, 15 ills., chart, Mar., 1916

BETHLEHEM and the Christmas Story. By John D. Whiting. LVI, pp. 699-735, 27 ills. in black and white, 14 ills. in color, Dec., 1929

BETIO ISLAND, Tarawa, Gilbert Islands:

Gilbert Islands in the Wake of Battle. By W. Robert Moore. LXXXVII, pp. 129-162, 11 ills. in black and white, 19 ills. in color, map, Feb., 1945

BETWEEN Massacres in Van (Armenian Capital). By Maynard Owen Williams. XXXVI, pp. 181-184, 3 ills., Aug., 1919

BETWEEN the Heather and the North Sea: Bold English Headlands Once Sheltered Sea Robbers, Later Were Ports of Wooden Ships, Centers of the Jet and Alum Trades, To-day Are Havens of Adventurous Fishing Fleets. By Leo Walmsley. LXIII, pp. 197-232, 41 ills., Feb., 1933

BEUKEMA, HERMAN:

West Point and the Grey-Clad Corps. By Lieut. Col. Herman Beukema. LXIX, pp. 777-788, 10 ills. in color, June, 1936

BEVAN, BERNARD:

Travels with a Donkey in Mexico: Three Adventurers Trudge from Oaxaca to Acapulco, 400 Miles, Through Back Country, Their Equipment Carried by Burros. By Bernard Bevan. LXVI, pp. 757-788, 36 ills., map, Dec., 1934

BEYOND Australia's Cities. By W. Robert Moore. LXX, pp. 709-747, 27 ills. in black and white, 12 ills. in color, Dec., 1936

BEYOND the Clay Hills: An Account of the National Geographic Society's Reconnaissance of a Previously Unexplored Section in Utah. By Neil M. Judd. XLV, pp. 275-302, 28 ills., map, Mar., 1924

BEYOND the Grand Atlas: Where the French Tricolor Flies Beside the Flag of the Sultan of Morocco. By V. C. Scott O'Connor. LXI, pp. 261-319, 52 ills. in black and white, 12 ills. in color, map, Mar., 1932

BEYROUTH, Lebanon. *See* Beirut

BHATGAON, Nepal:

Nepal: A Little-Known Kingdom. By John Claude White. XXXVIII, pp. 245-283, 32 ills., map, Oct., 1920

BHUTAN:
Castles in the Air: Experiences and Journeys in Unknown Bhutan. By John Claude White. XXV, pp. 365-455, 74 ills., map, Apr., 1914

BIBLE. *See* Bible Lands; Twenty-third Psalm

BIBLE LANDS:
American Alma Maters in the Near East. By Maynard Owen Williams. LXXXVIII, pp. 237-256, 16 ills., Aug., 1945
American Fighters Visit Bible Lands. By Maynard Owen Williams. With 23 color photos by author. LXXXIX, pp. 311-340, 10 ills. in black and white, Mar., 1946
Bombs over Bible Lands. By Frederick Simpich and W. Robert Moore. LXXX, pp. 141-180, 34 ills., two-page map, Aug., 1941
Change Comes to Bible Lands. By Frederick Simpich. LXXIV, pp. 695-750, 40 ills. in black and white, 25 ills. in color, map supplement, Dec., 1938
The Geography of the Jordan. By Nelson Glueck. LXXXVI, pp. 719-744, 23 ills., map, Dec., 1944
On the Trail of King Solomon's Mines: The Bible, in Addition to Its Spiritual Values, Continues to Prove a Rich Geography and Guide to Exploration of the Holy Land. By Nelson Glueck. LXXXV, pp. 233-256, 20 ills., map, Feb., 1944
The Society's Map of Bible Lands. By Gilbert Grosvenor. Text with map supplement. LXXIV, pp. 751-754, 3 ills., Dec., 1938
The Society's New Map of Bible Lands. Text with map supplement. XC, pp. 815-816, Dec., 1946
See also Arabian Peninsula; Egypt; Iraq; Lebanon; Levant States; Palestine; Syria; Trans-Jordan; Turkey

BICYCLE TRIPS:
An American Girl Cycles Across Romania: Two-wheel Pilgrim Pedals the Land of Castles and Gypsies, Where Roman Empire Traces Mingle With Remnants of Oriental Migration. By Dorothy Hosmer. LXXIV, pp. 557-588, 31 ills., map, Nov., 1938
On Danish By-Lanes: An American Cycles Through the Quaint City of Lace, the Curiosity Town Where Time Stands Still, and Even Finds a Frontier in the Farming Kingdom. By Willis Lindquist. LXXVII, pp. 1-34, 21 ills. in black and white, 10 ills. in color, map, Jan., 1940
Pedaling Through Poland: An American Girl Free-wheels Alone from Kraków, and Its Medieval Byways, Toward Ukraine's Restive Borderland. By Dorothy Hosmer. LXXV, pp. 739-775, 38 ills., maps, June, 1939

BIDENS PILOSA. *See* Shepherd's Needles

The **BIG** Game of Alaska. By Wilfred H. Osgood. XX, pp. 624-636, 10 ills., July, 1909

BIG Oklahoma. By Bird S. McGuire. XVII, pp. 103-105, Feb., 1906

BIG Things of the West. By Charles F. Holder. XIV, pp. 279-282, ills., July, 1903

BIG TREES:
Among the Big Trees of California. By John R. White. LXVI, pp. 219-232, 14 ills., Aug., 1934
The National Geographic Society Completes Its Gifts of Big Trees. XL, pp. 85-86, July, 1921

BIG TREES—*Continued*
The Oldest Living Thing ("General Sherman Tree"). XXIX, pictorial supplement, Apr., 1916
Our Big Trees Saved. XXXI, pp. 1-11, 10 ills., Jan., 1917
Our National Parks. By L. F. Schmeckebier. XXIII, pp. 531-579, 41 ills., map, June, 1912

BIGELOW, FRANK H.:
The International Cloud Work of the Weather Bureau. By Frank H. Bigelow. X, pp. 351-354, Sept., 1899
Scientific Work of Mount Weather Meteorological Research Observatory. By Professor Frank H. Bigelow. XV, pp. 442-445, Nov., 1904
Studies on the Rate of Evaporation at Reno, Nevada, and in the Salton Sink. By Professor Frank H. Bigelow. XIX, pp. 20-28, 5 ills., Jan., 1908
The Total Eclipse of the Sun, May 28, 1900. (By F. H. Bigelow). XI, pp. 33-34, Jan., 1900

BIGHORN MOUNTAINS, Wyoming:
Bighorn Mountains. By N. H. Darton. XVIII, pp. 355-364, 7 ills., map, June, 1907

BIGHORNS (Sheep):
Lords of the Rockies: Photographing Big Game Animals in Their Primeval Surroundings, from Arizona to Canada, Brings Adventure to Two Wilderness Wanderers. By Wendell and Lucie Chapman. LXXVI, pp. 87-128, 14 ills. in black and white, 28 ills. in color, July, 1939

BIKINI (Atoll), Marshall Islands:
American Pathfinders in the Pacific. By William H. Nicholas. LXXXIX, pp. 617-640, 17 ills., two-page map, May, 1946
Farewell to Bikini. By Carl Markwith. XC, pp. 97-116, 16 ills., July, 1946

BILBAO, Spain:
The Land of the Basques: Home of a Thrifty, Picturesque People, Who Take Pride in the Sobriquet, "The Yankees of Spain." By Harry A. McBride. XLI, pp. 63-87, 25 ills., map, Jan., 1922

BILLINGS, L. G.:
Some Personal Experiences with Earthquakes. By Rear Admiral L. G. Billings. XXVII, pp. 57-71, 7 ills., Jan., 1915

BILLIONS of Barrels of Oil Locked Up in Rocks. By Guy Elliott Mitchell. XXXIII, pp. 195-205, 10 ills., Feb., 1918

BIND the Wounds of France. By Herbert C. Hoover. XXXI, pp. 439-444, 5 ills., May, 1917

BINGHAM, HIRAM:
Awarded Jane M. Smith Life Membership. XXXVII, p. 342 (footnote), Apr., 1920
Building America's Air Army. By Hiram Bingham. XXXIII, pp. 48-86, 43 ills., Jan., 1918
Explorations in Peru. XXIII, pp. 417-422, 7 ills., map, Apr., 1912

BINGHAM, HIRAM—*Continued*

Further Explorations in the Land of the Incas: The Peruvian Expedition of 1915 of the National Geographic Society and Yale University. By Hiram Bingham. XXIX, pp. 431-473, 29 ills., maps, panorama, May, 1916

The Greatest Achievement of Ancient Man in America (Fortress of Sacsahuaman, Peru). Panorama from photo by author

Honors to Amundsen and Peary (Speech by Hiram Bingham). XXIV, pp. 113-130, 5 ills., Jan., 1913

In the Wonderland of Peru. By Hiram Bingham. XXIV, pp. 387-573, 250 ills., 3 diagrs., map, panorama, Apr., 1913

The Ruins of an Ancient Inca Capital, Machu Picchu. Panorama from photo by author

The Story of Machu Picchu: The Peruvian Expeditions of the National Geographic Society and Yale University. By Hiram Bingham. XXVII, pp. 172-217, 60 ills., Feb., 1915

BIOLOGY:

Report—Geography of Life. By C. Hart Merriam. I, pp. 160-162, Apr., 1889

See also U.S. Bureau of Biological Survey

BIRA, Celebes (Island):

Seafarers of South Celebes. By G. E. P. Collins. LXXXVII, pp. 53-78, 25 ills., map, Jan., 1945

BIRD, F. L.:

Modern Persia and Its Capital: And an Account of an Ascent of Mount Demavend, the Persian Olympus. By F. L. Bird. XXXIX, pp. 353-400, 47 ills., Apr., 1921

BIRD Banding, the Telltale of Migratory Flight: A Modern Method of Learning the Flight-Ways and Habits of Birds. By E. W. Nelson. LIII, pp. 91-131, 49 ills., map, Jan., 1928

BIRD Beauties of the Tanager and Finch Families. 55 portraits from paintings by Maj. Allan Brooks. LXVII, pp. 513-528, Apr., 1935

A **BIRD** City (Laysan Island, Hawaii). XV, pp. 494-498, 6 ills., Dec., 1904

BIRD Life Among Lava Rock and Coral Sand: The Chronicle of a Scientific Expedition in Little-known Islands of Hawaii. By Alexander Wetmore. XLVIII, pp. 77-108, 36 ills., map, July, 1925

BIRDS:

Adventures with Birds of Prey. By Frank and John Craighead. LXXII, pp. 109-134, 25 ills., July, 1937

Ambassadors of Good Will: Annual Messengers from Our Neighbor Republics to the South Bring Cheer and Add Interest to the Out-of-Doors. By Arthur A. Allen. LXXXI, pp. 786-796, 13 ills. in color, June, 1942

Contents: Belted Kingfisher, Bobolink, Cardinal, Prothonotary Warbler, Red-eyed Vireo, Red-headed Woodpecker, Redwing, Tree Swallow, Wood Thrush, Yellow-billed Cuckoo, Yellow-breasted Chat

BIRDS—*Continued*

American Birds of Prey—A Review of Their Value. XXXVIII, pp. 460-467, 6 ills., Dec., 1920

American Game Birds. By Henry Wetherbee Henshaw. Paintings by Louis Agassiz Fuertes. XXVIII, pp. 105-158, 4 ills. in black and white, 72 ills. in color, Aug., 1915

Contents: Cranes, Ducks, Geese, Grouse, Pheasants, Pigeons, Plovers, Quails, Rails, Sandpipers, Snipes, Stilts, Swans

Amid the Snow Peaks of the Equator: A Naturalist's Explorations Around Ruwenzori with an Excursion to the Congo State, and an Account of the Terrible Scourge of Sleeping Sickness. By A. F. R. Wollaston. XX, pp. 256-277, 11 ills., Mar., 1909

Around the World for Animals. By William M. and Lucile Q. Mann. LXXIII, pp. 665-714, 33 ills. in black and white, 23 ills. in color, map, June, 1938

Befriending Nature's Children: An Experiment With Some of California's Wild Folk. By Agnes Akin Atkinson. LXI, pp. 199-215, 26 ills., Feb., 1932

Bird Banding, the Telltale of Migratory Flight: A Modern Method of Learning the Flight-Ways and Habits of Birds. By E. W. Nelson. LIII, pp. 91-131, 49 ills., map, Jan., 1928

A Bird City (Laysan Island, Hawaii). XV, pp. 494-498, 6 ills., Dec., 1904

Bird Life Among Lava Rock and Coral Sand: The Chronicle of a Scientific Expedition to Little-known Islands of Hawaii. By Alexander Wetmore. XLVIII, pp. 77-108, 36 ills., map, July, 1925

Birds May Bring You More Happiness Than the Wealth of the Indies. By Frank M. Chapman. XXIV, pp. 699-714, 14 ills., June, 1913

Birds of the High Seas: Albatrosses and Petrels; Gannets, Man-o'-war-birds, and Tropic-birds. By Robert Cushman Murphy. Paintings by Major Allan Brooks. LXXIV, pp. 226-251, 7 ills. in black and white, 36 portraits in color, Aug., 1938

Birds of the Northern Seas. By Alexander Wetmore. Paintings by Maj. Allan Brooks. LXIX, pp. 95-122, 12 ills. in black and white, 34 portraits in color, Jan., 1936

Contents: Auklets, Auks, Dovekies, Guillemots, Murrelets, Murres, Puffins

Birds of Timberline and Tundra. By Arthur A. Allen. With 24 color photos by author. XC, pp. 313-339, 8 ills. in black and white, Sept., 1946

Contents: Arctic Loons, Arctic Terns, Blackpoll Warblers, Bonaparte's Gulls, Dowitchers, Golden Plovers, Harris's Sparrows, Herring Gulls, Horned Grebes, Hoyt's Horned Larks, Hudsonian Curlews, Lapland Longspurs, Least Sandpipers, Lesser Yellowlegs, Northern Phalaropes, Northern Shrikes, Parasitic Jaeger, Pintail Ducks, Pipits, Red-backed Sandpipers, Semipalmated Plovers, Semipalmated Sandpipers, Snow Buntings, Starlings, Stilt Sandpipers, Tree Sparrows, White-crowned Sparrows, Wild Geese, Willow Ptarmigans, Yellow Warblers

Birds of Town and Country. By Henry Wetherbee Henshaw. Paintings by Louis Agassiz Fuertes. XXV, pp. 494-531, 2 ills. in black and white, 64 ills. in color, May, 1914

Contents: Blackbirds, Eagles, Finches, Flycatchers, Gulls, Hawks, Herons, Hummingbirds, Jays, Kingfishers, Orioles, Owls, Sparrows, Starlings, Swallows, Swifts, Tanagers, Terns, Thrushes, Titmice, Vireos, Vultures, Waxwings, Whip-poor-wills, Wood Warblers, Woodpeckers

Birds on the Home Front. By Arthur A. Allen. LXXXIV, pp. 32-56, 7 ills. in black and white, 30 ills. in color, July, 1943
Contents: Canada Geese, Catbirds, Chickadees, Chuck-will's-widow, Cowbirds, Flickers, Flycatchers, Gallinules, Grebes, Grouse, Hummingbirds, Meadowlarks, Orioles, Owls, Peregrines, Plovers, Ptarmigans, Puffins, Rails, Redstarts, Shrikes, Skimmers, Swallows, Vireos, Warblers, Waxwings

Birds That Cruise the Coast and Inland Waters. By T. Gilbert Pearson. Paintings by Maj. Allan Brooks. LXV, pp. 299-328, 15 ills. in black and white, 24 portraits in color, Mar., 1934
Contents: Cormorants, Grebes, Loons, Pelicans, Water Turkeys

Blackbirds and Orioles. By Arthur A. Allen. Paintings by Major Allan Brooks. LXVI, pp. 111-130, 48 portraits in color, July, 1934
Contents: Blackbirds, Bobolinks, Cowbirds, Flycatchers, Grackles, Meadowlarks, Orioles, Shrikes, Vireos, Waxwings

Camps and Cruises of an Ornithologist. By George Shiras, 3d. XX, pp. 438-463, 30 ills., May, 1909

Canaries and Other Cage-Bird Friends. By Alexander Wetmore. Paintings by Major Allan Brooks. LXXIV, pp. 775-806, 19 ills. in black and white, 51 portraits in color, Dec., 1938

Crows, Magpies, and Jays: Unusual Intelligence Has Earned a Unique Position for These Birds. By T. Gilbert Pearson. Paintings by Maj. Allan Brooks. LXIII, pp. 51-79, 16 ills. in black and white, 17 ills. in color, Jan., 1933

Cruise of the *Kinkajou:* Among Desert Islands of Mexico Voyagers Find Outdoor Laboratories for the Naturalist and Ideal Fishing Grounds for the Sportsman. By Alfred M. Bailey. LXXX, pp. 339-366, 13 ills. in black and white, 12 ills. in color, map, Sept., 1941
Contents: Auklets, Belding's Plovers, Black Oyster-catchers, Black Turnstones, Black-vented Shearwaters, Blue-footed Boobies, Brewster's Boobies, Brown Towhees, Cactus Wrens, Cape Gilded Flickers, Caracaras, Cardinals, Cardon Woodpeckers, Cormorants, Frazar's Oyster-catchers, Gnat-catchers, Heermann's Gulls, Horned Larks, Hudsonian Curlews, Lark Buntings, Man-o'-war-birds, Mockingbirds, Noddy Terns, Ospreys, Pelicans, Petrels, Ravens, Red-billed Tropic-birds, Red-footed Boobies, Red Phalaropes, Rock Wrens, San Lucas Quail, San Lucas Sparrows, San Lucas Woodpeckers, Sooty Terns, Thrashers, Townsend's Shearwaters, Verdins, Vultures, Wandering Tattlers, White-winged Doves, Willets, Wyman's Gulls, Yellow-legged Gulls

The Eagle, King of Birds, and His Kin. By Alexander Wetmore. Paintings by Maj. Allan Brooks. LXIV, pp. 43-95, 23 ills. in black and white, 48 ills. in color, July, 1933

Encouraging Birds Around the Home. By Frederick H. Kennard. XXV, pp. 315-344, 36 ills., Mar., 1914

BIRDS—*Continued*

Far-Flying Wild Fowl and Their Foes. By Major Allan Brooks. With paintings from life by author. LXVI, pp. 487-528, 6 ills. in black and white, 93 portraits in color, Oct., 1934
Contents: Ducks, Geese, Swans

Fifty Common Birds of Farm and Orchard. By Henry Wetherbee Henshaw. Paintings by Louis Agassiz Fuertes. XXIV, pp. 669-697, 50 ills. in color, June, 1913
Included: Blackbirds, Creepers, Crows, Cuckoos, Doves, Flycatchers, Grouse, Gulls, Hawks, Jays, Kinglets, Larks, Nighthawks, Nuthatches, Orioles, Owls, Plovers, Quail, Shrikes, Sparrows, Swallows, Terns, Thrashers, Thrushes, Titmice, Wood Warblers, Woodpeckers, Wrens

Further Explorations in the Land of the Incas: The Peruvian Expedition of 1915 of the National Geographic Society and Yale University. By Hiram Bingham. XXIX, pp. 431-473, 29 ills., maps, panorama, May, 1916

Game Birds of Prairie, Forest, and Tundra. By Alexander Wetmore. Paintings by Maj. Allan Brooks. LXX, pp. 461-500, 5 ills. in black and white, 60 portraits in color, Oct., 1936
Contents: Chacalacas, Doves, Grouse, Partridges, Pheasants, Pigeons, Prairie Chickens, Ptarmigans, Quails, Turkeys

A Geographic Achievement (Reprint of Bird Bulletin). XXIV, pp. 667-668, June, 1913

Guillemot Eggs. XIV, pp. 386-388, ill., Oct., 1903

High Country of Colorado. By Alfred M. Bailey. With 23 color photos by author, Robert J. Niedrach, F. G. Brandenburg. XC, pp. 43-72, 9 ills. in black and white, July, 1946
Contents: Bluebirds, Flickers, Golden Eagles, Goshawks, Hawks, Hummingbirds, Juncos, Owls, Pine Grosbeaks, Ptarmigans, Robins, Sage Grouse, Sap-suckers, Sparrows, Vireos, Warblers, Woodpeckers

Hunting Birds With a Camera: A Record of Twenty Years of Adventure in Obtaining Photographs of Feathered Wild Life in America. By William L. Finley. XLIV, pp. 161-201, 37 ills., Aug., 1923

Hunting with a Microphone the Voices of Vanishing Birds. By Arthur A. Allen. LXXI, pp. 697-723, 32 ills., June, 1937

Hunting with the Lens. By Howard H. Cleaves. XXVI, pp. 1-35, 47 ills., July, 1914

A Journey by Jungle Rivers to the Home of the Cock-of-the-rock: Naturalists Enter the Amazon, Voyage Through the Heart of Tropical South America, and Emerge at the Mouth of the Orinoco. By Ernest G. Holt. LXIV, pp. 585-630, 4 ills., map, Nov., 1933

The Large Wading Birds: Long Legs and Remarkable Beaks, as Well as Size, Form, and Color, Distinguish the Herons, Ibises, and Flamingos. By T. Gilbert Pearson. Paintings by Maj. Allan Brooks. LXII, pp. 441-469, 13 ills. in black and white, 24 ills. in color, Oct., 1932

Life with an Indian Prince: As Guests of a Maharaja's Brother, Two Young American Naturalists Study Age-old Methods of Hunting with Trained Falcons and Cheetahs and Savor the Pomp of Royal India. By John and Frank Craighead. LXXXI, pp. 235-272, 38 ills., map, Feb., 1942

BIRDS—*Continued*

Lonely Australia: The Unique Continent. By Herbert E. Gregory. XXX, pp. 473-568, 68 ills., 5 maps (1 two-page), Dec., 1916

Masters of Flight. 8 ills. XXXVI, pp. 49-56, July, 1919

National Geographic Society's New "Book of Birds." LXXI, p. 723, June, 1937. LXXII, p. 183, Aug., 1937. LXXIV, p. 226, Aug., 1938; p. 775, Dec., 1938. LXXVII, p. 121, Jan., 1940

A Naturalist with MacMillan in the Arctic. By Walter N. Koelz. XLIX, pp. 299-318, 22 ills. in color, Mar., 1926

A Naturalist's Journey Around Vera Cruz and Tampico. By Frank M. Chapman. XXV, pp. 533-562, 31 ills., May, 1914

Notes on the Wild Fowl and Game Animals of Alaska. By E. W. Nelson. IX, pp. 121-132, 6 ills., Apr., 1898

One Season's Game-Bag with the Camera. By George Shiras, 3d. XIX, pp. 387-446, 70 ills., June, 1908

The Origin of West India Bird-Life. By Frank M. Chapman. IX, pp. 243-247, May, 1898

Our Greatest Travelers: Birds that Fly from Pole to Pole and Shun the Darkness: Birds that Make 2,500 Miles in a Single Flight. By Wells W. Cooke. XXII, pp. 346-365, 12 maps, Apr., 1911

Our Policemen of the Air. XXIV, p. 698, June, 1913

Parrots, Kingfishers, and Flycatchers: Strange Trogons and Curious Cuckoos are Pictured with these Other Birds of Color, Dash, and Courage. By Alexander Wetmore. Paintings by Maj. Allan Brooks. LXIX, pp. 801-828, 9 ills. in black and white, 36 portraits in color, June, 1936

Contents: Anis, Cuckoos, Flycatchers, Kingbirds, Kingfishers, Parakeets, Parrots, Pewees, Phoebes, Trogons

Peru's Wealth-Producing Birds: Vast Riches in the Guano Deposits of Cormorants, Pelicans, and Petrels which Nest on Her Barren, Rainless Coast. By R. E. Coker. XXXVII, pp. 537-566, 28 ills., June, 1920

Photographing Wild Game with Flashlight and Camera. By George Shiras, 3d. XVII, pp. 367-423, 74 ills., July, 1906

The Policemen of the Air. By Henry Wetherbee Henshaw. XIX, pp. 79-118, 38 ills., Feb., 1908

The Romance of Science in Polynesia: An Account of Five Years of Cruising Among the South Sea Islands. By Robert Cushman Murphy. Paintings by Hashime Murayama. XLVIII, pp. 355-426, 66 ills. in black and white, 16 ills. in color, 3 maps, Oct., 1925

Seeking the Smallest Feathered Creatures: Humming Birds, Peculiar to the New World, Are Found from Canada and Alaska to the Strait of Magellan. Swifts and Goatsuckers, Their Nearest Relatives. By Alexander Wetmore. Paintings by Maj. Allan Brooks. LXII, pp. 65-89, 9 ills. in black and white, 36 ills. in color, July, 1932

The Shore Birds, Cranes, and Rails: Willets, Plovers, Stilts, Phalaropes, Sandpipers, and Their Relatives Deserve Protection. By Arthur A. Allen. Paintings by Major Allan Brooks. LXXII, pp. 183-222, 4 ills. in black and white, 101 portraits in color, Aug., 1937

BIRDS—*Continued*

Sights and Sounds of the Winged World: Study of Birds to Make National Geographic Color Photographs Yields Rich Scientific Knowledge of Their Habits and Behavior. By Arthur A. Allen. LXXXVII, pp. 721-744, ill. in black and white, drawings, 26 ills. in color, June, 1945

Contents: Albino Rose-breasted Grosbeak, Baltimore Oriole, Bank Swallow, Black-billed Cuckoo, Black-capped Chickadee, Bronzed Grackle, Chestnut-sided Warbler, Crested Flycatcher, Downy Woodpecker, Forster's Tern, Hairy Woodpecker, Kingbird, Long-billed Marsh Wren, Marsh Hawk, Orchard Oriole, Pectoral Sandpiper, Pileated Woodpecker, Prairie Chicken, Redpoll, Rose-breasted Grosbeak, Rough-winged Swallow, Sharp-tailed Grouse, Wilson's Phalarope, Woodcock, Yellow-throat

Sindbads of Science: Narrative of a Windjammer's Specimen-Collecting Voyage to the Sargasso Sea, to Senegambian Africa and Among Islands of High Adventure in the South Atlantic. By George Finlay Simmons. LII, pp. 1-75, 89 ills., map, July, 1927

South Florida's Amazing Everglades: Encircled by Populous Places Is a Seldom-visited Area of Rare Birds, Prairies, Cowboys, and Teeming Wild Life of Big Cypress Swamp. By John O'Reilly. LXXVII, pp. 115-142, 26 ills., map, Jan., 1940

Contents: Burrowing Owl, Everglade Kite, Florida Cormorant, Florida Crane, Great White Heron, Limpkin, Pelican, Roseate Spoonbill, Snakebird, Snowy Egret, White Ibis, Wood Ibis

South Georgia, an Outpost of the Antarctic. By Robert Cushman Murphy. XLI, pp. 409-444, 41 ills., maps, Apr., 1922

Sparrows, Towhees, and Longspurs: These Happy Little Singers Make Merry in Field, Forest, and Desert Throughout North America. By T. Gilbert Pearson. Paintings by Allan Brooks and Walter A. Weber. LXXV, pp. 353-376, 5 ills. in black and white, 43 ills. in color, Mar., 1939

Stalking Birds With a Color Camera: An Expert in Avian Habits Persuades His Subjects to Sit Where He Wants Them, Even in His Hat. By Arthur A. Allen. LXXV, pp. 777-789, 3 ills. in black and white, 14 ills. in color, June, 1939

Contents: American Bittern, Blue Jay, Cedar Waxwing, Chipping Sparrow, Eastern Bluebird, Eastern Meadowlark, Goldfinch, Least Bittern, Purple Finch, Redwing, Robin, Scarlet Tanager, Wood Thrush

The Tanagers and Finches: Their Flashes of Color and Lilting Songs Gladden the Hearts of American Bird Lovers East and West. By Arthur A. Allen. Paintings by Maj. Allan Brooks. LXVII, pp. 505-532, 6 ills. in black and white, 55 portraits in color, Apr., 1935

Thrushes, Thrashers, and Swallows: Robins and Bluebirds are Familiar Members of a Famous Musical Family Which Includes the Hermit Thrush and European Nightingale. By T. Gilbert Pearson. Paintings by Maj. Allan Brooks. LXIX, pp. 523-546, 6 ills. in black and white, 42 paintings from life. Apr., 1936

Touring for Birds with Microphone and Color Cameras. By Arthur A. Allen. LXXXV, pp. 689-712, 3 ills. in black and white, 24 ills. in color, June, 1944

Note: Birds of Arizona, Texas, and Califor-

BIRDS—*Continued*

nia; and a discussion of the "Life Zone Theory" which treats of the distribution of bird fauna in relation to temperature

Contents: Burrowing Owl, California Blue Grosbeak, California Clapper Rail, California Woodpecker, Clark's Nutcracker, Coppery-tailed Trogon, Eastern Brown Pelican, Eastern Song Sparrow, Florida Ground Dove, Gambel's Quail, Hoyt's Horned Lark, Mourning Dove, Nighthawk, Purple Gallinule, Red-eyed Towhee, Reddish Egret, Sandhill Crane, Saw-whet Owl, Scissor-tailed Flycatcher, Sennett's Oriole, Snow Bunting, Snowy Egret, Western Gull, Western Horned Owl, Yellow Warbler

The Unique Island of Mount Desert. By George B. Dorr, Ernest Howe Forbush, M. L. Fernald. XXVI, pp. 75-89, 7 ills., July, 1914

Viking Life in the Storm-Cursed Faeroes. By Leo Hansen. LVIII, pp. 607-648, 49 ills., map, Nov., 1930

We Live Alone, and Like It—On an Island (Skokholm). By R. M. Lockley. LXXIV, pp. 252-278, 27 ills., Aug., 1938

Included: Auks, Cormorants, Gannets, Gulls, Petrels, Puffins, Shearwaters

What the Fighting Yanks See. By Wanda Burnett. LXXXVI, pp. 451-476, 27 ills., Oct., 1944

Included: Birds of Paradise, Cassowaries, Frogmouths, Grebes, Hornbills, Laughing Jack, Laughing Jackass, Lories, Love Terns, Parakeets, Parrots, Pink Cockatoos, White Cockatoos

Where Birds and Little Animals Find Haven (Eaton Canyon Bird and Game Sanctuary). By Agnes Akin Atkinson. LXX, pp. 232-241, 14 ills., Aug., 1936

Where Roosevelt Will Hunt (Africa). By Sir Harry Johnston. XX, pp. 207-256, 43 ills., map supplement, Mar., 1909

The White Sheep, Giant Moose, and Smaller Game of the Kenai Peninsula, Alaska. By George Shiras, 3d. XXIII, pp. 423-494, 59 ills., maps (1 two-page), May, 1912

The Wild Life of Lake Superior, Past and Present: The Habits of Deer, Moose, Wolves, Beavers, Muskrats, Trout, and Feathered Wood-Folk Studied with Camera and Flashlight. By George Shiras, 3d. XL, pp. 113-204, 76 ills., map, pictorial supplement, Aug., 1921

Wildlife of Tabasco and Veracruz (Mexico). By Walter A. Weber. With 19 ills. in color from paintings by author. LXXXVII, pp. 187-216, 7 ills. in black and white, map, Feb., 1945

Contents: Ant Tanager, Araçari Toucan, Black-bellied Tree Duck, Black-headed Trogon, Black Vulture, Blue Tanager, Crested Curassow, Crimson-collared Tanager, Finfoot, Forest Sparrow, Jacamar, King Vulture, Laughing Falcon, Least Kingfisher, Lesson's Oriole, Massena Trogon, Mexican Ant Thrush, Mexican Black Hawk, Mexican Jaçana, Mexican Motmot, Muscovy Duck, Oropendola, Plush Tanager, Quail Dove, Redstart, Ringed Kingfisher, Royal Flycatcher, Squirrel Cuckoo, Sulphur-breasted Toucan, Tiger Bittern, Veracruz Ivory-billed Woodpecker, White Snake Hawk, White-throated Bat Falcon, Yellow-headed Amazon, Yellow-tailed Oriole, Yellow-thighed Manakin

BIRDS—*Continued*

Wild Life of the Atlantic and Gulf Coasts: A Field Naturalist's Photographic Record of Nearly Half a Century of Fruitful Exploration. By George Shiras, 3d. LXII, pp. 261-309, 62 ills., Sept., 1932

Winged Denizens of Woodland, Stream, and Marsh. By Alexander Wetmore. Paintings by Major Allan Brooks. LXV, pp. 577-596, 37 portraits in color, May, 1934

Contents: Chickadees, Creepers, Dippers, Gnatcatchers, Kinglets, Nuthatches, Titmice, Wren-tits, Wrens

See also Cormorants; Crows; Ducks; Eagles; Falcons; Flamingos; Geese; Gulls; Hawks; Ibises; Ostriches; Owls; Pelicans; Penguins; Petrels; Pigeons; Poultry; Quetzals; Sparrows; Terns; Warblers; Woodpeckers; Wrens

BIRDS and Beasts of Mexico's Desert Islands. 12 color photos: 8 by Ed N. Harrison, 4 by Alfred M. Bailey and Robert J. Niedrach. LXXX, pp. 353-360, Sept., 1941

BIRD'S-EYE View of the Panama Canal. XXIII, panorama, Feb., 1912

BIRDS in Glossy Black and Vivid Color. 48 portraits from paintings by Major Allan Brooks. LXVI, pp. 113-128, July, 1934

BIRDS of Lake and Lagoon, Marsh and Seacoast. 24 portraits from paintings by Maj. Allan Brooks. LXV, pp. 313-328, Mar., 1934

BIRKINBINE, JOHN:

Our Neighbor, Mexico. By John Birkinbine. XXII, pp. 475-508, 26 ills., map supplement, May, 1911

BIRNIE, ROGERS, JR. *See* NGS: Board of Managers

BISHOP, WILLIAM A.:

Tales of the British Air Service. By Major William A. Bishop. XXXIII, pp. 27-37, 12 ills., Jan., 1918

BISKRA, the Ziban Queen. By Mrs. George C. Bosson, Jr. XIX, pp. 563-593, 29 ills., map, Aug., 1908

BISON:

Lords of the Rockies: Photographing Big Game Animals in Their Primeval Surroundings, from Arizona to Canada, Brings Adventure to Two Wilderness Wanderers. By Wendell and Lucie Chapman. LXXVI, pp. 87-128, 14 ills. in black and white, 28 ills. in color, July, 1939

A BIT of Elizabethan England in America: Fisher Folk of the Islands Off North Carolina Conserved the Speech and Customs of Sir Walter Raleigh's Colonists. By Blanch Nettleton Epler. LXIV, pp. 695-730, 43 ills., map, Dec., 1933

BITTER ROOT FOREST RESERVE, Idaho-Montana:

Bitter Root Forest Reserve. By Richard U. Goode. IX, pp. 387-400, 5 ills., foldout map, Sept., 1898

BITTERNS (Birds):

The Large Wading Birds: Long Legs and Remarkable Beaks, as Well as Size, Form, and Color, Distinguish the Herons, Ibises, and Flamingos. By T. Gilbert Pearson. Paintings by Maj. Allan Brooks. LXII, pp. 441-469, ill. in black and white, 3 ills. in color, Oct., 1932

BITTINGER, CHARLES:

Solar System's Eternal Show. 10 ills. in color from paintings by Charles Bittinger. LXXVI, pp. 16-24, July, 1939

Unfurling Old Glory on Canton Island. 11 ills. in color: painting of the eclipse by Charles Bittinger. LXXIII, pp. 753-760, June, 1938

BIZARRE Battleground—the Lonely Aleutians. By Lonnelle Davison. LXXXII, pp. 316-317, ill., Sept., 1942

BIZERTE, Tunisia:

Eastward from Gibraltar: Overland Route Across North Africa to Tunisia and Libia. By Cyrus French Wicker. LXXXIII, pp. 115-142, 28 ills., Jan., 1943

BLACK Acres (Mucklands of New York): A Thrilling Sketch in the Vast Volume of Who's Who Among the Peoples That Make America. By Dorothea D. and Fred Everett. LXXX, pp. 631-652, 13 ills. in black and white, 12 ills. in color, Nov., 1941

BLACK BEARS:

Once in a Lifetime: Black Bears Rarely Have Quadruplets, But Goofy Did—and the Camera Caught Her Nursing Her Remarkable Family. By Paul B. Kinney. LXXX, pp. 249-258, 11 ills., Aug., 1941

BLACK DEATH (Epidemic). *See* Bubonic Plague

BLACK FOREST, Germany:

Freiburg—Gateway to the Black Forest. By Alicia O'Reardon Overbeck. LXIV, pp. 213-252, 40 ills. in black and white, 11 ills. in color, Aug., 1933

Peasant Life in the Black Forest. By Karl Frederick Geiser. XIX, pp. 635-649, 12 ills., Sept., 1908

Wandering Through the Black Forest. 13 color photos by Hans Hildenbrand. LIV, pp. 659-666, Dec., 1928

BLACK-HEADED Gulls in London. By A. H. Hall. XLVII, pp. 664-672, 16 ills., June, 1925

The **BLACK** Hills (South Dakota), Once Hunting Grounds of the Red Men. LII, pp. 305-329, 18 ills. in black and white, 13 ills. in color, Sept., 1927

The **BLACK** Man's Continent. Text with map supplement. XX, p. 312, Mar., 1909

The **BLACK** Republic—Liberia. By Sir Harry Johnston and Ernest Lyon. XVIII, pp. 334-343, 9 ills., May, 1907

BLACK SEA:

The Gates to the Black Sea: The Dardanelles, the Bosphorus, and the Sea of Marmora. By Harry Griswold Dwight. XXVII, pp. 435-459, 27 ills., May, 1915

BLACKBIRDS:

Blackbirds and Orioles. By Arthur A. Allen. Paintings by Major Allan Brooks. LXVI, pp. 111-130, 12 portraits in color, July, 1934

BLACKER, L. V. S.:

The Aërial Conquest of Everest: Flying Over the World's Highest Mountain Realizes the Objective of Many Heroic Explorers. By Lieut. Col. L. V. S. Blacker. LXIV, pp. 127-162, 35 ills., map, Aug., 1933

BLACKMAN, LEOPOLD G.:

The Pacific: The Most-Explored and Least Known Region of the Globe. By Leopold G. Blackman. XIX, pp. 546-563, 11 ills., map, Aug., 1908

BLAKE, THOMAS EDWARD:

Waves and Thrills at Waikiki (Honolulu). 8 ills. in duotone by Thomas Edward Blake. LXVII, pp. 597-604, May, 1935

BLANC, Mont, France:

The Ascent of Mont Blanc. By Walter Woodburn Hyde. XXIV, pp. 861-942, 69 ills., Aug., 1913

A Woman's Climbs in the High Alps. By Dora Keen. XXII, pp. 643-675, 26 ills., July, 1911

BLANCHARD, C. J.:

The Call of the West. By C. J. Blanchard. XX, pp. 403-437, 20 ills., map, May, 1909

Home-Making by the Government: An Account of the Eleven Immense Irrigating Projects to be Opened in 1908. By C. J. Blanchard. XIX, pp. 250-287, 23 ills., Apr., 1908

Millions for Moisture: An Account of the Work of the U. S. Reclamation Service. By C. J. Blanchard. XVIII, pp. 217-243, 22 ills., Apr., 1907

The Spirit of the West (U. S.): The Wonderful Agricultural Development Since the Dawn of Irrigation. By C. J. Blanchard. XXI, pp. 333-360, 15 ills., Apr., 1910

Winning the West. By C. J. Blanchard. XVII, pp. 82-98, 10 ills., map, Feb., 1906

BLANCHARD, FRIEDA COBB:

Tuatara: "Living Fossils" Walk on Well-Nigh Inaccessible Rocky Islands off the Coast of New Zealand. By Frieda Cobb Blanchard. LXVII, pp. 649-662, 14 ills., map, May, 1935

BLAYNEY, THOMAS LINDSEY:

A Journey in Morocco: "The Land of the Moors." By Thomas Lindsey Blayney. XXII, pp. 750-775, 23 ills., map, Aug., 1911

BLIMPS:

Aboard a Blimp Hunting U-boats: A Day above the Atlantic Reveals Navy Talk and Navy Ways, Creeping Convoys, and Torpedoed Wrecks. By Mason Sutherland. LXXXIV, pp. 79-96, 18 ills., July, 1943

BLISS, HOWARD S.:

Sunshine in Turkey. By Howard S. Bliss. XX, pp. 66-76, ill., Jan., 1909

BLITHE Birds of Dooryard, Bush, and Brake. 37 portraits from paintings by Major Allan Brooks. LXV, pp. 579-594, May, 1934

BLOCH, SARA:
Sheep Dog Trials in Llangollen: Trained Collies Perform Marvels of Herding in the Cambrian Stakes, Open to the World. By Sara Bloch. LXXVII, pp. 559-574, 17 ills., Apr., 1940

BLODGETT, JAMES H.:
"Free Burghs" in the United States. By James H. Blodgett. VII, pp. 116-122, Mar., 1896
Geographic Literature. IX, pp. 478-480, Nov., 1898

"**BLOOD**, Toil, Tears, and Sweat": An American Tells the Story of Britain's War Effort, Summed up in Prime Minister Churchill's Unflinching Words. By Harvey Klemmer. LXXXII, pp. 141-166, 19 ills., Aug., 1942

BLOODWORMS:
The Worm Turns. By Samuel Sandrof. LXXXIX, pp. 775-786, 14 ills., June, 1946

BLOSSOM (Ship):
Sindbads of Science: Narrative of a Windjammer's Specimen-Collecting Voyage to the Sargasso Sea, to Senegambian Africa and Among Islands of High Adventure in the South Atlantic. By George Finlay Simmons. LII, pp. 1-75, 89 ills., map, July, 1927

BLOUNT, HENRY F.:
Resolution in memory of Col. Henry F. Blount. XXXIII, p. 371, Apr., 1918
See also NGS: Board of Managers

BLUE, RUPERT:
Conserving the Nation's Man-Power: Disease Weakens Armies, Cripples Industry, Reduces Production. How the Government is Sanitating the Civil Zones Around Cantonment Areas. A Nation-wide Campaign for Health. By Rupert Blue. XXXII, pp. 255-278, 17 ills., Sept., 1917

The **BLUE** Crab. XVII, p. 46, Jan., 1906

BLUE MOUNTAIN, Maryland:
The Geologist at Blue Mountain, Maryland. By Charles D. Walcott. V, pp. 84-88, July 10, 1893

BLUE RIDGE (Mountains), U. S.:
Spottswood's Expedition of 1716. By Dr. William M. Thornton. VII, pp. 265-269, Aug., 1896

BLUE Seas and Brilliant Costumes Along the Brittany Coast. 29 color photos by Gervais Courtellemont. LVI, pp. 143-174, Aug., 1929

BLUEBERRIES:
Taming the Wild Blueberry. By Frederick V. Coville. XXII, pp. 137-147, 5 ills., Feb., 1911
The Wild Blueberry Tamed: The New Industry of the Pine Barrens of New Jersey. By Frederick V. Coville. XXIX, pp. 535-546, 10 ills., June, 1916

BOARD OF MANAGERS. *See* NGS: Board of Managers

BOARD OF TRUSTEES. *See* NGS: Board of Trustees

BOARDMAN, MABEL:
The American Red Cross in Italy. By Mabel Boardman. XX, pp. 396-397, Apr., 1909

BOARDMAN, MABEL—*Continued*
Honors to the American Navy (Address by Mabel Boardman at NGS Banquet). XX, pp. 84-86, Jan., 1909
The National Geographic Society (Address by Mabel Boardman at Annual Banquet). XXIII, pp. 288-290, Mar., 1912

BOATS:
The "B B," experimental boat of Dr. Alexander Graham Bell, driven by aërial propellers. XVIII, ill. p. 671, Oct., 1907
China's Teeming Life on the Rivers and Sea. 18 photos in duotone by Paul De Gaston and W. Robert Moore. LXVI, pp. 625-640, Nov., 1934
Cosmopolitan Shanghai, Key Seaport of China. By W. Robert Moore. LXII, pp. 311-335, 19 ills., Sept., 1932
The Glass-Bottom Boat. By Charles Frederick Holder. XX, pp. 761-778, 17 ills., Sept., 1909
Ho for the Soochow Ho (China). By Mabel Craft Deering. LI, pp. 623-649, 32 ills., map, June, 1927
House-Boat Days in the Vale of Kashmir. By Florence H. Morden. LVI, pp. 437-463, 22 ills. in black and white, 30 ills. in color, Oct., 1929
Landing Craft for Invasion. By Melville Bell Grosvenor. LXXXVI, pp. 1-30, 26 ills., July, 1944
Life Afloat in China: Tens of Thousands of Chinese in Congested Ports Spend Their Entire Existence on Boats. By Robert F. Fitch. LI, pp. 665-686, 28 ills., June, 1927
Macao, "Land of Sweet Sadness": The Oldest European Settlement in the Far East, Long the Only Haven for Distressed Mariners in the China Sea. By Edgar Allen Forbes. LXII, pp. 337-357, 13 ills. in black and white, 11 ills. in color, Sept., 1932
Ore-Boat Unloaders. (By W. M. Gregory). XVIII, pp. 343-345, ill., May, 1907
Pirate-Fighters of the South China Sea. By Robert Cardwell. LXXXIX, pp. 787-796, 11 ills., June, 1946
Ships, from Dugouts to Dreadnoughts. By Captain Dudley W. Knox. LXXIII, pp. 57-98, 27 ills. in black and white, 16 ills. in gravure, Jan., 1938
The Speediest Boat. XXII, pp. 875-878, ills., Sept., 1911
Surveying the Grand Canyon of the Colorado: An Account of the 1923 Boating Expedition of the United States Geological Survey. By Lewis R. Freeman. XLV, pp. 471-548, 62 ills., map, May, 1924
Transporting a Navy Through the Jungles of Africa in War Time. By Frank J. Magee. XLII, pp. 331-362, 31 ills., Oct., 1922
The Tuna Harvest of the Sea: A Little-known Epic of the Ocean Is the Story of Southern California's Far-ranging Tuna Fleet. By John Degelman. LXXVIII, pp. 393-408, 17 ills., Sept., 1940
See also Canoes and Canoe Trips; Ships and Shipping; Voyages; *and* types of boats

BODINE, MARGARET L.:
Holidays with Humming Birds. By Margaret L. Bodine. LIII, pp. 731-742, 15 ills., June, 1928

BOERS:
A Critical Period in South African History. (By J. H.). VII, pp. 377-379, Nov., 1896
The Witwatersrand and the Revolt of the Uitlanders. By George F. Becker. VII, pp. 349-367, 4 ills., Nov., 1896

BOGHAZ KEOY, Turkey:
An Ancient Capital. By Isabel F. Dodd. XXI, pp. 111-124, 11 ills., Feb., 1910

BOGOSLOF (Volcanic Island), Aleutian Islands:
A Jack in the Box: An Account of the Strange Performances of the Most Wonderful Island in the World. By Captain F. M. Munger. XX, pp. 194-199, 8 ills., Feb., 1909
Riddle of the Aleutians: A Botanist Explores the Origin of Plants on Ever-misty Islands Now Enshrouded in the Fog of War. By Isobel Wylie Hutchison. LXXXII, pp. 769-792, 24 ills., Dec., 1942

BOGOTÁ, Colombia:
Hail Colombia! By Luis Marden. LXXVIII, pp. 505-536, 10 ills. in black and white, 18 ills. in color, map, Oct., 1940
Over the Andes to Bogotá. By Frank M. Chapman. XL, pp. 353-373, 19 ills., Oct., 1921
Round About Bogotá: A Hunt for New Fruits and Plants Among the Mountain Forests of Colombia's Unique Capital. By Wilson Popenoe. XLIX, pp. 127-160, 34 ills., map, Feb., 1926

BOHEMIA and the Czechs. By Aleš Hrdlička. XXXI, pp. 163-187, 18 ills., Feb., 1917

BOHLMAN, H. T.:
Successful Shots With a Friendly Camera. 16 photos by H. T. Bohlman, Irene Finley, William L. Finley. XLIV, pp. 165-180, Aug., 1923

BOLIVIA:
Bolivia—A Country Without a Debt. By Y. Calderon. XVIII, pp. 573-586, 4 ills., Sept., 1907
Bolivia, Land of Fiestas. By Alicia O'Reardon Overbeck. LXVI, pp. 645-660, 16 ills., map, Nov., 1934
Bolivia—Tin Roof of the Andes. By Henry Albert Phillips. LXXXIII, pp. 309-332, 5 ills. in black and white, 20 ills. in color, Mar., 1943
Buenos Aires to Washington by Horse: A Solitary Journey of Two and a Half Years, Through Eleven American Republics, Covers 9,600 Miles of Mountain and Plain, Desert and Jungle. By A. F. Tschiffely. LV, pp. 135-196, 75 ills., map, Feb., 1929
From Panama to Patagonia. By Charles M. Pepper. XVII, pp. 449-452, ill., Aug., 1906
The Heart of Aymará Land: A Visit to Tiahuanacu, Perhaps the Oldest City of the New World, Lost Beneath the Drifting Sand of Centuries in the Bolivian Highlands. By Stewart E. McMillin. LI, pp. 213-256, 23 ills. in black and white, 18 ills. in color, map, Feb., 1927

BOLIVIA—*Continued*
The Road to Bolivia. By William E. Curtis. XI, pp. 209-224, 7 ills., June, 1900; pp. 264-280, 6 ills., July, 1900
Some Wonderful Sights in the Andean Highlands: The Oldest City in America. Sailing on the Lake of the Clouds: The Yosemite of Peru. By Harriet Chalmers Adams. XIX, pp. 597-618, 19 ills., map, Sept., 1908
Tin, the Cinderella Metal. By Alicia O'Reardon Overbeck. LXXVIII, pp. 659-684, 24 ills., Nov., 1940
What the Latin American Republics Think of the Pan-American Conferences. XVII, pp. 474-479, Aug., 1906
See also La Paz

BOLL WEEVIL (Insect):
The Red Ant Versus the Boll Weevil. XV, pp. 262-264, June, 1904

BOMBAY, India:
The Parsees and the Towers of Silence at Bombay, India. By William Thomas Fee. XVI, pp. 529-554, 16 ills., Dec., 1905

BOMBERS:
Air Power for Peace. By General H. H. Arnold. LXXXIX, pp. 137-193, 35 ills. in black and white, 28 ills. in color, map supplement, Feb., 1946
American Bombers Attacking from Australia. By Howell Walker. LXXXIII, pp. 49-70, 19 ills., map, Jan., 1943
Cruise on an Escort Carrier. By Melville Bell Grosvenor. LXXXIV, pp. 513-546, 14 ills. in black and white, 20 ills. in color, Nov., 1943
8th Air Force in England. 10 ills. in color from U. S. Army Air Forces official photos. LXXXVII, pp. 297-304, Mar., 1945
Navy Wings over the Pacific. 12 ills. in color from U. S. Navy official photos. LXXXVI, pp. 241-248, Aug., 1944
The New Queen of the Seas. By Melville Bell Grosvenor. LXXXII, pp. 1-30, 27 ills., drawing, two-page map, July, 1942
Painting History in the Pacific. 19 ills. in color from paintings by Lt. William F. Draper, USNR. LXXXVI, pp. 408-424, Oct., 1944
Return to Florence (Italy). By 1st Lt. Benjamin C. McCartney. LXXXVII, pp. 257-296, 18 ills. in black and white, 18 ills. in color, Mar., 1945
Saga of the Carrier *Princeton.* By Capt. William H. Buracker, USN. LXXXVIII, pp. 189-218, 8 ills. in black and white, 22 ills. in color, map, Aug., 1945

BOMBS, Flying:
Air Power for Peace. By General H. H. Arnold. LXXXIX, pp. 137-193, 35 ills. in black and white, 28 ills. in color, map supplement, Feb., 1946
London Wins the Battle. By Marquis W. Childs. LXXXVIII, pp. 129-152, 21 ills., Aug., 1945

BOMBS over Bible Lands. By Frederick Simpich and W. Robert Moore. LXXX, pp. 141-180, 34 ills., two-page map, Aug., 1941

BONAIRE (Island), West Indies:
Curaçao and Aruba on Guard. By W. Robert Moore. LXXXIII, pp. 169-192, 12 ills. in black and white, 10 ills. in color, 4 maps, Feb., 1943

BONAPARTE, CHARLES J.:
Honors to Peary (Address by Charles J. Bonaparte). XVIII, pp. 49-60, ill., Jan., 1907

BONDS Between the Americas. By Frederick Simpich. LXXII, pp. 785-808, 22 ills., Dec., 1937

BONIN ISLANDS, Pacific Ocean. *See* Ogasawara Shoto

BONITA (Yawl):
Cruising to Crete: Four French Girls Set Sail in a Breton Yawl for the Island of the Legendary Minotaur. By Marthe Oulié and Mariel Jean-Brunhes. LV, pp. 249-272, 15 ills. in black and white, 14 ills. in color, map, Feb., 1929

BONIVARD, FRANÇOIS DE:
The Millennial City: The Romance of Geneva, Capital of the League of Nations. By Ralph A. Graves. XXXV, pp. 457-476, 13 ills., June, 1919

BONN, Germany:
War's Wake in the Rhineland. By Thomas R. Henry. LXXXVIII, pp. 1-32, 29 ills., map, July, 1945

BONNIE Scotland, Postwar Style. By Isobel Wylie Hutchison. LXXXIX, pp. 545-601, 14 ills. in black and white, 38 ills. in color, two-page map, May, 1946

A **BOOK** of Monsters (Insects). By David and Marian Fairchild. XXVI, pp. 89-98, 7 ills., July, 1914

BOOTH, EVANGELINE:
Around the World with the Salvation Army. By Evangeline Booth. XXXVII, pp. 347-368, 23 ills., Apr., 1920

BORAH, LEO A.:
Connecticut, Prodigy of Ingenuity: Factories Play a Symphony of Industry Amid Colonial Scenes in the State of Steady Habits. By Leo A. Borah. LXXIV, pp. 279-326, 25 ills. in black and white, 25 ills. in color, two-page map, Sept., 1938

Diamond Delaware, Colonial Still: Tradition Rules the "Three Lower Counties" Over Which William Penn and Lord Baltimore Went to Law. By Leo A. Borah. LXVIII, pp. 367-398, 25 ills. in black and white, 15 ills. in color, map, Sept., 1935

Home Folk around Historic Cumberland Gap. By Leo A. Borah. LXXXIV, pp. 741-768, 25 ills., map, Dec., 1943

Iowa, Abiding Place of Plenty: The State Where the Tall Corn Grows Provides the Nation with a Tenth of Its Food Supply. By Leo A. Borah. LXXVI, pp. 143-182, 15 ills. in black and white, 20 ills. in color, two-page map, Aug., 1939

Kentucky, Boone's Great Meadow: The Bluegrass State Celebrates Its Sesquicentennial As It Helps the Nation Gird for War. By Leo A. Borah. LXXXII, pp. 57-89, 13 ills. in black and white, 21 ills. in color, map, July, 1942

BORAH, LEO A.—*Continued*
Nebraska, the Cornhusker State. By Leo A. Borah. LXXXVII, pp. 513-542, 6 ills. in black and white, 23 ills. in color, map, May, 1945

New Map of the Atlantic Ocean: Foremost Sea of Commerce Becomes World's Battleground and Its Peaceful Islands Rise to Strategic Importance. By Leo A. Borah and Wellman Chamberlin. Text with map supplement. LXXX, pp. 407-418, 9 ills., Sept., 1941

Oregon Finds New Riches. By Leo A. Borah. XC, pp. 681-728, 15 ills. in black and white, 28 ills. in color, two-page map, Dec., 1946

A Patriotic Pilgrimage to Eastern National Parks: History and Beauty Live Along Paved Roads, Once Indian Trails, Through Virginia, North Carolina, Tennessee, Kentucky, and West Virginia. By Leo A. Borah. LXV, pp. 663-702, 18 ills. in black and white, 28 ills. in color, two-page map, June, 1934

Some Odd Pages from the Annals of the Tulip: A "Made" Flower of Unknown Origin Took Medieval Europe by Storm and Caused a Financial Panic in the Netherlands. By Leo A. Borah. LXIV, pp. 321-343, 13 ills. in black and white, 10 ills. in color, Sept., 1933

Utah, Carved by Winds and Waters: The Beehive State, Settled Only 89 Years Ago, Stands a Monument to the Courage of Its Founders. By Leo A. Borah. LXIX, pp. 577-623, 20 ills. in black and white, 22 ills. in color, two-page map, May, 1936

Washington, Home City and Show Place: To Residents and Visitors the Nation's Capital Presents Varied Sides as the City Steadily Grows in Beauty and Stature. By Leo A. Borah. LXXI, pp. 663-695, 11 ills. in black and white, 20 ills. in color, June, 1937

Washington, the Evergreen State: The Amazing Commonwealth of the Pacific Northwest Which Has Emerged from the Wilderness in a Span of Fifty Years. By Leo A. Borah. LXIII, pp. 131-196, 50 ills. in black and white, 26 ills. in color, two-page map, Feb., 1933

BORCHGREVINK, C. E.:
The National Geographic Society Expedition in the West Indies. XIII, pp. 209-213, maps, June, 1902

The National Geographic Society Expedition to Martinque and St. Vincent. XIII, pp. 183-184, ills., June, 1902

BORNEO:
Colonial Government in Borneo. By James M. Hubbard. XI, pp. 359-363, Sept., 1900

Keeping House in Borneo. By Virginia Hamilton. LXXXVIII, pp. 293-324, 28 ills., map, Sept., 1945

Notes on the Sea Dyaks of Borneo. By Edwin H. Gomes. XXII, pp. 695-723, 26 ills., Aug., 1911

Sarawak: The Land of the White Rajahs. By Harrison W. Smith. XXXV, pp. 110-167, 58 ills., map, Feb., 1919

BORNHOLM (Island), Denmark:
Bornholm—Denmark in a Nutshell. By Mason Sutherland. LXXXVII, pp. 239-256, 20 ills., map, Feb., 1945

"BORNHOLMERS" (Herring):

Bornholm—Denmark in a Nutshell. By Mason Sutherland. LXXXVII, pp. 239-256, 20 ills., map, Feb., 1945

BOSNIA:

East of the Adriatic: Notes on Dalmatia, Montenegro, Bosnia, and Herzegovina. By Kenneth McKenzie. XXIII, pp. 1159-1187, 1284, 37 ills., map, Dec., 1912

The Great Turk and His Lost Provinces. By William E. Curtis. XIV, pp. 45-61, 7 ills., Feb., 1903

Where East Meets West: Visit to Picturesque Dalmatia, Montenegro and Bosnia. By Marian Cruger Coffin. XIX, pp. 309-344, 26 ills., map, May, 1908

BOSPORUS (Strait):

Constantinople and Sancta Sophia. By Edwin A. Grosvenor. XXVII, pp. 459-482, 21 ills., May, 1915

The Gates to the Black Sea: The Dardanelles, the Bosphorus, and the Sea of Marmora. By Harry Griswold Dwight. XXVII, pp. 435-459, 27 ills., May, 1915

Seeing 3,000 Years of History in Four Hours: A Panorama of Ancient, Medieval, and Modern Events Against a Background of Mythology Unfolds During an Airplane Journey from Constantinople to Athens. By Maynard Owen Williams. LIV, pp. 719-739, 24 ills., map, Dec., 1928

Summer Holidays on the Bosporus. By Maynard Owen Williams. LVI, pp. 487-508, 13 ills. in black and white, 11 ills. in color, map, Oct., 1929

BOSQUE, FERNANDO DEL:

Expedition into Texas of Fernando del Bosque, Standard-Bearer of the King, Don Carlos II, in the Year 1675. Translated from an Old, Unpublished Spanish Manuscript. By Betty B. Brewster. XIV, pp. 339-348, Sept., 1903

BOSSHARD, W.:

Life on the Steppes and Oases of Chinese Turkestan. 32 color photos by W. Bosshard. LIX, pp. 333-356, Mar., 1931

BOSSON, MRS. GEORGE C., JR.:

Biskra, the Ziban Queen. By Mrs. George C. Bosson, Jr. XIX, pp. 563-593, 29 ills., map, Aug., 1908

Notes on Normandy. By Mrs. Geo. C. Bosson, Jr. XXI, pp. 775-782, 5 ills., Sept., 1910

Sicily, the Battle-Field of Nations and of Nature. By Mrs. George C. Bosson, Jr. XX, pp. 97-118, 25 ills., map, Jan., 1909

BOSTELMANN, ELSE:

Carnivores of a Lightless World (Fishes). 8 ills. in color from paintings by Else Bostelmann and E. J. Geske. LXVI, pp. 693-700, Dec., 1934

Exploring Neptune's Hidden World of Vivid Color. 8 ills. in color from paintings by E. Bostelmann. LXII, pp. 747-754, Dec., 1932

Fantastic Sea Life from Abyssal Depths. 8 ills. in color from paintings by E. Bostelmann. LXI, pp. 71-78, Jan., 1932

Flashes From Ocean Deeps. 8 ills. in color from paintings by Else Bostelmann and Helen D. Tee-Van. LXVI, pp. 677-684, Dec., 1934

BOSTELMANN, ELSE—*Continued*

Luminous Life in the Depths of the Sea. 8 ills. in color from paintings by E. Bostelmann. LIX, pp. 667-674, June, 1931

Monster and Midget Squid and Octopuses. 8 ills. in color from paintings by Else Bostelmann under direction Roy W. Miner. LXVIII, pp. 193-200, Aug., 1935

Multi-Hued Marvels of a Coral Reef. 8 ills. in color from paintings by Else Bostelmann. LXV, pp. 719-726, June, 1934

Sea Floor Aquarelles from Tongareva. 8 ills. in color from paintings by Else Bostelmann under direction Roy W. Miner. LXXIV, pp. 383-390, Sept., 1938

Strange Creatures of Sunny Seas (Mollusks, Crustaceans, etc.). 8 ills. in color from paintings by Else Bostelmann under direction Roy W. Miner. LXXI, pp. 211-218, Feb., 1937

Undersea Gardens of the North Atlantic Coast. 8 ills. in color from paintings by Else Bostelmann under direction Roy W. Miner. LXX, pp. 217-224, Aug., 1936

Whales, Porpoises, and Dolphins. 31 ills. in color from paintings by Else Bostelmann. LXXVII, pp. 41-80, Jan., 1940

BOSTON, Massachusetts:

Boston Through Midwest Eyes. By Frederick Simpich. LXX, pp. 37-82, 24 ills. in black and white, 31 ills. in color, July, 1936

BOSWORTH, ABBIE L.:

Life in a Norway Valley: An American Girl Is Welcomed Into the Homemaking and Haying of Happy Hallingdal. By Abbie L. Bosworth. LXVII, pp. 627-648, 21 ills., map, May, 1935

BOTANY. *See* Agricultural and Botanical Explorers; *and* Flowers; Plants; Trees

BOTFLIES (Insects):

Life Story of the Mosquito. By Graham Fairchild. With 10 ills. in color from paintings. LXXXV, pp. 180-195, 5 ills. in black and white, drawing, Feb., 1944

BOUGAINVILLE (Island), Solomon Islands:

Fiji Patrol on Bougainville. By David D. Duncan. LXXXVII, pp. 87-104, 9 ills. in black and white, 11 ills. in color, Jan., 1945

Jungle War: Bougainville and New Caledonia. 17 ills. in color from paintings by Lieut. William F. Draper. LXXXV, pp. 417-432, Apr., 1944

A Woman's Experiences among Stone Age Solomon Islanders: Primitive Life Remains Unchanged in Tropical Jungleland Where United States Forces Now Are Fighting. By Eleanor Schirmer Oliver. LXXXII, pp. 813-836, 26 ills., map, Dec., 1942

BOULTON, LAURA C.:

Timbuktu and Beyond: Desert City of Romantic Savor and Salt Emerges into World Life Again as Trading Post of France's Vast African Empire. By Laura C. Boulton. LXXIX, pp. 631-670, 18 ills. in black and white, 26 ills. in color, map, May, 1941

BOUNDARIES:

The Alaskan Boundary. By John W. Foster. X, pp. 425-456, 10 maps, map supplements, Nov., 1899

BOUNDARIES—*Continued*

Alaskan Boundary Decision. XIV, p. 423, Nov., 1903

Alaskan Boundary Dispute. XIV, p. 79, Feb., 1903

The Alaskan Boundary Survey. I—Introduction. By Dr. T. C. Mendenhall. II—The Boundary South of Fort Yukon. By J. E. McGrath. III—The Boundary North of Fort Yukon. By J. Henry Turner. IV, pp. 177-197, Feb. 8, 1893

The Alaskan Boundary Tribunal. By John W. Foster. XV, pp. 1-12, map, map supplement, Jan., 1904

Along Our Side of the Mexican Border. By Frederick Simpich. XXXVIII, pp. 61-80, 9 ills., map, July, 1920

The Anglo-Venezuelan Boundary Dispute. By Marcus Baker. XI, pp. 129-144, ills., map, Apr., 1900

Argentina-Chile Boundary. XIII, p. 117, Mar., 1902

Argentina-Chile Boundary Award. XIV, pp. 115-116, Mar., 1903

Argentine-Chile Boundary Dispute. XIII, pp. 27-28, Jan., 1902

The Battle-Line of Languages in Western Europe: A Problem in Human Geography More Perplexing Than That of International Boundaries. By A. L. Guerard. XLIII, pp. 145-180, 36 ills., Feb., 1923

Boundaries of Territorial Acquisitions. XII, pp. 373-377, chart, Oct., 1901

Brazil-French Guiana Boundary Decision. XII, p. 83, Feb., 1901

The California and Nevada Boundary. (By C. H. Sinclair). X, pp. 416-417, Oct., 1899

The Canadian Boundary. By John W. Foster. XIV, pp. 85-90, map, Mar., 1903

Charting a Coast-Line of 26,000 Miles (Alaska). XX, pp. 608-609, July, 1909

Chile-Argentina Boundary Dispute. XIII, p. 220, June, 1902

Decision of the Alaskan Boundary Tribunal. XV, pp. 12-14, Jan., 1904

The Geographic's New Map of Germany and Its Approaches: With a Review of The Society's Maps of Europe. By Gilbert Grosvenor. Text with map supplement. LXXXVI, pp. 66-72, ill., July, 1944

Included: Boundary changes in Europe (1912-1940)

How the United States Grew. By McFall Kerbey. LXIII, pp. 631-649, 17 ills., map, May, 1933

The Idaho and Montana Boundary Line. By Richard U. Goode. XI, pp. 23-29, ill., diagr., Jan., 1900

Location of the Boundary Between Nicaragua and Costa Rica. By Arthur P. Davis. XII, pp. 22-28, ill., map, Jan., 1901

The Lost Boundary of Texas. By Marcus Baker. XII, pp. 430-432, map, Dec., 1901

Marking the Alaskan Boundary. XIX, pp. 176-189, 16 ills., Mar., 1908

Marking the Alaskan Boundary. By Thomas Riggs, Jr. XX, pp. 593-607, 17 ills., July, 1909

The New Map of Europe: Showing the Boundaries Established by the Peace Conference at Paris and by Subsequent Decisions of the Supreme Council of the Allied and Associated Powers. By Ralph A. Graves. Text with map supplement. XXXIX, pp. 157-177, 18 ills., Feb., 1921

Oregon: Its History, Geography, and Resources. By John H. Mitchell, U. S. Senator from Oregon. VI, pp. 239-284, Apr. 20, 1895

The Original Boundary Stones of the District of Columbia. By Ernest A. Shuster, Jr. XX, pp. 356-359, 6 ills., map, Apr., 1909

Surveying the 141st Meridian (Boundary Line Between Canada and Alaska). By Thomas Riggs, Jr. XXIII, pp. 685-713, 46 ills., map, July, 1912

Surveys and Maps of the District of Columbia. By Marcus Baker. VI, pp. 149-178, diagr., tables, map, Nov. 1, 1894

Included: List of Maps of Washington and the District of Columbia

The Valley of the Orinoco. By T. H. Gignilliat. Text with map supplement. VII, p. 92, Feb., 1896

Venezuela: Her Government, People, and Boundary. By William E. Curtis. VII, pp. 49-58, 3 ills., map supplement, Feb., 1896

The Venezuelan Boundary Commission and Its Work. By Marcus Baker. VIII, pp. 193-201, July-Aug., 1897

Wandering Islands in the Rio Grande. By Mrs. Albert S. Burleson. XXIV, pp. 381-386, ills., map, Mar., 1913

BOUNDARY CHANGES IN EUROPE from 1912 to 1940. *See* The Geographic's New Map of Germany and Its Approaches, *above*

The **BOUNDARY** North of Fort Yukon. By J. Henry Turner. IV, pp. 189-197, Feb. 8, 1893

The **BOUNDARY** South of Fort Yukon. By J. E. McGrath. IV, pp. 181-188, Feb. 8, 1893

BOURCHIER, JAMES D.:

The Rise of Bulgaria. By James D. Bourchier. XXIII, pp. 1105-1118, 13 ills., Nov., 1912

BOURGES, France:

The Beauties of France. By Arthur Stanley Riggs. XXVIII, pp. 391-491, 73 ills. in black and white, 16 ills. in color, map, Nov., 1915

BOURLAY, REGINALD A.:

Wings Over Nature's Zoo in Africa. 20 photos in duotone by Reginald A. Bourlay. LXXVI, pp. 527-542, Oct., 1939

BOUTWELL, WILLIAM DOW:

The Mysterious Tomb of a Giant Meteorite (Meteor Crater, Arizona). By William D. Boutwell. LIII, pp. 721-730, 10 ills., June, 1928

Old World Charm in Modern Quebec. 9 color photos by William D. Boutwell. LVII, pp. 507-514, Apr., 1930

Quebec, Capital of French Canada. By William Dow Boutwell. LVII, pp. 515-522, 6 ills., Apr., 1930

BOUVET ISLAND, Antarctic Region:

The Definite Location of Bouvet Island. (By O. H. Tittmann). X, pp. 413-414, Oct., 1899

BOVEY, WILFRID:

The Gaspé Peninsula Wonderland. By Wilfrid Bovey. LXVIII, pp. 209-230, 13 ills. in black and white, 15 ills. in color, map, Aug., 1935

BOWDOIN (Ship):

The "Bowdoin" in North Greenland: Arctic Explorers Place Tablet to Commemorate Sacrifices of the Lady Franklin Bay Expedition. By Donald B. MacMillan. XLVII, pp. 677-722, 49 ills., June, 1925

BOWERS, GEORGE M.:

Planting Fishes in the Ocean. By George M. Bowers. XVIII, pp. 715-723, 5 ills., Nov., 1907

BOXER UPRISING: China:

The Causes that Led Up to the Siege of Pekin. By Dr. W. A. P. Martin. XII, pp. 53-63, ill., Feb., 1901

The Chinese "Boxers." By Llewellyn James Davies. XI, pp. 281-287, July, 1900

Shifting Scenes on the Stage of New China. XXXVIII, pp. 423-428, 4 ills., Nov., 1920

BOY SCOUTS:

Star and Crescent on Parade. 29 color photos by Maynard Owen Williams. LXXXVII, pp. 585-616, May, 1945

Youth Explores Its World. By Frederick Simpich. LXV, pp. 643-662, 21 ills., May, 1934

BOYDEN, AMANDA:

Changing Shanghai. By Amanda Boyden. LXXII, pp. 485-508, 21 ills., maps, Oct., 1937

BOYHOOD of Sir Walter Raleigh. Reproduction in color of the painting by Sir John Millais, Tate Gallery, London. XLIX, text, p. 596; supplement, May, 1926

BOYS' and Girls' Agricultural Clubs. XXII, pp. 639-641, 4 ills., July, 1911

BRACQ, JEAN C.:

The Colonial Expansion of France. By Professor Jean C. Bracq. XI, pp. 225-238, map, June, 1900

BRADLEY, LA VERNE:

San Francisco: Gibraltar of the West Coast. By La Verne Bradley. LXXXIII, pp. 279-308, 28 ills., Mar., 1943

Women at Work. By La Verne Bradley. LXXXVI, pp. 193-220, 23 ills., Aug., 1944

Women in Uniform. By La Verne Bradley. LXXXIV, pp. 445-458, 10 ills., Oct., 1943

BRADLEY, WALTER W.:

Some Mexican Transportation Scenes. By Walter W. Bradley. XXI, pp. 985-991, 10 ills., Dec., 1910

BRAEMAR, Scotland:

Clans in Kilt and Plaidie Gather at Braemar. 11 color photos by Maynard Owen Williams. LXVIII, pp. 153-160, Aug., 1935

BRAHMAPUTRA (River), India-Tibet:

The Tsangpo. By James Mascarene Hubbard. XII, pp. 32-35, Jan., 1901

BRANDES, E. W.:

Into Primeval Papua by Seaplane: Seeking Disease-resisting Sugar Cane, Scientists Find Neolithic Man in Unmapped Nooks of Sorcery and Cannibalism. By E. W. Brandes. LVI, pp. 253-332, 98 ills., map, Sept., 1929

BRANNER, J. C.:

The Recent Ascent of Itambé (Brazil). (By J. C. Branner). X, p. 183, May, 1899

BRAZIL:

Air Cruising Through New Brazil: A National Geographic Reporter Spots Vast Resources Which the Republic's War Declaration Adds to Strength of United Nations. By Henry Albert Phillips. LXXXII, pp. 503-536, 32 ills., Oct., 1942

The Amazon, Father of Waters: The Earth's Mightiest River Drains a Basin of More Than 2,700,000 Square Miles, from Which Came Originally the World's Finest Rubber. By W. L. Schurz. XLIX, pp. 445-463, 15 ills., Apr., 1926

Brazil and Peru. XVII, pp. 203-204, Apr., 1906

Brazil-French Guiana Boundary Decision. XII, p. 83, Feb., 1901

Brazil's Potent Weapons. By W. Robert Moore. LXXXV, pp. 41-78, 16 ills. in black and white, 18 ills. in color, two-page map, Jan., 1944

By Seaplane to Six Continents: Cruising 60,000 Miles, Italian Argonauts of the Air See World Geography Unroll, and Break New Sky Trails Over Vast Brazilian Jungles. By Commander Francesco de Pinedo. LIV, pp. 247-301, 60 ills., two-page map, Sept., 1928

Exploring the Valley of the Amazon in a Hydroplane: Twelve Thousand Miles of Flying Over the World's Greatest River and Greatest Forest to Chart the Unknown Parima River from the Sky. By Captain Albert W. Stevens. XLIX, pp. 353-420, 86 ills., map, Apr., 1926

The Falls of Iguazu. By Marie Robinson Wright. XVII, pp. 456-460, 4 ills., Aug., 1906

Fishing and Hunting Tales from Brazil. By Dewey Austin Cobb. XX, pp. 917-920, Oct., 1909

Gigantic Brazil and Its Glittering Capital. By Frederick Simpich. LVIII, pp. 733-778, 54 ills., map, Dec., 1930

How Latin America Looks from the Air: U. S. Army Airplanes Hurdle the High Andes, Brave Brazil Jungles, and Follow Smoking Volcanoes to Map New Sky Paths Around South America. By Major Herbert A. Dargue. LII, pp. 451-502, 52 ills., map, Oct., 1927

In Humboldt's Wake: Narrative of a National Geographic Society Expedition Up the Orinoco and Through the Strange Casiquiare Canal to Amazonian Waters. By Ernest G. Holt. LX, pp. 621-644, 27 ills., map, Nov., 1931

A Journey by Jungle Rivers to the Home of the Cock-of-the-rock: Naturalists Enter the Amazon, Voyage Through the Heart of Tropical South America, and Emerge at the Mouth of the Orinoco. By Ernest G. Holt. LXIV, pp. 585-630, 49 ills., map, Nov., 1933

The Peak of Itambé. IX, p. 476, Nov., 1898

The Recent Ascent of Itambé. (By J. C. Branner). X, p. 183, May, 1899

BRAZIL—*Continued*

Skypaths Through Latin America: Flying From Our Nation's Capital Southward Over Jungles, Remote Islands, and Great Cities on an Aërial Survey of the East Coast of South America. By Frederick Simpich. LIX, pp. 1-79, 77 ills., map, Jan., 1931

South America. Annual Address by the President, Gardiner G. Hubbard. III, pp. 1-29, foldout map, Mar. 28, 1891

South America Fifty Years Hence. By Charles M. Pepper. XVII, pp. 427-432, map supplement, Aug., 1906

Through Brazil to the Summit of Mount Roraima. By G. H. H. Tate. LVIII, pp. 585-605, 24 ills., map, Nov., 1930

Through Paraguay and Southern Matto Grosso. By Sir Christopher H. Gibson. LXXXIV, pp. 459-488, 20 ills. in black and white, 11 ills. in color, map, Oct., 1943

A Visit to the Brazilian Coffee Country. By Robert De C. Ward. XXII, pp. 908-931, 19 ills., map, Oct., 1911

Wonder Island of the Amazon Delta: On Marajó Cowboys Ride Oxen, Tree-dwelling Animals Throng Dense Forests, While Strange Fishes and Birds Help Make a Zoologist's Paradise. By Hugh B. Cott. LXXIV, pp. 635-670, 30 ills. in black and white, 12 ills. in color, map, Nov., 1938

The World's Great Waterfalls: Visits to Mighty Niagara, Wonderful Victoria, and Picturesque Iguazu. By Theodore W. Noyes. L, pp. 29-59, 29 ills., July, 1926

See also Rio de Janeiro; Santos; São Paulo

BRAZIL'S Potent Weapons. By W. Robert Moore. LXXXV, pp. 41-78, 16 ills. in black and white, 18 ills. in color, two-page map, Jan., 1944

BREAD MAKING:

Bread Making in Many Lands. 15 ills. XIX, pp. 165-179, Mar., 1908

How the World Is Fed. By William Joseph Showalter. XXIX, pp. 1-110, 101 ills., Jan., 1916

The **"BREAKING** Up" of the Yukon. By Captain George S. Gibbs. XVII, pp. 268-272, 6 ills., May, 1906

BREASTED, CHARLES:

Exploring the Secrets of Persepolis. By Charles Breasted. LXIV, pp. 381-420, 48 ills., plan, map, Oct., 1933

BREDIN, DEE:

Java Assignment. By Dee Bredin. LXXXI, pp. 89-119, 32 ills., map, Jan., 1942

BREED, AUSTIN A.:

Spain and Morocco. 6 color photos by Austin A. Breed. XXXI, pp. 257-270, Mar., 1917

BREED, JACK:

Flaming Cliffs of Monument Valley. By Lt. Jack Breed, USNR. With 9 color photos by author and Warren T. Mithoff. LXXXVIII, pp. 452-461, Oct., 1945

BREWER, ELIZABETH H.:

Peculiar Caves of Asia Minor. By Elizabeth H. Brewer. XXII, pp. 870-875, 5 ills., Sept., 1911

BREWSTER, BETTY B.:

Expedition into Texas of Fernando del Bosque, Standard-Bearer of the King, Don Carlos II, in the Year 1675. Translated from an Old, Unpublished Spanish Manuscript. By Betty B. Brewster. XIV, pp. 339-348, Sept., 1903

BRIDGES:

Bridges, from Grapevine to Steel. By Frederick Simpich. LXIX, pp. 391-406, 13 ills., Mar., 1936

California's Coastal Redwood Realm: Along a Belt of Tall Trees a Giant Bridge Speeds the Winning of Our Westernmost Frontier. By J. R. Hildebrand. LXXV, pp. 133-184, 31 ills. in black and white, 17 ills. in color, map, Feb., 1939

The Washington Aqueduct and Cabin John Bridge. By D. D. Gaillard. VIII, pp. 337-344, ills., Dec., 1897

BRIDGES, Natural:

Bursts of Color in Sculptured Utah. 22 ills. in color. LXIX, pp. 593-616, May, 1936

Colossal Natural Bridges of Utah. XV, pp. 367-369, ills., Sept., 1904

Encircling Navajo Mountain (Utah) with a Pack-Train: An Expedition to a Hitherto Untraversed Region of Our Southwest Discovers a New Route to Rainbow Natural Bridge. By Charles L. Bernheimer. XLIII, pp. 197-224, 33 ills., map, Feb., 1923

The Great Natural Bridges of Utah. XVIII, pp. 199-204, 3 ills., Mar., 1907

The Great Natural Bridges of Utah. By Byron Cummings. XXI, pp. 157-167, 7 ills., Feb., 1910

The Great Rainbow Natural Bridge of Southern Utah. By Joseph E. Pogue. XXII, pp. 1048-1056, 6 ills., Nov., 1911

The Natural Bridge of Virginia. By Charles D. Walcott. V, pp. 59-62, ill., diagr., July 10, 1893

BRIDGMAN, HERBERT L.:

The New British Empire of the Sudan. By Herbert L. Bridgman. XVII, pp. 241-267, 32 ills., map, May, 1906

Peary's Work and Prospects. (By H. L. Bridgman). X, pp. 414-415, Oct., 1899

Ten Years of the Peary Arctic Club. By Herbert L. Bridgman. XIX, pp. 661-668, 3 ills., Sept., 1908

A **BRIEF** Account of the Geographic Work of the U. S. Coast and Geodetic Survey. By T. C. Mendenhall and Otto H. Tittmann. VIII, pp. 294-299, Oct., 1897

BRIGHAM, ALBERT PERRY:

An Introduction to Physical Geography. (By Grove Karl Gilbert and Albert Perry Brigham). XIV, pp. 21-26, 6 ills., Jan., 1903

BRIGHT ANGEL TRAIL, Arizona:

Experiences in the Grand Canyon. By Ellsworth and Emery Kolb. XXVI, pp. 99-184, 70 ills., map, Aug., 1914

BRIGHT Bits in Poland's Mountainous South. 16 color photos by Hans Hildenbrand. LXVII, pp. 353-360, Mar., 1935

BRIGHT Corners of Time-Mellowed Germany. 11 color photos by Hans Hildenbrand and Wilhelm Tobien. LXIV, pp. 223-230, Aug., 1933

BRIGHT Facets of Brazil. 18 color photos by W. Robert Moore. LXXXV, pp. 49-72, Jan., 1944

BRIGHT Facets of Italy's Grandeur. 9 color photos: 8 by B. Anthony Stewart. LXXVII, pp. 355-362, Mar., 1940

BRIGHT Flashes from Pacific Corals (Fishes). 24 color photos by Walter H. Chute. LXXIX, pp. 349-372, Mar., 1941

BRIGHT-HUED Pets of Cage and Aviary. 51 portraits from paintings by Major Allan Brooks. LXXIV, pp. 783-790, Dec., 1938

BRIGHT Pages from an Asiatic Travel Log. 12 color photos by Maynard Owen Williams. LXII, pp. 545-552, Nov., 1932

BRIGHT Patterns of Long Island Life. 18 color photos: 14 by Willard R. Culver. LXXV, pp. 429-460, Apr., 1939

BRINGING the World to Our Foreign Language Soldiers: How a Military Training Camp is Solving a Seemingly Unsurmountable Problem by Using the Geographic. By Christina Krysto. XXXIV, pp. 81-90, 4 ills., Aug., 1918

BRIQUETS (Fuel):

An Ideal Fuel Manufactured Out of Waste Products: The American Coal Briquetting Industry. By Guy Elliott Mitchell. XXI, pp. 1067-1074, 4 ills., Dec., 1910

BRISBANE, Australia:

Capital Cities of Australia. By W. Robert Moore. LXVIII, pp. 667-722, 32 ills. in black and white, 24 ills. in color, two-page map, Dec., 1935

BRITAIN Fights in the Fields. By Francis A. Flood. LXXXVI, pp. 31-65, 17 ills. in black and white, 21 ills. in color, July, 1944

BRITAIN Just Before the Storm: A Canadian Canoe Threads Old English Waterways Athrob with the Midlands' Industrial Life. By Amos Burg. LXXVIII, pp. 185-212, 14 ills. in black and white, 9 ills. in color, map, Aug., 1940

The **BRITISH** Antarctic Expedition. XII, pp. 339-345, Sept., 1901

BRITISH Antarctic Expedition under Captain Robert F. Scott. 16 ills. XLV, pp. 255-270, Mar., 1924

BRITISH ASSOCIATION FOR THE ADVANCEMENT OF SCIENCE:

Geography at the British Association. XI, pp. 475-478, Dec., 1900

The Toronto Meeting of the British Association for the Advancement of Science. (By J. H.). VIII, pp. 247-251, Sept., 1897

BRITISH COLUMBIA (Province), Canada:

Alaskan Highway an Engineering Epic: Mosquitoes, Mud, and Muskeg Minor Obstacles of 1,671-mile Race to Throw the Alcan Life Line Through Thick Forests and Uninhabited Wilderness. By Froelich Rainey. LXXXIII, pp. 143-168, 21 ills., 3 maps, Feb., 1943

The Columbia (River) Turns on the Power. By Maynard Owen Williams. LXXIX, pp. 749-792, 25 ills. in black and white, 18 ills. in color, June, 1941

BRITISH COLUMBIA (Province), Canada—*Continued*

An Expedition through the Yukon District. By Charles Willard Hayes. IV, pp. 117-159, 3 maps (2 foldouts), May 15, 1892

Exploration in the Canadian Rockies. X, pp. 135-136, Apr., 1899

Factors Which Modify the Climate of Victoria. By Arthur W. McCurdy. XVIII, pp. 345-348, maps, May, 1907

The Forests of Canada. XIV, pp. 106-108, Mar., 1903

The Future of the Yukon Goldfields. By William H. Dall. IX, pp. 117-120, Apr., 1898

A Geologist's Paradise (Canadian Rockies). By Charles D. Walcott. XXII, pp. 509-536, 28 ills., panorama, June, 1911
Our Mountain Panorama (panorama)

Hunting the Grizzly in British Columbia. By Joseph Wendle. XVIII, pp. 612-615, 3 ills., Sept., 1907

An Interesting Rumor Concerning Andrée. (By J. H.). IX, pp. 102-103, Mar., 1898

Life on a Yukon Trail. By Alfred Pearce Dennis. X, pp. 377-391, 8 ills., map, Oct., 1899; pp. 457-466, 7 ills., Nov., 1899

The Monarch of the Canadian Rockies (Mount Robson). By Charles D. Walcott. XXIV, pp. 626-639, 13 ills., panorama, May, 1913
The Monarch of the Canadian Rockies—Robson Peak (panorama)

"Nakwasina" Goes North: A Man, a Woman, and a Pup Cruise from Tacoma to Juneau in a 17-Foot Canoe. By Jack Calvin. LXIV, pp. 1-42, 24 ills., map, July, 1933

On the Trail of a Horse Thief (Creek). By Herbert W. Gleason. XXXV, pp. 349-358, 6 ills., Apr., 1919

Overland Routes to the Klondike. By Hamlin Garland. IX, pp. 113-116, ill., Apr., 1898

Peaks and Parks of Western Canada. 11 photos: 5 by W. J. Oliver. LXXX, pp. 516-526, Oct., 1941

Peaks and Trails in the Canadian Alps. 16 photos in duotone by Byron Harmon and Clifford White. LXV, pp. 627-642, May, 1934

Recent Exploration in the Canadian Rockies. By Walter D. Wilcox. XIII, pp. 151-168, 12 ills., map, May, 1902; Part II, pp. 185-200, 9 ills., June, 1902

Some Tramps Across the Glaciers and Snowfields of British Columbia. By Howard Palmer. XXI, pp. 457-487, 25 ills., June, 1910

The Stikine River in 1898. By Eliza Ruhamah Scidmore. X, pp. 1-15, 4 ills., Jan., 1899

Tweedsmuir Park: The Diary of a Pilgrimage. By The Lady Tweedsmuir of Elsfield. LXXIII, pp. 451-476, 22 ills., maps, Apr., 1938

The Vast Timber Belts of Canada. XVII, pp. 509-511, Sept., 1906

Wartime in the Pacific Northwest. By Frederick Simpich. LXXXII, pp. 421-464, 25 ills. in black and white, 23 ills. in color, map, Oct., 1942

BRITISH COMMONWEALTH OF NATIONS:

The British Commonwealth of Nations: "Organized Freedom" Around the World. By Eric Underwood. LXXXIII, pp. 485-524, 31 ills., Apr., 1943

BRITISH COMMONWEALTH OF NATIONS— *Continued*

The Expansion of England. By Edwin D. Mead. XI, pp. 249-263, July, 1900

The Flags of the British Empire. By Byron McCandless and Gilbert Grosvenor. XXXII, pp. 378-385, 158 ills. in color, Oct., 1917

Great Britain's Bread Upon the Waters: Canada and Her Other Daughters. By William Howard Taft. XXIX, pp. 217-272, 56 ills., Mar., 1916

The United States and the British Empire. By Leonard David Gammans. LXXXVII, pp. 562-564, May, 1945

Yanks at Westminster. By Capt. Leonard David Gammans. XC, pp. 223-252, 6 ills. in black and white, 19 ills. in color, Aug., 1946

See also Great Britain; Northern Ireland; *and* names of dominions and colonies

BRITISH Dominions Scenes. 16 ills. XXIX, pp. 233-248, Mar., 1916

BRITISH EAST AFRICA:

Amid the Snow Peaks of the Equator: A Naturalist's Exploration Around Ruwenzori, with an Excursion to the Congo State, and an Account of the Terrible Scourge of Sleeping Sickness. By A. F. R. Wollaston. XX, pp. 256-277, 11 ills., Mar., 1909

The British Commonwealth of Nations: "Organized Freedom" Around the World. By Eric Underwood. LXXXIII, pp. 485-524, 31 ills., Apr., 1943

Elephant Hunting in Equatorial Africa with Rifle and Camera. By Carl E. Akeley. XXIII, pp. 779-810, 30 ills., Aug., 1912

A Great African Lake (Victoria). By Sir Henry M. Stanley. XIII, pp. 169-172, map, May, 1902

Uganda, "Land of Something New": Equatorial African Area Reveals Snow-crowned Peaks, Crater Lakes, Jungle-story Beasts, Human Giants, and Forest Pygmies. By Jay Marston. LXXI, pp. 109-130, 22 ills., map, Jan., 1937

When a Drought Blights Africa: Hippos and Elephants Are Driven Insane by Suffering, in the Lorian Swamp, Kenya Colony. By Capt. A. T. Curle. LV, pp. 521-528, 9 ills., Apr., 1929

Where Roosevelt Will Hunt. By Sir Harry Johnston. XX, pp. 207-256, 43 ills., map supplement, Mar., 1909

Wild Man and Wild Beast in Africa. By Theodore Roosevelt. XXII, pp. 1-33, 41 ills., map, Jan., 1911

Zanzibar. By Mrs. Harris R. Childs. XXIII, pp. 810-824, 11 ills., Aug., 1912

BRITISH EMPIRE. *See* British Commonwealth of Nations

BRITISH GUIANA:

The Anglo-Venezuelan Boundary Dispute. By Marcus Baker. XI, pp. 129-144, ills., map, Apr., 1900

An Impression of the Guiana Wilderness. By Angelo Heilprin. XVIII, pp. 373-381, 6 ills., June, 1907

Kaieteur and Roraima: The Great Falls and the Great Mountain of the Guianas. By Henry Edward Crampton. XXXVIII, pp. 227-244, 12 ills., map, Sept., 1920

BRITISH GUIANA—*Continued*

A New World to Explore: In the Tree-Roof of the British Guiana Forest Flourishes Much Hitherto-Unknown Life. By Maj. R. W. G. Hingston. LXII, pp. 617-642, 35 ills., Nov., 1932

Notes from a Naturalist's Experiences in British Guiana. By C. H. Eigenmann. XXII, pp. 859-870, 8 ills., Sept., 1911

South America. Annual Address by the President, Gardiner G. Hubbard. III, pp. 1-29, foldout map, Mar. 28, 1891

The Valley of the Orinoco. By T. H. Gignilliat. Text with map supplement. VII, p. 92, Feb., 1896

The Venezuelan Boundary Commission and Its Work. By Marcus Baker. VIII, pp. 193-201, July-Aug., 1897

The World's Greatest Waterfall: The Kaieteur Fall, in British Guiana. By Leonard Kennedy. XXII, pp. 846-859, 6 ills., map, Sept., 1911

BRITISH HONDURAS:

Notes on Central America. XVIII, pp. 272-279, ills., map, Apr., 1907

BRITISH ISLES:

A Geographical Description of the British Islands. (By W. M. Davis). VII, pp. 208-211, June, 1896

A Modern Pilgrim's Map of the British Isles. By Andrew H. Brown. Text with map supplement. LXXI, pp. 795-802, 3 ills., June, 1937

See also Channel Islands; Great Britain; Ireland; Man, Isle of; Orkneys; Scilly Isles; Shetland Islands; Skokholm; Wight, Isle of

BRITISH MALAYA:

The British Commonwealth of Nations: "Organized Freedom" Around the World. By Eric Underwood. LXXXIII, pp. 485-524, 31 ills., Apr., 1943

See also Singapore

BRITISH NEW GUINEA. *See* Papua

BRITISH Pacific Cable. XII, p. 78, Feb., 1901

BRITISH SOUTH AFRICA. *See* Union of South Africa

BRITISH South Africa and the Transvaal. By F. F. Hilder. XI, pp. 81-96, 7 ills., Mar., 1900

The **BRITISH** South Polar Expedition. XIV, pp. 210-212, May, 1903

The **BRITISH** Take Baku. XXXIV, pp. 163-164, ill., Aug., 1918

BRITISH WEST AFRICA:

The British Commonwealth of Nations: "Organized Freedom" Around the World. By Eric Underwood. LXXXIII, pp. 485-524, 31 ills., Apr., 1943

Notes on the Ekoi. By P. A. Talbot. XXIII, pp. 33-38, 8 ills., Jan., 1912

Three-Wheeling Through Africa: Two Adventurers Cross the So-called Dark Continent North of Lake Chad on Motorcycles with Side Cars. By James C. Wilson. LXV, pp. 37-92, 64 ills., two-page map, Jan., 1934

See also Gold Coast; Nigeria

BRITISH West Indian Interlude. By Anne Rainey Langley. LXXIX, pp. 1-46, 23 ills. in black and white, 21 ills. in color, maps, Jan., 1941

BRITISH WEST INDIES:

Americans in the Caribbean. By Luis Marden. LXXXI, pp. 723-758, 16 ills. in black and white, 22 ills. in color, map, June, 1942

The British Commonwealth of Nations: "Organized Freedom" Around the World. By Eric Underwood. LXXXIII, pp. 485-524, 31 ills., Apr., 1943

British West Indian Interlude. By Anne Rainey Langley. LXXIX, pp. 1-46, 23 ills. in black and white, 21 ills. in color, maps, Jan., 1941

See also Bahama Islands; Cayman Islands; Jamaica; St. Vincent; Trinidad

BRITISH Yukon Telegraph. XII, p. 164, Apr., 1901

BRITTANY (Region), France:

The Beauties of France. By Arthur Stanley Riggs. XXVIII, pp. 391-491, 73 ills. in black and white, 16 ills. in color, map, Nov., 1915

Brittany: The Land of the Sardine. By Hugh M. Smith. XX, pp. 541-573, 23 ills., June, 1909

The Coasts of Normandy and Brittany. By W. Robert Moore. LXXXIV, pp. 205-232, 5 ills. in black and white, 21 ills. in color, two-page map, Aug., 1943

The France of Today. By Major General A. W. Greely. XXVI, pp. 193-222, 27 ills., Sept., 1914

The Mysterious Prehistoric Monuments of Brittany. By Charles Buxton Going. XLIV, pp. 53-69, 16 ills., July, 1923

St. Malo, Ancient City of Corsairs: An Old Brittany Seaport Whose Past Bristles with Cannons and Cutlasses. By Junius B. Wood. LVI, pp. 131-177, 28 ills. in black and white, 29 ills. in color, map, Aug., 1929

Scenes from France. 16 ills. XL, pp. 29-44, July, 1921

Through the Back Doors of France: A Seven Weeks' Voyage in a Canadian Canoe from St. Malo, Through Brittany and the Château Country, to Paris. By Melville Chater. XLIV, pp. 1-51, 55 ills., map, July, 1923

Where Bretons Wrest a Living from the Sea. 23 photos by F. W. Goro. LXXI, pp. 751-766, June, 1937

BROAD, PHILIP:

Within the Halls of Cambridge (University). By Philip Broad. LXX, pp. 333-349, 7 ills. in black and white, 12 ills. in color, Sept., 1936

BROADBILL. *See* Swordfish

BROOKFIELD, CHARLES M.:

Cannon on Florida Reefs Solve Mystery of Sunken Ship. By Charles M. Brookfield. LXXX, pp. 807-824, 20 ills., map (on pen and ink drawing), Dec., 1941

BROOKLYN, New York:

Spin Your Globe to Long Island: Only Six States Have More People than the Insular Empire that Ranges from a World's Fair Through Potato Patches, Princely Estates, and Historic Shrines. By Frederick Simpich. LXXV, pp. 413-460, 25 ills. in black and white, 18 ills. in color, Apr., 1939

BROOKS, ALFRED H.:

Awarded Jane M. Smith Life Membership. XXXVII, p. 342 (footnote), Apr., 1920

The Brooks Alaskan Expedition. XIII, p. 389, Oct., 1902

The Geography of Alaska. By Alfred H. Brooks. XV, pp. 213-219, map supplement, May, 1904

How Much Is Known of Alaska. By Alfred H. Brooks. XVII, pp. 112-114, ill., map, Feb., 1906

Ice Cliffs on White River, Yukon Territory. By C. Willard Hayes and Alfred H. Brooks. XI, pp. 199-201, May, 1900

Plan for Climbing Mt. McKinley. By Alfred H. Brooks and D. L. Reaburn. XIV, pp. 30-35, map, Jan., 1903

Proposed Surveys in Alaska in 1902. By Alfred H. Brooks. XIII, pp. 133-135, map, Apr., 1902

Railway Routes in Alaska. By Alfred H. Brooks. XVIII, pp. 165-190, 9 ills., 8 maps, diagrs., Mar., 1907

Tribute to American Topographers. (By A. H. B.). XVI, p. 358, July, 1905

See also NGS: Board of Managers

BROOKS, ALLAN:

Auks and Their Northland Neighbors. 34 portraits from paintings by Maj. Allan Brooks. LXIX, pp. 101-116, Jan., 1936
Contents: Auklets, Auks, Dovekies, Guillemots, Murrelets, Murres, Puffins

Bird Beauties of the Tanager and Finch Families. 55 portraits from paintings by Maj. Allan Brooks. LXVII, pp. 513-528, Apr., 1935

Birds in Glossy Black and Vivid Color. 48 portraits from paintings by Major Allan Brooks. LXVI, pp. 113-128, July, 1934
Contents: Blackbirds, Bobolinks, Cowbirds, Flycatchers, Grackles, Meadowlarks, Orioles, Shrikes, Vireos, Waxwings

Birds of Lake and Lagoon, Marsh and Seacoast. 24 portraits from paintings by Maj. Allan Brooks. LXV, pp. 313-328, Mar., 1934
Contents: Cormorants, Grebes, Loons, Pelicans, Water Turkeys

Blithe Birds of Dooryard, Bush, and Brake. 37 portraits from paintings by Major Allan Brooks. LXV, pp. 579-594, May, 1934
Contents: Chickadees, Creepers, Dippers, Gnatcatchers, Kinglets, Nuthatches, Titmice, Wren-tits, Wrens

Bright-hued Pets of Cage and Aviary. 51 portraits from paintings by Major Allan Brooks. LXXIV, pp. 783-790, Dec., 1938

Crows, Magpies, and Jays. 17 ills. in color from paintings by Maj. Allan Brooks. LXIII, pp. 65-79, Jan., 1933

Eagles, Hawks, and Vultures. 48 ills. in color from paintings by Maj. Allan Brooks. LXIV, pp. 65-94, July, 1933

Far-Flying Wild Fowl and Their Foes. By Major Allan Brooks. With paintings from life by author. LXVI, pp. 487-528, 6 ills. in black and white, 93 portraits in color, Oct., 1934
Wild Geese, Ducks, and Swans. 93 portraits from paintings by author, pp. 493-524

Feathered Foragers of Swamp and Shore. 101 portraits from paintings by Major Allan Brooks. LXXII, pp. 191-222, Aug., 1937

BROOKS, ALLAN—*Continued*

Flycatchers and Other Friends in Feathers. 36 portraits from paintings by Maj. Allan Brooks. LXIX, pp. 807-822, June, 1936
Contents: Anis, Cuckoos, Flycatchers, Kingbirds, Kingfishers, Parakeets, Parrots, Pewees, Phoebes, Trogons

Humming Birds, Swifts and Goatsuckers. 36 ills. in color from paintings by Maj. Allan Brooks. LXII, pp. 75-88, July, 1932

Hunted Birds of Field and Wild. 60 portraits from paintings by Maj. Allan Brooks. LXX, pp. 469-500, Oct., 1936
Contents: Chacalacas, Doves, Grouse, Partridges, Pheasants, Pigeons, Prairie Chickens, Ptarmigans, Quails, Turkeys

Ibises, Herons, and Flamingos. 24 ills. in color from paintings by Maj. Allan Brooks. LXII, pp. 455-468, Oct., 1932

North American Woodpeckers. 25 ills. in color from paintings by Maj. Allan Brooks. LXIII, pp. 465-478, Apr., 1933

Silent-Winged Owls of North America. 21 portraits from paintings by Maj. Allan Brooks. LXVII, pp. 225-240, Feb., 1935

Some Songsters and Flyers of Wide Repute. 42 portraits from paintings by Maj. Allan Brooks. LXIX, pp. 529-544, Apr., 1936
Contents: Swallows, Thrashers, Thrushes

Sparrows, Towhees, and Longspurs. 43 paintings in color from life by Allan Brooks and Walter A. Weber. LXXV, pp. 361-375, Mar., 1939

Wings Over the Bounding Main (Ocean Birds). 36 portraits from paintings by Major Allan Brooks. LXXIV, pp. 237-251, Aug., 1938

BROOKS, SYDNEY:

What Great Britain Is Doing (The British War Effort). By Sydney Brooks. XXXI, pp. 193-210, 7 ills., Mar., 1917

BROUGHTON, VERA, LADY:

A Modern Dragon Hunt on Komodo: An English Yachting Party Traps and Photographs the Huge and Carnivorous Dragon Lizard of the Lesser Sundas. By Lady Broughton. LXX, pp. 321-331, 12 ills. in duotone, Sept., 1936

BROWN, ANDREW H.:

Americans Stand Guard in Greenland. By Andrew H. Brown. XC, pp. 457-500, 23 ills. in black and white, 19 ills. in color, map, Oct., 1946

Bekonscot, England's Toy-Size Town. By Andrew H. Brown and B. Anthony Stewart. LXXI, pp. 649-661, 2 ills. in black and white, 15 ills. in color, May, 1937

A Modern Pilgrim's Map of the British Isles. By Andrew H. Brown. Text with map supplement. LXXI, pp. 795-802, 3 ills., June, 1937

Salty Nova Scotia: In Friendly New Scotland Gaelic Songs Still Answer the Skirling Bagpipes. By Andrew H. Brown. LXXVII, pp. 575-624, 30 ills. in black and white, 21 ills. in color, two-page map, May, 1940

BROWN, BARNUM:

Hunting Big Game of Other Days: A Boating Expedition in Search of Fossils in Alberta, Canada. By Barnum Brown. XXXV, pp. 407-429, 24 ills., map, May, 1919

BROWN, G. M. L.:

Three Old Ports on the Spanish Main. By G. M. L. Brown. XVII, pp. 622-638, 12 ills., Nov., 1906

BROWN, H. C.:

The Indian Village of Baum (Ohio). (By H. C. Brown). XII, pp. 272-274, July 1901

BROWN, J. STANLEY. *See* Stanley-Brown, Joseph

BROWN, JOSEPHINE A.:

6,000 Miles over the Roads of Free China. By Josephine A. Brown. LXXXV, pp. 355-384, 30 ills., map, Mar., 1944

BROWN, ROBERT MARSHALL:

A Simple Method of Proving That the Earth Is Round. By Robert Marshall Brown. XVIII, pp. 771-774, 5 diagrs., Dec., 1907

BROWNE, JEFFERSON B.:

Across the Gulf by Rail to Key West (Florida). By Jefferson B. Browne. VII, pp. 203-207, June, 1896

BROWNSVILLE, Texas:

The Texas Delta of an American Nile: Orchards and Gardens Replace Thorny Jungle in the Southmost Tip of the Lone Star State. By McFall Kerbey. LXXV, pp. 51-96, 27 ills. in black and white, 24 ills. in color, map, Jan., 1939

BRUKKAROS, Mount, Africa:

Hunting an Observatory: A Successful Search for a Dry Mountain on Which to Establish the National Geographic Society's Solar Radiation Station. By C. G. Abbot. L, pp. 503-518, 13 ills., map, Oct., 1926

Keeping House for the "Shepherds of the Sun." By Mrs. William H. Hoover. LVII, pp. 483-506, 17 ills., map, Apr., 1930

BRUSSELS, Belgium:

Belgium—Europe in Miniature. By Douglas Chandler. LXXIII, pp. 397-450, 34 ills. in black and white, 20 ills. in color, Apr., 1938

BRYAN, WILLIAM JENNINGS:

Honors to Colonel Goethals: The Presentation, by President Woodrow Wilson, of the National Geographic Society Special Gold Medal, and Addresses by Secretary of State Bryan, the French Ambassador, the German Ambassador, and Congressman James R. Mann. XXV, pp. 677-690, 6 ills., June, 1914

BRYANT, HENRY G.:

A Traveler's Notes on Java. By Henry G. Bryant. XXI, pp. 91-111, 17 ills., Feb., 1910

BRYCE, JAMES:

The Discovery of the North Pole (Address by James Bryce). XXI, pp. 63-82, Jan., 1910

Honors for Amundsen (Address by James Bryce). XIX, pp. 55-76, 13 ills., Jan., 1908

Honors to Amundsen and Peary (Address by James Bryce). XXIV, pp. 113-130, 5 ills., Jan., 1913

Impressions of Palestine. By James Bryce. XXVII, pp. 293-317, 18 ills., map, Mar., 1915

In Honor of the Army and Aviation (Address by James Bryce). XXII, pp. 267-284, ill., Mar., 1911

BRYCE, JAMES—*Continued*

The National Geographic Society (Announcing the Election of James Bryce, British Ambassador, as an Honorary Member of the Society). XXIII, pp. 272-298, 5 ills., Mar., 1912

The Nation's Capital (Washington, D. C.). By James Bryce. XXIV, pp. 717-750, 26 ills., June, 1913

The Scenery of North America. By James Bryce. XLI, pp. 339-389, 45 ills., Apr., 1922

Two Possible Solutions for the Eastern Problem. By James Bryce. XXIII, pp. 1149-1157, 5 ills., map, Nov., 1912

Western Siberia and the Altai Mountains: With Some Speculations on the Future of Siberia. By James Bryce. XXXIX, pp. 469-507, 39 ills., May, 1921

BRYCE CANYON NATIONAL PARK, Utah:

Bursts of Color in Sculptured Utah. 22 ills. in color. LXIX, pp. 593-616, May, 1936

Photographing the Marvels of the West in Colors. By Fred Payne Clatworthy. LIII, pp. 694-719, 8 ills. in color, June, 1928

BUBONIC PLAGUE:

The Conquest of Bubonic Plague in the Philippines. XIV, pp. 185-195, 7 ills., May, 1903

Fearful Famines of the Past: History Will Repeat Itself Unless the American People Conserve Their Resources. By Ralph A. Graves. XXXII, pp. 69-90, 11 ills., July, 1917

Geographic Miscellanea. XI, p. 248, map, June, 1900

The History and Geographic Distribution of Bubonic Plague. By George M. Sternberg. XI, pp. 97-113, Mar., 1900

See also Rats

BUCHAN, SUSAN CHARLOTTE (Lady Tweedsmuir):

Tweedsmuir Park: The Diary of a Pilgrimage. By The Lady Tweedsmuir of Elsfield. LXXIII, pp. 451-476, 22 ills., maps, Apr., 1938

BUCHAREST, Romania:

Roumania, the Pivotal State. By James Howard Gore. XXVIII, pp. 360-390, 32 ills., Oct., 1915

Roumania and Its Rubicon. By John Oliver La Gorce. XXX, pp. 185-202, 11 ills., Sept., 1916

BUCKLE, H. T.:

The Geologic Atlas of the United States. (By W J M.). IX, pp. 339-342, July, 1898

BUDAPEST, Hungary:

Budapest, Twin City of the Danube. By J. R. Hildebrand. LXI, pp. 729-742, 3 ills. in black and white, 10 ills. in duotone, June, 1932

Hungary: A Land of Shepherd Kings. By C. Townley-Fullam. XXVI, pp. 311-393, 92 ills., map, Oct., 1914

Saint Stephen's Fete in Budapest. By De Witt Clinton Falls. XVIII, pp. 548-558, 9 ills., Aug., 1907

A Tale of Three Cities. By Thomas R. Henry. LXXXVIII, pp. 641-669, 23 ills., Dec., 1945

BUDDHISM:

Adam's Second Eden (Ceylon). By Eliza Ruhamah Scidmore. XXIII, pp. 105-173, 206, 61 ills., Feb., 1912

BUDDHISM—*Continued*

China's Great Wall of Sculpture: Man-hewn Caves and Countless Images Form a Colossal Art Wonder of Early Buddhism. By Mary Augusta Mullikin. Paintings by author and Anna M. Hotchkis. LXXIII, pp. 313-348, 23 ills. in black and white, 10 ills. in color, map, Mar., 1938

In the Diamond Mountains: Adventures Among the Buddhist Monasteries of Eastern Korea. By the Marquess Curzon of Kedleston. XLVI, pp. 353-374, 21 ills., map, Oct., 1924

Koyasan, the Japanese Valhalla. By Eliza R. Scidmore. XVIII, pp. 650-670, 14 ills., Oct., 1907

Puto, the Enchanted Island. By Robert F. Fitch. LXXXIX, pp. 373-384, 11 ills., map, Mar., 1946

The Sacred Tooth (of Buddha). XVIII, ill. p. 745, Nov., 1907

See also Lamaism

BUDDHIST Calm Survives Along China's Great Wall. 10 ills. in color: 4 paintings by Mary Augusta Mullikin and Anna M. Hotchkis. LXXIII, pp. 321-328, Mar., 1938

BUENOS AIRES, Argentina:

Buenos Aires: Queen of the River of Silver. By Maynard Owen Williams. LXXVI, pp. 561-600, 22 ills. in black and white, 24 ills. in color, map, Nov., 1939

Buenos Aires and Its River of Silver: A Journey Up the Paraná and Paraguay to the Chaco Cattle Country. By William R. Barbour. XL, pp. 393-432, 38 ills., Oct., 1921

Buenos Aires to Washington by Horse: A Solitary Journey of Two and a Half Years, Through Eleven American Republics, Covers 9,600 Miles of Mountain and Plain, Desert and Jungle. By A. F. Tschiffely. LV, pp. 135-196, 75 ills., map, Feb., 1929

The Fertile Pampas of Argentine. XVII, pp. 453-456, Aug., 1906

The First Transandine Railroad from Buenos Aires to Valparaiso. By Harriet Chalmers Adams. XXI, pp. 397-417, 14 ills., diagr., map, May, 1910

BUENOS AIRES—Metropolis of the Pampas. 24 color photos by Luis Marden, Maynard Owen Williams, W. Robert Moore. LXXVI, pp. 577-600, Nov., 1939

BUFFALO, New York:

The American Association (for the Advancement of Science) at Buffalo. VII, pp. 315-316, Sept., 1896

BUFFALO, American. *See* Bison

BUILDING America's Air Army. By Hiram Bingham. XXXIII, pp. 48-86, 43 ills., Jan., 1918

BUILDING the Alaskan Telegraph System. By Captain William Mitchell. XV, pp. 357-361, Sept., 1904

BUILDINGS. *See* Architecture; NGS: Buildings

BUKHARA, U. S. S. R.:

The Land of Lambskins: An Expedition to Bokhara, Russian Central Asia, to Study the Karakul Sheep Industry. By Robert K. Nabours. XXXVI, pp. 77-88, 15 ills., July, 1919

BUKHARA, U. S. S. R.—*Continued*

Russia's Orphan Races: Picturesque Peoples Who Cluster on the Southeastern Borderland of the Vast Slav Dominions. By Maynard Owen Williams. XXXIV, pp. 245-278, 26 ills., map, Oct., 1918

BULAWAYO, Southern Rhodesia:

Rhodesia, Hobby and Hope of Cecil Rhodes. By W. Robert Moore. LXXXVI, pp. 281-306, 13 ills. in black and white, 10 ills. in color, map, Sept., 1944

BULGARIA:

Bulgaria, Farm Land Without a Farmhouse: A Nation of Villagers Faces the Challenge of Modern Machinery and Urban Life. By Maynard Owen Williams. LXII, pp. 185-218, 19 ills. in black and white, 27 ills. in color, Aug., 1932

Bulgaria, the Peasant State. XIX, pp. 760-773, 14 ills., Nov., 1908

Bulgaria and Its Women. By Hester Donaldson Jenkins. XXVII, pp. 377-400, 22 ills., Apr., 1915

The Changing Map in the Balkans. By Frederick Moore. XXIV, pp. 199-226, 27 ills., map, Feb., 1913

Flags of Austria-Hungary, Bulgaria, Germany, and Turkey. By Byron McCandless and Gilbert Grosvenor. XXXII, pp. 386-388, 38 ills. in color, Oct., 1917

The Great Turk and His Lost Provinces. By William E. Curtis. XIV, pp. 45-61, 7 ills., Feb., 1903

The Races of Europe. By Edwin A. Grosvenor. XXXIV, pp. 441-534, 62 ills., diagr. and index, maps, map supplement, Dec., 1918

The Rise of Bulgaria. By James D. Bourchier. XXIII, pp. 1105-1118, 13 ills., Nov., 1912

The Whirlpool of the Balkans. By George Higgins Moses. XXXIX, pp. 179-197, 15 ills., Feb., 1921

See also Tirnova

BULGARIA'S Valley of Roses. 13 color photos by Wilhelm Tobien and Georg Paskoff. LXII, pp. 187-194, Aug., 1932

BULHAK, JAN:

Wilno, Stepchild of the Polish Frontier. 13 ills. in duotone: 8 by Jan Bulhak. LXXIII, pp. 777-784, June, 1938

BULL-FIGHTING:

Camargue, the Cowboy Country of Southern France. By Dr. André Vialles. XLII, pp. 1-34, 33 ills., map, July, 1922

BUMSTEAD, ALBERT H.:

Appointed Chief Cartographer, National Geographic Society. LXIX, p. 130, Jan., 1936

Inventor of the sun-compass, used by Admiral Richard E. Byrd on polar flights. XLVIII, p. 523, ill. p. 520, Nov., 1925. L, pp. 367, 381, ill. p. 378, Sept., 1926. LII, p. 238, ill. p. 242, Aug., 1927. LVIII, p. 233, Aug., 1930. LXIX, p. 130, Jan., 1936

BURACKER, WILLIAM H.:

Saga of the Carrier *Princeton*. By Capt. William H. Buracker, USN. LXXXVIII, pp. 189-218, 8 ills. in black and white, 22 ills. in color, map, Aug., 1945

BURBANK, J. E.:

The San Francisco Earthquake of April 18, 1906, as Recorded by the Coast and Geodetic Survey Magnetic Observatories. By L. A. Bauer and J. E. Burbank. XVII, pp. 298-300, tables, May, 1906

BURDEKIN, H. B.:

Shadowy London by Night. 8 ills. by H. B. Burdekin. LXVIII, pp. 177-184, Aug., 1935

BURDEN, W. DOUGLAS:

Stalking the Dragon Lizard on the Island of Komodo. By W. Douglas Burden. LII, pp. 216-232, 21 ills., Aug., 1927

The **BURDEN** France Has Borne. By Granville Fortescue. XXXI, pp. 323-344, 19 ills., Apr., 1917

BURDSALL, RICHARD L.:

Climbing Mighty Minya Konka: Americans First Scaled Mountain That Now Is Landmark of China's New Skyway. By Richard L. Burdsall and Terris Moore. LXXXIII, pp. 625-650, 23 ills., map, May, 1943

The **BUREAU** of Fisheries: How the Rich Fisheries of the United States Are Protected and New Fishing Grounds Discovered or Created. By Dr. Barton Warren Evermann. XV, pp. 191-212, 11 ills., 3 diagrs., May, 1904

BURG, AMOS:

Alaska—Our Northwestern Outpost. 16 color photos by Ernest H. Gruening, Amos Burg, Froelich Rainey. LXXXII, pp. 297-308, Sept., 1942

Britain Just Before the Storm: A Canadian Canoe Threads Old English Waterways Athrob with the Midlands' Industrial Life. By Amos Burg. LXXVIII, pp. 185-212, 14 ills. in black and white, 9 ills. in color, map, Aug., 1940

Canals and Pageants of Peacetime England. 9 color photos: 6 by author, pp. 197-204

Color Glimpses of the Changing South Seas. 14 color photos by Amos Burg. LXV, pp. 281-288, Mar., 1934

Inside Cape Horn. By Amos Burg. LXXII, pp. 743-783, 29 ills. in black and white, 10 ills. in color, two-page map, Dec., 1937

Land of the Horn, America's Tiptoe. 10 color photos by author, pp. 751-758

A Native Son's Rambles in Oregon. By Amos Burg. LXV, pp. 173-234, 39 ills. in black and white, 24 ills. in color, two-page map, Feb., 1934

Scenes and Round-Ups of the Beaver State. 24 color photos by author, pp. 181-212

On Mackenzie's Trail to the Polar Sea. By Amos Burg. LX, pp. 127-156, 32 ills., map, Aug., 1931

To-day on "The Yukon Trail of 1898." By Amos Burg. LVIII, pp. 85-126, 52 ills., map, July, 1930

BURIAL MOUNDS:

Indians of the Southeastern United States. By Matthew W. Stirling. Paintings by W. Langdon Kihn. LXXXIX, pp. 53-74, 8 ills. in black and white, 8 ills. in color, Jan., 1946

BURIAL SHIP:

Ancestor of the British Navy: England's Oldest Known War Vessel Is Unearthed, Laden with Remarkable Treasures of an Anglo-Saxon Ruler. By C. W. Phillips. LXXIX, pp. 247-268, 22 ills., 4 drawings, Feb., 1941

The **BURIED** Cities of Asia Minor. By Ernest L. Harris. XX, pp. 1-18, 10 ills., Jan., 1909

The **BURIED** City of Ceylon. By John M. Abbot. XVII, pp. 613-622, 8 ills., Nov., 1906

BURKE, ERIC KEAST:

Modern Life in the Cradle of Civilization (Iraq). 16 color photos by Eric Keast Burke. XLI, pp. 390-407, Apr., 1922

BURKE, WALTER:

Hurdle Racing in Canoes: A Thrilling and Spectacular Sport Among the Maoris of New Zealand. By Walter Burke. XXXVII, pp. 440-444, 6 ills., May, 1920

BURLESON, MRS. ALBERT S.:

Wandering Islands in the Rio Grande. By Mrs. Albert S. Burleson. XXIV, pp. 381-386, ills., map, Mar., 1913

BURMA:

The Aerial Invasion of Burma. By General H. H. Arnold. LXXXVI, pp. 129-148, 20 ills., Aug., 1944

Among the Hill Tribes of Burma—An Ethnological Thicket. By Sir George Scott. XLI, pp. 293-321, 22 ills., Mar., 1922

The British Commonwealth of Nations: "Organized Freedom" Around the World. By Eric Underwood. LXXXIII, pp. 485-524, 31 ills., Apr., 1943

Burma: Where India and China Meet: In the Massive Mountains of Southeast Asia, Swarming Road Builders Wage the "War of the Highways" for Free China and Her Allies. By John LeRoy Christian. LXXXIV, pp. 489-512, 18 ills., map, Oct., 1943

Burma Road, Back Door to China: Like the Great Wall of Ancient Times, This Mighty Mountain Highway Has Been Built by Myriad Chinese to Help Defend Their Homeland. By Frank Outram and G. E. Fane. LXXVIII, pp. 629-658, 26 ills., map, Nov., 1940

The Five Thousand Temples of Pagān: Burma's Sacred City Is a Place of Enchantment in the Midst of Ruins. By William H. Roberts. LX, pp. 445-454, 9 ills., Oct., 1931

Hunting the Chaulmoogra Tree. By Joseph F. Rock. XLI, pp. 243-276, 39 ills., map, Mar., 1922

Notes on Burma. By Thomas Barbour. XX, pp. 841-866, 34 ills., Oct., 1909

Shan Tribes Make Burma's Hills Flash with Color. 15 color photos by W. Robert Moore. LX, pp. 455-462, Oct., 1931

The Society's New Map of India and Burma. Text with map supplement. LXXXIX, p. 544, Apr., 1946

Stilwell Road—Land Route to China. By Nelson Grant Tayman. LXXXVII, pp. 681-698, 18 ills., June, 1945

Untoured Burma. By Charles H. Bartlett. XXIV, pp. 835-853, 17 ills., July, 1913

Working Teak in the Burma Forests: The Sagacious Elephant Is Man's Ablest Ally in the Logging Industry of the Far East. By A. W. Smith. LVIII, pp. 239-256, 5 ills. in black and white, 15 ills. in color, Aug., 1930

Yank Meets Native. By Wanda Burnett. LXXXVIII, pp. 105-128, 24 ills., July, 1945

BURMA ROAD:

Burma: Where India and China Meet: In the Massive Mountains of Southeast Asia, Swarming Road Builders Wage the "War of the Highways" for Free China and Her Allies. By John LeRoy Christian. LXXXIV, pp. 489-512, 18 ills., map, Oct., 1943

Burma Road, Back Door to China: Like the Great Wall of Ancient Times, This Mighty Mountain Highway Has Been Built by Myriad Chinese to Help Defend Their Homeland. By Frank Outram and G. E. Fane. LXXVIII, pp. 629-658, 26 ills., map, Nov., 1940

China Opens Her Wild West: In the Mountain-girt Heart of a Continent a New China Has Been Created During the Years of War. By Owen Lattimore. LXXXII, pp. 337-367, 21 ills. in black and white, 11 ills. in color, map, Sept., 1942

Stilwell Road—Land Route to China. By Nelson Grant Tayman. LXXXVII, pp. 681-698, 18 ills., June, 1945

BURNETT, WANDA:

Cape Cod People and Places. By Wanda Burnett. LXXXIX, pp. 737-774, 17 ills. in black and white, 24 ills. in color, map, June, 1946

What the Fighting Yanks See. By Wanda Burnett. LXXXVI, pp. 451-476, 27 ills., Oct., 1944

Yank Meets Native. By Wanda Burnett. LXXXVIII, pp. 105-128, 24 ills., July, 1945

BURNING the Roads. XVII, pp. 583-586, 4 ills., Oct., 1906

BURPEE, LAWRENCE J.:

Canada's Awakening North. By Lawrence J. Burpee. LXIX, pp. 749-768, 18 ills., June, 1936

New Brunswick Down by the Sea. By Lawrence J. Burpee. LXXIX, pp. 595-614, 14 ills., map, May, 1941

BURR, FRANKLIN L.:

Franklin L. Burr Prize established under the bequest of the late Mary C. Burr, in memory of her father, awarded to Capt. Albert W. Stevens. LXV, p. 626, May, 1934

BURR, MARY C.:

Fund bequeathed to the Society by Mary C. Burr. LXV, p. 626, May, 1934

BURR, WILLIAM H.:

The Republic of Panama. By Wm. H. Burr. XV, pp. 57-73, 7 ills., Feb., 1904

BURRALL, JESSIE L.:

Sight-Seeing in School: Taking Twenty Million Children on a Picture Tour of the World. By Jessie L. Burrall. XXXV, pp. 489-503, 14 ills., June, 1919

BURRITT, CHARLES H.:

The Mining Bureau of the Philippine Islands. By Charles H. Burritt. XIV, pp. 418-419, Nov., 1903

BURROUGHS, G. H. G.:

The Perahera Processions of Ceylon. By G. H. G. Burroughs. LXII, pp. 90-100, ill. in black and white, 8 ills. in duotone, July, 1932

BURSTS of Color in Sculptured Utah. 22 ills. in color. LXIX, pp. 593-616, May, 1936

BURTON, A. E.:

Organized scientific party, visiting Greenland, 1896. VIII, p. 97, Apr., 1897

BURTON, THEODORE:

Honors for Amundsen (Address by Theodore Burton). XIX, pp. 55-76, 13 ills., Jan., 1908

BURYAT-MONGOL AUTONOMOUS SOVIET SOCIALIST REPUBLIC, R. S. F. S. R.:

New Road to Asia. By Owen Lattimore. LXXXVI, pp. 641-676, 15 ills. in black and white, 26 ills. in color, Dec., 1944

BURYATS (People):

New Road to Asia. By Owen Lattimore. LXXXVI, pp. 641-676, 15 ills. in black and white, 26 ills. in color, Dec., 1944

BUSY Corner—the Cape of Good Hope: Ships Bound for Faraway Battlegrounds Stream Past Capetown, "Tavern of the Seas," and Other Ports of Virile South Africa. By W. Robert Moore. LXXXII, pp. 197-223, 11 ills. in black and white, 11 ills. in color, map, Aug., 1942

BUTTER Exports from Siberia. XIII, p. 34, Jan., 1902

BUTTER FESTIVAL:

Life Among the Lamas of Choni: Describing the Mystery Plays and Butter Festival in the Monastery of an Almost Unknown Tibetan Principality in Kansu Province, China. By Joseph F. Rock. LIV, pp. 569-619, 34 ills. in black and white, 16 ills. in color, map, Nov., 1928

BUTTERFLIES:

Butterflies—Try and Get Them. By Laurence Ilsley Hewes. LXIX, pp. 667-678, 10 ills., May, 1936

Butterfly Travelers: Some Varieties Migrate Thousands of Miles. By C. B. Williams. Paintings by Hashime Murayama. LXXI, pp. 568-585, ill. in black and white, 8 ills. in color, May, 1937

The Monsters of Our Back Yards. By David Fairchild. XXIV, pp. 575-626, 38 ills., May, 1913

Strange Habits of Familiar Moths and Butterflies. By William Joseph Showalter. LII, pp. 77-105, 19 ills. in black and white, drawing, 88 ills. in color, July, 1927

Contents: Danaidae, Hesperiidae, Lycaenidae, Nymphalidae, Papilionidae, Pieridae, Satyridae

Where Our Moths and Butterflies Roam. LII, pp. 105-126, 8 ills. in black and white, 81 ills. in color, July, 1927

Who's Who Among the Butterflies. By Austin H. Clark. Paintings by Hashime Murayama. LXIX, pp. 679-692, 5 ills. in black and white, 9 ills. in color, May, 1936

BUTTERFLY Travelers: Some Varieties Migrate Thousands of Miles. By C. B. Williams. Paintings by Hashime Murayama. LXXI, pp. 568-585, ill. in black and white, 8 ills. in color, May, 1937

BUXTON, B. H.:

A Corner of Old Württemberg (Germany). By B. H. Buxton. XXII, pp. 931-947, 17 ills., map, Oct., 1911

BUYSSENS, A.:

Beautiful Belgium, Restored by Peace. 5 color photos by A. Buyssens. LVI, pp. 555-562, Nov., 1929

Tulip Time in the Netherlands. 10 color photos by Wilhelm Tobien and A. Buyssens. LXIV, pp. 325-332, Sept., 1933

BW-1. *See* Weather Stations (Greenland)

BY Car and Steamer Around Our Inland Seas. By Maynard Owen Williams. LXV, pp. 451-491, 29 ills. in black and white, 8 ills. in duotone, two-page map, Apr., 1934

BY Coolie and Caravan Across Central Asia: Narrative of a 7,900-Mile Journey of Exploration and Research Over "the Roof of the World," from the Indian Ocean to the Yellow Sea. By William J. Morden. LII, pp. 369-431, 73 ills., map, Oct., 1927

BY Felucca Down the Nile: Giant Dams Rule Egypt's Lifeline River, Yet Village Life Goes On As It Did in the Time of the Pharaohs. By Willard Price. LXXVII, pp. 435-476, 21 ills. in black and white, 22 ills. in color, two-page map, Apr., 1940

BY Motor Through the East Coast and Batak Highlands of Sumatra. By Melvin A. Hall. XXXVII, pp. 69-102, 27 ills., Jan., 1920

BY Motor Trail Across French Indo-China. By Maynard Owen Williams. LXVIII, pp. 487-534, 31 ills. in black and white, 27 ills. in color, map, Oct., 1935

BY Sail Across Europe. By Merlin Minshall. LXXI, pp. 533-567, 38 ills., map, May, 1937

BY Seaplane to Six Continents: Cruising 60,000 Miles, Italian Argonauts of the Air See World Geography Unroll, and Break New Sky Trails Over Vast Brazilian Jungles. By Commander Francesco de Pinedo. LIV, pp. 247-301, 60 ills., two-page map, Sept., 1928

BYAGHA (Castle), Bhutan:

Castles in the Air: Experiences and Journeys in Unknown Bhutan. By John Claude White. XXV, pp. 365-455, 74 ills., map, Apr., 1914

BY-LAWS. *See* NGS: By-laws

BYRD, RICHARD EVELYN:

Admiral Byrd Receives New Honor From The Society (Presentation of Special Gold Medal). LVIII, pp. 228-238, 4 ills., Aug., 1930

Air Conquest: From the Early Days of Giant Kites and Birdlike Gliders, the National Geographic Society Has Aided and Encouraged the Growth of Aviation. LII, pp. 233-242, 13 ills., Aug., 1927

Commander Byrd at the North Pole. Reproduction in color of the painting by N. C. Wyeth, National Geographic Society, Washington, D. C. LIII, supplement, May, 1928

Commander Byrd Receives the Hubbard Gold Medal: The First Explorer to Reach the North Pole by Air Receives Coveted Honor at Brilliant National Geographic Society Reception (Address by Comdr. Byrd). L, pp. 377-388, 5 ills., chart, Sept., 1926

BYRD, RICHARD EVELYN—*Continued*

The Conquest of Antarctica by Air. By Richard Evelyn Byrd. LVIII, pp. 127-227, 71 ills. in black and white, 16 ills. in gravure, map, Aug., 1930

Exploring the Ice Age in Antarctica. By Richard Evelyn Byrd. LXVIII, pp. 399-474, 72 ills., maps (1 two-page), Oct., 1935

The First Flight to the North Pole. By Lieutenant Commander Richard Evelyn Byrd. L, pp. 357-376, 14 ills., Sept., 1926

Flying Over the Arctic. By Lieutenant Commander Richard E. Byrd. XLVIII, pp. 519-532, 10 ills., Nov., 1925

National Geographic Society Honors Byrd Antarctic Expedition. LXVIII, pp. 107-114, 6 ills., July, 1935

Our Transatlantic Flight. By Commander Richard Evelyn Byrd. LII, pp. 347-368, 17 ills., map, Sept., 1927

The Society Takes Part in Three Geographic Expeditions. LXV, pp. 625-626, May, 1934

See also NGS: Medals: Hubbard Medal

BYRD ANTARCTIC EXPEDITIONS:

Admiral Byrd Receives New Honor From The Society. LVIII, pp. 228-238, 4 ills., Aug., 1930

The Conquest of Antarctica by Air. By Richard Evelyn Byrd. LVIII, pp. 127-227, 71 ills. in black and white, 16 ills. in gravure, map, Aug., 1930

Antarctica by Sea, Land and Air. 16 ills. in gravure from photos by the Byrd Antarctic Expedition, pp. 159-206

Exploring the Ice Age in Antarctica. By Richard Evelyn Byrd. LXVIII, pp. 399-474, 72 ills., maps (1 two-page), Oct., 1935

Mapping the Antarctic from the Air: The Aërial Camera Earns Its Place as the Eyes and Memory of the Explorer. By Capt. Ashley C. McKinley. LXII, pp. 471-485, 13 ills., map supplement, Oct., 1932

The Society Takes Part in Three Geographic Expeditions. LXV, pp. 625-626, May, 1934

The Society's Special Medal Is Awarded to Dr. Thomas C. Poulter: Admiral Byrd's Second-in-Command and Senior Scientist Is Accorded High Geographic Honor. LXXII, pp. 105-108, ills., July, 1937

BYRNE, DONN:

Ireland: The Rock Whence I Was Hewn. By Donn Byrne. LI, pp. 257-326, 68 ills. in black and white, 11 ills. in color, map, Mar., 1927

BYROADS and Backwoods of Manchuria: Where Violent Contrasts of Modernism and Unaltered Ancient Tradition Clash. By Owen Lattimore. LXI, pp. 101-130, 27 ills., map, Jan., 1932

BYZANTIUM:

Constantinople Today. By Solita Solano. XLI, pp. 647-680, 40 ills., map, June, 1922

C

CABIN JOHN, Maryland:

The Washington Aqueduct and Cabin John Bridge. By D. D. Gaillard. VIII, pp. 337-344, ills., Dec., 1897

CABLES:

British Pacific Cable. XII, p. 78, Feb., 1901

The completion of the cable between Canada and Australia. XIII, p. 410, Nov., 1902

German Submarine Cable System. XII, p. 163, Apr., 1901

Girdling the Globe. XV, p. 236, May, 1904

The Influence of Submarine Cables Upon Military and Naval Supremacy. By Capt. George O. Squier. XII, pp. 1-12, Jan., 1901

New French Ocean Cables. XII, pp. 315-316, Aug., 1901

Peter Cooper and Submarine Telegraphy. VII, pp. 108-110, Mar., 1896

The Russo-American Telegraph Project of 1864-'67. By Professor William H. Dall. VII, pp. 110-111, ill., Mar., 1896

The Submarine Cables of the World. By Gustave Herrle. With chart compiled by U.S. Hydrographic Office. VII, pp. 102-107, Mar., 1896

The United States Government Telegraph and Cable Lines. XV, pp. 490-494, 3 maps, Dec., 1904

The World's Highest International Telephone Cable. LVIII, pp. 722-731, 8 ills., Dec., 1930

CABRILLO, JUAN RODRIGUEZ:

Early Voyages on the Northwestern Coast of America. By Professor George Davidson. V, pp. 235-256, Jan. 31, 1894

CACAO INDUSTRY:

São Tomé, the Chocolate Island. By William Leon Smyser. LXXXIX, pp. 657-680, 23 ills., map, May, 1946

CACTI:

Arizona Sands, Home of the Cactus King. 11 ills. LXXI, pp. 521-528, Apr., 1937

Canyons and Cacti of the American Southwest. 22 color photos by Edwin L. Wisherd, Jacob Gayer, Charles Martin. XLVIII, pp. 275-290, Sept., 1925

Fantastic Plants of Our Western Deserts. 8 ills. by Frank M. Campbell. XLV, pp. 33-40, Jan., 1924

A Land of Drought and Desert—Lower California: Two Thousand Miles on Horseback Through the Most Extraordinary Cacti Forests in the World. By E. W. Nelson. XXII, pp. 443-474, 25 ills., maps, May, 1911

Notes on the Deserts of the United States and Mexico (Extracted from a Publication of Dr. Daniel T. MacDougal). XXI, pp. 691-714, 16 ills., Aug., 1910

Utilizing the Desert. XVI, pp. 242-244, 3 ills., May, 1905

See also Saguaro

CADETS. *See* Aviation Cadets; West Point

CADIZ, Spain:

Adventurous Sons of Cádiz. By Harriet Chalmers Adams. XLVI, pp. 153-204, 37 ills. in black and white, 26 ills. in color, Aug., 1924

CAESAR'S City Today (Rome). 21 color photos by Bernard F. Rogers, Jr. and Luigi Pellerano. LXXI, pp. 285-316, Mar., 1937

CAETANI, GELASIO:

Redemption of the Pontine Marshes: By Draining the Malarial Wastes Around Rome, Italy Has Created a Promised Land. By Gelasio Caetani. LXVI, pp. 201-217, 9 ills. in black and white, 12 ills. in color, map, Aug., 1934

The Story and the Legends of the Pontine Marshes: After Many Centuries of Fruitless Effort, Italy Is to Inaugurate a Gigantic Enterprise to Drain the Fertile Region Southeast of Rome. By Don Gelasio Caetani. XLV, pp. 357-374, 18 ills., Apr., 1924

CAHALANE, VICTOR H.:

Deer of the World: As Workers, Pets, and Graceful "Living Statuary" in Parks and Estates, These Versatile Creatures Have Endeared Themselves to Mankind. By Victor H. Cahalane. Paintings by Walter A. Weber. LXXVI, pp. 463-510, 20 ills. in black and white, 23 ills. in color, Oct., 1939

King of Cats and His Court (Leopards, Lions, and Tigers). By Victor H. Cahalane. Paintings by Walter A. Weber. LXXXIII, pp. 217-259, 9 ills. in black and white, 20 ills. in color, Feb., 1943

CAHUILLA, Lake, California:

Lake Cahuilla: The Ancient Lake of the Colorado Desert. XVIII, p. 830, Dec., 1907

CAIRO, Egypt:

American Alma Maters in the Near East. By Maynard Owen Williams. LXXXVIII, pp. 237-256, 16 ills., Aug., 1945

American Fighters Visit Bible Lands. By Maynard Owen Williams. With 23 color photos by author. LXXXIX, pp. 311-340, 10 ills. in black and white, Mar., 1946

Cairo to Cape Town, Overland: An Adventurous Journey of 135 Days, Made by an American Man and His Wife, Through the Length of the African Continent. By Felix Shay. XLVII, pp. 123-260, 118 ills., map, Feb., 1925

Red Cross Girl Overseas. By Margaret Cotter. LXXXVI, pp. 745-768, 22 ills., Dec., 1944

CALABRIA (Department), Italy:

A Country Where Going to America Is an Industry (Sicily). By Arthur H. Warner. XX, pp. 1063-1102, 41 ills., Dec., 1909

Daily Life in Calabria. 16 ills. XLIII, pp. 181-196, Feb., 1923

CALCULATIONS of Population in June, 1900. By Henry Farquhar. X, pp. 406-413, Oct., 1899

CALCUTTA, India:

Through the Heart of Hindustan: A Teeming Highway Extending for Fifteen Hundred Miles, from the Khyber Pass to Calcutta. By Maynard Owen Williams. XL, pp. 433-467, 29 ills., Nov., 1921

CALDERON, ALFREDO ALVAREZ:

Peru—Its Resources, Development, and Future. By Alfredo Alvarez Calderon. XV, pp. 311-323, Aug., 1904

CALDERON, IGNACIO:

Bolivia—A Country Without a Debt. By Y. Calderon. XVIII, pp. 573-586, 4 ills., Sept., 1907

CALDERON, IGNACIO—*Continued*

What the Latin American Republics Think of the Pan-American Conferences (Address by Ignacio Calderon). XVII, pp. 474-479, Aug., 1906

CALI, Colombia:

Over the Andes to Bogotá. By Frank M. Chapman. XL, pp. 353-373, 19 ills., Oct., 1921

CALICUT, India:

The Pathfinder of the East: Setting Sail to Find "Christians and Spices," Vasco da Gama Met Amazing Adventures, Founded an Empire, and Changed the History of Western Europe. By J. R. Hildebrand. LII, pp. 503-550, 43 ills., map, pictorial supplement, Nov., 1927

Vasco da Gama at the Court of the Zamorin of Calicut. Reproduction in color of the painting by José Velloso Salgado, Sociedade de Geographia de Lisboa (supplement)

CALIFORNIA:

Among the Big Trees of California. By John R. White. LXVI, pp. 219-232, 14 ills., Aug., 1934

Befriending Nature's Children: An Experiment With Some of California's Wild Folk. By Agnes Akin Atkinson. LXI, pp. 199-215, 26 ills., Feb., 1932

Bringing the World to Our Foreign-Language Soldiers: How a Military Training Camp is Solving a Seemingly Unsurmountable Problem by Using the Geographic. By Christina Krysto. XXXIV, pp. 81-90, 4 ills., Aug., 1918

California. By the Hon. George C. Perkins. VII, pp. 317-327, Oct., 1896

California, Our Lady of Flowers. By Chapin Hall. LV, pp. 703-750, 20 ills. in black and white, 30 ills. in color, June, 1929

The California and Nevada Boundary. (By C. H. Sinclair). X, pp. 416-417, Oct., 1899

The California Earthquake. XVII, pp. 325-343, 27 ills., June, 1906

California Says It with Wild Flowers. By Francis Woodworth. With 9 color photos by B. Anthony Stewart. LXXXI, pp. 492-501, Apr., 1942

California's Coastal Redwood Realm: Along a Belt of Tall Trees a Giant Bridge Speeds the Winning of Our Westernmost Frontier. By J. R. Hildebrand. LXXV, pp. 133-184, 31 ills. in black and white, 17 ills. in color, map, Feb., 1939

Carrying Water Through a Desert: The Story of the Los Angeles Aqueduct. By Burt A. Heinly. XXI, pp. 568-596, 19 ills., map, July, 1910

The Colorado Desert. By David P. Barrows. XI, pp. 337-351, 4 ills., map, Sept., 1900

The Colorado Desert. By W. C. Mendenhall. XX, pp. 681-701, 16 ills., Aug., 1909

Crater Lake and Yosemite Through the Ages. By Wallace W. Atwood, Jr. Paintings by Eugene Kingman. LXXI, pp. 327-343, 7 ills. in black and white, 13 ills. in color, Mar., 1937

The Deserts of Nevada and the Death Valley. By Robert H. Chapman. XVII, pp. 483-497, 9 ills., map, Sept., 1906

Early Voyages on the Northwestern Coast of America. By Professor George Davidson. V, pp. 235-256, Jan. 31, 1894

CALIFORNIA—*Continued*

Forestry in California. XVI, pp. 480-481, Oct., 1905

The Glass-Bottom Boat. By Charles Frederick Holder. XX, pp. 761-778, 17 ills., Sept., 1909

Irrigation in California. By Wm. Hammond Hall. I, pp. 277-290, Oct., 1889

Lake Cahuilla: The Ancient Lake of the Colorado Desert. XVIII, p. 830, Dec., 1907

The Land of the Best. By Gilbert H. Grosvenor. XXIX, pp. 327-430, 71 ills. in black and white, 33 ills. in color, pictorial supplement, Apr., 1916

Lowest Point in the United States (Death Valley). XVIII, pp. 824-825, Dec., 1907

The Magic Mountain (Mount Wilson). By J. N. Patterson. XIX, pp. 457-468, 9 ills., July, 1908

The Man Without the Hoe. XXI, pp. 967-969, ills., Nov., 1910

A Mind's-Eye Map of America. By Franklin K. Lane. XXXVII, pp. 479-518, 25 ills. in black and white, 8 ills. in color, June, 1920

More Water for California's Great Central Valley. By Frederick Simpich. XC, pp. 645-664, 16 ills., map, Nov., 1946

The National Geographic Society Completes Its Gifts of Big Trees. XL, pp. 85-86, July, 1921

The New Inland Sea (Salton Sea). By Arthur P. Davis. XVIII, pp. 37-49, 8 ills., map, Jan., 1907

Northern California at Work. By Frederick Simpich. LXIX, pp. 309-389, 36 ills. in black and white, 41 ills. in color, maps (1 two-page), Mar., 1936

Oil Fields of Texas and California. XII, pp. 276-278, July, 1901

The Origin of Yosemite Valley. (By Henry Gannett). XII, pp. 86-87, Feb., 1901

Ostrich Farming in the United States. XVII, pp. 569-574, 6 ills., Oct., 1906

Our Big Trees Saved. XXXI, pp. 1-11, 10 ills., Jan., 1917

Our National Parks. By L. F. Schmeckebier. XXIII, pp. 531-579, 41 ills., map, June, 1912

Reclamation of Arid Land in California. XIV, pp. 78-79, Feb., 1903

The Redwood Forest of the Pacific Coast. By Henry Gannett. X, pp. 145-159, 6 ills., map, May, 1899

A Remarkable Salt Deposit (Salton Sea). By Charles F. Holder. XII, pp. 391-392, ills., Nov., 1901

Salton Sea and the Rainfall of the Southwest. By Alfred J. Henry. XVIII, pp. 244-248, Apr., 1907

Saving the Redwoods. By Madison Grant. XXXVII, pp. 519-536, 10 ills., June, 1920

Seed Farms in California. By A. J. Wells. XXIII, pp. 515-530, 14 ills., May, 1912

Seeing Our Spanish Southwest. By Frederick Simpich. LXXVII, pp. 711-756, 25 ills. in black and white, 17 ills. in duotone, map supplement, June, 1940

Sir Francis Drake's Anchorage. By Edward L. Berthoud. VI, pp. 208-214, Dec. 29, 1894

CALIFORNIA—*Continued*

Southern California at Work. By Frederick Simpich. LXVI, pp. 529-600, 39 ills. in black and white, 41 ills. in color, two-page map, Nov., 1934

The Southwest: Its Splendid Natural Resources, Agricultural Wealth, and Scenic Beauty. By N. H. Darton. XXI, pp. 631-665, 21 ills., map, Aug., 1910

Studies on the Rate of Evaporation at Reno, Nevada, and in the Salton Sink. By Professor Frank H. Bigelow. XIX, pp. 20-28, 5 ills., Jan., 1908

Surf-Boarders Capture California. 8 photos by J. H. Ball. LXXXVI, pp. 355-362, Sept., 1944

Topographic Work of the U. S. Geological Survey in 1902. XIII, pp. 326-328, Aug., 1902

Where Birds and Little Animals Find Haven (Eaton Canyon Bird and Game Sanctuary). By Agnes Akin Atkinson. LXX, pp. 232-241, 14 ills., Aug., 1936

Wild Ducks as Winter Guests in a City Park. By Joseph Dixon. XXXVI, pp. 331-343, 11 ills., Oct., 1919

The Wonderland of California. By Herman Whitaker. XXVIII, pp. 57-99, 34 ills., July, 1915

See also Berkeley; Colorado Desert; San Diego; San Francisco; Santa Catalina (Island)

CALIFORNIA—85 Years After the Gold Rush. 23 color photos by B. Anthony Stewart. LXIX, pp. 325-356, Mar., 1936

CALIFORNIA, Lower. *See* Baja California

CALIFORNIA Trapdoor Spider Performs Engineering Marvels. By Lee Passmore. LXIV, pp. 195-211, 23 ills., Aug., 1933

CALIFORNIA'S Coastal Redwood Realm: Along a Belt of Tall Trees a Giant Bridge Speeds the Winning of Our Westernmost Frontier. By J. R. Hildebrand. LXXV, pp. 133-184, 31 ills. in black and white, 17 ills. in color, map, Feb., 1939

The **CALL** of the West. By C. J. Blanchard. XX, pp. 403-437, 20 ills., map, May, 1909

The **CALL** to the Colors. 17 ills. XXXI, pp. 345-361, Apr., 1917

CALVIN, JACK:

"Nakwasina" Goes North: A Man, a Woman, and a Pup Cruise from Tacoma to Juneau in a 17-Foot Canoe. By Jack Calvin. LXIV, pp. 1-42, 24 ills., map, July, 1933

CALVIN, JOHN:

The Millennial City: The Romance of Geneva, Capital of the League of Nations. By Ralph A. Graves. XXXV, pp. 457-476, 11 ills., June, 1919

CALVO, JOAQUIN BERNARDO:

What the Latin American Republics Think of the Pan-American Conferences (Address by Joaquin Bernardo Calvo). XVII, pp. 474-479, Aug., 1906

CAMARGUE, the Cowboy Country of Southern France. By Dr. André Vialles. XLII, pp. 1-34, 33 ills., map, July, 1922

CAMBODIA (Protectorate), French Indo-China:
Along the Old Mandarin Road of Indo-China. By W. Robert Moore. LX, pp. 157-199, 32 ills. in black and white, 28 ills. in color, map, Aug., 1931
The Forgotten Ruins of Indo-China. By Jacob E. Conner. XXIII, pp. 209-272, 63 ills., maps, Mar., 1912
Four Faces of Siva: The Mystery of Angkor. By Robert J. Casey. LIV, pp. 303-332, 13 ills. in black and white, 27 ills. in color, map, Sept., 1928

CAMBRIAN STAKES (Sheep Dog Trials):
Sheep Dog Trials in Llangollen: Trained Collies Perform Marvels of Herding in the Cambrian Stakes, Open to the World. By Sara Bloch. LXXVII, pp. 559-574, 17 ills., Apr., 1940

CAMBRIDGE, England. *See* Cambridge University

CAMBRIDGE UNIVERSITY, England:
A Texan Teaches American History at Cambridge University. By J. Frank Dobie. LXXXIX, pp. 409-441, 9 ills. in black and white, 19 ills. in color, Apr., 1946
Within the Halls of Cambridge (University). By Philip Broad. LXX, pp. 333-349, 7 ills. in black and white, 12 ills. in color, Sept., 1936

The **CAMEL,** Man's Humpy, Grumpy Servant. 11 ills. in duotone. LXXXII, pp. 393-400, Sept., 1942

The **CAMEL** of the Frozen Desert (Reindeer). By Carl J. Lomen. XXXVI, pp. 539-556, 19 ills., Dec., 1919

CAMELS:
The Camel, Man's Humpy, Grumpy Servant. 11 ills. in duotone. LXXXII, pp. 393-400, Sept., 1942
Here and There in Northern Africa. By Frank Edward Johnson. XXV, pp. 1-132, 113 ills., Jan., 1914
The Road to Wang Ye Fu: An Account of the Work of the National Geographic Society's Central-China Expedition in the Mongol Kingdom of Ala Shan. By Frederick R. Wulsin. XLIX, pp. 197-234, 44 ills., map, Feb., 1926

CAMELS of the Clouds (Lamoids). By W. H. Hodge. LXXXIX, pp. 641-656, 15 ills., map, May, 1946

CAMERA Adventures in the African Wilds (Book Review). Photos by A. Radclyffe Dugmore. XXI, pp. 385-396, 11 ills., May, 1910

CAMERA Cruising in the Philippines. 12 color photos by J. Baylor Roberts, Fenno Jacobs, and others. LXXXVI, pp. 545-552, Nov., 1944

CAMERA Pastels in French Canada. 25 color photos by Harrison Howell Walker. LXXV, pp. 601-624, May, 1939

The **CAMERA'S** Color Records of North Africa. 16 color photos by Gervais Courtellemont. XLVII, pp. 333-340, Mar., 1925

CAMEROONS (Cameroun):
The Mandate of Cameroun: A Vast African Territory Ruled by Petty Sultans Under French Sway. By John W. Vandercook. LIX, pp. 225-260, 49 ills., map, Feb., 1931

CAMEROONS (Cameroun)—*Continued*
Trans-Africa Safari: A Motor Caravan Rolls Across Sahara and Jungle Through Realms of Dusky Potentates and the Land of Big-Lipped Women. By Lawrence Copley Thaw and Margaret Stout Thaw. LXXIV, pp. 327-364, 29 ills. in black and white, 14 ills. in color, map, Sept., 1938

CAMEROONS MOUNTAIN, Cameroons:
Timbuktu and Beyond: Desert City of Romantic Savor and Salt Emerges into World Life Again as Trading Post of France's Vast African Empire. By Laura C. Boulton. LXXIX, pp. 631-670, 18 ills. in black and white, 26 ills. in color, map, May, 1941

CAMP Fires on Desert and Lava (Book Review). XXI, pp. 715-718, 3 ills., Aug., 1910

CAMPBELL, ALFRED S.:
Guernsey, the Friendly Island. By Alfred S. Campbell. LXXIII, pp. 361-396, 28 ills. in black and white, 11 ills. in color, Mar., 1938

CAMPBELL, FRANK M.:
Fantastic Plants of Our Western Deserts. 8 ills. by Frank M. Campbell. XLV, pp. 33-40, Jan., 1924

CAMPBELL, MARIUS R.:
Geomorphology of the Southern Appalachians. By Charles Willard Hayes and Marius R. Campbell. VI, pp. 63-126, diagrs., 4 maps, May 23, 1894
How Long Will the Coal Reserves of the United States Last? By Marius R. Campbell. XVIII, pp. 129-138, 5 diagrs., map, Feb., 1907

CAMPHOR:
Formosa the Beautiful. By Alice Ballantine Kirjassoff. XXXVII, pp. 247-292, 60 ills., map, Mar., 1920

CAMPS and Cruises of an Ornithologist. By George Shiras, 3d. XX, pp. 438-463, 30 ills., May, 1909

CANADA:
Alaskan Highway an Engineering Epic: Mosquitoes, Mud, and Muskeg Minor Obstacles of 1,671-mile Race to Throw the Alcan Life Line Through Thick Forests and Uninhabited Wilderness. By Froelich Rainey. LXXXIII, pp. 143-168, 21 ills., 3 maps, Feb., 1943
Area and Drainage Basin of Lake Superior. By Dr. Mark W. Harrington. VIII, pp. 111-120, tables, Apr., 1897
Atlantic Coast Tides. By Mark S. W. Jefferson. IX, pp. 497-509, 3 charts, Dec., 1898
The British Commonwealth of Nations: "Organized Freedom" Around the World. By Eric Underwood. LXXXIII, pp. 485-524, 31 ills., Apr., 1943
Canada from the Air: Flights Aggregating 10,000 Miles Reveal the Marvelous Scenic Beauties and Amazing Natural Resources of the Dominion. By J. A. Wilson. L, pp. 389-466, 76 ills., map, Oct., 1926
Canada's Awakening North. By Lawrence J. Burpee. LXIX, pp. 749-768, 18 ills., June, 1936

CANADA—*Continued*

Canada's War Effort: A Canadian Pictures the Swift and Sweeping Transformation from a Peaceful Dominion to a Nation Geared for War. By Bruce Hutchison. LXXX, pp. 553-590, 40 ills., Nov., 1941

The Canadian Boundary. By John W. Foster. XIV, pp. 85-90, map, Mar., 1903

Canadian Immigration. XVII, p. 356, June, 1906

The Columbia (River) Turns on the Power. By Maynard Owen Williams. LXXIX, pp. 749-792, 25 ills. in black and white, 18 ills. in color, June, 1941

The completion of the cable between Canada and Australia. XIII, p. 410, Nov., 1902

The Conquest of Mount Logan: North America's Second Highest Peak Yields to the Intrepid Attack of Canadian Climbers. By H. F. Lambart. XLIX, pp. 597-631, 40 ills., June, 1926

Decision of the Alaskan Boundary Tribunal Under the Treaty of January 24, 1903, Between the United States and Great Britain. XV, pp. 12-14, Jan., 1904

An Expedition Through the Yukon District (pre-Yukon Territory). By Charles Willard Hayes. IV, pp. 117-159, 3 maps (2 foldouts), May 15, 1892

Exploring Yukon's Glacial Stronghold. By Bradford Washburn. LXIX, pp. 715-748, 29 ills., two-page map, June, 1936

The First Alaskan Air Expedition. By Captain St. Clair Streett. XLI, pp. 499-552, 37 ills., map, May, 1922

The Forests of Canada. XIV, pp. 106-108, Mar., 1903

The Forests of Canada. By Sir Wilfrid Laurier. XVII, pp. 504-509, Sept., 1906

The Future of the Yukon Goldfields. By William H. Dall. IX, pp. 117-120, Apr., 1898

Gentlemen Adventurers of the Air: Many Regions of Canada's Vast Wilderness, Long Hidden Even from Fur Trappers, Are Now Revealed by Exploring Airmen. By J. A. Wilson. LVI, pp. 597-642, 55 ills., map, Nov., 1929

Great Britain's Bread Upon the Waters: Canada and Her Other Daughters. By William Howard Taft. XXIX, pp. 217-272, 56 ills., Mar., 1916

How Canada Went to the Front. By T. B. Macaulay. XXXIV, pp. 297-307, 6 ills., Oct., 1918

The New Trans-Canada Railway. XIV, pp. 214-215, map, May, 1903

The Northwest Passes to the Yukon. By Eliza Ruhamah Scidmore. IX, pp. 105-112, 3 ills., Apr., 1898

On Mackenzie's Trail to the Polar Sea. By Amos Burg. LX, pp. 127-156, 32 ills., map, Aug., 1931

On the Trail of a Horse Thief (Columbia River). By Herbert W. Gleason. XXXV, pp. 349-358, 6 ills., Apr., 1919

The Origin of French-Canadians. IX, pp. 96-97, Mar., 1898

Origin of the Word Canada. (By N. H. Winchell). XVIII, p. 215, Mar., 1907

Overland Routes to the Klondike. By Hamlin Garland. IX, pp. 113-116, ill., Apr., 1898

CANADA—*Continued*

Peaks and Parks of Western Canada. 11 photos: 5 by W. J. Oliver. LXXX, pp. 516-526, Oct., 1941

Place Names in Canada. (By H. G.). X, pp. 519-520, Dec., 1899

The Possibilities of the Hudson Bay Country. XVIII, pp. 209-213, ill., Mar., 1907

The Society Maps Northwestern United States and Neighboring Canadian Provinces. Text with map supplement. LXXIX, pp. 805-806, June, 1941

The Society's New Map of Canada. Text with map supplement. LXIX, pp. 769-776, 9 ills., June, 1936

Sources of the Saskatchewan. By Walter D. Wilcox. X, pp. 113-134, 6 ills., chart, Apr., 1899

Surveying the 141st Meridian (Boundary Line Between Canada and Alaska). By Thomas Riggs, Jr. XXIII, pp. 685-713, 46 ills., map, July, 1912

To-day on "The Yukon Trail of 1898." By Amos Burg. LVIII, pp. 85-126, 52 ills., map, July, 1930

The Vast Timber Belts of Canada. XVII, pp. 509-511, Sept., 1906

See also Alberta; Anticosti Island; Baffin Island; British Columbia; Churchill; Gaspé Peninsula; Klondike; Labrador; New Brunswick; Newfoundland; Nova Scotia; Ontario; Passamaquoddy Bay; Quebec; Toronto; Yukon Territory

CANADA'S Awakening North. By Lawrence J. Burpee. LXIX, pp. 749-768, 18 ills., June, 1936

CANADA'S War Effort: A Canadian Pictures the Swift and Sweeping Transformation from a Peaceful Dominion to a Nation Geared for War. By Bruce Hutchison. LXXX, pp. 553-590, 40 ills., Nov., 1941

The **CANADIAN** Boundary. By John W. Foster. XIV, pp. 85-90, map, Mar., 1903

CANADIAN Immigration. XVII, p. 356, June, 1906

CANADIAN ROCKY MOUNTAINS:

Exploration in the Canadian Rockies. X, pp. 135-136, Apr., 1899

A Geologist's Paradise. By Charles D. Walcott. XXII, pp. 509-536, 28 ills., panorama, June, 1911

Our Mountain Panorama (panorama)

The Monarch of the Canadian Rockies (Mount Robson). By Charles D. Walcott. XXIV, pp. 626-639, 13 ills., panorama, May, 1913

The Monarch of the Canadian Rockies—Robson Peak (panorama)

The Mother of Rivers: An Account of a Photographic Expedition to the Great Columbia Ice Field of the Canadian Rockies. By Lewis R. Freeman. XLVII, pp. 377-446, 60 ills., maps, Apr., 1925

Peaks and Parks of Western Canada. 11 photos: 5 by W. J. Oliver. LXXX, pp. 516-526, Oct., 1941

Peaks and Trails in the Canadian Alps. 16 photos in duotone by Byron Harmon and Clifford White. LXV, pp. 627-642, May, 1934

CANADIAN ROCKY MOUNTAINS—*Continued*

Recent Exploration in the Canadian Rockies. By Walter D. Wilcox. XIII, pp. 151-168, 12 ills., map, May, 1902; Part II, pp. 185-200, 9 ills., June, 1902

Some Tramps Across the Glaciers and Snowfields of British Columbia. By Howard Palmer. XXI, pp. 457-487, 25 ills., June, 1910

The World's Highest Altitudes and First Ascents. By Charles E. Fay. XX, pp. 493-530, 25 ills., June, 1909

A **CANAL** from the Atlantic to the Mediterranean. XI, pp. 122-123, Mar., 1900

CANAL ZONE, Panama:

Who Treads Our Trails? A Camera Trapper Describes His Experiences on an Island in the Canal Zone, a Natural-History Laboratory in the American Tropics. By Frank M. Chapman. LII, pp. 331-345, 18 ills., map, Sept., 1927

See also Panama Canal

CANALS:

Across the Midi in a Canoe: Two Americans Paddle Along the Canals of Southern France from the Atlantic to the Mediterranean. By Melville Chater. LII, pp. 127-167, 49 ills., map, Aug., 1927

An Army Engineer Explores Nicaragua: Mapping a Route for a New Canal Through the Largest of Central American Republics. By Lieut. Col. Dan I. Sultan. LXI, pp. 593-627, 39 ills., map, May, 1932

Britain Just Before the Storm: A Canadian Canoe Threads Old English Waterways Athrob with the Midlands' Industrial Life. By Amos Burg. LXXVIII, pp. 185-212, 14 ills. in black and white, 9 ills. in color, map, Aug., 1940

By Sail Across Europe. By Merlin Minshall. LXXI, pp. 533-567, 38 ills., map, May, 1937

A Canal from the Atlantic to the Mediterranean. XI, pp. 122-123, Mar., 1900

The Cape Cod Canal. By Commodore J. W. Miller. XXVI, pp. 185-190, 3 ills., map, Aug., 1914

Completion of the La Boca Dock (Panama Canal). IX, p. 84, Mar., 1898

The Deep-Water Route from Chicago to the Gulf. XVIII, pp. 679-685, 3 ills., map, Oct., 1907

The Evolution of Commerce. Annual Address by the President, Hon. Gardiner G. Hubbard. IV, pp. 1-18, Mar. 26, 1892

Glimpses of Holland. By William Wisner Chapin. XXVII, pp. 1-29, 26 ills., Jan., 1915

Grand Canal Panorama (China). By Willard Price. LXXI, pp. 487-514, 31 ills., map, Apr., 1937

The Great Canals of the World. XVI, pp. 475-479, Oct., 1905

Ho for the Soochow Ho (China). By Mabel Craft Deering. LI, pp. 623-649, 32 ills., map, June, 1927

The Industrial Titan of America: Pennsylvania, Once the Keystone of the Original Thirteen, Now the Keystone of Forty-eight Sovereign States. By John Oliver La Gorce. XXXV, pp. 367-406, 33 ills., map, May, 1919

CANALS—*Continued*

The Isthmian Canal Commission. XI, p. 161, Apr., 1900

The Latest Route Proposed for the Isthmian Canal—Mandingo Route. XIII, pp. 64-70, chart, Feb., 1902

Life Afloat in China: Tens of Thousands of Chinese in Congested Ports Spend Their Entire Existence on Boats. By Robert F. Fitch. LI, pp. 665-686, 28 ills., June, 1927

The New Erie Canal. XVI, pp. 568-570, map, Dec., 1905

Nicaragua and the Isthmian Routes. By A. P. Davis. X, pp. 247-266, 7 ills., diagrs., July, 1899

Shantung—China's Holy Land. By Charles K. Edmunds. XXXVI, pp. 231-252, 21 ills., map, Sept., 1919

Surveying Through Khoresm: A Journey Into Parts of Asiatic Russia Which Have Been Closed to Western Travelers Since the World War. By Lyman D. Wilbur. LXI, pp. 753-780, 31 ills., map, June, 1932

Through the Back Doors of Belgium: Artist and Author Paddle for Three Weeks Along 200 Miles of Low-Countries Canals in a Canadian Canoe. By Melville Chater. XLVII, pp. 499-540, 39 ills., map, May, 1925

Through the Back Doors of France: A Seven Weeks' Voyage in a Canadian Canoe from St. Malo, Through Brittany and the Château Country, to Paris. By Melville Chater. XLIV, pp. 1-51, 55 ills., map, July, 1923

Through the Heart of England in a Canadian Canoe. By R. J. Evans. XLI, pp. 473-497, 26 ills., map, May, 1922

The Venice of Mexico (Aztec Lake Country). By Walter Hough. XXX, pp. 69-88, 18 ills., July, 1916

The Wonderful Canals of China. By F. H. King. XXIII, pp. 931-958, 35 ills., 5 maps, Oct., 1912

The Wonderful Canals of China. By George E. Anderson. XVI, pp. 68-69, Feb., 1905

See also Chesapeake and Ohio Canal; Florida Coast Line Canal; Nicaragua Canal; Panama Canal; Suez Canal; *and* Netherlands; Venice

CANALS and Pageants of Peacetime England. 9 color photos: 6 by Amos Burg. LXXVIII, pp. 197-204, Aug., 1940

CANARIES:

Canaries and Other Cage-Bird Friends. By Alexander Wetmore. Paintings by Major Allan Brooks. LXXIV, pp. 775-806, 19 ills. in black and white, 51 portraits in color, Dec., 1938

CANARY ISLANDS, Atlantic Ocean:

Hunting for Plants in the Canary Islands. By David Fairchild. LVII, pp. 607-652, 37 ills. in black and white, 39 ills. in color, map, May, 1930

New Map of the Atlantic Ocean: Foremost Sea of Commerce Becomes World's Battleground and Its Peaceful Islands Rise to Strategic Importance. By Leo A. Borah and Wellman Chamberlin. Text with map supplement. LXXX, pp. 407-418, 9 ills., Sept., 1941

CANBERRA, Australia:

Capital Cities of Australia. By W. Robert Moore. LXVIII, pp. 667-722, 32 ills. in black and white, 24 ills. in color, two-page map, Dec., 1935

CANCER:

The Discovery of Cancer in Plants. XXIV, pp. 53-70, 12 ills., Jan., 1913

CANDEE, HELEN CHURCHILL:

Life's Pattern on the Italian Riviera. By Helen Churchill Candee. LXVII, pp. 67-100, 25 ills. in black and white, 12 ills. in color, map, Jan., 1935

Normandy—Choice of the Vikings. By Helen Churchill Candee. LXIX, pp. 625-665, 25 ills. in black and white, 22 ills. in duotone, map, May, 1936

Summering in an English Cottage: Quiet and Loveliness Invite Contemplation in the Extra "Room," the Garden of the Thatched House. By Helen Churchill Candee. LXVII, pp. 429-456, 32 ills., Apr., 1935

CANDIA, Crete (Island):

Crete, Where Sea-Kings Reigned. By Agnes N. Stillwell. LXXXIV, pp. 547-568, 20 ills., map, Nov., 1943

CANEK (Mayan Hero):

The Home of a Forgotten Race: Mysterious Chichen Itza, in Yucatan, Mexico. By Edward H. Thompson. XXV, pp. 585-648, 59 ills., June, 1914

CANNIBALS:

Among the Cannibals of Belgian Kongo (Taken from Notes of E. Torday). XXI, pp. 969-971, 4 ills., Nov., 1910

Curious and Characteristic Customs of Central African Tribes (Belgian Congo). By E. Torday. XXXVI, pp. 342-368, 35 ills., Oct., 1919

Into Primeval Papua by Seaplane: Seeking Disease-resisting Sugar Cane, Scientists Find Neolithic Man in Unmapped Nooks of Sorcery and Cannibalism. By E. W. Brandes. LVI, pp. 253-332, 98 ills., map, Sept., 1929

The Luster of Ancient Mexico (Aztecs). By William H. Prescott. XXX, pp. 1-31, 22 ills., July, 1916

A Vanishing People of the South Seas: The Tragic Fate of the Marquesan Cannibals, Noted for Their Warlike Courage and Physical Beauty. By John W. Church. XXXVI, pp. 275-306, 22 ills., map, Oct., 1919

CANNING:

Forming New Fashions in Food: The Bearing of Taste on One of Our Great Food Economies, the Dried Vegetable, Which Is Developing into a Big War Industry. By David Fairchild. XXXIII, pp. 356-368, 11 ills., Apr., 1918

How the World Is Fed. By William Joseph Showalter. XXIX, pp. 1-110, 101 ills., Jan., 1916

CANNON, JOSEPH:

The Discovery of the North Pole (Speech by Joseph Cannon). XXI, pp. 63-82, Jan., 1910

CANNON:

Cannon on Florida Reefs Solve Mystery of Sunken Ship. By Charles M. Brookfield. LXXX, pp. 807-824, 20 ills., map (on pen and ink drawing), Dec., 1941

Pirate-Fighters of the South China Sea. By Robert Cardwell. LXXXIX, pp. 787-796, 11 ills., June, 1946

The Prevention of Hailstorms by the Use of Cannon. XI, pp. 239-241, June, 1900

CANOEING Down the River Jordan: Voyagers in Rubber Boats Find the Bible Stream Little Tamed Today as It Plunges to the Dead Sea Over the Earth's Lowest River Bed. By John D. Whiting. LXXVIII, pp. 781-808, 19 ills., map, Dec., 1940

CANOES AND CANOE TRIPS:

Across the Midi in a Canoe: Two Americans Paddle Along the Canals of Southern France from the Atlantic to the Mediterranean. By Melville Chater. LII, pp. 127-167, 49 ills., map, Aug., 1927

Britain Just Before the Storm: A Canadian Canoe Threads Old English Waterways Athrob with the Midlands' Industrial Life. By Amos Burg. LXXVIII, pp. 185-212, 14 ills. in black and white, 9 ills. in color, map, Aug., 1940

Canoeing Down the River Jordan: Voyagers in Rubber Boats Find the Bible Stream Little Tamed Today as It Plunges to the Dead Sea Over the Earth's Lowest River Bed. By John D. Whiting. LXXVIII, pp. 781-808, 19 ills., map, Dec., 1940

Entering the Front Doors of Medieval Towns: The Adventures of an American Woman and Her Daughter in a Folding Boat on Eight Rivers of Germany and Austria. By Cornelia Stratton Parker. LXI, pp. 365-394, 23 ills. in black and white, 11 ills. in color, map, Mar., 1932

An Expedition to Mount St. Elias, Alaska. By Israel C. Russell. III, pp. 53-191, 17 ills., 3 diagrs., tables, 7 maps (1 foldout), May 29, 1891

Hurdle Racing in Canoes: A Thrilling and Spectacular Sport Among the Maoris of New Zealand. By Walter Burke. XXXVII, pp. 440-444, 6 ills., May, 1920

"Nakwasina" Goes North: A Man, a Woman, and a Pup Cruise from Tacoma to Juneau in a 17-Foot Canoe. By Jack Calvin. LXIV, pp. 1-42, 24 ills., map, July, 1933

On Mackenzie's Trail to the Polar Sea. By Amos Burg. LX, pp. 127-156, 32 ills., map, Aug., 1931

Through the Back Doors of Belgium: Artist and Author Paddle for Three Weeks Along 200 Miles of Low-Countries Canals in a Canadian Canoe. By Melville Chater. XLVII, pp. 499-540, 39 ills., map, May, 1925

Through the Back Doors of France: A Seven Weeks' Voyage in a Canadian Canoe from St. Malo, Through Brittany and the Château Country, to Paris. By Melville Chater. XLIV, pp. 1-51, 55 ills., map, July, 1923

Through the Heart of England in a Canadian Canoe. By R. J. Evans. XLI, pp. 473-497, 26 ills., map, May, 1922

CANOES AND CANOE TRIPS—*Continued*

To-day on "The Yukon Trail of 1898." By Amos Burg. LVIII, pp. 85-126, 52 ills., map, July, 1930

CANOVA, ENRIQUE C.:

Cuba—The Isle of Romance. By Enrique C. Canova. LXIV, pp. 345-380, 34 ills., map, Sept., 1933

West Virginia: Treasure Chest of Industry. By Enrique C. Canova. LXXVIII, pp. 141-184, 19 ills. in black and white, 21 ills. in color, two-page map, Aug., 1940

CANTIGNY, France:

The National Geographic Society's Memorial to American Troops: Fountain and Water Supply System Presented to Historic French Town of Cantigny, Where Our Overseas Soldiers Won Their First Victory in the World War. XLIV, pp. 675-678, 4 ills., Dec., 1923

CANTON, China:

Changing Canton. 20 photos by Siukee Mack, Alfred T. Palmer, Kinchue Wong. LXXII, pp. 711-726, Dec., 1937

CANTON ISLAND, Phoenix Islands:

American Pathfinders in the Pacific. By William H. Nicholas. LXXXIX, pp. 617-640, 17 ills., two-page map, May, 1946

Crusoes of Canton Island: Life on a Tiny Pacific Atoll That Has Flashed Into World Importance. By Irvine C. Gardner. LXXIII, pp. 749-766, 7 ills. in black and white, 11 ills. in color, June, 1938

Eclipse Adventures on a Desert Isle. By Capt. J. F. Hellweg. LXXII, pp. 377-394, 14 ills., map, Sept., 1937

Nature's Most Dramatic Spectacle (Eclipse). By S. A. Mitchell. LXXII, pp. 361-376, 16 ills., map, Sept., 1937

CANTWELL, J. C.:

Ice-cliffs on the Kowak River. By Lieut. J. C. Cantwell. VII, pp. 345-346, Oct., 1896

CANYON OF DEATH, Arizona:

Exploring in the Canyon of Death: Remains of a People Who Dwelt in Our Southwest at Least 4,000 Years Ago Are Revealed. By Earl H. Morris. XLVIII, pp. 263-300, 24 ills. in black and white, 22 ills. in color, Sept., 1925

CANYONS and Cacti of the American Southwest. 22 color photos by Edwin L. Wisherd, Jacob Gayer, Charles Martin. XLVIII, pp. 275-290, Sept., 1925

CAPE BRETON ISLAND, Nova Scotia:

The Charm of Cape Breton Island: The Most Picturesque Portion of Canada's Maritime Provinces—A Land Rich in Historic Associations, Natural Resources, and Geographic Appeal. By Catherine Dunlop Mackenzie. XXXVIII, pp. 34-60, 22 ills., map, July, 1920

Salty Nova Scotia: In Friendly New Scotland Gaelic Songs Still Answer the Skirling Bagpipes. By Andrew H. Brown. LXXVII, pp. 575-624, 30 ills. in black and white, 21 ills. in color, two-page map, May, 1940

CAPE COD, Massachusetts:

The Cape Cod Canal. By Commodore J. W. Miller. XXVI, pp. 185-190, 3 ills., map, Aug., 1914

Cape Cod People and Places. By Wanda Burnett. LXXXIX, pp. 737-774, 17 ills. in black and white, 24 ills. in color, map, June, 1946

Collarin' Cape Cod: Experiences on Board a U. S. Navy Destroyer in a Wild Winter Storm. By Lieutenant H. R. Thurber. XLVIII, pp. 427-472, 46 ills., Oct., 1925

CAPE HORN, Chile:

The Cape Horn Grain-Ship Race: The Gallant "Parma" Leads the Vanishing Fleet of Square-Riggers Through Raging Gales and Irksome Calms 16,000 Miles, from Australia to England. By A. J. Villiers. LXIII, pp. 1-39, 38 ills., Jan., 1933

Inside Cape Horn. By Amos Burg. LXXII, pp. 743-783, 29 ills. in black and white, 10 ills. in color, two-page map, Dec., 1937

Rounding the Horn in a Windjammer. By A. J. Villiers. LIX, pp. 191-224, 36 ills., map, Feb., 1931

CAPE NOME, Alaska:

The Cape Nome Gold District. By F. C. Schrader. XI, pp. 15-23, 3 ills., map, Jan., 1900

Origin of the Name "Cape Nome." (By George Davidson). XII, p. 398, Nov., 1901

CAPE OF GOOD HOPE PROVINCE, Union of South Africa:

Busy Corner—the Cape of Good Hope: Ships Bound for Faraway Battlegrounds Stream Past Capetown, "Tavern of the Seas," and Other Ports of Virile South Africa. By W. Robert Moore. LXXXII, pp. 197-223, 11 ills. in black and white, 11 ills. in color, map, Aug., 1942

Cape of Good Hope: The Floral Province. By Melville Chater. LIX, pp. 391-430, 29 ills. in black and white, 11 ills. in color, two-page map, Apr., 1931

See also Capetown

CAPE-TO-CAIRO RAILWAY:

Transporting a Navy Through the Jungles of Africa in War Time. By Frank J. Magee. XLII, pp. 331-362, 31 ills., Oct., 1922

CAPE-TO-CAIRO TELEGRAPH:

Cape to Cairo Telegraph. XII, pp. 162-163, Apr., 1901

The Cape to Cairo Telegraph. XIII, pp. 76-77, Feb., 1902

CAPE VERDE ISLANDS, Atlantic Ocean:

New Map of the Atlantic Ocean: Foremost Sea of Commerce Becomes World's Battleground and Its Peaceful Islands Rise to Strategic Importance. By Leo A. Borah and Wellman Chamberlin. Text with map supplement. LXXX, pp. 407-418, 9 ills., Sept., 1941

Sindbads of Science: Narrative of a Windjammer's Specimen-Collecting Voyage to the Sargasso Sea, to Senegambian Africa and Among Islands of High Adventure in the South Atlantic. By George Finlay Simmons. LII, pp. 1-75, 89 ills., map, July, 1927

CAPETOWN, Union of South Africa:
Busy Corner—the Cape of Good Hope: Ships Bound for Faraway Battlegrounds Stream Past Capetown, "Tavern of the Seas," and Other Ports of Virile South Africa. By W. Robert Moore. LXXXII, pp. 197-223, 11 ills. in black and white, 11 ills. in color, map, Aug., 1942
Cairo to Cape Town, Overland: An Adventurous Journey of 135 Days, Made by an American Man and His Wife, Through the Length of the African Continent. By Felix Shay. XLVII, pp. 123-260, 118 ills., map, Feb., 1925
Sailing the Seven Seas in the Interest of Science: Adventures Through 157,000 Miles of Storm and Calm, from Arctic to Antarctic and Around the World, in the Non-magnetic Yacht "Carnegie." By J. P. Ault. XLII, pp. 631-690, 47 ills., chart, Dec., 1922
Under the South African Union. By Melville Chater. LIX, pp. 391-512, 97 ills. in black and white, 38 ills. in color, two-page map, Apr., 1931

CAPITAL and Chief Seaport of Chile (Santiago and Valparaíso). By W. Robert Moore. LXXXVI, pp. 477-500, 15 ills. in black and white, 8 ills. in color, map, Oct., 1944

CAPITAL and Country of Old Cathay. 16 ills. in duotone. LXIII, pp. 749-764, June, 1933

CAPITAL Cities of Australia. By W. Robert Moore. LXVIII, pp. 667-722, 32 ills. in black and white, 24 ills. in color, two-page map, Dec., 1935

The **CAPITOL** (U. S.), Wonder Building of the World. By Gilbert Grosvenor. XLIII, pp. 603-638, 17 ills. in black and white, 16 ills. in color, June, 1923

CAPPADOCIA:
The Cone-Dwellers of Asia Minor: A Primitive People Who Live in Nature-Made Apartment Houses, Fashioned by Volcanic Violence and Trickling Streams. By J. R. Sitlington Sterrett. XXXV, pp. 281-331, 52 ills., map, Apr., 1919
Peculiar Caves of Asia Minor. By Elizabeth H. Brewer. XXII, pp. 870-875, 5 ills., Sept., 1911
The Turkish Republic Comes of Age. By Maynard Owen Williams. LXXXVII, pp. 581-616, 4 ills. in black and white, 29 ills. in color, map, May, 1945
Where Early Christians Lived in Cones of Rock: A Journey to Cappadocia in Turkey Where Strange Volcanic Pinnacles Are Honeycombed with Hermit Cells and Monasteries. By John D. Whiting. LXXVI, pp. 763-802, 20 ills. in black and white, 20 ills. in color, map, Dec., 1939

CAPPS, STEPHEN R.:
A Game Country Without Rival in America: The Proposed Mount McKinley National Park. By Stephen R. Capps. XXXI, pp. 69-84, 14 ills., map, Jan., 1917

CAPRI (Island), Italy:
Capri, the Island Retreat of Roman Emperors. 12 photos by Morgan Heiskell. XLI, pp. 627-638, June, 1922

CAPRI (Island), Italy—*Continued*
Inexhaustible Italy. By Arthur Stanley Riggs. XXX, pp. 273-368, 76 ills., map, Oct., 1916
The Isle of Capri: An Imperial Residence and Probable Wireless Station of Ancient Rome. By John A. Kingman. XXXVI, pp. 213-231, 17 ills., Sept., 1919

CAPTAIN Charles D. Sigsbee, U. S. N. (By H. G.). IX, p. 250, ill. (front.), May, 1898

CAPTURING Giant Turtles in the Caribbean. By David D. Duncan. LXXXIV, pp. 177-190, 13 ills., map, Aug., 1943

CARACAS, Venezuela:
Caracas, Cradle of the Liberator: The Spirit of Simón Bolívar, South American George Washington, Lives On in the City of His Birth. By Luis Marden. LXXVII, pp. 477-513, 18 ills. in black and white, 19 ills. in color, Apr., 1940
I Kept House in a Jungle: The Spell of Primeval Tropics in Venezuela, Riotous With Strange Plants, Animals, and Snakes, Enthralls a Young American Woman. By Anne Rainey Langley. LXXV, pp. 97-132, 37 ills., map, Jan., 1939

A **CARAVAN** Journey Through Abyssinia: From Addis Ababa Through Lalibela, the Strange Jerusalem of Ethiopia, in Search of New Grains for American Farms. By Harry V. Harlan. XLVII, pp. 613-663, 46 ills., map, June, 1925

The **CARAVELS** of Columbus. By Victor Maria Concas. V, pp. 180-186, Jan. 31, 1894

The **CARAVELS** of Columbus. Reproduction in color of the painting by N. C. Wyeth, National Geographic Society, Washington, D. C. LIV, text, p. 55; supplement, July, 1928

CARCHEMISH (Ancient City):
Archeology, the Mirror of the Ages: Our Debt to the Humble Delvers in the Ruins at Carchemish and at Ur. By C. Leonard Woolley. LIV, pp. 207-226, 19 ills., Aug., 1928

CARDWELL, ROBERT:
Pirate-Fighters of the South China Sea. By Robert Cardwell. LXXXIX, pp. 787-796, 11 ills., June, 1946

CAREY, EDITH:
The Channel Islands. By Edith Carey. XXXVIII, pp. 143-164, 24 ills., map, Aug., 1920

CARIBBEAN REGIONS:
Americans in the Caribbean. By Luis Marden. LXXXI, pp. 723-758, 16 ills. in black and white, 22 ills. in color, map, June, 1942
Capturing Giant Turtles in the Caribbean. By David D. Duncan. LXXXIV, pp. 177-190, 13 ills., map, Aug., 1943
Fundamental Geographic Relation of the Three Americas. By Robert T. Hill. VII, pp. 175-181, map, May, 1896
The Haunts of the Caribbean Corsairs: The West Indies a Geographic Background for the Most Adventurous Episodes in the History of the Western Hemisphere. By Nell Ray Clarke. XLI, pp. 147-187, 43 ills., Feb., 1922

CARIBBEAN REGIONS—*Continued*
Heart of a Hemisphere: Of Vital Importance Is the Area Portrayed in The Society's New Map of Mexico, Central America, and the West Indies. Text with map supplement. LXXVI, pp. 739-740, ill., Dec., 1939
Hunting Useful Plants in the Caribbean. By David Fairchild. LXVI, pp. 705-737, 39 ills., Dec., 1934
Our Map of the Countries of the Caribbean. Text with map supplement. XLI, pp. 221-222, Feb., 1922
The Society's New Caribbean Map: Mexico, Central America, and the West Indies—Gateway of Discovery. Text with map supplement. LXVI, pp. 738-740, ill., Dec., 1934
See also West Indies; *and* names of countries and islands

CARIBOU (Animals):
The Big Game of Alaska. By Wilfred H. Osgood. XX, pp. 624-636, 10 ills., July, 1909
A Game Country Without Rival in America: The Proposed Mount McKinley National Park. By Stephen R. Capps. XXXI, pp. 69-84, 14 ills., map, Jan., 1917

CARILLONS:
The Singing Towers of Holland and Belgium. By William Gorham Rice. XLVII, pp. 357-376, 22 ills., Mar., 1925

CARIOCA Carnival (Rio de Janeiro). 34 color photos by W. Robert Moore. LXXVI, pp. 291-322, Sept., 1939

CARLSBAD CAVERNS, New Mexico:
Bats of the Carlsbad Cavern. By Vernon Bailey. XLVIII, pp. 321-330, 11 ills., Sept., 1925
New Discoveries in Carlsbad Cavern: Vast Subterranean Chambers with Spectacular Decorations are Explored, Surveyed, and Photographed. By Willis T. Lee. XLVIII, pp. 301-319, 19 ills., map, Sept., 1925
A Visit to Carlsbad Cavern: Recent Explorations of a Limestone Cave in the Guadalupe Mountains of New Mexico Reveal a Natural Wonder of the First Magnitude. By Willis T. Lee. XLV, pp. 1-40, 42 ills., Jan., 1924

CARNEGIE, ANDREW:
The Discovery of the North Pole (Speech by Andrew Carnegie). XXI, pp. 63-82, Jan., 1910

CARNEGIE (Yacht):
Most Curious Craft Afloat: The Compass in Navigation and the Work of the Non-Magnetic Yacht "Carnegie." By L. A. Bauer. XXI, pp. 223-245, 31 ills., Mar., 1910
Sailing the Seven Seas in the Interest of Science: Adventures Through 157,000 Miles of Storm and Calm, from Arctic to Antarctic and Around the World, in the Non-magnetic Yacht "Carnegie." By J. P. Ault. XLII, pp. 631-690, 47 ills., chart, Dec., 1922

CARNEGIE INSTITUTION OF WASHINGTON:
The Carnegie Institution. XIX, p. 124, Feb., 1908

CARNEGIE INSTITUTION OF WASHINGTON—*Continued*
Geologists in China. XVIII, pp. 640-644, 5 ills., Oct., 1907
Recent Magnetic Work by the Carnegie Institution of Washington. XVII, p. 648, Nov., 1906
See also Carnegie (Yacht)

CARNIVALS:
Carnival Days on the Riviera. By Maynard Owen Williams. L, pp. 467-501, 21 ills. in black and white, 21 ills. in color, Oct., 1926
Rio Panorama: Breath-taking Is This Fantastic City amid Peaks, Palms, and Sea, and in Carnival Time It Moves to the Rhythm of Music. By W. Robert Moore. LXXVI, pp. 283-324, 12 ills. in black and white, 34 ills. in color, Sept., 1939

CARNIVORES of a Lightless World (Fishes). 8 ills. in color from paintings by Else Bostelmann and E. J. Geske. LXVI, pp. 693-700, Dec., 1934

CAROLINE ISLANDS, North Pacific Ocean:
American Pathfinders in the Pacific. By William H. Nicholas. LXXXIX, pp. 617-640, 17 ills., two-page map, May, 1946
The Caroline Islands. X, p. 227, June, 1899
Hidden Key to the Pacific: Piercing the Web of Secrecy Which Long Has Veiled Japanese Bases in the Mandated Islands. By Willard Price. LXXXI, pp. 759-785, 28 ills., map, June, 1942
South from Saipan. By W. Robert Moore. LXXXVII, pp. 441-474, 11 ills. in black and white, 17 ills. in color, map, Apr., 1945
Yap and Other Pacific Islands under Japanese Mandate. By Junius B. Wood. XL, pp. 591-627, 34 ills., map supplement, Dec., 1921
See also Palau Islands; Yap

CARPENTER, FRANK G.:
Awarded Jane M. Smith Life Membership. XXXVII, p. 342, Apr., 1920

CARPENTER, RHYS:
Ancient Rome Brought to Life. By Rhys Carpenter. Paintings by H. M. Herget. XC, pp. 567-633, 2 ills. in black and white, 32 ills. in color, map, Nov., 1946

CARRIERS, Airplane. *See* Aircraft Carriers; Escort Carriers

CARRYING the Color Camera Through Unmapped China. 24 color photos by Joseph F. Rock. LVIII, pp. 403-434, Oct., 1930

CARRYING Water Through a Desert: The Story of the Los Angeles Aqueduct. By Burt A. Heinly. XXI, pp. 568-596, 19 ills., map, July, 1910

CARSON CITY, Nevada:
Nevada, Desert Treasure House. By W. Robert Moore. LXXXIX, pp. 1-38, 16 ills. in black and white, 20 ills. in color, map, Jan., 1946

CARTAGO, Costa Rica:
Costa Rica—Vulcan's Smithy. By H. Pittier. XXI, pp. 494-525, 30 ills., maps, June, 1910

CARTER, WILLIAM HARDING:
The Story of the Horse: The Development of Man's Companion in War Camp, on Farm, in the Marts of Trade, and in the Field of Sports. By Major General William Harding Carter. Paintings by Edward Herbert Miner. XLIV, pp. 455-566, 62 ills. in black and white, 24 ills. in color, Nov., 1923

CARTHAGE (Ancient City):
Ancient Carthage in the Light of Modern Excavation. By Count Byron Khun de Prorok. XLV, pp. 391-423, 27 ills. in black and white, 16 ills. in color, map, Apr., 1924

CARTOGRAPHY. *See* Map Articles; Map Making

The **CARTOGRAPHY** and Observations of Bering's First Voyage. By General A. W. Greely. III, pp. 205-230, map supplement, Jan. 28, 1892; Feb. 19, 1892

CARTS. *See* Oxcarts

CARTY, JOHN J.:
Voice Voyages by the National Geographic Society: A Tribute to the Geographical Achievements of the Telephone (Address by John J. Carty). XXIX, pp. 296-326, 15 ills., chart, Mar., 1916

CARVING, Wood. *See* Totem Poles

CARVINGS, Stone. *See* Archeology; Sculpture; Stone Faces (Monuments)

CASABLANCA, Morocco:
Casablanca Smiles. 10 color photos by Herbert P. MacNeal. LXXXIV, pp. 17-24, July, 1943
Eastward from Gibraltar: Overland Route Across North Africa to Tunisia and Libia. By Cyrus French Wicker. LXXXIII, pp. 115-142, 28 ills., Jan., 1943

CASASUS, JOAQUIN D.:
What the Latin American Republics Think of the Pan-American Conferences (Address by Joaquin D. Casasus). XVII, pp. 474-479, Aug., 1906

CASCADE RANGE, Canada-U. S.:
The Altitude of Mount Adams, Washington. By Edgar McClure. VII, pp. 151-153, tables, Apr., 1896
Mount St. Helens. By Lieut. Charles P. Elliott. VIII, pp. 226-230, foldout map, July-Aug., 1897
Recent Triangulation in the Cascades (Washington). By S. S. Gannett. VII, p. 150, Apr., 1896
Included: Elevation of Mount Adams; Mount Aix; Mount Rainier; Mount Stuart
Scenes Among the High Cascades in Central Oregon. By Ira A. Williams. XXIII, pp. 579-592, 11 ills., June, 1912

CASEY, ROBERT J.:
Four Faces of Siva: The Mystery of Angkor (Cambodia). By Robert J. Casey. LIV, pp. 303-332, 13 ills. in black and white, 27 ills. in color, map, Sept., 1928

CASO, ALFONSO:
Monte Albán, Richest Archeological Find in America: A Tomb in Oaxaca, Mexico, Yields Treasures Which Reveal the Splendid Culture of the Mixtecs. By Dr. Alfonso Caso. LXII, pp. 487-512, 28 ills., Oct., 1932

CASSAVA (Plant):
Dumboy, the National Dish of Liberia. By G. N. Collins. XXII, pp. 84-88, 5 ills., Jan., 1911

CASSERLY, GORDON:
Fez, Heart of Morocco: Africa's "Imperial City" Retains Its Teeming Streets, Cluttered Shops, Glamorous Moorish Homes and Mosques, Amid the Peace of French Rule. By Gordon Casserly. LXVII, pp. 663-694, 13 ills. in black and white, 27 ills. in color, June, 1935
Tripolitania (Africa), Where Rome Resumes Sway: The Ancient Trans-Mediterranean Empire, on the Fringe of the Libyan Desert, Becomes a Promising Modern Italian Colony. By Colonel Gordon Casserly. XLVIII, pp. 131-161, 27 ills. in black and white, 9 ills. in color, map, Aug., 1925
The White City of Algiers. By Lieut. Col. Gordon Casserly. LIII, pp. 206-232, 9 ills. in black and white, 32 ills. in color, Feb., 1928

CASTAWAYS:
They Survived at Sea. By Lt. Comdr. Samuel F. Harby. LXXXVII, pp. 617-640, 22 ills., May, 1945

CASTELROSSO (Island), Aegean Sea:
Rhodes, and Italy's Aegean Islands. By Dorothy Hosmer. LXXIX, pp. 449-480, 32 ills., map, Apr., 1941

CASTERET, NORBERT:
Discovering the Oldest Statues in the World: A Daring Explorer Swims Through a Subterranean River of the Pyrenees and Finds Rock Carvings Made 20,000 Years Ago. By Norbert Casteret. XLVI, pp. 123-152, 24 ills., maps, Aug., 1924

CASTLE, WILLIAM R.:
Hawaii, Then and Now: Boyhood Recollections and Recent Observations by An American Whose Grandfather Came to the Islands 102 Years Ago. By William R. Castle. LXXIV, pp. 419-462, 30 ills. in black and white, 10 ills. in color, map, Oct., 1938
Tokyo To-day. By William R. Castle, Jr. LXI, pp. 131-162, 33 ills., Feb., 1932

CASTLES:
Anticosti Island, Nugget of the North. By Eugene E. Wilson. LXXXI, pp. 121-140, 19 ills., map, Jan., 1942
Beyond the Grand Atlas: Where the French Tricolor Flies Beside the Flag of the Sultan of Morocco. By V. C. Scott O'Connor. LXI, pp. 261-319, 52 ills. in black and white, 12 ills. in color, map, Mar., 1932
Castles, Shrines, and Parks of Japanese Pilgrimage. 10 color photos by W. Robert Moore. LXIX, pp. 457-464, Apr., 1936
Castles in the Air: Experiences and Journeys in Unknown Bhutan. By John Claude White. XXV, pp. 365-455, 74 ills., map, Apr., 1914

CASTLES—*Continued*

Château Land—France's Pageant on the Loire. LVIII, pp. 466-475, 10 ills. in color, Oct., 1930

Country-House Life in Sweden: In Castle and Cottage the Landed Gentry Gallantly Keep the Old Traditions. By Amelie Posse-Brázdová. LXVI, pp. 1-64, 51 ills. in black and white, 13 ills. in color, map, July, 1934

Crusader Castles of the Near East. By William H. Hall. LIX, pp. 369-390, 19 ills., map, Mar., 1931

The Danube, Highway of Races: From the Black Forest to the Black Sea, Europe's Most Important River Has Borne the Traffic of Centuries. By Melville Chater. LVI, pp. 643-697, 54 ills., Dec., 1929

How Warwick Was Photographed in Color. By Maynard Owen Williams. LXX, pp. 83-93, 13 ills. in color, July, 1936

Hunting Castles in Italy. By Melville Chater. LXVIII, pp. 329-366, 25 ills. in black and white, 13 ills. in color, maps, Sept., 1935

Palaces and Peasants in Rome's Old Colony (Romania). 14 color photos by Wilhelm Tobien. LXV, pp. 439-446, Apr., 1934

The Road of the Crusaders: A Historian Follows the Steps of Richard the Lion Heart and Other Knights of the Cross Over the "Via Dei." By Harold Lamb. LXIV, pp. 645-693, 46 ills. in black and white, 13 ills. in color, map, Dec., 1933

Through the Back Doors of France: A Seven Weeks' Voyage in a Canadian Canoe from St. Malo, Through Brittany and the Château Country, to Paris. By Melville Chater. XLIV, pp. 1-51, 55 ills., map, July, 1923

Transylvania and Its Seven Castles: A Motor Circuit Through Rumania's New Province of Racial Complexity and Architectural Charm. By J. Theodore Marriner. XLIX, pp. 319-352, 35 ills., map, Mar., 1926

War's Wake in the Rhineland. By Thomas R. Henry. LXXXVIII, pp. 1-32, 29 ills., map, July, 1945

See also Palaces

CASTLES and Progress in Portugal. By W. Robert Moore. LXXIII, pp. 133-188, 36 ills. in black and white, 24 ills. in color, map, Feb., 1938

CATALINA ISLAND, California. *See* Santa Catalina

CATALPA (Tree):

The Hardy Catalpa. XIV, pp. 348-353, 4 ills., Sept., 1903

CATDOM'S Royalty Photographed in Color. 25 color photos by Willard R. Culver. LXXIV, pp. 597-628, Nov., 1938

CATERPILLARS:

Fighting Insects with Airplanes: An Account of the Successful Use of the Flying-Machine in Dusting Tall Trees Infected with Leaf-Eating Caterpillars. By C. R. Neillie and J. S. Houser. XLI, pp. 333-338, 6 ills., Mar., 1922

An Insect Community Lives in Flower Heads. By James G. Needham. XC, pp. 340-356, 5 ills. in black and white, 11 ills. in color, Sept., 1946

CATERPILLARS—*Continued*

Strange Habits of Familiar Moths and Butterflies. By William Joseph Showalter. LII, pp. 77-105, 19 ills. in black and white, drawing, 88 ills. in color, July, 1927

The **CATHEDRAL CHURCH OF SAINT PETER AND SAINT PAUL.** *See* Washington Cathedral

CATHEDRALS AND CHURCHES:

The Beauties of France. By Arthur Stanley Riggs. XXVIII, pp. 391-491, 73 ills. in black and white, 16 ills. in color, map, Nov., 1915

Cathedrals of England: An Artist's Pilgrimage to These Majestic Monuments of Man's Genius and Faith. By Norman Wilkinson. LXXVI, pp. 741-762, 3 ills. in black and white, 16 ills. in gravure from dry-point engravings by author, Dec., 1939

Cathedrals of the Old and New World. By J. Bernard Walker. XLII, pp. 61-114, 50 ills., July, 1922

The Clock Turns Back in Yugoslavia: The Fortified Monastery of Mountain-girt Dečani Survives Its Six Hundredth Birthday. By Ethel Chamberlain Porter. LXXXV, pp. 493-512, 20 ills., map, Apr., 1944

Constantinople and Sancta Sophia. By Edwin A. Grosvenor. XXVII, pp. 459-482, 21 ills., May, 1915

Constantinople Today. By Solita Solano. XLI, pp. 647-680, 40 ills., map, June, 1922

Glimpses of the Russian Empire. By William Wisner Chapin. XXIII, pp. 1043-1078, 51 ills. in color, map, Nov., 1912

Inexhaustible Italy. By Arthur Stanley Riggs. XXX, pp. 273-368, 76 ills., map, Oct., 1916

The Splendor of Rome. By Florence Craig Albrecht. XLI, pp. 593-626, 28 ills., June, 1922

Venice. By Karl Stieler. XXVII, pp. 587-630, 42 ills., maps, June, 1915

See also Chapels; St. Magnus Cathedral

CATS, Domestic:

The Panther of the Hearth: Lithe Grace and Independence of Spirit Contribute to the Appeal of Cats, "The Only Domestic Animal Man Has Never Conquered." By Frederick B. Eddy. LXXIV, pp. 589-634, 22 ills. in black and white, 25 ills. in color, Nov., 1938

CATS, Wild:

King of Cats and His Court. By Victor H. Cahalane. Paintings by Walter A. Weber. LXXXIII, pp. 217-259, 9 ills. in black and white, 20 ills. in color, Feb., 1943
Contents: African Wildcat, Bengal Tiger, Bobcat, Cheetah, Clouded Leopard, European Wildcat, Golden Cat, Jaguar, Jaguarundi, Leopard, Lion, Lynx, Marbled Cat, Ocelot, Pallas's Cat, Puma, Serval, Siberian Tiger, Snow Leopard, Tabby, Tiger Cat

CATSKILL AQUEDUCT, New York:

New York—The Metropolis of Mankind. By William Joseph Showalter. XXXIV, pp. 1-49, 39 ills., July, 1918

CATTLE AND CATTLE RAISING:

Beyond Australia's Cities. By W. Robert Moore. LXX, pp. 709-747, 27 ills. in black and white, 12 ills. in color, Dec., 1936

CATTLE AND CATTLE RAISING—*Continued*

Exploring a Grass Wonderland of Wild West China. By Ray G. Johnson. LXXXV, pp. 713-742, 24 ills., map, June, 1944

Grass Makes Wyoming Fat. By Frederick Simpich. LXXXVIII, pp. 153-188, 13 ills. in black and white, 19 ills. in color, two-page map, Aug., 1945

Life on the Argentine Pampa. By Frederick Simpich. LXIV, pp. 449-491, 41 ills. in black and white, 8 ills. in color, Oct., 1933

Lonely Australia: The Unique Continent. By Herbert E. Gregory. XXX, pp. 473-568, 68 ills., 5 maps (1 two-page), Dec., 1916

Nebraska, The Cornhusker State. By Leo A. Borah. LXXXVII, pp. 513-542, 6 ills. in black and white, 23 ills. in color, map, May, 1945

The Taurine World: Cattle and Their Place in the Human Scheme—Wild Types and Modern Breeds in Many Lands. By Alvin Howard Sanders. Paintings by Edward Herbert Miner. XLVIII, pp. 591-710, 76 ills. in black and white, 20 ills. in color, Dec., 1925

Included: Aberdeen-Angus, Ayrshire, Banteng, Brahman, Brown Swiss, Devon, Dutch Belted, Gaur, Guernsey, Hereford, Holstein-Friesian, Indian Buffalo, Jersey, Nivernais-Charolais, Red Africander, Red Polls, Shorthorn, Texas Longhorn, West Highlander, Wild White, Yak

Through Paraguay and Southern Matto Grosso. By Sir Christopher H. Gibson. LXXXIV, pp. 459-488, 20 ills. in black and white, 11 ills. in color, map, Oct., 1943

Wonder Island of the Amazon Delta: On Marajó Cowboys Ride Oxen, Tree-dwelling Animals Throng Dense Forests, While Strange Fishes and Birds Help Make a Zoologist's Paradise. By Hugh B. Cott. LXXIV, pp. 635-670, 30 ills. in black and white, 12 ills. in color, map, Nov., 1938

See also Forage; Meat Industry

The **CATTLE** of the World. 20 ills. in color from paintings by Edward Herbert Miner. XLVIII, pp. 639-678, Dec., 1925

CAUCA (River), Colombia:

Over the Andes to Bogotá. By Frank M. Chapman. XL, pp. 353-373, 19 ills., Oct., 1921

CAUCASUS (Mountains), U.S.S.R.:

An Island in the Sea of History: The Highlands of Daghestan. By George Kennan. XXIV, pp. 1087-1140, 49 ills., map, Oct., 1913

Roaming Russia's Caucasus: Rugged Mountains and Hardy Fighters Guard the Soviet Union's Caucasian Treasury of Manganese and Oil. By Rolf Singer. LXXXII, pp. 91-121, 33 ills., July, 1942

The World's Highest Altitudes and First Ascents. By Charles E. Fay. XX, pp. 493-530, 25 ills., June, 1909

The **CAUSE** of Earthquakes. By Robert F. Griggs. XLIV, pp. 443-451, 5 ills., map, Oct., 1923

The **CAUSE** of the Earth's Heat. XVI, pp. 124-125, ill., Mar., 1905

The **CAUSES** That Led Up to the Siege of Pekin. By Dr. W. A. P. Martin. XII, pp. 53-63, ill., Feb., 1901

CAVE DWELLERS. *See* Cliff Dwellers; Troglodytes and Christian "Troglodytes"

CAVE TEMPLES, China:

China's Great Wall of Sculpture: Man-hewn Caves and Countless Images Form a Colossal Art Wonder of Early Buddhism. By Mary Augusta Mullikin. Paintings by author and Anna M. Hotchkis. LXXIII, pp. 313-348, 23 ills. in black and white, 10 ills. in color, map, Mar., 1938

CAVES:

Discovering the Oldest Statues in the World: A Daring Explorer Swims Through a Subterranean River of the Pyrenees and Finds Rock Carvings Made 20,000 Years Ago. By Norbert Casteret. XLVI, pp. 123-152, 24 ills., maps, Aug., 1924

Ice Caves and Frozen Wells. (By W J McGee). XII, pp. 433-434, Dec., 1901

Impressions of Palestine. By James Bryce. XXVII, pp. 293-317, 18 ills., map, Mar., 1915

See also Carlsbad Caverns; Luray Caverns

CAVIAR Fishermen of Romania: From Vâlcov, "Little Venice" of the Danube Delta, Bearded Russian Exiles Go Down to the Sea. By Dorothy Hosmer. LXXVII, pp. 407-434, 29 ills., map, Mar., 1940

CAYENNE, French Guiana:

Color Glows in the Guianas, French and Dutch. By Nicol Smith. LXXXIII, pp. 459-480, 8 ills. in black and white, 13 ills. in color, map, Apr., 1943

CAYLEY, NEVILLE W.:

The Fairy Wrens of Australia: The Little Long-tailed "Blue Birds of Happiness" Rank High Among the Island Continent's Remarkable Birds. By Neville W. Cayley. With 8 ills. in color from paintings by author. LXXXVIII, pp. 488-498, ill. in black and white, Oct., 1945

Pastel Wrens from "Down Under." 8 ills. in color from paintings by author, pp. 489-496

CAYMAN ISLANDS, West Indies:

Capturing Giant Turtles in the Caribbean. By David D. Duncan. LXXXIV, pp. 177-190, 13 ills., map, Aug., 1943

CAYMANS (Alligators):

Wonder Island of the Amazon Delta: On Marajó Cowboys Ride Oxen, Tree-dwelling Animals Throng Dense Forests, While Strange Fishes and Birds Help Make a Zoologist's Paradise. By Hugh B. Cott. LXXIV, pp. 635-670, 30 ills. in black and white, 12 ills. in color, map, Nov., 1938

CEDARS OF LEBANON:

From Jerusalem to Aleppo. By John D. Whiting. XXIV, pp. 71-113, 30 ills., map, Jan., 1913

Syria and Lebanon Taste Freedom. By Maynard Owen Williams. With 21 color photos by author. XC, pp. 729-763, 16 ills. in black and white, Dec., 1946

CEDROS (Island), Mexico:

A Cruise Among Desert Islands. By G. Dallas Hanna and A. W. Anthony. XLIV, pp. 71-99, 32 ills., map, July, 1923

CELEBES (Island), Netherlands East Indies:

The Celebes: New Man's Land of the Indies. By Maynard Owen Williams. LXXVIII, pp. 51-82, 33 ills., map, July, 1940

Seafarers of South Celebes. By G. E. P. Collins. LXXXVII, pp. 53-78, 25 ills., map, Jan., 1945

CELEBRATING Christmas on the Meuse. By Captain Clifton Lisle. XXXVI, pp. 527-537, 5 ills., Dec., 1919

CEMETERIES:

Armistice Day and the American Battle Fields. By J. J. Jusserand. LVI, pp. 509-554, 32 ills. in black and white, 23 ills. in color, Nov., 1929

Fame's Eternal Camping Ground: Beautiful Arlington (Virginia), Burial Place of America's Illustrious Dead. By Enoch A. Chase. LIV, pp. 621-638, 19 ills., Nov., 1928

"The Glory That Was Greece." By Alexander Wilbourne Weddell. XLII, pp. 571-630, 51 ills., map, Dec., 1922

Our National War Memorials in Europe. By John J. Pershing. LXV, pp. 1-36, 24 ills. in black and white, 11 ills. in color, map, Jan., 1934

See also Koyasan

CENSUS:

The Census of 1900 (U. S.). By Dr. F. H. Wines. XI, pp. 34-36, Jan., 1900

The Great Populous Centers of the World. By General A. W. Greely. V, pp. 89-92, table, July 10, 1893

The Indian Census of 1911. By John J. Banninga. XXII, pp. 633-638, 4 ills., July, 1911

The Mexican Census. VII, p. 211, table, June, 1896

New United States Map Shows Census Changes. Text with map supplement. LXXVIII, pp. 821-824, ills., Dec., 1940

A Revelation of the Filipinos (Summary of Report of the First Census of the Philippines). (By Gilbert H. Grosvenor). XVI, pp. 139-192, 138 ills., Apr., 1905

The Russian Census of 1897. (By A. W. G.). VIII, pp. 335-336, Nov., 1897

See also Population; U.S. Bureau of the Census

CENTRAL AMERICA:

Buenos Aires to Washington by Horse: A Solitary Journey of Two and a Half Years, Through Eleven American Republics, Covers 9,600 Miles of Mountain and Plain, Desert and Jungle. By A. F. Tschiffely. LV, pp. 135-196, 75 ills., map, Feb., 1929

The Countries of the Caribbean. By William Joseph Showalter. XXIV, pp. 227-250, 23 ills., Feb., 1913

Fundamental Geographic Relation of the Three Americas. By Robert T. Hill. VII, pp. 175-181, map, May, 1896

CENTRAL AMERICA—*Continued*

The Great Unmapped Areas on the Earth's Surface Awaiting the Explorer and Geographer. By J. Scott Keltie. VIII, pp. 251-266, Sept., 1897

Heart of a Hemisphere: Of Vital Importance is the Area Portrayed in The Society's New Map of Mexico, Central America, and the West Indies. Text with map supplement. LXXVI, pp. 739-740, ill., Dec., 1939

How Latin America Looks from the Air: U. S. Army Airplanes Hurdle the High Andes, Brave Brazil Jungles, and Follow Smoking Volcanoes to Map New Sky Paths Around South America. By Major Herbert A. Dargue. LII, pp. 451-502, 52 ills., map, Oct., 1927

Notes on Central America. XVIII, pp. 272-279, ills., map, Apr., 1907

Our Map of the Countries of the Caribbean. Text with map supplement. XLI, pp. 221-222, Feb., 1922

Rubber Plantations in Mexico and Central America. XIV, pp. 409-414, 7 ills., Nov., 1903

Shattered Capitals of Central America. By Herbert J. Spinden. XXXVI, pp. 185-212, 32 ills., map, Sept., 1919

The Society's New Caribbean Map: Mexico, Central America, and the West Indies—Gateway of Discovery. Text with map supplement. LXVI, pp. 738-740, ill., Dec., 1934

To Bogotá and Back by Air: The Narrative of a 9,500-Mile Flight from Washington, Over Thirteen Latin-American Countries and Return, in the Single-Seater Airplane "Spirit of St. Louis." By Col. Charles A. Lindbergh. LIII, pp. 529-601, 98 ills., map, May, 1928

A Trip to Panama and Darien. By Richard U. Goode. I, pp. 301-314, diagr., foldout map, Oct., 1889

See also Costa Rica; El Salvador; Guatemala; Honduras; Nicaragua; Panama

CENTRAL ASIATIC EXPEDITION:

Explorations in the Gobi Desert. By Roy Chapman Andrews. LXIII, pp. 653-716, 50 ills. in black and white, 20 ills. in color, map, June, 1933

The **CENTRAL** Great Plains (U. S.). XVI, pp. 389-397, 8 ills., Aug., 1905

CENTRAL VALLEY, California:

More Water for California's Great Central Valley. By Frederick Simpich. XC, pp. 645-664, 16 ills., map, Nov., 1946

CEPHALOPODA:

Marauders of the Sea. By Roy Waldo Miner. Paintings by Else Bostelmann. LXVIII, pp. 185-207, 12 ills. in black and white, 8 ills. in color, Aug., 1935

See also Squid

CERAMEICUS (Cemetery), Athens:

"The Glory That Was Greece." By Alexander Wilbourne Weddell. XLII, pp. 571-630, 51 ills., map, Dec., 1922

CERAMICS:

The World's Ancient Porcelain Center (Kingtehchen, China). By Frank B. Lenz. XXXVIII, pp. 391-406, 17 ills., Nov., 1920

CERRO DE LAS MESAS, Mexico:

Expedition Unearths Buried Masterpieces of Carved Jade. By Matthew W. Stirling. LXXX, pp. 277-302, 14 ills. in black and white, 20 ills. in color, map, Sept., 1941

Jungle Housekeeping for a Geographic Expedition. By Marion Stirling. LXXX, pp. 303-327, 15 ills., Sept., 1941

CERTAIN Citizens of the Warm Sea. By Louis L. Mowbray. Paintings by Hashime Murayama. XLI, pp. 27-62, 18 ills. in black and white, 16 ills. in color, Jan., 1922

CETACEANS. *See* Dolphins; Porpoises; Whales

CETINJE, Yugoslavia:

East of the Adriatic: Notes on Dalmatia, Montenegro, Bosnia, and Herzegovina. By Kenneth McKenzie. XXIII, pp. 1159-1187, 1284, 37 ills., map, Dec., 1912

Greece and Montenegro. By George Higgins Moses. XXIV, pp. 281-310, 24 ills., Mar., 1913

The Whirlpool of the Balkans. By George Higgins Moses. XXXIX, pp. 179-197, 15 ills., Feb., 1921

CEYLON (Island), Indian Ocean:

Adam's Second Eden. By Eliza Ruhamah Scidmore. XXIII, pp. 105-173, 206, 61 ills., Feb., 1912

Archæology in the Air. By Eliza R. Scidmore. XVIII, pp. 151-163, 11 ills., Mar., 1907

The British Commonwealth of Nations: "Organized Freedom" Around the World. By Eric Underwood. LXXXIII, pp. 485-524, 31 ills., Apr., 1943

The Buried City of Ceylon. By John M. Abbot. XVII, pp. 613-622, 8 ills., Nov., 1906

Fishing for Pearls in the Indian Ocean. By Bella Sidney Woolf. XLIX, pp. 161-183, 24 ills., Feb., 1926

India and Ceylon. 8 color photos by Helen Messinger Murdoch. XXXIX, pp. 281-288, Mar., 1921

The Pearl Fisheries of Ceylon. By Hugh M. Smith. XXIII, pp. 173-194, 13 ills., map, Feb., 1912

The Perahera Processions of Ceylon. By G. H. G. Burroughs. LXII, pp. 90-100, ill. in black and white, 8 ills. in duotone, July, 1932

Sailing the Seven Seas in the Interest of Science: Adventures Through 157,000 Miles of Storm and Calm, from Arctic to Antarctic and Around the World, in the Non-magnetic Yacht "Carnegie." By J. P. Ault. XLII, pp. 631-690, 47 ills., chart, Dec., 1922

Sigiriya, "A Fortress in the Sky." By Wilson K. Norton. XC, pp. 665-680, 14 ills., map, Nov., 1946

CG-4A's (Cargo Gliders):

Gliders—Silent Weapons of the Sky. By William H. Nicholas. LXXXVI, pp. 149-160, 8 ills., Aug., 1944

CHACO (Region), South America:

Buenos Aires and Its Rivers of Silver: A Journey Up the Paraná and Paraguay to the Chaco Cattle Country. By William R. Barbour. XL, pp. 393-432, 38 ills., Oct., 1921

CHACO (Region), South America—*Continued*

Through Paraguay and Southern Matto Grosso. By Sir Christopher H. Gibson. LXXXIV, pp. 459-488, 20 ills. in black and white, 11 ills. in color, map, Oct., 1943

CHACO BOREAL (Region), Paraguay:

Through Paraguay and Southern Matto Grosso. By Sir Christopher H. Gibson. LXXXIV, pp. 459-488, 20 ills. in black and white, 11 ills. in color, map, Oct., 1943

CHACO CANYON, New Mexico:

Everyday Life in Pueblo Bonito: As Disclosed by the National Geographic Society's Archeologic Explorations in the Chaco Canyon National Monument, New Mexico. By Neil M. Judd. XLVIII, pp. 227-262, 37 ills., map, Sept., 1925

A New National Geographic Society Expedition: Ruins of Chaco Canyon, New Mexico, Nature-Made Treasure-Chest of Aboriginal American History, To Be Excavated and Studied; Work Begins This Month. XXXIX, pp. 637-643, 7 ills., June, 1921

Pueblo Bonito, the Ancient: The National Geographic Society's Third Expedition to the Southwest Seeks to Read in the Rings of Trees the Secret of the Age of Ruins. By Neil M. Judd. XLIV, pp. 99-108, 9 ills., diagr., July, 1923

The Pueblo Bonito Expedition of the National Geographic Society. By Neil M. Judd. XLI, pp. 323-331, 10 ills., diagr., Mar., 1922

CHAD TERRITORY:

Recent Geographic Advances, Especially in Africa. By Major General A. W. Greely. XXII, pp. 383-398, 5 ills., 5 maps, Apr., 1911

Three-Wheeling Through Africa: Two Adventurers Cross the So-called Dark Continent North of Lake Chad on Motorcycles with Side Cars. By James C. Wilson. LXV, pp. 37-92, 64 ills., two-page map, Jan., 1934

CHAMAN, India:

Back to Afghanistan. By Maynard Owen Williams. XC, pp. 517-544, 27 ills., map, Oct., 1946

CHAMBERLIN, ROLLIN T.:

Populous and Beautiful Szechuan: A Visit to the Restless Province of China, in which the Present Revolution Began. By Rollin T. Chamberlin. XXII, pp. 1094-1119, 26 ills., map, Dec., 1911

CHAMBERLIN, T. C.:

The Relations of Geology to Physiography in Our Educational System. By T. C. Chamberlin. V, pp. 154-160, Jan. 31, 1894

See also NGS: Board of Managers

CHAMBERLIN, WELLMAN:

New Map of the Atlantic Ocean: Foremost Sea of Commerce Becomes World's Battleground and Its Peaceful Islands Rise to Strategic Importance. By Leo A. Borah and Wellman Chamberlin. Text with map supplement. LXXX, pp. 407-418, 9 ills., Sept., 1941

CHAMONIX, France:

The Ascent of Mont Blanc. By Walter Woodburn Hyde. XXIV, pp. 861-942, 69 ills., Aug., 1913

CHAMORROS (Tribespeople):
South from Saipan. By W. Robert Moore. LXXXVII, pp. 441-474, 11 ills. in black and white, 17 ills. in color, map, Apr., 1945

CHAMP, W. S.:
The Annual Dinner of the National Geographic Society (Speech by W. S. Champ). XVII, pp. 22-37, Jan., 1906
Report Concerning Ziegler Polar Expedition. (By W. S. Champ). XV, pp. 427-428, Oct., 1904

CHAMPÉRY, Switzerland:
In Valais. By Louise Murray. XXI, pp. 249-256, 6 ills., Mar., 1910

CHANDLER, DOUGLAS:
Belgium—Europe in Miniature. By Douglas Chandler. LXXIII, pp. 397-450, 34 ills. in black and white, 20 ills. in color, Apr., 1938
Changing Berlin. By Douglas Chandler. LXXI, pp. 131-177, 30 ills. in black and white, 24 ills. in color, Feb., 1937
Flying Around the Baltic. By Douglas Chandler. LXXIII, pp. 767-806, 31 ills. in black and white, 13 ills. in duotone, map, June, 1938
Kaleidoscopic Land of Europe's Youngest King: Yugoslavia Holds a Mosaic of Slavs and the City Where Pistol Shots Touched Off the World War. By Douglas Chandler. LXXV, pp. 691-738, 18 ills. in black and white, 34 ills. in color, maps, June, 1939
The Transformation of Turkey: New Hats and New Alphabet Are the Surface Symbols of the Swiftest National Changes in Modern Times. By Douglas Chandler. LXXV, pp. 1-50, 27 ills. in black and white, 23 ills. in color, map, Jan., 1939

CHANDLER, J. S.:
The Madura Temples. By J. S. Chandler. XIX, pp. 218-222, 4 ills., Mar., 1908

CHANGE Comes to Bible Lands. By Frederick Simpich. LXXIV, pp. 695-750, 40 ills. in black and white, 25 ills. in color, map supplement, Dec., 1938

CHANGING Berlin. By Douglas Chandler. LXXI, pp. 131-177, 30 ills. in black and white, 24 ills. in color, Feb., 1937

CHANGING Canton (China). 20 photos by Siukee Mack, Alfred T. Palmer, Kinchue Wong. LXXII, pp. 711-726, Dec., 1937

The **CHANGING** Map in the Balkans. By Frederick Moore. XXIV, pp. 199-226, 27 ills., map, Feb., 1913

CHANGING Palestine. By Major Edward Keith-Roach. LXV, pp. 493-527, 43 ills., map, Apr., 1934

CHANGING Shanghai. By Amanda Boyden. LXXII, pp. 485-508, 21 ills., maps, Oct., 1937

CHANNEL INDIANS. *See* Alikuluf Indians; Yahgans

CHANNEL ISLANDS, English Channel:
The Channel Islands. By Edith Carey. XXXVIII, pp. 143-164, 24 ills., map, Aug., 1920

CHANNEL ISLANDS, English Channel—*Continued*
The Feudal Isle of Sark: Where Sixteenth-Century Laws Are Still Observed. By Sibyl Hathaway (La Dame de Serk). LXII, pp. 101-119, 21 ills., map, July, 1932
See also Guernsey

CHANNEL Ports—And Some Others (England). By Florence Craig Albrecht. XXVIII, pp. 1-55, 45 ills., July, 1915

CHANTIER (Ship):
The First Flight to the North Pole. By Lieutenant Commander Richard Evelyn Byrd. L, pp. 357-376, 14 ills., Sept., 1926

CHAPELS:
Our National War Memorials in Europe. By John J. Pershing. LXV, pp. 1-36, 24 ills. in black and white, 11 ills. in color, map, Jan., 1934
See also Cathedrals and Churches

CHAPIN, WILLIAM WISNER:
Empire of Romance—India. 16 color photos: 5 by William Wisner Chapin. XL, pp. 481-496, Nov., 1921
Glimpses of Holland. By William Wisner Chapin. XXVII, pp. 1-29, 26 ills., Jan., 1915
Glimpses of Japan. By William W. Chapin. XXII, pp. 965-1002, 10 ills. in black and white, 34 ills. in color, Nov., 1911
Japan. 34 photos, hand-tinted, by author, pp. 973-996
Glimpses of Korea and China. By William W. Chapin. XXI, pp. 895-934, 11 ills. in black and white, 39 ills. in color, Nov., 1910
Scenes in Korea and China. 39 photos, hand-tinted, by author, pp. 903-926
Glimpses of the Russian Empire. By William Wisner Chapin. XXIII, pp. 1043-1078, 51 ills. in color, map, Nov., 1912
Russian Empire. 51 photos, hand-tinted, by author, pp. 1047-1070

CHAPMAN, FRANK M.:
Birds May Bring You More Happiness Than the Wealth of the Indies. By Frank M. Chapman. XXIV, pp. 699-714, 14 ills., June, 1913
A Naturalist's Journey Around Vera Cruz and Tampico. By Frank M. Chapman. XXV, pp. 533-562, 31 ills., May, 1914
The Origin of West India Bird-Life. By Frank M. Chapman. IX, pp. 243-247, May, 1898
Over the Andes to Bogotá. By Frank M. Chapman. XL, pp. 353-373, 19 ills., Oct., 1921
Who Treads Our Trails? A Camera Trapper Describes His Experiences on an Island in the Canal Zone, a Natural-History Laboratory in the American Tropics. By Frank M. Chapman. LII, pp. 331-345, 18 ills., map, Sept., 1927

CHAPMAN, LUCIE:
Lords of the Rockies: Photographing Big Game Animals in Their Primeval Surroundings, from Arizona to Canada, Brings Adventure to Two Wilderness Wanderers. By Wendell and Lucie Chapman. LXXVI, pp. 87-128, 14 ills. in black and white, 28 ills. in color, July, 1939

CHAPMAN, LUCIE—*Continued*

With Wild Animals in the Rockies. By Lucie and Wendell Chapman. LXVIII, pp. 231-249, 26 ills. in duotone, Aug., 1935

CHAPMAN, ROBERT H.:

The Aberration of Sound as Illustrated by the Berkeley Powder Explosion. By Robert H. Chapman. VII, pp. 246-249, 3 diagrs., July, 1896

The Deserts of Nevada and the Death Valley. By Robert H. Chapman. XVII, pp. 483-497, 9 ills., map, Sept., 1906

A Drowned Empire (Swamp Drainage). By Robert H. Chapman. XIX, pp. 190-199, 10 ills., Mar., 1908

Our Northern Rockies. By R. H. Chapman. XIII, pp. 361-372, 10 ills., Oct., 1902

CHAPMAN, WENDELL:

Lords of the Rockies: Photographing Big Game Animals in Their Primeval Surroundings, from Arizona to Canada, Brings Adventure to Two Wilderness Wanderers. By Wendell and Lucie Chapman. LXXVI, pp. 87-128, 14 ills. in black and white, 28 ills. in color, July, 1939

Stalking Big Game with Color Camera. 28 color photos by Wendell Chapman, pp. 89-128

With Wild Animals in the Rockies. By Lucie and Wendell Chapman. LXVIII, pp. 231-249, 26 ills. in duotone, Aug., 1935

A **CHAPTER** from Japanese History. By Eki Hioki. XVI, pp. 220-228, May, 1905

A **CHAR-A-BANCS** in Cornwall. By Herbert Corey. XLVI, pp. 653-694, 44 ills., map, Dec., 1924

The **CHARACTER** of Our Immigration, Past and Present. By Z. F. McSweeny. XVI, pp. 1-15, chart, Jan., 1905

The **CHARACTERISTICS** of the Japanese People. By Baron Kentaro Kaneko. XVI, pp. 93-100, Mar., 1905

CHARCOT, JEAN:

Election of Dr. Jean Charcot as Honorary Member of the Society. XXIV, pp. 122, 124-125, Jan., 1913

CHARLES Francis Hall and Jones Sound. (By A. W. G.). VII, pp. 308-310, Sept., 1896

CHARLESTON: A Colonial Rhapsody. 24 color photos by B. Anthony Stewart. LXXV, pp. 289-312, Mar., 1939

CHARLESTON, South Carolina:

Charleston: Where Mellow Past and Present Meet. By DuBose Heyward. LXXV, pp. 273-312, 20 ills. in black and white, 24 ills. in color, map, Mar., 1939

Heroes' Return. By William H. Nicholas. LXXXVII, pp. 333-352, 19 ills., Mar., 1945

CHARLOTTESVILLE, Virginia:

Albemarle in Revolutionary Days. By Dr. G. Brown Goode. VII, pp. 271-281, Aug., 1896

Eighth Annual Field Meeting of the National Geographic Society. VII, pp. 259-260, ill., Aug., 1896

See also Monticello

CHARM and Color Distinguish Norman Byways. 13 color photos by Gervais Courtellemont. LXI, pp. 91-98, Jan., 1932

The **CHARM** of Cape Breton Island: The Most Picturesque Portion of Canada's Maritime Provinces—A Land Rich in Historic Associations, Natural Resources, and Geographic Appeal. By Catherine Dunlop Mackenzie. XXXVIII, pp. 34-60, 22 ills., map, July, 1920

CHARM Spots Along England's Harassed Coast. 16 ills. in duotone. LXXVIII, pp. 237-252, Aug., 1940

CHARTING a Coast-Line of 26,000 Miles (Alaska). XX, pp. 608-609, July, 1909

CHARTING a World at War. By William H. Nicholas. LXXXVI, pp. 617-640, 23 ills., drawing, Nov., 1944

CHARTS, Star. *See* Star Charts

CHASE, ENOCH A.:

Fame's Eternal Camping Ground: Beautiful Arlington (Virginia), Burial Place of America's Illustrious Dead. By Enoch A. Chase. LIV, pp. 621-638, 19 ills., Nov., 1928

CHASE, FRANCIS, JR.:

Palestine Today. By Francis Chase, Jr. XC, pp. 501-516, 16 ills., Oct., 1946

CHATEAU COUNTRY, France:

Château Land—France's Pageant on the Loire. LVIII, pp. 466-475, 10 ills. in color, Oct., 1930

Through the Back Doors of France: A Seven Weeks' Voyage in a Canadian Canoe from St. Malo, Through Brittany and the Château Country, to Paris. By Melville Chater. XLIV, pp. 1-51, 55 ills., map, July, 1923

CHATEAUX. *See* Anticosti Island, Canada; Château Country, France; *and* Castles

CHATER, MELVILLE:

Across the Midi in a Canoe: Two Americans Paddle Along the Canals of Southern France from the Atlantic to the Mediterranean. By Melville Chater. LII, pp. 127-167, 49 ills., map, Aug., 1927

Dalmatian Days: Coasting Along Debatable Shores Where Latin and Slav Meet. By Melville Chater. LIII, pp. 47-90, 26 ills. in black and white, 17 ills. in color, map, Jan., 1928

The Danube, Highway of Races: From the Black Forest to the Black Sea, Europe's Most Important River Has Borne the Traffic of Centuries. By Melville Chater. LVI, pp. 643-697, 54 ills., Dec., 1929

East of Constantinople: Glimpses of Village Life in Anatolia, the Battleground of East and West, Where the Turks Reorganized Their Forces After the World War. By Melville Chater. XLIII, pp. 509-534, 27 ills., map, May, 1923

Europe's Newest Kingdom: After Centuries of Struggle, Albania at Last Enjoys an Era of Peace and Stability. By Melville Chater. LIX, pp. 131-190, 37 ills. in black and white, 39 ills. in color, map, Feb., 1931

CHATER, MELVILLE—*Continued*

History's Greatest Trek: Tragedy Stalks Through the Near East as Greece and Turkey Exchange Two Million of Their People. By Melville Chater. XLVIII, pp. 533-590, 52 ills. in black and white, 32 ills. in color, Nov., 1925

Hunting Castles in Italy. By Melville Chater. LXVIII, pp. 329-366, 25 ills. in black and white, 13 ills. in color, maps, Sept., 1935

Jugoslavia—Ten Years After. By Melville Chater. LVIII, pp. 257-309, 44 ills. in black and white, 25 ills. in color, map, Sept., 1930

The Kizilbash Clans of Kurdistan. By Melville Chater. LIV, pp. 485-504, 22 ills., Oct., 1928

The Land of the Stalking Death: A Journey Through Starving Armenia on an American Relief Train. By Melville Chater. XXXVI, pp. 393-420, 23 ills., Nov., 1919

Michigan, Mistress of the Lakes. By Melville Chater. LIII, pp. 269-325, 65 ills., maps, Mar., 1928

Motor-Coaching Through North Carolina. By Melville Chater. XLIX, pp. 475-523, 43 ills., map, May, 1926

Ohio, the Gateway State. By Melville Chater. LXI, pp. 525-591, 58 ills. in black and white, 13 ills. in color, map, May, 1932

Rediscovering the Rhine: A Trip by Barge from the Sea to the Headwaters of Europe's Storied Stream. By Melville Chater. XLVIII, pp. 1-43, 44 ills., July, 1925

Rhodesia, the Pioneer Colony: In the Land of Sheba's Gold and Rhodes' Diamonds Emerge Model Towns and Modern Mines. By Melville Chater. LXVII, pp. 753-782, 31 ills., June, 1935

Skirting the Shores of Sunrise: Seeking and Finding "The Levant" in a Journey by Steamer, Motor-Car, and Train from Constantinople to Port Said. By Melville Chater. L, pp. 649-728, 60 ills. in black and white, 34 ills. in color, map, Dec., 1926

Through the Back Doors of Belgium: Artist and Author Paddle for Three Weeks Along 200 Miles of Low-Countries Canals in a Canadian Canoe. By Melville Chater. XLVII, pp. 499-540, 39 ills., map, May, 1925

Through the Back Doors of France: A Seven Weeks' Voyage in a Canadian Canoe, from St. Malo, Through Brittany and the Château Country, to Paris. By Melville Chater. XLIV, pp. 1-51, 55 ills., map, July, 1923

Under the South African Union. By Melville Chater. LIX, pp. 391-512, 97 ills. in black and white, 38 ills. in color, two-page map, Apr., 1931

Faces and Flowers Below the Tropics. 14 color photos by author, pp. 453-460

Scenes on High Veld and Low. 13 color photos by author, pp. 493-500

Trekking South Africa with a Color Camera. 11 color photos by author, pp. 413-420

Zigzagging Across Sicily. By Melville Chater. XLVI, pp. 303-352, 44 ills., map, Sept., 1924

CHATHAM, Massachusetts:

Cape Cod People and Places. By Wanda Burnett. LXXXIX, pp. 737-774, 17 ills. in black and white, 24 ills. in color, map, June, 1946

CHATTANOOGA AREA, Tennessee:

Geomorphology of the Southern Appalachians. By Charles Willard Hayes and Marius R. Campbell. VI, pp. 63-126, diagrs., 4 maps, May 23, 1894

CHAULMOOGRA OIL:

Hunting the Chaulmoogra Tree. By Joseph F. Rock. XLI, pp. 243-276, 39 ills., map, Mar., 1922

CHEESE:

An August First in Gruyères. By Melville Bell Grosvenor. LXX, pp. 137-168, 12 ills. in black and white, 23 ills. in color, Aug., 1936

Glimpses of Holland. By William Wisner Chapin. XXVII, pp. 1-29, 26 ills., Jan., 1915

A North Holland Cheese Market. By Hugh M. Smith. XXI, pp. 1051-1066, 17 ills., Dec., 1910

CHEKIANG (Province), China:

China's Wonderland—Yen Tang Shan. 8 ills. in color from camera paintings by Herbert Clarence White, Clarence C. Crisler, Deng Baoling, Hwang Yao-tso. LXXII, pp. 687-694, Dec., 1937

CHELAN, Lake, Washington:

Lake Chelan. By Henry Gannett. IX, pp. 417-428, 7 ills., map, Oct., 1898

CHELAN NATIONAL FOREST, Washington:

Forest Lookout. By Ella E. Clark. With 9 color photos by author. XC, pp. 73-96, 8 ills. in black and white, July, 1946

CHEMICAL Discussion of Analyses of Volcanic Ejecta from Martinique and St. Vincent. By W. F. Hillebrand. XIII, pp. 296-299, July, 1902

CHEMISTRY:

Chemists Make a New World: Creating Hitherto Unknown Raw Materials, Science Now Disrupts Old Trade Routes and Revamps the World Map of Industry. By Frederick Simpich. LXXVI, pp. 601-640, 22 ills. in black and white, 26 ills. in color, Nov., 1939

CHEMISTS Make a New World: Creating Hitherto Unknown Raw Materials, Science Now Disrupts Old Trade Routes and Revamps the World Map of Industry. By Frederick Simpich. LXXVI, pp. 601-640, 22 ills. in black and white, 26 ills. in color, Nov., 1939

CHENGTU, China:

The Eden of the Flowery Republic. By Dr. Joseph Beech. XXXVIII, pp. 355-390, 18 ills. in black and white, 16 ills. in color, Nov., 1920

Populous and Beautiful Szechuan: A Visit to the Restless Province of China, in which the Present Revolution Began. By Rollin T. Chamberlin. XXII, pp. 1094-1119, 26 ills., map, Dec., 1911

CHESAPEAKE AND OHIO CANAL:

Potomac, River of Destiny. By Albert W. Atwood. LXXXVIII, pp. 33-70, 15 ills. in black and white, 18 ills. in color, map, July, 1945

CHESAPEAKE BAY:

Atlantic Estuarine Tides. By Mark S. W. Jefferson. IX, pp. 400-409, diagrs., 7 tables, maps, Sept., 1898

Tides of Chesapeake Bay. By E. D. Preston. X, pp. 391-392, Oct., 1899

CHESAPEAKE BAY REGION:

Chesapeake Odyssey: An 18-foot Sailboat Follows the Course of Captain John Smith around This Spacious Bay of History, Commerce, Sea Food, and Nautical Lore. By John Maloney. LXXVI, pp. 357-392, 32 ills., map, Sept., 1939

CHESS (Game):

Ströbeck (Germany), Home of Chess: A Medieval Village in the Harz Mountains of Germany Teaches the Royal Game in Its Public School. By Harriet Geithmann. LIX, pp. 637-652, 8 ills. in black and white, 14 ills. in color, May, 1931

CHESTER, COLBY M.:

The American Eclipse Expedition. By Rear Admiral Colby M. Chester. XVII, pp. 589-612, 23 ills., col. pl., Nov., 1906

The Discovery of North Pole (Speech by Rear Admiral Colby M. Chester). XXI, pp. 63-82, Jan., 1910

Haiti: A Degenerating Island. By Rear Admiral Colby M. Chester. XIX, pp. 200-217, 5 ills., map, Mar., 1908

The Panama Canal. By Rear Admiral Colby M. Chester. XVI, pp. 445-467, 8 ills., Oct., 1905

Some Early Geographers of the United States. By Rear Admiral Colby M. Chester. XV, pp. 392-404, Oct., 1904

The Young Turk. By Rear-Admiral Colby M. Chester. XXIII, pp. 43-89, 39 ills., Jan., 1912

See also NGS: Board of Managers

CHÉTELAT, ELEANOR DE:

My Domestic Life in French Guinea: An American Woman Accompanies Her Husband, a French Geologist, on His Explorations in a Little-Known Region. By Eleanor de Chételat. LXVII, pp. 695-730, 48 ills., map, June, 1935

CHETELAT, ENZO DE:

Dusky Tribesmen of French West Africa. 26 color photos by Enzo de Chetelat. LXXIX, pp. 639-662, May, 1941

War Awakened New Caledonia: Swift Changes Take Place on the South Pacific Island of Mineral Wealth Defended by Free French and American Troops. By Enzo de Chetelat. LXXXII, pp. 31-55, 14 ills. in black and white, 12 ills. in color, map, July, 1942

South Sea Isle of Mineral Mountains. 12 color photos by author, pp. 33-40

CHETWODE, PENELOPE:

Nepal, the Sequestered Kingdom. By Penelope Chetwode. LXVII, pp. 319-352, 27 ills. in black and white, 15 ills. in color, map, Mar., 1935

CHEVERLANGE, ELIE:

The Manlike Apes of Jungle and Mountain. 10 ills. in color from paintings by Elie Cheverlange. LXXVIII, pp. 221-228, Aug., 1940

Who's Who in the Monkey World. 40 portraits from paintings by Elie Cheverlange. LXXIII, pp. 625-648, May, 1938

CHEYENNE, Wyoming:

Grass Makes Wyoming Fat. By Frederick Simpich. LXXXVIII, pp. 153-188, 13 ills. in black and white, 19 ills. in color, two-page map, Aug., 1945

CHIAPAS (State), Mexico:

Finding Jewels of Jade in a Mexican Swamp. By Matthew W. and Marion Stirling. LXXXII, pp. 635-661, 15 ills. in black and white, 12 ills. in color, map, Nov., 1942

CHICAGO, Illinois:

Chicago Today and Tomorrow: A City Whose Industries Have Changed the Food Status of the World and Transformed the Economic Situation of a Billion People. By William Joseph Showalter. XXXV, pp. 1-42, 28 ills., map, Jan., 1919

The Deep-Water Route from Chicago to the Gulf. XVIII, pp. 679-685, 3 ills., map, Oct., 1907

The Great Canals of the World. XVI, pp. 475-479, Oct., 1905

Illinois, Crossroads of the Continent. By Junius B. Wood. LIX, pp. 523-594, 51 ills. in black and white, 12 ills. in color, map supplement, May, 1931

CHICAGO, Titan of the Middle West. 12 color photos by Clifton Adams. LIX, pp. 585-592, May, 1931

CHICHEN ITZÁ, Mexico:

Chichen Itzá, an Ancient American Mecca: Recent Excavations in Yucatan Are Bringing to Light the Temples, Palaces, and Pyramids of America's Most Holy Native City. By Sylvanus Griswold Morley. XLVII, pp. 63-95, 34 ills., diagr., map, Jan., 1925

The Home of a Forgotten Race: Mysterious Chichen Itza, in Yucatan, Mexico. By Edward H. Thompson. XXV, pp. 585-648, 59 ills., June, 1914

Unearthing America's Ancient History: Investigation Suggests That the Maya May Have Designed the First Astronomical Observatory in the New World in Order to Cultivate Corn. By Sylvanus Griswold Morley. LX, pp. 99-126, 28 ills., July, 1931

Yucatán, Home of the Gifted Maya: Two Thousand Years of History Reach Back to Early American Temple Builders, Corn Cultivators, and Pioneers in Mathematics. By Sylvanus Griswold Morley. Paintings by H. M. Herget. LXX, pp. 591-644, 28 ills. in black and white, 35 ills. in color, map, Nov., 1936

CHICHI JIMA (Peel Island), Ogasawara Shoto:

Springboards to Tokyo. By Willard Price. LXXXVI, pp. 385-407, 16 ills., Oct., 1944

CHIENGMAL, Thailand:

Hunting the Chaulmoogra Tree. By Joseph F. Rock. XLI, pp. 243-276, 39 ills., map, Mar., 1922

CHIGNECTO SHIP RAILWAY. *See* Ship Railways

CHILDHOOD Scenes in Many Lands. 16 ills. XXXI, pp. 147-162, Feb., 1917

CHILDREN of the World. 15 ills. XIX, pp. 127-140, Feb., 1908

CHILDS, MRS. HARRIS R. (Eleanor Stuart):

Zanzibar. By Mrs. Harris R. Childs. XXIII, pp. 810-824, 11 ills., Aug., 1912

CHILDS, MARQUIS W.:

London Wins the Battle. By Marquis W. Childs. LXXXVIII, pp. 129-152, 21 ills., Aug., 1945

CHILE:

Argentina-Chile Boundary. XIII, p. 117, Mar., 1902

Argentina-Chile Boundary Award. XIV, pp. 115-116, Mar., 1903

Argentine-Chile Boundary Dispute. XIII, pp. 27-28, Jan., 1902

The Awakening of Argentina and Chile: Progress in the Lands That Lie Below Capricorn. By Bailey Willis. XXX, pp. 121-142, 14 ills., Aug., 1916

Capital and Chief Seaport of Chile (Santiago and Valparaíso). By W. Robert Moore. LXXXVI, pp. 477-500, 15 ills. in black and white, 8 ills. in color, map, Oct., 1944

Chile-Argentina Boundary Dispute. XIII, p. 220, June, 1902

Chile's Disputes with Peru and Bolivia. XII, pp. 401-402, Nov., 1901

Chile's Land of Fire and Water: Smoking Volcanoes and Ice-hooded Peaks Stand Sentinel Over Limpid Lakes in the Far Southern Andes. By W. Robert Moore. LXXX, pp. 91-110, 9 ills. in black and white, 10 ills. in color, map, July, 1941

The First Transandine Railroad from Buenos Aires to Valparaiso. By Harriet Chalmers Adams. XXI, pp. 397-417, 14 ills., diagr., map, May, 1910

Flying the "Hump" of the Andes. By Capt. Albert W. Stevens. LIX, pp. 595-636, 36 ills., map, May, 1931

Flying the World's Longest Air-Mail Route: From Montevideo, Uruguay, Over the Andes, Up the Pacific Coast, Across Central America and the Caribbean to Miami, Florida, in 67 Thrilling Flying Hours. By Junius B. Wood. LVII, pp. 261-325, 65 ills., map, Mar., 1930

From Panama to Patagonia. By Charles M. Pepper. XVII, pp. 449-452, ill., Aug., 1906

Hatcher's Work in Patagonia. (By W J McGee). VIII, pp. 319-322, Nov., 1897

The Indian Tribes of Southern Patagonia, Tierra del Fuego, and the Adjoining Islands. By J. B. Hatcher. XII, pp. 12-22, 4 ills., Jan., 1901

Inside Cape Horn. By Amos Burg. LXXII, pp. 743-783, 29 ills. in black and white, 10 ills. in color, two-page map, Dec., 1937

A Longitudinal Journey Through Chile. By Harriet Chalmers Adams. XLII, pp. 219-273, 60 ills., map, Sept., 1922

Patagonia. By J. B. Hatcher. VIII, pp. 305-319, 6 ills., map, Nov., 1897

Some Geographic Features of Southern Patagonia, with a Discussion of Their Origin. By J. B. Hatcher. XI, pp. 41-55, 4 ills., Feb., 1900

Some Personal Experiences with Earthquakes (Arica). By Rear Admiral L. G. Billings. XXVII, pp. 57-71, 7 ills., Jan., 1915

CHILE—*Continued*

Twin Stars of Chile: Valparaiso, the Gateway, and Santiago, the Capital—Key Cities with a Progressive Present and a Romantic Past. By William Joseph Showalter. LV, pp. 197-247, 35 ills. in black and white, 25 ills. in color, Feb., 1929

A Winter Voyage Through the Straits of Magellan. By the late Admiral R. W. Meade, U. S. N. VIII, pp. 129-141, ill., map, May, 1897

See also Easter Island; Juan Fernández Island

CHILE'S Disputes with Peru and Bolivia. XII, pp. 401-402, Nov., 1901

CHILE'S Land of Fire and Water: Smoking Volcanoes and Ice-hooded Peaks Stand Sentinel Over Limpid Lakes in the Far Southern Andes. By W. Robert Moore. LXXX, pp. 91-110, 9 ills. in black and white, 10 ills. in color, map, July, 1941

CHILKAT TLINGIT (Indian Tribe):

Indians of Our North Pacific Coast. By Matthew W. Stirling. Paintings by W. Langdon Kihn. LXXXVII, pp. 25-52, 3 ills. in black and white, 16 ills. in color, Jan., 1945

CHIMPANZEES:

Man's Closest Counterparts: Heavyweight of Monkeydom Is the "Old Man" Gorilla, by Far the Largest of the Four Great Apes. By William M. Mann. Paintings by Elie Cheverlange. LXXVIII, pp. 213-236, 10 ills. in black and white, 10 ills. in color, Aug., 1940

CHIMÚ CIVILIZATION:

Air Adventures in Peru: Cruising Among Andean Peaks, Pilots and Cameramen Discover Wondrous Works of an Ancient People. By Robert Shippee. LXIII, pp. 81-120, 40 ills., map, Jan., 1933

CHINA:

American Goods in China. XVII, pp. 173-175, 4 ills., Mar., 1906

Banishing the Devil of Disease Among the Nashi: Weird Ceremonies Performed by an Aboriginal Tribe in the Heart of Yünnan Province, China. By Joseph F. Rock. XLVI, pp. 473-499, 26 ills., map, Nov., 1924

Burma Road, Back Door to China: Like the Great Wall of Ancient Times, This Mighty Mountain Highway Has Been Built by Myriad Chinese to Help Defend Their Homeland. By Frank Outram and G. E. Fane. LXXVIII, pp. 629-658, 26 ills., map, Nov., 1940

Capital and Country of Old Cathay. 16 ills. in duotone. LXIII, pp. 749-764, June, 1933

Causes that Led Up to the Siege of Pekin. By Dr. W. A. P. Martin. XII, pp. 53-63, ill., Feb., 1901

China. By John W. Foster. XV, pp. 463-478, maps, Dec., 1904

China: Her History and Development. By John Barrett. XII, pp. 209-218, June, 1901; pp. 266-272, July, 1901

China and Her People—Some Reflections on Their Manners and Customs, Habits and Lives. By Commander Harrie Webster. XI, pp. 309-319, 3 ills., Aug., 1900

China and the United States. By Sir Chentung Liang-Cheng. XVI, pp. 554-557, Dec., 1905

CHINA—*Continued*

China Fights Erosion with U. S. Aid. By Walter C. Lowdermilk. LXXXVII, pp. 641-680, 10 ills. in black and white, 26 ills. in color, June, 1945

China Is Not Overpopulated. XVI, p. 572, Dec., 1905

China Opens Her Wild West (Yünnan): In the Mountain-girt Heart of a Continent a New China Has Been Created During the Years of War. By Owen Lattimore. LXXXII, pp. 337-367, 21 ills. in black and white, 11 ills. in color, map, Sept., 1942

China's Great Wall of Sculpture: Man-hewn Caves and Countless Images Form a Colossal Art Wonder of Early Buddhism. By Mary Augusta Mullikin. Paintings by author and Anna M. Hotchkis. LXXIII, pp. 313-348, 23 ills. in black and white, 10 ills. in color, map, Mar., 1938

China's Hand-built Air Bases. 9 ills. LXXXVIII, pp. 231-236, Aug., 1945

China's Treasures. By Frederick McCormick. XXIII, pp. 996-1040, 50 ills., Oct., 1912

The Chinese "Boxers." By Llewellyn James Davies. XI, pp. 281-287, July, 1900

The Chinese Jews. By Oliver Bainbridge. XVIII, pp. 621-632, 7 ills., Oct., 1907

The Chinese Paradox. By Harvey Maitland Watts. XI, pp. 352-358, ills., Sept., 1900

Chinese Pigeon Whistles. XXIV, pp. 715-716, ills., June, 1913

Climbing Mighty Minya Konka: Americans First Scaled Mountain That Now Is Landmark of China's New Skyway. By Richard L. Burdsall and Terris Moore. LXXXIII, pp. 625-650, 23 ills., map, May, 1943

Coastal Cities of China. By W. Robert Moore. LXVI, pp. 601-643, 12 ills. in black and white, 18 ills. in duotone, 14 ills. in color, map, Nov., 1934

Cotton and the Chinese Boycott (From an Address by President Roosevelt to the Citizens of Atlanta, October 20, 1905). XVI, pp. 516-517, Nov., 1905

Curious and Characteristic Customs of China. By Kenneth F. Junor. XXI, pp. 791-806, 7 ills., Sept., 1910

The Descendants of Confucius (Industries in Shantung). By Maynard Owen Williams. XXXVI, pp. 253-265, 16 ills., Sept., 1919

The Desert Road to Turkestan: Twentieth Century Travel Through Innermost Asia, Along Caravan Trails Over Which Oriental Commerce Was Once Borne from China to the Medieval Western World. By Owen Lattimore. LV, pp. 661-702, 45 ills., map, June, 1929

The Eden of the Flowery Republic. By Dr. Joseph Beech. XXXVIII, pp. 355-390, 18 ills. in black and white, 16 ills. in color, Nov., 1920

Experiences of a Lone Geographer: An American Agricultural Explorer Makes His Way Through Brigand-infested Central China en Route to the Amne Machin Range, Tibet. By Joseph F. Rock. XLVIII, pp. 331-347, 16 ills., map, Sept., 1925

Exploring a Grass Wonderland of Wild West China. By Ray G. Johnson. LXXXV, pp. 713-742, 24 ills., map, June, 1944

CHINA—*Continued*

Farmers Since the Days of Noah: China's Remarkable System of Agriculture Has Kept Alive the Densest Population in the World. By Adam Warwick. LI, pp. 469-500, 37 ills., Apr., 1927

Fearful Famines of the Past: History Will Repeat Itself Unless the American People Conserve Their Resources. By Ralph A. Graves. XXXII, pp. 69-90, 11 ills., July, 1917

Foreigners and Foreign Firms in China. XI, p. 330, Aug., 1900

Four Thousand Hours Over China. By Capt. Hans Koester. LXXIII, pp. 571-598, 25 ills., map, May, 1938

From the Mediterranean to the Yellow Sea by Motor: The Citroën-Haardt Expedition Successfully Completes Its Dramatic Journey. By Maynard Owen Williams. LXII, pp. 513-580, 45 ills. in black and white, 25 ills. in color, maps, Nov., 1932

Geographic Progress of Civilization. Annual Address by the President, Honorable Gardiner G. Hubbard. VI, pp. 1-22, Feb. 14, 1894

The Geography of China: The Influence of Physical Environment on the History and Character of the Chinese People. By Frank Johnson Goodnow. LI, pp. 651-664, 11 ills., June, 1927

Geologists in China. XVIII, pp. 640-644, 5 ills., Oct., 1907

Glimpses of Korea and China. By William W. Chapin. XXI, pp. 895-934, 11 ills. in black and white, 39 ills. in color, Nov., 1910

The Glories of the Minya Konka: Magnificent Snow Peaks of the China-Tibetan Border Are Photographed at Close Range by a National Geographic Society Expedition. By Joseph F. Rock. LVIII, pp. 385-437, 35 ills. in black and white, 24 ills. in color, map, Oct., 1930

Grand Canal Panorama. By Willard Price. LXXI, pp. 487-514, 31 ills., map, Apr., 1937

The Great Wall of China. (By James H. Wilson). XI, pp. 372-374, ill., Sept., 1900

The Hairnet Industry in North China. By H. W. Robinson. XLIV, pp. 327-336, 10 ills., Sept., 1923

Ho for the Soochow Ho. By Mabel Craft Deering. LI, pp. 623-649, 32 ills., map, June, 1927

How Half the World Works. By Alice Tisdale Hobart and Mary A. Nourse. LXI, pp. 509-524, 22 ills., Apr., 1932

Hunan—The Closed Province of China. By William Barclay Parsons. XI, pp. 393-400, ill., map, Oct., 1900

A Hunter of Plants. By David Fairchild. XXXVI, pp. 57-77, 18 ills., July, 1919

Jade. By S. E. Easter. XIV, pp. 9-17, maps, Jan., 1903

Japan, America, and the Orient. By Eki Hioki. XVII, pp. 498-504, Sept., 1906

Japan and China—Some Comparisons. By Commander Harrie Webster. XII, pp. 69-77, ills., Feb., 1901

The Kingdom of Flowers: An Account of the Wealth of Trees and Shrubs of China and of What the Arnold Arboretum, with China's Help, Is Doing to Enrich America. By Ernest H. Wilson. XXII, pp. 1003-1035, 24 ills., Nov., 1911

Konka Risumgongba, Holy Mountain of the Outlaws. By Joseph F. Rock. LX, pp. 1-65, 36 ills. in black and white, 43 ills. in color, map, July, 1931

The Lama's Motor-Car. By Ethan C. Le Munyon. XXIV, pp. 641-670, 34 ills., May, 1913

The Land of the Crossbow (Yünnan Province). By George Forrest. XXI, pp. 132-156, 15 ills., map, Feb., 1910

The Land of the Yellow Lama: National Geographic Society Explorer Visits the Strange Kingdom of Muli, Beyond the Likiang Snow Range of Yünnan Province, China. By Joseph F. Rock. XLVII, pp. 447-491, 39 ills., map, Apr., 1925

Landscaped Kwangsi, China's Province of Pictorial Art. By G. Weidman Groff and T. C. Lau. LXXII, pp. 671-710, 33 ills., map, Dec., 1937

Lessons from China (Forestry). XX, pp. 18-29, 8 ills., Jan., 1909

Life Afloat in China: Tens of Thousands of Chinese in Congested Ports Spend Their Entire Existence on Boats. By Robert F. Fitch. LI, pp. 665-686, 28 ills., June, 1927

Life Along the Central China Coast. 14 color photos by W. Robert Moore. LXII, pp. 317-324, Sept., 1932

Life Among the Lamas of Choni: Describing the Mystery Plays and Butter Festival in the Monastery of an Almost Unknown Tibetan Principality in Kansu Province, China. By Joseph F. Rock. LIV, pp. 569-619, 34 ills. in black and white, 16 ills. in color, map, Nov., 1928

"The Man in the Street" in China. By Guy Magee, Jr. XXXVIII, pp. 406-421, 15 ills., Nov., 1920

Map-Changing Medicine. By William Joseph Showalter. XLII, pp. 303-330, 26 ills., Sept., 1922

Mrs. Bishop's "The Yangtze Valley and Beyond." By Eliza Ruhamah Scidmore. XI, pp. 366-368, Sept., 1900

The National Geographic Society's Yünnan Province Expedition. By Gilbert Grosvenor. XLVII, pp. 493-498, 5 ills., Apr., 1925

New China and the Printed Page. By Paul Hutchinson. LI, pp. 687-722, 37 ills., June, 1927

Peacetime Plant Hunting About Peiping. By P. H. and J. H. Dorsett. LXXII, pp. 509-534, 21 ills., map, Oct., 1937

Pirate-Fighters of the South China Sea. By Robert Cardwell. LXXXIX, pp. 787-796, 11 ills., June, 1946

Populous and Beautiful Szechuan: A Visit to the Restless Province of China, in which the Present Revolution Began. By Rollin T. Chamberlin. XXII, pp. 1094-1119, 26 ills., map, Dec., 1911

Present Conditions in China. By Frederick McCormick. XXII, pp. 1120-1138, 13 ills., Dec., 1911

Present Conditions in China. By John W. Foster. XVII, pp. 651-672, 709-711, Dec., 1906

Problems in China. By James M. Hubbard. XI, pp. 297-308, 3 ills., map supplement, Aug., 1900

Race Prejudice in the Far East. By Melville E. Stone. XXI, pp. 973-985, 6 ills., Dec., 1910

Raft Life on the Hwang Ho. By W. Robert Moore. LXI, pp. 743-752, 14 ills., June, 1932

The Road to Wang Ye Fu: An Account of the Work of the National Geographic Society's Central-China Expedition in the Mongol Kingdom of Ala Shan. By Frederick R. Wulsin. XLIX, pp. 197-234, 44 ills., map, Feb., 1926

Salt for China's Daily Rice. 11 ills. LXXXVI, pp. 329-336, Sept., 1944

Seeking the Mountains of Mystery: An Expedition on the China-Tibet Frontier to the Unexplored Amnyi Machen Range, One of Whose Peaks Rivals Everest. By Joseph F. Rock. LVII, pp. 131-185, 54 ills., two-page map, Feb., 1930

Shantung—China's Holy Land. By Charles K. Edmunds. XXXVI, pp. 231-252, 21 ills., map, Sept., 1919

Shifting Scenes on the Stage of New China. XXXVIII, pp. 423-428, 4 ills., Nov., 1920

The Siberian Transcontinental Railroad. By General A. W. Greely. VIII, pp. 121-124, Apr., 1897

Singan—The Present Capital of the Chinese Empire. (By James Mascarene Hubbard). XII, pp. 63-66, ill., Feb., 1901

6,000 Miles over the Roads of Free China. By Josephine A. Brown. LXXXV, pp. 355-384, 30 ills., map, Mar., 1944

The Society's New Map of China. By James M. Darley. Text with map supplement. LXXXVII, pp. 745-746, June, 1945

Stilwell Road—Land Route to China. By Nelson Grant Tayman. LXXXVII, pp. 681-698, 18 ills., June, 1945

Taming "Flood Dragons" Along China's Hwang Ho (River). By Oliver J. Todd. LXXXI, pp. 205-234, 26 ills., map, Feb., 1942

A Thousand Miles Along the Great Wall of China: The Mightiest Barrier Ever Built by Man Has Stood Guard Over the Land of Chin for Twenty Centuries. By Adam Warwick. XLIII, pp. 113-143, 27 ills., maps, panorama, Feb., 1923
  The Great Wall of China Near Nankow Pass (panorama)

Through the Great River Trenches of Asia: National Geographic Society Explorer Follows the Yangtze, Mekong, and Salwin Through Mighty Gorges, Some of Whose Canyon Walls Tower to a Height of More Than Two Miles. By Joseph F. Rock. L, pp. 133-186, 47 ills., map, Aug., 1926

Today on the China Coast. By John B. Powell. LXXXVII, pp. 217-238, 17 ills., map, Feb., 1945

The Tsung-Li-Yamen (Foreign Office). (By Miss E. R. Scidmore). XI, pp. 291-292, diagr., map, July, 1900

Western Progress in China. XII, pp. 434-436, Dec., 1901

"Where the Mountains Walked": An Account of the Recent Earthquake in Kansu Province, China, Which Destroyed 100,000 Lives. By Upton Close and Elsie McCormick. XLI, pp. 445-464, 23 ills., map, May, 1922

CHINA—*Continued*

The Wonderful Canals of China. By F. H. King. XXIII, pp. 931-958, 35 ills., 5 maps, Oct., 1912

The Wonderful Canals of China. By George E. Anderson. XVI, pp. 68-69, Feb., 1905

The World's Ancient Porcelain Center (Kingtehchen). By Frank B. Lenz. XXXVIII, pp. 391-406, 17 ills., Nov., 1920

The World's Greatest Overland Explorer: How Marco Polo Penetrated Farthest Asia, "Discovered" Many Lands Unknown to Europe, and Added Numerous Minerals, Animals, Birds, and Plants to Man's Knowledge. By J. R. Hildebrand. LIV, pp. 505-568, 53 ills., two-page map, Nov., 1928

See also Canton; Hainan (Island); Hong Kong; Kunming; Macau; Manchuria (Manchukuo); Mongolia; Nanking; Peiping; Puto Shan (Island); Shanghai; Sinkiang; Tibet; Tsinghai; Yünnan

CHINA'S Great Wall of Sculpture: Man-hewn Caves and Countless Images Form a Colossal Art Wonder of Early Buddhism. By Mary Augusta Mullikin. Paintings by author and Anna M. Hotchkis. LXXIII, pp. 313-348, 23 ills. in black and white, 10 ills. in color, map, Mar., 1938

CHINA'S Hand-built Air Bases. 9 ills. LXXXVIII, pp. 231-236, Aug., 1945

CHINA'S Teeming Life on the Rivers and Sea. 18 photos in duotone by Paul De Gaston and W. Robert Moore. LXVI, pp. 625-640, Nov., 1934

CHINA'S Treasures. By Frederick McCormick. XXIII, pp. 996-1040, 50 ills., Oct., 1912

CHINA'S Wonderland—Yen Tang Shan (Chekiang Province). 8 ills. in color from camera paintings by Herbert Clarence White, Clarence C. Crisler, Deng Bao-ling, Hwang Yao-tso. LXXII, pp. 687-694, Dec., 1937

CHINCHA ISLANDS, Peru:

Peru's Wealth-Producing Birds: Vast Riches in the Guano Deposits of Cormorants, Pelicans, and Petrels which Nest on Her Barren, Rainless Coast. By R. E. Coker. XXXVII, pp. 537-566, 28 ills., June, 1920

CHINESE (People):

China and Her People—Some Reflections on Their Manners and Customs, Habits and Lives. By Commander Harrie Webster. XI, pp. 309-319, 3 ills., Aug., 1900

The Geography of China: The Influence of Physical Environment on the History and Character of the Chinese People. By Frank Johnson Goodnow. LI, pp. 651-664, 11 ills., June, 1927

I Lived on Formosa. By Joseph W. Ballantine. LXXXVII, pp. 1-24, 19 ills., maps, Jan., 1945

The **CHINESE** "Boxers." By Llewellyn James Davies. XI, pp. 281-287, July, 1900

The **CHINESE** Jews. By Oliver Bainbridge. XVIII, pp. 621-632, 7 ills., Oct., 1907

CHINESE Labor for Mexico. XVI, pp. 481-482, Oct., 1905

The **CHINESE** Paradox. By Harvey Maitland Watts. XI, pp. 352-358, ills., Sept., 1900

CHINESE Pigeon Whistles. XXIV, pp. 715-716, ills., June, 1913

CHINESE TURKISTAN. *See* Sinkiang

CHINGHAI (Province), China:

Seeking the Mountains of Mystery: An Expedition on the China-Tibet Frontier to the Unexplored Amnyi Machen Range, One of Whose Peaks Rivals Everest. By Joseph F. Rock. LVII, pp. 131-185, 54 ills., two-page map, Feb., 1930

CHINGTEHCHEN. *See* Kingtehchen

CHININI, Tunisia:

The Mole Men: An Account of the Troglodytes of Southern Tunisia. By Frank Edward Johnson. XXII, pp. 787-846, 60 ills., Sept., 1911

CHIOS (Island), Greece:

Historic Islands and Shores of the Ægean Sea. By Ernest Lloyd Harris. XXVIII, pp. 231-261, 28 ills., map, Sept., 1915

CHIPMUNKS:

Into the Land of the Chipmunk. By Ruth Alexander Nichols. LX, pp. 77-98, 28 ills., July, 1931

CHIPPEWA (Indian Tribe):

America's First Settlers, the Indians. By Matthew W. Stirling. Paintings by W. Langdon Kihn. LXXII, pp. 535-596, 34 ills. in black and white, 24 ills. in color, Nov., 1937

CHIPPEWA FOREST RESERVATION, Minnesota:

Summer Meeting of the American Forestry Association. XIII, pp. 352-358, Sept., 1902

CHITA, U. S. S. R.:

The Far Eastern Republic. By Junius B. Wood. XLI, pp. 565-592, 29 ills., map, June, 1922

"CHOCOLATE ISLAND." *See* São Tomé

CHOCOS (Indians):

The Land That Links the Americas (Panama). 22 color photos by Luis Marden. LXXX, pp. 601-624, Nov., 1941

Little-Known Parts of Panama. By Henry Pittier. XXIII, pp. 627-662, 35 ills., map, July, 1912

CHOLERA:

The Changing Map in the Balkans. By Frederick Moore. XXIV, pp. 199-226, 27 ills., map, Feb., 1913

CHONI, China:

Life Among the Lamas of Choni: Describing the Mystery Plays and Butter Festival in the Monastery of an Almost Unknown Tibetan Principality in Kansu Province, China. By Joseph F. Rock. LIV, pp. 569-619, 34 ills. in black and white, 16 ills. in color, map, Nov., 1928

CHOQQUEQUIRAU, Peru:

In the Wonderland of Peru. By Hiram Bingham. XXIV, pp. 387-573, 250 ills., 3 diagrs., map, Apr., 1913

CHOSEN. *See* Korea

CHOSEN—Land of Morning Calm. By Mabel Craft Deering. LXIV, pp. 421-448, 20 ills. in black and white, 13 ills. in color, map, Oct., 1933

CHOVAN, LUTHER M.:

American Soldier in Reykjavík. By Corporal Luther M. Chovan. LXXXVIII, pp. 536-568, 6 ills. in black and white, 34 ills. in color, Nov., 1945

Iceland Defrosted. 34 color photos by author, pp. 537-568

CHRIST OF THE ANDES, Argentina-Chile:

The First Transandine Railroad from Buenos Aires to Valparaiso. By Harriet Chalmers Adams. XXI, pp. 397-417, 14 ills., diagr., map, May, 1910

CHRISTIAN, JOHN LeROY:

Burma: Where India and China Meet: In the Massive Mountains of Southeast Asia, Swarming Road Builders Wage the "War of the Highways" for Free China and Her Allies. By John LeRoy Christian. LXXXIV, pp. 489-512, 18 ills., map, Oct., 1943

CHRISTIANITY:

The Pageant of Jerusalem: The Capital of the Land of Three Great Faiths Is Still the Holy City for Christian, Moslem, and Jew. By Major Edward Keith-Roach. LII, pp. 635-681, 57 ills., Dec., 1927

Recent Disclosures Concerning Pre-Columbian Voyages to America in the Archives of the Vatican. By William Eleroy Curtis. V, pp. 197-234, Jan. 31, 1894

CHRISTMAS:

Bethlehem and the Christmas Story. By John D. Whiting. LVI, pp. 699-735, 27 ills. in black and white, 14 ills. in color, Dec., 1929

Celebrating Christmas on the Meuse. By Captain Clifton Lisle. XXXVI, pp. 527-537, 5 ills., Dec., 1919

CHRISTMAS ISLAND, Indian Ocean:

At Home on the Oceans: Whales and Sharks Make Exciting Neighbors for a Professor's Wife, Turned Able Seaman, On a Three-year Voyage Around the World. By Edith Bauer Strout. LXXVI, pp. 33-86, 54 ills., map, July, 1939

CHRISTOPHE'S CITADEL, Haiti:

A Little-Known Marvel of the Western Hemisphere: Christophe's Citadel, a Monument to the Tyranny and Genius of Haiti's King of Slaves. By Major G. H. Osterhout, Jr. XXXVIII, pp. 469-482, 13 ills., Dec., 1920

CHROMATIC Highlights of Korea. 13 color photos by W. Robert Moore. LXIV, pp. 429-436, Oct., 1933

CHRONOMETER and Time Service of the U. S. Naval Observatory and the Present Status of Standard Time. By Lieut. Comdr. Edward Everett Hayden. XV, pp. 430-431, Oct., 1904

CHUAN, SHAOCHING H.:

The Most Extraordinary City in the World: Notes on Lhasa—The Mecca of the Buddhist Faith. By Shaoching H. Chuan. XXIII, pp. 959-995, 60 ills., Oct., 1912

CHUGACH MOUNTAINS, Alaska:

The National Geographic Society's Alaskan Expedition of 1909. By Ralph S. Tarr and Lawrence Martin. XXI, pp. 1-54, 42 ills., 12 maps, Jan., 1910

CHUNCHOS (Indians):

A New Peruvian Route to the Plain of the Amazon. By Solon I. Bailey. XVII, pp. 432-448, 12 ills., Aug., 1906

CHUNGKING, China:

The Eden of the Flowery Republic. By Dr. Joseph Beech. XXXVIII, pp. 355-390, 18 ills. in black and white, 16 ills. in color, Nov., 1920

CHURCH, D. B.:

The Valley of Ten Thousand Smokes: An Account of the Discovery and Exploration of the Most Wonderful Volcanic Region in the World. By Robert F. Griggs. XXXIII, pp. 115-169, 46 ills., map, panorama, Feb., 1918

CHURCH, JOHN W.:

A Vanishing People of the South Seas: The Tragic Fate of the Marquesan Cannibals, Noted for Their Warlike Courage and Physical Beauty. By John W. Church. XXXVI, pp. 275-306, 22 ills., map, Oct., 1919

CHURCHES. *See* Cathedrals and Churches; Chapels

CHURCHILL, Canada:

Birds of Timberline and Tundra. By Arthur A. Allen. With 24 color photos by author. XC, pp. 313-339, 8 ills. in black and white, Sept., 1946

CHUTE, WALTER H.:

Net Results from Oceania: Collecting Aquarium Specimens in Tropical Pacific Waters. By Walter H. Chute. LXXIX, pp. 347-372, 8 ills. in black and white, 24 ills. in color, Mar., 1941

Bright Flashes from Pacific Corals (Fishes). 24 color photos by author, pp. 349-372

Tropical Fish Immigrants Reveal New Nature Wonders. By Walter H. Chute. LXV, pp. 93-109, 8 ills. in black and white, 16 ills. in color, Jan., 1934

CINCHONA:

Quinine Hunters in Ecuador. By Froelich Rainey. LXXXIX, pp. 341-363, 21 ills., map, Mar., 1946

CINCINNATI, Ohio:

Ohio, the Gateway State. By Melville Chater. LXI, pp. 525-591, 58 ills. in black and white, 13 ills. in color, map, May, 1932

CINTRA, Portugal:

The Woods and Gardens of Portugal. By Martin Hume. XXI, pp. 883-894, 8 ills., Oct., 1910

CIRCUSES:
The Land of Sawdust and Spangles—A World in Miniature. By Francis Beverly Kelley. LX, pp. 463-516, 35 ills. in black and white, 29 ills. in color, Oct., 1931

CIRENAICA (District), Libia:
Cirenaica, Eastern Wing of Italian Libia. By Harriet Chalmers Adams. LVII, pp. 689-726, 35 ills. in black and white, 13 ills. in color, map, June, 1930
Crossing the Untraversed Libyan Desert: The Record of a 2,200-Mile Journey of Exploration Which Resulted in the Discovery of Two Oases of Strategic Importance on the Southwestern Frontier of Egypt. By A. M. Hassanein Bey. XLVI, pp. 233-277, 46 ills., map, Sept., 1924
Tripoli: A Land of Little Promise. By Adolf L. Vischer. XXII, pp. 1035-1047, 6 ills., map, Nov., 1911

CIRENAICA, On the Edge of the Saharan Sands. 13 color photos by Luigi Pellerano. LVII, pp. 693-700, June, 1930

The **CITIES** That Gold and Diamonds Built: Transvaal Treasures Have Created Bustling Johannesburg and Fostered Pretoria, Administrative Capital of the South African Union. By W. Robert Moore. LXXXII, pp. 735-766, 20 ills. in black and white, 9 ills. in color, map, Dec., 1942

The **CITIZEN** Army of Holland. By Henrik Willem Van Loon. XXIX, pp. 609-622, 9 ills., June, 1916

The **CITIZEN** Army of Switzerland. XXVIII, pp. 503-510, 7 ills., Nov., 1915

CITROËN CENTRAL AFRICAN EXPEDITION. *See* Africa

CITROËN-HAARDT TRANS-ASIATIC EXPEDITION:
The Citroën Trans-Asiatic Expedition Reaches Kashmir: Scientific Party Led by Georges-Marie Haardt Successfully Crosses Syria, Iraq, Persia, and Afghanistan to Arrive at the Pamir. By Maynard Owen Williams. LX, pp. 387-443, 62 ills., map, Oct., 1931
First Over the Roof of the World by Motor: The Trans-Asiatic Expedition Sets New Records for Wheeled Transport in Scaling Passes of the Himalayas. By Maynard Owen Williams. LXI, pp. 321-363, 45 ills., maps, Mar., 1932
From the Mediterranean to the Yellow Sea by Motor: The Citroën-Haardt Expedition Successfully Completes Its Dramatic Journey. By Maynard Owen Williams. LXII, pp. 513-580, 45 ills. in black and white, 25 ills. in color, maps, Nov., 1932
The Trans-Asiatic Expedition Starts. By Georges-Marie Haardt. LIX, pp. 776-782, 6 ills., June, 1931

A **CITY** Learns to Smile Again (Nancy, France). By Maj. Frederick G. Vosburgh. LXXXVII, pp. 361-384, 23 ills., map, Mar., 1945

The **CITY** of Jacqueline (Ter Goes, Netherlands). By Florence Craig Albrecht. XXVII, pp. 29-56, 31 ills., Jan., 1915

A **CITY** of Realized Dreams (San Francisco). By Franklin K. Lane. XXVII, pp. 169-171, Feb., 1915

A **CITY** That Refused to Die (Plymouth, England). By Harvey Klemmer. LXXXIX, pp. 211-236, 13 ills. in black and white, 9 ills. in color, map, Feb., 1946

CIUDAD TRUJILLO (Santo Domingo), Dominican Republic:
The Land Columbus Loved. By Oliver P. Newman. LXXXV, pp. 197-224, 15 ills. in black and white, 11 ills. in color, map, Feb., 1944

CIVIL AIR PATROL:
Heroes of Wartime Science and Mercy. By Elizabeth W. King. LXXXIV, pp. 715-740, 11 ills. in black and white, 334 ills. in color, Dec., 1943

The **CIVIL** Government of Alaska. By Hon. George C. Perkins. IX, pp. 172-178, Apr., 1898

CIVIL WAR (U. S.):
Fame's Eternal Camping Ground: Beautiful Arlington (Virginia), Burial Place of America's Illustrious Dead. By Enoch A. Chase. LIV, pp. 621-638, 19 ills., Nov., 1928
The Most Famous Battle Field in America (Gettysburg). 14 color photos by Clifton Adams and Orren R. Louden. LX, pp. 66-75, July, 1931

CIVILIZATION:
The Effects of Geographic Environment in the Development of Civilization in Primitive Man. By Hon. Gardiner G. Hubbard. VIII, pp. 161-176, June, 1897
Geographic Progress of Civilization. Annual Address by the President, Honorable Gardiner G. Hubbard. VI, pp. 1-22, Feb. 14, 1894
The National Geographic Society: Synopsis of a Course of Lectures on the Effects of Geographic Environment in Developing the Civilization of the World. (By Gardiner G. Hubbard). VIII, pp. 29-32, Jan., 1897

CLANS in Kilt and Plaidie Gather at Braemar (Scotland). 11 color photos by Maynard Owen Williams. LXVIII, pp. 153-160, Aug., 1935

CLARK, AUSTIN H.:
Potent Personalities—Wasps and Hornets: Though Often Painfully Stung, Mankind Profits Immeasurably from the Pest-killing Activities of These Fiery Little Flyers. By Austin H. Clark. Paintings by Hashime Murayama. LXXII, pp. 47-72, 18 ills. in black and white, 12 ills. in color, July, 1937
Who's Who Among the Butterflies. By Austin H. Clark. Paintings by Hashime Murayama. LXIX, pp. 679-692, 5 ills. in black and white, 9 ills. in color, May, 1936

CLARK, CHARLES UPSON:
Romantic Spain. By Charles Upson Clark. XXI, pp. 187-215, 40 ills., map, Mar., 1910

CLARK, D. WORTH:
Idaho Made the Desert Bloom. By D. Worth Clark. LXXXV, pp. 641-688, 21 ills. in black and white, 20 ills. in color, map, June, 1944

CLARK, ELLA E.:
Forest Lookout. By Ella E. Clark. With 9 color photos by author. XC, pp. 73-96, 8 ills. in black and white, July, 1946

CLARK, HUBERT LYMAN:

The Paradise of the Tasman (Lord Howe Island): A Pacific Island Provides the Palms Which Decorate Hotels, Churches, Steamships, and Homes. By Hubert Lyman Clark. LXVIII, pp. 115-136, 24 ills., map, July, 1935

CLARK, JAMES L.:

Morden-Clark Asiatic Expedition: By Coolie and Caravan Across Central Asia: Narrative of a 7,900-Mile Journey of Exploration and Research Over "the Roof of the World," from the Indian Ocean to the Yellow Sea. By William J. Morden. LII, pp. 369-431, 73 ills., map, Oct., 1927

CLARK, JOE:

Home Folk around Historic Cumberland Gap. By Leo A. Borah. LXXXIV, pp. 741-768, 25 ills., map, Dec., 1943

CLARK, LEONARD:

Among the Big Knot Lois of Hainan: Wild Tribesmen With Topknots Roam the Little-known Interior of This Big and Strategically Important Island in the China Sea. By Leonard Clark. LXXIV, pp. 391-418, 28 ills., map, Sept., 1938

CLARK, Lake, Alaska:

Lake Clark, a Little Known Alaskan Lake. By Wilfred H. Osgood. XV, pp. 326-331, ills., map, Aug., 1904

CLARKE, FREDERICK J.:

Ascension Island, an Engineering Victory. By Lt. Col. Frederick J. Clarke. LXXXV, pp. 623-640, 21 ills., May, 1944

CLARKE, NELL RAY:

The Haunts of the Caribbean Corsairs: The West Indies a Geographic Background for the Most Adventurous Episodes in the History of the Western Hemisphere. By Nell Ray Clarke. XLI, pp. 147-187, 43 ills., Feb., 1922

CLASSIC Greece Merges Into 1941 News. 19 photos: 15 by B. Anthony Stewart, 3 by Maynard Owen Williams. LXXIX, pp. 93-108, Jan., 1941

CLASSICAL LANDS:

Ancient Rome Brought to Life. By Rhys Carpenter. Paintings by H. M. Herget. XC, pp. 567-633, 2 ills. in black and white, 32 ills. in color, map, Nov., 1946

Classic Greece Merges Into 1941 News. 19 photos: 15 by B. Anthony Stewart, 3 by Maynard Owen Williams. LXXIX, pp. 93-108, Jan., 1941

Greece—the Birthplace of Science and Free Speech: Explorations on the Mainland and in Crete and the Aegean Isles Reveal Ancient Life Similar to That of the Present. By Richard Stillwell. Paintings by H. M. Herget. LXXXV, pp. 273-353, 13 ills. in black and white, 32 ills. in color, two-page map, Mar., 1944

Italy, From Roman Ruins to Radio: History of Ancient Bridge Building and Road Making Repeats Itself in Modern Public Works and Engineering Projects. By John Patric. LXXVII, pp. 347-394, 27 ills. in black and white, 9 ills. in color, Mar., 1940

CLASSICAL LANDS—*Continued*

Map Links Classic World with 1940. Text with map supplement. LXXVII, p. 338, Mar., 1940

Modern Odyssey in Classic Lands: Troy's Treasures, Athens' Parthenon, and Rome's First "Broad Way" Influence Today's Banks, Costumes, Jewelry, and Railroad Timetables. By Maynard Owen Williams. LXXVII, pp. 291-337, 27 ills. in black and white, 22 ills. in color, Mar., 1940

The Ruins at Selinus (Sicily). (By Marion Crawford). XX, p. 117, Jan., 1909

See also Athens; Carthage; Greece; Rome; Troy

The **CLASSIFICATION** of Geographic Forms by Genesis. By W J McGee. I, pp. 27-36, tables, Oct., 1888

CLATWORTHY, FRED PAYNE:

California: A Sunshine Land of Fruits, Flowers, Movies, and Sport. 14 color photos by Fred Payne Clatworthy. LXVI, pp. 585-592, Nov., 1934

Colorado: Among the Peaks and Parks of the Rockies. 11 color photos by Fred Payne Clatworthy. LXII, pp. 39-46, July, 1932

Mexico: Adventures in Color on Mexico's West Coast. 13 color photos by Fred Payne Clatworthy. LVIII, pp. 61-68, July, 1930

United States: Photographing the Marvels of the West in Colors. By Fred Payne Clatworthy. LIII, pp. 694-719, 30 ills. in color, June, 1928

United States: Scenic Glories of Western United States. 12 color photos by Fred Payne Clatworthy. LVI, pp. 223-230, Aug., 1929

United States: Western Views in the Land of the Best. 16 color photos by Fred Payne Clatworthy. XLIII, pp. 405-420, Apr., 1923

CLAY, ALBERT T.:

Pushing Back History's Horizon: How the Pick and Shovel Are Revealing Civilizations That Were Ancient When Israel Was Young. By Albert T. Clay. XXIX, pp. 162-216, 47 ills., map, Feb., 1916

CLAY HILLS, Utah:

Beyond the Clay Hills: An Account of the National Geographic Society's Reconnaissance of a Previously Unexplored Section of Utah. By Neil M. Judd. XLV, pp. 275-302, 28 ills., map, Mar., 1924

CLEAVES, HOWARD H.:

Hunting with the Lens (Birds). By Howard H. Cleaves. XXVI, pp. 1-35, 47 ills., July, 1914

CLEMENTS, EDITH S.:

Flower Pageant of the Midwest: From March to November Nature Embroiders an Ever-changing Pattern of Living Color. By Edith S. and Frederic E. Clements. Paintings by Edith S. Clements. LXXVI, pp. 219-271, ill. in black and white, 125 flower paintings in color, Aug., 1939

Floral Garlands of Prairie, Plain, and Woodland. 125 flower paintings in color by Edith S. Clements, pp. 225-271

Wild Flowers of the West (U.S.). By Edith S. Clements. Paintings from life by author. LI, pp. 566-622, 207 ills. in color, May, 1927

CLEMENTS, FREDERIC E.:

The Family Tree of the Flowers. By Frederic E. Clements and William Joseph Showalter. LI, pp. 555-563, ill. in black and white, ill. in color, May, 1927

Flower Pageant of the Midwest: From March to November Nature Embroiders an Ever-changing Pattern of Living Color. By Edith S. and Frederic E. Clements. LXXVI, pp. 219-271, ill. in black and white, 125 flower paintings in color, Aug., 1939

CLEVELAND, Ohio:

Ohio, the Gateway State. By Melville Chater. LXI, pp. 525-591, 58 ills. in black and white, 13 ills. in color, map, May, 1932

CLIFF DWELLERS:

The Isle of Frankincense (Socotra, Arabian Sea). By Charles K. Moser. XXXIII, pp. 267-278, 11 ills., Mar., 1918

The Prehistoric Ruin of Tsankawi (New Mexico). By George L. Beam. XX, pp. 807-822, 12 ills., Sept., 1909

CLIMATE:

The Antarctic Climate. X, pp. 520-521, Dec., 1899

Climatic Conditions of Alaska. By General A. W. Greely. IX, pp. 132-137, Apr., 1898

Deforestation and Climate. XVI, pp. 397-398, Aug., 1905

Do Volcanic Explosions Affect Our Climate? By C. G. Abbot. XXIV, pp. 181-198, 9 ills., diagr., Feb., 1913

Factors Which Modify the Climate of Victoria (British Columbia). By Arthur W. McCurdy. XVIII, pp. 345-348, maps, May, 1907

Further Explorations in the Land of the Incas: The Peruvian Expedition of 1915 of the National Geographic Society and Yale University. By Hiram Bingham. XXIX, pp. 431-473, 29 ills., maps, panorama, May, 1916

Geography. By Rear-Admiral Sir W. J. L. Wharton. XVI, pp. 483-498, Nov., 1905

Is Climatic Aridity Impending on the Pacific Slope? The Testimony of the Forest. By J. B. Leiberg. X, pp. 160-181, May, 1899

Laws of Temperature Control of the Geographic Distribution of Terrestrial Animals and Plants. Annual Address by Vice-President, Dr. C. Hart Merriam. VI, pp. 229-238, table, 3 maps, Dec. 29, 1894

The Southwest (U.S.): Its Splendid Natural Resources, Agricultural Wealth, and Scenic Beauty. By N. H. Darton. XXI, pp. 631-665, 21 ills., map, Aug., 1910

Weather Fights and Works for Man. By F. Barrows Colton. LXXXIV, pp. 641-670, 22 ills., 3 drawings, Dec., 1943

See also Meteorology

CLIMATIC Conditions of Alaska. By General A. W. Greely. IX, pp. 132-137, Apr., 1898

CLIMATIC LABORATORIES, U. S. Army:

Fit to Fight Anywhere. By Frederick Simpich. LXXXIV, pp. 233-256, 26 ills., Aug., 1943

CLIMBING Mighty Minya Konka: Americans First Scaled Mountain That Now Is Landmark of China's New Skyway. By Richard L. Burdsall and Terris Moore. LXXXIII, pp. 625-650, 23 ills., map, May, 1943

CLINIC, American Hospital, Deir ez Zor, Syria:

Ali Goes to the Clinic. By Herndon and Mary Hudson. XC, pp. 764-766, ills., Dec., 1946

CLIPPER SHIPS (Seaplanes):

Flying the Pacific. By William Burke Miller. LXX, pp. 665-707, 39 ills., Dec., 1936

Included: *China Clipper, Hawaii Clipper, Pan American Clipper, Philippine Clipper*

The **CLOCK** Turns Back in Yugoslavia: The Fortified Monastery of Mountain-girt Dečani Survives Its Six Hundredth Birthday. By Ethel Chamberlain Porter. LXXXV, pp. 493-512, 20 ills., map, Apr., 1944

CLOSE, UPTON (Pseudonym):

"Where the Mountains Walked": An Account of the Recent Earthquake in Kansu Province, China, Which Destroyed 100,000 Lives. By Upton Close and Elsie McCormick. XLI, pp. 445-464, 23 ills., map, May, 1922

CLOSE-UPS of a People Without a Country (Saar). 23 ills. in duotone. LXVII, pp. 249-264, Feb., 1935

CLOTHING AND COSTUMES:

Costumes of Czechoslovakia. 19 color photos by Hans Hildenbrand. LI, pp. 725-740, June, 1927

Rainbow Costumes of Poland's Peasants. 11 color photos by Hans Hildenbrand and Maynard Owen Williams. LXIII, pp. 329-336, Mar., 1933

The Restoration of Colonial Williamsburg. By W. A. R. Goodwin. LXXI, pp. 402-443, 21 ills. in black and white, 25 ills. in color, Apr., 1937

Snowy Peaks and Old Costumes of Switzerland. 12 color photos by Hans Hildenbrand. LXVI, pp. 147-154, Aug., 1934

Types and Costumes of Old Sweden. 30 color photos by Gustav Heurlin, G. W. Cronquist, Wilhelm Tobien, Charles Martin. LIV, pp. 425-440, Oct., 1928

See also Carnivals; Circuses; Coronations; Dances; Festivals; names of cities and countries; *and* the following: Arabs; Cowboys; East Indians; Eskimos; Gauchos; Indians of Central America; Indians of North America; Indians of South America; Lapps; names of tribes; *and* branches of the U. S. Armed Services

CLOTHING AND EQUIPMENT TESTS, U. S. Army:

Fit to Fight Anywhere. By Frederick Simpich. LXXXIV, pp. 233-256, 26 ills., Aug., 1943

CLOUDS:

Cloud Scenery of the High Plains. By Willard D. Johnson. IX, pp. 493-496, 3 ills., Dec., 1898

Forecasting the Weather. (By Alfred J. Henry). XV, pp. 285-292, 6 ills., chart, July, 1904

The International Cloud Work of the Weather Bureau. By Frank H. Bigelow. X, pp. 351-354, Sept., 1899

Our Heralds of Storm and Flood (U. S. Weather Bureau). By Gilbert H. Grosvenor. XVIII, pp. 586-601, 15 ills., chart, Sept., 1907

CLOUDS—*Continued*

Toilers of the Sky: Tenuous Clouds Perform the Mighty Task of Shaping the Earth and Sustaining Terrestrial Life. By McFall Kerbey. XLVIII, pp. 163-189, 33 ills., Aug., 1925

The Warfare on Our Eastern Coast. By John Oliver La Gorce. XXVIII, pp. 195-230, 29 ills., charts, Sept., 1915

Weather Fights and Works for Man. By F. Barrows Colton. LXXXIV, pp. 641-670, 22 ills., 3 drawings, Dec., 1943

CLOVELLY, England:

Channel Ports—And Some Others. By Florence Craig Albrecht. XXVIII, pp. 1-55, 45 ills., July, 1915

CNOSSUS, Crete (Island):

Crete, Where Sea-Kings Reigned. By Agnes N. Stillwell. LXXXIV, pp. 547-568, 20 ills., map, Nov., 1943

COAL AND COAL MINING:

Alaska and Its Mineral Resources. By Samuel Franklin Emmons. IX, pp. 139-172, 3 ills., map supplement, Apr., 1898

The Charm of Cape Breton Island: The Most Picturesque Portion of Canada's Maritime Provinces—A Land Rich in Historic Associations, Natural Resources, and Geographic Appeal. By Catherine Dunlop Mackenzie. XXXVIII, pp. 34-60, 22 ills., map, July, 1920

Coal—Ally of American Industry. By William Joseph Showalter. XXXIV, pp. 407-434, 23 ills., Nov., 1918

Coal: Prodigious Worker for Man. By Albert W. Atwood. LXXXV, pp. 569-592, 19 ills., drawing, May, 1944

The Coal-Fields of Alaska. XXI, pp. 83-87, 6 ills., Jan., 1910

Coal Resources of Alaska. XIII, pp. 172-174, May, 1902

The Course of the Retail Coal Trade. By Dr. David T. Day. XIII, pp. 394-398, Nov., 1902

Efforts to Obtain Greater Energy from Coal. XVIII, pp. 138-140, Feb., 1907

How Long Will the Coal Reserves of the United States Last? By Marius R. Campbell. XVIII, pp. 129-138, 5 diagrs., map, Feb., 1907

An Ideal Fuel (Briquets). By Guy Elliott Mitchell. XXI, pp. 1067-1074, 4 ills., Dec., 1910

The Nation's Undeveloped Resources (Alaska). By Franklin K. Lane. XXV, pp. 183-225, 32 ills., Feb., 1914

A New Source of Power (Lignite). By Guy Elliott Mitchell. XXI, pp. 935-944, 7 ills., Nov., 1910

Our Coal Lands. By Guy Elliott Mitchell. XXI, pp. 446-451, 5 ills., May, 1910

The Story of the Ruhr. By Frederick Simpich. XLI, pp. 553-564, 11 ills., map, May, 1922

The **COAST** and Geodetic Survey: Its Present Work. (By E. D. Preston). X, pp. 268-269, July, 1899

COAST Guard Patrol in Greenland. 9 color photos by Lieut. Thomas S. La Farge. LXXXIII, pp. 565-572, May, 1943

COASTAL Cities of China. By W. Robert Moore. LXVI, pp. 601-643, 12 ills. in black and white, 18 ills. in duotone, 14 ills. in color, map, Nov., 1934

COASTING Through the Bay State (Massachusetts). 12 color photos by Clifton Adams. LX, pp. 287-294, Sept., 1931

The **COASTS** of Corsica: Impressions of a Winter's Stay in the Island Birthplace of Napoleon. By Maynard Owen Williams. XLIV, pp. 221-312, 88 ills., maps, pictorial supplement, Sept., 1923

The **COASTS** of Normandy and Brittany (France). By W. Robert Moore. LXXXIV, pp. 205-232, 5 ills. in black and white, 21 ills. in color, two-page map, Aug., 1943

COBB, COLLIER:

Some Human Habitations. By Collier Cobb. XIX, pp. 509-515, 5 ills., July, 1908

Where the Wind Does the Work (Cape Hatteras). By Collier Cobb. XVII, pp. 310-317, 9 ills., map, June, 1906

COBB, DEWEY AUSTIN:

Fishing and Hunting Tales from Brazil. By Dewey Austin Cobb. XX, pp. 917-920, Oct., 1909

COBB, N. A.:

The House-Fly. By N. A. Cobb. XXI, pp. 371-380, 4 ills., May, 1910

Notes on the Distances Flies Can Travel. By N. A. Cobb. XXI, pp. 380-383, May, 1910

COBERN, CAMDEN M.:

The Sacred Ibis Cemetery and Jackal Catacombs at Abydos. By Camden M. Cobern. XXIV, pp. 1042-1056, 10 ills., Sept., 1913

COBHAM, SIR ALAN J.:

Seeing the World from the Air. By Sir Alan J. Cobham. LIII, pp. 349-384, 37 ills., map, Mar., 1928

COCHINAS BAY, Cuba:

Among the Mahogany Forests of Cuba. By Walter D. Wilcox. XIX, pp. 485-498, 6 ills., map, July, 1908

COCHRAN, DORIS M.:

Our Friend the Frog. By Doris M. Cochran. Paintings by Hashime Murayama. LXI, pp. 629-654, 16 ills. in black and white, 14 ills. in color, May, 1932

COCHRAN, PHILIP G.:

The Aerial Invasion of Burma. By General H. H. Arnold. LXXXVI, pp. 129-148, 20 ills., Aug., 1944

COCKFIGHTS:

The Races of Domestic Fowl. By M. A. Jull. Paintings by Hashime Murayama. LI, pp. 379-452, 67 ills. in black and white, 29 ills. in color, Apr., 1927

Sarawak: The Land of the White Rajahs. By Harrison W. Smith. XXXV, pp. 110-167, 58 ills., map, Feb., 1919

COCOANUTS. *See* Coconuts

COCONUT PALMS:

Nauru, the Richest Island in the South Seas. By Rosamond Dodson Rhone. XL, pp. 559-589, 24 ills., Dec., 1921

The Samoan Cocoanut (Article compiled by Gen. A. W. Greely). IX, pp. 12-24, Jan., 1898

COCONUTS:

Coconuts and Coral Islands (Ontong Java). By H. Ian Hogbin. LXV, pp. 265-298, 24 ills. in black and white, 14 ills. in color, map, Mar., 1934

The Samoan Cocoanut (Article compiled by Gen. A. W. Greely). IX, pp. 12-24, Jan., 1898

COCOS ISLAND, Pacific Ocean:

Costa Rica, Land of the Banana. By Paul B. Popenoe. XLI, pp. 201-220, 17 ills., Feb., 1922

COCOS ISLANDS, Indian Ocean:

At Home on the Oceans: Whales and Sharks Make Exciting Neighbors for a Professor's Wife, Turned Able Seaman, On a Three-year Voyage Around the World. By Edith Bauer Strout. LXXVI, pp. 33-86, 54 ills., map, July, 1939

COD, Cape, Massachusetts:

The Cape Cod Canal. By Commodore J. W. Miller. XXVI, pp. 185-190, 3 ills., map, Aug., 1914

Cape Cod People and Places. By Wanda Burnett. LXXXIX, pp. 737-774, 17 ills. in black and white, 24 ills. in color, map, June, 1946

Collarin' Cape Cod: Experiences on Board a U. S. Navy Destroyer in a Wild Winter Storm. By Lieutenant H. R. Thurber. XLVIII, pp. 427-472, 46 ills., Oct., 1925

CODFISH AND CODFISH INDUSTRY:

Fishes and Fisheries of Our North Atlantic Seaboard. By John Oliver La Gorce. Paintings by Hashime Murayama. XLIV, pp. 567-634, 35 ills. in black and white, 16 ills. in color, Dec., 1923

Islands Adrift: St. Pierre and Miquelon: In a Key Position on the North Atlantic Air Route, France's Oldest Colony Rides Out Another Storm. By Frederic K. Arnold. LXXX, pp. 743-768, 23 ills., map, Dec., 1941

Newfoundland, North Atlantic Rampart: From the "First Base of American Defense" Planes Fly to Britain's Aid over Stout Fishing Schooners of the Grand Banks. By George Whiteley, Jr. LXXX, pp. 111-140, 26 ills., map, July, 1941

Viking Life in the Storm-Cursed Faeroes. By Leo Hansen. LVIII, pp. 607-648, 49 ills., map, Nov., 1930

COFFEE:

As São Paulo Grows: Half the World's Coffee Beans Flavor the Life and Speed the Growth of an Inland Brazil City. By W. Robert Moore. LXXV, pp. 657-688, 33 ills., map, May, 1939

Coffee Is King in El Salvador. By Luis Marden. LXXXVI, pp. 575-616, 22 ills. in black and white, 27 ills. in color, map, Nov., 1944

Costa Rica, Land of the Banana. By Paul B. Popenoe. XLI, pp. 201-220, 17 ills., Feb., 1922

COFFEE—*Continued*

Guatemala, the Country of the Future. By Edine Frances Tisdel. XXI, pp. 596-624, 33 ills., map, July, 1910

Land of the Painted Oxcarts (Costa Rica). By Luis Marden. With 31 color photos by author. XC, pp. 409-456, 30 ills. in black and white, map, Oct., 1946

A Visit to the Brazilian Coffee Country. By Robert De C. Ward. XXII, pp. 908-931, 19 ills., map, Oct., 1911

COFFIN, MARIAN CRUGER:

Where East Meets West: Visit to Picturesque Dalmatia, Montenegro and Bosnia. By Marian Cruger Coffin. XIX, pp. 309-344, 26 ills., map, May, 1908

COIMBRA, Portugal:

The Woods and Gardens of Portugal. By Martin Hume. XXI, pp. 883-894, 8 ills., Oct., 1910

COINS AND COINAGE:

The Geography of Money. By William Atherton Du Puy. LII, pp. 745-768, 31 ills., Dec., 1927

Our Heterogeneous System of Weights and Measures. By Alexander Graham Bell. XVII, pp. 158-169, Mar., 1906

Pieces of Silver. By Frederick Simpich. LXIV, pp. 253-292, 49 ills., Sept., 1933

COKER, R. E.:

Peru's Wealth-Producing Birds: Vast Riches in the Guano Deposits of Cormorants, Pelicans, and Petrels which Nest on Her Barren, Rainless Coast. By R. E. Coker. XXXVII, pp. 537-566, 28 ills., June, 1920

COLBERT, L. O. *See* NGS: Board of Trustees

COLCA VALLEY, Peru:

A Forgotten Valley of Peru: Conquered by Incas, Scourged by Famine, Plagues, and Earthquakes, Colca Valley Shelters the Last Fragment of an Ancient Andean Tribe. By Robert Shippee. LXV, pp. 111-132, 22 ills., map, Jan., 1934

COLE, MABEL COOK:

The Island of Nias, at the Edge of the World. By Mabel Cook Cole. LX, pp. 201-224, 26 ills., map, Aug., 1931

COLLARIN' Cape Cod (Massachusetts): Experiences on Board a U. S. Navy Destroyer in a Wild Winter Storm. By Lieutenant H. R. Thurber. XLVIII, pp. 427-472, 46 ills., Oct., 1925

COLLECTIVE COMMUNITIES:

Palestine Today. By Francis Chase, Jr. XC, pp. 501-516, 16 ills., Oct., 1946

See also Ernst Thaelmann (Collective Farm)

COLLEGES. *See* Universities and Colleges

COLLIES (Dogs):

Sheep Dog Trials in Llangollen: Trained Collies Perform Marvels of Herding in the Cambrian Stakes, Open to the World. By Sara Bloch. LXXVII, pp. 559-574, 17 ills., Apr., 1940

COLLINS, G. E. P.:

Seafarers of South Celebes. By G. E. P. Collins. LXXXVII, pp. 53-78, 25 ills., map, Jan., 1945

COLLINS, G. N.:

Dumboy, the National Dish of Liberia. By G. N. Collins. XXII, pp. 84-88, 5 ills., Jan., 1911

Kboo, a Liberian Game. By G. N. Collins. XXI, pp. 944-948, 3 ills., Nov., 1910

Notes on Southern Mexico (Agricultural Products). By G. N. Collins and C. B. Doyle. XXII, pp. 301-320, 16 ills., map, Mar., 1911

A Primitive Gyroscope in Liberia. By G. N. Collins. XXI, pp. 531-535, 3 ills., June, 1910

COLLINS, HENRY B., JR.:

Exploring Frozen Fragments of American History: On the Trail of Early Eskimo Colonists Who Made a 55-Mile Crossing from the Old World to the New. By Henry B. Collins, Jr. LXXV, pp. 633-656, 24 ills., map, May, 1939

COLLINSON, SIR RICHARD:

Collinson's Arctic Journey. By General A. W. Greely. IV, pp. 198-200, Feb. 8, 1893

COLOGNE, Germany:

Cologne, Key City of the Rhineland. By Francis Woodworth. LXIX, pp. 829-848, 18 ills., map, June, 1936

War's Wake in the Rhineland. By Thomas R. Henry. LXXXVIII, pp. 1-32, 29 ills., map, July, 1945

COLOMBIA:

Hail Colombia! By Luis Marden. LXXVIII, pp. 505-536, 10 ills. in black and white, 18 ills. in color, map, Oct., 1940

Latin America and Colombia. By John Barrett. XVII, pp. 692-709, 10 ills., Dec., 1906

Notes on Panama and Colombia. XIV, pp. 458-466, 12 ills., Dec., 1903

Over the Andes to Bogotá. By Frank M. Chapman. XL, pp. 353-373, 19 ills., Oct., 1921

Round About Bogotá: A Hunt for New Fruits and Plants Among the Mountain Forests of Colombia's Unique Capital. By Wilson Popenoe. XLIX, pp. 127-160, 34 ills., map, Feb., 1926

Stone Idols of the Andes Reveal a Vanished People: Remarkable Relics of One of the Oldest Aboriginal Cultures of America are Unearthed in Colombia's San Agustín Region. By Hermann von Walde-Waldegg. LXXVII, pp. 627-647, 22 ills., map, May, 1940

The **COLONIAL** Expansion of France. By Professor Jean C. Bracq. XI, pp. 225-238, map, June, 1900

COLONIAL GOVERNMENT:

The British Commonwealth of Nations: "Organized Freedom" Around the World. By Eric Underwood. LXXXIII, pp. 485-524, 31 ills., Apr., 1943

Colonial Government in Borneo. By James M. Hubbard. XI, pp. 359-363, Sept., 1900

Colonial Systems of the World. By O. P. Austin. X, pp. 21-26, Jan., 1899

The United States and the British Empire. By Leonard David Gammans. LXXXVII, pp. 562-564, May, 1945

COLONIAL NATIONAL HISTORICAL PARK, Virginia:

The Restoration of Colonial Williamsburg. By W. A. R. Goodwin. LXXI, pp. 402-443, 21 ills. in black and white, 25 ills. in color, Apr., 1937

COLONIAL Systems of the World. By O. P. Austin. X, pp. 21-26, Jan., 1899

COLOPHON (Ancient City):

Some Ruined Cities of Asia Minor. By Ernest L. Harris. XIX, pp. 833-858, 19 ills., Dec., 1908

The **COLOR** and Customs of Sweden's Chateau Country. 13 color photos by Gustav Heurlin. LXVI, pp. 33-40, July, 1934

COLOR at Africa's Southern Tip. 11 color photos by W. Robert Moore. LXXXII, pp. 213-220, Aug., 1942

COLOR Brightens Rustic Life in Jugoslavia. 25 color photos by Hans Hildenbrand and Wilhelm Tobien. LVIII, pp. 273-304, Sept., 1930

The **COLOR** Camera Explores the Country That Moves by Night (Circus). 29 color photos by Richard H. Stewart, W. Robert Moore, Orren R. Louden, Jacob Gayer. LX, pp. 479-510, Oct., 1931

COLOR Camera Records of New Orleans. 15 color photos by Edwin L. Wisherd. LVII, pp. 459-466, Apr., 1930

The **COLOR** Camera Records Scenes in Eastern Spain. 13 color photos by Gervais Courtellemont. LV, pp. 365-372, Mar., 1929

The **COLOR** Camera's First Aërial Success. By Melville Bell Grosvenor. LVIII, pp. 344-353, 9 ills. in color, Sept., 1930

COLOR Close-ups of Europe's Corner Land (Portugal). 24 color photos by W. Robert Moore. LXXIII, pp. 149-180, Feb., 1938

COLOR Close-ups of Familiar Birds. 14 color photos by Arthur A. Allen. LXXV, pp. 779-786, June, 1939

COLOR Contrasts in Northern Spain. 14 color photos by Gervais Courtellemont. LIX, pp. 113-120, Jan., 1931

COLOR Cruising in Paraguay. 11 color photos by Fenno Jacobs. LXXXIV, pp. 465-472, Oct., 1943

COLOR Glimpses of the Changing South Seas. 14 color photos by Amos Burg. LXV, pp. 281-288, Mar., 1934

COLOR Glows in the Guianas, French and Dutch. By Nicol Smith. LXXXIII, pp. 459-480, 8 ills. in black and white, 13 ills. in color, map, Apr., 1943

COLOR Highlights of the Empire State. 35 color photos by Clifton Adams, James A. G. Davey, Edwin L. Wisherd. LXIV, pp. 529-576, Nov., 1933

The **COLOR** Palette of the Caribbean (Jamaica). 11 color photos by Jacob Gayer. LI, pp. 45-55, Jan., 1927

COLOR Records from the Changing Life of the Holy City (Jerusalem). By Maynard Owen Williams. LII, pp. 682-707, 27 ills. in color, Dec., 1927

COLORADO:

The Call of the West. By C. J. Blanchard. XX, pp. 403-437, 20 ills., map, May, 1909

Colorado, a Barrier That Became a Goal: Where Water Has Transformed Dry Plains Into Verdant Farms, and Highways Have Opened Up Mineral and Scenic Wealth. By McFall Kerbey. LXII, pp. 1-63, 56 ills. in black and white, 12 ills. in color, map, July, 1932

Down the Rio Grande: Tracing this Strange, Turbulent Stream on Its Long Course from Colorado to the Gulf of Mexico. By Frederick Simpich. LXXVI, pp. 415-462, 28 ills. in black and white, 24 ills. in color, 6 maps, Oct., 1939

High Country of Colorado. By Alfred M. Bailey. With 23 color photos by author, Robert J. Niedrach, F. G. Brandenburg. XC, pp. 43-72, 9 ills. in black and white, July, 1946

Home-Making by the Government: An Account of the Eleven Immense Irrigating Projects to be Opened in 1908. By C. J. Blanchard. XIX, pp. 250-287, 23 ills., Apr., 1908

Landslides and Rock Avalanches. By Guy Elliott Mitchell. XXI, pp. 277-287, 6 ills., Apr., 1910

Mesa Verde. By F. H. Newell. IX, pp. 431-434, Oct., 1898

A Mind's-Eye Map of America. By Franklin K. Lane. XXXVII, pp. 479-518, 25 ills. in black and white, 8 ills. in color, June, 1920

The Spirit of the West: The Wonderful Agricultural Development Since the Dawn of Irrigation. By C. J. Blanchard. XXI, pp. 333-360, 15 ills., Apr., 1910

The Wheeler National Monument. XX, pp. 837-840, 4 ills., Sept., 1909

COLORADO (River), U. S.-Mexico:

The Call of the West. By C. J. Blanchard. XX, pp. 403-437, 20 ills., map, May, 1909

The Colorado Desert. By W. C. Mendenhall. XX, pp. 681-701, 16 ills., Aug., 1909

Experiences in the Grand Canyon. By Ellsworth and Emery Kolb. XXVI, pp. 99-184, 70 ills., map, Aug., 1914

The Grand Canyon Bridge. By Harriet Chalmers Adams. XXXIX, pp. 645-650, 6 ills., June, 1921

The Man Without the Hoe. XXI, pp. 967-969, ills., Nov., 1910

More Changes of the Colorado River. By D. T. MacDougal. XIX, pp. 52-54, map, Jan., 1908

Surveying the Grand Canyon of the Colorado: An Account of the 1923 Boating Expedition of the United States Geological Survey. By Lewis R. Freeman. XLV, pp. 471-548, 62 ills., map, May, 1924

COLORADO DESERT, California:

The Colorado Desert. By David P. Barrows. XI, pp. 337-351, 4 ills., map, Sept., 1900

The Colorado Desert. By W. C. Mendenhall. XX, pp. 681-701, 16 ills., Aug., 1909

Lake Cahuilla: The Ancient Lake of the Colorado Desert. XVIII, p. 830, Dec., 1907

The New Inland Sea (Salton Sea). By Arthur P. Davis. XVIII, pp. 37-49, 8 ills., map, Jan., 1907

Pelican Profiles. By Lewis Wayne Walker. LXXXIV, pp. 589-598, 5 ills. in black and white, 8 ills. in color, Nov., 1943

COLORADO DESERT, California—*Continued*

A Remarkable Salt Deposit. By Charles F. Holder. XII, pp. 391-392, ills., Nov., 1901

Salton Sea and the Rainfall of the Southwest. By Alfred J. Henry. XVIII, pp. 244-248, Apr., 1907

Studies on the Rate of Evaporation at Reno, Nevada, and in the Salton Sink. By Professor Frank H. Bigelow. XIX, pp. 20-28, 5 ills., Jan., 1908

COLORFUL Corners of the City of Homes (Philadelphia). 13 color photos by Clifton Adams and Edwin L. Wisherd. LXII, pp. 675-682, Dec., 1932

COLORFUL Paths in Martinique and Guadeloupe. 13 color photos by Edwin L. Wisherd. LXXIII, pp. 281-288, Mar., 1938

COLORFUL Patinas of Northern Italy. 13 ills. in color. LXVIII, pp. 337-344, Sept., 1935

COLORFUL Porto Rico. 12 color photos by Charles Martin. XLVI, pp. 631-642, Dec., 1924

COLORFUL Wonders of the Hawaiian Islands. 21 color photos: 3 by Gilbert Grosvenor. XLV, pp. 191-206, Feb., 1924

COLOSSAL Natural Bridges of Utah. XV, pp. 367-369, ills., Sept., 1904

COLOSSAL Work in Baltimore. By Calvin W. Hendrick. XX, pp. 365-373, 6 ills., Apr., 1909

COLTON, F. BARROWS:

Aviation in Commerce and Defense. By F. Barrows Colton. LXXVIII, pp. 685-726, 39 ills., Dec., 1940

The Geography of a Hurricane: A Doughnut-shaped Storm Turned Back Time in New England to Candlelight Days, but Revealed Anew Yankee Courage and Ingenuity. By F. Barrows Colton. LXXV, pp. 529-552, 20 ills., map, Apr., 1939

How We Fight with Photographs. By F. Barrows Colton. LXXXVI, pp. 257-280, 22 ills., Sept., 1944

Lake Geneva: Cradle of Conferences. By F. Barrows Colton. LXXII, pp. 727-742, 12 ills., map, Dec., 1937

Life in Our Fighting Fleet. By F. Barrows Colton. LXXIX, pp. 671-702, 30 ills., June, 1941

Life with Our Fighting Coast Guard. By F. Barrows Colton. LXXXIII, pp. 557-588, 22 ills. in black and white, 9 ills. in color, May, 1943

The Miracle of Talking by Telephone. By F. Barrows Colton. LXXII, pp. 395-433, 41 ills., Oct., 1937

New Frontier in the Sky. By F. Barrows Colton. XC, pp. 379-408, 28 ills., diagr., Sept., 1946

News of the Universe: Mars Swings Nearer the Earth, Sunspots Wane, and a Giant New Telescopic Eye Soon Will Peer Into Unexplored Depths of Space. By F. Barrows Colton. Paintings by Charles Bittinger. LXXVI, pp. 1-32, 23 ills. in black and white, 10 ills. in color, July, 1939

Our Global Ocean—Last and Vast Frontier. By F. Barrows Colton. LXXXVII, pp. 105-128, 19 ills., drawing, Jan., 1945

COLTON, F. BARROWS—*Continued*

Ships That Guard Our Ocean Ramparts. By F. Barrows Colton. Paintings by Arthur Beaumont. LXXX, pp. 328-337, 8 ills. in color, Sept., 1941

Weather Fights and Works for Man. By F. Barrows Colton. LXXXIV, pp. 641-670, 22 ills., 3 drawings, Dec., 1943

Winged Words—New Weapon of War. By F. Barrows Colton. LXXXII, pp. 663-692, 29 ills., maps, Nov., 1942

Winning the War of Supply. By F. Barrows Colton. LXXXVIII, pp. 705-736, 32 ills., Dec., 1945

Your New World of Tomorrow. By F. Barrows Colton. LXXXVIII, pp. 385-410, 25 ills., Oct., 1945

COLUMBIA (River), U. S.-Canada:

The Columbia Turns on the Power. By Maynard Owen Williams. LXXIX, pp. 749-792, 25 ills. in black and white, 18 ills. in color, June, 1941

On the Trail of a Horse Thief. By Herbert W. Gleason. XXXV, pp. 349-358, 6 ills., Apr., 1919

Oregon Finds New Riches. By Leo A. Borah. XC, pp. 681-728, 15 ills. in black and white, 28 ills. in color, two-page map, Dec., 1946

COLUMBIA ICE FIELD, Canada:

The Mother of Rivers: An Account of a Photographic Expedition to the Great Columbia Ice Field of the Canadian Rockies. By Lewis R. Freeman. XLVII, pp. 377-446, 60 ills., maps, Apr., 1925

COLUMBIA NATIONAL FOREST, Washington:

Forest Lookout. By Ella E. Clark. With 9 color photos by author. XC, pp. 73-96, 8 ills. in black and white, July, 1946

COLUMBIAN EXPOSITION:

Proceedings of the International Geographic Conference, held in conjunction with the World's Columbian Exposition, Chicago, May 1-October 30, 1893. V, pp. 97-256, Jan. 31, 1894

COLUMBIAN GROUND SQUIRREL:

Tracking the Columbian Ground-Squirrel to Its Burrow: Loss of Millions to Crops and Danger of the Spread of Spotted Fever Necessitated Study of Peculiar Rodent of Western North America. By William T. Shaw. XLVII, pp. 587-596, 13 ills., May, 1925

COLUMBUS, CHRISTOPHER:

The Caravels of Columbus. By Victor Maria Concas. V, pp. 180-186, Jan. 31, 1894

The Caravels of Columbus. Reproduction in color of the painting by N. C. Wyeth, National Geographic Society, Washington, D. C. LIV, text, p. 55; supplement, July, 1928

The Countries of the Caribbean. By William Joseph Showalter. XXIV, pp. 227-250, 23 ills., Feb., 1913

Discoverers of America. Annual Address by the President, Hon. Gardiner G. Hubbard. V, pp. 1-20, charts, maps, 3 map supplements, Apr. 7, 1893

The First Landfall of Columbus. By Jacques W. Redway, F. R. G. S. VI, pp. 179-192, 4 maps, Dec. 29, 1894

COLUMBUS, CHRISTOPHER—*Continued*

Genoa, Where Columbus Learned to Love the Sea. By McFall Kerbey. LIV, pp. 333-352, 20 ills., pictorial supplement, Sept., 1928

Fate Directs the Faltering Footsteps of Columbus. Reproduction in color of the painting by Alfred Dehodencq, Paris (supplement)

In the Wake of Columbus. By Frederick A. Ober. V, pp. 187-196, Jan. 31, 1894

Jamaica, the Isle of Many Rivers. By John Oliver La Gorce. LI, pp. 1-55, 38 ills. in black and white, 11 ills. in color, map, Jan., 1927

COLUMBUS, Ohio:

Ohio, the Gateway State. By Melville Chater. LXI, pp. 525-591, 58 ills. in black and white, 13 ills. in color, map, May, 1932

The **COLUMBUS** of the Pacific: Captain James Cook, Foremost British Navigator, Expanded the Great Sea to Correct Proportions and Won for Albion an Insular Empire by Peaceful Exploration and Scientific Study. By J. R. Hildebrand. LI, pp. 85-132, 45 ills., maps, Jan., 1927

COMMANDOS, Air. *See* U. S. First Air Commando Force

COMMERCE:

Bonds Between the Americas. By Frederick Simpich. LXXII, pp. 785-808, 22 ills., Dec., 1937

Commerce of Mexico and the United States. By O. P. Austin. XIII, pp. 25-26, Jan., 1902

Commerce of the Philippine Islands. (By J. H.). IX, pp. 301-303, tables, June, 1898

The Evolution of Commerce. Annual Address by the President, Hon. Gardiner G. Hubbard. IV, pp. 1-18, Mar. 26, 1892

Foreign Commerce of the United States in 1903. XIV, pp. 359-360, Sept., 1903

Our Foreign Trade. (By H. G.). IX, pp. 27-28, Jan., 1898

Trade of the United States with Cuba. (By J. H.). IX, pp. 247-249, tables, May, 1898

COMMERCIAL and Financial Statistics of the Principal Countries of the World. XVIII, pp. 420-425, June, 1907

The **COMMERCIAL** Development of Japan. By O. P. Austin. X, pp. 329-337, Sept., 1899

COMMERCIAL GEOGRAPHY. *See* Industries; *and* names of products

The **COMMERCIAL** Importance of Samoa. (By O. P. Austin). X, pp. 218-220, June, 1899

COMMERCIAL Importance of the State of New York. XV, p. 429, Oct., 1904

COMMERCIAL Prize of the Orient. By O. P. Austin. XVI, pp. 399-423, 10 ills., 10 charts, map, Sept., 1905

The **COMMERCIAL** Valuation of Railway Operating Property in the United States. XVI, pp. 438-439, Sept., 1905

COMMITTEES. *See* NGS: Committees

COMMON American Wild Flowers. 17 ills. in color from paintings by Mary E. Eaton. XXIX, pp. 584-609, June, 1916

COMMON Mushrooms of the United States. By Louis C. C. Krieger. Paintings by author. XXXVII, pp. 387-439, 37 ills. in black and white, 16 ills. in color, May, 1920

COMMUNICATIONS:

Bonds Between the Americas. By Frederick Simpich. LXXII, pp. 785-808, 22 ills., Dec., 1937

The Miracle of Talking by Telephone. By F. Barrows Colton. LXXII, pp. 395-433, 41 ills., Oct., 1937

Winged Words—New Weapon of War (Radio). By F. Barrows Colton. LXXXII, pp. 663-692, 29 ills., maps, Nov., 1942

See also Cables; Radio; Telegraphy; Telephone; Television

COMMUNISM:

Russia of the Hour: Giant Battle Ground for Theories of Economy, Society, and Politics, as Observed by an Unbiased Correspondent. By Junius B. Wood. L, pp. 519-598, 81 ills., Nov., 1926

A **COMMUNITY** of Dwarfs (Insects). 11 color photos by Willard R. Culver. XC, pp. 345-352, Sept., 1946

COMO, Lake, Italy:

Frontier Cities of Italy. By Florence Craig Albrecht. XXVII, pp. 533-586, 45 ills., June, 1915

Gems of the Italian Lakes. By Arthur Ellis Mayer. XXIV, pp. 943-956, 13 ills., Aug., 1913

A **COMPARISON** of Norway and Sweden. XVI, pp. 429-431, Sept., 1905

A **COMPARISON** of Our Unprotected with Our Protected Forests. XIX, pp. 739-740, Oct., 1908

COMPASSES:

Charting a World at War. By William H. Nicholas. LXXXVI, pp. 617-640, 23 ills., drawing, Nov., 1944

The Compass in Modern Navigation. By G. W. Littlehales. VIII, pp. 266-272, Sept., 1897

The First Flight to the North Pole. By Lieutenant Commander Richard Evelyn Byrd. L, pp. 357-376, 14 ills., Sept., 1926

Most Curious Craft Afloat: The Compass in Navigation and the Work of the Non-Magnetic Yacht "Carnegie." By L. A. Bauer. XXI, pp. 223-245, 31 ills., Mar., 1910

See also Sun-compass

COMPIÈGNE, France:

The Maid of France Rides By: Compiègne, Where Joan of Arc Fought Her Last Battle, Celebrates Her Fifth Centenary. By Inez Buffington Ryan. LXII, pp. 607-616, 15 ills. in color, Nov., 1932

"COMPLEAT ANGLER" Fishes for Fossils. By Imogene Powell. LXVI, pp. 251-258, 7 ills., Aug., 1934

The **COMPLETED** report of the Isthmian Canal Commission. XII, p. 441, Dec., 1901

The **COMPLETION** of the cable between Canada and Australia. XIII, p. 410, Nov., 1902

COMPLETION of the La Boca Dock (Panama Canal). IX, p. 84, Mar., 1898

CONCARNEAU, France:

Brittany: The Land of the Sardine. By Hugh M. Smith. XX, pp. 541-573, 23 ills., June, 1909

CONCAS, VICTOR MARIA:

The Caravels of Columbus. By Victor Maria Concas. V, pp. 180-186, Jan. 31, 1894

CONCENTRATION CAMP: Norway. *See* Grini

CONCORD, Massachusetts:

Winter Rambles in Thoreau's Country. By Herbert W. Gleason. XXXVII, pp. 165-180, 15 ills., Feb., 1920

CONDITIONS in Cuba as Revealed by the Census. By Henry Gannett. XX, pp. 200-202, Feb., 1909

CONDITIONS in Liberia. By Roland P. Folkner, George Sale, Emmett J. Scott. XXI, pp. 729-741, 9 ills., Sept., 1910

CONDORS. *See* Vultures

CONDUITS. *See* Aqueducts

The **CONE-DWELLERS** of Asia Minor: A Primitive People Who Live in Nature-Made Apartment Houses, Fashioned by Volcanic Violence and Trickling Streams. By J. R. Sitlington Sterrett. XXXV, pp. 281-331, 52 ills., map, Apr., 1919

CONE DWELLINGS:

The Cone-Dwellers of Asia Minor: A Primitive People Who Live in Nature-Made Apartment Houses, Fashioned by Volcanic Violence and Trickling Streams. By J. R. Sitlington Sterrett. XXXV, pp. 281-331, 52 ills., map, Apr., 1919

Peculiar Caves of Asia Minor. By Elizabeth H. Brewer. XXII, pp. 870-875, 5 ills., Sept., 1911

The Turkish Republic Comes of Age. By Maynard Owen Williams. LXXXVII, pp. 581-616, 4 ills. in black and white, 29 ills. in color, map, May, 1945

Where Early Christians Lived in Cones of Rock: A Journey to Cappadocia in Turkey Where Strange Volcanic Pinnacles Are Honeycombed With Hermit Cells and Monasteries. By John D. Whiting. LXXVI, pp. 763-802, 20 ills. in black and white, 20 ills. in color, map, Dec., 1939

CONFERENCES. *See* International Geographic Conference; Pan-American Conferences; Peace Conference

CONFUCIANISM:

China: Her History and Development. By John Barrett. XII, pp. 209-218, June, 1901

Curious and Characteristic Customs of China. By Kenneth F. Junor. XXI, pp. 791-806, 7 ills., Sept., 1910

The Descendants of Confucius. By Maynard Owen Williams. XXXVI, pp. 253-265, 16 ills., Sept., 1919

CONFUCIANISM—*Continued*

The Geography of China: The Influence of Physical Environment on the History and Character of the Chinese People. By Frank Johnson Goodnow. LI, pp. 651-664, 11 ills., June, 1927

Shantung—China's Holy Land. By Charles K. Edmunds. XXXVI, pp. 231-252, 21 ills., map, Sept., 1919

CONGO. *See* Belgian Congo

CONGO (River), Africa:

Keeping House on the Congo. By Ruth Q. McBride. LXXII, pp. 643-670, 29 ills., Nov., 1937

Transporting a Navy Through the Jungles of Africa in War Time. By Frank J. Magee. XLII, pp. 331-362, 31 ills., Oct., 1922

CONGRESS OF EDUCATION. *See* World's Congress of Education

CONNECTICUT:

Connecticut, Prodigy of Ingenuity: Factories Play a Symphony of Industry Amid Colonial Scenes in the State of Steady Habits. By Leo A. Borah. LXXIV, pp. 279-326, 25 ills. in black and white, 25 ills. in color, two-page map, Sept., 1938

The Long River of New England: In War and Peace, from Mountain Wilderness to the Sea, Flows the Connecticut River, Through a Valley Abounding in History, Scenery, Inventive Genius, and Industry. By Albert W. Atwood. LXXXIII, pp. 401-434, 12 ills. in black and white, 24 ills. in color, map, Apr., 1943

CONNECTICUT (River), U. S.:

Atlantic Estuarine Tides. By Mark S. W. Jefferson. IX, pp. 400-409, diagrs., 7 tables, maps, Sept., 1898

The Long River of New England: In War and Peace, from Mountain Wilderness to the Sea, Flows the Connecticut River, Through a Valley Abounding in History, Scenery, Inventive Genius, and Industry. By Albert W. Atwood. LXXXIII, pp. 401-434, 12 ills. in black and white, 24 ills. in color, map, Apr., 1943

CONNER, JACOB E.:

The Forgotten Ruins of Indo-China. By Jacob E. Conner. XXIII, pp. 209-272, 63 ills., maps, Mar., 1912

Homer's Troy Today. By Jacob E. Conner. XXVII, pp. 521-532, 11 ills., map, May, 1915

The **CONQUEST** of Antarctica by Air. By Richard Evelyn Byrd. LVIII, pp. 127-227, 71 ills. in black and white, 16 ills. in gravure, map, Aug., 1930

The **CONQUEST** of Bubonic Plague in the Philippines. XIV, pp. 185-195, 7 ills., May, 1903

The **CONQUEST** of Mount Crillon (Alaska). By Bradford Washburn. LXVII, pp. 361-400, 40 ills., maps, Mar., 1935

The **CONQUEST** of Mount Logan: North America's Second Highest Peak Yields to the Intrepid Attack of Canadian Climbers. By H. F. Lambart. XLIX, pp. 597-631, 40 ills., June, 1926

The **CONQUEST** of the Sahara by the Automobile. XLV, pp. 87-93, 9 ills., map, Jan., 1924

CONRAD, JOSEPH:

Geography and Some Explorers. By Joseph Conrad. XLV, pp. 239-274, 28 ills., map, Mar., 1924

CONSERVATION League of America. By Henry Gannett. XIX, pp. 737-739, Oct., 1908

CONSERVATION of Our Natural Resources. XIX, p. 384, May, 1908

CONSERVING the Nation's Man Power: Disease Weakens Armies, Cripples Industry, Reduces Production. How the Government is Sanitating the Civil Zones Around Cantonment Areas. A Nation-wide Campaign for Health. By Rupert Blue. XXXII, pp. 255-278, 17 ills., Sept., 1917

CONSTANTINOPLE. *See* İstanbul

CONSTANTINOPLE and Sancta Sophia. By Edwin A. Grosvenor. XXVII, pp. 459-482, 21 ills., May, 1915

CONSTANTINOPLE Today. By Solita Solano. XLI, pp. 647-680, 40 ills., map, June, 1922

CONSTELLATIONS:

The Heavens Above: On Land, Sea, and in the Air the Stars Serve Modern Man as Map, Compass, and Clock. By Donald H. Menzel. With 12 charts, designed by author, showing star positions for each month, and 13 drawings of the constellations by Carlotta Gonzales Lahey. LXXXIV, pp. 97-128, map, July, 1943

CONSUL Skinner's Mission to Abyssinia. XV, pp. 165-166, ill., Apr., 1904

CONTENTED Guernsey (Island). 11 color photos by B. Anthony Stewart. LXXIII, pp. 377-384, Mar., 1938

CONTESTS. *See* Literary Contests; NGS: Essay Contests

CONTROLLING Sand Dunes in the United States and Europe. By A. S. Hitchcock. XV, pp. 43-47, 4 ills., Jan., 1904

The **CONVERSION** of Old Newspapers and Candle Ends into Fuel. XXXI, pp. 568-570, 3 ills., June, 1917

CONVOYS to Victory. By Harvey Klemmer. LXXXIII, pp. 193-216, 24 ills., Feb., 1943

COO (Island), Aegean Sea. *See* Cos

COOK, FREDERICK A.:

Committee members appointed by the University of Copenhagen to examine Cook's claims of having reached the North Pole. XXI, pp. 86-87, 6 ills., Jan., 1910

The Discovery of the Pole: First Report by Dr. Frederick A. Cook, Sept. 1, 1909. XX, pp. 892-916, 11 ills., map, Oct., 1909

Honors to Peary (Address by Dr. F. A. Cook). XVIII, pp. 49-60, ill., Jan., 1907

The North Pole. XX, pp. 921-922, Nov., 1909

Portrait. XIII, ill. p. 78, Feb., 1902

COOK, JAMES:

The Columbus of the Pacific: Captain James Cook, Foremost British Navigator, Expanded the Great Sea to Correct Proportions and Won for Albion an Insular Empire by Peaceful Exploration and Scientific Study. By J. R. Hildebrand. LI, pp. 85-132, 45 ills., maps, Jan., 1927

Revealing Earth's Mightiest Ocean (Pacific). By Albert W. Atwood. LXXXIV, pp. 291-306, 10 ills., map supplement, Sept., 1943

COOK, O. F.:

Awarded Jane M. Smith Life Membership. XXXVII, p. 342, Apr., 1920

Staircase Farms of the Ancients: Astounding Farming Skill of Ancient Peruvians, Who Were Among the Most Industrious and Highly Organized People in History. By O. F. Cook. XXIX, pp. 474-534, 48 ills., May, 1916

COOK ISLANDS, South Pacific Ocean. *See* Palmerston Island

COOKE, WELLS W.:

Our Greatest Travelers: Birds that Fly from Pole to Pole and Shun the Darkness: Birds that Make 2,500 Miles in a Single Flight. By Wells W. Cooke. XXII, pp. 346-365, 12 maps, Apr., 1911

Saving the Ducks and Geese. By Wells W. Cooke. XXIV, pp. 361-380, 7 ills., 7 maps, Mar., 1913

COOLIDGE, CALVIN:

Commander Byrd Receives the Hubbard Gold Medal: The First Explorer to Reach the North Pole by Air Receives Coveted Honor at Brilliant National Geographic Society Reception (Address by President Coolidge). L, pp. 377-388, 5 ills., chart, Sept., 1926

Massachusetts and Its Position in the Life of the Nation. By Calvin Coolidge. XLIII, pp. 337-352, 9 ills., Apr., 1923

Mr. Coolidge Becomes a Member of The Society's Board of Trustees. LV, p. 750, June, 1929

President Coolidge Bestows Lindbergh Award: The National Geographic Society's Hubbard Medal Is Presented to Aviator Before the Most Notable Gathering in the History of Washington (Address by President Coolidge). LIII, pp. 132-140, 4 ills., Jan., 1928

COONS (Animals). *See* Raccoons

COOPER, MERIAN C.:

Two Fighting Tribes of the Sudan. By Merian C. Cooper. Photos by Ernest B. Schoedsack. LVI, pp. 465-486, 27 ills., map, Oct., 1929

The Warfare of the Jungle Folk: Campaigning Against Tigers, Elephants, and Other Wild Animals in Northern Siam. By Merian C. Cooper. Photos by Ernest B. Schoedsack. LIII, pp. 233-268, 33 ills., Feb., 1928

COOPER, PETER:

Peter Cooper and Submarine Telegraphy. VII, pp. 108-110, Mar., 1896

COOPERATIVES. *See* Collective Communities

COOTIES and Courage. By Herbert Corey. XXXIII, pp. 495-509, 10 ills., June, 1918

COPENHAGEN, Denmark:

Denmark and the Danes. By Maurice Francis Egan. XLII, pp. 115-164, 38 ills., map, Aug., 1922

Royal Copenhagen, Capital of a Farming Kingdom: A Fifth of Denmark's Thrifty Population Resides in a Metropolis Famous for Its Porcelains, Its Silver, and Its Lace. By J. R. Hildebrand. LXI, pp. 217-250, 26 ills. in black and white, 14 ills. in color, Feb., 1932

COPIAPÓ, Chile:

A Longitudinal Journey Through Chile. By Harriet Chalmers Adams. XLII, pp. 219-273, 60 ills., map, Sept., 1922

The **COPPER** River Delta (Alaska). (By E. D. Preston). XI, pp. 29-31, Jan., 1900

COPRA:

The Samoan Cocoanut (Article compiled by Gen. A. W. Greely). IX, pp. 12-24, Jan., 1898

The **COPYRIGHT** of a Map or Chart. By William Alexander Miller. XIII, pp. 437-443, Dec., 1902

CORAL:

Bright Flashes from Pacific Corals. 24 color photos by Walter H. Chute. LXXIX, pp. 349-372, Mar., 1941

Coral Castle Builders of Tropic Seas. By Roy Waldo Miner. Paintings by Else Bostelmann. LXV, pp. 703-728, 15 ills. in black and white, 8 ills. in color, maps, June, 1934

The First Autochromes from the Ocean Bottom: Marine Life in Its Natural Habitat Along the Florida Keys Is Successfully Photographed in Colors. (Photographs by Dr. W. H. Longley and Charles Martin). LI, pp. 56-60, 8 ills. in color, Jan., 1927

The Great Barrier Reef and Its Isles: The Wonder and Mystery of Australia's World-Famous Geographical Feature. By Charles Barrett. LVIII, pp. 355-384, 38 ills., map, Sept., 1930

Life on a Coral Reef: The Fertility and Mystery of the Sea Studied Beneath the Waters Surrounding Dry Tortugas. By W. H. Longley. LI, pp. 61-83, 22 ills., Jan., 1927

On the Bottom of a South Sea Pearl Lagoon. By Roy Waldo Miner. Paintings by Else Bostelmann. LXXIV, pp. 365-390, 17 ills. in black and white, 8 ills. in color, Sept., 1938

Where Nature Runs Riot: On Australia's Great Barrier Reef Marine Animals Grow to Unusual Size, Develop Strange Weapons of Attack and Defense, and Acquire Brilliant Colors. By T. C. Roughley. LXXVII, pp. 823-850, 18 ills. in black and white, 15 ills. in color, map, June, 1940

CORAL FISHES:

Net Results from Oceania: Collecting Aquarium Specimens in Tropical Pacific Waters. By Walter H. Chute. LXXIX, pp. 347-372, 8 ills. in black and white, 24 ills. in color, Mar., 1941

COREY, CAROL:

A Day with Our Boys in the Geographic Wards. By Carol Corey. XXXIV, pp. 69-80, 8 ills., July, 1918

COREY, CAROL—*Continued*

From the Trenches to Versailles. By Carol Corey. XXXII, pp. 535-550, 12 ills., Nov.-Dec., 1917

Plain Tales from the Trenches: As Told Over the Tea Table in Blighty—A Soldier's "Home" in Paris. By Carol Corey. XXXIII, pp. 300-312, 7 ills., Mar., 1918

COREY, HERBERT:

Across the Equator with the American Navy. By Herbert Corey. XXXIX, pp. 571-624, 53 ills., June, 1921

Adventuring Down the West Coast of Mexico. By Herbert Corey. XLII, pp. 449-503, 44 ills., map, Nov., 1922

Along the Old Spanish Road in Mexico: Life Among the People of Nayarit and Jalisco, Two of the Richest States of the Southern Republic. By Herbert Corey. XLIII, pp. 225-281, 36 ills. in black and white, 16 ills. in color, map, Mar., 1923

Among the Zapotecs of Mexico: A Visit to the Indians of Oaxaca, Home State of the Republic's Great Liberator, Juárez, and Its Most Famous Ruler, Diaz. By Herbert Corey. LI, pp. 501-553, 59 ills., map, May, 1927

A Char-à-Bancs in Cornwall. By Herbert Corey. XLVI, pp. 653-694, 44 ills., map, Dec., 1924

Cooties and Courage. By Herbert Corey. XXXIII, pp. 495-509, 10 ills., June, 1918

Down Devon Lanes. By Herbert Corey. LV, pp. 529-568, 45 ills., map, May, 1929

The Green Mountain State (Vermont). By Herbert Corey. LI, pp. 333-369, 40 ills. in black and white, 6 ills. in color, map, Mar., 1927

The Isthmus of Tehuantepec (Mexico). By Herbert Corey. XLV, pp. 549-579, 25 ills., May, 1924

London from a Bus Top. By Herbert Corey. XLIX, pp. 551-596, 44 ills., May, 1926

On the Monastir Road. By Herbert Corey. XXXI, pp. 383-412, 31 ills., May, 1917

Shopping Abroad for Our Armies in France. By Herbert Corey. XXXIII, pp. 206-218, 6 ills., Feb., 1918

A Unique Republic, Where Smuggling Is an Industry (Andorra). By Herbert Corey. XXXIII, pp. 279-299, 16 ills., map, Mar., 1918

CORINTH CANAL, Greece:

The Great Canals of the World. XVI, pp. 475-479, Oct., 1905

CORK. XIX, pp. 690-693, 3 ills., Oct., 1908

CORMORANTS (Birds):

Birds That Cruise the Coast and Inland Waters. By T. Gilbert Pearson. Paintings by Maj. Allan Brooks. LXV, pp. 299-328, 5 ills. in black and white, 7 portraits in color, Mar., 1934

The Fisheries of Japan. By Hugh M. Smith. XVI, pp. 201-220, 13 ills., May, 1905

The Most Valuable Bird in the World. By Robert Cushman Murphy. XLVI, pp. 279-302, 25 ills., map, Sept., 1924

CORMORANTS (Birds)—*Continued*

Peru's Wealth-Producing Birds: Vast Riches in the Guano Deposits of Cormorants, Pelicans, and Petrels which Nest on Her Barren, Rainless Coast. By R. E. Coker. XXXVII, pp. 537-566, 28 ills., June, 1920

The White Sheep, Giant Moose, and Smaller Game of the Kenai Peninsula, Alaska. By George Shiras, 3d. XXIII, pp. 423-494, 59 ills., maps (1 two-page), May, 1912

CORN:

How the World Is Fed. By William Joseph Showalter. XXIX, pp. 1-110, 101 ills., Jan., 1916

Iowa, Abiding Place of Plenty: The State Where the Tall Corn Grows Provides the Nation with a Tenth of Its Food Supply. By Leo A. Borah. LXXVI, pp. 143-182, 15 ills. in black and white, 20 ills. in color, two-page map, Aug., 1939

Staircase Farms of the Ancients: Astounding Farming Skill of Ancient Peruvians, Who Were Among the Most Industrious and Highly Organized People in History. By O. F. Cook. XXIX, pp. 474-534, 48 ills., May, 1916

See also Indians of North America; Mayas

CORN and Color in the Hawkeye State (Iowa). 20 color photos: 19 by J. Baylor Roberts. LXXVI, pp. 151-174, Aug., 1939

CORNELIUS, S. A.:

A Vigorous Oil Well. By S. A. Cornelius. XVIII, pp. 348-349, ill., May, 1907

CORNELL UNIVERSITY, New York: Research:

Aurora Borealis research under the auspices of the National Geographic Society and Cornell University. LXXIX, p. 580, May, 1941. LXXXVI, p. 640, Nov., 1944. XC, p. 387, Sept., 1946

The Mystery of Auroras: National Geographic Society and Cornell University Study Spectacular Displays in the Heavens. LXXV, pp. 689-690, May, 1939

A **CORNER** of Old Württemberg (Germany). By B. H. Buxton. XXII, pp. 931-947, 17 ills., map, Oct., 1911

CORNHUSKER State Highlights (Nebraska). 23 color photos by B. Anthony Stewart. LXXXVII, pp. 521-536, May, 1945

CORNWALL, England:

Channel Ports—And Some Others. By Florence Craig Albrecht. XXVIII, pp. 1-55, 45 ills., July, 1915

A Char-à-Bancs in Cornwall. By Herbert Corey. XLVI, pp. 653-694, 44 ills., map, Dec., 1924

CORONA, Solar:

First natural-color photograph of an eclipse ever reproduced, showing the corona. By Irvine C. Gardner. LXXI, ill. p. 178, Feb., 1937

Nature's Most Dramatic Spectacle. By S. A. Mitchell. LXXII, pp. 361-376, 16 ills., map, Sept., 1937

CORONA, Solar—*Continued*

Observing an Eclipse in Asiatic Russia. By Irvine C. Gardner. LXXI, pp. 179-197, 19 ills. in black and white, ill. in color, Feb., 1937

Unfurling Old Glory on Canton Island. 11 ills. in color: painting by Charles Bittinger and color photo of the eclipse, showing the corona. LXXIII, pp. 753-760, June, 1938

CORONATIONS:

Along London's Coronation Route. By Maynard Owen Williams. LXXI, pp. 609-632, 22 ills., map, May, 1937

Coronation Days in Addis Ababa. By W. Robert Moore. LIX, pp. 738-746, 8 ills., June, 1931

The Coronation of His Majesty King Maha-Vajiravudh of Siam. By Colonel Lea Febiger. XXIII, pp. 389-416, 25 ills., Apr., 1912

Present Day Scenes in the World's Oldest Empire (Ethiopia). 27 color photos by W. Robert Moore. LIX, pp. 691-722, June, 1931

CORPUS CHRISTI CELEBRATION:

In the Canary Islands, Where Streets Are Carpeted With Flowers. 13 color photos by Wilhelm Tobien. LVII, pp. 615-622, May, 1930

The **CORRECT** Display of the Stars and Stripes. By Byron McCandless and Gilbert Grosvenor. XXXII, pp. 404-413, 8 ills., Oct., 1917

CORSICA (Island), Mediterranean Sea:

The Coasts of Corsica: Impressions of a Winter's Stay in the Island Birthplace of Napoleon. By Maynard Owen Williams. XLIV, pp. 221-312, 88 ills., maps, pictorial supplement, Sept., 1923

Peasant Home in Corsica (supplement)

CORTÉS, HERNANDO:

On the Cortés Trail. By Luis Marden. LXXVIII, pp. 335-375, 17 ills. in black and white, 22 ills. in color, map, Sept., 1940

CORTHELL, ELMER L.:

The Delta of the Mississippi River. By E. L. Corthell. VIII, pp. 351-354, Dec., 1897

The Tehuantepec Ship Railway. By Elmer L. Corthell. VII, pp. 64-72, maps, Feb., 1896

COS (Island), Aegean Sea:

Rhodes, and Italy's Aegean Islands. By Dorothy Hosmer. LXXIX, pp. 449-480, 32 ills., map, Apr., 1941

COSMIC RAYS:

Ballooning in the Stratosphere: Two Balloon Ascents to Ten-Mile Altitudes Presage New Mode of Aërial Travel. By Auguste Piccard. LXIII, pp. 353-384, 34 ills., Mar., 1933

New Frontier in the Sky. By F. Barrows Colton. XC, pp. 379-408, 28 ills., diagr., Sept., 1946

Series of flights under auspices of National Geographic Society, U. S. Army Air Forces, and Bartol Research Foundation of the Franklin Institute. XC, p. 387, ill. p. 388, Sept., 1946

COSMOPOLITAN Shanghai, Key Seaport of China. By W. Robert Moore. LXII, pp. 311-335, 19 ills., Sept., 1932

COSTA, GUIDO:

The Island of Sardinia and Its People: Traces of Many Civilizations to be Found in the Speech, Customs, and Costumes of This Picturesque Land. By Prof. Guido Costa. XLIII, pp. 1-75, 63 ills. in black and white, 16 ills. in color, maps, Jan., 1923

COSTA RICA:

Costa Rica. By Señor Ricardo Villafranca. VIII, pp. 143-151, May, 1897

Costa Rica, Land of the Banana. By Paul B. Popenoe. XLI, pp. 201-220, 17 ills., Feb., 1922

Costa Rica—Vulcan's Smithy. By H. Pittier. XXI, pp. 494-525, 30 ills., maps, June, 1910

The Countries of the Caribbean. By William Joseph Showalter. XXIV, pp. 227-250, 23 ills., Feb., 1913

Land of the Painted Oxcarts. By Luis Marden. With 31 color photos by author. XC, pp. 409-456, 30 ills. in black and white, map, Oct., 1946

Location of the Boundary Between Nicaragua and Costa Rica. By Arthur P. Davis. XII, pp. 22-28, ill., map, Jan., 1901

Methods of Obtaining Salt in Costa Rica. XIX, pp. 28-34, 7 ills., diagr., Jan., 1908

Notes on Central America. XVIII, pp. 272-279, ills., map, Apr., 1907

Shattered Capitals of Central America. By Herbert J. Spinden. XXXVI, pp. 185-212, 32 ills., map, Sept., 1919

Where Our Bananas Come From. By Edwin R. Fraser. XXIII, pp. 713-730, 14 ills., July, 1912

COSTUME Pageants in the French Pyrenees. 24 color photos by W. Robert Moore. LXXII, pp. 435-450, Oct., 1937

COSTUMES. *See* Clothing and Costumes

COSTUMES of Czechoslovakia. 19 color photos by Hans Hildenbrand. LI, pp. 725-740, June, 1927

COTIDAL Lines for the World. By R. A. Harris. XVII, pp. 303-309, 3 maps, map supplement, June, 1906

COTT, HUGH B.:

Wonder Island of the Amazon Delta: On Marajó Cowboys Ride Oxen, Tree-dwelling Animals Throng Dense Forests, While Strange Fishes and Birds Help Make a Zoologist's Paradise. By Hugh B. Cott. LXXIV, pp. 635-670, 30 ills. in black and white, 12 ills. in color, map, Nov., 1938

COTTER, MARGARET:

Red Cross Girl Overseas. By Margaret Cotter. LXXXVI, pp. 745-768, 22 ills., Dec., 1944

COTTON AND COTTON INDUSTRY:

Cotton: Foremost Fiber of the World. By J. R. Hildebrand. LXXIX, pp. 137-192, 31 ills. in black and white, 34 ills. in color, Feb., 1941

Cotton and the Chinese Boycott (From an Address by President Roosevelt to the Citizens of Atlanta, October 20, 1905). XVI, pp. 516-517, Nov., 1905

Cotton for England. XV, p. 39, Jan., 1904

The Farmers of the United States. XVI, pp. 39-46, Jan., 1905

COTTON AND COTTON INDUSTRY—*Continued*

Massachusetts—Beehive of Business. By William Joseph Showalter. XXXVII, pp. 203-245, 41 ills., Mar., 1920

The Modern Alchemist (Work of Department of Agriculture). By James Wilson. XVIII, pp. 781-795, 6 ills., Dec., 1907

Our Plant Immigrants. By David Fairchild. XVII, pp. 179-201, 29 ills., Apr., 1906

Paper From Cotton Stalks. XVII, p. 425, July, 1906

COTTONSEED OIL:

Cotton: Foremost Fiber of the World. By J. R. Hildebrand. LXXIX, pp. 137-192, 31 ills. in black and white, 34 ills. in color, Feb., 1941

The **COUNTRIES** of the Caribbean. By William Joseph Showalter. XXIV, pp. 227-250, 23 ills., Feb., 1913

COUNTRY-HOUSE Life in Sweden: In Castle and Cottage the Landed Gentry Gallantly Keep the Old Traditions. By Amelie Posse-Brázdová. LXVI, pp. 1-64, 51 ills. in black and white, 13 ills. in color, map, July, 1934

COUNTRY Life in Norway: The Beneficent Gulf Stream Enables One-third of the People in a Far-north, Mountainous Land to Prosper on Farms. By Axel H. Oxholm. LXXV, pp. 493-528, 17 ills. in black and white, 20 ills. in color, map, Apr., 1939

The **COUNTRY** of the Ant Men (Sahara). By Thomas H. Kearney. XXII, pp. 367-382, 13 ills., map, panorama, Apr., 1911

A **COUNTRY** Where Going to America Is an Industry (Sicily). By Arthur H. Warner. XX, pp. 1063-1102, 41 ills., Dec., 1909

The **COURSE** of the Retail Coal Trade. By Dr. David T. Day. XIII, pp. 394-398, Nov., 1902

COURTELLEMONT, GERVAIS:

Africa: The Camera's Color Records of North Africa. 16 color photos by Gervais Courtellemont. XLVII, pp. 333-340, Mar., 1925

Algeria: On the Fringe of the Great Desert. 32 color photos by Gervais Courtellemont. LIII, pp. 207-222, Feb., 1928

Asia: Sun-Painted Scenes in the Near East. 32 color photos by Gervais Courtellemont. XLVIII, pp. 541-556, Nov., 1925

Balearics: Spain's Enchanted Isles. 29 color photos by Gervais Courtellemont. LIV, pp. 183-198, Aug., 1928

Brittany: Blue Seas and Brilliant Costumes Along the Brittany Coast. 29 color photos by Gervais Courtellemont. LVI, pp. 143-174, Aug., 1929

Cambodia: The Enigma of Cambodia. 27 color photos by Gervais Courtellemont. LIV, pp. 307-322, Sept., 1928

Egypt: Along the Banks of the Colorful Nile. 23 color photos by Gervais Courtellemont. L, pp. 323-338, Sept., 1926

France: The Battle Fields of France Eleven Years After. 23 color photos by Gervais Courtellemont. LVI, pp. 523-538, Nov., 1929

COURTELLEMONT, GERVAIS—*Continued*

France: Beauty, History, and Romance Enrich the Château Country. 10 color photos by Gervais Courtellemont. LVIII, pp. 467-474, Oct., 1930

France: Charm and Color Distinguish Norman Byways. 13 color photos by Gervais Courtellemont. LXI, pp. 91-98, Jan., 1932

France: 15th-Century Vignettes of Compiègne. 15 color photos by Gervais Courtellemont. LXII, pp. 609-616, Nov., 1932

France: Flashes of Color Throughout France. 28 color photos by Gervais Courtellemont. XLVI, pp. 529-544, Nov., 1924

France: In Smiling Alsace, Where France Has Resumed Sway. 11 color photos by Gervais Courtellemont. LII, pp. 168-176, Aug., 1927

France: Versailles the Magnificent. 14 color photos by Gervais Courtellemont. XLVII, pp. 53-60, Jan., 1925

Holy Land: In the Birthplace of Christianity. 7 color photos by Gervais Courtellemont. L, pp. 697-720, Dec., 1926

India: Streets and Palaces of Colorful India. 34 color photos by Gervais Courtellemont. L, pp. 60-85, July, 1926

Morocco: In the Land of Cruel Desert and Majestic Mountain. 10 color photos by Gervais Courtellemont. LXI, pp. 307-314, Mar., 1932

Portugal: Rainbow Portraits of Portugal. 17 color photos by Gervais Courtellemont. LII, pp. 551-566, Nov., 1927

Spain: The Color Camera Records Scenes in Eastern Spain. 13 color photos by Gervais Courtellemont. LV, pp. 365-372, Mar., 1929

Spain: Color Contrasts in Northern Spain. 14 color photos by Gervais Courtellemont. LIX, pp. 113-120, Jan., 1931

Spain: Glories Past and Present of Northern Spain. 13 color photos by Gervais Courtellemont. LV, pp. 341-348, Mar., 1929

Spain: In Andalusia, Home of Song and Sunshine. 14 color photos by Gervais Courtellemont. LV, pp. 301-308, Mar., 1929

Spain: Moorish Spain. 26 color photos by Gervais Courtellemont. XLVI, pp. 163-178, Aug., 1924

Tunisia, Where Sea and Desert Meet. 16 color photos by Gervais Courtellemont. XLV, pp. 415-422, Apr., 1924

COVILLE, FREDERICK V.:

The Cultivation of the Mayflower. By Frederick V. Coville. XXVII, pp. 518-519, ill., May, 1915

Geographic Literature. VIII, p. 91, Mar., 1897

The National Geographic Society (Memorial Tribute to Frederick V. Coville). LXXI, p. 662, ill., May, 1937

The Quills of a Porcupine. By Frederick V. Coville. XXIII, pp. 25-31, 5 ills., Jan., 1912

The Sage Plains of Oregon. By Frederick V. Coville. VII, pp. 395-404, Dec., 1896

Taming the Wild Blueberry. By Frederick V. Coville. XXII, pp. 137-147, 5 ills., Feb., 1911

War, Patriotism, and the Food Supply. By Frederick V. Coville. XXXI, pp. 254-256, Mar., 1917

COVILLE, FREDERICK V.—*Continued*

The Wild Blueberry Tamed: The New Industry of the Pine Barrens of New Jersey. By Frederick V. Coville. XXIX, pp. 535-546, 10 ills., June, 1916

See also NGS: Board of Managers

COVILLE, LILIAN GROSVENOR:

Here in Manchuria: Many Thousand Lives Were Lost and More Than Half the Crops Destroyed by the Floods of 1932. By Lilian Grosvenor Coville. LXIII, pp. 233-256, 26 ills., Feb., 1933

COWBOYS:

Down the Rio Grande: Tracing this Strange, Turbulent Stream on Its Long Course from Colorado to the Gulf of Mexico. By Frederick Simpich. LXXVI, pp. 415-462, 28 ills. in black and white, 24 ills. in color, 6 maps, Oct., 1939

Grass Makes Wyoming Fat. By Frederick Simpich. LXXXVIII, pp. 153-188, 13 ills. in black and white, 19 ills. in color, two-page map, Aug., 1945

Life on the Argentine Pampa. By Frederick Simpich. Paintings by Cesâreo Bernaldo de Quirós. LXIV, pp. 449-491, 41 ills. in black and white, 8 ills. in color, Oct., 1933

On a Chilean Hacienda. 8 color photos by E. P. Haddon. LXXXVI, pp. 489-496, Oct., 1944

"Where Rolls the Oregon." 28 color photos by Ray Atkeson. XC, pp. 689-728, Dec., 1946

Wonder Island of the Amazon Delta: On Marajó Cowboys Ride Oxen, Tree-dwelling Animals Throng Dense Forests, While Strange Fishes and Birds Help Make a Zoologist's Paradise. By Hugh B. Cott. LXXIV, pp. 635-670, 30 ills. in black and white, 12 ills. in color, map, Nov., 1938

COWBOYS and Caymans of Marajó (Brazil). 12 color photos by Desmond Holdridge. LXXIV, pp. 645-652, Nov., 1938

COWES, Isle of Wight:

England's Sun Trap Isle of Wight. By J. R. Hildebrand. LXVII, pp. 1-33, 22 ills. in black and white, 14 ills. in color, map, Jan., 1935

CRABS:

The Blue Crab. XVII, p. 46, Jan., 1906

Crabs and Crablike Curiosities of the Sea. By William Crowder. Paintings by author. LIV, pp. 57-72, 10 ills. in black and white, 8 ills. in color, July, 1928
Contents: Blue, Fiddler, Hermit, Horseshoe, Mud, Rock, Spider, Swimming

Strange Sights in Far-Away Papua. By A. E. Pratt. XVIII, pp. 559-572, 7 ills., Sept., 1907

The **CRADLE** of Civilization: The Historic Lands Along the Euphrates and Tigris Rivers Where Briton Is Fighting Turk. By James Baikie. XXIX, pp. 127-162, 25 ills., Feb., 1916

CRADLES of English History. 15 color photos by Clifton Adams and Bernard Wakeman. LIX, pp. 269-276, Mar., 1931

CRAIGE, JOHN HOUSTON:

Haitian Vignettes. By Captain John Houston Craige. LXVI, pp. 435-485, 40 ills. in black and white, 13 ills. in color, map, Oct., 1934

CRAIGHEAD, FRANK:

Adventures with Birds of Prey. By Frank and John Craighead. LXXII, pp. 109-134, 25 ills., July, 1937

In Quest of the Golden Eagle: Over Lonely Mountain and Prairie Soars This Rare and Lordly Bird, But Three Youths from the East Catch Up With Him at Last. By John and Frank Craighead. LXXVII, pp. 693-710, 17 ills., May, 1940

Life with an Indian Prince: As Guests of a Maharaja's Brother, Two Young American Naturalists Study Age-old Methods of Hunting with Trained Falcons and Cheetahs and Savor the Pomp of Royal India. By John and Frank Craighead. LXXXI, pp. 235-272, 38 ills., map, Feb., 1942

CRAIGHEAD, JOHN:

Adventures with Birds of Prey. By Frank and John Craighead. LXXII, pp. 109-134, 25 ills., July, 1937

In Quest of the Golden Eagle: Over Lonely Mountain and Prairie Soars This Rare and Lordly Bird, But Three Youths from the East Catch Up With Him at Last. By John and Frank Craighead. LXXVII, pp. 693-710, 17 ills., May, 1940

Life with an Indian Prince: As Guests of a Maharaja's Brother, Two Young American Naturalists Study Age-old Methods of Hunting with Trained Falcons and Cheetahs and Savor the Pomp of Royal India. By John and Frank Craighead. LXXXI, pp. 235-272, 38 ills., map, Feb., 1942

CRAMPTON, HENRY EDWARD:

Kaieteur and Roraima: The Great Falls and the Great Mountain of the Guianas. By Henry Edward Crampton. XXXVIII, pp. 227-244, 12 ills., map, Sept., 1920

CRANE, ALICE ROLLINS:

The Midnight Sun in the Klondike. (By Alice Rollins Crane). XII, pp. 66-67, ill., Feb., 1901

The Northern Lights. (By Alice Rollins Crane). XII, p. 69, ill., Feb., 1901

CRANES:

The Shore Birds, Cranes, and Rails: Willets, Plovers, Stilts, Phalaropes, Sandpipers, and Their Relatives Deserve Protection. By Arthur A. Allen. Paintings by Major Allan Brooks. LXXII, pp. 183-222, 4 ills. in black and white, 101 portraits in color, Aug., 1937

CRATER LAKE, Oregon:

Crater Lake, Oregon. XIII, p. 221, June, 1902

Crater Lake, Oregon. By J. S. Diller. VIII, pp. 33-48, 6 ills., maps, Feb., 1897

The Mazamas. (By J. S. Diller). VIII, pp. 58-59, Feb., 1897

Oregon: Its History, Geography, and Resources. By John H. Mitchell, U. S. Senator from Oregon. VI, pp. 239-284, Apr. 20, 1895

"Where Rolls the Oregon." 28 color photos by Ray Atkeson. XC, pp. 689-728, Dec., 1946

CRATER LAKE NATIONAL PARK, Oregon:
Crater Lake and Yosemite Through the Ages. By Wallace W. Atwood, Jr. Paintings by Eugene Kingman. LXXI, pp. 327-343, 7 ills. in black and white, 13 ills. in color, Mar., 1937
Our National Parks. By L. F. Schmeckebier. XXIII, pp. 531-579, 41 ills., map, June, 1912

CRATERS OF THE MOON NATIONAL MONUMENT, Idaho:
Among the "Craters of the Moon": An Account of the First Expeditions Through the Remarkable Volcanic Lava Beds of Southern Idaho. By R. W. Limbert. XLV, pp. 303-328, 23 ills., map, Mar., 1924

CRAWFISH:
Certain Citizens of the Warm Sea. By Louis L. Mowbray. Paintings by Hashime Murayama. XLI, pp. 27-62, 18 ills. in black and white, 16 ills. in color, Jan., 1922

CRAWFORD, MARION:
The Ruins at Selinus (Sicily). (By Marion Crawford). XX, p. 117, Jan., 1909

CRAWFURD, OSWALD:
The Greatness of Little Portugal. By Oswald Crawfurd. XXI, pp. 867-883, 12 ills., Oct., 1910

CREEK INDIANS:
The Five Civilized Tribes and the Survey of Indian Territory. By C. H. Fitch. IX, pp. 481-491, 4 ills., map, Dec., 1898
Indians of the Southeastern United States. By Matthew W. Stirling. Paintings by W. Langdon Kihn. LXXXIX, pp. 53-74, 8 ills. in black and white, 8 ills. in color, Jan., 1946

CRESSON, W. P.:
Persia: The Awakening East. By W. P. Cresson. XIX, pp. 356-384, 21 ills., map, May, 1908

CRETE (Island), Greece:
Classic Greece Merges Into 1941 News. 19 photos: 15 by B. Anthony Stewart, 3 by Maynard Owen Williams. LXXIX, pp. 93-108, Jan., 1941
Crete, Where Sea-Kings Reigned. By Agnes N. Stillwell. LXXXIV, pp. 547-568, 20 ills., map, Nov., 1943
Cruising to Crete: Four French Girls Set Sail in a Breton Yawl for the Island of the Legendary Minotaur. By Marthe Oulié and Mariel Jean-Brunhes. LV, pp. 249-272, 15 ills. in black and white, 14 ills. in color, map, Feb., 1929
Explorations in Crete. By Edith H. Hall. XX, pp. 778-787, 15 ills., Sept., 1909
Greece—the Birthplace of Science and Free Speech: Explorations on the Mainland and in Crete and the Aegean Isles Reveal Ancient Life Similar to That of the Present. By Richard Stillwell. Paintings by H. M. Herget. LXXXV, pp. 273-353, 13 ills. in black and white, 32 ills. in color, two-page map, Mar., 1944
The Sea-Kings of Crete. By Rev. James Baikie. XXIII, pp. 1-25, 13 ills., Jan., 1912

CRILLON, Mount, Alaska:
The Conquest of Mount Crillon. By Bradford Washburn. LXVII, pp. 361-400, 40 ills., maps, Mar., 1935

CRIMEA Reborn. By Eddy Gilmore. LXXXVII, pp. 487-512, 23 ills., map, Apr., 1945

CRIMEAN AUTONOMOUS SOVIET SOCIALIST REPUBLIC, R. S. F. S. R.:
Crimea Reborn. By Eddy Gilmore. LXXXVII, pp. 487-512, 23 ills., map, Apr., 1945

CRITCHELL, LAURENCE SANFORD:
Crossroads of the Caribbean (Trinidad). By Laurence Sanford Critchell. LXXII, pp. 319-344, 18 ills. in black and white, 14 ills. in color, map, Sept., 1937

A **CRITICAL** Period in South African History. (By J. H.). VII, pp. 377-379, Nov., 1896

A **CRITICAL** Review of Bering's First Expedition, 1725-30, Together with a Translation of His Original Report Upon It. With a Map. By Wm. H. Dall. II, pp. 111-169, 8 tables, foldout map, May, 1890

CROATIA:
In Quaint Curious Croatia. By Felix J. Koch. XIX, pp. 809-832, 37 ills., Dec., 1908

CRONQUIST, G. W.:
Types and Costumes of Old Sweden. 30 color photos: 2 by G. W. Cronquist. LIV, pp. 425-440, Oct., 1928

CROSBY, OSCAR T.:
Abyssinia—The Country and People. By Oscar T. Crosby. XII, pp. 89-102, Mar., 1901
See also Crosby Expedition

The **CROSBY EXPEDITION** to Tibet. XV, pp. 229-231, 3 ills., May, 1904

CROSSING Asia Minor, the Country of the New Turkish Republic. By Major Robert Whitney Imbrie. XLVI, pp. 445-472, 31 ills., map, Oct., 1924

CROSSING the Untraversed Libyan Desert: The Record of a 2,200-Mile Journey of Exploration Which Resulted in the Discovery of Two Oases of Strategic Importance on the Southwestern Frontier of Egypt. By A. M. Hassanein Bey. XLVI, pp. 233-277, 46 ills., map, Sept., 1924

CROSSROADS of the Caribbean (Trinidad). By Laurence Sanford Critchell. LXXII, pp. 319-344, 18 ills. in black and white, 14 ills. in color, map, Sept., 1937

The **CROW,** Bird Citizen of Every Land: A Feathered Rogue Who Has Many Fascinating Traits and Many Admirable Qualities Despite His Marauding Propensities. By E. R. Kalmbach. XXXVII, pp. 322-337, 10 ills., Apr., 1920

CROW INDIANS:
The Friendly Crows in Festive Panoply. 13 color photos by Edwin L. Wisherd. LII, pp. 315-322, Sept., 1927

CROWDER, WILLIAM:

Crabs and Crablike Curiosities of the Sea. By William Crowder. Paintings by author. LIV, pp. 57-72, 10 ills. in black and white, 8 ills. in color, July, 1928

The Life of the Moon-Jelly. By William Crowder. Paintings by author. L, pp. 187-202, 6 ills. in black and white, 8 ills. in color, Aug., 1926

Jellyfishes—Living Draperies of Color. 8 ills. in color from paintings by author, pp. 193-200

Living Jewels of the Sea (Plankton). By William Crowder. Paintings by author. LII, pp. 290-304, 8 ills. in black and white, 8 ills. in color, Sept., 1927

Marvels of Mycetozoa: Exploration of a Long Island Swamp Reveals Some of the Secrets of the Slime Molds, Dwelling on the Borderland Between the Plant and Animal Kingdoms. By William Crowder. Paintings by author. XLIX, pp. 421-443, 5 ills. in black and white, 16 ills. in color, Apr., 1926

CROWS (Birds):

The Crow, Bird Citizen of Every Land: A Feathered Rogue Who Has Many Fascinating Traits and Many Admirable Qualities Despite His Marauding Propensities. By E. R. Kalmbach. XXXVII, pp. 322-337, 10 ills., Apr., 1920

Crows, Magpies, and Jays: Unusual Intelligence Has Earned a Unique Position for These Birds. By T. Gilbert Pearson. Paintings by Maj. Allan Brooks. LXIII, pp. 51-79, 16 ills. in black and white, 17 ills. in color, Jan., 1933

A **CRUISE** Among Desert Islands (Baja California). By G. Dallas Hanna and A. W. Anthony. XLIV, pp. 71-99, 32 ills., map, July, 1923

CRUISE of the *Kinkajou:* Among Desert Islands of Mexico Voyagers Find Outdoor Laboratories for the Naturalist and Ideal Fishing Grounds for the Sportsman. By Alfred M. Bailey. LXXX, pp. 339-366, 13 ills. in black and white, 12 ills. in color, map, Sept., 1941

CRUISE on an Escort Carrier. By Melville Bell Grosvenor. LXXXIV, pp. 513-546, 14 ills. in black and white, 20 ills. in color, Nov., 1943

CRUISES. *See* Voyages

CRUISING to Crete: Four French Girls Set Sail in a Breton Yawl for the Island of the Legendary Minotaur. By Marthe Oulié and Mariel Jean-Brunhes. LV, pp. 249-272, 15 ills. in black and white, 14 ills. in color, map, Feb., 1929

CRUSADER Castles of the Near East. By William H. Hall. LIX, pp. 369-390, 19 ills., map, Mar., 1931

CRUSADERS:

Crusader Castles of the Near East. By William H. Hall. LIX, pp. 369-390, 19 ills., map, Mar., 1931

The Road of the Crusaders: A Historian Follows the Steps of Richard the Lion Heart and Other Knights of the Cross Over the "Via Dei." By Harold Lamb. LXIV, pp. 645-693, 46 ills. in black and white, 13 ills. in color, map, Dec., 1933

CRUSOE, ROBINSON:

A Voyage to the Island Home of Robinson Crusoe (Juan Fernández). By Waldo L. Schmitt. LIV, pp. 353-370, 24 ills., Sept., 1928

CRUSOES of Canton Island: Life on a Tiny Pacific Atoll That Has Flashed Into World Importance. By Irvine C. Gardner. LXXIII, pp. 749-766, 7 ills. in black and white, 11 ills. in color, June, 1938

CRUSTACEANS:

America's Surpassing Fisheries: Their Present Condition and Future Prospects, and How the Federal Government Fosters Them. By Hugh M. Smith. XXIX, pp. 546-583, 35 ills., June, 1916

Certain Citizens of the Warm Sea. By Louis L. Mowbray. Paintings by Hashime Murayama. XLI, pp. 27-62, 18 ills. in black and white, 16 ills. in color, Jan., 1922

Denizens of Our Warm Atlantic Waters. By Roy Waldo Miner. Paintings by Else Bostelmann. LXXI, pp. 199-219, 10 ills. in black and white, 8 ills. in color, Feb., 1937

Fantastic Dwellers in a Coral Fairyland (Great Barrier Reef). 15 color photos by T. C. Roughley. LXXVII, pp. 831-838, June, 1940

Living Jewels of the Sea. By William Crowder. Paintings by author. LII, pp. 290-304, 8 ills. in black and white, 8 ills. in color, Sept., 1927

Sea Creatures of Our Atlantic Shores. By Roy Waldo Miner. Paintings by Else Bostelmann. LXX, pp. 209-231, 8 ills. in black and white, 8 ills. in color, chart, Aug., 1936

Treasures of the Pacific: Marine Fishes and Fisheries Yield Vast Wealth from Alaska to Baja California. By Leonard P. Schultz. Paintings by Hashime Murayama. LXXIV, pp. 463-498, 10 ills. in black and white, 31 portraits in color, Oct., 1938

See also Crabs; Lobsters; Shrimp

CRYPTOGAMS Collected by Dr. C. Willard Hayes in Alaska, 1891. By Clara E. Cummings. IV, pp. 160-162, May 15, 1892

CUBA:

Across the Equator with the American Navy. By Herbert Corey. XXXIX, pp. 571-624, 53 ills., June, 1921

American Progress in Cuba. XIII, p. 76, Feb., 1902

Among the Mahogany Forests of Cuba. By Walter D. Wilcox. XIX, pp. 485-498, 6 ills., map, July, 1908

Conditions in Cuba as Revealed by the Census. By Henry Gannett. XX, pp. 200-202, Feb., 1909

Cuba. By Robert T. Hill. IX, pp. 193-242, 12 ills., 7 diagrs., tables, 5 maps (1 foldout), May, 1898

Cuba—The Isle of Romance. By Enrique C. Canova. LXIV, pp. 345-380, 34 ills., map, Sept., 1933

Cuba—The Pearl of the Antilles. XVII, pp. 535-568, 24 ills., map supplement, Oct., 1906

Cuba—The Sugar Mill of the Antilles. By William Joseph Showalter. XXXVIII, pp. 1-33, 24 ills., map, July, 1920

Cuba and Porto Rico. XII, p. 80, Feb., 1901

The Cuban Census. XI, p. 205, 5 diagrs., May, 1900

CUBA—*Continued*

Cuban Railways. By Albert G. Robinson. XIII, pp. 108-110, Mar., 1902

Development of Cuba. XIV, pp. 112-113, map, Mar., 1903

The Influence of Submarine Cables upon Military and Naval Supremacy. By Capt. George O. Squier. XII, pp. 1-12, Jan., 1901

The Isle of Pines. XVII, pp. 105-108, ills., Feb., 1906

Our New Possessions and the Interest They Are Exciting. (By O. P. Austin). XI, pp. 32-33, Jan., 1900

Some Recent Instances of National Altruism: The Efforts of the United States to Aid the Peoples of Cuba, Porto Rico and the Philippines. By William H. Taft. XVIII, pp. 429-438, July, 1907

To Bogotá and Back by Air: The Narrative of a 9,500-Mile Flight from Washington, Over Thirteen Latin-American Countries and Return, in the Single-Seater Airplane "Spirit of St. Louis." By Col. Charles A. Lindbergh. LIII, pp. 529-601, 98 ills., map, May, 1928

Trade of the United States with Cuba. (By J. H.). IX, pp. 247-249, tables, May, 1898

Yellow Fever in Cuba. XII, p. 440, Dec., 1901

See also Havana

The **CUBAN** Census. XI, p. 205, 5 diagrs., May, 1900

CUBAN Railways. By Albert G. Robinson. XIII, pp. 108-110, Mar., 1902

CUCKOOS (Birds):

Parrots, Kingfishers, and Flycatchers: Strange Trogons and Curious Cuckoos Are Pictured with These Other Birds of Color, Dash, and Courage. By Alexander Wetmore. Paintings by Maj. Allan Brooks. LXIX, pp. 801-828, 9 ills. in black and white, 36 portraits in color, June, 1936

CUERNAVACA (Mexico), the Sun Child of the Sierras. By Russell Hastings Millward. XXII, pp. 291-301, 9 ills., Mar., 1911

CUICUILCO, Mexico:

Ruins of Cuicuilco May Revolutionize Our History of Ancient America: Lofty Mound Sealed and Preserved by Great Lava Flow for Perhaps Seventy Centuries Is Now Being Excavated in Mexico. By Byron Cummings. XLIV, pp. 203-220, 21 ills., map, Aug., 1923

CULIACAN, Mexico:

Adventuring Down the West Coast of Mexico. By Herbert Corey. XLII, pp. 449-503, 44 ills., map, Nov., 1922

CULTIVATION of Marine and Fresh-Water Animals in Japan. By K. Mitsukuri. XVII, pp. 524-531, 5 ills., Sept., 1906

The **CULTIVATION** of the Mayflower. By Frederick V. Coville. XXVII, pp. 518-519, ill., May, 1915

CULTURE Still Lights Our Wartime Capital (Washington, D. C.). 9 color photos by B. Anthony Stewart. LXXXI, pp. 337-344, Mar., 1942

CULVER, WILLARD R.:

Arkansas Traveler of 1946. 23 color photos by Willard R. Culver. XC, pp. 289-312, Sept., 1946

Butterflies: Nomads Among the Butterflies. 8 ills. in color: 3 paintings by Hashime Murayama, 5 color photos by Willard R. Culver. LXXI, pp. 569-584, May, 1937

Butterflies: Winged Jewels from Many Lands. 9 ills. in color: 3 paintings by Hashime Murayama, 6 color photos by Willard R. Culver. LXIX, pp. 673-688, May, 1936

Catdom's Royalty Photographed in Color. 25 color photos by Willard R. Culver. LXXIV, pp. 597-628, Nov., 1938

Chemistry: From Nature's Hidden Building Blocks. 26 color photos by Willard R. Culver. LXXVI, pp. 609-640, Nov., 1939

Connecticut: Old and New Blend in Yankeeland. 25 color photos: 7 by Willard R. Culver. LXXIV, pp. 295-326, Sept., 1938

Cotton: Golden Fleece of Dixie. 34 color photos by Willard R. Culver. LXXIX, pp. 153-192, Feb., 1941

Dogs in Toyland. 16 color photos by Willard R. Culver. LXXXV, pp. 473-480, Apr., 1944

Food: Flavor and Savor of American Foods. 25 color photos by J. Baylor Roberts, Willard R. Culver, and others. LXXXI, pp. 289-320, Mar., 1942

Glass: From Sand to Seer and Servant of Man. 22 color photos by Willard R. Culver. LXXXIII, pp. 17-48, Jan., 1943

Indiana: Hoosier Haunts and Holidays. 27 color photos by Willard R. Culver. LXX, pp. 283-314, Sept., 1936

Insects: A Community of Dwarfs. 11 color photos by Willard R. Culver. XC, pp. 345-352, Sept., 1946

New York: Bright Patterns of Long Island Life. 18 color photos: 14 by Willard R. Culver. LXXV, pp. 429-460, Apr., 1939

Potomac: George Washington's Historic River. 18 color photos by Willard R. Culver and Robert F. Sisson. LXXXVIII, pp. 41-64, July, 1945

Rubber: From Trees to Tires and Toys. 26 color photos by Willard R. Culver and J. Baylor Roberts. LXXVII, pp. 159-190, Feb., 1940

Virginia, Maryland, and Delaware: Tri-State Medley. 10 color photos by Willard R. Culver. LXXIV, pp. 33-40, July, 1938

Virginia's Colonial Heritage (Williamsburg). 25 color photos: 4 by Willard R. Culver. LXXI, pp. 417-440, Apr., 1937

Washington of Tradition (D. C.) Builds for the Future. 20 color photos: 3 by Willard R. Culver. LXXI, pp. 671-694, June, 1937

CUMANA, Venezuela:

Three Old Ports on the Spanish Main. By G. M. L. Brown. XVII, pp. 622-638, 12 ills., Nov., 1906

CUMBERLAND, Maryland:

Potomac, River of Destiny. By Albert W. Atwood. LXXXVIII, pp. 33-70, 15 ills. in black and white, 18 ills. in color, map, July, 1945

CUMBERLAND GAP, U. S.:

Home Folk around Historic Cumberland Gap. By Leo A. Borah. LXXXIV, pp. 741-768, 25 ills., map, Dec., 1943

CUMMINGS, BYRON:

The Great Natural Bridges of Utah. By Byron Cummings. XXI, pp. 157-167, 7 ills., Feb., 1910

Ruins of Cuicuilco May Revolutionize Our History of Ancient America: Lofty Mound Sealed and Preserved by Great Lava Flow for Perhaps Seventy Centuries Is Now Being Excavated in Mexico. By Byron Cummings. XLIV, pp. 203-220, 21 ills., map, Aug., 1923

CUMMINGS, CLARA E.:

Cryptogams Collected by Dr. C. Willard Hayes in Alaska, 1891. By Clara E. Cummings. IV, pp. 160-162, May 15, 1892

CUNA INDIANS. *See* San Blas Indians

CURAÇAO (Island), West Indies:

Curaçao and Aruba on Guard. By W. Robert Moore. LXXXIII, pp. 169-192, 12 ills. in black and white, 10 ills. in color, 4 maps, Feb., 1943

CURAÇAO and Aruba, Oil Isles of the Caribbean. 10 color photos by Philip Hanson Hiss and Robert Yarnall Richie. LXXXIII, pp. 175-182, Feb., 1943

CURARI (Poison). *See* Urari

CURIOUS and Characteristic Customs of Central African Tribes (Belgian Congo). By E. Torday. XXXVI, pp. 342-368, 35 ills., Oct., 1919

CURIOUS and Characteristic Customs of China. By Kenneth F. Junor. XXI, pp. 791-806, 7 ills., Sept., 1910

CURIOUS Scenes in Out-of-the-Way Places. 12 ills. XXIV, pp. 751-762, June, 1913

CURITYBA, Brazil:

Air Cruising Through New Brazil: A National Geographic Reporter Spots Vast Resources Which the Republic's War Declaration Adds to Strength of United Nations. By Henry Albert Phillips. LXXXII, pp. 503-536, 32 ills., Oct., 1942

CURLE, A. T.:

When a Drought Blights Africa: Hippos and Elephants Are Driven Insane by Suffering, in the Lorian Swamp, Kenya Colony. By Capt. A. T. Curle. LV, pp. 521-528, 9 ills., Apr., 1929

CURTIS, ASAHEL:

National Parks. 3 color photos by Asahel Curtis. XXXVII, pp. 511-518, June, 1920

Washington (State): Sunset Hues in the Pacific Northwest. 5 color photos by Asahel Curtis. LXIII, pp. 155-162, Feb., 1933

Washington (State): Where the Last of the West Was Won. 8 color photos by Asahel Curtis. LXIII, pp. 179-186, Feb., 1933

CURTIS, WILLIAM ELEROY:

The Great Turk and His Lost Provinces. By William E. Curtis. XIV, pp. 45-61, 7 ills., Feb., 1903

CURTIS, WILLIAM ELEROY—*Continued*

Honors to the American Navy (Address by William E. Curtis). XX, pp. 77-95, Jan., 1909

Recent Disclosures Concerning Pre-Columbian Voyages to America in the Archives of the Vatican. By William Eleroy Curtis. V, pp. 197-234, Jan. 31, 1894

The Revolution in Russia. By William Eleroy Curtis. XVIII, pp. 302-316, May, 1907

The Road to Bolivia. By William E. Curtis. XI, pp. 209-224, 7 ills., June, 1900; pp. 264-280, 6 ills., July, 1900

Venezuela: Her Government, People, and Boundary. By William E. Curtis. VII, pp. 49-58, 3 ills., map supplement, Feb., 1896

CURVATURE OF THE EARTH:

The first photograph ever made showing laterally the curvature of the earth. By Capt. A. W. Stevens. LIX, ill. p. 634, May, 1931. LXIX, p. 128, ill. p. 142, Jan., 1936

The First Photograph Ever Made Showing the Division Between the Troposphere and Stratosphere and also the Actual Curvature of the Earth. Aërial photo by Captain Albert W. Stevens. LXIX, supplement, May, 1936

CURZON, LADY MARY IRENE. *See* Ravensdale, Mary Irene, Baroness

CURZON OF KEDLESTON, MARQUESS:

In the Diamond Mountains: Adventures Among the Buddhist Monasteries of Eastern Korea. By the Marquess Curzon of Kedleston. XLVI, pp. 353-374, 21 ills., map, Oct., 1924

CUSHING, FRANK HAMILTON:

Frank Hamilton Cushing (Biography). XI, p. 206, May, 1900

CUSHING, H. P.:

Notes on the Geology of the Vicinity of Muir Glacier. By H. P. Cushing. IV, pp. 56-62, map, Mar. 21, 1892

CUSTOMS:

China and Her People—Some Reflections on Their Manners and Customs, Habits and Lives. By Commander Harrie Webster. XI, pp. 309-319, 3 ills., Aug., 1900

Curious and Characteristic Customs of Central African Tribes (Belgian Congo). By E. Torday. XXXVI, pp. 342-368, 35 ills., Oct., 1919

Curious and Characteristic Customs of China. By Kenneth F. Junor. XXI, pp. 791-806, 7 ills., Sept., 1910

Yank Meets Native. By Wanda Burnett. LXXXVIII, pp. 105-128, 24 ills., July, 1945

See also Carnivals; Coronations; Dances; Festivals; Marriage Customs; Religious Ceremonies; *and* names of countries

CUTLER, A. W.:

Announcement of the death and bequest of A. W. Cutler. XLII, p. 34, July, 1922

Portugal, the Land of Henry the Navigator. 16 color photos by A. W. Cutler. XLII, pp. 517-532, Nov., 1922

See also Scenes in the British Isles

CUTTING, C. SUYDAM:

Sky-high in Lama Land (Tibet). 12 photos by C. Suydam Cutting. XC, pp. 185-196, Aug., 1946

CUZCO, Peru:

Among the Snows and Flowers of Peru. 7 color photos by Jacob Gayer. LVII, pp. 733-764, June, 1930

Cuzco, America's Ancient Mecca. By Harriet Chalmers Adams. XIX, pp. 669-689, 19 ills., Oct., 1908

Further Explorations in the Land of the Incas: Peruvian Expedition of 1915 of the National Geographic Society and Yale University. By Hiram Bingham. XXIX, pp. 431-473, 29 ills., maps, panorama, May, 1916

In the Wonderland of Peru. By Hiram Bingham. XXIV, pp. 387-573, 250 ills., 3 diagrs., map, panorama, Apr., 1913

The Incas: Empire Builders of the Andes. By Philip Ainsworth Means. Paintings by H. M. Herget. LXXIII, pp. 225-264, 26 ills. in black and white, 10 ills. in color, Feb., 1938

The Story of Machu Picchu: The Peruvian Expeditions of the National Geographic Society and Yale University. By Hiram Bingham. XXVII, pp. 172-217, 60 ills., Feb., 1915

CVE's. *See* Escort Carriers

CYCLADES (Islands), Greece:

The Isles of Greece. By Lt. Richard Stillwell, USNR. LXXXV, pp. 593-622, 11 ills. in black and white, 20 ills. in color, map, May, 1944

Modern Odyssey in Classic Lands: Troy's Treasures, Athens' Parthenon, and Rome's First "Broad Way" Influence Today's Banks, Costumes, Jewelry, and Railroad Timetables. By Maynard Owen Williams. LXXVII, pp. 291-337, 27 ills. in black and white, 22 ills. in color, Mar., 1940

Santorin and Mýkonos, Aegean Gems. 8 color photos: 7 by B. Anthony Stewart. LXXVII, pp. 339-346, Mar., 1940

CYCLONES:

United States Daily Atmospheric Survey. By Prof. Willis L. Moore. VIII, pp. 299-303, Oct., 1897

See also Hurricanes

CYGNET (Kite):

Dr. Bell's Man-Lifting Kite. By Gilbert H. Grosvenor. XIX, pp. 35-52, 27 ills., Jan., 1908

CYPRUS (Island), Mediterranean Sea:

American Fighters Visit Bible Lands. By Maynard Owen Williams. With 23 color photos by author. LXXXIX, pp. 311-340, 10 ills. in black and white, Mar., 1946

Unspoiled Cyprus: The Traditional Island Birthplace of Venus Is One of the Least Sophisticated of Mediterranean Lands. By Maynard Owen Williams. LIV, pp. 1-55, 55 ills. in black and white, 10 ills. in color, map, July, 1928

CZECHOSLOVAKIA:

Bohemia and the Czechs. By Aleš Hrdlička. XXXI, pp. 163-187, 18 ills., Feb., 1917

Czechoslovakia, Key-Land to Central Europe. By Maynard Owen Williams. XXXIX, pp. 111-156, 45 ills., map, Feb., 1921

Czechoslovaks, Yankees of Europe. By John Patric. LXXIV, pp. 173-225, 23 ills. in black and white, 30 ills. in color, map, Aug., 1938

CZECHOSLOVAKIA—*Continued*

The Danube, Highway of Races: From the Black Forest to the Black Sea, Europe's Most Important River Has Borne the Traffic of Centuries. By Melville Chater. LVI, pp. 643-697, 54 ills., Dec., 1929

Hospitality of the Czechs. By Worth E. Shoults. LI, pp. 723-742, 19 ills. in color, June, 1927

The Land of Contrast: Austria-Hungary. By D. W. and A. S. Iddings. XXIII, pp. 1188-1217, 1284, 33 ills., map, Dec., 1912

The New Map of Europe: Showing the Boundaries Established by the Peace Conference at Paris and by Subsequent Decisions of the Supreme Council of the Allied and Associated Powers. By Ralph A. Graves. Text with map supplement. XXXIX, pp. 157-177, 18 ills., Feb., 1921

The Races of Europe. By Edwin A. Grosvenor. XXXIV, pp. 441-534, 62 ills., diagr. and index, maps, map supplement, Dec., 1918

When Czechoslovakia Puts a Falcon Feather in Its Cap. By Maynard Owen Williams. LXIII, pp. 40-49, 13 ills. in color, Jan., 1933

See also Prague

CZECHOSLOVAKIAN Cyclorama. 30 color photos by W. Robert Moore. LXXIV, pp. 181-220, Aug., 1938

CZECHOSLOVAKS, Yankees of Europe. By John Patric. LXXIV, pp. 173-225, 23 ills. in black and white, 30 ills. in color, map, Aug., 1938

D

DABNEY, CHARLES W., JR. *See* NGS: Board of Managers; Vice-President

DAGHESTAN AUTONOMOUS SOVIET SOCIALIST REPUBLIC, R. S. F. S. R.:

An Island in the Sea of History: The Highlands of Daghestan. By George Kennan. XXIV, pp. 1087-1140, 49 ills., map, Oct., 1913

Roaming Russia's Caucasus: Rugged Mountains and Hardy Fighters Guard the Soviet Union's Caucasian Treasury of Manganese and Oil. By Rolf Singer. LXXXII, pp. 91-121, 33 ills., July, 1942

DAILY Life in Ancient Egypt (Part I). Daily Life in Ancient Egypt: *The Later Period* (Part II). By William C. Hayes. Paintings by H. M. Herget. LXXX, pp. 419-515, 34 ills. in black and white, 32 ills. in color, map, Oct., 1941

DAILY Life in Calabria (Italy). 16 ills. XLIII, pp. 181-196, Feb., 1923

DAIREN (Dalny), Manchuria:

Building of Dalny. XIV, p. 360, Sept., 1903

Japan Faces Russia in Manchuria. By Willard Price. LXXXII, pp. 603-634, 30 ills., map, Nov., 1942

Mukden, the Manchu Home, and Its Great Art Museum. By Eliza R. Scidmore. XXI, pp. 289-320, 30 ills., Apr., 1910

DAITOTEI, Formosa:

Formosa the Beautiful. By Alice Ballantine Kirjassoff. XXXVII, pp. 247-292, 60 ills., map, Mar., 1920

DAKAR, Senegal:

French West Africa in Wartime. By Paul M. Atkins. LXXXI, pp. 371-408, 37 ills., maps, Mar., 1942

Timbuktu and Beyond: Desert City of Romantic Savor and Salt Emerges into World Life Again as Trading Post of France's Vast African Empire. By Laura C. Boulton. LXXIX, pp. 631-670, 18 ills. in black and white, 26 ills. in color, map, May, 1941

DALAI LAMA:

Across Tibet from India to China. By Lt. Col. Ilia Tolstoy, AUS. XC, pp. 169-222, 53 ills., map, Aug., 1946

DALARNE, Sweden:

In Beautiful Delecarlia (Dalecarlia). By Lillian Gore. XX, pp. 464-477, 13 ills., May, 1909

DALL, WILLIAM H.:

Awarded Jane M. Smith Life Membership. XXXVII, p. 342 (footnote), Apr., 1920

The Cartography and Observations of Bering's First Voyage. By General A. W. Greely. III, pp. 205-230, map supplement, Jan. 28, 1892; Feb. 19, 1892

A Critical Review of Bering's First Expedition, 1725-30, Together with a Translation of His Original Report Upon It. With a Map. By Wm. H. Dall. II, pp. 111-169, 8 tables, foldout map, May, 1890

Included: Supplementary Note by Marcus Baker, On the Alleged Observation of a Lunar Eclipse by Bering in 1728-9, pp. 167-169

The Future of the Yukon Gold Fields. By William H. Dall. IX, pp. 117-120, Apr., 1898

How Long a Whale May Carry a Harpoon. (By Wm. H. Dall). X, pp. 136-137, Apr., 1899

Marcus Baker (Address by Dr. Wm. H. Dall). XV, pp. 40-43, ill., Jan., 1904

The Metlakatla Mission in Danger. (By Wm. H. Dall). IX, pp. 187-189, Apr., 1898

Portrait. VII, pl. XII (opp. p. 110), Mar., 1896

The Russo-American Telegraph Project of 1864-'67. By Professor William H. Dall. VII, pp. 110-111, ill., Mar., 1896

The So-called "Jeannette Relics." By Professor William H. Dall. VII, pp. 93-98, Mar., 1896

A Yukon Pioneer, Mike Lebarge. (By Wm. H. Dall). IX, pp. 137-139, ill., Apr., 1898

See also NGS: Board of Managers; Vice-President

DALMATIA:

Dalmatian Days: Coasting Along Debatable Shores Where Latin and Slav Meet. By Melville Chater. LIII, pp. 47-90, 26 ills. in black and white, 17 ills. in color, map, Jan., 1928

East of the Adriatic: Notes on Dalmatia, Montenegro, Bosnia, and Herzegovina. By Kenneth McKenzie. XXIII, pp. 1159-1187, 1284, 37 ills., map, Dec., 1912

Where East Meets West: Visit to Picturesque Dalmatia, Montenegro and Bosnia. By Marian Cruger Coffin. XIX, pp. 309-344, 26 ills., map, May, 1908

DALMATIAN Days: Coasting Along Debatable Shores Where Latin and Slav Meet. By Melville Chater. LIII, pp. 47-90, 26 ills. in black and white, 17 ills. in color, map, Jan., 1928

DALNY, Manchuria. *See* Dairen

DAMASCUS, Syria:

Damascus, the Pearl of the Desert. By A. Forder. XXII, pp. 62-82, 19 ills., map, Jan., 1911

Syria and Lebanon Taste Freedom. By Maynard Owen Williams. With 21 color photos by author. XC, pp. 729-763, 16 ills. in black and white, Dec., 1946

DAMASCUS AND MECCA RAILWAY:

Damascus and Mecca Railway. XII, p. 408, Nov., 1901

One Thousand Miles of Railway Built for Pilgrims and Not for Dividends. By Colonel F. R. Maunsell. XX, pp. 156-172, 12 ills., map, Feb., 1909

DAMON, THERON J.:

The Albanians. By Theron J. Damon. XXIII, pp. 1090-1103, 14 ills., Nov., 1912

DAMPIER, WILLIAM:

Revealing Earth's Mightiest Ocean (Pacific). By Albert W. Atwood. LXXXIV, pp. 291-306, 10 ills., map supplement, Sept., 1943

DAMS:

By Felucca Down the Nile: Giant Dams Rule Egypt's Lifeline River, Yet Village Life Goes On As It Did in the Time of the Pharaohs. By Willard Price. LXXVII, pp. 435-476, 21 ills. in black and white, 22 ills. in color, two-page map, Apr., 1940

The Columbia (River) Turns on the Power. By Maynard Owen Williams. LXXIX, pp. 749-792, 25 ills. in black and white, 18 ills. in color, June, 1941

The Highest Dam in the World (Roosevelt Dam). XVI, pp. 440-441, Sept., 1905

The Marble Dams of Rajputana. By Eleanor Maddock. XL, pp. 469-499, 13 ills. in black and white, 16 ills. in color, Nov., 1921

More Water for California's Great Central Valley. By Frederick Simpich. XC, pp. 645-664, 16 ills., map, Nov., 1946

The Panama Canal. By Lieut. Colonel William L. Sibert. XXV, pp. 153-183, 24 ills., Feb., 1914

Taming the Outlaw Missouri River. By Frederick Simpich. LXXXVIII, pp. 569-598, 25 ills., two-page map, Nov., 1945

DANAKIL (Tribespeople):

Sailing Forbidden Coasts. By Ida Treat. LX, pp. 357-386, 31 ills., map, Sept., 1931

DANCES:

Artist Adventures on the Island of Bali. By Franklin Price Knott. LIII, pp. 326-347, 20 ills. in color, Mar., 1928

Bali and Points East: Crowded, Happy Isles of the Flores Sea Blend Rice Terraces, Dance Festivals, and Amazing Music in Their Pattern of Living. By Maynard Owen Williams. LXXV, pp. 313-352, 33 ills. in black and white, 11 ills. in color, map, Mar., 1939

DANCES—*Continued*

Costume Pageants in the French Pyrenees. 24 color photos by W. Robert Moore. LXXII, pp. 435-450, Oct., 1937

Field Sports Among the Wild Men of Northern Luzon. By Dean C. Worcester. XXII, pp. 215-267, 52 ills., map, Mar., 1911

The Forests and Deserts of Arizona. By Bernhard E. Fernow. VIII, pp. 203-226, 5 ills., July-Aug., 1897
Included: Snake Dance

Four Faces of Siva: The Mystery of Angkor (Cambodia). By Robert J. Casey. LIV, pp. 303-332, 13 ills. in black and white, 27 ills. in color, map, Sept., 1928

"The Glory That Was Greece." By Alexander Wilbourne Weddell. XLII, pp. 571-630, 51 ills., map, Dec., 1922

Head-Hunters of Northern Luzon. By Dean C. Worcester. XXIII, pp. 833-930, 102 ills., map, Sept., 1912

Here and There in Northern Africa. By Frank Edward Johnson. XXV, pp. 1-132, 113 ills., Jan., 1914

Impressions and Scenes of Mozambique. By O. W. Barrett. XXI, pp. 807-830, 31 ills., Oct., 1910

An Island in the Sea of History: The Highlands of Daghestan. By George Kennan. XXIV, pp. 1087-1140, 49 ills., map, Oct., 1913

Java, Queen of the East Indies. 10 color photos by W. Robert Moore and Tassilo Adam. LVI, pp. 335-358, Sept., 1929

The Land of the Basques: Home of a Thrifty, Picturesque People, Who Take Pride in the Sobriquet, "The Yankees of Spain." By Harry A. McBride. XLI, pp. 63-87, 25 ills., map, Jan., 1922

Life Among the Lamas of Choni: Describing the Mystery Plays and Butter Festival in the Monastery of an Almost Unknown Tibetan Principality in Kansu Province, China. By Joseph F. Rock. LIV, pp. 569-619, 34 ills. in black and white, 16 ills. in color, map, Nov., 1928

The Mexican Indian Flying Pole Dance. By Helga Larsen. LXXI, pp. 387-400, 13 ills., Mar., 1937

The Perahera Processions of Ceylon. By G. H. G. Burroughs. LXII, pp. 90-100, ill. in black and white, 8 ills. in duotone, July, 1932

Roumania and Its Rubicon. By John Oliver La Gorce. XXX, pp. 185-202, 11 ills., Sept., 1916

Samoa—South Sea Outpost of the U. S. Navy. 20 photos by Truman Bailey. LXXIX, pp. 615-630, May, 1941

The Snake Dance (Hopi Indians). By Marion L. Oliver. XXII, pp. 107-137, 31 ills., Feb., 1911

The Two Great Moorish Religious Dances. By George Edmund Holt. XXII, pp. 777-785, 6 ills., Aug., 1911

A Vanishing People of the South Seas: The Tragic Fate of the Marquesan Cannibals, Noted for Their Warlike Courage and Physical Beauty. By John W. Church. XXXVI, pp. 275-306, 22 ills., map, Oct., 1919

With the Devil Dancers of China and Tibet. 43 color photos by Joseph F. Rock. LX, pp. 19-58, July, 1931

DANIELS, JOSEPHUS:

The Gem of the Ocean: Our American Navy. By Josephus Daniels. XXXIII, pp. 313-335, 35 ills., Apr., 1918

Voice Voyages by the National Geographic Society: A Tribute to the Geographic Achievements of the Telephone (Address by Josephus Daniels). XXIX, pp. 296-326, 15 ills., chart, Mar., 1916

DANISH WEST INDIES. *See* Virgin Islands

The **DANISH** West Indies. XIII, pp. 72-73, Feb., 1902

DANUBE (River), Europe:

Budapest, Twin City of the Danube. By J. R. Hildebrand. LXI, pp. 729-742, 3 ills. in black and white, 10 ills. in duotone, June, 1932

The Danube, Highway of Races: From the Black Forest to the Black Sea, Europe's Most Important River Has Borne the Traffic of Centuries. By Melville Chater. LVI, pp. 643-697, 54 ills., Dec., 1929

DANUBE DELTA, Romania:

Caviar Fishermen of Romania: From Vâlcov, "Little Venice" of the Danube Delta, Bearded Russian Exiles Go Down to the Sea. By Dorothy Hosmer. LXXVII, pp. 407-434, 29 ills., map, Mar., 1940

DANZIG:

Flying Around the Baltic. By Douglas Chandler. LXXIII, pp. 767-806, 31 ills. in black and white, 13 ills. in duotone, map, June, 1938

Historic Danzig: Last of the City-States. By William and Alicelia Franklin. LXXVI, pp. 677-696, 26 ills., Nov., 1939

War Clouds Over Danzig and Poland's Port. 8 ills. LXXVI, pp. 551-558, Oct., 1939

DARDANELLES (Strait), Turkey:

The Gates to the Black Sea: The Dardanelles, the Bosphorus, and the Sea of Marmora. By Harry Griswold Dwight. XXVII, pp. 435-459, 27 ills., May, 1915

DARFUR (Province), Anglo-Egyptian Sudan:

Adventures Among the "Lost Tribes of Islam" In Eastern Darfur: A Personal Narrative of Exploring, Mapping, and Setting Up a Government in the Anglo-Egyptian Sudan Borderland. By Major Edward Keith-Roach. XLV, pp. 41-73, 32 ills., map, Jan., 1924

DARGUE, HERBERT A.:

How Latin America Looks from the Air: U. S. Army Airplanes Hurdle the High Andes, Brave Brazil Jungles, and Follow Smoking Volcanoes to Map New Sky Paths Around South America. By Major Herbert A. Dargue. LII, pp. 451-502, 52 ills., map, Oct., 1927

DARIEN (Province), Panama:

A Trip to Panama and Darien. By Richard U. Goode. I, pp. 301-314, diagr., foldout map, Oct., 1889

DARLEY, JAMES M.:

The Society Maps Northwestern United States and Neighboring Canadian Provinces. Text with map supplement. LXXIX, pp. 805-806, June, 1941

DARLEY, JAMES M.—*Continued*

The Society's New Map of China. By James M. Darley. Text with map supplement. LXXXVII, pp. 745-746, June, 1945

The World That Rims the Narrowing Atlantic: Latest Ten-color Map Supplement Shows Four Continents and New Transatlantic Air Routes Which Make This Ocean Only One Day Wide. By James M. Darley. Text with map supplement. LXXVI, pp. 139-142, ill., July, 1939

DARTMOUTH OUTING CLUB:

Skiing Over the New Hampshire Hills. By Fred H. Harris. XXXVII, pp. 151-164, 37 ills., Feb., 1920

DARTON, N. H.:

The Bad Lands of South Dakota. By N. H. Darton. X, pp. 339-343, 4 ills., Sept., 1899

Bighorn Mountains. By N. H. Darton. XVIII, pp. 355-364, 7 ills., map, June, 1907

Mexico—The Treasure House of the World. By N. H. Darton. XVIII, pp. 493-519, 23 ills., Aug., 1907

Our Pacific Northwest. By N. H. Darton. XX, pp. 645-663, 12 ills., maps, July, 1909

Shawangunk Mountain (New York). By N. H. Darton. VI, pp. 23-34, ills., 4 diagrs., Mar. 17, 1894

The Southwest (U. S.): Its Splendid Natural Resources, Agricultural Wealth, and Scenic Beauty. By N. H. Darton. XXI, pp. 631-665, 21 ills., map, Aug., 1910

Texas, Our Largest State. By N. H. Darton. XXIV, pp. 1330-1360, 22 ills., maps, Dec., 1913

DARWIN, Australia:

Life in Dauntless Darwin: A National Geographic Staff Writer Gives a Vivid Description of the Australian Town That Guards the Continent's Northern Door. By Howell Walker. LXXXII, pp. 123-138, 17 ills., map, July, 1942

DASARA CEREMONIES:

India Mosaic. By Peter Muir and Frances Muir. LXXXIX, pp. 443-470, 5 ills. in black and white, 22 ills. in color, map, Apr., 1946

DASHEEN (Vegetable):

In Honor of the Army and Aviation (NGS Banquet). XXII, pp. 267-284, 5 ills., Mar., 1911
Note: Dasheen, recently introduced into this country, served at banquet

The **DATE** Gardens of the Jerid. By Thomas H. Kearney. XXI, pp. 543-567, 20 ills., July, 1910

DATE PALMS:

The Country of the Ant Men (Souf, Algeria). By Thomas H. Kearney. XXII, pp. 367-382, 13 ills., map, panorama, Apr., 1911

The Date Gardens of the Jerid. By Thomas H. Kearney. XXI, pp. 543-567, 20 ills., July, 1910

Here and There in Northern Africa. By Frank Edward Johnson. XXV, pp. 1-132, 113 ills., Jan., 1914

The National Geographic Society (NGS Banquet). XXIII, p. 293, ill. pp. 278, 279, Mar., 1912
Note: First American-grown dates ever served at a public function; *and* information about date cultivation in this country

New Plant Immigrants. By David Fairchild. XXII, pp. 879-907, 34 ills., Oct., 1911

DATE PALMS—*Continued*

Our Plant Immigrants. By David Fairchild. XVII, pp. 179-210, 29 ills., Apr., 1906

DAVAO, Mindanao, Philippine Islands:

Mindanao, on the Road to Tokyo. By Frederick Simpich. LXXXVI, pp. 539-574, 26 ills. in black and white, 12 ills. in color, two-page map, Nov., 1944

DAVIDSON, GEORGE:

Early Voyages on the Northwestern Coast of America. By Professor George Davidson. V, pp. 235-256, Jan. 31, 1894

Origin of the Name "Cape Nome." (By George Davidson). XII, p. 398, Nov., 1901

DAVIES, LLEWELLYN JAMES:

The Chinese "Boxers." By Llewellyn James Davies. XI, pp. 281-287, July, 1900

DAVIS, ARTHUR P.:

Four Prominent Geographers. XVIII, pp. 425-428, 4 ills., June, 1907

The Kansas River. By Arthur P. Davis. VII, pp. 181-184, tables, May, 1896

Location of the Boundary Between Nicaragua and Costa Rica. By Arthur P. Davis. XII, pp. 22-28, ill., map, Jan., 1901

The New Inland Sea (Salton Sea). By Arthur P. Davis. XVIII, pp. 37-49, 8 ills., map, Jan., 1907

Nicaragua and the Isthmian Routes. By A. P. Davis. X, pp. 247-266, 7 ills., diagrs., July, 1899

The Water Supply for the Nicaragua Canal. By Arthur P. Davis. XI, pp. 363-365, Sept., 1900

DAVIS, NOEL:

The Removal of the North Sea Mine Barrage. By Lieutenant-Commander Noel Davis. XXXVII, pp. 103-133, 28 ills., maps, Feb., 1920

DAVIS, WILLIAM MORRIS:

Bearing of Physiography Upon Seuss' Theories. By W. M. Davis. XV, p. 430, Oct., 1904

Geographic Literature. VII, pp. 184-185, May, 1896; pp. 408-409, Dec., 1896

Geographic Methods in Geologic Investigation. By W. M. Davis. I, pp. 11-26, Oct., 1888

A Geographical Description of the British Islands. (By W. M. Davis). VII, pp. 208-211, June, 1896

The Improvement of Geographical Teaching. By Professor William Morris Davis. V, pp. 68-75, July 10, 1893

Practical Exercises in Geography. By W. M. Davis. XI, pp. 62-78, diagr., Feb., 1900

The Rational Element in Geography. By W. M. Davis. X, pp. 466-473, diagrs., Nov., 1899

The Rivers and Valleys of Pennsylvania. By William Morris Davis. I, pp. 183-253, 25 ills., map, July, 1889

The Rivers of Northern New Jersey, with Notes on the Classification of Rivers in General. By William Morris Davis. II, pp. 81-110, 6 diagrs., map drawing, May, 1890

The Seine, the Meuse, and the Moselle. (Part I). By William M. Davis. VII, pp. 189-202, ill., 7 maps, June, 1896

DAVIS, WILLIAM MORRIS—*Continued*

The Seine, the Meuse, and the Moselle. (Part) II. By William M. Davis. VII, pp. 228-238, table, 4 maps, July, 1896

See also NGS: Board of Managers

DAVISON, HENRY P.:

Our Armies of Mercy (American National Red Cross). By Henry P. Davison. XXXI, pp. 423-427, 3 ills., May, 1917

DAVISON, LONNELLE. *See* Aikman, Lonnelle Davison

DAWES, CHARLES G. *See* NGS: Board of Trustees

DAWSON, GEORGE M.:

George M. Dawson (Biography). (By H.G.). XII, p. 197, ill., May, 1901

DAY, CHARLES HEALY:

Flying the World: In a Homemade Airplane the Author and Her Husband Enjoy 16,000 Miles of Adventurous Flight Across Europe, Asia, and America. By Gladys M. Day. LXI, pp. 655-690, 41 ills., map, June, 1932

DAY, DAVID T.:

The Course of the Retail Coal Trade. By Dr. David T. Day. XIII, pp. 394-398, Nov., 1902

See also NGS: Board of Managers

DAY, GLADYS M.:

Flying the World: In a Homemade Airplane the Author and Her Husband Enjoy 16,000 Miles of Adventurous Flight Across Europe, Asia, and America. By Gladys M. Day. LXI, pp. 655-690, 41 ills., map, June, 1932

A **DAY** with Our Boys in the Geographic Wards. By Carol Corey. XXXIV, pp. 69-80, 8 ills., July, 1918

DAYAKS (Tribespeople). *See* Dyaks

The **DEAF:**

President Alexander Graham Bell on Japan. (By J. H.). IX, pp. 509-512, Dec., 1898

Included: Dr. Bell's discussion of the deaf and dumb in Japan

DEALINGS of the United States with the Nations of the World. XV, pp. 186-187, Apr., 1904

DEARBORN, N.:

The Pest of English Sparrows. By N. Dearborn. XXI, pp. 948-952, 4 ills., Nov., 1910

DEATH of G. Brown Goode. (By W J M.). VII, p. 316, Sept., 1896

DEATH VALLEY, California:

The Deserts of Nevada and the Death Valley. By Robert H. Chapman. XVII, pp. 483-497, 9 ills., map, Sept., 1906

Lowest Point in the United States. XVIII, pp. 824-825, Dec., 1907

DEĈANI MONASTERY, Yugoslavia:

The Clock Turns Back in Yugoslavia: The Fortified Monastery of Mountain-girt Dečani Survives Its Six Hundredth Birthday. By Ethel Chamberlain Porter. LXXXV, pp. 493-512, 20 ills., map, Apr., 1944

DECAPODS. *See* Crabs; Lobster; Shrimp

DE CHETELAT, ENZO. *See* Chetelat, Enzo de

DECISION of the Alaskan Boundary Tribunal. XV, pp. 12-14, Jan., 1904

DECORATIONS, Military and Naval:

American Decorations and Insignia of Honor and Service. By Col. Robert E. Wyllie. XXXVI, pp. 502-526, 6 ills. in black and white, 119 ills. in color, Dec., 1919

Decorations, Medals, Service Ribbons, Badges, and Women's Insignia. LXXXIV, pp. 414-444, 6 ills. in black and white, 376 ills. in color, Oct., 1943

The Heraldry of Heroism. By Arthur E. Du Bois. LXXXIV, pp. 409-413, ills., map, Oct., 1943

Insignia and Decorations of the United States Armed Forces. By Gilbert Grosvenor. LXXXVII, pp. 185-186, Feb., 1945

The Romance of Military Insignia: How the United States Government Recognizes Deeds of Heroism and Devotion to Duty. By Col. Robert E. Wyllie. XXXVI, pp. 463-501, 27 ills., Dec., 1919

DEEP-SEA Exploring Expedition of the Steamer "Albatross." By Hugh M. Smith. X, pp. 291-296, ills., diagr., Aug., 1899

The **DEEP-WATER** Route from Chicago to the Gulf. XVIII, pp. 679-685, 3 ills., map, Oct., 1907

DEEPS, Ocean. *See* Oceanography; Tuscarora Deep

DEER:

Deer Farming in the United States. XXI, pp. 269-276, ills., Mar., 1910

Deer of the World: As Workers, Pets, and Graceful "Living Statuary" in Parks and Estates, These Versatile Creatures Have Endeared Themselves to Mankind. By Victor H. Cahalane. Paintings by Walter A. Weber. LXXVI, pp. 463-510, 20 ills. in black and white, 23 ills. in color, Oct., 1939

Doe and Twin Fawns. Flashlight photo by George Shiras, 3d. XXIV, supplement, July, 1913. XL, ill. p. 136, Aug., 1921. LXXVI, ill. p. 475, Oct., 1939

The Larger North American Mammals. By E. W. Nelson. Paintings by Louis Agassiz Fuertes. XXX, pp. 385-472, 24 ills. in black and white, 49 ills. in color, pictorial supplement, Nov., 1916

Wild Animals That Took Their Own Pictures by Day and by Night. By George Shiras, 3d. XXIV, pp. 763-834, 68 ills., map, pictorial supplement, July, 1913

Doe and Twin Fawns. Flashlight photo by author (supplement)

The Wild Life of Lake Superior, Past and Present: The Habits of Deer, Moose, Wolves, Beavers, Muskrats, Trout, and Feathered Wood-Folk Studied with Camera and Flashlight. By George Shiras, 3d. XL, pp. 113-204, 76 ills., map, pictorial supplement, Aug., 1921

Hark! Flashlight photo of deer by author (supplement)

See also Mule Deer

DEERING, MABEL CRAFT:

Chosen—Land of Morning Calm. By Mabel Craft Deering. LXIV, pp. 421-448, 20 ills. in black and white, 13 ills. in color, map, Oct., 1933

Ho for the Soochow Ho. By Mabel Craft Deering. LI, pp. 623-649, 32 ills., map, June, 1927

DEFENSE BASES. *See* Air Bases; U. S. Defense Bases

The **DEFINITE** Location of Bouvet Island. (By O. H. Tittmann). X, pp. 413-414, Oct., 1899

DE FOREST, J. H.:

Why Nik-ko Is Beautiful. By J. H. De Forest. XIX, pp. 300-308, 8 ills., Apr., 1908

DEFORESTATION and Climate. XVI, pp. 397-398, Aug., 1905

DE GASTON, PAUL:

China's Teeming Life on the Rivers and Sea. 16 photos in duotone by Paul De Gaston. LXVI, pp. 625-640, Nov., 1934

DEGELMAN, JOHN:

The Tuna Harvest of the Sea: A Little-known Epic of the Ocean Is the Story of Southern California's Far-ranging Tuna Fleet. By John Degelman. LXXVIII, pp. 393-408, 17 ills., Sept., 1940

DEHODENCQ, ALFRED:

Fate Directs the Faltering Footsteps of Columbus. Reproduction in color of the painting by Alfred Dehodencq, Paris. LIV, supplement, Sept., 1928

DEIR-EL-BAHARI, Egypt:

Reconstructing Egypt's History. By Wallace N. Stearns. XXIV, pp. 1021-1042, 21 ills., Sept., 1913

The Resurrection of Ancient Egypt. By James Baikie. XXIV, pp. 957-1020, 46 ills., map, Sept., 1913

DEIR EZ ZOR, Syria:

Ali Goes to the Clinic. By Herndon and Mary Hudson. XC, pp. 764-766, ills., Dec., 1946

DELAWARE:

Diamond Delaware, Colonial Still: Tradition Rules the "Three Lower Counties" Over Which William Penn and Lord Baltimore Went to Law. By Leo A. Borah. LXVIII, pp. 367-398, 25 ills. in black and white, 15 ills. in color, map, Sept., 1935

DELAWARE (River), U. S.:

Atlantic Estuarine Tides. By Mark S. W. Jefferson. IX, pp. 400-409, diagrs., 7 tables, maps, Sept., 1898

The **DELECTABLE** Shrimp: Once a Culinary Stepchild, Today a Gulf Coast Industry. By Harlan Major. LXXXVI, pp. 501-512, 11 ills., map, Oct., 1944

DELHI, India:

India Mosaic. By Peter Muir and Frances Muir. LXXXIX, pp. 443-470, 5 ills. in black and white, 22 ills. in color, map, Apr., 1946

New Delhi Goes Full Time. By Maynard Owen Williams. LXXXII, pp. 465-494, 17 ills. in black and white, 13 ills. in color, map, Oct., 1942

DELHI, India—*Continued*

The Temples of India. 54 photos by W. M. Zumbro. XX, pp. 922-971, Nov., 1909

Through the Heart of Hindustan: A Teeming Highway Extending for Fifteen Hundred Miles, from the Khyber Pass to Calcutta. By Maynard Owen Williams. XL, pp. 433-467, 29 ills., Nov., 1921

DELI, Sumatra:

By Motor Through the East Coast and Batak Highlands of Sumatra. By Melvin A. Hall. XXXVII, pp. 69-102, 27 ills., Jan., 1920

DE L'ISLE, J. N.:

The Cartography and Observations of Bering's First Voyage. By General A. W. Greely. III, pp. 205-230, map supplement, Jan. 28, 1892; Feb. 19, 1892

DELOS (Island), Aegean Sea:

The Isles of Greece. By Lt. Richard Stillwell, USNR. LXXXV, pp. 593-622, 11 ills. in black and white, 20 ills. in color, map, May, 1944

DELPHI, Greece:

"The Glory That Was Greece." By Alexander Wilbourne Weddell. XLII, pp. 571-630, 51 ills., map, Dec., 1922

DELPHIC FESTIVAL (1930):

Festival Days on the Slopes of Mount Parnassus (Greece). 14 color photos by Maynard Owen Williams. LVIII, pp. 713-720, Dec., 1930

The **DELTA** of the Mississippi River. By E. L. Corthell. VIII, pp. 351-354, Dec., 1897

DEMAVEND, Mount, Iran:

Modern Persia and Its Capital: And an Account of an Ascent of Mount Demavend, the Persian Olympus. By F. L. Bird. XXXIX, pp. 353-400, 47 ills., Apr., 1921

DEMOCRACY'S Royal Palace (Westminster). 19 color photos by B. Anthony Stewart. XC, pp. 233-248, Aug., 1946

DEMOLISHING Germany's North Sea Ramparts. By Stuart E. Jones. XC, pp. 635-644, ill. in black and white, 10 ills. in color, Nov., 1946

DEMON DANCERS:

Demon Dancers and Butter Gods of Choni. 16 color photos by Joseph F. Rock. LIV, pp. 585-600, Nov., 1928

With the Devil Dancers of China and Tibet. 43 color photos by Joseph F. Rock. LX, pp. 19-58, July, 1931

DEMON-POSSESSED Tibetans and Their Incredible Feats. 12 ills. in color. LXVIII, pp. 479-486, Oct., 1935

DENBY, EDWIN:

A Memorial to Peary: The National Geographic Society Dedicates Monument in Arlington National Cemetery to Discoverer of the North Pole (Address by Edwin Denby). XLI, pp. 639-646, 4 ills., June, 1922

DENG BAO-LING:

China's Wonderland—Yen Tang Shan (Chekiang Province). 8 ills. in color from camera paint-

DENG BAO-LING—*Continued*
ings by Herbert Clarence White, Clarence C. Crisler, Deng Bao-ling, Hwang Yao-tso. LXXII, pp. 687-694, Dec., 1937

A Peiping Panorama in Vivid Pigments. 16 ills. in color from camera paintings by H. C. and J. H. White, Deng Bao-ling, Hwang Yao-tso. LXX, pp. 753-784, Dec., 1936

DENIZENS of Our Warm Atlantic Waters (Mollusks, Crustaceans, etc.). By Roy Waldo Miner. Paintings by Else Bostelmann. LXXI, pp. 199-219, 10 ills. in black and white, 8 ills. in color, Feb., 1937

DENMARK:

Denmark and the Danes. By Maurice Francis Egan. XLII, pp. 115-164, 38 ills., map, Aug., 1922

On Danish By-Lanes: An American Cycles Through the Quaint City of Lace, the Curiosity Town Where Time Stands Still, and Even Finds a Frontier in the Farming Kingdom. By Willis Lindquist. LXXVII, pp. 1-34, 21 ills. in black and white, 10 ills. in color, map, Jan., 1940

Royal Copenhagen, Capital of a Farming Kingdom: A Fifth of Denmark's Thrifty Population Resides in a Metropolis Famous for Its Porcelains, Its Silver, and Its Lace. By J. R. Hildebrand. LXI, pp. 217-250, 26 ills. in black and white, 14 ills. in color, Feb., 1932

See also Bornholm (Island)

DENMARK, Land of Farms and Fisheries. 14 color photos by Gustav Heurlin. LXI, pp. 223-230, Feb., 1932

DENMARK—Land of Tranquility. 10 ills. in color. LXXVII, pp. 17-24, Jan., 1940

DENNIS, ALFRED PEARCE:

The Land of Egypt: A Narrow Green Strip of Fertility Stretching for a Thousand Miles Through Walls of Desert. By Alfred Pearce Dennis. XLIX, pp. 271-298, 28 ills., map, Mar., 1926

Life on a Yukon Trail. By Alfred Pearce Dennis. X, pp. 377-391, 8 ills., map, Oct., 1899; pp. 457-466, 7 ills., Nov., 1899

Norway, A Land of Stern Reality: Where Descendants of the Sea Kings of Old Triumphed Over Nature and Wrought a Nation of Arts and Crafts. By Alfred Pearce Dennis. LVIII, pp. 1-44, 31 ills. in black and white, 27 ills. in color, July, 1930

DENT DU REQUIN (Mountain), France:

A Woman's Climbs in the High Alps. By Dora Keen. XXII, pp. 643-675, 26 ills., July, 1911

DENVER, Colorado:

Colorado, a Barrier That Became a Goal: Where Water Has Transformed Dry Plains Into Verdant Farms, and Highways Have Opened up Mineral and Scenic Wealth. By McFall Kerbey. LXII, pp. 1-63, 56 ills. in black and white, 12 ills. in color, map, July, 1932

The **DEPTHS** of the Sea: Strange Life Forms a Mile Below the Surface. By William Beebe. Paintings by E. Bostelmann. LXI, pp. 65-88, 15 ills. in black and white, 8 ills in color, map, Jan., 1932

The **DESCENDANTS** of Confucius (Industries in Shantung). By Maynard Owen Williams. XXXVI, pp. 253-265, 16 ills., Sept., 1919

DESCRIPTIVE Topographic Terms of Spanish America. By Robert T. Hill. VII, pp. 291-302, Sept., 1896

The **DESERT** Road to Turkestan: Twentieth Century Travel Through Innermost Asia, Along Caravan Trails Over Which Oriental Commerce Was Once Borne from China to the Medieval Western World. By Owen Lattimore. LV, pp. 661-702, 45 ills., map, June, 1929

DESERTS:

Africa: Cirenaica, Eastern Wing of Italian Libia. By Harriet Chalmers Adams. LVII, pp. 689-726, 35 ills. in black and white, 13 ills. in color, map, June, 1930

Africa: The Conquest of the Sahara by the Automobile. XLV, pp. 87-93, 9 ills., map, Jan., 1924

Africa: The Country of the Ant Men (Algeria). By Thomas H. Kearney. XXII, pp. 367-382, 13 ills., map, panorama, Apr., 1911

The Hour of Prayer: In the Sahara Desert (panorama)

Africa: Crossing the Untraversed Libyan Desert: The Record of a 2,200-Mile Journey of Exploration Which Resulted in the Discovery of Two Oases of Strategic Importance on the Southwestern Frontier of Egypt. By A. M. Hassanein Bey. XLVI, pp. 233-277, 46 ills., map, Sept., 1924

Africa: French Conquest of the Sahara. By Charles Rabot. XVI, pp. 76-80, ills., Feb., 1905

Africa: Here and There in Northern Africa (Sahara). By Frank Edward Johnson. XXV, pp. 1-132, 113 ills., Jan., 1914

Africa: The Mysteries of the Desert (Sahara). By Hanns Vischer. XXII, pp. 1056-1059, Nov., 1911

Africa: On the Fringe of the Great Desert (Algeria). 32 color photos by Gervais Courtellemont. LIII, pp. 207-222, Feb., 1928

Africa: Three-Wheeling Through Africa: Two Adventurers Cross the So-called Dark Continent North of Lake Chad on Motorcycles with Side Cars. By James C. Wilson. LXV, pp. 37-92, 64 ills., two-page map, Jan., 1934

Africa: Through the Deserts and Jungles of Africa by Motor: Caterpillar Cars Make 15,000-Mile Trip from Algeria to Madagascar in Nine Months. By Georges-Marie Haardt. XLIX, pp. 651-720, 95 ills., map, June, 1926

Africa: Timbuktu in the Sands of the Sahara. By Captain Cecil D. Priest. XLV, pp. 73-85, 16 ills., Jan., 1924

Africa: Time's Footprints in Tunisian Sands. By Maynard Owen Williams. LXXI, pp. 345-386, 43 ills., maps, Mar., 1937

Arabia, the Desert of the Sea. By Archibald Forder. XX, pp. 1039-1062, 1117, 20 ills., map, Dec., 1909

Arabian Peninsula: Guest in Saudi Arabia. By Maynard Owen Williams. LXXXVIII, pp. 463-487, 24 ills., map, Oct., 1945

Arizona: The Forests and Deserts of Arizona. By Bernhard E. Fernow. VIII, pp. 203-226, 5 ills., July-Aug., 1897

Asia: Life in the Great Desert of Central Asia. By Ellsworth Huntington. XX, pp. 749-760, 12 ills., Aug., 1909

DESERTS—*Continued*

Australia: Lonely Australia: The Unique Continent. By Herbert E. Gregory. XXX, pp. 473-568, 68 ills., 5 maps (1 two-page), Dec., 1916

Mexico: Camp Fires on Desert and Lava (Book Review). XXI, pp. 715-718, 3 ills., Aug., 1910

Mexico: The Land of Drought and Desert—Lower California: Two Thousand Miles on Horseback Through the Most Extraordinary Cacti Forests in the World. By E. W. Nelson. XXII, pp. 443-474, 25 ills., maps, May, 1911

Mongolia: The Desert Road to Turkestan: Twentieth Century Travel Through Innermost Asia, Along Caravan Trails Over Which Oriental Commerce Was Once Borne from China to the Medieval Western World. By Owen Lattimore. LV, pp. 661-702, 45 ills., map, June, 1929

Mongolia: The Lama's Motor-Car: A Trip Across the Gobi Desert by Motor-Car. By Ethan C. Le Munyon. XXIV, pp. 641-670, 34 ills., May, 1913

The North American Deserts. By Herr Professor Dr. Johannes Walther. IV, pp. 163-176, Feb. 8, 1893

Relations of Air and Water to Temperature and Life. By Honorable Gardiner G. Hubbard. V, pp. 112-124, Jan. 31, 1894

United States: The American Deserts. XV, pp. 153-163, 7 ills., map, Apr., 1904

United States: Canyons and Cacti of the American Southwest. 22 color photos by Edwin L. Wisherd, Jacob Gayer, Charles Martin. XLVIII, pp. 275-290, Sept., 1925

United States: Carrying Water Through a Desert: The Story of the Los Angeles Aqueduct. By Burt A. Heinly. XXI, pp. 568-596, 19 ills., map, July, 1910

United States: The Colorado Desert. By W. C. Mendenhall. XX, pp. 681-701, 16 ills., Aug., 1909

United States: The Deserts of Nevada and the Death Valley. By Robert H. Chapman. XVII, pp. 483-497, 9 ills., map, Sept., 1906

United States: Fantastic Plants of Our Western Deserts. 8 ills. by Frank M. Campbell. XLV, pp. 33-40, Jan., 1924

United States: Is Climatic Aridity Impending on the Pacific Slope? The Testimony of the Forest. By J. B. Leiberg. X, pp. 160-181, May, 1899

United States: Notes on the Deserts of the United States and Mexico (Extracted from a Publication of Dr. Daniel T. MacDougal). XXI, pp. 691-714, 16 ills., Aug., 1910

United States: The Saguaro, Cactus Camel of Arizona. By Forrest Shreve. LXXXVIII, pp. 695-704, 9 ills. in color, Dec., 1945

United States: The Saguaro Forest (Arizona). By H. L. Shantz. LXXI, pp. 515-532, 18 ills., Apr., 1937

United States: The Scenery of North America. By James Bryce. XLI, pp. 339-389, 45 ills., Apr., 1922

United States: The Southwest: Its Splendid Natural Resources, Agricultural Wealth, and Scenic Beauty. By N. H. Darton. XXI, pp. 631-665, 21 ills., map, Aug., 1910

See also Reclamation of Land; Sahara

DE SIEYES, JACQUES:

Aces of the Air. By Captain Jacques De Sieyes. XXXIII, pp. 5-9, ills., Jan., 1918

DESOLATE Greenland, Now an American Outpost. 17 photos: 12 by Willie Knutsen, 4 by F. Vogel. LXXX, pp. 393-406, Sept., 1941

DESTRUCTION of Pompeii as Interpreted by the Volcanic Eruptions of Martinique. By Angelo Heilprin. XV, p. 431, Oct., 1904

DETROIT, Michigan:

Michigan Fights. By Harvey Klemmer. LXXXVI, pp. 677-715, 20 ills. in black and white, 19 ills. in color, map, Dec., 1944

DEVASTATED Poland. By Frederic C. Walcott. XXXI, pp. 445-452, 6 ills., May, 1917

The **DEVELOPMENT** of Nevada. XV, p. 166, Apr., 1904

DEVIL-FISHING in the Gulf Stream. By John Oliver La Gorce. XXXV, pp. 476-488, 7 ills., June, 1919

DEVILLE NÉVÉ (Glacier), British Columbia:

Some Tramps Across the Glaciers and Snowfields of British Columbia. By Howard Palmer. XXI, pp. 457-487, 25 ills., June, 1910

DEVON (County), England:

Down Devon Lanes. By Herbert Corey. LV, pp. 529-568, 45 ills., map, May, 1929

See also Bampton; Clovelly

DEW:

The Magic Beauty of Snow and Dew. By Wilson A. Bentley. XLIII, pp. 103-112, 9 ills., Jan., 1923

DEWEY, GEORGE:

Election of Admiral Dewey as Honorary Member of the Society. XVIII, p. 51, Jan., 1907

DIAMOND Delaware, Colonial Still: Tradition Rules the "Three Lower Counties" Over Which William Penn and Lord Baltimore Went to Law. By Leo A. Borah. LXVIII, pp. 367-398, 25 ills. in black and white, 15 ills. in color, map, Sept., 1935

DIAMOND MINES:

Africa Since 1888, with Special Reference to South Africa and Abyssinia. By Hon. Gardiner G. Hubbard. VII, pp. 157-175, ill., foldout map, May, 1896

The Diamond Mines of South Africa. By Gardiner F. Williams. XVII, pp. 344-356, 11 ills., June, 1906

Under the South African Union. By Melville Chater. LIX, pp. 391-512, 97 ills. in black and white, 38 ills. in color, two-page map, Apr., 1931

DIAMOND MOUNTAINS, Korea:

In the Diamond Mountains: Adventures Among the Buddhist Monasteries of Eastern Korea. By the Marquess Curzon of Kedleston. XLVI, pp. 353-374, 21 ills., map, Oct., 1924

DIANA (Ship):

The Mission of the "Diana" (Peary Arctic Club). X, p. 273, July, 1899

DIANA (Ship)—*Continued*
Peary's Explorations in 1898-1899. X, pp. 415-416, Oct., 1899

DIARY of a Voyage from San Francisco to Tahiti and Return, 1901. By S. P. Langley. XII, pp. 413-429, 10 ills., maps, Dec., 1901

DICKEY, W. A.:
The Sushitna River, Alaska. By W. A. Dickey. VIII, pp. 322-327, map, Nov., 1897

DIEPPE, France:
Rehearsal at Dieppe. By W. Robert Moore. LXXXII, pp. 495-502, 6 ills., Oct., 1942

DIKES:
The Dikes of Holland. By Gerard H. Matthes. XII, pp. 219-234, 3 ills., 7 charts, June, 1901
Mending Dikes in the Netherlands. 20 photos by Lawrence Earl. XC, pp. 791-806, Dec., 1946

DILLER, J. S.:
Crater Lake, Oregon. By J. S. Diller. VIII, pp. 33-48, 6 ills., maps, Feb., 1897
The Mazamas. (By J. S. Diller). VIII, pp. 58-59, Feb., 1897
Our Youngest Volcano. By J. S. Diller. V, pp. 93-96, ill., July 10, 1893
Volcanic Rocks of Martinique and St. Vincent: Collected by Robert T. Hill and Israel C. Russell. By J. S. Diller. XIII, pp. 285-296, July, 1902

DILLON, RAYMOND A.:
War Finds Its Way to Gilbert Islands: United States Forces Dislodge Japanese from Enchanted Atolls Which Loom Now as Stepping Stones along South Sea Route from Australia to Hawaii. By Sir Arthur Grimble. Photos by Dr. Raymond A. Dillon. LXXXIII, pp. 71-92, 19 ills., map, Jan., 1943

DINKAS (Tribespeople):
Across Widest Africa. By A. Henry Savage Landor. XIX, pp. 694-737, 38 ills., map, Oct., 1908

DINKELSBÜHL (Germany), Romantic Vision from the Past. LX, pp. 689-702, 4 ills. in black and white, 12 ills. in color, Dec., 1931

DINOSAURS:
Hunting Big Game of Other Days: A Boating Expedition in Search of Fossils in Alberta, Canada. By Barnum Brown. XXXV, pp. 407-429, 24 ills., map, May, 1919
Parade of Life Through the Ages: Records in Rocks Reveal a Strange Procession of Prehistoric Creatures, from Jellyfish to Dinosaurs, Giant Sloths, Saber-toothed Tigers, and Primitive Man. By Charles R. Knight. With 24 ills. in color from paintings by author. LXXXI, pp. 141-184, 13 ills. in black and white, Feb., 1942
Contents: Ceratosaurus, Diplodocus, Parasaurolophus, Protoceratops, Stegosaurus, Styracosaurus, *Tyrannosaurus rex*

DIPO, the Little Desert "Kangaroo." By Walter E. Ketcham. LXXVIII, pp. 537-548, 14 ills., Oct., 1940

DIRECTORY of Officers and Councillors of Geographic Societies of the United States. XIV, pp. 392-394, Oct., 1903

DISCOVERERS, EXPLORERS, AND NAVIGATORS:
American Pathfinders in the Pacific. By William H. Nicholas. LXXXIX, pp. 617-640, 17 ills., two-page map, May, 1946
The Antarctic Continent (Geographic Notes). By Cyrus C. Babb. VI, pp. 217-223, map, Dec. 29, 1894
Boyhood of Sir Walter Raleigh. Reproduction in color of the painting by Sir John Millais, Tate Gallery, London. XLIX, text, p. 596; supplement, May, 1926
The Caravels of Columbus. By Victor Maria Concas. V, pp. 180-186, Jan. 31, 1894
The Caravels of Columbus. Reproduction in color of the painting by N. C. Wyeth, National Geographic Society, Washington, D.C. LIV, text, p. 55; supplement, July, 1928
Columbus, Christopher: Fate Directs the Faltering Footsteps of Columbus. Reproduction in color of the painting by Alfred Dehodencq, Paris. LIV, supplement, Sept., 1928
Cook, James: The Columbus of the Pacific: Captain James Cook, Foremost British Navigator, Expanded the Great Sea to Correct Proportions and Won for Albion an Insular Empire by Peaceful Exploration and Scientific Study. By J. R. Hildebrand. LI, pp. 85-132, 45 ills., maps, Jan., 1927
The Discoverer. Reproduction in color of the painting by N. C. Wyeth, National Geographic Society, Washington, D. C. LIII, text, p. 347; supplement, Mar., 1928
Discoverers of America. Annual Address by the President, Hon. Gardiner G. Hubbard. V, pp. 1-20, charts, maps, 3 map supplements, Apr. 7, 1893
The Discovery of Glacier Bay, Alaska. By Eliza Ruhamah Scidmore. VII, pp. 140-146, ill., map, Apr., 1896
Included: Muir, John; Wood, Lieut. C. E. S.
An Expedition to Mount St. Elias, Alaska. By Israel C. Russell. III, pp. 53-191, 17 ills., 3 diagrs., tables, 7 maps (1 foldout), May 29, 1891
Included: Belcher; Bering; Cook; Dixon; Douglas; La Pérouse; Malaspina; Schwatka; Tebenkof; Topham; Vancouver
The First Landfall of Columbus. By Jacques W. Redway, F. R. G. S. VI, pp. 179-192, 4 maps, Dec. 29, 1894
Gama, Vasco da: The Pathfinder of the East: Setting Sail to Find "Christians and Spices," Vasco da Gama Met Amazing Adventures, Founded an Empire, and Changed the History of Western Europe. By J. R. Hildebrand. LII, pp. 503-550, 43 ills., map, pictorial supplement, Nov., 1927
Vasco da Gama at the Court of the Zamorin of Calicut. Reproduction in color of the painting by José Velloso Salgado, Sociedade de Geographia de Lisboa (supplement)
Geography and Some Explorers. By Joseph Conrad. XLV, pp. 239-274, 28 ills., map, Mar., 1924
Henry Hudson, Magnificent Failure: Just 330 Years Ago He and His Mutinous Crew Found Manhattan Covered With "Goodly Oakes" and Fought Indians in New York Harbor. By Frederick G. Vosburgh. LXXV, pp. 461-490, 21 ills., Apr., 1939

DISCOVERERS, EXPLORERS, AND NAVIGATORS—*Continued*

In the Wake of Columbus. By Frederick A. Ober. V, pp. 187-196, Jan. 31, 1894

International Literary Contest (Madrid, Spain). I, pp. 273-276, July, 1889

Note: Held in conjunction with the Fourth Centennial Anniversary of the Discovery of America

Magellan, Ferdinand: The Greatest Voyage in the Annals of the Sea. By J. R. Hildebrand. LXII, pp. 699-739, 35 ills., maps, Dec., 1932

Revealing Earth's Mightiest Ocean (Pacific). By Albert W. Atwood. LXXXIV, pp. 291-306, 10 ills., map supplement, Sept., 1943

The Scope and Value of Arctic Explorations. By General A. W. Greely. VII, pp. 32-39, Jan., 1896

Sir Francis Drake's Anchorage. By Edward L. Berthoud. VI, pp. 208-214, Dec. 29, 1894

The World's Greatest Overland Explorer: How Marco Polo Penetrated Farthest Asia, "Discovered" Many Lands Unknown to Europe, and Added Numerous Minerals, Animals, Birds and Plants to Man's Knowledge. By J. R. Hildebrand. LIV, pp. 505-568, 53 ills., two-page map, Nov., 1928

See also Bering, Vitus; Gomez, Estevan; Hall, Charles Francis; Johansen, Frederic H.; Lebarge, Michel; Nansen, Fridtjof; Peary, Robert E.; Rock, Joseph F.; Stanley, Henry Morton; Sverdrup, Otto; *and* Agricultural and Botanical Explorers; Antarctic Regions; Arctic Regions; Expeditions; Geography; New World; Norsemen; Voyages

DISCOVERERS of America. Annual Address by the President, Hon. Gardiner G. Hubbard. V, pp. 1-20, charts, maps, 3 map supplements, Apr. 7, 1893

DISCOVERING Alaska's Oldest Arctic Town (Ipiutak): A Scientist Finds Ivory-eyed Skeletons of a Mysterious People and Joins Modern Eskimos in the Dangerous Spring Whale Hunt. By Froelich G. Rainey. LXXXII, pp. 319-336, 15 ills., Sept., 1942

DISCOVERING the New World's Oldest Dated Work of Man: A Maya Monument Inscribed 291 B. C. is Unearthed Near a Huge Stone Head by a Geographic-Smithsonian Expedition in Mexico. By Matthew W. Stirling. LXXVI, pp. 183-218, 40 ills., map, Aug., 1939

DISCOVERING the Oldest Statues in the World: A Daring Explorer Swims Through a Subterranean River of the Pyrenees and Finds Rock Carvings Made 20,000 Years Ago. By Norbert Casteret. XLVI, pp. 123-152, 24 ills., maps, Aug., 1924

DISCOVERY (Ship):

The Heart of the Antarctic. By Ernest H. Shackleton. XX, pp. 972-1007, 27 ills., map, Nov., 1909

DISCOVERY and Invention. By Alexander Graham Bell. XXV, pp. 649-655, June, 1914

The **DISCOVERY** of Cancer in Plants. XXIV, pp. 53-70, 12 ills., Jan., 1913

The **DISCOVERY** of Glacier Bay, Alaska. By Eliza Ruhamah Scidmore. VII, pp. 140-146, ill., map, Apr., 1896

The **DISCOVERY** of the North Pole. XXI, pp. 63-82, Jan., 1910

The **DISCOVERY** of the Pole (First Reports by Dr. Frederick A. Cook and Commander Robert E. Peary). XX, pp. 892-916, 11 ills., map, Oct., 1909

DISEASES:

Ali Goes to the Clinic. By Herndon and Mary Hudson. XC, pp. 764-766, ills., Dec., 1946

Amid the Snow Peaks of the Equator: A Naturalist's Explorations Around Ruwenzori, with an Excursion to the Congo State, and an Account of the Terrible Scourge of Sleeping Sickness. By A. F. R. Wollaston. XX, pp. 256-277, 11 ills., Mar., 1909

The Changing Map in the Balkans. By Frederick Moore. XXIV, pp. 199-226, 27 ills., map, Feb., 1913

Included: The cholera camps of the Turks

The Conquest of Bubonic Plague in the Philippines. XIV, pp. 185-195, 7 ills., May, 1903

The Discovery of Cancer in Plants. XXIV, pp. 53-70, 12 ills., Jan., 1913

Diseases of the Philippines. XI, pp. 123-124, Mar., 1900

Economic Loss to the People of the United States Through Insects That Carry Disease. By L. O. Howard. XX, pp. 735-749, Aug., 1909

Fearful Famines of the Past: History Will Repeat Itself Unless the American People Conserve Their Resources. By Ralph A. Graves. XXXII, pp. 69-90, 11 ills., July, 1917

Included: The Black Death

The History and Geographic Distribution of Bubonic Plague. By George M. Sternberg. XI, pp. 97-113, Mar., 1900

Life Story of the Mosquito. By Graham Fairchild. With 10 ills. in color from paintings. LXXXV, pp. 180-195, 5 ills. in black and white, drawing, Feb., 1944

Map-Changing Medicine. By William Joseph Showalter. XLII, pp. 303-330, 26 ills., Sept., 1922

Our Army Versus a Bacillus. By Alton G. Grinnell. XXIV, pp. 1146-1152, 5 ills., diagr., Oct., 1913

The Rat Pest: The Labor of 200,000 Men in the United States Required to Support Rats, Man's Most Destructive and Dangerous Enemy. By Edward W. Nelson. XXXII, pp. 1-23, 21 ills., July, 1917

Included: Bubonic plague

Redeeming the Tropics. By William Joseph Showalter. XXV, pp. 344-364, 13 ills., Mar., 1914

Saboteur Mosquitoes. By Harry H. Stage. LXXXV, pp. 165-179, 12 ills., Feb., 1944

Tracking the Columbian Ground-Squirrel to Its Burrow: Loss of Millions to Crops and Danger of the Spread of Spotted Fever Necessitated Study of Peculiar Rodent of Western North America. By William T. Shaw. XLVII, pp. 587-596, 13 ills., May, 1925

See also Sanitation

DISMAL Swamp in Legend and History: George Washington Owned Large Tracts in Region Which He Described as a "Glorious Paradise." By John Francis Ariza. LXII, pp. 121-130, 11 ills., July, 1932

The **DISPOSITION** of the Philippines. By Charles E. Howe. IX, p. 304, June, 1898

DISTRICT OF COLUMBIA. *See* Washington, D. C.

DITMARS, RAYMOND L.:

Reptiles of All Lands. By Raymond L. Ditmars. XXII, pp. 601-633, 32 ills., July, 1911

DIVING, Ocean:

On the Bottom of a South Sea Pearl Lagoon. By Roy Waldo Miner. Paintings by Else Bostelmann. LXXIV, pp. 365-390, 17 ills. in black and white, 8 ills. in color, Sept., 1938

A Round Trip to Davy Jones's Locker: Peering into Mysteries a Quarter Mile Down in the Open Sea, by Means of the Bathysphere. By William Beebe. Paintings by E. Bostelmann. LIX, pp. 653-678, 14 ills. in black and white, 8 ills. in color, map, June, 1931

Wonderer Under Sea. By William Beebe. Paintings by E. Bostelmann. LXII, pp. 741-758, 13 ills. in black and white, 8 ills. in color, Dec., 1932

DIXON, JOSEPH:

Wild Ducks as Winter Guests in a City Park. By Joseph Dixon. XXXVI, pp. 331-342, 11 ills., Oct., 1919

DJAKARTA, Java. *See* Batavia

DO Volcanic Explosions Affect Our Climate? By C. G. Abbot. XXIV, pp. 181-198, 9 ills., diagr., Feb., 1913

DO Your Bit for America: A Proclamation by President Wilson to the American People. XXXI, pp. 287-293, ills., Apr., 1917

DOBIE, J. FRANK:

A Texan Teaches American History at Cambridge University. By J. Frank Dobie. LXXXIX, pp. 409-441, 9 ills. in black and white, 19 ills. in color, Apr., 1946

DOCKS, Floating Dry:

Normandy's Made-in-England Harbors. LXXXVII, pp. 565-580, 16 ills., map, May, 1945

Your Navy as Peace Insurance. By Fleet Admiral Chester W. Nimitz. LXXXIX, pp. 681-736, 32 ills. in black and white, 26 ills. in color, June, 1946

DR. Bell's Man-Lifting Kite. By Gilbert H. Grosvenor. XIX, pp. 35-52, 27 ills., Jan., 1908

DR. Bell's Survey in Baffinland. (By W J McGee). XIII, p. 113, Mar., 1902

DR. Bell's Tetrahedral Tower. By Gilbert H. Grosvenor. XVIII, pp. 672-675, 5 ills., Oct., 1907

DOCUMENTS. *See* Vatican City

DODD, ISABEL F.:

An Ancient Capital (Boghaz Keoy, Turkey). By Isabel F. Dodd. XXI, pp. 111-124, 11 ills., Feb., 1910

DODECANESE ISLANDS, Aegean Sea:

Historic Islands and Shores of the Ægean Sea. By Ernest Lloyd Harris. XXVIII, pp. 231-261, 28 ills., map, Sept., 1915

DODECANESE ISLANDS, Aegean Sea—*Continued*

Rhodes, and Italy's Aegean Islands. By Dorothy Hosmer. LXXIX, pp. 449-480, 32 ills., map, Apr., 1941

See also Rhodes (Island)

DODGE, RICHARD E.:

The Teaching of Physical Geography in Elementary Schools. By Richard E. Dodge. XI, pp. 470-475, Dec., 1900

DOE and Twin Fawns. Flashlight photo by George Shiras, 3d. XXIV, supplement, July, 1913. XL, ill. p. 136, Aug., 1921. LXXVI, ill. p. 475, Oct., 1939

DOGS:

Animals Were Allies, Too. 16 ills. LXXXIX, pp. 75-88, Jan., 1946

Dogs of Duty and Devotion. By Frederick G. Vosburgh. LXXX, pp. 769-774, 3 ills., Dec., 1941

Field Dogs in Action. By Freeman Lloyd. Paintings by Edward Herbert Miner. LXXI, pp. 85-108, 8 ills. in black and white, 36 portraits in color, Jan., 1937

Contents: Chesapeake Bay Retriever, Clumber Spaniel, Cocker Spaniel, Curly-coated Retriever, Dachshund, English Setter, English Springer Spaniel, Field Spaniel, Flat-coated Retriever, German Short-haired Pointer, Golden Retriever, Gordon Setter, Irish Red Setter, Irish Water Spaniel, Labrador Retriever, Pointer, Sussex Spaniel, Wire-haired Pointing Griffon

Hark to the Hounds. By Freeman Lloyd. Paintings by Edward Herbert Miner. LXXII, pp. 453-484, 18 ills. in black and white, 31 portraits in color, Oct., 1937

Contents: Afghan Hound, American Foxhound, Basset Hound, Beagle, Bloodhound, Borzoi, or Russian Wolfhound, Deerhound, English Foxhound, Greyhound, Harrier, Irish Wolfhound, Otterhound, Rampur Hound, Saluki, Welsh Foxhound, Whippet

The Lure of the Frozen Desert (North Polar Regions). XXIII, panorama, Dec., 1912

Mankind's Best Friend: Companion of His Solitude, Advance Guard in the Hunt, and Ally of the Trenches. By Ernest Harold Baynes. XXXV, pp. 185-201, 11 ills., Mar., 1919

Man's Oldest Ally, the Dog: Since Cave-Dweller Days This Faithful Friend Has Shared the Work, Exploration, and Sport of Humankind. By Freeman Lloyd. Paintings by Edward Herbert Miner. LXIX, pp. 247-274, 13 ills. in black and white, 33 portraits in color, Feb., 1936

Contents: Airedale Terrier, Bedlington Terrier, Bull Terrier, Cairn Terrier, Dandie Dinmont Terrier, Irish Terrier, Kerry Blue Terrier, Lakeland Terrier, Manchester Terrier, Miniature Schnauzer, Scottish Terrier, Sealyham Terrier, Skye Terrier, Smooth Fox Terrier, Standard Schnauzer, Welsh Terrier, West Highland White Terrier, Wire-haired Fox Terrier

Non-sporting Dogs. By Freeman Lloyd. Paintings by Walter A. Weber. LXXXIV, pp. 569-588, 9 ills. in black and white, 8 ills. in color from paintings from life, Nov., 1943

DOGS—*Continued*

Contents: Boston Terrier, Chow, Dalmatian, English Bulldog, French Bulldog, Keeshond, Poodle, Schipperke

Other Working Dogs and the Wild Species. By Stanley P. Young. Paintings by Walter A. Weber. LXXXVI, pp. 363-384, 12 ills. in black and white, 9 ills. in color, Sept., 1944

Our Common Dogs. By Louis Agassiz Fuertes and Ernest Harold Baynes. Paintings by Louis Agassiz Fuertes. XXXV, pp. 201-253, 73 ills. in color, index p. 280, Mar., 1919

Contents: Basset, Beagle, Belgian Shepherd, Bloodhound, Brussels Griffon, Bulldogs, Chihuahua, Chow, Collies, Dachshund, Dalmatian, English Sheep-Dog, Eskimo, Foxhound, German Shepherd, Great Dane, Greyhound, Irish Wolfhound, Mastiff, Mexican Hairless, Newfoundland, Norwegian Elkhound, Otterhound, Pekingese, Persian Gazellehound, Pointer, Pomeranian, Poodles, Pug, Pyrenean Sheep-Dog, Retrievers, Russian Wolfhound, St. Bernard, Samoyed, Schipperke, Scottish Deerhound, Setters, Spaniels, Spitz, Terriers, Whippet

The Sagacity and Courage of Dogs: Instances of the Remarkable Intelligence and Unselfish Devotion of Man's Best Friend Among Dumb Animals. XXXV, pp. 253-275, 13 ills., Mar., 1919

Sheep Dog Trials in Llangollen: Trained Collies Perform Marvels of Herding in the Cambrian Stakes, Open to the World. By Sara Bloch. LXXVII, pp. 559-574, 17 ills., Apr., 1940

Sheep-Killers—The Pariahs of Dogkind. XXXV, pp. 275-280, 3 ills., Mar., 1919

Toy Dogs, Pets of Kings and Commoners. By Freeman Lloyd. LXXXV, pp. 459-480, 8 ills. in black and white, 16 ills. in color, Apr., 1944

Working Dogs of the World. By Freeman Lloyd. Paintings by Edward Herbert Miner. LXXX, pp. 776-806, 12 ills. in black and white, 20 ills. in color, Dec., 1941

Contents: Alaskan Malemute, Australian Kelpie, Belgian Sheep Dog, Bouvier de Flandres, Boxer, Briard, Bull Mastiff, Collie, Doberman Pinscher, Eskimo, German Shepherd, Giant Schnauzer, Great Dane, Great Pyrenees, Kuvasz, Mastiff, Newfoundland, Norwegian Elkhound, Old English Sheep Dog, Rottweiler, St. Bernard, Samoyede, Shetland Sheep Dog, Siberian Husky, Welsh Corgi

Your Dog Joins Up. By Frederick Simpich. LXXXIII, pp. 93-113, 25 ills., Jan., 1943

DOGS in Toyland. 16 color photos by Willard R. Culver. LXXXV, pp. 473-480, Apr., 1944

DOLAN, BROOKE, 2D:

Across Tibet from India to China. By Lt. Col. Ilia Tolstoy, AUS. XC, pp. 169-222, 41 ills., map, Aug., 1946

DOLLS, Miniature:

Cuernavaca, the Sun Child of the Sierras (Mexico). By Russell Hastings Millward. XXII, pp. 291-301, 9 ills., Mar., 1911

Included: Miniature dolls made by Isabel Belaunsaran

DOLOMITES (Mountains), Italy:

The Land of Contrast: Austria-Hungary. By D. W. and A. S. Iddings. XXIII, pp. 1188-1217, 1284, 33 ills., map, Dec., 1912

DOLPHINS (Mammals):

Whales, Giants of the Sea: Wonder Mammals, Biggest Creatures of All Time, Show Tender Affection for Young, But Can Maim or Swallow Human Hunters. By Remington Kellogg. Paintings by Else Bostelmann. LXXVII, pp. 35-90, 25 ills. in black and white, 31 ills. in color, Jan., 1940

Included: Porpoises and Dolphins

DOMESDAY BOOK:

The Ordnance Survey of Great Britain—Its History and Object. By Josiah Pierce, Jr. II, pp. 243-260, Aug., 1890

DOMESTIC Fowls of Field, Park, and Farmyard. 16 ills. in color from paintings by Hashime Murayama. LVII, pp. 329-360, Mar., 1930

DOMINICA (Island), West Indies:

British West Indian Interlude. By Anne Rainey Langley. LXXIX, pp. 1-46, 23 ills. in black and white, 21 ills. in color, maps, Jan., 1941

Report by Robert T. Hill on the Volcanic Disturbances in the West Indies. XIII, pp. 223-267, 12 ills., 3 maps, July, 1902

DOMINICAN REPUBLIC:

Arbitration Treaties. By William Howard Taft. XXII, pp. 1165-1172, Dec., 1911

Haiti: A Degenerating Island. By Rear Admiral Colby M. Chester. XIX, pp. 200-217, 5 ills., map, Mar., 1908

Haiti, the Home of Twin Republics. By Sir Harry Johnston. XXXVIII, pp. 483-496, 11 ills., map, Dec., 1920

Hispaniola Rediscovered. By Jacob Gayer. LIX, pp. 80-112, 12 ills. in black and white, 28 ills. in color, Jan., 1931

The Land Columbus Loved. By Oliver P. Newman. LXXXV, pp. 197-224, 15 ills. in black and white, 11 ills. in color, map, Feb., 1944

Wards of the United States: Notes on What Our Country Is Doing for Santo Domingo, Nicaragua, and Haiti. XXX, pp. 143-177, 36 ills., Aug., 1916

DOMINICAN Republic, Land of Plenty. 11 color photos by B. Anthony Stewart. LXXXV, pp. 209-216, Feb., 1944

DORJUN (Boat):

Inside Cape Horn. By Amos Burg. LXXII, pp. 743-783, 29 ills. in black and white, 10 ills. in color, two-page map, Dec., 1937

DORR, GEORGE B.:

The Unique Island of Mount Desert (Maine). By George B. Dorr, Ernest Howe Forbush, M. L. Fernald. XXVI, pp. 75-89, 7 ills., July, 1914

DORSETT, J. H.:

Mount Vernon: The Home of the First Farmer of America. 3 color photos by J. H. Dorsett. LIII, pp. 605-620, May, 1928

DORSETT, J. H.—*Continued*

Peacetime Plant Hunting About Peiping. By P. H. and J. H. Dorsett. LXXII, pp. 509-534, 21 ills., map, Oct., 1937

DORSETT, P. H.:

Peacetime Plant Hunting About Peiping. By P. H. and J. H. Dorsett. LXXII, pp. 509-534, 21 ills., map, Oct., 1937

A **DOUBTFUL** Island of the Pacific. By James D. Hague. XV, pp. 478-489, ill., maps, Dec., 1904

DOUGLASS, ANDREW ELLICOTT:

The Secret of the Southwest Solved by Talkative Tree Rings: Horizons of American History Are Carried Back to A. D. 700 and a Calendar for 1,200 Years Established by National Geographic Society Expeditions. By Andrew Ellicott Douglass. LVI, pp. 737-770, 33 ills., map, Dec., 1929

DOUIRAT, Tunisia:

The Mole Men: An Account of the Troglodytes of Southern Tunisia. By Frank Edward Johnson. XXII, pp. 787-846, 60 ills., Sept., 1911

DOVEKIES (Birds):

Birds of the Northern Seas. By Alexander Wetmore. Paintings by Maj. Allan Brooks. LXIX, pp. 95-122, 12 ills. in black and white, 34 portraits in color, Jan., 1936

DOVER, England:

Front-line Town of Britain's Siege. By Harvey Klemmer. LXXXV, pp. 105-128, 21 ills., Jan., 1944

DOVES:

Game Birds of Prairie, Forest, and Tundra. By Alexander Wetmore. Paintings by Maj. Allan Brooks. LXX, pp. 461-500, 5 ills. in black and white, 60 portraits in color, Oct., 1936

DOWN Devon Lanes. By Herbert Corey. LV, pp. 529-568, 45 ills., map, May, 1929

DOWN Idaho's River of No Return (Salmon River). By Philip J. Shenon and John C. Reed. LXX, pp. 95-136, 43 ills., maps, July, 1936

DOWN Mexico's Río Balsas. By John W. Webber. With 9 color photos by author, Kenneth Segerstrom, Jack Breed. XC, pp. 253-272, 5 ills. in black and white, map, Aug., 1946

DOWN the Rio Grande: Tracing this Strange, Turbulent Stream on Its Long Course from Colorado to the Gulf of Mexico. By Frederick Simpich. LXXVI, pp. 415-462, 28 ills. in black and white, 24 ills. in color, 6 maps, Oct., 1939

DOYLE, C. B.:

Notes on Southern Mexico (Agricultural Products). By G. N. Collins and C. B. Doyle. XXII, pp. 301-320, 16 ills., map, Mar., 1911

DRAGON LIZARDS:

A Modern Dragon Hunt on Komodo: An English Yachting Party Traps and Photographs the Huge and Carnivorous Dragon Lizard of the Lesser Sundas. By Lady Broughton. LXX, pp. 321-331, 12 ills. in duotone, Sept., 1936

DRAGON LIZARDS—*Continued*

Stalking the Dragon Lizard on the Island of Komodo. By W. Douglas Burden. LII, pp. 216-232, 21 ills., Aug., 1927

DRAINAGE:

Area and Drainage Basin of Lake Superior. By Dr. Mark W. Harrington. VIII, pp. 111-120, tables, Apr., 1897

Drainage of Wet Lands. XVII, pp. 713-714, Dec., 1906

Geomorphology of the Southern Appalachians. By Charles Willard Hayes and Marius R. Campbell. VI, pp. 63-126, diagrs., map, 3 foldout maps, May 23, 1894

See also Reclamation of Land

DRAKE, SIR FRANCIS:

Discoverers of America. Annual Address by the President, Hon. Gardiner G. Hubbard. V, pp. 1-20, charts, maps, 3 map supplements, Apr. 7, 1893

Sir Francis Drake's Anchorage. By Edward L. Berthoud. VI, pp. 208-214, Dec. 29, 1894

DRAPER, WILLIAM F.:

Jungle War: Bougainville and New Caledonia. 17 ills. in color from paintings by Lieut. William F. Draper. LXXXV, pp. 417-432, Apr., 1944

A Navy Artist Paints the Aleutians. 16 ills. in color from paintings by Lt. William F. Draper. LXXXIV, pp. 161-176, Aug., 1943

Painting History in the Pacific. 19 ills. in color from paintings by Lt. William F. Draper, USNR. LXXXVI, pp. 408-424, Oct., 1944

Victory's Portrait in the Marianas. By Lt. William Franklin Draper, USNR. With 17 ills. in color from paintings by author. LXXXVIII, pp. 599-616, Nov., 1945

The **DREAM** Ship: The Story of a Voyage of Adventure More Than Half Around the World in a 47-foot Lifeboat. By Ralph Stock. XXXIX, pp. 1-52, 43 ills., map, Jan., 1921

The **DRIFT** of Floating Bottles in the Pacific Ocean. By James Page. XII, pp. 337-339, Sept., 1901

DRIFTING Across the Pole. XVII, pp. 40-42, Jan., 1906

DRIGGS, LAURENCE LA TOURETTE:

Aces Among Aces (Aviators). By Laurence La Tourette Driggs. XXXIII, pp. 568-580, 9 ills., June, 1918

A **DROWNED** Empire (Swamp Drainage). By Robert H. Chapman. XIX, pp. 190-199, 10 ills., Mar., 1908

DRUSES (People):

Syria and Lebanon Taste Freedom. By Maynard Owen Williams. With 21 color photos by author. XC, pp. 729-763, 16 ills. in black and white, Dec., 1946

DRY TORTUGAS ISLANDS, Gulf of Mexico:

The First Autochromes from the Ocean Bottom: Marine Life in Its Natural Habitat Along the Florida Keys Is Successfully Photographed in Colors. By Dr. W. H. Longley and Charles Martin. LI, pp. 56-60, 8 ills. in color, Jan., 1927

DRY TORTUGAS ISLANDS, Gulf of Mexico—*Continued*

Life on a Coral Reef: The Fertility and Mystery of the Sea Studied Beneath the Waters Surrounding Dry Tortugas. By W. H. Longley. LI, pp. 61-83, 22 ills., Jan., 1927

DU BOIS, ARTHUR E.:

The Heraldry of Heroism. By Arthur E. Du Bois. LXXXIV, pp. 409-413, ills., map, Oct., 1943

The Traditions and Glamour of Insignia. By Arthur E. Du Bois. LXXXIII, pp. 652-655, 3 ills., June, 1943

DU CHAILLU, PAUL:

Paul Du Chaillu (Biography). XIV, pp. 282-285, ill., July, 1903

DUCKS:

American Game Birds. By Henry Wetherbee Henshaw. Paintings by Louis Agassiz Fuertes. XXVIII, pp. 105-158, 4 ills. in black and white, 72 ills. in color, Aug., 1915

Far-Flying Wild Fowl and Their Foes. By Major Allan Brooks. Paintings from life by author. LXVI, pp. 487-528, 6 ills. in black and white, 74 portraits in color, Oct., 1934

Fowls of Forest and Stream Tamed by Man. By Morley A. Jull. Paintings by Hashime Murayama. LVII, pp. 327-371, 27 ills. in black and white, 16 ills. in color, Mar., 1930
Contents: Aylesbury, Black East India, Blue Swedish, Buff, Cayuga, Crested White, Gray Call, Khaki Campbell, Muscovy, Pekin, Rouen, Runner

Saving the Ducks and Geese. By Wells W. Cooke. XXIV, pp. 361-380, 7 ills., 7 maps, Mar., 1913

Wild Ducks as Winter Guests in a City Park. By Joseph Dixon. XXXVI, pp. 331-342, 11 ills., Oct., 1919

Wild Life of the Atlantic and Gulf Coasts: A Field Naturalist's Photographic Record of Nearly Half a Century of Fruitful Exploration. By George Shiras, 3d. LXII, pp. 261-309, 62 ills., Sept., 1932

DUG-GYE JONG (Fort), Bhutan:

Castles in the Air—Experiences and Journeys in Unknown Bhutan. By John Claude White. XXV, pp. 365-455, 75 ills., map, Apr., 1914

DUGMORE, A. RADCLYFFE:

Camera Adventures in the African Wilds (Book Review). Photos by A. Radclyffe Dugmore. XXI, pp. 385-396, 11 ills., May, 1910

DUKE of the Abruzzi in the Himalayas. (By A.W.G.). XXI, pp. 245-249, Mar., 1910

DUMBOY, the National Dish of Liberia. By G. N. Collins. XXII, pp. 84-88, 5 ills., Jan., 1911

DUMONT D'URVILLE, JULES SÉBASTIEN CÉSAR:

Wilkes' and D'Urville's Discoveries in Wilkes Land. By Rear Admiral John E. Pillsbury. XXI, pp. 171-173, Feb., 1910

DUNANT, HENRI:

The Symbol of Service to Mankind. By Stockton Axson. XXXIII, pp. 375-390, 11 ills., Apr., 1918

DUNCAN, DAVID D.:

Capturing Giant Turtles in the Caribbean. By David D. Duncan. LXXXIV, pp. 177-190, 13 ills., map, Aug., 1943

Coffee Is King in El Salvador. 27 color photos by Luis Marden and David D. Duncan. LXXXVI, pp. 585-616, Nov., 1944

Fighting Giants of the Humboldt (Fish and Squid). By David D. Duncan. LXXIX, pp. 373-400, 28 ills., map, Mar., 1941

Fiji Patrol on Bougainville. By David D. Duncan. LXXXVII, pp. 87-104, 9 ills. in black and white, 11 ills. in color, Jan., 1945

Okinawa, Threshold to Japan. By Lt. David D. Duncan, USMC. With 22 color photos by author and others. LXXXVIII, pp. 411-428, Oct., 1945

Yap Meets the Yanks. By David D. Duncan, 1st Lt., USMC. With 11 color photos by author. LXXXIX, pp. 364-372, Mar., 1946

DUNCAN, WILLIAM:

The Metlakatla Mission in Danger. (By Wm. H. Dall). IX, pp. 187-189, Apr., 1898
Note: The Reverend William Duncan, missionary to the Tsimshian Indians at Metlakatla, Alaska

DUNDEE, Scotland:

Low Road, High Road, Around Dundee. By Maurice P. Dunlap. LXIX, pp. 547-576, 35 ills., map, Apr., 1936

DUNLAP, MAURICE PRATT:

Low Road, High Road, Around Dundee (Scotland). By Maurice P. Dunlap. LXIX, pp. 547-576, 35 ills., map, Apr., 1936

Outwitting the Water Demons of Kashmir. By Maurice Pratt Dunlap. XL, pp. 499-511, 9 ills., Nov., 1921

DU PUY, WILLIAM ATHERTON:

The Geography of Money. By William Atherton Du Puy. LII, pp. 745-768, 31 ills., Dec., 1927

DURBAN, Natal:

Natal: The Garden Colony. By Russell Hastings Millward. XX, pp. 278-291, 16 ills., Mar., 1909

Natal: The Garden Province. By Melville Chater. LIX, pp. 447-478, 29 ills. in black and white, 14 ills. in color, Apr., 1931

DURBARS:

Castles in the Air—Experiences and Journeys in Unknown Bhutan. By John Claude White. XXV, pp. 365-455, 74 ills., map, Apr., 1914

In the Realms of the Maharajas. By Lawrence Copley Thaw and Margaret S. Thaw. LXXVIII, pp. 727-780, 14 ills. in black and white, 40 ills. in color, map, Dec., 1940

DUSKY Tribesmen of French West Africa. 26 color photos by Enzo de Chetelat. LXXIX, pp. 639-662, May, 1941

DUTCH EAST INDIES. *See* Netherlands East Indies

DUTCH GUIANA. *See* Surinam

DUTCH NEW GUINEA. *See* Netherlands New Guinea

DWELLINGS. *See* Castles; Cliff Dwellers; Cone Dwellings; Estates; Houses; Housing; Huts

DWELLINGS of the Saga-Time in Iceland, Greenland, and Vineland. By Cornelia Horsford. IX, pp. 73-84, ill., 9 sketches, Mar., 1898

DWIGHT, HARRY GRISWOLD:
- The Gates to the Black Sea: The Dardanelles, the Bosphorus, and the Sea of Marmora. By Harry Griswold Dwight. XXVII, pp. 435-459, 27 ills., May, 1915
- The Hoary Monasteries of Mt. Athos (Greece). By H. G. Dwight. XXX, pp. 249-272, 24 ills., map, Sept., 1916
- Life in Constantinople. By H. G. Dwight. XXVI, pp. 521-545, 25 ills., Dec., 1914
- Saloniki (Greece). By H. G. Dwight. XXX, pp. 203-232, 28 ills., Sept., 1916

DYAKS (Tribespeople):
- Keeping House in Borneo. By Virginia Hamilton. LXXXVIII, pp. 293-324, 28 ills., map, Sept., 1945
- Notes on the Sea Dyaks of Borneo. By Edwin H. Gomes. XXII, pp. 695-723, 26 ills., Aug., 1911
- Sarawak: The Land of the White Rajahs. By Harrison W. Smith. XXXV, pp. 110-167, 58 ills., map, Feb., 1919

DYAR, HARRISON G.:
- Where Our Moths and Butterflies Roam. LII, pp. 105-126, 8 ills. in black and white, 81 ills. in color, July, 1927

DYER, GEORGE L.:
- Report—Geography of the Sea. By George L. Dyer. I, pp. 136-150, table, Apr., 1889
- *See also* NGS: Vice-President

DYOTT, G. M.:
- The Volcanoes of Ecuador, Guideposts in Crossing South America. By G. M. Dyott. LV, pp. 49-93, 42 ills. in black and white, 12 ills. in color, map, Jan., 1929

E

EADS SHIP RAILWAY:
- The Tehuantepec Ship Railway. By Elmer L. Corthell. VII, pp. 64-72, maps, Feb., 1896

The **EAGLE,** King of Birds, and His Kin. By Alexander Wetmore. Paintings by Maj. Allan Brooks. LXIV, pp. 43-95, 23 ills. in black and white, 48 ills. in color, July, 1933

The **EAGLE** in Action: An Intimate Study of the Eyrie Life of America's National Bird. By Francis H. Herrick. LV, pp. 635-660, 20 ills., May, 1929

EAGLES:
- The Eagle, King of Birds, and His Kin. By Alexander Wetmore. Paintings by Maj. Allan Brooks. LXIV, pp. 43-95, 23 ills. in black and white, 48 ills. in color, July, 1933

EAGLES—*Continued*
- The Eagle in Action: An Intimate Study of the Eyrie Life of America's National Bird. By Francis H. Herrick. LV, pp. 635-660, 20 ills., May, 1929
- In Quest of the Golden Eagle: Over Lonely Mountain and Prairie Soars This Rare and Lordly Bird, But Three Youths from the East Catch Up With Him at Last. By John and Frank Craighead. LXXVII, pp. 693-710, 17 ills., May, 1940

EAGLES, Hawks, and Vultures. 48 ills. in color from paintings by Maj. Allan Brooks. LXIV, pp. 65-94, July, 1933

EARHART, AMELIA:
- My Flight from Hawaii. By Amelia Earhart. LXVII, pp. 593-609, 4 ills. in black and white. 8 ills. in duotone, May, 1935
- The Society's Special Medal Awarded to Amelia Earhart: First Woman to Receive Geographic Distinction at Brilliant Ceremony in the National Capital (Address by Amelia Earhart). LXII, pp. 358-367, 7 ills., Sept., 1932
- *See also* NGS: Medals: Special Gold Medal

EARL, LAWRENCE:
- Mending Dikes in the Netherlands. 20 photos by Lawrence Earl. XC, pp. 791-806, Dec., 1946

EARLY Voyages on the Northwestern Coast of America. By Professor George Davidson. V, pp. 235-256, Jan. 31, 1894

EARTH:
- The first photograph ever made showing laterally the curvature of the earth. By Capt. A. W. Stevens. LIX, ill. p. 634, May, 1931. LXIX, p. 128, ill. p. 142, Jan., 1936
- The First Photograph Ever Made Showing the Division Between the Troposphere and Stratosphere and also the Actual Curvature of the Earth. Aërial photo by Captain Albert W. Stevens. LXIX, supplement, May, 1936

EARTHQUAKES:
- Antioch the Glorious. By William H. Hall. XXXVIII, pp. 81-103, 20 ills., map, Aug., 1920
- The California Earthquake (San Francisco). XVII, pp. 325-343, 27 ills., June, 1906
- The Cause of Earthquakes. By Robert F. Griggs. XLIV, pp. 443-451, 5 ills., map, Oct., 1923
- Charting a World at War. By William H. Nicholas. LXXXVI, pp. 617-640, 23 ills., drawing, Nov., 1944
- Costa Rica—Vulcan's Smithy. By H. Pittier. XXI, pp. 494-525, 30 ills., maps, June, 1910
- Echoes of the San Francisco Earthquake. By Robert E. C. Stearns. XVIII, pp. 351-353, ill., May, 1907
- The Geography of Japan: With Special Reference to Its Influence on the Character of the Japanese People. By Walter Weston. XL, pp. 45-84, 23 ills. in black and white, 16 ills. in color, July, 1921
- How the Earth Telegraphed Its Tokyo Quake to Washington. By the Rev. Francis A. Tondorf. XLIV, pp. 453-454, ill., Oct., 1923
- The Probable Cause of the San Francisco Earthquake. By Frederick Leslie Ransome. XVII, pp. 280-296, 9 ills., maps, May, 1906

EARTHQUAKES—*Continued*

The Recent Earthquake Wave on the Coast of Japan. By Eliza Ruhamah Scidmore. VII, pp. 285-289, 4 ills., foldout map, Sept., 1896

The Record of the Great Earthquake Written in Washington by the Seismograph of the U.S. Weather Bureau. By C. F. Marvin. XVII, pp. 296-298, May, 1906

Reelfoot—An Earthquake Lake (Tennessee). By Wilbur A. Nelson. XLV, pp. 95-114, 20 ills., Jan., 1924

Resolution Adopted by the Eighth International Geographic Congress, September, 1904. XV, pp. 415-418, Oct., 1904

Sakurajima, Japan's Greatest Volcanic Eruption: A Convulsion of Nature Whose Ravages Were Minimized by Scientific Knowledge, Compared with the Terrors and Destruction of the Recent Tokyo Earthquake. By Dr. Thomas Augustus Jaggar. XLV, pp. 441-470, 32 ills., map, Apr., 1924

The San Francisco Earthquake of April 18, 1906, as Recorded by the Coast and Geodetic Survey Magnetic Observatories. By L. A. Bauer and J. E. Burbank. XVII, pp. 298-300, tables, May, 1906

Shattered Capitals of Central America. By Herbert J. Spinden. XXXVI, pp. 185-212, 32 ills., map, Sept., 1919

Some Personal Experiences with Earthquakes (Chile-Peru). By Rear Admiral L. G. Billings. XXVII, pp. 57-71, 7 ills., Jan., 1915

Turkey, Where Earthquakes Followed Timur's Trail. 15 photos by Maynard Owen Williams. LXXVII, pp. 395-406, Mar., 1940
Photos showing area later devastated by earthquakes

"Where the Mountains Walked": An Account of the Recent Earthquake in Kansu Province, China, Which Destroyed 100,000 Lives. By Upton Close and Elsie McCormick. XLI, pp. 445-464, 23 ills., map, May, 1922

The World's Most Cruel Earthquake (Messina). By Charles W. Wright. XX, pp. 373-396, 22 ills., maps, Apr., 1909

EARTH'S Most Primitive People: A Journey with the Aborigines of Central Australia. By Charles P. Mountford. LXXXIX, pp. 89-112, 10 ills. in black and white, 8 ills. in color, map, Jan., 1946

EAST, BEN:

Winter Sky Roads to Isle Royal (Michigan). By Ben East. LX, pp. 759-774, 18 ills., map, Dec., 1931

EAST INDIANS:

The East Indians in the New World (Trinidad). By Harriet Chalmers Adams. XVIII, pp. 485-491, 6 ills., July, 1907

India Mosaic. By Peter Muir and Frances Muir. LXXXIX, pp. 443-470, 5 ills. in black and white, 22 ills. in color, map, Apr., 1946

EAST INDIES. *See* Netherlands East Indies

EAST of Constantinople: Glimpses of Village Life in Anatolia, the Battleground of East and West, Where the Turks Reorganized Their Forces After the World War. By Melville Chater. XLIII, pp. 509-534, 27 ills., map, May, 1923

EAST of Suez to the Mount of the Decalogue: Following the Trail Over Which Moses Led the Israelites from the Slave-Pens of Egypt to Sinai. By Maynard Owen Williams. LII, pp. 709-743, 32 ills., map, Dec., 1927

EAST of the Adriatic: Notes on Dalmatia, Montenegro, Bosnia, and Herzegovina. By Kenneth McKenzie. XXIII, pp. 1159-1187, 1284, 37 ills., map, Dec., 1912

EAST PRUSSIA:

Flying Around the Baltic. By Douglas Chandler. LXXIII, pp. 767-806, 31 ills. in black and white, 13 ills. in duotone, map, June, 1938

EASTER, S. E.:

Jade. By S. E. Easter. XIV, pp. 9-17, maps, Jan., 1903

EASTER ISLAND, South Pacific Ocean:

Great Stone Faces of Easter Island. 11 ills. LXXXV, pp. 225-232, Feb., 1944

The Mystery of Easter Island. By Mrs. Scoresby Routledge. XL, pp. 629-646, 13 ills., map, Dec., 1921

The Romance of Science in Polynesia: An Account of Five Years of Cruising Among the South Sea Islands. By Robert Cushman Murphy. Paintings by Hashime Murayama. XLVIII, pp. 355-426, 66 ills. in black and white, 16 ills. in color, 3 maps, Oct., 1925

Sailing the Seven Seas in the Interest of Science: Adventures Through 157,000 Miles of Storm and Calm, from Arctic to Antarctic and Around the World, in the Non-magnetic Yacht "Carnegie." By J. P. Ault. XLII, pp. 631-690, 47 ills., chart, Dec., 1922

Westward Bound in the *Yankee*. By Irving and Electa Johnson. LXXXI, pp. 1-44, 25 ills. in black and white, 20 ills. in color, map, Jan., 1942

EASTERN HEMISPHERE:

The "Map of Discovery." Reproduction in color of the painting by N. C. Wyeth, National Geographic Society, Washington, D.C. LIV, text, p. 568; supplement, Nov., 1928

The National Geographic Society's New Map of the World. Text with map supplement. LXVIII, pp. 796-798, Dec., 1935

New World Map Gives Backdrop for Headlines (Eastern and Western Hemispheres). Text with map supplement. LXXX, pp. 741-742, ill., Dec., 1941

EASTERN WOODLAND INDIANS:

America's First Settlers, the Indians. By Matthew W. Stirling. Paintings by W. Langdon Kihn. LXXII, pp. 535-596, 34 ills. in black and white, 24 ills. in color, Nov., 1937

EASTWARD from Gibraltar: Overland Route Across North Africa to Tunisia and Libia. By Cyrus French Wicker. LXXXIII, pp. 115-142, 28 ills., Jan., 1943

EATON, MARY E.:

Berries (American). 29 ills. in color from paintings by Mary E. Eaton. XXXV, pp. 173-180, Feb., 1919

Flowers. 47 ills. in color from paintings by Mary E. Eaton. XLV, pp. 613-628, June, 1924

EATON, MARY E.—*Continued*

Flowers (American Wild Flowers). 29 ills. in color from paintings by Mary E. Eaton. XXVII, pp. 483-506, May, 1915

Flowers (Common American Wild Flowers). 17 ills. in color from paintings by Mary E. Eaton. XXIX, pp. 591-606, June, 1916

Flowers (State Flowers). 30 ills. in color from paintings by Mary E. Eaton. XXXI, pp. 501-516, June, 1917

Midsummer Wild Flowers. 38 ills. in color from paintings by Mary E. Eaton. XLII, pp. 37-52, July, 1922

Pages From the Floral Life of America. 55 ills. in color from paintings by Mary E. Eaton. XLVIII, pp. 47-70, July, 1925

EATON CANYON BIRD AND GAME SANCTUARY, California:

Where Birds and Little Animals Find Haven. By Agnes Akin Atkinson. LXX, pp. 232-241, 14 ills., Aug., 1936

EBERLEIN, HAROLD DONALDSON:

Some Forgotten Corners of London: Many Places of Beauty and Historic Interest Repay the Search of the Inquiring Visitor. By Harold Donaldson Eberlein. LXI, pp. 163-198, 25 ills. in black and white, 13 ills. in color, Feb., 1932

Visits to the Old Inns of England: Historic Homes of Hospitality for the Wayfarer Dot the Length and Breadth of the Kingdom. By Harold Donaldson Eberlein. LIX, pp. 261-285, 17 ills. in black and white, 15 ills. in color, Mar., 1931

ECHAGÜE, J. ORTIZ:

Flashing Fashions of Old Spain. 26 ills. in duotone by J. Ortiz Echagüe. LXIX, pp. 413-428, Mar., 1936

ECHOES from Yugoslavia. 16 ills. LXXIX, pp. 793-804, June, 1941

ECHOES of the San Francisco Earthquake. By Robert E. C. Stearns. XVIII, pp. 351-353, ill., May, 1907

ECHOES of Whaling Days (Nantucket). 8 color photos by B. Anthony Stewart. LXXXV, pp. 449-456, Apr., 1944

ECKENER, HUGO:

The First Airship Flight Around the World: Dr. Hugo Eckener Tells of an Epochal Geographic Achievement upon the Occasion of the Bestowal of the National Geographic Society's Special Gold Medal. LVII, pp. 653-688, 37 ills., June, 1930

ECLIPSES:

The American Eclipse Expedition. By Rear Admiral Colby M. Chester. XVII, pp. 589-612, 23 ills., col. pl., Nov., 1906

The Cartography and Observations of Bering's First Voyage. By General A. W. Greely. III, pp. 205-230, map supplement, Jan. 28, 1892; Feb. 19, 1892

Eclipse Adventures on a Desert Isle (Canton). By Capt. J. F. Hellweg. LXXII, pp. 377-394, 14 ills., map, Sept., 1937

First natural-color photograph of an eclipse ever reproduced, showing the corona. By Irvine C. Gardner. LXXI, ill. p. 178, Feb., 1937

ECLIPSES—*Continued*

The National Geographic Society's Eclipse Expedition to Norfolk, Va. By Marcus Baker. XI, p. 320, Aug., 1900

Nature's Most Dramatic Spectacle. By S. A. Mitchell. LXXII, pp. 361-376, 16 ills., map, Sept., 1937

Observing a Total Eclipse of the Sun: Dimming Solar Light for a Few Seconds Entails Years of Work for Science and Attracts Throngs to "Nature's Most Magnificent Spectacle." By Paul A. McNally. LXII, pp. 597-605, 6 ills., Nov., 1932

Observing an Eclipse in Asiatic Russia. By Irvine C. Gardner. LXXI, pp. 179-197, 19 ills. in black and white, ill. in color, Feb., 1937

On the Alleged Observation of a Lunar Eclipse by Bering in 1728-9. By Marcus Baker. II, pp. 167-169, 4 tables, May, 1890

Photographing the Eclipse of 1932 from the Air: From Five Miles Above the Earth's Surface, the National Geographic Society-Army Air Corps Survey Obtains Successful Photographs of the Moon's Shadow. By Capt. Albert W. Stevens. LXII, pp. 581-596, 18 ills., Nov., 1932

The Scientific Work of the National Geographic Society's Eclipse Expedition to Norfolk, Va. By Simon Newcomb. XI, pp. 321-324, Aug., 1900

To Observe Solar Eclipse. XVI, p. 88, Feb., 1905

The Total Eclipse of the Sun, May 28, 1900. (By F. H. Bigelow). XI, pp. 33-34, Jan., 1900

Unfurling Old Glory on Canton Island. 11 ills. in color: painting by Charles Bittinger and color photo of the eclipse, showing the corona. LXXIII, pp. 753-760, June, 1938

The **ECONOMIC** Aspects of Soil Erosion. (Part I). By Dr. N. S. Shaler. VII, pp. 328-338, Oct., 1896

The **ECONOMIC** Aspects of Soil Erosion. (Part) II. By Dr. N. S. Shaler. VII, pp. 368-377, Nov., 1896

The **ECONOMIC** Condition of the Philippines. By Max L. Tornow. X, pp. 33-64, 10 ills., Feb., 1899

The **ECONOMIC** Evolution of Alaska. By Major General A. W. Greely. XX, pp. 585-593, 4 ills., July, 1909

ECONOMIC Loss to the People of the United States Through Insects That Carry Disease. By L. O. Howard. XX, pp. 735-749, Aug., 1909

ECUADOR:

Beautiful Ecuador. By Joseph Lee. XVIII, pp. 81-91, 9 ills., Feb., 1907

From Sea to Clouds in Ecuador. By W. Robert Moore. LXXX, pp. 717-740, 11 ills. in black and white, 9 ills. in color, Dec., 1941

A Journey in Ecuador. By Mark B. Kerr, C. E. VII, pp. 238-245, ills., map, July, 1896

Mrs. Robinson Crusoe in Ecuador. By Mrs. Richard C. Gill. LXV, pp. 133-172, 43 ills., map, Feb., 1934

Over Trail and Through Jungle in Ecuador: Indian Head-Hunters of the Interior, an Interesting Study in the South American Republic. By H. E. Anthony. XL, pp. 327-352, 28 ills., Oct., 1921

ECUADOR—*Continued*

Quinine Hunters in Ecuador. By Froelich Rainey. LXXXIX, pp. 341-363, 21 ills., map, Mar., 1946

The Road to Bolivia. By William E. Curtis. XI, pp. 209-224, 7 ills., June, 1900

The Volcanoes of Ecuador, Guideposts in Crossing South America. By G. M. Dyott. LV, pp. 49-93, 42 ills. in black and white, 12 ills. in color, map, Jan., 1929

EDAM CHEESE:

A North Holland Cheese Market. By Hugh M. Smith. XXI, pp. 1051-1066, 17 ills., Dec., 1910

EDDY, FREDERICK B.:

The Panther of the Hearth: Lithe Grace and Independence of Spirit Contribute to the Appeal of Cats, "The Only Domestic Animal Man Has Never Conquered." By Frederick B. Eddy. LXXIV, pp. 589-634, 22 ills. in black and white, 25 ills. in color, Nov., 1938

EDEN, Garden of:

The Cradle of Civilization: The Historic Lands Along the Euphrates and Tigris Rivers Where Briton Is Fighting Turk. By James Baikie. XXIX, pp. 127-162, 25 ills., Feb., 1916

Where Adam and Eve Lived. By Frederick and Margaret Simpich. XXVI, pp. 546-588, 35 ills., Dec., 1914

The **EDEN** of the Flowery Republic (Sze-chuan, China). By Dr. Joseph Beech. XXXVIII, pp. 355-390, 18 ills. in black and white, 16 ills. in color, Nov., 1920

EDGERTON, HAROLD E.:

Mystery Mammals of the Twilight (Bats). By Donald R. Griffin. XC, pp. 117-134, 19 ills., July, 1946

Included: Photographs taken by the high-speed camera developed by Prof. Harold E. Edgerton

EDINBURGH, Scotland:

Bonnie Scotland, Postwar Style. By Isobel Wylie Hutchison. LXXXIX, pp. 545-601, 14 ills. in black and white, 38 ills. in color, two-page map, May, 1946

Edinburgh, Athens of the North: Romantic History of Cramped Medieval City Vies With Austere Beauty of Newer Wide Streets and Stately Squares. By J. R. Hildebrand. LXII, pp. 219-246, 19 ills. in black and white, 8 ills. in duotone, Aug., 1932

Scotland in Wartime. By Isobel Wylie Hutchison. LXXXIII, pp. 723-743, 19 ills., June, 1943

Vagabonding in England: A Young American Works His Way Around the British Isles and Sees Sights from an Unusual Point of View. By John McWilliams. LXV, pp. 357-398, 39 ills., map, Mar., 1934

EDITORIAL DEPARTMENT. *See* NGM: Editorial Department

EDMUNDS, CHARLES K.:

Shantung—China's Holy Land. By Charles K. Edmunds. XXXVI, pp. 231-252, 21 ills., map, Sept., 1919

EDOM. *See* Trans-Jordan

EDSON, JOHN JOY. *See* NGS: Treasurer

EDUCATING the Filipinos. XVI, pp. 46-49, Jan., 1905

EDUCATION:

American Geographic Education. By W J McGee. IX, pp. 305-307, July, 1898

Bringing the World to Our Foreign-Language Soldiers: How a Military Training Camp is Solving a Seemingly Unsurmountable Problem by Using the Geographic. By Christina Krysto. XXXIV, pp. 81-90, 4 ills., Aug., 1918

Denmark and the Danes. By Maurice Francis Egan. XLII, pp. 115-164, 38 ills., map, Aug., 1922

Educating the Filipinos. XVI, pp. 46-49, Jan., 1905

For Teaching Physiography. XVIII, p. 353, May, 1907

Geographic Instruction in the Public Schools. By W. B. Powell. V, pp. 137-153, Jan. 31, 1894

Geographic Prizes (Gold Medal and certificates awarded annually to public high school students writing the best essay on geography). IV, pp. 206-208, Feb. 8, 1893

Important Announcement Concerning Essays (Gold Medal and certificates to be awarded for best essays on the River Systems of the United States). VI, pp. 227-228, Dec. 29, 1894

The Improvement of Geographical Teaching. By Professor William Morris Davis. V, pp. 68-75, July 10, 1893

Monographs of the National Geographic Society to be published for use in the public schools. VI, pp. 225-227, Dec. 29, 1894

New York—The Metropolis of Mankind. By William Joseph Showalter. XXXIV, pp. 1-49, 39 ills., July, 1918

Present Conditions in China. By John W. Foster. XVII, pp. 651-672, 709-711, Dec., 1906

President Alexander Graham Bell on Japan. (By J.H.). IX, pp. 509-512, Dec., 1898

The Relations of Geology to Physiography in Our Educational System. By T. C. Chamberlin. V, pp. 154-160, Jan. 31, 1894

Sight-Seeing in School: Taking Twenty Million Children on a Picture Tour of the World. By Jessie L. Burrall. XXXV, pp. 489-503, 14 ills., June, 1919

The Teaching of Physical Geography in the Elementary Schools. By Richard E. Dodge. XI, pp. 470-475, Dec., 1900

See also World's Congress of Education

EDWARDS, CLARENCE R.:

Governing the Philippine Islands. By Colonel Clarence R. Edwards. XV, pp. 273-284, 5 ills., July, 1904

The Work of the Bureau of Insular Affairs. By Colonel Clarence R. Edwards. XV, pp. 239-255, 8 ills., June, 1904

EDWARDS, WALTER M.:

Our Nation's Capital on Parade. 16 color photos by B. Anthony Stewart, Walter M. Edwards, and others. LXXXIV, pp. 265-288, Sept., 1943

Where the Winding Cam Mirrors Cambridge (University) Spires. 12 color photos by Bernard Wakeman and Walter M. Edwards. LXX, pp. 339-346, Sept., 1936

EELS:

The Mysterious Life of the Common Eel. By Hugh M. Smith. XXIV, pp. 1140-1146, 3 ills., Oct., 1913

EFATE (Island), New Hebrides:

Palms and Planes in the New Hebrides. By Maj. Robert D. Heinl, Jr. LXXXVI, pp. 229-256, 17 ills. in black and white, 12 ills. in color, map, Aug., 1944

The **EFFECTS** of Geographic Environment in the Development of Civilization in Primitive Man. By Hon. Gardiner G. Hubbard. VIII, pp. 161-176, June, 1897

EFFIE M. MORRISSEY (Schooner):

Servicing Arctic Airbases. By Robert A. Bartlett. LXXXIX, pp. 602-616, 3 ills. in black and white, 10 ills. in color, map, May, 1946

EFFORTS to Obtain Greater Energy from Coal. XVIII, pp. 138-140, Feb., 1907

EGAN, MAURICE FRANCIS:

Denmark and the Danes. By Maurice Francis Egan. XLII, pp. 115-164, 38 ills., map, Aug., 1922

Norway and the Norwegians. By Maurice Francis Egan. XLV, pp. 647-696, 45 ills., June, 1924

EGRETS (Birds):

The Large Wading Birds: Long Legs and Remarkable Beaks, as Well as Size, Form, and Color, Distinguish the Herons, Ibises, and Flamingos. By T. Gilbert Pearson. Paintings by Maj. Allan Brooks. LXII, pp. 441-469, 2 ills. in black and white, 4 ills. in color, Oct., 1932

EGYPT:

Along the Nile, Through Egypt and the Sudan. By Frederick Simpich. XLII, pp. 379-410, 29 ills., Oct., 1922

American Alma Maters in the Near East. By Maynard Owen Williams. LXXXVIII, pp. 237-256, 16 ills., Aug., 1945

American Discoveries in Egypt. XVIII, pp. 801-806, 8 ills., Dec., 1907

American Fighters Visit Bible Lands. By Maynard Owen Williams. With 23 color photos by author. LXXXIX, pp. 311-340, 10 ills. in black and white, Mar., 1946

At the Tomb of Tutankhamen: An Account of the Opening of the Royal Egyptian Sepulcher Which Contained the Most Remarkable Funeral Treasures Unearthed in Historic Times. By Maynard Owen Williams. XLIII, pp. 461-508, 53 ills., map, May, 1923

The Barrage of the Nile. By Day Allen Willey. XXI, pp. 175-184, 14 ills., Feb., 1910

The British Commonwealth of Nations: "Organized Freedom" Around the World. By Eric Underwood. LXXXIII, pp. 485-524, 31 ills., Apr., 1943

By Felucca Down the Nile: Giant Dams Rule Egypt's Lifeline River, Yet Village Life Goes On As It Did in the Time of the Pharaohs. By Willard Price. LXXVII, pp. 435-476, 21 ills. in black and white, 22 ills. in color, two-page map, Apr., 1940

EGYPT—*Continued*

Cairo to Cape Town, Overland: An Adventurous Journey of 135 Days, Made by an American Man and His Wife, Through the Length of the African Continent. By Felix Shay. XLVII, pp. 123-260, 118 ills., map, Feb., 1925

Change Comes to Bible Lands. By Frederick Simpich. LXXIV, pp. 695-750, 40 ills. in black and white, 25 ills. in color, map supplement, Dec., 1938

Crossing the Untraversed Libyan Desert: The Record of a 2,200-Mile Journey of Exploration Which Resulted in the Discovery of Two Oases of Strategic Importance on the Southwestern Frontier of Egypt. By A. M. Hassanein Bey. XLVI, pp. 233-277, 46 ills., map, Sept., 1924

Daily Life in Ancient Egypt (Part I). Daily Life in Ancient Egypt: *The Later Period* (Part II). By William C. Hayes. Paintings by H. M. Herget. LXXX, pp. 419-515, 34 ills. in black and white, 32 ills. in color, map, Oct., 1941

Contents: Life in Lower Egypt Before the Dawn of History.—A King of Upper Egypt Conquers the Delta and Unites the Two Kingdoms.—King Djoser and the Wise I-em-hotep Usher in the Old Kingdom.—The Builder of the Great Pyramid Receives a Visit from His Mother.—The Egyptian Farmer—Winter Sowing in the Pyramid Age.—Supplies of Food for a Resident of the City of the Dead—an Old Kingdom Maṣṭabeh Field Near Memphis.—Netting Wildfowl in the Marshes.—The Egyptian Scribe and His Equipment.—A "Dwarf of the Divine Dances from the Land of the Spirits" as a Gift to the Boy King of Egypt.—An Ancient Egyptian Brewery.—An XIth Dynasty Carpenter's Shop.—The Formal Gardens and Informal Children of Ancient Egypt.—The Egyptian Stonemason and His Craft—Construction Work on a XIIth Dynasty Pyramid Site.—An Ancient Egyptian River Fort on the Sudān Frontier.—An Egyptian Monarch Entertains a Bedawin Sheikh.—A King's Daughter and Her Personal Possessions.—The Founders of the New Kingdom.—The Family of King Ṭhut-mosĕ I.—A Sea Voyage to a Remote Land.—Amun-Rē', "King of the Gods," Pays His Yearly Visit to Queen Hatshepsūt's Temple in Western Thebes.—Egyptian Chariots at Armageddon.—The Vintage of 1400 B.C.—A Family Outing in the Papyrus Pools.—At Home with the Average Egyptian and His Wife.—The Aten Shines, King Akh-en-Aten Dreams, and the XVIIIth Dynasty Draws to a Close.—A Wealthy Theban Is Buried in His Tomb in the Western Cliffs.—User-ḥēt Entertains.—Preparation of a Painted Tomb-chapel—The Egyptian Artist and His Methods.—Ramesses "the Great."—The Manufacture and Use of Brick in Ancient Egypt.—The Largest Temple Ever Erected by Man—2,000 Years Building.—The Assyrians (and Others) Come Down Like a Wolf on the Fold.

East of Suez to the Mount of the Decalogue: Following the Trail Over Which Moses Led the Israelites from the Slave-Pens of Egypt to Sinai. By Maynard Owen Williams. LII, pp. 709-743, 32 ills., map, Dec., 1927

Excavations at Abydos. (By W. M. Flinders Petrie). XIV, pp. 358-359, Sept., 1903

EGYPT—*Continued*

Fearful Famines of the Past: History Will Repeat Itself Unless the American People Conserve Their Resources. By Ralph A. Graves. XXXII, pp. 69-90, 11 ills., July, 1917

Flying Over Egypt, Sinai, and Palestine: Looking Down Upon the Holy Land During an Air Journey of Two and a Half Hours from Cairo to Jerusalem. By Brigadier General P. R. C. Groves and Major J. R. McCrindle. L, pp. 313-355, 26 ills. in black and white, 23 ills. in color, map, Sept., 1926

Geographic Progress of Civilization. Annual Address by the President, Honorable Gardiner G. Hubbard. VI, pp. 1-22, Feb. 14, 1894

The Land of Egypt: A Narrow Green Strip of Fertility Stretching for a Thousand Miles Through Walls of Desert. By Alfred Pearce Dennis. XLIX, pp. 271-298, 28 ills., map, Mar., 1926

Old-New Battle Grounds of Egypt and Libia. By W. Robert Moore. LXXVIII, pp. 809-820, 8 ills., map, Dec., 1940

Recent Discoveries in Egypt. XII, pp. 396-397, Nov., 1901

Reconstructing Egypt's History. By Wallace N. Stearns. XXIV, pp. 1021-1042, 21 ills., Sept., 1913

Red Cross Girl Overseas. By Margaret Cotter. LXXXVI, pp. 745-768, 22 ills., Dec., 1944

The Resurrection of Ancient Egypt. By James Baikie. XXIV, pp. 957-1020, 46 ills., map, Sept., 1913

The Route Over Which Moses Led the Children of Israel Out of Egypt. By Franklin E. Hoskins. XX, pp. 1011-1038, 24 ills., map, Dec., 1909

The Sacred Ibis Cemetery and Jackal Catacombs at Abydos. By Camden M. Cobern. XXIV, pp. 1042-1056, 10 ills., Sept., 1913

The Suez Canal: Short Cut to Empires. By Maynard Owen Williams. LXVIII, pp. 611-632, 19 ills., map, Nov., 1935

Sunrise and Sunset from Mount Sinai. By Rev. Sartell Prentice, Jr. XXIII, pp. 1242-1282, 34 ills., map, Dec., 1912

War Meets Peace in Egypt. By Grant Parr and G. E. Janssen. LXXXI, pp. 503-526, 25 ills., map, Apr., 1942

EGYPT, Past and Present. 16 ills. XLIII, pp. 493-508, May, 1923

EIGENMANN, C. H.:

Notes from a Naturalist's Experiences in British Guiana. By C. H. Eigenmann. XXII, pp. 859-870, 8 ills., Sept., 1911

8TH Air Force in England. 10 ills. in color from U. S. Army Air Forces official photos. LXXXVII, pp. 297-304, Mar., 1945

EIGHTH Annual Field Meeting of the National Geographic Society (Monticello). VII, pp. 259-260, ill., Aug., 1896

EIGHTH INTERNATIONAL GEOGRAPHIC CONGRESS. *See* International Geographic Congress

EIGNER, JULIUS:

The Rise and Fall of Nanking. By Julius Eigner. LXXIII, pp. 189-224, 37 ills., Feb., 1938

EIRE:

The British Commonwealth of Nations: "Organized Freedom" Around the World. By Eric Underwood. LXXXIII, pp. 485-524, 31 ills., Apr., 1943

Old Ireland, Mother of New Eire: By Whatever Name, 'Tis the Same Fair Land With the Grass Growing Green on the Hills of Her and the Peat Smoke Hanging Low. By Harrison Howell Walker. LXXVII, pp. 649-691, 19 ills. in black and white, 18 ills. in color, map, May, 1940

See also Aran Islands

EKLINGI (Temple), India:

The Marble Dams of Rajputana. By Eleanor Maddock. XL, pp. 469-499, 13 ills. in black and white, 16 ills. in color, Nov., 1921

EKOI (Tribespeople):

Notes on the Ekoi (Nigeria). By P. A. Talbot. XXIII, pp. 33-38, 8 ills., Jan., 1912

ELBURZ MOUNTAINS, Iran:

Modern Persia and Its Capital: And an Account of an Ascent of Mount Demavend, the Persian Olympus. By F. L. Bird. XXXIX, pp. 353-400, 47 ills., Apr., 1921

ELECTRIC Street Railways (U. S.). (By J. H.). VIII, p. 284, Oct., 1897

ELECTRONICS:

Your New World of Tomorrow. By F. Barrows Colton. LXXXVIII, pp. 385-410, 25 ills., Oct., 1945

ELEPHANT Hunting in Equatorial Africa with Rifle and Camera. By Carl E. Akeley. XXIII, pp. 779-810, 30 ills., Aug., 1912

ELEPHANT SEALS:

Cruise of the *Kinkajou:* Among Desert Islands of Mexico Voyagers Find Outdoor Laboratories for the Naturalist and Ideal Fishing Grounds for the Sportsman. By Alfred M. Bailey. LXXX, pp. 339-366, 13 ills. in black and white, 12 ills. in color, map, Sept., 1941

South Georgia, an Outpost of the Antarctic. By Robert Cushman Murphy. XLI, pp. 409-444, 41 ills., maps, Apr., 1922

ELEPHANTS:

Elephant Hunting in Equatorial Africa with Rifle and Camera. By Carl E. Akeley. XXIII, pp. 779-810, 30 ills., Aug., 1912

The Greatest Hunt in the World. By Eliza Ruhamah Scidmore. XVII, pp. 673-692, 17 ills., Dec., 1906

The Land of Sawdust and Spangles—A World in Miniature. By Francis Beverly Kelley. LX, pp. 463-516, 35 ills. in black and white, 29 ills. in color, Oct., 1931

Nature's Most Amazing Mammal: Elephants, Unique Among Animals, Have Many Human Qualities When Wild That Make Them Foremost Citizens of Zoo and Circus. By Edmund Heller. LXV, pp. 729-759, 37 ills., June, 1934

ELEPHANTS—*Continued*

The Perahera Processions of Ceylon. By G. H. G. Burroughs. LXII, pp. 90-100, ill. in black and white, 8 ills. in duotone, July, 1932

The Warfare of the Jungle Folk: Campaigning Against Tigers, Elephants, and Other Wild Animals in Northern Siam. By Merian C. Cooper. Photos by Ernest B. Schoedsack. LIII, pp. 233-268, 33 ills., Feb., 1928

When a Drought Blights Africa: Hippos and Elephants Are Driven Insane by Suffering, in the Lorian Swamp, Kenya Colony. By Capt. A. T. Curle. LV, pp. 521-528, 9 ills., Apr., 1929

Where Roosevelt Will Hunt (Africa). By Sir Harry Johnston. XX, pp. 207-256, 43 ills., map supplement, Mar., 1909

Wild Man and Wild Beast in Africa. By Theodore Roosevelt. XXII, pp. 1-33, 41 ills., map, Jan., 1911

Wings Over Nature's Zoo in Africa. 20 photos in duotone by Reginald A. Bourlay. LXXVI, pp. 527-542, Oct., 1939

Working Teak in the Burma Forests: The Sagacious Elephant Is Man's Ablest Ally in the Logging Industry of the Far East. By A. W. Smith. LVIII, pp. 239-256, 5 ills. in black and white, 15 ills. in color, Aug., 1930

ELEVENTH Annual Report of the Interstate Commerce Commission (Review by H. T. Newcomb). IX, pp. 29-31, Jan., 1898

ELEVENTH International Congress of Orientalists. VIII, p. 303 (note), Oct., 1897

ELIOT, CHARLES W.:

The Need of Conserving the Beauty and Freedom of Nature in Modern Life. By Charles W. Eliot. XXVI, pp. 67-74, 4 ills., July, 1914

ELLICE ISLANDS, Pacific Ocean:

American Pathfinders in the Pacific. By William H. Nicholas. LXXXIX, pp. 617-640, 17 ills., two-page map, May, 1946

ELLIOTT, CHARLES P.:

Mount St. Helens. By Lieut. Charles P. Elliott. VIII, pp. 226-230, foldout map, July-Aug., 1897

ELLIS, WILLIAM T.:

Voyaging on the Volga Amid War and Revolution: War-time Sketches on Russia's Great Waterway. By William T. Ellis. XXXIII, pp. 245-265, 16 ills., Mar., 1918

ELLISON, NORMAN:

Shark Fishing—An Australian Industry. By Norman Ellison. LXII, pp. 369-386, 22 ills., Sept., 1932

ELLSWORTH, LINCOLN:

Ellsworth Awarded the Hubbard Medal. LXX, p. 36, July, 1936

My Flight Across Antarctica. By Lincoln Ellsworth. LXX, pp. 1-35, 37 ills., map, July, 1936

My Four Antarctic Expeditions: Explorations of 1933-39 Have Stricken Vast Areas from the Realm of the Unknown. By Lincoln Ellsworth. LXXVI, pp. 129-138, 9 ills., map, July, 1939

ELLSWORTH, LINCOLN—*Continued*

Navigating the "Norge" from Rome to the North Pole and Beyond: The Designer and Pilot of the First Dirigible to Fly Over the Top of the World Describes a Thrilling Voyage of More Than 8,000 Miles. By General Umberto Nobile. LII, pp. 177-215, 36 ills., map, Aug., 1927

EL OUED (Oasis), Algeria:

The Country of the Ant Men. By Thomas H. Kearney. XXII, pp. 367-382, 13 ills., map, panorama, Apr., 1911

EL PASO, Texas:

Along Our Side of the Mexican Border. By Frederick Simpich. XXXVIII, pp. 61-80, 9 ills., map, July, 1920

EL SALVADOR:

Coffee Is King in El Salvador. By Luis Marden. LXXXVI, pp. 575-616, 22 ills. in black and white, 27 ills. in color, map, Nov., 1944

The Countries of the Caribbean. By William Joseph Showalter. XXIV, pp. 227-250, 23 ills., Feb., 1913

Notes on Central America. XVIII, pp. 272-279, ills., map, Apr., 1907

Shattered Capitals of Central America. By Herbert J. Spinden. XXXVI, pp. 185-212, 32 ills., map, Sept., 1919

Volcano-Girded Salvador: A Prosperous Central American State with the Densest Rural Population in the Western World. By Harriet Chalmers Adams. XLI, pp. 189-200, 10 ills., Feb., 1922

ELSMORE, RAY T.:

New Guinea's Mountain and Swampland Dwellers. By Col. Ray T. Elsmore. LXXXVIII, pp. 671-694, 15 ills. in black and white, 7 ills. in color, map, Dec., 1945

"Shangri-la" in Panorama. 7 color photos by author, pp. 681-688

An **ELYSIUM** for the Beauty-Seeking Traveler (Canary Islands). 14 color photos by Wilhelm Tobien. LVII, pp. 631-638, May, 1930

The **EMANCIPATION** of Mohammedan Women. By Mary Mills Patrick. XX, pp. 42-66, 19 ills., Jan., 1909

EMERSON, HARRINGTON:

Opening of the Alaskan Territory. By Harrington Emerson. XIV, pp. 99-106, 5 ills., Mar., 1903

EMIGRATION from Siberia. XIII, pp. 32-33, Jan., 1902

EMIGRATION to America an Industry (Sicily). By Arthur H. Warner. XX, pp. 1063-1102, 41 ills., Dec., 1909

EMMONS, SAMUEL FRANKLIN:

Alaska and Its Mineral Resources. By Samuel Franklin Emmons. IX, pp. 139-172, 3 ills., map supplement, Apr., 1898

EMPEROR WORSHIP:

Behind the Mask of Modern Japan. By Willard Price. LXXXVIII, pp. 513-535, 14 ills., Nov., 1945

EMPIRE of Romance—India. 16 ills. in color. XL, pp. 481-496, Nov., 1921

The **EMPIRE** of the Risen Sun (Japan). By William Elliot Griffis. XLIV, pp. 415-443, 21 ills., Oct., 1923

EMPIRE State Onions and Pageantry (New York). 12 color photos by J. Baylor Roberts and Volkmar Wentzel. LXXX, pp. 641-648, Nov., 1941

EMU WRENS:

The Fairy Wrens of Australia: The Little Long-tailed "Blue Birds of Happiness" Rank High Among the Island Continent's Remarkable Birds. By Neville W. Cayley. With 8 ills. in color from paintings by author. LXXXVIII, pp. 488-498, ill. in black and white, Oct., 1945

The **ENCHANTED MESA** (New Mexico). By F. W. Hodge. VIII, pp. 273-284, 6 ills., map, Oct., 1897

ENCIRCLING Navajo Mountain (Utah) with a Pack-Train: An Expedition to a Hitherto Untraversed Region of Our Southwest Discovers a New Route to Rainbow Natural Bridge. By Charles L. Bernheimer. XLIII, pp. 197-224, 33 ills., map, Feb., 1923

ENCOURAGING Birds Around the Home. By Frederick H. Kennard. XXV, pp. 315-344, 36 ills., Mar., 1914

ENDEAVOUR (Ship):

The Columbus of the Pacific: Captain James Cook, Foremost British Navigator, Expanded the Great Sea to Correct Proportions and Won for Albion an Insular Empire by Peaceful Exploration and Scientific Study. By J. R. Hildebrand. LI, pp. 85-132, 45 ills., maps, Jan., 1927

ENGELN, O. D. VON:

Photography in Glacial Alaska. By O. D. von Engeln. XXI, pp. 54-62, 4 ills., Jan., 1910

ENGINEERING:

Alaskan Highway an Engineering Epic: Mosquitoes, Mud, and Muskeg Minor Obstacles of 1,671-mile Race to Throw the Alcan Life Line Through Thick Forests and Uninhabited Wilderness. By Froelich Rainey. LXXXIII, pp. 143-168, 21 ills., 3 maps, Feb., 1943

Ascension Island, an Engineering Victory. By Lt. Col. Frederick J. Clarke. LXXXV, pp. 623-640, 21 ills., May, 1944

Greens Grow for GI's on Soilless Ascension. By W. Robert Moore. LXXXVIII, pp. 219-230, 12 ills., Aug., 1945

Mending Dikes in the Netherlands. 20 photos by Lawrence Earl. XC, pp. 791-806, Dec., 1946

Normandy's Made-in-England Harbors. LXXXVII, pp. 565-580, 16 ills., map, May, 1945

Oil for Victory Piped under the Sea. 9 ills. LXXXVIII, pp. 721-726, Dec., 1945

See also Aqueducts; Bridges; Canals; Dams; Floods and Flood Control; Highways and Roads; Reclamation of Land

ENGLAND:

Ancestor of the British Navy: England's Oldest Known War Vessel Is Unearthed, Laden with Remarkable Treasures of an Anglo-Saxon Ruler. By C. W. Phillips. LXXIX, pp. 247-268, 22 ills., 4 drawings, Feb., 1941

Bathymetrical Survey of the Fresh-water Lakes of England. XII, p. 408, Nov., 1901

The Beauties of the Severn Valley. By Frank Wakeman. LXIII, pp. 417-452, 24 ills. in black and white, 15 ills. in color, map, Apr., 1933

Between the Heather and the North Sea: Bold English Headlands Once Sheltered Sea Robbers, Later Were Ports of Wooden Ships, Centers of the Jet and Alum Trades, To-day Are Havens of Adventurous Fishing Fleets. By Leo Walmsley. LXIII, pp. 197-232, 41 ills., Feb., 1933

"Blood, Toil, Tears, and Sweat": An American Tells the Story of Britain's War Effort, Summed up in Prime Minister Churchill's Unflinching Words. By Harvey Klemmer. LXXXII, pp. 141-166, 19 ills., Aug., 1942

Britain Fights in the Fields. By Francis A. Flood. LXXXVI, pp. 31-65, 17 ills. in black and white, 21 ills. in color, July, 1944

Britain Just Before the Storm: A Canadian Canoe Threads Old English Waterways Athrob with the Midlands' Industrial Life. By Amos Burg. LXXVIII, pp. 185-212, 14 ills. in black and white, 9 ills. in color, map, Aug., 1940

The British Commonwealth of Nations: "Organized Freedom" Around the World. By Eric Underwood. LXXXIII, pp. 485-524, 31 ills., Apr., 1943

British Isles. 16 ills. XXVIII, pp. 551-566, Dec., 1915

Cathedrals of England: An Artist's Pilgrimage to These Majestic Monuments of Man's Genius and Faith. By Norman Wilkinson. LXXVI, pp. 741-762, 3 ills. in black and white, 16 ills. in gravure from dry-point engravings by author, Dec., 1939

Channel Ports—And Some Others. By Florence Craig Albrecht. XXVIII, pp. 1-55, 45 ills., July, 1915

A Char-à-Bancs in Cornwall. By Herbert Corey. XLVI, pp. 653-694, 44 ills., map, Dec., 1924

Charm Spots Along England's Harassed Coast. 16 ills. in duotone. LXXVIII, pp. 237-252, Aug., 1940

Cotton for England. XV, p. 39, Jan., 1904

Down Devon Lanes. By Herbert Corey. LV, pp. 529-568, 45 ills., map, May, 1929

8th Air Force in England. 10 ills. in color from U. S. Army Air Forces official photos. LXXXVII, pp. 297-304, Mar., 1945

England's Sun Trap Isle of Wight. By J. R. Hildebrand. LXVII, pp. 1-33, 22 ills. in black and white, 14 ills. in color, map, Jan., 1935

Europe's Endangered Fish Supply: The War and the North Sea Fisheries. XXVII, pp. 141-152, 9 ills., map, Feb., 1915

Everyday Life in Wartime England. By Harvey Klemmer. LXXIX, pp. 497-534, 48 ills., Apr., 1941

A Geographical Description of the British Islands. (By W. M. Davis). VII, pp. 208-211, June, 1896

ENGLAND—*Continued*

Great Britain on Parade. By Maynard Owen Williams. LXVIII, pp. 137-184, 40 ills. in black and white, 11 ills. in color, Aug., 1935

Informal Salute to the English Lakes. By Maynard Owen Williams. LXIX, pp. 511-521, 10 ills. in color, Apr., 1936

King Herring: An Account of the World's Most Valuable Fish, the Industries It Supports, and the Part It Has Played in History. By Hugh M. Smith. XX, pp. 701-735, 21 ills., Aug., 1909

Included: Great Yarmouth; Lowestoft

Lend-Lease Is a Two-way Benefit: Innovation in Creative Statesmanship Pools Resources of United Nations, and Supplies American Forces Around the World. By Francis Flood. LXXXIII, pp. 745-761, 14 ills., June, 1943

A Modern Pilgrim's Map of the British Isles. By Andrew H. Brown. Text with map supplement. LXXI, pp. 795-802, 3 ills., June, 1937

Nooks and Bays of Storied England. 13 color photos by Clifton Adams and Bernard Wakeman. LXI, pp. 183-190, Feb., 1932

The Oldest Nation of Europe: Geographical Factors in the Strength of Modern England. By Roland G. Usher. XXVI, pp. 393-414, 11 ills., Oct., 1914

One Hundred British Seaports. XXXI, pp. 84-94, 10 ills., map, Jan., 1917

The Ordnance Survey of Great Britain—Its History and Object. By Josiah Pierce, Jr. II, pp. 243-260, Aug., 1890

The Penn Country in Sussex: Home of Pennsylvania's Founder Abounds in Quaker History and Memories of Adventurous Smugglers. By Col. P. T. Etherton. LXVIII, pp. 59-90, 32 ills., map, July, 1935

The Preservation of England's Historic and Scenic Treasures. By Eric Underwood. LXXXVII, pp. 413-440, 24 ills., two-page map, Apr., 1945

Rural Britain Carries On. By Harvey Klemmer. LXXX, pp. 527-552, 27 ills., Oct., 1941

Summering in an English Cottage: Quiet and Loveliness Invite Contemplation in the Extra "Room," the Garden of the Thatched House. By Helen Churchill Candee. LXVII, pp. 429-456, 32 ills., Apr., 1935

Through the English Lake District Afoot and Awheel. By Ralph A. Graves. LV, pp. 577-603, 19 ills. in black and white, 15 ills. in color, map, May, 1929

Through the Heart of England in a Canadian Canoe. By R. J. Evans. XLI, pp. 473-497, 26 ills., map, May, 1922

Time and Tide on the Thames. By Frederick Simpich. LXXV, pp. 239-272, 23 ills. in black and white, 10 ills. in color, map, Feb., 1939

A Tour in the English Fenland. By Christopher Marlowe. LV, pp. 605-634, 26 ills. in black and white, 16 ills. in color, map, May, 1929

Transportation in England. XVI, p. 88, Feb., 1905

A Vacation in a Fifteenth Century English Manor House. By George Alden Sanford. LIII, pp. 629-636, 8 ills., May, 1928

ENGLAND—*Continued*

Vagabonding in England: A Young American Works His Way Around the British Isles and Sees Sights from an Unusual Point of View. By John McWilliams. LXV, pp. 357-398, 39 ills., map, Mar., 1934

Visits to the Old Inns of England: Historic Homes of Hospitality for the Wayfarer Dot the Length and Breadth of the Kingdom. By Harold Donaldson Eberlein. LIX, pp. 261-285, 17 ills. in black and white, 15 ills. in color, Mar., 1931

When the Herring Fleet Comes to Great Yarmouth. By W. Robert Moore. LXVI, pp. 233-250, 19 ills., Aug., 1934

Yanks at Westminster. By Capt. Leonard David Gammans. XC, pp. 223-252, 6 ills. in black and white, 19 ills. in color, Aug., 1946

See also Bampton; Beaconsfield; Cambridge; Channel Islands; Dover; Great Britain; London; Man, Isle of; Oxford; Plymouth; Scilly Isles; Southampton; Warwick; Winchester

ENGLAND'S Island Garden of Rocks and Flowers (Isle of Wight). 14 color photos by W. Robert Moore. LXVII, pp. 17-24, Jan., 1935

ENGLAND'S Lake District, Fountainhead of Poetry. 10 ills. in color. LXIX, pp. 513-520, Apr., 1936

ENGLAND'S Wild Moorland Ponies. 10 ills. LXXXIX, pp. 129-136, Jan., 1946

ENGLISH CHANNEL:

Normandy's Made-in-England Harbors. LXXXVII, pp. 565-580, 16 ills., map, May, 1945

Oil for Victory Piped under the Sea. 9 ills. LXXXVIII, pp. 721-726, Dec., 1945

ENGRAVINGS AND ETCHINGS:

Cathedrals of England: An Artist's Pilgrimage to These Majestic Monuments of Man's Genius and Faith. By Norman Wilkinson. LXXVI, pp. 741-762, 3 ills. in black and white, 16 ills. in gravure from dry-point engravings by author, Dec., 1939

Ships of the Centuries. 16 ills. in gravure from original etchings by Norman Wilkinson. LXXIII, pp. 65-80; text, p. 98, Jan., 1938

The **ENIGMA** of Cambodia (French Indo-China). 27 color photos by Gervais Courtellemont. LIV, pp. 307-322, Sept., 1928

ENIWETOK (Atoll), Marshall Islands:

Our New Military Wards, the Marshalls. By W. Robert Moore. LXXXVIII, pp. 325-360, 14 ills. in black and white, 20 ills. in color, map, Sept., 1945

ENTERING the Front Doors of Medieval Towns: The Adventures of an American Woman and Her Daughter in a Folding Boat on Eight Rivers of Germany and Austria. By Cornelia Stratton Parker. LXI, pp. 365-394, 23 ills. in black and white, 11 ills. in color, map, Mar., 1932

ENTERPRISE, H. M. S.:

Collinson's Arctic Journey. By General A. W. Greely. IV, pp. 198-200, Feb. 8, 1893

ENTERTAINMENT. *See* Sports and Games

ENTOMOLOGY. *See* Insects

ENTRE RÍOS (Province), Argentina:

Pioneer Gaucho Days. 8 ills. in color from paintings by Cesáreo Bernaldo de Quirós. LXIV, pp. 453-460, Oct., 1933

EPHESUS (Ancient City):

Some Ruined Cities of Asia Minor. By Ernest L. Harris. XIX, pp. 833-858, 19 ills., Dec., 1908

EPLER, BLANCH NETTLETON:

A Bit of Elizabethan England in America: Fisher Folk of the Islands Off North Carolina Conserved the Speech and Customs of Sir Walter Raleigh's Colonists. By Blanch Nettleton Epler. LXIV, pp. 695-730, 43 ills., map, Dec., 1933

EQUATORIAL AFRICA:

Recent Explorations in Equatorial Africa. (By Ernest de Sasseville). VIII, pp. 88-91, Mar., 1897

See also Belgian Congo; French Equatorial Africa; Kenya; Uganda

EREBUS, Mount, Antarctica:

The Heart of the Antarctic. By Ernest H. Shackleton. XX, pp. 972-1007, 27 ills., map, Nov., 1909

ERG, El (Region), Algeria:

The Country of the Ant Men. By Thomas H. Kearney. XXII, pp. 367-382, 13 ills., map, panorama, Apr., 1911

ERICSSON, LEIF:

Discoverers of America. Annual Address by the President, Hon. Gardiner G. Hubbard. V, pp. 1-20, charts, maps, 3 map supplements, Apr. 7, 1893

Dwellings of the Saga-Time in Iceland, Greenland, and Vineland. By Cornelia Horsford. IX, pp. 73-84, ill., 9 sketches, Mar., 1898

ERIE, Lake, Canada-U. S.:

Rainfall and the Level of Lake Erie. (By E. L. Moseley). XIV, pp. 327-328, Aug., 1903

Submerged Valleys in Sandusky Bay. By Professor E. L. Moseley. XIII, pp. 398-403, 4 charts, Nov., 1902

Testing the Currents of Lake Erie. (By E. L. Moseley). XIV, pp. 41-42, Jan., 1903

ERIE, Pennsylvania:

The Industrial Titan of America: Pennsylvania, Once the Keystone of the Original Thirteen, Now the Keystone of Forty-eight Sovereign States. By John Oliver La Gorce. XXXV, pp. 367-406, 33 ills., map, May, 1919

ERIE CANAL, New York:

The New Erie Canal. XVI, pp. 568-570, map, Dec., 1905

ERIK THE RED:

Dwellings of the Saga-Time in Iceland, Greenland, and Vineland. By Cornelia Horsford. IX, pp. 73-84, ill., 9 sketches, Mar., 1898

ERITREA:

With the Italians in Eritrea: Torrid Colony Between the Red Sea and Ethiopia, 2,600 Miles by Sea from Rome, Is Mobilization Place of Fascist Troops and Planes. By Harald P. Lechenperg. LXVIII, pp. 265-295, 34 ills., two-page map, Sept., 1935

ERIVAN, U. S. S. R.:

The Land of the Stalking Death: A Journey Through Starving Armenia on an American Relief Train. By Melville Chater. XXXVI, pp. 393-420, 23 ills., Nov., 1919

The Old Post-Road from Tiflis to Erivan. By Esther Lancraft Hovey. XII, pp. 300-309, 9 ills., Aug., 1901

ERNST THAELMANN (Collective Farm), U. S. S. R.:

Sunny Siberia. 26 color photos by Owen Lattimore. LXXXVI, pp. 649-672, Dec., 1944

EROSION. *See* Marine Erosion; Peneplains; Soil Erosion

ERRANT (Airplane):

Flying the World: In a Homemade Airplane the Author and Her Husband Enjoy 16,000 Miles of Adventurous Flight Across Europe, Asia, and America. By Gladys M. Day. LXI, pp. 655-690, 41 ills., map, June, 1932

The **ERRATIC** (Geologic Formation of the United States). By O. A. Ljungstedt. XXI, pp. 525-531, 4 ills., map, June, 1910

The **ERUPTION** of Krakatoa. By Sir Robert Ball. XIII, pp. 200-204, June, 1902

The **ERUPTION** of Mount Vesuvius, April 7-8, 1906. By Thomas Augustus Jaggar, Jr. XVII, pp. 318-325, 6 ills., June, 1906

The **ERUPTIONS** of La Soufrière, St. Vincent, in May, 1902. By Edmund Otis Hovey. XIII, pp. 444-459, 4 ills., Dec., 1902

ERZURUM, Turkey:

The Turkish Republic Comes of Age. By Maynard Owen Williams. LXXXVII, pp. 581-616, 4 ills. in black and white, 29 ills. in color, map, May, 1945

ESCORT CARRIERS:

Cruise on an Escort Carrier. By Melville Bell Grosvenor. LXXXIV, pp. 513-546, 14 ills. in black and white, 20 ills. in color, Nov., 1943

Your Navy as Peace Insurance. By Fleet Admiral Chester W. Nimitz. LXXXIX, pp. 681-736, 32 ills. in black and white, 26 ills. in color, June, 1946

ESDRAELON (Plain), Palestine:

Impressions of Palestine. By James Bryce. XXVII, pp. 293-317, 18 ills., map, Mar., 1915

ESKIMOS:

Alaska—Our Northwestern Outpost. 16 color photos by Ernest H. Gruening, Amos Burg, Froelich Rainey. LXXXII, pp. 297-308, Sept., 1942

The Arctic Cruise of the U. S. S. Thetis in the Summer and Autumn of 1889. By Charles H. Stockton. II, pp. 171-198, ill., foldout map, July, 1890

ESKIMOS—*Continued*

Coast Guard Patrol in Greenland. 9 color photos by Lieut. Thomas S. La Farge. LXXXIII, pp. 565-572, May, 1943

Desolate Greenland, Now an American Outpost. 17 photos: 12 by Willie Knutsen, 4 by F. Vogel. LXXX, pp. 393-406, Sept., 1941

Discovering Alaska's Oldest Arctic Town (Ipiutak): A Scientist Finds Ivory-eyed Skeletons of a Mysterious People and Joins Modern Eskimos in the Dangerous Spring Whale Hunt. By Froelich G. Rainey. LXXXII, pp. 319-336, 15 ills., Sept., 1942

Exploring Frozen Fragments of American History: On the Trail of Early Eskimo Colonists Who Made a 55-Mile Crossing from the Old World to the New. By Henry B. Collins, Jr. LXXV, pp. 633-656, 24 ills., map, May, 1939

The First Natural-Color Photographs from the Arctic. 22 color photos by Jacob Gayer and Maynard Owen Williams. XLIX, pp. 301-316, Mar., 1926

Greenland from 1898 to Now: "Captain Bob," Who Went North with Peary, Tells of 42 Years of Exploration in the Orphan Island of New Aerial and Naval Interest. By Robert A. Bartlett. LXXVIII, pp. 111-140, 25 ills., two-page map, July, 1940

On Eskimo Geographic Names Ending in Miut. (By John Murdoch). IX, p. 190, Apr., 1898

The Origin of Stefansson's Blond Eskimo. By Major General A. W. Greely. XXIII, pp. 1225-1238, 10 ills., map, Dec., 1912

Peary as a Leader: Incidents from the Life of the Discoverer of the North Pole Told by One of His Lieutenants on the Expedition Which Reached the Goal. By Donald B. MacMillan. XXXVII, pp. 293-317, 20 ills., map, Apr., 1920

A Summer Voyage to the Arctic. By G. R. Putnam. VIII, pp. 97-110, 6 ills., map, Apr., 1897

Three Weeks in Hubbard Bay, West Greenland. By Robert Stein. IX, pp. 1-11, 6 ills., maps, Jan., 1898

Two Hundred Miles up the Kuskokwim. By Charles Hallock. IX, pp. 85-92, 6 ills., Mar., 1898

An Undiscovered Island Off the Northern Coast of Alaska. I—By Marcus Baker. II—By Captain Edward Perry Herendeen. III—By General A. W. Greely. V, pp. 76-83, July 10, 1893

ESPÍRITU SANTO (Island), New Hebrides:

Painting History in the Pacific. 19 ills. in color from paintings by Lt. William F. Draper, USNR. LXXXVI, pp. 408-424, Oct., 1944

ESSAYS. *See* Literary Contests; NGS: Essay Contests

ESTATES:

Channel Islands: The Feudal Isle of Sark: Where Sixteenth-Century Laws Are Still Observed. By Sibyl Hathaway (La Dame de Serk). LXII, pp. 101-119, 21 ills., map, July, 1932

England: Preservation of England's Historic and Scenic Treasures. By Eric Underwood. LXXXVII, pp. 413-440, 24 ills., two-page map, Apr., 1945

England: A Vacation in a Fifteenth Century English Manor House. By George Alden Sanford. LIII, pp. 629-636, 8 ills., May, 1928

ESTATES—*Continued*

A Mexican Hacienda. By J. E. Kirkwood. XXV, pp. 563-584, 18 ills., May, 1914

Monticello: Jefferson's Little Mountain: Romance Enfolds Monticello, the Restored Home of the Author of the Declaration of Independence. By Paul Wilstach. LV, pp. 481-503, 12 ills. in black and white, 12 ills. in color, Apr., 1929

Mount Vernon: The Home of the First Farmer of America. By Worth E. Shoults. LIII, pp. 603-628, 6 ills. in black and white, 26 ills. in color, May, 1928

South Carolina: The Ashley River and Its Gardens. By E. T. H. Shaffer. XLIX, pp. 525-550, 6 ills. in black and white, 7 ills. in color, May, 1926

Sweden: Country-House Life in Sweden: In Castle and Cottage the Landed Gentry Gallantly Keep the Old Traditions. By Amelie Posse-Brázdová. LXVI, pp. 1-64, 51 ills. in black and white, 13 ills. in color, map, July, 1934

Virginia—A Commonwealth That Has Come Back. By William Joseph Showalter. LV, pp. 403-472, 69 ills. in black and white, 13 ills. in color, map, Apr., 1929

Virginia: Tidewater Virginia, Where History Lives. By Albert W. Atwood. LXXXI, pp. 617-656, 18 ills. in black and white, 20 ills. in color, map, May, 1942

See also Haciendas

ESTONIA:

Estonia: At Russia's Baltic Gate: War Often Has Ravaged This Little Nation Whose Identity Was Long Submerged in the Vast Sea of Russian Peoples. By Baroness Irina Ungern-Sternberg. LXXVI, pp. 803-834, 33 ills., map, Dec., 1939

Flying Around the Baltic. By Douglas Chandler. LXXIII, pp. 767-806, 31 ills. in black and white, 13 ills. in duotone, map, June, 1938

The New Map of Europe: Showing the Boundaries Established by the Peace Conference at Paris and by Subsequent Decisions of the Supreme Council of Allied and Associated Powers. By Ralph A. Graves. Text with map supplement. XXXIX, pp. 157-177, 18 ills., Feb., 1921

The Races of Europe. By Edwin A. Grosvenor. XXXIV, pp. 441-534, 62 ills., diagr. and index, maps, map supplement, Dec., 1918

ESTUARY TIDES. *See* Tides and Tidal Waves

ETHERTON, P. T.:

The Penn Country in Sussex (England): Home of Pennsylvania's Founder Abounds in Quaker History and Memories of Adventurous Smugglers. By Col. P. T. Etherton. LXVIII, pp. 59-90, 32 ills., map, July, 1935

ETHIOPIA (Abyssinia):

Abyssinia—The Country and People. By Oscar T. Crosby. XII, pp. 89-102, Mar., 1901

Across Widest Africa. By A. Henry Savage Landor. XIX, pp. 694-737, 38 ills., map, Oct., 1908

ETHIOPIA (Abyssinia)—*Continued*

Africa Since 1888, with Special Reference to South Africa and Abyssinia. By Hon. Gardiner G. Hubbard. VII, pp. 157-175, ill., foldout map, May, 1896

A Caravan Journey Through Abyssinia: From Addis Ababa Through Lalibela, the Strange Jerusalem of Ethiopia, in Search of New Grains for American Farms. By Harry V. Harlan. XLVII, pp. 613-663, 46 ills., map, June, 1925

Consul Skinner's Mission to Abyssinia. XV, pp. 165-166, ill., Apr., 1904

Coronation Days in Addis Ababa. By W. Robert Moore. LIX, pp. 738-746, 8 ills., June, 1931

Explorations in Central East Africa. XII, pp. 42-43, Jan., 1901

The Geography of Abyssinia. XII, pp. 274-276, July, 1901

Life's Tenor in Ethiopia: Africa's Land of Early Christianity Now Yields Minerals for Modern Industry. By James Loder Park. LXVII, pp. 783-793, 8 ills., June, 1935

Modern Ethiopia: Haile Selassie the First, Formerly Ras Tafari, Succeeds to the World's Oldest Continuously Sovereign Throne. By Addison E. Southard. LIX, pp. 679-738, 47 ills. in black and white, 27 ills. in color, map, June, 1931

Nature and Man in Ethiopia. By Wilfred H. Osgood. LIV, pp. 121-176, 64 ills., map, Aug., 1928

Open-Air Law Courts of Ethiopia. With 18 photos by Harald P. Lechenperg. LXVIII, pp. 633-646, Nov., 1935

Traveling in the Highlands of Ethiopia. By Leo B. Roberts. LXVIII, pp. 297-328, 37 ills., Sept., 1935

ETHNOLOGY. *See* Anthropology; U. S. Bureau of American Ethnology

ETRUSCANS:

Ancient Rome Brought to Life. By Rhys Carpenter. Paintings by H. M. Herget. XC, pp. 567-633, 2 ills. in black and white, 32 ills. in color, map, Nov., 1946

EUCALYPTUS (Tree):

Lonely Australia: The Unique Continent. By Herbert E. Gregory. XXX, pp. 473-568, 68 ills., 5 maps (1 two-page), Dec., 1916

Notes on the Eucalyptus Tree from the United States Forest Service. XX, pp. 668-673, 4 ills., July, 1909

The Tallest Tree That Grows. By Edgerton R. Young. XX, pp. 664-667, 3 ills., July, 1909

EUGENICS:

A Few Thoughts Concerning Eugenics. By Alexander Graham Bell. XIX, pp. 119-123, Feb., 1908

Our Immigration Laws from the Viewpoint of National Eugenics. By Prof. Robert De C. Ward. XXIII, pp. 38-41, Jan., 1912

Who Shall Inherit Long Life? On the Existence of a Natural Process at Work Among Human Beings Tending to Improve the Vigor and Vitality of Succeeding Generations. By Dr. Alexander Graham Bell. XXXV, pp. 505-514, 13 ills., June, 1919

EUPHRATES (River), Asia:

The Cradle of Civilization: The Historic Lands Along the Euphrates and Tigris Rivers Where Briton Is Fighting Turk. By James Baikie. XXIX, pp. 127-162, 25 ills., Feb., 1916

The Mountaineers of the Euphrates. By Ellsworth Huntington. XX, pp. 142-156, 13 ills., Feb., 1909

Mystic Nedjef, the Shia Mecca. By Frederick Simpich. XXVI, pp. 589-598, 4 ills., Dec., 1914

Where Adam and Eve Lived. By Frederick and Margaret Simpich. XXVI, pp. 546-588, 35 ills., Dec., 1914

EUROPE:

Along the Old Silk Routes: A Motor Caravan with Air-conditioned Trailer Retraces Ancient Roads from Paris across Europe and Half of Asia to Delhi. By Lawrence Copley Thaw and Margaret S. Thaw. LXXVIII, pp. 453-486, 33 ills., map, Oct., 1940

Americans Help Liberated Europe Live Again. By Lt. Col. Frederick Simpich, Jr. LXXXVII, pp. 747-768, 17 ills., June, 1945

The Battle-Line of Languages in Western Europe: A Problem in Human Geography More Perplexing Than That of International Boundaries. By A. L. Guerard. XLIII, pp. 145-180, 36 ills., Feb., 1923

By Sail Across Europe. By Merlin Minshall. LXXI, pp. 533-567, 38 ills., map, May, 1937

Controlling Sand Dunes in the United States and Europe. By A. S. Hitchcock. XV, pp. 43-47, 4 ills., Jan., 1904

European Populations. (By Walter J. Ballard). XVI, p. 432, Sept., 1905

Europe's Endangered Fish Supply: The War and the North Sea Fisheries. XXVII, pp. 141-152, 9 ills., map, Feb., 1915

Europe's Looted Art. By John Walker. LXXXIX, pp. 39-52, 11 ills., Jan., 1946

The Evolution of Commerce. Annual Address by the President, Hon. Gardiner G. Hubbard. IV, pp. 1-18, Mar. 26, 1892

The Flags of Europe, Asia, and Africa. By Byron McCandless and Gilbert Grosvenor. XXXII, pp. 372-378, 101 ills. in color, Oct., 1917

Flying Around the Baltic. By Douglas Chandler. LXXIII, pp. 767-806, 31 ills. in black and white, 13 ills. in duotone, map, June, 1938

Flying Around the North Atlantic. By Anne Morrow Lindbergh. Foreword by Charles A. Lindbergh. LXVI, pp. 259-337, 82 ills., maps (1 two-page), Sept., 1934

From Africa to the Alps. 8 ills. in color from U. S. Army Air Forces official photos. LXXXIX, pp. 161-168, Feb., 1946

From England to India by Automobile: An 8,527-mile Trip Through Ten Countries, from London to Quetta, Requires Five and a Half Months. By Major F. A. C. Forbes-Leith. XLVIII, pp. 191-223, 33 ills., map, Aug., 1925

From London to Australia by Aëroplane: A Personal Narrative of the First Aërial Voyage Half Around the World. By Sir Ross Smith. XXXIX, pp. 229-339, 76 ills. in black and white, 8 ills. in color, map, Mar., 1921

EUROPE—*Continued*

Geographic Progress of Civilization. Annual Address by the President, Honorable Gardiner G. Hubbard. VI, pp. 1-22, Feb. 14, 1894
Included: Great Britain; Greece; Italy; Rome; Scandinavia; Spain

The Geographic's New Map of Europe and the Mediterranean. By Gilbert Grosvenor. Text with map supplement. LXXIII, pp. 525-528, ill., Apr., 1938

The Geographic's New Map of Germany and Its Approaches: With a Review of The Society's Maps of Europe. By Gilbert Grosvenor. Text with map supplement. LXXXVI, pp. 66-72, ill., July, 1944
Included: Boundary Changes in Europe from 1912 to 1940

Looking Down on Europe: The Thrills and Advantages of Sight-seeing by Airplane, as Demonstrated on a 6,500-mile Tour Over Commercial Aviation Routes. By Lieutenant J. Parker Van Zandt. XLVII, pp. 261-326, 67 ills., map, Mar., 1925

Looking Down on Europe Again: Crisscrossing Air Tracks Reveal Nature's Scenic Masterpieces and Man's Swift-changing Boundaries and Structures. By J. Parker Van Zandt. LXXV, pp. 791-822, 31 ills., map, June, 1939

Map of Europe Including the New Balkan States. Text with map supplement. XXVI, pp. 191-192, Aug., 1914

The National Geographic War-Zone Map. Text with map supplement. XXXIII, p. 494, May, 1918

New Map of Europe: Showing the Boundaries Established by the Peace Conference at Paris and by Subsequent Decisions of the Supreme Council of the Allied and Associated Powers. By Ralph A. Graves. Text with map supplement. XXXIX, pp. 157-177, 18 ills., Feb., 1921

New Map of Europe and the Near East. Text with map supplement. LXXXIII, pp. 762-763, ill., June, 1943

New Map of Europe Records War Changes. Text with map supplement. LXXVII, p. 625, May, 1940

Our Map of the Races of Europe. Text with map supplement. XXXIV, pp. 535-536, Dec., 1918

The Races of Europe. By Edwin A. Grosvenor. XXXIV, pp. 441-534, 62 ills., diagr. and index, maps, map supplement, Dec., 1918

The Remarkable Growth of Europe During 40 Years of Peace. (By O. P. Austin). XXVI, pp. 272-274, Sept., 1914

Russia in Europe. By Hon. Gardiner G. Hubbard. VII, pp. 3-26, map supplement, Jan., 1896

The Society's New Map of Central Europe and the Mediterranean. Text with map supplement. LXXVI, pp. 559-560, Oct., 1939

The Society's New Map of Europe. By Gilbert Grosvenor. Text with map supplement. LVI, pp. 771-774, Dec., 1929

A Tale of Three Cities (Prague; Vienna; Budapest). By Thomas R. Henry. LXXXVIII, pp. 641-669, 23 ills., Dec., 1945

Wayside Scenes in Europe. 16 ills. XXV, pp. 229-244, Feb., 1914

Wayside Scenes in Europe. 16 ills. XXVII, pp. 401-416, Apr., 1915

EUROPE—*Continued*

Western Front Map Embraces Three Continents (Europe, Africa, Asia). Text with map supplement. LXXXII, pp. 139-140, July, 1942

See also names of countries

EUROPEAN Outpost: The Azores. By Harriet Chalmers Adams. LXVII, pp. 35-66, 25 ills. in black and white, 13 ills. in color, map, Jan., 1935

EUROPEAN Populations. (By Walter J. Ballard). XVI, p. 432, Sept., 1905

EUROPEAN Tributes to Peary. XXI, pp. 536-540, 4 ills., June, 1910

EUROPEAN WAR. *See* World War I

EUROPE'S Endangered Fish Supply: The War and the North Sea Fisheries. XXVII, pp. 141-152, 9 ills., map, Feb., 1915

EUROPE'S Looted Art. By John Walker. LXXXIX, pp. 39-52, 11 ills., Jan., 1946

EUROPE'S Newest Kingdom: After Centuries of Struggle, Albania at Last Enjoys an Era of Peace and Stability. By Melville Chater. LIX, pp. 131-190, 37 ills. in black and white, 39 ills. in color, map, Feb., 1931

EUROPE'S Northern Nomads (Lapps). 12 color photos by Jack Kuhne. LXXVI, pp. 657-664, Nov., 1939

EVANS, SIR JOHN:

Portrait. VIII, pl. 38 (front.), Dec., 1897

Sir John Evans and Prof. W J McGee. (By J. H.). VIII, pp. 358-359, ills., Dec., 1897

EVANS, MALCOLM:

Storied Islands of the South Sea. 20 color photos: 5 by Malcolm Evans. LXXXI, pp. 9-40, Jan., 1942

EVANS, R. J.:

Through the Heart of England in a Canadian Canoe. By R. J. Evans. XLI, pp. 473-497, 26 ills., map, May, 1922

EVANS, ROBLEY D.:

Honors to the American Navy (Address by Rear Admiral Robley D. Evans). XX, pp. 77-95, Jan., 1909

EVANS, WALTER H.:

Some of the Conditions and Possibilities of Agriculture in Alaska. By Walter H. Evans. IX, pp. 178-187, Apr., 1898

EVER Changing California, Land of Startling Contrasts. 30 color photos by Charles Martin. LV, pp. 705-744, June, 1929

EVEREST, Mount, Nepal-Tibet:

The Aërial Conquest of Everest: Flying Over the World's Highest Mountain Realizes the Objective of Many Heroic Explorers. By Lieut. Col. L. V. S. Blacker. LXIV, pp. 127-162, 35 ills., map, Aug., 1933

EVERETT, DOROTHEA D.:

Black Acres: A Thrilling Sketch in the Vast Volume of Who's Who Among the Peoples That Make America. By Dorothea D. and Fred Everett. LXXX, pp. 631-652, 13 ills. in black and white, 12 ills. in color, Nov., 1941

EVERETT, FRED:

Black Acres: A Thrilling Sketch in the Vast Volume of Who's Who Among the Peoples That Make America. By Dorothea D. and Fred Everett. LXXX, pp. 631-652, 13 ills. in black and white, 12 ills. in color, Nov., 1941

EVERGLADES (Region), Florida:

The Geography of the Southern Peninsula of the United States. By the Rev. John N. MacGonigle. VII, pp. 381-394, 4 ills., Dec., 1896

South Florida's Amazing Everglades: Encircled by Populous Places Is a Seldom-visited Area of Rare Birds, Prairies, Cowboys, and Teeming Wild Life of Big Cypress Swamp. By John O'Reilly. LXXVII, pp. 115-142, 26 ills., map, Jan., 1940

EVERMANN, BARTON WARREN:

The Bureau of Fisheries. By Dr. Barton Warren Evermann. XV, pp. 191-212, 11 ills., 3 diagrs., May, 1904

EVERY-DAY Life in Afghanistan. By Frederick Simpich and "Haji Mirza Hussein." XXXIX, pp. 85-110, 26 ills., map, Jan., 1921

EVERYDAY Life in Pueblo Bonito: As Disclosed by the National Geographic Society's Archeologic Explorations in the Chaco Canyon National Monument, New Mexico. By Neil M. Judd. XLVIII, pp. 227-262, 37 ills., map, Sept., 1925

EVERYDAY Life in Wartime England. By Harvey Klemmer. LXXIX, pp. 497-534, 48 ills., Apr., 1941

EVIDENCE of Recent Volcanic Action in Southeast Alaska. XVII, pp. 173-176, Mar., 1906

The **EVOLUTION** of Commerce. Annual Address by the President, Hon. Gardiner G. Hubbard. IV, pp. 1-18, Mar. 26, 1892

EVOLUTION of Russian Government. By Edwin A. Grosvenor. XVI, pp. 309-332, 16 ills., July, 1905

EWING, HENRY E.:

Afield with the Spiders: Web Hunting in the Marshlands and Woodlands and Along the Lanes. By Henry E. Ewing. Paintings by Hashime Murayama. LXIV, pp. 163-194, 26 ills. in black and white, 64 ills. in color, Aug., 1933

EXCAVATIONS at Abydos. (By W. M. Flinders Petrie). XIV, pp. 358-359, Sept., 1903

EXCAVATIONS at Nippur (Iraq). XI, p. 392, Oct., 1900

EXCAVATIONS at Quirigua, Guatemala. By Sylvanus Griswold Morley. XXIV, pp. 339-361, 24 ills., diagr., Mar., 1913
Note. XXIV, p. 1056, Sept., 1913

EXCAVATIONS of M. de Morgan at Susa. XII, p. 315, Aug., 1901

EXCURSIONS. *See* NGS: Excursions and Field Meetings

EXMOOR PONIES:

England's Wild Moorland Ponies. 10 ills. LXXXIX, pp. 129-136, Jan., 1946

The **EXPANSION** of England. By Edwin D. Mead. XI, pp. 249-263, July, 1900

EXPEDITION into Texas of Fernando del Bosque, Standard-Bearer of the King, Don Carlos II, in the Year 1675. Translated from an Old, Unpublished Spanish Manuscript. By Betty B. Brewster. XIV, pp. 339-348, Sept., 1903

An **EXPEDITION** through the Yukon District. By Charles Willard Hayes. IV, pp. 117-159, 3 maps (2 foldouts), May 15, 1892

An **EXPEDITION** to Mount St. Elias, Alaska. By Israel C. Russell. III, pp. 53-191, 17 ills., 3 diagrs., tables, 7 maps (1 foldout), May 29, 1891

EXPEDITION to Turkestan. XIV, p. 215, May, 1903

EXPEDITION Unearths Buried Masterpieces of Carved Jade (Cerro de las Mesas, Mexico). By Matthew W. Stirling. LXXX, pp. 277-302, 14 ills. in black and white, 20 ills. in color, map, Sept., 1941

EXPEDITIONS:

Africa, Its Past and Future: Stanley Expedition. (By Gardiner G. Hubbard). I, pp. 99-124, foldout map, Apr., 1889

Alaska: Summary of Reports on the Mt. St. Elias Expedition. II, pp. 302-304, Apr., 1891

The Antarctic Continent (Geographic Notes. By Cyrus C. Babb). VI, pp. 217-223, map, Dec. 29, 1894

By Coolie and Caravan Across Central Asia: Narrative of a 7,900-Mile Journey of Exploration and Research Over the "Roof of the World," from the Indian Ocean to the Yellow Sea (Morden-Clark Asiatic Expedition). By William J. Morden. LII, pp. 369-431, 73 ills., map, Oct., 1927

The Cartography and Observations of Bering's First Voyage. By General A. W. Greely. III, pp. 205-230, map supplement, Jan. 28, 1892; Feb. 19, 1892

Charles Francis Hall and Jones Sound. (By A. W. G.). VII, pp. 308-310, Sept., 1896

Climbing Mighty Minya Konka: Americans First Scaled Mountain That Now Is Landmark of China's New Skyway. By Richard L. Burdsall and Terris Moore. LXXXIII, pp. 625-650, 23 ills., map, May, 1943

A Critical Review of Bering's First Expedition, 1725-30, Together with a Translation of His Original Report Upon It. With a Map. By Wm. H. Dall. II, pp. 111-169, 8 tables, foldout map, May, 1890
Included: Supplementary Note by Marcus Baker, On the Alleged Observation of a Lunar Eclipse by Bering in 1728-9, pp. 167-169

EXPEDITIONS—*Continued*

The Crosby Expedition to Tibet. XV, pp. 229-231, 3 ills., May, 1904

Earth's Most Primitive People: A Journey with the Aborigines of Central Australia. By Charles P. Mountford. LXXXIX, pp. 89-112, 10 ills. in black and white, 8 ills. in color, map, Jan., 1946

An Expedition through the Yukon District. By Charles Willard Hayes. IV, pp. 117-159, 3 maps (2 foldouts), May 15, 1892

An Expedition to Mount St. Elias, Alaska. By Israel C. Russell. III, pp. 53-191, 17 ills., 3 diagrs., tables, 7 maps (1 foldout), May 29, 1891

Introduction: The Southern Coast of Alaska, pp. 55-57

Part I: Previous Explorations in the St. Elias Region, pp. 58-74

Part II: Narrative of the St. Elias Expedition of 1890, pp. 75-166

Part III: Sketch of the Geology of the St. Elias Region, pp. 167-175

Part IV: Glaciers of the St. Elias Region, pp. 176-188

Part V: Height and Position of Mount St. Elias, pp. 189-191

Appendices: Official Instructions Governing the Expedition, pp. 192-194; Report on Topographic Work, p. 195; Report on Auriferous Sands from Yakutat Bay, pp. 196-198; Report on Fossil Plants, pp. 199-200

Expeditions in the Arctic and Antarctic. XIII, pp. 179-180, May, 1902

Fit to Fight Anywhere (Quartermaster Corps Expedition). By Frederick Simpich. LXXXIV, pp. 233-256, 26 ills., Aug., 1943

Hatcher's Work in Patagonia. (By J. H.). VIII, pp. 319-322, Nov., 1897

The Heart of Africa. By E. C. Hore. III, pp. 238-247, Feb. 19, 1892

The Mt. St. Elias Expedition of Prince Luigi Amadeo of Savoy, 1897. (By E. R. S.). IX, pp. 93-96, Mar., 1898

On the Telegraphic Determinations of Longitude by the Bureau of Navigation. By Lieut. J. A. Norris, U. S. N. II, pp. 1-30, Apr., 1890

Quinine Hunters in Ecuador. By Froelich Rainey. LXXXIX, pp. 341-363, 21 ills., map, Mar., 1946

Recent Explorations in Alaska. By Eliza Ruhamah Scidmore. V, pp. 173-179, Jan. 31, 1894

Report—Geography of the Land. By Herbert G. Ogden. II, pp. 31-48, Apr., 1890

Some Recent Geographic Events. (By J. H.). VIII, pp. 359-362, ill., Dec., 1897

Included: Andrée Balloon Expedition; de Gerlache Expedition; Jackson-Harmsworth Expedition; Peary Expedition to Greenland; Hedin Expedition to Central Asia; Duke of the Abruzzi Expedition to summit of Mount St. Elias; Mazama Expedition to summit of Mount Rainier

Spottswood's Expedition of 1716. By Dr. William M. Thornton. VII, pp. 265-269, Aug., 1896

Through the Deserts and Jungles of Africa by Motor: Caterpillar Cars Make 15,000-Mile Trip from Algeria to Madagascar in Nine Months (Citroën Central African Expedition). By Georges-Marie Haardt. XLIX, pp. 651-720, 95 ills., map, June, 1926

EXPEDITIONS—*Continued*

A Yukon Pioneer, Mike Lebarge. IX, pp. 137-139, ill., Apr., 1898

Note: First continuous trip from headwaters of the Yukon to the sea

See also American Museum of Natural History; Antarctic Regions; Arctic Regions; Citroën-Haardt Trans-Asiatic Expedition; Hourst Niger Expedition; Lady Franklin Bay Expedition; Lewis and Clark Expedition; MacMillan Arctic Expedition; Mountain Climbing; Nansen Polar Expedition; NGS: Expeditions; Shedd Aquarium; Smithsonian Institution; U.S. Bureau of American Ethnology; Wellman Polar Expedition; *and* names of expedition leaders

EXPERIENCES in the Grand Canyon. By Ellsworth and Emery Kolb. XXVI, pp. 99-184, 70 ills., map, Aug., 1914

EXPERIENCES of a Lone Geographer: An American Agricultural Explorer Makes His Way Through Brigand-infested Central China en Route to the Amne Machin Range, Tibet. By Joseph F. Rock. XLVIII, pp. 331-347, 16 ills., map, Sept., 1925

EXPLORATION:

Exploration During Victoria's Reign. XII, p. 160, Apr., 1901

Exploration in the Canadian Rockies. X, pp. 135-136, Apr., 1899

The Great Unmapped Areas on the Earth's Surface Awaiting the Explorer and Geographer. By J. Scott Keltie. VIII, pp. 251-266, Sept., 1897

The Scope and Value of Arctic Explorations. By General A. W. Greely. VII, pp. 32-39, Jan., 1896

See also Agricultural and Botanical Explorers; Discoverers, Explorers, and Navigators; Expeditions; *and* Africa; Alaska; Antarctic Regions; Arctic Regions; Asia; Greenland; New World; *and* the following articles

EXPLORATIONS by the Bureau of American Ethnology in 1895. By W J McGee. VII, pp. 77-80, Feb., 1896

EXPLORATIONS in Alaska. X, pp. 269-271, July, 1899

EXPLORATIONS in Central East Africa. XII, pp. 42-43, Jan., 1901

EXPLORATIONS in Crete. By Edith H. Hall. XX, pp. 778-787, 15 ills., Sept., 1909

EXPLORATIONS in Peru. XXIII, pp. 417-422, 7 ills., map, Apr., 1912

EXPLORATIONS in the Gobi Desert. By Roy Chapman Andrews. LXIII, pp. 653-716, 50 ills. in black and white, 20 ills. in color, map, June, 1933

EXPLORATIONS in Tibet. XIV, pp. 353-355, Sept., 1903

EXPLORER (Balloon):

Exploring the Stratosphere. By Captain Albert W. Stevens. LXVI, pp. 397-434, 43 ills., chart, Oct., 1934

See also Stratosphere

EXPLORER II (Balloon):
First natural-color photograph taken in the stratosphere. By Major Albert W. Stevens. LXXI, ill. p. 340, Mar., 1937
National Geographic Society-U. S. Army Air Corps Stratosphere Flight of 1935 in Balloon *Explorer II* (Contributed Technical Papers, *Stratosphere Series No. 2*). LXXI, p. 340, Mar., 1937; p. 802, June, 1937
See also Stratosphere

EXPLORERS. *See* Agricultural and Botanical Explorers; Discoverers, Explorers, and Navigators

EXPLORERS of a New Kind: Successful Introduction of Beetles and Parasites to Check Ravages of the Gipsy-moth and Brown-tail Moth. By L. O. Howard. XXVI, pp. 38-67, 11 ills. in black and white, 5 ills. in color, July, 1914

EXPLORING a Grass Wonderland of Wild West China. By Ray G. Johnson. LXXXV, pp. 713-742, 24 ills., map, June, 1944

EXPLORING Frozen Fragments of American History: On the Trail of Early Eskimo Colonists Who Made a 55-Mile Crossing from the Old World to the New. By Henry B. Collins, Jr. LXXV, pp. 633-656, 24 ills., map, May, 1939

EXPLORING in the Canyon of Death (Arizona): Remains of a People Who Dwelt in Our Southwest at Least 4,000 Years Ago Are Revealed. By Earl H. Morris. XLVIII, pp. 263-300, 24 ills. in black and white, 22 ills. in color, Sept., 1925

EXPLORING Neptune's Hidden World of Vivid Color. 8 ills. in color from paintings by E. Bostelmann. LXII, pp. 747-754, Dec., 1932

EXPLORING the Atlantic Seaboard with a Color Camera. 18 color photos by Charles Martin and Jacob Gayer. XLIX, pp. 533-548, May, 1926

EXPLORING the Earth's Stratosphere: The Holder of the American Altitude Record Describes His Experiences in Reaching the "Ceiling" of His Plane at an Elevation of Nearly Eight Miles. By First Lieutenant John A. Macready. L, pp. 755-776, 18 ills., Dec., 1926

EXPLORING the Glories of the Firmament. By William Joseph Showalter. XXXVI, pp. 153-181, 17 ills., diagr., 3 charts, Aug., 1919

EXPLORING the Ice Age in Antarctica. By Richard Evelyn Byrd. LXVIII, pp. 399-474, 72 ills., maps (1 two-page), Oct., 1935

EXPLORING the Mysteries of Plant Life. By William Joseph Showalter. XLV, pp. 581-646, 41 ills. in black and white, 47 ills. in color, June, 1924

EXPLORING the Secrets of Persepolis. By Charles Breasted. LXIV, pp. 381-420, 48 ills., plan, map, Oct., 1933

EXPLORING the Stratosphere. By Captain Albert W. Stevens. LXVI, pp. 397-434, 43 ills., chart, Oct., 1934

EXPLORING the Valley of the Amazon in a Hydroplane: Twelve Thousand Miles of Flying Over the World's Greatest River and Greatest Forest to Chart the Unknown Parima River from the Sky. By Captain Albert W. Stevens. XLIX, pp. 353-420, 86 ills., map, Apr., 1926

EXPLORING the Wonders of the Insect World. By William Joseph Showalter. Paintings by Hashime Murayama. LVI, pp. 1-90, 59 ills. in black and white, 269 ills. in color, July, 1929

EXPLORING Tibet. XII, pp. 403-404, Nov., 1901

EXPLORING Unknown Corners of the "Hermit Kingdom" (Korea). By Roy Chapman Andrews. XXXVI, pp. 25-48, 30 ills., map, July, 1919

EXPLORING Yukon's Glacial Stronghold. By Bradford Washburn. LXIX, pp. 715-748, 29 ills., two-page map, June, 1936

EXPLOSION:
The Aberration of Sound as Illustrated by the Berkeley Powder Explosion. By Robert H. Chapman. VII, pp. 246-249, 3 diagrs., July, 1896

EXPORTS AND IMPORTS. *See* Commerce; *and* name of product

EXPORTS of Manufactures. XVI, pp. 434-437, Sept., 1905

EXPOSITIONS:
An American Floating Exposition. XII, pp. 204-205, May, 1901
An Around-the-World American Exposition. By O. P. Austin. XII, pp. 49-53, chart, Feb., 1901
An Austro-Hungarian floating exposition. XII, p. 164, Apr., 1901
A City of Realized Dreams (San Francisco). By Franklin K. Lane. XXVII, pp. 169-171, Feb., 1915
The Philippine Exhibit at the Pan-American Exposition. By D. O. Noble Hoffmann. XII, pp. 119-122, Mar., 1901
Proceedings of the International Geographic Conference, held in conjunction with the World's Columbian Exposition, Chicago, May 1-October 30, 1893. V, pp. 97-256, Jan. 31, 1894
See also Ibero-American Exposition

EXTINCT Reptiles Found in Nodules. (By H. A. Largelamb). XVII, pp. 170-173, 9 ills., Mar., 1906

EYRE, EDWARD JOHN:
Edward John Eyre (Biography). XIII, p. 75, Feb., 1902

EYRE, LINCOLN:
Renascent Germany. By Lincoln Eyre. LIV, pp. 639-717, 59 ills. in black and white, 39 ills. in color, Dec., 1928

EZION-GEBER, Trans-Jordan:
On the Trail of King Solomon's Mines: The Bible, in Addition to Its Spiritual Values, Continues to Prove a Rich Geography and Guide to Exploration of the Holy Land. By Nelson Glueck. LXXXV, pp. 233-256, 20 ills., map, Feb., 1944

F

FABULOUS Yellowstone: Even Stranger Than the Tales of Early Trappers is the Truth About This Steaming Wonderland. By Frederick G. Vosburgh. LXXVII, pp. 769-794, 15 ills. in black and white, 9 ills. in color, map, June, 1940

FACE of Japan. By W. Robert Moore. LXXXVIII, pp. 753-768, 14 ills., map supplement, Dec., 1945

The **FACE** of the Netherlands Indies. 20 photos by Maynard Owen Williams and others. LXXXIX, pp. 261-276, Feb., 1946

FACES, Stone (Monuments). *See* Stone Faces

FACES and Fashions of Asia's Changeless Tribes. 26 ills. in color from paintings and drawings by Alexandre Iacovleff. LXIX, pp. 21-36, Jan., 1936

FACES and Flowers Below the Tropics (Union of South Africa). 14 color photos by Melville Chater. LIX, pp. 453-460, Apr., 1931

FACING War's Challenge "Down Under" (Australia and New Zealand). 20 color photos by Howell Walker. LXXXI, pp. 425-456, Apr., 1942

FACTORS Which Modify the Climate of Victoria (British Columbia). By Arthur W. McCurdy. XVIII, pp. 345-348, maps, May, 1907

FACTS about the Philippines. By Frederick Simpich. LXXXI, pp. 185-202, 17 ills., map, Feb., 1942

FAEROE ISLANDS, North Atlantic Ocean:

Viking Life in the Storm-Cursed Faeroes. By Leo Hansen. LVIII, pp. 607-648, 49 ills., map, Nov., 1930

FAIRBANKS, CHARLES W.:

Honors for Amundsen (Address by Charles W. Fairbanks). XIX, pp. 55-76, 13 ills., Jan., 1908

Honors to the American Navy (Address by Charles W. Fairbanks). XX, pp. 77-95, Jan., 1909

FAIRCHILD, DAVID:

A Book of Monsters (Insects). By David and Marian Fairchild. XXVI, pp. 89-98, 7 ills., July, 1914

Note: Announcement and summary of NGS publication, *A Book of Monsters,* p. 89

Forming New Fashions in Food: The Bearing of Taste on One of Our Great Food Economies, the Dried Vegetable, Which Is Developing Into a Big War Industry. By David Fairchild. XXXIII, pp. 356-368, 11 ills., Apr., 1918

A Hunter of Plants. By David Fairchild. XXXVI, pp. 57-77, 18 ills., July, 1919

Hunting for Plants in the Canary Islands. By David Fairchild. LVII, pp. 607-652, 37 ills. in black and white, 39 ills. in color, map, May, 1930

Hunting Useful Plants in the Caribbean. By David Fairchild. LXVI, pp. 705-737, 39 ills., Dec., 1934

The Jungles of Panama. By David Fairchild. XLI, pp. 131-145, 14 ills., Feb., 1922

FAIRCHILD, DAVID—*Continued*

Madeira, on the Way to Italy. By David Fairchild. XVIII, pp. 751-771, 18 ills., Dec., 1907

The Monsters of Our Back Yards. By David Fairchild. XXIV, pp. 575-626, 38 ills., May, 1913

New Plant Immigrants. By David Fairchild. XXII, pp. 879-907, 34 ills., Oct., 1911

Our Plant Immigrants. By David Fairchild. XVII, pp. 179-201, 29 ills., Apr., 1906

Sumatra's West Coast. By David G. Fairchild. IX, pp. 449-464, 8 ills., Nov., 1898

Travels in Arabia and Along the Persian Gulf. By David G. Fairchild. XV, pp. 139-151, 20 ills., Apr., 1904

FAIRCHILD, GRAHAM:

Life Story of the Mosquito. By Graham Fairchild. With 10 ills. in color from paintings. LXXXV, pp. 180-195, 5 ills. in black and white, drawing, Feb., 1944

FAIRCHILD, MARIAN:

A Book of Monsters (Insects). By David and Marian Fairchild. XXVI, pp. 89-98, 7 ills., July, 1914

Note: Announcement and summary of NGS publication, *A Book of Monsters,* p. 89

FAIRS:

England's Wild Moorland Ponies. 10 ills. LXXXIX, pp. 129-136, Jan., 1946

Peiping's Happy New Year: Lunar Celebration Attracts Throngs to Temple Fairs, Motley Bazaars, and Age-old Festivities. By George Kin Leung. LXX, pp. 749-792, 31 ills. in black and white, 16 ills. in color, Dec., 1936

FAIRY TERNS of the Atolls. By Lewis Wayne Walker. XC, pp. 807-814, 9 ills., Dec., 1946

FAIRY WRENS:

The Fairy Wrens of Australia: The Little Long-tailed "Blue Birds of Happiness" Rank High Among the Island Continent's Remarkable Birds. By Neville W. Cayley. With 8 ills. in color from paintings by author. LXXXVIII, pp. 488-498, ill. in black and white, Oct., 1945

FALCON ISLAND, Tonga Islands:

Falcon, the Pacific's Newest Island. By J. Edward Hoffmeister and Harry S. Ladd. LIV, pp. 757-766, 8 ills., map, Dec., 1928

FALCONRY:

Adventures with Birds of Prey. By Frank and John Craighead. LXXII, pp. 109-134, 25 ills., July, 1937

The Eagle, King of Birds, and His Kin. By Alexander Wetmore. Paintings by Maj. Allan Brooks. LXIV, pp. 43-95, 23 ills. in black and white, 28 ills. in color, July, 1933

Falconry, the Sport of Kings. By Louis Agassiz Fuertes. Paintings by author. XXXVIII, pp. 429-460, 13 ills. in black and white, 12 ills. in color, Dec., 1920

Life with an Indian Prince: As Guests of a Maharaja's Brother, Two Young American Naturalists Study Age-old Methods of Hunting with Trained Falcons and Cheetahs and Savor the Pomp of Royal India. By John and Frank Craighead. LXXXI, pp. 235-272, 38 ills., map, Feb., 1942

FALCONS:

American Birds of Prey—A Review of Their Value. XXXVIII, pp. 460-467, 6 ills., Dec., 1920

Eagles, Hawks, and Vultures. 28 ills. in color from paintings by Maj. Allan Brooks. LXIV, pp. 65-94, July, 1933

Falconry, the Sport of Kings. By Louis Agassiz Fuertes. Paintings by author. XXXVIII, pp. 429-460, 13 ills. in black and white, 12 ills. in color, Dec., 1920

In Quest of the Golden Eagle: Over Lonely Mountain and Prairie Soars This Rare and Lordly Bird, But Three Youths from the East Catch Up With Him at Last. By John and Frank Craighead. LXXVII, pp. 693-710, 17 ills., May, 1940

Life With an Indian Prince: As Guests of a Maharaja's Brother, Two Young American Naturalists Study Age-old Methods of Hunting with Trained Falcons and Cheetahs and Savor the Pomp of Royal India. By John and Frank Craighead. LXXXI, pp. 235-272, 38 ills., map, Feb., 1942

Week-Ends with the Prairie Falcon: A Commuter Finds Recreation in Scaling Cliffs to Observe the Nest Life and Flying Habits of These Elusive Birds. By Frederick Hall Fowler. LXVII, pp. 611-626, 21 ills., May, 1935

FALCONS. 12 ills. in color from paintings by Louis Agassiz Fuertes. XXXVIII, pp. 441-456, Dec., 1920

FALLING MOUNTAIN, Alaska:

The Valley of Ten Thousand Smokes: An Account of the Discovery and Exploration of the Most Wonderful Volcanic Region in the World. By Robert F. Griggs. XXXIII, pp. 115-169, 46 ills., map, panorama, Feb., 1918

FALLS, DE WITT CLINTON:

Saint Stephen's Fete in Budapest. By De Witt Clinton Falls. XVIII, pp. 548-558, 9 ills., Aug., 1907

FALLS. *See* Waterfalls

The **FALLS** of Iguazu. By Marie Robinson Wright. XVII, pp. 456-460, 4 ills., Aug., 1906

FALTBOATS:

Entering the Front Doors of Medieval Towns: The Adventures of an American Woman and Her Daughter in a Folding Boat on Eight Rivers of Germany and Austria. By Cornelia Stratton Parker. LXI, pp. 365-394, 23 ills., map, Mar., 1932

FAME'S Eternal Camping Ground: Beautiful Arlington (Virginia), Burial Place of America's Illustrious Dead. By Enoch A. Chase. LIV, pp. 621-638, 19 ills., Nov., 1928

FAMILIAR Grasses and Their Flowers. By E. J. Geske and W. J. Showalter. Paintings by E. J. Geske. XXXIX, pp. 625-636, 8 ills. in color, June, 1921

FAMILY Afoot in Yukon Wilds: Two Young Children and Their Parents Live Off the Country in the Northwest Canada Wilderness Now To Be Traversed by the Alaska Highway. By William Hamilton Albee, with Ruth Albee. LXXXI, pp. 589-616, 18 ills. in black and white, 14 ills. in color, May, 1942

The **FAMILY** Tree of the Flowers. By Frederic E. Clements and William Joseph Showalter. LI, pp. 555-563, ill. in black and white, ill. in color, May, 1927

FAMINES:

Fearful Famines of the Past: History Will Repeat Itself Unless the American People Conserve Their Resources. By Ralph A. Graves. XXXII, pp. 69-90, 11 ills., July, 1917

Forerunners of Famine. By Frederic C. Walcott. XXXIII, pp. 336-347, 4 ills., 4 diagrs., map, Apr., 1918

The Land of the Stalking Death: A Journey Through Starving Armenia on an American Relief Train. By Melville Chater. XXXVI, pp. 393-420, 23 ills., Nov., 1919

The **FAMOUS** Waldseemüller map of 1507. XV, p. 50, Jan., 1904

FANE, G. E.:

Burma Road, Back Door to China: Like the Great Wall of Ancient Times, This Mighty Mountain Highway Has Been Built by Myriad Chinese to Help Defend Their Homeland. By Frank Outram and G. E. Fane. LXXVIII, pp. 629-658, 26 ills., map, Nov., 1940

FANTASTIC Dwellers in a Coral Fairyland (Great Barrier Reef). 15 color photos by T. C. Roughley. LXXVII, pp. 831-838, June, 1940

FANTASTIC Plants of Our Western Deserts. 8 ills. by Frank M. Campbell. XLV, pp. 33-40, Jan., 1924

FANTASTIC Sea Life From Abyssal Depths. 8 ills. in color from paintings by E. Bostelmann. LXI, pp. 71-78, Jan., 1932

FANTIS (People):

The Gold Coast, Ashanti, and Kumassi. By George K. French. VIII, pp. 1-15, 9 ills., Jan., 1897

FAR EAST:

Indian Ocean Map Spans Far East News Centers. Text with map supplement. LXXIX, pp. 345-346, ill., Mar., 1941

See also Borneo; British Malaya; Celebes; China; Formosa; French Indo-China; Hong Kong; Japan; Java; Korea; Manchuria; Moluccas; New Guinea; Philippine Islands; Singapore; Sumatra; Thailand; Timor

The **FAR** Eastern Republic (U. S. S. R.). By Junius B. Wood. XLI, pp. 565-592, 29 ills., map, June, 1922

FAR-FLYING Wild Fowl and Their Foes. By Major Allan Brooks. With paintings from life by author. LXVI, pp. 487-528, 6 ills. in black and white, 93 portraits in color, Oct., 1934

FAREWELL to Bikini. By Carl Markwith. XC, pp. 97-116, 16 ills., July, 1946

FARMERS' Friends Among the Wasps and Hornets. 12 ills. in color from paintings by Hashime Murayama. LXXII, pp. 57-64, July, 1937

FARMERS Keep Them Eating. By Frederick Simpich. LXXXIII, pp. 435-458, 22 ills., Apr., 1943

The **FARMERS** of the United States. XVI, pp. 39-46, Jan., 1905

FARMERS Since the Days of Noah: China's Remarkable System of Agriculture Has Kept Alive the Densest Population in the World. By Adam Warwick. LI, pp. 469-500, 37 ills., Apr., 1927

FARMING. *See* Agriculture

FARMING on the Isthmus of Panama. By Dillwyn M. Hazlett. XVII, pp. 229-234, 5 ills., Apr., 1906

FARMS. *See* Ernst Thaelmann (Collective Farm); Gan Shemuel; Högakull

FARMS and Workshops of "The Garden State" (New Jersey). 13 color photos by Edwin L. Wisherd. LXIII, pp. 559-566, May, 1933

FAROE ISLANDS. *See* Faeroe Islands

FARQUHAR, HENRY:

Calculations of Population in June, 1900. By Henry Farquhar. X, pp. 406-413, Oct., 1899

FARTHEST North (Peary). XVII, pp. 638-644, 9 ills., Nov., 1906

The **FARTHEST-NORTH** Republic: Olympic Games and Arctic Flying Bring Sequestered Finland into New Focus of World Attention. By Alma Luise Olson. LXXIV, pp. 499-533, 25 ills. in black and white, 12 ills. in color, map, Oct., 1938

FATE Directs the Faltering Footsteps of Columbus. Reproduction in color of the painting by Alfred Dehodencq, Paris. LIV, supplement, Sept., 1928

FATU-HIVA (Island), Marquesas Islands:

Turning Back Time in the South Seas. By Thor Heyerdahl. LXXIX, pp. 109-136, 33 ills., maps, Jan., 1941

FAY, CHARLES E.:

The World's Highest Altitudes and First Ascents. By Charles E. Fay. XX, pp. 493-530, 25 ills., June, 1909

FAYETTEVILLE, Arkansas:

Arkansas Rolls Up Its Sleeves. By Frederick Simpich. XC, pp. 273-312, 16 ills. in black and white, 23 ills. in color, map, Sept., 1946

FEARFUL Famines of the Past: History Will Repeat Itself Unless the American People Conserve Their Resources. By Ralph A. Graves. XXXII, pp. 69-90, 11 ills., July, 1917

FEATHERED Foragers of Swamp and Shore. 101 portraits from paintings by Major Allan Brooks. LXXII, pp. 191-222, Aug., 1937

FEBIGER, LEA:

The Coronation of His Majesty King Maha-Vajiravudh of Siam. By Colonel Lea Febiger. XXIII, pp. 389-416, 25 ills., Apr., 1912

FEDERAL Fish Farming; or, Planting Fish by the Billion. By Hugh M. Smith. XXI, pp. 418-446, 22 ills., May, 1910

FEE, WILLIAM THOMAS:

The Parsees and the Towers of Silence at Bombay, India. By William Thomas Fee. XVI, pp. 529-554, 16 ills., Dec., 1905

FEENEY, CORINNE B.:

Arch-Isolationists, the San Blas Indians: Coconuts Serve as Cash on Islands Off the Panama Coast Where Tribesmen Cling to Their Ancient Ways and Discourage Visitors. By Corinne B. Feeney. LXXIX, pp. 193-220, 15 ills. in black and white, 12 ills. in color, map, Feb., 1941

FEN DISTRICT, England:

A Tour in the English Fenland. By Christopher Marlowe. LV, pp. 605-634, 26 ills. in black and white, 5 ills. in color, map, May, 1929

FERGUSON, ALBERT F.:

Report of the Annual Dinner of the National Geographic Society. By Albert F. Ferguson. XVII, pp. 22-23, Jan., 1906

FERNALD, M. L.:

The Unique Island of Mount Desert. By George B. Dorr, Ernest Howe Forbush, M. L. Fernald. XXVI, pp. 75-89, 7 ills., July, 1914

FERNOW, BERNHARD E.:

The Battle of the Forest. By B. E. Fernow. VI, pp. 127-148, 5 ills., map, June 22, 1894

The Forests and Deserts of Arizona. By Bernhard E. Fernow. VIII, pp. 203-226, 5 ills., July-Aug., 1897

FERNS:

Ferns as a Hobby. By William R. Maxon. Paintings by E. J. Geske. XLVII, pp. 541-586, 29 ills. in black and white, 16 ills. in color, May, 1925

Contents: Adder's-Tongue, Bracken, Bulblet Bladder, Christmas, Climbing, Common Wood, Dwarf Spleenwort, Eastern Lady, Interrupted, Maidenhair, Marginal, Marsh, Rattlesnake, Royal, Sensitive, Walking

FERNSWORTH, LAWRENCE A.:

Andorra—Mountain Museum of Feudal Europe. By Lawrence A. Fernsworth. LXIV, pp. 493-512, 21 ills., map, Oct., 1933

FERRARA, Italy:

Inexhaustible Italy. By Arthur Stanley Riggs. XXX, pp. 273-368, 76 ills., map, Oct., 1916

The **FERTILE** Pampas of Argentine. XVII, pp. 453-456, Aug., 1906

FERTILIZERS:

American Potash for America. By Guy Elliott Mitchell. XXII, pp. 399-405, 4 ills., Apr., 1911

Farmers Since the Days of Noah: China's Remarkable System of Agriculture Has Kept Alive the Densest Population in the World. By Adam Warwick. LI, pp. 469-500, 37 ills., Apr., 1927

Inoculating the Ground. XV, pp. 225-228, ills., May, 1904

The Most Valuable Bird in the World (Guanay). By Robert Cushman Murphy. XLVI, pp. 279-302, 25 ills., map, Sept., 1924

Our Greatest Plant Food (Phosphorus). By Guy Elliott Mitchell. XXI, pp. 783-791, 7 ills., diagr., Sept., 1910

FERTILIZERS—*Continued*

Peru's Wealth-Producing Birds: Vast Riches in the Guano Deposits of Cormorants, Pelicans, and Petrels which Nest on Her Barren, Rainless Coast. By R. E. Coker. XXXVII, pp. 537-566, 28 ills., June, 1920

FESTIVALS:

August First in Gruyères. By Melville Bell Grosvenor. LXX, pp. 137-168, 12 ills. in black and white, 23 ills. in color, Aug., 1936

Azores: Picturesque and Historic Half-way House of American Transatlantic Aviators. By Arminius T. Haeberle. XXXV, pp. 514-545, 26 ills., map, June, 1919

Bolivia, Land of Fiestas. By Alicia O'Reardon Overbeck. LXVI, pp. 645-660, 16 ills., map, Nov., 1934

Carnival Days on the Riviera. By Maynard Owen Williams. L, pp. 467-501, 21 ills., Oct., 1926

The Coronation of His Majesty King Maha-Vajiravudh of Siam. By Colonel Lea Febiger. XXIII, pp. 389-416, 25 ills., Apr., 1912

Costume Pageants in the French Pyrenees. 24 color photos by W. Robert Moore. LXXII, pp. 435-450, Oct., 1937

Czechoslovakia, Key-Land to Central Europe. By Maynard Owen Williams. XXXIX, pp. 111-156, 45 ills., map, Feb., 1921

Empire State Onions and Pageantry (New York). 12 color photos by J. Baylor Roberts and Volkmar Wentzel. LXXX, pp. 641-648, Nov., 1941

Festival Days on the Slopes of Mount Parnassus (Greece). 14 color photos by Maynard Owen Williams. LVIII, pp. 713-720, Dec., 1930

The Fire-Walking Hindus of Singapore. By L. Elizabeth Lewis. LIX, pp. 513-522, 12 ills., Apr., 1931

Great Britain on Parade. By Maynard Owen Williams. LXVIII, pp. 137-184, 40 ills. in black and white, 11 ills. in color, Aug., 1935

India at Work and Play. 22 color photos by Peter Upton Muir, Maynard Owen Williams, Frances Muir. LXXXIX, pp. 449-464, Apr., 1946

Life Among the Lamas of Choni: Describing the Mystery Plays and Butter Festival in the Monastery of an Almost Unknown Tibetan Principality in Kansu Province, China. By Joseph F. Rock. LIV, pp. 569-619, 34 ills. in black and white, 16 ills. in color, map, Nov., 1928

The Maid of France Rides By: Compiègne, Where Joan of Arc Fought Her Last Battle, Celebrates Her Fifth Centenary. By Inez Buffington Ryan. LXII, pp. 607-616, 15 ills. in color, Nov., 1932

The Marriage of the Gods (Madura, India). By John J. Banninga. XXIV, pp. 1314-1330, 16 ills., Dec., 1913

Medieval Pageantry in Modern Nördlingen (Germany). 12 color photos by Hans Hildenbrand. LIV, pp. 707-714, Dec., 1928

Merry Maskers of Imst (Austria). 14 photos by Francis C. Fuerst. LXX, pp. 201-208, Aug., 1936

FESTIVALS—*Continued*

The Mexican Indian Flying Pole Dance. By Helga Larsen. LXXI, pp. 387-400, 13 ills., Mar., 1937

North Carolina Colorcade. 21 color photos: 19 by J. Baylor Roberts. LXXX, pp. 189-220, Aug., 1941

Peiping's Happy New Year: Lunar Celebration Attracts Throngs to Temple Fairs, Motley Bazaars, and Age-old Festivities. By George Kin Leung. LXX, pp. 749-792, 31 ills. in black and white, 16 ills. in color, Dec., 1936

The Perahera Processions of Ceylon. By G. H. G. Burroughs. LXII, pp. 90-100, ill. in black and white, 8 ills. in duotone, July, 1932

Religious Penances and Punishments Self-Inflicted by the Holy Men of India. By W. M. Zumbro. XXIV, pp. 1257-1314, 69 ills., Dec., 1913

Rothenburg, the City Time Forgot. By Charles W. Beck, Jr. XLIX, pp. 184-194, 8 ills. in color, Feb., 1926

Saint Stephen's Fete in Budapest. By De Witt Clinton Falls. XVIII, pp. 548-558, 9 ills., Aug., 1907

Siena's Palio, an Italian Inheritance from the Middle Ages. By Marie Louise Handley. L, pp. 245-258, 3 ills., Aug., 1926

Some Aspects of Rural Japan. By Walter Weston. XLII, pp. 275-301, 12 ills. in black and white, 16 ills. in color, Sept., 1922

Sungmas, the Living Oracles of the Tibetan Church. By Joseph F. Rock. LXVIII, pp. 475-486, ill. in black and white, 12 ills. in color, Oct., 1935

When Czechoslovakia Puts a Falcon Feather in Its Cap. By Maynard Owen Williams. LXIII, pp. 40-49, 13 ills. in color, Jan., 1933

With the Devil Dancers of China and Tibet. 43 color photos by Joseph F. Rock. LX, pp. 19-58, July, 1931

See also Carnivals

The **FEUDAL** Isle of Sark: Where Sixteenth-Century Laws Are Still Observed. By Sibyl Hathaway (La Dame de Serk). LXII, pp. 101-119, 21 ills., map, July, 1932

FEVERS. *See* Malaria; Spotted Fever; Typhoid Fever; Yellow Fever

A **FEW** Glimpses into Russia. By Lieut. Zinovi Pechkoff. XXXII, pp. 238-253, 10 ills., Sept., 1917

A **FEW** Thoughts Concerning Eugenics. By Alexander Graham Bell. XIX, pp. 119-123, Feb., 1908

FEZ, Morocco:

Fez, Heart of Morocco: Africa's "Imperial City" Retains Its Teeming Streets, Cluttered Shops, Glamorous Moorish Homes and Mosques, Amid the Peace of French Rule. By Gordon Casserly. LXVII, pp. 663-694, 13 ills. in black and white, 27 ills. in color, June, 1935

Journey in Morocco: "The Land of the Moors." By Thomas Lindsey Blayney. XXII, pp. 750-775, 23 ills., map, Aug., 1911

FIALA, ANTHONY:

The Annual Dinner of the National Geographic Society (Speech by Anthony Fiala). XVII, pp. 22-37, Jan., 1906

The Lure of the Frozen Desert. Photo by Anthony Fiala. XXIII, panorama, Dec., 1912

Polar Photography. By Anthony Fiala. XVIII, pp. 140-142, Feb., 1907

The Ziegler Polar Expedition (Report by Anthony Fiala). XIV, pp. 414-417, 5 ills., Nov., 1903

FIELD Courses in Geology. XVI, p. 250, May, 1905

FIELD DOGS:

Field Dogs in Action. By Freeman Lloyd. Paintings by Edward Herbert Miner. LXXI, pp. 85-108, 8 ills. in black and white, 36 portraits in color, Jan., 1937

Contents: Chesapeake Bay Retriever, Clumber Spaniel, Cocker Spaniel, Curly-coated Retriever, Dachshund, English Setter, English Springer Spaniel, Field Spaniel, Flat-coated Retriever, German Short-haired Pointer, Golden Retriever, Gordon Setter, Irish Red Setter, Irish Water Spaniel, Labrador Retriever, Pointer, Sussex Spaniel, Wire-haired Pointing Griffon

FIELD MEETINGS. *See* NGS: Excursions and Field Meetings

FIELD Sports Among the Wild Men of Northern Luzon. By Dean C. Worcester. XXII, pp. 215-267, 52 ills., map, Mar., 1911

FIELDWORK of the United States Geological Survey for the Season 1902. XIII, pp. 322-325, Aug., 1902

15TH-CENTURY Vignettes of Compiègne (France). 15 color photos by Gervais Courtellemont. LXII, pp. 609-616, Nov., 1932

FIFTY Common Birds of Farm and Orchard. By Henry Wetherbee Henshaw. Paintings by Louis Agassiz Fuertes. XXIV, pp. 669-697, 50 ills. in color, June, 1913

The **FIGHT** Against Forest Fires. By Henry S. Graves. XXIII, pp. 662-683, 19 ills., July, 1912

The **FIGHT** at the Timber-Line. By John Oliver La Gorce. XLII, pp. 165-196, 32 ills., Aug., 1922

FIGHT the Flies. XXI, pp. 383-385, 452, 3 ills., May, 1910

FIGHTING Giants of the Humboldt (Fish and Squid). By David D. Duncan. LXXIX, pp. 373-400, 28 ills., map, Mar., 1941

FIGHTING Insects with Airplanes: An Account of the Successful Use of the Flying-Machine in Dusting Tall Trees Infested with Leaf-Eating Caterpillars. By C. R. Neillie and J. S. Houser. XLI, pp. 333-338, 6 ills., Mar., 1922

FIGHTING the Polar Ice (Book Review). XVIII, pp. 72-77, 7 ills., Jan., 1907

FIJI ISLANDS, South Pacific Ocean:

American Pathfinders in the Pacific. By William H. Nicholas. LXXXIX, pp. 617-640, 17 ills., two-page map, May, 1946

FIJI ISLANDS, South Pacific Ocean—*Continued*

The British Commonwealth of Nations: "Organized Freedom" Around the World. By Eric Underwood. LXXXIII, pp. 485-524, 31 ills., Apr., 1943

In the Savage South Seas. By Beatrice Grimshaw. XIX, pp. 1-19, 21 ills., Jan., 1908

Net Results from Oceania: Collecting Aquarium Specimens in Tropical Pacific Waters. By Walter H. Chute. LXXIX, pp. 347-372, 8 ills. in black and white, 24 ills. in color, Mar., 1941

Treasure Islands of Australasia: New Guinea, New Caledonia, and Fiji Trace across the South Pacific a Fertile Crescent Incredibly Rich in Minerals and Foods. By Douglas L. Oliver. LXXXI, pp. 691-722, 23 ills., two-page map, June, 1942

FIJI Patrol on Bougainville. By David D. Duncan. LXXXVII, pp. 87-104, 9 ills. in black and white, 11 ills. in color, Jan., 1945

FIJIANS:

Fiji Patrol on Bougainville. By David D. Duncan. LXXXVII, pp. 87-104, 9 ills. in black and white, 11 ills. in color, Jan., 1945

See also Fiji Islands

FINANCIAL STATISTICS:

Commercial and Financial Statistics of the Principal Countries of the World. XVIII, pp. 420-423, June, 1907

FINCHES (Birds):

Canaries and Otner Cage-Bird Friends. By Alexander Wetmore. Paintings by Major Allan Brooks. LXXIV, pp. 775-806, 19 ills. in black and white, 51 portraits in color, Dec., 1938

The Tanagers and Finches: Their Flashes of Color and Lilting Songs Gladden the Hearts of American Bird Lovers East and West. By Arthur A. Allen. Paintings by Maj. Allan Brooks. LXVII, pp. 505-532, 6 ills. in black and white, 55 portraits in color, Apr., 1935

FINDING Jewels of Jade in a Mexican Swamp (La Venta). By Matthew W. and Marion Stirling. LXXXII, pp. 635-661, 15 ills. in black and white, 12 ills. in color, map, Nov., 1942

FINGER LAKES REGION, New York:

Fruitful Shores of the Finger Lakes. By Harrison Howell Walker. LXXIX, pp. 559-594, 15 ills. in black and white, 22 ills. in color, map, May, 1941

FINLAND:

The Farthest-North Republic: Olympic Games and Arctic Flying Bring Sequestered Finland into New Focus of World Attention. By Alma Luise Olson. LXXIV, pp. 499-533, 25 ills. in black and white, 12 ills. in color, map, Oct., 1938

Flashes from Finland. 19 ills. LXXVII, pp. 239-254, Feb., 1940

Flying Around the Baltic. By Douglas Chandler. LXXIII, pp. 767-806, 31 ills. in black and white, 13 ills. in duotone, map, June, 1938

FINLAND—*Continued*

The New Map of Europe: Showing the Boundaries Established by the Peace Conference at Paris and by Subsequent Decisions of the Supreme Council of the Allied and Associated Powers. By Ralph A. Graves. Text with map supplement. XXXIX, pp. 157-177, 18 ills., Feb., 1921

Notes on Finland. (By Baroness Alletta Korff). XXI, pp. 493-494, June, 1910

The Races of Europe. By Edwin A. Grosvenor. XXXIV, pp. 441-534, 62 ills., diagr. and index, maps, map supplement, Dec., 1918

Where Women Vote. By Baroness Alletta Korff. XXI, pp. 487-493, June, 1910

See also Aland (Islands); Helsinki

FINLAND: Land of Sky-Blue Lakes. 12 color photos by Konstantin J. Kostich. LXXIV, pp. 515-522, Oct., 1938

FINLEY, IRENE:

Successful Shots With a Friendly Camera. 16 photos by H. T. Bohlman, Irene Finley, William L. Finley. XLIV, pp. 165-180, Aug., 1923

FINLEY, JOHN H.:

The Red Cross Spirit Speaks (Poem). By John H. Finley. XXXI, p. 474, May, 1917

FINLEY, WILLIAM L.:

Hunting Birds With a Camera: A Record of Twenty Years of Adventure in Obtaining Photographs of Feathered Wild Life in America. By William L. Finley. XLIV, pp. 161-201, 37 ills., Aug., 1923

Successful Shots With a Friendly Camera. 16 photos by author, H. T. Bohlman, Irene Finley. pp. 165-180

The **FIRE-WALKING** Hindus of Singapore. By L. Elizabeth Lewis. LIX, pp. 513-522, 12 ills., Apr., 1931

FIRST AIR COMMANDO FORCE, U. S.:

The Aerial Invasion of Burma. By General H. H. Arnold. LXXXVI, pp. 129-148, 20 ills., Aug., 1944

The **FIRST** Airship Flight Around the World: Dr. Hugo Eckener Tells of an Epochal Geographic Achievement upon the Occasion of the Bestowal of the National Geographic Society's Special Gold Medal. LVII, pp. 653-688, 37 ills., June, 1930

The **FIRST** Alaskan Air Expedition. By Captain St. Clair Streett. XLI, pp. 499-552, 37 ills., map, May, 1922

The **FIRST** American Census of Porto Rico. XI, p. 328, Aug., 1900

The **FIRST** Autochromes from the Ocean Bottom: Marine Life in Its Natural Habitat Along the Florida Keys Is Successfully Photographed in Colors. (Photographs by Dr. W. H. Longley and Charles Martin). LI, pp. 56-60, 8 ills. in color, Jan., 1927

1ST BATTALION, Fiji Infantry Regiment:

Fiji Patrol on Bougainville. By David D. Duncan. LXXXVII, pp. 87-104, 9 ills. in black and white, 11 ills. in color, Jan., 1945

FIRST Expedition of National Geographic Society. *See* NGS: Expeditions: Alaska: Mount St. Elias

FIRST Families of Southeastern America (Indians). 8 ills. in color from paintings by W. Langdon Kihn. LXXXIX, pp. 65-72, Jan., 1946

The **FIRST** Flight to the North Pole. By Lieutenant Commander Richard Evelyn Byrd. L, pp. 357-376, 14 ills., Sept., 1926

FIRST in Statehood, Delaware Retains Its Graciousness. 15 color photos by B. Anthony Stewart. LXVIII, pp. 377-384, Sept., 1935

FIRST Journey Across Alaska. XV, p. 267, June, 1904

The **FIRST** Landfall of Columbus. By Jacques W. Redway, F. R. G. S. VI, pp. 179-192, 4 maps, Dec. 29, 1894

The **FIRST** Meeting of the Poles (Photograph of the first meeting of Robert E. Peary, discoverer of the North Pole, and Roald Amundsen, discoverer of the South Pole, at the National Geographic Society, January 11, 1913). XXIV, ill. p. 114, Jan., 1913. LXIX, ill. p. 126, Jan., 1936

FIRST National Park East of Mississippi River (Mount Desert Island, Maine). XXIX, pp. 623-626, 5 ills., June, 1916

The **FIRST** Natural-Color Photographs from the Arctic. 22 color photos by Jacob Gayer and Maynard Owen Williams. XLIX, pp. 301-316, Mar., 1926

FIRST Over the Roof of the World by Motor: The Trans-Asiatic Expedition Sets New Records for Wheeled Transport in Scaling Passes of the Himalayas. By Maynard Owen Williams. LXI, pp. 321-363, 45 ills., maps, Mar., 1932

The **FIRST** Photograph Ever Made Showing the Division Between the Troposphere and the Stratosphere and also the Actual Curvature of the Earth—Photographed from an Elevation of 72,395 Feet, the Highest Point Ever Reached by Man. Aërial photo by Captain Albert W. Stevens. LXIX, supplement, May, 1936

The **FIRST** Transandine Railroad from Buenos Aires to Valparaiso. By Harriet Chalmers Adams. XXI, pp. 397-417, 14 ills., diagr., map, May, 1910

"FIRSTS," NGS, in Photography. *See* NGM: Photographs

FISCHER, HELENE:

Life and Death in Toradjaland. 22 photos: 8 by Helene Fischer. LXXVIII, pp. 65-80, July, 1940

A Mexican Land of Lakes and Lacquers (Pátzcuaro Region). 22 photos by Helene Fischer and Luis Marquez. LXXI, pp. 633-648, May, 1937

FISCHER, JOHN:

India's Treasures Helped the Allies. By John Fischer. LXXXIX, pp. 501-522, 18 ills., Apr., 1946

FISH HAWKS. *See* Ospreys

FISHER, CLYDE:

The Nomads of Arctic Lapland: Mysterious Little People of a Land of the Midnight Sun Live Off the Country Above the Arctic Circle. By Clyde Fisher. LXXVI, pp. 641-676, 28 ills. in black and white, 12 ills. in color, map, Nov., 1939

FISHER, FRANKLIN L.:

Insect Rivals of the Rainbow. (Text by Franklin L. Fisher). LVI, pp. 28-90, July, 1929

The Palace of Versailles, Its Park and the Trianons. By Franklin L. Fisher. XLVII, pp. 49-62, 4 ills. in black and white, 14 ills. in color, Jan., 1925

FISHER, WALTER L.:

Honors to Amundsen and Peary (Speech by Walter L. Fisher). XXIV, pp. 113-130, 5 ills., Jan., 1913

FISHES AND FISHERIES:

America's Most Valuable Fishes. By Hugh M. Smith. XXIII, pp. 494-514, 17 ills., May, 1912
Contents: Blueback Salmon, Chinook Salmon, Dog Salmon, Humpback Salmon, Silver Salmon

America's Surpassing Fisheries: Their Present Condition and Future Prospects, and How the Federal Government Fosters Them. By Hugh M. Smith. XXIX, pp. 546-583, 35 ills., June, 1916

Between the Heather and the North Sea: Bold English Headlands Once Sheltered Sea Robbers, Later Were Ports of Wooden Ships, Centers of the Jet and Alum Trades, To-day Are Havens of Adventurous Fishing Fleets. By Leo Walmsley. LXIII, pp. 197-232, 41 ills., Feb., 1933

Bornholm—Denmark in a Nutshell. By Mason Sutherland. LXXXVII, pp. 239-256, 20 ills., map, Feb., 1945
Included: The "Bornholmer" (Herring)

Brittany: The Land of the Sardine. By Hugh M. Smith. XX, pp. 541-573, 23 ills., June, 1909

The Bureau of Fisheries. By Dr. Barton Warren Evermann. XV, pp. 191-212, 11 ills., 3 diagrs., May, 1904

Caviar Fishermen of Romania: From Vâlcov, "Little Venice" of the Danube Delta, Bearded Russian Exiles Go Down to the Sea. By Dorothy Hosmer. LXXVII, pp. 407-434, 29 ills., map, Mar., 1940

Certain Citizens of the Warm Sea. By Louis L. Mowbray. Paintings by Hashime Murayama. XLI, pp. 27-62, 18 ills. in black and white, 16 ills. in color, Jan., 1922
Contents: Allison's Tuna, Amber Jack, Barracuda, Black Grouper, Bone-Fish, Crawfish, Dolphin, Gag, Green Turtle, Hawksbill Turtle, Kingfish, Margate Fish, Marlin, Moon Fish, Mutton Fish, Nassau Grouper, Red Grouper, Sailfish, Spanish Mackerel, Tarpon, Yellow Jack

Coffee Is King in El Salvador. By Luis Marden. LXXXVI, pp. 575-616, 22 ills. in black and white, 27 ills. in color, map, Nov., 1944
Included: The four-eyed fish, *Anableps dowei*

"Compleat Angler" Fishes for Fossils. By Imogene Powell. LXVI, pp. 251-258, 7 ills., Aug., 1934

FISHES AND FISHERIES—*Continued*

Cruise of the *Kinkajou:* Among Desert Islands of Mexico Voyagers Find Outdoor Laboratories for the Naturalist and Ideal Fishing Grounds for the Sportsman (Fishing for Marlin and Wahoo). By Alfred M. Bailey. LXXX, pp. 339-366, 13 ills. in black and white, 12 ills. in color, map, Sept., 1941

Cultivation of Marine and Fresh-Water Animals in Japan. By K. Mitsukuri. XVII, pp. 524-531, 5 ills., Sept., 1906
Included: Goldfish

The Depths of the Sea: Strange Life Forms a Mile Below the Surface. By William Beebe. Paintings by E. Bostelmann. LXI, pp. 65-88, 15 ills. in black and white, 8 ills. in color, map, Jan., 1932

Devil-Fishing in the Gulf Stream. By John Oliver La Gorce. XXXV, pp. 476-488, 7 ills., June, 1919

The Dream Ship: The Story of a Voyage of Adventure More Than Half Around the World in a 47-foot Lifeboat. By Ralph Stock. XXXIX, pp. 1-52, 43 ills., map, Jan., 1921

Europe's Endangered Fish Supply: The War and the North Sea Fisheries. XXVII, pp. 141-152, 9 ills., map, Feb., 1915

Federal Fish Farming; or, Planting Fish by the Billion. By Hugh M. Smith. XXI, pp. 418-446, 22 ills., May, 1910

Fighting Giants of the Humboldt. By David D. Duncan. LXXIX, pp. 373-400, 28 ills., map, Mar., 1941
Contents: Giant Manta Ray, Marlin, Squid, Swordfish, Whale

The First Autochromes from the Ocean Bottom: Marine Life in Its Natural Habitat Along the Florida Keys Is Successfully Photographed in Colors. (Photographs by Dr. W. H. Longley and Charles Martin). LI, pp. 56-60, 8 ills. in color, Jan., 1927
Contents: Common Grunt, French Grunt, Gray Snapper, Hogfish, Red Parrot Fish, Saucer-Eye Porgy, Yellow and Black Porkfish, Yellow Goatfish, Yellow Grunt

The Fisheries of Japan. By Hugh M. Smith. XV, pp. 362-364, Sept., 1904. XVI, pp. 201-220, 13 ills., May, 1905

Fishes and Fisheries of Our North Atlantic Seaboard. By John Oliver La Gorce. Paintings by Hashime Murayama. XLIV, pp. 567-634, 35 ills. in black and white, 16 ills. in color, Dec., 1923
Contents: Alewife, Atlantic Salmon, Butter-Fish, Codfish, Common Sturgeon, Cusk, Haddock, Halibut, Herring, Lobster, Mackerel, Pollock, Scup, Shad, Smelt, Squirrel Hake, Summer Flounder, Swordfish, Tautog, Tilefish, Tuna, Whiting, Winter Flounder

Fishes That Build Nests and Take Care of Their Young. XVIII, pp. 400-412, 16 ills., June, 1907

Fishes That Carry Lanterns. XXI, pp. 453-456, 5 ills., May, 1910

Fishing for Pearls in the Indian Ocean. By Bella Sidney Woolf. XLIX, pp. 161-183, 24 ills., Feb., 1926

Fishing in Pacific Coast Streams. By Leonard P. Schultz. Paintings by Hashime Murayama. LXXV, pp. 185-212, 10 ills. in black and white, 44 portraits in color, Feb., 1939
Contents: Chinook Salmon, Chum Salmon, Cutthroat Trout, Dolly Varden Trout, Eulachon, Golden Trout, Pink Salmon, Piute Trout, Rainbow Trout, Red Salmon, Sacramento Perch, Sacramento Pike, Sacramento Sucker, Silver Salmon, Steelhead Trout, Three-Spined Stickleback, White Sturgeon, Yellowstone Trout

The Glass-Bottom Boat. By Charles Frederick Holder. XX, pp. 761-778, 17 ills., Sept., 1909

The Golden Trout. XVII, p. 424, July, 1906

Goldfish and Their Cultivation in America. By Hugh M. Smith. Paintings by Hashime Murayama. XLVI, pp. 375-400, 14 ills. in black and white, 8 ills. in color, Oct., 1924

A Half Mile Down: Strange Creatures, Beautiful and Grotesque as Figments of Fancy, Reveal Themselves at Windows of the Bathysphere. By William Beebe. Paintings by Else Bostelmann, Helen D. Tee-Van, E. J. Geske. LXVI, pp. 661-704, 28 ills. in black and white, 16 ills. in color, map, Dec., 1934

Helping the Filipino Fisheries. XVIII, pp. 795-796, Dec., 1907

Interesting Citizens of the Gulf Stream. By Dr. John T. Nichols. XXXIX, pp. 69-84, 11 ills., Jan., 1921

Islands Adrift: St. Pierre and Miquelon: In a Key Position on the North Atlantic Air Route, France's Oldest Colony Rides Out Another Storm. By Frederic K. Arnold. LXXX, pp. 743-768, 23 ills., map, Dec., 1941

A Jumping Salmon. XIX, pp. 124-125, ill., Feb., 1908

King Herring: An Account of the World's Most Valuable Fish, the Industries It Supports, and the Part It Has Played in History. By Hugh M. Smith. XX, pp. 701-735, 21 ills., Aug., 1909

A Land of Lakes and Volcanoes. By Luis Marden. With 17 color photos by author. LXXXVI, pp. 161-192, 11 ills. in black and white, map, Aug., 1944

Life on a Coral Reef: The Fertility and Mystery of the Sea Studied Beneath the Waters Surrounding Dry Tortugas. By W. H. Longley. LI, pp. 61-83, 22 ills., Jan., 1927
Contents: Barracuda, Black Angel Fish, Gold-Browed Gnathypops, Gray Snapper, Nassau Grouper, Razor Fish, Red Parrot Fish, Squirrel Fish, Trunkfish, Yellow-Finned Grouper, Yellow Goatfish, Yellowtail

Life on the Grand Banks: An Account of the Sailor-Fishermen Who Harvest the Shoal Waters of North America's Eastern Coasts. By Frederick William Wallace. XL, pp. 1-28, 29 ills., July, 1921

The Maine American and the American Lobster. By John D. Lucas. LXXXIX, pp. 523-543, 19 ills., Apr., 1946

The Mysterious Life of the Common Eel. By Hugh M. Smith. XXIV, pp. 1140-1146, 3 ills., Oct., 1913

The Native Oysters of the West Coast. By Robert E. C. Stearns. XIX, pp. 224-226, Mar., 1908

Net Results from Oceania: Collecting Aquarium Specimens in Tropical Pacific Waters. By Walter H. Chute. LXXIX, pp. 347-372, 8 ills. in black and white, 24 ills. in color, Mar., 1941
Contents: Achilles Tang, *Balistapus aculeatus,* Banded Dascyllus, Bar Diagonal Butterflyfish, Birdfish, Black Tang, Black Triggerfish, Blackline Hawkfish, Blue Parrotfish, Bluegreen Chromide, Bluelined Wrasse, Bluespotted Niggerfish, Bluestriped Butterflyfish, Brown-spotted Grouper, *Chaetodon trifasciatus, Cheilinus bimaculatus,* Clown Goby, Clown Wrasse, Common Moray, Common Scorpion, Convict Tang, *Dascyllus albisella,* Fantail Filefish, Flying Gurnard, Gray Wrasse, Green Birdfish, Hawaiian Butterflyfish, *Hemitaurichthys zoster,* "Hinalea Hilu," "Hinalea Lolo," Lionfish, Longfin Butterflyfish, Longfin Razorfish, Longnose Butterflyfish, Moorish Idol, Moray Eel, Orangespot Tang, Orangestriped Triggerfish, Pinktail Triggerfish, Polkadot Moray, Polkadot Wrasse, "Pooú," Potter's Pomacentrid, Rectangular Triggerfish, Red Bigeye, Red Goatfish, Red Squirrelfish, Redline Wrasse, Ringed Hawkfish, Saddle Wrasse, Sailfin Tang, Sandfish, Sergeant Major, Spot Diagonal Butterflyfish, Spot Pomacentrid, Spot Wrasse, Spotted Rockfish, Spotted White Moray, Striped Apagon, Threadfish, Three-striped Coralfish, "Ulua," "Umauma Lei," Whiteline Hawkfish, Whiteline Squirrelfish, Whiteline Triggerfish, Yellow Blenny, Yellow Jack, Yellow Tang, Yelloweye Tang, Yellowspot Goatfish

Newfoundland, North Atlantic Rampart: From the "First Base of American Defense" Planes Fly to Britain's Aid over Stout Fishing Schooners of the Grand Banks. By George Whiteley, Jr. LXXX, pp. 111-140, 26 ills., map, July, 1941

Notes from a Naturalist's Experiences in British Guiana. By C. H. Eigenmann. XXII, pp. 859-870, 8 ills., Sept., 1911

Notes on the Sea Dyaks of Borneo. By Edwin H. Gomes. XXII, pp. 695-723, 26 ills., Aug., 1911

On the Bottom of a South Sea Pearl Lagoon. By Roy Waldo Miner. Paintings by Else Bostelmann. LXXIV, pp. 365-390, 17 ills. in black and white, 8 ills. in color, Sept., 1938

Oregon Finds New Riches. By Leo A. Borah. XC, pp. 681-728, 15 ills. in black and white, 28 ills. in color, two-page map, Dec., 1946

Our Fish Immigrants. By Hugh M. Smith. XVIII, pp. 383-400, 3 ills., June, 1907

Our Global Ocean—Last and Vast Frontier. By F. Barrows Colton. LXXXVII, pp. 105-128, 19 ills., drawing, Jan., 1945

Our Heritage of the Fresh Waters: Biographies of the Most Widely Distributed of the Important Food and Game Fishes of the United States. By Charles Haskins Townsend. Paintings by Hashime Murayama. XLIV, pp. 109-159, 25 ills. in black and white, 16 ills. in color, Aug., 1923
Contents: Black Bass, Brook Trout, Calico Bass, Common Bullhead, Common Eel, Common Whitefish, Crappie, Eastern Pickerel, Fresh-water Drum, Lake Chautauqua Muskellunge, Lake Sturgeon, Lake Trout, Pike, Pike-Perch, Rainbow Trout, Rock Bass, Sauger, Spotted Catfish, White Perch, Yellow Perch

FISHES AND FISHERIES—*Continued*

Our Smallest Possession—Guam. By William E. Safford. XVI, pp. 229-237, 5 ills., May, 1905

Oysters: The World's Most Valuable Water Crop. By Hugh M. Smith. XXIV, pp. 257-281, 21 ills., Mar., 1913

The Pearl Fisheries of Ceylon. By Hugh M. Smith. XXIII, pp. 173-194, 13 ills., map, Feb., 1912

Pearl Fishing in the Red Sea. By Henri de Monfreid. LXXII, pp. 597-626, 24 ills., map, Nov., 1937

Planting Fishes in the Ocean. By George M. Bowers. XVIII, pp. 715-723, 5 ills., Nov., 1907

The Purple Veil: A Romance of the Sea. (By H. A. L.). XVI, pp. 337-341, 9 ills., July, 1905

The Relations of the Gulf Stream and the Labrador Current. By William Libbey, Junior. V, pp. 161-166, Jan. 31, 1894

Restocking Our Rivers and Waters with Fish. XVII, pp. 424-425, July, 1906

The Rise of the New Arab Nation. By Frederick Simpich. XXXVI, pp. 369-393, 17 ills., map, Nov., 1919
Included: Pearl Fisheries

A Round Trip to Davy Jones's Locker: Peering into Mysteries a Quarter Mile Down in the Open Sea, by Means of the Bathysphere. By William Beebe. Paintings by E. Bostelmann. LIX, pp. 653-678, 14 ills. in black and white, 8 ills. in color, map, June, 1931

Sailing the Seven Seas in the Interest of Science: Adventures Through 157,000 Miles of Storm and Calm, from Arctic to Antarctic and Around the World, in the Non-magnetic Yacht "Carnegie." By J. P. Ault. XLII, pp. 631-690, 47 ills., chart, Dec., 1922

Shark Fishing—An Australian Industry. By Norman Ellison. LXII, pp. 369-386, 22 ills., Sept., 1932

Some Giant Fishes of the Seas. By Hugh M. Smith. XX, pp. 637-644, 6 ills., July, 1909
Contents: Basking Shark, "Devil-Fish," Jew-Fish, Man-Eater Shark, Ribbon-Fish, Saw-Fish, Sleeper Shark, Sun-Fish, Tunny, Whale Shark

Treasure-House of the Gulf Stream: The Completion and Opening of the New Aquarium and Biological Laboratory at Miami, Florida. By John Oliver La Gorce. Paintings by Hashime Murayama. XXXIX, pp. 53-68, 5 ills. in black and white, 16 ills. in color, Jan., 1921
Contents: Angel-Fish, Blue Striped Grunt, Buffalo Trunkfish, Butterfly Fish, Cow Pilot, Cowfish, Cuckold, Four-Eyed Fish, Green Moray, Pork Fish, Portuguese Man-of-War, Queen Trigger-Fish, Rainbow Parrot-Fish, Rock Hind, Sea Horse, Shark Sucker, Spade Fish, Squirrel Fish, Yellow Tail

Treasures of the Pacific: Marine Fishes and Fisheries Yield Vast Wealth from Alaska to Baja California. By Leonard P. Schultz. Paintings by Hashime Murayama. LXXIV, pp. 463-498, 10 ills. in black and white, 31 portraits in color, Oct., 1938

Tropical Fish Immigrants Reveal New Nature Wonders. By Walter H. Chute. LXV, pp. 93-109, 8 ills. in black and white, 16 ills. in color, Jan., 1934

FISHES AND FISHERIES—*Continued*

Tropical Toy Fishes: More Than 600 Varieties of Aquarium Pygmies Afford a Fascinating Field of Zoölogical Study in the Home. By Ida Mellen. Paintings by Hashime Murayama. LIX, pp. 287-317, 20 ills. in black and white, 8 ills. in color, Mar., 1931

The Tuna Harvest of the Sea: A Little-known Epic of the Ocean Is the Story of Southern California's Far-ranging Tuna Fleet. By John Degelman. LXXVIII, pp. 393-408, 17 ills., Sept., 1940

Viking Life in the Storm-Cursed Faeroes. By Leo Hansen. LVIII, pp. 607-648, 49 ills., map, Nov., 1930

The War and Ocean Geography. (By Gilbert Grosvenor). XXXIV, pp. 230-242, 6 ills., map, Sept., 1918

When the Father of Waters Goes on a Rampage: An Account of the Salvaging of Food-fishes from the Overflowed Lands of the Mississippi River. By Hugh M. Smith. XXXVII, pp. 369-386, 18 ills., Apr., 1920

When the Herring Fleet Comes to Great Yarmouth. By W. Robert Moore. LXVI, pp. 233-250, 19 ills., Aug., 1934

Where Bretons Wrest a Living from the Sea. 23 photos by F. W. Goro. LXXI, pp. 751-766, June, 1937

Where Nature Runs Riot: On Australia's Great Barrier Reef Marine Animals Grow to Unusual Size, Develop Strange Weapons of Attack and Defense, and Acquire Brilliant Colors. By T. C. Roughley. LXXVII, pp. 823-850, 18 ills. in black and white, 15 ills. in color, map, June, 1940

A Wonderer Under Sea. By William Beebe. Paintings by E. Bostelmann. LXII, pp. 741-758, 13 ills. in black and white, 8 ills. in color, Dec., 1932

FISHING. *See* Fishes and Fisheries

FISHING and Hunting Tales from Brazil. By Dewey Austin Cobb. XX, pp. 917-920, Oct., 1909

FISHING for Pearls in the Indian Ocean. By Bella Sidney Woolf. XLIX, pp. 161-183, 24 ills., Feb., 1926

FISHING in Pacific Coast Streams (Salmon, Trout, etc.). By Leonard P. Schultz. Paintings by Hashime Murayama. LXXV, pp. 185-212, 10 ills. in black and white, 44 portraits in color, Feb., 1939

FISSURE LAKE, Alaska:

The Valley of Ten Thousand Smokes: An Account of the Discovery and Exploration of the Most Wonderful Volcanic Region in the World. By Robert F. Griggs. XXXIII, pp. 115-169, 46 ills., map, panorama, Feb., 1918

FIT to Fight Anywhere (Army Quartermaster Tests). By Frederick Simpich. LXXXIV, pp. 233-256, 26 ills., Aug., 1943

FITA-FITAS (Samoan Soldiers):

America's South Sea Soldiers. By Lorena MacIntyre Quinn. XXXVI, pp. 267-274, 8 ills., Sept., 1919

FITCH, C. H.:

The Five Civilized Tribes and the Survey of Indian Territory. By C. H. Fitch. IX, pp. 481-491, 4 ills., map, Dec., 1898

FITCH, ROBERT F.:

China. 4 color photos by Robert F. Fitch. XXXVIII, pp. 377-389, Nov., 1920

Life Afloat in China: Tens of Thousands of Chinese in Congested Ports Spend Their Entire Existence on Boats. By Robert F. Fitch. LI, pp. 665-686, 28 ills., June, 1927

Puto, the Enchanted Island. By Robert F. Fitch. LXXXIX, pp. 373-384, 11 ills., map, Mar., 1946

The **FIVE** Civilized Tribes and the Survey of Indian Territory. By C. H. Fitch. IX, pp. 481-491, 4 ills., map, Dec., 1898

The **FIVE** Thousand Temples of Pagān: Burma's Sacred City Is a Place of Enchantment in the Midst of Ruins. By William H. Roberts. LX, pp. 445-454, 9 ills., Oct., 1931

FJORDS and Fjells of Viking Land (Norway). 27 color photos by Gustav Heurlin. LVIII, pp. 13-44, July, 1930

FLAGS:

The Correct Display of the Stars and Stripes. By Byron McCandless and Gilbert Grosvenor. XXXII, pp. 404-413, 8 ills., Oct., 1917

Flags Famous in American History. By Byron McCandless and Gilbert Grosvenor. XXXII, pp. 341-361, 92 ills. in color, Oct., 1917

Flags of Austria-Hungary, Bulgaria, Germany, and Turkey. By Byron McCandless and Gilbert Grosvenor. XXXII, pp. 386-388, 38 ills. in color, Oct., 1917

The Flags of Europe, Asia, and Africa. By Byron McCandless and Gilbert Grosvenor. XXXII, pp. 372-378, 101 ills. in color, Oct., 1917

The Flags of Our Army, Navy, and Government Departments. By Byron McCandless and Gilbert Grosvenor. XXXII, pp. 305-322, ill. in black and white, 300 ills. in color, diagrs., 4 tables, Oct., 1917

The Flags of Pan-America. By Byron McCandless and Gilbert Grosvenor. XXXII, pp. 361-369, 62 ills. in color, Oct., 1917

The Flags of the British Empire. By Byron McCandless and Gilbert Grosvenor. XXXII, pp. 378-385, 158 ills. in color, Oct., 1917

Flags of the World. By Gilbert Grosvenor and William J. Showalter. LXVI, pp. 339-396, 10 ills. in black and white, 808 ills. in color, Sept., 1934

Heroic Flags of the Middle Ages. By Byron McCandless and Gilbert Grosvenor. XXXII, pp. 388-399, 96 ills. in color, Oct., 1917

Index to Flags and Insignia (Our Flag Number). XXXII, p. 285, ill., Oct., 1917

The Makers of the Flag. By Franklin K. Lane. XXXII, p. 304, Oct., 1917

The Naval Flags of the World. By Byron McCandless and Gilbert Grosvenor. XXXII, text, p. 369; 214 ills. in color, Oct., 1917

Our Flag Number. By Gilbert Grosvenor. XXXII, pp. 281-284, ills., Oct., 1917

FLAGS—*Continued*

Our State Flags. By Byron McCandless and Gilbert Grosvenor. XXXII, pp. 325-341, 57 ills. in color, Oct., 1917

Pennants of Patriotism 200 Years Ago. By Byron McCandless and Gilbert Grosvenor. XXXII, pp. 399-403, 77 ills. in color, Oct., 1917

The Story of the American Flag. By Byron McCandless and Gilbert Grosvenor. XXXII, pp. 286-303, 12 ills., Oct., 1917

Unfurling Old Glory on Canton Island. 11 ills. in color: 10 color photos, and painting by Charles Bittinger. LXXIII, pp. 753-760, June, 1938

See also NGS: Flag

FLAME-FEATHERED Flamingos of Florida. By W. A. Watts. With 9 color photos by W. F. Gerecke. LXXIX, pp. 56-65, Jan., 1941

FLAMING Cliffs of Monument Valley. By Lt. Jack Breed, USNR. With 9 color photos by author and Warren T. Mithoff. LXXXVIII, pp. 452-461, Oct., 1945

FLAMINGOS:

Camps and Cruises of an Ornithologist. By George Shiras, 3d. XX, pp. 438-463, 30 ills., May, 1909

Flame-Feathered Flamingos of Florida. By W. A. Watts. With 9 color photos by W. F. Gerecke. LXXIX, pp. 56-65, Jan., 1941

The Large Wading Birds: Long Legs and Remarkable Beaks, as Well as Size, Form, and Color, Distinguish the Herons, Ibises, and Flamingos. By T. Gilbert Pearson. Paintings by Maj. Allan Brooks. LXII, pp. 441-469, 2 ills. in black and white, ill. in color, Oct., 1932

The Remarkable Photograph of Flamingo Nests. XV, p. 83, ill., Feb., 1904

The Story of the Flamingo. XVI, p. 50, Jan., 1905

FLANDRIN, M.:

Modern Life in Morocco, Western Outpost of Islam. 27 color photos by M. Flandrin. LXVII, pp. 679-694, June, 1935

FLASHES from Finland. 19 ills. LXXVII, pp. 239-254, Feb., 1940

FLASHES from Ocean Deeps. 8 ills. in color from paintings by Else Bostelmann and Helen D. Tee-Van. LXVI, pp. 677-684, Dec., 1934

FLASHES of Color in the Fifth Continent (Australia). 24 color photos by W. Robert Moore. LXVIII, pp. 681-704, Dec., 1935

FLASHES of Color Throughout France. 28 color photos by Gervais Courtellemont. XLVI, pp. 529-544, Nov., 1924

FLASHING Fashions of Old Spain. 26 ills. in duotone by J. Ortiz Echagüe. LXIX, pp. 413-428, Mar., 1936

A **FLASHLIGHT** Photo by George Shiras, 3d, of a Doe and Her Twin Fawns Feeding on a Lake in Northern Michigan. XXIV, supplement, July, 1913. XL, ill. p. 136, Aug., 1921. LXXVI, ill. p. 475, Oct., 1939

A **FLASHLIGHT** Story of an Albino Porcupine and of a Cunning but Unfortunate Coon. By George Shiras, 3d. XXII, pp. 572-596, 26 ills., June, 1911

FLASHLIGHTS from the Jungle. XVIII, pp. 534-548, 11 ills., Aug., 1907

FLAVOR and Savor of American Foods. 25 color photos by J. Baylor Roberts, Willard R. Culver, and others. LXXXI, pp. 289-320, Mar., 1942

FLECKS of Color in the Fertile Fields of Louisiana. 14 color photos by Edwin L. Wisherd. LVII, pp. 419-426, Apr., 1930

FLEISCHMAN, MAX:

Seventy-Five Days in the Arctics. By Max Fleischman. XVIII, pp. 439-446, 5 ills., July, 1907

FLEMING, ROBERT V. *See* NGS: Treasurer

FLIES:

A Book of Monsters. By David and Marian Fairchild. XXVI, pp. 89-98, 7 ills., July, 1914

Economic Loss to the People of the United States Through Insects That Carry Disease. By L. O. Howard. XX, pp. 735-749, Aug., 1909

Explorers of a New Kind: Successful Introduction of Beetles and Parasites to Check Ravages of the Gipsy-moth and Brown-tail Moth. By L. O. Howard. XXVI, pp. 38-67, 11 ills. in black and white, 5 ills. in color, July, 1914

Fight the Flies. XXI, pp. 383-385, 452, 3 ills., May, 1910

The House-Fly. By N. A. Cobb. XXI, pp. 371-380, 4 ills., May, 1910

An Insect Community Lives in Flower Heads. By James G. Needham. XC, pp. 340-356, 5 ills. in black and white, 11 ills. in color, Sept., 1946
Contents: Baccha Flies, Bandwing Flies, Clearwing Flies, Spotwing Flies

Marvels of Metamorphosis: A Scientific "G-man" Pursues Rare Trapdoor Spider Parasites for Three Years With a Spade and a Candid Camera. By George Elwood Jenks. LXXIV, pp. 807-828, 39 ills., Dec., 1938

Notes on the Distances Flies Can Travel. By N. A. Cobb. XXI, pp. 380-383, May, 1910

FLIGHTS from Arctic to Equator: Conquering the Alps, the Ice Peaks of Spitsbergen, of Persia, and Africa's Mountains of the Moon. By Walter Mittelholzer. LXI, pp. 445-498, 53 ills., map, Apr., 1932

FLOATING DRY DOCKS. *See* Docks

FLOATING EXPOSITIONS. *See* Expositions

FLOOD, FRANCIS A.:

Britain Fights in the Fields. By Francis A. Flood. LXXXVI, pp. 31-65, 17 ills. in black and white, 21 ills. in color, July, 1944

Lend-Lease Is a Two-way Benefit: Innovation in Creative Statesmanship Pools Resources of United Nations, and Supplies American Forces Around the World. By Francis Flood. LXXXIII, pp. 745-761, 14 ills., June, 1943

FLOOD, FRANCIS A.—*Continued*

Three-Wheeling Through Africa: Two Adventurers Cross the So-called Dark Continent North of Lake Chad on Motorcycles with Side Cars. By James C. Wilson. LXV, pp. 37-92, 64 ills., two-page map, Jan., 1934

FLOODS AND FLOOD CONTROL:

The Delta of the Mississippi River. By E. L. Corthell. VIII, pp. 351-354, Dec., 1897

Forecasting the Weather and Storms. By Professor Willis L. Moore. XVI, pp. 255-305, 5 ills., 20 charts, June, 1905

The Great Mississippi Flood of 1927: Since White Man's Discovery This Mighty River Has Served Him Well, Yet It Has Brought Widespread Devastation Along Its Lower Reaches. By Frederick Simpich. LII, pp. 243-289, 53 ills., map, Sept., 1927

Here in Manchuria: Many Thousand Lives Were Lost and More Than Half the Crops Destroyed by the Floods of 1932. By Lilian Grosvenor Coville. LXIII, pp. 233-256, 26 ills., Feb., 1933

Men Against the Rivers (Mississippi and Ohio Rivers). By Frederick Simpich. LXXI, pp. 767-794, 22 ills., maps, June, 1937

The Modern Mississippi Problem. By W J McGee. IX, pp. 24-27, Jan., 1898

More Water for California's Great Central Valley. By Frederick Simpich. XC, pp. 645-664, 16 ills., map, Nov., 1946

Our Heralds of Storm and Flood (U. S. Weather Bureau). By Gilbert H. Grosvenor. XVIII, pp. 586-601, 15 ills., chart, Sept., 1907

Taming "Flood Dragons" Along China's Hwang Ho (River). By Oliver J. Todd. LXXXI, pp. 205-234, 26 ills., map, Feb., 1942

Taming the Outlaw Missouri River. By Frederick Simpich. LXXXVIII, pp. 569-598, 25 ills., two-page map, Nov., 1945

The Weather Bureau. By Willis L. Moore. XII, pp. 362-369, Oct., 1901

The Weather Bureau and the Recent Floods. By H. C. Frankenfield. XIV, pp. 285-290, ills., July, 1903

The Weather Bureau River and Flood System. By Professor Willis L. Moore. VII, pp. 302-307, Sept., 1896

When the Father of Waters Goes on a Rampage: An Account of the Salvaging of Food-fishes from the Overflowed Lands of the Mississippi River. By Hugh M. Smith. XXXVII, pp. 369-386, 18 ills., Apr., 1920

FLORA. *See* Flowers; Plants; Shrubs; Trees

FLORAL CARPETS:

In the Canary Islands, Where Streets Are Carpeted with Flowers. 13 color photos by Wilhelm Tobien. LVII, pp. 615-622, May, 1930

FLORAL EMBLEMS:

Our State Flowers: The Floral Emblems Chosen by the Commonwealths. By Gilbert Grosvenor. Paintings by Mary E. Eaton. XXXI, pp. 481-517, 567, ill. in black and white, 30 ills. in color, June, 1917

FLORAL Garlands of Prairie, Plain, and Woodland. 125 flower paintings in color by Edith S. Clements. LXXVI, pp. 225-271, Aug., 1939

FLORENCE, Italy:

Inexhaustible Italy. By Arthur Stanley Riggs. XXX, pp. 273-368, 76 ills., map, Oct., 1916

Return to Florence. By 1st Lt. Benjamin C. McCartney. LXXXVII, pp. 257-296, 18 ills. in black and white, 18 ills. in color, Mar., 1945

FLORICULTURE:

The Garden Isles of Scilly: Geologists May Throw Stones at Legend of Lost Lyonnesse, But Natives Grow Flowers in Glass Houses for London. By W. Robert Moore. LXXIV, pp. 755-774, 9 ills. in black and white, 13 ills. in color, map, Dec., 1938

FLORIDA:

Certain Citizens of the Warm Sea. By Louis L. Mowbray. Paintings by Hashime Murayama. XLI, pp. 27-62, 18 ills. in black and white, 16 ills. in color, Jan., 1922

Devil-Fishing in the Gulf Stream. By John Oliver La Gorce. XXXV, pp. 476-488, 7 ills., June, 1919

Flame-Feathered Flamingos of Florida. By W. A. Watts. With 9 color photos by W. F. Gerecke. LXXIX, pp. 56-65, Jan., 1941

Florida—The Fountain of Youth. By John Oliver La Gorce. LVII, pp. 1-93, 73 ills. in black and white, 41 ills. in color, map supplement, Jan., 1930

The Geography of the Southern Peninsula of the United States. By the Rev. John N. MacGonigle. VII, pp. 381-394, 4 ills., Dec., 1896

Growth of Florida. XVII, p. 424, July, 1906

How We Use the Gulf of Mexico. By Frederick Simpich. LXXXV, pp. 1-40, 20 ills. in black and white, 19 ills. in color, two-page map, Jan., 1944

Interesting Citizens of the Gulf Stream. By Dr. John T. Nichols. XXXIX, pp. 69-84, 11 ills., Jan., 1921

South Florida's Amazing Everglades: Encircled by Populous Places Is a Seldom-visited Area of Rare Birds, Prairies, Cowboys, and Teeming Wild Life of Big Cypress Swamp. By John O'Reilly. LXXVII, pp. 115-142, 26 ills., map, Jan., 1940

Treasure-House of the Gulf Stream: The Completion and Opening of the New Aquarium and Biological Laboratory at Miami, Florida. By John Oliver La Gorce. Paintings by Hashime Murayama. XXXIX, pp. 53-68, 5 ills. in black and white, 16 ills. in color, Jan., 1921

Wild Life of the Atlantic and Gulf Coasts: A Field Naturalist's Photographic Record of Nearly Half a Century of Fruitful Exploration. By George Shiras, 3d. LXII, pp. 261-309, 62 ills., Sept., 1932

See also Florida Keys; Key West

FLORIDA COAST LINE CANAL:

The Florida Coast Line Canal. IX, p. 242, May, 1898

Miscellanea. IX, p. 480, Nov., 1898

FLORIDA KEYS, Florida:

Across the Gulf by Rail to Key West. By Jefferson B. Browne. VII, pp. 203-207, June, 1896

FLORIDA KEYS, Florida—*Continued*

Cannon on Florida Reefs Solve Mystery of Sunken Ship. By Charles M. Brookfield. LXXX, pp. 807-824, 20 ills., map (on pen and ink drawing), Dec., 1941

The First Autochromes from the Ocean Bottom: Marine Life in Its Natural Habitat Along the Florida Keys Is Successfully Photographed in Colors. (Photographs by Dr. W. H. Longley and Charles Martin). LI, pp. 56-60, 8 ills. in color, Jan., 1927

The Florida Keys. By John Gifford. XVII, pp. 5-16, 13 ills., map, Jan., 1906

Life on a Coral Reef: The Fertility and Mystery of the Sea Studied Beneath the Waters Surrounding Dry Tortugas. By W. H. Longley. LI, pp. 61-83, 22 ills., Jan., 1927

See also Key West

FLOW Onward, Connecticut! (River). 24 color photos: 22 by B. Anthony Stewart. LXXXIII, pp. 409-432, Apr., 1943

"The **FLOWER** of Paradise": The Part Which Khat Plays in the Life of the Yemen Arab. By Charles Moser. XXXII, pp. 173-186, 10 ills., map, Aug., 1917

FLOWER Pageant of the Midwest: From March to November Nature Embroiders an Ever-changing Pattern of Living Color. By Edith S. and Frederick E. Clements. Paintings by Edith S. Clements. LXXVI, pp. 219-271, ill. in black and white, 125 flower paintings in color, Aug., 1939

FLOWERS:

American Berries of Hill, Dale, and Wayside. Paintings by Mary E. Eaton. XXXV, pp. 168-184, ill. in black and white, 29 ills. in color, Feb., 1919

American Wild Flowers. Paintings by Mary E. Eaton. XXVII, pp. 507-517, 29 ills. in color, May, 1915

Included: American Holly, Bindweed, Bittersweet, Black Haw, Black-Eyed Susan, Blue Flag, Bluebell, Blue-Eyed Grass, Broad-Leaved Arrow-Head, Bulb-Bearing Loosestrife, Buttercup, Canada Lily, Cardinal Flower, Day Flower, Evening Primrose, Jewel Weed, Moth Mullen, Partridge Berry, Purple Flowering Raspberry, Purple Loosestrife, Showy Lady's-Slipper, Star Grass, Trailing Arbutus, Turk's Cap Lily, Virginia Strawberry, Wild Columbine, Wild Geranium, Wild Pink, Witch Hazel

The Ashley River and Its Gardens (South Carolina). By E. T. H. Shaffer. XLIX, pp. 525-550, 6 ills. in black and white, 18 ills. in color, May, 1926

California, Our Lady of Flowers. By Chapin Hall. LV, pp. 703-750, 20 ills. in black and white, 30 ills. in color, June, 1929

California Says It with Wild Flowers. By Francis Woodworth. With 9 color photos by B. Anthony Stewart. LXXXI, pp. 492-501, Apr., 1942

Contents: Babyblue-eyes, Blazingstar, Blueblossom, Collinsia, Coreopsis, Dandelion, Eveningprimrose, Farewell-to-spring, Flannel Bush, Ithuriel's Spear, Lupine, Monkeyflower, Mustard, Owlclover, Poppy, *Rosa californica,* Toyon, Yellowdaisy Tidytip

FLOWERS—*Continued*

Canyons and Cacti of the American Southwest. 22 color photos by Edwin L. Wisherd, Jacob Gayer, Charles Martin. XLVIII, pp. 275-290, Sept., 1925

Common American Wild Flowers. Paintings by Mary E. Eaton. XXIX, pp. 584-609, 17 ills. in color, June, 1916
Contents: Butter-and-Eggs, Butterfly-Weed, Button Bush, Chicory, Common Mullen, Fireweed, Forget-Me-Not, Fringed Gentian, Jack-in-the-Pulpit, New England Aster, Poison Ivy, Spotted Boneset, Steeple Bush, Swamp Rose-Mallow, Virginia Creeper, Wild Yellow Plum, Yarrow

The Cultivation of the Mayflower. By Frederick V. Coville. XXVII, pp. 518-519, ill., May, 1915

Exploring the Mysteries of Plant Life. By William Joseph Showalter. Paintings by Mary E. Eaton. XLV, pp. 581-646, 41 ills. in black and white, 47 ills. in color, June, 1924
Included: Alfalfa, Amsonia, Arethusa, Bindweed, Blackberry-Lily, Checkerbloom, Cobaea Pentstemon, Coneflower, Creeping Polemonium, Daylily, Goldmoss, Grays Lily, Ground-Ivy, Honeysuckle, Meadow-Parsnip, Phlox, Pitcher-plant, Poppy-Mallow, Rhododendron, Rose Pogonia, St.Johnswort, Shootingstar, Snow-on-the-Mountain, Spatterdock, Springbeauty, Wild-bergamot, Woodbetony, Woodsorrel, Yellow Ladyslipper

Familiar Grasses and Their Flowers. By E. J. Geske and W. J. Showalter. Paintings by E. J. Geske. XXXIX, pp. 625-636, 8 ills. in color, June, 1921

The Family Tree of the Flowers. By Frederic E. Clements and William Joseph Showalter. LI, pp. 555-563, ill. in black and white, ill. in color, May, 1927

Flower Pageant of the Midwest: From March to November Nature Embroiders an Ever-changing Pattern of Living Color. By Edith S. and Frederic E. Clements. Paintings by Edith S. Clements. LXXVI, pp. 219-271, ill. in black and white, 125 flower paintings in color, Aug., 1939
Contents: Acanthus, Amaryllis, Aster, Bluebell, Borage, Buckwheat, Buttercup, Cactus, Caper, Dogbane, Evening Primrose, Evening Star, Gentian, Geranium, Heath, Iris, Lily, Mallow, Meadow Beauty, Mint, Morning-Glory, Mustard, Orchid, Oxalis, Pea, Phlox, Pink, Poppy, Potato, Primrose, Purslane, Snapdragon, Spiderwort, Spurge, Touch-Me-Not, Verbena, Violet, Witch Hazel

The Garden Isles of Scilly: Geologists May Throw Stones at Legend of Lost Lyonnesse, But Natives Grow Flowers in Glass Houses for London. By W. Robert Moore. LXXIV, pp. 755-774, 9 ills. in black and white, 13 ills. in color, map, Dec., 1938

The Great White Monarch of the Pacific Northwest (Mount Rainier). By A. H. Barnes. XXIII, pp. 593-626, 31 ills., map, June, 1912

High Country of Colorado. By Alfred M. Bailey. With 23 color photos by author, Robert J. Niedrach, F. G. Brandenburg. XC, pp. 43-72, 9 ills. in black and white, July, 1946
Included: Arnica, Columbine, Marigolds, Shooting Stars, Snow Lily, Wild Onion, Wood Lilies

FLOWERS—*Continued*

In the Canary Islands, Where Streets Are Carpeted with Flowers. 13 color photos by Wilhelm Tobien. LVII, pp. 615-622, May, 1930

An Insect Community Lives in Flower Heads. By James G. Needham. XC, pp. 340-356, 5 ills. in black and white, 11 ills. in color, Sept., 1946

The Kingdom of Flowers: An Account of the Wealth of Trees and Shrubs of China and of What the Arnold Arboretum, with China's Help, Is Doing to Enrich America. By Ernest H. Wilson. XXII, pp. 1003-1035, 24 ills., Nov., 1911

Midsummer Wild Flowers. Paintings by Mary E. Eaton. XLII, pp. 35-59, 38 ills. in color, July, 1922
Included: American Waterlily, Beach Pea, Blue Vervain, Bluebell, Broom Flax, Closed Gentian, Corn Cockle, Corydalis, Dodder, Early Goldenrod, English Plaintain, False-Foxglove, Field Mustard, Gayfeather, Golden St. John's-Wort, Groundcherry, Hairy Pentstemon, Hyssop Skullcap, Milkweed, Milkwort, Mistflower, New York Aster, Pickerelweed, Pokeweed, Pricklepoppy, Purple Avens, Purple Wild-Bergamot, Rosemallow, Sheep Laurel, Sheep Sorrel, Silver Aster, Spiderwort, Sweetshrub, Tansy, Teasel, Turtlehead, Venus Looking-Glass, Yellow Fringed Orchid

Our State Flowers: The Floral Emblems Chosen by the Commonwealths. By Gilbert Grosvenor. Paintings by Mary E. Eaton. XXXI, pp. 481-517, 567, ill. in black and white, 30 ills. in color, June, 1917
Contents: Apple, Bitter Root, Cactus, Carnation, Colorado Columbine, Daisy, Golden Poppy, Goldenrod, Indian Paintbrush, Magnolia, Mistletoe, Moccasin Flower, Mountain Laurel, Orange, Oregon Grape, Pasque Flower, Peach, Pine, Red Clover, Rhododendron, Rose, Sagebrush, Sahuaro, Sego Lily, Sunflower, Syringa, Texas Bluebonnet, Trumpet Vine, Violet, Wild Prairie Rose, Wild Rose

Pages from the Floral Life of America. Paintings by Mary E. Eaton. XLVIII, pp. 44-75, 55 ills. in color, July, 1925
Contents: Acanthus, Amaranth, Amaryllis, Apple, Arum, Aster, Bicknell, Bladderwort, Borage, Broom-Rape, Buckthorn, Buckwheat, Bunchflower, Caper, Chicory, Diapensia, Dogwood, Evening-Primrose, Figwort, Four-O'Clock, Fumitory, Gentian, Ginseng, Gooseberry, Goosefoot, Gourd, Heath, Horsetail, Indianpipe, Lily-of-the-Valley, Logania, Madder, Magnolia, Meadowbeauty, Milkweed, Milkwort, Mimosa, Nettle, Olive, Parsley, Passionflower, Pea, Plantain, Pondweed, Ragweed, Rush, Saxifrage, Senna, Sundew, Waterlily

Photographing the Marvels of the West in Colors. 6 color photos by Fred Payne Clatworthy. LIII, pp. 694-719, June, 1928

Riddle of the Aleutians: A Botanist Explores the Origin of Plants on Ever-misty Islands Now Enshrouded in the Fog of War. By Isobel Wylie Hutchison. LXXXII, pp. 769-792, 24 ills., Dec., 1942

FLOWERS—*Continued*

Some Odd Pages from the Annals of the Tulip: A "Made" Flower of Unknown Origin Took Medieval Europe by Storm and Caused a Financial Panic in the Netherlands. By Leo A. Borah. LXIV, pp. 321-343, 13 ills. in black and white, 10 ills. in color, Sept., 1933

Spring's Gay Bouquets Deck the Nation's Capital. 10 color photos by Harrison Howell Walker. LXXIV, pp. 17-24, July, 1938

A Sunshine Land of Fruits, Flowers, Movies, and Sport (California). 41 color photos by Clifton Adams and Fred Payne Clatworthy. LXVI, pp. 545-592, Nov., 1934

Under the South African Union. By Melville Chater. LIX, pp. 391-512, 97 ills. in black and white, 38 ills. in color, two-page map, Apr., 1931

Where Spring Paints a State with Wild Flowers (California). 18 color photos by B. Anthony Stewart. LXIX, pp. 365-380, Mar., 1936

Wild Flowers of the West (U. S.). By Edith S. Clements. Paintings from life by author. LI, pp. 566-622, 207 ills. in color, May, 1927

Contents: Aster, Bellflower, Borage, Broom-Rape, Buckthorn, Buckwheat, Cactus, Caper, Chicory, Crowfoot, Dogbane, Evening-Primrose, Evening-Star, Figwort, Flax, Four-O'Clock, Fumitory, Gentian, Geranium, Gooseberry, Heath, Honeysuckle, Indianpipe, Iris, Leadwort, Lily, Lobelia, Mallow, Mesembryanthemum, Milkweed, Milkwort, Mint, Morning-Glory, Mustard, Orchid, Orpine, Parsley, Pea, Phlox, Pink, Poppy, Potato, Primrose, Purslane, Rockrose, Rose, St.Johnswort, Saxifrage, Violet, Waterleaf, Wintergreen, Woodsorrel

See also Gardens; Orchids

FLYCATCHERS (Birds):

Birds on the Home Front. By Arthur A. Allen. LXXXIV, pp. 32-56, 7 ills. in black and white, 30 ills. in color, July, 1943

Parrots, Kingfishers, and Flycatchers: Strange Trogons and Curious Cuckoos are Pictured with these Other Birds of Color, Dash, and Courage. By Alexander Wetmore. Paintings by Maj. Allan Brooks. LXIX, pp. 801-828, 9 ills. in black and white, 36 portraits in color, June, 1936

FLYCATCHERS and Other Friends in Feathers. 36 portraits from paintings by Maj. Allan Brooks. LXIX, pp. 807-822, June, 1936

FLYING. By Gilbert Grosvenor. LXIII, pp. 585-630, 33 ills. in black and white, 17 ills. in duotone, May, 1933

FLYING Around the Baltic. By Douglas Chandler. LXXIII, pp. 767-806, 31 ills. in black and white, 13 ills. in duotone, map, June, 1938

FLYING Around the North Atlantic. By Anne Morrow Lindbergh. Foreword by Charles A. Lindbergh. LXVI, pp. 259-337, 82 ills., maps (1 two-page), Sept., 1934

FLYING FORTRESSES:

American Bombers Attacking from Australia. By Howell Walker. LXXXIII, pp. 49-70, 19 ills., map, Jan., 1943

FLYING FORTRESSES—*Continued*

8th Air Force in England. 10 ills. in color from U. S. Army Air Forces official photos. LXXXVII, pp. 297-304, Mar., 1945

FLYING in France. By Captain André de Berroeta. XXXIII, pp. 9-26, 12 ills., Jan., 1918

FLYING Our Wounded Veterans Home. By Catherine Bell Palmer. LXXXVIII, pp. 363-384, 17 ills., Sept., 1945

FLYING Over Egypt, Sinai, and Palestine: Looking Down Upon the Holy Land During an Air Journey of Two and a Half Hours from Cairo to Jerusalem. By Brigadier General P. R. C. Groves and Major J. R. McCrindle. L, pp. 313-355, 26 ills. in black and white, 23 ills. in color, map, Sept., 1926

FLYING Over the Arctic. By Lieutenant Commander Richard E. Byrd. XLVIII, pp. 519-532, 10 ills., Nov., 1925

FLYING POLE DANCE:

The Mexican Indian Flying Pole Dance. By Helga Larsen. LXXI, pp. 387-400, 13 ills., Mar., 1937

FLYING the "Hump" of the Andes. By Capt. Albert W. Stevens. LIX, pp. 595-636, 36 ills., map, May, 1931

FLYING the Pacific. By William Burke Miller. LXX, pp. 665-707, 39 ills., Dec., 1936

FLYING the World: In a Homemade Airplane the Author and Her Husband Enjoy 16,000 Miles of Adventurous Flight Across Europe, Asia, and America. By Gladys M. Day. LXI, pp. 655-690, 41 ills., map, June, 1932

FLYING the World's Longest Air-Mail Route: From Montevideo, Uruguay, Over the Andes, Up the Pacific Coast, Across Central America and the Caribbean to Miami, Florida, in 67 Thrilling Flying Hours. By Junius B. Wood. LVII, pp. 261-325, 65 ills., map, Mar., 1930

FOEHN (Wind):

Americans Stand Guard in Greenland. By Andrew H. Brown. XC, pp. 457-500, 23 ills. in black and white, 19 ills. in color, map, Oct., 1946

FOLKNER, ROLAND P.:

Conditions in Liberia. By Roland P. Folkner, George Sale, Emmett J. Scott. XXI, pp. 729-741, 9 ills., Sept., 1910

FOLLIARD, EDWARD T.:

Martinique, Caribbean Question Mark. By Edward T. Folliard. LXXIX, pp. 47-55, 9 ills., Jan., 1941

FONCK, RENÉ:

Aces Among Aces (Aviators). By Laurence La Tourette Driggs. XXXIII, pp. 568-580, 9 ills., June, 1918

FOOD:

The Acorn, a Possibly Neglected Source of Food. By C. Hart Merriam. XXXIV, pp. 129-137, 8 ills., Aug., 1918

America's Debt to the Hen. By Harry R. Lewis. LI, pp. 453-467, 15 ills., Apr., 1927

FOOD—*Continued*

An Appeal to Members of the National Geographic Society (Food Conservation). XXXIII, pp. 347-348, ills., Apr., 1918

Britain Fights in the Fields. By Francis A. Flood. LXXXVI, pp. 31-65, 17 ills. in black and white, 21 ills. in color, July, 1944

Deer Farming in the United States. XXI, pp. 269-276, ills., Mar., 1910

The Delectable Shrimp: Once a Culinary Stepchild, Today a Gulf Coast Industry. By Harlan Major. LXXXVI, pp. 501-512, 11 ills., map, Oct., 1944

Dumboy, the National Dish of Liberia. By G. N. Collins. XXII, pp. 84-88, 5 ills., Jan., 1911

Farmers Keep Them Eating. By Frederick Simpich. LXXXIII, pp. 435-458, 22 ills., Apr., 1943

Farmers Since the Days of Noah: China's Remarkable System of Agriculture Has Kept Alive the Densest Population in the World. By Adam Warwick. LI, pp. 469-500, 37 ills., Apr., 1927

Fearful Famines of the Past: History Will Repeat Itself Unless the American People Conserve Their Resources. By Ralph A. Graves. XXXII, pp. 69-90, 11 ills., July, 1917

The Food Armies of Liberty. By Herbert Hoover. XXXII, pp. 187-196, 6 ills., Sept., 1917

Food for Our Allies in 1919. By Herbert Hoover. XXXIV, pp. 242-244, Sept., 1918

Forerunners of Famine. By Frederic C. Walcott. XXXIII, pp. 336-347, 4 ills., 4 diagrs., map, Apr., 1918

Forming New Fashions in Food: The Bearing of Taste on One of Our Great Food Economies, the Dried Vegetable, Which Is Developing Into a Big War Industry. By David Fairchild. XXXIII, pp. 356-368, 11 ills., Apr., 1918

Greens Grow for GI's on Soilless Ascension. By W. Robert Moore. LXXXVIII, pp. 219-230, 12 ills., Aug., 1945

Helping to Solve Our Allies' Food Problem: America Calls for a Million Young Soldiers of the Commissary to Volunteer for Service in 1918. By Ralph Graves. XXXIII, pp. 170-194, 23 ills., Feb., 1918

How the World Is Fed. By William Joseph Showalter. XXIX, pp. 1-110, 101 ills., Jan., 1916

Jungle Housekeeping for a Geographic Expedition (Cerro de las Mesas, Mexico). By Marion Stirling. LXXX, pp. 303-327, 15 ills., Sept., 1941

Lend-Lease Is a Two-way Benefit: Innovation in Creative Statesmanship Pools Resources of United Nations, and Supplies American Forces Around the World. By Francis Flood. LXXXIII, pp. 745-761, 14 ills., June, 1943

Nuts and Their Uses as Foods. XVIII, p. 800, Dec., 1907

Peacetime Plant Hunting About Peiping. By P. H. and J. H. Dorsett. LXXII, pp. 509-534, 21 ills., map, Oct., 1937

Reviving a Lost Art (Drying Fruits and Vegetables). XXXI, pp. 475-481, 9 ills., June, 1917

FOOD—*Continued*

Revolution in Eating: Machine Food Age—Born of Roads, Research, and Refrigeration—Makes the United States the Best-fed Nation in History. By J. R. Hildebrand. LXXXI, pp. 273-324, 33 ills. in black and white, 25 ills. in color, Mar., 1942

Round About Bogotá: A Hunt for New Fruits and Plants Among the Mountain Forests of Colombia's Unique Capital. By Wilson Popenoe. XLIX, pp. 127-160, 34 ills., map, Feb., 1926

War, Patriotism, and the Food Supply. By Frederick V. Coville. XXXI, pp. 254-256, Mar., 1917

The Weapon of Food. By Herbert Hoover. XXXII, pp. 197-212, 15 ills., Sept., 1917

Wokas, a Primitive Indian Food. XV, pp. 183-185, 3 ills., Apr., 1904

Your New World of Tomorrow. By F. Barrows Colton. LXXXVIII, pp. 385-410, 25 ills., Oct., 1945

See also Agriculture; Cheese; Corn; Fishes and Fisheries; Fruits; Meat Industry; Vegetables

FOOTE, JOHN:

The Geography of Medicines: War's Effect Upon the World's Sources of Supply. By John Foote. XXXII, pp. 213-238, 26 ills., Sept., 1917

Medicine Fakes and Fakers of All Ages: Strange Stories of Nostrums and Kingly Quacks in Every Era and Clime. By John Foote. XXXV, pp. 67-84, 14 ills., Jan., 1919

FORAGE:

The Sage Plains of Oregon. By Frederick V. Coville. VII, pp. 395-404, Dec., 1896

FORAN, W. ROBERT:

Tristan da Cunha, Isles of Contentment: On Lonely Sea Spots of Pirate Lore and Shipwrecks Seven Families Live Happily Far from War Rumors and World Changes. By W. Robert Foran. LXXIV, pp. 671-694, 23 ills., map, Nov., 1938

FORBES, EDGAR ALLEN:

Macao (China), "Land of Sweet Sadness": The Oldest European Settlement in the Far East, Long the Only Haven for Distressed Mariners in the China Sea. By Edgar Allen Forbes. LXII, pp. 337-357, 13 ills. in black and white, 11 ills. in color, Sept., 1932

Notes on the Only American Colony in the World (Liberia). By Edgar Allen Forbes. XXI, pp. 719-729, 14 ills., Sept., 1910

FORBES-LEITH, F. A. C.:

From England to India by Automobile: An 8,527-mile Trip Through Ten Countries, from London to Quetta, Requires Five and a Half Months. By Major F. A. C. Forbes-Leith. XLVIII, pp. 191-223, 33 ills., map, Aug., 1925

FORBUSH, ERNEST HOWE:

The Unique Island of Mount Desert. By George B. Dorr, Ernest Howe Forbush, M. L. Fernald. XXVI, pp. 75-89, 7 ills., July, 1914

FORD, RICHARD:

Seville, More Spanish Than Spain: The City of the Ibero-American Exposition, Which Opens This Spring, Presents a Tapestry of Many Ages and of Nations Old and New. By Richard Ford. LV, pp. 273-310, 35 ills. in black and white, 2 ills. in color, Mar., 1929

FORDER, ARCHIBALD:

Arabia, the Desert of the Sea. By Archibald Forder. XX, pp. 1039-1062, 1117, 20 ills., map, Dec., 1909

Damascus, the Pearl of the Desert. By A. Forder. XXII, pp. 62-82, 19 ills., map, Jan., 1911

FORECASTING the Weather. (By Alfred J. Henry). XV, pp. 285-292, 6 ills., chart, July, 1904

FORECASTING the Weather and Storms. By Professor Willis L. Moore. XVI, pp. 255-305, 5 ills., 20 charts, June, 1905

The **FOREIGN-BORN** of the United States. XXVI, pp. 265-271, 14 diagrs., Sept., 1914

FOREIGN Commerce of the United States in 1903. XIV, pp. 359-360, Sept., 1903

FOREIGNERS and Foreign Firms in China. XI, p. 330, Aug., 1900

The **FOREMOST** Intellectual Achievement of Ancient America: The Hieroglyphic Inscriptions on the Monuments in the Ruined Cities of Mexico, Guatemala, and Honduras Are Yielding the Secrets of the Maya Civilization. By Sylvanus Griswold Morley. XLI, pp. 109-130, 27 ills., 17 diagrs., map supplement, Feb., 1922

FORERUNNERS of Famine. By Frederic C. Walcott. XXXIII, pp. 336-347, 4 ills., 4 diagrs., map, Apr., 1918

"**FOREST** Fires in the Adirondacks in 1903." By H. M. Suter. XV, p. 224, May, 1904

FOREST Lookout. By Ella E. Clark. With 9 color photos by author. XC, pp. 73-96, 8 ills. in black and white, July, 1946

FOREST Reserves of the United States. (By Gifford Pinchot). XI, pp. 369-372, map, Sept., 1900

FORESTS AND FORESTRY:

The Amazon, Father of Waters: The Earth's Mightiest River Drains a Basin of More Than 2,700,000 Square Miles, from Which Came Originally the World's Finest Rubber. By W. L. Schurz. XLIX, pp. 445-463, 15 ills., Apr., 1926

Among the Big Trees of California. By John R. White. LXVI, pp. 219-232, 14 ills., Aug., 1934

Among the Mahogany Forests of Cuba. By Walter D. Wilcox. XIX, pp. 485-498, 6 ills., map, July, 1908

The Battle of the Forest. By B. E. Fernow. VI, pp. 127-148, 5 ills., map, June 22, 1894

Bitter Root Forest Reserve. By Richard U. Goode. IX, pp. 387-400, 5 ills., foldout map, Sept., 1898

FORESTS AND FORESTRY—*Continued*

By Seaplane to Six Continents: Cruising 60,000 Miles, Italian Argonauts of the Air See World Geography Unroll, and Break New Sky Trails Over Vast Brazilian Jungles. By Commander Francesco de Pinedo. LIV, pp. 247-301, 60 ills., two-page map, Sept., 1928

California's Coastal Redwood Realm: Along a Belt of Tall Trees a Giant Bridge Speeds the Winning of Our Westernmost Frontier. By J. R. Hildebrand. LXXV, pp. 133-184, 31 ills. in black and white, 17 ills. in color, map, Feb., 1939

A Comparison of Our Unprotected with Our Protected Forests. XIX, pp. 739-740, Oct., 1908

Deforestation and Climate. XVI, pp. 397-398, Aug., 1905

Exploring the Valley of the Amazon in a Hydroplane: Twelve Thousand Miles of Flying Over the World's Greatest River and Greatest Forest to Chart the Unknown Parima River from the Sky. By Captain Albert W. Stevens. XLIX, pp. 353-420, 86 ills., map, Apr., 1926

Exploring Unknown Corners of the "Hermit Kingdom" (Korea). By Roy Chapman Andrews. XXXVI, pp. 25-48, 30 ills., map, July, 1919

The Fight Against Forest Fires. By Henry S. Graves. XXIII, pp. 662-683, 19 ills., July, 1912

The Fight at the Timber-Line. By John Oliver La Gorce. XLII, pp. 165-196, 32 ills., Aug., 1922

The Forest Conditions and Standing Timber of the State of Washington. By Henry Gannett. IX, pp. 410-412, Sept., 1898

"Forest Fires in the Adirondacks in 1903." By H. M. Suter. XV, p. 224, May, 1904

Forest Lookout. By Ella E. Clark. With 9 color photos by author. XC, pp. 73-96, 8 ills. in black and white, July, 1946

Forest Reserves of the United States. (By Gifford Pinchot). XI, pp. 369-372, map, Sept., 1900

Forestry Abroad and at Home. By Gifford Pinchot. XVI, pp. 375-388, 8 ills., Aug., 1905

Forestry in California. XVI, pp. 480-481, Oct., 1905

The Forests and Deserts of Arizona. By Bernhard E. Fernow. VIII, pp. 203-226, 5 ills., July-Aug., 1897

The Forests of Canada. XIV, pp. 106-108, Mar., 1903

The Forests of Canada. By Sir Wilfrid Laurier. XVII, pp. 504-509, Sept., 1906

Forests Vital to Our Welfare (From an Address by President Roosevelt at Raleigh, N.C., October 19, 1905). XVI, pp. 515-516, Nov., 1905

Government Assistance in Handling Forest Lands. XV, pp. 450-452, Nov., 1904

An Impression of the Guiana Wilderness. By Angelo Heilprin. XVIII, pp. 373-381, 6 ills., June, 1907

Impressions of Asiatic Turkey. By Stephen van Rensselaer Trowbridge. XXVI, pp. 598-609, 6 ills., Dec., 1914

The Influence of Forestry upon the Lumber Industry of the United States. By Overton W. Price. XIV, pp. 381-386, ills., Oct., 1903

FORESTS AND FORESTRY—*Continued*

Is Climatic Aridity Impending on the Pacific Slope? The Testimony of the Forest. By J. B. Leiberg. X, pp. 160-181, May, 1899

The Jungles of Panama. By David Fairchild. XLI, pp. 131-145, 14 ills., Feb., 1922

Lessons from China (Forest Destruction). XX, pp. 18-29, 8 ills., Jan., 1909

The National Forest Reserves. By Frederick H. Newell. VIII, pp. 177-187, diagrs., tables, June, 1897

A New World to Explore: In the Tree-Roof of the British Guiana Forest Flourishes Much Hitherto-Unknown Life. By Maj. R. W. G. Hingston. LXII, pp. 617-642, 35 ills., Nov., 1932

Notes on the Eucalyptus Tree from the United States Forest Service. XX, pp. 668-673, 4 ills., July, 1909

Notes on the Forest Service. XVIII, pp. 142-145, 3 ills., Feb., 1907

Our Big Trees Saved. XXXI, pp. 1-11, 10 ills., Jan., 1917

Proposed Collection of Forestry Statistics. IX, p. 448, Oct., 1898

Protecting Our Forests from Fire. By James Wilson. XXII, pp. 98-106, 5 ills., Jan., 1911

The Redwood Forest of the Pacific Coast. By Henry Gannett. X, pp. 145-159, 6 ills., map, May, 1899

The Relation of Forests and Forest Fires. By Gifford Pinchot. X, pp. 393-403, 7 ills., Oct., 1899

Rubber Forests of Nicaragua and Sierra Leone. By General A. W. Greely. VIII, pp. 83-88, Mar., 1897

Saving the Forests. By Herbert A. Smith. XVIII, pp. 519-534, 7 ills., Aug., 1907

Studies of Muir Glacier, Alaska. By Harry Fielding Reid. IV, pp. 19-55, 13 ills., 6 diagrs., table, maps (1 foldout), Mar. 21, 1892
Included: The Buried Forest, p. 39
Supplement: Microscopical Examination of Wood from the Buried Forest, Muir Inlet, Alaska, by Francis H. Herrick, pp. 75-78

Summer Meeting of the American Forestry Association. XIII, pp. 352-358, Sept., 1902

The Tallest Tree That Grows (Eucalyptus). By Edgerton R. Young. XX, 664-667, 3 ills., July, 1909

Timber Lines. XIV, pp. 80-81, Feb., 1903

Timberlines. By Israel C. Russell. XV, pp. 47-49, Jan., 1904

Two Great Undertakings (Work of U. S. Bureau of Reclamation and U. S. Forest Service). XVII, pp. 645-647, Nov., 1906

The Value of the United States Forest Service. XX, pp. 29-41, 14 ills., Jan., 1909

The Vast Timber Belts of Canada. XVII, pp. 509-511, Sept., 1906

When Our Country Is Fifty Years Older. By Raphael Zon. XX, pp. 573-580, ills., diagr., June, 1909

Working Teak in the Burma Forests: The Sagacious Elephant Is Man's Ablest Ally in the Logging Industry of the Far East. By A. W. Smith. LVIII, pp. 239-256, 5 ills. in black and white, 15 ills. in color, Aug., 1930

See also Trees

The **FORGOTTEN** Ruins of Indo-China. By Jacob E. Conner. XXIII, pp. 209-272, 63 ills., maps, Mar., 1912

A **FORGOTTEN** Valley of Peru: Conquered by Incas, Scourged by Famine, Plagues, and Earthquakes, Colca Valley Shelters the Last Fragment of an Ancient Andean Tribe. By Robert Shippee. LXV, pp. 111-132, 22 ills., map, Jan., 1934

FORMING New Fashions in Food: The Bearing of Taste on One of Our Great Food Economies, the Dried Vegetable, Which Is Developing Into a Big War Industry. By David Fairchild. XXXIII, pp. 356-368, 11 ills., Apr., 1918

FORMOSA (Taiwan, Island):

Formosa the Beautiful. By Alice Ballantine Kirjassoff. XXXVII, pp. 247-292, 60 ills., map, Mar., 1920

I Lived on Formosa. By Joseph W. Ballantine. LXXXVII, pp. 1-24, 19 ills., maps, Jan., 1945

FORREST, GEORGE:

The Land of the Crossbow (Yünnan Province, China). By George Forrest. XXI, pp. 132-156, 15 ills., map, Feb., 1910

FORT PECK DAM, Montana:

Taming the Outlaw Missouri River. By Frederick Simpich. LXXXVIII, pp. 569-598, 25 ills., two-page map, Nov., 1945

FORT RELIANCE, Yukon District, Canada:

A Winter Weather Record From the Klondike Region. By E. W. Nelson. VIII, pp. 327-335, tables, Nov., 1897

FORT WRANGELL, Alaska:

The Stikine River in 1898. By Eliza Ruhamah Scidmore. X, pp. 1-15, 4 ills., Jan., 1899

FORT YUKON, Alaska:

The Alaskan Boundary Survey. I—Introduction. By Dr. T. C. Mendenhall. II—The Boundary South of Fort Yukon. By J. E. McGrath. III—The Boundary North of Fort Yukon. By J. Henry Turner. IV, pp. 177-197, Feb. 8, 1893

FORTESCUE, GRANVILLE:

The Burden France Has Borne. By Granville Fortescue. XXXI, pp. 323-344, 19 ills., Apr., 1917

Training the New Armies of Liberty: Camp Lee, Virginia's Home for the National Army. By Granville Fortescue. XXXII, pp. 421-437, 8 ills., map, Nov.-Dec., 1917

FORTS AND FORTRESSES:

Castles in the Air: Experiences and Journeys in Unknown Bhutan. By John Claude White. XXV, pp. 365-455, 74 ills., map, Apr., 1914

The Greatest Achievement of Ancient Man in America (Fortress of Sacsahuaman, Peru). XXIX, panorama, May, 1916

A Little Known Marvel of the Western Hemisphere: Christophe's Citadel, a Monument to the Tyranny and Genius of Haiti's King of Slaves. By Major G. H. Osterhout, Jr. XXXVIII, pp. 469-482, 13 ills., Dec., 1920

Sigiriya, "A Fortress in the Sky." By Wilson K. Norton. XC, pp. 665-680, 14 ills., map, Nov., 1946

See also Phyle

FORTY Years Among the Arabs. By John Van Ess. LXXXII, pp. 385-420, 27 ills., two-page map, Sept., 1942

FOSHAG, WILLIAM F.:

Paricutín, the Cornfield That Grew a Volcano (Mexico). By James A. Green. LXXXV, pp. 129-164, 16 ills. in black and white, 21 ills. in color, map, Feb., 1944

FOSSILS. *See* Paleontology

FOSTER, JOHN W.:

The Alaskan Boundary. By John W. Foster. X, pp. 425-456, 10 maps, map supplements, Nov., 1899

The Alaskan Boundary Tribunal. By John W. Foster. XV, pp. 1-12, map, map supplement, Jan., 1904

The Canadian Boundary. By John W. Foster. XIV, pp. 85-90, map, Mar., 1903

China. By John W. Foster. XV, pp. 463-478, maps, Dec., 1904

The Latin-American Constitutions and Revolutions. By John W. Foster. XII, pp. 169-175, May, 1901

The New Mexico. By John W. Foster. XIII, pp. 1-24, 11 ills., maps, Jan., 1902

Present Conditions in China. By John W. Foster. XVII, pp. 651-672, 709-711, Dec., 1906

FOUM TATAHOUINE, Tunisia:

The Mole Men: An Account of the Troglodytes of Southern Tunisia. By Frank Edward Johnson. XXII, pp. 787-846, 60 ills., Sept., 1911

FOUR Faces of Siva: The Mystery of Angkor (Cambodia). By Robert J. Casey. LIV, pp. 303-332, 13 ills. in black and white, 27 ills. in color, map, Sept., 1928

FOUR Prominent Geographers. XVIII, pp. 425-428, 4 ills., June, 1907

Biographies and portraits of the following: Arthur P. Davis, Frederick Haynes Newell, George Otis Smith, and Charles D. Walcott

FOUR Thousand Hours Over China. By Capt. Hans Koester. LXXIII, pp. 571-598, 25 ills., map, May, 1938

FOWL. *See* Poultry

FOWL of the Old and New World. 29 ills. in color from paintings by Hashime Murayama. LI, pp. 421-436, Apr., 1927

FOWLER, FREDERICK HALL:

Week-Ends with the Prairie Falcon: A Commuter Finds Recreation in Scaling Cliffs to Observe the Nest Life and Flying Habits of These Elusive Birds. By Frederick Hall Fowler. LXVII, pp. 611-626, 21 ills., May, 1935

FOWLIANG, China. *See* Kingtehchen

FOWLS of Forest and Stream Tamed by Man. By Morley A. Jull. Paintings by Hashime Murayama. LVII, pp. 327-371, 27 ills. in black and white, 16 ills. in color, Mar., 1930

Contents: Ducks, Geese, Guinea Fowl, Peafowl, Swans, Turkeys

FOX FARMING:

A Northern Crusoe's Island: Life on a Fox Farm Off the Coast of Alaska, Far from Contact with the World Eleven Months a Year. By Margery Pritchard Parker. XLIV, pp. 313-326, 15 ills., map, Sept., 1923

The Policemen of the Air: An Account of the Biological Survey of the Department of Agriculture. By Henry Wetherbee Henshaw. XIX, pp. 79-118, 38 ills., Feb., 1908

Included: Fox farming

FOX ISLAND PASSES, Alaska:

Some Notes on the Fox Island Passes, Alaska. By J. J. Gilbert. XVI, pp. 427-429, Sept., 1905

FRAM (Ship):

The Nansen Polar Expedititon. Special Report of the Hon. Ernest A. Man. VII, pp. 339-344, map supplement, Oct., 1896

Nansen's Polar Expedition. By General A. W. Greely. VII, pp. 98-101, ill., table, Mar., 1896

The Return of Dr. Nansen. VII, p. 290, Sept., 1896

FRANCE:

Aces Among Aces (Aviators). By Laurence La Tourette Driggs. XXXIII, pp. 568-580, 9 ills., June, 1918

Aces of the Air. By Captain Jacques De Sieyes. XXXIII, pp. 5-9, ills., Jan., 1918

Across the Midi in a Canoe: Two Americans Paddle Along the Canals of Southern France from the Atlantic to the Mediterranean. By Melville Chater. LII, pp. 127-167, 49 ills., map, Aug., 1927

Americans Help Liberated Europe Live Again. By Lt. Col. Frederick Simpich, Jr. LXXXVII, pp. 747-768, 17 ills., June, 1945

Armistice Day and the American Battle Fields. By J. J. Jusserand. LVI, pp. 509-554, 32 ills. in black and white, 23 ills. in color, Nov., 1929

The Ascent of Mont Blanc. By Walter Woodburn Hyde. XXIV, pp. 861-942, 69 ills., Aug., 1913

The Beauties of France. By Arthur Stanley Riggs. XXVIII, pp. 391-491, 73 ills. in black and white, 16 ills. in color, map, Nov., 1915

Bind the Wounds of France. By Herbert C. Hoover. XXXI, pp. 439-444, 5 ills., May, 1917

Brittany: The Land of the Sardine. By Hugh M. Smith. XX, pp. 541-573, 23 ills., June, 1909

The Burden France Has Borne. By Granville Fortescue. XXXI, pp. 323-344, 19 ills., Apr., 1917

Camargue, the Cowboy Country of Southern France. By Dr. André Vialles. XLII, pp. 1-34, 33 ills., map, July, 1922

A Canal from the Atlantic to the Mediterranean. XI, pp. 122-123, Mar., 1900

Carnival Days on the Riviera. By Maynard Owen Williams. L, pp. 467-501, 21 ills. in black and white, 21 ills. in color, Oct., 1926

Celebrating Christmas on the Meuse. By Captain Clifton Lisle. XXXVI, pp. 527-537, 5 ills., Dec., 1919

Château Land—France's Pageant on the Loire. LVIII, pp. 466-475, 10 ills. in color, Oct., 1930

A City Learns to Smile Again (Nancy). By Maj. Frederick G. Vosburgh. LXXXVII, pp. 361-384, 23 ills., map, Mar., 1945

FRANCE—*Continued*

The Coasts of Normandy and Brittany. By W. Robert Moore. LXXXIV, pp. 205-232, 5 ills. in black and white, 21 ills. in color, two-page map, Aug., 1943

The Colonial Expansion of France. By Professor Jean C. Bracq. XI, pp. 225-238, map, June, 1900

Cooties and Courage. By Herbert Corey. XXXIII, pp. 495-509, 10 ills., June, 1918

A Day with Our Boys in the Geographic Wards. By Carol Corey. XXXIV, pp. 69-80, 8 ills., July, 1918

Discovering the Oldest Statues in the World: A Daring Explorer Swims Through a Subterranean River of the Pyrenees and Finds Rock Carvings Made 20,000 Years Ago. By Norbert Casteret. XLVI, pp. 123-152, 24 ills., maps, Aug., 1924

Fearful Famines of the Past: History Will Repeat Itself Unless the American People Conserve Their Resources. By Ralph A. Graves. XXXII, pp. 69-90, 11 ills., July, 1917

Flashes of Color Throughout France. 28 color photos by Gervais Courtellemont. XLVI, pp. 529-544, Nov., 1924

Flying in France. By Captain André de Berroeta. XXXIII, pp. 9-26, 12 ills., Jan., 1918

France Farms as War Wages: An American Explores the Rich Rural Region of the Historic Paris Basin. By Harrison Howell Walker. LXXVII, pp. 201-238, 16 ills. in black and white, 18 ills. in color, map, Feb., 1940

The France of Today. By Major General A. W. Greely. XXVI, pp. 193-222, 27 ills., Sept., 1914

From the Trenches to Versailles. By Carol Corey. XXXII, pp. 535-550, 12 ills., Nov.-Dec., 1917

In French Lorraine: That Part of France Where the First American Soldiers Have Fallen. By Harriet Chalmers Adams. XXXII, pp. 499-518, 16 ills., Nov.-Dec., 1917

In Smiling Alsace, Where France Has Resumed Sway. LII, pp. 168-176, 11 ills. in color, Aug., 1927

The Land of William the Conqueror: Where Northmen Came to Build Castles and Cathedrals. By Inez Buffington Ryan. LXI, pp. 89-99, 13 ills. in color, Jan., 1932

The Life Story of an American Airman in France: Extracts from the Letters of Stuart Walcott, Who, Between July and December, 1917, Learned to Fly in French Schools of Aviation, Won Fame at the Front, and Fell Near Saint Souplet. XXXIII, pp. 86-106, 9 ills., Jan., 1918

Manless Alpine Climbing: The First Woman to Scale the Grépon, the Matterhorn, and Other Famous Peaks Without Masculine Support Relates Her Adventures. By Miriam O'Brien Underhill. LXVI, pp. 131-170, 30 ills. in black and white, 12 ills. in color, Aug., 1934

The Mysterious Prehistoric Monuments of Brittany. By Charles Buxton Going. XLIV, pp. 53-69, 16 ills., July, 1923

The National Geographic Society's Memorial to American Troops: Fountain and Water Supply System Presented to Historic French Town of Cantigny, Where Our Overseas Soldiers Won Their First Victory in the World War. XLIV, pp. 675-678, 4 ills., Dec., 1923

FRANCE—*Continued*

Normandy—Choice of the Vikings. By Helen Churchill Candee. LXIX, pp. 625-665, 25 ills. in black and white, 22 ills. in duotone, map, May, 1936

Normandy's Made-in-England Harbors. LXXXVII, pp. 565-580, 16 ills., map, May, 1945

Notes on Normandy. By Mrs. Geo. C. Bosson, Jr. XXI, pp. 775-782, 5 ills., Sept., 1910

Our First Alliance. By J. J. Jusserand. XXXI, pp. 518-548, 8 ills., June, 1917

Our Friends, the French: An Appraisal of the Traits and Temperament of the Citizens of Our Sister Republic. By Carl Holliday. XXXIV, pp. 345-377, 29 ills., Nov., 1918

Our Heritage of Liberty: An Address Before the United States Senate by M. Viviani, President of the French Commission to the United States, May 1, 1917. XXXI, pp. 365-367, ill., Apr., 1917

Our National War Memorials in Europe. By John J. Pershing. LXV, pp. 1-36, 24 ills. in black and white, 11 ills. in color, map, Jan., 1934

Our Second Alliance. By J. J. Jusserand. XXXI, pp. 565-566, ill., June, 1917

Our Transatlantic Flight. By Commander Richard Evelyn Byrd. LII, pp. 347-368, 17 ills., map, Sept., 1927

The Outspeaking of a Great Democracy: The Proceedings of the Chamber of Deputies of France on Friday, April 6, 1917, as Reported in the "Journal Officiel de La République Française." XXXI, pp. 362-365, ill., Apr., 1917

Plain Tales from the Trenches: As Told Over the Tea Table in Blighty—A Soldier's "Home" in Paris. By Carol Corey. XXXIII, pp. 300-312, 7 ills., Mar., 1918

The Price of Liberty, Equality, Fraternity. XXXIV, p. 377, Nov., 1918

The Races of Europe. By Edwin A. Grosvenor. XXXIV, pp. 441-534, 62 ills., diagr. and index, maps, map supplement, Dec., 1918

Republics—The Ladder to Liberty. By David Jayne Hill. XXXI, pp. 240-254, 5 ills., maps, Mar., 1917

Scenes from France. 16 ills. XL, pp. 29-44, July, 1921

The Seine, the Meuse, and the Moselle. (Part I). By William M. Davis. VII, pp. 189-202, ill., 7 maps, June, 1896

The Seine, the Meuse, and the Moselle. (Part) II. By William M. Davis. VII, pp. 228-238, table, 4 maps, July, 1896

Shopping Abroad for Our Armies in France. By Herbert Corey. XXXIII, pp. 206-218, 6 ills., Feb., 1918

A Skyline Drive in the Pyrenees. By W. Robert Moore. LXXII, pp. 434-452, 24 ills. in color, Oct., 1937

Through the Back Doors of France: A Seven Weeks' Voyage in a Canadian Canoe from St. Malo, Through Brittany and the Château Country, to Paris. By Melville Chater. XLIV, pp. 1-51, 55 ills., map, July, 1923

FRANCE—*Continued*

The Ties That Bind: Our Natural Sympathy with English Traditions, the French Republic, and the Russian Outburst for Liberty. By John Sharp Williams. XXXI, pp. 281-286, 4 ills., Mar., 1917

Where Bretons Wrest a Living from the Sea. 23 photos by F. W. Goro. LXXI, pp. 751-766, June, 1937

The World's Debt to France. XXVIII, pp. 491-501, 7 ills., Nov., 1915

See also Compiègne; Corsica (Island); Dieppe; Marseille; Paris; St. Malo; Versailles

The **FRANCE** of Sunshine and Flowers. 21 color photos by Maynard Owen Williams, Gervais Courtellemont, Hans Hildenbrand. L, pp. 481-496, Oct., 1926

FRANK, Alberta (Province), Canada:

Landslides and Rock Avalanches. By Guy Elliott Mitchell. XXI, pp. 277-287, 6 ills., Apr., 1910

FRANKENFIELD, H. C.:

Kite Work of the Weather Bureau. By H. C. Frankenfield. XI, pp. 55-62, Feb., 1900

The Weather Bureau and the Recent Floods. By H. C. Frankenfield. XIV, pp. 285-290, ills., July, 1903

FRANKINCENSE:

The Isle of Frankincense (Socotra, Arabian Sea). By Charles K. Moser. XXXIII, pp. 267-278, 11 ills., Mar., 1918

FRANKLIN, ALICELIA:

Historic Danzig: Last of the City-States. By William and Alicelia Franklin. LXXVI, pp. 677-696, 26 ills., Nov., 1939

FRANKLIN, BENJAMIN:

The Historic City of Brotherly Love: Philadelphia, Born of Penn and Strengthened by Franklin, a Metropolis of Industries, Homes, and Parks. By John Oliver La Gorce. LXII, pp. 643-697, 49 ills. in black and white, 13 ills. in color, Dec., 1932

FRANKLIN, SIR JOHN:

Location of the Sir John Franklin Monument. By James White. XIX, p. 596, Aug., 1908

FRANKLIN, WILLIAM:

Historic Danzig: Last of the City-States. By William and Alicelia Franklin. LXXVI, pp. 677-696, 26 ills., Nov., 1939

FRANKLIN INSTITUTE:

Series of flights under auspices of National Geographic Society, U. S. Army Air Forces, and Bartol Research Foundation of the Franklin Institute, to study cosmic rays. XC, p. 387, ill. p. 388, Sept., 1946

FRANZ JOSEF LAND, Arctic Region:

Through Franz Josef Land. X, p. 362, Sept., 1899

The Wellman Polar Expedition. By Walter Wellman. X, pp. 481-505, 10 ills., diagr., map, Dec., 1899

FRASER, EDWIN R.:

Where Our Bananas Come From (Costa Rica). By Edwin R. Fraser. XXIII, pp. 713-730, 14 ills., July, 1912

FREDERIC W. Putnam. (By J. H.). IX, pp. 429-431, ill. (front.), Oct., 1898

FREDERICKSBURG, Virginia:

Announcement of the Seventh Annual Excursion and Field Meeting, Saturday, May 4, 1895. VI, foldout, Apr. 20, 1895

"FREE BURGHS" in the United States. By James H. Blodgett. VII, pp. 116-122, Mar., 1896

FREEMAN, LEWIS R.:

The Mother of Rivers: An Account of a Photographic Expedition to the Great Columbia Ice Field of the Canadian Rockies. By Lewis R. Freeman. XLVII, pp. 377-446, 60 ills., maps, Apr., 1925

Surveying the Grand Canyon of the Colorado: An Account of the 1923 Boating Expedition of the United States Geological Survey. By Lewis R. Freeman. XLV, pp. 471-548, 62 ills., map, May, 1924

Trailing History Down the Big Muddy: In the Homeward Wake of Lewis and Clark, a Folding Steel Skiff Bears Its Lone Pilot on a 2,000-Mile Cruise on the Yellowstone-Missouri. By Lewis R. Freeman. LIV, pp. 73-120, 51 ills., map, July, 1928

FREIBURG (Germany)—Gateway to the Black Forest. By Alicia O'Reardon Overbeck. LXIV, pp. 213-252, 40 ills. in black and white, 11 ills. in color, Aug., 1933

FREIGHTERS of Fortune on our Great Lakes. 8 ills. in duotone by Maynard Owen Williams. LXV, pp. 463-470, Apr., 1934

FRENCH, GEORGE K.:

The Gold Coast, Ashanti, and Kumassi. By George K. French. VIII, pp. 1-15, 9 ills., Jan., 1897

FRENCH AND INDIAN WAR:

The Travels of George Washington: Dramatic Episodes in His Career as the First Geographer of the United States. By William Joseph Showalter. LXI, pp. 1-63, 50 ills., 5 maps, map supplement, Jan., 1932

FRENCH-CANADIANS:

The Origin of French-Canadians. IX, pp. 96-97, Mar., 1898

FRENCH Conquest of the Sahara. By Charles Rabot. XVI, pp. 76-80, ills., Feb., 1905

FRENCH EQUATORIAL AFRICA:

Three-Wheeling Through Africa: Two Adventurers Cross the So-called Dark Continent North of Lake Chad on Motorcycles with Side Cars. By James C. Wilson. LXV, pp. 37-92, 64 ills., two-page map, Jan., 1934

Through the Deserts and Jungles of Africa by Motor: Caterpillar Cars Make 15,000-Mile Trip from Algeria to Madagascar in Nine Months. By Georges-Marie Haardt. XLIX, pp. 651-720, 95 ills., map, June, 1926

See also Chad Territory

FRENCH GUIANA:
Brazil-French Guiana Boundary Decision. XII, p. 83, Feb., 1901
Color Glows in the Guianas, French and Dutch. By Nicol Smith. LXXXIII, pp. 459-480, 8 ills. in black and white, 13 ills. in color, map, Apr., 1943

FRENCH GUINEA:
Dusky Tribesmen of French West Africa. 26 color photos by Enzo de Chetelat. LXXIX, pp. 639-662, May, 1941
My Domestic Life in French Guinea: An American Woman Accompanies Her Husband, a French Geologist, on His Explorations in a Little-Known Region. By Eleanor de Chételat. LXVII, pp. 695-730, 48 ills., map, June, 1935

FRENCH INDO-CHINA:
Along the Old Mandarin Road of Indo-China. By W. Robert Moore. LX, pp. 157-199, 32 ills. in black and white, 28 ills. in color, map, Aug., 1931
By Motor Trail Across French Indo-China. By Maynard Owen Williams. LXVIII, pp. 487-534, 31 ills. in black and white, 27 ills. in color, map, Oct., 1935
The Forgotten Ruins of Indo-China. By Jacob E. Conner. XXIII, pp. 209-272, 63 ills., maps, Mar., 1912
Four Faces of Siva: The Mystery of Angkor. By Robert J. Casey. LIV, pp. 303-332, 13 ills. in black and white, 27 ills. in color, map, Sept., 1928
Glimpses of Asia. 16 ills. XXXIX, pp. 553-568, May, 1921

FRENCH MOROCCO. *See* Morocco

FRENCH NORTH AFRICA:
Americans on the Barbary Coast. By Willard Price. LXXXIV, pp. 1-31, 13 ills. in black and white, 10 ills. in color, map, July, 1943
Eastward from Gibraltar: Overland Route Across North Africa to Tunisia and Libia. By Cyrus French Wicker. LXXXIII, pp. 115-142, 28 ills., Jan., 1943
In Civilized French Africa. By James F. J. Archibald. XX, pp. 303-311, 14 ills., Mar., 1909
Through the Deserts and Jungles of Africa by Motor: Caterpillar Cars Make 15,000-Mile Trip from Algeria to Madagascar in Nine Months. By Georges-Marie Haardt. XLIX, pp. 651-720, 95 ills., map, June, 1926
Yank Meets Native. By Wanda Burnett. LXXXVIII, pp. 105-128, 24 ills., July, 1945
See also Algeria; Morocco; Tunisia

FRENCH SOMALILAND:
Across Widest Africa. By A. Henry Savage Landor. XIX, pp. 694-737, 38 ills., map, Oct., 1908
Sailing Forbidden Coasts. By Ida Treat. LX, pp. 357-386, 31 ills., map, Sept., 1931

FRENCH SUDAN:
Timbuktu, in the Sands of the Sahara. By Captain Cecil D. Priest. XLV, pp. 73-85, 16 ills., Jan., 1924

FRENCH SUDAN—*Continued*
Timbuktu and Beyond: Desert City of Romantic Savor and Salt Emerges into World Life Again as Trading Post of France's Vast African Empire. By Laura C. Boulton. LXXIX, pp. 631-670, 18 ills. in black and white, 26 ills. in color, map, May, 1941

FRENCH WEST AFRICA:
French Conquest of the Sahara. By Charles Rabot. XVI, pp. 76-80, ills., Feb., 1905
French West Africa in Wartime. By Paul M. Atkins. LXXXI, pp. 371-408, 37 ills., maps, Mar., 1942
My Domestic Life in French Guinea: An American Woman Accompanies Her Husband, a French Geologist, on His Explorations in a Little-Known Region. By Eleanor de Chételat. LXVII, pp. 695-730, 48 ills., map, June, 1935
Recent French Explorations in Africa. By Dr. Charles Rabot. XIII, pp. 119-132, 20 ills., Apr., 1902
Sindbads of Science: Narrative of a Windjammer's Specimen-Collecting Voyage to the Sargasso Sea, to Senegambian Africa and Among Islands of High Adventure in the South Atlantic. By George Finlay Simmons. LII, pp. 1-75, 89 ills., map, July, 1927
Three-Wheeling Through Africa: Two Adventurers Cross the So-called Dark Continent North of Lake Chad on Motorcycles with Side Cars. By James C. Wilson. LXV, pp. 37-92, 64 ills., two-page map, Jan., 1934
Through the Deserts and Jungles of Africa by Motor: Caterpillar Cars Make 15,000-Mile Trip from Algeria to Madagascar in Nine Months. By Georges-Marie Haardt. XLIX, pp. 651-720, 95 ills., map, June, 1926
Timbuktu, in the Sands of the Sahara. By Captain Cecil D. Priest. XLV, pp. 73-85, 16 ills., Jan., 1924
Timbuktu and Beyond: Desert City of Romantic Savor and Salt Emerges into World Life Again as Trading Post of France's Vast African Empire. By Laura C. Boulton. LXXIX, pp. 631-670, 18 ills. in black and white, 26 ills. in color, map, May, 1941

FRENCH WEST INDIES. *See* Guadeloupe; Martinique

FRESCOES:
Multicolored Cones of Cappadocia. 20 color photos by Eric Matson. LXXVI, pp. 769-800, Dec., 1939

FRESH-WATER Denizens of the Far West (Salmon, Trout, etc.). 44 portraits from paintings by Hashime Murayama. LXXV, pp. 193-204, Feb., 1939

FRESH-WATER Fishes of the United States. 16 ills. in color from paintings by Hashime Murayama. XLIV, pp. 133-148, Aug., 1923

FRIANT DAM, California:
More Water for California's Great Central Valley. By Frederick Simpich. XC, pp. 645-664, 16 ills., map, Nov., 1946

FRIENDLY BAY, Portugal:

Lisbon, the City of the Friendly Bay. By Clifford Albion Tinker. XLII, pp. 505-552, 30 ills. in black and white, 16 ills. in color, map, Nov., 1922

The **FRIENDLY** Crows (Indians) in Festive Panoply. 13 color photos by Edwin L. Wisherd. LII, pp. 315-322, Sept., 1927

FRIENDLY ISLANDS. *See* Tonga Islands

FRIENDLY Journeys in Japan: A Young American Finds a Ready Welcome in the Homes of the Japanese During Leisurely Travels Through the Islands. By John Patric. LXIX, pp. 441-480, 28 ills. in black and white, 10 ills. in color, map, Apr., 1936

FRIENDS of Our Forests. By Henry Wetherbee Henshaw. Paintings by Louis Agassiz Fuertes. XXXI, pp. 297-321, ill. in black and white, 32 ills. in color, Apr., 1917

The **FRINGE** of Verdure Around Asia Minor. By Ellsworth Huntington. XXI, pp. 761-775, 15 ills., Sept., 1910

FRISIAN ISLANDS. *See* North Frisian Islands

FRITHJOF (Ship):

The Wellman Polar Expedition. By Walter Wellman. X, pp. 481-505, 10 ills., diagr., map, Dec., 1899

A **FROG** That Eats Bats and Snakes: In Captivity, This Big Jungle Amphibian Exhibits an Extraordinary Appetite. By Kenneth W. Vinton. LXXIII, pp. 657-664, 11 ills., May, 1938

FROGS:

A Frog That Eats Bats and Snakes: In Captivity, This Big Jungle Amphibian Exhibits an Extraordinary Appetite. By Kenneth W. Vinton. LXXIII, pp. 657-664, 11 ills., May, 1938

Our Friend the Frog. By Doris M. Cochran. Paintings by Hashime Murayama. LXI, pp. 629-654, 16 ills. in black and white, 14 ills. in color, May, 1932

FROM Africa to the Alps. 8 ills. in color from U. S. Army Air Forces official photos. LXXXIX, pp. 161-168, Feb., 1946

FROM Chalet to Palace in Bavaria (Germany). 14 color photos by Hans Hildenbrand. LIV, pp. 683-690, Dec., 1928

FROM England to India by Automobile: An 8,527-mile Trip Through Ten Countries, from London to Quetta, Requires Five and a Half Months. By Major F. A. C. Forbes-Leith. XLVIII, pp. 191-223, 33 ills., map, Aug., 1925

FROM Granada to Gibraltar—A Tour of Southern Spain. By Harry A. McBride. XLVI, pp. 205-232, 23 ills., Aug., 1924

FROM Jerusalem to Aleppo. By John D. Whiting. XXIV, pp. 71-113, 30 ills., map, Jan., 1913

FROM London to Australia by Aëroplane: A Personal Narrative of the First Aërial Voyage Half Around the World. By Sir Ross Smith. XXXIX, pp. 229-339, 76 ills. in black and white, 8 ills. in color, map, Mar., 1921

FROM Nature's Hidden Building Blocks (Synthetic Products). 26 color photos by Willard R. Culver. LXXVI, pp. 609-640, Nov., 1939

FROM Notch to Notch in the White Mountains: Soaring Heights of New Hampshire Attract Multitudes to America's Oldest Mountain Recreation Area. By Leonard Cornell Roy. LXXII, pp. 73-104, 30 ills., map supplement, July, 1937

FROM Panama to Patagonia. By Charles M. Pepper. XVII, pp. 449-452, ill., Aug., 1906

FROM Sand to Seer and Servant of Man (Glassmaking). 22 color photos by Willard R. Culver. LXXXIII, pp. 17-48, Jan., 1943

FROM Sea to Clouds in Ecuador. By W. Robert Moore. LXXX, pp. 717-740, 11 ills. in black and white, 9 ills. in color, Dec., 1941

FROM Stratford to the North Sea (England). 16 color photos by Clifton Adams. LV, pp. 617-624, May, 1929

FROM the Halls of Montezuma (Mexico). 21 color photos by Richard H. Stewart and others. LXXXV, pp. 137-164, Feb., 1944

FROM the Mediterranean to the Yellow Sea by Motor: The Citroën-Haardt Expedition Successfully Completes Its Dramatic Journey. By Maynard Owen Williams. LXII, pp. 513-580, 45 ills. in black and white, 25 ills. in color, maps, Nov., 1932

FROM the Plains of Madras to the Snows of Kashmir. 16 ills. XLVI, pp. 561-576, Nov., 1924

FROM the Trenches to Versailles. By Carol Corey. XXXII, pp. 535-550, 12 ills., Nov.-Dec., 1917

FROM the War-Path to the Plow. By Franklin K. Lane. XXVII, pp. 73-87, 12 ills., Jan., 1915

FRONT-LINE Town of Britain's Siege (Dover). By Harvey Klemmer. LXXXV, pp. 105-128, 21 ills., Jan., 1944

FRONTIER Cities of Italy. By Florence Craig Albrecht. XXVII, pp. 533-586, 45 ills., June, 1915

FROST:

The Magic Beauty of Snow and Dew. By Wilson A. Bentley. XLIII, pp. 103-112, 9 ills., Jan., 1923

FROZEN FOODS:

Your New World of Tomorrow. By F. Barrows Colton. LXXXVIII, pp. 385-410, 25 ills., Oct., 1945

FRUITFUL Shores of the Finger Lakes (New York). By Harrison Howell Walker. LXXIX, pp. 559-594, 15 ills. in black and white, 22 ills. in color, map, May, 1941

FRUITS:

Agricultural Possibilities in Tropical Mexico. By Dr. Pehr Olsson-Seffer. XXI, pp. 1021-1040, 19 ills., Dec., 1910

American Berries of Hill, Dale, and Wayside. Paintings by Mary E. Eaton. XXXV, pp. 168-184, ill. in black and white, 29 ills. in color, Feb., 1919

FRUITS—*Continued*

Costa Rica, Land of the Banana. By Paul B. Popenoe. XLI, pp. 201-220, 17 ills., Feb., 1922

The Date Gardens of the Jerid (Northern Africa). By Thomas H. Kearney. XXI, pp. 543-567, 20 ills., July, 1910

Flavor and Savor of American Foods. 25 color photos by J. Baylor Roberts, Willard R. Culver, and others. LXXXI, pp. 289-320, Mar., 1942

Fruitful Shores of the Finger Lakes (New York). By Harrison Howell Walker. LXXIX, pp. 559-594, 15 ills. in black and white, 22 ills. in color, map, May, 1941

The Introduction of the Mango. XIV, pp. 320-327, 5 ills., Aug., 1903

More Water for California's Great Central Valley. By Frederick Simpich. XC, pp. 645-664, 16 ills., map, Nov., 1946

New Plant Immigrants. By David Fairchild. XXII, pp. 879-907, 34 ills., Oct., 1911

Peacetime Plant Hunting About Peiping. By P. H. and J. H. Dorsett. LXXII, pp. 509-534, 21 ills., map, Oct., 1937

Reviving a Lost Art (Drying Fruits and Vegetables). XXXI, pp. 475-481, 9 ills., June, 1917

Round About Bogotá: A Hunt for New Fruits and Plants Among the Mountain Forests of Colombia's Unique Capital. By Wilson Popenoe. XLIX, pp. 127-160, 34 ills., map, Feb., 1926

Taming the Wild Blueberry. By Frederick V. Coville. XXII, pp. 137-147, 5 ills., Feb., 1911

The Texas Delta of an American Nile: Orchards and Gardens Replace Thorny Jungle in the Southmost Tip of the Lone Star State. By McFall Kerbey. LXXV, pp. 51-96, 27 ills. in black and white, 24 ills. in color, map, Jan., 1939

The United States; Its Soils and Their Products. By H. W. Wiley. XIV, pp. 263-279, 11 ills., July, 1903

Where Our Bananas Come From (Costa Rica). By Edwin R. Fraser. XXIII, pp. 713-730, 14 ills., July, 1912

The Wild Blueberry Tamed: The New Industry of the Pine Barrens of New Jersey. By Frederick V. Coville. XXIX, pp. 535-546, 10 ills., June, 1916

FUEL:

The Conversion of Old Newspapers and Candle Ends into Fuel. XXXI, pp. 568-570, 3 ills., June, 1917

An Ideal Fuel Manufactured Out of Waste Products: The American Coal Briquetting Industry. By Guy Elliott Mitchell. XXI, pp. 1067-1074, 4 ills., Dec., 1910

See also Coal and Coal Mining; Petroleum

FUERST, FRANCIS C.:

Merry Maskers of Imst (Austria). 14 photos by Francis C. Fuerst. LXX, pp. 201-208, Aug., 1936

FUERTES, LOUIS AGASSIZ:

Birds (American Game Birds). 72 ills. in color from paintings by Louis Agassiz Fuertes. XXVIII, pp. 109-144, Aug., 1915

FUERTES, LOUIS AGASSIZ—*Continued*

Birds (Common Birds of Farm and Orchard). 50 ills. in color from paintings by Louis Agassiz Fuertes. XXIV, pp. 673-697, June, 1913

Birds (Common Birds of Town and Country). 64 ills. in color from paintings by Louis Agassiz Fuertes. XXV, pp. 499-530, May, 1914

Birds (The Warblers of North America). 32 ills. in color from paintings by Louis Agassiz Fuertes. XXXI, pp. 305-320, Apr., 1917

Dogs: Our Common Dogs. By Louis Agassiz Fuertes and Ernest Harold Baynes. XXXV, pp. 201-253, 73 ills. in color, index p. 280, Mar., 1919

Dogs. 73 ills. in color from paintings by Louis Agassiz Fuertes, pp. 202-263

Falconry, the Sport of Kings. By Louis Agassiz Fuertes. XXXVIII, pp. 429-460, 13 ills. in black and white, 12 ills. in color, Dec., 1920

Falcons. 12 ills. in color from paintings by author, pp. 441-456

Mammals: The Larger North American Mammals. 49 ills. in color from paintings by Louis Agassiz Fuertes. XXX, pp. 410-471, pictorial supplement, Nov., 1916

The Alaska Brown Bear: The Largest Carnivorous Animal Extant (supplement by artist)

Mammals: Smaller Mammals of North America. 59 ills. in color from paintings by Louis Agassiz Fuertes. XXXIII, pp. 404-465, May, 1918

FUJI (Peak), Japan:

The Geography of Japan: With Special Reference to Its Influence on the Character of the Japanese People. By Walter Weston. XL, pp. 45-84, 23 ills. in black and white, 16 ills. in color, July, 1921

FULAH (Tribespeople):

Dusky Tribesmen of French West Africa. 26 color photos by Enzo de Chetelat. LXXIX, pp. 639-662, May, 1941

FUMAROLES:

The Valley of Ten Thousand Smokes: An Account of the Discovery and Exploration of the Most Wonderful Volcanic Region in the World. By Robert F. Griggs. XXXIII, pp. 115-169, 46 ills., map, panorama, Feb., 1918

FUNCHAL, Madeira (Island):

Madeira the Florescent. By Harriet Chalmers Adams. LXVI, pp. 81-106, 19 ills. in black and white, 13 ills. in color, map, July, 1934

FUNDAMENTAL Geographic Relation of the Three Americas. By Robert T. Hill. VII, pp. 175-181, map, May, 1896

FUNDY, Bay of, Canada-U. S.:

Atlantic Coast Tides. By Mark S. W. Jefferson. IX, pp. 497-509, 3 charts, Dec., 1898

Tides in the Bay of Fundy. XVI, pp. 71-76, 4 ills., Feb., 1905

FUNGI:

Common Mushrooms of the United States. By Louis C. C. Krieger. Paintings by author. XXXVII, pp. 387-439, 37 ills. in black and white, 16 ills. in color, May, 1920

FUR FARMING. *See* Fox Farming

FURTHER Explorations in the Land of the Incas: The Peruvian Expedition of 1915 of the National Geographic Society and Yale University. By Hiram Bingham. XXIX, pp. 431-473, 29 ills., maps, panorama, May, 1916

FURTHER Notes on Dutch New Guinea. By Thomas Barbour. XIX, pp. 527-545, 19 ills., Aug., 1908

The **FUTURE** of the Airplane. By Rear Admiral Robert E. Peary. XXXIII, pp. 107-113, 4 ills., Jan., 1918

The **FUTURE** of the Yukon Goldfields. By William H. Dall. IX, pp. 117-120, Apr., 1898

FUZZY-WUZZIES (Tribespeople):
Two Fighting Tribes of the Sudan. By Merian C. Cooper. Photos by Ernest B. Schoedsack. LVI, pp. 465-486, 27 ills., map, Oct., 1929

G

GABERELL, JEAN:
Skiing in Switzerland's Realm of Winter Sports. 6 photos in duotone by Jean Gaberell. LXIII, pp. 345-352, Mar., 1933

GABES, Tunisia:
The Mole Men: An Account of the Troglodytes of Southern Tunisia. By Frank Edward Johnson. XXII, pp. 787-846, 60 ills., Sept., 1911

GADE, JOHN H.:
Belgium's Plight. By John H. Gade. XXXI, pp. 433-439, 3 ills., May, 1917

GADSDEN PURCHASE:
Boundaries of Territorial Acquisitions. XII, pp. 373-377, chart, Oct., 1901

GAILLARD, D. D.:
The Washington Aqueduct and Cabin John Bridge. By D. D. Gaillard. VIII, pp. 337-344, ills., Dec., 1897

GALÁPAGOS ISLANDS, Pacific Ocean:
At Home on the Oceans: Whales and Sharks Make Exciting Neighbors for a Professor's Wife, Turned Able Seaman, On a Three-year Voyage Around the World. By Edith Bauer Strout. LXXVI, pp. 33-86, 54 ills., map, July, 1939
The Dream Ship: The Story of a Voyage of Adventure More Than Half Around the World in a 47-foot Lifeboat. By Ralph Stock. XXXIX, pp. 1-52, 43 ills., map, Jan., 1921
Westward Bound in the *Yankee*. By Irving and Electa Johnson. LXXXI, pp. 1-44, 25 ills. in black and white, 20 ills. in color, map, Jan., 1942

GALICIA:
Partitioned Poland. By William Joseph Showalter. XXVII, pp. 88-106, 12 ills., Jan., 1915

GALILEE, Sea of, Palestine:
The Geography of the Jordan. By Nelson Glueck. LXXXVI, pp. 719-744, 23 ills., map, Dec., 1944

GALILEE, Sea of, Palestine—*Continued*
Impressions of Palestine. By James Bryce. XXVII, pp. 293-317, 18 ills., map, Mar., 1915

GALILEE (Ship):
The Work in the Pacific Ocean of the Magnetic Survey Yacht "Galilee." By L. A. Bauer. XVIII, pp. 601-611, 15 ills., Sept., 1907

GALL MIDGES. *See* Midges

GALLANT Little Sportsmen of the Terrier Tribe. 33 portraits from paintings by Edward Herbert Miner. LXIX, pp. 253-268, Feb., 1936

GALLOWAY, A. C.:
An Interesting Visit to the Ancient Pyramids of San Juan Teotihuacan. By A. C. Galloway. XXI, pp. 1041-1050, 8 ills., map, Dec., 1910

GALVESTON, Texas:
How We Use the Gulf of Mexico. By Frederick Simpich. LXXXV, pp. 1-40, 20 ills. in black and white, 19 ills. in color, two-page map, Jan., 1944
The Lessons of Galveston. By W J McGee. XI, pp. 377-383, Oct., 1900
Texas, Our Largest State. By N. H. Darton. XXIV, pp. 1330-1360, 22 ills., maps, Dec., 1913

GAMA, VASCO DA:
The Pathfinder of the East: Setting Sail to Find "Christians and Spices," Vasco da Gama Met Amazing Adventures, Founded an Empire, and Changed the History of Western Europe. By J. R. Hildebrand. LII, pp. 503-550, 43 ills., map, pictorial supplement, Nov., 1927
Vasco da Gama at the Court of the Zamorin of Calicut. Reproduction in color of the painting by José Velloso Salgado, Sociedade de Geographia de Lisboa (supplement)

GAME. *See* Mammals

GAME and Fur-Bearing Animals and Their Influence on the Indians of the Northwest. By Townsend W. Thorndike. XV, p. 431, Oct., 1904

GAME BIRDS:
American Game Birds. By Henry Wetherbee Henshaw. Paintings by Louis Agassiz Fuertes. XXVIII, pp. 105-158, 4 ills. in black and white, 72 ills. in color, Aug., 1915
Contents: Cranes, Ducks, Geese, Grouse, Pheasants, Pigeons, Plovers, Quails, Rails, Sandpipers, Snipes, Stilts, Swans
Birds on the Home Front. By Arthur A. Allen. LXXXIV, pp. 32-56, 7 ills. in black and white, 30 ills. in color, July, 1943
Far-Flying Wild Fowl and Their Foes. By Major Allan Brooks. Paintings from life by author. LXVI, pp. 487-528, 6 ills. in black and white, 93 portraits in color, Oct., 1934
Contents: Ducks, Geese, Swans
Game Birds of Prairie, Forest, and Tundra. By Alexander Wetmore. Paintings by Maj. Allan Brooks. LXX, pp. 461-500, 5 ills. in black and white, 60 portraits in color, Oct., 1936
Contents: Doves, Grouse, Partridges, Pheasants, Pigeons, Prairie Chickens, Ptarmigans, Quails, Turkeys

GAME BIRDS—*Continued*

Notes on the Wild Fowl and Game Animals of Alaska. By E. W. Nelson. IX, pp. 121-132, 6 ills., Apr., 1898

A **GAME** Country Without Rival in America: The Proposed Mount McKinley National Park. By Stephen R. Capps. XXXI, pp. 69-84, 14 ills., map, Jan., 1917

GAME FOWL (Game Cocks):

The Races of Domestic Fowl. By M. A. Jull. Paintings by Hashime Murayama. LI, pp. 379-452, 67 ills. in black and white, 29 ills. in color, Apr., 1927

Sarawak: The Land of the White Rajahs. By Harrison W. Smith. XXXV, pp. 110-167, 58 ills., map, Feb., 1919

GAME PRESERVES:

Africa the Largest Game Preserve in the World. (By John B. Torbert). XI, pp. 445-448, map, Nov., 1900

A Game Country Without Rival in America: The Proposed Mount McKinley National Park. By Stephen R. Capps. XXXI, pp. 69-84, 14 ills., map, Jan., 1917

The Policemen of the Air: An Account of the Biological Survey of the Department of Agriculture. By Henry Wetherbee Henshaw. XIX, pp. 79-118, 38 ills., Feb., 1908

Included: Big-game refuges and bird reservations

Where Birds and Little Animals Find Haven (Eaton Canyon Bird and Game Sanctuary). By Agnes Akin Atkinson. LXX, pp. 232-241, 14 ills., Aug., 1936

GAMES. *See* Sports and Games

GAMMANS, LEONARD DAVID:

The United States and the British Empire. By Leonard David Gammans. LXXXVII, pp. 562-564, May, 1945

Yanks at Westminster. By Capt. Leonard David Gammans. XC, pp. 223-252, 6 ills. in black and white, 19 ills. in color, Aug., 1946

GAN SHEMUEL, Palestine:

Palestine Today. By Francis Chase, Jr. XC, pp. 501-516, 16 ills., Oct., 1946

GANNETS:

Birds of the High Seas: Albatrosses and Petrels; Gannets, Man-o'-war-birds, and Tropic-birds. By Robert Cushman Murphy. Paintings by Major Allan Brooks. LXXIV, pp. 226-251, 7 ills. in black and white, 36 portraits in color, Aug., 1938

GANNETT, HENRY:

Agriculture in Alaska. (By Henry Gannett). XIII, p. 112, Mar., 1902

The Annexation Fever. (By Henry Gannett). VIII, pp. 354-358, Dec., 1897

Captain Charles D. Sigsbee, U. S. N. (By H. G.). IX, p. 250, ill. (front.), May, 1898

Chairman of Research Committee. XX, p. 486, May, 1909

Committee appointed to consider claims of Peary and Cook. XX, pp. 921-922, 1008, Nov., 1909

GANNETT, HENRY—*Continued*

Conditions in Cuba as Revealed by the Census. By Henry Gannett. XX, pp. 200-202, Feb., 1909

Conservation League of America. By Henry Gannett. XIX, pp. 737-739, Oct., 1908

Death notice. XXVI, p. 520, Nov., 1914

Elected member of the Geographical Society of Paris. XVIII, p. 428, June, 1907

The Forest Conditions and Standing Timber of the State of Washington. By Henry Gannett. IX, pp. 410-412, Sept., 1898

The General Geography of Alaska. By Henry Gannett. XII, pp. 180-196, 9 ills., May, 1901

Geographic Literature. VIII, pp. 60-61, Feb., 1897; pp. 230-232, July-Aug., 1897; p. 365, Dec., 1897. IX, pp. 71-72, Feb., 1898

Geographic Serials. VIII, pp. 25-26, Jan., 1897; pp. 61-63, Feb., 1897; pp. 92-94, Mar., 1897; pp. 127-128, Apr., 1897; pp. 158-159, May, 1897; pp. 190-191, June, 1897. IX, p. 256, May, 1898

Geographic Work of the General Government. By Henry Gannett. IX, pp. 329-338, July, 1898

The Great Ice Barrier (Antarctica). By Henry Gannett. XXI, pp. 173-174, ill., Feb., 1910

The Harriman Alaska Expedition. By Henry Gannett. X, pp. 507-512, chart, map, Dec., 1899

Henry Gannett (Biography). XXVI, pp. 609-613, ill., Dec., 1914

Honors to Amundsen and Peary (Speech by Henry Gannett). XXIV, pp. 113-130, 5 ills., Jan., 1913

In Honor of the Army and Aviation (Speech by Henry Gannett). XXII, pp. 267-284, ill., Mar., 1911

Judge of NGS prize essay contest. X, p. 32, Jan., 1899

Lake Chelan. By Henry Gannett. IX, pp. 417-428, 7 ills., map, Oct., 1898

Miscellanea. (By H. G.). VIII, p. 160, May, 1897

The Mother Maps of the United States. By Henry Gannett. IV, pp. 101-116, table, map supplement, Mar. 31, 1892

The Movements of Our Population. By Henry Gannett. V, pp. 21-44, 7 diagrs., 15 tables, 15 maps, Mar. 20, 1893

The National Geographic Society (Speech by Henry Gannett). XXIII, pp. 272-298, 5 ills., Mar., 1912

The Origin of Yosemite Valley. (By Henry Gannett). XII, pp. 86-87, Feb., 1901

Our Foreign Trade. (By H.G.). IX, pp. 27-28, Jan., 1898

The Philippine Islands and Their People. By Henry Gannett. XV, pp. 91-112, 13 ills., Mar., 1904

Place Names in Canada. (By H. G.). X, pp. 519-520, Dec., 1899

The Population of the United States. By Henry Gannett. XXII, pp. 34-48, 9 diagrs., 3 maps, Jan., 1911

Portraits. VII pl. XXVIII (front.), Aug., 1896. XII, ill. p. 195, May, 1901. XXVI, ill. p. 611, Dec., 1914

Recent Population Figures. By Henry Gannett. XXII, pp. 785-786, Aug., 1911

GANNETT, HENRY—*Continued*

The Redwood Forest of the Pacific Coast. By Henry Gannett. X, pp. 145-159, 6 ills., map, May, 1899

Statistics of Railways in the United States. (By H. G.). VII, pp. 406-407, Dec., 1896

The Survey and Map of Massachusetts. By Henry Gannett. I, pp. 78-86, Oct., 1888

Survey and Subdivision of Indian Territory. By Henry Gannett. VII, pp. 112-115, ill., map, Mar., 1896

The Topographic Atlas of the United States (Compiled by Henry Gannett). (By W J M.). IX, pp. 343-344, July, 1898

The Work of the United States Board on Geographic Names. By Henry Gannett. VII, pp. 221-227, July, 1896

See also NGS: Board of Managers; Founders; President; Secretary; Treasurer; Vice-President

GANNETT, S. S.:

Recent Triangulation in the Cascades (Washington). By S. S. Gannett. VII, p. 150, Apr., 1896

GARDENING in Northern Alaska. By Middleton Smith. XIV, pp. 355-357, Sept., 1903

GARDENS:

Bulgaria: Tirnova, the City of Hanging Gardens. By Felix J. Koch. XVIII, pp. 632-640, 7 ills., Oct., 1907

England: Bekonscot, England's Toy-Size Town. By Andrew H. Brown and B. Anthony Stewart. LXXI, pp. 649-661, 2 ills. in black and white, 15 ills. in color, May, 1937

England: Summering in an English Cottage: Quiet and Loveliness Invite Contemplation in the Extra "Room," the Garden of the Thatched House. By Helen Churchill Candee. LXVII, pp. 429-456, 32 ills., Apr., 1935

England: A Vacation in a Fifteenth Century English Manor House. By George Alden Sanford. LIII, pp. 629-636, 8 ills., May, 1928

England's Island Garden of Rocks and Flowers (Isle of Wight). 14 color photos by W. Robert Moore. LXVII, pp. 17-24, Jan., 1935

France: The Palace of Versailles, Its Park and the Trianons. By Franklin L. Fisher. XLVII, pp. 49-62, 4 ills. in black and white, 14 ills. in color, Jan., 1925

Maryland: Maytime in the Heart of Maryland (Sherwood Gardens). 10 color photos by B. Anthony Stewart and Charles Martin. LXXIX, pp. 441-448, Apr., 1941

Mount Vernon: The Home of the First Farmer of America. By Worth E. Shoults. LIII, pp. 603-628, 6 ills. in black and white, 26 ills. in color, May, 1928

Portugal: The Woods and Gardens of Portugal. By Martin Hume. XXI, pp. 883-894, 8 ills., Oct., 1910

Scilly Isles: The Garden Isles of Scilly: Geologists May Throw Stones at Legend of Lost Lyonnesse, But Natives Grow Flowers in Glass Houses for London. By W. Robert Moore. LXXIV, pp. 755-774, 9 ills. in black and white, 13 ills. in color, map, Dec., 1938

GARDENS—*Continued*

South Carolina: The Ashley River and Its Gardens. By E. T. H. Shaffer. XLIX, pp. 525-550, 6 ills. in black and white, 18 ills. in color, May, 1926

South Carolina: Charleston: Where Mellow Past and Present Meet. By DuBose Heyward. LXXV, pp. 273-312, 20 ills. in black and white, 24 ills. in color, map, Mar., 1939

Virginia: Gardens and Shrines of Old Virginia. 20 color photos by B. Anthony Stewart and J. Baylor Roberts. LXXXI, pp. 623-646, May, 1942

The **GARDENS** of the West. XVI, pp. 118-123, 7 ills., Mar., 1905

GARDINER Greene Hubbard. (Announcement of the Death of Mr. Hubbard). (By J. H.). VIII, p. 345, Dec., 1897

GARDINER Greene Hubbard: An Address delivered at the Memorial Services held at the Church of the Covenant, Washington, D. C., December 13, 1897. By Rev. Teunis S. Hamlin. IX, pp. 33-38, ill., Feb., 1898

GARDINER Greene Hubbard: Memorial Meeting, held in the City of Washington, January 21, 1898, Prof. Alexander Graham Bell, LL.D., President of the National Geographic Society, presiding. IX, pp. 39-70, Feb., 1898

GARDNER, IRVINE C.:

Crusoes of Canton Island: Life on a Tiny Pacific Atoll That Has Flashed Into World Importance. By Irvine C. Gardner. LXXIII, pp. 749-766, 7 ills. in black and white, 11 ills. in color, June, 1938

Natural-color photograph of 1937 eclipse, showing the corona. Photo by author, p. 756

Observing an Eclipse in Asiatic Russia. By Irvine C. Gardner. LXXI, pp. 179-197, 19 ills. in black and white, ill. in color, Feb., 1937

First natural-color photograph of an eclipse (1936) ever reproduced, showing the corona. Photo by author, p. 178

GARLAND, HAMLIN:

Overland Routes to the Klondike. By Hamlin Garland. IX, pp. 113-116, ill., Apr., 1898

GARRIOTT, E. B.:

The West Indian Hurricane of August 7-14, 1899. By E. B. Garriott. X, pp. 343-348, diagr., Sept., 1899

The West Indian Hurricane of September 1-12, 1900. By E. B. Garriott. XI, pp. 384-392, 4 charts, Oct., 1900

The West Indian Hurricane of September 10-11, 1898. By Prof. E. B. Garriott. X, pp. 17-20, Jan., 1899

GARRISON, C. L.:

Geography for Teachers. (By C. L. Garrison). X, pp. 223-225, June, 1899

GASES:

Helium, the New Balloon Gas. By G. Sherburne Rogers. XXXV, pp. 441-456, 11 ills., May, 1919

Natural-Gas, Oil, and Coal Supply of the United States. XV, p. 186, Apr., 1904

GASES—*Continued*

The Valley of Ten Thousand Smokes: An Account of the Discovery and Exploration of the Most Wonderful Volcanic Region in the World. By Robert F. Griggs. XXXIII, pp. 115-169, 46 ills., map, panorama, Feb., 1918

See also Helium

GASOLINE:

Oil for Victory Piped under the Sea. 9 ills. LXXXVIII, pp. 721-726, Dec., 1945

GASPÉ PENINSULA, Quebec, Canada:

The Gaspé Peninsula Wonderland. By Wilfrid Bovey. LXVIII, pp. 209-230, 13 ills. in black and white, 15 ills. in color, map, Aug., 1935

GATES AND GATEWAYS:

Sculptured Gates to English Learning (Cambridge University). 19 color photos by B. Anthony Stewart. LXXXIX, pp. 417-440, Apr., 1946

The **GATES** to the Black Sea: The Dardanelles, the Bosphorus, and the Sea of Marmora. By Harry Griswold Dwight. XXVII, pp. 435-459, 27 ills., May, 1915

GATSCHET, ALBERT S.:

All Around the Bay of Passamaquoddy. By Albert S. Gatschet. VIII, pp. 16-24, Jan., 1897

GATUN LAKE, Panama:

Nature's Transformation at Panama: Remarkable Changes in Faunal and Physical Conditions in the Gatun Lake Region. By George Shiras, 3d. XXVIII, pp. 159-194, 33 ills., maps, Aug., 1915

GATUN LOCKS AND DAM, Panama:

The Panama Canal. By Lieutenant Colonel William L. Sibert. XXV, pp. 153-183, 24 ills., Feb., 1914

GAUCHOS (Plainsmen):

Life on the Argentine Pampa. By Frederick Simpich. Paintings by Cesáreo Bernaldo de Quirós. LXIV, pp. 449-491, 41 ills. in black and white, 8 ills. in color, Oct., 1933

GAY Colors in the Land of Black Majesty (Haiti). 13 color photos by Clifton Adams. LXVI, pp. 445-452, Oct., 1934

GAYER, JACOB:

Arctic: The First Natural-Color Photographs from the Arctic. 19 color photos by Jacob Gayer. XLIX, pp. 301-316, Mar., 1926

Chile: Scenes of Beauty in Copper Land. 25 color photos by Jacob Gayer. LV, pp. 199-214, Feb., 1929

Dominican Republic: Hispaniola Rediscovered. By Jacob Gayer. LIX, pp. 80-112, 12 ills. in black and white, 28 ills. in color, Jan., 1931

Scenic Resources of the Dominican Republic. 28 color photos by author, pp. 81-104

Ecuador: Among the Highlands of the Equator Republic. 12 color photos by Jacob Gayer. LV, pp. 69-76, Jan., 1929

Guatemala: In the Land of the Quetzal. 20 color photos by Jacob Gayer. L, pp. 611-626, Nov., 1926

GAYER, JACOB—*Continued*

Jamaica: The Color Palette of the Caribbean. 11 color photos by Jacob Gayer. LI, pp. 45-55, Jan., 1927

Ohio: Where the Winning of the West Began. 13 color photos by Jacob Gayer. LXI, pp. 563-570, May, 1932

Peru: Among the Snows and Flowers of Peru. 25 color photos by Jacob Gayer. LVII, pp. 733-764, June, 1930

United States: Canyons and Cacti of the American Southwest. 14 color photos by Jacob Gayer. XLVIII, pp. 275-290, Sept., 1925

United States: Exploring the Atlantic Seaboard with a Color Camera. 8 color photos by Jacob Gayer. XLIX, pp. 533-548, May, 1926

Washington, D. C.: Our Colorful City of Magnificent Distances. 4 color photos by Jacob Gayer. LX, pp. 531-610, Nov., 1931

Washington, D. C.: Springtime Wreathes a Garland for the Nation's Capital. 13 color photos: 3 by Jacob Gayer. LXVII, pp. 473-480, Apr., 1935

GAZETTEERS:

A Dictionary of Universal Geography. XVII, p. 114, Feb., 1906

Gazetteers of the States. XV, pp. 369-370, Sept., 1904

GDYNIA, Poland:

War Clouds Over Danzig and Poland's Port. 8 ills. LXXVI, pp. 551-558, Oct., 1939

GEESE:

American Game Birds. By Henry Wetherbee Henshaw. Paintings by Louis Agassiz Fuertes. XXVIII, pp. 105-158, 4 ills. in black and white, 72 ills. in color, Aug., 1915

Far-Flying Wild Fowl and Their Foes. By Major Allan Brooks. Paintings from life by author. LXVI, pp. 487-528, 6 ills. in black and white, 16 portraits in color, Oct., 1934

Fowls of Forest and Stream Tamed by Man. By Morley A. Jull. Paintings by Hashime Murayama. LVII, pp. 327-371, 27 ills. in black and white, 16 ills. in color, Mar., 1930

Contents: Canadian, Chinese, Egyptian, Embden, Gray African, Sebastopol, Toulouse

Saving the Ducks and Geese. By Wells W. Cooke. XXIV, pp. 361-380, 7 ills., 7 maps, Mar., 1913

GEIKIE GLACIER, British Columbia:

Some Tramps Across the Glaciers and Snowfields of British Columbia. By Howard Palmer. XXI, pp. 457-487, 25 ills., June, 1910

GEISER, KARL FREDERICK:

Peasant Life in the Black Forest. By Karl Frederick Geiser. XIX, pp. 635-649, 12 ills., Sept., 1908

GEITHMANN, HARRIET:

Ströbeck, Home of Chess: A Medieval Village in the Harz Mountains of Germany Teaches the Royal Game in Its Public School. By Harriet Geithmann. LIX, pp. 637-652, 8 ills. in black and white, 14 ills. in color, May, 1931

The **GEM** of the Ocean: Our American Navy. By Josephus Daniels. XXXIII, pp. 313-335, 35 ills., Apr., 1918

GEMS:

The Diamond Mines of South Africa. By Gardiner F. Williams. XVII, pp. 344-356, 11 ills., June, 1906

Precious Stones. XIV, pp. 451-458, 4 ills., Dec., 1903

See also Jade; Jewels; Pearl Fisheries

GEMS from Scotland (Scenes in Scotland). 16 ills. XXXII, pp. 519-534, Nov.-Dec., 1917

GEMS of the Italian Lakes. By Arthur Ellis Mayer. XXIV, pp. 943-956, 13 ills., Aug., 1913

The **GENERAL** Geography of Alaska. By Henry Gannett. XII, pp. 180-196, 9 ills., May, 1901

GENERAL GRANT NATIONAL PARK, California:

Our National Parks. By L. F. Schmeckebier. XXIII, pp. 531-579, 41 ills., map, June, 1912

GENERAL LAND OFFICE (U. S.):

Geographic Work of the General Government. By Henry Gannett. IX, pp. 329-338, July, 1898

Geographical Research in the United States. By Gardiner G. Hubbard and Marcus Baker. VIII, pp. 285-293, Oct., 1897

See also Public Lands

"GENERAL SHERMAN TREE," Sequoia National Park, California:

The Oldest Living Thing. XXIX, pictorial supplement, Apr., 1916

GENESIS of the Williamsburg Restoration. By John D. Rockefeller, Jr. LXXI, p. 401, Apr., 1937

GENEVA, Lake, Switzerland-France:

Lake Geneva: Cradle of Conferences. By F. Barrows Colton. LXXII, pp. 727-742, 12 ills., map, Dec., 1937

GENEVA, Switzerland:

The Millennial City: The Romance of Geneva, Capital of the League of Nations. By Ralph A. Graves. XXXV, pp. 457-476, 13 ills., June, 1919

GENOA, Italy:

Frontier Cities of Italy. By Florence Craig Albrecht. XXVII, pp. 533-586, 45 ills., June, 1915

Genoa, Where Columbus Learned to Love the Sea. By McFall Kerbey. LIV, pp. 333-352, 20 ills., pictorial supplement, Sept., 1928

Inexhaustible Italy. By Arthur Stanley Riggs. XXX, pp. 273-368, 76 ills., map, Oct., 1916

GENTHE, ARNOLD:

Ageless Luster of Greece and Rhodes. 16 ills. in duotone by Arnold Genthe. LXXIII, pp. 477-492, Apr., 1938

GENTHE, MARTHA KRUG:

German Geographers and German Geography. By Martha Krug Genthe. XII, pp. 324-337, Sept., 1901

GENTLE Folk Settle Stern Saguenay: On French Canada's Frontier Homespun Colonists Keep the Customs of Old Norman Settlers. By Harrison Howell Walker. LXXV, pp. 595-632, 15 ills. in black and white, 25 ills. in color, map, May, 1939

GENTLEMEN Adventurers of the Air: Many Regions of Canada's Vast Wilderness, Long Hidden Even from Fur Trappers, Are Now Revealed by Exploring Airmen. By J. A. Wilson. LVI, pp. 597-642, 55 ills., map, Nov., 1929

GEODESY:

Charting a World at War. By William H. Nicholas. LXXXVI, pp. 617-640, 23 ills., drawing, Nov., 1944

Recent Contributions to Our Knowledge of the Earth's Shape and Size, by the United States Coast and Geodetic Survey. By C. A. Schott. XII, pp. 36-41, ill., chart, Jan., 1901

A Simple Method of Proving That the Earth Is Round. By Robert Marshall Brown. XVIII, pp. 771-774, 5 diagrs., Dec., 1907

GEOGRAPHERS:

Four Prominent Geographers. XVIII, pp. 425-428, 4 ills., June, 1907
Biographies and portraits of the following: Arthur P. Davis, Frederick Haynes Newell, George Otis Smith, and Charles D. Walcott

See also names of geographers, NGM editors, staff members, and contributors

A **GEOGRAPHIC** Achievement. XXIV, pp. 667-668, June, 1913

GEOGRAPHIC CONFERENCE. *See* International Geographic Conference

GEOGRAPHIC CONGRESS. *See* International Geographic Congress

GEOGRAPHIC Development of the District of Columbia. By W J McGee. IX, pp. 317-323, July, 1898

GEOGRAPHIC DISTRIBUTION OF LIFE:

Geography of Life. By C. Hart Merriam. I, pp. 160-162, Apr., 1889

Laws of Temperature Control of the Geographic Distribution of Terrestrial Animals and Plants. Annual Address by Vice-President, Dr. C. Hart Merriam. VI, pp. 229-238, table, 3 maps, Dec. 29, 1894

GEOGRAPHIC ENVIRONMENT:

The Effects of Geographic Environment in the Development of Civilization in Primitive Man. By Hon. Gardiner G. Hubbard. VIII, pp. 161-176, June, 1897

The National Geographic Society: Synopsis of a Course of Lectures on the Effects of Geographic Environment in Developing the Civilization of the World. (By Gardiner G. Hubbard). VIII, pp. 29-32, Jan., 1897

The Relation of Geography to History. By Francis W. Parker. V, pp. 125-131, Jan. 31, 1894

GEOGRAPHIC Facts from Report of the Taft Philippine Commission. XII, pp. 114-119, Mar., 1901

GEOGRAPHIC History of the Piedmont Plateau. By W J McGee. VII, pp. 261-265, Aug., 1896

GEOGRAPHIC Instruction in the Public Schools. By W. B. Powell. V, pp. 137-153, Jan. 31, 1894

GEOGRAPHIC Methods in Geologic Investigation. By W. M. Davis. I, pp. 11-26, Oct., 1888

GEOGRAPHIC NAMES:

All Around the Bay of Passamaquoddy. By Albert S. Gatschet. VIII, pp. 16-24, Jan., 1897
Included: A List of Indian Geographic Names Occurring Around Passamaquoddy Bay, Maine, with Their Derivations, pp. 21-24

Descriptive Topographic Terms of Spanish America. By Robert T. Hill. VII, pp. 291-302, Sept., 1896

Geographic Names in the United States and the Stories They Tell. By R. H. Whitbeck. XVI, pp. 100-104, Mar., 1905

Geographic Names in West Greenland. (By Ralph S. Tarr). IX, pp. 103-104, Mar., 1898

Geographic Nomenclature. (By E. W. Hilgard). XI, pp. 36-37, Jan., 1900

Geographic Nomenclature. Remarks by Herbert G. Ogden, Gustave Herrle, Marcus Baker, and A. H. Thompson. II, pp. 261-278, Aug., 1890

Geographical Aspects of the Monroe Doctrine. IX, pp. 476-477, Nov., 1898

Kodiak Not Kadiak. (By M. B.). XII, pp. 397-398, Nov., 1901

On Eskimo Geographic Names Ending in Miut. (By John Murdoch). IX, p. 190, Apr., 1898

The Origin of American State Names. By Frederick W. Lawrence. XXXVIII, pp. 105-143, 34 ills., Aug., 1920

Origin of the Name "Cape Nome." (By George Davidson). XII, p. 398, Nov., 1901

Origin of the Word Canada. (By N. H. Winchell). XVIII, p. 215, Mar., 1907

Place Names in Canada. (By H. G.). X, pp. 519-520, Dec., 1899

Place Names in Eastern Asia. XV, p. 136, Mar., 1904

Place Names of the United States. XIII, pp. 403-405, Nov., 1902

Porto Rico or Puerto Rico? (By R. T. Hill). X, pp. 516-517, Dec., 1899

Puerto Rico, Not Porto Rico. (By J. H.). XI, pp. 37-38, Jan., 1900

Rules for the Orthography of Geographic Names. Contributed by Mr. Herrle. II, pp. 279-285, 3 tables, Aug., 1890

Seriland (Mexico). By W J McGee and Willard D. Johnson. VII, pp. 125-133, ill., foldout map, Apr., 1896

Three Weeks in Hubbard Bay, West Greenland. By Robert Stein. IX, pp. 1-11, 6 ills., maps, Jan., 1898

See also U. S. Geographic Board

GEOGRAPHIC NOTES:

Geographic Notes. By Cyrus C. Babb. VI, pp. 217-228, table, map, Dec. 29, 1894
Included: The Antarctic Continent, pp. 217-223; Magnetic Observations in Iceland, Jan Mayen and Spitzbergen in 1892, pp. 223-224; A New Light on the Discovery of America, pp. 224-225; Monographs of the National Geographic Society, pp. 225-227; Important Announcement Concerning Essays, pp. 227-228

GEOGRAPHIC PRIZES. *See* NGS: Prizes

GEOGRAPHIC Progress of Civilization. Annual Address by the President, Honorable Gardiner G. Hubbard. VI, pp. 1-22, Feb. 14, 1894

GEOGRAPHIC SOCIETIES:

Directory of Officers and Councillors of Geographic Societies of the United States. XIV, pp. 392-394, Oct., 1903

See also National Geographic Society (NGS)

GEOGRAPHIC Work by the Bureau of American Ethnology. (By W J McGee). IX, pp. 98-100, Mar., 1898

GEOGRAPHIC Work in Peru. VII, p. 407, Dec., 1896

GEOGRAPHIC Work of the General Government (U. S.). By Henry Gannett. IX, pp. 329-338, July, 1898

GEOGRAPHICAL Aspects of the Monroe Doctrine. IX, pp. 476-477, Nov., 1898

GEOGRAPHICAL Congress at Berlin. X, p. 296, Aug., 1899

A **GEOGRAPHICAL** Description of the British Islands. (By W. M. Davis). VII, pp. 208-211, June, 1896

The **GEOGRAPHICAL** Distribution of Insanity in the United States. By Dr. William A. White. XIV, pp. 361-378, 6 maps, Oct., 1903

GEOGRAPHICAL Exploration: Its Moral and Material Results. By General A. W. Greely. XVII, pp. 1-5, Jan., 1906

The **GEOGRAPHICAL** Pivot of History (Steppes of Central Asia). (By H. J. Mackinder). XV, pp. 331-335, Aug., 1904

The **GEOGRAPHICAL** Position and Height of Mount Saint Elias. By Dr. T. C. Mendenhall. V, pp. 63-67, diagr., tables, July 10, 1893

GEOGRAPHICAL Research in the United States. By Gardiner G. Hubbard and Marcus Baker. VIII, pp. 285-293, Oct., 1897

The **GEOGRAPHIC'S** New Map of Europe and the Mediterranean. By Gilbert Grosvenor. Text with map supplement. LXXIII, pp. 525-528, ill., Apr., 1938

The **GEOGRAPHIC'S** New Map of Germany and Its Approaches: With a Review of The Society's Maps of Europe. By Gilbert Grosvenor. Text with map supplement. LXXXVI, pp. 66-72, ill., July, 1944

GEOGRAPHY:

Advances in Geographic Knowledge During the Nineteenth Century. By Brig.-Gen. A. W. Greely. XII, pp. 143-152, maps, Apr., 1901

American Geographic Education. By W J McGee. IX, pp. 305-307, July, 1898

Apperception in Geography. By M. E. Kelton. XI, pp. 192-199, May, 1900

Bearing of Physiography Upon Suess' Theories. By W. M. Davis. XV, p. 430, Oct., 1904

Cuba. By Robert T. Hill. IX, pp. 193-242, 12 ills., 7 diagrs., tables, 5 maps (1 foldout), May, 1898

Definitions of Geography. V, pp. 105, 125, 130, 159, Jan. 31, 1894

GEOGRAPHY—*Continued*

Geographic Development of the District of Columbia. By W J McGee. IX, pp. 317-323, July, 1898

Geographic Instruction in the Public Schools. By W. B. Powell. V, pp. 137-153, Jan. 31, 1894

Geographic Methods in Geologic Investigation. By W. M. Davis. I, pp. 11-26, Oct., 1888

Geographic Work in Peru. VII, p. 407, Dec., 1896

Geographic Work of the General Government (U. S.). By Henry Gannett. IX, pp. 329-338, July, 1898

A Geographical Description of the British Islands. (By W. M. Davis). VII, pp. 208-211, June, 1896

Geographical Exploration: Its Moral and Material Results. By General A. W. Greely. XVII, pp. 1-5, Jan., 1906

Geographical Research in the United States. By Gardiner G. Hubbard and Marcus Baker. VIII, pp. 285-293, Oct., 1897

Geography. By Rear Admiral Sir W. J. L. Wharton. XVI, pp. 483-498, Nov., 1905

Geography and Culture. XVI, pp. 70-71, Feb., 1905

Geography and Some Explorers. By Joseph Conrad. XLV, pp. 239-274, 28 ills., map, Mar., 1924

Geography at the British Association. XI, pp. 475-478, Dec., 1900

Geography for Teachers. (By C. L. Garrison). X, pp. 223-225, June, 1899

Geography in the University of Chicago. XIV, pp. 163-164, Apr., 1903

The Geography of Abyssinia. XII, pp. 274-276, July, 1901

The Geography of Alaska. By Alfred H. Brooks. XV, pp. 213-219, map supplement, May, 1904

The Geography of China: The Influence of Physical Environment on the History and Character of the Chinese People. By Frank Johnson Goodnow. LI, pp. 651-664, 11 ills., June, 1927

The Geography of Japan: With Special Reference to Its Influence on the Character of the Japanese People. By Walter Weston. XL, pp. 45-84, 23 ills. in black and white, 16 ills. in color, July, 1921

The Geography of Our Foreign Trade. By Frederick Simpich. XLI, pp. 89-108, 25 ills., Jan., 1922

Geography of the Air. Annual Address by the Vice-President, General A. W. Greely. VI, pp. 200-207, Dec. 29, 1894

Geography of the Land. Annual Report by Vice-President Herbert G. Ogden. III, pp. 31-40, Apr. 30, 1891

The Geography of the Southern Peninsula of the United States. By the Rev. John N. MacGonigle. VII, pp. 381-394, 4 ills., Dec., 1896

German Geographers and German Geography. By Martha Krug Genthe. XII, pp. 324-337, Sept., 1901

Imagination and Geography. XVIII, p. 825, Dec., 1907

The Improvement of Geographical Teaching. By Professor William Morris Davis. V, pp. 68-75, July 10, 1893

International Flat Globe and Geographical History. XVIII, pp. 281-282, Apr., 1907

GEOGRAPHY—*Continued*

An Introduction to Physical Geography. (By Grove Karl Gilbert and Albert Perry Brigham). XIV, pp. 21-26, 6 ills., Jan., 1903

Introductory Address. By the President, Mr. Gardiner G. Hubbard. I, pp. 3-10, Oct., 1888

Monographs of the National Geographic Society: Science manuals to be published for use in the public schools. VI, pp. 225-227, Dec. 29, 1894

Origin of the Physical Features of the United States. By G. K. Gilbert. IX, pp. 308-317, maps, July, 1898

Practical Exercises in Geography. By W. M. Davis. XI, pp. 62-78, diagr., Feb., 1900

The Probable Effect of the Panama Canal on the Commercial Geography of the World. By O. P. Austin. XXV, pp. 245-248, Feb., 1914

The Rational Element in Geography. By W. M. Davis. X, pp. 466-473, diagrs., Nov., 1899

Recent Geographic Advances, Especially in Africa. By Major General A. W. Greely. XXII, pp. 383-398, 5 ills., 5 maps, Apr., 1911

The Relation of Geography to History. By Francis W. Parker. V, pp. 125-131, Jan. 31, 1894

Report—Geography of the Land. By Herbert G. Ogden. I, pp. 125-135, Apr., 1889

Report—Geography of the Land. By Herbert G. Ogden. II, pp. 31-48, Apr., 1890

Sight-Seeing in School: Taking Twenty Million Children on a Picture Tour of the World. By Jessie L. Burrall. XXXV, pp. 489-503, 14 ills., June, 1919

Some Early Geographers of the United States. By Rear Admiral Colby M. Chester. XV, pp. 392-404, Oct., 1904

Some Lessons in Geography. By Edward Atkinson. XVI, pp. 193-198, Apr., 1905

The Teaching of Geography. By Ralph S. Tarr. XIII, pp. 55-64, Feb., 1902

The Teaching of Physical Geography in Elementary Schools. By Richard E. Dodge. XI, pp. 470-475, Dec., 1900

The Work of the National Geographic Society. (By W J McGee). VII, pp. 253-259, Aug., 1896

See also Discoverers, Explorers, and Navigators; Expeditions; NGS: Expeditions; Oceanography

The **GEOGRAPHY** of a Hurricane: A Doughnut-shaped Storm Turned Back Time in New England to Candlelight Days, but Revealed Anew Yankee Courage and Ingenuity. By F. Barrows Colton. LXXV, pp. 529-552, 20 ills., map, Apr., 1939

The **GEOGRAPHY** of Games: How the Sports of Nations Form a Gazetteer of the Habits and Histories of Their Peoples. By J. R. Hildebrand. XXXVI, pp. 89-144, 61 ills., Aug., 1919

GEOGRAPHY of Life. By C. Hart Merriam. I, pp. 160-162, Apr., 1889

The **GEOGRAPHY** of Medicines: War's Effect Upon the World's Sources of Supply. By John Foote. XXXII, pp. 213-238, 26 ills., Sept., 1917

The **GEOGRAPHY** of Money. By William Atherton Du Puy. LII, pp. 745-768, 31 ills., Dec., 1927

GEOGRAPHY of the Air. By A. W. Greely. I, pp. 151-159, Apr., 1889

GEOGRAPHY of the Air. By Gen. A. W. Greely. II, pp. 49-63, Apr., 1890

GEOGRAPHY of the Air. Annual Address by the Vice-President, General A. W. Greely. VI, pp. 200-207, Dec. 29, 1894

GEOGRAPHY of the Air. Annual Report by Vice-President A. W. Greely. III, pp. 41-52, May 1, 1891

GEOGRAPHY of the Air. Annual Report by Vice-President, General A. W. Greely. IV, pp. 85-100, Mar. 18, 1892

The **GEOGRAPHY** of the Jordan. By Nelson Glueck. LXXXVI, pp. 719-744, 23 ills., map, Dec., 1944

GEOGRAPHY of the Land. By Herbert G. Ogden. I, pp. 125-135, Apr., 1889

GEOGRAPHY of the Land. By Herbert G. Ogden. II, pp. 31-48, Apr., 1890

GEOGRAPHY of the Land. Annual Report by Vice-President Herbert G. Ogden. III, pp. 31-40, Apr. 30, 1891

GEOGRAPHY of the Sea. By George L. Dyer. I, pp. 136-150, table, Apr., 1889

The **GEOLOGIC** Atlas of the United States. (By W J M.). IX, pp. 339-342, July, 1898

GEOLOGIC Folios in Schools. XVI, pp. 244-247, May, 1905

The **GEOLOGIST** at Blue Mountain, Maryland. By Charles D. Walcott. V, pp. 84-88, July 10, 1893

GEOLOGISTS in China. XVIII, pp. 640-644, 5 ills., Oct., 1907

A **GEOLOGIST'S** Paradise (Canadian Rockies). By Charles D. Walcott. XXII, pp. 509-536, 28 ills., panorama, June, 1911

GEOLOGY:

Alaska and Its Mineral Resources. By Samuel Franklin Emmons. IX, pp. 139-172, 3 ills., map supplement, Apr., 1898

The Cause of the Earth's Heat. XVI, pp. 124-125, ill., Mar., 1905

The Central Great Plains (U. S.). XVI, pp. 389-397, 8 ills., Aug., 1905

The Classification of Geographic Forms by Genesis. By W J McGee. I, pp. 27-36, tables, Oct., 1888

Crater Lake, Oregon. By J. S. Diller. VIII, pp. 33-48, 6 ills., maps, Feb., 1897

Crater Lake and Yosemite Through the Ages. By Wallace W. Atwood, Jr. Paintings by Eugene Kingman. LXXI, pp. 327-343, 7 ills. in black and white, 13 ills. in color, Mar., 1937

Cuba. By Robert T. Hill. IX, pp. 193-242, 12 ills., 7 diagrs., tables, 5 maps (1 foldout), May, 1898

The Erratic. By O. A. Ljungstedt. XXI, pp. 525-531, 4 ills., map, June, 1910

GEOLOGY—*Continued*

An Expedition through the Yukon District. By Charles Willard Hayes. IV, pp. 117-159, 3 maps (2 foldouts), May 15, 1892

An Expedition to Mount St. Elias, Alaska. By Israel C. Russell. III, pp. 53-191, 17 ills., 3 diagrs., tables, 7 maps (1 foldout), May 29, 1891

Field Courses in Geology. XVI, p. 250, May, 1905

Geographic Development of the District of Columbia. By W J McGee. IX, pp. 317-323, July, 1898

Geographic History of the Piedmont Plateau. By W J McGee. VII, pp. 261-265, Aug., 1896

Geographic Methods in Geologic Investigation. By W. M. Davis. I, pp. 11-26, Oct., 1888

The Geologic Atlas of the United States. (By W J M.). IX, pp. 339-342, July, 1898

The Geologist at Blue Mountain, Maryland. By Charles D. Walcott. V, pp. 84-88, July 10, 1893

A Geologist's Paradise (Canadian Rockies). By Charles D. Walcott. XXII, pp. 509-536, 28 ills., panorama, June, 1911

Geomorphology of the Southern Appalachians. By Charles Willard Hayes and Marius R. Campbell. VI, pp. 63-126, diagrs., 4 maps, May 23, 1894

Landslides and Rock Avalanches. By Guy Elliott Mitchell. XXI, pp. 277-287, 6 ills., Apr., 1910

Limiting Width of Meander Belts. By Mark S. W. Jefferson. XIII, pp. 373-384, 6 charts, Oct., 1902

Notes on Some Eruptive Rocks from Alaska. By George H. Williams. IV, pp. 63-74, Mar. 21, 1892

Notes on the Geology of the Vicinity of Muir Glacier. By H. P. Cushing. IV, pp. 56-62, map, Mar. 21, 1892

Origin of the Physical Features of the United States. By G. K. Gilbert. IX, pp. 308-317, maps, July, 1898

Porto Rico. By Robert T. Hill. X, pp. 93-112, 13 ills., Mar., 1899

The Relations of Geology to Physiography in Our Educational System. By T. C. Chamberlin. V, pp. 154-160, Jan. 31, 1894

Report—Geography of the Land. By Herbert G. Ogden. I, pp. 125-135, Apr., 1889

Report by Robert T. Hill on the Volcanic Disturbances in the West Indies. XIII, pp. 223-267, 12 ills., 3 maps, July, 1902

The Rivers and Valleys of Pennsylvania. By William Morris Davis. I, pp. 183-253, 25 ills., map, July, 1889

The Rivers of Northern New Jersey, with Notes on the Classification of Rivers in General. By William Morris Davis. II, pp. 81-110, 6 diagrs., map drawing, May, 1890

Shawangunk Mountain (New York). By N. H. Darton. VI, pp. 23-34, ills., 4 diagrs., Mar. 17, 1894

Volcanic Rocks of Martinique and St. Vincent: Collected by Robert T. Hill and Israel C. Russell. By J. S. Diller. XIII, pp. 285-296, July, 1902

GEOLOGY—*Continued*

We Keep House on an Active Volcano: After Flying to Study a Spectacular Eruption in Belgian Congo, a Geologist Settles Down on a Newborn Craterless Vent for Eight Months' Study. By Dr. Jean Verhoogen. LXXVI, pp. 511-550, 28 ills., map, Oct., 1939

Where Early Christians Lived in Cones of Rock: A Journey to Cappadocia in Turkey Where Strange Volcanic Pinnacles Are Honeycombed With Hermit Cells and Monasteries. By John D. Whiting. LXXVI, pp. 763-802, 20 ills. in black and white, 20 ills. in color, map, Dec., 1939

See also Earthquakes; Geysers; Glaciers; Minerals; Mountains; Oceanography; Paleontology; Soil Erosion; U. S. Geological Survey; Volcanoes

GEOMAGNETISM:

Charting a World at War. By William H. Nicholas. LXXXVI, pp. 617-640, 23 ills., drawing, Nov., 1944

Magnetic Disturbances Caused by the Explosion of Mont Pelée. XIII, pp. 208-209, June, 1902

Magnetic Observations in Alaska. By Daniel L. Hazard. XX, pp. 675-676, map, July, 1909

Magnetic Observations in Iceland, Jan Mayen and Spitzbergen in 1892 (Geographic Notes. By Cyrus C. Babb). VI, pp. 223-224, table, Dec. 29, 1894

The Magnetic Survey of Africa. By Dr. L. A. Bauer. XX, pp. 291-297, 6 ills., Mar., 1909

Magnetic Survey of the Pacific. XIX, pp. 447-448, June, 1908

Magnetic Survey of the Pacific Ocean. (By L. A. Bauer). XVII, p. 237, Apr., 1906

Magnetic Survey of the United States. By Dr. L. A. Bauer. XIII, pp. 92-95, map, Mar., 1902

Magnetic Work of the Coast and Geodetic Survey. By L. A. Bauer. X, pp. 288-289, Aug., 1899

Most Curious Craft Afloat: The Compass in Navigation and the Work of the Non-Magnetic Yacht "Carnegie." By L. A. Bauer. XXI, pp. 223-245, 31 ills., Mar., 1910

Our Guardians on the Deep. By William Joseph Showalter. XXV, pp. 655-677, 15 ills., chart, June, 1914

Recent Magnetic Work by the Carnegie Institution of Washington. XVII, p. 648, Nov., 1906

Sailing the Seven Seas in the Interest of Science: Adventures Through 157,000 Miles of Storm and Calm, from Arctic to Antarctic and Around the World, in the Non-magnetic Yacht "Carnegie." By J. P. Ault. XLII, pp. 631-690, 47 ills., chart, Dec., 1922

Work in the Pacific Ocean of the Magnetic Survey Yacht "Galilee." By L. A. Bauer. XVIII, pp. 601-611, 15 ills., Sept., 1907

GEOMORPHOLOGY of the Southern Appalachians. By Charles Willard Hayes and Marius R. Campbell. VI, pp. 63-126, diagrs., 4 maps, May 23, 1894

GEORGE W. Melville, Engineer-in-chief, U. S. N. (By A. W. G.). VIII, pp. 187-190, ill., June, 1897

GEORGE Washington's Historic River (Potomac). 18 color photos by Willard R. Culver and Robert F. Sisson. LXXXVIII, pp. 41-64, July, 1945

GEORGESON, C. C.:

Agricultural Capacity of Alaska: What Population Can the Territory Support? By C. C. Georgeson. XX, pp. 676-679, July, 1909

The Possibilities of Alaska. By C. C. Georgeson. XIII, pp. 81-85, Mar., 1902

GEORGETOWN, Washington, D. C.:

Potomac, River of Destiny. By Albert W. Atwood. LXXXVIII, pp. 33-70, 15 ills. in black and white, 18 ills. in color, map, July, 1945

GEORGIA:

The Golden Isles of Guale. By W. Robert Moore. LXV, pp. 235-264, 35 ills., map, Feb., 1934

Marching Through Georgia Sixty Years After: Multifold Industries and Diversified Agriculture Are Restoring the Prosperity of America's Largest State East of the Mississippi. By Ralph A. Graves. L, pp. 259-311, 47 ills., map supplement, Sept., 1926

The Okefinokee Wilderness: Exploring the Mystery Land of the Suwannee River Reveals Natural Wonders and Fascinating Folklore. By Francis Harper. LXV, pp. 597-624, 35 ills., map, May, 1934

GEORGIAN SOVIET SOCIALIST REPUBLIC, U. S. S. R.:

The Land of the Stalking Death: A Journey Through Starving Armenia on an American Relief Train. By Melville Chater. XXXVI, pp. 393-420, 23 ills., Nov., 1919

Roaming Russia's Caucasus: Rugged Mountains and Hardy Fighters Guard the Soviet Union's Caucasian Treasury of Manganese and Oil. By Rolf Singer. LXXXII, pp. 91-121, 33 ills., July, 1942

Russia's Orphan Races: Picturesque Peoples Who Cluster on the Southeastern Borderland of the Vast Slav Dominions. By Maynard Owen Williams. XXXIV, pp. 245-278, 26 ills., map, Oct., 1918

The **GEOSPHERES.** By W J McGee. IX, pp. 435-447, Oct., 1898

GERBÉVILLER, France:

In French Lorraine: That Part of France Where the First American Soldiers Have Fallen. By Harriet Chalmers Adams. XXXII, pp. 499-518, 16 ills., Nov.-Dec., 1917

GERECKE, W. F.:

Flame-Feathered Flamingos of Florida. 9 color photos by W. F. Gerecke. LXXIX, pp. 57-64, Jan., 1941

GERIZIM (Mountain), Palestine:

The Last Israelitish Blood Sacrifice: How the Vanishing Samaritans Celebrate the Passover on Sacred Mount Gerizim. By John D. Whiting. XXXVII, pp. 1-46, 40 ills., map, Jan., 1920

GERMAN Geographers and German Geography. By Martha Krug Genthe. XII, pp. 324-337, Sept., 1901

The **GERMAN** Nation. XXVI, pp. 275-310, 28 ills., Sept., 1914

A GERMAN Route to India. (By Gilbert H. Grosvenor). XI, pp. 203-204, map, May, 1900

The **GERMAN** South Polar Expedition. XII, p. 311, Aug., 1901

The **GERMAN** South Polar Expedition. By Dr. Georg Kollm. XII, pp. 377-379, Oct., 1901

GERMAN Submarine Cable System. XII, p. 163, Apr., 1901

GERMANY:

Aces Among Aces (Aviators). By Laurence La Tourette Driggs. XXXIII, pp. 568-580, 9 ills., June, 1918

Americans Help Liberated Europe Live Again. By Lt. Col. Frederick Simpich, Jr. LXXXVII, pp. 747-768, 17 ills., June, 1945

The Beauty of the Bavarian Alps. By Colonel Fitzhugh Lee Minnigerode. XLIX, pp. 632-649, 16 ills. in color, June, 1926

Bright Corners of Time-Mellowed Germany. 11 color photos by Hans Hildenbrand and Wilhelm Tobien. LXIV, pp. 223-230, Aug., 1933

Cologne, Key City of the Rhineland. By Francis Woodworth. LXIX, pp. 829-848, 18 ills., map, June, 1936

A Corner of Old Württemberg. By B. H. Buxton. XXII, pp. 931-947, 17 ills., map, Oct., 1911

The Danube, Highway of Races: From the Black Forest to the Black Sea, Europe's Most Important River Has Borne the Traffic of Centuries. By Melville Chater. LVI, pp. 643-697, 54 ills., Dec., 1929

Emigrants, Diversion of, to South America. VIII, p. 336, Nov., 1897

Entering the Front Doors of Medieval Towns: The Adventures of an American Woman and Her Daughter in a Folding Boat on Eight Rivers of Germany and Austria. By Cornelia Stratton Parker. LXI, pp. 365-394, 23 ills. in black and white, 11 ills. in color, map, Mar., 1932

Flags of Austria-Hungary, Bulgaria, Germany, and Turkey. By Byron McCandless and Gilbert Grosvenor. XXXII, pp. 386-388, 38 ills. in color, Oct., 1917

The Geographic's New Map of Germany and Its Approaches: With a Review of The Society's Maps of Europe. By Gilbert Grosvenor. Text with map supplement. LXXXVI, pp. 66-72, ill., July, 1944

The German Nation. XXVI, pp. 275-310, 28 ills., Sept., 1914

German Submarine Cable System. XII, p. 163, Apr., 1901

Germany's Air Program. XXXIII, p. 114, Jan., 1918

Germany's Dream of World Domination. XXXIII, pp. 559-567, 3 ills., map, June, 1918

The Great Canals of the World. XVI, pp. 475-479, Oct., 1905

Grimm's Fairyland in Northwestern Germany. 14 color photos by Hans Hildenbrand and Wilhelm Tobien. LIX, pp. 641-648, May, 1931

The Industrial Training of the German People. XVI, pp. 111-114, ills., Mar., 1905

A Map of the New Germany. XXXV, pp. 545-546, map, June, 1919

GERMANY—*Continued*

The New Map of Europe: Showing the Boundaries Established by the Peace Conference at Paris and by Subsequent Decisions of the Supreme Council of the Allied and Associated Powers. By Ralph A. Graves. Text with map supplement. XXXIX, pp. 157-177, 18 ills., Feb., 1921

Peasant Life in the Black Forest. By Karl Frederick Geiser. XIX, pp. 635-649, 12 ills., Sept., 1908

Proposed Collection of Forestry Statistics (National Forest Association of Germany). IX, p. 448, Oct., 1898

Prussianism. By Robert Lansing. XXXIII, pp. 546-557, 5 ills., June, 1918

The Races of Europe. By Edwin A. Grosvenor. XXXIV, pp. 441-534, 62 ills., diagr. and index, maps, map supplement, Dec., 1918

Rediscovering the Rhine: A Trip by Barge from the Sea to the Headwaters of Europe's Storied Stream. By Melville Chater. XLVIII, pp. 1-43, 44 ills., July, 1925

Renascent Germany. By Lincoln Eyre. LIV, pp. 639-717, 59 ills. in black and white, 39 ills. in color, Dec., 1928

The Story of the Ruhr. By Frederick Simpich. XLI, pp. 553-564, 11 ills., map, May, 1922

The Town of Many Gables (Münster). By Florence Craig Albrecht. XXVII, pp. 107-140, 28 ills., Feb., 1915

War's Wake in the Rhineland. By Thomas R. Henry. LXXXVIII, pp. 1-32, 29 ills., map, July, 1945

The Wends of the Spreewald. By Frederick Simpich. XLIII, pp. 327-336, 12 ills., Mar., 1923

What Is the Saar? By Frederick Simpich. LXVII, pp. 241-264, 5 ills. in black and white, 23 ills. in duotone, maps, Feb., 1935

See also Berchtesgaden; Berlin; Dinkelsbühl; East Prussia; Freiburg; Hamburg; Helgoland (Island); Nördlingen; Oberammergau; Rothenburg; Ströbeck

GERMANY'S Air Program. XXXIII, p. 114, Jan., 1918

GERMANY'S Dream of World Domination. XXXIII, pp. 559-567, 3 ills., map, June, 1918

GESKE, E. J.:

Familiar Grasses and Their Flowers. By E. J. Geske and W. J. Showalter. Paintings by E. J. Geske. XXXIX, pp. 625-636, 8 ills. in color, June, 1921

Beauties of Our Common Grasses. 8 ills. in color from paintings by E. J. Geske, pp. 627-634

Marvels of Fern Life. 16 ills. in color from paintings by E. J. Geske. XLVII, pp. 547-562, May, 1925

GETTYSBURG, Pennsylvania:

The Most Famous Battle Field in America. 14 color photos by Clifton Adams and Orren R. Louden. LX, pp. 66-75, July, 1931

GEYSERS:

Costa Rica—Vulcan's Smithy. By H. Pittier. XXI, pp. 494-525, 30 ills., maps, June, 1910

GEYSERS—*Continued*
Fabulous Yellowstone: Even Stranger Than the Tales of Early Trappers is the Truth About This Steaming Wonderland. By Frederick G. Vosburgh. LXXVII, pp. 769-794, 15 ills. in black and white, 9 ills. in color, map, June, 1940
Waimangu and the Hot-Spring Country of New Zealand: The World's Greatest Geyser Is One of Many Natural Wonders in a Land of Inferno and Vernal Paradise. By Joseph C. Grew. XLVIII, pp. 109-130, 19 ills., map, Aug., 1925
See also Iceland

GHAZNI, Afghanistan:
Back to Afghanistan. By Maynard Owen Williams. XC, pp. 517-544, 27 ills., map, Oct., 1946

GIBBONS, A. ST. H.:
Methods of Exploration in Africa. By Major A. St. H. Gibbons. XV, pp. 408-410, Oct., 1904

GIBBONS:
Man's Closest Counterparts: Heavyweight of Monkeydom Is the "Old Man" Gorilla, by Far the Largest of the Four Great Apes. By William M. Mann. Paintings by Elie Cheverlange. LXXVIII, pp. 213-236, 10 ills. in black and white, 10 ills. in color, Aug., 1940

GIBBS, GEORGE S.:
The "Breaking Up" of the Yukon. By Captain George S. Gibbs. XVII, pp. 268-272, 6 ills., May, 1906
Transportation Methods in Alaska. By Captain George S. Gibbs. XVII, pp. 69-82, 19 ills., Feb., 1906

GIBRALTAR:
The American Eclipse Expedition. By Rear Admiral Colby M. Chester. XVII, pp. 589-612, 23 ills., col. pl., Nov., 1906
From Granada to Gibraltar—A Tour of Southern Spain. By Harry A. McBride. XLVI, pp. 205-232, 23 ills., Aug., 1924
The Rock of Gibraltar: Key to the Mediterranean. 17 ills. LXXVIII, pp. 376-391, Sept., 1940

GIBSON, SIR CHRISTOPHER H.:
Through Paraguay and Southern Matto Grosso. By Sir Christopher H. Gibson. LXXXIV, pp. 459-488, 20 ills. in black and white, 11 ills. in color, map, Oct., 1943

GIFFORD, JOHN:
The Florida Keys. By John Gifford. XVII, pp. 5-16, 13 ills., map, Jan., 1906

GIGANTIC Brazil and Its Glittering Capital. By Frederick Simpich. LVIII, pp. 733-778, 54 ills., map, Dec., 1930

GIGNILLIAT, T. HEYWARD:
The Valley of the Orinoco. By T. H. Gignilliat. Text with map supplement. VII, p. 92, Feb., 1896

GILBERT, GROVE KARL:
The Discovery of the North Pole (Presentation of Hubbard Gold Medal). XXI, pp. 63-82, Jan., 1910

GILBERT, GROVE KARL—*Continued*
The Glaciers of Alaska. (By Grove Karl Gilbert). XV, pp. 449-450, Nov., 1904
Grove Karl Gilbert (Biography). XI, p. 289, ill. (front.), July, 1900
An Introduction to Physical Geography. (By Grove Karl Gilbert and Albert Perry Brigham). XIV, pp. 21-26, 6 ills., Jan., 1903
Mr. Ziegler and the National Geographic Society. XIV, pp. 251-254, June, 1903
Included: Letter from G. K. Gilbert recommending types of research to be undertaken by the Ziegler Polar Expedition
Modification of the Great Lakes by Earth Movement. By G. K. Gilbert. VIII, pp. 233-247, 3 diagrs., table, 4 maps, Sept., 1897
Origin of the Physical Features of the United States. By G. K. Gilbert. IX, pp. 308-317, maps, July, 1898
Portrait. XI, pl. 7 (front.), July, 1900
Speech of welcome to Eighth International Geographic Congress. XV, p. 419, Oct., 1904
See also NGS: Board of Managers; President; Vice-President

GILBERT, J. J.:
Some Notes on the Fox Island Passes, Alaska. By J. J. Gilbert. XVI, pp. 427-429, Sept., 1905

GILBERT ISLANDS, Pacific Ocean:
American Pathfinders in the Pacific. By William H. Nicholas. LXXXIX, pp. 617-640, 17 ills., two-page map, May, 1946
Gilbert Islands in the Wake of Battle. By W. Robert Moore. LXXXVII, pp. 129-162, 11 ills. in black and white, 19 ills. in color, map, Feb., 1945
War Finds Its Way to Gilbert Islands: United States Forces Dislodge Japanese from Enchanted Atolls Which Loom Now as Stepping Stones along South Sea Route from Australia to Hawaii. By Sir Arthur Grimble. LXXXIII, pp. 71-92, 19 ills., map, Jan., 1943

GILDED Domes Against an Azure Sky (Iran). 13 color photos by Stephen H. Nyman. LXXVI, pp. 339-346, Sept., 1939

GILL, RICHARD C.:
Mrs. Robinson Crusoe in Ecuador. By Mrs. Richard C. Gill. LXV, pp. 133-172, 43 ills., map, Feb., 1934

GILL, MRS. RICHARD C.:
Mrs. Robinson Crusoe in Ecuador. By Mrs. Richard C. Gill. LXV, pp. 133-172, 43 ills., map, Feb., 1934

GILLES, HELEN TRYBULOWSKI:
Nigeria: From the Bight of Benin to Africa's Desert Sands. By Helen Trybulowski Gilles. LXXXV, pp. 537-568, 17 ills. in black and white, 10 ills. in color, map, May, 1944

GILMAN, DANIEL C.:
Gardiner Greene Hubbard: Memorial Meeting. Address by Dr. Daniel C. Gilman. IX, pp. 57-59, Feb., 1898
The Late Daniel C. Gilman (Biography). XIX, p. 883, ill., Dec., 1908

GILMAN, S. C.:

The Olympic Country. By the late S. C. Gilman, C. E. VII, pp. 133-140, foldout map, Apr., 1896

GILMORE, EDDY:

Crimea Reborn. By Eddy Gilmore. LXXXVII, pp. 487-512, 23 ills., map, Apr., 1945

I Learn About the Russians. By Eddy Gilmore. LXXXIV, pp. 619-640, 21 ills., Nov., 1943

Liberated Ukraine. By Eddy Gilmore. LXXXV, pp. 513-536, 22 ills., map, May, 1944

GILSON, MARTHA PHILLIPS:

A Woman's Winter on Spitsbergen. By Martha Phillips Gilson. LIV, pp. 227-246, 20 ills., map, Aug., 1928

GIPSON, HENRY CLAY:

Peru on Parade. 20 color photos by Henry Clay Gipson and Jack Kuhne. LXXXII, pp. 173-196, Aug., 1942

GIRAFFES:

Where Roosevelt Will Hunt (Africa). By Sir Harry Johnston. XX, pp. 207-256, 43 ills., map supplement, Mar., 1909

GIRDLING the Globe. XV, p. 236, May, 1904

GIRL SCOUTS:

Star and Crescent on Parade (Turkey). 29 color photos by Maynard Owen Williams. LXXXVII, pp. 585-616, May, 1945

GJOA (Ship):

A Modern Viking. XVII, pp. 38-41, ills., map, Jan., 1906

GLACIER BAY, Alaska:

The Discovery of Glacier Bay, Alaska. By Eliza Ruhamah Scidmore. VII, pp. 140-146, ill., map, Apr., 1896

The Recession of the Glaciers of Glacier Bay, Alaska. By Fremont Morse. XIX, pp. 76-78, map, Jan., 1908

GLACIER NATIONAL PARK, Montana:

A New National Park. By Guy Elliott Mitchell. XXI, pp. 215-223, 6 ills., Mar., 1910

Our National Parks. By L. F. Schmeckebier. XXIII, pp. 531-579, 41 ills., map, June, 1912

GLACIERS:

Among the Great Himalayan Glaciers. XIII, pp. 405-406, Nov., 1902

The Ascent of Mont Blanc. By Walter Woodburn Hyde. XXIV, pp. 861-942, 69 ills., Aug., 1913

The Conquest of Mount Logan: North America's Second Highest Peak Yields to the Intrepid Attack of Canadian Climbers. By H. F. Lambart. XLIX, pp. 597-631, 40 ills., June, 1926

Crater Lake and Yosemite Through the Ages. By Wallace W. Atwood, Jr. Paintings by Eugene Kingman. LXXI, pp. 327-343, 7 ills. in black and white, 13 ills. in color, Mar., 1937

An Expedition through the Yukon District. By Charles Willard Hayes. IV, pp. 117-159, 3 maps (2 foldouts), May 15, 1892

GLACIERS—*Continued*

An Expedition to Mount St. Elias, Alaska. By Israel C. Russell. III, pp. 53-191, 17 ills., 3 diagrs., tables, 7 maps (1 foldout), May 29, 1891

The Form of Glacier Terminals. XXII, p. 786, Aug., 1911

The Glaciers of Alaska. (By Grove Karl Gilbert). XV, pp. 449-450, Nov., 1904

Glaciers of the St. Elias Region (Part IV, from "An Expedition to Mount St. Elias, Alaska," by Israel C. Russell). III, pp. 176-188, May 29, 1891

The Great White Monarch of the Pacific Northwest (Mount Rainier). By A. H. Barnes. XXIII, pp. 593-626, 31 ills., map, June, 1912

Is Our Noblest Volcano Awakening to New Life: A Description of the Glaciers and Evidences of Volcanic Activity of Mount Hood. By A. H. Sylvester. XIX, pp. 515-525, 5 ills., map, July, 1908

Lake Chelan. By Henry Gannett. IX, pp. 417-428, 7 ills., map, Oct., 1898

The Monarch of the Canadian Rockies. By Charles D. Walcott. XXIV, pp. 626-639, 13 ills., panorama, May, 1913

Muir Glacier. (By C. L. Andrews). XIV, pp. 441-444, ills., map, Dec., 1903

The National Geographic Society Researches in Alaska. By Lawrence Martin. XXII, pp. 537-561, 17 ills., 5 maps, June, 1911

The National Geographic Society's Alaskan Expedition of 1909. By Ralph S. Tarr and Lawrence Martin. XXI, pp. 1-54, 42 ills., 12 maps, Jan., 1910

Note on Glacier Discovery. (By W. H. Jackson). XVII, p. 587, Oct., 1906

Photography in Glacial Alaska. By O. D. von Engeln. XXI, pp. 54-62, 4 ills., Jan., 1910

The Recession of the Glaciers of Glacier Bay, Alaska. By Fremont Morse. XIX, pp. 76-78, map, Jan., 1908

Scenes Among the High Cascades in Central Oregon. By Ira A. Williams. XXIII, pp. 579-592, 11 ills., June, 1912

Some Tramps Across the Glaciers and Snowfields of British Columbia. By Howard Palmer. XXI, pp. 457-487, 25 ills., June, 1910

The Stikine River in 1898 (British Columbia). By Eliza Ruhamah Scidmore. X, pp. 1-15, 4 ills., Jan., 1899

Studies of Muir Glacier, Alaska. By Harry Fielding Reid. IV, pp. 19-55, 13 ills., 6 diagrs., table, 2 maps (1 foldout), Mar. 21, 1892
See Muir Glacier, for Supplements and Appendices to this article

A Wonderland of Glaciers and Snow (Mount Rainier National Park). By Milnor Roberts. XX, pp. 530-537, 8 ills., June, 1909

See also Columbia Ice Field

The **GLAMOUR** of Historic Havana. 9 photos by F. S. Lincoln. LXIV, pp. 357-364, Sept., 1933

The **GLAMOUR** of Mexico—Old and New. 15 color photos: 13 by L. Pérez Parra. LXV, pp. 345-352, Mar., 1934

GLASGOW, Scotland:

Bonnie Scotland, Postwar Style. By Isobel Wylie Hutchison. LXXXIX, pp. 545-601, 14 ills. in black and white, 38 ills. in color, two-page map, May, 1946

GLASS AND GLASSMAKING:

Glass "Goes to Town." By J. R. Hildebrand. LXXXIII, pp. 1-48, 28 ills. in black and white, 22 ills. in color, Jan., 1943

The Industrial Titan of America: Pennsylvania, Once the Keystone of the Original Thirteen, Now the Keystone of Forty-eight Sovereign States. By John Oliver La Gorce. XXXV, pp. 367-406, 33 ills., map, May, 1919

The **GLASS-BOTTOM** Boat. By Charles Frederick Holder. XX, pp. 761-778, 17 ills., Sept., 1909

GLASSEY, FRANK P. S.:

Helsingfors (Finland)—A Contrast in Light and Shade. By Frank P. S. Glassey. XLVII, pp. 597-612, 20 ills., May, 1925

GLEAMING Fishes of Pacific Coastal Waters. 31 portraits in color from paintings by Hashime Murayama. LXXIV, pp. 467-498, Oct., 1938

GLEASON, HERBERT W.:

On the Trail of a Horse Thief (British Columbia). By Herbert W. Gleason. XXXV, pp. 349-358, 6 ills., Apr., 1919

Winter Rambles in Thoreau's Country. By Herbert W. Gleason. XXXVII, pp. 165-180, 15 ills., Feb., 1920

GLEN CANYON, Utah:

Experiences in the Grand Canyon. By Ellsworth and Emery Kolb. XXVI, pp. 99-184, 70 ills., map, Aug., 1914

GLENFINNAN, Scotland:

Heather Paints the Highlands. 38 color photos by B. Anthony Stewart. LXXXIX, pp. 561-600, May, 1946

GLENN, L. C.:

Applied Physiography in South Carolina. By L. C. Glenn. VIII, pp. 152-154, diagr., May, 1897

GLENORA, British Columbia:

The Stikine River in 1898. By Eliza Ruhamah Scidmore. X, pp. 1-15, 4 ills., Jan., 1899

GLIDE BOMBS:

Air Power for Peace. By General H. H. Arnold. LXXXIX, pp. 137-193, 35 ills. in black and white, 28 ills. in color, map supplement, Feb., 1946

GLIDERS:

The Aerial Invasion of Burma. By General H. H. Arnold. LXXXVI, pp. 129-148, 20 ills., Aug., 1944

Air Conquest: From the Early Days of Giant Kites and Birdlike Gliders, the National Geographic Society Has Aided and Encouraged the Growth of Aviation. LII, pp. 233-242, 13 ills., Aug., 1927

Gliders—Silent Weapons of the Sky. By William H. Nicholas. LXXXVI, pp. 149-160, 8 ills., Aug., 1944

GLIDERS—*Continued*

Men-Birds Soar on Boiling Air. By Frederick G. Vosburgh. LXXIV, pp. 123-140, 15 ills., July, 1938

On the Wings of the Wind: In Motorless Planes, Pilots Ride in Flying-Fox Fashion, Cruising on Upward Air Streams and Lifted by the Suction of Moving Clouds. By Howard Siepen. LV, pp. 751-780, 40 ills., June, 1929

Remarkable Photograph of Lilienthal's Gliding Machine. By R. W. Wood. XIX, p. 596, ill., Aug., 1908. XXII, ill. p. 271, Mar., 1911. LII, ill. p. 235, Aug., 1927

GLIMPSES East and West in America. 16 ills. XLV, pp. 531-546, May, 1924

GLIMPSES of Asia. 16 ills. XXXIX, pp. 553-568, May, 1921

GLIMPSES of Holland. By William Wisner Chapin. XXVII, pp. 1-29, 26 ills., Jan., 1915

GLIMPSES of Japan. By William W. Chapin. XXII, pp. 965-1002, 10 ills. in black and white, 34 ills. in color, Nov., 1911

GLIMPSES of Korea and China. By William W. Chapin. XXI, pp. 895-934, 11 ills. in black and white, 39 ills. in color, Nov., 1910

GLIMPSES of Siberia, the Russian "Wild East." By Cody Marsh. XXXVIII, pp. 513-536, 26 ills., Dec., 1920

GLIMPSES of the Russian Empire. By William Wisner Chapin. XXIII, pp. 1043-1078, 51 ills. in color, map, Nov., 1912

The **GLORIES** of the Minya Konka: Magnificent Snow Peaks of the China-Tibetan Border Are Photographed at Close Range by a National Geographic Society Expedition. By Joseph F. Rock. LVIII, pp. 385-437, 35 ills. in black and white, 24 ills. in color, map, Oct., 1930

GLORIES Past and Present of Northern Spain. 13 color photos by Gervais Courtellemont. LV, pp. 341-348, Mar., 1929

"The **GLORY** That Was Greece." By Alexander Wilbourne Weddell. XLII, pp. 571-630, 51 ills., map, Dec., 1922

"The **GLORY** That Was Greece." 32 ills. in color from paintings by H. M. Herget. LXXXV, pp. 290-352, Mar., 1944

The **GLORY** That Was Imperial Peking. By W. Robert Moore. LXIII, pp. 745-780, 18 ills. in black and white, 16 ills. in duotone, June, 1933

GLOUCESTER, Massachusetts:

Northeast of Boston. By Albert W. Atwood. LXXXVIII, pp. 257-292, 12 ills. in black and white, 17 ills. in color, map supplement, Sept., 1945

GLUECK, NELSON:

The Geography of the Jordan. By Nelson Glueck. LXXXVI, pp. 719-744, 23 ills., map, Dec., 1944

On the Trail of King Solomon's Mines: The Bible, in Addition to Its Spiritual Values, Continues to Prove a Rich Geography and Guide to Exploration of the Holy Land. By Nelson Glueck. LXXXV, pp. 233-256, 20 ills., map, Feb., 1944

GNATCATCHERS (Birds):

Winged Denizens of Woodland, Stream, and Marsh. By Alexander Wetmore. Paintings by Major Allan Brooks. LXV, pp. 577-596, 4 portraits in color, May, 1934

GOATS:

The Milch Goat. XVI, p. 237, ill. p. 241, May, 1905

GOATSUCKERS (Birds):

Seeking the Smallest Feathered Creatures: Humming Birds, Peculiar to the New World, Are Found from Canada and Alaska to the Strait of Magellan. Swifts and Goatsuckers, Their Nearest Relatives. By Alexander Wetmore. Paintings by Maj. Allan Brooks. LXII, pp. 65-89, ill. in black and white, 6 ills. in color, July, 1932

GOBI (Desert), Central Asia:

The Desert Road to Turkestan: Twentieth Century Travel Through Innermost Asia, Along Caravan Trails Over Which Oriental Commerce Was Once Borne from China to the Medieval Western World. By Owen Lattimore. LV, pp. 661-702, 45 ills., map, June, 1929

Explorations in the Gobi Desert. By Roy Chapman Andrews. LXIII, pp. 653-716, 50 ills. in black and white, 20 ills. in color, map, June, 1933

The Lama's Motor-Car. By Ethan C. Le Munyon. XXIV, pp. 641-670, 34 ills., May, 1913

GODDARD, GEORGE W.:

Aerial Color Photography Becomes a War Weapon. By H. H. Arnold. With 8 color photos by Major George W. Goddard. LXXVII, pp. 757-766, June, 1940

The Unexplored Philippines from the Air: Mapmaking Over Jungle Lands Never Before Seen By White Men. By Lieut. George W. Goddard. LVIII, pp. 311-343, 38 ills., map, Sept., 1930

GODESBERG, Bad, Germany:

War's Wake in the Rhineland. By Thomas R. Henry. LXXXVIII, pp. 1-32, 29 ills., map, July, 1945

GODTHAAB, Greenland:

Greenland Turns to America. By James K. Penfield. LXXXII, pp. 369-383, 7 ills. in black and white, 5 ills. in color, two-page map, Sept., 1942

GOES, Netherlands:

The City of Jacqueline. By Florence Craig Albrecht. XXVII, pp. 29-56, 31 ills., Jan., 1915

GOETHALS, GEORGE W.:

Honors to Colonel Goethals: The Presentation, by President Woodrow Wilson, of the National Geographic Society Special Gold Medal, and Addresses by Secretary of State Bryan, the French Ambassador, the German Ambassador, and Congressman James R. Mann. XXV, pp. 677-690, 6 ills., June, 1914

The Panama Canal. By Lieut. Col. Geo. W. Goethals. XX, pp. 334-355, 7 ills., diagr., map, Apr., 1909

The Panama Canal. By Colonel George W. Goethals. XXII, pp. 148-211, 49 ills., diagr., maps. Feb., 1911

GOING, CHARLES BUXTON:

The Mysterious Prehistoric Monuments of Brittany (France). By Charles Buxton Going. XLIV, pp. 53-69, 16 ills., July, 1923

GOLD AND GOLD MINING:

Alaska and Its Mineral Resources. By Samuel Franklin Emmons. IX, pp. 139-172, 3 ills., map supplement, Apr., 1898

Beyond Australia's Cities. By W. Robert Moore. LXX, pp. 709-747, 27 ills. in black and white, 12 ills. in color, Dec., 1936

The Cape Nome Gold District (Alaska). By F. C. Schrader. XI, pp. 15-23, 3 ills., map, Jan., 1900

The Cities That Gold and Diamonds Built: Transvaal Treasures Have Created Bustling Johannesburg and Fostered Pretoria, Administrative Capital of the South African Union. By W. Robert Moore. LXXXII, pp. 735-766, 20 ills. in black and white, 9 ills. in color, map, Dec., 1942

Colorado, a Barrier That Became a Goal: Where Water Has Transformed Dry Plains Into Verdant Farms, and Highways Have Opened up Mineral and Scenic Wealth. By McFall Kerbey. LXII, pp. 1-63, 56 ills. in black and white, 12 ills. in color, map, July, 1932

The Future of the Yukon Goldfields. By William H. Dall. IX, pp. 117-120, Apr., 1898

Gold in the Philippines. By F. F. Hilder. XI, pp. 465-470, Dec., 1900

A Growing Camp in the Tanana Gold Fields, Alaska. By Sidney Paige. XVI, pp. 104-111, 4 ills., Mar., 1905

Korea and the Koreans. By J. B. Bernadou. II, pp. 231-242, map, foldout map, Aug., 1890

Lonely Australia: The Unique Continent. By Herbert E. Gregory. XXX, pp. 473-568, 68 ills., 5 maps (1 two-page), Dec., 1916

Men and Gold. By Frederick Simpich. LXIII, pp. 481-518, 33 ills. in black and white, 11 ills. in duotone, Apr., 1933

The Nome Gold Fields. XIX, pp. 384-385, May, 1908

Report on Auriferous Sands from Yakutat Bay (Alaska). By J. Stanley-Brown. III, pp. 196-198, May 29, 1891

Under the South African Union. By Melville Chater. LIX, pp. 391-512, 97 ills. in black and white, 38 ills. in color, two-page map, Apr., 1931

Venezuela: Her Government, People, and Boundary. By William E. Curtis. VII, pp. 49-58, 3 ills., map supplement, Feb., 1896

The Witwatersrand and the Revolt of the Uitlanders. By George F. Becker. VII, pp. 349-367, 4 ills., Nov., 1896

The World's Production of Gold (From an Address to the American Bankers' Convention, by F. A. Vanderlip, October 11, 1905). XVI, pp. 571-572, Dec., 1905

GOLD COAST, West Africa:

The Gold Coast, Ashanti, and Kumassi. By George K. French. VIII, pp. 1-15, 9 ills., Jan., 1897

The Revolt of the Ashantis. XI, p. 244, map, June, 1900

GOLDEN EAGLES:

In Quest of the Golden Eagle: Over Lonely Mountain and Prairie Soars This Rare and Lordly Bird, But Three Youths from the East Catch Up With Him at Last. By John and Frank Craighead. LXXVII, pp. 693-710, 17 ills., May, 1940

GOLDEN Fleece of Dixie (Cotton). 34 color photos by Willard R. Culver. LXXIX, pp. 153-192, Feb., 1941

The **GOLDEN** Gate, and Redwood Evergreens (California). 17 color photos by B. Anthony Stewart. LXXV, pp. 149-160, Feb., 1939

The **GOLDEN** Isles of Guale (Sea Islands, Georgia). By W. Robert Moore. LXV, pp. 235-264, 35 ills., map, Feb., 1934

The **GOLDEN** Trout. XVII, p. 424, July, 1906

GOLDFISH:

The Fisheries of Japan. By Hugh M. Smith. XVI, pp. 201-220, 13 ills., May, 1905

Goldfish and Their Cultivation in America. By Hugh M. Smith. Paintings by Hashime Murayama. XLVI, pp. 375-400, 14 ills. in black and white, 8 ills. in color, Oct., 1924

GOMES, EDWIN H.:

Notes on the Sea Dyaks of Borneo. By Edwin H. Gomes. XXII, pp. 695-723, 26 ills., Aug., 1911

GOMEZ, ESTEVAN:

Gomez and the New York Gulf. (By L. D. Scisco). IX, pp. 371-373, Aug., 1898

GOOD HOPE, Cape of, South Africa:

Busy Corner—the Cape of Good Hope: Ships Bound for Faraway Battlegrounds Stream Past Capetown, "Tavern of the Seas," and Other Ports of Virile South Africa. By W. Robert Moore. LXXXII, pp. 197-223, 11 ills. in black and white, 11 ills. in color, map, Aug., 1942

Cape of Good Hope: The Floral Province. By Melville Chater. LIX, pp. 391-430, 29 ills. in black and white, 11 ills. in color, two-page map, Apr., 1931

GOODE, G. BROWN:

Albemarle in Revolutionary Days. By Dr. G. Brown Goode. VII, pp. 271-281, Aug., 1896

Death of G. Brown Goode. (By W J M.). VII, p. 316, Sept., 1896

See also NGS: Board of Managers

GOODE, RICHARD U.:

Bitter Root Forest Reserve. By Richard U. Goode. IX, pp. 387-400, 5 ills., foldout map, Sept., 1898

The Height of Mt. Rainier. By Richard U. Goode. IX, pp. 97-98, Mar., 1898

The Idaho and Montana Boundary Line. By Richard U. Goode. XI, pp. 23-29, ill., diagr., Jan., 1900

Portrait. XIV, ill. p. 424, Nov., 1903

Richard Urquhart Goode (Biography). XIV, pp. 424-425, ill., Nov., 1903

A Trip to Panama and Darien. By Richard U. Goode. I, pp. 301-314, diagr., foldout map, Oct., 1889

GOODING, PAUL:

Tahiti: A Playground of Nature. By Paul Gooding. XXXVIII, pp. 301-326, 16 ills., map, Oct., 1920

GOODNOW, FRANK JOHNSON:

The Geography of China: The Influence of Physical Environment on the History and Character of the Chinese People. By Frank Johnson Goodnow. LI, pp. 651-664, 11 ills., June, 1927

GOODWIN, W. A. R.:

The Restoration of Colonial Williamsburg. By W. A. R. Goodwin. LXXI, pp. 402-443, 21 ills. in black and white, 25 ills. in color, Apr., 1937

GOOSE FISH:

The Purple Veil: A Romance of the Sea. (By H. A. L.). XVI, pp. 337-341, 9 ills., July, 1905

GOPHERS:

Into the Land of the Chipmunk. By Ruth Alexander Nichols. LX, pp. 77-98, 28 ills., July, 1931

GORE, JAMES HOWARD:

As Seen from a Dutch Window. By James Howard Gore. XIX, pp. 619-634, 3 ills., Sept., 1908

The Discovery of the North Pole (Speech by James Howard Gore). XXI, pp. 63-82, Jan., 1910

Holland's War with the Sea. By James Howard Gore. XLIII, pp. 283-325, 39 ills., map, Mar., 1923

The Return of Wellman. By J. Howard Gore. X, pp. 348-351, ills., Sept., 1899

Roumania, the Pivotal State. By James Howard Gore. XXVIII, pp. 360-390, 32 ills., Oct., 1915

The Wellman Polar Expedition (Arctic). (By J. Howard Gore). X, pp. 267-268, July, 1899

See also NGS: Board of Managers

GORE, LILLIAN:

In Beautiful Delecarlia (Dalecarlia, Sweden). By Lillian Gore. XX, pp. 464-477, 13 ills., May, 1909

GORGONIANS (Coral):

The First Autochromes from the Ocean Bottom: Marine Life in Its Natural Habitat Along the Florida Keys Is Successfully Photographed in Colors. (Photographs by Dr. W. H. Longley and Charles Martin). LI, pp. 56-60, 8 ills. in color, Jan., 1927

Life on a Coral Reef: The Fertility and Mystery of the Sea Studied Beneath the Waters Surrounding Dry Tortugas. By W. H. Longley. LI, pp. 61-83, 22 ills., Jan., 1927

GORILLAS:

Man's Closest Counterparts: Heavyweight of Monkeydom Is the "Old Man" Gorilla, by Far the Largest of the Four Great Apes. By William M. Mann. Paintings by Elie Cheverlange. LXXVIII, pp. 213-236, 10 ills. in black and white, 10 ills. in color, Aug., 1940

GORKI (Nizhni Novgorod), R. S. F. S. R.:

Voyaging on the Volga Amid War and Revolution: War-time Sketches on Russia's Great Waterway. By William T. Ellis. XXXIII, pp. 245-265, 16 ills., Mar., 1918

GORMAN, MARTIN W.:

Ice-Cliffs on White River, Yukon Territory. By Martin W. Gorman. XI, pp. 113-117, Mar., 1900

GORO, F. W.:

Where Bretons Wrest a Living from the Sea. 23 photos by F. W. Goro. LXXI, pp. 751-766, June, 1937

GOULDER, HARVEY:

Honors for Amundsen (Address by Harvey Goulder). XIX, pp. 55-76, 13 ills., Jan., 1908

GOVERNING the Philippine Islands. By Colonel Clarence R. Edwards. XV, pp. 273-284, 5 ills., July, 1904

GOVERNMENT:

The British Commonwealth of Nations: "Organized Freedom" Around the World. By Eric Underwood. LXXXIII, pp. 485-524, 31 ills., Apr., 1943

The Civil Government of Alaska. By Hon. George C. Perkins. IX, pp. 172-178, Apr., 1898

Colonial Government in Borneo. By James M. Hubbard. XI, pp. 359-363, Sept., 1900

Colonial Systems of the World. By O. P. Austin. X, pp. 21-26, Jan., 1899

Cuba. By Robert T. Hill. IX, pp. 193-242, 12 ills., 7 diagrs., tables, 5 maps (1 foldout), May, 1898

Evolution of Russian Government. By Edwin A. Grosvenor. XVI, pp. 309-332, 16 ills., July, 1905

"Free Burghs" in the United States. By James H. Blodgett. VII, pp. 116-122, Mar., 1896

Geographic Work of the General Government. By Henry Gannett. IX, pp. 329-338, July, 1898

Great Britain's Bread Upon the Waters: Canada and Her Other Daughters. By William Howard Taft. XXIX, pp. 217-272, 56 ills., Mar., 1916

The Historical Development of the National Capital. By Marcus Baker. IX, pp. 323-329, July, 1898

Japan. By D. W. Stevens, Counselor of the Imperial Legation of Japan. VI, pp. 193-199, Dec. 29, 1894

The Oldest Free Assemblies: Address of Right Hon. Arthur J. Balfour, in the United States House of Representatives, May 5, 1917. XXXI, pp. 368-371, Apr., 1917

The United States and the British Empire. By Leonard David Gammans. LXXXVII, pp. 562-564, May, 1945

The Utilization of the Vacant Public Lands. By Emory F. Best. VIII, pp. 49-57, Feb., 1897
Included: Homestead Act

Yanks at Westminster. By Capt. Leonard David Gammans. XC, pp. 223-252, 6 ills. in black and white, 19 ills. in color, Aug., 1946

See also Allied Military Government; American Military Government; Communism

GOVERNMENT Assistance in Handling Forest Lands. XV, pp. 450-452, Nov., 1904

GRACE HARWAR (Ship):

Rounding the Horn in a Windjammer. By A. J. Villiers. LIX, pp. 191-224, 36 ills., map, Feb., 1931

GRAF ZEPPELIN (Airship):

The First Airship Flight Around the World: Dr. Hugo Eckener Tells of an Epochal Geographic Achievement upon the Occasion of the Bestowal of the National Geographic Society's Special Gold Medal. LVII, pp. 653-688, 37 ills., June, 1930

GRAHAM LAND, Antarctica:

American Discoverers of the Antarctic Continent. By Major General A. W. Greely. XXIII, pp. 298-312, 7 ills., map, Mar., 1912

GRANADA, Spain:

From Granada to Gibraltar—A Tour of Southern Spain. By Harry A. McBride. XLVI, pp. 205-232, 23 ills., Aug., 1924

GRAND BANKS, Newfoundland:

Life on the Grand Banks: An Account of the Sailor-Fishermen Who Harvest the Shoal Waters of North America's Eastern Coasts. By Frederick William Wallace. XL, pp. 1-28, 29 ills., July, 1921

GRAND CANAL, China:

Grand Canal Panorama. By Willard Price. LXXI, pp. 487-514, 31 ills., map, Apr., 1937

Shantung—China's Holy Land. By Charles K. Edmunds. XXXVI, pp. 231-252, 21 ills., map, Sept., 1919

GRAND CANYON, Arizona:

Experiences in the Grand Canyon. By Ellsworth and Emery Kolb. XXVI, pp. 99-184, 70 ills., map, Aug., 1914

The Forests and Deserts of Arizona. By Bernhard E. Fernow. VIII, pp. 203-226, 5 ills., July-Aug., 1897

The Grand Canyon Bridge. By Harriet Chalmers Adams. XXXIX, pp. 645-650, 6 ills., June, 1921

The North American Deserts. By Herr Professor Dr. Johannes Walther. IV, pp. 163-176, Feb. 8, 1893

Photographing the Marvels of the West in Colors. By Fred Payne Clatworthy. LIII, pp. 694-719, 5 ills. in color, June, 1928

The Scenery of North America. By James Bryce. XLI, pp. 339-389, 45 ills., Apr., 1922

Scenic Glories of Western United States. 12 color photos by Fred Payne Clatworthy. LVI, pp. 223-230, Aug., 1929

The Southwest: Its Splendid Natural Resources, Agricultural Wealth, and Scenic Beauty. By N. H. Darton. XXI, pp. 631-665, 21 ills., map, Aug., 1910

Surveying the Grand Canyon of the Colorado: An Account of the 1923 Boating Expedition of the United States Geological Survey. By Lewis R. Freeman. XLV, pp. 471-548, 62 ills., map, May, 1924

GRAND COULEE DAM, Washington:

The Columbia (River) Turns on the Power. By Maynard Owen Williams. LXXIX, pp. 749-792, 25 ills. in black and white, 18 ills. in color, June, 1941

The **GRAND** Duchy of Luxemburg: A Miniature Democratic State of Many Charms Against a Feudal Background. By Maynard Owen Williams. XLVI, pp. 501-528, 28 ills., map, Nov., 1924

GRAND UNION CANAL, England:
Britain Just Before the Storm: A Canadian Canoe Threads Old English Waterways Athrob with the Midlands' Industrial Life. By Amos Burg. LXXVIII, pp. 185-212, 14 ills. in black and white, 9 ills. in color, map, Aug., 1940

GRAND VALLEY, Netherlands New Guinea:
New Guinea's Mountain and Swampland Dwellers. By Col. Ray T. Elsmore. LXXXVIII, pp. 671-694, 15 ills. in black and white, 7 ills. in color, map, Dec., 1945
Unknown New Guinea: Circumnavigating the World in a Flying Boat, American Scientists Discover a Valley of 60,000 People Never Before Seen by White Men. By Richard Archbold. LXXIX, pp. 315-344, 28 ills., map, Mar., 1941

GRANDE BAIE, Canada:
Gentle Folk Settle Stern Saguenay: On French Canada's Frontier Homespun Colonists Keep the Customs of Old Norman Settlers. By Harrison Howell Walker. LXXV, pp. 595-632, 15 ills. in black and white, 25 ills. in color, map, May, 1939

The **GRANDEST** and Most Mighty Terrestrial Phenomenon: The Gulf Stream. By John Elliott Pillsbury. XXIII, pp. 767-778, ill., diagrs., 3 maps, Aug., 1912

The **GRANITE** City of the North: Austere Stockholm, Sweden's Prosperous Capital, Presents a Smiling Aspect in Summer. By Ralph A. Graves. LIV, pp. 403-424, 23 ills., Oct., 1928

GRANT, G. A.:
Western National Parks Invite America Out of Doors. 12 photos in duotone by G. A. Grant. LXVI, pp. 65-80, July, 1934

GRANT, MADISON:
Saving the Redwoods. By Madison Grant. XXXVII, pp. 519-536, 10 ills., June, 1920

GRAPE CULTURE:
Fruitful Shores of the Finger Lakes (New York). By Harrison Howell Walker. LXXIX, pp. 559-594, 15 ills. in black and white, 22 ills. in color, map, May, 1941
The Grape-Growing Industry in the United States. XIV, pp. 445-451, 5 ills., Dec., 1903

GRASS Makes Wyoming Fat. By Frederick Simpich. LXXXVIII, pp. 153-188, 13 ills. in black and white, 19 ills. in color, two-page map, Aug., 1945

"**GRASS** Never Grows Where the Turkish Hoof Has Trod." By Edwin Pears. XXIII, pp. 1132-1148, 19 ills., Nov., 1912

GRASSE, FRANÇOIS JOSEPH PAUL DE:
Our First Alliance. By J. J. Jusserand. XXXI, pp. 518-548, 8 ills., June, 1917

GRASSES:
American Wild Flowers. Paintings by Mary E. Eaton. XXVII, pp. 483-517, 29 ills. in color, May, 1915
Exploring a Grass Wonderland of Wild West China. By Ray G. Johnson. LXXXV, pp. 713-742, 24 ills., map, June, 1944

GRASSES—*Continued*
Familiar Grasses and Their Flowers. By E. J. Geske and W. J. Showalter. Paintings by E. J. Geske. XXXIX, pp. 625-636, 8 ills. in color, June, 1921
Contents: Barnyard Grass, Kentucky Bluegrass, Orchard Grass, Purple-Top, Redtop, Rye-Grass, Timothy, Yellow Foxtail

GRAVES, HENRY S.:
The Fight Against Forest Fires. By Henry S. Graves. XXIII, pp. 662-683, 19 ills., July, 1912

GRAVES, RALPH A.:
Fearful Famines of the Past: History Will Repeat Itself Unless the American People Conserve Their Resources. By Ralph A. Graves. XXXII, pp. 69-90, 11 ills., July, 1917
The Granite City of the North: Austere Stockholm, Sweden's Prosperous Capital, Presents a Smiling Aspect in Summer. By Ralph A. Graves. LIV, pp. 403-424, 23 ills., Oct., 1928
Helping to Solve Our Allies' Food Problem: America Calls for a Million Young Soldiers of the Commissary to Volunteer for Service in 1918. By Ralph Graves. XXXIII, pp. 170-194, 23 ills., Feb., 1918
Human Emotion Recorded by Photography. By Ralph A. Graves. XXXVIII, pp. 284-300, 16 ills., Oct., 1920
Louisiana, Land of Perpetual Romance. By Ralph A. Graves. LVII, pp. 393-482, 84 ills. in black and white, 29 ills. in color, map supplement, Apr., 1930
Marching Through Georgia Sixty Years After: Multifold Industries and Diversified Agriculture Are Restoring the Prosperity of America's Largest State East of the Mississippi. By Ralph A. Graves. L, pp. 259-311, 47 ills., map supplement, Sept., 1926
Memorial tribute of the Board of Trustees and Officers of the National Geographic Society to Ralph A. Graves, late Senior Assistant Editor of the National Geographic Magazine. LXII, p. 606, ill., Nov., 1932
The Millennial City: The Romance of Geneva, Capital of the League of Nations. By Ralph A. Graves. XXXV, pp. 457-476, 13 ills., June, 1919
The New Map of Europe: Showing the Boundaries Established by the Peace Conference at Paris and by Subsequent Decisions of the Supreme Council of the Allied and Associated Powers. By Ralph A. Graves. Text with map supplement. XXXIX, pp. 157-177, 18 ills., Feb., 1921
Ships for the Seven Seas: The Story of America's Maritime Needs, Her Capabilities and Her Achievements. By Ralph A. Graves. XXXIV, pp. 165-200, 24 ills., Sept., 1918
A Short Visit to Wales: Historic Associations and Scenic Beauties Contend for Interest in the Little Land Behind the Hills. By Ralph A. Graves. XLIV, pp. 635-675, 37 ills., map, Dec., 1923
Through the English Lake District Afoot and Awheel. By Ralph A. Graves. LV, pp. 577-603, 19 ills. in black and white, 15 ills. in color, map, May, 1929

GRAVOSA, Yugoslavia:

East of the Adriatic: Notes on Dalmatia, Montenegro, Bosnia, and Herzegovina. By Kenneth McKenzie. XXIII, pp. 1159-1187, 1284, 37 ills., map, Dec., 1912

A **GREAT** African Lake (Victoria). By Sir Henry M. Stanley. XIII, pp. 169-172, map, May, 1902

GREAT AMERICAN DESERT, Utah:

The Nation's Undeveloped Resources. By Franklin K. Lane. XXV, pp. 183-225, 32 ills., Feb., 1914

GREAT BARRIER REEF, Australia:

The Great Barrier Reef and Its Isles: The Wonder and Mystery of Australia's World-Famous Geographical Feature. By Charles Barrett. LVIII, pp. 355-384, 38 ills., map, Sept., 1930

Where Nature Runs Riot: On Australia's Great Barrier Reef Marine Animals Grow to Unusual Size, Develop Strange Weapons of Attack and Defense, and Acquire Brilliant Colors. By T. C. Roughley. LXXVII, pp. 823-850, 18 ills. in black and white, 15 ills. in color, map, June, 1940

GREAT BRITAIN:

Britain Fights in the Fields. By Francis A. Flood. LXXXVI, pp. 31-65, 17 ills. in black and white, 21 ills. in color, July, 1944

The British Commonwealth of Nations: "Organized Freedom" Around the World. By Eric Underwood. LXXXIII, pp. 485-524, 31 ills., Apr., 1943

British Isles. 16 ills. XXVIII, pp. 551-566, Dec., 1915

The Expansion of England. By Edwin D. Mead. XI, pp. 249-263, July, 1900

Fearful Famines of the Past: History Will Repeat Itself Unless the American People Conserve Their Resources. By Ralph A. Graves. XXXII, pp. 69-90, 11 ills., July, 1917
Included: Famines in England

The Flags of the British Empire. By Byron McCandless and Gilbert Grosvenor. XXXII, pp. 378-385, 158 ills. in color, Oct., 1917

A Geographical Description of the British Islands. (By W. M. Davis). VII, pp. 208-211, June, 1896

Great Britain in the Yangtze Valley. XII, p. 163, Apr., 1901

Great Britain on Parade. By Maynard Owen Williams. LXVIII, pp. 137-184, 40 ills. in black and white, 11 ills. in color, Aug., 1935

Great Britain's Bread Upon the Waters: Canada and Her Other Daughters. By William Howard Taft. XXIX, pp. 217-272, 56 ills., Mar., 1916

Lend-Lease Is a Two-way Benefit: Innovation in Creative Statesmanship Pools Resources of United Nations, and Supplies American Forces Around the World. By Francis Flood. LXXXIII, pp. 745-761, 14 ills., June, 1943

The Oldest Free Assemblies: Address of Right Hon. Arthur J. Balfour, in the United States House of Representatives, May 5, 1917. XXXI, pp. 368-371, Apr., 1917

One Hundred British Seaports. XXXI, pp. 84-94, 10 ills., map, Jan., 1917

GREAT BRITAIN—*Continued*

The Ordnance Survey of Great Britain—Its History and Object. By Josiah Pierce, Jr. II, pp. 243-260, Aug., 1890

The Races of Europe. By Edwin A. Grosvenor. XXXIV, pp. 441-534, 62 ills., diagr. and index, maps, map supplement, Dec., 1918

Shipbuilding in the United Kingdom in 1898. X, pp. 138-139, Apr., 1899

Some Significant Facts Concerning the Foreign Trade of Great Britain. XI, p. 480, Dec., 1900

Tales of the British Air Service. By Major William A. Bishop. XXXIII, pp. 27-37, 12 ills., Jan., 1918

The Ties that Bind: Our Natural Sympathy with English Traditions, the French Republic, and the Russian Outburst for Liberty. By John Sharp Williams. XXXI, pp. 281-286, 4 ills., Mar., 1917

What Great Britain Is Doing (The British War Effort). By Sydney Brooks. XXXI, pp. 193-210, 7 ills., Mar., 1917

What the War Has Done for Britain. By Judson C. Welliver. XXXIV, pp. 278-297, 13 ills., Oct., 1918

Yanks at Westminster. By Capt. Leonard David Gammans. XC, pp. 223-252, 6 ills. in black and white, 19 ills. in color, Aug., 1946

See also England; Scotland; Wales

GREAT Britain's Bread Upon the Waters: Canada and Her Other Daughters. By William Howard Taft. XXIX, pp. 217-272, 56 ills., Mar., 1916

The **GREAT** Canals of the World. XVI, pp. 475-479, Oct., 1905

GREAT FALLS, Potomac River:

The Great Falls of the Potomac. By Gilbert Grosvenor. LIII, pp. 385-400, 19 ills., Mar., 1928

Potomac, River of Destiny. By Albert W. Atwood. LXXXVIII, pp. 33-70, 15 ills. in black and white, 18 ills. in color, map, July, 1945

GREAT ICE BARRIER, Antarctica:

Geography. By Rear-Admiral Sir W. J. L. Wharton. XVI, pp. 483-498, Nov., 1905

The Great Ice Barrier. By Henry Gannett. XXI, pp. 173-174, ill., Feb., 1910

An Ice Wrapped Continent. (By G. H. G.). XVIII, pp. 95-117, 20 ills., map, Feb., 1907

GREAT LAKES, Canada-U. S.:

Area and Drainage Basin of Lake Superior. By Dr. Mark W. Harrington. VIII, pp. 111-120, tables, Apr., 1897

By Car and Steamer Around Our Inland Seas. By Maynard Owen Williams. LXV, pp. 451-491, 29 ills. in black and white, 8 ills. in duotone, two-page map, Apr., 1934

Great Lakes and Great Industries. 19 color photos by B. Anthony Stewart, Alfred T. Palmer, Willard R. Culver. LXXXVI, pp. 689-712, Dec., 1944

Honors for Amundsen (Address: "The Five Inland Seas," by Hon. Harvey Goulder). XIX, pp. 55-76, 13 ills., Jan., 1908

GREAT LAKES, Canada-U. S.—*Continued*

Modification of the Great Lakes by Earth Movement. By G. K. Gilbert. VIII, pp. 233-247, 3 diagrs., table, 4 maps, Sept., 1897

Rainfall and the Level of Lake Erie. (By E. L. Moseley). XIV, pp. 327-328, Aug., 1903

Submerged Valleys in Sandusky Bay. By Professor E. L. Moseley. XIII, pp. 398-403, 4 charts, Nov., 1902

Testing the Currents of Lake Erie. (By E. L. Moseley). XIV, pp. 41-42, Jan., 1903

Variations in Lake Levels and Atmospheric Precipitation. By Alfred J. Henry. X, pp. 403-406, diagr., Oct., 1899

See also Michigan; Superior, Lake

The **GREAT** Mississippi Flood of 1927: Since White Man's Discovery This Mighty River Has Served Him Well, Yet It Has Brought Widespread Devastation Along Its Lower Reaches. By Frederick Simpich. LII, pp. 243-289, 53 ills., map, Sept., 1927

The **GREAT** Natural Bridges of Utah. XVIII, pp. 199-204, 3 ills., Mar., 1907

The **GREAT** Natural Bridges of Utah. By Byron Cummings. XXI, pp. 157-167, 7 ills., Feb., 1910

The **GREAT** Populous Centers of the World. By General A. W. Greely. V, pp. 89-92, table, July 10, 1893

The **GREAT** Rainbow Natural Bridge of Southern Utah. By Joseph E. Pogue. XXII, pp. 1048-1056, 6 ills., Nov., 1911

GREAT RIFT VALLEY, Africa-Asia:

Where Roosevelt Will Hunt (Kenya). By Sir Harry Johnston. XX, pp. 207-256, 43 ills., map supplement, Mar., 1909

GREAT SMOKY MOUNTAINS, North Carolina-Tennessee:

Rambling Around the Roof of Eastern America. By Leonard C. Roy. LXX, pp. 243-266, 25 ills., map, Aug., 1936

GREAT Stone Faces of Easter Island. 11 ills. LXXXV, pp. 225-232, Feb., 1944

GREAT Stone Faces of the Mexican Jungle: Five Colossal Heads and Numerous Other Monuments of Vanished Americans Are Excavated by the Latest National Geographic-Smithsonian Expedition. By Matthew W. Stirling. LXXVIII, pp. 309-334, 26 ills., map, Sept., 1940

The **GREAT** Storm of March 11-14, 1888. By Brigadier-General A. W. Greely. I, pp. 37-39, Oct., 1888

The **GREAT** Storm Off the Atlantic Coast of the United States, March 11th-14th, 1888. By Everett Hayden. I, pp. 40-58, 6 charts, Oct., 1888

The **GREAT** Turk and His Lost Provinces. By William E. Curtis. XIV, pp. 45-61, 7 ills., Feb., 1903

The **GREAT** Unmapped Areas on the Earth's Surface Awaiting the Explorer and Geographer. By J. Scott Keltie. VIII, pp. 251-266, Sept., 1897

GREAT WALL OF CHINA:

China's Treasures. By Frederick McCormick. XXIII, pp. 996-1040, 50 ills., Oct., 1912

The Great Wall of China. (By James H. Wilson). XI, pp. 372-374, ill., Sept., 1900

Peking, the City of the Unexpected. By James Arthur Muller. XXXVIII, pp. 335-355, 18 ills., Nov., 1920

A Thousand Miles Along the Great Wall of China: The Mightiest Barrier Ever Built by Man Has Stood Guard Over the Land of Chin for Twenty Centuries. By Adam Warwick. XLIII, pp. 113-143, 27 ills., maps, panorama, Feb., 1923

The Great Wall of China Near Nankow Pass (panorama)

The **GREAT** Wall of China Near Nankow Pass. XLIII, panorama, Feb., 1923

The **GREAT** White Monarch of the Pacific Northwest (Mount Rainier). By A. H. Barnes. XXIII, pp. 593-626, 31 ills., map, June, 1912

GREAT YARMOUTH, England:

King Herring: An Account of the World's Most Valuable Fish, the Industries It Supports, and the Part It Has Played in History. By Hugh M. Smith. XX, pp. 701-735, 21 ills., Aug., 1909

When the Herring Fleet Comes to Great Yarmouth. By W. Robert Moore. LXVI, pp. 233-250, 19 ills., Aug., 1934

GREATER ANTILLES. *See* Cuba; Dominican Republic; Haiti; Jamaica; Puerto Rico

GREATER New York . . . Metropolis of Mankind. Aërial photo by Captain Albert W. Stevens. LXIV, supplement, Nov., 1933

GREATER SUNDA ISLANDS. *See* Borneo; Celebes; Java; Sumatra

The **GREATEST** Achievement of Ancient Man in America (Fortress of Sacsahuaman, Peru). XXIX, panorama, May, 1916

The **GREATEST** Hunt in the World (Elephant Hunting). By Eliza Ruhamah Scidmore. XVII, pp. 673-692, 17 ills., Dec., 1906

The **GREATEST** Volcanoes of Mexico. By A. Melgareio. XXI, pp. 741-760, 22 ills., Sept., 1910

The **GREATEST** Voyage in the Annals of the Sea. By J. R. Hildebrand. LXII, pp. 699-739, 35 ills., map, Dec., 1932

The **GREATNESS** of Little Portugal. By Oswald Crawfurd. XXI, pp. 867-883, 12 ills., Oct., 1910

GREBES (Birds):

Birds That Cruise the Coast and Inland Waters. By T. Gilbert Pearson. Paintings by Maj. Allan Brooks. LXV, pp. 299-328, 2 ills. in black and white, 9 portraits in color, Mar., 1934

GREECE:

Ageless Luster of Greece and Rhodes. 16 ills. in duotone by Arnold Genthe. LXXIII, pp. 477-492, Apr., 1938

The Changing Map in the Balkans. By Frederick Moore. XXIV, pp. 199-226, 27 ills., map, Feb., 1913

GREECE—*Continued*

Classic Greece Merges Into 1941 News. 19 photos: 15 by B. Anthony Stewart, 3 by Maynard Owen Williams. LXXIX, pp. 93-108, Jan., 1941

Geographic Progress of Civilization. Annual Address by the President, Honorable Gardiner G. Hubbard. VI, pp. 1-22, Feb. 14, 1894

"The Glory That Was Greece." By Alexander Wilbourne Weddell. XLII, pp. 571-630, 51 ills., map, Dec., 1922

"Grass Never Grows Where the Turkish Hoof Has Trod." By Edwin Pears. XXIII, pp. 1132-1148, 19 ills., Nov., 1912

The Great Turk and His Lost Provinces. By William E. Curtis. XIV, pp. 45-61, 7 ills., Feb., 1903

Greece—the Birthplace of Science and Free Speech: Explorations on the Mainland and in Crete and the Aegean Isles Reveal Ancient Life Similar to That of the Present. By Richard Stillwell. Paintings by H. M. Herget. LXXXV, pp. 273-353, 13 ills. in black and white, 32 ills. in color, two-page map, Mar., 1944

Contents: Boy and Girl Grappling Bulls at Cnossus: Crete.—Travelers at a Mycenaean Palace.—A Fountain House of 2,500 Years Ago.—Chariot Race at Olympia.—Athena's Gift to Greece Was the Precious Olive.—Fishermen in the Gulf of Corinth.—Hauling a Ship over the Isthmus.—The Famous Oracle at Delphi.—Young Spartans Were Tough.—Leonidas' Immortal Sacrifice at Thermopylae.—The Persians Storm the Acropolis.—Xerxes Watching the Battle of Salamis, 480 B. C.—To Greeks We Owe Our Love of Athletics.—An Athenian School.—Weaving and Spinning.—Herodotus—Geographer and Historian.—Pericles and Pheidias in the Parthenon.—The Panathenaic Procession Brings a New Robe to Athena.—Setting a Capital on the Erechtheum.—An Athenian Wedding Party.—Socrates Enjoys a Banquet.—Greek Women Used Mascara and Beauty Lotions.—Voting in the Market Place at Athens.—Potter Making Clay Figurines.—Hippocrates, Father of Medicine.—Phryne Poses for Praxiteles.—The Countryside Is Smiling; "Therefore, Ye Soft Pipes, Play on."—Alexander Calls on Diogenes the Cynic.—Alexander Defeats Darius the Persian at Issus, 333 B. C.—In Such a Theater Orestes and Electra Played Their Tragic Roles.—A Key to the Classic Sea Was the Port of Delos.—Archimedes Discovered the Law of Specific Gravity

Greece and Montenegro. By George Higgins Moses. XXIV, pp. 281-310, 24 ills., Mar., 1913

Greece of Today. By George Higgins Moses. XXVIII, pp. 295-329, 27 ills., Oct., 1915

The Greek Way. By Edith Hamilton. LXXXV, pp. 257-271, 12 ills., Mar., 1944

History's Greatest Trek: Tragedy Stalks Through the Near East as Greece and Turkey Exchange Two Million of Their People. By Melville Chater. XLVIII, pp. 533-590, 52 ills. in black and white, 32 ills. in color, Nov., 1925

The Hoary Monasteries of Mt. Athos. By H. G. Dwight. XXX, pp. 249-272, 24 ills., map, Sept., 1916

Megaspelæon, the Oldest Monastery in Greece. By Carroll Storrs Alden. XXIV, pp. 310-323, 11 ills., Mar., 1913

GREECE—*Continued*

Modern Odyssey in Classic Lands: Troy's Treasures, Athens' Parthenon, and Rome's First "Broad Way" Influence Today's Banks, Costumes, Jewelry, and Railroad Timetables. By Maynard Owen Williams. LXXVII, pp. 291-337, 27 ills. in black and white, 22 ills. in color, Mar., 1940

New Greece, the Centenarian, Forges Ahead. By Maynard Owen Williams. LVIII, pp. 649-721, 51 ills. in black and white, 40 ills. in color, map, Dec., 1930

The New Map of Europe: Showing the Boundaries Established by the Peace Conference at Paris and by Subsequent Decisions of the Supreme Council of the Allied and Associated Powers. By Ralph A. Graves. Text with map supplement. XXXIX, pp. 157-177, 18 ills., Feb., 1921

The Races of Europe. By Edwin A. Grosvenor. XXXIV, pp. 441-534, 62 ills., diagr. and index, maps, map supplement, Dec., 1918

Saloniki. By H. G. Dwight. XXX, pp. 203-232, 28 ills., Sept., 1916

Seeing 3,000 Years of History in Four Hours: A Panorama of Ancient, Medieval, and Modern Events Against a Background of Mythology Unfolds During an Airplane Journey from Constantinople to Athens. By Maynard Owen Williams. LIV, pp. 719-739, 24 ills., map, Dec., 1928

The Whirlpool of the Balkans. By George Higgins Moses. XXXIX, pp. 179-197, 15 ills., Feb., 1921

With the Monks at Meteora: The Monasteries of Thessaly. By Elizabeth Perkins. XX, pp. 799-807, 5 ills., Sept., 1909

See also Crete (Island); Cyclades (Islands); Dodecanese Islands

The **GREEK** Bronzes. Text regarding requests for photographs of bronzes. XXIII, p. 104, Jan., 1912

The **GREEK** Bronzes of Tunisia. By Frank Edward Johnson. XXIII, pp. 89-103, 11 ills., Jan., 1912

GREEK DRAMA:

Festival Days on the Slopes of Mount Parnassus. 6 color photos by Maynard Owen Williams. LVIII, pp. 713-720, Dec., 1930

The **GREEK** Way. By Edith Hamilton. LXXXV, pp. 257-271, 12 ills., Mar., 1944

GREEKS, Ancient:

Greece—the Birthplace of Science and Free Speech: Explorations on the Mainland and in Crete and the Aegean Isles Reveal Ancient Life Similar to That of the Present. By Richard Stillwell. Paintings by H. M. Herget. LXXXV, pp. 273-353, 13 ills. in black and white, 32 ills. in color, two-page map, Mar., 1944

See Greece, for contents note

The Greek Way. By Edith Hamilton. LXXXV, pp. 257-271, 12 ills., Mar., 1944

GREELY, A. W.:

Advances in Geographic Knowledge During the Nineteenth Century. By Brig.-Gen. A. W. Greely. XII, pp. 143-152, maps, Apr., 1901

GREELY, A. W.—*Continued*
American Discoverers of the Antarctic Continent. By Major General A. W. Greely. XXIII, pp. 298-312, 7 ills., map, Mar., 1912
The "Bowdoin" (Ship) in North Greenland: Arctic Explorers Place Tablet to Commemorate Sacrifices of the Lady Franklin Bay Expedition. By Donald B. MacMillan. XLVII, pp. 677-722, 49 ills., June, 1925
The Cartography and Observations of Bering's First Voyage. By General A. W. Greely. III, pp. 205-230, map supplement, Jan. 28, 1892; Feb. 19, 1892
Charles Francis Hall and Jones Sound. (By A. W. G.). VII, pp. 308-310, Sept., 1896
Climatic Conditions of Alaska. By General A. W. Greely. IX, pp. 132-137, Apr., 1898
Collinson's Arctic Journey. By General A. W. Greely. IV, pp. 198-200, Feb. 8, 1893
Duke of the Abruzzi in the Himalayas. (By A. W. G.). XXI, pp. 245-249, Mar., 1910
The Economic Evolution of Alaska. By Major General A. W. Greely. XX, pp. 585-593, 4 ills., July, 1909
Farthest north reached by General Greely. XVIII, p. 50, Jan., 1907
The France of Today. By Major General A. W. Greely. XXVI, pp. 193-222, 27 ills., Sept., 1914
Gardiner Greene Hubbard: Memorial Meeting. Address by General A. W. Greely. IX, pp. 68-70, Feb., 1898
Geographic Literature. IX, p. 191, Apr., 1898
Geographical Exploration: Its Moral and Material Results. By General A. W. Greely. XVII, pp. 1-5, Jan., 1906
Geography of the Air. Annual Address by the Vice-President, General A. W. Greely. VI, pp. 200-207, Dec. 29, 1894
Geography of the Air. Annual Report by Vice-President A. W. Greely. III, pp. 41-52, May 1, 1891
Geography of the Air. Annual Report by Vice-President, General A. W. Greely. IV, pp. 85-100, Mar. 18, 1892
George W. Melville, Engineer-in-chief, U. S. N. (By A. W. G.). VIII, pp. 187-190, ill., June, 1897
The Great Populous Centers of the World. By General A. W. Greely. V, pp. 89-92, table, July 10, 1893
The Great Storm of March 11-14, 1888. By Brigadier-General A. W. Greely. I, pp. 37-39, Oct., 1888
Greely's "Handbook of Alaska." By Gilbert H. Grosvenor. XX, pp. 491-492, May, 1909
Honors to the American Navy (Address by Maj. Gen. A. W. Greely). XX, pp. 77-95, Jan., 1909
Hurricanes on the Coast of Texas. By General A. W. Greely. XI, pp. 442-445, Nov., 1900
In Honor of the Army and Aviation (Address by Maj. Gen. A. W. Greely). XXII, pp. 267-284, Mar., 1911
Jefferson as a Geographer. By General A. W. Greely. VII, pp. 269-271, Aug., 1896
The Land of Promise (Siberia). By Major General A. W. Greely. XXIII, pp. 1078-1090, 7 ills., Nov., 1912

GREELY, A. W.—*Continued*
Miscellanea. VIII, p. 64, Feb., 1897
Nansen's Polar Expedition. By General A. W. Greely. VII, pp. 98-101, ill., table, Mar., 1896
The National Geographic Society in War Time. By Major-General A. W. Greely. XXXIII, pp. 369-375, 5 ills., Apr., 1918
National Geographic Society Notes (Election of Gen. Greely as Chairman of the Committee on Eighth International Geographic Congress). XIII, pp. 218-219, ill., June, 1902
The National Geographic Society's Notable Year (Address by Maj. Gen. A. W. Greely). XXXVII, pp. 338-345, ills., Apr., 1920
The Origin of Stefansson's Blond Eskimo. By Major General A. W. Greely. XXIII, pp. 1225-1238, 10 ills., map, Dec., 1912
Peary's Twenty Years Service in the Arctics. By Maj. Gen. A. W. Greely. XVIII, pp. 451-454, July, 1907
Portrait. VII, pl. XX (front.), June, 1896. XII, ill. p. 355, Oct., 1901
The Present State of the Nicaragua Canal. By General A. W. Greely. VII, pp. 73-76, Feb., 1896
Rainfall Types of the United States. Annual Report by Vice-President, General A. W. Greely. V, pp. 45-58, 5 tables, map, Apr. 29, 1893
Recent Geographic Advances, Especially in Africa. By Major General A. W. Greely. XXII, pp. 383-398, 5 ills., 5 maps, Apr., 1911
Report—Geography of the Air. By A. W. Greely. I, pp. 151-159, Apr., 1889
Report—Geography of the Air. By Gen. A. W. Greely. II, pp. 49-63, Apr., 1890
Rubber Forests of Nicaragua and Sierra Leone. By General A. W. Greely. VIII, pp. 83-88, Mar., 1897
Russia in Recent Literature. By General A. W. Greely. XVI, pp. 564-568, Dec., 1905
The Russian Census of 1897. (By A. W. G.). VIII, pp. 335-336, Nov., 1897
The Samoan Cocoanut (Article compiled by Gen. A. W. Greely). IX, pp. 12-24, Jan., 1898
The Scope and Value of Arctic Explorations. By General A. W. Greely. VII, pp. 32-39, Jan., 1896
The Siberian Transcontinental Railroad. By General A. W. Greely. VIII, pp. 121-124, Apr., 1897
Sixth International Geographical Congress. By A. W. G. VII, p. 380, Nov., 1896
An Undiscovered Island Off the Northern Coast of Alaska. III—By General A. W. Greely. V, pp. 80-83, July 10, 1893
See also NGS: Board of Managers; Founders; Vice-President

GREELY, JOHN N.:
Iran in Wartime: Through Fabulous Persia, Hub of the Middle East, Americans, Britons, and Iranians Keep Sinews of War Moving to the Embattled Soviet Union. By John N. Greely. LXXXIV, pp. 129-156, 26 ills., map, Aug., 1943

GREELY'S "Handbook of Alaska." By Gilbert H. Grosvenor. XX, pp. 491-492, May, 1909

GREEN, H. H.:

Bird's-Eye View of the Panama Canal. Map panorama by H. H. Green. XXIII, supplement, Feb., 1912

GREEN, JAMES A.:

Paricutín, the Cornfield That Grew a Volcano (Mexico). By James A. Green. LXXXV, pp. 129-164, 16 ills. in black and white, 21 ills. in color, map, Feb., 1944

GREEN, THOMAS E.:

The Making of a Japanese Newspaper. By Dr. Thomas E. Green. XXXVIII, pp. 327-334, 5 ills., Oct., 1920

GREEN Gruyère, Home of a Swiss Cheese. 23 color photos by Bernard F. Rogers, Jr. LXX, pp. 145-168, Aug., 1936

The **GREEN** Mountain State (Vermont). By Herbert Corey. LI, pp. 333-369, 40 ills. in black and white, 6 ills. in color, map, Mar., 1927

GREEN RIVER, Colorado-Utah-Wyoming:

Experiences in the Grand Canyon. By Ellsworth and Emory Kolb. XXVI, pp. 99-184, 70 ills., map, Aug., 1914

The Rivers of Northern New Jersey, with Notes on the Classification of Rivers in General. By William Morris Davis. II, pp. 81-110, 6 diagrs., map drawing, May, 1890
Included: Green River

GREENLAND:

Americans Stand Guard in Greenland. By Andrew H. Brown. XC, pp. 457-500, 23 ills. in black and white, 19 ills. in color, map, Oct., 1946

The "Bowdoin" (Ship) in North Greenland: Arctic Explorers Place Tablet to Commemorate Sacrifices of the Lady Franklin Bay Expedition. By Donald B. MacMillan. XLVII, pp. 677-722, 49 ills., June, 1925

Coast Guard Patrol in Greenland. 9 color photos by Lieut. Thomas S. La Farge. LXXXIII, pp. 565-572, May, 1943

Desolate Greenland, Now an American Outpost. 17 photos: 12 by Willie Knutsen, 4 by F. Vogel. LXXX, pp. 393-406, Sept., 1941

Dwellings of the Saga-Time in Iceland, Greenland, and Vineland. By Cornelia Horsford. IX, pp. 73-84, ill., 9 sketches, Mar., 1898

Flying Around the North Atlantic. By Anne Morrow Lindbergh. Foreword by Charles A. Lindbergh. LXVI, pp. 259-337, 82 ills., maps (1 two-page), Sept., 1934

Flying Over the Arctic. By Lieutenant Commander Richard E. Byrd. XLVIII, pp. 519-532, 10 ills., Nov., 1925

Geographic Names in West Greenland. (By Ralph S. Tarr). IX, pp. 103-104, Mar., 1898

Greenland from 1898 to Now: "Captain Bob," Who Went North with Peary, Tells of 42 Years of Exploration in the Orphan Island of New Aerial and Naval Interest. By Robert A. Bartlett. LXXVIII, pp. 111-140, 25 ills., two-page map, July, 1940

Greenland Turns to America. By James K. Penfield. LXXXII, pp. 369-383, 7 ills. in black and white, 5 ills. in color, two-page map, Sept., 1942

GREENLAND—*Continued*

A Hunting Trip to Northern Greenland. By Fullerton Merrill. XI, pp. 118-122, Mar., 1900

The MacMillan Arctic Expedition Returns: U. S. Navy Planes Make First Series of Overland Flights in the Arctic and National Geographic Society Staff Obtains Valuable Data and Specimens for Scientific Study. By Donald B. MacMillan. XLVIII, pp. 477-518, 42 ills., Nov., 1925

A Naturalist with MacMillan in the Arctic. By Walter N. Koelz. XLIX, pp. 299-318, 22 ills. in color, Mar., 1926

On Eskimo Geographic Names Ending in Miut. (By John Murdoch). IX, p. 190, Apr., 1898

The Origin of Stefansson's Blond Eskimo. By Major General A. W. Greely. XXIII, pp. 1225-1238, 10 ills., map, Dec., 1912

Recent Disclosures Concerning Pre-Columbian Voyages to America in the Archives of the Vatican. By William Eleroy Curtis. V, pp. 197-234, Jan. 31, 1894

Scenes from Greenland. 15 ills. XX, pp. 877-891, Oct., 1909

Servicing Arctic Airbases. By Robert A. Bartlett. LXXXIX, pp. 602-616, 3 ills. in black and white, 10 ills. in color, map, May, 1946

A Summer Voyage to the Arctic. By G. R. Putnam. VIII, pp. 97-110, 6 ills., map, Apr., 1897

Three Weeks in Hubbard Bay, West Greenland. By Robert Stein. IX, pp. 1-11, 6 ills., maps, Jan., 1898

GREENLAND—U. S. Base in the Arctic. 5 color photos by James K. Penfield. LXXXII, pp. 373-376, Sept., 1942

GREENS Grow for GI's on Soilless Ascension. By W. Robert Moore. LXXXVIII, pp. 219-230, 12 ills., Aug., 1945

GREGORY, HERBERT E.:

Lonely Australia: The Unique Continent. By Herbert E. Gregory. XXX, pp. 473-568, 68 ills., 5 maps (1 two-page), Dec., 1916

GREGORY, W. M.:

Ore-Boat Unloaders. (By W. M. Gregory). XVIII, pp. 343-345, ill., May, 1907

GRENADA (Island), West Indies:

British West Indian Interlude. By Anne Rainey Langley. LXXIX, pp. 1-46, 23 ills. in black and white, 21 ills. in color, maps, Jan., 1941

GRENFELL, SIR WILFRID T.:

A Land of Eternal Warring (Labrador). By Sir Wilfrid T. Grenfell. XXI, pp. 665-690, 24 ills., Aug., 1910

GREW, JOSEPH C.:

Japan and the Pacific. By Joseph C. Grew. LXXXV, pp. 385-414, 29 ills., 17 island maps, Apr., 1944

Waimangu and the Hot-Spring Country of New Zealand: The World's Greatest Geyser Is One of Many Natural Wonders in a Land of Inferno and Vernal Paradise. By Joseph C. Grew. XLVIII, pp. 109-130, 19 ills., map, Aug., 1925

GRIFFIN, DONALD R.:

Mystery Mammals of the Twilight (Bats). By Donald R. Griffin. XC, pp. 117-134, 19 ills., July, 1946

GRIFFIS, WILLIAM ELLIOT:

The Empire of the Risen Sun (Japan). By William Elliot Griffis. XLIV, pp. 415-443, 21 ills., Oct., 1923

Japan, Child of the World's Old Age: An Empire of Mountainous Islands, Whose Alert People Constantly Conquer Harsh Forces of Land, Sea, and Sky. By William Elliot Griffis. LXIII, pp. 257-301, 37 ills. in black and white, 12 ills. in color, Mar., 1933

GRIFFITHS, WILLIAM ARTHUR:

Malta: The Halting Place of Nations: First Account of Remarkable Prehistoric Tombs and Temples Recently Unearthed on the Island. By William Arthur Griffiths. XXXVII, pp. 445-478, 35 ills., map, May, 1920

GRIGGS, ROBERT F.:

Awarded Jane M. Smith Life Membership. XXXVII, p. 342, Apr., 1920

The Cause of Earthquakes. By Robert F. Griggs. XLIV, pp. 443-451, 5 ills., map, Oct., 1923

Our Greatest National Monument: The National Geographic Society Completes Its Explorations in the Valley of Ten Thousand Smokes. By Robert F. Griggs. XL, pp. 219-292, 73 ills. in black and white, 16 ills. in color, maps, Sept., 1921

The Valley of Ten Thousand Smokes: An Account of the Discovery and Exploration of the Most Wonderful Volcanic Region in the World. By Robert F. Griggs. XXXIII, pp. 115-169, 46 ills., map, panorama, Feb., 1918

The Awe-Inspiring Spectacle of the Valley of Ten Thousand Smokes, Discovered and Explored by National Geographic Society Expeditions. Panorama from photo by author

The Valley of Ten Thousand Smokes: National Geographic Society Explorations in the Katmai District of Alaska. By Robert F. Griggs. XXXI, pp. 13-68, 51 ills., map, Jan., 1917

GRIMBLE, SIR ARTHUR:

War Finds Its Way to Gilbert Islands: United States Forces Dislodge Japanese from Enchanted Atolls Which Loom Now as Stepping Stones along South Sea Route from Australia to Hawaii. By Sir Arthur Grimble. LXXXIII, pp. 71-92, 19 ills., map, Jan., 1943

GRIMES, S. A.:

Birds on the Home Front. 30 color photos by Dr. Arthur A. Allen, S. A. Grimes, and others. LXXXIV, pp. 33-56, July, 1943

GRIMM'S Fairyland in Northwestern Germany. 14 color photos by Hans Hildenbrand and Wilhelm Tobien. LIX, pp. 641-648, May, 1931

GRIMSBY, England:

Europe's Endangered Fish Supply: The War and the North Sea Fisheries. XXVII, pp. 141-152, 9 ills., map, Feb., 1915

GRIMSHAW, BEATRICE:

In the Savage South Seas. By Beatrice Grimshaw. XIX, pp. 1-19, 21 ills., Jan., 1908

GRINI (Concentration Camp), Norway:

The White War in Norway. By Thomas R. Henry. LXXXVIII, pp. 617-640, 23 ills., map, Nov., 1945

GRINNELL, ALTON G.:

Our Army Versus a Bacillus. By Alton G. Grinnell. XXIV, pp. 1146-1152, 5 ills., diagr., Oct., 1913

GRISCOM, LLOYD C.:

The Annual Dinner of the National Geographic Society (Speech by Lloyd C. Griscom). XVII, pp. 22-37, Jan., 1906

GROFF, G. WEIDMAN:

Landscaped Kwangsi, China's Province of Pictorial Art. By G. Weidman Groff and T. C. Lau. LXXII, pp. 671-710, 33 ills., map, Dec., 1937

GROSVENOR, EDWIN A.:

Constantinople and Sancta Sophia. By Edwin A. Grosvenor. XXVII, pp. 459-482, 21 ills., May, 1915

Evolution of Russian Government. By Edwin A. Grosvenor. XVI, pp. 309-332, 16 ills., July, 1905

The Growth of Russia. By Edwin A. Grosvenor. XI, pp. 169-185, 5 maps, May, 1900

Lectures, NGS. VIII, pp. 31-32, Jan., 1897; pp. 5-6 (insert), Feb., 1897; p. 159, May, 1897. IX, p. 32, Jan., 1898

The Races of Europe: The Graphic Epitome of a Never-ceasing Human Drama. The Aspirations, Failures, Achievements, and Conflicts of the Polyglot People of the Most Densely Populated Continent. By Edwin A. Grosvenor. XXXIV, pp. 441-534, 62 ills., diagr. and index, maps, map supplement, Dec., 1918

Siberia. By Prof. Edwin A. Grosvenor. XII, pp. 317-324, Sept., 1901

GROSVENOR, GILBERT H.:

Alexander Graham Bell's tribute to work of. XXIII, p. 274, Mar., 1912. LXIX, p. 148, Jan., 1936

Appointment of Gilbert H. Grosvenor as Editor, April 1, 1899. XXIII, p. 274, Mar., 1912

Chairman, committee of arrangements, for banquet honoring Peary. XVIII, p. 58, Jan., 1907

Cousin of President William Howard Taft. XVII, p. 25, Jan., 1906

Dr. J. Howard Gore praises the NGS President for aiding the Allied cause during World War I. XLIV, p. 676, Dec., 1923

Editorial Policy. *See* NGM: Editor: Policies; Editorial Department: Policies

Elected to the Board of Managers (Trustees). XVI, p. 87, Feb., 1905. Reelected, January 13, 1911. XXII, p. 211, Feb., 1911

Election of Gilbert Grosvenor as President of the Society. XXXVII, p. 345, Apr., 1920

Gilbert Grosvenor Trail, Antarctica. LVIII, pp. 184, 193, 198; air view p. 218, Aug., 1930

Growth of Society attributed to; certificate given in recognition. LXIX, pp. 148, 155, Jan., 1936

History of National Geographic Society. *See* NGS: History

Home, Boyhood. LXXXVII, p. 600, May, 1945. LXXXVIII, pp. 237-238, Aug., 1945

GROSVENOR, GILBERT H.—*Continued*

Home, Summer, Beinn Bhreagh. *See* Grosvenor, Gilbert H.: Photographs by: Nova Scotia

Home, Wild Acres, Maryland. LI, ill. p. 202, Feb., 1927. LVII, ill. p. 592, May, 1930

Lake Grosvenor, Alaska, named for Gilbert Grosvenor. XL, pp. 222, 287; ill. pp. 284, 288, Sept., 1921. L, ill. p. 89, July, 1926

Married Elsie May Bell. XXIII, p. 274, Mar., 1912. LXIX, p. 148, Jan., 1936

Mount Grosvenor, Alaska. XXII, p. 551, June, 1911

Mount Grosvenor, China. LVIII, p. 415; col. pls. VII, p. 409; X, p. 428, Oct., 1930

Nansen received by Dr. Grosvenor. LVIII, ill. p. 22, July, 1930

The National Geographic Society (Dr. Grosvenor's Work as Editor of the Magazine). XXIII, pp. 272-298, 5 ills., Mar., 1912

Office of the Editor. XXV, ill. p. 460, Apr., 1914

Paul Du Chaillu (Dr. Grosvenor's First Guest). XIV, pp. 282-285, ill., July, 1903

President Calvin Coolidge introduced by Dr. Grosvenor to members of the Society on the occasion of the presentation of the Hubbard Gold Medal to Commander Richard E. Byrd, and the Gold Medal to Floyd Bennett. L, p. 377, Sept., 1926

President Herbert Hoover introduced by Dr. Grosvenor to members of the Society on the occasion of the presentation of the Society's Special Gold Medal to Amelia Earhart. LXII, pp. 358, 359, 362, Sept., 1932

President Herbert Hoover introduced by Dr. Grosvenor to members of the Society on the occasion of the presentation of the Society's Special Gold Medal to Adm. Richard E. Byrd. LVIII, pp. 229, 231, Aug., 1930

Radio communications with stratosphere flyers. LXIX, p. 85, Jan., 1936

"Scenes from Every Land" (NGS Publication by Gilbert Grosvenor). XVIII, p. 348, May, 1907; p. 744, ill., Nov., 1907

Scientific Advisory Committee member, second stratosphere flight. LXVII, p. 272, Feb., 1935. LXIX, p. 94, Jan., 1936

Scientific committee to stratosphere flight appointed by. LXVI, p. 398, Oct., 1934

Society's New "Book of Birds." Edited by Gilbert Grosvenor and Alexander Wetmore. LXXI, p. 723, June, 1937. LXXII, p. 183, Aug., 1937. LXXIV, p. 226, Aug., 1938; p. 775, Dec., 1938. LXXVII, p. 121, Jan., 1940

Son-in-law of Alexander Graham Bell. XXIII, p. 274, Mar., 1912

Tribute by Admiral Byrd. LXXII, p. 106, July, 1937

War work of the Society directed by Gilbert Grosvenor. XXXIII, p. 375, Apr., 1918

See also NGM: Editor; NGS: Board of Trustees; President

Addresses by Gilbert H. Grosvenor:

Byrd, Commander Richard E., awarded the Hubbard Gold Medal. L, pp. 377, 383, Sept., 1926

Byrd, Adm. Richard E., awarded the Society's Special Gold Medal. LVIII, pp. 229, 231, Aug., 1930

Byrd, Adm. Richard E., honored at reception. LXVIII, pp. 107-108, July, 1935

GROSVENOR, GILBERT H.—*Continued*

Addresses by—*Continued*

Byrd, Adm. Richard E., Tribute to, heard via short-wave broadcast in Guatemala. LXX, p. 436, Oct., 1936

Earhart, Amelia, awarded the Society's Special Gold Medal. LXII, pp. 359, 362, Sept., 1932

Eckener, Dr. Hugo, awarded the Society's Special Gold Medal. LVII, pp. 653, 655, 681, 688, June, 1930

Ellsworth, Lincoln, awarded the Hubbard Medal. LXX, p. 36, July, 1936

Goethals, Col. George W., awarded the Society's Special Gold Medal. XXV, pp. 679-680, June, 1914

The Hawaiian Islands: America's Strongest Outpost of Defense—The Volcanic and Floral Wonderland of the World (Address Delivered before the Society). By Gilbert Grosvenor. XLV, pp. 115-238, 106 ills. in black and white, 21 ills. in color, diagr., 6 maps, Feb., 1924

Lindbergh, Anne Morrow, awarded the Hubbard Medal. LXV, pp. 791-792, June, 1934

Lindbergh, Charles A., awarded the Hubbard Medal. LIII, pp. 134, 137, Jan., 1928

Peary, Robert E., Memorial, unveiled in Arlington National Cemetery. XLI, pp. 641, 643, June, 1922

Poulter, Dr. Thomas C., awarded the Society's Special Gold Medal. LXXII, p. 105, July, 1937

Speech on opening of the Society's fifty-fifth annual series of lectures in Constitution Hall, Nov. 20, 1942. LXXXIII, pp. 277-278, Feb., 1943

Stevens, Capt. Albert W., and Anderson, Capt. Orvil A., awarded Hubbard Medals. LXIX, p. 713, May, 1936

Articles by Gilbert H. Grosvenor:

Admiral Byrd Receives New Honors From The Society (Address by Gilbert Grosvenor). LVIII, pp. 228-238, 4 ills., Aug., 1930

Air Conquest: From the Early Days of Giant Kites and Birdlike Gliders, the National Geographic Society Has Aided and Encouraged the Growth of Aviation. LII, pp. 233-242, 13 ills., Aug., 1927

Alaska's New Railway. XXVIII, pp. 567-589, 20 ills., Dec., 1915

America from the Air: No Such Series of Airplane Views Has Ever Before Been Printed. XLVI, pp. 85-92, 8 ills., July, 1924

The American Association for the Advancement of Science. (By G. H. G.). X, pp. 355-359, Sept., 1899

American Development of the Philippines. XIV, pp. 197-203, 4 ills., May, 1903

American Progress in Habana. XIII, pp. 97-108, 10 ills., Mar., 1902

Amundsen's Attainment of the South Pole. XXIII, pp. 205-208, map, Feb., 1912

The Annual Dinner of The National Geographic Society (Early History of the Society). XVII, pp. 22-37, Jan., 1906

An Appeal to Members of The National Geographic Society (Food Conservation). XXXIII, pp. 347-348, ills., Apr., 1918

The Belgian Antarctic Expedition. X, pp. 229-230, June, 1899

GROSVENOR, GILBERT H.—*Continued*

Articles by—*Continued*

Benguet—The Garden of the Philippines. XIV, pp. 203-210, 6 ills., May, 1903

A Bird City (Laysan Island, Hawaii). XV, pp. 494-498, 6 ills., Dec., 1904

The Black Hills (South Dakota), Once Hunting Grounds of the Red Men. LII, pp. 305-329, 18 ills. in black and white, 13 ills. in color, Sept., 1927

Boys' and Girls' Agricultural Clubs. XXII, pp. 639-641, 4 ills., July, 1911

The British Antarctic Expedition. XII, pp. 339-345, Sept., 1901

Bulgaria, the Peasant State. XIX, pp. 760-773, 14 ills., Nov., 1908

The Capitol (U. S.), Wonder Building of the World. By Gilbert Grosvenor. XLIII, pp. 603-638, 17 ills. in black and white, 16 ills. in color, June, 1923

Charting a Coast-Line of 26,000 Miles (Alaska). XX, pp. 608-609, July, 1909

Château Land—France's Pageant on the Loire. LVIII, pp. 466-475, 10 ills. in color, Oct., 1930

The Citizen Army of Switzerland. XXVIII, pp. 503-510, 7 ills., Nov., 1915

Colossal Natural Bridges of Utah. XV, pp. 367-369, ills., Sept., 1904

Commander Byrd Receives the Hubbard Gold Medal: The First Explorer to Reach the North Pole by Air Receives Coveted Honor at Brilliant National Geographic Society Reception (Address by Gilbert Grosvenor). L, pp. 377-388, 5 ills., chart, Sept., 1926

Commander Peary's New Vessel. XVI, p. 192, Apr., 1905

The Conquest of Bubonic Plague in the Philippines. XIV, pp. 185-195, 7 ills., May, 1903

The Conquest of the Sahara by the Automobile. XLV, pp. 87-93, 9 ills., map, Jan., 1924

The Correct Display of the Stars and Stripes. By Byron McCandless and Gilbert Grosvenor. XXXII, pp. 404-413, 8 ills., Oct., 1917

The Discovery of Cancer in Plants. XXIV, pp. 53-70, 12 ills., Jan., 1913

The Discovery of the North Pole. XXI, pp. 63-82, Jan., 1910

Dr. Bell's Man-Lifting Kite. By Gilbert H. Grosvenor. XIX, pp. 35-52, 27 ills., Jan., 1908

Dr. Bell's Tetrahedral Tower. By Gilbert H. Grosvenor. XVIII, pp. 672-675, 5 ills., Oct., 1907

Drifting Across the Pole. XVII, pp. 40-42, Jan., 1906

Editor of report of proceedings of Eighth International Geographic Congress. XVI, p. 199, Apr., 1905

Educating the Filipinos. XVI, pp. 46-49, Jan., 1905

European Tributes to Peary. XXI, pp. 536-540, 4 ills., June, 1910

Europe's Endangered Fish Supply: The War and the North Sea Fisheries. XXVII, pp. 141-152, 9 ills., map, Feb., 1915

Explorations in Alaska. X, pp. 269-271, July, 1899

Explorations in Central East Africa. XII, pp. 42-43, Jan., 1901

Explorations in Peru. XXIII, pp. 417-422, 7 ills., map, Apr., 1912

GROSVENOR, GILBERT H.—*Continued*

Articles by—*Continued*

Explorations in Tibet. XIV, pp. 353-355, Sept., 1903

Farthest North (Report from Commander Peary). XVII, pp. 638-644, 9 ills., Nov., 1906

The First Airship Flight Around the World: Dr. Hugo Eckener Tells of an Epochal Geographic Achievement upon the Occasion of the Bestowal of the National Geographic Society's Special Gold Medal (Presentation Address by Gilbert Grosvenor). LVII, pp. 653-688, 37 ills., June, 1930

Fishes That Build Nests and Take Care of Their Young. XVIII, pp. 400-412, 16 ills., June, 1907

Fishes That Carry Lanterns. XXI, pp. 453-456, 5 ills., May, 1910

Flags Famous in American History. By Byron McCandless and Gilbert Grosvenor. XXXII, pp. 341-361, 92 ills. in color, Oct., 1917

Flags of Austria-Hungary, Bulgaria, Germany, and Turkey. By Byron McCandless and Gilbert Grosvenor. XXXII, pp. 386-388, 38 ills. in color, Oct., 1917

The Flags of Europe, Asia, and Africa. By Byron McCandless and Gilbert Grosvenor. XXXII, pp. 372-378, 101 ills. in color, Oct., 1917

The Flags of Our Army, Navy, and Government Departments. By Byron McCandless and Gilbert Grosvenor. XXXII, pp. 305-322, ill. in black and white, 300 ills. in color, diagrs., 4 tables, Oct., 1917

The Flags of Pan-America. By Byron McCandless and Gilbert Grosvenor. XXXII, pp. 361-369, 62 ills. in color, Oct., 1917

The Flags of the British Empire. By Byron McCandless and Gilbert Grosvenor. XXXII, pp. 378-385, 158 ills. in color, Oct., 1917

Flags of the World. By Gilbert Grosvenor and William J. Showalter. LXVI, pp. 339-396, 10 ills. in black and white, 808 ills. in color, Sept., 1934

Flying. By Gilbert Grosvenor. LXIII, pp. 585-630, 33 ills. in black and white, 17 ills. in duotone, May, 1933

The Foreign-Born of the United States. XXVI, pp. 265-271, 14 diagrs., Sept., 1914

Four Prominent Geographers. XVIII, pp. 425-428, 4 ills., June, 1907

A Geographic Achievement. XXIV, pp. 667-668, June, 1913

Geographic Facts from Report of the Taft Philippine Commission. XII, pp. 114-119, Mar., 1901

The German Nation. XXVI, pp. 275-310, 28 ills., Sept., 1914

A German Route to India. (By Gilbert H. Grosvenor). XI, pp. 203-204, map, May, 1900

The German South Polar Expedition. XII, p. 311, Aug., 1901

Germany's Air Program. XXXIII, p. 114, Jan., 1918

Germany's Dream of World Domination. XXXIII, pp. 559-567, 3 ills., map, June, 1918

The Great Falls of the Potomac. By Gilbert Grosvenor. LIII, pp. 385-400, 19 ills., Mar., 1928

The Great Natural Bridges of Utah. XVIII, pp. 199-204, 3 ills., Mar., 1907

GROSVENOR, GILBERT H.—*Continued*

Articles by—*Continued*

The Greek Bronzes. Text regarding requests for photographs of bronzes. XXIII, p. 104, Jan., 1912

Greely's "Handbook of Alaska." By Gilbert H. Grosvenor. XX, pp. 491-492, May, 1909

Haiti and Its Regeneration by the United States. XXXVIII, pp. 497-511, 10 ills., Dec., 1920

The Harriman Alaska Expedition in Cooperation with the Washington Academy of Sciences. (By G. H. G.). X, pp. 225-227, June, 1899

The Hawaiian Islands: America's Strongest Outpost of Defense—The Volcanic and Floral Wonderland of the World (Address Delivered before the Society). By Gilbert Grosvenor. XLV, pp. 115-238, 106 ills. in black and white, 21 ills. in color, diagr., 6 maps, Feb., 1924

The Healer of Humanity's Wounds. XXXIV, pp. 308-324, 16 ills., Oct., 1918

Henry Gannett (Tribute to Late President of the Society). XXVI, pp. 609-613, ill., Dec., 1914

Heroic Flags of the Middle Ages. By Byron McCandless and Gilbert Grosvenor. XXXII, pp. 388-399, 96 ills. in color, Oct., 1917

Honors for Amundsen (Presentation of Hubbard Medal). XIX, pp. 55-76, 13 ills., Jan., 1908

Honors to Amundsen and Peary (Presentation of Special Gold Medal to Amundsen). XXIV, pp. 113-130, 5 ills., Jan., 1913

Honors to Colonel Goethals: The Presentation, by President Woodrow Wilson, of the National Geographic Society Special Gold Medal, and Addresses by Secretary of State Bryan, the French Ambassador, the German Ambassador, and Congressman James R. Mann (Address by Gilbert H. Grosvenor). XXV, pp. 677-690, 6 ills., June, 1914

Honors to Peary (Presentation of Hubbard Medal). XVIII, pp. 49-60, ill., Jan., 1907

Honors to the American Navy (Banquet). XX, pp. 77-95, Jan., 1909

Hospital Heroes Convict the Cootie. XXXIII, p. 510, June, 1918

How the World Is Shod. XIX, pp. 649-660, 12 ills., Sept., 1908

Hubbard Medals Awarded to Stratosphere Explorers: Presentation by General Pershing (Address by Gilbert Grosvenor). LXIX, p. 713, May, 1936

An Ice Wrapped Continent. (By G. H. G.). XVIII, pp. 95-117, 20 ills., map, Feb., 1907

Improvements in the City of Manila. XIV, pp. 195-197, ill., May, 1903

In Honor of the Army and Aviation (Banquet). XXII, pp. 267-284, ill., Mar., 1911

Inoculating the Ground. XV, pp. 225-228, ills., May, 1904

Insignia and Decorations of the United States Armed Forces. By Gilbert Grosvenor. LXXXVII, pp. 185-186, Feb., 1945

The Insignia of the Uniformed Forces of the United States. By Byron McCandless and Gilbert Grosvenor. XXXII, pp. 413-419, 318 ills., Oct., 1917

Insignia of the United States Armed Forces. By Gilbert Grosvenor. With 991 illustrations in color. LXXXIII, p. 651, June, 1943

GROSVENOR, GILBERT H.—*Continued*

Articles by—*Continued*

Introducing Reindeer into Labrador. XVIII, p. 686, Oct., 1907

The Italian Race. (By Gilbert Grosvenor). XXXIII, p. 47, Jan., 1918

John Wesley Powell. (By G. H. G.). XIII, pp. 393-394, ill., Nov., 1902

The Land of the Best (U. S.). By Gilbert H. Grosvenor. XXIX, pp. 327-430, 71 ills. in black and white, 33 ills. in color, pictorial supplement, Apr., 1916

Lessons from Japan. XV, pp. 221-225, 3 ills., May, 1904

Lloyd's Journey Across the Great Pygmy Forest (Belgian Congo). X, pp. 26-30, Jan., 1899

The MacMillan Arctic Expedition Sails. XLVIII, pp. 225-226, 3 ills., Aug., 1925

MacMillan in the Field. XLVIII, pp. 473-476, 3 ills., Oct., 1925

Marking the Alaskan Boundary. XIX, pp. 176-189, 16 ills., Mar., 1908

A Maryland Pilgrimage: Visits to Hallowed Shrines Recall the Major Rôle Played by This Prosperous State in the Development of Popular Government in America. By Gilbert Grosvenor. LI, pp. 133-212, 88 ills., map supplement, Feb., 1927

A Memorial to Peary: The National Geographic Society Dedicates Monument in Arlington National Cemetery to Discoverer of the North Pole (Address by Gilbert Grosvenor). XLI, pp. 639-645, 4 ills., June, 1922

The Mission of the "Diana." X, p. 273, July, 1899

Mr. Coolidge Becomes a Member of The Society's Board of Trustees. LV, p. 750, June, 1929

Mr. Roosevelt's "African Game Trails." XXI, pp. 953-962, 9 ills., Nov., 1910

Mr. Ziegler and The National Geographic Society. XIV, pp. 251-254, June, 1903

A Modern Viking (Amundsen). XVII, pp. 38-41, ills., map, Jan., 1906

The Most Historic Lands on Earth. XXVI, pp. 614-615, map, Dec., 1914

Muir Glacier. XIV, pp. 441-444, ills., map, Dec., 1903

Murman Coast: Arctic Gateway for American and Allied Expeditionary Forces in Northern European Russia. XXXV, pp. 331-348, 30 ills., map, Apr., 1919

The Mystery of Auroras: National Geographic Society and Cornell University Study Spectacular Displays in the Heavens. LXXV, pp. 689-690, May, 1939

Nansen's "Farthest North" Eclipsed. XI, pp. 411-413, ills., Oct., 1900

National Geographic Society (Discovery of the North Pole). XXI, p. 276, Mar., 1910

National Geographic Society (Early History of the Society). XXIII, pp. 272-298, 5 ills., Mar., 1912

National Geographic Society (Expeditions). XXXIII, p. 170, Feb., 1918

National Geographic Society (Jane M. Smith Bequest). XXIII, p. 104, Jan., 1912

National Geographic Society (Proceedings). (By G. H. G.). X, pp. 474-475, Nov., 1899

GROSVENOR, GILBERT H.—*Continued*

Articles by—*Continued*

The National Geographic Society (Proceedings). XXVII, p. 218, Feb., 1915

National Geographic Society (Roosevelt's African Expedition). XXI, pp. 365-370, 5 ills., Apr., 1910

National Geographic Society Alaska Expedition. XX, pp. 581-584, June, 1909

The National Geographic Society and Geographic Work. XX, pp. 485-487, May, 1909

The National Geographic Society and Its Magazine. By Gilbert Grosvenor. LXIX, pp. 123-164, 24 ills., Jan., 1936

The National Geographic Society and Its New Building. XXV, pp. 455-470, 11 ills., Apr., 1914

The National Geographic Society Completes Its Gifts of Big Trees. XL, pp. 85-86, July, 1921

The National Geographic Society Expedition in the West Indies. XIII, pp. 209-213, maps, June, 1902

The National Geographic Society Expedition to Martinique and St. Vincent. XIII, pp. 183-184, ills., June, 1902

National Geographic Society Expeditions in New Mexico. (By Gilbert Grosvenor). LVI, p. 737, Dec., 1929

National Geographic Society's Alaskan Expedition. XXI, p. 370, Apr., 1910

The National Geographic Society's Memorial to American Troops: Fountain and Water Supply System Presented to Historic French Town of Cantigny, Where Our Overseas Soldiers Won Their First Victory in the World War. XLIV, pp. 675-678, 4 ills., Dec., 1923

The National Geographic Society's Notable Year (Announcement of the Election of Gilbert Grosvenor as President of the Society). XXXVII, pp. 338-345, ills., Apr., 1920

The National Geographic Society's Yünnan Province Expedition. By Gilbert Grosvenor. XLVII, pp. 493-498, 5 ills., Apr., 1925

The Naval Flags of the World. By Byron McCandless and Gilbert Grosvenor. XXXII, text p. 369; 214 ills. in color, Oct., 1917

The New Cone of Mont Pelée. XIV, pp. 422-423, ills., Nov., 1903

The New English Province of Northern Nigeria. XV, pp. 433-442, 9 ills., Nov., 1904

The New National Geographic Society Expedition (Chaco Canyon). XXXIX, pp. 637-643, 7 ills., June, 1921

Next International Geographical Congress To Be Held in Washington. (By G. H. G.). XII, pp. 351-357, 4 ills., Oct., 1901

Nicaragua, Largest of Central American Republics. LI, pp. 370-378, 15 ills., Mar., 1927

The Nicaragua Canal. XII, pp. 28-32, ills., map, Jan., 1901

No Man's Land—Spitzbergen. XVIII, pp. 455-458, July, 1907

The North Pole (Appointment of Committee to Consider Claims of Peary and Cook). XX, pp. 921-922, Nov., 1909

The North Pole (Resolutions of the Society Acknowledging Peary's Discovery). XX, pp. 1008-1009, Nov., 1909

Notes on Macedonia. XIX, pp. 790-802, 15 ills., map, Nov., 1908

GROSVENOR, GILBERT H.—*Continued*

Articles by—*Continued*

Notes on Panama and Colombia. XIV, pp. 458-466, 12 ills., Dec., 1903

Notes on Turbulent Nicaragua. XX, pp. 1102-1116, 13 ills., map, Dec., 1909

One Hundred British Seaports. XXXI, pp. 84-94, 10 ills., map, Jan., 1917

Our Big Trees Saved. XXXI, pp. 1-11, 10 ills., Jan., 1917

Our Colored Pictures. XXI, pp. 965-967, Nov., 1910

Our Desert Panorama. Text with pictorial supplement. XXII, pp. 409-410, ill., Apr., 1911

Our Flag Number. By Gilbert Grosvenor. XXXII, pp. 281-284, ills., Oct., 1917

Our Foreign-Born Citizens. XXXI, pp. 95-130, 36 ills., 8 diagrs., map, Feb., 1917

Our Heralds of Storm and Flood (U. S. Weather Bureau). By Gilbert H. Grosvenor. XVIII, pp. 586-601, 15 ills., chart, Sept., 1907

Our Immigration During 1904. XVI, pp. 15-27, 6 ills., charts, Jan., 1905

Our Mountain Panorama (Canadian Rockies). XXII, text p. 521; ill. p. 520; panorama, June, 1911

Our Policemen of the Air (Birds). XXIV, p. 698, June, 1913

Our State Flags. By Byron McCandless and Gilbert Grosvenor. XXXII, pp. 325-341, 57 ills. in color, Oct., 1917

Our State Flowers: The Floral Emblems Chosen by the Commonwealths. By Gilbert Grosvenor. Paintings by Mary E. Eaton. XXXI, pp. 481-517, 567, ill. in black and white, 30 ills. in color, June, 1917

Peary on the North Pole. XIV, pp. 28-29, map, Jan., 1903

Peary to Try Again. XVIII, p. 281, Apr., 1907

Peary's Explorations in the Far North. By Gilbert Grosvenor. XXXVII, pp. 319-322, 3 ills., Apr., 1920

Peary's Polar Expedition. XIX, p. 447, June, 1908

Peary's Work in 1900 and 1901. XII, pp. 357-361, ills., Oct., 1901

Peary's Work in 1901-1902. (By G. H. G.). XIII, pp. 384-386, Oct., 1902

Pennants of Patriotism 200 Years Ago. By Byron McCandless and Gilbert Grosvenor. XXXII, pp. 399-403, 77 ills. in color, Oct., 1917

Plans for Reaching the South Pole. By Gilbert H. Grosvenor. X, pp. 316-319, map supplement, Aug., 1899

Practical Patriotism (National Geographic Society's War Work). XXXII, pp. 279-280, Sept., 1917

President Coolidge Bestows Lindbergh Award: The National Geographic Society's Hubbard Medal Is Presented to Aviator Before the Most Notable Gathering in the History of Washington (Address by Gilbert Grosvenor). LIII, pp. 132-140, 4 ills., Jan., 1928

The Price of Liberty, Equality, Fraternity. XXXIV, p. 377, Nov., 1918

Progress of The National Geographic Society (Report by Gilbert H. Grosvenor). XXIV, pp. 251-256, ill., Feb., 1913

Articles by—*Continued*

Progress on the Panama Canal. (By G. H. G.). XVI, pp. 467-475, map, Oct., 1905

Prosperous Porto Rico. XVII, p. 712, Dec., 1906

The Race for the South Pole (Presentation of Hubbard Medal to Shackleton). XXI, pp. 185-186, Mar., 1910

The "Races of Europe" Number. XXXIV, p. 440, Nov., 1918

Railways, Rivers, and Strategic Towns in Manchuria. (By G. H. G.). XI, pp. 326-327, Aug., 1900

Reindeer in Alaska. By Gilbert H. Grosvenor. XIV, pp. 127-149, 19 ills., map, Apr., 1903

Report of the Director and Editor of The National Geographic Society for the Year 1914. By Gilbert H. Grosvenor. XXVII, pp. 318-320, Mar., 1915

A Report of the Second Stratosphere Expedition. LXVIII, pp. 535-536, Oct., 1935

A Revelation of the Filipinos (Summary of Report of the First Census of the Philippines). (By Gilbert H. Grosvenor). XVI, pp. 139-192, 138 ills., Apr., 1905

The Sagacity and Courage of Dogs: Instances of the Remarkable Intelligence and Unselfish Devotion of Man's Best Friend Among Dumb Animals. XXXV, pp. 253-275, 13 ills., Mar., 1919

Scientific Aspects of the MacMillan Arctic Expedition. XLVIII, pp. 349-354, 5 ills., Sept., 1925

Servia and Montenegro. XIX, pp. 774-789, 24 ills., Nov., 1908

The Sex, Nativity, and Color of the People of the United States. (By G. H. G.). XII, pp. 381-389, 17 charts, Nov., 1901

Shackleton's Farthest South. XX, pp. 398-402, map, Apr., 1909

Sheep-Killers—The Pariahs of Dogkind. XXXV, pp. 275-280, 3 ills., Mar., 1919

Snow Crystals. XV, pp. 30-37, 31 ills., Jan., 1904

The Society Announces New Flight into the Stratosphere. By Gilbert Grosvenor. LXVII, pp. 265-272, ills., map, Feb., 1935

The Society Awards Hubbard Medal to Anne Morrow Lindbergh (Address by Gilbert Grosvenor). LXV, pp. 791-794, 4 ills., June, 1934

The Society Takes Part in Three Geographic Expeditions. LXV, pp. 625-626, May, 1934

The Society's Special Medal Awarded to Amelia Earhart: First Woman to Receive Geographic Distinction at Brilliant Ceremony in the National Capital (Address by Gilbert Grosvenor). LXII, pp. 358-367, 7 ills., Sept., 1932

The Society's Special Medal Is Awarded to Dr. Thomas C. Poulter: Admiral Byrd's Second-in-Command and Senior Scientist Is Accorded High Geographic Honor (Presentation by Gilbert Grosvenor). LXXII, pp. 105-108, ills., July, 1937

Some Facts About Japan. XV, pp. 446-448, Nov., 1904

Some of Our Immigrants. XVIII, pp. 317-334, 21 ills., May, 1907

The South Polar Expedition (Proposed by Peary for Consideration of the National Geographic Society). XXI, pp. 167-170, map, Feb., 1910

GROSVENOR, GILBERT H.—*Continued*

Articles by—*Continued*

South Polar Explorations. XXII, pp. 407-409, 4 ills., map, Apr., 1911

The Speediest Boat. XXII, pp. 875-878, ills., Sept., 1911

The Spirit of The Geographic. XXXIV, pp. 434-440, 4 ills., Nov., 1918

The Story of the American Flag. By Byron McCandless and Gilbert Grosvenor. XXXII, pp. 286-303, 12 ills., Oct., 1917

Streets and Palaces of Colorful India. L, pp. 60-85, 34 ills. in color, July, 1926

Studies Planned for New Stratosphere Flight with Helium. LXVII, pp. 795-800, 5 ills., June, 1935

A Suggested Field for Exploration (Volcanic Disturbances in Mexico, Central America, and the West Indies). XIV, pp. 290-291, July, 1903

The Supposed Birthplace of Civilizations. XVI, pp. 499-504, 6 ills., Nov., 1905

The Tailed People of Nigeria. XXIII, pp. 1239-1242, 3 ills., Dec., 1912

The Ten Thousand Smokes Now a National Monument. XXXV, pp. 359-366, 5 ills., Apr., 1919

To Seek the Unknown in the Arctic: United States Navy Fliers to Aid MacMillan Expedition Under the Auspices of the National Geographic Society in Exploring Vast Area. XLVII, pp. 673-675, ill., map, June, 1925

The United States Government Telegraph and Cable Lines. XV, pp. 490-494, 3 maps, Dec., 1904

The U. S. Signal Corps. (By Gilbert H. Grosvenor). XIV, pp. 467-468, Dec., 1903

The Value of the United States Forest Service. XX, pp. 29-41, 14 ills., Jan., 1909

Voice Voyages by the National Geographic Society: A Tribute to the Geographical Achievements of the Telephone. XXIX, pp. 296-326, 15 ills., chart, Mar., 1916

Volcanoes. (By G. H. G.). XIII, pp. 204-208, map, June, 1902

The War and Ocean Geography. By the Editor (Gilbert Grosvenor). XXXIV, pp. 230-242, 6 ills., map, Sept., 1918

Wards of the United States. XXX, pp. 143-177, 36 ills., Aug., 1916

Washington Through the Years: On Rolling Wooded Hills and Colonial Tobacco Fields, Where George Washington Dreamed Our Nation's Great Capital, His Gorgeous Vision Comes True. By Gilbert Grosvenor. LX, pp. 517-619, 67 ills. in black and white, 49 ills. in color, map, Nov., 1931

What the U. S. Geological Survey Has Done in Twenty-five Years. XV, pp. 365-366, ills., Sept., 1904

What the United States Government Does to Promote Agriculture. XIV, pp. 35-39, Jan., 1903

Where Our Moths and Butterflies Roam. LII, pp. 105-126, 8 ills. in black and white, 81 ills. in color, July, 1927

Where the Sard Holds Sway. XLIX, pp. 464-474, ill. in black and white, 9 ills. in color, Apr., 1926

Women and Children of the East. XVIII, pp. 248-271, 28 ills., Apr., 1907

GROSVENOR, GILBERT H.—*Continued*

Articles by—*Continued*

A Wonderland of Science. XXVII, pp. 153-169, 15 ills., Feb., 1915

Work in the Arctic and Antarctic. XI, pp. 164-165, Apr., 1900

The World's Debt to France. XXVIII, pp. 491-501, 7 ills., Nov., 1915

The World's Highest International Telephone Cable. LVIII, pp. 722-731, 8 ills., Dec., 1930

World's Largest Free Balloon to Explore Stratosphere. LXVI, pp. 107-110, ills., July, 1934

Young Russia: The Land of Unlimited Possibilities. By Gilbert H. Grosvenor. XXVI, pp. 421-520, 85 ills. in black and white, 17 ills. in color, Nov., 1914

Your Society Aids War Effort. LXXXIII, pp. 277-278, ill., Feb., 1943

Your Society Sponsors an Expedition to Explore the Stratosphere. LXV, pp. 528-530, ill., Apr., 1934

The Ziegler Polar Expedition. XIV, pp. 414-417, 5 ills., Nov., 1903

Map Articles:

The Geographic's New Map of Europe and the Mediterranean. By Gilbert Grosvenor. Text with map supplement. LXXIII, pp. 525-528, ill., Apr., 1938

The Geographic's New Map of Germany and Its Approaches: With a Review of The Society's Maps of Europe. By Gilbert Grosvenor. Text with map supplement. LXXXVI, pp. 66-72, ill., July, 1944

Heart of a Hemisphere: Of Vital Importance is the Area Portrayed in The Society's New Map of Mexico, Central America, and the West Indies. Text with map supplement. LXXVI, pp. 739-740, ill., Dec., 1939

Indian Ocean Map Spans Far East News Centers. Text with map supplement. LXXIX, pp. 345-346, ill., Mar., 1941

The Latest Map of Mexico. Text with map supplement. XXX, p. 88, July, 1916

Manchuria and Korea. Text with map supplement. XV, pp. 128-129, maps, Mar., 1904

Map Links Classic World with 1940. Text with map supplement. LXXVII, p. 338, Mar., 1940

Map of Europe Including the New Balkan States. Text with map supplement. XXVI, pp. 191-192, Aug., 1914

Map of Mediterranean Regions. Text with map supplement. XXIII, p. 104, Jan., 1912

A Map of the New Germany. XXXV, pp. 545-546, map, June, 1919

Map of the North Polar Regions. Text with map supplement. XVIII, pp. 454-455, July, 1907

Map of the Northern and Southern Hemispheres. Text with map supplement. LXXXIII, pp. 481-483, Apr., 1943

Map of the Philippines. Text with map supplement. XIII, p. 31, Jan., 1902

Maps for Victory: National Geographic Society's Charts Used in War on Land, Sea, and in the Air. By Gilbert Grosvenor. Text with map supplement. LXXXI, pp. 667-690, 28 ills., May, 1942

National Geographic Map of Japan, Regions of Asia, and the Pacific. Text with map supplement. LXXXV, pp. 415-416, Apr., 1944

GROSVENOR, GILBERT H.—*Continued*

Map Articles—*Continued*

The National Geographic Society's Map of Northeastern United States. Text with map supplement. LXXXVIII, pp. 361-362, Sept., 1945

The National Geographic Society's New Map of Africa. By Gilbert Grosvenor. Text with map supplement. LXVII, pp. 731-752, 20 ills. in duotone, June, 1935

The National Geographic Society's New Map of the World. Text with map supplement. LXVIII, pp. 796-798, Dec., 1935

The National Geographic War-Zone Map. Text with map supplement. XXXIII, p. 494, May, 1918

The New Map of Asia. Text with map supplement. XXXIX, pp. 552-570, 17 ills., May, 1921

The New Map of Europe: Showing the Boundaries Established by the Peace Conference at Paris and by Subsequent Decisions of the Supreme Council of the Allied and Associated Powers. By Ralph A. Graves. Text with map supplement. XXXIX, pp. 157-177, 18 ills., Feb., 1921

New Map of Europe Records War Changes. Text with map supplement. LXXVII, p. 625, May, 1940

New Map Reveals the Progress and Wonders of Our Country (U. S.). Text with map supplement. LXIII, pp. 650-652, ill., May, 1933

New Map Shows Asia's Role in Global Warfare. Text with map supplement. LXXXII, pp. 767-768, Dec., 1942

New Map Shows Immense Pacific Battleground. Text with map supplement. LXXXI, pp. 203-204, Feb., 1942

New National Geographic Society Map Charts South America's Wartime Importance. Text with map supplement. LXXXII, pp. 537-540, ills., Oct., 1942

New World Map Gives Backdrop for Headlines. Text with map supplement. LXXX, pp. 741-742, ill., Dec., 1941

North Polar Map. Text describing map compiled by Gilbert H. Grosvenor (July, 1907). XX, p. 915, Oct., 1909

Our Map of North America. Text with map supplement. XLV, p. 580, May, 1924

Our Map of the Countries of the Caribbean. Text with map supplement. XLI, pp. 221-222, Feb., 1922

Our Map of the Pacific. Text with map supplement. XL, pp. 647-648, map, Dec., 1921

Our Map of the Races of Europe. Text with map supplement. XXXIV, pp. 535-536, Dec., 1918

Our Map of the United States. Text with map supplement. XLIII, p. 460, Apr., 1923

Postwar Portrait of the United States. Text with map supplement. XC, pp. 135-136, July, 1946

The Society's Map of Bible Lands. By Gilbert Grosvenor. Text with map supplement. LXXIV, pp. 751-754, 3 ills., Dec., 1938

The Society's Map of South America. By Gilbert Grosvenor. Text with map supplement. LXXII, pp. 809-810, Dec., 1937

The Society's Map of the Antarctic. Text with map supplement. LXII, pp. 485-486, ill., Oct., 1932

GROSVENOR, GILBERT H.—*Continued*

Map Articles—*Continued*

The Society's Map of the Reaches of New York City. Text with map supplement. LXXV, pp. 491-492, Apr., 1939

The Society's New Caribbean Map: Mexico, Central America, and the West Indies—Gateway of Discovery. Text with map supplement. LXVI, pp. 738-740, ill., Dec., 1934

The Society's New Map of Africa. Text with map supplement. XLII, pp. 447-448, Oct., 1922

The Society's New Map of Asia. Text with map supplement. LXIV, pp. 770-772, ill., Dec., 1933

The Society's New Map of Bible Lands. Text with map supplement. XC, pp. 815-816, Dec., 1946

The Society's New Map of Central Europe and the Mediterranean. Text with map supplement. LXXVI, pp. 559-560, Oct., 1939

The Society's New Map of Europe. By Gilbert Grosvenor. Text with map supplement. LVI, pp. 771-774, Dec., 1929

The Society's New Map of India and Burma. Text with map supplement. LXXXIX, p. 544, Apr., 1946

The Society's New Map of South America. Text with map supplement. XL, pp. 374-392, 17 ills., Oct., 1921

The Society's New Map of Southeast Asia. Text with map supplement. LXXXVI, pp. 449-450, ill., Oct., 1944

The Society's New Map of Soviet Russia. Text with map supplement. LXXXVI, pp. 716-718, Dec., 1944

The Society's New Map of the Pacific. By Gilbert Grosvenor. Text with map supplement. LXX, pp. 793-796, Dec., 1936

The Society's New Map of the World. Text with map supplement. XLII, pp. 690-691, Dec., 1922

Southwest Trails from Horse to Motor. Text with map supplement. LXXVII, p. 767, June, 1940

The Story of the Map. Text with map supplement. LXII, pp. 759-774, 11 ills., Dec., 1932

The Travels of George Washington: Dramatic Episodes in His Career as the First Geographer of the United States. By William Joseph Showalter. Text with map supplement. LXI, pp. 1-63, 50 ills., 4 maps, Jan., 1932

Western Front Map Embraces Three Continents (Europe, Africa, Asia). Text with map supplement. LXXXII, pp. 139-140, July, 1942

Map Supplements edited by Gilbert Grosvenor:

Africa. Prepared from latest geographical data by Gilbert H. Grosvenor, Editor. XX, supplement, 15½ x 20 inches, Mar., 1909

Africa, with inset showing airways and relief. LXVII, supplement, 29 x 31½ inches, June, 1935

Africa, with insets of the Cape Verde Islands, relief map, and a table of airline distances in statute miles. LXXXIII, supplement, 29¼ x 31½ inches, Feb., 1943

Alaska. XV, supplement, 36 x 42 inches, May, 1904

Alaska. XXV, supplement, 15¼ x 20 inches, Feb., 1914

Alaska Boundary Tribunal. XV, supplement, 12 x 12½ inches, Jan., 1904

GROSVENOR, GILBERT H.—*Continued*

Map Supplements edited by—*Continued*

The Antarctic Regions, with inset maps showing Antarctic Archipelago, King Edward VII Land, and part of Marie Byrd Land, and Byrd's South Pole flight. LXII, supplement, 19½ x 26½ inches, Oct., 1932

The Arctic Regions. XLVIII, supplement, 19¼ x 18 inches, Nov., 1925

Asia and Adjacent Areas, with table of airline distances in statute miles. LXXXII, supplement, 40 x 26½ inches, Dec., 1942

Asia and Adjacent Regions. LXIV, supplement, 30¾ x 38 inches, Dec., 1933

Atlantic Ocean, with inset of Isthmus of Panama. LXXVI, supplement, 31 x 25 inches, July, 1939

Atlantic Ocean, with inset of Isthmus of Panama and a table of air-line distances in statute miles. LXXX, supplement, 31¼ x 25 inches, Sept., 1941

Bible Lands and the Cradle of Western Civilization; Insets: Holy Land Today, Holy Land in Biblical Times, Jerusalem, Traditional Route of the Exodus, St. Paul's Travels and the Seven Churches, The Crusades. XC, supplement, 32 x 22 inches, Dec., 1946

Bible Lands and the Cradle of Western Civilization; Insets: Jerusalem, The Holy Land, Economic Development, Route of the Exodus, St. Paul's Travels and the Seven Churches, The Crusades, Empire of Alexander the Great. LXXIV, supplement, 25 x 35 inches, Dec., 1938

Bird's-Eye View of the Panama Canal (Relief map painting). XXIII, supplement, 9 x 18 inches, Feb., 1912

Canada, with insets showing natural regions, precipitation and temperature, main natural resources, routes of explorers and time zones. LXIX, supplement, 27 x 40 inches, June, 1936

Central Europe and the Mediterranean as of September 1, 1939. LXXVI, supplement, 36½ x 26½ inches, Oct., 1939

Chart of the World on Mercator's Projection, showing Submarine Cables and Connections, and also Tracks for full-powered Steam Vessels. XVI, supplement, 25 x 45 inches, Feb., 1905

A Chart shewing part of the Coast of N. W. America (Vancouver's Chart No. I). X, supplement, 15½ x 18 inches, Nov., 1899

A Chart Shewing part of the Coast of N. W. America (Vancouver's Chart No. II). X, supplement, 15½ x 18 inches, Nov., 1899

China. LXXXVII, supplement, 37 x 26½ inches, June, 1945

Classical Lands of the Mediterranean. LXXVII, supplement, 35¼ x 26 inches, Mar., 1940

Cotidal Lines for the World; or, Lines of Simultaneous High Water at Each Hour and Half Hour of Greenwich Lunar Time. XVII, supplement, 8 x 14 inches, June, 1906

The Countries of the Caribbean, Including Mexico, Central America, the West Indies and the Panama Canal, with detailed insets of the Panama Canal and the Canal Zone, Porto Rico and the Virgin Islands, and Guantanamo Bay, Cuba. XLI, supplement, 25 x 44 inches, Feb., 1922

Map Supplements edited by—*Continued*

Cuba. XVII, supplement, 12 x 24 inches, Oct., 1906

Europe and the Mediterranean. LXXIII, supplement, 34 x 39 inches, Apr., 1938

Europe and the Near East. LVI, supplement, 34¼ x 39¼ inches, Dec., 1929

Europe and the Near East, as of April 1, 1940. LXXVII, supplement, 39 x 34 inches, May, 1940

Europe and the Near East, with inset map of the Middle East, and a table of distances between the principal ports via shortest navigable routes. LXXXIII, supplement, 39 x 34 inches, June, 1943

Florida, with insets of the following areas: Miami-Palm Beach, Pensacola, Jacksonville-St. Augustine, Tampa-St. Petersburg-Sarasota. LVII, supplement, 12½ x 13¼ inches, Jan., 1930

Germany and Its Approaches, with international boundaries as of September 1, 1939, the day Germany invaded Poland, and boundaries as of January 1, 1938, before Germany seized Austria and Czechoslovakia. LXXXVI, supplement, 33½ x 26½ inches, July, 1944

Greater New York . . . Metropolis of Mankind. Supplement from aërial photo by Captain Albert W. Stevens. LXIV, supplement, 22 x 17¼ inches, Nov., 1933

Historic and Scenic Reaches of the Nation's Capital. LXXIV, supplement, 26½ x 31¼ inches, July, 1938

Illinois, with inset of Chicago. LIX, supplement, 12½ x 19 inches, May, 1931

India and Burma, with insets of Bombay and Calcutta areas. Verso of map: Political Subdivisions; The Political Geography of India. LXXXIX, supplement, 30 x 25 inches, Apr., 1946

Indian Ocean, including Australia, New Zealand and Malaysia. LXXIX, supplement, 25½ x 32¾ inches, Mar., 1941

Japan and Adjacent Regions of Asia and the Pacific Ocean, with insets of industrial centers of Japan and the Marshall Islands. LXXXV, supplement, 26½ x 34½ inches, Apr., 1944

Japan and Korea, with insets of Kuril Islands, Pescadores, Karafuto, Ryukyu Islands, Okinawa, Formosa, Tokyo, and location of Japan in the western Pacific. LXXXVIII, supplement, 37 x 26½ inches, Dec., 1945

Kirin, Harbin, Vladivostok. Map showing seat of war in Manchuria, beginning just north of Mukden, and covering the country north to Harbin and east to Vladivostok; the map shows all roads, trails, and mountains over which the armies must pass. XVI, supplement, 18 x 44 inches, June, 1905

Louisiana, with inset of New Orleans. LVII, supplement, 13 x 13¼ inches, Apr., 1930

The Mall, Washington, D. C. XXVII, supplement, 18¼ x 9¾ inches, Mar., 1915

Map of Africa and Adjoining Portions of Europe and Asia. XLII, supplement, 27 x 30 inches, Oct., 1922

Map of Asia and Adjoining Europe with a Portion of Africa. XXXIX, supplement, 28 x 36 inches, May, 1921

GROSVENOR, GILBERT H.—*Continued*

Map Supplements edited by—*Continued*

Map of Central America, Cuba, Porto Rico, and the Islands of the Caribbean Sea, with inset of the Panama Canal and Canal Zone. XXIV, supplement, 12½ x 19 inches, Feb., 1913

Map of China and Its Territories. XXIII, supplement, 17 x 23 inches, Oct., 1912

Map of Discovery (Eastern Hemisphere). Reproduction in color of the painting by N. C. Wyeth, National Geographic Society, Washington, D. C. LIV, text, p. 568; supplement, 18½ x 16¾ inches, Nov., 1928

Map of Discovery (Western Hemisphere). Reproduction in color of the painting by N. C. Wyeth, National Geographic Society, Washington, D. C. LV, text, p. 93; supplement, 18½ x 16¾ inches, Jan., 1929

Map of Europe, Showing Countries as Established by the Peace Conference at Paris. XXXIX, supplement, 30 x 33 inches, Feb., 1921

Map of Europe and adjoining portions of Africa and Asia. XXVIII, supplement, 28 x 32 inches, July, 1915

Map of Korea and Manchuria. Prepared by the Second Division, General Staff (Military Information Division), War Department, Washington, U. S. A. Insets: Vladivostok; Port Arthur; and index map. XV, supplement, 36 x 42 inches, Mar., 1904

Map of Mexico. XXX, supplement, 20 x 29 inches, July, 1916

Map of North Eastern China. Prepared in the War Department, Adjutant General's Office, Military Information Division. XI, supplement, 18½ x 35½ inches, Sept., 1900

A Map of Northwestern United States and Neighboring Canadian Provinces. LXXIX, supplement, 24½ x 36 inches, June, 1941

Map of South America. XL, supplement, 26 x 36 inches, Oct., 1921

Map of the Countries Bordering the Mediterranean Sea. XXIII, supplement, 10 x 18 inches, Jan., 1912

Map of the New Balkan States and Central Europe. XXVI, supplement, 17 x 22½ inches, Aug., 1914

Map of the Races of Europe and Adjoining Portions of Asia and Africa. XXXIV, supplement, 19¾ x 31 inches, Dec., 1918

Map of the Region Adjacent to the Nicaragua Canal Route. By C. Willard Hayes. X, supplement, 7½ x 10½ inches, July, 1899

Map of the Seat of War in Africa. Prepared in the War Department, Adjutant General's Office, Military Information Division. Inset of South Africa. X, supplement, 33 x 45 inches, Dec., 1899

A Map of the Travels of George Washington. LXI, supplement, 20 x 29 inches, Jan., 1932

Map of the Western Theatre of War, with inset of France and Belgium. XXXIII, supplement, 26 x 31 inches, May, 1918

A Map of the World (in Eastern and Western Hemispheres), with insets showing land and water hemispheres, density of population, time zones, and world mapping. LXXX, supplement, 41 x 22 inches, Dec., 1941

Map Showing Location of Panama Canal, as recommended by the Isthmian Canal Com-

GROSVENOR, GILBERT H.—*Continued*

Map Supplements edited by—*Continued*

mission of 1899-1902. XVI, supplement, 24 x 33 inches, Oct., 1905

Maryland, Delaware, and District of Columbia. LI, supplement, 12 x 18 inches, Feb., 1927

Mexico. XXII, supplement, 17 x 24½ inches, May, 1911

Mexico. XXV, supplement, 17 x 24½ inches, May, 1914

Mexico, Central America, and the West Indies. LXVI, supplement, 23 x 40 inches, Dec., 1934

Mexico, Central America, and the West Indies. LXXVI, supplement, 24 x 41 inches, Dec., 1939

A Modern Pilgrim's Map of the British Isles or More Precisely the Kingdom of Great Britain and Northern Ireland and the Irish Free State. LXXI, supplement, 29 x 35 inches, June, 1937

North America. XLV, supplement, 27 x 37 inches, May, 1924

North America, with inset of the Aleutian Islands. LXXXI, supplement, 26½ x 33 inches, May, 1942

North Carolina, South Carolina, Georgia, and Eastern Tennessee. L, supplement, 14¾ x 19 inches, Sept., 1926

North Pole Regions. XVIII, supplement, 17½ x 17½ inches, July, 1907

Northeastern United States, with inset of southeastern New England. LXXXVIII, supplement, 41 x 26½ inches, Sept., 1945

Northern and Southern Hemispheres, with insets of time zones, world terrain, and tables of airline distances. LXXXIII, supplement, 41 x 22 inches, Apr., 1943

Northern Hemisphere, with tables showing airline distances in the Pacific, the Atlantic, the Arctic, and the Americas. LXXXIX, supplement, 21¾ x 24 inches, Feb., 1946

Pacific Ocean, with inset maps of important islands and island groups. LXX, supplement, 31 x 38 inches, Dec., 1936; revised in 1942

Pacific Ocean and the Bay of Bengal, with inset maps of important islands, and table of airline distances in statute miles. LXXXIV, supplement, 36½ x 26½ inches, Sept., 1943

The Philippine Islands as the Geographical Center of the Far East. XI, supplement, 7½ x 10¾ inches, Jan., 1900

The Philippines. Prepared by reduction from the map of the Bureau of Insular Affairs, War Department. Relief compiled from maps of the Corps of Engineers, U. S. Army, and from Spanish surveys. XVI, supplement, 23 x 36 inches, Aug., 1905

The Philippines. Progress map of Signal Corps telegraph lines and cables in the Military Division of the Philippines. XIII, supplement in two sheets, 34 x 35 and 33 x 35½ inches, Jan., 1902

The Philippines, with insets of Manila, Lingayen Gulf, and location map of the Philippines. LXXXVII, supplement, 17½ x 26 inches, Mar., 1945

Pilot Chart of the North Atlantic Ocean (February, 1903). XIV, supplement, 32 x 21¾ inches, Feb., 1903

The Reaches of New York City. LXXV, supplement, 26½ x 29 inches, Apr., 1939

South America. XVII, supplement, 8 x 11 inches, Aug., 1906

South America, with inset maps of the Galápagos Islands, airways and relief, chief natural resources, precipitation and temperature. Edited by Gilbert Grosvenor. LXXII, supplement, 26¾ x 37½ inches, Dec., 1937

South America, with insets of the Galapagos Islands, chief natural resources, precipitation and temperature, airways and relief, and a table of airline distances and flying times in hours. LXXXII, supplement, 26½ x 37¼ inches, Oct., 1942

South Polar Regions—Showing Routes of the Proposed Antarctic Expeditions. X, supplement, 8 x 8 inches, Aug., 1899

Southeast Asia and Pacific Islands from the Indies and the Philippines to the Solomons, with 22 inset maps of important cities and islands. LXXXVI, supplement, 41 x 26½ inches, Oct., 1944

The Southwestern United States. LXXVII, supplement, 35 x 26 inches, June, 1940

Sovereignty and Mandate Boundary Lines in 1921 of the Islands of the Pacific. XL, supplement, 19 x 25 inches, Dec., 1921

Theater of War in Europe, Africa, and Western Asia, with table of airline distances in statute miles. LXXXII, supplement, 26½ x 31 inches, July, 1942

Theater of War in the Pacific Ocean, with table of airline distances in statute miles. LXXXI, supplement, 20½ x 26½ inches, Feb., 1942

Theatre of Military Operations in Luzon, 1899. War Department, Adjutant General's Office, Military Information Division. X, supplement, 23½ x 38 inches, June, 1899

The Ultimate Washington (Plan laid out by the Commission of 1901 for the National Capital). XXVII, supplement, 18¼ x 9¾ inches, Mar., 1915

Union of Soviet Socialist Republics, with international boundaries according to Russian treaties and claims as of October 1, 1944. Boundaries of January 1, 1938, are shown in red. LXXXVI, supplement, 40 x 25 inches, Dec., 1944

United States and adjoining portions of Canada and Mexico. LXIII, supplement, 26 x 40 inches, May, 1933

The United States and adjoining portions of Canada and Mexico, with insets showing Army Corps areas and population of the States (1940). LXXVIII, supplement, 41 x 26½ inches, Dec., 1940

United States of America, with insets of important cities. XLIII, supplement, 26½ x 36¼ inches, Apr., 1923

The United States of America, with insets of United Nations area and East of Maine. XC, supplement, 26½ x 41 inches, July, 1946

The White Mountains of New Hampshire. LXXII, supplement, 17 x 20 inches, July, 1937

The World. XLII, supplement, 27½ x 40 inches, Dec., 1922

Map Supplements edited by—*Continued*

The World, with insets showing Arctic and Antarctic regions, natural vegetation and ocean currents, density of population and prevailing winds. LXII, supplement, 26 x 38½ inches, Dec., 1932

The World (in Eastern and Western Hemispheres), with insets showing land and water hemispheres, and time zones. LXVIII, supplement, 23 x 44 inches, Dec., 1935

The World Map, with insets of Arctic and Antarctic regions, territories occupied by belligerents in First and Second World Wars, and table of geographical equivalents and abbreviations. LXXXIV, supplement, 41 x 26½ inches, Dec., 1943

Photographs by Gilbert H. Grosvenor:

Bartlett, Captain Sam. XVII, p. 643, Nov., 1906

Bell, Alexander Graham, and Mrs. Bell, at Baddeck, Nova Scotia. XXXVIII, p. 41, July, 1920

Bell, Alexander Graham, and Mrs. Bell, with daughters and grandchildren, at Baddeck, Nova Scotia. XLI, p. 236, Mar., 1922

Bell, Alexander Graham, and Alexander Melville Bell. XLI, p. 233, Mar., 1922

Bell, Alexander Graham, and three grandchildren, Cape Breton, Nova Scotia. XXXVIII, p. 59, July, 1920

Bell, Alexander Graham, hauling down kite, Cape Breton Island, Nova Scotia. XXXVIII, p. 45, July, 1920. LXXVII, p. 612, May, 1940

Boat, "B B", driven by aerial propellers. XVIII, p. 671 (2 ills.), Oct., 1907

Bridgman, Herbert L. XVII, p. 643, Nov., 1906

Children, American. XXXI, p. 158, Feb., 1917

Grace Harwar, full-rigged at sea. LIX, p. 218, Feb., 1931

Grace Harwar, overhauled by a liner. LIX, p. 219, Feb., 1931

Grosvenor, Dr. Gilbert, at Tai Shan (mountain), China. LXXXVII, p. 717, June, 1945

Grosvenor, Dr. and Mrs. Gilbert, photographed before entrance to Shih Chia Fo temple. LXXIII, p. 319, Mar., 1938

Grosvenor, Mrs. Gilbert, at Tai Shan (mountain), China. LXXXVII, pp. 703, 704, 708, 716, 717, June, 1945

Kite, used in early aviation. XXXVIII, p. 38, July, 1920. LII, p. 235, Aug., 1927

Kites, Tetrahedral, of Dr. Alexander Graham Bell. XVIII, p. 24, Jan., 1907

Morrison family, Nine sons of, St. Ann's, Cape Breton, Nova Scotia. XXXV, p. 506, June, 1919

Morrison family, Parents and nine sons of, Baddeck, Nova Scotia. XXIX, p. 220, Mar., 1916

Peary, Commander Robert E., U. S. N. XVII, p. 639, Nov., 1906

Arizona

Arizona Comes of Age. By Frederick Simpich. LV, pp. 1-47, 40 ills. in black and white, 14 ills. in color, map, Jan., 1929
- Artificial lakes 40
- Cactus, Giant saguaro 10
- Canyon Lake 19

GROSVENOR, GILBERT H.—*Continued*

Photographs by—*Continued*

Cacti, Giant saguaro. LXXI, pp. 522, 527, Apr., 1937

Cactus, Barrel, or bisnaga. LXXI, p. 524, Apr., 1937

Bahama Islands

Fish catch: Fish bitten in half before landed. LXIX, p. 239, Feb., 1936

Brazil

São Paulo: Market place. LVIII, p. 770, Dec., 1930

California

General Sherman tree, Sequoia National Park. XXIX, p. 414, Apr., 1916. LXIX, p. 140, Jan., 1936

Sequoia National Park. XXXI, p. 8, Jan., 1917

China

Canton: Pagoda. LXXII, p. 724, Dec., 1937

Hong Kong: Junks. LXXIII, p. 91, Jan., 1938

Nanking: Crenelated wall. LXXIII, p. 207, Feb., 1938

Nanking: Sun Yat-sen Memorial. LXXIII, p. 195, Feb., 1938

Peiping: Peacetime Plant Hunting About Peiping. By P. H. and J. H. Dorsett. LXXII, pp. 509-534, 21 ills., map, Oct., 1937
- Great Wall 525
- Temple of Heaven 511
- U. S. Marines 518

Tai Shan, Sacred Mountain of the East. By Mary Augusta Mullikin. LXXXVII, pp. 699-719, 18 ills., map, June, 1945
- Chair bearers 702, 706, 708, 710
- Dragon's Throat Stairs 711
- Great Stone Road 704
- Halfway House 707
- Inscriptions 712
- Jade Emperor's Summit 717
- Pilgrim Way ...702, 706, 707, 708, 710, 711
- South Heavenly Gate 709
- Tablet Without Inscription 716
- Temple of the Jade Emperor......714, 716
- Temple of the Mother of the Great Bear 703
- Tower of Ten Thousand Fairies 702

Yun Kang Caves: China's Great Wall of Sculpture: Man-hewn Caves and Countless Images Form a Colossal Art Wonder of Early Buddhism. By Mary Augusta Mullikin. Paintings by author and Anna M. Hotchkis. LXXIII, pp. 313-348, 23 ills. in black and white, 10 ills. in color, map, Mar., 1938
- Amitabha 342
- Carved robes of Buddha 346
- Grosvenor, Dr. and Mrs. Gilbert, photographed before entrance to Shih Chia Fo temple 319
- Interior view of cave 330
- Lotus-bossed doorway 334
- Peking carts 314
- Restored figure 335
- Wu Chou Shan caves 317

Costa Rica

To Bogotá and Back by Air: The Narrative of a 9,500-Mile Flight from Washington, Over Thirteen Latin-American Countries and Return, in the Single-Seater Airplane "Spirit of St. Louis." By Col. Charles A. Lindbergh.

GROSVENOR, GILBERT H.—*Continued*
Photographs by—*Continued*
LIII, pp. 529-601, 98 ills., map, May, 1928
San José: Bullock team 563
Schoolboys 563
Volcanoes 562

Cuba

Havana: Morro Castle. LII, p. 497, Oct., 1927

Havana: Morro Castle. LVII, p. 582, May, 1930

Nuevitas: Seaplane docks. LXIII, p. 630, May, 1933

Denmark

Baltic Sea: Bathing at Bornholm. XLII, p. 158, Aug., 1922

Dominican Republic

San Pedro de Macorís: Refueling Clipper Ship. LXIII, p. 629, May, 1933

Finland

Helsingfors:
Coast near. XXXII, p. 28, July, 1917
Harbor. XXVI, p. 510, Nov., 1914
St. Nicholas Lutheran Church. XXVI, p. 511, Nov., 1914

Florida

St. Augustine: Reptiles of All Lands. By Raymond L. Ditmars. XXII, pp. 601-633, 32 ills., July, 1911
Alligators:
Big 611
King of 612
Young 610

Greece

Epidaurus: Greek Theater. LXXXV, p. 275, Mar., 1944

Hawaii

Ape-ape plants. LXXIV, p. 422, Oct., 1938

The Hawaiian Islands: America's Strongest Outpost of Defense—The Volcanic and Floral Wonderland of the World. By Gilbert Grosvenor. XLV, pp. 115-238, 106 ills. in black and white, 21 ills. in color, diagr., 6 maps, Feb., 1924
Colorful Wonders of the Hawaiian Islands. 3 color photos by author, pp. 198-203
Ape-ape and ferns on slopes of Haleakala 171
Ape-ape foliage: Puohokamoa Gulch, Island of Maui...................156
Fern, Bird's-nest...................126
Flame tree: Honolulu, col. pl. XIII....203
Haleakala Crater:
Floor and two dead cones, col. pl. IX.199
Small corner of 147
World's vastest extinct crater, col. pl. VIII....................198
Koa tree: Hawaii National Park......144
Lahaina Roadstead, Island of Maui.....165
Lava:
Aa on slopes of Loa...............188
Pahoehoe 210
Tunnel, through which lava river flowed from Halemaumau.........236
Mauna Loa:
Aa lava on upper slopes...........188
Dead cones on.....................208
Resthouse 182
Slopes of.........................209

GROSVENOR, GILBERT H.—*Continued*
Photographs by—*Continued*
Puna: Beach, Black sand.............148
Puna: Lava rock hurled above the cliff by a tidal wave...............148

Jamaica

Port Royal. LI, p. 3, Jan., 1927

Maryland

Cross Manor, oldest house in Maryland. LI, p. 138, Feb., 1927

Wild Acres. LI, p. 202, Feb., 1927

Massachusetts

Amherst College: Pigeons in garden of Dr. Edwin A. Grosvenor. XLIX, p. 97, Jan., 1926

Michigan

Houghton: Wharf scene. XXIX, p. 360, Apr., 1916

Montana

Glacier National Park. XXXVII, p. 484, June, 1920

Morocco

Beyond the Grand Atlas: Where the French Tricolor Flies Beside the Flag of the Sultan of Morocco. By V. C. Scott O'Connor. LXI, pp. 261-319, 52 ills. in black and white, 12 ills. in color, map, Mar., 1932
Blood-letting by Marrakech surgeons...289
Bou Jeloud, Gate of..................265
El Hassan, Chief of Zaian tribe.......270
Fortress, on the fringe of the Grand Atlas 286
Khenifra: Castle................268, 269
Stork's nest.........................301
Tent, Chief El Hassan's..............271

Fez, Heart of Morocco: Africa's "Imperial City" Retains Its Teeming Streets, Cluttered Shops, Glamorous Moorish Homes and Mosques, Amid the Peace of the French Rule. By Gordon Casserly. LXVII, pp. 663-694, 13 ills. in black and white, 27 ills. in color, June, 1935
Clock of Bou Inania..................670
Karouiine Mosque.....................668
Madrasah Bou Inania..................672
Market of Bab Mahrouk: Muffled figures dicker for wool.............664
Moulay Idris.........................674

New Mexico

Children of New Mexico. LXXIII, p. 557, May, 1938

White Sands, Alamogordo. LXVIII, pp. 252, 256, Aug., 1935

Nova Scotia

Baddeck Harbor. LIII, p. 508, Apr., 1928

Beinn Bhreagh, Baddeck: Summer home of Alexander Graham Bell. XLI, p. 238, Mar., 1922

Bras d'Or Lake, from Beinn Bhreagh. L, p. 426, Oct., 1926

Bras d'Or Lakes. XXIX, p. 226, Mar., 1916

Cape Breton Island: The Charm of Cape Breton Island: The Most Picturesque Portion of Canada's Maritime Provinces—A Land Rich in Historic Associations, Natural Resources, and Geographic Appeal. By Catherine Dunlop Mackenzie. With photos by Gilbert Grosvenor.

Photographs by—*Continued*
XXXVIII, pp. 34-60, 22 ills., map, July, 1920
Aspy Bay....................57
Baddeck....................36
Boat, submerged hydroplane type, Dr. Bell's "HD-4"............47, 48, 49
Bouleceet Harbor....................54
Bras d'Or Lakes....................36
Cape North....................57
Codfish drying....................56
Elsie's Harbor, Bras d'Or Lakes........54
Family pictures............38, 41, 45, 59
Kite, hauled down....................45
Kite, Man-lifting, over Bras d'Or Lakes..44
McAskill, Angus: Boot and waistcoat of Cape Breton's giant..............55
St. Anns, Bay of....................52
Sheep, Twin-bearing....................41
South Ingonish Harbor..............58
Tower, Beinn Bhreagh, Baddeck........43
Trout pool, near Cheticamp............56
Tuna, World's record, St. Anns Bay....51
Chéticamp: Barn dance. LXXVII, p. 611, May, 1940
Chéticamp: Picnic, game played. LXXVII, p. 605, May, 1940
Tuna fish, Landing: Cape Breton. XLIV, p. 592, Dec., 1923

Russia

Moscow:
The Great Imperial Theater. L, p. 581, Nov., 1926
Kremlin. L, p. 520, Nov., 1926
Russian schoolboys. XXXII, p. 30, July, 1917
Nizhni-Novgorod: Voyaging on the Volga Amid War and Revolution: War-time Sketches on Russia's Great Waterway. By William T. Ellis. XXXIII, pp. 245-265, 16 ills., Mar., 1918
Beggar....................250
Cab driver....................251
Policeman....................254
Petrograd: Shrine in a bazaar. XXXII, p. 45, July, 1917
Russia's Democrats. By Montgomery Schuyler. XXXI, pp. 210-240, 25 ills., Mar., 1917
Moscow: Schoolmaster and boys......235
Moscow: Street scene................225
Nizhni-Novgorod: Fair..............237
Russian group in street...............235
Young Russia: The Land of Unlimited Possibilities. By Gilbert H. Grosvenor. XXVI, pp. 421-520, 85 ills. in black and white, 17 ills. in color, Nov., 1914
Bazaar, Jewish....................460
Medals of Service, Russian errand boy's....................425
Moscow:
Bazaar....................462
Cannon captured from Napoleon.450, 451
Cathedral of Our Saviour......468, 469
Cathedral of St. Basil's......(col.) 493
Children....................447
Circassians..............(col.) 487
Coachman....................464
Funeral....................454
Girl, Russian, with glimpse of the University..............(col.) 492
Gypsies..................(col.) 491
Iberian Chapel....................467
Kremlin:
Battlements....................430

GROSVENOR, GILBERT H.—*Continued*

Photographs by—*Continued*
Bells................437, 438, 439
Boys visiting.............(col.) 488
Cathedral of Our Saviour Behind the Golden Gates..............441
Guards....................444
Inside Redeemer Gate...........434
Redeemer Gate.............432, 433
Russian mothers visit............446
Monastery of Miracles..............440
Nun....................457
Pigeons, Feeding, in Red Square.....452
Priest and wife....................444
Schoolboys and priest..............448
Shops, selling icons................461
Shrines................427, 458, 466
Workmen..............455, (col.) 489
Young Russian....................464
Nizhni-Novgorod:
Bells, Cart of....................424
Boys....................(col.) 492
Bridegroom....................478
Carts....................480
Fortune-teller with pet.......(col.) 497
Moujik....................479
Peasant....................478
Peasant woman....................479
Peasant woman and child..........479
Porter, Railway station............474
Prisoner....................476
Shrine....................477
Statue, Trial, in front of University..424
Tatar merchant at fair............475
Vodka saloon....................481
Waterfront....................473
Peddler of pictures................457
Petrograd:
Church of the Resurrection ...(col.) 499
Policeman....................426
Porter, in front of St. Isaac's Cathedral....................509
St. Isaac's golden dome...........485
Soldiers....................505
Statue, Peter the Great...........504
Priest, with wife and two children.....463
Priests....................465
Russian, making sign of the cross......443
Russian group, camera shy......(col.) 490
Schoolboys....................459
Volga River: Boat on................476
Volga River at Nizhni-Novgorod.......472

Scotland

Edinburgh Royal High School. XLI, p. 231, Mar., 1922

South Dakota

Stratobowl: Photographer's perch. LXIX, p. 696, May, 1936

Spain

Escorial, church-palace, near Madrid. LX, p. 251, Aug., 1931
On the Bypaths of Spain. By Harry A. McBride. LV, pp. 311-364, 50 ills. in black and white, 13 ills. in color, map, Mar., 1929
Algeciras: Docks....................318
Alhambra: Hall of the Ambassadors...327
Children, Andalusian................320
Cypress trees, garden of Palacio de Generalife, near Alhambra......328, 329
Fence of old ties, between Cordova and Toledo....................353
Málaga to Granada road.............315

GROSVENOR, GILBERT H.—*Continued*
Photographs by—*Continued*
Straw carried by donkeys............333
Záhara: Tower and battlements.......322

Sweden

Göta Canal. LIV, p. 454, Oct., 1928
Stockholm: Milkmaid. XXIX, p. 46, Jan., 1916

Washington

Olympic Forest. XXIX, p. 421, Apr., 1916

West Indies

Saba, volcanic cone. LIII, p. 583, May, 1928
St. Kitts. LIII, p. 582, May, 1928

Photographs of Gilbert Grosvenor. XXIV, p. 114, Jan., 1913. XXV, pp. 458, 460, Apr., 1914. XXIX, p. 298, Mar., 1916. XLI, p. 240, Mar., 1922; p. 640, June, 1922. XLVIII, p. 224, Aug., 1925; p. 476, Oct., 1925. L, p. 380, Sept., 1926. LIII, p. 135, Jan., 1928. LVII, pp. 583, 592, May, 1930. LVIII, p. 22, July, 1930; pp. 230, 233, Aug., 1930. LXII, p. 366, Sept., 1932. LXV, pp. 790, 792, June, 1934. LXVII, p. 137, Feb., 1935. LXVIII, pp. 112, 114, July, 1935. LXIX, pp. 126, 129, 132, 133, 134, 137, 139, 159, Jan., 1936; p. 712, May, 1936. LXXII, p. 107, July, 1937. LXXIII, p. 319, Mar., 1938. LXXXVII, p. 717, June, 1945. LXXXIX, p. 141, Feb., 1946

GROSVENOR, MELVILLE BELL:
An August First in Gruyères (Switzerland). By Melville Bell Grosvenor. LXX, pp. 137-168, 12 ills. in black and white, 23 ills. in color, Aug., 1936
The Color Camera's First Aërial Success. By Melville Bell Grosvenor. LVIII, pp. 344-353, 9 ills. in color, Sept., 1930
Cruise on an Escort Carrier. By Melville Bell Grosvenor. LXXXIV, pp. 513-546, 14 ills. in black and white, 20 ills. in color, Nov., 1943
Landing Craft for Invasion. By Melville Bell Grosvenor. LXXXVI, pp. 1-30, 26 ills., July, 1944
The New Queen of the Seas (Aircraft Carrier). By Melville Bell Grosvenor. LXXXII, pp. 1-30, 27 ills., drawing, two-page map, July, 1942
Poland, Land of the White Eagle. By Melville Bell Grosvenor. LXI, pp. 435-444, 12 ills. in color, Apr., 1932
Styria (Austria), a Favored Vacation Land of Central Europe. By Melville Bell Grosvenor. LXII, pp. 430-439, 14 ills. in color, Oct., 1932

GROUND CREWS, U. S. Army Air Forces:
They Sustain the Wings. By Frederick Simpich. LXXXIV, pp. 333-354, 19 ills., Sept., 1943

GROUSE (Bird):
Game Birds of Prairie, Forest, and Tundra. By Alexander Wetmore. Paintings by Maj. Allan Brooks. LXX, pp. 461-500, 5 ills. in black and white, 60 portraits in color, Oct., 1936
The Wild Life of Lake Superior, Past and Present: The Habits of Deer, Moose, Wolves, Beavers, Muskrats, Trout, and Feathered Wood-Folk Studied with Camera and Flashlight. By George Shiras, 3d. XL, pp. 113-204, 76 ills., map, pictorial supplement, Aug., 1921
See also Sage Grouse

GROVES, P. R. C.:
Flying Over Egypt, Sinai, and Palestine: Looking Down Upon the Holy Land During an Air Journey of Two and a Half Hours from Cairo to Jerusalem. By Brigadier General P. R. C. Groves and Major J. R. McCrindle. L, pp. 313-355, 26 ills. in black and white, 23 ills. in color, map, Sept., 1926

A **GROWING** Camp in the Tanana Gold Fields, Alaska. By Sidney Paige. XVI, pp. 104-111, 4 ills., Mar., 1905

GROWTH of Florida. XVII, p. 424, July, 1906

GROWTH of Maritime Commerce. (By J. H.). X, pp. 30-31, Jan., 1899

The **GROWTH** of Russia. By Edwin A. Grosvenor. XI, pp. 169-185, 5 maps, May, 1900

The **GROWTH** of the United States. By W J McGee. IX, pp. 377-386, diagr., table, Sept., 1898

GRUENING, ERNEST H.:
Strategic Alaska Looks Ahead: Our Vast Territory, Now Being More Closely Linked to Us by Road and Rail, Embodies the American Epic of Freedom, Adventure, and the Pioneer Spirit. By Ernest H. Gruening. LXXXII, pp. 281-315, 18 ills. in black and white, 16 ills. in color, two-page map, Sept., 1942
Alaska—Our Northwestern Outpost. 16 color photos by author, Amos Burg, Froelich Rainey, pp. 297-308

GRUNDTVIG, NIKOLAI FREDERIK SEVERIN:
Denmark and the Danes. By Maurice Francis Egan. XLII, pp. 115-164, 38 ills., map, Aug., 1922

GRUYÈRES, Switzerland:
An August First in Gruyères. By Melville Bell Grosvenor. LXX, pp. 137-168, 12 ills. in black and white, 23 ills. in color, Aug., 1936

GUADALAJARA, Mexico:
Vignettes of Guadalajara. By Frederick Simpich. LXV, pp. 329-356, 20 ills. in black and white, 15 ills. in color, map, Mar., 1934

GUADALCANAL (Island), Solomon Islands:
At Ease in the South Seas. By Maj. Frederick Simpich, Jr. LXXXV, pp. 79-104, 32 ills., Jan., 1944
What the Fighting Yanks See. By Wanda Burnett. LXXXVI, pp. 451-476, 27 ills., Oct., 1944

GUADALUPE (Island), Mexico:
A Cruise Among Desert Islands. By G. Dallas Hanna and A. W. Anthony. XLIV, pp. 71-99, 32 ills., map, July, 1923

GUADALUPE MOUNTAINS, New Mexico-Texas:
A Visit to Carlsbad Cavern: Recent Explorations of a Limestone Cave in the Guadalupe Mountains of New Mexico Reveal a Natural Wonder of the First Magnitude. By Willis T. Lee. XLV, pp. 1-40, 42 ills., Jan., 1924

GUADELOUPE (Islands), West Indies:
Colorful Paths in Martinique and Guadeloupe. 13 color photos by Edwin L. Wisherd. LXXIII, pp. 281-288, Mar., 1938

GUADELOUPE (Islands), West Indies—*Continued*

Report by Robert T. Hill on Volcanic Disturbances in the West Indies. XIII, pp. 223-267, 12 ills., 3 maps, July, 1902

GUALE. *See* Sea Islands, Georgia

GUAM (Island), Marianas Islands:

Guam—Perch of the China Clippers. By Margaret M. Higgins. LXXIV, pp. 99-122, 23 ills., map, July, 1938

Our Smallest Possession—Guam. By William E. Safford. XVI, pp. 229-237, 5 ills., May, 1905

Springboards to Tokyo. By Willard Price. LXXXVI, pp. 385-407, 16 ills., Oct., 1944

Victory's Portrait in the Marianas. By Lt. William Franklin Draper, USNR. With 17 ills. in color from paintings by author. LXXXVIII, pp. 599-616, Nov., 1945

GUANACOS:

Camels of the Clouds. By W. H. Hodge. LXXXIX, pp. 641-656, 15 ills., map, May, 1946

GUANAJUATO, Mexico:

The Treasure Chest of Mercurial Mexico (Silver Mines). By Frank H. Probert. XXX, pp. 33-68, 33 ills., July, 1916

GUANAYES (Birds):

The Most Valuable Bird in the World. By Robert Cushman Murphy. XLVI, pp. 279-302, 25 ills., map, Sept., 1924

GUANO (Fertilizer):

The Most Valuable Bird in the World (Guanay). By Robert Cushman Murphy. XLVI, pp. 279-302, 25 ills., map, Sept., 1924

Peru's Wealth-Producing Birds: Vast Riches in the Guano Deposits of Cormorants, Pelicans, and Petrels which Nest on Her Barren, Rainless Coast. By R. E. Coker. XXXVII, pp. 537-566, 28 ills., June, 1920

GUANTANAMO BAY, Cuba:

Across the Equator With the American Navy. By Herbert Corey. XXXIX, pp. 571-624, 53 ills., June, 1921

GUAREQUI (Plant):

Notes on the Deserts of the United States and Mexico (Extracted from a Publication by Dr. Daniel T. MacDougal). XXI, pp. 691-714, 16 ills., Aug., 1910

GUATEMALA:

Buenos Aires to Washington by Horse: A Solitary Journey of Two and a Half Years, Through Eleven American Republics, Covers 9,600 Miles of Mountain and Plain, Desert and Jungle. By A. F. Tschiffely. LV, pp. 135-196, 75 ills., map, Feb., 1929

The Countries of the Caribbean. By William Joseph Showalter. XXIV, pp. 227-250, 23 ills., Feb., 1913

Excavations at Quirigua, Guatemala. By Sylvanus Griswold Morley. XXIV, pp. 339-361, 24 ills., diagr., Mar., 1913
Note. XXIV, p. 1056, Sept., 1913

GUATEMALA—*Continued*

The Foremost Intellectual Achievement of Ancient America: The Hieroglyphic Inscriptions on the Monuments in the Ruined Cities of Mexico, Guatemala, and Honduras Are Yielding the Secrets of the Maya Civilization. By Sylvanus Griswold Morley. XLI, pp. 109-130, 27 ills., 17 diagrs., map supplement, Feb., 1922

Guatemala: Land of Volcanoes and Progress: Cradle of Ancient Mayan Civilization, Redolent With Its Later Spanish and Indian Ways, Now Reaping Prosperity from Bananas and Coffee. By Thomas F. Lee. L, pp. 599-648, 32 ills. in black and white, 20 ills. in color, map, Nov., 1926

Guatemala, the Country of the Future. By Edine Frances Tisdel. XXI, pp. 596-624, 33 ills., map, July, 1910

Guatemala Interlude: In the Land of the Quetzal a Modern Capital Contrasts With Primitive Indian Villages and the "Pompeii of America." By E. John Long. LXX, pp. 429-460, 22 ills. in black and white, 13 ills. in color, map, Oct., 1936

Mysterious Temples of the Jungle: The Prehistoric Ruins of Guatemala. By W. F. Sands. XXIV, pp. 325-338, 10 ills., Mar., 1913

Notes on Central America. XVIII, pp. 272-279, ills., map, Apr., 1907

Preserving Ancient America's Finest Sculptures. By J. Alden Mason. Paintings by H. M. Herget. LXVIII, pp. 537-570, 24 ills. in black and white, 10 ills. in color, Nov., 1935

Shattered Capitals of Central America. By Herbert J. Spinden. XXXVI, pp. 185-212, 32 ills., map, Sept., 1919

To Market in Guatemala. By Luis Marden. With 19 color photos by Giles Greville Healey and Charles S. Pineo. LXXXVIII, pp. 87-104, July, 1945

Unearthing America's Ancient History: Investigation Suggests That the Maya May Have Designed the First Astronomical Observatory in the New World in Order to Cultivate Corn. By Sylvanus Griswold Morley. LX, pp. 99-126, 28 ills., July, 1931

GUAYAQUIL, Ecuador:

Beautiful Ecuador. By Joseph Lee. XVIII, pp. 81-91, 9 ills., Feb., 1907

From Sea to Clouds in Ecuador. By W. Robert Moore. LXXX, pp. 717-740, 11 ills. in black and white, 9 ills. in color, Dec., 1941

Over Trail and Through Jungle in Ecuador: Indian Head-Hunters of the Interior, an Interesting Study in the South American Republic. By H. E. Anthony. XL, pp. 327-352, 28 ills., Oct., 1921

GUAYMAS, Mexico:

Adventuring Down the West Coast of Mexico. By Herbert Corey. XLII, pp. 449-503, 44 ills., map, Nov., 1922

GUAYMI INDIANS:

Little-Known Parts of Panama. By Henry Pittier. XXIII, pp. 627-662, 35 ills., map, July, 1912

GUELMA, Algeria:

The American Eclipse Expedition. By Rear Admiral Colby M. Chester. XVII, pp. 589-612, 23 ills., col. pl., Nov., 1906

GUÉRANDE (Peninsula), France:

Where Bretons Wrest a Living from the Sea. 23 photos by F. W. Goro. LXXI, pp. 751-766, June, 1937

GUERARD, A. L.:

The Battle-Line of Languages in Western Europe: A Problem in Human Geography More Perplexing Than That of International Boundaries. By A. L. Guerard. XLIII, pp. 145-180, 36 ills., Feb., 1923

GUERMESSA, Tunisia:

Here and There in Northern Africa. By Frank Edward Johnson. XXV, pp. 1-132, 113 ills., Jan., 1914

GUERNSEY (Island), Channel Islands:

The Channel Islands. By Edith Carey. XXXVIII, pp. 143-164, 24 ills., map, Aug., 1920

Guernsey, the Friendly Island. By Alfred S. Campbell. LXXIII, pp. 361-396, 28 ills. in black and white, 11 ills. in color, Mar., 1938

GUERRERO (State), Mexico:

Down Mexico's Río Balsas. By John W. Webber. With 9 color photos by author, Kenneth Segerstrom, Jack Breed. XC, pp. 253-272, 5 ills. in black and white, map, Aug., 1946

GUEST in Saudi Arabia. By Maynard Owen Williams. LXXXVIII, pp. 463-487, 24 ills., map, Oct., 1945

GUIANA, British. *See* British Guiana

GUIANA, Dutch. *See* Surinam

GUIANA, French. *See* French Guiana

GUILFORD (Suburb), Baltimore. *See* Sherwood Gardens

GUILLEMOT Eggs. XIV, pp. 386-388, ill., Oct., 1903

GUILLEMOTS (Birds):

Birds of the Northern Seas. By Alexander Wetmore. Paintings by Maj. Allan Brooks. LXIX, pp. 95-122, 12 ills. in black and white, 34 portraits in color, Jan., 1936

Guillemot Eggs. XIV, pp. 386-388, ill., Oct., 1903

GUILLUMETTE, PAUL G.:

Beautiful Belgium, Restored by Peace. 11 color photos by Paul G. Guillumette. LVI, pp. 555-562, Nov., 1929

GUINEA, French. *See* French Guinea

GUINEA FOWL:

Fowls of Forest and Stream Tamed by Man. By Morley A. Jull. Paintings by Hashime Murayama. LVII, pp. 327-371, 27 ills. in black and white, 16 ills. in color, Mar., 1930

GULF COAST, U. S.-Mexico:

The Delectable Shrimp: Once a Culinary Stepchild, Today a Gulf Coast Industry. By Harlan Major. LXXXVI, pp. 501-512, 11 ills., map, Oct., 1944

GULF COAST, U. S.-Mexico—*Continued*

How We Use the Gulf of Mexico. By Frederick Simpich. LXXXV, pp. 1-40, 20 ills. in black and white, 19 ills. in color, two-page map, Jan., 1944

GULF Coast Towns Get into the Fight. 19 color photos: 17 by J. Baylor Roberts. LXXXV, pp. 17-40, Jan., 1944

GULF STREAM:

Certain Citizens of the Warm Sea. By Louis L. Mowbray. Paintings by Hashime Murayama. XLI, pp. 27-62, 18 ills. in black and white, 16 ills. in color, Jan., 1922

Devil-Fishing in the Gulf Stream. By John Oliver La Gorce. XXXV, pp. 476-488, 7 ills., June, 1919

The Grandest and Most Mighty Terrestrial Phenomenon: The Gulf Stream. By John Elliott Pillsbury. XXIII, pp. 767-778, ill., diagrs., 3 maps, Aug., 1912

Interesting Citizens of the Gulf Stream. By Dr. John T. Nichols. XXXIX, pp. 69-84, 11 ills., Jan., 1921

Ocean Currents. By James Page. XIII, pp. 135-142, Apr., 1902

The Relations of the Gulf Stream and the Labrador Current. By William Libbey, Junior. V, pp. 161-166, Jan. 31, 1894

Treasure-House of the Gulf Stream: The Completion and Opening of the New Aquarium and Biological Laboratory at Miami, Florida. By John Oliver La Gorce. Paintings by Hashime Murayama. XXXIX, pp. 53-68, 5 ills. in black and white, 16 ills. in color, Jan., 1921

GULL-BILLED TERNS:

Pelican Profiles. By Lewis Wayne Walker. LXXXIV, pp. 589-598, 5 ills. in black and white, 8 ills. in color, Nov., 1943

Included: The Gull-billed Tern of the Salton Sea Area, California

GULLS (Birds):

Black-Headed Gulls in London. By A. H. Hall. XLVII, pp. 664-672, 16 ills., June, 1925

The White Sheep, Giant Moose, and Smaller Game of the Kenai Peninsula, Alaska. By George Shiras, 3d. XXIII, pp. 423-494, 59 ills., maps (1 two-page), May, 1912

GUNS. *See* Cannon; Weapons

GURKHAS:

Nepal: A Little-Known Kingdom. By John Claude White. XXXVIII, pp. 245-283, 32 ills., map, Oct., 1920

GUYNEMER, GEORGES:

Aces of the Air. By Captain Jacques De Sieyes. XXXIII, pp. 5-9, ills., Jan., 1918

GYANGTSE, Tibet:

Across Tibet from India to China. By Lt. Col. Ilia Tolstoy, AUS. XC, pp. 169-222, 41 ills., map, Aug., 1946

GYGIS ALBA. *See* Fairy Terns

GYPSIES:

An American Girl Cycles Across Romania: Two-wheel Pilgrim Pedals the Land of Castles and Gypsies, Where Roman Empire Traces Mingle With Remnants of Oriental Migration. By Dorothy Hosmer. LXXIV, pp. 557-588, 31 ills., map, Nov., 1938

Camargue, the Cowboy Country of Southern France. By Dr. André Vialles. XLII, pp. 1-34, 33 ills., map, July, 1922

Hungary: A Land of Shepherd Kings. By C. Townley-Fullam. XXVI, pp. 311-393, 92 ills., map, Oct., 1914

The Races of Europe. By Edwin A. Grosvenor. XXXIV, pp. 441-534, 62 ills., diagr. and index, maps, map supplement, Dec., 1918

GYPSUM:

The White Sands of Alamogordo (New Mexico): A Dry Ocean of Granular Gypsum Billows Under Desert Winds in a New National Playground. By Carl P. Russell. LXVIII, pp. 250-264, 12 ills., Aug., 1935

GYPSY-MOTH:

Explorers of a New Kind: Successful Introduction of Beetles and Parasites to Check Ravages of the Gipsy-moth and Brown-tail Moth. By L. O. Howard. XXVI, pp. 38-67, 11 ills. in black and white, 5 ills. in color, July, 1914

The Gypsy Moth. XVII, pp. 461-464, 5 ills., Aug., 1906

Pests and Parasites: Why We Need a National Law to Prevent the Importation of Insect-Infested and Diseased Plants. By Charles Lester Marlatt. XXII, pp. 321-346, 29 ills., maps, Apr., 1911

GYROSCOPE:

A Primitive Gyroscope in Liberia. By G. N. Collins. XXI, pp. 531-535, 3 ills., June, 1910

H

HAAKON VII (Norwegian King):

The White War in Norway. By Thomas R. Henry. LXXXVIII, pp. 617-640, 23 ills., map, Nov., 1945

HAARDT, GEORGES-MARIE:

The Citroën Trans-Asiatic Expedition Reaches Kashmir: Scientific Party Led by Georges-Marie Haardt Successfully Crosses Syria, Iraq, Persia, and Afghanistan to Arrive at the Pamir. By Maynard Owen Williams. LX, pp. 387-443, 62 ills., map, Oct., 1931

First Over the Roof of the World by Motor: The Trans-Asiatic Expedition Sets New Records for Wheeled Transport in Scaling Passes of the Himalayas. By Maynard Owen Williams. LXI, pp. 321-363, 45 ills., maps, Mar., 1932

From the Mediterranean to the Yellow Sea by Motor: The Citroën-Haardt Expedition Successfully Completes Its Dramatic Journey. By Maynard Owen Williams. LXII, pp. 513-580, 45 ills. in black and white, 25 ills. in color, maps, Nov., 1932

HAARDT, GEORGES-MARIE—*Continued*

Through the Deserts and Jungles of Africa by Motor: Caterpillar Cars Make 15,000-Mile Trip from Algeria to Madagascar in Nine Months. By Georges-Marie Haardt. XLIX, pp. 651-720, 95 ills., map, June, 1926

The Trans-Asiatic Expedition Starts. By Georges-Marie Haardt. LIX, pp. 776-782, 6 ills., June, 1931

HABANA, Cuba. *See* Havana

HACIENDAS:

A Mexican Hacienda. By J. E. Kirkwood. XXV, pp. 563-584, 18 ills., May, 1914

Mrs. Robinson Crusoe in Ecuador. By Mrs. Richard C. Gill. LXV, pp. 133-172, 43 ills., map, Feb., 1934

On a Chilean Hacienda. 8 color photos by E. P. Haddon. LXXXVI, pp. 489-496, Oct., 1944

HADDON, E. P.:

On a Chilean Hacienda. 8 color photos by E. P. Haddon. LXXXVI, pp. 489-496, Oct., 1944

HADHRAMAUT:

Into Burning Hadhramaut: The Arab Land of Frankincense and Myrrh, Ever a Lodestone of Western Exploration. By D. van der Meulen. LXII, pp. 387-429, 44 ills., map, Oct., 1932

HADJ (Pilgrimage):

An Unbeliever Joins the Hadj: On the Age-Old Pilgrimage to Mecca, Babies Are Born, Elders Die, and Families May Halt a Year to Earn Funds in Distant Lands. By Owen Tweedy. LXV, pp. 761-789, 30 ills., map, June, 1934

HAEBERLE, ARMINIUS T.:

The Azores: Picturesque and Historic Half-way House of American Transatlantic Aviators. By Arminius T. Haeberle. XXXV, pp. 514-545, 26 ills., map, June, 1919

HAGELBARGER, PAUL R.:

The Valley of Ten Thousand Smokes: An Account of the Discovery and Exploration of the Most Wonderful Volcanic Region in the World. By Robert F. Griggs. XXXIII, pp. 115-169, 46 ills., map, panorama, Feb., 1918

HAGERSTOWN, Maryland:

Potomac, River of Destiny. By Albert W. Atwood. LXXXVIII, pp. 33-70, 15 ills. in black and white, 18 ills. in color, map, July, 1945

HAGUE, JAMES D.:

A Doubtful Island of the Pacific. By James D. Hague. XV, pp. 478-489, ill., maps, Dec., 1904

A Recent Report from the "Doubtful Island Region." By James D. Hague. XVIII, pp. 205-208, maps, Mar., 1907

The **HAGUE,** Netherlands:

Glimpses of Holland. By William Wisner Chapin. XXVII, pp. 1-29, 26 ills., Jan., 1915

Holland Rises from War and Water. By Thomas R. Henry. LXXXIX, pp. 237-260, 18 ills., map, Feb., 1946

HAHA JIMA (Island), Ogasawara Shoto, Pacific Ocean:
Springboards to Tokyo. By Willard Price. LXXXVI, pp. 385-407, 16 ills., Oct., 1944

HAIDA (Indian Tribe):
Indians of Our North Pacific Coast. By Matthew W. Stirling. Paintings by W. Langdon Kihn. LXXXVII, pp. 25-52, 3 ills. in black and white, 16 ills. in color, Jan., 1945

HAIFA, Palestine:
Palestine Today. By Francis Chase, Jr. XC, pp. 501-516, 16 ills., Oct., 1946
Syria: The Land Link of History's Chain. By Maynard Owen Williams. XXXVI, pp. 437-462, 20 ills., map, Nov., 1919

HAIL Colombia! By Luis Marden. LXXVIII, pp. 505-536, 10 ills. in black and white, 18 ills. in color, map, Oct., 1940

HAILSTORMS:
The Prevention of Hailstorms by the Use of Cannon. XI, pp. 239-241, June, 1900

HAINAN (Island), China:
Among the Big Knot Lois of Hainan: Wild Tribesmen With Topknots Roam the Little-known Interior of This Big and Strategically Important Island in the China Sea. By Leonard Clark. LXXIV, pp. 391-418, 28 ills., map, Sept., 1938

The **HAIRNET** Industry in North China. By H. W. Robinson. XLIV, pp. 327-336, 10 ills., Sept., 1923

HAITI:
Bare Feet and Burros of Haiti. By Oliver P. Newman. LXXXVI, pp. 307-328, 10 ills. in black and white, 10 ills. in color, map, Sept., 1944
Haiti: A Degenerating Island. By Rear Admiral Colby M. Chester. XIX, pp. 200-217, 5 ills., map, Mar., 1908
Haiti, the Home of Twin Republics. By Sir Harry Johnston. XXXVIII, pp. 483-496, 11 ills., map, Dec., 1920
Haiti and Its Regeneration by the United States. XXXVIII, pp. 497-511, 10 ills., Dec., 1920
Haitian Vignettes. By Captain John Houston Craige. LXVI, pp. 435-485, 40 ills. in black and white, 13 ills. in color, map, Oct., 1934
A Little-Known Marvel of the Western Hemisphere: Christophe's Citadel, a Monument to the Tyranny and Genius of Haiti's King of Slaves. By Major G. H. Osterhout, Jr. XXXVIII, pp. 469-482, 13 ills., Dec., 1920
Wards of the United States: Notes on What Our Country Is Doing for Santo Domingo, Nicaragua, and Haiti. XXX, pp. 143-177, 36 ills., Aug., 1916

HAITI Goes to Market. 10 color photos by B. Anthony Stewart. LXXXVI, pp. 313-320, Sept., 1944

HAITIAN Vignettes. By Captain John Houston Craige. LXVI, pp. 435-485, 40 ills. in black and white, 13 ills. in color, map, Oct., 1934

HAL SAFLIENI (Temple), Malta:
Malta: The Halting Place of Nations: First Account of Remarkable Prehistoric Tombs and Temples Recently Unearthed on the Island. By William Arthur Griffiths. XXXVII, pp. 445-478, 35 ills., map, May, 1920

HALE, EDWARD E.:
Philip Nolan and the "Levant." (By Edward E. Hale). XVI, pp. 114-116, Mar., 1905

A **HALF** Mile Down: Strange Creatures, Beautiful and Grotesque as Figments of Fancy, Reveal Themselves at Windows of the Bathysphere. By William Beebe. Paintings by Else Bostelmann, Helen D. Tee-Van, E. J. Geske. LXVI, pp. 661-704, 28 ills. in black and white, 16 ills. in color, map, Dec., 1934

HALIFAX, LORD (Edward Frederick Lindley Wood):
India—Yesterday, Today, and Tomorrow. By Lord Halifax. LXXXIV, pp. 385-408, 20 ills., two-page map, Oct., 1943

HALL, A. H.:
Black-Headed Gulls in London. By A. H. Hall. XLVII, pp. 664-672, 16 ills., June, 1925
Aces of Aviation (Gulls). 16 photos by author, pp. 665-672

HALL, CHAPIN:
California, Our Lady of Flowers. By Chapin Hall. LV, pp. 703-750, 20 ills. in black and white, 30 ills. in color, June, 1929

HALL, CHARLES FRANCIS:
Charles Francis Hall and Jones Sound. (By A. W. G.). VII, pp. 308-310, Sept., 1896

HALL, EDITH H.:
Explorations in Crete. By Edith H. Hall. XX, pp. 778-787, 15 ills., Sept., 1909

HALL, JOSEF W. *See* Close, Upton

HALL, MELVIN A.:
By Motor Through the East Coast and Batak Highlands of Sumatra. By Melvin A. Hall. XXXVII, pp. 69-102, 27 ills., Jan., 1920

HALL, WILLIAM H.:
Antioch the Glorious. By William H. Hall. XXXVIII, pp. 81-103, 20 ills., map, Aug., 1920
Crusader Castles of the Near East. By William H. Hall. LIX, pp. 369-390, 19 ills., map, Mar., 1931
Under the Heel of the Turk: A Land with a Glorious Past, a Present of Abused Opportunities, and a Future of Golden Possibilities. By William H. Hall. XXXIV, pp. 51-69, 14 ills., July, 1918

HALL, WILLIAM HAMMOND:
Irrigation in California. By Wm. Hammond Hall. I, pp. 277-290, Oct., 1889

HALLINGDAL (Valley), Norway:
Life in a Norway Valley: An American Girl Is Welcomed Into the Homemaking and Haying of Happy Hallingdal. By Abbie L. Bosworth. LXVII, pp. 627-648, 21 ills., map, May, 1935

HALLOCK, CHARLES:

On Eskimo Geographic Names Ending in Miut. (Commentary by John Murdoch, on Kuskokwim River article written by Charles Hallock). IX, p. 190, Apr., 1898

Two Hundred Miles up the Kuskokwim. By Charles Hallock. IX, pp. 85-92, 6 ills., Mar., 1898

HAMA, Syria:

From Jerusalem to Aleppo. By John D. Whiting. XXIV, pp. 71-113, 30 ills., map, Jan., 1913

HAMADA EL HOMRA (Desert), Libia:

The Mysteries of the Desert. By Hanns Vischer. XXII, pp. 1056-1059, Nov., 1911

HAMADSHA (Dance):

The Two Great Moorish Religious Dances. By George Edmund Holt. XXII, pp. 777-785, 6 ills., Aug., 1911

HAMBLETON, JAMES I.:

Man's Winged Ally, the Busy Honeybee: Modern Research Adds a New Chapter to Usefulness of the Insect Which Has Symbolized Industry Since Early Bible Times. By James I. Hambleton. Paintings by Hashime Murayama. LXVII, pp. 401-428, 18 ills. in black and white, 16 ills. in color, Apr., 1935

HAMBURG, Germany:

Hamburg Speaks with Steam Sirens. By Frederick Simpich. LXIII, pp. 717-744, 32 ills., June, 1933

HAMILTON, EDITH:

The Greek Way. By Edith Hamilton. LXXXV, pp. 257-271, 12 ills., Mar., 1944

The Roman Way. By Edith Hamilton. XC, pp. 545-565, 14 ills., two-page map, Nov., 1946

HAMILTON, VIRGINIA:

Keeping House in Borneo. By Virginia Hamilton. LXXXVIII, pp. 293-324, 28 ills., map, Sept., 1945

HAMLIN, TEUNIS S.:

Gardiner Greene Hubbard: An Address delivered at the Memorial Services held at the Church of the Covenant, Washington, D. C., December 13, 1897. By Rev. Teunis S. Hamlin. IX, pp. 33-38, ill., Feb., 1898

HAMMERFEST, Norway:

Sailing the Seven Seas in the Interest of Science: Adventures Through 157,000 Miles of Storm and Calm, from Arctic to Antarctic and Around the World, in the Non-magnetic Yacht "Carnegie." By J. P. Ault. XLII, pp. 631-690, 47 ills., chart, Dec., 1922

HAMMOND, MRS. JOHN HAYS:

The National Geographic Society (Speech by Mrs. John Hays Hammond). XXIII, pp. 272-298, 5 ills., Mar., 1912

HAMMURABI, Code of:

Pushing Back History's Horizon: How the Pick and Shovel Are Revealing Civilizations That Were Ancient When Israel Was Young. By Albert T. Clay. XXIX, pp. 162-216, 47 ills., map, Feb., 1916

HANDLEY, MARIE LOUISE:

Siena's Palio, an Italian Inheritance from the Middle Ages. By Marie Louise Handley. L, pp. 245-258, 3 ills., Aug., 1926

HANGCHOW, China:

Ho for the Soochow Ho. By Mabel Craft Deering. LI, pp. 623-649, 32 ills., map, June, 1927

HANNA, G. DALLAS:

A Cruise Among Desert Islands (Baja California). By G. Dallas Hanna and A. W. Anthony. XLIV, pp. 71-99, 32 ills., map, July, 1923

HANSEN, LEO:

Viking Life in the Storm-Cursed Faeroes. By Leo Hansen. LVIII, pp. 607-648, 49 ills., map, Nov., 1930

HANSON, EARL:

The Island of the Sagas (Iceland). By Earl Hanson. LIII, pp. 499-511, 22 ills., Apr., 1928

HANSON, ELISHA:

Man's Feathered Friends of Longest Standing: Peoples of Every Clime and Age Have Lavished Care and Affection Upon Lovely Pigeons. By Elisha Hanson. Paintings by Hashime Murayama. XLIX, pp. 63-110, 35 ills. in black and white, 12 ills. in color, Jan., 1926

HANSON, GEORGE M.:

"As the Tuan Had Said." By George M. Hanson. LXIV, pp. 631-644, 19 ills., Nov., 1933

HAPPY Landing in Bermuda. By E. John Long. LXXV, pp. 213-238, 14 ills. in black and white, 12 ills. in color, Feb., 1939

HARBIN, Manchuria:

Here in Manchuria: Many Thousand Lives Were Lost and More Than Half the Crops Destroyed by the Floods of 1932. By Lilian Grosvenor Coville. LXIII, pp. 233-256, 26 ills., Feb., 1933

Japan Faces Russia in Manchuria. By Willard Price. LXXXII, pp. 603-634, 30 ills., map, Nov., 1942

The Land of Promise. By Major General A. W. Greely. XXIII, pp. 1078-1090, 7 ills., Nov., 1912

Russian Development of Manchuria. By Henry B. Miller. XV, pp. 113-127, 11 ills., map, Mar., 1904

HARBORS AND PORTS:

Between the Heather and the North Sea: Bold English Headlands Once Sheltered Sea Robbers, Later Were Ports of Wooden Ships, Centers of the Jet and Alum Trades, To-day Are Havens of Adventurous Fishing Fleets. By Leo Walmsley. LXIII, pp. 197-232, 41 ills., Feb., 1933

Capital and Chief Seaport of Chile. By W. Robert Moore. LXXXVI, pp. 477-500, 15 ills. in black and white, 8 ills. in color, map, Oct., 1944

Channel Ports—And Some Others. By Florence Craig Albrecht. XXVIII, pp. 1-55, 45 ills., July, 1915

HARBORS AND PORTS—*Continued*

Charm Spots Along England's Harassed Coast. 16 photos in duotone. LXXVIII, pp. 237-252, Aug., 1940

Cosmopolitan Shanghai, Key Seaport of China. By W. Robert Moore. LXII, pp. 311-335, 19 ills., Sept., 1932

Heroes' Return (Charleston, S. C.). By William H. Nicholas. LXXXVII, pp. 333-352, 19 ills., Mar., 1945

Jobos Harbor (Puerto Rico). (By O. H. Tittmann). X, p. 206, June, 1899

Marseille, Battle Port of Centuries. By a Staff Correspondent. LXXXVI, pp. 425-448, 24 ills., map, Oct., 1944

Normandy's Made-in-England Harbors. LXXXVII, pp. 565-580, 16 ills., map, May, 1945

One Hundred British Seaports. XXXI, pp. 84-94, 10 ills., map, Jan., 1917

Three Old Ports on the Spanish Main. By G. M. L. Brown. XVII, pp. 622-638, 12 ills., Nov., 1906

Today on the China Coast. By John B. Powell. LXXXVII, pp. 217-238, 17 ills., map, Feb., 1945

When the Herring Fleet Comes to Great Yarmouth. By W. Robert Moore. LXVI, pp. 233-250, 19 ills., Aug., 1934

HARBY, SAMUEL F.:

They Survived at Sea. By Lt. Comdr. Samuel F. Harby. LXXXVII, pp. 617-640, 22 ills., May, 1945

HARDING, WARREN G.:

President Harding present at unveiling of the Peary Memorial in Arlington National Cemetery, Apr. 6, 1922. XLI, p. 639, ill. pp. 640, 642, June, 1922

The **HARDY** Catalpa. XIV, pp. 348-353, 4 ills., Sept., 1903

HARGRAVE, LAURENCE:

The Tetrahedral Principle in Kite Structure. By Alexander Graham Bell. XIV, pp. 219-251, 89 ills., 15 diagrs., June, 1903

HARK! (Deer). Flashlight photo by George Shiras, 3d. XL, pictorial supplement, Aug., 1921

HARK to the Hounds. By Freeman Lloyd. Paintings by Edward Herbert Miner. LXXII, pp. 453-484, 18 ills. in black and white, 31 portraits in color, Oct., 1937

HARLAN, HARRY V.:

A Caravan Journey Through Abyssinia: From Addis Ababa Through Lalibela, the Strange Jerusalem of Ethiopia, in Search of New Grains for American Farms. By Harry V. Harlan. XLVII, pp. 613-663, 46 ills., map, June, 1925

HARMON, BYRON:

Peaks and Trails in the Canadian Alps. 13 photos in duotone by Byron Harmon. LXV, pp. 627-642, May, 1934

HARNDEN, PHOEBE BINNEY:

Keeping House in Majorca. By Phoebe Binney Harnden. XLV, pp. 425-440, 18 ills., map, Apr., 1924

HARPER, FRANCIS:

The Okefinokee Wilderness: Exploring the Mystery Land of the Suwannee River Reveals Natural Wonders and Fascinating Folklore. By Francis Harper. LXV, pp. 597-624, 35 ills., map, May, 1934

HARPERS FERRY, West Virginia:

Potomac, River of Destiny. By Albert W. Atwood. LXXXVIII, pp. 33-70, 15 ills. in black and white, 18 ills. in color, map, July, 1945

HARPUT, Turkey:

The Mountaineers of the Euphrates. By Ellsworth Huntington. XX, pp. 142-156, 13 ills., Feb., 1909

HARRIMAN, Pennsylvania:

Ships for the Seven Seas: The Story of America's Maritime Needs, Her Capabilities and Her Achievements. By Ralph A. Graves. XXXIV, pp. 165-200, 24 ills., Sept., 1918

The **HARRIMAN** Alaska Expedition. By Henry Gannett. X, pp. 507-512, chart, map, Dec., 1899

The **HARRIMAN** Alaska Expedition in Cooperation with the Washington Academy of Sciences. (By G. H. G.). X, pp. 225-227, June, 1899

HARRINGTON, MARK W.:

Area and Drainage Basin of Lake Superior. By Dr. Mark W. Harrington. VIII, pp. 111-120, tables, Apr., 1897

Weather Making, Ancient and Modern. By Mark W. Harrington. VI, pp. 35-62, Apr. 25, 1894

HARRIS, ERNEST LLOYD:

The Buried Cities of Asia Minor. By Ernest L. Harris. XX, pp. 1-18, 10 ills., Jan., 1909

Historic Islands and Shores of the Ægean Sea. By Ernest Lloyd Harris. XXVIII, pp. 231-261, 28 ills., map, Sept., 1915

Notes on Troy. (By Ernest L. Harris). XXVII, pp. 531-532, May, 1915

The Ruined Cities of Asia Minor. By Ernest L. Harris. XIX, pp. 741-760, 11 ills., Nov., 1908

Some Ruined Cities of Asia Minor. By Ernest L. Harris. XIX, pp. 833-858, 19 ills., Dec., 1908

HARRIS, FRED H.:

Skiing Over the New Hampshire Hills. By Fred H. Harris. XXXVII, pp. 151-164, 37 ills., Feb., 1920

HARRIS, JENNIE E.:

Living Casks of Honey (Ants). By Jennie E. Harris. LXVI, pp. 193-199, 4 ills., Aug., 1934

HARRIS, R. A.:

Cotidal Lines for the World. By R. A. Harris. XVII, pp. 303-309, 3 maps, map supplement, June, 1906

Some Indications of Land in the Vicinity of the North Pole. By R. A. Harris. XV, pp. 255-261, map, June, 1904

HARRISON, ED N.:

Birds and Beasts of Mexico's Desert Islands. 12 color photos: 8 by Ed N. Harrison, 4 by Alfred M. Bailey and Robert J. Niedrach. LXXX, pp. 353-360, Sept., 1941

HART, ALBERT BUSHNELL:

Judge of NGS prize essay contest. X, p. 32, Jan., 1899

HARTFORD, Connecticut:

Connecticut, Prodigy of Ingenuity: Factories Play a Symphony of Industry Amid Colonial Scenes in the State of Steady Habits. By Leo A. Borah. LXXIV, pp. 279-326, 25 ills. in black and white, 25 ills. in color, two-page map, Sept., 1938

HARVARD UNIVERSITY, Massachusetts: Biological Laboratories:

Mystery Mammals of the Twilight (Bats). By Donald R. Griffin. XC, pp. 117-134, 19 ills., July, 1946

HASANOĞLAN, Turkey: Village Institutes:

The Turkish Republic Comes of Age. By Maynard Owen Williams. LXXXVII, pp. 581-616, 4 ills. in black and white, 29 ills. in color, map, May, 1945

HASSANEIN BEY, A. M.:

Crossing the Untraversed Libyan Desert: The Record of a 2,200-Mile Journey of Exploration Which Resulted in the Discovery of Two Oases of Strategic Importance on the Southwestern Frontier of Egypt. By A. M. Hassanein Bey. XLVI, pp. 233-277, 46 ills., map, Sept., 1924

HATAY:

In the Land of Moses and Abraham. 25 color photos by W. Robert Moore. LXXIV, pp. 711-742, Dec., 1938

HATCHER, J. B.:

Hatcher's Work in Patagonia. (By W J M.). VIII, pp. 319-322, Nov., 1897

The Indian Tribes of Southern Patagonia, Tierra del Fuego, and the Adjoining Islands. By J. B. Hatcher. XII, pp. 12-22, 4 ills., Jan., 1901

Patagonia. By J. B. Hatcher. VIII, pp. 305-319, 6 ills., map, Nov., 1897

Some Geographic Features of Southern Patagonia, with a Discussion of Their Origin. By J. B. Hatcher. XI, pp. 41-55, 4 ills., Feb., 1900

HATHAWAY, SIBYL (La Dame de Serk):

The Feudal Isle of Sark: Where Sixteenth-Century Laws Are Still Observed. By Sibyl Hathaway (La Dame de Serk). LXII, pp. 101-119, 21 ills., map, July, 1932

HATTERAS, Cape, North Carolina. *See* articles, *following*

HATTERAS ISLAND, North Carolina:

A Bit of Elizabethan England in America: Fisher Folk of the Islands Off North Carolina Conserved the Speech and Customs of Sir Walter Raleigh's Colonists. By Blanch Nettleton Epler. LXIV, pp. 695-730, 43 ills., map, Dec., 1933

Where the Wind Does the Work. By Collier Cobb. XVII, pp. 310-317, 9 ills., map, June, 1906

HATTERIA (Reptile). *See* Tuatara

The **HAUNTS** of the Caribbean Corsairs: The West Indies a Geographic Background for the Most Adventurous Episodes in the History of the Western Hemisphere. By Nell Ray Clarke. XLI, pp. 147-187, 43 ills., Feb., 1922

HAVANA (Habana), Cuba:

American Progress in Habana. XIII, pp. 97-108, 10 ills., Mar., 1902

Cuba—The Isle of Romance. By Enrique C. Canova. LXIV, pp. 345-380, 34 ills., map, Sept., 1933

Cuba—The Sugar Mill of the Antilles. By William Joseph Showalter. XXXVIII, pp. 1-33, 24 ills., map, July, 1920

HAVASUPAI INDIANS:

Experiences in the Grand Canyon. By Ellsworth and Emery Kolb. XXVI, pp. 99-184, 70 ills., map, Aug., 1914

Indian Tribes of Pueblo Land. By Matthew W. Stirling. Paintings by W. Langdon Kihn. LXXVIII, pp. 549-596, 16 ills. in black and white, 25 ills. in color, Nov., 1940

HAWAII, Territory of:

American Pathfinders in the Pacific. By William H. Nicholas. LXXXIX, pp. 617-640, 17 ills., two-page map, May, 1946

A Bird City. XV, pp. 494-498, 6 ills., Dec., 1904

Bird Life Among Lava Rock and Coral Sand: The Chronicle of a Scientific Expedition to Little-known Islands of Hawaii. By Alexander Wetmore. XLVIII, pp. 77-108, 36 ills., map, July, 1925

Hawaii, Then and Now: Boyhood Recollections and Recent Observations by an American Whose Grandfather Came to the Islands 102 Years Ago. By William R. Castle. LXXIV, pp. 419-462, 30 ills. in black and white, 10 ills. in color, map, Oct., 1938

Hawaii for Homes. By H. P. Wood. XIX, pp. 298-299, Apr., 1908

The Hawaiian Islands: America's Strongest Outpost of Defense—The Volcanic and Floral Wonderland of the World. By Gilbert Grosvenor. XLV, pp. 115-238, 106 ills. in black and white, 21 ills. in color, diagr., 6 maps, Feb., 1924

The Key to the Pacific. By George C. Perkins. XIX, pp. 295-298, map, Apr., 1908

Life on the Hawaii "Front": All-out Defense and Belt Tightening of Pacific Outpost Foreshadow the Things to Come on Mainland. By Lieut. Frederick Simpich, Jr. LXXXII, pp. 541-560, 19 ills., map, Oct., 1942

My Flight from Hawaii. By Amelia Earhart. LXVII, pp. 593-609, 4 ills. in black and white, 8 ills. in duotone, May, 1935

Net Results from Oceania: Collecting Aquarium Specimens in Tropical Pacific Waters. By Walter H. Chute. LXXIX, pp. 347-372, 8 ills. in black and white, 24 ills. in color, Mar., 1941

HAWAIIAN Islands: America's Strongest Outpost of Defense—The Volcanic and Floral Wonderland of the World. By Gilbert Grosvenor. XLV, pp. 115-238, 106 ills. in black and white, 21 ills. in color, diagr., 6 maps, Feb., 1924

HAWKE (Cutter):

By Sail Across Europe. By Merlin Minshall. LXXI, pp. 533-567, 38 ills., map, May, 1937

HAWKS:

Adventures with Birds of Prey. By Frank and John Craighead. LXXII, pp. 109-134, 25 ills., July, 1937

American Birds of Prey—A Review of Their Value. XXXVIII, pp. 460-467, 6 ills., Dec., 1920

The Eagle, King of Birds, and His Kin. By Alexander Wetmore. Paintings by Maj. Allan Brooks. LXIV, pp. 43-95, 23 ills. in black and white, 48 ills. in color, July, 1933

Falconry, the Sport of Kings. By Louis Agassiz Fuertes. Paintings by author. XXXVIII, pp. 429-460, 13 ills. in black and white, 12 ills. in color, Dec., 1920

Hunting with the Lens. By Howard H. Cleaves. XXVI, pp. 1-35, 47 ills., July, 1914

In Quest of the Golden Eagle: Over Lonely Mountain and Prairie Soars This Rare and Lordly Bird, But Three Youths from the East Catch Up With Him at Last. By John and Frank Craighead. LXXVII, pp. 693-710, 17 ills., May, 1940

Life with an Indian Prince: As Guests of a Maharaja's Brother, Two Young American Naturalists Study Age-old Methods of Hunting with Trained Falcons and Cheetahs and Savor the Pomp of Royal India. By John and Frank Craighead. LXXXI, pp. 235-272, 38 ills., map, Feb., 1942

Photographing the Nest Life of the Osprey. By Capt. C. W. R. Knight. LXII, pp. 247-260, 25 ills., Aug., 1932

HAYDEN, EVERETT:

Chronometer and Time Service of the U. S. Naval Observatory and the Present Status of Standard Time. By Lieut. Comdr. Edward Everett Hayden. XV, pp. 430-431, Oct., 1904

The Great Storm Off the Atlantic Coast of the United States, March 11th-14th, 1888. By Everett Hayden. I, pp. 40-58, 6 charts, Oct., 1888

The Law of Storms, Considered with Special Reference to the North Atlantic. By Everett Hayden. II, pp. 199-211, ill., 3 diagrs., 3 foldout diagrs., foldout charts, July, 1890

See also NGS: Board of Managers; Secretary; Vice-President

HAYES, C. WILLARD:

An Assumed Inconstancy in the Level of Lake Nicaragua; A Question of Permanency of the Nicaragua Canal. By C. Willard Hayes. XI, pp. 156-161, Apr., 1900

Cryptogams Collected by Dr. C. Willard Hayes in Alaska, 1891. By Clara E. Cummings. IV, pp. 160-162, May 15, 1892

An Expedition Through the Yukon District. By Charles Willard Hayes. IV, pp. 117-159, 3 maps (2 foldouts), May 15, 1892

Geomorphology of the Southern Appalachians. By Charles Willard Hayes and Marius R. Campbell. VI, pp. 63-126, diagrs., 4 maps, May 23, 1894

HAYES, C. WILLARD—*Continued*

Ice Cliffs on White River, Yukon Territory. By C. Willard Hayes and Alfred H. Brooks. XI, pp. 199-201, May, 1900

Physiography of the Nicaragua Canal Route. By C. Willard Hayes. X, pp. 233-246, ill., diagr., maps, map supplement, July, 1899

HAYES, WILLIAM C.:

Daily Life in Ancient Egypt (Part I). Daily Life in Ancient Egypt: *The Later Period* (Part II). By William C. Hayes. Paintings by H. M. Herget. LXXX, pp. 419-515, 34 ills. in black and white, 32 ills. in color, map, Oct., 1941

HAZARD, DANIEL L.:

Magnetic Observations in Alaska. By Daniel L. Hazard. XX, pp. 675-676, map, July, 1909

HAZEN, HENRY ALLEN:

Professor Henry Allen Hazen (Biography). XI, pp. 78-79, Feb., 1900

HAZLETT, DILLWYN M.:

Farming on the Isthmus of Panama. By Dillwyn M. Hazlett. XVII, pp. 229-234, 5 ills., Apr., 1906

HEAD-HUNTERS:

Field Sports Among the Wild Men of Northern Luzon. By Dean C. Worcester. XXII, pp. 215-267, 52 ills., map, Mar., 1911

Formosa the Beautiful. By Alice Ballantine Kirjassoff. XXXVII, pp. 247-292, 60 ills., map, Mar., 1920

Head-Hunters of Northern Luzon. By Dean C. Worcester. XXIII, pp. 833-930, 102 ills., map, Sept., 1912

I Lived on Formosa. By Joseph W. Ballantine. LXXXVII, pp. 1-24, 19 ills., maps, Jan., 1945

Into Primeval Papua by Seaplane: Seeking Disease-resisting Sugar Cane, Scientists Find Neolithic Man in Unmapped Nooks of Sorcery and Cannibalism. By E. W. Brandes. LVI, pp. 253-332, 98 ills., map, Sept., 1929

New Guinea's Mountain and Swampland Dwellers. By Col. Ray T. Elsmore. LXXXVIII, pp. 671-694, 15 ills. in black and white, 7 ills. in color, map, Dec., 1945

Over Trail and Through Jungle in Ecuador: Indian Head-Hunters of the Interior, an Interesting Study in the South American Republic. By H. E. Anthony. XL, pp. 327-352, 28 ills., Oct., 1921

The **HEALER** of Humanity's Wounds (American Red Cross). XXXIV, pp. 308-324, 16 ills., Oct., 1918

HEALEY, GILES GREVILLE:

To Market in Guatemala. 19 color photos by Giles Greville Healey and Charles S. Pineo. LXXXVIII, pp. 89-104, July, 1945

The **HEALING** Arts in Global War: As Weapons Grow Deadlier, Scientific Medicine Pits Its Ever-rising Skill Against Them. By Albert W. Atwood. LXXXIV, pp. 599-618, 17 ills., Nov., 1943

The **HEALTH** and Morale of America's Citizen Army: Personal Observations of Conditions in Our Soldier Cities by a Former Commander-in-Chief of the United States Army and Navy. By William Howard Taft. XXXIII, pp. 219-245, 22 ills., Mar., 1918

HEARN, LAFCADIO:

Lafcadio Hearn on the Island and People of Martinique. XIII, pp. 214-216, June, 1902

HEART of a Hemisphere: Of Vital Importance is the Area Portrayed in The Society's New Map of Mexico, Central America, and the West Indies. Text with map supplement. LXXVI, pp. 739-740, ill., Dec., 1939

The **HEART** of Africa. By E. C. Hore. III, pp. 238-247, Feb. 19, 1892

The **HEART** of Aymará Land: A Visit to Tiahuanacu, Perhaps the Oldest City of the New World, Lost Beneath the Drifting Sand of Centuries in the Bolivian Highlands. By Stewart E. McMillin. LI, pp. 213-256, 23 ills. in black and white, 18 ills. in color, map, Feb., 1927

The **HEART** of the Antarctic. By Ernest H. Shackleton. XX, pp. 972-1007, 27 ills., map, Nov., 1909

HEATHER Paints the Highlands (Scotland). 38 color photos by B. Anthony Stewart. LXXXIX, pp. 561-600, May, 1946

The **HEAVENS** Above: On Land, Sea, and in the Air the Stars Serve Modern Man as Map, Compass, and Clock. By Donald H. Menzel. With 12 charts, designed by author, showing star positions for each month, and 13 drawings of the constellations by Carlotta Gonzales Lahey. LXXXIV, pp. 97-128, map, July, 1943

HEDIN, SVEN:

Dr. Sven Hedin (Biography). XIV, pp. 26-29, ill., Jan., 1903

Royal Geographical Society's Founders' Medal conferred on Dr. Sven Hedin. IX, p. 342, July, 1898

Sven Hedin in Tibet. XIII, pp. 96-97, Mar., 1902

Sven Hedin's Explorations in Central Asia. XII, pp. 393-395, Nov., 1901

HEIGHT and Position of Mount St. Elias. By Israel C. Russell. III, pp. 231-237, diagr., 7 tables, Feb. 19, 1892

HEIGHT and Position of Mount St. Elias (Part V, from "An Expedition to Mount St. Elias, Alaska," by Israel C. Russell). III, pp. 189-191, ill., table, May 29, 1891

The **HEIGHT** of Mt. Rainier. By Richard U. Goode. IX, pp. 97-98, Mar., 1898

HEILPRIN, ANGELO:

Destruction of Pompeii as Interpreted by the Volcanic Eruptions of Martinique. By Angelo Heilprin. XV, p. 431, Oct., 1904

An Impression of the Guiana Wilderness. By Angelo Heilprin. XVIII, pp. 373-381, 6 ills., June, 1907

HEILPRIN, ANGELO—*Continued*

The National Geographic Society Expedition in the West Indies. XIII, pp. 209-213, maps, June, 1902

The Shattered Obelisk of Mont Pelée. By Prof. Angelo Heilprin. XVII, pp. 465-474, 5 ills., Aug., 1906

See also NGS: Board of Managers

HEINICKE, ALFRED:

Persia. 4 color photos by Alfred Heinicke. XXXIX, pp. 401-416, Apr., 1921

HEINL, ROBERT D., JR.:

Palms and Planes in the New Hebrides. By Maj. Robert D. Heinl, Jr. LXXXVI, pp. 229-256, 17 ills. in black and white, 12 ills. in color, map, Aug., 1944

HEINLY, BURT A.:

Carrying Water Through a Desert: The Story of the Los Angeles Aqueduct. By Burt A. Heinly. XXI, pp. 568-596, 19 ills., map, July, 1910

HEISKELL, MORGAN:

Capri, the Island Retreat of Roman Emperors. 12 photos by Morgan Heiskell. XLI, pp. 627-638, June, 1922

HEJAZ (Arab Kingdom):

A Visit to Three Arab Kingdoms: Transjordania, Iraq, and the Hedjaz Present Many Problems to European Powers. By Junius B. Wood. XLIII, pp. 535-568, 30 ills., map, May, 1923

HELGOLAND (Island), Germany:

Demolishing Germany's North Sea Ramparts. By Stuart E. Jones. XC, pp. 635-644, ill. in black and white, 10 ills. in color, Nov., 1946

HELIUM:

Helium, the New Balloon Gas. By G. Sherburne Rogers. XXXV, pp. 441-456, 11 ills., May, 1919

Modern Transmutation of the Elements. By Sir William Ramsay. XVII, pp. 201-203, Apr., 1906

Studies Planned for New Stratosphere Flight with Helium. LXVII, pp. 795-800, 5 ills., June, 1935

HELL, Norway:

The White War in Norway. By Thomas R. Henry. LXXXVIII, pp. 617-640, 23 ills., map, Nov., 1945

HELLCATS (Airplanes):

Take-off for Japan. 22 ills. in color from U. S. Navy official photos. LXXXVIII, pp. 193-208, Aug., 1945

HELLER, EDMUND:

Nature's Most Amazing Mammal: Elephants, Unique Among Animals, Have Many Human Qualities When Wild That Make Them Foremost Citizens of Zoo and Circus. By Edmund Heller. LXV, pp. 729-759, 37 ills., June, 1934

HELLWEG, J. F.:

Eclipse Adventures on a Desert Isle (Canton). By Capt. J. F. Hellweg. LXXII, pp. 377-394, 14 ills., map, Sept., 1937

HELPING Navigation. XI, pp. 162-163, Apr., 1900

HELPING the Farmers. XVI, pp. 82-85, ill., Feb., 1905

HELPING the Farmers. XVIII, pp. 746-749, 7 ills., Nov., 1907

HELPING the Filipino Fisheries. XVIII, pp. 795-796, Dec., 1907

HELPING to Solve Our Allies' Food Problem: America Calls for a Million Young Soldiers of the Commissary to Volunteer for Service in 1918. By Ralph Graves. XXXIII, pp. 170-194, 23 ills., Feb., 1918

HELSINGFORS, Finland. *See* Helsinki

HELSINKI, Finland:

The Farthest-North Republic: Olympic Games and Arctic Flying Bring Sequestered Finland into New Focus of World Attention. By Alma Luise Olson. LXXIV, pp. 499-533, 25 ills. in black and white, 12 ills. in color, map, Oct., 1938

Flashes from Finland. 19 ills. LXXVII, pp. 239-254, Feb., 1940

Flying Around the Baltic. By Douglas Chandler. LXXIII, pp. 767-806, 31 ills. in black and white, 13 ills. in duotone, map, June, 1938

Helsingfors—A Contrast in Light and Shade. By Frank P. S. Glassey. XLVII, pp. 597-612, 20 ills., May, 1925

HEMISPHERE MAP ARTICLES:

The "Map of Discovery" of the Western Hemisphere With This Number. Announcement of map supplement. LV, p. 93, Jan., 1929

The "Map of Discovery" With This Number (Eastern Hemisphere). Announcement of map supplement. LIV, p. 568, Nov., 1928

Map of the Northern and Southern Hemispheres. Text with map supplement. LXXXIII, pp. 481-483, Apr., 1943

The National Geographic Society's New Map of the World (Eastern and Western Hemispheres). Text with map supplement. LXVIII, pp. 796-798, Dec., 1935

New World Map Gives Backdrop for Headlines (Eastern and Western Hemispheres). Text with map supplement. LXXX, pp. 741-742, ill., Dec., 1941

HENDERSON, ESTHER:

Saguaro, King of the Arizona Desert. 9 color photos by Esther Henderson, Jack Breed, Max Kegley. LXXXVIII, pp. 697-704, Dec., 1945

HENDRICK, CALVIN W.:

Colossal Work in Baltimore. By Calvin W. Hendrick. XX, pp. 365-373, 6 ills., Apr., 1909

HENEQUEN—The Yucatan Fiber. By E. H. Thompson. XIV, pp. 150-158, 6 ills., Apr., 1903

HENRY, ALFRED J.:

Forecasting the Weather. (By Alfred J. Henry). XV, pp. 285-292, 6 ills., chart, July, 1904

Salton Sea and the Rainfall of the Southwest. By Alfred J. Henry. XVIII, pp. 244-248, Apr., 1907

HENRY, ALFRED J.—*Continued*

The Storm of February 25-28, 1902. (By Alfred J. Henry). XIII, pp. 110-112, chart, Mar., 1902

Variations in Lake Levels and Atmospheric Precipitation. By Alfred J. Henry. X, pp. 403-406, diagr., Oct., 1899

See also NGS: Secretary

HENRY, THOMAS R.:

Holland Rises from War and Water. By Thomas R. Henry. LXXXIX, pp. 237-260, 18 ills., map, Feb., 1946

A Tale of Three Cities. By Thomas R. Henry. LXXXVIII, pp. 641-669, 23 ills., Dec., 1945

War's Wake in the Rhineland. By Thomas R. Henry. LXXXVIII, pp. 1-32, 29 ills., map, July, 1945

The White War in Norway. By Thomas R. Henry. LXXXVIII, pp. 617-640, 23 ills., map, Nov., 1945

HENRY Hudson, Magnificent Failure: Just 330 Years Ago He and His Mutinous Crew Found Manhattan Covered With "Goodly Oakes" and Fought Indians in New York Harbor. By Frederick G. Vosburgh. LXXV, pp. 461-490, 21 ills., Apr., 1939

HENSHAW, HENRY WETHERBEE:

American Game Birds. By Henry Wetherbee Henshaw. Paintings by Louis Agassiz Fuertes. XXVIII, pp. 105-158, 4 ills. in black and white, 72 ills. in color, Aug., 1915

Birds of Town and Country. By Henry Wetherbee Henshaw. Paintings by Louis Agassiz Fuertes. XXV, pp. 494-531, 2 ills. in black and white, 64 ills. in color, May, 1914

Fifty Common Birds of Farm and Orchard. By Henry Wetherbee Henshaw. Paintings by Louis Agassiz Fuertes. XXIV, pp. 669-697, 50 ills. in color, June, 1913

Friends of Our Forests. By Henry Wetherbee Henshaw. Paintings by Louis Agassiz Fuertes. XXXI, pp. 297-321, ill. in black and white, 32 ills. in color, Apr., 1917

The Policemen of the Air: An Account of the Biological Survey of the Department of Agriculture. By Henry Wetherbee Henshaw. XIX, pp. 79-118, 38 ills., Feb., 1908

Some of Nature's Scenic Gifts to Hawaii. 16 photos: 6 by Henry W. Henshaw. XLV, pp. 159-174, Feb., 1924

HĒRAKLEION, Crete (Island). *See* Candia

The **HERALDRY** of Heroism (Decorations and Medals). By Arthur E. Du Bois. LXXXIV, pp. 409-413, ills., map, Oct., 1943

HERBERT, CHARLES W.:

Island Treasures of the Caribbean. 23 color photos by Edwin L. Wisherd and C. W. Herbert. LXXVIII, pp. 281-304, Sept., 1940

Saba, Crater Treasure of the Indies. By Charles W. Herbert. LXXVIII, pp. 597-620, 14 ills. in black and white, 12 ills. in color, map (inset), Nov., 1940

Up and Down on Saba. 12 color photos by author, pp. 605-612

HERE and There in Northern Africa. By Frank Edward Johnson. XXV, pp. 1-132, 113 ills., Jan., 1914

HERE in Manchuria: Many Thousand Lives Were Lost and More Than Half the Crops Destroyed by the Floods of 1932. By Lilian Grosvenor Coville. LXIII, pp. 233-256, 26 ills., Feb., 1933

HERENDEEN, EDWARD PERRY:

An Undiscovered Island Off the Northern Coast of Alaska. II—By Captain Edward Perry Herendeen. V, pp. 78-80, July 10, 1893

HERGET, H. M.:

Aztecs Under the War God's Reign. 10 ills. in color from paintings by H. M. Herget. LXXI, pp. 735-742, June, 1937

Egyptians: Life, Culture, and History of the Egyptians. 32 ills. in color from paintings by H. M. Herget. LXXX, pp. 436-514, Oct., 1941

Greeks: "The Glory That Was Greece." 32 ills. in color from paintings by H. M. Herget. LXXXV, pp. 290-352, Mar., 1944

Incas: In the Realm of the Sons of the Sun. 10 ills. in color from paintings by H. M. Herget. LXXIII, pp. 229-236, Feb., 1938

Mayas: Life and Death in Ancient Maya Land. 10 ills. in color from paintings by H. M. Herget. LXX, pp. 623-630, Nov., 1936

Mayas: Portraits of Ancient Mayas, a Peace-Loving People. 10 ills. in color from paintings by H. M. Herget. LXVIII, pp. 553-560, Nov., 1935

Romans: Ancient Rome Brought to Life. 32 ills. in color from paintings by H. M. Herget. XC, pp. 570-633, Nov., 1946

HERKI (Tribespeople):

Mountain Tribes of Iran and Iraq. By Harold Lamb. LXXXIX, pp. 385-408, 15 ills., two-page map, Mar., 1946

HERM (Island), Channel Islands:

The Channel Islands. By Edith Carey. XXXVIII, pp. 143-164, 24 ills., map, Aug., 1920

HEROES of Wartime Science and Mercy. By Elizabeth W. King. LXXXIV, pp. 715-740, 11 ills. in black and white, 334 ills. in color, Dec., 1943

HEROES' Return. By William H. Nicholas. LXXXVII, pp. 333-352, 19 ills., Mar., 1945

HEROIC Flags of the Middle Ages. By Byron McCandless and Gilbert Grosvenor. XXXII, pp. 388-399, 96 ills. in color, Oct., 1917

HERONS:

The Large Wading Birds: Long Legs and Remarkable Beaks, as Well as Size, Form, and Color, Distinguish the Herons, Ibises, and Flamingos. By T. Gilbert Pearson. Paintings by Maj. Allan Brooks. LXII, pp. 441-469, 7 ills. in black and white, 11 ills. in color, Oct., 1932

HERRICK, FRANCIS H.:

The Eagle in Action: An Intimate Study of the Eyrie Life of America's National Bird. By Francis H. Herrick. LV, pp. 635-660, 20 ills., May, 1929

HERRICK, FRANCIS H.—*Continued*

Microscopical Examination of Wood from the Buried Forest, Muir Inlet, Alaska. By Francis H. Herrick. IV, pp. 75-78, drawings, Mar. 21, 1892

HERRING:

Bornholm—Denmark in a Nutshell. By Mason Sutherland. LXXXVII, pp. 239-256, 20 ills., map, Feb., 1945

Fishes and Fisheries of Our North Atlantic Seaboard. By John Oliver La Gorce. Paintings by Hashime Murayama. XLIV, pp. 567-634, 35 ills. in black and white, 16 ills. in color, Dec., 1923

King Herring: An Account of the World's Most Valuable Fish, the Industries It Supports, and the Part It Has Played in History. By Hugh M. Smith. XX, pp. 701-735, 21 ills., Aug., 1909

When the Herring Fleet Comes to Great Yarmouth. By W. Robert Moore. LXVI, pp. 233-250, 19 ills., Aug., 1934

HERRLE, GUSTAVE:

Geographic Nomenclature. Remarks by Herbert G. Ogden, Gustave Herrle, Marcus Baker, and A. H. Thompson. II, pp. 261-278, Aug., 1890

Rules for the Orthography of Geographic Names. Contributed by Mr. Herrle. II, pp. 279-285, 3 tables, Aug., 1890

The Submarine Cables of the World. By Gustave Herrle. With chart compiled by U. S. Hydrographic Office. VII, pp. 102-107, Mar., 1896

HERSEY, HENRY E.:

Member of Wellman Polar Expedition. XVII, p. 205, Apr., 1906; p. 712, Dec., 1906

HERZEGOVINA:

East of the Adriatic: Notes on Dalmatia, Montenegro, Bosnia, and Herzegovina. By Kenneth McKenzie. XXIII, pp. 1159-1187, 1284, 37 ills., map, Dec., 1912

Where East Meets West: Visit to Picturesque Dalmatia, Montenegro and Bosnia. By Marian Cruger Coffin. XIX, pp. 309-344, 26 ills., map, May, 1908

HERZFELD, ERNST EMIL:

Exploring the Secrets of Persepolis. By Charles Breasted. LXIV, pp. 381-420, 48 ills., plan, map, Oct., 1933

Note: Dr. Herzfeld, Field Director of the expedition sponsored by the Oriental Institute of the University of Chicago

HEURLIN, GUSTAV:

Denmark, Land of Farms and Fisheries. 14 color photos by Gustav Heurlin. LXI, pp. 223-230, Feb., 1932

Norway: Fjords and Fjells of Viking Land. 27 color photos by Gustav Heurlin. LVIII, pp. 13-44, July, 1930

Sweden: The Color and Customs of Sweden's Chateau Country. 13 color photos by Gustav Heurlin. LXVI, pp. 33-40, July, 1934

Sweden: Types and Costumes of Old Sweden. 23 color photos by Gustav Heurlin. LIV, pp. 425-440, Oct., 1928

HEWERS of Stone (Mitla, Mexico). By Jeremiah Zimmerman. XXI, pp. 1002-1020, 9 ills., Dec., 1910

HEWES, LAURENCE ILSLEY:

Butterflies—Try and Get Them. By Laurence Ilsley Hewes. LXIX, pp. 667-678, 10 ills., May, 1936

HEYERDAHL, THOR:

Turning Back Time in the South Seas (Fatu-Hiva Island). By Thor Heyerdahl. LXXIX, pp. 109-136, 33 ills., maps, Jan., 1941

HEYWARD, DuBOSE:

The American Virgins (Virgin Islands): After Dark Days, These Adopted Daughters of the United States Are Finding a New Place in the Caribbean Sun. By DuBose Heyward and Daisy Reck. LXXVIII, pp. 273-308, 15 ills. in black and white, 23 ills. in color, map, Sept., 1940

Charleston: Where Mellow Past and Present Meet. By DuBose Heyward. LXXV, pp. 273-312, 20 ills. in black and white, 24 ills. in color, map, Mar., 1939

HIALEAH PARK, Florida:

Flame-Feathered Flamingos of Florida. By W. A. Watts. With 9 color photos by W. F. Gerecke. LXXIX, pp. 56-65, Jan., 1941

HIDDEN GLACIER, Alaska:

The National Geographic Society's Alaska Expedition of 1909. By Ralph S. Tarr and Lawrence Martin. XXI, pp. 1-54, 42 ills., 12 maps, Jan., 1910

HIDDEN Key to the Pacific: Piercing the Web of Secrecy Which Long Has Veiled Japanese Bases in the Mandated Islands. By Willard Price. LXXXI, pp. 759-785, 28 ills., map, June, 1942

HIDDEN Perils of the Deep. By G. R. Putnam. XX, pp. 822-837, 19 diagrs., 3 charts, Sept., 1909

HIDDEN VALLEY, Netherlands New Guinea. *See* Grand Valley

HIERAPOLIS (Ancient City):

The Ruined Cities of Asia Minor. By Ernest L. Harris. XIX, pp. 741-760, 11 ills., Nov., 1908

HIGGINS, MARGARET M.:

Guam—Perch of the China Clippers. By Margaret M. Higgins. LXXIV, pp. 99-122, 23 ills., map, July, 1938

HIGH Country of Colorado. By Alfred M. Bailey. With 23 color photos by author, Robert J. Niedrach, F. G. Brandenburg. XC, pp. 43-72, 9 ills. in black and white, July, 1946

HIGH Road and Low through the Mountain State (West Virginia). 21 color photos by B. Anthony Stewart and Volkmar Wentzel. LXXVIII, pp. 157-180, Aug., 1940

HIGH Sierra. XVIII, pp. 213-214, ill., Mar., 1907

The **HIGHEST** Camp in the World. XVII, pp. 647-648, Nov., 1906

HIGHEST Camps and Climbs. By Edwin Swift Balch. XVII, p. 713, Dec., 1906

The **HIGHEST** Dam in the World (Roosevelt Dam). XVI, pp. 440-441, Sept., 1905

The **HIGHEST** Point in Each State. XX, pp. 539-541, ills., June, 1909

HIGH LIGHTS in the Peruvian and Bolivian Andes. 18 color photos by W. Robert Moore. LI, pp. 219-234, Feb., 1927

HIGH LIGHTS in the Sunshine State (Florida). 41 color photos by Clifton Adams and Charles Edward Hagle. LVII, pp. 27-82, Jan., 1930

HIGHLIGHTS of London Town. 15 color photos by Clifton Adams. LV, pp. 569-576, May, 1929

HIGHLIGHTS of the Volunteer State: Men and Industry in Tennessee Range from Pioneer Stages to Modern Machine Age. By Leonard Cornell Roy. LXXV, pp. 553-594, 20 ills. in black and white, 22 ills. in color, map, May, 1939

HIGHWAYS AND ROADS:

Alaskan Highway an Engineering Epic: Mosquitoes, Mud, and Muskeg Minor Obstacles of 1,671-mile Race to Throw the Alcan Life Line Through Thick Forests and Uninhabited Wilderness. By Froelich Rainey. LXXXIII, pp. 143-168, 21 ills., 3 maps, Feb., 1943

Burma: Where India and China Meet: In the Massive Mountains of Southeast Asia, Swarming Road Builders Wage the "War of the Highways" for Free China and Her Allies. By John LeRoy Christian. LXXXIV, pp. 489-512, 18 ills., map, Oct., 1943

Burma Road, Back Door to China: Like the Great Wall of Ancient Times, This Mighty Mountain Highway Has Been Built by Myriad Chinese to Help Defend Their Homeland. By Frank Outram and G. E. Fane. LXXVIII, pp. 629-658, 26 ills., map, Nov., 1940

Burma Road: China Opens Her Wild West: In the Mountain-girt Heart of a Continent a New China Has Been Created During the Years of War. By Owen Lattimore. LXXXII, pp. 337-367, 21 ills. in black and white, 11 ills. in color, map, Sept., 1942

Burning the Roads. XVII, pp. 583-586, 4 ills., Oct., 1906

The Immediate Necessity for Military Highways. By A. G. Batchelder. XXXII, pp. 477-499, 22 ills., Nov.-Dec., 1917

The Land of the Free in Africa. By Harry A. McBride. XLII, pp. 411-430, 22 ills., Oct., 1922

The Old Post-Road from Tiflis to Erivan. By Esther Lancraft Hovey. XII, pp. 300-309, 9 ills., Aug., 1901

6,000 Miles over the Roads of Free China. By Josephine A. Brown. LXXXV, pp. 355-384, 30 ills., map, Mar., 1944

Stilwell Road—Land Route to China. By Nelson Grant Tayman. LXXXVII, pp. 681-698, 18 ills., June, 1945

U. S. Roads in War and Peace. By Frederick Simpich. LXXX, pp. 687-716, 27 ills., Dec., 1941

HILDEBRAND, J. R.:

Budapest, Twin City of the Danube. By J. R. Hildebrand. LXI, pp. 729-742, 3 ills. in black and white, 10 ills. in duotone, June, 1932

California's Coastal Redwood Realm: Along a Belt of Tall Trees a Giant Bridge Speeds the Winning of Our Westernmost Frontier. By J. R. Hildebrand. LXXV, pp. 133-184, 31 ills. in black and white, 17 ills. in color, map, Feb., 1939

The Columbus of the Pacific: Captain James Cook, Foremost British Navigator, Expanded the Great Sea to Correct Proportions and Won for Albion an Insular Empire by Peaceful Exploration and Scientific Study. By J. R. Hildebrand. LI, pp. 85-132, 45 ills., maps, Jan., 1927

Cotton: Foremost Fiber of the World. By J. R. Hildebrand. LXXIX, pp. 137-192, 31 ills. in black and white, 34 ills. in color, Feb., 1941

Edinburgh, Athens of the North: Romantic History of Cramped Medieval City Vies With Austere Beauty of Newer Wide Streets and Stately Squares. By J. R. Hildebrand. LXII, pp. 219-246, 19 ills. in black and white, 8 ills. in duotone, Aug., 1932

England's Sun Trap Isle of Wight. By J. R. Hildebrand. LXVII, pp. 1-33, 22 ills. in black and white, 14 ills. in color, map, Jan., 1935

The Geography of Games: How the Sports of Nations Form a Gazetteer of the Habits and Histories of Their People. By J. R. Hildebrand. XXXVI, pp. 89-144, 61 ills., Aug., 1919

Glass "Goes to Town." By J. R. Hildebrand. LXXXIII, pp. 1-48, 28 ills. in black and white, 22 ills. in color, Jan., 1943

The Greatest Voyage in the Annals of the Sea. By J. R. Hildebrand. LXII, pp. 699-739, 35 ills., map, Dec., 1932

Machines Come to Mississippi. By J. R. Hildebrand. LXXII, pp. 263-318, 34 ills. in black and white, 26 ills. in color, two-page map, Sept., 1937

Man's Amazing Progress in Conquering the Air. By J. R. Hildebrand. XLVI, pp. 93-122, 28 ills., diagr., July, 1924

Our Most Versatile Vegetable Product: Rubber Drops from Millions of Tropical Trees Are Transformed by Genii Chemists into Myriad Articles, from Tires to Teething Rings. By J. R. Hildebrand. LXXVII, pp. 143-200, 51 ills. in black and white, 26 ills. in color, Feb., 1940

The Pathfinder of the East: Setting Sail to Find "Christians and Spices," Vasco da Gama Met Amazing Adventures, Founded an Empire, and Changed the History of Western Europe. By J. R. Hildebrand. LII, pp. 503-550, 43 ills., map, pictorial supplement, Nov., 1927

Revolution in Eating: Machine Food Age—Born of Roads, Research, and Refrigeration—Makes the United States the Best-fed Nation in History. By J. R. Hildebrand. LXXXI, pp. 273-324, 33 ills. in black and white, 25 ills. in color, Mar., 1942

Royal Copenhagen, Capital of a Farming Kingdom: A Fifth of Denmark's Thrifty Population Resides in a Metropolis Famous for Its Porcelains, Its Silver, and Its Lace. By J. R. Hildebrand. LXI, pp. 217-250, 26 ills. in black and white, 14 ills. in color, Feb., 1932

HILDEBRAND, J. R.—*Continued*

The Sources of Washington's Charm (D. C.). By J. R. Hildebrand. XLIII, pp. 639-680, 46 ills., June, 1923

Trains of Today—and Tomorrow. By J. R. Hildebrand. LXX, pp. 535-589, 51 ills., Nov., 1936

The World's Greatest Overland Explorer: How Marco Polo Penetrated Farthest Asia, "Discovered" Many Lands Unknown to Europe, and Added Numerous Minerals, Animals, Birds, and Plants to Man's Knowledge. By J. R. Hildebrand. LIV, pp. 505-568, 53 ills., two-page map, Nov., 1928

HILDENBRAND, HANS:

Austria: Alpine Villagers of Austria. 14 color photos by Hans Hildenbrand. LVI, pp. 669-676, Dec., 1929

Austria: Summering in Styria, Austria's Rural Playground. 14 color photos by Hans Hildenbrand. LXII, pp. 431-438, Oct., 1932

Austria: Tyrol, the Happy Mountain Land. 11 color photos by Hans Hildenbrand. LXI, pp. 371-378, Mar., 1932

An Austrian Album. 13 color photos by Hans Hildenbrand and Wilhelm Tobien. LXXI, pp. 457-464, Apr., 1937

Czechoslovakia: Costumes of Czechoslovakia. 19 color photos by Hans Hildenbrand. LI, pp. 725-740, June, 1927

Czechoslovakia: When Golden Praha Entertains the Majestic Sokol Festival. 13 color photos by Hans Hildenbrand. LXIII, pp. 41-48, Jan., 1933

The France of Sunshine and Flowers. 3 color photos by Hans Hildenbrand. L, pp. 481-496, Oct., 1926

Germany: The Beauty of the Bavarian Alps. 16 color photos by Hans Hildenbrand. XLIX, pp. 633-648, June, 1926

Germany: Bright Corners of Time-Mellowed Germany. 9 color photos by Hans Hildenbrand. LXIV, pp. 223-230, Aug., 1933

Germany: Dinkelsbühl, Romantic Vision from the Past. 12 color photos by Hans Hildenbrand. LX, pp. 693-700, Dec., 1931

Germany: From Chalet to Palace in Bavaria. 14 color photos by Hans Hildenbrand. LIV, pp. 683-690, Dec., 1928

Germany: Grimm's Fairyland in Northwestern Germany. 9 color photos by Hans Hildenbrand. LIX, pp. 641-648, May, 1931

Germany: Life and Luster of Berlin. 24 color photos by Wilhelm Tobien and Hans Hildenbrand. LXXI, pp. 147-177, Feb., 1937

Germany: Medieval Pageantry in Modern Nördlingen. 12 color photos by Hans Hildenbrand. LIV, pp. 707-714, Dec., 1928

Germany: Rothenburg, the City Time Forgot. 8 color photos by Hans Hildenbrand. XLIX, pp. 185-192, Feb., 1926

Germany: Wandering Through the Black Forest. 13 color photos by Hans Hildenbrand. LIV, pp. 659-666, Dec., 1928

Holy Land: In the Birthplace of Christianity. 10 color photos by Hans Hildenbrand. L, pp. 697-720, Dec., 1926

HILDENBRAND, HANS—*Continued*

Hungary: Rainbow Hues from Hungary. 26 color photos by Hans Hildenbrand. LXI, pp. 697-728, June, 1932

Hungary: Rural Hungarian Rhapsody. 20 color photos by Rudolf Balogh and Hans Hildenbrand. LXXIII, pp. 17-48, Jan., 1938

Italy: Colorful Patinas of Northern Italy. 13 color photos: 9 by Hans Hildenbrand. LXVIII, pp. 337-344, Sept., 1935

Italy: Man and Nature Paint Italian Scenes in Prodigal Colors. 33 color photos by Hans Hildenbrand. LIII, pp. 443-466, Apr., 1928

Italy: Neapolitan Blues and Imperial Purple of Roman Italy. 8 color photos by Hans Hildenbrand. LXVI, pp. 203-210, Aug., 1934

Italy: Under Radiant Italian Skies. 8 color photos: 7 by Hans Hildenbrand. L, pp. 249-256, Aug., 1926

Italy: Where the Blue Begins on the Italian Coast. 12 color photos by Hans Hildenbrand. LXVII, pp. 81-88, Jan., 1935

Poland: Bright Bits in Poland's Mountainous South. 16 color photos by Hans Hildenbrand. LXVII, pp. 353-360, Mar., 1935

Poland: In the Land of the White Eagle. 12 color photos by Hans Hildenbrand. LXI, pp. 437-444, Apr., 1932

Poland: Rainbow Costumes of Poland's Peasants. 10 color photos by Hans Hildenbrand. LXIII, pp. 329-336, Mar., 1933

Switzerland: Snowy Peaks and Old Costumes of Switzerland. 12 color photos by Hans Hildenbrand. LXVI, pp. 147-154, Aug., 1934

Yugoslavia: Color Brightens Rustic Life in Jugoslavia. 23 color photos by Hans Hildenbrand. LVIII, pp. 273-304, Sept., 1930

Yugoslavia: Medieval Glory Haunts the Eastern Adriatic. 17 color photos by Hans Hildenbrand. LIII, pp. 65-80, Jan., 1928

HILDER, FRANK FREDERICK:

British South Africa and the Transvaal. By F. F. Hilder. XI, pp. 81-96, 7 ills., Mar., 1900

Frank Frederick Hilder (Biography). (By W J M.). XII, pp. 85-86, ill., Feb., 1901

Gold in the Philippines. By F. F. Hilder. XI, pp. 465-470, Dec., 1900

The Philippine Islands. By F. F. Hilder. IX, pp. 257-284, 10 ills., table, maps, June, 1898

HILGARD, E. W.:

Geographic Nomenclature. (By E. W. Hilgard). XI, pp. 36-37, Jan., 1900

HILL, DAVID JAYNE:

The Original Territory of the United States. By David J. Hill. X, pp. 73-92, Mar., 1899

Republics—The Ladder to Liberty. By David Jayne Hill. XXXI, pp. 240-254, 5 ills., maps, Mar., 1917

HILL, EBENEZER J.:

A Trip Through Siberia. By Ebenezer J. Hill. XIII, pp. 37-54, 17 ills., map, Feb., 1902

HILL, ROBERT T.:

Cuba. By Robert T. Hill. IX, pp. 193-242, 12 ills., 7 diagrs., tables, 5 maps (1 foldout), May, 1898

HILL, ROBERT T.—*Continued*

Descriptive Topographic Terms of Spanish America. By Robert T. Hill. VII, pp. 291-302, Sept., 1896

Fundamental Geographic Relation of the Three Americas. By Robert T. Hill. VII, pp. 175-181, map, May, 1896

Geographic Literature. (By R. T. H.). IX, pp. 518-519, Dec., 1898

The National Geographic Society Expedition in the West Indies. XIII, pp. 209-213, maps, June, 1902

The National Geographic Society Expedition to Martinique and St. Vincent. XIII, pp. 183-184, ills., June, 1902

The Panama Canal Route. By Robert T. Hill. VII, pp. 59-64, ills., table, Feb., 1896

Porto Rico. By Robert T. Hill. X, pp. 93-112, 13 ills., Mar., 1899

Porto Rico or Puerto Rico? (By R. T. Hill). X, pp. 516-517, Dec., 1899

Portrait. XIII, ill. p. 183, June, 1902

Report by Robert T. Hill on the Volcanic Disturbances in the West Indies. XIII, pp. 223-267, 12 ills., 3 maps, July, 1902

Volcanic Rocks of Martinique and St. Vincent: Collected by Robert T. Hill and Israel C. Russell. By J. S. Diller. XIII, pp. 285-296, July, 1902

HILLEBRAND, W. F.:

Chemical Discussion of Analyses of Volcanic Ejecta from Martinique and St. Vincent. By W. F. Hillebrand. XIII, pp. 296-299, July, 1902

The **HILLS** and Dales of Erin. 11 color photos by Clifton Adams. LI, pp. 317-326, Mar., 1927

HIMALAYAS (Mountains), Asia:

The Aërial Conquest of Everest: Flying Over the World's Highest Mountain Realizes the Objective of Many Heroic Explorers. By Lieut. Col. L. V. S. Blacker. LXIV, pp. 127-162, 35 ills., map, Aug., 1933

Among the Great Himalayan Glaciers. XIII, pp. 405-406, Nov., 1902

Castles in the Air: Experiences and Journeys in Unknown Bhutan. By John Claude White. XXV, pp. 365-455, 74 ills., map, Apr., 1914

Duke of the Abruzzi in the Himalayas. (By A. W. G.). XXI, pp. 245-249, Mar., 1910

First Over the Roof of the World by Motor: The Trans-Asiatic Expedition Sets New Records for Wheeled Transport in Scaling Passes of the Himalayas. By Maynard Owen Williams. LXI, pp. 321-363, 45 ills., maps, Mar., 1932

The Highest Camp in the World. XVII, pp. 647-648, Nov., 1906

Nepal: A Little-Known Kingdom. By John Claude White. XXXVIII, pp. 245-283, 32 ills., map, Oct., 1920

A Pilgrimage to Amernath, Himalayan Shrine of the Hindu Faith. By Louise Ahl Jessop. XL, pp. 513-542, 29 ills., Nov., 1921

Record Ascents in the Himalayas. XIV, pp. 420-421, Nov., 1903

The World's Highest Altitudes and First Ascents. By Charles E. Fay. XX, pp. 493-530, 25 ills., June, 1909

HINDUS AND HINDUISM:

The Bathing and Burning Ghats at Benares. By Eliza R. Scidmore. XVIII, pp. 118-128, 7 ills., Feb., 1907

The Fire-Walking Hindus of Singapore. By L. Elizabeth Lewis. LIX, pp. 513-522, 12 ills., Apr., 1931

India—Yesterday, Today, and Tomorrow. By Lord Halifax. LXXXIV, pp. 385-408, 20 ills., two-page map, Oct., 1943

India Mosaic. By Peter Muir and Frances Muir. LXXXIX, pp. 443-470, 5 ills. in black and white, 22 ills. in color, map, Apr., 1946

The Marriage of the Gods (Festival at Madura, India). By John J. Banninga. XXIV, pp. 1314-1330, 16 ills., Dec., 1913

A Pilgrimage to Amernath, Himalayan Shrine of the Hindu Faith. By Louise Ahl Jessop. XL, pp. 513-542, 29 ills., Nov., 1921

Religious Penances and Punishments Self-Inflicted by the Holy Men of India. By W. M. Zumbro. XXIV, pp. 1257-1314, 69 ills., Dec., 1913

Yank Meets Native. By Wanda Burnett. LXXXVIII, pp. 105-128, 24 ills., July, 1945

HINDUSTAN (Region), India:

Through the Heart of Hindustan: A Teeming Highway Extending for Fifteen Hundred Miles, from the Khyber Pass to Calcutta. By Maynard Owen Williams. XL, pp. 443-467, 29 ills., Nov., 1921

HINE, JAMES S.:

The Valley of Ten Thousand Smokes: An Account of the Discovery and Exploration of the Most Wonderful Volcanic Region in the World. By Robert F. Griggs. XXXIII, pp. 115-169, 46 ills., map, panorama, Feb., 1918
Note: James S. Hine, Zoölogist of the Katmai Expedition

HINGSTON, R. W. G.:

A New World to Explore: In the Tree-Roof of the British Guiana Forest Flourishes Much Hitherto-Unknown Life. By Maj. R. W. G. Hingston. LXII, pp. 617-642, 35 ills., Nov., 1932

HIOKI, EKI:

A Chapter from Japanese History. By Eki Hioki. XVI, pp. 220-228, May, 1905

Japan, America, and the Orient. By Eki Hioki. XVII, pp. 498-504, Sept., 1906

The Purpose of the Anglo-Japanese Alliance. By Eki Hioki. XVI, pp. 333-337, July, 1905

HIPPOPOTAMUSES:

When a Drought Blights Africa: Hippos and Elephants Are Driven Insane by Suffering, in the Lorian Swamp, Kenya Colony. By Capt. A. T. Curle. LV, pp. 521-528, 9 ills., Apr., 1929

HIROHITO (Emperor):

Behind the Mask of Modern Japan. By Willard Price. LXXXVIII, pp. 513-535, 14 ills., Nov., 1945

HISPANIOLA (Island), West Indies. *See* Dominican Republic; Haiti

HISPANIOLA Rediscovered (Dominican Republic). By Jacob Gayer. LIX, pp. 80-112, 12 ills. in black and white, 28 ills. in color, Jan., 1931

HISS, PHILIP HANSON:

Curaçao and Aruba, Oil Isles of the Caribbean. 10 color photos by Philip Hanson Hiss and Robert Yarnall Richie. LXXXIII, pp. 175-182, Feb., 1943

Surinam Subjects of Queen Wilhelmina. 13 color photos by Philip Hanson Hiss. LXXXIII, pp. 465-472, Apr., 1943

The **HISTORIC** City of Brotherly Love: Philadelphia, Born of Penn and Strengthened by Franklin, a Metropolis of Industries, Homes, and Parks. By John Oliver La Gorce. LXII, pp. 643-697, 49 ills. in black and white, 13 ills. in color, Dec., 1932

HISTORIC Danzig: Last of the City-States. By William and Alicelia Franklin. LXXVI, pp. 677-696, 26 ills., Nov., 1939

HISTORIC Islands and Shores of the Ægean Sea. By Ernest Lloyd Harris. XXVIII, pp. 231-261, 28 ills., map, Sept., 1915

The **HISTORICAL** Development of the National Capital. By Marcus Baker. IX, pp. 323-329, July, 1898

HISTORY:

The Evolution of Commerce. Annual Address by the President, Hon. Gardiner G. Hubbard (Jan. 15, 1892). IV, pp. 1-18, Mar. 26, 1892

The Growth of the United States. By W J McGee. IX, pp. 377-386, diagr., table, Sept., 1898

The Historical Development of the National Capital. By Marcus Baker. IX, pp. 323-329, July, 1898

The Relation of Geography to History. By Francis W. Parker. V, pp. 125-131, Jan. 31, 1894

See also American Revolution; Civil War (U. S.); Discoverers, Explorers, and Navigators; Domesday Book; Flags; Homestead Land Law; Monroe Doctrine; NGS: History; Spanish Civil War; World War I; World War II; *and* names of people and places

The **HISTORY** and Geographic Distribution of Bubonic Plague. By George M. Sternberg. XI, pp. 97-113, Mar., 1900

HISTORY'S Greatest Trek: Tragedy Stalks Through the Near East as Greece and Turkey Exchange Two Million of Their People. By Melville Chater. XLVIII, pp. 533-590, 52 ills. in black and white, 32 ills. in color, Nov., 1925

HITCHCOCK, A. S.:

Controlling Sand Dunes in the United States and Europe. By A. S. Hitchcock. XV, pp. 43-47, 4 ills., Jan., 1904

HITTITES (People):

An Ancient Capital (Boghaz Keoy, Turkey). By Isabel F. Dodd. XXI, pp. 111-124, 11 ills., Feb., 1910

A Sketch of the Geographical History of Asia Minor. By Sir William Ramsay. XLII, pp. 553-570, 12 ills., Nov., 1922

Syria: The Land Link of History's Chain. By Maynard Owen Williams. XXXVI, pp. 437-462, 20 ills., map, Nov., 1919

HO for the Soochow Ho (China). By Mabel Craft Deering. LI, pp. 623-649, 32 ills., map, June, 1927

The **HOARY** Monasteries of Mt. Athos (Greece). By H. G. Dwight. XXX, pp. 249-272, 24 ills., map, Sept., 1916

HOBART, ALICE TISDALE:
How Half the World Works. By Alice Tisdale Hobart and Mary A. Nourse. LXI, pp. 509-524, 22 ills., Apr., 1932

HOBART, Tasmania:
Capital Cities of Australia. By W. Robert Moore. LXVIII, pp. 667-722, 32 ills. in black and white, 24 ills. in color, two-page map, Dec., 1935

HODGE, F. W.:
The Enchanted Mesa (New Mexico). By F. W. Hodge. VIII, pp. 273-284, 6 ills., map, Oct., 1897

HODGE, W. H.:
Camels of the Clouds (Lamoids). By W. H. Hodge. LXXXIX, pp. 641-656, 15 ills., map, May, 1946

HOFFMANN, D. O. NOBLE:
The Philippine Exhibit at the Pan-American Exposition. By D. O. Noble Hoffmann. XII, pp. 119-122, Mar., 1901

HOFFMEISTER, J. EDWARD:
Falcon, the Pacific's Newest Island. By J. Edward Hoffmeister and Harry S. Ladd. LIV, pp. 757-766, 8 ills., map, Dec., 1928

HOG ISLAND, Pennsylvania:
Ships for the Seven Seas: The Story of America's Maritime Needs, Her Capabilities and Her Achievements. By Ralph A. Graves. XXXIV, pp. 165-200, 24 ills., Sept., 1918

HÖGAKULL (Farm), Sweden:
Life's Flavor on a Swedish Farm: From the Rocky Hills of Småland Thousands of Sturdy Citizens Have Emigrated to the United States. By Willis Lindquist. LXXVI, pp. 393-414, 23 ills., map, Sept., 1939

HOGBIN, H. IAN:
Coconuts and Coral Islands (Ontong Java). By H. Ian Hogbin. LXV, pp. 265-298, 24 ills. in black and white, 14 ills. in color, map, Mar., 1934

HOLDER, CHARLES FREDERICK:
Big Things of the West. By Charles F. Holder. XIV, pp. 279-282, ills., July, 1903
The Glass-Bottom Boat. By Charles Frederick Holder. XX, pp. 761-778, 17 ills., Sept., 1909
A Remarkable Salt Deposit. By Charles F. Holder. XII, pp. 391-392, ills., Nov., 1901

HOLDING, FLORENCE POLK:
The Salzkammergut, a Playground of Austria. By Florence Polk Holding. LXXI, pp. 445-485, 34 ills. in black and white, 13 ills. in color, map, Apr., 1937

HOLDRIDGE, DESMOND:
Cowboys and Caymans of Marajó (Brazil). 12 color photos by Desmond Holdridge. LXXIV, pp. 645-652, Nov., 1938

HOLIDAYS Among the Hill Towns of Umbria and Tuscany. By Paul Wilstach. LIII, pp. 401-442, 40 ills., map, Apr., 1928

HOLIDAYS with Humming Birds. By Margaret L. Bodine. LIII, pp. 731-742, 15 ills., June, 1928

HOLLAND. *See* Netherlands

HOLLAND Rises from War and Water. By Thomas R. Henry. LXXXIX, pp. 237-260, 18 ills., map, Feb., 1946

HOLLAND'S War with the Sea. By James Howard Gore. XLIII, pp. 283-325, 39 ills., map, Mar., 1923

HOLLIDAY, CARL:
Our Friends, the French: An Appraisal of the Traits and Temperament of the Citizens of Our Sister Republic. By Carl Holliday. XXXIV, pp. 345-377, 29 ills., Nov., 1918

HOLMES, CHARLES H.:
Australia's Patchwork Creature, the Platypus: Man Succeeds in Making Friends with This Duck-billed, Fur-coated Paradox which Lays Eggs and Suckles Its Young. By Charles H. Holmes. LXXVI, pp. 273-282, 13 ills., Aug., 1939

HOLMES, HENRIETTA ALLEN:
The Spell of Romania: An American Woman's Narrative of Her Wanderings Among Colorful People and Long-Hidden Shrines. By Henrietta Allen Holmes. LXV, pp. 399-450, 37 ills. in black and white, 29 ills. in color, map, Apr., 1934

HOLMES, WILLIAM H.:
Awarded Jane M. Smith Life Membership. XXXVII, p. 342, Apr., 1920

HOLT, ERNEST G.:
In Humboldt's Wake: Narrative of a National Geographic Society Expedition Up the Orinoco and Through the Strange Casiquiare Canal to Amazonian Waters. By Ernest G. Holt. LX, pp. 621-644, 27 ills., map, Nov., 1931
A Journey by Jungle Rivers to the Home of the Cock-of-the-rock: Naturalists Enter the Amazon, Voyage Through the Heart of Tropical South America, and Emerge at the Mouth of the Orinoco. By Ernest G. Holt. LXIV, pp. 585-630, 49 ills., map, Nov., 1933

HOLT, GEORGE EDMUND:
The Two Great Moorish Religious Dances. By George Edmund Holt. XXII, pp. 777-785, 6 ills., Aug., 1911

HOLY LAND. *See* Palestine

HOME Folk around Historic Cumberland Gap. By Leo A. Borah. LXXXIV, pp. 741-768, 25 ills., map, Dec., 1943

HOME Life and Industry in the Netherlands. 11 photos in duotone. LXXVII, pp. 271-278, Feb., 1940

The **HOME** of a Forgotten Race: Mysterious Chichen Itza, in Yucatan, Mexico. By Edward H. Thompson. XXV, pp. 585-648, 59 ills., June, 1914

The **HOME** of the First Farmer of America (Mount Vernon). By Worth E. Shoults. LIII, pp. 603-628, 6 ills. in black and white, 26 ills. in color, May, 1928

The **HOME** of the National Geographic Society. XVI, p. 342, July, 1905

HOME-MAKING by the Government: An Account of the Eleven Immense Irrigating Projects to be Opened in 1908. By C. J. Blanchard. XIX, pp. 250-287, 23 ills., Apr., 1908

HOMER'S Troy Today. By Jacob E. Conner. XXVII, pp. 521-532, 11 ills., map, May, 1915

HOMESTEAD LAND LAWS:

The Civil Government of Alaska. By Hon. George C. Perkins. IX, pp. 172-178, Apr., 1898

The Utilization of the Vacant Public Lands. By Emory F. Best. VIII, pp. 49-57, Feb., 1897
Included: Homestead Act

HOMRA, Hamada el (Desert), Libia:

The Mysteries of the Desert. By Hanns Vischer. XXII, pp. 1056-1059, Nov., 1911

HONDURAN Highlights. With 11 color photos by H. C. Lanks. LXXXI, pp. 360-369, Mar., 1942

HONDURAS:

The Countries of the Caribbean. By William Joseph Showalter. XXIV, pp. 227-250, 23 ills., Feb., 1913

The Foremost Intellectual Achievement of Ancient America: The Hieroglyphic Inscriptions on the Monuments in the Ruined Cities of Mexico, Guatemala, and Honduras are Yielding the Secrets of the Maya Civilization. By Sylvanus Griswold Morley. XLI, pp. 109-130, 27 ills., 17 diagrs., map supplement, Feb., 1922

Honduran Highlights. With 11 color photos by H. C. Lanks. LXXXI, pp. 360-369, Mar., 1942

A Little Journey in Honduras. By F. J. Youngblood. XXX, pp. 177-184, 6 ills., Aug., 1916

Notes on Central America. XVIII, pp. 272-279, ills., map, Apr., 1907

HONDURAS, British. *See* British Honduras

HONEY ANTS:

Living Casks of Honey. By Jennie E. Harris. LXVI, pp. 193-199, 4 ills., Aug., 1934

HONEYBEES:

Man's Winged Ally, the Busy Honeybee: Modern Research Adds a New Chapter to Usefulness of the Insect Which Has Symbolized Industry Since Early Bible Times. By James I. Hambleton. Paintings by Hashime Murayama. LXVII, pp. 401-428, 18 ills. in black and white, 16 ills. in color, Apr., 1935

HONG KONG:

Hong Kong—Britain's Far-flung Outpost in China. 16 ills. LXXIII, pp. 349-360, Mar., 1938

1940 Paradox in Hong Kong. By Frederick Simpich. LXXVII, pp. 531-558, 24 ills., 3 maps, Apr., 1940

HONG KONG—*Continued*

Today on the China Coast. By John B. Powell. LXXXVII, pp. 217-238, 17 ills., map, Feb., 1945

HONOLULU, Oahu, Hawaii:

Hawaii, Then and Now: Boyhood Recollections and Recent Observations by an American Whose Grandfather Came to the Islands 102 Years Ago. By William R. Castle. LXXIV, pp. 419-462, 30 ills. in black and white, 10 ills. in color, map, Oct., 1938

Life on the Hawaii "Front": All-out Defense and Belt Tightening of Pacific Outpost Foreshadow the Things to Come on Mainland. By Lieut. Frederick Simpich, Jr. LXXXII, pp. 541-560, 19 ills., map, Oct., 1942

Waves and Thrills at Waikiki. 8 ills. in duotone by Thomas Edward Blake. LXVII, pp. 597-604, May, 1935

HONORARY MEMBERS. *See* NGS: Members and Membership: Honorary Members

HONORS for Amundsen. XIX, pp. 55-76, 13 ills., Jan., 1908

HONORS to Amundsen and Peary (National Geographic Society Banquet). XXIV, pp. 113-130, 5 ills., Jan., 1913

HONORS to Colonel Goethals: The Presentation, by President Woodrow Wilson, of the National Geographic Society Special Gold Medal, and Addresses by Secretary of State Bryan, the French Ambassador, the German Ambassador, and Congressman James R. Mann. XXV, pp. 677-690, 6 ills., June, 1914

HONORS to Peary (Presentation of Hubbard Medal). XVIII, pp. 49-60, ill., Jan., 1907

HONORS to the American Navy. XX, pp. 77-95, Jan., 1909

HOOD, Mount, Oregon:

Is Our Noblest Volcano Awakening to New Life: A Description of the Glaciers and Evidences of Volcanic Activity of Mount Hood. By A. H. Sylvester. XIX, pp. 515-525, 5 ills., map, July, 1908

Oregon Finds New Riches. By Leo A. Borah. XC, pp. 681-728, 15 ills. in black and white, 28 ills. in color, two-page map, Dec., 1946

HOOKWORM (Disease):

Map-Changing Medicine. By William Joseph Showalter. XLII, pp. 303-330, 26 ills., Sept., 1922

Redeeming the Tropics. By William Joseph Showalter. XXV, pp. 344-364, 13 ills., Mar., 1914

HOOSIER Haunts and Holidays (Indiana). 27 color photos by Willard R. Culver. LXX, pp. 283-314, Sept., 1936

HOOVER, HERBERT:

Admiral Byrd Receives New Honor From The Society (Address by Herbert Hoover). LVIII, pp. 228-238, 4 ills., Aug., 1930

Bind the Wounds of France. By Herbert C. Hoover. XXXI, pp. 439-444, 5 ills., May, 1917

The Food Armies of Liberty. By Herbert Hoover. XXXII, pp. 187-196, 6 ills., Sept., 1917

HOOVER, HERBERT—*Continued*

Food for Our Allies in 1919. By Herbert Hoover. XXXIV, pp. 242-244, Sept., 1918

The Great Mississippi Flood of 1927: Since White Man's Discovery This Mighty River Has Served Him Well, Yet It Has Brought Widespread Devastation Along Its Lower Reaches. By Frederick Simpich. LII, pp. 243-289, 53 ills., map, Sept., 1927

The Society's Special Medal Awarded to Amelia Earhart: First Woman to Receive Geographic Distinction at Brilliant Ceremony in the National Capital (Address by Herbert Hoover). LXII, pp. 358-367, 7 ills., Sept., 1932

The Weapon of Food. By Herbert Hoover. XXXII, pp. 197-212, 15 ills., Sept., 1917

HOOVER, MRS. HERBERT:

Member of National Geographic Society since 1902. LVIII, p. 231, Aug., 1930. LXII, p. 362, Sept., 1932

HOOVER, MRS. WILLIAM H.:

Keeping House for the "Shepherds of the Sun." By Mrs. William H. Hoover. LVII, pp. 483-506, 17 ills., map, Apr., 1930

HOPE (Ship):

A Summer Voyage to the Arctic. By G. R. Putnam. VIII, pp. 97-110, 6 ills., map, Apr., 1897

HOPEH (Province), China:

Grand Canal Panorama. By Willard Price. LXXI, pp. 487-514, 31 ills., map, Apr., 1937

Peacetime Plant Hunting About Peiping. By P. H. and J. H. Dorsett. LXXII, pp. 509-534, 21 ills., map, Oct., 1937

HOPI INDIANS:

Everyday Life in Pueblo Bonito: As Disclosed by the National Geographic Society's Archeologic Explorations in the Chaco Canyon National Monument, New Mexico. By Neil M. Judd. XLVIII, pp. 227-262, 37 ills., map, Sept., 1925

Exploring in the Canyon of Death: Remains of a People Who Dwelt in Our Southwest at Least 4,000 Years Ago Are Revealed. By Earl H. Morris. XLVIII, pp. 263-300, 24 ills. in black and white, 22 ills. in color, Sept., 1925

Indian Tribes of Pueblo Land. By Matthew W. Stirling. Paintings by W. Langdon Kihn. LXXVIII, pp. 549-596, 16 ills. in black and white, 25 ills. in color, Nov., 1940

The Land of the Best. By Gilbert H. Grosvenor. XXIX, pp. 327-430, 71 ills. in black and white, 33 ills. in color, pictorial supplement, Apr., 1916

North American Indians. XVIII, pp. 469-484, 14 ills., July, 1907

Photographing the Marvels of the West in Colors. By Fred Payne Clatworthy. LIII, pp. 694-719, 30 ills. in color, June, 1928

Scenes from America's Southwest. 14 ills. XXXIX, pp. 651-664, June, 1921

The Secret of the Southwest Solved by Talkative Tree Rings: Horizons of American History Are Carried Back to A. D. 700 and a Calendar for 1,200 Years Established by National Geographic Society Expeditions. By Andrew Ellicott Douglass. LVI, pp. 737-770, 33 ills., map, Dec., 1929

HOPI INDIANS—*Continued*

The Snake Dance. By Marion L. Oliver. XXII, pp. 107-137, 31 ills., Feb., 1911

HORACE—Classic Poet of the Countryside. By W. Coleman Nevils. LXVIII, pp. 771-795, 22 ills., map, Dec., 1935

HORE, E. C.:

The Heart of Africa. By E. C. Hore. III, pp. 238-247, Feb. 19, 1892

HORGAN, JAMES C.:

Bequest to the Society by James C. Horgan. XXXVII, p. 338, Apr., 1920

HORN, Cape, Chile:

The Cape Horn Grain-Ship Race: The Gallant "Parma" Leads the Vanishing Fleet of Square-Riggers Through Raging Gales and Irksome Calms 16,000 Miles, from Australia to England. By A. J. Villiers. LXIII, pp. 1-39, 38 ills., Jan., 1933

Inside Cape Horn. By Amos Burg. LXXII, pp. 743-783, 29 ills. in black and white, 10 ills. in color, two-page map, Dec., 1937

Rounding the Horn in a Windjammer. By A. J. Villiers. LIX, pp. 191-224, 36 ills., map, Feb., 1931

HORNETS:

Potent Personalities—Wasps and Hornets: Though Often Painfully Stung, Mankind Profits Immeasurably from the Pest-killing Activities of These Fiery Little Flyers. By Austin H. Clark. Paintings by Hashime Murayama. LXXII, pp. 47-72, 18 ills. in black and white, 12 ills. in color, July, 1937

HORSE CARS:

Electric Street Railways (U. S.). (By J. H.). VIII, p. 284, Oct., 1897

HORSE RACING:

Kentucky, Boone's Great Meadow: The Bluegrass State Celebrates Its Sesquicentennial As It Helps the Nation Gird for War. By Leo A. Borah. LXXXII, pp. 57-89, 13 ills. in black and white, 21 ills. in color, map, July, 1942

The People of the Wilderness: The Mongols, Once the Terror of All Christendom, Now a Primitive, Harmless Nomad Race. By Adam Warwick. XXXIX, pp. 507-551, 59 ills., May, 1921

Siena's Palio, an Italian Inheritance from the Middle Ages. By Marie Louise Handley. L, pp. 245-258, 3 ills., Aug., 1926

The Story of the Horse: The Development of Man's Companion in War Camp, on Farm, in the Marts of Trade, and in the Field of Sports. By Major General William Harding Carter. Paintings by Edward Herbert Miner. XLIV, pp. 455-566, 62 ills. in black and white, 24 ills. in color, Nov., 1923

HORSE THIEF CREEK, British Columbia:

On the Trail of a Horse Thief. By Herbert W. Gleason. XXXV, pp. 349-358, 6 ills., Apr., 1919

HORSEBACK JOURNEY:

Buenos Aires to Washington by Horse: A Solitary Journey of Two and a Half Years, Through Eleven American Republics, Covers 9,600 Miles of Mountain and Plain, Desert and Jungle. By A. F. Tschiffely. LV, pp. 135-196, 75 ills., map, Feb., 1929

HORSES:

Kentucky, Boone's Great Meadow: The Bluegrass State Celebrates Its Sesquicentennial As It Helps the Nation Gird for War. By Leo A. Borah. LXXXII, pp. 57-89, 13 ills. in black and white, 21 ills. in color, map, July, 1942

The People of the Wilderness: The Mongols, Once the Terror of All Christendom, Now a Primitive, Harmless Nomad Race. By Adam Warwick. XXXIX, pp. 507-551, 59 ills., May, 1921

Siena's Palio, an Italian Inheritance from the Middle Ages. By Marie Louise Handley. L, pp. 245-258, 3 ills., Aug., 1926

The Story of the Horse: The Development of Man's Companion in War Camp, on Farm, in the Marts of Trade, and in the Field of Sports. By Major General William Harding Carter. Paintings by Edward Herbert Miner. XLIV, pp. 455-566, 62 ills. in black and white, 24 ills. in color, Nov., 1923

See also Ponies

HORSES of the World. 24 ills. in color from paintings by Edward Herbert Miner. XLIV, pp. 479-526, Nov., 1923

HORSFORD, CORNELIA:

Dwellings of the Saga-Time in Iceland, Greenland, and Vineland. By Cornelia Horsford. IX, pp. 73-84, ill., 9 sketches, Mar., 1898

HORTICULTURE. *See* Floriculture; Fruits; Gardens; Plants

HOSKINS, FRANKLIN E.:

The Rock City of Petra. By Franklin E. Hoskins. XVIII, pp. 283-291, 5 ills., May, 1907

The Route Over Which Moses Led the Children of Israel Out of Egypt. By Franklin E. Hoskins. XX, pp. 1011-1038, 24 ills., map, Dec., 1909

HOSMER, DOROTHY:

An American Girl Cycles Across Romania: Two-wheel Pilgrim Pedals the Land of Castles and Gypsies, Where Roman Empire Traces Mingle With Remnants of Oriental Migration. By Dorothy Hosmer. LXXIV, pp. 557-588, 31 ills., map, Nov., 1938

Caviar Fishermen of Romania: From Vâlcov, "Little Venice" of the Danube Delta, Bearded Russian Exiles Go Down to the Sea. By Dorothy Hosmer. LXXVII, pp. 407-434, 29 ills., map, Mar., 1940

Pedaling Through Poland: An American Girl Free-wheels Alone from Kraków, and Its Medieval Byways, Toward Ukraine's Restive Borderland. By Dorothy Hosmer. LXXV, pp. 739-775, 38 ills., maps, June, 1939

Rhodes, and Italy's Aegean Islands. By Dorothy Hosmer. LXXIX, pp. 449-480, 32 ills., map, Apr., 1941

HOSPITAL, American: Deir ez Zor, Syria:

Ali Goes to the Clinic. By Herndon and Mary Hudson. XC, pp. 764-766, ills., Dec., 1946

HOSPITAL Heroes Convict the Cootie. XXXIII, p. 510, June, 1918

HOSPITAL SHIPS:

Heroes' Return. By William H. Nicholas. LXXXVII, pp. 333-352, 19 ills., Mar., 1945

HOSPITALITY of the Czechs. By Worth E. Shoults. LI, pp. 723-742, 19 ills. in color, June, 1927

HOT SPRINGS:

Fabulous Yellowstone: Even Stranger Than the Tales of Early Trappers is the Truth About This Steaming Wonderland. By Frederick G. Vosburgh. LXXVII, pp. 769-794, 15 ills. in black and white, 9 ills. in color, map, June, 1940

Our National Parks. By L. F. Schmeckebier. XXIII, pp. 531-579, 41 ills., map, June, 1912

Waimangu and the Hot-Spring Country of New Zealand: The World's Greatest Geyser Is One of Many Natural Wonders in a Land of Inferno and Vernal Paradise. By Joseph C. Grew. XLVIII, pp. 109-130, 19 ills., map, Aug., 1925

Why Nik-ko Is Beautiful. By J. H. De Forest. XIX, pp. 300-308, 8 ills., Apr., 1908

See also Hot Springs, Arkansas; Iceland

HOT SPRINGS, Arkansas:

Arkansas Rolls Up Its Sleeves. By Frederick Simpich. XC, pp. 273-312, 16 ills. in black and white, 23 ills. in color, map, Sept., 1946

HOTCHKIS, ANNA M.:

Buddhist Calm Survives Along China's Great Wall. 10 ills. in color: 4 paintings by Mary Augusta Mullikin and Anna M. Hotchkis. LXXIII, pp. 321-328, Mar., 1938

HOUGH, WALTER:

The Venice of Mexico (Aztec Lake Country). By Walter Hough. XXX, pp. 69-88, 18 ills., July, 1916

HOUMA, Louisiana:

The Delectable Shrimp: Once a Culinary Stepchild, Today a Gulf Coast Industry. By Harlan Major. LXXXVI, pp. 501-512, 11 ills., map, Oct., 1944

HOUNDS:

Hark to the Hounds. By Freeman Lloyd. Paintings by Edward Herbert Miner. LXXII, pp. 453-484, 18 ills. in black and white, 31 portraits in color, Oct., 1937

Contents: Afghan Hound, American Foxhound, Basset Hound, Beagle, Bloodhound, Borzoi, or Russian Wolfhound, Deerhound, English Foxhound, Greyhound, Harrier, Irish Wolfhound, Otterhound, Rampur Hound, Saluki, Welsh Foxhound, Whippet

The **HOUR** of Prayer: In the Sahara Desert. XXII, panorama, Apr., 1911

HOURST NIGER EXPEDITION:

Return of the Hourst Niger Expedition. (By Ernest de Sasseville). VIII, pp. 24-25, Jan., 1897

HOUSEBOATS:

China: Ho for the Soochow Ho. By Mabel Craft Deering. LI, pp. 623-649, 32 ills., map, June, 1927

China: Life Afloat in China: Tens of Thousands of Chinese in Congested Ports Spend Their Entire Existence on Boats. By Robert F. Fitch. LI, pp. 665-686, 28 ills., June, 1927

Kashmir: House-Boat Days in the Vale of Kashmir. By Florence H. Morden. LVI, pp. 437-463, 22 ills. in black and white, 30 ills. in color, Oct., 1929

The **HOUSE-FLY.** By N. A. Cobb. XXI, pp. 371-380, 4 ills., May, 1910

HOUSER, J. S.:

Fighting Insects with Airplanes: An Account of the Successful Use of the Flying-Machine in Dusting Tall Trees Infested with Leaf-Eating Caterpillars. By C. R. Neillie and J. S. Houser. XLI, pp. 333-338, 6 ills., Mar., 1922

HOUSES:

Alabama: Smoke Over Alabama. By Frederick Simpich. LX, pp. 703-758, 43 ills. in black and white, 26 ills. in color, map, Dec., 1931

Cape Cod People and Places. By Wanda Burnett. LXXXIX, pp. 737-774, 17 ills. in black and white, 24 ills. in color, map, June, 1946

Delaware: Diamond Delaware, Colonial Still: Tradition Rules the "Three Lower Counties" Over Which William Penn and Lord Baltimore Went to Law. By Leo A. Borah. LXVIII, pp. 367-398, 25 ills. in black and white, 15 ills. in color, map, Sept., 1935

Dwellings of the Saga-Time in Iceland, Greenland, and Vineland. By Cornelia Horsford. IX, pp. 73-84, ill., 9 sketches, Mar., 1898

England: Preservation of England's Historic and Scenic Treasures. By Eric Underwood. LXXXVII, pp. 413-440, 24 ills., two-page map, Apr., 1945

England: Summering in an English Cottage: Quiet and Loveliness Invite Contemplation in the Extra "Room," the Garden of the Thatched House. By Helen Churchill Candee. LXVII, pp. 429-456, 32 ills., Apr., 1935

England: A Vacation in a Fifteenth Century English Manor House. By George Alden Sanford. LIII, pp. 629-636, 8 ills., May, 1928

England's Island Garden of Rocks and Flowers (Isle of Wight). 14 color photos by W. Robert Moore. LXVII, pp. 17-24, Jan., 1935

Georgia: Marching Through Georgia Sixty Years After: Multifold Industries and Diversified Agriculture Are Restoring the Prosperity of America's Largest State East of the Mississippi. By Ralph A. Graves. L, pp. 259-311, 47 ills., map supplement, Sept., 1926

Indiana Journey. By Frederick Simpich. LXX, pp. 267-320, 32 ills. in black and white, 27 ills. in color, two-page map, Sept., 1936

Italy: The Stone Beehive Homes of the Italian Heel: In Trulli-Land the Native Builds His Dwelling and Makes His Field Arable in the Same Operation. By Paul Wilstach. LVII, pp. 229-260, 25 ills. in black and white, 12 ills. in color, map, Feb., 1930

HOUSES—*Continued*

Louisiana, Land of Perpetual Romance. By Ralph A. Graves. LVII, pp. 393-482, 84 ills. in black and white, 29 ills. in color, map supplement, Apr., 1930

Maryland Pilgrimage: Visits to Hallowed Shrines Recall the Major Rôle Played by This Prosperous State in the Development of Popular Government in America. By Gilbert Grosvenor. LI, pp. 133-212, 88 ills., map supplement, Feb., 1927

Massachusetts: Northeast of Boston. By Albert W. Atwood. LXXXVIII, pp. 257-292, 12 ills. in black and white, 17 ills. in color, map supplement, Sept., 1945

Mississippi: Machines Come to Mississippi. By J. R. Hildebrand. LXXII, pp. 263-318, 34 ills. in black and white, 26 ills. in color, two-page map, Sept., 1937

Ohio, the Gateway State. By Melville Chater. LXI, pp. 525-591, 58 ills. in black and white, 13 ills. in color, map, May, 1932

Pennsylvania: Penn's Land of Modern Miracles. By John Oliver La Gorce. LXVIII, pp. 1-58, 28 ills. in black and white, 39 ills. in color, two-page map, July, 1935

Sark: The Feudal Isle of Sark: Where Sixteenth-Century Laws Are Still Observed. By Sibyl Hathaway (La Dame de Serk). LXII, pp. 101-119, 21 ills., map, July, 1932

South Carolina: The Ashley River and Its Gardens. By E. T. H. Shaffer. XLIX, pp. 525-550, 6 ills. in black and white, 18 ills. in color, May, 1926

Sweden: Country-House Life in Sweden: In Castle and Cottage the Landed Gentry Gallantly Keep the Old Traditions. By Amelie Posse-Brázdová. LXVI, pp. 1-64, 51 ills. in black and white, 13 ills. in color, map, July, 1934

Tennessee: Highlights of the Volunteer State: Men and Industry in Tennessee Range from Pioneer Stages to Modern Machine Age. By Leonard Cornell Roy. LXXV, pp. 553-594, 20 ills. in black and white, 22 ills. in color, map, May, 1939

United States: Exploring the Atlantic Seaboard with a Color Camera. 11 color photos by Charles Martin and Jacob Gayer. XLIX, pp. 533-548, May, 1926

United States: Some Human Habitations. By Collier Cobb. XIX, pp. 509-515, 5 ills., July, 1908

Virginia—A Commonwealth That Has Come Back. By William Joseph Showalter. LV, pp. 403-472, 69 ills. in black and white, 13 ills. in color, map, Apr., 1929

Virginia: Fame's Eternal Camping Ground: Beautiful Arlington, Burial Place of America's Illustrious Dead. By Enoch A. Chase. LIV, pp. 621-638, 19 ills., Nov., 1928

Virginia: The Home of the First Farmer of America (Mount Vernon). By Worth E. Shoults. LIII, pp. 603-628, 6 ills. in black and white, 26 ills. in color, May, 1928

Virginia: Jefferson's Little Mountain: Romance Enfolds Monticello, the Restored Home of the Author of the Declaration of Independence. By Paul Wilstach. LV, pp. 481-503, 12 ills. in black and white, 12 ills. in color, Apr., 1929

HOUSES—*Continued*

Virginia: Tidewater Virginia, Where History Lives. By Albert W. Atwood. LXXXI, pp. 617-656, 18 ills. in black and white, 20 ills. in color, map, May, 1942

See also Castles; Cone Dwellings; Haciendas; Houseboats; Housing; Palaces

HOUSES OF PARLIAMENT. *See* Parliament

HOUSING, U. S. Government:

Wartime Washington. By William H. Nicholas. LXXXIV, pp. 257-290, 12 ills. in black and white, 16 ills. in color, Sept., 1943

HOUSTON, DAVID F.:

Soldiers of the Soil: Our Food Crops Must Be Greatly Increased. By David F. Houston. XXXI, pp. 273-280, 4 ills., Mar., 1917

HOUSTON-MOUNT EVEREST FLIGHT:

The Aërial Conquest of Everest: Flying over the World's Highest Mountain Realizes the Objective of Many Heroic Explorers. By Lieut. Col. L. V. S. Blacker. LXIV, pp. 127-162, 35 ills., map, Aug., 1933

HOVEY, EDMUND OTIS:

The Eruptions of La Soufrière, St. Vincent, in May, 1902. By Edmund Otis Hovey. XIII, pp. 444-459, 4 ills., Dec., 1902

HOVEY, ESTHER LANCRAFT:

The Old Post-Road from Tiflis to Erivan. By Esther Lancraft Hovey. XII, pp. 300-309, 9 ills., Aug., 1901

HOVEY, H. C.:

The Skeleton in Luray Cave. (By H. C. Hovey). XVII, pp. 425-426, July, 1906

HOW Canada Went to the Front. By T. B. Macaulay. XXXIV, pp. 297-307, 6 ills., Oct., 1918

HOW Half the World Works. By Alice Tisdale Hobart and Mary A. Nourse. LXI, pp. 509-524, 22 ills., Apr., 1932

HOW Latin America Looks from the Air: U. S. Army Airplanes Hurdle the High Andes, Brave Brazil Jungles, and Follow Smoking Volcanoes to Map New Sky Paths Around South America. By Major Herbert A. Dargue. LII, pp. 451-502, 52 ills., map, Oct., 1927

HOW Long a Whale May Carry a Harpoon. (By Wm. H. Dall). X, pp. 136-137, Apr., 1899

HOW Long Will the Coal Reserves of the United States Last? By Marius R. Campbell. XVIII, pp. 129-138, 5 diagrs., map, Feb., 1907

HOW Much is Known of Alaska. By Alfred H. Brooks. XVII, pp. 112-114, ill., map, Feb., 1906

HOW Old Is Man? By Theodore Roosevelt. XXIX, pp. 111-127, 12 ills., 3 maps, Feb., 1916

HOW the Earth Telegraphed Its Tokyo Quake to Washington. By the Rev. Francis A. Tondorf. XLIV, pp. 453-454, ill., Oct., 1923

HOW the United States Grew. By McFall Kerbey. LXIII, pp. 631-649, 17 ills., map, May, 1933

HOW the World Is Fed. By William Joseph Showalter. XXIX, pp. 1-110, 101 ills., Jan., 1916

HOW the World Is Shod. XIX, pp. 649-660, 12 ills., Sept., 1908

HOW to Use the Star Charts. Text with 12 star charts designed by Donald H. Menzel. LXXXIV, pp. 116-128, July, 1943

HOW Warwick (Castle) Was Photographed in Color. By Maynard Owen Williams. LXX, pp. 83-93, 13 ills. in color, July, 1936

HOW We Fight with Photographs. By F. Barrows Colton. LXXXVI, pp. 257-280, 22 ills., Sept., 1944

HOW We Use the Gulf of Mexico. By Frederick Simpich. LXXXV, pp. 1-40, 20 ills. in black and white, 19 ills. in color, two-page map, Jan., 1944

HOWARD, HENRY:

Southward Ho! In the "Alice." By Henry Howard. LXXIII, pp. 265-312, 38 ills. in black and white, 13 ills. in color, maps, Mar., 1938

HOWARD, L. O.:

Economic Loss to the People of the United States Through Insects That Carry Disease. By L. O. Howard. XX, pp. 735-749, Aug., 1909

Explorers of a New Kind: Successful Introduction of Beetles and Parasites to Check Ravages of the Gipsy-moth and Brown-tail Moth. By L. O. Howard. XXVI, pp. 38-67, 11 ills. in black and white, 5 ills. in color, July, 1914

HOWE, CHARLES E.:

The Disposition of the Philippines. By Charles E. Howe. IX, p. 304, June, 1898

HRDLIČKA, ALEŠ:

Bohemia and the Czechs. By Aleš Hrdlička. XXXI, pp. 163-187, 18 ills., Feb., 1917

HUAVE INDIANS:

The Isthmus of Tehuantepec: "The Bridge of the World's Commerce." By Helen Olsson-Seffer. XXI, pp. 991-1002, 7 ills., Dec., 1910

The **HUB** City (Boston), Cradle of American Liberty. 31 color photos by B. Anthony Stewart and Luis Marden. LXX, pp. 49-72, July, 1936

HUBBARD, BERNARD R.:

The Society Takes Part in Three Geographic Expeditions. LXV, pp. 625-626, May, 1934

A World Inside a Mountain: Aniakchak, the New Volcanic Wonderland of the Alaska Peninsula, Is Explored. By Bernard R. Hubbard. LX, pp. 319-345, 34 ills., map, Sept., 1931

HUBBARD, GARDINER GREENE:

First President of the Society. *See* NGS: President

Gardiner Greene Hubbard (Announcement of the Death of Gardiner Greene Hubbard). (By J. H.). VIII, p. 345, Dec., 1897

Gardiner Greene Hubbard: An Address delivered at the Memorial Services held at the Church of the Covenant, Washington, D. C., December 13, 1897. By Rev. Teunis S. Hamlin. IX, pp. 33-38, ill., Feb., 1898

Gardiner Greene Hubbard: Memorial Meeting, City of Washington, January 21, 1898. IX, pp. 39-70, Feb., 1898

HUBBARD, GARDINER GREENE—*Continued*

Hubbard Glacier, Alaska, named for Gardiner Greene Hubbard. III, pp. 99-100, ill. pl. 9, May, 1891. XXI, ill. pp. 7, 16, Jan., 1910. XLIX, ill. p. 599, June, 1926. LXIX, ill. p. 725, June, 1936. LXXXII, ill. p. 288, Sept., 1942

The Hubbard Memorial Building, National Geographic Society headquarters. XI, pp. 406-407, Oct., 1900. XIII, pp. 174-176, May, 1902. XIV, p. 217, May, 1903. XV, pp. 176-181, 5 ills., Apr., 1904. XVI, p. 342, July, 1905. XX, p. 1008, Nov., 1909. XXV, pp. 457, 459, ill. pp. 454, 458, 464, Apr., 1914

Hubbard Memorial Window, Church of the Covenant, Washington, D. C. XIII, pp. 174-175, May, 1902

Mount Hubbard, Alaska, named for Gardiner Greene Hubbard. XXI, ill. p. 16, Jan., 1910

Portrait. VII, pl. XVIII (front.), May, 1896. IX, pl. 2 (front.), Feb., 1898

Seal of the Society, designed under personal supervision of Gardiner Greene Hubbard. XC, p. 34, col. pl., p. 28, July, 1946

See also NGS: Founders; History; President

Addresses and Articles:

Africa, Its Past and Future. (By Gardiner G. Hubbard). I, pp. 99-124, foldout map, Apr., 1889

Africa Since 1888, with Special Reference to South Africa and Abyssinia. By Hon. Gardiner G. Hubbard. VII, pp. 157-175, ill., foldout map, May, 1896

Discoverers of America. Annual Address by the President, Hon. Gardiner G. Hubbard. V, pp. 1-20, charts, maps, 3 map supplements, Apr. 7, 1893

The Effects of Geographic Environment in the Development of Civilization in Primitive Man. By Hon. Gardiner G. Hubbard. VIII, pp. 161-176, June, 1897

The Evolution of Commerce. Annual Address by the President, Hon. Gardiner G. Hubbard. IV, pp. 1-18, Mar. 26, 1892

Geographic Progress of Civilization. Annual Address by the President, Honorable Gardiner G. Hubbard. VI, pp. 1-22, Feb. 14, 1894

Geographical Research in the United States. By Gardiner G. Hubbard and Marcus Baker. VIII, pp. 285-293, Oct., 1897

Introductory Address. By the President, Mr. Gardiner G. Hubbard. I, pp. 3-10, Oct., 1888

The National Geographic Society: Synopsis of a Course of Lectures on the Effects of Geographic Environment in Developing the Civilization of the World. (By Gardiner G. Hubbard). VIII, pp. 29-32, Jan., 1897

Relations of Air and Water to Temperature and Life. By Honorable Gardiner G. Hubbard. V, pp. 112-124, Jan. 31, 1894

Russia in Europe (Annual Address). By Hon. Gardiner G. Hubbard. VII, pp. 3-26, map supplement, Jan., 1896

South America. Annual Address by the President, Gardiner G. Hubbard. III, pp. 1-29, foldout map, Mar. 28, 1891

HUBBARD, MRS. GARDINER GREENE:

Tribute of respect to the memory of Mrs. Gardiner Greene Hubbard, adopted by the Board of Managers of the National Geographic Society at a special meeting held at Hubbard Memorial Hall, October 23, 1909. XX, p. 1008, Nov., 1909

HUBBARD, GERARD:

Aircraft Insignia, Spirit of Youth. By Gerard Hubbard. LXXXIII, pp. 710-722, 3 ills. in black and white, 337 ills. in color, June, 1943

HUBBARD, JAMES MASCARENE:

Colonial Government in Borneo. By James M. Hubbard. XI, pp. 359-363, Sept., 1900

Problems in China. By James M. Hubbard. XI, pp. 297-308, 3 ills., map supplement, Aug., 1900

Singan—The Present Capital of the Chinese Empire. (By James Mascarene Hubbard). XII, pp. 63-66, ill., Feb., 1901

The Tsangpo. By James Mascarene Hubbard. XII, pp. 32-35, Jan., 1901

HUBBARD, THOMAS H.:

The Discovery of the North Pole (Speech by General Thomas H. Hubbard). XXI, pp. 63-82, Jan., 1910

HUBBARD BAY, Greenland:

Three Weeks in Hubbard Bay, West Greenland. By Robert Stein. IX, pp. 1-11, 6 ills., maps, Jan., 1898

HUBBARD GLACIER, Alaska:

The National Geographic Society's Alaskan Expedition of 1909. By Ralph S. Tarr and Lawrence Martin. XXI, pp. 1-54, 42 ills., 12 maps, Jan., 1910

HUBBARD MEDAL:

Air Conquest: From the Early Days of Giant Kites and Birdlike Gliders, the National Geographic Society Has Aided and Encouraged the Growth of Aviation. LII, pp. 233-242, 13 ills., Aug., 1927

Included: Hubbard Medal recipients; Letter from Dr. Grosvenor to Col. Lindbergh, announcing award of Hubbard Medal to Col. Lindbergh

"Captain Bob" Bartlett awarded the Hubbard Medal. LXXXIX, p. 609, May, 1946

Commander Byrd Receives the Hubbard Gold Medal: The First Explorer to Reach the North Pole by Air Receives Coveted Honor at Brilliant National Geographic Society Reception. L, pp. 377-388, 5 ills., chart, Sept., 1926

The Discovery of the North Pole (Medal Awarded to Robert A. Bartlett and Grove Karl Gilbert). XXI, pp. 63-82, Jan., 1910

Ellsworth Awarded the Hubbard Medal. LXX, p. 36, July, 1936

Honors for Amundsen (Presentation of Hubbard Gold Medal by Charles W. Fairbanks). XIX, pp. 55-76, 13 ills., Jan., 1908

Honors to Peary (Presentation of Hubbard Gold Medal by President Roosevelt). XVIII, pp. 49-60, ill., Jan., 1907

Hubbard Medal winner, Roy Chapman Andrews. LXV, p. 792, June, 1934

HUBBARD MEDAL—*Continued*

Hubbard Medals Awarded to Stratosphere Explorers: Presentation by General Pershing. LXIX, pp. 713-714, ill. p. 712, May, 1936

The National Geographic Society's Notable Year (Medal Awarded to Stefansson). XXXVII, pp. 338-345, ills., Apr., 1920

President Coolidge Bestows Lindbergh Award: The National Geographic Society's Hubbard Medal Is Presented to Aviator Before the Most Notable Gathering in the History of Washington. LIII, pp. 132-140, 4 ills., Jan., 1928

President Truman presents Hubbard Medal to Gen. H. H. Arnold. LXXXIX, ill. p. 141, Feb., 1946

The Race for the South Pole (Presentation of Hubbard Gold Medal to Shackleton by President Taft). XXI, pp. 185-186, Mar., 1910

The Society Awards Hubbard Medal to Anne Morrow Lindbergh. LXV, pp. 791-794, 4 ills., June, 1934

See also NGS: Medals: Hubbard Medal, *for details*

HUBBARD MEMORIAL HALL:

The Home of the National Geographic Society. XVI, p. 342, July, 1905

The Hubbard Memorial Building (Laying of Cornerstone). XIII, pp. 174-176, May, 1902

The National Geographic Society and Its New Building. XXV, pp. 457, 459, ill. pp. 454, 464, Apr., 1914

The New Home of the National Geographic Society. XV, pp. 176-181, 5 ills., Apr., 1904

Opening of Building. XIV, p. 217, May, 1903

Plans for Memorial Building. XI, pp. 406-407, Oct., 1900

See also NGS: Buildings

HUDSON, HENRY:

Henry Hudson, Magnificent Failure: Just 330 Years Ago He and His Mutinous Crew Found Manhattan Covered With "Goodly Oakes" and Fought Indians in New York Harbor. By Frederick G. Vosburgh. LXXV, pp. 461-490, 21 ills., Apr., 1939

HUDSON, HERNDON:

Ali Goes to the Clinic. By Herndon and Mary Hudson. XC, pp. 764-766, ills., Dec., 1946

HUDSON, MARY:

Ali Goes to the Clinic. By Herndon and Mary Hudson. XC, pp. 764-766, ills., Dec., 1946

HUDSON (River), New York:

Atlantic Estuarine Tides. By Mark S. W. Jefferson. IX, pp. 400-409, diagrs., 7 tables, maps, Sept., 1898

Henry Hudson, Magnificent Failure: Just 330 Years Ago He and His Mutinous Crew Found Manhattan Covered With "Goodly Oakes" and Fought Indians in New York Harbor. By Frederick G. Vosburgh. LXXV, pp. 461-490, 21 ills., Apr., 1939

HUDSONIAN BIRDS:

Birds of Timberline and Tundra. By Arthur A. Allen. With 24 color photos by author. XC, pp. 313-339, 8 ills. in black and white, Sept., 1946

HUDSON'S BAY COMPANY:

The Northwest Passes to the Yukon. By Eliza Ruhamah Scidmore. IX, pp. 105-112, 3 ills., Apr., 1898

Oregon: Its History, Geography, and Resources. By John H. Mitchell, U. S. Senator from Oregon. VI, pp. 239-284, Apr. 20, 1895

Overland Routes to the Klondike. By Hamlin Garland. IX, pp. 113-116, ill., Apr., 1898

HUGHES, CHARLES EVANS. *See* NGS: Board of Trustees

HUMAN Emotions Recorded by Photography. By Ralph A. Graves. XXXVIII, pp. 284-300, 16 ills., Oct., 1920

HUMBOLDT CURRENT, Pacific Ocean:

Fighting Giants of the Humboldt (Fish and Squid). By David D. Duncan. LXXIX, pp. 373-400, 28 ills., map, Mar., 1941

HUME, MARTIN:

The Woods and Gardens of Portugal. By Martin Hume. XXI, pp. 883-894, 8 ills., Oct., 1910

HUMMINGBIRDS:

Holidays with Humming Birds. By Margaret L. Bodine. LIII, pp. 731-742, 15 ills., June, 1928

Seeking the Smallest Feathered Creatures: Humming Birds, Peculiar to the New World, Are Found from Canada and Alaska to the Strait of Magellan. Swifts and Goatsuckers, Their Nearest Relatives. By Alexander Wetmore. Paintings by Maj. Allan Brooks. LXII, pp. 65-89, 6 ills. in black and white, 25 ills. in color, July, 1932

HUMMING BIRDS, Swifts and Goatsuckers. 25 ills. in color from paintings by Maj. Allan Brooks. LXII, pp. 75-88, July, 1932

HUNAN—The Closed Province of China. By William Barclay Parsons. XI, pp. 393-400, ill., map, Oct., 1900

HUNGARY:

The Danube, Highway of Races: From the Black Forest to the Black Sea, Europe's Most Important River Has Borne the Traffic of Centuries. By Melville Chater. LVI, pp. 643-697, 54 ills., Dec., 1929

Flags of Austria-Hungary, Bulgaria, Germany, and Turkey. By Byron McCandless and Gilbert Grosvenor. XXXII, pp. 386-388, 38 ills. in color, Oct., 1917

Hungary, a Kingdom Without a King: A Tour from Central Europe's Largest Lake to the Fertile Plains of the Danube and the Tisza. By Elizabeth P. Jacobi. LXI, pp. 691-728, 22 ills. in black and white, 27 ills. in color, map, June, 1932

Hungary: A Land of Shepherd Kings. By C. Townley-Fullam. XXVI, pp. 311-393, 92 ills., map, Oct., 1914

The Land of Contrast: Austria-Hungary. By D. W. and A. S. Iddings. XXIII, pp. 1188-1217, 1284, 33 ills., map, Dec., 1912

Magyar Mirth and Melancholy. By John Patric. LXXIII, pp. 1-55, 33 ills. in black and white, 20 ills. in color, map, Jan., 1938

HUNGARY—*Continued*

A Sunday in Mezőkövesd. By Margery Rae. LXVII, pp. 489-504, 22 ills., Apr., 1935

See also Budapest

HUNTED Birds of Field and Wild. 60 portraits from paintings by Maj. Allan Brooks. LXX, pp. 469-500, Oct., 1936

A **HUNTER** of Plants. By David Fairchild. XXXVI, pp. 57-77, 18 ills., July, 1919

HUNTERS All: A Roll Call of the Hounds. 31 portraits from paintings by Edward Herbert Miner. LXXII, pp. 467-482, Oct., 1937

HUNTING an Observatory: A Successful Search for a Dry Mountain on Which to Establish the National Geographic Society's Solar Radiation Station. By C. G. Abbot. L, pp. 503-518, 13 ills., map, Oct., 1926

HUNTING Bears on Horseback (Wyoming). By Alan D. Wilson. XIX, pp. 350-356, 4 ills., May, 1908

HUNTING Big Game in Portuguese East Africa. (By R. C. F. Maugham). XVIII, pp. 723-730, 7 ills., Nov., 1907

HUNTING Big Game of Other Days: A Boating Expedition in Search of Fossils in Alberta, Canada. By Barnum Brown. XXXV, pp. 407-429, 24 ills., map, May, 1919

HUNTING Birds With a Camera: A Record of Twenty Years of Adventure in Obtaining Photographs of Feathered Wild Life in America. By William L. Finley. XLIV, pp. 161-201, 37 ills., Aug., 1923

HUNTING Castles in Italy. By Melville Chater. LXVIII, pp. 329-366, 25 ills. in black and white, 13 ills. in color, maps, Sept., 1935

HUNTING for Plants in the Canary Islands. By David Fairchild. LVII, pp. 607-652, 37 ills. in black and white, 39 ills. in color, map, May, 1930

HUNTING the Chaulmoogra Tree. By Joseph F. Rock. XLI, pp. 243-276, 39 ills., map, Mar., 1922

HUNTING the Great Brown Bear of Alaska. By George Mixter, 2d. XX, pp. 313-333, 35 ills., Apr., 1909

HUNTING the Grizzly in British Columbia. By Joseph Wendle. XVIII, pp. 612-615, 3 ills., Sept., 1907

HUNTING the Walrus. XXII, pp. 285-290, 10 ills., Mar., 1911

A **HUNTING** Trip to Northern Greenland. By Fullerton Merrill. XI, pp. 118-122, Mar., 1900

HUNTING Useful Plants in the Caribbean. By David Fairchild. LXVI, pp. 705-737, 39 ills., Dec., 1934

HUNTING with a Microphone the Voices of Vanishing Birds. By Arthur A. Allen. LXXI, pp. 697-723, 32 ills., June, 1937

HUNTING with the Lens (Birds). By Howard H. Cleaves. XXVI, pp. 1-35, 47 ills., July, 1914

HUNTINGTON, ELLSWORTH:

The Afghan Borderland. By Ellsworth Huntington. Part I: The Russian Frontier. XX, pp. 788-799, 14 ills., Sept., 1909. Part II: The Persian Frontier. XX, pp. 866-876, 12 ills., Oct., 1909

The Fringe of Verdure Around Asia Minor. By Ellsworth Huntington. XXI, pp. 761-775, 15 ills., Sept., 1910

Life in the Great Desert of Central Asia. By Ellsworth Huntington. XX, pp. 749-760, 12 ills., Aug., 1909

The Lost Wealth of the Kings of Midas. By Ellsworth Huntington. XXI, pp. 831-846, 15 ills., Oct., 1910

Medieval Tales of the Lop Basin in Central Asia. By Ellsworth Huntington. XIX, pp. 289-295, 9 ills., Apr., 1908

The Mountaineers of the Euphrates. By Ellsworth Huntington. XX, pp. 142-156, 13 ills., Feb., 1909

HUNTLEY, Montana:

The Call of the West. By C. J. Blanchard. XX, pp. 403-437, 20 ills., map, May, 1909

HUNZA (State), India:

First Over the Roof of the World by Motor. By Maynard Owen Williams. LXI, pp. 321-363, 45 ills., maps, Mar., 1932

HURDLE Racing in Canoes: A Thrilling and Spectacular Sport Among the Maoris of New Zealand. By Walter Burke. XXXVII, pp. 440-444, 6 ills., May, 1920

HURLEY, EDWARD N.:

The American People Must Become Ship-Minded. By Edward N. Hurley. XXXIV, pp. 201-211, 7 ills., Sept., 1918

HURLEY, FRANK:

Pictorial Jaunt Through Papua. 22 photos by Captain Frank Hurley. LI, pp. 109-124, Jan., 1927

HÜRLIMANN, MARTIN:

Remote Nepal, Land of Mystery. 15 color photos by Martin Hürlimann. LXVII, pp. 329-336, Mar., 1935

HURON (Indian Tribe):

America's First Settlers, the Indians. By Matthew W. Stirling. Paintings by W. Langdon Kihn. LXXII, pp. 535-596, 34 ills. in black and white, 24 ills. in color, Nov., 1937

HURRICANES:

Cape Cod People and Places. By Wanda Burnett. LXXXIX, pp. 737-774, 17 ills. in black and white, 24 ills. in color, map, June, 1946

Charting a World at War. By William H. Nicholas. LXXXVI, pp. 617-640, 23 ills., drawing, Nov., 1944

Forecasting the Weather and Storms. By Professor Willis L. Moore. XVI, pp. 255-306, 5 ills., 20 charts, June, 1905

The Geography of a Hurricane: A Doughnut-shaped Storm Turned Back Time in New England to Candlelight Days, but Revealed Anew Yankee Courage and Ingenuity. By F. Barrows Colton. LXXV, pp. 529-552, 20 ills., map, Apr., 1939

HURRICANES—*Continued*

Hurricanes on the Coast of Texas. By General A. W. Greely. XI, pp. 442-445, Nov., 1900

The Islands of Bermuda: A British Colony with a Unique Record in Popular Government. By William Howard Taft. XLI, pp. 1-26, 15 ills., map, Jan., 1922

The Law of Storms, Considered with Special Reference to the North Atlantic. By Everett Hayden. II, pp. 199-211, ill., 3 diagrs., 3 foldout diagrs., foldout charts, July, 1890

The Lessons of Galveston. By W J McGee. XI, pp. 377-383, Oct., 1900

United States Daily Atmospheric Survey. By Prof. Willis L. Moore. VIII, pp. 299-303, Oct., 1897

The West Indian Hurricane of August 7-14, 1899. By E. B. Garriott. X, pp. 343-348, diagr., Sept., 1899

The West Indian Hurricane of September 1-12, 1900. By E. B. Garriott. XI, pp. 384-392, 4 charts, Oct., 1900

The West Indian Hurricane of September 10-11, 1898. By Prof. E. B. Garriott. X, pp. 17-20, Jan., 1899

HUSSEIN, HAJI MIRZA (Col. Oscar Von Niedermeyer):

Every-Day Life in Afghanistan. By Frederick Simpich and "Haji Mirza Hussein." XXXIX, pp. 85-110, 26 ills., map, Jan., 1921

HUTCHINSON, PAUL:

New China and the Printed Page. By Paul Hutchinson. LI, pp. 687-722, 37 ills., June, 1927

HUTCHISON, BRUCE:

Canada's War Effort: A Canadian Pictures the Swift and Sweeping Transformation from a Peaceful Dominion to a Nation Geared for War. By Bruce Hutchison. LXXX, pp. 553-590, 40 ills., Nov., 1941

HUTCHISON, GEORGE W.:

Memorial tribute to George W. Hutchison. LXXXVII, p. 720, ill., June, 1945

See also NGS: Secretary

HUTCHISON, ISOBEL WYLIE:

Bonnie Scotland, Postwar Style. By Isobel Wylie Hutchison. LXXXIX, pp. 545-601, 14 ills. in black and white, 38 ills. in color, two-page map, May, 1946

Riddle of the Aleutians: A Botanist Explores the Origin of Plants on Ever-misty Islands Now Enshrouded in the Fog of War. By Isobel Wylie Hutchison. LXXXII, pp. 769-792, 24 ills., Dec., 1942

Scotland in Wartime. By Isobel Wylie Hutchison. LXXXIII, pp. 723-743, 19 ills., June, 1943

Wales in Wartime. By Isobel Wylie Hutchison. LXXXV, pp. 751-768, 16 ills., map, June, 1944

A Walking Tour Across Iceland. By Isobel Wylie Hutchison. LIII, pp. 467-497, 36 ills., map, Apr., 1928

HUTS:

Some Human Habitations. By Collier Cobb. XIX, pp. 509-515, 5 ills., July, 1908

HWANG HO (Yellow River), China:

Raft Life on the Hwang Ho. By W. Robert Moore. LXI, pp. 743-752, 14 ills., June, 1932

Shantung—China's Holy Land. By Charles K. Edmunds. XXXVI, pp. 231-252, 21 ills., map, Sept., 1919

Taming "Flood Dragons" Along China's Hwang Ho. By Oliver J. Todd. LXXXI, pp. 205-234, 26 ills., map, Feb., 1942

HWANG YAO-TSO:

China's Wonderland—Yen Tang Shan (Chekiang Province). 8 ills. in color from camera paintings by Herbert Clarence White, Clarence C. Crisler, Deng Bao-ling, Hwang Yao-tso. LXXII, pp. 687-694, Dec., 1937

A Peiping Panorama in Vivid Pigments. 16 ills. in color from camera paintings by H. C. and J. H. White, Deng Bao-ling, Hwang Yao-tso. LXX, pp. 753-784, Dec., 1936

HYANNIS, Massachusetts:

Cape Cod People and Places. By Wanda Burnett. LXXXIX, pp. 737-774, 17 ills. in black and white, 24 ills. in color, map, June, 1946

HYDE, JOHN:

Admiral R. W. Meade, U. S. N. (Obituary). (By J. H.). VIII, p. 142, May, 1897

American Association for the Advancement of Science. (By J. H.). IX, pp. 412-413, Sept., 1898

Commerce of the Philippine Islands. (By J. H.). IX, pp. 301-303, tables, June, 1898

A Critical Period in South African History. (By J. H.). VII, pp. 377-379, Nov., 1896

Electric Street Railways (U. S.). (By J. H.). VIII, p. 284, Oct., 1897

Frederic W. Putnam. (By J. H.). IX, pp. 429-431, ill. (front.), Oct., 1898

Gardiner Greene Hubbard. (By J. H.). VIII, p. 345, Dec., 1897

Geographic Literature. VII, pp. 212-214, June, 1896. VIII, pp. 156-157, May, 1897. IX, p. 192, Apr., 1898; p. 253, May, 1898; p. 514, Dec., 1898

Geographic Notes. VIII, p. 304, Oct., 1897

Growth of Maritime Commerce. (By J. H.). X, pp. 30-31, Jan., 1899

An Interesting Rumor Concerning Andrée. (By J. H.). IX, pp. 102-103, Mar., 1898

Introductory: The Editor. VII, pp. 1-2, Jan., 1896

Mineral Production in the United States. (By J. H.). VIII, pp. 201-202, July-Aug., 1897

Miscellanea. VIII, p. 64, Feb., 1897

The National Geographic Magazine and the U. S. Board on Geographic Names. (By J. H.). X, pp. 517-519, Dec., 1899

The National Geographic Society (Early History of the Society). (By John Hyde). X, pp. 220-223, June, 1899

President Alexander Graham Bell on Japan. (By J. H.). IX, pp. 509-512, Dec., 1898

Puerto Rico, Not Porto Rico. (By J. H.). XI, pp. 37-38, Jan., 1900

HYDE, JOHN—*Continued*
Reception to Captain C. D. Sigsbee, U. S. N. (By J. H.). IX, pp. 251-252, May, 1898
Sir John Evans and Prof. W J McGee. (By J. H.). VIII, pp. 358-359, ills., Dec., 1897
Some Recent Geographic Events. (By J. H.). VIII, pp. 359-362, ill., Dec., 1897
The Toronto Meeting of the British Association for the Advancement of Science. (By J. H.). VIII, pp. 247-251, Sept., 1897
Trade of the United States with Cuba. (By J. H.). IX, pp. 247-249, tables, May, 1898
The United States Department of Agriculture and Its Biological Survey. (By J. H.). VII, pp. 405-406, Dec., 1896
Wellman Polar Expedition. IX, pp. 373-375, Aug., 1898
See also NGS: Board of Managers

HYDE, WALTER WOODBURN:
The Ascent of Mont Blanc. By Walter Woodburn Hyde. XXIV, pp. 861-942, 69 ills., Aug., 1913

HYDROGRAPHIC Work of the U. S. Geological Survey. XI, pp. 324-325, ill., Aug., 1900

HYDROGRAPHY:
A Battle-Ground of Nature: The Atlantic Seaboard. By John Oliver La Gorce. XXXIII, pp. 511-546, 23 ills., 4 maps, June, 1918
Captain Charles D. Sigsbee, U. S. N. (By H. G.). IX, p. 250, ill. (front.), May, 1898
Charting a World at War. By William H. Nicholas. LXXXVI, pp. 617-640, 23 ills., drawing, Nov., 1944
Helping Navigation. XI, pp. 162-163, Apr., 1900
Hidden Perils of the Deep. By G. R. Putnam. XX, pp. 822-837, 19 diagrs., 3 charts, Sept., 1909
Hydrographic Work of the U. S. Geological Survey. XI, pp. 324-325, ill., Aug., 1900
Hydrography in the United States. By Frederick H. Newell. VII, pp. 146-150, Apr., 1896
Marine Hydrographic Surveys of the Coasts of the World. By George W. Littlehales. XVI, pp. 63-67, maps, Feb., 1905
Our Guardians on the Deep. By William Joseph Showalter. XXV, pp. 655-677, 15 ills., chart, June, 1914
Recent Hydrographic Work. (By F. H. N.). VII, pp. 347-348, Oct., 1896
Servicing Arctic Airbases. By Robert A. Bartlett. LXXXIX, pp. 602-616, 3 ills. in black and white, 10 ills. in color, map, May, 1946
Warfare on Our Eastern Coast. By John Oliver La Gorce. XXVIII, pp. 195-230, 29 ills., charts, Sept., 1915
The Work of the U. S. Hydrographic Office. By Commander W. H. H. Southerland. XIV, pp. 61-75, Feb., 1903
See also U. S. Geological Survey; U. S. Hydrographic Office

HYDROPLANES. *See* Seaplanes

HYDROPONICS:
Greens Grow for GI's on Soilless Ascension. By W. Robert Moore. LXXXVIII, pp. 219-230, 12 ills., Aug., 1945

I

I Kept House in a Jungle: The Spell of Primeval Tropics in Venezuela, Riotous With Strange Plants, Animals, and Snakes, Enthralls a Young American Woman. By Anne Rainey Langley. LXXV, pp. 97-132, 37 ills., map, Jan., 1939

I Learn About the Russians. By Eddy Gilmore. LXXXIV, pp. 619-640, 21 ills., Nov., 1943

I Lived on Formosa. By Joseph W. Ballantine. LXXXVII, pp. 1-24, 19 ills., maps, Jan., 1945

IACOVLEFF, ALEXANDRE:
Faces and Fashions of Asia's Changeless Tribes. 26 ills. in color from paintings and drawings by Alexandre Iacovleff. LXIX, pp. 21-36, Jan., 1936

IBERO-AMERICAN EXPOSITION:
Seville, More Spanish Than Spain: The City of the Ibero-American Exposition, Which Opens This Spring, Presents a Tapestry of Many Ages and of Nations Old and New. By Richard Ford. LV, pp. 273-310, 35 ills. in black and white, 2 ills. in color, Mar., 1929

IBISES (Birds):
The Large Wading Birds: Long Legs and Remarkable Beaks, as Well as Size, Form, and Color, Distinguish the Herons, Ibises, and Flamingos. By T. Gilbert Pearson. Paintings by Maj. Allan Brooks. LXII, pp. 441-469, ill. in black and white, 4 ills. in color, Oct., 1932
The Sacred Ibis Cemetery and Jackal Catacombs at Abydos. By Camden M. Cobern. XXIV, pp. 1042-1056, 10 ills., Sept., 1913

IBISES, Herons, and Flamingos. 24 ills. in color from paintings by Maj. Allan Brooks. LXII, pp. 455-468, Oct., 1932

IBN SAUD (King of Saudi Arabia). *See* Al Saud

IBU, Bougainville Island:
Fiji Patrol on Bougainville. By David D. Duncan. LXXXVII, pp. 87-104, 9 ills. in black and white, 11 ills. in color, Jan., 1945

ICE Caves and Frozen Wells. (By W J McGee). XII, pp. 433-434, Dec., 1901

ICE-CLIFFS on the Kowak River (Alaska). By Lieut. J. C. Cantwell. VII, pp. 345-346, Oct., 1896

ICE CLIFFS on White River, Yukon Territory. By C. Willard Hayes and Alfred H. Brooks. XI, pp. 199-201, May, 1900

ICE-CLIFFS on White River, Yukon Territory. By Martin W. Gorman. XI, pp. 113-117, Mar., 1900

ICE PATROL. *See* International Ice Patrol

An **ICE** Wrapped Continent (Antarctica). (By G. H. G.). XVIII, pp. 95-117, 20 ills., map, Feb., 1907

ICEBERGS:
Coast Guard Patrol in Greenland. 9 color photos by Lieut. Thomas S. La Farge. LXXXIII, pp. 565-572, May, 1943

ICEBERGS—*Continued*

Sailing the Seven Seas in the Interest of Science: Adventures Through 157,000 Miles of Storm and Calm, from Arctic to Antarctic and Around the World, in the Non-magnetic Yacht "Carnegie." By J. P. Ault. XLII, pp. 631-690, 47 ills., chart, Dec., 1922

Standing Iceberg Guard in the North Atlantic: International Patrol Safeguards the Lives of Thousands of Travelers and Protects Trans-Atlantic Liners from a "Titanic" Fate. By Lieutenant Commander F. A. Zeusler. L, pp. 1-28, 29 ills., map, July, 1926

ICELAND:

American Soldier in Reykjavík. By Corporal Luther M. Chovan. LXXXVIII, pp. 536-568, 6 ills. in black and white, 34 ills. in color, Nov., 1945

Ancient Iceland, New Pawn of War. 21 photos, map. LXXX, pp. 75-90, July, 1941

Dwellings of the Saga-Time in Iceland, Greenland, and Vineland. By Cornelia Horsford. IX, pp. 73-84, ill., 9 sketches, Mar., 1898

The Island of the Sagas. By Earl Hanson. LIII, pp. 499-511, 22 ills., Apr., 1928

The Land of Fire. By Jon Stefansson. XVIII, pp. 741-744, Nov., 1907

Magnetic Observations in Iceland, Jan Mayen and Spitzbergen in 1892 (Geographic Notes. By Cyrus C. Babb). VI, pp. 223-224, table, Dec. 29, 1894

Proposed Meteorological Station in Iceland. X, p. 228, June, 1899

Sailing the Seven Seas in the Interest of Science: Adventures Through 157,000 Miles of Storm and Calm, from Arctic to Antarctic and Around the World, in the Non-magnetic Yacht "Carnegie." By J. P. Ault. XLII, pp. 631-690, 47 ills., chart, Dec., 1922

A Visit to Lonely Iceland. By Perley H. Noyes. XVIII, pp. 731-741, 12 ills., Nov., 1907

A Walking Tour Across Iceland. By Isobel Wylie Hutchison. LIII, pp. 467-497, 36 ills., map, Apr., 1928

ICELAND Defrosted. 34 color photos by Luther M. Chovan. LXXXVIII, pp. 537-568, Nov., 1945

ID FESTIVAL:

India at Work and Play. 22 color photos by Peter Upton Muir, Maynard Owen Williams, Frances Muir. LXXXIX, pp. 449-464, Apr., 1946

IDAHO:

Among the "Craters of the Moon": An Account of the First Expeditions Through the Remarkable Volcanic Lava Beds of Southern Idaho. By R. W. Limbert. XLV, pp. 303-328, 23 ills., map, Mar., 1924

Bitter Root Forest Reserve. By Richard U. Goode. IX, pp. 387-400, 5 ills., foldout map, Sept., 1898

Down Idaho's River of No Return (Salmon River). By Philip J. Shenon and John C. Reed. LXX, pp. 95-136, 43 ills., maps, July, 1936

The Idaho and Montana Boundary Line. By Richard U. Goode. XI, pp. 23-29, ill., diagr., Jan., 1900

IDAHO—*Continued*

Idaho Made the Desert Bloom. By D. Worth Clark. LXXXV, pp. 641-688, 21 ills. in black and white, 20 ills. in color, map, June, 1944

A Mind's-Eye Map of America. By Franklin K. Lane. XXXVII, pp. 479-518, 25 ills. in black and white, 8 ills. in color, June, 1920

Prosperous Idaho (An Interview with Governor Gooding, of Idaho, Published in the New York *Sun*, December, 1905). XVII, pp. 16-22, Jan., 1906

IDDINGS, A. S.:

The Land of Contrast: Austria-Hungary. By D. W. and A. S. Iddings. XXIII, pp. 1188-1217, 1284, 33 ills., map, Dec., 1912

IDDINGS, D. W.:

The Land of Contrast: Austria-Hungary. By D. W. and A. S. Iddings. XXIII, pp. 1188-1217, 1284, 33 ills., map, Dec., 1912

An **IDEAL** Fuel Manufactured Out of Waste Products: The American Coal Briquetting Industry. By Guy Elliott Mitchell. XXI, pp. 1067-1074, 4 ills., Dec., 1910

IFITAMIN, North-East New Guinea:

New Guinea's Mountain and Swampland Dwellers. By Col. Ray T. Elsmore. LXXXVIII, pp. 671-694, 15 ills. in black and white, 7 ills. in color, map, Dec., 1945

IGDRASIL (Boat):

At Home on the Oceans: Whales and Sharks Make Exciting Neighbors for a Professor's Wife, Turned Able Seaman, On a Three-year Voyage Around the World. By Edith Bauer Strout. LXXVI, pp. 33-86, 54 ills., map, July, 1939

IGUAZU FALLS, Argentina-Brazil:

The Falls of Iguazu. By Marie Robinson Wright. XVII, pp. 456-460, 4 ills., Aug., 1906

The World's Great Waterfalls: Visits to Mighty Niagara, Wonderful Victoria, and Picturesque Iguazu. By Theodore W. Noyes. L, pp. 29-59, 29 ills., July, 1926

ILLINOIS:

Illinois, Crossroads of the Continent. By Junius B. Wood. LIX, pp. 523-594, 51 ills. in black and white, 27 ills. in color, map supplement, May, 1931

See also Chicago

IMAGINATION and Geography. XVIII, p. 825, Dec., 1907

IMBRIE, ROBERT WHITNEY:

Crossing Asia Minor, the Country of the New Turkish Republic. By Major Robert Whitney Imbrie. XLVI, pp. 445-472, 31 ills., map, Oct., 1924

The **IMMEDIATE** Necessity for Military Highways. By A. G. Batchelder. XXXII, pp. 477-499, 22 ills., Nov.-Dec., 1917

IMMIGRATION:

Canadian Immigration. XVII, p. 356, June, 1906

The Character of Our Immigration, Past and Present. By Z. F. McSweeny. XVI, pp. 1-15, chart, Jan., 1905

IMMIGRATION—*Continued*

The Foreign-Born of the United States. XXVI, pp. 265-271, 14 diagrs., Sept., 1914

Immigration and Naturalization. XVI, pp. 51-52, Jan., 1905

Immigration to the Southern States. XVI, pp. 517-519, Nov., 1905

The Movements of Our Population (U. S.). By Henry Gannett. V, pp. 21-44, 7 diagrs., 15 tables, 15 maps, Mar. 20, 1893

New York—The Metropolis of Mankind. By William Joseph Showalter. XXXIV, pp. 1-49, 39 ills., July, 1918

The Origin of French-Canadians. IX, pp. 96-97, Mar., 1898

Our Foreign-Born Citizens. XXXI, pp. 95-130, 36 ills., 8 diagrs., map, Feb., 1917

Our Immigration During 1904. XVI, pp. 15-27, 6 ills., charts, Jan., 1905

Our Immigration in 1905. XVI, pp. 434-435, Sept., 1905

Our Immigration Laws from the Viewpoint of National Eugenics. By Prof. Robert De C. Ward. XXIII, pp. 38-41, Jan., 1912

The Sex, Nativity, and Color of the People of the United States. (By G. H. G.). XII, pp. 381-389, 17 charts, Nov., 1901

Some of Our Immigrants. XVIII, pp. 317-334, 21 ills., May, 1907

South American Immigration. XVII, p. 587, Oct., 1906

IMPERIAL Rome Reborn. By John Patric. LXXI, pp. 269-325, 34 ills. in black and white, 21 ills. in color, Mar., 1937

IMPHAL, India:

Manipur—Where Japan Struck at India. 11 photos, map. LXXXV, pp. 743-750, June, 1944

IMPORTANT Announcement Concerning Essays. VI, pp. 227-228, Dec. 29, 1894

An **IMPORTANT** New Guide for Shipping: Navassa Light, on a Barren Island in the West Indies, is the First Signal for the Panama Canal. By George R. Putnam. XXXIV, pp. 401-406, 3 ills., map, Nov., 1918

An **IMPRESSION** of the Guiana Wilderness. By Angelo Heilprin. XVIII, pp. 373-381, 6 ills., June, 1907

IMPRESSIONS and Scenes of Mozambique. By O. W. Barrett. XXI, pp. 807-830, 31 ills., Oct., 1910

IMPRESSIONS of Asiatic Turkey. By Stephen van Rensselaer Trowbridge. XXVI, pp. 598-609, 6 ills., Dec., 1914

IMPRESSIONS of Palestine. By James Bryce. XXVII, pp. 293-317, 18 ills., map, Mar., 1915

The **IMPROVEMENT** of Geographical Teaching. By Professor William Morris Davis. V, pp. 68-75, July 10, 1893

IMPROVEMENTS in the City of Manila. XIV, pp. 195-197, ill., May, 1903

IMPROVEMENTS in the Republic of Panama. XVI, pp. 441-442, Sept., 1905

IMST, Austria:

Merry Maskers of Imst. 14 photos by Francis C. Fuerst. LXX, pp. 201-208, Aug., 1936

IN Andalusia, Home of Song and Sunshine. 14 color photos by Gervais Courtellemont. LV, pp. 301-308, Mar., 1929

IN Beautiful Delecarlia (Dalecarlia, Sweden). By Lillian Gore. XX, pp. 464-477, 13 ills., May, 1909

IN Civilized French Africa. By James F. J. Archibald. XX, pp. 303-311, 14 ills., Mar., 1909

IN Field and Hive with the Busy Honeybee. 16 ills. in color from paintings by Hashime Murayama. LXVII, pp. 417-424, Apr., 1935

IN French Lorraine: That Part of France Where the First American Soldiers Have Fallen. By Harriet Chalmers Adams. XXXII, pp. 499-518, 16 ills., Nov.-Dec., 1917

IN Honor of the Army and Aviation (National Geographic Society Banquet). XXII, pp. 267-284, 5 ills., Mar., 1911

IN Humboldt's Wake: Narrative of a National Geographic Society Expedition Up the Orinoco and Through the Strange Casiquiare Canal to Amazonian Waters. By Ernest G. Holt. LX, pp. 621-644, 27 ills., map, Nov., 1931

IN Montezuma's Painted Land (Mexico). 22 color photos: 21 by Luis Marden. LXXVIII, pp. 345-368, Sept., 1940

IN Quaint, Curious Croatia. By Felix J. Koch. XIX, pp. 809-832, 37 ills., Dec., 1908

IN Quest of the Golden Eagle: Over Lonely Mountain and Prairie Soars This Rare and Lordly Bird, But Three Youths from the East Catch Up With Him at Last. By John and Frank Craighead. LXXVII, pp. 693-710, 17 ills., May, 1940

IN Smiling Alsace, Where France Has Resumed Sway. 11 color photos by Gervais Courtellemont. LII, pp. 168-176, Aug., 1927

IN the Allagash Country (Maine). By Kenneth Fuller Lee. LV, pp. 505-520, 19 ills., Apr., 1929

IN the Birthplace of Christianity. 34 color photos by Hans Hildenbrand, Maynard Owen Williams, Gervais Courtellemont. L, pp. 697-720, Dec., 1926

IN the Canary Islands, Where Streets are Carpeted with Flowers. 13 color photos by Wilhelm Tobien. LVII, pp. 615-622, May, 1930

IN the Diamond Mountains: Adventures Among the Buddhist Monasteries of Eastern Korea. By the Marquess Curzon of Kedleston. XLVI, pp. 353-374, 21 ills., map, Oct., 1924

IN the Empire of the Aztecs: Mexico City Is Rich in Relics of a People Who Practiced Human Sacrifice, Yet Loved Flowers, Education, and Art. By Frank H. H. Roberts, Jr. Paintings by H. M. Herget. LXXI, pp. 725-750, 14 ills. in black and white, 10 ills. in color, June, 1937

IN the Land of Cruel Desert and Majestic Mountain (Morocco). 12 color photos by Gervais Courtellemont and M. Flandrin. LXI, pp. 307-314, Mar., 1932

IN the Land of Kublai Khan (Mongolia). 16 ills. in color. XLI, pp. 465-472, May, 1922

IN the Land of Moses and Abraham. 25 color photos by W. Robert Moore. LXXIV, pp. 711-742, Dec., 1938

IN the Land of the Montezumas. 16 color photos by Clifton Adams. XLIII, pp. 265-280, Mar., 1923

IN the Land of the Quetzal (Guatemala). 20 color photos by Jacob Gayer. L, pp. 611-626, Nov., 1926

IN the Land of the Vikings. 16 photos by Donald McLeish. XLV, pp. 661-676, June, 1924

IN the Land of the White Eagle (Poland). 12 color photos by Hans Hildenbrand. LXI, pp. 437-444, Apr., 1932

IN the Land of Windmills and Wooden Shoes. 16 photos by Donald McLeish. XLIII, pp. 297-312, Mar., 1923

IN the Pennsylvania Dutch Country. By Elmer C. Stauffer. LXXX, pp. 37-74, 20 ills. in black and white, 22 ills. in color, map (pen and ink drawing), July, 1941

IN the Realm of the Sons of the Sun (Incas). 10 ills. in color from paintings by H. M. Herget. LXXIII, pp. 229-236, Feb., 1938

IN the Realms of the Maharajas. By Lawrence Copley Thaw and Margaret S. Thaw. LXXVIII, pp. 727-780, 14 ills. in black and white, 40 ills. in color, map, Dec., 1940

IN the Savage South Seas. By Beatrice Grimshaw. XIX, pp. 1-19, 21 ills., Jan., 1908

IN the Shadow of Bulgarian Monasteries. 14 color photos by Wilhelm Tobien and Georg Paskoff. LXII, pp. 203-210, Aug., 1932

IN the Wake of Columbus. By Frederick A. Ober. V, pp. 187-196, Jan. 31, 1894

IN the Wonderland of Peru. By Hiram Bingham. XXIV, pp. 387-573, 250 ills., 3 diagrs., map, panorama, Apr., 1913

IN Valais (Switzerland). By Louise Murray. XXI, pp. 249-256, 6 ills., Mar., 1910

INCAS (Indians):

Air Adventures in Peru: Cruising Among Andean Peaks, Pilots and Cameramen Discover Wondrous Works of an Ancient People. By Robert Shippee. LXIII, pp. 81-120, 40 ills., map, Jan., 1933

Along the Old Inca Highway. By Harriet Chalmers Adams. XIX, pp. 231-250, 21 ills., Apr., 1908

Cuzco, America's Ancient Mecca. By Harriet Chalmers Adams. XIX, pp. 669-689, 19 ills., Oct., 1908

Explorations in Peru. XXIII, pp. 417-422, 7 ills., map, Apr., 1912

INCAS (Indians)—*Continued*

Further Explorations in the Land of the Incas: The Peruvian Expedition of 1915 of the National Geographic Society and Yale University. By Hiram Bingham. XXIX, pp. 431-473, 29 ills., maps, panorama, May, 1916
The Greatest Achievement of Ancient Man in America (Fortress of Sacsahuaman, Peru). Panorama from photo by author

The Heart of Aymará Land: A Visit to Tiahuanacu, Perhaps the Oldest City of the New World, Lost Beneath the Drifting Sand of Centuries in the Bolivian Highlands. By Stewart E. McMillin. LI, pp. 213-256, 23 ills. in black and white, 18 ills. in color, map, Feb., 1927

Honors to Amundsen and Peary (Banquet). XXIV, pp. 113-130, 5 ills., Jan., 1913
Included: Address by Hiram Bingham on the Peruvian Expedition

In the Wonderland of Peru. By Hiram Bingham. XXIV, pp. 387-573, 250 ills., 3 diagrs., map, panorama, Apr., 1913
The Ruins of an Ancient Inca Capital, Machu Picchu. Panorama from photo by author

The Incas: Empire Builders of the Andes. By Philip Ainsworth Means. Paintings by H. M. Herget. LXXIII, pp. 225-264, 26 ills. in black and white, 10 ills. in color, Feb., 1938

The Pith of Peru: A Journey from Talara to Machu Picchu, with Memorable Stopovers. By Henry Albert Phillips. LXXXII, pp. 167-196, 6 ills. in black and white, 20 ills. in color, map, Aug., 1942

Some Wonderful Sights in the Andean Highlands: The Oldest City in America. Sailing on the Lake of the Clouds: The Yosemite of Peru. By Harriet Chalmers Adams. XIX, pp. 579-618, 19 ills., map, Sept., 1908

South America. Annual Address by the President, Gardiner G. Hubbard (Dec. 19, 1890). III, pp. 1-29, foldout map, Mar. 28, 1891

Staircase Farms of the Ancients: Astounding Farming Skill of Ancient Peruvians, Who Were Among the Most Industrious and Highly Organized People in History. By O. F. Cook. XXIX, pp. 474-534, 48 ills., May, 1916

The Story of Machu Picchu: The Peruvian Expeditions of the National Geographic Society and Yale University. By Hiram Bingham. XXVII, pp. 172-217, 60 ills., Feb., 1915

***INDEPENDENCE*-class** Light Carrier. *See Princeton*

INDIA:

Across Tibet from India to China. By Lt. Col. Ilia Tolstoy, AUS. XC, pp. 169-222, 53 ills., map, Aug., 1946

The Aërial Conquest of Everest: Flying Over the World's Highest Mountain Realizes the Objective of Many Heroic Explorers. By Lieut. Col. L. V. S. Blacker. LXIV, pp. 127-162, 35 ills., map, Aug., 1933

Among the Great Himalayan Glaciers. XIII, pp. 405-406, Nov., 1902

The British Commonwealth of Nations: "Organized Freedom" Around the World. By Eric Underwood. LXXXIII, pp. 485-524, 31 ills., Apr., 1943

INDIA—*Continued*

Fearful Famines of the Past: History Will Repeat Itself Unless the American People Conserve Their Resources. By Ralph A. Graves. XXXII, pp. 69-90, 11 ills., July, 1917

First Over the Roof of the World by Motor: The Trans-Asiatic Expedition Sets New Records for Wheeled Transport in Scaling Passes of the Himalayas. By Maynard Owen Williams. LXI, pp. 321-363, 45 ills., maps, Mar., 1932

Flying the World: In a Homemade Airplane the Author and Her Husband Enjoy 16,000 Miles of Adventurous Flight Across Europe, Asia, and America. By Gladys M. Day. LXI, pp. 655-690, 41 ills., map, June, 1932

Geographic Progress of Civilization. Annual Address by the President, Honorable Gardiner G. Hubbard. VI, pp. 1-22, Feb. 14, 1894

In the Realms of the Maharajas. By Lawrence Copley Thaw and Margaret S. Thaw. LXXVIII, pp. 727-780, 14 ills. in black and white, 40 ills. in color, map, Dec., 1940

India—Yesterday, Today, and Tomorrow. By Lord Halifax. LXXXIV, pp. 385-408, 20 ills., two-page map, Oct., 1943

India and Ceylon. 8 color photos by Helen Messinger Murdoch. XXXIX, pp. 281-288, Mar., 1921

India Mosaic. By Peter Muir and Frances Muir. LXXXIX, pp. 443-470, 5 ills. in black and white, 22 ills. in color, map, Apr., 1946

The Indian Census of 1911. By John J. Banninga. XXII, pp. 633-638, 4 ills., July, 1911

India's Treasures Helped the Allies. By John Fischer. LXXXIX, pp. 501-522, 18 ills., Apr., 1946

Life with an Indian Prince: As Guests of a Maharaja's Brother, Two Young American Naturalists Study Age-old Methods of Hunting with Trained Falcons and Cheetahs and Savor the Pomp of Royal India. By John and Frank Craighead. LXXXI, pp. 235-272, 38 ills., map, Feb., 1942

Manipur—Where Japan Struck at India. 11 photos, map. LXXXV, pp. 743-750, June, 1944

The Marble Dams of Rajputana. By Eleanor Maddock. XL, pp. 469-499, 13 ills. in black and white, 16 ills. in color, Nov., 1921

The Marriage of the Gods (Religious Festival at Madura, India). By John J. Banninga. XXIV, pp. 1314-1330, 16 ills., Dec., 1913

Nature's Most Amazing Mammal: Elephants, Unique Among Animals, Have Many Human Qualities When Wild That Make Them Foremost Citizens of Zoo and Circus. By Edmund Heller. LXV, pp. 729-759, 37 ills., June, 1934

Old Mines and Mills in India. XX, pp. 489-490, ills., May, 1909

On the World's Highest Plateaus: Through an Asiatic No Man's Land to the Desert of Ancient Cathay. By Hellmut de Terra. LIX, pp. 319-367, 39 ills. in black and white, 32 ills. in color, map, Mar., 1931

The Oriental Pageantry of Northern India. 30 color photos by Franklin Price Knott. LVI, pp. 429-460, Oct., 1929

The Parsees and the Towers of Silence at Bombay, India. By William Thomas Fee. XVI, pp. 529-554, 16 ills., Dec., 1905

INDIA—*Continued*

The Pathfinder of the East: Setting Sail to Find "Christians and Spices," Vasco da Gama Met Amazing Adventures, Founded an Empire, and Changed the History of Western Europe. By J. R. Hildebrand. LII, pp. 503-550, 43 ills., map, pictorial supplement, Nov., 1927
  Vasco da Gama at the Court of Zamorin of Calicut. Reproduction in color of the painting by José Velloso Salgado, Sociedade de Geographia de Lisboa (supplement)

A Pilgrimage to Amernath, Himalayan Shrine of the Hindu Faith. By Louise Ahl Jessop. XL, pp. 513-542, 29 ills., Nov., 1921

Race Prejudice in the Far East. By Melville E. Stone. XXI, pp. 973-985, 6 ills., Dec., 1910

Religious Penances and Punishments Self-Inflicted by the Holy Men of India. By W. M. Zumbro. XXIV, pp. 1257-1314, 69 ills., Dec., 1913

The Society's New Map of India and Burma. Text with map supplement. LXXXIX, p. 544, Apr., 1946

South of Khyber Pass. By Maynard Owen Williams. LXXXIX, pp. 471-500, 31 ills., map supplement, Apr., 1946

Stilwell Road—Land Route to China. By Nelson Grant Tayman. LXXXVII, pp. 681-698, 18 ills., June, 1945

Streets and Palaces of Colorful India. 34 color photos by Gervais Courtellemont. L, pp. 60-85, July, 1926

The Temples of India. 54 photos by W. M. Zumbro. XX, pp. 922-971, Nov., 1909

Through the Heart of Hindustan: A Teeming Highway Extending for Fifteen Hundred Miles, from the Khyber Pass to Calcutta. By Maynard Owen Williams. XL, pp. 433-467, 29 ills., Nov., 1921

Tiger-Hunting in India. By Brigadier General William Mitchell. XLVI, pp. 545-598, 46 ills., map, Nov., 1924

The United States and the British Empire. By Leonard David Gammans. LXXXVII, pp. 562-564, May, 1945

Yank Meets Native. By Wanda Burnett. LXXXVIII, pp. 105-128, 24 ills., July, 1945

See also Benares; Delhi; Kashmir; Madura; New Delhi

INDIA at Work and Play. 22 color photos by Peter Upton Muir, Maynard Owen Williams, Frances Muir. LXXXIX, pp. 449-464, Apr., 1946

The **INDIAN** Census of 1911. By John J. Banninga. XXII, pp. 633-638, 4 ills., July, 1911

INDIAN Haven—Off the San Blas Coast (Mulatas Archipelago). 12 color photos by Lieutenant Dayton Seiler. LXXIX, pp. 209-216, Feb., 1941

INDIAN OCEAN:

Fishing for Pearls in the Indian Ocean. By Bella Sidney Woolf. XLIX, pp. 161-183, 24 ills., Feb., 1926

Indian Ocean Map Spans Far East News Centers. Text with map supplement. LXXIX, pp. 345-346, ill., Mar., 1941

INDIAN TERRITORY, U. S.:

The Five Civilized Tribes and the Survey of Indian Territory. By C. H. Fitch. IX, pp. 481-491, 4 ills., map, Dec., 1898

Survey and Subdivision of Indian Territory. By Henry Gannett. VII, pp. 112-115, ill., map, Mar., 1896

INDIAN Tribes of Pueblo Land. By Matthew W. Stirling. Paintings by W. Langdon Kihn. LXXVIII, pp. 549-596, 16 ills. in black and white, 25 ills. in color, Nov., 1940

The **INDIAN** Tribes of Southern Patagonia, Tierra del Fuego, and the Adjoining Islands. By J. B. Hatcher. XII, pp. 12-22, 4 ills., Jan., 1901

The **INDIAN** Village of Baum (Ohio). (By H. C. Brown). XII, pp. 272-274, July, 1901

INDIANA:

Indiana Journey. By Frederick Simpich. LXX, pp. 267-320, 32 ills. in black and white, 27 ills. in color, two-page map, Sept., 1936

Indiana's Unrivaled Sand-Dunes—A National Park Opportunity. By Orpheus Moyer Schantz. XXXV, pp. 430-441, 18 ills., May, 1919

INDIANS, East. *See* East Indians

INDIANS OF CENTRAL AMERICA:

Arch-Isolationists, the San Blas Indians: Coconuts Serve as Cash on Islands Off the Panama Coast Where Tribesmen Cling to Their Ancient Ways and Discourage Visitors. By Corinne B. Feeney. LXXIX, pp. 193-220, 15 ills. in black and white, 12 ills. in color, map, Feb., 1941

Costa Rica. By Señor Ricardo Villafranca. VIII, pp. 143-151, ill., May, 1897
Included: Talamanca Indians

Guatemala Interlude: In the Land of the Quetzal a Modern Capital Contrasts With Primitive Indian Villages and the "Pompeii of America." By E. John Long. LXX, pp. 429-460, 22 ills. in black and white, 13 ills. in color, map, Oct., 1936
Included: Cakchiquels, Quichés, Santo Tomás, Sololás, Todos Santos, and Tzutuhiles

The Land That Links the Americas (Panama). 22 color photos by Luis Marden. LXXX, pp. 601-624, Nov., 1941
Included: Choco and San Blas Indians

Little-Known Parts of Panama. By Henry Pittier. XXIII, pp. 627-662, 35 ills., map, July, 1912
Included: Chocoes, Guaymies, and San Blas Indians

To Market in Guatemala. By Luis Marden. With 19 color photos by Giles Greville Healey and Charles S. Pineo. LXXXVIII, pp. 87-104, July, 1945

See also Mayas; Quichés

INDIANS OF MEXICO:

Adventuring Down the West Coast of Mexico. By Herbert Corey. XLII, pp. 449-503, 44 ills., map, Nov., 1922
Included: Aztec and Seri Indians

Discovering the New World's Oldest Dated Work of Man: A Maya Monument Inscribed 291 B. C. is Unearthed Near a Huge Stone Head by a Geographic-Smithsonian Expedition in Mexico. By Matthew W. Stirling. LXXVI, pp. 183-218, 40 ills., map, Aug., 1939

INDIANS OF MEXICO—*Continued*

Expedition Unearths Buried Masterpieces of Carved Jade (Cerro de las Mesas). By Matthew W. Stirling. LXXX, pp. 277-302, 14 ills. in black and white, 20 ills. in color, map, Sept., 1941

Finding Jewels of Jade in a Mexican Swamp. By Matthew W. and Marion Stirling. LXXXII, pp. 635-661, 15 ills. in black and white, 12 ills. in color, map, Nov., 1942
Included: Zoque Indians, Zotzil Indians; and the Maya ruins at Palenque

Great Stone Faces of the Mexican Jungle: Five Colossal Heads and Numerous Other Monuments of Vanished Americans Are Excavated by the Latest National Geographic-Smithsonian Expedition. By Matthew W. Stirling. LXXVIII, pp. 309-334, 26 ills., map, Sept., 1940

The Isthmus of Tehuantepec: "The Bridge of the World's Commerce." By Helen Olsson-Seffer. XXI, pp. 991-1002, 7 ills., Dec., 1910
Included: Agualulcos, Aztecs, Huaves, Mijes, Zapotecs, Zoques

La Venta's Green Stone Tigers. By Matthew W. Stirling. LXXXIV, pp. 321-332, 4 ills. in black and white, 6 ills. in color, map, Sept., 1943

Paricutín, the Cornfield That Grew a Volcano. By James A. Green. LXXXV, pp. 129-164, 16 ills. in black and white, 21 ills. in color, map, Feb., 1944
Included: Tarascan Indians

See also Aztecs; Mayas; Mixtec Indians; Otomi Indians; Seri Indians; Tarascan Indians; Toltecs; Yaqui Indians; Zapotec Indians

INDIANS OF NORTH AMERICA:

The Acorn, a Possibly Neglected Source of Food. By C. Hart Merriam. XXXIV, pp. 129-137, 8 ills., Aug., 1918
Included: Indians of California

All Around the Bay of Passamaquoddy. By Albert S. Gatschet. VIII, pp. 16-24, Jan., 1897
Included: Abnâki Indian group; a List of Indian Geographic Names Occurring Around Passamaquoddy Bay, Maine, with Their Derivations, pp. 21-24

Along Our Side of the Mexican Border. By Frederick Simpich. XXXVIII, pp. 61-80, 9 ills., map, July, 1920
Included: Apache, Coahuila, Cocopah, Pima, Yuma

America's First Settlers, the Indians. By Matthew W. Stirling. Paintings by W. Langdon Kihn. LXXII, pp. 535-596, 34 ills. in black and white, 24 ills. in color, Nov., 1937
Included: Algonquian, Assiniboin, Cayuga, Chippewa, Huron, Iroquois, Malecite, Menominee, Mohawk, Mohican, Natchez, Oneida, Onondaga, Passamaquoddy, Penobscot, Pequot, Sauk and Fox, Seneca, Shawnee, Shoshoni, Tuscarora, Wampanoag

The Enchanted Mesa. By F. W. Hodge. VIII, pp. 273-284, 6 ills., map, Oct., 1897

Everyday Life in Pueblo Bonito: As Disclosed by the National Geographic Society's Archeologic Explorations in the Chaco Canyon National Monument, New Mexico. By Neil M. Judd. XLVIII, pp. 227-262, 37 ills., map, Sept., 1925

Explorations by the Bureau of American Ethnology in 1895. By W J McGee. VII, pp. 77-80, Feb., 1896

Included: Kiowa Indians, Papago Indians, Seri Indians, and the Pueblo Indians of New Mexico

Exploring in the Canyon of Death: Remains of a People Who Dwelt in Our Southwest at Least 4,000 Years Ago Are Revealed. By Earl H. Morris. XLVIII, pp. 263-300, 24 ills. in black and white, 22 ills. in color, Sept., 1925

The Five Civilized Tribes and the Survey of Indian Territory. By C. H. Fitch. IX, pp. 481-491, 4 ills., map, Dec., 1898
Included: Cherokee, Chickasaw, Choctaw, Creek, Seminole

The Forests and Deserts of Arizona. By Bernhard E. Fernow. VIII, pp. 203-226, 5 ills., July-Aug., 1897
Included: Hopi Indians

From the War-Path to the Plow. By Franklin K. Lane. XXVII, pp. 73-87, 12 ills., Jan., 1915
Included: Apache, Blackfeet, Cherokee, Crow, Osage

Game and Fur-Bearing Animals and Their Influence on the Indians of the Northwest. By Townsend W. Thorndike. XV, p. 431, Oct., 1904

Geographic Work by the Bureau of American Ethnology. (By W J McGee). IX, pp. 98-100, Mar., 1898

Grass Makes Wyoming Fat. By Frederick Simpich. LXXXVIII, pp. 153-188, 13 ills. in black and white, 19 ills. in color, two-page map, Aug., 1945
Included: Shoshoni

Indian Tribes of Pueblo Land. By Matthew W. Stirling. Paintings by W. Langdon Kihn. LXXVIII, pp. 549-596, 16 ills. in black and white, 25 ills. in color, Nov., 1940
Included: Acoma, Apache, Basket Makers, Cliff Dwellers, Cocopa, Comanche, Havasupai, Hohokam, Hopi, Kiowa, Laguna, Mojave, Navajo, Paiute, Papago, Pima, San Ildefonso, Tewa, Ute, Yaqui, Yavapai, Yuma, Zuni

The Indian Village of Baum (Ohio). (By H. C. Brown). XII, pp. 272-274, July, 1901

Indians of Our North Pacific Coast. By Matthew W. Stirling. Paintings by W. Langdon Kihn. LXXXVII, pp. 25-52, 3 ills. in black and white, 16 ills. in color, Jan., 1945
Included: Bellacoola, Haida, Kwakiutl, Niska, Nootka, Pomo, Tlingit, Tsimshian

Indians of Our Western Plains. By Matthew W. Stirling. Paintings by W. Langdon Kihn. LXXXVI, pp. 73-108, 14 ills. in black and white, 16 ills. in color, July, 1944
Included: Arapaho, Arikara, Bannock, Blackfeet, Caddo, Cheyenne, Chippewa, Comanche, Crow, Dakota, Hidatsa, Iowa, Kansas, Kiowa, Mandan, Missouri, Osage, Pawnee, Quapaw, Shoshoni, Sioux, Ute, Waco, Wichita

Indians of the Southeastern United States. By Matthew W. Stirling. Paintings by W. Langdon Kihn. LXXXIX, pp. 53-74, 8 ills. in black and white, 8 ills. in color, Jan., 1946
Included: Attacapan, Biloxi, Caddoan, Calusa, Catawba, Cheraw, Cherokee, Chickasaw, Chitmachan, Choctaw, Creek, Hitchiti, Muskhogean, Natchez, Pamunkey, Powhatan Confederacy, Seminole, Shawnee, Taensa, Timucuan, Tunican, Yuchi; Burial Mound and Temple Mound Periods

INDIANS OF NORTH AMERICA—*Continued*

The Land of the Best. By Gilbert H. Grosvenor. XXIX, pp. 327-430, 71 ills. in black and white, 33 ills. in color, pictorial supplement, Apr., 1916
Included: Acoma, Blackfeet, Hopi, Pueblo

Mesa Verde. By F. H. Newell. IX, pp. 431-434, Oct., 1898

New Mexico Melodrama. By Frederick Simpich. LXXIII, pp. 529-569, 19 ills. in black and white, 25 ills. in color, two-page map, May, 1938
Included: Isleta, Navajo, San Ildefonso, Santa Clara, Taos

The North American Indian. XIX, pp. 448-454, 5 ills., June, 1908
Included: Apache, Havasupai, Maricopa, Mojave, Navajo, Papago, Pima, Walapai, Yuma

North American Indians. XVIII, pp. 469-484, 14 ills., July, 1907
Included: Acoma, Apache, Crow, Hopi, Mohave, Navajo, San Ildefonso, Zuni

The Northwest Passes to the Yukon. By Eliza Ruhamah Scidmore. IX, pp. 105-112, 3 ills., Apr., 1898
Included: Chilkats, Chilkoots, Pellys, Tinnehs

The Origin of American State Names. By Frederick W. Lawrence. XXXVIII, pp. 105-143, 34 ills., Aug., 1920

Papagueria. By W J McGee. IX, pp. 345-371, 9 ills., Aug., 1898

Photographing the Marvels of the West in Colors. By Fred Payne Clatworthy. LIII, pp. 694-719, 4 ills. in color, June, 1928
Included: Hopis and Sioux; and text references to the Arapahoes, Cheyennes, and Utes

A Relic of the Lewis and Clarke Expedition. (By Cyrus C. Babb). IX, pp. 100-101, ill., Mar., 1898

Scenes from America's Southwest. 14 photos by Frederick I. Monsen and Charles Martin. XXXIX, pp. 651-664, June, 1921
Included: Hopi and Laguna Indians; and the following ruins and localities: Canyon De Chelly; Canyon Del Muerto; Mesa Verde; Painted Desert; Pueblo Bonito; Tyuonyi; Walpi

The Secret of the Southwest Solved by Talkative Tree Rings: Horizons of American History Are Carried Back to A. D. 700 and a Calendar for 1,200 Years Established by National Geographic Society Expeditions. By Andrew Ellicott Douglass. LVI, pp. 737-770, 33 ills., map, Dec., 1929

Survey and Subdivision of Indian Territory. By Henry Gannett. VII, pp. 112-115, ill., map, Mar., 1896
Included: Cherokees, Chickasaws, Choctaws, Creeks, Seminoles

The Sushitna River, Alaska. By W. A. Dickey. VIII, pp. 322-327, map, Nov., 1897
Included: Copper River, or Midnooskie, Indians, Kuskokwim Indians, Tanana Indians

Taming the Outlaw Missouri River. By Frederick Simpich. LXXXVIII, pp. 569-598, 25 ills., two-page map, Nov., 1945

The Travels of George Washington: Dramatic Episodes in His Career as the First Geographer of the United States. By William Joseph Showalter. LXI, pp. 1-63, 50 ills., 4 maps, map supplement, Jan., 1932

INDIANS OF NORTH AMERICA—*Continued*
Included: Washington's dealings with the Half-King
Weather Making, Ancient and Modern. By Mark W. Harrington. VI, pp. 35-62, Apr. 25, 1894
See also Crow Indians; Havasupai Indians; Hopi Indians; Klamath Indians; Navajos; Ojibways; Papago Indians; Seminole Indians; Seri Indians; Sioux Indians; Tahltan Indians; Tsimshian

INDIANS OF SOUTH AMERICA:
Bolivia—Tin Roof of the Andes. By Henry Albert Phillips. LXXXIII, pp. 309-332, 5 ills. in black and white, 20 ills. in color, Mar., 1943
Camels of the Clouds (Lamoids). By W. H. Hodge. LXXXIX, pp. 641-656, 15 ills., map, May, 1946
Included: Aymará and Quichua Indians
Chile's Land of Fire and Water: Smoking Volcanoes and Ice-hooded Peaks Stand Sentinel Over Limpid Lakes in the Far Southern Andes. By W. Robert Moore. LXXX, pp. 91-110, 9 ills. in black and white, 10 ills. in color, map, July, 1941
Included: Araucanian Indians
Further Explorations in the Land of the Incas: The Peruvian Expedition of 1915 of the National Geographic Society and Yale University. By Hiram Bingham. XXIX, pp. 431-473, 29 ills., maps, panorama, May, 1916
Included: Incas and the present-day Indians of the Lowlands and Highlands
High Lights in the Peruvian and Bolivian Andes. 12 color photos by W. Robert Moore. LI, pp. 218-235, Feb., 1927
In the Wonderland of Peru. By Hiram Bingham. XXIV, pp. 387-573, 250 ills., 3 diagrs., map, Apr., 1913
Included: Highland Indians of Southern Peru
The Indian Tribes of Southern Patagonia, Tierra del Fuego, and the Adjoining Islands. By J. B. Hatcher. XII, pp. 12-22, 4 ills., Jan., 1901
Included: Alaculoffs (Alikulufs), Onas, Tehuelches, Yahgans
Inside Cape Horn. By Amos Burg. LXXII, pp. 743-783, 29 ills. in black and white, 10 ills. in color, two-page map, Dec., 1937
Included: Alikulufs, Onas, Yahgans
A Journey in Ecuador. By Mark B. Kerr, C. E. VII, pp. 238-245, ills., map, July, 1896
Included: Alikulufs, Onas, Yahgans
A Longitudinal Journey Through Chile. By Harriet Chalmers Adams. XLII, pp. 219-273, 60 ills., map, Sept., 1922
Included: Alacaluf (Alikuluf) Indians, Araucanian Indians, Ona Indians, and Yahgan Indians
Patagonia. By J. B. Hatcher. VIII, pp. 305-319, 6 ills., map, Nov., 1897
Included: Channel Indians, Tehuelches
The Pith of Peru: A Journey from Talara to Machu Picchu, with Memorable Stopovers. By Henry Albert Phillips. LXXXII, pp. 167-196, 6 ills. in black and white, 20 ills. in color, map, Aug., 1942
Quinine Hunters in Ecuador. By Froelich Rainey. LXXXIX, pp. 341-363, 21 ills., map, Mar., 1946

INDIANS OF SOUTH AMERICA—*Continued*
South America. Annual Address by the President, Gardiner G. Hubbard. III, pp. 1-29, foldout map, Mar. 28, 1891
Stone Idols of the Andes Reveal a Vanished People: Remarkable Relics of One of the Oldest Aboriginal Cultures of America are Unearthed in Colombia's San Agustín Region. By Hermann von Walde-Waldegg. LXXVII, pp. 627-647, 22 ills., map, May, 1940
Where Snow Peaks Temper the Tropics (Ecuador). 9 color photos by W. Robert Moore. LXXX, pp. 727-734, Dec., 1941
A Winter Voyage Through the Straits of Magellan. By the late Admiral R. W. Meade, U. S. N. VIII, pp. 134-136, ill., map, May, 1897
Included: Fuegians, Patagonians
See also Arecuna Indians; Aymará Indians; Chunchos; Incas; Jivaro Indians; Quichua Indians

INDIA'S Treasures Helped the Allies. By John Fischer. LXXXIX, pp. 501-522, 18 ills., Apr., 1946

The **INDISPENSABLE** Sheep. LIII, pp. 512-528, 20 ills., Apr., 1928

INDO-CHINA. *See* French Indo-China

INDONESIA. *See* Netherlands East Indies

The **INDUSTRIAL** Titan of America: Pennsylvania, Once the Keystone of the Original Thirteen, Now the Keystone of Forty-eight Sovereign States. By John Oliver La Gorce. XXXV, pp. 367-406, 33 ills., map, May, 1919

The **INDUSTRIAL** Training of the German People. XVI, pp. 111-114, ills., Mar., 1905

INDUSTRIES:
The Automobile Industry: An American Art That Has Revolutionized Methods in Manufacturing and Transformed Transportation. By William Joseph Showalter. XLIV, pp. 337-414, 76 ills., Oct., 1923
Blueberry Culture: The Wild Blueberry Tamed: The New Industry of the Pine Barrens of New Jersey. By Frederick V. Coville. XXIX, pp. 535-546, 10 ills., June, 1916
Cacao: São Tomé, the Chocolate Island. By William Leon Smyser. LXXXIX, pp. 657-680, 23 ills., map, May, 1946
Cinchona: Quinine Hunters in Ecuador. By Froelich Rainey. LXXXIX, pp. 341-363, 21 ills., map, Mar., 1946
Coal—Ally of American Industry. By William Joseph Showalter. XXXIV, pp. 407-434, 23 ills., Nov., 1918
Coal: An Ideal Fuel Manufactured Out of Waste Products: The American Coal Briquetting Industry. By Guy Elliott Mitchell. XXI, pp. 1066-1074, 4 ills., Dec., 1910
Coal: Prodigious Worker for Man. By Albert W. Atwood. LXXXV, pp. 569-592, 19 ills., drawing, May, 1944
Coffee Is King in El Salvador. By Luis Marden. LXXXVI, pp. 575-616, 22 ills. in black and white, 27 ills. in color, map, Nov., 1944
Cork. XIX, pp. 690-693, 3 ills., Oct., 1908
Cotton: Foremost Fiber of the World. By J. R. Hildebrand. LXXIX, pp. 137-192, 31 ills. in black and white, 34 ills. in color, Feb., 1941

Floriculture: The Garden Isles of Scilly: Geologists May Throw Stones at Legend of Lost Lyonnesse, but Natives Grow Flowers in Glass Houses for London. By W. Robert Moore. LXXIV, pp. 755-774, 9 ills. in black and white, 13 ills. in color, map, Dec., 1938

Fruits and Vegetables: The Texas Delta of an American Nile: Orchards and Gardens Replace Thorny Jungle in the Southmost Tip of the Lone Star State. By McFall Kerbey. LXXV, pp. 51-96, 27 ills. in black and white, 24 ills. in color, map, Jan., 1939

Glass "Goes to Town." By J. R. Hildebrand. LXXXIII, pp. 1-48, 28 ills. in black and white, 22 ills. in color, Jan., 1943

The Grape-Growing Industry in the United States. XIV, pp. 445-451, 5 ills., Dec., 1903

The Hairnet Industry in North China. By H. W. Robinson. XLIV, pp. 327-336, 10 ills., Sept., 1923

Lobster Fishing: The Maine American and the American Lobster. By John D. Lucas. LXXXIX, pp. 523-543, 19 ills., Apr., 1946

Lumber: The Influence of Forestry upon the Lumber Industry of the United States. By Overton W. Price. XIV, pp. 381-386, ills., Oct., 1903

Lumber: The Lumber Business of the Government. XVII, pp. 531-533, Sept., 1906

Lumber: Lumbering in Manchuria. (By Henry B. Miller). XV, pp. 131-132, ills., Mar., 1904

Lumber: The Redwood Forest of the Pacific Coast. By Henry Gannett. X, pp. 145-159, 6 ills., map, May, 1899

Lumber: Working Teak in the Burma Forests: The Sagacious Elephant Is Man's Ablest Ally in the Logging Industry of the Far East. By A. W. Smith. LVIII, pp. 239-256, 5 ills. in black and white, 15 ills. in color, Aug., 1930

Metal Sinews of Strength: This Is a War of Many Metals, for We Live in an Age of Alloys. By Frederick G. Vosburgh. LXXXI, pp. 457-491, 35 ills., Apr., 1942

Nitrate: A Longitudinal Journey Through Chile. By Harriet Chalmers Adams. XLII, pp. 219-273, 60 ills., map, Sept., 1922

Paper: Lessons from Japan. XV, pp. 221-225, 3 ills., May, 1904

Paper from Cotton Stalks. XVII, p. 425, July, 1906

Pearl: Fishing for Pearls in the Indian Ocean. By Bella Sidney Woolf. XLIX, pp. 161-183, 24 ills., Feb., 1926

Petroleum: Curaçao and Aruba on Guard. By W. Robert Moore. LXXXIII, pp. 169-192, 12 ills. in black and white, 10 ills. in color, 4 maps, Feb., 1943

Petroleum: So Oklahoma Grew Up. By Frederick Simpich. LXXIX, pp. 269-314, 30 ills. in black and white, 19 ills. in color, map, Mar., 1941

Petroleum: Today's World Turns on Oil. By Frederick Simpich. LXXIX, pp. 703-748, 22 ills. in black and white, drawings, 21 ills. in color, June, 1941

Platinum in the World's Work. By Lonnelle Davison. LXXII, pp. 345-360, 17 ills., Sept., 1937

Porcelain: The World's Ancient Porcelain Center (Kingtehchen). By Frank B. Lenz. XXXVIII, pp. 391-406, 17 ills., Nov., 1920

Poultry: America's Debt to the Hen. By Harry R. Lewis. LI, pp. 453-467, 15 ills., Apr., 1927

Poultry: The Races of Domestic Fowl. By M. A. Jull. Paintings by Hashime Murayama. LI, pp. 379-452, 67 ills. in black and white, 29 ills. in color, Apr., 1927

Rose Oil: Bulgaria's Valley of Roses. 13 color photos by Wilhelm Tobien and Georg Paskoff. LXII, pp. 187-194, Aug., 1932

Rubber: Amazon, Father of Waters: The Earth's Mightiest River Drains a Basin of More than 2,700,000 Square Miles, from Which Came Originally the World's Finest Rubber. By W. L. Schurz. XLIX, pp. 445-463, 15 ills., Apr., 1926

Rubber: Our Most Versatile Vegetable Product: Rubber Drops from Millions of Tropical Trees Are Transformed by Genii Chemists into Myriad Articles, from Tires to Teething Rings. By J. R. Hildebrand. LXXVII, pp. 143-200, 51 ills. in black and white, 26 ills. in color, Feb., 1940

Rubber: Singapore, Crossroads of the East: The World's Greatest Mart for Rubber and Tin Was in Recent Times a Pirate-haunted, Tiger-infested Jungle Isle. By Frederick Simpich. XLIX, pp. 235-269, 32 ills., map, Mar., 1926

Rubber Plantations in Mexico and Central America. XIV, pp. 409-414, 7 ills., Nov., 1903

Salt for China's Daily Rice. 11 ills. LXXXVI, pp. 329-336, Sept., 1944

Sheep: The Indispensable Sheep. LIII, pp. 512-528, 20 ills., Apr., 1928

Sheep: The Land of Lambskins: An Expedition to Bokhara, Russian Central Asia, to Study the Karakul Sheep Industry. By Robert K. Nabours. XXXVI, pp. 77-88, 15 ills., July, 1919

Shipbuilding: As 2,000 Ships Are Born. By Frederick Simpich. LXXXI, pp. 551-588, 34 ills., May, 1942

Shipbuilding: Our Industrial Victory. By Charles M. Schwab. XXXIV, pp. 212-229, 17 ills., Sept., 1918

Shipbuilding in the United Kingdom in 1898. X, pp. 138-139, Apr., 1899

Shore-Whaling: A World Industry. By Roy Chapman Andrews. XXII, pp. 411-442, 34 ills., May, 1911

Shrimp: The Delectable Shrimp: Once a Culinary Stepchild, Today a Gulf Coast Industry. By Harlan Major. LXXXVI, pp. 501-512, 11 ills., map, Oct., 1944

Silk: How Half the World Works. By Alice Tisdale Hobart and Mary A. Nourse. LXI, pp. 509-524, 22 ills., Apr., 1932

Steel: Industry's Greatest Asset—Steel. By William Joseph Showalter. XXXII, pp. 121-156, 34 ills., Aug., 1917

Steel: "Magnetic City" (Magnitogorsk), Core of Valiant Russia's Industrial Might. By John Scott. LXXXIII, pp. 525-556, 27 ills., two-page map, May, 1943

Sugar: Agricultural Possibilities in Tropical Mexico. By Dr. Pehr Olsson-Seffer. XXI, pp. 1021-1040, 19 ills., Dec., 1910

Sugar: Cuba—The Sugar Mill of the Antilles. By William Joseph Showalter. XXXVIII, pp. 1-33, 24 ills., map, July, 1920

INDUSTRIES—*Continued*

Sugar: How the World Is Fed. By William Joseph Showalter. XXIX, pp. 1-110, 101 ills., Jan., 1916

Synthetic Products: Chemists Make a New World: Creating Hitherto Unknown Raw Materials, Science Now Disrupts Old Trade Routes and Revamps the World Map of Industry. By Frederick Simpich. LXXVI, pp. 601-640, 22 ills. in black and white, 26 ills. in color, Nov., 1939

Tin: Bolivia—Tin Roof of the Andes. By Henry Albert Phillips. LXXXIII, pp. 309-332, 5 ills. in black and white, 20 ills. in color, Mar., 1943

Tin, the Cinderella Metal. By Alicia O'Reardon Overbeck. LXXVIII, pp. 659-684, 24 ills., Nov., 1940

War Industries: American Industries Geared for War. By Thornton Oakley. With 16 ills. in color from paintings by author. LXXXII, pp. 716-734, ill. in black and white, Dec., 1942

War Industries: Brazil's Potent Weapons. By W. Robert Moore. LXXXV, pp. 41-78, 16 ills. in black and white, 18 ills. in color, two-page map, Jan., 1944

War Industries: India's Treasures Helped the Allies. By John Fischer. LXXXIX, pp. 501-522, 18 ills., Apr., 1946

War Industries: Michigan Fights. By Harvey Klemmer. LXXXVI, pp. 677-715, 20 ills. in black and white, 19 ills. in color, map, Dec., 1944

War Industries: The Miracle of War Production: For Victory the United States Transforms Its Complex Industry into the Biggest Factory and Mightiest Arsenal the World Has Ever Known. By Albert W. Atwood. With paintings by Thornton Oakley. LXXXII, pp. 693-715, 17 ills. in black and white, 16 ills. in color, Dec., 1942

War Industries: Women at Work. By La Verne Bradley. LXXXVI, pp. 193-220, 23 ills., Aug., 1944

War Industries: The Yield of Texas. By Frederick Simpich. LXXXVII, pp. 163-184, 15 ills., two-page map, Feb., 1945

Worm Digging (Fishing Bait): The Worm Turns. By Samuel Sandrof. LXXXIX, pp. 775-786, 14 ills., June, 1946

See also Agriculture; Bananas; Cattle and Cattle Raising; Codfish and Codfish Industry; Coffee; Meat Industry; Mines and Mining; Motion Picture Industry; Paper Industry; Rug Industry; Shark Fishing; Sheep and Sheep Raising; Shoes and Shoe Industry; Silk Industry; Tobacco Industry; Transportation; Turtling; *and* country and State articles describing local industries

INDUSTRY'S Greatest Asset—Steel. By William Joseph Showalter. XXXII, pp. 121-156, 34 ills., Aug., 1917

INEXHAUSTIBLE Italy. By Arthur Stanley Riggs. XXX, pp. 273-368, 76 ills., map, Oct., 1916

INFANTRYMEN—The Fighters of War. By Brigadier General W. H. Wilbur. LXXXVI, pp. 513-538, 22 ills., Nov., 1944

The **INFLUENCE** of Forestry upon the Lumber Industry of the United States. By Overton W. Price. XIV, pp. 381-386, ills., Oct., 1903

INFLUENCE of Geographical Conditions on Military Operations in South Africa. By Major W. A. Simpson. XI, pp. 186-192, ill., map, May, 1900

The **INFLUENCE** of Submarine Cables upon Military and Naval Supremacy. By Capt. George O. Squier. XII, pp. 1-12, Jan., 1901

INFORMAL Salute to the English Lakes. By Maynard Owen Williams. LXIX, pp. 511-521, 10 ills. in color, Apr., 1936

INNER MONGOLIA. *See* Mongolia

INNS:

England: Visits to the Old Inns of England: Historic Homes of Hospitality for the Wayfarer Dot the Length and Breadth of the Kingdom. By Harold Donaldson Eberlein. LIX, pp. 261-285, 17 ills. in black and white, 15 ills. in color, Mar., 1931

INOCULATING the Ground. XV, pp. 225-228, ills., May, 1904

INSANITY:

The Geographical Distribution of Insanity in the United States. By Dr. William A. White. XIV, pp. 361-378, 6 maps, Oct., 1903

An **INSECT** Community Lives in Flower Heads. By James G. Needham. XC, pp. 340-356, 5 ills. in black and white, 11 ills. in color, Sept., 1946

INSECT Rivals of the Rainbow. (Text by Franklin L. Fisher). 269 color photos by Edwin L. Wisherd and paintings by Hashime Murayama. LVI, pp. 28-90, July, 1929

INSECTS:

Amid the Snow Peaks of the Equator: A Naturalist's Explorations Around Ruwenzori, with an Excursion to the Congo State, and an Account of the Terrible Scourge of Sleeping Sickness. By A. F. R. Wollaston. XX, pp. 256-277, 11 ills., Mar., 1909

A Book of Monsters. By David and Marian Fairchild. XXVI, pp. 89-98, 7 ills., July, 1914

Cooties and Courage. By Herbert Corey. XXXIII, pp. 495-509, 10 ills., June, 1918

Economic Loss to the People of the United States Through Insects That Carry Disease. By L. O. Howard. XX, pp. 735-749, Aug., 1909

Explorers of a New Kind: Successful Introduction of Beetles and Parasites to Check Ravages of the Gipsy-moth and Brown-tail Moth. By L. O. Howard. XXVI, pp. 38-67, 11 ills. in black and white, 5 ills. in color, July, 1914

Exploring the Wonders of the Insect World. By William Joseph Showalter. Paintings by Hashime Murayama. LVI, pp. 1-90, 59 ills. in black and white, 269 ills. in color, July, 1929

Fighting Insects with Airplanes: An Account of the Successful Use of the Flying-Machine in Dusting Tall Trees Infested with Leaf-Eating Caterpillars. By C. R. Neillie and J. S. Houser. XLI, pp. 333-338, 6 ills., Mar., 1922

Hospital Heroes Convict the Cootie. XXXIII, p. 510, June, 1918

An Insect Community Lives in Flower Heads. By James G. Needham. XC, pp. 340-356, 5 ills. in black and white, 11 ills. in color, Sept., 1946

INSECTS—*Continued*

Included: Ants, Aphids, Baccha Flies, Bandwing Flies, Clearwing Flies, Mealy Bugs, Midges, Moths, Spotwing Flies

The Jungles of Panama. By David Fairchild. XLI, pp. 131-145, 14 ills., Feb., 1922

Marvels of Metamorphosis: A Scientific "G-man" Pursues Rare Trapdoor Spider Parasites for Three Years With a Spade and a Candid Camera. By George Elwood Jenks. LXXIV, pp. 807-828, 39 ills., Dec., 1938

The Monsters of Our Back Yards. By David Fairchild. XXIV, pp. 575-626, 38 ills., May, 1913

Included: Ant, Bee, Bee-Fly, Butterfly, Cicada, Cockroach, Cricket, Dragon-Fly, Grasshopper, Ground-Beetle, Hornet, Horse-Fly, June Beetle, June-Bug, Katydid, Long-Horned Beetle, Mosquito, Squash-Bug

Our Insect Fifth Column: Alien Enemies Take Steady Toll of Food, Trees, and Treasure by Boring from Within. By Frederick G. Vosburgh. Paintings by Hashime Murayama. LXXX, pp. 225-248, 14 ills. in black and white, 10 ills. in color, Aug., 1941

Included: Boll Weevil, *Centeter cinerea*, Digger Wasp, European Cabbage Butterfly, European Corn Borer, Gladiolus Thrips, Gypsy Moth, Japanese Beetle, Mexican Bean Beetle, Sweet Potato Weevil, White-fringed Beetle

Pests and Parasites: Why We Need a National Law to Prevent the Importation of Insect-Infested and Diseased Plants. By Charles Lester Marlatt. XXII, pp. 321-346, 29 ills., maps, Apr., 1911

Protecting the United States from Plant Pests. By Charles Lester Marlatt. XL, pp. 205-218, 16 ills., Aug., 1921

The Red Ant Versus the Boll Weevil. XV, pp. 262-264, June, 1904

See also Ants; Bees; Butterflies; Flies; Hornets; Locusts; Mosquitoes; Moths; Wasps

INSIDE Cape Horn. By Amos Burg. LXXII, pp. 743-783, 29 ills. in black and white, 10 ills. in color, two-page map, Dec., 1937

INSIGNIA:

Aircraft Insignia, Spirit of Youth. By Gerard Hubbard. LXXXIII, pp. 710-722, 3 ills. in black and white, 337 ills. in color, June, 1943

American Decorations and Insignia of Honor and Service. By Col. Robert E. Wyllie. XXXVI, pp. 502-526, 6 ills. in black and white, 119 ills. in color, Dec., 1919

Decorations, Medals, Service Ribbons, Badges, and Women's Insignia. LXXXIV, pp. 414-444, 6 ills. in black and white, 376 ills. in color, Oct., 1943

Heroes of Wartime Science and Mercy. By Elizabeth W. King. LXXXIV, pp. 715-740, 11 ills. in black and white, 334 ills. in color, Dec., 1943

Note: Insignia of the following organizations: Air Carrier Contract Personnel, American Red Cross, Civil Air Patrol, U. S. Army Transportation Corps Vessels, U. S. Coast and Geodetic Survey, U. S. Maritime Service, U. S. Public Health Service

Index to Flags and Insignia (Our Flag Number). XXXII, p. 285, ill., Oct., 1917

INSIGNIA—*Continued*

Insignia and Decorations of the United States Armed Forces. By Gilbert Grosvenor. LXXXVII, pp. 185-186, Feb., 1945

The Insignia of the Uniformed Forces of the United States. By Byron McCandless and Gilbert Grosvenor. XXXII, pp. 413-419, 318 ills., Oct., 1917

Insignia of the United States Armed Forces. By Gilbert Grosvenor. With 991 illustrations in color. LXXXIII, p. 651, June, 1943

The Romance of Military Insignia: How the United States Government Recognizes Deeds of Heroism and Devotion to Duty. By Col. Robert E. Wyllie. XXXVI, pp. 463-501, 27 ills., Dec., 1919

The Traditions and Glamour of Insignia. By Arthur E. Du Bois. LXXXIII, pp. 652-655, 3 ills., June, 1943

United States Military Insignia. LXXXIII, pp. 656-693, 7 ills. in black and white, 12 drawings, 311 ills. in color, June, 1943

United States Navy, Marine Corps, and Coast Guard Insignia. LXXXIII, pp. 694-709, 5 ills. in black and white, 343 ills. in color, June, 1943

See also Seals of Our Nation

INTERESTING Citizens of the Gulf Stream. By Dr. John T. Nichols. XXXIX, pp. 69-84, 11 ills., Jan., 1921

An **INTERESTING** Rumor Concerning Andrée. (By J. H.). IX, pp. 102-103, Mar., 1898

An **INTERESTING** Visit to the Ancient Pyramids of San Juan Teotihuacan. By A C. Galloway. XXI, pp. 1041-1050, 8 ills., map, Dec., 1910

INTERNATIONAL Arbitration and Its Possibilities. XI, p. 162, Apr., 1900

The **INTERNATIONAL** Cloud Work of the Weather Bureau. By Frank H. Bigelow. X, pp. 351-354, Sept., 1899

INTERNATIONAL CONGRESS OF ORIENTALISTS:

Eleventh International Congress of Orientalists. VIII, p. 303 (note), Oct., 1897

INTERNATIONAL Flat Globe and Geographical History. XVIII, pp. 281-282, Apr., 1907

INTERNATIONAL GEOGRAPHIC CONFERENCE:

Proceedings of the International Geographic Conference in Chicago, July 27-28, 1893. V, pp. 97-256, Jan. 31, 1894

Included: Minutes of the Conference; Memoirs and Addresses

INTERNATIONAL GEOGRAPHIC CONGRESS:

Address by Commander Robert E. Peary, U. S. N., On the Assembling of the Congress in Washington, September 8, 1904. XV, pp. 387-392, Oct., 1904

Chairman of Committee on Eighth Congress. XIII, p. 219, June, 1902. XIV, pp. 254-255, June, 1903

Delegates to Ninth Congress. XIX, pp. 385-386, May, 1908

Eighth International Geographic Congress. XIV, pp. 388-390, Oct., 1903

INTERNATIONAL GEOGRAPHIC CONGRESS
—*Continued*

Eighth International Geographic Congress. XV, pp. 419-426, ills., Oct., 1904

Eighth International Geographic Congress, Washington, 1904. XV, pp. 74-77, Feb., 1904

Eighth International Geographic Congress, Washington, 1904. XV, pp. 297-310, July, 1904

Geographic Congress Abstracts (Eighth). XV, pp. 502-503, Dec., 1904

Geographical Congress at Berlin. X, p. 296, Aug., 1899; p. 480, Nov., 1899

International Geographic Congress. XIV, p. 292, July, 1903

Next International Geographical Congress To Be Held in Washington. (By G. H. G.). XII, pp. 351-357, 4 ills., Oct., 1901

Ninth International Geographical Congress, Geneva, Switzerland, 1908. XVIII, p. 491, July, 1907

Program of Eighth International Geographic Congress. XV, pp. 373-386, map, Sept., 1904

Publication of Proceedings of Eighth Congress. XVI, pp. 198-199, Apr., 1905

Resolutions Adopted by the Eighth International Geographic Congress, September, 1904. XV, pp. 415-418, Oct., 1904

Sixth International Geographical Congress, London (1895). (By A. W. G.). VII, p. 380, Nov., 1896

The Special Telegraphic Time Signal from the Naval Observatory. XV, pp. 411-415, Oct., 1904

INTERNATIONAL ICE PATROL:

Coast Guard Patrol in Greenland. 9 color photos by Lieut. Thomas S. La Farge. LXXXIII, pp. 565-572, May, 1943

Standing Iceberg Guard in the North Atlantic: International Patrol Safeguards the Lives of Thousands of Travelers and Protects Trans-Atlantic Liners from a "Titanic" Fate. By Lieutenant Commander F. A. Zeusler. L, pp. 1-28, 29 ills., map, July, 1926

INTERNATIONAL Literary Contest (Madrid, Spain). I, pp. 273-276, July, 1889

The **INTERNATIONAL** Millionth Map of the World. By Bailey Willis. XXI, pp. 125-132, diagr., Feb., 1910

The **INTEROCEANIC** Canal. By Emory R. Johnson. X, pp. 311-316, Aug., 1899

INTERSTATE COMMERCE COMMISSION:

Eleventh Annual Report of the Interstate Commerce Commission (Review by H. T. Newcomb). IX, pp. 29-31, Jan., 1898

Statistics of Railways in the United States. (By H. G.). VII, pp. 406-407, Dec., 1896

INTERVIEWING the Stars: How Twentieth Century Astronomers Are Inducing the Heavens to Reveal Their Secrets. By William Joseph Showalter. XLVII, pp. 97-122, 18 ills., diagr., charts, Jan., 1925

INTO Burning Hadhramaut (Arabia): The Arab Land of Frankincense and Myrrh, Ever a Lodestone of Western Exploration. By D. van der Meulen. LXII, pp. 387-429, 44 ills., map, Oct., 1932

INTO Primeval Papua by Seaplane: Seeking Disease-resisting Sugar Cane, Scientists Find Neolithic Man in Unmapped Nooks of Sorcery and Cannibalism. By E. W. Brandes. LVI, pp. 253-332, 98 ills., map, Sept., 1929

INTO the Land of the Chipmunk. By Ruth Alexander Nichols. LX, pp. 77-98, 28 ills., July, 1931

INTRACOASTAL WATERWAY, U. S.:

The Florida Coast Line Canal. IX, p. 242, May, 1898

INTRODUCING Reindeer into Labrador. XVIII, p. 686, Oct., 1907

The **INTRODUCTION** of the Mango. XIV, pp. 320-327, 5 ills., Aug., 1903

An **INTRODUCTION** to Physical Geography. (By Grove Karl Gilbert and Albert Perry Brigham). XIV, pp. 21-26, 6 ills., Jan., 1903

INTRODUCTORY: The Editor (John Hyde). VII, pp. 1-2, Jan., 1896

INTRODUCTORY Address. By the President, Mr. Gardiner G. Hubbard. I, pp. 3-10, Oct., 1888

INVENTORS AND INVENTIONS:

Discovery and Invention. By Alexander Graham Bell. XXV, pp. 649-655, June, 1914

The Long River of New England: In War and Peace, from Mountain Wilderness to the Sea, Flows the Connecticut River, Through a Valley Abounding in History, Scenery, Inventive Genius, and Industry. By Albert W. Atwood. LXXXIII, pp. 401-434, 12 ills. in black and white, 24 ills. in color, map, Apr., 1943

Prizes for the Inventor: Some of the Problems Awaiting Solution. By Alexander Graham Bell. XXXI, pp. 131-146, 7 ills., Feb., 1917

Your New World of Tomorrow. By F. Barrows Colton. LXXXVIII, pp. 385-410, 25 ills., Oct., 1945

See also Bell, Alexander Graham; Bumstead, Albert; Edgerton, Harold E.; Wright, Orville; Wright, Wilbur

IOWA:

Iowa, Abiding Place of Plenty: The State Where the Tall Corn Grows Provides the Nation with a Tenth of Its Food Supply. By Leo A. Borah. LXXVI, pp. 143-182, 15 ills. in black and white, 20 ills. in color, two-page map, Aug., 1939

IOWA-class Battleship. *See Missouri*

IPIUTAK, Alaska:

Discovering Alaska's Oldest Arctic Town: A Scientist Finds Ivory-eyed Skeletons of a Mysterious People and Joins Modern Eskimos in the Dangerous Spring Whale Hunt. By Froelich G. Rainey. LXXXII, pp. 319-336, 15 ills., Sept., 1942

IRAN (Persia):

The Afghan Borderland. By Ellsworth Huntington. Part I: The Russian Frontier. XX, pp. 788-799, 14 ills., Sept., 1909. Part II: The Persian Frontier. XX, pp. 866-876, 12 ills., Oct., 1909

IRAN (Persia)—*Continued*

The Citroën Trans-Asiatic Expedition Reaches Kashmir: Scientific Party Led by Georges-Marie Haardt Successfully Crosses Syria, Iraq, Persia, and Afghanistan to Arrive at the Pamir. By Maynard Owen Williams. LX, pp. 387-443, 62 ills., map, Oct., 1931

Excavations of M. de Morgan at Susa. XII, p. 315, Aug., 1901

Exploring the Secrets of Persepolis. By Charles Breasted. LXIV, pp. 381-420, 48 ills., plan, map, Oct., 1933

Flights from Arctic to Equator: Conquering the Alps, the Ice Peaks of Spitsbergen, of Persia, and Africa's Mountains of the Moon. By Walter Mittelholzer. LXI, pp. 445-498, 53 ills., map, Apr., 1932

From England to India by Automobile: An 8,527-mile Trip Through Ten Countries, from London to Quetta, Requires Five and a Half Months. By Major F. A. C. Forbes-Leith. XLVIII, pp. 191-223, 33 ills., map, Aug., 1925

Geographic Progress of Civilization. Annual Address by the President, Honorable Gardiner G. Hubbard. VI, pp. 1-22, Feb. 14, 1894

A German Route to India. (By Gilbert H. Grosvenor). XI, pp. 203-204, map, May, 1900

Iran in Wartime: Through Fabulous Persia, Hub of the Middle East, Americans, Britons, and Iranians Keep Sinews of War Moving to the Embattled Soviet Union. By John N. Greely. LXXXIV, pp. 129-156, 26 ills., map, Aug., 1943

Modern Persia and Its Capital: And an Account of an Ascent of Mount Demavend, the Persian Olympus. By F. L. Bird. XXXIX, pp. 353-400, 47 ills., Apr., 1921

Mountain Tribes of Iran and Iraq. By Harold Lamb. LXXXIX, pp. 385-408, 15 ills., two-page map, Mar., 1946

The Mountaineers of the Euphrates. By Ellsworth Huntington. XX, pp. 142-156, 13 ills., Feb., 1909

Old and New in Persia: In This Ancient Land Now Called Iran a Modern Sugar Factory Rears Its Head Near the Palace of Darius the Great. By the Baroness Ravensdale. LXXVI, pp. 325-355, 20 ills. in black and white, 13 ills. in color, map, Sept., 1939

Persia—Past and Present. XVIII, pp. 91-95, 6 ills., Feb., 1907

Persia: The Awakening East. By W. P. Cresson. XIX, pp. 356-384, 21 ills., map, May, 1908

Persian Caravan Sketches: The Land of the Lion and the Sun as Seen on a Summer Caravan Trip. By Harold F. Weston. XXXIX, pp. 417-468, 46 ills. in black and white, 16 ills. in color, map, Apr., 1921

A Talk About Persia and Its Women. By Ella C. Sykes. XXI, pp. 847-866, 22 ills., Oct., 1910

Travels in Arabia and Along the Persian Gulf. By David G. Fairchild. XV, pp. 139-151, 20 ills., Apr., 1904

IRAQ:

Archeology, the Mirror of the Ages: Our Debt to the Humble Delvers in the Ruins at Carchemish and at Ur. By C. Leonard Woolley. LIV, pp. 207-226, 19 ills., Aug., 1928

Bombs over Bible Lands. By Frederick Simpich and W. Robert Moore. LXXX, pp. 141-180, 34 ills., two-page map, Aug., 1941

IRAQ—*Continued*

Change Comes to Bible Lands. By Frederick Simpich. LXXIV, pp. 695-750, 40 ills. in black and white, 25 ills. in color, map supplement, Dec., 1938

The Cradle of Civilization: The Historic Lands Along the Euphrates and Tigris Rivers Where Briton Is Fighting Turk. By James Baikie. XXIX, pp. 127-162, 25 ills., Feb., 1916

Excavations at Nippur. XI, p. 392, Oct., 1900

Forty Years Among the Arabs. By John Van Ess. LXXXII, pp. 385-420, 27 ills., two-page map, Sept., 1942

From England to India by Automobile: An 8,527-mile Trip Through Ten Countries, from London to Quetta, Requires Five and a Half Months. By Major F. A. C. Forbes-Leith. XLVIII, pp. 191-223, 33 ills., map, Aug., 1925

Modern Life in the Cradle of Civilization. XLI, pp. 390-407, 16 ills. in color, Apr., 1922

The Most Historic Lands on Earth. XXVI, pp. 614-615, map, Dec., 1914

Mountain Tribes of Iran and Iraq. By Harold Lamb. LXXXIX, pp. 385-408, 15 ills., two-page map, Mar., 1946

The Mountaineers of the Euphrates. By Ellsworth Huntington. XX, pp. 142-156, 13 ills., Feb., 1909

Mystic Nedjef, the Shia Mecca. By Frederick Simpich. XXVI, pp. 589-598, 4 ills., Dec., 1914

New Light on Ancient Ur: Excavations at the Site of the City of Abraham Reveal Geographical Evidence of the Biblical Story of the Flood. By M. E. L. Mallowan. LVII, pp. 95-130, 44 ills., map, Jan., 1930

Pushing Back History's Horizon: How the Pick and Shovel Are Revealing Civilizations That Were Ancient When Israel Was Young. By Albert T. Clay. XXIX, pp. 162-216, 47 ills., map, Feb., 1916

Travels in Arabia and Along the Persian Gulf. By David G. Fairchild. XV, pp. 139-151, 20 ills., Apr., 1904

Under the Heel of the Turk: A Land with a Glorious Past, a Present of Abused Opportunities, and a Future of Golden Possibilities. By William H. Hall. XXXIV, pp. 51-69, 14 ills., July, 1918

A Visit to Three Arab Kingdoms: Transjordania, Iraq, and the Hedjaz Present Many Problems to European Powers. By Junius B. Wood. XLIII, pp. 535-568, 30 ills., map, May, 1923

Where Adam and Eve Lived. By Frederick and Margaret Simpich. XXVI, pp. 546-588, 35 ills., Dec., 1914

IRELAND:

British Isles. 16 ills. XXVIII, pp. 551-566, Dec., 1915

Fearful Famines of the Past: History Will Repeat Itself Unless the American People Conserve Their Resources. By Ralph A. Graves. XXXII, pp. 69-90, 11 ills., July, 1917

Ireland: The Rock Whence I Was Hewn. By Donn Byrne. LI, pp. 257-326, 68 ills. in black and white, 11 ills. in color, map, Mar., 1927

The Mist and Sunshine of Ulster. By Bernard F. Rogers, Jr. LXVIII, pp. 571-610, 23 ills. in black and white, 21 ills. in color, map, Nov., 1935

IRELAND—*Continued*

Old Ireland, Mother of New Eire: By Whatever Name, 'Tis the Same Fair Land With the Grass Growing Green on the Hills of Her and the Peat Smoke Hanging Low. By Harrison Howell Walker. LXXVII, pp. 649-691, 19 ills. in black and white, 18 ills. in color, map, May, 1940

The Ordnance Survey of Great Britain—Its History and Object. By Josiah Pierce, Jr. II, pp. 243-260, Aug., 1890

The Races of Europe. By Edwin A. Grosvenor. XXXIV, pp. 441-534, 62 ills., diagr. and index, maps, map supplement, Dec., 1918

See also Aran Islands; Eire; Northern Ireland

The **IRIDESCENT** Beauty of Frogs and Toads. 14 ills. in color from paintings by Hashime Murayama. LXI, pp. 635-642, May, 1932

IRIDESCENT Denizens of the Miniature Aquarium. 8 ills. in color from paintings by Hashime Murayama. LIX, pp. 293-300, Mar., 1931

IRIDESCENT Isles of the South Seas. 16 ills. in color: 12 color photos; 4 paintings by Hashime Murayama. XLVIII, pp. 403-418, Oct., 1925

IROQUOIS INDIANS:

America's First Settlers, the Indians. By Matthew W. Stirling. Paintings by W. Langdon Kihn. LXXII, pp. 535-596, 34 ills. in black and white, 24 ills. in color, Nov., 1937

IRRAWADDY (River), Burma:

Untoured Burma. By Charles H. Bartlett. XXIV, pp. 835-853, 17 ills., July, 1913

IRRIGATION:

The Arid Regions of the United States. By F. H. Newell. V, pp. 167-172, Jan. 31, 1894

The Call of the West. By C. J. Blanchard. XX, pp. 403-437, 20 ills., map, May, 1909

China Fights Erosion with U. S. Aid. By Walter C. Lowdermilk. LXXXVII, pp. 641-680, 10 ills. in black and white, 26 ills. in color, June, 1945

Farmers Since the Days of Noah: China's Remarkable System of Agriculture Has Kept Alive the Densest Population in the World. By Adam Warwick. LI, pp. 469-500, 37 ills., Apr., 1927

Home-Making by the Government: An Account of the Eleven Immense Irrigating Projects to be Opened in 1908. By C. J. Blanchard. XIX, pp. 250-287, 23 ills., Apr., 1908

Irrigation in California. By Wm. Hammond Hall. I, pp. 277-290, Oct., 1889

The Irrigation Problem in Montana. By H. M. Wilson. II, pp. 212-229, 4 tables, July, 1890

More Water for California's Great Central Valley. By Frederick Simpich. XC, pp. 645-664, 16 ills., map, Nov., 1946

The Spirit of the West: The Wonderful Agricultural Development Since the Dawn of Irrigation. By C. J. Blanchard. XXI, pp. 333-360, 15 ills., Apr., 1910

See also U. S. Bureau of Reclamation

IS Climatic Aridity Impending on the Pacific Slope? The Testimony of the Forest. By J. B. Leiberg. X, pp. 160-181, May, 1899

IS Our Noblest Volcano Awakening to New Life: A Description of the Glaciers and Evidences of Volcanic Activity of Mount Hood. By A. H. Sylvester. XIX, pp. 515-525, 5 ills., map, July, 1908

ISABELA ISLAND, Mexico:

Cruise of the *Kinkajou:* Among Desert Islands of Mexico Voyagers Find Outdoor Laboratories for the Naturalist and Ideal Fishing Grounds for the Sportsman. By Alfred M. Bailey. LXXX, pp. 339-366, 13 ills. in black and white, 12 ills. in color, map, Sept., 1941

ISFAHAN, Iran:

Iran in Wartime: Through Fabulous Persia, Hub of the Middle East, Americans, Britons, and Iranians Keep Sinews of War Moving to the Embattled Soviet Union. By John N. Greely. LXXXIV, pp. 129-156, 26 ills., map, Aug., 1943

Persian Caravan Sketches: The Land of the Lion and the Sun as Seen on a Summer Caravan Trip. By Harold F. Weston. XXXIX, pp. 417-468, 46 ills. in black and white, 16 ills. in color, map, Apr., 1921

ISLAM. *See* Moslems

ISLAMABAD, India:

A Pilgrimage to Amernath, Himalayan Shrine of the Hindu Faith. By Louise Ahl Jessop. XL, pp. 513-542, 29 ills., Nov., 1921

An **ISLAND** in the Sea of History: The Highlands of Daghestan. By George Kennan. XXIV, pp. 1087-1140, 49 ills., map, Oct., 1913

The **ISLAND** of Nias, at the Edge of the World. By Mabel Cook Cole. LX, pp. 201-224, 26 ills., map, Aug., 1931

The **ISLAND** of Sardinia and Its People: Traces of Many Civilizations to Be Found in the Speech, Customs, and Costumes of This Picturesque Land. By Prof. Guido Costa. XLIII, pp. 1-75, 63 ills. in black and white, 16 ills. in color, maps, Jan., 1923

The **ISLAND** of the Sagas (Iceland). By Earl Hanson. LIII, pp. 499-511, 22 ills., Apr., 1928

ISLAND Treasures of the Caribbean (Virgin Islands). 23 color photos by Edwin L. Wisherd and C. W. Herbert. LXXVIII, pp. 281-304, Sept., 1940

ISLANDER (Yawl):

Around the World in the "Islander": A Narrative of the Adventures of a Solitary Voyager on His Four-Year Cruise in a Thirty-Four-Foot Sailing Craft. By Capt. Harry Pidgeon. LIII, pp. 141-205, 75 ills., two-page map, Feb., 1928

ISLANDS:

An Undiscovered Island Off the Northern Coast of Alaska. I—By Marcus Baker. II—By Captain Edward Perry Herendeen. III—By General A. W. Greely. V, pp. 76-83, July 10, 1893

See also Pacific Islands; *and* names of islands

ISLANDS Adrift: St. Pierre and Miquelon: In a Key Position on the North Atlantic Air Route, France's Oldest Colony Rides Out Another Storm. By Frederic K. Arnold. LXXX, pp. 743-768, 23 ills., map, Dec., 1941

The **ISLANDS** of Bermuda: A British Colony with a Unique Record in Popular Government. By William Howard Taft. XLI, pp. 1-26, 15 ills., map, Jan., 1922

The **ISLANDS** of the Pacific. By J. P. Thomson. XL, pp. 543-558, 15 ills., map supplement, Dec., 1921

The **ISLE** of Capri: An Imperial Residence and Probable Wireless Station of Ancient Rome. By John A. Kingman. XXXVI, pp. 213-231, 17 ills., Sept., 1919

The **ISLE** of Frankincense (Socotra, Arabian Sea). By Charles K. Moser. XXXIII, pp. 267-278, 11 ills., Mar., 1918

The **ISLE** of Man. By Captain F. H. Mellor. LXXI, pp. 587-608, 13 ills. in black and white, 12 ills. in color, map, May, 1937

The **ISLE** of Pines. XVII, pp. 105-108, ills., Feb., 1906

ISLE OF WIGHT. *See* Wight, Isle of

ISLE ROYALE, Michigan:

Winter Sky Roads to Isle Royal. By Ben East. LX, pp. 759-774, 18 ills., map, Dec., 1931

ISLES, Bay of, South Georgia:

South Georgia, an Outpost of the Antarctic. By Robert Cushman Murphy. XLI, pp. 409-444, 41 ills., maps, Apr., 1922

The **ISLES** of Greece. By Lt. Richard Stillwell, USNR. LXXXV, pp. 593-622, 11 ills. in black and white, 20 ills. in color, map, May, 1944

ISLES OF SPICE. *See* Moluccas

ISOLA BELLA (Island), Italy:

Gems of the Italian Lakes. By Arthur Ellis Mayer. XXIV, pp. 943-956, 13 ills., Aug., 1913

ISPAHAN, Iran. *See* Isfahan

ISRAEL. *See* Palestine

İSTANBUL, Turkey:

Alert Anatolia. 13 ills. LXXXV, pp. 481-492, Apr., 1944

Constantinople and Sancta Sophia. By Edwin A. Grosvenor. XXVII, pp. 459-482, 21 ills., May, 1915

Constantinople Today. By Solita Solano. XLI, pp. 647-680, 40 ills., map, June, 1922

Life in Constantinople. By H. G. Dwight. XXVI, pp. 521-545, 25 ills., Dec., 1914

The Transformation of Turkey: New Hats and New Alphabet are the Surface Symbols of the Swiftest National Changes in Modern Times. By Douglas Chandler. LXXV, pp. 1-50, 27 ills. in black and white, 23 ills. in color, map, Jan., 1939

The Turkish Republic Comes of Age. By Maynard Owen Williams. LXXXVII, pp. 581-616, 4 ills. in black and white, 29 ills. in color, map, May, 1945

İSTANBUL AMERIKAN KOLEJI, Turkey:

American Alma Maters in the Near East. By Maynard Owen Williams. LXXXVIII, pp. 237-256, 16 ills., Aug., 1945

İSTANBUL WOMAN'S COLLEGE, Arnautköy, Turkey:

American Alma Maters in the Near East. By Maynard Owen Williams. LXXXVIII, pp. 237-256, 16 ills., Aug., 1945

The **ISTHMIAN** Canal Commission. XI, p. 161, Apr., 1900

The **ISTHMIAN** Canal Problem. (By W J McGee). X, pp. 363-364, Sept., 1899

The **ISTHMUS** of Tehuantepec (Mexico). By Herbert Corey. XLV, pp. 549-579, 25 ills., May, 1924

The **ISTHMUS** of Tehuantepec (Mexico): "The Bridge of the World's Commerce." By Helen Olsson-Seffer. XXI, pp. 991-1002, 7 ills., Dec., 1910

ITALIAN ISLANDS OF THE AEGEAN. *See* Dodecanese Islands

The **ITALIAN** Race. (By Gilbert Grosvenor). XXXIII, p. 47, Jan., 1918

ITALY:

Aces Among Aces (Aviators). By Laurence La Tourette Driggs. XXXIII, pp. 568-580, 9 ills., June, 1918

The American Red Cross in Italy. By Mabel Boardman. XX, pp. 396-397, Apr., 1909

The Ascent of Mont Blanc. By Walter Woodburn Hyde. XXIV, pp. 861-942, 69 ills., Aug., 1913

Austro-Italian Mountain Frontiers. By Florence Craig Albrecht. XXVII, pp. 321-376, 60 ills., map, Apr., 1915

Behind the Lines in Italy. By Corporal Macon Reed, Jr. LXXXVI, pp. 109-128, 20 ills., July, 1944

Daily Life in Calabria. 16 ills. XLIII, pp. 181-196, Feb., 1923

The Eruption of Mount Vesuvius, April 7-8, 1906. By Thomas Augustus Jaggar, Jr. XVII, pp. 318-325, 6 ills., June, 1906

From Africa to the Alps. 8 ills. in color from U. S. Army Air Forces official photos. LXXXIX, pp. 161-168, Feb., 1946

From England to India by Automobile: An 8,527-mile Trip Through Ten Countries, from London to Quetta, Requires Five and a Half Months. By Major F. A. C. Forbes-Leith. XLVIII, pp. 191-223, 33 ills., map, Aug., 1925

Frontier Cities of Italy. By Florence Craig Albrecht. XXVII, pp. 533-586, 45 ills., June, 1915

Gems of the Italian Lakes. By Arthur Ellis Mayer. XXIV, pp. 943-956, 13 ills., Aug., 1913

Holidays Among the Hill Towns of Umbria and Tuscany. By Paul Wilstach. LIII, pp. 401-442, 40 ills., map, Apr., 1928

Horace—Classic Poet of the Countryside. By W. Coleman Nevils. LXVIII, pp. 771-795, 22 ills., map, Dec., 1935

Hunting Castles in Italy. By Melville Chater. LXVIII, pp. 329-366, 25 ills. in black and white, 13 ills. in color, maps, Sept., 1935

Inexhaustible Italy. By Arthur Stanley Riggs. XXX, pp. 273-368, 76 ills., map, Oct., 1916

Italian, French, and Swiss Scenes. 16 photos, hand-tinted, by Donald McLeish and Arthur Stanley Riggs. XXVIII, pp. 439-454, Nov., 1915

The Italian Race. (By Gilbert Grosvenor). XXXIII, p. 47, Jan., 1918

ITALY—*Continued*

Italy, From Roman Ruins to Radio: History of Ancient Bridge Building and Road Making Repeats Itself in Modern Public Works and Engineering Projects. By John Patric. LXXVII, pp. 347-394, 27 ills. in black and white, 9 ills. in color, Mar., 1940

Italy, Land of History and Romance. 16 ills. XLV, pp. 375-390, Apr., 1924

Italy's Eagles of Combat and Defense: Heroic Achievements of Aviators Above the Adriatic, the Apennines, and the Alps. By General P. Tozzi. XXXIII, pp. 38-47, 8 ills., Jan., 1918

Letters from the Italian Front. By Marchesa Louise de Rosales to Ethel Mather Bagg. XXXII, pp. 47-67, 22 ills., July, 1917

Life's Pattern on the Italian Riviera. By Helen Churchill Candee. LXVII, pp. 67-100, 25 ills. in black and white, 12 ills. in color, map, Jan., 1935

The Majesty of the Matterhorn. XXIII, text p. 514; pictorial supplement, May, 1912

Man and Nature Paint Italian Scenes in Prodigal Colors. 33 color photos by Hans Hildenbrand. LIII, pp. 443-466, Apr., 1928

Mount Vesuvius. XVII, pp. 272-279, 7 ills., map, May, 1906

The New Map of Europe: Showing the Boundaries Established by the Peace Conference at Paris and by Subsequent Decisions of the Supreme Council of the Allied and Associated Powers. By Ralph A. Graves. Text with map supplement. XXXIX, pp. 157-177, 18 ills., Feb., 1921

Northern Italy: Scenic Battleground. 18 color photos: 13 by B. Anthony Stewart, 3 by Lt. Benjamin C. McCartney. LXXXVII, pp. 265-288, Mar., 1945

Over the Alps to Brenner Pass. 15 photos, two-page map. LXXXIV, pp. 701-714, Dec., 1943

The Perennial Geographer: After 2,000 Years Vergil Is Still the Most Widely Read of Latin Poets—First to Popularize the Geography of the Roman Empire. By W. Coleman Nevils. LVIII, pp. 439-465, 29 ills., Oct., 1930

The Races of Europe. By Edwin A. Grosvenor. XXXIV, pp. 441-534, 62 ills., diagr. and index, maps, map supplement, Dec., 1918

Redemption of the Pontine Marshes: By Draining the Malarial Wastes Around Rome, Italy Has Created a Promised Land. By Gelasio Caetani. LXVI, pp. 201-217, 9 ills. in black and white, 12 ills. in color, map, Aug., 1934

Scenes in Italy. 12 ills. XXI, pp. 321-332, Apr., 1910

Sojourning in the Italy of Today. By Mrs. Kenneth Roberts. LXX, pp. 351-396, 46 ills., map, Sept., 1936

The Stone Beehive Homes of the Italian Heel: In Trulli-Land the Native Builds His Dwelling and Makes His Field Arable in the Same Operation. By Paul Wilstach. LVII, pp. 229-260, 25 ills. in black and white, 12 ills. in color, map, Feb., 1930

The Story and the Legends of the Pontine Marshes: After Many Centuries of Fruitless Effort, Italy Is to Inaugurate a Gigantic Enterprise to Drain the Fertile Region Southeast of Rome. By Don Gelasio Caetani. XLV, pp. 357-374, 18 ills., Apr., 1924

ITALY—*Continued*

Under Radiant Italian Skies. 8 color photos by Hans Hildenbrand and Luigi Pellerano. L, pp. 249-256, Aug., 1926

See also Capri (Island); Florence; Genoa; Rome; Sardinia (Island); Sicily (Island); Siena; Vatican City; Venice

ITALY'S Eagles of Combat and Defense: Heroic Achievements of Aviators Above the Adriatic, the Apennines, and the Alps. By General P. Tozzi. XXXIII, pp. 38-47, 8 ills., Jan., 1918

ITALY'S Monuments Tell Rome's Magnificence. 8 photos: 7 by B. Anthony Stewart. LXXVII, pp. 371-378, Mar., 1940

ITAMBÉ (Peak), Brazil:

The Peak of Itambé. IX, p. 476, Nov., 1898

The Recent Ascent of Itambé. (By J. C. Branner). X, p. 183, May, 1899

ITHERA (Oasis), Arabia:

Arabia, the Desert of the Sea. By Archibald Forder. XX, pp. 1039-1062, 1117, 20 ills., map, Dec., 1909

IVAN IV, The Terrible:

Young Russia: The Land of Unlimited Possibilities. By Gilbert H. Grosvenor. XXVI, pp. 421-520, 85 ills. in black and white, 17 ills. in color, Nov., 1914

IZALCO VOLCANO, El Salvador:

Coffee Is King in El Salvador. By Luis Marden. LXXXVI, pp. 575-616, 22 ills. in black and white, 27 ills. in color, map, Nov., 1944

İZMIR (Smyrna), Turkey:

History's Greatest Trek: Tragedy Stalks Through the Near East as Greece and Turkey Exchange Two Million of Their People. By Melville Chater. XLVIII, pp. 533-590, 52 ills. in black and white, 32 ills. in color, Nov., 1925

Some Ruined Cities of Asia Minor. By Ernest L. Harris. XIX, pp. 833-858, 19 ills., Dec., 1908

The Turkish Republic Comes of Age. By Maynard Owen Williams. LXXXVII, pp. 581-616, 4 ills. in black and white, 29 ills. in color, map, May, 1945

J

A **JACK** in the Box: An Account of the Strange Performances of the Most Wonderful Island in the World (Bogoslof Volcano, Alaska). By Captain F. M. Munger. XX, pp. 194-199, 8 ills., Feb., 1909

JACKALS:

The Sacred Ibis Cemetery and Jackal Catacombs at Abydos. By Camden M. Cobern. XXIV, pp. 1042-1056, 10 ills., Sept., 1913

JACKSON, SHELDON:

Agriculture in the Yukon Valley. IX, pp. 189-190, Apr., 1898

The Arctic Cruise of the United States Revenue Cutter "Bear." By Dr. Sheldon Jackson. VII, pp. 27-31, 3 ills., Jan., 1896

Introducing Reindeer into Labrador. XVIII, p. 686, Oct., 1907

JACKSON, SHELDON—*Continued*
Reindeer in Alaska. By Gilbert H. Grosvenor. XIV, pp. 127-149, 19 ills., map, Apr., 1903
Note: Dr. Jackson's introduction of reindeer into Alaska
Some of the Conditions and Possibilities of Agriculture in Alaska. By Walter H. Evans. IX, pp. 178-187, Apr., 1898

JACKSON, W. H.:
Note on Glacier Discovery. (By W. H. Jackson). XVII, p. 587, Oct., 1906

JACKSON, Mississippi:
Machines Come to Mississippi. By J. R. Hildebrand. LXXII, pp. 263-318, 34 ills. in black and white, 26 ills. in color, two-page map, Sept., 1937

JACOBI, ELIZABETH P.:
Hungary, a Kingdom Without a King: A Tour from Central Europe's Largest Lake to the Fertile Plains of the Danube and the Tisza. By Elizabeth P. Jacobi. LXI, pp. 691-728, 22 ills. in black and white, 27 ills. in color, map, June, 1932

JACOBINS (Pigeons):
Man's Feathered Friends of Longest Standing: Peoples of Every Clime and Age Have Lavished Care and Affection Upon Lovely Pigeons. By Elisha Hanson. Paintings by Hashime Murayama. XLIX, pp. 63-110, 35 ills. in black and white, 12 ills. in color, Jan., 1926

JACOBS, FENNO:
Bolivia—Tin Roof of the Andes. 20 color photos by Carl S. Bell and Fenno Jacobs. LXXXIII, pp. 311-326, Mar., 1943
Paraguay: Color Cruising in Paraguay. 11 color photos by Fenno Jacobs. LXXXIV, pp. 465-472, Oct., 1943
Philippines: Camera Cruising in the Philippines. 12 color photos by J. Baylor Roberts, Fenno Jacobs, and others. LXXXVI, pp. 545-552, Nov., 1944

JACQUELINE, COUNTESS OF HOLLAND:
The City of Jacqueline (Ter Goes, Netherlands). By Florence Craig Albrecht. XXVII, pp. 29-56, 31 ills., Jan., 1915

JADE:
Expedition Unearths Buried Masterpieces of Carved Jade (Cerro de las Mesas, Mexico). By Matthew W. Stirling. LXXX, pp. 277-302, 14 ills. in black and white, 20 ills. in color, map, Sept., 1941
Finding Jewels of Jade in a Mexican Swamp (La Venta). By Matthew W. and Marion Stirling. LXXXII, pp. 635-661, 15 ills. in black and white, 12 ills. in color, map, Nov., 1942
Jade. By S. E. Easter. XIV, pp. 9-17, maps, Jan., 1903
La Venta's Green Stone Tigers. By Matthew W. Stirling. LXXXIV, pp. 321-332, 4 ills. in black and white, 6 ills. in color, map, Sept., 1943

JAGGAR, THOMAS AUGUSTUS:
The Eruption of Mount Vesuvius, April 7-8, 1906. By Thomas Augustus Jaggar, Jr. XVII, pp. 318-325, 6 ills., June, 1906

JAGGAR, THOMAS AUGUSTUS—*Continued*
Living on a Volcano: An Unspoiled Patch of Polynesia Is Niuafoō, Nicknamed "Tin Can Island" by Stamp Collectors. By Thomas A. Jaggar. LXVIII, pp. 91-106, 17 ills., map, July, 1935
Mapping the Home of the Great Brown Bear: Adventures of the National Geographic Society's Pavlof Volcano Expedition to Alaska. By Dr. Thomas A. Jaggar. LV, pp. 109-134, 30 ills., map, Jan., 1929
Sakurajima, Japan's Greatest Volcanic Eruption: A Convulsion of Nature Whose Ravages Were Minimized by Scientific Knowledge, Compared with the Terrors and Destruction of the Recent Tokyo Earthquake. By Dr. Thomas Augustus Jaggar. XLV, pp. 441-470, 32 ills., map, Apr., 1924

JAIPUR, India:
The Oriental Pageantry of Northern India. 8 color photos by Franklin Price Knott. LVI, pp. 429-460, Oct., 1929

JALISCO (State), Mexico:
Along the Old Spanish Road in Mexico: Life Among the People of Nayarit and Jalisco, Two of the Richest States of the Southern Republic. By Herbert Corey. XLIII, pp. 225-281, 36 ills. in black and white, 16 ills. in color, map, Mar., 1923
See also Guadalajara

JAMAICA:
Jamaica, the Isle of Many Rivers. By John Oliver La Gorce. LI, pp. 1-55, 38 ills. in black and white, 11 ills. in color, map, Jan., 1927
See also Cayman Islands

JAMMU AND KASHMIR. *See* Kashmir

JAN MAYEN (Island), Greenland Sea-Norwegian Sea:
Magnetic Observations in Iceland, Jan Mayen and Spitzbergen in 1892 (Geographic Notes. By Cyrus C. Babb). VI, pp. 223-224, table, Dec. 29, 1894

JANSSEN, G. E.:
War Meets Peace in Egypt. By Grant Parr and G. E. Janssen. LXXXI, pp. 503-526, 25 ills., map, Apr., 1942

JANSSEN OBSERVATORY, Mont Blanc:
The Ascent of Mont Blanc. By Walter Woodburn Hyde. XXIV, pp. 861-942, 69 ills., Aug., 1913

JAP Rule in the Hermit Nation (Korea). By Willard Price. LXXXVIII, pp. 429-451, 19 ills., map, Oct., 1945

JAPAN:
Agriculture in Japan. By Consul-General Bellows. XV, pp. 323-326, Aug., 1904
Behind the Mask of Modern Japan. By Willard Price. LXXXVIII, pp. 513-535, 14 ills., Nov., 1945
A Chapter from Japanese History. By Eki Hioki. XVI, pp. 220-228, May, 1905
The Characteristics of the Japanese People. By Baron Kentaro Kaneko. XVI, pp. 93-100, Mar., 1905
The Commercial Development of Japan. By O. P. Austin. X, pp. 329-337, Sept., 1899

JAPAN—*Continued*

Cultivation of Marine and Fresh-Water Animals in Japan. By K. Mitsukuri. XVII, pp. 524-531, 5 ills., Sept., 1906

The Empire of the Risen Sun. By William Elliot Griffis. XLIV, pp. 415-443, 21 ills., Oct., 1923

Face of Japan. By W. Robert Moore. LXXXVIII, pp. 753-768, 14 ills., map supplement, Dec., 1945

The Fisheries of Japan. By Hugh M. Smith. XV, pp. 362-364, Sept., 1904. XVI, pp. 201-220, 13 ills., May, 1905

Friendly Journeys in Japan: A Young American Finds a Ready Welcome in the Homes of the Japanese During Leisurely Travels Through the Islands. By John Patric. LXIX, pp. 441-480, 28 ills. in black and white, 10 ills. in color, map, Apr., 1936

The Geography of Japan: With Special Reference to Its Influence on the Character of the Japanese People. By Walter Weston. XL, pp. 45-84, 23 ills. in black and white, 16 ills. in color, July, 1921

Glimpses of Japan. By William W. Chapin. XXII, pp. 965-1002, 10 ills. in black and white, 34 ills. in color, Nov., 1911

How the Earth Telegraphed Its Tokyo Quake to Washington. By the Rev. Francis A. Tondorf. XLIV, pp. 453-454, ill., Oct., 1923

Japan. XXVI, pp. 415-420, 3 ills., Oct., 1914

Japan. By D. W. Stevens, Counselor of the Imperial Legation of Japan. VI, pp. 193-199, Dec. 29, 1894

Japan, America, and the Orient. By Eki Hioki. XVII, pp. 498-504, Sept., 1906

Japan, Child of the World's Old Age: An Empire of Mountainous Islands, Whose Alert People Constantly Conquer Harsh Forces of Land, Sea, and Sky. By William Elliot Griffis. LXIII, pp. 257-301, 37 ills. in black and white, 12 ills. in color, Mar., 1933

Japan and China—Some Comparisons. By Commander Harrie Webster. XII, pp. 69-77, ills., Feb., 1901

Japan and the Pacific. By Joseph C. Grew. LXXXV, pp. 385-414, 29 ills., 17 island maps, Apr., 1944

Japan and the United States. XVI, pp. 432-434, ill., Sept., 1905

Japan Faces Russia in Manchuria. By Willard Price. LXXXII, pp. 603-634, 30 ills., map, Nov., 1942

Koyasan, the Japanese Valhalla. By Eliza R. Scidmore. XVIII, pp. 650-670, 14 ills., Oct., 1907

Lessons from Japan. XV, pp. 221-225, 3 ills., May, 1904

The Making of a Japanese Newspaper. By Dr. Thomas E. Green. XXXVIII, pp. 327-334, 5 ills., Oct., 1920

Motor Trails in Japan. By W. Robert Moore. LXIII, pp. 303-318, 17 ills., Mar., 1933

National Geographic Map of Japan, Regions of Asia, and the Pacific. Text with map supplement. LXXXV, pp. 415-416, Apr., 1944

Observations on the Russo-Japanese War, in Japan and Manchuria. By Dr. Louis Livingston Seaman. XVI, pp. 80-82, Feb., 1905

The Population of Japan. (By Walter J. Ballard). XVI, p. 482, Oct., 1905

JAPAN—*Continued*

President Alexander Graham Bell on Japan. (By J. H.). IX, pp. 509-512, Dec., 1898

The Purpose of the Anglo-Japanese Alliance. By Eki Hioki. XVI, pp. 333-337, July, 1905

Race Prejudice in the Far East. By Melville E. Stone. XXI, pp. 973-985, 6 ills., Dec., 1910

The Recent Earthquake Wave on the Coast of Japan. By Eliza Ruhamah Scidmore. VII, pp. 285-289, 4 ills., foldout map, Sept., 1896

Sakurajima, Japan's Greatest Volcanic Eruption: A Convulsion of Nature Whose Ravages Were Minimized by Scientific Knowledge, Compared with the Terrors and Destruction of the Recent Tokyo Earthquake. By Dr. Thomas Augustus Jaggar. XLV, pp. 441-470, 32 ills., map, Apr., 1924

Some Aspects of Rural Japan. By Walter Weston. XLII, pp. 275-301, 12 ills. in black and white, 16 ills. in color, Sept., 1922

Some Facts About Japan. XV, pp. 446-448, Nov., 1904

Some Impressions of 150,000 Miles of Travel. By William Howard Taft. LVII, pp. 523-598, 80 ills., May, 1930

Sunset in the East. By Blair A. Walliser. LXXXIX, pp. 797-812, 17 ills., June, 1946

Tokyo To-day. By William R. Castle, Jr. LXI, pp. 131-162, 33 ills., Feb., 1932

Torii Gate. XXII, col. pl. p. 982, Nov., 1911; enlargement for framing

Unknown Japan: A Portrait of the People Who Make Up One of the Two Most Fanatical Nations in the World. By Willard Price. LXXXII, pp. 225-252, 30 ills., Aug., 1942

Why Nik-ko Is Beautiful. By J. H. De Forest. XIX, pp. 300-308, 8 ills., Apr., 1908

Women's Work in Japan. By Mary A. Nourse. LXXIII, pp. 99-132, 32 ills. in black and white, 11 ills. in color, Jan., 1938

Young Japan. By Eliza R. Scidmore. XXVI, pp. 36-38, 54-64, 11 ills. in color, July, 1914

See also Kazan Retto; Ogasawara Shoto; Okinawa; Ryukyu Retto; *and* the following mandated and occupied territories: Caroline Islands; Formosa; Korea; Manchuria (Manchukuo); Marianas Islands; Marshall Islands; Palau Islands

JAPANESE (People):

The Characteristics of the Japanese People. By Baron Kentaro Kaneko. XVI, pp. 93-100, Mar., 1905

The Geography of Japan: With Special Reference to Its Influence on the Character of the Japanese People. By Walter Weston. XL, pp. 45-84, 23 ills. in black and white, 16 ills. in color, July, 1921

Unknown Japan: A Portrait of the People Who Make Up One of the Two Most Fanatical Nations in the World. By Willard Price. LXXXII, pp. 225-252, 30 ills., Aug., 1942

JAUF (Al Jawf), Saudi Arabia:

Arabia, the Desert of the Sea. By Archibald Forder. XX, pp. 1039-1062, 1117, 20 ills., map, Dec., 1909

JAVA:

The Face of the Netherlands Indies. 20 photos by Maynard Owen Williams and others. LXXXIX, pp. 261-276, Feb., 1946

JAVA—*Continued*
Java Assignment. By Dee Bredin. LXXXI, pp. 89-119, 32 ills., map, Jan., 1942
Through Java in Pursuit of Color. By W. Robert Moore. LVI, pp. 333-362, 9 ills. in black and white, 29 ills. in color, map, Sept., 1929
A Traveler's Notes on Java. By Henry G. Bryant. XXI, pp. 91-111, 17 ills., Feb., 1910

JAVA, Queen of the East Indies. 29 color photos by W. Robert Moore and Tassilo Adam. LVI, pp. 335-358, Sept., 1929

JAYS:
Crows, Magpies, and Jays: Unusual Intelligence Has Earned a Unique Position for These Birds. By T. Gilbert Pearson. Paintings by Maj. Allan Brooks. LXIII, pp. 51-79, 16 ills. in black and white, 17 ills. in color, Jan., 1933
The White Sheep, Giant Moose, and Smaller Game of the Kenai Peninsula, Alaska. By George Shiras, 3d. XXIII, pp. 423-494, 59 ills., maps (1 two-page), May, 1912

JEAN-BRUNHES, MARIEL:
Cruising to Crete: Four French Girls Set Sail in a Breton Yawl for the Island of the Legendary Minotaur. By Marthe Oulié and Mariel Jean-Brunhes. LV, pp. 249-272, 15 ills. in black and white, 14 ills. in color, map, Feb., 1929

JEANNETTE (Ship):
The So-called "Jeannette Relics." By Professor William H. Dall. VII, pp. 93-98, Mar., 1896

JEFFERSON, MARK S. W.:
Atlantic Coast Tides. By Mark S. W. Jefferson. IX, pp. 497-509, 3 charts, Dec., 1898
Atlantic Estuarine Tides. By Mark S. W. Jefferson. IX, pp. 400-409, diagrs., 7 tables, maps, Sept., 1898
Limiting Width of Meander Belts. By Mark S. W. Jefferson. XIII, pp. 373-385, 6 charts, Oct., 1902
What Is the Tide of the Open Atlantic? By Mark S. W. Jefferson. IX, pp. 465-475, 6 charts, Nov., 1898

JEFFERSON, THOMAS:
Jefferson as a Geographer. By General A. W. Greely. VII, pp. 269-271, Aug., 1896
Jefferson's Little Mountain: Romance Enfolds Monticello, the Restored Home of the Author of the Declaration of Independence. By Paul Wilstach. LV, pp. 481-503, 12 ills. in black and white, 12 ills. in color, Apr., 1929

JEFFERSON'S Little Mountain: Romance Enfolds Monticello, the Restored Home of the Author of the Declaration of Independence. By Paul Wilstach. LV, pp. 481-503, 12 ills. in black and white, 12 ills. in color, Apr., 1929

JELLYFISHES:
The Life of the Moon-Jelly. By William Crowder. Paintings by author. L, pp. 187-202, 6 ills. in black and white, 8 ills. in color, Aug., 1926
Included: Aurelia Aurita, Beroe Cucumis, Cunoctantha Octonaria, Cyanea Capillata, Dactylometra Quinquecirra, Eutima Variabilis, Gonionemus Murbachii, Linerges Mercurius, Mnemiopsis Leidyi, Pelagia Cyanella, Pleurobrachia Rhododactyla, Sarsia Mirabilis, Stomolophus Meleagris, Zygodactyla Groenlandica

JELLYFISHES—Living Draperies of Color. 8 ills. in color from paintings by William Crowder. L, pp. 193-200, Aug., 1926

JENKINS, HESTER DONALDSON:
Armenia and the Armenians. By Hester Donaldson Jenkins. XXVIII, pp. 329-360, 27 ills., map, Oct., 1915
Bulgaria and Its Women. By Hester Donaldson Jenkins. XXVII, pp. 377-400, 22 ills., Apr., 1915

JENKS, GEORGE ELWOOD:
Marvels of Metamorphosis: A Scientific "G-man" Pursues Rare Trapdoor Spider Parasites for Three Years With a Spade and a Candid Camera. By George Elwood Jenks. LXXIV, pp. 807-828, 39 ills., Dec., 1938

JERICHO, Palestine:
The Geography of the Jordan. By Nelson Glueck. LXXXVI, pp. 719-744, 23 ills., map, Dec., 1944

JERID (Region), Algeria-Tunisia:
The Date Gardens of the Jerid. By Thomas H. Kearney. XXI, pp. 543-567, 20 ills., July, 1910

JERSEY (Island), Channel Islands:
The Channel Islands. By Edith Carey. XXXVIII, pp. 143-164, 24 ills., map, Aug., 1920

JERUSALEM, Holy Land:
American Fighters Visit Bible Lands. By Maynard Owen Williams. With 23 color photos by author. LXXXIX, pp. 311-340, 10 ills. in black and white, Mar., 1946
Changing Palestine. By Major Edward Keith-Roach. LXV, pp. 493-527, 43 ills., map, Apr., 1934
Color Records from the Changing Life of the Holy City. By Maynard Owen Williams. LII, pp. 682-707, 27 ills. in color, Dec., 1927
Crusader Castles of the Near East. By William H. Hall. LIX, pp. 369-390, 19 ills., map, Mar., 1931
In the Birthplace of Christianity. 8 color photos by Hans Hildenbrand and Gervais Courtellemont. L, pp. 697-720, Dec., 1926
Jerusalem's Locust Plague: Being a Description of the Recent Locust Influx into Palestine, and Comparing Same with Ancient Locust Invasions as Narrated in the Old World's History Book, the Bible. By John D. Whiting. XXVIII, pp. 511-550, 25 ills., map, Dec., 1915
An Old Jewel in the Proper Setting: An Eyewitness's Account of the Reconquest of the Holy Land by Twentieth Century Crusaders. By Charles W. Whitehair. XXXIV, pp. 325-344, 17 ills., Oct., 1918
The Pageant of Jerusalem: The Capital of the Land of Three Great Faiths Is Still the Holy City for Christian, Moslem, and Jew. By Major Edward Keith-Roach. LII, pp. 635-681, 57 ills., Dec., 1927
Palestine Today. By Francis Chase, Jr. XC, pp. 501-516, 16 ills., Oct., 1946
Village Life in the Holy Land. By John D. Whiting. XXV, pp. 249-314, 27 ills. in black and white, 21 ills. in color, Mar., 1914

JERUSALEM'S Locust Plague: Being a Description of the Recent Locust Influx into Palestine, and Comparing Same with Ancient Locust Invasions as Narrated in the Old World's History Book, the Bible. By John D. Whiting. XXVIII, pp. 511-550, 25 ills., map, Dec., 1915

JESSOP, LOUISE AHL:

A Pilgrimage to Amernath, Himalayan Shrine of the Hindu Faith. By Louise Ahl Jessop. XL, pp. 513-542, 29 ills., Nov., 1921

JESUP, MORRIS K.:

Election of Morris K. Jesup as Honorary Member of the Society. XVIII, p. 51, Jan., 1907

JET PROPULSION:

Air Power for Peace. By General H. H. Arnold. LXXXIX, pp. 137-193, 35 ills. in black and white, 28 ills. in color, map supplement, Feb., 1946

New Frontier in the Sky. By F. Barrows Colton. XC, pp. 379-408, 28 ills., diagr., Sept., 1946

Your New World of Tomorrow. By F. Barrows Colton. LXXXVIII, pp. 385-410, 25 ills., Oct., 1945

JEWELS:

Princely India, Resplendent with Jewels and Gold. 40 color photos by Lawrence Copley Thaw. LXXVIII, pp. 733-780, Dec., 1940

See also Gems; Jade; Pearl Fisheries

JEWS:

American Fighters Visit Bible Lands. By Maynard Owen Williams. With 23 color photos by author. LXXXIX, pp. 311-340, 10 ills. in black and white, Mar., 1946

The Chinese Jews. By Oliver Bainbridge. XVIII, pp. 621-632, 7 ills., Oct., 1907

Palestine Today. By Francis Chase, Jr. XC, pp. 501-516, 16 ills., Oct., 1946

Pedaling Through Poland: An American Girl Free-wheels Alone from Kraków, and Its Medieval Byways, Toward Ukraine's Restive Borderland. By Dorothy Hosmer. LXXV, pp. 739-775, 38 ills., maps, June, 1939

The Progressive World Struggle of the Jews for Civil Equality. By William Howard Taft. XXXVI, pp. 1-23, 14 ills., July, 1919

The Races of Europe. By Edwin A. Grosvenor. XXXIV, pp. 441-534, 62 ills., diagr. and index, maps, map supplement, Dec., 1918

JHELUM (River), India:

A Pilgrimage to Amernath, Himalayan Shrine of the Hindu Faith. By Louise Ahl Jessop. XL, pp. 513-542, 29 ills., Nov., 1921

JIDDA, Saudi Arabia:

Guest in Saudi Arabia. By Maynard Owen Williams. LXXXVIII, pp. 463-487, 24 ills., map, Oct., 1945

Mecca the Mystic: A New Kingdom Within Arabia. By S. M. Zwemer. XXXII, pp. 157-172, 13 ills., Aug., 1917

The Rise of the New Arab Nation. By Frederick Simpich. XXXVI, pp. 369-393, 17 ills., map, Nov., 1919

An Unbeliever Joins the Hadj: On the Age-Old Pilgrimage to Mecca, Babies Are Born, Elders Die, and Families May Halt a Year to Earn Funds in Distant Lands. By Owen Tweedy. LXV, pp. 761-789, 30 ills., map, June, 1934

JIVARO INDIANS:

Over Trail and Through Jungle in Ecuador: Indian Head-Hunters of the Interior, an Interesting Study in the South American Republic. By H. E. Anthony. XL, pp. 327-352, 28 ills., Oct., 1921

JOAN OF ARC:

The Maid of France Rides By: Compiègne, Where Joan of Arc Fought Her Last Battle, Celebrates Her Fifth Centenary. By Inez Buffington Ryan. LXII, pp. 607-616, 15 ills. in color, Nov., 1932

JOBOS Harbor (Puerto Rico). (By O. H. Tittmann). X, p. 206, June, 1899

JOHANNESBURG, Transvaal:

The Cities That Gold and Diamonds Built: Transvaal Treasures Have Created Bustling Johannesburg and Fostered Pretoria, Administrative Capital of the South African Union. By W. Robert Moore. LXXXII, pp. 735-766, 20 ills. in black and white, 9 ills. in color, map, Dec., 1942

Transvaal: The Treasure-House Province. By Melville Chater. LIX, pp. 479-512, 28 ills. in black and white, 13 ills. in color, Apr., 1931

JOHANSEN, FREDERIC H.:

The Nansen Polar Expedition. Special Report of the Hon. Ernest A. Man. VII, pp. 339-344, map supplement, Oct., 1896

JOHN G. SHEDD AQUARIUM, Chicago. *See* Shedd Aquarium

JOHNS HOPKINS UNIVERSITY, Baltimore, Maryland:

A Maryland Pilgrimage: Visits to Hallowed Shrines Recall the Major Rôle Played by This Prosperous State in the Development of Popular Government in America. By Gilbert Grosvenor. LI, pp. 133-212, 88 ills., map supplement, Feb., 1927

JOHNSON, ELECTA:

Westward Bound in the *Yankee*. By Irving and Electa Johnson. LXXXI, pp. 1-44, 25 ills. in black and white, 20 ills. in color, map, Jan., 1942

JOHNSON, EMORY R.:

The Interoceanic Canal. By Emory R. Johnson. X, pp. 311-316, Aug., 1899

JOHNSON, FRANK EDWARD:

The Greek Bronzes of Tunisia. By Frank Edward Johnson. XXIII, pp. 89-103, 11 ills., Jan., 1912

Here and There in Northern Africa. By Frank Edward Johnson. XXV, pp. 1-132, 113 ills., Jan., 1914

The Mole Men: An Account of the Troglodytes of Southern Tunisia. By Frank Edward Johnson. XXII, pp. 787-846, 60 ills., Sept., 1911

The Sacred City of the Sands (Kairouan, Tunisia). By Frank Edward Johnson. XXII, pp. 1061-1093, 25 ills., map, Dec., 1911

Tunis of Today. By Frank Edward Johnson. XXII, pp. 723-749, 24 ills., Aug., 1911

JOHNSON, IRVING:

Westward Bound in the *Yankee*. By Irving and Electa Johnson. LXXXI, pp. 1-44, 25 ills. in black and white, 20 ills. in color, map, Jan., 1942

Storied Islands of the South Sea. 20 color photos: 13 by Irving Johnson, pp. 9-40

JOHNSON, RAY G.:

Exploring a Grass Wonderland of Wild West China. By Ray G. Johnson. LXXXV, pp. 713-742, 24 ills., map, June, 1944

JOHNSON, WILLARD D.:
Cloud Scenery of the High Plains. By Willard D. Johnson. IX, pp. 493-496, 3 ills., Dec., 1898
Seriland. By W J McGee and Willard D. Johnson. VII, pp. 125-133, ill., foldout map, Apr., 1896
See also NGS: Board of Managers

JOHNSTON, SIR HARRY:
The Black Republic—Liberia. By Sir Harry Johnston and Ernest Lyon. XVIII, pp. 334-343, 9 ills., May, 1907
Haiti, the Home of Twin Republics. By Sir Harry Johnston. XXXVIII, pp. 483-496, 11 ills., map, Dec., 1920
Where Roosevelt Will Hunt (Africa). By Sir Harry Johnston. XX, pp. 207-256, 43 ills., map supplement, Mar., 1909

JONAS, LUCIEN:
Three Drawings of the World War. 3 ills. from drawings by Lucien Jonas. XXXIII, pp. 355-355b, Apr., 1918

JONES, E. LESTER. *See* NGS: Board of Trustees

JONES, FRANK I.:
Katmai. 16 color photos by Frank I. Jones. XL, pp. 271-278, Sept., 1921

JONES, STUART E.:
Demolishing Germany's North Sea Ramparts. By Stuart E. Jones. XC, pp. 635-644, ill. in black and white, 10 ills. in color, Nov., 1946

JONES SOUND, Northwest Territories:
Charles Francis Hall and Jones Sound. (By A. W. G.). VII, pp. 308-310, Sept., 1896

JORDAN. *See* Trans-Jordan

JORDAN (River), Palestine:
Canoeing Down the River Jordan: Voyagers in Rubber Boats Find the Bible Stream Little Tamed Today as It Plunges to the Dead Sea Over the Earth's Lowest River Bed. By John D. Whiting. LXXVIII, pp. 781-808, 19 ills., map, Dec., 1940
The Geography of the Jordan. By Nelson Glueck. LXXXVI, pp. 719-744, 23 ills., map, Dec., 1944

JOSEPH CONRAD (Ship):
North About. By Alan J. Villiers. LXXI, pp. 221-250, 24 ills., Feb., 1937

JOSEPHINE FORD (Airplane):
The First Flight to the North Pole. By Lieutenant Commander Richard Evelyn Byrd. L, pp. 357-376, 14 ills., Sept., 1926

JOURNALISM:
China: New China and the Printed Page. By Paul Hutchinson. LI, pp. 687-722, 37 ills., June, 1927
Japan: The Making of a Japanese Newspaper. By Dr. Thomas E. Green. XXXVIII, pp. 327-334, 5 ills., Oct., 1920

A **JOURNEY** by Jungle Rivers to the Home of the Cock-of-the-rock: Naturalists Enter the Amazon, Voyage Through the Heart of Tropical South America, and Emerge at the Mouth of the Orinoco. By Ernest G. Holt. LXIV, pp. 585-630, 49 ills., map, Nov., 1933

A **JOURNEY** in Ecuador. By Mark B. Kerr, C. E. VII, pp. 238-245, ills., map, July, 1896

A **JOURNEY** in Morocco: "The Land of the Moors." By Thomas Lindsey Blayney. XXII, pp. 750-775, 23 ills., map, Aug., 1911

A **JOURNEY** Through the Eastern Portion of the Congo State. By Major P. H. G. Powell-Cotton. XIX, pp. 155-163, 9 ills., Mar., 1908

JUAN FERNANDEZ ISLAND, Pacific Ocean:
A Voyage to the Island Home of Robinson Crusoe. By Waldo L. Schmitt. LIV, pp. 353-370, 24 ills., Sept., 1928

JUÁREZ, BENITO:
Among the Zapotecs of Mexico: A Visit to the Indians of Oaxaca, Home State of the Republic's Great Liberator, Juárez, and Its Most Famous Ruler, Diaz. By Herbert Corey. LI, pp. 501-553, 59 ills., map, May, 1927

JUDAISM:
The Pageant of Jerusalem: The Capital of the Land of Three Great Faiths Is Still the Holy City for Christian, Moslem, and Jew. By Major Edward Keith-Roach. LII, pp. 635-681, 57 ills., Dec., 1927
See also Jews

JUDD, NEIL M.:
Beyond the Clay Hills: An Account of the National Geographic Society's Reconnaissance of a Previously Unexplored Section in Utah. By Neil M. Judd. XLV, pp. 275-302, 28 ills., map, Mar., 1924
Everyday Life in Pueblo Bonito: As Disclosed by the National Geographic Society's Archeologic Explorations in the Chaco Canyon National Monument, New Mexico. By Neil M. Judd. XLVIII, pp. 227-262, 37 ills., map, Sept., 1925
Pueblo Bonito, the Ancient: The National Geographic Society's Third Expedition to the Southwest Seeks to Read in the Rings of Trees the Secret of the Age of Ruins. By Neil M. Judd. XLIV, pp. 99-108, 9 ills., diagr., July, 1923
The Pueblo Bonito Expedition of the National Geographic Society. By Neil M. Judd. XLI, pp. 323-331, 10 ills., diagr., Mar., 1922

JUGOSLAVIA. *See* Yugoslavia

JUGOSLAVIA—Ten Years After. By Melville Chater. LVIII, pp. 257-309, 44 ills. in black and white, 25 ills. in color, map, Sept., 1930

JULL, MORLEY A.:
Fowls of Forest and Stream Tamed by Man. By Morley A. Jull. Paintings by Hashime Murayama. LVII, pp. 327-371, 27 ills. in black and white, 16 ills. in color, Mar., 1930
The Races of Domestic Fowl. By M. A. Jull. Paintings by Hashime Murayama. LI, pp. 379-452, 67 ills. in black and white, 29 ills. in color, Apr., 1927

A **JUMPING** Salmon. XIX, pp. 124-125, ill., Feb., 1908

JUNE Week at Annapolis, Cradle of the Navy. 13 ills. in color. LXIX, pp. 791-798, June, 1936

JUNGLE Housekeeping for a Geographic Expedition (Cerro de las Mesas). By Marion Stirling. LXXX, pp. 303-327, 15 ills., Sept., 1941

JUNGLE War: Bougainville and New Caledonia. 17 ills. in color from paintings by Lieut. William F. Draper. LXXXV, pp. 417-432, Apr., 1944

JUNGLES:

Africa: Flashlights from the Jungle. XVIII, pp. 534-548, 11 ills., Aug., 1907

Africa: Through the Deserts and Jungles of Africa by Motor: Caterpillar Cars Make 15,000-Mile Trip from Algeria to Madagascar in Nine Months. By Georges-Marie Haardt. XLIX, pp. 651-720, 95 ills., map, June, 1926

Brazil: By Seaplane to Six Continents: Cruising 60,000 Miles, Italian Argonauts of the Air See World Geography Unroll, and Break New Sky Trails Over Vast Brazilian Jungles. By Commander Francesco de Pinedo. LIV, pp. 247-301, 60 ills., two-page map, Sept., 1928

Brazil: Exploring the Valley of the Amazon in a Hydroplane: Twelve Thousand Miles of Flying Over the World's Greatest River and Greatest Forest to Chart the Unknown Parima River from the Sky. By Captain Albert W. Stevens. XLIX, pp. 353-420, 86 ills., map, Apr., 1926

British Guiana: A New World to Explore: In the Tree-Roof of the British Guiana Forest Flourishes Much Hitherto-Unknown Life. By Maj. R. W. G. Hingston. LXII, pp. 617-642, 35 ills., Nov., 1932

Burma: Working Teak in the Burma Forests: The Sagacious Elephant Is Man's Ablest Ally in the Logging Industry of the Far East. By A. W. Smith. LVIII, pp. 239-256, 5 ills. in black and white, 15 ills. in color, Aug., 1930

Ecuador: Mrs. Robinson Crusoe in Ecuador. By Mrs. Richard C. Gill. LXV, pp. 133-172, 43 ills., map, Feb., 1934

Guatemala: Mysterious Temples of the Jungle: The Prehistoric Ruins of Guatemala. By W. F. Sands. XXIV, pp. 325-338, 10 ills., Mar., 1913

Mexico: Great Stone Faces of the Mexican Jungle: Five Colossal Heads and Numerous Other Monuments of Vanished Americans Are Excavated by the Latest National Geographic-Smithsonian Expedition. By Matthew W. Stirling. LXXVIII, pp. 309-334, 26 ills., map, Sept., 1940

Mexico: Jungle Housekeeping for a Geographic Expedition. By Marion Stirling. LXXX, pp. 303-327, 15 ills., Sept., 1941

Panama: The Jungles of Panama. By David Fairchild. XLI, pp. 131-145, 14 ills., Feb., 1922

Tanganyika: Flashlights from the Jungle. XVIII, pp. 534-548, 11 ills., Aug., 1907

Thailand: The Warfare of the Jungle Folk: Campaigning Against Tigers, Elephants, and Other Wild Animals in Northern Siam. By Merian C. Cooper. Photos by Ernest B. Schoedsack. LIII, pp. 233-268, 33 ills., Feb., 1928

Venezuela: I Kept House in a Jungle: The Spell of Primeval Tropics in Venezuela, Riotous With Strange Plants, Animals, and Snakes, Enthralls a Young American Woman. By Anne Rainey Langley. LXXV, pp. 97-132, 37 ills., map, Jan., 1939

JUNKS (Boats):

Cosmopolitan Shanghai, Key Seaport of China. By W. Robert Moore. LXII, pp. 311-335, 19 ills., Sept., 1932

Life Afloat in China: Tens of Thousands of Chinese in Congested Ports Spend Their Entire Existence on Boats. By Robert F. Fitch. LI, pp. 665-686, 28 ills., June, 1927

Macao, "Land of Sweet Sadness": The Oldest European Settlement in the Far East, Long the Only Haven for Distressed Mariners in the China Sea. By Edgar Allen Forbes. LXII, pp. 337-357, 13 ills. in black and white, 11 ills. in color, Sept., 1932

Pirate-Fighters of the South China Sea. By Robert Cardwell. LXXXIX, pp. 787-796, 11 ills., June, 1946

JUNOR, KENNETH F.:

Curious and Characteristic Customs of China. By Kenneth F. Junor. XXI, pp. 791-806, 7 ills., Sept., 1910

JUSSERAND, JEAN ADRIEN ANTOINE JULES:

Armistice Day and the American Battlefields. By J. J. Jusserand. LVI, pp. 509-554, 32 ills. in black and white, 23 ills. in color, Nov., 1929

The Discovery of the North Pole (Address by J. J. Jusserand). XXI, pp. 63-80, Jan., 1910

Honors for Amundsen (Address by J. J. Jusserand). XIX, pp. 55-76, 13 ills., Jan., 1908

Honors to Amundsen and Peary (Address by J. J. Jusserand). XXIV, pp. 113-130, 5 ills., Jan., 1913

Honors to Colonel Goethals: The Presentation, by President Woodrow Wilson, of the National Geographic Society Special Gold Medal, and Addresses by Secretary of State Bryan, the French Ambassador, the German Ambassador, and Congressman James R. Mann (Election of J. J. Jusserand as Honorary Member of the Society). XXV, pp. 677-690, 6 ills., June, 1914

Our First Alliance. By J. J. Jusserand. XXXI, pp. 518-548, 8 ills., June, 1917

Our Second Alliance. By J. J. Jusserand. XXXI, pp. 565-566, ill., June, 1917

JUTE:

India's Treasures Helped the Allies. By John Fischer. LXXXIX, pp. 501-522, 18 ills., Apr., 1946

JYEKUNDO (Yushu), China:

Across Tibet from India to China. By Lt. Col. Ilia Tolstoy, AUS. XC, pp. 169-222, 41 ills., map, Aug., 1946

K

KABUL, Afghanistan:

Back to Afghanistan. By Maynard Owen Williams. XC, pp. 517-544, 27 ills., map, Oct., 1946

KAF, Arabian Peninsula:

Arabia, the Desert of the Sea. By Archibald Forder. XX, pp. 1039-1062, 1117, 20 ills., map, Dec., 1909

KAFIRS (Tribespeople):

Impressions and Scenes of Mozambique. By O. W. Barrett. XXI, pp. 807-830, 31 ills., Oct., 1910

KAHN, MIRZA ALI KULI:
The National Geographic Society (Speech by Mirza Ali Kuli Kahn). XXIII, pp. 272-298, 5 ills., Mar., 1912

KAIETEUR FALLS, British Guiana:
Kaieteur and Roraima: The Great Falls and the Great Mountain of the Guianas. By Henry Edward Crampton. XXXVIII, pp. 227-244, 12 ills., map, Sept., 1920
The World's Greatest Waterfall: The Kaieteur Fall, in British Guiana. By Leonard Kennedy. XXII, pp. 846-859, 6 ills., map, Sept., 1911

KAIJO (Songdo), Korea:
Chosen—Land of Morning Calm. By Mabel Craft Deering. LXIV, pp. 421-448, 20 ills. in black and white, 13 ills. in color, map, Oct., 1933

KAIROUAN, Tunisia:
Eastward from Gibraltar: Overland Route Across North Africa to Tunisia and Libia. By Cyrus French Wicker. LXXXIII, pp. 115-142, 28 ills., Jan., 1943
The Sacred City of the Sands. By Frank Edward Johnson. XXII, pp. 1061-1093, 25 ills., map, Dec., 1911

KAISER WILHELM CANAL, Germany:
The Great Canals of the World. XVI, pp. 475-479, Oct., 1905

KALEIDOSCOPIC Land of Europe's Youngest King: Yugoslavia Holds a Mosaic of Slavs and the City Where Pistol Shots Touched Off the World War. By Douglas Chandler. LXXV, pp. 691-738, 18 ills. in black and white, 34 ills. in color, maps, June, 1939

KALEIDOSCOPIC La Paz: The City of the Clouds. By Harriet Chalmers Adams. XX, pp. 119-141, 23 ills., Feb., 1909

KALMBACH, E. R.:
The Crow, Bird Citizen of Every Land: A Feathered Rogue Who Has Many Fascinating Traits and Many Admirable Qualities Despite His Marauding Propensities. By E. R. Kalmbach. XXXVII, pp. 322-337, 10 ills., Apr., 1920

KALMUCKS (Tribespeople):
With the Nomads of Central Asia: A Summer's Sojourn in the Tekes Valley, Plateau Paradise of Mongol and Turkic Tribes. By Edward Murray. Paintings and drawings by Alexandre Iacovleff. LXIX, pp. 1-57, 43 ills. in black and white, 26 ills. in color, map, Jan., 1936

KAMCHATKA (Region), U. S. S. R.:
A Critical Review of Bering's First Expedition, 1725-30, Together with a Translation of His Original Report Upon It. With a Map. By Wm. H. Dall. II, pp. 111-169, 8 tables, foldout map, May, 1890
Included: Supplementary Note by Marcus Baker, On the Alleged Observation of a Lunar Eclipse by Bering in 1728-9, pp. 167-169

KAMPANZAN, Formosa (Island):
Formosa the Beautiful. By Alice Ballantine Kirjassoff. XXXVII, pp. 247-292, 60 ills., map, Mar., 1920

KANDAHAR, Afghanistan:
Back to Afghanistan. By Maynard Owen Williams. XC, pp. 517-544, 27 ills., map, Oct., 1946

KANDY, Ceylon:
Adam's Second Eden. By Eliza Ruhamah Scidmore. XXIII, pp. 105-173, 206, 61 ills., Feb., 1912
The Perahera Processions of Ceylon. By G. H. G. Burroughs. LXII, pp. 90-100, ill. in black and white, 8 ills. in duotone, July, 1932

KANEKO, KENTARO, BARON:
The Characteristics of the Japanese People. By Baron Kentaro Kaneko. XVI, pp. 93-100, Mar., 1905

KANGAROO RAT:
Dipo, the Little Desert "Kangaroo." By Walter E. Ketcham. LXXVIII, pp. 537-548, Oct., 1940

KANO, Mud-made City. 10 color photos by George W. Scott and K. S. Twitchell. LXXXV, pp. 545-552, May, 1944

KANO, Nigeria:
Nigeria: From the Bight of Benin to Africa's Desert Sands. By Helen Trybulowski Gilles. LXXXV, pp. 537-568, 17 ills. in black and white, 10 ills. in color, map, May, 1944

KANSAS:
Cloud Scenery of the High Plains. By Willard D. Johnson. IX, pp. 493-496, 3 ills., Dec., 1898
The Kansas River. By Arthur P. Davis. VII, pp. 181-184, tables, May, 1896
Speaking of Kansas. By Frederick Simpich. LXXII, pp. 135-182, 37 ills. in black and white, 12 ills. in color, two-page map, Aug., 1937

KANSAS CITY, Missouri:
Taming the Outlaw Missouri River. By Frederick Simpich. LXXXVIII, pp. 569-598, 25 ills., two-page map, Nov., 1945
These Missourians. By Frederick Simpich. LXXXIX, pp. 277-310, 12 ills. in black and white, 22 ills. in color, map, Mar., 1946

The **KANSAS** River. By Arthur P. Davis. VII, pp. 181-184, tables, May, 1896

KANSU (Province), China:
China Fights Erosion with U. S. Aid. By Walter C. Lowdermilk. LXXXVII, pp. 641-680, 10 ills. in black and white, 26 ills. in color, June, 1945
"Where the Mountains Walked": An Account of the Recent Earthquake in Kansu Province, China, Which Destroyed 100,000 Lives. By Upton Close and Elsie McCormick. XLI, pp. 445-464, 23 ills., map, May, 1922
See also Choni

KARAGANDA, U. S. S. R.:
New Road to Asia. By Owen Lattimore. LXXXVI, pp. 641-676, 15 ills. in black and white, 26 ills. in color, Dec., 1944

KARAKUL SHEEP:
The Land of Lambskins: An Expedition to Bokhara, Russian Central Asia, to Study the Karakul Sheep Industry. By Robert K. Nabours. XXXVI, pp. 77-88, 15 ills., July, 1919

KARBALA (Kerbela), Iraq:
Mystic Nedjef, the Shia Mecca. By Frederick Simpich. XXVI, pp. 589-598, 4 ills., Dec., 1914

KARENS (Tribespeople):

Among the Hill Tribes of Burma—An Ethnological Thicket. By Sir George Scott. XLI, pp. 293-321, 22 ills., Mar., 1922

Burma: Where India and China Meet: In the Massive Mountains of Southeast Asia, Swarming Road Builders Wage the "War of the Highways" for Free China and Her Allies. By John LeRoy Christian. LXXXIV, pp. 489-512, 18 ills., map, Oct., 1943

Notes on Burma. By Thomas Barbour. XX, pp. 841-866, 34 ills., Oct., 1909

KARNAK, Egypt:

The Resurrection of Ancient Egypt. By James Baikie. XXIV, pp. 957-1020, 46 ills., map, Sept., 1913

KÄRNTEN (Austrian Province):

Entering the Front Doors of Medieval Towns: The Adventures of an American Woman and Her Daughter in a Folding Boat on Eight Rivers of Germany and Austria. By Cornelia Stratton Parker. LXI, pp. 365-394, 23 ills. in black and white, 11 ills. in color, map, Mar., 1932

KARYÉS, Greece:

The Hoary Monasteries of Mt. Athos. By H. G. Dwight. XXX, pp. 249-272, 24 ills., map, Sept., 1916

KASHGAIS (Tribespeople):

Mountain Tribes of Iran and Iraq. By Harold Lamb. LXXXIX, pp. 385-408, 15 ills., two-page map, Mar., 1946

KASHMIR:

First Over the Roof of the World by Motor: The Trans-Asiatic Expedition Sets New Records for Wheeled Transport in Scaling Passes of the Himalayas. By Maynard Owen Williams. LXI, pp. 321-363, 45 ills., maps, Mar., 1932

House-Boat Days in the Vale of Kashmir. By Florence H. Morden. LVI, pp. 437-463, 22 ills. in black and white, 10 ills. in color, Oct., 1929

On the World's Highest Plateaus: Through an Asiatic No Man's Land to the Desert of Ancient Cathay. By Hellmut de Terra. LIX, pp. 319-367, 39 ills. in black and white, 32 ills. in color, map, Mar., 1931

Outwitting the Water Demons of Kashmir. By Maurice Pratt Dunlap. XL, pp. 499-511, 9 ills., Nov., 1921

A Pilgrimage to Amernath, Himalayan Shrine of the Hindu Faith. By Louise Ahl Jessop. XL, pp. 513-542, 29 ills., Nov., 1921

KATMAI, Mount, Alaska:

Our Greatest National Monument: The National Geographic Society Completes Its Explorations in the Valley of Ten Thousand Smokes. By Robert F. Griggs. XL, pp. 219-292, 73 ills. in black and white, 16 ills. in color, maps, Sept., 1921

The Recent Eruption of Katmai Volcano in Alaska. By George C. Martin. XXIV, pp. 131-181, 45 ills., diagr., map, Feb., 1913

The Ten Thousand Smokes Now a National Monument: The President of the United States Sets Aside for the American People the Extraordinary Valley Discovered and Explored by the National Geographic Society. XXXV, pp. 359-366, 5 ills., Apr., 1919

KATMAI, Mount, Alaska—*Continued*

The Valley of Ten Thousand Smokes: An Account of the Discovery and Exploration of the Most Wonderful Volcanic Region in the World. By Robert F. Griggs. XXXIII, pp. 115-169, 46 ills., map, panorama, Feb., 1918

The Valley of Ten Thousand Smokes: National Geographic Society's Explorations in the Katmai District of Alaska. By Robert F. Griggs. XXXI, pp. 13-68, 51 ills., map, Jan., 1917

Volcanoes of Alaska (Report by Capt. K. W. Perry). XXIII, pp. 824-832, 11 ills., Aug., 1912

KATZIMO. *See* Enchanted Mesa

KAUFFMANN, RUDOLPH. *See* NGS: Board of Managers

KAWS (Tribespeople):

Burma: Where India and China Meet: In the Massive Mountains of Southeast Asia, Swarming Road Builders Wage the "War of the Highways" for Free China and Her Allies. By John LeRoy Christian. LXXXIV, pp. 489-512, 18 ills., map, Oct., 1943

Shan Tribes Make Burma's Hills Flash With Color. 15 color photos by W. Robert Moore. LX, pp. 455-462, Oct., 1931

Strange Tribes in the Shan States of Burma. 15 color photos by W. Robert Moore. LVIII, pp. 247-254, Aug., 1930

KAYANS (Tribespeople):

Sarawak: The Land of the White Rajahs. By Harrison W. Smith. XXXV, pp. 110-167, 28 ills., map, Feb., 1919

KAZAKH SOVIET SOCIALIST REPUBLIC, U. S. S. R.:

New Road to Asia. By Owen Lattimore. LXXXVI, pp. 641-676, 15 ills. in black and white, 26 ills. in color, Dec., 1944

See also Ak Bulak

KAZAKHS:

New Road to Asia. By Owen Lattimore. LXXXVI, pp. 641-676, 15 ills. in black and white, 26 ills. in color, Dec., 1944

KAZAN RETTO (Volcano Islands), Pacific Ocean:

Springboards to Tokyo. By Willard Price. LXXXVI, pp. 385-407, 16 ills., Oct., 1944

KBOO, a Liberian Game. By G. N. Collins. XXI, pp. 944-948, 3 ills., Nov., 1910

KEARNEY, THOMAS H.:

The Country of the Ant Men. By Thomas H. Kearney. XXII, pp. 367-382, 13 ills., map, panorama, Apr., 1911

The Date Gardens of the Jerid. By Thomas H. Kearney. XXI, pp. 543-567, 20 ills., July, 1910

KEARNY, Camp, California:

Bringing the World to Our Foreign-Language Soldiers: How a Military Training Camp is Solving a Seemingly Unsurmountable Problem by Using the Geographic. By Christina Krysto. XXXIV, pp. 81-90, 4 ills., Aug., 1918

KEBON DJAHE, Sumatra:
By Motor Through the East Coast and Batak Highlands of Sumatra. By Melvin A. Hall. XXXVII, pp. 69-102, 27 ills., Jan., 1920

KEEN, DORA:
A Woman's Climbs in the High Alps. By Dora Keen. XXII, pp. 643-675, 26 ills., July, 1911

KEEPING House for the "Shepherds of the Sun." By Mrs. William H. Hoover. LVII, pp. 483-506, 17 ills., map, Apr., 1930

KEEPING House in Borneo. By Virginia Hamilton. LXXXVIII, pp. 293-324, 28 ills., map, Sept., 1945

KEEPING House in Majorca. By Phoebe Binney Harnden. XLV, pp. 425-440, 18 ills., map, Apr., 1924

KEEPING House on the Congo. By Ruth Q. McBride. LXXII, pp. 643-670, 29 ills., Nov., 1937

KEIJO, Korea. *See* Seoul

KEITH-ROACH, EDWARD:
Adventures Among the "Lost Tribes of Islam" in Eastern Darfur: A Personal Narrative of Exploring, Mapping, and Setting Up a Government in the Anglo-Egyptian Sudan Borderland. By Major Edward Keith-Roach. XLV, pp. 41-73, 32 ills., map, Jan., 1924
Changing Palestine. By Major Edward Keith-Roach. LXV, pp. 493-527, 43 ills., map, Apr., 1934
The Pageant of Jerusalem: The Capital of the Land of Three Great Faiths Is Still the Holy City for Christian, Moslem, and Jew. By Major Edward Keith-Roach. LII, pp. 635-681, 57 ills., Dec., 1927

KĚKAWNGDU (Tribespeople):
Among the Hill Tribes of Burma—An Ethnological Thicket. By Sir George Scott. XLI, pp. 293-321, 22 ills., Mar., 1922

KELLEY, FRANCIS BEVERLY:
The Land of Sawdust and Spangles—A World in Miniature. By Francis Beverly Kelley. LX, pp. 463-516, 35 ills. in black and white, 29 ills. in color, Oct., 1931

KELLOGG, REMINGTON:
Whales, Giants of the Sea: Wonder Mammals, Biggest Creatures of All Time, Show Tender Affection for Young, But Can Maim or Swallow Human Hunters. By Remington Kellogg. Paintings by Else Bostelmann. LXXVII, pp. 35-90, 25 ills. in black and white, 31 ills. in color, Jan., 1940

KELTIE, J. SCOTT:
The Great Unmapped Areas on the Earth's Surface Awaiting the Explorer and Geographer. By J. Scott Keltie. VIII, pp. 251-266, Sept., 1897

KELTON, M. E.:
Apperception in Geography. By M. E. Kelton. XI, pp. 192-199, May, 1900

KEMAL ATATÜRK. *See* Mustapha Kemal

KENAI PENINSULA, Alaska:
The White Sheep, Giant Moose, and Smaller Game of the Kenai Peninsula, Alaska. By George Shiras, 3d. XXIII, pp. 423-494, 59 ills., maps (1 two-page), May, 1912

KENASTON, C. A. *See* NGS: Board of Managers; Secretary

KENNAN, GEORGE:
Awarded Jane M. Smith Life Membership. XXXVII, p. 342 (footnote), Apr., 1920
An Island in the Sea of History: The Highlands of Daghestan. By George Kennan. XXIV, pp. 1087-1140, 49 ills., map, Oct., 1913
See also NGS: Secretary

KENNARD, FREDERICK H.:
Encouraging Birds Around the Home. By Frederick H. Kennard. XXV, pp. 315-344, 36 ills., Mar., 1914

KENNEBEC (River), Maine:
Atlantic Estuarine Tides. By Mark S. W. Jefferson. IX, pp. 400-409, diagrs., 7 tables, maps, Sept., 1898

KENNEDY, LEONARD:
The World's Greatest Waterfall: The Kaieteur Fall, in British Guiana. By Leonard Kennedy. XXII, pp. 846-859, 6 ills., map, Sept., 1911

KENT (County), England:
Britain Fights in the Fields. By Francis A. Flood. LXXXVI, pp. 31-65, 17 ills. in black and white, 21 ills. in color, July, 1944
Charm Spots Along England's Harassed Coast. 16 ills. in duotone. LXXVIII, pp. 237-252, Aug., 1940
See also Dover

KENTUCKY:
Home Folk around Historic Cumberland Gap. By Leo A. Borah. LXXXIV, pp. 741-768, 25 ills., map, Dec., 1943
Kentucky, Boone's Great Meadow: The Bluegrass State Celebrates Its Sesquicentennial As It Helps the Nation Gird for War. By Leo A. Borah. LXXXII, pp. 57-89, 13 ills. in black and white, 21 ills. in color, map, July, 1942
A Patriotic Pilgrimage to Eastern National Parks: History and Beauty Live Along Paved Roads, Once Indian Trails, Through Virginia, North Carolina, Tennessee, Kentucky, and West Virginia. By Leo A. Borah. LXV, pp. 663-702, 18 ills. in black and white, 28 ills. in color, two-page map, June, 1934

KENYA:
When a Drought Blights Africa: Hippos and Elephants Are Driven Insane by Suffering, in the Lorian Swamp, Kenya Colony. By Capt. A. T. Curle. LV, pp. 521-528, 9 ills., Apr., 1929
Where Roosevelt Will Hunt. By Sir Harry Johnston. XX, pp. 207-256, 43 ills., map supplement, Mar., 1909

KEPNER, WILLIAM E.:
Exploring the Stratosphere. By Captain Albert W. Stevens. LXVI, pp. 397-434, 43 ills., chart, Oct., 1934

KERBELA, Iraq. *See* Karbala

KERBEY, McFALL:
Behind Netherlands Sea Ramparts: Dikes and Pumps Keep Ocean and Rivers at Bay While a Busy People Carries on Peacetime Work. By McFall Kerbey. LXXVII, pp. 255-290, 26 ills. in black and white, 11 ills. in duotone, map, Feb., 1940
Colorado, a Barrier That Became a Goal: Where Water Has Transformed Dry Plains Into Verdant Farms, and Highways Have Opened up Mineral and Scenic Wealth. By McFall Kerbey. LXII, pp. 1-63, 56 ills. in black and white, 12 ills. in color, map, July, 1932
Genoa, Where Columbus Learned to Love the Sea. By McFall Kerbey. LIV, pp. 333-352, 20 ills., pictorial supplement, Sept., 1928
How the United States Grew. By McFall Kerbey. LXIII, pp. 631-649, 17 ills., map, May, 1933
The Texas Delta of an American Nile: Orchards and Gardens Replace Thorny Jungle in the Southmost Tip of the Lone Star State. By McFall Kerbey. LXXV, pp. 51-96, 27 ills. in black and white, 24 ills. in color, map, Jan., 1939
Toilers of the Sky: Tenuous Clouds Perform the Mighty Task of Shaping the Earth and Sustaining Terrestrial Life. By McFall Kerbey. XLVIII, pp. 163-189, 33 ills., Aug., 1925

KERENSKY, ALEXANDER:
Russia from Within: Her War of Yesterday, Today, and Tomorrow. By Stanley Washburn. XXXII, pp. 91-120, 30 ills., Aug., 1917
Russia's Man of the Hour: Alexander Kerensky's First Speeches and Proclamations. XXXII, pp. 24-45, 17 ills., July, 1917

KERR, MARK B.:
A Journey in Ecuador. By Mark B. Kerr, C. E. VII, pp. 238-245, ills., map, July, 1896
Report on Topographic Work (Mount St. Elias Expedition). By Mark B. Kerr. III, p. 195, map, May 29, 1891

KETCHAM, WALTER E.:
Dipo, the Little Desert "Kangaroo." By Walter E. Ketcham. LXXVIII, pp. 537-548, 14 ills., Oct., 1940

KETCHIKAN, Alaska:
Ketchikan. XVI, pp. 508-509, ill., Nov., 1905

KETTERING, CHARLES F. *See* NGS: Board of Trustees

The **KEY** to the Pacific (Territory of Hawaii). By George C. Perkins. XIX, pp. 295-298, map, Apr., 1908

KEY WEST, Florida:
Across the Gulf by Rail to Key West. By Jefferson B. Browne. VII, pp. 203-207, June, 1896
Capturing Giant Turtles in the Caribbean. By David D. Duncan. LXXXIV, pp. 177-190, 13 ills., map, Aug., 1943

KEYHOE, DONALD E.:
Seeing America With Lindbergh: The Record of a Tour of More Than 20,000 Miles by Airplane Through Forty-eight States on Schedule Time. By Lieutenant Donald E. Keyhoe. LIII, pp. 1-46, 46 ills., map, Jan., 1928

KHARKOV, U. S. S. R.:
Liberated Ukraine. By Eddy Gilmore. LXXXV, pp. 513-536, 22 ills., map, May, 1944
Ukraine, Past and Present. By Nevin O. Winter. XXXIV, pp. 114-128, 14 ills., Aug., 1918

KHAT (Flower):
"The Flower of Paradise": The Part Which Khat Plays in the Life of the Yemen Arab. By Charles Moser. XXXII, pp. 173-186, 10 ills., map, Aug., 1917

KHATMANDU, Nepal:
Nepal: A Little-Known Kingdom. By John Claude White. XXXVIII, pp. 245-283, 32 ills., map, Oct., 1920

KHORESM:
Surveying Through Khoresm: A Journey Into Parts of Asiatic Russia Which Have Been Closed to Western Travelers Since the World War. By Lyman D. Wilbur. LXI, pp. 753-780, 31 ills., map, June, 1932

KHUN, BYRON, COUNT DE PROROK. *See* Prorok, Byron Khun, Count de

KHUN (Tribespeople):
Strange Tribes in the Shan States of Burma. 15 color photos by W. Robert Moore. LVIII, pp. 247-254, Aug., 1930

KHYBER PASS, India:
Through the Heart of Hindustan: A Teeming Highway Extending for Fifteen Hundred Miles, from the Khyber Pass to Calcutta. By Maynard Owen Williams. XL, pp. 433-467, 29 ills., Nov., 1921

KIANGSI (Province), China:
The World's Ancient Porcelain Center. By Frank B. Lenz. XXXVIII, pp. 391-406, 17 ills., Nov., 1920

KIENLUNG (Emperor of China):
Mukden, the Manchu Home and Its Great Art Museum. By Eliza R. Scidmore. XXI, pp. 289-320, 30 ills., Apr., 1910

KIEV, U. S. S. R.:
Liberated Ukraine. By Eddy Gilmore. LXXXV, pp. 513-536, 22 ills., map, May, 1944
Ukraine, Past and Present. By Nevin O. Winter. XXXIV, pp. 114-128, 14 ills., Aug., 1918

KIHN, W. LANGDON:
First Families of Southeastern America (Indians). 8 ills. in color from paintings by W. Langdon Kihn. LXXXIX, pp. 65-72, Jan., 1946
Indians of Our Western Plains. 16 ills. in color from paintings by W. Langdon Kihn. LXXXVI, pp. 81-96, July, 1944
A Palette from Spain. By W. Langdon Kihn. LXIX, pp. 407-440, 16 ills. in black and white, 26 ills. in duotone, map, Mar., 1936
Red Men of the Southwest. 25 ills. in color from paintings by W. Langdon Kihn. LXXVIII, pp. 557-596, Nov., 1940
Totem-pole Builders. 16 ills. in color from paintings by W. Langdon Kihn. LXXXVII, pp. 33-48, Jan., 1945
When Red Men Ruled Our Forests. 24 ills. in color from paintings by W. Langdon Kihn. LXXII, pp. 551-590, Nov., 1937

KILLDEER (Bird):
Hunting with the Lens. By Howard H. Cleaves. XXVI, pp. 1-35, 47 ills., July, 1914

KILLIN, BENTON:
Some of the Conditions and Possibilities of Agriculture in Alaska. By Walter H. Evans. IX, pp. 178-187, Apr., 1898

KINALING, Sumatra:
By Motor Through the East Coast and Batak Highlands of Sumatra. By Melvin A. Hall. XXXVII, pp. 69-102, 27 ills., Jan., 1920

KING, ELIZABETH W.:
Heroes of Wartime Science and Mercy. By Elizabeth W. King. LXXXIV, pp. 715-740, 11 ills. in black and white, 334 ills. in color, Dec., 1943
Seals of Our Nation, States, and Territories. By Elizabeth W. King. Paintings by Carlotta Gonzales Lahey, Irvin E. Alleman, Theodora Price. XC, pp. 1-42, 14 ills. in black and white, 84 ills. in color, July, 1946

KING, F. H.:
Awarded Grant Squires Prize. XXIV, p. 115, Jan., 1913
The Wonderful Canals of China. By F. H. King. XXIII, pp. 931-958, 35 ills., 5 maps, Oct., 1912

KING Herring: An Account of the World's Most Valuable Fish, the Industries It Supports, and the Part It Has Played in History. By Hugh M. Smith. XX, pp. 701-735, 21 ills., Aug., 1909

KING of Cats and His Court (Leopards, Lions, and Tigers). By Victor H. Cahalane. Paintings by Walter A. Weber. LXXXIII, pp. 217-259, 9 ills. in black and white, 20 ills. in color, Feb., 1943

The **KINGDOM** of Flowers: An Account of the Wealth of Trees and Shrubs of China and of What the Arnold Arboretum, with China's Help, Is Doing to Enrich America. By Ernest H. Wilson. XXII, pp. 1003-1035, 24 ills., Nov., 1911

A **KINGDOM** of Many Tribes (Afghanistan). 12 color photos by Maynard Owen Williams. LXIV, pp. 745-752, Dec., 1933

The **KINGDOM** of Servia. By William Joseph Showalter. XXVII, pp. 417-432, 12 ills., map, Apr., 1915

KINGFISHERS (Birds):
Parrots, Kingfishers, and Flycatchers: Strange Trogons and Curious Cuckoos are Pictured with these Other Birds of Color, Dash, and Courage. By Alexander Wetmore. Paintings by Maj. Allan Brooks. LXIX, pp. 801-828, 9 ills. in black and white, 36 portraits in color, June, 1936

KINGLETS (Birds):
Winged Denizens of Woodland, Stream, and Marsh. By Alexander Wetmore. Paintings by Major Allan Brooks. LXV, pp. 577-596, 4 portraits in color, May, 1934

KINGMAN, EUGENE:
Crater Lake and Yosemite Through the Ages. 13 ills. in color from paintings by Eugene Kingman. LXXI, pp. 333-339, Mar., 1937

KINGMAN, JOHN A.:
The Isle of Capri: An Imperial Residence and Probable Wireless Station of Ancient Rome. By John A. Kingman. XXXVI, pp. 213-231, 17 ills., Sept., 1919

KINGSFORD-SMITH, CHARLES E.:
Our Conquest of the Pacific: The Narrative of the 7,400-Mile Flight from San Francisco to Brisbane in Three Ocean Hops. By Squadron-Leader Charles E. Kingsford-Smith and Flight-Lieut. Charles T. P. Ulm. LIV, pp. 371-402, 27 ills., map, Oct., 1928

KINGSTON, Jamaica:
Jamaica, the Isle of Many Rivers. By John Oliver La Gorce. LI, pp. 1-55, 38 ills. in black and white, 11 ills. in color, map, Jan., 1927

KINGTEHCHEN, China:
The World's Ancient Porcelain Center. By Frank B. Lenz. XXXVIII, pp. 391-406, 17 ills., Nov., 1920

KINKAJOU (Yacht):
Cruise of the *Kinkajou:* Among Desert Islands of Mexico Voyagers Find Outdoor Laboratories for the Naturalist and Ideal Fishing Grounds for the Sportsman. By Alfred M. Bailey. LXXX, pp. 339-366, 13 ills. in black and white, 12 ills. in color, map, Sept., 1941

KINNEY, PAUL B.:
Once in a Lifetime: Black Bears Rarely Have Quadruplets, But Goofy Did—and the Camera Caught Her Nursing Her Remarkable Family. By Paul B. Kinney. LXXX, pp. 249-258, 11 ills., Aug., 1941

KINNEY, WILLIAM A.:
American Wings Soar Around the World: Epic Story of the Air Transport Command of the U. S. Army Is a Saga of Yankee Daring and Doing. By Donald H. Agnew and William A. Kinney. LXXXIV, pp. 57-78, 22 ills., July, 1943

KIRCHHOFF, C.:
The United States—Her Mineral Resources. By C. Kirchhoff. XIV, pp. 331-339, Sept., 1903

KIRGHIZ (Tribespeople):
First Over the Roof of the World by Motor: The Trans-Asiatic Expedition Sets New Records for Wheeled Transport in Scaling Passes of the Himalayas. By Maynard Owen Williams. LXI, pp. 321-363, 45 ills., maps, Mar., 1932
With the Nomads of Central Asia: A Summer's Sojourn in the Tekes Valley, Plateau Paradise of Mongol and Turkic Tribes. By Edward Murray. Paintings and drawings by Alexandre Iacovleff. LXIX, pp. 1-57, 43 ills. in black and white, 26 ills. in color, map, Jan., 1936

KIRJASSOFF, ALICE BALLANTINE:
Formosa the Beautiful. By Alice Ballantine Kirjassoff. XXXVII, pp. 247-292, 60 ills., map, Mar., 1920

KIRKWOOD, J. E.:
A Mexican Hacienda. By J. E. Kirkwood. XXV, pp. 563-584, 18 ills., May, 1914

KITE Work of the Weather Bureau. By H. C. Frankenfield. XI, pp. 55-62, Feb., 1900

KITES:
Aërial Locomotion: With a Few Notes of Progress in the Construction of an Aërodrome. By Alexander Graham Bell. XVIII, pp. 1-34, 36 ills., Jan., 1907
Air Conquest: From the Early Days of Giant Kites and Birdlike Gliders, the National Geographic Society Has Aided and Encouraged the Growth of Aviation. LII, pp. 233-242, 13 ills., Aug., 1927
The Charm of Cape Breton Island: The Most Picturesque Portion of Canada's Maritime Provinces—A Land Rich in Historic Associations, Natural Resources, and Geographic Appeal. By Catherine Dunlop Mackenzie. XXXVIII, pp. 34-60, 22 ills., map, July, 1920
Included: Alexander Graham Bell's kites
Dr. Bell's Man-Lifting Kite. By Gilbert H. Grosvenor. XIX, pp. 35-52, 27 ills., Jan., 1908
Kite Work of the Weather Bureau. By H. C. Frankenfield. XI, pp. 55-62, Feb., 1900
The Tetrahedral Kite. XIV, p. 294, ill., July, 1903
The Tetrahedral Principle in Kite Structure. By Alexander Graham Bell. XIV, pp. 219-251, 79 ills., 15 diagrs., June, 1903

KITES (Birds):
The Eagle, King of Birds, and His Kin. By Alexander Wetmore. Paintings by Maj. Allan Brooks. LXIV, pp. 43-95, 2 ills. in black and white, 6 ills. in color, July, 1933

The **KIZILBASH** Clans of Kurdistan. By Melville Chater. LIV, pp. 485-504, 22 ills., Oct., 1928

KLAMATH INDIANS:
Wokas, a Primitive Indian Food. XV, pp. 183-185, 3 ills., Apr., 1904

KLEMMER, HARVEY:
"Blood, Toil, Tears, and Sweat": An American Tells the Story of Britain's War Effort, Summed up in Prime Minister Churchill's Unflinching Words. By Harvey Klemmer. LXXXII, pp. 141-166, 19 ills., Aug., 1942
A City That Refused to Die (Plymouth, England). By Harvey Klemmer. LXXXIX, pp. 211-236, 13 ills. in black and white, 9 ills. in color, map, Feb., 1946
Convoys to Victory. By Harvey Klemmer. LXXXIII, pp. 193-216, 24 ills., Feb., 1943
Everyday Life in Wartime England. By Harvey Klemmer. LXXIX, pp. 497-534, 48 ills., Apr., 1941
Front-line Town of Britain's Siege (Dover). By Harvey Klemmer. LXXXV, pp. 105-128, 21 ills., Jan., 1944
Lend-Lease and the Russian Victory. By Harvey Klemmer. LXXXVIII, pp. 499-512, 6 ills., Oct., 1945
Lisbon—Gateway to Warring Europe. By Harvey Klemmer. LXXX, pp. 259-276, 18 ills., Aug., 1941
Michigan Fights. By Harvey Klemmer. LXXXVI, pp. 677-715, 20 ills. in black and white, 19 ills. in color, map, Dec., 1944
Rural Britain Carries On. By Harvey Klemmer. LXXX, pp. 527-552, 27 ills., Oct., 1941

KLONDIKE (Region), Canada:
Climatic Conditions of Alaska. By General A. W. Greely. IX, pp. 132-137, Apr., 1898
Included: Temperature recordings at Dawson and Fort Reliance
Overland Routes to the Klondike. By Hamlin Garland. IX, pp. 113-116, ill., Apr., 1898
A Winter Weather Record From the Klondike Region. By E. W. Nelson. VIII, pp. 327-335, tables, Nov., 1897

KNIGHT, C. W. R.:
Photographing the Nest Life of the Osprey. By Capt. C. W. R. Knight. LXII, pp. 247-260, 25 ills., Aug., 1932

KNIGHT, CHARLES R.:
Parade of Life Through the Ages: Records in Rocks Reveal a Strange Procession of Prehistoric Creatures, from Jellyfish to Dinosaurs, Giant Sloths, Saber-toothed Tigers, and Primitive Man. By Charles R. Knight. With 24 ills. in color from paintings by author. LXXXI, pp. 141-184, 13 ills. in black and white, Feb., 1942

KNIGHT, WILBUR C.:
The Wyoming Fossil Fields Expedition of July, 1899. By Wilbur C. Knight. XI, pp. 449-465, 8 ills., Dec., 1900

"KNIGHTS OF THE GOLDEN HORSESHOE":
Spottswood's Expedition of 1716. By Dr. William M. Thornton. VII, pp. 265-269, Aug., 1896

KNOSSOS, Crete (Island). *See* Cnossus

KNOTT, FRANKLIN PRICE:
Bali: Artist Adventures on the Island of Bali. By Franklin Price Knott. LIII, pp. 326-347, 20 ills. in color, Mar., 1928
India: The Oriental Pageantry of Northern India. 30 color photos by Franklin Price Knott. LVI, pp. 429-460, Oct., 1929
United States: Beauty Spots in the United States. 23 color photos by Franklin Price Knott. XXIX, pp. 379-405, Apr., 1916
World: People and Places. 16 color photos by Franklin Price Knott. XXX, pp. 233-248, Sept., 1916

KNOX, DUDLEY W.:
Ships, from Dugouts to Dreadnoughts. By Captain Dudley W. Knox. LXXIII, pp. 57-98, 27 ills. in black and white, 16 ills. in gravure, Jan., 1938

KNUTSEN, WILLIE:
Desolate Greenland, Now an American Outpost. 17 photos: 12 by Willie Knutsen, 4 by F. Vogel. LXXX, pp. 393-406, Sept., 1941

The **KOALA,** or Australian Teddy Bear. By F. Lewis. LX, pp. 346-355, 13 ills., Sept., 1931

KOCH, FELIX J.:
In Quaint, Curious Croatia. By Felix J. Koch. XIX, pp. 809-832, 37 ills., Dec., 1908
Tirnova, the City of Hanging Gardens. By Felix J. Koch. XVIII, pp. 632-640, 7 ills., Oct., 1907

KODIAK (Island), Alaska:
Kodiak Not Kadiak. (By M. B.). XII, pp. 397-398, Nov., 1901

KODIAK (Island), Alaska—*Continued*

A Navy Artist Paints the Aleutians. By Mason Sutherland. Paintings by Lt. William F. Draper. LXXXIV, pp. 157-176, 4 ills. in black and white, 16 ills. in color, Aug., 1943

The Recent Eruption of Katmai Volcano in Alaska. By George C. Martin. XXIV, pp. 131-181, 45 ills., diagr., map, Feb., 1913

The Valley of Ten Thousand Smokes: National Geographic Society Explorations in the Katmai District of Alaska. By Robert F. Griggs. XXXI, pp. 13-68, 51 ills., map, Jan., 1917

Volcanoes of Alaska (Report by Capt. K. W. Perry on the Eruption of Mt. Katmai in June, 1912). XXIII, pp. 824-832, 11 ills., Aug., 1912

KOELZ, WALTER N.:

A Naturalist with MacMillan in the Arctic. By Walter N. Koelz. XLIX, pp. 299-318, 22 ills. in color, Mar., 1926

KOESTER, HANS:

Four Thousand Hours Over China. By Capt. Hans Koester. LXXIII, pp. 571-598, 25 ills., map, May, 1938

KOKSOAK (Big River), Quebec, Canada:

Servicing Arctic Airbases. By Robert A. Bartlett. LXXXIX, pp. 602-616, 3 ills. in black and white, 10 ills. in color, map, May, 1946

KOLB, ELLSWORTH:

Experiences in the Grand Canyon. By Ellsworth and Emery Kolb. XXVI, pp. 99-184, 70 ills., map, Aug., 1914

KOLB, EMERY:

Experiences in the Grand Canyon. By Ellsworth and Emery Kolb. XXVI, pp. 99-184, 70 ills., map, Aug., 1914

KOLD, KRISTEN:

Denmark and the Danes. By Maurice Francis Egan. XLII, pp. 115-164, 38 ills., map, Aug., 1922

KOLLM, GEORG:

The German South Polar Expedition. By Dr. Georg Kollm. XII, pp. 377-379, Oct., 1901

KOMENSKY, JAN AMOS:

Bohemia and the Czechs. By Aleš Hrdlička. XXXI, pp. 163-187, 18 ills., Feb., 1917

KOMODO (Island), Netherlands East Indies:

A Modern Dragon Hunt on Komodo: An English Yachting Party Traps and Photographs the Huge and Carnivorous Dragon Lizard of the Lesser Sundas. By Lady Broughton. LXX, pp. 321-331, 12 ills. in duotone, Sept., 1936

Stalking the Dragon Lizard on the Island of Komodo. By W. Douglas Burden. LII, pp. 216-232, 21 ills., Aug., 1927

KOMSOMOLSK, U. S. S. R.:

New Road to Asia. By Owen Lattimore. LXXXVI, pp. 641-676, 15 ills. in black and white, 26 ills. in color, Dec., 1944

KONKA RISUMGONGBA, Holy Mountain of the Outlaws. By Joseph F. Rock. LX, pp. 1-65, 36 ills. in black and white, 43 ills. in color, map, July, 1931

KOREA:

Chosen—Land of Morning Calm. By Mabel Craft Deering. LXIV, pp. 421-448, 20 ills. in black and white, 13 ills. in color, map, Oct., 1933

Exploring the Unknown Corners of the "Hermit Kingdom." By Roy Chapman Andrews. XXXVI, pp. 25-48, 30 ills., map, July, 1919

Glimpses of Korea and China. By William W. Chapin. XXI, pp. 895-934, 11 ills. in black and white, 39 ills. in color, Nov., 1910

A Hunter of Plants. By David Fairchild. XXXVI, pp. 57-77, 18 ills., July, 1919

In the Diamond Mountains: Adventures Among the Buddhist Monasteries of Eastern Korea. By the Marquess Curzon of Kedleston. XLVI, pp. 353-374, 21 ills., map, Oct., 1924

Jap Rule in the Hermit Nation. By Willard Price. LXXXVIII, pp. 429-451, 19 ills., map, Oct., 1945

Korea—The Hermit Nation. By Commander Harrie Webster. XI, pp. 145-155, 7 ills., Apr., 1900

Korea and the Koreans. By J. B. Bernadou. II, pp. 231-242, map, foldout map, Aug., 1890

Manchuria and Korea. Text with map supplement. XV, pp. 128-129, maps, Mar., 1904

Notes and Scenes from Korea. XIX, pp. 498-508, 14 ills., July, 1908

The Passing of Korea. XVII, pp. 575-581, 6 ills., Oct., 1906

Scenes from the Land Where Everybody Dresses in White. Photos by Rev. J. Z. Moore. XIX, pp. 871-877, 10 ills., Dec., 1908

Some Facts About Korea. XV, p. 79, Feb., 1904

KORFF, ALLETTA, BARONESS:

Notes on Finland. (By Baroness Alletta Korff). XXI, pp. 493-494, June, 1910

Where Women Vote (Finland). By Baroness Alletta Korff. XXI, pp. 487-493, June, 1910

KOSTICH, KONSTANTIN J.:

Finland: Land of Sky-Blue Lakes. 12 color photos by Konstantin J. Kostich. LXXIV, pp. 515-522, Oct., 1938

Yugoslavia: Where Oriental Hues Splash Europe. 34 color photos by Konstantin J. Kostich and Rudolph Balogh. LXXV, pp. 699-738, June, 1939

KOWAK RIVER, Alaska:

Ice-cliffs on the Kowak River. By Lieut. J. C. Cantwell. VII, pp. 345-346, Oct., 1896

KOYASAN, the Japanese Valhalla. By Eliza R. Scidmore. XVIII, pp. 650-670, 14 ills., Oct., 1907

KPWESIS (Tribespeople):

The Land of the Free in Africa. By Harry A. McBride. XLII, pp. 411-430, 22 ills., Oct., 1922

KRAKATAU (Island), Netherlands East Indies:

Do Volcanic Explosions Affect Our Climate? By C. G. Abbot. XXIV, pp. 181-198, 9 ills., diagr., Feb., 1913

The Eruption of Krakatoa. By Sir Robert Ball. XIII, pp. 200-204, June, 1902

KRAKÓW, Poland:

Pedaling Through Poland: An American Girl Free-wheels Alone from Kraków, and Its Medieval Byways, Toward Ukraine's Restive Borderland. By Dorothy Hosmer. LXXV, pp. 739-775, 38 ills., maps, June, 1939

Poland, Land of the White Eagle. By Melville Bell Grosvenor. With 12 color photos by Hans Hildenbrand. LXI, pp. 435-444, Apr., 1932

KREIDER, HERMAN H.:

Looking in on the Everyday Life of New Turkey. 7 color photos by Herman H. Kreider. LXI, pp. 501-508, Apr., 1932

KREMLIN, Moscow:

The Rebirth of Religion in Russia: The Church Reorganized While Bolshevik Cannon Spread Destruction in the Nation's Holy of Holies. By Thomas Whittemore. XXXIV, pp. 379-401, 16 ills., Nov., 1918

Russia of the Hour: Giant Battle Ground for Theories of Economy, Society, and Politics, as Observed by an Unbiased Correspondent. By Junius B. Wood. L, pp. 519-598, 81 ills., Nov., 1926

Young Russia: The Land of Unlimited Possibilities. By Gilbert H. Grosvenor. XXVI, pp. 421-520, 85 ills. in black and white, 17 ills. in color, Nov., 1914

KRIEGER, LOUIS C. C.:

Common Mushrooms of the United States. By Louis C. C. Krieger. Paintings by author. XXXVII, pp. 387-439, 37 ills. in black and white, 16 ills. in color, May, 1920

KRUISINGA, J. C. M.:

A New Country Awaits Discovery: The Draining of the Zuider Zee Makes Room for the Excess Population of the Netherlands. By J. C. M. Kruisinga. LXIV, pp. 293-320, 20 ills. in black and white, 13 ills. in color, maps, Sept., 1933

KRUNG THEP, Thailand. *See* Bangkok

KRUS (Tribespeople):

The Land of the Free in Africa. By Harry A. McBride. XLII, pp. 411-430, 22 ills., Oct., 1922

KRYSTO, CHRISTINA:

Bringing the World to Our Foreign-Language Soldiers: How a Military Training Camp is Solving a Seemingly Unsurmountable Problem by Using the Geographic. By Christina Krysto. XXXIV, pp. 81-90, 4 ills., Aug., 1918

KUBLAI KHAN:

The World's Greatest Overland Explorer: How Marco Polo Penetrated Farthest Asia, "Discovered" Many Lands Unknown to Europe, and Added Numerous Minerals, Animals, Birds, and Plants to Man's Knowledge. By J. R. Hildebrand. LIV, pp. 505-568, 53 ills., two-page map, Nov., 1928

KUHNE, JACK:

Europe's Northern Nomads (Lapps). 12 color photos by Jack Kuhne. LXXVI, pp. 657-664, Nov., 1939

Norwegian Fjords and Folkways. 20 color photos: 19 by Jack Kuhne. LXXV, pp. 501-524, Apr., 1939

KUHNE, JACK—*Continued*

Peru on Parade. 20 color photos by Henry Clay Gipson and Jack Kuhne. LXXXII, pp. 173-196, Aug., 1942

KUIBYSHEV, U. S. S. R.:

Mother Volga Defends Her Own. By Maynard Owen Williams. LXXXII, pp. 793-811, 21 ills., Dec., 1942

KULUSUK, Greenland:

Uncle Sam's Icebox Outposts. 19 color photos by John E. Schneider and Robert B. Sykes, Jr. XC, pp. 473-496, Oct., 1946

KUMASSI:

The Gold Coast, Ashanti, and Kumassi. By George K. French. VIII, pp. 1-15, 9 ills., Jan., 1897

KUNMING, China:

Kunming, Southwestern Gateway to China. By Joseph E. Passantino. With 18 color photos by author. XC, pp. 137-168, 12 ills. in black and white, Aug., 1946

KURDS (People):

The Kizilbash Clans of Kurdistan. By Melville Chater. LIV, pp. 485-504, 22 ills., Oct., 1928

Mountain Tribes of Iran and Iraq. By Harold Lamb. LXXXIX, pp. 385-408, 15 ills., two-page map, Mar., 1946

The Mountaineers of the Euphrates. By Ellsworth Huntington. XX, pp. 142-156, 13 ills., Feb., 1909

Persian Caravan Sketches: The Land of the Lion and the Sun as Seen on a Summer Caravan Trip. By Harold F. Weston. XXXIX, pp. 417-468, 46 ills. in black and white, 16 ills. in color, map, Apr., 1921

KUSAIE (Island), Caroline Islands:

Hidden Key to the Pacific: Piercing the Web of Secrecy Which Long Has Veiled Japanese Bases in the Mandated Islands. By Willard Price. LXXXI, pp. 759-785, 28 ills., map, June, 1942

KUSKOKWIM (River), Alaska:

Two Hundred Miles up the Kuskokwim. By Charles Hallock. IX, pp. 85-92, 6 ills., Mar., 1898

KUZZILILAR, Turkey:

The Fringe of Verdure Around Asia Minor. By Ellsworth Huntington. XXI, pp. 761-775, 15 ills., Sept., 1910

KWAJALEIN (Atoll), Marshall Islands:

Our New Military Wards, the Marshalls. By W. Robert Moore. LXXXVIII, pp. 325-360, 14 ills. in black and white, 20 ills. in color, map, Sept., 1945

KWAKIUTL (Indian Tribe):

Indians of Our North Pacific Coast. By Matthew W. Stirling. Paintings by W. Langdon Kihn. LXXXVII, pp. 25-52, 3 ills. in black and white, 16 ills. in color, Jan., 1945

KWANGSI (Province), China:

Landscaped Kwangsi, China's Province of Pictorial Art. By G. Weidman Groff and T. C. Lau. LXXII, pp. 671-710, 33 ills., map, Dec., 1937

KYOTO, Japan:

Glimpses of Japan. By William W. Chapin. XXII, pp. 965-1002, 10 ills. in black and white, 34 ills. in color, Nov., 1911

L

LA BOCA, Canal Zone:

Completion of the La Boca Dock (Panama Canal). IX, p. 84, Mar., 1898

LABORATORIES. *See* Climatic Laboratories; Harvard University; Miami Aquarium; Science

LABRADOR:

Introducing Reindeer into Labrador. XVIII, p. 686, Oct., 1907

Labrador Expedition. XV, p. 185, Apr., 1904

A Land of Eternal Warring. By Sir Wilfrid T. Grenfell. XXI, pp. 665-690, 24 ills., Aug., 1910

The MacMillan Arctic Expedition Returns: U. S. Navy Planes Make First Series of Overhead Flights in the Arctic and National Geographic Society Staff Obtains Valuable Data and Specimens for Scientific Study. By Donald B. MacMillan. XLVIII, pp. 477-518, 42 ills., Nov., 1925

Origin of "Labrador." XVII, pp. 587-588, Oct., 1906

LABRADOR CURRENT:

The Relations of the Gulf Stream and the Labrador Current. By William Libbey, Junior. V, pp. 161-166, Jan. 31, 1894

LADD, HARRY S.:

Falcon, the Pacific's Newest Island. By J. Edward Hoffmeister and Harry S. Ladd. LIV, pp. 757-766, 8 ills., map, Dec., 1928

LADRONES ISLANDS, Pacific Ocean. *See* Marianas Islands

LADY FRANKLIN BAY EXPEDITION:

The "Bowdoin" (Ship) in North Greenland: Arctic Explorers Place Tablet to Commemorate Sacrifices of the Lady Franklin Bay Expedition. By Donald B. MacMillan. XLVII, pp. 677-722, 49 ills., June, 1925

LA FARGE, THOMAS S.:

Coast Guard Patrol in Greenland. 9 color photos by Lieut. Thomas S. La Farge. LXXXIII, pp. 565-572, May, 1943

LAFAYETTE, MARQUIS DE:

Our First Alliance. By J. J. Jusserand. XXXI, pp. 518-548, 8 ills., June, 1917

LAFAYETTE ESCADRILLE:

Armistice Day and the American Battle Fields. By J. J. Jusserand. LVI, pp. 509-554, 32 ills. in black and white, 23 ills. in color, Nov., 1929

The Life Story of an American Airman in France: Extracts from the Letters of Stuart Walcott, Who, Between July and December, 1917, Learned to Fly in French Schools of Aviation, Won Fame at the Front, and Fell Near Saint Souplet. XXXIII, pp. 86-106, 9 ills., Jan., 1918

LAFAYETTE NATIONAL PARK, Maine:

The Unique Island of Mount Desert. By George B. Dorr, Ernest Howe Forbush, M. L. Fernald. XXVI, pp. 75-89, 7 ills., July, 1914

LAFCADIO Hearn on the Island and People of Martinique. XIII, pp. 214-216, June, 1902

LA GORCE, JOHN OLIVER:

Employed by National Geographic Society. LXIX, p. 152, Jan., 1936

Expedition to the Bahamas led by Doctors Fuertes and La Gorce. LXII, p. 452, Oct., 1932

Meteorological station, Antarctica, named for Dr. La Gorce. LVIII, p. 184, ill. p. 193, Aug., 1930

Mount La Gorce, Alaska, named for Dr. La Gorce. XL, pp. 222, 287, Sept., 1921

The National Geographic Society's Notable Year (Announcement of the Election of Dr. La Gorce to the Board of Managers). XXXVII, pp. 338-345, ills., Apr., 1920

Tribute by Dr. Gilbert H. Grosvenor. LXIX, pp. 152-153, Jan., 1936

See also NGM: Editorial Department, for Associate Editor; NGS: Board of Managers; Vice-President

Articles and Photographs by:

The Argosy of Geography (Sailing Ship). Photo by John Oliver La Gorce. XXXIX, pictorial supplement, Jan., 1921

A Battle-Ground of Nature: The Atlantic Seaboard. By John Oliver La Gorce. XXXIII, pp. 511-546, 23 ills., 4 maps, June, 1918

Devil-Fishing in the Gulf Stream. By John Oliver La Gorce. XXXV, pp. 476-488, 7 ills., June, 1919

The Fight at the Timber-Line. By John Oliver La Gorce. XLII, pp. 165-196, 32 ills., Aug., 1922

Fishes and Fisheries of Our North Atlantic Seaboard. By John Oliver La Gorce. Paintings by Hashime Murayama. XLIV, pp. 567-634, 35 ills. in black and white, 16 ills. in color, Dec., 1923

Florida—The Fountain of Youth. By John Oliver La Gorce. LVII, pp. 1-93, 73 ills. in black and white, 41 ills. in color, map supplement, Jan., 1930

The Historic City of Brotherly Love: Philadelphia, Born of Penn and Strengthened by Franklin, a Metropolis of Industries, Homes, and Parks. By John Oliver La Gorce. LXII, pp. 643-697, 49 ills. in black and white, 13 ills. in color, Dec., 1932

The Industrial Titan of America: Pennsylvania, Once the Keystone of the Original Thirteen, Now the Keystone of Forty-eight Sovereign States. By John Oliver La Gorce. XXXV, pp. 367-406, 33 ills., map, May, 1919

Jamaica, the Isle of Many Rivers. By John Oliver La Gorce. LI, pp. 1-55, 38 ills. in black and white, 11 ills. in color, map, Jan., 1927

Penn's Land of Modern Miracles (Pennsylvania). By John Oliver La Gorce. LXVIII, pp. 1-58, 28 ills. in black and white, 39 ills. in color, two-page map, July, 1935

Pirate Rivers and Their Prizes: The Warfare of Waterways Has Sometimes Changed the Geography of Our Continents. By John Oliver La Gorce. L, pp. 87-132, 48 ills., map, July, 1926

LA GORCE, JOHN OLIVER—*Continued*

Articles and Photographs by—*Continued*

Porto Rico, the Gate of Riches: Amazing Prosperity Has Been the Lot of Ponce de León's Isle Under American Administration. By John Oliver La Gorce. XLVI, pp. 599-651, 46 ills. in black and white, 12 ills. in color, map, Dec., 1924

Roumania and Its Rubicon. By John Oliver La Gorce. XXX, pp. 185-202, 11 ills., Sept., 1916

Treasure-House of the Gulf Stream: The Completion and Opening of the New Aquarium and Biological Laboratory at Miami, Florida. By John Oliver La Gorce. Paintings by Hashime Murayama. XXXIX, pp. 53-68, 5 ills. in black and white, 16 ills. in color, Jan., 1921

The Warfare on Our Eastern Coast. By John Oliver La Gorce. XXVIII, pp. 195-230, 29 ills., charts, Sept., 1915

LAGOS, Nigeria:

Nigeria: From the Bight of Benin to Africa's Desert Sands. By Helen Trybulowski Gilles. LXXXV, pp. 537-568, 17 ills. in black and white, 10 ills. in color, map, May, 1944

LAHEY, CARLOTTA GONZALES:

The Heavens Above: On Land, Sea, and in the Air the Stars Serve Modern Man as Map, Compass, and Clock. By Donald H. Menzel. With 12 charts, designed by author, showing star positions for each month, and 13 drawings of the constellations by Carlotta Gonzales Lahey. LXXXIV, pp. 97-128, map, July, 1943

Seals of Our Nation, States, and Territories. 84 ills. in color from paintings by Carlotta Gonzales Lahey, Irvin E. Alleman, Theodora Price. XC, pp. 17-32, July, 1946

LAHORE, India:

Through the Heart of Hindustan: A Teeming Highway Extending for Fifteen Hundred Miles, from the Khyber Pass to Calcutta. By Maynard Owen Williams. XL, pp. 433-467, 29 ills., Nov., 1921

LAKE Cahuilla: The Ancient Lake of the Colorado Desert. XVIII, p. 830, Dec., 1907

LAKE Chelan. By Henry Gannett. IX, pp. 417-428, 7 ills., map, Oct., 1898

LAKE Clark, a Little Known Alaskan Lake. By Wilfred H. Osgood. XV, pp. 326-331, ills., map, Aug., 1904

LAKE DISTRICT, Chile:

Chile's Land of Fire and Water: Smoking Volcanoes and Ice-hooded Peaks Stand Sentinel Over Limpid Lakes in the Far Southern Andes. By W. Robert Moore. LXXX, pp. 91-110, 9 ills. in black and white, 10 ills. in color, map, July, 1941

LAKE DISTRICT, England:

Informal Salute to the English Lakes. By Maynard Owen Williams. LXIX, pp. 511-521, 10 ills. in color, Apr., 1936

Through the English Lake District Afoot and Awheel. By Ralph A. Graves. LV, pp. 577-603, 19 ills. in black and white, 15 ills. in color, map, May, 1929

LAKE Geneva: Cradle of Conferences. By F. Barrows Colton. LXXII, pp. 727-742, 12 ills., map, Dec., 1937

LAKEHURST, New Jersey: U. S. Naval Air Station:

Aboard a Blimp Hunting U-boats: A Day above the Atlantic Reveals Navy Talk and Navy Ways, Creeping Convoys, and Torpedoed Wrecks. By Mason Sutherland. LXXXIV, pp. 79-96, 18 ills., July, 1943

LAKELAND, Home of England's Nature Poets. 15 color photos by Clifton Adams. LV, pp. 593-600, May, 1929

LAKES:

Bathymetrical Survey of the Fresh-water Lakes of England. XII, p. 408, Nov., 1901

Gems of the Italian Lakes. By Arthur Ellis Mayer. XXIV, pp. 943-956, 13 ills., Aug., 1913

Contents: Como; Lugano; Maggiore

Lake Chelan. By Henry Gannett. IX, pp. 417-428, 7 ills., map, Oct., 1898

A Land of Lakes and Volcanoes (Nicaragua). By Luis Marden. With 17 color photos by author. LXXXVI, pp. 161-192, 11 ills. in black and white, map, Aug., 1944

Modification of the Great Lakes by Earth Movement. By G. K. Gilbert. VIII, pp. 233-247, 3 diagrs., table, 4 maps, Sept., 1897

Shawangunk Mountain (New York). By N. H. Darton. VI, pp. 23-34, ills., 4 diagrs., Mar. 17, 1894

Included: Lake Awosting; Lake Maratanza; Lake Minnewaska; Lake Mohonk

Variations in Lake Levels and Atmospheric Precipitation. By Alfred J. Henry. X, pp. 403-406, diagr., Oct., 1899

See also Atitlan; Baikal; Balaton; Cahuilla; Clark; Como; Crater Lake; Erie; Finger Lakes Region; Fissure Lake; Gatun Lake; Geneva; Great Lakes; Lake District, Chile; Lake District, England; Lugano; Maggiore; Merritt; Naivasha; Raj Samand; Superior; Titicaca; Toba; Victoria Lake; Windermere; Xochimilco

LALIBELA, Ethiopia:

A Caravan Journey Through Abyssinia: From Addis Ababa Through Lalibela, the Strange Jerusalem of Ethiopia, in Search of New Grains for American Farms. By Harry V. Harlan. XLVII, pp. 613-663, 46 ills., map, June, 1925

LAMAISM:

Across Tibet from India to China. By Lt. Col. Ilia Tolstoy, AUS. XC, pp. 169-222, 53 ills., map, Aug., 1946

Castles in the Air: Experiences and Journeys in Unknown Bhutan. By John Claude White. XXV, pp. 365-455, 74 ills., map, Apr., 1914

Konka Risumgongba, Holy Mountain of the Outlaws. By Joseph F. Rock. LX, pp. 1-65, 36 ills. in black and white, 43 ills. in color, map, July, 1931

The Lama's Motor-Car. By Ethan C. Le Munyon. XXIV, pp. 641-670, 34 ills., May, 1913

The Land of the Yellow Lama: National Geographic Society Explorer Visits the Strange Kingdom of Muli, Beyond the Likiang Snow Range of Yünnan Province, China. By Joseph F. Rock. XLVII, pp. 447-491, 39 ills., map, Apr., 1925

LAMAISM—*Continued*

Life Among the Lamas of Choni: Describing the Mystery Plays and Butter Festival in the Monastery of an Almost Unknown Tibetan Principality in Kansu Province, China. By Joseph F. Rock. LIV, pp. 569-619, 34 ills. in black and white, 16 ills. in color, map, Nov., 1928

The Most Extraordinary City in the World: Notes on Lhasa—The Mecca of the Buddhist Faith. By Shaoching H. Chuan. XXIII, pp. 959-995, 60 ills., Oct., 1912

Seeking the Mountains of Mystery: An Expedition on the China-Tibet Frontier to the Unexplored Amnyi Machen Range, One of Whose Peaks Rivals Everest. By Joseph F. Rock. LVII, pp. 131-185, 54 ills., two-page map, Feb., 1930

Sungmas, the Living Oracles of the Tibetan Church. By Joseph F. Rock. LXVIII, pp. 475-486, ill. in black and white, 12 ills. in color, Oct., 1935

The World's Strangest Capital (Lhasa, Tibet). By John Claude White. XXIX, pp. 273-295, 19 ills., panorama, Mar., 1916

See also Lhasa

The **LAMA'S** Motor-Car: A Trip Across the Gobi Desert by Motor-Car. By Ethan C. Le Munyon. XXIV, pp. 641-670, 34 ills., May, 1913

LAMB, HAROLD:

Mountain Tribes of Iran and Iraq. By Harold Lamb. LXXXIX, pp. 385-408, 15 ills., two-page map, Mar., 1946

The Road of the Crusaders: A Historian Follows the Steps of Richard the Lion Heart and Other Knights of the Cross Over the "Via Dei." By Harold Lamb. LXIV, pp. 645-693, 46 ills. in black and white, 13 ills. in color, map, Dec., 1933

LAMBART, H. F.:

The Conquest of Mount Logan: North America's Second Highest Peak Yields to the Intrepid Attack of Canadian Climbers. By H. F. Lambart. XLIX, pp. 597-631, 40 ills., June, 1926

LAMOIDS:

Camels of the Clouds. By W. H. Hodge. LXXXIX, pp. 641-656, 15 ills., map, May, 1946
Included: Alpacas, Guanacas, Llamas, Vicuñas

LANCASTER (County), Pennsylvania:

Pennsylvania Dutch—In a Land of Milk and Honey. 10 color photos by J. Baylor Roberts. LXXIV, pp. 49-56, July, 1938

The **LAND** Columbus Loved (Dominican Republic). By Oliver P. Newman. LXXXV, pp. 197-224, 15 ills. in black and white, 11 ills. in color, map, Feb., 1944

LAND of a Million Smiles (Ozarks). By Frederick Simpich. LXXXIII, pp. 589-623, 14 ills. in black and white, 20 ills. in color, map, May, 1943

The **LAND** of Contrast: Austria-Hungary. By D. W. and A. S. Iddings. XXIII, pp. 1188-1217, 1284, 33 ills., map, Dec., 1912

A **LAND** of Drought and Desert—Lower California: Two Thousand Miles on Horseback Through the Most Extraordinary Cacti Forests in the World. By E. W. Nelson. XXII, pp. 443-474, 25 ills., maps, May, 1911

The **LAND** of Egypt: A Narrow Green Strip of Fertility Stretching for a Thousand Miles Through Walls of Desert. By Alfred Pearce Dennis. XLIX, pp. 271-298, 28 ills., map, Mar., 1926

A **LAND** of Eternal Warring (Labrador). By Sir Wilfrid T. Grenfell. XXI, pp. 665-690, 24 ills., Aug., 1910

The **LAND** of Fire (Iceland). By Jon Stefansson. XVIII, pp. 741-744, Nov., 1907

The **LAND** of Genghis Khan in Its True Colors. 13 color photos by Maynard Owen Williams. LXII, pp. 569-576, Nov., 1932

A **LAND** of Giants and Pygmies (Ruanda). By the Duke Adolphus Frederick of Mecklenburg. XXIII, pp. 369-388, 16 ills., map, Apr., 1912

A **LAND** of Lakes and Volcanoes (Nicaragua). By Luis Marden. With 17 color photos by author. LXXXVI, pp. 161-192, 11 ills. in black and white, map, Aug., 1944

The **LAND** of Lambskins: An Expedition to Bokhara, Russian Central Asia, to Study the Karakul Sheep Industry. By Robert K. Nabours. XXXVI, pp. 77-88, 15 ills., July, 1919

The **LAND** of Promise (Siberia). By Major General A. W. Greely. XXIII, pp. 1078-1090, 7 ills., Nov., 1912

LAND of Sagebrush and Silver (Nevada). 20 color photos by W. Robert Moore. LXXXIX, pp. 9-32, Jan., 1946

The **LAND** of Sawdust and Spangles—A World in Miniature. By Francis Beverly Kelley. LX, pp. 463-516, 35 ills. in black and white, 29 ills. in color, Oct., 1931

The **LAND** of the Basques: Home of a Thrifty, Picturesque People, Who Take Pride in the Sobriquet, "The Yankees of Spain." By Harry A. McBride. XLI, pp. 63-87, 25 ills., map, Jan., 1922

The **LAND** of the Best (U. S.). By Gilbert H. Grosvenor. XXIX, pp. 327-430, 71 ills. in black and white, 33 ills. in color, pictorial supplement, Apr., 1916

The **LAND** of the Crossbow (Yünnan Province, China). By George Forrest. XXI, pp. 132-156, 15 ills., map, Feb., 1910

The **LAND** of the Free in Africa. By Harry A. McBride. XLII, pp. 411-430, 22 ills., Oct., 1922

"**LAND** of the Free" in Asia: Siam Has Blended New With Old in Her Progressive March to Modern Statehood in the Family of Nations. By W. Robert Moore. LXV, pp. 531-576, 28 ills. in black and white, 26 ills. in color, map, May, 1934

LAND of the Horn, America's Tiptoe. 10 color photos by Amos Burg. LXXII, pp. 751-758, Dec., 1937

LAND of the Painted Oxcarts (Costa Rica). By Luis Marden. With 31 color photos by author. XC, pp. 409-456, 30 ills. in black and white, map, Oct., 1946

The **LAND** of the Stalking Death: A Journey Through Starving Armenia on an American Relief Train. By Melville Chater. XXXVI, pp. 393-420, 23 ills., Nov., 1919

The **LAND** of the Yellow Lama: National Geographic Society Explorer Visits the Strange Kingdom of Muli, Beyond the Likiang Snow Range of Yünnan Province, China. By Joseph F. Rock. XLVII, pp. 447-491, 39 ills., map, Apr., 1925

The **LAND** of William the Conqueror (Normandy): Where Northmen Came to Build Castles and Cathedrals. By Inez Buffington Ryan. LXI, pp. 89-99, 13 ills. in color, Jan., 1932

The **LAND** That Links the Americas (Panama). 22 color photos by Luis Marden. LXXX, pp. 601-624, Nov., 1941

LANDING Craft for Invasion. By Melville Bell Grosvenor. LXXXVI, pp. 1-30, 26 ills., July, 1944

LANDOR, A. HENRY SAVAGE:

Across Widest Africa. By A. Henry Savage Landor. XIX, pp. 694-737, 38 ills., map, Oct., 1908

LANDSCAPE ARCHITECTURE:

The Need of Conserving the Beauty and Freedom of Nature in Modern Life. By Charles W. Eliot. XXVI, pp. 67-74, 4 ills., July, 1914

LANDSCAPED Kwangsi, China's Province of Pictorial Art. By G. Weidman Groff and T. C. Lau. LXXII, pp. 671-710, 33 ills., map, Dec., 1937

LANDSLIDES:

Landslides and Rock Avalanches. By Guy Elliott Mitchell. XXI, pp. 277-287, 6 ills., Apr., 1910

"Where the Mountains Walked": An Account of the Recent Earthquake in Kansu Province, China, Which Destroyed 100,000 Lives. By Upton Close and Elsie McCormick. XLI, pp. 445-464, 23 ills., map, May, 1922

LANE, FRANKLIN K.:

A City of Realized Dreams (San Francisco). By Franklin K. Lane. XXVII, pp. 169-171, Feb., 1915

From the War-Path to the Plow. By Franklin K. Lane. XXVII, pp. 73-87, 12 ills., Jan., 1915

The Makers of the Flag. By Franklin K. Lane. XXXII, p. 304, Oct., 1917

A Mind's-Eye Map of America. By Franklin K. Lane. XXXVII, pp. 479-518, 25 ills. in black and white, 8 ills. in color, June, 1920

The Nation's Pride (Natural Resources). By Franklin K. Lane. XXVIII, pp. 589-606, 6 ills., Dec., 1915

The Nation's Undeveloped Resources (U. S.). By Franklin K. Lane. XXV, pp. 183-225, 32 ills., Feb., 1914

Voice Voyages by the National Geographic Society: A Tribute to the Geographical Achievements of the Telephone (Address by Franklin K. Lane). XXIX, pp. 296-326, 15 ills., chart, Mar., 1916

LANE, FRANKLIN K.—*Continued*

What Is It To Be an American? By Franklin K. Lane. XXXIII, pp. 348-354, 4 ills., diagr., Apr., 1918

See also NGS: Board of Managers

LANG, ANTON, JR.:

Where Bible Characters Live Again: Everyday Life in Oberammergau, World Famous for Its Passion Play, Reaches a Climax at Christmas. By Anton Lang, Jr. LXVIII, pp. 743-769, 19 ills. in black and white, 11 ills. in color, map, Dec., 1935

LANGLADE ISLAND (Petite Miquelon). *See* Miquelon

LANGLEY, ANNE RAINEY:

British West Indian Interlude. By Anne Rainey Langley. LXXIX, pp. 1-46, 23 ills. in black and white, 21 ills. in color, maps, Jan., 1941

I Kept House in a Jungle: The Spell of Primeval Tropics in Venezuela, Riotous With Strange Plants, Animals, and Snakes, Enthralls a Young American Woman. By Anne Rainey Langley. LXXV, pp. 97-132, 37 ills., map, Jan., 1939

LANGLEY, S. P.:

Aërial Locomotion. By Alexander Graham Bell. XVIII, pp. 1-34, 33 ills., Jan., 1907

Biography of S. P. Langley. XVII, p. 170, Mar., 1906

Diary of a Voyage from San Francisco to Tahiti and Return, 1901. By S. P. Langley. XII, pp. 413-429, 10 ills., maps, Dec., 1901

Gardiner Greene Hubbard: Memorial Meeting. Address by Prof. S. P. Langley. IX, p. 43, Feb., 1898

LANGUAGES:

All Around the Bay of Passamaquoddy. By Albert S. Gatschet. VIII, pp. 16-24, Jan., 1897
Included: A List of Indian Geographic Names Occurring Around Passamaquoddy Bay, Maine, with Their Derivations, pp. 21-24

The Battle-Line of Languages in Western Europe: A Problem in Human Geography More Perplexing Than That of International Boundaries. By A. L. Guerard. XLIII, pp. 145-180, 36 ills., Feb., 1923

Descriptive Topographic Terms of Spanish America. By Robert T. Hill. VII, pp. 291-302, Sept., 1896

A New Alphabet of the Ancients Is Unearthed: An Inconspicuous Mound in Northern Syria Yields Archeological Treasures of Far-reaching Significance. By F. A. Schaeffer. LVIII, pp. 477-516, 47 ills., map, Oct., 1930

New China and the Printed Page. By Paul Hutchinson. LI, pp. 687-722, 37 ills., June, 1927

The Origin of French-Canadians. IX, pp. 96-97, Mar., 1898

Rules for the Orthography of Geographic Names. Contributed by Mr. Herrle. II, pp. 279-285, 3 tables, Aug., 1890
Included: British System—French System—German System—Alphabets, Russian-English; English-Russian

LANGUAGES—*Continued*

Secrets from Syrian Hills: Explorations Reveal World's Earliest Known Alphabet, Deciphered from Schoolboy Slates and Dictionaries of 3,000 Years Ago. By Claude F. A. Schaeffer. LXIV, pp. 97-126, 40 ills., map, July, 1933

Turkey Goes to School. By Maynard Owen Williams. LV, pp. 95-108, 17 ills., Jan., 1929

The World's Words. By William H. Nicholas. LXXXIV, pp. 689-700, 8 ills., two-page map, map supplement, Dec., 1943

See also Geographic Names

LANKS, H. C.:

Honduran Highlights. With 11 color photos by H. C. Lanks. LXXXI, pp. 360-369, Mar., 1942

LANSING, ROBERT:

Prussianism. By Robert Lansing. XXXIII, pp. 546-557, 5 ills., June, 1918

LAODICEA (Ancient City):

The Ruined Cities of Asia Minor. By Ernest L. Harris. XIX, pp. 741-760, 11 ills., Nov., 1908

LA PAZ, Bolivia:

Bolivia—Tin Roof of the Andes. By Henry Albert Phillips. LXXXIII, pp. 309-332, 5 ills. in black and white, 20 ills. in color, Mar., 1943

Kaleidoscopic La Paz: The City of the Clouds. By Harriet Chalmers Adams. XX, pp. 119-141, 23 ills., Feb., 1909

LA PAZ, Mexico:

Adventuring Down the West Coast of Mexico. By Herbert Corey. XLII, pp. 449-503, 44 ills., map, Nov., 1922

LAPLAND:

The Nomads of Arctic Lapland: Mysterious Little People of a Land of the Midnight Sun Live Off the Country Above the Arctic Circle. By Clyde Fisher. LXXVI, pp. 641-676, 28 ills. in black and white, 12 ills. in color, map, Nov., 1939

LAPPS:

The Nomads of Arctic Lapland: Mysterious Little People of a Land of the Midnight Sun Live Off the Country Above the Arctic Circle. By Clyde Fisher. LXXVI, pp. 641-676, 28 ills. in black and white, 12 ills. in color, map, Nov., 1939

The **LARGE** Wading Birds: Long Legs and Remarkable Beaks, as Well as Size, Form, and Color, Distinguish the Herons, Ibises, and Flamingos. By T. Gilbert Pearson. Paintings by Maj. Allan Brooks. LXII, pp. 441-469, 13 ills. in black and white, 24 ills. in color, Oct., 1932

LARGELAMB, H. A. (Pseudonym):

Extinct Reptiles Found in Nodules. (By H. A. Largelamb). XVII, pp. 170-173, 9 ills., Mar., 1906

Notes on the Remarkable Habits of Certain Turtles and Lizards. By H. A. Largelamb. XVIII, pp. 413-419, 12 ills., June, 1907

The Purple Veil: A Romance of the Sea. (By H. A. L.). XVI, pp. 337-341, 9 ills., July, 1905

See also Bell, Alexander Graham

The **LARGER** North American Mammals. By E. W. Nelson. Paintings by Louis Agassiz Fuertes. XXX, pp. 385-472, 24 ills. in black and white, 49 ills. in color, pictorial supplement, Nov., 1916

LARSEN, HELGA:

The Mexican Indian Flying Pole Dance. By Helga Larsen. LXXI, pp. 387-400, 13 ills., Mar., 1937

The **LAST** Israelitish Blood Sacrifice: How the Vanishing Samaritans Celebrate the Passover on Sacred Mount Gerizim. By John D. Whiting. XXXVII, pp. 1-46, 40 ills., map, Jan., 1920

LATAKIA:

Antioch the Glorious. By William H. Hall. XXXVIII, pp. 81-103, 20 ills., map, Aug., 1920

Crusader Castles of the Near East. By William H. Hall. LIX, pp. 369-390, 19 ills., map, Mar., 1931

A New Alphabet of the Ancients Is Unearthed: An Inconspicuous Mound in Northern Syria Yields Archeological Treasures of Far-reaching Significance. By F. A. Schaeffer. LVIII, pp. 477-516, 47 ills., map, Oct., 1930

The Road of the Crusaders: A Historian Follows the Steps of Richard the Lion Heart and Other Knights of the Cross Over the "Via Dei." By Harold Lamb. LXIV, pp. 645-693, 46 ills. in black and white, 13 ills. in color, map, Dec., 1933

Secrets from Syrian Hills: Explorations Reveal World's Earliest Known Alphabet, Deciphered from Schoolboy Slates and Dictionaries of 3,000 Years Ago. By Claude F. A. Schaeffer. LXIV, pp. 97-126, 40 ills., map, July, 1933

The **LATEST** Map of Mexico. Text with map supplement. XXX, p. 88, July, 1916

The **LATEST** Route Proposed for the Isthmian Canal—Mandingo Route. XIII, pp. 64-70, chart, Feb., 1902

LATIN AMERICA:

Buenos Aires to Washington by Horse: A Solitary Journey of Two and a Half Years, Through Eleven American Republics, Covers 9,600 Miles of Mountain and Plain, Desert and Jungle. By A. F. Tschiffely. LV, pp. 135-196, 75 ills., map, Feb., 1929

The Flags of Pan-America. By Byron McCandless and Gilbert Grosvenor. XXXII, pp. 361-369, 62 ills. in color, Oct., 1917

Flying the World's Longest Air-Mail Route: From Montevideo, Uruguay, Over the Andes, Up the Pacific Coast, Across Central America and the Caribbean to Miami, Florida, in 67 Thrilling Flying Hours. By Junius B. Wood. LVII, pp. 261-325, 65 ills., map, Mar., 1930

How Latin America Looks from the Air: U. S. Army Airplanes Hurdle the High Andes, Brave Brazil Jungles, and Follow Smoking Volcanoes to Map New Sky Paths Around South America. By Major Herbert A. Dargue. LII, pp. 451-502, 42 ills., map, Oct., 1927

Latin America and Colombia. By John Barrett. XVII, pp. 692-709, 10 ills., Dec., 1906

The Latin-American Constitutions and Revolutions. By John W. Foster. XII, pp. 169-175, May, 1901

The Peace of Latin America. XVI, pp. 479-480, Oct., 1905

LATIN AMERICA—*Continued*

Skypaths Through Latin America: Flying From Our Nation's Capital Southward Over Jungles, Remote Islands, and Great Cities on an Aërial Survey of the East Coast of South America. By Frederick Simpich. LIX, pp. 1-79, 77 ills., map, Jan., 1931

To Bogotá and Back by Air: The Narrative of a 9,500-Mile Flight from Washington, Over Thirteen Latin-American Countries and Return, in the Single-Seater Airplane "Spirit of St. Louis." By Col. Charles A. Lindbergh. LIII, pp. 529-601, 98 ills., map, May, 1928

What the Latin American Republics Think of the Pan-American Conferences. XVII, pp. 474-479, Aug., 1906

See also names of countries

The **LATIN-AMERICAN** Constitutions and Revolutions. By John W. Foster. XII, pp. 169-175, May, 1901

LATTIMORE, OWEN:

Byroads and Backwoods of Manchuria: Where Violent Contrasts of Modernism and Unaltered Ancient Tradition Clash. By Owen Lattimore. LXI, pp. 101-130, 27 ills., map, Jan., 1932

China Opens Her Wild West (Yünnan): In the Mountain-girt Heart of a Continent a New China Has Been Created During the Years of War. By Owen Lattimore. LXXXII, pp. 337-367, 21 ills. in black and white, 11 ills. in color, map, Sept., 1942

South of the Clouds—Yünnan. 11 color photos by author and Frank Outram, pp. 349-356

The Desert Road to Turkestan: Twentieth Century Travel Through Innermost Asia, Along Caravan Trails Over Which Oriental Commerce Was Once Borne from China to the Medieval Western World. By Owen Lattimore. LV, pp. 661-702, 45 ills., map, June, 1929

New Road to Asia. By Owen Lattimore. LXXXVI, pp. 641-676, 15 ills. in black and white, 26 ills. in color, Dec., 1944

Sunny Siberia. 26 color photos by author, pp. 649-672

LATVIA:

Flying Around the Baltic. By Douglas Chandler. LXXIII, pp. 767-806, 31 ills. in black and white, 13 ills. in duotone, map, June, 1938

Latvia, Home of the Letts: One of the Baltic Republics Which Is Successfully Working Its Way to Stability. By Maynard Owen Williams. XLVI, pp. 401-443, 48 ills., map, Oct., 1924

The Races of Europe. By Edwin A. Grosvenor. XXXIV, pp. 441-534, 62 ills., diagr. and index, maps, map supplement, Dec., 1918

LAU, T. C.:

Landscaped Kwangsi, China's Province of Pictorial Art. By G. Weidman Groff and T. C. Lau. LXXII, pp. 671-710, 33 ills., map, Dec., 1937

LAURIER, SIR WILFRID:

The Forests of Canada. By Sir Wilfrid Laurier. XVII, pp. 504-509, Sept., 1906

LAURINBURG-MAXTON ARMY AIR BASE, North Carolina:

Gliders—Silent Weapons of the Sky. By William H. Nicholas. LXXXVI, pp. 149-160, 8 ills., Aug., 1944

LA VENTA, Mexico:

Finding Jewels of Jade in a Mexican Swamp. By Matthew W. and Marion Stirling. LXXXII, pp. 635-661, 15 ills. in black and white, 12 ills. in color, map, Nov., 1942

Great Stone Faces of the Mexican Jungle: Five Colossal Heads and Numerous Other Monuments of Vanished Americans Are Excavated by the Latest National Geographic-Smithsonian Expedition. By Matthew W. Stirling. LXXVIII, pp. 309-334, 26 ills., map, Sept., 1940

La Venta's Green Stone Tigers. By Matthew W. Stirling. LXXXIV, pp. 321-332, 4 ills. in black and white, 6 ills. in color, map, Sept., 1943

Wildlife of Tabasco and Veracruz. By Walter A. Weber. With 19 ills. in color from paintings by author. LXXXVII, pp. 187-216, 7 ills. in black and white, map, Feb., 1945

LA VENTA'S Green Stone Tigers. By Matthew W. Stirling. LXXXIV, pp. 321-332, 4 ills. in black and white, 6 ills. in color, map, Sept., 1943

LAW COURTS:

Open-Air Law Courts of Ethiopia. With 18 ills. by Harald P. Lechenperg. LXVIII, pp. 633-646, Nov., 1935

The **LAW** of Storms, Considered with Special Reference to the North Atlantic. By Everett Hayden. II, pp. 199-211, ill., 3 diagrs., 3 foldout diagrs., foldout charts, July, 1890

LAWRENCE, FREDERICK W.:

The Origin of American State Names. By Frederick W. Lawrence. XXXVIII, pp. 105-143, 34 ills., Aug., 1920

LAWS:

The Civil Government of Alaska. By Hon. George C. Perkins. IX, pp. 172-178, Apr., 1898

Our Immigration Laws from the Viewpoint of National Eugenics. By Prof. Robert De C. Ward. XXIII, pp. 38-41, Jan., 1912

The Utilization of the Vacant Public Lands. By Emory F. Best. VIII, pp. 49-57, Feb., 1897

Included: Homestead Act

See also Hammurabi, Code of

LAWS of Temperature Control of the Geographic Distribution of Terrestrial Animals and Plants. Annual Address by Vice-President, Dr. C. Hart Merriam. VI, pp. 229-238, table, 3 maps, Dec. 29, 1894

LAYSAN (Island), Hawaii:

A Bird City. XV, pp. 494-498, 6 ills., Dec., 1904

Bird Life Among Lava Rock and Coral Sand: The Chronicle of a Scientific Expedition to Little-known Islands of Hawaii. By Alexander Wetmore. XLVIII, pp. 77-108, 36 ills., map, July, 1925

LCIs (Landing Craft, Infantry):

Landing Craft for Invasion. By Melville Bell Grosvenor. LXXXVI, pp. 1-30, 26 ills., July, 1944

LCTs (Landing Craft, Tank):

Landing Craft for Invasion. By Melville Bell Grosvenor. LXXXVI, pp. 1-30, 26 ills., July, 1944

The **LEACH'S** Petrel: His Nursery on Little Duck Island. By Arnold Wood. XX, pp. 360-365, 7 ills., Apr., 1909

LEAF-CUTTING ANTS. *See* Atta Ants

LEAGUE OF NATIONS:

The League of Nations, What It Means and Why It Must Be. By William Howard Taft. XXXV, pp. 43-66, 15 ills., Jan., 1919

The Millennial City: The Romance of Geneva, Capital of the League of Nations. By Ralph A. Graves. XXXV, pp. 457-476, 11 ills., June, 1919

LEBANON:

American Alma Maters in the Near East. By Maynard Owen Williams. LXXXVIII, pp. 237-256, 16 ills., Aug., 1945

Crusader Castles of the Near East. By William H. Hall. LIX, pp. 369-390, 19 ills., map, Mar., 1931

From Jerusalem to Aleppo. By John D. Whiting. XXIV, pp. 71-113, 30 ills., map, Jan., 1913

In the Land of Moses and Abraham. 25 color photos by W. Robert Moore. LXXIV, pp. 711-742, Dec., 1938

The Road of the Crusaders: A Historian Follows the Steps of Richard the Lion Heart and Other Knights of the Cross Over the "Via Dei." By Harold Lamb. LXIV, pp. 645-693, 46 ills. in black and white, 13 ills. in color, map, Dec., 1933

Skirting the Shores of Sunrise: Seeking and Finding "The Levant" in a Journey by Steamer, Motor-Car, and Train from Constantinople to Port Said. By Melville Chater. L, pp. 649-728, 60 ills. in black and white, 34 ills. in color, map, Dec., 1926

Syria and Lebanon Taste Freedom. By Maynard Owen Williams. With 21 color photos by author. XC, pp. 729-763, 16 ills. in black and white, Dec., 1946

See also Beirut

LEBARGE, MICHEL:

A Yukon Pioneer, Mike Lebarge. (By Wm. H. Dall). IX, pp. 137-139, ill., Apr., 1898

LECHENPERG, HARALD P.:

Open-Air Law Courts of Ethiopia. With 18 ills. by Harald P. Lechenperg. LXVIII, pp. 633-646, Nov., 1935

With the Italians in Eritrea: Torrid Colony Between the Red Sea and Ethiopia, 2,600 Miles by Sea from Rome, Is Mobilization Place of Fascist Troops and Planes. By Harald P. Lechenperg. LXVIII, pp. 265-295, 34 ills., two-page map, Sept., 1935

LE CONTE, JOSEPH:

Joseph Le Conte (Biography). (By W J M.). XII, pp. 309-311, ill., Aug., 1901

LEDO-BURMA ROAD. *See* Stilwell Road

LEDO ROAD:

Stilwell Road—Land Route to China. By Nelson Grant Tayman. LXXXVII, pp. 681-698, 18 ills., June, 1945

LEE, J. R.:

Transporting a Navy Through the Jungles of Africa in War Time. By Frank J. Magee. XLII, pp. 331-362, 31 ills., Oct., 1922

Note: J. R. Lee, originator of the plan

LEE, JOSEPH:

Beautiful Ecuador. By Joseph Lee. XVIII, pp. 81-91, 9 ills., Feb., 1907

LEE, KENNETH FULLER:

In the Allagash Country (Maine). By Kenneth Fuller Lee. LV, pp. 505-520, 19 ills., Apr., 1929

LEE, THOMAS F.:

Guatemala: Land of Volcanoes and Progress: Cradle of Ancient Mayan Civilization, Redolent With Its Later Spanish and Indian Ways, Now Reaping Prosperity from Bananas and Coffee. By Thomas F. Lee. L, pp. 599-648, 32 ills. in black and white, 20 ills. in color, map, Nov., 1926

LEE, WILLIS T.:

New Discoveries in Carlsbad Cavern (New Mexico): Vast Subterranean Chambers with Spectacular Decorations Are Explored, Surveyed, and Photographed. By Willis T. Lee. XLVIII, pp. 301-319, 19 ills., map, Sept., 1925

A Visit to Carlsbad Cavern: Recent Explorations of a Limestone Cave in the Guadalupe Mountains of New Mexico Reveal a Natural Wonder of the First Magnitude. By Willis T. Lee. XLV, pp. 1-40, 42 ills., Jan., 1924

LEE, Camp, Virginia:

Training the New Armies of Liberty: Camp Lee, Virginia's Home for the National Army. By Granville Fortescue. XXXII, pp. 421-437, 8 ills., map, Nov.-Dec., 1917

LEEWARD ISLANDS, Hawaii:

Bird Life Among Lava Rock and Coral Sand: The Chronicle of a Scientific Expedition to Little-known Islands of Hawaii. By Alexander Wetmore. XLVIII, pp. 77-108, 36 ills., map, July, 1925

LEEWARD ISLANDS, West Indies:

British West Indian Interlude. By Anne Rainey Langley. LXXIX, pp. 1-46, 23 ills. in black and white, 21 ills. in color, maps, Jan., 1941

See also Antigua; Dominica; Guadeloupe; Martinique; Saba; St. Kitts; Virgin Islands

LEFFINGWELL, E. DE K.:

The Anglo-American Polar Expedition. (By E. de K. Leffingwell). XVIII, p. 796, Dec., 1907

LEGENDS:

The Story and Legends of the Pontine Marshes: After Many Centuries of Fruitless Effort, Italy Is to Inaugurate a Gigantic Enterprise to Drain the Fertile Region Southeast of Rome. By Don Gelasio Caetani. XLV, pp. 357-374, 18 ills., Apr., 1924

War's Wake in the Rhineland. By Thomas R. Henry. LXXXVIII, pp. 1-32, 29 ills., map, July, 1945

LEIBERG, J. B.:

Is Climatic Aridity Impending on the Pacific Slope? The Testimony of the Forest. By J. B. Leiberg. X, pp. 160-181, May, 1899

LEIS from Aloha Land (Hawaii). 10 color photos: 8 by Richard H. Stewart. LXXIV, pp. 435-442, Oct., 1938

LE MUNYON, ETHAN C.:

The Lama's Motor-Car. By Ethan C. Le Munyon. XXIV, pp. 641-670, 34 ills., May, 1913

LEND-LEASE:

Iran in Wartime: Through Fabulous Persia, Hub of the Middle East, Americans, Britons, and Iranians Keep Sinews of War Moving to the Embattled Soviet Union. By John N. Greely. LXXXIV, pp. 129-156, 26 ills., map, Aug., 1943

Lend-Lease and the Russian Victory. By Harvey Klemmer. LXXXVIII, pp. 499-512, 6 ills., Oct., 1945

Lend-Lease Is a Two-way Benefit: Innovation in Creative Statesmanship Polls Resources of United Nations, and Supplies American Forces Around the World. By Francis Flood. LXXXIII, pp. 745-761, 14 ills., June, 1943

LENINGRAD, R. S. F. S. R.:

Glimpses of the Russian Empire. By William Wisner Chapin. XXIII, pp. 1043-1078, 51 ills. in color, map, Nov., 1912

Young Russia: The Land of Unlimited Possibilities. By Gilbert H. Grosvenor. XXVI, pp. 421-520, 85 ills. in black and white, 17 ills. in color, Nov., 1914

LENZ, FRANK B.:

The World's Ancient Porcelain Center (Kingtehchen). By Frank B. Lenz. XXXVIII, pp. 391-406, 17 ills., Nov., 1920

LEOPARDS:

King of Cats and His Court. By Victor H. Cahalane. Paintings by Walter A. Weber. LXXXIII, pp. 217-259, 9 ills. in black and white, 20 ills. in color, Feb., 1943

LEPROSY:

Hunting the Chaulmoogra Tree. By Joseph F. Rock. XLI, pp. 243-276, 39 ills., map, Mar., 1922

LESBOS (Island). *See* Mytilene

LESSER ANTILLES. *See* Antigua; Aruba; Bonaire; Curaçao; Dominica; Guadeloupe; Martinique; Saba; St. Kitts; St. Lucia; St. Vincent; Trinidad; Virgin Islands

LESSER SUNDA ISLANDS. *See* Bali; Timor

LESSONS from China (Forestry). XX, pp. 18-29, 8 ills., Jan., 1909

LESSONS from Japan. XV, pp. 221-225, 3 ills., May, 1904

The **LESSONS** of Galveston. By W J McGee. XI, pp. 377-383, Oct., 1900

LETTERS from the Italian Front. By Marchesa Louise de Rosales to Ethel Mather Bagg. XXXII, pp. 47-67, 22 ills., July, 1917

LEUANIUA (Island), Solomon Islands:

Coconuts and Coral Islands. By H. Ian Hogbin. LXV, pp. 265-298, 24 ills. in black and white, 14 ills. in color, map, Mar., 1934

LEUNG, GEORGE KIN:

Peiping's Happy New Year: Lunar Celebration Attracts Throngs to Temple Fairs, Motley Bazaars, and Age-old Festivities. By George Kin Leung. LXX, pp. 749-792, 31 ills. in black and white, 16 ills. in color, Dec., 1936

LEVANT (Ship):

A Doubtful Island of the Pacific. By James D. Hague. XV, pp. 478-489, ill., maps, Dec., 1904

Philip Nolan and the "Levant." (By Edward E. Hale). XVI, pp. 114-116, Mar., 1905

A Recent Report from the "Doubtful Island Region." By James D. Hague. XVIII, pp. 205-208, maps, Mar., 1907

LEVANT STATES:

Change Comes to Bible Lands. By Frederick Simpich. LXXIV, pp. 695-750, 40 ills. in black and white, 25 ills. in color, map supplement, Dec., 1938

Crusader Castles of the Near East. By William H. Hall. LIX, pp. 369-390, 19 ills., map, Mar., 1931

Damascus, the Pearl of the Desert. By A. Forder. XXII, pp. 62-82, 19 ills., map, Jan., 1911

Damascus and Mecca Railway. XII, p. 408, Nov., 1901

From Jerusalem to Aleppo. By John D. Whiting. XXIV, pp. 71-113, 30 ills., map, Jan., 1913

Impressions of Asiatic Turkey. By Stephen van Rensselaer Trowbridge. XXVI, pp. 598-609, 6 ills., Dec., 1914

A New Alphabet of the Ancients Is Unearthed: An Inconspicuous Mound in Northern Syria Yields Archeological Treasures of Far-reaching Significance. By F. A. Schaeffer. LVIII, pp. 477-516, 47 ills., map, Oct., 1930

One Thousand Miles of Railway Built for Pilgrims and Not for Dividends. By Colonel F. R. Maunsell. XX, pp. 156-172, 12 ills., map, Feb., 1909

The Road of the Crusaders: A Historian Follows the Steps of Richard the Lion Heart and Other Knights of the Cross Over the "Via Dei." By Harold Lamb. LXIV, pp. 645-693, 46 ills. in black and white, 13 ills. in color, map, Dec., 1933

Scenes in Asia Minor. 35 ills., map. XX, pp. 173-193, Feb., 1909

Secrets from Syrian Hills: Explorations Reveal World's Earliest Known Alphabet, Deciphered from Schoolboy Slates and Dictionaries of 3,000 Years Ago. By Claude F. A. Schaeffer. LXIV, pp. 97-126, 40 ills., map, July, 1933

Skirting the Shores of Sunrise: Seeking and Finding "The Levant" in a Journey by Steamer, Motor-Car, and Train from Constantinople to Port Said. By Melville Chater. L, pp. 649-728, 60 ills. in black and white, 34 ills. in color, map, Dec., 1926

Under the Heel of the Turk: A Land with a Glorious Past, a Present of Abused Opportunities, and a Future of Golden Possibilities. By William H. Hall. XXXIV, pp. 51-69, 14 ills., July, 1918

LEVEES:
The Delta of the Mississippi River. By E. L. Corthell. VIII, pp. 351-354, Dec., 1897
The Great Mississippi Flood of 1927: Since White Man's Discovery This Mighty River Has Served Him Well, Yet It Has Brought Widespread Devastation Along Its Lower Reaches. By Frederick Simpich. LII, pp. 243-289, 53 ills., map., Sept., 1927

LEWIS, F.:
The Koala, or Australian Teddy Bear. By F. Lewis. LX, pp. 346-355, 13 ills., Sept., 1931

LEWIS, HARRY R.:
America's Debt to the Hen. By Harry R. Lewis. LI, pp. 453-467, 15 ills., Apr., 1927

LEWIS, L. ELIZABETH:
The Fire-Walking Hindus of Singapore. By L. Elizabeth Lewis. LIX, pp. 513-522, 12 ills., Apr., 1931

LEWIS AND CLARK EXPEDITION:
Oregon: Its History, Geography, and Resources. By John H. Mitchell, U. S. Senator from Oregon. VI, pp. 239-284, Apr. 20, 1895
A Relic of the Lewis and Clarke Expedition. (By Cyrus C. Babb). IX, pp. 100-101, ill., Mar., 1898

LEWIS AND CLARK EXPEDITION ROUTE:
Trailing History Down the Big Muddy: In the Homeward Wake of Lewis and Clark, a Folding Steel Skiff Bears Its Lone Pilot on a 2,000-Mile Cruise on the Yellowstone-Missouri. By Lewis R. Freeman. LIV, pp. 73-120, 51 ills., map, July, 1928

LHASA, Tibet:
Across Tibet from India to China. By Lt. Col. Ilia Tolstoy, AUS. XC, pp. 169-222, 53 ills., map, Aug., 1946
Explorations in Tibet. XIV, pp. 353-355, Sept., 1903
The Most Extraordinary City in the World: Notes on Lhasa—The Mecca of the Buddhist Faith. By Shaoching H. Chuan. XXIII, pp. 959-995, 60 ills., Oct., 1912
Notes on Tibet. XV, pp. 292-294, ill., July, 1904
Views of Lhasa. 11 ills. XVI, pp. 27-38, Jan., 1905
The World's Strangest Capital. By John Claude White. XXIX, pp. 273-295, 19 ills., panorama, Mar., 1916
Lhasa—The Mecca of the Buddhist Faith (panorama)

LIANG-CHENG, SIR CHENTUNG:
China and the United States. By Sir Chentung Liang-Cheng. XVI, pp. 554-557, Dec., 1905

LIBBEY, WILLIAM, JR.:
The Relations of the Gulf Stream and the Labrador Current. By William Libbey, Junior. V, pp. 161-166, Jan. 31, 1894

LIBERATED Ukraine. By Eddy Gilmore. LXXXV, pp. 513-536, 22 ills., map, May, 1944

LIBERATORS (Bombers):
8th Air Force in England. 10 ills. in color from U. S. Army Air Forces official photos. LXXXVII, pp. 297-304, Mar., 1945

LIBERIA:
The Black Republic—Liberia. By Sir Harry Johnston and Ernest Lyon. XVIII, pp. 334-343, 9 ills., May, 1907
Conditions in Liberia. By Roland P. Folkner, George Sale, Emmett J. Scott. XXI, pp. 729-741, 9 ills., Sept., 1910
Dumboy, the National Dish of Liberia. By G. N. Collins. XXII, pp. 84-88, 5 ills., Jan., 1911
Kboo, a Liberian Game. By G. N. Collins. XXI, pp. 944-948, 3 ills., Nov., 1910
The Land of the Free in Africa. By Harry A. McBride. XLII, pp. 411-430, 22 ills., Oct., 1922
Notes on the Only American Colony in the World. By Edgar Allen Forbes. XXI, pp. 719-729, 14 ills., Sept., 1910
A Primitive Gyroscope in Liberia. By G. N. Collins. XXI, pp. 531-535, 3 ills., June, 1910
Scene in Liberia. 4 ills. XX, pp. 298-301, Mar., 1909

LIBERIA, Costa Rica:
Land of the Painted Oxcarts. By Luis Marden. With 31 color photos by author. XC, pp. 409-456, 30 ills. in black and white, map, Oct., 1946

LIBIA:
Cirenaica, Eastern Wing of Italian Libia. By Harriet Chalmers Adams. LVII, pp. 689-726, 35 ills. in black and white, 13 ills. in color, map, June, 1930
Crossing the Untraversed Libyan Desert: The Record of a 2,200-Mile Journey of Exploration Which Resulted in the Discovery of Two Oases of Strategic Importance on the Southwestern Frontier of Egypt. By A. M. Hassanein Bey. XLVI, pp. 233-277, 46 ills., map, Sept., 1924
Here and There in Northern Africa. By Frank Edward Johnson. XXV, pp. 1-132, 113 ills., Jan., 1914
The Mysteries of the Desert. By Hanns Vischer. XXII, pp. 1056-1059, Nov., 1911
Old-New Battle Grounds of Egypt and Libia. By W. Robert Moore. LXXVIII, pp. 809-820, 8 ills., map, Dec., 1940
Tripoli: A Land of Little Promise. By Adolf L. Vischer. XXII, pp. 1035-1047, 6 ills., map, Nov., 1911
Tripolitania, Where Rome Resumes Sway: The Ancient Trans-Mediterranean Empire, on the Fringe of the Libyan Desert, Becomes a Promising Modern Italian Colony. By Colonel Gordon Casserly. XLVIII, pp. 131-161, 27 ills. in black and white, 9 ills. in color, map, Aug., 1925
See also Bengasi; Tripoli

LIBIAN DESERT, Africa:
Crossing the Untraversed Libyan Desert: The Record of a 2,200-Mile Journey of Exploration Which Resulted in the Discovery of Two Oases of Strategic Importance on the Southwestern Frontier of Egypt. By A. M. Hassanein Bey. XLVI, pp. 233-277, 46 ills., map, Sept., 1924
See also Tripolitania

LIBRARIES. *See* NGS: Library; *and* Washington, D.C., for Library of Congress

LIECHTENSTEIN:

Round About Liechtenstein: A Tiny Principality Which the Visitor May Encompass in a Single View Affords Adventurous Climbs Among Steep Pastures and Quaint Villages. By Maynard Owen Williams. LII, pp. 611-634, 18 ills., map, Nov., 1927

LIFE, Culture, and History of the Egyptians. 32 ills. in color from paintings by H. M. Herget. LXXX, pp. 436-514, Oct., 1941

LIFE Afloat in China: Tens of Thousands of Chinese in Congested Ports Spend Their Entire Existence on Boats. By Robert F. Fitch. LI, pp. 665-686, 28 ills., June, 1927

LIFE Along the Central China Coast. 14 color photos by W. Robert Moore. LXII, pp. 317-324, Sept., 1932

LIFE Among the Lamas of Choni: Describing the Mystery Plays and Butter Festival in the Monastery of an Almost Unknown Tibetan Principality in Kansu Province, China. By Joseph F. Rock. LIV, pp. 569-619, 34 ills. in black and white, 16 ills. in color, map, Nov., 1928

LIFE Among the People of Eastern Tibet. By Dr. A. L. Shelton. XL, pp. 293-326, 35 ills., map, Sept., 1921

LIFE and Color Under the Rising Sun (Japan). 12 color photos by W. Robert Moore and Kiyoshi Sakamoto. LXIII, pp. 289-296, Mar., 1933

LIFE and Death in Ancient Maya Land (Yucatán). 10 ills. in color from paintings by H. M. Herget. LXX, pp. 623-630, Nov., 1936

LIFE and Death in Toradjaland. 22 photos: 11 by Maynard Owen Williams, 8 by Helene Fischer. LXXVIII, pp. 65-80, July, 1940

LIFE and Luster of Berlin. 24 color photos by Wilhelm Tobien and Hans Hildenbrand. LXXI, pp. 147-177, Feb., 1937

LIFE Grows Grim in Singapore. By H. Gordon Minnigerode. LXXX, pp. 661-686, 17 ills. in black and white, 9 ills. in color, map, Nov., 1941

LIFE in a Norway Valley: An American Girl Is Welcomed Into the Homemaking and Haying of Happy Hallingdal. By Abbie L. Bosworth. LXVII, pp. 627-648, 21 ills., map, May, 1935

LIFE in Constantinople. By H. G. Dwight. XXVI, pp. 521-545, 25 ills., Dec., 1914

LIFE in Dauntless Darwin: A National Geographic Staff Writer Gives a Vivid Description of the Australian Town That Guards the Continent's Northern Door. By Howell Walker. LXXXII, pp. 123-138, 17 ills., map, July, 1942

LIFE in Our Fighting Fleet (U. S. Navy). By F. Barrows Colton. LXXIX, pp. 671-702, 30 ills., June, 1941

LIFE in the Antarctic. 8 ills. XLII, pp. 655-662, Dec., 1922

LIFE in the Great Desert of Central Asia. By Ellsworth Huntington. XX, pp. 749-760, 12 ills., Aug., 1909

LIFE MEMBERS. *See* NGS: Members and Membership: Life Members

The **LIFE** of the Moon-Jelly. By William Crowder. Paintings by author. L, pp. 187-202, 6 ills. in black and white, 8 ills. in color, Aug., 1926

LIFE on a Coral Reef: The Fertility and Mystery of the Sea Studied Beneath the Waters Surrounding Dry Tortugas. By W. H. Longley. LI, pp. 61-83, 22 ills., Jan., 1927

LIFE on a Yukon Trail. By Alfred Pearce Dennis. X, pp. 377-391, 8 ills., map, Oct., 1899; pp. 457-466, 7 ills., Nov., 1899

LIFE on the Argentine Pampa. By Frederick Simpich. Paintings by Cesáreo Bernaldo de Quirós. LXIV, pp. 449-491, 41 ills. in black and white, 8 ills. in color, Oct., 1933

LIFE on the Grand Banks: An Account of the Sailor-Fishermen Who Harvest the Shoal Waters of North America's Eastern Coasts. By Frederick William Wallace. XL, pp. 1-28, 29 ills., July, 1921

LIFE on the Hawaii "Front": All-out Defense and Belt Tightening of Pacific Outpost Foreshadow the Things to Come on Mainland. By Lieut. Frederick Simpich, Jr. LXXXII, pp. 541-560, 19 ills., map, Oct., 1942

LIFE on the Steppes and Oases of Chinese Turkestan. 32 color photos by W. Bosshard. LIX, pp. 333-356, Mar., 1931

The **LIFE** Story of an American Airman in France: Extracts from the Letters of Stuart Walcott, Who, Between July and December, 1917, Learned to Fly in French Schools of Aviation, Won Fame at the Front, and Fell Near Saint Souplet. XXXIII, pp. 86-106, 9 ills., Jan., 1918

LIFE Story of the Mosquito. By Graham Fairchild. With 10 ills. in color from paintings. LXXXV, pp. 180-195, 5 ills. in black and white, drawing, Feb., 1944

LIFE with an Indian Prince: As Guests of a Maharajah's Brother, Two Young American Naturalists Study Age-old Methods of Hunting with Trained Falcons and Cheetahs and Savor the Pomp of Royal India. By John and Frank Craighead. LXXXI, pp. 235-272, 38 ills., map, Feb., 1942

LIFE with Our Fighting Coast Guard. By F. Barrows Colton. LXXXIII, pp. 557-588, 22 ills. in black and white, 9 ills. in color, May, 1943

LIFE ZONES:

Laws of Temperature Control of the Geographic Distribution of Terrestrial Animals and Plants. Annual Address by Vice-President, Dr. C. Hart Merriam. VI, pp. 229-238, table, 3 maps, Dec. 29, 1894

LIFE'S Color in Wisconsin. 27 color photos: 23 by B. Anthony Stewart. LXXII, pp. 17-40, July, 1937

LIFE'S Flavor on a Swedish Farm: From the Rocky Hills of Småland Thousands of Sturdy Citizens Have Emigrated to the United States. By Willis Lindquist. LXXVI, pp. 393-414, 23 ills., map, Sept., 1939

LIFE'S Pattern on the Italian Riviera. By Helen Churchill Candee. LXVII, pp. 67-100, 25 ills. in black and white, 12 ills. in color, map, Jan., 1935

LIFE'S Tenor in Ethiopia : Africa's Land of Early Christianity Now Yields Minerals for Modern Industry. By James Loder Park. LXVII, pp. 783-793, 8 ills., June, 1935

LIGHTHOUSES:

A Battle-Ground of Nature: The Atlantic Seaboard. By John Oliver La Gorce. XXXIII, pp. 511-546, 23 ills., 4 maps, June, 1918

Beacons of the Sea. By George R. Putnam. XXIV, pp. 1-53, 65 ills., diagrs., map, Jan., 1913

An Important New Guide for Shipping: Navassa Light, on a Barren Island in the West Indies, is the First Signal for the Panama Canal. By George R. Putnam. XXXIV, pp. 401-406, 3 ills., map, Nov., 1918

The Isle of Capri: An Imperial Residence and Probable Wireless Station of Ancient Rome. By John A. Kingman. XXXVI, pp. 213-231, 17 ills., Sept., 1919

New Safeguards for Ships in Fog and Storm. By George R. Putnam. LXX, pp. 169-200, 28 ills., charts, Aug., 1936

Warfare on Our Eastern Coast. By John Oliver La Gorce. XXVIII, pp. 195-230, 29 ills., charts, Sept., 1915

LIGHTSHIPS:

New Safeguards for Ships in Fog and Storm. By George R. Putnam. LXX, pp. 169-200, 28 ills., charts, Aug., 1936

LIGNITE:

Alaska and Its Mineral Resources. By Samuel Franklin Emmons. IX, pp. 139-172, 3 ills., map supplement, Apr., 1898

LILIENTHAL, OTTO:

Aërial Locomotion. By Alexander Graham Bell. XVIII, pp. 1-34, 33 ills., Jan., 1907

Remarkable Photograph of Lilienthal's Gliding Machine. By R. W. Wood. XIX, p. 596, ill., Aug., 1908. XXII, ill. p. 271, Mar., 1911. LII, ill. p. 235, Aug., 1927

LIMA, Peru:

The Lure of Lima, City of the Kings. By William Joseph Showalter. LVII, pp. 727-784, 41 ills. in black and white, 25 ills. in color, June, 1930

LIMBERT, R. W.:

Among the "Craters of the Moon": An Account of the First Expeditions Through the Remarkable Volcanic Lava Beds of Southern Idaho. By R. W. Limbert. XLV, pp. 303-328, 23 ills., map, Mar., 1924

The **LIMITED** Water Supply of the Arid Region. By Frederick H. Newell. XI, pp. 438-442, Nov., 1900

LIMITING Width of Meander Belts. By Mark S. W. Jefferson. XIII, pp. 373-384, 6 charts, Oct., 1902

LIMÓN, Costa Rica:

Land of the Painted Oxcarts. By Luis Marden. With 31 color photos by author. XC, pp. 409-456, 30 ills. in black and white, map, Oct., 1946

LINCOLN, F. S.:

The Glamour of Historic Havana. 9 photos by F. S. Lincoln. LXIV, pp. 357-364, Sept., 1933

LINCOLN, Nebraska:

Nebraska, the Cornhusker State. By Leo A. Borah. LXXXVII, pp. 513-542, 6 ills. in black and white, 23 ills. in color, map, May, 1945

LINCOLN MEMORIAL, Washington, D. C.:

The Lincoln Memorial. By William Howard Taft. XLIII, pp. 597-602, 5 ills., June, 1923

Views of the Lincoln Memorial in Washington. 8 ills. XLII, pp. 197-204, Aug., 1922

LINDBERGH, ANNE MORROW:

Flying Around the North Atlantic. By Anne Morrow Lindbergh. Foreword by Charles A. Lindbergh. LXVI, pp. 259-337, 82 ills., maps (1 two-page), Sept., 1934

The Society Awards Hubbard Medal to Anne Morrow Lindbergh. LXV, pp. 791-794, 4 ills., June, 1934

See also NGS: Medals: Hubbard Medal

LINDBERGH, CHARLES A.:

Air Conquest: From the Early Days of Giant Kites and Birdlike Gliders, the National Geographic Society Has Aided and Encouraged the Growth of Aviation. LII, pp. 233-242, 13 ills., Aug., 1927

Flying Around the North Atlantic. By Anne Morrow Lindbergh. Foreword by Charles A. Lindbergh. LXVI, pp. 259-337, 82 ills., maps (1 two-page), Sept., 1934

President Coolidge Bestows Lindbergh Award: The National Geographic Society's Hubbard Medal Is Presented to Aviator Before the Most Notable Gathering in the History of Washington (Address by Colonel Lindbergh). LIII, pp. 132-140, 4 ills., Jan., 1928

Seeing America with Lindbergh: The Record of a Tour of More Than 20,000 Miles by Airplane Through Forty-eight States on Schedule Time. By Lieutenant Donald E. Keyhoe. LIII, pp. 1-46, 46 ills., map, Jan., 1928

To Bogotá and Back by Air: The Narrative of a 9,500-Mile Flight from Washington, Over Thirteen Latin-American Countries and Return, in the Single-Seater Airplane "Spirit of St. Louis." By Col. Charles A. Lindbergh. LIII, pp. 529-601, 98 ills., map, May, 1928

See also NGS: Medals: Hubbard Medal

LINDQUIST, WILLIS:

Life's Flavor on a Swedish Farm: From the Rocky Hills of Småland Thousands of Sturdy Citizens Have Emigrated to the United States. By Willis Lindquist. LXXVI, pp. 393-414, 23 ills., map, Sept., 1939

On Danish By-Lanes: An American Cycles Through the Quaint City of Lace, the Curiosity Town Where Time Stands Still, and Even Finds a Frontier in the Farming Kingdom. By Willis Lindquist. LXXVII, pp. 1-34, 21 ills. in black and white, 10 ills. in color, map, Jan., 1940

LINDSAY ISLAND, Antarctic Region:
Sailing the Seven Seas in the Interest of Science: Adventures Through 157,000 Miles of Storm and Calm, from Arctic to Antarctic and Around the World, in the Non-magnetic Yacht "Carnegie." By J. P. Ault. XLII, pp. 631-690, 47 ills., chart, Dec., 1922

LINGNAN UNIVERSITY, Canton, China: Expedition:
Landscaped Kwangsi, China's Province of Pictorial Art. By G. Weidman Groff and T. C. Lau. LXXII, pp. 671-710, 33 ills., map, Dec., 1937

The **LINK** Relations of Southwestern Asia. By Talcott Williams. XII, pp. 249-265, 12 maps, July, 1901; pp. 291-299, maps, Aug., 1901

LIONS:
King of Cats and His Court. By Victor H. Cahalane. Paintings by Walter A. Weber. LXXXIII, pp. 217-259, 9 ills. in black and white, 20 ills. in color, Feb., 1943
Wild Man and Wild Beast in Africa. By Theodore Roosevelt. XXII, pp. 1-33, 41 ills., map, Jan., 1911

LIPOVAN FISHERMEN:
Caviar Fishermen of Romania: From Vâlcov, "Little Venice" of the Danube Delta, Bearded Russian Exiles Go Down to the Sea. By Dorothy Hosmer. LXXVII, pp. 407-434, 29 ills., map, Mar., 1940

LISBON, Portugal:
Castles and Progress in Portugal. By W. Robert Moore. LXXIII, pp. 133-188, 36 ills. in black and white, 24 ills. in color, map, Feb., 1938
Lisbon—Gateway to Warring Europe. By Harvey Klemmer. LXXX, pp. 259-276, 18 ills., Aug., 1941
Lisbon, the City of the Friendly Bay. By Clifford Albion Tinker. XLII, pp. 505-552, 30 ills. in black and white, 16 ills. in color, map, Nov., 1922
The Woods and Gardens of Portugal. By Martin Hume. XXI, pp. 883-894, 8 ills., Oct., 1910

LISLE, CLIFTON:
Celebrating Christmas on the Meuse. By Captain Clifton Lisle. XXXVI, pp. 527-537, 5 ills., Dec., 1919

A **LIST** of Indian Geographic Names Occurring Around Passamaquoddy Bay, Maine, with Their Derivations. VIII, pp. 21-24, Jan., 1897

LIST of Maps of Washington and the District of Columbia, with Notes Thereon. By Marcus Baker. VI, pp. 167-178, Nov. 1, 1894

LIST of Plants Collected near Muir Glacier, determined by W. W. Rowlee. IV, p. 79, Mar. 21, 1892

LIST of References to the Literature on the Artificial Production of Rainfall. VI, pp. 60-62, Apr. 25, 1894

LITERARY CONTESTS:
International Literary Contest (Madrid, Spain). I, pp. 273-276, July, 1889
See also NGS: Essay Contests

LITHUANIA:
Flying Around the Baltic. By Douglas Chandler. LXXIII, pp. 767-806, 31 ills. in black and white, 13 ills. in duotone, map, June, 1938

LITTLE AMERICA, Antarctica:
The Conquest of Antarctica by Air. By Richard Evelyn Byrd. LVIII, pp. 127-227, 71 ills. in black and white, 16 ills. in gravure, map, Aug., 1930
Mapping the Antarctic from the Air: The Aërial Camera Earns Its Place as the Eyes and Memory of the Explorer. By Capt. Ashley C. McKinley. LXII, pp. 471-485, 13 ills., map supplement, Oct., 1932

LITTLE DUCK ISLAND, Maine:
The Leach's Petrel: His Nursery on Little Duck Island. By Arnold Wood. XX, pp. 360-365, 7 ills., Apr., 1909

"LITTLE GRAY LADY." *See* Nantucket (Island)

A **LITTLE** Journey in Honduras. By F. J. Youngblood. XXX, pp. 177-184, 6 ills., Aug., 1916

A **LITTLE-KNOWN** Marvel of the Western Hemisphere: Christophe's Citadel, a Monument to the Tyranny and Genius of Haiti's King of Slaves. By Major G. H. Osterhout, Jr. XXXVIII, pp. 469-482, 13 ills., Dec., 1920

LITTLE-KNOWN Parts of Panama. By Henry Pittier. XXIII, pp. 627-662, 35 ills., map, July, 1912

LITTLE-KNOWN Sardinia. By Helen Dunstan Wright. XXX, pp. 97-120, 23 ills., map, Aug., 1916

LITTLE NORWAY (Training Center), Toronto, Canada:
Norway, an Active Ally. By Wilhelm Morgenstierne. LXXXIII, pp. 333-357, 24 ills., map, Mar., 1943

LITTLE ROCK, Arkansas:
Arkansas Rolls Up Its Sleeves. By Frederick Simpich. XC, pp. 273-312, 16 ills. in black and white, 23 ills. in color, map, Sept., 1946

LITTLEHALES, GEORGE W.:
The Compass in Modern Navigation. By G. W. Littlehales. VIII, pp. 266-272, Sept., 1897
Marine Hydrographic Surveys of the Coasts of the World. By George W. Littlehales. XVI, pp. 63-67, maps, Feb., 1905

LIVESTOCK:
Britain Fights in the Fields. By Francis A. Flood. LXXXVI, pp. 31-65, 17 ills. in black and white, 21 ills. in color, July, 1944
Exploring a Grass Wonderland of Wild West China. By Ray G. Johnson. LXXXV, pp. 713-742, 24 ills., map, June, 1944
Grass Makes Wyoming Fat. By Frederick Simpich. LXXXVIII, pp. 153-188, 13 ills. in black and white, 19 ills. in color, two-page map, Aug., 1945
Idaho Made the Desert Bloom. By D. Worth Clark. LXXXV, pp. 641-688, 21 ills. in black and white, 20 ills. in color, map, June, 1944

LIVESTOCK—*Continued*

Nebraska, the Cornhusker State. By Leo A. Borah. LXXXVII, pp. 513-542, 6 ills. in black and white, 23 ills. in color, map, May, 1945

See also Cattle and Cattle Raising; Goats; Sheep and Sheep Raising

LIVING Casks of Honey (Ants). By Jennie E. Harris. LXVI, pp. 193-199, 4 ills., Aug., 1934

LIVING Jewels of the Sea (Plankton). By William Crowder. Paintings by author. LII, pp. 290-304, 8 ills. in black and white, 8 ills. in color, Sept., 1927

LIVING on a Volcano: An Unspoiled Patch of Polynesia Is Niuafoō, Nicknamed "Tin Can Island" by Stamp Collectors. By Thomas A. Jaggar. LXVIII, pp. 91-106, 17 ills., map, July, 1935

LIZARDS:

Lonely Australia: The Unique Continent. By Herbert E. Gregory. XXX, pp. 473-568, 68 ills., 5 maps (1 two-page), Dec., 1916
Included: Monitor, Skink, Slow-worm

A Modern Dragon Hunt on Komodo: An English Yachting Party Traps and Photographs the Huge and Carnivorous Dragon Lizard of the Lesser Sundas. By Lady Broughton. LXX, pp. 321-331, 12 ills. in duotone, Sept., 1936

Notes on the Remarkable Habits of Certain Turtles and Lizards. By H. A. Largelamb. XVIII, pp. 413-419, 12 ills., June, 1907
Included: Glass "Snake," Mexican Horned Lizard, Pacific Horned Lizard, Plated Lizard, Regal Horned Lizard, Two-Footed Worm Lizard

Reptiles of All Lands. By Raymond L. Ditmars. XXII, pp. 601-633, 32 ills., July, 1911
Included: Black Tegu, Flying Dragon, Gecko, Gila Monster, Horned Lizard, Iguana, Malayan Kabara-Goya, Monitor, Spiny Lizard

Stalking the Dragon Lizard on the Island of Komodo. By W. Douglas Burden. LII, pp. 216-232, 21 ills., Aug., 1927

LJUNGSTEDT, O. A.:

The Erratic (Geologic Formation of the United States). By O. A. Ljungstedt. XXI, pp. 525-531, 4 ills., map, June, 1910

LLAMAS:

Camels of the Clouds. By W. H. Hodge. LXXXIX, pp. 641-656, 15 ills., map, May, 1946

LLANGOLLEN, Wales:

Sheep Dog Trials in Llangollen: Trained Collies Perform Marvels of Herding in the Cambrian Stakes, Open to the World. By Sarah Bloch. LXXVII, pp. 559-574, 17 ills., Apr., 1940

LLOYD, ALBERT B.:

Lloyd's Journey Across the Great Pygmy Forest (Belgian Congo). X, pp. 26-30, Jan., 1899

LLOYD, FREEMAN:

Field Dogs in Action. By Freeman Lloyd. Paintings by Edward Herbert Miner. LXXI, pp. 85-108, 8 ills. in black and white, 36 portraits in color, Jan., 1937

LLOYD, FREEMAN—*Continued*

Hark to the Hounds. By Freeman Lloyd. Paintings by Edward Herbert Miner. LXXII, pp. 453-484, 18 ills. in black and white, 31 portraits in color, Oct., 1937

Man's Oldest Ally, the Dog: Since Cave-Dweller Days This Faithful Friend Has Shared the Work, Exploration, and Sport of Humankind. By Freeman Lloyd. Paintings by Edward Herbert Miner. LXIX, pp. 247-274, 13 ills. in black and white, 33 portraits in color, Feb., 1936

Non-sporting Dogs. By Freeman Lloyd. Paintings by Walter A. Weber. LXXXIV, pp. 569-588, 9 ills. in black and white, 8 ills. in color from paintings from life, Nov., 1943

Toy Dogs, Pets of Kings and Commoners. By Freeman Lloyd. LXXXV, pp. 459-480, 8 ills. in black and white, 16 ills. in color, Apr., 1944

Working Dogs of the World. By Freeman Lloyd. Paintings by Edward Herbert Miner. LXXX, pp. 776-806, 12 ills. in black and white, 20 ills. in color, Dec., 1941

LLOYD, HENRY DEMAREST:

Problems of the Pacific—New Zealand. By Henry Demarest Lloyd. XIII, pp. 342-352, Sept., 1902

LLOYD'S Journey Across the Great Pygmy Forest (Belgian Congo). X, pp. 26-30, Jan., 1899

LOANDA, Angola:

Angola, the Last Foothold of Slavery. XXI, pp. 625-630, 6 ills., July, 1910

LOBOS ISLANDS, Peru:

Peru's Wealth-Producing Birds: Vast Riches in the Guano Deposits of Cormorants, Pelicans, and Petrels which Nest on Her Barren, Rainless Coast. By R. E. Coker. XXXVII, pp. 537-566, 28 ills., June, 1920

LOBSTERS:

The Maine American and the American Lobster. By John D. Lucas. LXXXIX, pp. 523-543, 19 ills., Apr., 1946

LOCATION of the Boundary Between Nicaragua and Costa Rica. By Arthur P. Davis. XII, pp. 22-28, ill., map, Jan., 1901

LOCKLEY, R. M.:

We Live Alone, and Like It—On an Island (Skokholm). By R. M. Lockley. LXXIV, pp. 252-278, 27 ills., Aug., 1938

LOCUSTS:

Here and There in Northern Africa. By Frank Edward Johnson. XXV, pp. 1-132, 113 ills., Jan., 1914

Jerusalem's Locust Plague: Being a Description of the Recent Locust Influx into Palestine, and Comparing Same with Ancient Locust Invasions as Narrated in the Old World's History Book, the Bible. By John D. Whiting. XXVIII, pp. 511-550, 25 ills., map, Dec., 1915

Life in the Great Desert of Central Asia. By Ellsworth Huntington. XX, pp. 749-760, 12 ills., Aug., 1909

LODORE CANYON, Colorado:

Experiences in the Grand Canyon. By Ellsworth and Emery Kolb. XXVI, pp. 99-184, 70 ills., map, Aug., 1914

LOGAN, Mount, Canada:

The Conquest of Mount Logan: North America's Second Highest Peak Yields to the Intrepid Attack of Canadian Climbers. By H. F. Lambart. XLIX, pp. 597-631, 40 ills., June, 1926

LOIRE (River), France:

Château Land—France's Pageant on the Loire. LVIII, pp. 466-475, 10 ills. in color, Oct., 1930

LOIS (Tribespeople):

Among the Big Knot Lois of Hainan: Wild Tribesmen With Topknots Roam the Little-known Interior of This Big and Strategically Important Island in the China Sea. By Leonard Clark. LXXIV, pp. 391-418, 28 ills., map, Sept., 1938

LOJA, Ecuador:

Over Trail and Through Jungle in Ecuador: Indian Head-Hunters of the Interior, an Interesting Study in the South American Republic. By H. E. Anthony. XL, pp. 327-352, 28 ills., Oct., 1921

LOMBARDY (Department), Italy:

Inexhaustible Italy. By Arthur Stanley Riggs. XXX, pp. 273-368, 76 ills., map, Oct., 1916

LOMEN, CARL J.:

The Camel of the Frozen Desert (Reindeer). By Carl J. Lomen. XXXVI, pp. 539-556, 19 ills., Dec., 1919

LONDON, England:

Along London's Coronation Route. By Maynard Owen Williams. LXXI, pp. 609-632, 22 ills., map, May, 1937

As London Toils and Spins. By Frederick Simpich. LXXI, pp. 1-57, 38 ills. in black and white, 23 ills. in color, Jan., 1937

Black-Headed Gulls in London. By A. H. Hall. XLVII, pp. 664-672, 16 ills., June, 1925

Everyday Life in Wartime England. By Harvey Klemmer. LXXIX, pp. 497-534, 48 ills., Apr., 1941

Highlights of London Town. 15 color photos by Clifton Adams. LV, pp. 569-576, May, 1929

London. By Florence Craig Albrecht. XXVIII, pp. 263-294, 29 ills., Sept., 1915

London from a Bus Top. By Herbert Corey. XLIX, pp. 551-596, 44 ills., May, 1926

London Wins the Battle. By Marquis W. Childs. LXXXVIII, pp. 129-152, 21 ills., Aug., 1945

Shadowy London by Night. 8 ills. by H. B. Burdekin. LXVIII, pp. 177-184, Aug., 1935

Some Forgotten Corners of London: Many Places of Beauty and Historic Interest Repay the Search of the Inquiring Visitor. By Harold Donaldson Eberlein. LXI, pp. 163-198, 25 ills. in black and white, 13 ills. in color, Feb., 1932

Vagabonding in England: A Young American Works His Way Around the British Isles and Sees Sights from an Unusual Point of View. By John McWilliams. LXV, pp. 357-398, 39 ills., map, Mar., 1934

When GI Joes Took London. By Maj. Frederick Simpich, Jr. LXXXVI, pp. 337-354, 18 ills., Sept., 1944

Yanks at Westminster. By Capt. Leonard David Gammans. XC, pp. 223-252, 6 ills. in black and white, 19 ills. in color, Aug., 1946

LONELY Australia: The Unique Continent. By Herbert E. Gregory. XXX, pp. 473-568, 68 ills., 5 maps (1 two-page), Dec., 1916

LONG, E. JOHN:

Guatemala Interlude: In the Land of the Quetzal a Modern Capital Contrasts With Primitive Indian Villages and the "Pompeii of America." By E. John Long. LXX, pp. 429-460, 22 ills. in black and white, 13 ills. in color, map, Oct., 1936

Happy Landing in Bermuda. By E. John Long. LXXV, pp. 213-238, 14 ills. in black and white, 12 ills. in color, Feb., 1939

Mid-ocean Color Log. 12 color photos: 9 by author, pp. 221-228

Montserrat, Spain's Mountain Shrine. By E. John Long. LXIII, pp. 121-130, 10 ills., Jan., 1933

New Jersey Now! By E. John Long. LXIII, pp. 519-584, 49 ills. in black and white, 24 ills. in color, maps, May, 1933

Oxford, Mother of Anglo-Saxon Learning. By E. John Long. LVI, pp. 563-596, 31 ills., Nov., 1929

Puerto Rico: Watchdog of the Caribbean: Venerable Domain Under American Flag Has New Role as West Indian Stronghold and Sentinel of the Panama Canal. By E. John Long. LXXVI, pp. 697-738, 24 ills. in black and white, 23 ills. in color, Dec., 1939

LONG ISLAND, New York:

Marvels of Mycetozoa: Exploration of a Long Island Swamp Reveals Some of the Secrets of the Slime Molds, Dwelling on the Borderland Between the Plant and Animal Kingdoms. By William Crowder. Paintings by author. XLIX, pp. 421-443, 5 ills. in black and white, 16 ills. in color, Apr., 1926

Spin Your Globe to Long Island: Only Six States Have More People than the Insular Empire that Ranges from a World's Fair Through Potato Patches, Princely Estates, and Historic Shrines. By Frederick Simpich. LXXV, pp. 413-460, 25 ills. in black and white, 18 ills. in color, Apr., 1939

LONG ISLAND SOUND, Connecticut-New York:

Atlantic Coast Tides. By Mark S. W. Jefferson. IX, pp. 497-509, 3 charts, Dec., 1898

LONG PALEI (Village), Sarawak:

Sarawak: The Land of the White Rajahs. By Harrison W. Smith. XXXV, pp. 110-167, 58 ills., map, Feb., 1919

The **LONG** River of New England: In War and Peace, from Mountain Wilderness to the Sea, Flows the Connecticut River, Through a Valley Abounding in History, Scenery, Inventive Genius, and Industry. By Albert W. Atwood. LXXXIII, pp. 401-434, 12 ills. in black and white, 24 ills. in color, map, Apr., 1943

LONGEVITY:

Who Shall Inherit Long Life? On the Existence of a Natural Process at Work Among Human Beings Tending to Improve the Vigor and Vitality of Succeeding Generations. By Dr. Alexander Graham Bell. XXXV, pp. 505-514, 13 ills., June, 1919

LONGITUDE:

On the Telegraphic Determinations of Longitude by the Bureau of Navigation. By Lieut. J. A. Norris, U. S. N. II, pp. 1-30, Apr., 1890

A **LONGITUDINAL** Journey Through Chile. By Harriet Chalmers Adams. XLII, pp. 219-273, 60 ills., map, Sept., 1922

LONGLEY, W. H.:

The First Autochromes from the Ocean Bottom: Marine Life in Its Natural Habitat Along the Florida Keys Is Successfully Photographed in Colors. (Photographs by Dr. W. H. Longley and Charles Martin). LI, pp. 56-60, 8 ills. in color, Jan., 1927

Life on a Coral Reef: The Fertility and Mystery of the Sea Studied Beneath the Waters Surrounding Dry Tortugas. By W. H. Longley. LI, pp. 61-83, 22 ills., Jan., 1927

LOOKING Down on Europe: The Thrills and Advantages of Sight-seeing by Airplane, as Demonstrated on a 6,500-mile Tour Over Commercial Aviation Routes. By Lieutenant J. Parker Van Zandt. XLVII, pp. 261-326, 67 ills., map, Mar., 1925

LOOKING Down on Europe Again: Crisscrossing Air Tracks Reveal Nature's Scenic Masterpieces and Man's Swift-changing Boundaries and Structures. By J. Parker Van Zandt. LXXV, pp. 791-822, 31 ills., map, June, 1939

LOOKING in on New Turkey. LXI, pp. 499-508, 12 ills. in color, Apr., 1932

LOOKING in on the Everyday Life of New Turkey. 12 color photos by Herman H. Kreider, Maynard Owen Williams, Gervais Courtellemont. LXI, pp. 501-508, Apr., 1932

LOONS (Birds):

Birds of Timberline and Tundra. By Arthur A. Allen. With 24 color photos by author. XC, pp. 313-339, 8 ills. in black and white, Sept., 1946

Birds That Cruise the Coast and Inland Waters. By T. Gilbert Pearson. Paintings by Maj. Allan Brooks. LXV, pp. 299-328, ill. in black and white, 6 portraits in color, Mar., 1934

LOP BASIN, Sinkiang:

Medieval Tales of the Lop Basin in Central Asia. By Ellsworth Huntington. XIX, pp. 289-295, 9 ills., Apr., 1908

LORD HOWE (Island), Tasman Sea:

The Paradise of the Tasman: A Pacific Island Provides the Palms Which Decorate Hotels, Churches, Steamships, and Homes. By Hubert Lyman Clark. LXVIII, pp. 115-136, 24 ills., map, July, 1935

LORD HOWE GROUP. *See* Ontong Java

LORDS of the Rockies: Photographing Big Game Animals in Their Primeval Surroundings, from Arizona to Canada, Brings Adventure to Two Wilderness Wanderers. By Wendell and Lucie Chapman. LXXVI, pp. 87-128, 14 ills. in black and white, 28 ills. in color, July, 1939

LORIAN SWAMP, Kenya:

When a Drought Blights Africa: Hippos and Elephants Are Driven Insane by Suffering, in the Lorian Swamp, Kenya Colony. By Capt. A. T. Curle. LV, pp. 521-528, 9 ills., Apr., 1929

LORRAINE (Region), France:

A City Learns to Smile Again (Nancy). By Maj. Frederick G. Vosburgh. LXXXVII, pp. 361-384, 23 ills., map, Mar., 1945

In French Lorraine: That Part of France Where the First American Soldiers Have Fallen. By Harriet Chalmers Adams. XXXII, pp. 499-518, 16 ills., Nov.-Dec., 1917

LOS ANGELES, California:

Carrying Water Through a Desert: The Story of the Los Angeles Aqueduct. By Burt A. Heinly. XXI, pp. 568-596, 19 ills., map, July, 1910

Southern California at Work. By Frederick Simpich. LXVI, pp. 529-600, 39 ills. in black and white, 41 ills. in color, two-page map, Nov., 1934

LOSS of Life by Lightning. XIII, p. 115, Mar., 1902

LOSS of Property from Lightning. XII, p. 82, Feb., 1901

The **LOST** Boundary of Texas. By Marcus Baker. XII, pp. 430-432, map, Dec., 1901

The **LOST** Wealth of the Kings of Midas. By Ellsworth Huntington. XXI, pp. 831-846, 15 ills., Oct., 1910

LOUDEN, ORREN R.:

Circus: The Color Camera Explores the Country That Moves by Night. 5 color photos by Orren R. Louden. LX, pp. 479-510, Oct., 1931

Gettysburg: The Most Famous Battle Field in America. 5 color photos by Orren R. Louden. LX, pp. 66-75, July, 1931

Washington, D. C.: Our Colorful City of Magnificent Distances. 7 color photos by Orren R. Louden. LX, pp. 531-610, Nov., 1931

Washington, D. C.: Secrets of Washington's Lure. 7 color photos by Orren R. Louden. LVII, pp. 377-384, Mar., 1930

Washington, D. C.: Springtime Wreathes a Garland for the Nation's Capital. 13 color photos: 3 by Orren R. Louden. LXVII, pp. 473-480, Apr., 1935

LOUISIANA:

The Delectable Shrimp: Once a Culinary Stepchild, Today a Gulf Coast Industry. By Harlan Major. LXXXVI, pp. 501-512, 11 ills., map, Oct., 1944

The Delta of the Mississippi River. By E. L. Corthell. VIII, pp. 351-354, Dec., 1897

The Great Mississippi Flood of 1927: Since White Man's Discovery This Mighty River Has Served Him Well, Yet It Has Brought Widespread Devastation Along Its Lower Reaches. By Frederick Simpich. LII, pp. 243-289, 53 ills., map, Sept., 1927

How We Use the Gulf of Mexico. By Frederick Simpich. LXXXV, pp. 1-40, 20 ills. in black and white, 19 ills. in color, two-page map, Jan., 1944

Louisiana, Land of Perpetual Romance. By Ralph A. Graves. LVII, pp. 393-482, 84 ills. in black and white, 29 ills. in color, map supplement, Apr., 1930

LOUISIANA PURCHASE:
Boundaries of Territorial Acquisitions. XII, pp. 373-377, chart, Oct., 1901

LOVE TERNS (Birds). *See* Fairy Terns

LOW Countries Await Liberation (Belgium and Netherlands). 10 ills. LXXXVI, pp. 221-228, Aug., 1944

LOW Road, High Road, Around Dundee (Scotland). By Maurice P. Dunlap. LXIX, pp. 547-576, 35 ills., map, Apr., 1936

LOWDERMILK, WALTER C.:
China Fights Erosion with U. S. Aid. By Walter C. Lowdermilk. LXXXVII, pp. 641-680, 10 ills. in black and white, 26 ills. in color, June, 1945

LOWER CALIFORNIA. *See* Baja California

LOWEST Point in the United States (Death Valley, California). XVIII, pp. 824-825, Dec., 1907

LSTs (Landing Ship, Tank):
Landing Craft for Invasion. By Melville Bell Grosvenor. LXXXVI, pp. 1-30, 26 ills., July, 1944

LUALABA (Congo River), Belgian Congo:
Transporting a Navy Through the Jungles of Africa in War Time. By Frank J. Magee. XLII, pp. 331-362, 31 ills., Oct., 1922

LUCAS, JOHN D.:
The Maine American and the American Lobster. By John D. Lucas. LXXXIX, pp. 523-543, 19 ills., Apr., 1946

LUCIA GLACIER, Alaska:
The National Geographic Society's Alaskan Expedition of 1909. By Ralph S. Tarr and Lawrence Martin. XXI, pp. 1-54, 42 ills., 12 maps, Jan., 1910

LUGANO, Lake, Italy-Switzerland:
Frontier Cities of Italy. By Florence Craig Albrecht. XXVII, pp. 533-586, 45 ills., June, 1915
Gems of the Italian Lakes. By Arthur Ellis Mayer. XXIV, pp. 943-956, 13 ills., Aug., 1913

LUIGI AMADEO, DUKE OF THE ABRUZZI. *See* Abruzzi, Duke of the

LUKE, SIR HARRY:
The Maltese Islands: Cicero's Land of "Honey and Roses," and Stronghold of the Knights, Again Is Focus of Naval Strategy. By Sir Harry Luke. LXVIII, pp. 647-666, 20 ills., maps, Nov., 1935

The **LUMBER** Business of the Government. XVII, pp. 531-533, Sept., 1906

LUMBERING:
The Influence of Forestry upon the Lumber Industry of the United States. By Overton W. Price. XIV, pp. 381-386, ills., Oct., 1903
The Lumber Business of the Government. XVII, pp. 531-533, Sept., 1906
Lumbering in Manchuria. (By Henry B. Miller). XV, pp. 131-132, ills., Mar., 1904

LUMBERING—*Continued*
The Redwood Forest of the Pacific Coast. By Henry Gannett. X, pp. 145-159, 6 ills., map, May, 1899
Working Teak in the Burma Forests: The Sagacious Elephant Is Man's Ablest Ally in the Logging Industry of the Far East. By A. W. Smith. LVIII, pp. 239-256, 5 ills. in black and white, 15 ills. in color, Aug., 1930

LUMINOUS Life in the Depths of the Sea. 8 ills. in color from paintings by E. Bostelmann. LIX, pp. 667-674, June, 1931

LUNAR ECLIPSES. *See* Eclipses

LUNÉVILLE, France:
In French Lorraine: That Part of France Where the First American Soldiers Have Fallen. By Harriet Chalmers Adams. XXXII, pp. 499-518, 16 ills., Nov.-Dec., 1917

LURAY CAVERNS, Virginia:
The Luray Caverns. XVII, pp. 358-362, 3 ills., June, 1906
The Skeleton in Luray Cave. (By H. C. Hovey). XVII, pp. 425-426, July, 1906

The **LURE** of Lima, City of the Kings. By William Joseph Showalter. LVII, pp. 727-784, 41 ills. in black and white, 25 ills. in color, June, 1930

The **LURE** of the Frozen Desert (Arctic Region). XXIII, panorama, Dec., 1912

The **LURE** of the Land of Ice (Antarctic Region). 16 ills. XLV, pp. 255-270, Mar., 1924

LURS (Tribespeople):
Mountain Tribes of Iran and Iraq. By Harold Lamb. LXXXIX, pp. 385-408, 15 ills., two-page map, Mar., 1946

The **LUSTER** of Ancient Mexico (Aztecs). By William H. Prescott. XXX, pp. 1-32, 22 ills., July, 1916

LUXEMBOURG (Grand Duchy):
The Grand Duchy of Luxemburg: A Miniature Democratic State of Many Charms Against a Feudal Background. By Maynard Owen Williams. XLVI, pp. 501-528, 28 ills., map, Nov., 1924

LUXOR, Egypt:
The Resurrection of Ancient Egypt. By James Baikie. XXIV, pp. 957-1020, 46 ills., map, Sept., 1913

LUZON (Island), Philippine Islands:
Camera Cruising in the Philippines. 12 color photos by J. Baylor Roberts, Fenno Jacobs, and others. LXXXVI, pp. 545-552, Nov., 1944
Field Sports Among the Wild Men of Northern Luzon. By Dean C. Worcester. XXII, pp. 215-267, 52 ills., map, Mar., 1911
Head-Hunters of Northern Luzon. By Dean C. Worcester. XXIII, pp. 833-930, 102 ills., map, Sept., 1912
The Non-Christian Peoples of the Philippine Islands. By Dean C. Worcester. XXIV, pp. 1157-1256, 41 ills. in black and white, 48 ills. in color, Nov., 1913

LUZON (Island), Philippine Islands—*Continued*

Taal Volcano and Its Recent Destructive Eruption. By Dean C. Worcester. XXIII, pp. 313-367, 40 ills., diagr., 4 maps, Apr., 1912

What Luzon Means to Uncle Sam. By Frederick Simpich. LXXXVII, pp. 305-332, 25 ills., map supplement, Mar., 1945

LYON, ERNEST:

The Black Republic—Liberia. By Sir Harry Johnston and Ernest Lyon. XVIII, pp. 334-343, 9 ills., May, 1907

LYTTELTON, New Zealand:

Sailing the Seven Seas in the Interest of Science: Adventures Through 157,000 Miles of Storm and Calm, from Arctic to Antarctic and Around the World, in the Non-magnetic Yacht "Carnegie." By J. P. Ault. XLII, pp. 631-690, 47 ills., chart, Dec., 1922

M

MACAO, "Land of Sweet Sadness": The Oldest European Settlement in the Far East, Long the Only Haven for Distressed Mariners in the China Sea. By Edgar Allen Forbes. LXII, pp. 337-357, 13 ills. in black and white, 11 ills. in color, Sept., 1932

MacASKILL, W. R.:

Tartan Tints New Scotland (Nova Scotia). 21 color photos by John Mills, Jr., W. R. MacAskill, and others. LXXVII, pp. 591-622, May, 1940

MACAU, China:

Macao, "Land of Sweet Sadness": The Oldest European Settlement in the Far East, Long the Only Haven for Distressed Mariners in the China Sea. By Edgar Allen Forbes. LXII, pp. 337-357, 13 ills. in black and white, 11 ills. in color, Sept., 1932

MACAULAY, T. B.:

How Canada Went to the Front. By Hon. T. B. Macaulay, of Montreal. XXXIV, pp. 297-307, 6 ills., Oct., 1918

McBRIDE, HARRY A.:

From Granada to Gibraltar—A Tour of Southern Spain. By Harry A. McBride. XLVI, pp. 205-232, 23 ills., Aug., 1924

The Land of the Basques: Home of a Thrifty, Picturesque People, Who Take Pride in the Sobriquet, "The Yankees of Spain." By Harry A. McBride. XLI, pp. 63-87, 25 ills., map, Jan., 1922

The Land of the Free in Africa. By Harry A. McBride. XLII, pp. 411-430, 22 ills., Oct., 1922

On the Bypaths of Spain. By Harry A. McBride. LV, pp. 311-364, 50 ills. in black and white, 13 ills. in color, map, Mar., 1929

Pursuing Spanish Bypaths Northwest of Madrid. By Harry A. McBride. LIX, pp. 121-130, 6 ills. in black and white, 14 ills. in color, map, Jan., 1931

McBRIDE, RUTH Q.:

Keeping House on the Congo. By Ruth Q. McBride. LXXII, pp. 643-670, 29 ills., Nov., 1937

McBRIDE, RUTH Q.—*Continued*

Old Masters in a New National Gallery. By Ruth Q. McBride. LXXVIII, pp. 1-50, 11 ills. in black and white, 32 color reproductions of masterpieces, July, 1940

Turbulent Spain. By Ruth Q. McBride. LXX, pp. 397-427, 25 ills., two-page map, Oct., 1936

McCANDLESS, BYRON:

The Correct Display of the Stars and Stripes. By Byron McCandless and Gilbert Grosvenor. XXXII, pp. 404-413, 8 ills., Oct., 1917

Flags Famous in American History. By Byron McCandless and Gilbert Grosvenor. XXXII, pp. 341-361, 92 ills. in color, Oct., 1917

Flags of Austria-Hungary, Bulgaria, Germany, and Turkey. By Byron McCandless and Gilbert Grosvenor. XXXII, pp. 386-388, 38 ills. in color, Oct., 1917

The Flags of Europe, Asia, and Africa. By Byron McCandless and Gilbert Grosvenor. XXXII, pp. 372-378, 101 ills. in color, Oct., 1917

The Flags of Our Army, Navy, and Government Departments. By Byron McCandless and Gilbert Grosvenor. XXXII, pp. 305-322, ill. in black and white, 300 ills. in color, diagr., 4 tables, Oct., 1917

The Flags of Pan-America. By Byron McCandless and Gilbert Grosvenor. XXXII, pp. 361-369, 62 ills. in color, Oct., 1917

The Flags of the British Empire. By Byron McCandless and Gilbert Grosvenor. XXXII, pp. 378-385, 158 ills. in color, Oct., 1917

Heroic Flags of the Middle Ages. By Byron McCandless and Gilbert Grosvenor. XXXII, pp. 388-399, 96 ills. in color, Oct., 1917

The Insignia of the Uniformed Forces of the United States. By Byron McCandless and Gilbert Grosvenor. XXXII, pp. 413-419, 318 ills., Oct., 1917

The Naval Flags of the World. By Byron McCandless and Gilbert Grosvenor. XXXII, text p. 369; 214 ills. in color, Oct., 1917

Our State Flags. By Byron McCandless and Gilbert Grosvenor. XXXII, pp. 325-341, 57 ills. in color, Oct., 1917

Pennants of Patriotism 200 Years Ago. By Byron McCandless and Gilbert Grosvenor. XXXII, pp. 399-403, 77 ills. in color, Oct., 1917

The Story of the American Flag. By Byron McCandless and Gilbert Grosvenor. XXXII, pp. 286-303, 12 ills., Oct., 1917

McCARTNEY, BENJAMIN C.:

Return to Florence. By 1st Lt. Benjamin C. McCartney. LXXXVII, pp. 257-296, 18 ills. in black and white, 18 ills. in color, Mar., 1945

Northern Italy: Scenic Battleground. 18 color photos: 13 by B. Anthony Stewart, 3 by author, pp. 265-288

McCLURE, EDGAR:

The Altitude of Mount Adams, Washington. By Edgar McClure. VII, pp. 151-153, tables, Apr., 1896

McCLURE, HENRY HERBERT:

Shortening Time Across the Continent. By Henry Herbert McClure. XIII, pp. 319-321, Aug., 1902

McCORMICK, ELSIE:

"Where the Mountains Walked": An Account of the Recent Earthquake in Kansu Province, China, Which Destroyed 100,000 Lives. By Upton Close and Elsie McCormick. XLI, pp. 445-464, 23 ills., map, May, 1922

McCORMICK, FREDERICK:

China's Treasures. By Frederick McCormick. XXIII, pp. 996-1040, 50 ills., Oct., 1912

Present Conditions in China. By Frederick McCormick. XXII, pp. 1120-1138, 13 ills., Dec., 1911

MacCRACKEN, WILLIAM P.:

President Coolidge Bestows Lindbergh Award: The National Geographic Society's Hubbard Medal Is Presented to Aviator Before the Most Notable Gathering in the History of Washington (Address by Secretary MacCracken). LIII, pp. 132-140, 4 ills., Jan., 1928

McCRINDLE, J. R.:

Flying Over Egypt, Sinai, and Palestine: Looking Down Upon the Holy Land During an Air Journey of Two and a Half Hours from Cairo to Jerusalem. By Brigadier General P. R. C. Groves and Major J. R. McCrindle. L, pp. 313-355, 26 ills. in black and white, 23 ills. in color, map, Sept., 1926

McCUDDEN, JAMES BYFORD:

Aces Among Aces (Aviators). By Laurence La Tourette Driggs. XXXIII, pp. 568-580, 9 ills., June, 1918

McCURDY, ARTHUR W.:

Factors Which Modify the Climate of Victoria (British Columbia). By Arthur W. McCurdy. XVIII, pp. 345-348, maps, May, 1907

MACDONALD, T. L. *See* NGS: Board of Managers

MacDOUGAL, DANIEL T.:

More Changes of the Colorado River. By D. T. MacDougal. XIX, pp. 52-54, map, Jan., 1908

Notes on the Deserts of the United States and Mexico (Extracted from a Publication of Dr. Daniel T. MacDougal). XXI, pp. 691-714, 16 ills., Aug., 1910

MACEDONIA:

"Grass Never Grows Where the Turkish Hoof Has Trod." By Edwin Pears. XXIII, pp. 1132-1148, 19 ills., Nov., 1912

The Great Turk and His Lost Provinces. By William E. Curtis. XIV, pp. 45-61, 7 ills., Feb., 1903

The Hoary Monasteries of Mt. Athos. By H. G. Dwight. XXX, pp. 249-272, 24 ills., map, Sept., 1916

New Greece, the Centenarian, Forges Ahead. By Maynard Owen Williams. LVIII, pp. 649-721, 51 ills. in black and white, 40 ills. in color, map, Dec., 1930

Notes on Macedonia. XIX, pp. 790-802, 15 ills., map, Nov., 1908

On the Monastir Road. By Herbert Corey. XXXI, pp. 383-412, 31 ills., May, 1917

The Races and Religions of Macedonia. By Luigi Villari. XXIII, pp. 1118-1132, 14 ills., Nov., 1912

MACEDONIA—*Continued*

Saloniki. By H. G. Dwight. XXX, pp. 203-232, 28 ills., Sept., 1916

The Whirlpool of the Balkans. By George Higgins Moses. XXXIX, pp. 179-197, 15 ills., Feb., 1921

McGEE, ANITA NEWCOMB:

Judge of NGS prize essay contest. X, p. 32, Jan., 1899

McGEE, W J:

American Geographic Education. By W J McGee. IX, pp. 305-307, July, 1898

Asia, the Cradle of Humanity. By W J McGee. XII, pp. 281-290, Aug., 1901

Chairman of Committee on Eighth International Geographic Congress. XIV, pp. 254-255, June, 1903

The Classification of Geographic Forms by Genesis. By W J McGee. I, pp. 27-36, tables, Oct., 1888

Death of G. Brown Goode. (By W J M.). VII, p. 316, Sept., 1896

Dr. Bell's Survey in Baffinland. (By W J McGee). XIII, p. 113, Mar., 1902

Explorations by the Bureau of American Ethnology in 1895. By W J McGee. VII, pp. 77-80, Feb., 1896

Frank Frederick Hilder (Biography). (By W J M.). XII, pp. 85-86, ill., Feb., 1901

Geographic Development of the District of Columbia. By W J McGee. IX, pp. 317-323, July, 1898

Geographic History of the Piedmont Plateau. By W J McGee. VII, pp. 261-265, Aug., 1896

Geographic Literature. VIII, pp. 59-60, Feb., 1897; pp. 91-92, Mar., 1897; pp. 124-127, Apr., 1897; pp. 362-364, Dec., 1897. IX, pp. 477-478, Nov., 1898; pp. 512-514, 515-518, Dec., 1898

Geographic Work by the Bureau of American Ethnology. (By W J McGee). IX, pp. 98-100, Mar., 1898

The Geologic Atlas of the United States. (By W J M.). IX, pp. 339-342, July, 1898

The Geospheres. By W J McGee. IX, pp. 435-447, Oct., 1898

The Growth of the United States. By W J McGee. IX, pp. 377-386, diagr., table, Sept., 1898

Hatcher's Work in Patagonia. (By W J M.). VIII, pp. 319-322, Nov., 1897

Ice Caves and Frozen Wells. (By W J McGee). XII, pp. 433-434, Dec., 1901

The Isthmian Canal Problem. (By W J McGee). X, pp. 363-364, Sept., 1899

Joseph Le Conte (Biography). (By W J M.). XII, pp. 309-311, ill., Aug., 1901

The Lessons of Galveston. (By W J McGee). XI, pp. 377-383, Oct., 1900

The Modern Mississippi Problem. By W J McGee. IX, pp. 24-27, Jan., 1898

National Growth and National Character. By W J McGee. X, pp. 185-206, June, 1899

The New Home of the National Geographic Society (Election of Dr. W J McGee as President of the Society). XV, pp. 176-181, 5 ills., Apr., 1904

The Old Yuma Trail. By W J McGee. XII, pp. 103-107, Mar., 1901; pp. 129-143, 7 ills., map, Apr., 1901

McGEE, W J—*Continued*

Papagueria. By W J McGee. IX, pp. 345-371, 9 ills., Aug., 1898

Portrait. VIII, pl. 38 (front.), Dec., 1897. XII, ill. p. 354, Oct., 1901

Problems of the Pacific—The Great Ocean in World Growth. By W J McGee. XIII, pp. 333-342, Sept., 1902

Professor O. C. Marsh (Biography). (By W J M.). X, pp. 181-182, May, 1899

Seriland. By W J McGee and Willard D. Johnson. VII, pp. 125-133, ill., foldout map, Apr., 1896

Sir John Evans and Prof. W J McGee. (By J. H.). VIII, pp. 358-359, ills., Dec., 1897

The Topographic Atlas of the United States. (By W J M.). IX, pp. 343-344, July, 1898

Work of the Bureau of American Ethnology. By W J McGee. XII, pp. 369-372, Oct., 1901

The Work of the National Geographic Society. (By W J McGee). VII, pp. 253-259, Aug., 1896

See also NGS: Board of Managers; Secretary; Vice-President

MacGILLIVRAY, JAMES:

Mickey the Beaver: An Animal Engineer Performs for the Camera as a Star in the Activities of His Species. By James MacGillivray. LIV, pp. 741-756, 23 ills., Dec., 1928

MacGONIGLE, JOHN N.:

The Geography of the Southern Peninsula of the United States. By the Rev. John N. MacGonigle. VII, pp. 381-394, 4 ills., Dec., 1896

McGRATH, J. E.:

The Alaskan Boundary Survey. II—The Boundary South of Fort Yukon. By J. E. McGrath. IV, pp. 181-188, Feb. 8, 1893

McGREGOR MOUNTAIN, Washington:

Forest Lookout. By Ella E. Clark. With 9 color photos by author. XC, pp. 73-96, 8 ills. in black and white, July, 1946

McGUIRE, BIRD S.:

Big Oklahoma. By Bird S. McGuire. XVII, pp. 103-105, Feb., 1906

MACHINES Come to Mississippi. By J. R. Hildebrand. LXXII, pp. 263-318, 34 ills. in black and white, 26 ills. in color, two-page map, Sept., 1937

MACHU PICCHU, Peru:

Further Explorations in the Land of the Incas: The Peruvian Expedition of 1915 of the National Geographic Society and Yale University. By Hiram Bingham. XXIX, pp. 431-473, 29 ills., maps, panorama, May, 1916

Honors to Amundsen and Peary (National Geographic Society Banquet: Address by Hiram Bingham). XXIV, pp. 113-130, 5 ills., Jan., 1913

In the Wonderland of Peru. By Hiram Bingham. XXIV, pp. 387-573, 250 ills., 3 diagrs., map, panorama, Apr., 1913

Ruins of an Ancient Inca Capital, Machu Picchu. Panorama from photo by author

The Pith of Peru: A Journey from Talara to Machu Picchu, with Memorable Stopovers. By Henry Albert Phillips. LXXXII, pp. 167-196, 6 ills. in black and white, 20 ills. in color, map, Aug., 1942

The Story of Machu Picchu: The Peruvian Expeditions of the National Geographic Society and Yale University. By Hiram Bingham. XXVII, pp. 172-217, 60 ills., Feb., 1915

MACK, SIUKEE:

Changing Canton (China). 20 photos by Siukee Mack, Alfred T. Palmer, Kinchue Wong. LXXII, pp. 711-726, Dec., 1937

MACKENZIE, CATHERINE DUNLOP:

The Charm of Cape Breton Island: The Most Picturesque Portion of Canada's Maritime Provinces—A Land Rich in Historic Associations, Natural Resources, and Geographic Appeal. By Catherine Dunlop Mackenzie. XXXVIII, pp. 34-60, 22 ills., map, July, 1920

McKENZIE, KENNETH:

East of the Adriatic: Notes on Dalmatia, Montenegro, Bosnia, and Herzegovina. By Kenneth McKenzie. XXIII, pp. 1159-1187, 1284, 37 ills., map, Dec., 1912

MACKENZIE (River), Canada:

On Mackenzie's Trail to the Polar Sea. By Amos Burg. LX, pp. 127-156, 32 ills., map, Aug., 1931

MACKINDER, H. J.:

Geographical Pivot of History (Steppes of Central Asia). (By H. J. Mackinder). XV, pp. 331-335, Aug., 1904

McKINLEY, ASHLEY C.:

Mapping the Antarctic from the Air: The Aërial Camera Earns Its Place as the Eyes and Memory of the Explorer. By Capt. Ashley C. McKinley. LXII, pp. 471-485, 13 ills., map supplement, Oct., 1932

McKINLEY, WILLIAM:

Announcement of the death of. XII, front., Oct., 1901

Proceedings of the National Geographic Society, Session 1898-'99 (Election of President McKinley to Honorary Membership in the Society). X, pp. 143-144, Apr., 1899

McKINLEY, Mount, Alaska:

Fit to Fight Anywhere (Quartermaster Corps Expedition). By Frederick Simpich. LXXXIV, pp. 233-256, 26 ills., Aug., 1943

A Game Country Without Rival in America: The Proposed Mount McKinley National Park. By Stephen R. Capps. XXXI, pp. 69-84, 14 ills., map, Jan., 1917

The Monarchs of Alaska. By R. H. Sargent. XX, pp. 610-623, 9 ills., July, 1909

Mount Huntington and Mount McKinley. XXII, pp. 597-600, 4 ills., June, 1911

Mount McKinley. (By Robert Muldrow). XII, pp. 312-313, map, Aug., 1901

Over the Roof of Our Continent. By Bradford Washburn. LXXIV, pp. 78-98, 17 ills. in duotone, map, July, 1938

Plan for Climbing Mt. McKinley. By Alfred H. Brooks and D. L. Reaburn. XIV, pp. 30-35, map, Jan., 1903

McKINLEY, Mount, Alaska—*Continued*

The Sushitna River, Alaska. By W. A. Dickey. VIII, pp. 322-327, map, Nov., 1897

McKNEW, THOMAS W.:

Impressing the Society's Seal on Membership Certificate. XC, ill. p. 39, July, 1946

See also NGS: Secretary

McLEISH, DONALD:

In the Land of the Vikings. 16 photos by Donald McLeish. XLV, pp. 661-676, June, 1924

In the Land of Windmills and Wooden Shoes. 16 photos by Donald McLeish. XLIII, pp. 297-312, Mar., 1923

Italy, France, Switzerland. 10 photos, hand-tinted, by Donald McLeish. XXVIII, pp. 439-450, Nov., 1915

A Vacation in Holland. 8 color photos by Donald McLeish. LVI, pp. 367-374, Sept., 1929

McMASTER, JOHN BACH:

Judge of NGS prize essay contest. X, p. 32, Jan., 1899

MacMILLAN, DONALD B.:

The "Bowdoin" (Ship) in North Greenland: Arctic Explorers Place Tablet to Commemorate Sacrifices of the Lady Franklin Bay Expedition. By Donald B. MacMillan. XLVII, pp. 677-722, 49 ills., June, 1925

Note: The National Geographic Society was the donor of the bronze tablet erected at Cape Sabine, Ellesmere Island, in memory of the brave men of the Lady Franklin Bay Expedition who perished in the spring of 1884

The MacMillan Arctic Expedition Returns: U. S. Navy Planes Make First Series of Overland Flights in the Arctic and National Geographic Society Staff Obtains Valuable Data and Specimens for Scientific Study. By Donald B. MacMillan. XLVIII, pp. 477-518, 42 ills., Nov., 1925

Peary as a Leader: Incidents from the Life of the Discoverer of the North Pole Told by One of His Lieutenants on the Expedition Which Reached the Goal. By Donald B. MacMillan. XXXVII, pp. 293-317, 20 ills., map, Apr., 1920

MacMILLAN ARCTIC EXPEDITION:

Flying Over the Arctic. By Lieutenant Commander Richard E. Byrd. XLVIII, pp. 519-532, 10 ills., Nov., 1925

The MacMillan Arctic Expedition Returns: U. S. Navy Planes Make First Series of Overland Flights in the Arctic and National Geographic Society Staff Obtains Valuable Data and Specimens for Scientific Study. By Donald B. MacMillan. XLVIII, pp. 477-518, 42 ills., Nov., 1925

The MacMillan Arctic Expedition Sails. XLVIII, pp. 225-226, 3 ills., Aug., 1925

MacMillan in the Field. XLVIII, pp. 473-476, 3 ills., Oct., 1925

A Naturalist with MacMillan in the Arctic. By Walter N. Koelz. XLIX, pp. 299-318, 22 ills. in color, Mar., 1926

Scientific Aspects of the MacMillan Arctic Expedition. XLVIII, pp. 349-354, 5 ills., Sept., 1925

MacMILLAN ARCTIC EXPEDITION—*Continued*

To Seek the Unknown in the Arctic: United States Navy Flyers to Aid MacMillan Expedition Under the Auspices of the National Geographic Society in Exploring Vast Area. XLVII, pp. 673-675, ill., map, June, 1925

McMILLIN, STEWART E.:

The Heart of Aymará Land: A Visit to Tiahuanacu, Perhaps the Oldest City of the New World, Lost Beneath the Drifting Sand of Centuries in the Bolivian Highlands. By Stewart E. McMillin. LI, pp. 213-256, 23 ills. in black and white, 18 ills. in color, map, Feb., 1927

McNALLY, PAUL A.:

Observing a Total Eclipse of the Sun: Dimming Solar Light for a Few Seconds Entails Years of Work for Science and Attracts Throngs to "Nature's Most Magnificent Spectacle." By Paul A. McNally. LXII, pp. 597-605, 6 ills., Nov., 1932

MacNEAL, HERBERT P.:

Casablanca Smiles. 10 color photos by Herbert P. MacNeal. LXXXIV, pp. 17-24, July, 1943

McQUESTEN, L. N.:

A Winter Weather Record From the Klondike Region. By E. W. Nelson. VIII, pp. 327-335, tables, Nov., 1897

MACREADY, JOHN A.:

Exploring the Earth's Stratosphere: The Holder of the American Altitude Record Describes His Experiences in Reaching the "Ceiling" of His Plane at an Elevation of Nearly Eight Miles. By First Lieutenant John A. Macready. L, pp. 755-776, 18 ills., Dec., 1926

The Non-Stop Flight Across America. By Lieutenant John A. Macready. Photos by Lieutenant Albert W. Stevens. XLVI, pp. 1-83, 68 ills., maps, July, 1924

McSWEENY, Z. F.:

The Character of Our Immigration, Past and Present. By Z. F. McSweeny. XVI, pp. 1-15, chart, Jan., 1905

McWILLIAMS, JOHN:

Vagabonding in England: A Young American Works His Way Around the British Isles and Sees Sights from an Unusual Point of View. By John McWilliams. LXV, pp. 357-398, 39 ills., map, Mar., 1934

MADAGASCAR:

Across Madagascar by Boat, Auto, Railroad, and Filanzana. By Charles F. Swingle. LVI, pp. 179-211, 42 ills., maps, Aug., 1929

Madagascar: Mystery Island: Japan's Push into the Indian Ocean Swings the Searchlight of World Attention to This Huge French Sentinel off the African Coast. By Paul Almasy. LXXXI, pp. 797-830, 37 ills., 3 maps, June, 1942

See also Expeditions (Through the Deserts)

MA'DAN (Tribespeople):

Forty Years Among the Arabs. By John Van Ess. LXXXII, pp. 385-420, 27 ills., two-page map, Sept., 1942

MADDOCK, ELEANOR:

The Marble Dams of Rajputana. By Eleanor Maddock. XL, pp. 469-499, 13 ills. in black and white, 16 ills. in color, Nov., 1921

MADEIRA (Islands), Atlantic Ocean:

Madeira, on the Way to Italy. By David Fairchild. XVIII, pp. 751-771, 18 ills., Dec., 1907

Madeira the Florescent. By Harriet Chalmers Adams. LXVI, pp. 81-106, 19 ills. in black and white, 13 ills. in color, map, July, 1934

MADRID, Spain:

International Literary Contest to be held in Madrid. I, pp. 273-276, July, 1889

Madrid Out-of-Doors. By Harriet Chalmers Adams. LX, pp. 225-256, 35 ills., Aug., 1931

We Escape from Madrid. By Gretchen Schwinn. LXXI, pp. 251-268, 15 ills., Feb., 1937

MADURA, India:

The Madura Temples. By J. S. Chandler. XIX, pp. 218-222, 4 ills., Mar., 1908

The Marriage of the Gods (Religious Festival). By John J. Banninga. XXIV, pp. 1314-1330, 16 ills., Dec., 1913

The Temples of India. 54 photos by W. M. Zumbro. XX, pp. 922-971, Nov., 1909

MAGDALENA (River), Colombia:

Over the Andes to Bogotá. By Frank M. Chapman. XL, pp. 353-373, 19 ills., Oct., 1921

MAGDALENA BAY, Mexico:

A Land of Drought and Desert—Lower California: Two Thousand Miles on Horseback Through the Most Extraordinary Cacti Forests in the World. By E. W. Nelson. XXII, pp. 443-474, 25 ills., maps, May, 1911

MAGEE, FRANK J.:

Transporting a Navy Through the Jungles of Africa in War Time. By Frank J. Magee. XLII, pp. 331-362, 31 ills., Oct., 1922

MAGEE, GUY, JR.:

"The Man in the Street" in China. By Guy Magee, Jr. XXXVIII, pp. 406-421, 15 ills., Nov., 1920

MAGEIK, Mount, Alaska:

The Valley of Ten Thousand Smokes: An Account of the Discovery and Exploration of the Most Wonderful Volcanic Region in the World. By Robert F. Griggs. XXXIII, pp. 115-169, 46 ills., map, panorama, Feb., 1918

The Valley of Ten Thousand Smokes: National Geographic Society Explorations in the Katmai District of Alaska. By Robert F. Griggs. XXXI, pp. 13-68, 51 ills., map, Jan., 1917

MAGELLAN, FERDINAND:

Discoverers of America. Annual Address by the President, Hon. Gardiner G. Hubbard. V, pp. 1-20, charts, maps, 3 map supplements, Apr. 7, 1893

The Greatest Voyage in the Annals of the Sea. By J. R. Hildebrand. LXII, pp. 699-739, 35 ills., map, Dec., 1932

MAGELLAN, Strait of:

A Winter Voyage Through the Straits of Magellan. By the late Admiral R. W. Meade, U. S. N. VIII, pp. 129-141, ill., map, May, 1897

MAGGIORE, Lake, Italy-Switzerland:

Frontier Cities of Italy. By Florence Craig Albrecht. XXVII, pp. 533-586, 45 ills., June, 1915

Gems of the Italian Lakes. By Arthur Ellis Mayer. XXIV, pp. 943-956, 13 ills., Aug., 1913

The **MAGIC** Beauty of Snow and Dew. By Wilson A. Bentley. XLIII, pp. 103-112, 9 ills., Jan., 1923

The **MAGIC** Mountain (Mount Wilson, California). By J. N. Patterson. XIX, pp. 457-468, 9 ills., July, 1908

MAGNESIA (Ancient City):

The Buried Cities of Asia Minor. By Ernest L. Harris. XX, pp. 1-18, 10 ills., Jan., 1909

Some Ruined Cities of Asia Minor. By Ernest L. Harris. XIX, pp. 833-858, 19 ills., Dec., 1908

"MAGNETIC CITY" (Magnitogorsk), Core of Valiant Russia's Industrial Might. By John Scott. LXXXIII, pp. 525-556, 27 ills., two-page map, May, 1943

MAGNETIC Disturbance Caused by the Explosion of Mont Pelée. XIII, pp. 208-209, June, 1902

MAGNETIC Observations (Muir Glacier, Alaska). By Harry Fielding Reid. IV, p. 82, table, Mar. 21, 1892

MAGNETIC Observations in Alaska. By Daniel L. Hazard. XX, pp. 675-676, map, July, 1909

MAGNETIC Observations in Iceland, Jan Mayen and Spitzbergen in 1892 (Geographic Notes. By Cyrus C. Babb). VI, pp. 223-224, table, Dec. 29, 1894

The **MAGNETIC** Survey of Africa. By Dr. L. A. Bauer. XX, pp. 291-297, 6 ills., Mar., 1909

MAGNETIC Survey of the Pacific. XIX, pp. 447-448, June, 1908

MAGNETIC Survey of the Pacific Ocean. (By L. A. Bauer). XVII, p. 237, Apr., 1906

MAGNETIC Survey of the United States. By Dr. L. A. Bauer. XIII, pp. 92-95, map, Mar., 1902

MAGNETIC Work of the Coast and Geodetic Survey. By L. A. Bauer. X, pp. 288-289, Aug., 1899

MAGNETISM:

The Compass in Modern Navigation. By G. W. Littlehales. VIII, pp. 266-272, Sept., 1897

MAGNETISM, Terrestrial. *See* Geomagnetism

MAGNITOGORSK, R. S. F. S. R.:

"Magnetic City," Core of Valiant Russia's Industrial Might. By John Scott. LXXXIII, pp. 525-556, 27 ills., two-page map, May, 1943

The **MAGNITUDE** of the New World Metropolis (New York City). 8 ills. in gravure. LVIII, pp. 523-530, Nov., 1930

MAGNOLIA GARDENS, South Carolina:

The Ashley River and Its Gardens. By E. T. H. Shaffer. XLIX, pp. 525-550, 6 ills. in black and white. 18 ills. in color, May, 1926

MAGNOLIA State Mosaic (Mississippi). 26 color photos by J. Baylor Roberts. LXXII, pp. 279-310, Sept., 1937

MAGPIES (Birds):
Crows, Magpies, and Jays: Unusual Intelligence Has Earned a Unique Position for These Birds. By T. Gilbert Pearson. Paintings by Maj. Allan Brooks. LXIII, pp. 51-79, 2 ills. in color, Jan., 1933

MAGYAR Mirth and Melancholy. By John Patric. LXXIII, pp. 1-55, 33 ills. in black and white, 20 ills. in color, map, Jan., 1938

MAGYARS (People):
Hungary: A Land of Shepherd Kings. By C. Townley-Fullam. XXVI, pp. 311-393, 92 ills., map, Oct., 1914
The Land of Contrast: Austria-Hungary. By D. W. and A. S. Iddings. XXIII, pp. 1188-1217, 1284, 33 ills., map, Dec., 1912
Magyar Mirth and Melancholy. By John Patric. LXXIII, pp. 1-55, 33 ills. in black and white, 20 ills. in color, map, Jan., 1938
The Races of Europe. By Edwin A. Grosvenor. XXXIV, pp. 441-534, 62 ills., diagr. and index, maps, map supplement, Dec., 1918

MAHA-VAJIRAVUDH (King of Siam):
The Coronation of His Majesty King Maha-Vajiravudh of Siam. By Colonel Lea Febiger. XXIII, pp. 389-416, 25 ills., Apr., 1912

MAHDIA, Tunisia:
The Greek Bronzes of Tunisia. By Frank Edward Johnson. XXIII, pp. 89-103, 11 ills., Jan., 1912

MAHOGANIES (Trees):
Among the Mahogany Forests of Cuba. By Walter D. Wilcox. XIX, pp. 485-498, 6 ills., map, July, 1908

The **MAID** of France Rides By: Compiègne, Where Joan of Arc Fought Her Last Battle, Celebrates Her Fifth Centenary. By Inez Buffington Ryan. LXII, pp. 607-616, 15 ills. in color, Nov., 1932

MAINE:
All Around the Bay of Passamaquoddy. By Albert S. Gatschet. VIII, pp. 16-24, Jan., 1897
Included: A List of Indian Geographic Names Occurring Around Passamaquoddy Bay, Maine, with Their Derivations, pp. 21-24
First National Park East of Mississippi River (Mount Desert Island). XXIX, pp. 623-626, 5 ills., June, 1916
In the Allagash Country. By Kenneth Fuller Lee. LV, pp. 505-520, 19 ills., Apr., 1929
The Leach's Petrel: His Nursery on Little Duck Island. By Arnold Wood. XX, pp. 360-365, 7 ills., Apr., 1909
Maine, the Outpost State: Some Forgotten Incidents in the Life of an Old and Stout-Hearted Commonwealth. By George Otis Smith. LXVII, pp. 533-592, 35 ills. in black and white, 39 ills. in color, two-page map, May, 1935
The Maine American and the American Lobster. By John D. Lucas. LXXXIX, pp. 523-543, 19 ills., Apr., 1946
Northeast of Boston. By Albert W. Atwood. LXXXVIII, pp. 257-292, 12 ills. in black and white, 17 ills. in color, map supplement, Sept., 1945

MAINE—*Continued*
The Unique Island of Mount Desert. By George B. Dorr, Ernest Howe Forbush, M. L. Fernald. XXVI, pp. 75-89, 7 ills., July, 1914
The Worm Turns. By Samuel Sandrof. LXXXIX, pp. 775-786, 14 ills., June, 1946
Included: Worm-digging industry

MAINE (Battleship):
Reception to Captain C. D. Sigsbee, U.S.N. (By J. H.). IX, pp. 251-252, May, 1898

The **MAJESTY** of the Matterhorn. XXIII, text p. 514; pictorial supplement, May, 1912

MAJOR, HARLAN:
The Delectable Shrimp: Once a Culinary Stepchild, Today a Gulf Coast Industry. By Harlan Major. LXXXVI, pp. 501-512, 11 ills., map, Oct., 1944

MAJORCA (Island), Balearic Islands:
Keeping House in Majorca. By Phoebe Binney Harnden. XLV, pp. 425-440, 18 ills., map, Apr., 1924

MAJURO (Atoll), Marshall Islands:
Our New Military Wards, the Marshalls. By W. Robert Moore. LXXXVIII, pp. 325-360, 14 ills. in black and white, 20 ills. in color, map, Sept., 1945

The **MAKERS** of the Flag. By Franklin K. Lane. XXXII, p. 304, Oct., 1917

MAKIN (Atoll), Gilbert Islands:
Gilbert Islands in the Wake of Battle. By W. Robert Moore. LXXXVII, pp. 129-162, 11 ills. in black and white, 19 ills. in color, map, Feb., 1945

The **MAKING** of a Japanese Newspaper. By Dr. Thomas E. Green. XXXVIII, pp. 327-334, 5 ills., Oct., 1920

The **MAKING** of an Anzac. By Howell Walker. LXXXI, pp. 409-456, 31 ills. in black and white, 20 ills. in color, two-page map, Apr., 1942

The **MAKING** of Military Maps. By William H. Nicholas. LXXXIII, pp. 765-778, 17 ills., June, 1943

MAKING the Fur Seal Abundant. By Hugh M. Smith. XXII, pp. 1139-1165, 18 ills., map, Dec., 1911

MALARIA:
Economic Loss to the People of the United States Through Insects That Carry Disease. By L. O. Howard. XX, pp. 735-749, Aug., 1909
Life Story of the Mosquito. By Graham Fairchild. With 10 ills. in color from paintings. LXXXV, pp. 180-195, 5 ills. in black and white, drawing, Feb., 1944
Map-Changing Medicine. By William Joseph Showalter. XLII, pp. 303-330, 26 ills., Sept., 1922
Redeeming the Tropics. By William Joseph Showalter. XXV, pp. 344-364, 13 ills., Mar., 1914
Saboteur Mosquitoes. By Harry H. Stage. LXXXV, pp. 165-179, 12 ills., Feb., 1944

MALASPINA GLACIER, Alaska:
The National Geographic Society's Alaskan Expedition of 1909. By Ralph S. Tarr and Lawrence Martin. XXI, pp. 1-54, 42 ills., 12 maps, Jan., 1910

MALAY ARCHIPELAGO. *See* Bali; Borneo; Celebes; Java; Moluccas; Netherlands East Indies; New Guinea; Philippine Islands; Sumatra; Timor

MALAY PENINSULA. *See* British Malaya; Singapore; Thailand

MALCOLM, IAN:
The Needs Abroad. By Ian Malcolm. XXXI, pp. 427-433, 5 ills., May, 1917

The **MALL,** Washington, D. C. XXVII, plan, Mar., 1915

MALLOWAN, M. E. L.:
New Light on Ancient Ur: Excavations at the Site of the City of Abraham Reveal Geographical Evidence of the Biblical Story of the Flood. By M. E. L. Mallowan. LVII, pp. 95-130, 44 ills., map, Jan., 1930

MALONEY, JOHN:
Chesapeake Odyssey: An 18-foot Sailboat Follows the Course of Captain John Smith around This Spacious Bay of History, Commerce, Sea Food, and Nautical Lore. By John Maloney. LXXVI, pp. 357-392, 32 ills., map, Sept., 1939

MALTA (Islands), Mediterranean Sea:
Malta: The Halting Place of Nations: First Account of Remarkable Prehistoric Tombs and Temples Recently Unearthed on the Island. By William Arthur Griffiths. XXXVII, pp. 445-478, 35 ills., map, May, 1920
Malta Invicta. By Bartimeus (A Captain in the Royal Navy). LXXXIII, pp. 375-400, 27 ills., map, Mar., 1943
The Maltese Islands: Cicero's Land of "Honey and Roses," and Stronghold of the Knights, Again Is Focus of Naval Strategy. By Sir Harry Luke. LXVIII, pp. 647-666, 20 ills., maps, Nov., 1935
The Races of Europe. By Edwin A. Grosvenor. XXXIV, pp. 441-534, 62 ills., diagr. and index, maps, map supplement, Dec., 1918
Wanderers Awheel in Malta: British Stronghold Has Been a Steppingstone of Conquest Since Phoenicians Cruised the Mediterranean and St. Paul Was Shipwrecked There. By Richard Walter. LXXVIII, pp. 253-272, 17 ills., maps, Aug., 1940

The **MALTESE** Islands: Cicero's Land of "Honey and Roses," and Stronghold of the Knights, Again Is Focus of Naval Strategy. By Sir Harry Luke. LXVIII, pp. 647-666, 20 ills., maps, Nov., 1935

MAMMALS:
Animal Wealth of the United States. By Francis E. Warren. XVII, pp. 511-524, 6 ills., diagrs., Sept., 1906
Animals Were Allies, Too. 16 ills. LXXXIX, pp. 75-88, Jan., 1946
Contents: Camels, Carabaos, Cattle, Dogs, Donkeys, Elephants, Horses, Monkeys, Mules, Oxen

MAMMALS—*Continued*
Around the World for Animals. By William M. and Lucile Q. Mann. LXXIII, pp. 665-714, 33 ills. in black and white, 23 ills. in color, map, June, 1938
Befriending Nature's Children: An Experiment With Some of California's Wild Folk. By Agnes Akin Atkinson. LXI, pp. 199-215, 26 ills., Feb., 1932
The Big Game of Alaska. By Wilfred H. Osgood. XX, pp. 624-636, 10 ills., July, 1909
Camera Adventures in the African Wilds (Book Review). Photos by A. Radclyffe Dugmore. XXI, pp. 385-396, 11 ills., May, 1910
A Flashlight Story of an Albino Porcupine and of a Cunning but Unfortunate Coon. By George Shiras, 3d. XXII, pp. 572-596, 26 ills., June, 1911
Flashlights from the Jungle. XVIII, pp. 534-548, 11 ills., Aug., 1907
Game and Fur-Bearing Animals and Their Influence on the Indians of the Northwest. By Townsend W. Thorndike. XV, p. 431, Oct., 1904
A Game Country Without Rival in America: The Proposed Mount McKinley National Park. By Stephen R. Capps. XXXI, pp. 69-84, 14 ills., map, Jan., 1917
Hunting Big Game in Portuguese East Africa. (By R. C. F. Maugham). XVIII, pp. 723-730, 7 ills., Nov., 1907
A Land of Eternal Warring (Labrador). By Sir Wilfrid T. Grenfell. XXI, pp. 665-690, 24 ills., Aug., 1910
The Land of Sawdust and Spangles A World in Miniature. By Francis Beverly Kelley. LX, pp. 463-516, 35 ills. in black and white, 29 ills. in color, Oct., 1931
The Larger North American Mammals. By E. W. Nelson. Paintings by Louis Agassiz Fuertes. XXX, pp. 385-472, 24 ills. in black and white, 49 ills. in color, pictorial supplement, Nov., 1916
Contents: Antelope, Badger, Bear, Beaver, Buffalo, Caribou, Coyote, Deer, Elk, Eyra, Fisher, Fox, Goat, Jaguar, Lynx, Manati, Moose, Mountain Lion, Musk-Ox, Ocelot, Opossum, Otter, Peccary, Raccoon, Seal, Sheep, Walrus, Whale, Wolf, Wolverine
Lords of the Rockies: Photographing Big Game Animals in Their Primeval Surroundings, from Arizona to Canada, Brings Adventure to Two Wilderness Wanderers. By Wendell and Lucie Chapman. LXXVI, pp. 87-128, 14 ills. in black and white, 28 ills. in color, July, 1939
Mr. Roosevelt's "African Game Trails." XXI, pp. 953-962, 9 ills., Nov., 1910
A Naturalist's Journey Around Vera Cruz and Tampico. By Frank M. Chapman. XXV, pp. 533-562, 31 ills., May, 1914
Nature's Transformation at Panama: Remarkable Changes in Faunal and Physical Conditions in the Gatun Lake Region. By George Shiras, 3d. XXVIII, pp. 159-194, 33 ills., maps, Aug., 1915
Notes on the Wild Fowl and Game Animals of Alaska. By E. W. Nelson. IX, pp. 121-132, 6 ills., Apr., 1898
One Season's Game-Bag with the Camera. By George Shiras, 3d. XIX, pp. 387-446, 70 ills., June, 1908

MAMMALS—*Continued*

Photographing Wild Game with Flashlight and Camera. By George Shiras, 3d. XVII, pp. 367-423, 74 ills., July, 1906

The Policemen of the Air: An Account of the Biological Survey of the Department of Agriculture. By Henry Wetherbee Henshaw. XIX, pp. 79-118, 38 ills., Feb., 1908

Contents: Many of the Small Mammals Become Pests.—Wolves Cause Millions of Dollars of Loss Yearly.—Fox Farming.—Life and Crop Zones.—Game Protection and Kindred Subjects.—Big-Game Refuges

The Quills of a Porcupine. By Frederick V. Coville. XXIII, pp. 25-31, 5 ills., Jan., 1912

Scenes in Scotland. 16 ills. XXXII, pp. 519-534, Nov.-Dec., 1917

Smaller Mammals of North America. By E. W. Nelson. Paintings by Louis Agassiz Fuertes. XXXIII, pp. 371*-493, 29 ills. in black and white, 59 ills. in color, May, 1918

Contents: Armadillo, Bat, Beaver, Cat, Chipmunk, Ferret, Gopher, Hare, Lemming, Marmot, Marten, Mink, Mole, Mouse, Muskrat, Porcupine, Prairie-dog, Rabbit, Rat, Shrew, Skunk, Squirrel, Weasel, Woodrat

Tiger-Hunting in India. By Brig. Gen. William Mitchell. XLVI, pp. 545-598, 46 ills., map, Nov., 1924

The Warfare of the Jungle Folk: Campaigning Against Tigers, Elephants, and Other Wild Animals in Northern Siam. By Merian C. Cooper. Photos by Ernest B. Schoedsack. LIII, pp. 233-268, 33 ills., Feb., 1928

What the Fighting Yanks See. By Wanda Burnett. LXXXVI, pp. 451-476, 27 ills., Oct., 1944

When a Drought Blights Africa: Hippos and Elephants Are Driven Insane by Suffering, in the Lorian Swamp, Kenya Colony. By Capt. A. T. Curle. LV, pp. 521-528, 9 ills., Apr., 1929

Where Birds and Little Animals Find Haven (Eaton Canyon Bird and Game Sanctuary). By Agnes Akin Atkinson. LXX, pp. 232-241, 14 ills., Aug., 1936

Where Roosevelt Will Hunt (Africa). By Sir Harry Johnston. XX, pp. 207-256, 43 ills., map supplement, Mar., 1909

The White Sheep, Giant Moose, and Smaller Game of the Kenai Peninsula, Alaska. By George Shiras, 3d. XXIII, pp. 423-494, 59 ills., maps (1 two-page), May, 1912

Who Treads Our Trails? A Camera Trapper Describes His Experiences on an Island in the Canal Zone, a Natural-History Laboratory in the American Tropics. By Frank M. Chapman. LII, pp. 331-345, 18 ills., map, Sept., 1927

Wild Animals That Took Their Own Pictures by Day and by Night. By George Shiras, 3d. XXIV, pp. 763-834, 68 ills., map, pictorial supplement, July, 1913

The Wild Life of Lake Superior, Past and Present: The Habits of Deer, Moose, Wolves, Beavers, Muskrats, Trout, and Feathered Wood-Folk Studied with Camera and Flashlight. By George Shiras, 3d. XL, pp. 113-204, 76 ills., map, pictorial supplement, Aug., 1921

Wild Life of the Atlantic and Gulf Coasts: A Field Naturalist's Photographic Record of Nearly Half a Century of Fruitful Exploration. By George Shiras, 3d. LXII, pp. 261-309, 62 ills., Sept., 1932

MAMMALS—*Continued*

Wild Man and Wild Beast in Africa. By Theodore Roosevelt. XXII, pp. 1-33, 41 ills., map, Jan., 1911

Wings Over Nature's Zoo in Africa. 20 photos in duotone by Reginald A. Bourlay. LXXVI, pp. 527-542, Oct., 1939

With Wild Animals in the Rockies. By Lucie and Wendell Chapman. LXVIII, pp. 231-249, 26 ills. in duotone, Aug., 1935

Wonder Island of the Amazon Delta: On Marajó Cowboys Ride Oxen, Tree-dwelling Animals Throng Dense Forests, While Strange Fishes and Birds Help Make a Zoologist's Paradise. By Hugh B. Cott. LXXIV, pp. 635-670, 30 ills. in black and white, 12 ills. in color, map, Nov., 1938

See also Apes; Bats; Bears; Camels; Cats; Cattle and Cattle Raising; Deer; Dogs; Dolphins; Elephant Seals; Elephants; Goats; Horses; Jackals; Lamoids; Marsupials; Monkeys; Platypus; Porcupines; Porpoises; Reindeer; Rodents; Seals; Sheep and Sheep Raising; Walruses; Whales; Wild Cats; Wolves; *and* Paleontology

MAMMOTH:

A Strange and Remarkable Beast. XVIII, p. 620, ill., Sept., 1907

MAN, ERNEST A.:

The Nansen Polar Expedition. Special Report of the Hon. Ernest A. Man. VII, pp. 339-344, map supplement, Oct., 1896

MAN, Isle of, England:

The Isle of Man. By Captain F. H. Mellor. LXXI, pp. 587-608, 13 ills. in black and white, 12 ills. in color, map, May, 1937

MAN and Nature Paint Italian Scenes in Prodigal Colors. 33 color photos by Hans Hildenbrand. LIII, pp. 443-466, Apr., 1928

"The **MAN** in the Street" in China. By Guy Magee, Jr. XXXVIII, pp. 406-421, 15 ills., Nov., 1920

The **MAN** Without the Hoe. XXI, pp. 967-969, ills., Nov., 1910

MANAGUA, Nicaragua:

A Land of Lakes and Volcanoes. By Luis Marden. With 17 color photos by author. LXXXVI, pp. 161-192, 11 ills. in black and white, map, Aug., 1944

MANAMA, Bahrein Islands:

Bahrein: Port of Pearls and Petroleum. By Maynard Owen Williams. LXXXIX, pp. 195-210, 6 ills. in black and white, 11 ills. in color, map, Feb., 1946

MANAOS, Brazil:

Air Cruising Through New Brazil: A National Geographic Reporter Spots Vast Resources Which the Republic's War Declaration Adds to Strength of United Nations. By Henry Albert Phillips. LXXXII, pp. 503-536, 32 ills., Oct., 1942

MANCHESTER SHIP CANAL, England:

The Great Canals of the World. XVI, pp. 475-479, Oct., 1905

MANCHUKUO. *See* Manchuria

MANCHURIA:
Building of Dalny (Dairen). XIV, p. 360, Sept., 1903
Byroads and Backwoods of Manchuria: Where Violent Contrasts of Modernism and Unaltered Ancient Tradition Clash. By Owen Lattimore. LXI, pp. 101-130, 27 ills., map, Jan., 1932
Here in Manchuria: Many Thousand Lives Were Lost and More than Half the Crops Destroyed by the Floods of 1932. By Lilian Grosvenor Coville. LXIII, pp. 233-256, 26 ills., Feb., 1933
Japan Faces Russia in Manchuria. By Willard Price. LXXXII, pp. 603-634, 30 ills., map, Nov., 1942
The Land of Promise. By Major General A. W. Greely. XXIII, pp. 1078-1090, 7 ills., Nov., 1912
Lumbering in Manchuria. (By Henry B. Miller). XV, pp. 131-132, ills., Mar., 1904
Manchuria, Promised Land of Asia: Invaded by Railways and Millions of Settlers, This Vast Region Now Recalls Early Boom Days in the American West. By Frederick Simpich. LVI, pp. 379-428, 58 ills., map, Oct., 1929
Manchuria and Korea. Text with map supplement. XV, pp. 128-129, maps, Mar., 1904
Mukden, the Manchu Home, and Its Great Art Museum. By Eliza R. Scidmore. XXI, pp. 289-320, 30 ills., Apr., 1910
Notes on Manchuria. By Henry B. Miller. XV, pp. 261-262, June, 1904
Observations on the Russo-Japanese War, in Japan and Manchuria. By Dr. Louis Livingston Seaman. XVI, pp. 80-82, Feb., 1905
Railways, Rivers, and Strategic Towns in Manchuria. XI, pp. 326-327, Aug., 1900
Russian Development of Manchuria. By Henry B. Miller. XV, pp. 113-127, 11 ills., map, Mar., 1904

MANDALAY, Burma:
Notes on Burma. By Thomas Barbour. XX, pp. 841-866, 34 ills., Oct., 1909

MANDARIN ROAD, French Indo-China:
Along the Old Mandarin Road of Indo-China. By W. Robert Moore. LX, pp. 157-199, 32 ills. in black and white, 28 ills. in color, map, Aug., 1931

The **MANDATE** of Cameroun: A Vast African Territory Ruled by Petty Sultans Under French Sway. By John W. Vandercook. LIX, pp. 225-260, 49 ills., map, Feb., 1931

MANEUVERS of Military Planes Disclose Majestic Aërial Views. 17 ills. in duotone from U. S. Army and Navy official photos. LXIII, pp. 599-614, May, 1933

MANGANESE:
India's Treasures Helped the Allies. By John Fischer. LXXXIX, pp. 501-522, 18 ills., Apr., 1946

MANGBETTU (Tribespeople):
Trans-Africa Safari: A Motor Caravan Rolls Across Sahara and Jungle Through Realms of Dusky Potentates and the Land of Big-Lipped Women. By Lawrence Copley Thaw and Margaret Stout Thaw. LXXIV, pp. 327-364, 29 ills. in black and white, 14 ills. in color, map, Sept., 1938

MANGOES (Trees):
The Introduction of the Mango. XIV, pp. 320-327, 5 ills., Aug., 1903
New Plant Immigrants. By David Fairchild. XXII, pp. 879-907, 34 ills., Oct., 1911

MANGYANS (Tribespeople):
Notes on Some Primitive Philippine Tribes. By Dean C. Worcester. IX, pp. 284-301, 11 ills., June, 1898

MANIHIKI (Atoll), South Pacific Ocean:
Sailing the Seven Seas in the Interest of Science: Adventures Through 157,000 Miles of Storm and Calm, from Arctic to Antarctic and Around the World, in the Non-magnetic Yacht "Carnegie." By J. P. Ault. XLII, pp. 631-690, 47 ills., chart, Dec., 1922

MANILA, Luzon, Philippine Islands:
The Economic Condition of the Philippines. By Max L. Tornow. X, pp. 33-64, 10 ills., Feb., 1899
Facts about the Philippines. By Frederick Simpich. LXXXI, pp. 185-202, 17 ills., map, Feb., 1942
Improvements in the City of Manila. XIV, pp. 195-197, ill., May, 1903
Manila and the Philippines. By Major A. Falkner von Sonnenburg. X, pp. 65-72, Feb., 1899
The Manila Observatory. By Rev. Father José Algué. XI, pp. 427-438, ills., Nov., 1900
Return to Manila. By Frederick Simpich. LXXVIII, pp. 409-451, 21 ills. in black and white, 21 ills. in color, map, Oct., 1940
What Luzon Means to Uncle Sam. By Frederick Simpich. LXXXVII, pp. 305-332, 25 ills., map supplement, Mar., 1945

MANIPUR (State), India:
Manipur—Where Japan Struck at India. 11 photos, map. LXXXV, pp. 743-750, June, 1944

MANITOBA (Province), Canada. *See* Churchill

MANKIND'S Best Friend (Dog): Companion of His Solitude, Advance Guard in the Hunt, and Ally of the Trenches. By Ernest Harold Baynes. XXXV, pp. 185-201, 11 ills., Mar., 1919

MANLESS Alpine Climbing: The First Woman to Scale the Grépon, the Matterhorn, and Other Famous Peaks Without Masculine Support Relates Her Adventures. By Miriam O'Brien Underhill. LXVI, pp. 131-170, 30 ills. in black and white, 12 ills. in color, Aug., 1934

The **MANLIKE** Apes of Jungle and Mountain. 10 ills. in color from paintings by Elie Cheverlange. LXXVIII, pp. 221-228, Aug., 1940

MANN, JAMES R.:
Honors to Colonel Goethals: The Presentation, by President Woodrow Wilson, of the National Geographic Society Special Gold Medal, and Addresses by Secretary of State Bryan, the French Ambassador, the German Ambassador, and Congressman James R. Mann. XXV, pp. 677-690, 6 ills., June, 1914

MANN, LUCILE Q.:
Around the World for Animals. By William M. and Lucile Q. Mann. LXXIII, pp. 665-714, 33 ills. in black and white, 23 ills. in color, map, June, 1938

MANN, WILLIAM M.:
Around the World for Animals. By William M. and Lucile Q. Mann. LXXIII, pp. 665-714, 33 ills. in black and white, 23 ills. in color, map, June, 1938

Man's Closest Counterparts: Heavyweight of Monkeydom Is the "Old Man" Gorilla, by Far the Largest of the Four Great Apes. By William M. Mann. Paintings by Elie Cheverlange. LXXVIII, pp. 213-236, 10 ills. in black and white, 10 ills. in color, Aug., 1940

Monkey Folk. By William M. Mann. Paintings by Elie Cheverlange. LXXIII, pp. 615-655, 24 ills. in black and white, 40 portraits in color, May, 1938

Stalking Ants, Savage and Civilized: A Naturalist Braves Bites and Stings in Many Lands to Learn the Story of an Insect Whose Ways Often Parallel Those of Man. By W. M. Mann. Paintings by Hashime Murayama. LXVI, pp. 171-192, 7 ills. in black and white, 18 ills. in color, Aug., 1934

MAN-O'-WAR-BIRDS:
Birds of the High Seas: Albatrosses and Petrels; Gannets, Man-o'-war-birds, and Tropic-birds. By Robert Cushman Murphy. Paintings by Major Allan Brooks. LXXIV, pp. 226-251, 7 ills. in black and white, 36 portraits in color, Aug., 1938

MAN'S Amazing Progress in Conquering the Air. By J. R. Hildebrand. XLVI, pp. 93-122, 28 ills., diagr., July, 1924

MAN'S Closest Counterparts: Heavyweight of Monkeydom Is the "Old Man" Gorilla, by Far the Largest of the Four Great Apes. By William M. Mann. Paintings by Elie Cheverlange. LXXVIII, pp. 213-236, 10 ills. in black and white, 10 ills. in color, Aug., 1940

MAN'S Farthest Aloft: Rising to 13.71 Miles, the National Geographic Society-U. S. Army Stratosphere Expedition Gathers Scientific Data at Record Altitude. By Capt. Albert W. Stevens. LXIX, pp. 59-94, 39 ills., map, Jan., 1936
Included: Action Photographs of the Balloon's Perfect Landing

MAN'S Feathered Friends of Longest Standing: Peoples of Every Clime and Age Have Lavished Care and Affection Upon Lovely Pigeons. By Elisha Hanson. Paintings by Hashime Murayama. XLIX, pp. 63-110, 35 ills. in black and white, 12 ills. in color, Jan., 1926

MAN'S Hunting Partner, the Field Dog. 36 portraits from paintings by Edward Herbert Miner. LXXI, pp. 89-104, Jan., 1937

MAN'S Oldest Ally, the Dog: Since Cave-Dweller Days This Faithful Friend Has Shared the Work, Exploration, and Sport of Humankind. By Freeman Lloyd. Paintings by Edward Herbert Miner. LXIX, pp. 247-274, 13 ills. in black and white, 33 portraits in color, Feb., 1936

MAN'S Winged Ally, the Busy Honeybee: Modern Research Adds a New Chapter to Usefulness of the Insect Which Has Symbolized Industry Since Early Bible Times. By James I. Hambleton. Paintings by Hashime Murayama. LXVII, pp. 401-428, 18 ills. in black and white, 16 ills. in color, Apr., 1935

MAORIS (Tribespeople):
Hurdle Racing in Canoes: A Thrilling and Spectacular Sport Among the Maoris of New Zealand. By Walter Burke. XXXVII, pp. 440-444, 6 ills., May, 1920

The Maoris of New Zealand. XVIII, pp. 198-199, 8 ills., Mar., 1907

MAP (Island), Caroline Islands:
Mysterious Micronesia: Yap, Map, and Other Islands Under Japanese Mandate are Museums of Primitive Man. By Willard Price. LXIX, pp. 481-510, 37 ills., map, Apr., 1936

MAP ARTICLES; MAP MAKING:
Bitter Root Forest Reserve. By Richard U. Goode. IX, pp. 387-400, 5 ills., foldout map, Sept., 1898
Included: U. S. Geological Survey's mapping of forest reserves

The Cartography and Observations of Bering's First Voyage. By General A. W. Greely. III, pp. 205-230, map supplement, Jan. 28, 1892; Feb. 19, 1892

Charting a World at War. By William H. Nicholas. LXXXVI, pp. 617-640, 23 ills., drawing, Nov., 1944

The Copyright of a Map or Chart. By William Alexander Miller. XIII, pp. 437-443, Dec., 1902

A Critical Review of Bering's First Expedition, 1725-30, Together with a Translation of His Original Report Upon It. With a Map. By Wm. H. Dall. II, pp. 111-169, 8 tables, foldout map, May, 1890

Discoverers of America. Annual Address by the President, Hon. Gardiner G. Hubbard. V, pp. 1-20, charts, maps, 3 map supplements, Apr. 7, 1893

The famous Waldseemüller map of 1507. XV, p. 50, Jan., 1904

The First Landfall of Columbus. By Jacques W. Redway, F. R. G. S. VI, pp. 179-192, 4 maps, Dec. 29, 1894

Geographic Work of the General Government. By Henry Gannett. IX, pp. 329-338, July, 1898

A Geographical Description of the British Islands. (By W. M. Davis). VII, pp. 208-211, June, 1896

The Geography of Alaska: Illustrated by a New Map. By Alfred H. Brooks. XV, pp. 213-219, map supplement, May, 1904

The Geologic Atlas of the United States. (By W J M.). IX, pp. 339-342, July, 1898

Gomez and the New York Gulf. (By L. D. Scisco). IX, pp. 371-373, Aug., 1898

International Flat Globe and Geographical History. XVIII, pp. 281-282, Apr., 1907

The International Millionth Map of the World. By Bailey Willis. XXI, pp. 125-132, diagr., Feb., 1910

Korea and the Koreans. By J. B. Bernadou. II, pp. 231-242, map, foldout map, Aug., 1890

The Making of Military Maps. By William H. Nicholas. LXXXIII, pp. 765-778, 17 ills., June, 1943

A Map of the New Germany. Text with map. XXXV, pp. 545-546, map, June, 1919

Maps for Victory: National Geographic Society's Charts Used in War on Land, Sea, and in the Air. By Gilbert Grosvenor. LXXXI, pp. 667-690, 28 ills., May, 1942

Maps Recently Published by the U. S. Geological Survey. XVI, pp. 423-427, Sept., 1905

The Mother Maps of the United States. By Henry Gannett. IV, pp. 101-116, table, map supplement, Mar. 31, 1892

The Ordnance Survey of Great Britain—Its History and Object. By Josiah Pierce, Jr. II, pp. 243-260, Aug., 1890

Plan of a Map of the World. By Dr. Albrecht Penck. XV, pp. 405-408, Oct., 1904

Report on Topographic Work (Mount St. Elias Expedition). By Mark B. Kerr. III, p. 195, map, May 29, 1891

Sarichef's Atlas, 1826. By Marcus Baker. XIII, pp. 86-92, Mar., 1902

The Story of the Map. Text with map supplement. LXII, pp. 759-774, 11 ills., Dec., 1932

The Submarine Cables of the World. By Gustave Herrle. With chart compiled by U. S. Hydrographic Office. VII, pp. 102-107, Mar., 1896

The Survey and Map of Massachusetts. By Henry Gannett. I, pp. 78-86, Oct., 1888

Surveys and Maps of the District of Columbia. By Marcus Baker. VI, pp. 149-178, diagr., tables, map, Nov. 1, 1894
Included: List of Maps of Washington and the District of Columbia

The Topographic Atlas of the United States. (By W J M.). IX, pp. 343-344, July, 1898

Topographic Maps Issued by the Geological Survey in 1907. XIX, pp. 226-227, Mar., 1908

Topographic Models. By Cosmos Mindeleff. I, pp. 254-268, 7 diagrs., map, July, 1889

Two Famous Maps of America. XIII, p. 72, Feb., 1902

An Undiscovered Island Off the Northern Coast of Alaska. I—By Marcus Baker. II—By Captain Edward Perry Herendeen. III—By General A. W. Greely. V, pp. 76-83, July 10, 1893

The Unexplored Philippines from the Air: Mapmaking over Jungle Lands Never Before Seen By White Men. By Lieut. George W. Goddard. LVIII, pp. 311-343, 38 ills., map, Sept., 1930

Your Society Aids War Effort. LXXXIII, pp. 277-278, ill., Feb., 1943

See also Surveying; *and* the following NGS articles and announcements

NGS Map Supplement Articles and Announcements:

Africa

Africa First of 1943 Global Warfare Maps. By William H. Nicholas. Text with map supplement. LXXXIII, pp. 261-276, 13 ills., Feb., 1943

The Black Man's Continent. Text with map supplement. XX, p. 312, Mar., 1909

NGS Map Supplement Articles and Announcements—*Continued*

Map of Africa. Announcement of map supplement (The Black Man's Continent, Mar., 1909). XVIII, p. 640, Oct., 1907

The National Geographic Society's New Map of Africa. By Gilbert Grosvenor. Text with map supplement. LXVII, pp. 731-752, 20 ills. in duotone, June, 1935

The Society's New Map of Africa. Text with map supplement. XLII, pp. 447-448, Oct., 1922

Western Front Map Embraces Three Continents (Europe, Africa, Asia). Text with map supplement. LXXXII, pp. 139-140, July, 1942

Alaska

Map of Alaska. Announcement of map supplement (May, 1904). XV, p. 188, Apr., 1904; p. 236, May, 1904

See also North America

Antarctic Regions

The Society's Map of the Antarctic. Text with map supplement. LXII, pp. 485-486, ill., Oct., 1932

Arctic Regions

Map of the North Polar Regions. Text with map supplement. XVIII, pp. 454-455, July, 1907

North Polar Map. Text describing map compiled by Gilbert H. Grosvenor (July, 1907). XX, p. 915, Oct., 1909

A Polar Map. Announcement of map supplement (July, 1907). XVII, p. 533, Sept., 1906

Asia

Face of Japan (Map of Japan and Korea). By W. Robert Moore. Text with map supplement. LXXXVIII, pp. 753-768, 14 ills., Dec., 1945

Indian Ocean Map Spans Far East News Centers. Text with map supplement. LXXIX, pp. 345-346, ill., Mar., 1941

Manchuria and Korea. Text with map supplement. XV, pp. 128-129, maps, Mar., 1904

Map of the Philippines. Announcement of map supplement (Aug., 1905). XVI, p. 434, Sept., 1905

Map of the Philippines. Text with map supplement. XIII, p. 31, Jan., 1902

National Geographic Map of Japan, Regions of Asia, and the Pacific. Text with map supplement. LXXXV, pp. 415-416, Apr., 1944

The New Map of Asia. Text with map supplement. XXXIX, pp. 552-570, 17 ills., May, 1921

New Map Shows Asia's Role in Global Warfare. Text with map supplement. LXXXII, pp. 767-768, Dec., 1942

New National Geographic Map Shows Strategic Philippines (What Luzon Means to Uncle Sam). By Frederick Simpich. Text with map supplement. LXXXVII, pp. 305-307, 312, 332, Mar., 1945

The Society's New Map of Asia. Text with map supplement. LXIV, pp. 770-772, ill., Dec., 1933

The Society's New Map of China. By James M. Darley. Text with map supplement. LXXXVII, pp. 745-746, June, 1945

The Society's New Map of India and Burma. Text with map supplement. LXXXIX, p. 544, Apr., 1946

The Society's New Map of Southeast Asia. Text with map supplement. LXXXVI, pp. 449-450, ill., Oct., 1944

The Society's New Map of Soviet Russia. Text with map supplement. LXXXVI, pp. 716-718, Dec., 1944

Western Front Map Embraces Three Continents (Europe, Africa, Asia). Text with map supplement. LXXXII, pp. 139-140, July, 1942

Atlantic Ocean

New Map of the Atlantic Ocean: Foremost Sea of Commerce Becomes World's Battleground and Its Peaceful Islands Rise to Strategic Importance. By Leo A. Borah and Wellman Chamberlin. Text with map supplement. LXXX, pp. 407-418, 9 ills., Sept., 1941

The World That Rims the Narrowing Atlantic: Latest Ten-color Map Supplement Shows Four Continents and New Transatlantic Air Routes Which Make This Ocean Only One Day Wide. By James M. Darley. Text with map supplement. LXXVI, pp. 139-142, ill., July, 1939

Bible Lands

The Society's Map of Bible Lands. By Gilbert Grosvenor. Text with map supplement. LXXIV, pp. 751-754, 3 ills., Dec., 1938

The Society's New Map of Bible Lands. Text with map supplement. XC, pp. 815-816, Dec., 1946

Canada

The Society Maps Northwestern United States and Neighboring Canadian Provinces. Text with map supplement. LXXIX, pp. 805-806, June, 1941

The Society's New Map of Canada. Text with map supplement. LXIX, pp. 769-776, 9 ills., June, 1936

See also North America

Caribbean Regions

Heart of a Hemisphere: Of Vital Importance is the Area Portrayed in The Society's New Map of Mexico, Central America, and the West Indies. Text with map supplement. LXXVI, pp. 739-740, ill., Dec., 1939

Our Map of the Countries of the Caribbean. Text with map supplement. XLI, pp. 221-222, Feb., 1922

The Society's New Caribbean Map: Mexico, Central America, and the West Indies—Gateway of Discovery. Text with map supplement. LXVI, pp. 738-740, ill., Dec., 1934

Central America

Bird's-Eye View of the Panama Canal. Announcement of map supplement. XXIII, p. 208, Feb., 1912

Map of Panama Canal. Announcement of map supplement (Oct., 1905). XVI, p. 441, Sept., 1905

See also Caribbean Regions

Europe

The Geographic's New Map of Europe and the Mediterranean. By Gilbert Grosvenor. Text with map supplement. LXXIII, pp. 525-528, ill., Apr., 1938

MAP ARTICLES; MAP MAKING—*Continued*

NGS Map Supplement Articles and Announcements—*Continued*

The Geographic's New Map of Germany and Its Approaches: With a Review of The Society's Maps of Europe. By Gilbert Grosvenor. Text with map supplement. LXXXVI, pp. 66-72, ill., July, 1944

Map Links Classic World with 1940. Text with map supplement. LXXVII, p. 338, Mar., 1940

Map of Europe Including the New Balkan States. Text with map supplement. XXVI, pp. 191-192, Aug., 1914

A Modern Pilgrim's Map of the British Isles. By Andrew H. Brown. Text with map supplement. LXXI, pp. 795-802, 3 ills., June, 1937

The National Geographic War-Zone Map. Text with map supplement. XXXIII, p. 494, May, 1918

The New Map of Europe: Showing the Boundaries Established by the Peace Conference at Paris and by Subsequent Decisions of the Supreme Council of the Allied and Associated Powers. By Ralph A. Graves. Text with map supplement. XXXIX, pp. 157-177, 18 ills., Feb., 1921

New Map of Europe and the Near East. Text with map supplement. LXXXIII, pp. 762-763, ill., June, 1943

New Map of Europe Records War Changes. Text with map supplement. LXXVII, p. 625, May, 1940

Our Map of the Races of Europe. Text with map supplement. XXXIV, pp. 535-536, Dec., 1918

The Society's New Map of Central Europe and the Mediterranean. Text with map supplement. LXXVI, pp. 559-560, Oct., 1939

The Society's New Map of Europe. By Gilbert Grosvenor. Text with map supplement. LVI, pp. 771-774, Dec., 1929

The Society's New Map of Soviet Russia. Text with map supplement. LXXXVI, pp. 716-718, Dec., 1944

Western Front Map Embraces Three Continents (Europe, Africa, Asia). Text with map supplement. LXXXII, pp. 139-140, July, 1942

Mediterranean Regions

Map of Mediterranean Regions. Announcement of map supplement. XXIII, p. 104, Jan., 1912

See also Bible Lands; Europe

Mexico

The Latest Map of Mexico. Text with map supplement. XXX, p. 88, July, 1916

Map of Mexico. Announcement of map supplement (May, 1911). XXII, p. 410, Apr., 1911

See also North America

Near East

New Map of Europe and the Near East. Text with map supplement. LXXXIII, pp. 762-763, ill., June, 1943

North America

Maps for Victory: National Geographic Society's Charts Used in War on Land, Sea, and in the Air. By Gilbert Grosvenor. Text with map supplement. LXXXI, pp. 667-690, 28 ills., May, 1942

Our Map of North America. Text with map supplement. XLV, p. 580, May, 1924

MAP ARTICLES; MAP MAKING—*Continued*

NGS Map Supplement Articles and Announcements—*Continued*

Pacific Ocean

New Map Shows Immense Pacific Battleground. Text with map supplement. LXXXI, pp. 203-204, Feb., 1942

Our Map of the Pacific. Text with map supplement. XL, pp. 647-648, map, Dec., 1921

Revealing Earth's Mightiest Ocean. By Albert W. Atwood. Announcement of map supplement. LXXXIV, p. 291, Sept., 1943

The Society's New Map of the Pacific. By Gilbert Grosvenor. Text with map supplement. LXX, pp. 793-796, Dec., 1936

South America

New National Geographic Society Map Charts South America's Wartime Importance. Text with map supplement. LXXXII, pp. 537-540, ills., Oct., 1942

The Society's Map of South America. By Gilbert Grosvenor. Text with map supplement. LXXII, pp. 809-810, Dec., 1937

The Society's New Map of South America. Text with map supplement. XL, pp. 374-392, 17 ills., Oct., 1921

South America Map. Announcement of map supplement (Aug., 1906). XVII, p. 424, July, 1906

The Valley of the Orinoco. By T. H. Gignilliat. Text with map supplement. VII, p. 92, Feb., 1896

United States

Another Important Map (U. S.). Announcement of map supplement (Apr., 1923). XLIII, p. 336, Mar., 1923

The National Geographic Society's Map of Northeastern United States. Text with map supplement. LXXXVIII, pp. 361-362, Sept., 1945

New Map Reveals the Progress and Wonders of Our Country. Text with map supplement. LXIII, pp. 650-652, ill., May, 1933

New United States Map Shows Census Changes. Text with map supplement. LXXVIII, pp. 821-824, ills., Dec., 1940

Our Map of the United States. Text with map supplement. XLIII, p. 460, Apr., 1923

Postwar Portrait of the United States. Text with map supplement. XC, pp. 135-136, July, 1946

The Society Maps Northwestern United States and Neighboring Canadian Provinces. Text with map supplement. LXXIX, pp. 805-806, June, 1941

The Society's Map of Historic and Scenic Reaches of the Nation's Capital. Text with map supplement. LXXIV, pp. 57-58, July, 1938

The Society's Map of the Reaches of New York City. Text with map supplement. LXXV, pp. 491-492, Apr., 1939

The Society's Map of the White Mountains of New Hampshire. Note describing map supplement. LXXII, p. 73, July, 1937

Southwest Trails from Horse to Motor. Text with map supplement. LXXVII, p. 767, June, 1940

The Travels of George Washington. By William Joseph Showalter. Text with map supplement. LXI, pp. 1-63, 50 ills., 4 maps, Jan., 1932

MAP ARTICLES; MAP MAKING—*Continued*

NGS Map Supplement Articles and Announcements—*Continued*

World

Chart of the World. Announcement of map supplement (Feb., 1905). XV, p. 500, Dec., 1904. XVI, p. 50, Jan., 1905

The "Map of Discovery" of the Western Hemisphere with This Number. Announcement of map supplement. LV, p. 93, Jan., 1929

The "Map of Discovery" with This Number (Eastern Hemisphere). Announcement of map supplement. LIV, p. 568, Nov., 1928

Map of the Northern and Southern Hemispheres. Text with map supplement. LXXXIII, pp. 481-483, Apr., 1943

The National Geographic Society's New Map of the World. Text with map supplement. LXVIII, pp. 796-798, Dec., 1935

New World Map Gives Backdrop for Headlines. Text with map supplement. LXXX, pp. 741-742, ill., Dec., 1941

The Society's New Map of the World. Text with map supplement. XLII, pp. 690-691, Dec., 1922

The Story of the Map. Text with map supplement. LXII, pp. 759-774, 11 ills., Dec., 1932

The World's Words (Map of the World). By William H. Nicholas. Text with map supplement. LXXXIV, p. 689, Dec., 1943

MAP-CHANGING Medicine. By William Joseph Showalter. XLII, pp. 303-330, 26 ills., Sept., 1922

MAP Links Classic World with 1940. Text with map supplement. LXXVII, p. 338, Mar., 1940

MAPPING the Antarctic from the Air: The Aërial Camera Earns Its Place as the Eyes and Memory of the Explorer. By Capt. Ashley C. McKinley. LXII, pp. 471-485, 13 ills., map supplement, Oct., 1932

MAPPING the Home of the Great Brown Bear: Adventures of the National Geographic Society's Pavlof Volcano Expedition to Alaska. By Dr. Thomas A. Jaggar. LV, pp. 109-134, 30 ills., map, Jan., 1929

MAPS. *See* Map Index, *following this index*

MAPS, Sky. *See* Star Charts; *and* Map Index: Heavens

MAPS for Victory: National Geographic Society's Charts Used in War on Land, Sea, and in the Air. By Gilbert Grosvenor. Text with map supplement. LXXXI, pp. 667-690, 28 ills., May, 1942

MAPS OF DISCOVERY:

Eastern Hemisphere. Reproduction in color of the painting by N. C. Wyeth, National Geographic Society, Washington, D. C. LIV, text, p. 568; supplement, Nov., 1928

Western Hemisphere. Reproduction in color of the painting by N. C. Wyeth, National Geographic Society, Washington, D. C. LV, text, p. 93; supplement, Jan., 1929

MAPUCHES (Indians). *See* Araucanian Indians

MARAJÓ ISLAND, Brazil:

Wonder Island of the Amazon Delta: On Marajó Cowboys Ride Oxen, Tree-dwelling Animals Throng Dense Forests, While Strange Fishes and Birds Help Make a Zoologist's Paradise.

MARAJÓ ISLAND, Brazil—*Continued*
By Hugh B. Cott. LXXIV, pp. 635-670, 30 ills. in black and white, 12 ills. in color, map, Nov., 1938

MARAKEI (Atoll), Gilbert Islands:
Gilbert Islands in the Wake of Battle. By W. Robert Moore. LXXXVII, pp. 129-162, 11 ills. in black and white, 19 ills. in color, map, Feb., 1945

MARATHON (Plain), Greece:
"The Glory That Was Greece." By Alexander Wilbourne Weddell. XLII, pp. 571-630, 51 ills., map, Dec., 1922

MARAUDERS (Bombers):
Return to Florence. By 1st Lt. Benjamin C. McCartney. LXXXVII, pp. 257-296, 18 ills. in black and white, 18 ills. in color, Mar., 1945

MARAUDERS of the Sea (Squid and Octopuses). By Roy Waldo Miner. Paintings by Else Bostelmann. LXVIII, pp. 185-207, 12 ills. in black and white, 8 ills. in color, Aug., 1935

MARBLE CANYON, Arizona:
Experiences in the Grand Canyon. By Ellsworth and Emory Kolb. XXVI, pp. 99-184, 70 ills., map, Aug., 1914

The **MARBLE** Dams of Rajputana. By Eleanor Maddock. XL, pp. 469-499, 13 ills. in black and white, 16 ills. in color, Nov., 1921

MARBLEHEAD, Massachusetts:
Northeast of Boston. By Albert W. Atwood. LXXXVIII, pp. 257-292, 12 ills. in black and white, 17 ills. in color, map supplement, Sept., 1945

MARCHING Through Georgia Sixty Years After: Multifold Industries and Diversified Agriculture Are Restoring the Prosperity of America's Largest State East of the Mississippi. By Ralph A. Graves. L, pp. 259-311, 47 ills., map supplement, Sept., 1926

MARCUS, OSCAR:
Pilgrims' Progress to Mecca. 22 ills. in duotone: 18 by Oscar Marcus. LXXII, pp. 627-642, Nov., 1937

MARDEN, LUIS:
Americans in the Caribbean. By Luis Marden. LXXXI, pp. 723-758, 16 ills. in black and white, 22 ills. in color, map, June, 1942
War Echoes in the West Indies. 22 color photos by author, pp. 731-754

Buenos Aires—Metropolis of the Pampas. 24 color photos by Luis Marden, Maynard Owen Williams, W. Robert Moore. LXXVI, pp. 577-600, Nov., 1939

Caracas, Cradle of the Liberator: The Spirit of Simón Bolívar, South American George Washington, Lives On in the City of His Birth. By Luis Marden. LXXVII, pp. 477-513, 18 ills. in black and white, 19 ills. in color, Apr., 1940
Venezuela's Capital—City of Contrasts. 19 color photos by author, pp. 483-506

Coffee Is King in El Salvador. By Luis Marden. With 27 color photos by author and David D. Duncan. LXXXVI, pp. 575-616, 22 ills. in black and white, map, Nov., 1944

MARDEN, LUIS—*Continued*
Hail Colombia! By Luis Marden. LXXVIII, pp. 505-536, 10 ills. in black and white, 18 ills. in color, map, Oct., 1940
Beneath Colombia's Azure Skies. 18 color photos: 17 by author, pp. 513-536

The Hub City (Boston), Cradle of American Liberty. 31 color photos: 26 by Luis Marden. LXX, pp. 49-72, July, 1936

A Land of Lakes and Volcanoes (Nicaragua). By Luis Marden. With 17 color photos by author. LXXXVI, pp. 161-192, 11 ills. in black and white, map, Aug., 1944

Land of the Painted Oxcarts (Costa Rica). By Luis Marden. With 31 color photos by author. XC, pp. 409-456, 30 ills. in black and white, map, Oct., 1946

Old and New Blend in Yankeeland (Connecticut). 25 color photos: 10 by Luis Marden. LXXIV, pp. 295-326, Sept., 1938

On the Cortés Trail (Mexico). By Luis Marden. LXXVIII, pp. 335-375, 17 ills. in black and white, 22 ills. in color, map, Sept., 1940
In Montezuma's Painted Land. 22 color photos: 21 by author, pp. 345-368

Panama, Bridge of the World. By Luis Marden. LXXX, pp. 591-630, 23 ills. in black and white, 22 ills. in color, map, Nov., 1941
The Land That Links the Americas. 22 color photos by author, pp. 601-624

Riatas and Romance on the Rio Grande. 24 color photos: 23 by Luis Marden. LXXVI, pp. 431-462, Oct., 1939

To Market in Guatemala. By Luis Marden. With 19 color photos by Giles Greville Healey and Charles S. Pineo. LXXXVIII, pp. 87-104, July, 1945

Today in the Feathered Serpent's City (Chichen Itzá). 25 color photos by Luis Marden. LXX, pp. 599-614, Nov., 1936

Virginia's Colonial Heritage (Williamsburg). 25 color photos: 8 by Luis Marden. LXXI, pp. 417-440, Apr., 1937

Where Man's Garb Rivals the Quetzal (Guatemala). 13 color photos by Luis Marden. LXX, pp. 437-444, Oct., 1936

MARIANAS ISLANDS, West Pacific Ocean:
American Pathfinders in the Pacific. By William H. Nicholas. LXXXIX, pp. 617-640, 17 ills., two-page map, May, 1946

Hidden Key to the Pacific: Piercing the Web of Secrecy Which Long Has Veiled Japanese Bases in the Mandated Islands. By Willard Price. LXXXI, pp. 759-785, 28 ills., map, June, 1942

South from Saipan. By W. Robert Moore. LXXXVII, pp. 441-474, 11 ills. in black and white, 17 ills. in color, map, Apr., 1945

Springboards to Tokyo. By Willard Price. LXXXVI, pp. 385-407, 16 ills., Oct., 1944

Victory's Portrait in the Marianas. By Lt. William Franklin Draper, USNR. With 17 ills. in color from paintings by author. LXXXVIII, pp. 599-616, Nov., 1945

See also Guam

MARINE BIOLOGY:
America's Most Valuable Fishes. By Hugh M. Smith. XXIII, pp. 494-514, 17 ills., May, 1912

MARINE BIOLOGY—*Continued*

Certain Citizens of the Warm Sea. By Louis L. Mowbray. Paintings by Hashime Murayama. XLI, pp. 27-62, 18 ills. in black and white, 16 ills. in color, Jan., 1922

Coral Castle Builders of Tropic Seas. By Roy Waldo Miner. Paintings by Else Bostelmann. LXV, pp. 703-728, 15 ills. in black and white, 8 ills. in color, maps, June, 1934

Crabs and Crablike Curiosities of the Sea. By William Crowder. Paintings by author. LIV, pp. 57-72, 10 ills. in black and white, 8 ills. in color, July, 1928

Cultivation of Marine and Fresh-Water Animals in Japan. By K. Mitsukuri. XVII, pp. 524-531, 5 ills., Sept., 1906

Deep-Sea Exploring Expedition of the Steamer "Albatross." By Hugh M. Smith. X, pp. 291-296, ills., diagr., Aug., 1899

Denizens of Our Warm Atlantic Waters. By Roy Waldo Miner. Paintings by Else Bostelmann. LXXI, pp. 199-219, 10 ills. in black and white, 8 ills. in color, Feb., 1937

The Depths of the Sea: Strange Life Forms a Mile Below the Surface. By William Beebe. Paintings by E. Bostelmann. LXI, pp. 65-88, 15 ills. in black and white, 8 ills. in color, map, Jan., 1932

The First Autochromes from the Ocean Bottom: Marine Life in Its Natural Habitat Along the Florida Keys Is Successfully Photographed in Colors. (Photographs by Dr. W. H. Longley and Charles Martin). LI, pp. 56-60, 8 ills. in color, Jan., 1927

Fishes and Fisheries of Our North Atlantic Seaboard. By John Oliver La Gorce. Paintings by Hashime Murayama. XLIV, pp. 567-634, 35 ills. in black and white, 16 ills. in color, Dec., 1923

Fishes That Build Nests and Take Care of Their Young. XVIII, pp. 400-412, 16 ills., June, 1907

Fishes That Carry Lanterns. XXI, pp. 453-456, 5 ills., May, 1910

Fishing in Pacific Coast Streams. By Leonard P. Schultz. Paintings by Hashime Murayama. LXXV, pp. 185-212, 10 ills. in black and white, 54 portraits in color, Feb., 1939

The Glass-Bottom Boat. By Charles Frederick Holder. XX, pp. 761-778, 17 ills., Sept., 1909

The Great Barrier Reef and Its Isles: The Wonder and Mystery of Australia's World-Famous Geographical Feature. By Charles Barrett. LVIII, pp. 355-384, 38 ills., map, Sept., 1930

A Half Mile Down: Strange Creatures, Beautiful and Grotesque as Figments of Fancy, Reveal Themselves at Windows of the Bathysphere. By William Beebe. Paintings by Else Bostelmann, Helen D. Tee-Van, E. J. Geske. LXVI, pp. 661-704, 28 ills. in black and white, 16 ills. in color, map, Dec., 1934

Interesting Citizens of the Gulf Stream. By Dr. John T. Nichols. XXXIX, pp. 69-84, 11 ills., Jan., 1921

King Herring: An Account of the World's Most Valuable Fish, the Industries It Supports, and the Part It Has Played in History. By Hugh M. Smith. XX, pp. 701-735, 21 ills., Aug., 1909

The Life of the Moon-Jelly. By William Crowder. Paintings by author. L, pp. 187-202, 6 ills. in black and white, 8 ills. in color, Aug., 1926

MARINE BIOLOGY—*Continued*

Life on a Coral Reef: The Fertility and Mystery of the Sea Studied Beneath the Waters Surrounding Dry Tortugas. By W. H. Longley. LI, pp. 61-83, 22 ills., Jan., 1927

Living Jewels of the Sea (Plankton). By William Crowder. Paintings by author. LII, pp. 290-304, 8 ills. in black and white, 8 ills. in color, Sept., 1927

The Mysterious Life of the Common Eel. By Hugh M. Smith. XXIV, pp. 1140-1146, 3 ills., Oct., 1913

The Native Oysters of the West Coast. By Robert E. C. Stearns. XIX, pp. 224-226, Mar., 1908

Notes from a Naturalist's Experiences in British Guiana. By C. H. Eigenmann. XXII, pp. 859-870, 8 ills., Sept., 1911

On the Bottom of a South Sea Pearl Lagoon. By Roy Waldo Miner. Paintings by Else Bostelmann. LXXIV, pp. 365-390, 17 ills. in black and white, 8 ills. in color, Sept., 1938

Oysters: The World's Most Valuable Water Crop. By Hugh M. Smith. XXIV, pp. 257-281, 21 ills., Mar., 1913

Planting Fishes in the Ocean. By George M. Bowers. XVIII, pp. 715-723, 5 ills., Nov., 1907

The Purple Veil: A Romance of the Sea. (By H.A.L.). XVI, pp. 337-341, 9 ills., July, 1905

A Round Trip to Davy Jones's Locker: Peering into Mysteries a Quarter Mile Down in the Open Sea, by Means of the Bathysphere. By William Beebe. Paintings by E. Bostelmann. LIX, pp. 653-678, 14 ills. in black and white, 8 ills. in color, map, June, 1931

Sea Creatures of Our Atlantic Shores. By Roy Waldo Miner. Paintings by Else Bostelmann. LXX, pp. 209-231, 8 ills. in black and white, 8 ills. in color, chart, Aug., 1936

Some Giant Fishes of the Seas. By Hugh M. Smith. XX, pp. 637-644, 6 ills., July, 1909

Treasure-House of the Gulf Stream: The Completion and Opening of the New Aquarium and Biological Laboratory at Miami, Florida. By John Oliver La Gorce. Paintings by Hashime Murayama. XXXIX, pp. 53-68, 5 ills. in black and white, 16 ills. in color, Jan., 1921

Treasures of the Pacific: Marine Fishes and Fisheries Yield Vast Wealth from Alaska to Baja California. By Leonard P. Schultz. Paintings by Hashime Murayama. LXXIV, pp. 463-498, 10 ills. in black and white, 31 portraits in color, Oct., 1938

Tropical Fish Immigrants Reveal New Nature Wonders. By Walter H. Chute. LXV, pp. 93-109, 8 ills. in black and white, 16 ills. in color, Jan., 1934

Tropical Toy Fishes: More Than 600 Varieties of Aquarium Pygmies Afford a Fascinating Field of Zoölogical Study in the Home. By Ida Mellen. Paintings by Hashime Murayama. LIX, pp. 287-317, 20 ills. in black and white, 8 ills. in color, Mar., 1931

Where Nature Runs Riot: On Australia's Great Barrier Reef Marine Animals Grow to Unusual Size, Develop Strange Weapons of Attack and Defense, and Acquire Brilliant Colors. By T. C. Roughley. LXXVII, pp. 823-850, 18 ills. in black and white, 15 ills. in color, map, June, 1940

MARINE BIOLOGY—*Continued*
A Wonderer Under Sea. By William Beebe. Paintings by E. Bostelmann. LXII, pp. 741-758, 13 ills. in black and white, 8 ills. in color, Dec., 1932

MARINE EROSION:
The Economic Aspects of Soil Erosion. (Part I). By Dr. N. S. Shaler. VII, pp. 328-338, Oct., 1896

MARINE Hydrographic Surveys of the Coasts of the World. By George W. Littlehales. XVI, pp. 63-67, maps, Feb., 1905

MARINE WORMS:
The Worm Turns. By Samuel Sandrof. LXXXIX, pp. 775-786, 14 ills., June, 1946

MARINES, U. S. *See* U. S. Marine Corps

MARKEN (Island), Netherlands:
Glimpses of Holland. By William Wisner Chapin. XXVII, pp. 1-29, 26 ills., Jan., 1915

MARKETS:
Down Mexico's Río Balsas. 9 color photos by John W. Webber, Kenneth Segerstrom, Jack Breed. XC, pp. 257-264, Aug., 1946
Haiti Goes to Market. 10 color photos by B. Anthony Stewart. LXXXVI, pp. 313-320, Sept., 1944
Kano (Nigeria), Mud-made City. 10 color photos by George W. Scott and K. S. Twitchell. LXXXV, pp. 545-552, May, 1944
Manipur—Where Japan Struck at India. 11 photos, map. LXXXV, pp. 743-750, June, 1944
A North Holland Cheese Market. By Hugh M. Smith. XXI, pp. 1051-1066, 17 ills., Dec., 1910
Oil Comes to Bahrein, Port of Pearls. 11 color photos by Maynard Owen Williams. LXXXIX, pp. 201-208, Feb., 1946
Syria and Lebanon Taste Freedom. By Maynard Owen Williams. With 21 color photos by author. XC, pp. 729-763, 16 ills. in black and white, Dec., 1946
To Market in Guatemala. By Luis Marden. With 19 color photos by Giles Greville Healey and Charles S. Pineo. LXXXVIII, pp. 87-104, July, 1945

MARKING the Alaskan Boundary. XIX, pp. 176-189, 16 ills., Mar., 1908

MARKING the Alaskan Boundary. By Thomas Riggs, Jr. XX, pp. 593-607, 17 ills., July, 1909

MARKWITH, CARL:
Farewell to Bikini. By Carl Markwith. XC, pp. 97-116, 16 ills., July, 1946

MARLATT, CHARLES LESTER:
Pests and Parasites: Why We Need a National Law to Prevent the Importation of Insect-Infested and Diseased Plants. By Charles Lester Marlatt. XXII, pp. 321-346, 29 ills., maps, Apr., 1911
Protecting the United States from Plant Pests. By Charles Lester Marlatt. XL, pp. 205-218, 16 ills., Aug., 1921

MARLIN (Fish):
Fighting Giants of the Humboldt. By David D. Duncan. LXXIX, pp. 373-400, 28 ills., map, Mar., 1941

MARLOWE, CHRISTOPHER:
A Tour in the English Fenland. By Christopher Marlowe. LV, pp. 605-634, 26 ills. in black and white, 16 ills. in color, map, May, 1929

MARMORA, Sea of:
The Gates to the Black Sea: The Dardanelles, the Bosphorus, and the Sea of Marmora. By Harry Griswold Dwight. XXVII, pp. 435-459, 27 ills., May, 1915

MARQUEEN ISLANDS. *See* Tauu Islands

MARQUESAS ISLANDS, South Pacific Ocean:
At Home on the Oceans: Whales and Sharks Make Exciting Neighbors for a Professor's Wife, Turned Able Seaman, On a Three-year Voyage Around the World. By Edith Bauer Strout. LXXVI, pp. 33-86, 54 ills., map, July, 1939
Diary of a Voyage from San Francisco to Tahiti and Return, 1901. By S. P. Langley. XII, pp. 413-429, 10 ills., maps, Dec., 1901
The Dream Ship: The Story of a Voyage of Adventure More Than Half Around the World in a 47-foot Lifeboat. By Ralph Stock. XXXIX, pp. 1-52, 43 ills., map, Jan., 1921
The Romance of Science in Polynesia: An Account of Five Years of Cruising Among the South Sea Islands. By Robert Cushman Murphy. Paintings by Hashime Murayama. XLVIII, pp. 355-426, 66 ills. in black and white, 16 ills. in color, 3 maps, Oct., 1925
A Vanishing People of the South Seas: The Tragic Fate of the Marquesan Cannibals, Noted for Their Warlike Courage and Physical Beauty. By John W. Church. XXXVI, pp. 275-306, 22 ills., map, Oct., 1919
See also Fatu-Hiva (Island)

MARQUEZ, LUIS:
A Mexican Land of Lakes and Lacquers (Pátzcuaro Region). 22 photos by Helene Fischer and Luis Marquez. LXXI, pp. 633-648, May, 1937

MARRAK POINT, Greenland:
Uncle Sam's Icebox Outposts. 19 color photos by John E. Schneider and Robert B. Sykes, Jr. XC, pp. 473-496, Oct., 1946

MARRAKECH, Morocco:
Americans on the Barbary Coast. By Willard Price. LXXXIV, pp. 1-31, 13 ills. in black and white, 10 ills. in color, map, July, 1943

MARRIAGE CUSTOMS:
Among the Hill Tribes of Burma—An Ethnological Thicket. By Sir George Scott. XLI, pp. 293-321, 22 ills., Mar., 1922
The Beauties of France. By Arthur Stanley Riggs. XXVIII, pp. 391-491, 73 ills. in black and white, 16 ills. in color, map, Nov., 1915
"The Flower of Paradise": The Part Which Khat Plays in the Life of the Yemen Arab. By Charles Moser. XXXII, pp. 173-186, 10 ills., map, Aug., 1917
In the Realms of the Maharajas. By Lawrence Copley Thaw and Margaret S. Thaw. LXXVIII, pp. 727-780, 14 ills. in black and white, 40 ills. in color, map, Dec., 1940

MARRIAGE CUSTOMS—*Continued*

A Journey in Morocco: "The Land of the Moors." By Thomas Lindsey Blayney. XXII, pp. 750-775, 23 ills., map, Aug., 1911

Pushing Back History's Horizon: How the Pick and Shovel Are Revealing Civilizations That Were Ancient When Israel Was Young. By Albert T. Clay. XXIX, pp. 162-216, 47 ills., map, Feb., 1916

Roumania and Its Rubicon. By John Oliver La Gorce. XXX, pp. 185-202, 11 ills., Sept., 1916

A Vanishing People of the South Seas: The Tragic Fate of the Marquesan Cannibals, Noted for Their Warlike Courage and Physical Beauty. By John W. Church. XXXVI, pp. 275-306, 22 ills., map, Oct., 1919

Village Life in the Holy Land. By John D. Whiting. XXV, pp. 249-314, 27 ills. in black and white, 21 ills. in color, Mar., 1914

The **MARRIAGE** of the Gods (Religious Festival, Madura, India). By John J. Banninga. XXIV, pp. 1314-1330, 16 ills., Dec., 1913

MARRINER, J. THEODORE:

Transylvania and Its Seven Castles: A Motor Circuit Through Rumania's New Province of Racial Complexity and Architectural Charm. By J. Theodore Marriner. XLIX, pp. 319-352, 35 ills., map, Mar., 1926

MARSEILLE (France), Battle Port of Centuries. By a Staff Correspondent. LXXXVI, pp. 425-448, 24 ills., map, Oct., 1944

MARSH, CODY:

Glimpses of Siberia, the Russian "Wild East." By Cody Marsh. XXXVIII, pp. 513-536, 26 ills., Dec., 1920

MARSH, O. C.:

Professor O. C. Marsh (Biography). (By W J M.). X, pp. 181-182, May, 1899

MARSHALL ISLANDS, Pacific Ocean:

American Pathfinders in the Pacific. By William H. Nicholas. LXXXIX, pp. 617-640, 17 ills., two-page map, May, 1946

Farewell to Bikini. By Carl Markwith. XC, pp. 97-116, 16 ills., July, 1946

Hidden Key to the Pacific: Piercing the Web of Secrecy Which Long Has Veiled Japanese Bases in the Mandated Islands. By Willard Price. LXXXI, pp. 759-785, 28 ills., map, June, 1942

Our New Military Wards, the Marshalls. By W. Robert Moore. LXXXVIII, pp. 325-360, 14 ills. in black and white, 20 ills. in color, map, Sept., 1945

Yap and Other Pacific Islands Under Japanese Mandate. By Junius B. Wood. XL, pp. 591-627, 34 ills., map supplement, Dec., 1921

MARSHALLESE Are Happy Again. 20 color photos by W. Robert Moore. LXXXVIII, pp. 337-360, Sept., 1945

MARSTON, JAY:

Uganda, "Land of Something New": Equatorial African Area Reveals Snow-crowned Peaks, Crater Lakes, Jungle-story Beasts, Human Giants, and Forest Pygmies. By Jay Marston. LXXI, pp. 109-130, 22 ills., map, Jan., 1937

MARSUPIALS:

Koala, or Australian Teddy Bear. By F. Lewis. LX, pp. 346-355, 13 ills., Sept., 1931

What the Fighting Yanks See. By Wanda Burnett. LXXXVI, pp. 451-476, 27 ills., Oct., 1944

MARTIN, CHARLES:

California: Ever Changing California, Land of Startling Contrasts. 30 color photos by Charles Martin. LV, pp. 705-744, June, 1929

Fish: The First Autochromes from the Ocean Bottom: Marine Life in Its Natural Habitat Along the Florida Keys Is Successfully Photographed in Colors. (Photographs by Dr. W. H. Longley and Charles Martin). LI, pp. 56-60, 8 ills. in color, Jan., 1927

Monticello, One of America's Most Historic Shrines. 3 color photos by Charles Martin. LV, pp. 489-496, Apr., 1929

Philippines. 48 photos, hand-tinted, by Dean C. Worcester and Charles Martin. XXIV, pp. 1161-1192, Nov., 1913

Puerto Rico: Colorful Porto Rico. 12 color photos by Charles Martin. XLVI, pp. 631-642, Dec., 1924

Sungmas (Oracles): Demon-Possessed Tibetans and Their Incredible Feats. 12 color photos: 3 by Charles Martin. LXVIII, pp. 479-486, Oct., 1935

United States: Exploring the Atlantic Seaboard with a Color Camera. 10 color photos by Charles Martin. XLIX, pp. 533-548, May, 1926

Virginia: Scenes and Shrines of the Cavalier Country. 7 color photos by Charles Martin. LV, pp. 425-432, Apr., 1929

Washington, D. C.: Our Colorful City of Magnificent Distances. 10 color photos by Charles Martin. LX, pp. 531-610, Nov., 1931

Washington, D. C.: Secrets of Washington's Lure. 3 color photos by Charles Martin. LVII, pp. 377-384, Mar., 1930

Washington, D. C.: Unique Gifts of Washington to the Nation. 5 color photos by Charles Martin. LV, pp. 473-480, Apr., 1929

Washington, D. C.: Winter Lights and Shadows in the Nation's Capital. 21 ills. in duotone: 3 by Charles Martin. LXVII, pp. 201-216, Feb., 1935

Washington (D. C.), the Pride of the Nation. 16 color photos by Charles Martin. XLIII, pp. 617-632, June, 1923

MARTIN, GEORGE C.:

The Recent Eruption of Katmai Volcano in Alaska. By George C. Martin. XXIV, pp. 131-181, 45 ills., diagr., map, Feb., 1913

MARTIN, LAWRENCE:

The National Geographic Society Researches in Alaska. By Lawrence Martin. XXII, pp. 537-561, 17 ills., 5 maps, June, 1911

The National Geographic Society's Alaskan Expedition of 1909. By Ralph S. Tarr and Lawrence Martin. XXI, pp. 1-54, 42 ills., 12 maps, Jan., 1910

MARTIN, W. A. P.:

The Causes That Led Up to the Siege of Pekin. By Dr. W. A. P. Martin. XII, pp. 53-63, ill., Feb., 1901

MARTIN, Mount, Alaska:
Our Greatest National Monument: The National Geographic Society Completes Its Explorations in the Valley of Ten Thousand Smokes. By Robert F. Griggs. XL, pp. 219-292, 73 ills. in black and white, 16 ills. in color, maps, Sept., 1921
The Valley of Ten Thousand Smokes: National Geographic Society Explorations in the Katmai District of Alaska. By Robert F. Griggs. XXXI, pp. 13-68, 51 ills., map, Jan., 1917

MARTINIQUE (Island), West Indies:
Chemical Discussion of Analyses of Volcanic Ejecta from Martinique and St. Vincent. By W. F. Hillebrand. XIII, pp. 296-299, July, 1902
Destruction of Pompeii as Interpreted by the Volcanic Eruptions of Martinique. By Angelo Heilprin. XV, p. 431, Oct., 1904
Lafcadio Hearn on the Island and People of Martinique. XIII, pp. 214-216, June, 1902
Magnetic Disturbance Caused by the Explosion of Mont Pelée. XIII, pp. 208-209, June, 1902
Martinique, Caribbean Question Mark. By Edward T. Folliard. LXXIX, pp. 47-55, 9 ills., Jan., 1941
The National Geographic Society Expedition in the West Indies. XIII, pp. 209-213, maps, June, 1902
The National Geographic Society Expedition to Martinique and St. Vincent. XIII, pp. 183-184, ills., June, 1902
The New Cone of Mont Pelée. XIV, pp. 422-423, ills., Nov., 1903
The Recent Volcanic Eruptions in the West Indies. By Israel C. Russell. XIII, pp. 267-285, 7 ills., map, July, 1902
Report by Robert T. Hill on the Volcanic Disturbances in the West Indies. XIII, pp. 223-267, 12 ills., 3 maps, July, 1902
Reports of Vessels as to the Range of Volcanic Dust. By James Page. XIII, pp. 299-301, July, 1902
The Shattered Obelisk of Mont Pelée. By Prof. Angelo Heilprin. XVII, pp. 465-474, 5 ills., Aug., 1906
Southward Ho! In the "Alice." By Henry Howard. LXXIII, pp. 265-312, 38 ills. in black and white, 13 ills. in color, maps, Mar., 1938
Volcanic Eruptions on Martinique and St. Vincent. By Israel C. Russell. XIII, pp. 415-436, 10 ills., Dec., 1902
Volcanic Rocks of Martinique and St. Vincent: Collected by Robert T. Hill and Israel C. Russell. By J. S. Diller. XIII, pp. 285-296, July, 1902

MARTINSBURG, West Virginia:
Potomac, River of Destiny. By Albert W. Atwood. LXXXVIII, pp. 33-70, 15 ills. in black and white, 18 ills. in color, map, July, 1945

The **MARVELOUS** Prosperity of the South. XVIII, p. 685, Oct., 1907

MARVELS of Fern Life. 16 ills. in color from paintings by E. J. Geske. XLVII, pp. 547-562, May, 1925

MARVELS of Metamorphosis: A Scientific "G-man" Pursues Rare Trapdoor Spider Parasites for Three Years With a Spade and a Candid Camera. By George Elwood Jenks. LXXIV, pp. 807-828, 39 ills., Dec., 1938

MARVELS of Mycetozoa: Exploration of a Long Island Swamp Reveals Some of the Secrets of the Slime Molds, Dwelling on the Borderland Between the Plant and Animal Kingdoms. By William Crowder. Paintings by author. XLIX, pp. 421-443, 5 ills. in black and white, 16 ills. in color, Apr., 1926

MARVIN, C. F.:
The Record of the Great Earthquake Written in Washington by the Seismograph of the U. S. Weather Bureau. By C. F. Marvin. XVII, pp. 296-298, May, 1906

MARYLAND:
Approaching Washington by Tidewater Potomac. By Paul Wilstach. LVII, pp. 372-392, 7 ills. in black and white, 15 ills. in color, Mar., 1930
Chesapeake Odyssey: An 18-foot Sailboat Follows the Course of Captain John Smith around This Spacious Bay of History, Commerce, Sea Food, and Nautical Lore. By John Maloney. LXXVI, pp. 357-392, 32 ills., map, Sept., 1939
Colossal Work in Baltimore. By Calvin W. Hendrick. XX, pp. 365-373, 6 ills., Apr., 1909
The Geologist at Blue Mountain, Maryland. By Charles D. Walcott. V, pp. 84-88, July 10, 1893
A Maryland Pilgrimage: Visits to Hallowed Shrines Recall the Major Rôle Played by This Prosperous State in the Development of Popular Government in America. By Gilbert Grosvenor. LI, pp. 133-212, 88 ills., map supplement, Feb., 1927
Maryland Presents—. By W. Robert Moore. LXXIX, pp. 401-448, 17 ills. in black and white, 32 ills. in color, map, Apr., 1941
Potomac, River of Destiny. By Albert W. Atwood. LXXXVIII, pp. 33-70, 15 ills. in black and white, 18 ills. in color, map, July, 1945
Roads from Washington. By John Patric. LXXIV, pp. 1-56, 27 ills. in black and white, 30 ills. in color, map supplement, July, 1938
The Society's Map of Historic and Scenic Reaches of the Nation's Capital. Text with map supplement. LXXIV, pp. 57-58, July, 1938
The Travels of George Washington: Dramatic Episodes in His Career as the First Geographer of the United States. By William Joseph Showalter. LXI, pp. 1-63, 50 ills., 4 maps, map supplement, Jan., 1932
Wartime Washington. By William H. Nicholas. LXXXIV, pp. 257-290, 12 ills. in black and white, 16 ills. in color, Sept., 1943
See also Annapolis; Cabin John; Solomons Island

MASAI (Tribespeople):
Where Roosevelt Will Hunt. By Sir Harry Johnston. XX, pp. 207-256, 43 ills., map supplement, Mar., 1909
Wild Man and Wild Beast in Africa. By Theodore Roosevelt. XXII, pp. 1-33, 41 ills., map, Jan., 1911

MASKS:
Merry Maskers of Imst (Austria). 14 photos by Francis C. Fuerst. LXX, pp. 201-208, Aug., 1936

MASON, J. ALDEN:
Preserving Ancient America's Finest Sculptures (Guatemala). By J. Alden Mason. Paintings by H. M. Herget. LXVIII, pp. 537-570, 24 ills. in black and white, 10 ills. in color, Nov., 1935

MASSACHUSETTS:
The Cape Cod Canal. By Commodore J. W. Miller. XXVI, pp. 185-190, 3 ills., map, Aug., 1914
Cape Cod People and Places. By Wanda Burnett. LXXXIX, pp. 737-774, 17 ills. in black and white, 24 ills. in color, map, June, 1946
Coasting Through the Bay State. 12 color photos by Clifton Adams. LX, pp. 287-294, Sept., 1931
Collarin' Cape Cod: Experiences on Board a U. S. Navy Destroyer in a Wild Winter Storm. By Lieutenant H. R. Thurber. XLVIII, pp. 427-472, 46 ills., Oct., 1925
The Long River of New England: In War and Peace, from Mountain Wilderness to the Sea, Flows the Connecticut River, Through a Valley Abounding in History, Scenery, Inventive Genius, and Industry. By Albert W. Atwood. LXXXIII, pp. 401-434, 12 ills. in black and white, 24 ills. in color, map, Apr., 1943
Massachusetts—Beehive of Business. By William Joseph Showalter. XXXVII, pp. 203-245, 41 ills., Mar., 1920
Massachusetts and Its Position in the Life of the Nation. By Calvin Coolidge. XLIII, pp. 337-352, 9 ills., Apr., 1923
Northeast of Boston. By Albert W. Atwood. LXXXVIII, pp. 257-292, 12 ills. in black and white, 17 ills. in color, map supplement, Sept., 1945
Sauntering Through the Land of Roger Williams. 5 color photos by Clifton Adams. LX, pp. 311-318, Sept., 1931
The Survey and Map of Massachusetts. By Henry Gannett. I, pp. 78-86, Oct., 1888
Winter Rambles in Thoreau's Country. By Herbert W. Gleason. XXXVII, pp. 165-180, 15 ills., Feb., 1920
See also Boston; Nantucket (Island)

MASTERS of Flight (Birds). 8 ills. XXXVI, pp. 49-56, July, 1919

MATHER, STEPHEN T.:
Awarded Jane M. Smith Life Membership. XXXVII, p. 342, Apr., 1920
See also NGS: Board of Trustees

MATMATA, Tunisia:
The Mole Men: An Account of the Troglodytes of Southern Tunisia. By Frank Edward Johnson. XXII, pp. 787-846, 60 ills., Sept., 1911

MATSANG TSANGPO (River), Tibet:
The Tsangpo. By James Mascarene Hubbard. XII, pp. 32-35, Jan., 1901

MATSON, G. E.:
Multicolored Cones of Cappadocia. 20 color photos by Eric Matson. LXXVI, pp. 769-800, Dec., 1939
The Rose-Red City of Rock (Petra, Trans-Jordan). 21 color photos by G. E. Matson. LXVII, pp. 145-160, Feb., 1935

MATTERHORN (Peak), Alps:
The Majesty of the Matterhorn. XXIII, text p. 514; pictorial supplement, May, 1912
Manless Alpine Climbing: The First Woman to Scale the Grépon, the Matterhorn, and Other Famous Peaks Without Masculine Support Relates Her Adventures. By Miriam O'Brien Underhill. LXVI, pp. 131-170, 30 ills. in black and white, 12 ills. in color, Aug., 1934
A Woman's Climbs in the High Alps. By Dora Keen. XXII, pp. 643-675, 26 ills., July, 1911

MATTHES, GERARD H.:
The Dikes of Holland. By Gerard H. Matthes. XII, pp. 219-234, 3 ills., 7 charts, June, 1901

MATTO GROSSO (State), Brazil:
Through Paraguay and Southern Matto Grosso. By Sir Christopher H. Gibson. LXXXIV, pp. 459-488, 20 ills. in black and white, 11 ills. in color, map, Oct., 1943

MAUGHAM, R. C. F.:
Hunting Big Game in Portuguese East Africa. (By R. C. F. Maugham). XVIII, pp. 723-730, 7 ills., Nov., 1907

MAUNSELL, F. R.:
One Thousand Miles of Railway Built for Pilgrims and Not for Dividends (Damascus to Mecca). By Colonel F. R. Maunsell. XX, pp. 156-172, 12 ills., map, Feb., 1909

MAURY, MATTHEW FONTAINE:
The Gem of the Ocean: Our American Navy. By Josephus Daniels. XXXIII, pp. 313-335, 35 ills., Apr., 1918

MAXEY, ROBERT F.:
Pine-Scented, Harbor-Dented Maine. 39 color photos by B. Anthony Stewart and Robert F. Maxey. LXVII, pp. 549-588, May, 1935

MAXON, WILLIAM R.:
Ferns as a Hobby. By William R. Maxon. Paintings by E. J. Geske. XLVII, pp. 541-586, 29 ills. in black and white, 16 ills. in color, May, 1925

MAYAS (Indians):
Chichen Itzá, an Ancient American Mecca: Recent Excavations in Yucatan Are Bringing to Light the Temples, Palaces, and Pyramids of America's Most Holy Native City. By Sylvanus Griswold Morley. XLVII, pp. 63-95, 34 ills., diagr., map, Jan., 1925
Discovering the New World's Oldest Dated Work of Man: A Maya Monument Inscribed 291 B. C. is Unearthed Near a Huge Stone Head by a Geographic-Smithsonian Expedition in Mexico. By Matthew W. Stirling. LXXVI, pp. 183-218, 40 ills., map, Aug., 1939
Excavations at Quirigua, Guatemala. By Sylvanus Griswold Morley. XXIV, pp. 339-361, 24 ills., diagr., Mar., 1913
Note. XXIV, p. 1056, Sept., 1913

MAYAS (Indians)—*Continued*

Finding Jewels of Jade in a Mexican Swamp (Palenque Ruins). By Matthew W. and Marion Stirling. LXXXII, pp. 635-661, 15 ills. in black and white, 12 ills. in color, map, Nov., 1942

The Foremost Intellectual Achievement of Ancient America: The Hieroglyphic Inscriptions on the Monuments in the Ruined Cities of Mexico, Guatemala, and Honduras Are Yielding the Secrets of the Maya Civilization. By Sylvanus Griswold Morley. XLI, pp. 109-130, 27 ills., 17 diagrs., map supplement, Feb., 1922

The Home of a Forgotten Race: Mysterious Chichen Itza, in Yucatan, Mexico. By Edward H. Thompson. XXV, pp. 585-648, 59 ills., June, 1914

Mysterious Temples of the Jungle: The Prehistoric Ruins of Guatemala. By W. F. Sands. XXIV, pp. 325-338, 10 ills., Mar., 1913

Preserving Ancient America's Finest Sculptures (Guatemala). By J. Alden Mason. Paintings by H. M. Herget. LXVIII, pp. 537-570, 24 ills. in black and white, 10 ills. in color, Nov., 1935

To Market in Guatemala. By Luis Marden. With 19 color photos by Giles Greville Healey and Charles S. Pineo. LXXXVIII, pp. 87-104, July, 1945

Unearthing America's Ancient History: Investigation Suggests That the Maya May Have Designed the First Astronomical Observatory in the New World in Order to Cultivate Corn. By Sylvanus Griswold Morley. LX, pp. 99-126, 28 ills., July, 1931

Yucatán, Home of the Gifted Maya: Two Thousand Years of History Reach Back to Early American Temple Builders, Corn Cultivators, and Pioneers in Mathematics. By Sylvanus Griswold Morley. Paintings by H. M. Herget. LXX, pp. 591-644, 28 ills. in black and white, 35 ills. in color, map, Nov., 1936

MAYER, ALFRED GOLDSBOROUGH:

Our Neglected Southern Coast. By Alfred Goldsborough Mayer. XIX, pp. 859-871, 10 ills., Dec., 1908

MAYER, ARTHUR ELLIS:

Gems of the Italian Lakes. By Arthur Ellis Mayer. XXIV, pp. 943-956, 13 ills., Aug., 1913

MAYFLOWER. *See* Arbutus

MAYNARD, CLARENCE F.:

The Valley of Ten Thousand Smokes: An Account of the Discovery and Exploration of the Most Wonderful Volcanic Region in the World. By Robert F. Griggs. XXXIII, pp. 115-169, 46 ills., map, panorama, Feb., 1918

MAYTIME in the Heart of Maryland (Sherwood Gardens). 10 color photos by B. Anthony Stewart and Charles Martin. LXXIX, pp. 441-448, Apr., 1941

MAZAMAS (Association of Mountain Climbers):

The Altitude of Mount Adams, Washington. By Edgar McClure. VII, pp. 151-153, tables, Apr., 1896

The Mazamas. (By J. S. Diller). VIII, pp. 58-59, Feb., 1897

MAZATLAN, Mexico:

Adventuring Down the West Coast of Mexico. By Herbert Corey. XLII, pp. 449-503, 44 ills., map, Nov., 1922

M'CHOPIS (Tribespeople):

Impressions and Scenes of Mozambique. By O. W. Barrett. XXI, pp. 807-830, 31 ills., Oct., 1910

MEAD, EDWIN D.:

The Expansion of England. By Edwin D. Mead. XI, pp. 249-263, July, 1900

MEADE, R. W.:

Admiral R. W. Meade, U. S. N. (Obituary). (By J. H.). VIII, p. 142, May, 1897

Portrait. VIII, pl. 27 (front.), May, 1897

A Winter Voyage Through the Straits of Magellan. By the late Admiral R. W. Meade, U. S. N. VIII, pp. 129-141, ill., map, May, 1897

MEALY BUGS:

An Insect Community Lives in Flower Heads. By James G. Needham. XC, pp. 340-356, 5 ills. in black and white, 11 ills. in color, Sept., 1946

MEANS, PHILIP AINSWORTH:

The Incas: Empire Builders of the Andes. By Philip Ainsworth Means. Paintings by H. M. Herget. LXXIII, pp. 225-264, 26 ills. in black and white, 10 ills. in color, Feb., 1938

MEASURING the Sun's Heat and Forecasting the Weather: The National Geographic Society to Maintain a Solar Station in a Remote Part of the World to Coöperate with Smithsonian Institution Stations in California and Chile. By C. G. Abbot. XLIX, pp. 111-126, 15 ills., chart, Jan., 1926

MEAT INDUSTRY:

Farmers Keep Them Eating. By Frederick Simpich. LXXXIII, pp. 435-458, 22 ills., Apr., 1943

Nebraska, the Cornhusker State. By Leo A. Borah. LXXXVII, pp. 513-542, 6 ills. in black and white, 23 ills. in color, map, May, 1945

Revolution in Eating: Machine Food Age—Born of Roads, Research, and Refrigeration—Makes the United States the Best-fed Nation in History. By J. R. Hildebrand. LXXXI, pp. 273-324, 33 ills. in black and white, 25 ills. in color, Mar., 1942

MECCA, Saudi Arabia:

Damascus and Mecca Railway. XII, p. 408, Nov., 1901

Mecca the Mystic: A New Kingdom Within Arabia (Hejaz). By S. M. Zwemer. XXXII, pp. 157-172, 13 ills., Aug., 1917

One Thousand Miles of Railway Built for Pilgrims and Not for Dividends (Damascus to Mecca). By Colonel F. R. Maunsell. XX, pp. 156-172, 12 ills., map, Feb., 1909

Pilgrims' Progress to Mecca. 22 ills. in duotone: 18 by Oscar Marcus. LXXII, pp. 627-642, Nov., 1937

MECHANICS, Airplane:

They Sustain the Wings. By Frederick Simpich. LXXXIV, pp. 333-354, 19 ills., Sept., 1943

MEDALS:

American Decorations and Insignia of Honor and Service. By Col. Robert E. Wyllie. XXXVI, pp. 502-526, 6 ills. in black and white, 119 ills. in color, Dec., 1919

Decorations, Medals, Service Ribbons, Badges, and Women's Insignia. LXXXIV, pp. 414-444, 6 ills. in black and white, 376 ills. in color, Oct., 1943

The Heraldry of Heroism. By Arthur E. Du Bois. LXXXIV, pp. 409-413, ills., map, Oct., 1943

The Romance of Military Insignia: How the United States Government Recognizes Deeds of Heroism and Devotion to Duty. By Col. Robert E. Wyllie. XXXVI, pp. 463-501, 27 ills., Dec., 1919

See also NGS: Medals

MEDAN, Sumatra:

By Motor Through the East Coast and Batak Highlands of Sumatra. By Melvin A. Hall. XXXVII, pp. 69-102, 27 ills., Jan., 1920

MÉDENINE, Tunisia:

The Mole Men: An Account of the Troglodytes of Southern Tunisia. By Frank Edward Johnson. XXII, pp. 787-846, 60 ills., Sept., 1911

MEDICINE AND HEALTH:

Ali Goes to the Clinic. By Herndon and Mary Hudson. XC, pp. 764-766, ills., Dec., 1946

Flying Our Wounded Veterans Home. By Catherine Bell Palmer. LXXXVIII, pp. 363-384, 17 ills., Sept., 1945

The Geography of Medicines: War's Effect Upon the World's Sources of Supply. By John Foote. XXXII, pp. 213-238, 26 ills., Sept., 1917

The Healing Arts in Global War: As Weapons Grow Deadlier, Scientific Medicine Pits Its Ever-rising Skill Against Them. By Albert W. Atwood. LXXXIV, pp. 599-618, 17 ills., Nov., 1943

Life Story of the Mosquito. By Graham Fairchild. With 10 ills. in color from paintings. LXXXV, pp. 180-195, 5 ills. in black and white, drawing, Feb., 1944

Map-Changing Medicine. By William Joseph Showalter. XLII, pp. 303-330, 26 ills., Sept., 1922

Medicine Fakes and Fakers of All Ages: Strange Stories of Nostrums and Kingly Quacks in Every Era and Clime. By John Foote. XXXV, pp. 67-84, 14 ills., Jan., 1919

New Frontier in the Sky. By F. Barrows Colton. XC, pp. 379-408, 28 ills., diagr., Sept., 1946

1940 Paradox in Hong Kong. By Frederick Simpich. LXXVII, pp. 531-558, 24 ills., 3 maps, Apr., 1940

Redeeming the Tropics. By William Joseph Showalter. XXV, pp. 344-364, 13 ills., Mar., 1914

Saboteur Mosquitoes. By Harry H. Stage. LXXXV, pp. 165-179, 12 ills., Feb., 1944

Your New World of Tomorrow. By F. Barrows Colton. LXXXVIII, pp. 385-410, 25 ills., Oct., 1945

See also Chaulmoogra Oil; Diseases; Sanitation

MEDIEVAL Glory Haunts the Eastern Adriatic. 17 color photos by Hans Hildenbrand. LIII, pp. 65-80, Jan., 1928

MEDIEVAL Pageantry in Modern Nördlingen (Germany). 12 color photos by Hans Hildenbrand. LIV, pp. 707-714, Dec., 1928

MEDIEVAL Tales of the Lop Basin in Central Asia. By Ellsworth Huntington. XIX, pp. 289-295, 9 ills., Apr., 1908

MEDITERRANEAN REGIONS:

From Africa to the Alps. 8 ills. in color from U. S. Army Air Forces official photos. LXXXIX, pp. 161-168, Feb., 1946

The Geographic's New Map of Europe and the Mediterranean. By Gilbert Grosvenor. Text with map supplement. LXXIII, pp. 525-528, ill., Apr., 1938

Map of Mediterranean Regions. Announcement of map supplement. XXIII, p. 104, Jan., 1912

Mediterranean Checkerboard. By Frederick Simpich. LXXXI, pp. 527-550, 20 ills., map, Apr., 1942

The Society's New Map of Central Europe and the Mediterranean. Text with map supplement. LXXVI, pp. 559-560, Oct., 1939

See also Balearic Islands; Corsica; Crete; Cyprus; Malta; Sardinia; Sicily; *and* names of countries

MEETINGS. *See* names of international and Pan American conferences; NGS: Meetings; Peace Conference

MEGASPELÆON, the Oldest Monastery in Greece. By Carroll Storrs Alden. XXIV, pp. 310-323, 11 ills., Mar., 1913

MEIGS, MONTGOMERY C.:

The Washington Aqueduct and Cabin John Bridge. By D. D. Gaillard. VIII, pp. 337-344, ills., Dec., 1897

MEKONG (River), Asia:

Through the Great River Trenches of Asia: National Geographic Society Explorer Follows the Yangtze, Mekong, and Salwin Through Mighty Gorges, Some of Whose Canyon Walls Tower to a Height of More Than Two Miles. By Joseph F. Rock. L, pp. 133-186, 47 ills., map, Aug., 1926

MELANESIA:

In the Savage South Seas. By Beatrice Grimshaw. XIX, pp. 1-19, 21 ills., Jan., 1908

The Islands of the Pacific. By J. P. Thomson. XL, pp. 543-558, 15 ills., map supplement, Dec., 1921

North About. By Alan J. Villiers. LXXI, pp. 221-250, 24 ills., Feb., 1937

Treasure Islands of Australasia: New Guinea, New Caledonia, and Fiji Trace across the South Pacific a Fertile Crescent Incredibly Rich in Minerals and Foods. By Douglas L. Oliver. LXXXI, pp. 691-722, 23 ills., two-page map, June, 1942

See also Bougainville; Fiji Islands; Munda; New Caledonia; New Guinea; New Hebrides; Solomon Islands

MELBOURNE, Australia:

Capital Cities of Australia. By W. Robert Moore. LXVIII, pp. 667-722, 32 ills. in black and white, 24 ills. in color, two-page map, Dec., 1935

Lonely Australia: The Unique Continent. By Herbert E. Gregory. XXX, pp. 473-568, 68 ills., 5 maps (1 two-page), Dec., 1916

MELGAREIO, A.:
The Greatest Volcanoes of Mexico. By A. Melgareio. XXI, pp. 741-760, 22 ills., Sept., 1910

MELLEN, IDA:
Tropical Toy Fishes: More Than 600 Varieties of Aquarium Pygmies Afford a Fascinating Field of Zoölogical Study in the Home. By Ida Mellen. Paintings by Hashime Murayama. LIX, pp. 287-317, 20 ills. in black and white, 8 ills. in color, Mar., 1931

MELLOR, F. H.:
The Isle of Man. By Captain F. H. Mellor. LXXI, pp. 587-608, 13 ills. in black and white, 12 ills. in color, map, May, 1937

MELVILLE, GEORGE W.:
Geographic Literature. VII, p. 212, June, 1896
George W. Melville, Engineer-in-chief, U. S. N. (By A. W. G.). VIII, pp. 187-190, ill., June, 1897
Portrait. VIII, pl. 28 (front.), June, 1897
See also NGS: Vice-President

A **MEMORIAL** to Peary: The National Geographic Society Dedicates Monument in Arlington National Cemetery to Discoverer of the North Pole. XLI, pp. 639-646, 4 ills., June, 1922

MEMORIALS:
Our National War Memorials in Europe. By John J. Pershing. LXV, pp. 1-36, 24 ills. in black and white, 11 ills. in color, map, Jan., 1934
See also Cemeteries; NGS: Memorials

MEN Against the Rivers (Mississippi and Ohio). By Frederick Simpich. LXXI, pp. 767-794, 22 ills., maps, June, 1937

MEN and Gold. By Frederick Simpich. LXIII, pp. 481-518, 33 ills. in black and white, 11 ills. in duotone, Apr., 1933

MEN-BIRDS Soar on Boiling Air (Sailplanes). By Frederick G. Vosburgh. LXXIV, pp. 123-140, 15 ills., July, 1938

MEN of the Eagle in Their Mountain Eyrie (Albania). 39 color photos by Luigi Pellerano. LIX, pp. 143-190, Feb., 1931

MENDAÑA, ALVARO DE:
Revealing Earth's Mightiest Ocean (Pacific). By Albert W. Atwood. LXXXIV, pp. 291-306, 10 ills., map supplement, Sept., 1943

MENDENHALL, T. C.:
The Alaskan Boundary Survey. I—Introduction. By Dr. T. C. Mendenhall. IV, pp. 177-180, Feb. 8, 1893
A Brief Account of the Geographic Work of the U. S. Coast and Geodetic Survey. By T. C. Mendenhall and Otto H. Tittmann. VIII, pp. 294-299, Oct., 1897
The Geographical Position and Height of Mount Saint Elias. By Dr. T. C. Mendenhall. V, pp. 63-67, diagr., tables, July 10, 1893
See also NGS: Board of Managers; Vice-President

MENDENHALL, WALTER C.:
The Colorado Desert. By W. C. Mendenhall. XX, pp. 681-701, 16 ills., Aug., 1909
The Wrangell Mountains, Alaska. By Walter C. Mendenhall. XIV, pp. 395-407, 3 ills., panorama, Nov., 1903
The Wrangell Mountains. Panorama taken by author from ridge east of the Dadina River

MENDING Dikes in the Netherlands. 20 photos by Lawrence Earl. XC, pp. 791-806, Dec., 1946

MENGO, Uganda:
Where Roosevelt Will Hunt. By Sir Harry Johnston. XX, pp. 207-256, 43 ills., map supplement, Mar., 1909

MENOMINEE (Indian Tribe):
America's First Settlers, the Indians. By Matthew W. Stirling. Paintings by W. Langdon Kihn. LXXII, pp. 535-596, 34 ills. in black and white, 24 ills. in color, Nov., 1937

MENZEL, DONALD H.:
The Heavens Above: On Land, Sea, and in the Air the Stars Serve Modern Man as Map, Compass, and Clock. By Donald H. Menzel. With 12 charts, designed by author, showing star positions for each month, and 13 drawings of the constellations by Carlotta Gonzales Lahey. LXXXIV, pp. 97-128, map, July, 1943
Note: How to Use the Star Charts. Text with 12 star charts designed by author, pp. 116-128

MERRIAM, C. HART:
The Acorn, a Possibly Neglected Source of Food. By C. Hart Merriam. XXXIV, pp. 129-137, 8 ills., Aug., 1918
Director of newly-formed U. S. Division of Biological Survey. VII, p. 405, Dec., 1896
Laws of Temperature Control of the Geographic Distribution of Terrestrial Animals and Plants. Annual Address by Vice-President, Dr. C. Hart Merriam. VI, pp. 229-238, table, 3 maps, Dec. 29, 1894
Report—Geography of Life. By C. Hart Merriam. I, pp. 160-162, Apr., 1889
See also NGS: Board of Managers; Vice-President

MERRILL, FULLERTON:
A Hunting Trip to Northern Greenland. By Fullerton Merrill. XI, pp. 118-122, Mar., 1900

MERRITT, Lake, Oakland, California:
Wild Ducks as Winter Guests in a City Park. By Joseph Dixon. XXXVI, pp. 331-342, 11 ills., Oct., 1919

MERRY Maskers of Imst (Austria). 14 photos by Francis C. Fuerst. LXX, pp. 201-208, Aug., 1936

MESA VERDE (Colorado). By F. H. Newell. IX, pp. 431-434, Oct., 1898

MESA VERDE NATIONAL PARK, Colorado:
Our National Parks. By L. F. Schmeckebier. XXIII, pp. 531-579, 41 ills., map, June, 1912

MESHED, Iran:

Gilded Domes Against an Azure Sky. 13 color photos by Stephen H. Nyman. LXXVI, pp. 339-346, Sept., 1939

MESOPOTAMIA:

The Effects of Geographic Environment in the Development of Civilization in Primitive Man. By Hon. Gardiner G. Hubbard. VIII, pp. 161-176, June, 1897

Geographic Progress of Civilization. Annual Address by the President, Honorable Gardiner G. Hubbard. VI, pp. 1-22, Feb. 14, 1894

Pushing Back History's Horizon: How the Pick and Shovel Are Revealing Civilizations That Were Ancient When Israel Was Young. By Albert T. Clay. XXIX, pp. 162-216, 47 ills., map, Feb., 1916

See also Iraq

MESSERIAS (Tribespeople):

Two Fighting Tribes of the Sudan. By Merian C. Cooper. Photos by Ernest B. Schoedsack. LVI, pp. 465-486, 27 ills., map, Oct., 1929

MESSINA, Sicily:

The World's Most Cruel Earthquake. By Charles W. Wright. XX, pp. 373-396, 22 ills., maps, Apr., 1909

METAL Sinews of Strength: This Is a War of Many Metals, for We Live in an Age of Alloys. By Frederick G. Vosburgh. LXXXI, pp. 457-491, 35 ills., Apr., 1942

METALS:

Metal Sinews of Strength: This Is a War of Many Metals, for We Live in an Age of Alloys. By Frederick G. Vosburgh. LXXXI, pp. 457-491, 35 ills., Apr., 1942

Mineral Production in the United States. VII, p. 250, July, 1896; p. 310, Sept., 1896. VIII, pp. 201-202, July-Aug., 1897

See also Gold and Gold Mining; Platinum; Radium; Silver and Silver Mining; Tin

METAMORPHOSIS:

Marvels of Metamorphosis: A Scientific "G-man" Pursues Rare Trapdoor Spider Parasites for Three Years With a Spade and a Candid Camera. By George Elwood Jenks. LXXIV, pp. 807-828, 39 ills., Dec., 1938

METEORITES:

The Mysterious Tomb of a Giant Meteorite (Meteor Crater, Arizona). By William D. Boutwell. LIII, pp. 721-730, 10 ills., June, 1928

METEOROLOGICAL Observations (Muir Glacier, Alaska). By Harry Fielding Reid. IV, pp. 80-81, tables, Mar. 21, 1892

The **METEOROLOGICAL** Observations of the Second Wellman Expedition. By Evelyn B. Baldwin. X, pp. 512-516, Dec., 1899

METEOROLOGY:

Americans Stand Guard in Greenland. By Andrew H. Brown. XC, pp. 457-500, 23 ills. in black and white, 19 ills. in color, map, Oct., 1946

Climatic Conditions of Alaska. By General A. W. Greely. IX, pp. 132-137, Apr., 1898

METEOROLOGY—*Continued*

Forecasting the Weather. (By Alfred J. Henry). XV, pp. 285-292, 6 ills., chart, July, 1904

Forecasting the Weather and Storms. By Professor Willis L. Moore. XVI, pp. 255-305, 5 ills., 20 charts, June, 1905

Geography of the Air. Annual Report by Vice-President A. W. Greely. III, pp. 41-52, May 1, 1891

Geography of the Air. Annual Report by Vice-President, General A. W. Greely. IV, pp. 85-100, Mar. 18, 1892

The Great Storm of March 11-14, 1888. By Brigadier-General A. W. Greely. I, pp. 37-39, Oct., 1888

The Great Storm Off the Atlantic Coast of the United States, March 11th-14th, 1888. By Everett Hayden. I, pp. 40-58, 6 charts, Oct., 1888

Hurricanes on the Coast of Texas. By General A. W. Greely. XI, pp. 442-445, Nov., 1900

Ice Caves and Frozen Wells. (By W J McGee). XII, pp. 433-434, Dec., 1901

The International Cloud Work of the Weather Bureau. By Frank H. Bigelow. X, pp. 351-354, Sept., 1899

Kite Work of the Weather Bureau. By H. C. Frankenfield. XI, pp. 55-62, Feb., 1900

The Law of Storms, Considered with Special Reference to the North Atlantic. By Everett Hayden. II, pp. 199-211, ill., 3 diagrs., 3 foldout diagrs., foldout charts, July, 1890

Loss of Life by Lightning. XIII, p. 115, Mar., 1902

Loss of Property from Lightning. XII, p. 82, Feb., 1901

The Magic Beauty of Snow and Dew. By Wilson A. Bentley. XLIII, pp. 103-112, 9 ills., Jan., 1923

The Manila Observatory. By Rev. Father José Algué. XI, pp. 427-438, ills., Nov., 1900

Measuring the Sun's Heat and Forecasting the Weather: The National Geographic Society to Maintain a Solar Station in a Remote Part of the World to Coöperate with Smithsonian Institution Stations in California and Chile. By C. G. Abbot. XLIX, pp. 111-126, 15 ills., chart, Jan., 1926

Men-Birds Soar on Boiling Air. By Frederick G. Vosburgh. LXXIV, pp. 123-140, 15 ills., July, 1938

Meteorological Observations (Muir Glacier, Alaska). By Harry Fielding Reid. IV, pp. 80-81, tables, Mar. 21, 1892

The Meteorological Observations of the Second Wellman Expedition. By Evelyn B. Baldwin. X, pp. 512-516, Dec., 1899

Meteorology in the Philippines. X, pp. 271-272, July, 1899

The Mystery of Auroras: National Geographic Society and Cornell University Study Spectacular Displays in the Heavens. LXXV, pp. 689-690, May, 1939

New Frontier in the Sky. By F. Barrows Colton. XC, pp. 379-408, 28 ills., diagr., Sept., 1946

Our Heralds of Storm and Flood. By Gilbert H. Grosvenor. XVIII, pp. 586-601, 15 ills., chart, Sept., 1907

METEOROLOGY—*Continued*

The Philippine Weather Service. XV, pp. 77-78, Feb., 1904

The Prevention of Hailstorms by the Use of Cannon. XI, pp. 239-241, June, 1900

Project for the Exploration of the Atmosphere Over the Tropical Oceans. By A. Lawrence Rotch. XV, p. 430, Oct., 1904

Proposed Meteorological Station in Iceland. X, p. 228, June, 1899

Relations of Air and Water to Temperature and Life. By Honorable Gardiner G. Hubbard. V, pp. 112-124, Jan. 31, 1894

Report—Geography of the Air. By A. W. Greely. I, pp. 151-159, Apr., 1889

Report—Geography of the Air. By Gen. A. W. Greely. II, pp. 49-63, Apr., 1890

Salton Sea and the Rainfall of the Southwest. By Alfred J. Henry. XVIII, pp. 244-248, Apr., 1907

Scientific Work of Mount Weather Meteorological Observatory. By Professor Frank H. Bigelow. XV, pp. 442-445, Nov., 1904

Snow Crystals. (By Wilson A. Bentley). XV, pp. 30-37, 31 ills., Jan., 1904

The Storm of February 25-28, 1902. (By Alfred J. Henry). XIII, pp. 110-112, chart, Mar., 1902

Storms and Weather Forecasts. By Professor Willis L. Moore. VIII, pp. 65-82, 25 charts, Mar., 1897

Studies on the Rate of Evaporation at Reno, Nevada, and in the Salton Sink. By Professor Frank H. Bigelow. XIX, pp. 20-28, 5 ills., Jan., 1908

Toilers of the Sky: Tenuous Clouds Perform the Mighty Task of Shaping the Earth and Sustaining Terrestrial Life. By McFall Kerbey. XLVIII, pp. 163-189, 33 ills., Aug., 1925

United States Daily Atmospheric Survey. By Prof. Willis L. Moore. VIII, pp. 299-303, Oct., 1897

U. S. Weather Bureau. XIII, pp. 71-72, Feb., 1902

The U. S. Weather Bureau. By James Wilson. XV, pp. 37-39, Jan., 1904

The U. S. Weather Bureau at the Paris Exposition. XII, pp. 81-82, Feb., 1901

Variations in Lake Levels and Atmospheric Precipitation. By Alfred J. Henry. X, pp. 403-406, diagr., Oct., 1899

The Weather Bureau. By Willis L. Moore. XII, pp. 362-369, Oct., 1901

The Weather Bureau and the Recent Floods. By H. C. Frankenfield. XIV, pp. 285-290, ills., July, 1903

Weather Fights and Works for Man. By F. Barrows Colton. LXXXIV, pp. 641-670, 22 ills., 3 drawings, Dec., 1943

Weather Making, Ancient and Modern. By Mark W. Harrington. VI, pp. 35-62, Apr. 25, 1894

The West Indian Hurricane of August 7-14, 1899. By E. B. Garriott. X, pp. 343-348, diagr., Sept., 1899

The West Indian Hurricane of September 1-12, 1900. By E. B. Garriott. XI, pp. 384-392, 4 charts, Oct., 1900

METEOROLOGY—*Continued*

The West Indian Hurricane of September 10-11, 1898. By Prof. E. B. Garriott. X, pp. 17-20, Jan., 1899

A Winter Weather Record From the Klondike Region. By E. W. Nelson. VIII, pp. 327-335, tables, Nov., 1897

See also Climate; Hurricanes; Rainfall; Temperature; Winds

METHODS of Exploration in Africa. By Major A. St. H. Gibbons. XV, pp. 408-410, Oct., 1904

METHODS of Obtaining Salt in Costa Rica. XIX, pp. 28-34, 7 ills., diagr., Jan., 1908

The **METLAKATLA** Mission in Danger. (By Wm. H. Dall). IX, pp. 187-189, Apr., 1898

MEULEN, D. VAN DER. *See* Van der Meulen, D.

MEUSE (River), France:

The Seine, the Meuse, and the Moselle. (Part I). By William M. Davis. VII, pp. 189-202, ill., 7 maps, June, 1896

The Seine, the Meuse, and the Moselle. (Part) II. By William M. Davis. VII, pp. 228-238, table, 4 maps, July, 1896

MEWAR (State), India. *See* Udaipur

The **MEXICAN** Census. VII, p. 211, table, June, 1896

A **MEXICAN** Hacienda: Life on one of the Baronial Estates of our Southern Neighbor. By J. E. Kirkwood. XXV, pp. 563-584, 18 ills., May, 1914

The **MEXICAN** Indian Flying Pole Dance. By Helga Larsen. LXXI, pp. 387-400, 13 ills., Mar., 1937

A **MEXICAN** Land of Canaan: Marvelous Riches of the Wonderful West Coast of Our Neighbor Republic. By Frederick Simpich. XXXVI, pp. 307-330, 16 ills., map, Oct., 1919

A **MEXICAN** Land of Lakes and Lacquers (Pátzcuaro Region). 22 photos by Helene Fischer and Luis Marquez. LXXI, pp. 633-648, May, 1937

MEXICO:

Adventures in Color on Mexico's West Coast. 13 color photos by Fred Payne Clatworthy. LVIII, pp. 61-68, July, 1930

Adventuring Down the West Coast of Mexico. By Herbert Corey. XLII, pp. 449-503, 44 ills., map, Nov., 1922

Agricultural Possibilities in Tropical Mexico. By Dr. Pehr Olsson-Seffer. XXI, pp. 1021-1040, 19 ills., Dec., 1910

Along Our Side of the Mexican Border. By Frederick Simpich. XXXVIII, pp. 61-80, 9 ills., map, July, 1920

Along the Old Spanish Road in Mexico: Life Among the People of Nayarit and Jalisco, Two of the Richest States of the Southern Republic. By Herbert Corey. XLIII, pp. 225-281, 36 ills. in black and white, 16 ills. in color, map, Mar., 1923

Among the Zapotecs of Mexico: A Visit to the Indians of Oaxaca, Home State of the Republic's Great Liberator, Juárez, and Its Most Famous Ruler, Diaz. By Herbert Corey. LI, pp. 501-553, 59 ills., map, May, 1927

Baja California Wakes Up. By Frederick Simpich. LXXXII, pp. 253-275, 19 ills., map, Aug., 1942

Boundaries of Territorial Acquisitions. XII, pp. 373-377, chart, Oct., 1901

Buenos Aires to Washington by Horse: A Solitary Journey of Two and a Half Years, Through Eleven American Republics, Covers 9,600 Miles of Mountain and Plain, Desert and Jungle. By A. F. Tschiffely. LV, pp. 135-196, 75 ills., map, Feb., 1929

Camp Fires on Desert and Lava (Book Review). XXI, pp. 715-718, 3 ills., Aug., 1910

Chichen Itzá, an Ancient American Mecca: Recent Excavations in Yucatan Are Bringing to Light the Temples, Palaces, and Pyramids of America's Most Holy Native City. By Sylvanus Griswold Morley. XLVII, pp. 63-95, 34 ills., diagr., map, Jan., 1925

Chinese Labor for Mexico. XVI, pp. 481-482, Oct., 1905

The Colorado Desert. By W. C. Mendenhall. XX, pp. 681-701, 16 ills., Aug., 1909

Commerce of Mexico and the United States. By O. P. Austin. XIII, pp. 25-26, Jan., 1902

A Cruise Among Desert Islands (Baja California). By G. Dallas Hanna and A. W. Anthony. XLIV, pp. 71-99, 32 ills., map, July, 1923

Cruise of the *Kinkajou:* Among Desert Islands of Mexico Voyagers Find Outdoor Laboratories for the Naturalist and Ideal Fishing Grounds for the Sportsman. By Alfred M. Bailey. LXXX, pp. 339-366, 13 ills. in black and white, 12 ills. in color, map, Sept., 1941

Cuernavaca, the Sun Child of the Sierras. By Russell Hastings Millward. XXII, pp. 291-301, 9 ills., Mar., 1911

Descriptive Topographic Terms of Spanish America. By Robert T. Hill. VII, pp. 291-302, Sept., 1896

Discovering the New World's Oldest Dated Work of Man: A Maya Monument Inscribed 291 B. C. is Unearthed Near a Huge Stone Head by a Geographic-Smithsonian Expedition in Mexico. By Matthew W. Stirling. LXXVI, pp. 183-218, 40 ills., map, Aug., 1939

Down Mexico's Río Balsas. By John W. Webber. With 9 color photos by author, Kenneth Segerstrom, Jack Breed. XC, pp. 253-272, 5 ills. in black and white, map, Aug., 1946

Down the Rio Grande: Tracing this Strange, Turbulent Stream on Its Long Course from Colorado to the Gulf of Mexico. By Frederick Simpich. LXXVI, pp. 415-462, 28 ills. in black and white, 24 ills. in color, 6 maps, Oct., 1939

Expedition into Texas of Fernando del Bosque, Standard-Bearer of the King, Don Carlos II, in the Year 1675. Translated from an Old, Unpublished Spanish Manuscript. By Betty B. Brewster. XIV, pp. 339-348, Sept., 1903

MEXICO—*Continued*

Expedition Unearths Buried Masterpieces of Carved Jade (Cerro de las Mesas). By Matthew W. Stirling. LXXX, pp. 277-302, 14 ills. in black and white, 20 ills. in color, map, Sept., 1941

Finding Jewels of Jade in a Mexican Swamp (La Venta). By Matthew W. and Marion Stirling. LXXXII, pp. 635-661, 15 ills. in black and white, 12 ills. in color, map, Nov., 1942

The Foremost Intellectual Achievement of Ancient America: The Hieroglyphic Inscriptions on the Monuments in the Ruined Cities of Mexico, Guatemala, and Honduras Are Yielding the Secrets of the Maya Civilization. By Sylvanus Griswold Morley. XLI, pp. 109-130, 27 ills., 17 diagrs., map supplement, Feb., 1922

Great Stone Faces of the Mexican Jungle: Five Colossal Heads and Numerous Other Monuments of Vanished Americans Are Excavated by the Latest National Geographic-Smithsonian Expedition. By Matthew W. Stirling. LXXVIII, pp. 309-334, 26 ills., map, Sept., 1940

The Greatest Volcanoes of Mexico. By A. Melgareio. XXI, pp. 741-760, 22 ills., Sept., 1910

Heart of a Hemisphere: Of Vital Importance is the Area Portrayed in The Society's New Map of Mexico, Central America, and the West Indies. Text with map supplement. LXXVI, pp. 739-740, ill., Dec., 1939

Henequen—The Yucatan Fiber. By E. H. Thompson. XIV, pp. 150-158, 6 ills., Apr., 1903

Hewers of Stone. By Jeremiah Zimmerman. XXI, pp. 1002-1020, 9 ills., Dec., 1910

The Home of a Forgotten Race: Mysterious Chichen Itza, in Yucatan, Mexico. By Edward H. Thompson. XXV, pp. 585-648, 59 ills., June, 1914

An Interesting Visit to the Ancient Pyramids of San Juan Teotihuacan. By A. C. Galloway. XXI, pp. 1041-1050, 8 ills., map, Dec., 1910

The Isthmus of Tehuantepec. By Herbert Corey. XLV, pp. 549-579, 25 ills., May, 1924

The Isthmus of Tehuantepec: "The Bridge of the World's Commerce." By Helen Olsson-Seffer. XXI, pp. 991-1002, 7 ills., Dec., 1910

Jungle Housekeeping for a Geographic Expedition (Cerro de las Mesas). By Marion Stirling. LXXX, pp. 303-327, 15 ills., Sept., 1941

The Land of Drought and Desert—Lower California: Two Thousand Miles on Horseback Through the Most Extraordinary Cacti Forests in the World. By E. W. Nelson. XXII, pp. 443-474, 25 ills., maps, May, 1911

The Latest Map of Mexico. Text with map supplement. XXX, p. 88, July, 1916

La Venta's Green Stone Tigers. By Matthew W. Stirling. LXXXIV, pp. 321-332, 4 ills. in black and white, 6 ills. in color, map, Sept., 1943

The Luster of Ancient Mexico (Aztecs). By William H. Prescott. XXX, pp. 1-32, 22 ills., July, 1916

Map of Mexico. Announcement of map supplement (May, 1911). XXII, p. 410, Apr., 1911

The Mexican Census. VII, p. 211, table, June, 1896

A Mexican Hacienda. By J. E. Kirkwood. XXV, pp. 563-584, 18 ills., May, 1914

MEXICO—*Continued*

The Mexican Indian Flying Pole Dance. By Helga Larsen. LXXI, pp. 387-400, 13 ills., Mar., 1937

A Mexican Land of Canaan: Marvelous Riches of the Wonderful West Coast of Our Neighbor Republic. By Frederick Simpich. XXXVI, pp. 307-330, 16 ills., map, Oct., 1919

A Mexican Land of Lakes and Lacquers (Pátzcuaro Region). 22 photos by Helene Fischer and Luis Marquez. LXXI, pp. 633-648, May, 1937

Mexico—The Treasure House of the World. By N. H. Darton. XVIII, pp. 493-519, 23 ills., Aug., 1907

Mexico and Mexicans. By William Joseph Showalter. XXV, pp. 471-493, 17 ills., map supplement, May, 1914

Mexico of Today. By Dr. Don Juan N. Navarro. XII, pp. 152-157, Apr., 1901; pp. 176-179, May, 1901; pp. 235-238, June, 1901

Modern Progress and Age-Old Glamour in Mexico. 22 ills. in duotone. LXVI, pp. 741-756, Dec., 1934

Monte Albán, Richest Archeological Find in America: A Tomb in Oaxaca, Mexico, Yields Treasures Which Reveal the Splendid Culture of the Mixtecs. By Dr. Alfonso Caso. LXII, pp. 487-512, 28 ills., Oct., 1932

More Changes of the Colorado River. By D. T. MacDougal. XIX, pp. 52-54, map, Jan., 1908

A Naturalist's Journey Around Vera Cruz and Tampico. By Frank M. Chapman. XXV, pp. 533-562, 31 ills., May, 1914

The New Mexico. By John W. Foster. XIII, pp. 1-24, 11 ills., maps, Jan., 1902

Notes on Southern Mexico (Agricultural Products). By G. N. Collins and C. B. Doyle. XXII, pp. 301-320, 16 ills., map, Mar., 1911

Notes on the Deserts of the United States and Mexico (Extracted from a Publication by Dr. Daniel T. MacDougal). XXI, pp. 691-714, 16 ills., Aug., 1910

The Oil Treasure of Mexico. By Russell Hastings Millward. XIX, pp. 803-805, ill., Nov., 1908

The Old Yuma Trail. By W J McGee. XII, pp. 103-107, Mar., 1901; pp. 129-143, 7 ills., map, Apr., 1901

On the Cortés Trail. By Luis Marden. LXXVIII, pp. 335-375, 17 ills. in black and white, 22 ills. in color, map, Sept., 1940

Our Map of the Countries of the Caribbean. Text with map supplement. XLI, pp. 221-222, Feb., 1922

Our Neighbor, Mexico. By John Birkinbine. XXII, pp. 475-508, 26 ills., map supplement, May, 1911

Paricutín, the Cornfield That Grew a Volcano. By James A. Green. LXXXV, pp. 129-164, 16 ills. in black and white, 21 ills. in color, map, Feb., 1944

Rubber Plantations in Mexico and Central America. XIV, pp. 409-414, 7 ills., Nov., 1903

Ruins of Cuicuilco May Revolutionize Our History of Ancient America: Lofty Mound Sealed and Preserved by Great Lava Flow for Perhaps Seventy Centuries Is Now Being Excavated in Mexico. By Byron Cummings. XLIV, pp. 203-220, 21 ills., map, Aug., 1923

MEXICO—*Continued*

Seriland. By W J McGee and Willard D. Johnson. VII, pp. 125-133, ill., foldout map, Apr., 1896

The Society's New Caribbean Map: Mexico, Central America, and the West Indies—Gateway of Discovery. Text with map supplement. LXVI, pp. 738-740, ill., Dec., 1934

Some Mexican Transportation Scenes. By Walter W. Bradley. XXI, pp. 985-991, 10 ills., Dec., 1910

The Tehuantepec Ship Railway. By Elmer L. Corthell. VII, pp. 64-72, maps, Feb., 1896

To Bogotá and Back by Air: The Narrative of a 9,500-Mile Flight from Washington, Over Thirteen Latin-American Countries and Return, in the Single-Seater Airplane "Spirit of St. Louis." By Col. Charles A. Lindbergh. LIII, pp. 529-601, 98 ills., map, May, 1928

Travels with a Donkey in Mexico: Three Adventurers Trudge from Oaxaca to Acapulco, 400 Miles, Through Back Country, Their Equipment Carried by Burros. By Bernard Bevan. LXVI, pp. 757-788, 36 ills., map, Dec., 1934

The Treasure Chest of Mercurial Mexico (Silver Mines in Guanajuato). By Frank H. Probert. XXX, pp. 33-68, 33 ills., July, 1916

Unearthing America's Ancient History: Investigation Suggests That the Maya May Have Designed the First Astronomical Observatory in the New World in Order to Cultivate Corn. By Sylvanus Griswold Morley. LX, pp. 99-126, 28 ills., July, 1931

The Venice of Mexico (Aztec Lake Country). By Walter Hough. XXX, pp. 69-88, 18 ills., July, 1916

Vignettes of Guadalajara. By Frederick Simpich. LXV, pp. 329-356, 20 ills. in black and white, 15 ills. in color, map, Mar., 1934

Wandering Islands in the Rio Grande. By Mrs. Albert S. Burleson. XXIV, pp. 381-386, ills., map, Mar., 1913

Wildlife of Tabasco and Veracruz. By Walter A. Weber. With 19 ills. in color from paintings by author. LXXXVII, pp. 187-216, 7 ills. in black and white, map, Feb., 1945

A Winter Expedition in Southwestern Mexico. By E. W. Nelson. XV, pp. 341-356, 14 ills., Sept., 1904

Yucatán, Home of the Gifted Maya: Two Thousand Years of History Reach Back to Early American Temple Builders, Corn Cultivators, and Pioneers in Mathematics. By Sylvanus Griswold Morley. Paintings by H. M. Herget. LXX, pp. 591-644, 28 ills. in black and white, 35 ills. in color, map, Nov., 1936

Yucatan in 1895. VII, pp. 83-85, Feb., 1896

See also Mexico, D. F.

MEXICO, D. F. (Mexico City):

From the Halls of Montezuma. 21 color photos by Richard H. Stewart and others. LXXXV, pp. 137-164, Feb., 1944

In the Empire of the Aztecs: Mexico City Is Rich in Relics of a People Who Practiced Human Sacrifice, Yet Loved Flowers, Education, and Art. By Frank H. H. Roberts, Jr. Paintings by H. M. Herget. LXXI, pp. 725-750, 14 ills. in black and white, 10 ills. in color, June, 1937

MEXICO, D. F. (Mexico City)—*Continued*
Mexico and Mexicans. By William Joseph Showalter. XXV, pp. 471-493, 17 ills., map supplement, May, 1914
Modern Progress and Age-Old Glamour in Mexico. 22 ills. in duotone. LXVI, pp. 741-756, Dec., 1934
North America's Oldest Metropolis: Through 600 Melodramatic Years, Mexico City Has Grown in Splendor and Achievement. By Frederick Simpich. LVIII, pp. 45-84, 34 ills., July, 1930

MEXICO, Gulf of:
The Delectable Shrimp: Once a Culinary Stepchild, Today a Gulf Coast Industry. By Harlan Major. LXXXVI, pp. 501-512, 11 ills., map, Oct., 1944
The Delta of the Mississippi River. By E. L. Corthell. VIII, pp. 351-354, Dec., 1897
How We Use the Gulf of Mexico. By Frederick Simpich. LXXXV, pp. 1-40, 20 ills. in black and white, 19 ills. in color, two-page map, Jan., 1944
See also Florida Keys; Gulf Stream

MEXICO'S Deep South Yields New Treasure (Tabasco and Chiapas). 12 color photos by Richard H. Stewart. LXXXII, pp. 649-656, Nov., 1942

MEYER, FRANK N.:
A Hunter of Plants. By David Fairchild. XXXVI, pp. 57-77, 18 ills., July, 1919

MEZŐKÖVESD, Hungary:
A Sunday in Mezőkövesd. By Margery Rae. LXVII, pp. 489-504, 22 ills., Apr., 1935

MIAMI, Florida. *See* Hialeah Park; Miami Aquarium

MIAMI AQUARIUM, Miami, Florida:
Treasure-House of the Gulf Stream: The Completion and Opening of the New Aquarium and Biological Laboratory at Miami. Florida. By John Oliver La Gorce. Paintings by Hashime Murayama. XXXIX, pp. 53-68, 5 ills. in black and white, 16 ills. in color, Jan., 1921

MICA (Sheet Mica):
India's Treasures Helped the Allies. By John Fischer. LXXXIX, pp. 501-522, 18 ills., Apr., 1946

MICE:
A Plague of Mice. XX, pp. 479-485, 7 ills., May, 1909

MICHIGAN:
By Car and Steamer Around Our Inland Seas. By Maynard Owen Williams. LXV, pp. 451-491, 29 ills. in black and white, 8 ills. in duotone, two-page map, Apr., 1934
Michigan, Mistress of the Lakes. By Melville Chater. LIII, pp. 269-325, 65 ills., maps, Mar., 1928
Michigan Fights. By Harvey Klemmer. LXXXVI, pp. 677-715, 20 ills. in black and white, 19 ills. in color, map, Dec., 1944
Summer Meeting of the American Forestry Association. XIII, pp. 352-358, Sept., 1902
Winter Sky Roads to Isle Royal. By Ben East. LX, pp. 759-774, 18 ills., map, Dec., 1931

MICHOACAN (State), Mexico:
Down Mexico's Río Balsas. By John W. Webber. With 9 color photos by author, Kenneth Segerstrom, Jack Breed. XC, pp. 253-272, 5 ills. in black and white, map, Aug., 1946
A Mexican Land of Lakes and Lacquers (Pátzcuaro Region). 22 photos by Helene Fischer and Luis Marquez. LXXI, pp. 633-648, May, 1937
Paricutín, the Cornfield That Grew a Volcano. By James A. Green. LXXXV, pp. 129-164, 16 ills. in black and white, 21 ills. in color, map, Feb., 1944

MICKEY the Beaver: An Animal Engineer Performs for the Camera as a Star in the Activities of His Species. By James MacGillivray. LIV, pp. 741-756, 23 ills., Dec., 1928

MICRONESIA:
Hidden Key to the Pacific: Piercing the Web of Secrecy Which Long Has Veiled Japanese Bases in the Mandated Islands. By Willard Price. LXXXI, pp. 759-785, 28 ills., map, June, 1942
Mysterious Micronesia: Yap, Map, and Other Islands Under Japanese Mandate are Museums of Primitive Man. By Willard Price. LXIX, pp. 481-510, 37 ills., map, Apr., 1936
Nauru, the Richest Island in the South Seas. By Rosamond Dodson Rhone. XL, pp. 559-589, 24 ills., Dec., 1921
Yap and Other Pacific Islands Under Japanese Mandate. By Junius B. Wood. XL, pp. 591-627, 34 ills., map, Dec., 1921
See also Caroline Islands; Gilbert Islands; Guam; Marianas Islands; Marshall Islands; Palau Islands

MICROSCOPICAL Examination of Wood from the Buried Forest, Muir Inlet, Alaska. By Francis H. Herrick. IV, pp. 75-78, drawings, Mar. 21, 1892

MIDDLE EAST. *See* Map Index, *following this index*

MIDDLETON GARDENS, South Carolina:
The Ashley River and Its Gardens. By E. T. H. Shaffer. XLIX, pp. 525-550, 6 ills. in black and white, 18 ills. in color, May, 1926

MIDDLETON ISLAND, Alaska:
A Northern Crusoe's Island: Life on a Fox Farm Off the Coast of Alaska, Far from Contact with the World Eleven Months a Year. By Margery Pritchard Parker. XLIV, pp. 313-326, 15 ills., map, Sept., 1923

MIDDLETON PLACE, South Carolina:
The Ashley River and Its Gardens. By E. T. H. Shaffer. XLIX, pp. 525-550, 6 ills. in black and white, 18 ills. in color, May, 1926

MIDGES:
An Insect Community Lives in Flower Heads. By James G. Needham. XC, pp. 340-356, 5 ills. in black and white, 11 ills. in color, Sept., 1946

MIDI (Region), France:
Across the Midi in a Canoe: Two Americans Paddle Along the Canals of Southern France from the Atlantic to the Mediterranean. By Melville Chater. LII, pp. 127-167, 49 ills., map, Aug., 1927

The **MIDNIGHT** Sun in the Klondike. (By Alice Rollins Crane). XII, pp. 66-67, ill., Feb., 1901

MID-OCEAN Color Log (Bermuda Islands). 12 color photos: 9 by E. John Long. LXXV, pp. 221-228, Feb., 1939

MIDSUMMER Wild Flowers. Paintings by Mary E. Eaton. XLII, pp. 35-59, 38 ills. in color, July, 1922

MIDWAY ISLANDS, Pacific Ocean:
American Pathfinders in the Pacific. By William H. Nicholas. LXXXIX, pp. 617-640, 17 ills., two-page map, May, 1946

MIJES (Indians):
The Isthmus of Tehuantepec: "The Bridge of the World's Commerce." By Helen Olsson-Seffer. XXI, pp. 991-1002, 7 ills., Dec., 1910

MILAN, Italy:
Frontier Cities of Italy. By Florence Craig Albrecht. XXVII, pp. 533-586, 45 ills., June, 1915

The **MILCH** Goat. XVI, p. 237, ill. p. 241, May, 1905

MILETUS (Ancient City):
Some Ruined Cities of Asia Minor. By Ernest L. Harris. XIX, pp. 833-858, 19 ills., Dec., 1908

MILITARY GOVERNMENT AND OCCUPATION. *See* Allied Military Government

MILITARY MAPS:
The Making of Military Maps. By William H. Nicholas. LXXXIII, pp. 765-778, 17 ills., June, 1943

MILL, H. R.:
A Geographical Description of the British Islands. (By W. M. Davis). VII, pp. 208-211, June, 1896
Note: From the article in the London *Geographical Journal*, by Dr. H. R. Mill

MILLAIS, SIR JOHN:
Boyhood of Sir Walter Raleigh. Reproduction in color of the painting by Sir John Millais, Tate Gallery, London. XLIX, text, p. 596; supplement, May, 1926

The **MILLENNIAL** City: The Romance of Geneva, Capital of the League of Nations. By Ralph A. Graves. XXXV, pp. 457-476, 13 ills., June, 1919

MILLER, HENRY B.:
Lumbering in Manchuria. (By Henry B. Miller). XV, pp. 131-132, ills., Mar., 1904
Notes on Manchuria. By Henry B. Miller. XV, pp. 261-262, June, 1904
Russian Development of Manchuria. By Henry B. Miller. XV, pp. 113-127, 11 ills., map, Mar., 1904

MILLER, J. W.:
The Cape Cod Canal. By Commodore J. W. Miller. XXVI, pp. 185-190, 3 ills., map, Aug., 1914

MILLER, WILLIAM ALEXANDER:
The Copyright of a Map or Chart. By William Alexander Miller. XIII, pp. 437-443, Dec., 1902

MILLER, WILLIAM BURKE:
Flying the Pacific. By William Burke Miller. LXX, pp. 665-707, 39 ills., Dec., 1936

MILLIONS for Moisture: An Account of the Work of the U. S. Reclamation Service. By C. J. Blanchard. XVIII, pp. 217-243, 22 ills., Apr., 1907

MILLS, JOHN, JR.:
Tartan Tints New Scotland (Nova Scotia). 21 color photos by John Mills, Jr., W. R. MacAskill, and others. LXXVII, pp. 591-622, May, 1940

MILLWARD, RUSSELL HASTINGS:
Cuernavaca, the Sun Child of the Sierras (Mexico). By Russell Hastings Millward. XXII, pp. 291-301, 9 ills., Mar., 1911
Natal: The Garden Colony. By Russell Hastings Millward. XX, pp. 278-291, 16 ills., Mar., 1909
The Oil Treasure of Mexico. By Russell Hastings Millward. XIX, pp. 803-805, ill., Nov., 1908

MINAS GERAIS (State), Brazil:
Brazil's Potent Weapons. By W. Robert Moore. LXXXV, pp. 41-78, 16 ills. in black and white, 18 ills. in color, two-page map, Jan., 1944

MINDANAO (Island), Philippine Islands:
Mindanao, on the Road to Tokyo. By Frederick Simpich. LXXXVI, pp. 539-574, 26 ills. in black and white, 12 ills. in color, two-page map, Nov., 1944

MINDELEFF, COSMOS:
Topographic Models. By Cosmos Mindeleff. I, pp. 254-268, 7 diagrs., map, July, 1889

A **MIND'S-EYE** Map of America. By Franklin K. Lane. XXXVII, pp. 479-518, 25 ills. in black and white, 8 ills. in color, June, 1920

MINER, EDWARD HERBERT:
Announcement of the death of. LXXX, p. 769, Dec., 1941
The Cattle of the World. 20 ills. in color from paintings by Edward Herbert Miner. XLVIII, pp. 639-678, Dec., 1925
Dogs: Gallant Little Sportsmen of the Terrier Tribe. 33 portraits from paintings by Edward Herbert Miner. LXIX, pp. 253-268, Feb., 1936
Dogs: Hunters All: A Roll Call of the Hounds. 31 portraits from paintings by Edward Herbert Miner. LXXII, pp. 467-482, Oct., 1937
Dogs: Man's Hunting Partner, the Field Dog. 36 portraits from paintings by Edward Herbert Miner. LXXI, pp. 89-104, Jan., 1937
Dogs: Working Dogs of the World. 20 ills. in color from paintings by Edward Herbert Miner. LXXX, pp. 775-806, Dec., 1941
Horses of the World. 24 ills. in color from paintings by Edward Herbert Miner. XLIV, pp. 479-526, Nov., 1923
Painting the Terrier Series (Acknowledgments). By Edward Herbert Miner. LXIX, pp. 273-274, Feb., 1936

MINER, ROY WALDO:
Coral Castle Builders of Tropic Seas. By Roy Waldo Miner. Paintings by Else Bostelmann. LXV, pp. 703-728, 15 ills. in black and white, 8 ills. in color, maps, June, 1934

MINER, ROY WALDO—*Continued*

Denizens of Our Warm Atlantic Waters (Mollusks, Crustaceans, etc.). By Roy Waldo Miner. Paintings by Else Bostelmann. LXXI, pp. 199-219, 10 ills. in black and white, 8 ills. in color, Feb., 1937

Marauders of the Sea. By Roy Waldo Miner. Paintings by Else Bostelmann. LXVIII, pp. 185-207, 12 ills. in black and white, 8 ills. in color, Aug., 1935

On the Bottom of a South Sea Pearl Lagoon. By Roy Waldo Miner. Paintings by Else Bostelmann. LXXIV, pp. 365-390, 17 ills. in black and white, 8 ills. in color, Sept., 1938

Sea Creatures of Our Atlantic Shores (Mollusks, Crustaceans, etc.). By Roy Waldo Miner. Paintings by Else Bostelmann. LXX, pp. 209-231, 8 ills. in black and white, 8 ills. in color, chart, Aug., 1936

MINERAL Production in the United States. VII, p. 250, July, 1896; p. 310, Sept., 1896. VIII, pp. 201-202, July-Aug., 1897

MINERALS:

Alaska and Its Mineral Resources. By Samuel Franklin Emmons. IX, pp. 139-172, 3 ills., map supplement, Apr., 1898

Brazil's Potent Weapons. By W. Robert Moore. LXXXV, pp. 41-78, 16 ills. in black and white, 18 ills. in color, two-page map, Jan., 1944

Cuba. By Robert T. Hill. IX, pp. 193-242, 12 ills., 7 diagrs., tables, 5 maps (1 foldout), May, 1898

An Expedition Through the Yukon District. By Charles Willard Hayes. IV, pp. 117-159, 3 maps (2 foldouts), May 15, 1892

India's Treasures Helped the Allies. By John Fischer. LXXXIX, pp. 501-522, 18 ills., Apr., 1946

Mineral Production in the United States. VII, p. 250, July, 1896; p. 310, Sept., 1896. VIII, pp. 201-202, July-Aug., 1897

The Philippine Islands. By F. F. Hilder. IX, pp. 257-284, 10 ills., table, maps, June, 1898

Report on Auriferous Sands from Yakutat Bay (Alaska). By J. Stanley-Brown. III, pp. 196-198, May 29, 1891

See also Metals; Mines and Mining

MINES, Submarine:

The North Sea Mine Barrage. By Capt. Reginald R. Belknap. XXXV, pp. 85-110, 23 ills., diagr., map, Feb., 1919

The Removal of the North Sea Mine Barrage. By Lieutenant-Commander Noel Davis. XXXVII, pp. 103-133, 28 ills., maps, Feb., 1920

MINES AND MINING:

Beyond Australia's Cities. By W. Robert Moore. LXX, pp. 709-747, 27 ills. in black and white, 12 ills. in color, Dec., 1936

Bolivia—Tin Roof of the Andes. By Henry Albert Phillips. LXXXIII, pp. 309-332, 5 ills. in black and white, 20 ills. in color, Mar., 1943

Brazil's Potent Weapons. By W. Robert Moore. LXXXV, pp. 41-78, 16 ills. in black and white, 18 ills. in color, two-page map, Jan., 1944

MINES AND MINING—*Continued*

Burma: Where India and China Meet: In the Massive Mountains of Southeast Asia, Swarming Road Builders Wage the "War of the Highways" for Free China and Her Allies. By John LeRoy Christian. LXXXIV, pp. 489-512, 18 ills., map, Oct., 1943

California. By the Hon. George C. Perkins. VII, pp. 317-327, Oct., 1896

The Cities That Gold and Diamonds Built: Transvaal Treasures Have Created Bustling Johannesburg and Fostered Pretoria, Administrative Capital of the South African Union. By W. Robert Moore. LXXXII, pp. 735-766, 20 ills. in black and white, 9 ills. in color, map, Dec., 1942

Coal—Ally of American Industry. By William Joseph Showalter. XXXIV, pp. 407-434, 23 ills., Nov., 1918

Coal: Prodigious Worker for Man. By Albert W. Atwood. LXXXV, pp. 569-592, 19 ills., drawing, May, 1944

Coal-Fields of Alaska. XXI, pp. 83-87, 6 ills., Jan., 1910

Colorado, a Barrier That Became a Goal: Where Water Has Transformed Dry Plains Into Verdant Farms, and Highways Have Opened up Mineral and Scenic Wealth. By McFall Kerbey. LXII, pp. 1-63, 56 ills. in black and white, 12 ills. in color, map, July, 1932

The Diamond Mines of South Africa. By Gardiner F. Williams. XVII, pp. 344-356, 11 ills., June, 1906

India's Treasures Helped the Allies. By John Fischer. LXXXIX, pp. 501-522, 18 ills., Apr., 1946

Industry's Greatest Asset—Steel. By William Joseph Showalter. XXXII, pp. 121-156, 34 ills., Aug., 1917

Lonely Australia: The Unique Continent. By Herbert E. Gregory. XXX, pp. 473-568, 68 ills., 5 maps (1 two-page), Dec., 1916

Men and Gold. By Frederick Simpich. LXIII, pp. 481-518, 33 ills. in black and white, 11 ills. in duotone, Apr., 1933

A Mexican Hacienda. By J. E. Kirkwood. XXV, pp. 563-584, 18 ills., May, 1914

Mexico—The Treasure House of the World. By N. H. Darton. XVIII, pp. 493-519, 23 ills., Aug., 1907

The Mining Bureau of the Philippine Islands. By Charles H. Burritt. XIV, pp. 418-419, Nov., 1903

Nevada, Desert Treasure House. By W. Robert Moore. LXXXIX, pp. 1-38, 16 ills. in black and white, 20 ills. in color, map, Jan., 1946

Old Mines and Mills in India. XX, pp. 489-490, ills., May, 1909

Ore-Boat Unloaders. (By W. M. Gregory). XVIII, pp. 343-345, ill., May, 1907

Pieces of Silver. By Frederick Simpich. LXIV, pp. 253-292, 49 ills., Sept., 1933

Platinum in the World's Work. By Lonnelle Davison. LXXII, pp. 345-360, 17 ills., Sept., 1937

Precious Stones. XIV, pp. 451-458, 4 ills., Dec., 1903

MINES AND MINING—*Continued*

Rhodesia, Hobby and Hope of Cecil Rhodes. By W. Robert Moore. LXXXVI, pp. 281-306, 13 ills. in black and white, 10 ills. in color, map, Sept., 1944

The Story of the Ruhr. By Frederick Simpich. XLI, pp. 553-564, 11 ills., map, May, 1922

Tin, the Cinderella Metal. By Alicia O'Reardon Overbeck. LXXVIII, pp. 659-684, 24 ills., Nov., 1940

The Treasure Chest of Mercurial Mexico. By Frank H. Probert. XXX, pp. 33-68, 33 ills., July, 1916

Under the South African Union. By Melville Chater. LIX, pp. 391-512, 97 ills. in black and white, 38 ills. in color, two-page map, Apr., 1931

The United States—Her Mineral Resources. By C. Kirchhoff. XIV, pp. 331-339, Sept., 1903

War Awakened New Caledonia: Swift Changes on the South Pacific Island of Mineral Wealth Defended by Free French and American Troops. By Enzo de Chetelat. LXXXII, pp. 31-55, 14 ills. in black and white, 12 ills. in color, map, July, 1942

MINIATURES of Macao (China). 11 color photos by W. Robert Moore. LXII, pp. 341-348, Sept., 1932

MINNEAPOLIS, Minnesota: Northwestern Aeronautical Corporation:

Gliders—Silent Weapons of the Sky. By William H. Nicholas. LXXXVI, pp. 149-160, 8 ills., Aug., 1944

MINNESOTA:

Minnesota, Mother of Lakes and Rivers. By Glanville Smith. LXVII, pp. 273-318, 42 ills. in black and white, 11 ills. in color, two-page map, Mar., 1935

The Wild Life of Lake Superior, Past and Present: The Habits of Deer, Moose, Wolves, Beavers, Muskrats, Trout, and Feathered Wood-Folk Studied with Camera and Flashlight. By George Shiras, 3d. XL, pp. 113-204, 76 ills., map, pictorial supplement, Aug., 1921

See also Minneapolis

MINNIGERODE, FITZHUGH LEE:

The Beauty of the Bavarian Alps. By Colonel Fitzhugh Lee Minnigerode. XLIX, pp. 632-649, 16 ills. in color, June, 1926

MINNIGERODE, H. GORDON:

Life Grows Grim in Singapore. By H. Gordon Minnigerode. LXXX, pp. 661-686, 17 ills. in black and white, 9 ills. in color, map, Nov., 1941

MINSHALL, MERLIN:

By Sail Across Europe. By Merlin Minshall. LXXI, pp. 533-567, 38 ills., map, May, 1937

MINYA KONKA (Mountain), China:

Climbing Mighty Minya Konka: Americans First Scaled Mountain That Now Is Landmark of China's New Skyway. By Richard L. Burdsall and Terris Moore. LXXXIII, pp. 625-650, 23 ills., map, May, 1943

MINYA KONKA (Mountain), China—*Continued*

The Glories of the Minya Konka: Magnificent Snow Peaks of the China-Tibetan Border Are Photographed at Close Range by a National Geographic Society Expedition. By Joseph F. Rock. LVIII, pp. 385-437, 35 ills. in black and white, 24 ills. in color, map, Oct., 1930

MIQUELON (Island), St. Pierre and Miquelon:

Islands Adrift: St. Pierre and Miquelon: In a Key Position on the North Atlantic Air Route, France's Oldest Colony Rides Out Another Storm. By Frederic K. Arnold. LXXX, pp. 743-768, 23 ills., map, Dec., 1941

The **MIRACLE** of Talking by Telephone. By F. Barrows Colton. LXXII, pp. 395-433, 41 ills., Oct., 1937

The **MIRACLE** of War Production: For Victory the United States Transforms Its Complex Industry into the Biggest Factory and Mightiest Arsenal the World Has Ever Known. By Albert W. Atwood. With paintings by Thornton Oakley. LXXXII, pp. 693-715, 17 ills. in black and white, 16 ills. in color, Dec., 1942

MIRAM SHAH, India:

South of Khyber Pass. By Maynard Owen Williams. LXXXIX, pp. 471-500, 31 ills., map supplement, Apr., 1946

MIRRORS of Madeira, Rock Garden of the Atlantic. 13 color photos by Wilhelm Tobien. LXVI, pp. 89-96, July, 1934

The **MISSION** of the "Diana" (Peary Arctic Club). X, p. 273, July, 1899

MISSIONARIES. *See* Duncan, William; Moore, J. Z.; Whitman, Marcus; *and* Moravian Missionaries

MISSIONS:

Agriculture in the Yukon Valley. IX, pp. 189-190, Apr., 1898

The Metlakatla Mission in Danger. (By Wm. H. Dall). IX, pp. 187-189, Apr., 1898

MISSISSIPPI:

Burning the Roads. XVII, pp. 583-586, 4 ills., Oct., 1906

Machines Come to Mississippi. By J. R. Hildebrand. LXXII, pp. 263-318, 34 ills. in black and white, 26 ills. in color, two-page map, Sept., 1937

MISSISSIPPI (River), U. S.:

The Deep-Water Route from Chicago to the Gulf. XVIII, pp. 679-685, 3 ills., map, Oct., 1907

The Delta of the Mississippi River. By E. L. Corthell. VIII, pp. 351-354, Dec., 1897

The Great Mississippi Flood of 1927: Since White Man's Discovery This Mighty River Has Served Him Well, Yet It Has Brought Widespread Devastation Along Its Lower Reaches. By Frederick Simpich. LII, pp. 243-289, 53 ills., map, Sept., 1927

Honors for Amundsen (National Geographic Society Banquet: Address by Hon. Theodore Burton on the Mississippi). XIX, pp. 55-76, 13 ills., Jan., 1908

MISSISSIPPI (River), U. S.—*Continued*
Louisiana, Land of Perpetual Romance. By Ralph A. Graves. LVII, pp. 393-482, 84 ills. in black and white, 29 ills. in color, map supplement, Apr., 1930
Men Against the Rivers. By Frederick Simpich. LXXI, pp. 767-794, 22 ills., maps, June, 1937
The Modern Mississippi Problem. By W J McGee. IX, pp. 24-27, Jan., 1898
Report—Geography of the Land. By Herbert G. Ogden. II, pp. 31-48, Apr., 1890
When the Father of Waters Goes on a Rampage: An Account of the Salvaging of Food-fishes from the Overflowed Lands of the Mississippi River. By Hugh M. Smith. XXXVII, pp. 369-386, 18 ills., Apr., 1920

MISSOURI:
Land of a Million Smiles (Ozarks). By Frederick Simpich. LXXXIII, pp. 589-623, 14 ills. in black and white, 20 ills. in color, map, May, 1943
Missouri, Mother of the West. By Frederick Simpich. XLIII, pp. 421-460, 35 ills., Apr., 1923
Taming the Outlaw Missouri River. By Frederick Simpich. LXXXVIII, pp. 569-598, 25 ills., two-page map, Nov., 1945
These Missourians. By Frederick Simpich. LXXXIX, pp. 277-310, 12 ills. in black and white, 22 ills. in color, map, Mar., 1946

MISSOURI (River), U. S.:
Taming the Outlaw Missouri River. By Frederick Simpich. LXXXVIII, pp. 569-598, 25 ills., two-page map, Nov., 1945
Trailing History Down the Big Muddy: In the Homeward Wake of Lewis and Clark, a Folding Steel Skiff Bears Its Lone Pilot on a 2,000-Mile Cruise on the Yellowstone-Missouri. By Lewis R. Freeman. LIV, pp. 73-120, 51 ills., map, July, 1928

MISSOURI RIVER BASIN:
Taming the Outlaw Missouri River. By Frederick Simpich. LXXXVIII, pp. 569-598, 25 ills., two-page map, Nov., 1945

MISSOURI (Battleship):
Battleship *Missouri* Comes of Age. 11 ills. in color. LXXXVII, pp. 353-360, Mar., 1945

MISSOURI Mirrors of 1946. 22 color photos by Richard H. Stewart. LXXXIX, pp. 285-308, Mar., 1946

The **MIST** and Sunshine of Ulster (Northern Ireland). By Bernard F. Rogers, Jr. LXVIII, pp. 571-610, 23 ills. in black and white, 21 ills. in color, map, Nov., 1935

MR. Coolidge Becomes a Member of The Society's Board of Trustees. LV, p. 750, June, 1929

MR. Roosevelt's "African Game Trails." XXI, pp. 953-962, 9 ills., Nov., 1910

MR. Ziegler and the National Geographic Society. XIV, pp. 251-254, June, 1903

The **MISTLETOE.** XXI, p. 965, 3 ills., Nov., 1910

MISTRAL, FRÉDÉRIC:
Camargue, the Cowboy Country of Southern France. By Dr. André Vialles. XLII, pp. 1-34, 33 ills., map, July, 1922

MRS. Bishop's "The Yangtze Valley and Beyond." By Eliza Ruhamah Scidmore. XI, pp. 366-368, Sept., 1900

MRS. Robinson Crusoe in Ecuador. By Mrs. Richard C. Gill. LXV, pp. 133-172, 43 ills., map, Feb., 1934

MITCHELL, GUY ELLIOTT:
American Potash for America. By Guy Elliott Mitchell. XXII, pp. 399-405, 4 ills., Apr., 1911
Billions of Barrels of Oil Locked Up in Rocks. By Guy Elliott Mitchell. XXXIII, pp. 195-205, 10 ills., Feb., 1918
An Ideal Fuel Manufactured Out of Waste Products: The American Coal Briquetting Industry. By Guy Elliott Mitchell. XXI, pp. 1067-1074, 4 ills., Dec., 1910
Landslides and Rock Avalanches. By Guy Elliott Mitchell. XXI, pp. 277-287, 6 ills., Apr., 1910
A New National Park (Glacier National Park). By Guy Elliott Mitchell. XXI, pp. 215-223, 6 ills., Mar., 1910
A New Source of Power (Lignite). By Guy Elliott Mitchell. XXI, pp. 935-944, 7 ills., Nov., 1910
Our Coal Lands. By Guy Elliott Mitchell. XXI, pp. 446-451, 5 ills., May, 1910
Our Greatest Plant Food (Phosphorus). By Guy Elliott Mitchell. XXI, pp. 783-791, 5 ills., diagrs., Sept., 1910

MITCHELL, HENRY. *See* NGS: Board of Managers

MITCHELL, JOHN H.:
Oregon: Its History, Geography, and Resources. By John H. Mitchell, U. S. Senator from Oregon. VI, pp. 239-284, Apr. 20, 1895

MITCHELL, S. A.:
Nature's Most Dramatic Spectacle (Eclipse). By S. A. Mitchell. LXXII, pp. 361-376, 16 ills., map, Sept., 1937

MITCHELL, WILLIAM:
America in the Air: The Future of Airplane and Airship, Economically and as Factors in National Defense. By Brigadier-General William Mitchell. XXXIX, pp. 339-352, 8 ills., map, Mar., 1921
Building the Alaskan Telegraph System. By Captain William Mitchell. XV, pp. 357-361, Sept., 1904
Tiger-Hunting in India. By Brigadier General William Mitchell. XLVI, pp. 545-598, 46 ills., map, Nov., 1924

MITLA, Mexico:
Hewers of Stone. By Jeremiah Zimmerman. XXI, pp. 1002-1020, 9 ills., Dec., 1910

MITSUKURI, K.:
Cultivation of Marine and Fresh-Water Animals in Japan. By K. Mitsukuri. XVII, pp. 524-531, 5 ills., Sept., 1906

MITTELHOLZER, WALTER:

Flights from Arctic to Equator: Conquering the Alps, the Ice Peaks of Spitsbergen, of Persia, and Africa's Mountains of the Moon. By Walter Mittelholzer. LXI, pp. 445-498, 53 ills., map, Apr., 1932

MIXTEC INDIANS:

Monte Albán, Richest Archeological Find in America: A Tomb in Oaxaca, Mexico, Yields Treasures Which Reveal the Splendid Culture of the Mixtecs. By Dr. Alfonso Caso. LXII, pp. 487-512, 28 ills., Oct., 1932

MIXTER, GEORGE, 2D:

Hunting the Great Brown Bear of Alaska. By George Mixter, 2d. XX, pp. 313-333, 35 ills., Apr., 1909

The **MODERN** Alchemist (U. S. Department of Agriculture). By James Wilson. XVIII, pp. 781-795, 6 ills., Dec., 1907

A **MODERN** Dragon Hunt on Komodo: An English Yachting Party Traps and Photographs the Huge and Carnivorous Dragon Lizard of the Lesser Sundas. By Lady Broughton. LXX, pp. 321-331, 12 ills. in duotone, Sept., 1936

MODERN Ethiopia: Haile Selassie the First, Formerly Ras Tafari, Succeeds to the World's Oldest Continuously Sovereign Throne. By Addison E. Southard. LIX, pp. 679-738, 47 ills. in black and white, 27 ills. in color, map, June, 1931

MODERN Life in Morocco, Western Outpost of Islam. 27 color photos by M. Flandrin. LXVII, pp. 679-694, June, 1935

MODERN Life in the Cradle of Civilization (Iraq). XLI, pp. 390-407, 16 ills. in color, Apr., 1922

The **MODERN** Mississippi Problem. By W J McGee. IX, pp. 24-27, Jan., 1898

MODERN Odyssey in Classic Lands: Troy's Treasures, Athens' Parthenon, and Rome's First "Broad Way" Influence Today's Banks, Costumes, Jewelry, and Railroad Timetables. By Maynard Owen Williams. LXXVII, pp. 291-337, 27 ills. in black and white, 22 ills. in color, Mar., 1940

MODERN Persia and Its Capital: And an Account of an Ascent of Mount Demavend, the Persian Olympus. By F. L. Bird. XXXIX, pp. 353-400, 47 ills., Apr., 1921

A **MODERN** Pilgrim's Map of the British Isles. By Andrew H. Brown. Text with map supplement. LXXI, pp. 795-802, 3 ills., June, 1937

MODERN Progress and Age-Old Glamour in Mexico. 22 ills. in duotone. LXVI, pp. 741-756, Dec., 1934

A **MODERN** Saga of the Seas: The Narrative of a 17,000-Mile Cruise on a 40-Foot Sloop by the Author, His Wife, and a Baby, Born on the Voyage. By Erling Tambs. LX, pp. 645-688, 49 ills., map, Dec., 1931

MODERN Scenes in the Land of Lincoln's Birth (Kentucky). 15 color photos by Edwin L. Wisherd. LXV, pp. 695-702, June, 1934

MODERN Transmutation of the Elements. By Sir William Ramsay. XVII, pp. 201-203, Apr., 1906

MODERN Venezuelan Vignettes. 9 ills. LXXV, pp. 113-120, Jan., 1939

A **MODERN** Viking (Amundsen). XVII, pp. 38-41, ills., map, Jan., 1906

MODIFICATION of the Great Lakes by Earth Movement. By G. K. Gilbert. VIII, pp. 233-247, 3 diagrs., table, 4 maps, Sept., 1897

MOHAWK (Indian Tribe):

America's First Settlers, the Indians. By Matthew W. Stirling. Paintings by W. Langdon Kihn. LXXII, pp. 535-596, 34 ills. in black and white, 24 ills. in color, Nov., 1937

MOHONK, Lake, New York:

Shawangunk Mountain. By N. H. Darton. VI, pp. 23-34, ills., 4 diagrs., Mar. 17, 1894

MOJAVE DESERT, California:

Carrying Water Through a Desert: The Story of the Los Angeles Aqueduct. By Burt A. Heinly. XXI, pp. 568-596, 19 ills., map, July, 1910

The **MOLE** Men: An Account of the Troglodytes of Southern Tunisia. By Frank Edward Johnson. XXII, pp. 787-846, 60 ills., Sept., 1911

MOLLUSKS:

America's Surpassing Fisheries: Their Present Condition and Future Prospects, and How the Federal Government Fosters Them. By Hugh M. Smith. XXIX, pp. 546-583, 35 ills., June, 1916

Cultivation of Marine and Fresh-Water Animals in Japan. By K. Mitsukuri. XVII, pp. 524-531, 5 ills., Sept., 1906

Denizens of Our Warm Atlantic Waters. By Roy Waldo Miner. Paintings by Else Bostelmann. LXXI, pp. 199-219, 10 ills. in black and white, 8 ills. in color, Feb., 1937

The Dream Ship: The Story of a Voyage of Adventure More Than Half Around the World in a 47-foot Lifeboat. By Ralph Stock. XXXIX, pp. 1-52, 43 ills., map, Jan., 1921

Fantastic Dwellers in a Coral Fairyland (Great Barrier Reef). 15 color photos by T. C. Roughley. LXXVII, pp. 831-838, June, 1940

Marauders of the Sea. By Roy Waldo Miner. Paintings by Else Bostelmann. LXVIII, pp. 185-207, 12 ills. in black and white, 8 ills. in color, Aug., 1935

The Native Oysters of the West Coast. By Robert E. C. Stearns. XIX, pp. 224-226, Mar., 1908

Oysters: The World's Most Valuable Water Crop. By Hugh M. Smith. XXIV, pp. 257-281, 21 ills., Mar., 1913

The Pearl Fisheries of Ceylon. By Hugh M. Smith. XXIII, pp. 173-194, 13 ills., map, Feb., 1912

The Rise of the New Arab Nation. By Frederick Simpich. XXXVI, pp. 369-393, 17 ills., map, Nov., 1919

Included: Arabia's pearl fisheries

Sea Creatures of Our Atlantic Shores. By Roy Waldo Miner. Paintings by Else Bostelmann. LXX, pp. 209-231, 8 ills. in black and white, 8 ills. in color, chart, Aug., 1936

MOLUCCAS (Islands), Netherlands East Indies:
Airplanes Come to the Isles of Spice: Once Magnet of World Explorers, the Moluccas Again Stand at Crossroads of History in the Netherlands Indies. By Maynard Owen Williams. LXXIX, pp. 535-558, 26 ills., map, May, 1941

MOMBASA, Kenya:
Where Roosevelt Will Hunt. By Sir Harry Johnston. XX, pp. 207-256, 43 ills., map supplement, Mar., 1909

The **MONARCH** of the Canadian Rockies (Mount Robson). By Charles D. Walcott. XXIV, pp. 626-639, 13 ills., panorama, May, 1913

The **MONARCH** of the Canadian Rockies—Robson Peak. XXIV, panorama, May, 1913

The **MONARCHS** of Alaska (Mountains). By R. H. Sargent. XX, pp. 610-623, 9 ills., July, 1909

MONASTERIES:
Across Tibet from India to China. By Lt. Col. Ilia Tolstoy, AUS. XC, pp. 169-222, 53 ills., map, Aug., 1946
Castles in the Air: Experiences and Journeys in Unknown Bhutan. By John Claude White. XXV, pp. 365-455, 74 ills., map, Apr., 1914
The Clock Turns Back in Yugoslavia: The Fortified Monastery of Mountain-girt Dečani Survives Its Six Hundredth Birthday. By Ethel Chamberlain Porter. LXXXV, pp. 493-512, 20 ills., map, Apr., 1944
Frontier Cities of Italy. By Florence Craig Albrecht. XXVII, pp. 533-586, 45 ills., June, 1915
The Hoary Monasteries of Mt. Athos (Greece). By H. G. Dwight. XXX, pp. 249-272, 24 ills., map, Sept., 1916
In the Diamond Mountains: Adventures Among the Buddhist Monasteries of Eastern Korea. By the Marquess Curzon of Kedleston. XLVI, pp. 353-374, 21 ills., map, Oct., 1924
In the Shadow of Bulgarian Monasteries. 14 color photos by Wilhelm Tobien and Georg Paskoff. LXII, pp. 203-210, Aug., 1932
The Land of the Yellow Lama: National Geographic Society Explorer Visits the Strange Kingdom of Muli, Beyond the Likiang Snow Range of Yünnan Province, China. By Joseph F. Rock. XLVII, pp. 447-491, 39 ills., map, Apr., 1925
Megaspelæon, the Oldest Monastery in Greece. By Carroll Storrs Alden. XXIV, pp. 310-323, 11 ills., Mar., 1913
Montserrat, Spain's Mountain Shrine. By E. John Long. LXIII, pp. 121-130, 10 ills., Jan., 1933
The Most Extraordinary City in the World: Notes on Lhasa—The Mecca of the Buddhist Faith. By Shaoching H. Chuan. XXIII, pp. 959-995, 60 ills., Oct., 1912
Puto, the Enchanted Island. By Robert F. Fitch. LXXXIX, pp. 373-384, 11 ills., map, Mar., 1946
The Route Over Which Moses Led the Children of Israel Out of Egypt. By Franklin E. Hoskins. XX, pp. 1011-1038, 24 ills., map, Dec., 1909

MONASTERIES—*Continued*
Sunrise and Sunset from Mount Sinai. By Rev. Sartell Prentice, Jr. XXIII, pp. 1242-1282, 34 ills., map, Dec., 1912
Where Early Christians Lived in Cones of Rock: A Journey to Cappadocia in Turkey Where Strange Volcanic Pinnacles Are Honeycombed With Hermit Cells and Monasteries. By John D. Whiting. LXXVI, pp. 763-802, 20 ills. in black and white, 20 ills. in color, map, Dec., 1939
The Whirlpool of the Balkans. By George Higgins Moses. XXXIX, pp. 179-197, 15 ills., Feb., 1921
With the Monks at Meteora: The Monasteries of Thessaly. By Elizabeth Perkins. XX, pp. 799-807, 5 ills., Sept., 1909
The World's Strangest Capital (Lhasa, Tibet). By John Claude White. XXIX, pp. 273-295, 19 ills., panorama, Mar., 1916
See also Al Qosh

MONASTIR, Yugoslavia:
On the Monastir Road. By Herbert Corey. XXXI, pp. 383-412, 31 ills., May, 1917

MONEY:
The Geography of Money. By William Atherton Du Puy. LII, pp. 745-768, 31 ills., Dec., 1927
Our Heterogeneous System of Weights and Measures. By Alexander Graham Bell. XVII, pp. 158-169, Mar., 1906
Pieces of Silver. By Frederick Simpich. LXIV, pp. 253-292, 49 ills., Sept., 1933

MONFREID, HENRI DE:
Pearl Fishing in the Red Sea. By Henri de Monfreid. LXXII, pp. 597-626, 24 ills., map, Nov., 1937

MONGOLIA:
By Coolie and Caravan Across Central Asia: Narrative of a 7,900-Mile Journey of Exploration and Research Over "the Roof of the World," from the Indian Ocean to the Yellow Sea. By William J. Morden. LII, pp. 369-431, 73 ills., map, Oct., 1927
The Desert Road to Turkestan: Twentieth Century Travel Through Innermost Asia, Along Caravan Trails Over Which Oriental Commerce Was Once Borne from China to the Medieval Western World. By Owen Lattimore. LV, pp. 661-702, 45 ills., map, June, 1929
Explorations in the Gobi Desert. By Roy Chapman Andrews. LXIII, pp. 653-716, 50 ills. in black and white, 20 ills. in color, map, June, 1933
In the Land of Kublai Khan. 16 color photos by M. Stéphane Passet. XLI, pp. 465-472, May, 1922
The Lama's Motor-Car. By Ethan C. Le Munyon. XXIV, pp. 641-670, 34 ills., May, 1913
The Land of Genghis Khan in Its True Colors. 6 color photos by Maynard Owen Williams. LXII, pp. 569-576, Nov., 1932
The People of the Wilderness: The Mongols, Once the Terror of All Christendom, Now a Primitive, Harmless Nomad Race. By Adam Warwick. XXXIX, pp. 507-551, 59 ills., May, 1921

MONGOLIA—*Continued*

The Road to Wang Ye Fu: An Account of the Work of the National Geographic Society's Central-China Expedition in the Mongol Kingdom of Ala Shan. By Frederick R. Wulsin. XLIX, pp. 197-234, 44 ills., map, Feb., 1926

A Thousand Miles Along the Great Wall of China: The Mightiest Barrier Ever Built by Man Has Stood Guard Over the Land of Chin for Twenty Centuries. By Adam Warwick. XLIII, pp. 113-143, 27 ills., maps, panorama, Feb., 1923

The World's Greatest Overland Explorer: How Marco Polo Penetrated Farthest Asia, "Discovered" Many Lands Unknown to Europe, and Added Numerous Minerals, Animals, Birds, and Plants to Man's Knowledge. By J. R. Hildebrand. LIV, pp. 505-568, 53 ills., two-page map, Nov., 1928

MONGOLS:

Japan Faces Russia in Manchuria. By Willard Price. LXXXII, pp. 603-634, 30 ills., map, Nov., 1942

New Road to Asia. By Owen Lattimore. LXXXVI, pp. 641-676, 15 ills. in black and white, 26 ills. in color, Dec., 1944

Nomad Life and Fossil Treasures of Mongolia. 20 color photos by J. B. Shackelford. LXIII, pp. 669-700, June, 1933

The People of the Wilderness: The Mongols, Once the Terror of All Christendom, Now a Primitive, Harmless Nomad Race. By Adam Warwick. XXXIX, pp. 507-551, 59 ills., May, 1921

With the Nomads of Central Asia: A Summer's Sojourn in the Tekes Valley, Plateau Paradise of Mongol and Turkic Tribes. By Edward Murray. Paintings and drawings by Alexandre Iacovleff. LXIX, pp. 1-57, 43 ills. in black and white, 26 ills. in color, map, Jan., 1936

MONKEYS:

Monkey Folk. By William M. Mann. Paintings by Elie Cheverlange. LXXIII, pp. 615-655, 24 ills. in black and white, 40 portraits in color, May, 1938

See also Apes

MONOGRAPHS of the National Geographic Society, to be published for use in the public schools. VI, pp. 225-227, Dec. 29, 1894

MONROE DOCTRINE:

Geographical Aspects of the Monroe Doctrine. IX, pp. 476-477, Nov., 1898

MONROVIA, Liberia:

The Land of the Free in Africa. By Harry A. McBride. XLII, pp. 411-430, 22 ills., Oct., 1922

Notes on the Only American Colony in the World. By Edgar Allen Forbes. XXI, pp. 719-729, 14 ills., Sept., 1910

MONSTER and Midget Squid and Octopuses. 8 ills. in color from paintings by Else Bostelmann under direction Roy W. Miner. LXVIII, pp. 193-200, Aug., 1935

The **MONSTERS** of Our Back Yards (Insects). By David Fairchild. XXIV, pp. 575-626, 38 ills., May, 1913

MONT St. Michel (France), a Medieval Masterpiece. 22 ills. in duotone. LXIX, pp. 633-648, May, 1936

MONTANA:

A Bear Hunt in Montana. By Arthur Alvord Stiles. XIX, pp. 149-154, 5 ills., Feb., 1908

Bitter Root Forest Reserve. By Richard U. Goode. IX, pp. 387-400, 5 ills., foldout map, Sept., 1898

The Call of the West. By C. J. Blanchard. XX, pp. 403-437, 20 ills., map, May, 1909

The Friendly Crows (Indians) in Festive Panoply. 13 color photos by Edwin L. Wisherd. LII, pp. 315-322, Sept., 1927

The Idaho and Montana Boundary Line. By Richard U. Goode. XI, pp. 23-29, ill., diagr., Jan., 1900

The Irrigation Problem in Montana. By H. M. Wilson. II, pp. 212-229, 4 tables, July, 1890

A New National Park (Glacier National Park). By Guy Elliott Mitchell. XXI, pp. 215-223, 6 ills., Mar., 1910

Our National Parks. By L. F. Schmeckebier. XXIII, pp. 531-579, 41 ills., map, June, 1912

Our Northern Rockies. By R. H. Chapman. XIII, pp. 361-372, 10 ills., Oct., 1902

Taming the Outlaw Missouri River. By Frederick Simpich. LXXXVIII, pp. 569-598, 25 ills., two-page map, Nov., 1945

MONTE Albân, Richest Archeological Find in America: A Tomb in Oaxaca, Mexico, Yields Treasures Which Reveal the Splendid Culture of the Mixtecs. By Dr. Alfonso Caso. LXII, pp. 487-512, 28 ills., Oct., 1932

MONTENEGRO:

East of the Adriatic: Notes on Dalmatia, Montenegro, Bosnia, and Herzegovina. By Kenneth McKenzie. XXIII, pp. 1159-1187, 1284, 37 ills., map, Dec., 1912

Greece and Montenegro. By George Higgins Moses. XXIV, pp. 281-310, 24 ills., Mar., 1913

The New Map of Europe: Showing the Boundaries Established by the Peace Conference at Paris and by Subsequent Decisions of the Supreme Council of the Allied and Associated Powers. By Ralph A. Graves. Text with map supplement. XXXIX, pp. 157-177, 18 ills., Feb., 1921

The Races of Europe. By Edwin A. Grosvenor. XXXIV, pp. 441-534, 62 ills., diagr. and index, maps, map supplement, Dec., 1918

Servia and Montenegro. XIX, pp. 774-789, 24 ills., Nov., 1908

Where East Meets West: Visit to Picturesque Dalmatia, Montenegro and Bosnia. By Marian Cruger Coffin. XIX, pp. 309-344, 26 ills., map, May. 1908

The Whirlpool of the Balkans. By George Higgins Moses. XXXIX, pp. 179-197, 15 ills., Feb., 1921

MONTESPAN GROTTO, France:

Discovering the Oldest Statues in the World: A Daring Explorer Swims Through a Subterranean River of the Pyrenees and Finds Rock Carvings Made 20,000 Years Ago. By Norbert Casteret. XLVI, pp. 123-152, 24 ills., maps, Aug., 1924

MONTICELLO, Albemarle County, Virginia:
Eighth Annual Field Meeting of the National Geographic Society. VII, pp. 259-260, ill., Aug., 1896
Jefferson's Little Mountain: Romance Enfolds Monticello, the Restored Home of the Author of the Declaration of Independence. By Paul Wilstach. LV, pp. 481-503, 12 ills. in black and white, 12 ills. in color, Apr., 1929

MONTICELLO, One of America's Most Historic Shrines. 12 color photos by Edwin L. Wisherd, Charles Martin, Jacob Gayer. LV, pp. 489-496, Apr., 1929

MONTSERRAT, Spain's Mountain Shrine. By E. John Long. LXIII, pp. 121-130, 10 ills., Jan., 1933

MONUMENT VALLEY, Arizona-Utah:
Flaming Cliffs of Monument Valley. By Lt. Jack Breed, USNR. With 9 color photos by author and Warren T. Mithoff. LXXXVIII, pp. 452-461, Oct., 1945

MONUMENTS. *See* Memorials

MONUMENTS, Archeological. *See* Archeology

MONUMENTS, FINE ARTS, AND ARCHIVES BRANCH, Military Government:
Europe's Looted Art. By John Walker. LXXXIX, pp. 39-52, 11 ills., Jan., 1946

MOON. *See* Eclipses

MOON JELLYFISH:
The Life of the Moon-Jelly. By William Crowder. Paintings by author. L, pp. 187-202, 6 ills. in black and white, 8 ills. in color, Aug., 1926

MOORE, CHARLES:
The Transformation of Washington (D.C.): A Glance at the History and Along the Vista of the Future of the Nation's Capital. By Charles Moore. XLIII, pp. 569-595, 16 ills., maps, June, 1923

MOORE, FREDERICK:
The Changing Map in the Balkans. By Frederick Moore. XXIV, pp. 199-226, 27 ills., map, Feb., 1913
Rumania and Her Ambitions. By Frederick Moore. XXIV, pp. 1057-1085, 34 ills., Oct., 1913

MOORE, J. HAMPTON:
Honors for Amundsen (Address by J. Hampton Moore). XIX, pp. 55-76, 13 ills., Jan., 1908
National Geographic Society (Pamphlet by J. Hampton Moore on Discovery of North Pole). XXI, p. 276, Mar., 1910

MOORE, J. Z.:
Scenes from the Land Where Everybody Dresses in White (Korea). Photos by Rev. J. Z. Moore. XIX, pp. 871-877, 10 ills., Dec., 1908

MOORE, TERRIS:
Climbing Mighty Minya Konka: Americans First Scaled Mountain That Now Is Landmark of China's New Skyway. By Richard L. Burdsall and Terris Moore. LXXXIII, pp. 625-650, 23 ills., map, May, 1943

MOORE, W. ROBERT:
Along the Old Mandarin Road of Indo-China. By W. Robert Moore. LX, pp. 157-199, 32 ills. in black and white, 28 ills. in color, map, Aug., 1931
Under the French Tricolor in Indo-China. 28 color photos by author, pp. 167-198
Among the Hill Tribes of Sumatra. By W. Robert Moore. LVII, pp. 187-227, 31 ills. in black and white, 25 ills. in color, map, Feb., 1930
Sumatra, a Ribbon of Color on the Equator. 25 color photos by author, pp. 195-218
As São Paulo Grows: Half the World's Coffee Beans Flavor the Life and Speed the Growth of an Inland Brazil City. By W. Robert Moore. LXXV, pp. 657-688, 33 ills., map, May, 1939
Austrian August—and September. By W. Robert Moore. LXXIII, pp. 493-524, 11 ills. in black and white, 19 ills. in color, Apr., 1938
Austrian Kodachromes from a Candid Camera. 19 color photos by author, pp. 501-524
Beyond Australia's Cities. By W. Robert Moore. LXX, pp. 709-747, 27 ills. in black and white, 12 ills. in color, Dec., 1936
Sunny Corners of Kangaroo Land. 12 color photos by author, pp. 713-720
Bombs over Bible Lands. By Frederick Simpich and W. Robert Moore. LXXX, pp. 141-180, 34 ills., two-page map, Aug., 1941
Brazil's Potent Weapons. By W. Robert Moore. LXXXV, pp. 41-78, 16 ills. in black and white, 18 ills. in color, two-page map, Jan., 1944
Bright Facets of Brazil. 18 color photos by author, pp. 49-72
Buddhist Calm Survives Along China's Great Wall. 10 ills. in color: 3 by W. Robert Moore. LXXIII, pp. 321-328, Mar., 1938
Busy Corner—the Cape of Good Hope: Ships Bound for Faraway Battlegrounds Stream Past Capetown, "Tavern of the Seas," and Other Ports of Virile South Africa. By W. Robert Moore. LXXXII, pp. 197-223, 11 ills. in black and white, 11 ills. in color, map, Aug., 1942
Color at Africa's Southern Tip. 11 color photos by author, pp. 213-220
Capital and Chief Seaport of Chile. By W. Robert Moore. LXXXVI, pp. 477-500, 15 ills. in black and white, 8 ills. in color, map, Oct., 1944
Capital Cities of Australia. By W. Robert Moore. LXVIII, pp. 667-722, 32 ills. in black and white, 24 ills. in color, two-page map, Dec., 1935
Flashes of Color in the Fifth Continent. 24 color photos by author, pp. 681-704
Castles, Shrines, and Parks of Japanese Pilgrimage. 10 color photos by W. Robert Moore. LXIX, pp. 457-464, Apr., 1936
Castles and Progress in Portugal. By W. Robert Moore. LXXIII, pp. 133-188, 36 ills. in black and white, 24 ills. in color, map, Feb., 1938
Color Close-ups of Europe's Corner Land. 24 color photos by author, pp. 149-180
Chile's Land of Fire and Water: Smoking Volcanoes and Ice-hooded Peaks Stand Sentinel Over Limpid Lakes in the Far Southern Andes. By W. Robert Moore. LXXX, pp. 91-110, 9 ills. in black and white, 10 ills. in color, map, July, 1941

Sunshine Over the Chilean Lakes. 10 color photos by author and John Swope, pp. 97-104

Chromatic Highlights of Korea. 13 color photos by W. Robert Moore. LXIV, pp. 429-436, Oct., 1933

The Cities That Gold and Diamonds Built: Transvaal Treasures Have Created Bustling Johannesburg and Fostered Pretoria, Administrative Capital of the South African Union. By W. Robert Moore. LXXXII, pp. 735-766, 20 ills. in black and white, 9 ills. in color, map, Dec., 1942

Sunny South Africa. 9 color photos by author, pp. 749-756

Coastal Cities of China. By W. Robert Moore. LXVI, pp. 601-643, 12 ills. in black and white, 18 ills. in duotone, 14 ills. in color, map, Nov., 1934

Peiping, City of Dust and Color. 13 color photos by author, pp. 609-616

The Coasts of Normandy and Brittany. By W. Robert Moore. LXXXIV, pp. 205-232, 5 ills. in black and white, 21 ills. in color, two-page map, Aug., 1943

Normandy and Brittany in Brighter Days. 21 color photos by author, Peter Upton Muir, and others, pp. 209-232

The Color Camera Explores the Country That Moves by Night. 8 color photos by W. Robert Moore. LX, pp. 479-510, Oct., 1931

Coronation Days in Addis Ababa (Ethiopia). By W. Robert Moore. LIX, pp. 738-746, 8 ills., June, 1931

Cosmopolitan Shanghai, Key Seaport of China. By W. Robert Moore. LXII, pp. 311-335, 19 ills., Sept., 1932

Curaçao and Aruba on Guard. By W. Robert Moore. LXXXIII, pp. 169-192, 12 ills. in black and white, 10 ills. in color, 4 maps, Feb., 1943

Czechoslovakian Cyclorama. 30 color photos by W. Robert Moore. LXXIV, pp. 181-220, Aug., 1938

England's Island Garden of Rocks and Flowers (Isle of Wight). 14 color photos by W. Robert Moore. LXVII, pp. 17-24, Jan., 1935

Face of Japan. By W. Robert Moore. LXXXVIII, pp. 753-768, 14 ills., map supplement, Dec., 1945

From Sea to Clouds in Ecuador. By W. Robert Moore. LXXX, pp. 717-740, 11 ills. in black and white, 9 ills. in color, Dec., 1941

Where Snow Peaks Temper the Tropics. 9 color photos by author, pp. 727-734

The Garden Isles of Scilly: Geologists May Throw Stones at Legend of Lost Lyonnesse, But Natives Grow Flowers in Glass Houses for London. By W. Robert Moore. LXXIV, pp. 755-774, 9 ills. in black and white, 13 ills. in color, map, Dec., 1938

Gilbert Islands in the Wake of Battle. By W. Robert Moore. LXXXVII, pp. 129-162, 11 ills. in black and white, 19 ills. in color, map, Feb., 1945

Round About Grim Tarawa. 19 color photos by author, pp. 137-160

The Glory That Was Imperial Peking. By W. Robert Moore. LXIII, pp. 745-780, 18 ills. in black and white, 16 ills. in duotone, June, 1933

Capital and Country of Old Cathay. 16 ills. in duotone: 9 by author, pp. 749-764

The Golden Isles of Guale (Sea Islands, Georgia). By W. Robert Moore. LXV, pp. 235-264, 35 ills., map, Feb., 1934

Greens Grow for GI's on Soilless Ascension. By W. Robert Moore. LXXXVIII, pp. 219-230, 12 ills., Aug., 1945

High Lights in the Peruvian and Bolivian Andes. 18 color photos by W. Robert Moore. LI, pp. 219-234, Feb., 1927

In the Land of Moses and Abraham. 25 color photos by W. Robert Moore. LXXIV, pp. 711-742, Dec., 1938

"Land of the Free" in Asia: Siam Has Blended New With Old in Her Progressive March to Modern Statehood in the Family of Nations. By W. Robert Moore. LXV, pp. 531-576, 28 ills. in black and white, 26 ills. in color, map, May, 1934

Among the Plains and Hill People of Siam. 12 color photos by author, pp. 563-570

Temples and Ceremonies of Kaleidoscopic Bangkok. 9 color photos by author, pp. 547-554

Life Along the Central China Coast. 14 color photos by W. Robert Moore. LXII, pp. 317-324, Sept., 1932

Life and Color Under the Rising Sun. 9 color photos by W. Robert Moore and Kiyoshi Sakamoto. LXIII, pp. 289-296, Mar., 1933

Maryland Presents—. By W. Robert Moore. LXXIX, pp. 401-448, 17 ills. in black and white, 32 ills. in color, map, Apr., 1941

Old Line State Cyclorama. 22 color photos: 17 by author, pp. 409-432

Miniatures of Macao (China). 11 color photos by W. Robert Moore. LXII, pp. 341-348, Sept., 1932

Motor Trails in Japan. By W. Robert Moore. LXIII, pp. 303-318, 17 ills., Mar., 1933

Nevada, Desert Treasure House. By W. Robert Moore. LXXXIX, pp. 1-38, 16 ills. in black and white, 20 ills. in color, map, Jan., 1946

Land of Sagebrush and Silver. 20 color photos by author, pp. 9-32

New Zealand "Down Under." By W. Robert Moore. LXIX, pp. 165-218, 31 ills. in black and white, 23 ills. in color, two-page map, Feb., 1936

Alpine Peaks and Pastures of South Island. 11 color photos by author, pp. 205-212

North Island of New Zealand: A Vulcan's Playground. 12 color photos by author, pp. 181-188

Old-New Battle Grounds of Egypt and Libia. By W. Robert Moore. LXXVIII, pp. 809-820, 8 ills., map, Dec., 1940

Our New Military Wards, the Marshalls. By W. Robert Moore. LXXXVIII, pp. 325-360, 14 ills. in black and white, 20 ills. in color, map, Sept., 1945

Marshallese Are Happy Again. 20 color photos by author, pp. 337-360

Present Day Scenes in the World's Oldest Empire (Ethiopia). 27 color photos by W. Robert Moore. LIX, pp. 691-722, June, 1931

MOORE, W. ROBERT—*Continued*

Raft Life on the Hwang Ho. By W. Robert Moore. LXI, pp. 743-752, 14 ills., June, 1932

Rehearsal at Dieppe (France). By W. Robert Moore. LXXXII, pp. 495-502, 6 ills., Oct., 1942

Rhodesia, Hobby and Hope of Cecil Rhodes. By W. Robert Moore. LXXXVI, pp. 281-306, 13 ills. in black and white, 10 ills. in color, map, Sept., 1944

African Rainbow. 10 color photos by author, pp. 289-296

Rio Panorama: Breath-taking Is This Fantastic City amid Peaks, Palms, and Sea, and in Carnival Time It Moves to the Rhythm of Music. By W. Robert Moore. LXXVI, pp. 283-324, 12 ills. in black and white, 34 ills. in color, Sept., 1939

Carioca Carnival. 34 color photos by author, pp. 291-322

Shan Tribes Make Burma's Hills Flash With Color. 15 color photos by W. Robert Moore. LX, pp. 455-462, Oct., 1931

A Skyline Drive in the Pyrenees. By W. Robert Moore. LXXII, pp. 434-452, 24 ills. in color, Oct., 1937

Costume Pageants in the French Pyrenees. 24 color photos by author, pp. 435-450

South from Saipan. By W. Robert Moore. LXXXVII, pp. 441-474, 11 ills. in black and white, 17 ills. in color, map, Apr., 1945

Saipan and Tinian, Take-offs to Tokyo. 17 color photos: 15 by author, pp. 453-468

Strange Tribes in the Shan States of Burma. 15 color photos by W. Robert Moore. LVIII, pp. 247-254, Aug., 1930

Through Java in Pursuit of Color. By W. Robert Moore. LVI, pp. 333-362, 9 ills. in black and white, 29 ills. in color, map, Sept., 1929

Java, Queen of the East Indies. 26 color photos by author, pp. 335-358

"Time Will Not Dim the Glory of Their Deeds" (World War Memorials). 11 color photos by W. Robert Moore. LXV, pp. 17-24, Jan., 1934

Tradition Lingers in Modern Japan. 11 color photos by W. Robert Moore. LXXIII, pp. 117-124, Jan., 1938

When the Herring Fleet Comes to Great Yarmouth. By W. Robert Moore. LXVI, pp. 233-250, 19 ills., Aug., 1934

MOORE, WILLIS L.:

The Annual Dinner of the National Geographic Society (Speeches by Willis L. Moore). XVII, pp. 22-37, Jan., 1906

The Discovery of the North Pole (Speeches by Willis L. Moore). XXI, pp. 63-82, Jan., 1910

Forecasting the Weather and Storms. By Professor Willis L. Moore. XVI, pp. 255-305, 5 ills., 20 charts, June, 1905

Honors for Amundsen (Speeches by Willis L. Moore). XIX, pp. 55-76, 13 ills., Jan., 1908

Honors to Peary (Speeches by Willis L. Moore). XVIII, pp. 49-60, ill., Jan., 1907

Honors to the American Navy (Speeches by Willis L. Moore). XX, pp. 77-95, Jan., 1909

National Geographic Society (Announcement of the Election of Willis L. Moore as President of the Society). XVI, p. 87, Feb., 1905

MOORE, WILLIS L.—*Continued*

Portrait. XVIII, ill. p. 587, Sept., 1907

Storms and Weather Forecasts. By Professor Willis L. Moore. VIII, pp. 65-82, 25 charts, Mar., 1897

United States Daily Atmospheric Survey. By Prof. Willis L. Moore. VIII, pp. 299-303, Oct., 1897

The Weather Bureau. By Willis L. Moore. XII, pp. 362-369, Oct., 1901

The Weather Bureau River and Flood System. By Professor Willis L. Moore. VII, pp. 302-307, Sept., 1896

See also NGS: Board of Managers

MOORISH Spain. 26 color photos by Gervais Courtellemont. XLVI, pp. 163-178, Aug., 1924

MOOSE:

The Big Game of Alaska. By Wilfred H. Osgood. XX, pp. 624-636, 10 ills., July, 1909

Deer of the World: As Workers, Pets, and Graceful "Living Statuary" in Parks and Estates, These Versatile Creatures Have Endeared Themselves to Mankind. By Victor H. Cahalane. Paintings by Walter A. Weber. LXXVI, pp. 463-510, 20 ills. in black and white, 23 ills. in color, Oct., 1939

Lords of the Rockies: Photographing Big Game Animals in Their Primeval Surroundings, from Arizona to Canada, Brings Adventure to Two Wilderness Wanderers. By Wendell and Lucie Chapman. LXXVI, pp. 87-128, 14 ills. in black and white, 28 ills. in color, July, 1939

One Season's Game-Bag with the Camera. By George Shiras, 3d. XIX, pp. 387-446, 70 ills., June, 1908

The White Sheep, Giant Moose, and Smaller Game of the Kenai Peninsula, Alaska. By George Shiras, 3d. XXIII, pp. 423-494, 59 ills., maps (1 two-page), May, 1912

Wild Animals That Took Their Own Pictures by Day and by Night. By George Shiras, 3d. XXIV, pp. 763-834, 68 ills., map, pictorial supplement, July, 1913

The Wild Life of Lake Superior, Past and Present: The Habits of Deer, Moose, Wolves, Beavers, Muskrats, Trout, and Feathered Wood-Folk Studied with Camera and Flashlight. By George Shiras, 3d. XL, pp. 113-204, 76 ills., map, pictorial supplement, Aug., 1921

MORAVIAN MISSIONARIES:

Two Hundred Miles up the Kuskokwim. By Charles Hallock. IX, pp. 85-92, 6 ills., Mar., 1898

Note: Messrs. Hartmann and Weinland, missionaries

MORDEN, FLORENCE H.:

House-Boat Days in the Vale of Kashmir. By Florence H. Morden. LVI, pp. 437-463, 22 ills. in black and white, 30 ills. in color, Oct., 1929

MORDEN, WILLIAM J.:

By Coolie and Caravan Across Central Asia: Narrative of a 7,900-Mile Journey of Exploration and Research Over "the Roof of the World," from the Indian Ocean to the Yellow Sea. By William J. Morden. LII, pp. 369-431, 73 ills., map, Oct., 1927

MORDEN-CLARK ASIATIC EXPEDITION. *See* article, *above*

MORE Changes of the Colorado River. By D. T. MacDougal. XIX, pp. 52-54, map, Jan., 1908

MORE Water for California's Great Central Valley. By Frederick Simpich. XC, pp. 645-664, 16 ills., map, Nov., 1946

MORGAN, EDWIN V.:

The Samoan Islands. By Edwin V. Morgan. XI, pp. 417-426, Nov., 1900

MORGAN, SIR HENRY:

The Haunts of the Caribbean Corsairs: The West Indies a Geographic Background for the Most Adventurous Episodes in the History of the Western Hemisphere. By Nell Ray Clarke. XLI, pp. 147-187, 27 ills., Feb., 1922

MORGAN, JACQUES DE:

Excavations of M. de Morgan at Susa. XII, p. 315, Aug., 1901

MORGENSTIERNE, WILHELM:

Norway, an Active Ally. By Wilhelm Morgenstierne. LXXXIII, pp. 333-357, 24 ills., map, Mar., 1943

MORLEY, SYLVANUS GRISWOLD:

Chichen Itzá, an Ancient American Mecca: Recent Excavations in Yucatan Are Bringing to Light the Temples, Palaces, and Pyramids of America's Most Holy Native City. By Sylvanus Griswold Morley. XLVII, pp. 63-95, 34 ills., diagr., map, Jan., 1925

Excavations at Quirigua, Guatemala. By Sylvanus Griswold Morley. XXIV, pp. 339-361, 24 ills., diagr., Mar., 1913
Note. XXIV, p. 1056, Sept., 1913

The Foremost Intellectual Achievement of Ancient America: The Hieroglyphic Inscriptions on the Monuments in the Ruined Cities of Mexico, Guatemala, and Honduras Are Yielding the Secrets of the Maya Civilization. By Sylvanus Griswold Morley. XLI, pp. 109-130, 27 ills., 17 diagrs., map supplement, Feb., 1922

Unearthing America's Ancient History: Investigation Suggests That the Maya May Have Designed the First Astronomical Observatory in the New World in Order to Cultivate Corn. By Sylvanus Griswold Morley. LX, pp. 99-126, 28 ills., July, 1931

Yucatán, Home of the Gifted Maya: Two Thousand Years of History Reach Back to Early American Temple Builders, Corn Cultivators, and Pioneers in Mathematics. By Sylvanus Griswold Morley. Paintings by H. M. Herget. LXX, pp. 591-644, 28 ills. in black and white, 35 ills. in color, map, Nov., 1936

MOROCCO:

Across French and Spanish Morocco. By Harriet Chalmers Adams. XLVII, pp. 327-356, 19 ills. in black and white, 16 ills. in color, map, Mar., 1925

Americans on the Barbary Coast. By Willard Price. LXXXIV, pp. 1-31, 13 ills. in black and white, 10 ills. in color, map, July, 1943

Beyond the Grand Atlas: Where the French Tricolor Flies Beside the Flag of the Sultan of Morocco. By V. C. Scott O'Connor. LXI, pp. 261-319, 52 ills. in black and white, 12 ills. in color, map, Mar., 1932

MOROCCO—*Continued*

Eastward from Gibraltar: Overland Route Across North Africa to Tunisia and Libia. By Cyrus French Wicker. LXXXIII, pp. 115-142, 28 ills., Jan., 1943

Fez, Heart of Morocco: Africa's "Imperial City" Retains Its Teeming Streets, Cluttered Shops, Glamorous Moorish Homes and Mosques, Amid the Peace of French Rule. By Gordon Casserly. LXVII, pp. 663-694, 13 ills. in black and white, 27 ills. in color, June, 1935

A Journey in Morocco: "The Land of the Moors." By Thomas Lindsey Blayney. XXII, pp. 750-775, 23 ills., map, Aug., 1911

Morocco, "The Land of the Extreme West" and the Story of My Captivity. By Ion Perdicaris. XVII, pp. 117-157, 24 ills., Mar., 1906

Notes on Morocco. XVII, p. 157, Mar., 1906

The People of Morocco. XVII, pp. 108-109, ill., Feb., 1906

Scenes from North Africa. XVIII, pp. 615-619, 4 ills., Sept., 1907

The Two Great Moorish Religious Dances. By George Edmund Holt. XXII, pp. 777-785, 6 ills., Aug., 1911

See also Casablanca

MOROS (People):

Mindanao, on the Road to Tokyo. By Frederick Simpich. LXXXVI, pp. 539-574, 26 ills. in black and white, 12 ills. in color, two-page map, Nov., 1944

MORRIS, EARL H.:

Exploring in the Canyon of Death (Arizona): Remains of a People Who Dwelt in Our Southwest at Least 4,000 Years Ago Are Revealed. By Earl H. Morris. XLVIII, pp. 263-300, 24 ills. in black and white, 22 ills. in color, Sept., 1925

MORRISSEY (Schooner). *See Effie M. Morrissey*

MORRISTOWN, New Jersey: Seeing Eye School:

Dogs of Duty and Devotion. By Frederick G. Vosburgh. LXXX, pp. 769-774, 3 ills., Dec., 1941

MORSE, FREMONT:

The Recession of the Glaciers of Glacier Bay, Alaska. By Fremont Morse. XIX, pp. 76-78, map, Jan., 1908

MOSCOW, U. S. S. R.:

Glimpses of the Russian Empire. By William Wisner Chapin. XXIII, pp. 1043-1078, 51 ills. in color, map, Nov., 1912

I Learn About the Russians. By Eddy Gilmore. LXXXIV, pp. 619-640, 21 ills., Nov., 1943

The Rebirth of Religion in Russia: The Church Reorganized While Bolshevik Cannon Spread Destruction in the Nation's Holy of Holies. By Thomas Whittemore. XXXIV, pp. 379-401, 16 ills., Nov., 1918

Russia of the Hour: Giant Battle Ground for Theories of Economy, Society, and Politics, as Observed by an Unbiased Correspondent. By Junius B. Wood. L, pp. 519-598, 81 ills., Nov., 1926

MOSCOW, U. S. S. R.—*Continued*
Young Russia: The Land of Unlimited Possibilities. By Gilbert H. Grosvenor. XXVI, pp. 421-520, 85 ills. in black and white, 17 ills. in color, Nov., 1914

MOSELEY, E. L.:
Rainfall and the Level of Lake Erie. (By E. L. Moseley). XIV, pp. 327-328, Aug., 1903
Submerged Valleys in Sandusky Bay (Ohio). By Professor E. L. Moseley. XIII, pp. 398-403, 4 charts, Nov., 1902
Testing the Currents of Lake Erie. (By E. L. Moseley). XIV, pp. 41-42, Jan., 1903

MOSELLE (River), France:
The Seine, the Meuse, and the Moselle. (Part I). By William M. Davis. VII, pp. 189-202, ill., 7 maps, June, 1896
The Seine, the Meuse, and the Moselle. (Part) II. By William M. Davis. VII, pp. 228-238, table, 4 maps, July, 1896

MOSER, CHARLES K.:
"The Flower of Paradise": The Part Which Khat Plays in the Life of the Yemen Arab. By Charles K. Moser. XXXII, pp. 173-186, 10 ills., map, Aug., 1917
The Isle of Frankincense (Socotra, Arabian Sea). By Charles K. Moser. XXXIII, pp. 267-278, 11 ills., Mar., 1918

MOSES, GEORGE HIGGINS:
Greece and Montenegro. By George Higgins Moses. XXIV, pp. 281-310, 24 ills., Mar., 1913
Greece of Today. By George Higgins Moses. XXVIII, pp. 295-329, 27 ills., Oct., 1915
New Hampshire, the Granite State. By George Higgins Moses. LX, pp. 257-310, 47 ills. in black and white, 5 ills. in color, map. Sept., 1931
The Whirlpool of the Balkans. By George Higgins Moses. XXXIX, pp. 179-197, 15 ills., Feb., 1921

MOSLEMS:
Color Records from the Changing Life of the Holy City (Jerusalem). By Maynard Owen Williams. LII, pp. 682-707, 27 ills. in color, Dec., 1927
The Emancipation of Mohammedan Women. By Mary Mills Patrick. XX, pp. 42-66, 19 ills., Jan., 1909
India—Yesterday, Today, and Tomorrow. By Lord Halifax. LXXXIV, pp. 385-408, 20 ills., two-page map, Oct., 1943
India Mosaic. By Peter Muir and Frances Muir. LXXXIX, pp. 443-470, 5 ills. in black and white, 22 ills. in color, map, Apr., 1946
Mecca the Mystic: A New Kingdom Within Arabia (Hejaz). By S. M. Zwemer. XXXII, pp. 157-172, 13 ills., Aug., 1917
Mystic Nedjef, the Shia Mecca. By Frederick Simpich. XXVI, pp. 589-598, 4 ills., Dec., 1914
The Pageant of Jerusalem: The Capital of the Land of Three Great Faiths Is Still the Holy City for Christian, Moslem, and Jew. By Major Edward Keith-Roach. LII, pp. 635-681, 57 ills., Dec., 1927

MOSLEMS—*Continued*
Pilgrims' Progress to Mecca. 22 ills. in duotone: 18 by Oscar Marcus. LXXII, pp. 627-642, Nov., 1937
The Races and Religions of Macedonia. By Luigi Villari. XXIII, pp. 1118-1132, 14 ills., Nov., 1912
The Sacred City of the Sands (Kairouan, Tunisia). By Frank Edward Johnson. XXII, pp. 1061-1093, 25 ills., map, Dec., 1911
An Unbeliever Joins the Hadj: On the Age-Old Pilgrimage to Mecca, Babies Are Born, Elders Die, and Families May Halt a Year to Earn Funds in Distant Lands. By Owen Tweedy. LXV, pp. 761-789, 30 ills., map, June, 1934
See also Moros

MOSQUES:
Gilded Domes Against an Azure Sky. 13 color photos by Stephen H. Nyman. LXXVI, pp. 339-346, Sept., 1939
See also Sancta Sophia

MOSQUITO CAYS, Caribbean Sea:
Capturing Giant Turtles in the Caribbean. By David D. Duncan. LXXXIV, pp. 177-190, 13 ills., map, Aug., 1943

MOSQUITOES:
Life Story of the Mosquito. By Graham Fairchild. With 10 ills. in color from paintings. LXXXV, pp. 180-195, 5 ills. in black and white, drawing, Feb., 1944
Saboteur Mosquitoes. By Harry H. Stage. LXXXV, pp. 165-179, 12 ills., Feb., 1944

MOST Curious Craft Afloat: The Compass in Navigation and the Work of the Non-Magnetic Yacht "Carnegie." By L. A. Bauer. XXI, pp. 223-245, 31 ills., Mar., 1910

The **MOST** Extraordinary City in the World: Notes on Lhasa—The Mecca of the Buddhist Faith. By Shaoching H. Chuan. XXIII, pp. 959-995, 60 ills., Oct., 1912

The **MOST** Famous Battle Field in America (Gettysburg). 14 color photos by Clifton Adams and Orren R. Louden. LX, pp. 66-75, July, 1931

The **MOST** Historic Lands on Earth. XXVI, p. 615, map, Dec., 1914

The **MOST** Valuable Bird in the World (Guanay). By Robert Cushman Murphy. XLVI, pp. 279-302, 25 ills., map, Sept., 1924

The **MOTHER MAPS** of the United States. By Henry Gannett. IV, pp. 101-116, table, map supplement, Mar. 31, 1892

The **MOTHER** of Rivers: An Account of a Photographic Expedition to the Great Columbia Ice Field of the Canadian Rockies. By Lewis R. Freeman. XLVII, pp. 377-446, 60 ills., maps, Apr., 1925

MOTHER Volga Defends Her Own (U. S. S. R.). By Maynard Owen Williams. LXXXII, pp. 793-811, 21 ills., Dec., 1942

MOTHERS of Many Lands. 16 ills. XXXI, pp. 549-564, June, 1917

MOTHS:

Explorers of a New Kind: Successful Introduction of Beetles and Parasites to Check Ravages of the Gipsy-moth and Brown-tail Moth. By L. O. Howard. XXVI, pp. 38-67, 11 ills. in black and white, 5 ills. in color, July, 1914

Exploring the Wonders of the Insect World. By William Joseph Showalter. Paintings by Hashime Murayama. LVI, pp. 1-90, 59 ills. in black and white, 269 ills. in color, July, 1929

The Gypsy Moth. XVII, pp. 461-464, 5 ills., Aug., 1906

An Insect Community Lives in Flower Heads. By James G. Needham. XC, pp. 340-356, 5 ills. in black and white, 11 ills. in color, Sept., 1946

Pests and Parasites: Why We Need a National Law to Prevent the Importation of Insect-Infested and Diseased Plants. By Charles Lester Marlatt. XXII, pp. 321-346, 29 ills., maps, Apr., 1911

Strange Habits of Familiar Moths and Butterflies. By William Joseph Showalter. LII, pp. 77-105, 19 ills. in black and white, drawing, 88 ills. in color, July, 1927

Where Our Moths and Butterflies Roam. LII, pp. 105-126, 8 ills. in black and white, 81 ills. in color, July, 1927
Contents: Arctiidae, Ceratocampidae, Lithosiidae Noctuidae, Saturniidae, Sphingidae

MOTION PICTURE INDUSTRY:

Southern California at Work. By Frederick Simpich. LXVI, pp. 529-600, 39 ills. in black and white, 41 ills. in color, two-page map, Nov., 1934

MOTOR-COACHING Through North Carolina. By Melville Chater. XLIX, pp. 475-523, 43 ills., map, May, 1926

MOTOR Trails in Japan. By W. Robert Moore. LXIII, pp. 303-318, 17 ills., Mar., 1933

MOUND BUILDERS:

The Indian Village of Baum (Ohio). (By H. C. Brown). XII, pp. 272-274, July, 1901

Indians of the Southeastern United States. By Matthew W. Stirling. Paintings by W. Langdon Kihn. LXXXIX, pp. 53-74, 8 ills. in black and white, 8 ills. in color, Jan., 1946

Ohio, the Gateway State. By Melville Chater. LXI, pp. 525-591, 58 ills. in black and white, 13 ills. in color, map, May, 1932

MOUNT DESERT ISLAND, Maine:

First National Park East of Mississippi River. XXIX, pp. 623-626, 5 ills., June, 1916

The Need of Conserving the Beauty and Freedom of Nature in Modern Life. By Charles W. Eliot. XXVI, pp. 67-74, 4 ills., July, 1914

Northeast of Boston. By Albert W. Atwood. LXXXVIII, pp. 257-292, 12 ills. in black and white, 17 ills. in color, map supplement, Sept., 1945

The Unique Island of Mount Desert. By George B. Dorr, Ernest Howe Forbush, M. L. Fernald. XXVI, pp. 75-89, 7 ills., July, 1914

MOUNT McKinley. (By Robert Muldrow). XII, pp. 312-313, map, Aug., 1901

MOUNT McKINLEY NATIONAL PARK, Alaska:

A Game Country Without Rival in America: The Proposed Mount McKinley National Park. By Stephen R. Capps. XXXI, pp. 69-84, 14 ills., map, Jan., 1917

MOUNT RAINIER NATIONAL PARK, Washington:

The Great White Monarch of the Pacific Northwest. By A. H. Barnes. XXIII, pp. 593-626, 31 ills., map, June, 1912

Our National Parks. By L. F. Schmeckebier. XXIII, pp. 531-579, 41 ills., map, June, 1912

A Wonderland of Glaciers and Snow. By Milnor Roberts. XX, pp. 530-537, 8 ills., June, 1909

The **MT.** St. Elias Expedition of Prince Luigi Amadeo of Savoy, 1897. (By E.R.S.). IX, pp. 93-96, Mar., 1898

MOUNT St. Helens. By Lieut. Charles P. Elliott. VIII, pp. 226-230, foldout map, July-Aug., 1897

MOUNT VERNON, Virginia:

The Home of the First Farmer of America. By Worth E. Shoults. LIII, pp. 603-628, 6 ills. in black and white, 26 ills. in color, May, 1928

MOUNT Vesuvius. XVII, pp. 272-279, 7 ills., map, May, 1906

MOUNT WEATHER METEOROLOGICAL OBSERVATORY, Virginia:

Scientific Work of Mount Weather Meteorological Observatory. By Professor Frank H. Bigelow. XV, pp. 442-445, Nov., 1904

MOUNTAIN CLIMBING:

Amid the Snow Peaks of the Equator: A Naturalist's Explorations Around Ruwenzori, with an Excursion to the Congo State, and an Account of the Terrible Scourge of Sleeping Sickness. By A. F. R. Wollaston. XX, pp. 256-277, 11 ills., Mar., 1909

The Ascent of Mont Blanc. By Walter Woodburn Hyde. XXIV, pp. 861-942, 69 ills., Aug., 1913

Climbing Mighty Minya Konka: Americans First Scaled Mountain That Now Is Landmark of China's New Skyway. By Richard L. Burdsall and Terris Moore. LXXXIII, pp. 625-650, 23 ills., map, May, 1943

The Conquest of Mount Crillon (Alaska). By Bradford Washburn. LXVII, pp. 361-400, 40 ills., maps, Mar., 1935

The Conquest of Mount Logan: North America's Second Highest Peak Yields to the Intrepid Attack of Canadian Climbers. By H. F. Lambart. XLIX, pp. 597-631, 40 ills., June, 1926

Duke of the Abruzzi in the Himalayas. (By A. W. G.). XXI, pp. 245-249, Mar., 1910

An Expedition to Mount St. Elias, Alaska. By Israel C. Russell. III, pp. 53-191, 17 ills., 3 diagrs., tables, 7 maps (1 foldout), May 29, 1891

The Glories of the Minya Konka: Magnificent Snow Peaks of the China-Tibetan Border Are Photographed at Close Range by a National Geographic Society Expedition. By Joseph F. Rock. LVIII, pp. 385-437, 35 ills. in black and white, 24 ills. in color, map, Oct., 1930

MOUNTAIN CLIMBING—*Continued*

The Highest Camp in the World. XVII, pp. 647-648, Nov., 1906

Highest Camps and Climbs. By Edwin Swift Balch. XVII, p. 713, Dec., 1906

Konka Risumgongba, Holy Mountain of the Outlaws. By Joseph F. Rock. LX, pp. 1-65, 36 ills. in black and white, 43 ills. in color, map, July, 1931

Manless Alpine Climbing: The First Woman to Scale the Grépon, the Matterhorn, and Other Famous Peaks Without Masculine Support Relates Her Adventures. By Miriam O'Brien Underhill. LXVI, pp. 131-170, 30 ills. in black and white, 12 ills. in color, Aug., 1934

Modern Persia and Its Capital: And an Account of an Ascent of Mount Demavend, the Persian Olympus. By F. L. Bird. XXXIX, pp. 353-400, 47 ills., Apr., 1921

The Monarch of the Canadian Rockies (Mount Robson). By Charles D. Walcott. XXIV, pp. 626-639, 13 ills., panorama, May, 1913

The Mt. St. Elias Expedition of Prince Luigi Amadeo of Savoy, 1897. (By E.R.S.). IX, pp. 93-96, Mar., 1898

The Peak of Itambé. IX, p. 476, Nov., 1898

Plan for Climbing Mt. McKinley. By Alfred H. Brooks and D. L. Reaburn. XIV, pp. 30-35, map, Jan., 1903

The Recent Ascent of Itambé. (By J. C. Branner). X, p. 183, May, 1899

Record Ascents in the Himalayas. XIV, pp. 420-421, Nov., 1903

Seeking the Mountains of Mystery: An Expedition on the China-Tibet Frontier to the Unexplored Amnyi Machen Range, One of Whose Peaks Rivals Everest. By Joseph F. Rock. LVII, pp. 131-185, 54 ills., two-page map, Feb., 1930

Through Brazil to the Summit of Mount Roraima. By G. H. H. Tate. LVIII, pp. 585-605, 24 ills., map, Nov., 1930

The Volcanoes of Ecuador, Guideposts in Crossing South America. By G. M. Dyott. LV, pp. 49-93, 42 ills. in black and white, 12 ills. in color, map, Jan., 1929

A Woman's Climbs in the High Alps. By Dora Keen. XXII, pp. 643-675, 26 ills., July, 1911

The World's Highest Altitudes and First Ascents. By Charles E. Fay. XX, pp. 493-530, 25 ills., June, 1909

See also Mazamas

MOUNTAIN SHEEP:

Lords of the Rockies: Photographing Big Game Animals in Their Primeval Surroundings, from Arizona to Canada, Brings Adventure to Two Wilderness Wanderers. By Wendell and Lucie Chapman. LXXVI, pp. 87-128, 14 ills. in black and white, 28 ills. in color, July, 1939

MOUNTAIN Tribes of Iran and Iraq. By Harold Lamb. LXXXIX, pp. 385-408, 15 ills., two-page map, Mar., 1946

MOUNTAINEERS: Tennessee-Kentucky:

Home Folk around Historic Cumberland Gap. By Leo A. Borah. LXXXIV, pp. 741-768, 25 ills., map, Dec., 1943

The **MOUNTAINEERS** of the Euphrates. By Ellsworth Huntington. XX, pp. 142-156, 13 ills., Feb., 1909

MOUNTAINS:

Fundamental Geographic Relation of the Three Americas. By Robert T. Hill. VII, pp. 175-181, map, May, 1896

Geomorphology of the Southern Appalachians. By Charles Willard Hayes and Marius R. Campbell. VI, pp. 63-126, diagrs., 4 maps, May 23, 1894

Relations of Air and Water to Temperature and Life. By Honorable Gardiner G. Hubbard. V, pp. 112-124, Jan. 31, 1894

Round About Asheville. By Bailey Willis. I, pp. 291-300, map supplement, Oct., 1889

See also Adirondack Mountains; Alps; Altai Mountains; Amne Machin Shan; Andes; Argaeus, Mount; Athos, Mount; Atlas Mountains; Bandai-San; Bighorn Mountains; Blanc, Mont; Blue Mountain; Blue Ridge; Brukkaros, Mount; Cameroons Mountain; Canadian Rocky Mountains; Cascade Range; Caucasus; Chugach; Crillon; Demavend, Mount; Dent du Requin; Diamond Mountains; Dolomites; Elburz Mountains; Erebus, Mount; Everest, Mount; Falling Mountain; Gerizim; Great Smoky Mountains; Guadalupe Mountains; Himalayas; Hood, Mount; Itambé; Izalco Volcano; Katmai; Konka Risumgongba; Logan, Mount; McKinley, Mount; Martin, Mount; Matterhorn; Minya Konka; Mulu, Mount; Navajo Mountain; Novarupta; Nyamlagira; Olympic Mountains; Orizaba; Parnassus; Pavlof Volcano; Pelée, Mont; Perry Peak; Poás; Popocatepetl; Pyrenees; Rainier, Mount; Robson, Mount; Rocky Mountains; Roraima; Rosa, Monte; Ruwenzori; St. Elias; St. Helens, Mount; Sakurajima; San Juan Mountains; San Salvador Volcano; Selkirk Mountains; Shawangunk Mountain; Shishaldin; Soufrière; Tai Shan; Vesuvius; Volcanoes; Weisshorn; White Mountains; Wilson, Mount; Wrangell Mountains

MOUNTAINS OF THE MOON. *See* Ruwenzori

MOUNTAINS on Unimak Island, Alaska. By Ferdinand Westdahl. XIV, pp. 91-99, 4 ills., map, Mar., 1903

MOUNTFORD, CHARLES P.:

Earth's Most Primitive People: A Journey with the Aborigines of Central Australia. By Charles P. Mountford. LXXXIX, pp. 89-112, 10 ills. in black and white, 8 ills. in color, map, Jan., 1946

Australia's Stone Age Men. 8 color photos by author, pp. 105-112

The **MOVEMENTS** of Our Population (U. S.). By Henry Gannett. V, pp. 21-44, 7 diagrs., 15 tables, 15 maps, Mar. 20, 1893

MOWBRAY, LOUIS L.:

Certain Citizens of the Warm Sea. By Louis L. Mowbray. Paintings by Hashime Murayama. XLI, pp. 27-62, 18 ills. in black and white, 16 ills. in color, Jan., 1922

MOZAMBIQUE:

Hunting Big Game in Portugese East Africa. (By R. C. F. Maugham). XVIII, pp. 723-730, 7 ills., Nov., 1907

MOZAMBIQUE—*Continued*
Impressions and Scenes of Mozambique. By O. W. Barrett. XXI, pp. 807-830, 31 ills., Oct., 1910

Wings Over Nature's Zoo in Africa. 20 photos in duotone by Reginald A. Bourlay. LXXVI, pp. 527-542, Oct., 1939

MTZKHET, U. S. S. R.:
Russia's Orphan Races: Picturesque Peoples Who Cluster on the Southeastern Borderland of the Vast Slav Dominions. By Maynard Owen Williams. XXXIV, pp. 245-278, 26 ills., map, Oct., 1918

MUGHS (Tribespeople):
India's Treasures Helped the Allies. By John Fischer. LXXXIX, pp. 501-522, 18 ills., Apr., 1946

MUHARRAQ (Town and Island), Bahrein Islands:
Bahrein: Port of Pearls and Petroleum. By Maynard Owen Williams. LXXXIX, pp. 195-210, 6 ills. in black and white, 11 ills. in color, map, Feb., 1946

MUIR, FRANCES:
India Mosaic. By Peter Muir and Frances Muir. LXXXIX, pp. 443-470, 5 ills. in black and white, 22 ills. in color, map, Apr., 1946
India at Work and Play. 22 color photos by authors and Maynard Owen Williams, pp. 449-464

MUIR, JOHN:
The Discovery of Glacier Bay, Alaska. By Eliza Ruhamah Scidmore. VII, pp. 140-146, ill., map, Apr., 1896
Included: John Muir's discovery of Glacier Bay

Portrait. XII, ill. p. 188, May, 1901

MUIR, PETER UPTON:
India Mosaic. By Peter Muir and Frances Muir. LXXXIX, pp. 443-470, 5 ills. in black and white, 22 ills. in color, map, Apr., 1946
India at Work and Play. 22 color photos by authors and Maynard Owen Williams, pp. 449-464

Normandy and Brittany in Brighter Days. 21 color photos by W. Robert Moore, Peter Upton Muir, and others. LXXXIV, pp. 209-232, Aug., 1943

MUIR GLACIER, Alaska:
The Discovery of Glacier Bay, Alaska. By Eliza Ruhamah Scidmore. VII, pp. 140-146, ill., map, Apr., 1896

Muir Glacier. (By C. L. Andrews). XIV, pp. 441-444, ills., map, Dec., 1903

Studies of Muir Glacier, Alaska. By Harry Fielding Reid. IV, pp. 19-55, 13 ills., 6 diagrs., table, 2 maps (1 foldout), Mar. 21, 1892
Appendices: List of Plants Collected near Muir Glacier, determined by W. W. Rowlee, p. 79; Meteorological Observations, by Harry Fielding Reid, pp. 80-81; Magnetic Observations, by Harry Fielding Reid, p. 82; Suggestions to Future Observers, by H. F. Reid, pp. 83-84

MUIR GLACIER, Alaska—*Continued*
Supplements: Notes on the Geology of the Vicinity of Muir Glacier, by H. P. Cushing, pp. 56-62, map; Notes on Some Eruptive Rocks from Alaska, by George H. Williams, pp. 63-74; Microscopical Examination of Wood from the Buried Forest, Muir Inlet, Alaska, by Francis H. Herrick, pp. 75-78, drawings

MUIR INLET, Alaska:
Studies of Muir Glacier, Alaska. By Harry Fielding Reid. IV, pp. 19-55, 13 ills., 6 diagrs., table, 2 maps (1 foldout), Mar. 21, 1892
Supplement: Microscopical Examination of Wood from the Buried Forest, Muir Inlet, Alaska, by Francis H. Herrick, pp. 75-78, drawings

MUKDEN, Manchuria:
Japan Faces Russia in Manchuria. By Willard Price. LXXXII, pp. 603-634, 30 ills., map, Nov., 1942

Mukden, the Manchu Home, and Its Great Art Museum. By Eliza R. Scidmore. XXI, pp. 289-320, 30 ills., Apr., 1910

MULA MULAI (Ship):
Seafarers of South Celebes. By G. E. P. Collins. LXXXVII, pp. 53-78, 25 ills., map, Jan., 1945

MULATAS ARCHIPELAGO, Panama:
Arch-Isolationists, the San Blas Indians: Coconuts Serve as Cash on Islands Off the Panama Coast Where Tribesmen Cling to Their Ancient Ways and Discourage Visitors. By Corine B. Feeney. LXXIX, pp. 193-220, 15 ills. in black and white, 12 ills. in color, map, Feb., 1941

MULBERRY (Artificial Harbor), Normandy Coast, France:
Normandy's Made-in-England Harbors. LXXXVII, pp. 565-580, 16 ills., map, May, 1945

MULDROW, ROBERT:
Mount McKinley. (By Robert Muldrow). XII, pp. 312-313, map, Aug., 1901

MULE DEER:
High Country of Colorado. By Alfred M. Bailey. With 23 color photos by author, Robert J. Niedrach, F. G. Brandenburg. XC, pp. 43-72, 9 ills. in black and white, July, 1946

MULI (Lama Kingdom):
The Land of the Yellow Lama: National Geographic Society Explorer Visits the Strange Kingdom of Muli, Beyond the Likiang Snow Range of Yünnan Province, China. By Joseph F. Rock. XLVII, pp. 447-491, 39 ills., map, Apr., 1925

MULLER, JAMES ARTHUR:
Peking, the City of the Unexpected. By James Arthur Muller. XXXVIII, pp. 335-355, 18 ills., Nov., 1920

MULLIKIN, MARY AUGUSTA:
China's Great Wall of Sculpture: Man-hewn Caves and Countless Images Form a Colossal Art Wonder of Early Buddhism. By Mary Augusta Mullikin. Paintings by author and Anna M. Hotchkis. LXXIII, pp. 313-348, 23 ills. in black and white, 10 ills. in color, map, Mar., 1938

MULLIKIN, MARY AUGUSTA—*Continued*
Buddhist Calm Survives Along China's Great Wall. 10 ills. in color: 4 paintings by author and Anna M. Hotchkis, pp. 321-328
Tai Shan, Sacred Mountain of the East. By Mary Augusta Mullikin. LXXXVII, pp. 699-719, 18 ills., map, June, 1945

MULTICOLORED Cones of Cappadocia. 20 color photos by Eric Matson. LXXVI, pp. 769-800, Dec., 1939

MULTI-HUED Marvels of a Coral Reef. 8 ills. in color from paintings by Else Bostelmann. LXV, pp. 719-726, June, 1934

MULU, Mount, Borneo:
Sarawak: The Land of the White Rajahs. By Harrison W. Smith. XXXV, pp. 110-167, 58 ills., map, Feb., 1919

MUNDA, New Georgia (Island), Solomon Islands:
Painting History in the Pacific. 19 ills. in color from paintings by Lt. William F. Draper, USNR. LXXXVI, pp. 408-424, Oct., 1944

MUNGER, F. M.:
A Jack in the Box: An Account of the Strange Performances of the Most Wonderful Island in the World (Bogoslof Volcano, Alaska). By Captain F. M. Munger. XX, pp. 194-199, 8 ills., Feb., 1909

MÜNSTER, Germany:
The Town of Many Gables. By Florence Craig Albrecht. XXVII, pp. 107-140, 28 ills., Feb., 1915

MURAYAMA, HASHIME:
Ants: Work and War in the World of Ants. 18 ills. in color from paintings by Hashime Murayama. LXVI, pp. 179-186, Aug., 1934
Bees: In Field and Hive with the Busy Honeybee. 16 ills. in color from paintings by Hashime Murayama. LXVII, pp. 417-424, Apr., 1935
Birds: Iridescent Isles of the South Seas. 16 ills. in color: 4 paintings by Hashime Murayama. XLVIII, pp. 403-418, Oct., 1925
Birds: Pigeons of Resplendent Plumage. 12 ills. in color from paintings by Hashime Murayama. XLIX, pp. 65-76, Jan., 1926
Butterflies: Nomads Among the Butterflies. 8 ills. in color: 3 paintings by Hashime Murayama, 5 color photos by Willard R. Culver. LXXI, pp. 569-584, May, 1937
Butterflies: Winged Jewels from Many Lands. 9 ills. in color: 3 paintings by Hashime Murayama, 6 color photos by Willard R. Culver. LXIX, pp. 673-688, May, 1936
Fish. 16 ills. in color from paintings by Hashime Murayama. XXXIX, pp. 61-68, Jan., 1921
Fish. 16 ills. in color from paintings by Hashime Murayama. XLI, pp. 37-52, Jan., 1922
Fish: Fresh-Water Denizens of the Far West. 44 portraits from paintings by Hashime Murayama. LXXV, pp. 193-204, Feb., 1939
Fish: Fresh-Water Fishes of the United States. 16 ills. in color from paintings by Hashime Murayama. XLIV, pp. 133-148, Aug., 1923

MURAYAMA, HASHIME—*Continued*
Fish: Gleaming Fishes of Pacific Coastal Waters. 31 portraits from paintings by Hashime Murayama. LXXIV, pp. 467-498, Oct., 1938
Fish: Goldfish and Their Cultivation. 8 ills. in color from paintings by Hashime Murayama. XLVI, pp. 385-392, Oct., 1924
Fish: Iridescent Denizens of the Miniature Aquarium. 8 ills. in color from paintings by Hashime Murayama. LIX, pp. 293-300, Mar., 1931
Fish: North Atlantic Fishes. 16 ills in color from paintings by Hashime Murayama. XLIV, pp. 613-628, Dec., 1923
Fowl: Domestic Fowls of Field, Park, and Farmyard. 16 ills. in color from paintings by Hashime Murayama. LVII, pp. 329-360, Mar., 1930
Fowl of the Old and New World. 29 ills. in color from paintings by Hashime Murayama. LI, pp. 421-436, Apr., 1927
Frogs and Toads: The Iridescent Beauty of Frogs and Toads. 14 ills. in color from paintings by Hashime Murayama. LXI, pp. 635-642, May, 1932
Insect Rivals of the Rainbow. 3 ills. in color from paintings by Hashime Murayama. LVI, pp. 29, 53, 77, July, 1929
Insects: Rogues' Gallery of Imported Pests. 10 ills. in color from paintings by Hashime Murayama. LXXX, pp. 237-244, Aug., 1941
Spiders: Nature's Ingenious Spinners. 64 ills. in color from paintings by Hashime Murayama. LXIV, pp. 167-174, Aug., 1933
Wasps and Hornets: Farmers' Friends Among the Wasps and Hornets. 12 ills. in color from paintings by Hashime Murayama. LXXII, pp. 57-64, July, 1937

MURDOCH, HELEN MESSINGER:
India and Ceylon. 8 color photos by Helen Messinger Murdoch. XXXIX, pp. 281-288, Mar., 1921

MURDOCH, JOHN:
On Eskimo Geographic Names Ending in Miut. (By John Murdoch). IX, p. 190, Apr., 1898

MURDOCH, L. H.:
Why Great Salt Lake Has Fallen. By L. H. Murdoch. XIV, pp. 75-77, Feb., 1903

The **MURMAN COAST:** Arctic Gateway for American and Allied Expeditionary Forces in Northern European Russia. XXXV, pp. 331-348, 30 ills., map, Apr., 1919

MURPHY, ROBERT CUSHMAN:
Birds of the High Seas: Albatrosses and Petrels; Gannets, Man-o'-war-birds, and Tropic-birds. By Robert Cushman Murphy. Paintings by Major Allan Brooks. LXXIV, pp. 226-251, 7 ills. in black and white, 36 portraits in color, Aug., 1938
The Most Valuable Bird in the World (Guanay). By Robert Cushman Murphy. XLVI, pp. 279-302, 25 ills., map, Sept., 1924

MURPHY, ROBERT CUSHMAN—*Continued*

The Romance of Science in Polynesia: An Account of Five Years of Cruising Among the South Sea Islands. By Robert Cushman Murphy. Paintings by Hashime Murayama. XLVIII, pp. 355-426, 66 ills. in black and white, 16 ills. in color, 3 maps, Oct., 1925

South Georgia, an Outpost of the Antarctic. By Robert Cushman Murphy. XLI, pp. 409-444, 41 ills., maps, Apr., 1922

The Timeless Arans: The Workaday World Lies Beyond the Horizon of Three Rocky Islets Off the Irish Coast. By Robert Cushman Murphy. LIX, pp. 747-775, 35 ills., map, June, 1931

MURRAY, EDWARD STEVENSON:

On the Turks' Russian Frontier: Everyday Life in the Fastnesses between the Black Sea and Ararat, Borderland of Oil and Minerals that Hitler Covets. By Edward Stevenson Murray. LXXX, pp. 367-392, 21 ills., map, Sept., 1941

With the Nomads of Central Asia: A Summer's Sojourn in the Tekes Valley, Plateau Paradise of Mongol and Turkic Tribes. By Edward Murray. Paintings and drawings by Alexandre Iacovleff. LXIX, pp. 1-57, 43 ills. in black and white, 26 ills. in color, map, Jan., 1936

MURRAY, SIR JOHN:

Sir John Murray (Biography). XII, pp. 238-240, ill., June, 1901

MURRAY, LOUISE:

In Valais (Switzerland). By Louise Murray. XXI, pp. 249-256, 6 ills., Mar., 1910

MURRELETS (Birds):

Birds of the Northern Seas. By Alexander Wetmore. Paintings by Maj. Allan Brooks. LXIX, pp. 95-122, 12 ills. in black and white, 34 portraits in color, Jan., 1936

MURRES (Birds):

Birds of the Northern Seas. By Alexander Wetmore. Paintings by Maj. Allan Brooks. LXIX, pp. 95-122, 12 ills. in black and white, 34 portraits in color, Jan., 1936

MURZUCH, Libia:

The Mysteries of the Desert. By Hanns Vischer. XXII, pp. 1056-1059, Nov., 1911

MUSAN, Korea:

Exploring Unknown Corners of the "Hermit Kingdom." By Roy Chapman Andrews. XXXVI, pp. 25-48, 30 ills., map, July, 1919

MUSHROOMS:

Common Mushrooms of the United States. By Louis C. C. Krieger. Paintings by author. XXXVII, pp. 387-439, 37 ills. in black and white, 16 ills. in color, May, 1920

MUSKRATS:

Wild Animals That Took Their Own Pictures by Day and by Night. By George Shiras, 3d. XXIV, pp. 763-834, 68 ills., map, pictorial supplement, July, 1913

The Wild Life of Lake Superior, Past and Present: The Habits of Deer, Moose, Wolves, Beavers, Muskrats, Trout, and Feathered Wood-Folk Studied with Camera and Flashlight. By George Shiras, 3d. XL, pp. 113-204, 76 ills., map, pictorial supplement, Aug., 1921

MUSTAPHA KEMAL (President of Turkey):

The Turkish Republic Comes of Age. By Maynard Owen Williams. LXXXVII, pp. 581-616, 4 ills. in black and white, 29 ills. in color, map, May, 1945

MY Domestic Life in French Guinea: An American Woman Accompanies Her Husband, a French Geologist, on His Explorations in a Little-Known Region. By Eleanor de Chételat. LXVII, pp. 695-730, 48 ills., map, June, 1935

MY Flight Across Antarctica. By Lincoln Ellsworth. LXX, pp. 1-35, 37 ills., map, July, 1936

MY Flight from Hawaii. By Amelia Earhart. LXVII, pp. 593-609, 4 ills. in black and white, 8 ills. in duotone, May, 1935

MY Four Antarctic Expeditions: Explorations of 1933-39 Have Stricken Vast Areas from the Realm of the Unknown. By Lincoln Ellsworth. LXXVI, pp. 129-138, 9 ills., map, July, 1939

MYCETOZOA:

Marvels of Mycetozoa: Exploration of a Long Island Swamp Reveals Some of the Secrets of the Slime Molds, Dwelling on the Borderland Between the Plant and Animal Kingdoms. By William Crowder. Paintings by author. XLIX, pp. 421-443, 5 ills. in black and white, 16 ills. in color, Apr., 1926

Contents: Arcyria denudata, Arcyria ferruginea, Badhamia papaveracea, Comatricha pulchella, Diachea leucopoda, Dictydium cancellatum, Diderma testaceum, Fuligo septica, Globuliferum, Lamproderma arcyrionema, Lamproderma violaceum, Leocarpus fragilis, Physarum lateritium, Physarum viride, Stemonitis splendens, Trichia persimilis

MÝKONOS (Island), Aegean Sea:

The Isles of Greece. By Lt. Richard Stillwell, USNR. LXXXV, pp. 593-622, 11 ills. in black and white, 20 ills. in color, map, May, 1944

Santorin and Mýkonos, Aegean Gems. 8 color photos: 7 by B. Anthony Stewart. LXXVII, pp. 339-346, Mar., 1940

MYSORE, India:

India Mosaic. By Peter Muir and Frances Muir. LXXXIX, pp. 443-470, 5 ills. in black and white, 22 ills. in color, map, Apr., 1946

The **MYSTERIES** of the Desert (Sahara). By Hanns Vischer. XXII, pp. 1056-1059, Nov., 1911

The **MYSTERIOUS** Life of the Common Eel. By Hugh M. Smith. XXIV, pp. 1140-1146, 3 ills., Oct., 1913

MYSTERIOUS Micronesia: Yap, Map, and Other Islands Under Japanese Mandate are Museums of Primitive Man. By Willard Price. LXIX, pp. 481-510, 37 ills., map, Apr., 1936

The **MYSTERIOUS** Prehistoric Monuments of Brittany (France). By Charles Buxton Going. XLIV, pp. 53-69, 16 ills., July, 1923

MYSTERIOUS Temples of the Jungle: The Prehistoric Ruins of Guatemala. By W. F. Sands. XXIV, pp. 325-338, 10 ills., Mar., 1913

The **MYSTERIOUS** Tomb of a Giant Meteorite (Meteor Crater, Arizona). By William D. Boutwell. LIII, pp. 721-730, 10 ills., June, 1928

MYSTERY Mammals of the Twilight (Bats). By Donald R. Griffin. XC, pp. 117-134, 19 ills., July, 1946

The **MYSTERY** of Auroras: National Geographic Society and Cornell University Study Spectacular Displays in the Heavens. LXXV, pp. 689-690, May, 1939

The **MYSTERY** of Easter Island. By Mrs. Scoresby Routledge. XL, pp. 629-646, 13 ills., map, Dec., 1921

MYSTIC Nedjef, the Shia Mecca. By Frederick Simpich. XXVI, pp. 589-598, 4 ills., Dec., 1914

MYTILENE (Island), Greece:

Some Ruined Cities of Asia Minor. By Ernest L. Harris. XIX, pp. 833-858, 19 ills., Dec., 1908

N

NABLUS (Shechem), Palestine:

The Last Israelitish Blood Sacrifice: How the Vanishing Samaritans Celebrate the Passover on Sacred Mount Gerizim. By John D. Whiting. XXXVII, pp. 1-46, 40 ills., map, Jan., 1920

NABOURS, ROBERT K.:

The Land of Lambskins: An Expedition to Bokhara, Russian Central Asia, to Study the Karakul Sheep Industry. By Robert K. Nabours. XXXVI, pp. 77-88, 15 ills., July, 1919

NABUCO, JOAQUIM:

What the Latin American Republics Think of the Pan-American Conferences (Address by the Brazilian Ambassador). XVII, pp. 474-479, Aug., 1906

NAGAS (Tribespeople):

Women of All Nations. XXII, pp. 49-61, 12 ills., Jan., 1911

NAGEOMA (Canoe):

Across the Midi in a Canoe: Two Americans Paddle Along the Canals of Southern France from the Atlantic to the Mediterranean. By Melville Chater. LII, pp. 127-167, 49 ills., map, Aug., 1927

Note: *Nageoma,* used by the author in his travels through Europe, named after the *National Geographic Magazine*

Through the Back Doors of Belgium: Artist and Author Paddle for Three Weeks Along 200 Miles of Low-Countries Canals in a Canadian Canoe. By Melville Chater. XLVII, pp. 499-540, 39 ills., map, May, 1925

Through the Back Doors of France: A Seven Weeks' Voyage in a Canadian Canoe from St. Malo, Through Brittany and the Chateau Country, to Paris. By Melville Chater. XLIV, pp. 1-51, 55 ills., map, July, 1923

NAGEOMA, giraffe named after the *National Geographic Magazine.* LXXIII, ill. p. 714, June, 1938

NAHA, Okinawa (Island), Ryukyu Retto:

Peacetime Rambles in the Ryukyus. By William Leonard Schwartz. LXXXVII, pp. 543-561, 12 ills., maps, May, 1945

NAIVASHA (Lake), Kenya:

Where Roosevelt Will Hunt. By Sir Harry Johnston. XX, pp. 207-256, 43 ills., map supplement, Mar., 1909

NAJAF, An, Iraq:

Mystic Nedjef, the Shia Mecca. By Frederick Simpich. XXVI, pp. 589-598, 4 ills., Dec., 1914

"NAKWASINA" Goes North: A Man, a Woman, and a Pup Cruise from Tacoma to Juneau in a 17-Foot Canoe. By Jack Calvin. LXIV, pp. 1-42, 24 ills., map, July, 1933

NANCY, France:

A City Learns to Smile Again. By Maj. Frederick G. Vosburgh. LXXXVII, pp. 361-384, 23 ills., map, Mar., 1945

In French Lorraine: That Part of France Where the First American Soldiers Have Fallen. By Harriet Chalmers Adams. XXXII, pp. 499-518, 16 ills., Nov.-Dec., 1917

NANKING, China:

The Rise and Fall of Nanking. By Julius Eigner. LXXIII, pp. 189-224, 37 ills., Feb., 1938

NANSEI SHOTO (Islands). *See* Ryukyu Retto

NANSEN, FRIDTJOF:

Portrait. VII, pl. XI (opp. p. 98), Mar., 1896

See also articles, *following*

NANSEN POLAR EXPEDITION:

The Nansen Polar Expedition. Special Report of the Hon. Ernest A. Man. VII, pp. 339-344, map supplement, Oct., 1896

Nansen's Polar Expedition. By General A. W. Greely. VII, pp. 98-101, ill., table, Mar., 1896

The Return of Dr. Nansen. VII, p. 290, Sept., 1896

NANSEN'S "Farthest North" Eclipsed. XI, pp. 411-413, ills., Oct., 1900

NANTUCKET (Island), Massachusetts:

Nantucket—Little Gray Lady. By William H. Nicholas. LXXXV, pp. 433-458, 14 ills. in black and white, 8 ills. in color, map, Apr., 1944

NAPLES, Italy:

Inexhaustible Italy. By Arthur Stanley Riggs. XXX, pp. 273-368, 76 ills., map, Oct., 1916

NAPOLEON I:

The Coasts of Corsica: Impressions of a Winter's Stay in the Island Birthplace of Napoleon. By Maynard Owen Williams. XLIV, pp. 221-312, 88 ills., maps, pictorial supplement, Sept., 1923

NARRATIVE of the St. Elias Expedition of 1890 (Part II, from "An Expedition to Mount St. Elias, Alaska," by Israel C. Russell). III, pp. 75-166, 14 ills., 3 diagrs., map, May 29, 1891

NARSAK, Greenland:

Americans Stand Guard in Greenland. By Andrew H. Brown. XC, pp. 457-500, 23 ills. in black and white, 19 ills. in color, map, Oct., 1946

NARSARSSUAK, Greenland:
Americans Stand Guard in Greenland. By Andrew H: Brown. XC, pp. 457-500, 23 ills. in black and white, 19 ills. in color, map, Oct., 1946

NASHI (Tribespeople):
Banishing the Devil of Disease Among the Nashi: Weird Ceremonies Performed by an Aboriginal Tribe in the Heart of Yünnan Province, China. By Joseph F. Rock. XLVI, pp. 473-499, 26 ills., map, Nov., 1924

NATAL (Province), Union of South Africa:
Natal: The Garden Colony. By Russell Hastings Millward. XX, pp. 278-291, 16 ills., Mar., 1909
Natal: The Garden Province. By Melville Chater. LIX, pp. 447-478, 29 ills. in black and white, 14 ills. in color, Apr., 1931

NATCHEZ INDIANS:
Indians of the Southeastern United States. By Matthew W. Stirling. Paintings by W. Langdon Kihn. LXXXIX, pp. 53-74, 8 ills. in black and white, 8 ills. in color, Jan., 1946

NATIONAL EDUCATIONAL ASSOCIATION:
American Geographic Education. By W J McGee. IX, pp. 305-307, July, 1898

NATIONAL FOREST ASSOCIATION OF GERMANY:
Proposed Collection of Forestry Statistics. IX, p. 448, Oct., 1898

NATIONAL FORESTS:
Forest Lookout. By Ella E. Clark. With 9 color photos by author. XC, pp. 73-96, 8 ills. in black and white, July, 1946
The National Forest Reserves. By Frederick H. Newell. VIII, pp. 177-187, diagrs., tables, June, 1897
Saving the Forests. By Herbert A. Smith. XVIII, pp. 519-534, 7 ills., tables, Aug., 1907

NATIONAL GALLERY OF ART, Washington, D. C.:
Old Masters in a New National Gallery. By Ruth Q. McBride. LXXVIII, pp. 1-50, 11 ills. in black and white, 32 color reproductions of masterpieces, July, 1940

NATIONAL GEOGRAPHIC MAGAZINE (NGM):

Articles:
First extensive article in America on gliders (On the Wings of the Wind), published in the National Geographic Magazine, June, 1929. LXXIV, p. 123, July, 1938. LXXXVI, p. 150, Aug., 1944
Flag number: Letter from President Woodrow Wilson to Gilbert H. Grosvenor, congratulating him on the flag number. XXXII, p. 549, Nov.-Dec., 1917

Associate Editor. *See* La Gorce, John Oliver; NGM: Editorial Department; NGS: Vice-President; *and* names of Associate Editors on *National Geographic Magazine* mastheads, 1896-1945

Censorship of the Magazine. LXXXIV, p. 280, Sept., 1943

NATIONAL GEOGRAPHIC MAGAZINE—*Continued*

Circulation: Increase in circulation. XXIII, p. 208, Feb., 1912; p. 274, Mar., 1912. XXIV, pp. 252-253, Feb., 1913. XXV, p. 680, June, 1914. XXVII, p. 318, Mar., 1915. XXXVII, p. 343, Apr., 1920. LXIX, p. 123, Jan., 1936

Correspondence Department. XVII, p. 37, Jan., 1906. XXV, p. 465, Apr., 1914

Editor:

Gannett, Henry

Editor and Associate Editor. *See* Gannett, Henry, for Articles

Grosvenor, Gilbert H.

Alexander Graham Bell's appreciation of. XXIII, p. 274, Mar., 1912. LXIX, p. 148, Jan., 1936
Engaged as Assistant Editor in 1899. XXIII, p. 274, Mar., 1912. LXIX, pp. 123, 136-137, 139, 148, Jan., 1936
Policies, Editorial, adopted: the seven guiding principles. XXVII, p. 319, Mar., 1915
President Taft's appreciation of. XXII, p. 276, Mar., 1911
Private office of Editor. XXV, ill. p. 460, Apr., 1914
Report of the Director and Editor of the National Geographic Society for the Year 1914. By Gilbert H. Grosvenor. XXVII, pp. 318-320, Mar., 1915
Dr. Grosvenor's first years as Editor..318-319
Growth of the Society since 1899...319, 320
Magazine policy 319
Report of the Editor for 1912. XXIV, pp. 251-255, Feb., 1913
Advertising policy 253
Appreciation in *Boston Herald*......253, 255
Educational purposes 253
Increase in circulation 252-253
See also Grosvenor, Gilbert H., for Addresses, Articles, Map Supplements, Photographs; NGS: President

Hyde, John

Editor and Honorary Editor. *See* Hyde, John, for Articles

Editorial Department:
Announcement of the death of Ralph A. Graves, Senior Assistant Editor. LXII, p. 606, Nov., 1932
Assistant Editor appointed. X, p. 222, June, 1899
Borah, Leo. LXXXV, p. 677, June, 1944
Editorial Committee. X, p. 222, June, 1899
La Gorce, John Oliver: Private office of Associate Editor. XXV, ill. p. 461, Apr., 1914. LXIX, ill. p. 156, Jan., 1936
Nygaard, Arnvid, Chief Translator. LXXXIV, ill. p. 695, Dec., 1943
Policies regarding the Magazine. XX, p. 486, May, 1909. XXIII, pp. 273-274, Mar., 1912. XXIV, p. 253, Feb., 1913. XXVII, p. 319, Mar., 1915. LXIX, pp. 123, 135, 145, 148, 149, Jan., 1936
Staff members' service records. LXIX, pp. 162-163, Jan., 1936
See also NGM: Editor; NGS: President; Vice-President

NATIONAL GEOGRAPHIC MAGAZINE—*Continued*

Educational Usage:

Bringing the World to Our Foreign-Language Soldiers: How a Military Training Camp is Solving a Seemingly Unsurmountable Problem by Using the Geographic. By Christina Krysto. XXXIV, pp. 81-90, 4 ills., Aug., 1918

The Magazine, instructive for adults and children. XXV, pp. 468-469, Apr., 1914

See also NGS: News Service; School Service

Engravings and Etchings:

Cathedrals of England. 16 ills. in gravure from dry-point engravings by Norman Wilkinson. LXXVI, pp. 745-760; text, p. 762, Dec., 1939

Ships of the Centuries. 16 ills. in gravure from etchings by Norman Wilkinson. LXXIII, pp. 65-80; text, p. 98, Jan., 1938

History:

Early years of the Magazine. X, pp. 221-222, June, 1899

History of the Magazine (Speech by Alexander Graham Bell). XXIII, pp. 273-274, Mar., 1912

The National Geographic Society and Its Magazine. By Gilbert Grosvenor. LXIX, pp. 123-164, 24 ills., Jan., 1936

See also NGS: History, *for details*

Illustrations. *See* NGM: Engravings and Etchings; Paintings; Photographs

Increase in circulation of the Magazine. *See* NGM: Circulation

Map Supplement Articles and Announcements:

Africa

Africa First of 1943 Global Warfare Maps. By William H. Nicholas. Text with map supplement. LXXXIII, pp. 261-276, 13 ills., Feb., 1943

The Black Man's Continent. Text with map supplement. XX, p. 312, Mar., 1909

Map of Africa. Announcement of map supplement (The Black Man's Continent, Mar., 1909). XVIII, p. 640, Oct., 1907

The National Geographic Society's New Map of Africa. By Gilbert Grosvenor. Text with map supplement. LXVII, pp. 731-752, 20 ills. in duotone, June, 1935

The Society's New Map of Africa. Text with map supplement. XLII, pp. 447-448, Oct., 1922

Western Front Map Embraces Three Continents (Europe, Africa, Asia). Text with map supplement. LXXXII, pp. 139-140, July, 1942

Alaska

Map of Alaska. Announcement of map supplement (May, 1904). XV, p. 188, Apr., 1904; p. 236, May, 1904

See also North America

Antarctic Regions

The Society's Map of the Antarctic. Text with map supplement. LXII, pp. 485-486, ill., Oct., 1932

Arctic Regions

Map of the North Polar Regions. Text with map supplement. XVIII, pp. 454-455, July, 1907

North Polar Map. Text describing map compiled by Gilbert H. Grosvenor (July, 1907). XX, p. 915, Oct., 1909

NATIONAL GEOGRAPHIC MAGAZINE—*Continued*

Map Supplement Articles and Announcements—*Continued*

A Polar Map. Announcement of map supplement (July, 1907). XVII, p. 533, Sept., 1906

Asia

Face of Japan (Map of Japan and Korea). By W. Robert Moore. Text with map supplement. LXXXVIII, pp. 753-768, 14 ills., Dec., 1945

Indian Ocean Map Spans Far East News Centers. Text with map supplement. LXXIX, pp. 345-346, ill., Mar., 1941

Manchuria and Korea. Text with map supplement. XV, pp. 128-129, maps, Mar., 1904

Map of the Philippines. Announcement of map supplement (Aug., 1905). XVI, p. 434, Sept., 1905

Map of the Philippines. Text with map supplement. XIII, p. 31, Jan., 1902

National Geographic Map of Japan, Regions of Asia, and the Pacific. Text with map supplement. LXXXV, pp. 415-416, Apr., 1944

The New Map of Asia. Text with map supplement. XXXIX, pp. 552-570, 17 ills., May, 1921

New Map Shows Asia's Role in Global Warfare. Text with map supplement. LXXXII, pp. 767-768, Dec., 1942

New National Geographic Map Shows Strategic Philippines (What Luzon Means to Uncle Sam). By Frederick Simpich. Text with map supplement. LXXXVII, pp. 305-307, 312, 332, Mar., 1945

The Society's New Map of Asia. Text with map supplement. LXIV, pp. 770-772, ill., Dec., 1933

The Society's New Map of China. By James M. Darley. Text with map supplement. LXXXVII, pp. 745-746, June, 1945

The Society's New Map of India and Burma. Text with map supplement. LXXXIX, p. 544, Apr., 1946

The Society's New Map of Southeast Asia. Text with map supplement. LXXXVI, pp. 449-450, ill., Oct., 1944

The Society's New Map of Soviet Russia. Text with map supplement. LXXXVI, pp. 716-718, Dec., 1944

Western Front Map Embraces Three Continents (Europe, Africa, Asia). Text with map supplement. LXXXII, pp. 139-140, July, 1942

Atlantic Ocean

New Map of the Atlantic Ocean: Foremost Sea of Commerce Becomes World's Battleground and Its Peaceful Islands Rise to Strategic Importance. By Leo A. Borah and Wellman Chamberlin. Text with map supplement. LXXX, pp. 407-418, 9 ills., Sept., 1941

The World That Rims the Narrowing Atlantic: Latest Ten-color Map Supplement Shows Four Continents and New Transatlantic Air Routes Which Make This Ocean Only One Day Wide. By James M. Darley. Text with map supplement. LXXVI, pp. 139-142, ill., July, 1939

Bible Lands

The Society's Map of Bible Lands. By Gilbert Grosvenor. Text with map supplement. LXXIV, pp. 751-754, 3 ills., Dec., 1938

Map Supplement Articles and Announcements—*Continued*

The Society's New Map of Bible Lands. Text with map supplement. XC, pp. 815-816, Dec., 1946

Canada

The Society Maps Northwestern United States and Neighboring Canadian Provinces. Text with map supplement. LXXIX, pp. 805-806, June, 1941

The Society's New Map of Canada. Text with map supplement. LXIX, pp. 769-776, 9 ills., June, 1936

See also North America

Caribbean Regions

Heart of a Hemisphere: Of Vital Importance is the Area Portrayed in The Society's New Map of Mexico, Central America, and the West Indies. Text with map supplement. LXXVI, pp. 739-740, ill., Dec., 1939

Our Map of the Countries of the Caribbean. Text with map supplement. XLI, pp. 221-222, Feb., 1922

The Society's New Caribbean Map: Mexico, Central America, and the West Indies—Gateway of Discovery. Text with map supplement. LXVI, pp. 738-740, ill., Dec., 1934

Central America

Bird's-Eye View of the Panama Canal. Announcement of map supplement. XXIII, p. 208, Feb., 1912

Map of Panama Canal. Announcement of map supplement (Oct., 1905). XVI, p. 441, Sept., 1905

See also Caribbean Regions

Europe

The Geographic's New Map of Europe and the Mediterranean. By Gilbert Grosvenor. Text with map supplement. LXXIII, pp. 525-528, ill., Apr., 1938

The Geographic's New Map of Germany and Its Approaches: With a Review of The Society's Maps of Europe. By Gilbert Grosvenor. Text with map supplement. LXXXVI, pp. 66-72, ill., July, 1944

Map Links Classic World with 1940. Text with map supplement. LXXVII, p. 338, Mar., 1940

Map of Europe Including the New Balkan States. Text with map supplement. XXVI, pp. 191-192, Aug., 1914

A Modern Pilgrim's Map of the British Isles. By Andrew H. Brown. Text with map supplement. LXXI, pp. 795-802, 3 ills., June, 1937

The National Geographic War-Zone Map. Text with map supplement. XXXIII, p. 494, May, 1918

The New Map of Europe: Showing the Boundaries Established by the Peace Conference at Paris and by Subsequent Decisions of the Supreme Council of the Allied and Associated Powers. By Ralph A. Graves. Text with map supplement. XXXIX, pp. 157-177, 18 ills., Feb., 1921

New Map of Europe and the Near East. Text with map supplement. LXXXIII, pp. 762-763, ill., June, 1943

Map Supplement Articles and Announcements—*Continued*

New Map of Europe Records War Changes. Text with map supplement. LXXVII, p. 625, May, 1940

Our Map of the Races of Europe. Text with map supplement. XXXIV, pp. 535-536, Dec., 1918

The Society's New Map of Central Europe and the Mediterranean. Text with map supplement. LXXVI, pp. 559-560, Oct., 1939

The Society's New Map of Europe. By Gilbert Grosvenor. Text with map supplement. LVI, pp. 771-774, Dec., 1929

The Society's New Map of Soviet Russia. Text with map supplement. LXXXVI, pp. 716-718, Dec., 1944

Western Front Map Embraces Three Continents (Europe, Africa, Asia). Text with map supplement. LXXXII, pp. 139-140, July, 1942

Mediterranean Regions

Map of Mediterranean Regions. Announcement of map supplement. XXIII, p. 104, Jan., 1912

See also Bible Lands; Europe

Mexico

Heart of a Hemisphere: Of Vital Importance is the Area Portrayed in The Society's New Map of Mexico, Central America, and the West Indies. Text with map supplement. LXXVI, pp. 739-740, ill., Dec., 1939

The Latest Map of Mexico. Text with map supplement. XXX, p. 88, July, 1916

Map of Mexico. Announcement of map supplement (May, 1911). XXII, p. 410, Apr., 1911

Our Map of the Countries of the Caribbean. Text with map supplement. XLI, pp. 221-222, Feb., 1922

The Society's New Caribbean Map: Mexico, Central America, and the West Indies—Gateway of Discovery. Text with map supplement. LXVI, pp. 738-740, ill., Dec., 1934

See also North America

Near East

New Map of Europe and the Near East. Text with map supplement. LXXXIII, pp. 762-763, ill., June, 1943

North America

Maps for Victory: National Geographic Society's Charts Used in War on Land, Sea, and in the Air. By Gilbert Grosvenor. Text with map supplement. LXXXI, pp. 667-690, 28 ills., May, 1942

Our Map of North America. Text with map supplement. XLV, p. 580, May, 1924

Pacific Ocean

New Map Shows Immense Pacific Battleground. Text with map supplement. LXXXI, pp. 203-204, Feb., 1942

Our Map of the Pacific. Text with map supplement. XL, pp. 647-648, map, Dec., 1921

Revealing Earth's Mightiest Ocean. By Albert W. Atwood. Announcement of map supplement. LXXXIV, p. 291, Sept., 1943

The Society's New Map of the Pacific. By Gilbert Grosvenor. Text with map supplement. LXX, pp. 793-796, Dec., 1936

NATIONAL GEOGRAPHIC MAGAZINE—*Continued*

Map Supplement Articles and Announcements—*Continued*

South America

New National Geographic Society Map Charts South America's Wartime Importance. Text with map supplement. LXXXII, pp. 537-540, ills., Oct., 1942

The Society's Map of South America. By Gilbert Grosvenor. Text with map supplement. LXXII, pp. 809-810, Dec., 1937

The Society's New Map of South America. Text with map supplement. XL, pp. 374-392, 17 ills., Oct., 1921

South America Map. Announcement of map supplement (Aug., 1906). XVII, p. 424, July, 1906

The Valley of the Orinoco. By T. H. Gignilliat. Text with map supplement. VII, p. 92, Feb., 1896

United States

Another Important Map (U. S.). Announcement of map supplement (Apr., 1923). XLIII, p. 336, Mar., 1923

The National Geographic Society's Map of Northeastern United States. Text with map supplement. LXXXVIII, pp. 361-362, Sept., 1945

New Map Reveals the Progress and Wonders of Our Country. Text with map supplement. LXIII, pp. 650-652, ill., May, 1933

New United States Map Shows Census Changes. Text with map supplement. LXXVIII, pp. 821-824, ills., Dec., 1940

Our Map of the United States. Text with map supplement. XLIII, p. 460, Apr., 1923

Postwar Portrait of the United States. Text with map supplement. XC, pp. 135-136, July, 1946

The Society Maps Northwestern United States and Neighboring Canadian Provinces. Text with map supplement. LXXIX, pp. 805-806, June, 1941

The Society's Map of Historic and Scenic Reaches of the Nation's Capital. Text with map supplement. LXXIV, pp. 57-58, July, 1938

The Society's Map of the Reaches of New York City. Text with map supplement. LXXV, pp. 491-492, Apr., 1939

The Society's Map of the White Mountains of New Hampshire. Note describing map supplement. LXXII, p. 73, July, 1937

Southwest Trails from Horse to Motor. Text with map supplement. LXXVII, p. 767, June, 1940

The Travels of George Washington. Text with map supplement. LXI, pp. 1-63, 50 ills., 4 maps, Jan., 1932

World

Announcement of map of the Northern Hemisphere. LXXXIX, text and footnote, p. 160, Feb., 1946

Chart of the World. Announcement of map supplement (Feb., 1905). XV, p. 500, Dec., 1904. XVI, p. 50, Jan., 1905

NATIONAL GEOGRAPHIC MAGAZINE—*Continued*

Map Supplement Articles and Announcements—*Continued*

The "Map of Discovery" of the Western Hemisphere with This Number. Announcement of map supplement. LV, p. 93, Jan., 1929

The "Map of Discovery" with This Number (Eastern Hemisphere). Announcement of map supplement. LIV, p. 568, Nov., 1928

Map of the Northern and Southern Hemispheres. Text with map supplement. LXXXIII, pp. 481-483, Apr., 1943

The National Geographic Society's New Map of the World. Text with map supplement. LXVIII, pp. 796-798, Dec., 1935

New World Map Gives Backdrop for Headlines. Text with map supplement. LXXX, pp. 741-742, ill., Dec., 1941

The Society's New Map of the World. Text with map supplement. XLII, pp. 690-691, Dec., 1922

The Story of the Map. Text with map supplement. LXII, pp. 759-774, 11 ills., Dec., 1932

The World's Words (Map of the World). By William H. Nicholas. Text with map supplement. LXXXIV, p. 689, Dec., 1943

Map Supplements (Text and Illustrations):

Date of issue printed on each Geographic map. LXXXVI, p. 69, July, 1944

Key to foreign names for physical features. LXXXVI, p. 68, July, 1944

Map supplement of Canada used by Sir Hubert Wilkins in air navigation. LXXIV, p. 142, Aug., 1938

Master drawing, Tacking highway routes over. LXXIX, ill. p. 436, Apr., 1941

Number, Total, of maps printed since December, 1941. LXXXVI, p. 450, Oct., 1944

Number of maps printed annually. LXXIX, p. 419, Apr., 1941

Number of supplements for 1941. LXXXI, p. 333, Mar., 1942

Printed by A. Hoen and Company, Inc. LXXIX, pp. 419, 436, Apr., 1941. LXXXI, ill. p. 679, May, 1942

"Rediscovering America" series of decorated charts on sections of the United States. LXXIX, p. 805, June, 1941. LXXXVIII, p. 362, Sept., 1945

Various uses of the Society's map supplements by Army and Navy, Government Departments, embassies, clubs, offices, and private citizens. LXXIII, p. 525, Apr., 1938. LXXXI, p. 333, Mar., 1942; pp. 671-673, 674, ill. pp. 668-674, 682-684, 686-690, May, 1942; p. 691, June, 1942. LXXXII, ill. pp. 670, 671, Nov., 1942. LXXXIII, p. 265, ill. p. 278, Feb., 1943. LXXXV, p. 83, ill. p. 93, Jan., 1944; p. 415, Apr., 1944. LXXXVI, pp. 66-67, 71, 72, ill. p. 69, July, 1944; ill. p. 279, Sept., 1944; p. 450, ill. p. 450, Oct., 1944. LXXXVIII, ill. p. 7, July, 1945; pp. 709, 753, Dec., 1945

Wartime map series. LXXXI, p. 203, Feb., 1942. LXXXII, p. 139, July, 1942; pp. 767-768, Dec., 1942. LXXXV, pp. 415, 416, Apr., 1944. LXXXVI, pp. 449, 450, Oct., 1944; p. 716, Dec., 1944. LXXXVII, p. 745, June, 1945

Maps. *See* Map Index, *following this index*

NATIONAL GEOGRAPHIC MAGAZINE—*Continued*

Paintings:

Aleutians

A Navy Artist Paints the Aleutians. 16 ills. in color from paintings by Lt. William F. Draper. LXXXIV, pp. 161-176, Aug., 1943

Ants

Work and War in the World of Ants. 18 ills. in color from paintings by Hashime Murayama. LXVI, pp. 179-186, Aug., 1934

Asia

Faces and Fashions of Asia's Changeless Tribes. 26 ills. in color from paintings and drawings by Alexandre Iacovleff. LXIX, pp. 21-36, Jan., 1936

Bees

In Field and Hive With the Busy Honeybee. 16 ills. in color from paintings by Hashime Murayama. LXVII, pp. 417-424, Apr., 1935

Berries

American Berries of Hill, Dale, and Wayside. 29 ills. in color from paintings by Mary E. Eaton. XXXV, pp. 173-180, Feb., 1919

Birds

American Game Birds. 72 ills. in color from paintings by Louis Agassiz Fuertes. XXVIII, pp. 109-144, Aug., 1915

Auks and Their Northland Neighbors. 34 portraits from paintings by Maj. Allan Brooks. LXIX, pp. 101-116, Jan., 1936

Bird Beauties of the Tanager and Finch Families. 55 portraits from paintings by Maj. Allan Brooks. LXVII, pp. 513-528, Apr., 1935

Birds in Glossy Black and Vivid Color. 48 portraits from paintings by Major Allan Brooks. LXVI, pp. 113-128, July, 1934

Birds of Lake and Lagoon, Marsh and Seacoast. 24 portraits from paintings by Maj. Allan Brooks. LXV, pp. 313-328, Mar., 1934

Birds of Town and Country. 64 ills. in color from paintings by Louis Agassiz Fuertes. XXV, pp. 499-530, May, 1914

Blithe Birds of Dooryard, Bush, and Brake. 37 portraits from paintings by Major Allan Brooks. LXV, pp. 579-594, May, 1934

Bright-hued Pets of Cage and Aviary. 51 portraits from paintings by Major Allan Brooks. LXXIV, pp. 783-790, Dec., 1938

Common Birds of Farm and Orchard. 50 ills. in color from paintings by Louis Agassiz Fuertes. XXIV, pp. 673-697, June, 1913

Crows, Magpies, and Jays. 17 ills. in color from paintings by Maj. Allan Brooks. LXIII, pp. 65-78, Jan., 1933

Eagles, Hawks, and Vultures. 48 ills. in color from paintings by Maj. Allan Brooks. LXIV, pp. 65-94, July, 1933

Falconry, the Sport of Kings. 12 ills. in color from paintings by Louis Agassiz Fuertes. XXXVIII, pp. 441-456, Dec., 1920

Feathered Foragers of Swamp and Shore. 101 portraits from paintings by Major Allan Brooks. LXXII, pp. 191-222, Aug., 1937

NATIONAL GEOGRAPHIC MAGAZINE—*Continued*

Paintings—*Continued*

Flycatchers and Other Friends in Feathers. 36 portraits from paintings by Maj. Allan Brooks. LXIX, pp. 807-822, June, 1936

Humming Birds, Swifts and Goatsuckers. 36 ills. in color from paintings by Maj. Allan Brooks. LXII, pp. 75-88, July, 1932

Hunted Birds of Field and Wild. 60 portraits from paintings by Maj. Allan Brooks. LXX, pp. 469-500, Oct., 1936

Ibises, Herons, and Flamingos. 24 ills. in color from paintings by Maj. Allan Brooks. LXII, pp. 455-468, Oct., 1932

Iridescent Isles of the South Seas. 16 ills. in color: 4 paintings of birds by Hashime Murayama. XLVIII, pp. 403-418, Oct., 1925

North American Woodpeckers. 25 ills. in color from paintings by Maj. Allan Brooks. LXIII, pp. 465-478, Apr., 1933

Pastel Wrens from "Down Under." 8 ills. in color from paintings by N. W. Cayley. LXXXVIII, pp. 489-496, Oct., 1945

Pigeons of Resplendent Plumage. 12 ills. in color from paintings by Hashime Murayama. XLIX, pp. 65-76, Jan., 1926

Silent-Winged Owls of North America. 21 portraits from paintings by Maj. Allan Brooks. LXVII, pp. 225-240, Feb., 1935

Some Songsters and Flyers of Wide Repute (Thrushes, Thrashers, and Swallows). 42 portraits from paintings by Maj. Allan Brooks. LXIX, pp. 529-544, Apr., 1936

Sparrows, Towhees, and Longspurs. 43 portraits from paintings by Allan Brooks and Walter A Weber. LXXV, pp. 361-375, Mar., 1939

Warblers of North America. 32 ills. in color from paintings by Louis Agassiz Fuertes. XXXI, pp. 305-320, Apr., 1917

Wild Geese, Ducks, and Swans. 93 portraits from paintings by Major Allan Brooks. LXVI, pp. 493-524, Oct., 1934

Wings Over the Bounding Main (Ocean Birds). 36 portraits from paintings by Major Allan Brooks. LXXIV, pp. 237-251, Aug., 1938

Butterflies

Nomads Among the Butterflies. 8 ills. in color: 3 paintings by Hashime Murayama. LXXI, pp. 569-584, May, 1937

Winged Jewels From Many Lands. 9 ills. in color: 3 paintings by Hashime Murayama. LXIX, pp. 673-688, May, 1936

California

Crater Lake and Yosemite Through the Ages. 13 ills. in color from paintings by Eugene Kingman. LXXI, pp. 333-339, Mar., 1937

Cats

King of Cats and His Court. 20 ills. in color from paintings by Walter A. Weber. LXXXIII, pp. 223-254, Feb., 1943

Cattle

The Cattle of the World. 20 ills. in color from paintings by Edward Herbert Miner. XLVIII, pp. 639-678, Dec., 1925

National Geographic

Cephalopoda

Monster and Midget Squid and Octopuses. 8 ills. in color from paintings by Else Bostelmann under direction Roy W. Miner. LXVIII, pp. 193-200, Aug., 1935

China

Buddhist Calm Survives Along China's Great Wall. 10 ills. in color: 4 paintings by Mary Augusta Mullikin and Anna M. Hotchkis. LXXIII, pp. 321-328, Mar., 1938

China's Wonderland—Yen Tang Shan (Chekiang Province). 8 ills. in color from camera paintings by Herbert Clarence White, Clarence C. Crisler, Deng Bao-ling, Hwang Yao-tso. LXXII, pp. 687-694, Dec., 1937

A Peiping Panorama in Vivid Pigments. 16 ills. in color from camera paintings by H. C. and J. H. White, Deng Bao-ling, Hwang Yao-tso. LXX, pp. 753-784, Dec., 1936

Coral

Multi-Hued Marvels of a Coral Reef. 8 ills. in color from paintings by Else Bostelmann. LXV, pp. 719-726, June, 1934

Crabs

Crabs and Crablike Curiosities of the Sea. 8 ills. in color from paintings by William Crowder. LIV, pp. 63-70, July, 1928

Deer

Antlered Majesties of Many Lands. 23 ills. in color from paintings by Walter A. Weber. LXXVI, pp. 479-510, Oct., 1939

Dogs

Gallant Little Sportsmen of the Terrier Tribe. 33 portraits from paintings by Edward Herbert Miner. LXIX, pp. 253-268, Feb., 1936

Hunters All: A Roll Call of the Hounds. 31 portraits from paintings by Edward Herbert Miner. LXXII, pp. 467-482, Oct., 1937

Man's Hunting Partner, the Field Dog. 36 portraits from paintings by Edward Herbert Miner. LXXI, pp. 89-104, Jan., 1937

Non-sporting Dogs. 8 ills. in color from paintings from life by Walter A. Weber. LXXXIV, pp. 577-584, Nov., 1943

Our Common Dogs. 73 ills. in color from paintings by Louis Agassiz Fuertes. XXXV, pp. 202-263, Mar., 1919

Wild Dogs and Working Dogs. 9 ills. in color from paintings by Walter A. Weber. LXXXVI, pp. 369-376, Sept., 1944

Working Dogs of the World. 20 ills. in color from paintings by Edward Herbert Miner. LXXX, pp. 775-806, Dec., 1941

Egypt

Life, Culture, and History of the Egyptians. 32 ills. in color from paintings by H. M. Herget. LXXX, pp. 436-514, Oct., 1941

Ferns

Marvels of Fern Life. 16 ills. in color from paintings by E. J. Geske. XLVII, pp. 547-562, May, 1925

NATIONAL GEOGRAPHIC MAGAZINE—*Continued*

Paintings—*Continued*

Fishes

Carnivores of a Lightless World. 8 ills. in color from paintings by Else Bostelmann and E. J. Geske. LXVI, pp. 693-700, Dec., 1934

Certain Citizens of the Warm Sea. 16 ills. in color from paintings by Hashime Murayama. XLI, pp. 37-52, Jan., 1922

Fishes of Our North Atlantic Seaboard. 16 ills. in color from paintings by Hashime Murayama. XLIV, pp. 613-628, Dec., 1923

Flashes From Ocean Deeps. 8 ills. in color from paintings by Else Bostelmann and Helen D. Tee-Van. LXVI, pp. 677-684, Dec., 1934

Fresh-Water Denizens of the Far West (Salmon, Trout, etc.). 44 portraits from paintings by Hashime Murayama. LXXV, pp. 193-204, Feb., 1939

Fresh-Water Fishes of the United States. 16 ills. in color from paintings by Hashime Murayama. XLIV, pp. 133-148, Aug., 1923

Gleaming Fishes of Pacific Coastal Waters. 31 portraits from paintings by Hashime Murayama. LXXIV, pp. 467-498, Oct., 1938

Goldfish and Their Cultivation in America. 8 ills. in color from paintings by Hashime Murayama. XLVI, pp. 385-392, Oct., 1924

Iridescent Denizens of the Miniature Aquarium. 8 ills. in color from paintings by Hashime Murayama. LIX, pp. 293-300, Mar., 1931

Luminous Life in the Depths of the Sea. 8 ills. in color from paintings by E. Bostelmann. LIX, pp. 667-674, June, 1931

Treasure-House of the Gulf Stream. 16 ills. in color from paintings by Hashime Murayama. XXXIX, pp. 61-68, Jan., 1921

Flowers

American Wild Flowers. 29 ills. in color from paintings by Mary E. Eaton. XXVII, pp. 483-506, May, 1915

Common American Wild Flowers. 17 ills. in color from paintings by Mary E. Eaton. XXIX, pp. 591-606, June, 1916

Exploring the Mysteries of Plant Life. 47 ills. in color from paintings by Mary E. Eaton. XLV, pp. 613-628, June, 1924

Floral Garlands of Prairie, Plain, and Woodland. 125 flower paintings in color by Edith S. Clements. LXXVI, pp. 225-271, Aug., 1939

Midsummer Wild Flowers. 38 ills. in color from paintings by Mary E. Eaton. XLII, pp. 37-52, July, 1922

Our State Flowers. 30 ills. in color from paintings by Mary E. Eaton. XXXI, pp. 501-516, June, 1917

Pages From the Floral Life of America. 55 ills. in color from paintings by Mary E. Eaton. XLVIII, pp. 47-70, July, 1925

Wild Flowers of the West. 207 ills. in color from paintings by Edith S. Clements. LI, pp. 566-620, May, 1927

Fowl

Domestic Fowls of Field, Park, and Farmyard. 16 ills. in color from paintings by Hashime Murayama. LVII, pp. 329-360, Mar., 1930

Paintings—*Continued*

Fowl of the Old and New World. 29 ills. in color from paintings by Hashime Murayama. LI, pp. 421-436, Apr., 1927

Frogs and Toads

The Iridescent Beauty of Frogs and Toads. 14 ills. in color from paintings by Hashime Murayama. LXI, pp. 635-642, May, 1932

Gauchos

Pioneer Gaucho Days. 8 ills. in color from paintings by Cesáreo Bernaldo de Quirós. LXIV, pp. 453-460, Oct., 1933

Grasses

Beauties of Our Common Grasses. 8 ills. in color from paintings by E. J. Geske. XXXIX, pp. 627-634, June, 1921

Greece

"The Glory That Was Greece." 32 ills. in color from paintings by H. M. Herget. LXXXV, pp. 290-352, Mar., 1944

Horses

Horses of the World. 24 ills. in color from paintings by Edward Herbert Miner. XLIV, pp. 479-526, Nov., 1923

Indians

Aztecs Under the War God's Reign. 10 ills. in color from paintings by H. M. Herget. LXXI, pp. 735-742, June, 1937

First Families of Southeastern America. 8 ills. in color from paintings by W. Langdon Kihn. LXXXIX, pp. 65-72, Jan., 1946

In the Realm of the Sons of the Sun (Incas). 10 ills. in color from paintings by H. M. Herget. LXXIII, pp. 229-236, Feb., 1938

Indians of Our Western Plains. 16 ills. in color from paintings by W. Langdon Kihn. LXXXVI, pp. 81-96, July, 1944

Life and Death in Ancient Maya Land (Yucatán). 10 ills. in color from paintings by H. M. Herget. LXX, pp. 623-630, Nov., 1936

Portraits of Ancient Mayas, a Peace-Loving People. 10 ills. in color from paintings by H. M. Herget. LXVIII, pp. 553-560, Nov., 1935

Red Men of the Southwest. 25 ills. in color from paintings by W. Langdon Kihn. LXXVIII, pp. 557-596, Nov., 1940

Totem-pole Builders. 16 ills. in color from paintings by W. Langdon Kihn. LXXXVII, pp. 33-48, Jan., 1945

When Red Men Ruled Our Forests. 24 ills. in color from paintings by W. Langdon Kihn. LXXII, pp. 551-590, Nov., 1937

Insects

Insect Rivals of the Rainbow. 24 ills. in color: 3 paintings by Hashime Murayama. LVI, pp. 29-84, July, 1929

Rogues' Gallery of Imported Pests. 10 ills. in color from paintings by Hashime Murayama. LXXX, pp. 237-244, Aug., 1941

Jellyfishes

Jellyfishes—Living Draperies of Color. 8 ills. in color from paintings by William Crowder. L, pp. 193-200, Aug., 1926

NATIONAL GEOGRAPHIC MAGAZINE—*Continued*

Paintings—*Continued*

Mammals

The Larger North American Mammals. 49 ills. in color from paintings by Louis Agassiz Fuertes. XXX, pp. 410-471, Nov., 1916

Smaller Mammals of North America. 59 ills. in color from paintings by Louis Agassiz Fuertes. XXXIII, pp. 404-465, May, 1918

Marianas

Victory's Portrait in the Marianas. 17 ills. in color from paintings by Lt. William F. Draper, USNR. LXXXVIII, pp. 601-616, Nov., 1945

Marine Biology

Carnivores of a Lightless World. 8 ills. in color from paintings by Else Bostelmann and E. J. Geske. LXVI, pp. 693-700, Dec., 1934

Exploring Neptune's Hidden World of Vivid Color. 8 ills. in color from paintings by E. Bostelmann. LXII, pp. 747-754, Dec., 1932

Fantastic Sea Life From Abyssal Depths. 8 ills. in color from paintings by E. Bostelmann. LXI, pp. 71-78, Jan., 1932

Flashes From Ocean Deeps. 8 ills. in color from paintings by Else Bostelmann and Helen D. Tee-Van. LXVI, pp. 677-684, Dec., 1934

Luminous Life in the Depths of the Sea. 8 ills. in color from paintings by E. Bostelmann. LIX, pp. 667-674, June, 1931

Sea Floor Aquarelles from Tongareva. 8 ills. in color from paintings by Else Bostelmann under direction Roy W. Miner. LXXIV, pp. 383-390, Sept., 1938

Strange Creatures of Sunny Seas. 8 ills. in color from paintings by Else Bostelmann under direction Roy W. Miner. LXXI, pp. 211-218, Feb., 1937

Undersea Gardens of the North Atlantic Coast. 8 ills. in color from paintings by Else Bostelmann under direction Roy W. Miner. LXX, pp. 217-224, Aug., 1936

Mexico

Wildlife of Tabasco and Veracruz. 19 ills. in color from paintings by Walter A. Weber. LXXXVII, pp. 193-208, Feb., 1945

Monkeys

The Manlike Apes of Jungle and Mountain. 10 ills. in color from paintings by Elie Cheverlange. LXXVIII, pp. 221-228, Aug., 1940

Who's Who in the Monkey World. 40 portraits from paintings by Elie Cheverlange. LXXIII, pp. 625-648, May, 1938

Mosquitoes

Life Story of the Mosquito. 10 ills. in color from paintings. LXXXV, pp. 181-188, Feb., 1944

Mushrooms

Common Mushrooms of the United States. 16 ills. in color from paintings by Louis C. C. Krieger. XXXVII, pp. 423-438, May, 1920

Mycetozoa

Marvels of Mycetozoa. 16 ills. in color from paintings by William Crowder. XLIX, pp. 425-440, Apr., 1926

Oregon

Crater Lake and Yosemite Through the Ages. 13 ills. in color from paintings by Eugene Kingman. LXXI, pp. 333-339, Mar., 1937

Pacific War

Jungle War: Bougainville and New Caledonia. 17 ills. in color from paintings by Lieut. William F. Draper. LXXXV, pp. 417-432, Apr., 1944

Painting History in the Pacific. 19 ills. in color from paintings by Lt. William F. Draper, USNR. LXXXVI, pp. 409-424, Oct., 1944

See also Aleutians; Marianas, *above*

Paleontology

Parade of Life Through the Ages. 24 ills. in color from paintings by Charles R. Knight. LXXXI, pp. 149-180, Feb., 1942

Plankton

Living Jewels of the Sea. 8 ills. in color from paintings by William Crowder. LII, pp. 291-298, Sept., 1927

Porpoises and Dolphins

Whales, Porpoises, and Dolphins. 31 ills. in color from paintings by Else Bostelmann. LXXVII, pp. 41-80, Jan., 1940

Rome

Ancient Rome Brought to Life. 32 ills. in color from paintings by H. M. Herget. XC, pp. 570-633, Nov., 1946

Science

Science Works for Mankind. 16 ills. in color from paintings by Thornton Oakley. LXXXVIII, pp. 737-752, Dec., 1945

Seals (Symbols)

Seals of Our Nation, States, and Territories. 84 ills. in color from paintings by Carlotta Gonzales Lahey, Irvin E. Alleman, Theodora Price. XC, pp. 17-32, July, 1946

Solar System

Solar System's Eternal Show. 10 ills. in color from paintings by Charles Bittinger. LXXVI, pp. 17-24, July, 1939

Spiders

Nature's Ingenious Spinners. 64 ills. in color from paintings by Hashime Murayama. LXIV, pp. 167-174, Aug., 1933

Transportation

American Transportation Vital to Victory. 16 ills. in color from paintings by Thornton Oakley. LXXXIV, pp. 673-688, Dec., 1943

U. S. Army

Painting the Army on Maneuvers. 16 ills. in color from paintings by Arthur Beaumont. LXXXII, pp. 577-600, Nov., 1942

U. S. Navy

Ships of Our Navy. 8 ills. in color from paintings by Arthur Beaumont. LXXX, pp. 329-336, Sept., 1941

NATIONAL GEOGRAPHIC MAGAZINE—*Continued*

Paintings—*Continued*

War Industries

American Industries Geared for War. 16 ills. in color from paintings by Thornton Oakley. LXXXII, pp. 717-732, Dec., 1942

Wasps and Hornets

Farmers' Friends Among the Wasps and Hornets. 12 ills. in color from paintings by Hashime Murayama. LXXII, pp. 57-64, July, 1937

Whales

Whales, Porpoises, and Dolphins. 31 ills. in color from paintings by Else Bostelmann. LXXVII, pp. 41-80, Jan., 1940

Paintings (Supplements):

Boyhood of Sir Walter Raleigh. Reproduction in color of the painting by Sir John Millais, Tate Gallery, London. XLIX, text, p. 596; supplement, May, 1926

The Caravels of Columbus. Reproduction in color of the painting by N. C. Wyeth, National Geographic Society, Washington, D. C. LIV, text, p. 55; supplement, July, 1928

Commander Byrd at the North Pole (Through Pathless Skies to the North Pole). Reproduction in color of the painting by N. C. Wyeth, National Geographic Society, Washington, D. C. LIII, supplement, May, 1928

The Discoverer. Reproduction in color of the painting by N. C. Wyeth, National Geographic Society, Washington, D. C. LIII, text, p. 347; supplement, Mar., 1928

Fate Directs the Faltering Footsteps of Columbus. Reproduction in color of the painting by Alfred Dehodencq, Paris. LIV, supplement, Sept., 1928

The "Map of Discovery" (Eastern Hemisphere). Reproduction in color of the painting by N. C. Wyeth, National Geographic Society, Washington, D. C. LIV, text, p. 568; supplement, Nov., 1928

The "Map of Discovery" (Western Hemisphere). Reproduction in color of the painting by N. C. Wyeth, National Geographic Society, Washington, D. C. LV, text, p. 93; supplement, Jan., 1929

Vasco da Gama at the Court of the Zamorin of Calicut. Reproduction in color of the painting by José Velloso Salgado, Sociedade de Geographia de Lisboa. LII, supplement, Nov., 1927

Paintings (Text):

American Industries Geared for War. By Thornton Oakley. Text with 16 colored illustrations from paintings by author. LXXXII, pp. 716-734, ill. in black and white, Dec., 1942

American Transportation Vital to Victory. By Thornton Oakley. Text with 16 colored illustrations from paintings by author. LXXXIV, pp. 671-672, Dec., 1943

First color portraits of birds ("Fifty Common Birds of Farm and Orchard"). XXIV, p. 667, ill. pp. 673-697, June, 1913

NATIONAL GEOGRAPHIC MAGAZINE—*Continued*

Paintings—*Continued*

First to publish a complete set of full-color pictures (31 paintings) of the better-known whales, porpoises, and dolphins. LXXVII, p. 35, Jan., 1940

A Navy Artist Paints the Aleutians. By Mason Sutherland. Text with 16 colored illustrations from paintings by Lt. William F. Draper. LXXXIV, pp. 157-160, 4 ills. in black and white, Aug., 1943

Painting History in the Pacific. Text with 19 colored illustrations from paintings by Lt. William F. Draper, USNR. LXXXVI, p. 408, Oct., 1944

Painting the Army on Maneuvers. By Arthur Beaumont. Text with 16 colored illustrations from paintings by author. LXXXII, pp. 601-602, Nov., 1942

Painting the Field Dog Series (Acknowledgments). LXXI, p. 108, Jan., 1937

Painting the Hound Series (Acknowledgments). LXXII, p. 484, Oct., 1937

Paintings by Alexandre Iacovleff owned by the Society. LXIX, col. pls. IV, p. 24, V, p. 25, Jan., 1936

Paper:

Clay added to coating of paper gives greater luster to photographs. LXXIV, p. 753, Dec., 1938

Paper manufactured for the Magazine. XXXVII, pp. 234-245, 9 ills., Mar., 1920

Photographs:

First aerial color photographs published, September, 1930 (The Color Camera's First Aërial Success). LVIII, p. 344, Sept., 1930. LXIX, p. 128, Jan., 1936. LXXI, p. 340, Mar., 1937. LXXVII, p. 757, June, 1940

First appearance of hand-tinted illustrations in the Magazine (Across Nicaragua with Transit and Machéte). I, pp. 315-335, 3 ills. in color, Oct., 1889

First natural-color photograph (Lumiere Autochrome plate) in the Magazine (Ghent Flower Garden). XXVI, ill. p. 49, July, 1914

First natural-color photograph of an eclipse ever reproduced, showing the corona. By Irvine C. Gardiner. LXXI, ill. p. 178, Feb., 1937

First natural-color photograph taken in the stratosphere (*Explorer II* balloon). By Major Albert W. Stevens. LXXI, ill. p. 340, Mar., 1937

First natural-color photographs to be made of undersea life, reproduced in the Magazine, January, 1927 (The First Autochromes from the Ocean Bottom). LI, p. 56, Jan., 1927. LVIII, p. 344, Sept., 1930. LXIX, p. 128, Jan., 1936. LXXI, p. 340, Mar., 1937

First natural-color series of photographs (Autochromes) in the Magazine (The Land of the Best). XXIX, pp. 379-405, 23 ills. in color, Apr., 1916

First photograph ever made showing laterally the curvature of the earth. By Capt. A. W. Stevens. LIX, ill. p. 634, May, 1931. LXIX, p. 128, ill. p. 142, Jan., 1936

NATIONAL GEOGRAPHIC MAGAZINE—*Continued*

Photographs—*Continued*

First Photograph Ever Made Showing the Division Between the Troposphere and Stratosphere and also the Actual Curvature of the Earth. Aërial photo by Captain Albert W. Stevens. LXIX, supplement, May, 1936

First series of hand-tinted illustrations appear in the Magazine (Scenes in Korea and China). XXI, pp. 903-926, 39 ills. in color, Nov., 1910. LXIX, p. 154, Jan., 1936

First series of natural-color photographs of the Arctic regions made by the Society's staff photographers (The First Natural-Color Photographs from the Arctic), published, March, 1926. XLIX, p. 301, Mar., 1926. LVIII, p. 344, Sept., 1930. LXIX, p. 128, Jan., 1936. LXXI, p. 340, Mar., 1937

List of pioneering achievements in photography. LXIX, p. 128, Jan., 1936

See also Photography; Pictorial Supplements

Policies regarding the Magazine. XX, p. 486, May, 1909. XXIII, pp. 273-274, Mar., 1912. XXIV, p. 253, Feb., 1913. XXVII, p. 319, Mar., 1915. LXIX, pp. 123, 135, 145, 148, 149, Jan., 1936

Printing:

Judd & Detweiler, printers of the Magazine (since 1891). XXV, ill. p. 465, Apr., 1914

Printing the Magazine. LXXXI, p. 484, ill. p. 474, Apr., 1942

Publication Rules:

Address of the President to the Board of Managers, June 1, 1900 (National Expansion through Regular Publication Schedule). (By Alexander Graham Bell). XI, pp. 401-408, Oct., 1900

Reports:

Report by Gilbert H. Grosvenor for the year 1912. XXIV, pp. 251-255, Feb., 1913

Report of the Director and Editor of the National Geographic Society for the year 1914. By Gilbert H. Grosvenor. XXVII, pp. 318-320, Mar., 1915

NATIONAL GEOGRAPHIC SOCIETY (NGS):

Abstract of Minutes. *See* NGS: Meetings: Proceedings

Aeronautics:

Admiral Byrd Receives New Honor From The Society (Presentation by President Hoover of Special Gold Medal). LVIII, pp. 228-238, 4 ills., Aug., 1930
- Achievements of Byrd Antarctic Expedition 231–232
- Bumstead sun-compass praised by Byrd.. 233
- Byrd Antarctic Expedition aided by the Society 232

Aëronautics promoted by the Society. XLVI, p. 122, July, 1924

Air Conquest: From the Early Days of Giant Kites and Birdlike Gliders, the National Geographic Society Has Aided and Encouraged the Growth of Aviation. LII, pp. 233-242, 13 ills., Aug., 1927
- Aërial photography sponsored by the Society 240

NATIONAL GEOGRAPHIC SOCIETY—*Continued*

Aeronautics—*Continued*

Articles on aviation published in the Magazine 233–234, 240–242
Banquet celebrating progress in aviation. 233
Bell, Alexander Graham: Kite experiments of ....233; ill. pp. 235, 236
Bumstead sun-compass, Byrd's use of 238; ill. p. 242
Expeditions aided by the Society....234, 238; ill. p. 239
Gold Medal awarded Floyd Bennett..... 238
Hubbard Gold Medal awarded Comdr. Byrd ....238; ill. p. 239
Hubbard Gold Medal awarded Lindbergh 241–242; ill. p. 234
Peary's prophecy regarding aviation.... 234

The First Airship Flight Around the World: Dr. Hugo Eckener Tells of an Epochal Geographic Achievement upon the Occasion of the Bestowal of the National Geographic Society's Special Gold Medal. LVII, pp. 653-688, 37 ills., June, 1930
Four aviators awarded Society's medals.. 655
Presentation of medal to Dr. Eckener by Dr. Grosvenor..................653–655
Service of aviation to geography........ 655

In Honor of the Army and Aviation. XXII, pp. 267-284, 5 ills., Mar., 1911
Appreciation of S. P. Langley........... 279
Aviation in Germany....270-271; ill. p. 271
Importance of aviation in warfare...278–280
Wright, Wilbur: Address by........279–281

President Coolidge Bestows Lindbergh Award: The National Geographic Society's Hubbard Medal Is Presented to Aviator Before the Most Notable Gathering in the History of Washington. LIII, pp. 132-140, 4 ills., Jan., 1928
Aviation aided by the Society........... 135
Aviators at ceremony................. 132
Contributions of U. S. to aviation...... 138
Lindbergh's achievements..........134–135
Motion picture of aviation history...139–140

The Society Awards Hubbard Medal to Anne Morrow Lindbergh. LXV, pp. 791-794, 4 ills., June, 1934
Aërial photography sponsored by the Society 794
Aviation sponsored by the Society...... 791
Tribute to Mrs. Lindbergh by Dr. Grosvenor 791–792

The Society's Special Medal Awarded to Amelia Earhart: First Woman to Receive Geographic Distinction at Brilliant Ceremony in the National Capital. LXII, pp. 358-367, 7 ills., Sept., 1932
Aviation sponsored by the Society...... 362
Earhart, Amelia: Account of Transatlantic flight..358, 363-367; ill. pp. 359, 360
Tribute to Miss Earhart by Dr. Grosvenor 359
Tribute to Miss Earhart by President Hoover 362–363

See also Aeronautics; NGS: Expeditions: Stratosphere

Air-raid wardens, Demonstrations given for. LXXXI, ill. p. 460, Apr., 1942

Air travel by the Society's staff. LXIII, pp. 587, 628, May, 1933

Annex (Eckington). *See* NGS: Buildings

NATIONAL GEOGRAPHIC SOCIETY—*Continued*

Announcements:

The organization and purpose of the Society, the publication of its magazine, and the furthering of geographic knowledge through education and exploration. I, pp. i-ii, Oct., 1888. II, pp. 287-289, Apr., 1891

Annual Reports. *See* NGS: Committees: Auditing Committee; Secretary; Treasurer; *and* names of NGS Presidents and Vice-Presidents

Aquariums. LXV, ill. p. 107, Jan., 1934

Auditing Committee. *See* NGS: Committees

Banquets:

Announcement of Annual Banquet. XVII, p. 714, Dec., 1906
Guests 714

Announcement of Annual Banquet. XIX, p. 805, Nov., 1908; p. 888, Dec., 1908

Announcement of Annual Dinner, December 20, 1905. XVI, p. 570, Dec., 1905
Guests 570

Annual Banquet, January 26, 1912. XXIII, pp. 272-298, 5 ills., Mar., 1912
American Red Cross................288–290
Announcement of election of James Bryce as Honorary Member.........272, 275–276
Bell, Alexander Graham: Speeches by 272-276, 280, 282, 284, 287, 290, 292, 293
Boardman, Mabel: Speech by.......288–290
Bryce, James: Speech by...........276–280
Date-growing experiments in America... 293
Expeditions of the Society............. 275
Gannett, Henry: Speech by............ 272
Geography of food.................... 283
Growth of the Society..............272–274
Guests 272, 293–298
Hammond, Mrs. John Hays: Speech by 292–293
Importance of trigonometrical surveys 284, 287
Kahn, Mirza Ali Kuli: Speech by....281–282
Nitobe, Dr. Inazu: Speech by.......290–292
Progress of the Magazine under its Editor, Gilbert H. Grosvenor............ 274
Taft, William H.: Message from....... 282
Tittmann, O. H.: Speech by.........284, 287
Wiley, Dr. Harvey W.: Speech by....282–284

The Annual Dinner of the National Geographic Society. XVII, pp. 22-37, Jan., 1906
Achievements of the American press...29–32
Champ, W. S.: Speech by.............35–36
Committee for banquet................ 37
Definition of geography............... 24
Fiala, Anthony: Speech by...........32–34
Greely, Brig. Gen. A. W.: Speech by.... 36
Griscom, Floyd C.: Speech by.........27–29
Guests 22–23, 36–37
History of the Society...............23–24
Newspaper account of dinner.........22–23
Scott, Charles F.: Speech by..........29–32
Taft, William H.: Speech by..........25–26
Taft, Mr. and Mrs. William H.: Guests of honor.......................... 22

Banquets—*Continued*

Toast in memory of Gardiner Greene Hubbard 24
Toast to the President and the Flag...25–26
Toastmaster (Willis L. Moore)...23–25, 26–27, 29, 32, 34–35
Wellman, Walter: Speech by 36
Ziegler Polar Expedition..............32–36

The Discovery of the North Pole (Presentation of Special Gold Medal to Peary by Willis L. Moore, and Hubbard Gold Medal to Bartlett by James Bryce). XXI, pp. 63-82, Jan., 1910

Abruzzi, Duke of the: Message from.... 64
Barrett, John: Speech by............. 79
Bartlett, Capt. Robert A.: Acceptance speech by 77–78
Bryce, James: Presentation speech by..75–77
Cannon, Joseph: Speech by...........66–67
Carnegie, Andrew: Speech by.........68–69
Chester, Rear Adm. Colby M.: Speech by 69–73
Guests 63, 79–82
History of Peary's explorations........69–73
Hubbard, Gen. Thomas H.: Speech by 78–79
Hubbard Gold Medal awarded to Grove Karl Gilbert 63, 75
Hubbard Gold Medal presented to Capt. Robert A. Bartlett by James Bryce 63, 75–77
Jusserand, J. J.: Speech by...........64–66
Medals received by Peary............. 73
Moore, Willis L.: Presentation speech by 73–74
Peary, Robert E.: Acceptance speech by 74–75
Peary Arctic Club..................78–79
Planches, Baron Mayor des: Speech by.. 64
Purpose and organization of the Society 67–68
Roosevelt, Theodore: Message from..... 63
Special Gold Medal presented to Peary by Willis L. Moore.............63, 74–75
Toastmaster (Willis L. Moore)......63, 66–69, 73–75, 78–79

Honors for Amundsen (Presentation of Hubbard Gold Medal by Charles W. Fairbanks). XIX, pp. 55-76, 13 ills., Jan., 1908

Amundsen, Roald: Speech by.......... 57
Bryce, James: Speech by.............62–64
Burton, Theodore: Speech by.........66–68
Fairbanks, Charles W.: Presentation speech by 55–57
Forestry in America.................64–65
Goulder, Harvey: Speech by..........69–72
Great Lakes 69–72
Guests 55, 57, 74–76
Importance of geography.............62–64
Jusserand, J. J.: Speech by...........57–61
McGee, W J: Speech by............... 69
Mississippi River 66–68
Moore, J. Hampton: Speech by........72–74
Norse explorations 58
Rivers of the Atlantic coast..........72–74
Toastmaster (Willis L. Moore)...55, 57, 61–62, 64, 68–69, 72

Honors to Amundsen and Peary (Presentation of Special Gold Medal to Amundsen by Peary). XXIV, pp. 113-130, 6 ills., Jan., 1913

NATIONAL GEOGRAPHIC SOCIETY—*Continued*

Banquets—*Continued*

Amundsen, Roald: Speech of acceptance 129–130
Award of Grant Squires Prize to F. H. King 115
Bingham, Hiram: Account of Peruvian Expedition 116–117
Bryce, James: Speech and farewell..117–119
Buildings of the Society...........ill. p. 126
Election of Jean Charcot as Honorary Member 122, 124–125
Fields of exploration..............118–119
Finances 115
Fisher, Walter L.: Speech on Alaska and Hawaii 125, 127
Gannett, Henry: Speech by............ 115
Guests 113
Jusserand, J. J.: Speech by..........122–125
Membership 113, 115
Need of instruction in geography....121–122
Photograph of distinguished guests and officers of the Society...........ill. p. 114
Polar exploration 127–130
Presentation of Special Gold Medal to Amundsen by Peary..129; ill. pp. 120, 128
Redfield, William C.: Speech by......121–122
Toastmaster (Robert E. Peary)......115, 117, 119, 122, 125, 127–129, 130

Honors to Colonel Goethals: The Presentation, by President Woodrow Wilson, of the National Geographic Society Special Gold Medal. XXV, pp. 677-690, 6 ills., June, 1914

Announcement of the election of J. J. Jusserand as Honorary Member......679, 688
Bernstorff, Johann Heinrich, Count von: Speech by 684
Goethals, Col. George W.: Acceptance speech by 683–684
Grosvenor, Gilbert: Address by......679–680
Guests 677
Jusserand, J. J.: Speech by........688, 690
Magazine circulation 679
Mann, James R.: Speech by 687
Membership statistics 679
Panama Canal............679, 680, 683, 687
Toastmaster (William Jennings Bryan) 679, 680, 684, 687, 688, 690
Wilson, Woodrow: Presentation speech by 679, 680, 683

Honors to Peary (Presentation of Hubbard Gold Medal by President Roosevelt). XVIII, pp. 49-60, ill., Jan., 1907

Abruzzi, Duke of the: Tribute to......50–51
Achievements of members............. 50
Bell, Alexander Graham: Speech by....53–54
Bonaparte, Charles J.: Speech by......51–52
Committee for banquet................ 58
Cook, Frederick A.: Speech by........54–56
Expeditions by Frederick A. Cook......54–56
Guests 49, 58–60
History of the Society................ 49
Honorary Members 51
Peary, Robert E.: Speeches by.....50, 57–58
Planches, Baron Mayor des: Speech by.. 50
Roosevelt, Theodore: Presentation speech by 56–57

NATIONAL GEOGRAPHIC SOCIETY—*Continued*
Banquets—*Continued*

Toastmaster (Willis L. Moore)....49-50, 51, 53, 56
U. S. Navy..........................51-53

Honors to the American Navy. XX, pp. 77-95, Jan., 1909
Achievements of the Society........... 77
Boardman, Mabel: Speech by..........84-86
Curtis, William Eleroy: Speech by....82-84
Evans, Rear Adm. Robley D.: Speech by 91-93
Exploration and research promoted by the Navy 79-80, 90
Fairbanks, Charles W.: Speech by....77-78
Geographic research 89-90
Greely, Maj. Gen. A. W.: Speech by..89-90
Guests 93-95
Newberry, Truman H.: Speech by......79-81
Theme of speeches................... 77
Toastmaster (Willis L. Moore)...77-78, 82, 84, 86, 89, 91
Weeks, John M.: Speech by..........86-89
Work of the Red Cross..............84-86

In Honor of the Army and Aviation. XXII, pp. 267-284, 5 ills., Mar., 1911
Announcement of the election of President Taft as Honorary Member........267, 276
Appreciation of S. P. Langley.......... 279
Aviation in Germany...............270-271
Barra, Francisco Leon de la: Speech by 272-273
Bernstorff, Johann Heinrich, Count von: Speech by......................270-271
Bryce, James: Speech by............275-276
Commercial routes of the world......272-273
Committee for banquet................ 281
Fields of exploration..............275-276
Greely, Maj. Gen. A. W.: Speech by..278-279
Guests.....................267, 281-284
Introduction of dasheen (vegetable) 267; ill. pp. 268, 269
Taft, William Howard: Speech by....276-277
Toastmaster (Gen. John M. Wilson).268, 270-272, 275-279
Wood, Maj. Gen. Leonard: Speech by.. 278
Work of the Society.................. 267
Wright, Wilbur: Speech by..........279-281

Voice Voyages by the National Geographic Society: A Tribute to the Geographical Achievements of the Telephone. XXIX, pp. 296-326, 15 ills., chart, Mar., 1916
Bell, Alexander Graham: Speech by..315-316
Bell, Alexander Graham: Telephone invented by..296, 297, 306, 310, 316-318, 320
Bethell, Union Noble: Speech by....319-322
Carty, John J.: Speech by............. 316
Carty, John J.: Telephone demonstration by 297-302
Daniels, Josephus: Speech by........322-326
Geographical census of telephones....320-321
Geographical importance of telephone.310, 312
Guests .... 296-297; ill. p. 298
History of the telephone and telegraph 306-310, 315-318, 324
Long distance telephone demonstration 297-302; map, p. 297; ill. p. 301
Setting telephone poles...........ill. p. 307
Speakers' table ....ill. p. 298
Telephone Building, Buffalo, New York ill. p. 308
Telephone Building, El Paso, Texas ill. p. 303

NATIONAL GEOGRAPHIC SOCIETY—*Continued*
Banquets—*Continued*

Telephone cables ....ill. p. 311
Toastmaster (Franklin K. Lane)....305-306
U. S. Navy wireless system.........324, 326
Vail, Theodore N.: Speech by.......306-315
Wireless telephone demonstration....302-305

See also NGS: Receptions

Bequests:

A. W. Cutler, photographic artist, leaves his entire collection of negatives to the Society. XLII, p. 34, July, 1922

Fund bequeathed by Mary C. Burr. LXV, p. 626, May, 1934

James C. Horgan bequest. XXXVII, p. 338, Apr., 1920

Jane M. Smith bequest for life memberships. XXIII, p. 104, Jan., 1912. XXXVII, pp. 342-343, Apr., 1920

Recent Bequests by Members of the National Geographic Society. XLIX, p. 474, Apr., 1926
Designated use of funds................ 474
Nealley, George True: Fund given by.... 474
White, Abbie M.: Fund given by...... 474

Board of Managers:

Amendment of by-laws. XVI, p. 53, Jan., 1905

Claims of Peary and Cook referred to Committee on Research. XX, pp. 921-922, Nov., 1909

Committee appointed to advise Wellman Polar Expedition. IX, pp. 373-374, Aug., 1898

Election, and reelection, of members of Board. *See* names of Managers, *below*

Election of new members of the Society. *See* NGS: Members and Membership

International Geographic Conference, in conjunction with the World's Columbian Exposition, of 1893, sponsored by the Board. V. pp. 98-99, Jan. 31, 1894

Monographs on the physical features of the United States, to be prepared for use in the public schools. VI, pp. 225-227, Dec. 29, 1894

The National Geographic Society in War Time. By Major-General A. W. Greely. XXXIII, pp. 369-375, 5 ills., Apr., 1918
Committee to present Honorary Membership to President Wilson............ 369
Election of Woodrow Wilson as Honorary Member 369
Resolution in memory of Col. Henry F. Blount 371
William Howard Taft elected to the Board of Managers...................... 371

North Pole. XX, pp. 1008-1009, Nov., 1909
Committee appointed to consider claims of Cook..........................1009
Report of committee on claims of Cook and Peary.......................1008
Resolution acknowledging Peary's discovery 1008
Resolution awarding medals to Peary and Bartlett 1008-1009

NATIONAL GEOGRAPHIC SOCIETY—*Continued*

Board of Managers—*Continued*

Photograph of Board of Managers. XXIV, ill. p. 114, Jan., 1913. LXIX, ill. p. 126, Jan., 1936

Research fund established. XX, p. 486, May, 1909

Resolution authorizing purchase of Big Trees. XXXI, p. 5, Jan., 1917

Resolution concerning Wellman Polar Expedition. XVII, p. 205, Apr., 1906

Resolution subscribing to Peary Expedition of 1907-1908. XVIII, p. 281, Apr., 1907

Resolution withdrawing subscription to South Polar Expedition of Peary Arctic Club. XXI, p. 365, Apr., 1910

Resolutions concerning medals. XX, p. 487, May, 1909

Retirement: Regrouping of Board members for retirement. VII, p. 215, June, 1896

Rules:

Standing Rules of the Board of Managers (Jan. 16, 1891). II, pp. 308-310, Apr., 1891

See also NGM: Publication Rules

Tribute of respect to the memory of Mrs. Gardiner Greene Hubbard. XX, p. 1008, Nov., 1909

See also NGS: Board of Trustees; By-laws; Certificate of Incorporation; History

Managers

Year of:

1888. I, p. 93, Oct., 1888; p. 165, Apr., 1889

1889. I, p. 168, Apr., 1889

1890. II, p. ii (publ. Apr., 1891); p. 69, Apr., 1890

1891. II, p. 315, Apr., 1891. III, p. ii, Feb. 19, 1892

1892. III, p. xiv, Feb. 19, 1892. IV, p. ii, Feb. 20, 1893

1893. V, p. ii, May 5, 1894

1894. V, p. xxvii, May 5, 1894

1894 and to May 31, 1895. VI, p. ii, Oct. 31, 1895

1895-96. VI, p. xxxii, Oct. 31, 1895

1903-1905. XV, p. II, 1904

1906-1907. XVI, p. II, 1905

Abbe, Cleveland

Election of. I, p. 165, Apr., 1889; p. 270, July, 1889. II, p. 68, Apr., 1890

Baker, Marcus

Appreciation of. XV, pp. 40-43, ill., Jan., 1904

Election of. I, p. 165, Apr., 1889; p. 270, July, 1889. II, p. 68, Apr., 1890. III, p. xii, Feb. 19, 1892. IV, p. xix, Feb. 20, 1893. V, p. xix, May 5, 1894. VIII, p. 191, June, 1897

Bell, Alexander Graham

Election of. IX, p. 414, Sept., 1898. XVI, p. 87, Feb., 1905. XXII, p. 211, Feb., 1911

Bell, Charles J.

Election of. VII, p. 216, June, 1896

Birnie, Rogers, Jr.

Election of. I, p. 165, Apr., 1889; p. 270, July, 1889. II, p. 68, Apr., 1890; p. 294, Apr., 1891

NATIONAL GEOGRAPHIC SOCIETY—*Continued*

Board of Managers—*Continued*

Resignation of. IV, p. vii, Feb. 20, 1893

Blount, Henry F.

Election of. III, p. xii, Feb. 19, 1892. IV, p. xix, Feb. 20, 1893. V, p. xix, May 5, 1894. VIII, p. 191, June, 1897. XXI, p. 88, Jan., 1910

Resolution in memory of. XXXIII, p. 371, Apr., 1918

Brooks, Alfred H.

Election of. XVI, p. 87, Feb., 1905

Chamberlin, T. C.

Election of. XVI, p. 87, Feb., 1905

Chester, Colby M.

Election of. XXI, p. 88, Jan., 1910

Coville, Frederick V.

Election of. VIII, p. 191, June, 1897. XXI, p. 88, Jan., 1910

Memorial tribute to. LXXI, p. 662, ill., May, 1937

Dabney, Charles W., Jr.

Election of. VII, p. 216, June, 1896

Dall, William H.

Election of. VII, p. 216, June, 1896

Davis, William M.

Resignation of. XVI, p. 87, Feb., 1905

Day, David T.

Election of. VII, p. 216, June, 1896

Gannett, Henry

Election of. II, p. 297, Apr., 1891. III, p. xii, Feb. 19, 1892. IV, p. xix, Feb. 20, 1893. IX, p. 414, Sept., 1898. XVI, p. 87, Feb., 1905. XXII, p. 211, Feb., 1911

Naming of Electric Peak, Yellowstone National Park. LXXVII, p. 794, June, 1940

Resolution in memory of. XXVI, pp. 609-613, ill., Dec., 1914

Gilbert, Grove Karl

Election of. II, p. 294, Apr., 1891. III, p. xii, Feb. 19, 1892. IV, p. xix, Feb. 20, 1893. V, p. xix, May 5, 1894. VII, p. 216, June, 1896

Resignation of. IX, p. 520, Dec., 1898

Goode, G. Brown

Election of. I, p. 165, Apr., 1889; p. 270, July, 1889. II, p. 68, Apr., 1890; p. 294, Apr., 1891

Gore, James Howard

Charter member of the Society. LXV, p. 793, June, 1934

Election of. XXII, p. 211, Feb., 1911

Greely, A. W.

Charter member of the Society. LXV, p. 793, June, 1934

Election of. IX, p. 414, Sept., 1898. XVI, p. 87, Feb., 1905. XXII, p. 211, Feb., 1911

Founder and life trustee. LXXXIV, p. 133, Aug., 1943

Photograph of. LXIX, ill. p. 129, Jan., 1936

NATIONAL GEOGRAPHIC SOCIETY—*Continued*
Board of Managers—*Continued*
Grosvenor, Gilbert H.
Election of. XVI, p. 87, Feb., 1905
Reelection of. XXII, p. 211, Feb., 1911
Hayden, Everett
Election of. V, p. xix, May 5, 1894. VIII, p. 191, June, 1897
Termination of office, by transfer to another city. IX, p. 520, Dec., 1898
Heilprin, Angelo
Election of. XVI, p. 87, Feb., 1905
Hyde, John
Election of. III, p. xii, Feb. 19, 1892. IV, p. xix, Feb. 20, 1893. V, p. xix, May 5, 1894. IX, p. 414, Sept., 1898
Johnson, Willard D.
Election of. I, p. 270, July, 1889. II, p. 68, Apr., 1890; p. 294, Apr., 1891
Resignation of. I, p. 270, July, 1889
Kauffmann, Rudolph
Election of. XXI, p. 88, Jan., 1910
Kenaston, C. A.
Election of. I, p. 270, July, 1889. II, p. 68, Apr., 1890
La Gorce, John Oliver
Election of. XXXVII, p. 345, Apr., 1920
Lane, Franklin K.
Member of. LXIX, p. 343, Mar., 1936
Macdonald, T. L.
Election of. XXI, p. 88, Jan., 1910
McGee, W J
Election of. II, p. 294, Apr., 1891. III, p. xii, Feb. 19, 1892. IV, p. xix, Feb. 20, 1893. V, p. xix, May 5, 1894. IX, p. 414, Sept., 1898
Mendenhall, T. C.
Election of. II, p. 294, Apr., 1891. III, p. xii, Feb. 19, 1892. IV, p. xix, Feb. 20, 1893
Member of. LXXXVI, p. 640, Nov., 1944
Merriam, C. Hart
Charter member of the Society. LXV, pp. 792-793, June, 1934
Member for 54 years, 1888-1942. LXXXV, p. 694, June, 1944
Reelection of. VIII, p. 191, June, 1897
Mitchell, Henry
Election of. I, p. 165, Apr., 1889
Resignation of. I, p. 270, July, 1889
Moore, Willis L.
Election of. IX, p. 520, Dec., 1898. XXI, p. 88, Jan., 1910
Newell, Frederick H.
Election of. V, pp. ii, xix, May 5, 1894. IX, p. 414, Sept., 1898
North, S. N. D.
Election of. XXI, p. 88, Jan., 1910
Ogden, Herbert G.
Election of. VII, p. 216, June, 1896

NATIONAL GEOGRAPHIC SOCIETY—*Continued*
Board of Managers—*Continued*
Peary, Robert E.
Announcement of the death of. XXXVII, p. 345, Apr., 1920
Election of. XLI, p. 643, June, 1922
Pillsbury, John Elliott
Announcement of the death of. XXXVII, p. 345, Apr., 1920
Election of. XXI, p. 88, Jan., 1910
Powell, W. B.
Election of. I, p. 165, Apr., 1889; p. 270, July, 1889. II, p. 68, Apr., 1890; p. 294, Apr., 1891. III, p. xii, Feb. 19, 1892. IV, p. xix, Feb. 20, 1893. VIII, p. 191, June, 1897
Pritchett, Henry S.
Election of. IX, p. 520, Dec., 1898
Member of. LXXXVI, p. 640, Nov., 1944
Russell, Israel C.
Election of. XIII, pp. 218-219, ill., June, 1902
Shiras, George, 3d
Member of. LXV, p. 793, June, 1934. LXIX, p. 128, Jan., 1936
Smith, George Otis
Election of. XXII, p. 211, Feb., 1911
Taft, William Howard
Birthplace. LXI, ill. p. 591, May, 1932
Election of. XXXVII, p. 371, Apr., 1918
Funeral. LVII, ill. p. 597, May, 1930
Member for 13 years (1917-1930). LXIX, p. 153, Jan., 1936. LXXIV, p. 312, Sept., 1938
Tittmann, O. H.
Charter member of the Society. LXV, p. 793, June, 1934
Election of. I, p. 270, July, 1889. XVI, p. 87, Feb., 1905. XXII, p. 211, Feb., 1911
Member of. LXXXVI, p. 640, Nov., 1944
Warder, B. H.
Election of. II, p. 294, Apr., 1891
Welling, James C.
Election of. I, p. 165, Apr., 1889; p. 270, July, 1889. II, p. 68, Apr., 1890
Resignation of. II, p. 297, Apr., 1891
Willits, Edwin
Election of. III, p. xii, Feb. 19, 1892. IV, p. xix, Feb. 20, 1893. V, p. xix, May 5, 1894
Wilson, John M.
Announcement of the death of. XXXVII, p. 345, Apr., 1920
Election of. XVI, p. 87, Feb., 1905. XXII, p. 211, Feb., 1911
Photograph of. LXIX, ill. p. 129, Jan., 1936
See also Board of Trustees, *following*

Board of Trustees:
Photograph of members of the Board of Trustees, June, 1929. LVII, ill. p. 592, May, 1930
Photograph of the Board of Trustees, December 14, 1921. XLI, ill. p. 240, Mar., 1922. LXIX, ill. p. 133, Jan., 1936

NATIONAL GEOGRAPHIC SOCIETY—*Continued*
Board of Trustees—*Continued*
Photograph of Trustees and Officers of the Society in 1930. LXIX, ill. p. 159, Jan., 1936
Presentation of Hubbard Medal by President Truman to Gen. H. H. Arnold. LXXXIX, ill. p. 141, Feb., 1946
Proposed amendment to by-laws regarding Trustees. XXXVII, p. 292, Mar., 1920
Redwood groves, California, named for Franklin K. Lane and Stephen T. Mather. LXIX, p. 343, Mar., 1936
U. S. Coast and Geodetic Survey Directors, members of the Board of Trustees. LXXXVI, p. 640, ill. p. 618, Nov., 1944

Colbert, L. O.

Member of. LXXXVI, p. 640, ill. p. 618, Nov., 1944
Presents wings to a flying daughter (Women's AirForce Service Pilots). LXXXIV, ill. p. 458, Oct., 1943

Coolidge, Calvin

Election of. LV, p. 750, June, 1929
Member of. LXII, p. 362, Sept., 1932

Dawes, Charles G.

Member of. LXV, p. 793, June, 1934

Hughes, Charles Evans

Chief Justice of the United States, a Board member. LXV, p. 792, June, 1934

Jones, E. Lester

Member of. L, p. 384, Sept., 1926. LXXXVI, p. 640, Nov., 1944

Kettering, Charles F.

Member of. LXXXVI, ill. p. 703, Dec., 1944

Mather, Stephen T.

Member of. LXIX, p. 343, Mar., 1936

Patton, Raymond S.

Member of. LXXXVI, p. 640, Nov., 1944

Payne, John Barton

Member of. LXV, p. 793, June, 1934

Pershing, John J.

Member of. LXV, p. 793, June, 1934. LXIX, p. 713, ill. p. 712, May, 1936
Photograph of. LXXI, ill. p. 517, Apr., 1937

Pratt, William V.

Member of. LXV, p. 793, June, 1934. LXVII, p. 591, May, 1935

Wetmore, Alexander

Member of. LXXXVI, p. 161, Aug., 1944
See also NGS: Board of Managers, for Board members prior to 1920; History

Buildings:

Annex (Eckington)

Location. XLI, air view, p. 522, May, 1922. XLIII, air view, p. 390, Apr., 1923
Photograph of. LXIX, ill. p. 125, Jan., 1936

Hubbard Memorial Hall

A gift to the Society by the family of the first President, Gardiner Greene Hubbard. XVII, p. 24, Jan., 1906. XX, p. 1008, Nov., 1909. XXIV, p. 251, Feb., 1913. LXIX, pp. 124, 152, Jan., 1936

NATIONAL GEOGRAPHIC SOCIETY—*Continued*
Buildings—*Continued*
The Home of the National Geographic Society. XVI, p. 342, July, 1905
- Deed of trust for Hubbard Memorial Hall 342
- Resolution of thanks to donors of building 342

The Hubbard Memorial Building. XIII, pp. 174-176, May, 1902
- Cornerstone contents 174–176
- Dedication to Gardiner Greene Hubbard 175
- Laying of cornerstone 174–175

Mural, "The Discoverer." LXXIV, p. 77, July, 1938
Mural paintings by the noted artist, N. C. Wyeth. LIV, p. 568, Nov., 1928. LV, p. 93, Jan., 1929. LXXIV, p. 77, July, 1938
The New Home of the National Geographic Society. XV, pp. 176-181, 5 ills., Apr., 1904
- Entrance hall .... ill. p. 178
- Exterior .... ill. p. 177
- Fireplace .... ill. p. 180
- Formal opening 176
- Library and meeting hall ....176; ill. pp. 179–181

Opening of Hubbard Memorial Hall. XIV, p. 217, May, 1903. XV, p. 176, Apr., 1904
Photographs and sketch of. XV, ill. pp. 177-181, Apr., 1904. XXIV, ill. p. 126, Jan., 1913. XXV, ill. pp. 454, 464, Apr., 1914. XLIII, ill. pp. 669, 670, June, 1923. LIII, ill. p. 133, Jan., 1928. LVII, ill. p. 597, May, 1930. LXIX, ill. p. 124, Jan., 1936
Plans for. XI, pp. 406-407, Oct., 1900

New Building, 16th Street (1913)

Board of Managers, in December, 1912, authorized the construction of a building, on the property adjacent to Hubbard Memorial Hall. XXIV, p. 251, Feb., 1913
Funeral cortege of William Howard Taft passes the Society's headquarters. LVII, ill. p. 597, May, 1930
The National Geographic Society and Its New Building. XXV, pp. 455-470, 11 ills., Apr., 1914
- Architecture and plan 459
- Correspondence 465
- Editorial rooms ....459; ill. pp. 460, 461
- Exterior .... ill. p. 454
- General office .... ill. p. 456
- Hubbard Memorial Hall 457; ill. pp. 454, 464
- Index Department .... ill. p. 463
- Library ....459; ill. pp. 454, 458, 464
- Mail room .... ill. p. 462

Office of Gilbert H. Grosvenor. XXV, ill. p. 460, Apr., 1914
Office of John Oliver La Gorce. XXV, ill. p. 461, Apr., 1914. LXIX, ill. p. 156, Jan., 1936
Photographs and sketch of. XXIV, ill. p. 126, Jan., 1913. XLIII, ill. pp. 669, 670, June, 1923. LIII, ill. p. 133, Jan., 1928. LVII, ill. p. 597, May, 1930. LXIX, ill. p. 124, Jan., 1936
Plans for. XXIV, pp. 251-252, Feb., 1913

New Building, 16th Street (1932)
Addition

Air-conditioning plant. LXIII, p. 574, May, 1933

Aquariums. LXV, ill. p. 107, Jan., 1934

Architect. LX, p. 544, Nov., 1931

Building stone used. LXVII, p. 486, Apr., 1935

Cafeteria. LXXXII, p. 209, Aug., 1942

Cartographic Department. LXIII, ill. p. 651, June, 1933. LXXXI, ill. p. 333, Mar., 1942; ill. pp. 675, 680, May, 1942

Explorers' Hall. LXV, pp. 791, 794, June, 1934. LXXXI, col. pl. II, p. 338, Mar., 1942; p. 657, May, 1942

Façade of executive and editorial offices, illuminated. LXVII, duotone pl. XVI, p. 216, Feb., 1935

Foyer of the Society's headquarters. LXIX, ill. p. 157, Jan., 1936. XC, ill. p. 11, July, 1946

Photographic Laboratory. LXIV, ill. p. 277, Sept., 1933. LXVII, p. 486, Apr., 1935. LXXI, p. 670, June, 1937

Photographic Library. LXXXIV, p. 289, ill. p. 274, Sept., 1943

Photographs and sketch of. LX, ill. p. 544, Nov., 1931. LXV, ill. p. 794, June, 1934. LXVII, duotone pl. XVI, p. 216, Feb., 1935. LXIX, ill. p. 124, Jan., 1936

Seal, Bronze, in lobby floor. LXIX, ill. p. 157, Jan., 1936. XC, ill. p. 11, July, 1946

By-laws:

Adoption of by-laws. XII, p. 208, May, 1901

Amendments to by-laws. I, p. 271, July, 1889. II, pp. 290, 294, Apr., 1891. IV, pp. xiii, xv, Feb. 20, 1893. V, pp. xiv, xvii, xix, xxi, May 5, 1894. VII, p. 86, Feb., 1896; p. 215, June, 1896. IX, pp. 414-416, Sept., 1898

Copy of by-laws. I, pp. 90-92, Oct., 1888; pp. 169-171, Apr., 1889. XVI, pp. 137-138, Mar., 1905

Copy of by-laws, as adopted with amendments up to January 9, 1891. II, pp. 305-307, Apr., 1891

Copy of by-laws, as adopted with amendments up to January 6, 1894. V, pp. xxv-xxvi, May 5, 1894

Copy of by-laws, as adopted with amendments up to May 31, 1895. VI, pp. xxix-xxxi, Oct. 31, 1895

Copy of by-laws, as adopted with amendments, May 20, 1898. IX, pp. 414-416, Sept., 1898

Copy of by-laws adopted May 16, 1902. XIV, pp. 123-124, Mar., 1903.

Creation of a class of Fellows. XIII, p. 220, June, 1902

Notice of proposed amendments. XIII, p. 182, May, 1902

Proposed change in by-laws. XVI, p. 53, Jan., 1905. XVIII, pp. 826-829, Dec., 1907

NATIONAL GEOGRAPHIC SOCIETY—*Continued*

Proposed changes in by-laws. XXXVII, p. 292, Mar., 1920
Amendments 292
Board of Trustees.................... 292
Dues 292

Proposed changes in by-laws, especially regarding membership. XI, p. 404, Oct., 1900. XII, pp. 167-168, Apr., 1901

Calendar:

Program of lectures and meetings for the years:
1894-1895. VI, pp. xviii-xx, Oct. 31, 1895
1896-1897. VII, foldout, Dec., 1896. VIII, foldout, Mar., 1897
1901-1902. XII, p. 379, Oct., 1901; pp. 411-412, Nov., 1901
1903-1904. XIV, p. 428, Nov., 1903
1904-1905. XV, pp. 461-462, Nov., 1904
1905. XVI, p. 54, Jan., 1905
1905-1906. XVI, pp. 527-528, Nov., 1905
1906-1907. XVII, pp. 649-650, Nov., 1906
1909-1910. XX, pp. 1009-1010, Nov., 1909

See also NGS: Meetings

Cartographic Department. *See* NGS: Buildings: New Building (1932)

Certificate of Incorporation. I, p. 80, Oct., 1888; pp. 165, 167, Apr., 1889

Certificates:

Geographic Prizes: Certificates to be awarded to the best essayist of each state, and to the second-best essayist of the country, in the geographic essay contest held annually for students in the public high schools. IV, pp. 206-207, Feb. 8, 1893

Important Announcement Concerning Essays (Certificate Awards). VI, pp. 227-228, Dec. 29, 1894

See also NGS: Prizes

Character and Scope. I, p. 1, Oct., 1888. II, p. 288, Apr., 1891. VII, p. 2, Jan., 1896. LXIX, pp. 123-124, 134-135, 145, 148, Jan., 1936

Committees:

Advisory Committee for Stratosphere Flight. LXVI, pp. 109-110, July, 1934; pp. 398, 411, Oct., 1934

Appointment of committee to nominate President. XIV, p. 254, June, 1903

Auditing Committee: Members of, and reports submitted, for the years, 1888-1898. I, p. 163, Apr., 1889. II, p. 65, Apr., 1890; p. 301, Apr., 1891. III, p. xii, Feb. 19, 1892. IV, pp. xii, xxiv, Feb. 20, 1893. V, pp. xix, xxiv, May 5, 1894. VI, p. xxviii, Oct. 31, 1895. VIII, pp. 191, 192, June, 1897. IX, pp. 31-32, Jan., 1898; p. 414, Sept., 1898

Chairman of Committee on Eighth International Geographic Congress. XIII, p. 219, June, 1902. XIV, p. 254, June, 1903

Committee appointed to advise with Mr. Wellman on the forthcoming expedition to the Arctic. IX, pp. 373-374, Aug., 1898

NATIONAL GEOGRAPHIC SOCIETY—*Continued*

Committees—*Continued*

Committee appointed to consider claims of Cook. XX, p. 1009, Nov., 1909

Committee appointed to consider claims of Peary and Cook. XX, pp. 921-922, 1008, Nov., 1909

Committee appointed to examine records of Byrd Arctic Expedition. L, pp. 377, 384-388, Sept., 1926
- Members of committee.................. 384
- Reports approving records......377, 384–388

Committee of five appointed to devise plans for carrying out the purposes of the Society. II, p. 292, Apr., 1891

Committee to present Honorary Membership to President Wilson. XXXIII, p. 369, Apr., 1918

Committees for 1906. XVII, p. 240, Apr., 1906

Committees of 1907. XVIII, p. 216, Mar., 1907

Communications and Publications. II, p. 294, Apr., 1891

Communications Committee. II, p. 308, Apr., 1891. IX, pp. 415-416, Sept., 1898

Editorial Committee. X, p. 222, June, 1899

Essay Committee. *See* Prize Committee, *below*

Exploration: Report of Committee on Exploration in Alaska. (By G. K. Gilbert, Everett Hayden, Willard D. Johnson). III, pp. 248-250, Feb. 19, 1892

Finance Committee. XXIV, p. 251, Feb., 1913

Prize Committee. IV, p. 208, Feb. 8, 1893. VI, p. 228, Dec. 29, 1894. X, p. 32, Jan., 1899. XI, p. 246, June, 1900

See also NGS: Essay Contests

Publications Committee. II, pp. 294, 308, Apr., 1891. IV, p. i, Feb. 20, 1893. V, p. i, May 5, 1894. VI, p. i, Oct. 31, 1895. IX, pp. 415-416, Sept., 1898

Research Committee. XVII, p. 205, Apr., 1906. XX, p. 486, May, 1909; pp. 921-922, Nov., 1909

Standing committees appointed by Alexander Graham Bell. XIII, p. 118, Mar., 1902; p. 150, Apr., 1902

See also NGS: Rules

Cruises. *See* NGS: Excursions and Field Meetings; Expeditions

Dues. XI, p. 406, Oct., 1900. XXXVIII, p. 80, July, 1920

See also NGS: By-laws

Editorial Department. *See* National Geographic Magazine

Engravings and Etchings. *See* National Geographic Magazine

Essay Contests:

Geographic Prizes (Certificates and medals awarded annually to public high school students writing the best essay on geography). IV, pp. 206-208, Feb. 8, 1893

NATIONAL GEOGRAPHIC SOCIETY—*Continued*

Essay Contests—*Continued*

Important Announcement Concerning Essays (Subject: River Systems of the United States). VI, pp. 227-228, Dec. 29, 1894

Prizes for Essays on Norse Discoveries in America. X, pp. 31-32, Jan., 1899. XI, p. 246, June, 1900

Excursions and Field Meetings:

Annapolis, Maryland, May 9, 1903. XIV, p. 217, May, 1903

Annapolis, Maryland: State House, Naval Academy, Chase Mansion, visited, May 27, 1892. IV, p. xvii, Feb. 20, 1893

Brandywine, Delaware, May 18, 1901. XII, p. 208, May, 1901

Cabin John Bridge, Maryland, October 2, 1897. VIII, pp. 365-366, Dec., 1897

Charlottesville, Virginia: Eighth Annual Field Meeting of the National Geographic Society: Monticello and University of Virginia, visited, May 16, 1896. VII, p. 216, June, 1896; pp. 259-260, ill., Aug., 1896

Eclipse: The National Geographic Society's Eclipse Expedition to Norfolk, Va., May 27-28, 1900. XI, p. 320, Aug., 1900

Eclipse: The Scientific Work of the National Geographic Society's Eclipse Expedition to Norfolk, Va., May 27-28, 1900. By Simon Newcomb. XI, pp. 321-324, Aug., 1900

Fredericksburg, Virginia: Announcement of the Seventh Annual Excursion and Field Meeting, Saturday, May 4, 1895. VI, foldout, Apr. 20, 1895

Gettysburg, Pennsylvania, May 17, 1902. XIII, p. 150, Apr., 1902

Harpers Ferry, West Virginia, May 14, 1898. IX, p. 414, Sept., 1898

High Island, Potomac River, Maryland, November 6, 1897. VIII, p. 366, Dec., 1897

Luray Caverns, Virginia, May 19, 1906. XVII, p. 302, May, 1906; pp. 358-362, 3 ills., June, 1906

Luray Caverns, Virginia, May 26, 1906. XVII, pp. 358-362, 3 ills., June, 1906

Manassas Gap, Virginia, May 22, 1897. VIII, p. 192, June, 1897

Naval Observatory, Washington, D. C., November 13, 1897. IX, p. 31, Jan., 1898

Potomac River cruise to Indian Head and Marshall Hall, May 1, 1893. V, p. xiii, May 5, 1894

Shendun, Virginia: Caves visited, June 3-4, 1891. III, p. x, Feb. 19, 1892

Virginia Beach and the Dismal Swamp, April 20, 1894. VI, p. xvi, Oct. 31, 1895

Expeditions:

Expeditions of 1912. XXIV, p. 251, Feb., 1913

First expedition. *See* NGS: **Expeditions: Alaska**: Mount St. Elias

See also NGS: History

Expeditions—*Continued*

Africa

Hunting an Observatory: A Successful Search for a Dry Mountain on Which to Establish the National Geographic Society's Solar Radiation Station. By C. G. Abbot. L, pp. 503-518, 13 ills., map, Oct., 1926

Keeping House for the "Shepherds of the Sun." By Mrs. William H. Hoover. LVII, pp. 483-506, 17 ills., map, Apr., 1930

Measuring the Sun's Heat and Forecasting the Weather: The National Geographic Society to Maintain a Solar Station in a Remote Part of the World to Coöperate with Smithsonian Institution Stations in California and Chile. By C. G. Abbot. XLIX, pp. 111-126, 15 ills., chart, Jan., 1926

National Geographic Society (Report and Cables concerning Roosevelt's African Expedition sponsored by the Smithsonian Institution). XXI, pp. 365-370, 5 ills., Apr., 1910

Under the South African Union. By Melville Chater. LIX, pp. 391-512, 97 ills. in black and white, 38 ills. in color, two-page map, Apr., 1931

Alaska

Appropriation for, and personnel of, 1919 Katmai Expedition. XXXV, p. 366, Apr., 1919

Appropriation for fifth expedition to the Valley of Ten Thousand Smokes. XXXIII, p. 372, Apr., 1918

Contributors to Alaskan Expedition of 1909. XXI, p. 88, Jan., 1910

An Expedition to Mount St. Elias, Alaska. By Israel C. Russell. III, pp. 53-191, 17 ills., 3 diagrs., tables, 7 maps (1 foldout), May 29, 1891

Expeditions of 1912. XXIV, p. 251, Feb., 1913

Exploring Frozen Fragments of American History: On the Trail of Early Eskimo Colonists Who Made a 55-Mile Crossing from the Old World to the New. By Henry B. Collins, Jr. LXXV, pp. 633-656, 24 ills., map, May, 1939

Father Hubbard's Alaskan Explorations. LXV, pp. 625-626, May, 1934

Mapping the Home of the Great Brown Bear: Adventures of the National Geographic Society's Pavlof Volcano Expedition to Alaska. By Dr. Thomas A. Jaggar. LV, pp. 109-134, 30 ills., map, Jan., 1929

Mount St. Elias Expedition, the Society's first scientific exploration, under the leadership of Israel C. Russell. II, p. 288, Apr., 1891. III, pp. 39-40, Apr. 30, 1891. IV, pp. vii-ix, Feb. 20, 1893. V, p. 177, Jan. 31, 1894

National Geographic Society Alaska Expedition. XX, pp. 581-584, June, 1909

National Geographic Society-Harvard University Alaska Expedition (1938). LXXXI, p. 675, May, 1942

Expeditions—*Continued*

National Geographic Society-Harvard University Mount McKinley Flight Expedition (1936). LXXXII, p. 310, Sept., 1942

The National Geographic Society Researches in Alaska. By Lawrence Martin. XXII, pp. 537-561, 17 ills., 5 maps, June, 1911

The National Geographic Society's Alaskan Expedition. XXI, p. 370, Apr., 1910

The National Geographic Society's Alaskan Expedition of 1909. By Ralph S. Tarr and Lawrence Martin. XXI, pp. 1-54, 42 ills., 12 maps, Jan., 1910

Our Greatest National Monument: The National Geographic Society Completes Its Explorations in the Valley of Ten Thousand Smokes. By Robert F. Griggs. XL, pp. 219-292, 73 ills. in black and white, 16 ills. in color, maps, Sept., 1921

Over the Roof of Our Continent (Mount McKinley). By Bradford Washburn. LXXIV, pp. 78-98, 17 ills. in duotone, map, July, 1938

Photography in Glacial Alaska. By O. D. von Engeln. XXI, pp. 54-62, 4 ills., Jan., 1910

The Recent Eruption of Katmai Volcano in Alaska. By George C. Martin. XXIV, pp. 131-181, 45 ills., diagr., map, Feb., 1913

Recent Explorations in Alaska. By Eliza Ruhamah Scidmore. V, pp. 173-179, Jan. 31, 1894

Report of Committee on Exploration in Alaska. III, pp. 248-250, Feb. 19, 1892

Report of sixth Katmai Expedition. XXXVII, p. 338, Apr., 1920

Summary of Reports on the Mt. St. Elias Expedition. II, pp. 302-304, Apr., 1891

The Ten Thousand Smokes Now a National Monument: The President of the United States Sets Aside for the American People the Extraordinary Valley Discovered and Explored by the National Geographic Society. XXXV, pp. 359-366, 5 ills., Apr., 1919

The Valley of Ten Thousand Smokes: An Account of the Discovery and Exploration of the Most Wonderful Volcanic Region in the World. By Robert F. Griggs. XXXIII, pp. 115-169, 46 ills., map, panorama, Feb., 1918

The Valley of Ten Thousand Smokes: National Geographic Society Explorations in the Katmai District of Alaska. By Robert F. Griggs. XXXI, pp. 13-68, 51 ills., map, Jan., 1917

Volcanoes of Alaska (Report by Capt. K. W. Perry). XXIII, pp. 824-832, 11 ills., Aug., 1912

Antarctic Regions

The Conquest of Antarctica by Air. By Richard Evelyn Byrd. LVIII, pp. 127-227, 71 ills. in black and white, 16 ills. in gravure, map, Aug., 1930

Exploring the Ice Age in Antarctica. By Richard Evelyn Byrd. LXVIII, pp. 399-474, 72 ills., maps (1 two-page), Oct., 1935

NATIONAL GEOGRAPHIC SOCIETY—*Continued*

Expeditions—*Continued*

Mapping the Antarctic from the Air: The Aërial Camera Earns Its Place as the Eyes and Memory of the Explorer. By Capt. Ashley C. McKinley. LXII, pp. 471-485, 13 ills., map supplement, Oct., 1932

Second Byrd Antarctic Expedition. LXV, p. 626, May, 1934

The Society's Special Medal Is Awarded to Dr. Thomas C. Poulter: Admiral Byrd's Second-in-Command and Senior Scientist Is Accorded High Geographic Honor. LXXII, pp. 105-108, ills., July, 1937

The South Polar Expedition (Proposed by Peary for Consideration by NGS). XXI, pp. 167-170, map, Feb., 1910

Arctic Regions

The "Bowdoin" in North Greenland: Arctic Explorers Place Tablet to Commemorate Sacrifices of the Lady Franklin Bay Expedition. By Donald B. MacMillan. XLVII, pp. 677-722, 49 ills., June, 1925
Note: MacMillan Expedition of 1923-24 transports and erects memorial tablet, a gift of NGS

Farthest North (Peary Expedition). XVII, pp. 638-644, 9 ills., Nov., 1906

Fighting the Polar Ice (Ziegler Polar Expedition). XVIII, pp. 72-78, 7 ills., Jan., 1907

Flying Over the Arctic. By Lieutenant Commander Richard E. Byrd. XLVIII, pp. 519-532, 10 ills., Nov., 1925

The MacMillan Arctic Expedition Returns: U. S. Navy Planes Make First Series of Overland Flights in the Arctic and National Geographic Society Staff Obtains Valuable Data and Specimens for Scientific Study. By Donald B. MacMillan. XLVIII, pp. 477-518, 42 ills., Nov., 1925

The MacMillan Arctic Expedition Sails. XLVIII, pp. 225-226, 3 ills., Aug., 1925

MacMillan in the Field. XLVIII, pp. 473-476, 3 ills., Oct., 1925

The Meteorological Observations of the Second Wellman Expedition. By Evelyn B. Baldwin. X, pp. 512-516, Dec., 1899

Mr. Ziegler and the National Geographic Society. XIV, pp. 251-254, June, 1903

A Naturalist with MacMillan in the Arctic. By Walter N. Koelz. XLIX, pp. 299-318, 22 ills. in color, Mar., 1926

Nearest the Pole (Address by Robert E. Peary to the Society). XVIII, pp. 446-450, July, 1907

Peary to Try Again. XVIII, p. 281, Apr., 1907

Peary's Polar Expedition. XIX, p. 447, June, 1908

The Polar Airship (Wellman Expedition). By Walter Wellman. XVII, pp. 208-228, 5 diagrs., Apr., 1906

Polar Photography (Ziegler Polar Expedition). By Anthony Fiala. XVIII, pp. 140-142, Feb., 1907

The Return of Wellman. By J. Howard Gore. X, pp. 348-351, ills., Sept., 1899

NATIONAL GEOGRAPHIC SOCIETY—*Continued*

Expeditions—*Continued*

Scientific Aspects of the MacMillan Arctic Expedition. XLVIII, pp. 349-354, 5 ills., Sept., 1925

To Seek the Unknown in the Arctic: United States Navy Flyers to Aid MacMillan Expedition Under the Auspices of the National Geographic Society in Exploring Vast Area. XLVII, pp. 673-675, ill., map, June, 1925

Walter Wellman's Expedition to the North Pole. XVII, pp. 205-207, chart, Apr., 1906

Wellman Expedition. LIV, p. 242, Aug., 1928

Wellman Polar Expedition. IX, pp. 373-375, Aug., 1898

The Wellman Polar Expedition. X, pp. 361-362, Sept., 1899

The Wellman Polar Expedition. XVII, p. 712, Dec., 1906

The Wellman Polar Expedition. (By J. Howard Gore). X, pp. 267-268, July, 1899

The Wellman Polar Expedition. By Walter Wellman. X, pp. 481-505, 10 ills., diagr., map, Dec., 1899

The Ziegler Polar Expedition. XIV, pp. 414-417, 5 ills., Nov., 1903

Ziegler Polar Expedition. XV, pp. 427-428, Oct., 1904

The Ziegler Polar Expedition. XVI, p. 198, Apr., 1905

Ziegler Polar Expedition. XVI, p. 355, July, 1905

The Ziegler Polar Expedition. XVI, pp. 439-440, Sept., 1905

Ziegler Polar Expedition. Speeches by Anthony Fiala and W. S. Champ at the NGS Annual Dinner, Dec. 20, 1905. XVII, pp. 32-36, Jan., 1906

Arizona

Exploring in the Canyon of Death: Remains of a People Who Dwelt in Our Southwest at Least 4,000 Years Ago Are Revealed. By Earl H. Morris. XLVIII, pp. 263-300, 24 ills. in black and white, 22 ills. in color, Sept., 1925
Included: NGS photographic party in Cañon del Muerto. ill. p. 265

The Secret of the Southwest Solved by Talkative Tree Rings: Horizons of American History Are Carried Back to A. D. 700 and a Calendar for 1,200 Years Established by National Geographic Society Expeditions. By Andrew Ellicott Douglass. LVI, pp. 737-770, 33 ills., map, Dec., 1929

Asia

Citroën-Haardt Trans-Asiatic and Thaw Expeditions followed Abraham's trail, in crossing the desert. LXXX, p. 157, Aug., 1941

The Citroën Trans-Asiatic Expedition Reaches Kashmir: Scientific Party Led by Georges-Marie Haardt Successfully Crosses Syria, Iraq, Persia, and Afghanistan to Arrive at the Pamir. By Maynard Owen Williams. LX, pp. 387-443, 62 ills., map, Oct., 1931

NATIONAL GEOGRAPHIC SOCIETY—*Continued*

Expeditions—*Continued*

First Over the Roof of the World by Motor: The Trans-Asiatic Expedition Sets New Records for Wheeled Transport in Scaling Passes of the Himalayas. By Maynard Owen Williams. LXI, pp. 321-363, 45 ills., maps, Mar., 1932

From the Mediterranean to the Yellow Sea by Motor: The Citroën-Haardt Expedition Successfully Completes Its Dramatic Journey. By Maynard Owen Williams. LXII, pp. 513-580, 45 ills. in black and white, 25 ills. in color, maps, Nov., 1932

The Trans-Asiatic Expedition Starts. By Georges-Marie Haardt. LIX, pp. 776-782, 6 ills., June, 1931

Aviation

Air Conquest: From the Early Days of Giant Kites and Birdlike Gliders, the National Geographic Society Has Aided and Encouraged the Growth of Aviation. LII, pp. 233-242, 13 ills., Aug., 1927

Bahamas

Flamingos studied by the Society's expedition led by Dr. Fuertes and Dr. La Gorce. LXII, ill. p. 452, Oct., 1932

Brazil-Venezuela

In Humboldt's Wake: Narrative of a National Geographic Society Expedition Up the Orinoco and Through the Strange Casiquiare Canal to Amazonian Waters. By Ernest G. Holt. LX, pp. 621-644, 27 ills., map, Nov., 1931

A Journey by Jungle Rivers to the Home of the Cock-of-the-rock: Naturalists Enter the Amazon, Voyage Through the Heart of Tropical South America, and Emerge at the Mouth of the Orinoco. By Ernest G. Holt. LXIV, pp. 585-630, 49 ills., map, Nov., 1933

Canada

Exploring Yukon's Glacial Stronghold. By Bradford Washburn. LXIX, pp. 715-748, 29 ills., two-page map, June, 1936

National Geographic Society-U. S. Geological Survey Expedition. XLIX, p. 597, ill. pp. 598, 599, June, 1926

National Geographic Society Yukon Expedition (1935). LXXIV, p. 79, July, 1938

Cape Horn

Inside Cape Horn. By Amos Burg. LXXII, pp. 743-783, 29 ills. in black and white, 10 ills. in color, two-page map, Dec., 1937

China

Banishing the Devil of Disease Among the Nashi: Weird Ceremonies Performed by an Aboriginal Tribe in the Heart of Yünnan Province, China. By Joseph F. Rock. XLVI, pp. 473-499, 26 ills., map, Nov., 1924

Expeditions of Joseph F. Rock. LXIV, p. 279, Sept., 1933

The Glories of the Minya Konka: Magnificent Snow Peaks of the China-Tibetan Border Are Photographed at Close Range by a National Geographic Society Expedition. By Joseph F. Rock. LVIII, pp. 385-437, 35 ills. in black and white, 24 ills. in color, map, Oct., 1930

Konka Risumgongba, Holy Mountain of the Outlaws. By Joseph F. Rock. LX, pp. 1-65, 36 ills. in black and white, 43 ills. in color, map, July, 1931

The Land of the Yellow Lama: National Geographic Society Explorer Visits the Strange Kingdom of Muli, Beyond the Likiang Snow Range of Yünnan Province, China. By Joseph F. Rock. XLVII, pp. 447-491, 39 ills., map, Apr., 1925

Landscaped Kwangsi, China's Province of Pictorial Art. By G. Weidman Groff and T. C. Lau. LXXII, pp. 671-710, 33 ills., map, Dec., 1937

National Geographic Society Expeditions led by Dr. Joseph F. Rock. LXXXI, p. 331, Mar., 1942

The National Geographic Society's Yünnan Province Expedition. By Gilbert Grosvenor. XLVII, pp. 493-498, 5 ills., Apr., 1925

The Road to Wang Ye Fu: An Account of the Work of the National Geographic Society's Central-China Expedition in the Mongol Kingdom of Ala Shan. By Frederick R. Wulsin. XLIX, pp. 197-234, 44 ills., map, Feb., 1926

Seeking the Mountains of Mystery: An Expedition on the China-Tibet Frontier to the Unexplored Amnyi Machen Range, One of Whose Peaks Rivals Everest. By Joseph F. Rock. LVII, pp. 131-185, 54 ills., two-page map, Feb., 1930

Through the Great River Trenches of Asia: National Geographic Society Explorer Follows the Yangtze, Mekong, and Salwin Through Mighty Gorges, Some of Whose Canyon Walls Tower to a Height of More Than Two Miles. By Joseph F. Rock. L, pp. 133-186, 47 ills., map, Aug., 1926

Cosmic Rays

Series of flights under auspices of National Geographic Society, U. S. Army Air Forces, and Bartol Research Foundation of the Franklin Institute. XC, p. 387, ill. p. 388, Sept., 1946

Deep Sea

Cruise sponsored by the National Geographic Society and Woods Hole Oceanographic Institution, to photograph the ocean floor. LXXXVII, p. 106, Jan., 1945

Deep-sea diving record of National Geographic Society-William Beebe Expedition. LXXII, p. 419, Oct., 1937. LXXVI, p. 140, July, 1939

A Half Mile Down: Strange Creatures, Beautiful and Grotesque as Figments of Fancy, Reveal Themselves at Windows of the Bathysphere. By William Beebe. Paintings by Else Bostelmann, Helen D. Tee-Van, E. J. Geske. LXVI, pp. 661-704, 28 ills. in black and white, 16 ills. in color, map, Dec., 1934

NATIONAL GEOGRAPHIC SOCIETY—*Continued*

Expeditions—*Continued*

The National Geographic Society-William Beebe Expedition. LXV, p. 625, May, 1934

East Indies

Around the World for Animals. By William M. and Lucile Q. Mann. LXXIII, pp. 665-714, 33 ills. in black and white, 23 ills. in color, map, June, 1938

National Geographic Society-Smithsonian Institution Expedition to the Netherlands Indies. LXXI, p. 668, June, 1937. LXXIII, pp. 647, 650, 651, May, 1938

Eclipse

Camera of National Geographic Society-Bureau of Standards Eclipse Expedition of 1936. LXXII, ill. p. 374, Sept., 1937

Eclipse Adventures on a Desert Isle (Canton). By Capt. J. F. Hellweg. LXXII, pp. 377-394, 14 ills., map, Sept., 1937

First natural-color photograph of an eclipse (1936) ever reproduced, showing the corona. By Irvine C. Gardner. LXXI, ill. p. 178, Feb., 1937

National Geographic Society-National Bureau of Standards Expedition (1940). LXXIX, p. 163, Feb., 1941

National Geographic Society-U. S. Navy Eclipse Expedition (1937). LXXIII, p. 749, ill. p. 764, June, 1938. LXXX, p. 741, Dec., 1941

The National Geographic Society's Eclipse Expedition to Norfolk, Va. By Marcus Baker. XI, p. 320, Aug., 1900

Nature's Most Dramatic Spectacle. By S. A. Mitchell. LXXII, pp. 361-376, 16 ills., map, Sept., 1937

Observing an Eclipse in Asiatic Russia. By Irvine C. Gardner. LXXI, pp. 179-197, 19 ills. in black and white, ill. in color, Feb., 1937

Photographing the Eclipse of 1932 from the Air: From Five Miles Above the Earth's Surface, the National Geographic Society-Army Air Corps Survey Obtains Successful Photographs of the Moon's Shadow. By Capt. Albert W. Stevens. LXII, pp. 581-596, 18 ills., Nov., 1932

The Scientific Work of the National Geographic Society's Eclipse Expedition to Norfolk, Va. By Simon Newcomb. XI, pp. 321-324, Aug., 1900

Unfurling Old Glory on Canton Island. 11 ills. in color: painting by Charles Bittinger and photo of the eclipse, showing the corona. LXXIII, pp. 753-760, June, 1938

Hudson Bay

Expeditions of 1912. XIV, p. 251, Feb., 1913

Idaho

Down Idaho's River of No Return (Salmon River). By Philip J. Shenon and John C. Reed. LXX, pp. 95-136, 43 ills., maps, July, 1936

Latin America

Flamingos photographed from air. LXII, ill. p. 453, Oct., 1932

NATIONAL GEOGRAPHIC SOCIETY—*Continued*

Expeditions—*Continued*

Skypaths Through Latin America: Flying From Our Nation's Capital Southward Over Jungles, Remote Islands, and Great Cities on an Aërial Survey of the East Coast of South America. By Frederick Simpich. LIX, pp. 1-79, 77 ills., map, Jan., 1931

Mexico

A Cruise Among Desert Islands. By G. Dallas Hanna and A. W. Anthony. XLIV, pp. 71-99, 32 ills., map, July, 1923

Discovering the New World's Oldest Dated Work of Man: A Maya Monument Inscribed 291 B. C. is Unearthed Near a Huge Stone Head by a Geographic-Smithsonian Expedition in Mexico. By Matthew W. Stirling. LXXVI, pp. 183-218, 40 ills., map, Aug., 1939

Excavations at Cuicuilco. LX, p. 107, July, 1931

Expedition Unearths Buried Masterpieces of Carved Jade (Cerro de las Mesas). By Matthew W. Stirling. LXXX, pp. 277-302, 14 ills. in black and white, 20 ills. in color, map, Sept., 1941

Great Stone Faces of the Mexican Jungle: Five Colossal Heads and Numerous Other Monuments of Vanished Americans Are Excavated by the Latest National Geographic-Smithsonian Expedition. By Matthew W. Stirling. LXXVIII, pp. 309-334, 26 ills., map, Sept., 1940

Jungle Housekeeping for a Geographic Expedition (Cerro de las Mesas). By Marion Stirling. LXXX, pp. 303-327, 15 ills., Sept., 1941

La Venta's Green Stone Tigers. By Matthew W. Stirling. LXXXIV, pp. 321-332, 4 ills. in black and white, 6 ills. in color, map, Sept., 1943

National Geographic Society-Smithsonian Institution Archeological Expedition to Cerro de las Mesas, Veracruz (1941). LXXXII, pp. 635, 642, 649, Nov., 1942. LXXXIV, p. 323, Sept., 1943

National Geographic Society-Smithsonian Institution Archeological Expedition to La Venta, Tabasco (1940). LXXXII, pp. 635, 642, Nov., 1942

National Geographic Society-Smithsonian Institution Archeological Expedition to La Venta, Tabasco (1942). LXXXIV, pp. 321, 323, Sept., 1943

National Geographic Society-Smithsonian Institution Archeological Expedition to La Venta, Tabasco (1943). LXXXVII, pp. 187, 193, ill. p. 190, Feb., 1945

National Geographic Society-Smithsonian Institution Expedition to Mexico (1936). LXXXIV, pp. 699-700, Dec., 1943

National Geographic Society-Smithsonian Institution Expedition to Veracruz (1938-1939). LXXXI, p. 338, Mar., 1942

NATIONAL GEOGRAPHIC SOCIETY—*Continued*

Expeditions—*Continued*

Ruins of Cuicuilco May Revolutionize Our History of Ancient America: Lofty Mound Sealed and Preserved by Great Lava Flow for Perhaps Seventy Centuries Is Now Being Excavated in Mexico. By Byron Cummings. XLIV, pp. 203-220, 21 ills., map, Aug., 1923

Wildlife of Tabasco and Veracruz. By Walter A. Weber. With 19 ills. in color from paintings by author. LXXXVII, pp. 187-216, 7 ills. in black and white, map, Feb., 1945

New Mexico

Carlsbad Caverns. LXXIII, pp. 530, 560, May, 1938. LXXVII, pp. 718, 724, June, 1940

Everyday Life in Pueblo Bonito: As Disclosed by the National Geographic Society's Archeologic Explorations in the Chaco Canyon National Monument, New Mexico. By Neil M. Judd. XLVIII, pp. 227-262, 37 ills., map, Sept., 1925

New Discoveries in Carlsbad Cavern: Vast Subterranean Chambers with Spectacular Decorations Are Explored, Surveyed, and Photographed. By Willis T. Lee. XLVIII, pp. 301-319, 19 ills., map, Sept., 1925

A New National Geographic Society Expedition: Ruins of Chaco Canyon, New Mexico, Nature-Made Treasure-Chest of Aboriginal American History, To Be Excavated and Studied; Work Begins This Month. XXXIX, pp. 637-643, 7 ills., June, 1921

Pueblo Bonito. LXXIII, pp. 547, 551, May, 1938. LXXVII, p. 767, June, 1940

Pueblo Bonito, the Ancient: The National Geographic Society's Third Expedition to the Southwest Seeks to Read in the Rings of Trees the Secret of the Age of Ruins. By Neil M. Judd. XLIV, pp. 99-108, 9 ills., diagr., July, 1923

The Pueblo Bonito Expedition of the National Geographic Society. By Neil M. Judd. XLI, pp. 323-331, 10 ills., diagr., Mar., 1922

The Secret of the Southwest Solved by Talkative Tree Rings: Horizons of American History Are Carried Back to A. D. 700 and a Calendar for 1,200 Years Established by National Geographic Society Expeditions. By Andrew Ellicott Douglass. LVI, pp. 737-770, 33 ills., map, Dec., 1929

Peru

Expeditions of 1912. XXIV, p. 251, Feb., 1913

Explorations in Peru. XXIII, pp. 417-422, 7 ills., map, Apr., 1912

Further Explorations in the Land of the Incas: The Peruvian Expedition of 1915 of the National Geographic Society and Yale University. By Hiram Bingham. XXIX, pp. 431-473, 29 ills., maps, panorama, May, 1916

Honors to Amundsen and Peary (Address by Hiram Bingham). XXIV, pp. 116-117, Jan., 1913

NATIONAL GEOGRAPHIC SOCIETY—*Continued*

Expeditions—*Continued*

In the Wonderland of Peru. By Hiram Bingham. XXIV, pp. 387-573, 250 ills., 3 diagrs., map, panorama, Apr., 1913

National Geographic Society-Yale University Peruvian Expeditions. LXXIII, pp. 244, 256, 258, Feb., 1938. LXXXII, pp. 187, 192, Aug., 1942

Staircase Farms of the Ancients: Astounding Farming Skill of Ancient Peruvians, Who Were Among the Most Industrious and Highly Organized People in History. By O. F. Cook. XXIX, pp. 474-534, 48 ills., May, 1916

The Story of Machu Picchu: The Peruvian Expeditions of the National Geographic Society and Yale University. By Hiram Bingham. XXVII, pp. 172-217, 60 ills., Feb., 1915

Salmon River

National Geographic Society-United States Geological Survey Expedition. LXXXV, p. 643, June, 1944

Sicily

Announcement of Messina Expedition. XX, p. 118, map, Jan., 1909

Messina earthquake (1909). LXXXIV, p. 314, Sept., 1943

The World's Most Cruel Earthquake. By Charles W. Wright. XX, pp. 373-396, 22 ills., maps, Apr., 1909

South Dakota

National Geographic Society-South Dakota School of Mines Paleontological Expedition to the Badlands of South Dakota (1940). LXXXI, p. 161, Feb., 1942

Stratosphere

Capt. Albert W. Stevens (now Lt. Col., ret.) and Capt. Orvil A. Anderson (now Brig. Gen.) photographed with Sioux Indians in front of gondola. LXXXVI, ill. p. 106, July, 1944

Exploring the Stratosphere. By Captain Albert W. Stevens. LXVI, pp. 397-434, 43 ills., chart, Oct., 1934

First natural-color photograph taken in the stratosphere. By Major Albert W. Stevens. LXXI, ill. p. 340, Mar., 1937

Helium used by National Geographic Society-U. S. Army Air Corps Expedition, 1935, to inflate *Explorer II*. LXXII, p. 363, Sept., 1937

Infrared sensitive plates used in photographing curvature of the earth from record altitude of 72,395 feet. LXXXVI, p. 265, Sept., 1944

Man's Farthest Aloft: Rising to 13.71 Miles, the National Geographic Society-U. S. Army Stratosphere Expedition Gathers Scientific Data at Record Altitude. By Capt. Albert W. Stevens. LXIX, pp. 59-94, 39 ills., map, Jan., 1936

Included: Action Photographs of the Balloon's Perfect Landing

National Geographic Society-U. S. Army Air Corps Flight insured by Lloyd's. LXXI, p. 34, Jan., 1937

Expeditions—*Continued*

National Geographic Society-U. S. Army Air Corps Stratosphere Flight of 1935 in Balloon *Explorer II* (Contributed Technical Papers, *Stratosphere Series No. 2*). LXXI, p. 340, Mar., 1937; p. 802, June, 1937

National Geographic Society-U. S. Army Air Corps Stratosphere Flights. LXXXII, p. 444, Oct., 1942. XC, p. 379, Sept., 1946

A Report of the Second Stratosphere Expedition. LXVIII, pp. 535-536, Oct., 1935

The Scientific Results of the World-Record Stratosphere Flight. By Capt. Albert W. Stevens. LXIX, pp. 693-712, 15 ills., May, 1936

The Society Announces New Flight into the Stratosphere. By Gilbert Grosvenor. LXVII, pp. 265-272, ills., map, Feb., 1935

Spectograph carried on National Geographic Society-U. S. Army Air Corps Expedition, 1935. LXXII, p. 372, Sept., 1937

Studies Planned for New Stratosphere Flight with Helium. LXVII, pp. 795-800, 5 ills., June, 1935

World's Largest Free Balloon to Explore Stratosphere. LXVI, pp. 107-110, ills., July, 1934

Your Society Sponsors an Expedition to Explore the Stratosphere. LXV, pp. 528-530, ill., Apr., 1934

See also NGS: Stratosphere Balloon

Utah

Beyond the Clay Hills: An Account of the National Geographic Society's Reconnaissance of a Previously Unexplored Section in Utah. By Neil M. Judd. XLV, pp. 275-302, 28 ills., map, Mar., 1924

Expedition to Moki Canyon (1923). LXXIX, p. 143, Feb., 1941

Venezuela-Brazil

In Humboldt's Wake: Narrative of a National Geographic Society Expedition Up the Orinoco and Through the Strange Casiquiare Canal to Amazonian Waters. By Ernest G. Holt. LX, pp. 621-644, 27 ills., map, Nov., 1931

A Journey by Jungle Rivers to the Home of the Cock-of-the-rock: Naturalists Enter the Amazon, Voyage Through the Heart of Tropical South America, and Emerge at the Mouth of the Orinoco. By Ernest G. Holt. LXIV, pp. 585-630, 49 ills., map, Nov., 1933

West Indies

Martinique Island (1902). LXXIII, p. 292, Mar., 1938. LXXIX, p. 48, Jan., 1941

Members of the Society on Expedition to Martinique and St. Vincent. XIII, p. 219, June, 1902

The National Geographic Society Expedition in the West Indies. XIII, pp. 209-213, maps, June, 1902

The National Geographic Society Expedition to Martinique and St. Vincent. XIII, pp. 183-184, ills., June, 1902

Expeditions—*Continued*

The Recent Volcanic Eruptions in the West Indies. By Israel C. Russell. XIII, pp. 267-285, 7 ills., map, July, 1902

Report by Robert T. Hill on the Volcanic Disturbances in the West Indies. XIII, pp. 223-267, 12 ills., 3 maps, July, 1902

Volcanic Eruptions on Martinique and St. Vincent. By Israel C. Russell. XIII, pp. 415-436, 10 ills., Dec., 1902

Volcanic Rocks of Martinique and St. Vincent: Collected by Robert T. Hill and Israel C. Russell. By J. S. Diller. XIII, pp. 285-296, July, 1902

Fellows:

Alexander Graham Bell's proposal regarding Fellows. XI, pp. 404-405, Oct., 1900

Change in by-laws instituting a class of Fellows. XIII, p. 220, June, 1902

Notice of proposed amendment to the by-laws of the National Geographic Society. XIII, p. 182, May, 1902

Proposal to elect Fellows. XXIII, p. 274, Mar., 1912

Proposed amendment creating a class of Fellows and Honorary Fellows. VI, p. xv, Oct. 31, 1895

Finances:

Contribution to the Wellman Polar Expedition. IX, pp. 373-374, Aug., 1898

Finances. II, p. 308, Apr., 1891. X, p. 222, June, 1899. XI, p. 405, Oct., 1900. XVII, pp. 23-24, Jan., 1906. XXI, p. 365, Apr., 1910. XXIII, pp. 273, 275, Mar., 1912. XXIV, p. 115, Jan., 1913; pp. 251, 252, Feb., 1913. XXVII, pp. 318, 320, Mar., 1915. XXXVII, p. 292, Mar., 1920

Research fund established. XX, p. 486, May, 1909

Treasurer's Reports. I, p. 163, Apr., 1889. II, p. 64, Apr., 1890; pp. 299-300, Apr., 1891. IV, pp. x-xi, xxii-xxiii, Feb. 20, 1893. V, pp. xxii-xxiii, May 5, 1894. VI, pp. xxvi-xxvii, Oct. 31, 1895. XIII, p. 80, Feb., 1902. XXI, pp. 89-90, Jan., 1910. XXII, p. 214, Feb., 1911. XXIV, p. 256, Feb., 1913

See also NGS: Bequests; Dues; Prizes

Flag, National (U. S.):

Flag, gift of Miss Ulrica Dahlgren, presented by the President of the Society to Lieut. Robert E. Peary for his trip to Greenland. III, p. viii, Feb. 19, 1892

National flag belonging to the Society, displayed on northeast coast of Greenland, after Lieutenant Peary's crossing of the northern Greenland ice. IV, p. 205, Feb. 8, 1893

Flag, NGS:

Bathysphere cable. LXVI, ill. pp. 662, 663, 665, Dec., 1934. LXIX, ill. p. 153, Jan., 1936

NATIONAL GEOGRAPHIC SOCIETY—*Continued*

Flag, NGS—*Continued*

Canton Island: National Geographic Society-U. S. Navy Eclipse Expedition (1937). LXXII, p. 388, ill. p. 385, Sept., 1937. LXXIII, ill. p. 764; col. pls. I, p. 753, II, p. 754, VI, p. 758, June, 1938

Dundee Island, Antarctic: Ellsworth Antarctic Expedition. LXX, ill. p. 34, July, 1936. LXXXIV, ill. p. 301, Sept., 1943

The Flag of the National Geographic Society (Flags of the World). LXVI, p. 364, col. pl., p. 367, Sept., 1934

The Flag of the National Geographic Society (Our Flag Number). XXXII, p. 340, ill. in color, p. 335, Oct., 1917

Hubbard Gold Medal presentation to Anne Morrow Lindbergh. LXIX, ill. p. 137, Jan., 1936

Katmai mast on Naknek Lake, Alaska. XL, ill. p. 291, Sept., 1921

Silverash (Ship). LXXIII, ill. p. 700, June, 1938

Special Gold Medal presentation to Dr. Thomas C. Poulter. LXXII, ill. p. 107, July, 1937

Stratocamp, South Dakota. LXVI, ill. p. 404, Oct., 1934

Stratosphere balloon rigging. LXIX, ill. p. 70, Jan., 1936

Sumatra: National Geographic Society-Smithsonian Institution East Indies Expedition. LXXIII, col. pls. VIII, p. 688, XIII, p. 709, June, 1938

Travel-stained flag, to be taken on aërial survey to Latin America. LIX, ill. p. 2, Jan., 1931

Valley of Ten Thousand Smokes. XL, ill. p. 238, Sept., 1921

World travels made by the Society's flag. LVII, p. 655, June, 1930

Yukon flight of Bradford Washburn. LXIX, ill. p. 717, June, 1936

Founders:

Gannett, Henry. XVII, p. 23, Jan., 1906

Gore, James Howard. LXV, p. 793, June, 1934

Greely, Maj. Gen. Adolphus W. XVII, p. 23, Jan., 1906. LXV, p. 793, June, 1934. LXXXIV, p. 133, Aug., 1943

Hubbard, Gardiner Greene. XVII, pp. 23, 24, Jan., 1906

Merriam, C. Hart. LXV, pp. 792-793, June, 1934

Tittmann, O. H. LXV, p. 793, June, 1934

Founding:

Announcements of the organization and aims of the Society and the publication of its magazine. I, pp. i-ii, Oct., 1888. II, pp. 287-289, Apr., 1891

Date of. I, p. ii. Oct., 1888. II, pp. 287, 296, Apr., 1891. IV, p. vii, Feb. 20, 1893. VI, p. xxi, Oct. 31, 1895. XXIII, p. 273, Mar., 1912. LXIX, p. 131, Jan., 1936

NATIONAL GEOGRAPHIC SOCIETY—*Continued*

Founding—*Continued*

Invitation to a meeting at the Cosmos Club, January 13, 1888, for the purpose of organizing a geographic society. I, p. 164, Apr., 1889. LXIX, p. 131, Jan., 1936

Resolution adopted, for organizing a geographic society. I, p. 164, Apr., 1889. LXIX, p. 131, Jan., 1936

See also NGS: By-laws; Certificate of Incorporation; Founders; Meetings

Funds. *See* NGS: Bequests; Finances

History:

Achievements of the Society. XXXIII, p. 170, Feb., 1918

Address, Introductory, by the first President. I, pp. 3-10, Oct., 1888

Address of the President to the Board of Managers, June 1, 1900. (By Alexander Graham Bell). XI, pp. 401-408, chart, Oct., 1900

Announcements of the organization and aims of the Society and the publication of its magazine. I, pp. i-ii, Oct., 1888. II, pp. 287-289, Apr., 1891

The Annual Dinner of the National Geographic Society. XVII, pp. 22-37, Jan., 1906
- Finances 23–24
- Founders 23
- Hubbard Memorial Hall.... 24
- Membership 23

Founding of the Society. *See* NGS: Founding

The National Geographic Society. (By John Hyde). X, pp. 220-223, June, 1899
- Assistant Editor appointed 222
- Editorial Committee 222
- Influence of the Society 222
- Magazine 221–222
- Members 221, 223
- Object 221
- Presidents 222

The National Geographic Society and Its Magazine. By Gilbert Grosvenor. LXIX, pp. 123-164, 24 ills., Jan., 1936
- Aid rendered scientific exploration and research 123, 124–125, 140, 141, 143, 150, 154
- Banquets ....150; ill. p. 127
- Board of Managers...135, 138, 139, 144, 148, 152, 155; ill. pp. 126, 129
- Board of Trustees ...129, 131, 152, 153, 154, 155, 162; ill. pp. 129, 133, 138, 159
- Buildings ...131, 148, 152, 155; ill. pp. 124, 125, 126, 133, 156, 157
- Certificate presented Gilbert Grosvenor.. 155
- Committees 136, 139, 144, 152, 154
- Cumulative Index 123, 125, 161, 162
- Employees 125, 131, 162
- Expeditions ....124–125, 126, 141, 147; ill. pp. 143, 146, 151, 153, 158
- Flag ....124; ill. pp. 137, 153
- History and organization ..131, 134–135, 136–137, 138, 144–145, 148, 150, 152, 154, 155, 162
- Library ....128; ill. p. 124
- Luncheon in honor of Col. Theodore Roosevelt ....ill. p. 129

NATIONAL GEOGRAPHIC SOCIETY—*Continued*
History—*Continued*
Medals and medal presentations ....127, 149, 154, 161; ill. pp. 127, 134, 136, 137, 138, 139
Membership 123–124, 125, 130, 134, 135, 145, 148, 152, 155, 161, 163–164
Officers and staff members.128, 131, 134, 138, 139, 148, 152, 154, 155, 162; ill. pp. 126, 156, 157, 159
Offices ....ill. p. 156
Photographic achievements.128–129, 143, 150, 153–154, 155, 157, 158; ill. p. 142
Purpose and policies of the Society..123, 134–135, 145, 148, 162
Seal of the Society ....ill. p. 157
Unveiling of Peary Memorial......ill. p. 132

The National Geographic Society and Its New Building. XXV, pp. 455-470, 11 ills., Apr., 1914
Expeditions 459, 465
Geographic distribution of membership 468–470
Growth of the Society............455, 457
Photograph of officers and members ill. p. 458

The National Geographic Society's Notable Year. XXXVII, pp. 338–345, ills., Apr., 1920
Announcement of the deaths of Brig. Gen. John M. Wilson, Rear Adm. John E. Pillsbury, and Rear Adm. Robert E. Peary 345
Award of eight Jane M. Smith Life Memberships 342–343
Election of Gilbert Grosvenor as President 345
Election of John Oliver La Gorce to Board of Managers 345
Geographic News Bulletins and School Service 343
Greely, Maj. Gen. A. W.: Presentation of medal to Stefansson by........339-342
Hubbard Gold Medal awarded to Stefansson 338–342
James C. Horgan bequest 338
Magazine circulation 343
Peary, Rear Adm. Robert E.: Last public appearance of 339
Photograph of Peary, Stefansson, and Greely ....ill. p. 318
Previous recipients of Jane M. Smith Life Memberships 342
Purpose of the Society 345
Sixth Katmai Expedition 338

Report of the Director and Editor of the National Geographic Society for the Year 1914. By Gilbert H. Grosvenor. XXVII, pp. 318-320, Mar., 1915
Appropriations for research 320
Assets 318–320
Bell, Alexander Graham: Funds contributed by 318
Early history of the Society 319
Growth of the Society since 1907 320
Lecturers 320
Magazine policy adopted by G. Grosvenor 319
Membership 318

NATIONAL GEOGRAPHIC SOCIETY—*Continued*
History—*Continued*
Report of the Editor for 1912. XXIV, pp. 251–255, Feb., 1913
Expeditions 251
Funds 251–252
Growth of the Magazine 252
Growth of the Society 252
Membership 255

Speech by Alexander Graham Bell at Annual Banquet, January, 1912. XXIII, pp. 272–275, Mar., 1912
Buildings 273
Change in membership policy.......... 273
Committee on Research............... 275
Early history of the Society.........273–274
Expeditions 275
Fellows 274
Finances 273, 275
Founding 273
Gilbert H. Grosvenor engaged as Assistant Editor of Magazine in 1899.......... 274
Magazine policy and growth........273–274

Speech by James Howard Gore at Annual Banquet, January, 1910. XXI, pp. 67-68, Jan., 1910
Membership 67
Organization 67–68
Purpose 67

See also NGS: Banquets; Board of Managers; Board of Trustees; Buildings; By-laws; Certificate of Incorporation; Founders; Meetings; Members and Membership; Officers; Receptions

Honorary Members. *See* NGS: Members and Membership

Incorporation. *See* NGS: Certificate of Incorporation

Insignia Publications. *See* NGS: Publications

International Geographic Conference:
International Geographic Conference, Chicago, Illinois, July 27-28, 1893. V, pp. 97-256, Jan. 31, 1894
Delegates 99–100
Headquarters 98
Memoirs and addresses............112–256
Sessions 101–111
World's Columbian Exposition........98–99

International Geographic Congress:
Address by Commander Peary at Eighth Congress. XV, pp. 387-392, Oct., 1904
Chairman of Committee on Eighth Congress. XIII, p. 219, June, 1902. XIV, pp. 254-255, June, 1903
Eighth International Geographic Congress. XIV, pp. 388-390, Oct., 1903
Committee on arrangements............ 390
Plans 388, 390
Eighth International Geographic Congress. XV, pp. 74-77, Feb., 1904
American societies coöperating......... 74
Discussion subjects..................75–76
Membership 75
Officers and committees..............76–77
Publications 75
Sessions and excursions.............. 74

NATIONAL GEOGRAPHIC SOCIETY—*Continued*

International Geographic Congress—*Continued*

Eighth International Geographic Congress. XV, pp. 297-310, July, 1904
American societies coöperating......... 297
Headquarters 298
Lectures and papers...............306–310
Meetings 297–298
Membership 301–302
Officers and committees.............304–305
Program 299–301
Publications 303
Registration 298
Subjects for discussion.............302–303
Transportation 301

Eighth International Geographic Congress. XV, pp. 419-426, ills., Oct., 1904
Entertainment 420, 423, 424–425
Gilbert, Grove Karl: Speech by......... 419
Meetings and papers..............420, 424
Photographs of members.....ill. pp. 421, 422
Telegram sent to President Roosevelt... 420
Walcott, Charles D.: Speech by........ 419

Geographic Congress Abstracts (Eighth). XV, pp. 502-503, Dec., 1904

International Geographic Congress. XIV, p. 292, July, 1903
Appointment of committees............ 292
Plans for Eighth Congress............. 292

Next International Geographical Congress to be Held in Washington. (By G. H. G.). XII, pp. 351-357, 4 ills., Oct., 1901
Delegates to Seventh Congress......... 352
Delegates to Sixth Congress............ 352
Invitation for Eighth Congress extended by the Society...................352–353
Plans for entertainment of Congress..356–357

Ninth International Geographic Congress, Geneva, Switzerland, 1908. XVIII, p. 491, July, 1907

Ninth International Geographic Congress, Geneva, Switzerland, 1908. XIX, pp. 385-386, May, 1908
Delegates 386

Program of Eighth International Geographic Congress. XV, pp. 373-386, map, Sept., 1904
Map of Washington, D. C............. 375
Officers and committees..............384–386
Washington sessions................. 383

Publication of Proceedings of Eighth International Geographic Congress. XVI, pp. 198-199, Apr., 1905
Editors 199
Resolutions 199

Resolutions Adopted by the Eighth International Geographic Congress. XV, pp. 415-418, Oct., 1904

Seventh International Geographical Congress, Berlin, Germany, 1899. X, p. 296, Aug., 1899
Delegates 296
Discussions and papers................ 296

Seventh International Geographical Congress, Berlin, Germany, 1899. X, p. 480, Nov., 1899
Delegates 480
Papers 480

NATIONAL GEOGRAPHIC SOCIETY—*Continued*

International Geographic Congress—*Continued*

Sixth International Geographical Congress, London, England, 1895. (By A. W. G.). VII, p. 380, Nov., 1896
Report edited by Messrs. J. Scott Keltie and Hugh Robert Mill............... 380

Inventions. *See* Sun-compass

Lectures:

Lecture courses, defined. VII, pp. 257-258, Aug., 1896

Lecture courses, self-supporting. XXVII, p. 320, Mar., 1915

Lectures, Public, in Washington, D. C. II, p. 289, Apr., 1891

The National Geographic Society: Synopsis of a Course of Lectures on the Effects of Geographic Environment in Developing the Civilization of the World. (By Gardiner G. Hubbard). VIII, pp. 29-32, Jan., 1897

The National Geographic Society: The Forthcoming Course of Lectures on the Effects of Geographic Environment in Developing the Civilization of the World. VIII, insert (pp. 1-6), Feb., 1897

See also NGS: Calendar

Grosvenor, Edwin A.

Constantinople. VIII, pp. 31-32, Jan., 1897; insert (pp. 5-6), Feb., 1897; p. 159, May, 1897

The Greek and the Turk: the Product of Geographic Environment. IX, p. 32, Jan., 1898

Peary, Robert E.

Addresses the Society on his proposed Greenland expedition of 1891-92. III, p. viii, Feb. 19, 1892

Lecture, on the results of his recent expedition to Greenland. V, p. ix, May 5, 1894

Peary, Mrs. Robert E.

Lecture, under the auspices of the Society, to raise funds to equip an expedition for the return of Lieutenant Peary. VI, pp. xxii-xxiii, Oct. 31, 1895

Library:

Fund bequeathed to the Society by George True Nealley to be used in purchasing books for the Library. XLIX, p. 474, Apr., 1926

Gifts received. V, p. xxi, May 5, 1894. VI, pp. xxiii-xxiv, Oct. 31, 1895

Nouvelles Annales des Voyages, from 1819 to 1865, 184 volumes, gift of Gardiner G. Hubbard. VII, p. 348, Oct., 1896

Photographs of. XV, ill. pp. 177, 179-181, Apr., 1904. XXV, ill. pp. 454, 458, 464, Apr., 1914. XLIII, ill. p. 670, June, 1923. LXV, ill. p. 794, June, 1934. LXIX, ill. p. 124, Jan., 1936

Short History of Cyprus (Philip Newman), obtained by Maynard Owen Williams. LXXXIX, p. 331, Mar., 1946

See also NGS: Buildings: Hubbard Memorial Hall

Life Members. *See* NGS: Members and Membership

Managers. *See* NGS: Board of Managers

Map Department. *See* NGS: Buildings: New Building (1932): Cartographic Department

Map Rack presented to President Truman. LXXXIX, p. 290, Mar., 1946

Map Supplement Articles. *See* National Geographic Magazine

Maps. *See* Map Index, *following this index*

Medals:

The National Geographic Society and Its Magazine. By Gilbert Grosvenor. LXIX, pp. 123-164, 24 ills., Jan., 1936

Resolution awarding medals to Peary and Bartlett. XX, pp. 1008-1009, Nov., 1909

Resolutions concerning medals (The National Geographic Society and Geographic Work). XX, pp. 486-487, May, 1909
- Basis of awards.................... 487
- Endowment of awards................ 487
- Purpose of medals.................. 486
- Recommendations for awards.......... 487
- Society medals..................... 487
- Special medals..................... 487
- Squires, Grant: Endowment by......... 487

Essay Contest Awards

Gold Medal to be awarded best essayist of the country (U. S.). IV, p. 207, Feb. 8, 1893

Important Announcement Concerning Essays (Gold Medal Award for best essay on the River Systems of the United States). VI, pp. 227-228, Dec. 29, 1894

Hubbard Medal

Amundsen, Roald:

Honors for Amundsen (Presentation of Hubbard Gold Medal by Charles W. Fairbanks). XIX, pp. 55-76, 13 ills., Jan., 1908
- Basis of award..................... 56
- Presentation 56–57

Hubbard Medal presented to Amundsen by the Vice-President of the United States, Charles W. Fairbanks. LXIX, p. 149, Jan., 1936

Anderson, Orvil A.:

Hubbard Medals Awarded to Stratosphere Explorers: Presentation by General Pershing. LXIX, pp. 713-714, May, 1936
- Address by Gilbert Grosvenor.......... 713
- Presentation ....713–714; ill. p. 712

Andrews, Roy Chapman:

Hubbard Medal winner. LXV, p. 792, June, 1934

Arnold, H. H.:

President Truman presents Hubbard Medal to Gen. H. H. Arnold, Nov. 16, 1945. LXXXIX, ill. p. 141, Feb., 1946

Bartlett, Robert A.:

"Captain Bob" Bartlett awarded the Hubbard Medal. LXXXIX, p. 609, May, 1946

NATIONAL GEOGRAPHIC SOCIETY—*Continued*

Medals—*Continued*

The Discovery of the North Pole. XXI, pp. 63-82, Jan., 1910
- Basis of awards...................63, 75
- Hubbard Gold Medal awarded to Grove Karl Gilbert....................63, 75
- Hubbard Gold Medal presented to Capt. Robert A. Bartlett by James Bryce...63, 75–77
- Inscriptions 63
- Special Gold Medal presented to Peary by Willis L. Moore............63, 73–74
- Telegrams of congratulation.........63, 64

Resolution awarding medal to Captain Bartlett. XX, p. 1009, Nov., 1909

Byrd, Richard E.:

Commander Byrd Receives the Hubbard Gold Medal: The First Explorer to Reach the North Pole by Air Receives Coveted Honor at Brilliant National Geographic Society Reception (Also Presentation of Gold Medal to Floyd Bennett). L, pp. 377-388, 5 ills., chart, Sept., 1926
- Acceptance of medal by Comdr. Byrd.379–383
- Basis of awards..................378–379
- Bennett, Floyd: Gold Medal presented to 377–379
- Comparison of Peary's and Byrd's achievements 377–378
- Photographs of medals.......ill. pp. 382, 385
- Presentation of medals by President Coolidge ....377–379; ill. p. 380
- Previous recipients.................. 377

President Coolidge presents Commander Byrd with the Hubbard Gold Medal. LII, p. 238, ill. p. 239, Aug., 1927. LXIX, ill. p. 139, Jan., 1936

Ellsworth, Lincoln:

Ellsworth Awarded the Hubbard Medal. LXX, p. 36, July, 1936
- Acceptance speech.................. 36
- Grosvenor, Gilbert: Exploits of Lincoln Ellsworth related by............... 36
- Presentation speech by President Franklin D. Roosevelt.................. 36

Gilbert, Grove Karl:

The Discovery of the North Pole. XXI, pp. 63-82, Jan., 1910
- Basis of awards..................63, 75
- Hubbard Gold Medal awarded to Grove Karl Gilbert....................63, 75
- Hubbard Gold Medal presented to Capt. Robert A. Bartlett by James Bryce.63, 75–77
- Inscriptions 63
- Special Gold Medal presented to Peary by Willis L. Moore............63, 73–74
- Telegrams of congratulation..........63, 64

Lindbergh, Anne Morrow:

Hubbard Gold Medal presented to Anne Morrow Lindbergh by Dr. Grosvenor. LXIX, ill. pp. 136, 137, Jan., 1936

The Society Awards Hubbard Medal to Anne Morrow Lindbergh. LXV, pp. 791-794, 4 ills., June, 1934
- Acceptance by Mrs. Lindbergh.......... 792
- Basis of award...................... 791
- Bumstead, Albert H.: Medal designed by. 793

Medals—*Continued*

Design and inscription........791, 792, 793
Messages of congratulation............ 793
Photograph of medal............ill. p. 793
Presentation by Dr. Grosvenor..791–792; ill. p. 792
Previous recipients...............791, 792
Projection used for map design on medal. 793

Lindbergh, Charles A.:

Air Conquest: From the Early Days of Giant Kites and Birdlike Gliders the National Geographic Society Has Aided and Encouraged the Growth of Aviation (Hubbard Gold Medal Awarded Lindbergh). LII, pp. 233-242, 13 ills., Aug., 1927
Basis of award..................241, 242
Byrd, Comdr. Richard E.: Lindbergh notified by........................ 241
Inscription ....ill. p. 234
Letter from Gilbert Grosvenor announcing award........................ 242
Photograph of medal............ill. p. 234
Previous recipients.................. 242

Hubbard Medal awarded to Colonel Lindbergh. LXIX, p. 137, ill. p. 138, Jan., 1936

President Coolidge Bestows Lindbergh Award: The National Geographic Society's Hubbard Medal Is Presented to Aviator Before the Most Notable Gathering in the History of Washington. LIII, pp. 132-140, 4 ills., Jan., 1928
Acceptance by Lindbergh..........135, 137
Inscription 139
Presentation by President Coolidge..134–135; ill. p. 139

Peary, Robert E.:

Honors to Peary (Presentation of Hubbard Gold Medal by President Roosevelt). XVIII, pp. 49-60, ill., Jan., 1907
Basis of award...................... 56
Design and inscription.........49; ill. p. 48
Presentation 57

Hubbard Medal presented to Robert E. Peary. LXIX, pp. 137, 149, Jan., 1936

Shackleton, Sir Ernest H.:

The Race for the South Pole (Presentation of Hubbard Gold Medal to Sir Ernest H. Shackleton). XXI, pp. 185-186, Mar., 1910
Acceptance speech by Shackleton....... 186
Basis of award...................... 185
Distinguished audience............... 185
Presentation speech by President Taft... 186

Stefansson, Vilhjalmur:

The National Geographic Society's Notable Year (Award of Hubbard Gold Medal to Stefansson). XXXVII, pp. 338-345, ills., Apr., 1920
Achievements of Stefansson.........339–342
Basis of award...................... 340
Peary, Rear Adm. Robert E.: Tribute to Stefansson by..................... 339
Photograph of Peary, Stefansson, and Greely ....ill. p. 318
Presentation of medal by Maj. Gen. A. W. Greely 339–342
Tribute to Stefansson by members of Greely International Polar Expedition. 342

Medals—*Continued*

Stevens, Albert W.:

Hubbard Medals Awarded to Stratosphere Explorers: Presentation by General Pershing. LXIX, pp. 713-714, May, 1936
Address by Gilbert Grosvenor........... 713
Presentation ....713–714; ill. p. 712

Special Gold Medal

Amundsen, Roald:

Admiral Robert E. Peary presents the Special Gold Medal to Amundsen. LXIX, p. 149, ill. p. 127, Jan., 1936

Honors to Amundsen and Peary (Special Gold Medal Presented to Amundsen by Peary). XXIV, pp. 113-130, 5 ills., Jan., 1913
Amundsen's acceptance speech.......129–130
Photograph of medal............ill. p. 128
Photograph of presentation ceremony ill. p. 120
Presentation by Peary.......129; ill. p. 120

Bennett, Floyd:

Awarded Gold Medal. LII, p. 238, Aug., 1927

Commander Byrd Receives the Hubbard Gold Medal: The First Explorer to Reach the North Pole by Air Receives Coveted Honor at Brilliant National Geographic Society Reception (Also Presentation of Gold Medal to Floyd Bennett). L, pp. 377-388, 5 ills., chart, Sept., 1926
Acceptance of medal by Comdr. Byrd.379–383
Basis of awards....................378–379
Bennett, Floyd: Gold Medal presented to 377–379
Comparison of Peary's and Byrd's achievements 377–378
Photographs of medals......ill. pp. 382, 385
Presentation of medals by President Coolidge ....377–379; ill. p. 380
Previous recipients.................. 377

Byrd, Richard E.:

Admiral Byrd Receives New Honor From The Society (Presentation by President Hoover of Special Medal of Honor). LVIII, pp. 228-238, 4 ills., Aug., 1930
Basis of award...................... 232
Photograph of medal...........ill. p. 235
Presentation by President Hoover..231–232; ill. p. 233
Two of the Society's medals awarded Byrd 229

Earhart, Amelia:

President Hoover presents medal to Amelia Earhart. LXIX, ill. p. 134, Jan., 1936

The Society's Special Medal Awarded to Amelia Earhart: First Woman to Receive Geographic Distinction at Brilliant Ceremony in the National Capital. LXII, pp. 358-367, 7 ills., Sept., 1932
Acceptance by Miss Earhart....363, 365, 367
Inscription 359
Photograph of medal............ill. p. 366
Presentation by President Hoover...358, 362–363; ill. p. 366
Presidents of the U. S. who have presented the Society's medals.......... 362
Previous recipients...............359, 362

NATIONAL GEOGRAPHIC SOCIETY—*Continued*
Medals—*Continued*

Eckener, Hugo:

The First Airship Flight Around the World: Dr. Hugo Eckener Tells of an Epochal Geographic Achievement upon the Occasion of the Bestowal of the National Geographic Society's Special Gold Medal. LVII, pp. 653-688, 37 ills., June, 1930
Acceptance speech by Dr. Eckener....655–681
Basis of award...................... 653
Inscription 655
Presentation by Gilbert Grosvenor...653–655
Previous recipients.................. 655
Telegram of congratulation from Byrd.. 688

Goethals, George W.:

Honors to Colonel Goethals: The Presentation, by President Woodrow Wilson, of the National Geographic Society Special Gold Medal, and Addresses by Secretary of State Bryan, the French Ambassador, the German Ambassador, and Congressman James R. Mann. XXV, pp. 677-690, 6 ills., June, 1914
Acceptance speech................683–684
Basis of award..............679, 680, 683
Inscription 679
Presentation speech..........679, 680, 683
Previous recipients.................. 679

Peary, Robert E.:

The Discovery of the North Pole. XXI, pp. 63-82, Jan., 1910
Basis of awards.....................63, 75
Hubbard Gold Medal awarded to Grove Karl Gilbert.....................63, 75
Hubbard Gold Medal presented to Capt. Robert A. Bartlett by James Bryce..63, 75–77
Inscriptions 63
Special Gold Medal presented to Peary by Willis L. Moore................63, 73–74
Telegrams of congratulation..........63, 64

Peary awarded Special Gold Medal for reaching the North Pole. LXIX, pp. 149, 154, Jan., 1936

Resolution awarding a special medal to Commander Peary. XX, p. 1008, Nov., 1909

Special Gold Medal presented to Peary. XXI, ill. p. 540, June, 1910

Poulter, Thomas C.:

The Society's Special Medal Is Awarded to Dr. Thomas C. Poulter: Admiral Byrd's Second-in-Command and Senior Scientist Is Accorded High Geographic Honor. LXXII, pp. 105-108, ills., July, 1937
Acceptance by Dr. Poulter..........105–106
Basis of award...................... 105
Byrd, Rear Adm. R. E.: Tribute to Dr. Poulter by 106–108
Photograph of medal............ill. p. 107
Presentation by Dr. Grosvenor.105; ill. p. 107

Meetings:

Annual Meeting, January 10, 1902. XIII, p. 80, Feb., 1902
Report of Secretary concerning membership 80
Treasurer's report.................. 80

NATIONAL GEOGRAPHIC SOCIETY—*Continued*
Meetings—*Continued*

Annual Meeting, January 13, 1905. XVI, p. 87, Feb., 1905
Board of Managers: Election of members. 87
Henry Gannett elected Vice-President... 87
Secretary's report.................... 87
Willis L. Moore elected President....... 87

Annual Meeting, January 14, 1910. XXI, pp. 88-90, Jan., 1910
Board of Managers: Election of members. 88
Election of officers.................. 88
Secretary's report..................88–89
Treasurer's report..................89–90

Annual Meeting, January 13, 1911. XXII, pp. 211, 214, Feb., 1911
Board of Managers: Election of members. 211
Election of officers.................. 211
Membership 211, 214
President Taft elected Honorary Member. 214
Secretary's report................211, 214
Treasurer's report.................. 214

First meeting:
For organizing a geographic society, January 13, 1888, Cosmos Club. I, p. 164, Apr., 1889. LXIX, p. 131, Jan., 1936
For the purpose of incorporating, January 20, 1888. I, p. 165, Apr., 1889. LXIX, p. 131, Jan., 1936
Of the Society, after incorporation, January 27, 1888: Election of officers and adoption of by-laws. I, p. 165, Apr., 1889. LXIX, pp. 131, 134, Jan., 1936
Regular meeting, February 17, 1888, Law Lecture Room, Columbian University: Inaugural address, by the President of the Society. I, p. 87, Oct., 1888

Meeting of Board of Managers. XIV, pp. 254-255, June, 1903
Appointment of Chairman of Committee on Eighth International Geographic Congress 254–255
Appointment of Presidential Nominating Committee 254
Resignation of Alexander Graham Bell as President 254

Meeting of Board of Managers. XVII, p. 205, Apr., 1906
Maj. Henry E. Hersey appointed representative of the Society on Wellman Polar Expedition 205
Resolution concerning the expedition.... 205

Meeting of Board of Managers. XXVI, pp. 281, Apr., 1907
Resolution subscribing to Peary Expedition of 1907-1908................. 281

Meeting of Board of Managers (The National Geographic Society and Geographic Work). XX, pp. 486-487, May, 1909
Research fund established............. 486
Resolutions concerning medals......... 487

Meeting of Board of Managers. XX, pp. 921-922, Nov., 1909
Claims of Peary and Cook referred to Committee on Research............. 921

Meeting of Board of Managers. XX, pp. 1008-1009, Nov., 1909
Report of committee on claims of Cook and Peary........................1008

NATIONAL GEOGRAPHIC SOCIETY—*Continued*

Meetings—*Continued*

Resolution appointing committee to consider claims of Cook................1009

Resolution awarding medals to Peary and Bartlett 1008–1009

Tribute in memory of Mrs. Gardiner Greene Hubbard....................1008

Meeting of Board of Managers. XXI, p. 365, Apr., 1910

Resolution withdrawing subscription to South Polar Expedition.............. 365

Meeting of Board of Managers. XXVI, pp. 609-610, Dec., 1914

Tribute to Henry Gannett..........609–610

Meeting of Board of Managers. XXVII, p. 218, Feb., 1915

John E. Pillsbury elected Vice-President. 218

O. H. Tittmann elected President....... 218

Notice of Annual Meeting, January 13, 1905. XVI, p. 53, Jan., 1905

100th meeting: Letters of congratulation read. VI, p. xvii, Oct. 31, 1895

Order of business. II, p. 309, Apr., 1891

Proceedings of the National Geographic Society: Abstract of Minutes (Feb. 17, 1888-Apr. 13, 1888). I, pp. 87-88, Oct., 1888

Proceedings of the National Geographic Society: Abstract of Minutes (Oct. 5, 1888-May 17, 1889). I, pp. 269-272, July, 1889

Proceedings of the National Geographic Society: Abstract of Minutes (Nov. 1, 1889-Mar. 7, 1890). II, pp. 67-68, Apr., 1890

Proceedings of the National Geographic Society: Abstract of Minutes (Mar. 21, 1890-Feb. 27, 1891). II, pp. 290-295, Apr., 1891

Proceedings of the National Geographic Society: Abstract of Minutes (Mar. 6, 1891-Jan. 15, 1892). III, pp. vii-xiii, Feb. 19, 1892

Proceedings of the National Geographic Society: Abstract of Minutes (Jan. 22, 1892-Dec. 23, 1892). IV, pp. xiii-xix, Feb. 20, 1893

Proceedings of the National Geographic Society: Abstract of Minutes (Dec. 30, 1892-Jan. 5, 1894). V, pp. ix-xix, May 5, 1894

Proceedings of the National Geographic Society: Abstract of Minutes (Jan., 1894, to May, 1895). VI, pp. xiii-xvii, Oct. 31, 1895

Proceedings of the National Geographic Society, Session 1895-'96. VII, pp. 46-48, Jan., 1896; pp. 86-87, Feb., 1896; pp. 122-123, Mar., 1896; pp. 155-156, Apr., 1896; pp. 214-216, June, 1896

Proceedings of the National Geographic Society, Session of 1896-'97. VII, p. 379, Nov., 1896; p. 410, Dec., 1896. VIII, pp. 28-29, Jan., 1897; pp. 63-64, Feb., 1897; pp. 94-95, Mar., 1897; p. 128, Apr., 1897; pp. 159-160, May, 1897; pp. 191-192, June, 1897

NATIONAL GEOGRAPHIC SOCIETY—*Continued*

Meetings—*Continued*

Proceedings of the National Geographic Society, Session 1897-'98. VIII, pp. 365-367, Dec., 1897. IX, pp. 31-32, Jan., 1898; pp. 70-71, Feb., 1898; p. 104, Mar., 1898; pp. 375-376, Aug., 1898; pp. 414-416, Sept., 1898

Proceedings of the National Geographic Society, Session 1898-'99. IX, pp. 519-520, Dec., 1898. X, pp. 143-144, Apr., 1899; pp. 327-328, Aug., 1899

Annual reception.................... 328

Election of new members.............. 144

President McKinley elected Honorary Member 143

Proceedings of the National Geographic Society, with abstract of the address by Hon. William F. Willoughby, "Some of the Administrative and Industrial Problems of Porto Rico." (By G. H. G.). XIII, pp. 466-470, Dec., 1902

See also NGS: Board of Managers; Board of Trustees; By-laws; Calendar; Excursions and Field Meetings

Members and Membership:

Achievements of members. XVIII, p. 50, Jan., 1907

Certificate of newly elected member. XC, ill. p. 39, July, 1946

Change in membership policy. XI, p. 289, July, 1900; pp. 403-404, Oct., 1900. XXIII, p. 273, Mar., 1912

Chart of membership, 1888-1900. XI, p. 402, Oct., 1900

Classes, Five, of members proposed. VI, p. xv, Oct. 31, 1895

Diagram of membership (Jan., 1888, to May 31, 1895). VI, pl. 15 (insert), Oct. 31, 1895

Election of new members. VII, pp. 47-48, Jan., 1896; pp. 86-87, Feb., 1896; p. 123, Mar., 1896; p. 156, Apr., 1896; p. 216, June, 1896; p. 379, Nov., 1896; p. 410, Dec., 1896. VIII, pp. 28-29, Jan., 1897; pp. 63-64, Feb., 1897; p. 95, Mar., 1897; p. 128, Apr., 1897; p. 160, May, 1897; p. 192, June, 1897; pp. 366-367, Dec., 1897. IX, p. 32, Jan., 1898; p. 71, Feb., 1898; p. 376, Aug., 1898; p. 416, Sept., 1898; p. 520, Dec., 1898. X, p. 144, Apr., 1899. XC, p. 39, July, 1946

See also NGS: Rules

Geographic distribution. II, p. 288, Apr., 1891. XIV, 75-page supplement (following p. 44), Jan., 1903. XXI, pp. 88-89, Jan., 1910. XXII, pp. 211, 214, Feb., 1911. XXIV, p. 255, Feb., 1913. XXV, pp. 468-470, Apr., 1914; p. 679, June, 1914. LIII, p. 137, Jan., 1928; pp. 173, 192, Feb., 1928. LXIX, pp. 163-164, Jan., 1936. LXXVIII, p. 61, July, 1940

By Place

Africa. LXVII, pp. 731-732, June, 1935

Argentina. LXXI, p. 31, Jan., 1937

Ascension Island: 2 members. LXXXV, p. 635, May, 1944

Members and Membership—*Continued*

Bahrein Island: 26 members. LXXXIX, p. 209, Feb., 1946

Belgian merchant, a member for fifteen years. LXXIII, p. 446, Apr., 1938

Buenos Aires: 1,527 members. LXXVI, p. 585, Nov., 1939

Canada. LXIX, p. 769, June, 1936

El Salvador: 7 members of Alvarez family. LXXXVI, p. 577, Nov., 1944

Europe. LVI, p. 771, Dec., 1929

Iceland. LXXI, pp. 30-31, Jan., 1937

Idaho: Uncle Dave ("Cougar Dave" Lewis). LXXXV, p. 679, June, 1944

Lord Howe Island: 2 members. LXVIII, pp. 126, 136, July, 1935

Malacca. LV, col. pl. XIV, p. 478, Apr., 1929

Martinique member. LXXIII, ill. p. 297, Mar., 1938

Mauritius Island: 55 members. LXXVI, p. 73, July, 1939

Nicaragua: Chinese merchant of Bluefields. LXXXVI, pp. 177-178, Aug., 1944

Ohio: Members in Conneaut. LXV, p. 458, Apr., 1934

Peru: Sociedad Geográfica de Lima membership includes several NGS members. VII, p. 407, Dec., 1896

Scotland. LXXXIX, p. 550, May, 1946

South American members—farthest south. LXXII, p. 750, ill. p. 761, Dec., 1937

Tibetan member. XC, p. 198, ill. p. 179, Aug., 1946

Increase in membership. I, p. 165, Apr., 1889. II, p. 66, Apr., 1890; pp. 293, 296, Apr., 1891. IV, pp. vii, xx, Feb. 20, 1893. V, p. xx, May 5, 1894. VI, p. xxi, Oct. 31, 1895. XI, p. 289, July, 1900; p. 403, Oct., 1900. XXI, p. 88, Jan., 1910. XXII, p. 211, Feb., 1911. XXIII, pp. 272-273, Mar., 1912. XXIV, pp. 252, 255, Feb., 1913. XXVII, p. 318, Mar., 1915

Intellectual caliber of members. XVII, p. 23, Jan., 1906

List of members, with addresses. I, pp. 94-98, Oct., 1888; pp. 172-181, Apr., 1889. II, pp. 70-80, Apr., 1890; pp. 316-334, Apr., 1891. III, pp. xv-xxxv, Feb. 19, 1892. V, pp. xxix-lxviii, May 5, 1894. VI, pp. xxiii-lxxxiii, Oct. 31, 1895. XIV, 75-page supplement (following p. 44), Jan., 1903

Members—By Name:

Fuad I, King. LXV, p. 658, May, 1934

Hoover, Mrs. Herbert. LVIII, p. 231, Aug., 1930. LXII, p. 362, Sept., 1932

Peary, Robert E. XLI, p. 641, June, 1922

Tungwenuk, Louis, westernmost member on the American Continent. LXXV, pp. 650-651, ill. p. 646, May, 1939

See also NGS: Honorary Members

Members use Geographic map to follow text of Franklin D. Roosevelt's address. LXXXI, p. 667, ill. p. 669, May, 1942

Notice of proposed amendments to the by-laws of the National Geographic Society. XIII, p. 182, May, 1902

NATIONAL GEOGRAPHIC SOCIETY—*Continued*

Members and Membership—*Continued*

Number of members. I, p. ii, Oct., 1888; pp. 165, 166, Apr., 1889. II, p. 66, Apr., 1890; pp. 287, 296, 334, Apr., 1891. III, p. xxxv, Feb. 19, 1892. IV, pp. vii, xx, Feb. 20, 1893. V, pp. xx, lxviii, May 5, 1894. VI, pp. xxi, lxxxiii, Oct. 31, 1895. VII, inserts, Jan., 1896, and Dec., 1896. X, p. 221, June, 1899. XIII, p. 80, Feb., 1902. XIV, p. 217, May, 1903. XVI, p. 87, Feb., 1905; p. 241, May, 1905. XVII, p. 23, Jan., 1906. XXI, p. 67, Jan., 1910. XXII, p. 267, Mar., 1911. XXIV, p. 113, Jan., 1913. XXV, p. 679, June, 1914. L, p. 377, Sept., 1926. LXXIII, p. 525, Apr., 1938. LXXVII, p. 625, May, 1940; p. 767, June, 1940. LXXVIII, p. 61, July, 1940. LXXIX, p. 345, Mar., 1941. LXXX, p. 741, Dec., 1941. LXXXI, p. 203, Feb., 1942; p. 333, Mar., 1942; p. 667, May, 1942. LXXXII, p. 139, July, 1942; p. 276, Aug., 1942; p. 537, Oct., 1942; p. 767, Dec., 1942. LXXXIII, p. 261, Feb., 1943. LXXXV, p. 415, Apr., 1944. LXXXVI, p. 66, July, 1944; p. 716, Dec., 1944. LXXXVII, p. 745, June, 1945. LXXXVIII, p. 361, Sept., 1945. XC, pp. 34, 39, 135, July, 1946; p. 815, Dec., 1946

Proposed change in by-laws. XII, p. 167, Apr., 1901

Rules of the Board of Managers regarding new members. II, pp. 308, 309, Apr., 1891

Active Members

Number of, listed by Government Department, club, and profession. VII, inserts, Jan., 1896, and Dec., 1896

See also List of members, *above*

Corresponding Members

Classification of members by profession, career, and occupation. VII, insert, Dec., 1896

List of, with addresses. II, pp. 316-334, Apr., 1891. III, pp. xv-xxxv, Feb. 19, 1892. V, pp. xxix-lxviii, May 5, 1894. VI, pp. lxxii-lxxxiii, Oct. 31, 1895

Honorary Members

List of. V, p. xxviii, May 5, 1894. VI, p. xxxiii, Oct. 31, 1895. XVIII, p. 51, Jan., 1907. XXII, p. 214, Feb., 1911

Number of. V, pp. xx, lxviii, May 5, 1894. VI, pp. xxi, lxxxiii, Oct. 31, 1895. VII, inserts, Jan., 1896, and Dec., 1896

President of the United States. VII, inserts, Jan., 1896, and Dec., 1896

See also names of U. S. Presidents, *below*

Honorary Members

By Name

Abruzzi, Duke of the. XVIII, p. 51, Jan., 1907

Amundsen, Roald. XVIII, p. 51, Jan., 1907. XIX, p. 57, Jan., 1908

Bonaparte, Prince Roland. XVIII, p. 51, 1907

Bryce, James. XXIII, pp. 272, 275-276, Mar., 1912

Charcot, Jean. XXIV, p. 122, Jan., 1913

Cleveland, Grover. XVIII, p. 51, Jan., 1907

NATIONAL GEOGRAPHIC SOCIETY—*Continued*

Members and Membership—*Continued*

Dewey, George. XVIII, p. 51, Jan., 1907. XXII, p. 214, Feb., 1911

Jesup, Morris K. XVIII, p. 51, Jan., 1907; ill. p. 460, July, 1907

Jusserand, Jules. XXV, pp. 679, 688, June. 1914

McKinley, William. IX, p. 520, Dec., 1898. X, p. 143, Apr., 1899

Nansen, Frithjof (Fridtjof). XVIII, p. 51, Jan., 1907. XXII, p. 214, Feb., 1911

Peary, Robert E. XVIII, p. 51, Jan., 1907. XXII, p. 214, Feb., 1911. XLI, p. 643, June, 1922

Roosevelt, Theodore. XVIII, p. 51, Jan., 1907. XXII, p. 214, Feb., 1911

Taft, William H. XXII, p. 214, Feb., 1911; pp. 267, 276, Mar., 1911

Truman, Harry S. LXXXIX, p. 141, Feb., 1946

Wilson, Woodrow. XXXIII, p. 369, Apr., 1918

Life Members

Award of eight Jane M. Smith Life Memberships. XXXVII, pp. 342-343, Apr., 1920
- List and account of recipients.......342–343
- Previous recipients.................. 342
- Reasons for awards...............342–343

51 new life members elected in 1910. XXII, p. 211, Feb., 1911

55 new life members elected in 1912. XXIV, p. 255, Feb., 1913

Jane M. Smith bequest for life memberships. XXIII, p. 104, Jan., 1912

List of, with addresses. I, pp. 94-98, Oct., 1888; pp. 172-181, Apr., 1889. II, pp. 70-80, Apr., 1890; pp. 316-334, Apr., 1891. III, pp. xv-xxxv, Feb. 19, 1892. V, pp. xxix-lxviii, May 5, 1894

See also Honorary Members, *above*

Original Members

List of, with addresses. I, pp. 94-98, Oct., 1888; pp. 172-181, Apr., 1889. II, pp. 70-80, Apr., 1890; pp. 316-334, Apr., 1891. III, pp. xv-xxxv, Feb. 19, 1892. V, pp. xxix-lxviii, May 5, 1894

Number of (165). II, p. 296, Apr., 1891. IV, p. vii, Feb. 20, 1893

See also NGS: By-laws; Founders

Memorials:

The "Bowdoin" (Ship) in North Greenland: Arctic Explorers Place Tablet to Commemorate Sacrifices of the Lady Franklin Bay Expedition. By Donald B. MacMillan. XLVII, pp. 677-722, 49 ills., June, 1925
- Christmas message from Greely to MacMillan 684
- History of Lady Franklin Bay Expedition 677–679
- Photographs of memorial....ill. pp. 700, 706
- Site of memorial..................... 688
- Unveiling ceremony...............688, 700

Memorial Fountain, Cantigny, France. LVI, ill. p. 548, Nov., 1929. LXV, ill. p. 34, Jan., 1934

NATIONAL GEOGRAPHIC SOCIETY—*Continued*

Memorials—*Continued*

Monument to Rear Adm. Charles Wilkes. LIV, ill. p. 633, Nov., 1928

The National Geographic Society's Memorial to American Troops: Fountain and Water Supply System Presented to Historic French Town of Cantigny, Where Our Overseas Soldiers Won Their First Victory in the World War. XLIV, pp. 675-678, 4 ills., Dec., 1923
- American Legion color guard......ill. p. 676
- Dedication of...................... 675
- Fund for memorial.................. 676
- Gore, James Howard: Presentation address by......................675–676

Robert E. Peary Memorial

A Memorial to Peary: The National Geographic Society Dedicates Monument in Arlington National Cemetery to Discoverer of the North Pole. XLI, pp. 639-646, 4 ills., June, 1922
- Design 646
- Inscriptions 645–646
- Photographs ....ill. pp. 644, 646
- Unveiling ....639; ill. pp. 640, 644

Photograph of. LIV, ill. p. 632, Nov., 1928

Unveiling of. LVII, ill. p. 583, May, 1930. LXIX, ill. p. 132, Jan., 1936

Museum:

Exhibit case. LX, col. pl. XVII, p. 579, Nov., 1931

Hebrew shekel presented to. LXIV, ill. p. 259, Sept., 1933

Varied exhibits. LXXI, p. 670, June, 1937

Yünnan Expedition exhibit. LXVII, col. pl. VII, p. 479, Apr., 1935. LXVIII, col. pls., III, p. 481, VII, p. 485, Oct., 1935

Musical Composition:

The "National Geographic Society March," composed and dedicated by Captain Thomas F. Darcy, leader of the United States Army Band, Washington. LXIX, p. 122, Jan., 1936

Name of the Society. *See* NGS: By-laws

News Service:

Current newspaper maps, a special feature of the News Service. LXXX, p. 741, Dec., 1941

Geographic News Bulletins reach twelve million readers. XXXVII, p. 343, Apr., 1920

North Pole Discovery:

The Discovery of the North Pole. XXI, pp. 63-82, Jan., 1910
- Account of Peary's explorations.......69–73
- Hubbard Gold Medal presented to Capt. Robert A. Bartlett..............63, 75–77
- Special Gold Medal presented to Peary 63, 74–75

The Discovery of the Pole. XX, pp. 892-916, 11 ills., map, Oct., 1909
- Cook, Frederick A.: Report by......892–896
- Peary, Robert E.: Report by 896–915

NATIONAL GEOGRAPHIC SOCIETY—*Continued*

North Pole Discovery—*Continued*

A Memorial to Peary: The National Geographic Society Dedicates Monument in Arlington National Cemetery to Discoverer of the North Pole. XLI, pp. 639-646, 4 ills., June, 1922
Denby, Edwin: Speech by.643–645; ill. p. 642
Grosvenor, Gilbert: Address by......641–643
Members and guests present...639, 641; ill. pp. 640, 642
Peary, a member of the Society........ 641
Peary's career....................643–645
Peary's first address to the Society..... 641
Peary's last public appearance, last article, and last photograph were for the Society 641
Recognition of Peary by the Society..... 643
Roosevelt, Col. Theodore: Speech by.... 645
Stafford, Mrs. Edward (Marie Peary): Monument unveiled by......639; ill. p. 644

The North Pole. XX, pp. 921-922, Nov., 1909
Committee appointed to consider claims of Peary and Cook...............921–922

The North Pole. XX, pp. 1008-1009, Nov., 1909
Committee appointed to consider claims of Cook..........................1009
Medals awarded Peary and Bartlett 1008–1009
Recognition of Peary's discovery.......1008

"Peary's Discovery of the North Pole" (Pamphlet by J. Hampton Moore), presented to members of the Society. XXI, p. 276, Mar., 1910

See also NGS: Expeditions: Arctic Regions

Notary Public. XC, ill. p. 7, July, 1946

Object. *See* NGS: Purpose

Officers:

Election of. *See* NGS: By-laws; Meetings: Proceedings; Rules

First officers elected. I, p. 165, Apr., 1889

Photograph of Officers and Board of Managers in 1913. XXIV, ill. p. 114, Jan., 1913. LXIX, ill. p. 126, Jan., 1936

Photograph of Officers and Trustees in 1930. LXIX, ill. p. 159, Jan., 1936

Presentation of Hubbard Medal by President Truman to Gen. H. H. Arnold: Officers attending. LXXXIX, ill. p. 141, Feb., 1946

Year of:
1888. I, p. 93, Oct., 1888
1889. I, p. 168, Apr., 1889
1890. II, p. 69, Apr., 1890; p. ii, Apr., 1891
1891. II, p. 315, Apr., 1891. III, p. ii, Feb. 19, 1892
1892. III, p. xiv, Feb. 19, 1892. IV, p. ii, Feb. 20, 1893
1893. V, p. ii, May 5, 1894
1894. V, p. xxvii, May 5, 1894
1894 and to May 31, 1895. VI, p. ii, Oct. 31, 1895
1895–96. VI, p. xxxii, Oct. 31, 1895
1904 (Dec. 1). XV, p. II, 1904
1905 (Dec. 1). XVI, p. II, 1905

NATIONAL GEOGRAPHIC SOCIETY—*Continued*

Officers—*Continued*

See also NGS: President; Secretary; Treasurer; Vice-President; *and* NGS: Rules

Offices. *See* NGS: Buildings

Paintings. *See* NGM: Paintings; NGS: Buildings: Hubbard Memorial Hall: Mural Paintings

Photographic Exhibits, Newspaper:

The American Scene. 29 winning photos in the Sixth Annual Newspaper National Snapshot Awards (1940), with explanatory note. LXXIX, pp. 220-246, Feb., 1941

Americana. 11 winning photos in the Seventh Annual Newspaper National Snapshot Awards (1941). LXXXI, pp. 657-666, May, 1942

Photographic Laboratory. *See* NGS: Buildings: New Building (1932)

Photographic Library. *See* NGS: Buildings: New Building (1932)

Photography. *See* NGM: Photographs; Photography; Pictorial Supplements

Preservation of wildlife encouraged by the Society. LXII, p. 263, Sept., 1932

President:

Bell, Alexander Graham

Address delivered before the International Journalists' Association, Tokyo. IX, pp. 509-512, Dec., 1898

Announcement of the death of. XLII, p. 302, Sept., 1922

Contributed generously to the Society in time, energy, and money. X, pp. 222-223, June, 1899. LXIX, pp. 138, 144, 152, Jan., 1936

Election of. IX, p. 28, Jan., 1898; p. 416, Sept., 1898

Photograph of: Inaugurates telephone service, New York to Chicago. LXXII, ill. p. 397, Oct., 1937

Portraits. IX, pl. 3 (front.); text, p. 104, Mar., 1898. XII, ill. p. 353, Oct., 1901. XLII, ill. p. 302, Sept., 1922

Reception to Captain C. D. Sigsbee, U.S.N. (By J.H.). IX, pp. 251-252, May, 1898

Resignation of. XIV, p. 254, June, 1903

Gannett, Henry

Biography of. XXVI, pp. 609-613, ill., Dec., 1914

Chief Geographer, U. S. Geological Survey, and President of the Society from 1910 to 1914. XC, p. 95, July, 1946

Death of. XXVI, p. 520, Nov., 1914

Election of. XXI, p. 88, Jan., 1910

Speeches by. XXII, p. 267, Mar., 1911. XXIII, p. 272, Mar., 1912. XXIV, p. 115, Jan., 1913

Gilbert, Grove Karl

Acting President: Eighth International Geographic Congress welcomed by. XV, p. 419, Oct., 1904

Biographical sketch of. XI, p. 289; portrait, pl. 7 (front.), July, 1900

NATIONAL GEOGRAPHIC SOCIETY—*Continued*

President—*Continued*

Grosvenor, Gilbert H.

Addresses:

Opening of the Society's fifty-fifth annual series of lectures in Constitution Hall, November 20, 1942. LXXXIII, pp. 277-278, Feb., 1943

Presentation of Hubbard Gold Medal to Anne Morrow Lindbergh. LXV, pp. 791-792, June, 1934

Presentation of Hubbard Gold Medal to Charles A. Lindbergh. LIII, pp. 132, 134, 137, Jan., 1928

Presentation of Hubbard Gold Medal to Commander Richard E. Byrd. L, pp. 377, 383, Sept., 1926

Presentation of Hubbard Gold Medal to Lincoln Ellsworth. LXX, p. 36, July, 1936

Presentation of Hubbard Gold Medals to Captain Albert W. Stevens and Captain Orvil A. Anderson. LXIX, p. 713, May, 1936

Presentation of Special Gold Medal to Admiral Richard E. Byrd. LVIII, pp. 229-231, Aug., 1930

Presentation of Special Gold Medal to Amelia Earhart. LXII, pp. 359, 362, Sept., 1932

Presentation of Special Gold Medal to Dr. Thomas C. Poulter. LXXII, p. 105, July, 1937

Presentation of Special Gold Medal to Hugo Eckener. LVII, pp. 653-655, 681, 688, June, 1930

Reception for Admiral Richard E. Byrd. LXVIII, pp. 107-108, July, 1935

Unveiling of Robert E. Peary Memorial. XLI, pp. 641, 643, June, 1922

Air travel by. LXIII, p. 628, May, 1933

Alexander Graham Bell pays tribute to. XXIII, p. 274, Mar., 1912. LXIX, p. 148, Jan., 1936

Boyhood, spent in Turkey. LXXXVII, p. 600, May, 1945. LXXXVIII, pp. 237, 238, Aug., 1945

Byrd's North Pole flight aided by. L, p. 381, Sept., 1926

Cornerstone document of Hubbard Memorial Hall, signed by. LXIX, p. 152, Jan., 1936

Election of. XXXVII, p. 345, Apr., 1920

Engaged as Assistant Editor, April 1, 1889. XXIII, p. 274, Mar., 1912. LXIX, pp. 123, 136-137, 139, 148, Jan., 1936

Gilbert Grosvenor Trail, Antarctica. LVIII, pp. 184, 193, 198, ill. p. 218, Aug., 1930

Home of. LI, ill. p. 202, Feb., 1927. LVII, ill. p. 592, May, 1930

Lake, Alaskan, named for. XL, pp. 222, 287, ill. pp. 284, 288, Sept., 1921. L, ill. p. 89, July, 1926

Letter to Colonel Lindbergh, announcing award of Hubbard Medal. LII, p. 242, Aug., 1927

MacMillan Arctic Expedition: Dr. Grosvenor accompanies expedition from Maine to Labrador. XLVIII, p. 226, ill. p. 224, Aug., 1925; ill. p. 476, Oct., 1925

NATIONAL GEOGRAPHIC SOCIETY—*Continued*

President—*Continued*

Mount Grosvenor, Alaska. XXII, p. 551, June, 1911

Mount Grosvenor, China. LVIII, p. 415, col. pls., VII, p. 409, X, p. 428, Oct., 1930

Nansen received by. LVIII, ill. p. 22, July, 1930

Photographs of. XLI, ill. p. 240, Mar., 1922; ill. p. 640, June, 1922. XLVIII, ill. p. 224, Aug., 1925; ill. p. 476, Oct., 1925. L, ill. p. 380, Sept., 1926. LIII, ill. p. 135, Jan., 1928. LVII, ill. pp. 583, 592, May, 1930. LVIII, ill. p. 22, July, 1930; ill. pp. 230, 233, Aug., 1930. LXII, ill. p. 366, Sept., 1932. LXV, ill. pp. 790, 792, June, 1934. LXVII, ill. p. 137, Feb., 1935. LXVIII, ill. pp. 112, 114, July, 1935. LXIX, ill. pp. 126, 129, 132, 133, 134, 137, 139, 159, Jan., 1936; ill. p. 712, May, 1936. LXXII, ill. p. 107, July, 1937. LXXIII, ill. p. 319, Mar., 1938. LXXXVII, ill. p. 717, June, 1945

Presentation of Hubbard Medal by President Truman to Gen. H. H. Arnold. LXXXIX, ill. p. 141, Feb., 1946

See also Grosvenor, Gilbert H., for Addresses, Articles, and Tributes; NGM: Editor; NGS: History

Hubbard, Gardiner Greene

Alaskan glacier named for. III, pp. 99-100, ill. pl. 9, May, 1891. XXI, ill. pp. 7, 16, Jan., 1910. XLIX, ill. p. 599, June, 1926. LXIX, ill. p. 725, June, 1936. LXXXII, ill. p. 288, Sept., 1942

Contributed generously to the Society. X, pp. 222-223, June, 1899

Dedication of Hubbard Memorial Hall. XIII, pp. 174-176, May, 1902

Election of. I, p. 165, Apr., 1889; p. 270, July, 1889. II, p. 68, Apr., 1890; p. 294, Apr., 1891. III, p. xii, Feb. 19, 1892. IV, p. xix, Feb. 20, 1893. V, p. xix, May 5, 1894. VII, p. 216, June, 1896. LXIX, p. 134, Jan., 1936

First Regular Meeting, Feb. 17, 1888, the President, Mr. Hubbard, in the chair. I, p. 87, Oct., 1888

A founder of the Society. XVII, pp. 23, 24, Jan., 1906. LXIX, p. 131, Jan., 1936

Portrait. VII, pl. XVIII (front.), May, 1896. IX, pl. 2 (front.), Feb., 1898

Seal of the Society, designed under personal supervision of Gardiner Greene Hubbard. XC, p. 34, col. pl., p. 28, July, 1946

Toast to the memory of Gardiner Greene Hubbard, the first President. XVII, p. 24, Jan., 1906

See also Hubbard, Gardiner Greene, for Addresses, Articles, and Memorial Tributes; NGS: History

McGee, W J

Election of. XV, p. 176, Apr., 1904

Moore, Willis L.

Election of. XVI, p. 87, Feb., 1905

Photograph of. XVIII, ill. p. 587, Sept., 1907

NATIONAL GEOGRAPHIC SOCIETY—*Continued*

President—*Continued*

Special Gold Medal presented to Peary by. XXI, pp. 73-74, Jan., 1910

Speeches by. XVII, pp. 23-27, 29, 32, 34-35, Jan., 1906. XVIII, pp. 49-51, 53, 56, Jan., 1907. XIX, pp. 55, 57, 61-62, 64, 68-69, 72, Jan., 1908. XX, pp. 77, 78, 82, 84, 86, 89, 91, Jan., 1909. XXI, pp. 63, 67-69, 73-74, 78-79, Jan., 1910

Pillsbury, John Elliott

Death of. XXXVII, p. 345, Apr., 1920

Election to NGS Presidency in 1919. XXXVII, pp. 341, 345, Apr., 1920

Photograph of. XXXVII, ill. p. 341, Apr., 1920

Tittmann, O. H.

Election of. XXVII, p. 218, Feb., 1915

See also NGS: Rules; *and* names of NGS Presidents

Presidents of the United States Address National Geographic Society:

Presidents of the United States who have presented the Society's medals. LXII, p. 362, Sept., 1932

Coolidge, Calvin

Presentation of Hubbard Gold Medal to Commander Byrd and Gold Medal to Floyd Bennett. L, pp. 377-379, ill. p. 380, Sept., 1926. LII, ill. p. 239, Aug., 1927. LXIX, ill. p. 139, Jan., 1936

Presentation of Hubbard Medal to Charles Lindbergh. LIII, pp. 134-135, ill. p. 139, Jan., 1928. LXV, p. 791, June, 1934. LXIX, ill. p. 138, Jan., 1936

Hoover, Herbert

Presentation of Society's Gold Medal to Amelia Earhart. LXII, pp. 358, 362-363, ill. p. 366, Sept., 1932

Presentation of Special Medal of Honor to Admiral Byrd. LVIII, pp. 231-232, ill. p. 233, Aug., 1930

Roosevelt, Franklin D.

Presentation of Hubbard Gold Medal to Lincoln Ellsworth. LXX, p. 36, July, 1936

Roosevelt, Theodore

Address, "Wild Man and Wild Beast in Africa," delivered before the Society, Nov. 18, 1910. XXII, pp. 1-33, Jan., 1911. LXII, p. 358, Sept., 1932

Presentation of Hubbard Gold Medal to Robert Peary. XVIII, pp. 56-57, Jan., 1907. XXXVII, pp. 293, 322, Apr., 1920. LXII, p. 362, Sept., 1932. LXIX, p. 149, Jan., 1936

Taft, William Howard

Address at Annual Dinner of the Society. XVII, pp. 22-37, Jan., 1906

Address upon election as Honorary Member of the Society. XXII, pp. 267-284, ill., Mar., 1911

Presentation of Hubbard Gold Medal to Sir Ernest H. Shackleton. XXI, p. 186, Mar., 1910

NATIONAL GEOGRAPHIC SOCIETY—*Continued*

Presidents of the United States Address National Geographic Society—*Continued*

Truman, Harry S

Presentation of Hubbard Medal by President Truman to Gen. H. H. Arnold. LXXXIX, ill. p. 141, Feb., 1946

Wilson, Woodrow

Presentation of Gold Medal to Colonel Goethals. XXV, pp. 679, 680, 683, June, 1914

See also, for articles and additional information, the following names: Coolidge, Calvin; Harding, Warren G.; Hoover, Herbert; McKinley, William; Roosevelt, Theodore; Taft, William Howard; Truman, Harry S; Wilson, Woodrow; *and* NGS: Banquets; Members and Membership: Honorary Members

Press Reports:

Article on the Society in Boston *Herald*, November 23, 1907. XVIII, p. 825, Dec., 1907

Prizes:

Essay Contest on Norse Discoveries in America. X, pp. 31-32, Jan., 1899
Chairman of Prize Committee.......... 32
Judges of contest.................... 32
Rules of contest....................31–32

Essay Contest on Norse Discoveries in America. XI, p. 246, June, 1900
Award of prizes...................... 246

Essay Contests: Certificates and medals awarded annually to public high school students writing the best essay on geography. IV, pp. 206-208, Feb. 8, 1893. VI, pp. 227-228, Dec. 29, 1894

Franklin L. Burr Prize awarded to Capt. Albert W. Stevens. LXV, p. 626, May, 1934

Grant Squires Prize awarded to F. H. King. XXIV, p. 115, Jan., 1913

Proceedings. *See* NGS: Meetings

Property:

Purchase of lot adjoining Hubbard Memorial Hall. XX, p. 487, May, 1909

Publication Rules:

Rules Relating to Publication. Adopted by the Board of Managers, February 6, 1891. II, pp. 311-314, Apr., 1891

Publications:

Atlas, Physical, of the United States, in preparation. I, p. i, Oct., 1888; p. 166, Apr., 1889. II, p. 289, Apr., 1891

Book of Fishes. LXXXI, p. 730, June, 1942

Book of Flags. LXXIX, p. 162, Feb., 1941

Book of Monsters. By David and Marian Fairchild. XXVI, p. 89, July, 1914

Cumulative Index to NGM. LXIX, pp. 123, 125, 161, 162, Jan., 1936

Hunting Wild Life with Camera and Flashlight. By George Shiras, 3d. LXXVI, p. 87, July, 1939. LXXIX, p. 612, May, 1941. LXXXIII, p. 248, Feb., 1943

Insignia and Decorations of the United States Armed Forces (Revised). LXXXVII, pp. 185, 186, Feb., 1945

NATIONAL GEOGRAPHIC SOCIETY—*Continued*

Publications—*Continued*

Insignia and Decorations of the United States Armed Forces. By Gilbert Grosvenor. LXXXVII, pp. 185-186, Feb., 1945

Monographs of the National Geographic Society, to be published for use in the public schools. VI, pp. 225-227, Dec. 29, 1894

National Geographic Monographs. VII, p. 42, Jan., 1896

National Geographic Society-U. S. Army Air Corps Stratosphere Flight of 1935 in Balloon *Explorer II* (Contributed Technical Papers, *Stratosphere Series No. 2*). LXXI, p. 340, Mar., 1937; p. 802, June, 1937

National Geographic Society's New "Book of Birds." LXXI, p. 723, June, 1937. LXXII, p. 183, Aug., 1937. LXXIV, p. 226, Aug., 1938; p. 775, Dec., 1938. LXXVII, p. 121, Jan., 1940

Reprints Available for Mosquito, Classic Greece, and Insignia Articles. LXXXV, p. 536, May, 1944

Reprints of Insignia Article. LXXXIV, col. pl. XVI, p. 288, Sept., 1943; p. 488, Oct., 1943; p. 740, Dec., 1943. LXXXV, p. 536, May, 1944

Valley of Ten Thousand Smokes. LXXXIV, p. 157, Aug., 1943. LXXXV, p. 154, Feb., 1944

See also National Geographic Magazine; NGS: By-laws

Purpose of the Society. I, p. i, Oct., 1888. II, pp. 287, 302, Apr., 1891. V, p. 105, Jan. 31, 1894. VII, pp. 253, 256-257, Aug., 1896. X, p. 221, June, 1899. XXI, pp. 67-68, Jan., 1910. XXIII, p. 273, Mar., 1912. XXXVII, p. 345, Apr., 1920. LXIX, pp. 123, 134, Jan., 1936

See also NGS: By-laws (Copy); Certificate of Incorporation

Receptions:

Admiral Byrd Receives New Honor From The Society. LVIII, pp. 228-238, 4 ills., Aug., 1930
- Article for the Magazine prepared by Byrd ....228; ill. p. 229
- Audience and distinguished guests...228, 234–238
- Byrd, Rear Adm. Richard E.: Address by 228, 232–233
- Decorations 228
- Grosvenor, Gilbert: Introduction of President Hoover...................229–231
- Guests on platform.................. 228
- Luncheon in honor of Byrd and his party 232–233
- Members of Byrd Expedition guests of the Society ....232, 238; ill. p. 230
- Mrs. Hoover, long a member of the Society 231
- Motion pictures of Byrd Expedition..... 232
- Presentation of Special Gold Medal by President Hoover.....231–232; ill. p. 233
- Reception by President Hoover at White House ....ill. p. 230
- Travels of President Hoover........... 231

NATIONAL GEOGRAPHIC SOCIETY—*Continued*

Receptions—*Continued*

Annual Reception, March 15, 1893. V, p. xi, May 5, 1894

Annual Reception, March 20, 1895. VI, pp. xix, xxii, Oct. 31, 1895

Annual Reception, March 25, 1897. VIII, p. 128, Apr., 1897

Annual Reception, March 16, 1898. IX, p. 375, Aug., 1898

Annual Reception, March 22, 1899. X, p. 328, Aug., 1899

Annual Reception, April 12, 1901. XII, p. 167, Apr., 1901; p. 208, May, 1901

Commander Byrd Receives the Hubbard Gold Medal: The First Explorer to Reach the North Pole by Air Receives Coveted Honor at Brilliant National Geographic Society Reception (Also Presentation of Gold Medal to Floyd Bennett). L, pp. 377-388, 5 ills., chart, Sept., 1926
- Byrd, Comdr. Richard E.: Acceptance speech by......................379–383
- Chart of route of flight.............. 386
- Committee appointed to examine Byrd's records 377, 384–385
- Coolidge, Calvin: Presentation speech by 377–379
- Finances and equipment of Byrd Arctic Expedition 382
- Grosvenor, Gilbert: Byrd Arctic Expedition aided by...................... 381
- Grosvenor, Gilbert: Speeches by.....377, 383
- Importance of aviation in Arctic exploration 382–383
- Instruments used by Byrd Arctic Expedition ....ill. pp. 378, 379
- Introduction of President Coolidge by Dr. Grosvenor 377
- MacMillan Expedition aided by the Society 379, 381
- Members and guests present........... 377
- Personnel of Byrd Arctic Expedition.... 381
- Presentation ceremony............ill. p. 380
- Record of flight....................385–388
- Reports of committee approving Byrd's records 377, 384–388
- Tribute to Bumstead sun-compass...381; ill. p. 378
- Wilbur, Curtis D.: Speech by.......383–384

Cuban delegation, received, informally, December 2, 1898. IX, pp. 519-520, Dec., 1898

The First Airship Flight Around the World: Dr. Hugo Eckener Tells of an Epochal Geographic Achievement upon the Occasion of the Bestowal of the National Geographic Society's Special Gold Medal. LVII, pp. 653-688, 37 ills., June, 1930
- Byrd, Rear Adm. Richard E.: Telegram of congratulation from.............. 688
- Eckener, Dr. Hugo: Acceptance speech by 655–681
- Grosvenor, Gilbert: Presentation speech 653–655
- Members of audience.................. 653
- Tribute to Dr. Eckener.............653, 655
- World travels of the Society's flag...... 655

National Geographic Society Honors Byrd Antarctic Expedition. LXVIII, pp. 107-114, 6 ills., July, 1935

NATIONAL GEOGRAPHIC SOCIETY—*Continued*

Receptions—*Continued*

Byrd, Rear Adm. Richard E.: Address by ....107, 108-109; ill. p. 111
Grosvenor, Gilbert: Address by......107–108
Grosvenor, Gilbert: Scroll presented by 107, 108; ill. pp. 112, 114
Tribute to men of the Expedition....... 109

President Coolidge Bestows Lindbergh Award: The National Geographic Society's Hubbard Medal Is Presented to Aviator Before the Most Notable Gathering in the History of Washington. LIII, pp. 132-140, 4 ills., Jan., 1928
Contributions of U. S. to aviation...... 138
Coolidge, Calvin: Presentation speech by 132, 134–135; ill. p. 135
Geographical distribution of the Society's members 137
Grosvenor, Gilbert: Speech presenting President Coolidge........132, 134
Grosvenor, Gilbert: Speech presenting Secretary MacCracken........ 137
Guests of honor on platform..132; ill. p. 135
Lindbergh introduced by President Coolidge 133–134
Lindbergh's speech of acceptance...135, 137
MacCracken, William P.: Speech by..137–139
Members and guests present...132, 140; ill. p. 135
Motion picture of history of aviation.139–140
Presentation ceremony.........132–133, 134–135; ill. p. 139
Radio broadcast of ceremony........... 139
Ticket lines.....................ill. p. 133

Reception to Captain C. D. Sigsbee, U.S.N., April 2, 1898. IX, pp. 251-252, May, 1898; p. 376, Aug., 1898

Reception to Dr. Nansen, October 26, 1897, Arlington Hotel. VIII, p. 366, Dec., 1897

The Society Awards Hubbard Medal to Anne Morrow Lindbergh. LXV, pp. 791-794, 4 ills., June, 1934
Grosvenor, Gilbert: Presentation speech by 791–792
Guests 791, 792–793
Lindbergh, Anne Morrow: Acceptance speech by........ 792
Photograph of Officers and Mrs. Lindbergh ....ill. p. 790

The Society's Special Medal Awarded to Amelia Earhart: First Woman to Receive Geographic Distinction at Brilliant Ceremony in the National Capital. LXII, pp. 358-367, 7 ills., Sept., 1932
Arrival of Miss Earhart..........ill. p. 364
Audience 358–359
Decorations 358
Earhart, Amelia: Account of transatlantic flight..358, 363-367; ill. pp. 359, 360
First accounts of explorers in the Magazine 358
Grosvenor, Gilbert: Address introducing President Hoover..........359, 362
Guests on platform..........358–359
Hoover, Herbert: Presentation by..358, 362–363
Luncheon in honor of Miss Earhart.... 358
Reception of Miss Earhart by President Hoover at the White House....ill. p. 366
Tribute to Mrs. Hoover........ 362

NATIONAL GEOGRAPHIC SOCIETY—*Continued*

Receptions—*Continued*

Venezuelan Boundary Commission, received, March 12, 1896, Arlington Hotel. VII, p. 155, Apr., 1896

See also NGS: Banquets

Reprints. *See* NGS: Publications

Research:

Appropriations for research. XXVII, p. 320, Mar., 1915

Aurora Borealis: The Mystery of Auroras: National Geographic Society and Cornell University Study Spectacular Displays in the Heavens. LXXV, pp. 689-690, May, 1939

Aurora Borealis: Research under the auspices of the National Geographic Society and Cornell University. LXXIX, p. 580, May, 1941. LXXXVI, p. 640, Nov., 1944. XC, p. 387, Sept., 1946

Cosmic Rays: Series of flights under auspices of National Geographic Society, U. S. Army Air Forces, and Bartol Research Foundation. XC, p. 387, ill. p. 388, Sept., 1946

Promotion of research by the Society. XX, pp. 486-487, May, 1909

Solar Radiation: Hunting an Observatory: A Successful Search for a Dry Mountain on Which to Establish the National Geographic Society's Solar Radiation Station. By C. G. Abbot. L, pp. 503-518, 13 ills., map, Oct., 1926

Solar Radiation: Measuring the Sun's Heat and Forecasting the Weather: The National Geographic Society to Maintain a Solar Station in a Remote Part of the World to Coöperate with Smithsonian Institution Stations in California and Chile. By C. G. Abbot. XLIX, pp. 111-126, 15 ills., chart, Jan., 1926

Solar Radiation: National Geographic Society-Smithsonian Institution Solar Radiation Station, Mount Brukkaros, South-West Africa. LVII, p. 483, Apr., 1930

See also NGS: Expeditions

Rhododendrons:

Rhododendron seeds presented to Golden Gate Park, San Francisco, by the Society. LV, p. 729, June, 1929. LXI, p. 428, Apr., 1932

Rhododendrons presented to Kew Gardens, London, by the Society. LV, col. pl. IV, p. 572, May, 1929. LXVIII, pp. 143, 147, ill. p. 146, Aug., 1935

Rules:

Standing Rules of the Board of Managers. Adopted January 16, 1891. II, pp. 308-310, Apr., 1891

See also NGS: By-laws; Publication Rules

School Service:

Schoolroom aids provided by the National Geographic Society. XXV, p. 468, Apr., 1914. XXXVII, p. 343, Apr., 1920. LXIX, pp. 161-162, Jan., 1936. LXXX, p. 366, Sept., 1941; p. 824, Dec., 1941

NATIONAL GEOGRAPHIC SOCIETY—*Continued*

School Service—*Continued*

Sight-seeing in School: Taking Twenty Million Children on a Picture Tour of the World. By Jessie L. Burrall. XXXV, pp. 489-503, 14 ills., June, 1919
- Educational value of the Society's photographs ... 499
- Pictorial Geography series ... 503
- Separate picture sets for schools ... 501
- Use of the National Geographic in schools ... 497, 499

Seal:

Authorization and design of the Society's new seal. VII, p. 215, June, 1896. XC, p. 34, col. pl., p. 28, July, 1946

Bronze seal of the Society, set in lobby floor. LXIX, ill. p. 157, Jan., 1936. XC, ill. p. 11, July, 1946

First seal of the Society, on Magazine covers. I, Oct., 1888, through VII, May, 1896

Secretary impressing the Society's seal on membership certificate. XC, ill. p. 39, July, 1946

Society's seal on marker erected by Eclipse Expedition on Canton Island. LXXII, ill. p. 376, Sept., 1937

Secretary:

Corresponding Secretary. *See* Gannett, Henry; Kenaston, C. A.; Kennan, George; Moore, Willis L.; Scidmore, Eliza Ruhamah; Tittmann, O. H.

Employment of a permanent Secretary, November 1, 1893. V, pp. xvii, xxi, May 5, 1894

Recording Secretary. *See* Babb, Cyrus C.; Baker, Marcus; Gannett, Henry; Hayden, Everett; Henry, A. J.; Newell, Frederick H.; Stanley-Brown, Joseph

See also NGS: Rules; *and* names of NGS Secretaries

Austin, O. P.

Election of. XIV, p. 425, Nov., 1903

Reports by. XVI, p. 87, Feb., 1905. XXI, pp. 88-89, Jan., 1910. XXII, pp. 211, 214, Feb., 1911. XXIV, p. 255, Feb., 1913

Babb, Cyrus C.

Election of. V, pp. ii, xix, May 5, 1894

Employed as a permanent Secretary. V, p. xvii, May 5, 1894

Report by. V, pp. xx-xxi, May 5, 1894

Resignation of. VI, p. ii, Oct. 31, 1895

Baker, Marcus

Correspondence addressed to. II, p. 289, Apr., 1891

Election of. II, pp. 294, 297, Apr., 1891

Reports by. II, pp. 296-298, Apr., 1891. IV, pp. vii-ix, Feb. 20, 1893

Gannett, Henry

Election of. I, p. 165, Apr., 1889; p. 270, July, 1889. II, p. 68, Apr., 1890. VII, p. 216, June, 1896. LXIX, p. 134, Jan., 1936

NATIONAL GEOGRAPHIC SOCIETY—*Continued*

Secretary—*Continued*

Reports by. I, pp. 164-166, Apr., 1889. II, p. 66, Apr., 1890

Resignation of. II, p. 297, Apr., 1891

Hayden, Everett

Election of, VI, p. ii, Oct. 31, 1895. VII, p. 216, June, 1896

Report by. VI, pp. xxi-xxv, Oct. 31, 1895

Resignation of. IX, p. 70, Feb., 1898

Henry, Alfred J.

Report by. XIII, p. 80, Feb., 1902

Resignation of. XIV, p. 425, Nov., 1903

Hutchison, George W.

Memorial tribute to. LXXXVII, p. 720, ill., June, 1945

Photographs of. LXV, ill. p. 790, June, 1934. LXIX, ill. p. 157, Jan., 1936. LXXIX, col. pl., p. 432, Apr., 1941. LXXXVII, ill. p. 720, June, 1945

Tribute by Dr. Grosvenor. LXIX, p. 154, Jan., 1936

Kenaston, C. A.

Election of. II, p. 294, Apr., 1891

Reports by. II, pp. 296-298, Apr., 1891. IV, pp. vii-ix, Feb. 20, 1893

Kennan, George

Correspondence addressed to. I, p. ii, Oct., 1888

Election of. I, p. 165, Apr., 1889; p. 270, July, 1889. LXIX, p. 134, Jan., 1936

Report by. I, pp. 164-166, Apr., 1889

McGee, W J

Speech by. XIX, p. 69, Jan., 1908

McKnew, Thomas W.

Impressing the Society's seal on membership certificate. XC, ill. p. 39, July, 1946

Presentation of Hubbard Medal by President Truman to Gen. H. H. Arnold. LXXXIX, ill. p. 141, Feb., 1946

Newell, Frederick H.

Designated to fill vacancy of office of Recording Secretary (Dec., 1897). IX, p. 70, Feb., 1898

Election of. III, p. xii, Feb. 19, 1892. IV, p. xix, Feb. 20, 1893. IX, p. 416, Sept., 1898

Report by. IV, pp. xx-xxi, Feb. 20, 1893

Resignation of (Nov., 1893). V, p. ii, May 5, 1894

Resignation of (Oct., 1899). X, p. 474, Nov., 1899

Scidmore, Eliza Ruhamah

Elected Corresponding Secretary. III, p. xii, Feb. 19, 1892. IV, p. xix, Feb. 20, 1893. V, p. xix, May 5, 1894. IX, p. 416, Sept., 1898

Reports by. IV, pp. xx-xxi, Feb. 20, 1893. V, pp. xx-xxi, May 5, 1894

Stanley-Brown, Joseph

Election of. X, p. 475, Nov., 1899

NATIONAL GEOGRAPHIC SOCIETY—*Continued*

Secretary—*Continued*

Tittmann, O. H.

Election of. II, p. 68, Apr., 1890

Resignation of. II, p. 297, Apr., 1891

See also NGS: Rules; *and* names of NGS Secretaries, for Articles

Sequoia National Park:

The National Geographic Society Completes Its Gifts of Big Trees. XL, pp. 85-86, July, 1921
- Amount of funds subscribed..........85–86
- Area of purchase....................85–86
- Contributors to fund................. 85
- Fall, Albert B.: Letter acknowledging gift 86

Our Big Trees Saved. XXXI, pp. 1-11, 10 ills., Jan., 1917
- Letter from Gilbert H. Grosvenor to Secretary Lane announcing gift.......... 5, 7
- Letter from Secretary Lane acknowledging gift........................... 7
- Resolution of Board of Managers appropriating purchase fund............. 5
- Tablet, commemorating the Society, to be placed on one of the trees............ 7

Photograph of Sequoia National Park. LXIV, duotone pl. V, p. 21, July, 1933

Society's gift of Big Trees. LXVI, p. 231, Aug., 1934

Tablet commemorating Society's gift. XXXI, p. 7, Jan., 1917. LV, ill. pp. 719, 733, June, 1929. LXVI, ill. p. 225, Aug., 1934

Staff Members. *See* NGM: Editorial Department

Stratosphere Balloon:

Explorer II: LXXIX, p. 168, Feb., 1941. LXXXI, p. 471, Apr., 1942

See also NGS: Expeditions: Stratosphere

Supplements. *See* Map Index, *following this index; and* Pictorial Supplements: Enlargements and Panoramas

Translators. LXXXIV, p. 698, ill. p. 695, Dec., 1943

Treasurer:

Bell, Charles J.

Election of. I, p. 165, Apr., 1889; p. 270, July, 1889. II, p. 68, Apr., 1890; p. 294, Apr., 1891. III, p. xii, Feb. 19, 1892. IV, p. xix, Feb. 20, 1893. V, p. xix, May 5, 1894. VII, p. 216, June, 1896. LXIX, p. 134, Jan., 1936

Reports by. I, p. 163, Apr., 1889. II, p. 64, Apr., 1890; pp. 299-300, Apr., 1891. IV, pp. x-xi, xxii-xxiii, Feb. 20, 1893. V, pp. xxii-xxiii, May 5, 1894. VI, pp. xxvi-xxvii, Oct. 31, 1895

Tribute by Dr. Grosvenor. LXIX, p. 152, Jan., 1936

Edson, John Joy

Photograph of. LXV, ill. p. 790, June, 1934

Reports by. XIII, p. 80, Feb., 1902. XXI, pp. 89-90, Jan., 1910. XXII, p. 214, Feb., 1911. XXIV, p. 256, Feb., 1913

NATIONAL GEOGRAPHIC SOCIETY—*Continued*

Treasurer—*Continued*

Tribute by Dr. Grosvenor. LXIX, p. 162, Jan., 1936

Fleming, Robert V.

Elected in 1935. LXIX, p. 159, Jan., 1936

Presentation of Hubbard Medal by President Truman to Gen. H. H. Arnold. LXXXIX, ill. p. 141, Feb., 1946

Gannett, Henry

Election of. IX, p. 416, Sept., 1898

See also NGS: Rules; *and* names of NGS Treasurers

Vice-President:

Baker, Marcus

Election of. VII, p. 216, June, 1896

Bartlett, John R.

Election of. I, p. 165, Apr., 1889. LXIX, p. 134, Jan., 1936

Resignation of. I, p. 270, July, 1889

Batchelder, R. N.

Election of. IV, p. xix, Feb. 20, 1893

Dabney, Charles W., Jr.

Election of. VI, p. ii, Oct. 31, 1895

Dall, William H.

Election of. VII, p. 216, June, 1896

Dyer, George L.

Election of. I, p. 270, July, 1889

Gannett, Henry

Chairman of committee appointed to consider claims of Cook and Peary. XX, pp. 921, 922, 1008, Nov., 1909

Chairman of Research Committee. XX, p. 486, May, 1909

Elected member of Geographical Society of Paris. XVIII, p. 428, June, 1907

Election of. V, p. xix, May 5, 1894. XVI, p. 87, Feb., 1905

Gilbert, Grove Karl

Election of. VII, p. 216, June, 1896. XV, p. 176, Apr., 1904

Greely, A. W.

Election of. I, p. 165, Apr., 1889; p. 270, July, 1889. II, p. 68, Apr., 1890; p. 294, Apr., 1891. III, p. xii, Feb. 19, 1892. IV, p. xix, Feb. 20, 1893. V, p. xix, May 5, 1894. VII, p. 216, June, 1896. LXIX, p. 134, Jan., 1936

Hayden, Everett

Election of. II, p. 68, Apr., 1890; p. 294, Apr., 1891. III, p. xii, Feb. 19, 1892. IV, p. xix, Feb. 20, 1893

La Gorce, John Oliver

Expedition to the Bahamas. LXII, p. 452, Oct., 1932

Meteorological station, Antarctica, named for. LVIII, p. 184, ill. p. 193, Aug., 1930

Mountain, Alaskan, named for. XL, pp. 222, 287, Sept., 1921

NATIONAL GEOGRAPHIC SOCIETY—*Continued*

Vice-President—*Continued*

Photographs of. XLVIII, ill. p. 352, Sept., 1925. LVIII, ill. p. 230, Aug., 1930. LIX, ill. p. 2, Jan., 1931. LX, ill. p. 391, Oct., 1931. LXII, ill. p. 366, Sept., 1932. LXV, ill. p. 790, June, 1934. LXIX, ill. pp. 126, 133, 134, 156, 159, Jan., 1936. LXXXIV, ill. p. 336, Sept., 1943

Presentation of Hubbard Medal by President Truman to Gen. H. H. Arnold. LXXXIX, ill. p. 141, Feb., 1946

Tribute by Dr. Grosvenor. LXIX, pp. 152-153, Jan., 1936

McGee, W J

Election of. IX, p. 416, Sept., 1898

Photograph of. XII, ill. p. 354, Oct., 1901

Melville, George W.

Election of. V, p. xix, May 5, 1894

Mendenhall, T. C.

Election of. V, p. xix, May 5, 1894

Resignation of. VI, p. ii, Oct. 31, 1895

Merriam, C. Hart

Election of. I, p. 165, Apr., 1889; p. 270, July, 1889. II, p. 68, Apr., 1890; p. 294, Apr., 1891. III, p. xii, Feb. 19, 1892. IV, p. xix, Feb. 20, 1893. V, p. xix, May 5, 1894. VII, p. 216, June, 1896. LXIX, p. 134, Jan., 1936

Ogden, Herbert G.

Election of. I, p. 165, Apr., 1889; p. 270, July, 1889. II, p. 68, Apr., 1890; p. 294, Apr., 1891. III, p. xii, Feb. 19, 1892. IV, p. xix. Feb. 20, 1893. VII, p. 216, June, 1896. LXIX, p. 134, Jan., 1936

Pillsbury, John Elliott

Election of. XXVII, p. 218, Feb., 1915

Powell, W. B.

Election of. V, p. xix, May 5, 1894

Thompson, A. H.

Election of. I, p. 165, Apr., 1889; p. 270, July, 1889. II, p. 68, Apr., 1890. LXIX, p. 134, Jan., 1936

Tittmann, O. H.

Election of. XXI, p. 88, Jan., 1910

Speech by. XXIII, pp. 284, 287, Mar., 1912

See also NGS: Rules; *and* names of NGS Vice-Presidents

War Work:

World War I

An Appeal to Members of the National Geographic Society. XXXIII, pp. 347-348, ills., Apr., 1918

Bringing the World to Our Foreign Language Soldiers: How a Military Training Camp is Solving a Seemingly Unsurmountable Problem by Using the Geographic. By Christina Krysto. XXXIV, pp. 81-90, 4 ills., Aug., 1918

A Day With Our Boys in the Geographic Wards. By Carol Corey. XXXIV, pp. 69-80, 8 ills., July, 1918

NATIONAL GEOGRAPHIC SOCIETY—*Continued*

War Work—*Continued*

Maps published: *Map of the New Balkan States and Central Europe,* Aug., 1914; *Map of the Western Theatre of War,* May, 1918. LXIX, p. 155, Jan., 1936

The National Geographic Society in War Time. By Major-General A. W. Greely. XXXIII, pp. 369-375, 5 ills., Apr., 1918
- Liberty Loan investment...........372–373
- National Geographic wards..........373, 375
- President Wilson's suggestions regarding the Society's war work............. 369
- Society's war work directed by Gilbert Grosvenor 375
- U.S. Military Hospitals......ill. pp. 370, 371, 372, 373
- War Savings Stamp club............. 373

Practical Patriotism. XXXII, pp. 279-280, Sept., 1917; p. 476, Nov.-Dec., 1917
- Addressing Department, NGS, donates services 279
- American Red Cross campaign aided by.. 279
- Food conservation promoted............ 280
- Liberty Loan campaigns aided by....279, 280
- National Geographic Society Ward...... 280
- Patriotic flag number of the Magazine 279, 280
- Red Cross work by members of staff.... 279
- Subscriptions donated to Army and Navy 280

The Spirit of the Geographic. XXXIV, pp. 434-440, 4 ills., Nov., 1918
- Contributions received.........434–435, 437
- Geographic wards.........434–435, 437, 440
- Message from a soldier in a Geographic ward 440

World War II

Army, Navy, Government Departments, and private organizations use the Society's maps, photographs, and publications. LXXXI, p. 333, Mar., 1942. LXXXII, p. 767, Dec., 1942. LXXXIII, p. 265, Feb., 1943; p. 482, Apr., 1943; pp. 763, 766, ill. p. 763, June, 1943. LXXXIV, pp. 288, 289, ill. p. 274, Sept., 1943. LXXXV, p. 83, ill. p. 93, Jan., 1944; p. 415, Apr., 1944. LXXXVI, pp. 66-67, 71, 72, ill. p. 69, July, 1944; p. 263, ill. p. 279, Sept., 1944; p. 450, ill. p. 450, Oct., 1944. LXXXVIII, ill. p. 7, July, 1945; pp. 709, 753, Dec., 1945

Blood donors. LXXXIV, ill. p. 610, Nov., 1943

Your Society Aids War Effort. LXXXIII, pp. 277-278, ill., Feb., 1943

The **Work** of the National Geographic Society. (By W J McGee). VII, pp. 253-259, Aug., 1896
- Character of the Society.............. 253
- Development of geography............. 253
- Future of geography.................. 255
- Purposes and methods of the Society.... 256

The **NATIONAL** Geographic Society and Geographic Work. XX, pp. 485-487, May, 1909

The **NATIONAL** Geographic Society and Its Magazine. By Gilbert Grosvenor. LXIX, pp. 123-164, 24 ills., Jan., 1936

The **NATIONAL** Geographic Society's Map of Northeastern United States. Text with map supplement. LXXXVIII, pp. 361-362, Sept., 1945

The **NATIONAL** Geographic Society's Notable Year. XXXVII, pp. 338-345, ills., Apr., 1920

NATIONAL Growth and National Character. By W J McGee. X, pp. 185-206, June, 1899

NATIONAL MONUMENTS:

Among the "Craters of the Moon": An Account of the First Expeditions Through the Remarkable Volcanic Lava Beds of Southern Idaho. By R. W. Limbert. XLV, pp. 303-328, 23 ills., map, Mar., 1924

Note: Craters of the Moon became a national monument, May 2, 1924

Arizona Sands, Home of the Cactus King. 11 ills. LXXI, pp. 521-528, Apr., 1937

Bats of the Carlsbad Cavern (New Mexico). By Vernon Bailey. XLVIII, pp. 321-330, 11 ills., Sept., 1925

Bursts of Color in Sculptured Utah. 22 ills. in color. LXIX, pp. 593-616, May, 1936

Colossal Natural Bridges of Utah. XV, pp. 367-369, ills., Sept., 1904

Everyday Life in Pueblo Bonito: As Disclosed by the National Geographic Society's Archeologic Explorations in the Chaco Canyon National Monument, New Mexico. By Neil M. Judd. XLVIII, pp. 227-262, 37 ills., map, Sept., 1925

The Great Natural Bridges of Utah. XVIII, pp. 199-204, 3 ills., Mar., 1907

The Great Natural Bridges of Utah. By Byron Cummings. XXI, pp. 157-167, 7 ills., Feb., 1910

The Great Rainbow Natural Bridge of Southern Utah. By Joseph E. Pogue. XXII, pp. 1048-1056, 6 ills., Nov., 1911

New Discoveries in Carlsbad Cavern (New Mexico): Vast Subterranean Chambers with Spectacular Decorations Are Explored, Surveyed, and Photographed. By Willis T. Lee. XLVIII, pp. 301-319, 19 ills., map, Sept., 1925

Note: Carlsbad Caverns a national monument from 1923 to 1930, when it became a national park

New Mexico Melodrama. By Frederick Simpich. LXXIII, pp. 529-569, 19 ills. in black and white, 25 ills. in color, two-page map, May, 1938

Included: Aztec Ruins; Bandelier; El Morro; Pueblo Bonito; White Sands

A New National Geographic Society Expedition: Ruins of Chaco Canyon, New Mexico, Nature-Made Treasure-Chest of Aboriginal American History, To Be Excavated and Studied; Work Begins This Month. XXXIX, pp. 637-643, 7 ills., June, 1921

Our Greatest National Monument: The National Geographic Society Completes Its Explorations in the Valley of Ten Thousand Smokes. By Robert F. Griggs. XL, pp. 219-292, 73 ills. in black and white, 16 ills. in color, maps, Sept., 1921

Our National Parks. By L. F. Schmeckebier. XXIII, pp. 531-579, 41 ills., map, June, 1912

Photographing the Marvels of the West in Colors. By Fred Payne Clatworthy. LIII, pp. 694-719, 30 ills. in color, June, 1928

NATIONAL MONUMENTS—*Continued*

The Pueblo Bonito Expedition of the National Geographic Society. By Neil M. Judd. XLI, pp. 323-331, 10 ills., diagr., Mar., 1922

The Recent Eruption of Katmai Volcano in Alaska. By George C. Martin. XXIV, pp. 131-181, 45 ills., diagr., map, Feb., 1913

The Saguaro Forest (Arizona). By H. L. Shantz. LXXI, pp. 515-532, 18 ills., Apr., 1937

The Scenery of North America. By James Bryce. XLI, pp. 339-389, 45 ills., Apr., 1922

The Ten Thousand Smokes Now a National Monument: The President of the United States Sets Aside for the American People the Extraordinary Valley Discovered and Explored by the National Geographic Society. XXXV, pp. 359-366, 5 ills., Apr., 1919

The Valley of Ten Thousand Smokes: An Account of the Discovery and Exploration of the Most Wonderful Volcanic Region in the World. By Robert F. Griggs. XXXIII, pp. 115-169, 46 ills., map, panorama, Feb., 1918

The Valley of Ten Thousand Smokes: National Geographic Society's Explorations in the Katmai District of Alaska. By Robert F. Griggs. XXXI, pp. 13-68, 51 ills., map, Jan., 1917

A Visit to Carlsbad Cavern: Recent Explorations of a Limestone Cave in the Guadalupe Mountains of New Mexico Reveal a Natural Wonder of the First Magnitude. By Willis T. Lee. XLV, pp. 1-40, 42 ills., Jan., 1924

Volcanoes of Alaska (Report by Capt. K. W. Perry on the Eruption of Mt. Katmai in June, 1912). XXIII, pp. 824-832, 11 ills., Aug., 1912

The Wheeler National Monument. XX, pp. 837-840, 4 ills., Sept., 1909

The White Sands of Alamogordo (New Mexico): A Dry Ocean of Granular Gypsum Billows Under Desert Winds in a New National Playground. By Carl P. Russell. LXVIII, pp. 250-264, 12 ills., Aug., 1935

See also Chesapeake and Ohio Canal

NATIONAL PARKS:

Among the Big Trees of California. By John R. White. LXVI, pp. 219-232, 14 ills., Aug., 1934

Bursts of Color in Sculptured Utah. 22 ills. in color. LXIX, pp. 593-616, May, 1936

Crater Lake and Yosemite Through the Ages. By Wallace W. Atwood, Jr. Paintings by Eugene Kingman. LXXI, pp. 327-343, 7 ills. in black and white, 13 ills. in color, Mar., 1937

Fabulous Yellowstone: Even Stranger Than the Tales of Early Trappers is the Truth About This Steaming Wonderland. By Frederick G. Vosburgh. LXXVII, pp. 769-794, 15 ills. in black and white, 9 ills. in color, map, June, 1940

First National Park East of Mississippi River (Mount Desert Island). XXIX, pp. 623-626, 5 ills., June, 1916

A Game Country Without Rival in America: The Proposed Mount McKinley National Park. By Stephen R. Capps. XXXI, pp. 69-84, 14 ills., map, Jan., 1917

The Grand Canyon Bridge. By Harriet Chalmers Adams. XXXIX, pp. 645-650, 6 ills., June, 1921

NATIONAL PARKS—*Continued*

The Great White Monarch of the Pacific Northwest (Mount Rainier). By A. H. Barnes. XXIII, pp. 593-626, 31 ills., map, June, 1912

Indiana's Unrivaled Sand-Dunes—A National Park Opportunity. By Orpheus Moyer Schantz. XXXV, pp. 430-441, 18 ills., May, 1919

The Land of the Best (U. S.). By Gilbert H. Grosvenor. XXIX, pp. 327-430, 71 ills. in black and white, 33 ills. in color, pictorial supplement, Apr., 1916

A Mind's-Eye Map of America. By Franklin K. Lane. XXXVII, pp. 479-518, 25 ills. in black and white, 8 ills. in color, June, 1920

The National Geographic Society Completes Its Gifts of Big Trees. XL, pp. 85-86, July, 1921

Nature's Scenic Marvels of the West. 17 ills. in duotone. LXIV, pp. 17-32, July, 1933

A New National Park (Glacier National Park). By Guy Elliott Mitchell. XXI, pp. 215-223, 6 ills., Mar., 1910

Our Big Trees Saved. XXXI, pp. 1-11, 10 ills., Jan., 1917

Our National Parks. By L. F. Schmeckebier. XXIII, pp. 531-579, 41 ills., map, June, 1912

A Patriotic Pilgrimage to Eastern National Parks: History and Beauty Live Along Paved Roads, Once Indian Trails, Through Virginia, North Carolina, Tennessee, Kentucky, and West Virginia. By Leo A. Borah. LXV, pp. 663-702, 18 ills. in black and white, 28 ills. in color, two-page map, June, 1934

Peaks and Parks of Western Canada. 11 photos: 5 by W. J. Oliver. LXXX, pp. 516-526, Oct., 1941

Photographing the Marvels of the West in Colors. By Fred Payne Clatworthy. LIII, pp. 694-719, 30 ills. in color, June, 1928

Rambling Around the Roof of Eastern America (Great Smoky Mountains). By Leonard C. Roy. LXX, pp. 243-266, 25 ills., map, Aug., 1936

The Scenery of North America. By James Bryce. XLI, pp. 339-389, 45 ills., Apr., 1922

Scenic Glories of Western United States. 12 color photos by Fred Payne Clatworthy. LVI, pp. 223-230, Aug., 1929

Surveying the Grand Canyon of the Colorado: An Account of the 1923 Boating Expedition of the United States Geological Survey. By Lewis R. Freeman. XLV, pp. 471-548, 62 ills., map, May, 1924

The Unique Island of Mount Desert. By George B. Dorr, Ernest Howe Forbush, M. L. Fernald. XXVI, pp. 75-89, 7 ills., July, 1914

Western National Parks Invite America Out of Doors. 17 photos in duotone by G. A. Grant, W. M. Rush, Merl La Voy, J. S. Dixon. LXVI, pp. 65-80, July, 1934

Western Views in the Land of the Best (U. S.). 16 color photos by Fred Payne Clatworthy. XLIII, pp. 405-420, Apr., 1923

The Wonderland of California. By Herman Whitaker. XXVIII, pp. 57-99, 34 ills., July, 1915

A Wonderland of Glaciers and Snow (Mount Rainier National Park). By Milnor Roberts. XX, pp. 530-537, 8 ills., June, 1909

See also National Monuments

NATIONAL TRUST FOR PLACES OF HISTORIC INTEREST OR NATURAL BEAUTY:

The Preservation of England's Historic and Scenic Treasures. By Eric Underwood. LXXXVII, pp. 413-440, 24 ills., two-page map, Apr., 1945

The **NATION'S** Capital (Washington, D. C.). By James Bryce. XXIV, pp. 717-750, 26 ills., June, 1913

The **NATION'S** Capital by Night (Washington, D. C.). By Volkmar Wentzel. With 16 photos in duotone by author. LXXVII, pp. 514-530, Apr., 1940

The **NATION'S** Pride (Natural Resources). By Franklin K. Lane. XXVIII, pp. 589-606, 6 ills., Dec., 1915

The **NATION'S** Undeveloped Resources. By Franklin K. Lane. XXV, pp. 183-225, 32 ills., Feb., 1914

The **NATIVE** Oysters of the West Coast. By Robert E. C. Stearns. XIX, pp. 224-226, Mar., 1908

A **NATIVE** Son's Rambles in Oregon. By Amos Burg. LXV, pp. 173-234, 39 ills. in black and white, 24 ills. in color, two-page map, Feb., 1934

NATURAL BRIDGES. *See* Bridges, Natural

NATURAL-COLOR photograph of 1936 eclipse, showing the corona. By Irvine C. Gardner. LXXI, ill. p. 178, Feb., 1937

NATURAL-COLOR photograph of 1937 eclipse, showing the corona. By Irvine C. Gardner. LXXIII, ill. p. 756, June, 1938

NATURAL-GAS, Oil, and Coal Supply of the United States. XV, p. 186, Apr., 1904

NATURAL HISTORY:

What the Fighting Yanks See. By Wanda Burnett. LXXXVI, pp. 451-476, 27 ills., Oct., 1944

Wildlife of Tabasco and Veracruz (Mexico). By Walter A. Weber. With 19 ills. in color from paintings by author. LXXXVII, pp. 187-216, 7 ills. in black and white, map, Feb., 1945

See also Biology; Birds; Crustaceans; Fishes and Fisheries; Flowers; Geographic Distribution of Life; Geology; Insects; Mammals; Marine Biology; Minerals; Mollusks; Paleontology; Plants; Reptiles; Trees; Wildlife

A **NATURALIST** with MacMillan in the Arctic. By Walter N. Koelz. XLIX, pp. 299-318, 22 ills. in color, Mar., 1926

A **NATURALIST'S** Journey Around Vera Cruz and Tampico. By Frank M. Chapman. XXV, pp. 533-562, 31 ills., May, 1914

NATURE and Man in Ethiopia. By Wilfred H. Osgood. LIV, pp. 121-176, 64 ills., map, Aug., 1928

NATURE Paints New Mexico. 25 color photos by Richard H. Stewart. LXXIII, pp. 537-568, May, 1938

NATURE'S Ingenious Spinners (Spiders). 64 ills. in color from paintings by Hashime Murayama. LXIV, pp. 167-174, Aug., 1933

NATURE'S Most Amazing Mammal: Elephants, Unique Among Animals, Have Many Human Qualities When Wild That Make Them Foremost Citizens of Zoo and Circus. By Edmund Heller. LXV, pp. 729-759, 37 ills., June, 1934

NATURE'S Most Dramatic Spectacle (Eclipse). By S. A. Mitchell. LXXII, pp. 361-376, 16 ills., map, Sept., 1937

NATURE'S Scenic Marvels of the West. 17 ills. in duotone. LXIV, pp. 17-32, July, 1933

NATURE'S Transformation at Panama: Remarkable Changes in Faunal and Physical Conditions in the Gatun Lake Region. By George Shiras, 3d. XXVIII, pp. 159-194, 33 ills., maps, Aug., 1915

NAURU, the Richest Island in the South Seas. By Rosamond Dodson Rhone. XL, pp. 559-589, 24 ills., Dec., 1921

NAVAJO INDIAN RESERVATION, Utah-Arizona:

Flaming Cliffs of Monument Valley. By Lt. Jack Breed, USNR. With 9 color photos by author and Warren T. Mithoff. LXXXVIII, pp. 452-461, Oct., 1945

NAVAJO MOUNTAIN, Utah:

Encircling Navajo Mountain with a Pack-Train: An Expedition to a Hitherto Untraversed Region of Our Southwest Discovers a New Route to Rainbow Natural Bridge. By Charles L. Bernheimer. XLIII, pp. 197-224, 33 ills., map, Feb., 1923

NAVAJOS (Indians):

Flaming Cliffs of Monument Valley. By Lt. Jack Breed, USNR. With 9 color photos by author and Warren T. Mithoff. LXXXVIII, pp. 452-461, Oct., 1945

Indian Tribes of Pueblo Land. By Matthew W. Stirling. Paintings by W. Langdon Kihn. LXXVIII, pp. 549-596, 16 ills. in black and white, 25 ills. in color, Nov., 1940

New Mexico Melodrama. By Frederick Simpich. LXXIII, pp. 529-569, 19 ills. in black and white, 25 ills. in color, two-page map, May, 1938

NAVAL AFRICA EXPEDITION:

Transporting a Navy Through the Jungles of Africa in War Time. By Frank J. Magee. XLII, pp. 331-362, 31 ills., Oct., 1922

NAVAL AIR TRANSPORT SERVICE:

Flying Our Wounded Veterans Home. By Catherine Bell Palmer. LXXXVIII, pp. 363-384, 17 ills., Sept., 1945

The **NAVAL** Flags of the World. By Byron McCandless and Gilbert Grosvenor. XXXII, text, p. 369; 214 ills. in color, Oct., 1917

NAVARRO, DON JUAN N.:

Mexico of Today. By Dr. Don Juan N. Navarro. XII, pp. 152-157, Apr., 1901; pp. 176-179, May, 1901; pp. 235-238, June, 1901

NAVASSA ISLAND, West Indies:

An Important New Guide for Shipping: Navassa Light, on a Barren Island in the West Indies, is the First Signal for the Panama Canal. By George R. Putnam. XXXIV, pp. 401-406, 3 ills., map, Nov., 1918

NAVIGATING the "Norge" from Rome to the North Pole and Beyond: The Designer and Pilot of the First Dirigible to Fly Over the Top of the World Describes a Thrilling Voyage of More Than 8,000 Miles. By General Umberto Nobile. LII, pp. 177-215, 36 ills., map, Aug., 1927

NAVIGATION:

The Compass in Modern Navigation. By G. W. Littlehales. VIII, pp. 266-272, Sept., 1897

The Heavens Above: On Land, Sea, and in the Air the Stars Serve Modern Man as Map, Compass, and Clock. By Donald H. Menzel. With 12 charts, designed by author, showing star positions for each month, and 13 drawings of the constellations by Carlotta Gonzales Lahey. LXXXIV, pp. 97-128, map, July, 1943

Revealing Earth's Mightiest Ocean (Pacific). By Albert W. Atwood. LXXXIV, pp. 291-306, 10 ills., map supplement, Sept., 1943

See also U. S. Bureau of Navigation

NAVIGATORS. *See* Discoverers, Explorers, and Navigators

A **NAVY** Artist Paints the Aleutians. By Mason Sutherland. Paintings by Lt. William F. Draper. LXXXIV, pp. 157-176, 4 ills. in black and white, 16 ills. in color, Aug., 1943

NAVY Wings over the Pacific. 12 ills. in color from U. S. Navy official photos. LXXXVI, pp. 241-248, Aug., 1944

NAYARIT (State), Mexico:

Along the Old Spanish Road in Mexico: Life Among the People of Nayarit and Jalisco, Two of the Richest States of the Southern Republic. By Herbert Corey. XLIII, pp. 225-281, 36 ills. in black and white, 16 ills. in color, map, Mar., 1923

NEALLEY, GEORGE TRUE:

Recent Bequests by Members of the National Geographic Society. XLIX, p. 474, Apr., 1926

NEAPOLITAN Blues and Imperial Purple of Roman Italy. 12 color photos by Hans Hildenbrand, Luigi Pellerano, Gervais Courtellemont. LXVI, pp. 203-210, Aug., 1934

NEAR EAST:

American Alma Maters in the Near East. By Maynard Owen Williams. LXXXVIII, pp. 237-256, 16 ills., Aug., 1945

New Map of Europe and the Near East. Text with map supplement. LXXXIII, pp. 762-763, ill., June, 1943

See also Balkan Peninsula; names of countries; *and* Map Index, *following this index*

NEAREST the Pole (Commander Robert E. Peary's Address to the Society). XVIII, pp. 446-450, July, 1907

NEBAJ, Guatemala:

To Market in Guatemala. By Luis Marden. With 19 color photos by Giles Greville Healey and Charles S. Pineo. LXXXVIII, pp. 87-104, July, 1945

NEBRASKA:

Nebraska, the Cornhusker State. By Leo A. Borah. LXXXVII, pp. 513-542, 6 ills. in black and white, 23 ills. in color, map, May, 1945

Taming the Outlaw Missouri River. By Frederick Simpich. LXXXVIII, pp. 569-598, 25 ills., two-page map, Nov., 1945

NEDJEF. *See* Najaf

The **NEED** of Conserving the Beauty and Freedom of Nature in Modern Life. By Charles W. Eliot. XXVI, pp. 67-74, 4 ills., July, 1914

NEEDHAM, JAMES G.:

An Insect Community Lives in Flower Heads. By James G. Needham. XC, pp. 340-356, 5 ills. in black and white, 11 ills. in color, Sept., 1946

The **NEEDS** Abroad. By Ian Malcolm. XXXI, pp. 427-433, 5 ills., May, 1917

NEILLIE, C. R.:

Fighting Insects With Airplanes: An Account of the Successful Use of the Flying-Machine in Dusting Tall Trees Infested With Leaf-Eating Caterpillars. By C. R. Neillie and J. S. Houser. XLI, pp. 333-338, 6 ills., Mar., 1922

NEJD. *See* Saudi Arabia

NELSON, E. W.:

Awarded Jane M. Smith Life Membership. XXXVII, p. 342, Apr., 1920

Bird Banding, the Telltale of Migratory Flight: A Modern Method of Learning the Flight-Ways and Habits of Birds. By E. W. Nelson. LIII, pp. 91-131, 49 ills., map, Jan., 1928

A Land of Drought and Desert—Lower California: Two Thousand Miles on Horseback Through the Most Extraordinary Cacti Forests in the World. By E. W. Nelson. XXII, pp. 443-474, 25 ills., maps, May, 1911

The Larger North American Mammals. By E. W. Nelson. Paintings by Louis Agassiz Fuertes. XXX, pp. 385-472, 24 ills. in black and white, 49 ills. in color, pictorial supplement, Nov., 1916

Notes on the Wild Fowl and Game Animals of Alaska. By E. W. Nelson. IX, pp. 121-132, 6 ills., Apr., 1898

The Rat Pest: The Labor of 200,000 Men in the United States Required to Support Rats, Man's Most Destructive and Dangerous Enemy. By Edward W. Nelson. XXXII, pp. 1-23, 21 ills., July, 1917

Smaller Mammals of North America. By E. W. Nelson. Paintings by Louis Agassiz Fuertes. XXXIII, pp. 371*-493, 29 ills. in black and white, 59 ills. in color, May, 1918

A Winter Expedition in Southwestern Mexico. By E. W. Nelson. XV, pp. 341-356, 14 ills., Sept., 1904

A Winter Weather Record from the Klondike Region. By E. W. Nelson. VIII, pp. 327-335, tables, Nov., 1897

NELSON, WILBUR A.:

Reelfoot—An Earthquake Lake (Tennessee). By Wilbur A. Nelson. XLV, pp. 95-114, 20 ills., Jan., 1924

NEPAL:

The Aërial Conquest of Everest: Flying Over the World's Highest Mountain Realizes the Objective of Many Heroic Explorers. By Lieut. Col. L. V. S. Blacker. LXIV, pp. 127-162, 35 ills., map, Aug., 1933

Nepal: A Little-Known Kingdom. By John Claude White. XXXVIII, pp. 245-283, 32 ills., map, Oct., 1920

Nepal, the Sequestered Kingdom. By Penelope Chetwode. LXVII, pp. 319-352, 27 ills. in black and white, 15 ills. in color, map, Mar., 1935

NERVION RIVER, Spain:

The Land of the Basques: Home of a Thrifty, Picturesque People, Who Take Pride in the Sobriquet, "The Yankees of Spain." By Harry A. McBride. XLI, pp. 63-87, 25 ills., map, Jan., 1922

NET Results from Oceania: Collecting Aquarium Specimens in Tropical Pacific Waters. By Walter H. Chute. LXXIX, pp. 347-372, 8 ills. in black and white, 24 ills. in color, Mar., 1941

NETHERLANDS:

As Seen from a Dutch Window. By James Howard Gore. XIX, pp. 619-634, 8 ills., Sept., 1908

Behind Netherlands Sea Ramparts: Dikes and Pumps Keep Ocean and Rivers at Bay While a Busy People Carries on Peacetime Work. By McFall Kerbey. LXXVII, pp. 255-290, 26 ills. in black and white, 11 ills. in duotone, map, Feb., 1940

The Citizen Army of Holland. By Henrik Willem Van Loon. XXIX, pp. 609-622, 9 ills., June, 1916

The City of Jacqueline (Goes). By Florence Craig Albrecht. XXVII, pp. 29-56, 31 ills., Jan., 1915

The Dikes of Holland. By Gerard H. Matthes. XII, pp. 219-234, 3 ills., 7 charts, June, 1901

Glimpses of Holland. By William Wisner Chapin. XXVII, pp. 1-29, 26 ills., Jan., 1915

Holland Rises from War and Water. By Thomas R. Henry. LXXXIX, pp. 237-260, 18 ills., map, Feb., 1946

Holland's War with the Sea. By James Howard Gore. XLIII, pp. 283-325, 39 ills., map, Mar., 1923

Low Countries Await Liberation. 10 ills. LXXXVI, pp. 221-228, Aug., 1944

Mending Dikes in the Netherlands. 20 photos by Lawrence Earl. XC, pp. 791-806, Dec., 1946

A New Country Awaits Discovery: The Draining of the Zuider Zee Makes Room for the Excess Population of the Netherlands. By J. C. M. Kruisinga. LXIV, pp. 293-320, 20 ills. in black and white, 13 ills. in color, maps, Sept., 1933

A North Holland Cheese Market. By Hugh M. Smith. XXI, pp. 1051-1066, 17 ills., Dec., 1910

The Races of Europe. By Edwin A. Grosvenor. XXXIV, pp. 441-534, 62 ills., diagr. and index, maps, map supplement, Dec., 1918

NETHERLANDS—*Continued*

Rediscovering the Rhine: A Trip by Barge from the Sea to the Headwaters of Europe's Storied Stream. By Melville Chater. XLVIII, pp. 1-43, 44 ills., July, 1925

The Singing Towers of Holland and Belgium. By William Gorham Rice. XLVII, pp. 357-376, 22 ills., Mar., 1925

Some Odd Pages from the Annals of the Tulip: A "Made" Flower of Unknown Origin Took Medieval Europe by Storm and Caused a Financial Panic in the Netherlands. By Leo A. Borah. LXIV, pp. 321-343, 13 ills. in black and white, 10 ills. in color, Sept., 1933

A Vacation in Holland. By George Alden Sanford. LVI, pp. 363-378, 6 ills. in black and white, 8 ills. in color, map, Sept., 1929

NETHERLANDS EAST INDIES:

Around the World for Animals. By William M. and Lucile Q. Mann. LXXIII, pp. 665-714, 33 ills. in black and white, 23 ills. in color, map, June, 1938

The Face of the Netherlands Indies. 20 photos by Maynard Owen Williams and others. LXXXIX, pp. 261-276, Feb., 1946

From London to Australia by Aëroplane: A Personal Narrative of the First Aërial Voyage Half Around the World. By Sir Ross Smith. XXXIX, pp. 229-339, 76 ills. in black and white, 8 ills. in color, map, Mar., 1921

The Greatest Voyage in the Annals of the Sea. By J. R. Hildebrand. LXII, pp. 699-739, 35 ills., maps, Dec., 1932

See also Bali; Borneo; Celebes; Java; Komodo; Krakatau; Moluccas; Netherlands New Guinea; Nias; Sumatra; Timor

NETHERLANDS Indies: Patchwork of Peoples. 23 color photos by Maynard Owen Williams. LXXIII, pp. 681-712, June, 1938

NETHERLANDS NEW GUINEA:

Further Notes on Dutch New Guinea. By Thomas Barbour. XIX, pp. 527-545, 19 ills., Aug., 1908

New Guinea's Mountain and Swampland Dwellers. By Col. Ray T. Elsmore. LXXXVIII, pp. 671-694, 15 ills. in black and white, 7 ills. in color, map, Dec., 1945

Notes on a Zoological Collecting Trip to Dutch New Guinea. By Thomas Barbour. XIX, pp. 469-484, 12 ills., maps, July, 1908

Unknown New Guinea: Circumnavigating the World in a Flying Boat, American Scientists Discover a Valley of 60,000 People Never Before Seen by White Men. By Richard Archbold. LXXIX, pp. 315-344, 28 ills., map, Mar., 1941

NETHERLANDS WEST INDIES. *See* Aruba; Bonaire; Curaçao; Saba

NEVADA:

The California and Nevada Boundary. (By C. H. Sinclair). X, pp. 416-417, Oct., 1899

The Deserts of Nevada and the Death Valley. By Robert H. Chapman. XVII, pp. 483-497, 9 ills., map, Sept., 1906

The Development of Nevada. XV, p. 166, Apr., 1904

NEVADA—*Continued*

Nevada, Desert Treasure House. By W. Robert Moore. LXXXIX, pp. 1-38, 16 ills. in black and white, 20 ills. in color, map, Jan., 1946

A Plague of Mice (Abstracted from "The Nevada Mouse Plague of 1907-08"). XX, pp. 479-485, 7 ills., May, 1909

Studies on the Rate of Evaporation at Reno, Nevada, and in the Salton Sink. By Professor Frank H. Bigelow. XIX, pp. 20-28, 5 ills., Jan., 1908

Sulphur Mine in Nevada. XV, p. 498, Dec., 1904

NEVILS, W. COLEMAN:

Augustus—Emperor and Architect: Two Thousand Years Ago Was Born the Physically Frail But Spiritually Great Roman Who Became the Master of His World. By W. Coleman Nevils. LXXIV, pp. 535-556, 17 ills., map, Oct., 1938

Horace—Classic Poet of the Countryside. By W. Coleman Nevils. LXVIII, pp. 771-795, 22 ills., map, Dec., 1935

The Perennial Geographer: After 2,000 Years Vergil Is Still the Most Widely Read of Latin Poets—First to Popularize the Geography of the Roman Empire. By W. Coleman Nevils. LVIII, pp. 439-465, 29 ills., Oct., 1930

The Smallest State in the World: Vatican City on Its 108 Acres Is a Complete Sovereignty Internationally Recognized. By W. Coleman Nevils. LXXV, pp. 377-412, 37 ills., two-page map, Mar., 1939

A **NEW** Alphabet of the Ancients Is Unearthed: An Inconspicuous Mound in Northern Syria Yields Archeological Treasures of Far-reaching Significance. By F. A. Schaeffer. LVIII, pp. 477-516, 47 ills., map, Oct., 1930

NEW BRITAIN (Island), Bismarck Archipelago:

The Islands of the Pacific. By J. P. Thomson. XL, pp. 543-558, 15 ills., map supplement, Dec., 1921

The **NEW** British Empire of the Sudan. By Herbert L. Bridgman. XVII, pp. 241-267, 32 ills., map, May, 1906

NEW BRUNSWICK (Province), Canada:

All Around the Bay of Passamaquoddy. By Albert S. Gatschet. VIII, pp. 16-24, Jan., 1897

New Brunswick Down by the Sea. By Lawrence J. Burpee. LXXIX, pp. 595-614, 14 ills., map, May, 1941

NEW CALEDONIA (Island), South Pacific Ocean:

At Ease in the South Seas. By Maj. Frederick Simpich, Jr. LXXXV, pp. 79-104, 32 ills., Jan., 1944

Jungle War: Bougainville and New Caledonia. 17 ills. in color from paintings by Lieut. William F. Draper. LXXXV, pp. 417-432, Apr., 1944

Treasure Islands of Australasia: New Guinea, New Caledonia, and Fiji Trace across the South Pacific a Fertile Crescent Incredibly Rich in Minerals and Foods. By Douglas L. Oliver. LXXXI, pp. 691-722, 23 ills., two-page map, June, 1942

NEW CALEDONIA (Island), South Pacific Ocean—*Continued*

War Awakened New Caledonia: Swift Changes Take Place on the South Pacific Island of Mineral Wealth Defended by Free French and American Troops. By Enzo de Chetelat. LXXXII, pp. 31-55, 14 ills. in black and white, 12 ills. in color, map, July, 1942

Yank Meets Native. By Wanda Burnett. LXXXVIII, pp. 105-128, 24 ills., July, 1945

NEW China and the Printed Page. By Paul Hutchinson. LI, pp. 687-722, 37 ills., June, 1927

The **NEW** Cone of Mont Pelée. XIV, pp. 422-423, ills., Nov., 1903

A **NEW** Country Awaits Discovery: The Draining of the Zuider Zee Makes Room for the Excess Population of the Netherlands. By J. C. M. Kruisinga. LXIV, pp. 293-320, 20 ills. in black and white, 13 ills. in color, maps, Sept., 1933

NEW DELHI, India:

New Delhi Goes Full Time. By Maynard Owen Williams. LXXXII, pp. 465-494, 17 ills. in black and white, 13 ills. in color, map, Oct., 1942

NEW Discoveries in Carlsbad Cavern (New Mexico): Vast Subterranean Chambers with Spectacular Decorations Are Explored, Surveyed, and Photographed. By Willis T. Lee. XLVIII, pp. 301-319, 19 ills., map, Sept., 1925

NEW ENGLAND (Region), U. S.:

Cape Cod People and Places. By Wanda Burnett. LXXXIX, pp. 737-774, 17 ills. in black and white, 24 ills. in color, map, June, 1946

From Notch to Notch in the White Mountains: Soaring Heights of New Hampshire Attract Multitudes to America's Oldest Mountain Recreation Area. By Leonard Cornell Roy. LXXII, pp. 73-104, 30 ills., map supplement, July, 1937

The Geography of a Hurricane: A Doughnut-shaped Storm Turned Back Time in New England to Candlelight Days, but Revealed Anew Yankee Courage and Ingenuity. By F. Barrows Colton. LXXV, pp. 529-552, 20 ills., map, Apr., 1939

Gomez and the New York Gulf. (By L. D. Scisco). IX, pp. 371-373, Aug., 1898

The Improvement of Geographical Teaching. By Professor William Morris Davis. V, pp. 68-75, July 10, 1893

The Long River of New England: In War and Peace, from Mountain Wilderness to the Sea, Flows the Connecticut River, Through a Valley Abounding in History, Scenery, Inventive Genius, and Industry. By Albert W. Atwood. LXXXIII, pp. 401-434, 12 ills. in black and white, 24 ills. in color, map, Apr., 1943

New England Ski Trails: Snow and Ice Sports Transform Whittier's Winters of Snowbound Seclusion Into Seasons of Outdoor Recreation. By Daniel Rochford. LXX, pp. 645-664, 11 ills. in black and white, 13 ills. in color, Nov., 1936

New England's Wonderland of Mountain, Lake, and Seascape. 14 color photos by Clifton Adams. LX, pp. 263-270, Sept., 1931

NEW ENGLAND (Region), U. S.—*Continued*

Northeast of Boston. By Albert W. Atwood. LXXXVIII, pp. 257-292, 12 ills. in black and white, 17 ills. in color, map supplement, Sept., 1945

See also Connecticut; Maine; Massachusetts; New Hampshire; Rhode Island; Vermont

NEW England's Wonderland of Mountain, Lake, and Seascape. 14 color photos by Clifton Adams. LX, pp. 263-270, Sept., 1931

The **NEW** English Province of Northern Nigeria. XV, pp. 433-442, 9 ills., Nov., 1904

The **NEW** Erie Canal. XVI, pp. 568-570, map, Dec., 1905

NEW French Ocean Cables. XII, pp. 315-316, Aug., 1901

NEW Frontier in the Sky. By F. Barrows Colton. XC, pp. 379-408, 28 ills., diagr., Sept., 1946

NEW GEORGIA (Island), Solomon Islands. *See* Munda

NEW Greece, the Centenarian, Forges Ahead. By Maynard Owen Williams. LVIII, pp. 649-721, 51 ills. in black and white, 40 ills. in color, map, Dec., 1930

NEW GUINEA:

Further Notes on Dutch New Guinea. By Thomas Barbour. XIX, pp. 527-545, 19 ills., Aug., 1908

Into Primeval Papua by Seaplane: Seeking Disease-resisting Sugar Cane, Scientists Find Neolithic Man in Unmapped Nooks of Sorcery and Cannibalism. By E. W. Brandes. LVI, pp. 253-332, 98 ills., map, Sept., 1929

The Islands of the Pacific. By J. P. Thomson. XL, pp. 543-558, 15 ills., map supplement, Dec., 1921

New Guinea's Mountain and Swampland Dwellers. By Col. Ray T. Elsmore. LXXXVIII, pp. 671-694, 15 ills. in black and white, 7 ills. in color, map, Dec., 1945

Notes on a Zoological Collecting Trip to Dutch New Guinea. By Thomas Barbour. XIX, pp. 469-484, 12 ills., maps, July, 1908

Pictorial Jaunt Through Papua. 22 photos by Captain Frank Hurley. LI, pp. 109-124, Jan., 1927

Strange Sights in Far-Away Papua. By A. E. Pratt. XVIII, pp. 559-572, 7 ills., Sept., 1907

Treasure Islands of Australasia: New Guinea, New Caledonia, and Fiji Trace across the South Pacific a Fertile Crescent Incredibly Rich in Minerals and Foods. By Douglas L. Oliver. LXXXI, pp. 691-722, 23 ills., two-page map, June, 1942

Unknown New Guinea: Circumnavigating the World in a Flying Boat, American Scientists Discover a Valley of 60,000 People Never Before Seen by White Men. By Richard Archbold. LXXIX, pp. 315-344, 28 ills., map, Mar., 1941

NEW GUINEA—*Continued*

What the Fighting Yanks See. By Wanda Burnett. LXXXVI, pp. 451-476, 27 ills., Oct., 1944

Yank Meets Native. By Wanda Burnett. LXXXVIII, pp. 105-128, 24 ills., July, 1945

NEW Guinea's Mountain and Swampland Dwellers. By Col. Ray T. Elsmore. LXXXVIII, pp. 671-694, 15 ills. in black and white, 7 ills. in color, map, Dec., 1945

NEW HAMPSHIRE:

From Notch to Notch in the White Mountains: Soaring Heights of New Hampshire Attract Multitudes to America's Oldest Mountain Recreation Area. By Leonard Cornell Roy. LXXII, pp. 73-104, 30 ills., map supplement, July, 1937

The Long River of New England: In War and Peace, from Mountain Wilderness to the Sea, Flows the Connecticut River, Through a Valley Abounding in History, Scenery, Inventive Genius, and Industry. By Albert W. Atwood. LXXXIII, pp. 401-434, 12 ills. in black and white, 24 ills. in color, map, Apr., 1943

New Hampshire, the Granite State. By George Higgins Moses. LX, pp. 257-310, 47 ills. in black and white, 5 ills. in color, map, Sept., 1931

Skiing Over the New Hampshire Hills. By Fred H. Harris. XXXVII, pp. 151-164, 37 ills., Feb., 1920

See also Portsmouth

NEW HEBRIDES (Islands), South Pacific Ocean:

In the Savage South Seas. By Beatrice Grimshaw. XIX, pp. 1-19, 21 ills., Jan., 1908

Palms and Planes in the New Hebrides. By Maj. Robert D. Heinl, Jr. LXXXVI, pp. 229-256, 17 ills. in black and white, 12 ills. in color, map, Aug., 1944

See also Espíritu Santo

The **NEW** Home of the National Geographic Society. XV, pp. 176-181, 5 ills., Apr., 1904

The **NEW** Inland Sea (Salton Sea). By Arthur P. Davis. XVIII, pp. 37-49, 8 ills., map, Jan., 1907

NEW JERSEY:

New Jersey Now! By E. John Long. LXIII, pp. 519-584, 49 ills. in black and white, 24 ills. in color, maps, May, 1933

The Rivers of Northern New Jersey, with Notes on the Classification of Rivers in General. By William Morris Davis. II, pp. 81-110, 6 diagrs., map drawing, May, 1890

The Wild Blueberry Tamed: The New Industry of the Pine Barrens of New Jersey. By Frederick V. Coville. XXIX, pp. 535-546, 10 ills., June, 1916

See also Lakehurst; Morristown

NEW Light on Ancient Ur: Excavations at the Site of the City of Abraham Reveal Geographical Evidence of the Biblical Story of the Flood. By M. E. L. Mallowan. LVII, pp. 95-130, 44 ills., map, Jan., 1930

A **NEW** Light on the Discovery of America (Geographic Notes. By Cyrus C. Babb). VI, pp. 224-225, Dec. 29, 1894

The **NEW** Map of Asia. Text with map supplement. XXXIX, pp. 552-570, 17 ills., May, 1921

The **NEW** Map of Europe: Showing the Boundaries Established by the Peace Conference at Paris and by Subsequent Decisions of the Supreme Council of the Allied and Associated Powers. By Ralph A. Graves. Text with map supplement. XXXIX, pp. 157-177, 18 ills., Feb., 1921

NEW Map of Europe and the Near East. Text with map supplement. LXXXIII, pp. 762-763, ill., June, 1943

NEW Map of Europe Records War Changes. Text with map supplement. LXXVII, p. 625, May, 1940

NEW Map of the Atlantic Ocean: Foremost Sea of Commerce Becomes World's Battleground and Its Peaceful Islands Rise to Strategic Importance. By Leo A. Borah and Wellman Chamberlin. Text with map supplement. LXXX, pp. 407-418, 9 ills., Sept., 1941

NEW Map Reveals the Progress and Wonders of Our Country. Text with map supplement. LXIII, pp. 650-652, ill., May, 1933

NEW Map Shows Asia's Role in Global Warfare. Text with map supplement. LXXXII, pp. 767-768, Dec., 1942

NEW Map Shows Immense Pacific Battleground. Text with map supplement. LXXXI, pp. 203-204, Feb., 1942

NEW MEXICO:

Arizona and New Mexico. By B. S. Rodey. XVII, pp. 100-102, ills., Feb., 1906

Bats of the Carlsbad Cavern. By Vernon Bailey. XLVIII, pp. 321-330, 11 ills., Sept., 1925

The Call of the West. By C. J. Blanchard. XX, pp. 403-437, 20 ills., map, May, 1909

Canyons and Cacti of the American Southwest. 22 color photos by Edwin L. Wisherd, Jacob Gayer, Charles Martin. XLVIII, pp. 275-290, Sept., 1925

Descriptive Topographic Terms of Spanish America. By Robert T. Hill. VII, pp. 291-302, Sept., 1896

Down the Rio Grande: Tracing this Strange, Turbulent Stream on Its Long Course from Colorado to the Gulf of Mexico. By Frederick Simpich. LXXVI, pp. 415-462, 28 ills. in black and white, 24 ills. in color, 6 maps, Oct., 1939

The Enchanted Mesa. By F. W. Hodge. VIII, pp. 273-284, 6 ills., map, Oct., 1897

Everyday Life in Pueblo Bonito: As Disclosed by the National Geographic Society's Archeologic Explorations in the Chaco Canyon National Monument, New Mexico. By Neil M. Judd. XLVIII, pp. 227-262, 37 ills., map, Sept., 1925

New Discoveries in Carlsbad Cavern: Vast Subterranean Chambers with Spectacular Decorations Are Explored, Surveyed, and Photographed. By Willis T. Lee. XLVIII, pp. 301-319, 19 ills., map, Sept., 1925

NEW MEXICO—*Continued*

New Mexico Melodrama. By Frederick Simpich. LXXIII, pp. 529-569, 19 ills. in black and white, 25 ills. in color, two-page map, May, 1938

A New National Geographic Society Expedition: Ruins of Chaco Canyon, New Mexico, Nature-Made Treasure-Chest of Aboriginal American History, To Be Excavated and Studied; Work Begins This Month. XXXIX, pp. 637-643, 7 ills., June, 1921

Notes on the Deserts of the United States and Mexico (Extracted from a Publication of Dr. Daniel T. MacDougal). XXI, pp. 691-714, 16 ills., Aug., 1910

The Prehistoric Ruin of Tsankawi. By George L. Beam. XX, pp. 807-822, 12 ills., Sept., 1909

Pueblo Bonito, the Ancient: The National Geographic Society's Third Expedition to the Southwest Seeks to Read in the Rings of Trees the Secret of the Age of Ruins. By Neil M. Judd. XLIV, pp. 99-108, 9 ills., diagr., July, 1923

The Pueblo Bonito Expedition of the National Geographic Society. By Neil M. Judd. XLI, pp. 323-331, 10 ills., diagr., Mar., 1922

Scenes from America's Southwest. 14 ills. XXXIX, pp. 651-664, June, 1921

The Secret of the Southwest Solved by Talkative Tree Rings: Horizons of American History Are Carried Back to A. D. 700 and a Calendar for 1,200 Years Established by National Geographic Society Expeditions. By Andrew Ellicott Douglass. LVI, pp. 737-770, 33 ills., map, Dec., 1929

Seeing Our Spanish Southwest. By Frederick Simpich. LXXVII, pp. 711-756, 25 ills. in black and white, 17 ills. in duotone, map supplement, June, 1940

The Southwest: Its Splendid Natural Resources, Agricultural Wealth, and Scenic Beauty. By N. H. Darton. XXI, pp. 631-665, 21 ills., map, Aug., 1910

A Visit to Carlsbad Cavern: Recent Explorations of a Limestone Cave in the Guadalupe Mountains of New Mexico Reveal a Natural Wonder of the First Magnitude. By Willis T. Lee. XLV, pp. 1-40, 42 ills., Jan., 1924

The White Sands of Alamogordo: A Dry Ocean of Granular Gypsum Billows Under Desert Winds in a New National Playground. By Carl P. Russell. LXVIII, pp. 250-264, 12 ills., Aug., 1935

A **NEW** National Geographic Society Expedition: Ruins of Chaco Canyon, New Mexico, Nature-Made Treasure-Chest of Aboriginal American History, To Be Excavated and Studied; Work Begins This Month. XXXIX, pp. 637-643, 7 ills., June, 1921

NEW National Geographic Society Map Charts South America's Wartime Importance. Text with map supplement. LXXXII, pp. 537-540, ills., Oct., 1942

A **NEW** National Park (Glacier National Park). By Guy Elliott Mitchell. XXI, pp. 215-223, 6 ills., Mar., 1910

NEW ORLEANS, Louisiana:

Louisiana, Land of Perpetual Romance. By Ralph A. Graves. LVII, pp. 393-482, 84 ills. in black and white, 29 ills. in color, map supplement, Apr., 1930

A **NEW** Peruvian Route to the Plain of the Amazon. By Solon I. Bailey. XVII, pp. 432-448, 12 ills., Aug., 1906

NEW Plant Immigrants. By David Fairchild XXII, pp. 879-907, 34 ills., Oct., 1911

The **NEW** Queen of the Seas (Aircraft Carrier). By Melville Bell Grosvenor. LXXXII, pp. 1-30, 27 ills., drawing, two-page map, July, 1942

NEW Road to Asia (U. S. S. R.). By Owen Lattimore. LXXXVI, pp. 641-676, 15 ills. in black and white, 26 ills. in color, Dec., 1944

NEW Safeguards for Ships in Fog and Storm. By George R. Putnam. LXX, pp. 169-200, 28 ills., charts, Aug., 1936

A **NEW** Source of Power: Billions of Tons of Lignite, Previously Thought Too Poor Coal for Commercial Use, Are Made Easily Available. By Guy Elliott Mitchell. XXI, pp. 935-944, 7 ills., Nov., 1910

NEW SOUTH WALES (State), Australia:

Shark Fishing—An Australian Industry. By Norman Ellison. LXII, pp. 369-386, 22 ills., Sept., 1932

See also Lord Howe (Island)

The **NEW** Trans-Canada Railway. XIV, pp. 214-215, map, May, 1903

NEW United States Map Shows Census Changes. Text with map supplement. LXXVIII, pp. 821-824, ills., Dec., 1940

NEW WORLD:

Early Voyages on the Northwestern Coast of America. By Professor George Davidson. V, pp. 235-256, Jan. 31, 1894

The First Landfall of Columbus. By Jacques W. Redway, F. R. G. S. VI, pp. 179-192, 4 maps, Dec. 29, 1894

In the Wake of Columbus. By Frederick A. Ober. V, pp. 187-196, Jan. 31, 1894

A New Light on the Discovery of America (Geographic Notes. By Cyrus C. Babb). VI, pp. 224-225, Dec. 29, 1894

Recent Disclosures Concerning Pre-Columbian Voyages to America in the Archives of the Vatican. By William Eleroy Curtis. V, pp. 197-234, Jan. 31, 1894

Sir Francis Drake's Anchorage. By Edward L. Berthoud. VI, pp. 208-214, Dec. 29, 1894

NEW World Map Gives Backdrop for Headlines. Text with map supplement. LXXX, pp. 741-742, ill., Dec., 1941

A **NEW** World to Explore: In the Tree-Roof of the British Guiana Forest Flourishes Much Hitherto-Unknown Life. By Maj. R. W. G. Hingston. LXII, pp. 617-642, 35 ills., Nov., 1932

NEW YEAR CELEBRATIONS:

Peiping's Happy New Year: Lunar Celebration Attracts Throngs to Temple Fairs, Motley Bazaars, and Age-old Festivities. By George Kin Leung. LXX, pp. 749-792, 31 ills. in black and white, 16 ills. in color, Dec., 1936

NEW YORK (City):

Greater New York . . . Metropolis of Mankind. Aërial photo by Captain Albert W. Stevens. LXIV, supplement, Nov., 1933

New York—The Metropolis of Mankind. By William Joseph Showalter. XXXIV, pp. 1-49, 39 ills., July, 1918

The Society's Map of the Reaches of New York City. Text with map supplement. LXXV, pp. 491-492, Apr., 1939

Spin Your Globe to Long Island: Only Six States Have More People than the Insular Empire that Ranges from a World's Fair Through Potato Patches, Princely Estates, and Historic Shrines. By Frederick Simpich. LXXV, pp. 413-460, 25 ills. in black and white, 18 ills. in color, Apr., 1939

This Giant That Is New York. By Frederick Simpich. LVIII, pp. 517-583, 26 ills. in black and white, 8 ills. in gravure, 42 ills. in color, Nov., 1930

NEW YORK (State):

Black Acres: A Thrilling Sketch in the Vast Volume of Who's Who Among the Peoples that Make America. By Dorothea D. and Fred Everett. LXXX, pp. 631-652, 13 ills. in black and white, 12 ills. in color, Nov., 1941

Commercial Importance of the State of New York. XV, p. 429, Oct., 1904

Fruitful Shores of the Finger Lakes. By Harrison Howell Walker. LXXIX, pp. 559-594, 15 ills. in black and white, 22 ills. in color, map, May, 1941

The New Erie Canal. XVI, pp. 568-570, map, Dec., 1905

New York—An Empire Within a Republic. By William Joseph Showalter. LXIV, pp. 513-584, 47 ills. in black and white, 35 ills. in color, two-page map, pictorial supplement, Nov., 1933

Greater New York . . . Metropolis of Mankind. Supplement from aërial photo by Captain Albert W. Stevens

New York State's Air-Conditioned Roof (Adirondacks). By Frederick G. Vosburgh. LXXIII, pp. 715-748, 23 ills. in black and white, 10 ills. in color, map, June, 1938

Niagara at the Battle Front. By William Joseph Showalter. XXXI, pp. 413-422, 6 ills., May, 1917

Shawangunk Mountain. By N. H. Darton. VI, pp. 23-34, ills., 4 diagrs., Mar. 17, 1894

The Society's Map of the Reaches of New York City. Text with map supplement. LXXV, pp. 491-492, Apr., 1939

Spin Your Globe to Long Island: Only Six States Have More People than the Insular Empire that Ranges from a World's Fair Through Potato Patches, Princely Estates, and Historic Shrines. By Frederick Simpich. LXXV, pp. 413-460, 25 ills. in black and white, 18 ills. in color, Apr., 1939

See also Buffalo; New York (City); West Point

NEW YORK GULF:

Gomez and the New York Gulf. (By L. D. Scisco). IX, pp. 371-373, Aug., 1898

NEW ZEALAND:

At Home on the Oceans: Whales and Sharks Make Exciting Neighbors for a Professor's Wife, Turned Able Seaman, On a Three-year Voyage Around the World. By Edith Bauer Strout. LXXVI, pp. 33-86, 54 ills., map, July, 1939

The British Commonwealth of Nations: "Organized Freedom" Around the World. By Eric Underwood. LXXXIII, pp. 485-524, 31 ills., Apr., 1943

Great Britain's Bread Upon the Waters: Canada and Her Other Daughters. By William Howard Taft. XXIX, pp. 217-272, 56 ills., Mar., 1916

Hurdle Racing in Canoes: A Thrilling and Spectacular Sport Among the Maoris of New Zealand. By Walter Burke. XXXVII, pp. 440-444, 6 ills., May, 1920

The Making of an Anzac. By Howell Walker. LXXXI, pp. 409-456, 31 ills. in black and white, 20 ills. in color, two-page map, Apr., 1942

The Maoris of New Zealand. XVIII, pp. 198-199, 8 ills., Mar., 1907

New Zealand "Down Under." By W. Robert Moore. LXIX, pp. 165-218, 31 ills. in black and white, 23 ills. in color, two-page map, Feb., 1936

Problems of the Pacific—New Zealand. By Henry Demarest Lloyd. XIII, pp. 342-352, Sept., 1902

Tuatara: "Living Fossils" Walk on Well-Nigh Inaccessible Rocky Islands off the Coast of New Zealand. By Frieda Cobb Blanchard. LXVII, pp. 649-662, 14 ills., map, May, 1935

Waimangu and the Hot-Spring Country of New Zealand: The World's Greatest Geyser Is One of Many Natural Wonders in a Land of Inferno and Vernal Paradise. By Joseph C. Grew. XLVIII, pp. 109-130, 19 ills., map, Aug., 1925

The World's Highest Altitudes and First Ascents. By Charles E. Fay. XX, pp. 493-530, 25 ills., June, 1909

NEWBERRY, TRUMAN H.:

Honors to the American Navy (Address by Truman H. Newberry). XX, pp. 77-95, Jan., 1909

NEWBURYPORT, Massachusetts:

Northeast of Boston. By Albert W. Atwood. LXXXVIII, pp. 257-292, 12 ills. in black and white, 17 ills. in color, map supplement, Sept., 1945

NEWCOMB, H. T.:

Geographic Literature. IX, pp. 29-31, Jan., 1898; pp. 253-256, May, 1898

NEWCOMB, SIMON:

The Scientific Work of the National Geographic Society's Eclipse Expedition to Norfolk, Va. By Simon Newcomb. XI, pp. 321-324, Aug., 1900

NEWELL, FREDERICK H.:

The Arid Regions of the United States. By F. H. Newell. V, pp. 167-172, Jan. 31, 1894

Four Prominent Geographers. XVIII, pp. 425-428, 4 ills., June, 1907

Hydrography in the United States. By Frederick H. Newell. VII, pp. 146-150, Apr., 1896

International Geographic Conference in Chicago, July 27-28, 1893: Minutes of the Conference. F. H. Newell and Eliza R. Scidmore, Secretaries. V, pp. 101-111, Jan. 31, 1894

The Limited Water Supply of the Arid Region. By Frederick H. Newell. XI, pp. 438-442, Nov., 1900

Mesa Verde. By F. H. Newell. IX, pp. 431-434, Oct., 1898

The National Forest Reserves. By Frederick H. Newell. VIII, pp. 177-187, diagrs., tables, June, 1897

National Geographic Society (Resignation of Frederick H. Newell as Secretary of the Society). (By G. H. Grosvenor). X, pp. 474-475, Nov., 1899

Pollution of the Potomac River. By F. H. Newell. VIII, pp. 346-351, Dec., 1897

Portrait. XVIII, ill. p. 427, June, 1907

Recent Hydrographic Work. (By F. H. N.). VII, pp. 347-348, Oct., 1896

The Reclamation of the West. By F. H. Newell. XV, pp. 15-30, 6 ills., 7 maps, Jan., 1904

See also NGS: Board of Managers; Secretary

NEWFOUNDLAND:

King Herring: An Account of the World's Most Valuable Fish, the Industries It Supports, and the Part It Has Played in History. By Hugh M. Smith. XX, pp. 701-735, 21 ills., Aug., 1909

Life on the Grand Banks: An Account of the Sailor-Fishermen Who Harvest the Shoal Waters of North America's Eastern Coasts. By Frederick William Wallace. XL, pp. 1-28, 29 ills., July, 1921

Newfoundland, North Atlantic Rampart: From the "First Base of American Defense" Planes Fly to Britain's Aid over Stout Fishing Schooners of the Grand Banks. By George Whiteley, Jr. LXXX, pp. 111-140, 26 ills., map, July, 1941

The Sealing Saga of Newfoundland. By Captain Robert A. Bartlett. LVI, pp. 91-130, 44 ills., July, 1929

NEWMAN, OLIVER P.:

Bare Feet and Burros of Haiti. By Oliver P. Newman. LXXXVI, pp. 307-328, 10 ills. in black and white, 10 ills. in color, map, Sept., 1944

The Land Columbus Loved (Dominican Republic). By Oliver P. Newman. LXXXV, pp. 197-224, 15 ills. in black and white, 11 ills. in color, map, Feb., 1944

NEWS of the Universe: Mars Swings Nearer the Earth, Sunspots Wane, and a Giant New Telescopic Eye Soon Will Peer Into Unexplored Depths of Space. By F. Barrows Colton. Paintings by Charles Bittinger. LXXVI, pp. 1-32, 23 ills. in black and white, 10 ills. in color, July, 1939

NEWSPAPERS:

The American Scene. 29 winning photos in the Sixth Annual Newspaper National Snapshot Awards, with explanatory note. LXXIX, pp. 220-246, Feb., 1941

Americana. 11 winning photos in the Seventh Annual Newspaper National Snapshot Awards. LXXXI, pp. 657-666, May, 1942

The Making of a Japanese Newspaper. By Dr. Thomas E. Green. XXXVIII, pp. 327-334, 5 ills., Oct., 1920

New China and the Printed Page. By Paul Hutchinson. LI, pp. 687-722, 37 ills., June, 1927

NEXT International Geographical Congress To Be Held in Washington (D. C.). (By G. H. G.). XII, pp. 351-357, 4 ills., Oct., 1901

NIAGARA FALLS, Canada-U. S.:

The American Association (for the Advancement of Science) at Buffalo. VII, pp. 315-316, Sept., 1896

Niagara at the Battle Front. By William Joseph Showalter. XXXI, pp. 413-422, 6 ills., May, 1917

The World's Great Waterfalls: Visits to Mighty Niagara, Wonderful Victoria, and Picturesque Iguazu. By Theodore W. Noyes. L, pp. 29-59, 29 ills., July, 1926

NIAGARAS of Five Continents. 16 ills. XXXVIII, pp. 211-226, Sept., 1920

NIAS (Island), Netherlands East Indies:

The Island of Nias, at the Edge of the World. By Mable Cook Cole. LX, pp. 201-224, 26 ills., map, Aug., 1931

NICARAGUA:

Across Nicaragua with Transit and Machéte. By R. E. Peary. I, pp. 315-335, 3 ills. (tinted), foldout map, Oct., 1889

An Army Engineer Explores Nicaragua: Mapping a Route for a New Canal Through the Largest of Central American Republics. By Lieut. Col. Dan I. Sultan. LXI, pp. 593-627, 39 ills., map, May, 1932

The Countries of the Caribbean. By William Joseph Showalter. XXIV, pp. 227-250, 23 ills., Feb., 1913

Flying the World's Longest Air-Mail Route: From Montevideo, Uruguay, Over the Andes, Up the Pacific Coast, Across Central America and the Caribbean to Miami, Florida, in 67 Thrilling Flying Hours. By Junius B. Wood. LVII, pp. 261-325, 65 ills., map, Mar., 1930

A Land of Lakes and Volcanoes. By Luis Marden. With 17 color photos by author. LXXXVI, 161-192, 11 ills. in black and white, map, Aug., 1944

Location of the Boundary Between Nicaragua and Costa Rica. By Arthur P. Davis. XII, pp. 22-28, ill., map, Jan., 1901

Nicaragua, Largest of Central American Republics. LI, pp. 370-378, 15 ills., Mar., 1927

Nicaragua and the Isthmian Routes. By Arthur P. Davis. X, pp. 247-266, 7 ills., diagrs., July, 1899

Notes on Central America. XVIII, pp. 272-279, ills., map, Apr., 1907

NICARAGUA—*Continued*

Notes on Turbulent Nicaragua. XX, pp. 1102-1116, 13 ills., map, Dec., 1909

Rubber Forests of Nicaragua and Sierra Leone. By General A. W. Greely. VIII, pp. 83-88, Mar., 1897

Shattered Capitals of Central America. By Herbert J. Spinden. XXXVI, pp. 185-212, 32 ills., map, Sept., 1919

Wards of the United States: Notes on What Our Country Is Doing for Santo Domingo, Nicaragua, and Haiti. XXX, pp. 143-177, 36 ills., Aug., 1916

See also Nicaragua Canal

NICARAGUA CANAL:

Across Nicaragua with Transit and Machéte. By R. E. Peary. I, pp. 315-335, 3 ills. (tinted), foldout map, Oct., 1889

An Army Engineer Explores Nicaragua: Mapping a Route for a New Canal Through the Largest of Central American Republics. By Lieut. Col. Dan I. Sultan. LXI, pp. 593-627, 39 ills., map, May, 1932

An Assumed Inconstancy in the Level of Lake Nicaragua; A Question of Permanency of the Nicaragua Canal. By C. Willard Hayes. XI, pp. 156-161, Apr., 1900

The completed report of the Isthmian Canal Commission. XII, p. 441, Dec., 1901

The Evolution of Commerce. Annual Address by the President, Hon. Gardiner G. Hubbard. IV, pp. 1-18, Mar. 26, 1892

Geography of the Land. Annual Report by Vice-President Herbert G. Ogden. III, pp. 31-40, Apr. 30, 1891

The Isthmian Canal Problem. (By W J McGee). X, pp. 363-364, Sept., 1899

Nicaragua and the Isthmian Routes. By A. P. Davis. X, pp. 247-266, 7 ills., diagrs., July, 1899

The Nicaragua Canal. XII, pp. 28-32, ills., map, Jan., 1901

Oregon: Its History, Geography, and Resources. By John H. Mitchell, U. S. Senator from Oregon. VI, pp. 239-284, Apr. 20, 1895
  Included: Demand for the Nicaragua Canal

Physiography of the Nicaragua Canal Route. By C. Willard Hayes. X, pp. 233-246, ill., diagr., maps, map supplement, July, 1899

The Present State of the Nicaragua Canal. By General A. W. Greely. VII, pp. 73-76, Feb., 1896

The Proposed American Interoceanic Canal in Its Commercial Aspects. By Joseph Nimmo, Jr. X, pp. 297-310, Aug., 1899

The Water Supply for the Nicaragua Canal. By Arthur P. Davis. XI, pp. 363-365, Sept., 1900

NICE, France:

Carnival Days on the Riviera. By Maynard Owen Williams. L, pp. 467-501, 21 ills. in black and white, 21 ills. in color, Oct., 1926

NICHOLAS, WILLIAM H.:

Africa First of 1943 Global Warfare Maps. By William H. Nicholas. Text with map supplement. LXXXIII, pp. 261-276, 13 ills., Feb., 1943

NICHOLAS, WILLIAM H.—*Continued*

American Pathfinders in the Pacific. By William H. Nicholas. LXXXIX, pp. 617-640, 17 ills., two-page map, May, 1946

Charting a World at War. By William H. Nicholas. LXXXVI, pp. 617-640, 23 ills., drawing, Nov., 1944

Gliders—Silent Weapons of the Sky. By William H. Nicholas. LXXXVI, pp. 149-160, 8 ills., Aug., 1944

Heroes' Return. By William H. Nicholas. LXXXVII, pp. 333-352, 19 ills., Mar., 1945

The Making of Military Maps. By William H. Nicholas. LXXXIII, pp. 765-778, 17 ills., June, 1943

Nantucket—Little Gray Lady. By William H. Nicholas. LXXXV, pp. 433-458, 14 ills. in black and white, 8 ills. in color, map, Apr., 1944

Wartime Washington. By William H. Nicholas. LXXXIV, pp. 257-290, 12 ills. in black and white, 16 ills. in color, Sept., 1943

The World's Words. By William H. Nicholas. LXXXIV, pp. 689-700, 8 ills., two-page map, map supplement, Dec., 1943

NICHOLS, JOHN T.:

Interesting Citizens of the Gulf Stream. By Dr. John T. Nichols. XXXIX, pp. 69-84, 11 ills., Jan., 1921

NICHOLS, RUTH ALEXANDER:

Into the Land of the Chipmunk. By Ruth Alexander Nichols. LX, pp. 77-98, 28 ills., July, 1931

NIEDERMEYER, OSCAR VON ("Haji Mirza Hussein"):

Every-Day Life in Afghanistan. By Frederick Simpich and "Haji Mirza Hussein." XXXIX, pp. 85-110, 26 ills., map, Jan., 1921

NIEDRACH, ROBERT J.:

Birds and Beasts of Mexico's Desert Islands. 12 color photos: 8 by Ed N. Harrison, 4 by Alfred M. Bailey and Robert J. Niedrach. LXXX, pp. 353-360, Sept., 1941

High Country of Colorado. 23 color photos by Alfred M. Bailey, Robert J. Niedrach, F. G. Brandenburg. XC, pp. 49-64, July, 1946

NIGER (River), and Valley, Africa:

In the Valley of the Niger. XIX, p. 164, ill., Mar., 1908

Return of the Hourst Niger Expedition. (By Ernest de Sasseville). VIII, pp. 24-25, Jan., 1897

NIGER COLONY:

Three-Wheeling Through Africa: Two Adventurers Cross the So-called Dark Continent North of Lake Chad on Motorcycles with Side Cars. By James C. Wilson. LXV, pp. 37-92, 64 ills., two-page map, Jan., 1934

NIGERIA:

The British Commonwealth of Nations: "Organized Freedom" Around the World. By Eric Underwood. LXXXIII, pp. 485-524, 31 ills., Apr., 1943

The New English Province of Northern Nigeria. XV, pp. 433-442, 9 ills., Nov., 1904

NIGERIA—*Continued*

Nigeria: From the Bight of Benin to Africa's Desert Sands. By Helen Trybulowski Gilles. LXXXV, pp. 537-568, 17 ills. in black and white, 10 ills. in color, map, May, 1944

Notes on the Ekoi. By P. A. Talbot. XXIII, pp. 33-38, 8 ills., Jan., 1912

The Tailed People of Nigeria. XXIII, pp. 1239-1242, 3 ills., Dec., 1912

Three-Wheeling Through Africa: Two Adventurers Cross the So-called Dark Continent North of Lake Chad on Motorcycles with Side Cars. By James C. Wilson. LXV, pp. 37-92, 64 ills., two-page map, Jan., 1934

Timbuktu and Beyond: Desert City of Romantic Savor and Salt Emerges into World Life Again as Trading Post of France's Vast African Empire. By Laura C. Boulton. LXXIX, pp. 631-670, 18 ills. in black and white, 26 ills. in color, map, May, 1941

Trans-Africa Safari: A Motor Caravan Rolls Across Sahara and Jungle Through Realms of Dusky Potentates and the Land of Big-Lipped Women. By Lawrence Copley Thaw and Margaret Stout Thaw. LXXIV, pp. 327-364, 29 ills. in black and white, 14 ills. in color, map, Sept., 1938

NIGHTINGALE, FLORENCE:

The Symbol of Service to Mankind. By Stockton Axson. XXXIII, pp. 375-390, 11 ills., Apr., 1918

NIKKO, Japan:

Glimpses of Japan. By William W. Chapin. XXII, pp. 965-1002, 10 ills. in black and white, 34 ills. in color, Nov., 1911

Why Nik-ko Is Beautiful. By J. H. De Forest. XIX, pp. 300-308, 8 ills., Apr., 1908

NILE (River), Africa:

Along the Nile, Through Egypt and the Sudan. By Frederick Simpich. XLII, pp. 379-410, 29 ills., Oct., 1922

The Barrage of the Nile. By Day Allen Willey. XXI, pp. 175-184, 14 ills., Feb., 1910

By Felucca Down the Nile: Giant Dams Rule Egypt's Lifeline River, Yet Village Life Goes On As It Did in the Time of the Pharaohs. By Willard Price. LXXVII, pp. 435-476, 21 ills. in black and white, 22 ills. in color, two-page map, Apr., 1940

The Land of Egypt: A Narrow Green Strip of Fertility Stretching for a Thousand Miles Through Walls of Desert. By Alfred Pearce Dennis. XLIX, pp. 271-298, 28 ills., map, Mar., 1926

NILSON, ELIZABETH W.:

Rural Sweden Through American Eyes: A Visitor in Peacetime Finds Warmth, Welcome, and Strange Folkways On a Century-old Farm. By Elizabeth W. Nilson. LXXVII, pp. 795-822, 8 ills. in black and white, 22 ills. in color, June, 1940

NIMITZ, CHESTER W.:

Your Navy as Peace Insurance. By Fleet Admiral Chester W. Nimitz. LXXXIX, pp. 681-736, 32 ills. in black and white, 26 ills. in color, June, 1946

NIMMO, JOSEPH, JR.:

The Proposed American Interoceanic Canal in Its Commercial Aspects. By Joseph Nimmo, Jr. X, pp. 297-310, Aug., 1899

1940 Paradox in Hong Kong. By Frederick Simpich. LXXVII, pp. 531-558, 24 ills., 3 maps, Apr., 1940

NIPPUR, Iraq:

Excavations at Nippur. XI, p. 392, Oct., 1900

NITOBE, INAZU:

The National Geographic Society (Speech by Dr. Inazu Nitobe). XXIII, pp. 272-298, 5 ills., Mar., 1912

NITRATE INDUSTRY:

A Longitudinal Journey Through Chile. By Harriet Chalmers Adams. XLII, pp. 219-273, 60 ills., map, Sept., 1922

NIUAFOŌ (Island), Tonga Islands:

Living on a Volcano: An Unspoiled Patch of Polynesia Is Niuafoō, Nicknamed "Tin Can Island" by Stamp Collectors. By Thomas A. Jaggar. LXVIII, pp. 91-106, 17 ills., map, July, 1935

NIZHNI NOVGOROD. *See* Gorki

NO Man's Land—Spitzbergen. XVIII, pp. 455-458, July, 1907

NOBILE, UMBERTO:

Navigating the "Norge" from Rome to the North Pole and Beyond: The Designer and Pilot of the First Dirigible to Fly Over the Top of the World Describes a Thrilling Voyage of More Than 8,000 Miles. By General Umberto Nobile. LII, pp. 177-215, 36 ills., map, Aug., 1927

NOMAD Life and Fossil Treasures of Mongolia. 20 color photos by J. B. Shackelford. LXIII, pp. 669-700, June, 1933

NOMADS:

Mountain Tribes of Iran and Iraq. By Harold Lamb. LXXXIX, pp. 385-408, 15 ills., two-page map, Mar., 1946

New Road to Asia. By Owen Lattimore. LXXXVI, pp. 641-676, 15 ills. in black and white, 26 ills. in color, Dec., 1944

The Nomads of Arctic Lapland: Mysterious Little People of a Land of the Midnight Sun Live Off the Country Above the Arctic Circle. By Clyde Fisher. LXXVI, pp. 641-676, 28 ills. in black and white, 12 ills. in color, map, Nov., 1939

The People of the Wilderness: The Mongols, Once the Terror of All Christendom, Now a Primitive, Harmless, Nomad Race. By Adam Warwick. XXXIX, pp. 507-551, 59 ills., May, 1921

With the Nomads of Central Asia: A Summer's Sojourn in the Tekes Valley, Plateau Paradise of Mongol and Turkic Tribes. By Edward Murray. Paintings and drawings by Alexandre Iacovleff. LXIX, pp. 1-57, 43 ills. in black and white, 26 ills. in color, map, Jan., 1936

See also Bedouin; Gypsies

NOMADS Among the Butterflies. 8 ills. in color: 3 paintings by Hashime Murayama, 5 color photos by Willard R. Culver. LXXI, pp. 569-584, May, 1937

The **NOMADS** of Arctic Lapland: Mysterious Little People of a Land of the Midnight Sun Live Off the Country Above the Arctic Circle. By Clyde Fisher. LXXVI, pp. 641-676, 28 ills. in black and white, 12 ills. in color, map, Nov., 1939

NOME, Alaska:

The Cape Nome Gold District. By F. C. Schrader. XI, pp. 15-23, 3 ills., map, Jan., 1900

The Nome Gold Fields. XIX, pp. 384-385, May, 1908

NOME, Cape, Alaska:

The Cape Nome Gold District. By F. C. Schrader. XI, pp. 15-23, 3 ills., map, Jan., 1900

Origin of the Name "Cape Nome." (By George Davidson). XII, p. 398, Nov., 1901

The **NON-CHRISTIAN** Peoples of the Philippine Islands. By Dean C. Worcester. XXIV, pp. 1157-1256, 41 ills. in black and white, 48 ills. in color, Nov., 1913

NONSATONG, Korea:

Exploring Unknown Corners of the "Hermit Kingdom." By Roy Chapman Andrews. XXXVI, pp. 25-48, 30 ills., map, July, 1919

NON-SPORTING Dogs. By Freeman Lloyd. Paintings by Walter A. Weber. LXXXIV, pp. 569-588, 9 ills. in black and white, 8 ills. in color from paintings from life, Nov., 1943

The **NON-STOP** Flight Across America. By Lieutenant John A. Macready. Photos by Lieutenant Albert W. Stevens. XLVI, pp. 1-83, 68 ills., maps, July, 1924

NONSUCH ISLAND, Bermuda:

The Depths of the Sea: Strange Life Forms a Mile Below the Surface. By William Beebe. Paintings by Else Bostelmann. LXI, pp. 65-88, 15 ills. in black and white, 8 ills. in color, map, Jan., 1932

A Round Trip to Davy Jones's Locker: Peering into Mysteries a Quarter Mile Down in the Open Sea, by Means of the Bathysphere. By William Beebe. Paintings by Else Bostelmann. LIX, pp. 653-678, 14 ills. in black and white, 8 ills. in color, map, June, 1931

NOOKS and Bays Around the Zuider Zee. 13 color photos by Wilhelm Tobien, Gervais Courtellemont, Franklin Price Knott. LXIV, pp. 301-308, Sept., 1933

NOOKS and Bays of Storied England. 13 color photos by Clifton Adams and Bernard Wakeman. LXI, pp. 183-190, Feb., 1932

NOOTKA (Indian Tribe):

Indians of Our North Pacific Coast. By Matthew W. Stirling. Paintings by W. Langdon Kihn. LXXXVII, pp. 25-52, 3 ills. in black and white, 16 ills. in color, Jan., 1945

NÖRDLINGEN, Germany:

Medieval Pageantry in Modern Nördlingen. 12 color photos by Hans Hildenbrand. LIV, pp. 707-714, Dec., 1928

NORGE (Airship):

Navigating the "Norge" from Rome to the North Pole and Beyond: The Designer and Pilot of the First Dirigible to Fly Over the Top of the World Describes a Thrilling Voyage of More Than 8,000 Miles. By General Umberto Nobile. LII, pp. 177-215, 36 ills., map, Aug., 1927

NORMANDY (Region), France:

The Beauties of France. By Arthur Stanley Riggs. XXVIII, pp. 391-491, 73 ills. in black and white, 16 ills. in color, map, Nov., 1915

The Coasts of Normandy and Brittany. By W. Robert Moore. LXXXIV, pp. 205-232, 5 ills. in black and white, 21 ills. in color, two-page map, Aug., 1943

France Farms as War Wages: An American Explores the Rich Rural Region of the Historic Paris Basin. By Harrison Howell Walker. LXXVII, pp. 201-238, 16 ills. in black and white, 18 ills. in color, map, Feb., 1940

The Land of William the Conqueror: Where Northmen Came to Build Castles and Cathedrals. By Inez Buffington Ryan. LXI, pp. 89-99, 13 ills. in color, Jan., 1932

Normandy—Choice of the Vikings. By Helen Churchill Candee. LXIX, pp. 625-665, 25 ills. in black and white, 22 ills. in duotone, map, May, 1936

Normandy's Made-in-England Harbors. LXXXVII, pp. 565-580, 16 ills., map, May, 1945

Notes on Normandy. By Mrs. Geo. C. Bosson, Jr. XXI, pp. 775-782, 5 ills., Sept., 1910

NORMANDY and Brittany in Brighter Days. 21 color photos by W. Robert Moore, Peter Upton Muir, and others. LXXXIV, pp. 209-232, Aug., 1943

NORMANDY'S Made-in-England Harbors. LXXXVII, pp. 565-580, 16 ills., map, May, 1945

NORRIS, J. A.:

On the Telegraphic Determinations of Longitude by the Bureau of Navigation. By Lieut. J. A. Norris, U.S.N. II, pp. 1-30, Apr., 1890

NORSEMEN:

Discoverers of America. Annual Address by the President, Hon. Gardiner G. Hubbard. V, pp. 1-20, charts, maps, 3 map supplements, Apr. 7, 1893

Dwellings of the Saga-Time in Iceland, Greenland, and Vineland. By Cornelia Horsford. IX, pp. 73-84, ill., 9 sketches, Mar., 1898

Norway and the Vikings. By Captain Magnus Andersen. V, pp. 132-136, Jan. 31, 1894

Recent Disclosures Concerning Pre-Columbian Voyages to America in the Archives of the Vatican. By William Eleroy Curtis. V, pp. 197-234, Jan. 31, 1894

NORTH, S. N. D. *See* NGS: Board of Managers

NORTH About (Sailing Ship, *Joseph Conrad*). By Alan J. Villiers. LXXI, pp. 221-250, 24 ills., Feb., 1937

NORTH AMERICA:
The Battle of the Forest. By B. E. Fernow. VI, pp. 127-148, 5 ills., map, June 22, 1894
Fundamental Geographic Relation of the Three Americas. By Robert T. Hill. VII, pp. 175-181, map, May, 1896
Geographic Progress of Civilization. Annual Address by the President, Honorable Gardiner G. Hubbard. VI, pp. 1-22, Feb. 14, 1894
The Great Unmapped Areas on the Earth's Surface Awaiting the Explorer and Geographer. By J. Scott Keltie. VIII, pp. 251-266, Sept., 1897
Maps for Victory: National Geographic Society's Charts Used in War on Land, Sea, and in the Air. By Gilbert Grosvenor. Text with map supplement. LXXXI, pp. 667-690, 28 ills., May, 1942
The North American Deserts. By Herr Professor Dr. Johannes Walther. IV, pp. 163-176, Feb. 8, 1893
Our Map of North America. Text with map supplement. XLV, p. 580, May, 1924
See also New World; *and* names of countries

The **NORTH** American Deserts. By Herr Professor Dr. Johannes Walther. IV, pp. 163-176, Feb. 8, 1893

The **NORTH** American Indian. XIX, pp. 448-454, 5 ills., June, 1908

NORTH American Indians. XVIII, pp. 469-484, 14 ills., July, 1907

NORTH American Woodpeckers. 25 ills. in color from paintings by Maj. Allan Brooks. LXIII, pp. 465-478, Apr., 1933

NORTH America's Oldest Metropolis: Through 600 Melodramatic Years, Mexico City Has Grown in Splendor and Achievement. By Frederick Simpich. LVIII, pp. 45-84, 34 ills., July, 1930

NORTH CAROLINA:
A Bit of Elizabethan England in America: Fisher Folk of the Islands Off North Carolina Conserved the Speech and Customs of Sir Walter Raleigh's Colonists. By Blanch Nettleton Epler. LXIV, pp. 695-730, 43 ills., map, Dec., 1933
Dismal Swamp in Legend and History: George Washington Owned Large Tracts in Region Which He Described as a "Glorious Paradise." By John Francis Ariza. LXII, pp. 121-130, 11 ills., July, 1932
Gliders—Silent Weapons of the Sky (Laurinburg-Maxton Army Air Base). By William H. Nicholas. LXXXVI, pp. 149-160, 8 ills., Aug., 1944
Motor-Coaching Through North Carolina. By Melville Chater. XLIX, pp. 475-523, 43 ills., map, May, 1926
A Patriotic Pilgrimage to Eastern National Parks: History and Beauty Live Along Paved Roads, Once Indian Trails, Through Virginia, North Carolina, Tennessee, Kentucky, and West Virginia. By Leo A. Borah. LXV, pp. 663-702, 18 ills. in black and white, 28 ills. in color, two-page map, June, 1934

NORTH CAROLINA—*Continued*
Rambling Around the Roof of Eastern America (Great Smoky Mountains). By Leonard C. Roy. LXX, pp. 243-266, 25 ills., map, Aug., 1936
Round About Asheville. By Bailey Willis. I, pp. 291-300, map supplement, Oct., 1889
Some Human Habitations. By Collier Cobb. XIX, pp. 509-515, 5 ills., July, 1908
Tarheelia on Parade: Versatile and Vibrant, North Carolina in a Generation Has Climbed New Economic Heights. By Leonard C. Roy. LXXX, pp. 181-224, 24 ills. in black and white, 21 ills. in color, map, Aug., 1941
Where the Wind Does the Work (Cape Hatteras). By Collier Cobb. XVII, pp. 310-317, 9 ills., map, June, 1906

NORTH Carolina Colorcade. 21 color photos: 19 by J. Baylor Roberts. LXXX, pp. 189-220, Aug., 1941

NORTH DAKOTA:
A New Source of Power: Billions of Tons of Lignite, Previously Thought Too Poor Coal for Commercial Use, Are Made Easily Available. By Guy Elliott Mitchell. XXI, pp. 935-944, 7 ills., Nov., 1910
Taming the Outlaw Missouri River. By Frederick Simpich. LXXXVIII, pp. 569-598, 25 ills., two-page map, Nov., 1945

NORTH FRISIAN ISLANDS, Denmark-Germany:
Demolishing Germany's North Sea Ramparts (Helgoland). By Stuart E. Jones. XC, pp. 635-644, ill. in black and white, 10 ills. in color, Nov., 1946

A **NORTH** Holland Cheese Market. By Hugh M. Smith. XXI, pp. 1051-1066, 17 ills., Dec., 1910

NORTH Island of New Zealand: A Vulcan's Playground. 12 color photos by W. Robert Moore. LXIX, pp. 181-188, Feb., 1936

NORTH POLE:
Commander Byrd at the North Pole (Through Pathless Skies to the North Pole). Reproduction in color of the painting by N. C. Wyeth, National Geographic Society, Washington, D. C. LIII, supplement, May, 1928
Commander Byrd Receives the Hubbard Gold Medal: The First Explorer to Reach the North Pole by Air Receives Coveted Honor at Brilliant National Geographic Society Reception. L, pp. 377-388, 5 ills., chart, Sept., 1926
The Discovery of the North Pole (National Geographic Society Banquet: Medals Presented). XXI, pp. 63-82, Jan., 1910
The Discovery of the Pole (First Reports by Peary and Cook). XX, pp. 892-916, 11 ills., map, Oct., 1909
European Tributes to Peary. XXI, pp. 536-540, 4 ills., June, 1910
Farthest North. XVII, pp. 638-644, 9 ills., Nov., 1906
The First Flight to the North Pole. By Lieutenant Commander Richard Evelyn Byrd. L, pp. 357-376, 14 ills., Sept., 1926

NORTH POLE—*Continued*

Honors to Peary (Presentation of Hubbard Gold Medal). XVIII, pp. 49-60, ill., Jan., 1907

Included: Commander Peary's reasons, methods, and desires to reach the Pole. Medal presented for arctic exploration farthest north, 87° 6′, Dec. 15, 1906

A Memorial to Peary: The National Geographic Society Dedicates Monument in Arlington National Cemetery to Discoverer of the North Pole. XLI, pp. 639-646, 4 ills., June, 1922

Nansen's Polar Expedition. By General A. W. Greely. VII, pp. 98-101, ill., table, Mar., 1896

National Geographic Society (Records of North Pole Discovery). XXI, p. 276, Mar., 1910

Navigating the "Norge" from Rome to the North Pole and Beyond: The Designer and Pilot of the First Dirigible to Fly Over the Top of the World Describes a Thrilling Voyage of More than 8,000 Miles. By General Umberto Nobile. LII, pp. 177-215, 36 ills., map, Aug., 1927

Nearest the Pole (Commander Robert E. Peary's Address to the Society). XVIII, pp. 446-450, July, 1907

The North Pole (Appointment of a Committee by the Society to Consider Claims of Peary and Cook). XX, pp. 921-922, Nov., 1909

The North Pole (Resolutions of the Society Acknowledging Peary's Discovery). XX, pp. 1008-1009, Nov., 1909

Peary and the North Pole. XIV, pp. 379-381, Oct., 1903

Peary as a Leader: Incidents from the Life of the Discoverer of the North Pole Told by One of His Lieutenants on the Expedition Which Reached the Goal. By Donald B. MacMillan. XXXVII, pp. 293-317, 20 ills., map, Apr., 1920

Peary on the North Pole. XIV, p. 29, map, Jan., 1903

Peary to Try Again. XVIII, p. 281, Apr., 1907

Peary's Explorations in the Far North. By Gilbert Grosvenor. XXXVII, pp. 319-322, 3 ills., Apr., 1920

Peary's Polar Expedition. XIX, p. 447, June, 1908

Peary's Twenty Years' Service in the Arctics. By Maj. Gen. A. W. Greely. XVIII, pp. 451-454, July, 1907

Some Indications of Land in the Vicinity of the North Pole. By R. A. Harris. XV, pp. 255-261, map, June, 1904

The Value of Arctic Exploration. By Commander Robert E. Peary. XIV, pp. 429-436, Dec., 1903

See also Arctic Regions

NORTH SEA:

Demolishing Germany's North Sea Ramparts (Helgoland). By Stuart E. Jones. XC, pp. 635-644, ill. in black and white, 10 ills. in color, Nov., 1946

Europe's Endangered Fish Supply: The War and the North Sea Fisheries. XXVII, pp. 141-152, 9 ills., map, Feb., 1915

The North Sea Mine Barrage. By Capt. Reginald R. Belknap. XXXV, pp. 85-110, 23 ills., diagr., map, Feb., 1919

The Removal of the North Sea Mine Barrage. By Lieutenant-Commander Noel Davis. XXXVII, pp. 103-133, 28 ills., maps, Feb., 1920

NORTH-EAST NEW GUINEA. *See* Ifitamin

NORTHEAST of Boston. By Albert W. Atwood. LXXXVIII, pp. 257-292, 12 ills. in black and white, 17 ills. in color, map supplement, Sept., 1945

NORTHEASTERN WOODLAND INDIANS. *See* Eastern Woodland Indians

NORTHERN California at Work. By Frederick Simpich. LXIX, pp. 309-389, 36 ills. in black and white, 41 ills. in color, maps (1 two-page), Mar., 1936

A **NORTHERN** Crusoe's Island: Life on a Fox Farm Off the Coast of Alaska, Far from Contact with the World Eleven Months a Year. By Margery Pritchard Parker. XLIV, pp. 313-326, 15 ills., map, Sept., 1923

NORTHERN HEMISPHERE:

Map of the Northern and Southern Hemispheres. Text with map supplement. LXXXIII, pp. 481-483, Apr., 1943

Northern Hemisphere. Announcement of map supplement. LXXXIX, text and footnote, p. 160, Feb., 1946

NORTHERN IRELAND:

The British Commonwealth of Nations: "Organized Freedom" Around the World. By Eric Underwood. LXXXIII, pp. 485-524, 31 ills., Apr., 1943

The Mist and Sunshine of Ulster. By Bernard F. Rogers, Jr. LXVIII, pp. 571-610, 23 ills. in black and white, 21 ills. in color, map, Nov., 1935

Yanks in Northern Ireland. 15 ills. LXXXIV, pp. 191-204, Aug., 1943

NORTHERN Italy: Scenic Battleground. 18 color photos: 13 by B. Anthony Stewart, 3 by Lt. Benjamin C. McCartney. LXXXVII, pp. 265-288, Mar., 1945

The **NORTHERN** Lights. (By Alice Rollins Crane). XII, p. 69, ill., Feb., 1901

NORTHWEST COAST INDIANS:

Indians of Our North Pacific Coast. By Matthew W. Stirling. Paintings by W. Langdon Kihn. LXXXVII, pp. 25-52, 3 ills. in black and white, 16 ills. in color, Jan., 1945

NORTH-WEST FRONTIER PROVINCE, India:

South of Khyber Pass. By Maynard Owen Williams. LXXXIX, pp. 471-500, 31 ills., map supplement, Apr., 1946

NORTHWEST PASSAGE:

Honors for Amundsen. XIX, pp. 55-76, 13 ills., Jan., 1908

A Modern Viking (Amundsen). XVII, pp. 38-41, ills., map, Jan., 1906

The **NORTHWEST** Passes to the Yukon. By Eliza Ruhamah Scidmore. IX, pp. 105-112, 3 ills., Apr., 1898

NORTHWEST TERRITORIES, Canada:

Canada's Awakening North. By Lawrence J. Burpee. LXIX, pp. 749-768, 18 ills., June, 1936

Charles Francis Hall and Jones Sound. (By A. W. G.). VII, pp. 308-310, Sept., 1896

See also Yukon District (pre-Yukon Territory)

NORTHWESTERN AERONAUTICAL CORPORATION, Minneapolis, Minnesota:
Gliders—Silent Weapons of the Sky. By William H. Nicholas. LXXXVI, pp. 149-160, 8 ills., Aug., 1944

NORTON, WILSON K.:
Sigiriya, "A Fortress in the Sky." By Wilson K. Norton. XC, pp. 665-680, 14 ills., map, Nov., 1946

NORWAY:
A Comparison of Norway and Sweden. XVI, pp. 429-431, Sept., 1905
Country Life in Norway: The Beneficent Gulf Stream Enables One-third of the People in a Far-north, Mountainous Land to Prosper on Farms. By Axel H. Oxholm. LXXV, pp. 493-528, 17 ills. in black and white, 20 ills. in color, map, Apr., 1939
Europe's Northern Nomads (Lapps). 12 color photos by Jack Kuhne. LXXVI, pp. 657-664, Nov., 1939
King Herring: An Account of the World's Most Valuable Fish, the Industries It Supports, and the Part It Has Played in History. By Hugh M. Smith. XX, pp. 701-735, 21 ills., Aug., 1909
Life in a Norway Valley: An American Girl Is Welcomed Into the Homemaking and Haying of Happy Hallingdal. By Abbie L. Bosworth. LXVII, pp. 627-648, 21 ills., map, May, 1935
Norway, A Land of Stern Reality: Where Descendants of the Sea Kings of Old Triumphed Over Nature and Wrought a Nation of Arts and Crafts. By Alfred Pearce Dennis. LVIII, pp. 1-44, 31 ills. in black and white, 27 ills. in color, July, 1930
Norway, an Active Ally. By Wilhelm Morgenstierne. LXXXIII, pp. 333-357, 24 ills., map, Mar., 1943
Norway and the Norwegians. By Maurice Francis Egan. XLV, pp. 647-696, 45 ills., June, 1924
Norway and the Vikings. By Captain Magnus Andersen. V, pp. 132-136, Jan. 31, 1894
A Notable Norwegian Publication. (By Charles Rabot). XV, pp. 370-371, Sept., 1904
Sailing the Seven Seas in the Interest of Science: Adventures Through 157,000 Miles of Storm and Calm, from Arctic to Antarctic and Around the World, in the Non-magnetic Yacht "Carnegie." By J. P. Ault. XLII, pp. 631-690, 47 ills., chart, Dec., 1922
The White War in Norway. By Thomas R. Henry. LXXXVIII, pp. 617-640, 23 ills., map, Nov., 1945

NORWEGIAN Expedition to the Magnetic North Pole by Roald Amundsen. XIV, pp. 293-294, July, 1903

NORWEGIAN Fjords and Folkways. 20 color photos: 19 by Jack Kuhne. LXXV, pp. 501-524, Apr., 1939

NORWEGIAN SEAMEN AND SHIPS:
Convoys to Victory. By Harvey Klemmer. LXXXIII, pp. 193-216, 24 ills., Feb., 1943

NOTE on the Height of Mount Saint Elias. By Professor Israel C. Russell. VI, pp. 215-216, Dec. 29, 1894

NOTES About Ants and Their Resemblance to Man. By William Morton Wheeler. XXIII, pp. 731-766, 32 ills., diagrs., Aug., 1912

NOTES and Scenes from Korea. XIX, pp. 498-508, 14 ills., July, 1908

NOTES from a Naturalist's Experiences in British Guiana. By C. H. Eigenmann. XXII, pp. 859-870, 8 ills., Sept., 1911

NOTES on a Zoological Collecting Trip to Dutch New Guinea. By Thomas Barbour. XIX, pp. 469-484, 12 ills., maps, July, 1908

NOTES on Burma. By Thomas Barbour. XX, pp. 841-866, 34 ills., Oct., 1909

NOTES on Central America. XVIII, pp. 272-279, ills., map, Apr., 1907

NOTES on Finland. (By Baroness Alletta Korff). XXI, pp. 493-494, June, 1910

NOTES on Macedonia. XIX, pp. 790-802, 15 ills., map, Nov., 1908

NOTES on Manchuria. By Henry B. Miller. XV, pp. 261-262, June, 1904

NOTES on Morocco. XVII, p. 157, Mar., 1906

NOTES on Normandy. By Mrs. Geo. C. Bosson, Jr. XXI, pp. 775-782, 5 ills., Sept., 1910

NOTES on Oman. By S. M. Zwemer. XXII, pp. 89-98, 8 ills., map, Jan., 1911

NOTES on Panama and Colombia. XIV, pp. 458-466, 12 ills., Dec., 1903

NOTES on Rumania. XXIII, pp. 1219-1225, 1239, 9 ills., Dec., 1912

NOTES on Some Eruptive Rocks from Alaska. By George H. Williams. IV, pp. 63-74, Mar. 21, 1892

NOTES on Some Primitive Philippine Tribes. By Dean C. Worcester. IX, pp. 284-301, 11 ills., June, 1898

NOTES on Southern Mexico (Agricultural Products). By G. N. Collins and C. B. Doyle. XXII, pp. 301-320, 16 ills., map, Mar., 1911

NOTES on Tahiti. By H. W. Smith. XXII, pp. 947-963, 17 ills., Oct., 1911

NOTES on the Deserts of the United States and Mexico (Extracted from a Publication of Dr. Daniel T. MacDougal). XXI, pp. 691-714, 16 ills., Aug., 1910

NOTES on the Distances Flies Can Travel. By N. A. Cobb. XXI, pp. 380-383, May, 1910

NOTES on the Ekoi (Nigeria). By P. A. Talbot. XXIII, pp. 33-38, 8 ills., Jan., 1912

NOTES on the Eucalyptus Tree from the United States Forest Service. XX, pp. 668-673, 4 ills., July, 1909

NOTES on the Forest Service. XVIII, pp. 142-145, 3 ills., Feb., 1907

NOTES on the Geology of the Vicinity of Muir Glacier. By H. P. Cushing. IV, pp. 56-62, map, Mar. 21, 1892

NOTES on the Only American Colony in the World (Liberia). By Edgar Allen Forbes. XXI, pp. 719-729, 14 ills., Sept., 1910

NOTES on the Panama Canal. (By Theodore P. Shonts). XVII, pp. 362-363, June, 1906

NOTES on the Remarkable Habits of Certain Turtles and Lizards. By H. A. Largelamb. XVIII, pp. 413-419, 12 ills., June, 1907

NOTES on the Sea Dyaks of Borneo. By Edwin H. Gomes. XXII, pp. 695-723, 26 ills., Aug., 1911

NOTES on the Wild Fowl and Game Animals of Alaska. By E. W. Nelson. IX, pp. 121-132, 6 ills., Apr., 1898

NOTES on Tibet. XV, pp. 292-294, ill., July, 1904

NOTES on Troy. (By Ernest L. Harris). XXVII, pp. 531-532, May, 1915

NOTES on Turbulent Nicaragua. XX, pp. 1102-1116, 13 ills., map, Dec., 1909

NOURSE, MARY A.:

How Half the World Works. By Alice Tisdale Hobart and Mary A. Nourse. LXI, pp. 509-524, 22 ills., Apr., 1932

Women's Work in Japan. By Mary A. Nourse. LXXIII, pp. 99-132, 32 ills. in black and white, 11 ills. in color, Jan., 1938

NOVA SCOTIA (Province), Canada:

The Charm of Cape Breton Island: The Most Picturesque Portion of Canada's Maritime Provinces—A Land Rich in Historic Associations, Natural Resources, and Geographic Appeal. By Catherine Dunlop Mackenzie. XXXVIII, pp. 34-60, 22 ills., map, July, 1920

Salty Nova Scotia: In Friendly New Scotland Gaelic Songs Still Answer the Skirling Bagpipes. By Andrew H. Brown. LXXVII, pp. 575-624, 30 ills. in black and white, 21 ills. in color, two-page map, May, 1940

Tides in the Bay of Fundy. XVI, pp. 71-76, 4 ills., Feb., 1905

NOVARUPTA (Volcano), Alaska:

The Valley of Ten Thousand Smokes: An Account of the Discovery and Exploration of the Most Wonderful Volcanic Region in the World. By Robert F. Griggs. XXXIII, pp. 115-169, 46 ills., map, panorama, Feb., 1918

NOYES, PERLEY H.:

A Visit to Lonely Iceland. By Perley H. Noyes. XVIII, pp. 731-741, 12 ills., Nov., 1907

NOYES, THEODORE W.:

The World's Great Waterfalls: Visits to Mighty Niagara, Wonderful Victoria, and Picturesque Iguazu. By Theodore W. Noyes. L, pp. 29-59, 29 ills., July, 1926

NUBAS (Tribespeople):

Two Fighting Tribes of the Sudan. By Merian C. Cooper. Photos by Ernest B. Schoedsack. LVI, pp. 465-486, 27 ills., map, Oct., 1929

NUERS (Tribespeople):

Across Widest Africa. By A. Henry Savage Landor. XIX, pp. 694-737, 38 ills., map, Oct., 1908

NUNIVAK (Island), Bering Sea:

Alaska—Our Northwestern Outpost. 16 color photos by Ernest H. Gruening, Amos Burg, Froelich Rainey. LXXXII, pp. 297-308, Sept., 1942

NURSING:

Flying Our Wounded Veterans Home. By Catherine Bell Palmer. LXXXVIII, pp. 363-384, 17 ills., Sept., 1945

Heroes' Return. By William H. Nicholas. LXXXVII, pp. 333-352, 19 ills., Mar., 1945

The Symbol of Service to Mankind. By Stockton Axson. XXXIII, pp. 375-390, 11 ills., Apr., 1918

See also Red Cross; *and* American National Red Cross

NUTHATCHES (Birds):

Winged Denizens of Woodland, Stream, and Marsh. By Alexander Wetmore. Paintings by Major Allan Brooks. LXV, pp. 577-596, 5 portraits in color, May, 1934

NUTS and Their Uses as Foods. XVIII, p. 800, Dec., 1907

NYAMLAGIRA (Volcano), Belgian Congo:

We Keep House on an Active Volcano: After Flying to Study a Spectacular Eruption in Belgian Congo, a Geologist Settles Down on a Newborn Craterless Vent for Eight Months' Study. By Dr. Jean Verhoogen. LXXVI, pp. 511-550, 28 ills., map, Oct., 1939

NYMAN, STEPHEN H.:

Gilded Domes Against an Azure Sky (Iran). 13 color photos by Stephen H. Nyman. LXXVI, pp. 339-346, Sept., 1939

O

OAKLAND, California:

Wild Ducks as Winter Guests in a City Park. By Joseph Dixon. XXXVI, pp. 331-342, 11 ills., Oct., 1919

OAKLEY, THORNTON:

Industries: American Industries Geared for War. By Thornton Oakley. With 16 ills. in color from paintings by author. LXXXII, pp. 716-734, ill. in black and white, Dec., 1942

Science Works for Mankind. 16 ills. in color from paintings by Thornton Oakley. LXXXVIII, pp. 737-752, Dec., 1945

Transportation: American Transportation Vital to Victory. By Thornton Oakley. With 16 ills. in color from paintings by author. LXXXIV, pp. 671-688, Dec., 1943

OAXACA (State), Mexico:

Among the Zapotecs of Mexico: A Visit to the Indians of Oaxaca, Home State of the Republic's Great Liberator, Juárez, and Its Most Famous Ruler, Diaz. By Herbert Corey. LI, pp. 501-553, 59 ills., map, May, 1927

OAXACA (State), Mexico—*Continued*

Hewers of Stone. By Jeremiah Zimmerman. XXI, pp. 1002-1020, 9 ills., Dec., 1910

Monte Albán, Richest Archeological Find in America: A Tomb in Oaxaca, Mexico, Yields Treasures Which Reveal the Splendid Culture of the Mixtecs. By Dr. Alfonso Caso. LXII, pp. 487-512, 28 ills., Oct., 1932

OBER, FREDERICK A.:

In the Wake of Columbus. By Frederick A. Ober. V, pp. 187-196, Jan. 31, 1894

OBERAMMERGAU, Germany:

Where Bible Characters Live Again: Everyday Life in Oberammergau, World Famous for Its Passion Play, Reaches a Climax at Christmas. By Anton Lang, Jr. LXVIII, pp. 743-769, 19 ills. in black and white, 11 ills. in color, map, Dec., 1935

OBSERVATIONS on the Russo-Japanese War, in Japan and Manchuria. By Dr. Louis Livingston Seaman. XVI, pp. 80-82, Feb., 1905

OBSERVING a Total Eclipse of the Sun: Dimming Solar Light for a Few Seconds Entails Years of Work for Science and Attracts Throngs to "Nature's Most Magnificent Spectacle." By Paul A. McNally. LXII, pp. 597-605, 6 ills., Nov., 1932

OBSERVING an Eclipse in Asiatic Russia. By Irvine C. Gardner. LXXI, pp. 179-197, 19 ills. in black and white, ill. in color, Feb., 1937

OCEANIA. *See* Pacific Islands

OCEANOGRAPHY:

Captain Charles D. Sigsbee, U.S.N. (By H. G.). IX, p. 250, ill. (front.), May, 1898

Charting a World at War. By William H. Nicholas. LXXXVI, pp. 617-640, 23 ills., drawing, Nov., 1944

Cotidal Lines for the World. By R. A. Harris. XVII, pp. 303-309, 3 maps, map supplement, June, 1906

The Drift of Floating Bottles in the Pacific Ocean. By James Page. XII, pp. 337-339, Sept., 1901

The Grandest and Most Mighty Terrestrial Phenomenon: The Gulf Stream. By John Elliott Pillsbury. XXIII, pp. 767-778, ill., diagrs., 3 maps, Aug., 1912

The Great Unmapped Areas on the Earth's Surface Awaiting the Explorer and Geographer. By J. Scott Keltie. VIII, pp. 251-266, Sept., 1897

Introductory Address. By the President, Mr. Gardiner G. Hubbard. I, pp. 3-10, Oct., 1888

Ocean Currents. By James Page. XIII, pp. 135-142, Apr., 1902

Our Global Ocean—Last and Vast Frontier. By F. Barrows Colton. LXXXVII, pp. 105-128, 19 ills., drawing, Jan., 1945

Our Guardians on the Deep. By William Joseph Showalter. XXV, pp. 655-677, 15 ills., chart, June, 1914

Relations of Air and Water to Temperature and Life. By Honorable Gardiner G. Hubbard. V, pp. 112-124, Jan. 31, 1894

OCEANOGRAPHY—*Continued*

The Relations of the Gulf Stream and the Labrador Current. By William Libbey, Junior. V, pp. 161-166, Jan. 31, 1894

Report—Geography of the Sea. By George L. Dyer. I, pp. 136-150, table, Apr., 1889

Reports of Sealing Schooners Cruising in the Neighborhood of Tuscarora Deep in May and June, 1896. (By Eliza Ruhamah Scidmore). VII, pp. 310-312, Sept., 1896

Tides in the Bay of Fundy. XVI, pp. 71-76, 4 ills., Feb., 1905

Tides of Chesapeake Bay. By E. D. Preston. X, pp. 391-392, Oct., 1899

The War and Ocean Geography. By the Editor (Gilbert Grosvenor). XXXIV, pp. 230-242, 6 ills., map, Sept., 1918

See also Hydrography; Marine Biology; Marine Erosion; Tides and Tidal Waves

O'CONNOR, V. C. SCOTT:

Beyond the Grand Atlas: Where the French Tricolor Flies Beside the Flag of the Sultan of Morocco. By V. C. Scott O'Connor. LXI, pp. 261-319, 52 ills. in black and white, 12 ills. in color, map, Mar., 1932

Old France in Modern Canada. By V. C. Scott O'Connor. LXVII, pp. 167-200, 36 ills., map, Feb., 1935

OCTOPUSES:

Marauders of the Sea. By Roy Waldo Miner. Paintings by Else Bostelmann. LXVIII, pp. 185-207, 12 ills. in black and white, 8 ills. in color, Aug., 1935

ODESSA, U. S. S. R.:

Ukraine, Past and Present. By Nevin O. Winter. XXXIV, pp. 114-128, 14 ills., Aug., 1918

OGASAWARA SHOTO (Bonin Islands), Pacific Ocean:

American Pathfinders in the Pacific. By William H. Nicholas. LXXXIX, pp. 617-640, 17 ills., two-page map, May, 1946

Hidden Key to the Pacific: Piercing the Web of Secrecy Which Long Has Veiled Japanese Bases in the Mandated Islands. By Willard Price. LXXXI, pp. 759-785, 28 ills., map, June, 1942

Springboards to Tokyo. By Willard Price. LXXXVI, pp. 385-407, 16 ills., Oct., 1944

OGDEN, HERBERT G.:

Annual Report of the Superintendent of the United States Coast and Geodetic Survey (Summary by Herbert G. Ogden). VII, pp. 186-188, May, 1896

Geographic Nomenclature. Remarks by Herbert G. Ogden, Gustave Herrle, Marcus Baker, and A. H. Thompson. II, pp. 261-278, Aug., 1890

Geography of the Land. Annual Report by Vice-President Herbert G. Ogden. III, pp. 31-40, Apr. 30, 1891

Report—Geography of the Land. By Herbert G. Ogden. I, pp. 125-135, Apr., 1889

Report—Geography of the Land. By Herbert G. Ogden. II, pp. 31-48, Apr., 1890

The Survey of the Coast. By Herbert G. Ogden. I, pp. 59-77, Oct., 1888

See also NGS: Board of Managers; Vice-President

OHIO:
The Indian Village of Baum. (By H. C. Brown). XII, pp. 272-274, July, 1901
Ohio, the Gateway State. By Melville Chater. LXI, pp. 525-591, 58 ills. in black and white, 13 ills. in color, map, May, 1932
Submerged Valleys in Sandusky Bay. By Professor E. L. Moseley. XIII, pp. 398-403, 4 charts, Nov., 1902
See also Wright Field

OHIO (River), U. S.:
Men Against the Rivers. By Frederick Simpich. LXXI, pp. 767-794, 22 ills., maps, June, 1937
Ohio, the Gateway State. By Melville Chater. LXI, pp. 525-591, 58 ills. in black and white, 13 ills. in color, map, May, 1932
The Travels of George Washington: Dramatic Episodes in His Career as the First Geographer of the United States. By William Joseph Showalter. LXI, pp. 1-63, 50 ills., 4 maps, map supplement, Jan., 1932

OIL. *See* Petroleum

OIL Comes to Bahrein, Port of Pearls. 11 color photos by Maynard Owen Williams. LXXXIX, pp. 201-208, Feb., 1946

OIL Fields of Texas and California. XII, pp. 276-278, July, 1901

OIL for Victory Piped under the Sea. 9 ills. LXXXVIII, pp. 721-726, Dec., 1945

The **OIL** Treasure of Mexico. By Russell Hastings Millward. XIX, pp. 803-805, ill., Nov., 1908

OILS, Plant. *See* Chaulmoogra Oil; Coconuts; Cottonseed Oil; Rose Oil Industry

OJIBWAYS (Indians):
The Wild Life of Lake Superior, Past and Present: The Habits of Deer, Moose, Wolves, Beavers, Muskrats, Trout, and Feathered Wood-Folk Studied with Camera and Flashlight. By George Shiras, 3d. XL, pp. 113-204, 76 ills., map, pictorial supplement, Aug., 1921

OKEFINOKEE (Swamp), Georgia-Florida:
The Okefinokee Wilderness: Exploring the Mystery Land of the Suwannee River Reveals Natural Wonders and Fascinating Folklore. By Francis Harper. LXV, pp. 597-624, 35 ills., map, May, 1934

OKINAWA (Island), Okinawa Gunto, Ryukyu Retto:
American Pathfinders in the Pacific. By William H. Nicholas. LXXXIX, pp. 617-640, 17 ills., two-page map, May, 1946
Okinawa, Threshold to Japan. By Lt. David D. Duncan, USMC. With 22 color photos by author and others. LXXXVIII, pp. 411-428, Oct., 1945
Peacetime Rambles in the Ryukyus. By William Leonard Schwartz. LXXXVII, pp. 543-561, 12 ills., maps, May, 1945

OKLAHOMA:
Big Oklahoma. By Bird S. McGuire. XVII, pp. 103-105, Feb., 1906
The Five Civilized Tribes and the Survey of Indian Territory. By C. H. Fitch. IX, pp. 481-491, 4 ills., map, Dec., 1898

OKLAHOMA—*Continued*
So Oklahoma Grew Up. By Frederick Simpich. LXXIX, pp. 269-314, 30 ills. in black and white, 19 ills. in color, map, Mar., 1941
Survey and Subdivision of Indian Territory. By Henry Gannett. VII, pp. 112-115, ill., map, Mar., 1896

OKLAHOMA CITY, Oklahoma:
So Oklahoma Grew Up. By Frederick Simpich. LXXIX, pp. 269-314, 30 ills. in black and white, 19 ills. in color, map, Mar., 1941

OLCOTT, CHARLES S.:
The Orkneys and Shetlands—A Mysterious Group of Islands. By Charles S. Olcott. XXXIX, pp. 197-228, 33 ills., Feb., 1921

OLD and New Blend in Yankeeland (Connecticut). 25 ills. in color. LXXIV, pp. 295-326, Sept., 1938

OLD and New in Persia: In This Ancient Land Now Called Iran a Modern Sugar Factory Rears Its Head Near the Palace of Darius the Great. By the Baroness Ravensdale. LXXVI, pp. 325-355, 20 ills. in black and white, 13 ills. in color, map, Sept., 1939

OLD France in Modern Canada. By V. C. Scott O'Connor. LXVII, pp. 167-200, 36 ills., map, Feb., 1935

OLD Ireland, Mother of New Eire: By Whatever Name, 'Tis the Same Fair Land With the Grass Growing Green on the Hills of Her and the Peat Smoke Hanging Low. By Harrison Howell Walker. LXXVII, pp. 649-691, 19 ills. in black and white, 18 ills. in color, map, May, 1940

An **OLD** Jewel in the Proper Setting: An Eyewitness's Account of the Reconquest of the Holy Land by Twentieth Century Crusaders. By Charles W. Whitehair. XXXIV, pp. 325-344, 17 ills., Oct., 1918

OLD Line State Cyclorama (Maryland). 22 color photos by W. Robert Moore, B. Anthony Stewart, and others. LXXIX, pp. 409-432, Apr., 1941

OLD Masters in a New National Gallery. By Ruth Q. McBride. LXXVIII, pp. 1-50, 11 ills. in black and white, 32 color reproductions of masterpieces, July, 1940

OLD Mines and Mills in India. XX, pp. 489-490, ills., May, 1909

OLD-NEW Battle Grounds of Egypt and Libia. By W. Robert Moore. LXXVIII, pp. 809-820, 8 ills., map, Dec., 1940

OLD Pattern and New in Turkey. 23 color photos by Bernard F. Rogers, Jr. LXXV, pp. 17-48, Jan., 1939

The **OLD** Post-Road from Tiflis to Erivan. By Esther Lancraft Hovey. XII, pp. 300-309, 9 ills., Aug., 1901

OLD World Charm in Modern Quebec. 12 color photos by William D. Boutwell, Jacob Gayer, Edwin L. Wisherd, Clifton Adams. LVII, pp. 507-514, Apr., 1930

The **OLD** Yuma Trail. By W J McGee. XII, pp. 103-107, Mar., 1901; pp. 129-143, 7 ills., map, Apr.. 1901

The **OLDEST** Free Assemblies: Address of Right Hon. Arthur J. Balfour, in the United States House of Representatives, May 5, 1917. XXXI, pp. 368-371, Apr., 1917

The **OLDEST** Living Thing ("General Sherman Tree"). XXIX, pictorial supplement, Apr., 1916

The **OLDEST** Nation of Europe: Geographical Factors in the Strength of Modern England. By Roland G. Usher. XXVI, pp. 393-414, 11 ills., Oct., 1914

OLIVER, DOUGLAS L.:

Treasure Islands of Australasia: New Guinea, New Caledonia, and Fiji Trace across the South Pacific a Fertile Crescent Incredibly Rich in Minerals and Foods. By Douglas L. Oliver. LXXXI, pp. 691-722, 23 ills., two-page map, June, 1942

OLIVER, ELEANOR SCHIRMER:

A Woman's Experiences among Stone Age Solomon Islanders: Primitive Life Remains Unchanged in Tropical Jungleland Where United States Forces Now Are Fighting. By Eleanor Schirmer Oliver. LXXXII, pp. 813-836, 26 ills., map, Dec., 1942

OLIVER, MARION L.:

The Snake Dance (Hopi Indians). By Marion L. Oliver. XXII, pp. 107-137, 31 ills., Feb., 1911

OLIVER, R. L.:

Yucatan in 1895 (Report by R. L. Oliver). VII, pp. 83-85, Feb., 1896

OLIVER, W. J.:

Peaks and Parks of Western Canada. 11 photos: 5 by W. J. Oliver. LXXX, pp. 516-526, Oct., 1941

OLMEC CIVILIZATION:

Discovering the New World's Oldest Dated Work of Man: A Maya Monument Inscribed 291 B. C. is Unearthed Near a Huge Stone Head by a Geographic-Smithsonian Expedition in Mexico. By Matthew W. Stirling. LXXVI, pp. 183-218, 40 ills., map, Aug., 1939

Expedition Unearths Buried Masterpieces of Carved Jade (Cerro de las Mesas, Mexico). By Matthew W. Stirling. LXXX, pp. 277-302, 14 ills. in black and white, 20 ills. in color, map, Sept., 1941

Finding Jewels of Jade in a Mexican Swamp (La Venta). By Matthew W. and Marion Stirling. LXXXII, pp. 635-661, 15 ills. in black and white, 12 ills. in color, map, Nov., 1942

Great Stone Faces of the Mexican Jungle: Five Colossal Heads and Numerous Other Monuments of Vanished Americans Are Excavated by the Latest National Geographic-Smithsonian Expedition. By Matthew W. Stirling. LXXVIII, pp. 309-334, 26 ills., map, Sept., 1940

La Venta's Green Stone Tigers. By Matthew W. Stirling. LXXXIV, pp. 321-332, 4 ills. in black and white, 6 ills. in color, map, Sept., 1943

OLSON, ALMA LUISE:

The Farthest-North Republic: Olympic Games and Arctic Flying Bring Sequestered Finland into New Focus of World Attention. By Alma Luise Olson. LXXIV, pp. 499-533, 25 ills. in black and white, 12 ills. in color, map, Oct., 1938

Sweden, Land of White Birch and White Coal. By Alma Luise Olson. LIV, pp. 441-484, 51 ills., Oct., 1928

OLSSON-SEFFER, HELEN:

The Isthmus of Tehuantepec (Mexico): "The Bridge of the World's Commerce." By Helen Olsson-Seffer. XXI, pp. 991-1002, 7 ills., Dec., 1910

OLSSON-SEFFER, PEHR:

Agricultural Possibilities in Tropical Mexico. By Dr. Pehr Olsson-Seffer. XXI, pp. 1021-1040, 19 ills., Dec., 1910

The **OLYMPIC** Country (Washington). By the late S. C. Gilman, C. E. VII, pp. 133-140, foldout map, Apr., 1896

OLYMPIC MOUNTAINS, Washington:

The Olympic Country. By the late S. C. Gilman, C. E. VII, pp. 133-140, foldout map, Apr., 1896

OMAHA, Nebraska:

Nebraska, the Cornhusker State. By Leo A. Borah. LXXXVII, pp. 513-542, 6 ills. in black and white, 23 ills. in color, map, May, 1945

OMAHA BEACH (Artificial Harbor), Normandy Coast, France:

Normandy's Made-in-England Harbors. LXXXVII, pp. 565-580, 16 ills., map, May, 1945

OMAN (Sultanate), Arabian Peninsula:

Notes on Oman. By S. M. Zwemer. XXII, pp. 89-98, 8 ills., map, Jan., 1911

OMSK, R. S. F. S. R.:

The Land of Promise (Siberia). By Major General A. W. Greely. XXIII, pp. 1078-1090, 7 ills., Nov., 1912

ON a Chilean Hacienda. 8 color photos by E. P. Haddon. LXXXVI, pp. 489-496, Oct., 1944

ON Danish By-Lanes: An American Cycles Through the Quaint City of Lace, the Curiosity Town Where Time Stands Still, and Even Finds a Frontier in the Farming Kingdom. By Willis Lindquist. LXXVII, pp. 1-34, 21 ills. in black and white, 10 ills. in color, map, Jan., 1940

ON Eskimo Geographic Names Ending in Miut. (By John Murdoch). IX, p. 190, Apr., 1898

ON Goes Wisconsin: Strength and Vigor Mark This Midwestern State, With Its Woods and Lakes and Its Blend of Sturdy Nationalities. By Glanville Smith. LXXII, pp. 1-46, 25 ills. in black and white, 27 ills. in color, two-page map, July, 1937

ON Mackenzie's Trail to the Polar Sea. By Amos Burg. LX, pp. 127-156, 32 ills., map, Aug., 1931

ON the Alleged Observation of a Lunar Eclipse by Bering in 1728-9. By Marcus Baker. II, pp. 167-169, 4 tables, May, 1890

ON the Bottom of a South Sea Pearl Lagoon. By Roy Waldo Miner. Paintings by Else Bostelmann. LXXIV, pp. 365-390, 17 ills. in black and white, 8 ills. in color, Sept., 1938

ON the Bypaths of Spain. By Harry A. McBride. LV, pp. 311-364, 50 ills. in black and white, 13 ills. in color, map, Mar., 1929

ON the Cortés Trail. By Luis Marden. LXXVIII, pp. 335-375, 17 ills. in black and white, 22 ills. in color, map, Sept., 1940

ON the Fringe of the Great Desert (Algeria). 32 color photos by Gervais Courtellemont. LIII, pp. 207-222, Feb., 1928

ON the Monastir Road. By Herbert Corey. XXXI, pp. 383-412, 31 ills., May, 1917

ON the Shores of the Caribbean. 16 ills. XLI, pp. 157-172, Feb., 1922

ON the Telegraphic Determinations of Longitude by the Bureau of Navigation. By Lieut. J. A. Norris, U.S.N. II, pp. 1-30, Apr., 1890

ON the Trail of a Horse Thief (British Columbia). By Herbert W. Gleason. XXXV, pp. 349-358, 6 ills., Apr., 1919

ON the Trail of King Solomon's Mines: The Bible, in Addition to Its Spiritual Values, Continues to Prove a Rich Geography and Guide to Exploration of the Holy Land. By Nelson Glueck. LXXXV, pp. 233-256, 20 ills., map, Feb., 1944

ON the Trail of the Air Mail: A Narrative of the Experiences of the Flying Couriers Who Relay the Mail Across America at a Speed of More than 2,000 Miles a Day. By Lieut. J. Parker Van Zandt. XLIX, pp. 1-61, 67 ills., map, Jan., 1926

ON the Turks' Russian Frontier: Everyday Life in the Fastnesses between the Black Sea and Ararat, Borderland of Oil and Minerals that Hitler Covets. By Edward Stevenson Murray. LXXX, pp. 367-392, 21 ills., map, Sept., 1941

ON the Wings of the Wind: In Motorless Planes, Pilots Ride in Flying-Fox Fashion, Cruising on Upward Air Streams and Lifted by the Suction of Moving Clouds. By Howard Siepen. LV, pp. 751-780, 40 ills., June, 1929

ON the World's Highest Plateaus: Through an Asiatic No Man's Land to the Desert of Ancient Cathay. By Hellmut de Terra. LIX, pp. 319-367, 39 ills. in black and white, 32 ills. in color, map, Mar., 1931

ONA INDIANS:

The Indian Tribes of Southern Patagonia, Tierra del Fuego, and the Adjoining Islands. By J. B. Hatcher. XII, pp. 12-22, 4 ills., Jan., 1901

ONCE in a Lifetime: Black Bears Rarely Have Quadruplets, But Goofy Did—and the Camera Caught Her Nursing Her Remarkable Family. By Paul B. Kinney. LXXX, pp. 249-258, 11 ills., Aug., 1941

ONE Hundred British Seaports. XXXI, pp. 84-94, 10 ills., map, Jan., 1917

ONE Season's Game-Bag with the Camera. By George Shiras, 3d. XIX, pp. 387-446, 70 ills., June, 1908

ONE Thousand Miles of Railway Built for Pilgrims and Not for Dividends (Damascus to Mecca). By Colonel F. R. Maunsell. XX, pp. 156-172, 12 ills., map, Feb., 1909

ONIONS AND ONION GROWING:

Black Acres (Mucklands of New York): A Thrilling Sketch in the Vast Volume of Who's Who Among the Peoples That Make America. By Dorothea D. and Fred Everett. LXXX, pp. 631-652, 13 ills. in black and white, 12 ills. in color, Nov., 1941

ONTARIO (Province), Canada:

Ontario, Next Door: Alert, Energetic, and Resourceful, Its British Pluck and Skill in Arts and Trades Gain for This Province a High Place Under the Union Jack. By Frederick Simpich. LXII, pp. 131-183, 54 ills., map, Aug., 1932

ONTONG JAVA (Islands), Solomon Islands:

Coconuts and Coral Islands. By H. Ian Hogbin. LXV, pp. 265-298, 24 ills. in black and white, 14 ills. in color, map, Mar., 1934

OPEN-AIR Law Courts of Ethiopia. 18 photos by Harald P. Lechenperg. LXVIII, pp. 633-646, Nov., 1935

OPENING of the Alaskan Territory. By Harrington Emerson. XIV, pp. 99-106, 5 ills., Mar., 1903

OPERATION CROSSROADS (Atomic Bomb Tests):

Farewell to Bikini. By Carl Markwith. XC, pp. 97-116, 16 ills., July, 1946

OPERATION PLUTO: World War II:

Oil for Victory Piped under the Sea. 9 ills. LXXXVIII, pp. 721-726, Dec., 1945

ORAIBI, Arizona:

The Snake Dance (Hopi Indians). By Marion L. Oliver. XXII, pp. 107-137, 31 ills., Feb., 1911

ORAN, Algeria:

Eastward from Gibraltar: Overland Route Across North Africa to Tunisia and Libia. By Cyrus French Wicker. LXXXIII, pp. 115-142, 28 ills., Jan., 1943

ORANGE COUNTY, New York:

Black Acres: A Thrilling Sketch in the Vast Volume of Who's Who Among the Peoples That Make America. By Dorothea D. and Fred Everett. LXXX, pp. 631-652, 13 ills. in black and white, 12 ills. in color, Nov., 1941

ORANGE FREE STATE, Union of South Africa:

Orange Free State: The Prairie Province. By Melville Chater. LIX, pp. 431-444, 11 ills., Apr., 1931

ORANGUTANS:

Man's Closest Counterparts: Heavyweight of Monkeydom Is the "Old Man" Gorilla, by Far the Largest of the Four Great Apes. By William M. Mann. Paintings by Elie Cheverlange. LXXVIII, pp. 213-236, 10 ills. in black and white, 10 ills. in color, Aug., 1940

ORCHIDS:

Land of the Painted Oxcarts (Costa Rica). By Luis Marden. With 31 color photos by author. XC, pp. 409-456, 30 ills. in black and white, map, Oct., 1946

The **ORDNANCE** Survey of Great Britain—Its History and Object. By Josiah Pierce, Jr. II, pp. 243-260, Aug., 1890

ORE-BOAT Unloaders. (By W. M. Gregory). XVIII, pp. 343-345, ill., May, 1907

OREGON:

The Columbia (River) Turns on the Power. By Maynard Owen Williams. LXXIX, pp. 749-792, 25 ills. in black and white, 18 ills. in color, June, 1941

Crater Lake, Oregon. XIII, p. 221, June, 1902

Crater Lake, Oregon. By J. S. Diller. VIII, pp. 33-48, 6 ills., maps, Feb., 1897

Crater Lake and Yosemite Through the Ages. By Wallace W. Atwood, Jr. Paintings by Eugene Kingman. LXXI, pp. 327-343, 7 ills. in black and white, 13 ills. in color, Mar., 1937

Is Our Noblest Volcano Awakening to New Life: A Description of the Glaciers and Evidences of Volcanic Activity of Mount Hood. By A. H. Sylvester. XIX, pp. 515-525, 5 ills., map, July, 1908

A Native Son's Rambles in Oregon. By Amos Burg. LXV, pp. 173-234, 39 ills. in black and white, 24 ills. in color, two-page map, Feb., 1934

Oregon: Its History, Geography, and Resources. By John H. Mitchell, U. S. Senator from Oregon. VI, pp. 239-284, Apr. 20, 1895

Oregon Finds New Riches. By Leo A. Borah. XC, pp. 681-728, 15 ills. in black and white, 28 ills. in color, two-page map, Dec., 1946

Our Pacific Northwest. By N. H. Darton. XX, pp. 645-663, 12 ills., maps, July, 1909

A Relic of the Lewis and Clarke Expedition. (By Cyrus C. Babb). IX, pp. 100-101, ill., Mar., 1898

The Sage Plains of Oregon. By Frederick V. Coville. VII, pp. 395-404, Dec., 1896

Scenes Among the High Cascades in Central Oregon. By Ira A. Williams. XXIII, pp. 579-592, 11 ills., June, 1912

Topographic Work of the U. S. Geological Survey in 1902. XIII, pp. 326-328, Aug., 1902

Wartime in the Pacific Northwest. By Frederick Simpich. LXXXII, pp. 421-464, 25 ills. in black and white, 23 ills. in color, map, Oct., 1942

OREGON TERRITORY:

Boundaries of Territorial Acquisitions. XII, pp. 373-377, chart, Oct., 1901

Oregon: Its History, Geography, and Resources. By John H. Mitchell, U. S. Senator from Oregon. VI, pp. 239-284, Apr. 20, 1895

OREGON TRAIL:

Grass Makes Wyoming Fat. By Frederick Simpich. LXXXVIII, pp. 158-188, 13 ills. in black and white, 19 ills. in color, two-page map, Aug., 1945

Idaho Made the Desert Bloom. By D. Worth Clark. LXXXV, pp. 641-688, 21 ills. in black and white, 20 ills. in color, map, June, 1944

Nebraska, the Cornhusker State. By Leo A. Borah. LXXXVII, pp. 513-542, 6 ills. in black and white, 23 ills. in color, map, May, 1945

O'REILLY, JOHN:

South Florida's Amazing Everglades: Encircled by Populous Places Is a Seldom-visited Area of Rare Birds, Prairies, Cowboys, and Teeming Wild Life of Big Cypress Swamp. By John O'Reilly. LXXVII, pp. 115-142, 26 ills., map, Jan., 1940

The **ORIENTAL** Pageantry of Northern India. 30 color photos by Franklin Price Knott. LVI, pp. 429-460, Oct., 1929

The **ORIGIN** of American State Names. By Frederick W. Lawrence. XXXVIII, pp. 105-143, 34 ills., Aug., 1920

The **ORIGIN** of French-Canadians. IX, pp. 96-97, Mar., 1898

ORIGIN of "Labrador." XVII, pp. 587-588, Oct., 1906

The **ORIGIN** of Stefansson's Blond Eskimo. By Major General A. W. Greely. XXIII, pp. 1225-1238, 10 ills., map, Dec., 1912

ORIGIN of the Name "Cape Nome." (By George Davidson). XII, p. 398, Nov., 1901

ORIGIN of the Physical Features of the United States. By G. K. Gilbert. IX, pp. 308-317, maps, July, 1898

The **ORIGIN** of West India Bird-Life. By Frank M. Chapman. IX, pp. 243-247, May, 1898

The **ORIGIN** of Yosemite Valley. (By Henry Gannett). XII, pp. 86-87, Feb., 1901

The **ORIGINAL** Boundary Stones of the District of Columbia. By Ernest A. Shuster, Jr. XX, pp. 356-359, 6 ills., map, Apr., 1909

The **ORIGINAL** Territory of the United States. By David J. Hill. X, pp. 73-92, Mar., 1899

ORINOCO (River), Venezuela:

In Humboldt's Wake: Narrative of a National Geographic Society Expedition Up the Orinoco and Through the Strange Casiquiare Canal to Amazonian Waters. By Ernest G. Holt. LX, pp. 621-644, 27 ills., map, Nov., 1931

South America. Annual Address by the President, Gardiner G. Hubbard. III, pp. 1-29, fold-out map, Mar. 28, 1891

The Valley of the Orinoco. By T. H. Gignilliat. Text with map supplement. VII, p. 92, Feb., 1896

Venezuela: Her Government, People, and Boundary. By William E. Curtis. VII, pp. 49-58, 3 ills., map supplement, Feb., 1896

ORIOLES:

Blackbirds and Orioles. By Arthur A. Allen. Paintings by Major Allan Brooks. LXVI, pp. 111-130, 12 portraits in color, July, 1934

ORIZABA (Volcano), Mexico:

The Greatest Volcanoes of Mexico. By A. Melgareio. XXI, pp. 741-760, 22 ills., Sept., 1910

A Naturalist's Journey Around Vera Cruz and Tampico. By Frank M. Chapman. XXV, pp. 533-562, 31 ills., May, 1914

The **ORKNEYS** and Shetlands—A Mysterious Group of Islands. By Charles S. Olcott. XXXIX, pp. 197-228, 33 ills., Feb., 1921

ORTHOGRAPHY. *See* Geographic Names; Languages

OSGOOD, WILFRED H.:

The Alaskan Brown Bear. (By Wilfred H. Osgood). XX, pp. 332-333, Apr., 1909

The Big Game of Alaska. By Wilfred H. Osgood. XX, pp. 624-636, 10 ills., July, 1909

Lake Clark, a Little Known Alaskan Lake. By Wilfred H. Osgood. XV, pp. 326-331, ills., map, Aug., 1904

Nature and Man in Ethiopia. By Wilfred H. Osgood. LIV, pp. 121-176, 64 ills., map, Aug., 1928

OSLO, Norway:

The White War in Norway. By Thomas R. Henry. LXXXVIII, pp. 617-640, 23 ills., map, Nov., 1945

OSPREYS:

Cruise of the *Kinkajou:* Among Desert Islands of Mexico Voyagers Find Outdoor Laboratories for the Naturalist and Ideal Fishing Grounds for the Sportsman. By Alfred M. Bailey. LXXX, pp. 339-366, 13 ills. in black and white, 12 ills. in color, map, Sept., 1941

The Eagle, King of Birds, and His Kin. By Alexander Wetmore. Paintings by Maj. Allan Brooks. LXIV, pp. 43-95, 23 ills. in black and white, 48 ills. in color, July, 1933

Photographing the Nest Life of the Osprey. By Capt. C. W. R. Knight. LXII, pp. 247-260, 25 ills., Aug., 1932

OSTERHOUT, G. H., JR.:

A Little-Known Marvel of the Western Hemisphere: Christophe's Citadel, a Monument to the Tyranny and Genius of Haiti's King of Slaves. By Major G. H. Osterhout, Jr. XXXVIII, pp. 469-482, 13 ills., Dec., 1920

OSTRICH Farming in the United States. XVII, pp. 569-574, 6 ills., Oct., 1906

OSTRICHES:

Ostrich Farming in the United States. XVII, pp. 569-574, 6 ills., Oct., 1906

OTHER Working Dogs and the Wild Species. By Stanley P. Young. Paintings by Walter A. Weber. LXXXVI, pp. 363-384, 12 ills. in black and white, 9 ills. in color, Sept., 1944

OTOMI INDIANS:

The Mexican Indian Flying Pole Dance. By Helga Larsen. LXXI, pp. 387-400, 13 ills., Mar., 1937

OTTAWA, Ontario, Canada:

Ontario, Next Door: Alert, Energetic, and Resourceful, Its British Pluck and Skill in Arts and Trades Gain for This Province a High Place Under the Union Jack. By Frederick Simpich. LXII, pp. 131-183, 54 ills., map, Aug., 1932

OUED SOUF (Region), Algeria:

The Country of the Ant Men. By Thomas H. Kearney. XXII, pp. 367-382, 13 ills., map, panorama, Apr., 1911

OULIÉ, MARTHE:

Cruising to Crete: Four French Girls Set Sail in a Breton Yawl for the Island of the Legendary Minotaur. By Marthe Oulié and Mariel Jean-Brunhes. LV, pp. 249-272, 15 ills. in black and white, 14 ills. in color, map, Feb., 1929

OUR Air Frontier in Alaska. By Major General H. H. Arnold. LXXVIII, pp. 487-504, 15 ills., map, Oct., 1940

OUR Armies of Mercy (Red Cross). By Henry P. Davison. XXXI, pp. 423-427, 3 ills., May, 1917

OUR Army Versus a Bacillus. By Alton G. Grinnell. XXIV, pp. 1146-1152, 5 ills., diagr., Oct., 1913

OUR Big Trees Saved. XXXI, pp. 1-11, 10 ills., Jan., 1917

OUR Coal Lands. By Guy Elliott Mitchell. XXI, pp. 446-451, 5 ills., May, 1910

OUR Colored Pictures (Scenes in Korea and China). Text with 39 photos, hand-tinted. XXI, pp. 965, 967, Nov., 1910

OUR Colorful City of Magnificent Distances (Washington, D. C.). 49 color photos by Staff Photographers and Capt. A. W. Stevens. LX, pp. 531-610, Nov., 1931

OUR Common Dogs. By Louis Agassiz Fuertes and Ernest Harold Baynes. Paintings by Louis Agassiz Fuertes. XXXV, pp. 201-253, 73 ills. in color, index p. 280, Mar., 1919

OUR Conquest of the Pacific: The Narrative of the 7,400-Mile Flight from San Francisco to Brisbane in Three Ocean Hops. By Squadron-Leader Charles E. Kingsford-Smith and Flight-Lieut. Charles T. P. Ulm. LIV, pp. 371-402, 27 ills., map, Oct., 1928

OUR Desert Panorama. Text with pictorial supplement. XXII, pp. 409-410, Apr., 1911

OUR First Alliance. By J. J. Jusserand. XXXI, pp. 518-548, 8 ills., June, 1917

OUR Fish Immigrants. By Hugh M. Smith. XVIII, pp. 383-400, 3 ills., June, 1907

OUR Flag Number. By Gilbert Grosvenor. XXXII, pp. 281-284, ills., Oct., 1917

OUR Foreign-Born Citizens. XXXI, pp. 95-130, 36 ills., 8 diagrs., map, Feb., 1917

OUR Foreign Trade. (By H. G.). IX, pp. 27-28, Jan., 1898

OUR Friend the Frog. By Doris M. Cochran. Paintings by Hashime Murayama. LXI, pp. 629-654, 16 ills. in black and white, 14 ills. in color, May, 1932

OUR Friends, the Bees. By A. I. and E. R. Root. XXII, pp. 675-694, 21 ills., July, 1911

OUR Friends, the French: An Appraisal of the Traits and Temperament of the Citizens of Our Sister Republic. By Carl Holliday. XXXIV, pp. 345-377, 29 ills., Nov., 1918

OUR Global Ocean—Last and Vast Frontier. By F. Barrows Colton. LXXXVII, pp. 105-128, 19 ills., drawing, Jan., 1945

OUR Global Strong Arm (Air Power). 10 ills. in color from U. S. Army Air Forces official photos. LXXXIX, pp. 145-152, Feb., 1946

OUR Greatest National Monument: The National Geographic Society Completes Its Explorations in the Valley of Ten Thousand Smokes. By Robert F. Griggs. XL, pp. 219-292, 73 ills. in black and white, 16 ills. in color, maps, Sept., 1921

OUR Greatest Plant Food (Phosphorus). By Guy Elliott Mitchell. XXI, pp. 783-791, 5 ills., diagrs., Sept., 1910

OUR Greatest Travelers: Birds that Fly from Pole to Pole and Shun the Darkness: Birds that Make 2,500 Miles in a Single Flight. By Wells W. Cooke. XXII, pp. 346-365, 12 maps, Apr., 1911

OUR Guardians on the Deep (U. S. Coast and Geodetic Survey). By William Joseph Showalter. XXV, pp. 655-677, 15 ills., chart, June, 1914

OUR Heralds of Storm and Flood (U. S. Weather Bureau). By Gilbert H. Grosvenor. XVIII, pp. 586-601, 15 ills., chart, Sept., 1907

OUR Heritage of Liberty: An Address Before the United States Senate by M. Viviani, President of the French Commission to the United States, May 1, 1917. XXXI, pp. 365-367, ill., Apr., 1917

OUR Heritage of the Fresh Waters: Biographies of the Most Widely Distributed of the Important Food and Game Fishes of the United States. By Charles Haskins Townsend. Paintings by Hashime Murayama. XLIV, pp. 109-159, 25 ills. in black and white, 16 ills. in color, Aug., 1923

OUR Heterogeneous System of Weights and Measures. By Alexander Graham Bell. XVII, pp. 158-169, Mar., 1906

OUR Immigration During 1904. XVI, pp. 15-27, 6 ills., charts, Jan., 1905

OUR Immigration in 1905. XVI, pp. 434-435, Sept., 1905

OUR Immigration Laws from the Viewpoint of National Eugenics. By Prof. Robert De C. Ward. XXIII, pp. 38-41, Jan., 1912

OUR Industrial Victory. By Charles M. Schwab. XXXIV, pp. 212-229, 17 ills., Sept., 1918

OUR Insect Fifth Column: Alien Enemies Take Steady Toll of Food, Trees, and Treasure by Boring from Within. By Frederick G. Vosburgh. Paintings by Hashime Murayama. LXXX, pp. 225-248, 14 ills. in black and white, 10 ills. in color, Aug., 1941

OUR Littlest Ally (San Marino). By Alice Rohe. XXXIV, pp. 139-163, 17 ills., Aug., 1918

OUR Map of North America. Text with map supplement. XLV, p. 580, May, 1924

OUR Map of the Countries of the Caribbean. Text with map supplement. XLI, pp. 221-222, Feb., 1922

OUR Map of the Pacific. Text with map supplement. XL, pp. 647-648, map, Dec., 1921

OUR Map of the Races of Europe. Text with map supplement. XXXIV, pp. 535-536, Dec., 1918

OUR Map of the United States. Text with map supplement. XLIII, p. 460, Apr., 1923

OUR Most Versatile Vegetable Product: Rubber Drops from Millions of Tropical Trees Are Transformed by Genii Chemists into Myriad Articles, from Tires to Teething Rings. By J. R. Hildebrand. LXXVII, pp. 143-200, 51 ills. in black and white, 26 ills. in color, Feb., 1940

OUR Mountain Panorama (Canadian Rockies). XXII, text, p. 521; ill. p. 520; panorama, June, 1911

OUR National Parks. By L. F. Schmeckebier. XXIII, pp. 531-579, 41 ills., map, June, 1912

OUR National War Memorials in Europe. By John J. Pershing. LXV, pp. 1-36, 24 ills. in black and white, 11 ills. in color, map, Jan., 1934

OUR Nation's Capital (Washington, D. C.) on Parade. 16 color photos by B. Anthony Stewart, Walter M. Edwards, and others. LXXXIV, pp. 265-288, Sept., 1943

OUR Neglected Southern Coast. By Alfred Goldsborough Mayer. XIX, pp. 859-871, 10 ills., Dec., 1908

OUR Neighbor, Mexico. By John Birkinbine. XXII, pp. 475-508, 26 ills., map supplement, May, 1911

OUR New Military Wards, the Marshalls. By W. Robert Moore. LXXXVIII, pp. 325-360, 14 ills. in black and white, 20 ills. in color, map, Sept., 1945

OUR New Possessions and the Interest They Are Exciting. (By O. P. Austin). XI, pp. 32-33, Jan., 1900

OUR Northern Rockies. By R. H. Chapman. XIII, pp. 361-372, 10 ills., Oct., 1902

OUR Pacific Northwest. By N. H. Darton. XX, pp. 645-663, 12 ills., maps, July, 1909

OUR Plant Immigrants. By David Fairchild. XVII, pp. 179-201, 29 ills., Apr., 1906

OUR Policemen of the Air (Birds). XXIV, p. 698, June, 1913

OUR Present Population. XV, p. 232, May, 1904

OUR Search for the Lost Aviators: An Arctic Area Larger Than Montana First Explored in Hunt for Missing Russians. By Sir Hubert Wilkins. LXXIV, pp. 141-172, 29 ills., two-page map, Aug., 1938

OUR Second Alliance. By J. J. Jusserand. XXXI, pp. 565-566, ill., June, 1917

OUR Smallest Possession—Guam. By William E. Safford. XVI, pp. 229-237, 5 ills., May, 1905

OUR State Flags. By Byron McCandless and Gilbert Grosvenor. XXXII, pp. 325-341, 57 ills. in color, Oct., 1917

OUR State Flowers: The Floral Emblems Chosen by the Commonwealths. By Gilbert Grosvenor. Paintings by Mary E. Eaton. XXXI, pp. 481-517, 567, ill. in black and white, 30 ills. in color, June, 1917

OUR Transatlantic Flight. By Commander Richard Evelyn Byrd. LII, pp. 347-368, 17 ills., map, Sept., 1927

OUR Youngest Volcano. By J. S. Diller. V, pp. 93-96, ill., July 10, 1893

OUT in San Francisco: Fed on Gold Dust and Fattened by Sea Trade, a Pioneer Village Becomes a Busy World Port. By Frederick Simpich. LXI, pp. 395-434, 38 ills., Apr., 1932

OUTRAM, FRANK:

Burma Road, Back Door to China: Like the Great Wall of Ancient Times, This Mighty Mountain Highway Has Been Built by Myriad Chinese to Help Defend Their Homeland. By Frank Outram and G. E. Fane. LXXVIII, pp. 629-658, 26 ills., map, Nov., 1940

The **OUTSPEAKING** of a Great Democracy: The Proceedings of the Chamber of Deputies of France on Friday, April 6, 1917, as Reported in the "Journal Officiel de La République Française." XXXI, pp. 362-365, ill., Apr., 1917

OUTWITTING the Water Demons of Kashmir. By Maurice Pratt Dunlap. XL, pp. 499-511, 9 ills., Nov., 1921

OVER the Alps to Brenner Pass. 15 photos, two-page map. LXXXIV, pp. 701-714, Dec., 1943

OVER the Andes to Bogotá. By Frank M. Chapman. XL, pp. 353-373, 19 ills., Oct., 1921

OVER the Roof of Our Continent (Mount McKinley). By Bradford Washburn. LXXIV, pp. 78-98, 17 ills. in duotone, map, July, 1938

OVER Trail and Through Jungle in Ecuador: Indian Head-Hunters of the Interior, an Interesting Study in the South American Republic. By H. E. Anthony. XL, pp. 327-352, 28 ills., Oct., 1921

OVERBECK, ALICIA O'REARDON:

Bolivia, Land of Fiestas. By Alicia O'Reardon Overbeck. LXVI, pp. 645-660, 16 ills., map, Nov., 1934

Freiburg (Germany)—Gateway to the Black Forest. By Alicia O'Reardon Overbeck. LXIV, pp. 213-252, 40 ills. in black and white, 11 ills. in color, Aug., 1933

Tin, the Cinderella Metal. By Alicia O'Reardon Overbeck. LXXVIII, pp. 659-684, 24 ills., Nov., 1940

OVERLAND Routes to the Klondike. By Hamlin Garland. IX, pp. 113-116, ill., Apr., 1898

OVIS POLI (Sheep):

By Coolie and Caravan Across Central Asia: Narrative of a 7,900-Mile Journey of Exploration and Research Over "the Roof of the World," from the Indian Ocean to the Yellow Sea. By William J. Morden. LII, pp. 369-431, 73 ills., map, Oct., 1927

OWLS:

American Birds of Prey—A Review of Their Value. XXXVIII, pp. 460-467, 6 ills., Dec., 1920

In Quest of the Golden Eagle: Over Lonely Mountain and Prairie Soars This Rare and Lordly Bird, But Three Youths from the East Catch Up With Him at Last. By John and Frank Craighead. LXXVII, pp. 693-710, 17 ills., May, 1940

Included: Barn Owl, Burrowing Owl, Great Horned Owl

Photoflashing Western Owls. By Lewis W. Walker. LXXXVII, pp. 475-486, 6 ills. in black and white, 7 ills. in color, Apr., 1945

Contents: Elf Owl, Great Horned Owl, Long-eared Owl, Screech Owl

Shadowy Birds of the Night. By Alexander Wetmore. Paintings by Maj. Allan Brooks. LXVII, pp. 217-240, 5 ills. in black and white, 21 portraits in color, Feb., 1935

OXCARTS:

Land of the Painted Oxcarts (Costa Rica). By Luis Marden. With 31 color photos by author. XC, pp. 409-456, 30 ills. in black and white, map, Oct., 1946

OXFORD, England:

Through the Heart of England in a Canadian Canoe. By R. J. Evans. XLI, pp. 473-497, 26 ills., map, May, 1922

See also Oxford University

OXFORD UNIVERSITY, England:

Oxford, Mother of Anglo-Saxon Learning. By E. John Long. LVI, pp. 563-596, 31 ills., Nov., 1929

See also article, *above*

OXHOLM, AXEL H.:

Country Life in Norway: The Beneficent Gulf Stream Enables One-third of the People in a Far-north, Mountainous Land to Prosper on Farms. By Axel H. Oxholm. LXXV, pp. 493-528, 17 ills. in black and white, 20 ills. in color, map, Apr., 1939

OXUS (River), Central Asia. *See* Amu Darya

OYSTERS:

America's Surpassing Fisheries: Their Present Condition and Future Prospects, and How the Federal Government Fosters Them. By Hugh M. Smith. XXIX, pp. 546-583, 35 ills., June, 1916

Cultivation of Marine and Fresh-Water Animals in Japan. By K. Mitsukuri. XVII, pp. 524-531, 5 ills., Sept., 1906

The Dream Ship: The Story of a Voyage of Adventure More Than Half Around the World in a 47-foot Lifeboat. By Ralph Stock. XXXIX, pp. 1-52, 43 ills., map, Jan., 1921

OYSTERS—*Continued*

A Maryland Pilgrimage: Visits to Hallowed Shrines Recall the Major Rôle Played by This Prosperous State in the Development of Popular Government in America. By Gilbert Grosvenor. LI, pp. 133-212, 88 ills., map supplement, Feb., 1927

The Native Oysters of the West Coast. By Robert E. C. Stearns. XIX, pp. 224-226, Mar., 1908

Oysters: The World's Most Valuable Water Crop. By Hugh M. Smith. XXIV, pp. 257-281, 21 ills., Mar., 1913

The Pearl Fisheries of Ceylon. By Hugh M. Smith. XXIII, pp. 173-194, 13 ills., map, Feb., 1912

The Rise of the New Arab Nation. By Frederick Simpich. XXXVI, pp. 369-393, 17 ills., map, Nov., 1919

OZARKS (Plateau), U. S.:

Arkansas Rolls Up Its Sleeves. By Frederick Simpich. XC, pp. 273-312, 16 ills. in black and white, 23 ills. in color, map, Sept., 1946

Land of a Million Smiles. By Frederick Simpich. LXXXIII, pp. 589-623, 14 ills. in black and white, 20 ills. in color, map, May, 1943

P

PACIFIC ISLANDS:

American Pathfinders in the Pacific. By William H. Nicholas. LXXXIX, pp. 617-640, 17 ills., two-page map, May, 1946

Around the World in the "Islander" (Yawl): A Narrative of the Adventures of a Solitary Voyager on His Four-Year Cruise in a Thirty-Four-Foot Sailing Craft. By Capt. Harry Pidgeon. LIII, pp. 141-205, 75 ills., two-page map, Feb., 1928

At Ease in the South Seas. By Maj. Frederick Simpich, Jr. LXXXV, pp. 79-104, 32 ills., Jan., 1944

At Home on the Oceans: Whales and Sharks Make Exciting Neighbors for a Professor's Wife, Turned Able Seaman, On a Three-year Voyage Around the World. By Edith Bauer Strout. LXXVI, pp. 33-86, 54 ills., map, July, 1939

Color Glimpses of the Changing South Seas. 14 color photos by Amos Burg. LXV, pp. 281-288, Mar., 1934

Diary of a Voyage from San Francisco to Tahiti and Return, 1901. By S. P. Langley. XII, pp. 413-429, 10 ills., maps, Dec., 1901

The Dream Ship: The Story of a Voyage of Adventure More Than Half Around the World in a 47-foot Lifeboat. By Ralph Stock. XXXIX, pp. 1-52, 43 ills., map, Jan., 1921

Fairy Terns of the Atolls. By Lewis Wayne Walker. XC, pp. 807-814, 9 ills., Dec., 1946

The Greatest Voyage in the Annals of the Sea. By J. R. Hildebrand. LXII, pp. 699-739, 35 ills., maps, Dec., 1932

Hidden Key to the Pacific: Piercing the Web of Secrecy Which Long Has Veiled Japanese Bases in the Mandated Islands. By Willard Price. LXXXI, pp. 759-785, 28 ills., map, June, 1942

PACIFIC ISLANDS—*Continued*

In the Savage South Seas. By Beatrice Grimshaw. XIX, pp. 1-19, 21 ills., Jan., 1908

The Islands of the Pacific. By J. P. Thomson. XL, pp. 543-558, 15 ills., map supplement, Dec., 1921

Jungle War: Bougainville and New Caledonia. 17 ills. in color from paintings by Lieut. William F. Draper. LXXXV, pp. 417-432, Apr., 1944

Living on a Volcano: An Unspoiled Patch of Polynesia Is Niuafoō, Nicknamed "Tin Can Island" by Stamp Collectors. By Thomas A. Jaggar. LXVIII, pp. 91-106, 17 ills., map, July, 1935

A Modern Saga of the Seas: The Narrative of a 17,000-Mile Cruise on a 40-Foot Sloop by the Author, His Wife, and a Baby, Born on the Voyage. By Erling Tambs. LX, pp. 645-688, 49 ills., map, Dec., 1931

Mysterious Micronesia: Yap, Map, and Other Islands Under Japanese Mandate are Museums of Primitive Man. By Willard Price. LXIX, pp. 481-510, 37 ills., map, Apr., 1936

New Map Shows Immense Pacific Battleground. Text with map supplement. LXXXI, pp. 203-204, Feb., 1942

North About. By Alan J. Villiers. LXXI, pp. 221-250, 24 ills., Feb., 1937

Included: Balabac, Philippines; Balimbing, Philippines; Barahun, Solomons; Bongao, Philippines; Florida, Solomons; Guadalcanal, Solomons; Kawio, Pacific Ocean; Kiriwina, Trobriand Islands; Lusancay Islands, Pacific Ocean; Mambahenauhan, Sulu Sea; Nissan, Solomons; Santa Ana, Solomons; Santa Catalina, Solomons; Tawitawi, Philippines

Our New Possessions and the Interest They Are Exciting. (By O. P. Austin). XI, pp. 32-33, Jan., 1900

Painting History in the Pacific. 19 ills. in color from paintings by Lt. William F. Draper, USNR. LXXXVI, pp. 408-424, Oct., 1944

The "Pilgrim" Sails the Seven Seas: A Schooner Yacht Out of Boston Drops in at Desert Isles and South Sea Edens in a Leisurely Two-Year Voyage. By Harold Peters. LXXII, pp. 223-262, 36 ills., Aug., 1937

Revealing Earth's Mightiest Ocean. By Albert W. Atwood. LXXXIV, pp. 291-306, 10 ills., map supplement, Sept., 1943

The Romance of Science in Polynesia: An Account of Five Years of Cruising Among the South Sea Islands. By Robert Cushman Murphy. Paintings by Hashime Murayama. XLVIII, pp. 355-426, 66 ills. in black and white, 16 ills. in color, 3 maps, Oct., 1925

The Society's New Map of Southeast Asia. Text with map supplement. LXXXVI, pp. 449-450, ill., Oct., 1944

South from Saipan. By W. Robert Moore. LXXXVII, pp. 441-474, 11 ills. in black and white, 17 ills. in color, map, Apr., 1945

Springboards to Tokyo. By Willard Price. LXXXVI, pp. 385-407, 16 ills., Oct., 1944

Treasure Islands of Australasia: New Guinea, New Caledonia, and Fiji Trace across the South Pacific a Fertile Crescent Incredibly Rich in Minerals and Foods. By Douglas L. Oliver. LXXXI, pp. 691-722, 23 ills., two-page map, June, 1942

PACIFIC ISLANDS—*Continued*

Westward Bound in the *Yankee.* By Irving and Electa Johnson. LXXXI, pp. 1-44, 25 ills. in black and white, 20 ills. in color, map, Jan., 1942
Included: Easter Island; Galápagos Islands; Pitcairn; Samoa; Santa Cruz; Solomon Islands

What the Fighting Yanks See. By Wanda Burnett. LXXXVI, pp. 451-476, 27 ills., Oct., 1944

Yap and Other Pacific Islands Under Japanese Mandate. By Junius B. Wood. XL, pp. 591-627, 34 ills., map supplement, Dec., 1921

See also Aleutian Islands; Canton Island; Caroline Islands; Easter Island; Falcon Island; Fatu-Hiva; Fiji Islands; Gilbert Islands; Guam; Hawaii; Marianas Islands; Marquesas Islands; Marshall Islands; Nauru; New Caledonia; New Guinea; New Hebrides; Niuafoō; Okinawa; Philippine Islands; Ryukyu Retto; Samoa; Society Islands; Solomon Islands; Tahiti; Tongareva; Wake

PACIFIC NORTHWEST, U. S.:

The Columbia (River) Turns on the Power. By Maynard Owen Williams. LXXIX, pp. 749-792, 25 ills. in black and white, 18 ills. in color, June, 1941

The Great White Monarch of the Pacific Northwest (Mount Rainier). By A. H. Barnes. XXIII, pp. 593-626, 31 ills., map, June, 1912

Our Pacific Northwest. By N. H. Darton. XX, pp. 645-663, 12 ills., maps, July, 1909

The Society Maps Northwestern United States and Neighboring Canadian Provinces. Text with map supplement. LXXIX, pp. 805-806, June, 1941

Wartime in the Pacific Northwest. By Frederick Simpich. LXXXII, pp. 421-464, 25 ills. in black and white, 23 ills. in color, map, Oct., 1942

See also Oregon; Washington

PACIFIC OCEAN:

The Columbus of the Pacific: Captain James Cook, Foremost British Navigator, Expanded the Great Sea to Correct Proportions and Won for Albion an Insular Empire by Peaceful Exploration and Scientific Study. By J. R. Hildebrand. LI, pp. 85-132, 45 ills., maps, Jan., 1927

Deep-Sea Exploring Expedition of the Steamer "Albatross." By Hugh M. Smith. X, pp. 291-296, ills., diagr., Aug., 1899

A Doubtful Island of the Pacific. By James D. Hague. XV, pp. 478-489, ill., maps, Dec., 1904

The Drift of Floating Bottles in the Pacific Ocean. By James Page. XII, pp. 337-339, Sept., 1901

Flying the Pacific. By William Burke Miller. LXX, pp. 665-707, 39 ills., Dec., 1936

The Islands of the Pacific. By J. P. Thomson. XL, pp. 543-558, 15 ills., map supplement, Dec., 1921

Magnetic Survey of the Pacific. XIX, pp. 447-448, June, 1908

Magnetic Survey of the Pacific Ocean. (By L. A. Bauer). XVII, p. 237, Apr., 1906

PACIFIC OCEAN—*Continued*

New Map Shows Immense Pacific Battleground. Text with map supplement. LXXXI, pp. 203-204, Feb., 1942

Our Global Ocean—Last and Vast Frontier. By F. Barrows Colton. LXXXVII, pp. 105-128, 19 ills., drawing, Jan., 1945

Our Map of the Pacific. Text with map supplement. XL, pp. 647-648, map, Dec., 1921

The Pacific: The Most Explored and Least Known Region of the Globe. By Leopold G. Blackman. XIX, pp. 546-563, 11 ills., map, Aug., 1908

Problems of the Pacific—The Commerce of the Great Ocean. By O. P. Austin. XIII, pp. 303-318, 7 maps, Aug., 1902

Problems of the Pacific—The Great Ocean in World Growth. By W J McGee. XIII, pp. 333-342, Sept., 1902

A Recent Report from the "Doubtful Island Region." By James D. Hague. XVIII, pp. 205-208, maps, Mar., 1907

Revealing Earth's Mightiest Ocean. By Albert W. Atwood. LXXXIV, pp. 291-306, 10 ills., map supplement, Sept., 1943

The Romance of Science in Polynesia: An Account of Five Years of Cruising Among the South Sea Islands. By Robert Cushman Murphy. Paintings by Hashime Murayama. XLVIII, pp. 355-426, 66 ills. in black and white, 16 ills. in color, 3 maps, Oct., 1925

Sailing the Seven Seas in the Interest of Science: Adventures Through 157,000 Miles of Storm and Calm, from Arctic to Antarctic and Around the World, in the Non-magnetic Yacht "Carnegie." By J. P. Ault. XLII, pp. 631-690, 47 ills., chart, Dec., 1922

Search for the Lost Island of the Pacific. XV, pp. 425-426, Oct., 1904

The Society's New Map of the Pacific. By Gilbert Grosvenor. Text with map supplement. LXX, pp. 793-796, Dec., 1936

The Work in the Pacific Ocean of the Magnetic Survey Yacht "Galilee." By L. A. Bauer. XVIII, pp. 601-611, 15 ills., Sept., 1907

See also Pacific Islands; Tuscarora Deep

PADAUNGS (Tribespeople):

Among the Hill Tribes of Burma—An Ethnological Thicket. By Sir George Scott. XLI, pp. 293-321, 22 ills., Mar., 1922

Burma: Where India and China Meet: In the Massive Mountains of Southeast Asia, Swarming Road Builders Wage the "War of the Highways" for Free China and Her Allies. By John LeRoy Christian. LXXXIV, pp. 489-512, 18 ills., map, Oct., 1943

PAGAN, Burma:

The Five Thousand Temples of Pagān: Burma's Sacred City Is a Place of Enchantment in the Midst of Ruins. By William H. Roberts. LX, pp. 445-454, 9 ills., Oct., 1931

Untoured Burma. By Charles H. Bartlett. XXIV, pp. 835-853, 17 ills., July, 1913

PAGE, JAMES:

The Drift of Floating Bottles in the Pacific Ocean. By James Page. XII, pp. 337-339, Sept., 1901

PAGE, JAMES—*Continued*

Ocean Currents. By James Page. XIII, pp. 135-142, Apr., 1902

Reports of Vessels as to the Range of Volcanic Dust. By James Page. XIII, pp. 299-301, July, 1902

The Sailing Ship and the Panama Canal. By James Page. XV, pp. 167-176, charts, Apr., 1904

The **PAGEANT** of Jerusalem: The Capital of the Land of Three Great Faiths Is Still the Holy City for Christian, Moslem, and Jew. By Major Edward Keith-Roach. LII, pp. 635-681, 57 ills., Dec., 1927

PAGES from the Floral Life of America. Paintings by Mary E. Eaton. XLVIII, pp. 44-75, 55 ills. in color, July, 1925

PAGO PAGO, Samoa:

America's South Sea Soldiers. By Lorena MacIntyre Quinn. XXXVI, pp. 267-274, 8 ills., Sept., 1919

Sailing the Seven Seas in the Interest of Science: Adventures Through 157,000 Miles of Storm and Calm, from Arctic to Antarctic and Around the World, in the Non-magnetic Yacht "Carnegie." By J. P. Ault. XLII, pp. 631-690, 47 ills., chart, Dec., 1922

Samoa—South Sea Outpost of the U. S. Navy. 20 photos by Truman Bailey. LXXIX, pp. 615-630, May, 1941

PAHUATLAN, Mexico:

The Mexican Indian Flying Pole Dance. By Helga Larsen. LXXI, pp. 387-400, 13 ills., Mar., 1937

PAIGE, SIDNEY:

A Growing Camp in the Tanana Gold Fields, Alaska. By Sidney Paige. XVI, pp. 104-111, 4 ills., Mar., 1905

PAINTING History in the Pacific. 19 ills. in color from paintings by Lt. William F. Draper, USNR. LXXXVI, pp. 408-424, Oct., 1944

PAINTING the Army on Maneuvers. By Arthur Beaumont. Text with 16 ills. in color from paintings by author. LXXXII, pp. 601-602, Nov., 1942

PAINTING the Terrier Series (Acknowledgments). By Edward Herbert Miner. LXIX, pp. 273-274, Feb., 1936

PAINTINGS:

Democracy's Royal Palace (Westminster). 19 color photos by B. Anthony Stewart. XC, pp. 233-248, Aug., 1946

Europe's Looted Art. By John Walker. LXXXIX, pp. 39-52, 11 ills., Jan., 1946

Faces and Fashions of Asia's Changeless Tribes. 26 ills. in color from paintings and drawings by Alexandre Iacovleff. LXIX, pp. 21-36, Jan., 1936

How Warwick (Castle) Was Photographed in Color. By Maynard Owen Williams. LXX, pp. 83-93, 13 ills. in color, July, 1936

PAINTINGS—*Continued*

Old Masters in a New National Gallery. By Ruth Q. McBride. LXXVIII, pp. 1-50, 11 ills. in black and white, 32 color reproductions of masterpieces, July, 1940

Contents: Mellon and Kress Collections

Pioneer Gaucho Days. 8 ills. in color from paintings by Cesáreo Bernaldo de Quirós. LXIV, pp. 453-460, Oct., 1933

See also NGM: Paintings

The **PALACE** of Versailles, Its Park and the Trianons. By Franklin L. Fisher. XLVII, pp. 49-62, 4 ills. in black and white, 14 ills. in color, Jan., 1925

PALACE OF WESTMINSTER (Parliament), London:

Yanks at Westminster. By Capt. Leonard David Gammans. XC, pp. 223-252, 6 ills. in black and white, 19 ills. in color, Aug., 1946

PALACES:

India: Streets and Palaces of Colorful India. L, pp. 60-85, 34 ills. in color, July, 1926

Mexico: Chichen Itzá, an Ancient American Mecca: Recent Excavations in Yucatan Are Bringing to Light the Temples, Palaces, and Pyramids of America's Most Holy Native City. By Sylvanus Griswold Morley. XLVII, pp. 63-95, 34 ills., diagr., map, Jan., 1925

Persia (Iran): Exploring the Secrets of Persepolis. By Charles Breasted. LXIV, pp. 381-420, 48 ills., plan, map, Oct., 1933

Romania: Palaces and Peasants in Rome's Old Colony. 14 color photos by Wilhelm Tobien. LXV, pp. 439-446, Apr., 1934

See also Castles; Château Country; Potala; Versailles; *and* Palace of Westminster

PALARIS (Ships):

Seafarers of South Celebes. By G. E. P. Collins. LXXXVII, pp. 53-78, 25 ills., map, Jan., 1945

PALAU ISLANDS, Caroline Islands:

Hidden Key to the Pacific: Piercing the Web of Secrecy Which Long Has Veiled Japanese Bases in the Mandated Islands. By Willard Price. LXXXI, pp. 759-785, 28 ills., map, June, 1942

Painting History in the Pacific. 19 ills. in color from paintings by Lt. William F. Draper, USNR. LXXXVI, pp. 409-424, Oct., 1944

South from Saipan. By W. Robert Moore. LXXXVII, pp. 441-474, 11 ills. in black and white, 17 ills. in color, map, Apr., 1945

Yap and Other Pacific Islands Under Japanese Mandate. By Junius B. Wood. XL, pp. 591-627, 34 ills., map supplement, Dec., 1921

PALENQUE RUINS, Mexico:

Finding Jewels of Jade in a Mexican Swamp. By Matthew W. and Marion Stirling. LXXXII, pp. 635-661, 15 ills. in black and white, 12 ills. in color, map, Nov., 1942

PALEONTOLOGY:

Birds May Bring You More Happiness Than the Wealth of the Indies. By Frank M. Chapman. XXIV, pp. 699-714, 14 ills., June, 1913

"Compleat Angler" Fishes for Fossils. By Imogene Powell. LXVI, pp. 251-258, 7 ills., Aug., 1934

PALEONTOLOGY—*Continued*

Explorations in the Gobi Desert. By Roy Chapman Andrews. LXIII, pp. 653-716, 50 ills. in black and white, 20 ills. in color, map, June, 1933

Extinct Reptiles Found in Nodules. (By H. A. Largelamb). XVII, pp. 170-173, 9 ills., Mar., 1906

How Old Is Man? By Theodore Roosevelt. XXIX, pp. 111-127, 12 ills., 3 maps, Feb., 1916

Hunting Big Game of Other Days: A Boating Expedition in Search of Fossils in Alberta, Canada. By Barnum Brown. XXXV, pp. 407-429, 24 ills., map, May, 1919

The Larger North American Mammals. By E. W. Nelson. Paintings by Louis Agassiz Fuertes. XXX, pp. 385-472, 24 ills. in black and white, 49 ills. in color, pictorial supplement, Nov., 1916

Our Coal Lands. By Guy Elliott Mitchell. XXI, pp. 446-451, 5 ills., May, 1910

Parade of Life Through the Ages: Records in Rocks Reveal a Strange Procession of Prehistoric Creatures, from Jellyfish to Dinosaurs, Giant Sloths, Saber-toothed Tigers, and Primitive Man. By Charles R. Knight. With 24 ills. in color from paintings by author. LXXXI, pp. 141-184, 13 ills. in black and white, Feb., 1942

Contents: American Mastodon, Archaeopteryx, Arsinoitherium, Ceratosaurus, Cladoselache, Cro-Magnon Man, Dimetrodon, Dinichthys, Diplodocus, Eohippus, Eryops, Eurypterid, Folsom Man, Glyptodon, Hyaenodon, Lake Dwellers, Macrauchenia, Megaceros, Megatherium, Moa, Mosasaurus, Naosaurus, Neanderthal Man, Parasaurolophus, Protoceratops, Pteranodon, Pterodactyl, Saber-toothed Tiger, Stegosaurus, Styracosaurus, Titanotherium, Toxodon, *Tyrannosaurus rex,* Uintatherium, Woolly Mammoth

Report on Fossil Plants (Mount St. Elias Expedition). By Lester F. Ward. III, pp. 199-200, May 29, 1891

Reptiles of All Lands. By Raymond L. Ditmars. XXII, pp. 601-633, 32 ills., July, 1911

Contents: Brontosaurus, Diplodocus, Stegosaurus

A Strange and Remarkable Beast (Mammoth). XVIII, p. 620, ill., Sept., 1907

The Wyoming Fossil Fields Expedition of July, 1899. By Wilbur C. Knight. XI, pp. 449-465, 8 ills., Dec., 1900

PALERMO, Sicily:

Sicily, the Battle-Field of Nations and of Nature. By Mrs. George C. Bosson, Jr. XX, pp. 97-118, 25 ills., map, Jan., 1909

Sicily Again in the Path of War. By Maynard Owen Williams. LXXXIV, pp. 307-320, 7 ills., map, Sept., 1943

PALESTINE:

American Fighters Visit Bible Lands. By Maynard Owen Williams. With 23 color photos by author. LXXXIX, pp. 311-340, 10 ills. in black and white, Mar., 1946

Among the Bethlehem Shepherds: A Visit to the Valley Which David Probably Recalled When He Wrote the Twenty-third Psalm. By John D. Whiting. L, pp. 729-753, 19 ills., Dec., 1926

PALESTINE—*Continued*

Bethlehem and the Christmas Story. By John D. Whiting. LVI, pp. 699-735, 27 ills. in black and white, 14 ills. in color, Dec., 1929

Bombs over Bible Lands. By Frederick Simpich and W. Robert Moore. LXXX, pp. 141-180, 34 ills., two-page map, Aug., 1941

Canoeing Down the River Jordan: Voyagers in Rubber Boats Find the Bible Stream Little Tamed Today as It Plunges to the Dead Sea Over the Earth's Lowest River Bed. By John D. Whiting. LXXVIII, pp. 781-808, 19 ills., map, Dec., 1940

Change Comes to Bible Lands. By Frederick Simpich. LXXIV, pp. 695-750, 40 ills. in black and white, 25 ills. in color, map supplement, Dec., 1938

Changing Palestine. By Major Edward Keith-Roach. LXV, pp. 493-527, 43 ills., map, Apr., 1934

Crusader Castles of the Near East. By William H. Hall. LIX, pp. 369-390, 19 ills., map, Mar., 1931

Flying Over Egypt, Sinai, and Palestine: Looking Down Upon the Holy Land During an Air Journey of Two and a Half Hours from Cairo to Jerusalem. By Brigadier General P. R. C. Groves and Major J. R. McCrindle. L, pp. 313-355, 26 ills. in black and white, 23 ills. in color, map, Sept., 1926

The Geography of the Jordan. By Nelson Glueck. LXXXVI, pp. 719-744, 23 ills., map, Dec., 1944

Impressions of Palestine. By James Bryce. XXVII, pp. 293-317, 18 ills., map, Mar., 1915

Jerusalem's Locust Plague: Being a Description of the Recent Locust Influx into Palestine, and Comparing Same with Ancient Locust Invasions as Narrated in the Old World's History Book, the Bible. By John D. Whiting. XXVIII, pp. 511-550, 25 ills., map, Dec., 1915

The Last Israelitish Blood Sacrifice: How the Vanishing Samaritans Celebrate the Passover on Sacred Mount Gerizim. By John D. Whiting. XXXVII, pp. 1-46, 40 ills., map, Jan., 1920

An Old Jewel in the Proper Setting: An Eyewitness's Account of the Reconquest of the Holy Land by Twentieth Century Crusaders. By Charles W. Whitehair. XXXIV, pp. 325-344, 17 ills., Oct., 1918

On the Trail of King Solomon's Mines: The Bible, in Addition to Its Spiritual Values, Continues to Prove a Rich Geography and Guide to Exploration of the Holy Land. By Nelson Glueck. LXXXV, pp. 233-256, 20 ills., map, Feb., 1944

Palestine Today. By Francis Chase, Jr. XC, pp. 501-516, 16 ills., Oct., 1946

The Road of the Crusaders: A Historian Follows the Steps of Richard the Lion Heart and Other Knights of the Cross Over the "Via Dei." By Harold Lamb. LXIV, pp. 645-693, 46 ills. in black and white, 13 ills. in color, map, Dec., 1933

Skirting the Shores of Sunrise: Seeking and Finding "The Levant" in a Journey by Steamer, Motor-Car, and Train from Constantinople to Port Said. By Melville Chater. L, pp. 649-728, 60 ills. in black and white, 34 ills. in color, map, Dec., 1926

PALESTINE—*Continued*

Village Life in the Holy Land. By John D. Whiting. XXV, pp. 249-314, 27 ills. in black and white, 21 ills. in color, Mar., 1914

See also Jerusalem

PALESTINE. 21 photos, hand-tinted, by the American Colony, Jerusalem. XXV, pp. 265-313, Mar., 1914

A **PALETTE** from Spain. By W. Langdon Kihn. LXIX, pp. 407-440, 16 ills. in black and white, 26 ills. in duotone, map, Mar., 1936

PALIO (Horse Race):

Siena's Palio, an Italian Inheritance from the Middle Ages. By Marie Louise Handley. L, pp. 245-258, 3 ills., Aug., 1926

PALMER, ALFRED T.:

China: Changing Canton. 20 photos by Siukee Mack, Alfred T. Palmer, Kinchue Wong. LXXII, pp. 711-726, Dec., 1937

Great Lakes and Great Industries. 19 color photos by B. Anthony Stewart, Alfred T. Palmer, Willard R. Culver. LXXXVI, pp. 689-712, Dec., 1944

PALMER, CATHERINE BELL:

Flying Our Wounded Veterans Home. By Catherine Bell Palmer. LXXXVIII, pp. 363-384, 17 ills., Sept., 1945

PALMER, HOWARD:

Some Tramps Across the Glaciers and Snowfields of British Columbia. By Howard Palmer. XXI, pp. 457-487, 25 ills., June, 1910

PALMERSTON ISLAND, South Pacific Ocean:

The Dream Ship: The Story of a Voyage of Adventure More Than Half Around the World in a 47-foot Lifeboat. By Ralph Stock. XXXIX, pp. 1-52, 43 ills., map, Jan., 1921

PALMS (Plants):

The Palms. XXII, pictorial supplement, Dec., 1911

The Paradise of the Tasman (Lord Howe Island): A Pacific Island Provides the Palms Which Decorate Hotels, Churches, Steamships, and Homes. By Hubert Lyman Clark. LXVIII, pp. 115-136, 24 ills., map, July, 1935

See also Coconut Palms; Date Palms

PALMS and Planes in the New Hebrides. By Maj. Robert D. Heinl, Jr. LXXXVI, pp. 229-256, 17 ills. in black and white, 12 ills. in color, map, Aug., 1944

PANAMA:

Farming on the Isthmus of Panama. By Dillwyn M. Hazlett. XVII, pp. 229-234, 5 ills., Apr., 1906

Improvements in the Republic of Panama. XVI, pp. 441-442, Sept., 1905

The Jungles of Panama. By David Fairchild. XLI, pp. 131-145, 14 ills., Feb., 1922

The Latest Route Proposed for the Isthmian Canal—Mandingo Route. XIII, pp. 64-70, chart, Feb., 1902

Little-Known Parts of Panama. By Henry Pittier. XXIII, pp. 627-662, 35 ills., map, July, 1912

PANAMA—*Continued*

Nature's Transformation at Panama: Remarkable Changes in Faunal and Physical Conditions in the Gatun Lake Region. By George Shiras, 3d. XXVIII, pp. 159-194, 33 ills., maps, Aug., 1915

Notes on Panama and Colombia. XIV, pp. 458-466, 12 ills., Dec., 1903

Panama, Bridge of the World. By Luis Marden. LXXX, pp. 591-630, 23 ills. in black and white, 22 ills. in color, map, Nov., 1941

The Panama Canal Route. By Robert T. Hill. VII, pp. 59-64, ills., table, Feb., 1896

Redeeming the Tropics. By William Joseph Showalter. XXV, pp. 344-364, 13 ills., Mar., 1914

The Republic of Panama. By Wm. H. Burr. XV, pp. 57-73, 7 ills., Feb., 1904

A Trip to Panama and Darien. By Richard U. Goode. I, pp. 301-314, diagr., foldout map, Oct., 1889

Who Treads Our Trails? A Camera Trapper Describes His Experiences on an Island in the Canal Zone, a Natural-History Laboratory in the American Tropics. By Frank M. Chapman. LII, pp. 331-345, 18 ills., map, Sept., 1927

See also Mulatas Archipelago

PANAMA CANAL:

Battling with the Panama Slides. By William Joseph Showalter. XXV, pp. 133-153, 15 ills., Feb., 1914

Bird's-Eye View of Panama Canal. Announcement of map supplement. XXIII, p. 208, Feb., 1912

The completed report of the Isthmian Canal Commission. XII, p. 441, Dec., 1901

Completion of the La Boca Dock. IX, p. 84, Mar., 1898

The Dream Ship: The Story of a Voyage of Adventure More Than Half Around the World in a 47-foot Lifeboat. By Ralph Stock. XXXIX, pp. 1-52, 43 ills., map, Jan., 1921

Geography of the Land. Annual Report by Vice-President Herbert G. Ogden. III, pp. 31-40, Apr. 30, 1891

Honors to Colonel Goethals: The Presentation, by President Woodrow Wilson, of the National Geographic Society Special Gold Medal. XXV, pp. 677-690, 6 ills., June, 1914

The Interoceanic Canal. By Emory R. Johnson. X, pp. 311-316, Aug., 1899

Map of Panama Canal. Announcement of map supplement (Oct., 1905). XVI, p. 441, Sept., 1905

Nicaragua and the Isthmian Routes. By Arthur P. Davis. X, pp. 247-266, 7 ills., diagrs., July, 1899

Notes on the Panama Canal. (By Theodore P. Shonts). XVII, pp. 362-363, June, 1906

Panama, Bridge of the World. By Luis Marden. LXXX, pp. 591-630, 23 ills. in black and white, 22 ills. in color, map, Nov., 1941

The Panama Canal. By Rear Admiral Colby M. Chester. XVI, pp. 445-467, 8 ills., Oct., 1905

The Panama Canal. By Lieut. Col. Geo. W. Goethals. XX, pp. 334-355, 7 ills., diagr., map, Apr., 1909

PANAMA CANAL—*Continued*

The Panama Canal. By Colonel George W. Goethals. XXII, pp. 148-211, 49 ills., diagr., maps, Feb., 1911

The Panama Canal. By Theodore P. Shonts. XVII, pp. 55-68, 5 ills., Feb., 1906

The Panama Canal. By William Joseph Showalter. XXIII, pp. 195-205, map supplement, Feb., 1912

Bird's-Eye View of the Panama Canal. Map supplement (panorama by H. H. Green) ; text, p. 208

The Panama Canal. By Lieut. Colonel William L. Sibert. XXV, pp. 153-183, 24 ills., Feb., 1914

The Panama Canal Route. By Robert T. Hill. VII, pp. 59-64, ills., table, Feb., 1896

The Probable Effect of the Panama Canal on the Commercial Geography of the World. By O. P. Austin. XXV, pp. 245-248, Feb., 1914

Progress on the Panama Canal. (By G. H. G.). XVI, pp. 467-475, map, Oct., 1905

The Proposed American Interoceanic Canal in Its Commercial Aspects. By Joseph Nimmo, Jr. X, pp. 297-310, Aug., 1899

The Republic of Panama. By Wm. H. Burr. XV, pp. 57-73, 7 ills., Feb., 1904

A Trip to Panama and Darien. By Richard U. Goode. I, pp. 301-314, diagr., foldout map, Oct., 1889

What Has Been Accomplished by the United States Toward Building the Panama Canal. By Theodore P. Shonts. XVI, pp. 558-564, Dec., 1905

The Work on the Isthmus. XVII, pp. 586-587, Oct., 1906

PANAMA-PACIFIC INTERNATIONAL EXPOSITION:

A City of Realized Dreams (San Francisco). By Franklin K. Lane. XXVII, pp. 169-171, Feb., 1915

PANAMA RAILROAD:

A Trip to Panama and Darien. By Richard U. Goode. I, pp. 301-314, diagr., foldout map, Oct., 1889

PAN AMERICAN AIRWAYS:

Flight Expedition: Over the Roof of Our Continent (Mount McKinley). By Bradford Washburn. LXXIV, pp. 78-98, 17 ills. in duotone, map, July, 1938

Flying the Pacific. By William Burke Miller. LXX, pp. 665-707, 39 ills., Dec., 1936

PAN-AMERICAN CONFERENCES:

Reasons Why the United States in Particular Should Encourage the Pan-American Conferences. (By Elihu Root). XVII, pp. 479-480, Aug., 1906

What the Latin American Republics Think of the Pan-American Conferences. XVII, pp. 474-479, Aug., 1906

PAN-AMERICAN EXPOSITION:

The Philippine Exhibit at the Pan-American Exposition. By D. O. Noble Hoffmann. XII, pp. 119-122, Mar., 1901

PAN AMERICAN GOOD WILL FLYERS:

How Latin America Looks from the Air: U. S. Army Airplanes Hurdle the High Andes, Brave Brazil Jungles, and Follow Smoking Volcanoes to Map New Sky Paths Around South America. By Major Herbert A. Dargue. LII, pp. 451-502, 52 ills., map, Oct., 1927

PAN-AMERICAN RAILWAY:

Pan-American Railway. XV, pp. 232-233, May, 1904

South America. Annual Address by the President, Gardiner G. Hubbard. III, pp. 1-29, foldout map, Mar. 28, 1891

PANORAMAS. *See* Pictorial Supplements: Enlargements and Panoramas

PANORAMIC View from the west side of Burgess Pass, 3280 feet above Field, British Columbia, in the Canadian Rockies. XXII, text p. 521; ill. p. 520; panorama, June, 1911

The **PANTHER** of the Hearth: Lithe Grace and Independence of Spirit Contribute to the Appeal of Cats, "The Only Domestic Animal Man Has Never Conquered." By Frederick B. Eddy. LXXIV, pp. 589-634, 22 ills. in black and white, 25 ills. in color, Nov., 1938

PAPAGO INDIANS:

The Old Yuma Trail. By W J McGee. XII, pp. 103-107, Mar., 1901; pp. 129-143, 7 ills., map, Apr., 1901

Papagueria. By W J McGee. IX, pp. 345-371, 9 ills., Aug., 1898

PAPAGUERIA (U. S.-Mexico). By W J McGee. IX, pp. 345-371, 9 ills., Aug., 1898

PAPEETE, Tahiti:

Notes on Tahiti. By H. W. Smith. XXII, pp. 947-963, 17 ills., Oct., 1911

Tahiti: A Playground of Nature. By Paul Gooding. XXXVIII, pp. 301-326, 16 ills., map, Oct., 1920

PAPER INDUSTRY:

Lessons from Japan. XV, pp. 221-225, 3 ills., May, 1904

Massachusetts—Beehive of Business. By William Joseph Showalter. XXXVII, pp. 203-245, 41 ills., Mar., 1920

Paper From Cotton Stalks. XVII, p. 425, July, 1906

PAPUA (Territory), New Guinea:

Further Notes on Dutch New Guinea. By Thomas Barbour. XIX, pp. 527-545, 19 ills., Aug., 1908

Into Primeval Papua by Seaplane: Seeking Disease-resisting Sugar Cane, Scientists Find Neolithic Man in Unmapped Nooks of Sorcery and Cannibalism. By E. W. Brandes. LVI, pp. 253-332, 98 ills., map, Sept., 1929

Notes on a Zoological Collecting Trip to Dutch New Guinea. By Thomas Barbour. XIX, pp. 469-484, 12 ills., maps, July, 1908

Pictorial Jaunt Through Papua. 22 photos by Captain Frank Hurley. LI, pp. 109-124, Jan., 1927

Strange Sights in Far-Away Papua. By A. E. Pratt. XVIII, pp. 559-572, 7 ills., Sept., 1907

PARADE of Life Through the Ages: Records in Rocks Reveal a Strange Procession of Prehistoric Creatures, from Jellyfish to Dinosaurs, Giant Sloths, Saber-toothed Tigers, and Primitive Man. By Charles R. Knight. With 24 ills. in color from paintings by author. LXXXI, pp. 141-184, 13 ills. in black and white, Feb., 1942

The **PARADISE** of the Tasman (Lord Howe Island): A Pacific Island Provides the Palms Which Decorate Hotels, Churches, Steamships, and Homes. By Hubert Lyman Clark. LXVIII, pp. 115-136, 24 ills., map, July, 1935

PARAGUAY:

Buenos Aires and Its River of Silver: A Journey Up the Paraná and Paraguay to the Chaco Cattle Country. By William R. Barbour. XL, pp. 393-432, 38 ills., Oct., 1921

The Falls of Iguazu. By Marie Robinson Wright. XVII, pp. 456-460, 4 ills., Aug., 1906

River-Encircled Paraguay. By Harriet Chalmers Adams. LXIII, pp. 385-416, 35 ills., map, Apr., 1933

Through Paraguay and Southern Matto Grosso. By Sir Christopher H. Gibson. LXXXIV, pp. 459-488, 20 ills. in black and white, 11 ills. in color, map, Oct., 1943

PARAGUAY (River), Paraguay:

Buenos Aires and Its River of Silver: A Journey Up the Paraná and Paraguay to the Chaco Cattle Country. By William R. Barbour. XL, pp. 393-432, 38 ills., Oct., 1921

Through Paraguay and Southern Matto Grosso. By Sir Christopher H. Gibson. LXXXIV, pp. 459-488, 20 ills. in black and white, 11 ills. in color, map, Oct., 1943

PARAMARIBO, Surinam:

Color Glows in the Guianas, French and Dutch. By Nicol Smith. LXXXIII, pp. 459-480, 8 ills. in black and white, 13 ills. in color, map, Apr., 1943

Picturesque Paramaribo. By Harriet Chalmers Adams. XVIII, pp. 365-373, 7 ills., June, 1907

PARANÁ (River), South America:

Buenos Aires and Its River of Silver: A Journey Up the Paraná and Paraguay to the Chaco Cattle Country. By William R. Barbour. XL, pp. 393-432, 38 ills., Oct., 1921

Through Paraguay and Southern Matto Grosso. By Sir Christopher H. Gibson. LXXXIV, pp. 459-488, 20 ills. in black and white, 11 ills. in color, map, Oct., 1943

PARICUTÍN, the Cornfield That Grew a Volcano (Mexico). By James A. Green. LXXXV, pp. 129-164, 16 ills. in black and white, 21 ills. in color, map, Feb., 1944

PARIMA (River), Brazil:

Exploring the Valley of the Amazon in a Hydroplane: Twelve Thousand Miles of Flying Over the World's Greatest River and Greatest Forest to Chart the Unknown Parima River from the Sky. By Captain Albert W. Stevens. XLIX, pp. 353-420, 86 ills., map, Apr., 1926

PARIS, France:

Paris Delivered. 10 ills. LXXXVII, pp. 79-86, Jan., 1945

Paris Freed. By Maj. Frederick Simpich, Jr. LXXXVII, pp. 385-412, 14 ills. in black and white, 12 ills. in color, Apr., 1945

Paris in Spring. By Maynard Owen Williams. LXX, pp. 501-534, 30 ills., Oct., 1936

Paris Lives Again. By M. O. Williams. XC, pp. 767-790, 24 ills., Dec., 1946

PARIS BASIN, France:

France Farms as War Wages: An American Explores the Rich Rural Region of the Historic Paris Basin. By Harrison Howell Walker. LXXVII, pp. 201-238, 16 ills. in black and white, 18 ills. in color, map, Feb., 1940

PARK, JAMES LODER:

Life's Tenor in Ethiopia: Africa's Land of Early Christianity Now Yields Minerals for Modern Industry. By James Loder Park. LXVII, pp. 783-793, 8 ills., June, 1935

PARKER, CORNELIA STRATTON:

Entering the Front Doors of Medieval Towns: The Adventures of an American Woman and Her Daughter in a Folding Boat on Eight Rivers of Germany and Austria. By Cornelia Stratton Parker. LXI, pp. 365-394, 23 ills. in black and white, 11 ills. in color, map, Mar., 1932

PARKER, FRANCIS W.:

The Relation of Geography to History. By Francis W. Parker. V, pp. 125-131, Jan. 31, 1894

PARKER, MARGERY PRITCHARD:

A Northern Crusoe's Island: Life on a Fox Farm Off the Coast of Alaska, Far from Contact with the World Eleven Months a Year. By Margery Pritchard Parker. XLIV, pp. 313-326, 15 ills., map, Sept., 1923

PARKS. *See* National Parks

PARLIAMENT (British):

The Oldest Free Assemblies: Address of Right Hon. Arthur J. Balfour, in the United States House of Representatives, May 5, 1917. XXXI, pp. 368-371, Apr., 1917

Yanks at Westminster. By Capt. Leonard David Gammans. XC, pp. 223-252, 6 ills. in black and white, 19 ills. in color, Aug., 1946

PARMA (Ship):

The Cape Horn Grain-Ship Race: The Gallant "Parma" Leads the Vanishing Fleet of Square-Riggers Through Raging Gales and Irksome Calms 16,000 Miles, from Australia to England. By A. J. Villiers. LXIII, pp. 1-39, 38 ills., Jan., 1933

PARNASSUS, Mount, Greece:

Festival Days on the Slopes of Mount Parnassus. 14 color photos by Maynard Owen Williams. LVIII, pp. 713-720, Dec., 1930

PARO JONG (Fort), Bhutan:

Castles in the Air: Experiences and Journeys in Unknown Bhutan. By John Claude White. XXV, pp. 365-455, 74 ills., map, Apr., 1914

PARO-TA-TSHANG (Monastery), Bhutan:

Castles in the Air: Experiences and Journeys in Unknown Bhutan. By John Claude White. XXV, pp. 365-455, 74 ills., map, Apr., 1914

PARR, GRANT:

War Meets Peace in Egypt. By Grant Parr and G. E. Janssen. LXXXI, pp. 503-526, 25 ills., map, Apr., 1942

PARRA, L. PÉREZ:

The Glamour of Mexico—Old and New. 15 color photos: 13 by L. Pérez Parra. LXV, pp. 345-352, Mar., 1934

PARROTS:

Parrots, Kingfishers, and Flycatchers: Strange Trogons and Curious Cuckoos are Pictured with these Other Birds of Color, Dash, and Courage. By Alexander Wetmore. Paintings by Maj. Allan Brooks. LXIX, pp. 801-828, 9 ills. in black and white, 36 portraits in color, June, 1936

The **PARSEES** and the Towers of Silence at Bombay, India. By William Thomas Fee. XVI, pp. 529-554, 16 ills., Dec., 1905

PARSONS, WILLIAM BARCLAY:

Hunan—The Closed Province of China. By William Barclay Parsons. XI, pp. 393-400, ill., map, Oct., 1900

PARTITIONED Poland. By William Joseph Showalter. XXVII, pp. 88-106, 12 ills., Jan., 1915

PASHPATI, Nepal:

Nepal: A Little-Known Kingdom. By John Claude White. XXXVIII, pp. 245-283, 32 ills., map, Oct., 1920

PASSAMAQUODDY BAY, Canada-U. S.:

All Around the Bay of Passamaquoddy. By Albert S. Gatschet. VIII, pp. 16-24, Jan., 1897
Included: A List of Indian Geographic Names Occurring Around Passamaquoddy Bay, Maine, with Their Derivations, pp. 21-24

PASSANTINO, JOSEPH E.:

Kunming, Southwestern Gateway to China. By Joseph E. Passantino. With 18 color photos by author. XC, pp. 137-168, 12 ills. in black and white, Aug., 1946

PASSET, STÉPHANE:

Mongolia: In the Land of Kublai Khan. 16 color photos by M. Stéphane Passet. XLI, pp. 465-472, May, 1922

The **PASSING** of Korea. XVII, pp. 575-581, 6 ills., Oct., 1906

PASSION PLAY: Oberammergau, Germany:

Where Bible Characters Live Again: Everyday Life in Oberammergau, World Famous for Its Passion Play, Reaches a Climax at Christmas. By Anton Lang, Jr. LXVIII, pp. 743-769, 19 ills. in black and white, 11 ills. in color, map, Dec., 1935

PASSMORE, LEE:

California Trapdoor Spider Performs Engineering Marvels. By Lee Passmore. LXIV, pp. 195-211, 23 ills., Aug., 1933

PASSOVER:

The Last Israelitish Blood Sacrifice: How the Vanishing Samaritans Celebrate the Passover on Sacred Mount Gerizim. By John D. Whiting. XXXVII, pp. 1-46, 40 ills., map, Jan., 1920

PASTEL Wrens from "Down Under." 8 ills. in color from paintings by N. W. Cayley. LXXXVIII, pp. 489-496, Oct., 1945

PATAGONIA (Region), South America:

Hatcher's Work in Patagonia. (By W J M.). VIII, pp. 319-322, Nov., 1897

The Indian Tribes of Southern Patagonia, Tierra del Fuego, and the Adjoining Islands. By J. B. Hatcher. XII, pp. 12-22, 4 ills., Jan., 1901

Patagonia. By J. B. Hatcher. VIII, pp. 305-319, 6 ills., map, Nov., 1897

Some Geographic Features of Southern Patagonia, with a Discussion of Their Origin. By J. B. Hatcher. XI, pp. 41-55, 4 ills., Feb., 1900

PATAN, Nepal:

Nepal: A Little-Known Kingdom. By John Claude White. XXXVIII, pp. 245-283, 32 ills., map, Oct., 1920

PATHANS:

South of Khyber Pass (India). By Maynard Owen Williams. LXXXIX, pp. 471-500, 31 ills., map supplement, Apr., 1946

The **PATHFINDER** of the East: Setting Sail to Find "Christians and Spices," Vasco da Gama Met Amazing Adventures, Founded an Empire, and Changed the History of Western Europe. By J. R. Hildebrand. LII, pp. 503-550, 43 ills., map, pictorial supplement, Nov., 1927

PATMOS (Island), Aegean Sea:

Rhodes, and Italy's Aegean Islands. By Dorothy Hosmer. LXXIX, pp. 449-480, 32 ills., map, Apr., 1941

PATRIC, JOHN:

Czechoslovaks, Yankees of Europe. By John Patric. LXXIV, pp. 173-225, 23 ills. in black and white, 30 ills. in color, map, Aug., 1938

Friendly Journeys in Japan: A Young American Finds a Ready Welcome in the Homes of the Japanese During Leisurely Travels Through the Islands. By John Patric. LXIX, pp. 441-480, 28 ills. in black and white, 10 ills. in color, map, Apr., 1936

Imperial Rome Reborn. By John Patric. LXXI, pp. 269-325, 34 ills. in black and white, 21 ills. in color, Mar., 1937

Italy, From Roman Ruins to Radio: History of Ancient Bridge Building and Road Making Repeats Itself in Modern Public Works and Engineering Projects. By John Patric. LXXVII, pp. 347-394, 27 ills. in black and white, 9 ills. in color, Mar., 1940

Magyar Mirth and Melancholy. By John Patric. LXXIII, pp. 1-55, 33 ills. in black and white, 20 ills. in color, map, Jan., 1938

Roads from Washington (D. C.). By John Patric. LXXIV, pp. 1-56, 27 ills. in black and white, 30 ills. in color, map supplement, July, 1938

PATRICK, MARY MILLS:
Asia Minor in the Time of the Seven Wise Men. By Mary Mills Patrick. XXXVII, pp. 47-67, 19 ills., Jan., 1920
The Emancipation of Mohammedan Women. By Mary Mills Patrick. XX, pp. 42-66, 19 ills., Jan., 1909

A **PATRIOTIC** Pilgrimage to Eastern National Parks: History and Beauty Live Along Paved Roads, Once Indian Trails, Through Virginia, North Carolina, Tennessee, Kentucky, and West Virginia. By Leo A. Borah. LXV, pp. 663-702, 18 ills. in black and white, 28 ills. in color, two-page map, June, 1934

PATTERSON, J. N.:
The Magic Mountain (Mount Wilson, California). By J. N. Patterson. XIX, pp. 457-468, 9 ills., July, 1908

PATTON, RAYMOND S. *See* NGS: Board of Trustees

PÁTZCUARO, Mexico:
A Mexican Land of Lakes and Lacquers. 22 photos by Helene Fischer and Luis Marquez. LXXI, pp. 633-648, May, 1937

PAUL du Chaillu (Biography). XIV, pp. 282-285, ill., July, 1903

PAVIA, Italy:
Frontier Cities of Italy. By Florence Craig Albrecht. XXVII, pp. 533-586, 45 ills., June, 1915

PAVLOF VOLCANO, Alaska:
Mapping the Home of the Great Brown Bear: Adventures of the National Geographic Society's Pavlof Volcano Expedition to Alaska. By Dr. Thomas A. Jaggar. LV, pp. 109-134, 30 ills., map, Jan., 1929

PAYNE, JOHN BARTON. *See* NGS: Board of Trustees

PEACE CONFERENCE: Paris, France:
Paris Lives Again. By M. O. Williams. XC, pp. 767-790, 24 ills., Dec., 1946

The **PEACE** of Latin America. XVI, pp. 479-480, Oct., 1905

PEACETIME Plant Hunting About Peiping. By P. H. and J. H. Dorsett. LXXII, pp. 509-534, 21 ills., map, Oct., 1937

PEACETIME Rambles in the Ryukyus. By William Leonard Schwartz. LXXXVII, pp. 543-561, 12 ills., maps, May, 1945

PEAFOWL:
Fowls of Forest and Stream Tamed by Man. By Morley A. Jull. Paintings by Hashime Murayama. LVII, pp. 327-371, 27 ills. in black and white, 16 ills. in color, Mar., 1930

The **PEAK** of Itambé (Brazil). IX, p. 476, Nov., 1898

PEAKS and Parks of Western Canada. 11 photos: 5 by W. J. Oliver. LXXX, pp. 516-526, Oct., 1941

PEAKS and Trails in the Canadian Alps. 16 photos in duotone by Byron Harmon and Clifford White. LXV, pp. 627-642, May, 1934

PEARL FISHERIES:
Bahrein: Port of Pearls and Petroleum. By Maynard Owen Williams. LXXXIX, pp. 195-210, 6 ills. in black and white, 11 ills. in color, map, Feb., 1946
Cultivation of Marine and Fresh-Water Animals in Japan. By K. Mitsukuri. XVII, pp. 524-531, 5 ills., Sept., 1906
The Dream Ship: The Story of a Voyage of Adventure More Than Half Around the World in a 47-foot Lifeboat. By Ralph Stock. XXXIX, pp. 1-52, 43 ills., map, Jan., 1921
Fishing for Pearls in the Indian Ocean. By Bella Sidney Woolf. XLIX, pp. 161-183, 24 ills., Feb., 1926
On the Bottom of a South Sea Pearl Lagoon. By Roy Waldo Miner. Paintings by Else Bostelmann. LXXIV, pp. 365-390, 17 ills. in black and white, 8 ills. in color, Sept., 1938
Pearl and Turtle Farms in Japan. XV, p. 427, Oct., 1904
The Pearl Fisheries of Ceylon. By Hugh M. Smith. XXIII, pp. 173-194, 13 ills., map, Feb., 1912
The Rise of the New Arab Nation. By Frederick Simpich. XXXVI, pp. 369-393, 17 ills., map, Nov., 1919
Included: Pearl fisheries of Bahrein; Pearl diving; Pearl trade

PEARL Fishing in the Red Sea. By Henri de Monfreid. LXXII, pp. 597-626, 24 ills., map, Nov., 1937

PEARL HARBOR, Oahu, Hawaii:
Hawaii, Then and Now: Boyhood Recollections by an American Whose Grandfather Came to the Islands 102 Years Ago. By William R. Castle. LXXIV, pp. 419-462, 30 ills. in black and white, 10 ills. in color, map, Oct., 1938
Life on the Hawaii "Front": All-out Defense and Belt Tightening of Pacific Outpost Foreshadow the Things to Come on Mainland. By Lieut. Frederick Simpich, Jr. LXXXII, pp. 541-560, 19 ills., map, Oct., 1942

PEARS, EDWIN:
"Grass Never Grows Where the Turkish Hoof Has Trod." By Edwin Pears. XXIII, pp. 1132-1148, 19 ills., Nov., 1912

PEARSON, T. GILBERT:
Birds That Cruise the Coast and Inland Waters. By T. Gilbert Pearson. Paintings by Maj. Allan Brooks. LXV, pp. 299-328, 15 ills. in black and white, 24 portraits in color, Mar., 1934
Crows, Magpies, and Jays: Unusual Intelligence Has Earned a Unique Position for These Birds. By T. Gilbert Pearson. Paintings by Maj. Allan Brooks. LXIII, pp. 51-79, 16 ills. in black and white, 17 ills. in color, Jan., 1933

PEARSON, T. GILBERT—*Continued*

The Large Wading Birds: Long Legs and Remarkable Beaks, as Well as Size, Form, and Color, Distinguish the Herons, Ibises, and Flamingos. By T. Gilbert Pearson. Paintings by Maj. Allan Brooks. LXII, pp. 441-469, 13 ills. in black and white, 24 ills. in color, Oct., 1932

Sparrows, Towhees, and Longspurs: These Happy Little Singers Make Merry in Field, Forest, and Desert Throughout North America. By T. Gilbert Pearson. Paintings by Allan Brooks and Walter A. Weber. LXXV, pp. 353-376, 5 ills. in black and white, 43 ills. in color, Mar., 1939

Thrushes, Thrashers, and Swallows: Robins and Bluebirds are Familiar Members of a Famous Musical Family Which Includes the Hermit Thrush and European Nightingale. By T. Gilbert Pearson. Paintings by Maj. Allan Brooks. LXIX, pp. 523-546, 6 ills. in black and white, 42 paintings from life, Apr., 1936

Woodpeckers, Friends of Our Forests. By T. Gilbert Pearson. Paintings by Maj. Allan Brooks. LXIII, pp. 453-479, 12 ills. in black and white, 25 ills. in color, Apr., 1933

PEARY, ROBERT E.:

Across Nicaragua with Transit and Machéte. By R. E. Peary. I, pp. 315-335, 3 ills. (tinted), foldout map, Oct., 1889

Address by Commander Robert E. Peary, U. S. N., On the Assembling of the Congress in Washington, September 8, 1904. XV, pp. 387-392, Oct., 1904

Commander Peary's New Vessel. XVI, p. 192, Apr., 1905

The Discovery of the North Pole (Presentation of Special Gold Medal). XXI, pp. 63-82, Jan., 1910

The Discovery of the Pole: First Report by Commander Robert E. Peary, September 6, 1909. XX, pp. 892-916, 11 ills., map, Oct., 1909

European Tributes to Peary. XXI, pp. 536-540, 4 ills., June, 1910

Farthest North. XVII, pp. 638-644, 9 ills., Nov., 1906

The First Meeting of the Poles (Photograph of the first meeting of Robert E. Peary, discoverer of the North Pole, and Roald Amundsen, discoverer of the South Pole, at the National Geographic Society, January 11, 1913). XXIV, ill. p. 114, Jan., 1913. LXIX, ill. p. 126, Jan., 1936

The Future of the Airplane. By Rear Admiral Robert E. Peary. XXXIII, pp. 107-113, 4 ills., Jan., 1918

Honors to Amundsen and Peary (Speeches by Robert E. Peary). XXIV, pp. 113-130, 5 ills., Jan., 1913

Honors to Peary (Presentation of Hubbard Medal by President Roosevelt). XVIII, pp. 49-60, ill., Jan., 1907

Leader of scientific party, visiting Greenland, 1896. VIII, p. 97, Apr., 1897

A Memorial to Peary: The National Geographic Society Dedicates Monument in Arlington National Cemetery to Discoverer of the North Pole. XLI, pp. 639-646, 4 ills., June, 1922

PEARY, ROBERT E.—*Continued*

National Geographic Society (Records of North Pole Discovery). XXI, p. 276, Mar., 1910

The National Geographic Society's Notable Year (Address by Rear Admiral Robert E. Peary). XXXVII, pp. 338-345, ills., Apr., 1920

Nearest the Pole (Commander Robert E. Peary's Address to the Society). XVIII, pp. 446-450, July, 1907

The North Pole (Appointment of a Committee by the Society to Consider Claims of Peary and Cook). XX, pp. 921-922, Nov., 1909

The North Pole (Resolutions of the Society Acknowledging Peary's Discovery). XX, pp. 1008-1009, Nov., 1909

Peary and the North Pole. XIV, pp. 379-381, Oct., 1903

Peary as a Leader: Incidents from the Life of the Discoverer of the North Pole Told by One of His Lieutenants on the Expedition Which Reached the Goal. By Donald B. MacMillan. XXXVII, pp. 293-317, 20 ills., map, Apr., 1920

Peary on the North Pole. XIV, p. 29, map, Jan., 1903

Peary to Try Again. XVIII, p. 281, Apr., 1907

Peary's Explorations in 1898-1899. X, pp. 415-416, Oct., 1899

Peary's Explorations in the Far North. By Gilbert Grosvenor. XXXVII, pp. 319-322, 3 ills., Apr., 1920

Peary's Polar Expedition. XIX, p. 447, June, 1908

Peary's Twenty Years' Service in the Arctics. By Maj. Gen. A. W. Greely. XVIII, pp. 451-454, July, 1907

Peary's Work and Prospects. (By H. L. Bridgman). X, pp. 414-415, Oct., 1899

Peary's Work in 1900 and 1901. XII, pp. 357-361, ills., Oct., 1901

Peary's Work in 1901-1902. (By G. H. G.). XIII, pp. 384-386, Oct., 1902

Portrait. XII, ill. p. 359, Oct., 1901. XVIII, ill. p. 459, July, 1907

Royal Geographical Society's Patrons' Medal conferred on Lieut. Robert E. Peary. IX, p. 342, July, 1898

The South Polar Expedition (Proposed by Peary for Consideration of the National Geographic Society). XXI, pp. 167-170, map, Feb., 1910

The Value of Arctic Exploration. By Commander Robert E. Peary. XIV, pp. 429-436, Dec., 1903

See also NGS: Board of Managers; Lectures; Medals: Hubbard Medal; Special Gold Medal

PEARY, MRS. ROBERT E.:

Portrait. XII, ill. p. 360, Oct., 1901

See also NGS: Lectures

PEARY ARCTIC CLUB:

Letter of appreciation to Commander Robert E. Peary, signed by Theodore Roosevelt. XIV, p. 330, Aug., 1903

The Mission of the "Diana." X, p. 273, July, 1899

Peary Arctic Club. XIII, p. 146, Apr., 1902

Ten Years of the Peary Arctic Club. By Herbert L. Bridgman. XIX, pp. 661-668, 3 ills., Sept., 1908

PEASANT Home in Corsica. XLIV, pictorial supplement, Sept., 1923

PEASANT Life in the Black Forest. By Karl Frederick Geiser. XIX, pp. 635-649, 12 ills., Sept., 1908

PECHKOFF, ZINOVI:

A Few Glimpses into Russia. By Lieut. Zinovi Pechkoff. XXXII, pp. 238-253, 10 ills., Sept., 1917

PECULIAR Caves of Asia Minor. By Elizabeth H. Brewer. XXII, pp. 870-875, 5 ills., Sept., 1911

PEDALING Through Poland: An American Girl Free-wheels Alone from Kraków, and Its Medieval Byways, Toward Ukraine's Restive Borderland. By Dorothy Hosmer. LXXV, pp. 739-775, 38 ills., maps, June, 1939

PEEL ISLAND, Bonin Islands. *See* Chichi Jima

PEIPING (Peking), China:

Approach to Peiping. By Major John W. Thomason, Jr. LXIX, pp. 275-308, 24 ills., map, Feb., 1936

The Causes That Led Up to the Siege of Pekin. By Dr. W. A. P. Martin. XII, pp. 53-63, ill., Feb., 1901

Glimpses of Korea and China. By William W. Chapin. XXI, pp. 895-934, 11 ills. in black and white, 39 ills. in color, Nov., 1910

The Glory That Was Imperial Peking. By W. Robert Moore. LXIII, pp. 745-780, 18 ills. in black and white, 16 ills. in duotone, June, 1933

Map-Changing Medicine. By William Joseph Showalter. XLII, pp. 303-330, 26 ills., Sept., 1922

Peacetime Plant Hunting About Peiping. By P. H. and J. H. Dorsett. LXXII, pp. 509-534, 21 ills., map, Oct., 1937

Peiping, City of Dust and Color. 14 color photos by W. Robert Moore and Owen Lattimore. LXVI, pp. 609-616, Nov., 1934

Peiping's Happy New Year: Lunar Celebration Attracts Throngs to Temple Fairs, Motley Bazaars, and Age-old Festivities. By George Kin Leung. LXX, pp. 749-792, 31 ills. in black and white, 16 ills. in color, Dec., 1936

Peking, the City of the Unexpected. By James Arthur Muller. XXXVIII, pp. 335-355, 18 ills., Nov., 1920

A **PEIPING** Panorama in Vivid Pigments. 16 ills. in color from camera paintings by H. C. and J. H. White, Deng Bao-ling, Hwang Yao-tso. LXX, pp. 753-784, Dec., 1936

PEKING, China. *See* Peiping

PEKING, the City of the Unexpected. By James Arthur Muller. XXXVIII, pp. 335-355, 18 ills., Nov., 1920

PELÉE, Mont (Volcano), Martinique:

Magnetic Disturbance Caused by the Explosion of Mont Pelée. XIII, pp. 208-209, June, 1902

The National Geographic Society Expedition in the West Indies. XIII, pp. 209-213, maps, June, 1902

PELÉE, Mont (Volcano), Martinique—*Continued*

The New Cone of Mont Pelée. XIV, pp. 422-423, ills., Nov., 1903

The Recent Volcanic Eruptions in the West Indies. By Israel C. Russell. XIII, pp. 267-285, 7 ills., map, July, 1902

Report by Robert T. Hill on the Volcanic Disturbances in the West Indies. XIII, pp. 223-267, 12 ills., 3 maps, July, 1902

The Shattered Obelisk of Mont Pelée. By Prof. Angelo Heilprin. XVII, pp. 465-474, 5 ills., Aug., 1906

Volcanic Eruptions on Martinique and St. Vincent. By Israel C. Russell. XIII, pp. 415-436, 10 ills., Dec., 1902

PELELIU (Island), Palau Islands, Carolines:

South from Saipan. By W. Robert Moore. LXXXVII, pp. 441-474, 11 ills. in black and white, 17 ills. in color, map, Apr., 1945

PELICAN Profiles. By Lewis Wayne Walker. LXXXIV, pp. 589-598, 5 ills. in black and white, 8 ills. in color, Nov., 1943

PELICANS:

Birds That Cruise the Coast and Inland Waters. By T. Gilbert Pearson. Paintings by Maj. Allan Brooks. LXV, pp. 299-328, 7 ills. in black and white, portraits in color, Mar., 1934

Pelican Profiles. By Lewis Wayne Walker. LXXXIV, pp. 589-598, 5 ills. in black and white, 8 ills. in color, Nov., 1943

Peru's Wealth-Producing Birds: Vast Riches in the Guano Deposits of Cormorants, Pelicans, and Petrels which Nest on Her Barren, Rainless Coast. By R. E. Coker. XXXVII, pp. 537-566, 28 ills., June, 1920

PELLERANO, LUIGI:

Albania: Men of the Eagle in Their Mountain Eyrie. 39 color photos by Luigi Pellerano. LIX, pp. 143-190, Feb., 1931

Cirenaica, On the Edge of the Saharan Sands. 13 color photos by Luigi Pellerano. LVII, pp. 693-700, June, 1930

Italy: Caesar's City Today (Rome). 21 color photos by Bernard F. Rogers, Jr. and Luigi Pellerano. LXXI, pp. 285-316, Mar., 1937

Italy: Stone Beehive Homes of Italian Peasants. 5 color photos by Luigi Pellerano. LVII, pp. 235-242, Feb., 1930

Libia: Under Italian Libya's Burning Sun. 9 color photos by Luigi Pellerano. XLVIII, pp. 141-148, Aug., 1925

Rhodes: Souvenirs of Knighthood in Rhodes. 13 color photos by Luigi Pellerano. LXIV, pp. 665-672, Dec., 1933

Sardinia: Where the Sard Holds Sway. 9 color photos by Colonel Luigi Pellerano. XLIX, pp. 464-474, Apr., 1926

Sicily: Island of Vivid Beauty and Crumbling Glory. 22 color photos: 21 by Luigi Pellerano. LII, pp. 432-449, Oct., 1927

PENCK, ALBRECHT:

Plan of a Map of the World. By Dr. Albrecht Penck. XV, pp. 405-408, Oct., 1904

PENDLETON, Oregon:
"Where Rolls the Oregon." 28 color photos by Ray Atkeson. XC, pp. 689-728, Dec., 1946

PENEPLAINS:
Geomorphology of the Southern Appalachians. By Charles Willard Hayes and Marius R. Campbell. VI, pp. 63-126, diagrs., 4 maps, May 23, 1894
The Rivers of Northern New Jersey, with Notes on the Classification of Rivers in General. By William Morris Davis. II, pp. 81-110, 6 diagrs., map drawing, May, 1890

PENFIELD, JAMES K.:
Greenland Turns to America. By James K. Penfield. LXXXII, pp. 369-383, 7 ills. in black and white, 5 ills. in color, two-page map, Sept., 1942
Greenland—U. S. Base in the Arctic. 5 color photos by author, pp. 373-376

PENGUINS:
Antarctica's Most Interesting Citizen: The Comical Penguin Is Both Romantic and Bellicose. By Worth E. Shoults. LXI, pp. 251-260, 8 ills., Feb., 1932
South Georgia, an Outpost of the Antarctic. By Robert Cushman Murphy. XLI, pp. 409-444, 41 ills., maps, Apr., 1922

PENN, WILLIAM:
The Historic City of Brotherly Love: Philadelphia, Born of Penn and Strengthened by Franklin, a Metropolis of Industries, Homes, and Parks. By John Oliver La Gorce. LXII, pp. 643-697, 49 ills. in black and white, 13 ills. in color, Dec., 1932

The **PENN** Country in Sussex (England): Home of Pennsylvania's Founder Abounds in Quaker History and Memories of Adventurous Smugglers. By Col. P. T. Etherton. LXVIII, pp. 59-90, 32 ills., map, July, 1935

PENNANTS of Patriotism 200 Years Ago. By Byron McCandless and Gilbert Grosvenor. XXXII, pp. 399-403, 77 ills. in color, Oct., 1917

PENN'S Land of Modern Miracles (Pennsylvania). By John Oliver La Gorce. LXVIII, pp. 1-58, 28 ills. in black and white, 39 ills. in color, two-page map, July, 1935

PENNSYLVANIA:
In the Pennsylvania Dutch Country. By Elmer C. Stauffer. LXXX, pp. 37-74, 20 ills. in black and white, 22 ills. in color, map (pen and ink drawing), July, 1941
The Industrial Titan of America: Pennsylvania, Once the Keystone of the Original Thirteen, Now the Keystone of Forty-eight Sovereign States. By John Oliver La Gorce. XXXV, pp. 367-406, 33 ills., map, May, 1919
Penn's Land of Modern Miracles. By John Oliver La Gorce. LXVIII, pp. 1-58, 28 ills. in black and white, 39 ills. in color, two-page map, July, 1935
The Rivers and Valleys of Pennsylvania. By William Morris Davis. I, pp. 183-253, 25 ills., map, July, 1889

PENNSYLVANIA—*Continued*
Roads from Washington. By John Patric. LXXIV, pp. 1-56, 27 ills. in black and white, 30 ills. in color, map supplement, July, 1938
The Travels of George Washington: Dramatic Episodes in His Career as the First Geographer of the United States. By William Joseph Showalter. LXI, pp. 1-63, 50 ills., 4 maps, map supplement, Jan., 1932
See also Gettysburg; Philadelphia

PENNSYLVANIA DUTCH (People):
In the Pennsylvania Dutch Country. By Elmer C. Stauffer. LXXX, pp. 37-74, 20 ills. in black and white, 22 ills. in color, map (pen and ink drawing), July, 1941
Pennsylvania Dutch—In a Land of Milk and Honey. 10 color photos by J. Baylor Roberts. LXXIV, pp. 49-56, July, 1938

PENNSYLVANIA Dutch—In a Land of Milk and Honey. 10 color photos by J. Baylor Roberts. LXXIV, pp. 49-56, July, 1938

PENNSYLVANIA'S Land of Plenty. 22 color photos by Harrison Howell Walker. LXXX, pp. 41-64, July, 1941

PENOBSCOT (Indian Tribe):
America's First Settlers, the Indians. By Matthew W. Stirling. Paintings by W. Langdon Kihn. LXXII, pp. 535-596, 34 ills. in black and white, 24 ills. in color, Nov., 1937

PENOBSCOT BAY, Maine:
Atlantic Estuarine Tides. By Mark S. W. Jefferson. IX, pp. 400-409, diagrs., 7 tables, maps, Sept., 1898

PENRHYN (Atoll), South Pacific Ocean. *See* Tongareva

PENROSE, C. B.:
The Bear Hunt. XIX, p. 222, Mar., 1908
A Bear Hunt in Montana. By Arthur Alvord Stiles. XIX, pp. 149-154, 5 ills., Feb., 1908

The **PEOPLE** of Morocco. XVII, pp. 108-109, ill., Feb., 1906

The **PEOPLE** of the Wilderness: The Mongols, Once the Terror of All Christendom, Now a Primitive, Harmless Nomad Race. By Adam Warwick. XXXIX, pp. 507-551, 59 ills., May, 1921

PEOPLES and Places of Northern Africa. 16 ills. XLII, pp. 363-378, Oct., 1922

The **PEOPLE'S** Fight Against Slavery. By Hon. Henry A. Wallace. Reprint of address delivered at a dinner of the Free World Association, May 8, 1942. LXXXII, pp. 276-280, ill., Aug., 1942

PEPPER, CHARLES M.:
From Panama to Patagonia. By Charles M. Pepper. XVII, pp. 449-452, ill., Aug., 1906
South America Fifty Years Hence. By Charles M. Pepper. XVII, pp. 427-432, map supplement, Aug., 1906

PEQUOT (Indian Tribe):

America's First Settlers, the Indians. By Matthew W. Stirling. Paintings by W. Langdon Kihn. LXXII, pp. 535-596, 34 ills. in black and white, 24 ills. in color, Nov., 1937

The **PERAHERA** Processions of Ceylon. By G. H. G. Burroughs. LXII, pp. 90-100, ill. in black and white, 8 ills. in duotone, July, 1932

PERDICARIS, ION:

Morocco, "The Land of the Extreme West" and the Story of My Captivity. By Ion Perdicaris. XVII, pp. 117-157, 24 ills., Mar., 1906

The **PERENNIAL** Geographer: After 2,000 Years Vergil Is Still the Most Widely Read of Latin Poets—First to Popularize the Geography of the Roman Empire. By W. Coleman Nevils. LVIII, pp. 439-465, 29 ills., Oct., 1930

PERGAMUS (Ancient City):

The Buried Cities of Asia Minor. By Ernest L. Harris. XX, pp. 1-18, 10 ills., Jan., 1909

PERIGUEUX, France:

The Beauties of France. By Arthur Stanley Riggs. XXVIII, pp. 391-491, 73 ills. in black and white, 16 ills. in color, map, Nov., 1915

PERKINS, ELIZABETH:

With the Monks at Meteora: The Monasteries of Thessaly. By Elizabeth Perkins. XX, pp. 799-807, 5 ills., Sept., 1909

PERKINS, GEORGE C.:

California. By the Hon. George C. Perkins. VII, pp. 317-327, Oct., 1896

The Civil Government of Alaska. By Hon. George C. Perkins. IX, pp. 172-178, Apr., 1898

The Key to the Pacific (Territory of Hawaii). By George C. Perkins. XIX, pp. 295-298, map, Apr., 1908

PERNAMBUCO, Brazil. *See* Recife

PERRY, K. W.:

Volcanoes of Alaska (Report by Capt. K. W. Perry on the Eruption of Mt. Katmai in June, 1912). XXIII, pp. 824-832, 11 ills., Aug., 1912

PERRY, MATTHEW CALBRAITH:

A Chapter from Japanese History. By Eki Hioki. XVI, pp. 220-228, May, 1905

The Gem of the Ocean: Our American Navy. By Josephus Daniels. XXXIII, pp. 313-335, 35 ills., Apr., 1918

Some Early Geographers of the United States. By Rear Admiral Colby M. Chester. XV, pp. 392-404, Oct., 1904

PERRY PEAK (Volcano), Alaska:

A Jack in the Box: An Account of the Strange Performances of the Most Wonderful Island in the World. By Captain F. M. Munger. XX, pp. 194-199, 8 ills., Feb., 1909

PERSEPOLIS, Iran:

Exploring the Secrets of Persepolis. By Charles Breasted. LXIV, pp. 381-420, 48 ills., plan, map, Oct., 1933

PERSHING, JOHN J.:

Hubbard Medals Awarded to Stratosphere Explorers: Presentation by General Pershing. LXIX, pp. 713-714, ill. p. 712, May, 1936

Our National War Memorials in Europe. By John J. Pershing. LXV, pp. 1-36, 24 ills. in black and white, 11 ills. in color, map, Jan., 1934

Shopping Abroad for Our Armies in France. By Herbert Corey. XXXIII, pp. 206-218, 6 ills., Feb., 1918

Stand by the Soldier. By Major General John J. Pershing. XXXI, pp. 457-459, ill., May, 1917

See also NGS: Board of Trustees

PERSIA. *See* Iran

PERSIA—Past and Present. XVIII, pp. 91-95, 6 ills., Feb., 1907

PERSIA: The Awakening East. By W. P. Cresson. XIX, pp. 356-384, 21 ills., map, May, 1908

PERSIAN Caravan Sketches: The Land of the Lion and the Sun as Seen on a Summer Caravan Trip. By Harold F. Weston. XXXIX, pp. 417-468, 46 ills. in black and white, 16 ills. in color, map, Apr., 1921

PERSIAN CATS:

The Panther of the Hearth: Lithe Grace and Independence of Spirit Contribute to the Appeal of Cats, "The Only Domestic Animal Man Has Never Conquered." By Frederick B. Eddy. LXXIV, pp. 589-634, 22 ills. in black and white, 25 ills. in color, Nov., 1938

PERTH, Australia:

Capital Cities of Australia. By W. Robert Moore. LXVIII, pp. 667-722, 32 ills. in black and white, 24 ills. in color, two-page map, Dec., 1935

PERU:

Air Adventures in Peru: Cruising Among Andean Peaks, Pilots and Cameramen Discover Wondrous Works of an Ancient People. By Robert Shippee. LXIII, pp. 81-120, 40 ills., map, Jan., 1933

Along the Old Inca Highway. By Harriet Chalmers Adams. XIX, pp. 231-250, 21 ills., Apr., 1908

Brazil and Peru. XVII, pp. 203-204, Apr., 1906

Buenos Aires to Washington by Horse: A Solitary Journey of Two and a Half Years, Through Eleven American Republics, Covers 9,600 Miles of Mountain and Plain, Desert and Jungle. By A. F. Tschiffely. LV, pp. 135-196, 75 ills., map, Feb., 1929

Camels of the Clouds (Lamoids). By W. H. Hodge. LXXXIX, pp. 641-656, 15 ills., map, May, 1946

Chile's Disputes with Peru and Bolivia. XII, pp. 401-402, Nov., 1901

Cuzco, America's Ancient Mecca. By Harriet Chalmers Adams. XIX, pp. 669-689, 19 ills., Oct., 1908

Explorations in Peru. XXIII, pp. 417-422, 7 ills., map, Apr., 1912

PERU—*Continued*

Flying the World's Longest Air-Mail Route: From Montevideo, Uruguay, Over the Andes, Up the Pacific Coast, Across Central America and the Caribbean to Miami, Florida, in 67 Thrilling Flying Hours. By Junius B. Wood. LVII, pp. 261-325, 65 ills., map, Mar., 1930

A Forgotten Valley of Peru: Conquered by Incas, Scourged by Famine, Plagues, and Earthquakes, Colca Valley Shelters the Last Fragment of an Ancient Andean Tribe. By Robert Shippee. LXV, pp. 111-132, 22 ills., map, Jan., 1934

From Panama to Patagonia. By Charles M. Pepper. XVII, pp. 449-452, ill., Aug., 1906

Further Exploration in the Land of the Incas: The Peruvian Expedition of 1915 of the National Geographic Society and Yale University. By Hiram Bingham. XXIX, pp. 431-473, 29 ills., maps, panorama, May, 1916

The Greatest Achievement of Ancient Man in America (Fortress of Sacsahuaman). Panorama from photo by author

Geographic Work in Peru. VII, p. 407, Dec., 1896

High Lights in the Peruvian and Bolivian Andes. 18 color photos by W. Robert Moore. LI, pp. 219-234, Feb., 1927

Honors to Amundsen and Peary (Banquet: Address by Hiram Bingham, "The Expedition to Peru"). XXIV, pp. 113-130, 5 ills., Jan., 1913

How Latin America Looks from the Air: U. S. Army Airplanes Hurdle the High Andes, Brave Brazil Jungles, and Follow Smoking Volcanoes to Map New Sky Paths Around South America. By Major Herbert A. Dargue. LII, pp. 451-502, 52 ills., map, Oct., 1927

In the Wonderland of Peru. By Hiram Bingham. XXIV, pp. 387-573, 250 ills., 3 diagrs., map, panorama, Apr., 1913

The Ruins of an Ancient Inca Capital, Machu Picchu. Panorama from photo by author

The Incas: Empire Builders of the Andes. By Philip Ainsworth Means. Paintings by H. M. Herget. LXXIII, pp. 225-264, 26 ills. in black and white, 10 ills. in color, Feb., 1938

The Lure of Lima, City of the Kings. By William Joseph Showalter. LVII, pp. 727-784, 41 ills. in black and white, 25 ills. in color, June, 1930

The Most Valuable Bird in the World (Guanay). By Robert Cushman Murphy. XLVI, pp. 279-302, 25 ills., map, Sept., 1924

A New Peruvian Route to the Plain of the Amazon. By Solon I. Bailey. XVII, pp. 432-448, 12 ills., Aug., 1906

Peru—Its Resources, Development, and Future. By Alfredo Alvarez Calderon. XV, pp. 311-323, Aug., 1904

Peru's Wealth-Producing Birds: Vast Riches in the Guano Deposits of Cormorants, Pelicans, and Petrels which Nest on Her Barren, Rainless Coast. By R. E. Coker. XXXVII, pp. 537-566, 28 ills., June, 1920

PERU—*Continued*

The Pith of Peru: A Journey from Talara to Machu Picchu, with Memorable Stopovers. By Henry Albert Phillips. LXXXII, pp. 167-196, 6 ills. in black and white, 20 ills. in color, map, Aug., 1942

The Road to Bolivia. By William E. Curtis. XI, pp. 209-224, 7 ills., June, 1900; pp. 264-280, 6 ills., July, 1900

Some Personal Experiences with Earthquakes (Arica). By Rear Admiral L. G. Billings. XXVII, pp. 57-71, 7 ills., Jan., 1915

Some Wonderful Sights in the Andean Highlands: The Oldest City in America. Sailing on the Lake of the Clouds: The Yosemite of Peru. By Harriet Chalmers Adams. XIX, pp. 597-618, 19 ills., map, Sept., 1908

South America. Annual Address by the President, Gardiner G. Hubbard. III, pp. 1-29, foldout map, Mar. 28, 1891

Staircase Farms of the Ancients: Astounding Farming Skill of Ancient Peruvians, Who Were Among the Most Industrious and Highly Organized People in History. By O. F. Cook. XXIX, pp. 474-534, 48 ills., May, 1916

The Story of Machu Picchu: The Peruvian Expeditions of the National Geographic Society and Yale University. By Hiram Bingham. XXVII, pp. 172-217, 60 ills., Feb., 1915

PERU CURRENT. *See* Humboldt Current

PERU on Parade. 20 color photos by Henry Clay Gipson and Jack Kuhne. LXXXII, pp. 173-196, Aug., 1942

PERUGIA, Italy:

Inexhaustible Italy. By Arthur Stanley Riggs. XXX, pp. 273-368, 76 ills., map, Oct., 1916

PERU'S Wealth-Producing Birds: Vast Riches in the Guano Deposits of Cormorants, Pelicans, and Petrels which Nest on Her Barren, Rainless Coast. By R. E. Coker. XXXVII, pp. 537-566, 28 ills., June, 1920

PESHAWAR, India:

South of Khyber Pass. By Maynard Owen Williams. LXXXIX, pp. 471-500, 31 ills., map supplement, Apr., 1946

Through the Heart of Hindustan: A Teeming Highway Extending for Fifteen Hundred Miles, from the Khyber Pass to Calcutta. By Maynard Owen Williams. XL, pp. 433-467, 29 ills., Nov., 1921

The **PEST** of English Sparrows. By N. Dearborn. XXI, pp. 948-952, 4 ills., Nov., 1910

PESTS and Parasites: Why We Need a National Law to Prevent the Importation of Insect-Infested and Diseased Plants. By Charles Lester Marlatt. XXII, pp. 321-346, 29 ills., maps, Apr., 1911

PETER I, The Great:

Young Russia: The Land of Unlimited Possibilities. By Gilbert H. Grosvenor. XXVI, pp. 421-520, 85 ills. in black and white, 17 ills. in color, Nov., 1914

PETER Cooper and Submarine Telegraphy. VII, pp. 108-110, Mar., 1896

PETERS, HAROLD:

The "Pilgrim" Sails the Seven Seas: A Schooner Yacht Out of Boston Drops in at Desert Isles and South Sea Edens in a Leisurely Two-Year Voyage. By Harold Peters. LXXII, pp. 223-262, 36 ills., Aug., 1937

PETERS, WILLIAM J.:

Mr. Ziegler and the National Geographic Society. XIV, pp. 251-254, June, 1903

PETRA (Ruins), Trans-Jordan:

Arabia, the Desert of the Sea. By Archibald Forder. XX, pp. 1039-1062, 1117, 20 ills., map, Dec., 1909

Petra, Ancient Caravan Stronghold: Mysterious Temples and Tombs, Carved in Glowing Cliffs of Eroded Sandstone, Are Remnants of a City David Longed to Storm. By John D. Whiting. LXVII, pp. 129-165, 15 ills. in black and white, 21 ills. in color, maps, Feb., 1935

The Rock City of Petra. By Franklin E. Hoskins. XVIII, pp. 283-291, 5 ills., May, 1907

PETRELS (Birds):

Birds of the High Seas: Albatrosses and Petrels; Gannets, Man-o'-war-birds, and Tropic-birds. By Robert Cushman Murphy. Paintings by Major Allan Brooks. LXXIV, pp. 226-251, 7 ills. in black and white, 36 portraits in color, Aug., 1938

The Leach's Petrel: His Nursery on Little Duck Island. By Arnold Wood. XX, pp. 360-365, 7 ills., Apr., 1909

Peru's Wealth-Producing Birds: Vast Riches in the Guano Deposits of Cormorants, Pelicans, and Petrels which Nest on Her Barren, Rainless Coast. By R. E. Coker. XXXVII, pp. 537-566, 28 ills., June, 1920

PETRIE, W. M. FLINDERS:

Excavations at Abydos. (By W. M. Flinders Petrie). XIV, pp. 358-359, Sept., 1903

PETROGRAD. *See* Leningrad

PETROLEUM:

Bahrein: Port of Pearls and Petroleum. By Maynard Owen Williams. LXXXIX, pp. 195-210, 6 ills. in black and white, 11 ills. in color, map, Feb., 1946

Billions of Barrels of Oil Locked up in Rocks. By Guy Elliott Mitchell. XXXIII, pp. 195-205, 10 ills., Feb., 1918

Bombs over Bible Lands. By Frederick Simpich and W. Robert Moore. LXXX, pp. 141-180, 34 ills., two-page map, Aug., 1941

Curaçao and Aruba on Guard. By W. Robert Moore. LXXXIII, pp. 169-192, 12 ills. in black and white, 10 ills. in color, 4 maps, Feb., 1943

Guest in Saudi Arabia. By Maynard Owen Williams. LXXXVIII, pp. 463-487, 24 ills., map, Oct., 1945

The Nation's Undeveloped Resources. By Franklin K. Lane. XXV, pp. 183-225, 32 ills., Feb., 1914

Natural-Gas, Oil, and Coal Supply of the United States. XV, p. 186, Apr., 1904

Oil Fields of Texas and California. XII, pp. 276-278, July, 1901

Oil for Victory Piped under the Sea. 9 ills. LXXXVIII, pp. 721-726, Dec., 1945

PETROLEUM—*Continued*

The Oil Treasure of Mexico. By Russell Hastings Millward. XIX, pp. 803-805, ill., Nov., 1908

So Oklahoma Grew Up. By Frederick Simpich. LXXIX, pp. 269-314, 30 ills. in black and white, 19 ills. in color, map, Mar., 1941

Today's World Turns on Oil. By Frederick Simpich. LXXIX, pp. 703-748, 22 ills. in black and white, drawings, 21 ills. in color, June, 1941

A Vigorous Oil Well. By S. A. Cornelius. XVIII, pp. 348-349, ill., May, 1907

Where the World Gets Its Oil: But Where Will Our Children Get It When American Wells Cease to Flow? By George Otis Smith. XXXVII, pp. 181-202, 21 ills., 3 maps, Feb., 1920

PETROLEUM Serves—From Lamps to Wheels. 21 color photos: 20 by B. Anthony Stewart. LXXIX, pp. 707-738, June, 1941

PFINGSTL, W.:

Behind the Scenes in the Home of the Passion Play (Oberammergau, Germany). 11 color photos: 4 by W. Pfingstl. LXVIII, pp. 753-760, Dec., 1935

PHILADELPHIA (Ancient City):

The Buried Cities of Asia Minor. By Ernest L. Harris. XX, pp. 1-18, 10 ills., Jan., 1909

PHILADELPHIA, Pennsylvania:

The Historic City of Brotherly Love: Philadelphia, Born of Penn and Strengthened by Franklin, a Metropolis of Industries, Homes, and Parks. By John Oliver La Gorce. LXII, pp. 643-697, 49 ills. in black and white, 13 ills. in color, Dec., 1932

PHILAE (Island), Egypt:

The Resurrection of Ancient Egypt. By James Baikie. XXIV, pp. 957-1020, 46 ills., map, Sept., 1913

PHILIP Nolan and the "Levant." (By Edward E. Hale). XVI, pp. 114-116, Mar., 1905

PHILIPPINE CLIPPER (Seaplane):

Flying the Pacific. By William Burke Miller. LXX, pp. 665-707, 39 ills., Dec., 1936

PHILIPPINE ISLANDS (Republic of the Philippines):

American Development of the Philippines. XIV, pp. 197-203, 4 ills., May, 1903

The Area of the Philippines. X, pp. 182-183, May, 1899

"As the Tuan Had Said." By George M. Hanson. LXIV, pp. 631-644, 19 ills., Nov., 1933

Benguet—The Garden of the Philippines. XIV, pp. 203-210, 6 ills., May, 1903

Commerce of the Philippine Islands. (By J. H.). IX, pp. 301-303, tables, June, 1898

The Conquest of Bubonic Plague in the Philippines. XIV, pp. 185-195, 7 ills., May, 1903

Diseases of the Philippines. XI, pp. 123-124, Mar., 1900

The Disposition of the Philippines. By Charles E. Howe. IX, p. 304, June, 1898

PHILIPPINE ISLANDS (Republic of the Philippines)—*Continued*

The Economic Condition of the Philippines. By Max L. Tornow. X, pp. 33-64, 10 ills., Feb., 1899

Educating the Filipinos. XVI, pp. 46-49, Jan., 1905

Facts about the Philippines. By Frederick Simpich. LXXXI, pp. 185-202, 17 ills., map, Feb., 1942

Field Sports Among the Wild Men of Northern Luzon. By Dean C. Worcester. XXII, pp. 215-267, 52 ills., map, Mar., 1911

Geographic Facts from Report of the Taft Philippine Commission. XII, pp. 114-119, Mar., 1901

Gold in the Philippines. By F. F. Hilder. XI, pp. 465-470, Dec., 1900

Governing the Philippine Islands. By Colonel Clarence R. Edwards. XV, pp. 273-284, 5 ills., July, 1904

Head-Hunters of Northern Luzon. By Dean C. Worcester. XXIII, pp. 833-930, 102 ills., map, Sept., 1912

Helping the Filipino Fisheries. XVIII, pp. 795-796, Dec., 1907

Map of the Philippines. Text with map supplement. XIII, p. 31, Jan., 1902

Meteorology in the Philippines. X, pp. 271-272, July, 1899

Mindanao, on the Road to Tokyo. By Frederick Simpich. LXXXVI, pp. 539-574, 26 ills. in black and white, 12 ills. in color, two-page map, Nov., 1944

The Mining Bureau of the Philippine Islands. By Charles H. Burritt. XIV, pp. 418-419, Nov., 1903

The Non-Christian Peoples of the Philippine Islands. By Dean C. Worcester. XXIV, pp. 1157-1256, 41 ills. in black and white, 48 ills. in color, Nov., 1913

Notes on Some Primitive Philippine Tribes. By Dean C. Worcester. IX, pp. 284-301, 11 ills., June, 1898

Our New Possessions and the Interest They Are Exciting. (By O. P. Austin). XI, pp. 32-33, Jan., 1900

The Philippine Exhibit at the Pan-American Exposition. By D. O. Noble Hoffmann. XII, pp. 119-122, Mar., 1901

The Philippine Islands. By F. F. Hilder. IX, pp. 257-284, 10 ills., table, maps, June, 1898

The Philippine Islands and Their Environment. By John Barrett. XI, pp. 1-14, map supplement, Jan., 1900

The Philippine Islands and Their People. By Henry Gannett. XV, pp. 91-112, 13 ills., Mar., 1904

The Philippine Weather Service. XV, pp. 77-78, Feb., 1904

The Philippines. By William H. Taft. XVI, pp. 361-375, 3 ills., map supplement, Aug., 1905

Progress in the Philippines. XVI, pp. 116-118, Mar., 1905

Progress in the Philippines. XVI, pp. 511-514, ills., Nov., 1905

PHILIPPINE ISLANDS (Republic of the Philippines)—*Continued*

Return to Manila. By Frederick Simpich. LXXVIII, pp. 409-451, 21 ills. in black and white, 21 ills. in color, map, Oct., 1940

A Revelation of the Filipinos (Summary of Report of the First Census of the Philippines). (By Gilbert H. Grosvenor). XVI, pp. 139-192, 138 ills., Apr., 1905

Some Impressions of 150,000 Miles of Travel. By William Howard Taft. LVII, pp. 523-598, 80 ills., May, 1930

Some Recent Instances of National Altruism: The Efforts of the United States to Aid the Peoples of Cuba, Porto Rico, and the Philippines. By William H. Taft. XVIII, pp. 429-438, July, 1907

Surveying the Philippine Islands. By George H. Putnam. XIV, pp. 437-441, 4 ills., Dec., 1903

Surveys in the Philippines. (By P. A. Welker). XXII, p. 82, map, Jan., 1911

Taal Volcano and Its Recent Destructive Eruption. By Dean C. Worcester. XXIII, p. 313-367, 40 ills., diagr., 4 maps, Apr., 1912

Ten Years in the Philippires. By William Howard Taft. XIX, pp. 141-148, Feb., 1908

The Unexplored Philippines from the Air: Mapmaking Over Jungle Lands Never Before Seen By White Men. By Lieut. George W. Goddard. LVIII, pp. 311-343, 38 ills., map, Sept., 1930

What Luzon Means to Uncle Sam. By Frederick Simpich. LXXXVII, pp. 305-332, 25 ills., map supplement, Mar., 1945

The Work of the Bureau of Insular Affairs. By Colonel Clarence R. Edwards. XV, pp. 239-255, 8 ills., June, 1904

See also Manila

PHILLIPS, C. W.:

Ancestor of the British Navy: England's Oldest Known War Vessel Is Unearthed, Laden with Remarkable Treasures of an Anglo-Saxon Ruler. By C. W. Phillips. LXXIX, pp. 247-268, 22 ills., 4 drawings, Feb., 1941

PHILLIPS, HENRY ALBERT:

Air Cruising Through New Brazil: A National Geographic Reporter Spots Vast Resources Which the Republic's War Declaration Adds to Strength of United Nations. By Henry Albert Phillips. LXXXII, pp. 503-536, 32 ills., Oct., 1942

Bolivia—Tin Roof of the Andes. By Henry Albert Phillips. LXXXIII, pp. 309-332, 5 ills. in black and white, 20 ills. in color, Mar., 1943

The Pith of Peru: A Journey from Talara to Machu Picchu, with Memorable Stopovers. By Henry Albert Phillips. LXXXII, pp. 167-196, 6 ills. in black and white, 20 ills. in color, map, Aug., 1942

PHOENIX ISLANDS, South Pacific Ocean:

American Pathfinders in the Pacific. By William H. Nicholas. LXXXIX, pp. 617-640, 17 ills., two-page map, May, 1946

See also Canton Island

PHOSPHATES:

Nauru, the Richest Island in the South Seas. By Rosamond Dodson Rhone. XL, pp. 559-589, 24 ills., Dec., 1921

Our Greatest Plant Food. By Guy Elliott Mitchell. XXI, pp. 783-791, 5 ills., diagrs., Sept., 1910

PHOTOFLASHING Western Owls. By Lewis W. Walker. LXXXVII, pp. 475-486, 6 ills. in black and white, 7 ills. in color, Apr., 1945

PHOTOGRAPHING the Eclipse of 1932 from the Air: From Five Miles Above the Earth's Surface, the National Geographic Society-Army Air Corps Survey Obtains Successful Photographs of the Moon's Shadow. By Capt. Albert W. Stevens. LXII, pp. 581-596, 18 ills., Nov., 1932

PHOTOGRAPHING the Marvels of the West in Colors. By Fred Payne Clatworthy. LIII, pp. 694-719, 30 ills. in color, June, 1928

PHOTOGRAPHING the Nest Life of the Osprey. By Capt. C. W. R. Knight. LXII, pp. 247-260, 25 ills., Aug., 1932

PHOTOGRAPHING Wild Game with Flashlight and Camera. By George Shiras, 3d. XVII, pp. 367-423, 74 ills., July, 1906

PHOTOGRAPHY:

Adventures with Birds of Prey. By Frank and John Craighead. LXXII, pp. 109-134, 25 ills., July, 1937

The American Scene. 29 winning photos in the Sixth Annual Newspaper National Snapshot Awards, with explanatory note. LXXIX, pp. 220-246, Feb., 1941

Americana. 11 winning photos in the Seventh Annual Newspaper National Snapshot Awards. LXXXI, pp. 657-666, May, 1942

First natural-color photograph of an eclipse ever reproduced, showing the corona. By Irvine C. Gardner. LXXI, ill. p. 178, Feb., 1937

How Warwick (Castle) Was Photographed in Color. By Maynard Owen Williams. LXX, pp. 83-93, 13 ills. in color, July, 1936

How We Fight with Photographs. By F. Barrows Colton. LXXXVI, pp. 257-280, 22 ills., Sept., 1944

Hunting Birds With a Camera: A Record of Twenty Years of Adventure in Obtaining Photographs of Feathered Wild Life in America. By William L. Finley. XLIV, pp. 161-201, 37 ills., Aug., 1923

Hunting with the Lens. By Howard H. Cleaves. XXVI, pp. 1-35, 47 ills., July, 1914

In Quest of the Golden Eagle: Over Lonely Mountain and Prairie Soars This Rare and Lordly Bird, But Three Youths from the East Catch Up With Him at Last. By John and Frank Craighead. LXXVII, pp. 693-710, 17 ills., May, 1940

Lords of the Rockies: Photographing Big Game Animals in Their Primeval Surroundings, from Arizona to Canada, Brings Adventure to Two Wilderness Wanderers. By Wendell and Lucie Chapman. LXXVI, pp. 87-128, 14 ills. in black and white, 28 ills. in color, July, 1939

PHOTOGRAPHY—*Continued*

Mystery Mammals of the Twilight (Bats). By Donald R. Griffin. XC, pp. 117-134, 19 ills., July, 1946

Included: Photographs taken by the high-speed camera developed by Prof. Harold E. Edgerton

The Nation's Capital by Night. By Volkmar Wentzel. With 16 photos in duotone by author. LXXVII, pp. 514-530, Apr., 1940

Natural-color photograph of 1937 eclipse, showing the corona. By Irvine C. Gardner. LXXIII, ill. p. 756, June, 1938

Nature's Most Dramatic Spectacle (Eclipse). By S. A. Mitchell. LXXII, pp. 361-376, 16 ills., map, Sept., 1937

Net Results from Oceania: Collecting Aquarium Specimens in Tropical Pacific Waters. By Walter H. Chute. LXXIX, pp. 347-372, 8 ills. in black and white, 24 ills. in color, Mar., 1941

Observing an Eclipse in Asiatic Russia. By Irvine C. Gardner. LXXI, pp. 179-197, 19 ills. in black and white, ill. in color, Feb., 1937

One Season's Game-Bag with the Camera. By George Shiras, 3d. XIX, pp. 387-446, 70 ills., June, 1908

Photographing the Marvels of the West in Colors. By Fred Payne Clatworthy. LIII, pp. 694-719, 30 ills. in color, June, 1928

Photography in Glacial Alaska. By O. D. von Engeln. XXI, pp. 54-62, 4 ills., Jan., 1910

Polar Photography. By Anthony Fiala. XVIII, pp. 140-142, Feb., 1907

Stalking Birds With a Color Camera: An Expert in Avian Habits Persuades His Subjects to Sit Where He Wants Them, Even in His Hat. By Arthur A. Allen. LXXV, pp. 777-789, 3 ills. in black and white, 14 ills. in color, June, 1939

PHOTOGRAPHY, Aerial:

Aerial Color Photography Becomes a War Weapon. By H. H. Arnold. LXXVII, pp. 757-766, 8 ills. in color, June, 1940

The Aërial Conquest of Everest: Flying Over the World's Highest Mountain Realizes the Objective of Many Heroic Explorers. By Lieut. Col. L. V. S. Blacker. LXIV, pp. 127-162, 35 ills., map, Aug., 1933

Air Adventures in Peru: Cruising Among Andean Peaks, Pilots and Cameramen Discover Wondrous Works of an Ancient People. By Robert Shippee. LXIII, pp. 81-120, 40 ills., map, Jan., 1933

America from the Air: No Such Series of Airplane Views Has Ever Before Been Printed. 8 photos by Lieutenant A. W. Stevens. XLVI, pp. 85-92, July, 1924

By Seaplane to Six Continents: Cruising 60,000 Miles, Italian Argonauts of the Air See World Geography Unroll, and Break New Sky Trails Over Vast Brazilian Jungles. By Commander Francesco de Pinedo. LIV, pp. 247-301, 60 ills., two-page map, Sept., 1928

Canada from the Air: Flights Aggregating 10,000 Miles Reveal the Marvelous Scenic Beauties and Amazing Natural Resources of the Dominion. By J. A. Wilson. L, pp. 389-466, 76 ills., map, Oct., 1926

PHOTOGRAPHY, Aerial—*Continued*

The Color Camera's First Aërial Success. By Melville Bell Grosvenor. LVIII, pp. 344-353, 9 ills. in color, Sept., 1930

The Conquest of Antarctica by Air. By Richard Evelyn Byrd. LVIII, pp. 127-227, 71 ills. in black and white, 16 ills. in gravure, map, Aug., 1930

Curvature of the Earth: The first photograph ever made showing laterally the curvature of the earth. By Capt. A. W. Stevens. LIX, ill. p. 634, May, 1931. LXIX, p. 128, ill. p. 142, Jan., 1936

Curvature of the Earth: The First Photograph Ever Made Showing the Division Between the Troposphere and Stratosphere and also the Actual Curvature of the Earth. Aërial photo by Captain Albert W. Stevens. LXIX, supplement, May, 1936

Exploring the Stratosphere. By Captain Albert W. Stevens. LXVI, pp. 397-434, 43 ills., chart, Oct., 1934

Exploring the Valley of the Amazon in a Hydroplane: Twelve Thousand Miles of Flying Over the World's Greatest River and Greatest Forest to Chart the Unknown Parima River from the Sky. By Captain Albert W. Stevens. XLIX, pp. 353-420, 86 ills., map, Apr., 1926

The First Airship Flight Around the World: Dr. Hugo Eckener Tells of an Epochal Geographic Achievement upon the Occasion of the Bestowal of the National Geographic Society's Special Gold Medal. LVII, pp. 653-688, 37 ills., June, 1930

The First Alaskan Air Expedition. By Captain St. Clair Streett. XLI, pp. 499-552, 37 ills., map, May, 1922

First natural-color photograph taken in the stratosphere. By Major Albert W. Stevens. LXXI, ill. p. 340, Mar., 1937

Flying Around the North Atlantic. By Anne Morrow Lindbergh. Foreword by Charles A. Lindbergh. LXVI, pp. 259-337, 82 ills., maps (1 two-page), Sept., 1934

Flying Over Egypt, Sinai, and Palestine: Looking Down Upon the Holy Land During an Air Journey of Two and a Half Hours from Cairo to Jerusalem. By Brigadier General P. R. C. Groves and Major J. R. McCrindle. L, pp. 313-355, 26 ills. in black and white, 23 ills. in color, map, Sept., 1926

Flying the "Hump" of the Andes. By Capt. Albert W. Stevens. LIX, pp. 595-636, 36 ills., map, May, 1931

Flying the World's Longest Air-Mail Route: From Montevideo, Uruguay, Over the Andes, Up the Pacific Coast, Across Central America and the Caribbean to Miami, Florida, in 67 Thrilling Flying Hours. By Junius B. Wood. LVII, pp. 261-325, 65 ills., map, Mar., 1930

From London to Australia by Aëroplane: A Personal Narrative of the First Aërial Voyage Half Around the World. By Sir Ross Smith. XXXIX, pp. 229-339, 76 ills. in black and white, 8 ills. in color, map, Mar., 1921

Greater New York . . . Metropolis of Mankind. Aërial photo by Captain Albert W. Stevens. LXIV, supplement, Nov., 1933

PHOTOGRAPHY, Aerial—*Continued*

How Latin America Looks from the Air: U. S. Army Airplanes Hurdle the High Andes, Brave Brazil Jungles, and Follow Smoking Volcanoes to Map New Sky Paths Around South America. By Major Herbert A. Dargue. LII, pp. 451-502, 52 ills., map, Oct., 1927

Looking Down on Europe: The Thrills and Advantages of Sight-seeing by Airplane, as Demonstrated on a 6,500-mile Tour Over Commercial Aviation Routes. By Lieutenant J. Parker Van Zandt. XLVII, pp. 261-326, 67 ills., map, Mar., 1925

Mapping the Antarctic from the Air: The Aërial Camera Earns Its Place as the Eyes and Memory of the Explorer. By Capt. Ashley C. McKinley. LXII, pp. 471-485, 13 ills., map supplement, Oct., 1932

The Non-Stop Flight Across America. By Lieutenant John A. Macready. Photos by Lieutenant Albert W. Stevens. XLVI, pp. 1-83, 68 ills., maps, July, 1924

On the Trail of the Air Mail: A Narrative of the Experiences of the Flying Couriers Who Relay the Mail Across America at a Speed of More than 2,000 Miles a Day. By Lieut. J. Parker Van Zandt. XLIX, pp. 1-61, 67 ills., map, Jan., 1926

Over the Roof of Our Continent (Mount McKinley). By Bradford Washburn. LXXIV, pp. 78-98, 17 ills. in duotone, map, July, 1938

Photographing the Eclipse of 1932 from the Air: From Five Miles Above the Earth's Surface, the National Geographic Society-Army Air Corps Survey Obtains Successful Photographs of the Moon's Shadow. By Capt. Albert W. Stevens. LXII, pp. 581-596, 18 ills., Nov., 1932

Seeing America from the "Shenandoah": An Account of the Record-making 9,000-mile Flight from the Atlantic to the Pacific Coast and Return in the Navy's American-built, American-manned Airship. By Junius B. Wood. XLVII, pp. 1-47, 39 ills., diagr., map, Jan., 1925

Seeing America with Lindbergh: The Record of a Tour of More than 20,000 Miles by Airplane Through Forty-eight States on Schedule Time. By Lieutenant Donald E. Keyhoe. LIII, pp. 1-46, 46 ills., map, Jan., 1928

Seeing the World from the Air. By Sir Alan J. Cobham. LIII, pp. 349-384, 37 ills., map, Mar., 1928

Seeing 3,000 Years of History in Four Hours: A Panorama of Ancient, Medieval, and Modern Events Against a Background of Mythology Unfolds During an Airplane Journey from Constantinople to Athens. By Maynard Owen Williams. LIV, pp. 719-739, 24 ills., map, Dec., 1928

Skypaths Through Latin America: Flying From Our Nation's Capital Southward Over Jungles, Remote Islands, and Great Cities on an Aërial Survey of the East Coast of South America. By Frederick Simpich. LIX, pp. 1-79, 77 ills., map, Jan., 1931

To Bogotá and Back by Air: The Narrative of a 9,500-Mile Flight from Washington, Over Thirteen Latin-American Countries and Return, in the Single-Seater Airplane "Spirit of St. Louis." By Col. Charles A. Lindbergh. LIII, pp. 529-601, 98 ills., map, May, 1928

PHOTOGRAPHY, Aerial—*Continued*

The Unexplored Philippines from the Air: Map-making Over Jungle Lands Never Before Seen By White Men. By Lieut. George W. Goddard. LVIII, pp. 311-343, 38 ills., map, Sept., 1930

Wings Over Nature's Zoo in Africa. 20 photos in duotone by Reginald A. Bourlay. LXXVI, pp. 527-542, Oct., 1939

PHOTOGRAPHY, Color. *See* NGM: Photographs; names of photographers; *and* subject-heading listings

PHOTOGRAPHY, Flashlight:

Doe and Twin Fawns. Flashlight photo by George Shiras, 3d. XXIV, supplement, July, 1913. XL, ill. p. 136, Aug., 1921. LXXVI, ill. p. 475, Oct., 1939

A Flashlight Story of an Albino Porcupine and of a Cunning but Unfortunate Coon. By George Shiras, 3d. XXII, pp. 572-596, 26 ills., June, 1911

Flashlights from the Jungle. XVIII, pp. 534-548, 11 ills., Aug., 1907

Nature's Transformation at Panama: Remarkable Changes in Faunal and Physical Conditions in the Gatun Lake Region. By George Shiras, 3d. XXVIII, pp. 159-194, 33 ills., maps, Aug., 1915

Photographing Wild Game with Flashlight and Camera. By George Shiras, 3d. XVII, pp. 367-423, 74 ills., July, 1906

Who Treads Our Trails? A Camera Trapper Describes His Experiences on an Island in the Canal Zone, a Natural-History Laboratory in the American Tropics. By Frank M. Chapman. LII, pp. 331-345, 18 ills., map, Sept., 1927

Wild Animals That Took Their Own Pictures by Day and by Night. By George Shiras, 3d. XXIV, pp. 763-834, 68 ills., map, pictorial supplement, July, 1913

Doe and Twin Fawns. Flashlight photo by author (supplement)

The Wild Life of Lake Superior, Past and Present: The Habits of Deer, Moose, Wolves, Beavers, Muskrats, Trout, and Feathered Wood-Folk Studied with Camera and Flashlight. By George Shiras, 3d. XL, pp. 113-204, 76 ills., map, pictorial supplement, Aug., 1921

Hark! Flashlight photo of deer by author (supplement)

PHOTOGRAPHY, High-Speed Flash:

Mystery Mammals of the Twilight (Bats). By Donald R. Griffin. XC, pp. 117-134, 19 ills., July, 1946

Included: Photographs taken by the high-speed camera developed by Prof. Harold E. Edgerton

PHOTOGRAPHY, Underwater:

The First Autochromes from the Ocean Bottom: Marine Life in Its Natural Habitat Along the Florida Keys Is Successfully Photographed in Colors. (Photographs by Dr. W. H. Longley and Charles Martin). LI, pp. 56-60, 8 ills. in color, Jan., 1927

On the Bottom of a South Sea Pearl Lagoon. By Roy Waldo Miner. Paintings by Else Bostelmann. LXXIV, pp. 365-390, 17 ills. in black and white, 8 ills. in color, Sept., 1938

PHRYGIA (Ancient Kingdom):

The Lost Wealth of the Kings of Midas. By Ellsworth Huntington. XXI, pp. 831-846, 15 ills., Oct., 1910

PHYLE (Fortress), Greece:

"The Glory That Was Greece." By Alexander Wilbourne Weddell. XLII, pp. 571-630, 51 ills., map, Dec., 1922

PHYSALIA (Yacht):

Our Neglected Southern Coast. By Alfred Goldsborough Mayer. XIX, pp. 859-871, 10 ills., Dec., 1908

PHYSICAL Features of the United States. By G. K. Gilbert. IX, pp. 308-317, maps, July, 1898

PHYSIOGRAPHY:

Applied Physiography in South Carolina. By L. C. Glenn. VIII, pp. 152-154, diagr., May, 1897

Physiography of the Nicaragua Canal Route. By C. Willard Hayes. X, pp. 233-246, ill., diagr., maps, map supplement, July, 1899

The Relations of Geology to Physiography in Our Educational System. By T. C. Chamberlin. V, pp. 154-160, Jan. 31, 1894

See also Geology

PICCARD, AUGUSTE:

Ballooning in the Stratosphere: Two Balloon Ascents to Ten-Mile Altitudes Presage New Mode of Aërial Travel. By Auguste Piccard. LXIII, pp. 353-384, 34 ills., Mar., 1933

PICTORIAL Jaunt Through Papua. 22 photos by Captain Frank Hurley. LI, pp. 109-124, Jan., 1927

PICTORIAL SUPPLEMENTS: Enlargements and Panoramas:

The Alaska Brown Bear: The Largest Carnivorous Animal Extant. XXX, pictorial supplement, Nov., 1916

The Argosy of Geography (Sailing Ship). XXXIX, pictorial supplement, Jan., 1921

The Awe-Inspiring Spectacle of the Valley of Ten Thousand Smokes, Discovered and Explored by National Geographic Society Expeditions. XXXIII, panorama, Feb., 1918

"Babes in the Wood" (Bears). XXXII, pictorial supplement, Aug., 1917

Bird's-Eye View of the Panama Canal. XXIII, panorama, Feb., 1912

Boyhood of Sir Walter Raleigh. Reproduction in color of the painting by Sir John Millais, Tate Gallery, London. XLIX, text, p. 596; supplement, May, 1926

The Caravels of Columbus. Reproduction in color of the painting by N. C. Wyeth, National Geographic Society, Washington, D. C. LIV, text, p. 55; supplement, July, 1928

Cathedrals of England. 16 ills. in gravure from dry-point engravings by Norman Wilkinson. LXXVI, pp. 745-760; text, p. 762, Dec., 1939

PICTORIAL SUPPLEMENTS: Enlargements and Panoramas—*Continued*

Commander Byrd at the North Pole (Through Pathless Skies to the North Pole). Reproduction in color of the painting by N. C. Wyeth, National Geographic Society, Washington, D. C. LIII, supplement, May, 1928

Curvature of the Earth: The First Photograph Ever Made Showing the Division Between the Troposphere and Stratosphere and also the Actual Curvature of the Earth. Aërial photo by Captain Albert W. Stevens. LXIX, supplement, May, 1936

The Discoverer. Reproduction in color of the painting by N. C. Wyeth, National Geographic Society, Washington, D. C. LIII, text, p. 347; supplement, Mar., 1928

Doe and Twin Fawns. Flashlight photo by George Shiras, 3d. XXIV, supplement, July, 1913. XL, ill. p. 136, Aug., 1921. LXXVI, ill. p. 475, Oct., 1939

Fate Directs the Faltering Footsteps of Columbus. Reproduction in color of the painting by Alfred Dehodencq, Paris. LIV, supplement, Sept., 1928

The Great Wall of China Near Nankow Pass. XLIII, panorama, Feb., 1923

Greater New York . . . Metropolis of Mankind. Aërial photo by Captain Albert W. Stevens. LXIV, supplement, Nov., 1933

The Greatest Achievement of Ancient Man in America (Fortress of Sacsahuaman, Peru). XXIX, panorama, May, 1916

Hark! (Deer). XL, pictorial supplement, Aug., 1921

The Hour of Prayer: In the Sahara Desert. XXII, panorama, Apr., 1911

The House of the Rich Man—Jerusalem. Pictorial supplement for framing

Lhasa—The Mecca of the Buddhist Faith. XXIX, panorama, Mar., 1916

The Lure of the Frozen Desert (Arctic Regions). XXIII, panorama, Dec., 1912

The Majesty of the Matterhorn. XXIII, text, p. 514; pictorial supplement, May, 1912

The Mall, Washington, D. C. XXVII, plan, Mar., 1915

The "Map of Discovery" (Eastern Hemisphere). Reproduction in color of the painting by N. C. Wyeth, National Geographic Society, Washington, D. C. LIV, text, p. 568; supplement, Nov., 1928

The "Map of Discovery" (Western Hemisphere). Reproduction in color of the painting by N. C. Wyeth, National Geographic Society, Washington, D. C. LV, text, p. 93; supplement, Jan., 1929

The Monarch of the Canadian Rockies—Robson Peak. XXIV, panorama, May, 1913

The Oldest Living Thing ("General Sherman Tree"). XXIX, pictorial supplement, Apr., 1916

Our Mountain Panorama (Canadian Rockies). XXII, text, p. 521; ill. p. 520; panorama, June, 1911

The Palms (Trees). XXII, pictorial supplement, Dec., 1911

Peasant Home in Corsica. XLIV, pictorial supplement, Sept., 1923

PICTORIAL SUPPLEMENTS: Enlargements and Panoramas—*Continued*

The Ruins of an Ancient Inca Capital, Machu Picchu. XXIV, panorama, Apr., 1913

Rumanian Peasant Girl. XXIV, ill. p. 1084, Oct., 1913. XXXIV, ill. p. 467, Dec., 1918; enlargement for framing

Ships of the Centuries. 16 ills. in gravure from etchings by Norman Wilkinson. LXXIII, pp. 65-80; text, p. 98, Jan., 1938

Torii Gate, Japan. XXII, col. pl., p. 982, Nov., 1911; enlargement for framing

The Ultimate Washington (Plan laid out by the Commission of 1901 for the National Capital). XXVII, panorama, Mar., 1915

Vasco da Gama at the Court of the Zamorin of Calicut. Reproduction in color of the painting by José Velloso Salgado, Sociedade de Geographia de Lisboa. LII, supplement, Nov., 1927

The Wrangell Mountains (Alaska). Panorama taken by W. C. Mendenhall from the ridge east of the Dadina River. XIV, panorama, Nov., 1903

PICTURESQUE Paramaribo (Surinam). By Harriet Chalmers Adams. XVIII, pp. 365-373, 7 ills., June, 1907

The **PICTURESQUE** Side of Japanese Life. 16 color photos: 12 by Kiyoshi Sakamoto. XLII, pp. 283-298, Sept., 1922

PIDGEON, HARRY:

Around the World in the "Islander" (Yawl): A Narrative of the Adventures of a Solitary Voyager on His Four-Year Cruise in a Thirty-Four-Foot Sailing Craft. By Capt. Harry Pidgeon. LIII, pp. 141-205, 75 ills., two-page map, Feb., 1928

PIECES of Silver. By Frederick Simpich. LXIV, pp. 253-292, 49 ills., Sept., 1933

PIEDMONT PLATEAU, U. S.:

Geographic History of the Piedmont Plateau. By W J McGee. VII, pp. 261-265, Aug., 1896

PIERCE, JOSIAH, JR.:

The Ordnance Survey of Great Britain—Its History and Object. By Josiah Pierce, Jr. II, pp. 243-260, Aug., 1890

PIGEONS:

American Game Birds. By Henry Wetherbee Henshaw. Paintings by Louis Agassiz Fuertes. XXVIII, pp. 105-158, 4 ills. in black and white, 72 ills. in color, Aug., 1915

Chinese Pigeon Whistles. XXIV, pp. 715-716, ills., June, 1913

Game Birds of Prairie, Forest, and Tundra. By Alexander Wetmore. Paintings by Maj. Allan Brooks. LXX, pp. 461-500, 5 ills. in black and white, 60 portraits in color, Oct., 1936

Man's Feathered Friends of Longest Standing: Peoples of Every Clime and Age Have Lavished Care and Affection Upon Lovely Pigeons. By Elisha Hanson. Paintings by Hashime Murayama. XLIX, pp. 63-110, 35 ills. in black and white, 12 ills. in color, Jan., 1926

Contents: Barb, Carneau, Carrier, Dragoon, Fantail, Helmet, Homer, Jacobin, King, Magpie, Mondaine, Nun, Oriental Frill, Park, Pouter, Swallow, Tumbler, Victoria Crowned

PIGEONS—*Continued*

The Wild Life of Lake Superior, Past and Present: The Habits of Deer, Moose, Wolves, Beavers, Muskrats, Trout, and Feathered Wood-Folk Studied with Camera and Flashlight. By George Shiras, 3d. XL, pp. 113-204, 76 ills., map, pictorial supplement, Aug., 1921

PIGEONS of Resplendent Plumage. 12 ills. in color from paintings by Hashime Murayama. XLIX, pp. 65-76, Jan., 1926

The **"PILGRIM"** Sails the Seven Seas: A Schooner-Yacht Out of Boston Drops in at Desert Isles and South Sea Edens in a Leisurely Two-Year Voyage. By Harold Peters. LXXII, pp. 223-262, 36 ills., Aug., 1937

A **PILGRIMAGE** to Amernath, Himalayan Shrine of the Hindu Faith. By Louise Ahl Jessop. XL, pp. 513-542, 29 ills., Nov., 1921

PILGRIMS AND PILGRIMAGES:

A Pilgrimage to Amernath, Himalayan Shrine of the Hindu Faith. By Louise Ahl Jessop. XL, pp. 513-542, 29 ills., Nov., 1921

Pilgrims' Progress to Mecca. 22 ills. in duotone: 18 by Oscar Marcus. LXXII, pp. 627-642, Nov., 1937

Puto, the Enchanted Island. By Robert F. Fitch. LXXXIX, pp. 373-384, 11 ills., map, Mar., 1946

Religious Penances and Punishments Self-Inflicted by the Holy Men of India. By W. M. Zumbro. XXIV, pp. 1257-1314, 69 ills., Dec., 1913

Tai Shan, Sacred Mountain of the East. By Mary Augusta Mullikin. LXXXVII, pp. 699-719, 18 ills., map, June, 1945

An Unbeliever Joins the Hadj: On the Age-Old Pilgrimage to Mecca, Babies Are Born, Elders Die, and Families May Halt a Year to Earn Funds in Distant Lands. By Owen Tweedy. LXV, pp. 761-789, 30 ills., map, June, 1934

PILGRIMS Still Stop at Plymouth (England). By Maynard Owen Williams. LXXIV, pp. 59-77, 19 ills., July, 1938

PILLSBURY, JOHN ELLIOTT:

Announcement of the death of. XXXVII, p. 345, Apr., 1920

Election of Rear Admiral Pillsbury as Vice-President of the Society. XXVII, p. 218, Feb., 1915

Election to NGS Presidency in 1919. XXXVII, pp. 341, 345, Apr., 1920

The Grandest and Most Mighty Terrestrial Phenomenon: The Gulf Stream. By John Elliott Pillsbury. XXIII, pp. 767-778, ill., diagrs., 3 maps, Aug., 1912

Photograph of. XXXVII, ill. p. 341, Apr., 1920

Wilkes' and D'Urville's Discoveries in Wilkes Land. By Rear Admiral John E. Pillsbury. XXI, pp. 171-173, Feb., 1910

See also NGS: Board of Managers

PINCHOT, GIFFORD:

An American Fable (Conservation of Resources). By Gifford Pinchot. XIX, pp. 345-350, May, 1908

PINCHOT, GIFFORD—*Continued*

Forest Reserves of the United States. (By Gifford Pinchot). XI, pp. 369-372, map, Sept., 1900

Forestry Abroad and at Home. By Gifford Pinchot. XVI, pp. 375-388, 8 ills., Aug., 1905

The Relation of Forests and Forest Fires. By Gifford Pinchot. X, pp. 393-403, 7 ills., Oct., 1899

PINE-SCENTED, Harbor-Dented Maine. 39 color photos by B. Anthony Stewart and Robert F. Maxcy. LXVII, pp. 549-588, May, 1935

PINEDO, FRANCESCO DE:

By Seaplane to Six Continents: Cruising 60,000 Miles, Italian Argonauts of the Air See World Geography Unroll and Break New Sky Trails Over Vast Brazilian Jungles. By Commander Francesco de Pinedo. LIV, pp. 247-301, 60 ills., two-page map, Sept., 1928

PINEO, CHARLES S.:

To Market in Guatemala. 19 color photos by Giles Greville Healey and Charles S. Pineo. LXXXVIII, pp. 89-104, July, 1945

PINES, Isle of, Cuba:

Cuba. By Robert T. Hill. IX, pp. 193-242, 12 ills., 7 diagrs., tables, 5 maps (1 foldout), May, 1898

The Isle of Pines. XVII, pp. 105-108, ills., Feb., 1906

PIONEER Gaucho Days. 8 ills. in color from paintings by Cesáreo Bernaldo de Quirós. LXIV, pp. 453-460, Oct., 1933

PIPELINES:

Oil for Victory Piped under the Sea. 9 ills. LXXXVIII, pp. 721-726, Dec., 1945

PIRATE-FIGHTERS of the South China Sea. By Robert Cardwell. LXXXIX, pp. 787-796, 11 ills., June, 1946

PIRATE Rivers and Their Prizes: The Warfare of Waterways Has Sometimes Changed the Geography of Our Continents. By John Oliver La Gorce. L, pp. 87-132, 48 ills., map, July, 1926

PIRATES:

The Haunts of the Caribbean Corsairs: The West Indies a Geographic Background for the Most Adventurous Episodes in the History of the Western Hemisphere. By Nell Ray Clarke. XLI, pp. 147-187, 43 ills., Feb., 1922

Pirate-Fighters of the South China Sea. By Robert Cardwell. LXXXIX, pp. 787-796, 11 ills., June, 1946

See also Tristan da Cunha

PISA, Italy:

From London to Australia by Aëroplane: A Personal Narrative of the First Aërial Voyage Half Around the World. By Sir Ross Smith. XXXIX, pp. 229-339, 76 ills. in black and white, 8 ills. in color, map, Mar., 1921

Inexhaustible Italy. By Arthur Stanley Riggs. XXX, pp. 273-368, 76 ills., map, Oct., 1916

PISAC (Fortress), Pisac, Peru:
Some Wonderful Sights in the Andean Highlands: The Oldest City in America. Sailing on the Lake of the Clouds: The Yosemite of Peru. By Harriet Chalmers Adams. XIX, pp. 597-618, 19 ills., map, Sept., 1908

PITCAIRN ISLAND, South Pacific Ocean:
Westward Bound in the *Yankee*. By Irving and and Electa Johnson. LXXXI, pp. 1-44, 25 ills. in black and white, 20 ills. in color, map, Jan., 1942

The **PITH** of Peru: A Journey from Talara to Machu Picchu, with Memorable Stopovers. By Henry Albert Phillips. LXXXII, pp. 167-196, 6 ills. in black and white, 20 ills. in color, map, Aug., 1942

PITTIER, HENRY:
Awarded Jane M. Smith Life Membership. XXXVII, p. 342 (footnote), Apr., 1920
Costa Rica—Vulcan's Smithy. By H. Pittier. XXI, pp. 494-525, 30 ills., maps, June, 1910
Little-Known Parts of Panama. By Henry Pittier. XXIII, pp. 627-662, 35 ills., map, July, 1912

PLACE NAMES. *See* Geographic Names

PLACE Names in Canada. (By H. G.). X, pp. 519-520, Dec., 1899

PLACE Names in Eastern Asia. XV, p. 136, Mar., 1904

PLACE Names of the United States. XIII, pp. 403-405, Nov., 1902

A **PLAGUE** of Mice. XX, pp. 479-485, 7 ills., May, 1909

PLAIN Tales from the Trenches: As Told Over the Tea Table in Blighty—A Soldier's "Home" in Paris. By Carol Corey. XXXIII, pp. 300-312, 7 ills., Mar., 1918

PLAINS:
Cloud Scenery of the High Plains (Kansas). By Willard D. Johnson. IX, pp. 493-496, 3 ills., Dec., 1898
The Sage Plains of Oregon. By Frederick V. Coville. VII, pp. 395-404, Dec., 1896
See also Peneplains

PLAINS INDIANS: United States:
Indians of Our Western Plains. By Matthew W. Stirling. Paintings by W. Langdon Kihn. LXXXVI, pp. 73-108, 14 ills. in black and white, 16 ills. in color, July, 1944

PLAN for Climbing Mt. McKinley. By Alfred H. Brooks and D. L. Reaburn. XIV, pp. 30-35, map, Jan., 1903

PLAN of a Map of the World. By Dr. Albrecht Penck. XV, pp. 405-408, Oct., 1904

PLANCHES, EDMOND MAYOR, BARON DES:
The Discovery of the North Pole (Address by Baron Mayor des Planches). XXI, pp. 63-82, Jan., 1910
Honors to Peary (Address by Baron Mayor des Planches). XVIII, pp. 49-60, ill., Jan., 1907

PLANKTON:
Living Jewels of the Sea. By William Crowder. Paintings by author. LII, pp. 290-304, 8 ills. in black and white, 8 ills. in color, Sept., 1927
Contents: Crustaceans, Diatoms, Dinoflagellates, Foraminifers, Radiolarians

PLANS for Reaching the South Pole. By Gilbert H. Grosvenor. X, pp. 316-319, map supplement, Aug., 1899

PLANTING Fishes in the Ocean. By George M. Bowers. XVIII, pp. 715-723, 5 ills., Nov., 1907

PLANTS:
The American Deserts. XV, pp. 153-163, 7 ills., map, Apr., 1904
Big Things of the West. By Charles F. Holder. XIV, pp. 279-282, ills., July, 1903
Canyons and Cacti of the American Southwest. 22 color photos by Edwin L. Wisherd, Jacob Gayer, Charles Martin. XLVIII, pp. 275-290, Sept., 1925
Common Mushrooms of the United States. By Louis C. C. Krieger. Paintings by author. XXXVII, pp. 387-439, 37 ills. in black and white, 16 ills. in color, May, 1920
Cryptogams Collected by Dr. C. Willard Hayes in Alaska, 1891. By Clara E. Cummings. IV, pp. 160-162, May 15, 1892
The Discovery of Cancer in Plants. XXIV, pp. 53-70, 12 ills., Jan., 1913
Exploring a Grass Wonderland of Wild West China. By Ray G. Johnson. LXXXV, pp. 713-742, 24 ills., map, June, 1944
Exploring the Mysteries of Plant Life. By William Joseph Showalter. Paintings by Mary E. Eaton. XLV, pp. 581-646, 41 ills. in black and white, 47 ills. in color, June, 1924
Familiar Grasses and Their Flowers. By E. J. Geske and W. J. Showalter. Paintings by E. J. Geske. XXXIX, pp. 625-636, 8 ills. in color, June, 1921
Fantastic Plants of Our Western Deserts. 8 ills. by Frank M. Campbell. XLV, pp. 33-40, Jan., 1924
Ferns as a Hobby. By William R. Maxon. Paintings by E. J. Geske. XLVII, pp. 541-586, 29 ills. in black and white, 16 ills. in color, May, 1925
Goldfish and Their Cultivation in America. By Hugh M. Smith. Paintings by Hashime Murayama. XLVI, pp. 375-400, 14 ills. in black and white, 8 ills. in color, Oct., 1924
Included: The following ornamental plants grown in aquaria: Fanwort, Spatterdock, Water Seedbox, Waterweed
Henequen—The Yucatan Fiber. By E. H. Thompson. XIV, pp. 150-158, 6 ills., Apr., 1903
A Hunter of Plants. By David Fairchild. XXXVI, pp. 57-77, 18 ills., July, 1919
Hunting for Plants in the Canary Islands. By David Fairchild. LVII, pp. 607-652, 37 ills. in black and white, 39 ills. in color, map, May, 1930
Hunting Useful Plants in the Caribbean. By David Fairchild. LXVI, pp. 705-737, 39 ills., Dec., 1934

PLANTS—*Continued*

An Insect Community Lives in Flower Heads (Shepherd's Needles). By James G. Needham. XC, pp. 340-356, 5 ills. in black and white, 11 ills. in color, Sept., 1946

The Kingdom of Flowers: An Account of the Wealth of Trees and Shrubs of China and of What the Arnold Arboretum, with China's Help, Is Doing to Enrich America. By Ernest H. Wilson. XXII, pp. 1003-1035, 24 ills., Nov., 1911

Laws of Temperature Control of the Geographic Distribution of Terrestrial Animals and Plants. Annual Address by Vice-President, Dr. C. Hart Merriam. VI, pp. 229-238, table, 3 maps, Dec. 29, 1894

List of Plants Collected near Muir Glacier, determined by W. W. Rowlee. IV, p. 79, Mar. 21, 1892

The Mistletoe. XXI, p. 965, Nov., 1910

New Plant Immigrants. By David Fairchild. XXII, pp. 879-907, 34 ills., Oct., 1911

Our Plant Immigrants. By David Fairchild. XVII, pp. 179-201, 29 ills., Apr., 1906

Peacetime Plant Hunting About Peiping. By P. H. and J. H. Dorsett. LXXII, pp. 509-534, 21 ills., map, Oct., 1937

Pests and Parasites: Why We Need a National Law to Prevent the Importation of Insect-Infested and Diseased Plants. By Charles Lester Marlatt. XXII, pp. 321-346, 29 ills., maps, Apr., 1911

Protecting the United States from Plant Pests. By Charles Lester Marlatt. XL, pp. 205-218, 16 ills., Aug., 1921

Report on Fossil Plants (Mount St. Elias Expedition). By Lester F. Ward. III, pp. 199-200, May 29, 1891

Riddle of the Aleutians: A Botanist Explores the Origin of Plants on Ever-misty Islands Now Enshrouded in the Fog of War. By Isobel Wylie Hutchison. LXXXII, pp. 769-792, 24 ills., Dec., 1942

Round About Bogotá: A Hunt for New Fruits and Plants Among the Mountain Forests of Colombia's Unique Capital. By Wilson Popenoe. XLIX, pp. 127-160, 34 ills., map, Feb., 1926

The Sage Plains of Oregon. By Frederick V. Coville. VII, pp. 395-404, Dec., 1896

See also Agricultural and Botanical Explorers; Agriculture; Cacti; Flowers; Fruits; Gardens; Seaweeds; Shrubs; Trees

PLASTICS:

Chemists Make a New World: Creating Hitherto Unknown Raw Materials, Science Now Disrupts Old Trade Routes and Revamps the World Map of Industry. By Frederick Simpich. LXXVI, pp. 601-640, 22 ills. in black and white, 26 ills. in color, Nov., 1939

PLATINUM:

Platinum in the World's Work. By Lonnelle Davison. LXXII, pp. 345-360, 17 ills., Sept., 1937

PLATYPUS:

Australia's Patchwork Creature, the Platypus: Man Succeeds in Making Friends with This Duck-billed, Fur-coated Paradox which Lays Eggs and Suckles Its Young. By Charles H. Holmes. LXXVI, pp. 273-282, 13 ills., Aug., 1939

PLOVERS (Birds):

Birds of Timberline and Tundra. By Arthur A. Allen. With 24 color photos by author. XC, pp. 313-339, 8 ills. in black and white, Sept., 1946

Our Greatest Travelers: Birds that Fly from Pole to Pole and Shun the Darkness: Birds that Make 2,500 Miles in a Single Flight. By Wells W. Cooke. XXII, pp. 346-366, 12 maps, Apr., 1911

The Shore Birds, Cranes, and Rails: Willets, Plovers, Stilts, Phalaropes, Sandpipers, and Their Relatives Deserve Protection. By Arthur A. Allen. Paintings by Major Allan Brooks. LXXII, pp. 183-222, 4 ills. in black and white, 101 portraits in color, Aug., 1937

PLUTO, Operation, World War II. *See* Operation Pluto

PLYMOUTH, England:

Channel Ports—And Some Others. By Florence Craig Albrecht. XXVIII, pp. 1-55, 45 ills., July, 1915

A City That Refused to Die. By Harvey Klemmer. LXXXIX, pp. 211-236, 13 ills. in black and white, 9 ills. in color, map, Feb., 1946

Pilgrims Still Stop at Plymouth. By Maynard Owen Williams. LXXIV, pp. 59-77, 19 ills., July, 1938

POAS (Volcano), Costa Rica:

Costa Rica—Vulcan's Smithy. By H. Pittier. XXI, pp. 494-525, 30 ills., maps, June, 1910

POCKET Carriers Fight the Submarines. 20 ills. in color from U. S. Navy official photos. LXXXIV, pp. 521-544, Nov., 1943

POGUE, JOSEPH E.:

The Great Rainbow Natural Bridge of Southern Utah. By Joseph E. Pogue. XXII, pp. 1048-1056, 6 ills., Nov., 1911

A **POISONED** World. By William Howard Taft. XXXI, pp. 459-467, 7 ills., May, 1917

POITOU (French Province):

The Beauties of France. By Arthur Stanley Riggs. XXVIII, pp. 391-491, 73 ills. in black and white, 16 ills. in color, map, Nov., 1915

POLAND:

Bright Bits in Poland's Mountainous South. 16 color photos by Hans Hildenbrand. LXVII, pp. 353-360, Mar., 1935

Devastated Poland. By Frederic C. Walcott. XXXI, pp. 445-452, 6 ills., May, 1917

The New Map of Europe: Showing the Boundaries Established by the Peace Conference at Paris and by Subsequent Decisions of the Supreme Council of the Allied and Associated Powers. By Ralph A. Graves. Text with map supplement. XXXIX, pp. 157-177, 18 ills., Feb., 1921

POLAND—*Continued*

Partitioned Poland. By William Joseph Showalter. XXVII, pp. 88-106, 12 ills., Jan., 1915

Pedaling Through Poland: An American Girl Free-wheels Alone from Kraków, and Its Medieval Byways, Toward Ukraine's Restive Borderland. By Dorothy Hosmer. LXXV, pp. 739-775, 38 ills., maps, June, 1939

Poland, Land of the White Eagle. By Melville Bell Grosvenor. With 12 color photos by Hans Hildenbrand. LXI, pp. 435-444, Apr., 1932

The Poland of the Present. By Maynard Owen Williams. LXIII, pp. 319-344, 19 ills. in black and white, 11 ills. in color, Mar., 1933

The Races of Europe. By Edwin A. Grosvenor. XXXIV, pp. 441-534, 62 ills., diagr. and index, maps, map supplement, Dec., 1918

Struggling Poland: A Journey in Search of the Picturesque Through the Most Populous of the New States of Europe. By Maynard Owen Williams. L, pp. 203-244, 48 ills., map, Aug., 1926

Wilno, Stepchild of the Polish Frontier. 13 ills. in duotone. LXXIII, pp. 777-784, June, 1938

See also Gdynia

The **POLAR** Airship. By Walter Wellman. XVII, pp. 208-228, 5 diagrs., Apr., 1906

POLAR EXPEDITIONS. *See* Antarctic Regions; Arctic Regions; *and* NGS: Expeditions: Antarctic Regions; Arctic Regions

POLAR Exploration. XVI, p. 482, Oct., 1905

POLAR Photography. By Anthony Fiala. XVIII, pp. 140-142, Feb., 1907

POLAR REGIONS. *See* Antarctic Regions; Arctic Regions

POLAR STAR (Airplane):

My Flight Across Antarctica. By Lincoln Ellsworth. LXX, pp. 1-35, 37 ills., map, July, 1936

POLES (People):

Black Acres: A Thrilling Sketch in the Vast Volume of Who's Who Among the Peoples That Make America. By Dorothea D. and Fred Everett. LXXX, pp. 631-652, 13 ills. in black and white, 12 ills. in color, Nov., 1941

The **POLICEMEN** of the Air (Birds): An Account of the Biological Survey of the Department of Agriculture. By Henry Wetherbee Henshaw. XIX, pp. 79-118, 38 ills., Feb., 1908

POLLUTION of the Potomac River. By F. H. Newell. VIII, pp. 346-351, Dec., 1897

POLO, MARCO:

The World's Greatest Overland Explorer: How Marco Polo Penetrated Farthest Asia, "Discovered" Many Lands Unknown to Europe, and Added Numerous Minerals, Animals, Birds, and Plants to Man's Knowledge. By J. R. Hildebrand. LIV, pp. 505-568, 53 ills., two-page map, Nov., 1928

POLPERRO, England:

Channel Ports—And Some Others. By Florence Craig Albrecht. XXVIII, pp. 1-55, 45 ills., July, 1915

POLYNESIA:

Around the World in the "Islander" (Yawl): A Narrative of the Adventures of a Solitary Voyager on His Four-Year Cruise in a Thirty-Four-Foot Sailing Craft. By Capt. Harry Pidgeon. LIII, pp. 141-205, 75 ills., two-page map, Feb., 1928

At Home on the Oceans: Whales and Sharks Make Exciting Neighbors for a Professor's Wife, Turned Able Seaman, on a Three-year Voyage Around the World. By Edith Bauer Strout. LXXVI, pp. 33-86, 54 ills., map, July, 1939

Color Glimpses of the Changing South Seas. 14 color photos by Amos Burg. LXV, pp. 281-288, Mar., 1934

Diary of a Voyage from San Francisco to Tahiti and Return, 1901. By S. P. Langley. XII, pp. 413-429, 10 ills., maps, Dec., 1901

The Dream Ship: The Story of a Voyage of Adventure More Than Half Around the World in a 47-foot Lifeboat. By Ralph Stock. XXXIX, pp. 1-52, 43 ills., map, Jan., 1921

The Greatest Voyage in the Annals of the Sea. By J. R. Hildebrand. LXII, pp. 699-739, 35 ills., maps, Dec., 1932

The Islands of the Pacific. By J. P. Thomson. XL, pp. 543-558, 15 ills., map supplement, Dec., 1921

Living on a Volcano: An Unspoiled Patch of Polynesia Is Niuafoō, Nicknamed "Tin Can Island" by Stamp Collectors. By Thomas A. Jaggar. LXVIII, pp. 91-106, 17 ills., map, July, 1935

A Modern Saga of the Seas: The Narrative of a 17,000-Mile Cruise on a 40-Foot Sloop by the Author, His Wife, and a Baby, Born on the Voyage. By Erling Tambs. LX, pp. 645-688, 49 ills., map, Dec., 1931

The "Pilgrim" Sails the Seven Seas: A Schooner Yacht Out of Boston Drops in at Desert Isles and South Sea Edens in a Leisurely Two-Year Voyage. By Harold Peters. LXXII, pp. 223-262, 36 ills., Aug., 1937

The Romance of Science in Polynesia: An Account of Five Years of Cruising Among the South Sea Islands. By Robert Cushman Murphy. Paintings by Hashime Murayama. XLVIII, pp. 355-426, 66 ills. in black and white, 16 ills. in color, 3 maps, Oct., 1925

See also Canton Island; Easter Island; Falcon Island; Fatu-Hiva; Hawaii; Marquesas Islands; Pitcairn Island; Samoa; Society Islands; Tongareva

POLYPS (Marine Animals):

Coral Castle Builders of Tropic Seas. By Roy Waldo Miner. Paintings by Else Bostelmann. LXV, pp. 703-728, 15 ills. in black and white, 8 ills. in color, maps, June, 1934

The **POMP** and Pulse of Modern London. 23 color photos by B. Anthony Stewart. LXXI, pp. 17-48, Jan., 1937

POMPEII, Italy:

Destruction of Pompeii as Interpreted by the Volcanic Eruptions of Martinique. By Angelo Heilprin. XV, p. 431, Oct., 1904

PONAPE (Island), Caroline Islands:
Hidden Key to the Pacific: Piercing the Web of Secrecy Which Long Has Veiled Japanese Bases in the Mandated Islands. By Willard Price. LXXXI, pp. 759-785, 28 ills., map, June, 1942
Yap and Other Pacific Islands Under Japanese Mandate. By Junius B. Wood. XL, pp. 591-627, 34 ills., map, Dec., 1921

PONIES:
England's Wild Moorland Ponies. 10 ills. LXXXIX, pp. 129-136, Jan., 1946

PONTA DELGADA, Azores:
The Azores: Picturesque and Historic Half-way House of American Transatlantic Aviators. By Arminius T. Haeberle. XXXV, pp. 514-545, 26 ills., map, June, 1919

PONTINE MARSHES, Italy:
Redemption of the Pontine Marshes: By Draining the Malarial Wastes Around Rome, Italy Has Created a Promised Land. By Gelasio Caetani. LXVI, pp. 201-217, 9 ills. in black and white, 12 ills. in color, map, Aug., 1934
The Story and the Legends of the Pontine Marshes: After Many Centuries of Fruitless Effort, Italy Is to Inaugurate a Gigantic Enterprise to Drain the Fertile Region Southeast of Rome. By Don Gelasio Caetani. XLV, pp. 357-374, 18 ills., Apr., 1924

PONTING, HERBERT G.:
Life in the Antarctic. 8 photos by Herbert G. Ponting, official photographer of the British Antarctic Expedition under Capt. Robert F. Scott. XLII, pp. 655-662, Dec., 1922
The Lure of the Land of Ice. 16 photos by Herbert G. Ponting, official photographer of the British Antarctic Expedition under Capt. Robert F. Scott. XLV, pp. 255-270, Mar., 1924

POPENOE, PAUL B.:
Costa Rica, Land of the Banana. By Paul B. Popenoe. XLI, pp. 201-220, 17 ills., Feb., 1922

POPENOE, WILSON:
Round About Bogotá: A Hunt for New Fruits and Plants Among the Mountain Forests of Colombia's Unique Capital. By Wilson Popenoe. XLIX, pp. 127-160, 34 ills., map, Feb., 1926

POPOCATEPETL (Volcano), Mexico:
The Greatest Volcanoes of Mexico. By A. Melgareio. XXI, pp. 741-760, 22 ills., Sept., 1910

POPULATION:
Calculations of Population in June, 1900. By Henry Farquhar. X, pp. 406-413, Oct., 1899
European Populations. (By Walter J. Ballard). XVI, p. 432, Sept., 1905
The Geographical Distribution of Insanity in the United States. By Dr. William A. White. XIV, pp. 361-378, 6 maps, Oct., 1903
The Great Populous Centers of the World. By General A. W. Greely. V, pp. 89-92, table, July 10, 1893
The Growth of the United States. By W J McGee. IX, pp. 377-386, diagr., table, Sept., 1898

POPULATION—*Continued*
The Indian Census of 1911. By John J. Banninga. XXII, pp. 633-638, 4 ills., July, 1911
The Mexican Census. VII, p. 211, table, June, 1896
The Movements of Our Population (U. S.). By Henry Gannett. V, pp. 21-44, 7 diagrs., 15 tables, 15 maps, Mar. 20, 1893
The Population of Japan. (By Walter J. Ballard). XVI, p. 482, Oct., 1905
The Population of the United States. By Henry Gannett. XXII, pp. 34-48, 9 diagrs., 3 maps, Jan., 1911
Proportion of Children in the United States. XVI, pp. 504-508, charts, Nov., 1905
Recent Population Figures. By Henry Gannett. XXII, pp. 785-786, Aug., 1911
The Remarkable Growth of Europe During 40 Years of Peace. (By O. P. Austin). XXVI, pp. 272-274, Sept., 1914
The Russian Census of 1897. (By A. W. G.). VIII, pp. 335-336, Nov., 1897
Urban Population of United States. XII, pp. 345-346, Sept., 1901
White Population of the Chief British Colonies. XIV, p. 360, Sept., 1903
See also Census; Immigration

POPULOUS and Beautiful Szechuan: A Visit to the Restless Province of China, in which the Present Revolution Began. By Rollin T. Chamberlin. XXII, pp. 1094-1119, 26 ills., map, Dec., 1911

PORCELAIN:
The World's Ancient Porcelain Center (Kingtehchen). By Frank B. Lenz. XXXVIII, pp. 391-406, 17 ills., Nov., 1920

PORCUPINES:
A Flashlight Story of an Albino Porcupine and of a Cunning but Unfortunate Coon. By George Shiras, 3d. XXII, pp. 572-596, 26 ills., June, 1911
The Quills of a Porcupine. By Frederick V. Coville. XXIII, pp. 25-31, 5 ills., Jan., 1912
Smaller Mammals of North America. By E. W. Nelson. Paintings by Louis Agassiz Fuertes. XXXIII, pp. 371*-493, 29 ills. in black and white, 59 ills. in color, May, 1918
Wild Animals That Took Their Own Pictures by Day and by Night. By George Shiras, 3d. XXIV, pp. 763-834, 68 ills., map, pictorial supplement, July, 1913

PORPOISES:
Whales, Giants of the Sea: Wonder Mammals, Biggest Creatures of All Time, Show Tender Affection for Young, But Can Maim or Swallow Human Hunters. By Remington Kellogg. Paintings by Else Bostelmann. LXXVII, pp. 35-90, 25 ills. in black and white, 31 ills. in color, Jan., 1940
Included: Porpoises and Dolphins

PORT-AU-PRINCE, Haiti:
Bare Feet and Burros of Haiti. By Oliver P. Newman. LXXXVI, pp. 307-328, 10 ills. in black and white, 10 ills. in color, map, Sept., 1944

PORT-AU-PRINCE, Haiti—*Continued*

Haiti, the Home of Twin Republics. By Sir Harry Johnston. XXXVIII, pp. 483-496, 11 ills., map, Dec., 1920

Haitian Vignettes. By Captain John Houston Craige. LXVI, pp. 435-485, 40 ills. in black and white, 13 ills. in color, map, Oct., 1934

PORT-OF-SPAIN, Trinidad:

Crossroads of the Caribbean. By Laurence Sanford Critchell. LXXII, pp. 319-344, 18 ills. in black and white, 14 ills. in color, map, Sept., 1937

PORTER, ETHEL CHAMBERLAIN:

The Clock Turns Back in Yugoslavia: Fortified Monastery of Mountain-girt Dečani Survives Its Six Hundredth Birthday. By Ethel Chamberlain Porter. LXXXV, pp. 493-512, 20 ills., map, Apr., 1944

PORTER, RUSSELL W.:

Member of Ziegler Polar Expedition. XVII, p. 35, Jan., 1906

PORTLAND, Oregon:

Oregon Finds New Riches. By Leo A. Borah. XC, pp. 681-728, 15 ills. in black and white, 28 ills. in color, two-page map, Dec., 1946

PORTO ALEGRE, Rio Grande do Sul, Brazil:

Air Cruising Through New Brazil: A National Geographic Reporter Spots Vast Resources Which the Republic's War Declaration Adds to Strength of United Nations. By Henry Albert Phillips. LXXXII, pp. 503-536, 32 ills., Oct., 1942

PORTO RICO. *See* Puerto Rico

PORTO Rico. By Robert T. Hill. X, pp. 93-112, 13 ills., Mar., 1899

PORTO Rico, the Gate of Riches: Amazing Prosperity Has Been the Lot of Ponce de León's Isle Under American Administration. By John Oliver La Gorce. XLVI, pp. 599-651, 46 ills. in black and white, 12 ills. in color, map, Dec., 1924

PORTO Rico or Puerto Rico? (By R. T. Hill). X, pp. 516-517, Dec., 1899

PORTRAITS of Ancient Mayas, a Peace-Loving People. 10 ills. in color from paintings by H. M. Herget. LXVIII, pp. 553-560, Nov., 1935

PORTS. *See* Harbors and Ports

PORTSMOUTH, New Hampshire:

Northeast of Boston. By Albert W. Atwood. LXXXVIII, pp. 257-292, 12 ills. in black and white, 17 ills. in color, map supplement, Sept., 1945

PORTUGAL:

An Altitudinal Journey Through Portugal: Rugged Scenic Beauty, Colorful Costumes, and Ancient Castles Abound in Tiny Nation That Once Ruled a Vast Empire. By Harriet Chalmers Adams. LII, pp. 567-610, 44 ills., map, Nov., 1927

Castles and Progress in Portugal. By W. Robert Moore. LXXIII, pp. 133-188, 36 ills. in black and white, 24 ills. in color, map, Feb., 1938

PORTUGAL—*Continued*

The Greatness of Little Portugal. By Oswald Crawfurd. XXI, pp. 867-883, 12 ills., Oct., 1910

The Pathfinder of the East: Setting Sail to Find "Christians and Spices," Vasco da Gama Met Amazing Adventures, Founded an Empire, and Changed the History of Western Europe. By J. R. Hildebrand. LII, pp. 503-550, 43 ills., map, pictorial supplement, Nov., 1927

Portugal, the Land of Henry the Navigator. 16 color photos by A. W. Cutler. XLII, pp. 517-532, Nov., 1922

The Races of Europe. By Edwin A. Grosvenor. XXXIV, pp. 441-534, 62 ills., diagr. and index, maps, map supplement, Dec., 1918

Rainbow Portraits of Portugal. 17 color photos by Gervais Courtellemont. LII, pp. 551-566, Nov., 1927

The Woods and Gardens of Portugal. By Martin Hume. XXI, pp. 883-894, 8 ills., Oct., 1910

See also Azores (Islands); Lisbon; Madeira (Islands); São Tomé (Island)

PORTUGUESE EAST AFRICA. *See* Mozambique

PORTUGUESE TIMOR:

Timor a Key to the Indies. By Stuart St. Clair. LXXXIV, pp. 355-384, 33 ills., map, Sept., 1943

PORTUGUESE WEST AFRICA. *See* Angola

POSSE-BRÁZDOVÁ, AMELIE:

Country-House Life in Sweden: In Castle and Cottage the Landed Gentry Gallantly Keep the Old Traditions. By Amelie Posse-Brázdová. LXVI, pp. 1-64, 51 ills. in black and white, 13 ills. in color, map, July, 1934

The **POSSIBILITIES** of Alaska. By C. C. Georgeson. XIII, pp. 81-85, Mar., 1902

The **POSSIBILITIES** of the Hudson Bay Country. XVIII, pp. 209-213, ill., Mar., 1907

POSTWAR Portrait of the United States. Text with map supplement. XC, pp. 135-136, July, 1946

POTALA (Monastery), Tibet:

Sky-high in Lama Land. 12 photos by C. Suydam Cutting. XC, pp. 185-196, Aug., 1946

The World's Strangest Capital (Lhasa, Tibet). By John Claude White. XXIX, pp. 273-295, 19 ills., panorama, Mar., 1916

POTASH:

American Potash for America. By Guy Elliott Mitchell. XXII, pp. 399-405, 4 ills., Apr., 1911

POTENT Personalities—Wasps and Hornets: Though Often Painfully Stung, Mankind Profits Immeasurably from the Pest-killing Activities of These Fiery Little Flyers. By Austin H. Clark. Paintings by Hashime Murayama. LXXII, pp. 47-72, 18 ills. in black and white, 12 ills. in color, July, 1937

POTOMAC (River), Maryland-West Virginia-D. C.:

Approaching Washington by Tidewater Potomac. By Paul Wilstach. LVII, pp. 372-392, 7 ills. in black and white, 15 ills. in color, Mar., 1930

POTOMAC (River), Maryland-West Virginia-D.C. —*Continued*

Atlantic Estuarine Tides. By Mark S. W. Jefferson. IX, pp. 400-409, diagrs., 7 tables, maps, Sept., 1898

The Great Falls of the Potomac. By Gilbert Grosvenor. LIII, pp. 385-400, 19 ills., Mar., 1928

Pollution of the Potomac River. By F. H. Newell. VIII, pp. 346-351, Dec., 1897

Potomac, River of Destiny. By Albert W. Atwood. LXXXVIII, pp. 33-70, 15 ills. in black and white, 18 ills. in color, map, July, 1945

The Washington Aqueduct and Cabin John Bridge. By D. D. Gaillard. VIII, pp. 337-344, ills., Dec., 1897

POTOSI, Bolivia:

Bolivia—Tin Roof of the Andes. By Henry Albert Phillips. LXXXIII, pp. 309-332, 5 ills. in black and white, 20 ills. in color, Mar., 1943

POTTERY:

The World's Ancient Porcelain Center (Kingtehchen, China). By Frank B. Lenz. XXXVIII, pp. 391-406, 17 ills., Nov., 1920

POULTER, THOMAS C.:

The Society's Special Medal Is Awarded to Dr. Thomas C. Poulter: Admiral Byrd's Second-in-Command and Senior Scientist Is Accorded High Geographic Honor. LXXII, pp. 105-108, ills., July, 1937

POULTRY:

America's Debt to the Hen. By Harry R. Lewis. LI, pp. 453-467, 15 ills., Apr., 1927

Fowls of Forest and Stream Tamed by Man. By Morley A. Jull. Paintings by Hashime Murayama. LVII, pp. 327-371, 27 ills. in black and white, 16 ills. in color, Mar., 1930

Contents: Ducks, Geese, Guinea Fowl, Peafowl, Swans, Turkeys

The Races of Domestic Fowl. By M. A. Jull. Paintings by Hashime Murayama. LI, pp. 379-452, 67 ills. in black and white, 29 ills. in color, Apr., 1927

Included: Ancona, Andalusian, Araucana, Bantam, Brahma, Campine, Cochin, Cornish, Dominique, Frizzle, Hamburg, Houdan, Jersey Black Giant, Langshan, Leghorn, Minorca, Plymouth Rock, Polish, Red Jungle Fowl, Rhode Island Red, Silkie, Sussex, Wyandotte, Yokohama

POWDER EXPLOSION:

The Aberration of Sound as Illustrated by the Berkeley Powder Explosion. By Robert H. Chapman. VII, pp. 246-249, 3 diagrs., July, 1896

POWELL, IMOGENE:

"Compleat Angler" Fishes for Fossils. By Imogene Powell. LXVI, pp. 251-258, 7 ills., Aug., 1934

POWELL, JOHN B.:

Today on the China Coast. By John B. Powell. LXXXVII, pp. 217-238, 17 ills., map, Feb., 1945

POWELL, JOHN WESLEY:

Gardiner Greene Hubbard: Memorial Meeting. Address by Major John W. Powell. IX, pp. 59-63, Feb., 1898

John Wesley Powell (Biography). (By G. H. G.). XIII, pp. 393-394, ill., Nov., 1902

Surveying the Grand Canyon of the Colorado: An Account of the 1923 Boating Expedition of the United States Geological Survey. By Lewis R. Freeman. XLV, pp. 471-548, 62 ills., map, May, 1924

Included: Expeditions of John Wesley Powell in the Grand Canyon area

POWELL, W. B.:

Chairman of National Geographic Society Prize Committee. X, p. 32, Jan., 1899

Geographic Instruction in the Public Schools. By W. B. Powell. V, pp. 137-153, Jan. 31, 1894

See also NGS: Board of Managers; Vice-President

POWELL-COTTON, P. H. G.:

A Journey Through the Eastern Portion of the Congo State. By Major P. H. G. Powell-Cotton. XIX, pp. 155-163, 9 ills., Mar., 1908

POWHATAN CONFEDERACY:

Indians of the Southeastern United States. By Matthew W. Stirling. Paintings by W. Langdon Kihn. LXXXIX, pp. 53-74, 8 ills. in black and white, 8 ills. in color, Jan., 1946

PRACTICAL Exercises in Geography. By W. M. Davis. XI, pp. 62-78, diagr., Feb., 1900

PRACTICAL Patriotism (National Geographic Society's War Work). XXXII, pp. 279-280, Sept., 1917; p. 476, Nov.-Dec., 1917

PRAGUE (Praha), Czechoslovakia:

Czechoslovakia, Key-Land to Central Europe. By Maynard Owen Williams. XXXIX, pp. 111-156, 45 ills., map, Feb., 1921

Czechoslovaks, Yankees of Europe. By John Patric. LXXIV, pp. 173-225, 23 ills. in black and white, 30 ills. in color, map, Aug., 1938

A Tale of Three Cities. By Thomas R. Henry. LXXXVIII, pp. 641-669, 23 ills., Dec., 1945

When Czechoslovakia Puts a Falcon Feather in Its Cap. By Maynard Owen Williams. LXIII, pp. 40-49, 13 ills. in color, Jan., 1933

PRAHA, Czechoslovakia. *See* Prague

PRAIRIE FALCONS:

In Quest of the Golden Eagle: Over Lonely Mountain and Prairie Soars This Rare and Lordly Bird, But Three Youths from the East Catch Up With Him at Last. By John and Frank Craighead. LXXVII, pp. 693-710, 17 ills., May, 1940

Week-Ends With the Prairie Falcon: A Commuter Finds Recreation in Scaling Cliffs to Observe the Nest Life and Flying Habits of These Elusive Birds. By Frederick Hall Fowler. LXVII, pp. 611-626, 21 ills., May, 1935

PRATT, A. E.:

Strange Sights in Far-Away Papua. By A. E. Pratt. XVIII, pp. 559-572, 7 ills., Sept., 1907

PRATT, WILLIAM V. *See* NGS: Board of Trustees

PRAUS (Ships):
Seafarers of South Celebes. By G. E. P. Collins. LXXXVII, pp. 53-78, 25 ills., map, Jan., 1945

PRECIOUS Stones. XIV, pp. 451-458, 4 ills., Dec., 1903

PREHISTORIC ANIMALS. *See* Paleontology

The **PREHISTORIC** Ruin of Tsankawi (New Mexico). By George L. Beam. XX, pp. 807-822, 12 ills., Sept., 1909

PREHISTORIC Telephone Days. By Alexander Graham Bell. XLI, pp. 223-241, 17 ills., Mar., 1922

PRENTICE, SARTELL, JR.:
Sunrise and Sunset from Mount Sinai. By Rev. Sartell Prentice, Jr. XXIII, pp. 1242-1282, 34 ills., map, Dec., 1912

PRESCOTT, WILLIAM H.:
The Luster of Ancient Mexico (Aztecs). By William H. Prescott. XXX, pp. 1-32, 22 ills., July, 1916

PRESENT Conditions in China. By Frederick McCormick. XXII, pp. 1120-1138, 13 ills., Dec., 1911

PRESENT Conditions in China. By John W. Foster. XVII, pp. 651-672, 709-711, Dec., 1906

PRESENT Day Scenes in the World's Oldest Empire (Ethiopia). 27 color photos by W. Robert Moore. LIX, pp. 691-722, June, 1931

The **PRESENT** State of the Nicaragua Canal. By General A. W. Greely. VII, pp. 73-76, Feb., 1896

The **PRESERVATION** of England's Historic and Scenic Treasures. By Eric Underwood. LXXXVII, pp. 413-440, 24 ills., two-page map, Apr., 1945

PRESERVING Ancient America's Finest Sculptures (Guatemala). By J. Alden Mason. Paintings by H. M. Herget. LXVIII, pp. 537-570, 24 ills. in black and white, 10 ills. in color, Nov., 1935

The **PRESIDENCY** of the National Geographic Society. IX, p. 28, Jan., 1898
See also NGS: President

PRESIDENT Alexander Graham Bell on Japan. (By J. H.). IX, pp. 509-512, Dec., 1898

PRESIDENT Coolidge Bestows Lindbergh Award: The National Geographic Society's Hubbard Medal Is Presented to Aviator Before the Most Notable Gathering in the History of Washington. LIII, pp. 132-140, 4 ills., Jan., 1928

PRESTON, E. D.:
The Coast and Geodetic Survey: Its Present Work. (By E. D. Preston). X, pp. 268-269, July, 1899
The Copper River Delta (Alaska). (By E. D. Preston). XI, pp. 29-31, Jan., 1900
Tides of Chesapeake Bay. By E. D. Preston. X, pp. 391-392, Oct., 1899

PRETORIA, Transvaal, Union of South Africa:
The Cities That Gold and Diamonds Built: Transvaal Treasures Have Created Bustling Johannesburg and Fostered Pretoria, Administrative Capital of the South African Union. By W. Robert Moore. LXXXII, pp. 735-766, 20 ills. in black and white, 9 ills. in color, map, Dec., 1942
The Transvaal: The Treasure-House Province. By Melville Chater. LIX, pp. 479-512, 28 ills. in black and white, 13 ills. in color, Apr., 1931

The **PREVENTION** of Hailstorms by the Use of Cannon. XI, pp. 239-241, June, 1900

PREVIOUS Explorations in the St. Elias Region (Part I, from "An Expedition to Mount St. Elias, Alaska," by Israel C. Russell). III, pp. 58-74, 5 maps, May 29, 1891

PRIBILOF ISLANDS, Alaska:
Making the Fur Seal Abundant. By Hugh M. Smith. XXII, pp. 1139-1165, 18 ills., map, Dec., 1911

PRICE, OVERTON W.:
The Influence of Forestry upon the Lumber Industry of the United States. By Overton W. Price. XIV, pp. 381-386, ills., Oct., 1903

PRICE, THEODORA:
Seals of Our Nation, States, and Territories. 84 ills. in color from paintings by Carlotta Gonzales Lahey, Irvin E. Alleman, Theodora Price. XC, pp. 17-32, July, 1946

PRICE, WILLARD:
Americans on the Barbary Coast (Africa). By Willard Price. LXXXIV, pp. 1-31, 13 ills. in black and white, 10 ills. in color, map, July, 1943
Behind the Mask of Modern Japan. By Willard Price. LXXXVIII, pp. 513-535, 14 ills., Nov., 1945
By Felucca Down the Nile: Giant Dams Rule Egypt's Lifeline River, Yet Village Life Goes On As It Did in the Time of the Pharaohs. By Willard Price. LXXVII, pp. 435-476, 21 ills. in black and white, 22 ills. in color, two-page map, Apr., 1940
Grand Canal Panorama (China). By Willard Price. LXXI, pp. 487-514, 31 ills., map, Apr., 1937
Hidden Key to the Pacific: Piercing the Web of Secrecy Which Long Has Veiled Japanese Bases in the Mandated Islands. By Willard Price. LXXXI, pp. 759-785, 28 ills., map, June, 1942
Jap Rule in the Hermit Nation (Korea). By Willard Price. LXXXVIII, pp. 429-451, 19 ills., map, Oct., 1945
Japan Faces Russia in Manchuria. By Willard Price. LXXXII, pp. 603-634, 30 ills., map, Nov., 1942
Mysterious Micronesia: Yap, Map, and Other Islands Under Japanese Mandate are Museums of Primitive Man. By Willard Price. LXIX, pp. 481-510, 37 ills., map, Apr., 1936
Springboards to Tokyo. By Willard Price. LXXXVI, pp. 385-407, 16 ills., Oct., 1944
Unknown Japan: A Portrait of the People Who Make Up One of the Two Most Fanatical Nations in the World. By Willard Price. LXXXII, pp. 225-252, 30 ills., Aug., 1942

PRICE of Free World Victory (Title of Address Delivered by the Honorable Henry A. Wallace at a Dinner of the Free World Association, May 8, 1942). LXXXII, pp. 276-280, ill., Aug., 1942

The **PRICE** of Liberty, Equality, Fraternity. XXXIV, p. 377, Nov., 1918

PRIENE, Turkey:

Some Ruined Cities of Asia Minor. By Ernest L. Harris. XIX, pp. 833-858, 19 ills., Dec., 1908

PRIEST, CECIL D.:

Timbuktu, in the Sands of the Sahara. By Captain Cecil D. Priest. XLV, pp. 73-85, 16 ills., Jan., 1924

A **PRIMITIVE** Gyroscope in Liberia. By G. N. Collins. XXI, pp. 531-535, 3 ills., June, 1910

PRINCELY India, Resplendent with Jewels and Gold. 40 color photos by Lawrence Copley Thaw. LXXVIII, pp. 733-780, Dec., 1940

PRINCETON (Aircraft Carrier):

Saga of the Carrier *Princeton.* By Capt. William H. Buracker, USN. LXXXVIII, pp. 189-218, 8 ills. in black and white, 22 ills. in color, map, Aug., 1945

PRITCHETT, HENRY S.:

Judge of prize essay contest. X, p. 32, Jan., 1899

See also NGS: Board of Managers

PRIZES. *See* NGS: Prizes

PRIZES for the Inventor: Some of the Problems Awaiting Solution. By Alexander Graham Bell. XXXI, pp. 131-146, 7 ills., Feb., 1917

The **PROBABLE** Cause of the San Francisco Earthquake. By Frederick Leslie Ransome. XVII, pp. 280-296, 9 ills., maps, May, 1906

The **PROBABLE** Effect of the Panama Canal on the Commercial Geography of the World. By O. P. Austin. XXV, pp. 245-248, Feb., 1914

PROBERT, FRANK H.:

The Treasure Chest of Mercurial Mexico (Silver Mines in Guanajuato). By Frank H. Probert. XXX, pp. 33-68, 33 ills., July, 1916

PROBLEMS in China. By James M. Hubbard. XI, pp. 297-308, 3 ills., map supplement, Aug., 1900

PROBLEMS of the Pacific—New Zealand. By Henry Demarest Lloyd. XIII, pp. 342-352, Sept., 1902

PROBLEMS of the Pacific—The Commerce of the Great Ocean. By O. P. Austin. XIII, pp. 303-318, 7 maps, Aug., 1902

PROBLEMS of the Pacific—The Great Ocean in World Growth. By W J McGee. XIII, pp. 333-342, Sept., 1902

PROBOSCIS WORM. *See* Bloodworms

PROCEEDINGS of the International Geographic Conference in Chicago, July 27-28, 1893. V, pp. 97-256, Jan. 31, 1894

Included: Minutes of the Conference; Memoirs and Addresses

PROCEEDINGS of the National Geographic Society. *See* NGS: Meetings

The **PRODUCTION** of Whalebone. XIX, pp. 883-885, ill. pp. 878, 879, Dec., 1908

PROGRESS in Surveying the United States. By O. H. Tittmann. XVII, pp. 110-112, ill., Feb., 1906

PROGRESS in the Philippines. XVI, pp. 116-118, Mar., 1905

PROGRESS in the Philippines. XVI, pp. 511-514, ills., Nov., 1905

PROGRESS of the National Geographic Society. XXIV, pp. 251-256, ill., Feb., 1913

PROGRESS on the Panama Canal. (By G. H. G.). XVI, pp. 467-475, map, Oct., 1905

The **PROGRESSIVE** World Struggle of the Jews for Civil Equality. By William Howard Taft. XXXVI, pp. 1-23, 14 ills., July, 1919

PROJECT for the Exploration of the Atmosphere Over the Tropical Oceans. By A. Lawrence Rotch. XV, p. 430, Oct., 1904

PRONGHORNS:

Stalking Big Game with Color Camera. 28 color photos by Wendell Chapman. LXXVI, pp. 89-128, July, 1939

PROPORTION of Children in the United States. XVI, pp. 504-508, charts, Nov., 1905

The **PROPOSED** American Interoceanic Canal in Its Commercial Aspects. By Joseph Nimmo, Jr. X, pp. 297-310, Aug., 1899

PROPOSED Collection of Forestry Statistics. IX, p. 448, Oct., 1898

PROPOSED Meteorological Station in Iceland. X, p. 228, June, 1899

PROPOSED Surveys in Alaska in 1902. By Alfred H. Brooks. XIII, pp. 133-135, map, Apr., 1902

PROROK, BYRON KHUN, COUNT DE:

Ancient Carthage in the Light of Modern Excavation. By Count Byron Khun de Prorok. XLV, pp. 391-423, 27 ills. in black and white, 16 ills. in color, map, Apr., 1924

PROSPEROUS Idaho (An Interview with Governor Gooding, of Idaho, Published in the New York *Sun,* December, 1905). XVII, pp. 16-22, Jan., 1906

PROSPEROUS Porto Rico. XVII, p. 712, Dec., 1906

PROTECTING Our Forests from Fire. By James Wilson. XXII, pp. 98-106, 5 ills., Jan., 1911

PROTECTING the United States from Plant Pests. By Charles Lester Marlatt. XL, pp. 205-218, 16 ills., Aug., 1921

PROVENCE (French Province):

Camargue, the Cowboy Country of Southern France. By Dr. André Vialles. XLII, pp. 1-34, 33 ills., map, July, 1922

PROVINCETOWN, Massachusetts:

Cape Cod People and Places. By Wanda Burnett. LXXXIX, pp. 737-774, 17 ills. in black and white, 24 ills. in color, map, June, 1946

PRUSSIA. *See* East Prussia

PRUSSIANISM. By Robert Lansing. XXXIII, pp. 546-557, 5 ills., June, 1918

PSALMS. *See* Twenty-third Psalm

PTARMIGANS (Birds):

Birds of Timberline and Tundra. By Arthur A. Allen. With 24 color photos by author. XC, pp. 313-339, 8 ills. in black and white, Sept., 1946

Game Birds of Prairie, Forest, and Tundra. By Alexander Wetmore. Paintings by Maj. Allan Brooks. LXX, pp. 461-500, 5 ills. in black and white, 60 portraits in color, Oct., 1936

The White Sheep, Giant Moose, and Smaller Game of the Kenai Peninsula, Alaska. By George Shiras, 3d. XXIII, pp. 423-494, 59 ills., maps (1 two-page), May, 1912

PUBLIC LANDS:

The National Forest Reserves. By Frederick H. Newell. VIII, pp. 177-187, diagrs., tables, June, 1897

The Utilization of the Vacant Public Lands. By Emory F. Best. VIII, pp. 49-57, Feb., 1897

See also National Forests; National Monuments; National Parks; *and* Homestead Land Laws

PUBLIC SCHOOLS:

Geographic Instruction in the Public Schools. By W. B. Powell. V, pp. 137-153, Jan. 31, 1894

Geographic Prizes (Gold Medal and certificates awarded annually to public high school students writing the best essay on geography). IV, pp. 206-208, Feb. 8, 1893

Important Announcement Concerning Essays (Gold Medal and certificates to be awarded for best essays on the River Systems of the United States). VI, pp. 227-228, Dec. 29, 1894

Monographs of the National Geographic Society, to be published for use in the public schools. VI, pp. 225-227, Dec. 29, 1894

Sight-Seeing in School: Taking Twenty Million Children on a Picture Tour of the World. By Jessie L. Burrall. XXXV, pp. 489-503, 14 ills., June, 1919

See also Education

PUEBLA (State), Mexico:

The Mexican Indian Flying Pole Dance. By Helga Larsen. LXXI, pp. 387-400, 13 ills., Mar., 1937

PUEBLO BONITO, New Mexico:

Everyday Life in Pueblo Bonito: As Disclosed by the National Geographic Society's Archeologic Explorations in the Chaco Canyon National Monument, New Mexico. By Neil M. Judd. XLVIII, pp. 227-262, 37 ills., map, Sept., 1925

A New National Geographic Society Expedition: Ruins of Chaco Canyon, New Mexico, Nature-Made Treasure-Chest of Aboriginal American History, To Be Excavated and Studied; Work Begins This Month. XXXIX, pp. 637-643, 7 ills., June, 1921

PUEBLO BONITO, New Mexico—*Continued*

Pueblo Bonito, the Ancient: The National Geographic Society's Third Expedition to the Southwest Seeks to Read in the Rings of Trees the Secret of the Age of Ruins. By Neil M. Judd. XLIV, pp. 99-108, 9 ills., diagr., July, 1923

The Pueblo Bonito Expedition of the National Geographic Society. By Neil M. Judd. XLI, pp. 323-331, 10 ills., diagr., Mar., 1922

See also Tree Rings

PUEBLO INDIANS:

Everyday Life in Pueblo Bonito: As Disclosed by the National Geographic Society's Archeologic Explorations in the Chaco Canyon National Monument, New Mexico. By Neil M. Judd. XLVIII, pp. 227-262, 37 ills., map, Sept., 1925

Indian Tribes of Pueblo Land. By Matthew W. Stirling. Paintings by W. Langdon Kihn. LXXVIII, pp. 549-596, 16 ills. in black and white, 25 ills. in color, Nov., 1940

New Mexico Melodrama. By Frederick Simpich. LXXIII, pp. 529-569, 19 ills. in black and white, 25 ills. in color, two-page map, May, 1938

Scenes from America's Southwest. 14 ills. XXXIX, pp. 651-664, June, 1921

See also Hopi Indians

PUEBLO VIEJO (Ruins), Mexico:

La Venta's Green Stone Tigers. By Matthew W. Stirling. LXXXIV, pp. 321-332, 4 ills. in black and white, 6 ills. in color, map, Sept., 1943

PUERTO RICO:

The Countries of the Caribbean. By William Joseph Showalter. XXIV, pp. 227-250, 23 ills., Feb., 1913

The First American Census of Porto Rico. XI, p. 328, Aug., 1900

Geographic Nomenclature. (By E. W. Hilgard). XI, pp. 36-37, Jan., 1900

Jobos Harbor. (By O. H. Tittmann). X, p. 206, June, 1899

Our New Possessions and the Interest They Are Exciting. (By O. P. Austin). XI, pp. 32-33, Jan., 1900

Porto Rico. By Robert T. Hill. X, pp. 93-112, 13 ills., Mar., 1899

Porto Rico, the Gate of Riches: Amazing Prosperity Has Been the Lot of Ponce de León's Isle Under American Administration. By John Oliver La Gorce. XLVI, pp. 599-651, 46 ills. in black and white, 12 ills. in color, map, Dec., 1924

Porto Rico or Puerto Rico? (By R. T. Hill). X, pp. 516-517, Dec., 1899

Proceedings of the National Geographic Society (Abstract of Address on Puerto Rico by Hon. William F. Willoughby). XIII, pp. 466-470, Dec., 1902

Prosperous Porto Rico. XVII, p. 712, Dec., 1906

Puerto Rico: Watchdog of the Caribbean: Venerable Domain Under American Flag Has New Role as West Indian Stronghold and Sentinel of the Panama Canal. By E. John Long. LXXVI, pp. 697-738, 24 ills. in black and white, 23 ills. in color, Dec., 1939

Puerto Rico, Not Porto Rico. (By J. H.). XI, pp. 37-38, Jan., 1900

PUERTO RICO—*Continued*
The Rediscovery of Puerto Rico. X, pp. 359-360, Sept., 1899
Some Recent Instances of National Altruism: The Efforts of the United States to Aid the Peoples of Cuba, Porto Rico and the Philippines. By William H. Taft. XVIII, pp. 429-438, July, 1907
The U. S. Signal Corps in Porto Rico. XI, p. 243, map, June, 1900

PUERTO Rico Polychromes. 23 color photos by Edwin L. Wisherd. LXXVI, pp. 713-736, Dec., 1939

PUFFINS (Birds):
Birds of the Northern Seas. By Alexander Wetmore. Paintings by Maj. Allan Brooks. LXIX, pp. 95-122, 12 ills. in black and white, 34 portraits in color, Jan., 1936

PUGET SOUND, Washington:
Our Pacific Northwest. By N. H. Darton. XX, pp. 645-663, 12 ills., maps, July, 1909

PUNTA ARENAS, Chile:
A Longitudinal Journey Through Chile. By Harriet Chalmers Adams. XLII, pp. 219-273, 60 ills., map, Sept., 1922

The **PURPLE** Veil: A Romance of the Sea. (By H. A. L.). XVI, pp. 337-341, 9 ills., July, 1905

The **PURPOSE** of the Anglo-Japanese Alliance. By Eki Hioki. XVI, pp. 333-337, July, 1905

PURSUING Spanish Bypaths Northwest of Madrid. By Harry A. McBride. LIX, pp. 121-130, 6 ills. in black and white, 14 ills. in color, map, Jan., 1931

PUSHING Back History's Horizon: How the Pick and Shovel Are Revealing Civilizations That Were Ancient When Israel Was Young. By Albert T. Clay. XXIX, pp. 162-216, 47 ills., map, Feb., 1916

PUTNAM, AMELIA EARHART. *See* Earhart, Amelia

PUTNAM, FREDERIC W.:
Frederic W. Putnam. (By J. H.). IX, pp. 429-431, ill. (front.), Oct., 1898
Portrait. IX, pl. 13 (front.), Oct., 1898

PUTNAM, GEORGE R.:
Beacons of the Sea. By George R. Putnam. XXIV, pp. 1-53, 65 ills., diagrs., map, Jan., 1913
Hidden Perils of the Deep. By George R. Putnam. XX, pp. 822-837, 19 diagrs., 3 charts, Sept., 1909
An Important New Guide for Shipping: Navassa Light, on a Barren Island in the West Indies, is the First Signal for the Panama Canal. By George R. Putnam. XXXIV, pp. 401-406, 3 ills., map, Nov., 1918
New Safeguards for Ships in Fog and Storm. By George R. Putnam. LXX, pp. 169-200, 28 ills., charts, Aug., 1936
A Summer Voyage to the Arctic. By G. R. Putnam. VIII, pp. 97-110, 6 ills., map, Apr., 1897
Surveying the Philippine Islands. By George R. Putnam. XIV, pp. 437-441, 4 ills., Dec., 1903

PUTO SHAN (Island), East China Sea:
Puto, the Enchanted Island. By Robert F. Fitch. LXXXIX, pp. 373-384, 11 ills., map, Mar., 1946

PYGMIES (People):
Into Primeval Papua by Seaplane: Seeking Disease-resisting Sugar Cane, Scientists Find Neolithic Man in Unmapped Nooks of Sorcery and Cannibalism. By E. W. Brandes. LVI, pp. 253-332, 98 ills., map, Sept., 1929
A Journey Through the Eastern Portion of the Congo State. By Major P. H. G. Powell-Cotton. XIX, pp. 155-163, 9 ills., Mar., 1908
A Land of Giants and Pygmies (Ruanda). By the Duke Adolphus Frederick of Mecklenburg. XXIII, pp. 369-388, 16 ills., map, Apr., 1912
Lloyd's Journey Across the Great Pygmy Forest (Belgian Congo). X, pp. 26-30, Jan., 1899
See also Uganda

PYRAMIDS:
Chichen Itzá, an Ancient American Mecca: Recent Excavations in Yucatan Are Bringing to Light the Temples, Palaces, and Pyramids of America's Most Holy Native City. By Sylvanus Griswold Morley. XLVII, pp. 63-95, 34 ills., diagr., map, Jan., 1925
An Interesting Visit to the Ancient Pyramids of San Juan Teotihuacan. By A. C. Galloway. XXI, pp. 1041-1050, 8 ills., map, Dec., 1910
The Resurrection of Ancient Egypt. By James Baikie. XXIV, pp. 957-1020, 46 ills., map, Sept., 1913
See also Egypt

PYRENEES (Mountains), France-Spain:
Andorra—Mountain Museum of Feudal Europe. By Lawrence A. Fernsworth. LXIV, pp. 493-512, 21 ills., map, Oct., 1933
Discovering the Oldest Statues in the World: A Daring Explorer Swims Through a Subterranean River of the Pyrenees and Finds Rock Carvings Made 20,000 Years Ago. By Norbert Casteret. XLVI, pp. 123-152, 24 ills., maps, Aug., 1924
A Skyline Drive in the Pyrenees (France). By W. Robert Moore. LXXII, pp. 434-452, 24 ills. in color, Oct., 1937

Q

QM, the Fighting Storekeeper. By Frederick Simpich. Paintings by Arthur Beaumont. LXXXII, pp. 561-600, 22 ills. in black and white, 16 ills. in color, Nov., 1942

QUAILS (Birds):
Game Birds of Prairie, Forest, and Tundra. By Alexander Wetmore. Paintings by Maj. Allan Brooks. LXX, pp. 461-500, 5 ills. in black and white, 60 portraits in color, Oct., 1936

QUARTERMASTER CORPS, U. S. Army. *See* U. S. Army Quartermaster Corps

QUEBEC (Province), Canada:
Gaspé Peninsula Wonderland. By Wilfrid Bovey. LXVIII, pp. 209-230, 13 ills. in black and white, 15 ills. in color, map, Aug., 1935

QUEBEC (Province), Canada—*Continued*
Gentle Folk Settle Stern Saguenay: On French Canada's Frontier Homespun Colonists Keep the Customs of Old Norman Settlers. By Harrison Howell Walker. LXXV, pp. 595-632, 15 ills. in black and white, 25 ills. in color, map, May, 1939
Old France in Modern Canada. By V. C. Scott O'Connor. LXVII, pp. 167-200, 36 ills., map, Feb., 1935
Contents: St. Lawrence and Saguenay Regions
Quebec, Capital of French Canada. By William Dow Boutwell. LVII, pp. 515-522, 6 ills. in black and white, 12 ills. in color, Apr., 1930
Servicing Arctic Airbases. By Robert A. Bartlett. LXXXIX, pp. 602-616, 3 ills. in black and white, 10 ills. in color, map, May, 1946
See also Anticosti Island

QUEBEC (City), Quebec, Canada:
Old France in Modern Canada. By V. C. Scott O'Connor. LXVII, pp. 167-200, 36 ills., map, Feb., 1935
Quebec, Capital of French Canada. By William Dow Boutwell. LVII, pp. 515-522, 6 ills. in black and white, 12 ills. in color, Apr., 1930

QUEENSLAND (State), Australia. *See* Great Barrier Reef

QUEER Methods of Travel in Curious Corners of the World. By O. P. Austin. XVIII, pp. 687-715, 29 ills., Nov., 1907

The **QUEST** of Gold and the Goldsmith's Art. 11 ills. in duotone. LXIII, pp. 489-496, Apr., 1933

QUETZALS (Birds):
Land of the Painted Oxcarts (Costa Rica). By Luis Marden. With 31 color photos by author. XC, pp. 409-456, 30 ills. in black and white, map, Oct., 1946
See also Guatemala; *and* Mayas (Yucatán)

QUICHÉS (Indians):
Guatemala: Land of Volcanoes and Progress: Cradle of Ancient Mayan Civilization, Redolent With Its Later Spanish and Indian Ways, Now Reaping Prosperity from Bananas and Coffee. By Thomas F. Lee. L, pp. 599-648, 32 ills. in black and white, 20 ills. in color, map, Nov., 1926
Guatemala Interlude: In the Land of the Quetzal a Modern Capital Contrasts With Primitive Indian Villages and the "Pompeii of America." By E. John Long. LXX, pp. 429-460, 22 ills. in black and white, 13 ills. in color, map, Oct., 1936

QUICHUA INDIANS:
Along the Old Inca Highway. By Harriet Chalmers Adams. XIX, pp. 231-250, 21 ills., Apr., 1908
Cuzco, America's Ancient Mecca. By Harriet Chalmers Adams. XIX, pp. 669-689, 19 ills., Oct., 1908
Over Trail and Through Jungle in Ecuador: Indian Head-Hunters of the Interior, an Interesting Study in the South American Republic. By H. E. Anthony. XL, pp. 327-352, 28 ills., Oct., 1921

The **QUILLS** of a Porcupine. By Frederick V. Coville. XXIII, pp. 25-31, 5 ills., Jan., 1912

QUININE Hunters in Ecuador. By Froelich Rainey. LXXXIX, pp. 341-363, 21 ills., map, Mar., 1946

QUINN, LORENA MacINTYRE:
America's South Sea Soldiers (American Samoa). By Lorena MacIntyre Quinn. XXXVI, pp. 267-274, 8 ills., Sept., 1919

QUIRIGUA, Guatemala:
Excavations at Quirigua, Guatemala. By Sylvanus Griswold Morley. XXIV, pp. 339-361, 24 ills., diagr., Mar., 1913
Note. XXIV, p. 1056, Sept., 1913
Mysterious Temples of the Jungle: The Prehistoric Ruins of Guatemala. By W. F. Sands. XXIV, pp. 325-338, 10 ills., Mar., 1913

QUIRÓS, CESÁREO BERNALDO DE:
Pioneer Gaucho Days. 8 ills. in color from paintings by Cesáreo Bernaldo de Quirós. LXIV, pp. 453-460, Oct., 1933

QUIRÓS, PEDRO FERNÁNDEZ DE:
Revealing Earth's Mightiest Ocean (Pacific). By Albert W. Atwood. LXXXIV, pp. 291-306, 10 ills., map supplement, Sept., 1943

QUITO, Ecuador:
From Sea to Clouds in Ecuador. By W. Robert Moore. LXXX, pp. 717-740, 11 ills. in black and white, 9 ills. in color, Dec., 1941
Over Trail and Through Jungle in Ecuador: Indian Head-Hunters of the Interior, an Interesting Study in the South American Republic. By H. E. Anthony. XL, pp. 327-352, 28 ills., Oct., 1921

R

RABAT, Morocco:
Eastward from Gibraltar: Overland Route Across North Africa to Tunisia and Libia. By Cyrus French Wicker. LXXXIII, pp. 115-142, 28 ills., Jan., 1943

RABBITS:
Lonely Australia: The Unique Continent. By Herbert E. Gregory. XXX, pp. 473-568, 68 ills., 5 maps (1 two-page), Dec., 1916
Smaller Mammals of North America. By E. W. Nelson. Paintings by Louis Agassiz Fuertes. XXXIII, pp. 371*-493, 29 ills. in black and white, 59 ills. in color, May, 1918
Wild Animals That Took Their Own Pictures by Day and by Night. By George Shiras, 3d. XXIV, pp. 763-834, 68 ills., map, pictorial supplement, July, 1913

RABOT, CHARLES:
French Conquest of the Sahara. By Charles Rabot. XVI, pp. 76-80, ills., Feb., 1905
A Notable Norwegian Publication. (By Charles Rabot). XV, pp. 370-371, Sept., 1904
Recent French Explorations in Africa. By Dr. Charles Rabot. XIII, pp. 119-132, 20 ills., Apr., 1902

RACCOONS:

A Flashlight Story of an Albino Porcupine and of a Cunning but Unfortunate Coon. By George Shiras, 3d. XXII, pp. 572-596, 26 ills., June, 1911

The **RACE** for the South Pole (Presentation of Hubbard Medal to Shackleton). XXI, pp. 185-186, Mar., 1910

RACE Prejudice in the Far East. By Melville E. Stone. XXI, pp. 973-985, 6 ills., Dec., 1910

RACES:

Geographic Progress of Civilization. Annual Address by the President, Honorable Gardiner G. Hubbard. VI, pp. 1-22, Feb. 14, 1894

The Movements of Our Population (U. S.). By Henry Gannett. V, pp. 21-44, 7 diagrs., 15 tables, 15 maps, Mar. 20, 1893

The Races and Religions of Macedonia. By Luigi Villari. XXIII, pp. 1118-1132, 14 ills., Nov., 1912

The Races of Europe: The Graphic Epitome of a Never-ceasing Human Drama. The Aspirations, Failures, Achievements, and Conflicts of the Polyglot People of the Most Densely Populated Continent. By Edwin A. Grosvenor. XXXIV, pp. 441-534, 62 ills., diagr. and index, maps, map supplement, Dec., 1918

The **RACES** of Domestic Fowl. By M. A. Jull. Paintings by Hashime Murayama. LI, pp. 379-452, 67 ills. in black and white, 29 ills. in color, Apr., 1927

RADAR:

Air Power for Peace. By General H. H. Arnold. LXXXIX, pp. 137-193, 35 ills. in black and white, 28 ills. in color, map supplement, Feb., 1946

New Frontier in the Sky. By F. Barrows Colton. XC, pp. 379-408, 28 ills., diagr., Sept., 1946

Your New World of Tomorrow. By F. Barrows Colton. LXXXVIII, pp. 385-410, 25 ills., Oct., 1945

RADIO:

Air Power for Peace. By General H. H. Arnold. LXXXIX, pp. 137-193, 35 ills. in black and white, 28 ills. in color, map supplement, Feb., 1946

The Miracle of Talking by Telephone. By F. Barrows Colton. LXXII, pp. 395-433, 41 ills., Oct., 1937

New Frontier in the Sky. By F. Barrows Colton. XC, pp. 379-408, 28 ills., diagr., Sept., 1946

New Safeguards for Ships in Fog and Storm. By George R. Putnam. LXX, pp. 169-200, 28 ills., charts, Aug., 1936

Voice Voyages by the National Geographic Society: A Tribute to the Geographic Achievements of the Telephone. XXIX, pp. 296-326, 15 ills., chart, Mar., 1916

Winged Words—New Weapon of War. By F. Barrows Colton. LXXXII, pp. 663-692, 29 ills., maps, Nov., 1942

Your New World of Tomorrow. By F. Barrows Colton. LXXXVIII, pp. 385-410, 25 ills., Oct., 1945

RADIO STATIONS:

Americans Stand Guard in Greenland. By Andrew H. Brown. XC, pp. 457-500, 23 ills. in black and white, 19 ills. in color, map, Oct., 1946

RADIUM:

The Cause of the Earth's Heat. XVI, pp. 124-125, ill., Mar., 1905

Helium, the New Balloon Gas. By G. Sherburne Rogers. XXXV, pp. 441-456, 11 ills., May, 1919

Prizes for the Inventor: Some of the Problems Awaiting Solution. By Alexander Graham Bell. XXXI, pp. 131-146, 7 ills., Feb., 1917

RAE, MARGERY:

A Sunday in Mezőkövesd (Hungary). By Margery Rae. LXVII, pp. 489-504, 22 ills., Apr., 1935

RAFT Life on the Hwang Ho. By W. Robert Moore. LXI, pp. 743-752, 14 ills., June, 1932

RAILROADS:

Across the Gulf by Rail to Key West (Florida). By Jefferson B. Browne. VII, pp. 203-207, June, 1896

Alaska's New Railway. XXVIII, pp. 567-589, 20 ills., Dec., 1915

America's Amazing Railway Traffic. By William Joseph Showalter. XLIII, pp. 353-404, 46 ills., map, Apr., 1923

The Commercial Valuation of Railway Operating Property in the United States. XVI, pp. 438-439, Sept., 1905

Cuban Railways. By Albert G. Robinson. XIII, pp. 108-110, Mar., 1902

The First Transandine Railroad from Buenos Aires to Valparaiso. By Harriet Chalmers Adams. XXI, pp. 397-417, 14 ills., diagr., map, May, 1910

Manchuria, Promised Land of Asia: Invaded by Railways and Millions of Settlers, This Vast Region Now Recalls Early Boom Days in the American West. By Frederick Simpich. LVI, pp. 379-428, 58 ills., map, Oct., 1929

A Maryland Pilgrimage: Visits to Hallowed Shrines Recall the Major Rôle Played by This Prosperous State in the Development of Popular Government in America. By Gilbert Grosvenor. LI, pp. 133-212, 88 ills., map supplement, Feb., 1927

Pan-American Railway. XV, pp. 232-233, May, 1904

Railroads and Canals. X, p. 420, Oct., 1899

Railway Construction and Improvements. XI, p. 163, Apr., 1900

Railway Routes in Alaska. By Alfred H. Brooks. XVIII, pp. 165-190, 9 ills., diagrs., 8 maps, Mar., 1907

Railways, Rivers, and Strategic Towns in Manchuria. (By G. H. G.). XI, pp. 326-327, Aug., 1900

Russian Railways. XI, p. 243, June, 1900

Shortening Time Across the Continent. By Henry Herbert McClure. XIII, pp. 319-321, Aug., 1902

South America. Annual Address by the President, Gardiner G. Hubbard. III, pp. 1-29, foldout map, Mar. 28, 1891

RAILROADS—*Continued*

Statistics of Railways in the United States. (By H. G.). VII, pp. 406-407, Dec., 1896

The Tehuantepec Ship Railway. By Elmer L. Corthell. VII, pp. 64-72, maps, Feb., 1896
Included: National Railroad of Tehuantepec

Trains of Today—and Tomorrow. By J. R. Hildebrand. LXX, pp. 535-589, 51 ills., Nov., 1936

Winning the War of Supply. By F. Barrows Colton. LXXXVIII, pp. 705-736, 32 ills., Dec., 1945

See also Damascus and Mecca Railway; Trans-Siberian Railway

RAILS (Birds):

The Shore Birds, Cranes, and Rails: Willets, Plovers, Stilts, Phalaropes, Sandpipers, and Their Relatives Deserve Protection. By Arthur A. Allen. Paintings by Major Allan Brooks. LXXII, pp. 183-222, 4 ills. in black and white, 101 portraits in color, Aug., 1937

RAILWAY Construction and Improvements. XI, p. 163, Apr., 1900

RAILWAY Routes in Alaska. By Alfred H. Brooks. XVIII, pp. 165-190, 9 ills., diagrs., 8 maps, Mar., 1907

RAILWAYS. *See* Electric Street Railways; Railroads; Ship Railways

RAILWAYS, Rivers, and Strategic Towns in Manchuria. (By G. H. G.). XI, pp. 326-327, Aug., 1900

RAINBOW Costumes of Poland's Peasants. 11 color photos by Hans Hildenbrand and Maynard Owen Williams. LXIII, pp. 329-336, Mar., 1933

RAINBOW Denizens of the Aquarium. 16 color photos by Edwin L. Wisherd. LXV, pp. 97-104, Jan., 1934

RAINBOW Hues from Hungary. 27 color photos: 26 by Hans Hildenbrand. LXI, pp. 697-728, June, 1932

RAINBOW NATURAL BRIDGE, Utah:

Encircling Navajo Mountain with a Pack-Train: An Expedition to a Hitherto Untraversed Region of Our Southwest Discovers a New Route to Rainbow Natural Bridge. By Charles L. Bernheimer. XLIII, pp. 197-224, 33 ills., map, Feb., 1923

The Great Rainbow Natural Bridge of Southern Utah. By Joseph E. Pogue. XXII, pp. 1048-1056, 6 ills., Nov., 1911

RAINBOW Portraits of Portugal. 17 color photos by Gervais Courtellemont. LII, pp. 551-566, Nov., 1927

RAINEY, FROELICH G.:

Alaskan Highway an Engineering Epic: Mosquitoes, Mud, and Muskeg Minor Obstacles of 1,671-mile Race to Throw the Alcan Life Line Through Thick Forests and Uninhabited Wilderness. By Froelich Rainey. LXXXIII, pp. 143-168, 21 ills., 3 maps, Feb., 1943

RAINEY, FROELICH G.—*Continued*

Discovering Alaska's Oldest Arctic Town: A Scientist Finds Ivory-eyed Skeletons of a Mysterious People and Joins Modern Eskimos in the Dangerous Spring Whale Hunt. By Froelich G. Rainey. LXXXII, pp. 319-336, 15 ills., Sept., 1942

Quinine Hunters in Ecuador. By Froelich Rainey. LXXXIX, pp. 341-363, 21 ills., map, Mar., 1946

RAINFALL:

The Economic Aspects of Soil Erosion. (Part I). By Dr. N. S. Shaler. VII, pp. 328-338, Oct., 1896

The Economic Aspects of Soil Erosion. (Part) II. By Dr. N. S. Shaler. VII, pp. 368-377, Nov., 1896

Rainfall and the Level of Lake Erie. (By E. L. Moseley). XIV, pp. 327-328, Aug., 1903

Rainfall Types of the United States. Annual Report by Vice-President, General A. W. Greely. V, pp. 45-58, 5 tables, map, Apr. 29, 1893

Relations of Air and Water to Temperature and Life. By Honorable Gardiner G. Hubbard. V, pp. 112-124, Jan. 31, 1894

Report—Geography of the Air. By Gen. A. W. Greely. II, pp. 49-63, Apr., 1890

Salton Sea and the Rainfall of the Southwest. By Alfred J. Henry. XVIII, pp. 244-248, Apr., 1907

See also Floods and Flood Control; Meteorology; Rainmaking; Storms; Water Supply

RAINIER, Mount, Washington:

The Great White Monarch of the Pacific Northwest. By A. H. Barnes. XXIII, pp. 593-626, 31 ills., map, June, 1912

The Height of Mt. Rainier. By Richard U. Goode. IX, pp. 97-98, Mar., 1898

Our National Parks. By L. F. Schmeckebier. XXIII, pp. 531-579, 41 ills., map, June, 1912

A Wonderland of Glaciers and Snow. By Milnor Roberts. XX, pp. 530-537, 8 ills.. June, 1909

RAINMAKING:

Weather Making, Ancient and Modern. By Mark W. Harrington. VI, pp. 35-62, Apr. 25, 1894
Included: Bibliography on artificial production of rain

RAJPUTANA (States), India:

The Marble Dams of Rajputana. By Eleanor Maddock. XL, pp. 469-499, 13 ills. in black and white, 16 ills. in color, Nov., 1921

RAJ SAMAND (Lake), India:

The Marble Dams of Rajputana. By Eleanor Maddock. XL, pp. 469-499, 13 ills. in black and white, 16 ills. in color, Nov., 1921

RALEIGH, SIR WALTER:

Boyhood of Sir Walter Raleigh. Reproduction in color of the painting by Sir John Millais, Tate Gallery, London. XLIX, text, p. 596; supplement, May, 1926

RALEIGH Rock (Akao Sho, Japan). XIV, p. 148, ill., Apr., 1903

RALIK CHAIN, Marshall Islands. *See* Bikini; Rongerik

RAMBLES Through the Prairie State (Illinois). 15 color photos by Clifton Adams. LIX, pp. 545-552, May, 1931

RAMBLES Through Ulster, Northern Tip of the Shamrock Isle. 21 color photos by Bernard F. Rogers, Jr. LXVIII, pp. 577-600, Nov., 1935

RAMBLING Around the Roof of Eastern America (Great Smoky Mountains). By Leonard C. Roy. LXX, pp. 243-266, 25 ills., map, Aug., 1936

RAMSAY, SIR WILLIAM:

Modern Transmutation of the Elements. By Sir William Ramsay. XVII, pp. 201-203, Apr., 1906

A Sketch of the Geographical History of Asia Minor. By Sir William Ramsay. XLII, pp. 553-570, 12 ills., Nov., 1922

RANCHES:

On a Chilean Hacienda. 8 color photos by E. P. Haddon. LXXXVI, pp. 489-496, Oct., 1944

RAND DISTRICT, South Africa. *See* Witwatersrand

RANGOON, Burma:

Notes on Burma. By Thomas Barbour. XX, pp. 841-866, 34 ills., Oct., 1909

RANSOME, FREDERICK LESLIE:

The Probable Cause of the San Francisco Earthquake. By Frederick Leslie Ransome. XVII, pp. 280-296, 9 ills., maps, May, 1906

RAPA NUI (Island), South Pacific Ocean. *See* Easter Island

RAS AT TANNURA, Saudi Arabia:

Guest in Saudi Arabia. By Maynard Owen Williams. LXXXVIII, pp. 463-487, 24 ills., map, Oct., 1945

RAS SHAMRA, Syria:

A New Alphabet of the Ancients Is Unearthed: An Inconspicuous Mound in Northern Syria Yields Archeological Treasures of Far-reaching Significance. By F. A. Schaeffer. LVIII, pp. 477-516, 47 ills., map, Oct., 1930

Secrets from Syrian Hills: Explorations Reveal World's Earliest Known Alphabet, Deciphered from Schoolboy Slates and Dictionaries of 3,000 Years Ago. By Claude F. A. Schaeffer. LXIV, pp. 97-126, 40 ills., map, July, 1933

The **RAT** Pest: The Labor of 200,000 Men in the United States Required to Support Rats, Man's Most Destructive and Dangerous Enemy. By Edward W. Nelson. XXXII, pp. 1-23, 21 ills., July, 1917

The **RATIONAL** Element in Geography. By W. M. Davis. X, pp. 466-473, diagrs., Nov., 1899

RATS:

The Rat Pest: The Labor of 200,000 Men in the United States Required to Support Rats, Man's Most Destructive and Dangerous Enemy. By Edward W. Nelson. XXXII, pp. 1-23, 21 ills., July, 1917

Smaller Mammals of North America. By E. W. Nelson. Paintings by Louis Agassiz Fuertes. XXXIII, pp. 371*-493, 29 ills. in black and white, 59 ills. in color, May, 1918

RAVENS (Birds):

Crows, Magpies, and Jays: Unusual Intelligence Has Earned a Unique Position for These Birds. By T. Gilbert Pearson. Paintings by Maj. Allan Brooks. LXIII, pp. 51-79, 16 ills. in black and white, 17 ills. in color, Jan., 1933

RAVENSDALE, MARY IRENE, BARONESS:

Old and New in Persia: In This Ancient Land Now Called Iran a Modern Sugar Factory Rears Its Head Near the Palace of Darius the Great. By the Baroness Ravensdale. LXXVI, pp. 325-355, 20 ills. in black and white, 13 ills. in color, map, Sept., 1939

REABURN, D. L.:

Plan for Climbing Mt. McKinley. By Alfred H. Brooks and D. L. Reaburn. XIV, pp. 30-35, map, Jan., 1903

The **REBIRTH** of Religion in Russia: The Church Reorganized While Bolshevik Cannon Spread Destruction in the Nation's Holy of Holies. By Thomas Whittemore. XXXIV, pp. 379-401, 16 ills., Nov., 1918

The **RECENT** Ascent of Itambé (Brazil). (By J. C. Branner). X, p. 183, May, 1899

RECENT Bequests by Members of the National Geographic Society. XLIX, p. 474, Apr., 1926

RECENT Contributions to Our Knowledge of the Earth's Shape and Size, by the United States Coast and Geodetic Survey. By C. A. Schott. XII, pp. 36-41, ill., chart, Jan., 1901

RECENT Disclosures Concerning Pre-Columbian Voyages to America in the Archives of the Vatican. By William Eleroy Curtis. V, pp. 197-234, Jan. 31, 1894

RECENT Discoveries in Egypt. XII, pp. 396-397, Nov., 1901

The **RECENT** Earthquake Wave on the Coast of Japan. By Eliza Ruhamah Scidmore. VII, pp. 285-289, 4 ills., foldout map, Sept., 1896

The **RECENT** Eruption of Katmai Volcano in Alaska. By George C. Martin. XXIV, pp. 131-181, 45 ills., diagr., map, Feb., 1913

RECENT Exploration in the Canadian Rockies. By Walter D. Wilcox. XIII, pp. 151-168, 12 ills., map, May, 1902; Part II, pp. 185-200, 9 ills., June, 1902

RECENT Explorations in Alaska. By Eliza Ruhamah Scidmore. V, pp. 173-179, Jan. 31, 1894

RECENT Explorations in Equatorial Africa. (By Ernest de Sasseville). VIII, pp. 88-91, Mar., 1897

RECENT French Explorations in Africa. By Dr. Charles Rabot. XIII, pp. 119-132, 20 ills., Apr., 1902

RECENT Geographic Advances, Especially in Africa. By Major General A. W. Greely. XXII, pp. 383-398, 5 ills., 5 maps, Apr., 1911

RECENT Hydrographic Work. (By F. H. N.). VII, pp. 347-348, Oct., 1896

RECENT Magnetic Work by the Carnegie Institution of Washington. XVII, p. 648, Nov., 1906

RECENT Observations in Albania. By Brig. Gen. George P. Scriven. XXXIV, pp. 90-114, 21 ills., map, Aug., 1918

RECENT Population Figures. By Henry Gannett. XXII, pp. 785-786, Aug., 1911

A **RECENT** Report from the "Doubtful Island Region." By James D. Hague. XVIII, pp. 205-208, maps, Mar., 1907

RECENT Triangulation in the Cascades (Washington). By S. S. Gannett. VII, p. 150, Apr., 1896

The **RECENT** Volcanic Eruptions in the West Indies. By Israel C. Russell. XIII, pp. 267-285, 7 ills., map, July, 1902

RECEPTION to Captain C. D. Sigsbee, U. S. N. (By J. H.). IX, pp. 251-252, May, 1898

RECEPTIONS. *See* NGS: Receptions

The **RECESSION** of the Glaciers of Glacier Bay, Alaska. By Fremont Morse. XIX, pp. 76-78, map, Jan., 1908

RECIFE (Pernambuco), Brazil:

Air Cruising Through New Brazil: A National Geographic Reporter Spots Vast Resources Which the Republic's War Declaration Adds to Strength of United Nations. By Henry Albert Phillips. LXXXII, pp. 503-536, 32 ills., Oct., 1942

RECK, DAISY:

The American Virgins (Virgin Islands): After Dark Days, These Adopted Daughters of the United States Are Finding a New Place in the Caribbean Sun. By DuBose Heyward and Daisy Reck. LXXVIII, pp. 273-308, 15 ills. in black and white, 23 ills. in color, map, Sept., 1940

RECLAIMING the Swamp Lands of the United States. By Herbert M. Wilson. XVIII, pp. 292-301, ills., diagr., map, May, 1907

RECLAMATION OF LAND:

The Call of the West. By C. J. Blanchard. XX, pp. 403-437, 20 ills., map, May, 1909

China Fights Erosion with U. S. Aid. By Walter C. Lowdermilk. LXXXVII, pp. 641-680, 10 ills. in black and white, 26 ills. in color, June, 1945

The Dikes of Holland. By Gerard H. Matthes. XII, pp. 219-234, 3 ills., 7 charts, June, 1901

Drainage of Wet Lands. XVII, pp. 713-714, Dec., 1906

A Drowned Empire. By Robert H. Chapman. XIX, pp. 190-199, 10 ills., Mar., 1908

Farmers Since the Days of Noah: China's Remarkable System of Agriculture Has Kept Alive the Densest Population in the World. By Adam Warwick. LI, pp. 469-500, 37 ills., Apr., 1927

Holland's War With the Sea. By James Howard Gore. XLIII, pp. 283-325, 39 ills., map, Mar., 1923

Home-Making by the Government: An Account of the Eleven Immense Irrigating Projects to be Opened in 1908. By C. J. Blanchard. XIX, pp. 250-287, 23 ills., Apr., 1908

RECLAMATION OF LAND—*Continued*

The Land of Egypt: A Narrow Green Strip of Fertility Stretching for a Thousand Miles Through Walls of Desert. By Alfred Pearce Dennis. XLIX, pp. 271-298, 28 ills., map, Mar., 1926

The Limited Water Supply of the Arid Region. By Frederick H. Newell. XI, pp. 438-442, Nov., 1900

Mending Dikes in the Netherlands. 20 photos by Lawrence Earl. XC, pp. 791-806, Dec., 1946

Millions for Moisture: An Account of the Work of the U. S. Reclamation Service. By C. J. Blanchard. XVIII, pp. 217-243, 22 ills., Apr., 1907

More Water for California's Great Central Valley. By Frederick Simpich. XC, pp. 645-664, 16 ills., map, Nov., 1946

The Nation's Undeveloped Resources. By Franklin K. Lane. XXV, pp. 183-225, 32 ills., Feb., 1914

A New Country Awaits Discovery: The Draining of the Zuider Zee Makes Room for the Excess Population of the Netherlands. By J. C. M. Kruisinga. LXIV, pp. 293-320, 20 ills. in black and white, 13 ills. in color, maps, Sept., 1933

New Mexico (Drainage of the Valley of Mexico). By John W. Foster. XIII, pp. 1-24, 11 ills., maps, Jan., 1902

Reclaiming the Swamp Lands of the United States. By Herbert M. Wilson. XVIII, pp. 292-301, ills., diagr., map, May, 1907

Reclamation: Drainage; Planting Denuded State Land; Control of the Boll Weevil. 6 ills. XVIII, pp. 778-780, Dec., 1907

Reclamation in Wyoming and Colorado. XIV, p. 166, Apr., 1903

The Reclamation of the West. By F. H. Newell. XV, pp. 15-30, 6 ills., 7 maps, Jan., 1904

Redemption of the Pontine Marshes: By Draining the Malarial Wastes Around Rome, Italy Has Created a Promised Land. By Gelasio Caetani. LXVI, pp. 201-217, 9 ills. in black and white, 12 ills. in color, map, Aug., 1934

The Spirit of the West: The Wonderful Agricultural Development Since the Dawn of Irrigation. By C. J. Blanchard. XXI, pp. 333-360, 15 ills., Apr., 1910

Staircase Farms of the Ancients: Astounding Farming Skill of Ancient Peruvians, Who Were Among the Most Industrious and Highly Organized People in History. By O. F. Cook. XXIX, pp. 474-534, 48 ills., May, 1916

The Story and the Legends of the Pontine Marshes: After Many Centuries of Fruitless Effort, Italy Is to Inaugurate a Gigantic Enterprise to Drain the Fertile Region Southeast of Rome. By Don Gelasio Caetani. XLV, pp. 357-374, 18 ills., Apr., 1924

Surveying Through Khoresm: A Journey into Parts of Asiatic Russia Which Have Been Closed to Western Travelers Since the World War. By Lyman D. Wilbur. LXI, pp. 753-780, 31 ills., map, June, 1932

Taming the Outlaw Missouri River. By Frederick Simpich. LXXXVIII, pp. 569-598, 25 ills., two-page map, Nov., 1945

Two Great Undertakings (Work of U. S. Bureau of Reclamation and U. S. Forest Service). XVII, pp. 645-647, Nov., 1906

RECLAMATION OF LAND—*Continued*
Winning the West. By C. J. Blanchard. XVII, pp. 82-98, 10 ills., map, Feb., 1906

RECONSTRUCTING Egypt's History. By Wallace N. Stearns. XXIV, pp. 1021-1042, 21 ills., Sept., 1913

RECORD Ascents in the Himalayas. XIV, pp. 420-421, Nov., 1903

RECORD of the Great Earthquake Written in Washington by the Seismograph of the U. S. Weather Bureau. By C. F. Marvin. XVII, pp. 296-298, May, 1906

The **RED** Ant Versus the Boll Weevil. XV, pp. 262-264, June, 1904

RED CROSS:
The Needs Abroad. By Ian Malcolm. XXXI, pp. 427-433, 5 ills., May, 1917
The Red Cross Spirit. By Eliot Wadsworth. XXXI, pp. 467-474, 8 ills., May, 1917
The Red Cross Spirit Speaks (Poem). By John H. Finley. XXXI, p. 474, May, 1917
The Symbol of Service to Mankind. By Stockton Axson. XXXIII, pp. 375-390, 11 ills., Apr., 1918
See also American National Red Cross

RED Cross Girl Overseas. By Margaret Cotter. LXXXVI, pp. 745-768, 22 ills., Dec., 1944

RED Men of the Southwest (Pueblo Indians). 25 ills. in color from paintings by W. Langdon Kihn. LXXVIII, pp. 557-596, Nov., 1940

RED SEA:
Pearl Fishing in the Red Sea. By Henri de Monfreid. LXXII, pp. 597-626, 24 ills., map, Nov., 1937

REDEEMING the Tropics. By William Joseph Showalter. XXV, pp. 344-364, 13 ills., Mar., 1914

REDEMPTION of the Pontine Marshes: By Draining the Malarial Wastes Around Rome, Italy Has Created a Promised Land. By Gelasio Caetani. LXVI, pp. 201-217, 9 ills. in black and white, 12 ills. in color, map, Aug., 1934

REDFIELD, WILLIAM C.:
Honors to Amundsen and Peary (Speech by William C. Redfield). XXIV, pp. 113-130, 5 ills., Jan., 1913

REDISCOVERING the Rhine: A Trip by Barge from the Sea to the Headwaters of Europe's Storied Stream. By Melville Chater. XLVIII, pp. 1-43, 44 ills., July, 1925

The **REDISCOVERY** of Puerto Rico. X, pp. 359-360, Sept., 1899

REDWAY, JACQUES W.:
The First Landfall of Columbus. By Jacques W. Redway, F. R. G. S. VI, pp. 179-192, 4 maps, Dec. 29, 1894

The **REDWOOD** Forest of the Pacific Coast. By Henry Gannett. X, pp. 145-159, 6 ills., map, May, 1899

REDWOODS (Trees):
California's Coastal Redwood Realm: Along a Belt of Tall Trees a Giant Bridge Speeds the Winning of Our Westernmost Frontier. By J. R. Hildebrand. LXXV, pp. 133-184, 31 ills. in black and white, 17 ills. in color, map, Feb., 1939
The Redwood Forest of the Pacific Coast. By Henry Gannett. X, pp. 145-159, 6 ills., map, May, 1899
Saving the Redwoods. By Madison Grant. XXXVII, pp. 519-536, 10 ills., June, 1920

REED, JOHN C.:
Down Idaho's River of No Return (Salmon River). By Philip J. Shenon and John C. Reed. LXX, pp. 95-136, 43 ills., maps, July, 1936

REED, MACON, JR.:
Behind the Lines in Italy. By Corporal Macon Reed, Jr. LXXXVI, pp. 109-128, 20 ills., July, 1944

REELFOOT—An Earthquake Lake (Tennessee). By Wilbur A. Nelson. XLV, pp. 95-114, 20 ills., Jan., 1924

REHABILITATION:
Americans Help Liberated Europe Live Again. By Lt. Col. Frederick Simpich, Jr. LXXXVII, pp. 747-768, 17 ills., June, 1945

REHEARSAL at Dieppe (France). By W. Robert Moore. LXXXII, pp. 495-502, 6 ills., Oct., 1942

REY BOUBA, Cameroons:
Trans-Africa Safari: A Motor Caravan Rolls Across Sahara and Jungle Through Realms of Dusky Potentates and the Land of Big-Lipped Women. By Lawrence Copley Thaw and Margaret Stout Thaw. LXXIV, pp. 327-364, 29 ills. in black and white, 14 ills. in color, map, Sept., 1938

REID, HARRY FIELDING:
Studies of Muir Glacier, Alaska. By Harry Fielding Reid. IV, pp. 19-55, 13 ills., 6 diagrs., table, 2 maps (1 foldout), Mar. 21, 1892
Appendices: List of Plants Collected near Muir Glacier, determined by W. W. Rowlee, p. 79; Meteorological Observations, by Harry Fielding Reid, pp. 80-81; Magnetic Observations, by Harry Fielding Reid, p. 82; Suggestions to Future Observers, by H. F. Reid, pp. 83-84

REINDEER:
The Camel of the Frozen Desert. By Carl J. Lomen. XXXVI, pp. 539-556, 19 ills., Dec., 1919
Introducing Reindeer into Labrador. XVIII, p. 686, Oct., 1907
Reindeer in Alaska. By Gilbert H. Grosvenor. XIV, pp. 127-149, 19 ills., map, Apr., 1903

The **RELATION** of Forests and Forest Fires. By Gifford Pinchot. X, pp. 393-403, 7 ills., Oct., 1899

The **RELATION** of Geography to History. By Francis W. Parker. V, pp. 125-131, Jan. 31, 1894

RELATIONS of Air and Water to Temperature and Life. By Honorable Gardiner G. Hubbard. V, pp. 112-124, Jan. 31, 1894

The **RELATIONS** of Geology to Physiography in Our Educational System. By T. C. Chamberlin. V, pp. 154-160, Jan. 31, 1894

A **RELIC** of the Lewis and Clarke Expedition. (By Cyrus C. Babb). IX, pp. 100-101, ill., Mar., 1898

RELIGIONS:

Behind the Mask of Modern Japan. By Willard Price. LXXXVIII, pp. 513-535, 14 ills., Nov., 1945

Included: Buddhism, Shinto, Emperor Worship

The Rebirth of Religion in Russia: The Church Reorganized While Bolshevik Cannon Spread Destruction in the Nation's Holy of Holies. By Thomas Whittemore. XXXIV, pp. 379-401, 16 ills., Nov., 1918

See also Buddhism; Christianity; Confucianism; Hindus and Hinduism; Judaism; Lamaism; Moslems; Samaritans; Zoroastrianism; *and* Taoist Shrines

RELIGIOUS CEREMONIES:

Banishing the Devil of Disease Among the Nashi: Weird Ceremonies Performed by an Aboriginal Tribe in the Heart of Yünnan Province, China. By Joseph F. Rock. XLVI, pp. 473-499, 26 ills., map, Nov., 1924

The Fire-Walking Hindus of Singapore. By L. Elizabeth Lewis. LIX, pp. 513-522, 12 ills., Apr., 1931

In the Canary Islands, Where Streets are Carpeted with Flowers. 13 color photos by Wilhelm Tobien. LVII, pp. 615-622, May, 1930

India Mosaic. By Peter Muir and Frances Muir. LXXXIX, pp. 443-470, 5 ills. in black and white, 22 ills. in color, map, Apr., 1946

The Last Israelitish Blood Sacrifice: How the Vanishing Samaritans Celebrate the Passover on Sacred Mount Gerizim. By John D. Whiting. XXXVII, pp. 1-46, 40 ills., map, Jan., 1920

Life Among the Lamas of Choni: Describing the Mystery Plays and Butter Festival in the Monastery of an Almost Unknown Tibetan Principality in Kansu Province, China. By Joseph F. Rock. LIV, pp. 569-619, 34 ills. in black and white, 16 ills. in color, map, Nov., 1928

The Marriage of the Gods. By John J. Banninga. XXIV, pp. 1314-1330, 16 ills., Dec., 1913

The Pageant of Jerusalem: The Capital of the Land of Three Great Faiths Is Still the Holy City for Christian, Moslem, and Jew. By Major Edward Keith-Roach. LII, pp. 635-681, 57 ills., Dec., 1927

The Perahera Processions of Ceylon. By G. H. G. Burroughs. LXII, pp. 90-100, ill. in black and white, 8 ills. in duotone, July, 1932

The Sacred City of the Sands (Kairouan, Tunisia). By Frank Edward Johnson. XXII, pp. 1061-1093, 25 ills., map, Dec., 1911

The Snake Dance (Hopi Indians). By Marion L. Oliver. XXII, pp. 107-137, 31 ills., Feb., 1911

Sungmas, the Living Oracles of the Tibetan Church. By Joseph F. Rock. LXVIII, pp. 475-486, ill. in black and white, 12 ills. in color, Oct., 1935

RELIGIOUS CEREMONIES—*Continued*

Syria: The Land Link of History's Chain. By Maynard Owen Williams. XXXVI, pp. 437-462, 20 ills., map, Nov., 1919

The Two Great Moorish Religious Dances. By George Edmund Holt. XXII, pp. 777-785, 6 ills., Aug., 1911

RELIGIOUS Penances and Punishments Self-Inflicted by the Holy Men of India. By W. M. Zumbro. XXIV, pp. 1257-1314, 69 ills., Dec., 1913

REMAGEN, Germany:

War's Wake in the Rhineland. By Thomas R. Henry. LXXXVIII, pp. 1-32, 29 ills., map, July, 1945

The **REMARKABLE** Growth of Europe During 40 Years of Peace. (By O. P. Austin). XXVI, pp. 272-274, Sept., 1914

A **REMARKABLE** Salt Deposit. By Charles F. Holder. XII, pp. 391-392, ills., Nov., 1901

REMNANTS of Royal France in Canada. 15 color photos by B. Anthony Stewart. LXVIII, pp. 217-224, Aug., 1935

REMOTE Nepal, Land of Mystery. 15 color photos by Martin Hürlimann. LXVII, pp. 329-336, Mar., 1935

The **REMOVAL** of the North Sea Mine Barrage. By Lieutenant-Commander Noel Davis. XXXVII, pp. 103-133, 28 ills., maps, Feb., 1920

RENASCENT Germany. By Lincoln Eyre. LIV, pp. 639-717, 59 ills. in black and white, 39 ills. in color, Dec., 1928

RENO, Nevada:

Nevada, Desert Treasure House. By W. Robert Moore. LXXXIX, pp. 1-38, 16 ills. in black and white, 20 ills. in color, map, Jan., 1946

Studies on the Rate of Evaporation at Reno, Nevada, and in the Salton Sink. By Professor Frank H. Bigelow. XIX, pp. 20-28, 5 ills., Jan., 1908

REPORT—Geography of Life. By C. Hart Merriam. I, pp. 160-162, Apr., 1889

REPORT—Geography of the Air. By A. W. Greely. I, pp. 151-159, Apr., 1889

REPORT—Geography of the Air. By Gen. A. W. Greely. II, pp. 49-63, Apr., 1890

REPORT—Geography of the Land. By Herbert G. Ogden. I, pp. 125-135, Apr., 1889

REPORT—Geography of the Land. By Herbert G. Ogden. II, pp. 31-48, Apr., 1890

REPORT—Geography of the Sea. By George L. Dyer. I, pp. 136-150, table, Apr., 1889

REPORT by Robert T. Hill on the Volcanic Disturbances in the West Indies. XIII, pp. 223-267, 12 ills., 3 maps, July, 1902

REPORT of Committee on Exploration in Alaska. III, pp. 248-250, Feb. 19, 1892

REPORT of the Director and Editor of the National Geographic Society for the Year 1914. By Gilbert H. Grosvenor. XXVII, pp. 318-320, Mar., 1915

A **REPORT** of the Eruption of the Soufrière of St. Vincent, 1812. XIV, pp. 158-161, Apr., 1903

A **REPORT** of the Second Stratosphere Expedition. LXVIII, pp. 535-536, Oct., 1935

REPORT on Auriferous Sands from Yakutat Bay (Alaska). By J. Stanley-Brown. III, pp. 196-198, May 29, 1891

REPORT on Fossil Plants (Mount St. Elias Expedition). By Lester F. Ward. III, pp. 199-200, May 29, 1891

REPORT on Topographic Work (Mount St. Elias Expedition). By Mark B. Kerr. III, p. 195, map, May 29, 1891

REPORTS. *See* NGM: Editor: Grosvenor, Gilbert H.; NGS: Committees; Secretary; Treasurer; *and* names of NGS Presidents and Vice-Presidents

REPORTS of Sealing Schooners Cruising in the Neighborhood of Tuscarora Deep in May and June, 1896. (By Eliza Ruhamah Scidmore). VII, pp. 310-312, Sept., 1896

REPORTS of Vessels as to the Range of Volcanic Dust (Martinique). By James Page. XIII, pp. 299-301, July, 1902

REPTILES:

Certain Citizens of the Warm Sea. By Louis L. Mowbray. Paintings by Hashime Murayama. XLI, pp. 27-62, 18 ills. in black and white, 16 ills. in color, Jan., 1922

Cultivation of Marine and Fresh-Water Animals in Japan. By K. Mitsukuri. XVII, pp. 524-531, 5 ills., Sept., 1906

Extinct Reptiles Found in Nodules. (By H. A. Largelamb). XVII, pp. 170-173, 9 ills., Mar., 1906
Contents: Inostransevia and Pariasaurus

Hunting Big Game of Other Days: A Boating Expedition in Search of Fossils in Alberta, Canada. By Barnum Brown. XXXV, pp. 407-429, 24 ills., map, May, 1919

Lonely Australia: The Unique Continent. By Herbert E. Gregory. XXX, pp. 473-568, 68 ills., 5 maps (1 two-page), Dec., 1916

A Modern Dragon Hunt on Komodo: An English Yachting Party Traps and Photographs the Huge and Carnivorous Dragon Lizard of the Lesser Sundas. By Lady Broughton. LXX, pp. 321-331, 12 ills. in duotone, Sept., 1936

Notes on the Remarkable Habits of Certain Turtles and Lizards. By H. A. Largelamb. XVIII, pp. 413-419, 12 ills., June, 1907

Parade of Life Through the Ages: Records in Rocks Reveal a Strange Procession of Prehistoric Creatures, from Jellyfish to Dinosaurs, Giant Sloths, Saber-toothed Tigers, and Primitive Man. By Charles R. Knight. With 24 ills. in color from paintings by author. LXXXI, pp. 141-184, 13 ills. in black and white, Feb., 1942
Contents: Ceratosaurus, Dimetrodon, Diplodocus, Mosasaurus, Naosaurus, Parasaurolophus, Protoceratops, Pteranodon, Pterodactyl, Stegosaurus, Styracosaurus, *Tyrannosaurus rex*

REPTILES—*Continued*

Reptiles of All Lands. By Raymond L. Ditmars. XXII, pp. 601-633, 32 ills., July, 1911
Contents: Crocodiles and Alligators.—The Tortoises and Turtles.—The Lizards.—Snakes.—The Vipers

Stalking the Dragon Lizard on the Island of Komodo. By W. Douglas Burden. LII, pp. 216-232, 21 ills., Aug., 1927

Tuatara: "Living Fossils" Walk on Well-Nigh Inaccessible Rocky Islands off the Coast of New Zealand. By Frieda Cobb Blanchard. LXVII, pp. 649-662, 14 ills., map, May, 1935

Wonder Island of the Amazon Delta: On Marajó Cowboys Ride Oxen, Tree-dwelling Animals Throng Dense Forests, While Strange Fishes and Birds Help Make a Zoologist's Paradise. By Hugh B. Cott. LXXIV, pp. 635-670, 30 ills. in black and white, 12 ills. in color, map, Nov., 1938

See also Turtles

The **REPUBLIC** of Panama. By Wm. H. Burr. XV, pp. 57-73, 7 ills., Feb., 1904

REPUBLICS—The Ladder to Liberty. By David Jayne Hill. XXXI, pp. 240-254, 5 ills., maps, Mar., 1917

RESCUE WORK:

New Guinea's Mountain and Swampland Dwellers. By Col. Ray T. Elsmore. LXXXVIII, pp. 671-694, 15 ills. in black and white, 7 ills. in color, map, Dec., 1945
Included: References to the U. S. Army plane crash (May, 1945) and illustrations of the survivors

They Survived at Sea. By Lt. Comdr. Samuel F. Harby. LXXXVII, pp. 617-640, 22 ills., May, 1945

See also U. S. Revenue Cutter Service

RESOLUTION (Ship):

The Columbus of the Pacific: Captain James Cook, Foremost British Navigator, Expanded the Great Sea to Correct Proportions and Won for Albion an Insular Empire by Peaceful Exploration and Scientific Study. By J. R. Hildebrand. LI, pp. 85-132, 45 ills., maps, Jan., 1927

The **RESTORATION** of Colonial Williamsburg. By W. A. R. Goodwin. LXXI, pp. 402-443, 21 ills. in black and white, 25 ills. in color, Apr., 1937

The **RESURRECTION** of Ancient Egypt. By James Baikie. XXIV, pp. 957-1020, 46 ills., map, Sept., 1913

The **RETURN** of Dr. Nansen. VII, p. 290, Sept., 1896

The **RETURN** of Wellman. By J. Howard Gore. X, pp. 348-351, ills., Sept., 1899

RETURN to Florence (Italy). By 1st Lt. Benjamin C. McCartney. LXXXVII, pp. 257-296, 18 ills. in black and white, 18 ills. in color, Mar., 1945

RETURN to Manila. By Frederick Simpich. LXXVIII, pp. 409-451, 21 ills. in black and white, 21 ills. in color, map, Oct., 1940

The **RETURNS** from Alaska. XVI, p. 513, map, Nov., 1905

REVEALING Earth's Mightiest Ocean (Pacific). By Albert W. Atwood. LXXXIV, pp. 291-306, 10 ills., map supplement, Sept., 1943

A **REVELATION** of the Filipinos (Summary of Report of the First Census of the Philippines). (By Gilbert H. Grosvenor). XVI, pp. 139-192, 138 ills., Apr., 1905

REVENUE CUTTER. *See Bear*

REVIEW OF THE SOCIETY'S MAPS OF EUROPE:

The Geographic's New Map of Germany and Its Approaches: With a Review of The Society's Maps of Europe. By Gilbert Grosvenor. Text with map supplement. LXXXVI, pp. 66-72, ill., July, 1944

REVIVING a Lost Art (Drying Fruits and Vegetables). XXXI, pp. 475-481, 9 ills., June, 1917

The **REVOLT** of the Ashantis (Gold Coast). XI, p. 244, map, June, 1900

REVOLUTION in Eating: Machine Food Age—Born of Roads, Research, and Refrigeration—Makes the United States the Best-fed Nation in History. By J. R. Hildebrand. LXXXI, pp. 273-324, 33 ills. in black and white, 25 ills. in color, Mar., 1942

The **REVOLUTION** in Russia. By William Eleroy Curtis. XVIII, pp. 302-316, May, 1907

REVOLUTIONARY WAR. *See* American Revolution

REYKJAVÍK, Iceland:

American Soldier in Reykjavík. By Corporal Luther M. Chovan. LXXXVIII, pp. 536-568, 6 ills. in black and white, 34 ills. in color, Nov., 1945

RHINE (River), Europe:

Rediscovering the Rhine: A Trip by Barge from the Sea to the Headwaters of Europe's Storied Stream. By Melville Chater. XLVIII, pp. 1-43, 44 ills., July, 1925

The Story of the Ruhr. By Frederick Simpich. XLI, pp. 553-564, 11 ills., map, May, 1922

See also Rhineland, *below*

RHINELAND (Region), Germany:

Cologne, Key City of the Rhineland. By Francis Woodworth. LXIX, pp. 829-848, 18 ills., map, June, 1936

War's Wake in the Rhineland. By Thomas R. Henry. LXXXVIII, pp. 1-32, 29 ills., map, July, 1945

See also Rhine, *above*

RHODE ISLAND:

Sauntering Through the Land of Roger Williams. 8 color photos by Clifton Adams. LX, pp. 311-318, Sept., 1931

RHODES, CECIL:

Rhodesia, Hobby and Hope of Cecil Rhodes. By W. Robert Moore. LXXXVI, pp. 281-306, 13 ills. in black and white, 10 ills. in color, map, Sept., 1944

RHODES (Island), Aegean Sea:

Ageless Luster of Greece and Rhodes. 16 ills. in duotone by Arnold Genthe. LXXIII, pp. 477-492, Apr., 1938

Historic Islands and Shores of the Ægean Sea. By Ernest Lloyd Harris. XXVIII, pp. 231-261, 28 ills., map, Sept., 1915

Rhodes, and Italy's Aegean Islands. By Dorothy Hosmer. LXXIX, pp. 449-480, 32 ills., map, Apr., 1941

Souvenirs of Knighthood in Rhodes. 13 color photos by Luigi Pellerano. LXIV, pp. 665-672, Dec., 1933

RHODESIA:

Rhodesia, Hobby and Hope of Cecil Rhodes. By W. Robert Moore. LXXXVI, pp. 281-306, 13 ills. in black and white, 10 ills. in color, map, Sept., 1944

Rhodesia, the Pioneer Colony: In the Land of Sheba's Gold and Rhodes' Diamonds Emerge Model Towns and Modern Mines. By Melville Chater. LXVII, pp. 753-782, 31 ills., June, 1935

The Wonders of the Mosi-oa-Tunga: The Falls of the Zambesi. By Louis Livingston Seaman. XXII, pp. 561-571, 6 ills., June, 1911

The World's Great Waterfalls: Visits to Mighty Niagara, Wonderful Victoria, and Picturesque Iguazu. By Theodore W. Noyes. L, pp. 29-59, 29 ills., July, 1926

RHODODENDRONS, Black:

Through the Great River Trenches of Asia: National Geographic Society Explorer Follows the Yangtze, Mekong, and Salwin Through Mighty Gorges, Some of Whose Canyon Walls Tower to a Height of More Than Two Miles. By Joseph F. Rock. L, pp. 133-186, 47 ills., map, Aug., 1926

RHONE, ROSAMOND DODSON:

Nauru, the Richest Island in the South Seas. By Rosamond Dodson Rhone. XL, pp. 559-589, 24 ills., Dec., 1921

RIATAS and Romance on the Rio Grande. 24 color photos: 23 by Luis Marden. LXXVI, pp. 431-462, Oct., 1939

RICE, WILLIAM GORHAM:

The Singing Towers of Holland and Belgium. By William Gorham Rice. XLVII, pp. 357-376, 22 ills., Mar., 1925

RICE:

How Half the World Works. By Alice Tisdale Hobart and Mary A. Nourse. LXI, pp. 509-524, 22 ills., Apr., 1932

Some Aspects of Rural Japan. By Walter Weston. XLII, pp. 275-301, 12 ills. in black and white, 16 ills. in color, Sept., 1922

RICHMOND, Virginia:

Virginia—A Commonwealth That Has Come Back. By William Joseph Showalter. LV, pp. 403-472, 5 ills. in black and white, ill. in color, Apr., 1929

RICHTHOFEN, MANFRED VON:

Aces Among Aces (Aviators). By Laurence La Tourette Driggs. XXXIII, pp. 568-580, 9 ills., June, 1918

RIDDLE of the Aleutians: A Botanist Explores the Origin of Plants on Ever-misty Islands Now Enshrouded in the Fog of War. By Isobel Wylie Hutchison. LXXXII, pp. 769-792, 24 ills., Dec., 1942

RIFT VALLEY (Great Rift Valley), Africa-Asia:

Where Roosevelt Will Hunt. By Sir Harry Johnston. XX, pp. 207-256, 43 ills., map supplement, Mar., 1909

RIGA, Latvia:

Flying Around the Baltic. By Douglas Chandler. LXXIII, pp. 767-806, 31 ills. in black and white, 13 ills. in duotone, map, June, 1938

RIGGS, ARTHUR STANLEY:

The Beauties of France. By Arthur Stanley Riggs. XXVIII, pp. 391-491, 73 ills. in black and white, 16 ills. in color, map, Nov., 1915

Inexhaustible Italy. By Arthur Stanley Riggs. XXX, pp. 273-368, 76 ills., map, Oct., 1916

RIGGS, THOMAS, JR.:

Marking the Alaskan Boundary. By Thomas Riggs, Jr. XX, pp. 593-607, 17 ills., July, 1909

Surveying the 141st Meridian (Boundary Line Between Canada and Alaska). By Thomas Riggs, Jr. XXIII, pp. 685-713, 46 ills., map, July, 1912

RIO DE JANEIRO, Brazil:

Air Cruising Through New Brazil: A National Geographic Reporter Spots Vast Resources Which the Republic's War Declaration Adds to Strength of United Nations. By Henry Albert Phillips. LXXXII, pp. 503-536, 32 ills., Oct., 1942

Brazil's Potent Weapons. By W. Robert Moore. LXXXV, pp. 41-78, 16 ills. in black and white, 18 ills. in color, two-page map, Jan., 1944

Gigantic Brazil and Its Glittering Capital. By Frederick Simpich. LVIII, pp. 733-778, 54 ills., map, Dec., 1930

Rio de Janeiro, in the Land of Lure. By Harriet Chalmers Adams. XXXVIII, pp. 165-210, 39 ills., map, Sept., 1920

Rio Panorama: Breath-taking Is This Fantastic City amid Peaks, Palms, and Sea, and in Carnival Time It Moves to the Rhythm of Music. By W. Robert Moore. LXXVI, pp. 283-324, 12 ills. in black and white, 34 ills. in color, Sept., 1939

RIO GRANDE (River), U. S.-Mexico:

Down the Rio Grande: Tracing this Strange, Turbulent Stream on Its Long Course from Colorado to the Gulf of Mexico. By Frederick Simpich. LXXVI, pp. 415-462, 28 ills. in black and white, 24 ills. in color, 6 maps, Oct., 1939

Wandering Islands in the Rio Grande. By Mrs. Albert S. Burleson. XXIV, pp. 381-386, ills., map, Mar., 1913

RIO Grande Cornucopia Under a Winter Sun (Texas). 24 color photos by B. Anthony Stewart. LXXV, pp. 65-96, Jan., 1939

RIO GRANDE NATIONAL FOREST, Colorado:

The Wheeler National Monument. XX, pp. 837-840, 4 ills., Sept., 1909

The **RISE** and Fall of Nanking. By Julius Eigner. LXXIII, pp. 189-224, 37 ills., Feb., 1938

The **RISE** of Bulgaria. By James D. Bourchier. XXIII, pp. 1105-1118, 13 ills., Nov., 1912

The **RISE** of the New Arab Nation. By Frederick Simpich. XXXVI, pp. 369-393, 17 ills., map, Nov., 1919

RITTER, HOMER P.:

Note on the Activity of Shishaldin Volcano. (By Homer P. Ritter). XVI, p. 249, May, 1905

RIVER-ENCIRCLED Paraguay. By Harriet Chalmers Adams. LXIII, pp. 385-416, 35 ills., map, Apr., 1933

RIVERS:

Alaska and Its Mineral Resources. By Samuel Franklin Emmons. IX, pp. 139-172, 3 ills., map supplement, Apr., 1898

The Amazon, Father of Waters: The Earth's Mightiest River Drains a Basin of More Than 2,700,000 Square Miles, from Which Came Originally the World's Finest Rubber. By W. L. Schurz. XLIX, pp. 445-463, 15 ills., Apr., 1926

Atlantic Estuarine Tides. By Mark S. W. Jefferson. IX, pp. 400-409, diagrs., 7 tables, maps, Sept., 1898

The Barrage of the Nile. By Day Allen Willey. XXI, pp. 175-184, 14 ills., Feb., 1910

The "Breaking Up" of the Yukon. By Captain George S. Gibbs. XVII, pp. 268-272, 6 ills., May, 1906

By Sail Across Europe. By Merlin Minshall. LXXI, pp. 533-567, 38 ills., map, May, 1937

China Fights Erosion with U. S. Aid. By Walter C. Lowdermilk. LXXXVII, pp. 641-680, 10 ills. in black and white, 26 ills. in color, June, 1945

The Columbia Turns on the Power. By Maynard Owen Williams. LXXIX, pp. 749-792, 25 ills. in black and white, 18 ills. in color, June, 1941

The Deep-Water Route from Chicago to the Gulf. XVIII, pp. 679-685, 3 ills., map, Oct., 1907

Down Mexico's Río Balsas. By John W. Webber. With 9 color photos by author, Kenneth Segerstrom, Jack Breed. XC, pp. 253-272, 5 ills. in black and white, map, Aug., 1946

The Geography of the Jordan. By Nelson Glueck. LXXXVI, pp. 719-744, 23 ills., map, Dec., 1944

Geomorphology of the Southern Appalachians. By Charles Willard Hayes and Marius R. Campbell. VI, pp. 63-126, diagrs., 4 maps, May 23, 1894

The Great Falls of the Potomac. By Gilbert Grosvenor. LIII, pp. 385-400, 19 ills., Mar., 1928

The Great Mississippi Flood of 1927: Since White Man's Discovery This Mighty River Has Served Him Well, Yet It Has Brought Widespread Devastation Along Its Lower Reaches. By Frederick Simpich. LII, pp. 243-289, 53 ills., map, Sept., 1927

Important Announcement Concerning Essays (Subject: River Systems of the United States). VI, pp. 227-228, Dec. 29, 1894

RIVERS—*Continued*

The Kansas River. By Arthur P. Davis. VII, pp. 181-184, tables, May, 1896
Included: Tributaries of the Kansas

Lake Chelan. By Henry Gannett. IX, pp. 417-428, 7 ills., map, Oct., 1898

Limiting Width of Meander Belts. By Mark S. W. Jefferson. XIII, pp. 373-384, 6 charts, Oct., 1902

The Long River of New England: In War and Peace, from Mountain Wilderness to the Sea, Flows the Connecticut River, Through a Valley Abounding in History, Scenery, Inventive Genius, and Industry. By Albert W. Atwood. LXXXIII, pp. 401-434, 12 ills. in black and white, 24 ills. in color, map, Apr., 1943

Men Against the Rivers (Mississippi and Ohio). By Frederick Simpich. LXXI, pp. 767-794, 22 ills., maps, June, 1937

The Modern Mississippi Problem. By W J McGee. IX, pp. 24-27, Jan., 1898

More Changes of the Colorado River. By D. T. MacDougal. XIX, pp. 52-54, map, Jan., 1908

The Mother of Rivers: An Account of a Photographic Expedition to the Great Columbia Ice Field of the Canadian Rockies. By Lewis R. Freeman. XLVII, pp. 377-446, 60 ills., maps, Apr., 1925
Included: Alexandra; Athabaska; Bow; Bush; Castleguard; Chaba; Cline; Columbia; Howse; Mackenzie; Mistaya; North Fork; Saskatchewan; Sunwapta; Wood

Mother Volga Defends Her Own. By Maynard Owen Williams. LXXXII, pp. 793-811, 21 ills., Dec., 1942

Pirate Rivers and Their Prizes: The Warfare of Waterways Has Sometimes Changed the Geography of Our Continents. By John Oliver La Gorce. L, pp. 87-132, 48 ills., map, July, 1926

Potomac, River of Destiny. By Albert W. Atwood. LXXXVIII, pp. 33-70, 15 ills. in black and white, 18 ills. in color, map, July, 1945

Rediscovering the Rhine: A Trip by Barge from the Sea to the Headwaters of Europe's Storied Stream. By Melville Chater. XLVIII, pp. 1-43, 44 ills., July, 1925

Report—Geography of the Air. By Gen. A. W. Greely. II, pp. 49-63, Apr., 1890
Included: Inter-relation of rainfall and river outflows

The Rivers and Valleys of Pennsylvania. By William Morris Davis. I, pp. 183-253, 25 ills., map, July, 1889

The Rivers of Northern New Jersey, with Notes on the Classification of Rivers in General. By William Morris Davis. II, pp. 81-110, 6 diagrs., map drawing, May, 1890

The Seine, the Meuse, and the Moselle. (Part I). By William M. Davis. VII, pp. 189-202, ill., 7 maps, June, 1896

The Seine, the Meuse, and the Moselle. (Part) II. By William M. Davis. VII, pp. 228-238, table, 4 maps, July, 1896

South America. Annual Address by the President, Gardiner G. Hubbard. III, pp. 1-29, foldout map, Mar. 28, 1891
Included: Amazon; Orinoco; Rio de la Plata; San Francisco

RIVERS—*Continued*

The Stikine River in 1898. By Eliza Ruhamah Scidmore. X, pp. 1-15, 4 ills., Jan., 1899

Taming "Flood Dragons" Along China's Hwang Ho (Yellow River). By Oliver J. Todd. LXXXI, pp. 205-234, 26 ills., map, Feb., 1942

Taming the Outlaw Missouri River. By Frederick Simpich. LXXXVIII, pp. 569-598, 25 ills., two-page map, Nov., 1945

Through Paraguay and Southern Matto Grosso (Paraguay and Paraná Rivers). By Sir Christopher H. Gibson. LXXXIV, pp. 459-488, 20 ills. in black and white, 11 ills. in color, map, Oct., 1943

The Tsangpo (Brahmaputra River). By James Mascarene Hubbard. XII, pp. 32-35, Jan., 1901

Two Hundred Miles up the Kuskokwim (Alaska). By Charles Hallock. IX, pp. 85-92, 6 ills., Mar., 1898

The Weather Bureau River and Flood System. By Professor Willis L. Moore. VII, pp. 302-307, Sept., 1896

When the Father of Waters Goes on a Rampage: An Account of the Salvaging of Food-fishes from the Overflowed Lands of the Mississippi River. By Hugh M. Smith. XXXVII, pp. 369-386, 18 ills., Apr., 1920

See also the following names of rivers: Amazon; Amu Darya; Avon; Balim; Cauca; Colorado; Columbia; Congo; Danube; Euphrates; Green; Hwang Ho; Irrawaddy; Jhelum; Jordan; Koksoak; Kowak; Loire; Mackenzie; Magdalena; Mekong; Mississippi; Missouri; Nervion; Nile; Ohio; Orinoco; Paraguay; Paraná; Parima; Potomac; Rhine; Rio Grande; Ruhr; Sacramento; Salmon; Salween; San Joaquin; San Juan; Saskatchewan; Seine; Stikine; Sungari; Sushitna; Suwannee; Tejo; Thames; Tigris; Tumen; Volga; White River; Yangtze; Yellowstone; Yukon; Zambezi

RIVIERA (Region), France-Italy:

Carnival Days on the Riviera. By Maynard Owen Williams. L, pp. 467-501, 21 ills. in black and white, 21 ills. in color, Oct., 1926

Life's Pattern on the Italian Riviera. By Helen Churchill Candee. LXVII, pp. 67-100, 25 ills. in black and white, 12 ills. in color, map, Jan., 1935

RIYADH, Saudi Arabia:

Guest in Saudi Arabia. By Maynard Owen Williams. LXXXVIII, pp. 463-487, 24 ills., map, Oct., 1945

The **ROAD** of the Crusaders: A Historian Follows the Steps of Richard the Lion Heart and Other Knights of the Cross Over the "Via Dei." By Harold Lamb. LXIV, pp. 645-693, 46 ills. in black and white, 13 ills. in color, map, Dec., 1933

The **ROAD** to Bolivia. By William E. Curtis. XI, pp. 209-224, 7 ills., June, 1900; pp. 264-280, 6 ills., July, 1900

The **ROAD** to Wang Ye Fu: An Account of the Work of the National Geographic Society's Central-China Expedition in the Mongol Kingdom of Ala Shan. By Frederick R. Wulsin. XLIX, pp. 197-234, 44 ills., map, Feb., 1926

ROADS. *See* Highways and Roads

ROADS from Washington (D. C.). By John Patric. LXXIV, pp. 1-56, 27 ills. in black and white, 30 ills. in color, map supplement, July, 1938

ROAMING Russia's Caucasus: Rugged Mountains and Hardy Fighters Guard the Soviet Union's Caucasian Treasury of Manganese and Oil. By Rolf Singer. LXXXII, pp. 91-121, 33 ills., July, 1942

ROANOKE ISLAND, North Carolina:

A Bit of Elizabethan England in America: Fisher Folk of the Islands Off North Carolina Conserved the Speech and Customs of Sir Walter Raleigh's Colonists. By Blanch Nettleton Epler. LXIV, pp. 695-730, 43 ills., map, Dec., 1933

ROBERT COLLEGE, Turkey:

American Alma Maters in the Near East. By Maynard Owen Williams. LXXXVIII, pp. 237-256, 16 ills., Aug., 1945

ROBERTS, FRANK H. H., JR.:

In the Empire of the Aztecs: Mexico City Is Rich in Relics of a People Who Practiced Human Sacrifice, Yet Loved Flowers, Education, and Art. By Frank H. H. Roberts, Jr. Paintings by H. M. Herget. LXXI, pp. 725-750, 14 ills. in black and white, 10 ills. in color, June, 1937

ROBERTS, J. BAYLOR:

America on the Move. 26 photos by J. Baylor Roberts, B. Anthony Stewart, and others. XC, pp. 357-378, Sept., 1946

Food: Flavor and Savor of American Foods. 25 color photos by J. Baylor Roberts, Willard R. Culver, and others. LXXXI, pp. 289-320, Mar., 1942

Gulf Coast Towns Get into the Fight. 19 color photos: 17 by J. Baylor Roberts. LXXXV, pp. 17-40, Jan., 1944

Iowa: Corn and Color in the Hawkeye State. 20 color photos: 19 by J. Baylor Roberts. LXXVI, pp. 151-174, Aug., 1939

Mississippi: Magnolia State Mosaic. 26 color photos by J. Baylor Roberts. LXXII, pp. 279-310, Sept., 1937

New York: Empire State Onions and Pageantry. 12 color photos by J. Baylor Roberts and Volkmar Wentzel. LXXX, pp. 641-648, Nov., 1941

North Carolina Colorcade. 21 color photos: 19 by J. Baylor Roberts. LXXX, pp. 189-220, Aug., 1941

Ozarks (Plateau): Work and Play in the Ozarks. 20 color photos by B. Anthony Stewart and J. Baylor Roberts. LXXXIII, pp. 597-620, May, 1943

Pacific Northwest: Where Fog and Sun Paint the Pacific. 23 color photos by J. Baylor Roberts. LXXXII, pp. 437-460, Oct., 1942

Pennsylvania Dutch—In a Land of Milk and Honey. 10 color photos by J. Baylor Roberts. LXXIV, pp. 49-56, July, 1938

Philippines: Camera Cruising in the Philippines. 12 color photos by J. Baylor Roberts, Fenno Jacobs, and others. LXXXVI, pp. 545-552, Nov., 1944

ROBERTS, J. BAYLOR—*Continued*

Philippines: Smiling, Happy Philippines. 21 color photos: 19 by J. Baylor Roberts. LXXVIII, pp. 425-448, Oct., 1940

Rubber: From Trees to Tires and Toys. 26 color photos by Willard R. Culver and J. Baylor Roberts. LXXVII, pp. 159-190, Feb., 1940

Singapore—Britain's Outpost of Empire. 9 color photos by J. Baylor Roberts. LXXX, pp. 665-672, Nov., 1941

Tennessee Tableaux. 22 color photos: 19 by J. Baylor Roberts. LXXV, pp. 569-592, May, 1939

The Washington of Tradition Builds for the Future. 20 color photos: 13 by J. Baylor Roberts. LXXI, pp. 671-694, June, 1937

ROBERTS, MRS. KENNETH:

Sojourning in the Italy of Today. By Mrs. Kenneth Roberts. LXX, pp. 351-396, 46 ills., map, Sept., 1936

ROBERTS, LEO B.:

Traveling in the Highlands of Ethiopia. By Leo B. Roberts. LXVIII, pp. 297-328, 37 ills., Sept., 1935

ROBERTS, MILNOR:

A Wonderland of Glaciers and Snow. By Milnor Roberts. XX, pp. 530-537, 8 ills., June, 1909

ROBERTS, WILLIAM H.:

The Five Thousand Temples of Pagān: Burma's Sacred City Is a Place of Enchantment in the Midst of Ruins. By William H. Roberts. LX, pp. 445-454, 9 ills., Oct., 1931

ROBIN HOOD'S BAY, England:

Between the Heather and the North Sea: Bold English Headlands Once Sheltered Sea Robbers, Later Were Ports of Wooden Ships, Centers of the Jet and Alum Trades, To-day Are Havens of Adventurous Fishing Fleets. By Leo Walmsley. LXIII, pp. 197-232, 41 ills., Feb., 1933

ROBINSON, ALBERT G.:

Cuban Railways. By Albert G. Robinson. XIII, pp. 108-110, Mar., 1902

ROBINSON, H. W.:

The Hairnet Industry in North China. By H. W. Robinson. XLIV, pp. 327-336, 10 ills., Sept., 1923

ROBOT AIRPLANES:

Air Power for Peace. By General H. H. Arnold. LXXXIX, pp. 137-193, 35 ills. in black and white, 28 ills. in color, map supplement, Feb., 1946

ROBOT BOMBS:

Air Power for Peace. By General H. H. Arnold. LXXXIX, pp. 137-193, 35 ills. in black and white, 28 ills. in color, map supplement, Feb., 1946

London Wins the Battle. By Marquis W. Childs. LXXXVIII, pp. 129-152, 21 ills., Aug., 1945

ROBSON, Mount, British Columbia:

The Monarch of the Canadian Rockies. By Charles D. Walcott. XXIV, pp. 626-639, 13 ills., panorama, May, 1913

The Monarch of the Canadian Rockies—Robson Peak (panorama)

ROCHAMBEAU, JEAN-BAPTISTE DONATIEN DE VIMEUR, COMTE DE:

Our First Alliance. By J. J. Jusserand. XXXI, pp. 518-548, 8 ills., June, 1917

ROCHFORD, DANIEL:

New England Ski Trails: Snow and Ice Sports Transform Whittier's Winters of Snowbound Seclusion Into Seasons of Outdoor Recreation. By Daniel Rochford. LXX, pp. 645-664, 11 ills. in black and white, 13 ills. in color, Nov., 1936

ROCK, JOSEPH F.:

Banishing the Devil of Disease Among the Nashi: Weird Ceremonies Performed by an Aboriginal Tribe in the Heart of Yünnan Province, China. By Joseph F. Rock. XLVI, pp. 473-499, 26 ills., map, Nov., 1924

Experiences of a Lone Geographer: An American Agricultural Explorer Makes His Way Through Brigand-infested Central China en Route to the Amne Machin Range, Tibet. By Joseph F. Rock. XLVIII, pp. 331-347, 16 ills., map, Sept., 1925

The Glories of the Minya Konka: Magnificent Snow Peaks of the China-Tibetan Border Are Photographed at Close Range by a National Geographic Society Expedition. By Joseph F. Rock. LVIII, pp. 385-437, 35 ills. in black and white, 24 ills. in color, map, Oct., 1930

Carrying the Color Camera Through Unmapped China. 24 color photos by author, pp. 403-434

Hunting the Chaulmoogra Tree. By Joseph F. Rock. XLI, pp. 243-276, 39 ills., map, Mar., 1922

Konka Risumgongba, Holy Mountain of the Outlaws. By Joseph F. Rock. LX, pp. 1-65, 36 ills. in black and white, 43 ills. in color, map, July, 1931

With the Devil Dancers of China and Tibet. 43 color photos by author, pp. 19-58

The Land of the Yellow Lama: National Geographic Society Explorer Visits the Strange Kingdom of Muli, Beyond the Likiang Snow Range of Yünnan Province, China. By Joseph F. Rock. XLVII, pp. 447-491, 39 ills., map, Apr., 1925

Life Among the Lamas of Choni: Describing the Mystery Plays and Butter Festival in the Monastery of an Almost Unknown Tibetan Principality in Kansu Province, China. By Joseph F. Rock. LIV, pp. 569-619, 34 ills. in black and white, 16 ills. in color, map, Nov., 1928

Demon Dancers and Butter Gods of Choni. 16 color photos by author, pp. 585-600

Seeking the Mountains of Mystery: An Expedition on the China-Tibet Frontier to the Unexplored Amnyi Machen Range, One of Whose Peaks Rivals Everest. By Joseph F. Rock. LVII, pp. 131-185, 54 ills., two-page map, Feb., 1930

Sungmas, the Living Oracles of the Tibetan Church. By Joseph F. Rock. LXVIII, pp. 475-486, ill. in black and white, 12 ills. in color, Oct., 1935

Demon-Possessed Tibetans and Their Incredible Feats. 12 color photos: 8 by author, pp. 479-486

ROCK, JOSEPH F.—*Continued*

Through the Great River Trenches of Asia: National Geographic Society Explorer Follows the Yangtze, Mekong, and Salwin Through Mighty Gorges, Some of Whose Canyon Walls Tower to a Height of More Than Two Miles. By Joseph F. Rock. L, pp. 133-186, 47 ills., map, Aug., 1926

The **ROCK** City of Petra. By Franklin E. Hoskins. XVIII, pp. 283-291, 5 ills., May, 1907

The **ROCK** of Aden: The Volcanic Mountain Fortress, on the Sea Route from Suez to India, Assumes New Importance. By H. G. C. Swayne. LXVIII, pp. 723-742, 24 ills., map, Dec., 1935

The **ROCK** of Gibraltar: Key to the Mediterranean. 17 ills. LXXVIII, pp. 376-391, Sept., 1940

ROCKEFELLER, JOHN D., JR.:

The Genesis of the Williamsburg Restoration. By John D. Rockefeller, Jr. LXXI, p. 401, Apr., 1937

ROCKET BOMBS:

London Wins the Battle. By Marquis W. Childs. LXXXVIII, pp. 129-152, 21 ills., Aug., 1945

ROCKETS:

Air Power for Peace. By General H. H. Arnold. LXXXIX, pp. 137-193, 35 ills. in black and white, 28 ills. in color, map supplement, Feb., 1946

New Frontier in the Sky. By F. Barrows Colton. XC, pp. 379-408, 28 ills., diagr., Sept., 1946

Your New World of Tomorrow. By F. Barrows Colton. LXXXVIII, pp. 385-410, 25 ills., Oct., 1945

ROCKY MOUNTAIN NATIONAL PARK, Colorado:

Photographing the Marvels of the West in Colors. By Fred Payne Clatworthy. LIII, pp. 694-719, 30 ills. in color, June, 1928

ROCKY MOUNTAIN SHEEP:

High Country of Colorado. By Alfred M. Bailey. With 23 color photos by author, Robert J. Niedrach, F. G. Brandenburg. XC, pp. 43-72, 9 ills. in black and white, July, 1946

ROCKY MOUNTAINS, Canada-U. S.:

Bighorn Mountains. By N. H. Darton. XVIII, pp. 355-364, 7 ills., map, June, 1907

Colorado, a Barrier That Became a Goal: Where Water Has Transformed Dry Plains Into Verdant Farms, and Highways Have Opened up Mineral and Scenic Wealth. By McFall Kerbey. LXII, pp. 1-63, 56 ills. in black and white, 12 ills. in color, map, July, 1932

Exploration in the Canadian Rockies. X, pp. 135-136, Apr., 1899

A Geologist's Paradise. By Charles D. Walcott. XXII, pp. 509-536, 28 ills., panorama, June, 1911

Our Mountain Panorama (panorama)

Lords of the Rockies: Photographing Big Game Animals in Their Primeval Surroundings, from Arizona to Canada, Brings Adventure to Two Wilderness Wanderers. By Wendell and Lucie Chapman. LXXVI, pp. 87-128, 14 ills. in black and white, 28 ills. in color, July, 1939

ROCKY MOUNTAINS, Canada-U. S.—*Continued*

The Monarch of the Canadian Rockies (Mount Robson). By Charles D. Walcott. XXIV, pp. 626-639, 13 ills., panorama, May, 1913

The Monarch of the Canadian Rockies—Robson Peak (panorama)

The Mother of Rivers: An Account of a Photographic Expedition to the Great Columbia Ice Field of the Canadian Rockies. By Lewis R. Freeman. XLVII, pp. 377-446, 60 ills., maps, Apr., 1925

Our Northern Rockies. By R. H. Chapman. XIII, pp. 361-372, 10 ills., Oct., 1902

Peaks and Parks of Western Canada. 11 photos: 5 by W. J. Oliver. LXXX, pp. 516-526, Oct., 1941

Peaks and Trails in the Canadian Alps. 16 photos in duotone by Byron Harmon and Clifford White. LXV, pp. 627-642, May, 1934

Photographing the Marvels of the West in Colors. By Fred Payne Clatworthy. LIII, pp. 694-719, 30 ills. in color, June, 1928

Recent Exploration in the Canadian Rockies. By Walter D. Wilcox. XIII, pp. 151-168, 12 ills., map, May, 1902; Part II, pp. 185-200, 9 ills., June, 1902

Some Tramps Across the Glaciers and Snowfields of British Columbia. By Howard Palmer. XXI, pp. 457-487, 25 ills., June, 1910

With Wild Animals in the Rockies. By Lucie and Wendell Chapman. LXVIII, pp. 231-249, 26 ills. in duotone, Aug., 1935

The World's Highest Altitudes and First Ascents. By Charles E. Fay. XX, pp. 493-530, 25 ills., June, 1909

RODENTS:

Dipo, the Little Desert "Kangaroo." By Walter E. Ketcham. LXXVIII, pp. 537-548, 14 ills., Oct., 1940

Into the Land of the Chipmunk. By Ruth Alexander Nichols. LX, pp. 77-98, 28 ills., July, 1931

Mickey the Beaver: An Animal Engineer Performs for the Camera as a Star in the Activities of His Species. By James MacGillivray. LIV, pp. 741-756, 23 ills., Dec., 1928

A Plague of Mice. XX, pp. 479-485, 7 ills., May, 1909

The Policemen of the Air: An Account of the Biological Survey of the Department of Agriculture. By Henry Wetherbee Henshaw. XIX, pp. 79-118, 38 ills., Feb., 1908

Included: Crop damage by rodents and methods of combating

The Rat Pest: The Labor of 200,000 Men in the United States Required to Support Rats, Man's Most Destructive and Dangerous Enemy. By Edward W. Nelson. XXXII, pp. 1-23, 21 ills., July, 1917

Smaller Mammals of North America. By E. W. Nelson. Paintings by Louis Agassiz Fuertes. XXXIII, pp. 371*-493, 29 ills. in black and white, 59 ills. in color, May, 1918

Tracking the Columbian Ground-Squirrel to Its Burrow: Loss of Millions to Crops and Danger of the Spread of Spotted Fever Necessitated Study of Peculiar Rodent of Western North America. By William T. Shaw. XLVII, pp. 587-596, 13 ills., May, 1925

RODEY, B. S.:

Arizona and New Mexico. By B. S. Rodey. XVII, pp. 100-102, ills., Feb., 1906

ROGERS, BERNARD F., JR.:

Ireland: The Mist and Sunshine of Ulster. By Bernard F. Rogers, Jr. LXVIII, pp. 571-610, 23 ills. in black and white, 21 ills. in color, map, Nov., 1935

Rambles Through Ulster, Northern Tip of the Shamrock Isle. 21 color photos by author, pp. 577-600

Italy: Caesar's City Today (Rome). 21 color photos by Bernard F. Rogers, Jr. and Luigi Pellerano. LXXI, pp. 285-316, Mar., 1937

Switzerland: Green Gruyère, Home of a Swiss Cheese. 23 color photos by Bernard F. Rogers, Jr. LXX, pp. 145-168, Aug., 1936

Turkey: Old Pattern and New in Turkey. 23 color photos by Bernard F. Rogers, Jr. LXXV, pp. 17-48, Jan., 1939

ROGERS, G. SHERBURNE:

Helium, the New Balloon Gas. By G. Sherburne Rogers. XXXV, pp. 441-456, 11 ills., May, 1919

ROGUES' Gallery of Imported Pests (Insects). 10 ills. in color from paintings by Hashime Murayama. LXXX, pp. 237-244, Aug., 1941

ROHE, ALICE:

Our Littlest Ally (San Marino). By Alice Rohe. XXXIV, pp. 139-163, 17 ills., Aug., 1918

ROMAN EMPIRE. *See* Rome, Ancient

The **ROMAN** Way. By Edith Hamilton. XC, pp. 545-565, 14 ills., two-page map, Nov., 1946

ROMANCE OF DISCOVERY SERIES:

The Caravels of Columbus. Reproduction in color of the painting by N. C. Wyeth, National Geographic Society, Washington, D. C. LIV, text, p. 55; supplement, July, 1928

Commander Byrd at the North Pole (Through Pathless Skies to the North Pole). Reproduction in color of the painting by N. C. Wyeth, National Geographic Society, Washington, D. C. LIII, supplement, May, 1928

The Discoverer. Reproduction in color of the painting by N. C. Wyeth, National Geographic Society, Washington, D. C. LIII, text, p. 347; supplement, Mar., 1928

The "Map of Discovery" (Eastern Hemisphere). Reproduction in color of the painting by N. C. Wyeth, National Geographic Society, Washington, D. C. LIV, text, p. 568; supplement, Nov., 1928

The "Map of Discovery" (Western Hemisphere). Reproduction in color of the painting by N. C. Wyeth, National Geographic Society, Washington, D. C. LV, text, p. 93; supplement, Jan., 1929

The **ROMANCE** of Military Insignia: How the United States Government Recognizes Deeds of Heroism and Devotion to Duty. By Col. Robert E. Wyllie. XXXVI, pp. 463-501, 27 ills., Dec., 1919

The **ROMANCE** of Science in Polynesia: An Account of Five Years of Cruising Among the South Sea Islands. By Robert Cushman Murphy. Paintings by Hashime Murayama. XLVIII, pp. 355-426, 66 ills. in black and white, 16 ills. in color, 3 maps, Oct., 1925

ROMANIA (Rumania):

An American Girl Cycles Across Romania: Two-wheel Pilgrim Pedals the Land of Castles and Gypsies, Where Roman Empire Traces Mingle With Remnants of Oriental Migration. By Dorothy Hosmer. LXXIV, pp. 557-588, 31 ills., map, Nov., 1938

Caviar Fishermen of Romania: From Vâlcov, "Little Venice" of the Danube Delta, Bearded Russian Exiles Go Down to the Sea. By Dorothy Hosmer. LXXVII, pp. 407-434, 29 ills., map, Mar., 1940

The Changing Map in the Balkans. By Frederick Moore. XXIV, pp. 199-226, 27 ills., map, Feb., 1913

The New Map of Europe: Showing the Boundaries Established by the Peace Conference at Paris and by Subsequent Decisions of the Supreme Council of the Allied and Associated Powers. By Ralph A. Graves. Text with map supplement. XXXIX, pp. 157-177, 18 ills., Feb., 1921

Notes on Rumania. XXIII, pp. 1219-1225, 1239, 9 ills., Dec., 1912

The Races of Europe. By Edwin A. Grosvenor. XXXIV, pp. 441-534, 62 ills., diagr. and index, maps, map supplement, Dec., 1918

Roumania, the Pivotal State. By James Howard Gore. XXVIII, pp. 360-390, 32 ills., Oct., 1915

Roumania and Its Rubicon. By John Oliver La Gorce. XXX, pp. 185-202, 11 ills., Sept., 1916

Rumania and Her Ambitions. By Frederick Moore. XXIV, pp. 1057-1085, 34 ills., Oct., 1913

Rumanian Peasant Girl. XXIV, ill. p. 1084, Oct., 1913. XXXIV, ill. p. 467, Dec., 1918; enlargement for framing

The Spell of Romania: An American Woman's Narrative of Her Wanderings Among Colorful People and Long-Hidden Shrines. By Henrietta Allen Holmes. LXV, pp. 399-450, 37 ills. in black and white, 29 ills. in color, map, Apr., 1934

Transylvania and Its Seven Castles: A Motor Circuit Through Rumania's New Province of Racial Complexity and Architectural Charm. By J. Theodore Marriner. XLIX, pp. 319-352, 35 ills., map, Mar., 1926

The Whirlpool of the Balkans. By George Higgins Moses. XXXIX, pp. 179-197, 15 ills., Feb., 1921

ROMANIA, Land of Color and Contrast. 15 color photos by Wilhelm Tobien. LXV, pp. 415-422, Apr., 1934

ROMANS, Ancient:

Ancient Rome Brought to Life. By Rhys Carpenter. Paintings by H. M. Herget. XC, pp. 567-633, 2 ills. in black and white, 32 ills. in color, map, Nov., 1946

See Rome, Ancient, for detailed contents

The Roman Way. By Edith Hamilton. XC, pp. 545-565, 14 ills., two-page map, Nov., 1946

ROMANTIC Spain. By Charles Upson Clark. XXI, pp. 187-215, 40 ills., map, Mar., 1910

ROME, Ancient:

Ancient Rome Brought to Life. By Rhys Carpenter. Paintings by H. M. Herget. XC, pp. 567-633, 2 ills. in black and white, 32 ills. in color, map, Nov., 1946

Contents: Before Rome Was Founded.—Etruscan Funeral.—Etruscan Festival.—Bridge over the Tiber.—Market and Wharf at a Roman Port.—At the Slave Market.—The Roman Army Crosses Alcântara in Spain.—Siege of a Walled City.—Triumphal Procession.—Unconditional Surrender.—An Embassy to Caligula.—An Empress Makes Ready.—In the Gardens of Lucullus.—A Distinguished Dinner Party.—Horace's Villa in the Sabine Hills.—Interior of a Rich Man's House.—Vegetable Market.—Tunisian Farm.—Street Scene in Pompeii.—In a Pompeian Tavern.—Seaside Villas.—Roman Baths: Tepidarium.—Furnaces Beneath the Baths.—Worship of Isis.—Rehearsal for the Mysteries.—Sacrifice of the "Suovetaurilia."—In a Court of Law.—The Library in Timgad.—At the Theater.—Sea Battle in the Arena.—Diocletian's Palace at Spalato.—Dusk on the Street of Tombs.

Augustus—Emperor and Architect: Two Thousand Years Ago Was Born the Physically Frail But Spiritually Great Roman Who Became the Master of His World. By W. Coleman Nevils. LXXIV, pp. 535-556, 17 ills., map, Oct., 1938

Fearful Famines of the Past: History Will Repeat Itself Unless the American People Conserve Their Resources. By Ralph A. Graves. XXXII, pp. 69-90, 11 ills., July, 1917

Geographic Progress of Civilization. Annual Address by the President, Honorable Gardiner G. Hubbard. VI, pp. 1-22, Feb. 14, 1894

Inexhaustible Italy. By Arthur Stanley Riggs. XXX, pp. 273-368, 76 ills., map, Oct., 1916

The Isle of Capri: An Imperial Residence and Probable Wireless Station of Ancient Rome. By John A. Kingman. XXXVI, pp. 213-231, 17 ills., Sept., 1919

Italy's Monuments Tell Rome's Magnificence. 8 photos: 7 by B. Anthony Stewart. LXXVII, pp. 371-378, Mar., 1940

The Perennial Geographer: After 2,000 Years Vergil Is Still the Most Widely Read of Latin Poets—First to Popularize the Geography of the Roman Empire. By W. Coleman Nevils. LVIII, pp. 439-465, 29 ills., Oct., 1930

The Roman Way. By Edith Hamilton. XC, pp. 545-565, 14 ills., two-page map, Nov., 1946

The Splendor of Rome. By Florence Craig Albrecht. XLI, pp. 593-626, 28 ills., June, 1922

ROME, Italy:

Imperial Rome Reborn. By John Patric. LXXI, pp. 269-325, 34 ills. in black and white, 21 ills. in color, Mar., 1937

Inexhaustible Italy. By Arthur Stanley Riggs. XXX, pp. 273-368, 76 ills., map, Oct., 1916

Italy's Monuments Tell Rome's Magnificence. 8 photos: 7 by B. Anthony Stewart. LXXVII, pp. 371-378, Mar., 1940

ROME, Italy—*Continued*

The Perennial Geographer: After 2,000 Years Vergil Is Still the Most Widely Read of Latin Poets—First to Popularize the Geography of the Roman Empire. By W. Coleman Nevils. LVIII, pp. 439-465, 29 ills., Oct., 1930

The Splendor of Rome. By Florence Craig Albrecht. XLI, pp. 593-626, 28 ills., June, 1922

See also Rome, Ancient; Vatican City

RONGERIK (Atoll), Marshall Islands:

Farewell to Bikini. By Carl Markwith. XC, pp. 97-116, 16 ills., July, 1946

ROOSEVELT, FRANKLIN D.:

Ellsworth Awarded the Hubbard Medal (Presentation by Franklin D. Roosevelt). LXX, p. 36, July, 1936

ROOSEVELT, THEODORE:

Cotton and the Chinese Boycott (From an Address by President Roosevelt). XVI, pp. 516-517, Nov., 1905

Forests Vital to Our Welfare (From an Address by President Roosevelt). XVI, pp. 515-516, Nov., 1905

Honors to Peary (Address by President Roosevelt). XVIII, pp. 49-60, ill., Jan., 1907

How Old Is Man? By Theodore Roosevelt. XXIX, pp. 111-127, 12 ills., 3 maps, Feb., 1916

Lessons from China (From President Roosevelt's Message to Congress, December 8, 1908). XX, pp. 18-29, 8 ills., Jan., 1909

Mr. Roosevelt's "African Game Trails." XXI, pp. 953-962, 9 ills., Nov., 1910

National Geographic Society (Cables and Report by Theodore Roosevelt on the African Expedition). XXI, pp. 365-370, 5 ills., Apr., 1910

The Roosevelt African Trophies. XXII, pp. 103-106, 4 ills., Jan., 1911

Where Roosevelt Will Hunt (Africa). By Sir Harry Johnston. XX, pp. 207-256, 43 ills., map supplement, Mar., 1909

Wild Man and Wild Beast in Africa. By Theodore Roosevelt. XXII, pp. 1-33, 41 ills., map, Jan., 1911

ROOSEVELT (Ship):

Commander Peary's New Vessel. XVI, p. 192, Apr., 1905

ROOSEVELT DAM, Arizona:

The Highest Dam in the World. XVI, pp. 440-441, Sept., 1905

Home-Making by the Government: An Account of the Eleven Immense Irrigating Projects to be Opened in 1908. By C. J. Blanchard. XIX, pp. 250-287, 23 ills., Apr., 1908

The Spirit of the West: The Wonderful Agricultural Development Since the Dawn of Irrigation. By C. J. Blanchard. XXI, pp. 333-360, 15 ills., Apr., 1910

ROOT, A. I.:

Our Friends, the Bees. By A. I. and E. R. Root. XXII, pp. 675-694, 21 ills., July, 1911

ROOT, E. R.:

Our Friends, the Bees. By A. I. and E. R. Root. XXII, pp. 675-694, 21 ills., July, 1911

ROOT, ELIHU:

An Awakened Continent to the South of Us. By Elihu Root. XVIII, pp. 61-72, Jan., 1907

Reasons Why the United States in Particular Should Encourage the Pan-American Conferences. (By Elihu Root). XVII, pp. 479-480, Aug., 1906

RORAIMA, Mount, South America:

Kaieteur and Roraima: The Great Falls and the Great Mountain of the Guianas. By Henry Edward Crampton. XXXVIII, pp. 227-244, 12 ills., map, Sept., 1920

Through Brazil to the Summit of Mount Roraima. By G. H. H. Tate. LVIII, pp. 585-605, 24 ills., map, Nov., 1930

ROSA, Monte, Alps:

A Woman's Climbs in the High Alps. By Dora Keen. XXII, pp. 643-675, 26 ills., July, 1911

ROSALES, LOUISE, MARCHESA DE:

Letters from the Italian Front. By Marchesa Louise de Rosales to Ethel Mather Bagg. XXXII, pp. 47-67, 22 ills., July, 1917

ROSE OIL INDUSTRY:

Bulgaria's Valley of Roses. 13 color photos by Wilhelm Tobien and Georg Paskoff. LXII, pp. 187-194, Aug., 1932

The **ROSE-RED** City of Rock (Petra, Trans-Jordan). 21 color photos by G. E. Matson. LXVII, pp. 145-160, Feb., 1935

ROSEATE SPOONBILLS:

The Large Wading Birds: Long Legs and Remarkable Beaks, as Well as Size, Form, and Color, Distinguish the Herons, Ibises, and Flamingos. By T. Gilbert Pearson. Painting by Maj. Allan Brooks. LXII, pp. 441-469, ill. in color, Oct., 1932

ROSS, JOHN W.:

Gardiner Greene Hubbard: Memorial Meeting. Address by Honorable John W. Ross. IX, pp. 66-67, Feb., 1898

ROTCH, A. LAWRENCE:

Project for the Exploration of the Atmosphere Over the Tropical Oceans. By A. Lawrence Rotch. XV, p. 430, Oct., 1904

ROTHENBURG, Bavaria, Germany:

Rothenburg, the City Time Forgot. By Charles W. Beck, Jr. XLIX, pp. 184-194. 8 ills. in color, Feb., 1926

ROTTERDAM, Netherlands:

Holland Rises from War and Water. By Thomas R. Henry. LXXXIX, pp. 237-260, 18 ills., map, Feb., 1946

ROUEN, France:

The Beauties of France. By Arthur Stanley Riggs. XXVIII, pp. 391-491, 73 ills. in black and white, 16 ills. in color, map, Nov., 1915

The Coasts of Normandy and Brittany. By W. Robert Moore. LXXXIV, pp. 205-232, 5 ills. in black and white, 21 ills. in color, two-page map, Aug., 1943

ROUGHLEY, T. C.:

Where Nature Runs Riot: On Australia's Great Barrier Reef Marine Animals Grow to Unusual Size, Develop Strange Weapons of Attack and Defense, and Acquire Brilliant Colors. By T. C. Roughley. LXXVII, pp. 823-850, 18 ills. in black and white, 15 ills. in color, map, June, 1940

Fantastic Dwellers in a Coral Fairyland. 15 color photos by author, pp. 831-838

ROUMANIA. *See* Romania

ROUMANIA, the Pivotal State. By James Howard Gore. XXVIII, pp. 360-390, 32 ills., Oct., 1915

ROUMANIA and Its Rubicon. By John Oliver La Gorce. XXX, pp. 185-202, 11 ills., Sept., 1916

ROUND About Asheville. By Bailey Willis. I, pp. 291-300, map supplement, Oct., 1889

ROUND About Bogotá: A Hunt for New Fruits and Plants Among the Mountain Forests of Colombia's Unique Capital. By Wilson Popenoe. XLIX, pp. 127-160, 34 ills., map, Feb., 1926

ROUND About Grim Tarawa. 19 color photos by W. Robert Moore. LXXXVII, pp. 137-160, Feb., 1945

ROUND About Liechtenstein: A Tiny Principality Which the Visitor May Encompass in a Single View Affords Adventurous Climbs Among Steep Pastures and Quaint Villages. By Maynard Owen Williams. LII, pp. 611-634, 18 ills., map, Nov., 1927

A **ROUND** Trip to Davy Jones's Locker: Peering into Mysteries a Quarter Mile Down in the Open Sea, by Means of the Bathysphere. By William Beebe. Paintings by E. Bostelmann. LIX, pp. 653-678, 14 ills. in black and white, 8 ills. in color, map, June, 1931

ROUNDING the Horn in a Windjammer. By A. J. Villiers. LIX, pp. 191-224, 36 ills., map, Feb., 1931

The **ROUTE** Over Which Moses Led the Children of Israel Out of Egypt. By Franklin E. Hoskins. XX, pp. 1011-1038. 24 ills., map, Dec., 1909

ROUTLEDGE, MRS. SCORESBY:

The Mystery of Easter Island. By Mrs. Scoresby Routledge. XL, pp. 629-646, 13 ills., map, Dec., 1921

ROWLEE, W. W.:

List of Plants Collected near Muir Glacier, determined by W. W. Rowlee. IV, p. 79, Mar. 21, 1892

ROY, LEONARD C.:

From Notch to Notch in the White Mountains: Soaring Heights of New Hampshire Attract Multitudes to America's Oldest Mountain Recreation Area. By Leonard Cornell Roy. LXXII, pp. 73-104, 30 ills., map supplement, July, 1937

Highlights of the Volunteer State: Men and Industry in Tennessee Range from Pioneer Stages to Modern Machine Age. By Leonard Cornell Roy. LXXV, pp. 553-594, 20 ills. in black and white, 22 ills. in color, map, May, 1939

ROY, LEONARD C.—*Continued*

Rambling Around the Roof of Eastern America (Great Smoky Mountains). By Leonard C. Roy. LXX, pp. 243-266, 25 ills., map, Aug., 1936

Tarheelia on Parade: Versatile and Vibrant, North Carolina in a Generation Has Climbed New Economic Heights. By Leonard C. Roy. LXXX, pp. 181-224, 24 ills. in black and white, 21 ills. in color, map, Aug., 1941

ROYAL Copenhagen, Capital of a Farming Kingdom: A Fifth of Denmark's Thrifty Population Resides in a Metropolis Famous for Its Porcelains, Its Silver, and Its Lace. By J. R. Hildebrand. LXI, pp. 217-250, 26 ills. in black and white, 14 ills. in color, Feb., 1932

ROYAL GEOGRAPHICAL SOCIETY, London:

The British Antarctic Expedition (Instructions Given by the Presidents of the Royal Society and the Royal Geographical Society to Capt. Scott and Dr. George Murray). XII, pp. 339-345, Sept., 1901

A Geographical Description of the British Islands. (By W. M. Davis). VII, pp. 208-211, June, 1896

Medal presented to Gen. A. W. Greely, U. S. Army. VII, front., June, 1896. XII, ill. p. 355, Oct., 1901

Medals presented to Sven Hedin and Robert E. Peary. IX, p. 342, July, 1898

ROYALE, Isle, Michigan:

Winter Sky Roads to Isle Royal. By Ben East. LX, pp. 759-774, 18 ills., map, Dec., 1931

RUANDA (Region), Belgian Congo:

A Land of Giants and Pygmies. By the Duke Adolphus Frederick of Mecklenburg. XXIII, pp. 369-388, 16 ills., map, Apr., 1912

RUBBER:

The Amazon, Father of Waters: The Earth's Mightiest River Drains a Basin of More Than 2,700,000 Square Miles, from Which Came Originally the World's Finest Rubber. By W. L. Schurz. XLIX, pp. 445-463, 15 ills., Apr., 1926

Our Most Versatile Vegetable Product: Rubber Drops from Millions of Tropical Trees Are Transformed by Genii Chemists into Myriad Articles, from Tires to Teething Rings. By J. R. Hildebrand. LXXVII, pp. 143-200, 51 ills. in black and white, 26 ills. in color, Feb., 1940

Rubber Forests of Nicaragua and Sierra Leone. By General A. W. Greely. VIII, pp. 83-88, Mar., 1897

Rubber Plantations in Mexico and Central America. XIV, pp. 409-414, 7 ills., Nov., 1903

Singapore, Crossroads of the East: The World's Greatest Mart for Rubber and Tin Was in Recent Times a Pirate-haunted, Tiger-infested Jungle Isle. By Frederick Simpich. XLIX, pp. 235-269, 32 ills., map, Mar., 1926

RUBBER: From Trees to Tires and Toys. 26 color photos by Willard R. Culver and J. Baylor Roberts. LXXVII, pp. 159-190, Feb., 1940

RUG INDUSTRY:
Russia's Orphan Races: Picturesque Peoples Who Cluster on the Southeastern Borderland of the Vast Slav Dominions. By Maynard Owen Williams. XXXIV, pp. 245-278, 26 ills., map, Oct., 1918

RUHR (Region), Germany:
The Story of the Ruhr. By Frederick Simpich. XLI, pp. 553-564, 11 ills., map, May, 1922

RUHR (River), Germany. *See* article, *above*

The **RUINED** Cities of Asia Minor. By Ernest L. Harris. XIX, pp. 741-760, 11 ills., Nov., 1908

RUINS. *See* Archeology

The **RUINS** at Selinus (Sicily). (By Marion Crawford). XX, p. 117, Jan., 1909

The **RUINS** of an Ancient Inca Capital, Machu Picchu. XXIV, panorama, Apr., 1913

RUINS of Cuicuilco May Revolutionize Our History of Ancient America: Lofty Mound Sealed and Preserved by Great Lava Flow for Perhaps Seventy Centuries Is Now Being Excavated in Mexico. By Byron Cummings. XLIV, pp. 203-220, 21 ills., map, Aug., 1923

RULES for the Orthography of Geographic Names. Contributed by Mr. Herrle. II, pp. 279-285, 3 tables, Aug., 1890

RUMANIA. *See* Romania

RUMANIA and Her Ambitions. By Frederick Moore. XXIV, pp. 1057-1085, 34 ills., Oct., 1913

RUMANIAN Peasant Girl. XXIV, ill. p. 1084, Oct., 1913. XXXIV, ill. p. 467, Dec., 1918; enlargement for framing

RUMELI HISSAR (Castle), Turkey:
American Alma Maters in the Near East. By Maynard Owen Williams. LXXXVIII, pp. 237-256, 16 ills., Aug., 1945

RURAL Britain Carries On. By Harvey Klemmer. LXXX, pp. 527-552, 27 ills., Oct., 1941

RURAL Hungarian Rhapsody. 20 color photos by Rudolf Balogh and Hans Hildenbrand. LXXIII, pp. 17-48, Jan., 1938

RURAL Scenes in Brittany. 16 ills. XLIV, pp. 11-26, July, 1923

RURAL Sweden Through American Eyes: A Visitor in Peacetime Finds Warmth, Welcome, and Strange Folkways On a Century-old Farm. By Elizabeth W. Nilson. LXXVII, pp. 795-822, 8 ills. in black and white, 22 ills. in color, June, 1940

RUSSELL, CARL P.:
The White Sands of Alamogordo (New Mexico): A Dry Ocean of Granular Gypsum Billows Under Desert Winds in a New National Playground. By Carl P. Russell. LXVIII, pp. 250-264, 12 ills., Aug., 1935

RUSSELL, ISRAEL C.:
An Expedition to Mount St. Elias, Alaska. By Israel C. Russell. III, pp. 53-191, 17 ills., 3 diagrs., tables, 7 maps (1 foldout), May 29, 1891

RUSSELL, ISRAEL C.—*Continued*
Height and Position of Mount St. Elias. By Israel C. Russell. III, pp. 231-237, diagr., 7 tables, Feb. 19, 1892

Mount St. Elias Expedition, the Society's first scientific exploration, under the leadership of I. C. Russell. III, pp. 39-40, Apr. 30, 1891

The National Geographic Society Expedition in the West Indies. XIII, pp. 209-213, maps, June, 1902

The National Geographic Society Expedition to Martinique and St. Vincent. XIII, pp. 183-184, ills., June, 1902

National Geographic Society Notes (Election of Dr. Russell to Board of Managers). XIII, pp. 218-219, ill., June, 1902

Note on the Height of Mount Saint Elias. By Professor Israel C. Russell. VI, pp. 215-216, Dec. 29, 1894

The Recent Volcanic Eruptions in the West Indies. By Israel C. Russell. XIII, pp. 267-285, 7 ills., map, July, 1902

Timberlines. By Israel C. Russell. XV, pp. 47-49, Jan., 1904

Volcanic Eruptions on Martinique and St. Vincent. By Israel C. Russell. XIII, pp. 415-436, 10 ills., Dec., 1902

Volcanic Rocks of Martinique and St. Vincent: Collected by Robert T. Hill and Israel C. Russell. By J. S. Diller. XIII, pp. 285-296, July, 1902

RUSSIA. *See* Union of Soviet Socialist Republics

RUSSIA. By Charles Emory Smith. XVI, pp. 55-63, Feb., 1905

RUSSIA from Within: Her War of Yesterday, Today, and Tomorrow. By Stanley Washburn. XXXII, pp. 91-120, 30 ills., Aug., 1917

RUSSIA in Europe. By Hon. Gardiner G. Hubbard. VII, pp. 3-26, map supplement, Jan., 1896

RUSSIA in Recent Literature. By General A. W. Greely. XVI, pp. 564-568, Dec., 1905

RUSSIA of the Hour: Giant Battle Ground for Theories of Economy, Society, and Politics, as Observed by an Unbiased Correspondent. By Junius B. Wood. L, pp. 519-598, 81 ills., Nov., 1926

The **RUSSIAN** Census of 1897. (By A. W. G.). VIII, pp. 335-336, Nov., 1897

RUSSIAN Development of Manchuria. By Henry B. Miller. XV, pp. 113-127, 11 ills., map, Mar., 1904

The **RUSSIAN** Expedition to Spitzbergen. XII, p. 404, Nov., 1901

The **RUSSIAN** Situation and Its Significance to America. By Stanley Washburn. XXXI, pp. 371-382, 8 ills., Apr., 1917

RUSSIAN SOVIET FEDERATED SOCIALIST REPUBLIC, U. S. S. R.:
I Learn About the Russians. By Eddy Gilmore. LXXXIV, pp. 619-640, 21 ills., Nov., 1943

Mother Volga Defends Her Own. By Maynard Owen Williams. LXXXII, pp. 793-811, 21 ills., Dec., 1942

RUSSIAN SOVIET FEDERATED SOCIALIST REPUBLIC, U. S. S. R.—*Continued*

New Road to Asia. By Owen Lattimore. LXXXVI, pp. 641-676, 15 ills. in black and white, 26 ills. in color, Dec., 1944

Roaming Russia's Caucasus: Rugged Mountains and Hardy Fighters Guard the Soviet Union's Caucasian Treasury of Manganese and Oil. By Rolf Singer. LXXXII, pp. 91-121, 33 ills., July, 1942

The Society's New Map of Soviet Russia. Text with map supplement. LXXXVI, pp. 716-718, Dec., 1944

See also Crimea; Daghestan Autonomous Soviet Socialist Republic; Siberia

RUSSIAN TURKISTAN. *See* Soviet Central Asia

RUSSIANS:

I Learn About the Russians. By Eddy Gilmore. LXXXIV, pp. 619-640, 21 ills., Nov., 1943

"Magnetic City" (Magnitogorsk), Core of Valiant Russia's Industrial Might. By John Scott. LXXXIII, pp. 525-556, 27 ills., two-page map, May, 1943

New Road to Asia. By Owen Lattimore. LXXXVI, pp. 641-676, 15 ills. in black and white, 26 ills. in color, Dec., 1944

Roaming Russia's Caucasus: Rugged Mountains and Hardy Fighters Guard the Soviet Union's Caucasian Treasury of Manganese and Oil. By Rolf Singer. LXXXII, pp. 91-121, 33 ills., July, 1942

RUSSIA'S Democrats. By Montgomery Schuyler. XXXI, pp. 210-240, 25 ills., Mar., 1917

RUSSIA'S Man of the Hour: Alexander Kerensky's First Speeches and Proclamations. XXXII, pp. 24-45, 17 ills., July, 1917

RUSSIA'S Orphan Races: Picturesque Peoples Who Cluster on the Southeastern Borderland of the Vast Slav Dominions. By Maynard Owen Williams. XXXIV, pp. 245-278, 26 ills., map, Oct., 1918

RUSSIA'S Wheat Surplus. XVII, pp. 580-583, Oct., 1906

The **RUSSO-AMERICAN** Telegraph Project of 1864-'67. By Professor William H. Dall. VII, pp. 110-111, ill., Mar., 1896

RUWENZORI (Mountains), Central Africa:

Amid the Snow Peaks of the Equator: A Naturalist's Explorations Around Ruwenzori, with an Excursion to the Congo State, and an Account of the Terrible Scourge of Sleeping Sickness. By A. F. R. Wollaston. XX, pp. 256-277, 11 ills., Mar., 1909

Flights from Arctic to Equator: Conquering the Alps, the Ice Peaks of Spitsbergen, of Persia, and Africa's Mountains of the Moon. By Walter Mittelholzer. LXI, pp. 445-498, 53 ills., map, Apr., 1932

The World's Highest Altitudes and First Ascents. By Charles E. Fay. XX, pp. 493-530, 25 ills., June, 1909

RYAN, INEZ BUFFINGTON:

The Land of William the Conqueror (Normandy): Where Northmen Came to Build Castles and Cathedrals. By Inez Buffington Ryan. LXI, pp. 89-99, 13 ills. in color, Jan., 1932

RYAN, INEZ BUFFINGTON—*Continued*

The Maid of France Rides By: Compiègne, Where Joan of Arc Fought Her Last Battle, Celebrates Her Fifth Centenary. By Inez Buffington Ryan. LXII, pp. 607-616, 15 ills. in color, Nov., 1932

RYDER, C. H.:

Three Weeks in Hubbard Bay, West Greenland. By Robert Stein. IX, pp. 1-11, 6 ills., maps, Jan., 1898

RYUKYU RETTO (Nansei Shoto), Japan:

Peacetime Rambles in the Ryukyus. By William Leonard Schwartz. LXXXVII, pp. 543-561, 12 ills., maps, May, 1945

See also Okinawa

S

SAAR (Region), Germany:

What Is the Saar? By Frederick Simpich. LXVII, pp. 241-264, 5 ills. in black and white, 23 ills. in duotone, maps, Feb., 1935

SABA (Island), Leeward Islands:

Saba, Crater Treasure of the Indies. By Charles W. Herbert. LXXVIII, pp. 597-620, 14 ills. in black and white, 12 ills. in color, map (inset), Nov., 1940

SABOTEUR Mosquitoes. By Harry H. Stage. LXXXV, pp. 165-179, 12 ills., Feb., 1944

SACRAMENTO (River), California:

More Water for California's Great Central Valley. By Frederick Simpich. XC, pp. 645-664, 16 ills., map, Nov., 1946

The **SACRED** City of the Sands (Kairouan, Tunisia). By Frank Edward Johnson. XXII, pp. 1061-1093, 25 ills., map, Dec., 1911

The **SACRED** Ibis Cemetery and Jackal Catacombs at Abydos. By Camden M. Cobern. XXIV, pp. 1042-1056, 10 ills., Sept., 1913

The **SACRED** Tooth (of Buddha). XVIII, ill. p. 745, Nov., 1907

SACSAHUAMAN (Fortress), Peru:

The Greatest Achievement of Ancient Man in America (Fortress of Sacsahuaman). XXIX, panorama, May, 1916

SAFFORD, WILLIAM E.:

Our Smallest Possession—Guam. By William E. Safford. XVI, pp. 229-237, 5 ills., May, 1905

SAGA of the Carrier *Princeton.* By Capt. William H. Buracker, USN. LXXXVIII, pp. 189-218, 8 ills. in black and white, 22 ills. in color, map, Aug., 1945

The **SAGACITY** and Courage of Dogs: Instances of the Remarkable Intelligence and Unselfish Devotion of Man's Best Friend Among Dumb Animals. XXXV, pp. 253-275, 13 ills., Mar., 1919

SAGAS:

Dwellings of the Saga-Time in Iceland, Greenland, and Vineland. By Cornelia Horsford. IX, pp. 73-84, ills., 9 sketches, Mar., 1898

SAGE BRUSH. *See* Sage Plains, *below*

SAGE GROUSE:

High Country of Colorado. By Alfred M. Bailey. With 23 color photos by author, Robert J. Niedrach, F. G. Brandenburg. XC, pp. 43-72, 9 ills. in black and white, July, 1946

The **SAGE PLAINS** of Oregon. By Frederick V. Coville. VII, pp. 395-404, Dec., 1896

SAGUARO:

The Saguaro, Cactus Camel of Arizona. By Forrest Shreve. LXXXVIII, pp. 695-704, 9 ills. in color, Dec., 1945

The Saguaro Forest (Arizona). By H. L. Shantz. LXXI, pp. 515-532, 18 ills., Apr., 1937

SAGUARO, King of the Arizona Desert. 9 color photos by Esther Henderson, Jack Breed, Max Kegley. LXXXVIII, pp. 697-704, Dec., 1945

SAGUARO NATIONAL MONUMENT, Arizona:

The Saguaro Forest. By H. L. Shantz. LXXI, pp. 515-532, 18 ills., Apr., 1937

SAGUENAY RIVER REGION, Canada. *See* Quebec (Province)

SAHARA (Desert), Africa:

The Conquest of the Sahara by the Automobile. XLV, pp. 87-93, 9 ills., map, Jan., 1924

The Country of the Ant Men. By Thomas H. Kearney. XXII, pp. 367-382, 13 ills., map, panorama, Apr., 1911

The Date Gardens of the Jerid. By Thomas H. Kearney. XXI, pp. 543-567, 20 ills., July, 1910

French Conquest of the Sahara. By Charles Rabot. XVI, pp. 76-80, ills., Feb., 1905

Here and There in Northern Africa. By Frank Edward Johnson. XXV, pp. 1-132, 113 ills., Jan., 1914

The Mysteries of the Desert. By Hanns Vischer. XXII, pp. 1056-1059, Nov., 1911

Our Desert Panorama. Text with panorama. XXII, pp. 409-410, Apr., 1911

The Hour of Prayer: In the Sahara Desert (panorama)

Three-Wheeling Through Africa: Two Adventurers Cross the So-called Dark Continent North of Lake Chad on Motorcycles with Side Cars. By James C. Wilson. LXV, pp. 37-92, 64 ills., two-page map, Jan., 1934

Trans-Africa Safari: A Motor Caravan Rolls Across Sahara and Jungle Through Realms of Dusky Potentates and the Land of Big-Lipped Women. By Lawrence Copley Thaw and Margaret Stout Thaw. LXXIV, pp. 327-364, 29 ills. in black and white, 14 ills. in color, map, Sept., 1938

SAHUARO (Cactus). *See* Saguaro

SAILING Forbidden Coasts (Africa). By Ida Treat. LX, pp. 357-386, 31 ills., map, Sept., 1931

The **SAILING** Ship and the Panama Canal. By James Page. XV, pp. 167-176, charts, Apr., 1904

SAILING the Seven Seas in the Interest of Science: Adventures Through 157,000 Miles of Storm and Calm, from Arctic to Antarctic and Around the World, in the Non-magnetic Yacht "Carnegie." By J. P. Ault. XLII, pp. 631-690, 47 ills., chart, Dec., 1922

SAILORS, U. S. *See* U. S. Navy

SAILPLANES:

Men-Birds Soar on Boiling Air. By Frederick G. Vosburgh. LXXIV, pp. 123-140, 15 ills., July, 1938

On the Wings of the Wind: In Motorless Planes, Pilots Ride in Flying-Fox Fashion, Cruising on Upward Air Streams and Lifted by the Suction of Moving Clouds. By Howard Siepen. LV, pp. 751-780, 40 ills., June, 1929

ST. ANDREWS, Scotland:

Bonnie Scotland, Postwar Style. By Isobel Wylie Hutchison. LXXXIX, pp. 545-601, 14 ills. in black and white, 38 ills. in color, two-page map, May, 1946

ST. CATHERINE, Monastery of, Sinai, Egypt:

The Route Over Which Moses Led the Children of Israel Out of Egypt. By Franklin E. Hoskins. XX, pp. 1011-1038, 24 ills., map, Dec., 1909

ST. CHRISTOPHER (Island). *See* St. Kitts

ST. CLAIR, STUART:

Timor a Key to the Indies. By Stuart St. Clair. LXXXIV, pp. 355-384, 33 ills., map, Sept., 1943

ST. CROIX (Island), Virgin Islands:

An American Gibraltar: Notes on the Danish West Indies. XXX, pp. 89-96, 4 ills., map, July, 1916

The American Virgins: After Dark Days, These Adopted Daughters of the United States Are Finding a New Place in the Caribbean Sun. By DuBose Heyward and Daisy Reck. LXXVIII, pp. 273-308, 15 ills. in black and white, 23 ills. in color, map, Sept., 1940

ST. ELIAS, Mount, Canada-Alaska:

The Conquest of Mount Logan: North America's Second Highest Peak Yields to the Intrepid Attack of Canadian Climbers. By H. F. Lambart. XLIX, pp. 597-631, 40 ills., June, 1926

An Expedition to Mount St. Elias, Alaska. By Israel C. Russell. III, pp. 53-191, 17 ills., 3 diagrs., tables, 7 maps (1 foldout), May 29, 1891

Introduction: The Southern Coast of Alaska, pp. 55-57

Part I: Previous Explorations in the St. Elias Region, pp. 58-74

Part II: Narrative of the St. Elias Expedition of 1890, pp. 75-166

Part III: Sketch of the Geology of the St. Elias Region, pp. 167-175

Part IV: Glaciers of the St. Elias Region, pp. 176-188

Part V: Height and Position of Mount St. Elias, pp. 189-191

Appendices: Official Instructions Governing the Expedition, pp. 192-194; Report on Topographic Work, p. 195; Report on Auriferous Sands from Yakutat Bay, pp. 196-198; Report on Fossil Plants, pp. 199-200

ST. ELIAS, Mount, Canada-Alaska—*Continued*

The Geographical Position and Height of Mount Saint Elias. By Dr. T. C. Mendenhall. V, pp. 63-67, diagr., tables, July 10, 1893

Height and Position of Mount St. Elias. By Israel C. Russell. III, pp. 231-237, diagr., 7 tables, Feb. 19, 1892

The Monarchs of Alaska. By R. H. Sargent. XX, pp. 610-623, 9 ills., July, 1909

Mount St. Elias expedition, the Society's first scientific exploration, under the leadership of I. C. Russell. III, pp. 39-40, Apr. 30, 1891

The Mt. St. Elias Expedition of Prince Luigi Amadeo of Savoy, 1897. (By E.R.S.). IX, pp. 93-96, Mar., 1898

The National Geographic Society's Alaskan Expedition of 1909. By Ralph S. Tarr and Lawrence Martin. XXI, pp. 1-54, 42 ills., 12 maps, Jan., 1910

Note on the Height of Mount Saint Elias. By Professor Israel C. Russell. VI, pp. 215-216, Dec. 29, 1894

Recent Explorations in Alaska. By Eliza Ruhamah Scidmore. V, pp. 173-179, Jan. 31, 1894

Summary of Reports on the Mt. St. Elias Expedition. II, pp. 302-304, Apr., 1891

ST. HELENA (Island), South Atlantic Ocean:

Sailing the Seven Seas in the Interest of Science: Adventures Through 157,000 Miles of Storm and Calm, from Arctic to Antarctic and Around the World, in the Non-magnetic Yacht "Carnegie." By J. P. Ault. XLII, pp. 631-690, 47 ills., chart, Dec., 1922

ST. HELENS, Mount, Washington:

Mount St. Helens. By Lieut. Charles P. Elliott. VIII, pp. 226-230, foldout map, July-Aug., 1897

ST. IVES, Cornwall, England:

Channel Ports—And Some Others. By Florence Craig Albrecht. XXVIII, pp. 1-55, 45 ills., July, 1915

SAINT JOHN, New Brunswick:

New Brunswick Down by the Sea. By Lawrence J. Burpee. LXXIX, pp. 595-614, 14 ills., map, May, 1941

ST. JOHN (River), New Brunswick:

Atlantic Estuarine Tides. By Mark S. W. Jefferson. IX, pp. 400-409, diagrs., 7 tables, maps, Sept., 1898

ST. JOHN (Island), Virgin Islands:

An American Gilbraltar: Notes on the Danish West Indies. XXX, pp. 89-96, 4 ills., map, July, 1916

The American Virgins: After Dark Days, These Adopted Daughters of the United States Are Finding a New Place in the Caribbean Sun. By DuBose Heyward and Daisy Reck. LXXVIII, pp. 273-308, 15 ills. in black and white, 23 ills. in color, map, Sept., 1940

ST. JOHN'S, Newfoundland:

Newfoundland, North Atlantic Rampart: From the "First Base of American Defense" Planes Fly to Britain's Aid over Stout Fishing Schooners of the Grand Banks. By George Whiteley, Jr. LXXX, pp. 111-140, 26 ills., map, July, 1941

ST. KITTS (St. Christopher, Island), West Indies:

British West Indian Interlude. By Anne Rainey Langley. LXXIX, pp. 1-46, 23 ills. in black and white, 21 ills. in color, maps, Jan., 1941

ST. LAWRENCE (River), Canada-U. S.:

Atlantic Estuarine Tides. By Mark S. W. Jefferson. IX, pp. 400-409, diagrs., 7 tables, maps, Sept., 1898

See also Quebec (Province)

ST. LAWRENCE, Gulf of:

Atlantic Coast Tides. By Mark S. W. Jefferson. IX, pp. 497-509, 3 charts, Dec., 1898

ST. LOUIS, Missouri:

These Missourians. By Frederick Simpich. LXXXIX, pp. 277-310, 12 ills. in black and white, 22 ills. in color, map, Mar., 1946

ST. LUCIA (Island), West Indies:

Americans in the Caribbean. By Luis Marden. LXXXI, pp. 723-758, 16 ills. in black and white, 22 ills. in color, map, June, 1942

British West Indian Interlude. By Anne Rainey Langley. LXXIX, pp. 1-46, 23 ills. in black and white, 21 ills. in color, maps, Jan., 1941

ST. MAGNUS CATHEDRAL, Orkney Islands:

The Orkneys and Shetlands—A Mysterious Group of Islands. By Charles S. Olcott. XXXIX, pp. 197-228, 33 ills., Feb., 1921

ST. MALO, France:

St. Malo, Ancient City of Corsairs: An Old Brittany Seaport Whose Past Bristles with Cannons and Cutlasses. By Junius B. Wood. LVI, pp. 131-177, 28 ills. in black and white, 29 ills. in color, map, Aug., 1929

ST. MARK'S CATHEDRAL, Venice:

Venice. By Karl Stieler. XXVII, pp. 587-630, 42 ills., maps, June, 1915

ST. MICHAEL'S (São Miguel, Island), Azores:

The Azores: Picturesque and Historic Half-way House of American Transatlantic Aviators. By Arminius T. Haeberle. XXXV, pp. 514-545, 26 ills., map, June, 1919

ST. PETER'S CATHEDRAL, Rome:

Inexhaustible Italy. By Arthur Stanley Riggs. XXX, pp. 273-368, 76 ills., map, Oct., 1916

The Splendor of Rome. By Florence Craig Albrecht. XLI, pp. 593-626, 28 ills., June, 1922

ST. PIERRE, Martinique:

Lafcadio Hearn on the Island and People of Martinique. XIII, pp. 214-216, June, 1902

The Recent Volcanic Eruptions in the West Indies. By Israel C. Russell. XIII, pp. 267-285, 7 ills., map, July, 1902

ST. PIERRE AND MIQUELON, Atlantic Ocean:
Islands Adrift: St. Pierre and Miquelon: In a Key Position on the North Atlantic Air Route, France's Oldest Colony Rides Out Another Storm. By Frederic K. Arnold. LXXX, pp. 743-768, 23 ills., map, Dec., 1941

ST. SIMONS ISLAND, Sea Islands, Georgia:
The Golden Isles of Guale. By W. Robert Moore. LXV, pp. 235-264, 35 ills., map, Feb., 1934

SAINT Stephen's Fete in Budapest. By De Witt Clinton Falls. XVIII, pp. 548-558, 9 ills., Aug., 1907

ST. THOMAS (Island), Virgin Islands:
An American Gibraltar: Notes on the Danish West Indies. XXX, pp. 89-96, 4 ills., map, July, 1916
The American Virgins: After Dark Days, These Adopted Daughters of the United States Are Finding a New Place in the Caribbean Sun. By DuBose Heyward and Daisy Reck. LXXVIII, pp. 273-308, 15 ills. in black and white, 23 ills. in color, map, Sept., 1940
The Haunts of the Caribbean Corsairs: The West Indies a Geographic Background for the Most Adventurous Episodes in the History of the Western Hemisphere. By Nell Ray Clarke. XLI, pp. 147-187, 27 ills., Feb., 1922

ST. VINCENT (Island), West Indies:
British West Indian Interlude. By Anne Rainey Langley. LXXIX, pp. 1-46, 23 ills. in black and white, 21 ills. in color, maps, Jan., 1941
Chemical Discussion of Analyses of Volcanic Ejecta from Martinique and St. Vincent. By W. F. Hillebrand. XIII, pp. 296-299, July, 1902
The Eruptions of La Soufrière, St. Vincent, in May, 1902. By Edmund Otis Hovey. XIII, pp. 444-459, 4 ills., Dec., 1902
The National Geographic Society Expedition to Martinique and St. Vincent. XIII, pp. 183-184, ills., June, 1902
The Recent Volcanic Eruptions in the West Indies. By Israel C. Russell. XIII, pp. 267-285, 7 ills., map, July, 1902
Report by Robert T. Hill on the Volcanic Disturbances in the West Indies. XIII, pp. 223-267, 12 ills., 3 maps, July, 1902
A Report of the Eruption of the Soufrière of St. Vincent, 1812 (From the *Evening News* of June 30, 1812). XIV, pp. 158-161, Apr., 1903
Reports of Vessels as to the Range of Volcanic Dust. By James Page. XIII, pp. 299-301, July, 1902
Volcanic Eruptions on Martinique and St. Vincent. By Israel C. Russell. XIII, pp. 415-436, 10 ills., Dec., 1902
Volcanic Rocks of Martinique and St. Vincent: Collected by Robert T. Hill and Israel C. Russell. By J. S. Diller. XIII, pp. 285-296, July, 1902

SAIPAN (Island), Marianas Islands:
Hidden Key to the Pacific: Piercing the Web of Secrecy Which Long Has Veiled Japanese Bases in the Mandated Islands. By Willard Price. LXXXI, pp. 759-785, 28 ills., map, June, 1942

SAIPAN (Island), Marianas Islands—*Continued*
South from Saipan. By W. Robert Moore. LXXXVII, pp. 441-474, 11 ills. in black and white, 17 ills. in color, map, Apr., 1945
Springboards to Tokyo. By Willard Price. LXXXVI, pp. 385-407, 16 ills., Oct., 1944
Victory's Portrait in the Marianas. By Lt. William Franklin Draper, USNR. With 17 ills. in color from paintings by author. LXXXVIII, pp. 599-616, Nov., 1945

SAIPAN and Tinian, Take-offs to Tokyo. 17 color photos: 15 by W. Robert Moore. LXXXVII, pp. 453-468, Apr., 1945

SAKAMOTO, KIYOSHI:
Japan. 11 color photos by Kiyoshi Sakamoto. XL, pp. 61-76, July, 1921
The Picturesque Side of Japanese Life. 12 color photos by Kiyoshi Sakamoto. XLII, pp. 283-298, Sept., 1922

SAKURAJIMA, Japan's Greatest Volcanic Eruption: A Convulsion of Nature Whose Ravages Were Minimized by Scientific Knowledge, Compared with the Terrors and Destruction of the Recent Tokyo Earthquake. By Dr. Thomas Augustus Jaggar. XLV, pp. 441-470, 32 ills., map, Apr., 1924

SALE, GEORGE:
Conditions in Liberia. By Roland P. Folkner, George Sale, Emmett J. Scott. XXI, pp. 729-741, 9 ills., Sept., 1910

SALE, Morocco:
Eastward from Gibraltar: Overland Route Across North Africa to Tunisia and Libia. By Cyrus French Wicker. LXXXIII, pp. 115-142, 28 ills., Jan., 1943

SALEM, Massachusetts:
Northeast of Boston. By Albert W. Atwood. LXXXVIII, pp. 257-292, 12 ills. in black and white, 17 ills. in color, map supplement, Sept., 1945

SALEM, Oregon:
Oregon Finds New Riches. By Leo A. Borah. XC, pp. 681-728, 15 ills. in black and white, 28 ills. in color, two-page map, Dec., 1946

SALGADO, JOSÉ VELLOSO:
Vasco da Gama at the Court of the Zamorin of Calicut. Reproduction in color of the painting by José Velloso Salgado, Sociedade de Geographia de Lisboa. LII, supplement, Nov., 1927

SALISBURY, Southern Rhodesia:
Rhodesia, Hobby and Hope of Cecil Rhodes. By W. Robert Moore. LXXXVI, pp. 281-306, 13 ills. in black and white, 10 ills. in color, map, Sept., 1944

SALMON (River), Idaho:
Down Idaho's River of No Return. By Philip J. Shenon and John C. Reed. LXX, pp. 95-136, 43 ills., maps, July, 1936

SALMON (Fish):
America's Most Valuable Fishes. By Hugh M. Smith. XXIII, pp. 494-514, 17 ills., May, 1912

SALMON (Fish)—*Continued*
Federal Fish Farming; or, Planting Fish by the Billion. By Hugh M. Smith. XXI, pp. 418-446, 22 ills., May, 1910
Fishing in Pacific Coast Streams. By Leonard P. Schultz. Paintings by Hashime Murayama. LXXV, pp. 185-212, 10 ills. in black and white, 44 portraits in color, Feb., 1939
A Jumping Salmon. XIX, pp. 124-125, ill., Feb., 1908
The White Sheep, Giant Moose, and Smaller Game of the Kenai Peninsula, Alaska. By George Shiras, 3d. XXIII, pp. 423-494, 59 ills., maps (1 two-page), May, 1912

SALONIKI (Greece). By H. G. Dwight. XXX, pp. 203-232, 28 ills., Sept., 1916

SALT:
The Eden of the Flowery Republic. By Dr. Joseph Beech. XXXVIII, pp. 355-390, 18 ills. in black and white, 16 ills. in color, Nov., 1920
An Interesting Photograph (Salt Deposit, Athabasca District, Alberta). XVII, pp. 236-237, ill., Apr., 1906
Methods of Obtaining Salt in Costa Rica. XIX, pp. 28-34, 7 ills., diagr., Jan., 1908
A Remarkable Salt Deposit. By Charles F. Holder. XII, pp. 391-392, ills., Nov., 1901
Salt for China's Daily Rice. 11 ills. LXXXVI, pp. 329-336, Sept., 1944

SALTON SEA, California:
The Colorado Desert. By W. C. Mendenhall. XX, pp. 681-701, 16 ills., Aug., 1909
The New Inland Sea. By Arthur P. Davis. XVIII, pp. 37-49, 8 ills., map, Jan., 1907
A Remarkable Salt Deposit. By Charles F. Holder. XII, pp. 391-392, ills., Nov., 1901
Salton Sea and the Rainfall of the Southwest. By Alfred J. Henry. XVIII, pp. 244-248, Apr., 1907
Studies on the Rate of Evaporation at Reno, Nevada, and in the Salton Sink. By Professor Frank H. Bigelow. XIX, pp. 20-28, 5 ills., Jan., 1908

SALTON SEA BIRD REFUGE, California:
Pelican Profiles. By Lewis Wayne Walker. LXXXIV, pp. 589-598, 5 ills. in black and white, 8 ills. in color, Nov., 1943

SALTY Nova Scotia: In Friendly New Scotland Gaelic Songs Still Answer the Skirling Bagpipes. By Andrew H. Brown. LXXVII, pp. 575-624, 30 ills. in black and white, 21 ills. in color, two-page map, May, 1940

SALVADOR. *See* El Salvador

SALVADOR (Bahia), Brazil:
Air Cruising Through New Brazil: A National Geographic Reporter Spots Vast Resources Which the Republic's War Declaration Adds to Strength of United Nations. By Henry Albert Phillips. LXXXII, pp. 503-536, 32 ills., Oct., 1942

SALVATION ARMY:
Around the World with the Salvation Army. By Evangeline Booth. XXXVII, pp. 347-368, 23 ills., Apr., 1920

SALWEEN (River), Tibet-Burma-China:
The Land of the Crossbow (Yünnan Province). By George Forrest. XXI, pp. 132-156, 15 ills., map, Feb., 1910
Through the Great River Trenches of Asia: National Geographic Society Explorer Follows the Yangtze, Mekong, and Salwin Through Mighty Gorges, Some of Whose Canyon Walls Tower to a Height of More Than Two Miles. By Joseph F. Rock. L, pp. 133-186, 47 ills., map, Aug., 1926

SALZBURG (Province), Austria:
The Salzkammergut, a Playground of Austria. By Florence Polk Holding. LXXI, pp. 445-485, 34 ills. in black and white, 13 ills. in color, map, Apr., 1937
This Was Austria. 18 ills. LXXXVIII, pp. 71-86, July, 1945

SALZKAMMERGUT (Region), Austria:
The Salzkammergut, a Playground of Austria. By Florence Polk Holding. LXXI, pp. 445-485, 34 ills. in black and white, 13 ills. in color, map, Apr., 1937

SAMANA (Island). *See* Bahama Islands

SAMARITANISM. *See* Samaritans

SAMARITANS (Sect):
The Last Israelitish Blood Sacrifice: How the Vanishing Samaritans Celebrate the Passover on Sacred Mount Gerizim. By John D. Whiting. XXXVII, pp. 1-46, 40 ills., map, Jan., 1920

SAMARKAND, Uzbek, U. S. S. R.:
Russia's Orphan Races: Picturesque Peoples Who Cluster on the Southeastern Borderland of the Vast Slav Dominions. By Maynard Owen Williams. XXXIV, pp. 245-278, 26 ills., map, Oct., 1918

SAMOA (Islands), South Pacific Ocean:
America's South Sea Soldiers. By Lorena MacIntyre Quinn. XXXVI, pp. 267-274, 8 ills., Sept., 1919
The Commercial Importance of Samoa. (By O. P. Austin). X, pp. 218-220, June, 1899
Sailing the Seven Seas in the Interest of Science: Adventures Through 157,000 Miles of Storm and Calm, from Arctic to Antarctic and Around the World, in the Non-magnetic Yacht "Carnegie." By J. P. Ault. XLII, pp. 631-690, 47 ills., chart, Dec., 1922
Samoa: Navigators Islands. By Commander H. Webster. X, pp. 207-217, 9 ills., June, 1899
Samoa—South Sea Outpost of the U. S. Navy. 20 photos by Truman Bailey. LXXIX, pp. 615-630, May, 1941
The Samoan Cocoanut (Article compiled by Gen. A. W. Greely). IX, pp. 12-24, Jan., 1898
The Samoan Islands. By Edwin V. Morgan. XI, pp. 417-426, Nov., 1900

The **SAMOAN** Cocoanut (Article compiled by Gen. A. W. Greely). IX, pp. 12-24, Jan., 1898

SAMOS (Island), Aegean Sea:
Historic Islands and Shores of the Ægean Sea. By Ernest Lloyd Harris. XXVIII, pp. 231-261, 28 ills., map, Sept., 1915

SAN AGUSTÍN REGION, Colombia:
Stone Idols of the Andes Reveal a Vanished People: Remarkable Relics of One of the Oldest Aboriginal Cultures of America are Unearthed in Colombia's San Agustín Region. By Hermann von Walde-Waldegg. LXXVII, pp. 627-647, 22 ills., map, May, 1940

SAN BENITO ISLANDS, Mexico:
Cruise of the *Kinkajou:* Among Desert Islands of Mexico Voyagers Find Outdoor Laboratories for the Naturalist and Ideal Fishing Grounds for the Sportsman. By Alfred M. Bailey. LXXX, pp. 339-366, 13 ills. in black and white, 12 ills. in color, map, Sept., 1941

SAN BLAS INDIANS:
Arch-Isolationists, the San Blas Indians: Coconuts Serve as Cash on Islands Off the Panama Coast Where Tribesmen Cling to Their Ancient Ways and Discourage Visitors. By Corinne B. Feeney. LXXIX, pp. 193-220, 15 ills. in black and white, 12 ills. in color, map, Feb., 1941
The Land That Links the Americas (Panama). 22 color photos by Luis Marden. LXXX, pp. 601-624, Nov., 1941
Little-Known Parts of Panama. By Henry Pittier. XXIII, pp. 627-662, 35 ills., map, July, 1912

SAN CRISTOBAL (Island), Galápagos Islands:
The Dream Ship: The Story of a Voyage of Adventure More Than Half Around the World in a 47-foot Lifeboat. By Ralph Stock. XXXIX, pp. 1-52, 43 ills., map, Jan., 1921

SAN DIEGO, California:
San Diego Can't Believe It. By Frederick Simpich. LXXXI, pp. 45-80, 26 ills. in black and white, 9 ills. in color, Jan., 1942

SAN FRANCISCO, California:
The California Earthquake. XVII, pp. 325-343, 27 ills., June, 1906
A City of Realized Dreams. By Franklin K. Lane. XXVII, pp. 169-171, Feb., 1915
Echoes of the San Francisco Earthquake. By Robert E. C. Stearns. XVIII, pp. 351-353, ill., May, 1907
Out in San Francisco: Fed on Gold Dust and Fattened by Sea Trade, a Pioneer Village Becomes a Busy World Port. By Frederick Simpich. LXI, pp. 395-434, 38 ills., Apr., 1932
The Probable Cause of the San Francisco Earthquake. By Frederick Leslie Ransome. XVII, pp. 280-296, 9 ills., maps, May, 1906
The Record of the Great Earthquake Written in Washington by the Seismograph of the U. S. Weather Bureau. By C. F. Marvin. XVII, pp. 296-298, May, 1906
San Francisco: Gibraltar of the West Coast. By La Verne Bradley. LXXXIII, pp. 279-308, 28 ills., Mar., 1943
The San Francisco Earthquake of April 18, 1906, as Recorded by the Coast and Geodetic Survey Magnetic Observatories. By L. A. Bauer and J. E. Burbank. XVII, pp. 298-300, tables, May, 1906
The Sea Fogs of San Francisco. XII, pp. 108-114, 5 ills., Mar., 1901

SAN FRANCISCO, California—*Continued*
The Wonderland of California. By Herman Whitaker. XXVIII, pp. 57-104, 45 ills., July, 1915

SAN Francisco Earthquake. 27 ills. XVII, pp. 326-343, June, 1906

SAN JOAQUIN (River), California:
More Water for California's Great Central Valley. By Frederick Simpich. XC, pp. 645-664, 16 ills., map, Nov., 1946

SAN JOSÉ, Costa Rica:
Costa Rica, Land of the Banana. By Paul B. Popenoe. XLI, pp. 201-220, 17 ills., Feb., 1922
Costa Rica—Vulcan's Smithy. By H. Pittier. XXI, pp. 494-525, 30 ills., maps, June, 1910
Land of the Painted Oxcarts. By Luis Marden. With 31 color photos by author. XC, pp. 409-456, 30 ills. in black and white, map, Oct., 1946

SAN JUAN, Puerto Rico:
Puerto Rico: Watchdog of the Caribbean: Venerable Domain Under American Flag Has New Role as West Indian Stronghold and Sentinel of the Panama Canal. By E. John Long. LXXVI, pp. 697-738, 24 ills. in black and white, 23 ills. in color, Dec., 1939

SAN JUAN (River), Colorado-New Mexico-Utah:
Beyond the Clay Hills: An Account of the National Geographic Society's Reconnaissance of a Previously Unexplored Section in Utah. By Neil M. Judd. XLV, pp. 275-302, 28 ills., map, Mar., 1924

SAN JUAN MOUNTAINS, Colorado-New Mexico:
Landslides and Rock Avalanches. By Guy Elliott Mitchell. XXI, pp. 277-287, 6 ills., Apr., 1910

SAN JUAN TEOTIHUACAN, Mexico:
An Interesting Visit to the Ancient Pyramids of San Juan Teotihuacan. By A. C. Galloway. XXI, pp. 1041-1050, 8 ills., map, Dec., 1910

SAN MARINO:
Our Littlest Ally. By Alice Rohe. XXXIV, pp. 139-163, 17 ills., Aug., 1918

SAN SALVADOR (Watling, Island). *See* Bahama Islands

SAN SALVADOR, El Salvador:
Coffee Is King in El Salvador. By Luis Marden. LXXXVI, pp. 575-616, 22 ills. in black and white, 27 ills. in color, map, Nov., 1944
Volcano-Girded Salvador: A Prosperous Central American State with the Densest Rural Population in the Western World. By Harriet Chalmers Adams. XLI, pp. 189-200, 10 ills., Feb., 1922

SAN SALVADOR VOLCANO, El Salvador:
Coffee Is King in El Salvador. By Luis Marden. LXXXVI, pp. 575-616, 22 ills. in black and white, 27 ills. in color, map, Nov., 1944

SAN VICENTE (Hacienda), Chile:
On a Chilean Hacienda. 8 color photos by E. P. Haddon. LXXXVI, pp. 489-496, Oct., 1944

SANCTA SOPHIA (Mosque), İstanbul:

Constantinople and Sancta Sophia. By Edwin A. Grosvenor. XXVII, pp. 459-482, 21 ills., May, 1915

Constantinople Today. By Solita Solano. XLI, pp. 647-680, 40 ills., map, June, 1922

SAND DUNES:

A Battle-Ground of Nature: The Atlantic Seaboard. By John Oliver La Gorce. XXXIII, pp. 511-546, 23 ills., 4 maps, June, 1918

Controlling Sand Dunes in the United States and Europe. By A. S. Hitchcock. XV, pp. 43-47, 4 ills., Jan., 1904

Indiana's Unrivaled Sand-Dunes—A National Park Opportunity. By Orpheus Moyer Schantz. XXXV, pp. 430-441, 18 ills., May, 1919

Our Neglected Southern Coast. By Alfred Goldsborough Mayer. XIX, pp. 859-871, 10 ills., Dec., 1908

The Warfare on Our Eastern Coast. By John Oliver La Gorce. XXVIII, pp. 195-230, 29 ills., charts, Sept., 1915

Where the Wind Does the Work (Cape Hatteras, North Carolina). By Collier Cobb. XVII, pp. 310-317, 9 ills., map, June, 1906

The White Sands of Alamogordo (New Mexico): A Dry Ocean of Granular Gypsum Billows Under Desert Winds in a New National Playground. By Carl P. Russell. LXVIII, pp. 250-264, 12 ills., Aug., 1935

See also Deserts

SANDERS, ALVIN HOWARD:

The Taurine World: Cattle and Their Place in the Human Scheme—Wild Types and Modern Breeds in Many Lands. By Alvin Howard Sanders. Paintings by Edward Herbert Miner. XLVIII, pp. 591-710, 76 ills. in black and white, 20 ills. in color, Dec., 1925

SANDPIPERS:

Birds of Timberline and Tundra. By Arthur A. Allen. With 24 color photos by author. XC, pp. 313-339, 8 ills. in black and white, Sept., 1946

The Shore Birds, Cranes, and Rails: Willets, Plovers, Stilts, Phalaropes, Sandpipers, and Their Relatives Deserve Protection. By Arthur A. Allen. Paintings by Major Allan Brooks. LXXII, pp. 183-222, 4 ills. in black and white, 101 portraits in color, Aug., 1937

SANDROF, SAMUEL:

The Worm Turns. By Samuel Sandrof. LXXXIX, pp. 775-786, 14 ills., June, 1946

SANDS, W. F.:

Mysterious Temples of the Jungle: The Prehistoric Ruins of Guatemala. By W. F. Sands. XXIV, pp. 325-338, 10 ills., Mar., 1913

SANDS:

Report on Auriferous Sands from Yakutat Bay (Alaska). By J. Stanley-Brown. III, pp. 196-198, May 29, 1891

See also Sand Dunes

SANDUSKY BAY, Ohio:

Submerged Valleys in Sandusky Bay. By Professor E. L. Moseley. XIII, pp. 398-403, 4 charts, Nov., 1902

SANDWICH, Massachusetts:

Cape Cod People and Places. By Wanda Burnett. LXXXIX, pp. 737-774, 17 ills. in black and white, 24 ills. in color, map, June, 1946

SANDWORMS:

The Worm Turns. By Samuel Sandrof. LXXXIX, pp. 775-786, 14 ills., June, 1946

SANFORD, GEORGE ALDEN:

A Vacation in a Fifteenth Century English Manor House. By George Alden Sanford. LIII, pp. 629-636, 8 ills., May, 1928

A Vacation in Holland. By George Alden Sanford. LVI, pp. 363-378, 6 ills. in black and white, 8 ills. in color, map, Sept., 1929

SANITATION:

Colossal Work in Baltimore. By Calvin W. Hendrick. XX, pp. 365-373, 6 ills., Apr., 1909

Conserving the Nation's Man Power: Disease Weakens Armies, Cripples Industry, Reduces Production. How the Government is Sanitating the Civil Zones Around Cantonment Areas. A Nation-wide Campaign for Health. By Rupert Blue. XXXII, pp. 255-278, 17 ills., Sept., 1917

Cooties and Courage. By Herbert Corey. XXXIII, pp. 495-509, 10 ills., June, 1918

Economic Loss to the People of the United States Through Insects That Carry Disease. By L. O. Howard. XX, pp. 735-749. Aug., 1909

Hospital Heroes Convict the Cootie. XXXIII, p. 510, June, 1918

New York—The Metropolis of Mankind. By William Joseph Showalter. XXXIV, pp. 1-49, 39 ills., July, 1918

Our Army Versus a Bacillus. By Alton G. Grinnell. XXIV, pp. 1146-1152, 5 ills., diagr., Oct., 1913

The Panama Canal. By Rear Admiral Colby M. Chester. XVI, pp. 445-467, 8 ills., Oct., 1905

Redeeming the Tropics. By William Joseph Showalter. XXV, pp. 344-364, 13 ills., Mar., 1914

SANTA BARBARA ISLANDS, California:

Early Voyages on the Northwestern Coast of America. By Professor George Davidson. V, pp. 235-256, Jan. 31, 1894

SANTA CATALINA (Island), California:

Santa Catalina—400 Years a Lure to California Travelers. 11 color photos by B. Anthony Stewart. LXXXI, pp. 81-88, Jan., 1942

SANTA FE, New Mexico:

New Mexico Melodrama. By Frederick Simpich. LXXIII, pp. 529-569, 19 ills. in black and white, 25 ills. in color, two-page map, May, 1938

The **SANTA FE TRAIL,** Path to Empire. By Frederick Simpich. LVI, pp. 213-252, 35 ills. in black and white, 12 ills. in color, map, Aug., 1929

SANTA MARIÁ (Seaplane):

By Seaplane to Six Continents: Cruising 60,000 Miles, Italian Argonauts of the Air See World Geography Unroll, and Break New Sky Trails Over Vast Brazilian Jungles. By Commander Francesco de Pinedo. LIV, pp. 247-301, 60 ills., two-page map, Sept., 1928

SANTA TECLA, El Salvador:

Coffee Is King in El Salvador. By Luis Marden. LXXXVI, pp. 575-616, 22 ills. in black and white, 27 ills. in color, map, Nov., 1944

SANTAREM, Brazil:

Air Cruising Through New Brazil: A National Geographic Reporter Spots Vast Resources Which the Republic's War Declaration Adds to Strength of United Nations. By Henry Albert Phillips. LXXXII, pp. 503-536, 32 ills., Oct., 1942

SANTIAGO, Chile:

Capital and Chief Seaport of Chile. By W. Robert Moore. LXXXVI, pp. 477-500, 15 ills. in black and white, 8 ills. in color, map, Oct., 1944

Twin Stars of Chile: Valparaiso, the Gateway, and Santiago, the Capital—Key Cities with a Progressive Present and a Romantic Past. By William Joseph Showalter. LV, pp. 197-247, 35 ills. in black and white, 25 ills. in color, Feb., 1929

SANTIAGO ATITLAN, Guatemala:

To Market in Guatemala. By Luis Marden. With 19 color photos by Giles Greville Healey and Charles S. Pineo. LXXXVIII, pp. 87-104, July, 1945

SANTO DOMINGO. *See* Dominican Republic

SANTORIN (Island), Aegean Sea:

The Isles of Greece. By Lt. Richard Stillwell, USNR. LXXXV, pp. 593-622, 11 ills. in black and white, 20 ills. in color, map, May, 1944

Santorin and Mýkonos, Aegean Gems. 8 color photos: 7 by B. Anthony Stewart. LXXVII, pp. 339-346, Mar., 1940

SANTOS, Brazil:

As São Paulo Grows: Half the World's Coffee Beans Flavor the Life and Speed the Growth of an Inland Brazil City. By W. Robert Moore. LXXV, pp. 657-688, 33 ills., map, May, 1939

SÃO PAULO (City), São Paulo, Brazil:

As São Paulo Grows: Half the World's Coffee Beans Flavor the Life and Speed the Growth of an Inland Brazil City. By W. Robert Moore. LXXV, pp. 657-688, 33 ills., map, May, 1939

See also São Paulo (State)

SÃO PAULO (State), Brazil:

Air Cruising Through New Brazil: A National Geographic Reporter Spots Vast Resources Which the Republic's War Declaration Adds to Strength of United Nations. By Henry Albert Phillips. LXXXII, pp. 503-536, 32 ills., Oct., 1942

Brazil's Potent Weapons. By W. Robert Moore. LXXXV, pp. 41-78, 16 ills. in black and white, 18 ills. in color, two-page map, Jan., 1944

SÃO PAULO (State), Brazil—*Continued*

A Visit to the Brazilian Coffee Country. By Robert De C. Ward. XXII, pp. 908-931, 19 ills., map, Oct., 1911

See also São Paulo (City)

SÃO TOMÉ (Island), Gulf of Guinea:

São Tomé, the Chocolate Island. By William Leon Smyser. LXXXIX, pp. 657-680, 23 ills., map, May, 1946

SAPELO ISLAND, Sea Islands, Georgia:

The Golden Isles of Guale. By W. Robert Moore. LXV, pp. 235-264, 35 ills., map, Feb., 1934

SARAWAK:

Colonial Government in Borneo. By James M. Hubbard. XI, pp. 359-363, Sept., 1900

Keeping House in Borneo. By Virginia Hamilton. LXXXVIII, pp. 293-324, 28 ills., map, Sept., 1945

Notes on the Sea Dyaks of Borneo. By Edwin H. Gomes. XXII, pp. 695-723, 26 ills., Aug., 1911

Sarawak: The Land of the White Rajahs. By Harrison W. Smith. XXXV, pp. 110-167, 58 ills., map, Feb., 1919

SARDINES:

Brittany: The Land of the Sardine. By Hugh M. Smith. XX, pp. 541-573, 23 ills., June, 1909

SARDINIA (Island), Mediterranean Sea:

The Island of Sardinia and Its People: Traces of Many Civilizations to Be Found in the Speech, Customs, and Costumes of This Picturesque Land. By Prof. Guido Costa. XLIII, pp. 1-75, 63 ills. in black and white, 16 ills. in color, maps, Jan., 1923

Little-Known Sardinia. By Helen Dunstan Wright. XXX, pp. 97-120, 23 ills., map, Aug., 1916

Where the Sard Holds Sway. By Colonel Luigi Pellerano. XLIX, pp. 464-474, ill. in black and white, 9 ills. in color, Apr., 1926

SARDINIAN Smiles. 16 color photos by Clifton Adams. XLIII, pp. 31-46, Jan., 1923

SARDIS (Ancient City):

The Buried Cities of Asia Minor. By Ernest L. Harris. XX, pp. 1-18, 10 ills., Jan., 1909

SARGASSO SEA:

Sindbads of Science: Narrative of a Windjammer's Specimen-Collecting Voyage to the Sargasso Sea, to Senegambian Africa and Among Islands of High Adventure in the South Atlantic. By George Finlay Simmons. LII, pp. 1-75, 89 ills., map, July, 1927

SARGENT, R. H.:

The Monarchs of Alaska. By R. H. Sargent. XX, pp. 610-623, 9 ills., July, 1909

SARICHEF'S Atlas, 1826. By Marcus Baker. XIII, pp. 86-92, Mar., 1902

SARK (Island), Channel Islands:

The Channel Islands. By Edith Carey. XXXVIII, pp. 143-164, 24 ills., map, Aug., 1920

SARK (Island), Channel Islands—*Continued*
The Feudal Isle of Sark: Where Sixteenth-Century Laws Are Still Observed. By Sibyl Hathaway (La Dame de Serk). LXII, pp. 101-119, 21 ills., map, July, 1932

SASKATCHEWAN (River), Canada:
The Mother of Rivers: An Account of a Photographic Expedition to the Great Columbia Ice Field of the Canadian Rockies. By Lewis R. Freeman. XLVII, pp. 377-446, 60 ills., maps, Apr., 1925
Included: Saskatchewan River
Sources of the Saskatchewan. By Walter D. Wilcox. X, pp. 113-134, 6 ills., chart, Apr., 1899

SASKATOON, Saskatchewan, Canada:
The First Alaskan Air Expedition. By Captain St. Clair Streett. XLI, pp. 499-552, 37 ills., map, May, 1922

SASSEVILLE, ERNEST DE:
Recent Explorations in Equatorial Africa. (By Ernest de Sasseville). VIII, pp. 88-91, Mar., 1897
Return of the Hourst Niger Expedition. (By Ernest de Sasseville). VIII, pp. 24-25, Jan., 1897
Sheik Said. (By Ernest de Sasseville). VIII, pp. 155-156, May, 1897

AL SAUD, ABDUL AZIZ (King of Saudi Arabia):
Guest in Saudi Arabia. By Maynard Owen Williams. LXXXVIII, pp. 463-487, 24 ills., map, Oct., 1945

SAUDI ARABIA:
Damascus and Mecca Railway. XII, p. 408, Nov., 1901
Guest in Saudi Arabia. By Maynard Owen Williams. LXXXVIII, pp. 463-487, 24 ills., map, Oct., 1945
Mecca the Mystic: A New Kingdom Within Arabia. By S. M. Zwemer. XXXII, pp. 157-172, 13 ills., Aug., 1917
One Thousand Miles of Railway Built for Pilgrims and Not for Dividends (Damascus to Mecca). By Colonel F. R. Maunsell. XX, pp. 156-172, 12 ills., map, Feb., 1909
Pilgrims' Progress to Mecca. 22 ills. in duotone: 18 by Oscar Marcus. LXXII, pp. 627-642, Nov., 1937
The Rise of the New Arab Nation. By Frederick Simpich. XXXVI, pp. 369-393, 17 ills., map, Nov., 1919
An Unbeliever Joins the Hadj: On the Age-Old Pilgrimage to Mecca, Babies Are Born, Elders Die, and Families May Halt a Year to Earn Funds in Distant Lands. By Owen Tweedy. LXV, pp. 761-789, 30 ills., map, June, 1934
A Visit to Three Arab Kingdoms: Transjordania, Iraq, and the Hedjaz Present Many Problems to European Powers. By Junius B. Wood. XLIII, pp. 535-568, 30 ills., map, May, 1923
See also Jauf (Al Jawf)

SAUK AND FOX (Indian Tribe):
America's First Settlers, the Indians. By Matthew W. Stirling. Paintings by W. Langdon Kihn. LXXII, pp. 535-596, 34 ills. in black and white, 24 ills. in color, Nov., 1937

SAUNTERING Through the Land of Roger Williams. 14 color photos by Clifton Adams. LX, pp. 311-318, Sept., 1931

SAUSSURE, H. B. DE:
The Ascent of Mont Blanc. By Walter Woodburn Hyde. XXIV, pp. 861-942, 69 ills., Aug., 1913

SAVING the Ducks and Geese. By Wells W. Cooke. XXIV, pp. 361-380, 7 ills., 7 maps, Mar., 1913

SAVING the Forests. By Herbert A. Smith. XVIII, pp. 519-534, 7 ills., Aug., 1907

SAVING the Redwoods. By Madison Grant. XXXVII, pp. 519-536, 10 ills., June, 1920

SAVOY, PRINCE OF. *See* Abruzzi, Duke of the

SAYRE, J. D.:
The Valley of Ten Thousand Smokes: An Account of the Discovery and Exploration of the Most Wonderful Volcanic Region in the World. By Robert F. Griggs. XXXIII, pp. 115-169, 46 ills., map, panorama, Feb., 1918

SCAT. *See* South Pacific Combat Air Transport

SCENE in Liberia. 4 ills. XX, pp. 298-301, Mar., 1909

The **SCENERY** of North America. By James Bryce. XLI, pp. 339-389, 45 ills., Apr., 1922

SCENES Along the Byways of Hellas. 13 color photos by Maynard Owen Williams. LVIII, pp. 689-696, Dec., 1930

SCENES Among the High Cascades in Central Oregon. By Ira A. Williams. XXIII, pp. 579-592, 11 ills., June, 1912

SCENES and Round-Ups of the Beaver State (Oregon). 24 color photos by Amos Burg. LXV, pp. 181-212, Feb., 1934

SCENES and Shrines of the Cavalier Country (Virginia). 13 color photos by Charles Martin, Edwin L. Wisherd, Jacob Gayer, Clifton Adams. LV, pp. 425-432, Apr., 1929

SCENES from America's Southwest. 14 ills. XXXIX, pp. 651-664, June, 1921

"**SCENES** from Every Land" (National Geographic Society Publication). XVIII, p. 348, May, 1907; p. 744, ill., Nov., 1907

SCENES from France. 16 ills. XL, pp. 29-44, July, 1921

SCENES from Greenland. 15 ills. XX, pp. 877-891, Oct., 1909

SCENES from North Africa. XVIII, pp. 615-619, 4 ills. from David Fairchild, Sept., 1907

SCENES from the Land Where Everybody Dresses in White (Korea). Photos by Rev. J. Z. Moore. XIX, pp. 871-877, 10 ills., Dec., 1908

SCENES in Asia Minor. 35 ills., map. XX, pp. 173-193, Feb., 1909

SCENES in Italy. 12 ills. XXI, pp. 321-332, Apr., 1910

SCENES in Korea and China. 39 photos, hand-tinted, by William W. Chapin. XXI, pp. 903-926, Nov., 1910

SCENES in Many Lands (People and Places). 16 ills. in color by Franklin Price Knott. XXX, pp. 233-248, Sept., 1916

SCENES in Out-of-the-Way Places. 7 ills. XXIV, pp. 854-860, July, 1913

SCENES in Scotland (Gems from Scotland). 16 ills. XXXII, pp. 519-534, Nov.-Dec., 1917

SCENES in South America. 16 ills. XL, pp. 375-390, Oct., 1921

SCENES in Switzerland. 13 ills. XXI, pp. 257-268, Mar., 1910

SCENES in the British Isles. 16 ills. in duotone by A. W. Cutler. XXVIII, pp. 551-566, Dec., 1915

SCENES in the Celestial Republic (China). 16 ills. in duotone. XLIX, pp. 217-232, Feb., 1926

SCENES in the Fortunate Isles (Canary Islands). 12 color photos by Wilhelm Tobien. LVII, pp. 599-606, May, 1930

SCENES of Beauty in Copper Land (Chile). 25 color photos by Jacob Gayer. LV, pp. 199-214, Feb., 1929

SCENES of Sunny Africa. 20 ills. in duotone. LXVII, pp. 735-750, June, 1935

SCENES on High Veld and Low (Union of South Africa). 13 color photos by Melville Chater. LIX, pp. 493-500, Apr., 1931

SCENIC Glories of Western United States. 12 color photos by Fred Payne Clatworthy. LVI, pp. 223-230, Aug., 1929

SCENIC Resources of the Dominican Republic. 28 color photos by Jacob Gayer. LIX, pp. 81-104, Jan., 1931

SCHAEFFER, CLAUDE F. A.:

A New Alphabet of the Ancients Is Unearthed: An Inconspicuous Mound in Northern Syria Yields Archeological Treasures of Far-reaching Significance. By F. A. Schaeffer. LVIII, pp. 477-516, 47 ills., map, Oct., 1930

Secrets from Syrian Hills: Explorations Reveal World's Earliest Known Alphabet, Deciphered from Schoolboy Slates and Dictionaries of 3,000 Years Ago. By Claude F. A. Schaeffer. LXIV, pp. 97-126, 40 ills., map, July, 1933

SCHANTZ, ORPHEUS MOYER:

Indiana's Unrivaled Sand-Dunes—A National Park Opportunity. By Orpheus Moyer Schantz. XXXV, pp. 430-441, 18 ills., May, 1919

SCHILLINGS, C. G.:

Flashlights from the Jungle (Extracted from a Publication by C. G. Schillings). XVIII, pp. 534-548, 11 ills., Aug., 1907

SCHLESWIG-HOLSTEIN (Region), Germany. *See* Helgoland

SCHMECKEBIER, L. F.:

Our National Parks (U. S.). By L. F. Schmeckebier. XXIII, pp. 531-579, 41 ills., map, June, 1912

SCHMITT, WALDO L.:

A Voyage to the Island Home of Robinson Crusoe (Juan Fernández). By Waldo L. Schmitt. LIV, pp. 353-370, 24 ills., Sept., 1928

SCHNEIDER, JOHN E.:

Uncle Sam's Icebox Outposts. 19 color photos by John E. Schneider and Robert B. Sykes, Jr. XC, pp. 473-496, Oct., 1946

SCHOEDSACK, ERNEST B.:

Two Fighting Tribes of the Sudan. By Merian C. Cooper. Photos by Ernest B. Schoedsack. LVI, pp. 465-486, 27 ills., map, Oct., 1929

The Warfare of the Jungle Folk: Campaigning Against Tigers, Elephants, and Other Wild Animals in Northern Siam. By Merian C. Cooper. Photos by Ernest B. Schoedsack LIII, pp. 233-268, 33 ills., Feb., 1928

SCHOOLS:

Turkey Goes to School. By Maynard Owen Williams. LV, pp. 95-108, 17 ills., Jan., 1929

See also Public Schools; Training Schools; U. S. Military Academy; U. S. Naval Academy; Universities and Colleges; *and* Education

SCHOONERS:

Life on the Grand Banks: An Account of the Sailor-Fishermen Who Harvest the Shoal Waters of North America's Eastern Coasts. By Frederick William Wallace. XL, pp. 1-28, 29 ills., July, 1921

Newfoundland, North Atlantic Rampart: From the "First Base of American Defense" Planes Fly to Britain's Aid over Stout Fishing Schooners of the Grand Banks. By George Whiteley, Jr. LXXX, pp. 111-140, 26 ills., map, July, 1941

See also Sealing Schooners; *and Adams; Bowdoin; Effie M. Morrissey; Kinkajou; Yankee*

SCHOTT, C. A.:

Recent Contributions to Our Knowledge of the Earth's Shape and Size, by the United States Coast and Geodetic Survey. By C. A. Schott. XII, pp. 36-41, ill., chart, Jan., 1901

SCHRADER, F. C.:

The Cape Nome Gold District (Alaska). By F. C. Schrader. XI, pp. 15-23, 3 ills., map, Jan., 1900

SCHULTZ, LEONARD P.:

Fishing in Pacific Coast Streams. By Leonard P. Schultz. Paintings by Hashime Murayama. LXXV, pp. 185-212, 10 ills. in black and white, 44 portraits in color, Feb., 1939

Treasures of the Pacific: Marine Fishes and Fisheries Yield Vast Wealth from Alaska to Baja California. By Leonard P. Schultz. Paintings by Hashime Murayama. LXXIV, pp. 463-498, 10 ills. in black and white, 31 portraits in color, Oct., 1938

SCHURZ, W. L.:

The Amazon, Father of Waters: The Earth's Mightiest River Drains a Basin of More Than 2,700,000 Square Miles, from Which Came Originally the World's Finest Rubber. By W. L. Schurz. XLIX, pp. 445-463, 15 ills., Apr., 1926

SCHUYLER, MONTGOMERY:

Russia's Democrats. By Montgomery Schuyler. XXXI, pp. 210-240, 25 ills., Mar., 1917

SCHWAB, CHARLES M.:

Our Industrial Victory. By Charles M. Schwab. XXXIV, pp. 212-229, 17 ills., Sept., 1918

SCHWARTZ, WILLIAM LEONARD:

Peacetime Rambles in the Ryukyus. By William Leonard Schwartz. LXXXVII, pp. 543-561, 12 ills., maps, May, 1945

SCHWINN, GRETCHEN:

We Escape from Madrid. By Gretchen Schwinn. LXXI, pp. 251-268, 15 ills., Feb., 1937

SCIDMORE, ELIZA RUHAMAH:

Adam's Second Eden (Ceylon). By Eliza Ruhamah Scidmore. XXIII, pp. 105-173, 206, 61 ills., Feb., 1912

Archæology in the Air. By Eliza R. Scidmore. XVIII, pp. 151-163, 11 ills., Mar., 1907

The Bathing and Burning Ghats at Benares. By Eliza R. Scidmore. XVIII, pp. 118-128, 7 ills., Feb., 1907

The Discovery of Glacier Bay, Alaska. By Eliza Ruhamah Scidmore. VII, pp. 140-146, ill., map, Apr., 1896

The Greatest Hunt in the World (Elephant Hunting). By Eliza Ruhamah Scidmore. XVII, pp. 673-692, 17 ills., Dec., 1906

International Geographic Conference in Chicago, July 27-28, 1893: Minutes of the Conference. F. H. Newell and Eliza R. Scidmore, Secretaries. V, pp. 101-111, Jan. 31, 1894

Koyasan, the Japanese Valhalla. By Eliza R. Scidmore. XVIII, pp. 650-670, 14 ills., Oct., 1907

Mrs. Bishop's "The Yangtze Valley and Beyond." By Eliza Ruhamah Scidmore. XI, pp. 366-368, Sept., 1900

The Mt. St. Elias Expedition of Prince Luigi Amadeo of Savoy, 1897. (By E.R.S.). IX, pp. 93-96, Mar., 1898

Mukden, the Manchu Home, and Its Great Art Museum. By Eliza R. Scidmore. XXI, pp. 289-320, 30 ills., Apr., 1910

The Northwest Passes to the Yukon. By Eliza Ruhamah Scidmore. IX, pp. 105-112, 3 ills., Apr., 1898

The Recent Earthquake Wave on the Coast of Japan. By Eliza Ruhamah Scidmore. VII, pp. 285-289, 4 ills., foldout map, Sept., 1896

Recent Explorations in Alaska. By Eliza Ruhamah Scidmore. V, pp. 173-179, Jan. 31, 1894

Reports of Sealing Schooners Cruising in the Neighborhood of Tuscarora Deep in May and June, 1896. (By Eliza Ruhamah Scidmore). VII, pp. 310-312, Sept., 1896

SCIDMORE, ELIZA RUHAMAH—*Continued*

The Stikine River in 1898 (British Columbia). By Eliza Ruhamah Scidmore. X, pp. 1-15, 4 ills., Jan., 1899

The Tsung-Li-Yamen (Foreign Office, China). (By Miss E. R. Scidmore). XI, pp. 291-292, diagr., map, July, 1900

Young Japan. By Eliza R. Scidmore. XXVI, pp. 36-38, 54-64, 11 ills. in color, July, 1914

Japan. 11 photos, hand-tinted, by author, pp. 54-64

See also NGS: Secretary

SCIENCE:

The American Association for the Advancement of Science. (By G. H. G.). X, pp. 355-359, Sept., 1899

Chemists Make a New World: Creating Hitherto Unknown Raw Materials, Science Now Disrupts Old Trade Routes and Revamps the World Map of Industry. By Frederick Simpich. LXXVI, pp. 601-640, 22 ills. in black and white, 26 ills. in color, Nov., 1939

Discovery and Invention. By Alexander Graham Bell. XXV, pp. 649-655, June, 1914

Prizes for the Inventor: Some of the Problems Awaiting Solution. By Alexander Graham Bell. XXXI, pp. 131-146, 7 ills., Feb., 1917

Science Works for Mankind. 16 ills. in color from paintings by Thornton Oakley. LXXXVIII, pp. 737-752, Dec., 1945

A Wonderland of Science. XXVII, pp. 153-169, 15 ills., Feb., 1915

Your New World of Tomorrow. By F. Barrows Colton. LXXXVIII, pp. 385-410, 25 ills., Oct., 1945

See also the various branches of science

SCIENTIFIC Aspects of the MacMillan Arctic Expedition. XLVIII, pp. 349-354, 5 ills., Sept., 1925

The **SCIENTIFIC** Results of the World-Record Stratosphere Flight. By Capt. Albert W. Stevens. LXIX, pp. 693-712, 15 ills., pictorial supplement, May, 1936

SCIENTIFIC Work of Mount Weather Meteorological Research Observatory. By Professor Frank H. Bigelow. XV, pp. 442-445, Nov., 1904

SCIENTIFIC Work of the National Geographic Society's Eclipse Expedition to Norfolk, Va. By Simon Newcomb. XI, pp. 321-324, Aug., 1900

The **SCILLIES:** Isles of Wrecks and Golden Daffodils. 13 color photos by B. Anthony Stewart, Maynard Owen Williams, W. Robert Moore. LXXIV, pp. 759-766, Dec., 1938

SCILLY ISLES, England:

The Garden Isles of Scilly: Geologists May Throw Stones at Legend of Lost Lyonnesse, But Natives Grow Flowers in Glass Houses for London. By W. Robert Moore. LXXIV, pp. 755-774, 9 ills. in black and white, 13 ills. in color, map, Dec., 1938

SCISCO, L. D.:

Gomez and the New York Gulf. (By L. D. Scisco). IX, pp. 371-373, Aug., 1898

The **SCOPE** and Value of Arctic Explorations. By General A. W. Greely. VII, pp. 32-39, Jan., 1896

SCOTLAND:

Bonnie Scotland, Postwar Style. By Isobel Wylie Hutchison. LXXXIX, pp. 545-601, 14 ills. in black and white, 38 ills. in color, two-page map, May, 1946

Gems from Scotland. 16 ills. XXXII, pp. 519-534, Nov.-Dec., 1917

Great Britain on Parade. By Maynard Owen Williams. LXVIII, pp. 137-184, 40 ills. in black and white, 11 ills. in color, Aug., 1935

Low Road, High Road, Around Dundee. By Maurice P. Dunlap. LXIX, pp. 547-576, 35 ills., map, Apr., 1936

The Ordnance Survey of Great Britain—Its History and Object. By Josiah Pierce, Jr. II, pp. 243-260, Aug., 1890

The Orkneys and Shetlands—A Mysterious Group of Islands. By Charles S. Olcott. XXXIX, pp. 197-228, 33 ills., Feb., 1921

The Races of Europe. By Edwin A. Grosvenor. XXXIV, pp. 441-534, 62 ills., diagr. and index, maps, map supplement, Dec., 1918

Scotland in Wartime. By Isobel Wylie Hutchison. LXXXIII, pp. 723-743, 19 ills., June, 1943

See also Edinburgh

SCOTT, CHARLES F.:

The Annual Dinner of the National Geographic Society (Speech by Charles F. Scott). XVII, pp. 22-37, Jan., 1906

SCOTT, EMMETT J.:

Conditions in Liberia. By Roland P. Folkner, George Sale, Emmett J. Scott. XXI, pp. 729-741, 9 ills., Sept., 1910

SCOTT, SIR GEORGE:

Among the Hill Tribes of Burma—An Ethnological Thicket. By Sir George Scott. XLI, pp. 293-321, 22 ills., Mar., 1922

SCOTT, GEORGE W.:

Kano, Mud-made City. 10 color photos by George W. Scott and K. S. Twitchell. LXXXV, pp. 545-552, May, 1944

SCOTT, JOHN:

"Magnetic City" (Magnitogorsk), Core of Valiant Russia's Industrial Might. By John Scott. LXXXIII, pp. 525-556, 27 ills., two-page map, May, 1943

SCOTT, ROBERT F.:

The British Antarctic Expedition. XII, pp. 339-345, Sept., 1901

The British South Polar Expedition. XIV, pp. 210-212, May, 1903

An Ice Wrapped Continent. (By G. H. G.). XVIII, pp. 95-117, 20 ills., map, Feb., 1907

The Lure of the Land of Ice. 16 photos by Herbert G. Ponting, official photographer of the British Antarctic Expedition under Capt. Robert F. Scott. XLV, pp. 255-270, Mar., 1924

Some Recent English Statements About the Antarctic. (By Edwin Swift Balch). XV, p. 266, June, 1904

SCOUTS. *See* Boy Scouts; Girl Scouts

SCRIVEN, GEORGE P.:

Recent Observations in Albania. By Brig. Gen. George P. Scriven. XXXIV, pp. 90-114, 21 ills., map, Aug., 1918

SCULPTURE:

China's Great Wall of Sculpture: Man-hewn Caves and Countless Images Form a Colossal Art Wonder of Early Buddhism. By Mary Augusta Mullikin. Paintings by author and Anna M. Hotchkis. LXXIII, pp. 313-348, 23 ills. in black and white, 10 ills. in color, map, Mar., 1938

Discovering the New World's Oldest Dated Work of Man: A Maya Monument Inscribed 291 B. C. is Unearthed Near a Huge Stone Head by a Geographic-Smithsonian Expedition in Mexico. By Matthew W. Stirling. LXXVI, pp. 183-218, 40 ills., map, Aug., 1939

Discovering the Oldest Statues in the World: A Daring Explorer Swims Through a Subterranean River of the Pyrenees and Finds Rock Carvings Made 20,000 Years Ago. By Norbert Casteret. XLVI, pp. 123-152, 24 ills., maps, Aug., 1924

Exploring the Secrets of Persepolis. By Charles Breasted. LXIV, pp. 381-420, 48 ills., plan, map, Oct., 1933

Great Stone Faces of Easter Island. 11 ills. LXXXV, pp. 225-232, Feb., 1944

Great Stone Faces of the Mexican Jungle: Five Colossal Heads and Numerous Other Monuments of Vanished Americans Are Excavated by the Latest National Geographic-Smithsonian Expedition. By Matthew W. Stirling. LXXVIII, pp. 309-334, 26 ills., map, Sept., 1940

The Greek Bronzes of Tunisia. By Frank Edward Johnson. XXIII, pp. 89-103, 11 ills., Jan., 1912

Italy's Monuments Tell Rome's Magnificence. 8 photos: 7 by B. Anthony Stewart. LXXVII, pp. 371-378, Mar., 1940

Modern Odyssey in Classic Lands: Troy's Treasures, Athens' Parthenon, and Rome's First "Broad Way" Influence Today's Banks, Costumes, Jewelry, and Railroad Timetables. By Maynard Owen Williams. LXXVII, pp. 291-337, 27 ills. in black and white, 22 ills. in color, Mar., 1940

The Mystery of Easter Island. By Mrs. Scoresby Routledge. XL, pp. 629-646, 13 ills., map, Dec., 1921

The Nation's Capital by Night. By Volkmar Wentzel. With 16 photos in duotone by author. LXXVII, pp. 514-530, Apr., 1940

The Smallest State in the World: Vatican City on Its 108 Acres Is a Complete Sovereignty Internationally Recognized. By W. Coleman Nevils. LXXV, pp. 377-412, 37 ills., two-page map, Mar., 1939

Stone Idols of the Andes Reveal a Vanished People: Remarkable Relics of One of the Oldest Aboriginal Cultures of America Are Unearthed in Colombia's San Agustín Region. By Hermann von Walde-Waldegg. LXXVII, pp. 627-647, 22 ills., map, May, 1940

Storied Islands of the South Sea. 20 color photos by Irving Johnson, Malcolm Evans, and others. LXXXI, pp. 9-40, Jan., 1942

SCULPTURED Gates to English Learning (Cambridge University). 19 color photos by B. Anthony Stewart. LXXXIX, pp. 417-440, Apr., 1946

SEA CAPTAINS:

American Pathfinders in the Pacific. By William H. Nicholas. LXXXIX, pp. 617-640, 17 ills., two-page map, May, 1946

SEA Creatures of Our Atlantic Shores (Mollusks, Crustaceans, etc.). By Roy Waldo Miner. Paintings by Else Bostelmann. LXX, pp. 209-231, 8 ills. in black and white, 8 ills. in color, chart, Aug., 1936

SEA ELEPHANTS. *See* Elephant Seals

SEA Floor Aquarelles from Tongareva. 8 ills. in color from paintings by Else Bostelmann under direction Roy W. Miner. LXXIV, pp. 383-390, Sept., 1938

The **SEA** Fogs of San Francisco. XII, pp. 108-114, 5 ills., Mar., 1901

SEA ISLANDS, Georgia:

The Golden Isles of Guale. By W. Robert Moore. LXV, pp. 235-264, 35 ills., map, Feb., 1934

The **SEA-KINGS** of Crete. By Rev. James Baikie. XXIII, pp. 1-25, 13 ills., Jan., 1912

SEA RESCUES:

They Survived at Sea. By Lt. Comdr. Samuel F. Harby. LXXXVII, pp. 617-640, 22 ills., May, 1945

SEABEES:

Your Navy as Peace Insurance. By Fleet Admiral Chester W. Nimitz. LXXXIX, pp. 681-736, 32 ills. in black and white, 26 ills. in color, June, 1946

SEAFARERS of South Celebes. By G. E. P. Collins. LXXXVII, pp. 53-78, 25 ills., map, Jan., 1945

The **SEALING** Saga of Newfoundland. By Captain Robert A. Bartlett. LVI, pp. 91-130, 44 ills., July, 1929

SEALING SCHOONERS:

Reports of Sealing Schooners Cruising in the Neighborhood of Tuscarora Deep in May and June, 1896. (By Eliza Ruhamah Scidmore). VII, pp. 310-312, Sept., 1896

The Sealing Saga of Newfoundland. By Captain Robert A. Bartlett. LVI, pp. 91-130, 44 ills., July, 1929

SEALS (Mammals):

Cruise of the *Kinkajou:* Among Desert Islands of Mexico Voyagers Find Outdoor Laboratories for the Naturalist and Ideal Fishing Grounds for the Sportsman. By Alfred M. Bailey. LXXX, pp. 339-366, 13 ills. in black and white, 12 ills. in color, map, Sept., 1941

A Land of Eternal Warring (Labrador). By Sir Wilfrid T. Grenfell. XXI, pp. 665-690, 24 ills., Aug., 1910

Making the Fur Seal Abundant. By Hugh M. Smith. XXII, pp. 1139-1165, 18 ills., map, Dec., 1911

SEALS (Mammals)—*Continued*

The Sealing Saga of Newfoundland. By Captain Robert A. Bartlett. LVI, pp. 91-130, 44 ills., July, 1929

South Georgia, an Outpost of the Antarctic. By Robert Cushman Murphy. XLI, pp. 409-444, 41 ills., maps, Apr., 1922

SEALS of Our Nation, States, and Territories. By Elizabeth W. King. Paintings by Carlotta Gonzales Lahey, Irvin E. Alleman, Theodora Price. XC, pp. 1-42, 14 ills. in black and white, 84 ills. in color, July, 1946

Contents: Seals of the States and the District of Columbia; Seals of the Territories, Island Possessions, the Canal Zone, and the Philippine Commonwealth; Great Seal of the United States and Other Federal Seals; Seals of the President and of the Government Departments

SEAMAN, LOUIS LIVINGSTON:

Observations on the Russo-Japanese War, in Japan and Manchuria. By Dr. Louis Livingston Seaman. XVI, pp. 80-82, Feb., 1905

The Wonders of the Mosi-oa-Tunga: The Falls of the Zambesi. By Louis Livingston Seaman. XXII, pp. 561-571, 6 ills., June, 1911

SEAMANSHIP:

The Law of Storms, Considered with Special Reference to the North Atlantic. By Everett Hayden. II, pp. 199-211, ill., 3 diagrs., 3 foldout diagrs., foldout charts, July, 1890

SEAPLANES:

The Azores: Picturesque and Historic Half-way House of American Transatlantic Aviators. By Arminius T. Haeberle. XXXV, pp. 514-545, 26 ills., map, June, 1919

Seaplane to Six Continents: Cruising 60,000 Miles, Italian Argonauts of the Air See World Geography Unroll, and Break New Sky Trails Over Vast Brazilian Jungles. By Commander Francesco de Pinedo. LIV, pp. 247-301, 60 ills., two-page map, Sept., 1928

Exploring the Valley of the Amazon in a Hydroplane: Twelve Thousand Miles of Flying Over the World's Greatest River and Greatest Forest to Chart the Unknown Parima River from the Sky. By Captain Albert W. Stevens. XLIX, pp. 353-420, 86 ills., map, Apr., 1926

Flying. By Gilbert Grosvenor. LXIII, pp. 585-630, 33 ills. in black and white, 17 ills. in duotone, May, 1933

Flying Around the North Atlantic. By Anne Morrow Lindbergh. Foreword by Charles A. Lindbergh. LXVI, pp. 259-337, 82 ills., maps (1 two-page), Sept., 1934

Flying Over the Arctic. By Lieutenant Commander Richard E. Byrd. XLVIII, pp. 519-532, 10 ills., Nov., 1925

Note: Loening Amphibians used in exploratory flights

Flying the Pacific. By William Burke Miller. LXX, pp. 665-707, 39 ills., Dec., 1936

How the United States Grew. By McFall Kerbey. LXIII, pp. 631-649, 17 ills., map, May, 1933

SEAPLANES—*Continued*

Into Primeval Papua by Seaplane: Seeking Disease-resisting Sugar Cane, Scientists Find Neolithic Man in Unmapped Nooks of Sorcery and Cannibalism. By E. W. Brandes. LVI, pp. 253-332, 98 ills., map, Sept., 1929

Seeing 3,000 Years of History in Four Hours: A Panorama of Ancient, Medieval, and Modern Events Against a Background of Mythology Unfolds During an Airplane Journey from Constantinople to Athens. By Maynard Owen Williams. LIV, pp. 719-739, 24 ills., map, Dec., 1928

Unknown New Guinea: Circumnavigating the World in a Flying Boat, American Scientists Discover a Valley of 60,000 People Never Before Seen by White Men. By Richard Archbold. LXXIX, pp. 315-344, 28 ills., map, Mar., 1941

SEATTLE, Washington:

Washington, the Evergreen State: The Amazing Commonwealth of the Pacific Northwest Which Has Emerged from the Wilderness in a Span of Fifty Years. By Leo A. Borah. LXIII, pp. 131-196, 50 ills. in black and white, 26 ills. in color, two-page map, Feb., 1933

SEAWEEDS:

The Fisheries of Japan. By Hugh M. Smith. XVI, pp. 201-220, 13 ills., May, 1905

Seaweeds of the United States. XVI, p. 244, ills., May, 1905

Undersea Gardens of the North Atlantic Coast. 8 ills. in color from paintings by Else Bostelmann under direction Roy W. Miner. LXX, pp. 217-224, Aug., 1936

SECOND MARINE DIVISION, U. S.:

Gilbert Islands in the Wake of Battle. By W. Robert Moore. LXXXVII, pp. 129-162, 11 ills. in black and white, 19 ills. in color, map, Feb., 1945

The **SECRET** of the Southwest Solved by Talkative Tree Rings: Horizons of American History Are Carried Back to A. D. 700 and a Calendar for 1,200 Years Established by National Geographic Society Expeditions. By Andrew Ellicott Douglass. LVI, pp. 737-770, 33 ills., map, Dec., 1929

SECRETS from Syrian Hills: Explorations Reveal World's Earliest Known Alphabet, Deciphered from Schoolboy Slates and Dictionaries of 3,000 Years Ago. By Claude F. A. Schaeffer. LXIV, pp. 97-126, 40 ills., map, July, 1933

SECRETS of Washington's Lure. 15 color photos by Staff Photographers. LVII, pp. 377-384, Mar., 1930

SEED Farms in California. By A. J. Wells. XXIII, pp. 515-530, 14 ills., May, 1912

SEEING America from the "Shenandoah": An Account of the Record-making 9,000-mile Flight from the Atlantic to the Pacific Coast and Return in the Navy's American-built American-manned Airship. By Junius B. Wood. XLVII, pp. 1-47, 39 ills., diagr., map, Jan., 1925

SEEING America with Lindbergh: The Record of a Tour of More than 20,000 Miles by Airplane Through Forty-eight States on Schedule Time. By Lieutenant Donald E. Keyhoe. LIII, pp. 1-46, 46 ills., map, Jan., 1928

SEEING EYE (School), Morristown, New Jersey:

Dogs of Duty and Devotion. By Frederick G. Vosburgh. LXXX, pp. 769-774, 3 ills., Dec., 1941

SEEING Our Spanish Southwest. By Frederick Simpich. LXXVII, pp. 711-756, 25 ills. in black and white, 17 ills. in duotone, map supplement, June, 1940

SEEING Paris on a 48-Hour Pass. 12 ills. in color from U. S. Army official photos. LXXXVII, pp. 401-412, Apr., 1945

SEEING the World from the Air. By Sir Alan J. Cobham. LIII, pp. 349-384, 37 ills., map, Mar., 1928

SEEING 3,000 Years of History in Four Hours: A Panorama of Ancient, Medieval, and Modern Events Against a Background of Mythology Unfolds During an Airplane Journey from Constantinople to Athens. By Maynard Owen Williams. LIV, pp. 719-739, 24 ills., map, Dec., 1928

SEEKING the Mountains of Mystery: An Expedition on the China-Tibet Frontier to the Unexplored Amnyi Machen Range, One of Whose Peaks Rivals Everest. By Joseph F. Rock. LVII, pp. 131-185, 54 ills., two-page map, Feb., 1930

SEEKING the Smallest Feathered Creatures: Humming Birds, Peculiar to the New World, Are Found from Canada and Alaska to the Straits of Magellan. Swifts and Goatsuckers, Their Nearest Relatives. By Alexander Wetmore. Paintings by Maj. Allan Brooks. LXII, pp. 65-89, 9 ills. in black and white, 36 ills. in color, July, 1932

SEGERSTROM, KENNETH:

Down Mexico's Río Balsas. 9 color photos by John W. Webber, Kenneth Segerstrom, Jack Breed. XC, pp. 257-264, Aug., 1946

SEILER, DAYTON:

Indian Haven—Off the San Blas Coast (Mulatas Archipelago). 12 color photos by Lieutenant Dayton Seiler. LXXIX, pp. 209-216, Feb., 1941

SEINE (River), France:

The Beauties of France. By Arthur Stanley Riggs. XXVIII, pp. 391-491, 73 ills. in black and white, 16 ills. in color, map, Nov., 1915

The Seine, the Meuse, and the Moselle. (Part I). By William M. Davis. VII, pp. 189-202, ill., 7 maps, June, 1896

The Seine, the Meuse, and the Moselle. (Part) II. By William M. Davis. VII, pp. 228-238, table, 4 maps, July, 1896

SEISMOLOGY:

Charting a World at War. By William H. Nicholas. LXXXVI, pp. 617-640, 23 ills., drawing, Nov., 1944

SEISMOLOGY—*Continued*

How the Earth Telegraphed Its Tokyo Quake to Washington. By the Rev. Francis A. Tondorf. XLIV, pp. 453-454, ill., Oct., 1923

The Record of the Great Earthquake Written in Washington by the Seismograph of the U. S. Weather Bureau. By C. F. Marvin. XVII, pp. 296-298, May, 1906

The San Francisco Earthquake of April 18, 1906, as Recorded by the Coast and Geodetic Survey Magnetic Observatories. By L. A. Bauer and J. E. Burbank. XVII, pp. 298-300, tables, May, 1906

See also Earthquakes

SELENIUM (Chemical Element):

Discovery and Invention. By Alexander Graham Bell. XXV, pp. 649-655, June, 1914

SELEUCUS I (King of Syria):

Antioch the Glorious. By William H. Hall. XXXVIII, pp. 81-103, 20 ills., map, Aug., 1920

SELINUS, Sicily:

The Ruins at Selinus. (By Marion Crawford). XX, p. 117, Jan., 1909

SELKIRK MOUNTAINS, British Columbia-U. S.:

Some Tramps Across the Glaciers and Snowfields of British Columbia. By Howard Palmer. XXI, pp. 457-487, 25 ills., June, 1910

SELLA, VITTORIO:

Africa: Cairo to Cape Town, Overland: An Adventurous Journey of 135 Days, Made by an American and His Wife, Through the Length of the African Continent. By Felix Shay. XLVII, pp. 123-260, 118 ills., map, Feb., 1925

Amid the Snows and Swamps of Tropical Africa. 16 photos: 7 by Vittorio Sella, pp. 163-178

African Scenes from the Equator to the Cape. 16 photos: 5 by Vittorio Sella. XLII, pp. 431-446, Oct., 1922

Daghestan: An Island in the Sea of History: The Highlands of Daghestan. By George Kennan. XXIV, pp. 1087-1140, 49 ills., map, Oct., 1913

Included: 6 photos by Vittorio Sella

The Fight at the Timber-Line. By John Oliver La Gorce. XLII, pp. 165-196, 32 ills., Aug., 1922

Included: 9 photos by Vittorio Sella

Mountain Scenes. 16 photos: 11 by Vittorio Sella. XXVII, pp. 187-202, Feb., 1915

U. S. S. R.: Young Russia: The Land of Unlimited Possibilities. By Gilbert H. Grosvenor. XXVI, pp. 421-520, 85 ills. in black and white, 17 ills. in color, Nov., 1914

Included: 4 photos by Vittorio Sella

The World's Highest Altitudes and First Ascents. By Charles E. Fay. XX, pp. 493-530, 25 ills., June, 1909

Included: 9 photos by Vittorio Sella

SEMINOLE INDIANS:

The Five Civilized Tribes and the Survey of Indian Territory. By C. H. Fitch. IX, pp. 481-491, 4 ills., map, Dec., 1898

SEMINOLE INDIANS—*Continued*

Indians of the Southeastern United States. By Matthew W. Stirling. Paintings by W. Langdon Kihn. LXXXIX, pp. 53-74, 8 ills. in black and white, 8 ills. in color, Jan., 1946

South Florida's Amazing Everglades: Encircled by Populous Places Is a Seldom-visited Area of Rare Birds, Prairies, Cowboys, and Teeming Wild Life of Big Cypress Swamp. By John O'Reilly. LXXVII, pp. 115-142, 26 ills., map, Jan., 1940

SENECA (Indian Tribe):

America's First Settlers, the Indians. By Matthew W. Stirling. Paintings by W. Langdon Kihn. LXXII, pp. 535-596, 34 ills. in black and white, 24 ills. in color, Nov., 1937

SENEGAL:

French West Africa in Wartime. By Paul M. Atkins. LXXXI, pp. 371-408, 37 ills., maps, Mar., 1942

See also Dakar

SEOUL (Keijo), Korea:

Chosen—Land of Morning Calm. By Mabel Craft Deering. LXIV, pp. 421-448, 20 ills. in black and white, 13 ills. in color, map, Oct., 1933

Glimpses of Korea and China. By William W. Chapin. XXI, pp. 895-934, 11 ills. in black and white, 39 ills. in color, Nov., 1910

Jap Rule in the Hermit Nation. By Willard Price. LXXXVIII, pp. 429-451, 19 ills., map, Oct., 1945

SEQUOIA NATIONAL PARK, California:

Among the Big Trees of California. By John R. White. LXVI, pp. 219-232, 14 ills., Aug., 1934

The Land of the Best. By Gilbert H. Grosvenor. XXIX, pp. 327-430, 71 ills. in black and white, 33 ills. in color, pictorial supplement, Apr., 1916

The Oldest Living Thing ("General Sherman Tree") (supplement)

The National Geographic Society Completes Its Gifts of Big Trees. XL, pp. 85-86, July, 1921

Our Big Trees Saved. XXXI, pp. 1-11, 10 ills., Jan., 1917

Our National Parks. By L. F. Schmeckebier. XXIII, pp. 531-579, 41 ills., map, June, 1912

SEQUOIAS (Trees):

Among the Big Trees of California. By John R. White. LXVI, pp. 210-232, 14 ills., Aug., 1934

California's Coastal Redwood Realm: Along a Belt of Tall Trees a Giant Bridge Speeds the Winning of Our Westernmost Frontier. By J. R. Hildebrand. LXXV, pp. 133-184, 31 ills. in black and white, 17 ills. in color, map, Feb., 1939

The National Geographic Society Completes Its Gifts of Big Trees. XL, pp. 85-86, July, 1921

The Oldest Living Thing ("General Sherman Tree"). XXIX, pictorial supplement, Apr., 1916

Our Big Trees Saved. XXXI, pp. 1-11, 10 ills., Jan., 1917

Our National Parks. By L. F. Schmeckebier. XXIII, pp. 531-579, 41 ills., map, June, 1912

SEQUOIAS (Trees)—*Continued*
The Redwood Forest of the Pacific Coast. By Henry Gannett. X, pp. 145-159, 6 ills., map, May, 1899
Saving the Redwoods. By Madison Grant. XXXVII, pp. 519-536, 10 ills., June, 1920

SERBIA:
The Changing Map in the Balkans. By Frederick Moore. XXIV, pp. 199-226, 27 ills., map, Feb., 1913
The Clock Turns Back in Yugoslavia: The Fortified Monastery of Mountain-girt Dečani Survives Its Six Hundredth Birthday. By Ethel Chamberlain Porter. LXXXV, pp. 493-512, 20 ills., map, Apr., 1944
The Great Turk and His Lost Provinces. By William E. Curtis. XIV, pp. 45-61, 7 ills., Feb., 1903
The Kingdom of Servia. By William Joseph Showalter. XXVII, pp. 417-432, 12 ills., map, Apr., 1915
The Land of Contrast: Austria-Hungary. By D. W. and A. S. Iddings. XXIII, pp. 1188-1217, 1284, 33 ills., map, Dec., 1912
The Races of Europe. By Edwin A. Grosvenor. XXXIV, pp. 441-534, 62 ills., diagr. and index, maps, map supplement, Dec., 1918
Servia and Montenegro. XIX, pp. 774-789, 24 ills., Nov., 1908

SERI INDIANS:
Adventuring Down the West Coast of Mexico. By Herbert Corey. XLII, pp. 449-503, 44 ills., map, Nov., 1922
A Mexican Land of Canaan: Marvelous Riches of the Wonderful West Coast of Our Neighbor Republic. By Frederick Simpich. XXXVI, pp. 307-330, 16 ills., map, Oct., 1919
The Seri Indians. XII, pp. 278-280, July, 1901
Seriland. By W J McGee and Willard D. Johnson. VII, pp. 125-133, ill., foldout map, Apr., 1896

SERILAND (Mexico). By W J McGee and Willard D. Johnson. VII, pp. 125-133, ill., foldout map, Apr., 1896

SERVIA and Montenegro. XIX, pp. 774-789, 24 ills., Nov., 1908

SERVICE RIBBONS, Military and Naval:
Decorations, Medals, Service Ribbons, Badges, and Women's Insignia. LXXXIV, pp. 414-444, 6 ills. in black and white, 376 ills. in color, Oct., 1943

SERVICING Arctic Airbases. By Robert A. Bartlett. LXXXIX, pp. 602-616, 3 ills. in black and white, 10 ills. in color, map, May, 1946

SETON, ERNEST THOMPSON:
Smaller Mammals of North America. By E. W. Nelson. Paintings by Louis Agassiz Fuertes. XXXIII, pp. 371*-493, 29 ills. in black and white, 59 ills. in color, May, 1918
Included: Drawings of animal tracks by Ernest Thompson Seton

SEVASTOPOL, U. S. S. R.:
Crimea Reborn. By Eddy Gilmore. LXXXVII, pp. 487-512, 23 ills., map, Apr., 1945

SEVENTH ANNUAL NEWSPAPER NATIONAL SNAPSHOT AWARDS:
Americana. 11 winning photos in the Seventh Annual Newspaper National Snapshot Awards. LXXXI, pp. 657-666, May, 1942

SEVENTY-FIVE Days in the Arctics. By Max Fleischman. XVIII, pp. 439-446, 5 ills., July, 1907

SEVERN VALLEY, England:
The Beauties of the Severn Valley. By Frank Wakeman. LXIII, pp. 417-452, 24 ills. in black and white, 15 ills. in color, map, Apr., 1933

SEVILLE, Spain:
Seville, More Spanish Than Spain: The City of the Ibero-American Exposition, Which Opens This Spring, Presents a Tapestry of Many Ages and of Nations Old and New. By Richard Ford. LV, pp. 273-310, 35 ills. in black and white, 2 ills. in color, Mar., 1929

The **SEX,** Nativity, and Color of the People of the United States. (By G. H. G.). XII, pp. 381-389, 17 charts, Nov., 1901

SHACKELFORD, J. B.:
Nomad Life and Fossil Treasures of Mongolia. 20 color photos by J. B. Shackelford. LXIII, pp. 669-700, June, 1933

SHACKLETON, SIR ERNEST H.:
The Heart of the Antarctic. By Ernest H. Shackleton. XX, pp. 972-1007, 27 ills., map, Nov., 1909
The Race for the South Pole (Presentation of Hubbard Medal by President Taft). XXI, pp. 185-186, Mar., 1910
Shackleton's Farthest South. XX, pp. 398-402, map, Apr., 1909
South Georgia, an Outpost of the Antarctic. By Robert Cushman Murphy. XLI, pp. 409-444, 41 ills., maps, Apr., 1922

SHACKLETON'S Farthest South. XX, pp. 398-402, map, Apr., 1909

SHAD (Fish):
Federal Fish Farming; or, Planting Fish by the Billion. By Hugh M. Smith. XXI, pp. 418-446, 22 ills., May, 1910

SHADOWY Birds of the Night (Owls). By Alexander Wetmore. Paintings by Maj. Allan Brooks. LXVII, pp. 217-240, 5 ills. in black and white, 21 portraits in color, Feb., 1935

SHADOWY London by Night. 8 ills. by H. B. Burdekin. LXVIII, pp. 177-184, Aug., 1935

SHAFFER, E. T. H.:
The Ashley River and Its Gardens (South Carolina). By E. T. H. Shaffer. XLIX, pp. 525-550, 6 ills. in black and white, 18 ills. in color, May, 1926

SHAHR KURD, Iran:
Mountain Tribes of Iran and Iraq. By Harold Lamb. LXXXIX, pp. 385-408, 15 ills., two-page map, Mar., 1946

SHALER, N. S.:
The Economic Aspects of Soil Erosion. (Part I). By Dr. N. S. Shaler. VII, pp. 328-338, Oct., 1896
The Economic Aspects of Soil Erosion. (Part) II. By Dr. N. S. Shaler. VII, pp. 368-377, Nov., 1896

SHAN (Tribespeople):
Burma: Where India and China Meet: In the Massive Mountains of Southeast Asia, Swarming Road Builders Wage the "War of the Highways" for Free China and Her Allies. By John LeRoy Christian. LXXXIV, pp. 489-512, 18 ills., map, Oct., 1943
Shan Tribes Make Burma's Hills Flash With Color. 15 color photos by W. Robert Moore. LX, pp. 455-462, Oct., 1931
Strange Tribes in the Shan States of Burma. 15 color photos by W. Robert Moore. LVIII, pp. 247-254, Aug., 1930

SHAN STATES, Burma:
Burma: Where India and China Meet: In the Massive Mountains of Southeast Asia, Swarming Road Builders Wage the "War of the Highways" for Free China and Her Allies. By John LeRoy Christian. LXXXIV, pp. 489-512, 18 ills., map, Oct., 1943
Shan Tribes Make Burma's Hills Flash With Color. 15 color photos by W. Robert Moore. LX, pp. 455-462, Oct., 1931
Strange Tribes in the Shan States of Burma. 15 color photos by W. Robert Moore. LVIII, pp. 247-254, Aug., 1930

SHANGHAI, China:
Changing Shanghai. By Amanda Boyden. LXXII, pp. 485-508, 21 ills., maps, Oct., 1937
Cosmopolitan Shanghai, Key Seaport of China. By W. Robert Moore. LXII, pp. 311-335, 19 ills., Sept., 1932
Today on the China Coast. By John B. Powell. LXXXVII, pp. 217-238, 17 ills., map., Feb., 1945

"SHANGRI-LA," Netherlands New Guinea. *See* Grand Valley

"SHANGRI-LA" in Panorama (New Guinea). 7 color photos by Ray T. Elsmore. LXXXVIII, pp. 681-688, Dec., 1945

SHANSI (Province), China:
China's Great Wall of Sculpture: Man-hewn Caves and Countless Images Form a Colossal Art Wonder of Early Buddhism. By Mary Augusta Mullikin. Paintings by author and Anna M. Hotchkis. LXXIII, pp. 313-348, 23 ills. in black and white, 10 ills. in color, map, Mar., 1938

SHANTUNG (Province), China:
The Descendants of Confucius. By Maynard Owen Williams. XXXVI, pp. 253-265, 16 ills., Sept., 1919
Shantung—China's Holy Land. By Charles K. Edmunds. XXXVI, pp. 231-252, 21 ills., map, Sept., 1919
Tai Shan, Sacred Mountain of the East. By Mary Augusta Mullikin. LXXXVII, pp. 699-719, 18 ills., map, June, 1945

SHANTZ, H. L.:
The Saguaro Forest (Arizona). By H. L. Shantz. LXXI, pp. 515-532, 18 ills., Apr., 1937

SHARK FISHING—An Australian Industry. By Norman Ellison. LXII, pp. 369-386, 22 ills., Sept., 1932

SHASTA DAM, California:
More Water for California's Great Central Valley. By Frederick Simpich. XC, pp. 645-664, 16 ills., map, Nov., 1946

SHATTERED Capitals of Central America. By Herbert J. Spinden. XXXVI, pp. 185-212, 32 ills., map, Sept., 1919

SHATTERED Obelisk of Mont Pelée. By Prof. Angelo Heilprin. XVII, pp. 465-474, 5 ills., Aug., 1906

SHAW, WILLIAM T.:
Tracking the Columbian Ground-Squirrel to Its Burrow: Loss of Millions to Crops and Danger of the Spread of Spotted Fever Necessitated Study of Peculiar Rodent of Western North America. By William T. Shaw. XLVII, pp. 587-596, 13 ills., May, 1925

SHAWANGUNK Mountain (Ulster County, New York). By N. H. Darton. VI, pp. 23-34, ills., 4 diagrs., Mar. 17, 1894

SHAWNEE (Indian Tribe):
America's First Settlers, the Indians. By Matthew W. Stirling. Paintings by W. Langdon Kihn. LXXII, pp. 535-596, 34 ills. in black and white, 24 ills. in color, Nov., 1937

SHAY, FELIX:
Cairo to Cape Town, Overland: An Adventurous Journey of 135 Days, Made by an American Man and His Wife, Through the Length of the African Continent. By Felix Shay. XLVII, pp. 123-260, 118 ills., map, Feb., 1925

SHEARWATERS:
Birds of the High Seas: Albatrosses and Petrels; Gannets, Man-o'-war-birds, and Tropic-birds. By Robert Cushman Murphy. Paintings by Major Allan Brooks. LXXIV, pp. 226-251, 7 ills. in black and white, 36 portraits in color, Aug., 1938

SHECHEM, Palestine. *See* Nablus

SHEDD AQUARIUM, Chicago: Expedition:
Net Results from Oceania: Collecting Aquarium Specimens in Tropical Pacific Waters. By Walter H. Chute. LXXIX, pp. 347-372, 8 ills. in black and white, 24 ills. in color, Mar., 1941

SHEEP AND SHEEP RAISING:
Among the Bethlehem Shepherds: A Visit to the Valley Which David Probably Recalled When He Wrote the Twenty-third Psalm. By John D. Whiting. L, pp. 729-753, 19 ills., Dec., 1926
Beyond Australia's Cities. By W. Robert Moore. LXX, pp. 709-747, 27 ills. in black and white, 12 ills. in color, Dec., 1936

SHEEP AND SHEEP RAISING—*Continued*

By Coolie and Caravan Across Central Asia: Narrative of a 7,900-Mile Journey of Exploration and Research Over "the Roof of the World," from the Indian Ocean to the Yellow Sea. By William J. Morden. LII, pp. 369-431, 73 ills., map, Oct., 1927

Included: Marco Polo sheep, or *Ovis poli*

Grass Makes Wyoming Fat. By Frederick Simpich. LXXXVIII, pp. 153-188, 13 ills. in black and white, 19 ills. in color, two-page map, Aug., 1945

The Indispensable Sheep. LIII, pp. 512-528, 20 ills., Apr., 1928

The Land of Lambskins: An Expedition to Bokhara, Russian Central Asia, to Study the Karakul Sheep Industry. By Robert H. Nabours. XXXVI, pp. 77-88, 15 ills., July, 1919

Lonely Australia: The Unique Continent. By Herbert E. Gregory. XXX, pp. 473-568, 68 ills., 5 maps (1 two-page), Dec., 1916

The White Sheep, Giant Moose, and Smaller Game of the Kenai Peninsula, Alaska. By George Shiras, 3d. XXIII, pp. 423-494, 59 ills., maps (1 two-page), May, 1912

See also Mountain Sheep

SHEEP DOGS:

Sheep Dog Trials in Llangollen: Trained Collies Perform Marvels of Herding in the Cambrian Stakes, Open to the World. By Sara Bloch. LXXVII, pp. 559-574, 17 ills., Apr., 1940

Working Dogs of the World. By Freeman Lloyd. Paintings by Edward Herbert Miner. LXXX, pp. 776-806, 12 ills. in black and white, 20 ills. in color, Dec., 1941

SHEEP-KILLERS—The Pariahs of Dogkind. XXXV, pp. 275-280, 3 ills., Mar., 1919

SHEIK Said. (By Ernest de Sasseville). VIII, pp. 155-156, May, 1897

SHELLFISH. *See* Crabs; Crustaceans; Lobsters; Mollusks; Oysters; Shrimp

SHELTON, A. L.:

Life Among the People of Eastern Tibet. By Dr. A. L. Shelton. XL, pp. 293-326, 35 ills., map, Sept., 1921

SHENANDOAH (Airship):

Man's Amazing Progress in Conquering the Air. By J. R. Hildebrand. XLVI, pp. 93-122, 28 ills., diagr., July, 1924

Included: Cross-section and end-on diagram of the "Shenandoah"

Seeing America from the "Shenandoah": An Account of the Record-making 9,000-mile Flight from the Atlantic to the Pacific Coast and Return in the Navy's American-built, American-manned Airship. By Junius B. Wood. XLVII, pp. 1-47, 39 ills., diagr., map, Jan., 1925

SHENON, PHILIP J.:

Down Idaho's River of No Return (Salmon River). By Philip J. Shenon and John C. Reed. LXX, pp. 95-136, 43 ills., maps, July, 1936

SHENSI (Province), China:

China Fights Erosion with U. S. Aid. By Walter C. Lowdermilk. LXXXVII, pp. 641-680, 10 ills. in black and white, 26 ills. in color, June, 1945

See also Siking

SHEPHERD'S NEEDLES (Plants):

An Insect Community Lives in Flower Heads. By James G. Needham. XC, pp. 340-356, 5 ills. in black and white, 11 ills. in color, Sept., 1946

SHERWOOD GARDENS, Baltimore, Maryland:

Maytime in the Heart of Maryland. 10 color photos by B. Anthony Stewart and Charles Martin. LXXIX, pp. 441-448, Apr., 1941

SHETLAND ISLANDS, Scotland:

The Orkneys and Shetlands—A Mysterious Group of Islands. By Charles S. Olcott. XXXIX, pp. 197-228, 33 ills., Feb., 1921

SHIAS (Tribespeople):

Mystic Nedjef, the Shia Mecca. By Frederick Simpich. XXVI, pp. 589-598, 4 ills., Dec., 1914

SHIFTING Scenes on the Stage of New China. XXXVIII, pp. 423-428, 4 ills., Nov., 1920

SHIGATSE, Tibet:

Sky-high in Lama Land. 12 photos by C. Suydam Cutting. XC, pp. 185-196, Aug., 1946

SHINTO:

Behind the Mask of Modern Japan. By Willard Price. LXXXVIII, pp. 513-535, 14 ills., Nov., 1945

SHIP BURIAL:

Ancestor of the British Navy: England's Oldest Known War Vessel Is Unearthed, Laden with Remarkable Treasures of an Anglo-Saxon Ruler. By C. W. Phillips. LXXIX, pp. 247-268, 22 ills., 4 drawings, Feb., 1941

SHIP RAILWAYS:

The Tehuantepec Ship Railway (Mexico). By Elmer L. Corthell. VII, pp. 64-72, maps, Feb., 1896

Included: Chignecto Ship Railway, Canada

SHIPBUILDING:

American Industries Geared for War. By Thornton Oakley. With 16 ills. in color from paintings by author. LXXXII, pp. 716-734, ill. in black and white, Dec., 1942

The American People Must Become Ship-Minded. By Edward N. Hurley. XXXIV, pp. 201-211, 7 ills., Sept., 1918

As 2,000 Ships Are Born. By Frederick Simpich. LXXXI, pp. 551-588, 34 ills., May, 1942

Our Industrial Victory. By Charles M. Schwab. XXXIV, pp. 212-229, 17 ills., Sept., 1918

Shipbuilding in the United Kingdom in 1898. X, pp. 138-139, Apr., 1899

Ships for the Seven Seas: The Story of America's Maritime Needs, Her Capabilities and Her Achievements. By Ralph A. Graves. XXXIV, pp. 165-200, 24 ills., Sept., 1918

SHIPLEY, L. W.:

The Valley of Ten Thousand Smokes: An Account of the Discovery and Exploration of the Most Wonderful Volcanic Region in the World. By Robert F. Griggs. XXXIII, pp. 115-169, 46 ills., map, panorama, Feb., 1918

SHIPPEE, ROBERT:

Air Adventures in Peru: Cruising Among Andean Peaks, Pilots and Cameramen Discover Wondrous Works of an Ancient People. By Robert Shippee. LXIII, pp. 81-120, 40 ills., map, Jan., 1933

A Forgotten Valley of Peru: Conquered by Incas, Scourged by Famine, Plagues, and Earthquakes, Colca Valley Shelters the Last Fragment of an Ancient Andean Tribe. By Robert Shippee. LXV, pp. 111-132, 22 ills., map, Jan., 1934

SHIPS AND SHIPPING:

American Industries Geared for War. By Thornton Oakley. With 16 ills. in color from paintings by author. LXXXII, pp. 716-734, ill. in black and white, Dec., 1942

American Pathfinders in the Pacific. By William H. Nicholas. LXXXIX, pp. 617-640, 17 ills., two-page map, May, 1946

Ancestor of the British Navy: England's Oldest Known War Vessel Is Unearthed, Laden with Remarkable Treasures of an Anglo-Saxon Ruler. By C. W. Phillips. LXXIX, pp. 247-268, 22 ills., 4 drawings, Feb., 1941

The Argosy of Geography (Sailing Ship). XXXIX, pictorial supplement, Jan., 1921

As 2,000 Ships Are Born. By Frederick Simpich. LXXXI, pp. 551-588, 34 ills., May, 1942

Battleship *Missouri* Comes of Age. 11 ills. LXXXVII, pp. 353-369, Mar., 1945

By Car and Steamer Around Our Inland Seas. By Maynard Owen Williams. LXV, pp. 451-491, 29 ills. in black and white, 8 ills. in duotone, two-page map, Apr., 1934

Cannon on Florida Reefs Solve Mystery of Sunken Ship. By Charles M. Brookfield. LXXX, pp. 807-824, 20 ills., map (on pen and ink drawing), Dec., 1941

The Caravels of Columbus. Reproduction in color of the painting by N. C. Wyeth, National Geographic Society, Washington, D. C. LIV, text, p. 55; supplement, July, 1928

Convoys to Victory. By Harvey Klemmer. LXXXIII, pp. 193-216, 24 ills., Feb., 1943

Growth of Maritime Commerce. (By J.H.). X, pp. 30-31, Jan., 1899

Heroes' Return. By William H. Nicholas. LXXXVII, pp. 333-352, 19 ills., Mar., 1945

Landing Craft for Invasion. By Melville Bell Grosvenor. LXXXVI, pp. 1-30, 26 ills., July, 1944

Life in Our Fighting Fleet. By F. Barrows Colton. LXXIX, pp. 671-702, 30 ills., June, 1941

Life with Our Fighting Coast Guard. By F. Barrows Colton. LXXXIII, pp. 557-588, 22 ills. in black and white, 9 ills. in color, May, 1943

SHIPS AND SHIPPING—*Continued*

Most Curious Craft Afloat: The Compass in Navigation and the Work of the Non-Magnetic Yacht "Carnegie." By L. A. Bauer. XXI, pp. 223-245, 31 ills., Mar., 1910

New Safeguards for Ships in Fog and Storm. By George R. Putnam. LXX, pp. 169-200, 28 ills., charts, Aug., 1936

Normandy's Made-in-England Harbors. LXXXVII, pp. 565-580, 16 ills., map, May, 1945

North About. By Alan J. Villiers. LXXI, pp. 221-250, 24 ills., Feb., 1937

Norway, an Active Ally. By Wilhelm Morgenstierne. LXXXIII, pp. 333-357, 24 ills., map, Mar., 1943

Norway and the Vikings. By Captain Magnus Andersen. V, pp. 132-136, Jan. 31, 1894
Note: Voyage of the *Viking,* Bergen to New London

The Sailing Ship and the Panama Canal. By James Page. XV, pp. 167-176, charts, Apr., 1904

Seafarers of South Celebes. By G. E. P. Collins. LXXXVII, pp. 53-78, 25 ills., map, Jan., 1945

Shipbuilding in the United Kingdom in 1898. X, pp. 138-139, Apr., 1899

Ships, from Dugouts to Dreadnoughts. By Captain Dudley W. Knox. LXXIII, pp. 57-98, 27 ills. in black and white, 16 ills. in gravure, Jan., 1938

Ships That Guard Our Ocean Ramparts. By F. Barrows Colton. Paintings by Arthur Beaumont. LXXX, pp. 328-337, 8 ills. in color, Sept., 1941

Time and Tide on the Thames. By Frederick Simpich. LXXV, pp. 239-272, 23 ills. in black and white, 10 ills. in color, map, Feb., 1939

Victory's Portrait in the Marianas. By Lt. William Franklin Draper, USNR. With 17 ills. in color from paintings by author. LXXXVIII, pp. 599-616, Nov., 1945

Where the Sailing Ship Survives (Aland Islands). By A. J. Villiers. LXVII, pp. 101-128, 31 ills., map, Jan., 1935

Your Navy as Peace Insurance. By Fleet Admiral Chester W. Nimitz. LXXXIX, pp. 681-736, 32 ills. in black and white, 26 ills. in color, June, 1946

See also Aircraft Carriers; Boats; Caravels; Escort Carriers; Junks; Lighthouses; Schooners; Shipbuilding; Shipwrecks; U. S. Army Transportation Corps; U. S. Coast Guard; U. S. Maritime Service; U. S. Navy; Voyages; Windjammers; Yachts

SHIPS of the Centuries. 16 ills. in gravure from etchings by Norman Wilkinson. LXXIII, pp. 65-80; text, p. 98, Jan., 1938

SHIPS That Won the Greatest Naval War. 26 ills. in color from U. S. Navy official photos. LXXXIX, pp. 697-736, June, 1946

SHIPTON, JAMES A.:

The Peak of Itambé (Brazil). IX, p. 476, Nov., 1898

SHIPWRECKS:

Where the Wind Does the Work (Cape Hatteras). By Collier Cobb. XVII, pp. 310-317, 9 ills., map, June, 1906

SHIPWRECKS—*Continued*

See also Jeannette; Winchester; and St. Pierre and Miquelon

SHIRAS, GEORGE, 3D:

Camps and Cruises of an Ornithologist. By George Shiras, 3d. XX, pp. 438-463, 30 ills., May, 1909

Doe and Twin Fawns. Flashlight photo by George Shiras, 3d. XXIV, supplement, July, 1913. XL, ill. p. 136, Aug., 1921. LXXVI, ill. p. 475, Oct., 1939

A Flashlight Story of an Albino Porcupine and of a Cunning but Unfortunate Coon. By George Shiras, 3d. XXII, pp. 572-596, 26 ills., June, 1911

Nature's Transformation at Panama: Remarkable Changes in Faunal and Physical Conditions in the Gatun Lake Region. By George Shiras, 3d. XXVIII, pp. 159-194, 33 ills., maps, Aug., 1915

One Season's Game-Bag with the Camera. By George Shiras, 3d. XIX, pp. 387-446, 70 ills., June, 1908

Photographing Wild Game with Flashlight and Camera. By George Shiras, 3d. XVII, pp. 367-423, 74 ills., July, 1906

The White Sheep, Giant Moose, and Smaller Game of the Kenai Peninsula, Alaska. By George Shiras, 3d. XXIII, pp. 423-494, 59 ills., maps (1 two-page), May, 1912

Wild Animals That Took Their Own Pictures by Day and by Night. By George Shiras, 3d. XXIV, pp. 763-834, 68 ills., map, pictorial supplement, July, 1913

Doe and Twin Fawns. Flashlight photo by author (supplement)

The Wild Life of Lake Superior, Past and Present: The Habits of Deer, Moose, Wolves, Beavers, Muskrats, Trout, and Feathered Wood-Folk Studied with Camera and Flashlight. By George Shiras, 3d. XL, pp. 113-204, 76 ills., map, pictorial supplement, Aug., 1921

Hark! Flashlight photo of deer by author (supplement)

Wild Life of the Atlantic and Gulf Coasts: A Field Naturalist's Photographic Record of Nearly Half a Century of Fruitful Exploration. By George Shiras, 3d. LXII, pp. 261-309, 62 ills., Sept., 1932

See also NGS: Board of Managers

SHISHALDIN (Volcano), Aleutian Islands:

Mountains on Unimak Island, Alaska. By Ferdinand Westdahl. XIV, pp. 91-99, 4 ills., map, Mar., 1903

Note on the Activity of Shishaldin Volcano. (By Homer P. Ritter). XVI, p. 249, May, 1905

Shishaldin as a Field for Exploration. By Joseph Stanley-Brown. X, pp. 281-288, 3 ills., map, Aug., 1899

SHOES AND SHOE INDUSTRY:

Czechoslovaks, Yankees of Europe. By John Patric. LXXIV, pp. 173-225, 23 ills. in black and white, 30 ills. in color, map, Aug., 1938

How the World Is Shod. XIX, pp. 649-660, 12 ills., Sept., 1908

Massachusetts—Beehive of Business. By William Joseph Showalter. XXXVII, pp. 203-245, 41 ills., Mar., 1920

SHONTS, THEODORE P.:

Notes on the Panama Canal. (By Theodore P. Shonts). XVII, pp. 362-363, June, 1906

The Panama Canal. By Theodore P. Shonts. XVII, pp. 55-68, 5 ills., Feb., 1906

What Has Been Accomplished by the United States Toward Building the Panama Canal. By Theodore P. Shonts. XVI, pp. 558-564, Dec., 1905

SHOPPING Abroad for Our Armies in France. By Herbert Corey. XXXIII, pp. 206-218, 6 ills., Feb., 1918

The **SHORE BIRDS,** Cranes, and Rails: Willets, Plovers, Stilts, Phalaropes, Sandpipers, and Their Relatives Deserve Protection. By Arthur A. Allen. Paintings by Major Allan Brooks. LXXII, pp. 183-222, 4 ills. in black and white, 101 portraits in color, Aug., 1937

SHORE-WHALING: A World Industry. By Roy Chapman Andrews. XXII, pp. 411-442, 34 ills., May, 1911

A **SHORT** Visit to Wales: Historic Associations and Scenic Beauties Contend for Interest in the Little Land Behind the Hills. By Ralph A. Graves. XLIV, pp. 635-675, 37 ills., map, Dec., 1923

SHORTENING Time Across the Continent. By Henry Herbert McClure. XIII, pp. 319-321, Aug., 1902

SHOSHONE DAM, Wyoming:

The Call of the West. By C. J. Blanchard. XX, pp. 403-437, 20 ills., map, May, 1909

The Spirit of the West: The Wonderful Agricultural Development Since the Dawn of Irrigation. By C. J. Blanchard. XXI, pp. 333-360, 15 ills., Apr., 1910

SHOULTS, WORTH E.:

Antarctica's Most Interesting Citizen: The Comical Penguin Is Both Romantic and Bellicose. By Worth E. Shoults. LXI, pp. 251-260, 8 ills., Feb., 1932

The Home of the First Farmer of America (Mount Vernon). By Worth E. Shoults. LIII, pp. 603-628, 6 ills. in black and white, 26 ills. in color, May, 1928

Hospitality of the Czechs. By Worth E. Shoults. LI, pp. 723-742, 19 ills. in color, June, 1927

SHOWALTER, WILLIAM JOSEPH:

America's Amazing Railway Traffic. By William Joseph Showalter. XLIII, pp. 353-404, 46 ills., map, Apr., 1923

America's New Soldier Cities: The Geographical and Historical Environment of the National Army Cantonments and National Guard Camps. By William Joseph Showalter. XXXII, pp. 439-476, 18 ills., map, Nov.-Dec., 1917

The Automobile Industry: An American Art That Has Revolutionized Methods in Manufacturing and Transformed Transportation. By William Joseph Showalter. XLIV, pp. 337-414, 76 ills., Oct., 1923

Battling with the Panama Slides. By William Joseph Showalter. XXV, pp. 133-153, 15 ills., Feb., 1914

Belgium: The Innocent Bystander. By William Joseph Showalter. XXVI, pp. 223-264, 35 ills., Sept., 1914

Chicago Today and Tomorrow: A City Whose Industries Have Changed the Food Status of the World and Transformed the Economic Situation of a Billion People. By William Joseph Showalter. XXXV, pp. 1-42, 28 ills., map, Jan., 1919

Coal—Ally of American Industry. By William Joseph Showalter. XXXIV, pp. 407-434, 23 ills., Nov., 1918

The Countries of the Caribbean. By William Joseph Showalter. XXIV, pp. 227-250, 23 ills., Feb., 1913

Cuba—The Sugar Mill of the Antilles. By William Joseph Showalter. XXXVIII, pp. 1-33, 24 ills., map, July, 1920

Exploring the Glories of the Firmament. By William Joseph Showalter. XXXVI, pp. 153-181, 17 ills., diagr., 3 charts, Aug., 1919

Exploring the Mysteries of Plant Life. By William Joseph Showalter. Paintings by Mary E. Eaton. XLV, pp. 581-646, 41 ills. in black and white, 47 ills. in color, June, 1924

Exploring the Wonders of the Insect World. By William Joseph Showalter. Paintings by Hashime Murayama. LVI, pp. 1-90, 59 ills. in black and white, 269 ills. in color, July, 1929

Familiar Grasses and Their Flowers. By E. J. Geske and W. J. Showalter. Paintings by E. J. Geske. XXXIX, pp. 625-636, 8 ills. in color, June, 1921

The Family Tree of the Flowers. By Frederic E. Clements and William Joseph Showalter. LI, pp. 555-563, ill. in black and white, ill. in color, May, 1927

Flags of the World. By Gilbert Grosvenor and William J. Showalter. LXVI, pp. 339-396, 10 ills. in black and white, 808 ills. in color, Sept., 1934

How the World Is Fed. By William Joseph Showalter. XXIX, pp. 1-110, 101 ills., Jan., 1916

Industry's Greatest Asset—Steel. By William Joseph Showalter. XXXII, pp. 121-156, 34 ills., Aug., 1917

Interviewing the Stars: How Twentieth Century Astronomers Are Inducing the Heavens to Reveal Their Secrets. By William Joseph Showalter. XLVII, pp. 97-122, 18 ills., diagr., charts, Jan., 1925

The Kingdom of Servia. By William Joseph Showalter. XXVII, pp. 417-432, 12 ills., map, Apr., 1915

The Lure of Lima, City of the Kings. By William Joseph Showalter. LVII, pp. 727-784, 41 ills. in black and white, 25 ills. in color, June, 1930

Map-Changing Medicine. By William Joseph Showalter. XLII, pp. 303-330, 26 ills., Sept., 1922

Massachusetts—Beehive of Business. By William Joseph Showalter. XXXVII, pp. 203-245, 41 ills., Mar., 1920

Mexico and Mexicans. By William Joseph Showalter. XXV, pp. 471-493, 17 ills., map supplement, May, 1914

New York—An Empire Within a Republic. By William Joseph Showalter. LXIV, pp. 513-584, 47 ills. in black and white, 35 ills. in color, two-page map, pictorial supplement, Nov., 1933

New York—The Metropolis of Mankind. By William Joseph Showalter. XXXIV, pp. 1-49, 39 ills., July, 1918

Niagara at the Battle Front. By William Joseph Showalter. XXXI, pp. 413-422, 6 ills., May, 1917

Our Guardians on the Deep. By William Joseph Showalter. XXV, pp. 655-677, 15 ills., chart, June, 1914

The Panama Canal. By William Joseph Showalter. XXIII, pp. 195-205, map supplement, Feb., 1912

Partitioned Poland. By William Joseph Showalter. XXVII, pp. 88-106, 12 ills., Jan., 1915

Redeeming the Tropics. By William Joseph Showalter. XXV, pp. 344-364, 13 ills., Mar., 1914

Strange Habits of Familiar Moths and Butterflies. By William Joseph Showalter. LII, pp. 77-105, 19 ills. in black and white, drawing, 88 ills. in color, July, 1927

The Travels of George Washington: Dramatic Episodes in His Career as the First Geographer of the United States. By William Joseph Showalter. LXI, pp. 1-63, 50 ills., 4 maps, map supplement, Jan., 1932

Twin Stars of Chile: Valparaiso, the Gateway, and Santiago, the Capital—Key Cities with a Progressive Present and a Romantic Past. By William Joseph Showalter. LV, pp. 197-247, 35 ills. in black and white, 25 ills. in color, Feb., 1929

Virginia—A Commonwealth That Has Come Back. By William Joseph Showalter. LV, pp. 403-472, 69 ills. in black and white, 13 ills. in color, map, Apr., 1929

SHREVE, FORREST:

The Saguaro, Cactus Camel of Arizona. By Forrest Shreve. LXXXVIII, pp. 695-704, 9 ills. in color, Dec., 1945

SHRIMP:

The Delectable Shrimp: Once a Culinary Stepchild, Today a Gulf Coast Industry. By Harlan Major. LXXXVI, pp. 501-512, 11 ills., map, Oct., 1944

SHRINES:

Behind the Mask of Modern Japan. By Willard Price. LXXXVIII, pp. 513-535, 14 ills., Nov., 1945

Castles, Shrines, and Parks of Japanese Pilgrimage. 10 color photos by W. Robert Moore. LXIX, pp. 457-464, Apr., 1936

Gilded Domes Against an Azure Sky (Iran). 13 color photos by Stephen H. Nyman. LXXVI, pp. 339-346, Sept., 1939

A Pilgrimage to Amernath, Himalayan Shrine of the Hindu Faith. By Louise Ahl Jessop. XL, pp. 513-542, 29 ills., Nov., 1921

Pilgrims' Progress to Mecca. 22 ills. in duotone: 18 by Oscar Marcus. LXXII, pp. 627-642, Nov., 1937

SHRINES—*Continued*

Puto, the Enchanted Island. By Robert F. Fitch. LXXXIX, pp. 373-384, 11 ills., map, Mar., 1946

Tai Shan, Sacred Mountain of the East. By Mary Augusta Mullikin. LXXXVII, pp. 699-719, 18 ills., map, June, 1945

See also Montserrat

SHRUBS:

American Berries of Hill, Dale, and Wayside. Paintings by Mary E. Eaton. XXXV, pp. 168-184, ill. in black and white, 28 ills. in color, Feb., 1919

The Kingdom of Flowers: An Account of the Wealth of Trees and Shrubs of China and of What the Arnold Arboretum, with China's Help, Is Doing to Enrich America. By Ernest H. Wilson. XXII, pp. 1003-1035, 24 ills., Nov., 1911

See also Rhododendrons

SHURI, Okinawa (Island), Ryukyu Retto:

Peacetime Rambles in the Ryukyus. By William Leonard Schwartz. LXXXVII, pp. 543-561, 12 ills., maps, May, 1945

SHUSH, Iran. *See* Susa

SHUSTER, ERNEST A., JR.:

The Original Boundary Stones of the District of Columbia. By Ernest A. Shuster, Jr. XX, pp. 356-359, 6 ills., map, Apr., 1909

SIAM. *See* Thailand

SIAMESE CATS:

The Panther of the Hearth: Lithe Grace and Independence of Spirit Contribute to the Appeal of Cats, "The Only Domestic Animal Man Has Never Conquered." By Frederick B. Eddy. LXXIV, pp. 589-634, 22 ills. in black and white, 25 ills. in color, Nov., 1938

SIAN (Siking), China:

Singan—The Present Capital of the Chinese Empire. (By James Mascarene Hubbard). XII, pp. 63-66, ill., Feb., 1901

SIASCONSET, Nantucket (Island):

Nantucket—Little Gray Lady. By William H. Nicholas. LXXXV, pp. 433-458, 14 ills. in black and white, 8 ills. in color, map, Apr., 1944

SIBERIA:

Butter Exports from Siberia. XIII, p. 34, Jan., 1902

A Critical Review of Bering's First Expedition, 1725-30, Together with a Translation of His Original Report Upon It. With a Map. By Wm. H. Dall. II, pp. 111-169, 8 tables, foldout map, May, 1890

The Far Eastern Republic. By Junius B. Wood. XLI, pp. 565-592, 29 ills., map, June, 1922

Glimpses of Siberia, the Russian "Wild East." By Cody Marsh. XXXVIII, pp. 513-536, 26 ills., Dec., 1920

The Land of Promise. By Major General A. W. Greely. XXIII, pp. 1078-1090, 7 ills., Nov., 1912

SIBERIA—*Continued*

"Magnetic City" (Magnitogorsk), Core of Valiant Russia's Industrial Might. By John Scott. LXXXIII, pp. 525-556, 27 ills., two-page map, May, 1943

New Road to Asia. By Owen Lattimore. LXXXVI, pp. 641-676, 15 ills. in black and white, 26 ills. in color, Dec., 1944

Siberia. By Prof. Edwin A. Grosvenor. XII, pp. 317-324, Sept., 1901

The Siberian Transcontinental Railroad. By General A. W. Greely. VIII, pp. 121-124, Apr., 1897

A Strange and Remarkable Beast (Mammoth). XVIII, p. 620, ill., Sept., 1907

A Trip Through Siberia. By Ebenezer J. Hill. XIII, pp. 37-54, 17 ills., map, Feb., 1902

Western Siberia and the Altai Mountains: With Some Speculations on the Future of Siberia. By James Bryce. XXXIX, pp. 469-507, 39 ills., May, 1921

With an Exile in Arctic Siberia: The Narrative of a Russian Who Was Compelled to Turn Polar Explorer for Two Years. By Vladimir M. Zenzinov. XLVI, pp. 695-718, 30 ills., map, Dec., 1924

SIBERIAN TRANSCONTINENTAL RAILROAD. *See* Trans-Siberian Railway

The **SIBERIAN** Transcontinental Railroad. By General A. W. Greely. VIII, pp. 121-124, Apr., 1897

SIBERT, WILLIAM L.:

The Panama Canal. By Lieut. Colonel William L. Sibert. XXV, pp. 153-183, 24 ills., Feb., 1914

SICILY (Island), Mediterranean Sea:

Africa First of 1943 Global Warfare Maps. By William H. Nicholas. Text with map supplement. LXXXIII, pp. 261-276, 13 ills., Feb., 1943

A Country Where Going to America Is an Industry. By Arthur H. Warner. XX, pp. 1063-1102, 41 ills., Dec., 1909

Inexhaustible Italy. By Arthur Stanley Riggs. XXX, pp. 273-368, 76 ills., map, Oct., 1916

The Ruins at Selinus. (By Marion Crawford). XX, p. 117, Jan., 1909

Sicily: Island of Vivid Beauty and Crumbling Glory. LII, pp. 432-449, 22 ills. in color, Oct., 1927

Sicily, the Battle-Field of Nations and of Nature. By Mrs. George C. Bosson, Jr. XX, pp. 97-118, 25 ills., map, Jan., 1909

Sicily Again in the Path of War. By Maynard Owen Williams. LXXXIV, pp. 307-320, 7 ills., map, Sept., 1943

The World's Most Cruel Earthquake (Messina). By Charles W. Wright. XX, pp. 373-396, 22 ills., maps, Apr., 1909

Zigzagging Across Sicily. By Melville Chater. XLVI, pp. 303-352, 44 ills., map, Sept., 1924

SIENA, Italy:

Inexhaustible Italy. By Arthur Stanley Riggs. XXX, pp. 273-368, 76 ills., map, Oct., 1916

Siena's Palio, an Italian Inheritance from the Middle Ages. By Marie Louise Handley. L, pp. 245-258, 3 ills., Aug., 1926

SIEPEN, HOWARD:

On the Wings of the Wind: In Motorless Planes, Pilots Ride in Flying-Fox Fashion, Cruising on Upward Air Streams and Lifted by the Suction of Moving Clouds. By Howard Siepen. LV, pp. 751-780, 40 ills., June, 1929

SIERRA LEONE:

Rubber Forests of Nicaragua and Sierra Leone. By General A. W. Greely. VIII, pp. 83-88, Mar., 1897

SIEUR DE MONTS NATIONAL MONUMENT, Maine. *See* Mount Desert Island

SIGHT-SEEING in School: Taking Twenty Million Children on a Picture Tour of the World. By Jessie L. Burrall. XXXV, pp. 489-503, 14 ills., June, 1919

SIGHTS and Sounds of the Winged World: Study of Birds to Make National Geographic Color Photographs Yields Rich Scientific Knowledge of Their Habits and Behavior. By Arthur A. Allen. LXXXVII, pp. 721-744, ill. in black and white, drawings, 26 ills. in color, June, 1945

SIGIRI (Fortress Rock), Ceylon. *See* Sigiriya

SIGIRIYA (Fortress Rock), Ceylon:

Archæology in the Air. By Eliza R. Scidmore. XVIII, pp. 151-163, 11 ills., Mar., 1907

Sigiriya, "A Fortress in the Sky." By Wilson K. Norton. XC, pp. 665-680, 14 ills., map, Nov., 1946

SIGNAL CORPS, U. S. Army. *See* U. S. Army Signal Corps

SIGSBEE, CHARLES D.:

Captain Charles D. Sigsbee, U. S. N. (By H.G.). IX, p. 250, ill. (front.), May, 1898

Portrait. IX, pl. 5 (front.), May, 1898

Reception to Captain C. D. Sigsbee, U. S. N. (By J.H.). IX, pp. 251-252, May, 1898

SIKANG (Province), China:

Climbing Mighty Minya Konka: Americans First Scaled Mountain That Now Is Landmark of China's New Skyway. By Richard L. Burdsall and Terris Moore. LXXXIII, pp. 625-650, 23 ills., map, May, 1943

Experiences of a Lone Geographer: An American Agricultural Explorer Makes His Way Through Brigand-infested Central China en Route to the Amne Machin Range, Tibet. By Joseph F. Rock. XLVIII, pp. 331-347, 16 ills., map, Sept., 1925

Exploring a Grass Wonderland of Wild West China. By Ray G. Johnson. LXXXV, pp. 713-742, 24 ills., map, June, 1944

The Glories of the Minya Konka: Magnificent Snow Peaks of the China-Tibetan Border Are Photographed at Close Range by a National Geographic Society Expedition. By Joseph F. Rock. LVIII, pp. 385-437, 35 ills. in black and white, 24 ills. in color, map, Oct., 1930

SIKANG (Province), China—*Continued*

Konka Risumgongba, Holy Mountain of the Outlaws. By Joseph F. Rock. LX, pp. 1-65, 36 ills. in black and white, 43 ills. in color, map, July, 1931

The Land of the Yellow Lama: National Geographic Society Explorer Visits the Strange Kingdom of Muli, Beyond the Likiang Snow Range of Yünnan Province, China. By Joseph F. Rock. XLVII, pp. 447-491, 39 ills., map, Apr., 1925

Populous and Beautiful Szechuan: A Visit to the Restless Province of China, in which the Present Revolution Began. By Rollin T. Chamberlin. XXII, pp. 1094-1119, 26 ills., map, Dec., 1911

SIKANG EXPEDITION:

Climbing Mighty Minya Konka: Americans First Scaled Mountain That Now Is Landmark of China's New Skyway. By Richard L. Burdsall and Terris Moore. LXXXIII, pp. 625-650, 23 ills., map, May, 1943

SIKING (Sian), China:

Singan—The Present Capital of the Chinese Empire. (By James Mascarene Hubbard). XII, pp. 63-66, ill., Feb., 1901

SILENT-WINGED Owls of North America. 21 portraits from paintings by Maj. Allan Brooks. LXVII, pp. 225-240, Feb., 1935

SILK INDUSTRY:

How Half the World Works. By Alice Tisdale Hobart and Mary A. Nourse. LXI, pp. 509-524, 22 ills., Apr., 1932

The Industrial Titan of America: Pennsylvania, Once the Keystone of the Original Thirteen, Now the Keystone of Forty-eight Sovereign States. By John Oliver La Gorce. XXXV, pp. 367-406, 33 ills., map, May, 1919

Massachusetts—Beehive of Business. By William Joseph Showalter. XXXVII, pp. 203-245, 41 ills., Mar., 1920

Strange Habits of Familiar Moths and Butterflies. By William Joseph Showalter. LII, pp. 77-105, 19 ills. in black and white, drawing, 88 ills. in color, July, 1927

SILVER AND SILVER MINING:

Pieces of Silver. By Frederick Simpich. LXIV, pp. 253-292, 49 ills., Sept., 1933

The Treasure Chest of Mercurial Mexico. By Frank H. Probert. XXX, pp. 33-68, 33 ills., July, 1916

SILVERWARE:

Pieces of Silver. By Frederick Simpich. LXIV, pp. 253-292, 49 ills., Sept., 1933

SIMI (Island), Aegean Sea:

Rhodes, and Italy's Aegean Islands. By Dorothy Hosmer. LXXIX, pp. 449-480, 32 ills., map, Apr., 1941

SIMMONS, GEORGE FINLAY:

Sindbads of Science: Narrative of a Windjammer's Specimen-Collecting Voyage to the Sargasso Sea, to Senegambian Africa and Among Islands of High Adventure in the South Atlantic. By George Finlay Simmons. LII, pp. 1-75, 89 ills., map, July, 1927

SIMPICH, FREDERICK:

Along Our Side of the Mexican Border. By Frederick Simpich. XXXVIII, pp. 61-80, 9 ills., map, July, 1920

Along the Nile Through Egypt and the Sudan. By Frederick Simpich. XLII, pp. 379-410, 29 ills., Oct., 1922

Arizona Comes of Age. By Frederick Simpich. LV, pp. 1-47, 40 ills. in black and white, 14 ills. in color, map, Jan., 1929

Arkansas Rolls Up Its Sleeves. By Frederick Simpich. XC, pp. 273-312, 16 ills. in black and white, 23 ills. in color, map, Sept., 1946

Around the Clock with Your Soldier Boy. By Frederick Simpich. LXXX, pp. 1-36, 42 ills., July, 1941

As London Toils and Spins. By Frederick Simpich. LXXI, pp. 1-57, 38 ills. in black and white, 23 ills. in color, Jan., 1937

As 2,000 Ships Are Born. By Frederick Simpich. LXXXI, pp. 551-588, 34 ills., May, 1942

Bahama Holiday. By Frederick Simpich. LXIX, pp. 219-245, 29 ills., map, Feb., 1936

Baja California Wakes Up. By Frederick Simpich. LXXXII, pp. 253-275, 19 ills., map, Aug., 1942

Behind the News in Singapore. By Frederick Simpich. LXXVIII, pp. 83-110, 26 ills., map, July, 1940

Bombs Over Bible Lands. By Frederick Simpich and W. Robert Moore. LXXX, pp. 141-180, 34 ills., two-page map, Aug., 1941

Bonds Between the Americas. By Frederick Simpich. LXXII, pp. 785-808, 22 ills., Dec., 1937

Boston Through Midwest Eyes. By Frederick Simpich. LXX, pp. 37-82, 24 ills. in black and white, 31 ills. in color, July, 1936

Bridges, from Grapevine to Steel. By Frederick Simpich. LXIX, pp. 391-406, 13 ills., Mar., 1936

Change Comes to Bible Lands. By Frederick Simpich. LXXIV, pp. 695-750, 40 ills. in black and white, 25 ills. in color, map supplement, Dec., 1938

Chemists Make a New World: Creating Hitherto Unknown Raw Materials, Science Now Disrupts Old Trade Routes and Revamps the World Map of Industry. By Frederick Simpich. LXXVI, pp. 601-640, 22 ills. in black and white, 26 ills. in color, Nov., 1939

Down the Rio Grande: Tracing this Strange, Turbulent Stream on Its Long Course from Colorado to the Gulf of Mexico. By Frederick Simpich. LXXVI, pp. 415-462, 28 ills. in black and white, 24 ills. in color, 6 maps, Oct., 1939

Every-Day Life in Afghanistan. By Frederick Simpich and "Haji Mirza Hussein." XXXIX, pp. 85-110, 26 ills., map, Jan., 1921

Facts about the Philippines. By Frederick Simpich. LXXXI, pp. 185-202, 17 ills., map, Feb., 1942

Farmers Keep Them Eating. By Frederick Simpich. LXXXIII, pp. 435-458, 22 ills., Apr., 1943

Fit to Fight Anywhere (Army Quartermaster Tests). By Frederick Simpich. LXXXIV, pp. 233-256, 26 ills., Aug., 1943

SIMPICH, FREDERICK—*Continued*

The Geography of Our Foreign Trade. By Frederick Simpich. XLI, pp. 89-108, 25 ills., Jan., 1922

Gigantic Brazil and Its Glittering Capital. By Frederick Simpich. LVIII, pp. 733-778, 54 ills., map, Dec., 1930

Grass Makes Wyoming Fat. By Frederick Simpich. LXXXVIII, pp. 153-188, 13 ills. in black and white, 19 ills. in color, two-page map, Aug., 1945

The Great Mississippi Flood of 1927: Since White Man's Discovery This Mighty River Has Served Him Well, Yet It Has Brought Widespread Devastation Along Its Lower Reaches. By Frederick Simpich. LII, pp. 243-289, 53 ills., map, Sept., 1927

Hamburg Speaks with Steam Sirens. By Frederick Simpich. LXIII, pp. 717-744, 32 ills., June, 1933

How We Use the Gulf of Mexico. By Frederick Simpich. LXXXV, pp. 1-40, 20 ills. in black and white, 19 ills. in color, two-page map, Jan., 1944

Indiana Journey. By Frederick Simpich. LXX, pp. 267-320, 32 ills. in black and white, 27 ills. in color, two-page map, Sept., 1936

Land of a Million Smiles (Ozarks). By Frederick Simpich. LXXXIII, pp. 589-623, 14 ills. in black and white, 20 ills. in color, map, May, 1943

Life on the Argentine Pampa. By Frederick Simpich. Paintings by Cesáreo Bernaldo de Quirós. LXIV, pp. 449-491, 41 ills. in black and white, 8 ills. in color, Oct., 1933

Manchuria, Promised Land of Asia: Invaded by Railways and Millions of Settlers, This Vast Region Now Recalls Early Boom Days in the American West. By Frederick Simpich. LVI, pp. 379-428, 58 ills., map, Oct., 1929

Mediterranean Checkerboard. By Frederick Simpich. LXXXI, pp. 527-550, 20 ills., map, Apr., 1942

Men Against the Rivers (Mississippi and Ohio). By Frederick Simpich. LXXI, pp. 767-794, 22 ills., maps, June, 1937

Men and Gold. By Frederick Simpich. LXIII, pp. 481-518, 33 ills. in black and white, 11 ills. in duotone, Apr., 1933

A Mexican Land of Canaan: Marvelous Riches of the Wonderful West Coast of Our Neighbor Republic. By Frederick Simpich. XXXVI, pp. 307-330, 16 ills., map, Oct., 1919

Mindanao, on the Road to Tokyo. By Frederick Simpich. LXXXVI, pp. 539-574, 26 ills. in black and white, 12 ills. in color, two-page map, Nov., 1944

Missouri, Mother of the West. By Frederick Simpich. XLIII, pp. 421-460, 35 ills., Apr., 1923

More Water for California's Great Central Valley. By Frederick Simpich. XC, pp. 645-664, 16 ills., map, Nov., 1946

Mystic Nedjef, the Shia Mecca. By Frederick Simpich. XXVI, pp. 589-598, 4 ills., Dec., 1914

New Mexico Melodrama. By Frederick Simpich. LXXIII, pp. 529-569, 19 ills. in black and white, 25 ills. in color, two-page map, May, 1938

1940 Paradox in Hong Kong. By Frederick Simpich. LXXVII, pp. 531-558, 24 ills., 3 maps, Apr., 1940

North America's Oldest Metropolis: Through 600 Melodramatic Years, Mexico City Has Grown in Splendor and Achievement. By Frederick Simpich. LVIII, pp. 45-84, 34 ills., July, 1930

Northern California at Work. By Frederick Simpich. LXIX, pp. 309-389, 36 ills. in black and white, 41 ills. in color, maps (1 two-page), Mar., 1936

Ontario, Next Door: Alert, Energetic, and Resourceful, Its British Pluck and Skill in Arts and Trades Gain for This Province a High Place Under the Union Jack. By Frederick Simpich. LXII, pp. 131-183, 54 ills., map, Aug., 1932

Out in San Francisco: Fed on Gold Dust and Fattened by Sea Trade, a Pioneer Village Becomes a Busy World Port. By Frederick Simpich. LXI, pp. 395-434, 38 ills., Apr., 1932

Pieces of Silver. By Frederick Simpich. LXIV, pp. 253-292, 49 ills., Sept., 1933

QM, the Fighting Storekeeper. By Frederick Simpich. Paintings by Arthur Beaumont. LXXXII, pp. 561-600, 22 ills. in black and white, 16 ills. in color, Nov., 1942

Return to Manila. By Frederick Simpich. LXXVIII, pp. 409-451, 21 ills. in black and white, 21 ills. in color, map, Oct., 1940

The Rise of the New Arab Nation. By Frederick Simpich. XXXVI, pp. 369-393, 17 ills., map, Nov., 1919

San Diego Can't Believe It. By Frederick Simpich. LXXXI, pp. 45-80, 26 ills. in black and white, 9 ills. in color, Jan., 1942

The Santa Fe Trail, Path to Empire. By Frederick Simpich. LVI, pp. 213-252, 35 ills. in black and white, 12 ills. in color, map, Aug., 1929

Seeing Our Spanish Southwest. By Frederick Simpich. LXXVII, pp. 711-756, 25 ills. in black and white, 17 ills. in duotone, map supplement, June, 1940

Singapore, Crossroads of the East: The World's Greatest Mart for Rubber and Tin Was in Recent Times a Pirate-haunted, Tiger-infested Jungle Isle. By Frederick Simpich. XLIX, pp. 235-269, 32 ills., Mar., 1926

Skypaths Through Latin America: Flying From Our Nation's Capital Southward Over Jungles, Remote Islands, and Great Cities on an Aërial Survey of the East Coast of South America. By Frederick Simpich. LIX, pp. 1-79, 77 ills., map, Jan., 1931

Smoke Over Alabama. By Frederick Simpich. LX, pp. 703-758, 43 ills. in black and white, 26 ills. in color, map, Dec., 1931

So Big Texas. By Frederick Simpich. LIII, pp. 637-693, 72 ills., two-page map, June, 1928

So Oklahoma Grew Up. By Frederick Simpich. LXXIX, pp. 269-314, 30 ills. in black and white, 19 ills. in color, map, Mar., 1941

Southern California at Work. By Frederick Simpich. LXVI, pp. 529-600, 39 ills. in black and white, 41 ills. in color, two-page map, Nov., 1934

Speaking of Kansas. By Frederick Simpich. LXXII, pp. 135-182, 37 ills. in black and white, 12 ills. in color, two-page map, Aug., 1937

Spin Your Globe to Long Island: Only Six States Have More People than the Insular Empire that Ranges from a World's Fair Through Potato Patches, Princely Estates, and Historic Shrines. By Frederick Simpich. LXXV, pp. 413-460, 25 ills. in black and white, 18 ills. in color, Apr., 1939

The Story of the Ruhr. By Frederick Simpich. XLI, pp. 553-564, 11 ills., map, May, 1922

Taming the Outlaw Missouri River. By Frederick Simpich. LXXXVIII, pp. 569-598, 25 ills., two-page map, Nov., 1945

These Missourians. By Frederick Simpich. LXXXIX, pp. 277-310, 12 ills. in black and white, 22 ills. in color, map, Mar., 1946

They Sustain the Wings (Ground Crews). By Frederick Simpich. LXXXIV, pp. 333-354, 19 ills., Sept., 1943

This Giant That Is New York. By Frederick Simpich. LVIII, pp. 517-583, 26 ills. in black and white, 8 ills. in gravure, 42 ills. in color, Nov., 1930

Time and Tide on the Thames. By Frederick Simpich. LXXV, pp. 239-272, 23 ills. in black and white, 10 ills. in color, map, Feb., 1939

Today's World Turns on Oil. By Frederick Simpich. LXXIX, pp. 703-748, 22 ills. in black and white, drawings, 21 ills. in color, June, 1941

U. S. Roads in War and Peace. By Frederick Simpich. LXXX, pp. 687-716, 27 ills., Dec., 1941

Vignettes of Guadalajara (Mexico). By Frederick Simpich. LXV, pp. 329-356, 20 ills. in black and white, 15 ills. in color, map, Mar., 1934

Wartime in the Pacific Northwest. By Frederick Simpich. LXXXII, pp. 421-464, 25 ills. in black and white, 23 ills. in color, map, Oct., 1942

The Wends of the Spreewald. By Frederick Simpich. XLIII, pp. 327-336, 12 ills., Mar., 1923

What Is the Saar? By Frederick Simpich. LXVII, pp. 241-264, 5 ills. in black and white, 23 ills. in duotone, maps, Feb., 1935

What Luzon Means to Uncle Sam. By Frederick Simpich. LXXXVII, pp. 305-332, 25 ills., map supplement, Mar., 1945

Where Adam and Eve Lived (Baghdad). By Frederick and Margaret Simpich. XXVI, pp. 546-588, 35 ills., Dec., 1914

Winchester, England's Early Capital. By Frederick Simpich. LXXIX, pp. 67-92, 25 ills., map, Jan., 1941

The Yield of Texas. By Frederick Simpich. LXXXVII, pp. 163-184, 15 ills., two-page map, Feb., 1945

Your Dog Joins Up. By Frederick Simpich. LXXXIII, pp. 93-113, 25 ills., Jan., 1943

Youth Explores Its World (Boy Scouts). By Frederick Simpich. LXV, pp. 643-662, 21 ills., May, 1934

SIMPICH, FREDERICK, JR.:

Americans Help Liberated Europe Live Again. By Lt. Col. Frederick Simpich, Jr. LXXXVII, pp. 747-768, 17 ills., June, 1945

At Ease in the South Seas. By Maj. Frederick Simpich, Jr. LXXXV, pp. 79-104, 32 ills., Jan., 1944

Life on the Hawaii "Front": All-out Defense and Belt Tightening of Pacific Outpost Foreshadow the Things to Come on Mainland. By Lieut. Frederick Simpich, Jr. LXXXII, pp. 541-560, 19 ills., map, Oct., 1942

Paris Freed. By Maj. Frederick Simpich, Jr. LXXXVII, pp. 385-412, 14 ills. in black and white, 12 ills. in color, Apr., 1945

When GI Joes Took London. By Maj. Frederick Simpich, Jr. LXXXVI, pp. 337-354, 18 ills., Sept., 1944

SIMPICH, MARGARET:

Where Adam and Eve Lived (Baghdad). By Frederick and Margaret Simpich. XXVI, pp. 546-588, 35 ills., Dec., 1914

A **SIMPLE** Method of Proving That the Earth Is Round. By Robert Marshall Brown. XVIII, pp. 771-774, 5 diagrs., Dec., 1907

SIMPSON, W. A.:

Influence of Geographical Conditions on Military Operations in South Africa. By Major W. A. Simpson. XI, pp. 186-192, ill., map, May, 1900

SIMSON, SPICER:

Transporting a Navy Through the Jungles of Africa in War Time. By Frank J. Magee. XLII, pp. 331-362, 31 ills., Oct., 1922
Note: Commander Spicer Simson, R. N., organizer and leader of the expedition

SINAI (Peninsula), Egypt:

East of Suez to the Mount of the Decalogue: Following the Trail Over Which Moses Led the Israelites from the Slave-Pens of Egypt to Sinai. By Maynard Owen Williams. LII, pp. 709-743, 32 ills., map, Dec., 1927

Flying Over Egypt, Sinai, and Palestine: Looking Down Upon the Holy Land During an Air Journey of Two and a Half Hours from Cairo to Jerusalem. By Brigadier General P. R. C. Groves and Major J. R. McCrindle. L, pp. 313-355, 26 ills. in black and white, 23 ills. in color, map, Sept., 1926

The Route Over Which Moses Led the Children of Israel Out of Egypt. By Franklin E. Hoskins. XX, pp. 1011-1038, 24 ills., map, Dec., 1909

Sunrise and Sunset from Mount Sinai. By Rev. Sartell Prentice, Jr. XXIII, pp. 1242-1282, 34 ills., map, Dec., 1912

SINCLAIR, C. H.:

The California and Nevada Boundary. (By C. H. Sinclair). X, pp. 416-417, Oct., 1899

SINDBADS of Science: Narrative of a Windjammer's Specimen-Collecting Voyage to the Sargasso Sea, to Senegambian Africa and Among Islands of High Adventure in the South Atlantic. By George Finlay Simmons. LII, pp. 1-75, 89 ills., map, July, 1927

SINGAN—The Present Capital of the Chinese Empire. (By James Mascarene Hubbard). XII, pp. 63-66, ill., Feb., 1901

SINGAPORE—Britain's Outpost of Empire. 9 color photos by J. Baylor Roberts. LXXX, pp. 665-672, Nov., 1941

SINGAPORE, Straits Settlements:

Behind the News in Singapore. By Frederick Simpich. LXXVIII, pp. 83-110, 26 ills., map, July, 1940

The Fire-Walking Hindus of Singapore. By L. Elizabeth Lewis. LIX, pp. 513-522, 12 ills., Apr., 1931

Life Grows Grim in Singapore. By H. Gordon Minnigerode. LXXX, pp. 661-686, 17 ills. in black and white, 9 ills. in color, map, Nov., 1941

Singapore, Crossroads of the East: The World's Greatest Mart for Rubber and Tin Was in Recent Times a Pirate-haunted, Tiger-infested Jungle Isle. By Frederick Simpich. XLIX, pp. 235-269, 32 ills., map, Mar., 1926

Singapore: Far East Gibraltar in the Malay Jungle. 23 ills. LXXIII, pp. 599-614, May, 1938

SINGER, ROLF:

Roaming Russia's Caucasus: Rugged Mountains and Hardy Fighters Guard the Soviet Union's Caucasian Treasury of Manganese and Oil. By Rolf Singer. LXXXII, pp. 91-121, 33 ills., July, 1942

The **SINGING** Towers of Holland and Belgium. By William Gorham Rice. XLVII, pp. 357-376, 22 ills., Mar., 1925

SINKIANG (Chinese Turkistan):

By Coolie and Caravan Across Central Asia: Narrative of a 7,900-Mile Journey of Exploration and Research Over "the Roof of the World," from the Indian Ocean to the Yellow Sea. By William J. Morden. LII, pp. 369-431, 73 ills., map, Oct., 1927

The Desert Road to Turkestan: Twentieth Century Travel Through Innermost Asia, Along Caravan Trails Over Which Oriental Commerce Was Once Borne from China to the Medieval Western World. By Owen Lattimore. LV, pp. 661-702, 45 ills., map, June, 1929

First Over the Roof of the World by Motor: The Trans-Asiatic Expedition Sets New Records for Wheeled Transport in Scaling Passes of the Himalayas. By Maynard Owen Williams. LXI, pp. 321-363, 45 ills., maps, Mar., 1932

From the Mediterranean to the Yellow Sea by Motor: The Citroën-Haardt Expedition Successfully Completes Its Dramatic Journey. By Maynard Owen Williams. LXII, pp. 513-580, 45 ills. in black and white, 25 ills. in color, maps, Nov., 1932

Medieval Tales of the Lop Basin in Central Asia. By Ellsworth Huntington. XIX, pp. 289-295, 9 ills., Apr., 1908

On the World's Highest Plateaus: Through an Asiatic No Man's Land to the Desert of Ancient Cathay. By Hellmut de Terra. LIX, pp. 319-367, 39 ills. in black and white, 32 ills. in color, map, Mar., 1931

Sven Hedin's Explorations in Central Asia. XII, pp. 393-395, Nov., 1901

SINKIANG (Chinese Turkistan)—*Continued*
With the Nomads of Central Asia: A Summer's Sojourn in the Tekes Valley, Plateau Paradise of Mongol and Turkic Tribes. By Edward Murray. Paintings and drawings by Alexandre Iacovleff. LXIX, pp. 1-57, 43 ills. in black and white, 26 ills. in color, map, Jan., 1936

SIOUX INDIANS:
The Black Hills, Once Hunting Grounds of the Red Men. LII, pp. 305-329, 18 ills. in black and white, 13 ills. in color, Sept., 1927

SIR Francis Drake's Anchorage. By Edward L. Berthoud. VI, pp. 208-214, Dec. 29, 1894

SIR John Evans and Prof. W J McGee. (By J. H.). VIII, pp. 358-359, ills., Dec., 1897

SIRACUSA (Syracuse), Sicily:
Sicily, the Battle-Field of Nations and of Nature. By Mrs. George C. Bosson, Jr. XX, pp. 97-118, 25 ills., map, Jan., 1909

SISAL HEMP. *See* Henequen

SISSON, ROBERT F.:
Cape Cod People and Places. 24 color photos: 23 by Robert F. Sisson. LXXXIX, pp. 753-768, June, 1946
Potomac: George Washington's Historic River. 18 color photos by Willard R. Culver and Robert F. Sisson. LXXXVIII, pp. 41-64, July, 1945

SIVAS, Turkey:
The Turkish Republic Comes of Age. By Maynard Owen Williams. LXXXVII, pp. 581-616, 4 ills. in black and white, 29 ills. in color, map, May, 1945

SIWAI (Tribespeople):
A Woman's Experiences among Stone Age Solomon Islanders: Primitive Life Remains Unchanged in Tropical Jungleland Where United States Forces Now Are Fighting. By Eleanor Schirmer Oliver. LXXXII, pp. 813-836, 26 ills., map, Dec., 1942

6,000 Miles over the Roads of Free China. By Josephine A. Brown. LXXXV, pp. 355-384, 30 ills., map, Mar., 1944

SIXTH ANNUAL NEWSPAPER NATIONAL SNAPSHOT AWARDS:
The American Scene. 29 winning photos in the Sixth Annual Newspaper National Snapshot Awards, with explanatory note. LXXIX, pp. 220-246, Feb., 1941

The **SKELETON** in Luray Cave. (By H. C. Hovey). XVII, pp. 425-426, July, 1906

A **SKETCH** of the Geographical History of Asia Minor. By Sir William Ramsay. XLII, pp. 553-570, 12 ills., Nov., 1922

SKETCH of the Geology of the St. Elias Region (Part III, from "An Expedition to Mount St. Elias, Alaska," by Israel C. Russell). III, pp. 167-175, ills., May 29, 1891

SKIING (Sport):
New England Ski Trails: Snow and Ice Sports Transform Whittier's Winters of Snowbound Seclusion Into Seasons of Outdoor Recreation. By Daniel Rochford. LXX, pp. 645-664, 11 ills. in black and white, 13 ills. in color, Nov., 1936

SKIING (Sport)—*Continued*
Skiing in Switzerland's Realm of Winter Sports. 10 photos in duotone by Jean Gaberell, E. Gyger, A. Klopfenstein. LXIII, pp. 345-352, Mar., 1933
Skiing Over the New Hampshire Hills. By Fred H. Harris. XXXVII, pp. 151-164, 37 ills., Feb., 1920

SKINNER, ROBERT P.:
Consul Skinner's Mission to Abyssinia. XV, pp. 165-166, ill., Apr., 1904

SKIRTING the Shores of Sunrise: Seeking and Finding "The Levant" in a Journey by Steamer, Motor-Car, and Train from Constantinople to Port Said. By Melville Chater. L, pp. 649-728, 60 ills. in black and white, 34 ills. in color, map, Dec., 1926

SKOKHOLM (Island), Wales:
We Live Alone, and Like It—On an Island. By R. M. Lockley. LXXIV, pp. 252-278, 27 ills., Aug., 1938

SKUAS (Birds):
South Georgia, an Outpost of the Antarctic. By Robert Cushman Murphy. XLI, pp. 409-444, 41 ills., maps, Apr., 1922

SKUNKS:
Wild Animals That Took Their Own Pictures by Day and by Night. By George Shiras, 3d. XXIV, pp. 763-834, 68 ills., map, pictorial supplement, July, 1913

SKY CHARTS. *See* Star Charts

SKY-HIGH in Lama Land (Tibet). 12 photos by C. Suydam Cutting. XC, pp. 185-196, Aug., 1946

A **SKYLINE** Drive in the Pyrenees (France). By W. Robert Moore. LXXII, pp. 434-452, 24 ills. in color, Oct., 1937

SKYPATHS Through Latin America: Flying From Our Nation's Capital Southward Over Jungles, Remote Islands, and Great Cities on an Aërial Survey of the East Coast of South America. By Frederick Simpich. LIX, pp. 1-79, 77 ills., map, Jan., 1931

SKÝROS (Island), Aegean Sea:
The Isles of Greece. By Lt. Richard Stillwell, USNR. LXXXV, pp. 593-622, 11 ills. in black and white, 20 ills. in color, map, May, 1944

SLAVE TRADE:
Africa, Its Past and Future. (By Gardiner G. Hubbard). I, pp. 99-124, foldout map, Apr., 1889

SLEDGE DOGS:
Dogs of Duty and Devotion. By Frederick G. Vosburgh. LXXX, pp. 769-774, 3 ills., Dec., 1941
Working Dogs of the World. By Freeman Lloyd. Paintings by Edward Herbert Miner. LXXX, pp. 776-806, 12 ills. in black and white, 20 ills. in color, Dec., 1941

SLEEPING SICKNESS:
Amid the Snow Peaks of the Equator: A Naturalist's Explorations Around Ruwenzori, with an Excursion to the Congo State, and an Account of the Terrible Scourge of Sleeping Sickness. By A. F. R. Wollaston. XX, pp. 256-277, 11 ills., Mar., 1909

SLIME MOLDS. *See* Mycetozoa

SMALAND (Region), Sweden:
Life's Flavor on a Swedish Farm: From the Rocky Hills of Småland Thousands of Sturdy Citizens Have Emigrated to the United States. By Willis Lindquist. LXXVI, pp. 393-414, 23 ills., map, Sept., 1939

SMALLER Mammals of North America. By E. W. Nelson. Paintings by Louis Agassiz Fuertes. XXXIII, pp. 371*-493, 29 ills. in black and white, 59 ills. in color, May, 1918

The **SMALLEST** State in the World: Vatican City on Its 108 Acres Is a Complete Sovereignty Internationally Recognized. By W. Coleman Nevils. LXXV, pp. 377-412, 37 ills., two-page map, Mar., 1939

SMILING, Happy Philippines. 21 color photos: 19 by J. Baylor Roberts. LXXVIII, pp. 425-448, Oct., 1940

SMITH, A. W.:
Working Teak in the Burma Forests: The Sagacious Elephant Is Man's Ablest Ally in the Logging Industry of the Far East. By A. W. Smith. LVIII, pp. 239-256, 5 ills. in black and white, 15 ills. in color, Aug., 1930

SMITH, CHARLES EMORY:
Russia. By Charles Emory Smith. XVI, pp. 55-63, Feb., 1905

SMITH, GEORGE OTIS:
Four Prominent Geographers. XVIII, pp. 425-428, 4 ills., June, 1907
Maine, the Outpost State: Some Forgotten Incidents in the Life of an Old and Stout-Hearted Commonwealth. By George Otis Smith. LXVII, pp. 533-592, 35 ills. in black and white, 39 ills. in color, two-page map, May, 1935
Where the World Gets Its Oil: But Where Will Our Children Get It When American Wells Cease to Flow? By George Otis Smith. XXXVII, pp. 181-202, 21 ills., 3 maps, Feb., 1920
See also NGS: Board of Managers

SMITH, GLANVILLE:
Minnesota, Mother of Lakes and Rivers. By Glanville Smith. LXVII, pp. 273-318, 42 ills. in black and white, 11 ills. in color, two-page map, Mar., 1935
On Goes Wisconsin: Strength and Vigor Mark This Midwestern State, With Its Woods and Lakes and Its Blend of Sturdy Nationalities. By Glanville Smith. LXXII, pp. 1-46, 25 ills. in black and white, 27 ills. in color, two-page map, July, 1937

SMITH, HARRISON W.:
Notes on Tahiti. By H. W. Smith. XXII, pp. 947-963, 17 ills., Oct., 1911
Sarawak: The Land of the White Rajahs. By Harrison W. Smith. XXXV, pp. 110-167, 58 ills., map, Feb., 1919

SMITH, HERBERT A.:
Saving the Forests. By Herbert A. Smith. XVIII, pp. 519-534, 7 ills., Aug., 1907

SMITH, HUGH M.:
America's Most Valuable Fishes. By Hugh M. Smith. XXIII, pp. 494-514, 17 ills., May, 1912
America's Surpassing Fisheries: Their Present Condition and Future Prospects, and How the Federal Government Fosters Them. By Hugh M. Smith. XXIX, pp. 546-583, 35 ills., June, 1916
Brittany: The Land of the Sardine. By Hugh M. Smith. XX, pp. 541-573, 23 ills., June, 1909
Deep-Sea Exploring Expedition of the Steamer "Albatross." By Hugh M. Smith. X, pp. 291-296, ills., diagr., Aug., 1899
Federal Fish Farming; or, Planting Fish by the Billion. By Hugh M. Smith. XXI, pp. 418-446, 22 ills., May, 1910
The Fisheries of Japan. By Hugh M. Smith. XV, pp. 362-364, Sept., 1904. XVI, pp. 201-220, 13 ills., May, 1905
Goldfish and Their Cultivation in America. By Hugh M. Smith. Paintings by Hashime Murayama. XLVI, pp. 375-400, 14 ills. in black and white, 8 ills. in color, Oct., 1924
King Herring: An Account of the World's Most Valuable Fish, the Industries It Supports, and the Part It Has Played in History. By Hugh M. Smith. XX, pp. 701-735, 21 ills., Aug., 1909
Making the Fur Seal Abundant. By Hugh M. Smith. XXII, pp. 1139-1165, 18 ills., map, Dec., 1911
The Mysterious Life of the Common Eel. By Hugh M. Smith. XXIV, pp. 1140-1146, 3 ills., Oct., 1913
A North Holland Cheese Market. By Hugh M. Smith. XXI, pp. 1051-1066, 17 ills., Dec., 1910
Our Fish Immigrants. By Hugh M. Smith. XVIII, pp. 383-400, 3 ills., June, 1907
Oysters: The World's Most Valuable Water Crop. By Hugh M. Smith. XXIV, pp. 257-281, 21 ills., Mar., 1913
The Pearl Fisheries of Ceylon. By Hugh M. Smith. XXIII, pp. 173-194, 13 ills., map, Feb., 1912
Some Giant Fishes of the Seas. By Hugh M. Smith. XX, pp. 637-644, 6 ills., July, 1909
When the Father of Waters Goes on a Rampage: An Account of the Salvaging of Food-fishes from the Overflowed Lands of the Mississippi River. By Hugh M. Smith. XXXVII, pp. 369-386, 18 ills., Apr., 1920

SMITH, JANE M.:
Fund for Life Memberships in the Society bequeathed by Jane M. Smith. XXIII, p. 104, Jan., 1912
The National Geographic Society's Notable Year (Award of Life Memberships Under Jane M. Smith Endowment Fund). XXXVII, pp. 338-345, ills., Apr., 1920

SMITH, MIDDLETON:
Gardening in Northern Alaska. By Middleton Smith. XIV, pp. 355-357, Sept., 1903

SMITH, NICOL:
Color Glows in the Guianas, French and Dutch. By Nicol Smith. LXXXIII, pp. 459-480, 8 ills. in black and white, 13 ills. in color, map, Apr., 1943

SMITH, SIR ROSS:
From London to Australia by Aëroplane: A Personal Narrative of the First Aërial Voyage Half Around the World. By Sir Ross Smith. XXXIX, pp. 229-339, 76 ills. in black and white, 8 ills. in color, map, Mar., 1921

SMITHSONIAN INSTITUTION, Washington, D. C.:
Geographic Work of the General Government. By Henry Gannett. IX, pp. 329-338, July, 1898

Expeditions
Around the World for Animals. By William M. and Lucile Q. Mann. LXXIII, pp. 665-714, 33 ills. in black and white, 23 ills. in color, map, June, 1938
Discovering the New World's Oldest Dated Work of Man: A Maya Monument Inscribed 291 B. C. is Unearthed Near a Huge Stone Head by a Geographic-Smithsonian Expedition in Mexico. By Matthew W. Stirling. LXXVI, pp. 183-218, 40 ills., map, Aug., 1939
Expedition Unearths Buried Masterpieces of Carved Jade. By Matthew W. Stirling. LXXX, pp. 277-302, 14 ills. in black and white, 20 ills. in color, map, Sept., 1941
Exploring Frozen Fragments of American History: On the Trail of Early Eskimo Colonists Who Made a 55-Mile Crossing from the Old World to the New. By Henry B. Collins, Jr. LXXV, pp. 633-656, 24 ills., map, May, 1939
Great Stone Faces of the Mexican Jungle: Five Colossal Heads and Numerous Other Monuments of Vanished Americans Are Excavated by the Latest National Geographic-Smithsonian Expedition. By Matthew W. Stirling. LXXVIII, pp. 309-334, 26 ills., map, Sept., 1940
Jungle Housekeeping for a Geographic Expedition. By Marion Stirling. LXXX, pp. 303-327, 15 ills., Sept., 1941
La Venta's Green Stone Tigers. By Matthew W. Stirling. LXXXIV, pp. 321-332, 4 ills. in black and white, 6 ills. in color, map, Sept., 1943
Measuring the Sun's Heat and Forecasting the Weather: The National Geographic Society to Maintain a Solar Station in a Remote Part of the World to Coöperate with Smithsonian Institution Stations in California and Chile. By C. G. Abbot. XLIX, pp. 111-126, 15 ills., chart, Jan., 1926
National Geographic Society (Cables and Report by Theodore Roosevelt on the African Expedition Sponsored by the Smithsonian Institution). XXI, pp. 365-370, 5 ills., Apr., 1910
Wild Man and Wild Beast in Africa. By Theodore Roosevelt. XXII, pp. 1-33, 41 ills., map, Jan., 1911
See also Africa (Mr. Roosevelt's)
Wildlife of Tabasco and Veracruz (Mexico). By Walter A. Weber. With 19 ills. in color from paintings by author. LXXXVII, pp. 187-216, 7 ills. in black and white, map, Feb., 1945

SMOKE Over Alabama. By Frederick Simpich. LX, pp. 703-758, 43 ills. in black and white, 26 ills. in color, map, Dec., 1931

SMOKY JUNGLE FROG:
A Frog That Eats Bats and Snakes: In Captivity, This Big Jungle Amphibian Exhibits an Extraordinary Appetite. By Kenneth W. Vinton. LXXIII, pp. 657-664, 11 ills., May, 1938

SMOKY MOUNTAINS, North Carolina-Tennessee. *See* Great Smoky Mountains

SMYRNA, Turkey. *See* İzmir

SMYSER, WILLIAM LEON:
São Tomé, the Chocolate Island. By William Leon Smyser. LXXXIX, pp. 657-680, 23 ills., map, May, 1946

SNAKE DANCE:
The Forests and Deserts of Arizona. By Bernhard E. Fernow. VIII, pp. 203-226, 5 ills., July-Aug., 1897
The Snake Dance (Hopi Indians). By Marion L. Oliver. XXII, pp. 107-137, 31 ills., Feb., 1911

SNAKES. *See* Reptiles

SNOW:
The Magic Beauty of Snow and Dew. By Wilson A. Bentley. XLIII, pp. 103-112, 9 ills., Jan., 1923
Snow Crystals. (By Wilson A. Bentley). XV, pp. 30-37, 31 ills., Jan., 1904
Snow Scenes. 5 ills. XXIX, pp. 60-64, Jan., 1916

SNOW STORM ("Blizzard of '88"). *See* Storms

SNOWY Peaks and Old Costumes of Switzerland. 12 color photos by Hans Hildenbrand. LXVI, pp. 147-154, Aug., 1934

SO Big Texas. By Frederick Simpich. LIII, pp. 637-693, 72 ills., two-page map, June, 1928

The **SO-CALLED** "Jeannette Relics." By Professor William H. Dall. VII, pp. 93-98, Mar., 1896

SO Oklahoma Grew Up. By Frederick Simpich. LXXIX, pp. 269-314, 30 ills. in black and white, 19 ills. in color, map, Mar., 1941

The **SOCIETY** Announces New Flight into the Stratosphere. By Gilbert Grosvenor. LXVII, pp. 265-272, ills., map, Feb., 1935

The **SOCIETY** Awards Hubbard Medal to Anne Morrow Lindbergh. LXV, pp. 791-794, 4 ills., June, 1934

SOCIETY ISLANDS, South Pacific Ocean:
Diary of a Voyage from San Francisco to Tahiti and Return, 1901. By S. P. Langley. XII, pp. 413-429, 10 ills., maps, Dec., 1901
The Dream Ship: The Story of a Voyage of Adventure More Than Half Around the World in a 47-foot Lifeboat. By Ralph Stock. XXXIX, pp. 1-52, 43 ills., map, Jan., 1921
Notes on Tahiti. By H. W. Smith. XXII, pp. 947-963, 17 ills., Oct., 1911
Tahiti: A Playground of Nature. By Paul Gooding. XXXVIII, pp. 301-326, 16 ills., map, Oct., 1920

The **SOCIETY** Maps Northwestern United States and Neighboring Canadian Provinces. Text with map supplement. LXXIX, pp. 805-806, June, 1941

The **SOCIETY** Takes Part in Three Geographic Expeditions. LXV, pp. 625-626, May, 1934

The **SOCIETY'S** Map of Bible Lands. By Gilbert Grosvenor. Text with map supplement. LXXIV, pp. 751-754, 3 ills., Dec., 1938

The **SOCIETY'S** Map of Historic and Scenic Reaches of the Nation's Capital. Text with map supplement. LXXIV, pp. 57-58, July, 1938

The **SOCIETY'S** Map of South America. By Gilbert Grosvenor. Text with map supplement. LXXII, pp. 809-810, Dec., 1937

The **SOCIETY'S** Map of the Antarctic. Text with map supplement. LXII, pp. 485-486, ill., Oct., 1932

The **SOCIETY'S** Map of the Reaches of New York City. Text with map supplement. LXXV, pp. 491-492, Apr., 1939

The **SOCIETY'S** New Caribbean Map: Mexico, Central America, and the West Indies—Gateway of Discovery. Text with map supplement. LXVI, pp. 738-740, ill., Dec., 1934

The **SOCIETY'S** New Map of Africa. Text with map supplement. XLII, pp. 447-448, Oct., 1922

The **SOCIETY'S** New Map of Asia. Text with map supplement. LXIV, pp. 770-772, ill., Dec., 1933

The **SOCIETY'S** New Map of Bible Lands. Text with map supplement. XC, pp. 815-816, Dec., 1946

The **SOCIETY'S** New Map of Canada. Text with map supplement. LXIX, pp. 769-776, 9 ills., June, 1936

The **SOCIETY'S** New Map of Central Europe and the Mediterranean. Text with map supplement. LXXVI, pp. 559-560, Oct., 1939

The **SOCIETY'S** New Map of China. By James M. Darley. Text with map supplement. LXXXVII, pp. 745-746, June, 1945

The **SOCIETY'S** New Map of Europe. By Gilbert Grosvenor. Text with map supplement. LVI, pp. 771-774, Dec., 1929

The **SOCIETY'S** New Map of India and Burma. Text with map supplement. LXXXIX, p. 544, Apr., 1946

The **SOCIETY'S** New Map of South America. Text with map supplement. XL, pp. 374-392, 17 ills., Oct., 1921

The **SOCIETY'S** New Map of Southeast Asia. Text with map supplement. LXXXVI, pp. 449-450, ill., Oct., 1944

The **SOCIETY'S** New Map of Soviet Russia. Text with map supplement. LXXXVI, pp. 716-718, Dec., 1944

The **SOCIETY'S** New Map of the Pacific. By Gilbert Grosvenor. Text with map supplement. LXX, pp. 793-796, Dec., 1936

The **SOCIETY'S** New Map of the World. Text with map supplement. XLII, p. 690, Dec., 1922

The **SOCIETY'S** Special Medal Awarded to Amelia Earhart: First Woman to Receive Geographic Distinction at Brilliant Ceremony in the National Capital. LXII, pp. 358-367, 7 ills., Sept., 1932

The **SOCIETY'S** Special Medal Is Awarded to Dr. Thomas C. Poulter: Admiral Byrd's Second-in-Command and Senior Scientist Is Accorded High Geographic Honor. LXXII, pp. 105-108, ills., July, 1937

SOCIOLOGY. *See* Civilization

SOCOTRA (Island), Arabian Sea:

The Isle of Frankincense. By Charles K. Moser. XXXIII, pp. 267-278, 11 ills., Mar., 1918

SOFIA, Bulgaria:

Bulgaria, Farm Land Without a Farmhouse: A Nation of Villagers Faces the Challenge of Modern Machinery and Urban Life. By Maynard Owen Williams. LXII, pp. 185-218, 19 ills. in black and white, 27 ills. in color, map, Aug., 1932

SOIL. *See* Agriculture; Soil Erosion

SOIL EROSION:

China Fights Erosion with U. S. Aid. By Walter C. Lowdermilk. LXXXVII, pp. 641-680, 10 ills. in black and white, 26 ills. in color, June, 1945

The Economic Aspects of Soil Erosion. (Part I). By Dr. N. S. Shaler. VII, pp. 328-338, Oct., 1896

The Economic Aspects of Soil Erosion. (Part) II. By Dr. N. S. Shaler. VII, pp. 368-377, Nov., 1896

Taming "Flood Dragons" Along China's Hwang Ho (River). By Oliver J. Todd. LXXXI, pp. 205-234, 26 ills., map, Feb., 1942

Taming the Outlaw Missouri River. By Frederick Simpich. LXXXVIII, pp. 569-598, 25 ills., two-page map, Nov., 1945

SOJOURNING in the Italy of Today. By Mrs. Kenneth Roberts. LXX, pp. 351-396, 46 ills., map, Sept., 1936

SOKOL FESTIVAL:

Czechoslovakia, Key-Land to Central Europe. By Maynard Owen Williams. XXXIX, pp. 111-156, 45 ills., map, Feb., 1921

When Czechoslovakia Puts a Falcon Feather in Its Cap. By Maynard Owen Williams. LXIII, pp. 40-49, 13 ills. in color, Jan., 1933

SOLANO, SOLITA:

Constantinople Today. By Solita Solano. XLI, pp. 647-680, 40 ills., map, June, 1922

Vienna—A Capital Without a Nation. By Solita Solano. XLIII, pp. 77-102, 27 ills., Jan., 1923

SOLAR ECLIPSES. *See* Eclipses

SOLAR RADIATION:

Hunting an Observatory: A Successful Search for a Dry Mountain on Which to Establish the National Geographic Society's Solar Radiation Station. By C. G. Abbot. L, pp. 503-518, 13 ills., map, Oct., 1926

SOLAR RADIATION—*Continued*

Keeping House for the "Shepherds of the Sun." By Mrs. William H. Hoover. LVII, pp. 483-506, 17 ills., map, Apr., 1930

Measuring the Sun's Heat and Forecasting the Weather: The National Geographic Society to Maintain a Solar Station in a Remote Part of the World to Coöperate with Smithsonian Institution Stations in California and Chile. By C. G. Abbot. XLIX, pp. 111-126, 15 ills., chart, Jan., 1926

SOLAR System's Eternal Show. 10 ills. in color from paintings by Charles Bittinger. LXXVI, pp. 16-24, July, 1939

SOLDIER CRABS:

Strange Sights in Far-Away Papua. By A. E. Pratt. XVIII, pp. 559-572, 7 ills., Sept., 1907

SOLDIERS:

The Aerial Invasion of Burma. By General H. H. Arnold. LXXXVI, pp. 129-148, 20 ills., Aug., 1944

Included: Allied troops who served with Major General Orde Charles Wingate

American Fighters Visit Bible Lands. By Maynard Owen Williams. With 23 color photos by author. LXXXIX, pp. 311-340, 10 ills. in black and white, Mar., 1946

American Soldier in Reykjavík. By Corporal Luther M. Chovan. LXXXVIII, pp. 536-568, 6 ills. in black and white, 34 ills. in color, Nov., 1945

Americans Stand Guard in Greenland. By Andrew H. Brown. XC, pp. 457-500, 23 ills. in black and white, 19 ills. in color, map, Oct., 1946

Around the Clock with Your Soldier Boy. By Frederick Simpich. LXXX, pp. 1-36, 42 ills., July, 1941

Fiji Patrol on Bougainville. By David D. Duncan. LXXXVII, pp. 87-104, 9 ills. in black and white, 11 ills. in color, Jan., 1945

Flying Our Wounded Veterans Home. By Catherine Bell Palmer. LXXXVIII, pp. 363-384, 17 ills., Sept., 1945

Heroes' Return. By William H. Nicholas. LXXXVII, pp. 333-352, 19 ills., Mar., 1945

Infantrymen—The Fighters of War. By Brigadier General W. H. Wilbur. LXXXVI, pp. 513-538, 22 ills., Nov., 1944

Painting the Army on Maneuvers. By Arthur Beaumont. Text with 16 ills. in color from paintings by author. LXXXII, pp. 601-602, Nov., 1942

Paris Delivered. 10 ills. LXXXVII, pp. 79-86, Jan., 1945

Paris Freed. By Maj. Frederick Simpich, Jr. LXXXVII, pp. 385-412, 14 ills. in black and white, 12 ills. in color, Apr., 1945

This Is My Own: How the United States Seems to a Citizen Soldier Back from Three Years Overseas. By Frederick G. Vosburgh. LXXXIX, pp. 113-128, 14 ills., Jan., 1946

When GI Joes Took London. By Maj. Frederick Simpich, Jr. LXXXVI, pp. 337-354, 18 ills., Sept., 1944

The White War in Norway. By Thomas R. Henry. LXXXVIII, pp. 617-640, 23 ills., map, Nov., 1945

SOLDIERS—*Continued*

Yank Meets Native. By Wanda Burnett. LXXXVIII, pp. 105-128, 24 ills., July, 1945

Yanks in Northern Ireland. 15 ills. LXXXIV, pp. 191-204, Aug., 1943

See also Anzacs; Fita-Fitas; Fuzzy-Wuzzies; U. S. Army; U. S. Army Air Forces; U. S. Army Engineers; U. S. Army Quartermaster Corps; U. S. Army Signal Corps; World War I; World War II

SOLDIERS of the Soil: Our Food Crops Must Be Greatly Increased. By David F. Houston. XXXI, pp. 273-280, 4 ills., Mar., 1917

SOLOMON (King of Israel):

On the Trail of King Solomon's Mines: The Bible, in Addition to Its Spiritual Values, Continues to Prove a Rich Geography and Guide to Exploration of the Holy Land. By Nelson Glueck. LXXXV, pp. 233-256, 20 ills., map, Feb., 1944

SOLOMON ISLANDS, South Pacific Ocean:

American Pathfinders in the Pacific. By William H. Nicholas. LXXXIX, pp. 617-640, 17 ills., two-page map, May, 1946

Coconuts and Coral Islands. By H. Ian Hogbin. LXV, pp. 265-298, 24 ills. in black and white, 14 ills. in color, map, Mar., 1934

The Islands of the Pacific. By J. P. Thomson. XL, pp. 543-558, 15 ills., map supplement, Dec., 1921

What the Fighting Yanks See. By Wanda Burnett. LXXXVI, pp. 451-476, 27 ills., Oct., 1944

A Woman's Experiences among Stone Age Solomon Islanders: Primitive Life Remains Unchanged in Tropical Jungleland Where United States Forces Now Are Fighting. By Eleanor Schirmer Oliver. LXXXII, pp. 813-836, 26 ills., map, Dec., 1942

See also Bougainville; Guadalcanal; Munda

SOLOMONS ISLAND, Maryland: Amphibious Training Base:

Landing Craft for Invasion. By Melville Bell Grosvenor. LXXXVI, pp. 1-30, 26 ills., July, 1944

SOLUKA CREEK, Alaska:

The Valley of Ten Thousand Smokes: National Geographic Society Explorations in the Katmai District of Alaska. By Robert F. Griggs. XXXI, pp. 13-68, 51 ills., map, Jan., 1917

SOMALILAND. *See* French Somaliland

SOME Aspects of Rural Japan. By Walter Weston. XLII, pp. 275-301, 12 ills. in black and white, 16 ills. in color, Sept., 1922

SOME Early Geographers of the United States. By Rear Admiral Colby M. Chester. XV, pp. 392-404, Oct., 1904

SOME Facts About Japan. XV, pp. 446-448, Nov., 1904

SOME Forgotten Corners of London: Many Places of Beauty and Historic Interest Repay the Search of the Inquiring Visitor. By Harold Donaldson Eberlein. LXI, pp. 163-198, 25 ills. in black and white, 13 ills. in color, Feb., 1932

SOME French Pastorals. 18 color photos by Harrison Howell Walker. LXXVII, pp. 207-230, Feb., 1940

SOME Geographic Features of Southern Patagonia, with a Discussion of Their Origin. By J. B. Hatcher. XI, pp. 41-55, 4 ills., Feb., 1900

SOME Giant Fishes of the Seas. By Hugh M. Smith. XX, pp. 637-644, 6 ills., July, 1909

SOME Human Habitations. By Collier Cobb. XIX, pp. 509-515, 5 ills., July, 1908

SOME Impressions of 150,000 Miles of Travel. By William Howard Taft. LVII, pp. 523-598, 80 ills., May, 1930

SOME Indications of Land in the Vicinity of the North Pole. By R. A. Harris. XV, pp. 255-261, map, June, 1904

SOME Lessons in Geography. By Edward Atkinson. XVI, pp. 193-198, Apr., 1905

SOME Mexican Transportation Scenes. By Walter W. Bradley. XXI, pp. 985-991, 10 ills., Dec., 1910

SOME Notes on the Fox Island Passes, Alaska. By J. J. Gilbert. XVI, pp. 427-429, Sept., 1905

SOME Notes on Venezuela. XIV, pp. 17-21, 3 ills., map, Jan., 1903

SOME Odd Pages from the Annals of the Tulip: A "Made" Flower of Unknown Origin Took Medieval Europe by Storm and Caused a Financial Panic in the Netherlands. By Leo A. Borah. LXIV, pp. 321-343, 13 ills. in black and white, 10 ills. in color, Sept., 1933

SOME of Nature's Scenic Gifts to Hawaii. 16 photos: 6 by Henry W. Henshaw. XLV, pp. 159-174, Feb., 1924

SOME of Our Immigrants. XVIII, pp. 317-334, 21 ills., May, 1907

SOME of the Conditions and Possibilities of Agriculture in Alaska. By Walter H. Evans. IX, pp. 178-187, Apr., 1898

SOME Peculiar Features of Central African Geography. (By Samuel P. Verner). XV, p. 448, Nov., 1904

SOME Personal Experiences with Earthquakes (Arica, Peru). By Rear Admiral L. G. Billings. XXVII, pp. 57-71, 7 ills., Jan., 1915

SOME Recent Geographic Events. (By J. H.). VIII, pp. 359-362, ill., Dec., 1897

SOME Recent Instances of National Altruism: The Efforts of the United States to Aid the Peoples of Cuba, Porto Rico and the Philippines. By William H. Taft. XVIII, pp. 429-438, July, 1907

SOME Ruined Cities of Asia Minor. By Ernest L. Harris. XIX, pp. 833-858, 19 ills., Dec., 1908

SOME Songsters and Flyers of Wide Repute. 42 portraits from paintings by Maj. Allan Brooks. LXIX, pp. 529-544, Apr., 1936

SOME Tramps Across the Glaciers and Snowfields of British Columbia. By Howard Palmer. XXI, pp. 457-487, 25 ills., June, 1910

SOME Wonderful Sights in the Andean Highlands: The Oldest City in America. Sailing on the Lake of the Clouds: The Yosemite of Peru. By Harriet Chalmers Adams. XIX, pp. 597-618, 19 ills., map, Sept., 1908

SOMERS, SIR GEORGE:

The Islands of Bermuda: A British Colony with a Unique Record in Popular Government. By William Howard Taft. XLI, pp. 1-26, 15 ills., map, Jan., 1922

SONGDO (Kaijo), Korea:

Chosen—Land of Morning Calm. By Mabel Craft Deering. LXIV, pp. 421-448, 20 ills. in black and white, 13 ills. in color, map, Oct., 1933

SONNENBURG, A. FALKNER VON:

Manila and the Philippines. By Major A. Falkner von Sonnenburg. X, pp. 65-72, Feb., 1899

SONORA (State), Mexico:

Adventuring Down the West Coast of Mexico. By Herbert Corey. XLII, pp. 449-503, 44 ills., map, Nov., 1922

A Mexican Land of Canaan: Marvelous Riches of the Wonderful West Coast of Our Neighbor Republic. By Frederick Simpich. XXXVI, pp. 307-330, 16 ills., map, Oct., 1919

Papagueria. By W J McGee. IX, pp. 345-371, 9 ills., Aug., 1898

Seriland. By W J McGee and Willard D. Johnson. VII, pp. 125-133, ill., foldout map, Apr., 1896

SOOCHOW CREEK, China:

Ho for the Soochow Ho. By Mabel Craft Deering. LI, pp. 623-649, 32 ills., map, June, 1927

SORATA, Bolivia:

Bolivia—Tin Roof of the Andes. By Henry Albert Phillips. LXXXIII, pp. 309-332, 5 ills. in black and white, 20 ills. in color, Mar., 1943

SOUF (Region), Algeria:

The Country of the Ant Men. By Thomas H. Kearney. XXII, pp. 367-382, 13 ills., map, panorama, Apr., 1911

SOUFRIÈRE (Volcano), St. Vincent:

The Eruptions of La Soufrière, St. Vincent, in May, 1902. By Edmund Otis Hovey. XIII, pp. 444-459, 4 ills., Dec., 1902

The National Geographic Society Expedition in the West Indies. XIII, pp. 209-213, maps, June, 1902

The Recent Volcanic Eruptions in the West Indies. By Israel C. Russell. XIII, pp. 267-285, 7 ills., map, July, 1902

A Report of the Eruption of the Soufrière of St. Vincent, 1812 (From the *Evening News* of June 30, 1812). XIV, pp. 158-161, Apr., 1903

SOUND:

The Aberration of Sound as Illustrated by the Berkeley Powder Explosion. By Robert H. Chapman. VII, pp. 246-249, 3 diagrs., July, 1896

SOURCES of the Saskatchewan. By Walter D. Wilcox. X, pp. 113-134, 6 ills., chart, Apr., 1899

The **SOURCES** of Washington's Charm (D. C.). By J. R. Hildebrand. XLIII, pp. 639-680, 46 ills., June, 1923

SOUTH AFRICA. *See* Union of South Africa

SOUTH AMERICA:

An Awakened Continent to the South of Us. By Elihu Root. XVIII, pp. 61-72, Jan., 1907

Bonds Between the Americas. By Frederick Simpich. LXXII, pp. 785-808, 22 ills., Dec., 1937

Buenos Aires and Its River of Silver: A Journey Up the Paraná and Paraguay to the Chaco Cattle Country. By William R. Barbour. XL, pp. 393-432, 38 ills., Oct., 1921

Buenos Aires to Washington by Horse: A Solitary Journey of Two and a Half Years, Through Eleven American Republics, Covers 9,600 Miles of Mountain and Plain, Desert and Jungle. By A. F. Tschiffely. LV, pp. 135-196, 75 ills., map, Feb., 1929

By Seaplane to Six Continents: Cruising 60,000 Miles, Italian Argonauts of the Air See World Geography Unroll, and Break New Sky Trails Over Vast Brazilian Jungles. By Commander Francesco de Pinedo. LIV, pp. 247-301, 60 ills., two-page map, Sept., 1928

The Flags of Pan-America. By Byron McCandless and Gilbert Grosvenor. XXXII, pp. 361-369, 62 ills. in color, Oct., 1917

Flying the "Hump" of the Andes. By Capt. Albert W. Stevens. LIX, pp. 595-636, 36 ills., map, May, 1931

Flying the World's Longest Air-Mail Route: From Montevideo, Uruguay, Over the Andes, Up the Pacific Coast, Across Central America and the Caribbean to Miami, Florida, in 67 Thrilling Flying Hours. By Junius B. Wood. LVII, pp. 261-325, 65 ills., map, Mar., 1930

From Panama to Patagonia. By Charles M. Pepper. XVII, pp. 449-452, ill., Aug., 1906

Fundamental Geographic Relation of the Three Americas. By Robert T. Hill. VII, pp. 175-181, map, May, 1896

Geographic Progress of Civilization. Annual Address by the President, Honorable Gardiner G. Hubbard. VI, pp. 1-22, Feb. 14, 1894

The Great Unmapped Areas on the Earth's Surface Awaiting the Explorer and Geographer. By J. Scott Keltie. VIII, pp. 251-266, Sept., 1897

Hatcher's Work in Patagonia. (By W J M.). VIII, pp. 319-322, Nov., 1897

How Latin America Looks from the Air: U. S. Army Airplanes Hurdle the High Andes, Brave Brazil Jungles, and Follow Smoking Volcanoes to Map New Sky Paths Around South America. By Major Herbert A. Dargue. LII, pp. 451-502, 52 ills., map, Oct., 1927

In Humboldt's Wake: Narrative of a National Geographic Society Expedition Up the Orinoco and Through the Strange Casiquiare Canal to Amazonian Waters. By Ernest G. Holt. LX, pp. 621-644, 27 ills., map, Nov., 1931

Latin America and Colombia. By John Barrett. XVII, pp. 692-709, 10 ills., Dec., 1906

The Latin-American Constitutions and Revolutions. By John W. Foster. XII, pp. 169-175, May, 1901

A New Light on the Discovery of America (Geographic Notes. By Cyrus C. Babb). VI, pp. 224-225, Dec. 29, 1894

New National Geographic Society Map Charts South America's Wartime Importance. Text with map supplement. LXXXII, pp. 537-540, ills., Oct., 1942

SOUTH AMERICA—*Continued*

Over the Andes to Bogotá. By Frank M. Chapman. XL, pp. 353-373, 19 ills., Oct., 1921

Patagonia. By J. B. Hatcher. VIII, pp. 305-319, 6 ills., map, Nov., 1897

The Peace of Latin America. XVI, pp. 479-480, Oct., 1905

Skypaths Through Latin America: Flying From Our Nation's Capital Southward Over Jungles, Remote Islands, and Great Cities on an Aërial Survey of the East Coast of South America. By Frederick Simpich. LIX, pp. 1-79, 77 ills., map, Jan., 1931

The Society's Map of South America. By Gilbert Grosvenor. Text with map supplement. LXXII, pp. 809-810, Dec., 1937

The Society's New Map of South America. Text with map supplement. XL, pp. 374-392, 17 ills., Oct., 1921

South America. Annual Address by the President, Gardiner G. Hubbard. III, pp. 1-29, foldout map, Mar. 28, 1891

South America Fifty Years Hence. By Charles M. Pepper. XVII, pp. 427-432, map supplement, Aug., 1906

South America Map. Announcement of map supplement (Aug., 1906). XVII, p. 424, July, 1906

South American Immigration. XVII, p. 587, Oct., 1906

To Bogotá and Back by Air: The Narrative of a 9,500-Mile Flight from Washington, Over Thirteen Latin-American Countries and Return, in the Single-Seater Airplane "Spirit of St. Louis." By Col. Charles A. Lindbergh. LIII, pp. 529-601, 98 ills., map, May, 1928

What the Latin American Republics Think of the Pan-American Conferences. XVII, pp. 474-479, Aug., 1906

A Winter Voyage Through the Straits of Magellan. By the late Admiral R. W. Meade, U. S. N. VIII, pp. 129-141, ill., map, May, 1897

The World's Highest International Telephone Cable. LVIII, pp. 722-731, 8 ills., Dec., 1930

See also Argentina; Bolivia; Brazil; British Guiana; Buenos Aires; Chile; Colombia; Ecuador; French Guiana; Marajó Island; Paraguay; Peru; Rio de Janeiro; Santos; São Paulo; Surinam; Tierra del Fuego (Archipelago); Venezuela

SOUTH American Immigration. XVII, p. 587, Oct., 1906

SOUTH CAROLINA:

Applied Physiography in South Carolina. By L. C. Glenn. VIII, pp. 152-154, diagr., May, 1897

The Ashley River and Its Gardens. By E. T. H. Shaffer. XLIX, pp. 525-550, 6 ills. in black and white, 18 ills. in color, May, 1926

See also Charleston

SOUTH DAKOTA:

The Bad Lands of South Dakota. By N. H. Darton. X. pp. 339-343, 4 ills., Sept., 1899

The Black Hills, Once Hunting Grounds of the Red Men. LII, pp. 305-329, 18 ills. in black and white, 13 ills. in color, Sept., 1927

The Call of the West. By C. J. Blanchard. XX, pp. 403-437, 20 ills., map, May, 1909

SOUTH DAKOTA—*Continued*

Exploring the Stratosphere. By Captain Albert W. Stevens. LXVI, pp. 397-434, 43 ills., chart, Oct., 1934

Man's Farthest Aloft: Rising to 13.71 Miles, the National Geographic Society-U. S. Army Stratosphere Expedition Gathers Scientific Data at Record Altitude. By Capt. Albert W. Stevens. LXIX, pp. 59-94, 39 ills., map, Jan., 1936

Included: Action Photographs of the Balloon's Perfect Landing

Taming the Outlaw Missouri River. By Frederick Simpich. LXXXVIII, pp. 569-598, 25 ills., two-page map, Nov., 1945

SOUTH Florida's Amazing Everglades: Encircled by Populous Places Is a Seldom-visited Area of Rare Birds, Prairies, Cowboys, and Teeming Wild Life of Big Cypress Swamp. By John O'Reilly. LXXVII, pp. 115-142, 26 ills., map, Jan., 1940

SOUTH from Saipan. By W. Robert Moore. LXXXVII, pp. 441-474, 11 ills. in black and white, 17 ills. in color, map, Apr., 1945

SOUTH GEORGIA (Island), South Atlantic Ocean:

Sailing the Seven Seas in the Interest of Science: Adventures Through 157,000 Miles of Storm and Calm, from Arctic to Antarctic and Around the World, in the Non-magnetic Yacht "Carnegie." By J. P. Ault. XLII, pp. 631-690, 47 ills., chart, Dec., 1922

South Georgia, an Outpost of the Antarctic. By Robert Cushman Murphy. XLI, pp. 409-444, 41 ills., maps, Apr., 1922

SOUTH ISLAND, New Zealand:

Alpine Peaks and Pastures of South Island. 11 color photos by W. Robert Moore. LXIX, pp. 205-212, Feb., 1936

SOUTH of Khyber Pass (India). By Maynard Owen Williams. LXXXIX, pp. 471-500, 31 ills., map supplement, Apr., 1946

SOUTH of the Clouds—Yünnan (China). 11 color photos by Owen Lattimore and Frank Outram. LXXXII, pp. 349-356, Sept., 1942

SOUTH PACIFIC COMBAT AIR TRANSPORT (SCAT):

Flying Our Wounded Veterans Home. By Catherine Bell Palmer. LXXXVIII, pp. 363-384, 17 ills., Sept., 1945

SOUTH PACIFIC ISLANDS. *See* Pacific Islands

The **SOUTH** Polar Expedition (Proposed by Peary for Consideration by the Society). XXI, pp. 167-170, map, Feb., 1910

SOUTH Polar Explorations. XXII, pp. 407-409, 4 ills., map, Apr., 1911

SOUTH POLE. *See* Antarctic Regions

SOUTH SEA ISLANDS. *See* Melanesia; Micronesia; Polynesia

SOUTH Sea Isle of Mineral Mountains (New Caledonia). 12 color photos by Enzo de Chetelat. LXXXII, pp. 33-40, July, 1942

SOUTHAMPTON—Gateway to London: The Port of Double Tides Where the "Mayflower" Moored is Rich in Sea History and Lore of Early England. By Stanley Toogood. LXXVII, pp. 91-114, 21 ills., map, Jan., 1940

SOUTHARD, ADDISON E.:

Modern Ethiopia: Haile Selassie the First, Formerly Ras Tafari, Succeeds to the World's Oldest Continuously Sovereign Throne. By Addison E. Southard. LIX, pp. 679-738, 47 ills. in black and white, 27 ills. in color, map, June, 1931

SOUTHERLAND, W. H. H.:

The Work of the U. S. Hydrographic Office. By Commander W. H. H. Southerland. XIV, pp. 61-75, Feb., 1903

SOUTHERN California at Work. By Frederick Simpich. LXVI, pp. 529-600, 39 ills. in black and white, 41 ills. in color, two-page map, Nov., 1934

The **SOUTHERN** Coast of Alaska. Introduction to "An Expedition to Mount St. Elias, Alaska," by Israel C. Russell. III, pp. 55-57, May 29, 1891

SOUTHERN CROSS (Airplane):

Our Conquest of the Pacific: The Narrative of the 7,400-Mile Flight from San Francisco to Brisbane in Three Ocean Hops. By Squadron-Leader Charles E. Kingsford-Smith and Flight-Leader Charles T. P. Ulm. LIV, pp. 371-402, 27 ills., map, Oct., 1928

SOUTHERN HEMISPHERE:

Map of the Northern and Southern Hemispheres. Text with map supplement. LXXXIII, pp. 481-483, Apr., 1943

SOUTHERN RHODESIA:

Rhodesia, Hobby and Hope of Cecil Rhodes. By W. Robert Moore. LXXXVI, pp. 281-306, 13 ills. in black and white, 10 ills. in color, map, Sept., 1944

SOUTHWARD Ho! In the "Alice" (Atlantic and Caribbean Cruise). By Henry Howard. LXXIII, pp. 265-312, 38 ills. in black and white, 13 ills. in color, maps, Mar., 1938

SOUTHWEST (Region), U. S.:

The Southwest: Its Splendid Natural Resources, Agricultural Wealth, and Scenic Beauty. By N. H. Darton. XXI, pp. 631-665, 21 ills., map, Aug., 1910

Southwest Trails from Horse to Motor. Text with map supplement. LXXVII, p. 767, June, 1940

See also the following southwestern and neighboring states: Arizona; California; Colorado; Nevada; New Mexico; Oklahoma; Texas; Utah

SOUTH-WEST AFRICA:

Hunting an Observatory: A Successful Search For a Dry Mountain on Which to Establish the National Geographic Society's Solar Radiation Station. By C. G. Abbot. L, pp. 503-518, 13 ills., map, Oct., 1926

Keeping House for the "Shepherds of the Sun." By Mrs. William H. Hoover. LVII, pp. 483-506, 17 ills., map, Apr., 1930

SOUVENIRS of Knighthood in Rhodes. 13 color photos by Luigi Pellerano. LXIV, pp. 665-672, Dec., 1933

SOVIET CENTRAL ASIA:

The Afghan Borderland. By Ellsworth Huntington. Part I: The Russian Frontier. XX, pp. 788-799, 14 ills., Sept., 1909

The Land of Lambskins: An Expedition to Bokhara, Russian Central Asia, to Study the Karakul Sheep Industry. By Robert K. Nabours. XXXVI, pp. 77-88, 15 ills., July, 1919

Life in the Great Desert of Central Asia. By Ellsworth Huntington. XX, pp. 749-760, 12 ills., Aug., 1909

New Road to Asia. By Owen Lattimore. LXXXVI, pp. 641-676, 15 ills. in black and white, 26 ills. in color, Dec., 1944

Observing an Eclipse in Asiatic Russia. By Irvine C. Gardner. LXXI, pp. 179-197, 19 ills. in black and white, ill. in color, Feb., 1937

Russia's Orphan Races: Picturesque People Who Cluster on the Southeastern Borderland of the Vast Slav Dominions. By Maynard Owen Williams. XXXIV, pp. 245-278, 26 ills., map, Oct., 1918

The Supposed Birthplace of Civilizations. XVI, pp. 499-504, 6 ills., Nov., 1905

Surveying Through Khoresm: A Journey Into Parts of Asiatic Russia Which Have Been Closed to Western Travelers Since the World War. By Lyman D. Wilbur. LXI, pp. 753-780, 31 ills., map, June, 1932

Where Slav and Mongol Meet. 16 ills. in color. XXXVI, pp. 421-436, Nov., 1919

SPAIN:

Adventurous Sons of Cádiz. By Harriet Chalmers Adams. XLVI, pp. 153-204, 37 ills. in black and white, 26 ills. in color, Aug., 1924

The American Eclipse Expedition. By Rear Admiral Colby M. Chester. XVII, pp. 589-612, 23 ills., col. pl., Nov., 1906

The Color Camera Records Scenes in Eastern Spain. 13 color photos by Gervais Courtellemont. LV, pp. 365-372, Mar., 1929

From Granada to Gibraltar—A Tour of Southern Spain. By Harry A. McBride. XLVI, pp. 205-232, 23 ills., Aug., 1924

In Andalusia, Home of Song and Sunshine. 14 color photos by Gervais Courtellemont. LV, pp. 301-308, Mar., 1929

International Literary Contest (Madrid). I, pp. 273-276, July, 1889

The Land of the Basques: Home of a Thrifty, Picturesque People, Who Take Pride in the Sobriquet, "The Yankees of Spain." By Harry A. McBride. XLI, pp. 63-87, 25 ills., map, Jan., 1922

Montserrat, Spain's Mountain Shrine. By E. John Long. LXIII, pp. 121-130, 10 ills., Jan., 1933

On the Bypaths of Spain. By Harry A. McBride. LV, pp. 311-364, 50 ills. in black and white, 13 ills. in color, map, Mar., 1929

A Palette from Spain. By W. Langdon Kihn. LXIX, pp. 407-440, 16 ills. in black and white, 26 ills. in duotone, map, Mar., 1936

SPAIN—*Continued*

Pursuing Spanish Bypaths Northwest of Madrid. By Harry A. McBride. LIX, pp. 121-130, 6 ills. in black and white, 14 ills. in color, map, Jan., 1931

The Races of Europe. By Edwin A. Grosvenor. XXXIV, pp. 441-534, 62 ills., diagr. and index, maps, map supplement, Dec., 1918

The Rock of Gibraltar: Key to the Mediterranean. 17 ills. LXXVIII, pp. 376-391, Sept., 1940

Romantic Spain. By Charles Upson Clark. XXI, pp. 187-215, 40 ills., map, Mar., 1910

Turbulent Spain. By Ruth Q. McBride. LXX, pp. 397-427, 25 ills., two-page map, Oct., 1936

See also Balearic Islands; Barcelona; Madrid; Seville

SPAIN'S Enchanted Isles (Balearic Islands). 29 color photos by Gervais Courtellemont. LIV, pp. 183-198, Aug., 1928

SPANIELS:

Toy Dogs, Pets of Kings and Commoners. By Freeman Lloyd. LXXXV, pp. 459-480, 8 ills. in black and white, 16 ills. in color, Apr., 1944

SPANISH AMERICA:

Descriptive Topographic Terms of Spanish America. By Robert T. Hill. VII, pp. 291-302, Sept., 1896

Included: Mexico; New Mexico; Texas

See also Latin America

SPANISH-AMERICAN WAR:

The Disposition of the Philippines. By Charles E. Howe. IX, p. 304, June, 1898

Manila and the Philippines. By Major A. Falkner von Sonnenburg. X, pp. 65-72, Feb., 1899

SPANISH CIVIL WAR:

Turbulent Spain. By Ruth Q. McBride. LXX, pp. 397-427, 25 ills., two-page map, Oct., 1936

We Escape from Madrid. By Gretchen Schwinn. LXXI, pp. 251-268, 15 ills., Feb., 1937

SPANISH MOROCCO:

Across French and Spanish Morocco. By Harriet Chalmers Adams. XLVII, pp. 327-356, 19 ills. in black and white, 16 ills. in color, map, Mar., 1925

SPARROWS:

Birds of Timberline and Tundra. By Arthur A. Allen. With 24 color photos by author. XC, pp. 313-339, 8 ills. in black and white, Sept., 1946

The Pest of English Sparrows. By N. Dearborn. XXI, pp. 948-952, 4 ills., Nov., 1910

Sparrows, Towhees, and Longspurs: These Happy Little Singers Make Merry in Field, Forest, and Desert Throughout North America. By T. Gilbert Pearson. Paintings by Allan Brooks and Walter A. Weber. LXXV, pp. 353-376, 5 ills. in black and white, 43 ills. in color, Mar., 1939

SPARROWS, Towhees, and Longspurs. 43 paintings in color from life by Allan Brooks and Walter A. Weber. LXXV, pp. 361-375, Mar., 1939

SPARS. *See* Women's Reserve of the U. S. Coast Guard Reserve

SPEAKING of Kansas. By Frederick Simpich. LXXII, pp. 135-182, 37 ills. in black and white, 12 ills. in color, two-page map, Aug., 1937

The **SPECIAL** Telegraphic Time Signal from the Naval Observatory. XV, pp. 411-415, Oct., 1904

SPECTROSCOPES:

Exploring the Glories of the Firmament. By William Joseph Showalter. XXXVI, pp. 153-181, 17 ills., diagr., 3 charts, Aug., 1919

The **SPEEDIEST** Boat. XXII, pp. 875-878, ills., Sept., 1911

The **SPELL** of Romania: An American Woman's Narrative of Her Wanderings Among Colorful People and Long-Hidden Shrines. By Henrietta Allen Holmes. LXV, pp. 399-450, 37 ills. in black and white, 29 ills. in color, map, Apr., 1934

SPICES:

Airplanes Come to the Isles of Spice: Once Magnet of World Explorers, the Moluccas Again Stand at Crossroads of History in the Netherlands Indies. By Maynard Owen Williams. LXXIX, pp. 535-558, 26 ills., map, May, 1941

The Greatest Voyage in the Annals of the Sea. By J. R. Hildebrand. LXII, pp. 699-739, 35 ills., map, Dec., 1932

How the World Is Fed. By William Joseph Showalter. XXIX, pp. 1-110, 101 ills., Jan., 1916

The Pathfinder of the East: Setting Sail to Find "Christians and Spices," Vasco da Gama Met Amazing Adventures, Founded an Empire, and Changed the History of Western Europe. By J. R. Hildebrand. LII, pp. 503-550, 43 ills., map, pictorial supplement, Nov., 1927

SPIDER CRABS:

Crabs and Crablike Curiosities of the Sea. By William Crowder. Paintings by author. LIV, pp. 57-72, 10 ills. in black and white, 8 ills. in color, July, 1928

SPIDERS:

Afield with the Spiders: Web Hunting in the Marshlands and Woodlands and Along the Lanes. By Henry E. Ewing. Paintings by Hashime Murayama. LXIV, pp. 163-194, 26 ills. in black and white, 64 ills. in color, Aug., 1933

California Trapdoor Spider Performs Engineering Marvels. By Lee Passmore. LXIV, pp. 195-211, 23 ills., Aug., 1933

Marvels of Metamorphosis: A Scientific "G-man" Pursues Rare Trapdoor Spider Parasites for Three Years with a Spade and a Candid Camera. By George Elwood Jenks. LXXIV, pp. 807-828, 39 ills., Dec., 1938

The Monsters of Our Back Yards. By David Fairchild. XXIV, pp. 575-626, 38 ills., May, 1913

SPIN Your Globe to Long Island: Only Six States Have More People than the Insular Empire that Ranges from a World's Fair Through Potato Patches, Princely Estates, and Historic Shrines. By Frederick Simpich. LXXV, pp. 413-460, 25 ills. in black and white, 18 ills. in color, Apr., 1939

SPINDEN, HERBERT J.:

Shattered Capitals of Central America. By Herbert J. Spinden. XXXVI, pp. 185-212, 32 ills., map, Sept., 1919

SPIRIT OF ST. LOUIS (Airplane):

Seeing America with Lindbergh: The Record of a Tour of More Than 20,000 Miles by Airplane Through Forty-eight States on Schedule Time. By Lieutenant Donald E. Keyhoe. LIII, pp. 1-46, 46 ills., map, Jan., 1928

To Bogotá and Back by Air: The Narrative of a 9,500-Mile Flight from Washington, Over Thirteen Latin-American Countries and Return, in the Single-Seater Airplane "Spirit of St. Louis." By Col. Charles A. Lindbergh. LIII, pp. 529-601, 98 ills., map, May, 1928

The **SPIRIT** of the Geographic (World War I). XXXIV, pp. 434-440, 4 ills., Nov., 1918

The **SPIRIT** of the West (U. S.): The Wonderful Agricultural Development Since the Dawn of Irrigation. By C. J. Blanchard. XXI, pp. 333-360, 15 ills., Apr., 1910

SPITSBERGEN (Svalbard, Archipelago), Arctic Ocean:

Flights from Arctic to Equator: Conquering the Alps, the Ice Peaks of Spitsbergen, of Persia, and Africa's Mountains of the Moon. By Walter Mittelholzer. LXI, pp. 445-498, 53 ills., map, Apr., 1932

Magnetic Observations in Iceland, Jan Mayen and Spitzbergen in 1892 (Geographic Notes. By Cyrus C. Babb). VI, pp. 223-224, table, Dec. 29, 1894

No Man's Land—Spitzbergen. XVIII, pp. 455-458, July, 1907

The Russian Expedition to Spitzbergen. XII, p. 404, Nov., 1901

A Woman's Winter on Spitsbergen. By Martha Phillips Gilson. LIV, pp. 227-246, 20 ills., map, Aug., 1928

The **SPLENDOR** of Rome. By Florence Craig Albrecht. XLI, pp. 593-626, 28 ills., June, 1922

SPOFFORD, A. R.:

Gardiner Greene Hubbard: Memorial Meeting. Address by the Honorable A. R. Spofford. IX, pp. 63-65, Feb., 1898

SPONGES:

Federal Fish Farming; or, Planting Fish by the Billion. By Hugh M. Smith. XXI, pp. 418-446, 22 ills., May, 1910

Here and There in Northern Africa. By Frank Edward Johnson. XXV, pp. 1-132, 113 ills., Jan., 1914

SPOONBILLS, Roseate:

The Large Wading Birds: Long Legs and Remarkable Beaks, as Well as Size, Form, and Color, Distinguish the Herons, Ibises, and Flamingos. By T. Gilbert Pearson. Painting by Maj. Allan Brooks. LXII, pp. 441-469, ill. in color, Oct., 1932

SPORADES, Northern (Islands). *See* Skýros

SPORADES, Southern (Islands). *See* Dodecanese Islands

SPORT and Color Amid New England Snows. 13 color photos by B. Anthony Stewart. LXX, pp. 647-654, Nov., 1936

SPORTS AND GAMES:

Clans in Kilt and Plaidie Gather at Braemar (Scotland). 11 color photos by Maynard Owen Williams. LXVIII, pp. 153-160, Aug., 1935

Devil-Fishing in the Gulf Stream. By John Oliver La Gorce. XXXV, pp. 476-488, 7 ills., June, 1919

Field Sports Among the Wild Men of Northern Luzon. By Dean C. Worcester. XXII, pp. 215-267, 52 ills., map, Mar., 1911

The Geography of Games: How the Sports of Nations Form a Gazetteer of the Habits and Histories of Their Peoples. By J. R. Hildebrand. XXXVI, pp. 89-144, 61 ills., Aug., 1919

Hurdle Racing in Canoes: A Thrilling and Spectacular Sport Among the Maoris of New Zealand. By Walter Burke. XXXVII, pp. 440-444, 6 ills., May, 1920

New England Ski Trails: Snow and Ice Sports Transform Whittier's Winters of Snowbound Seclusion Into Seasons of Outdoor Recreation. By Daniel Rochford. LXX, pp. 645-664, 11 ills. in black and white, 13 ills. in color, Nov., 1936

When Czechoslovakia Puts a Falcon Feather in Its Cap (Gymnastics). By Maynard Owen Williams. LXIII, pp. 40-49, 13 ills. in color, Jan., 1933

See also Chess; Cock-fighting; Falconry; Horse Racing; Kboo; Skiing; Surfboarding; Tops

SPOTTED FEVER:

Tracking the Columbian Ground-Squirrel to Its Burrow: Loss of Millions to Crops and Danger of the Spread of Spotted Fever Necessitated Study of Peculiar Rodent of Western North America. By William T. Shaw. XLVII, pp. 587-596, 13 ills., May, 1925

SPOTTSWOOD, ALEXANDER:

Spottswood's Expedition of 1716. By Dr. William M. Thornton. VII, pp. 265-269, Aug., 1896

SPREEWALD (Region), Germany:

The Wends of the Spreewald. By Frederick Simpich. XLIII, pp. 327-336, 12 ills., Mar., 1923

SPRINGBOARDS to Tokyo. By Willard Price. LXXXVI, pp. 385-407, 16 ills., Oct., 1944

SPRING'S Gay Bouquets Deck the Nation's Capital (Washington, D. C.). 10 color photos by Harrison Howell Walker. LXXIV, pp. 17-24, July, 1938

SPRINGTIME Wreathes a Garland for the Nation's Capital (Washington, D. C.). 13 ills. in color. LXVII, pp. 473-480, Apr., 1935

SQUID:

Fighting Giants of the Humboldt. By David D. Duncan. LXXIX, pp. 373-400, 28 ills., map, Mar., 1941

Marauders of the Sea. By Roy Waldo Miner. Paintings by Else Bostelmann. LXVIII, pp. 185-207, 12 ills. in black and white, 8 ills. in color, Aug., 1935

SQUIER, GEORGE O.:

The Influence of Submarine Cables Upon Military and Naval Supremacy. By Capt. George O. Squier. XII, pp. 1-12, Jan., 1901

SQUIRES, GRANT:

First award by the Society from the Grant Squires fund, to Mr. F. H. King, author of "Farmers of Forty Centuries" (China). XXIV, p. 115, Jan., 1913

SQUIRRELS:

Tracking the Columbian Ground-Squirrel to Its Burrow: Loss of Millions to Crops and Danger of the Spread of Spotted Fever Necessitated Study of Peculiar Rodent of Western North America. By William T. Shaw. XLVII, pp. 587-596, 13 ills., May, 1925

SRINAGAR, Kashmir:

Outwitting the Water Demons of Kashmir. By Maurice Pratt Dunlap. XL, pp. 499-511, 9 ills., Nov., 1921

A Pilgrimage to Amernath, Himalayan Shrine of the Hindu Faith. By Louise Ahl Jessop. XL, pp. 513-542, 29 ills., Nov., 1921

STAGE, HARRY H.:

Saboteur Mosquitoes. By Harry H. Stage. LXXXV, pp. 165-179, 12 ills., Feb., 1944

STAIRCASE Farms of the Ancients: Astounding Farming Skill of Ancient Peruvians, Who Were Among the Most Industrious and Highly Organized People in History. By O. F. Cook. XXIX, pp. 474-534, 48 ills., May, 1916

STALKING Ants, Savage and Civilized: A Naturalist Braves Bites and Stings in Many Lands to Learn the Story of an Insect Whose Ways Often Parallel Those of Man. By W. M. Mann. Paintings by Hashime Murayama. LXVI, pp. 171-192, 7 ills. in black and white, 18 ills. in color, Aug., 1934

STALKING Big Game with Color Camera. 28 color photos by Wendell Chapman. LXXVI, pp. 89-128, July, 1939

STALKING Birds With a Color Camera: An Expert in Avian Habits Persuades His Subjects to Sit Where He Wants Them, Even in His Hat. By Arthur A. Allen. LXXV, pp. 777-789, 3 ills. in black and white, 14 ills. in color, June, 1939

STALKING the Dragon Lizard on the Island of Komodo. By W. Douglas Burden. LII, pp. 216-232, 21 ills., Aug., 1927

STAND by the Soldier. By Major General John J. Pershing. XXXI, pp. 457-459, ill., May, 1917

STANDING Iceberg Guard in the North Atlantic: International Patrol Safeguards the Lives of Thousands of Travelers and Protects Trans-Atlantic Liners from a "Titanic" Fate. By Lieutenant Commander F. A. Zeusler. L, pp. 1-28, 29 ills., map, July, 1926

STANLEY, SIR HENRY MORTON:

Africa, Its Past and Future. (By Gardiner G. Hubbard). I, pp. 99-124, foldout map, Apr., 1889

STANLEY, SIR HENRY MORTON—*Continued*
A Great African Lake (Victoria). By Sir Henry M. Stanley. XIII, pp. 169-172, map, May, 1902
Report—Geography of the Land. By Herbert G. Ogden. II, pp. 31-48, Apr., 1890

STANLEY-BROWN, JOSEPH:
Report on Auriferous Sands from Yakutat Bay. By J. Stanley-Brown. III, pp. 196-198, May 29, 1891
Shishaldin as a Field for Exploration (Alaska). By Joseph Stanley-Brown. X, pp. 281-288, 3 ills., map, Aug., 1899
See also NGS: Secretary

STAR and Crescent on Parade (Turkey). 29 color photos by Maynard Owen Williams. LXXXVII, pp. 585-616, May, 1945

STAR CHARTS:
How to Use the Star Charts. Text with 12 star charts designed by Donald H. Menzel. LXXXIV, pp. 116-128, July, 1943

STARS. *See* Astronomy

STATE FLAGS. *See* Flags

STATE FLOWERS. *See* Flowers

The **STATE** of Sky-Blue Water and Verdure (Minnesota). 11 color photos by Clifton Adams and Edwin L. Wisherd. LXVII, pp. 289-296, Mar., 1935

STATE SEALS. *See* Seals

STATE SURVEY ARTICLES: United States:
Alabama: Smoke Over Alabama. By Frederick Simpich. LX, pp. 703-758, 43 ills. in black and white, 26 ills. in color, map, Dec., 1931
Arizona Comes of Age. By Frederick Simpich. LV, pp. 1-47, 40 ills. in black and white, 14 ills. in color, map, Jan., 1929
Arkansas Rolls Up Its Sleeves. By Frederick Simpich. XC, pp. 273-312, 16 ills. in black and white, 23 ills. in color, map, Sept., 1946
California: Northern California at Work. By Frederick Simpich. LXIX, pp. 309-389, 36 ills. in black and white, 41 ills. in color, maps (1 two-page), Mar., 1936
California: Southern California at Work. By Frederick Simpich. LXVI, pp. 529-600, 39 ills. in black and white, 41 ills. in color, two-page map, Nov., 1934
Colorado, a Barrier That Became a Goal: Where Water Has Transformed Dry Plains Into Verdant Farms, and Highways Have Opened Up Mineral and Scenic Wealth. By McFall Kerbey. LXII, pp. 1-63, 56 ills. in black and white, 12 ills. in color, map, July, 1932
Connecticut, Prodigy of Ingenuity: Factories Play a Symphony of Industry Amid Colonial Scenes in the State of Steady Habits. By Leo A. Borah. LXXIV, pp. 279-326, 25 ills. in black and white, 25 ills. in color, two-page map, Sept., 1938
Delaware: Diamond Delaware, Colonial Still: Tradition Rules the "Three Lower Counties" Over Which William Penn and Lord Baltimore Went to Law. By Leo A. Borah. LXVIII, pp. 367-398, 25 ills. in black and white, 15 ills. in color, map, Sept., 1935

STATE SURVEY ARTICLES: United States—*Continued*
Florida—The Fountain of Youth. By John Oliver La Gorce. LVII, pp. 1-93, 73 ills. in black and white, 41 ills. in color, map supplement, Jan., 1930
Georgia: Marching Through Georgia Sixty Years After: Multifold Industries and Diversified Agriculture Are Restoring the Prosperity of America's Largest State East of the Mississippi. By Ralph A. Graves. L, pp. 259-311, 47 ills., map supplement, Sept., 1926
Idaho Made the Desert Bloom. By D. Worth Clark. LXXXV, pp. 641-688, 21 ills. in black and white, 20 ills. in color, map, June, 1944
Illinois, Crossroads of the Continent. By Junius B. Wood. LIX, pp. 523-594, 51 ills. in black and white, 27 ills. in color, map supplement, May, 1931
Indiana Journey. By Frederick Simpich. LXX, pp. 267-320, 32 ills. in black and white, 27 ills. in color, two-page map, Sept., 1936
Iowa, Abiding Place of Plenty: The State Where the Tall Corn Grows Provides the Nation With a Tenth of Its Food Supply. By Leo A. Borah. LXXVI, pp. 143-182, 15 ills. in black and white, 20 ills. in color, two-page map, Aug., 1939
Kansas: Speaking of Kansas. By Frederick Simpich. LXXII, pp. 135-182, 37 ills. in black and white, 12 ills. in color, two-page map, Aug., 1937
Kentucky, Boone's Great Meadow: The Bluegrass State Celebrates Its Sesquicentennial As It Helps the Nation Gird for War. By Leo A. Borah. LXXXII, pp. 57-89, 13 ills. in black and white, 21 ills. in color, map, July, 1942
Louisiana, Land of Perpetual Romance. By Ralph A. Graves. LVII, pp. 393-482, 84 ills. in black and white, 29 ills. in color, map supplement, Apr., 1930
Maine, the Outpost State: Some Forgotten Incidents in the Life of an Old and Stout-Hearted Commonwealth. By George Otis Smith. LXVII, pp. 533-592, 35 ills. in black and white, 39 ills. in color, two-page map, May, 1935
A Maryland Pilgrimage: Visits to Hallowed Shrines Recall the Major Rôle Played by This Prosperous State in the Development of Popular Government in America. By Gilbert Grosvenor. LI, pp. 133-212, 88 ills., map supplement, Feb., 1927
Maryland Presents—. By W. Robert Moore. LXXIX, pp. 401-448, 17 ills. in black and white, 32 ills. in color, map, Apr., 1941
Massachusetts—Beehive of Business. By William Joseph Showalter. XXXVII, pp. 203-245, 41 ills., Mar., 1920
Michigan, Mistress of the Lakes. By Melville Chater. LIII, pp. 269-325, 65 ills., maps, Mar., 1928
Minnesota, Mother of Lakes and Rivers. By Glanville Smith. LXVII, pp. 273-318, 42 ills. in black and white, 11 ills. in color, two-page map, Mar., 1935
Mississippi: Machines Come to Mississippi. By J. R. Hildebrand. LXXII, pp. 263-318, 34 ills. in black and white, 26 ills. in color, two-page map, Sept., 1937
Missouri, Mother of the West. By Frederick Simpich. XLIII, pp. 421-460, 35 ills., Apr., 1923

STATE SURVEY ARTICLES: United States—*Continued*

Missouri: These Missourians. By Frederick Simpich. LXXXIX, pp. 277-310, 12 ills. in black and white, 22 ills. in color, map, Mar., 1946

Nebraska, the Cornhusker State. By Leo A. Borah. LXXXVII, pp. 513-542, 6 ills. in black and white, 23 ills. in color, map, May, 1945

Nevada, Desert Treasure House. By W. Robert Moore. LXXXIX, pp. 1-38, 16 ills. in black and white, 20 ills. in color, map, Jan., 1946

New Hampshire, the Granite State. By George Higgins Moses. LX, pp. 257-310, 47 ills. in black and white, 5 ills. in color, map, Sept., 1931

New Jersey Now! By E. John Long. LXIII, pp. 519-584, 49 ills. in black and white, 24 ills. in color, maps, May, 1933

New Mexico Melodrama. By Frederick Simpich. LXXIII, pp. 529-569, 19 ills. in black and white, 25 ills. in color, two-page map, May, 1938

New York—An Empire Within a Republic. By William Joseph Showalter. LXIV, pp. 513-584, 47 ills. in black and white, 35 ills. in color, two-page map, pictorial supplement, Nov., 1933

North Carolina: Motor-Coaching Through North Carolina. By Melville Chater. XLIX, pp. 475-523, 43 ills., map, May, 1926

North Carolina: Tarheelia on Parade: Versatile and Vibrant, North Carolina in a Generation Has Climbed New Economic Heights. By Leonard C. Roy. LXXX, pp. 181-224, 24 ills. in black and white, 21 ills. in color, map, Aug., 1941

Ohio, the Gateway State. By Melville Chater. LXI, pp. 525-591, 58 ills. in black and white, 13 ills. in color, map, May, 1932

Oklahoma: So Oklahoma Grew Up. By Frederick Simpich. LXXIX, pp. 269-314, 30 ills. in black and white, 19 ills. in color, map, Mar., 1941

Oregon: A Native Son's Rambles in Oregon. By Amos Burg. LXV, pp. 173-234, 39 ills. in black and white, 24 ills. in color, two-page map, Feb., 1934

Oregon Finds New Riches. By Leo A. Borah. XC, pp. 681-728, 15 ills. in black and white, 28 ills. in color, two-page map, Dec., 1946

Pennsylvania: The Industrial Titan of America: Pennsylvania, Once the Keystone of the Original Thirteen, Now the Keystone of Forty-eight Sovereign States. By John Oliver La Gorce. XXXV, pp. 367-406, 33 ills., map, May, 1919

Pennsylvania: Penn's Land of Modern Miracles. By John Oliver La Gorce. LXVIII, pp. 1-58, 28 ills. in black and white, 39 ills. in color, two-page map, July, 1935

Tennessee: Highlights of the Volunteer State: Men and Industry in Tennessee Range from Pioneer Stages to Modern Machine Age. By Leonard Cornell Roy. LXXV, pp. 553-594, 20 ills. in black and white, 22 ills. in color, map, May, 1939

Texas: So Big Texas. By Frederick Simpich. LIII, pp. 637-693, 72 ills., two-page map, June, 1928

STATE SURVEY ARTICLES: United States—*Continued*

Utah, Carved by Winds and Waters: The Beehive State, Settled Only 89 Years Ago, Stands a Monument to the Courage of Its Founders. By Leo A. Borah. LXIX, pp. 577-623, 20 ills. in black and white, 22 ills. in color, two-page map, May, 1936

Vermont: The Green Mountain State. By Herbert Corey. LI, pp. 333-369, 40 ills. in black and white, 6 ills. in color, map, Mar., 1927

Virginia—A Commonwealth That Has Come Back. By William Joseph Showalter. LV, pp. 403-472, 69 ills. in black and white, 13 ills. in color, map, Apr., 1929

Washington, the Evergreen State: The Amazing Commonwealth of the Pacific Northwest Which Has Emerged from the Wilderness in a Span of Fifty Years. By Leo A. Borah. LXIII, pp. 131-196, 50 ills. in black and white, 26 ills. in color, two-page map, Feb., 1933

West Virginia: Treasure Chest of Industry. By Enrique C. Canova. LXXVIII, pp. 141-184, 19 ills. in black and white, 21 ills. in color, two-page map, Aug., 1940

Wisconsin: On Goes Wisconsin: Strength and Vigor Mark This Midwestern State, With Its Woods and Lakes and Its Blend of Sturdy Nationalities. By Glanville Smith. LXXII, pp. 1-46, 25 ills. in black and white, 27 ills. in color, two-page map, July, 1937

Wyoming: Grass Makes Wyoming Fat. By Frederick Simpich. LXXXVIII, pp. 153-188, 13 ills. in black and white, 19 ills. in color, two-page map, Aug., 1945

STATISTICAL Atlas of the United States. XV, pp. 50-52, diagrs., Jan., 1904

STATISTICS:

Commercial and Financial Statistics of the Principal Countries of the World. XVIII, pp. 420-423, June, 1907

Shipbuilding in the United Kingdom in 1898. X, pp. 138-139, Apr., 1899

Some Significant Facts Concerning the Foreign Trade of Great Britain. XI, p. 480, Dec., 1900

Statistics of Cities (U. S.). XVI, p. 437, Sept., 1905

Statistics of Railways in the United States. (By H. G.). VII, pp. 406-407, Dec., 1896

Useful Facts About the Countries of the World. XVIII, pp. 424-425, June, 1907

See also Census; Population; Railroads; Ships and Shipping; Street Cars

STATUES. *See* Archeology; Sculpture; Stone Faces (Monuments); *and* names of cities

STAUFFER, ELMER C.:

In the Pennsylvania Dutch Country. By Elmer C. Stauffer. LXXX, pp. 37-74, 20 ills. in black and white, 22 ills. in color, map (pen and ink drawing), July, 1941

STEARNS, ROBERT E. C.:

Echoes of the San Francisco Earthquake. By Robert E. C. Stearns. XVIII, pp. 351-353, ill., May, 1907

The Native Oysters of the West Coast. By Robert E. C. Stearns. XIX, pp. 224-226, Mar., 1908

STEARNS, WALLACE N.:

Reconstructing Egypt's History. By Wallace N. Stearns. XXIV, pp. 1021-1042, 21 ills., Sept., 1913

STEEL INDUSTRY:

India's Treasures Helped the Allies. By John Fischer. LXXXIX, pp. 501-522, 18 ills., Apr., 1946

Industry's Greatest Asset—Steel. By William Joseph Showalter. XXXII, pp. 121-156, 34 ills., Aug., 1917

"Magnetic City" (Magnitogorsk), Core of Valiant Russia's Industrial Might. By John Scott. LXXXIII, pp. 525-556, 27 ills., two-page map, May, 1943

STEFANSSON, JON:

The Land of Fire (Iceland). By Jon Stefansson. XVIII, pp. 741-744, Nov., 1907

STEFANSSON, VILHJALMUR:

The Arctic as an Air Route of the Future. By Vilhjalmur Stefansson. XLII, pp. 205-218, 8 ills., map, Aug., 1922

The National Geographic Society's Notable Year (Award of Hubbard Gold Medal). XXXVII, pp. 338-345, ills., Apr., 1920

The Origin of Stefansson's Blond Eskimo. By Major General A. W. Greely. XXIII, pp. 1225-1238, 10 ills., map, Dec., 1912

STEIN, ROBERT:

Geographic Names in West Greenland. (By Ralph S. Tarr). IX, pp. 103-104, Mar., 1898

Three Weeks in Hubbard Bay, West Greenland. By Robert Stein. IX, pp. 1-11, 6 ills., maps, Jan., 1898

STEINER, ALBERT:

Amid the Snows of Switzerland. 16 ills. in duotone by Albert Steiner. XLI, pp. 277-292, Mar., 1922

STERNBERG, GEORGE M.:

Gardiner Greene Hubbard: Memorial Meeting. Address by Dr. George M. Sternberg, Surgeon-General, U.S.A. IX, pp. 41-43, Feb., 1898

The History and Geographic Distribution of Bubonic Plague. By George M. Sternberg. XI, pp. 97-113, Mar., 1900

STERRETT, J. R. SITLINGTON:

The Cone-Dwellers of Asia Minor: A Primitive People Who Live in Nature-Made Apartment Houses, Fashioned by Volcanic Violence and Trickling Streams. By J. R. Sitlington Sterrett. XXXV, pp. 281-331, 52 ills., map, Apr., 1919

STEVENS, ALBERT W.:

America from the Air: No Such Series of Airplane Views Has Ever Before Been Printed. 8 ills. from photos by Lieutenant A. W. Stevens. XLVI, pp. 85-92, July, 1924

Curvature of the Earth: The First Photograph Ever Made Showing the Division Between the Troposphere and Stratosphere and also the Actual Curvature of the Earth. Aërial photo by Captain Albert W. Stevens. LXIX, supplement, May, 1936

STEVENS, ALBERT W.—*Continued*

Exploring the Stratosphere. By Captain Albert W. Stevens. LXVI, pp. 397-434, 43 ills., chart, Oct., 1934

Exploring the Valley of the Amazon in a Hydroplane: Twelve Thousand Miles of Flying Over the World's Greatest River and Greatest Forest to Chart the Unknown Parima River from the Sky. By Captain Albert W. Stevens. XLIX, pp. 353-420, 86 ills., map, Apr., 1926

First natural-color photograph taken in the stratosphere. By Major Albert W. Stevens. LXXI, ill. p. 340, Mar., 1937

Flying the "Hump" of the Andes. By Capt. Albert W. Stevens. LIX, pp. 595-636, 36 ills., map, May, 1931

The first photograph ever made showing laterally the curvature of the earth. Aërial photo by author, ill. p. 634 (Reprint: LXIX, ill. p. 142, Jan., 1936)

Franklin L. Burr Prize awarded to Captain Stevens. LXV, p. 626, May, 1934

Greater New York . . . Metropolis of Mankind. Aërial photo by Captain Albert W. Stevens. LXIV, supplement, Nov., 1933

Hubbard Medals Awarded to Stratosphere Explorers: Presentation by General Pershing. LXIX, pp. 713-714, ill. p. 712, May, 1936

Man's Farthest Aloft: Rising to 13.71 Miles, the National Geographic Society-U. S. Army Stratosphere Expedition Gathers Scientific Data at Record Altitude. By Capt. Albert W. Stevens. LXIX, pp. 59-94, 39 ills., map, Jan., 1936

Included: Action Photographs of the Balloon's Perfect Landing

National Geographic Society-U. S. Army Air Corps Stratosphere Flight of 1935 in Balloon *Explorer II* (Contributed Technical Papers, *Stratosphere Series No. 2*). LXXI, p. 340, Mar., 1937; p. 802, June, 1937

The Non-Stop Flight Across America. By Lieutenant John A. Macready. Photos by Lieutenant Albert W. Stevens. XLVI, pp. 1-83, 68 ills., maps, July, 1924

Our Colorful City of Magnificent Distances (Washington, D. C.). 5 color photos by Capt. A. W. Stevens. LX, pp. 531-610, Nov., 1931

Photographing the Eclipse of 1932 from the Air: From Five Miles Above the Earth's Surface, the National Geographic Society-Army Air Corps Survey Obtains Successful Photographs of the Moon's Shadow. By Capt. Albert W. Stevens. LXII, pp. 581-596, 18 ills., Nov., 1932

The Scientific Results of the World-Record Stratosphere Flight. By Capt. Albert W. Stevens. LXIX, pp. 693-712, 15 ills., pictorial supplement, May, 1936

The First Photograph Ever Made Showing the Division Between the Troposphere and Stratosphere and also the Actual Curvature of the Earth. Supplement from aërial photo by author

The Society Takes Part in Three Geographic Expeditions. LXV, pp. 625-626, May, 1934

Your Society Sponsors an Expedition to Explore the Stratosphere. LXV, pp. 528-530, ill., Apr., 1934

STEVENS, D. W.:

Japan. By D. W. Stevens, Counselor of the Imperial Legation of Japan. VI, pp. 193-199, Dec. 29, 1894

STEWART, B. ANTHONY:

Aegean Islands: The Isles of Greece. 20 color photos by Maynard Owen Williams and B. Anthony Stewart. LXXXV, pp. 601-616, May, 1944

America on the Move. 26 photos by J. Baylor Roberts, B. Anthony Stewart, and others. XC, pp. 357-378, Sept., 1946

Bekonscot, England's Toy-Size Town. By Andrew H. Brown and B. Anthony Stewart. LXXI, pp. 649-661, 2 ills. in black and white, 15 ills. in color, May, 1937

Tableaux in an English Lilliput. 15 color photos by B. Anthony Stewart, pp. 653-660

Belgian Portraits. 20 color photos by B. Anthony Stewart. LXXIII, pp. 413-444, Apr., 1938

Boston, Massachusetts: The Hub City, Cradle of American Liberty. 31 color photos: 5 by B. Anthony Stewart. LXX, pp. 49-72, July, 1936

California—85 Years After the Gold Rush. 23 color photos by B. Anthony Stewart. LXIX, pp. 325-356, Mar., 1936

California: The Golden Gate, and Redwood Evergreens. 17 color photos by B. Anthony Stewart. LXXV, pp. 149-160, Feb., 1939

California: The Sun Shines on San Diego. 9 color photos by B. Anthony Stewart. LXXXI, pp. 57-64, Jan., 1942

California: Where Spring Paints a State with Wild Flowers. 18 color photos by B. Anthony Stewart. LXIX, pp. 365-380, Mar., 1936

California Says It With Wild Flowers. 9 color photos by B. Anthony Stewart. LXXXI, pp. 493-500, Apr., 1942

Cambridge University: Sculptured Gates to English Learning. 19 color photos by B. Anthony Stewart. LXXXIX, pp. 417-440, Apr., 1946

Canada: Remnants of Royal France in Canada. 15 color photos by B. Anthony Stewart. LXVIII, pp. 217-224, Aug., 1935

Charleston, South Carolina: A Colonial Rhapsody. 24 color photos by B. Anthony Stewart. LXXV, pp. 289-312, Mar., 1939

Connecticut: Old and New Blend in Yankeeland. 25 color photos: 4 by B. Anthony Stewart. LXXIV, pp. 295-326, Sept., 1938

Delaware: First in Statehood, Delaware Retains Its Graciousness. 15 color photos by B. Anthony Stewart. LXVIII, pp. 377-384, Sept., 1935

Dominican Republic, Land of Plenty. 11 color photos by B. Anthony Stewart. LXXXV, pp. 209-216, Feb., 1944

Egypt: Under Egypt's Golden Sun. 22 color photos by B. Anthony Stewart. LXXVII, pp. 451-466, Apr., 1940

England: Democracy's Royal Palace (Westminster). 19 color photos by B. Anthony Stewart. XC, pp. 233-248, Aug., 1946

England: The Pomp and Pulse of Modern London. 23 color photos by B. Anthony Stewart. LXXI, pp. 17-48, Jan., 1937

STEWART, B. ANTHONY—*Continued*

England: The Thames, England's Gateway to the World. 10 color photos by B. Anthony Stewart. LXXV, pp. 253-260, Feb., 1939

Great Lakes and Great Industries. 19 color photos by B. Anthony Stewart, Alfred T. Palmer, Willard R. Culver. LXXXVI, pp. 689-712, Dec., 1944

Greece: Classic Greece Merges Into 1941 News. 19 photos: 15 by B. Anthony Stewart, 3 by Maynard Owen Williams. LXXIX, pp. 93-108, Jan., 1941

Greece: Today's Evidence of Grecian Glory. 22 color photos by B. Anthony Stewart. LXXVII, pp. 307-322, Mar., 1940

Guernsey (Island): Contented Guernsey. 11 color photos by B. Anthony Stewart. LXXIII, pp. 377-384, Mar., 1938

Haiti Goes to Market. 10 color photos by B. Anthony Stewart. LXXXVI, pp. 313-320, Sept., 1944

Italy: Bright Facets of Italy's Grandeur. 9 color photos: 8 by B. Anthony Stewart. LXXVII, pp. 355-362, Mar., 1940

Italy: Northern Italy: Scenic Battleground. 18 color photos: 13 by B. Anthony Stewart, 3 by Lt. Benjamin C. McCartney. LXXXVII, pp. 265-288, Mar., 1945

Italy's Monuments Tell Rome's Magnificence. 8 photos: 7 by B. Anthony Stewart. LXXVII, pp. 371-378, Mar., 1940

Kentucky: The Sun Shines Bright in Kentucky. 21 color photos by B. Anthony Stewart, Volkmar Wentzel, Ray Scott. LXXXII, pp. 65-88, July, 1942

Maine: Pine-Scented, Harbor-Dented Maine. 39 color photos by B. Anthony Stewart and Robert F. Maxcy. LXVII, pp. 549-588, May, 1935

Man, Isle of: Sunny Corners in a Friendly Isle. 12 color photos by B. Anthony Stewart. LXXI, pp. 601-608, May, 1937

Maryland: Maytime in the Heart of Maryland. 10 color photos by B. Anthony Stewart and Charles Martin. LXXIX, pp. 441-448, Apr., 1941

Maryland: Old Line State Cyclorama. 22 color photos: 3 by B. Anthony Stewart. LXXIX, pp. 409-432, Apr., 1941

Nantucket: Echoes of Whaling Days. 8 color photos by B. Anthony Stewart. LXXXV, pp. 449-456, Apr., 1944

Nebraska: Cornhusker State Highlights. 23 color photos by B. Anthony Stewart. LXXXVII, pp. 521-536, May, 1945

New England: Flow Onward, Connecticut! (River). 24 color photos: 22 by B. Anthony Stewart. LXXXIII, pp. 409-432, Apr., 1943

New England: Sport and Color Amid New England Snows. 13 color photos by B. Anthony Stewart. LXX, pp. 647-654, Nov., 1936

New England: Where New England Meets the Sea. 17 color photos by B. Anthony Stewart. LXXXVIII, pp. 265-288, Sept., 1945

Oklahoma: Sunshine over Oklahoma. 19 color photos by B. Anthony Stewart. LXXIX, pp. 277-308, Mar., 1941

Ozarks (Plateau): Work and Play in the Ozarks. 20 color photos by B. Anthony Stewart and J. Baylor Roberts. LXXXIII, pp. 597-620, May, 1943

STEWART, B. ANTHONY—*Continued*

Petroleum Serves—From Lamps to Wheels. 21 color photos: 20 by B. Anthony Stewart. LXXIX, pp. 707-738, June, 1941

Plymouth, England: A City That Refused to Die. 9 color photos by B. Anthony Stewart. LXXXIX, pp. 225-232, Feb., 1946

Santa Catalina—400 Years a Lure to California Travelers. 11 color photos by B. Anthony Stewart. LXXXI, pp. 81-88, Jan., 1942

Santorin and Mýkonos, Aegean Gems. 8 color photos: 7 by B. Anthony Stewart. LXXVII, pp. 339-346, Mar., 1940

The Scillies: Isles of Wrecks and Golden Daffodils. 13 color photos: 9 by B. Anthony Stewart. LXXIV, pp. 759-766, Dec., 1938

Scotland: Heather Paints the Highlands. 38 color photos by B. Anthony Stewart. LXXXIX, pp. 561-600, May, 1946

Texas: Rio Grande Cornucopia Under a Winter Sun. 24 color photos by B. Anthony Stewart. LXXV, pp. 65-96, Jan., 1939

Virginia: Gardens and Shrines of Old Virginia. 20 color photos by B. Anthony Stewart and J. Baylor Roberts. LXXXI, pp. 623-646, May, 1942

Washington, D. C.: Culture Still Lights Our Wartime Capital. 9 color photos by B. Anthony Stewart. LXXXI, pp. 337-344, Mar., 1942

Washington, D. C.: Our Nation's Capital on Parade. 16 color photos by B. Anthony Stewart, Walter M. Edwards, and others. LXXXIV, pp. 265-288, Sept., 1943

Washington, D. C.: Winter Lights and Shadows in the Nation's Capital. 21 ills. in duotone: 6 by B. Anthony Stewart. LXVII, pp. 201-216, Feb., 1935

West Virginia: High Road and Low through the Mountain State. 21 color photos by B. Anthony Stewart and Volkmar Wentzel. LXXVIII, pp. 157-180, Aug., 1940

Wisconsin: Life's Color in Wisconsin. 27 color photos: 23 by B. Anthony Stewart. LXXII, pp. 17-40, July, 1937

Wyoming: Welcome to Wyoming. 19 color photos: 18 by B. Anthony Stewart. LXXXVIII, pp. 161-184, Aug., 1945

STEWART, RICHARD H.:

Canton Island: Unfurling Old Glory on Canton Island. 11 ills. in color: 7 color photos by Richard H. Stewart. LXXIII, pp. 753-760, June, 1938

Circus: The Color Camera Explores the Country That Moves by Night. 15 color photos by Richard H. Stewart. LX, pp. 479-510, Oct., 1931

Hawaii: Leis from Aloha Land. 10 color photos: 8 by Richard H. Stewart. LXXIV, pp. 435-442, Oct., 1938

Kansas: Views and Hues of the Sunflower State. 12 color photos by Richard H. Stewart. LXXII, pp. 151-158, Aug., 1937

Mexico: From the Halls of Montezuma. 21 color photos by Richard H. Stewart and others. LXXXV, pp. 137-164, Feb., 1944

Mexico: La Venta's Green Stone Tigers. 6 color photos by Richard H. Stewart. LXXXIV, pp. 329-332, Sept., 1943

STEWART, RICHARD H.—*Continued*

Mexico: Treasure-trove of Old Mexican Jade (Cerro de las Mesas). 20 color photos by Richard H. Stewart. LXXX, pp. 293-316, Sept., 1941

Mexico's Deep South Yields New Treasure (Tabasco and Chiapas). 12 color photos by Richard H. Stewart. LXXXII, pp. 649-656, Nov., 1942

Missouri Mirrors of 1946. 22 color photos by Richard H. Stewart. LXXXIX, pp. 285-308, Mar., 1946

New Mexico: Nature Paints New Mexico. 25 color photos by Richard H. Stewart. LXXIII, pp. 537-568, May, 1938

Utah: Bursts of Color in Sculptured Utah. 22 color photos: 18 by Richard H. Stewart. LXIX, pp. 593-616, May, 1936

STIELER, KARL:

Venice. By Karl Stieler. XXVII, pp. 587-630, 42 ills., maps, June, 1915

STIKINE RIVER, Alaska-Canada:

Life on a Yukon Trail. By Alfred Pearce Dennis. X, pp. 377-391, 8 ills., map, Oct., 1899; pp. 457-466, 7 ills., Nov., 1899

The Stikine River in 1898. By Eliza Ruhamah Scidmore. X, pp. 1-15, 4 ills., Jan., 1899

STILES, ARTHUR ALVORD:

A Bear Hunt in Montana. By Arthur Alvord Stiles. XIX, pp. 149-154, 5 ills., Feb., 1908

STILLWELL, AGNES N.:

Crete, Where Sea-Kings Reigned. By Agnes N. Stillwell. LXXXIV, pp. 547-568, 20 ills., map, Nov., 1943

STILLWELL, RICHARD:

Greece—the Birthplace of Science and Free Speech: Explorations on the Mainland and in Crete and the Aegean Isles Reveal Ancient Life Similar to That of the Present. By Richard Stillwell. Paintings by H. M. Herget. LXXXV, pp. 273-353, 13 ills. in black and white, 32 ills. in color, two-page map, Mar., 1944

The Isles of Greece. By Lt. Richard Stillwell, USNR. LXXXV, pp. 593-622, 11 ills. in black and white, 20 ills. in color, map, May, 1944

STILWELL Road—Land Route to China. By Nelson Grant Tayman. LXXXVII, pp. 681-698, 18 ills., June, 1945

STIRLING, MARION:

Finding Jewels of Jade in a Mexican Swamp (La Venta). By Matthew W. and Marion Stirling. LXXXII, pp. 635-661, 15 ills. in black and white, 12 ills. in color, map, Nov., 1942

Jungle Housekeeping for a Geographic Expedition (Cerro de las Mesas, Mexico). By Marion Stirling. LXXX, pp. 303-327, 15 ills., Sept., 1941

STIRLING, MATTHEW W.:

America's First Settlers, the Indians. By Matthew W. Stirling. Paintings by W. Langdon Kihn. LXXII, pp. 535-596, 34 ills. in black and white, 24 ills. in color, Nov., 1937

STIRLING, MATTHEW W.—*Continued*

Discovering the New World's Oldest Dated Work of Man: A Maya Monument Inscribed 291 B.C. Is Unearthed Near a Huge Stone Head by a Geographic-Smithsonian Expedition in Mexico. By Matthew W. Stirling. LXXVI, pp. 183-218, 40 ills., map, Aug., 1939

Expedition Unearths Buried Masterpieces of Carved Jade (Cerro de las Mesas, Mexico). By Matthew W. Stirling. LXXX, pp. 277-302, 14 ills. in black and white, 20 ills. in color, map, Sept., 1941

Finding Jewels of Jade in a Mexican Swamp (La Venta). By Matthew W. and Marion Stirling. LXXXII, pp. 635-661, 15 ills. in black and white, 12 ills. in color, map, Nov., 1942

Great Stone Faces of the Mexican Jungle: Five Colossal Heads and Numerous Other Monuments of Vanished Americans Are Excavated by the Latest National Geographic-Smithsonian Expedition. By Matthew W. Stirling. LXXVIII, pp. 309-334, 26 ills., map, Sept., 1940

Indian Tribes of Pueblo Land. By Matthew W. Stirling. Paintings by W. Langdon Kihn. LXXVIII, pp. 549-596, 16 ills. in black and white, 25 ills. in color, Nov., 1940

Indians of Our North Pacific Coast. By Matthew W. Stirling. Paintings by W. Langdon Kihn. LXXXVII, pp. 25-52, 3 ills. in black and white, 16 ills. in color, Jan., 1945

Indians of Our Western Plains. By Matthew W. Stirling. Paintings by W. Langdon Kihn. LXXXVI, pp. 73-108, 14 ills. in black and white, 16 ills. in color, July, 1944

Indians of the Southeastern United States. By Matthew W. Stirling. Paintings by W. Langdon Kihn. LXXXIX, pp. 53-74, 8 ills. in black and white, 8 ills. in color, Jan., 1946

La Venta's Green Stone Tigers. By Matthew W. Stirling. LXXXIV, pp. 321-332, 4 ills. in black and white, 6 ills. in color, map, Sept., 1943

STOCK, RALPH:

The Dream Ship: The Story of a Voyage of Adventure More Than Half Around the World in a 47-foot Lifeboat. By Ralph Stock. XXXIX, pp. 1-52, 43 ills., map, Jan., 1921

STOCKHOLM, Sweden:

Flying Around the Baltic. By Douglas Chandler. LXXIII, pp. 767-806, 31 ills. in black and white, 13 ills. in duotone, map, June, 1938

The Granite City of the North: Austere Stockholm, Sweden's Prosperous Capital, Presents a Smiling Aspect in Summer. By Ralph A. Graves. LIV, pp. 403-424, 23 ills., Oct., 1928

Types and Costumes of Old Sweden. 30 color photos by Gustav Heurlin, G. W. Cronquist, Wilhelm Tobien, Charles Martin. LIV, pp. 425-440, Oct., 1928

STOCKTON, CHARLES H.:

The Arctic Cruise of the U. S. S. Thetis in the Summer and Autumn of 1889. By Charles H. Stockton. II, pp. 171-198, ill., foldout map, July, 1890

STOCKTON, CHARLES H.—*Continued*

Collinson's Arctic Journey. By General A. W. Greely. IV, pp. 198-200, Feb. 8, 1893

Note: References to the Arctic voyage of Lieutenant Commander Charles H. Stockton, U.S.N., in the *Thetis*, in 1889

STONE, MELVILLE E.:

Race Prejudice in the Far East. By Melville E. Stone. XXI, pp. 973-985, 6 ills., Dec., 1910

STONE Beehive Homes of Italian Peasants. 12 color photos by Luigi Pellerano and L.U.C.E. LVII, pp. 235-242, Feb., 1930

The **STONE** Beehive Homes of the Italian Heel: In Trulli-Land the Native Builds His Dwelling and Makes His Field Arable in the Same Operation. By Paul Wilstach. LVII, pp. 229-260, 25 ills. in black and white, 12 ills. in color, map, Feb., 1930

STONE FACES (Monuments):

Discovering the New World's Oldest Dated Work of Man: A Maya Monument Inscribed 291 B.C. Is Unearthed Near a Huge Stone Head by a Geographic-Smithsonian Expedition in Mexico. By Matthew W. Stirling. LXXVI, pp. 183-218, 40 ills., map, Aug., 1939

Great Stone Faces of Easter Island. 11 ills. LXXXV, pp. 225-232, Feb., 1944

Great Stone Faces of the Mexican Jungle: Five Colossal Heads and Numerous Other Monuments of Vanished Americans Are Excavated by the Latest National Geographic-Smithsonian Expedition. By Matthew W. Stirling. LXXVIII, pp. 309-334, 26 ills., map, Sept., 1940

The Mystery of Easter Island. By Mrs. Scoresby Routledge. XL, pp. 629-646, 13 ills., map, Dec., 1921

Stone Idols of the Andes Reveal a Vanished People: Remarkable Relics of One of the Oldest Aboriginal Cultures of America are Unearthed in Colombia's San Agustín Region. By Hermann von Walde-Waldegg. LXXVII, pp. 627-647, 22 ills., map, May, 1940

Storied Islands of the South Sea. 20 color photos by Irving Johnson, Malcolm Evans, and others. LXXXI, pp. 9-40, Jan., 1942

STONE Idols of the Andes Reveal a Vanished People: Remarkable Relics of One of the Oldest Aboriginal Cultures of America are Unearthed in Colombia's San Agustín Region. By Hermann von Walde-Waldegg. LXXVII, pp. 627-647, 22 ills., map, May, 1940

STORIED Islands of the South Sea. 20 color photos by Irving Johnson, Malcolm Evans, and others. LXXXI, pp. 9-40, Jan., 1942

STORMS:

Forecasting the Weather and Storms. By Willis L. Moore. XVI, pp. 255-306, 5 ills., 20 charts, June, 1905

The Great Storm of March 11-14, 1888. By Brigadier-General A. W. Greely. I, pp. 37-39, Oct., 1888

The Great Storm Off the Atlantic Coast of the United States, March 11th-14th, 1888. By Everett Hayden. I, pp. 40-58, 6 charts, Oct., 1888

STORMS—*Continued*

The Law of Storms, Considered with Special Reference to the North Atlantic. By Everett Hayden. II, pp. 199-211, ill., 3 diagrs., 3 foldout diagrs., foldout charts, July, 1890

Our Heralds of Storm and Flood. By Gilbert H. Grosvenor. XVIII, pp. 586-601, 15 ills., chart, Sept., 1907

Report—Geography of the Air. By Gen. A. W. Greely. II, pp. 49-63, Apr., 1890

The Storm of February 25-28, 1902. (By Alfred J. Henry). XIII, pp. 110-112, chart, Mar., 1902

Storms and Weather Forecasts. By Professor Willis L. Moore. VIII, pp. 65-82, 25 charts, Mar., 1897

United States Daily Atmospheric Survey. By Professor Willis L. Moore. VIII, pp. 299-303, Oct., 1897

See also Hurricanes; Meteorology; Rainfall

The **STORY** and the Legends of the Pontine Marshes: After Many Centuries of Fruitless Effort, Italy Is to Inaugurate a Gigantic Enterprise to Drain the Fertile Region Southeast of Rome. By Don Gelasio Caetani. XLV, pp. 357-374, 18 ills., Apr., 1924

The **STORY** of Machu Picchu: The Peruvian Expeditions of the National Geographic Society and Yale University. By Hiram Bingham. XXVII, pp. 172-217, 60 ills., Feb., 1915

The **STORY** of the American Flag. By Byron McCandless and Gilbert Grosvenor. XXXII, pp. 286-303, 12 ills., Oct., 1917

The **STORY** of the Flamingo. XVI, p. 50, Jan., 1905

The **STORY** of the Horse: The Development of Man's Companion in War Camp, on Farm, in the Marts of Trade, and in the Field of Sports. By Major General William Harding Carter. Paintings by Edward Herbert Miner. XLIV, pp. 455-566, 62 ills. in black and white, 24 ills. in color, Nov., 1923

The **STORY** of the Map. Text with map supplement. LXII, pp. 759-774, 11 ills., Dec., 1932

The **STORY** of the Ruhr. By Frederick Simpich. XLI, pp. 553-564, 11 ills., map, May, 1922

STRAITS SETTLEMENTS, Malay Peninsula. *See* Christmas Island; Cocos Islands; Singapore

A **STRANGE** and Remarkable Beast (Mammoth). XVIII, p. 620, ill., Sept., 1907

STRANGE Creatures of Sunny Seas (Mollusks, Crustaceans, etc.). 8 ills. in color from paintings by Else Bostelmann under direction Roy W. Miner. LXXI, pp. 211-218, Feb., 1937

STRANGE Habits of Familiar Moths and Butterflies. By William Joseph Showalter. LII, pp. 77-105, 19 ills. in black and white, drawing, 88 ills. in color, July, 1927

STRANGE Sights in Far-Away Papua. By A. E. Pratt. XVIII, pp. 559-572, 7 ills., Sept., 1907

STRANGE Tribes in the Shan States of Burma. 15 color photos by W. Robert Moore. LVIII, pp. 247-254, Aug., 1930

STRATEGIC Alaska Looks Ahead: Our Vast Territory, Now Being More Closely Linked to Us by Road and Rail, Embodies the American Epic of Freedom, Adventure, and the Pioneer Spirit. By Ernest H. Gruening. LXXXII, pp. 281-315, 18 ills. in black and white, 16 ills. in color, two-page map, Sept., 1942

STRATFORD UPON AVON, England:

Through the Heart of England in a Canadian Canoe. By R. J. Evans. XLI, pp. 473-497, 26 ills., map, May, 1922

STRATOSPHERE:

Ballooning in the Stratosphere: Two Balloon Ascents to Ten-Mile Altitudes Presage New Mode of Aërial Travel. By Auguste Piccard. LXIII, pp. 353-384, 34 ills., Mar., 1933

Exploring the Earth's Stratosphere: The Holder of the American Altitude Record Describes His Experiences in Reaching the "Ceiling" of His Plane at an Elevation of Nearly Eight Miles. By First Lieutenant John A. Macready. L, pp. 755-776, 18 ills., Dec., 1926

Exploring the Stratosphere. By Captain Albert W. Stevens. LXVI, pp. 397-434, 43 ills., chart, Oct., 1934

First natural-color photograph taken in the stratosphere. By Major Albert W. Stevens. LXXI, ill. p. 340, Mar., 1937

The First Photograph Ever Made Showing the Division Between the Troposphere and Stratosphere and also the Actual Curvature of the Earth. Aërial photo by Captain Albert W. Stevens. LXIX, supplement, May, 1936

Man's Farthest Aloft: Rising to 13.71 Miles, the National Geographic Society-U. S. Army Stratosphere Expedition Gathers Scientific Data at Record Altitude. By Capt. Albert W. Stevens. LXIX, pp. 59-94, 39 ills., map, Jan., 1936

Included: Action Photographs of the Balloon's Perfect Landing

National Geographic Society-U. S. Army Air Corps Stratosphere Flight of 1935 in Balloon *Explorer II* (Contributed Technical Papers, *Stratosphere Series No. 2*). LXXI, p. 340, Mar., 1937; p. 802, June, 1937

A Report of the Second Stratosphere Expedition. LXVIII, pp. 535-536, Oct., 1935

The Scientific Results of the World-Record Stratosphere Flight. By Capt. Albert W. Stevens. LXIX, pp. 693-712, 15 ills., pictorial supplement, May, 1936

The First Photograph Ever Made Showing the Division Between the Troposphere and Stratosphere and also the Actual Curvature of the Earth. Supplement from aërial photo by author

The Society Announces New Flight into the Stratosphere. By Gilbert Grosvenor. LXVII, pp. 265-272, ills., map, Feb., 1935

Studies Planned for New Stratosphere Flight with Helium. LXVII, pp. 795-800, 5 ills., June, 1935

World's Largest Free Balloon to Explore Stratosphere. LXVI, pp. 107-110, ills., July, 1934

Your Society Sponsors an Expedition to Explore the Stratosphere. LXV, pp. 528-530, ill., Apr., 1934

STRAUSS, JOSEPH:
Awarded Jane M. Smith Life Membership. XXXVII, p. 342, Apr., 1920

STREET CARS:
Electric Street Railways (U. S.). (By J. H.). VIII, p. 284, Oct., 1897

STREETS and Palaces of Colorful India. 34 color photos by Gervais Courtellemont. L, pp. 60-85, July, 1926

STREETT, ST. CLAIR:
The First Alaskan Air Expedition. By Captain St. Clair Streett. XLI, pp. 499-552, 37 ills., map, May, 1922

STRÖBECK, Germany:
Ströbeck, Home of Chess: A Medieval Village in the Harz Mountains of Germany Teaches the Royal Game in Its Public School. By Harriet Geithmann. LIX, pp. 637-652, 8 ills. in black and white, 14 ills. in color, May, 1931

STROUT, EDITH BAUER:
At Home on the Oceans: Whales and Sharks Make Exciting Neighbors for a Professor's Wife, Turned Able Seaman, On a Three-year Voyage Around the World. By Edith Bauer Strout. LXXVI, pp. 33-86, 54 ills., map, July, 1939

STRUGGLING Poland: A Journey in Search of the Picturesque Through the Most Populous of the New States of Europe. By Maynard Owen Williams. L, pp. 203-244, 48 ills., map, Aug., 1926

STUART, ELEANOR (Mrs. Harris R. Childs):
Zanzibar. By Mrs. Harris R. Childs. XXIII, pp. 810-824, 11 ills., Aug., 1912

STUDIES of Muir Glacier, Alaska. By Harry Fielding Reid. IV, pp. 19-55, 13 ills., 6 diagrs., table, 2 maps (1 foldout), Mar. 21, 1892

STUDIES on the Rate of Evaporation at Reno, Nevada, and in the Salton Sink. By Professor Frank H. Bigelow. XIX, pp. 20-28, 5 ills., Jan., 1908

STUDIES Planned for New Stratosphere Flight with Helium. LXVII, pp. 795-800, 5 ills., June, 1935

STYRIA (Province), Austria:
Styria, a Favored Vacation Land of Central Europe. By Melville Bell Grosvenor. LXII, pp. 430-439, 14 ills. in color, Oct., 1932
This Was Austria. 18 ills. LXXXVIII, pp. 71-86, July, 1945

The **SUBMARINE** Cables of the World. By Gustave Herrle. With chart compiled by U.S. Hydrographic Office. VII, pp. 102-107, Mar., 1896

SUBMARINES:
Your Navy as Peace Insurance. By Fleet Admiral Chester W. Nimitz. LXXXIX, pp. 681-736, 32 ills. in black and white, 26 ills. in color, June, 1946

SUBMERGED Valleys in Sandusky Bay (Ohio). By Professor E. L. Moseley. XIII, pp. 398-403, 4 charts, Nov., 1902

SUCCESSFUL Shots With a Friendly Camera. 16 photos by H. T. Bohlman, Irene Finley, William L. Finley. XLIV, pp. 165-180, Aug., 1923

SUDAN (Region), Africa:
Three-Wheeling Through Africa: Two Adventurers Cross the So-called Dark Continent North of Lake Chad on Motorcycles with Side Cars. By James C. Wilson. LXV, pp. 37-92, 64 ills., two-page map, Jan., 1934
See also Anglo-Egyptian Sudan; French Sudan

SUEZ CANAL, Egypt:
The Evolution of Commerce. Annual Address by the President, Hon. Gardiner G. Hubbard. IV, pp. 1-18, Mar. 26, 1892
The Suez Canal: Short Cut to Empires. By Maynard Owen Williams. LXVIII, pp. 611-632, 19 ills., map, Nov., 1935
Traffic on the Suez Canal. XII, p. 380, Oct., 1901

SUGAR CANE:
Into Primeval Papua by Seaplane: Seeking Disease-resisting Sugar Cane, Scientists Find Neolithic Man in Unmapped Nooks of Sorcery and Cannibalism. By E. W. Brandes. LVI, pp. 253-332, 98 ills., map, Sept., 1929
See also Sugar Industry

SUGAR INDUSTRY:
Agricultural Possibilities in Tropical Mexico. By Dr. Pehr Olsson-Seffer. XXI, pp. 1021-1040, 19 ills., Dec., 1910
Cuba—The Sugar Mill of the Antilles. By William Joseph Showalter. XXXVIII, pp. 1-33, 24 ills., map, July, 1920
How the World Is Fed. By William Joseph Showalter. XXIX, pp. 1-110, 101 ills., Jan., 1916

A **SUGGESTED** Field for Exploration (Caribbean Regions). XIV, pp. 290-291, July, 1903

SUGGESTIONS to Future Observers (Muir Glacier, Alaska). By H. F. Reid. IV, pp. 83-84, Mar. 21, 1892

SULAIMANIYA, Iraq:
Mountain Tribes of Iran and Iraq. By Harold Lamb. LXXXIX, pp. 385-408, 15 ills., two-page map, Mar., 1946

SULPHUR Mine in Nevada. XV, p. 498, Dec., 1904

SULTAN, DAN I.:
An Army Engineer Explores Nicaragua: Mapping a Route for a New Canal Through the Largest of Central American Republics. By Lieut. Col. Dan I. Sultan. LXI, pp. 593-627, 39 ills., map, May, 1932

SULU ARCHIPELAGO, Philippine Islands:
"As the Tuan Had Said." By George M. Hanson. LXIV, pp. 631-644, 19 ills., Nov., 1933

SUMATRA:
Among the Hill Tribes of Sumatra. By W. Robert Moore. LVII, pp. 187-227, 31 ills. in black and white, 25 ills. in color, map, Feb., 1930

SUMATRA—*Continued*

Around the World for Animals. By William M. and Lucile Q. Mann. LXXIII, pp. 665-714, 33 ills. in black and white, 23 ills. in color, map, June, 1938

By Motor Through the East Coast and Batak Highlands of Sumatra. By Melvin A. Hall. XXXVII, pp. 69-102, 27 ills., Jan., 1920

The Face of the Netherlands Indies. 20 photos by Maynard Owen Williams and others. LXXXIX, pp. 261-276, Feb., 1946

Sumatra's West Coast. By David G. Fairchild. IX, pp. 449-464, 8 ills., Nov., 1898

SUMATRA, a Ribbon of Color on the Equator. 25 color photos by W. Robert Moore. LVII, pp. 195-218, Feb., 1930

SUMERIANS (People):

New Light on Ancient Ur: Excavations at the Site of the City of Abraham Reveal Geographical Evidence of the Biblical Story of the Flood. By M. E. L. Mallowan. LVII, pp. 95-130, 44 ills., map, Jan., 1930

SUMMARY of Reports on the Mt. St. Elias Expedition. II, pp. 302-304, Apr., 1891

SUMMER Holidays on the Bosporus. By Maynard Owen Williams. LVI, pp. 487-508, 13 ills. in black and white, 11 ills. in color, map, Oct., 1929

SUMMER Meeting of the American Forestry Association. XIII, pp. 352-358, Sept., 1902

A **SUMMER** Voyage to the Arctic. By G. R. Putnam. VIII, pp. 97-110, 6 ills., map, Apr., 1897

SUMMERING in an English Cottage: Quiet and Loveliness Invite Contemplation in the Extra "Room," the Garden of the Thatched House. By Helen Churchill Candee. LXVII, pp. 429-456, 32 ills., Apr., 1935

SUMMERING in Styria, Austria's Rural Playground. 14 color photos by Hans Hildenbrand. LXII, pp. 431-438, Oct., 1932

SUN. *See* Astronomy; Solar Radiation

SUN-COMPASS, Bumstead:

Albert H. Bumstead, inventor of the sun-compass which Admiral Byrd used on polar flights. XLVIII, p. 523, ill. p. 520, Nov., 1925. L, pp. 367, 381, ill. p. 378, Sept., 1926. LII, p. 238, ill. p. 242, Aug., 1927. LVIII, p. 233, Aug., 1930. LXIX, p. 130, Jan., 1936

The First Flight to the North Pole. By Lieutenant Commander Richard Evelyn Byrd. L, pp. 357-376, 14 ills., Sept., 1926

SUN-PAINTED Scenes in the Near East. 32 color photos by Gervais Courtellemont. XLVIII, pp. 541-556, Nov., 1925

The **SUN** Shines Bright in Kentucky. 21 color photos by B. Anthony Stewart, Volkmar Wentzel, Ray Scott. LXXXII, pp. 65-88, July, 1942

The **SUN** Shines on San Diego (California). 9 color photos by B. Anthony Stewart. LXXXI, pp. 57-64, Jan., 1942

SUNDA ISLANDS, Greater. *See* Borneo; Celebes; Java; Sumatra

SUNDA ISLANDS, Lesser. *See* Bali; Timor

A **SUNDAY** in Mezőkövesd (Hungary). By Margery Rae. LXVII, pp. 489-504, 22 ills., Apr., 1935

SUNGARI (River), Manchuria:

Here in Manchuria: Many Thousand Lives Were Lost and More Than Half the Crops Destroyed by the Floods of 1932. By Lilian Grosvenor Coville. LXIII, pp. 233-256, 26 ills., Feb., 1933

SUNGMAS, the Living Oracles of the Tibetan Church. By Joseph F. Rock. LXVIII, pp. 475-486, ill. in black and white, 12 ills. in color, Oct., 1935

SUNNY Corners in a Friendly Isle (Isle of Man). 12 color photos by B. Anthony Stewart. LXXI, pp. 601-608, May, 1937

SUNNY Corners of Kangaroo Land (Australia). 12 color photos by W. Robert Moore. LXX, pp. 713-720, Dec., 1936

SUNNY Siberia. 26 color photos by Owen Lattimore. LXXXVI, pp. 649-672, Dec., 1944

SUNNY South Africa. 9 color photos by W. Robert Moore. LXXXII, pp. 749-756, Dec., 1942

SUNRISE and Sunset from Mount Sinai. By Rev. Sartell Prentice, Jr. XXIII, pp. 1242-1282, 34 ills., map, Dec., 1912

SUNSET Hues in the Pacific Northwest (Washington). 13 color photos by Clifton Adams and Asahel Curtis. LXIII, pp. 155-162, Feb., 1933

SUNSET in the East (Japan). By Blair A. Walliser. LXXXIX, pp. 797-812, 17 ills., June, 1946

SUNSHINE in Turkey. By Howard S. Bliss. XX, pp. 66-76, ill., Jan., 1909

A **SUNSHINE** Land of Fruits, Flowers, Movies, and Sport (California). 41 color photos by Clifton Adams and Fred Payne Clatworthy. LXVI, pp. 545-592, Nov., 1934

SUNSHINE over Oklahoma. 19 color photos by B. Anthony Stewart. LXXIX, pp. 277-308, Mar., 1941

SUNSHINE Over the Chilean Lakes. 10 color photos by W. Robert Moore and John Swope. LXXX, pp. 97-104, July, 1941

SUPERIOR, Lake, Canada-U. S.:

Area and Drainage Basin of Lake Superior. By Dr. Mark W. Harrington. VIII, pp. 111-120, tables, Apr., 1897

The Wild Life of Lake Superior, Past and Present: The Habits of Deer, Moose, Wolves, Beavers, Muskrats, Trout, and Feathered Wood-Folk Studied with Camera and Flashlight. By George Shiras, 3d. XL, pp. 113-204, 76 ills., map, pictorial supplement, Aug., 1921

Winter Sky Roads to Isle Royal. By Ben East. LX, pp. 759-774, 18 ills., map, Dec., 1931

SUPERSTITIONS. *See* Rainmaking

SUPPLEMENTARY Note by Marcus Baker. On the Alleged Observation of a Lunar Eclipse by Bering in 1728-9. II, pp. 167-169, 4 tables, May, 1890

SUPPLEMENTS. *See* NGM: Map Supplement Articles and Announcements; Map Supplements (Text and Illustrations); Pictorial Supplements; *and* Map Index, *following this index*

SUPPLY:
War, Patriotism, and the Food Supply. By Frederick V. Coville. XXXI, pp. 254-256, Mar., 1917
Winning the War of Supply. By F. Barrows Colton. LXXXVIII, pp. 705-736, 32 ills., Dec., 1945
See also Lend-Lease; U. S. Army Quartermaster Corps; Water Supply

The **SUPPOSED** Birthplace of Civilizations. XVI, pp. 499-504, 6 ills., Nov., 1905

SURF-BOARDERS Capture California. 8 photos by J. H. Ball. LXXXVI, pp. 355-362, Sept., 1944

SURFBOARDING:
Surf-Boarders Capture California. 8 photos by J. H. Ball. LXXXVI, pp. 355-362, Sept., 1944
Waves and Thrills at Waikiki (Honolulu). 8 ills. in duotone by Thomas Edward Blake. LXVII, pp. 597-604, May, 1935

SURINAM (Dutch Guiana):
Color Glows in the Guianas, French and Dutch. By Nicol Smith. LXXXIII, pp. 459-480, 8 ills. in black and white, 13 ills. in color, map, Apr., 1943
Picturesque Paramaribo. By Harriet Chalmers Adams. XVIII, pp. 365-373, 7 ills., June, 1907

SURINAM Subjects of Queen Wilhelmina. 13 color photos by Philip Hanson Hiss. LXXXIII, pp. 465-472, Apr., 1943

The **SURVEY** and Map of Massachusetts. By Henry Gannett. I, pp. 78-86, Oct., 1888

SURVEY and Subdivision of Indian Territory. By Henry Gannett. VII, pp. 112-115, ill., map, Mar., 1896

The **SURVEY** of the Coast (U.S.). By Herbert G. Ogden. I, pp. 59-77, Oct., 1888

SURVEY of the Grand Canyon. XIV, pp. 162-163, Apr., 1903

SURVEYING:
Across Nicaragua with Transit and Machête. By R. E. Peary. I, pp. 315-335, 3 ills. (tinted), foldout map, Oct., 1889
The Alaskan Boundary Survey. I—Introduction. By Dr. T. C. Mendenhall. II—The Boundary South of Fort Yukon. By J. E. McGrath. III—The Boundary North of Fort Yukon. By J. Henry Turner. IV, pp. 177-197, Feb. 8, 1893
The Five Civilized Tribes and the Survey of Indian Territory. By C. H. Fitch. IX, pp. 481-491, 4 ills., map, Dec., 1898

SURVEYING—*Continued*
Geographical Research in the United States. By Gardiner G. Hubbard and Marcus Baker. VIII, pp. 285-293, Oct., 1897
The Mother Maps of the United States. By Henry Gannett. IV, pp. 101-116, table, map supplement, Mar. 31, 1892
The Ordnance Survey of Great Britain—Its History and Object. By Josiah Pierce, Jr. II, pp. 243-260, Aug., 1890
The Survey and Map of Massachusetts. By Henry Gannett. I, pp. 78-86, Oct., 1888
Survey and Subdivision of Indian Territory. By Henry Gannett. VII, pp. 112-115, ill., map, Mar., 1896
The Survey of the Coast (U.S.). By Herbert G. Ogden. I, pp. 59-77, Oct., 1888
Survey of the Grand Canyon. XIV, pp. 162-163, Apr., 1903
Surveying the Grand Canyon of the Colorado: An Account of the 1923 Boating Expedition of the United States Geological Survey. By Lewis R. Freeman. XLV, pp. 471-548, 62 ills., map, May, 1924
Surveying the 141st Meridian (Boundary Line Between Canada and Alaska). By Thomas Riggs, Jr. XXIII, pp. 685-713, 46 ills., map, July, 1912
Surveying the Philippine Islands. By George H. Putnam. XIV, pp. 437-441, 4 ills., Dec., 1903
Surveying Through Khoresm: A Journey Into Parts of Asiatic Russia Which Have Been Closed to Western Travelers Since the World War. By Lyman D. Wilbur. LXI, pp. 753-780, 31 ills., map, June, 1932
Surveys and Maps of the District of Columbia. By Marcus Baker. VI, pp. 149-178, diagr., tables, map, Nov. 1, 1894
Included: List of Maps of Washington and the District of Columbia
Surveys in the Philippines. (By P. A. Welker). XXII, p. 82, map, Jan., 1911
See also Triangulation

SURVEYING, Hydrographic. *See* Hydrography; U. S. Coast and Geodetic Survey

SURVEYS. *See* Surveying

SURVIVAL:
The Nansen Polar Expedition. Special Report of the Hon. Ernest A. Man. VII, pp. 339-344, map supplement, Oct., 1896
They Survived at Sea. By Lt. Comdr. Samuel F. Harby. LXXXVII, pp. 617-640, 22 ills., May, 1945

SUSA (Shush), Iran:
Excavations of M. de Morgan at Susa. XII, p. 315, Aug., 1901

The **SUSHITNA** River, Alaska. By W. A. Dickey. VIII, pp. 322-327, map, Nov., 1897

SUSSEX (County), England:
The Penn Country in Sussex: Home of Pennsylvania's Founder Abounds in Quaker History and Memories of Adventurous Smugglers. By Col. P. T. Etherton. LXVIII, pp. 59-90, 32 ills., map, July, 1935

SUSU (Tribespeople):

Dusky Tribesmen of French West Africa. 26 color photos by Enzo de Chetelat. LXXIX, pp. 639-662, May, 1941

SUTER, H. M.:

"Forest Fires in the Adirondacks in 1903." By H. M. Suter. XV, p. 224, May, 1904

SUTHERLAND, MASON:

Aboard a Blimp Hunting U-boats: A Day above the Atlantic Reveals Navy Talk and Navy Ways, Creeping Convoys, and Torpedoed Wrecks. By Mason Sutherland. LXXXIV, pp. 79-96, 18 ills., July, 1943

Bornholm—Denmark in a Nutshell. By Mason Sutherland. LXXXVII, pp. 239-256, 20 ills., map, Feb., 1945

A Navy Artist Paints the Aleutians. By Mason Sutherland. Paintings by Lt. William F. Draper. LXXXIV, pp. 157-176, 4 ills. in black and white, 16 ills. in color, Aug., 1943

SUTTON COURTENAY (Manor), England:

A Vacation in a Fifteenth Century English Manor House. By George Alden Sanford. LIII, pp. 629-636, 8 ills., May, 1928

SUTTON HOO SHIP BURIAL:

Ancestor of the British Navy: England's Oldest Known War Vessel Is Unearthed, Laden with Remarkable Treasures of an Anglo-Saxon Ruler. By C. W. Phillips. LXXIX, pp. 247-268, 22 ills., 4 drawings, Feb., 1941

SUWANNEE (River), Georgia:

The Okefinokee Wilderness: Exploring the Mystery Land of the Suwannee River Reveals Natural Wonders and Fascinating Folklore. By Francis Harper. LXV, pp. 597-624, 35 ills., map, May, 1934

SVALBARD (Archipelago). *See* Spitsbergen

SVANS (People):

Roaming Russia's Caucasus: Rugged Mountains and Hardy Fighters Guard the Soviet Union's Caucasian Treasury of Manganese and Oil. By Rolf Singer. LXXXII, pp. 91-121, 33 ills., July, 1942

SVEN Hedin in Tibet. XIII, pp. 96-97, Mar., 1902

SVEN Hedin's Explorations in Central Asia. XII, pp. 393-395, Nov., 1901

SVERDRUP, OTTO:

The Nansen Polar Expedition. Special Report of the Hon. Ernest A. Man. VII, pp. 339-344, map supplement, Oct., 1896

The Return of Dr. Nansen. VII, p. 290, Sept., 1896

Sverdrup's Work in the Arctics. XIII, p. 461, map, Dec., 1902

SWALLOWS:

Thrushes, Thrashers, and Swallows: Robins and Bluebirds are Familiar Members of a Famous Musical Family Which Includes the Hermit Thrush and European Nightingale. By T. Gilbert Pearson. Paintings by Maj. Allan Brooks. LXIX, pp. 523-546, 6 ills. in black and white, 42 paintings from life, Apr., 1936

SWAMP DRAINAGE. *See* Reclamation of Land

SWANS:

Far-Flying Wild Fowl and Their Foes. By Major Allan Brooks. Paintings from life by author. LXVI, pp. 487-528, 6 ills. in black and white, 3 portraits in color, Oct., 1934

Fowls of Forest and Stream Tamed by Man. By Morley A. Jull. Paintings by Hashime Murayama. LVII, pp. 327-371, 27 ills. in black and white, 16 ills. in color, Mar., 1930

SWAYNE, H. G. C.:

The Rock of Aden: The Volcanic Mountain Fortress, on the Sea Route from Suez to India, Assumes New Importance. By H. G. C. Swayne. LXVIII, pp. 723-742, 24 ills., map, Dec., 1935

SWEDEN:

A Comparison of Norway and Sweden. XVI, pp. 429-431, Sept., 1905

Country-House Life in Sweden: In Castle and Cottage the Landed Gentry Gallantly Keep the Old Traditions. By Amelie Posse-Brázdová. LXVI, pp. 1-64, 51 ills. in black and white, 13 ills. in color, map, July, 1934

Flying Around the Baltic. By Douglas Chandler. LXXIII, pp. 767-806, 31 ills. in black and white, 13 ills. in duotone, map, June, 1938

In Beautiful Delecarlia (Dalecarlia). By Lillian Gore. XX, pp. 464-477, 13 ills., May, 1909

King Herring: An Account of the World's Most Valuable Fish, the Industries It Supports, and the Part It Has Played in History. By Hugh M. Smith. XX, pp. 701-735, 21 ills., Aug., 1909

Life's Flavor on a Swedish Farm: From the Rocky Hills of Småland Thousands of Sturdy Citizens Have Emigrated to the United States. By Willis Lindquist. LXXVI, pp. 393-414, 23 ills., map, Sept., 1939

The Nomads of Arctic Lapland: Mysterious Little People of a Land of the Midnight Sun Live Off the Country Above the Arctic Circle. By Clyde Fisher. LXXVI, pp. 641-676, 28 ills. in black and white, 12 ills. in color, map, Nov., 1939

Rural Sweden Through American Eyes: A Visitor in Peacetime Finds Warmth, Welcome, and Strange Folkways On a Century-old Farm. By Elizabeth W. Nilson. LXXVII, pp. 795-822, 8 ills. in black and white, 22 ills. in color, June, 1940

Sweden, Land of White Birch and White Coal. By Alma Luise Olson. LIV, pp. 441-484, 51 ills., Oct., 1928

Types and Costumes of Old Sweden. 30 color photos by Gustav Heurlin, G. W. Cronquist, Wilhelm Tobien, Charles Martin. LIV, pp. 425-440, Oct., 1928

See also Stockholm

SWIFTS (Birds):

Seeking the Smallest Feathered Creatures: Humming Birds, Peculiar to the New World, Are Found from Canada and Alaska to the Strait of Magellan. Swifts and Goatsuckers, Their Nearest Relatives. By Alexander Wetmore. Paintings by Maj. Allan Brooks. LXII, pp. 65-89, 2 ills. in black and white, 5 ills. in color, July, 1932

SWINGLE, CHARLES F.:

Across Madagascar by Boat, Auto, Railroad, and Filanzana. By Charles F. Swingle. LVI, pp. 179-211, 42 ills., maps, Aug., 1929

SWINGLE, WALTER T.:

Awarded Jane M. Smith Life Membership. XXXVII, p. 342, Apr., 1920

SWISS Cherish Their Ancient Liberties. 21 ills. LXXIX, pp. 481-496, Apr., 1941

SWITZERLAND:

Amid the Snows of Switzerland. 16 ills. in duotone by Albert Steiner. XLI, pp. 277-292, Mar., 1922

The Ascent of Mont Blanc. By Walter Woodburn Hyde. XXIV, pp. 861-942, 69 ills., Aug., 1913

The Citizen Army of Switzerland. XXVIII, pp. 503-510, 7 ills., Nov., 1915

Flights from Arctic to Equator: Conquering the Alps, the Ice Peaks of Spitsbergen, of Persia, and Africa's Mountains of the Moon. By Walter Mittelholzer. LXI, pp. 445-498, 53 ills., map, Apr., 1932

In Valais. By Louise Murray. XXI, pp. 249-256, 6 ills., Mar., 1910

Italian, French, and Swiss Scenes. 16 photos, hand-tinted, by Donald McLeish and Arthur Stanley Riggs. XXVIII, pp. 439-454, Nov., 1915

Lake Geneva: Cradle of Conferences. By F. Barrows Colton. LXXII, pp. 727-742, 12 ills., map, Dec., 1937

Landslides and Rock Avalanches. By Guy Elliott Mitchell. XXI, pp. 277-287, 6 ills., Apr., 1910

The Majesty of the Matterhorn. XXIII, text p. 514; pictorial supplement, May, 1912

Manless Alpine Climbing: The First Woman to Scale the Grépon, the Matterhorn, and Other Famous Peaks Without Masculine Support Relates Her Adventures. By Miriam O'Brien Underhill. LXVI, pp. 131-170, 30 ills. in black and white, 12 ills. in color, Aug., 1934

The Races of Europe. By Edwin A. Grosvenor. XXXIV, pp. 441-534, 62 ills., diagr. and index, maps, map supplement, Dec., 1918

Republics—The Ladder to Liberty. By David Jayne Hill. XXXI, pp. 240-254, 5 ills., maps, Mar., 1917

Scenes in Switzerland. 13 ills. XXI, pp. 257-268, Mar., 1910

Skiing in Switzerland's Realm of Winter Sports. 10 photos in duotone by Jean Gaberell, E. Gyger, A. Klopfenstein. LXIII, pp. 345-352, Mar., 1933

Swiss Cherish Their Ancient Liberties. 21 ills. LXXIX, pp. 481-496, Apr., 1941

A Woman's Climbs in the High Alps. By Dora Keen. XXII, pp. 643-675, 26 ills., July, 1911

See also Geneva; Gruyères

SWOPE, JOHN:

Sunshine Over the Chilean Lakes. 10 color photos by W. Robert Moore and John Swope. LXXX, pp. 97-104, July, 1941

SWORDFISH:

Fighting Giants of the Humboldt. By David D. Duncan. LXXIX, pp. 373-400, 28 ills., map, Mar., 1941

SYDNEY, Australia:

Capital Cities of Australia. By W. Robert Moore. LXVIII, pp. 667-722, 32 ills. in black and white, 24 ills. in color, two-page map, Dec., 1935

Lonely Australia: The Unique Continent. By Herbert E. Gregory. XXX, pp. 473-568, 68 ills., 5 maps (1 two-page), Dec., 1916

Sydney Faces the War Front Down Under. By Howell Walker. LXXXIII, pp. 359-374, 8 ills. in black and white, 10 ills. in color, Mar., 1943

SYKES, ELLA C.:

A Talk About Persia and Its Women. By Ella C. Sykes. XXI, pp. 847-866, 22 ills., Oct., 1910

SYKES, ROBERT B., JR.:

Uncle Sam's Icebox Outposts. 19 color photos by John E. Schneider and Robert B. Sykes, Jr. XC, pp. 473-496, Oct., 1946

SYLVESTER, A. H.:

Is Our Noblest Volcano Awakening to New Life: A Description of the Glaciers and Evidences of Volcanic Activity of Mount Hood. By A. H. Sylvester. XIX, pp. 515-525, 5 ills., map, July, 1908

The **SYMBOL** of Service to Mankind (American National Red Cross). By Stockton Axson. XXXIII, pp. 375-390, 11 ills., Apr., 1918

SYNTHETIC PRODUCTS:

Chemists Make a New World: Creating Hitherto Unknown Raw Materials, Science Now Disrupts Old Trade Routes and Revamps the World Map of Industry. By Frederick Simpich. LXXVI, pp. 601-640, 22 ills. in black and white, 26 ills. in color, Nov., 1939

SYRACUSE, Sicily. *See* Siracusa

SYRIA:

Antioch the Glorious. By William H. Hall. XXXVIII, pp. 81-103, 20 ills., map, Aug., 1920

Bombs over Bible Lands. By Frederick Simpich and W. Robert Moore. LXXX, pp. 141-180, 34 ills., two-page map, Aug., 1941

Change Comes to Bible Lands. By Frederick Simpich. LXXIV, pp. 695-750, 40 ills. in black and white, 25 ills. in color, map supplement, Dec., 1938

Damascus, the Pearl of the Desert. By A. Forder. XXII, pp. 62-82, 19 ills., map, Jan., 1911

Damascus and Mecca Railway. XII, p. 408, Nov., 1901

From Jerusalem to Aleppo. By John D. Whiting. XXIV, pp. 71-113, 30 ills., map, Jan., 1913

Geographic Progress of Civilization. Annual Address by the President, Honorable Gardiner G. Hubbard. VI, pp. 1-22, Feb. 14, 1894

Impressions of Asiatic Turkey. By Stephen van Rensselaer Trowbridge. XXVI, pp. 598-609, 6 ills., Dec., 1914

SYRIA—*Continued*

A New Alphabet of the Ancients Is Unearthed: An Inconspicuous Mound in Northern Syria Yields Archeological Treasures of Far-reaching Significance. By F. A. Schaeffer. LVIII, pp. 477-516, 47 ills., map, Oct., 1930

One Thousand Miles of Railway Built for Pilgrims and Not for Dividends. By Colonel F. R. Maunsell. XX, pp. 156-172, 12 ills., map, Feb., 1909

Secrets from Syrian Hills: Explorations Reveal World's Earliest Known Alphabet, Deciphered from Schoolboy Slates and Dictionaries of 3,000 Years Ago. By Claude F. A. Schaeffer. LXIV, pp. 97-126, 40 ills., map, July, 1933

Skirting the Shores of Sunrise: Seeking and Finding "The Levant" in a Journey by Steamer, Motor-Car, and Train from Constantinople to Port Said. By Melville Chater. L, pp. 649-728, 60 ills. in black and white, 34 ills. in color, map, Dec., 1926

Syria: The Land Link of History's Chain. By Maynard Owen Williams. XXXVI, pp. 437-462, 20 ills., map, Nov., 1919

Syria and Lebanon Taste Freedom. By Maynard Owen Williams. With 21 color photos by author. XC, pp. 729-763, 16 ills. in black and white, Dec., 1946

See also Dèir ez Zor

SZECHWAN (Province), China:

China Fights Erosion with U. S. Aid. By Walter C. Lowdermilk. LXXXVII, pp. 641-680, 10 ills. in black and white, 26 ills. in color, June, 1945

The Eden of the Flowery Republic. By Dr. Joseph Beech. XXXVIII, pp. 355-390, 18 ills. in black and white, 16 ills. in color, Nov., 1920

Populous and Beautiful Szechuan: A Visit to the Restless Province of China, in which the Present Revolution Began. By Rollin T. Chamberlin. XXII, pp. 1094-1119, 26 ills., map, Dec., 1911

Salt for China's Daily Rice. 11 ills. LXXXVI, pp. 329-336, Sept., 1944

T

T-2 (Airplane):

The Non-Stop Flight Across America. By Lieutenant John A. Macready. Photos by Lieutenant Albert W. Stevens. XLVI, pp. 1-83, 68 ills., maps, July, 1924

TAAL Volcano and Its Recent Destructive Eruption (Philippine Islands). By Dean C. Worcester. XXIII, pp. 313-367, 40 ills., diagr., 4 maps, Apr., 1912

TABASCO (State), Mexico:

Wildlife of Tabasco and Veracruz. By Walter A. Weber. With 19 ills. in color from paintings by author. LXXXVII, pp. 187-216, 7 ills. in black and white, map, Feb., 1945

See also La Venta

TABLEAUX in an English Lilliput (Bekonscot). 15 color photos by B. Anthony Stewart. LXXI, pp. 653-660, May, 1937

TACOMA, Washington:

Our Pacific Northwest. By N. H. Darton. XX, pp. 645-663, 12 ills., maps, July, 1909

TAFT, WILLIAM HOWARD:

The Annual Dinner of the National Geographic Society (Speech by William Howard Taft). XVII, pp. 22-37, Jan., 1906

The Arbitration Treaties. By William Howard Taft. XXII, pp. 1165-1172, Dec., 1911

Great Britain's Bread Upon the Waters: Canada and Her Other Daughters. By William Howard Taft. XXIX, pp. 217-272, 56 ills., Mar., 1916

The Health and Morale of America's Citizen Army: Personal Observations of Conditions in Our Soldier Cities by a Former Commander-in-Chief of the United States Army and Navy. By William Howard Taft. XXXIII, pp. 219-245, 22 ills., Mar., 1918

In Honor of the Army and Aviation (Address upon Election as Honorary Member of the Society). XXII, pp. 267-284, ill., Mar., 1911

The Islands of Bermuda: A British Colony with a Unique Record in Popular Government. By William Howard Taft. XLI, pp. 1-26, 15 ills., map, Jan., 1922

The League of Nations, What It Means and Why It Must Be. By William Howard Taft. XXXV, pp. 43-66, 15 ills., Jan., 1919

The Lincoln Memorial (Washington, D. C.). By William Howard Taft. XLIII, pp. 597-602, 5 ills., June, 1923

The Philippines. By William H. Taft. XVI, pp. 361-375, 3 ills., map supplement, Aug., 1905

A Poisoned World. By William Howard Taft. XXXI, pp. 459-467, 7 ills., May, 1917

The Progressive World Struggle of the Jews for Civil Equality. By William Howard Taft. XXXVI, pp. 1-23, 14 ills., July, 1919

The Race for the South Pole (Presentation of Hubbard Gold Medal to Sir Ernest H. Shackleton by President Taft). XXI, pp. 185-186, Mar., 1910

Some Impressions of 150,000 Miles of Travel. By William Howard Taft. LVII, pp. 523-598, 80 ills., May, 1930

Some Recent Instances of National Altruism: The Efforts of the United States to Aid the Peoples of Cuba, Porto Rico and the Philippines. By William H. Taft. XVIII, pp. 429-438, July, 1907

Ten Years in the Philippines. By William Howard Taft. XIX, pp. 141-148, Feb., 1908

Washington (D. C.): Its Beginning, Its Growth, and Its Future. By William Howard Taft. XXVII, pp. 221-292, 33 ills. in black and white, 32 ills. in color, map, panoramas, Mar., 1915

See also NGS: Board of Managers

TAG. *See* Transport Air Group

TAGBANUAS (People):

Notes on Some Primitive Philippine Tribes. By Dean C. Worcester. IX, pp. 284-301, 11 ills., June, 1898

TAGUS (River), Spain-Portugal. *See* Tejo

TAHITI (Island), Society Islands:

Diary of a Voyage from San Francisco to Tahiti and Return, 1901. By S. P. Langley. XII, pp. 413-429, 10 ills., maps, Dec., 1901

The Dream Ship: The Story of a Voyage of Adventure More Than Half Around the World in a 47-foot Lifeboat. By Ralph Stock. XXXIX, pp. 1-52, 43 ills., map, Jan., 1921

Notes on Tahiti. By H. W. Smith. XXII, pp. 947-963, 17 ills., Oct., 1911

Tahiti: A Playground of Nature. By Paul Gooding. XXXVIII, pp. 301-326, 16 ills., map, Oct., 1920

TAHLTAN INDIANS:

Life on a Yukon Trail. By Alfred Pearce Dennis. X, pp. 377-391, 8 ills., map, Oct., 1899

TAI PUSAM (Hindu Festival):

The Fire-Walking Hindus of Singapore. By L. Elizabeth Lewis. LIX, pp. 513-522, 12 ills., Apr., 1931

TAI SHAN, Sacred Mountain of the East (China). By Mary Augusta Mullikin. LXXXVII, pp. 699-719, 18 ills., map, June, 1945

TAIAN, China:

Tai Shan, Sacred Mountain of the East. By Mary Augusta Mullikin. LXXXVII, pp. 699-719, 18 ills., map, June, 1945

TAIHOKU (Taipei), Formosa:

Formosa the Beautiful. By Alice Ballantine Kirjassoff. XXXVII, pp. 247-292, 60 ills., map, Mar., 1920

I Lived on Formosa. By Joseph W. Ballantine. LXXXVII, pp. 1-24, 19 ills., maps, Jan., 1945

The **TAILED** People of Nigeria. XXIII, pp. 1239-1242, 3 ills., Dec., 1912

TAIPEI, Formosa. *See* Taihoku

TAIREN, Manchuria. *See* Dairen

TAIWAN (Island). *See* Formosa

TAJ MAHAL (Mausoleum), Agra, India:

Through the Heart of Hindustan: A Teeming Highway Extending for Fifteen Hundred Miles, from the Khyber Pass to Calcutta. By Maynard Owen Williams. XL, pp. 433-467, 29 ills., Nov., 1921

TAKE-OFF for Japan. 22 ills. in color from U.S. Navy official photos. LXXXVIII, pp. 193-208, Aug., 1945

TALBOT, P. A.:

Notes on the Ekoi (Nigeria). By P. A. Talbot. XXIII, pp. 33-38, 8 ills., Jan., 1912

TALC (Block Talc):

India's Treasures Helped the Allies. By John Fischer. LXXXIX, pp. 501-522, 18 ills., Apr., 1946

A **TALE** of Three Cities (Prague, Vienna, Budapest). By Thomas R. Henry. LXXXVIII, pp. 641-669, 23 ills., Dec., 1945

TALES of the British Air Service. By Major William A. Bishop. XXXIII, pp. 27-37, 12 ills., Jan., 1918

A **TALK** About Persia and Its Women. By Ella C. Sykes. XXI, pp. 847-866, 22 ills., Oct., 1910

The **TALLEST** Tree That Grows (Eucalyptus). By Edgerton R. Young. XX, pp. 664-667, 3 ills., July, 1909

TALLINN, Estonia:

Estonia: At Russia's Baltic Gate: War Often Has Ravaged This Little Nation Whose Identity Was Long Submerged in the Vast Sea of Russian Peoples. By Baroness Irina Ungern-Sternberg. LXXVI, pp. 803-834, 33 ills., map, Dec., 1939

Flying Around the Baltic. By Douglas Chandler. LXXIII, pp. 767-806, 31 ills. in black and white, 13 ills. in duotone, map, June, 1938

TAMBS, ERLING:

A Modern Saga of the Seas: The Narrative of a 17,000-Mile Cruise on a 40-Foot Sloop by the Author, His Wife, and a Baby, Born on the Voyage. By Erling Tambs. LX, pp. 645-688, 49 ills., map, Dec., 1931

TAMING "Flood Dragons" Along China's Hwang Ho (River). By Oliver J. Todd. LXXXI, pp. 205-234, 26 ills., map, Feb., 1942

TAMING the Outlaw Missouri River. By Frederick Simpich. LXXXVIII, pp. 569-598, 25 ills., two-page map, Nov., 1945

TAMING the Wild Blueberry. By Frederick V. Coville. XXII, pp. 137-147, 5 ills., Feb., 1911

TAMPICO, Mexico:

A Naturalist's Journey Around Vera Cruz and Tampico. By Frank M. Chapman. XXV, pp. 533-562, 31 ills., May, 1914

TANAGER (Ship):

Bird Life Among Lava Rock and Coral Sand: The Chronicle of a Scientific Expedition to Little-known Islands of Hawaii. By Alexander Wetmore. XLVIII, pp. 77-108, 36 ills., map, July, 1925

TANAGERS (Birds):

The Tanagers and Finches: Their Flashes of Color and Lilting Songs Gladden the Hearts of American Bird Lovers East and West. By Arthur A. Allen. Paintings by Maj. Allan Brooks. LXVII, pp. 505-532, 6 ills. in black and white, 55 portraits in color, Apr., 1935

TANAHMERAH, Netherlands New Guinea:

New Guinea's Mountain and Swampland Dwellers. By Col. Ray T. Elsmore. LXXXVIII, pp. 671-694, 15 ills. in black and white, 7 ills. in color, map, Dec., 1945

TANGANYIKA:

Flashlights from the Jungle. XVIII, pp. 534-548, 11 ills., Aug., 1907

The Heart of Africa. By E. C. Hore. III, pp. 238-247, Feb. 19, 1892

Wings Over Nature's Zoo in Africa. 20 photos in duotone by Reginald A. Bourlay. LXXVI, pp. 527-542, Oct., 1939

TANGANYIKA LAKE, Belgian Congo-Tanganyika:

Where Exploration Is Needed (Africa). XI, pp. 163-164, Apr., 1900

TANGIER, International Zone, Morocco:

Eastward from Gibraltar: Overland Route Across North Africa to Tunisia and Libia. By Cyrus French Wicker. LXXXIII, pp. 115-142, 28 ills., Jan., 1943

A Journey in Morocco: "The Land of the Moors." By Thomas Lindsey Blayney. XXII, pp. 750-775, 23 ills., Aug., 1911

Morocco, "the Land of the Extreme West" and the Story of My Captivity. By Ion Perdicaris. XVII, pp. 117-157, 24 ills., Mar., 1906

The Two Great Moorish Religious Dances. By George Edmund Holt. XXII, pp. 777-785, 6 ills., Aug., 1911

TANKERS:

Ships That Won the Greatest Naval War. 26 ills. in color from U. S. Navy official photos. LXXXIX, pp. 697-736, June, 1946

TANNURA, Ras at (Sandspit), Saudi Arabia:

Guest in Saudi Arabia. By Maynard Owen Williams. LXXXVIII, pp. 463-487, 24 ills., map, Oct., 1945

TAOIST SHRINES:

Tai Shan, Sacred Mountain of the East. By Mary Augusta Mullikin. LXXXVII, pp. 699-719, 18 ills., map, June, 1945

TARASCAN INDIANS:

A Mexican Land of Lakes and Lacquers (Pâtzcuaro Region). 22 photos by Helene Fischer and Luis Marquez. LXXI, pp. 633-648, May, 1937

Paricutín, the Cornfield That Grew a Volcano (Mexico). By James A. Green. LXXXV, pp. 129-164, 16 ills. in black and white, 21 ills. in color, map, Feb., 1944

TARAWA (Atoll), Gilbert Islands:

Gilbert Islands in the Wake of Battle. By W. Robert Moore. LXXXVII, pp. 129-162, 11 ills. in black and white, 19 ills. in color, map, Feb., 1945

TARHEELIA on Parade: Versatile and Vibrant, North Carolina in a Generation Has Climbed New Economic Heights. By Leonard C. Roy. LXXX, pp. 181-224, 24 ills. in black and white, 21 ills. in color, map, Aug., 1941

TARR, RALPH S.:

Geographic Names in West Greenland. (By Ralph S. Tarr). IX, pp. 103-104, Mar., 1898

The National Geographic Society's Alaskan Expedition of 1909. By Ralph S. Tarr and Lawrence Martin. XXI, pp. 1-54, 42 ills., 12 maps, Jan., 1910

The Teaching of Geography. By Ralph S. Tarr. XIII, pp. 55-64, Feb., 1902

TARTAN Tints New Scotland (Nova Scotia). 21 color photos: 12 by John Mills, Jr., 7 by W. R. MacAskill. LXXVII, pp. 591-622, May, 1940

TARXIEN TEMPLE, Malta:

Malta: The Halting Place of Nations: First Account of Remarkable Prehistoric Tombs and Temples Recently Unearthed on the Island. By William Arthur Griffiths. XXXVII, pp. 445-478, 35 ills., map, May, 1920

TASHI-CHO-JONG (Fort), Bhutan:

Castles in the Air: Experiences and Journeys in Unknown Bhutan. By John Claude White. XXV, pp. 365-455, 74 ills., map, Apr., 1914

TATARS (People):

Young Russia: The Land of Unlimited Possibilities. By Gilbert H. Grosvenor. XXVI, pp. 421-520, 85 ills. in black and white, 17 ills. in color, Nov., 1914

TATE, G. H. H.:

Through Brazil to the Summit of Mount Roraima. By G. H. H. Tate. LVIII, pp. 585-605, 24 ills., map, Nov., 1930

The **TAURINE** World: Cattle and Their Place in the Human Scheme—Wild Types and Modern Breeds in Many Lands. By Alvin Howard Sanders. Paintings by Edward Herbert Miner. XLVIII, pp. 591-710, 76 ills. in black and white, 20 ills. in color, Dec., 1925

TAUTIRA, Tahiti, Society Islands:

Notes on Tahiti. By H. W. Smith. XXII, pp. 947-963, 17 ills., Oct., 1911

TAUU ISLANDS, South Pacific Ocean:

American Pathfinders in the Pacific. By William H. Nicholas. LXXXIX, pp. 617-640, 17 ills., two-page map, May, 1946

TAYMAN, NELSON GRANT:

Stilwell Road—Land Route to China. By Nelson Grant Tayman. LXXXVII, pp. 681-698, 18 ills., June, 1945

TEACHING. *See* Education; Public Schools

The **TEACHING** of Geography. By Ralph S. Tarr. XIII, pp. 55-64, Feb., 1902

The **TEACHING** of Physical Geography in Elementary Schools. By Richard E. Dodge. XI, pp. 470-475, Dec., 1900

TEAK (Trees):

Working Teak in the Burma Forests: The Sagacious Elephant Is Man's Ablest Ally in the Logging Industry of the Far East. By A. W. Smith. LVIII, pp. 239-256, 5 ills. in black and white, 15 ills. in color, Aug., 1930

TECHNICAL TRAINING SCHOOLS, U. S. Army Air Forces. *See* Army Air Forces Training Command

TEDDY (Sloop):

A Modern Saga of the Seas: The Narrative of a 17,000-Mile Cruise on a 40-Foot Sloop by the Author, His Wife, and a Baby, Born on the Voyage. By Erling Tambs. LX, pp. 645-688, 49 ills., map, Dec., 1931

TEHRAN, Iran:

Iran in Wartime: Through Fabulous Persia, Hub of the Middle East, Americans, Britons, and Iranians Keep Sinews of War Moving to the Embattled Soviet Union. By John N. Greely. LXXXIV, pp. 129-156, 26 ills., map, Aug., 1943

Modern Persia and Its Capital: And an Account of an Ascent of Mount Demavend, the Persian Olympus. By F. L. Bird. XXXIX, pp. 353-400, 47 ills., Apr., 1921

TEHUANTEPEC (Isthmus), Mexico:

In Honor of the Army and Aviation (Banquet: Speech by the Mexican Ambassador Concerning the Isthmian Canal). XXII, pp. 267-284, ill., Mar., 1911

The Isthmus of Tehuantepec. By Herbert Corey. XLV, pp. 549-579, 25 ills., May, 1924

The Isthmus of Tehuantepec: "The Bridge of the World's Commerce." By Helen Olsson-Seffer. XXI, pp. 991-1002, 7 ills., Dec., 1910

See also Tehuantepec Ship Railway

The **TEHUANTEPEC** Ship Railway. By Elmer L. Corthell. VII, pp. 64-72, maps, Feb., 1896

TEHUELCHE INDIANS:

The Indian Tribes of Southern Patagonia, Tierra del Fuego, and the Adjoining Islands. By J. B. Hatcher. XII, pp. 12-22, 4 ills., Jan., 1901

TEJO (River), Portugal:

Lisbon, the City of the Friendly Bay. By Clifford Albion Tinker. XLII, pp. 505-552, 30 ills. in black and white, 16 ills. in color, map, Nov., 1922

TEKES VALLEY, Sinkiang:

With the Nomads of Central Asia: A Summer's Sojourn in the Tekes Valley, Plateau Paradise of Mongol and Turkic Tribes. By Edward Murray. Paintings and drawings by Alexandre Iacovleff. LXIX, pp. 1-57, 43 ills. in black and white, 26 ills. in color, map, Jan., 1936

TEL AVIV, Palestine:

American Fighters Visit Bible Lands. By Maynard Owen Williams. With 23 color photos by author. LXXXIX, pp. 311-340, 10 ills. in black and white, Mar., 1946

Palestine Today. By Francis Chase, Jr. XC, pp. 501-516, 16 ills., Oct., 1946

TELEGRAPHY:

Building the Alaskan Telegraph System. By Captain William Mitchell. XV, pp. 357-361, Sept., 1904

Cape to Cairo Telegraph. XII, pp. 162-163, Apr., 1901

The Cape to Cairo Telegraph. XIII, pp. 76-77, Feb., 1902

On the Telegraphic Determinations of Longitude by the Bureau of Navigation. By Lieut. J. A. Norris, U. S. N. II, pp. 1-30, Apr., 1890

Peter Cooper and Submarine Telegraphy. VII, pp. 108-110, Mar., 1896

The Russo-American Telegraph Project of 1864-'67. By Professor William H. Dall. VII, pp. 110-111, ill., Mar., 1896

The Special Telegraphic Time Signal from the Naval Observatory. XV, pp. 411-415, Oct., 1904

The United States Government Telegraph and Cable Lines. XV, pp. 490-494, 3 maps, Dec., 1904

See also Cables

TELEPHONE:

The Miracle of Talking by Telephone. By F. Barrows Colton. LXXII, pp. 395-433, 41 ills., Oct., 1937

TELEPHONE—*Continued*

Prehistoric Telephone Days. By Alexander Graham Bell. XLI, pp. 223-241, 17 ills., Mar., 1922

Voice Voyages by the National Geographic Society: A Tribute to the Geographical Achievements of the Telephone. XXIX, pp. 296-326, 15 ills., chart, Mar., 1916

The World's Highest International Telephone Cable. LVIII, pp. 722-731, 8 ills., Dec., 1930

TELESCOPES:

Exploring the Glories of the Firmament. By William Joseph Showalter. XXXVI, pp. 153-181, 17 ills., diagr., 3 charts, Aug., 1919

News of the Universe: Mars Swings Nearer the Earth, Sunspots Wane, and a Giant New Telescopic Eye Soon Will Peer Into Unexplored Depths of Space. By F. Barrows Colton. Paintings by Charles Bittinger. LXXVI, pp. 1-32, 23 ills. in black and white, 10 ills. in color, July, 1939

See also Astronomy

TELEVISION:

Your New World of Tomorrow. By F. Barrows Colton. LXXXVIII, pp. 385-410, 25 ills., Oct., 1945

TELL EL-KHELEIFEH (Ezion-geber), Trans-Jordan:

On the Trail of King Solomon's Mines: The Bible, in Addition to Its Spiritual Values, Continues to Prove a Rich Geography and Guide to Exploration of the Holy Land. By Nelson Glueck. LXXXV, pp. 233-256, 20 ills., map, Feb., 1944

TEMPERATURE:

Climatic Conditions of Alaska. By General A. W. Greely. IX, pp. 132-137, Apr., 1898

Laws of Temperature Control of the Geographic Distribution of Terrestrial Animals and Plants. Annual Address by Vice-President, Dr. C. Hart Merriam. VI, pp. 229-238, table, 3 maps, Dec. 29, 1894

Relations of Air and Water to Temperature and Life. By Honorable Gardiner G. Hubbard. V, pp. 112-124, Jan. 31, 1894

TEMPLE MOUNDS:

Indians of the Southeastern United States. By Matthew W. Stirling. Paintings by W. Langdon Kihn. LXXXIX, pp. 53-74, 8 ills. in black and white, 8 ills. in color, Jan., 1946

TEMPLES:

Chichen Itzá, an Ancient American Mecca: Recent Excavations in Yucatan Are Bringing to Light the Temples, Palaces, and Pyramids of America's Most Holy Native City. By Sylvanus Griswold Morley. XLVII, pp. 63-95, 34 ills., diagr., map, Jan., 1925

Excavations at Quirigua, Guatemala. By Sylvanus Griswold Morley. XXIV, pp. 339-361, 24 ills., diagr., Mar., 1913
Note. XXIV, p. 1056, Sept., 1913

The Five Thousand Temples of Pagān: Burma's Sacred City Is a Place of Enchantment in the Midst of Ruins. By William H. Roberts. LX, pp. 445-454, 9 ills., Oct., 1931

TEMPLES—*Continued*

"The Glory That Was Greece." By Alexander Wilbourne Weddell. XLII, pp. 571-630, 51 ills., map, Dec., 1922

The Home of a Forgotten Race: Mysterious Chichen Itza, in Yucatan, Mexico. By Edward H. Thompson. XXV, pp. 585-648, 59 ills., June, 1914

The Madura Temples. By J. S. Chandler. XIX, pp. 218-222, 4 ills., Mar., 1908

Malta: The Halting Place of Nations: First Account of Remarkable Prehistoric Tombs and Temples Recently Unearthed on the Island. By William Arthur Griffiths. XXXVII, pp. 445-478, 35 ills., map, May, 1920

The Marble Dams of Rajputana. By Eleanor Maddock. XL, pp. 469-499, 13 ills. in black and white, 16 ills. in color, Nov., 1921

Mysterious Temples of the Jungle: The Prehistoric Ruins of Guatemala. By W. F. Sands. XXIV, pp. 325-338, 10 ills., Mar., 1913

Peiping's Happy New Year: Lunar Celebration Attracts Throngs to Temple Fairs, Motley Bazaars, and Age-old Festivities. By George Kin Leung. LXX, pp. 749-792, 31 ills. in black and white, 16 ills. in color, Dec., 1936

Puto, the Enchanted Island. By Robert F. Fitch. LXXXIX, pp. 373-384, 11 ills., map, Mar., 1946

Tai Shan, Sacred Mountain of the East (China). By Mary Augusta Mullikin. LXXXVII, pp. 699-719, 18 ills., map, June, 1945

Temples and Ceremonies of Kaleidoscopic Bangkok. 12 color photos by Amos Burg, Gervais Courtellemont, W. Robert Moore. LXV, pp. 547-554, May, 1934

The Temples of India. 54 photos by W. M. Zumbro. XX, pp. 922-971, Nov., 1909

See also Cave Temples; Temple Mounds

TEMPO and Color of a Great City (New York City). 42 color photos by Clifton Adams and Edwin L. Wisherd. LVIII, pp. 539-578, Nov., 1930

The **TEN** Thousand Smokes Now a National Monument: The President of the United States Sets Aside for the American People the Extraordinary Valley Discovered and Explored by the National Geographic Society. XXXV, pp. 359-366, 5 ills., Apr., 1919

TEN Years in the Philippines. By William Howard Taft. XIX, pp. 141-148, Feb., 1908

TEN Years of the Peary Arctic Club. By Herbert L. Bridgman. XIX, pp. 661-668, 3 ills., Sept., 1908

TENNESSEE:

Highlights of the Volunteer State: Men and Industry in Tennessee Range from Pioneer Stages to Modern Machine Age. By Leonard Cornell Roy. LXXV, pp. 553-594, 20 ills. in black and white, 22 ills. in color, map, May, 1939

Home Folk Around Historic Cumberland Gap. By Leo A. Borah. LXXXIV, pp. 741-768, 25 ills., map, Dec., 1943

TENNESSEE—*Continued*

Rambling Around the Roof of Eastern America (Great Smoky Mountains). By Leonard C. Roy. LXX, pp. 243-266, 25 ills., map, Aug., 1936

Reelfoot—An Earthquake Lake. By Wilbur A. Nelson. XLV, pp. 95-114, 20 ills., Jan., 1924

TENNESSEE (Battleship):

Victory's Portrait in the Marianas. By Lt. William Franklin Draper, USNR. With 17 ills. in color from paintings by author. LXXXVIII, pp. 599-616, Nov., 1945

TENNESSEE Tableaux. 22 color photos: 19 by J. Baylor Roberts. LXXV, pp. 569-592, May, 1939

TENOS (Island), Aegean Sea:

The Isles of Greece. By Lt. Richard Stillwell, USNR. LXXXV, pp. 593-622, 11 ills. in black and white, 20 ills. in color, map, May, 1944

TER GOES, Netherlands. *See* Goes

TERCEIRA (Island), Azores:

American Airmen in the Azores. 10 ills. in color. LXXXIX, pp. 177-184, Feb., 1946

TERMINATION Land (Antarctica). (By Edwin Swift Balch). XV, pp. 220-221, May, 1904

TERNS (Birds):

Fairy Terns of the Atolls. By Lewis Wayne Walker. XC, pp. 807-814, 9 ills., Dec., 1946

Pelican Profiles. By Lewis Wayne Walker. LXXXIV, pp. 589-598, 5 ills. in black and white, 8 ills. in color, Nov., 1943

Included: The Gull-billed Tern of the Salton Sea Area, California

TERRA, HELLMUT DE:

On the World's Highest Plateaus: Through an Asiatic No Man's Land to the Desert of Ancient Cathay. By Hellmut de Terra. LIX, pp. 319-367, 39 ills. in black and white, 32 ills. in color, map, Mar., 1931

TERRESTRIAL MAGNETISM. *See* Geomagnetism

TERRIERS:

Man's Oldest Ally, the Dog: Since Cave-Dweller Days This Faithful Friend Has Shared the Work, Exploration, and Sport of Humankind. By Freeman Lloyd. Paintings by Edward Herbert Miner. LXIX, pp. 247-274, 13 ills. in black and white, 33 portraits in color, Feb., 1936

Contents: Airedale Terrier, Bedlington Terrier, Bull Terrier, Cairn Terrier, Dandie Dinmont Terrier, Irish Terrier, Kerry Blue Terrier, Lakeland Terrier, Manchester Terrier, Miniature Schnauzer, Scottish Terrier, Sealyham Terrier, Skye Terrier, Smooth Fox Terrier, Standard Schnauzer, Welsh Terrier, West Highland White Terrier, Wire-haired Fox Terrier

Toy Dogs, Pets of Kings and Commoners. By Freeman Lloyd. LXXXV, pp. 459-480, 8 ills. in black and white, 16 ills. in color, Apr., 1944

The **TESTING** of Arctic Currents. XII, p. 404, Nov., 1901

TESTING the Currents of Lake Erie. (By E. L. Moseley). XIV, pp. 41-42, Jan., 1903

TETRAHEDRAL KITES:

Aërial Locomotion: With a Few Notes of Progress in the Construction of an Aërodrome. By Alexander Graham Bell. XVIII, pp. 1-34, 36 ills., Jan., 1907

The Tetrahedral Kite. XIV, p. 294, ill., July, 1903

The Tetrahedral Principle in Kite Structure. By Alexander Graham Bell. XIV, pp. 219-251, 79 ills., 15 diagrs., June, 1903

TETRAHEDRAL TOWER:

Dr. Bell's Tetrahedral Tower. By Gilbert H. Grosvenor. XVIII, pp. 672-675, 5 ills., Oct., 1907

A **TEXAN** Teaches American History at Cambridge University. By J. Frank Dobie. LXXXIX, pp. 409-441, 9 ills. in black and white, 19 ills. in color, Apr., 1946

TEXAS:

Along Our Side of the Mexican Border. By Frederick Simpich. XXXVIII, pp. 61-80, 9 ills., map, July, 1920

Boundaries of Territorial Acquisitions. XII, pp. 373-377, chart, Oct., 1901

Descriptive Topographic Terms of Spanish America. By Robert T. Hill. VII, pp. 291-302, Sept., 1896

Down the Rio Grande: Tracing this Strange, Turbulent Stream on Its Long Course from Colorado to the Gulf of Mexico. By Frederick Simpich. LXXVI, pp. 415-462, 28 ills. in black and white, 24 ills. in color, 6 maps, Oct., 1939

Expedition into Texas of Fernando del Bosque, Standard-Bearer of the King, Don Carlos II, in the Year 1675. Translated from an Old, Unpublished Spanish Manuscript. By Betty B. Brewster. XIV, pp. 339-348, Sept., 1903

How We Use the Gulf of Mexico. By Frederick Simpich. LXXXV, pp. 1-40, 20 ills. in black and white, 19 ills. in color, two-page map, Jan., 1944

Hurricanes on the Coast of Texas. By General A. W. Greely. XI, pp. 442-445, Nov., 1900

The Lessons of Galveston. By W J McGee. XI, pp. 377-383, Oct., 1900

The Lost Boundary of Texas. By Marcus Baker. XII, pp. 430-432, map, Dec., 1901

Oil Fields of Texas and California. XII, pp. 276-278, July, 1901

So Big Texas. By Frederick Simpich. LIII, pp. 637-693, 72 ills., two-page map, June, 1928

Texas, Our Largest State. By N. H. Darton. XXIV, pp. 1330-1360, 22 ills., maps, Dec., 1913

The Texas Delta of an American Nile: Orchards and Gardens Replace Thorny Jungle in the Southmost Tip of the Lone Star State. By McFall Kerbey. LXXV, pp. 51-96, 27 ills. in black and white, 24 ills. in color, map, Jan., 1939

Wandering Islands in the Rio Grande. By Mrs. Albert S. Burleson. XXIV, pp. 381-386, ills., map, Mar., 1913

TEXAS—*Continued*

The Yield of Texas. By Frederick Simpich. LXXXVII, pp. 163-184, 15 ills., two-page map, Feb., 1945

TEXTILES:

Chemists Make a New World: Creating Hitherto Unknown Raw Materials, Science Now Disrupts Old Trade Routes and Revamps the World Map of Industry. By Frederick Simpich. LXXVI, pp. 601-640, 22 ills. in black and white, 26 ills. in color, Nov., 1939

Massachusetts—Beehive of Business. By William Joseph Showalter. XXXVII, pp. 203-245, 41 ills., Mar., 1920

See also Cotton and Cotton Industry; Silk Industry

THAELMANN COLLECTIVE FARM, U. S. S. R. *See* Ernst Thaelmann (Collective Farm)

THAILAND (Siam):

Ancient Temples and Modern Guns in Thailand. 10 photos: 6 by Maynard Owen Williams. LXXX, pp. 653-660, Nov., 1941

The Coronation of His Majesty King Maha-Vajiravudh of Siam. By Colonel Lea Febiger. XXIII, pp. 389-416, 25 ills., Apr., 1912

The Greatest Hunt in the World (Elephant Hunting). By Eliza Ruhamah Scidmore. XVII, pp. 673-692, 17 ills., Dec., 1906

Hunting the Chaulmoogra Tree. By Joseph F. Rock. XLI, pp. 243-276, 39 ills., map, Mar., 1922

"Land of the Free" in Asia: Siam Has Blended New With Old in Her Progressive March to Modern Statehood in the Family of Nations. By W. Robert Moore. LXV, pp. 531-576, 28 ills. in black and white, 26 ills. in color, map, May, 1934

The Warfare of the Jungle Folk: Campaigning Against Tigers, Elephants, and Other Wild Animals in Northern Siam. By Merian C. Cooper. Photos by Ernest B. Schoedsack. LIII, pp. 233-268, 33 ills., Feb., 1928

THAMES (River), England:

Through the Heart of England in a Canadian Canoe. By R. J. Evans. XLI, pp. 473-497, 26 ills., map, May, 1922

Time and Tide on the Thames. By Frederick Simpich. LXXV, pp. 239-272, 23 ills. in black and white, 10 ills. in color, map, Feb., 1939

The **THAMES,** England's Gateway to the World. 10 color photos by B. Anthony Stewart. LXXV, pp. 253-260, Feb., 1939

THAW, LAWRENCE COPLEY:

Along the Old Silk Routes: A Motor Caravan with Air-conditioned Trailer Retraces Ancient Roads from Paris across Europe and Half of Asia to Delhi. By Lawrence Copley Thaw and Margaret S. Thaw. LXXVIII, pp. 453-486, 33 ills., map, Oct., 1940

In the Realms of the Maharajas. By Lawrence Copley Thaw and Margaret S. Thaw. LXXVIII, pp. 727-780, 14 ills. in black and white, 40 ills. in color, map, Dec., 1940

Princely India, Resplendent with Jewels and Gold. 40 color photos by Lawrence Copley Thaw, pp. 733-780

THAW, LAWRENCE COPLEY—*Continued*

Trans-Africa Safari: A Motor Caravan Rolls Across Sahara and Jungle Through Realms of Dusky Potentates and the Land of Big-Lipped Women. By Lawrence Copley Thaw and Margaret Stout Thaw. LXXIV, pp. 327-364, 29 ills. in black and white, 14 ills. in color, map, Sept., 1938

Africa on Parade. 14 color photos by Lawrence Thaw, pp. 343-350

THAW, MARGARET S.:

Along the Old Silk Routes: A Motor Caravan with Air-conditioned Trailer Retraces Ancient Roads from Paris across Europe and Half of Asia to Delhi. By Lawrence Copley Thaw and Margaret S. Thaw. LXXVIII, pp. 453-486, 33 ills., map, Oct., 1940

In the Realms of the Maharajas. By Lawrence Copley Thaw and Margaret S. Thaw. LXXVIII, pp. 727-780, 14 ills. in black and white, 40 ills. in color, map, Dec., 1940

Trans-Africa Safari: A Motor Caravan Rolls Across Sahara and Jungle Through Realms of Dusky Potentates and the Land of Big-Lipped Women. By Lawrence Copley Thaw and Margaret Stout Thaw. LXXIV, pp. 327-364, 29 ills. in black and white, 14 ills. in color, map, Sept., 1938

THEBES, Egypt:

Reconstructing Egypt's History. By Wallace N. Stearns. XXIV, pp. 1021-1042, 21 ills., Sept., 1913

The Resurrection of Ancient Egypt. By James Baikie. XXIV, pp. 957-1020, 46 ills., map, Sept., 1913

THEIR Monument Is in Our Hearts: Address by M. Viviani Before the Tomb of Washington, at Mount Vernon, April 29, 1917. XXXI, p. 367, Apr., 1917

THEORIES of Volcanic Action. XIV, pp. 110-111, Mar., 1903

THĒRA (Island), Aegean Sea. *See* Santorin

THERMOPYLAE (Pass), Greece:

"The Glory That Was Greece." By Alexander Wilbourne Weddell. XLII, pp. 571-630, 51 ills., map, Dec., 1922

THESE Missourians. By Frederick Simpich. LXXXIX, pp. 277-310, 12 ills. in black and white, 22 ills. in color, map, Mar., 1946

THESSALY (Division), Greece:

With the Monks at Meteora: The Monasteries of Thessaly. By Elizabeth Perkins. XX, pp. 799-807, 5 ills., Sept., 1909

THETIS, U. S. S.:

The Arctic Cruise of the U. S. S. Thetis in the Summer and Autumn of 1889. By Charles H. Stockton. II, pp. 171-198, ill., foldout map, July, 1890

Collinson's Arctic Journey. By General A. W. Greely. IV, pp. 198-200, Feb. 8, 1893

Note: References to the Arctic voyage of Lieutenant-Commander Charles H. Stockton, U. S. N., in the *Thetis,* in 1889

THEY Survived at Sea. By Lt. Comdr. Samuel F. Harby. LXXXVII, pp. 617-640, 22 ills., May, 1945

THEY Sustain the Wings (Ground Crews). By Frederick Simpich. LXXXIV, pp. 333-354, 19 ills., Sept., 1943

38TH ENGINEERS, U. S. Army:

Ascension Island, an Engineering Victory. By Lt. Col. Frederick J. Clarke. LXXXV, pp. 623-640, 21 ills., May, 1944

THIS Giant That Is New York. By Frederick Simpich. LVIII, pp. 517-583, 26 ills. in black and white, 8 ills. in gravure, 42 ills. in color, Nov., 1930

THIS Is My Own: How the United States Seems to a Citizen Soldier Back from Three Years Overseas. By Frederick G. Vosburgh. LXXXIX, pp. 113-128, 14 ills., Jan., 1946

THIS Was Austria. 18 ills. LXXXVIII, pp. 71-86, July, 1945

THOMASON, JOHN W., JR.:

Approach to Peiping. By Major John W. Thomason, Jr. LXIX, pp. 275-308, 24 ills., map, Feb., 1936

THOMPSON, A. H.:

Geographic Nomenclature. Remarks by Herbert G. Ogden, Gustave Herrle, Marcus Baker, and A. H. Thompson. II, pp. 261-278, Aug., 1890

See also NGS: Vice-President

THOMPSON, EDWARD H.:

Henequen—The Yucatan Fiber. By Edward H. Thompson. XIV, pp. 150-158, 6 ills., Apr., 1903

The Home of a Forgotten Race: Mysterious Chichen Itza, in Yucatan, Mexico. By Edward H. Thompson. XXV, pp. 585-648, 59 ills., June, 1914

THOMSON, J. P.:

The Islands of the Pacific. By J. P. Thomson. XL, pp. 543-558, 15 ills., map supplement, Dec., 1921

THOREAU, HENRY DAVID:

Winter Rambles in Thoreau's Country. By Herbert W. Gleason. XXXVII, pp. 165-180, 15 ills., Feb., 1920

THORNDIKE, TOWNSEND W.:

Game and Fur-Bearing Animals and Their Influence on the Indians of the Northwest. By Townsend W. Thorndike. XV, p. 431, Oct., 1904

THORNTON, WILLIAM M.:

Spottswood's Expedition of 1716. By Dr. William M. Thornton. VII, pp. 265-269, Aug., 1896

A **THOUSAND** Miles Along the Great Wall of China: The Mightiest Barrier Ever Built by Man Has Stood Guard Over the Land of Chin for Twenty Centuries. By Adam Warwick. XLIII, pp. 113-143, 27 ills., maps, panorama, Feb., 1923

THRASHERS (Birds):

Thrushes, Thrashers, and Swallows: Robins and Bluebirds are Familiar Members of a Famous Musical Family Which Includes the Hermit Thrush and European Nightingale. By T. Gilbert Pearson. Paintings by Maj. Allan Brooks. LXIX, pp. 523-546, 6 ills. in black and white, 42 paintings from life, Apr., 1936

THREE Drawings of the World War. 3 ills. from drawings by Lucien Jonas. XXXIII, pp. 355-355b, Apr., 1918

THREE Old Ports on the Spanish Main. By G. M. L. Brown. XVII, pp. 622-638, 12 ills., Nov., 1906

THREE SISTERS (Peaks), Oregon:

Scenes Among the High Cascades in Central Oregon. By Ira A. Williams. XXIII, pp. 579-592, 11 ills., June, 1912

THREE Weeks in Hubbard Bay, West Greenland. By Robert Stein. IX, pp. 1-11, 6 ills., maps, Jan., 1898

THREE-WHEELING Through Africa: Two Adventurers Cross the So-called Dark Continent North of Lake Chad on Motorcycles with Side Cars. By James C. Wilson. LXV, pp. 37-92, 64 ills., two-page map, Jan., 1934

THROUGH Brazil to the Summit of Mount Roraima. By G. H. H. Tate. LVIII, pp. 585-605, 24 ills., map, Nov., 1930

THROUGH Franz Josef Land. X, p. 362, Sept., 1899

THROUGH Java in Pursuit of Color. By W. Robert Moore. LVI, pp. 333-362, 9 ills. in black and white, 29 ills. in color, map, Sept., 1929

THROUGH Paraguay and Southern Matto Grosso. By Sir Christopher H. Gibson. LXXXIV, pp. 459-488, 20 ills. in black and white, 11 ills. in color, map, Oct., 1943

THROUGH Pathless Skies to the North Pole (Commander Byrd). Reproduction in color of the painting by N. C. Wyeth, National Geographic Society, Washington, D. C. LIII, supplement, May, 1928

THROUGH the Back Doors of Belgium: Artist and Author Paddle for Three Weeks Along 200 Miles of Low-Countries Canals in a Canadian Canoe. By Melville Chater. XLVII, pp. 499-540, 39 ills., map, May, 1925

THROUGH the Back Doors of France: A Seven Weeks' Voyage in a Canadian Canoe from St. Malo, Through Brittany and the Château Country, to Paris. By Melville Chater. XLIV, pp. 1-51, 55 ills., map, July, 1923

THROUGH the Deserts and Jungles of Africa by Motor: Caterpillar Cars Make 15,000-Mile Trip from Algeria to Madagascar in Nine Months. By Georges-Marie Haardt. XLIX, pp. 651-720, 95 ills., map, June, 1926

THROUGH the English Lake District Afoot and Awheel. By Ralph A. Graves. LV, pp. 577-603, 19 ills. in black and white, 15 ills. in color, map, May, 1929

THROUGH the Great River Trenches of Asia: National Geographic Society Explorer Follows the Yangtze, Mekong, and Salwin Through Mighty Gorges, Some of Whose Canyon Walls Tower to a Height of More Than Two Miles. By Joseph F. Rock. L, pp. 133-186, 47 ills., map, Aug., 1926

THROUGH the Heart of Africa. XI, pp. 408-411, map, Oct., 1900

THROUGH the Heart of England in a Canadian Canoe. By R. J. Evans. XLI, pp. 473-497, 26 ills., map, May, 1922

THROUGH the Heart of Hindustan: A Teeming Highway Extending for Fifteen Hundred Miles, from the Khyber Pass to Calcutta. By Maynard Owen Williams. XL, pp. 433-467, 29 ills., Nov., 1921

THRUSHES (Birds):

Thrushes, Thrashers, and Swallows: Robins and Bluebirds are Familiar Members of a Famous Musical Family Which Includes the Hermit Thrush and European Nightingale. By T. Gilbert Pearson. Paintings by Maj. Allan Brooks. LXIX, pp. 523-546, 6 ills. in black and white, 42 paintings from life, Apr., 1936

THURBER, H. R.:

Collarin' Cape Cod (Massachusetts): Experiences on Board a U. S. Navy Destroyer in a Wild Winter Storm. By Lieutenant H. R. Thurber. XLVIII, pp. 427-472, 46 ills., Oct., 1925

TIAHUANACU, Bolivia:

The Heart of Aymará Land: A Visit to Tiahuanacu, Perhaps the Oldest City of the New World, Lost Beneath the Drifting Sand of Centuries in the Bolivian Highlands. By Stewart E. McMillin. LI, pp. 213-256, 23 ills. in black and white, 18 ills. in color, map, Feb., 1927

Some Wonderful Sights in the Andean Highlands: The Oldest City in America. Sailing on the Lake of the Clouds: The Yosemite of Peru. By Harriet Chalmers Adams. XIX, pp. 597-618, 19 ills., map, Sept., 1908

TIBET:

Across Tibet from India to China. By Lt. Col. Ilia Tolstoy, AUS. XC, pp. 169-222, 53 ills., map, Aug., 1946

The Crosby Expedition to Tibet. XV, pp. 229-231, 3 ills., May, 1904

Life Among the People of Eastern Tibet. By Dr. A. L. Shelton. XL, pp. 293-326, 35 ills., map, Sept., 1921

Sven Hedin in Tibet. XIII, pp. 96-97, Mar., 1902

The Tsangpo (Matsang). By James Mascarene Hubbard. XII, pp. 32-35, Jan., 1901

See also Lhasa

TIBETAN HIGHLAND:

Climbing Mighty Minya Konka: Americans First Scaled Mountain That Now Is Landmark of China's New Skyway. By Richard L. Burdsall and Terris Moore. LXXXIII, pp. 625-650, 23 ills., map, May, 1943

TIBETANS:

Exploring a Grass Wonderland of Wild West China. By Ray G. Johnson. LXXXV, pp. 713-742, 24 ills., map, June, 1944

Life Among the People of Eastern Tibet. By Dr. A. L. Shelton. XL, pp. 293-326, 35 ills., map, Sept., 1921

Sungmas, the Living Oracles of the Tibetan Church. By Joseph F. Rock. LXVIII, pp. 475-486, ill. in black and white, 12 ills. in color, Oct., 1935

TIBURON (Island), Mexico:

A Mexican Land of Canaan: Marvelous Riches of the Wonderful West Coast of our Neighbor Republic. By Frederick Simpich. XXXVI, pp. 307-330, 16 ills., map, Oct., 1919

Seriland. By W J McGee and Willard D. Johnson. VII, pp. 125-133, ill., foldout map, Apr., 1896

TIDES AND TIDAL WAVES:

Atlantic Coast Tides. By Mark S. W. Jefferson. IX, pp. 497-509, 3 charts, Dec., 1898

Atlantic Estuarine Tides. By Mark S. W. Jefferson. IX, pp. 400-409, diagrs., 7 tables, maps, Sept., 1898

Charting a World at War. By William H. Nicholas. LXXXVI, pp. 617-640, 23 ills., drawing, Nov., 1944

Cotidal Lines for the World. By R. A. Harris. XVII, pp. 303-309, 3 maps, map supplement, June, 1906

The Lessons of Galveston. By W J McGee. XI, pp. 377-383, Oct., 1900

Our Guardians on the Deep. By William Joseph Showalter. XXV, pp. 655-677, 15 ills., chart, June, 1914

The Recent Earthquake Wave on the Coast of Japan. By Eliza Ruhamah Scidmore. VII, pp. 285-289, 4 ills., foldout map, Sept., 1896

Reports of Sealing Schooners Cruising in the Neighborhood of Tuscarora Deep in May and June, 1896. (By Eliza Ruhamah Scidmore). VII, pp. 310-312, Sept., 1896

Some Personal Experiences with Earthquakes (Arica). By Rear Adm. L. G. Billings. XXVII, pp. 57-71, 7 ills., Jan., 1915

Tides in the Bay of Fundy. XVI, pp. 71-76, 4 ills., Feb., 1905

Tides of Chesapeake Bay. By E. D. Preston. X, pp. 391-392, Oct., 1899

What Is the Tide of the Open Atlantic? By Mark S. W. Jefferson. IX, pp. 465-475, 6 charts, Nov., 1898

The World's Most Cruel Earthquake (Messina). By Charles W. Wright. XX, pp. 373-396, 22 ills., maps, Apr., 1909

See also Nova Scotia; Southampton (England); Wight, Isle of

TIDEWATER Virginia, Where History Lives. By Albert W. Atwood. LXXXI, pp. 617-656, 18 ills. in black and white, 20 ills. in color, map, May, 1942

TIERRA DEL FUEGO (Archipelago), South America:

The Indian Tribes of Southern Patagonia, Tierra del Fuego, and the Adjoining Islands. By J. B. Hatcher. XII, pp. 12-22, 4 ills., Jan., 1901

Inside Cape Horn. By Amos Burg. LXXII, pp. 743-783, 29 ills. in black and white, 10 ills. in color, two-page map, Dec., 1937

A Longitudinal Journey Through Chile. By Harriet Chalmers Adams. XLII, pp. 219-273, 60 ills., map, Sept., 1922

The **TIES** That Bind: Our Natural Sympathy with English Traditions, the French Republic, and the Russian Outburst for Liberty. By John Sharp Williams. XXXI, pp. 281-286, 4 ills., Mar., 1917

TIFLIS, Georgian Soviet Socialist Republic:

The Land of the Stalking Death: A Journey Through Starving Armenia on an American Relief Train. By Melville Chater. XXXVI, pp. 393-420, 23 ills., Nov., 1919

TIGARA, Alaska:

Discovering Alaska's Oldest Arctic Town: A Scientist Finds Ivory-eyed Skeletons of a Mysterious People and Joins Modern Eskimos in the Dangerous Spring Whale Hunt. By Froelich G. Rainey. LXXXII, pp. 319-336, 15 ills., Sept., 1942

TIGER-HUNTING in India. By Brigadier General William Mitchell. XLVI, pp. 545-598, 46 ills., map, Nov., 1924

TIGERS:

King of Cats and His Court. By Victor H. Cahalane. Paintings by Walter A. Weber. LXXXIII, pp. 217-259, 9 ills. in black and white, 20 ills. in color, Feb., 1943

Tiger-Hunting in India. By Brigadier General William Mitchell. XLVI, pp. 545-598, 46 ills., map, Nov., 1924

The Warfare of the Jungle Folk: Campaigning Against Tigers, Elephants, and Other Wild Animals in Northern Siam. By Merian C. Cooper. Photos by Ernest B. Schoedsack. LIII, pp. 233-268, 33 ills., Feb., 1928

TIGRIS (River), Turkey-Iraq:

The Cradle of Civilization: The Historic Lands Along the Euphrates and Tigris Rivers Where Briton Is Fighting Turk. By James Baikie. XXIX, pp. 127-162, 25 ills., Feb., 1916

Where Adam and Eve Lived. By Frederick and Margaret Simpich. XXVI, pp. 546-588, 35 ills., Dec., 1914

TILE-FISH:

The Relations of the Gulf Stream and the Labrador Current. By William Libbey, Junior. V, pp. 161-166, Jan. 31, 1894

TIMBER. *See* Forests and Forestry

TIMBER LINES. XIV, pp. 80-81, Feb., 1903

TIMBERLINES. By Israel C. Russell. XV, pp. 47-49, Jan., 1904

TIMBUKTU (Tombouctou), French Sudan:

Timbuktu, in the Sands of the Sahara. By Captain Cecil D. Priest. XLV, pp. 73-85, 16 ills., Jan., 1924

Timbuktu and Beyond: Desert City of Romantic Savor and Salt Emerges into World Life Again as Trading Post of France's Vast African Empire. By Laura C. Boulton. LXXIX, pp. 631-670, 18 ills. in black and white, 26 ills. in color, map, May, 1941

TIME and Tide on the Thames (England). By Frederick Simpich. LXXV, pp. 239-272, 23 ills. in black and white, 10 ills. in color, map, Feb., 1939

"**TIME** Will Not Dim the Glory of Their Deeds" (World War Memorials). 11 color photos by W. Robert Moore. LXV, pp. 17-24, Jan., 1934

The **TIMELESS** Arans: The Workaday World Lies Beyond the Horizon of Three Rocky Islets Off the Irish Coast. By Robert Cushman Murphy. LIX, pp. 747-775, 35 ills., map, June, 1931

TIMELY Articles and Maps Give Geographic Members Background of European Drama. LXXVI, p. 550, Oct., 1939

TIME'S Footprints in Tunisian Sands. By Maynard Owen Williams. LXXI, pp. 345-386, 43 ills., maps, Mar., 1937

TIMOR a Key to the Indies. By Stuart St. Clair. LXXXIV, pp. 355-384, 33 ills., map, Sept., 1943

TIN:

Bolivia—Tin Roof of the Andes. By Henry Albert Phillips. LXXXIII, pp. 309-332, 5 ills. in black and white, 20 ills. in color, Mar., 1943

Tin, the Cinderella Metal. By Alicia O'Reardon Overbeck. LXXVIII, pp. 659-684, 24 ills., Nov., 1940

TIN CAN ISLAND. *See* Niuafoō

TINAJAS ALTAS (Water Basins). *See* Yuma Trail

TINGMISSARTOQ (Seaplane):

Flying Around the North Atlantic. By Anne Morrow Lindbergh. Foreword by Charles A. Lindbergh. LXVI, pp. 259-337, 82 ills., maps (1 two-page), Sept., 1934

TINIAN (Island), Marianas Islands:

South from Saipan. By W. Robert Moore. LXXXVII, pp. 441-474, 11 ills. in black and white, 17 ills. in color, map, Apr., 1945

Springboards to Tokyo. By Willard Price. LXXXVI, pp. 385-407, 16 ills., Oct., 1944

TINKER, CLIFFORD ALBION:

Lisbon, the City of the Friendly Bay. By Clifford Albion Tinker. XLII, pp. 505-552, 30 ills. in black and white, 16 ills. in color, map, Nov., 1922

TINTAGEL, England:

Channel Ports—And Some Others. By Florence Craig Albrecht. XXVIII, pp. 1-55, 45 ills., July, 1915

TIRNOVA, Bulgaria:

Tirnova, the City of Hanging Gardens. By Felix J. Koch. XVIII, pp. 632-640, 7 ills., Oct., 1907

TIROL (Region). *See* Tyrol

TISDEL, EDINE FRANCES:

Guatemala, the Country of the Future. By Edine Frances Tisdel. XXI, pp. 596-624, 33 ills., map, July, 1910

TITICACA, Lake, Bolivia-Peru:

The Heart of Aymará Land: A Visit to Tiahuanacu, Perhaps the Oldest City of the New World, Lost Beneath the Drifting Sand of Centuries in the Bolivian Highlands. By Stewart E. McMillin. LI, pp. 213-256, 23 ills. in black and white, 18 ills. in color, map, Feb., 1927

TITICACA, Lake, Bolivia-Peru—*Continued*

Some Wonderful Sights in the Andean Highlands: The Oldest City in America. Sailing on the Lake of the Clouds: The Yosemite of Peru. By Harriet Chalmers Adams. XIX, pp. 597-618, 19 ills., map, Sept., 1908

TITMICE (Birds):

Winged Denizens of Woodland, Stream, and Marsh. By Alexander Wetmore. Paintings by Major Allan Brooks. LXV, pp. 577-596, 11 portraits in color, May, 1934

TITTMANN, O. H.:

A Brief Account of the Geographic Work of the U. S. Coast and Geodetic Survey. By T. C. Mendenhall and Otto H. Tittmann. VIII, pp. 294-299, Oct., 1897

The Definite Location of Bouvet Island. (By O. H. Tittmann). X, pp. 413-414, Oct., 1899

Jobos Harbor. (By O. H. Tittmann). X, p. 206, June, 1899

Ketchikan. XVI, pp. 508-509, ill., Nov., 1905

The National Geographic Society (Election of O. H. Tittmann as President of the Society). XXVII, p. 218, Feb., 1915

The National Geographic Society (Speech by O. H. Tittmann). XXIII, pp. 272-298, 5 ills., Mar., 1912

Portrait. XII, ill. p. 37, Jan., 1901

Progress in Surveying the United States. By O. H. Tittmann. XVII, pp. 110-112, ill., Feb., 1906

The U. S. Coast and Geodetic Survey. By O. H. Tittmann. XIV, pp. 1-9, Jan., 1903

See also NGS: Board of Managers; Secretary; Vice-President

TLAPEHUALA, Mexico:

Down Mexico's Río Balsas. By John W. Webber. With 9 color photos by author, Kenneth Segerstrom, Jack Breed. XC, pp. 253-272, 5 ills. in black and white, map, Aug., 1946

TLINGIT (Indian Tribe):

Indians of Our North Pacific Coast. By Matthew W. Stirling. Paintings by W. Langdon Kihn. LXXXVII, pp. 25-52, 3 ills. in black and white, 16 ills. in color, Jan., 1945

TO Bogotá and Back by Air: The Narrative of a 9,500-Mile Flight from Washington, Over Thirteen Latin-American Countries and Return, in the Single-Seater Airplane "Spirit of St. Louis." By Col. Charles A. Lindbergh. LIII, pp. 529-601, 98 ills., map, May, 1928

TO Market in Guatemala. By Luis Marden. With 19 color photos by Giles Greville Healey and Charles S. Pineo. LXXXVIII, pp. 87-104, July, 1945

TO Seek the Unknown in the Arctic: United States Navy Fliers to Aid MacMillan Expedition Under the Auspices of the National Geographic Society in Exploring Vast Area. XLVII, pp. 673-675, ill., map, June, 1925

TOADS:

Our Friend the Frog. By Doris M. Cochran. Paintings by Hashime Murayama. LXI, pp. 629-654, 16 ills. in black and white, 14 ills. in color, May, 1932

TOBA (Lake), Sumatra:
By Motor Through the East Coast and Batak Highlands of Sumatra. By Melvin A. Hall. XXXVII, pp. 69-102, 27 ills., Jan., 1920

TOBACCO INDUSTRY:
Cuba—The Sugar Mill of the Antilles. By William Joseph Showalter. XXXVIII, pp. 1-33, 24 ills., map, July, 1920
Included: Tobacco lands of Pinar del Rio
Helping the Farmers. XVI, pp. 82-85, ill., Feb., 1905

TOBIEN, WILHELM:
The Azores, Communications Hub of the Atlantic. 13 color photos by Wilhelm Tobien. LXVII, pp. 41-48, Jan., 1935
Bulgaria: In the Shadow of Bulgarian Monasteries. 13 color photos by Wilhelm Tobien. LXII, pp. 203-210, Aug., 1932
Bulgaria's Valley of Roses. 12 color photos by Wilhelm Tobien. LXII, pp. 187-194, Aug., 1932
Canary Islands: An Elysium for the Beauty-Seeking Traveler. 14 color photos by Wilhelm Tobien. LVII, pp. 631-638, May, 1930
Canary Islands: In the Canary Islands, Where Streets Are Carpeted With Flowers. 13 color photos by Wilhelm Tobien. LVII, pp. 615-622, May, 1930
Canary Islands: Scenes in the Fortunate Isles. 12 color photos by Wilhelm Tobien. LVII, pp. 599-606, May, 1930
Frisian Islands, North: Demolishing Germany's North Sea Ramparts. 10 color photos by Wilhelm Tobien. XC, pp. 637-644, Nov., 1946
Germany: Grimm's Fairyland in Northwestern Germany. 5 color photos by Wilhelm Tobien. LIX, pp. 641-648, May, 1931
Germany: Life and Luster of Berlin. 24 color photos by Wilhelm Tobien and Hans Hildenbrand. LXXI, pp. 147-177, Feb., 1937
Madeira: Mirrors of Madeira, Rock Garden of the Atlantic. 13 color photos by Wilhelm Tobien. LXVI, pp. 89-96, July, 1934
Netherlands: Nooks and Bays Around the Zuider Zee. 11 color photos by Wilhelm Tobien. LXIV, pp. 301-308, Sept., 1933
Netherlands: Tulip Time in the Netherlands. 9 color photos by Wilhelm Tobien. LXIV, pp. 325-332, Sept., 1933
Romania: Palaces and Peasants in Rome's Old Colony. 14 color photos by Wilhelm Tobien. LXV, pp. 439-446, Apr., 1934
Romania, Land of Color and Contrast. 15 color photos by Wilhelm Tobien. LXV, pp. 415-422, Apr., 1934
Sweden: Types and Costumes of Old Sweden. 4 color photos by Wilhelm Tobien. LIV, pp. 425-440, Oct., 1928

TODAY in the Feathered Serpent's City (Chichen Itzá). 25 color photos by Luis Marden. LXX, pp. 599-614, Nov., 1936

TODAY in the Land of Penn and Franklin (Pennsylvania). 39 color photos by Edwin L. Wisherd. LXVIII, pp. 13-52, July, 1935

TODAY on the China Coast. By John B. Powell. LXXXVII, pp. 217-238, 17 ills., map, Feb., 1945

TO-DAY on "The Yukon Trail of 1898." By Amos Burg. LVIII, pp. 85-126, 52 ills., map, July, 1930

TODAY'S Evidence of Grecian Glory. 22 color photos by B. Anthony Stewart. LXXVII, pp. 307-322, Mar., 1940

TODAY'S World Turns on Oil. By Frederick Simpich. LXXIX, pp. 703-748, 22 ills. in black and white, drawings, 21 ills. in color, June, 1941

TODD, OLIVER J.:
Taming "Flood Dragons" Along China's Hwang Ho (River). By Oliver J. Todd. LXXXI, pp. 205-234, 26 ills., map, Feb., 1942

TOILERS of the Sky: Tenuous Clouds Perform the Mighty Task of Shaping the Earth and Sustaining Terrestrial Life. By McFall Kerbey. XLVIII, pp. 163-189, 33 ills., Aug., 1925

TOKYO, Japan:
Behind the Mask of Modern Japan. By Willard Price. LXXXVIII, pp. 513-535, 14 ills., Nov., 1945
Japan, Child of the World's Old Age: An Empire of Mountainous Islands, Whose Alert People Constantly Conquer Harsh Forces of Land, Sea, and Sky. By William Elliott Griffis. LXIII, pp. 257-301, 37 ills. in black and white, 12 ills. in color, Mar., 1933
Sakurajima, Japan's Greatest Volcanic Eruption: A Convulsion of Nature Whose Ravages Were Minimized by Scientific Knowledge, Compared with the Terrors and Destruction of the Recent Tokyo Earthquake. By Dr. Thomas Augustus Jaggar. XLV, pp. 441-470, 32 ills., map, Apr., 1924
South from Saipan. By W. Robert Moore. LXXXVII, pp. 441-474, 11 ills. in black and white, 17 ills. in color, map, Apr., 1945
Included: Aerial photo of Tokyo
Sunset in the East. By Blair A. Walliser. LXXXIX, pp. 797-812, 17 ills., June, 1946
Tokyo To-day. By William R. Castle, Jr. LXI, pp. 131-162, 33 ills., Feb., 1932

TOLSTOY, ILIA:
Across Tibet from India to China. By Lt. Col. Ilia Tolstoy, AUS. XC, pp. 169-222, 53 ills., map, Aug., 1946

TOLTECS (Indians):
An Interesting Visit to the Ancient Pyramids of San Juan Teotihuacan. By A. C. Galloway. XXI, pp. 1041-1050, 8 ills., map, Dec., 1910
The Luster of Ancient Mexico. By William H. Prescott. XXX, pp. 1-32, 22 ills., July, 1916

TOMBOUCTOU, French Sudan. *See* Timbuktu

TOMBS:
At the Tomb of Tutankhamen: An Account of the Opening of the Royal Egyptian Sepulcher Which Contained the Most Remarkable Funeral Treasures Unearthed in Historic Times. By Maynard Owen Williams. XLIII, pp. 461-508, 53 ills., map, May, 1923
China's Treasures. By Frederick McCormick. XXIII, pp. 996-1040, 50 ills., Oct., 1912

TOMBS—*Continued*

Malta: The Halting Place of Nations: First Account of Remarkable Prehistoric Tombs and Temples Recently Unearthed on the Island. By William Arthur Griffiths. XXXVII, pp. 445-478, 35 ills., map, May, 1920

Monte Albán, Richest Archeological Find in America: A Tomb in Oaxaca, Mexico, Yields Treasures Which Reveal the Splendid Culture of the Mixtecs. By Dr. Alfonso Caso. LXII, pp. 487-512, 28 ills., Oct., 1932

Mukden, the Manchu Home, and Its Great Art Museum. By Eliza R. Scidmore. XXI, pp. 289-320, 30 ills., Apr., 1910

Secrets from Syrian Hills: Explorations Reveal World's Earliest Known Alphabet, Deciphered from Schoolboy Slates and Dictionaries of 3,000 Years Ago. By Claude F. A. Schaeffer. LXIV, pp. 97-126, 40 ills., map, July, 1933

See also Taj Mahal; *and* Egypt

TOMSK, Siberia, U. S. S. R.:

Western Siberia and the Altai Mountains: With Some Speculations on the Future of Siberia. By James Bryce. XXXIX, pp. 469-507, 39 ills., May, 1921

TONDORF, FRANCIS A.:

How the Earth Telegraphed Its Tokyo Quake to Washington. By the Rev. Francis A. Tondorf. XLIV, pp. 453-454, ill., Oct., 1923

TONGA ISLANDS, South Pacific Ocean:

The Dream Ship: The Story of a Voyage of Adventure More Than Half Around the World in a 47-foot Lifeboat. By Ralph Stock. XXXIX, pp. 1-52, 43 ills., map, Jan., 1921

Falcon, the Pacific's Newest Island. By J. Edward Hoffmeister and Harry S. Ladd. LIV, pp. 757-766, 8 ills., map, Dec., 1928

Living on a Volcano: An Unspoiled Patch of Polynesia Is Niuafoō, Nicknamed "Tin Can Island" by Stamp Collectors. By Thomas A. Jaggar. LXVIII, pp. 91-106, 17 ills., map, July, 1935

TONGAREVA (Penrhyn, Atoll), South Pacific Ocean:

On the Bottom of a South Sea Pearl Lagoon. By Roy Waldo Miner. Paintings by Else Bostelmann. LXXIV, pp. 365-390, 17 ills. in black and white, 8 ills. in color, Sept., 1938

Sailing the Seven Seas in the Interest of Science: Adventures Through 157,000 Miles of Storm and Calm, from Arctic to Antarctic and Around the World, in the Non-magnetic Yacht "Carnegie." By J. P. Ault. XLII, pp. 631-690, 47 ills., chart, Dec., 1922

TONGSA JONG (Fort), Bhutan:

Castles in the Air: Experiences and Journeys in Unknown Bhutan. By John Claude White. XXV, pp. 365-455, 74 ills., map, Apr., 1914

TONKIN, French Indo-China:

Along the Old Mandarin Road of Indo-China. By W. Robert Moore. LX, pp. 157-199, 32 ills. in black and white, 28 ills. in color, map, Aug., 1931

TOOGOOD, STANLEY:

Southampton—Gateway to London: The Port of Double Tides Where the "Mayflower" Moored is Rich in Sea History and Lore of Early England. By Stanley Toogood. LXXVII, pp. 91-114, 21 ills., map, Jan., 1940

The **TOPOGRAPHIC** Atlas of the United States. (By W J M.). IX, pp. 343-344, July, 1898

TOPOGRAPHIC Maps Issued by the Geological Survey in 1907. XIX, pp. 226-227, Mar., 1908

TOPOGRAPHIC Models. By Cosmos Mindeleff. I, pp. 254-268, 7 diagrs., map, July, 1889

TOPOGRAPHIC SURVEYS. *See* Surveying

TOPOGRAPHIC Work of the U. S. Geological Survey in 1902. XIII, pp. 326-328, Aug., 1902

TOPOGRAPHY:

The Classification of Geographic Forms by Genesis. By W J McGee. I, pp. 27-36, tables, Oct., 1888

Cuba. By Robert T. Hill. IX, pp. 193-242, 12 ills., 7 diagrs., tables, 5 maps (1 foldout), May, 1898

Descriptive Topographic Terms of Spanish America. By Robert T. Hill. VII, pp. 291-302, Sept., 1896

An Expedition through the Yukon District. By Charles Willard Hayes. IV, pp. 117-159, 3 maps (2 foldouts), May 15, 1892

Geographic Methods in Geologic Investigation. By W. M. Davis. I, pp. 11-26, Oct., 1888

The Improvement of Geographical Teaching. By Professor William Morris Davis. V, pp. 68-75, July 10, 1893

Report on Topographic Work (Mount St. Elias Expedition). By Mark B. Kerr. III, p. 195, map, May 29, 1891

The Rivers and Valleys of Pennsylvania. By William Morris Davis. I, pp. 183-253, 25 ills., map, July, 1889

Round About Asheville (N. C.). By Bailey Willis. I, pp. 291-300, map supplement, Oct., 1889

The Topographic Atlas of the United States. (By W J M.). IX, pp. 343-344, July, 1898

Topographic Maps Issued by the Geological Survey in 1907. XIX, pp. 226-227, Mar., 1908

Topographic Models. By Cosmos Mindeleff. I, pp. 254-268, 7 diagrs., map, July, 1889

Topographic Work of the U. S. Geological Survey in 1902. XIII, pp. 326-328, Aug., 1902

TOPS:

A Primitive Gyroscope in Liberia. By G. N. Collins. XXI, pp. 531-535, 3 ills., June, 1910

TORADJA (Tribe):

Life and Death in Toradjaland (Celebes). 22 photos: 11 by Maynard Owen Williams, 8 by Helene Fischer. LXXVIII, pp. 65-80, July, 1940

TORBERT, JOHN B.:

Africa the Largest Game Preserve in the World. (By John B. Torbert). XI, pp. 445-448, map, Nov., 1900

TORDAY, E.:

Among the Cannibals of Belgian Kongo (Taken from the Notes of E. Torday). XXI, pp. 969-971, 4 ills., Nov., 1910

Curious and Characteristic Customs of Central African Tribes (Belgian Congo). By E. Torday. XXXVI, pp. 342-368, 35 ills., Oct., 1919

TORII Gate, Japan. XXII, col. pl., p. 982, Nov., 1911; enlargement for framing

TORLANINI, ENRICO:

The Speediest Boat. XXII, pp. 875-878, ills., Sept., 1911

TORNADOES:

Forecasting the Weather and Storms. By Professor Willis L. Moore. XVI, pp. 255-305, 5 ills., 20 charts, June, 1905

TORNOW, MAX L.:

The Economic Condition of the Philippines. By Max L. Tornow. X, pp. 33-64, 10 ills., Feb., 1899

TORONTO, Ontario, Canada:

Ontario, Next Door: Alert, Energetic, and Resourceful, Its British Pluck and Skill in Arts and Trades Gain for This Province a High Place Under the Union Jack. By Frederick Simpich. LXII, pp. 131-183, 54 ills., map, Aug., 1932

The Toronto Meeting of the British Association for the Advancement of Science. (By J. H.). VIII, pp. 247-251, Sept., 1897

See also Little Norway (Training Center)

The **TOTAL** Eclipse of the Sun, May 28, 1900. (By F. H. Bigelow). XI, pp. 33-34, Jan., 1900

TOTEM-POLE Builders (Indians). 16 ills. in color from paintings by W. Langdon Kihn. LXXXVII, pp. 33-48, Jan., 1945

TOTEM POLES:

Indians of Our North Pacific Coast. By Matthew W. Stirling. Paintings by W. Langdon Kihn. LXXXVII, pp. 25-52, 3 ills. in black and white, 16 ills. in color, Jan., 1945

A **TOUR** in the English Fenland. By Christopher Marlowe. LV, pp. 605-634, 26 ills. in black and white, 5 ills. in color, map, May, 1929

TOURING for Birds with Microphone and Color Cameras. By Arthur A. Allen. LXXXV, pp. 689-712, 3 ills. in black and white, 24 ills. in color, June, 1944

TOWERS:

Dr. Bell's Tetrahedral Tower. By Gilbert H. Grosvenor. XVIII, pp. 672-675, 5 ills., Oct., 1907

The Parsees and the Towers of Silence at Bombay, India. By William Thomas Fee. XVI, pp. 529-554, 16 ills., Dec., 1905

The Singing Towers of Holland and Belgium. By William Gorham Rice. XLVII, pp. 357-376, 22 ills., Mar., 1925

TOWHEES:

Sparrows, Towhees, and Longspurs: These Happy Little Singers Make Merry in Field, Forest, and Desert Throughout North America. By T. Gilbert Pearson. Paintings by Allan Brooks and Walter A. Weber. LXXV, pp. 353-376, 5 ills. in black and white, 43 ills. in color, Mar., 1939

The **TOWN** of Many Gables (Münster, Germany). By Florence Craig Albrecht. XXVII, pp. 107-140, 28 ills., Feb., 1915

TOWNLEY-FULLAM, C.:

Hungary: A Land of Shepherd Kings. By C. Townley-Fullam. XXVI, pp. 311-393, 92 ills., map, Oct., 1914

TOWNSEND, CHARLES HASKINS:

Our Heritage of the Fresh Waters: Biographies of the Most Widely Distributed of the Important Food and Game Fishes of the United States. By Charles Haskins Townsend. Paintings by Hashime Murayama. XLIV, pp. 109-159, 25 ills. in black and white, 16 ills. in color, Aug., 1923

TOY DOGS, Pets of Kings and Commoners. By Freeman Lloyd. LXXXV, pp. 459-480, 8 ills. in black and white, 16 ills. in color, Apr., 1944

TOY FISHES:

Tropical Toy Fishes: More Than 600 Varieties of Aquarium Pygmies Afford a Fascinating Field of Zoölogical Study in the Home. By Ida Mellen. Paintings by Hashime Murayama. LIX, pp. 287-317, 20 ills. in black and white, 8 ills. in color, Mar., 1931

TOYS. *See* Tops; *and* Bekonscot (Toy Town)

TOZEUR, Tunisia:

The Date Gardens of the Jerid. By Thomas H. Kearney. XXI, pp. 543-567, 20 ills., July, 1910

TOZZI, PASQUALE:

Italy's Eagles of Combat and Defense: Heroic Achievements of Aviators Above the Adriatic, the Apennines, and the Alps. By General P. Tozzi. XXXIII, pp. 38-47, 8 ills., Jan., 1918

TRACKING the Columbian Ground-Squirrel to Its Burrow: Loss of Millions to Crops and Danger of the Spread of Spotted Fever Necessitated Study of Peculiar Rodent of Western North America. By William T. Shaw. XLVII, pp. 587-596, 13 ills., May, 1925

TRADE. *See* Commerce

TRADE of the United States with Cuba. (By J.H.). IX, pp. 247-249, tables, May, 1898

TRADITION Lingers in Modern Japan. 11 color photos by W. Robert Moore. LXXIII, pp. 117-124, Jan., 1938

The **TRADITIONS** and Glamour of Insignia. By Arthur E. Du Bois. LXXXIII, pp. 652-655, 3 ills., June, 1943

TRAFFIC on the Suez Canal. XII, p. 380, Oct., 1901

TRAILER CAMPS:

America on the Move. 26 photos by J. Baylor Roberts, B. Anthony Stewart, and others. XC, pp. 357-378, Sept., 1946

TRAILING History Down the Big Muddy: In the Homeward Wake of Lewis and Clark, a Folding Steel Skiff Bears Its Lone Pilot on a 2,000-Mile Cruise on the Yellowstone-Missouri. By Lewis R. Freeman. LIV, pp. 73-120, 51 ills., map, July, 1928

TRAINING CENTER (Little Norway), Toronto, Canada:

Norway, an Active Ally. By Wilhelm Morgenstierne. LXXXIII, pp. 333-357, 24 ills., map, Mar., 1943

TRAINING SCHOOLS:

Aviation Cadet: Pocket Carriers Fight the Submarines. 20 ills. in color from U. S. Navy official photos. LXXXIV, pp. 521-544, Nov., 1943

Blimp: Aboard a Blimp Hunting U-boats: A Day above the Atlantic Reveals Navy Talk and Navy Ways, Creeping Convoys, and Torpedoed Wrecks. By Mason Sutherland. LXXXIV, pp. 79-96, 18 ills., July, 1943

U. S. Army Air Forces: They Sustain the Wings (Ground Crews). By Frederick Simpich. LXXXIV, pp. 333-354, 19 ills., Sept., 1943

TRAINING the New Armies of Liberty: Camp Lee, Virginia's Home for the National Army. By Granville Fortescue. XXXII, pp. 421-437, 8 ills., map, Nov.-Dec., 1917

TRAINS:

Trains of Today—and Tomorrow. By J. R. Hildebrand. LXX, pp. 535-589, 51 ills., Nov., 1936

Your New World of Tomorrow. By F. Barrows Colton. LXXXVIII, pp. 385-410, 25 ills., Oct., 1945

See also Railroads

TRALEE (Boat):

Chesapeake Odyssey: An 18-foot Sailboat Follows the Course of Captain John Smith around This Spacious Bay of History, Commerce, Sea Food, and Nautical Lore. By John Maloney. LXXVI, pp. 357-392, 32 ills., map, Sept., 1939

TRALLES (Ancient City):

The Ruined Cities of Asia Minor. By Ernest L. Harris. XIX, pp. 741-760, 11 ills., Nov., 1908

TRANS-AFRICA Safari: A Motor Caravan Rolls Across Sahara and Jungle Through Realms of Dusky Potentates and the Land of Big-Lipped Women. By Lawrence Copley Thaw and Margaret Stout Thaw. LXXIV, pp. 327-364, 29 ills. in black and white, 14 ills. in color, map, Sept., 1938

TRANSANDINE RAILWAY, Argentina-Chile:

The First Transandine Railroad from Buenos Aires to Valparaiso. By Harriet Chalmers Adams. XXI, pp. 397-417, 14 ills., diagr., map, May, 1910

TRANS-ASIATIC EXPEDITIONS:

The Citroën Trans-Asiatic Expedition Reaches Kashmir: Scientific Party Led by Georges-Marie Haardt Successfully Crosses Syria, Iraq, Persia, and Afghanistan to Arrive at the Pamir. By Maynard Owen Williams. LX, pp. 387-443, 62 ills., map, Oct., 1931

First Over the Roof of the World by Motor: The Trans-Asiatic Expedition Sets New Records for Wheeled Transport in Scaling Passes of the Himalayas. By Maynard Owen Williams. LXI, pp. 321-363, 45 ills., maps, Mar., 1932

From the Mediterranean to the Yellow Sea by Motor: The Citroën-Haardt Expedition Successfully Completes Its Dramatic Journey. By Maynard Owen Williams. LXII, pp. 513-580, 45 ills. in black and white, 25 ills. in color, maps, Nov., 1932

The Trans-Asiatic Expedition Starts. By Georges-Marie Haardt. LIX, pp. 776-782, 6 ills., June, 1931

See also the following names of explorers and expedition leaders: Clark, James L.; Lattimore, Owen; Morden, William J.; Thaw, Lawrence Copley; Thaw, Margaret S.; *and* Polo, Marco

TRANSCAUCASIA (Region), U. S. S. R.:

Armenia and the Armenians. By Hester Donaldson Jenkins. XXVIII, pp. 329-360, 27 ills., map, Oct., 1915

The British Take Baku. XXXIV, pp. 163-164, ill., Aug., 1918

An Island in the Sea of History: The Highlands of Daghestan. By George Kennan. XXIV, pp. 1087-1140, 49 ills., map, Oct., 1913

The Land of the Stalking Death: A Journey Through Starving Armenia on an American Relief Train. By Melville Chater. XXXVI, pp. 393-420, 23 ills., Nov., 1919

The Old Post-Road from Tiflis to Erivan. By Esther Lancraft Hovey. XII, pp. 300-309, 9 ills., Aug., 1901

The Races of Europe. By Edwin A. Grosvenor. XXXIV, pp. 441-534, 62 ills., diagr. and index, maps, map supplement, Dec., 1918

Roaming Russia's Caucasus: Rugged Mountains and Hardy Fighters Guard the Soviet Union's Caucasian Treasury of Manganese and Oil. By Rolf Singer. LXXXII, pp. 91-121, 33 ills., July, 1942

Russia's Orphan Races: Picturesque Peoples Who Cluster on the Southeastern Borderland of the Vast Slav Dominions. By Maynard Owen Williams. XXXIV, pp. 245-278, 26 ills., map, Oct., 1918

The **TRANSFORMATION** of Turkey: New Hats and New Alphabet are the Surface Symbols of the Swiftest National Changes in Modern Times. By Douglas Chandler. LXXV, pp. 1-50, 27 ills. in black and white, 23 ills. in color, map, Jan., 1939

The **TRANSFORMATION** of Washington (D. C.): A Glance at the History and Along the Vista of the Future of the Nation's Capital. By Charles Moore. XLIII, pp. 569-595, 16 ills., maps, June, 1923

TRANS-JORDAN:

Bedouin Life in Bible Lands: The Nomads of the "House of Hair" Offer Unstinted Hospitality to an American. By John D. Whiting. LXXI, pp. 59-83, 27 ills., map, Jan., 1937

The Geography of the Jordan. By Nelson Glueck. LXXXVI, pp. 719-744, 23 ills., map, Dec., 1944

On the Trail of King Solomon's Mines: The Bible, in Addition to Its Spiritual Values, Continues to Prove a Rich Geography and Guide to Exploration of the Holy Land. By Nelson Glueck. LXXXV, pp. 233-256, 20 ills., map, Feb., 1944

One Thousand Miles of Railway Built for Pilgrims and Not for Dividends (Damascus to Mecca). By Colonel F. R. Maunsell. XX, pp. 156-172, 12 ills., map, Feb., 1909

A Visit to Three Arab Kingdoms: Transjordania, Iraq, and the Hedjaz Present Many Problems to European Powers. By Junius B. Wood. XLIII, pp. 535-568, 30 ills., map, May, 1923

See also Petra

TRANSPORT AIR GROUP (TAG):

Flying Our Wounded Veterans Home. By Catherine Bell Palmer. LXXXVIII, pp. 363-384, 17 ills., Sept., 1945

TRANSPORTATION:

America on the Move. 26 photos by J. Baylor Roberts, B. Anthony Stewart, and others. XC, pp. 357-378, Sept., 1946

American Transportation Vital to Victory. By Thornton Oakley. With 16 ills. in color from paintings by author. LXXXIV, pp. 671-688, Dec., 1943

Animals Were Allies, Too. 16 ills. LXXXIX, pp. 75-88, Jan., 1946

The Automobile Industry: An American Art That Has Revolutionized Methods in Manufacturing and Transformed Transportation. By William Joseph Showalter. XLIV, pp. 337-414, 76 ills., Oct., 1923

Bonds Between the Americas. By Frederick Simpich. LXXII, pp. 785-808, 22 ills., Dec., 1937

Burma: Where India and China Meet: In the Massive Mountains of Southeast Asia, Swarming Road Builders Wage the "War of the Highways" for Free China and Her Allies. By John LeRoy Christian. LXXXIV, pp. 489-512, 18 ills., map, Oct., 1943

Burma Road: China Opens Her Wild West: In the Mountain-girt Heart of a Continent a New China Has Been Created During the Years of War. By Owen Lattimore. LXXXII, pp. 337-367, 21 ills. in black and white, 11 ills. in color, map, Sept., 1942

The Future of the Yukon Goldfields. By William H. Dall. IX, pp. 117-120, Apr., 1898

Kunming, Southwestern Gateway to China. By Joseph E. Passantino. With 18 color photos by author. XC, pp. 137-168, 12 ills. in black and white, Aug., 1946

Landing Craft for Invasion. By Melville Bell Grosvenor. LXXXVI, pp. 1-30, 26 ills., July, 1944

TRANSPORTATION—*Continued*

Mother Volga Defends Her Own. By Maynard Owen Williams. LXXXII, pp. 793-811, 21 ills., Dec., 1942

Queer Methods of Travel in Curious Corners of the World. By O. P. Austin. XVIII, pp. 687-715, 29 ills., Nov., 1907

6,000 Miles over the Roads of Free China. By Josephine A. Brown. LXXXV, pp. 355-384, 30 ills., map, Mar., 1944

Some Mexican Transportation Scenes. By Walter W. Bradley. XXI, pp. 985-991, 10 ills., Dec., 1910

This Is My Own: How the United States Seems to a Citizen Soldier Back from Three Years Overseas. By Frederick G. Vosburgh. LXXXIX, pp. 113-128, 14 ills., Jan., 1946

Transportation in England. XVI, p. 88, Feb., 1905

Transportation Methods in Alaska. By Captain George S. Gibbs. XVII, pp. 69-82, 19 ills., Feb., 1906

U. S. Roads in War and Peace. By Frederick Simpich. LXXX, pp. 687-716, 27 ills., Dec., 1941

Winning the War of Supply. By F. Barrows Colton. LXXXVIII, pp. 705-736, 32 ills., Dec., 1945

Your New World of Tomorrow. By F. Barrows Colton. LXXXVIII, pp. 385-410, 25 ills., Oct., 1945

See also Air Carrier Contract Personnel; Air Transport Command; Boats; Commerce; Highways and Roads; Railroads; Ship Railways; Ships and Shipping; Street Cars; Trains; U. S. Army Transportation Corps

TRANSPORTING a Navy Through the Jungles of Africa in War Time. By Frank J. Magee. XLII, pp. 331-362, 31 ills., Oct., 1922

TRANS-SIBERIAN RAILWAY, U. S. S. R.:

The Land of Promise (Siberia). By Major General A. W. Greely. XXIII, pp. 1078-1090, 7 ills., Nov., 1912

Manchuria, Promised Land of Asia: Invaded by Railways and Millions of Settlers, This Vast Region Now Recalls Early Boom Days in the American West. By Frederick Simpich. LVI, pp. 379-428, 58 ills., map, Oct., 1929

Railways, Rivers, and Strategic Towns in Manchuria. (By G. H. G.). XI, pp. 326-327, Aug., 1900

Siberia. By Prof. Edwin A. Grosvenor. XII, pp. 317-324, Sept., 1901

The Siberian Transcontinental Railroad. By General A. W. Greely. VIII, pp. 121-124, Apr., 1897

Western Siberia and the Altai Mountains: With Some Speculations on the Future of Siberia. By James Bryce. XXXIX, pp. 469-507, 39 ills., May, 1921

TRANSVAAL (Province), Union of South Africa:

Africa Since 1888, with Special Reference to South Africa and Abyssinia. By Hon. Gardiner G. Hubbard. VII, pp. 157-175, ill., foldout map, May, 1896

British South Africa and the Transvaal. By F. F. Hilder. XI, pp. 81-96, 7 ills., Mar., 1900

TRANSVAAL (Province), Union of South Africa —*Continued*

The Cities That Gold and Diamonds Built: Transvaal Treasures Have Created Bustling Johannesburg and Fostered Pretoria, Administrative Capital of the South African Union. By W. Robert Moore. LXXXII, pp. 735-766, 20 ills. in black and white, 9 ills. in color, map, Dec., 1942

A Critical Period in South African History. (By J. H.). VII, pp. 377-379, Nov., 1896

The Transvaal: The Treasure-House Province. By Melville Chater. LIX, pp. 479-512, 28 ills. in black and white, 13 ills. in color, Apr., 1931

The Witwatersrand and the Revolt of the Uitlanders. By George F. Becker. VII, pp. 349-367, 4 ills., Nov., 1896

TRANSYLVANIA (Region), Romania:

An American Girl Cycles Across Romania: Two-wheel Pilgrim Pedals the Land of Castles and Gypsies, Where Roman Empire Traces Mingle With Remnants of Oriental Migration. By Dorothy Hosmer. LXXIV, pp. 557-588, 31 ills., map, Nov., 1938

Roumania and Its Rubicon. By John Oliver La Gorce. XXX, pp. 185-202, 11 ills., Sept., 1916

Transylvania and Its Seven Castles: A Motor Circuit Through Rumania's New Province of Racial Complexity and Architectural Charm. By J. Theodore Marriner. XLIX, pp. 319-352, 35 ills., map, Mar., 1926

TRAPDOOR SPIDERS:

California Trapdoor Spider Performs Engineering Marvels. By Lee Passmore. LXIV, pp. 195-211, 23 ills., Aug., 1933

Marvels of Metamorphosis: A Scientific "G-man" Pursues Rare Trapdoor Spider Parasites for Three Years With a Spade and a Candid Camera. By George Elwood Jenks. LXXIV, pp. 807-828, 39 ills., Dec., 1938

A **TRAVELER'S** Notes on Java. By Henry G. Bryant. XXI, pp. 91-111, 17 ills., Feb., 1910

TRAVELING in the Highlands of Ethiopia. By Leo B. Roberts. LXVIII, pp. 297-328, 37 ills., Sept., 1935

TRAVELS in Arabia and Along the Persian Gulf. By David G. Fairchild. XV, pp. 139-151, 20 ills., Apr., 1904

The **TRAVELS** of George Washington: Dramatic Episodes in His Career as the First Geographer of the United States. By William Joseph Showalter. LXI, pp. 1-63, 50 ills., 4 maps, map supplement, Jan., 1932

TRAVELS with a Donkey in Mexico: Three Adventurers Trudge from Oaxaca to Acapulco, 400 Miles, Through Back Country, Their Equipment Carried by Burros. By Bernard Bevan. LXVI, pp. 757-788, 36 ills., map, Dec., 1934

The **TREASURE** Chest of Mercurial Mexico (Silver Mines in Guanajuato). By Frank H. Probert. XXX, pp. 33-68, 33 ills., July, 1916

TREASURE-HOUSE of the Gulf Stream: The Completion and Opening of the New Aquarium and Biological Laboratory at Miami, Florida. By John Oliver La Gorce. Paintings by Hashime Murayama. XXXIX, pp. 53-68, 5 ills. in black and white, 16 ills. in color, Jan., 1921

TREASURE Islands of Australasia: New Guinea, New Caledonia, and Fiji Trace across the South Pacific a Fertile Crescent Incredibly Rich in Minerals and Foods. By Douglas L. Oliver. LXXXI, pp. 691-722, 23 ills., two-page map, June, 1942

TREASURE-TROVE of Old Mexican Jade (Cerro de las Mesas). 20 color photos by Richard H. Stewart. LXXX, pp. 293-316, Sept., 1941

TREASURES of the Pacific: Marine Fishes and Fisheries Yield Vast Wealth from Alaska to Baja California. By Leonard P. Schultz. Paintings by Hashime Murayama. LXXIV, pp. 463-498, 10 ills. in black and white, 31 portraits in color, Oct., 1938

TREAT, IDA:

Sailing Forbidden Coasts. By Ida Treat. LX, pp. 357-386, 31 ills., map, Sept., 1931

TREE RINGS:

Pueblo Bonito, the Ancient: The National Geographic Society's Third Expedition to the Southwest Seeks to Read in the Rings of Trees the Secret of the Age of Ruins. By Neil M. Judd. XLIV, pp. 99-108, 9 ills., diagr., July, 1923

The Secret of the Southwest Solved by Talkative Tree Rings: Horizons of American History Are Carried Back to A. D. 700 and a Calendar for 1,200 Years Established by National Geographic Society Expeditions. By Andrew Ellicott Douglass. LVI, pp. 737-770, 33 ills., map, Dec., 1929

TREES:

American Berries of Hill, Dale, and Wayside. Paintings by Mary E. Eaton. XXXV, pp. 168-184, ill. in black and white, 28 ills. in color, Feb., 1919

Among the Big Trees of California. By John R. White. LXVI, pp. 219-232, 14 ills., Aug., 1934

The Battle of the Forest. By B. E. Fernow. VI, pp. 127-148, 5 ills., map, June 22, 1894

California's Coastal Redwood Realm: Along a Belt of Tall Trees a Giant Bridge Speeds the Winning of Our Westernmost Frontier. By J. R. Hildebrand. LXXV, pp. 133-184, 31 ills. in black and white, 17 ills. in color, map, Feb., 1939

Cork. XIX, pp. 690-693, 3 ills., Oct., 1908

The Fight at the Timber-Line. By John Oliver La Gorce. XLII, pp. 165-196, 32 ills., Aug., 1922

Formosa the Beautiful (Camphor). By Alice Ballantine Kirjassoff. XXXVII, pp. 247-292, 60 ills., map, Mar., 1920

The Hardy Catalpa. XIV, pp. 348-353, 4 ills., Sept., 1903

Hunting the Chaulmoogra Tree. By Joseph F. Rock. XLI, pp. 243-276, 39 ills., map, Mar., 1922

The Introduction of the Mango. XIV, pp. 320-327, 5 ills., Aug., 1903

The Isle of Frankincense (Socotra, Arabian Sea). By Charles K. Moser. XXXIII, pp. 267-278, 11 ills., Mar., 1918

TREES—*Continued*

The Kingdom of Flowers: An Account of the Wealth of Trees and Shrubs of China and of What the Arnold Arboretum, with China's Help, Is Doing to Enrich America. By Ernest H. Wilson. XXII, pp. 1003-1035, 24 ills., Nov., 1911

Lonely Australia: The Unique Continent. By Herbert E. Gregory. XXX, pp. 473-568, 68 ills., 5 maps (1 two-page), Dec., 1916

The National Geographic Society Completes Its Gifts of Big Trees. XL, pp. 85-86, July, 1921

A New World to Explore: In the Tree-Roof of the British Guiana Forest Flourishes Much Hitherto-Unknown Life. By Maj. R. W. G. Hingston. LXII, pp. 617-642, 35 ills., Nov., 1932

Notes on the Eucalyptus Tree from the United States Forest Service. XX, pp. 668-673, 4 ills., July, 1909

The Oldest Living Thing ("General Sherman Tree"). XXIX, pictorial supplement, Apr., 1916

Our Big Trees Saved. XXXI, pp. 1-11, 10 ills., Jan., 1917

Our National Parks. By L. F. Schmeckebier. XXIII, pp. 531-579, 41 ills., map, June, 1912

The Palms. XXII, pictorial supplement, Dec., 1911

Quinine Hunters in Ecuador (Cinchona Tree). By Froelich Rainey. LXXXIX, pp. 341-363, 21 ills., map, Mar., 1946

The Redwood Forest of the Pacific Coast. By Henry Gannett. X, pp. 145-159, 6 ills., map, May, 1899

Rubber Plantations in Mexico and Central America. XIV, pp. 409-414, 7 ills., Nov., 1903

The Samoan Cocoanut (Article compiled by Gen. A. W. Greely). IX, pp. 12-24, Jan., 1898

Saving the Redwoods. By Madison Grant. XXXVII, pp. 519-536, 10 ills., June, 1920

Strange Sights in Far-Away Papua (Stinging Trees). By A. E. Pratt. XVIII, pp. 559-572, 7 ills., Sept., 1907

The Tallest Tree That Grows (Eucalyptus). By Edgerton R. Young. XX, pp. 664-667, 3 ills., July, 1909

The Wonderland of California. By Herman Whitaker. XXVIII, pp. 57-104, 45 ills., July, 1915

See also Forests and Forestry; *and* Coconut Palms; Date Palms

TREKKING South Africa with a Color Camera. 11 color photos by Melville Chater. LIX, pp. 413-420, Apr., 1931

TRES ZAPOTES, Mexico:

Discovering the New World's Oldest Dated Work of Man: A Maya Monument Inscribed 291 B. C. is Unearthed Near a Huge Stone Head by a Geographic-Smithsonian Expedition in Mexico. By Matthew W. Stirling. LXXVI, pp. 183-218, 40 ills., map, Aug., 1939

Great Stone Faces of the Mexican Jungle: Five Colossal Heads and Numerous Other Monuments of Vanished Americans Are Excavated by the Latest National Geographic-Smithsonian Expedition. By Matthew W. Stirling. LXXVIII, pp. 309-334, 26 ills., map, Sept., 1940

TRIANGULATION:

Recent Triangulation in the Cascades (Washington). By S. S. Gannett. VII, p. 150, Apr., 1896

A **TRIBUTE** to America. By Herbert Henry Asquith. XXXI, pp. 295-296, ills., Apr., 1917

TRIBUTE to American Topographers. (By A. H. B.). XVI, p. 358, July, 1905

The **TRICOLOR** Rules the Rainbow in French Indo-China. 27 color photos by Maynard Owen Williams. LXVIII, pp. 495-518, Oct., 1935

TRINIDAD (Island), West Indies:

Americans in the Caribbean. By Luis Marden. LXXXI, pp. 723-758, 16 ills. in black and white, 22 ills. in color, map, June, 1942

Crossroads of the Caribbean. By Laurence Sanford Critchell. LXXII, pp. 319-344, 18 ills. in black and white, 14 ills. in color, map, Sept., 1937

The East Indians in the New World. By Harriet Chalmers Adams. XVIII, pp. 485-491, 6 ills., July, 1907

A **TRIP** Through Siberia. By Ebenezer J. Hill. XIII, pp. 37-54, 17 ills., map, Feb., 1902

A **TRIP** to Panama and Darien. By Richard U. Goode. I, pp. 301-314, diagr., foldout map, Oct., 1889

TRIPOLI, Lebanon:

From Jerusalem to Aleppo. By John D. Whiting. XXIV, pp. 71-113, 30 ills., map, Jan., 1913

TRIPOLI, Libia:

Americans on the Barbary Coast. By Willard Price. LXXXIV, pp. 1-31, 13 ills. in black and white, 10 ills. in color, map, July, 1943

Tripoli: A Land of Little Promise. By Adolf L. Vischer. XXII, pp. 1035-1047, 6 ills., map, Nov., 1911

TRIPOLITANIA (Region), North Africa:

Here and There in Northern Africa. By Frank Edward Johnson. XXV, pp. 1-132, 113 ills., Jan., 1914

The Mysteries of the Desert. By Hanns Vischer. XXII, pp. 1056-1059, Nov., 1911

Tripoli: A Land of Little Promise. By Adolf L. Vischer. XXII, pp. 1035-1047, 6 ills., map, Nov., 1911

Tripolitania, Where Rome Resumes Sway: The Ancient Trans-Mediterranean Empire, on the Fringe of the Libyan Desert, Becomes a Promising Modern Italian Colony. By Colonel Gordon Casserly. XLVIII, pp. 131-161, 27 ills. in black and white, 9 ills. in color, map, Aug., 1925

See also Tripoli, Libia

TRISTAN DA CUNHA, Isles of Contentment: On Lonely Sea Spots of Pirate Lore and Shipwrecks Seven Families Live Happily Far from War Rumors and World Changes. By W. Robert Foran. LXXIV, pp. 671-694, 23 ills., map, Nov., 1938

TRI-STATE Medley (Virginia, Maryland, and Delaware). 10 color photos by Willard R. Culver. LXXIV, pp. 33-40, July, 1938

TROGLODYTES AND CHRISTIAN "TROGLODYTES":
The Cone-Dwellers of Asia Minor: A Primitive People Who Live in Nature-Made Apartment Houses, Fashioned by Volcanic Violence and Trickling Streams. By J. R. Sitlington Sterrett. XXXV, pp. 281-331, 52 ills., map, Apr., 1919
Here and There in Northern Africa. By Frank Edward Johnson. XXV, pp. 1-132, 113 ills., Jan., 1914
The Mole Men: An Account of the Troglodytes of Southern Tunisia. By Frank Edward Johnson. XXII, pp. 787-846, 60 ills., Sept., 1911
Peculiar Caves of Asia Minor. By Elizabeth H. Brewer. XXII, pp. 870-875, 5 ills., Sept., 1911
The Turkish Republic Comes of Age. By Maynard Owen Williams. LXXXVII, pp. 581-616, 4 ills. in black and white, 29 ills. in color, map, May, 1945
Where Early Christians Lived in Cones of Rock: A Journey to Cappadocia in Turkey Where Strange Volcanic Pinnacles Are Honeycombed with Hermit Cells and Monasteries. By John D. Whiting. LXXVI, pp. 763-802, 20 ills. in black and white, 20 ills. in color, map, Dec., 1939

TRONDHEIM, Norway:
The White War in Norway. By Thomas R. Henry. LXXXVIII, pp. 617-640, 23 ills., map, Nov., 1945

TROOP CARRIER COMMAND, U. S. Army Air Forces:
Flying Our Wounded Veterans Home. By Catherine Bell Palmer. LXXXVIII, pp. 363-384, 17 ills., Sept., 1945

TROPIC-BIRDS:
Birds of the High Seas: Albatrosses and Petrels; Gannets, Man-o'-war-birds, and Tropic-birds. By Robert Cushman Murphy. Paintings by Major Allan Brooks. LXXIV, pp. 226-251, 7 ills. in black and white, 36 portraits in color, Aug., 1938

TROPIC Color in Trinidad. 14 color photos by Edwin L. Wisherd. LXXII, pp. 327-334, Sept., 1937

TROPICAL Fish Immigrants Reveal New Nature Wonders. By Walter H. Chute. LXV, pp. 93-109, 8 ills. in black and white, 16 ills. in color, Jan., 1934

TROPICAL Toy Fishes: More Than 600 Varieties of Aquarium Pygmies Afford a Fascinating Field of Zoölogical Study in the Home. By Ida Mellen. Paintings by Hashime Murayama. LIX, pp. 287-317, 20 ills. in black and white, 8 ills. in color, Mar., 1931

TROUTS (Fishes):
Fishing in Pacific Coast Streams. By Leonard P. Schultz. Paintings by Hashime Murayama. LXXV, pp. 185-212, 10 ills. in black and white, 44 portraits in color, Feb., 1939
The Golden Trout. XVII, p. 424, July, 1906
The Wild Life of Lake Superior, Past and Present: The Habits of Deer, Moose, Wolves, Beavers, Muskrats, Trout, and Feathered Wood-Folk Studied with Camera and Flashlight. By George Shiras, 3d. XL, pp. 113-204, 76 ills., map, pictorial supplement, Aug., 1921

TROWBRIDGE, STEPHEN VAN RENSSELAER:
Impressions of Asiatic Turkey. By Stephen van Rensselaer Trowbridge. XXVI, pp. 598-609, 6 ills., Dec., 1914

TROY (Ancient City):
Homer's Troy Today. By Jacob E. Conner. XXVII, pp. 521-532, 11 ills., map, May, 1915
Notes on Troy. (By Ernest L. Harris). XXVII, pp. 531-532, May, 1915

TRUJILLO (City), Dominican Republic. *See* Ciudad Trujillo

TRUK ISLANDS, Caroline Islands:
Hidden Key to the Pacific: Piercing the Web of Secrecy Which Long Has Veiled Japanese Bases in the Mandated Islands. By Willard Price. LXXXI, pp. 759-785, 28 ills., map, June, 1942
Yap and Other Pacific Islands Under Japanese Mandate. By Junius B. Wood. XL, pp. 591-627, 34 ills., map, Dec., 1921

TRULLI (Dwellings): Italy:
The Stone Beehive Homes of the Italian Heel: In Trulli-Land the Native Builds His Dwelling and Makes His Field Arable in the Same Operation. By Paul Wilstach. LVII, pp. 229-260, 25 ills. in black and white, 12 ills. in color, map, Feb., 1930

TRUMAN, HARRY S:
Map rack presented to. LXXXIX, p. 290, Mar., 1946
President Truman presents Hubbard Medal to General H. H. Arnold, Nov. 16, 1945. LXXXIX, ill. p. 141, Feb., 1946

The **TRUTH** About the Congo. XVIII, pp. 811-813, 6 ills., Dec., 1907

The **TSANGPO** (Brahmaputra River). By James Mascarene Hubbard. XII, pp. 32-35, Jan., 1901

TSANKAWI, New Mexico:
The Prehistoric Ruin of Tsankawi. By George L. Beam. XX, pp. 807-822, 12 ills., Sept., 1909

TSCHIFFELY, A. F.:
Buenos Aires to Washington by Horse: A Solitary Journey of Two and a Half Years, Through Eleven American Republics, Covers 9,600 Miles of Mountain and Plain, Desert and Jungle. By A. F. Tschiffely. LV, pp. 135-196, 75 ills., map, Feb., 1929

TSIMSHIAN (Indians):
Indians of Our North Pacific Coast. By Matthew W. Stirling. Paintings by W. Langdon Kihn. LXXXVII, pp. 25-52, 3 ills. in black and white, 16 ills. in color, Jan., 1945
The Metlakatla Mission in Danger. (By Wm. H. Dall). IX, pp. 187-189, Apr., 1898

TSINGHAI (Province), China:
Across Tibet from India to China. By Lt. Col. Ilia Tolstoy, AUS. XC, pp. 169-222, 53 ills., map, Aug., 1946
China Fights Erosion with U. S. Aid. By Walter C. Lowdermilk. LXXXVII, pp. 641-680, 10 ills. in black and white, 26 ills. in color, June, 1945

TSINGNING, China:

"Where the Mountains Walked": An Account of the Recent Earthquake in Kansu Province, China, Which Destroyed 100,000 Lives. By Upton Close and Elsie McCormick. XLI, pp. 445-464, 23 ills., map, May, 1922

The **TSUNG-LI-YAMEN** (Foreign Office, China). (By Miss E. R. Scidmore). XI, pp. 291-292, diagr., map, July, 1900

TUAMOTU (Archipelago), South Pacific Ocean:

The Romance of Science in Polynesia: An Account of Five Years of Cruising Among the South Sea Islands. By Robert Cushman Murphy. Paintings by Hashime Murayama. XLVIII, pp. 355-426, 66 ills. in black and white, 16 ills. in color, 3 maps, Oct., 1925

TUAREG (Tribespeople):

The Mysteries of the Desert (Sahara). By Hanns Vischer. XXII, pp. 1056-1059, Nov., 1911

Trans-Africa Safari: A Motor Caravan Rolls Across Sahara and Jungle Through Realms of Dusky Potentates and the Land of Big-Lipped Women. By Lawrence Copley Thaw and Margaret Stout Thaw. LXXIV, pp. 327-364, 29 ills. in black and white, 14 ills. in color, map, Sept., 1938

TUATARA (Reptile):

Tuatara: "Living Fossils" Walk on Well-Nigh Inaccessible Rocky Islands off the Coast of New Zealand. By Frieda Cobb Blanchard. LXVII, pp. 649-662, 14 ills., map, May, 1935

TUGERI (Tribespeople):

Strange Sights in Far-Away Papua. By A. E. Pratt. XVIII, pp. 559-572, 7 ills., Sept., 1907

TULASNE, JOSEPH:

America's Part in the Allies' Mastery of the Air. By Major Joseph Tulasne. XXXIII, pp. 1-5, ills., Jan., 1918

TULES (Indians). *See* San Blas Indians

TULIP Time in the Netherlands. 10 color photos by Wilhelm Tobien and A. Buyssens. LXIV, pp. 325-332, Sept., 1933

TULIPS:

Some Odd Pages from the Annals of the Tulip: A "Made" Flower of Unknown Origin Took Medieval Europe by Storm and Caused a Financial Panic in the Netherlands. By Leo A. Borah. LXIV, pp. 321-343, 13 ills. in black and white, 10 ills. in color, Sept., 1933

TULSA, Oklahoma:

So Oklahoma Grew Up. By Frederick Simpich. LXXIX, pp. 269-314, 30 ills. in black and white, 19 ills. in color, map, Mar., 1941

TUMEN (River), China-Korea:

Exploring Unknown Corners of the "Hermit Kingdom." By Roy Chapman Andrews. XXXVI, pp. 25-48, 30 ills., map, July, 1919

The **TUNA** Harvest of the Sea: A Little-known Epic of the Ocean Is the Story of Southern California's Far-ranging Tuna Fleet. By John Degelman. LXXVIII, pp. 393-408, 17 ills., Sept., 1940

TUNIS, Tunisia:

Eastward from Gibraltar: Overland Route Across North Africa to Tunisia and Libia. By Cyrus French Wicker. LXXXIII, pp. 115-142, 28 ills., Jan., 1943

Tunis of Today. By Frank Edward Johnson. XXII, pp. 723-749, 24 ills., Aug., 1911

TUNISIA:

Americans on the Barbary Coast. By Willard Price. LXXXIV, pp. 1-31, 13 ills. in black and white, 10 ills. in color, map, July, 1943

Ancient Carthage in the Light of Modern Excavation. By Count Byron Khun de Prorok. XLV, pp. 391-423, 27 ills. in black and white, 16 ills. in color, map, Apr., 1924

The Country of the Ant Men. By Thomas H. Kearney. XXII, pp. 367-382, 13 ills., map, panorama, Apr., 1911

The Date Gardens of the Jerid. By Thomas H. Kearney. XXI, pp. 543-567, 20 ills., July, 1910

Eastward from Gibraltar: Overland Route Across North Africa to Tunisia and Libia. By Cyrus French Wicker. LXXXIII, pp. 115-142, 28 ills., Jan., 1943

From Africa to the Alps. 8 ills. in color from U. S. Army Air Forces official photos. LXXXIX, pp. 161-168, Feb., 1946

The Greek Bronzes of Tunisia. By Frank Edward Johnson. XXIII, pp. 89-103, 11 ills., Jan., 1912

Here and There in Northern Africa. By Frank Edward Johnson. XXV, pp. 1-132, 113 ills., Jan., 1914

In Civilized French Africa. By James F. J. Archibald. XX, pp. 303-311, 14 ills., Mar., 1909

The Mole Men: An Account of the Troglodytes of Southern Tunisia. By Frank Edward Johnson. XXII, pp. 787-846, 60 ills., Sept., 1911

The Sacred City of the Sands (Kairouan). By Frank Edward Johnson. XXII, pp. 1061-1093, 25 ills., map, Dec., 1911

Scenes in Many Lands (People and Places). 16 photos in color by Franklin Price Knott. XXX, pp. 233-248, Sept., 1916

Time's Footprints in Tunisian Sands. By Maynard Owen Williams. LXXI, pp. 345-386, 43 ills., maps, Mar., 1937

Tunis of Today. By Frank Edward Johnson. XXII, pp. 723-749, 24 ills., Aug., 1911

TUNISIA, Where Sea and Desert Meet. 16 color photos by Gervais Courtellemont. XLV, pp. 415-422, Apr., 1924

TURBULENT Spain. By Ruth Q. McBride. LXX, pp. 397-427, 25 ills., two-page map, Oct., 1936

TURCIANSKY SVATY MARTIN (Turocz Szent Martin), Czechoslovakia:

Czechoslovakia, Key-Land to Central Europe. By Maynard Owen Williams. XXXIX, pp. 111-156, 45 ills., map, Feb., 1921

TURKESTAN. *See* Sinkiang; Soviet Central Asia

TURKEY:

Alert Anatolia. 13 ills. LXXXV, pp. 481-492, Apr., 1944

American Alma Maters in the Near East. By Maynard Owen Williams. LXXXVIII, pp. 237-256, 16 ills., Aug., 1945

An Ancient Capital (Boghaz Keoy). By Isabel F. Dodd. XXI, pp. 111-124, 11 ills., Feb., 1910

Archeology, the Mirror of the Ages: Our Debt to the Humble Delvers in the Ruins at Carchemish and at Ur. By C. Leonard Woolley. LIV, pp. 207-226, 19 ills., Aug., 1928

Armenia and the Armenians. By Hester Donaldson Jenkins. XXVIII, pp. 329-360, 27 ills., map, Oct., 1915

Asia Minor in the Time of the Seven Wise Men. By Mary Mills Patrick. XXXVII, pp. 47-67, 19 ills., Jan., 1920

The Buried Cities of Asia Minor. By Ernest Lloyd Harris. XX, pp. 1-18, 10 ills., Jan., 1909

The Changing Map in the Balkans. By Frederick Moore. XXIV, pp. 199-226, 27 ills., map, Feb., 1913

The Cone-Dwellers of Asia Minor: A Primitive People Who Live in Nature-Made Apartment Houses, Fashioned by Volcanic Violence and Trickling Streams. By J. R. Sitlington Sterrett. XXXV, pp. 281-331, 52 ills., map, Apr., 1919

Crossing Asia Minor, the Country of the New Turkish Republic. By Major Robert Whitney Imbrie. XLVI, pp. 445-472, 31 ills., map, Oct., 1924

East of Constantinople: Glimpses of Village Life in Anatolia, the Battleground of East and West, Where the Turks Reorganized Their Forces After the World War. By Melville Chater. XLIII, pp. 509-534, 27 ills., map, May, 1923

The Emancipation of Mohammedan Women. By Mary Mills Patrick. XX, pp. 42-66, 19 ills., Jan., 1909

Flags of Austria-Hungary, Bulgaria, Germany, and Turkey. By Byron McCandless and Gilbert Grosvenor. XXXII, pp. 386-388, 38 ills. in color, Oct., 1917

The Fringe of Verdure Around Asia Minor. By Ellsworth Huntington. XXI, pp. 761-775, 15 ills., Sept., 1910

From England to India by Automobile: An 8,527-mile Trip Through Ten Countries, from London to Quetta, Requires Five and a Half Months. By Major F. A. C. Forbes-Leith. XLVIII, pp. 191-223, 33 ills., map, Aug., 1925

The Gates to the Black Sea: The Dardanelles, the Bosphorus, and the Sea of Marmora. By Harry Griswold Dwight. XXVII, pp. 435-459, 27 ills., May, 1915

A German Route to India. (By Gilbert H. Grosvenor). XI, pp. 203-204, map, May, 1900

"Grass Never Grows Where the Turkish Hoof Has Trod." By Edwin Pears. XXIII, pp. 1132-1148, 19 ills., Nov., 1912

Historic Islands and Shores of the Ægean Sea. By Ernest Lloyd Harris. XXVIII, pp. 231-261, 28 ills., map, Sept., 1915

Homer's Troy Today. By Jacob E. Conner. XXVII, pp. 521-532, 11 ills., map, May, 1915

TURKEY—*Continued*

Impressions of Asiatic Turkey. By Stephen van Rensselaer Trowbridge. XXVI, pp. 598-609, 6 ills., Dec., 1914

The Kizilbash Clans of Kurdistan. By Melville Chater. LIV, pp. 485-504, 22 ills., Oct., 1928

The Land of the Stalking Death: A Journey Through Starving Armenia on an American Relief Train. By Melville Chater. XXXVI, pp. 393-420, 23 ills., Nov., 1919

Looking in on New Turkey. LXI, pp. 499-508, 12 ills. in color, Apr., 1932

The Lost Wealth of the Kings of Midas. By Ellsworth Huntington. XXI, pp. 831-846, 15 ills., Oct., 1910

The Most Historic Lands on Earth. XXVI, p. 615, map, Dec., 1914

The Mountaineers of the Euphrates. By Ellsworth Huntington. XX, pp. 142-156, 13 ills., Feb., 1909

The New Map of Europe: Showing the Boundaries Established by the Peace Conference at Paris and by Subsequent Decisions of the Supreme Council of the Allied and Associated Powers. By Ralph A. Graves. Text with map supplement. XXXIX, pp. 157-177, 18 ills., Feb., 1921

Notes on Troy. (By Ernest L. Harris). XXVII, pp. 531-532, May, 1915

On the Turks' Russian Frontier: Everyday Life in the Fastnesses between the Black Sea and Ararat, Borderland of Oil and Minerals that Hitler Covets. By Edward Stevenson Murray. LXXX, pp. 367-392, 21 ills., map, Sept., 1941

Peculiar Caves of Asia Minor. By Elizabeth H. Brewer. XXII, pp. 870-875, 5 ills., Sept., 1911

The Races of Europe. By Edwin A. Grosvenor. XXXIV, pp. 441-534, 62 ills., diagr. and index, maps, map supplement, Dec., 1918

The Road of the Crusaders: A Historian Follows the Steps of Richard the Lion Heart and Other Knights of the Cross over the "Via Dei." By Harold Lamb. LXIV, pp. 645-693, 46 ills. in black and white, 13 ills. in color, map, Dec., 1933

The Ruined Cities of Asia Minor. By Ernest L. Harris. XIX, pp. 741-760, 11 ills., Nov., 1908

Scenes in Asia Minor. 35 ills., map. XX, pp. 173-193, Feb., 1909

Seeing 3,000 Years of History in Four Hours: A Panorama of Ancient, Medieval, and Modern Events Against a Background of Mythology Unfolds During an Airplane Journey from Constantinople to Athens. By Maynard Owen Williams. LIV, pp. 719-739, 24 ills., map, Dec., 1928

A Sketch of the Geographical History of Asia Minor. By Sir William Ramsay. XLII, pp. 553-570, 12 ills., Nov., 1922

Skirting the Shores of Sunrise: Seeking and Finding "The Levant" in a Journey by Steamer, Motor-Car, and Train from Constantinople to Port Said. By Melville Chater. L, pp. 649-728, 60 ills. in black and white, 34 ills. in color, map, Dec., 1926

Some Ruined Cities of Asia Minor. By Ernest L. Harris. XIX, pp. 833-858, 19 ills., Dec., 1908

TURKEY—*Continued*

Summer Holidays on the Bosporus. By Maynard Owen Williams. LVI, pp. 487-508, 13 ills. in black and white, 11 ills. in color, map, Oct., 1929

Sunshine in Turkey. By Howard S. Bliss. XX, pp. 66-76, ill., Jan., 1909

The Transformation of Turkey: New Hats and New Alphabet are the Surface Symbols of the Swiftest National Changes in Modern Times. By Douglas Chandler. LXXV, pp. 1-50, 27 ills. in black and white, 23 ills. in color, map, Jan., 1939

Turkey, Where Earthquakes Followed Timur's Trail. 15 photos by Maynard Owen Williams. LXXVII, pp. 395-406, Mar., 1940

Turkey Goes to School. By Maynard Owen Williams. LV, pp. 95-108, 17 ills., Jan., 1929

The Turkish Republic Comes of Age. By Maynard Owen Williams. LXXXVII, pp. 581-616, 4 ills. in black and white, 29 ills. in color, map, May, 1945

Two Possible Solutions for the Eastern Problem. By James Bryce. XXIII, pp. 1149-1157, 5 ills., map, Nov., 1912

Under the Heel of the Turk: A Land with a Glorious Past, a Present of Abused Opportunities, and a Future of Golden Possibilities. By William H. Hall. XXXIV, pp. 51-69, 14 ills., July, 1918

Where Early Christians Lived in Cones of Rock: A Journey to Cappadocia in Turkey Where Strange Volcanic Pinnacles Are Honeycombed With Hermit Cells and Monasteries. By John D. Whiting. LXXVI, pp. 763-802, 20 ills. in black and white, 20 ills. in color, map, Dec., 1939

The Young Turk. By Rear-Admiral Colby M. Chester. XXIII, pp. 43-89, 39 ills., Jan., 1912

See also Istanbul; Van

TURKEYS:

Fowls of Forest and Stream Tamed by Man. By Morley A. Jull. Paintings by Hashime Murayama. LVII, pp. 327-371, 27 ills. in black and white, 16 ills. in color, Mar., 1930

TURKIC TRIBES:

With the Nomads of Central Asia: A Summer's Sojourn in the Tekes Valley, Plateau Paradise of Mongol and Turkic Tribes. By Edward Murray. Paintings and drawings by Alexandre Iacovleff. LXIX, pp. 1-57, 43 ills. in black and white, 26 ills. in color, map, Jan., 1936

See also Tatars; Turkomans

The **TURKISH** Republic Comes of Age. By Maynard Owen Williams. LXXXVII, pp. 581-616, 4 ills. in black and white, 29 ills. in color, map, May, 1945

TURKISTAN. *See* Sinkiang; Soviet Central Asia

TURKMEN SOVIET SOCIALIST REPUBLIC:

The Afghan Borderland. By Ellsworth Huntington. Part I: The Russian Frontier. XX, pp. 788-799, 14 ills., Sept., 1909

Life in the Great Desert of Central Asia. By Ellsworth Huntington. XX, pp. 749-760, 12 ills., Aug., 1909

TURKOMANS (Tribespeople):

Life in the Great Desert of Central Asia. By Ellsworth Huntington. XX, pp. 749-760, 12 ills., Aug., 1909

Russia's Orphan Races: Picturesque Peoples Who Cluster on the Southeastern Borderland of the Vast Slav Dominions. By Maynard Owen Williams. XXXIV, pp. 245-278, 26 ills., map, Oct., 1918

TURNER, DANIEL S.:

Voyage of the *Morrissey*. 10 color photos by Daniel S. Turner and Sherman A. Wengerd. LXXXIX, pp. 609-616, May, 1946

TURNER, J. HENRY:

The Alaskan Boundary Survey. III—The Boundary North of Fort Yukon. By J. Henry Turner. IV, pp. 189-197, Feb. 8, 1893

TURNING Back Time in the South Seas (Fatu-Hiva Island). By Thor Heyerdahl. LXXIX, pp. 109-136, 33 ills., maps, Jan., 1941

TUROCZ SZENT MARTIN, Czechoslovakia. *See* Turciansky Svaty Martin

TURTLES:

Capturing Giant Turtles in the Caribbean. By David D. Duncan. LXXXIV, pp. 177-190, 13 ills., map, Aug., 1943

Certain Citizens of the Warm Sea. By Louis L. Mowbray. Paintings by Hashime Murayama. XLI, pp. 27-62, 18 ills. in black and white, 16 ills. in color, Jan., 1922

Cultivation of Marine and Fresh-Water Animals in Japan. By K. Mitsukuri. XVII, pp. 524-531, 5 ills., Sept., 1906

Notes on the Remarkable Habits of Certain Turtles and Lizards. By H. A. Largelamb. XVIII, pp. 413-419, 12 ills., June, 1907

Reptiles of All Lands. By Raymond L. Ditmars. XXII, pp. 601-633, 32 ills., July, 1911

TURTLING:

Capturing Giant Turtles in the Caribbean. By David D. Duncan. LXXXIV, pp. 177-190, 13 ills., map, Aug., 1943

TUSCANY (Region), Italy:

Holidays Among the Hill Towns of Umbria and Tuscany. By Paul Wilstach. LIII, pp. 401-442, 40 ills., map, Apr., 1928

Inexhaustible Italy. By Arthur Stanley Riggs. XXX, pp. 273-368, 76 ills., map, Oct., 1916

Italy, From Roman Ruins to Radio: History of Ancient Bridge Building and Road Making Repeats Itself in Modern Public Works and Engineering Projects. By John Patric. LXXVII, pp. 347-394, 27 ills. in black and white, 9 ills. in color, Mar., 1940

TUSCARORA DEEP, North Pacific Ocean:

The Recent Earthquake Wave on the Coast of Japan. By Eliza Ruhamah Scidmore. VII, pp. 285-289, 4 ills., foldout map, Sept., 1896

Reports of Sealing Schooners Cruising in the Neighborhood of Tuscarora Deep in May and June, 1896. (By Eliza Ruhamah Scidmore). VII, pp. 310-312, Sept., 1896

TUTANKHAMEN (Pharaoh):
At the Tomb of Tutankhamen: An Account of the Opening of the Royal Egyptian Sepulcher Which Contained the Most Remarkable Funeral Treasures Unearthed in Historic Times. By Maynard Owen Williams. XLIII, pp. 461-508, 53 ills., map, May, 1923

TUTUILA (Island), Samoa:
America's South Sea Soldiers. By Lorena MacIntyre Quinn. XXXVI, pp. 267-274, 8 ills., Sept., 1919

TWEEDSMUIR OF ELSFIELD, SUSAN CHARLOTTE BUCHAN, LADY. *See* article, *below*

TWEEDSMUIR PARK (British Columbia): The Diary of a Pilgrimage. By The Lady Tweedsmuir of Elsfield. LXXIII, pp. 451-476, 22 ills., maps, Apr., 1938

TWEEDY, OWEN:
An Unbeliever Joins the Hadj: On the Age-Old Pilgrimage to Mecca, Babies Are Born, Elders Die, and Families May Halt a Year to Earn Funds in Distant Lands. By Owen Tweedy. LXV, pp. 761-789, 30 ills., map, June, 1934

TWENTY-THIRD PSALM:
Among the Bethlehem Shepherds: A Visit to the Valley Which David Probably Recalled When He Wrote the Twenty-third Psalm. By John D. Whiting. L, pp. 729-753, 19 ills., Dec., 1926

TWIN Stars of Chile: Valparaiso, the Gateway, and Santiago, the Capital—Key Cities with a Progressive Present and a Romantic Past. By William Joseph Showalter. LV, pp. 197-247, 35 ills. in black and white, 25 ills. in color, Feb., 1929

TWITCHELL, K. S.:
Kano, Mud-made City. 10 color photos by George W. Scott and K. S. Twitchell. LXXXV, pp. 545-552, May, 1944

TWO Fighting Tribes of the Sudan. By Merian C. Cooper. Photos by Ernest B. Schoedsack. LVI, pp. 465-486, 27 ills., map, Oct., 1929

The **TWO** Great Moorish Religious Dances. By George Edmund Holt. XXII, pp. 777-785, 6 ills., Aug., 1911

TWO Great Undertakings (Work of U. S. Bureau of Reclamation and U. S. Forest Service). XVII, pp. 645-647, Nov., 1906

TWO Hundred Miles up the Kuskokwim (Alaska). By Charles Hallock. IX, pp. 85-92, 6 ills., Mar., 1898

TWO Possible Solutions for the Eastern Problem. By James Bryce. XXIII, pp. 1149-1157, 5 ills., map, Nov., 1912

TYOSEN. *See* Korea

TYPES and Costumes of Old Sweden. 30 color photos by Gustav Heurlin, G. W. Cronquist, Wilhelm Tobien, Charles Martin. LIV, pp. 425-440, Oct., 1928

TYPHOID FEVER:
Economic Loss to the People of the United States Through Insects That Carry Disease. By L. O. Howard. XX, pp. 735-749, Aug., 1909
Our Army Versus a Bacillus. By Alton G. Grinnell. XXIV, pp. 1146-1152, 5 ills., diagr., Oct., 1913
Redeeming the Tropics. By William Joseph Showalter. XXV, pp. 344-364, 13 ills., Mar., 1914

TYROL (Region), Austria-Italy:
Austro-Italian Mountain Frontiers. By Florence Craig Albrecht. XXVII, pp. 321-376, 60 ills., map, Apr., 1915
Entering the Front Doors of Medieval Towns: The Adventures of an American Woman and Her Daughter in a Folding Boat on Eight Rivers of Germany and Austria. By Cornelia Stratton Parker. LXI, pp. 365-394, 23 ills. in black and white, 11 ills. in color, map, Mar., 1932
The Land of Contrast: Austria-Hungary. By D. W. and A. S. Iddings. XXIII, pp. 1188-1217, 1284, 33 ills., map, Dec., 1912
Merry Maskers of Imst. 14 photos by Francis C. Fuerst. LXX, pp. 201-208, Aug., 1936
Over the Alps to Brenner Pass. 15 photos, two-page map. LXXXIV, pp. 701-714, Dec., 1943
This Was Austria. 18 ills. LXXXVIII, pp. 71-86, July, 1945

TYROL, the Happy Mountain Land. 11 color photos by Hans Hildenbrand. LXI, pp. 371-378, Mar., 1932

TZELIUTSING, China:
Salt for China's Daily Rice. 11 ills. LXXXVI, pp. 329-336, Sept., 1944

TZOTZILS (Indians). *See* Zotzils

U

UAXACTUN, Guatemala:
Unearthing America's Ancient History: Investigation Suggests That the Maya May Have Designed the First Astronomical Observatory in the New World in Order to Cultivate Corn. By Sylvanus Griswold Morley. LX, pp. 99-126, 28 ills., July, 1931

UDAIPUR (State), India:
The Marble Dams of Rajputana. By Eleanor Maddock. XL, pp. 469-499, 13 ills. in black and white, 16 ills. in color, Nov., 1921

UGANDA:
Amid the Snow Peaks of the Equator: A Naturalist's Explorations Around Ruwenzori, with an Excursion to the Congo State, and an Account of the Terrible Scourge of Sleeping Sickness. By A. F. R. Wollaston. XX, pp. 256-277, 11 ills., Mar., 1909
Elephant Hunting in Equatorial Africa with Rifle and Camera. By Carl E. Akeley. XXIII, pp. 779-810, 30 ills., Aug., 1912
A Great African Lake (Victoria). By Sir Henry M. Stanley. XIII, pp. 169-172, map, May, 1902

UGANDA—*Continued*

Uganda, "Land of Something New": Equatorial African Area Reveals Snow-crowned Peaks, Crater Lakes, Jungle-story Beasts, Human Giants, and Forest Pygmies. By Jay Marston. LXXI, pp. 109-130, 22 ills., map, Jan., 1937

Where Roosevelt Will Hunt. By Sir Harry Johnston. XX, pp. 207-256, 43 ills., map supplement, Mar., 1909

Wild Man and Wild Beast in Africa. By Theodore Roosevelt. XXII, pp. 1-33, 41 ills., map, Jan., 1911

UITLANDERS:

Africa Since 1888, with Special Reference to South Africa and Abyssinia. By Hon. Gardiner G. Hubbard. VII, pp. 157-175, ill., foldout map, May, 1896

The Witwatersrand and the Revolt of the Uitlanders. By George F. Becker. VII, pp. 349-367, 4 ills., Nov., 1896

The **UKRAINE,** Past and Present. By Nevin O. Winter. XXXIV, pp. 114-128, 14 ills., Aug., 1918

UKRAINIAN SOVIET SOCIALIST REPUBLIC, U. S. S. R.:

Liberated Ukraine. By Eddy Gilmore. LXXXV, pp. 513-536, 22 ills., map, May, 1944

The Races of Europe. By Edwin A. Grosvenor. XXXIV, pp. 441-534, 62 ills., diagr. and index, maps, map supplement, Dec., 1918

The Society's New Map of Soviet Russia. Text with map supplement. LXXXVI, pp. 716-718, Dec., 1944

The Ukraine, Past and Present. By Nevin O. Winter. XXXIV, pp. 114-128, 14 ills., Aug., 1918

ULITHI (Atoll), Caroline Islands:

American Pathfinders in the Pacific. By William H. Nicholas. LXXXIX, pp. 617-640, 17 ills., two-page map, May, 1946

ULM, CHARLES T. P.:

Our Conquest of the Pacific: The Narrative of the 7,400-Mile Flight from San Francisco to Brisbane in Three Ocean Hops. By Squadron-Leader Charles E. Kingsford-Smith and Flight-Lieut. Charles T. P. Ulm. LIV, pp. 371-402, 27 ills., map, Oct., 1928

ULSTER. *See* Ireland; Northern Ireland

ULSTER COUNTY, New York:

Shawangunk Mountain. By N. H. Darton. VI, pp. 23-34, ills., 4 diagrs., Mar. 17, 1894

The **ULTIMATE** Washington (Plan Laid Out by the Commission of 1901 for the National Capital). XXVII, panorama, Mar., 1915

UMBRELLA ANTS. *See* Atta Ants

UMBRIA (Region), Italy:

Holidays Among the Hill Towns of Umbria and Tuscany. By Paul Wilstach. LIII, pp. 401-442, 40 ills., map, Apr., 1928

UMNAK (Island), Aleutian Islands:

A Navy Artist Paints the Aleutians. By Mason Sutherland. Paintings by Lt. William F. Draper. LXXXIV, pp. 157-176, 4 ills. in black and white, 16 ills. in color, Aug., 1943

UNALASKA (Island), Aleutian Islands:

Shishaldin as a Field for Exploration. By Joseph Stanley-Brown. X, pp. 281-288, 3 ills., map, Aug., 1899

An **UNBELIEVER** Joins the Hadj: On the Age-Old Pilgrimage to Mecca, Babies Are Born, Elders Die, and Families May Halt a Year to Earn Funds in Distant Lands. By Owen Tweedy. LXV, pp. 761-789, 30 ills., map, June, 1934

UNCLE Sam's Icebox Outposts (Greenland). 19 color photos by John E. Schneider and Robert B. Sykes, Jr. XC, pp. 473-496, Oct., 1946

UNCOMPAHGRE VALLEY, Colorado:

Home-Making by the Government: An Account of the Eleven Immense Irrigating Projects to be Opened in 1908. By C. J. Blanchard. XIX, pp. 250-287, 23 ills., Apr., 1908

The Spirit of the West: The Wonderful Agricultural Development Since the Dawn of Irrigation. By C. J. Blanchard. XXI, pp. 333-360, 15 ills., Apr., 1910

UNDER Egypt's Golden Sun. 22 color photos by B. Anthony Stewart. LXXVII, pp. 451-466, Apr., 1940

UNDER Italian Libya's Burning Sun. 9 color photos by Luigi Pellerano. XLVIII, pp. 141-148, Aug., 1925

UNDER Radiant Italian Skies. 8 color photos by Hans Hildenbrand and Luigi Pellerano. L, pp. 249-256, Aug., 1926

UNDER Swedish Roofs and Skies. 22 color photos by Volkmar Wentzel. LXXVII, pp. 799-822, June, 1940

UNDER the French Tricolor in Indo-China. 28 color photos by W. Robert Moore. LX, pp. 167-198, Aug., 1931

UNDER the Heel of the Turk: A Land with a Glorious Past, a Present of Abused Opportunities, and a Future of Golden Possibilities. By William H. Hall. XXXIV, pp. 51-69, 14 ills., July, 1918

UNDER the South African Union. By Melville Chater. LIX, pp. 391-512, 97 ills. in black and white, 38 ills. in color, two-page map, Apr., 1931

The **UNDERGROUND:**

The White War in Norway. By Thomas R. Henry. LXXXVIII, pp. 617-640, 23 ills., map, Nov., 1945

UNDERHILL, MIRIAM O'BRIEN:

Manless Alpine Climbing: The First Woman to Scale the Grépon, the Matterhorn, and Other Famous Peaks Without Masculine Support Relates Her Adventures. By Miriam O'Brien Underhill. LXVI, pp. 131-170, 30 ills. in black and white, 12 ills. in color, Aug., 1934

UNDERSEA Gardens of the North Atlantic Coast. 8 ills. in color from paintings by Else Bostelmann under direction Roy W. Miner. LXX, pp. 217-224, Aug., 1936

UNDERWOOD, ERIC:

The British Commonwealth of Nations: "Organized Freedom" Around the World. By Eric Underwood. LXXXIII, pp. 485-524, 31 ills., Apr., 1943

The Preservation of England's Historic and Scenic Treasures. By Eric Underwood. LXXXVII, pp. 413-440, 24 ills., two-page map, Apr., 1945

An **UNDISCOVERED** Island Off the Northern Coast of Alaska. I—By Marcus Baker. II—By Captain Edward Perry Herendeen. III—By General A. W. Greely. V, pp. 76-83, July 10, 1893

UNEARTHING America's Ancient History: Investigation Suggests That the Maya May Have Designed the First Astronomical Observatory in the New World in Order to Cultivate Corn. By Sylvanus Griswold Morley. LX, pp. 99-126, 28 ills., July, 1931

The **UNEXPLORED** Philippines from the Air: Map-making Over Jungle Lands Never Before Seen By White Men. By Lieut. George W. Goddard. LVIII, pp. 311-343, 38 ills., map, Sept., 1930

UNFURLING Old Glory on Canton Island. 11 ills. in color: painting by Charles Bittinger and 10 color photos by Richard H. Stewart and others. LXXIII, pp. 753-760, June, 1938

UNGERN-STERNBERG, IRINA, BARONESS:

Estonia: At Russia's Baltic Gate: War Often Has Ravaged This Little Nation Whose Identity Was Long Submerged in the Vast Sea of Russian Peoples. By Baroness Irina Ungern-Sternberg. LXXVI, pp. 803-834, 33 ills., map, Dec., 1939

UNIMAK (Island), Aleutian Islands:

Mountains on Unimak Island, Alaska. By Ferdinand Westdahl. XIV, pp. 91-99, 4 ills., map, Mar., 1903

UNION OF SOUTH AFRICA:

Africa Since 1888, with Special Reference to South Africa and Abyssinia. By Hon. Gardiner G. Hubbard. VII, pp. 157-175, ill., foldout map, May, 1896

The British Commonwealth of Nations: "Organized Freedom" Around the World. By Eric Underwood. LXXXIII, pp. 485-524, 31 ills., Apr., 1943

British South Africa and the Transvaal. By F. F. Hilder. XI, pp. 81-96, 7 ills., Mar., 1900

Busy Corner—the Cape of Good Hope: Ships Bound for Faraway Battlegrounds Stream Past Capetown, "Tavern of the Seas," and Other Ports of Virile South Africa. By W. Robert Moore. LXXXII, pp. 197-223, 11 ills. in black and white, 11 ills. in color, map, Aug., 1942

Cairo to Cape Town, Overland: An Adventurous Journey of 135 Days, Made by an American Man and His Wife, Through the Length of the African Continent. By Felix Shay. XLVII, pp. 123-260, 118 ills., map, Feb., 1925

UNION OF SOUTH AFRICA—*Continued*

The Cities That Gold and Diamonds Built: Transvaal Treasures Have Created Bustling Johannesburg and Fostered Pretoria, Administrative Capital of the South African Union. By W. Robert Moore. LXXXII, pp. 735-766, 20 ills. in black and white, 9 ills. in color, map, Dec., 1942

A Critical Period in South African History. (By J. H.). VII, pp. 377-379, Nov., 1896

The Diamond Mines of South Africa. By Gardiner F. Williams. XVII, pp. 344-356, 11 ills., June, 1906

Great Britain's Bread Upon the Waters: Canada and Her Other Daughters. By William Howard Taft. XXIX, pp. 217-272, 56 ills., Mar., 1916

Influence of Geographical Conditions on Military Operations in South Africa. By Major W. A. Simpson. XI, pp. 186-192, ill., map, May, 1900

Natal: The Garden Colony. By Russell Hastings Millward. XX, pp. 278-291, 16 ills., Mar., 1909

Under the South African Union. By Melville Chater. LIX, pp. 391-512, 97 ills. in black and white, 38 ills. in color, two-page map, Apr., 1931

Contents: Cape of Good Hope: The Floral Province.—Orange Free State: The Prairie Province.—Natal: The Garden Province.—The Transvaal: The Treasure-House Province

The Witwatersrand and the Revolt of the Uitlanders. By George F. Becker. VII, pp. 349-367, 4 ills., Nov., 1896

UNION OF SOVIET SOCIALIST REPUBLICS:

The Afghan Borderland. By Ellsworth Huntington. Part I: The Russian Frontier. XX, pp. 788-799, 14 ills., Sept., 1909

Armenia and the Armenians. By Hester Donaldson Jenkins. XXVIII, pp. 329-360, 27 ills., map, Oct., 1915

The British Take Baku. XXXIV, pp. 163-164, ill., Aug., 1918

Butter Exports from Siberia. XIII, p. 34, Jan., 1902

A Critical Review of Bering's First Expedition, 1725-30, Together with a Translation of His Original Report Upon It. With a Map. By Wm. H. Dall. II, pp. 111-169, 8 tables, foldout map, May, 1890

Included: Supplementary Note by Marcus Baker, On the Alleged Observation of a Lunar Eclipse by Bering in 1728-9, pp. 167-169

Evolution of Russian Government. By Edwin A. Grosvenor. XVI, pp. 309-332, 16 ills., July, 1905

The Far Eastern Republic. By Junius B. Wood. XLI, pp. 565-592, 29 ills., map, June, 1922

A Few Glimpses into Russia. By Lieut. Zinovi Pechkoff. XXXII, pp. 238-253, 10 ills., Sept., 1917

The First Airship Flight Around the World: Dr. Hugo Eckener Tells of an Epochal Geographic Achievement Upon the Occasion of the Bestowal of the National Geographic Society's Special Gold Medal. LVII, pp. 653-688, 37 ills., June, 1930

The Geographical Pivot of History (Steppes of Central Asia). (By H. J. Mackinder). XV, pp. 331-335, Aug., 1904

UNION OF SOVIET SOCIALIST REPUBLICS —*Continued*

Glimpses of Siberia, the Russian "Wild East." By Cody Marsh. XXXVIII, pp. 513-536, 26 ills., Dec., 1920

Glimpses of the Russian Empire. By William Wisner Chapin. XXIII, pp. 1043-1078, 51 ills. in color, map, Nov., 1912

The Growth of Russia. By Edwin A. Grosvenor. XI, pp. 169-185, 5 maps, May, 1900

I Learn About the Russians. By Eddy Gilmore. LXXXIV, pp. 619-640, 21 ills., Nov., 1943

An Island in the Sea of History: The Highlands of Daghestan. By George Kennan. XXIV, pp. 1087-1140, 49 ills., map, Oct., 1913

Japan Faces Russia in Manchuria. By Willard Price. LXXXII, pp. 603-634, 30 ills., map, Nov., 1942

The Land of Lambskins: An Expedition to Bokhara, Russian Central Asia, to Study the Karakul Sheep Industry. By Robert K. Nabours. XXXVI, pp. 77-88, 15 ills., July, 1919

The Land of Promise (Siberia). By Major General A. W. Greely. XXIII, pp. 1078-1090, 7 ills., Nov., 1912

The Land of the Stalking Death: A Journey Through Starving Armenia on an American Relief Train. By Melville Chater. XXXVI, pp. 393-420, 23 ills., Nov., 1919

Lend-Lease and the Russian Victory. By Harvey Klemmer. LXXXVIII, pp. 499-512, 6 ills., Oct., 1945

Life in the Great Desert of Central Asia. By Ellsworth Huntington. XX, pp. 749-760, 12 ills., Aug., 1909

"Magnetic City" (Magnitogorsk), Core of Valiant Russia's Industrial Might. By John Scott. LXXXIII, pp. 525-556, 27 ills., two-page map, May, 1943

Mother Volga Defends Her Own. By Maynard Owen Williams. LXXXII, pp. 793-811, 21 ills., Dec., 1942

The Murman Coast: Arctic Gateway for American and Allied Expeditionary Forces in Northern European Russia. XXXV, pp. 331-348, 30 ills., map, Apr., 1919

The New Map of Europe: Showing the Boundaries Established by the Peace Conference at Paris and by Subsequent Decisions of the Supreme Council of the Allied and Associated Powers. By Ralph A. Graves. Text with map supplement. XXXIX, pp. 157-177, 18 ills., Feb., 1921

New Road to Asia. By Owen Lattimore. LXXXVI, pp. 641-676, 15 ills. in black and white, 26 ills. in color, Dec., 1944

Observations on the Russo-Japanese War, in Japan and Manchuria. By Dr. Louis Livingston Seaman. XVI, pp. 80-82, Feb., 1905

Observing an Eclipse in Asiatic Russia. By Irvine C. Gardner. LXXI, pp. 179-197, 19 ills. in black and white, ill. in color, Feb., 1937

The Old Post-Road from Tiflis to Erivan. By Esther Lancraft Hovey. XII, pp. 300-309, 9 ills., Aug., 1901

The Races of Europe. By Edwin A. Grosvenor. XXXIV, pp. 441-534, 62 ills., diagr. and index, maps, map supplement, Dec., 1918

UNION OF SOVIET SOCIALIST REPUBLICS —*Continued*

The Rebirth of Religion in Russia: The Church Reorganized While Bolshevik Cannon Spread Destruction in the Nation's Holy of Holies. By Thomas Whittemore. XXXIV, pp. 379-401, 16 ills., Nov., 1918

The Revolution in Russia. By William Eleroy Curtis. XVIII, pp. 302-316, May, 1907

Roaming Russia's Caucasus: Rugged Mountains and Hardy Fighters Guard the Soviet Union's Caucasian Treasury of Manganese and Oil. By Rolf Singer. LXXXII, pp. 91-121, 33 ills., July, 1942

Russia. By Charles Emory Smith. XVI, pp. 55-63, Feb., 1905

Russia from Within: Her War of Yesterday, Today, and Tomorrow. By Stanley Washburn. XXXII, pp. 91-120, 30 ills., Aug., 1917

Russia in Europe. By Hon. Gardiner G. Hubbard. VII, pp. 3-26, map supplement, Jan., 1896

Russia in Recent Literature. By General A. W. Greely. XVI, pp. 564-568, Dec., 1905

Russia of the Hour: Giant Battle Ground for Theories of Economy, Society, and Politics, as Observed by an Unbiased Correspondent. By Junius B. Wood. L, pp. 519-598, 81 ills., Nov., 1926

The Russian Census of 1897. (By A. W. G.). VIII, pp. 335-336, Nov., 1897

The Russian Situation and Its Significance to America. By Stanley Washburn. XXXI, pp. 371-382, 8 ills., Apr., 1917

Russia's Democrats. By Montgomery Schuyler. XXXI, pp. 210-240, 25 ills., Mar., 1917

Russia's Man of the Hour: Alexander Kerensky's First Speeches and Proclamations. XXXII, pp. 24-45, 17 ills., July, 1917

Russia's Orphan Races: Picturesque Peoples Who Cluster on the Southeastern Borderland of the Vast Slav Dominions. By Maynard Owen Williams. XXXIV, pp. 245-278, 26 ills., map, Oct., 1918

Russia's Wheat Surplus. XVII, pp. 580-583, Oct., 1906

The Russo-American Telegraph Project of 1864-'67. By Professor William H. Dall. VII, pp. 110-111, ill., Mar., 1896

Siberia. By Prof. Edwin A. Grosvenor. XII, pp. 317-324, Sept., 1901

The Siberian Transcontinental Railroad. By General A. W. Greely. VIII, pp. 121-124, Apr., 1897

The Society's New Map of Soviet Russia. Text with map supplement. LXXXVI, pp. 716-718, Dec., 1944

Some Impressions of 150,000 Miles of Travel. By William Howard Taft. LVII, pp. 523-598, 80 ills., May, 1930

A Strange and Remarkable Beast. XVIII, p. 620, ill., Sept., 1907
Note: The mammoth recovered from the frozen tundra of northern Siberia

The Supposed Birthplace of Civilizations. XVI, pp. 499-504, 6 ills., Nov., 1905

UNION OF SOVIET SOCIALIST REPUBLICS
—Continued

Surveying Through Khoresm: A Journey Into Parts of Asiatic Russia Which Have Been Closed to Western Travelers Since the World War. By Lyman D. Wilbur. LXI, pp. 753-780, 31 ills., map, June, 1932

The Ties That Bind: Our Natural Sympathy with English Traditions, the French Republic, and the Russian Outburst for Liberty. By John Sharp Williams. XXXI, pp. 281-286, 4 ills., Mar., 1917

A Trip Through Siberia. By Ebenezer J. Hill. XIII, pp. 37-54, 17 ills., map, Feb., 1902

Voyaging on the Volga Amid War and Revolution: War-time Sketches on Russia's Great Waterway. By William T. Ellis. XXXIII, pp. 245-265, 16 ills., Mar., 1918

Western Siberia and the Altai Mountains: With Some Speculations on the Future of Siberia. By James Bryce. XXXIX, pp. 469-507, 39 ills., May, 1921

Where Slav and Mongol Meet. 16 ills. in color. XXXVI, pp. 421-436, Nov., 1919

With an Exile in Arctic Siberia: The Narrative of a Russian Who Was Compelled to Turn Polar Explorer for Two Years. By Vladimir M. Zenzinov. XLVI, pp. 695-718, 30 ills., map, Dec., 1924

Young Russia: The Land of Unlimited Possibilities. By Gilbert H. Grosvenor. XXVI, pp. 421-520, 85 ills. in black and white, 17 ills. in color, Nov., 1914

See also Crimea; Ukrainian Soviet Socialist Republic; *and* Trans-Siberian Railway

UNIQUE Gifts of Washington (D. C.) to the Nation. 11 color photos by Charles Martin, Edwin L. Wisherd, Jacob Gayer, Clifton Adams. LV, pp. 473-480, Apr., 1929

The **UNIQUE** Island of Mount Desert (Maine). By George B. Dorr, Ernest Howe Forbush, M. L. Fernald. XXVI, pp. 75-89, 7 ills., July, 1914

A **UNIQUE** Republic, Where Smuggling Is an Industry (Andorra). By Herbert Corey. XXXIII, pp. 279-299, 16 ills., map, Mar., 1918

UNITED NATIONS. *See* Index to Maps, *following this index*

UNITED STATES:

Aces Among Aces (Aviators). By Laurence La Tourette Driggs. XXXIII, pp. 568-580, 9 ills., June, 1918

Aerial Color Photography Becomes a War Weapon. By H. H. Arnold. LXXVII, pp. 757-766, 8 ills. in color, June, 1940

Along Our Side of the Mexican Border. By Frederick Simpich. XXXVIII, pp. 61-80, 9 ills., map, July, 1920

America Fights on the Farms. 21 ills. in color. LXXXVI, pp. 33-48, July, 1944

America from the Air: No Such Series of Airplane Views Has Ever Before Been Printed. (Photos by Lieutenant Albert W. Stevens). XLVI, pp. 85-92, 8 ills., July, 1924

UNITED STATES—*Continued*

America in the Air: The Future of Airplane and Airship, Economically and as Factors in National Defense. By Brigadier-General William Mitchell. XXXIX, pp. 339-352, 8 ills., map, Mar., 1921

America on the Move. 26 photos by J. Baylor Roberts, B. Anthony Stewart, and others. XC, pp. 357-378, Sept., 1946

The American Deserts. XV, pp. 153-163, 7 ills., map, Apr., 1904

An American Fable (Conservation of Natural Resources). By Gifford Pinchot. XIX, pp. 345-350, May, 1908

American Industries Geared for War. By Thornton Oakley. With 16 ills. in color from paintings by author. LXXXII, pp. 716-734, ill. in black and white, Dec., 1942

The American People Must Become Ship-Minded. By Edward N. Hurley. XXXIV, pp. 201-211, 7 ills., Sept., 1918

The American Scene. 29 winning photos in the Sixth Annual Newspaper National Snapshot Awards, with explanatory note. LXXIX, pp. 220-246, Feb., 1941

American Transportation Vital to Victory. By Thornton Oakley. With 16 ills. in color from paintings by author. LXXXIV, pp. 671-688, Dec., 1943

Americana. 11 winning photos in the Seventh Annual Newspaper National Snapshot Awards. LXXXI, pp. 657-666, May, 1942

America's Amazing Railway Traffic. By William Joseph Showalter. XLIII, pp. 353-404, 46 ills., map, Apr., 1923

America's Duty. By Newton D. Baker. XXXI, pp. 453-457, 5 ills., May, 1917

America's Part in the Allies' Mastery of the Air. By Major Joseph Tulasne. XXXIII, pp. 1-5, ills., Jan., 1918

Animal Wealth of the United States. By Francis E. Warren. XVII, pp. 511-524, 6 ills., 4 diagrs., Sept., 1906

The Annexation Fever. (By Henry Gannett). VIII, pp. 354-358, Dec., 1897

Another Important Map (U. S.). Announcement of map supplement (Apr., 1923). XLIII, p. 336, Mar., 1923

Area and Drainage Basin of Lake Superior. By Dr. Mark W. Harrington. VIII, pp. 111-120, tables, Apr., 1897

The Arid Regions of the United States. By F. H. Newell. V, pp. 167-172, Jan. 31, 1894

As 2,000 Ships Are Born. By Frederick Simpich. LXXXI, pp. 551-588, 34 ills., May, 1942

Atlantic Coast Tides. By Mark S. W. Jefferson. IX, pp. 497-509, 3 charts, Dec., 1898

The Automobile Industry: An American Art That Has Revolutionized Methods in Manufacturing and Transformed Transportation. By William Joseph Showalter. XLIV, pp. 337-414, 76 ills., Oct., 1923

The Battle of the Forest. By B. E. Fernow. VI, pp. 127-148, 5 ills., map, June 22, 1894

A Battle-Ground of Nature: The Atlantic Seaboard. By John Oliver La Gorce. XXXIII, pp. 511-546, 23 ills., 4 maps, June, 1918

UNITED STATES—*Continued*

Big Things of the West. By Charles F. Holder. XIV, pp. 279-282, ills., July, 1903

Billions of Barrels of Oil Locked Up in Rocks. By Guy Elliott Mitchell. XXXIII, pp. 195-205, 10 ills., Feb., 1918

Bitter Root Forest Reserve. By Richard U. Goode. IX, pp. 387-400, 5 ills., foldout map, Sept., 1898

Boundaries of Territorial Acquisitions. XII, pp. 373-377, chart, Oct., 1901

Building America's Air Army. By Hiram Bingham. XXXIII, pp. 48-86, 43 ills., Jan., 1918

By Car and Steamer Around Our Inland Seas. By Maynard Owen Williams. LXV, pp. 451-491, 29 ills. in black and white, 8 ills. in duotone, two-page map, Apr., 1934

Calculations of Population in June, 1900. By Henry Farquhar. X, pp. 406-413, Oct., 1899

The Call of the West. By C. J. Blanchard. XX, pp. 403-437, 20 ills., map, May, 1909

Canyons and Cacti of the American Southwest. 22 color photos by Edwin L. Wisherd, Jacob Gayer, Charles Martin. XLVIII, pp. 275-290, Sept., 1925

The Census of 1900. By Dr. F. H. Wines. XI, pp. 34-36, Jan., 1900

The Center of Population of the United States. XII, p. 241, June, 1901

The Central Great Plains. XVI, pp. 389-397, 8 ills., Aug., 1905

The Character of Our Immigration, Past and Present. By Z. F. McSweeny. XVI, pp. 1-15, chart, Jan., 1905

China and the United States. By Sir Chentung Liang-Cheng. XVI, pp. 554-557, Dec., 1905

Cloud Scenery of the High Plains. By Willard D. Johnson. IX, pp. 493-496, 3 ills., Dec., 1898

Coal, Prodigious Worker for Man. By Albert W. Atwood. LXXXV, pp. 569-592, 19 ills., drawing, May, 1944

The Columbia (River) Turns on the Power. By Maynard Owen Williams. LXXIX, pp. 749-792, 25 ills. in black and white, 18 ills. in color, June, 1941

Commerce of Mexico and the United States. By O. P. Austin. XIII, pp. 25-26, Jan., 1902

Conservation League of America. By Henry Gannett. XIX, pp. 737-739, Oct., 1908

Conservation of Our Natural Resources. XIX, p. 384, May, 1908

Controlling Sand Dunes in the United States and Europe. By A. S. Hitchcock. XV, pp. 43-47, 4 ills., Jan., 1904

The Correct Display of the Stars and Stripes. By Byron McCandless and Gilbert Grosvenor. XXXII, pp. 404-413, 8 ills., Oct., 1917

Cotton: Foremost Fiber of the World. By J. R. Hildebrand. LXXIX, pp. 137-192, 31 ills. in black and white, 34 ills. in color, Feb., 1941

Dealings of the United States with the Nations of the World. XV, pp. 186-187, Apr., 1904

The Deep-Water Route from Chicago to the Gulf. XVIII, pp. 679-685, 3 ills., map, Oct., 1907

UNITED STATES—*Continued*

Down the Rio Grande: Tracing this Strange, Turbulent Stream on Its Long Course from Colorado to the Gulf of Mexico. By Frederick Simpich. LXXVI, pp. 415-462, 28 ills. in black and white, 24 ills. in color, 6 maps, Oct., 1939

A Drowned Empire (Swamp Drainage). By Robert H. Chapman. XIX, pp. 190-199, 10 ills., Mar., 1908

Economic Loss of the People of the United States Through Insects That Carry Disease. By L. O. Howard. XX, pp. 735-749, Aug., 1909

Electric Street Railways. (By J. H.). VIII, p. 284, Oct., 1897

The Evolution of Commerce. Annual Address by the President, Hon. Gardiner G. Hubbard. IV, pp. 1-18, Mar. 26, 1892

Exploring the Atlantic Seaboard with a Color Camera. 18 color photos by Charles Martin and Jacob Gayer. XLIX, pp. 533-548, May, 1926

Exports of Manufactures. XVI, pp. 434-437, Sept., 1905

Fantastic Plants of Our Western Deserts. 8 ills. by Frank M. Campbell. XLV, pp. 33-40, Jan., 1924

Farmers Keep Them Eating. By Frederick Simpich. LXXXIII, pp. 435-458, 22 ills., Apr., 1943

Fearful Famines of the Past: History Will Repeat Itself Unless the American People Conserve Their Resources. By Ralph A. Graves. XXXII, pp. 69-90, 11 ills., July, 1917

The First Alaskan Air Expedition. By Captain St. Clair Streett. XLI, pp. 499-552, 37 ills., map, May, 1922

Fishes and Fisheries of Our North Atlantic Seaboard. By John Oliver La Gorce. Paintings by Hashime Murayama. XLIV, pp. 567-634, 35 ills. in black and white, 16 ills. in color, Dec., 1923

Flags Famous in American History. By Byron McCandless and Gilbert Grosvenor. XXXII, pp. 341-361, 92 ills. in color, Oct., 1917

The Flags of Our Army, Navy, and Government Departments. By Byron McCandless and Gilbert Grosvenor. XXXII, pp. 305-322, ill. in black and white, 300 ills. in color, diagrs., 4 tables, Oct., 1917

Flags of the World. By Gilbert Grosvenor and William J. Showalter. LXVI, pp. 339-396, 10 ills. in black and white, 808 ills. in color, Sept., 1934

Flaming Cliffs of Monument Valley. By Lt. Jack Breed, USNR. With 9 color photos by author and Warren T. Mithoff. LXXXVIII, pp. 452-461, Oct., 1945

Flying. By Gilbert Grosvenor. LXIII, pp. 585-630, 33 ills. in black and white, 17 ills. in duotone, May, 1933

The Foreign-Born of the United States. XXVI, pp. 265-271, 14 diagrs., Sept., 1914

Foreign Commerce of the United States in 1903. XIV, pp. 359-360, Sept., 1903

Forest Reserves of the United States. (By Gifford Pinchot). XI, pp. 369-372, map, Sept., 1900

"Free Burghs" in the United States. By James H. Blodgett. VII, pp. 116-122, Mar., 1896

UNITED STATES—*Continued*

From the War-Path to the Plow. By Franklin K. Lane. XXVII, pp. 73-87, 12 ills., Jan., 1915

The Gardens of the West. XVI, pp. 118-123, 7 ills., Mar., 1905

Gazetteers of the States. XV, pp. 369-370, Sept., 1904

Geographic History of the Piedmont Plateau. By W J McGee. VII, pp. 261-265, Aug., 1896

Geographic Names in the United States and the Stories They Tell. By R. H. Whitbeck. XVI, pp. 100-104, Mar., 1905

Geographic Progress of Civilization. Annual Address by the President, Honorable Gardiner G. Hubbard. VI, pp. 1-22, Feb. 14, 1894

Geographic Work of the General Government. By Henry Gannett. IX, pp. 329-338, July, 1898

The Geographical Distribution of Insanity in the United States. By Dr. William A. White. XIV, pp. 361-378, 6 maps, Oct., 1903

Geographical Research in the United States. By Gardiner G. Hubbard and Marcus Baker. VIII, pp. 285-293, Oct., 1897

The Geography of a Hurricane: A Doughnut-shaped Storm Turned Back Time in New England to Candlelight Days, but Revealed Anew Yankee Courage and Ingenuity. By F. Barrows Colton. LXXV, pp. 529-552, 20 ills., map, Apr., 1939

The Geography of Our Foreign Trade. By Frederick Simpich. XLI, pp. 89-108, 25 ills., Jan., 1922

The Geography of the Southern Peninsula of the United States. By the Rev. John N. MacGonigle. VII, pp. 381-394, 4 ills., Dec., 1896

The Geologic Atlas of the United States. (By W J M.). IX, pp. 339-342, July, 1898

Geomorphology of the Southern Appalachians. By Charles Willard Hayes and Marius R. Campbell. VI, pp. 63-126, diagrs., 4 maps, May 23, 1894

Glass "Goes to Town." By J. R. Hildebrand. LXXXIII, pp. 1-48, 28 ills. in black and white, 22 ills. in color, Jan., 1943

Glimpses East and West in America. 16 ills. XLV, pp. 531-546, May, 1924

The Grape-Growing Industry in the United States. XIV, pp. 445-451, 5 ills., Dec., 1903

The Great Canals of the World. XVI, pp. 475-479, Oct., 1905

The Great Mississippi Flood of 1927: Since White Man's Discovery This Mighty River Has Served Him Well, Yet It Has Brought Widespread Devastation Along Its Lower Reaches. By Frederick Simpich. LII, pp. 243-289, 53 ills., map, Sept., 1927

The Great Storm of March 11-14, 1888. By Brigadier-General A. W. Greely. I, pp. 37-39, Oct., 1888

The Great Storm Off the Atlantic Coast of the United States, March 11th-14th, 1888. By Everett Hayden. I, pp. 40-58, 6 charts, Oct., 1888

The Growth of the United States. By W J McGee. IX, pp. 377-386, diagr., table, Sept., 1898

The Highest Point in Each State. XX, pp. 539-541, ills., June, 1909

UNITED STATES—*Continued*

Home Folk around Historic Cumberland Gap. By Leo A. Borah. LXXXIV, pp. 741-768, 25 ills., map, Dec., 1943

Home-Making by the Government: An Account of the Eleven Immense Irrigating Projects to be Opened in 1908. By C. J. Blanchard. XIX, pp. 250-287, 23 ills., Apr., 1908

How Long Will the Coal Reserves of the United States Last? By Marius R. Campbell. XVIII, pp. 129-138, 5 diagrs., map, Feb., 1907

How the United States Grew. By McFall Kerbey. LXIII, pp. 631-649, 17 ills., map, May, 1933

How We Use the Gulf of Mexico. By Frederick Simpich. LXXXV, pp. 1-40, 20 ills. in black and white, 19 ills. in color, two-page map, Jan., 1944

Hydrography in the United States. By Frederick H. Newell. VII, pp. 146-150, Apr., 1896

Immigration and Naturalization. XVI, pp. 517-519, Jan., 1905

Immigration to the Southern States. XVI, pp. 517-519, Nov., 1905

The Improvement of Geographical Teaching. By Professor William Morris Davis. V, pp. 68-75, July 10, 1893

The Influence of Forestry upon the Lumber Industry of the United States. By Overton W. Price. XIV, pp. 381-386, ills., Oct., 1903

Is Climatic Aridity Impending on the Pacific Slope? The Testimony of the Forest. By J. B. Leiberg. X, pp. 160-181, May, 1899

Japan, America, and the Orient. By Eki Hioki. XVII, pp. 498-504, Sept., 1906

Japan and the United States. XVI, pp. 432-434, ill., Sept., 1905

Land of a Million Smiles (Ozarks). By Frederick Simpich. LXXXIII, pp. 589-623, 14 ills. in black and white, 20 ills. in color, map, May, 1943

The Land of the Best. By Gilbert H. Grosvenor. XXIX, pp. 327-430, 71 ills. in black and white, 33 ills. in color, pictorial supplement, Apr., 1916

Lend-Lease and the Russian Victory. By Harvey Klemmer. LXXXVIII, pp. 499-512, 6 ills., Oct., 1945

Life on the Grand Banks: An Account of the Sailor-Fishermen Who Harvest the Shoal Waters of North America's Eastern Coasts. By Frederick William Wallace. XL, pp. 1-28, 29 ills., July, 1921

The Limited Water Supply of the Arid Region. By Frederick H. Newell. XI, pp. 438-442, Nov., 1900

The Long River of New England: In War and Peace, from Mountain Wilderness to the Sea, Flows the Connecticut River, Through a Valley Abounding in History, Scenery, Inventive Genius, and Industry. By Albert W. Atwood. LXXXIII, pp. 401-434, 12 ills. in black and white, 24 ills. in color, map, Apr., 1943

Magnetic Survey of the United States. By Dr. L. A. Bauer. XIII, pp. 92-95, map, Mar., 1902

The Marvelous Prosperity of the South. XVIII, p. 685, Oct., 1907

Men Against the Rivers (Mississippi and Ohio Rivers). By Frederick Simpich. LXXI, pp. 767-794, 22 ills., maps, June, 1937

Metal Sinews of Strength: This Is a War of Many Metals, for We Live in an Age of Alloys. By Frederick G. Vosburgh. LXXXI, pp. 457-491, 35 ills., Apr., 1942

A Mind's-Eye Map of America. By Franklin K. Lane. XXXVII, pp. 479-518, 25 ills. in black and white, 8 ills. in color, June, 1920

Mineral Production in the United States. VII, p. 250, July, 1896

Mineral Production in the United States. VII, p. 310, Sept., 1896

Mineral Production in the United States. (By J. H.). VIII, pp. 201-202, July-Aug., 1897

The Miracle of War Production: For Victory the United States Transforms Its Complex Industry into the Biggest Factory and Mightiest Arsenal the World Has Ever Known. By Albert W. Atwood. With paintings by Thornton Oakley. LXXXII, pp. 693-715, 17 ills. in black and white, 16 ills. in color, Dec., 1942

The Mother Maps of the United States. By Henry Gannett. IV, pp. 101-116, table, map supplement, Mar. 31, 1892

The Movements of Our Population. By Henry Gannett. V, pp. 21-44, 7 diagrs., 15 tables, 15 maps, Mar. 20, 1893

The National Forest Reserves. By Frederick H. Newell. VIII, pp. 177-187, diagrs., tables, June, 1897

The National Geographic Society's Map of Northeastern United States. Text with map supplement. LXXXVIII, pp. 361-362, Sept., 1945

National Growth and National Character. By W J McGee. X, pp. 185-206, June, 1899

The Nation's Pride (Natural Resources). By Franklin K. Lane. XXVIII, pp. 589-606, 6 ills., Dec., 1915

The Nation's Undeveloped Resources. By Franklin K. Lane. XXV, pp. 183-225, 32 ills., Feb., 1914

The Native Oysters of the West Coast. By Robert E. C. Stearns. XIX, pp. 224-226, Mar., 1908

Nature's Scenic Marvels of the West. 17 ills. in duotone. LXIV, pp. 17-32, July, 1933

New Map Reveals the Progress and Wonders of Our Country. Text with map supplement. LXIII, pp. 650-652, ill., May, 1933

New United States Map Shows Census Changes. Text with map supplement. LXXVIII, pp. 821-824, ills., Dec., 1940

The Non-Stop Flight Across America. By Lieutenant John A. Macready. Photos by Lieutenant Albert W. Stevens. XLVI, pp. 1-83, 68 ills., maps, July, 1924

The North American Deserts. By Herr Professor Dr. Johannes Walther. IV, pp. 163-176, Feb. 8, 1893

Northeast of Boston. By Albert W. Atwood. LXXXVIII, pp. 257-292, 12 ills. in black and white, 17 ills. in color, map supplement, Sept., 1945

Notes on the Deserts of the United States and Mexico (Extracted from a Publication of Dr. Daniel T. MacDougal). XXI, pp. 691-714, 16 ills., Aug., 1910

The Oldest Free Assemblies: Address of Right Hon. Arthur J. Balfour, in the United States House of Representatives, May 5, 1917. XXXI, pp. 368-371, Apr., 1917

The Origin of American State Names. By Frederick W. Lawrence. XXXVIII, pp. 105-143, 34 ills., Aug., 1920

Origin of the Physical Features of the United States. By G. K. Gilbert. IX, pp. 308-317, maps, July, 1898

The Original Territory of the United States. By David J. Hill. X, pp. 73-92, Mar., 1899

Our Coal Lands. By Guy Elliott Mitchell. XXI, pp. 446-451, 5 ills., May, 1910

Our First Alliance. By J. J. Jusserand. XXXI, pp. 518-548, 8 ills., June, 1917

Our Foreign-Born Citizens. XXXI, pp. 95-130, 36 ills., 8 diagrs., map, Feb., 1917

Our Immigration During 1904. XVI, pp. 15-27, 6 ills., charts, Jan., 1905

Our Immigration in 1905. XVI, pp. 434-435, Sept., 1905

Our Immigration Laws from the Viewpoint of National Eugenics. By Prof. Robert De C. Ward. XXIII, pp. 38-41, Jan., 1912

Our Industrial Victory. By Charles M. Schwab. XXXIV, pp. 212-229, 17 ills., Sept., 1918

Our Map of the United States. Text with map supplement. XLIII, p. 460, Apr., 1923

Our National Parks. By L. F. Schmeckebier. XXIII, pp. 531-579, 41 ills., map, June, 1912

Our Neglected Southern Coast. By Alfred Goldsborough Mayer. XIX, pp. 859-871, 10 ills., Dec., 1908

Our New Possessions and the Interest They Are Exciting. (By O. P. Austin). XI, pp. 32-33, Jan., 1900

Our Present Population. XV, p. 232, May, 1904

Our State Flags. By Byron McCandless and Gilbert Grosvenor. XXXII, pp. 325-341, 57 ills. in color, Oct., 1917

Our State Flowers: The Floral Emblems Chosen by the Commonwealths. By Gilbert Grosvenor. Paintings by Mary E. Eaton. XXXI, pp. 481-517, 567, ill. in black and white, 30 ills. in color, June, 1917

Our Youngest Volcano. By J. S. Diller. V, pp. 93-96, ill., July 10, 1893

Pages from the Floral Life of America. Paintings by Mary E. Eaton. XLVIII, pp. 44-75, 55 ills. in color, July, 1925

A Patriotic Pilgrimage to Eastern National Parks: History and Beauty Live Along Paved Roads, Once Indian Trails, Through Virginia, North Carolina, Tennessee, Kentucky, and West Virginia. By Leo A. Borah. LXV, pp. 663-702, 18 ills. in black and white, 28 ills. in color, two-page map, June, 1934

Photographing the Marvels of the West in Colors. By Fred Payne Clatworthy. LIII, pp. 694-719, 30 ills. in color, June, 1928

Pirate Rivers and Their Prizes: The Warfare of Waterways Has Sometimes Changed the Geography of Our Continents. By John Oliver La Gorce. L, pp. 87-132, 48 ills., map, July, 1926

UNITED STATES—*Continued*

Place Names of the United States. XIII, pp. 403-405, Nov., 1902

The Population of the United States. By Henry Gannett. XXII, pp. 34-48, 9 diagrs., 3 maps, Jan., 1911

Postwar Portrait of the United States. Text with map supplement. XC, pp. 135-136, July, 1946

Proportion of Children in the United States. XVI, pp. 504-508, charts, Nov., 1905

Protecting the United States from Plant Pests. By Charles Lester Marlatt. XL, pp. 205-218, 16 ills., Aug., 1921

Rainfall Types of the United States. Annual Report by Vice-President, General A. W. Greely. V, pp. 45-58, 5 tables, map, Apr. 29, 1893

Reclaiming the Swamp Lands of the United States. By Herbert M. Wilson. XVIII, pp. 292-301, diagr., map, May, 1907

Reclamation: Drainage; Planting Denuded State Land; Control of the Boll Weevil. 6 ills. XVIII, pp. 778-780, Dec., 1907

The Reclamation of the West. By F. H. Newell. XV, pp. 15-30, 6 ills., 7 maps, Jan., 1904

Report—Geography of the Land. By Herbert G. Ogden. II, pp. 31-48, Apr., 1890

Republics—The Ladder to Liberty. By David Jayne Hill. XXXI, pp. 240-254, 5 ills., maps, Mar., 1917

Revolution in Eating: Machine Food Age—Born of Roads, Research, and Refrigeration—Makes the United States the Best-fed Nation in History. By J. R. Hildebrand. LXXXI, pp. 273-324, 33 ills. in black and white, 25 ills. in color, Mar., 1942

The Rivers of Northern New Jersey, with Notes on the Classification of Rivers in General. By William Morris Davis. II, pp. 81-110, drawing, 6 diagrs., map, May, 1890

The Russo-American Telegraph Project of 1864-'67. By Professor William H. Dall. VII, pp. 110-111, ill., Mar., 1896

The Sage Plains of Oregon. By Frederick V. Coville. VII, pp. 395-404, Dec., 1896

Salton Sea and the Rainfall of the Southwest. By Alfred J. Henry. XVIII, pp. 244-248, Apr., 1907

The Santa Fe Trail, Path to Empire. By Frederick Simpich. LVI, pp. 213-252, 35 ills. in black and white, 12 ills. in color, map, Aug., 1929

The Scenery of North America. By James Bryce. XLI, pp. 339-389, 45 ills., Apr., 1922

Seals of Our Nation, States, and Territories. By Elizabeth W. King. Paintings by Carlotta Gonzales Lahey, Irvin E. Alleman, Theodora Price. XC, pp. 1-42, 14 ills. in black and white, 84 ills. in color, July, 1946

Contents: Seals of the States and District of Columbia; Seals of the Territories, Island Possessions, the Canal Zone, and the Philippine Commonwealth; Great Seal of the United States and Other Federal Seals; Seals of the President and of the Government Departments

UNITED STATES—*Continued*

The Secret of the Southwest Solved by Talkative Tree Rings: Horizons of American History Are Carried Back to A. D. 700 and a Calendar for 1,200 Years Established by National Geographic Society Expeditions. By Andrew Ellicott Douglass. LVI, pp. 737-770, 33 ills., map, Dec., 1929

Seeing America from the "Shenandoah": An Account of the Record-making 9,000-mile Flight from the Atlantic to the Pacific Coast and Return in the Navy's American-built, American-manned Airship. By Junius B. Wood. XLVII, pp. 1-47, 39 ills., diagr., map, Jan., 1925

Seeing America with Lindbergh: The Record of a Tour of More Than 20,000 Miles by Airplane Through Forty-eight States on Schedule Time. By Lieutenant Donald E. Keyhoe. LIII, pp. 1-46, 46 ills., map, Jan., 1928

Seeing Our Spanish Southwest. By Frederick Simpich. LXXVII, pp. 711-756, 25 ills. in black and white, 17 ills. in duotone, map supplement, June, 1940

The Sex, Nativity, and Color of the People of the United States. (By G. H. G.). XII, pp. 361-389, 17 charts, Nov., 1901

Ships for the Seven Seas: The Story of America's Maritime Needs, Her Capabilities and Her Achievements. By Ralph A. Graves. XXXIV, pp. 165-200, 24 ills., Sept., 1918

Shortening Time Across the Continent. By Henry Herbert McClure. XIII, pp. 319-321, Aug., 1902

The Society Maps Northwestern United States and Neighboring Canadian Provinces. Text with map supplement. LXXIX, pp. 805-806, June, 1941

Some Early Geographers of the United States. By Rear Admiral Colby M. Chester. XV, pp. 392-404, Oct., 1904

Some of Our Immigrants. XVIII, pp. 317-334, 21 ills., May, 1907

The Southwest: Its Splendid Natural Resources, Agricultural Wealth, and Scenic Beauty. By N. H. Darton. XXI, pp. 631-665, 21 ills., map, Aug., 1910

Southwest Trails from Horse to Motor. Text with map supplement. LXXVII, p. 767, June, 1940

The Spirit of the West: The Wonderful Agricultural Development Since the Dawn of Irrigation. By C. J. Blanchard. XXI, pp. 333-360, 15 ills., Apr., 1910

Statistical Atlas of the United States. XV, pp. 50-52, diagrs., Jan., 1904

Statistics of Cities. XVI, p. 437, Sept., 1905

Statistics of Railways in the United States. (By H. G.). VII, pp. 406-407, Dec., 1896

The Storm of February 25-28, 1902. (By Alfred J. Henry). XIII, pp. 110-112, chart, Mar., 1902

The Story of the American Flag. By Byron McCandless and Gilbert Grosvenor. XXXII, pp. 286-303, 12 ills., Oct., 1917

Survey and Subdivision of Indian Territory. By Henry Gannett. VII, pp. 112-115, ill., map, Mar., 1896

UNITED STATES—*Continued*

Taming the Outlaw Missouri River. By Frederick Simpich. LXXXVIII, pp. 569-598, 25 ills., two-page map, Nov., 1945

This Is My Own: How the United States Seems to a Citizen Soldier Back from Three Years Overseas. By Frederick G. Vosburgh. LXXXIX, pp. 113-128, 14 ills., Jan., 1946

The Topographic Atlas of the United States. (By W J M.). IX, pp. 343-344, July, 1898

Trade of the United States with Cuba. (By J. H.). IX, pp. 247-249, tables, May, 1898

Trailing History Down the Big Muddy: In the Homeward Wake of Lewis and Clark, a Folding Steel Skiff Bears Its Lone Pilot on a 2,000-Mile Cruise on the Yellowstone-Missouri. By Lewis R. Freeman. LIV, pp. 73-120, 51 ills., map, July, 1928

A Tribute to America. By Herbert Henry Asquith. XXXI, pp. 295-296, ills., Apr., 1917

The United States: Her Industries. By O. P. Austin. XIV, pp. 301-320, 24 diagrs., Aug., 1903

The United States—Her Mineral Resources. By C. Kirchhoff. XIV, pp. 331-339, Sept., 1903

The United States; Its Soils and Their Products. By H. W. Wiley. XIV, pp. 263-279, 11 ills., July, 1903

"The United States—Land and Waters." By Cyrus C. Adams. XIV, pp. 171-185, 8 ills., map, May, 1903

The United States and the British Empire. By Leonard David Gammans. LXXXVII, pp. 562-564, May, 1945

United States Daily Atmospheric Survey. By Prof. Willis L. Moore. VIII, pp. 299-303, Oct., 1897

The United States Government Telegraph and Cable Lines. XV, pp. 490-494, 3 maps, Dec., 1904

U. S. Roads in War and Peace. By Frederick Simpich. LXXX, pp. 687-716, 27 ills., Dec., 1941

Urban Population of the United States. XII, pp. 345-346, Sept., 1901

The Utilization of the Vacant Public Lands. By Emory F. Best. VIII, pp. 49-57, Feb., 1897

The Warfare on Our Eastern Coast. By John Oliver La Gorce. XXVIII, pp. 195-230, 29 ills., charts, Sept., 1915

Wartime in the Pacific Northwest. By Frederick Simpich. LXXXII, pp. 421-464, 25 ills. in black and white, 23 ills. in color, map, Oct., 1942

A Wasteful Nation (Report of Conservation Commission). XX, pp. 203-206, Feb., 1909

Western National Parks Invite America Out of Doors. 17 photos in duotone by G. A. Grant, W. M. Rush, Merl La Voy, J. S. Dixon. LXVI, pp. 65-80, July, 1934

Western Views in the Land of the Best. 16 color photos by Fred Payne Clatworthy. XLIII, pp. 405-420, Apr., 1923

What Is It To Be an American? By Franklin K. Lane. XXXIII, pp. 348-354, 4 ills., diagr., Apr., 1918

UNITED STATES—*Continued*

What the Latin American Republics Think of the Pan-American Conferences. XVII, pp. 474-479, Aug., 1906

When Our Country Is Fifty Years Older. By Raphael Zon. XX, pp. 573-580, ills., diagr., June, 1909

Where the World Gets Its Oil: But Where Will Our Children Get It When American Wells Cease to Flow? By George Otis Smith. XXXVII, pp. 181-202, 21 ills., 3 maps, Feb., 1920

Winning the West. By C. J. Blanchard. XVII, pp. 82-98, 10 ills., map, Feb., 1906

See also names of States; Washington, D. C.; *and* subject headings beginning with U. S.

U. S. AIR MAIL SERVICE:

Flying. By Gilbert Grosvenor. LXIII, pp. 585-630, 33 ills. in black and white, 17 ills. in duotone, May, 1933

Flying the World's Longest Air-Mail Route: From Montevideo, Uruguay, Over the Andes, Up the Pacific Coast, Across Central America and the Caribbean to Miami, Florida, in 67 Thrilling Flying Hours. By Junius B. Wood. LVII, pp. 261-325, 65 ills., map, Mar., 1930

On the Trail of the Air Mail: A Narrative of the Experiences of the Flying Couriers Who Relay the Mail Across America at a Speed of More than 2,000 Miles a Day. By Lieut. J. Parker Van Zandt. XLIX, pp. 1-61, 67 ills., map, Jan., 1926

U. S. ARMED FORCES:

At Ease in the South Seas. By Maj. Frederick Simpich, Jr. LXXXV, pp. 79-104, 32 ills., Jan., 1944

Insignia and Decorations of the United States Armed Forces. By Gilbert Grosvenor. LXXXVII, pp. 185-186, Feb., 1945

Insignia of the United States Armed Forces. By Gilbert Grosvenor. With 991 illustrations in color. LXXXIII, p. 651, June, 1943

A Navy Artist Paints the Aleutians. By Mason Sutherland. Paintings by Lt. William F. Draper. LXXXIV, pp. 157-176, 4 ills. in black and white, 16 ills. in color, Aug., 1943

See also U. S. Army; U. S. Coast Guard; U. S. Marine Corps; U. S. Navy; *and* other branches of service

U. S. ARMY:

American Decorations and Insignia of Honor and Service. By Col. Robert E. Wyllie. XXXVI, pp. 502-526, 6 ills. in black and white, 119 ills. in color, Dec., 1919

Americans Help Liberated Europe Live Again. By Lt. Col. Frederick Simpich, Jr. LXXXVII, pp. 747-768, 17 ills., June, 1945

America's New Soldier Cities: The Geographical and Historical Environment of the National Army Cantonments and National Guard Camps. By William Joseph Showalter. XXXII, pp. 439-476, 18 ills., map, Nov.-Dec., 1917

Animals Were Allies, Too. 16 ills. LXXXIX, pp. 75-88, Jan., 1946

Around the Clock with Your Soldier Boy. By Frederick Simpich. LXXX, pp. 1-36, 42 ills., July, 1941

U. S. ARMY—*Continued*

Bringing the World to Our Foreign Language Soldiers: How a Military Training Camp is Solving a Seemingly Unsurmountable Problem by Using the Geographic. By Christina Krysto. XXXIV, pp. 81-90, 4 ills., Aug., 1918

Celebrating Christmas on the Meuse. By Captain Clifton Lisle. XXXVI, pp. 527-537, 5 ills., Dec., 1919

A City Learns to Smile Again (Nancy, France). By Maj. Frederick G. Vosburgh. LXXXVII, pp. 361-384, 23 ills., map, Mar., 1945

Conserving the Nation's Man-Power: Disease Weakens Armies, Cripples Industry, Reduces Production. How the Government is Sanitating the Civil Zones Around Cantonment Areas. A Nation-wide Campaign for Health. By Rupert Blue. XXXII, pp. 255-278, 17 ills., Sept., 1917

Cooties and Courage. By Herbert Corey. XXXIII, pp. 495-509, 10 ills., June, 1918

Europe's Looted Art. By John Walker. LXXXIX, pp. 39-52, 11 ills., Jan., 1946

The Flags of Our Army, Navy, and Government Departments. By Byron McCandless and Gilbert Grosvenor. XXXII, pp. 305-322, ill. in black and white, 300 ills. in color, diagrs., 4 tables, Oct., 1917

The Health and Morale of America's Citizen Army: Personal Observations of Conditions in Our Soldier Cities by a Former Commander-in-Chief of the United States Army and Navy. By William Howard Taft. XXXIII, pp. 219-245, 22 ills., Mar., 1918

Heroes' Return. By William H. Nicholas. LXXXVII, pp. 333-352, 19 ills., Mar., 1945

In Honor of the Army and Aviation (Banquet). XXII, pp. 267-284, 5 ills., Mar., 1911

Infantrymen—The Fighters of War. By Brigadier General W. H. Wilbur. LXXXVI, pp. 513-538, 22 ills., Nov., 1944

The Insignia of the Uniformed Forces of the United States. By Byron McCandless and Gilbert Grosvenor. XXXII, pp. 413-419, 318 ills., Oct., 1917

Lend-Lease Is a Two-way Benefit: Innovation in Creative Statesmanship Pools Resources of United Nations, and Supplies American Forces Around the World. By Francis Flood. LXXXIII, pp. 745-761, 14 ills., June, 1943

Our Army Versus a Bacillus. By Alton G. Grinnell. XXIV, pp. 1146-1152, 5 ills., diagr., Oct., 1913

Painting the Army on Maneuvers. By Arthur Beaumont. Text with 16 ills. in color from paintings by author. LXXXII, pp. 601-602, Nov., 1942

The Romance of Military Insignia: How the United States Government Recognizes Deeds of Heroism and Devotion to Duty. By Col. Robert E. Wyllie. XXXVI, pp. 463-501, 27 ills., Dec., 1919

San Francisco: Gibraltar of the West Coast. By La Verne Bradley. LXXXIII, pp. 279-308, 28 ills., Mar., 1943

Shopping Abroad for Our Armies in France. By Herbert Corey. XXXIII, pp. 206-218, 6 ills., Feb., 1918

U. S. ARMY—*Continued*

Training the New Armies of Liberty: Camp Lee, Virginia's Home for the National Army. By Granville Fortescue. XXXII, pp. 421-437, 8 ills., map, Nov.-Dec., 1917

United States Military Insignia. LXXXIII, pp. 656-693, 7 ills. in black and white, 12 drawings, 311 ills. in color, June, 1943

Winning the War of Supply. By F. Barrows Colton. LXXXVIII, pp. 705-736, 23 ills., Dec., 1945

Your Dog Joins Up. By Frederick Simpich. LXXXIII, pp. 93-113, 25 ills., Jan., 1943

See also U. S. Military Academy; Women's Army Corps (WAC)

U. S. ARMY AIR FORCES:

Aerial Color Photography Becomes a War Weapon. By H. H. Arnold. LXXVII, pp. 757-766, 8 ills. in color, June, 1940

The Aerial Invasion of Burma. By General H. H. Arnold. LXXXVI, pp. 129-148, 20 ills., Aug., 1944

Air Power for Peace. By General H. H. Arnold. LXXXIX, pp. 137-193, 35 ills. in black and white, 28 ills. in color, map supplement, Feb., 1946

Aircraft Insignia, Spirit of Youth. By Gerard Hubbard. LXXXIII, pp. 710-722, 3 ills. in black and white, 337 ills. in color, June, 1943

American Bombers Attacking from Australia. By Howell Walker. LXXXIII, pp. 49-70, 19 ills., map, Jan., 1943

American Wings Soar Around the World: Epic Story of the Air Transport Command of the U. S. Army Is a Saga of Yankee Daring and Doing. By Donald H. Agnew and William A. Kinney. LXXXIV, pp. 57-78, 22 ills., July, 1943

Americans Stand Guard in Greenland. By Andrew H. Brown. XC, pp. 457-500, 23 ills. in black and white, 19 ills. in color, map, Oct., 1946

Cosmic Rays: Series of flights under auspices of National Geographic Society, U. S. Army Air Forces, and Bartol Research Foundation of the Franklin Institute. XC, p. 387, ill. p. 388, Sept., 1946

8th Air Force in England. 10 ills. in color from U. S. Army Air Forces official photos. LXXXVII, pp. 297-304, Mar., 1945

Exploring the Stratosphere. By Captain Albert W. Stevens. LXVI, pp. 397-434, 43 ills., chart, Oct., 1934

First natural-color photograph taken in the stratosphere. By Major Albert W. Stevens. LXXI, ill. p. 340, Mar., 1937

The First Photograph Ever Made Showing the Division Between the Troposphere and Stratosphere and also the Actual Curvature of the Earth. Aërial photo by Captain Albert W. Stevens. LXIX, supplement, May, 1936

Flying Our Wounded Veterans Home. By Catherine Bell Palmer. LXXXVIII, pp. 363-384, 17 ills., Sept., 1945

Gliders—Silent Weapons of the Sky. By William H. Nicholas. LXXXVI, pp. 149-160, 8 ills., Aug., 1944

U. S. ARMY AIR FORCES—*Continued*

Greens Grow for GI's on Soilless Ascension. By W. Robert Moore. LXXXVIII, pp. 219-230, 12 ills., Aug., 1945

How Latin America Looks from the Air: U. S. Army Airplanes Hurdle the High Andes, Brave Brazil Jungles, and Follow Smoking Volcanoes to Map New Sky Paths Around South America. By Major Herbert A. Dargue. LII, pp. 451-502, 52 ills., map, Oct., 1927

How We Fight with Photographs. By F. Barrows Colton. LXXXVI, pp. 257-280, 22 ills., Sept., 1944

Maneuvers of Military Planes Disclose Majestic Aërial Views. 7 ills. in duotone from U. S. Army official photos. LXIII, pp. 599-614, May, 1933

Man's Farthest Aloft: Rising to 13.71 Miles, the National Geographic Society-U. S. Army Stratosphere Expedition Gathers Scientific Data at Record Altitude. By Capt. Albert W. Stevens. LXIX, pp. 59-94, 39 ills., map, Jan., 1936

Included: Action Photographs of the Balloon's Perfect Landing

National Geographic Society-U. S. Army Air Corps Stratosphere Flight of 1935 in Balloon *Explorer II* (Contributed Technical Papers, *Stratosphere Series No. 2*). LXXI, p. 340, Mar., 1937; p. 802, June, 1937

New Frontier in the Sky. By F. Barrows Colton. XC, pp. 379-408, 28 ills., diagr., Sept., 1946

New Guinea's Mountain and Swampland Dwellers. By Col. Ray T. Elsmore. LXXXVIII, pp. 671-694, 15 ills. in black and white, 7 ills. in color, map, Dec., 1945

Included: References to the U. S. Army plane crash (May, 1945) and illustrations of the survivors

Our Air Frontier in Alaska. By Major General H. H. Arnold. LXXVIII, pp. 487-504, 15 ills., map, Oct., 1940

Photographing the Eclipse of 1932 from the Air: From Five Miles Above the Earth's Surface, the National Geographic Society-Army Air Corps Survey Obtains Successful Photographs of the Moon's Shadow. By Capt. Albert W. Stevens. LXII, pp. 581-596, 18 ills., Nov., 1932

Return to Florence (Italy). By 1st Lt. Benjamin C. McCartney. LXXXVII, pp. 257-296, 18 ills. in black and white, 18 ills. in color, Mar., 1945

They Sustain the Wings (Ground Crews). By Frederick Simpich. LXXXIV, pp. 333-354, 19 ills., Sept., 1943

World's Largest Free Balloon to Explore Stratosphere. LXVI, pp. 107-110, ills., July, 1934

Your Society Sponsors an Expedition to Explore the Stratosphere. LXV, pp. 528-530, ill., Apr., 1934

See also Air Carrier Contract Personnel; Civil Air Patrol; Women's AirForce Service Pilots (WASPS)

U. S. ARMY ENGINEERS:

Alaskan Highway an Engineering Epic: Mosquitoes, Mud, and Muskeg Minor Obstacles of 1,671-mile Race to Throw the Alcan Life Line Through Thick Forests and Uninhabited Wilderness. By Froelich Rainey. LXXXIII, pp. 143-168, 21 ills., 3 maps, Feb., 1943

U. S. ARMY ENGINEERS—*Continued*

An Army Engineer Explores Nicaragua: Mapping a Route for a New Canal Through the Largest of Central American Republics. By Lieut. Col. Dan I. Sultan. LXI, pp. 593-627, 39 ills., map, May, 1932

Ascension Island, an Engineering Victory. By Lt. Col. Frederick J. Clarke. LXXXV, pp. 623-640, 21 ills., May, 1944

Geographic Work of the General Government. By Henry Gannett. IX, pp. 329-338, July, 1898

Geographical Research in the United States. By Gardiner G. Hubbard and Marcus Baker. VIII, pp. 285-293, Oct., 1897

Greens Grow for GI's on Soilless Ascension. By W. Robert Moore. LXXXVIII, pp. 219-230, 12 ills., Aug., 1945

Men Against the Rivers (Mississippi and Ohio Rivers). By Frederick Simpich. LXXI, pp. 767-794, 22 ills., maps, June, 1937

More Water for California's Great Central Valley. By Frederick Simpich. XC, pp. 645-664, 16 ills., map, Nov., 1946

Stilwell Road—Land Route to China. By Nelson Grant Tayman. LXXXVII, pp. 681-698, 18 ills., June, 1945

Taming the Outlaw Missouri River. By Frederick Simpich. LXXXVIII, pp. 569-598, 25 ills., two-page map, Nov., 1945

U. S. ARMY MAP SERVICE:

The Making of Military Maps. By William H. Nicholas. LXXXIII, pp. 765-778, 17 ills., June, 1943

U. S. ARMY NURSE CORPS:

Flying Our Wounded Veterans Home. By Catherine Bell Palmer. LXXXVIII, pp. 363-384, 17 ills., Sept., 1945

Heroes' Return. By William H. Nicholas. LXXXVII, pp. 333-352, 19 ills., Mar., 1945

Women in Uniform. By La Verne Bradley. LXXXIV, pp. 445-458, 10 ills., Oct., 1943

U. S. ARMY QUARTERMASTER CORPS:

Fit to Fight Anywhere (Equipment Tests). By Frederick Simpich. LXXXIV, pp. 233-256, 26 ills., Aug., 1943

QM, the Fighting Storekeeper. By Frederick Simpich. Paintings by Arthur Beaumont. LXXXII, pp. 561-600, 22 ills. in black and white, 16 ills. in color, Nov., 1942

U. S. ARMY SIGNAL CORPS:

Geography of the Air. Annual Report by Vice-President, General A. W. Greely. IV, pp. 85-100, Mar. 18, 1892

U. S. Signal Corps. XIII, p. 407, Nov., 1902

The U. S. Signal Corps. (By Gilbert H. Grosvenor). XIV, pp. 467-468, Dec., 1903

The U. S. Signal Corps in Porto Rico. XI, p. 243, map, June, 1900

Winged Words—New Weapon of War. By F. Barrows Colton. LXXXII, pp. 663-692, 29 ills., maps, Nov., 1942

See also U. S. Signal Service, for Meteorological Work

U. S. ARMY TRANSPORTATION CORPS:

Heroes' Return. By William H. Nicholas. LXXXVII, pp. 333-352, 19 ills., Mar., 1945

U. S. ARMY TRANSPORTATION CORPS VESSELS:

Heroes of Wartime Science and Mercy. By Elizabeth W. King. LXXXIV, pp. 715-740, 11 ills. in black and white, 334 ills. in color, Dec., 1943

U. S. BOARD ON GEOGRAPHIC NAMES. *See* U. S. Geographic Board

U. S. BUREAU OF AMERICAN ETHNOLOGY:

Explorations by the Bureau of American Ethnology in 1895. By W J McGee. VII, pp. 77-80, Feb., 1896

Geographic Work by the Bureau of American Ethnology. (By W J McGee). IX, pp. 98-100, Mar., 1898

Seriland. By W J McGee and Willard D. Johnson. VII, pp. 125-133, ill., foldout map, Apr., 1896

Work of the Bureau of American Ethnology. By W J McGee. XII, pp. 369-372, Oct., 1901

U. S. BUREAU OF BIOLOGICAL SURVEY:

Bird Life Among Lava Rock and Coral Sand: The Chronicle of a Scientific Expedition to Little-known Islands of Hawaii. By Alexander Wetmore. XLVIII, pp. 77-108, 36 ills., map, July, 1925

Our Policemen of the Air. XXIV, p. 698, June, 1913

A Plague of Mice. XX, pp. 479-485, 7 ills., May, 1909

The Policemen of the Air: An Account of the Biological Survey of the Department of Agriculture. By Henry Wetherbee Henshaw. XIX, pp. 79-118, 38 ills., Feb., 1908

The United States Department of Agriculture and Its Biological Survey. (By J. H.). VII, pp. 405-406, Dec., 1896

U. S. BUREAU OF FISHERIES:

America's Surpassing Fisheries: Their Present Condition and Future Prospects, and How the Federal Government Fosters Them. By Hugh M. Smith. XXIX, pp. 546-583, 35 ills., June, 1916

The Bureau of Fisheries. By Dr. Barton Warren Evermann. XV, pp. 191-212, 11 ills., 3 diagrs., May, 1904

Federal Fish Farming; or, Planting Fish by the Billion. By Hugh M. Smith. XXI, pp. 418-446, 22 ills., May, 1910

Our Fish Immigrants. By Hugh M. Smith. XVIII, pp. 383-400, 3 ills., June, 1907

Planting Fishes in the Ocean. By George M. Bowers. XVIII, pp. 715-723, 5 ills., Nov., 1907

When the Father of Waters Goes on a Rampage: An Account of the Salvaging of Food-fishes from the Overflowed Lands of the Mississippi River. By Hugh M. Smith. XXXVII, pp. 369-386, 18 ills., Apr., 1920

U. S. BUREAU OF INSULAR AFFAIRS:

The Work of the Bureau of Insular Affairs. By Colonel Clarence R. Edwards. XV, pp. 239-255, 8 ills., June, 1904

U. S. BUREAU OF NAVIGATION:

On the Telegraphic Determinations of Longitude by the Bureau of Navigation. By Lieut. J. A. Norris, U.S.N. II, pp. 1-30, Apr., 1890

U. S. BUREAU OF RECLAMATION:

The Call of the West. By C. J. Blanchard. XX, pp. 403-437, 20 ills., map, May, 1909

Four Prominent Geographers. XVIII, pp. 425-428, 4 ills., June, 1907

Home-Making by the Government: An Account of the Eleven Immense Irrigating Projects to be Opened in 1908. By C. J. Blanchard. XIX, pp. 250-287, 23 ills., Apr., 1908

Millions for Moisture. By C. J. Blanchard. XVIII, pp. 217-243, 22 ills., Apr., 1907

More Water for California's Great Central Valley. By Frederick Simpich. XC, pp. 645-664, 16 ills., map, Nov., 1946

The Reclamation of the West. By F. H. Newell. XV, pp. 15-30, 6 ills., maps, Jan., 1904

The Spirit of the West: The Wonderful Agricultural Development Since the Dawn of Irrigation. By C. J. Blanchard. XXI, pp. 333-360, 15 ills., Apr., 1910

Two Great Undertakings (Work of U. S. Bureau of Reclamation and U. S. Forest Service). XVII, pp. 645-647, Nov., 1906

Winning the West. By C. J. Blanchard. XVII, pp. 82-98, 10 ills., map, Feb., 1906

U. S. BUREAU OF STANDARDS:

Observing an Eclipse in Asiatic Russia. By Irvine C. Gardner. LXXI, pp. 179-197, 19 ills. in black and white, ill. in color, Feb., 1937
First natural-color photo of an eclipse, showing the corona, by author, p. 178

A Wonderland of Science. XXVII, pp. 153-169, 15 ills., Feb., 1915

U. S. BUREAU OF THE CENSUS:

The Census of 1900. By Dr. F. H. Wines. XI, pp. 34-36, Jan., 1900

Geographic Work of the General Government. By Henry Gannett. IX, pp. 329-338, July, 1898

Statistics of Cities. XVI, p. 437, Sept., 1905

See also Census; Population

U. S. COAST AND GEODETIC SURVEY:

Annual Report of the Superintendent of the United States Coast and Geodetic Survey. VII, pp. 186-188, May, 1896

A Brief Account of the Geographic Work of the U. S. Coast and Geodetic Survey. By T. C. Mendenhall and Otto H. Tittmann. VIII, pp. 294-299, Oct., 1897

Charting a Coast-Line of 26,000 Miles (Alaska). XX, pp. 608-609, July, 1909

Charting a World at War. By William H. Nicholas. LXXXVI, pp. 617-640, 23 ills., drawing, Nov., 1944

The Coast and Geodetic Survey: Its Present Work. (By E. D. Preston). X, pp. 268-269, July, 1899

Geographic Work of the General Government. By Henry Gannett. IX, pp. 329-338, July, 1898

Geographical Research in the United States. By Gardiner G. Hubbard and Marcus Baker. VIII, pp. 285-293, Oct., 1897

Heroes of Wartime Science and Mercy. By Elizabeth W. King. LXXXIV, pp. 715-740, 11 ills. in black and white, 334 ills. in color, Dec., 1943

U. S. COAST AND GEODETIC SURVEY—*Continued*

Hidden Perils of the Deep. By G. R. Putnam. XX, pp. 822-837, 19 diagrs., 3 charts, Sept., 1909

Magnetic Work of the Coast and Geodetic Survey. By L. A. Bauer. X, pp. 288-289, Aug., 1899

Our Guardians on the Deep. By William Joseph Showalter. XXV, pp. 655-677, 15 ills., chart, June, 1914

Progress in Surveying the United States. By O. H. Tittmann. XVII, pp. 110-112, ill., Feb., 1906

Recent Contributions to Our Knowledge of the Earth's Shape and Size, by the United States Coast and Geodetic Survey. By C. A. Schott. XII, pp. 36-41, ill., chart, Jan., 1901

The San Francisco Earthquake of April 18, 1906, as Recorded by the Coast and Geodetic Survey Magnetic Observatories. By L. A. Bauer and J. E. Burbank. XVII, pp. 298-300, tables, May, 1906

The Survey of the Coast. By Herbert G. Ogden. I, pp. 59-77, Oct., 1888

Surveys and Maps of the District of Columbia. By Marcus Baker. VI, pp. 149-178, diagr., tables, map, Nov. 1, 1894
Included: List of Maps of Washington and the District of Columbia

The U. S. Coast and Geodetic Survey. By O. H. Tittmann. XIV, pp. 1-9, Jan., 1903

U. S. COAST GUARD:

The Great Mississippi Flood of 1927: Since White Man's Discovery This Mighty River Has Served Him Well, Yet It Has Brought Widespread Devastation Along Its Lower Reaches. By Frederick Simpich. LII, pp. 243-289, 53 ills., map, Sept., 1927

Life with Our Fighting Coast Guard. By F. Barrows Colton. LXXXIII, pp. 557-588, 22 ills. in black and white, 9 ills. in color, May, 1943

Standing Iceberg Guard in the North Atlantic: International Patrol Safeguards the Lives of Thousands of Travelers and Protects Trans-Atlantic Liners from a "Titanic" Fate. By Lieutenant Commander F. A. Zeusler. L, pp. 1-28, 29 ills., map, July, 1926

Uncle Sam's Icebox Outposts (Greenland). 19 color photos by John E. Schneider and Robert B. Sykes, Jr. XC, pp. 473-496, Oct., 1946

United States Navy, Marine Corps, and Coast Guard Insignia. LXXXIII, pp. 694-709, 5 ills. in black and white, 343 ills. in color, June, 1943

Your Dog Joins Up. By Frederick Simpich. LXXXIII, pp. 93-113, 25 ills., Jan., 1943

See also U. S. Revenue Cutter Service; Women's Reserve of the U. S. Coast Guard Reserve (SPARS)

U. S. COMMISSION OF FINE ARTS:

Washington, D. C. 32 ills. and 2 panoramas in color from illustrations from the Commission of Fine Arts. XXVII, pp. 245-276, map, Mar., 1915

U. S. DEFENSE BASES:

Alaska—Our Northwestern Outpost. 16 color photos by Ernest H. Gruening, Amos Burg, Froelich Rainey. LXXXII, pp. 297-308, Sept., 1942

Alaskan Highway an Engineering Epic: Mosquitoes, Mud, and Muskeg Minor Obstacles of 1,671-mile Race to Throw the Alcan Life Line Through Thick Forests and Uninhabited Wilderness. By Froelich Rainey. LXXXIII, pp. 143-168, 21 ills., 3 maps, Feb., 1943

American Soldier in Reykjavík. By Corporal Luther M. Chovan. LXXXVIII, pp. 536-568, 6 ills. in black and white, 34 ills. in color, Nov., 1945

Americans in the Caribbean. By Luis Marden. LXXXI, pp. 723-758, 16 ills. in black and white, 22 ills. in color, map, June, 1942

Americans Stand Guard in Greenland. By Andrew H. Brown. XC, pp. 457-500, 23 ills. in black and white, 19 ills. in color, map, Oct., 1946

America's New Crescent of Defense. 8 photos, map. LXXVIII, pp. 621-628, Nov., 1940

Ancient Iceland, New Pawn of War. 21 photos, map. LXXX, pp. 75-90, July, 1941

Ascension Island, an Engineering Victory. By Lt. Col. Frederick J. Clarke. LXXXV, pp. 623-640, 21 ills., May, 1944

Bizarre Battleground—the Lonely Aleutians. By Lonnelle Davison. LXXXII, pp. 316-317, ill., Sept., 1942

Coast Guard Patrol in Greenland. 9 color photos by Lieut. Thomas S. La Farge. LXXXIII, pp. 565-572, May, 1943

Desolate Greenland, Now an American Outpost. 17 photos: 12 by Willie Knutsen, 4 by F. Vogel. LXXX, pp. 393-406, Sept., 1941

Greenland Turns to America. By James K. Penfield. LXXXII, pp. 369-383, 7 ills. in black and white, 5 ills. in color, two-page map, Sept., 1942

Greens Grow for GI's on Soilless Ascension. By W. Robert Moore. LXXXVIII, pp. 219-230, 12 ills., Aug., 1945

Life on the Hawaii "Front": All-out Defense and Belt Tightening of Pacific Outposts Foreshadow the Things to Come on Mainland. By Lieut. Frederick Simpich, Jr. LXXXII, pp. 541-560, 19 ills., map, Oct., 1942

A Navy Artist Paints the Aleutians. By Mason Sutherland. Paintings by Lt. William F. Draper. LXXXIV, pp. 157-176, 4 ills. in black and white, 16 ills. in color, Aug., 1943

Newfoundland, North Atlantic Rampart: From the "First Base of American Defense" Planes Fly to Britain's Aid over Stout Fishing Schooners of the Grand Banks. By George Whiteley, Jr. LXXX, pp. 111-140, 26 ills., map, July, 1941

Our Air Frontier in Alaska. By Major General H. H. Arnold. LXXVIII, pp. 487-504, 15 ills., map, Oct., 1940

Servicing Arctic Airbases. By Robert A. Bartlett. LXXXIX, pp. 602-616, 3 ills. in black and white, 10 ills. in color, map, May, 1946

West Indies Links in a Defense Chain. 21 color photos: 20 by Edwin L. Wisherd. LXXIX, pp. 9-32, Jan., 1941

U. S. DEPARTMENT OF AGRICULTURE:

The Discovery of Cancer in Plants. XXIV, pp. 53-70, 12 ills., Jan., 1913

Geographic Work of the General Government. By Henry Gannett. IX, pp. 329-338, July, 1898

A Hunter of Plants. By David Fairchild. XXXVI, pp. 57-77, 18 ills., July, 1919

Hunting Useful Plants in the Caribbean. By David Fairchild. LXVI, pp. 705-737, 39 ills., Dec., 1934

Into Primeval Papua by Seaplane: Seeking Disease-resisting Sugar Cane, Scientists Find Neolithic Man in Unmapped Nooks of Sorcery and Cannibalism. By E. W. Brandes. LVI, pp. 253-332, 98 ills., map, Sept., 1929

The Modern Alchemist. By James Wilson. XVIII, pp. 781-795, 6 ills., Dec., 1907

New Plant Immigrants. By David Fairchild. XXII, pp. 879-907, 34 ills., Oct., 1911

Our Plant Immigrants. By David Fairchild. XVII, pp. 179-201, 29 ills., Apr., 1906

Peacetime Plant Hunting About Peiping. By P. H. and J. H. Dorsett. LXXII, pp. 509-534, 21 ills., map, Oct., 1937

Pests and Parasites. By Charles Lester Marlatt. XXII, pp. 321-346, 29 ills., maps, Apr., 1911

Protecting the United States from Plant Pests. By Charles Lester Marlatt. XL, pp. 205-218, 16 ills., Aug., 1921

Some of the Conditions and Possibilities of Agriculture in Alaska. By Walter H. Evans. IX, pp. 178-187, Apr., 1898

The United States Department of Agriculture and Its Biological Survey. (By J. H.). VII, pp. 405-406, Dec., 1896

What the United States Government Does to Promote Agriculture. XIV, pp. 35-39, Jan., 1903

See also U. S. Bureau of Biological Survey

U. S. FIRST AIR COMMANDO FORCE:

The Aerial Invasion of Burma. By General H. H. Arnold. LXXXVI, pp. 129-148, 20 ills., Aug., 1944

U. S. FOREST SERVICE:

Government Assistance in Handling Forest Lands. XV, pp. 450-452, Nov., 1904

Notes on the Eucalyptus Tree from the United States Forest Service. XX, pp. 668-673, 4 ills., July, 1909

Notes on the Forest Service. XVIII, pp. 142-145, 3 ills., Feb., 1907

Saving the Forests. By Herbert A. Smith. XVIII, pp. 519-534, 7 ills., tables, Aug., 1907

Two Great Undertakings (Work of U. S. Bureau of Reclamation and U. S. Forest Service). XVII, pp. 645-647, Nov., 1906

The Value of the United States Forest Service. XX, pp. 29-41, 14 ills., Jan., 1909

U. S. GEOGRAPHIC BOARD:

The American Board on Geographic Names. III, p. 39, Apr. 30, 1891

Decisions of the U. S. Board on Geographic Names. XI, pp. 478-480, Dec., 1900

Decisions of the U. S. Board on Geographic Names. XIII, pp. 178-179, May, 1902

U. S. GEOGRAPHIC BOARD—*Continued*

Decisions of the U. S. Board on Geographic Names. XIII, p. 329, Aug., 1902

Decisions of the U. S. Board on Geographic Names. XIII, p. 409, Nov., 1902

Decisions of the U. S. Board on Geographic Names. XIV, pp. 82-83, Feb., 1903

Decisions of the U. S. Board on Geographic Names. XIV, pp. 258-259, June, 1903

Decisions of the United States Board on Geographic Names. XV, pp. 49-50, Jan., 1904

Decisions of the U. S. Board on Geographic Names. XV, p. 501, Dec., 1904

Decisions of the U. S. Board on Geographic Names. XVI, pp. 358-359, July, 1905

Decisions of the United States Geographic Board. XVIII, p. 216, Mar., 1907

Decisions of U. S. Board on Geographic Names. XVI, pp. 131-132, Mar., 1905

Geographic Names. XII, p. 87, Feb., 1901

Geographic Names. XII, p. 125, Mar., 1901

Geographic Names. XII, p. 242, June, 1901

Geographic Nomenclature. Remarks by Herbert G. Ogden, Gustave Herrle, Marcus Baker, and A. H. Thompson. II, pp. 261-278, Aug., 1890

Geographical Aspects of the Monroe Doctrine. IX, pp. 476-477, Nov., 1898

The National Geographic Magazine and the U. S. Board on Geographic Names. (By J. H.). X, pp. 517-519, Dec., 1899

Recent Decisions of U. S. Board on Geographic Names. XIII, pp. 28-30, Jan., 1902

U. S. Board on Geographic Names. XI, pp. 329-330, Aug., 1900

The U. S. Board on Geographic Names. XII, p. 316, Aug., 1901

U. S. Board on Geographic Names. (By Theodore Roosevelt). XVII, p. 177, Mar., 1906

The U. S. Board on Geographic Names and Its Foreign Critics. (By H. G.). X, p. 16, Jan., 1899

United States Board on Geographic Names Changed to *United States Geographic Board* by executive order of President Theodore Roosevelt. XVII, p. 588, Oct., 1906

The Work of the United States Board on Geographic Names. By Henry Gannett. VII, pp. 221-227, July, 1896

U. S. GEOLOGICAL SURVEY:

The Central Great Plains. XVI, pp. 389-397, 8 ills., Aug., 1905

Down Idaho's River of No Return (Salmon River). By Philip J. Shenon and John C. Reed. LXX, pp. 95-136, 43 ills., maps, July, 1936

A Drowned Empire. By Robert H. Chapman. XIX, pp. 190-199, 10 ills., Mar., 1908

An Expedition to Mount St. Elias, Alaska. By Israel C. Russell. III, pp. 53-191, 17 ills., 3 diagrs., tables, 7 maps (1 foldout), May 29, 1891

Fieldwork of the United States Geological Survey for the Season 1902. XIII, pp. 322-325, Aug., 1902

The Five Civilized Tribes and the Survey of Indian Territory. By C. H. Fitch. IX, pp. 481-491, 4 ills., map, Dec., 1898

U. S. GEOLOGICAL SURVEY—*Continued*

For Teaching Physiography. XVIII, p. 353, May, 1907

Four Prominent Geographers. XVIII, pp. 425-428, 4 ills., June, 1907

Geographic Work of the General Government. By Henry Gannett. IX, pp. 329-338, July, 1898

Geographical Research in the United States. By Gardiner G. Hubbard and Marcus Baker. VIII, pp. 285-293, Oct., 1897

The Geologic Atlas of the United States. (By W J M.). IX, pp. 339-342, July, 1898

Geologic Folios in Schools. XVI, pp. 244-247, May, 1905

Hydrographic Work of the U. S. Geological Survey. XI, pp. 324-325, ill., Aug., 1900

Maps Recently Published by the U. S. Geological Survey. XVI, pp. 423-427, Sept., 1905

New Topographic Maps. XVIII, pp. 353-354, May, 1907; p. 686, Oct., 1907. XIX, p. 386, May, 1908

Recent Hydrographic Work. (By F. H. N.). VII, pp. 347-348, Oct., 1896

The Survey and Map of Massachusetts. By Henry Gannett. I, pp. 78-86, Oct., 1888

Survey of the Grand Canyon. XIV, pp. 162-163, Apr., 1903

Surveying the Grand Canyon of the Colorado: An Account of the 1923 Boating Expedition of the United States Geological Survey. By Lewis R. Freeman. XLV, pp. 471-548, 62 ills., map, May, 1924

The Topographic Atlas of the United States. (By W J M.). IX, pp. 343-344, July, 1898

Topographic Maps Issued by the Geological Survey in 1907. XIX, pp. 226-227, Mar., 1908

Topographic Work of the U. S. Geological Survey. XIII, pp. 326-328, Aug., 1902

Twenty-fifth Anniversary of the U. S. Geological Survey. XV, pp. 234-235, ill., May, 1904

What the U. S. Geological Survey Has Done in Twenty-five Years. XV, pp. 365-366, Sept., 1904

U. S. GOVERNMENT AGENCIES AND EMPLOYEES:

The Flags of Our Army, Navy, and Government Departments. By Byron McCandless and Gilbert Grosvenor. XXXII, pp. 305-322, ill. in black and white, 300 ills. in color, diagrs., 4 tables, Oct., 1917

Geographic Work of the General Government. By Henry Gannett. IX, pp. 329-338, July, 1898

Geographical Research in the United States. By Gardiner G. Hubbard and Marcus Baker. VIII, pp. 285-293, Oct., 1897

Wartime Washington. By William H. Nicholas. LXXXIV, pp. 257-290, 12 ills. in black and white, 16 ills. in color, Sept., 1943

See also National Geographic Magazine: Map Supplements (Various uses of the Society's map supplements)

U. S. HYDROGRAPHIC OFFICE:

The Drift of Floating Bottles in the Pacific Ocean. By James Page. XII, pp. 337-339, Sept., 1901

U. S. HYDROGRAPHIC OFFICE—*Continued*

Note: Research by this office concerning the surface currents of the sea

Geographic Work of the General Government. By Henry Gannett. IX, pp. 329-338, July, 1898

Geographical Research in the United States. By Gardiner G. Hubbard and Marcus Baker. VIII, pp. 285-293, Oct., 1897

The Work of the U. S. Hydrographic Office. By Commander W. H. H. Southerland. XIV, pp. 61-75, Feb., 1903

U. S. MARINE CORPS:

Aircraft Insignia, Spirit of Youth. By Gerard Hubbard. LXXXIII, pp. 710-722, 3 ills. in black and white, 337 ills. in color, June, 1943

Animals Were Allies, Too. 16 ills. LXXXIX, pp. 75-88, Jan., 1946

Flying Our Wounded Veterans Home. By Catherine Bell Palmer. LXXXVIII, pp. 363-384, 17 ills., Sept., 1945

Gilbert Islands in the Wake of Battle. By W. Robert Moore. LXXXVII, pp. 129-162, 11 ills. in black and white, 19 ills. in color, map, Feb., 1945

Jungle War: Bougainville and New Caledonia. 17 ills. in color from paintings by Lieut. William F. Draper. LXXXV, pp. 417-432, Apr., 1944

Okinawa, Threshold to Japan. By Lt. David D. Duncan, USMC. With 22 color photos by author and others. LXXXVIII, pp. 411-428, Oct., 1945

Palms and Planes in the New Hebrides. By Maj. Robert D. Heinl, Jr. LXXXVI, pp. 229-256, 17 ills. in black and white, 12 ills. in color, map, Aug., 1944

United States Navy, Marine Corps, and Coast Guard Insignia. LXXXIII, pp. 694-709, 5 ills. in black and white, 343 ills. in color, June, 1943

Victory's Portrait in the Marianas. By Lt. William Franklin Draper, USNR. With 17 ills. in color from paintings by author. LXXXVIII, pp. 599-616, Nov., 1945

Your Navy as Peace Insurance. By Fleet Admiral Chester W. Nimitz. LXXXIX, pp. 681-736, 32 ills. in black and white, 26 ills. in color, June, 1946

See also U. S. Marine Corps Women's Reserve

U. S. MARINE CORPS WOMEN'S RESERVE:

Decorations, Medals, Service Ribbons, Badges, and Women's Insignia. LXXXIV, pp. 414-444, 6 ills. in black and white, 376 ills. in color, Oct., 1943

Women in Uniform. By La Verne Bradley. LXXXIV, pp. 445-458, 10 ills., Oct., 1943

U. S. MARITIME SERVICE:

Heroes of Wartime Science and Mercy. By Elizabeth W. King. LXXXIV, pp. 715-740, 11 ills. in black and white, 334 ills. in color, Dec., 1943

U. S. MILITARY ACADEMY:

West Point and the Gray-Clad Corps. By Lieut. Col. Herman Beukema. LXIX, pp. 777-788, 10 ills. in color, June, 1936

UNITED States Military Insignia. LXXXIII, pp. 656-693, 7 ills. in black and white, 12 drawings, 311 ills. in color, June, 1943

U. S. NAVAL ACADEMY:

Annapolis, Cradle of the Navy. By Lieutenant Arthur A. Ageton. LXIX, pp. 789-800, 13 ills. in color, June, 1936

Old Line State Cyclorama. 22 color photos by W. Robert Moore, B. Anthony Stewart, and others. LXXIX, pp. 409-432, Apr., 1941

U. S. NAVAL AIR STATION, Lakehurst, New Jersey:

Aboard a Blimp Hunting U-boats: A Day above the Atlantic Reveals Navy Talk and Navy Ways, Creeping Convoys, and Torpedoed Wrecks. By Mason Sutherland. LXXXIV, pp. 79-96, 18 ills., July, 1943

U. S. NAVAL OBSERVATORY:

Chronometer and Time Service of the U. S. Naval Observatory and the Present Status of Standard Time. By Lieut. Comdr. Edward Everett Hayden. XV, pp. 430-431, Oct., 1904

The Special Telegraphic Time Signal from the Naval Observatory. XV, pp. 411-415, Oct., 1904

U. S. NAVY:

Aboard a Blimp Hunting U-boats: A Day above the Atlantic Reveals Navy Talk and Navy Ways, Creeping Convoys, and Torpedoed Wrecks. By Mason Sutherland. LXXXIV, pp. 79-96, 18 ills., July, 1943

Across the Equator with the American Navy. By Herbert Corey. XXXIX, pp. 571-624, 53 ills., June, 1921

Aircraft Insignia, Spirit of Youth. By Gerard Hubbard. LXXXIII, pp. 710-722, 3 ills. in black and white, 337 ills. in color, June, 1943

American Decoration, and Insignia of Honor and Service. By Col. Robert E. Wyllie. XXXVI, pp. 502-526, 6 ills. in black and white, 119 ills. in color, Dec., 1919

The Arctic Cruise of the U. S. S. Thetis in the Summer and Autumn of 1889. By Charles H. Stockton. II, pp. 171-198, ill., foldout map, July, 1890

The Azores: Picturesque and Historic Half-way House of American Transatlantic Aviators. By Arminius T. Haeberle. XXXV, pp. 514-545, 26 ills., map, June, 1919
Note: References to recent transatlantic flights; map showing route of the American seaplane NC-4; also, routes of the NC-1, NC-3, and the Hawker-Grieve Expedition

Battleship *Missouri* Comes of Age. 11 ills. in color from U. S. Navy official photos. LXXXVII, pp. 353-360, Mar., 1945

The Call to the Colors. 17 ills. XXXI, pp. 345-361, Apr., 1917

Collarin' Cape Cod (Massachusetts): Experiences on Board a U. S. Navy Destroyer in a Wild Winter Storm. By Lieutenant H. R. Thurber. XLVIII, pp. 427-472, 46 ills., Oct., 1925

Cruise on an Escort Carrier. By Melville Bell Grosvenor. LXXXIV, pp. 513-546, 14 ills. in black and white, 20 ills. in color, Nov., 1943

U. S. NAVY—*Continued*

Eclipse Adventures on a Desert Isle (Canton). By Capt. J. F. Hellweg. LXXII, pp. 377-394, 14 ills., map, Sept., 1937

Farewell to Bikini. By Carl Markwith. XC, pp. 97-116, 16 ills., July, 1946

The Flags of Our Army, Navy, and Government Departments. By Byron McCandless and Gilbert Grosvenor. XXXII, pp. 305-322, ill. in black and white, 300 ills. in color, diagrs., 4 tables, Oct., 1917

Flying Over the Arctic. By Lieutenant Commander Richard E. Byrd. XLVIII, pp. 519-532, 10 ills., Nov., 1925

The Gem of the Ocean: Our American Navy. By Josephus Daniels. XXXIII, pp. 313-335, 35 ills., Apr., 1918

Honors to the American Navy (National Geographic Society Banquet). XX, pp. 77-95, Jan., 1909

How We Fight with Photographs. By F. Barrows Colton. LXXXVI, pp. 257-280, 22 ills., Sept., 1944

The Insignia of the Uniformed Forces of the United States. By Byron McCandless and Gilbert Grosvenor. XXXII, pp. 413-419, 318 ills., Oct., 1917

Jungle War: Bougainville and New Caledonia. 17 ills. in color from paintings by Lieut. William F. Draper. LXXXV, pp. 417-432, Apr., 1944

Landing Craft for Invasion. By Melville Bell Grosvenor. LXXXVI, pp. 1-30, 26 ills., July, 1944

Life in Our Fighting Fleet. By F. Barrows Colton. LXXIX, pp. 671-702, 30 ills., June, 1941

The MacMillan Arctic Expedition Returns: U. S. Navy Planes Make First Series of Overland Flights in the Arctic and National Geographic Society Staff Obtains Valuable Data and Specimens for Scientific Study. By Donald B. MacMillan. XLVIII, pp. 477-518, 42 ills., Nov., 1925

Maneuvers of Military Planes Disclose Majestic Aërial Views. 10 ills. in duotone from U. S. Navy official photos. LXIII, pp. 599-614, May, 1933

Nature's Most Dramatic Spectacle (Eclipse). By S. A. Mitchell. LXXII, pp. 361-376, 16 ills., map, Sept., 1937

A Navy Artist Paints the Aleutians. By Mason Sutherland. Paintings by Lt. William F. Draper. LXXXIV, pp. 157-176, 4 ills. in black and white, 16 ills. in color, Aug., 1943

The New Queen of the Seas (Aircraft Carrier). By Melville Bell Grosvenor. LXXXII, pp. 1-30, 27 ills., drawing, two-page map, July, 1942

The North Sea Mine Barrage. By Capt. Reginald R. Belknap. XXXV, pp. 85-110, 23 ills., diagr., map, Feb., 1919

Painting History in the Pacific. 19 ills. in color from paintings by Lt. William F. Draper, USNR. LXXXVI, pp. 408-424, Oct., 1944

Palms and Planes in the New Hebrides. By Maj. Robert D. Heinl, Jr. LXXXVI, pp. 229-256, 17 ills. in black and white, 12 ills. in color, map, Aug., 1944

U. S. NAVY—*Continued*

The Removal of the North Sea Mine Barrage. By Lieutenant-Commander Noel Davis. XXXVII, pp. 103-133, 28 ills., maps, Feb., 1920

The Romance of Military Insignia: How the United States Government Recognizes Deeds of Heroism and Devotion to Duty. By Col. Robert E. Wyllie. XXXVI, pp. 463-501, 27 ills., Dec., 1919

Saga of the Carrier *Princeton*. By Capt. William H. Buracker, USN. LXXXVIII, pp. 189-218, 8 ills. in black and white, 22 ills. in color, map, Aug., 1945

San Francisco: Gibraltar of the West Coast. By La Verne Bradley. LXXXIII, pp. 279-308, 28 ills., Mar., 1943

Seeing America from the "Shenandoah": An Account of the Record-making 9,000-mile Flight from the Atlantic to the Pacific Coast and Return in the Navy's American-built, American-manned Airship. By Junius B. Wood. XLVII, pp. 1-47, 39 ills., diagr., map, Jan., 1925

Ships That Guard Our Ocean Ramparts. By F. Barrows Colton. Paintings by Arthur Beaumont. LXXX, pp. 328-337, 8 ills. in color, Sept., 1941

They Survived at Sea. By Lt. Comdr. Samuel F. Harby. LXXXVII, pp. 617-640, 22 ills., May, 1945

To Seek the Unknown in the Arctic: United States Navy Fliers to Aid MacMillan Expedition Under the Auspices of the National Geographic Society in Exploring Vast Area. XLVII, pp. 673-675, ill., map, June, 1925

Unfurling Old Glory on Canton Island. 11 ills. in color: 10 color photos and painting by Charles Bittinger. LXXIII, pp. 753-760, June, 1938

United States Navy, Marine Corps, and Coast Guard Insignia. LXXXIII, pp. 694-709, 5 ills. in black and white, 343 ills. in color, June, 1943

Victory's Portrait in the Marianas. By Lt. William Franklin Draper, USNR. With 17 ills. in color from paintings by author. LXXXVIII, pp. 599-616, Nov., 1945

Your Navy as Peace Insurance. By Fleet Admiral Chester W. Nimitz. LXXXIX, pp. 681-736, 32 ills. in black and white, 26 ills. in color, June, 1946

See also Naval Air Transport Service; U. S. Bureau of Navigation; U. S. Coast Guard; U. S. Hydrographic Office; U. S. Marine Corps; U. S. Naval Academy; U. S. Naval Observatory; U. S. Navy Nurse Corps; Women's Reserve of the U. S. Naval Reserve (WAVES)

UNITED States Navy, Marine Corps, and Coast Guard Insignia. LXXXIII, pp. 694-709, 5 ills. in black and white, 343 ills. in color, June, 1943

U. S. NAVY NURSE CORPS:

Flying Our Wounded Veterans Home. By Catherine Bell Palmer. LXXXVIII, pp. 363-384, 17 ills., Sept., 1945

Women in Uniform. By La Verne Bradley. LXXXIV, pp. 445-458, 10 ills., Oct., 1943

U. S. PUBLIC HEALTH SERVICE:

Heroes of Wartime Science and Mercy. By Elizabeth W. King. LXXXIV, pp. 715-740, 11 ills. in black and white, 334 ills. in color, Dec., 1943

U. S. RECLAMATION SERVICE. *See* U. S. Bureau of Reclamation

U. S. REVENUE CUTTER SERVICE:

The Arctic Cruise of the United States Revenue Cutter "Bear." By Dr. Sheldon Jackson. VII, pp. 27-31, 3 ills., Jan., 1896

U. S. Roads in War and Peace. By Frederick Simpich. LXXX, pp. 687-716, 27 ills., Dec., 1941

U. S. SHIPPING BOARD:

The American People Must Become Ship-Minded. By Edward N. Hurley. XXXIV, pp. 201-211, 7 ills., Sept., 1918

Ships for the Seven Seas: The Story of America's Maritime Needs, Her Capabilities and Her Achievements. By Ralph A. Graves. XXXIV, pp. 165-200, 24 ills., Sept., 1918

U. S. SIGNAL CORPS. *See* U. S. Army Signal Corps; *and* articles *following,* for Meteorological Work

U. S. SIGNAL SERVICE:

Geography of the Air. Annual Report by Vice-President A. W. Greely. III, pp. 41-52, May 1, 1891

Geography of the Air. Annual Report by Vice-President, General A. W. Greely. IV, pp. 85-100, Mar. 18, 1892

The Weather Bureau River and Flood System. By Professor Willis L. Moore. VII, pp. 302-307, Sept., 1896

See also U. S. Army Signal Corps; U. S. Weather Bureau

U. S. WAR AGENCIES. *See* War Agencies

U. S. WEATHER BUREAU:

Forecasting the Weather and Storms. By Professor Willis L. Moore. XVI, pp. 255-305, 5 ills., 20 charts, June, 1905

Geographic Work of the General Government. By Henry Gannett. IX, pp. 329-338, July, 1898

Geographical Research in the United States. By Gardiner G. Hubbard and Marcus Baker. VIII, pp. 285-293, Oct., 1897

The International Cloud Work of the Weather Bureau. By Frank H. Bigelow. X, pp. 351-354, Sept., 1899

Kite Work of the Weather Bureau. By H. C. Frankenfield. XI, pp. 55-62, Feb., 1900

Loss of Life by Lightning. XIII, p. 115, Mar., 1902

Loss of Property from Lightning. XII, p. 82, Feb., 1901

Our Heralds of Storm and Flood. By Gilbert H. Grosvenor. XVIII, pp. 586-601, 15 ills., chart, Sept., 1907

The Record of the Great Earthquake Written in Washington by the Seismograph of the U. S. Weather Bureau. By C. F. Marvin. XVII, pp. 296-298, May, 1906

Scientific Work of Mount Weather Meteorological Research Observatory. By Professor Frank H. Bigelow. XV, pp. 442-445, Nov., 1904

U. S. WEATHER BUREAU—*Continued*

United States Daily Atmospheric Survey. By Prof. Willis L. Moore. VIII, pp. 299-303, Oct., 1897

U. S. Weather Bureau. XIII, pp. 71-72, Feb., 1902

The U. S. Weather Bureau. By James Wilson. XV, pp. 37-39, Jan., 1904

The U. S. Weather Bureau at the Paris Exposition. XII, pp. 81-82, Feb., 1901

The Weather Bureau. By Willis L. Moore. XII, pp. 362-369, Oct., 1901

The Weather Bureau and the Recent Floods. By H. C. Frankenfield. XIV, pp. 285-290, ills., July, 1903

The Weather Bureau River and Flood System. By Professor Willis L. Moore. VII, pp. 302-307, Sept., 1896

See also U. S. Signal Service

UNIVERSITIES AND COLLEGES:

American Alma Maters in the Near East. By Maynard Owen Williams. LXXXVIII, pp. 237-256, 16 ills., Aug., 1945

Contents: American University at Cairo; American University of Beirut; Istanbul Woman's College; Robert College

Geography in the University of Chicago. XIV, pp. 163-164, Apr., 1903

The Long River of New England: In War and Peace, from Mountain Wilderness to the Sea, Flows the Connecticut River, Through a Valley Abounding in History, Scenery, Inventive Genius, and Industry. By Albert W. Atwood. LXXXIII, pp. 401-434, 12 ills. in black and white, 24 ills. in color, map, Apr., 1943

Included: Amherst College; Dartmouth College; Mount Holyoke College; Smith College; Wesleyan University; Yale University

Oxford, Mother of Anglo-Saxon Learning. By E. John Long. LVI, pp. 563-596, 31 ills., Nov., 1929

A Texan Teaches American History at Cambridge University. By J. Frank Dobie. LXXXIX, pp. 409-441, 9 ills. in black and white, 19 ills. in color, Apr., 1946

Within the Halls of Cambridge (England). By Philip Broad. LXX, pp. 333-349, 7 ills. in black and white, 12 ills. in color, Sept., 1936

See also Cornell University; Harvard University; Johns Hopkins University; Lingnan University; *and* State Survey Articles

UNKNOWN Japan: A Portrait of the People Who Make Up One of the Two Most Fanatical Nations of the World. By Willard Price. LXXXII, pp. 225-252, 30 ills., Aug., 1942

UNKNOWN New Guinea: Circumnavigating the World in a Flying Boat, American Scientists Discover a Valley of 60,000 People Never Before Seen by White Men. By Richard Archbold. LXXIX, pp. 315-344, 28 ills., map, Mar., 1941

UNSPOILED Cyprus: The Traditional Island Birthplace of Venus Is One of the Least Sophisticated of Mediterranean Lands. By Maynard Owen Williams. LIV, pp. 1-55, 55 ills. in black and white, 10 ills. in color, map, July, 1928

UNTOUCHABLES:

India Mosaic. By Peter Muir and Frances Muir. LXXXIX, pp. 409-441, 9 ills. in black and white, 22 ills. in color, map, Apr., 1946

UNTOURED Burma. By Charles H. Bartlett. XXIV, pp. 835-853, 17 ills., July, 1913

UP and Down on Saba (Island). 12 color photos by Charles W. Herbert. LXXVIII, pp. 605-612, Nov., 1940

UR (Ancient City):

Archeology, the Mirror of the Ages: Our Debt to the Humble Delvers in the Ruins at Carchemish and at Ur. By C. Leonard Woolley. LIV, pp. 207-226, 19 ills., Aug., 1928

New Light on Ancient Ur: Excavations at the Site of the City of Abraham Reveal Geographical Evidence of the Biblical Story of the Flood. By M. E. L. Mallowan. LVII, pp. 95-130, 44 ills., map, Jan., 1930

URARI (Poison):

Fishing and Hunting Tales from Brazil. By Dewey Austin Cobb. XX, pp. 917-920, Oct., 1909

URBAN Population of United States. XII, pp. 345-346, Sept., 1901

URGA, Outer Mongolia:

The Lama's Motor-Car: A Trip Across the Gobi Desert by Motor-Car. By Ethan C. Le Munyon. XXIV, pp. 641-670, 34 ills., May, 1913

URGUB, Turkey:

Peculiar Caves of Asia Minor. By Elizabeth H. Brewer. XXII, pp. 870-875, 5 ills., Sept., 1911

USBR. *See* U. S. Bureau of Reclamation

USEFUL Facts About the Countries of the World. XVIII, pp. 424-425, June, 1907

USHER, ROLAND G.:

The Oldest Nation of Europe: Geographical Factors in the Strength of Modern England. By Roland G. Usher. XXVI, pp. 393-414, 11 ills., Oct., 1914

UTAH:

Beyond the Clay Hills: An Account of the National Geographic Society's Reconnaissance of a Previously Unexplored Section in Utah. By Neil M. Judd. XLV, pp. 275-302, 28 ills., map, Mar., 1924

Colossal Natural Bridges of Utah. XV, pp. 367-369, ills., Sept., 1904

Encircling Navajo Mountain with a Pack-Train: An Expedition to a Hitherto Untraversed Region of Our Southwest Discovers a New Route to Rainbow Natural Bridge. By Charles L. Bernheimer. XLIII, pp. 197-224, 33 ills., map, Feb., 1923

Experiences in the Grand Canyon. By Ellsworth and Emery Kolb. XXVI, pp. 99-184, 70 ills., map, Aug., 1914

Flaming Cliffs of Monument Valley. By Lt. Jack Breed, USNR. With 9 color photos by author and Warren T. Mithoff. LXXXVIII, pp. 452-461, Oct., 1945

UTAH—*Continued*

The Great Natural Bridges of Utah. XVIII, pp. 199-204, 3 ills., Mar., 1907

The Great Natural Bridges of Utah. By Byron Cummings. XXI, pp. 157-167, 7 ills., Feb., 1910

The Great Rainbow Natural Bridge of Southern Utah. By Joseph E. Pogue. XXII, pp. 1048-1056, 6 ills., Nov., 1911

Utah, Carved by Winds and Waters: The Beehive State, Settled Only 89 Years Ago, Stands a Monument to the Courage of Its Founders. By Leo A. Borah. LXIX, pp. 577-623, 20 ills. in black and white, 22 ills. in color, two-page map, May, 1936

Why Great Salt Lake Has Fallen. By L. H. Murdoch. XIV, pp. 75-77, Feb., 1903

The **UTILIZATION** of the Vacant Public Lands. By Emory F. Best. VIII, pp. 49-57, Feb., 1897

UTRECHT, Netherlands:

Holland Rises from War and Water. By Thomas R. Henry. LXXXIX, pp. 237-260, 18 ills., map, Feb., 1946

UZBEK SOVIET SOCIALIST REPUBLIC, U. S. S. R.:

The Land of Lambskins: An Expedition to Bokhara, Russian Central Asia, to Study the Karakul Sheep Industry. By Robert K. Nabours. XXXVI, pp. 77-88, 15 ills., July, 1919

New Road to Asia. By Owen Lattimore. LXXXVI, pp. 641-676, 15 ills. in black and white, 26 ills. in color, Dec., 1944

Russia's Orphan Races: Picturesque Peoples Who Cluster on the Southeastern Borderland of the Vast Slav Dominions. By Maynard Owen Williams. XXXIV, pp. 245-278, 26 ills., map, Oct., 1918

Where Slav and Mongol Meet. 16 ills. in color. XXXVI, pp. 421-436, Nov., 1919

V

V-1 (Buzz Bomb):

Air Power for Peace. By General H. H. Arnold. LXXXIX, pp. 137-193, 35 ills. in black and white, 28 ills. in color, map supplement, Feb., 1946

London Wins the Battle. By Marquis W. Childs. LXXXVIII, pp. 129-152, 21 ills., Aug., 1945

V-2 (Rocket):

Air Power for Peace. By General H. H. Arnold. LXXXIX, pp. 137-193, 35 ills. in black and white, 28 ills. in color, map supplement, Feb., 1946

London Wins the Battle. By Marquis W. Childs. LXXXVIII, pp. 129-152, 21 ills., Aug., 1945

New Frontier in the Sky. By F. Barrows Colton. XC, pp. 379-408, 28 ills., diagr., Sept., 1946

A **VACATION** in a Fifteenth Century English Manor House. By George Alden Sanford. LIII, pp. 629-636, 8 ills., May, 1928

A **VACATION** in Holland. By George Alden Sanford. LVI, pp. 363-378, 6 ills. in black and white, 8 ills. in color, map, Sept., 1929

VAGABONDING in England: A Young American Works His Way Around the British Isles and Sees Sights from an Unusual Point of View. By John McWilliams. LXV, pp. 357-398, 39 ills., map, Mar., 1934

VAI (Tribespeople):

The Land of the Free in Africa. By Harry A. McBride. XLII, pp. 411-430, 22 ills., Oct., 1922

VAIL, THEODORE N.:

Voice Voyages by the National Geographic Society: A Tribute to the Geographical Achievements of the Telephone (Address by Theodore N. Vail). XXIX, pp. 296-326, 15 ills., chart, Mar., 1916

VALAIS (Canton), Switzerland:

In Valais. By Louise Murray. XXI, pp. 249-256, 6 ills., Mar., 1910

VÂLCOV, Romania:

Caviar Fishermen of Romania: From Vâlcov, "Little Venice" of the Danube Delta, Bearded Russian Exiles Go Down to the Sea. By Dorothy Hosmer. LXXVII, pp. 407-434, 29 ills., map, Mar., 1940

VALDEZ, Alaska:

The National Geographic Society's Alaskan Expedition of 1909. By Ralph S. Tarr and Lawrence Martin. XXI, pp. 1-54, 42 ills., 12 maps, Jan., 1910

VALLEY OF TEN THOUSAND SMOKES, Alaska:

Our Greatest National Monument: The National Geographic Society Completes Its Explorations in the Valley of Ten Thousand Smokes. By Robert F. Griggs. XL, pp. 219-292, 73 ills. in black and white, 16 ills. in color, maps, Sept., 1921

The Ten Thousand Smokes Now a National Monument: The President of the United States Sets Aside for the American People the Extraordinary Valley Discovered and Explored by the National Geographic Society. XXXV, pp. 359-366, 5 ills., Apr., 1919

The Valley of Ten Thousand Smokes: An Account of the Discovery and Exploration of the Most Wonderful Volcanic Region in the World. By Robert F. Griggs. XXXIII, pp. 115-169, 46 ills., map, panorama, Feb., 1918

The Awe-Inspiring Spectacle of the Valley of Ten Thousand Smokes, Discovered and Explored by National Geographic Society Expeditions (panorama)

The Valley of Ten Thousand Smokes: National Geographic Society Explorations in the Katmai District of Alaska. By Robert F. Griggs. XXXI, pp. 13-68, 51 ills., map, Jan., 1917

The **VALLEY** of the Orinoco (Venezuela). By T. H. Gignilliat. Text with map supplement. VII, p. 92, Feb., 1896

VALLEYS:

The Rivers and Valleys of Pennsylvania. By William Morris Davis. I, pp. 183-253, 25 ills., map, July, 1889

See also names of countries and rivers

VALPARAISO, Chile:
Capital and Chief Seaport of Chile. By W. Robert Moore. LXXXVI, pp. 477-500, 15 ills. in black and white, 8 ills. in color, map, Oct., 1944
From Panama to Patagonia. By Charles M. Pepper. XVII, pp. 449-452, ill., Aug., 1906
A Longitudinal Journey Through Chile. By Harriet Chalmers Adams. XLII, pp. 219-273, 60 ills., map, Sept., 1922
Twin Stars of Chile: Valparaiso, the Gateway, and Santiago, the Capital—Key Cities with a Progressive Present and a Romantic Past. By William Joseph Showalter. LV, pp. 197-247, 35 ills. in black and white, 25 ills. in color, Feb., 1929

The **VALUE** of Arctic Exploration. By Commander Robert E. Peary. XIV, pp. 429-436, Dec., 1903

The **VALUE** of the United States Forest Service. XX, pp. 29-41, 14 ills., Jan., 1909

VAN, Turkey:
Between Massacres in Van (Armenia). By Maynard Owen Williams. XXXVI, pp. 181-184, 3 ills., Aug., 1919

VANDERCOOK, JOHN W.:
The Mandate of Cameroun: A Vast African Territory Ruled by Petty Sultans Under French Sway. By John W. Vandercook. LIX, pp. 225-260, 49 ills., map, Feb., 1931

VANDERLIP, F. A.:
The World's Production of Gold (From an Address to the American Bankers' Convention by F. A. Vanderlip, October 11, 1905). XVI, pp. 571-572, Dec., 1905

VAN DER MEULEN, D.:
Into Burning Hadhramaut: The Arab Land of Frankincense and Myrrh, Ever a Lodestone of Western Explorations. By D. van der Meulen. LXII, pp. 387-429, 44 ills., map, Oct., 1932

VAN ESS, JOHN:
Forty Years Among the Arabs. By John Van Ess. LXXXII, pp. 385-420, 27 ills., two-page map, Sept., 1942

VAN HORN RANGE (Canadian Rockies), Summits above 9500 Ft. Panorama from photo by Charles D. Walcott. XXII, text, p. 521; ill. p. 520; panorama, June, 1911

A VANISHING People of the South Seas: The Tragic Fate of the Marquesan Cannibals, Noted for their Warlike Courage and Physical Beauty. By John W. Church. XXXVI, pp. 275-306, 22 ills., map, Oct., 1919

VAN LOON, HENRIK WILLEM:
The Citizen Army of Holland. By Henrik Willem Van Loon. XXIX, pp. 609-622, 9 ills., June, 1916

VAN ZANDT, J. PARKER:
Looking Down on Europe: The Thrills and Advantages of Sight-seeing by Airplane, as Demonstrated on a 6,500-mile Tour Over Commercial Aviation Routes. By Lieutenant J. Parker Van Zandt. XLVII, pp. 261-326, 67 ills., map, Mar., 1925

VAN ZANDT, J. PARKER—*Continued*
Looking Down on Europe Again: Crisscrossing Air Tracks Reveal Nature's Scenic Masterpieces and Man's Swift-changing Boundaries and Structures. By J. Parker Van Zandt. LXXV, pp. 791-822, 31 ills., map, June, 1939
On the Trail of the Air Mail. A Narrative of the Experiences of the Flying Couriers Who Relay the Mail Across America at a Speed of More than 2,000 Miles a Day. By Lieut. J. Parker Van Zandt. XLIX, pp. 1-61, 67 ills., map, Jan., 1926

VARIATIONS in Lake Levels and Atmospheric Precipitation. By Alfred J. Henry. X, pp. 403-406, diagr., Oct., 1899

VASCO DA GAMA. *See* Gama, Vasco da

VASCO da Gama at the Court of the Zamorin of Calicut. Reproduction in color of the painting by José Velloso Salgado, Sociedade de Geographia de Lisboa. LII, supplement, Nov., 1927

The **VAST** Timber Belts of Canada. XVII, pp. 509-511, Sept., 1906

VATICAN CITY:
Recent Disclosures Concerning Pre-Columbian Voyages to America in the Archives of the Vatican. By William Eleroy Curtis. V, pp. 197-234, Jan. 31, 1894
The Smallest State in the World: Vatican City on Its 108 Acres Is a Complete Sovereignty Internationally Recognized. By W. Coleman Nevils. LXXV, pp. 377-412, 37 ills., two-page map, Mar., 1939

VATICAN City: Treasure House of the Ages. 8 ills. LXXV, pp. 393-400, Mar., 1939

VATOPÉTHI (Monastery), Greece:
The Hoary Monasteries of Mt. Athos. By H. G. Dwight. XXX, pp. 249-272, 24 ills., map, Sept., 1916

VEGETABLES:
America Fights on the Farms. 21 ills. in color. LXXXVI, pp. 33-48, July, 1944
Black Acres (Mucklands of New York): A Thrilling Sketch in the Vast Volume of Who's Who Among the Peoples That Make America. By Dorothea D. and Fred Everett. LXXX, pp. 631-652, 13 ills. in black and white, 12 ills. in color, Nov., 1941
Farmers Keep Them Eating. By Frederick Simpich. LXXXIII, pp. 435-458, 22 ills., Apr., 1943
Fruitful Shores of the Finger Lakes (New York). By Harrison Howell Walker. LXXIX, pp. 559-594, 15 ills. in black and white, 22 ills. in color, map, May, 1941
Greens Grow for GI's on Soilless Ascension. By W. Robert Moore. LXXXVIII, pp. 219-230, 12 ills., Aug., 1945
More Water for California's Great Central Valley. By Frederick Simpich. XC, pp. 645-664, 16 ills., map, Nov., 1946
The Texas Delta of an American Nile: Orchards and Gardens Replace Thorny Jungle in the Southmost Tip of the Lone Star State. By McFall Kerbey. LXXV, pp. 51-96, 27 ills. in black and white, 24 ills. in color, map, Jan., 1939

VEGETABLES, Dried:

Forming New Fashions in Food: The Bearing of Taste on One of Our Great Food Economies, the Dried Vegetable, Which Is Developing Into a Big War Industry. By David Fairchild. XXXIII, pp. 356-368, 11 ills., Apr., 1918

Reviving a Lost Art (Drying Fruits and Vegetables). XXXI, pp. 475-481, 9 ills., June, 1917

VENEZUELA:

The Anglo-Venezuelan Boundary Dispute. By Marcus Baker. XI, pp. 129-144, ills., map, Apr., 1900

The Countries of the Caribbean. By William Joseph Showalter. XXIV, pp. 227-250, 23 ills., Feb., 1913

I Kept House in a Jungle: The Spell of Primeval Tropics in Venezuela, Riotous With Strange Plants, Animals, and Snakes, Enthralls a Young American Woman. By Anne Rainey Langley. LXXV, pp. 97-132, 37 ills., map, Jan., 1939

In Humboldt's Wake: Narrative of a National Geographic Society Expedition Up the Orinoco and Through the Strange Casiquiare Canal to Amazonian Waters. By Ernest G. Holt. LX, pp. 621-644, 27 ills., map, Nov., 1931

A Journey by Jungle Rivers to the Home of the Cock-of-the-rock: Naturalists Enter the Amazon, Voyage Through the Heart of Tropical South America, and Emerge at the Mouth of the Orinoco. By Ernest G. Holt. LXIV, pp. 585-630, 49 ills., map, Nov., 1933

Some Notes on Venezuela. XIV, pp. 17-21, 3 ills., map, Jan., 1903

Three Old Ports on the Spanish Main. By G. M. L. Brown. XVII, pp. 622-638, 12 ills., Nov., 1906

The Valley of the Orinoco. By T. H. Gignilliat. Text with map supplement. VII, p. 92, Feb., 1896

Venezuela: Her Government, People, and Boundary. By William E. Curtis. VII, pp. 49-58, 3 ills., map supplement, Feb., 1896

The Venezuelan Boundary Commission and Its Work. By Marcus Baker. VIII, pp. 193-201, July-Aug., 1897

See also Caracas

The **VENEZUELAN** Boundary Commission and Its Work. By Marcus Baker. VIII, pp. 193-201, July-Aug., 1897

VENEZUELA'S Capital—City of Contrasts. 19 color photos by Luis Marden. LXXVII, pp. 483-506, Apr., 1940

VENICE, Italy:

Frontier Cities of Italy. By Florence Craig Albrecht. XXVII, pp. 533-586, 45 ills., June, 1915

The Geography of Medicines: War's Effect Upon the World's Sources of Supply. By John Foote. XXXII, pp. 213-238, 26 ills., Sept., 1917

Northern Italy: Scenic Battleground. 18 color photos: 13 by B. Anthony Stewart, 3 by Lt. Benjamin C. McCartney. LXXXVII, pp. 265-288, Mar., 1945

Republics—The Ladder to Liberty. By David Jayne Hill. XXXI, pp. 240-254, 5 ills., maps, Mar., 1917

VENICE, Italy—*Continued*

Venice. By Karl Stieler. XXVII, pp. 587-630, 42 ills., maps, June, 1915

Venice: Home City of Marco Polo. 8 ills. LIV, pp. 559-566, Nov., 1928

The **VENICE** of Mexico (Aztec Lake Country). By Walter Hough. XXX, pp. 69-88, 18 ills., July, 1916

VENIZELOS, ELEUTHERIOS:

Greece and Montenegro. By George Higgins Moses. XXIV, pp. 281-310, 24 ills., Mar., 1913

VERACRUZ (State), Mexico:

Discovering the New World's Oldest Dated Work of Man: A Mayan Monument Inscribed 291 B. C. is Unearthed Near a Huge Stone Head by a Geographic-Smithsonian Expedition in Mexico. By Matthew W. Stirling. LXXVI, pp. 183-218, 40 ills., map, Aug., 1939

Expedition Unearths Buried Masterpieces of Carved Jade. By Matthew W. Stirling. LXXX, pp. 277-302, 14 ills. in black and white, 20 ills. in color, map, Sept., 1941

Great Stone Faces of the Mexican Jungle: Five Colossal Heads and Numerous Other Monuments of Vanished Americans Are Excavated by the Latest National Geographic-Smithsonian Expedition. By Matthew W. Stirling. LXXVIII, pp. 309-334, 26 ills., map, Sept., 1940

Jungle Housekeeping for a Geographic Expedition. By Marion Stirling. LXXX, pp. 303-327, 15 ills., Sept., 1941

A Naturalist's Journey Around Vera Cruz and Tampico. By Frank M. Chapman. XXV, pp. 533-562, 31 ills., May, 1914

Wildlife of Tabasco and Vera Cruz. By Walter A. Weber. With 19 ills. in color from paintings by author. LXXXVII, pp. 187-216, 7 ills. in black and white, map, Feb., 1945

VERGIL:

The Perennial Geographer: After 2,000 Years Vergil Is Still the Most Widely Read of Latin Poets—First to Popularize the Geography of the Roman Empire. By W. Coleman Nevils. LVIII, pp. 439-465, 29 ills., Oct., 1930

VERHOOGEN, JEAN:

We Keep House on an Active Volcano: After Flying to Study a Spectacular Eruption in Belgian Congo, a Geologist Settles Down on a Newborn Craterless Vent for Eight Months' Study. By Dr. Jean Verhoogen. LXXVI, pp. 511-550, 28 ills., map, Oct., 1939

VERMONT:

The Green Mountain State. By Herbert Corey. LI, pp. 333-369, 40 ills. in black and white, 6 ills. in color, map, Mar., 1927

The Long River of New England: In War and Peace, from Mountain Wilderness to the Sea, Flows the Connecticut River, Through a Valley Abounding in History, Scenery, Inventive Genius, and Industry. By Albert W. Atwood. LXXXIII, pp. 401-434, 12 ills. in black and white, 24 ills. in color, map, Apr., 1943

New England's Wonderland of Mountain, Lake, and Seascape. 5 color photos by Clifton Adams. LX, pp. 263-270, Sept., 1931

VERNER, SAMUEL P.:
Some Peculiar Features of Central African Geography. (By Samuel P. Verner). XV, p. 448, Nov., 1904

VERONA, Italy:
Frontier Cities of Italy. By Florence Craig Albrecht. XXVII, pp. 533-586, 45 ills., June, 1915

VERSAILLES (Palace), France:
From the Trenches to Versailles. By Carol Corey. XXXII, pp. 535-550, 12 ills., Nov.-Dec., 1917
The Palace of Versailles, Its Park and the Trianons. By Franklin L. Fisher. XLVII, pp. 49-62, 4 ills. in black and white, 14 ills. in color, Jan., 1925

VERSAILLES the Magnificent. 14 color photos by Gervais Courtellemont. XLVII, pp. 53-60, Jan., 1925

VEST SPITSBERGEN (Island). *See* Spitsbergen

VESUVIUS (Volcano), Italy:
Behind the Lines in Italy. By Corporal Macon Reed, Jr. LXXXVI, pp. 109-128, 20 ills., July, 1944
The Eruption of Mount Vesuvius, April 7-8, 1906. By Thomas Augustus Jaggar, Jr. XVII, pp. 318-325, 6 ills., June, 1906
Mount Vesuvius. XVII, pp. 272-279, 7 ills., map, May, 1906

VIALLES, ANDRÉ:
Camargue, the Cowboy Country of Southern France. By Dr. André Vialles. XLII, pp. 1-34, 33 ills., map, July, 1922

VICTORIA, British Columbia, Canada:
Factors Which Modify the Climate of Victoria. By Arthur W. McCurdy. XVIII, pp. 345-348, maps, May, 1907

VICTORIA, Lake, East Africa:
A Great African Lake. By Sir Henry M. Stanley. XIII, pp. 169-172, map, May, 1902
Where Roosevelt Will Hunt. By Sir Harry Johnston. XX, pp. 207-256, 43 ills., map supplement, Mar., 1909

VICTORIA FALLS, South Central Africa:
Rhodesia, Hobby and Hope of Cecil Rhodes. By W. Robert Moore. LXXXVI, pp. 281-306, 13 ills. in black and white, 10 ills. in color, map, Sept., 1944
The Wonders of the Mosi-oa-Tunga: The Falls of the Zambesi. By Louis Livingston Seaman. XXII, pp. 561-571, 6 ills., June, 1911
The World's Great Waterfalls: Visits to Mighty Niagara, Wonderful Victoria, and Picturesque Iguazu. By Theodore W. Noyes. L, pp. 29-59, 29 ills., July, 1926

VICTORIA ISLAND, N.W.T., Canada:
The Origin of Stefansson's Blond Eskimo. By Major General A. W. Greely. XXIII, pp. 1225-1238, 10 ills., map, Dec., 1912

VICTORY'S Portrait in the Marianas. By Lt. William Franklin Draper, USNR. With 17 ills. in color from paintings by author. LXXXVIII, pp. 599-616, Nov., 1945

VICUÑAS:
Camels of the Clouds. By W. H. Hodge. LXXXIX, pp. 641-656, 15 ills., map, May, 1946

VIENNA, Austria:
A Tale of Three Cities. By Thomas R. Henry. LXXXVIII, pp. 641-669, 23 ills., Dec., 1945
Vienna—A Capital Without a Nation. By Solita Solano. XLIII, pp. 77-102, 27 ills., Jan., 1923

VIEWS and Hues of the Sunflower State (Kansas). 12 color photos by Richard H. Stewart. LXXII, pp. 151-158, Aug., 1937

VIEWS from Mexico. 8 ills. XLII, pp. 461-468, Nov., 1922

VIEWS of Lhasa (Tibet). 11 ills. XVI, pp. 27-38, Jan., 1905

VIEWS of the Lincoln Memorial in Washington. 8 ills. XLII, pp. 197-204, Aug., 1922

VIGNETTES of Guadalajara (Mexico). By Frederick Simpich. LXV, pp. 329-356, 20 ills. in black and white, 15 ills. in color, map, Mar., 1934

VIKING Life in the Storm-Cursed Faeroes. By Leo Hansen. LVIII, pp. 607-648, 49 ills., map, Nov., 1930

VIKINGS. *See* Norsemen

VILA, Efate (Island), New Hebrides:
Palms and Planes in the New Hebrides. By Maj. Robert D. Heinl, Jr. LXXXVI, pp. 229-256, 17 ills. in black and white, 12 ills. in color, map, Aug., 1944

VILLAFRANCA, RICARDO:
Costa Rica. By Señor Ricardo Villafranca. VIII, pp. 143-151, 4 ills., May, 1897

VILLAGE Life in the Holy Land. By John D. Whiting. XXV, pp. 249-314, 27 ills. in black and white, 21 ills. in color, Mar., 1914

VILLARI, LUIGI:
The Races and Religions of Macedonia. By Luigi Villari. XXIII, pp. 1118-1132, 14 ills., Nov., 1912

VILLIERS, ALAN J.:
The Cape Horn Grain-Ship Race: The Gallant "Parma" Leads the Vanishing Fleet of Square-Riggers Through Raging Gales and Irksome Calms 16,000 Miles, from Australia to England. By A. J. Villiers. LXIII, pp. 1-39, 38 ills., Jan., 1933
North About (*Joseph Conrad*). By Alan J. Villiers. LXXI, pp. 221-250, 24 ills., Feb., 1937
Rounding the Horn in a Windjammer (*Grace Harwar*). By A. J. Villiers. LIX, pp. 191-224, 36 ills., map, Feb., 1931
Where the Sailing Ship Survives (Aland Islands). By A. J. Villiers. LXVII, pp. 101-128, 31 ills., map, Jan., 1935

VINELAND:
Dwellings of the Saga-Time in Iceland, Greenland, and Vineland. By Cornelia Horsford. IX, pp. 73-84, ill., 9 sketches, Mar., 1898

VINEYARDS. *See* Grape Culture

VINTON, KENNETH W.:

A Frog That Eats Bats and Snakes: In Captivity, This Big Jungle Amphibian Exhibits an Extraordinary Appetite. By Kenneth W. Vinton. LXXIII, pp. 657-664, 11 ills., May, 1938

VINTON, S. R.:

China. 3 color photos by S. R. Vinton. XXXVIII, pp. 382-390, Nov., 1920

VIREOS:

Blackbirds and Orioles. By Arthur A. Allen. Paintings by Major Allan Brooks. LXVI, pp. 111-130, 7 portraits in color, July, 1934

VIRGIL. *See* Vergil

VIRGIN ISLANDS, West Indies:

An American Gibraltar: Notes on the Danish West Indies. XXX, pp. 89-96, 4 ills., map, July, 1916

The American Virgins: After Dark Days, These Adopted Daughters of the United States Are Finding a New Place in the Caribbean Sun. By DuBose Heyward and Daisy Reck. LXXVIII, pp. 273-308, 15 ills. in black and white, 23 ills. in color, map, Sept., 1940

The Danish West Indies. XIII, pp. 72-73, Feb., 1902

The Haunts of the Caribbean Corsairs: The West Indies a Geographic Background for the Most Adventurous Episodes in the History of the Western Hemisphere. By Nell Ray Clarke. XLI, pp. 147-187, 27 ills., Feb., 1922

Is Germany the Cause of Denmark's Refusal to Sell Her West Indian Possessions? XIV, p. 39, Jan., 1903

Southward Ho! In the "Alice." By Henry Howard. LXXIII, pp. 265-312, 38 ills. in black and white, 13 ills. in color, maps, Mar., 1938

VIRGINIA:

Albemarle in Revolutionary Days. By Dr. G. Brown Goode. VII, pp. 271-281, Aug., 1896

Approaching Washington by Tidewater Potomac. By Paul Wilstach. LVII, pp. 372-392, 7 ills. in black and white, 15 ills. in color, Mar., 1930

Chesapeake Odyssey: An 18-foot Sailboat Follows the Course of Captain John Smith around This Spacious Bay of History, Commerce, Sea Food, and Nautical Lore. By John Maloney. LXXVI, pp. 357-392, 32 ills., map, Sept., 1939

Dismal Swamp in Legend and History: George Washington Owned Large Tracts in Region Which He Described as a "Glorious Paradise." By John Francis Ariza. LXII, pp. 121-130, 11 ills., July, 1932

Eighth Annual Field Meeting of the National Geographic Society (Monticello). VII, pp. 259-260, ill., Aug., 1896

Fame's Eternal Camping Ground: Beautiful Arlington, Burial Place of America's Illustrious Dead. By Enoch A. Chase. LIV, pp. 621-638, 19 ills., Nov., 1928

"Free Burghs" in the United States. By James H. Blodgett. VII, pp. 116-122, Mar., 1896

Geographic History of the Piedmont Plateau. By W J McGee. VII, pp. 261-265, Aug., 1896

VIRGINIA—*Continued*

The Home of the First Farmer of America (Mount Vernon). By Worth E. Shoults. LIII, pp. 603-628, 6 ills. in black and white, 26 ills. in color, May, 1928

Jefferson's Little Mountain: Romance Enfolds Monticello, the Restored Home of the Author of the Declaration of Independence. By Paul Wilstach. LV, pp. 481-503, 12 ills. in black and white, 12 ills. in color, Apr., 1929

The Luray Caverns. XVII, pp. 358-362, 3 ills., June, 1906

The National Geographic Society's Eclipse Expedition to Norfolk, Va. By Marcus Baker. XI, p. 320, Aug., 1900

The Natural Bridge of Virginia. By Charles D. Walcott. V, pp. 59-62, ill., diagr., July 10, 1893

A Patriotic Pilgrimage to Eastern National Parks: History and Beauty Live Along Paved Roads, Once Indian Trails, Through Virginia, North Carolina, Tennessee, Kentucky, and West Virginia. By Leo A. Borah. LXV, pp. 663-702, 18 ills. in black and white, 28 ills. in color, two-page map, June, 1934

Potomac, River of Destiny. By Albert W. Atwood. LXXXVIII, pp. 33-70, 15 ills. in black and white, 18 ills. in color, map, July, 1945

The Restoration of Colonial Williamsburg. By W. A. R. Goodwin. LXXI, pp. 402-443, 21 ills. in black and white, 25 ills. in color, Apr., 1937

Roads from Washington. By John Patric. LXXIV, pp. 1-56, 27 ills. in black and white, 30 ills. in color, map supplement, July, 1938

Scientific Work of Mount Weather Meteorological Observatory. By Professor Frank H. Bigelow. XV, pp. 442-445, Nov., 1904

The Skeleton in Luray Cave. (By H. C. Hovey). XVII, pp. 425-426, July, 1906

The Society's Map of Historic and Scenic Reaches of the Nation's Capital. Text with map supplement. LXXIV, pp. 57-58, July, 1938

Spottswood's Expedition of 1716. By Dr. William M. Thornton. VII, pp. 265-269, Aug., 1896

Tidewater Virginia, Where History Lives. By Albert W. Atwood. LXXXI, pp. 617-656, 18 ills. in black and white, 20 ills. in color, map, May, 1942

Training the New Armies of Liberty: Camp Lee, Virginia's Home for the National Army. By Granville Fortescue. XXXII, pp. 421-437, 8 ills., map, Nov.-Dec., 1917

The Travels of George Washington: Dramatic Episodes in His Career as the First Geographer of the United States. By William Joseph Showalter. LXI, pp. 1-63, 50 ills., 4 maps, map supplement, Jan., 1932

Virginia—A Commonwealth That Has Come Back. By William Joseph Showalter. LV, pp. 403-472, 69 ills. in black and white, 13 ills. in color, map, Apr., 1929

See also Arlington County; Cumberland Gap; Fredericksburg

VIRGINIA'S Colonial Heritage (Williamsburg). 25 ills. in color. LXXI, pp. 417-440, Apr., 1937

VISCHER, ADOLF L.:

Tripoli: A Land of Little Promise (Libia). By Adolf L. Vischer. XXII, pp. 1035-1047, 6 ills., map, Nov., 1911

VISCHER, HANNS:

The Mysteries of the Desert (Sahara). By Hanns Vischer. XXII, pp. 1056-1059, Nov., 1911

A **VISIT** to Carlsbad Cavern: Recent Explorations of a Limestone Cave in the Guadalupe Mountains of New Mexico Reveal a Natural Wonder of the First Magnitude. By Willis T. Lee. XLV, pp. 1-40, 42 ills., Jan., 1924

A **VISIT** to Lonely Iceland. By Perley H. Noyes. XVIII, pp. 731-741, 12 ills., Nov., 1907

A **VISIT** to the Brazilian Coffee Country. By Robert De C. Ward. XXII, pp. 908-931, 19 ills., map, Oct., 1911

A **VISIT** to Three Arab Kingdoms: Transjordania, Iraq, and the Hedjaz Present Many Problems to European Powers. By Junius B. Wood. XLIII, pp. 535-568, 30 ills., map, May, 1923

VISITS to the Old Inns of England: Historic Homes of Hospitality for the Wayfarer Dot the Length and Breadth of the Kingdom. By Harold Donaldson Eberlein. LIX, pp. 261-285, 17 ills. in black and white, 15 ills. in color, Mar., 1931

VISOKI DEČANI (Monastery), Yugoslavia:

The Clock Turns Back in Yugoslavia: The Fortified Monastery of Mountain-girt Dečani Survives Its Six Hundredth Birthday. By Ethel Chamberlain Porter. LXXXV, pp. 493-512, 20 ills., map, Apr., 1944

VIVIANI, RENÉ RAPHAËL:

Our Heritage of Liberty: An Address Before the United States Senate by M. Viviani, President of the French Commission to the United States. XXXI, pp. 365-367, ill., Apr., 1917

Their Monument Is in Our Hearts: Address by M. Viviani Before the Tomb of Washington, at Mount Vernon, April 29, 1917. XXXI, p. 367, Apr., 1917

VLADIVOSTOK, U. S. S. R.:

Glimpses of Siberia, the Russian "Wild East." By Cody Marsh. XXXVIII, pp. 513-536, 26 ills., Dec., 1920

Japan Faces Russia in Manchuria. By Willard Price. LXXXII, pp. 603-634, 30 ills., map, Nov., 1942

The Land of Promise (Siberia). By Major General A. W. Greely. XXIII, pp. 1078-1090, 7 ills., Nov., 1912

Siberia. By Prof. Edwin A. Grosvenor. XII, pp. 317-324, Sept., 1901

VOGEL, F.:

Desolate Greenland, Now an American Outpost. 17 photos: 12 by Willie Knutsen, 4 by F. Vogel. LXXX, pp. 393-406, Sept., 1941

VOICE Voyages by the National Geographic Society: A Tribute to the Geographical Achievements of the Telephone. XXIX, pp. 296-326, 15 ills., chart, Mar., 1916

VOLCANIC Eruptions on Martinique and St. Vincent. By Professor Israel C. Russell. XIII, pp. 415-436, 10 ills., Dec., 1902

VOLCANIC Rocks of Martinique and St. Vincent: Collected by Robert T. Hill and Israel C. Russell. By J. S. Diller. XIII, pp. 285-296, July, 1902

VOLCANO-GIRDED Salvador: A Prosperous Central American State with the Densest Rural Population in the Western World. By Harriet Chalmers Adams. XLI, pp. 189-200, 10 ills., Feb., 1922

VOLCANO ISLANDS, Pacific Ocean. *See* Kazan Retto

VOLCANOES:

Africa: We Keep House on an Active Volcano: After Flying to Study a Spectacular Eruption in Belgian Congo, a Geologist Settles Down on a Newborn Craterless Vent for Eight Months' Study. By Dr. Jean Verhoogen. LXXVI, pp. 511-550, 28 ills., map, Oct., 1939

Alaska: Evidence of Recent Volcanic Action in Southeast Alaska. XVII, pp. 173-176, Mar., 1906

Alaska: Mapping the Home of the Great Brown Bear: Adventures of the National Geographic Society's Pavlof Volcano Expedition to Alaska. By Dr. Thomas A. Jaggar. LV, pp. 109-134, 30 ills., map, Jan., 1929

Alaska: The Monarchs of Alaska. By R. H. Sargent. XX, pp. 610-623, 9 ills., July, 1909

Alaska: Our Greatest National Monument: The National Geographic Society Completes Its Explorations in the Valley of Ten Thousand Smokes. By Robert F. Griggs. XL, pp. 219-292, 73 ills. in black and white, 16 ills. in color, maps, Sept., 1921

Alaska: The Recent Eruption of Katmai Volcano in Alaska. By George C. Martin. XXIV, pp. 131-181, 45 ills., diagr., map, Feb., 1913

Alaska: The Valley of Ten Thousand Smokes: An Account of the Discovery and Exploration of the Most Wonderful Volcanic Region in the World. By Robert F. Griggs. XXXIII, pp. 115-169, 46 ills., map, panorama, Feb., 1918

Alaska: The Valley of Ten Thousand Smokes: National Geographic Society Explorations in the Katmai District of Alaska. By Robert F. Griggs. XXXI, pp. 13-68, 51 ills., map, Jan., 1917

Alaska: Volcanoes of Alaska (Report by Capt. K. W. Perry on the Eruption of Mt. Katmai in June, 1912). XXIII, pp. 824-832, 11 ills., Aug., 1912

Alaska: A World Inside a Mountain: Aniakchak, the New Volcanic Wonderland of the Alaska Peninsula, Is Explored. By Bernard R. Hubbard. LX, pp. 319-345, 34 ills., map, Sept., 1931

Aleutians: A Jack in the Box: An Account of the Strange Performances of the Most Wonderful Island in the World (Bogoslof Volcano). By Captain F. M. Munger. XX, pp. 194-199, 8 ills., Feb., 1909

VOLCANOES—*Continued*

Aleutians: Mountains on Unimak Island, Alaska. By Ferdinand Westdahl. XIV, pp. 91-99, 4 ills., map, Mar., 1903

Aleutians: Riddle of the Aleutians: A Botanist Explores the Origin of Plants on Ever-misty Islands Now Enshrouded in the Fog of War. By Isobel Wylie Hutchison. LXXXII, pp. 769-792, 24 ills., Dec., 1942

Aleutians: Shishaldin as a Field for Exploration. By Joseph Stanley-Brown. X, pp. 281-288, 3 ills., map, Aug., 1899

Americas: Fundamental Geographic Relation of the Three Americas. By Robert T. Hill. VII, pp. 175-181, map, May, 1896

Caribbean Regions: A Suggested Field for Exploration. XIV, pp. 290-291, July, 1903

Central America: Shattered Capitals of Central America. By Herbert J. Spinden. XXXVI, pp. 185-212, 32 ills., map, Sept., 1919

Chile's Land of Fire and Water: Smoking Volcanoes and Ice-hooded Peaks Stand Sentinel Over Limpid Lakes in the Far Southern Andes. By W. Robert Moore. LXXX, pp. 91-110, 9 ills. in black and white, 10 ills. in color, map, July, 1941

Costa Rica: Land of the Painted Oxcarts. By Luis Marden. With 31 color photos by author. XC, pp. 409-456, 30 ills. in black and white, map, Oct., 1946

Costa Rica—Vulcan's Smithy. By H. Pittier. XXI, pp. 494-525, 30 ills., maps, June, 1910

Do Volcanic Explosions Affect Our Climate? By C. G. Abbot. XXIV, pp. 181-198, 9 ills., diagr., Feb., 1913

Ecuador: The Volcanoes of Ecuador, Guideposts in Crossing South America. By G. M. Dyott. LV, pp. 49-93, 42 ills. in black and white, 12 ills. in color, map, Jan., 1929

El Salvador: Coffee Is King in El Salvador. By Luis Marden. LXXXVI, pp. 575-616, 22 ills. in black and white, 27 ills. in color, map, Nov., 1944

Falcon, the Pacific's Newest Island. By J. Edward Hoffmeister and Harry S. Ladd. LIV, pp. 757-766, 8 ills., map, Dec., 1928

Guatemala: Land of Volcanoes and Progress: Cradle of Ancient Mayan Civilization, Redolent With Its Later Spanish and Indian Ways, Now Reaping Prosperity from Bananas and Coffee. By Thomas F. Lee. L, pp. 599-648, 32 ills. in black and white, 20 ills. in color, map, Nov., 1926

Hawaii, Then and Now: Boyhood Recollections and Recent Observations by an American Whose Grandfather Came to the Islands 102 Years Ago. By William R. Castle. LXXIV, pp. 419-462, 30 ills. in black and white, 10 ills. in color, map, Oct., 1938

The Hawaiian Islands: America's Strongest Outpost of Defense—The Volcanic and Floral Wonderland of the World. By Gilbert Grosvenor. XLV, pp. 115-238, 106 ills. in black and white, 21 ills. in color, 6 maps, diagr., Feb., 1924

Iceland: The Land of Fire. By Jon Stefansson. XVIII, pp. 741-744, Nov., 1907

VOLCANOES—*Continued*

Italy: Behind the Lines in Italy. By Corporal Macon Reed, Jr. LXXXVI, pp. 109-128, 20 ills., July, 1944
Included: The 1944 eruption of Vesuvius

Italy: The Eruption of Mount Vesuvius, April 7-8, 1906. By Thomas Augustus Jaggar, Jr. XVII, pp. 318-325, 6 ills., June, 1906

Italy: Mount Vesuvius. XVII, pp. 272-279, 7 ills., map, May, 1906

Japan: Face of Japan. By W. Robert Moore. LXXXVIII, pp. 753-768, 14 ills., map supplement, Dec., 1945

Japan: The Geography of Japan: With Special Reference to Its Influence on the Character of the Japanese People. By Walter Weston. XL, pp. 45-84, 23 ills. in black and white, 16 ills. in color, July, 1921

Japan: Sakurajima, Japan's Greatest Volcanic Eruption: A Convulsion of Nature Whose Ravages Were Minimized by Scientific Knowledge, Compared with the Terrors and Destruction of the Recent Tokyo Earthquake. By Dr. Thomas Augustus Jaggar. XLV, pp. 441-470, 32 ills., map, Apr., 1924

Krakatau: The Eruption of Krakatoa. By Sir Robert Ball. XIII, pp. 200-204, June, 1902

Mexico: The Greatest Volcanoes of Mexico. By A. Melgareio. XXI, pp. 741-760, 22 ills., Sept., 1910

Mexico: Paricutín, the Cornfield That Grew a Volcano. By James A. Green. LXXXV, pp. 129-164, 16 ills. in black and white, 21 ills. in color, map, Feb., 1944

Nicaragua: A Land of Lakes and Volcanoes. By Luis Marden. With 17 color photos by author. LXXXVI, pp. 161-192, 11 ills. in black and white, map, Aug., 1944

Niuafoō: Living on a Volcano: An Unspoiled Patch of Polynesia Is Niuafoō, Nicknamed "Tin Can Island" by Stamp Collectors. By Thomas A. Jaggar. LXVIII, pp. 91-106, 17 ills., map, July, 1935

Pacific Ocean: Reports of Sealing Schooners Cruising in the Neighborhood of Tuscarora Deep in May and June, 1896. (By Eliza Ruhamah Scidmore). VII, pp. 310-312, Sept., 1896

Philippine Islands: Taal Volcano and Its Recent Destructive Eruption. By Dean C. Worcester. XXIII, pp. 313-367, 40 ills., diagr., 4 maps, Apr., 1912

Theories of Volcanic Action. XIV, pp. 110-111, Mar., 1903

United States: Crater Lake, Oregon. By J. S. Diller. VIII, pp. 33-48, 6 ills., maps, Feb., 1897

United States: Crater Lake and Yosemite Through the Ages. By Wallace W. Atwood, Jr. Paintings by Eugene Kingman. LXXI, pp. 327-343, 7 ills. in black and white, 13 ills. in color, Mar., 1937

United States: Is Our Noblest Volcano Awakening to New Life: A Description of the Glaciers and Evidences of Volcanic Activity of Mount Hood. By A. H. Sylvester. XIX, pp. 515-525, 5 ills., map, July, 1908

United States: Mount St. Helens. By Lieut. Charles P. Elliott. VIII, pp. 226-230, foldout map, July-Aug., 1897

VOLCANOES—*Continued*

United States: Our Youngest Volcano. By J. S. Diller. V, pp. 93-96, ill., July 10, 1893

Volcanoes. (By G. H. G.). XIII, pp. 204-208, map, June, 1902

West Indies: Chemical Discussion of Analyses of Volcanic Ejecta from Martinique and St. Vincent. By W. F. Hillebrand. XIII, pp. 296-299, July, 1902

West Indies: Destruction of Pompeii as Interpreted by the Volcanic Eruptions of Martinique. By Angelo Heilprin. XV, p. 431, Oct., 1904

West Indies: The Eruptions of La Soufrière, St. Vincent, in May, 1902. By Edmund Otis Hovey. XIII, pp. 444-459, 4 ills., Dec., 1902

West Indies: Magnetic Disturbance Caused by the Explosion of Mont Pelée (Martinique). XIII, pp. 208-209, June, 1902

West Indies: The National Geographic Society Expedition in the West Indies. XIII, pp. 209-213, maps, June, 1902

West Indies: The New Cone of Mont Pelée (Martinique). XIV, pp. 422-423, ills., Nov., 1903

West Indies: The Recent Volcanic Eruptions in the West Indies (Martinique and St. Vincent). By Israel C. Russell. XIII, pp. 267-285, 7 ills., map, July, 1902

West Indies: Report by Robert T. Hill on the Volcanic Disturbances in the West Indies. XIII, pp. 223-267, 12 ills., 3 maps, July, 1902

West Indies: A Report of the Eruption of the Soufrière of St. Vincent, 1812 (From the *Evening News* of June 30, 1812). XIV, pp. 158-161, Apr., 1903

West Indies: Reports of Vessels as to the Range of Volcanic Dust (Martinique and St. Vincent). By James Page. XIII, pp. 299-301, July, 1902

West Indies: The Shattered Obelisk of Mont Pelée (Martinique). By Prof. Angelo Heilprin. XVII, pp. 465-474, 5 ills., Aug., 1906

West Indies: Volcanic Eruptions on Martinique and St. Vincent. By Israel C. Russell. XIII, pp. 415-436, 10 ills., Dec., 1902

West Indies: Volcanic Rocks of Martinique and St. Vincent: Collected by Robert T. Hill and Israel C. Russell. By J. S. Diller. XIII, pp. 285-296, July, 1902

Yukon: An Expedition through the Yukon District. By Charles Willard Hayes. IV, pp. 117-159, 3 maps (2 foldouts), May 15, 1892

VOLENDAM, Netherlands:

Glimpses of Holland. By William Wisner Chapin. XXVII, pp. 1-29, 26 ills., Jan., 1915

VOLGA (River), U. S. S. R.:

Mother Volga Defends Her Own. By Maynard Owen Williams. LXXXII, pp. 793-811, 21 ills., Dec., 1942

Voyaging on the Volga Amid War and Revolution: War-time Sketches on Russia's Great Waterway. By William T. Ellis. XXXIII, pp. 245-265, 16 ills., Mar., 1918

VOSBURGH, FREDERICK G.:

A City Learns to Smile Again (Nancy, France). By Maj. Frederick G. Vosburgh. LXXXVII, pp. 361-384, 23 ills., map, Mar., 1945

Dogs of Duty and Devotion. By Frederick G. Vosburgh. LXXX, pp. 769-774, 3 ills., Dec., 1941

Fabulous Yellowstone: Even Stranger Than the Tales of Early Trappers is the Truth About This Steaming Wonderland. By Frederick G. Vosburgh. LXXVII, pp. 769-794, 15 ills. in black and white, 9 ills. in color, map, June, 1940

Henry Hudson, Magnificent Failure: Just 330 Years Ago He and His Mutinous Crew Found Manhattan Covered With "Goodly Oakes" and Fought Indians in New York Harbor. By Frederick G. Vosburgh. LXXV, pp. 461-490, 21 ills., Apr., 1939

Men-Birds Soar on Boiling Air. By Frederick G. Vosburgh. LXXIV, pp. 123-140, 15 ills., July, 1938

Metal Sinews of Strength: This Is a War of Many Metals, for We Live in an Age of Alloys. By Frederick G. Vosburgh. LXXXI, pp. 457-491, 35 ills., Apr., 1942

New York State's Air-Conditioned Roof (Adirondacks). By Frederick G. Vosburgh. LXXIII, pp. 715-748, 23 ills. in black and white, 10 ills. in color, map, June, 1938

Our Insect Fifth Column: Alien Enemies Take Steady Toll of Food, Trees, and Treasure by Boring from Within. By Frederick G. Vosburgh. Paintings by Hashime Murayama. LXXX, pp. 225-248, 14 ills. in black and white, 10 ills. in color, Aug., 1941

This Is My Own: How the United States Seems to a Citizen Soldier Back from Three Years Overseas. By Frederick G. Vosburgh. LXXXIX, pp. 113-128, 14 ills., Jan., 1946

Wonders of the New Washington: Efficient Modern Structures Rise in the Biggest Government Building Program Since the Capital City Was Founded in a Wilderness. By Frederick G. Vosburgh. LXVII, pp. 457-488, 20 ills. in black and white, 13 ills. in color, Apr., 1935

VOYAGE of the *Morrissey*. 10 color photos by Daniel S. Turner and Sherman A. Wengerd. LXXXIX, pp. 609-616, May, 1946

A **VOYAGE** to the Island Home of Robinson Crusoe (Juan Fernández). By Waldo L. Schmitt. LIV, pp. 353-370, 24 ills., Sept., 1928

VOYAGES:

American Pathfinders in the Pacific. By William H. Nicholas. LXXXIX, pp. 617-640, 17 ills., two-page map, May, 1946

The Antarctic Continent (Geographic Notes. By Cyrus C. Babb). VI, pp. 217-223, map, Dec. 29, 1894

Note: A resumé of the expeditions and discoveries in the Antarctic from 1567 through 1894

The Arctic Cruise of the United States Revenue Cutter "Bear." By Dr. Sheldon Jackson. VII, pp. 27-31, 3 ills., Jan., 1896

The Arctic Cruise of the U. S. S. Thetis in the Summer and Autumn of 1889. By Charles H. Stockton. II, pp. 171-198, ill., foldout map, July, 1890

Around the World for Animals. By William M. and Lucile Q. Mann. LXXIII, pp. 665-714, 33 ills. in black and white, 23 ills. in color, map, June, 1938

Around the World in the "Islander": A Narrative of the Adventures of a Solitary Voyager on His Four-Year Cruise in a Thirty-Four-Foot Sailing Craft. By Capt. Harry Pidgeon. LIII, pp. 141-205, 75 ills., two-page map, Feb., 1928

At Home on the Oceans: Whales and Sharks Make Exciting Neighbors for a Professor's Wife, Turned Able Seaman, On a Three-year Voyage Around the World. By Edith Bauer Strout. LXXVI, pp. 33-86, 54 ills., map, July, 1939

Bird Life Among Lava Rock and Coral Sand: The Chronicle of a Scientific Expedition to Little-known Islands of Hawaii. By Alexander Wetmore. XLVIII, pp. 77-108, 36 ills., map, July, 1925

By Felucca Down the Nile: Giant Dams Rule Egypt's Lifeline River, Yet Village Life Goes On As It Did in the Time of the Pharaohs. By Willard Price. LXXVII, pp. 435-476, 21 ills. in black and white, 22 ills. in color, two-page map, Apr., 1940

By Sail Across Europe. By Merlin Minshall. LXXI, pp. 533-567, 38 ills., map, May, 1937

The Cape Horn Grain-Ship Race: The Gallant "Parma" Leads the Vanishing Fleet of Square-Riggers Through Raging Gales and Irksome Calms 16,000 Miles, from Australia to England. By A. J. Villiers. LXIII, pp. 1-39, 38 ills., Jan., 1933

Capturing Giant Turtles in the Caribbean. By David D. Duncan. LXXXIV, pp. 177-190, 13 ills., map, Aug., 1943

The Cartography and Observations of Bering's First Voyage. By General A. W. Greely. III, pp. 205-230, map supplement, Jan. 28, 1892; Feb. 19, 1892

Chesapeake Odyssey: An 18-foot Sailboat Follows the Course of Captain John Smith around This Spacious Bay of History, Commerce, Sea Food, and Nautical Lore. By John Maloney. LXXVI, pp. 357-392, 32 ills., map, Sept., 1939

Collinson's Arctic Journey. By General A. W. Greely. IV, pp. 198-200, Feb. 8, 1893
Note: References to the Arctic voyage of Lieutenant-Commander Charles H. Stockton, U. S. N., in the *Thetis*, in 1889

The Columbus of the Pacific: Captain James Cook, Foremost British Navigator, Expanded the Great Sea to Correct Proportions and Won for Albion an Insular Empire by Peaceful Exploration and Scientific Study. By J. R. Hildebrand. LI, pp. 85-132, 45 ills., maps, Jan., 1927

Convoys to Victory. By Harvey Klemmer. LXXXIII, pp. 193-216, 24 ills., Feb., 1943

A Critical Review of Bering's First Expedition, 1725-30, Together with a Translation of His Original Report Upon It. With a Map. By Wm. H. Dall. II, pp. 111-169, 8 tables, foldout map, May, 1890

A Cruise Among Desert Islands (Baja California). By G. Dallas Hanna and A. W. Anthony. XLIV, pp. 71-99, 32 ills., map, July, 1923

Cruise of the *Kinkajou:* Among Desert Islands of Mexico Voyagers Find Outdoor Laboratories for the Naturalist and Ideal Fishing Grounds for the Sportsman. By Alfred M. Bailey. LXXX, pp. 339-366, 13 ills. in black and white, 12 ills. in color, map, Sept., 1941

Cruising to Crete: Four French Girls Set Sail in a Breton Yawl for the Island of the Legendary Minotaur. By Marthe Oulié and Mariel Jean-Brunhes. LV, pp. 249-272, 15 ills. in black and white, 14 ills. in color, map, Feb., 1929

The Danube, Highway of Races: From the Black Forest to the Black Sea, Europe's Most Important River Has Borne the Traffic of Centuries. By Melville Chater. LVI, pp. 643-697, 54 ills., Dec., 1929

Deep-Sea Exploring Expedition of the Steamer "Albatross." By Hugh M. Smith. X, pp. 291-296, ills., diagr., Aug., 1899

Diary of a Voyage from San Francisco to Tahiti and Return, 1901. By S. P. Langley. XII, pp. 413-429, 10 ills., maps, Dec., 1901

Discoverers of America. Annual Address by the President, Hon. Gardiner G. Hubbard. V, pp. 1-20, charts, maps, 3 map supplements, Apr. 7, 1893

The Dream Ship: The Story of a Voyage of Adventure More Than Half Around the World in a 47-foot Lifeboat. By Ralph Stock. XXXIX, pp. 1-52, 43 ills., map, Jan., 1921

Early Voyages on the Northwestern Coast of America. By Professor George Davidson. V, pp. 235-256, Jan. 31, 1894

The Greatest Voyage in the Annals of the Sea. By J. R. Hildebrand. LXII, pp. 699-739, 35 ills., map, Dec., 1932

Greenland from 1898 to Now: "Captain Bob," Who Went North with Peary, Tells of 42 Years of Exploration in the Orphan Island of New Aerial and Naval Interest. By Robert A. Bartlett. LXXVIII, pp. 111-140, 25 ills., two-page map, July, 1940

Henry Hudson, Magnificent Failure: Just 330 Years Ago He and His Mutinous Crew Found Manhattan Covered With "Goodly Oakes" and Fought Indians in New York Harbor. By Frederick G. Vosburgh. LXXV, pp. 461-490, 21 ills., Apr., 1939

Inside Cape Horn. By Amos Burg. LXXII, pp. 743-783, 29 ills. in black and white, 10 ills. in color, two-page map, Dec., 1937

The Isles of Greece. By Lt. Richard Stillwell, USNR. LXXXV, pp. 593-622, 11 ills. in black and white, 20 ills. in color, map, May, 1944

A Journey by Jungle Rivers to the Home of the Cock-of-the-rock: Naturalists Enter the Amazon, Voyage Through the Heart of Tropical South America, and Emerge at the Mouth of the Orinoco. By Ernest G. Holt. LXIV, pp. 585-630, 49 ills., map, Nov., 1933

A Modern Saga of the Seas: The Narrative of a 17,000-Mile Cruise on a 40-Foot Sloop by the Author, His Wife, and a Baby, Born on the Voyage. By Erling Tambs. LX, pp. 645-688, 49 ills., map, Dec., 1931

North About. By Alan J. Villiers. LXXI, pp. 221-250, 24 ills., Feb., 1937

Norway and the Vikings. By Captain Magnus Andersen. V, pp. 132-136, Jan. 31, 1894
Included: Viking ship replica, sailed from Bergen, Norway, to New London, Connecticut

The Pathfinder of the East: Setting Sail to Find "Christians and Spices," Vasco da Gama Met Amazing Adventures, Founded an Empire, and Changed the History of Western Europe. By J. R. Hildebrand. LII, pp. 503-550, 43 ills., map, pictorial supplement, Nov., 1927

The "Pilgrim" Sails the Seven Seas: A Schooner Yacht Out of Boston Drops in at Desert Isles and South Sea Edens in a Leisurely Two-Year Voyage. By Harold Peters. LXXII, pp. 223-262, 36 ills., Aug., 1937

Recent Disclosures Concerning Pre-Columbian Voyages to America in the Archives of the Vatican. By William Eleroy Curtis. V, pp. 197-234, Jan. 31, 1894

Rediscovering the Rhine: A Trip by Barge from the Sea to the Headwaters of Europe's Storied Stream. By Melville Chater. XLVIII, pp. 1-43, 44 ills., July, 1925

Revealing Earth's Mightiest Ocean (Pacific). By Albert W. Atwood. LXXXIV, pp. 291-306, 10 ills., map supplement, Sept., 1943

The Road to Bolivia. By William E. Curtis. XI, pp. 209-224, 7 ills., June, 1900

The Romance of Science in Polynesia: An Account of Five Years of Cruising Among the South Sea Islands. By Robert Cushman Murphy. Paintings by Hashime Murayama. XLVIII, pp. 355-426, 66 ills. in black and white, 16 ills. in color, 3 maps, Oct., 1925

Rounding the Horn in a Windjammer. By A. J. Villiers. LIX, pp. 191-224, 36 ills., map, Feb., 1931

Sailing Forbidden Coasts (Africa). By Ida Treat. LX, pp. 357-386, 31 ills., map, Sept., 1931

Sailing the Seven Seas in the Interest of Science: Adventures Through 157,000 Miles of Storm and Calm, from Arctic to Antarctic and Around the World, in the Non-magnetic Yacht "Carnegie." By J. P. Ault. XLII, pp. 631-690, 47 ills., chart, Dec., 1922

Seafarers of South Celebes. By G. E. P. Collins. LXXXVII, pp. 53-78, 25 ills., map, Jan., 1945

Servicing Arctic Airbases. By Robert A. Bartlett. LXXXIX, pp. 602-616, 3 ills. in black and white, 10 ills. in color, map, May, 1946

Sindbads of Science: Narrative of a Windjammer's Specimen-Collecting Voyage to the Sargasso Sea, to Senegambian Africa and Among Islands of High Adventure in the South Atlantic. By George Finlay Simmons. LII, pp. 1-75, 89 ills., map, July, 1927

Sir Francis Drake's Anchorage. By Edward L. Berthoud. VI, pp. 208-214, Dec. 29, 1894

Skirting the Shores of Sunrise: Seeking and Finding "The Levant" in a Journey by Steamer, Motor-Car, and Train from Constantinople to Port Said. By Melville Chater. L, pp. 649-728, 60 ills. in black and white, 34 ills. in color, map, Dec., 1926

Southward Ho! In the "Alice." By Henry Howard. LXXIII, pp. 265-312, 38 ills. in black and white, 13 ills. in color, maps, Mar., 1938

A Summer Voyage to the Arctic. By G. R. Putnam. VIII, pp. 97-110, 6 ills., map, Apr., 1897

Surveying the Grand Canyon of the Colorado: An Account of the 1923 Boating Expedition of the United States Geological Survey. By Lewis R. Freeman. XLV, pp. 471-548, 62 ills., map, May, 1924

A Voyage to the Island Home of Robinson Crusoe (Juan Fernández). By Waldo L. Schmitt. LIV, pp. 353-370, 24 ills., Sept., 1928

Voyaging on the Volga Amid War and Revolution: War-time Sketches on Russia's Great Waterway. By William T. Ellis. XXXIII, pp. 245-265, 16 ills., Mar., 1918

Westward Bound in the *Yankee*. By Irving and Electa Johnson. LXXXI, pp. 1-44, 25 ills. in black and white, 20 ills. in color, map, Jan., 1942
Included: Easter Island; Galápagos Islands; Pitcairn; Samoa; Santa Cruz; Solomon Islands

See also Antarctic Regions; Arctic Regions; Canoes and Canoe Trips; Discoverers, Explorers, and Navigators

VOYAGING on the Volga Amid War and Revolution: War-time Sketches on Russia's Great Waterway. By William T. Ellis. XXXIII, pp. 245-265, 16 ills., Mar., 1918

VULTURES (Birds):

The Eagle, King of Birds, and His Kin. By Alexander Wetmore. Paintings by Maj. Allan Brooks. LXIV, pp. 43-95, 23 ills. in black and white, 48 ills. in color, July, 1933

W

WAC. *See* Women's Army Corps

WADSWORTH, ELIOT:

The Red Cross Spirit. By Eliot Wadsworth. XXXI, pp. 464-474, 8 ills., May, 1917

WAIKIKI BEACH, Honolulu, Hawaii:

Waves and Thrills at Waikiki. 8 ills. in duotone by Thomas Edward Blake. LXVII, pp. 597-604, May, 1935

WAIMANGU and the Hot-Spring Country of New Zealand: The World's Greatest Geyser Is One of Many Natural Wonders in a Land of Inferno and Vernal Paradise. By Joseph C. Grew. XLVIII, pp. 109-130, 19 ills., map, Aug., 1925

WAKE (Island), North Pacific Ocean:

Navy Wings over the Pacific. 12 ills. in color from U. S. Navy official photos. LXXXVI, pp. 241-248, Aug., 1944

WAKEMAN, BERNARD:

Wayfaring Down the Winding Severn. 9 color photos by Bernard Wakeman. LXIII, pp. 433-440, Apr., 1933

Where the Winding Cam Mirrors Cambridge (University) Spires. 12 color photos by Bernard Wakeman and Walter M. Edwards. LXX, pp. 339-346, Sept., 1936

WAKEMAN, FRANK:

The Beauties of the Severn Valley. By Frank Wakeman. LXIII, pp. 417-452, 24 ills. in black and white, 15 ills. in color, map, Apr., 1933
Wayfaring Down the Winding Severn. 6 color photos by author, pp. 433-440

WALCHEREN (Island), Netherlands:

Holland Rises from War and Water. By Thomas R. Henry. LXXXIX, pp. 237-260, 18 ills., map, Feb., 1946

Mending Dikes in the Netherlands. 20 photos by Lawrence Earl. XC, pp. 791-806, Dec., 1946

WALCOTT, CHARLES D.:

Four Prominent Geographers. XVIII, pp. 425-428, 4 ills., June, 1907

The Geologist at Blue Mountain, Maryland. By Charles D. Walcott. V, pp. 84-88, July 10, 1893

A Geologist's Paradise (Canadian Rockies). By Charles D. Walcott. XXII, pp. 509-536, 28 ills., panorama, June, 1911
Our Mountain Panorama. Panorama from photo by author

The Monarch of the Canadian Rockies (Mount Robson). By Charles D. Walcott. XXIV, pp. 626-639, 13 ills., panorama, May, 1913
The Monarch of the Canadian Rockies—Robson Peak. Panorama from photo by author

The Natural Bridge of Virginia. By Charles D. Walcott. V, pp. 59-62, ill., diagr., July 10, 1893

Portrait. XV, ill. p. 235, May, 1904. XVIII, ill. p. 426, June, 1907

WALCOTT, FREDERIC C.:

Devastated Poland. By Frederic C. Walcott. XXXI, pp. 445-452, 6 ills., May, 1917

Forerunners of Famine. By Frederic C. Walcott. XXXIII, pp. 336-347, 4 ills., 4 diagrs., map, Apr., 1918

WALCOTT, STUART:

The Life Story of an American Airman in France: Extracts from Letters of Stuart Walcott, Who, Between July and December, 1917, Learned to Fly in French Schools of Aviation, Won Fame at the Front, and Fell Near Saint Souplet. XXXIII, pp. 86-106, 9 ills., Jan., 1918

WALDE-WALDEGG, HERMANN VON:

Stone Idols of the Andes Reveal a Vanished People: Remarkable Relics of One of the Oldest Aboriginal Cultures of America are Unearthed in Colombia's San Agustín Region. By Hermann von Walde-Waldegg. LXXVII, pp. 627-647, 22 ills., map, May, 1940

WALDSEEMÜLLER MAPS:

The famous Waldseemüller map of 1507. XV, p. 50, Jan., 1904

Two Famous Maps of America. XIII, p. 72, Feb., 1902

WALES:

The Races of Europe. By Edwin A. Grosvenor. XXXIV, pp. 441-534, 62 ills., diagr. and index, maps, map supplement, Dec., 1918

Sheep Dog Trials in Llangollen: Trained Collies Perform Marvels of Herding in the Cambrian Stakes, Open to the World. By Sara Bloch. LXXVII, pp. 559-574, 17 ills., Apr., 1940

A Short Visit to Wales: Historic Associations and Scenic Beauties Contend for Interest in the Little Land Behind the Hills. By Ralph A. Graves. XLIV, pp. 635-675, 37 ills., map, Dec., 1923

Wales in Wartime. By Isobel Wylie Hutchison. LXXXV, pp. 751-768, 16 ills., map, June, 1944

See also Skokholm (Island)

WALES, Alaska:

Exploring Frozen Fragments of American History: On the Trail of Early Eskimo Colonists Who Made a 55-Mile Crossing from the Old World to the New. By Henry B. Collins, Jr. LXXV, pp. 633-656, 24 ills., map, May, 1939

WALKER, HARRISON HOWELL:

Adirondack Idyls. 10 color photos by Harrison Howell Walker. LXXIII, pp. 729-736, June, 1938

American Bombers Attacking from Australia. By Howell Walker. LXXXIII, pp. 49-70, 19 ills., map, Jan., 1943

France Farms as War Wages: An American Explores the Rich Rural Region of the Historic Paris Basin. By Harrison Howell Walker. LXXVII, pp. 201-238, 16 ills. in black and white, 18 ills. in color, map, Feb., 1940
Some French Pastorals. 18 color photos by author, pp. 207-230

Fruitful Shores of the Finger Lakes. By Harrison Howell Walker. LXXIX, pp. 559-594, 15 ills. in black and white, 22 ills. in color, map, May, 1941

Gentle Folk Settle Stern Saguenay: On French Canada's Frontier Homespun Colonists Keep the Customs of Old Norman Settlers. By Harrison Howell Walker. LXXV, pp. 595-632, 15 ills. in black and white, 25 ills. in color, map, May, 1939
Camera Pastels in French Canada. 25 color photos by author, pp. 601-624

Life in Dauntless Darwin: A National Geographic Staff Writer Gives a Vivid Description of the Australian Town That Guards the Continent's Northern Door. By Howell Walker. LXXXII, pp. 123-138, 17 ills., map, July, 1942

The Making of an Anzac. By Howell Walker. LXXXI, pp. 409-456, 31 ills. in black and white, 20 ills. in color, two-page map, Apr., 1942
Facing War's Challenge "Down Under." 20 color photos by author, pp. 425-456

WALKER, HARRISON HOWELL—*Continued*

Old Ireland, Mother of New Eire: By Whatever Name, 'Tis the Same Fair Land With the Grass Growing Green on the Hills of Her and the Peat Smoke Hanging Low. By Harrison Howell Walker. LXXVII, pp. 649-691, 19 ills. in black and white, 18 ills. in color, map, May, 1940

When Irish Skies Are Smiling. 18 color photos by author, pp. 663-686

Pennsylvania's Land of Plenty. 22 color photos by Harrison Howell Walker. LXXX, pp. 41-64, July, 1941

Spring's Gay Bouquets Deck the Nation's Capital. 10 color photos by Harrison Howell Walker. LXXIV, pp. 17-24, July, 1938

Sydney Faces the War Front Down Under. By Howell Walker. LXXXIII, pp. 359-374, 8 ills. in black and white, 10 ills. in color, Mar., 1943

WALKER, J. BERNARD:

Cathedrals of the Old and New World. By J. Bernard Walker. XLII, pp. 61-114, 50 ills., July, 1922

WALKER, JOHN:

Europe's Looted Art. By John Walker. LXXXIX, pp. 39-52, 11 ills., Jan., 1946

WALKER, LEWIS WAYNE:

Fairy Terns of the Atolls. By Lewis Wayne Walker. XC, pp. 807-814, 9 ills., Dec., 1946

Pelican Profiles. By Lewis Wayne Walker. LXXXIV, pp. 589-598, 5 ills. in black and white, 8 ills. in color, Nov., 1943

Photoflashing Western Owls. By Lewis W. Walker. LXXXVII, pp. 475-486, 6 ills. in black and white, 7 ills. in color, Apr., 1945

A **WALKING** Tour Across Iceland. By Isobel Wylie Hutchison. LIII, pp. 467-497, 36 ills., map, Apr., 1928

WALL OF CHINA. *See* Great Wall of China

WALLACE, FREDERICK WILLIAM:

Life on the Grand Banks: An Account of the Sailor-Fishermen Who Harvest the Shoal Waters of North America's Eastern Coasts. By Frederick William Wallace. XL, pp. 1-28, 29 ills., July, 1921

WALLACE, HENRY A.:

The People's Fight Against Slavery. By Hon. Henry A. Wallace. Reprint of address delivered at a dinner of the Free World Association, May 8, 1942. LXXXII, pp. 276-280, ill., Aug., 1942

WALLISER, BLAIR A.:

Sunset in the East (Japan). By Blair A. Walliser. LXXXIX, pp. 797-812, 17 ills., June, 1946

WALMSLEY, LEO:

Between the Heather and the North Sea: Bold English Headlands Once Sheltered Sea Robbers, Later Were Ports of Wooden Ships, Centers of the Jet and Alum Trades, To-day Are Havens of Adventurous Fishing Fleets. By Leo Walmsley. LXIII, pp. 197-232, 41 ills., Feb., 1933

WALRUSES:

Hunting the Walrus. XXII, pp. 285-290, 10 ills., Mar., 1911

WALTER, RICHARD:

Wanderers Awheel in Malta: British Stronghold Has Been a Steppingstone of Conquest Since Phoenicians Cruised the Mediterranean and St. Paul Was Shipwrecked There. By Richard Walter. LXXVIII, pp. 253-272, 17 ills., maps, Aug., 1940

WALTER Wellman's Expedition to the North Pole. XVII, pp. 205-207, chart, Apr., 1906

WALTHER, JOHANNES:

The North American Deserts. By Herr Professor Dr. Johannes Walther. IV, pp. 163-176, Feb. 8, 1893

WANDERERS Awheel in Malta: British Stronghold Has Been a Steppingstone of Conquest Since Phoenicians Cruised the Mediterranean and St. Paul Was Shipwrecked There. By Richard Walter. LXXVIII, pp. 253-272, 17 ills., maps, Aug., 1940

WANDERING Islands in the Rio Grande. By Mrs. Albert S. Burleson. XXIV, pp. 381-386, ills., map, Mar., 1913

WANDERING Through the Black Forest (Germany). 13 color photos by Hans Hildenbrand. LIV, pp. 659-666, Dec., 1928

WANG YE FU, China:

The Road to Wang Ye Fu: An Account of the Work of the National Geographic Society's Central-China Expedition in the Mongol Kingdom of Ala Shan. By Frederick R. Wulsin. XLIX, pp. 197-234, 44 ills., map, Feb., 1926

WAR, Patriotism, and the Food Supply. By Frederick V. Coville. XXXI, pp. 254-256, Mar., 1917

WAR AGENCIES, Washington, D. C.:

Wartime Washington. By William H. Nicholas. LXXXIV, pp. 257-290, 12 ills. in black and white, 16 ills. in color, Sept., 1943

The **WAR** and Ocean Geography. By the Editor (Gilbert Grosvenor). XXXIV, pp. 230-242, 6 ills., map, Sept., 1918

WAR Awakened New Caledonia: Swift Changes Take Place on the South Pacific Island of Mineral Wealth Defended by Free French and American Troops. By Enzo de Chetelat. LXXXII, pp. 31-55, 14 ills. in black and white, 12 ills. in color, map, July, 1942

WAR Clouds Over Danzig and Poland's Port (Gdynia). 8 ills. LXXVI, pp. 551-558, Oct., 1939

WAR DOGS:

Animals Were Allies, Too. 16 ills. LXXXIX, pp. 75-88, Jan., 1946

Mankind's Best Friend: Companion of His Solitude, Advance Guard in the Hunt, and Ally of the Trenches. By Ernest Harold Baynes. XXXV, pp. 185-201, 11 ills., Mar., 1919

WAR DOGS—*Continued*

The Sagacity and Courage of Dogs: Instances of the Remarkable Intelligence and Unselfish Devotion of Man's Best Friend Among Dumb Animals. XXXV, pp. 253-275, 13 ills., Mar., 1919

Your Dog Joins Up. By Frederick Simpich. LXXXIII, pp. 93-113, 25 ills., Jan., 1943

WAR Echoes in the West Indies. 22 color photos by Luis Marden. LXXXI, pp. 731-754, June, 1942

WAR Finds Its Way to Gilbert Islands: United States Forces Dislodge Japanese from Enchanted Atolls Which Loom Now as Stepping Stones along South Sea Route from Australia to Hawaii. By Sir Arthur Grimble. LXXXIII, pp. 71-92, 19 ills., map, Jan., 1943

WAR INDUSTRIES. *See* Industries

WAR Meets Peace in Egypt. By Grant Parr and G. E. Janssen. LXXXI, pp. 503-526, 25 ills., map, Apr., 1942

WARBLERS (Birds):

Birds of Timberline and Tundra. By Arthur A. Allen. With 24 color photos by author. XC, pp. 313-339, 8 ills. in black and white, Sept., 1946

Birds on the Home Front. By Arthur A. Allen. LXXXIV, pp. 32-56, 7 ills. in black and white, 31 ills. in color, July, 1943

Friends of Our Forests. By Henry Wetherbee Henshaw. Paintings by Louis Agassiz Fuertes. XXXI, pp. 297-321, ill. in black and white, 32 ills. in color, Apr., 1917

The **WARBLERS** of North America. 32 ills. in color from paintings by Louis Agassiz Fuertes. XXXI, pp. 305-320, Apr., 1917

WARD, LESTER F.:

Report on Fossil Plants (Mount St. Elias Expedition). By Lester F. Ward. III, pp. 199-200, May 29, 1891

WARD, ROBERT DE C.:

Our Immigration Laws from the Viewpoint of National Eugenics. By Prof. Robert De C. Ward. XXIII, pp. 38-41, Jan., 1912

A Visit to the Brazilian Coffee Country. By Robert De C. Ward. XXII, pp. 908-931, 19 ills., map, Oct., 1911

WARDER, B. H. *See* NGS: Board of Managers

WARDS of the United States: Notes on What Our Country Is Doing for Santo Domingo, Nicaragua, and Haiti. XXX, pp. 143-177, 36 ills., Aug., 1916

The **WARFARE** of the Jungle Folk: Campaigning Against Tigers, Elephants, and Other Wild Animals in Northern Siam. By Merian C. Cooper. Photos by Ernest B. Schoedsack. LIII, pp. 233-268, 33 ills., Feb., 1928

The **WARFARE** on Our Eastern Coast. By John Oliver La Gorce. XXVIII, pp. 195-230, 29 ills., charts, Sept., 1915

WARNER, ARTHUR H.:

A Country Where Going to America Is an Industry (Sicily). By Arthur H. Warner. XX, pp. 1063-1102, 41 ills., Dec., 1909

WARREN, FRANCIS E.:

Animal Wealth of the United States. By Francis E. Warren. XVII, pp. 511-524, 6 ills., 4 diagrs., Sept., 1906

WAR'S Wake in the Rhineland. By Thomas R. Henry. LXXXVIII, pp. 1-32, 29 ills., map, July, 1945

WARSAW, Poland:

Partitioned Poland. By William Joseph Showalter. XXVII, pp. 88-106, 12 ills., Jan., 1915

WARTIME in the Pacific Northwest (U. S. and Canada). By Frederick Simpich. LXXXII, pp. 421-464, 25 ills. in black and white, 23 ills. in color, map, Oct., 1942

WARTIME Washington (D. C.). By William H. Nicholas. LXXXIV, pp. 257-290, 12 ills. in black and white, 16 ills. in color, Sept., 1943

WARWICK, ADAM:

Farmers Since the Days of Noah: China's Remarkable System of Agriculture Has Kept Alive the Densest Population in the World. By Adam Warwick. LI, pp. 469-500, 37 ills., Apr., 1927

The People of the Wilderness: The Mongols, Once the Terror of All Christendom, Now a Primitive, Harmless Nomad Race. By Adam Warwick. XXXIX, pp. 507-551, 59 ills., May, 1921

A Thousand Miles Along the Great Wall of China: The Mightiest Barrier Ever Built by Man Has Stood Guard Over the Land of Chin for Twenty Centuries. By Adam Warwick. XLIII, pp. 113-143, 27 ills., maps, panorama, Feb., 1923

WARWICK, England:

How Warwick (Castle) Was Photographed in Color. By Maynard Owen Williams. LXX, pp. 83-93, 13 ills. in color, July, 1936

WARWICK Castle, Stage for Old England's Pageantry. 13 color photos by Maynard Owen Williams. LXX, pp. 85-92, July, 1936

WASHBURN, BRADFORD:

The Conquest of Mount Crillon (Alaska). By Bradford Washburn. LXVII, pp. 361-400, 40 ills., map, Mar., 1935

Exploring Yukon's Glacial Stronghold. By Bradford Washburn. LXIX, pp. 715-748, 29 ills., two-page map, June, 1936

Over the Roof of Our Continent (Mount McKinley). By Bradford Washburn. LXXIV, pp. 78-98, 17 ills. in duotone, map, July, 1938

WASHBURN, STANLEY:

Russia from Within: Her War of Yesterday, Today, and Tomorrow. By Stanley Washburn. XXXII, pp. 91-120, 30 ills., Aug., 1917

The Russian Situation and Its Significance to America. By Stanley Washburn. XXXI, pp. 371-382, 8 ills., Apr., 1917

WASHINGTON, GEORGE:

Dismal Swamp in Legend and History: George Washington Owned Large Tracts in Region Which He Described as a "Glorious Paradise." By John Francis Ariza. LXII, pp. 121-130, 11 ills., July, 1932

The Home of the First Farmer of America (Mount Vernon). By Worth E. Shoults. LIII, pp. 603-628, 6 ills. in black and white, 26 ills. in color, May, 1928

Our First Alliance. By J. J. Jusserand. XXXI, pp. 518-548, 8 ills., June, 1917

Their Monument Is in Our Hearts: Address by M. Viviani Before the Tomb of Washington, at Mount Vernon, April 29, 1917. XXXI, p. 367, Apr., 1917

The Travels of George Washington: Dramatic Episodes in His Career as the First Geographer of the United States. By William Joseph Showalter. LXI, pp. 1-63, 50 ills., 4 maps, map supplement, Jan., 1932

WASHINGTON (State):

The Altitude of Mount Adams, Washington. By Edgar McClure. VII, pp. 151-153, tables, Apr., 1896

The Call of the West. By C. J. Blanchard. XX, pp. 403-437, 20 ills., map, May, 1909

The Columbia (River) Turns on the Power. By Maynard Owen Williams. LXXIX, pp. 749-792, 25 ills. in black and white, 18 ills. in color, June, 1941

The Forest Conditions and Standing Timber of the State of Washington. By Henry Gannett. IX, pp. 410-412, Sept., 1898

Forest Lookout. By Ella E. Clark. With 9 color photos by author. XC, pp. 73-96, 8 ills. in black and white, July, 1946

The Great White Monarch of the Pacific Northwest (Mount Rainier). By A. H. Barnes. XXIII, pp. 593-626, 31 ills., map, June, 1912

Home-Making by the Government: An Account of the Eleven Immense Irrigating Projects to be Opened in 1908. By C. J. Blanchard. XIX, pp. 250-287, 23 ills., Apr., 1908

Lake Chelan. By Henry Gannett. IX, pp. 417-428, 7 ills., map, Oct., 1898

The Olympic Country. By the late S. C. Gilman, C. E. VII, pp. 133-140, foldout map, Apr., 1896

Our Pacific Northwest. By N. H. Darton. XX, pp. 645-663, 12 ills., maps, July, 1909

Recent Triangulation in the Cascades. By S. S. Gannett. VII, p. 150, Apr., 1896
Included: Mount Adams; Mount Aix; Mount Rainier; Mount Stuart

The Spirit of the West: The Wonderful Agricultural Development Since the Dawn of Irrigation. By C. J. Blanchard. XXI, pp. 333-360, 15 ills., Apr., 1910

Wartime in the Pacific Northwest. By Frederick Simpich. LXXXII, pp. 421-464, 25 ills. in black and white, 23 ills. in color, map, Oct., 1942

WASHINGTON (State)—*Continued*

Washington, the Evergreen State: The Amazing Commonwealth of the Pacific Northwest Which Has Emerged from the Wilderness in a Span of Fifty Years. By Leo A. Borah. LXIII, pp. 131-196, 50 ills. in black and white, 26 ills. in color, two-page map, Feb., 1933

A Wonderland of Glaciers and Snow. By Milnor Roberts. XX, pp. 530-537, 8 ills., June, 1909

WASHINGTON, D. C.:

American Geographic Education. By W J McGee. IX, pp. 305-307, July, 1898

Approaching Washington by Tidewater Potomac. By Paul Wilstach. LVII, pp. 372-392, 7 ills. in black and white, 15 ills. in color, Mar., 1930

The Capitol, Wonder Building of the World. By Gilbert Grosvenor. XLIII, pp. 603-638, 17 ills. in black and white, 16 ills. in color, June, 1923
Included: Library of Congress; Lincoln Memorial; Pan American Union; Washington Monument; White House

The Color Camera's First Aërial Success. 5 color photos by Melville Bell Grosvenor. LVIII, pp. 344-353, Sept., 1930
Included: Capitol; Library of Congress; Lincoln Memorial; Potomac and Anacostia Rivers; Washington Monument

Geographic Development of the District of Columbia. By W J McGee. IX, pp. 317-323, July, 1898

The Historical Development of the National Capital. By Marcus Baker. IX, pp. 323-329, July, 1898

How the Earth Telegraphed Its Tokyo Quake to Washington. By the Rev. Francis A. Tondorf. XLIV, pp. 453-454, ill., Oct., 1923

The Lincoln Memorial. By William Howard Taft. XLIII, pp. 597-602, 5 ills., June, 1923

The Nation's Capital. By James Bryce. XXIV, pp. 717-750, 26 ills., June, 1913

The Nation's Capital by Night. By Volkmar Wentzel. With 16 photos in duotone by author. LXXVII, pp. 514-530, Apr., 1940

Next International Geographical Congress To Be Held in Washington. (By G. H. G.). XII, pp. 351-357, 4 ills., Oct., 1901

Old Masters in a New National Gallery. By Ruth Q. McBride. LXXVIII, pp. 1-50, 11 ills. in black and white, 32 color reproductions of masterpieces, July, 1940

The Original Boundary Stones of the District of Columbia. By Ernest A. Shuster, Jr. XX, pp. 356-359, 6 ills., map, Apr., 1909

Potomac, River of Destiny. By Albert W. Atwood. LXXXVIII, pp. 33-70, 15 ills. in black and white, 18 ills. in color, map, July, 1945

The Sources of Washington's Charm. By J. R. Hildebrand. XLIII, pp. 639-680, 46 ills., June, 1923

Spring's Gay Bouquets Deck the Nation's Capital. 10 color photos by Harrison Howell Walker. LXXIV, pp. 17-24, July, 1938

WASHINGTON, D. C.—*Continued*

Surveys and Maps of the District of Columbia. By Marcus Baker. VI, pp. 149-178, diagr., tables, map, Nov. 1, 1894
Included: List of Maps of Washington and the District of Columbia

The Transformation of Washington: A Glance at the History and Along the Vista of the Future of the Nation's Capital. By Charles Moore. XLIII, pp. 569-595, 16 ills., maps, June, 1923

Unique Gifts of Washington to the Nation. 11 color photos by Charles Martin, Edwin L. Wisherd, Jacob Gayer, Clifton Adams. LV, pp. 473-481, Apr., 1929

Views of the Lincoln Memorial in Washington. 8 ills. XLII, pp. 197-204, Aug., 1922

Wartime Washington. By William H. Nicholas. LXXXIV, pp. 257-290, 12 ills. in black and white, 16 ills. in color, Sept., 1943

Washington, Home City and Show Place: To Residents and Visitors the Nation's Capital Presents Varied Sides as the City Steadily Grows in Beauty and Stature. By Leo A. Borah. LXXI, pp. 663-695, 11 ills. in black and white, 20 ills. in color, June, 1937

Washington: Its Beginning, Its Growth, and Its Future. By William Howard Taft. XXVII, pp. 221-292, 33 ills. in black and white, 32 ills. in color, map, panoramas, Mar., 1915
The Mall (panorama)
The Ultimate Washington: Plan Laid Out by the Commission of 1901 for the National Capital (panorama)

Washington—Storehouse of Knowledge. By Albert W. Atwood. LXXXI, pp. 325-359, 20 ills. in black and white, 9 ills. in color, Mar., 1942

The Washington Aqueduct and Cabin John Bridge. By D. D. Gaillard. VIII, pp. 337-344, ills., Dec., 1897

Washington Through the Years: On Rolling Wooded Hills and Colonial Tobacco Fields, Where George Washington Dreamed Our Nation's Great Capital, His Gorgeous Vision Comes True. By Gilbert Grosvenor. LX, pp. 517-619, 67 ills. in black and white, 49 ills. in color, map, Nov., 1931

Winter Lights and Shadows in the Nation's Capital. 21 ills. in duotone. LXVII, pp. 201-216, Feb., 1935

Wonders of the New Washington: Efficient Modern Structures Rise in the Biggest Government Building Program Since the Capital City Was Founded in a Wilderness. By Frederick G. Vosburgh. LXVII, pp. 457-488, 20 ills. in black and white, 13 ills. in color, Apr., 1935

See also Washington Cathedral; *and* near-by sites: Arlington National Cemetery; Great Falls; Mount Vernon

WASHINGTON, the Pride of the Nation. 16 color photos by Charles Martin. XLIII, pp. 617-632, June, 1923

WASHINGTON ACADEMY OF SCIENCES:

The Harriman Alaska Expedition in Cooperation with the Washington Academy of Sciences. (By G. H. G.). X, pp. 225-227, June, 1899

The **WASHINGTON** Aqueduct and Cabin John Bridge. By D. D. Gaillard. VIII, pp. 337-344, ills., Dec., 1897

WASHINGTON CATHEDRAL, Washington, D. C.:

Cathedrals of the Old and New World. By J. Bernard Walker. XLII, pp. 61-114, 50 ills., July, 1922

The **WASHINGTON** of Tradition Builds for the Future. 20 ills. in color. LXXI, pp. 671-694, June, 1937

WASPS. *See* Women's AirForce Service Pilots

WASPS (Insects):

Marvels of Metamorphosis: A Scientific "G-man" Pursues Rare Trapdoor Spider Parasites for Three Years With a Spade and a Candid Camera. By George Elwood Jenks. LXXIV, pp. 807-828, 39 ills., Dec., 1938

Potent Personalities—Wasps and Hornets: Though Often Painfully Stung, Mankind Profits Immeasurably from the Pest-killing Activities of These Fiery Little Flyers. By Austin H. Clark. Paintings by Hashime Murayama. LXXII, pp. 47-72, 18 ills. in black and white, 12 ills. in color, July, 1937

A **WASTEFUL** Nation (Report of Conservation Commission). XX, pp. 203-206, Feb., 1909

WATER SUPPLY:

The Arid Regions of the United States. By F. H. Newell. V, pp. 167-172, Jan. 31, 1894

Artesian Water Predictions. XXI, pp. 361-363, ill., Apr., 1910

Carrying Water Through a Desert: The Story of the Los Angeles Aqueduct. By Burt A. Heinly. XXI, pp. 568-596, 19 ills., map, July, 1910

The Central Great Plains. XVI, pp. 389-397, 8 ills., Aug., 1905

Irrigation in California. By Wm. Hammond Hall. I, pp. 277-290, Oct., 1889

The Irrigation Problem in Montana. By H. M. Wilson. II, pp. 212-229, 4 tables, July, 1890

The Limited Water Supply of the Arid Region. By Frederick H. Newell. XI, pp. 438-442, Nov., 1900

More Water for California's Great Central Valley. By Frederick Simpich. XC, pp. 645-664, 16 ills., map, Nov., 1946

The National Geographic Society's Memorial to American Troops: Fountain and Water Supply System Presented to Historic French Town of Cantigny, Where Our Overseas Soldiers Won Their First Victory in the World War. XLIV, pp. 675-678, 4 ills., Dec., 1923

New York—The Metropolis of Mankind. By William Joseph Showalter. XXXIV, pp. 1-49, 39 ills., July, 1918

An Old Jewel in the Proper Setting: An Eyewitness's Account of the Reconquest of the Holy Land by Twentieth Century Crusaders. By Charles W. Whitehair. XXXIV, pp. 325-344, 17 ills., Oct., 1918

Pollution of the Potomac River. By F. H. Newell. VIII, pp. 346-351, Dec., 1897

WATER SUPPLY—*Continued*
Recent Hydrographic Work. (By F. H. N.). VII, pp. 347-348, Oct., 1896
The Water Supply for the Nicaragua Canal. By Arthur P. Davis. XI, pp. 363-365, Sept., 1900
See also Aqueducts

WATEREE (Ship):
Some Personal Experiences with Earthquakes (Arica). By Rear Admiral L. G. Billings. XXVII, pp. 57-71, 7 ills., Jan., 1915

WATERFALLS:
The Falls of Iguazu. By Marie Robinson Wright. XVII, pp. 456-460, 4 ills., Aug., 1906
The Geography of Japan: With Special Reference to Its Influence on the Character of the Japanese People. By Walter Weston. XL, pp. 45-84, 23 ills. in black and white, 16 ills. in color, July, 1921
The Great Falls of the Potomac. By Gilbert Grosvenor. LIII, pp. 385-400, 19 ills., Mar., 1928
Kaieteur and Roraima: The Great Falls and the Great Mountain of the Guianas. By Henry Edward Crampton. XXXVIII, pp. 227-244, 12 ills., map, Sept., 1920
Niagara at the Battle Front. By William Joseph Showalter. XXXI, pp. 413-422, 6 ills., May, 1917
Niagaras of Five Continents. 16 ills. XXXVIII, pp. 211-226, Sept., 1920
Potomac, River of Destiny. By Albert W. Atwood. LXXXVIII, pp. 33-70, 15 ills. in black and white, 18 ills. in color, map, July, 1945
Rhodesia, Hobby and Hope of Cecil Rhodes. By W. Robert Moore. LXXXVI, pp. 281-306, 13 ills. in black and white, 10 ills. in color, map, Sept., 1944
The Wonders of the Mosi-oa-Tunga: The Falls of the Zambesi. By Louis Livingston Seaman. XXII, pp. 561-571, 6 ills., June, 1911
The World's Great Waterfalls: Visits to Mighty Niagara, Wonderful Victoria, and Picturesque Iguazu. By Theodore W. Noyes. L, pp. 29-59, 29 ills., July, 1926
The World's Greatest Waterfall: The Kaieteur Fall, in British Guiana. By Leonard Kennedy. XXII, pp. 846-859, 6 ills., map, Sept., 1911

WATERWAYS. *See* Canals; Rivers; *and* Intracoastal Waterway

WATLING (San Salvador, Island). *See* Bahama Islands

WATSON, THOMAS:
Voice Voyages by the National Geographic Society: A Tribute to the Geographical Achievements of the Telephone (Address by Thomas Watson). XXIX, pp. 296-326, 15 ills., chart, Mar., 1916

WATTS, HARVEY MAITLAND:
The Chinese Paradox. By Harvey Maitland Watts. XI, pp. 352-358, ills., Sept., 1900

WATTS, W. A.:
Flame-Feathered Flamingos of Florida. By W. A. Watts. With 9 color photos by W. F. Gerecke. LXXIX, pp. 56-65, Jan., 1941

WATUSSI (Tribespeople):
A Land of Giants and Pygmies (Ruanda). By the Duke Adolphus Frederick of Mecklenburg. XXIII, pp. 369-388, 16 ills., map, Apr., 1912
Uganda, "Land of Something New": Equatorial African Area Reveals Snow-crowned Peaks, Crater Lakes, Jungle-story Beasts, Human Giants, and Forest Pygmies. By Jay Marston. LXXI, pp. 109-130, 22 ills., map, Jan., 1937

WAVES. *See* Women's Reserve of the U. S. Naval Reserve

WAVES, Ocean:
The Economic Aspects of Soil Erosion. (Part I). By Dr. N. S. Shaler. VII, pp. 328-338, Oct., 1896
Included: Marine erosion
See also Tides and Tidal Waves

WAVES and Thrills at Waikiki (Honolulu). 8 ills. in duotone by Thomas Edward Blake. LXVII, pp. 597-604, May, 1935

WAYFARING Down the Winding Severn. 15 color photos by Frank and Bernard Wakeman. LXIII, pp. 433-440, Apr., 1933

WAYS and Byways of an Island Paradise (Bali). 9 ills. LXXV, pp. 345-352, Mar., 1939

WAYSIDE Scenes in Europe. 16 ills. in duotone. XXV, pp. 229-244, Feb., 1914

WAYSIDE Scenes in Europe. 16 ills. in duotone. XXVII, pp. 401-416, Apr., 1915

WAXEL, SWEN:
The Cartography and Observations of Bering's First Voyage. By General A. W. Greely. III, pp. 205-230, map supplement, Jan. 28, 1892; Feb. 19, 1892

WAZIRISTAN (Region), India:
South of Khyber Pass. By Maynard Owen Williams. LXXXIX, pp. 471-500, 31 ills., map supplement, Apr., 1946

WE Escape from Madrid. By Gretchen Schwinn. LXXI, pp. 251-268, 15 ills., Feb., 1937

WE Keep House on an Active Volcano: After Flying to Study a Spectacular Eruption in Belgian Congo, a Geologist Settles Down on a Newborn Craterless Vent for Eight Months' Study. By Dr. Jean Verhoogen. LXXVI, pp. 511-550, 28 ills., map, Oct., 1939

WE Live Alone and Like It—On an Island (Skokholm). By R. M. Lockley. LXXIV, pp. 252-278, 27 ills., Aug., 1938

WE Occupy the Best Position on the Map. XVI, pp. 514-515, Nov., 1905

The **WEALTH** of Nations. XIII, p. 145, Apr., 1902

The **WEAPON** of Food. By Herbert Hoover. XXXII, pp. 197-212, 15 ills., Sept., 1917

WEAPONS:
Air Power for Peace. By General H. H. Arnold. LXXXIX, pp. 137-193, 35 ills. in black and white, 28 ills. in color, map supplement, Feb., 1946

WEAPONS—*Continued*

Infantrymen—The Fighters of War. By Brigadier General W. H. Wilbur. LXXXVI, pp. 513-538, 22 ills., Nov., 1944

Pirate-Fighters of the South China Sea. By Robert Cardwell. LXXXIX, pp. 787-796, 11 ills., June, 1946

See also Bombs; Rockets; World War I; World War II

WEATHER. *See* Meteorology

WEATHER BUREAU. *See* U. S. Weather Bureau

The **WEATHER** Bureau. By Willis L. Moore. XII, pp. 362-369, Oct., 1901

The **WEATHER** Bureau and the Recent Floods. By H. C. Frankenfield. XIV, pp. 285-290, ills., July, 1903

The **WEATHER** Bureau River and Flood System. By Professor Willis L. Moore. VII, pp. 302-307, Sept., 1896

WEATHER Fights and Works for Man. By F. Barrows Colton. LXXXIV, pp. 641-670, 22 ills., 3 drawings, Dec., 1943

WEATHER Making, Ancient and Modern. By Mark W. Harrington. VI, pp. 35-62, Apr. 25, 1894

WEATHER Proverbs. XV, p. 133, Mar., 1904

WEATHER STATIONS:

Americans Stand Guard in Greenland. By Andrew H. Brown. XC, pp. 457-500, 23 ills. in black and white, 19 ills. in color, map, Oct., 1946

New Frontier in the Sky. By F. Barrows Colton. XC, pp. 379-408, 28 ills., diagr., Sept., 1946

Servicing Arctic Airbases. By Robert A. Bartlett. LXXXIX, pp. 602-616, 3 ills. in black and white, 10 ills. in color, map, May, 1946

See also Solar Radiation

WEAVER BIRDS:

Canaries and Other Cage-Bird Friends. By Alexander Wetmore. Paintings by Major Allan Brooks. LXXIV, pp. 775-806, 19 ills. in black and white, 51 portraits in color, Dec., 1938

WEAVERS of the World. 8 ills. in duotone. XXXVI, pp. 145-152, Aug., 1919

WEAVING:

Totem-pole Builders. 16 ills. in color from paintings by W. Langdon Kihn. LXXXVII, pp. 33-48, Jan., 1945

Weavers of the World. 8 ills. in duotone. XXXVI, pp. 145-152, Aug., 1919

See also Textiles

WEBBER, JOHN W.:

Down Mexico's Río Balsas. By John W. Webber. With 9 color photos by author, Kenneth Segerstrom, Jack Breed. XC, pp. 253-272, 5 ills. in black and white, map, Aug., 1946

WEBER, WALTER A.:

Birds: Sparrows, Towhees, and Longspurs. 43 paintings in color from life by Allan Brooks and Walter A. Weber. LXXV, pp. 361-375, Mar., 1939

Cats: King of Cats and His Court. 20 ills. in color from paintings by Walter A. Weber. LXXXIII, pp. 223-254, Feb., 1943

Deer: Antlered Majesties of Many Lands. 23 ills. in color from paintings by Walter A. Weber. LXXVI, pp. 479-510, Oct., 1939

Dogs: Non-sporting Dogs. 8 ills. in color from paintings from life by Walter A. Weber. LXXXIV, pp. 577-584, Nov., 1943

Dogs: Wild Dogs and Working Dogs. 9 ills. in color from paintings by Walter A. Weber. LXXXVI, pp. 369-376, Sept., 1944

Wildlife of Tabasco and Veracruz (Mexico). By Walter A. Weber. With 19 ills. in color from paintings by author. LXXXVII, pp. 187-216, 7 ills. in black and white, map, Feb., 1945

WEBSTER, HARRIE:

China and Her People—Some Reflections on Their Manners and Customs, Habits and Lives. By Commander Harrie Webster. XI, pp. 309-319, 3 ills., Aug., 1900

Japan and China—Some Comparisons. By Commander Harrie Webster. XII, pp. 69-77, ills., Feb., 1901

Korea—The Hermit Nation. By Commander Harrie Webster. XI, pp. 145-155, 7 ills., Apr., 1900

Samoa: Navigators Islands. By Commander H. Webster. X, pp. 207-217, 9 ills., June, 1899

WEDDELL, ALEXANDER WILBOURNE:

"The Glory That Was Greece." By Alexander Wilbourne Weddell. XLII, pp. 571-630, 51 ills., map, Dec., 1922

WEEK-ENDS with the Prairie Falcon: A Commuter Finds Recreation in Scaling Cliffs to Observe the Nest Life and Flying Habits of These Elusive Birds. By Frederick Hall Fowler. LXVII, pp. 611-626, 21 ills., May, 1935

WEEKS, JOHN M.:

Honors to the American Navy (Address by John M. Weeks). XX, pp. 77-95, Jan., 1909

WEIGHTS AND MEASURES:

Our Heterogeneous System of Weights and Measures. By Alexander Graham Bell. XVII, pp. 158-169, Mar., 1906

A Wonderland of Science. XXVII, pp. 153-169, 15 ills., Feb., 1915

WEISSHORN (Peak), Switzerland:

A Woman's Climbs in the High Alps. By Dora Keen. XXII, pp. 643-675, 26 ills., July, 1911

WELCOME to Wyoming. 19 color photos: 18 by B. Anthony Stewart. LXXXVIII, pp. 161-184, Aug., 1945

WELKER, P. A.:

Surveys in the Philippines. (By P. A. Welker). XXII, pp. 82-83, map, Jan., 1911

WELLFLEET, Massachusetts:

Cape Cod People and Places. By Wanda Burnett. LXXXIX, pp. 737-774, 17 ills. in black and white, 24 ills. in color, map, June, 1946

WELLING, JAMES C. *See* NGS: Board of Managers

WELLIVER, JUDSON C.:

What the War Has Done for Britain. By Judson C. Welliver. XXXIV, pp. 278-297, 13 ills., Oct., 1918

WELLMAN, WALTER:

The Polar Airship. By Walter Wellman. XVII, pp. 208-228, 5 diagrs., Apr., 1906

Portraits. X, ill. p. 349, Sept., 1899. XVII, ill. p. 237, Apr., 1906

WELLMAN POLAR EXPEDITIONS:

The Meteorological Observations of the Second Wellman Expedition. By Evelyn B. Baldwin. X, pp. 512-516, Dec., 1899

No Man's Land—Spitzbergen. XVIII, pp. 455-458, July, 1907

The Return of Wellman. By J. Howard Gore. X, pp. 348-351, ills., Sept., 1899

Walter Wellman's Expedition to the North Pole. XVII, pp. 205-207, chart, Apr., 1906

Wellman Polar Expedition. IX, pp. 373-375, Aug., 1898

The Wellman Polar Expedition. X, pp. 361-362, Sept., 1899

The Wellman Polar Expedition. XVII, p. 712, Dec., 1906

The Wellman Polar Expedition. (By J. Howard Gore). X, pp. 267-268, July, 1899

The Wellman Polar Expedition. By Walter Wellman. X, pp. 481-505, 10 ills., diagr., map, Dec., 1899

WELLS, A. J.:

Seed Farms in California. By A. J. Wells. XXIII, pp. 515-530, 14 ills., May, 1912

WENDLE, JOSEPH:

Hunting the Grizzly in British Columbia. By Joseph Wendle. XVIII, pp. 612-615, 3 ills., Sept., 1907

The **WENDS** of the Spreewald (Germany). By Frederick Simpich. XLIII, pp. 327-336, 12 ills., Mar., 1923

WENTZEL, VOLKMAR:

Kentucky: The Sun Shines Bright in Kentucky. 21 color photos by B. Anthony Stewart, Volkmar Wentzel, Ray Scott. LXXXII, pp. 65-88, July, 1942

New York: Empire State Onions and Pageantry. 12 color photos by J. Baylor Roberts and Volkmar Wentzel. LXXX, pp. 641-648, Nov., 1941

Sweden: Under Swedish Roofs and Skies. 22 color photos by Volkmar Wentzel. LXXVII, pp. 799-822, June, 1940

Washington, D. C.: The Nation's Capital by Night. By Volkmar Wentzel. With 16 photos in duotone by author. LXXVII, pp. 514-530, Apr., 1940

WENTZEL, VOLKMAR—*Continued*

West Virginia: High Road and Low through the Mountain State. 21 color photos by B. Anthony Stewart and Volkmar Wentzel. LXXVIII, pp. 157-180, Aug., 1940

WEST AFRICA:

The Gold Coast, Ashanti, and Kumassi. By George K. French. VIII, pp. 1-15, 9 ills., Jan., 1897

See also French West Africa

The **WEST** Indian Hurricane of August 7-14, 1899. By E. B. Garriott. X, pp. 343-348, diagr., Sept., 1899

The **WEST** Indian Hurricane of September 1-12, 1900. By E. B. Garriott. XI, pp. 384-392, 4 charts, Oct., 1900

The **WEST** Indian Hurricane of September 10-11, 1898. By Prof. E. B. Garriott. X, pp. 17-20, Jan., 1899

WEST INDIES:

Americans in the Caribbean. By Luis Marden. LXXXI, pp. 723-758, 16 ills. in black and white, 22 ills. in color, map, June, 1942

America's New Crescent of Defense. 8 photos, map. LXXVIII, pp. 621-628, Nov., 1940

The British Commonwealth of Nations: "Organized Freedom" Around the World. By Eric Underwood. LXXXIII, pp. 485-524, 31 ills., Apr., 1943

British West Indian Interlude. By Anne Rainey Langley. LXXIX, pp. 1-46, 23 ills. in black and white, 21 ills. in color, maps, Jan., 1941

The Countries of the Caribbean. By William Joseph Showalter. XXIV, pp. 227-250, 23 ills., Feb., 1913

The First Landfall of Columbus. By Jacques W. Redway, F. R. G. S. VI, pp. 179-192, 4 maps, Dec. 29, 1894

Included: Mariguana (Mayaguana); Samana; Watling (San Salvador)

Geographic Progress of Civilization. Annual Address by the President, Honorable Gardiner G. Hubbard. VI, pp. 1-22, Feb. 14, 1894

Included: Jamaica; San Domingo

The Haunts of the Caribbean Corsairs: The West Indies a Geographic Background for the Most Adventurous Episodes in the History of the Western Hemisphere. By Nell Ray Clarke. XLI, pp. 147-187, 43 ills., Feb., 1922

Heart of a Hemisphere: Of Vital Importance is the Area Portrayed in The Society's New Map of Mexico, Central America, and the West Indies. Text with map supplement. LXXVI, pp. 739-740, ill., Dec., 1939

How Latin America Looks from the Air: U. S. Army Airplanes Hurdle the High Andes, Brave Brazil Jungles, and Follow Smoking Volcanoes to Map New Sky Paths Around South America. By Major Herbert A. Dargue. LII, pp. 451-502, 52 ills., map, Oct., 1927

Hunting Useful Plants in the Caribbean. By David Fairchild. LXVI, pp. 705-737, 39 ills., Dec., 1934

WEST INDIES—*Continued*

An Important New Guide for Shipping: Navassa Light, on a Barren Island in the West Indies, is the First Signal for the Panama Canal. By George R. Putnam. XXXIV, pp. 401-406, 3 ills., map, Nov., 1918

In the Wake of Columbus. By Frederick A. Ober. V, pp. 187-196, Jan. 31, 1894

The Law of Storms, Considered with Special Reference to the North Atlantic. By Everett Hayden. II, pp. 199-211, ill., 3 diagrs., 3 foldout diagrs., foldout charts, July, 1890

On the Shores of the Caribbean. 16 ills. XLI, pp. 157-172, Feb., 1922

The Origin of West India Bird-Life. By Frank M. Chapman. IX, pp. 243-247, May, 1898

Our Map of the Countries of the Caribbean. Text with map supplement. XLI, pp. 221-222, Feb., 1922

Report by Robert T. Hill on the Volcanic Disturbances in the West Indies. XIII, pp. 223-267, 12 ills., 3 maps, July, 1902

Skypaths Through Latin America: Flying From Our Nation's Capital Southward Over Jungles, Remote Islands, and Great Cities on an Aërial Survey of the East Coast of South America. By Frederick Simpich. LIX, pp. 1-79, 77 ills., map, Jan., 1931

The Society's New Caribbean Map: Mexico, Central America, and the West Indies—Gateway of Discovery. Text with map supplement. LXVI, pp. 738-740, ill., Dec., 1934

Southward Ho! In the "Alice." By Henry Howard. LXXIII, pp. 265-312, 38 ills. in black and white, 13 ills. in color, maps, Mar., 1938

To Bogotá and Back by Air: The Narrative of a 9,500-Mile Flight from Washington, Over Thirteen Latin-American Countries and Return, in the Single-Seater Airplane "Spirit of St. Louis." By Col. Charles A. Lindbergh. LIII, pp. 529-601, 98 ills., map, May, 1928

The West Indian Hurricane of August 7-14, 1899. By E. B. Garriott. X, pp. 343-348, diagr., Sept., 1899

The West Indian Hurricane of September 1-12, 1900. By E. B. Garriott. XI, pp. 384-392, 4 charts, Oct., 1900

The West Indian Hurricane of September 10-11, 1898. By Prof. E. B. Garriott. X, pp. 17-20, Jan., 1899

See also Aruba; Bahama Islands; Bonaire; Cayman Islands; Cuba; Curaçao; Dominican Republic; Guadeloupe; Haiti; Jamaica; Martinique; Puerto Rico; Saba; St. Vincent; Trinidad; Virgin Islands

WEST Indies Links in a Defense Chain. 21 color photos: 20 by Edwin L. Wisherd. LXXIX, pp. 9-32, Jan., 1941

WEST Point, Mother of Army Men. 10 color photos by Edwin L. Wisherd. LXIX, pp. 779-786, June, 1936

WEST POINT, New York:

West Point and the Gray-Clad Corps. By Lieut. Col. Herman Beukema. LXIX, pp. 777-788, 10 ills. in color, June, 1936

WEST VIRGINIA:

Potomac, River of Destiny. By Albert W. Atwood. LXXXVIII, pp. 33-70, 15 ills. in black and white, 18 ills. in color, map, July, 1945

Roads from Washington. By John Patric. LXXIV, pp. 1-56, 27 ills. in black and white, 30 ills. in color, map supplement, July, 1938

The Travels of George Washington: Dramatic Episodes in His Career as the First Geographer of the United States. By William Joseph Showalter. LXI, pp. 1-63, 50 ills., 4 maps, map supplement, Jan., 1932

West Virginia: Treasure Chest of Industry. By Enrique C. Canova. LXXVIII, pp. 141-184, 19 ills. in black and white, 21 ills. in color, two-page map, Aug., 1940

WESTDAHL, FERDINAND:

Mountains on Unimak Island, Alaska. By Ferdinand Westdahl. XIV, pp. 91-99, 4 ills., map, Mar., 1903

WESTERN Front Map Embraces Three Continents (Europe, Africa, Asia). Text with map supplement. LXXXII, pp. 139-140, July, 1942

WESTERN HEMISPHERE:

The "Map of Discovery." Reproduction in color of the painting by N. C. Wyeth, National Geographic Society, Washington, D. C. LV, text, p. 93; supplement, Jan., 1929

The National Geographic Society's New Map of the World. Text with map supplement. LXVIII, pp. 796-798, Dec., 1935

New World Map Gives Backdrop for Headlines (Eastern and Western Hemispheres). Text with map supplement. LXXX, pp. 741-742, ill., Dec., 1941

WESTERN National Parks Invite America Out of Doors. 17 photos in duotone by G. A. Grant, W. M. Rush, Merl La Voy, J. S. Dixon. LXVI, pp. 65-80, July, 1934

WESTERN Progress in China. XII, pp. 434-436, Dec., 1901

WESTERN Siberia and the Altai Mountains: With Some Speculations on the Future of Siberia. By James Bryce. XXXIX, pp. 469-507, 39 ills., May, 1921

WESTERN Views in the Land of the Best (U. S.). 16 color photos by Fred Payne Clatworthy. XLIII, pp. 405-420, Apr., 1923

WESTMINSTER, Palace of, London, England:

Yanks at Westminster. By Capt. Leonard David Gammans. XC, pp. 223-252, 6 ills. in black and white, 19 ills. in color, Aug., 1946

WESTON, HAROLD F.:

Persian Caravan Sketches: The Land of the Lion and the Sun as Seen on a Summer Caravan Trip. By Harold F. Weston. XXXIX, pp. 417-468, 46 ills. in black and white, 16 ills. in color, map, Apr., 1921

Persia. 16 color photos: 11 by author, pp. 401-416

WESTON, WALTER:

The Geography of Japan: With Special Reference to Its Influence on the Character of the Japanese People. By Walter Weston. XL, pp. 45-84, 23 ills. in black and white, 16 ills. in color, July, 1921

Some Aspects of Rural Japan. By Walter Weston. XLII, pp. 275-301, 12 ills. in black and white, 16 ills. in color, Sept., 1922

WESTWARD Bound in the *Yankee*. By Irving and Electa Johnson. LXXXI, pp. 1-44, 25 ills. in black and white, 20 ills. in color, map, Jan., 1942

WETMORE, ALEXANDER:

Bird Life Among Lava Rock and Coral Sand: The Chronicle of a Scientific Expedition to Little-known Islands of Hawaii. By Alexander Wetmore. XLVIII, pp. 77-108, 36 ills., map, July, 1925

Birds of the Northern Seas. By Alexander Wetmore. Paintings by Maj. Allan Brooks. LXIX, pp. 95-122, 12 ills. in black and white, 34 portraits in color, Jan., 1936

Canaries and Other Cage-Bird Friends. By Alexander Wetmore. Paintings by Major Allan Brooks. LXXIV, pp. 775-806, 19 ills. in black and white, 51 portraits in color, Dec., 1938

The Eagle, King of Birds, and His Kin. By Alexander Wetmore. Paintings by Maj. Allan Brooks. LXIV, pp. 43-95, 23 ills. in black and white, 48 ills. in color, July, 1933

Game Birds of Prairie, Forest, and Tundra. By Alexander Wetmore. Paintings by Maj. Allan Brooks. LXX, pp. 461-500, 5 ills. in black and white, 60 portraits in color, Oct., 1936

Parrots, Kingfishers, and Flycatchers; Strange Trogons and Curious Cuckoos are Pictured with these Other Birds of Color, Dash, and Courage. By Alexander Wetmore. Paintings by Maj. Allan Brooks. LXIX, pp. 801-828, 9 ills. in black and white, 36 portraits in color, June, 1936

Seeking the Smallest Feathered Creatures: Humming Birds, Peculiar to the New World, Are Found from Canada and Alaska to the Strait of Magellan. Swifts and Goatsuckers, Their Nearest Relatives. By Alexander Wetmore. Paintings by Maj. Allan Brooks. LXII, pp. 65-89, 9 ills. in black and white, 36 ills. in color, July, 1932

Shadowy Birds of the Night (Owls). By Alexander Wetmore. Paintings by Maj. Allan Brooks. LXVII, pp. 217-240, 5 ills. in black and white, 21 portraits in color, Feb., 1935

Winged Denizens of Woodland, Stream, and Marsh (Birds). By Alexander Wetmore. Paintings by Major Allan Brooks. LXV, pp. 577-596, 37 portraits in color, May, 1934

See also NGS: Board of Trustees

WHALEBONE:

The Production of Whalebone. XIX, pp. 883-885, ill. pp. 878, 879, Dec., 1908

WHALERS (Men):

American Pathfinders in the Pacific. By William H. Nicholas. LXXXIX, pp. 617-640, 17 ills., two-page map, May, 1946

WHALERS (Ships):

American Pathfinders in the Pacific. By William H. Nicholas. LXXXIX, pp. 617-640, 17 ills., two-page map, May, 1946

WHALES:

Discovering Alaska's Oldest Arctic Town: A Scientist Finds Ivory-eyed Skeletons of a Mysterious People and Joins Modern Eskimos in the Dangerous Spring Whale Hunt. By Froelich G. Rainey. LXXXII, pp. 319-336, 15 ills., Sept., 1942

The Production of Whalebone. XIX, pp. 883-885, ill. pp. 878, 879, Dec., 1908

South Georgia, an Outpost of the Antarctic. By Robert Cushman Murphy. XLI, pp. 409-444, 41 ills., maps, Apr., 1922

Whales, Giants of the Sea: Wonder Mammals, Biggest Creatures of All Time, Show Tender Affection for Young, But Can Maim or Swallow Human Hunters. By Remington Kellogg. Paintings by Else Bostelmann. LXXVII, pp. 35-90, 25 ills. in black and white, 31 ills. in color, Jan., 1940

WHALES, Porpoises, and Dolphins. 31 ills. in color from paintings by Else Bostelmann. LXXVII, pp. 41-80, Jan., 1940

WHALING:

Discovering Alaska's Oldest Arctic Town: A Scientist Finds Ivory-eyed Skeletons of a Mysterious People and Joins Modern Eskimos in the Dangerous Spring Whale Hunt. By Froelich G. Rainey. LXXXII, pp. 319-336, 15 ills., Sept., 1942

How Long a Whale May Carry a Harpoon. (By Wm. H. Dall). X, pp. 136-137, Apr., 1899

Indians of Our North Pacific Coast. By Matthew W. Stirling. Paintings by W. Langdon Kihn. LXXXVII, pp. 25-52, 3 ills. in black and white, 16 ills. in color, Jan., 1945

Shore-Whaling: A World Industry. By Roy Chapman Andrews. XXII, pp. 411-442, 34 ills., May, 1911

South Georgia, an Outpost of the Antarctic. By Robert Cushman Murphy. XLI, pp. 409-444, 41 ills., maps, Apr., 1922

WHARTON, SIR W. J. L.:

Geography. By Rear-Admiral Sir W. J. L. Wharton. XVI, pp. 483-498, Nov., 1905

WHAT Great Britain Is Doing (The British War Effort). By Sydney Brooks. XXXI, pp. 193-210, 7 ills., Mar., 1917

WHAT Has Been Accomplished by the United States Toward Building the Panama Canal. By Theodore P. Shonts. XVI, pp. 558-564, Dec., 1905

WHAT Is It To Be an American? By Franklin K. Lane. XXXIII, pp. 348-354, 4 ills., diagr., Apr., 1918

WHAT Is the Saar? By Frederick Simpich. LXVII, pp. 241-264, 5 ills. in black and white, 23 ills. in duotone, maps, Feb., 1935

WHAT Is the Tide of the Open Atlantic? By Mark S. W. Jefferson. IX, pp. 465-475, 6 charts, Nov., 1898

WHAT Luzon Means to Uncle Sam. By Frederick Simpich. LXXXVII, pp. 305-332, 25 ills., map supplement, Mar., 1945

WHAT the Fighting Yanks See. By Wanda Burnett. LXXXVI, pp. 451-476, 27 ills., Oct., 1944

WHAT the Latin American Republics Think of the Pan-American Conferences. XVII, pp. 474-479, Aug., 1906

WHAT the U. S. Geological Survey Has Done in Twenty-five Years. XV, pp. 365-366, Sept., 1904

WHAT the United States Government Does to Promote Agriculture. XIV, pp. 35-39, Jan., 1903

WHAT the War Has Done for Britain. By Judson C. Welliver. XXXIV, pp. 278-297, 13 ills., Oct., 1918

WHEAT:

How the World Is Fed. By William Joseph Showalter. XXIX, pp. 1-110, 101 ills., Jan., 1916

Russia's Wheat Surplus. XVII, pp. 580-583, Oct., 1906

Speaking of Kansas. By Frederick Simpich. LXXII, pp. 135-182, 37 ills. in black and white, 12 ills. in color, two-page map, Aug., 1937

WHEELER, WILLIAM MORTON:

Notes About Ants and Their Resemblance to Man. By William Morton Wheeler. XXIII, pp. 731-766, 32 ills., diagrs., Aug., 1912

WHEELER NATIONAL MONUMENT, Colorado:

The Wheeler National Monument. XX, pp. 837-840, 4 ills., Sept., 1909

WHEN a Drought Blights Africa: Hippos and Elephants Are Driven Insane by Suffering, in the Lorian Swamp, Kenya Colony. By Capt. A. T. Curle. LV, pp. 521-528, 9 ills., Apr., 1929

WHEN Czechoslovakia Puts a Falcon Feather in Its Cap. By Maynard Owen Williams. LXIII, pp. 40-49, 13 ills. in color, Jan., 1933

WHEN GI Joes Took London. By Maj. Frederick Simpich, Jr. LXXXVI, pp. 337-354, 18 ills., Sept., 1944

WHEN Golden Praha Entertains the Majestic Sokol Festival. 13 color photos by Hans Hildenbrand. LXIII, pp. 41-48, Jan., 1933

WHEN Irish Skies Are Smiling. 18 color photos by Harrison Howell Walker. LXXVII, pp. 663-686, May, 1940

WHEN Our Country Is Fifty Years Older. By Raphael Zon. XX, pp. 573-580, ills., diagr., June, 1909

WHEN Red Men Ruled Our Forests (Northeastern Indians). 24 ills. in color from paintings by W. Langdon Kihn. LXXII, pp. 551-590, Nov., 1937

WHEN the Father of Waters Goes on a Rampage: An Account of the Salvaging of Food-fishes from the Overflowed Lands of the Mississippi River. By Hugh M. Smith. XXXVII, pp. 369-386, 18 ills., Apr., 1920

WHEN the Herring Fleet Comes to Great Yarmouth. By W. Robert Moore. LXVI, pp. 233-250, 19 ills., Aug., 1934

WHERE Adam and Eve Lived. By Frederick and Margaret Simpich. XXVI, pp. 546-588, 35 ills., Dec., 1914

WHERE Ancient Sea Kings Held Sway (Crete). 14 color photos by Maynard Owen Williams. LV, pp. 255-262, Feb., 1929

WHERE Bible Characters Live Again: Everyday Life in Oberammergau, World Famous for Its Passion Play, Reaches a Climax at Christmas. By Anton Lang, Jr. LXVIII, pp. 743-769, 19 ills. in black and white, 11 ills. in color, map, Dec., 1935

WHERE Birds and Little Animals Find Haven (Eaton Canyon Bird and Game Sanctuary). By Agnes Akin Atkinson. LXX, pp. 232-241, 14 ills., Aug., 1936

WHERE Bretons Wrest a Living from the Sea (Guérande Peninsula). 23 photos by F. W. Goro. LXXI, pp. 751-766, June, 1937

WHERE Early Christians Lived in Cones of Rock: A Journey to Cappadocia in Turkey Where Strange Volcanic Pinnacles Are Honeycombed With Hermit Cells and Monasteries. By John D. Whiting. LXXVI, pp. 763-802, 20 ills. in black and white, 20 ills. in color, map, Dec., 1939

WHERE East Meets West: Visit to Picturesque Dalmatia, Montenegro and Bosnia. By Marian Cruger Coffin. XIX, pp. 309-344, 26 ills., map, May, 1908

WHERE Everybody Dresses in White (Korea). 10 photos by Rev. J. Z. Moore. XIX, pp. 872-877, Dec., 1908

WHERE Exploration Is Needed (Africa). XI, pp. 163-164, Apr., 1900

WHERE Fog and Sun Paint the Pacific (Pacific Northwest). 23 color photos by J. Baylor Roberts. LXXXII, pp. 437-460, Oct., 1942

WHERE Hot Pools Seethe and Geysers Spout (Yellowstone). 9 color photos by Edwin L. Wisherd. LXXVII, pp. 775-782, June, 1940

WHERE Man's Garb Rivals the Quetzal (Guatemala). 13 color photos by Luis Marden. LXX, pp. 437-444, Oct., 1936

WHERE Nature Runs Riot: On Australia's Great Barrier Reef Marine Animals Grow to Unusual Size, Develop Strange Weapons of Attack and Defense, and Acquire Brilliant Colors. By T. C. Roughley. LXXVII, pp. 823-850, 18 ills. in black and white, 15 ills. in color, map, June, 1940

WHERE New England Meets the Sea. 17 color photos by B. Anthony Stewart. LXXXVIII, pp. 265-288, Sept., 1945

WHERE Our Bananas Come From (Costa Rica). By Edwin R. Fraser. XXIII, pp. 713-730, 14 ills., July, 1912

WHERE Our Moths and Butterflies Roam. LII, pp. 105-126, 8 ills. in black and white, 81 ills. in color, July, 1927

"**WHERE** Rolls the Oregon." 28 color photos by Ray Atkeson. XC, pp. 689-728, Dec., 1946

WHERE Roosevelt Will Hunt (Africa). By Sir Harry Johnston. XX, pp. 207-256, 43 ills., map supplement, Mar., 1909

WHERE Slav and Mongol Meet. 16 ills. in color. XXXVI, pp. 421-436, Nov., 1919

WHERE Snow Peaks Temper the Tropics (Ecuador). 9 color photos by W. Robert Moore. LXXX, pp. 727-734, Dec., 1941

WHERE Spring Paints a State with Wild Flowers (California). 18 color photos by B. Anthony Stewart. LXIX, pp. 365-380, Mar., 1936

WHERE the Blue Begins on the Italian Coast. 12 color photos by Hans Hildenbrand. LXVII, pp. 81-88, Jan., 1935

WHERE the Last of the West Was Won (Washington). 13 color photos by Clifton Adams and Asahel Curtis. LXIII, pp. 179-186, Feb., 1933

"**WHERE** the Mountains Walked": An Account of the Recent Earthquake in Kansu Province, China, Which Destroyed 100,000 Lives. By Upton Close and Elsie McCormick. XLI, pp. 445-464, 23 ills., map, May, 1922

WHERE the New South Challenges the Old (Alabama). 26 color photos by Edwin L. Wisherd. LX, pp. 717-748, Dec., 1931

WHERE the Sailing Ship Survives (Aland Islands). By A. J. Villiers. LXVII, pp. 101-128, 31 ills., map, Jan., 1935

WHERE the Sard Holds Sway. By Colonel Luigi Pellerano. XLIX, pp. 464-474, ill. in black and white, 9 ills. in color, Apr., 1926

WHERE the Wind Does the Work (Cape Hatteras). By Collier Cobb. XVII, pp. 310-317, 9 ills., map, June, 1906

WHERE the Winding Cam Mirrors Cambridge (University) Spires. 12 color photos by Bernard Wakeman and Walter M. Edwards. LXX, pp. 339-346, Sept., 1936

WHERE the Winning of the West Began (Ohio). 13 color photos by Jacob Gayer LXI, pp. 563-570, May, 1932

WHERE the World Gets Its Oil: But Where Will Our Children Get It When American Wells Cease to Flow? By George Otis Smith. XXXVII, pp. 181-202, 21 ills., 3 maps, Feb., 1920

WHERE Women Vote (Finland). By Baroness Alletta Korff. XXI, pp. 487-493, June, 1910

The **WHIRLPOOL** of the Balkans. By George Higgins Moses. XXXIX, pp. 179-197, 15 ills., Feb., 1921

WHITAKER, HERMAN:

The Wonderland of California. By Herman Whitaker. XXVIII, pp. 57-99, 34 ills., July, 1915

WHITBECK, R. H.:

Geographic Names in the United States and the Stories They Tell. By R. H. Whitbeck. XVI, pp. 100-104, Mar., 1905

WHITBY, England:

Between the Heather and the North Sea: Bold English Headlands Once Sheltered Sea Robbers, Later Were Ports of Wooden Ships, Centers of the Jet and Alum Trades, To-day Are Havens of Adventurous Fishing Fleets. By Leo Walmsley. LXIII, pp. 197-232, 41 ills., Feb., 1933

WHITE, ABBIE M.:

Recent Bequests by Members of the National Geographic Society. XLIX, p. 474, Apr., 1926

WHITE, CLIFFORD:

Peaks and Trails in the Canadian Alps. 3 photos in duotone by Clifford White. LXV, pp. 627-642, May, 1934

WHITE, H. C.:

China's Wonderland—Yen Tang Shan (Chekiang Province). 8 ills. in color from camera paintings by Herbert Clarence White, Clarence C. Crisler, Deng Bao-ling, Hwang Yao-tso. LXXII, pp. 687-694, Dec., 1937

A Peiping Panorama in Vivid Pigments. 16 ills. in color from camera paintings by H. C. and J. H. White, Deng Bao-ling, Hwang Yao-tso. LXX, pp. 753-784, Dec., 1936

WHITE, J. H.:

A Peiping Panorama in Vivid Pigments. 16 ills. in color from camera paintings by H. C. and J. H. White, Deng Bao-ling, Hwang Yao-tso. LXX, pp. 753-784, Dec., 1936

WHITE, JAMES:

Location of the Sir John Franklin Monument. By James White. XIX, p. 596, Aug., 1908

WHITE, JOHN CLAUDE:

Castles in the Air: Experiences and Journeys in Unknown Bhutan. By John Claude White. XXV, pp. 365-455, 74 ills., map, Apr., 1914

Nepal: A Little-Known Kingdom. By John Claude White. XXXVIII, pp. 245-283, 32 ills., map, Oct., 1920

The World's Strangest Capital (Lhasa, Tibet). By John Claude White. XXIX, pp. 273-295, 19 ills., panorama, Mar., 1916

WHITE, JOHN R.:

Among the Big Trees of California. By John R. White. LXVI, pp. 219-232, 14 ills., Aug., 1934

WHITE, WILLIAM A.:

The Geographical Distribution of Insanity in the United States. By Dr. William A. White. XIV, pp. 361-378, 6 maps, Oct., 1903

The **WHITE** City of Algiers. By Lieut. Col. Gordon Casserly. LIII, pp. 206-232, 9 ills. in black and white, 32 ills. in color, Feb., 1928

WHITE HOUSE. *See* Washington, D. C.

WHITE MOUNTAINS, New Hampshire:

From Notch to Notch in the White Mountains: Soaring Heights of New Hampshire Attract Multitudes to America's Oldest Mountain Recreation Area. By Leonard Cornell Roy. LXXII, pp. 73-104, 30 ills., map supplement, July, 1937

WHITE PELICANS:
Pelican Profiles. By Lewis Wayne Walker. LXXXIV, pp. 589-598, 5 ills. in black and white, 8 ills. in color, Nov., 1943

WHITE Population of the Chief British Colonies. XIV, p. 360, Sept., 1903

WHITE RIVER, Yukon Territory:
Ice Cliffs on White River, Yukon Territory. By C. Willard Hayes and Alfred H. Brooks. XI, pp. 199-201, May, 1900
Ice-Çliffs on White River, Yukon Territory. By Martin W. Gorman. XI, pp. 113-117, Mar., 1900

WHITE RUSSIAN SOVIET SOCIALIST REPUBLIC, U. S. S. R.:
The Society's New Map of Soviet Russia. Text with map supplement. LXXXVI, pp. 716-718, Dec., 1944

The **WHITE** Sands of Alamogordo (New Mexico): A Dry Ocean of Granular Gypsum Billows Under Desert Winds in a New National Playground. By Carl P. Russell. LXVIII, pp. 250-264, 12 ills., Aug., 1935

The **WHITE** Sheep, Giant Moose, and Smaller Game of the Kenai Peninsula, Alaska. By George Shiras, 3d. XXIII, pp. 423-494, 59 ills., maps (1 two-page), May, 1912

The **WHITE** War in Norway. By Thomas R. Henry. LXXXVIII, pp. 617-640, 23 ills., map, Nov., 1945

WHITEHAIR, CHARLES W.:
An Old Jewel in the Proper Setting: An Eyewitness's Account of the Reconquest of the Holy Land by Twentieth Century Crusaders. By Charles W. Whitehair. XXXIV, pp. 325-344, 17 ills., Oct., 1918

WHITELEY, GEORGE, JR.:
Newfoundland, North Atlantic Rampart: From the "First Base of American Defense" Planes Fly to Britain's Aid over Stout Fishing Schooners of the Grand Banks. By George Whiteley, Jr. LXXX, pp. 111-140, 26 ills., map, July, 1941

WHITING, JOHN D.:
Among the Bethlehem Shepherds: A Visit to the Valley Which David Probably Recalled When He Wrote the Twenty-third Psalm. By John D. Whiting. L, pp. 729-753, 19 ills., Dec., 1926
Bedouin Life in Bible Lands: The Nomads of the "Houses of Hair" Offer Unstinted Hospitality to an American. By John D. Whiting. LXXI, pp. 59-83, 27 ills., map, Jan., 1937
Bethlehem and the Christmas Story. By John D. Whiting. LVI, pp. 699-735, 27 ills. in black and white, 14 ills. in color, Dec., 1929
Canoeing Down the River Jordan: Voyagers in Rubber Boats Find the Bible Stream Little Tamed Today as It Plunges to the Dead Sea Over the Earth's Lowest River Bed. By John D. Whiting. LXXVIII, pp. 781-808, 19 ills., map, Dec., 1940
From Jerusalem to Aleppo. By John D. Whiting. XXIV, pp. 71-113, 30 ills., map, Jan., 1913

WHITING, JOHN D.—*Continued*
Jerusalem's Locust Plague: Being a Description of the Recent Locust Influx into Palestine, and Comparing Same with Ancient Locust Invasions as Narrated in the Old World's History Book, the Bible. By John D. Whiting. XXVIII, pp. 511-550, 25 ills., map, Dec., 1915
The Last Israelitish Blood Sacrifice: How the Vanishing Samaritans Celebrate the Passover on Sacred Mount Gerizim. By John D. Whiting. XXXVII, pp. 1-46, 40 ills., map, Jan., 1920
Petra, Ancient Caravan Stronghold: Mysterious Temples and Tombs, Carved in Glowing Cliffs of Eroded Sandstone, Are Remnants of a City David Longed to Storm. By John D. Whiting. LXVII, pp. 129-165, 15 ills. in black and white, 21 ills. in color, maps, Feb., 1935
Village Life in the Holy Land. By John D. Whiting. XXV, pp. 249-314, 27 ills. in black and white, 21 ills. in color, Mar., 1914
Where Early Christians Lived in Cones of Rock: A Journey to Cappadocia in Turkey Where Strange Volcanic Pinnacles Are Honeycombed With Hermit Cells and Monasteries. By John D. Whiting. LXXVI, pp. 763-802, 20 ills. in black and white, 20 ills. in color, map, Dec., 1939

WHITMAN, B. L.:
Gardiner Greene Hubbard: Memorial Meeting. Address by Dr. B. L. Whitman. IX, pp. 50-53, Feb., 1898

WHITMAN, MARCUS:
Oregon: Its History, Geography, and Resources. By John H. Mitchell, U. S. Senator from Oregon. VI, pp. 239-284, Apr. 20, 1895

WHITTEMORE, THOMAS:
The Rebirth of Religion in Russia: The Church Reorganized While Bolshevik Cannon Spread Destruction in the Nation's Holy of Holies. By Thomas Whittemore. XXXIV, pp. 379-401, 16 ills., Nov., 1918

WHO Shall Inherit Long Life? On the Existence of a Natural Process at Work Among Human Beings Tending to Improve the Vigor and Vitality of Succeeding Generations. By Dr. Alexander Graham Bell. XXXV, pp. 505-514, 13 ills., June, 1919

WHO Treads Our Trails? A Camera Trapper Describes His Experiences on an Island in the Canal Zone, a Natural-History Laboratory in the American Tropics. By Frank M. Chapman. LII, pp. 331-345, 18 ills., map, Sept., 1927

WHO'S Who Among the Butterflies. By Austin H. Clark. Paintings by Hashime Murayama. LXIX, pp. 679-692, 5 ills. in black and white, 9 ills. in color, May, 1936

WHO'S Who in the Monkey World. 40 portraits from paintings by Elie Cheverlange. LXXIII, pp. 625-648, May, 1938

WHY Great Salt Lake Has Fallen. By L. H. Murdoch. XIV, pp. 75-77, Feb., 1903

WHY Nik-ko (Japan) Is Beautiful. By J. H. De Forest. XIX, pp. 300-308, 8 ills., Apr., 1908

WICKER, CYRUS FRENCH:

Eastward from Gibraltar: Overland Route Across North Africa to Tunisia and Libia. By Cyrus French Wicker. LXXXIII, pp. 115-142, 28 ills., Jan., 1943

WIDEAWAKE FIELD, Ascension Island:

Ascension Island, an Engineering Victory. By Lt. Col. Frederick J. Clarke. LXXXV, pp. 623-640, 21 ills., May, 1944

WIGHT, Isle of, England:

England's Sun Trap Isle of Wight. By J. R. Hildebrand. LXVII, pp. 1-33, 22 ills. in black and white, 14 ills. in color, map, Jan., 1935

WILBUR, CURTIS D.:

Commander Byrd Receives the Hubbard Gold Medal: The First Explorer to Reach the North Pole by Air Receives Coveted Honor at Brilliant National Geographic Society Reception (Address by Secretary Wilbur). L, pp. 377-388, 5 ills., chart, Sept., 1926

WILBUR, LYMAN D.:

Surveying Through Khoresm: A Journey Into Parts of Asiatic Russia Which Have Been Closed to Western Travelers Since the World War. By Lyman D. Wilbur. LXI, pp. 753-780, 31 ills., map, June, 1932

WILBUR, W. H.:

Infantrymen—The Fighters of War. By Brigadier General W. H. Wilbur. LXXXVI, pp. 513-538, 22 ills., Nov., 1944

WILCOX, WALTER D.:

Among the Mahogany Forests of Cuba. By Walter D. Wilcox. XIX, pp. 485-498, 6 ills., map, July, 1908

Recent Exploration in the Canadian Rockies. By Walter D. Wilcox. XIII, pp. 151-168, 12 ills., map, May, 1902; Part II, pp. 185-200, 9 ills., June, 1902

Sources of the Saskatchewan. By Walter D. Wilcox. X, pp. 113-134, 6 ills., chart, Apr., 1899

WILD Animals That Took Their Own Pictures by Day and by Night. By George Shiras, 3d. XXIV, pp. 763-834, 68 ills., map, pictorial supplement, July, 1913

The **WILD** Blueberry Tamed: The New Industry of the Pine Barrens of New Jersey. By Frederick V. Coville. XXIX, pp. 535-546, 10 ills., June, 1916

WILD CATS:

King of Cats and His Court. By Victor H. Cahalane. Paintings by Walter A. Weber. LXXXIII, pp. 217-259, 9 ills. in black and white, 20 ills. in color, Feb., 1943

WILD DOGS:

Other Working Dogs and the Wild Species. By Stanley P. Young. Paintings by Walter A. Weber. LXXXVI, pp. 363-384, 12 ills. in black and white, 9 ills. in color, Sept., 1944

WILD Dogs and Working Dogs. 9 ills. in color from paintings by Walter A. Weber. LXXXVI, pp. 369-376, Sept., 1944

WILD Ducks as Winter Guests in a City Park. By Joseph Dixon. XXXVI, pp. 331-342, 11 ills., Oct., 1919

WILD FLOWERS. *See* Flowers

WILD Flowers of the West (U. S.). By Edith S. Clements. Paintings from life by author. LI, pp. 566-622, 206 ills. in color, May, 1927

The **WILD** Fowl and Game Animals of Alaska. By E. W. Nelson. IX, pp. 121-132, 6 ills., Apr., 1898

WILD Gardens of the Southern Appalachians. 13 color photos by Edwin L. Wisherd, Laurence V. Jolliffe, Clifton Adams. LXV, pp. 679-686, June, 1934

WILD Geese, Ducks, and Swans. 93 portraits from paintings by Major Allan Brooks. LXVI, pp. 493-524, Oct., 1934

WILD Man and Wild Beast in Africa. By Theodore Roosevelt. XXII, pp. 1-33, 41 ills., map, Jan., 1911

WILDLIFE:

High Country of Colorado. By Alfred M. Bailey. With 23 color photos by author, Robert J. Niedrach, F. G. Brandenburg. XC, pp. 43-72, 9 ills. in black and white, July, 1946

Notes on the Wild Fowl and Game Animals of Alaska. By E. W. Nelson. IX, pp. 121-132, 6 ills., Apr., 1898

The Wild Life of Lake Superior, Past and Present: The Habits of Deer, Moose, Wolves, Beavers, Muskrats, Trout, and Feathered Wood-Folk Studied with Camera and Flashlight. By George Shiras, 3d. XL, pp. 113-204, 76 ills., map, pictorial supplement, Aug., 1921

Wildlife of Tabasco and Veracruz (Mexico). By Walter A. Weber. With 19 ills. in color from paintings by author. LXXXVII, pp. 187-216, 7 ills. in black and white, map, Feb., 1945

Wild Life of the Atlantic and Gulf Coasts: A Field Naturalist's Photographic Record of Nearly Half a Century of Fruitful Exploration. By George Shiras, 3d. LXII, pp. 261-309, 62 ills., Sept., 1932

See also Birds; Fishes and Fisheries; Mammals; Reptiles; *and* Game Preserves; National Parks

WILEY, HARVEY W.:

The National Geographic Society (Speech by Doctor Harvey W. Wiley). XXIII, pp. 272-298, 5 ills., Mar., 1912

The United States; Its Soils and Their Products. By H. W. Wiley. XIV, pp. 263-279, 11 ills., July, 1903

WILKES, CHARLES:

American Discoverers of the Antarctic Continent. By Major General A. W. Greely. XXIII, pp. 298-312, 7 ills., map, Mar., 1912

The Gem of the Ocean: Our American Navy. By Josephus Daniels. XXXIII, pp. 313-335, 35 ills., Apr., 1918

Memorial Monument to, erected by National Geographic Society. LIV, ill. p. 633, Nov., 1928

Revealing Earth's Mightiest Ocean (Pacific). By Albert W. Atwood. LXXXIV, pp. 291-306, 10 ills., map supplement, Sept. 1943

WILKES, CHARLES—*Continued*

Some Early Geographers of the United States. By Rear Admiral Colby M. Chester. XV, pp. 392-404, Oct., 1904

Termination Land (Antarctica). (By Edwin Swift Balch). XV, pp. 220-221, May, 1904

Wilkes' and D'Urville's Discoveries in Wilkes Land. By Rear Admiral John E. Pillsbury. XXI, pp. 171-173, Feb., 1910

WILKINS, SIR HUBERT:

Our Search for the Lost Aviators: An Arctic Area Larger Than Montana First Explored in Hunt for Missing Russians. By Sir Hubert Wilkins. LXXIV, pp. 141-172, 29 ills., two-page map, Aug., 1938

WILKINSON, NORMAN:

Cathedrals of England: An Artist's Pilgrimage to These Majestic Monuments of Man's Genius and Faith. By Norman Wilkinson. LXXVI, pp. 741-762, 3 ills. in black and white, 16 ills. in gravure from dry-point engravings by author, Dec., 1939

Ships of the Centuries. 16 ills. in gravure from etchings by Norman Wilkinson. LXXIII, pp. 65-80; text, p. 98, Jan., 1938

WILLEMSTAD, Curaçao (Island):

Curaçao and Aruba on Guard. By W. Robert Moore. LXXXIII, pp. 169-192, 12 ills. in black and white, 10 ills. in color, 4 maps, Feb., 1943

WILLEY, DAY ALLEN:

The Barrage of the Nile. By Day Allen Willey. XXI, pp. 175-184, 14 ills., Feb., 1910

WILLIAM I, The Conqueror:

The Land of William the Conqueror (Normandy): Where Northmen Came to Build Castles and Cathedrals. By Inez Buffington Ryan. LXI, pp. 89-99, 13 ills. in color, Jan., 1932

WILLIAMS, C. B.:

Butterfly Travelers: Some Varieties Migrate Thousands of Miles. By C. B. Williams. Paintings by Hashime Murayama. LXXI, pp. 568-585, ill. in black and white, 8 ills. in color, May, 1937

WILLIAMS, GARDINER F.:

The Diamond Mines of South Africa. By Gardiner F. Williams. XVII, pp. 344-356, 11 ills., June, 1906

WILLIAMS, GEORGE H.:

Notes on Some Eruptive Rocks from Alaska. By George H. Williams. IV, pp. 63-74, Mar. 21, 1892

WILLIAMS, IRA A.:

Scenes Among the High Cascades in Central Oregon. By Ira A. Williams. XXIII, pp. 579-592, 11 ills., June, 1912

WILLIAMS, JOHN SHARP:

The Ties That Bind: Our Natural Sympathy with English Traditions, the French Republic, and the Russian Outburst for Liberty. By John Sharp Williams. XXXI, pp. 281-286, 4 ills., Mar., 1917

WILLIAMS, MAYNARD OWEN:

Adventures with a Camera in Many Lands. By Maynard Owen Williams. XL, pp. 87-112, 24 ills., July, 1921

Afghanistan Makes Haste Slowly. By Maynard Owen Williams. LXIV, pp. 731-769, 33 ills. in black and white, 12 ills. in color, map, Dec., 1933

A Kingdom of Many Tribes. 12 color photos by author, pp. 745-752

Airplanes Come to the Isles of Spice: Once Magnet of World Explorers, the Moluccas Again Stand at Crossroads of History in the Netherlands Indies. By Maynard Owen Williams. LXXIX, pp. 535-558, 26 ills., map, May, 1941

Along London's Coronation Route. By Maynard Owen Williams. LXXI, pp. 609-632, 22 ills., map, May, 1937

American Alma Maters in the Near East. By Maynard Owen Williams. LXXXVIII, pp. 237-256, 16 ills., Aug., 1945

American Fighters Visit Bible Lands. By Maynard Owen Williams. With 23 color photos by author. LXXXIX, pp. 311-340, 10 ills. in black and white, Mar., 1946

Ancient Temples and Modern Guns in Thailand. 10 photos: 6 by Maynard Owen Williams. LXXX, pp. 653-660, Nov., 1941

At the Tomb of Tutankhamen: An Account of the Opening of the Royal Egyptian Sepulcher Which Contained the Most Remarkable Funeral Treasures Unearthed in Historic Times. By Maynard Owen Williams. XLIII, pp. 461-508, 53 ills., map, May, 1923

Back to Afghanistan. By Maynard Owen Williams. XC, pp. 517-544, 27 ills., map, Oct., 1946

Bahrein: Port of Pearls and Petroleum. By Maynard Owen Williams. LXXXIX, pp. 195-210, 6 ills. in black and white, 11 ills. in color, map, Feb., 1946

Oil Comes to Bahrein, Port of Pearls. 11 color photos by author, pp. 201-208

Bali and Points East: Crowded, Happy Isles of the Flores Sea Blend Rice Terraces, Dance Festivals, and Amazing Music in Their Pattern of Living. By Maynard Owen Williams. LXXV, pp. 313-352, 33 ills. in black and white, 11 ills. in color, map, Mar., 1939

Bali, Gem of the Netherlands Indies. 11 color photos: 10 by author, pp. 329-336

Between Massacres in Van. By Maynard Owen Williams. XXXVI, pp. 181-184, 3 ills., Aug., 1919

Buddhist Calm Survives Along China's Great Wall. 10 ills. in color: 3 color photos by Maynard Owen Williams. LXXIII, pp. 321-328, Mar., 1938

Buenos Aires: Queen of the River of Silver. By Maynard Owen Williams. LXXVI, pp. 561-600, 22 ills. in black and white, 24 ills. in color, map, Nov., 1939

Buenos Aires—Metropolis of the Pampas. 24 color photos by author, Luis Marden, W. Robert Moore, pp. 577-600

Bulgaria, Farm Land Without a Farmhouse: A Nation of Villagers Faces the Challenge of Modern Machinery and Urban Life. By Maynard Owen Williams. LXII, pp. 185-218, 19 ills. in black and white, 27 ills. in color, map, Aug., 1932

By Car and Steamer Around Our Inland Seas. By Maynard Owen Williams. LXV, pp. 451-491, 29 ills. in black and white, 8 ills. in duotone, two-page map, Apr., 1934
  Freighters of Fortune on Our Great Lakes. 8 ills. in duotone by author, pp. 463-470

By Motor Trail Across French Indo-China. By Maynard Owen Williams. LXVIII, pp. 487-534, 31 ills. in black and white, 27 ills. in color, map, Oct., 1935
  The Tricolor Rules the Rainbow in French Indo-China. 27 color photos by author, pp. 495-518

Carnival Days on the Riviera. By Maynard Owen Williams. L, pp. 467-501, 21 ills. in black and white, 21 ills. in color, Oct., 1926
  The France of Sunshine and Flowers. 16 color photos by author, pp. 481-496

The Celebes: New Man's Land of the Indies. By Maynard Owen Williams. LXXVIII, pp. 51-82, 33 ills., map, July, 1940
  Life and Death in Toradjaland. 22 photos: 11 by author, 8 by Helene Fischer, pp. 65-80

The Citroën Trans-Asiatic Expedition Reaches Kashmir: Scientific Party Led by Georges-Marie Haardt Successfully Crosses Syria, Iraq, Persia, and Afghanistan to Arrive at the Pamir. By Maynard Owen Williams. LX, pp. 387-443, 62 ills., map, Oct., 1931

Classic Greece Merges Into 1941 News. 19 photos: 15 by B. Anthony Stewart, 3 by Maynard Owen Williams. LXXIX, pp. 93-108, Jan., 1941

The Coasts of Corsica: Impressions of a Winter's Stay in the Island Birthplace of Napoleon. By Maynard Owen Williams. XLIV, pp. 221-312, 88 ills., maps, pictorial supplement, Sept., 1923

Color Records from the Changing Life of the Holy City (Jerusalem). By Maynard Owen Williams. LII, pp. 682-707, 27 ills. in color, Dec., 1927

The Columbia (River) Turns on the Power. By Maynard Owen Williams. LXXIX, pp. 749-792, 25 ills. in black and white, 18 ills. in color, June, 1941

Czechoslovakia, Key-Land to Central Europe. By Maynard Owen Williams. XXXIX, pp. 111-156, 45 ills., map, Feb., 1921

The Descendants of Confucius (Industries in Shantung). By Maynard Owen Williams. XXXVI, pp. 253-265, 16 ills., Sept., 1919

East of Suez to the Mount of the Decalogue: Following the Trail Over Which Moses Led the Israelites from the Slave-Pens of Egypt to Sinai. By Maynard Owen Williams. LII, pp. 709-743, 32 ills., map, Dec., 1927

Empire of Romance—India. 16 color photos by Maynard Owen Williams and others. XL, pp. 481-496, Nov., 1921

The Face of the Netherlands Indies. 20 photos by Maynard Owen Williams and others. LXXXIX, pp. 261-276, Feb., 1946

The First Natural-Color Photographs from the Arctic. 3 color photos by Maynard Owen Williams. XLIX, pp. 301-316, Mar., 1926

WILLIAMS, MAYNARD OWEN—*Continued*

First Over the Roof of the World by Motor: The Trans-Asiatic Expedition Sets New Records for Wheeled Transport in Scaling Passes of the Himalayas. By Maynard Owen Williams. LXI, pp. 321-363, 45 ills., maps, Mar., 1932

From the Mediterranean to the Yellow Sea by Motor: The Citroën-Haardt Expedition Successfully Completes Its Dramatic Journey. By Maynard Owen Williams. LXII, pp. 513-580, 45 ills. in black and white, 25 ills. in color, maps, Nov., 1932
  Bright Pages from an Asiatic Travel Log. 12 color photos by author, pp. 545-552
  The Land of Genghis Khan in Its True Colors. 13 color photos by author, pp. 569-576

The Grand Duchy of Luxemburg: A Miniature Democratic State of Many Charms Against a Feudal Background. By Maynard Owen Williams. XLVI, pp. 501-528, 28 ills., map, Nov., 1924

Great Britain on Parade. By Maynard Owen Williams. LXVIII, pp. 137-184, 40 ills. in black and white, 11 ills. in color, Aug., 1935
  Clans in Kilt and Plaidie Gather at Braemar (Scotland). 11 color photos by author, pp. 153-160

Guest in Saudi Arabia. By Maynard Owen Williams. LXXXVIII, pp. 463-487, 24 ills., map, Oct., 1945

How Warwick (Castle) Was Photographed in Color. By Maynard Owen Williams. LXX, pp. 83-93, 13 ills. in color, July, 1936
  Warwick Castle, Stage for Old England's Pageantry. 13 color photos by author, pp. 85-92

Idaho Made the Desert Bloom. 20 color photos: 17 by Dr. Maynard Owen Williams. LXXXV, pp. 657-688, June, 1944

In the Birthplace of Christianity. 17 color photos by Maynard Owen Williams. L, pp. 697-720, Dec., 1926

India at Work and Play. 22 color photos by Peter Upton Muir, Maynard Owen Williams, Frances Muir. LXXXIX, pp. 449-464, Apr., 1946

Informal Salute to the English Lakes. By Maynard Owen Williams. LXIX, pp. 511-521, 10 ills. in color, Apr., 1936

The Isles of Greece. 20 color photos by Maynard Owen Williams and B. Anthony Stewart. LXXXV, pp. 601-616, May, 1944

Latvia, Home of the Letts: One of the Baltic Republics Which Is Successfully Working Its Way to Stability. By Maynard Owen Williams. XLVI, pp. 401-443, 48 ills., map, Oct., 1924

Looking in on the Everyday Life of New Turkey. 4 color photos by Maynard Owen Williams. LXI, pp. 501-508, Apr., 1932

Modern Odyssey in Classic Lands: Troy's Treasures, Athens' Parthenon, and Rome's First "Broad Way" Influence Today's Banks, Costumes, Jewelry, and Railroad Timetables. By Maynard Owen Williams. LXXVII, pp. 291-337, 27 ills. in black and white, 22 ills. in color, Mar., 1940

Mother Volga Defends Her Own. By Maynard Owen Williams. LXXXII, pp. 793-811, 21 ills., Dec., 1942

WILLIAMS, MAYNARD OWEN—*Continued*

Netherlands Indies: Patchwork of Peoples. 23 color photos by Maynard Owen Williams. LXXIII, pp. 681-712, June, 1938

New Delhi (India) Goes Full Time. By Maynard Owen Williams. LXXXII, pp. 465-494, 17 ills. in black and white, 13 ills. in color, map, Oct., 1942

Behind New Delhi's News. 13 color photos by author, pp. 477-484

New Greece, the Centenarian, Forges Ahead. By Maynard Owen Williams. LVIII, pp. 649-721, 51 ills. in black and white, 40 ills. in color, map, Dec., 1930

Amidst the Templed Hills of Greece. 13 color photos by author, pp. 665-672

Festival Days on the Slopes of Mount Parnassus. 14 color photos by author, pp. 713-720

Scenes Along the Byways of Hellas. 13 color photos by author, pp. 689-696

Paris in Spring. By Maynard Owen Williams. LXX, pp. 501-534, 30 ills., Oct., 1936

Paris Lives Again. By M. O. Williams. XC, pp. 767-790, 24 ills., Dec., 1946

Pilgrims Still Stop at Plymouth (England). By Maynard Owen Williams. LXXIV, pp. 59-77, 19 ills., July, 1938

The Poland of the Present. By Maynard Owen Williams. LXIII, pp. 319-344, 19 ills. in black and white, 11 ills. in color, Mar., 1933

Round About Liechtenstein: A Tiny Principality Which the Visitor May Encompass in a Single View Affords Adventurous Climbs Among Steep Pastures and Quaint Villages. By Maynard Owen Williams. LII, pp. 611-634, 18 ills., map, Nov., 1927

Russia's Orphan Races: Picturesque Peoples Who Cluster on the Southeastern Borderland of the Vast Slav Dominions. XXXIV, pp. 245-278, 26 ills., map, Oct., 1918

The Scillies: Isles of Wrecks and Golden Daffodils. 13 color photos: 3 by Maynard Owen Williams. LXXIV, pp. 759-766, Dec., 1938

Seeing 3,000 Years of History in Four Hours: A Panorama of Ancient, Medieval, and Modern Events Against a Background of Mythology Unfolds During an Airplane Journey from Constantinople to Athens. By Maynard Owen Williams. LIV, pp. 719-739, 24 ills., map, Dec., 1928

Sicily Again in the Path of War. By Maynard Owen Williams. LXXXIV, pp. 307-320, 7 ills., map, Sept., 1943

Singapore: Far East Gibraltar in the Malay Jungle. 23 photos: 5 by Maynard Owen Williams. LXXIII, pp. 599-614, May, 1938

South of Khyber Pass (India). By Maynard Owen Williams. LXXXIX, pp. 471-500, 31 ills., map supplement, Apr., 1946

Struggling Poland: A Journey in Search of the Picturesque Through the Most Populous of the New States of Europe. By Maynard Owen Williams. L, pp. 203-244, 48 ills., map, Aug., 1926

The Suez Canal: Short Cut to Empires. By Maynard Owen Williams. LXVIII, pp. 611-632, 19 ills., map, Nov., 1935

WILLIAMS, MAYNARD OWEN—*Continued*

Summer Holidays on the Bosporus. By Maynard Owen Williams. LVI, pp. 487-508, 13 ills. in black and white, 11 ills. in color, map, Oct., 1929

Beside the Bosporus, Divider of Continents. 11 color photos by author, pp. 493-500

Syria: The Land Link of History's Chain. By Maynard Owen Williams. XXXVI, pp. 437-462, 20 ills., map, Nov., 1919

Syria and Lebanon Taste Freedom. By Maynard Owen Williams. With 21 color photos by author. XC, pp. 729-763, 16 ills. in black and white, Dec., 1946

Through the Heart of Hindustan: A Teeming Highway Extending for Fifteen Hundred Miles, from the Khyber Pass to Calcutta. By Maynard Owen Williams. XL, pp. 433-467, 29 ills., Nov., 1921

Time's Footprints in Tunisian Sands. By Maynard Owen Williams. LXXI, pp. 345-386, 43 ills., maps, Mar., 1937

Turkey, Where Earthquakes Followed Timur's Trail. 15 photos by Maynard Owen Williams. LXXVII, pp. 395-406, Mar., 1940

Turkey Goes to School. By Maynard Owen Williams. LV, pp. 95-108, 17 ills., Jan., 1929

The Turkish Republic Comes of Age. By Maynard Owen Williams. LXXXVII, pp. 581-616, 4 ills. in black and white, 29 ills. in color, map, May, 1945

Star and Crescent on Parade. 29 color photos by author, pp. 585-616

Unspoiled Cyprus: The Traditional Island Birthplace of Venus Is One of the Least Sophisticated of Mediterranean Lands. By Maynard Owen Williams. LIV, pp. 1-55, 55 ills. in black and white, 10 ills. in color, map, July, 1928

When Czechoslovakia Puts a Falcon Feather in Its Cap. By Maynard Owen Williams. LXIII, pp. 40-49, 13 ills. in color, Jan., 1933

Where Ancient Sea Kings Held Sway (Crete). 14 color photos by Maynard Owen Williams. LV, pp. 255-262, Feb., 1929

Where Slav and Mongol Meet. 16 color photos by Maynard Owen Williams. XXXVI, pp. 421-436, Nov., 1919

Wilno, Stepchild of the Polish Frontier. 13 ills. in duotone: 3 by Maynard Owen Williams. LXXIII, pp. 777-784, June, 1938

WILLIAMS, TALCOTT:

The Link Relations of Southwestern Asia. By Talcott Williams. XII, pp. 249-265, 12 maps, July, 1901; pp. 291-299, maps, Aug., 1901

WILLIAMSBURG, Virginia:

The Genesis of the Williamsburg Restoration. By John D. Rockefeller, Jr. LXXI, p. 401, Apr., 1937

The Restoration of Colonial Williamsburg. By W. A. R. Goodwin. LXXI, pp. 402-443, 21 ills. in black and white, 25 ills. in color, Apr., 1937

WILLIS, BAILEY:

The Awakening of Argentina and Chile: Progress in the Lands That Lie Below Capricorn. By Bailey Willis. XXX, pp. 121-142, 14 ills., Aug., 1916

WILLIS, BAILEY—*Continued*

The International Millionth Map of the World. By Bailey Willis. XXI, pp. 125-132, diagr., Feb., 1910

Round About Asheville. By Bailey Willis. I, pp. 291-300, map supplement, Oct., 1889

WILLITS, EDWIN. *See* NGS: Board of Managers

WILLOUGHBY, WILLIAM F.:

Proceedings of the National Geographic Society (Abstract of Address on Puerto Rico by Hon. William F. Willoughby). XIII, pp. 466-470, Dec., 1902

WILLOW RUN, Michigan: Bomber Plant:

Michigan Fights. By Harvey Klemmer. LXXXVI, pp. 677-715, 20 ills. in black and white, 19 ills. in color, map, Dec., 1944

WILNO, Stepchild of the Polish Frontier. 13 ills. in duotone. LXXIII, pp. 777-784, June, 1938

WILSON, ALAN D.:

Hunting Bears on Horseback. By Alan D. Wilson. XIX, pp. 350-356, 4 ills., May, 1908

WILSON, ERNEST H.:

The Kingdom of Flowers: An Account of the Wealth of Trees and Shrubs of China and of What the Arnold Arboretum, with China's Help, Is Doing to Enrich America. By Ernest H. Wilson. XXII, pp. 1003-1035, 24 ills., Nov., 1911

WILSON, EUGENE E.:

Anticosti Island, Nugget of the North. By Eugene E. Wilson. LXXXI, pp. 121-140, 19 ills., map, Jan., 1942

WILSON, HERBERT M.:

The Irrigation Problem in Montana. By H. M. Wilson. II, pp. 212-229, 4 tables, July, 1890

Reclaiming the Swamp Lands of the United States. By Herbert M. Wilson. XVIII, pp. 292-301, ills., diagr., map, May, 1907

WILSON, J. A.:

Canada from the Air: Flights Aggregating 10,000 Miles Reveal the Marvelous Scenic Beauties and Amazing Natural Resources of the Dominion. By J. A. Wilson. L, pp. 389-466, 76 ills., map, Oct., 1926

Gentlemen Adventurers of the Air: Many Regions of Canada's Vast Wilderness, Long Hidden Even from Fur Trappers, Are Now Revealed by Exploring Airmen. By J. A. Wilson. LVI, pp. 597-642, 55 ills., map, Nov., 1929

WILSON, JAMES:

The Modern Alchemist (Work of the Department of Agriculture). By James Wilson. XVIII, pp. 781-795, 6 ills., Dec., 1907

Protecting Our Forests from Fire. By James Wilson. XXII, pp. 98-106, 5 ills., Jan., 1911

The U. S. Weather Bureau. By James Wilson. XV, pp. 37-39, Jan., 1904

WILSON, JAMES C.:

Three-Wheeling Through Africa: Two Adventurers Cross the So-called Dark Continent North of Lake Chad on Motorcycles with Side Cars. By James C. Wilson. LXV, pp. 37-92, 64 ills., two-page map, Jan., 1934

WILSON, JAMES H.:

The Great Wall of China. (By James H. Wilson). XI, pp. 372-374, ill., Sept., 1900

WILSON, JOHN M.:

Announcement of the death of Brigadier-General John M. Wilson. XXXVII, p. 345, Apr., 1920

In Honor of the Army and Aviation (Speeches by Gen. John M. Wilson). XXII, pp. 267-284, ill., Mar., 1911

See also NGS: Board of Managers

WILSON, WILLIAM L.:

Gardiner Greene Hubbard: Memorial Meeting. Address by Honorable William L. Wilson. IX, pp. 43-45, Feb., 1898

WILSON, WOODROW:

Do Your Bit for America: A Proclamation by President Wilson to the American People. XXXI, pp. 287-293, ills., Apr., 1917

Election of Woodrow Wilson as Honorary Member of the Society. XXXIII, p. 369, Apr., 1918

Help Our Red Cross. By Woodrow Wilson. XXXI, p. 422, May, 1917

Honors to Colonel Goethals: The Presentation, by President Woodrow Wilson, of the National Geographic Society Special Gold Medal, and Addresses by Secretary of State Bryan, the French Ambassador, the German Ambassador, and Congressman James R. Mann. XXV, pp. 677-690, 6 ills., June, 1914

Letter to Gilbert H. Grosvenor (Flag Number). XXXII, p. 549, Nov.-Dec., 1917

WILSON, Mount, California:

The Magic Mountain. By J. N. Patterson. XIX, pp. 457-468, 9 ills., July, 1908

WILSTACH, PAUL:

Approaching Washington by Tidewater Potomac. By Paul Wilstach. LVII, pp. 372-392, 7 ills. in black and white, 15 ills. in color, Mar., 1930

Holidays Among the Hill Towns of Umbria and Tuscany. By Paul Wilstach. LIII, pp. 401-442, 40 ills., map, Apr., 1928

Jefferson's Little Mountain: Romance Enfolds Monticello, the Restored Home of the Author of the Declaration of Independence. By Paul Wilstach. LV, pp. 481-503, 12 ills. in black and white, 12 ills. in color, Apr., 1929

The Stone Beehive Homes of the Italian Heel: In Trulli-Land the Native Builds His Dwelling and Makes His Field Arable in the Same Operation. By Paul Wilstach. LVII, pp. 229-260, 25 ills. in black and white, 12 ills. in color, map, Feb., 1930

WINCHELL, N. H.:

Origin of the Word Canada. (By N. H. Winchell). XVIII, p. 215, Mar., 1907

WINCHESTER, England:

Winchester, England's Early Capital. By Frederick Simpich. LXXIX, pp. 67-92, 25 ills., map, Jan., 1941

WINCHESTER (Ship):

Cannon on Florida Reefs Solve Mystery of Sunken Ship. By Charles M. Brookfield. LXXX, pp. 807-824, 20 ills., map (on pen and ink drawing), Dec., 1941

WINDERMERE (Lake), British Columbia:

On the Trail of a Horse Thief. By Herbert W. Gleason. XXXV, pp. 349-358, 6 ills., Apr., 1919

WINDJAMMERS:

The Cape Horn Grain-Ship Race: The Gallant "Parma" Leads the Vanishing Fleet of Square-Riggers Through Raging Gales and Irksome Calms 16,000 Miles, from Australia to England. By A. J. Villiers. LXIII, pp. 1-39, 38 ills., Jan., 1933

Rounding the Horn in a Windjammer. By A. J. Villiers. LIX, pp. 191-224, 36 ills., map, Feb., 1931

Sindbads of Science: Narrative of a Windjammer's Specimen-Collecting Voyage to the Sargasso Sea, to Senegambian Africa and Among Islands of High Adventure in the South Atlantic. By George Finlay Simmons. LII, pp. 1-75, 89 ills., map, July, 1927

WINDS:

Americans Stand Guard in Greenland. By Andrew H. Brown. XC, pp. 457-500. 23 ills. in black and white, 19 ills. in color, map, Oct., 1946

Forecasting the Weather. (By Alfred J. Henry). XV, pp. 285-292, 6 ills., chart, July, 1904

The Polar Airship. By Walter Wellman. XVII, pp. 208-228, 5 diagrs., Apr., 1906

Relations of Air and Water to Temperature and Life. By Honorable Gardiner G. Hubbard. V, pp. 112-124, Jan. 31, 1894

Report—Geography of the Air. By Gen. A. W. Greely. II, pp. 49-63, Apr., 1890

The Sailing Ship and the Panama Canal. By James Page. XV, pp. 167-176, charts, Apr., 1904

Weather Fights and Works for Man. By F. Barrows Colton. LXXXIV, pp. 641-670, 22 ills., 3 drawings, Dec., 1943

Weather Making, Ancient and Modern. By Mark W. Harrington. VI, pp. 35-62, Apr. 25, 1894

Where the Wind Does the Work (Cape Hatteras). By Collier Cobb. XVII, pp. 310-317, 9 ills., map, June, 1906

See also Hurricanes; Tornadoes; *and* Marine Erosion

WINDWARD ISLANDS, West Indies:

British West Indian Interlude. By Anne Rainey Langley. LXXIX, pp. 1-46, 23 ills. in black and white, 21 ills. in color, maps, Jan., 1941

See also St. Lucia; St. Vincent

WINES, F. H.:

The Census of 1900 (U. S.). By Dr. F. H. Wines. XI, pp. 34-36, Jan., 1900

WINGATE, ORDE C.:

The Aerial Invasion of Burma. By General H. H. Arnold. LXXXVI, pp. 129-148, 20 ills., Aug., 1944

WINGED Denizens of Woodland, Stream, and Marsh (Birds). By Alexander Wetmore. Paintings by Major Allan Brooks. LXV, pp. 577-596, 37 portraits in color, May, 1934

WINGED Jewels from Many Lands (Butterflies). 9 ills. in color: 3 paintings by Hashime Murayama, 6 color photos by Willard R. Culver. LXIX, pp. 673-688, May, 1936

WINGED Words—New Weapon of War (Radio). By F. Barrows Colton. LXXXII, pp. 663-692, 29 ills., maps, Nov., 1942

WINGS Over Nature's Zoo in Africa. 20 photos in duotone by Reginald A. Bourlay. LXXVI, pp. 527-542, Oct., 1939

WINGS Over the Bounding Main (Ocean Birds). 36 portraits from paintings by Major Allan Brooks. LXXIV, pp. 237-251, Aug., 1938

WINNING the War of Supply. By F. Barrows Colton. LXXXVIII, pp. 705-736, 32 ills., Dec., 1945

WINNING the West. By C. J. Blanchard. XVII, pp. 82-98, 10 ills., map, Feb., 1906

WINTER, NEVIN O.:

The Ukraine, Past and Present. By Nevin O. Winter. XXXIV, pp. 114-128, 14 ills., Aug., 1918

A **WINTER** Expedition in Southwestern Mexico. By E. W. Nelson. XV, pp. 341-356, 14 ills., Sept., 1904

WINTER Lights and Shadows in the Nation's Capital. 21 ills. in duotone. LXVII, pp. 201-216, Feb., 1935

WINTER Rambles in Thoreau's Country. By Herbert W. Gleason. XXXVII, pp. 165-180, 15 ills., Feb., 1920

WINTER Scenes. 16 ills. XXXVII, pp. 135-150, Feb., 1920

WINTER Sky Roads to Isle Royal (Michigan). By Ben East. LX, pp. 759-774, 18 ills., map, Dec., 1931

A **WINTER** Voyage Through the Straits of Magellan. By the late Admiral R. W. Meade, U. S. N. VIII, pp. 129-141, ill., map, May, 1897

A **WINTER** Weather Record from the Klondike Region. By E. W. Nelson. VIII, pp. 327-335, tables, Nov., 1897

WISCASSET, Maine:

The Worm Turns. By Samuel Sandrof. LXXXIX, pp. 775-786, 14 ills., June, 1946

WISCONSIN:

On Goes Wisconsin: Strength and Vigor Mark This Midwestern State, With Its Woods and Lakes and Its Blend of Sturdy Nationalities. By Glanville Smith. LXXII, pp. 1-46, 25 ills. in black and white, 27 ills. in color, two-page map, July, 1937

WISHERD, EDWIN L.:

Alabama: Where the New South Challenges the Old. 26 color photos by Edwin L. Wisherd. LX, pp. 717-748, Dec., 1931

Connecticut: Old and New Blend in Yankeeland. 25 color photos: 4 by Edwin L. Wisherd. LXXIV, pp. 295-326, Sept., 1938

Fish: Rainbow Denizens of the Aquarium. 16 color photos by Edwin L. Wisherd. LXV, pp. 97-104, Jan., 1934

Indians: The Friendly Crows in Festive Panoply. 13 color photos by Edwin L. Wisherd. LII, pp. 315-322, Sept., 1927

Insect Rivals of the Rainbow. 21 color photos by Edwin L. Wisherd. LVI, pp. 28-90, July, 1929

Kentucky: Modern Scenes in the Land of Lincoln's Birth. 15 color photos by Edwin L. Wisherd. LXV, pp. 695-702, June, 1934

Louisiana: Color Camera Records of New Orleans. 15 color photos by Edwin L. Wisherd. LVII, pp. 459-466, Apr., 1930

Louisiana: Flecks of Color in the Fertile Fields of Louisiana. 14 color photos by Edwin L. Wisherd. LVII, pp. 419-426, Apr., 1930

Minnesota: The State of Sky-Blue Water and Verdure. 11 color photos by Clifton Adams and Edwin L. Wisherd. LXVII, pp. 289-296, Mar., 1935

Monticello, One of America's Most Historic Shrines. 8 color photos by Edwin L. Wisherd. LV, pp. 489-496, Apr., 1929

New Jersey: Beaches and Bathers of the Jersey Shore. 11 color photos by Edwin L. Wisherd. LXIII, pp. 535-542, May, 1933

New Jersey: Farms and Workshops of "The Garden State." 13 color photos by Edwin L. Wisherd. LXIII, pp. 559-566, May, 1933

New York (City): Tempo and Color of a Great City. 42 color photos by Clifton Adams and Edwin L. Wisherd. LVIII, pp. 539-578, Nov., 1930

New York (State): Color Highlights of the Empire State. 4 color photos by Edwin L. Wisherd. LXIV, pp. 569-576, Nov., 1933

Pennsylvania: Today in the Land of Penn and Franklin. 39 color photos by Edwin L. Wisherd. LXVIII, pp. 13-52, July, 1935

Philadelphia: Colorful Corners of the City of Homes. 13 color photos by Clifton Adams and Edwin L. Wisherd. LXII, pp. 675-682, Dec., 1932

Puerto Rico Polychromes. 23 color photos by Edwin L. Wisherd. LXXVI, pp. 713-736, Dec., 1939

United States: Canyons and Cacti of the American Southwest. 7 color photos by Edwin L. Wisherd. XLVIII, pp. 275-290, Sept., 1925

United States: Wild Gardens of the Southern Appalachians. 10 color photos by Edwin L. Wisherd. LXV, pp. 679-686, June, 1934

Virgin Islands: Island Treasures of the Caribbean. 23 color photos by Edwin L. Wisherd and C. W. Herbert. LXXVIII, pp. 281-304, Sept., 1940

Virginia: Scenes and Shrines of the Cavalier Country. 2 color photos by Edwin L. Wisherd. LV, pp. 425-432, Apr., 1929

WISHERD, EDWIN L.—*Continued*

Virginia's Colonial Heritage (Williamsburg). 25 color photos: 12 by Edwin L. Wisherd. LXXI, pp. 417-440, Apr., 1937

Washington, D. C.: Springtime Wreathes a Garland for the Nation's Capital. 13 color photos: 3 by Edwin L. Wisherd. LXVII, pp. 473-480, Apr., 1935

Washington, D. C.: Unique Gifts of Washington to the Nation. 2 color photos by Edwin L. Wisherd. LV, pp. 473-480, Apr., 1929

Washington, D. C.: Winter Lights and Shadows in the Nation's Capital. 21 ills. in duotone: 9 by Edwin L. Wisherd. LXVII, pp. 201-216, Feb., 1935

West Indies: Colorful Paths in Martinique and Guadeloupe. 13 color photos by Edwin L. Wisherd. LXXIII, pp. 281-288, Mar., 1938

West Indies: Tropic Color in Trinidad. 14 color photos by Edwin L. Wisherd. LXXII, pp. 327-334, Sept., 1937

West Indies Links in a Defense Chain. 21 color photos: 20 by Edwin L. Wisherd. LXXIX, pp. 9-32, Jan., 1941

West Point, Mother of Army Men. 10 color photos by Edwin L. Wisherd. LXIX, pp. 779-786, June, 1936

Wyoming: Where Hot Pools Seethe and Geysers Spout (Yellowstone). 9 color photos by Edwin L. Wisherd. LXXVII, pp. 775-782, June, 1940

WITH an Exile in Arctic Siberia: The Narrative of a Russian Who Was Compelled to Turn Polar Explorer for Two Years. By Vladimir M. Zenzinov. XLVI, pp. 695-718, 30 ills., map, Dec., 1924

WITH the Devil Dancers of China and Tibet. 43 color photos by Joseph F. Rock. LX, pp. 19-58, July, 1931

WITH the Italians in Eritrea: Torrid Colony Between the Red Sea and Ethiopia, 2,600 Miles by Sea from Rome, Is Mobilization Place of Fascist Troops and Planes. By Harald P. Lechenperg. LXVIII, pp. 265-295, 34 ills., two-page map, Sept., 1935

WITH the Monks at Meteora: The Monasteries of Thessaly. By Elizabeth Perkins. XX, pp. 799-807, 5 ills., Sept., 1909

WITH the Nomads of Central Asia: A Summer's Sojourn in the Tekes Valley, Plateau Paradise of Mongol and Turkic Tribes. By Edward Murray. Paintings and drawings by Alexandre Iacovleff. LXIX, pp. 1-57, 43 ills. in black and white, 26 ills. in color, map, Jan., 1936

WITH Wild Animals in the Rockies. By Lucie and Wendell Chapman. LXVIII, pp. 231-249, 26 ills. in duotone, Aug., 1935

WITHIN the Halls of Cambridge (University). By Philip Broad. LXX, pp. 333-349, 7 ills. in black and white, 12 ills. in color, Sept., 1936

WITWATERSRAND (Region), Transvaal:

A Critical Period in South African History. (By J. H.). VII, pp. 377-379, Nov., 1896

The Transvaal: The Treasure-House Province. By Melville Chater. LIX, pp. 479-512, 28 ills. in black and white, 13 ills. in color, Apr., 1931

WITWATERSRAND (Region), Transvaal—*Continued*

The Witwatersrand and the Revolt of the Uitlanders. By George F. Becker. VII, pp. 349-367, 4 ills., Nov., 1896

WOKAS, a Primitive Indian Food. XV, pp. 183-185, 3 ills., Apr., 1904

WOLLASTON, A. F. R.:

Amid the Snow Peaks of the Equator: A Naturalist's Explorations Around Ruwenzori, with an Excursion to the Congo State, and an Account of the Terrible Scourge of Sleeping Sickness. By A. F. R. Wollaston. XX, pp. 256-277, 11 ills., Mar., 1909

WOLLASTON LAND (Wollaston Peninsula), Victoria Island, Canada:

The Origin of Stefansson's Blond Eskimo. By Major General A. W. Greely. XXIII, pp. 1225-1238, 10 ills., map, Dec., 1912

WOLVES:

Other Working Dogs and the Wild Species. By Stanley P. Young. Paintings by Walter A. Weber. LXXXVI, pp. 363-384, 12 ills. in black and white, 9 ills. in color, Sept., 1944

The Wild Life of Lake Superior, Past and Present: The Habits of Deer, Moose, Wolves, Beavers, Muskrats, Trout, and Feathered Wood-Folk Studied with Camera and Flashlight. By George Shiras, 3d. XL, pp. 113-204, 76 ills., map, pictorial supplement, Aug., 1921

Wolves. XVIII, pp. 145-147, ills., Feb., 1907

A **WOMAN'S** Climbs in the High Alps. By Dora Keen. XXII, pp. 643-675, 26 ills., July, 1911

A **WOMAN'S** Experiences among Stone Age Solomon Islanders: Primitive Life Remains Unchanged in Tropical Jungleland Where United States Forces Now Are Fighting. By Eleanor Schirmer Oliver. LXXXII, pp. 813-836, 26 ills., map, Dec., 1942

A **WOMAN'S** Winter on Spitsbergen. By Martha Phillips Gilson. LIV, pp. 227-246, 20 ills., map, Aug., 1928

WOMEN and Children of the East. XVIII, pp. 248-271, 28 ills., Apr., 1907

WOMEN at Work. By La Verne Bradley. LXXXVI, pp. 193-220, 23 ills., Aug., 1944

WOMEN in Uniform. By La Verne Bradley. LXXXIV, pp. 445-458, 10 ills., Oct., 1943

WOMEN of All Nations. XXII, pp. 49-61, 12 ills., Jan., 1911

WOMEN'S AIRFORCE SERVICE PILOTS (WASPS):

Women in Uniform. By La Verne Bradley. LXXXIV, pp. 445-458, 10 ills., Oct., 1943

WOMEN'S ARMY CORPS (WAC):

Decorations, Medals, Service Ribbons, Badges, and Women's Insignia. LXXXIV, pp. 414-444, 6 ills. in black and white, 376 ills. in color, Oct., 1943

Paris Freed. By Maj. Frederick Simpich, Jr. LXXXVII, pp. 385-412, 14 ills. in black and white, 12 ills. in color, Apr., 1945

Women in Uniform. By La Verne Bradley. LXXXIV, pp. 445-458, 10 ills., Oct., 1943

WOMEN'S INSIGNIA:

Decorations, Medals, Service Ribbons, Badges, and Women's Insignia. LXXXIV, pp. 414-444, 6 ills. in black and white, 376 ills. in color, Oct., 1943

WOMEN'S RESERVE OF THE U. S. COAST GUARD RESERVE (SPARS):

Decorations, Medals, Service Ribbons, Badges, and Women's Insignia. LXXXIV, pp. 414-444, 6 ills. in black and white, 376 ills. in color, Oct., 1943

Women in Uniform. By La Verne Bradley. LXXXIV, pp. 445-458, 10 ills., Oct., 1943

WOMEN'S RESERVE OF THE U. S. NAVAL RESERVE (WAVES):

Decorations, Medals, Service Ribbons, Badges, and Women's Insignia. LXXXIV, pp. 414-444, 6 ills. in black and white, 376 ills. in color, Oct., 1943

Women in Uniform. By La Verne Bradley. LXXXIV, pp. 445-458, 10 ills., Oct., 1943

WOMEN'S Work in Japan. By Mary A. Nourse. LXXIII, pp. 99-132, 32 ills. in black and white, 11 ills. in color, Jan., 1938

WONDER Island of the Amazon Delta: On Marajó Cowboys Ride Oxen, Tree-dwelling Animals Throng Dense Forests, While Strange Fishes and Birds Help Make a Zoologist's Paradise. By Hugh B. Cott. LXXIV, pp. 635-670, 30 ills. in black and white, 12 ills. in color, map, Nov., 1938

A **WONDERER** Under Sea. By William Beebe. Paintings by E. Bostelmann. LXII, pp. 741-758, 13 ills. in black and white, 8 ills. in color, Dec., 1932

The **WONDERFUL** Canals of China. By F. H. King. XXIII, pp. 931-958, 35 ills., 5 maps, Oct., 1912

The **WONDERFUL** Canals of China. By George E. Anderson. XVI, pp. 68-69, Feb., 1905

WONDERFUL Strides of Africa. XVII, pp. 176-177, Mar., 1906

The **WONDERLAND** of California. By Herman Whitaker. XXVIII, pp. 57-99, 34 ills., July, 1915

A **WONDERLAND** of Glaciers and Snow (Mount Rainier National Park). By Milnor Roberts. XX, pp. 530-537, 8 ills., June, 1909

A **WONDERLAND** of Science. XXVII, pp. 153-169, 15 ills., Feb., 1915

The **WONDERS** of the Mosi-oa-Tunga: The Falls of the Zambesi. By Louis Livingston Seaman. XXII, pp. 561-571, 6 ills., June, 1911

WONDERS of the New Washington: Efficient Modern Structures Rise in the Biggest Government Building Program Since the Capital City Was Founded in a Wilderness. By Frederick G. Vosburgh. LXVII, pp. 457-488, 20 ills. in black and white, 13 ills. in color, Apr., 1935

WONG, KINCHUE:

Changing Canton (China). 20 photos by Siukee Mack, Alfred T. Palmer, Kinchue Wong. LXXII, pp. 711-726, Dec., 1937

WOOD, ARNOLD:

The Leach's Petrel: His Nursery on Little Duck Island. By Arnold Wood. XX, pp. 360-365, 7 ills., Apr., 1909

WOOD, EDWARD FREDERICK LINDLEY. *See* Halifax, Lord

WOOD, H. P.:

Hawaii for Homes. By H. P. Wood. XIX, pp. 298-299, Apr., 1908

WOOD, JUNIUS B.:

The Far Eastern Republic (U. S. S. R.). By Junius B. Wood. XLI, pp. 565-592, 29 ills., map, June, 1922

Flying the World's Longest Air-Mail Route: From Montevideo, Uruguay, Over the Andes, Up the Pacific Coast, Across Central America and the Caribbean to Miami, Florida, in 67 Thrilling Flying Hours. By Junius B. Wood. LVII, pp. 261-325, 65 ills., map, Mar., 1930

Illinois, Crossroads of the Continent. By Junius B. Wood. LIX, pp. 523-594, 51 ills. in black and white, 27 ills. in color, map supplement, May, 1931

Russia of the Hour: Giant Battleground for Theories of Economy, Society, and Politics, as Observed by an Unbiased Correspondent. By Junius B. Wood. L, pp. 519-598, 81 ills., Nov., 1926

St. Malo (France), Ancient City of Corsairs: An Old Brittany Seaport Whose Past Bristles with Cannons and Cutlasses. By Junius B. Wood. LVI, pp. 131-177, 28 ills. in black and white, 29 ills. in color, map, Aug., 1929

Seeing America from the "Shenandoah": An Account of the Record-making 9,000-mile Flight from the Atlantic to the Pacific Coast and Return in the Navy's American-built, American-manned Airship. By Junius B. Wood. XLVII, pp. 1-47, 39 ills., diagr., map, Jan., 1925

A Visit to Three Arab Kingdoms: Transjordania, Iraq, and the Hedjaz Present Many Problems to European Powers. By Junius B. Wood. XLIII, pp. 535-568, 30 ills., map, May, 1923

Yap and Other Pacific Islands Under Japanese Mandate. By Junius B. Wood. XL, pp. 591-627, 34 ills., map supplement, Dec., 1921

WOOD, LEONARD:

In Honor of the Army and Aviation (Speech by Maj. Gen. Leonard Wood). XXII, pp. 267-284, ill., Mar., 1911

WOOD, R. W.:

Remarkable Photograph of Lilienthal's Gliding Machine. By R. W. Wood. XIX, p. 596, ill., Aug., 1908. XXII, ill. p. 271, Mar., 1911. LII, ill. p. 235, Aug., 1927

WOOD:

Microscopical Examination of Wood from the Buried Forest, Muir Inlet, Alaska. By Francis H. Herrick. IV, pp. 75-78, drawings, Mar. 21, 1892

See also Lumbering

WOODPECKERS (Birds):

Woodpeckers, Friends of Our Forests. By T. Gilbert Pearson. Paintings by Maj. Allan Brooks. LXIII, pp. 453-479, 12 ills. in black and white, 25 ills. in color, Apr., 1933

The **WOODS** and Gardens of Portugal. By Martin Hume. XXI, pp. 883-894, 8 ills., Oct., 1910

WOODWORTH, FRANCIS:

California Says It with Wild Flowers. By Francis Woodworth. With 9 color photos by B. Anthony Stewart. LXXXI, pp. 492-501, Apr., 1942

Cologne, Key City of the Rhineland. By Francis Woodworth. LXIX, pp. 829-848, 18 ills., map, June, 1936

WOOL:

Beyond Australia's Cities. By W. Robert Moore. LXX, pp. 709-747, 27 ills. in black and white, 12 ills. in color, Dec., 1936

The Indispensable Sheep. LIII, pp. 512-528, 20 ills., Apr., 1928

WOOLF, BELLA SIDNEY:

Fishing for Pearls in the Indian Ocean. By Bella Sidney Woolf. XLIX, pp. 161-183, 24 ills., Feb., 1926

WOOLLEY, C. LEONARD:

Archeology, the Mirror of the Ages: Our Debt to the Humble Delvers in the Ruins at Carchemish and at Ur. By C. Leonard Woolley. LIV, pp. 207-226, 19 ills., Aug., 1928

WORCESTER, DEAN C.:

Field Sports Among the Wild Men of Northern Luzon. By Dean C. Worcester. XXII, pp. 215-267, 52 ills., map, Mar., 1911

Head-Hunters of Northern Luzon. By Dean C. Worcester. XXIII, pp. 833-930, 102 ills., map, Sept., 1912

The Non-Christian Peoples of the Philippine Islands. By Dean C. Worcester. XXIV, pp. 1157-1256, 41 ills. in black and white, 48 ills. in color, Nov., 1913

Philippines. 48 photos, hand-tinted, by author and Charles Martin, pp. 1161-1192

Notes on Some Primitive Philippine Tribes. By Dean C. Worcester. IX, pp. 284-301, 11 ills., June, 1898

Taal Volcano and Its Recent Destructive Eruption (Philippine Islands). By Dean C. Worcester. XXIII, pp. 313-367, 40 ills., diagr., 4 maps, Apr., 1912

WORK and Play in the Ozarks. 20 color photos by B. Anthony Stewart and J. Baylor Roberts. LXXXIII, pp. 597-620, May, 1943

WORK and War in the World of Ants. 18 ills. in color from paintings by Hashime Murayama. LXVI, pp. 179-186, Aug., 1934

WORK in the Arctic and Antarctic. XI, pp. 164-165, Apr., 1900

WORK in the Far South. XIV, p. 109, map, Mar., 1903

The **WORK** in the Pacific Ocean of the Magnetic Survey Yacht "Galilee." By L. A. Bauer. XVIII, pp. 601-611, 15 ills., Sept., 1907

WORK of the Bureau of American Ethnology. By W J McGee. XII, pp. 369-372, Oct., 1901

The **WORK** of the Bureau of Insular Affairs. By Colonel Clarence R. Edwards. XV, pp. 239-255, 8 ills., June, 1904

The **WORK** of the National Geographic Society. (By W J McGee). VII, pp. 253-259, Aug., 1896

The **WORK** of the United States Board on Geographic Names. By Henry Gannett. VII, pp. 221-227, July, 1896

The **WORK** of the U. S. Hydrographic Office. By Commander W. H. H. Southerland. XIV, pp. 61-75, Feb., 1903

The **WORK** on the Isthmus (Panama). XVII, pp. 586-587, Oct., 1906

WORKING DOGS:

Dogs of Duty and Devotion. By Frederick G. Vosburgh. LXXX, pp. 769-774, 3 ills., Dec., 1941

Other Working Dogs and the Wild Species. By Stanley P. Young. Paintings by Walter A. Weber. LXXXVI, pp. 363-384, 12 ills. in black and white, 9 ills. in color, Sept., 1944

Working Dogs of the World. By Freeman Lloyd. Paintings by Edward Herbert Miner. LXXX, pp. 776-806, 12 ills. in black and white, 20 ills. in color, Dec., 1941

WORKING Teak in the Burma Forests: The Sagacious Elephant Is Man's Ablest Ally in the Logging Industry of the Far East. By A. W. Smith. LVIII, pp. 239-256, 5 ills. in black and white, 15 ills. in color, Aug., 1930

WORLD:

Advances in Geographic Knowledge During the Nineteenth Century. By Brig.-Gen. A. W. Greely. XII, pp. 143-152, maps, Apr., 1901

Cotidal Lines for the World. By R. A. Harris. XVII, pp. 303-309, 3 maps, map supplement, June, 1906

The Great Populous Centers of the World. By General A. W. Greely. V, pp. 89-92, table, July 10, 1893

The Great Unmapped Areas on the Earth's Surface Awaiting the Explorer and Geographer. By J. Scott Keltie. VIII, pp. 251-266, Sept., 1897

Marine Hydrographic Surveys of the Coasts of the World. By George W. Littlehales. XVI, pp. 63-67, maps, Feb., 1905

Recent Contributions to Our Knowledge of the Earth's Shape and Size, by the United States Coast and Geodetic Survey. By C. A. Schott. XII, pp. 36-41, ill., chart, Jan., 1901

WORLD COMMUNICATIONS. *See* Cables; Radio; Telegraphy; Telephone; Television

WORLD CONGRESSES. *See* International Congress of Orientalists; International Geographic Congress; World's Congress of Education

WORLD FAIRS AND EXPOSITIONS. *See* Expositions

WORLD FLIGHTS. *See* Aeronautics

A **WORLD** Inside a Mountain: Aniakchak, the New Volcanic Wonderland of the Alaska Peninsula, Is Explored. By Bernard R. Hubbard. LX, pp. 319-345, 34 ills., map, Sept., 1931

WORLD MAP ARTICLES:

Chart of the World. Announcement of map supplement (Feb., 1905). XV, p. 500, Dec., 1904. XVI, p. 50, Jan., 1905

The "Map of Discovery" of the Western Hemisphere with This Number. Announcement of pictorial map supplement, a reproduction in color of the mural painting by N. C. Wyeth. LV, p. 93, Jan., 1929

The "Map of Discovery" with This Number (Eastern Hemisphere). Announcement of pictorial map supplement, a reproduction in color of the mural painting by N. C. Wyeth. LIV, p. 568, Nov., 1928

Map of the Northern and Southern Hemispheres. Text with map supplement. LXXXIII, pp. 481-483, Apr., 1943

The National Geographic Society's New Map of the World. Text with map supplement. LXVIII, pp. 796-798, Dec., 1935

New World Map Gives Backdrop for Headlines. Text with map supplement. LXXX, pp. 741-742, ill., Dec., 1941

The Society's New Map of the World. Text with map supplement. XLII, p. 690, Dec., 1922

The Story of the Map. Text with map supplement. LXII, pp. 759-774, 11 ills., Dec., 1932

The World That Rims the Narrowing Atlantic: Latest Ten-color Map Supplement Shows Four Continents and New Transatlantic Air Routes Which Make This Ocean Only One Day Wide. By James M. Darley. Text with map supplement. LXXVI, pp. 139-142, ill., July, 1939

The World's Words (Map of the World). By William H. Nicholas. Text with map supplement. LXXXIV, p. 689, Dec., 1943

WORLD TRAVEL. *See* Voyages

WORLD WAR I:

Aces Among Aces. By Laurence La Tourette Driggs. XXXIII, pp. 568-580, 9 ills., June, 1918

Aces of the Air. By Captain Jacques De Sieyes. XXXIII, pp. 5-9, ills., Jan., 1918

America's Duty. By Newton D. Baker. XXXI, pp. 453-457, 5 ills., May, 1917

America's Part in the Allies' Mastery of the Air. By Major Joseph Tulasne. XXXIII, pp. 1-5, ills., Jan., 1918

An Appeal to Members of the National Geographic Society (Food Conservation). XXXIII, pp. 347-348, ills., Apr., 1918

Armistice Day and the American Battle Fields. By J. J. Jusserand. LVI, pp. 509-554, 32 ills. in black and white, 23 ills. in color, Nov., 1929

Belgium: The Innocent Bystander. By William Joseph Showalter. XXVI, pp. 223-264, 35 ills., Sept., 1914

Belgium's Plight. By John H. Gade. XXXI, pp. 433-439, 3 ills., May, 1917

Bind the Wounds of France. By Herbert C. Hoover. XXXI, pp. 439-444, 5 ills., May, 1917

The British Take Baku. XXXIV, pp. 163-164, ill., Aug., 1918

WORLD WAR I—*Continued*

Building America's Air Army. By Hiram Bingham. XXXIII, pp. 48-86, 43 ills., Mar., 1918

The Burden France Has Borne. By Granville Fortescue. XXXI, pp. 323-344, 19 ills., Apr., 1917

The Call to the Colors. 17 ills. XXXI, pp. 345-361, Apr., 1917

Celebrating Christmas on the Meuse. By Captain Clifton Lisle. XXXVI, pp. 527-537, 5 ills., Dec., 1919

Conserving the Nation's Man Power: Disease Weakens Armies, Cripples Industry, Reduces Production. How the Government is Sanitating the Civil Zones Around Cantonment Areas. A Nation-wide Campaign for Health. By Rupert Blue. XXXII, pp. 255-278, 17 ills., Sept., 1917

Cooties and Courage. By Herbert Corey. XXXIII, pp. 495-509, 10 ills., June, 1918

A Day with Our Boys in the Geographic Wards. By Carol Corey. XXXIV, pp. 69-80, 8 ills., July, 1918

Devastated Poland. By Frederic C. Walcott. XXXI, pp. 445-452, 6 ills., May, 1917

Do Your Bit for America: A Proclamation by President Wilson to the American People. XXXI, pp. 287-293, ills., Apr., 1917

Flying in France. By Captain André de Berroeta. XXXIII, pp. 9-26, 12 ills., Jan., 1918

The Food Armies of Liberty. By Herbert Hoover. XXXII, pp. 187-196, 6 ills., Sept., 1917

Food for Our Allies in 1919. By Herbert Hoover. XXXIV, pp. 242-244, Sept., 1918

Forerunners of Famine. By Frederic C. Walcott. XXXIII, pp. 336-347, 4 ills., 4 diagrs., map, Apr., 1918

From the Trenches to Versailles. By Carol Corey. XXXII, pp. 535-550, 12 ills., Nov.-Dec., 1917

The Geography of Medicines: War's Effect Upon the World's Sources of Supply. By John Foote. XXXII, pp. 213-238, 26 ills., Sept., 1917

Germany's Air Program. XXXIII, p. 114, Jan., 1918

Germany's Dream of World Domination. XXXIII, pp. 559-567, 3 ills., June, 1918

The Healer of Humanity's Wounds. XXXIV, pp. 308-324, 16 ills., Oct., 1918

The Health and Morale of America's Citizen Army. By William Howard Taft. XXXIII, pp. 219-245, 22 ills., Mar., 1918

Helping to Solve Our Allies' Food Problem: America Calls for a Million Young Soldiers of the Commissary to Volunteer for Service in 1918. By Ralph Graves. XXXIII, pp. 170-194, 23 ills., Feb., 1918

Hospital Heroes Convict the Cootie. XXXIII, p. 510, June, 1918

How Canada Went to the Front. By T. B. Macaulay. XXXIV, pp. 297-307, 6 ills., Oct., 1918

The Immediate Necessity for Military Highways. By A. G. Batchelder. XXXII, pp. 477-499, 22 ills., Nov.-Dec., 1917

In French Lorraine: That Part of France Where the First American Soldiers Have Fallen. By Harriet Chalmers Adams. XXXII, pp. 499-518, 16 ills., Nov.-Dec., 1917

WORLD WAR I—*Continued*

Italy's Eagles of Combat and Defense: Heroic Achievements of Aviators Above the Adriatic, the Apennines, and the Alps. By General P. Tozzi. XXXIII, pp. 38-47, 8 ills., Jan., 1918

Letters from the Italian Front. By Marchesa Louise de Rosales to Ethel Mather Bagg. XXXII, pp. 47-67, 22 ills., July, 1917

The Life Story of an American Airman in France: Extracts from the Letters of Stuart Walcott, Who, Between July and December, 1917, Learned to Fly in French Schools of Aviation, Won Fame at the Front, and Fell Near Saint Souplet. XXXIII, pp. 86-106, 9 ills., Jan., 1918

Map of Europe Including the New Balkan States. Text with map supplement. XXVI, pp. 191-192, Aug., 1914

The Murman Coast: Arctic Gateway for American and Allied Expeditionary Forces in Northern European Russia. XXXV, pp. 331-348, 30 ills., map, Apr., 1919

The National Geographic Society in War Time. By Major-General A. W. Greely. XXXIII, pp. 369-375, 5 ills., Apr., 1918

The National Geographic Society's Memorial to American Troops: Fountain and Water Supply System Presented to Historic French Town of Cantigny, Where Our Overseas Soldiers Won Their First Victory in the World War. XLIV, pp. 675-678, 4 ills., Dec., 1923

The National Geographic War-Zone Map. Text with map supplement. XXXIII, p. 494, May, 1918

The Needs Abroad. By Ian Malcolm. XXXI, pp. 427-433, 5 ills., May, 1917

The New Map of Europe: Showing the Boundaries Established by the Peace Conference at Paris and by Subsequent Decisions of the Supreme Council of the Allied and Associated Powers. By Ralph A. Graves. Text with map supplement. XXXIX, pp. 157-177, 18 ills., Feb., 1921

Niagara at the Battle Front. By William Joseph Showalter. XXXI, pp. 413-422, 6 ills., May, 1917

The North Sea Mine Barrage. By Capt. Reginald R. Belknap. XXXV, pp. 85-110, 23 ills., diagr., map, Feb., 1919

An Old Jewel in the Proper Setting: An Eyewitness's Account of the Reconquest of the Holy Land by Twentieth Century Crusaders. By Charles W. Whitehair. XXXIV, pp. 325-344, 14 ills., Oct., 1918

On the Monastir Road. By Herbert Corey. XXXI, pp. 383-412, 31 ills., May, 1917

Our Armies of Mercy (American National Red Cross). By Henry P. Davison. XXXI, pp. 423-427, 3 ills., May, 1917

Our Industrial Victory. By Charles M. Schwab. XXXIV, pp. 212-229, 17 ills., Sept., 1918

Our National War Memorials in Europe. By John J. Pershing. LXV, pp. 1-36, 24 ills. in black and white, 11 ills. in color, map, Jan., 1934

Our Second Alliance. By J. J. Jusserand. XXXI, pp. 565-566, ill., June, 1917

WORLD WAR I—*Continued*

The Outspeaking of a Great Democracy: The Proceedings of the Chamber of Deputies of France on Friday, April 6, 1917, As Reported in the "Journal Officiel de La République Française." XXXI, pp. 362-365, ill., Apr., 1917

Plain Tales from the Trenches: As Told Over the Tea Table in Blighty—A Soldier's "Home" in Paris. By Carol Corey. XXXIII, pp. 300-312, 7 ills., Mar., 1918

A Poisoned World. By William Howard Taft. XXXI, pp. 459-467, 7 ills., May, 1917

Practical Patriotism (National Geographic Society's War Work). XXXII, pp. 279-280, Sept., 1917; p. 476, Nov.-Dec., 1917

The Price of Liberty, Equality, Fraternity. XXXIV, p. 377, Nov., 1918

Prussianism. By Robert Lansing. XXXIII, pp. 546-557, 5 ills., June, 1918

The Removal of the North Sea Mine Barrage. By Lieutenant-Commander Noel Davis. XXXVII, pp. 103-133, 28 ills., maps, Feb., 1920

Russia from Within: Her War of Yesterday, Today, and Tomorrow. By Stanley Washburn. XXXII, pp. 91-120, 30 ills., Aug., 1917

The Russian Situation and Its Significance to America. By Stanley Washburn. XXXI, pp. 371-382, 8 ills., Apr., 1917

Russia's Man of the Hour: Alexander Kerensky's First Speeches and Proclamations. XXXII, pp. 24-45, 17 ills., July, 1917

Shopping Abroad for Our Armies in France. By Herbert Corey. XXXIII, pp. 206-218, 6 ills., Feb., 1918

The Spirit of the Geographic. XXXIV, pp. 434-440, 4 ills., Nov., 1918

Stand by the Soldier. By Major General John J. Pershing. XXXI, pp. 457-459, ill., May, 1917

Tales of the British Air Service. By Major William A. Bishop. XXXIII, pp. 27-37, 12 ills., Jan., 1918

Three Drawings of the World War. 3 ills. from drawings by Lucien Jonas. XXXIII, pp. 355-355b, Apr., 1918

The Ties That Bind: Our Natural Sympathy with English Traditions, the French Republic, and the Russian Outburst for Liberty. By John Sharp Williams. XXXI, pp. 281-286, 4 ills., Mar., 1917

Transporting a Navy Through the Jungles of Africa in War Time. By Frank J. Magee. XLII, pp. 331-362, 31 ills., Oct., 1922

A Tribute to America. By Herbert Henry Asquith. XXXI, pp. 295-296, ills., Apr., 1917

War, Patriotism, and the Food Supply. By Frederick V. Coville. XXXI, pp. 254-256, Mar., 1917

The War and Ocean Geography. By the Editor (Gilbert Grosvenor). XXXIV, pp. 230-242, 6 ills., map, Sept., 1918

The Weapon of Food. By Herbert Hoover. XXXII, pp. 197-212, 15 ills., Sept., 1917

What Great Britain Is Doing. By Sydney Brooks. XXXI, pp. 193-210, 7 ills., Mar., 1917

What the War Has Done for Britain. By Judson C. Welliver. XXXIV, pp. 278-297, 13 ills., Oct., 1918

See also Red Cross

WORLD WAR II:

Aboard a Blimp Hunting U-boats: A Day above the Atlantic Reveals Navy Talk and Navy Ways, Creeping Convoys, and Torpedoed Wrecks. By Mason Sutherland. LXXXIV, pp. 79-96, 18 ills., July, 1943

The Aerial Invasion of Burma. By General H. H. Arnold. LXXXVI, pp. 129-148, 20 ills., Aug., 1944

America Fights on the Farms. 21 ills. in color. LXXXVI, pp. 33-48, July, 1944

American Bombers Attacking from Australia. By Howell Walker. LXXXIII, pp. 49-70, 19 ills., map, Jan., 1943

American Industries Geared for War. By Thornton Oakley. With 16 ills. in color from paintings by author. LXXXII, pp. 716-734, ill. in black and white, Dec., 1942

American Soldier in Reykjavík. By Corporal Luther M. Chovan. LXXXVIII, pp. 536-568, 6 ills. in black and white, 34 ills. in color, Nov., 1945

American Transportation Vital to Victory. By Thornton Oakley. With 16 ills. in color from paintings by author. LXXXIV, pp. 671-688, Dec., 1943

American Wings Soar Around the World: Epic Story of the Air Transport Command of the U. S. Army Is a Saga of Yankee Daring and Doing. By Donald H. Agnew and William A. Kinney. LXXXIV, pp. 57-78, 22 ills., July, 1943

Americans Help Liberated Europe Live Again. By Lt. Col. Frederick Simpich, Jr. LXXXVII, pp. 747-768, 17 ills., June, 1945

Americans on the Barbary Coast (Africa). By Willard Price. LXXXIV, pp. 1-31, 13 ills. in black and white, 10 ills. in color, map, July, 1943

Ancient Iceland, New Pawn of War. 21 photos, map. LXXX, pp. 75-90, July, 1941

Animals Were Allies, Too. 16 ills. LXXXIX, pp. 75-88, Jan., 1946

As 2,000 Ships Are Born. By Frederick Simpich. LXXXI, pp. 551-588, 34 ills., May, 1942

At Ease in the South Seas. By Maj. Frederick Simpich, Jr. LXXXV, pp. 79-104, 32 ills., Jan., 1944

Battleship *Missouri* Comes of Age. 11 ills. in color from U. S. Navy official photos. LXXXVII, pp. 353-360, Mar., 1945

Behind the Lines in Italy. By Corporal Macon Reed, Jr. LXXXVI, pp. 109-128, 20 ills., July, 1944

"Blood, Toil, Tears, and Sweat": An American Tells the Story of Britain's War Effort, Summed up in Prime Minister Churchill's Unflinching Words. By Harvey Klemmer. LXXXII, pp. 141-166, 19 ills., Aug., 1942

Bombs over Bible Lands. By Frederick Simpich and W. Robert Moore. LXXX, pp. 141-180, 34 ills., two-page map, Aug., 1941

Britain Fights in the Fields. By Francis A. Flood. LXXXVI, pp. 31-65, 17 ills. in black and white, 21 ills. in color, July, 1944

Canada's War Effort: A Canadian Pictures the Swift and Sweeping Transformation from a Peaceful Dominion to a Nation Geared for War. By Bruce Hutchison. LXXX, pp. 553-590, 40 ills., Nov., 1941

WORLD WAR II—*Continued*

China Opens Her Wild West: In the Mountain-girt Heart of a Continent a New China Has Been Created During the Years of War. By Owen Lattimore. LXXXII, pp. 337-367, 21 ills. in black and white, 11 ills. in color, map, Sept., 1942

A City Learns to Smile Again (Nancy, France). By Maj. Frederick G. Vosburgh. LXXXVII, pp. 361-384, 23 ills., map, Mar., 1945

A City That Refused to Die (Plymouth, England). By Harvey Klemmer. LXXXIX, pp. 211-236, 13 ills. in black and white, 9 ills. in color, map, Feb., 1946

The Coasts of Normandy and Brittany. By W. Robert Moore. LXXXIV, pp. 205-232, 5 ills. in black and white, 21 ills. in color, two-page map, Aug., 1943

Convoys to Victory. By Harvey Klemmer. LXXXIII, pp. 193-216, 24 ills., Feb., 1943

Crimea Reborn. By Eddy Gilmore. LXXXVII, pp. 487-512, 23 ills., map, Apr., 1945

Cruise on an Escort Carrier. By Melville Bell Grosvenor. LXXXIV, pp. 513-546, 14 ills. in black and white, 20 ills. in color, Nov., 1943

Demolishing Germany's North Sea Ramparts (Helgoland). By Stuart E. Jones. XC, pp. 635-644, ill. in black and white, 10 ills. in color, Nov., 1946

8th Air Force in England. 10 ills. in color from U. S. Army Air Forces official photos. LXXXVII, pp. 297-304, Mar., 1945

Europe's Looted Art. By John Walker. LXXXIX, pp. 39-52, 11 ills., Jan., 1946

Everyday Life in Wartime England. By Harvey Klemmer. LXXIX, pp. 497-534, 48 ills., Apr., 1941

Fiji Patrol on Bougainville. By David D. Duncan. LXXXVII, pp. 87-104, 9 ills. in black and white, 11 ills. in color, Jan., 1945

Flying Our Wounded Veterans Home. By Catherine Bell Palmer. LXXXVIII, pp. 363-384, 17 ills., Sept., 1945

French West Africa in Wartime. By Paul M. Atkins. LXXXI, pp. 371-408, 37 ills., maps, Mar., 1942

From Africa to the Alps. 8 ills. in color from U. S. Army Air Forces official photos. LXXXIX, pp. 161-168, Feb., 1946

Front-line Town of Britain's Siege (Dover). By Harvey Klemmer. LXXXV, pp. 105-128, 21 ills., Jan., 1944

Gilbert Islands in the Wake of Battle. By W. Robert Moore. LXXXVII, pp. 129-162, 11 ills. in black and white, 19 ills. in color, map, Feb., 1945

Gliders—Silent Weapons of the Sky. By William H. Nicholas. LXXXVI, pp. 149-160, 8 ills., Aug., 1944

Greens Grow for GI's on Soilless Ascension. By W. Robert Moore. LXXXVIII, pp. 219-230, 12 ills., Aug., 1945

The Healing Arts in Global War: As Weapons Grow Deadlier, Scientific Medicine Pits Its Ever-rising Skill Against Them. By Albert W. Atwood. LXXXIV, pp. 599-618, 17 ills., Nov., 1943

Heroes of Wartime Science and Mercy. By Elizabeth W. King. LXXXIV, pp. 715-740, 11 ills. in black and white, 334 ills. in color, Dec., 1943

Heroes' Return. By William H. Nicholas. LXXXVII, pp. 333-352, 19 ills., Mar., 1945

Holland Rises from War and Water. By Thomas R. Henry. LXXXIX, pp. 237-260, 18 ills., map, Feb., 1946

How We Fight with Photographs. By F. Barrows Colton. LXXXVI, pp. 257-280, 22 ills., Sept., 1944

How We Use the Gulf of Mexico. By Frederick Simpich. LXXXV, pp. 1-40, 20 ills. in black and white, 19 ills. in color, two-page map, Jan., 1944

India's Treasures Helped the Allies. By John Fischer. LXXXIX, pp. 501-522, 18 ills., Apr., 1946

Infantrymen—The Fighters of War. By Brigadier General W. H. Wilbur. LXXXVI, pp. 513-538, 22 ills., Nov., 1944

Japan Faces Russia in Manchuria. By Willard Price. LXXXII, pp. 603-634, 30 ills., map, Nov., 1942

Jungle War: Bougainville and New Caledonia. 17 ills. in color from paintings by Lieut. William F. Draper. LXXXV, pp. 417-432, Apr., 1944

Landing Craft for Invasion. By Melville Bell Grosvenor. LXXXVI, pp. 1-30, 26 ills., July, 1944

Lend-Lease and the Russian Victory. By Harvey Klemmer. LXXXVIII, pp. 499-512, 6 ills., Oct., 1945

Lend-Lease Is a Two-way Benefit: Innovation in Creative Statesmanship Pools Resources of United Nations, and Supplies American Forces Around the World. By Francis Flood. LXXXIII, pp. 745-761, 14 ills., June, 1943

Liberated Ukraine. By Eddy Gilmore. LXXXV, pp. 513-536, 22 ills., map, May, 1944

Life Grows Grim in Singapore. By H. Gordon Minnigerode. LXXX, pp. 661-686, 17 ills. in black and white, 9 ills. in color, map, Nov., 1941

Life in Dauntless Darwin: A National Geographic Staff Writer Gives a Vivid Description of the Australian Town That Guards the Continent's Northern Door. By Howell Walker. LXXXII, pp. 123-138, 17 ills., map, July, 1942

Life on the Hawaii "Front": All-out Defense and Belt Tightening of Pacific Outpost Foreshadow the Things to Come on Mainland. By Lieut. Frederick Simpich, Jr. LXXXII, pp. 541-560, 19 ills., map, Oct., 1942

Lisbon—Gateway to Warring Europe. By Harvey Klemmer. LXXX, pp. 259-276, 18 ills., Aug., 1941

London Wins the Battle. By Marquis W. Childs. LXXXVIII, pp. 129-152, 21 ills., Aug., 1945

The Making of an Anzac. By Howell Walker. LXXXI, pp. 409-456, 31 ills. in black and white, 20 ills. in color, two-page map, Apr., 1942

Malta Invicta. By Bartimeus (A Captain in the Royal Navy). LXXXIII, pp. 375-400, 27 ills., map, Mar., 1943

Mediterranean Checkerboard. By Frederick Simpich. LXXXI, pp. 527-550, 20 ills., map, Apr., 1942

Metal Sinews of Strength: This Is a War of Many Metals, for We Live in an Age of Alloys. By Frederick G. Vosburgh. LXXXI, pp. 457-491, 35 ills., Apr., 1942

Michigan Fights. By Harvey Klemmer. LXXXVI, pp. 677-715, 20 ills. in black and white, 19 ills. in color, map, Dec., 1944

Mindanao, on the Road to Tokyo. By Frederick Simpich. LXXXVI, pp. 539-574, 26 ills. in black and white, 12 ills. in color, two-page map, Nov., 1944

The Miracle of War Production: For Victory the United States Transforms Its Complex Industry into the Biggest Factory and Mightiest Arsenal the World Has Ever Known. By Albert W. Atwood. With paintings by Thornton Oakley. LXXXII, pp. 693-715, 17 ills. in black and white, 16 ills. in color, Dec., 1942

A Navy Artist Paints the Aleutians. By Mason Sutherland. Paintings by Lt. William F. Draper. LXXXIV, pp. 157-176, 4 ills. in black and white, 16 ills. in color, Aug., 1943

The New Queen of the Seas (Aircraft Carrier). By Melville Bell Grosvenor. LXXXII, pp. 1-30, 27 ills., drawing, two-page map, July, 1942

Newfoundland, North Atlantic Rampart: From the "First Base of American Defense" Planes Fly to Britain's Aid over Stout Fishing Schooners of the Grand Banks. By George Whiteley, Jr. LXXX, pp. 111-140, 26 ills., map, July, 1941

Normandy's Made-in-England Harbors. LXXXVII, pp. 565-580, 16 ills., map, May, 1945

Norway, an Active Ally. By Wilhelm Morgenstierne. LXXXIII, pp. 333-357, 24 ills., map, Mar., 1943

Okinawa, Threshold to Japan. By Lt. David D. Duncan, USMC. With 22 color photos by author and others. LXXXVIII, pp. 411-428, Oct., 1945

Our Global Strong Arm. 10 ills. in color from U. S. Army Air Forces official photos. LXXXIX, pp. 145-152, Feb., 1946

Painting History in the Pacific. 19 ills. in color from paintings by Lt. William F. Draper, USNR. LXXXVI, pp. 408-424, Oct., 1944

Palms and Planes in the New Hebrides. By Maj. Robert D. Heinl, Jr. LXXXVI, pp. 229-256, 17 ills. in black and white, 12 ills. in color, map, Aug., 1944

Paris Delivered. 10 ills. LXXXVII, pp. 79-86, Jan., 1945

Paris Freed. By Maj. Frederick Simpich, Jr. LXXXVII, pp. 385-412, 14 ills. in black and white, 12 ills. in color, Apr., 1945

Paris Lives Again. By M. O. Williams. XC, pp. 767-790, 24 ills., Dec., 1946

The People's Fight Against Slavery. By Hon. Henry A. Wallace. Reprint of address delivered at a dinner of the Free World Association, May 8, 1942. LXXXII, pp. 276-280, ill., Aug., 1942

WORLD WAR II—*Continued*

QM, the Fighting Storekeeper. By Frederick Simpich. Paintings by Arthur Beaumont. LXXXII, pp. 561-600, 22 ills. in black and white, 16 ills. in color, Nov., 1942

Red Cross Girl Overseas. By Margaret Cotter. LXXXVI, pp. 745-768, 22 ills., Dec., 1944

Rehearsal at Dieppe (France). By W. Robert Moore. LXXXII, pp. 495-502, 6 ills., Oct., 1942

Return to Florence (Italy). By 1st Lt. Benjamin C. McCartney. LXXXVII, pp. 257-296, 18 ills. in black and white, 18 ills. in color, Mar., 1945

Rural Britain Carries On. By Harvey Klemmer. LXXX, pp. 527-552, 27 ills., Oct., 1941

Saga of the Carrier *Princeton*. By Capt. William H. Buracker, USN. LXXXVIII, pp. 189-218, 8 ills. in black and white, 22 ills. in color, map, Aug., 1945

San Diego Can't Believe It. By Frederick Simpich. LXXXI, pp. 45-80, 26 ills. in black and white, 9 ills. in color, Jan., 1942

San Francisco: Gibraltar of the West Coast. By La Verne Bradley. LXXXIII, pp. 279-308, 28 ills., Mar., 1943

Scotland in Wartime. By Isobel Wylie Hutchison. LXXXIII, pp. 723-743, 19 ills., June, 1943

South from Saipan. By W. Robert Moore. LXXXVII, pp. 441-474, 11 ills. in black and white, 17 ills. in color, map, Apr., 1945

Springboards to Tokyo. By Willard Price. LXXXVI, pp. 385-407, 16 ills., Oct., 1944

Sydney Faces the War Front Down Under. By Howell Walker. LXXXIII, pp. 359-374, 8 ills. in black and white, 10 ills. in color, Mar., 1943

A Tale of Three Cities (Prague, Vienna, Budapest). By Thomas R. Henry. LXXXVIII, pp. 641-669, 23 ills., Dec., 1945

They Sustain the Wings (Ground Crews). By Frederick Simpich. LXXXIV, pp. 333-354, 19 ills., Sept., 1943

This Is My Own: How the United States Seems to a Citizen Soldier Back from Three Years Overseas. By Frederick G. Vosburgh. LXXXIX, pp. 113-128, 14 ills., Jan., 1946

This Was Austria. 18 ills. LXXXVIII, pp. 71-86, July, 1945

Today on the China Coast. By John B. Powell. LXXXVII, pp. 217-238, 17 ills., map, Feb., 1945

Victory's Portrait in the Marianas. By Lt. William Franklin Draper, USNR. With 17 ills. in color from paintings by author. LXXXVIII, pp. 599-616, Nov., 1945

War Meets Peace in Egypt. By Grant Parr and G. E. Janssen. LXXXI, pp. 503-526, 25 ills., map, Apr., 1942

War's Wake in the Rhineland. By Thomas R. Henry. LXXXVIII, pp. 1-32, 29 ills., map, July, 1945

Wartime in the Pacific Northwest (U. S. and Canada). By Frederick Simpich. LXXXII, pp. 421-464, 25 ills. in black and white, 23 ills. in color, map, Oct., 1942

WORLD WAR II—*Continued*

What Luzon Means to Uncle Sam. By Frederick Simpich. LXXXVII, pp. 305-332, 25 ills., map supplement, Mar., 1945

What the Fighting Yanks See. By Wanda Burnett. LXXXVI, pp. 451-476, 27 ills., Oct., 1944

When GI Joes Took London. By Maj. Frederick Simpich, Jr. LXXXVI, pp. 337-354, 18 ills., Sept., 1944

The White War in Norway. By Thomas R. Henry. LXXXVIII, pp. 617-640, 23 ills., map, Nov., 1945

Winning the War of Supply. By F. Barrows Colton. LXXXVIII, pp. 705-736, 32 ills., Dec., 1945

Women at Work. By La Verne Bradley. LXXXVI, pp. 193-220, 23 ills., Aug., 1944

Women in Uniform. By La Verne Bradley. LXXXIV, pp. 445-458, 10 ills., Oct., 1943

Yank Meets Native. By Wanda Burnett. LXXXVIII, pp. 105-128, 24 ills., July, 1945

Yanks in Northern Ireland. 15 ills. LXXXIV, pp. 191-204, Aug., 1943

Your Dog Joins Up. By Frederick Simpich. LXXXIII, pp. 93-113, 25 ills., Jan., 1943

Your Navy as Peace Insurance. By Fleet Admiral Chester W. Nimitz. LXXXIX, pp. 681-736, 32 ills. in black and white, 26 ills. in color, June, 1946

Your Society Aids War Effort. LXXXIII, pp. 277-278, ill., Feb., 1943

See also articles of the war years (1939-1945) under the following headings: Alaska; Aleutian Islands; Algeria; Baja California; Belgium; Berchtesgaden; Borneo; Brazil; China; Danzig; Fiji Islands; Formosa; Gilbert Islands; Greenland; Iran; Japan; Java; Madagascar; Manipur (State), India; Marseille; Marshall Islands; Micronesia; Morocco; Netherlands; New Caledonia; New Guinea; Philippine Islands; Ryukyu Retto; Sicily; Singapore; Solomon Islands; Timor; Tunisia; Union of Soviet Socialist Republics; West Indies; *and* U. S. Army; U. S. Army Air Forces; U. S. Army Engineers; U. S. Army Map Service; U. S. Army Quartermaster Corps; U. S. Army Signal Corps; U. S. Coast Guard; U. S. Defense Bases; U. S. Marine Corps; U. S. Navy; *and* Insignia; Map Articles; War Agencies

The **WORLD'S** Ancient Porcelain Center (Kingtehchen, China). By Frank B. Lenz. XXXVIII, pp. 391-406, 17 ills., Nov., 1920

WORLD'S COLUMBIAN EXPOSITION:

Proceedings of the International Geographic Conference, held in conjunction with the World's Columbian Exposition, Chicago, May 1-October 30, 1893. V, pp. 97-256, Jan. 31, 1894

WORLD'S CONGRESS OF EDUCATION:

The International Geographic Conference, Chicago, July 27-28, 1893, sponsored by National Geographic Society, held in conjunction with the World's Congress of Education. V, pp. 98-100, Jan. 31, 1894

The **WORLD'S** Debt to France. XXVIII, pp. 491-501, 7 ills., Nov., 1915

The **WORLD'S** Great Waterfalls: Visits to Mighty Niagara, Wonderful Victoria, and Picturesque Iguazu. By Theodore W. Noyes. L, pp. 29-59, 29 ills., July, 1926

The **WORLD'S** Greatest Overland Explorer: How Marco Polo Penetrated Farthest Asia, "Discovered" Many Lands Unknown to Europe, and Added Numerous Minerals, Animals, Birds, and Plants to Man's Knowledge. By J. R. Hildebrand. LIV, pp. 505-568, 53 ills., two-page map, Nov., 1928

The **WORLD'S** Greatest Waterfall: The Kaieteur Fall, in British Guiana. By Leonard Kennedy. XXII, pp. 846-859, 6 ills., map, Sept., 1911

The **WORLD'S** Highest Altitudes and First Ascents. By Charles E. Fay. XX, pp. 493-530, 25 ills., June, 1909

The **WORLD'S** Highest International Telephone Cable. LVIII, pp. 722-731, 8 ills., Dec., 1930

WORLD'S Largest Free Balloon to Explore Stratosphere. LXVI, pp. 107-110, ills., July, 1934

The **WORLD'S** Most Cruel Earthquake (Messina, Sicily). By Charles W. Wright. XX, pp. 373-396, 22 ills., maps, Apr., 1909

The **WORLD'S** Production of Gold (From an Address to the American Bankers' Convention, by F. A. Vanderlip, October 11, 1905). XVI, pp. 571-572, Dec., 1905

The **WORLD'S** Strangest Capital (Lhasa, Tibet). By John Claude White. XXIX, pp. 273-295, 19 ills., panorama, Mar., 1916

The **WORLD'S** Words. By William H. Nicholas. LXXXIV, pp. 689-700, 8 ills., two-page map, map supplement, Dec., 1943

The **WORM** Turns. By Samuel Sandrof. LXXXIX, pp. 775-786, 14 ills., June, 1946

WORMS, Marine:

The Worm Turns. By Samuel Sandrof. LXXXIX, pp. 775-786, 14 ills., June, 1946

WOUNDED, Evacuation of. *See* Aerial Invasion of Burma; Air Evacuation of Wounded; Healing Arts in Global War; Heroes' Return

WRANGELL MOUNTAINS, Alaska:

The Wrangell Mountains. By Walter C. Mendenhall. XIV, pp. 395-407, 3 ills., panorama, Nov., 1903

The Wrangell Mountains. Panorama taken by author from the ridge east of the Dadina River

WRENS:

The Fairy Wrens of Australia: The Little Long-tailed "Blue Birds of Happiness" Rank High Among the Island Continent's Remarkable Birds. By Neville W. Cayley. With 8 ills. in color from paintings by author. LXXXVIII, pp. 488-498, ill. in black and white, Oct., 1945

Winged Denizens of Woodland, Stream, and Marsh. By Alexander Wetmore. Paintings by Major Allan Brooks. LXV, pp. 577-596, 10 portraits in color, May, 1934

WRIGHT, CHARLES W.:

The World's Most Cruel Earthquake (Messina, Sicily). By Charles W. Wright. XX, pp. 373-396, 22 ills., maps, Apr., 1909

WRIGHT, HELEN DUNSTAN:

Little-Known Sardinia. By Helen Dunstan Wright. XXX, pp. 97-120, 23 ills., map, Aug., 1916

WRIGHT, MARIE ROBINSON:

The Falls of Iguazu. By Marie Robinson Wright. XVII, pp. 456-460, 4 ills., Aug., 1906

WRIGHT, ORVILLE:

Air Conquest: From the Early Days of Giant Kites and Birdlike Gliders, the National Geographic Society Has Aided and Encouraged the Growth of Aviation. LII, pp. 233-242, 13 ills., Aug., 1927

WRIGHT, WILBUR:

Air Conquest: From the Early Days of Giant Kites and Birdlike Gliders, the National Geographic Society Has Aided and Encouraged the Growth of Aviation. LII, pp. 233-242, 13 ills., Aug., 1927

In Honor of the Army and Aviation (Speech by Wilbur Wright). XXII, pp. 267-284, ill., Mar., 1911

WRIGHT FIELD, Ohio:

New Frontier in the Sky. By F. Barrows Colton. XC, pp. 379-408, 28 ills., diagr., Sept., 1946

WULSIN, FREDERICK R.:

The Road to Wang Ye Fu: An Account of the Work of the National Geographic Society's Central-China Expedition in the Mongol Kingdom of Ala Shan. By Frederick R. Wulsin. XLIX, pp. 197-234, 44 ills., map, Feb., 1926

WÜRTTEMBERG (Former State), Germany:

A Corner of Old Württemberg. By B. H. Buxton. XXII, pp. 931-947, 17 ills., map, Oct., 1911

WYATT EARP (Ship):

My Four Antarctic Expeditions: Explorations of 1933-1939 Have Stricken Vast Areas from the Realm of the Unknown. By Lincoln Ellsworth. LXXVI, pp. 129-138, 9 ills., map, July, 1939

WYETH, N. C.:

The Caravels of Columbus. Reproduction in color of the painting by N. C. Wyeth, National Geographic Society, Washington, D. C. LIV, text, p. 55; supplement, July, 1928

Commander Byrd at the North Pole (Through Pathless Skies to the North Pole). Reproduction in color of the painting by N. C. Wyeth, National Geographic Society, Washington, D. C. LIII, supplement, May, 1928

The Discoverer. Reproduction in color of the painting by N. C. Wyeth, National Geographic Society, Washington, D. C. LIII, text, p. 347; supplement, Mar., 1928

The "Map of Discovery" (Eastern Hemisphere). Reproduction in color of the painting by N. C. Wyeth, National Geographic Society, Washington, D. C. LIV, text, p. 568; supplement, Nov., 1928

WYETH, N. C.—*Continued*

The "Map of Discovery" (Western Hemisphere). Reproduction in color of the painting by N. C. Wyeth, National Geographic Society, Washington, D. C. LV, text, p. 93; supplement, Jan., 1929

WYLLIE, ROBERT E.:

American Decorations and Insignia of Honor and Service. By Col. Robert E. Wyllie. XXXVI, pp. 502-526, 6 ills. in black and white, 119 ills. in color, Dec., 1919

The Romance of Military Insignia: How the United States Government Recognizes Deeds of Heroism and Devotion to Duty. By Col. Robert E. Wyllie. XXXVI, pp. 463-501, 27 ills., Dec., 1919

WYOMING:

Bighorn Mountains. By N. H. Darton. XVIII, pp. 355-364, 7 ills., map, June, 1907

The Call of the West. By C. J. Blanchard. XX, pp. 403-437, 20 ills., map, May, 1909

"Compleat Angler" Fishes for Fossils. By Imogene Powell. LXVI, pp. 251-258, 7 ills., Aug., 1934

Fabulous Yellowstone: Even Stranger Than the Tales of Early Trappers is the Truth About This Steaming Wonderland. By Frederick G. Vosburgh. LXXVII, pp. 769-794, 15 ills. in black and white, 9 ills. in color, map, June, 1940

Grass Makes Wyoming Fat. By Frederick Simpich. LXXXVIII, pp. 153-188, 13 ills. in black and white, 19 ills. in color, two-page map, Aug., 1945

Hunting Bears on Horseback. By Alan D. Wilson. XIX, pp. 350-356, 4 ills., May, 1908

The Land of the Best. By Gilbert H. Grosvenor. XXIX, pp. 327-430, 71 ills. in black and white, 33 ills. in color, pictorial supplement, Apr., 1916

Our National Parks. By L. F. Schmeckebier. XXIII, pp. 531-579, 41 ills., map, June, 1912

Wild Animals That Took Their Own Pictures by Day and by Night. By George Shiras, 3d. XXIV, pp. 763-834, 68 ills., map, pictorial supplement, July, 1913

The Wyoming Fossil Fields Expedition of July, 1899. By Wilbur C. Knight. XI, pp. 449-465, 8 ills., Dec., 1900

X

XOCHIMILCO (City and Lake), Mexico:

The Venice of Mexico (Aztec Lake Country). By Walter Hough. XXX, pp. 69-88, 18 ills., July, 1916

Y

YACHTS:

Most Curious Craft Afloat: The Compass in Navigation and the Work of the Non-Magnetic Yacht "Carnegie." By L. A. Bauer. XXI, pp. 223-245, 31 ills., Mar., 1910

YACHTS—*Continued*

Sailing the Seven Seas in the Interest of Science: Adventures Through 157,000 Miles of Storm and Calm, from Arctic to Antarctic and Around the World, in the Non-magnetic Yacht "Carnegie." By J. P. Ault. XLII, pp. 631-690, 47 ills., chart, Dec., 1922

See also Alice; Bonita; Galilee; Kinkajou; Physalia; Pilgrim; Yankee

YAHGANS (Indians):

The Indian Tribes of Southern Patagonia, Tierra del Fuego, and the Adjoining Islands. By J. B. Hatcher. XII, pp. 12-22, 4 ills., Jan., 1901

Inside Cape Horn. By Amos Burg. LXXII, pp. 743-783, 29 ills. in black and white, 10 ills. in color, two-page map, Dec., 1937

YAKUTAT BAY, Alaska:

The National Geographic Society's Alaskan Expedition of 1909. By Ralph S. Tarr and Lawrence Martin. XXI, pp. 1-54, 42 ills., 12 maps, Jan., 1910

Report on Auriferous Sands from Yakutat Bay. By J. Stanley-Brown. III, pp. 196-198, May 29, 1891

YAKUTS (People):

New Road to Asia. By Owen Lattimore. LXXXVI, pp. 641-676, 15 ills. in black and white, 26 ills. in color, Dec., 1944

YALE, CAROLINE A.:

Gardiner Greene Hubbard: Memorial Meeting. Address by Miss Caroline A. Yale, LL.D. IX, pp. 46-50, Feb., 1898

YALU (River), Korea-Manchuria:

Exploring Unknown Corners of the "Hermit Kingdom." By Roy Chapman Andrews. XXXVI, pp. 25-48, 30 ills., map, July, 1919

YAMBOS (Tribespeople):

Across Widest Africa. By A. Henry Savage Landor. XIX, pp. 694-737, 38 ills., map, Oct., 1908

YANGTZE (River), China:

The Eden of the Flowery Republic. By Dr. Joseph Beech. XXXVIII, pp. 355-390, 18 ills. in black and white, 16 ills. in color, Nov., 1920

Mrs. Bishop's "The Yangtze Valley and Beyond." By Eliza Ruhamah Scidmore. XI, pp. 366-368, Sept., 1900

Through the Great River Trenches of Asia: National Geographic Society Explorer Follows the Yangtze, Mekong, and Salwin Through Mighty Gorges, Some of Whose Canyon Walls Tower to a Height of More than Two Miles. By Joseph F. Rock. L, pp. 133-186, 47 ills., map, Aug., 1926

YANK Meets Native. By Wanda Burnett. LXXXVIII, pp. 105-128, 24 ills., July, 1945

YANKEE (Schooner):

Westward Bound in the *Yankee*. By Irving and Electa Johnson. LXXXI, pp. 1-44, 25 ills. in black and white, 20 ills. in color, map, Jan., 1942

YANKOVSKY, GEORGE M.:

Jap Rule in the Hermit Nation (Korea). By Willard Price. LXXXVIII, pp. 429-451, 19 ills., map, Oct., 1945

YANKS at Westminster. By Capt. Leonard David Gammans. XC, pp. 223-252, 6 ills. in black and white, 19 ills. in color, Aug., 1946

YANKS in Northern Ireland. 15 ills. LXXXIV, pp. 191-204, Aug., 1943

YAP (Islands), Caroline Islands:

Hidden Key to the Pacific: Piercing the Web of Secrecy Which Long Has Veiled Japanese Bases in the Mandated Islands. By Willard Price. LXXXI, pp. 759-785, 28 ills., map, June, 1942

Mysterious Micronesia: Yap, Map, and Other Islands Under Japanese Mandate are Museums of Primitive Man. By Willard Price. LXIX, pp. 481-510, 37 ills., map, Apr., 1936

Yap and Other Pacific Islands Under Japanese Mandate. By Junius B. Wood. XL, pp. 591-627, 34 ills., map supplement, Dec., 1921

Yap Meets the Yanks. By David D. Duncan, 1st Lt., USMC. With 11 color photos by author. LXXXIX, pp. 364-372, Mar., 1946

YAPANESE (People). *See* articles, *preceding*

YAQUI INDIANS:

Adventuring Down the West Coast of Mexico. By Herbert Corey. XLII, pp. 449-503, 44 ills., map, Nov., 1922

A Mexican Land of Canaan: Marvelous Riches of the Wonderful West Coast of Our Neighbor Republic. By Frederick Simpich. XXXVI, pp. 307-330, 16 ills., map, Oct., 1919

YARMOUTH (Great Yarmouth), England:

King Herring: An Account of the World's Most Valuable Fish, the Industries It Supports, and the Part It Has Played in History. By Hugh M. Smith. XX, pp. 701-735, 21 ills., Aug., 1909

When the Herring Fleet Comes to Great Yarmouth. By W. Robert Moore. LXVI, pp. 233-250, 19 ills., Aug., 1934

YARMOUTH PORT, Massachusetts:

Cape Cod People and Places. By Wanda Burnett. LXXXIX, pp. 737-774, 17 ills. in black and white, 24 ills. in color, map, June, 1946

YAWL (Boat):

Cruising to Crete: Four French Girls Set Sail in a Breton Yawl (*Bonita*) for the Island of the Legendary Minotaur. By Marthe Oulié and Mariel Jean-Brunhes. LV, pp. 249-272, 15 ills. in black and white, 14 ills. in color, map, Feb., 1929

See also Islander

YELLOW FEVER:

Economic Loss to the People of the United States Through Insects That Carry Disease. By L. O. Howard. XX, pp. 735-749, Aug., 1909

Map-Changing Medicine. By William Joseph Showalter. XLII, pp. 303-330, 26 ills., Sept., 1922

YELLOW RIVER, China. *See* Hwang Ho

YELLOWSTONE (River), Wyoming-Montana-North Dakota:

Trailing History Down the Big Muddy: In the Homeward Wake of Lewis and Clark, a Folding Steel Skiff Bears Its Lone Pilot on a 2,000-Mile Cruise on the Yellowstone-Missouri. By Lewis R. Freeman. LIV, pp. 73-120, 51 ills., map, July, 1928

YELLOWSTONE NATIONAL PARK, Wyoming-Montana-Idaho:

Fabulous Yellowstone: Even Stranger Than the Tales of Early Trappers is the Truth About This Steaming Wonderland. By Frederick G. Vosburgh. LXXVII, pp. 769-794, 15 ills. in black and white, 9 ills. in color, map, June, 1940

The Land of the Best. By Gilbert H. Grosvenor. XXIX, pp. 327-430, 71 ills. in black and white, 33 ills. in color, pictorial supplement, Apr., 1916

Our National Parks. By L. F. Schmeckebier. XXIII, pp. 531-579, 41 ills., map, June, 1912

Wild Animals That Took Their Own Pictures by Day and by Night. By George Shiras, 3d. XXIV, pp. 763-834, 68 ills., map, pictorial supplement, July, 1913

YEMEN:

"The Flower of Paradise": The Part Which Khat Plays in the Life of the Yemen Arab. By Charles Moser. XXXII, pp. 173-186, 10 ills., map, Aug., 1917

YEN TANG SHAN, Chekiang Province, China:

China's Wonderland—Yen Tang Shan. 8 ills. in color from camera paintings by Herbert Clarence White, Clarence C. Crisler, Deng Bao-ling, Hwang Yao-tso. LXXII, pp. 687-694, Dec., 1937

YEZDIKHAST, Iran:

Persian Caravan Sketches: The Land of the Lion and the Sun as Seen on a Summer Caravan Trip. By Harold F. Weston. XXXIX, pp. 417-468, 46 ills. in black and white, 16 ills. in color, map, Apr., 1921

YEZIDIS (Tribespeople):

Mountain Tribes of Iran and Iraq. By Harold Lamb. LXXXIX, pp. 385-408, 15 ills., two-page map, Mar., 1946

The **YIELD** of Texas. By Frederick Simpich. LXXXVII, pp. 163-184, 15 ills., two-page map, Feb., 1945

YORKSHIRE, England:

Between the Heather and the North Sea: Bold English Headlands Once Sheltered Sea Robbers, Later Were Ports of Wooden Ships, Centers of the Jet and Alum Trades, To-day Are Havens of Adventurous Fishing Fleets. By Leo Walmsley. LXIII, pp. 197-232, 41 ills., Feb., 1933

YORKTOWN (Aircraft Carrier):

Victory's Portrait in the Marianas. By Lt. William Franklin Draper, USNR. With 17 ills. in color from paintings by author. LXXXVIII, pp. 599-616, Nov., 1945

YOSEMITE NATIONAL PARK, California:

Crater Lake and Yosemite Through the Ages. By Wallace W. Atwood, Jr. Paintings by Eugene Kingman. LXXI, pp. 327-343, 7 ills. in black and white, 13 ills. in color, Mar., 1937

The Land of the Best. By Gilbert H. Grosvenor. XXIX, pp. 327-430, 71 ills. in black and white, 33 ills. in color, pictorial supplement, Apr., 1916

Our National Parks. By L. F. Schmeckebier. XXIII, pp. 531-579, 41 ills., map, June, 1912

The Wonderland of California. By Herman Whitaker. XXVIII, pp. 57-104, 45 ills., July, 1915

YOUNG, EDGERTON R.:

The Tallest Tree That Grows (Eucalyptus). By Edgerton R. Young. XX, pp. 664-667, 3 ills., July, 1909

YOUNG, STANLEY P.:

Other Working Dogs and the Wild Species. By Stanley P. Young. Paintings by Walter A. Weber. LXXXVI, pp. 363-384, 12 ills. in black and white, 9 ills. in color, Sept., 1944

YOUNG Japan. By Eliza R. Scidmore. XXVI, pp. 36-38, 54-64, 11 ills. in color, July, 1914

YOUNG Russia: The Land of Unlimited Possibilities. By Gilbert H. Grosvenor. XXVI, pp. 421-520, 85 ills. in black and white, 17 ills. in color, Nov., 1914

The **YOUNG** Turk. By Rear-Admiral Colby M. Chester. XXIII, pp. 43-89, 39 ills., Jan., 1912

YOUNGBLOOD, F. J.:

A Little Journey in Honduras. By F. J. Youngblood. XXX, pp. 177-184, 6 ills., Aug., 1916

YOUR Dog Joins Up. By Frederick Simpich. LXXXIII, pp. 93-113, 25 ills., Jan., 1943

YOUR Navy as Peace Insurance. By Fleet Admiral Chester W. Nimitz. LXXXIX, pp. 681-736, 32 ills. in black and white, 26 ills. in color, June, 1946

YOUR New World of Tomorrow. By F. Barrows Colton. LXXXVIII, pp. 385-410, 25 ills., Oct., 1945

YOUR Society (NGS) Aids War Effort. LXXXIII, pp. 277-278, ill., Feb., 1943

YOUR Society (NGS) Sponsors an Expedition to Explore the Stratosphere. LXV, pp. 528-530, ill., Apr., 1934

YOUTH Explores Its World (Boy Scouts). By Frederick Simpich. LXV, pp. 643-662, 21 ills., May, 1934

YUCATAN (State), Mexico:

Chichen Itzá, an Ancient American Mecca: Recent Excavations in Yucatan Are Bringing to Light the Temples, Palaces, and Pyramids of America's Most Holy Native City. By Sylvanus Griswold Morley. XLVII, pp. 63-95, 34 ills., diagr., map, Jan., 1925

Henequen—The Yucatan Fiber. By E. H. Thompson. XIV, pp. 150-158, 6 ills., Apr., 1903

YUCATAN (State), Mexico—*Continued*

The Home of a Forgotten Race: Mysterious Chichen Itza, in Yucatan, Mexico. By Edward H. Thompson. XXV, pp. 585-648, 59 ills., June, 1914

Yucatán, Home of the Gifted Maya: Two Thousand Years of History Reach Back to Early American Temple Builders, Corn Cultivators, and Pioneers in Mathematics. By Sylvanus Griswold Morley. Paintings by H. M. Herget. LXX, pp. 591-644, 28 ills. in black and white, 35 ills. in color, map, Nov., 1936

Yucatan in 1895. VII, pp. 83-85, Feb., 1896

YUCAY VALLEY, Peru:

Some Wonderful Sights in the Andean Highlands: The Oldest City in America. Sailing on the Lake of the Clouds: The Yosemite of Peru. By Harriet Chalmers Adams. XIX, pp. 597-618, 19 ills., map, Sept., 1908

YUGOSLAVIA:

The Changing Map in the Balkans. By Frederick Moore. XXIV, pp. 199-226, 27 ills., map, Feb., 1913

The Clock Turns Back in Yugoslavia: The Fortified Monastery of Mountain-girt Dečani Survives Its Six Hundredth Birthday. By Ethel Chamberlain Porter. LXXXV, pp. 493-512, 20 ills., map, Apr., 1944

Dalmatian Days: Coasting Along Debatable Shores Where Latin and Slav Meet. By Melville Chater. LIII, pp. 47-90, 26 ills. in black and white, 17 ills. in color, map, Jan., 1928

The Danube, Highway of Races: From the Black Forest to the Black Sea, Europe's Most Important River Has Borne the Traffic of Centuries. By Melville Chater. LVI, pp. 643-697, 54 ills., Dec., 1929

East of the Adriatic: Notes on Dalmatia, Montenegro, Bosnia, and Herzegovina. By Kenneth McKenzie. XXIII, pp. 1159-1187, 1284, 37 ills., map, Dec., 1912

Echoes from Yugoslavia. 16 ills. LXXIX, pp. 793-804, June, 1941

From England to India by Automobile: An 8,527-mile Trip Through Ten Countries, from London to Quetta, Requires Five and a Half Months. By Major F. A. C. Forbes-Leith. XLVIII, pp. 191-223, 33 ills., map, Aug., 1925

The Great Turk and His Lost Provinces. By William E. Curtis. XIV, pp. 45-61, 7 ills., Feb., 1903

Greece and Montenegro. By George Higgins Moses. XXIV, pp. 281-310, 24 ills., Mar., 1913

In Quaint, Curious Croatia. By Felix J. Koch. XIX, pp. 809-832, 37 ills., Dec., 1908

Jugoslavia—Ten Years After. By Melville Chater. LVIII, pp. 257-309, 44 ills. in black and white, 25 ills. in color, map, Sept., 1930

Kaleidoscopic Land of Europe's Youngest King: Yugoslavia Holds a Mosaic of Slavs and the City Where Pistol Shots Touched Off the World War. By Douglas Chandler. LXXV, pp. 691-738, 18 ills. in black and white, 34 ills. in color, maps, June, 1939

The Kingdom of Servia. By William Joseph Showalter. XXVII, pp. 417-432, 12 ills., map, Apr., 1915

YUGOSLAVIA—*Continued*

The Land of Contrast: Austria-Hungary. By D. W. and A. S. Iddings. XXIII, pp. 1188-1217, 1284, 33 ills., map, Dec., 1912

The New Map of Europe: Showing the Boundaries Established by the Peace Conference at Paris and by Subsequent Decisions of the Supreme Council of the Allied and Associated Powers. By Ralph A. Graves. Text with map supplement. XXXIX, pp. 157-177, 18 ills., Feb., 1921

The Races of Europe. By Edwin A. Grosvenor. XXXIV, pp. 441-534, 62 ills., diagr. and index, maps, map supplement, Dec., 1918

Servia and Montenegro. XIX, pp. 774-789, 24 ills., Nov., 1908

Where East Meets West: A Visit to Picturesque Dalmatia, Montenegro and Bosnia. By Marian Cruger Coffin. XIX, pp. 309-344, 26 ills., map, May, 1908

The Whirlpool of the Balkans. By George Higgins Moses. XXXIX, pp. 179-197, 15 ills., Feb., 1921

YUGOSLAVIA: Where Oriental Hues Splash Europe. 34 color photos by Konstantin J. Kostich and Rudolf Balogh. LXXV, pp. 699-738, June, 1939

YUKON (River), Canada-Alaska:

Alaska and Its Mineral Resources. By Samuel Franklin Emmons. IX, pp. 139-172, 3 ills., map supplement, Apr., 1898

The "Breaking Up" of the Yukon. By Captain George S. Gibbs. XVII, pp. 268-272, 6 ills., May, 1906

Climatic Conditions of Alaska. By General A. W. Greely. IX, pp. 132-137, Apr., 1898

The Future of the Yukon Goldfields. By William H. Dall. IX, pp. 117-120, Apr., 1898

To-day on "The Yukon Trail of 1898." By Amos Burg. LVIII, pp. 85-126, 52 ills., map, July, 1930

A Winter Weather Record From the Klondike Region. By E. W. Nelson. VIII, pp. 327-335, tables, Nov., 1897

A Yukon Pioneer, Mike Lebarge. (By Wm. H. Dall). IX, pp. 137-139, ill., Apr., 1898

YUKON DISTRICT (pre-Yukon Territory), Canada. *See* Yukon Territory, articles prior to June, 1898

A **YUKON** Pioneer, Mike Lebarge. (By Wm. H. Dall). IX, pp. 137-139, ill., Apr., 1898

YUKON TERRITORY, Canada:

Alaskan Highway an Engineering Epic: Mosquitoes, Mud, and Muskeg Minor Obstacles of 1,671-mile Race to Throw the Alcan Life Line Through Thick Forests and Uninhabited Wilderness. By Froelich Rainey. LXXXIII, pp. 143-168, 21 ills., 3 maps, Feb., 1943

Climatic Conditions of Alaska. By General A. W. Greely. IX, pp. 132-137, Apr., 1898
Included: Dawson and Fort Selkirk in the Klondike Region

An Expedition Through the Yukon District. By Charles Willard Hayes. IV, pp. 117-159, 3 maps (2 foldouts), May 15, 1892

YUKON TERRITORY, Canada—*Continued*

Exploring Yukon's Glacial Stronghold. By Bradford Washburn. LXIX, pp. 715-748, 29 ills., two-page map, June, 1936

Family Afoot in Yukon Wilds: Two Young Children and Their Parents Live Off the Country in the Northwest Canada Wilderness Now To Be Traversed by the Alaska Highway. By William Hamilton Albee, with Ruth Albee. LXXXI, pp. 589-616, 18 ills. in black and white, 14 ills. in color, May, 1942

The Future of the Yukon Goldfields. By William H. Dall. IX, pp. 117-120, Apr., 1898

Geographical Aspects of the Monroe Doctrine. IX, pp. 476-477, Nov., 1898

Ice Cliffs on White River, Yukon Territory. By C. Willard Hayes and Alfred H. Brooks. XI, pp. 199-201, May, 1900

Ice-Cliffs on White River, Yukon Territory. By Martin W. Gorman. XI, pp. 113-117, Mar., 1900

Life on a Yukon Trail. By Alfred Pearce Dennis. X, pp. 377-391, 8 ills., map, Oct., 1899; pp. 457-466, 7 ills., Nov., 1899

The Northwest Passes to the Yukon. By Eliza Ruhamah Scidmore. IX, pp. 105-113, 3 ills., Apr., 1898

To-day on "The Yukon Trail of 1898." By Amos Burg. LVIII, pp. 85-126, 52 ills., map, July, 1930

A Winter Weather Record From the Klondike Region. By E. W. Nelson. VIII, pp. 327-335, tables, Nov., 1897

YUMA TRAIL, Arizona-Mexico:

The Old Yuma Trail. By W J McGee. XII, pp. 103-107, Mar., 1901; pp. 129-143, 7 ills., map, Apr., 1901

YUN KANG CAVES, Shansi Province, China:

China's Great Wall of Sculpture: Man-hewn Caves and Countless Images Form a Colossal Art Wonder of Early Buddhism. By Mary Augusta Mullikin. Paintings by author and Anna M. Hotchkis. LXXIII, pp. 313-348, 23 ills. in black and white, 10 ills. in color, map, Mar., 1938

YÜNNAN (Province), China:

Banishing the Devil of Disease Among the Nashi: Weird Ceremonies Performed by an Aboriginal Tribe in the Heart of Yünnan Province, China. By Joseph F. Rock. XLVI, pp. 473-499, 26 ills., map, Nov., 1924

Burma Road, Back Door to China: Like the Great Wall of Ancient Times, This Mighty Mountain Highway Has Been Built by Myriad Chinese to Help Defend Their Homeland. By Frank Outram and G. E. Fane. LXXVIII, pp. 629-658, 26 ills., map, Nov., 1940

China Opens Her Wild West: In the Mountain-girt Heart of a Continent a New China Has Been Created During the Years of War. By Owen Lattimore. LXXXII, pp. 337-367, 21 ills. in black and white, 11 ills. in color, map, Sept., 1942

Kunming, Southwestern Gateway to China. By Joseph E. Passantino. With 18 color photos by author. XC, pp. 137-168, 12 ills. in black and white, Aug., 1946

YÜNNAN (Province), China—*Continued*

The Land of the Crossbow. By George Forrest. XXI, pp. 132-156, 15 ills., map, Feb., 1910

The National Geographic Society's Yünnan Province Expedition. By Gilbert Grosvenor. XLVII, pp. 493-498, 5 ills., Apr., 1925

Stilwell Road—Land Route to China. By Nelson Grant Tayman. LXXXVII, pp. 681-698, 18 ills., June, 1945

Sungmas, the Living Oracles of the Tibetan Church. By Joseph F. Rock. LXVIII, pp. 475-486, ill. in black and white, 12 ills. in color, Oct., 1935

Through the Great River Trenches of Asia: National Geographic Society Explorer Follows the Yangtze, Mekong, and Salwin Through Mighty Gorges, Some of Whose Canyon Walls Tower to a Height of More Than Two Miles. By Joseph F. Rock. L, pp. 133-186, 47 ills., map, Aug., 1926

YUSHU, China. *See* Jyekundo

Z

ZAANDAM, Netherlands:

Glimpses of Holland. By William Wisner Chapin. XXVII, pp. 1-29, 26 ills., Jan., 1915

ZACATECAS (State), Mexico:

A Mexican Hacienda. By J. E. Kirkwood. XXV, pp. 563-584, 18 ills., May, 1914

ZAMBEZI (River), Africa:

Impressions and Scenes of Mozambique. By O. W. Barrett. XXI, pp. 807-830, 31 ills., Oct., 1910

The Wonders of the Mosi-oa-Tunga: The Falls of the Zambesi. By Louis Livingston Seaman. XXII, pp. 561-571, 6 ills., June, 1911

ZANZIBAR (Island), Africa:

Zanzibar. By Mrs. Harris R. Childs. XXIII, pp. 810-824, 11 ills., Aug., 1912

ZAPOTEC INDIANS:

Among the Zapotecs of Mexico: A Visit to the Indians of Oaxaca, Home State of the Republic's Great Liberator, Juárez, and Its Most Famous Ruler, Diaz. By Herbert Corey. LI, pp. 501-553, 59 ills., map, May, 1927

Hewers of Stone (Mitla, Mexico). By Jeremiah Zimmerman. XXI, pp. 1002-1020, 9 ills., Dec., 1910

The Isthmus of Tehuantepec: "The Bridge of the World's Commerce." By Helen Olsson-Seffer. XXI, pp. 991-1002, 7 ills., Dec., 1910

Monte Albán, Richest Archeological Find in America: A Tomb in Oaxaca, Mexico, Yields Treasures Which Reveal the Splendid Culture of the Mixtecs. By Dr. Alfonso Caso. LXII, pp. 487-512, 28 ills., Oct., 1932

ZARA, Dalmatia:

East of the Adriatic: Notes on Dalmatia, Montenegro, Bosnia, and Herzegovina. By Kenneth McKenzie. XXIII, pp. 1159-1187, 1284, 37 ills., map, Dec., 1912

ZEELAND (Province), Netherlands:
The City of Jacqueline (Goes, Netherlands). By Florence Craig Albrecht. XXVII, pp. 29-56, 31 ills., Jan., 1915
See also Walcheren (Island)

ZENZINOV, VLADIMIR M.:
With an Exile in Arctic Siberia: The Narrative of a Russian Who Was Compelled to Turn Polar Explorer for Two Years. By Vladimir M. Zenzinov. XLVI, pp. 695-718, 30 ills., map, Dec., 1924

ZEUSLER, F. A.:
Standing Iceberg Guard in the North Atlantic: International Patrol Safeguards the Lives of Thousands of Travelers and Protects Trans-Atlantic Liners from a "Titanic" Fate. By Lieutenant Commander F. A. Zeusler. L, pp. 1-28, 29 ills., map, July, 1926

ZIEGLER, WILLIAM:
Biography of William Ziegler. XVI, pp. 355-357, ill., July, 1905

ZIEGLER POLAR EXPEDITIONS:
The Annual Dinner of the National Geographic Society (The Arctic: Speeches by Anthony Fiala and W. S. Champ). XVII, pp. 32-36, Jan., 1906
The Baldwin-Ziegler Arctic Expedition. XIII, pp. 358-359, Sept., 1902
Fighting the Polar Ice. XVIII, pp. 72-77, 7 ills., Jan., 1907
Mr. Ziegler and the National Geographic Society. XIV, pp. 251-254, June, 1903
Polar Photography. By Anthony Fiala. XVIII, pp. 140-142, Feb., 1907
The Ziegler Polar Expedition. XIV, pp. 414-417, 5 ills., Nov., 1903
Ziegler Polar Expedition. XV, pp. 427-428, Oct., 1904
The Ziegler Polar Expedition. XVI, p. 198, Apr., 1905
The Ziegler Polar Expedition. XVI, pp. 439-440, Sept., 1905

ZIGZAGGING Across Sicily. By Melville Chater. XLVI, pp. 303-352, 44 ills., map, Sept., 1924

ZIMBABWE (Ruins), Southern Rhodesia:
Rhodesia, Hobby and Hope of Cecil Rhodes. By W. Robert Moore. LXXXVI, pp. 281-306, 13 ills. in black and white, 10 ills. in color, map, Sept., 1944

ZIMMERMAN, JEREMIAH:
Hewers of Stone (Mitla, Mexico). By Jeremiah Zimmerman. XXI, pp. 1002-1020, 9 ills., Dec., 1910

ZION NATIONAL PARK, Utah:
Bursts of Color in Sculptured Utah. 22 ills. in color. LXIX, pp. 593-616, May, 1936
Photographing the Marvels of the West in Colors. By Fred Payne Clatworthy. LIII, pp. 694-719, 30 ills. in color, June, 1928

ZON, RAPHAEL:
When Our Country Is Fifty Years Older. By Raphael Zon. XX, pp. 573-580, ills., diagr., June, 1909

ZOQUES (Indians):
Finding Jewels of Jade in a Mexican Swamp. By Matthew W. and Marion Stirling. LXXXII, pp. 635-661, 15 ills. in black and white, 12 ills. in color, map, Nov., 1942
The Isthmus of Tehuantepec: "The Bridge of the World's Commerce." By Helen Olsson-Seffer. XXI, pp. 991-1002, 7 ills., Dec., 1910

ZOROASTRIANISM:
The Parsees and the Towers of Silence at Bombay, India. By William Thomas Fee. XVI, pp. 529-554, 16 ills., Dec., 1905

ZOTZILS (Indians):
Finding Jewels of Jade in a Mexican Swamp. By Matthew W. and Marion Stirling. LXXXII, pp. 635-661, 15 ills. in black and white, 12 ills. in color, map, Nov., 1942

ZUIDER ZEE, Netherlands:
Glimpses of Holland. By William Wisner Chapin. XXVII, pp. 1-29, 26 ills., Jan., 1915
A New Country Awaits Discovery: The Draining of the Zuider Zee Makes Room for the Excess Population of the Netherlands. By J. C. M. Kruisinga. LXIV, pp. 293-320, 20 ills. in black and white, 13 ills. in color, maps, Sept., 1933

ZULULAND, Natal:
Natal: The Garden Colony. By Russell Hastings Millward. XX, pp. 278-291, 16 ills., Mar., 1909
Natal: The Garden Province. By Melville Chater. LIX, pp. 447-478, 29 ills. in black and white, 14 ills. in color, Apr., 1931

ZULUS (Tribespeople):
The Diamond Mines of South Africa. By Gardiner F. Williams. XVII, pp. 344-356, 11 ills., June, 1906
See also Zululand

ZUMBRO, W. M.:
Religious Penances and Punishments Self-Inflicted by the Holy Men of India. By W. M. Zumbro. XXIV, pp. 1257-1314, 69 ills., Dec., 1913
The Temples of India. 54 photos by W. M. Zumbro. XX, pp. 922-971, Nov., 1909

ZUÑI INDIANS:
Everyday Life in Pueblo Bonito: As Disclosed by the National Geographic Society's Archeologic Explorations in the Chaco Canyon National Monument, New Mexico. By Neil M. Judd. XLVIII, pp. 227-262, 37 ills., map, Sept., 1925
Indian Tribes of Pueblo Land. By Matthew W. Stirling. Paintings by W. Langdon Kihn. LXXVIII, pp. 549-596, 16 ills. in black and white, 25 ills. in color, Nov., 1940

ZWEMER, S. M.:
Mecca the Mystic: A New Kingdom Within Arabia. By S. M. Zwemer. XXXII, pp. 157-172, 13 ills., Aug., 1917
Notes on Oman. By S. M. Zwemer. XXII, pp. 89-98, 8 ills., map, Jan., 1911

NATIONAL GEOGRAPHIC MAP INDEX

Large color maps issued as supplements to the NATIONAL GEOGRAPHIC MAGAZINE are listed by title in *italics,* and sizes are shown.

A

ABYSSINIA. *See* Ethiopia

ACKLIN (ACKLINS) ISLAND. *See* Bahama Islands

ADEN, Arabian Peninsula:

Map showing position of Aden and Little Aden Peninsulas. LXVIII, p. 726, Dec., 1935

ADIRONDACK STATE PARK, New York:

Adirondack State Park. LXXIII, p. 720, June, 1938

AEGEAN REGIONS:

Aegean regions, and an inset of the Bosphorus. LVI, p. 489, Oct., 1929

Aegean regions, showing the isles of Greece and the Italian islands of the Aegean. LXXXV, p. 596, May, 1944

Asia Minor, the Dardanelles, and the islands of the Ægean Sea. XLII, p. 554, Nov., 1922

Asia Minor and the Holy Land. XXXVII, p. 46, Jan., 1920

Classical Lands of the Mediterranean. LXXVII, supplement, 35¼ x 26 inches, Mar., 1940

Crete and Greece. LV, p. 250, Feb., 1929

Gates to the Black Sea. XXVII, p. 532, May, 1915

Gates to the Black Sea. XXVIII, p. 232, Sept., 1915

Greece, and inset showing expansion of Greece. LVIII, p. 652, Dec., 1930

Greece, Asia Minor, and Mediterranean regions, showing route of the "Bonita." LV, p. 250, Feb., 1929

Greece, Bulgaria, Turkey. XXX, p. 271, Sept., 1916

Greece and the Aegean, showing sites of antiquity and the necklace of Hellenic cities that adorned the coast of Asia Minor. LXXXV, pp. 280-281, Mar., 1944

Italian islands of the Aegean. LXXIX, p. 451, Apr., 1941

"Shores of Sunrise" (The Levant). L, p. 652, Dec., 1926

Shores of the Aegean, which have provided the geographic panorama for much of the history of civilization. LIV, p. 725, Dec., 1928

AFGHANISTAN:

Afghanistan, buffer between Russia and India. XC, p. 521, Oct., 1946

Afghanistan and adjacent regions. LXIV, p. 742, Dec., 1933

Afghanistan and its border lands. XXXIX, p. 90, Jan., 1921

AFRICA:

Africa. Prepared from latest geographical data by Gilbert H. Grosvenor, Editor. XX, supplement, 15½ x 20 inches, Mar., 1909

Africa, as described by Ptolemy in the second century. By Mattiolo, Venice, 1548. XXII, p. 390, Apr., 1911

Africa, showing Darfur. XLV, p. 46, Jan., 1924

Africa, showing possessions of each European power. XXII, p. 393, Apr., 1911

Africa, showing territory within which the Convention of May 19, 1900, places restrictions on the killing of wild animals. XI, p. 447, Nov., 1900

Africa, showing the homes of the fighting tribes of the Sudan. LVI, p. 466, Oct., 1929

Africa, showing Vasco da Gama's first voyage around Cape of Good Hope. LII, p. 504, Nov., 1927

Africa, with Da Gama's discoveries, 1498. By Mattiolo, 1548. XXII, p. 391, Apr., 1911

Africa, with inset showing airways and relief. LXVII, supplement, 29 x 31½ inches, June, 1935

Africa, with insets of the Cape Verde Islands, relief map, and a table of airline distances in statute miles. LXXXIII, supplement, 29¼ x 31½ inches, Feb., 1943

Appropriation of Africa by Europeans. I, foldout (opp. p. 124), Apr., 1889

Atlantic Ocean, showing west coast of Africa. LXXVI, supplement, 31 x 25 inches, July, 1939

Atlantic Ocean, showing west coast of Africa, and a table of air-line distances in statute miles. LXXX, supplement, 31¼ x 25 inches, Sept., 1941

Europe and northern Africa, showing extent of Roman Empire, with table of historical facts. XC, pp. 552-553, Nov., 1946

French West Africa, with pictographs, showing route followed by Mrs. Boulton. LXXIX, pp. 636-637, May, 1941

Geographic relation of France and her African colonies. XI, p. 233, June, 1900

Gulf of Guinea region, with enlargement of São Tomé, the Chocolate Island. LXXXIX, p. 659, May, 1946

Indian Ocean, including Australia, New Zealand and Malaysia, showing east coast of Africa and Suez Canal. LXXIX, supplement, 25½ x 32¾ inches, Mar., 1941

Madagascar, in its relation to Africa and compared with the eastern United States. LVI, p. 183, Aug., 1929

AFRICA—*Continued*

Map of Africa and Adjoining Portions of Europe and Asia. XLII, supplement, 27 x 30 inches, Oct., 1922

Map of the Countries Bordering the Mediterranean Sea. XXIII, supplement, 10 x 18 inches, Jan., 1912

Map of the Seat of War in Africa. Prepared in the War Department, Adjutant General's Office, Military Information Division. Inset of South Africa. X, supplement, 33 x 45 inches, Dec., 1899

Mediterranean coast of Libia and Egypt. LXXVIII, p. 810, Dec., 1940

North Africa. XXII, p. 751, Aug., 1911

North Africa, showing countries bordering on the Mediterranean and bombing ranges from Bizerte, Tunisia. LXXXIV, pp. 8-9, July, 1943

North-central Africa, showing route of Flood-Wilson Expedition. LXV, pp. 40-41, Jan., 1934

Northwest Africa, showing mileage between Dakar, French West Africa, and important points in the Eastern and Western Hemispheres. LXXXI, p. 374, Mar., 1942

Railways in South Africa. XI, p. 188, May, 1900

Roosevelt's route and hunting trips in Africa (British East Africa). XXII, p. 2, Jan., 1911

Route of Felix Shay from Cairo to Capetown. XLVII, p. 128, Feb., 1925

Route of Hassanein Bey through the Libyan Desert. XLVI, p. 236, Sept., 1924

Route of the Citroën African Expedition. XLIX, p. 652, June, 1926

Route of the Thaw Expedition from Algiers to Nairobi. LXXIV, p. 330, Sept., 1938

Sketch map of Africa, showing principal political divisions. VII, pl. XIX (opp. p. 164), foldout, May, 1896

South-West Africa, showing Mount Brukkaros and neighboring region. LVII, p. 489, Apr., 1930

Southwest Africa in the vicinity of the new observatory (National Geographic Society's solar radiation station). L, p. 504, Oct., 1926

Sudan. XVII, p. 245, May, 1906

Sudan, French West Africa, and British East Africa. XIX, p. 736, Oct., 1908

Theater of War in Europe, Africa, and Western Asia, with table of airline distances in statute miles. LXXXII, supplement, 26½ x 31 inches, July, 1942

Uganda Railway. XIII, p. 170, May, 1902

Western Africa, showing strategic position of Dakar. LXXXI, p. 377, Mar., 1942

Western Rift Valley and surrounding country, with inset of the Virunga Mountains, Belgian Congo. LXXVI, p. 515, Oct., 1939

See also Algeria; Anglo-Egyptian Sudan; Belgian Congo; Cameroons; Egypt; Gold Coast; Kenya; Libia; Morocco; Nigeria; Rhodesia; Suez Canal; Tunisia; Uganda; Union of South Africa; *and* island: Madagascar

AIR CURRENTS. *See* Pacific Ocean; Weather Charts

AIR ROUTES:

Airway routes of the United States. LXIII, p. 634, May, 1933

AIR ROUTES—*Continued*

Atlantic Ocean, showing air routes to Norway, Britain, and Portugal from Newfoundland, Greenland, and Iceland. LXXX, p. 77, July, 1941

Burma to China as the crow flies. LXXXIV, p. 492, Oct., 1943

Canada, showing the route flown by the author (J. A. Wilson) in his air survey of the Dominion. L, pp. 392-393, Oct., 1926

Europe, showing route followed by Lieutenant J. Parker Van Zandt in his 6,500-mile airplane tour. XLVII, p. 275, Mar., 1925

Europe, showing routes of J. Parker Van Zandt's flights. LXXV, p. 794, June, 1939

Flying around the North Atlantic: Route of the Lindberghs in the *Tingmissartoq*. LXVI, pp. 266-267, Sept., 1934

Four years of aerial trail blazing in ancient China (routes flown by Capt. Hans Koester). LXXIII, p. 574, May, 1938

How Commander Byrd plots a new transatlantic route along which future flyers may cross on schedule. LII, p. 348, Sept., 1927

How the "Southern Cross" (airplane) blazed an aërial trail across the Pacific. LIV, p. 373, Oct., 1928

Northern Hemisphere, showing proposed routes of aircraft over the Arctic zone. XLII, p. 206, Aug., 1922

Pacific islands, showing route of Flying Clippers. LXXIV, p. 102, July, 1938

Pinedo's 60,000-mile air cruise in the "Santa María" (seaplane) to six continents. LIV, pp. 248-249, Sept., 1928

Route flown by the Days. LXI, p. 656, June, 1932

Route flown by the National Geographic aërial survey party from Washington to Buenos Aires. LIX, p. 4, Jan., 1931

Route followed by air-mail planes from Montevideo to Miami. LVII, p. 264, Mar., 1930

Route followed by Capt. Harry Pidgeon in his circumnavigation of the globe. LIII, pp. 144-145, Feb., 1928

Route followed by Lindbergh in his flight over 13 Latin-American countries. LIII, p. 532, May, 1928

Route followed by Sir Ross Smith from London to Australia. XXXIX, pp. 230-231, Mar., 1921

Route followed by U. S. Army aviators on the first Alaskan Air Expedition from New York to Nome. XLI, pp. 500-501, May, 1922

Route of the flight from Purnea, India, across Nepal, to the summit of Everest. LXIV, p. 130, Aug., 1933

Route of the "Norge" (airship) from Rome to Alaska: A flight of 8,500 miles across the top of the world. LII, pp. 188-189, Aug., 1927

Route of the trail-blazing flight of U. S. Army airplanes through 20 countries of Latin America. LII, p. 452, Oct., 1927

Route of transandean mail and passenger planes. LIX, p. 596, May, 1931

Routes flown by Sir Alan J. Cobham over Europe, Asia, Australia, and Africa. LIII, p. 350, Mar., 1928

AIR ROUTES—*Continued*

Routes followed by Lieutenant John A. Macready and Lieutenant Oakley G. Kelly in their transcontinental, non-stop flights, and by Lieutenant Macready and Lieutenant A. W. Stevens on their later photographic flights. XLVI, p. 6, July, 1924

Southern Greenland: Route of the Lindberghs. LXVI, p. 262, Sept., 1934

Territory covered in flights of Walter Mittelholzer. LXI, p. 466, Apr., 1932

Territory observed by Brigadier General P. R. C. Groves and Major J. R. McCrindle in their flight over Egypt, Sinai, and Palestine. L, p. 315, Sept., 1926

Three groups of the Azores and the routes of the successful American aviators in their transatlantic flight; also, the route chosen by the ill-fated Hawker-Grieve Expedition. XXXV, p. 515, June, 1919

United States, showing route followed by Lindbergh in the "Spirit of St. Louis," and its companion plane. LIII, p. 5, Jan., 1928

United States, showing transcontinental routes of the "Shenandoah" on its record-making voyage. XLVII, p. 5, Jan., 1925

United States air mail routes in operation and proposed. XLIX, p. 5, Jan., 1926

See also Antarctic Regions; Arctic Regions

ALABAMA:

Alabama. LX, p. 706, Dec., 1931

ALAND (Islands), Finland:

Aland. LXVII, p. 105, Jan., 1935

ALASKA:

Alaska. XV, supplement, 36 x 42 inches, May, 1904

Alaska. XX, p. 674, July, 1909

Alaska. XXV, supplement, 15¼ x 20 inches, Feb., 1914

Alaska, showing Alcan Highway. LXXXIII, pp. 150-151, Feb., 1943

Alaska, showing distribution of timber. XVIII, p. 172, Mar., 1907

Alaska, showing mineral deposits so far as known. XVI, p. 512, Nov., 1905

Alaska, showing navigable waters and railroads. XVIII, p. 164, Mar., 1907

Alaska, showing railway routes and known occurrences of economically important minerals. XVIII, p. 181, Mar., 1907

Alaska, showing so far as known, the distribution of metamorphic rocks and the localities where gold has been mined. XVIII, p. 168, Mar., 1907

Alaska, showing the distribution of the coal-bearing rocks so far as known. XVIII, p. 170, Mar., 1907

Alaska, showing the sections that have been mapped and surveyed. XXIII, p. 424, May, 1912

Alaska, showing unexplored areas in 1905. XVII, p. 112, Feb., 1906

Alaska—springboard for attack on Japan and key to continental defense. LXXXII, pp. 286-287, Sept., 1942

ALASKA—*Continued*

Alaska and adjoining Yukon Territory. LVIII, p. 89, July, 1930

Alaska boundary in Portland Canal. XV, p. 5, Jan., 1904

Alaska Boundary Tribunal. XV, supplement, 12 x 12½ inches, Jan., 1904

Alaska-British Northwest Territory-British Columbia, showing route of expedition of 1891, northern limit of glaciation, and volcanic tufa; an index map of the Yukon district, for pls. 19 and 20. IV, pls. 18-20, 2 foldouts, May 15, 1892

Alaska-Canada boundary line. XXIII, p. 693, July, 1912

Alaska telegraph and cable lines. XV, p. 491, Dec., 1904

Alaskan boundary lines claimed by the United States and Canada. XIV, p. 90, Mar., 1903

The Arctic cruise of the U. S. S. "Thetis," Lieut. Comdr. Chas. H. Stockton, U. S. N., Comdg. in the summer and autumn of 1889. II, foldout, July, 1890

Base of the Alaska Peninsula, showing the major features of the Katmai district and the adjoining country. XL, p. 222, Sept., 1921

Bay de Monti, after Malaspina. III, pl. 6 (opp. p. 66), May 29, 1891

British map, 1832. X, p. 438, Nov., 1899

Canadian map of 1831. X, p. 441, Nov., 1899

Canadian map of 1857. X, p. 442, Nov., 1899

A Chart shewing part of the Coast of N. W. America (Vancouver's chart, No. I). X, supplement, 15½ x 18 inches, Nov., 1899

A Chart Shewing part of the Coast of N. W. America (Vancouver's chart, No. II). X, supplement, 15½ x 18 inches, Nov., 1899

Coastal region, mapped by the International Boundary Commission in 1906-1908, and adjoining Yukon and British Columbia, surveyed by Bradford Washburn in 1935. LXIX, pp. 720-721, June, 1936

Columbia Glacier, Prince William Sound. XXI, p. 10, Jan., 1910

Copper-bearing areas of Alaska, so far as known. XVIII, p. 169, Mar., 1907

Copper River and Northwestern Railway. XXI, p. 25, Jan., 1910

Disenchantment Bay, after Malaspina. III, pl. 7 (opp. p. 68), May 29, 1891

Eastern shore of Yakutat Bay, after Dixon. III, pl. 4 (opp. p. 62), May 29, 1891

Fairweather peninsula with inset showing location of Mount Crillon. LXVII, p. 363, Mar., 1935

French map, 1844. X, p. 445, Nov., 1899

Fronts of the Johns Hopkins, Grand Pacific, and Muir Glaciers. XIX, p. 77, Jan., 1908

Geographic provinces of northwestern North America. XVIII, p. 176, Mar., 1907

Geologic map of Muir Glacier Basin. By H. P. Cushing. IV, pl. 16 (opp. p. 62), Mar. 21, 1892

Glacier Bay and Muir Glacier. By Harry Fielding Reid. VII, p. 144, Apr., 1896

Glaciers of Prince William Sound and Copper River. XXII, p. 540, June, 1911

ALASKA—*Continued*

The Gold and Coal Fields of Alaska, Together with the Principal Steamer Routes and Trails; Insets: Trails from Tide Water to the Headwaters of the Yukon River; The Klondike Gold Region, Canada. IX, pl. 4, supplement, 25 x 30 inches, Apr., 1898

Golofnin Bay and Cape Nome gold fields. XI, p. 16, Jan., 1900

Government reindeer stations in Alaska. XIV, p. 131, Apr., 1903

Hidden Glacier in 1899, 1905, 1906, and 1909. XXI, p. 45, Jan., 1910

Hudson's Bay Company map, 1857. X, pl. xi (opp. p. 425), Nov., 1899

Katmai Volcano and vicinity. XXXI, p. 23, Jan., 1917

Kenai Peninsula, showing the best portion of the sheep country and location of Seward and Resurrection Bay. XXIII, pp. 428-429, May, 1912

Lake Clark and vicinity. XV, p. 330, Aug., 1904

Location of Aniakchak Crater and topographical detail. LX, p. 322, Sept., 1931

Location of Mount McKinley. XII, p. 312, Aug., 1901

Lower Copper River, Controller Bay region. XXI, p. 24, Jan., 1910

Lower Hubbard Glacier. XXI, p. 5, Jan., 1910

Malaspina Glacier. XXI, p. 9, Jan., 1910

Malaspina Glacier, showing Marvine lobe; Atrevida; and Lucia. XXI, p. 34, Jan., 1910

Model of the Valley of Ten Thousand Smokes and vicinity. XL, p. 227, Sept., 1921

Mount McKinley. XII, p. 312, Aug., 1901

Mt. McKinley area; Sushitna River. VIII, p. 323, Nov., 1897

Mt. McKinley region, Alaska. XIV, p. 32, Jan., 1903

Muir Glacier, Alaska. Surveyed with Plane Table in 1890, by Harry Fielding Reid. IV, supplement, 19½ x 17¾ inches, Mar. 21, 1892

Muir Inlet and front of Muir Glacier, showing positions of the ice front in 1890 and in May, 1903. XIV, p. 444, Dec., 1903

Northern part of Muir Inlet. IV, pl. 15 (opp. p. 55), Mar. 21, 1892

Nunatak Glacier in 1895, 1899, and 1909. XXI, p. 44, Jan., 1910

Pacific coast of the Gulf of Alaska. XXI, p. 3, Jan., 1910

Port Wells, Prince William Sound, in 1899. XXII, p. 550, June, 1911

Port Wells in 1910, showing the extraordinary retreat of Barry and Surprise Glaciers. XXII, p. 550, June, 1911

Probable summer migration route of Alaska geese. LIII, p. 116, Jan., 1928

Proposed Mount McKinley National Park from surveys by the United States Geological Survey. XXXI, p. 71, Jan., 1917

Region affected by the Katmai eruption, showing the ash fall at varying distances. XXIV, p. 132, Feb., 1913

Route followed by Bradford Washburn up Mount Crillon in the Fairweather Range. LXVII, p. 385, Mar., 1935

ALASKA—*Continued*

Route followed by the *Nakwasina* from Washington State to Alaska, by way of the Inside Passage. LXIV, p. 6, July, 1933

Route of Harriman Alaska Expedition. X, p. 506, Dec., 1899

Russian imperial map, 1827. X, p. 437, Nov., 1899

St. Elias region, after La Pérouse. III, pl. 3 (opp. p. 60), May 29, 1891

St. Elias region, after Malaspina. III, pl. 5 (opp. p. 64), May 29, 1891

Scottish Geographical Magazine map, 1898. X, p. 448, Nov., 1899

Seward Peninsula. LXXV, p. 638, May, 1939

Sketch map of Alaska. III, pl. 2 (opp. p. 53), foldout, May 29, 1891

Sketch map of Mount St. Elias region, Alaska. By Mark B. Kerr. III, pl. 8 (opp. p. 75), May 29, 1891

Soundings in Port Wells, Prince William Sound. XXII, p. 559, June, 1911

Southeastern Alaska. LXXIV, p. 79, July, 1938

South eastern Alaska, 1824. X, p. 428, Nov., 1899

South eastern Alaska, showing boundary lines of American and British claims. X, p. 454, Nov., 1899

South eastern Alaska and Klondike region. X, pl. 10 (opp. p. 377), Oct., 1899

State Department map, 1867. X, p. 446, Nov., 1899

Sushitna river area; Mt. McKinley, shown. VIII, p. 323, Nov., 1897

Territory mapped by the Pavlof Expedition of 1928, and an inset showing the location of the peninsula. LV, p. 112, Jan., 1929

Topographic reconnaissance map from Controller Bay to Prince William Sound. XVIII, p. 178, Mar., 1907

Unexplored areas of Alaska. XIII, p. 132, Apr., 1902

United States Army and Navy air bases in Alaska. LXXVIII, p. 490, Oct., 1940

Upper part of Port Wells, Prince Williams Sound, Alaska. X, p. 511, Dec., 1899

Valdez Glacier Highway. XXI, p. 11, Jan., 1910

Valley of Ten Thousand Smokes. XXXIII, p. 155, Feb., 1918

Variegated and Haenke Glaciers. XXI, p. 35, Jan., 1910

Volcanic axes and structure lines in eastern Asia and Alaska and why Japan is subject to frequent destructive earthquakes. XLIV, p. 446, Oct., 1923

See also Aleutian Islands

ALASKAN-CANADIAN MILITARY HIGHWAY:

Alaska, showing Alcan Highway. LXXXIII, pp. 150-151, Feb., 1943

Western Canada, showing Alcan Highway. LXXXIII, p. 148, Feb., 1943

ALBANIA:

Albania. LIX, p. 133, Feb., 1931

Albania and its border countries of the Balkan Peninsula. XXXIV, p. 95, Aug., 1918

ALBERTA (Province), Canada:

A Map of Northwestern United States and Neighboring Canadian Provinces. LXXIX, supplement, 24½ x 36 inches, June, 1941

Sources of the Saskatchewan. X, p. 115, Apr., 1899

"ALCAN" HIGHWAY. *See* Alaskan-Canadian Military Highway

ALEUTIAN ISLANDS, Alaska:

Alaska—springboard for attack on Japan and key to continental defense. LXXXII, pp. 286-287, Sept., 1942

Detailed map of the Aleutian Islands. LXXXIII, pp. 152-153, Feb., 1943

North America, with inset of Aleutian Islands. LXXXI, supplement, 26½ x 33 inches, May, 1942

See also Attu; Bogoslof; Kiska; Unimak

ALGERIA:

Sketch map of Algeria. XIX, p. 564, Aug., 1908

Souf country. XXII, p. 377, Apr., 1911

ALPS (Mountains), Europe:

Austro-Italo Alpine region, with surrounding territory. XXVII, p. 374, Apr., 1915

Bavarian Alps, Germany. LXVIII, p. 746, Dec., 1935

Julian Alps, showing frontiers of Yugoslavia, Germany, and Italy. LXXV, p. 695, June, 1939

AMAMI GUNTO (Islands), Ryukyu Retto, Japan:

Southeast Asia and Pacific Islands from the Indies and the Philippines to the Solomons, with inset of Nansei Islands, Amami to Okinawa. LXXXVI, supplement, 41 x 26½ inches, Oct., 1944

AMERICA. *See* New World

"AMERICAN MEDITERRANEAN." *See* Caribbean Regions

ANATOLIA. *See* Asia Minor

ANDORRA:

Andorra. LXIV, p. 495, Oct., 1933

ANGLO-EGYPTIAN SUDAN:

Eastern Anglo-Egyptian Sudan, Egypt, Ethiopia, western Arabia, and adjacent countries. LXV, p. 765, June, 1934

ANTARCTIC REGIONS:

The Antarctic Continent: Outline according to John Murray. VI, p. 221, Dec. 29, 1894

Antarctic regions, showing explorations of the American discoverers of the continent, Palmer and Wilkes. XXIII, p. 308, Mar., 1912

The Antarctic Regions, with inset maps showing Antarctic Archipelago, King Edward VII Land, and part of Marie Byrd Land, and Byrd's South Pole flight. LXII, supplement, 19½ x 26½ inches, Oct., 1932

Antarctica, showing course followed by Lincoln Ellsworth in the *Polar Star* from Cape Eielson to Little America. LXX, p. 4, July, 1936

Antarctica, showing routes of Lincoln Ellsworth's flights, 1935 and 1939. LXXVI, p. 132, July, 1939

ANTARCTIC REGIONS—*Continued*

Island of South Georgia, outpost of the Antarctic. XLI, p. 412, Apr., 1922

Location of Byrd Antarctic Expedition activities, with details of Antarctic continent and Little America. LVIII, p. 132, Aug., 1930

Map of the continent, showing airplane, dog, and tractor party trails made by Byrd Antarctic Expedition. Inset of Alexandra and Rockefeller Mountains. LXVIII, pp. 450-451, Oct., 1935

Northern and Southern Hemispheres, with insets of time zones, world terrain, and tables of airline distances in four hemispheres. LXXXIII, supplement, 41 x 22 inches, Apr., 1943

Route of Amundsen to South Pole. XXIII, p. 207, Feb., 1912

Routes followed by ships and planes of Byrd Antarctic Expedition in the South Pacific. LXVIII, p. 405, Oct., 1935

South Polar regions. XVIII, p. 114, Feb., 1907

South Polar regions. XX, p. 399, Apr., 1909

South Polar regions. XX, p. 1007, Nov., 1909

South Polar regions. XXI, p. 168, Feb., 1910

South Polar regions. XXII, p. 406, Apr., 1911

South Polar Regions—Showing Routes of the Proposed Antarctic Expeditions. X, supplement, 8 x 8 inches, Aug., 1899

Work in the far south. XIV, p. 109, Mar., 1903

The World, with insets showing Arctic and Antarctic regions, natural vegetation and ocean currents, and density of population and prevailing winds. LXII, supplement, 26 x 38½ inches, Dec., 1932

The World Map, with insets of Arctic and Antarctic regions, territories occupied by belligerents in first and second World Wars, and table of geographical equivalents and abbreviations. LXXXIV, supplement, 41 x 26½ inches, Dec., 1943

ANTICOSTI ISLAND, Canada:

Southeastern Canada, with enlargement of Anticosti Island. LXXXI, p. 122, Jan., 1942

ANTILLES, Greater. *See* Cuba; Dominican Republic; Haiti; Jamaica; Puerto Rico

ANTILLES, Lesser. *See* Aruba; Bonaire; Curaçao; Leeward Islands; Martinique; Saba; St. Vincent; Tobago; Trinidad; Windward Islands; *and* Virgin Islands

ANVILLE, JEAN BAPTISTE BOURGUIGNON D': Atlas:

Bering's chart of his first voyage. From D'Anville's Atlas, 1737. The first published map of his explorations. II, foldout (opp. p. 111), May, 1890

APPALACHIAN MOUNTAINS, U. S.:

Southern Appalachians, showing the deformed Cretaceous Peneplain and the areas not reduced to baselevel. VI, pl. 5, May 23, 1894; reprint, foldout map, 1965

Southern Appalachians, showing the deformed Tertiary Peneplain and the areas not reduced to baselevel. VI, pl. 6, May 23, 1894; reprint, foldout map, 1965

ARABIAN PENINSULA:

Arabia. XX, p. 1117, Dec., 1909

Arabia. XXIV, p. 72, Jan., 1913

Arabia. XXXII, p. 181, Aug., 1917

Arabia, showing the geographical relation of the new kingdom of Hejaz to Syria, Mesopotamia, and Armenia. XXXVI, p. 374, Nov., 1919

Arabia, Turkey, and Egypt. XXII, p. 63, Jan., 1911

Arabia, with inset of Hadhramaut Province. LXII, p. 389, Oct., 1932

Asia Minor and the Damascus to Mecca Railway. XX, p. 173, Feb., 1909

Near East, showing Egypt, Anatolia, and the Arab kingdoms of Hedjaz, Transjordania, and Iraq. XLIII, p. 534, May, 1923

Railway survey from Mecca to Damascus. XI, p. 247, June, 1900

Western Arabia, adjacent countries, and northeastern Africa. LXV, p. 765, June, 1934

See also Aden; Oman; Saudi Arabia

ARAN ISLANDS, Ireland:

Aran Islands, with inset of Ireland. LIX, p. 752, June, 1931

ARCTIC OCEAN. *See* Arctic Regions

ARCTIC REGIONS:

Amundsen's route (Northwest Passage). XVII, p. 39, Jan., 1906

The Arctic cruise of the U. S. S. "Thetis," Lieut. Comdr. Chas. H. Stockton, U. S. N., Comdg. in the summer and autumn of 1889. II, foldout, July, 1890

The Arctic Regions. XLVIII, supplement, 19¼ x 18 inches, Nov., 1925

Arctic regions, showing Captain Bob Bartlett's world, as seen from 10,000 miles in space. LXXXIX, p. 604, May, 1946

Arctic regions, showing outline of indicated North Polar land. XV, p. 256, June, 1904

The Arctic Regions, showing routes traversed by the Nansen Expedition of 1893-96. VII, pl. xxxiv, supplement, 9¼ x 15 inches, Oct., 1896; reprint, 10 x 14¼ inches, 1965

Arctic regions, showing the known route of the lost Soviet aviators and the network of Sir Hubert Wilkins' search flights. LXXIV, pp. 144-145, Aug., 1938

Canada, Alaska, Greenland, showing distribution of blond eskimo. XXIII, p. 1224, Dec., 1912

Capt. O. Sverdrup's explorations, 1898-1902. XIII, p. 460, Dec., 1902

Field of activity of the MacMillan Arctic Expedition under the auspices of the National Geographic Society. XLVII, p. 674, June, 1925

Franz Josef Land archipelago, showing explorations by the Wellman Expedition. X, p. 502, Dec., 1899

Global map of Arctic regions, showing Greenland, important for weather stations and air bases. XC, p. 459, Oct., 1946

Greenland—an aerial stepping stone to Europe. LXXXII, pp. 370-371, Sept., 1942

ARCTIC REGIONS—*Continued*

Greenland, as seen from the North Pole. LXXVIII, pp. 118-119, July, 1940

Hubbard Bay and Alison Bay, west Greenland. South of 74° 30′ after C. H. Ryder; North of 74° 30′ after J. A. Björling. IX, p. 3, Jan., 1898

Lapland. LXXVI, p. 645, Nov., 1939

North Polar regions. XX, p. 916, Oct., 1909

North Pole Regions. XVIII, supplement, 17½ x 17½ inches, July, 1907

Northern and Southern Hemispheres, with insets of time zones, world terrain, and tables of airline distances in four hemispheres. LXXXIII, supplement, 41 x 22 inches, Apr., 1943

Northern Hemisphere, showing proposed routes of aircraft over the Arctic zone. XLII, p. 206, Aug., 1922

Northern Hemisphere, with tables showing airline distances in the Pacific, the Atlantic, the Arctic, and the Americas. LXXXIX, supplement, 21¾ x 24 inches, Feb., 1946

Peary's sledge routes and surveys. XIV, p. 28, Jan., 1903

Plan of Arctic exploration from a base near Jones Sound or at Cape Sabine. IX, p. 2, Jan., 1898

Record of Rear Admiral Peary's 20 years of polar exploration, finally crowned with success, April 6, 1909. XXXVII, p. 297, Apr., 1920

Route of the *Frithjof,* 1898. X, p. 483, Dec., 1899

Route of the "Hope" from Sydney, Nova Scotia, as far as Umanak, Greenland, showing magnetic stations. VIII, p. 99, Apr., 1897

Route of the "Norge" (airship) from Rome to Alaska: A flight of 8,500 miles across the top of the world. LII, pp. 188-189, Aug., 1927

The World, with insets showing Arctic and Antarctic regions, natural vegetation and ocean currents, and density of population and prevailing winds. LXII, supplement, 26 x 38½ inches, Dec., 1932

The World Map, with insets of Arctic and Antarctic regions, territories occupied by belligerents in first and second World Wars, and table of geographical equivalents and abbreviations. LXXXIV, supplement, 41 x 26½ inches, Dec., 1943

See also Spitsbergen

ARGENTINA:

Buenos Aires region. LXXVI, p. 565, Nov., 1939

Patagonia, illustrating explorations of J. B. Hatcher, 1896–'97. VIII, p. 311, Nov., 1896

Route of transandean mail and passenger planes. LIX, p. 596, May, 1931

ARIZONA:

Arizona. LV, p. 8, Jan., 1929

Arizona and New Mexico, showing location of Indian ruins. LVI, p. 743, Dec., 1929

Grand Canyon, from Green River, Wyoming, to Mexico. XXVI, p. 153, Aug., 1914

Grand Canyon of the Colorado River: 1923 Expedition of the U. S. Geological Survey. XLV, p. 474, May, 1924

ARIZONA—*Continued*

Old Yuma Trail region. XII, p. 132, Apr., 1901

Route to Rainbow Natural Bridge. XLIII, p. 198, Feb., 1923

Southwestern United States. XXI, p. 632, Aug., 1910

The Southwestern United States. LXXVII, supplement, 35 x 26 inches, June, 1940

ARKANSAS:

Arkansas. XC, pp. 280-281, Sept., 1946

Ozark Plateau, showing Missouri and Arkansas with portions of bordering States. LXXXIII, p. 593, May, 1943

ARMENIA:

Ancient Armenia and the country where the Armenians now live. XXVIII, p. 359, Oct., 1915

See also Turkey

ARUBA (Island), West Indies:

Caribbean regions, with enlargements of Aruba, Bonaire, and Curaçao. LXXXIII, p. 172, Feb., 1943

ASHEVILLE. *See* North Carolina

ASIA:

Arabia, Turkey, Persia, Egypt. XXIV, p. 72, Jan., 1913

Arid regions and closed basins of Asia. XII, p. 254, July, 1901

Asia, from "Theatrum Orbis Terrarum," 16th century. LXIV, p. 771, Dec., 1933

Asia, showing route flown by the Days. LXI, p. 656, June, 1932

Asia and Adjacent Areas, with table of airline distances in statute miles. LXXXII, supplement, 40 x 26½ inches, Dec., 1942

Asia and Adjacent Regions. LXIV, supplement, 30¾ x 38 inches, Dec., 1933

Central Asia. LXIX, p. 7, Jan., 1936

Central Asia, showing the route of the Morden-Clark Asiatic Expedition. LII, p. 374, Oct., 1927

Central Asia and the route followed by Mr. and Mrs. Owen Lattimore, Peiping to India. LV, p. 664, June, 1929

China-India war route, with enlargement showing Minya Konka and the route followed by the Sikang Expedition. LXXXIII, p. 628, May, 1943

Citroën-Haardt Trans-Asiatic Expedition route. LX, p. 388, Oct., 1931

Citroën-Haardt Trans-Asiatic Expedition route from Beyrouth to Peiping. LXI, p. 324, Mar., 1932

Citroën-Haardt Trans-Asiatic Expedition route from Beyrouth to Peiping. LXII, p. 522, Nov., 1932

Citroën-Haardt Trans-Asiatic Expedition route from Beyrouth to Srinagar. LX, p. 388, Oct., 1931

Citroën-Haardt Trans-Asiatic Expedition route from Kashgar to Peiping. LXII, p. 522, Nov., 1932

Citroën-Haardt Trans-Asiatic Expedition route from Srinagar to Kashgar. LXI, p. 323, Mar., 1932

ASIA—*Continued*

Eastern Hemisphere, showing interrelation of the races. XII, p. 264, July, 1901

Europe and the Near East. LVI, supplement, 34¼ x 39¼ inches, Dec., 1929

The Far East. XI, p. 290, July, 1900

India, from "Geographia Universalis," 1552 (Ptolemy's map). LXII, p. 765, Dec., 1932

Indian Ocean, including Australia, New Zealand and Malaysia, with insets of Singapore and Canton-Hong Kong area. LXXIX, supplement, 25½ x 32¾ inches, Mar., 1941

Japan and Adjacent Regions of Asia and the Pacific Ocean, with insets of industrial centers of Japan and the Marshall Islands. LXXXV, supplement, 26½ x 34½ inches, Apr., 1944

Map of Asia and Adjoining Europe with a Portion of Africa. XXXIX, supplement, 28 x 36 inches, May, 1921

Map of China and Its Territories. Included: Mongolia, Manchuria, Chosen, East Turkestan, Tibet, Northern India. XXIII, supplement, 17 x 23 inches, Oct., 1912

Marco Polo's travels through Asia. LIV, pp. 508-509, Nov., 1928

Near East, showing Egypt, Anatolia, and the Arabs kingdoms of Hedjaz, Transjordania, and Iraq. XLIII, p. 534, May, 1923

Northern Europe and Asia, showing advance of Russia in Asia. XVI, p. 404, Sept., 1905

The Philippine Islands as the Geographical Center of the Far East. XI, supplement, 7½ x 10¾ inches, Jan., 1900

Physical map of Asia, illustrating the obstacles to land transportation which rendered early commerce between Occident and Orient extremely difficult. XVI, p. 400, Sept., 1905

Relief map of Eurasia, Lambert's projection. XII, p. 251, July, 1901

Route followed by Major F. A. C. Forbes-Leith from England to India. XLVIII, p. 193, Aug., 1925

Route followed by Sir Ross Smith in first aëroplane voyage from London to Australia. XXXIX, pp. 230-231, Mar., 1921

Routes flown by Sir Alan J. Cobham over Europe, Asia, Australia, and Africa. LIII, p. 350, Mar., 1928

Southeast Asia and Pacific Islands from the Indies and the Philippines to the Solomons, with 22 inset maps of important cities and islands. LXXXVI, supplement, 41 x 26½ inches, Oct., 1944

Telegraph lines of China, 1904. XVI, p. 409, Sept., 1905

Thaw Trans-Asia Expedition following the old silk routes. LXXVIII, pp. 456-457, Oct., 1940

Theater of War in Europe, Africa, and Western Asia, with table of airline distances in statute miles. LXXXII, supplement, 26½ x 31 inches, July, 1942

Trade routes from the East to Egypt. XII, p. 293, Aug., 1901

Turkey, Persia, Afghanistan, and southern Russia. XXXIV, p. 277, Oct., 1918

ASIA—*Continued*

Union of Soviet Socialist Republics, with international boundaries according to Russian treaties and claims as of October 1, 1944. Boundaries of January 1, 1938, are shown in red. LXXXVI, supplement, 40 x 25 inches, Dec., 1944

Volcanic axes and structure lines in eastern Asia and Alaska and why Japan is subject to frequent destructive earthquakes. XLIV, p. 446, Oct., 1923

See also Siberia; *and* names of countries

ASIA MINOR:

Asia Minor. XLVI, p. 450, Oct., 1924

Asia Minor, the Dardanelles, and the islands of the Ægean Sea. XLII, p. 554, Nov., 1922

Crusader trails and castles. LXIV, p. 654, Dec., 1933

Greece and the Aegean, showing sites of antiquity and the necklace of Hellenic cities that adorned the coast of Asia Minor. LXXXV, pp. 280-281, Mar., 1944

Near East, showing Egypt, Anatolia, and the Arab kingdoms of Hedjaz, Transjordania, and Iraq. XLIII, p. 534, May, 1923

Railways constructed and proposed in Asia Minor and Persia. XI, p. 202, May, 1900

"Shores of Sunrise" (The Levant). L, p. 652, Dec., 1926

See also Turkey

ASTRONOMY. *See* Heavens

ATAFU (Atoll), Tokelau Islands:

Pacific Ocean and the Bay of Bengal, with inset of Atafu. LXXXIV, supplement, 36½ x 26½ inches, Sept., 1943

ATHENS, Greece:

Classical Lands of the Mediterranean, with inset of Ancient Athens. LXXVII, supplement, 35¼ x 26 inches, Mar., 1940

ATLANTIC OCEAN:

Atlantic coast tides. IX, p. 498, Dec., 1898

Atlantic Ocean, showing mileage of air routes to Norway, Britain, and Portugal from Newfoundland, Greenland, and Iceland. LXXX, p. 77, July, 1941

Atlantic Ocean, with inset of Isthmus of Panama. LXXVI, supplement, 31 x 25 inches, July, 1939

Atlantic Ocean, with inset of Isthmus of Panama and a table of air-line distances in statute miles. LXXX, supplement, 31¼ x 25 inches, Sept., 1941

Cotidal chart (1833) by Dr. William Whewell. IX, p. 468, Nov., 1898

East coast of United States, showing a shelf of shallow water. LXX, p. 212, Aug., 1936

General direction of the Gulf Stream and other currents in the North Atlantic Ocean. XXIII, p. 772, Aug., 1912

How Commander Byrd plots a new transatlantic route along which future flyers may cross on schedule. LII, p. 348, Sept., 1927

Hurricanes in the North Atlantic. II, foldout charts (bet. pp. 210-211), July, 1890

ATLANTIC OCEAN—*Continued*

Iceberg danger zone in the North Atlantic. L, p. 4, July, 1926

Pilot Chart of the North Atlantic Ocean (February, 1903). XIV, supplement, 32 x 21¾ inches, Feb., 1903

Route of the "Alice" (yacht). LXXIII, p. 268, Mar., 1938

Route of the "Blossom" (ship). LII, p. 5, July, 1927

Route of the Lindberghs in the *Tingmissartoq.* LXVI, pp. 266-267, Sept., 1934

Route of the *Yankee,* from Gloucester, Massachusetts, through the Panama Canal to Pitcairn Island. LXXXI, p. 4, Jan., 1942

The St. Thomas-Hatteras hurricane of September 3-12, 1889. II, foldout charts (bet. pp. 210-211), July, 1890

South Atlantic Ocean, showing location of Tristan da Cunha. LXXIV, p. 674, Nov., 1938

Submarine Cables of the World, with the Principal Connecting Land Lines, also Coaling, Docking, and Repairing Stations. Compiled in the U. S. Hydrographic Office. VII, pl. X, supplement, 48 x 30 inches, Mar., 1896

Western Atlantic Ocean and Caribbean Sea, showing location of new United States defense bases leased from Britain. LXXVIII, p. 621, Nov., 1940

World globe, showing submarine mountain ranges and deeps of Atlantic Ocean. LXXXVII, p. 112, Jan., 1945

See also Tides

ATTU (Island), Aleutian Islands:

Pacific Ocean and the Bay of Bengal, with inset of Attu. LXXXIV, supplement, 36½ x 26½ inches, Sept., 1943

AUSTRAL ISLANDS, South Pacific Ocean:

Marquesas, Tuamotu, and Austral Islands. XLVIII, p. 366, Oct., 1925

See also Vavitao

AUSTRALIA:

Australia, with enlargement of central primordial lands inhabited by aborigines. LXXXIX, p. 91, Jan., 1946

Australia, with inset of Tasmania. XXX, pp. 480-481, Dec., 1916

Australia, with inset of Tasmania. LXVIII, pp. 672-673, Dec., 1935

Australia and neighboring islands. LXXXII, p. 124, July, 1942

Australia superimposed on outline of North America of same scale, in correct latitude. XXX, p. 477, Dec., 1916

Australia superimposed on outline of the United States, to show relative sizes. XXX, p. 476, Dec., 1916

Distribution of the population of Australia. XXX, p. 512, Dec., 1916

East coast of Australia, showing Great Barrier Reef. LVIII, p. 359, Sept., 1930

Great Barrier Reef, with inset of Australia. LXXVII, p. 827, June, 1940

Indian Ocean, including Australia, New Zealand and Malaysia. LXXIX, supplement, 25½ x 32¾ inches, Mar., 1941

AUSTRALIA—*Continued*

Isolation of Australia. XXX, p. 475, Dec., 1916

New Guinea, New Caledonia, and Fiji command the shortest supply routes from America to Australia, with table of airline distances. LXXXI, pp. 698-699, June, 1942

Northwest coast of Australia. XLV, p. 332, Mar., 1924

Pacific islands, showing limit of long-range bombing from northern Australia, with table of airline distances in statute miles. LXXXIII, pp. 56-57, Jan., 1943

Pacific war area, showing Australia, New Zealand, Netherlands Indies, and surrounding islands. LXXXI, pp. 416-417, Apr., 1942

The Philippine Islands as the Geographical Center of the Far East. XI, supplement, 7½ x 10¾ inches, Jan., 1900

Physical map of Australia. XXX, p. 489, Dec., 1916

Railroad map of Australia. XXX, p. 559, Dec., 1916

Rainfall in Australia. XXX, p. 488, Dec., 1916

See also Lord Howe (Island)

AUSTRIA:

Austria-Hungary. XXIII, p. 1284, Dec., 1912

Austria-Hungary. XXVI, p. 392, Oct., 1914

Austro-Italo Alpine region, with surrounding territory. XXVII, p. 374, Apr., 1915

Frontier cities of Italy and Austria-Hungary. XXVII, p. 628, June, 1915

Rivers paddled by Cornelia Stratton Parker. LXI, p. 368, Mar., 1932

Salzkammergut (district). LXXI, p. 446, Apr., 1937

AZORES (Islands), Atlantic Ocean:

Azores, with inset of Atlantic Ocean. LXVII, p. 36, Jan., 1935

Three groups of the Azores and the routes of the successful American aviators in their transatlantic flight; also, the route chosen by the ill-fated Hawker-Grieve Expedition. XXXV, p. 515, June, 1919

B

BAFFIN ISLAND, N.W.T., Canada:

Arctic regions, showing Captain Bob Bartlett's world, as seen from 10,000 miles in space. LXXXIX, p. 604, May, 1946

BAHAMA ISLANDS, West Indies:

Bahama Islands, with inset of New Providence Island. LXIX, p. 223, Feb., 1936

Cuba and Bahama Islands. LXIV, p. 348, Sept., 1933

Herrera map, 1601, with vignette of Watling Island from a modern chart. Samana and Guanahani, shown. VI, p. 187, Dec. 29, 1894

Juan de la Cosa map, 1500, with vignette of Samana from a modern chart. VI, pl. 10 (opp. p. 186), Dec. 29, 1894

Mappa Munde Peinte sur Parchemin par Ordre de Henri II, Roi de France—1532; Samana (Guanahani), shown. VI, pl. 11 (opp. p. 188), Dec. 29, 1894

BAHAMA ISLANDS, West Indies—*Continued*

Modern map of Samana, Crooked and Acklin Islands. VI, p. 191, Dec. 29, 1894

BAHREIN ISLANDS, Persian Gulf:

Bahrein, with inset of Middle East. LXXXIX, p. 199, Feb., 1946

BAILY GROUP, Pacific Ocean. *See* Haha Jima Retto

BAJA CALIFORNIA (Lower California), Mexico:

Baja California, with inset showing relationship to Mexico and States of the U. S. Southwest. LXXXII, p. 258, Aug., 1942

Cruise of the *Kinkajou* to desert islands of Mexico. LXXX, p. 340, Sept., 1941

Desert islands of Lower California. XLIV, p. 73, July, 1923

Lower California, showing route of E. W. Nelson. XXII, p. 446, May, 1911

Mexico and the peninsula of Lower California. XXXVI, p. 310, Oct., 1919

BAKER (Island), Pacific Ocean:

Pacific Ocean and the Bay of Bengal, with inset of Baker Island. LXXXIV, supplement, 36½ x 26½ inches, Sept., 1943

BALEARIC ISLANDS, Spain:

Balearic Islands. LIV, p. 179, Aug., 1928

Majorca, Balearic Islands. XLV, p. 431, Apr., 1924

BALI (Island), Netherlands East Indies:

Bali. LXXV, p. 316, Mar., 1939

BALKAN PENINSULA:

Balkan States. XXIV, p. 224, Feb., 1913

Bulgaria, Servia, Albania, Montenegro, and Turkey in Europe. XXVII, p. 421, Apr., 1915

Bulgaria, Servia, and Turkey in Europe. XXIII, p. 1152, Nov., 1912

Map of the New Balkan States and Central Europe. XXVI, supplement, 17 x 22½ inches, Aug., 1914

Southeastern Europe, showing the Balkan States and European Turkey. XIX, p. 799, Nov., 1908

See also names of countries

BALSAS, Río, Mexico:

Río Balsas region. XC, p. 254, Aug., 1946

BALTIC REGIONS:

Baltic region, with inset of Bornholm (island). LXXXVII, p. 240, Feb., 1945

Estonia, with inset of the Baltic region. LXXVI, p. 805, Dec., 1939

Southeast Baltic coast. LXXIII, p. 770, June, 1938

BAR (River), France:

The Lower Valley of the Bar. VII, pl. XXVI (opp. p. 236), July, 1896

Sketch map of the Meuse, showing the Bar, the Aire, and the Aisne. VII, p. 232, July, 1896

BARRO COLORADO ISLAND, Canal Zone:

Barro Colorado, the largest island in the Canal Zone. LII, p. 332, Sept., 1927

BAVARIA (Region), Germany:

Map showing location of Oberammergau. LXVIII, p. 746, Dec., 1935

BEECHEY GROUP, Pacific Ocean. *See* Chichi Jima Retto

BELGIAN CONGO:

Ruanda, "The Land of Giants and Pygmies." XXIII, p. 388, Apr., 1912

Western Rift Valley and surrounding country, with inset of the Virunga Mountains. LXXVI, p. 515, Oct., 1939

BELGIUM:

Map of the Western Theatre of War, with inset of France and Belgium. XXXIII, supplement, 26 x 31 inches, May, 1918

Route of the "Nageoma" (canoe). XLVII, p. 507, May, 1925

BENGAL, Bay of:

Pacific Ocean and the Bay of Bengal, with inset maps of important islands, and table of air-line distances in statute miles. LXXXIV, supplement, 36½ x 26½ inches, Sept., 1943

BERING, VITUS: Voyages:

Bering's chart of his first voyage. From D'Anville's Atlas, 1737. The first published map of his explorations. II, foldout (opp. p. 111), May, 1890

Carte Généralè des Découvertes de l'Amiral de Fonte, et autres Navigateurs Espagnols, Anglois et Russes pour la recherche du Passage à la Mer du Sud. Par M. De l'Isle. Voyages of Bering, included. III, supplement, 16¼ x 13 inches, Jan. 28, 1892; Feb. 19, 1892

BERING SEA AND BERING STRAIT:

The Arctic cruise of the U. S. S. "Thetis," Lieut. Comdr. Chas. H. Stockton, U. S. N., Comdg. in the summer and autumn of 1889. II, foldout, July, 1890

Bering Sea, showing location of Pribilof Islands. XXII, p. 1141, Dec., 1911

Bering Sea region. LXXV, p. 638, May, 1939

BERMUDA (Islands), Atlantic Ocean:

Bermuda Islands. XLI, p. 2, Jan., 1922

Bermuda Islands, showing location of Beebe deep-sea dives. LXVI, p. 670, Dec., 1934

Location of Nonsuch Island and deep-sea explorations off Bermuda. LIX, p. 656, June, 1931

Location of Nonsuch Island and deep-sea explorations off Bermuda. LXI, p. 66, Jan., 1932

Mexico, Central America, and the West Indies, with inset of the Bermuda Islands. LXVI, supplement, 23 x 40 inches, Dec., 1934

Mexico, Central America, and the West Indies, with inset of the Bermuda Islands. LXXVI, supplement, 24 x 41 inches, Dec., 1939

Military outposts leased from Britain put new teeth in Uncle Sam's defenses. LXXVIII, p. 621, Nov., 1940

BHUTAN:

Bhutan, showing journeys by John Claude White. XXV, p. 453, Apr., 1914

BIBLE LANDS:

Bible Lands, showing Palestine, Trans-Jordan, and Egypt. LXXXV, p. 236, Feb., 1944

Bible Lands, showing Palestine, Trans-Jordan, and Syria. LXXXVI, p. 722, Dec., 1944

Bible Lands and the Cradle of Western Civilization; Insets: Holy Land Today, Holy Land in Biblical Times, Jerusalem, Traditional Route of the Exodus, St. Paul's Travels and the Seven Churches, The Crusades. XC, supplement, 32 x 22 inches, Dec., 1946

Bible Lands and the Cradle of Western Civilization; Insets: Jerusalem, The Holy Land, Economic Development, Route of the Exodus, St. Paul's Travels and the Seven Churches, The Crusades, Empire of Alexander the Great. LXXIV, supplement, 25 x 35 inches, Dec., 1938

Jordan River from Galilee to Dead Sea. LXXVIII, p. 784, Dec., 1940

World trouble spot, the oil-rich Middle East. LXXXIX, pp. 396-397, Mar., 1946

World's deepest land depression separates Palestine from Trans-Jordan. LXXI, p. 72, Jan., 1937

BIRD MIGRATION ROUTES AND HABITATS:

Bird migration routes from South America to North America converge funnel-like in Central America. Inset of Veracruz and Tabasco, Mexico, showing La Venta region, a natural bird observatory. LXXXVII, p. 188, Feb., 1945

Breeding ground, winter home, and curious migration routes of the white-winged scoter. XXIV, p. 365, Mar., 1913

Breeding ground and winter home of the Ross goose. XXIV, p. 367, Mar., 1913

Breeding ground of the ducks and geese in northern Canada. XXIV, p. 364, Mar., 1913

Breeding grounds of wild ducks and geese. XXIV, p. 362, Mar., 1913

The Connecticut warbler chooses a different route to return to its winter home than it used when leaving in spring. XXII, p. 353, Apr., 1911

Evolution of the present migration route of the golden plover. XXII, p. 357, Apr., 1911

How the golden plover is able to navigate to the Hawaiian Islands in the Mid-Pacific. XXII, p. 359, Apr., 1911

Location of 46 out of the 56 national bird reservations. XXIV, p. 369, Mar., 1913

Longest single flight made by any bird—2,500 miles across the ocean from Nova Scotia to South America. XXII, p. 354, Apr., 1911

Migration route of the black-poll warblers that nest in Alaska. XXII, p. 348, Apr., 1911

Migration route of the bobolink is changing. XXII, p. 365, Apr., 1911

Migration route of the cliff swallows that nest in Nova Scotia. XXII, p. 349, Apr., 1911

Peruvian coast, showing the islands on which the guanayes have their rookeries. XLVI, p. 282, Sept., 1924

Principal routes used by birds in their migrations between North and South America. XXII, p. 347, Apr., 1911

Principal winter resorts of the wild ducks and geese. XXIV, p. 368, Mar., 1913

BIRD MIGRATION ROUTES AND HABITATS —Continued
Probable summer migration route of Alaska geese. LIII, p. 116, Jan., 1928
The robin moves much more quickly on the Pacific than on the Atlantic. XXII, p. 362, Apr., 1911
The scarlet tanager. XXII, p. 363, Apr., 1911
Summer and winter homes of the bird that hates darkness. XXII, p. 360, Apr., 1911
Two of the principal migration routes of the palm warbler. XXII, p. 352, Apr., 1911
The Ward-McIlhenny and the Louisiana refuges for game birds. XXIV, p. 373, Mar., 1913

BISMARCK ARCHIPELAGO, South Pacific Ocean. *See* New Britain; New Ireland

BITTER ROOT FOREST RESERVE, Idaho-Montana:
Bitter Root Forest Reserve. IX, pl. 12 (opp. p. 394), foldout, Sept., 1898

BOER WAR. *See* South African War

BOGOSLOF (Volcanic Island), Aleutian Islands:
Bogoslof Island in September, 1908. XX, p. 194, Feb., 1909

BOLABOLA (Island), Society Islands:
Topography of two coral-ringed volcanic isles: Bolabola of the Society group and Vavitao of the Austral group. XLVIII, p. 369, Oct., 1925

BOLIVIA:
Lake Titicaca region. LI, p. 214, Feb., 1927
Western Bolivia. LXVI, p. 649, Nov., 1934

BONAIRE (Island), West Indies:
Caribbean regions, with enlargements of Aruba, Bonaire, and Curaçao. LXXXIII, p. 172, Feb., 1943

BONIN ISLANDS, Pacific Ocean. *See* Ogasawara Shoto

BORNEO:
Borneo and Java. LXXXVIII, p. 297, Sept., 1945
Sarawak (State), Borneo. XXXV, p. 161, Feb., 1919

BORNHOLM (Island), Denmark:
Baltic region, with inset of Bornholm. LXXXVII, p. 240, Feb., 1945

BOSPORUS (Strait). *See* Turkey

BOUGAINVILLE (Island), Solomon Islands:
Solomon Islands, with inset maps showing Guadalcanal-Tulagi area and Bougainville area. LXXXII, p. 815, Dec., 1942

BRAZIL:
Basin of the Amazon, the world's greatest river. XLIX, p. 354, Apr., 1926
Brazil. LXXXV, pp. 44-45, Jan., 1944
Brazil, showing state boundaries. LVIII, p. 738, Dec., 1930
Brazil, Venezuela, and British Guiana, showing Roraima. LVIII, p. 588, Nov., 1930
Marajó Island. LXXIV, p. 638, Nov., 1938
North-central South America, showing Brazil-Venezuela boundary. LXIV, p. 589, Nov., 1933

BRAZIL—*Continued*
Rio de Janeiro, its famous bay and surrounding hills. XXXVIII, p. 173, Sept., 1920
Southern Matto Grosso (State) and Paraguay, with inset showing river system. LXXXIV, p. 461, Oct., 1943
See also São Paulo

BRITISH COLUMBIA (Province), Canada:
Alaska-British Northwest Territory (pre-Yukon Territory)-British Columbia, showing route of expedition of 1891, northern limit of glaciation, and volcanic tufa; an index map of the Yukon district for pls. 19 and 20. IV, pls. 18-20, 2 foldouts, May 15, 1892
Coastline of British Columbia. LXIV, p. 6, July, 1933
Columbia Ice Field Photographic Expedition; location map. XLVII, pp. 382, 383, Apr., 1925
Columbia River entrance, showing movement of Sand Island, and changes from 1792 to 1905. XX, p. 834, Sept., 1909
Kananaskis Lakes. XIII, p. 167, May, 1902
A Map of Northwestern United States and Neighboring Canadian Provinces. LXXIX, supplement, 24½ x 36 inches, June, 1941
Pacific coast defense area. LXXXII, p. 425, Oct., 1942
Summer and winter isothermal lines of Victoria, British Columbia. XVIII, p. 346, May, 1907
Tweedsmuir Park. LXXIII, p. 454, Apr., 1938
Unexplored territory of British Columbia. LXXIII, p. 452, Apr., 1938
Victoria, British Columbia. XVIII, p. 347, May, 1907
Yukon-British Columbia, area surveyed by Bradford Washburn in 1935, and adjoining Alaska, mapped by the International Boundary Commission in 1906-1908. LXIX, pp. 720-721, June, 1936

BRITISH EAST AFRICA:
Roosevelt's route and hunting trips in Africa. XXII, p. 2, Jan., 1911
See also Kenya; Uganda

BRITISH GUIANA:
Boundaries as claimed by Great Britain and Venezuela and as awarded by the Paris Tribunal, 1899. XI, pl. 4 (opp. p. 129), Apr., 1900
British Guiana. XXII, p. 847, Sept., 1911
Guianas, with an inset showing the territory traversed by the "Kaieteur and Roraima" Expedition. XXXVIII, p. 229, Sept., 1920
Roraima and contiguous territory. LVIII, p. 588, Nov., 1930

BRITISH ISLES:
British harbors. XXXI, p. 85, Jan., 1917
British Isles and North Sea, showing fishing banks and war zone. XXVII, p. 149, Feb., 1915
Cotidal chart (1807) by Dr. Thomas Young. IX, p. 470, Nov., 1898
Cotidal charts by Dr. William Whewell. IX, p. 470, Nov., 1898
Isle of Man, with inset of the British Isles. LXXI, p. 588, May, 1937

BRITISH ISLES—*Continued*

A Modern Pilgrim's Map of the British Isles or More Precisely the Kingdom of Great Britain and Northern Ireland and the Irish Free State. LXXI, supplement, 29 x 35 inches, June, 1937

Scilly Isles, with inset of the British Isles. LXXIV, p. 757, Dec., 1938

See also Channel Islands; Ireland; Wight, Isle of; *and* England, Scotland, Wales, for Great Britain

BRITISH MALAYA. *See* Singapore

BRITISH SOUTH AFRICA. *See* Union of South Africa

BRITISH WEST AFRICA. *See* Gold Coast; Nigeria

BRITISH WEST INDIES. *See* Bahama Islands; Jamaica; St. Vincent; Trinidad

BRITTANY (Region), France:

Northwest France, including Normandy and Brittany. LXXXIV, pp. 218-219, Aug., 1943

BROWN (Atoll), Marshall Islands. *See* Eniwetok

BULGARIA:

Bulgaria. LXII, p. 197, Aug., 1932

Bulgaria, Servia, and Macedonia. XXIII, p. 1152, Nov., 1912

Bulgaria and Servia. XXVII, p. 421, Apr., 1915

BURMA:

Burma, home of the Chaulmoogra oil tree. XLI, p. 242, Mar., 1922

Burma and eastern India, showing Manipur, scene of battle for Upper Burma. LXXXV, p. 750, June, 1944

Burma to China as the crow flies. LXXXIV, p. 492, Oct., 1943

India and Burma, with insets of Bombay and Calcutta areas. Verso of map: Political Subdivisions; The Political Geography of India. LXXXIX, supplement, 30 x 25 inches, Apr., 1946

Southwestern China and Burma, showing route of the Burma Road. LXXVIII, p. 631, Nov., 1940

BUTLER'S COMPLETE GEOGRAPHY:

Photo-engraving of topographic model of North America, from Butler's Complete Geography. I, insert (bet. pp. 268-269), July, 1889

BUZZARDS BAY. *See* Massachusetts

C

CABLES:

Alaska telegraph and cable lines. XV, p. 491, Dec., 1904

Chart of the World on Mercator's Projection, showing Submarine Cables and Connections, and also Tracks for full-powered Steam Vessels. XVI, supplement, 25 x 45 inches, Feb., 1905

CABLES—*Continued*

Military telegraph lines in Porto Rico operated by the Signal Corps, U. S. Army; military posts; ports of entry; and area (of Porto Rico) compared with that of the State of Connecticut. XI, p. 242, June, 1900

The Philippines. Progress Map of Signal Corps Telegraph Lines and Cables in the Military Division of the Philippines. XIII, supplement in two sheets, 34 x 35, and 33 x 35½ inches, Jan., 1902

Proposed routes for Pacific cables. XIII, p. 312, Aug., 1902

Relief map of Porto Rico, showing telegraph lines. XV, p. 493, Dec., 1904

Relief map of the Philippine Islands, showing telegraph and cable lines. XV, p. 492, Dec., 1904

Submarine Cables of the World, with the Principal Connecting Land Lines, also Coaling, Docking, and Repairing Stations. Compiled in the U. S. Hydrographic Office. VII, pl. X, supplement, 48 x 30 inches, Mar., 1896

Telegraph lines of China in 1904. XVI, p. 409, Sept., 1905

CALIFORNIA:

Central Valley. XC, p. 648, Nov., 1946

Changes in the estuary of the Colorado River. XIX, p. 54, Jan., 1908

Colorado Desert region. XI, p. 339, Sept., 1900

Geographical distribution of redwood on the Pacific coast. X, p. 146, May, 1899

Los Angeles Aqueduct. XXI, p. 595, July, 1910

Lower Colorado River, showing irrigable lands. XVII, p. 94, Feb., 1906

Lower Colorado River, showing the great new lake rising in Salton Sink. XVIII, p. 36, Jan., 1907

Northern California, with inset of San Francisco Bay and vicinity. LXIX, pp. 312-313, Mar., 1936

Northern coast, showing route of Redwood Highway. LXXV, pp. 138-139, Feb., 1939

San Francisco Bay and vicinity. XVII, p. 281, May, 1906

San Francisco peninsula (showing principal fault lines). XVII, p. 287, May, 1906

Southern California. LXVI, pp. 534-535, Nov., 1934

The Southwestern United States. LXXVII, supplement, 35 x 26 inches, June, 1940

United States of America, with inset maps of San Francisco and Los Angeles. XLIII, supplement, 26½ x 36¼ inches, Apr., 1923

Yosemite National Park. LXIX, p. 344, Mar., 1936

CAMBODIA. *See* French Indo-China

CAMEROONS (Cameroun):

Cameroun. LIX, p. 228, Feb., 1931

CAMPBELL, MARIUS R.: Maps:

Southern Appalachians, showing the deformed Cretaceous Peneplain and the areas not reduced to baselevel. By C. Willard Hayes and Marius R. Campbell. VI, pl. 5, May 23, 1894; reprint, foldout map, 1965

CAMPBELL, MARIUS R.: Maps—*Continued*

Southern Appalachians, showing the deformed Tertiary Peneplain and the areas not reduced to baselevel. By C. Willard Hayes and Marius R. Campbell. VI, pl. 6, May 23, 1894; reprint, foldout map, 1965

CANADA:

Alaska-British Northwest Territory (pre-Yukon Territory)-British Columbia, showing route of expedition of 1891, northern limit of glaciation, and volcanic tufa; an index map of the Yukon district, for pls. 19 and 20. IV, pls. 18-20, 2 foldouts, May 15, 1892

Alaska-Canada boundary line. XXIII, p. 693, July, 1912

Atlantic coast tides. IX, p. 498, Dec., 1898

Breeding ground of the ducks and geese in northern Canada. XXIV, p. 364, Mar., 1913

British map, 1832. X, p. 438, Nov., 1899

Canada. LVI, p. 600, Nov., 1929

Canada, showing the route flown by the author (J. A. Wilson) in his air survey of the Dominion. L, pp. 392-393, Oct., 1926

Canada, with insets showing natural regions, precipitation and temperature, main natural resources, routes of explorers and time zones. LXIX, supplement, 27 x 40 inches, June, 1936

Canadian map of 1831. X, p. 441, Nov., 1899

Canadian map of 1857. X, p. 442, Nov., 1899

Chignecto Ship Railway to connect the Gulf of St. Lawrence and the Bay of Fundy. VII, p. 70, Feb., 1896

Columbia Ice Field Photographic Expedition. XLVII, p. 382, Apr., 1925

Cotidals from St. Johns, Newfoundland. IX, p. 502, Dec., 1898

French map, 1844. X, p. 445, Nov., 1899

The Gold and Coal Fields of Alaska, Together with the Principal Steamer Routes and Trails; Insets: Trails from Tide Water to the Headwaters of the Yukon River; The Klondike Gold Region, Canada. IX, pl. 4, supplement, 25 x 30 inches, Apr., 1898

Hudson's Bay Company map, 1857. X, pl. xi (opp. p. 425), Nov., 1899

Mackenzie River and Basin, with an inset showing Amos Burg's route from McPherson, Northwest Territories, to Fort Yukon, Alaska. LX, p. 132, Aug., 1931

A Map of Northwestern United States and Neighboring Canadian Provinces. LXXIX, supplement, 24½ x 36 inches, June, 1941

Natural divisions of the North American forests, exclusive of Mexico. VI, pl. 8 (opp. p. 139), June 22, 1894

New Brunswick faces strategic Newfoundland across the Gulf of St. Lawrence. LXXIX, p. 597, May, 1941

North America. XLV, supplement, 27 x 37 inches, May, 1924

North America, with inset of the Aleutian Islands. LXXXI, supplement, 26½ x 33 inches, May, 1942

Provinces of northwestern North America. XVIII, p. 176, Mar., 1907

CANADA—*Continued*

Route and landing fields of the first air expedition from New York to Alaska, completed in 53 hours and 30 minutes flying time. XLI, pp. 500-501, May, 1922

Route of new trans-canadian railway. XIV, p. 214, May, 1903

Scottish Geographical Magazine map, 1898. X, p. 448, Nov., 1899

South eastern Alaska, showing boundary lines of American and British claims. X, p. 454, Nov., 1899

Southeastern Canada, with enlargement of Anticosti Island. LXXXI, p. 122, Jan., 1942

Southeastern Canada, with inset of Gaspé Peninsula. LXVIII, p. 210, Aug., 1935

The southern part of the prehistoric Canadian ice-sheet. Photograph from a model. The glacial data are on the authority of T. C. Chamberlin. IX, pl. 9 (opp. p. 314), July, 1898

Unexplored territory, British Columbia-Yukon. LXXIII, p. 452, Apr., 1938

United States and adjoining portions of Canada and Mexico. LXIII, supplement, 26 x 40 inches, May, 1933

The United States and adjoining portions of Canada and Mexico. LXXVIII, supplement, 41 x 26½ inches, Dec., 1940

Western Canada, showing Alcan Highway. LXXXIII, p. 148, Feb., 1943

Yukon-British Columbia, area surveyed by Bradford Washburn in 1935, and adjoining Alaska, mapped by the International Boundary Commission in 1906-1908. LXIX, pp. 720-721, June, 1936

See also Alberta; British Columbia; Newfoundland; Northwest Territories: Nova Scotia; Ontario; Quebec; Yukon Territory

CANAL ZONE. *See* Panama

CANALS:

Canals in 718 square miles of Chekiang Province. XXIII, p. 932, Oct., 1912

Cape Cod Canal. XXVI, p. 186, Aug., 1914

Chekiang and Kiangsu Provinces, showing canals. XXIII, p. 933, Oct., 1912

Grand Canal stretches 1,000 miles southward from Peiping. LXXI, p. 488, Apr., 1937

Mexico: Area drained by the Great Canal. XIII, p. 7, Jan., 1902

Northeast China, showing Grand Canal. XXIII, p. 934, Oct., 1912

Route of the new Erie Canal. XVI, p. 569, Dec., 1905

Shanghai, China, showing canals. XXIII, p. 958, Oct., 1912

Southeastern United States: Showing the expanse of country that would be traversed, if a canal were built to correspond with the Grand Canal of China. XXIII, p. 933, Oct., 1912

See also Grand Union Canal; Nicaragua; Panama; Suez Canal

CANARY ISLANDS, Atlantic Ocean:

Canary Islands and an inset showing their location in relation to Africa and Spain. LVII, p. 612, May, 1930

CANTON ISLAND, Phoenix Islands:

Pacific Ocean and the Bay of Bengal, with inset of Canton Island. LXXXIV, supplement, 36½ x 26½ inches, Sept., 1943

South Pacific, showing Date Line and Canton Island, site of 1937 eclipse expedition. LXXII, p. 380, Sept., 1937

CAPE BRETON ISLAND, Nova Scotia:

Cape Breton Island. XXXVIII, p. 35, July, 1920

CAPE COD. *See* Massachusetts

CAPE VERDE ISLANDS, Atlantic Ocean:

Africa, with insets of the Cape Verde Islands, relief map, and a table of airline distances in statute miles. LXXXIII, supplement, 29¼ x 31½ inches, Feb., 1943

CAPPADOCIA:

Location of Mt. Argæus and of the Troglodytes. XXXV, p. 315, Apr., 1919

Turkey and the Near East, with inset of Cappadocia. LXXVI, p. 767, Dec., 1939

CARIBBEAN REGIONS:

American bases in the Lesser Antilles protect the Panama Canal. LXXXI, p. 729, June, 1942

Caribbean regions, showing airline distances in statute miles, with enlargements of Aruba, Bonaire, and Curaçao. LXXXIII, p. 172, Feb., 1943

Central America and neighboring islands, showing turtling areas. LXXXIV, p. 181, Aug., 1943

The Countries of the Caribbean, Including Mexico, Central America, the West Indies and the Panama Canal, with detailed insets of the Panama Canal and the Canal Zone, Porto Rico and the Virgin Islands, and Guantanamo Bay, Cuba. XLI, supplement, 25 x 44 inches, Feb., 1922

Geographical relation of Venezuela to the Isthmian canal routes, to the West Indies and Florida. XIV, p. 18, Jan., 1903

Map of Central America, Cuba, Porto Rico and the Islands of the Caribbean Sea, with inset of the Panama Canal and Canal Zone. XXIV, supplement, 12½ x 19 inches, Feb., 1913

Mexico, Central America, and the West Indies. LXVI, supplement, 23 x 40 inches, Dec., 1934

Mexico, Central America, and the West Indies. LXXVI, supplement, 24 x 41 inches, Dec., 1939

Route followed by Lindbergh in his flight over 13 Latin-American countries. LIII, p. 532, May, 1928

Salient geographic features of the American Mediterranean and surrounding lands. VII, p. 177, May, 1896

Western Atlantic Ocean and Caribbean Sea, showing location of new United States defense bases leased from Britain. LXXVIII, p. 621, Nov., 1940

See also West Indies; *and* names of countries and islands

CAROLINE ISLAND, Line Islands:

Pacific Ocean and the Bay of Bengal, with inset of Caroline Island. LXXXIV, supplement, 36½ x 26½ inches, Sept., 1943

CAROLINE ISLANDS, North Pacific Ocean:

Strategic isles of the Pacific: Chichi Jima, Eniwetok, Guam, Hachijo, Haha Jima, Jaluit, Kusaie, Kwajalein, Marcus, Palau, Paramushiro, Ponape, Rota, Saipan, Tinian, Truk, Wake, Yap. LXXXV, pp. 392-393, 17 island maps, Apr., 1944

The taking of Saipan opens the gate in Japan's wall of island defenses. LXXXVII, p. 447, Apr., 1945

Truk, Ruk, and Hogolu islands, of the Caroline group, showing encircling coral reef. XL, p. 648, Dec., 1921

See also Palau Islands; Ponape; Truk Islands; Yap

CASCADE RANGE, Canada-U. S.:

Mount Saint Helens, compiled from original surveys and field notes by Lieut. Charles P. Elliott, U.S.A. VIII, pl. 31 (opp. p. 228), July-Aug., 1897

CELEBES (Island), Netherlands East Indies:

Celebes. LXXVIII, p. 56, July, 1940

South Celebes. LXXXVII, p. 58, Jan., 1945

CENTRAL AMERICA:

Atlantic Ocean, with inset of Isthmus of Panama. LXXVI, supplement, 31 x 25 inches, July, 1939

Bird migration routes from South America to North America converge funnel-like in Central America. Inset of Veracruz and Tabasco, Mexico, showing La Venta region, a natural bird observatory. LXXXVII, p. 188, Feb., 1945

Central America. XVIII, p. 273, Apr., 1907

Central America, showing the principal volcanoes whose eruptions have for centuries levied a heavy toll on life and property. XXXVI, p. 194, Sept., 1919

Central America, with special reference to Nicaragua. XX, p. 1104, Dec., 1909

Central America and neighboring islands, showing turtling areas. LXXXIV, p. 181, Aug., 1943

Central America and southern Mexico. XLVII, p. 64, Jan., 1925

The Countries of the Caribbean, Including Mexico, Central America, the West Indies and the Panama Canal, with detailed insets of the Panama Canal and the Canal Zone, Porto Rico and the Virgin Islands, and Guantanamo Bay, Cuba. XLI, supplement, 25 x 44 inches, Feb., 1922

Map of Central America, Cuba, Porto Rico, and the Islands of the Caribbean Sea, with inset of the Panama Canal and Canal Zone. XXIV, supplement, 12½ x 19 inches, Feb., 1913

Mexico, Central America, and the West Indies. LXVI, supplement, 23 x 40 inches, Dec., 1934

Mexico, Central America, and the West Indies. LXXVI, supplement, 24 x 41 inches, Dec., 1939

Panama Rail Road, Panama Canal, and tributary drainage. I, foldout (bet. pp. 314-315), Oct., 1889

Route followed by Lindbergh in his flight over 13 Latin-American countries. LIII, p. 532, May, 1928

CENTRAL AMERICA—*Continued*

Route of A. F. Tschiffely on his horseback journey from Buenos Aires to Washington. LV, p. 140, Feb., 1929

Route of the trail-blazing flight of U. S. Army airplanes through 20 countries of Latin America. LII, p. 452, Oct., 1927

Salient geographic features of the American Mediterranean and surrounding lands. VII, p. 177, May, 1896

See also Costa Rica; El Salvador; Guatemala; Nicaragua; Panama

CEYLON (Island), Indian Ocean:

Ceylon, with location map. XC, p. 666, Nov., 1946

Outline of Ceylon. XXIII, p. 193, Feb., 1912

CHACO (Region), South America:

Paraguay, showing part of Chaco area. LXIII, p. 387, Apr., 1933

CHANNEL ISLANDS, English Channel:

Channel Islands. LXII, p. 104, July, 1932

Channel Islands, showing their geographical relation to France and England. XXXVIII, p. 151, Aug., 1920

CHARLESTON, South Carolina:

Streets and historic sights of Charleston. LXXV, p. 279, Mar., 1939

CHATTANOOGA AREA, Tennessee:

Relief map of the Chattanooga district. VI, pl. 4, May 23, 1894; reprint, foldout map, 1965

CHELAN, Lake, Washington:

Lake Chelan and vicinity. IX, p. 418, Oct., 1898

CHESAPEAKE BAY:

Chesapeake Bay region, showing route of the "Tralee." LXXVI, p. 361, Sept., 1939

Tidal hours in the Chesapeake. IX, p. 403, Sept., 1898

CHICHI JIMA RETTO, Ogasawara Shoto, Pacific Ocean:

Pacific Ocean and the Bay of Bengal, with inset of Chichi Jima. LXXXIV, supplement, 36½ x 26½ inches, Sept., 1943

Southeast Asia and Pacific Islands from the Indies and the Philippines to the Solomons, with inset of Chichi Jima Retto. LXXXVI, supplement, 41 x 26½ inches, Oct., 1944

Strategic isles of the Pacific. LXXXV, pp. 392-393, 17 island maps, Apr., 1944

CHIGNECTO SHIP RAILWAY, Canada:

Chignecto Ship Railway, to connect the Gulf of St. Lawrence and the Bay of Fundy. VII, p. 70, Feb., 1896

CHILE:

Central Chile, showing Valparaíso-Santiago region. LXXXVI, p. 481, Oct., 1944

Chile. XLII, p. 223, Sept., 1922

Lake District. LXXX, p. 94, July, 1941

Patagonia, illustrating explorations of J. B. Hatcher, 1896-'97. VIII, p. 311, Nov., 1897

Route of A. F. Tschiffely on his horseback journey from Buenos Aires to Washington. LV, p. 140, Feb., 1929

CHILE—*Continued*

Route of transandean mail and passenger planes. LIX, p. 596, May, 1931

See also Easter Island

CHINA:

Aerial routes blazed by Capt. Hans Koester, in four years. LXXIII, p. 574, May, 1938

Canals in 718 square miles of Chekiang Province. XXIII, p. 932, Oct., 1912

Chekiang and Kiangsu Provinces (showing canals). XXIII, p. 933, Oct., 1912

China. LI, p. 625, June, 1927

China. LXXXVII, supplement, 37 x 26½ inches, June, 1945

China, showing areas of Japanese penetration. LXXXV, p. 359, Mar., 1944

China, showing location of Choni in Kansu Province. LIV, p. 576, Nov., 1928

China, showing Szechuan. XXII, p. 1097, Dec., 1911

China coast, showing extent of Japanese penetration. LXXXVII, p. 223, Feb., 1945

China-India war route, with enlargement showing Minya Konka and the route followed by the Sikang Expedition. LXXXIII, p. 628, May, 1943

China-Tibetan border, showing route of Joseph F. Rock to the Amnyi Machen Mountains. LVII, pp. 138-139, Feb., 1930

The Chinese Empire and Japan: Showing the provinces, treaty ports, railways, etc., and the present condition of the Russian railway through Manchuria to Port Arthur. XI, pl. 8, foldout (opp. p. 297), Aug., 1900

Country from Ta-ku to Pekin. XI, p. 292, July, 1900

Eastern China. LXIX, p. 278, Feb., 1936

Eastern China, with inset of Hong Kong. LXVI, p. 603, Nov., 1934

Eastern part of Hunan as delineated by William B. Parsons. XI, p. 394, Oct., 1900

Foreign concessions in North China. XV, p. 469, Dec., 1904

Foreign concessions in South China. XV, p. 470, Dec., 1904

Grand Canal, represented by black line, superimposed on map of the Southeastern United States. XXIII, p. 933, Oct., 1912

Grand Canal stretches 1,000 miles southward from Peiping. LXXI, p. 488, Apr., 1937

Great Wall, superimposed on United States map, extends from Philadelphia to Topeka, Kansas. XLIII, p. 118, Feb., 1923

Hong Kong Island. LXXVII, p. 534, Apr., 1940

Indian Ocean, including Australia, New Zealand and Malaysia, with inset of the Canton-Hong Kong area. LXXIX, supplement, 25½ x 32¾ inches, Mar., 1941

Joseph F. Rock's route from Tungchwan to Choni. XLVIII, p. 334, Sept., 1925

Kwangsi, one of China's least-known provinces. LXXII, p. 674, Dec., 1937

Land of the Nashi, in Yünnan Province, China. XLVI, p. 478, Nov., 1924

Map of China and Its Territories. XXIII, supplement, 17 x 23 inches, Oct., 1912

CHINA—*Continued*

Map of North Eastern China. Prepared in the War Department, Adjutant General's Office, Military Information Division. XI, supplement, 18½ x 35½ inches, Sept., 1900

Northeast China. LXXII, p. 489, Oct., 1937

Northeast China, showing Grand Canal. XXIII, p. 934, Oct., 1912

Northeast China, showing strategic position of Peiping and Tientsin. LXXII, p. 512, Oct., 1937

Northeastern China, showing location of Yun Kang Caves. LXXIII, p. 315, Mar., 1938

Northern China, showing route of Hwang Ho (Yellow River) across the Great Plain. LXXXI, p. 207, Feb., 1942

Northern China, showing the meanderings of the Great Wall. XLIII, p. 116, Feb., 1923

Photograph of model relief map showing China's supply roads and the territories now occupied by Japan. LXXXII, pp. 344-345, Sept., 1942

Portion of the route of the National Geographic Society's Central-China Expedition. XLIX, p. 199, Feb., 1926

Railways constructed and proposed in China. XVI, p. 408, Sept., 1905

Route of Joseph F. Rock from Muli to the Konkaling Peaks. LX, p. 7, July, 1931

Shanghai, China, and adjacent regions. XXIII, p. 958, Oct., 1912

Shanghai's geographic position makes it the major seaport of the Yangtze Valley. LXXII, p. 491, Oct., 1937

Shantung. XXXVI, p. 235, Sept., 1919

Sikang's mountain grasslands, route followed by Ray G. Johnson and party. LXXXV, p. 718, June, 1944

Southeast China, showing Pearl River Delta. LXXVII, p. 534, Apr., 1940

Southeastern China, showing Hainan (island). LXXIV, p. 394, Sept., 1938

Southwestern China and Burma, showing route of the Burma Road. LXXVIII, p. 631, Nov., 1940

Szechwan, Yünnan, and Sikang Provinces. LVIII, p. 388, Oct., 1930

Telegraph lines of China in 1904. XVI, p. 409, Sept., 1905

Tibet, showing adjacent areas of India and China. XC, p. 172, Aug., 1946

Upper Salwin. XXI, p. 147, Feb., 1910

See also Kansu; Manchuria; Mongolia; Puto Shan (Island); Sikang; Sinkiang; Tai Shan (Mountain); Tibet; Yünnan

CHINESE TURKISTAN. *See* Sinkiang

CHISHIMA RETTO (Kuril Islands), Japan:

Japan and Adjacent Regions of Asia and the Pacific Ocean, with insets of industrial centers of Japan and the Marshall Islands. LXXXV, supplement, 26½ x 34½ inches, Apr., 1944

Japan and Korea, with insets of Kuril Islands, Pescadores, Karafuto, Ryukyu Islands, Okinawa, Formosa, Tokyo, and location of Japan in the western Pacific. LXXXVIII, supplement, 37 x 26½ inches, Dec., 1945

See also Paramushiro Jima

"CHOCOLATE ISLAND." *See* São Tomé

CHOSEN. *See* Korea

CHRISTMAS ISLAND, Line Islands:

Pacific Ocean and the Bay of Bengal, with inset of Christmas Island. LXXXIV, supplement, 36½ x 26½ inches, Sept., 1943

CLASSICAL LANDS:

Classical Lands of the Mediterranean. LXXVII, supplement, 35¼ x 26 inches, Mar., 1940

Europe and northern Africa, showing extent of Roman Empire, with table of historical facts. XC, pp. 552-553, Nov., 1946

Extent of the Empire, at the death of Augustus (A.D. 14). LXXIV, p. 538, Oct., 1938

Greece and the Aegean, showing sites of antiquity and the necklace of Hellenic cities that adorned the coast of Asia Minor. LXXXV, pp. 280-281, Mar., 1944

Rome-Naples area, showing main arteries and important sites of antiquity. XC, p. 569, Nov., 1946

See also Greece

CLIMATE. *See* Temperature Maps; Weather Charts; *and* United States

COAL FIELDS:

Alaska, showing so far as known, the distribution of the coal-bearing rocks. XVIII, p. 170, Mar., 1907

Coal areas of the United States. XVIII, p. 135, Feb., 1907

The Gold and Coal Fields of Alaska, Together with the Principal Steamer Routes and Trails; Insets: Trails from Tide Water to the Headwaters of the Yukon River; The Klondike Gold Region, Canada. IX, pl. 4, supplement, 25 x 30 inches, Apr., 1898

COD, Cape. *See* Massachusetts

COFFIN GROUP, Pacific Ocean. *See* Haha Jima Retto

COLOMBIA:

Northwestern Colombia. LXXVII, p. 629, May, 1940

Republic of Colombia. XLIX, p. 132, Feb., 1926

Western Colombia. LXXVIII, p. 509, Oct., 1940

COLONIZATION:

Appropriation of Africa by Europeans. I, foldout (opp. p. 124), Apr., 1889

COLORADO:

Colorado. LXII, p. 6, July, 1932

Course of the Rio Grande (river) from its source in Colorado through northern New Mexico. LXXVI, p. 419, Oct., 1939

The Southwestern United States. LXXVII, supplement, 35 x 26 inches, June, 1940

COLORADO (River), U. S.-Mexico:

Changes in the estuary of the Colorado River. XIX, p. 54, Jan., 1908

Grand Canyon, from Green River, Wyoming, to mouth of Colorado, in Mexico. XXVI, p. 153, Aug., 1914

COLORADO (River), U. S.-Mexico—*Continued*
Grand Canyon of the Colorado River: 1923 Expedition of the U. S. Geological Survey. XLV, p. 474, May, 1924
Lower Colorado River, showing irrigable lands. XVII, p. 94, Feb., 1906
Lower Colorado River, showing the great new lake rising in Salton Sink. XVIII, p. 36, Jan., 1907

CONGO. *See* Belgian Congo

CONNECTICUT:
Connecticut. LXXIV, pp. 282-283, Sept., 1938
Northeastern United States. LXXXVIII, supplement, 41 x 26½ inches, Sept., 1945
The Reaches of New York City. LXXV, supplement, 26½ x 29 inches, Apr., 1939

CONNECTICUT (River), U. S.:
Route of the Connecticut River through New England. LXXXIII, p. 405, Apr., 1943

CONSTELLATIONS. *See* Heavens

CORAL SEA:
Coral Sea area, showing the Solomons and New Hebrides, with an inset of Efate. LXXXVI, p. 233, Aug., 1944

CORSICA (Island), Mediterranean Sea:
Corsica. XLIV, p. 224, Sept., 1923
Geographical relation of Corsica to the mother country, France. XLIV, p. 223, Sept., 1923

COSA, JUAN DE LA: Maps:
Juan de la Cosa map, 1500, with vignette of Samana from a modern chart. VI, pl. 10 (opp. p. 186), Dec. 29, 1894
World: *Juan de la Cosa Map, 1500.* V, pl. 4, supplement, 20 x 9½ inches, Apr. 7, 1893

COSTA RICA:
Boundary between Nicaragua and Costa Rica. XII, p. 27, Jan., 1901
Costa Rica, with location map of the Caribbean. XC, p. 412, Oct., 1946
Part of Costa Rica which was overwhelmed by the earthquake of May 4, 1910. XXI, p. 516, June, 1910
Volcanoes of Costa Rica, showing location of Poas. XXI, p. 495, June, 1910

CRATER LAKE. *See* Oregon

CRETE (Island), Greece:
Eastern Mediterranean, with an enlargement of Crete. LXXXIV, p. 550, Nov., 1943
Island of Crete, and map showing route of the "Bonita" (Breton yawl) on its Mediterranean voyage. LV, p. 250, Feb., 1929

CRIMEA (Peninsula), U. S. S. R.:
Crimea. LXXXVII, p. 496, Apr., 1945

CROOKED ISLAND. *See* Bahama Islands

CUBA:
Bay of Cochinas (Cochinos). XIX, p. 497, July, 1908
The Countries of the Caribbean, Including Mexico, Central America, the West Indies and the Panama Canal, with detailed insets of the Panama Canal and the Canal Zone, Porto Rico and the Virgin Islands, and Guantanamo Bay, Cuba. XLI, supplement, 25 x 44 inches, Feb., 1922
Cuba. XVII, supplement, 12 x 24 inches, Oct., 1906
Cuba; compiled from best known authorities by Robert T. Hill. IX, pl. 6 (opp. p. 208), foldout, May, 1898
Cuba, showing Spanish strongholds and Cuban outposts; Cuba Libre and devastated Cuba. IX, p. 234, May, 1898
Cuba and Bahama Islands. LXIV, p. 348, Sept., 1933
Cuba and the neighboring Bahama Islands. XXXVIII, p. 4, July, 1920
The Cuban hurricane of September, 1888. II, 3 maps, p. 208, foldout charts (bet. pp. 210-211), July, 1890
Geologic map of the island of Cuba. Adapted from map of de Castro and Salterain. IX, p. 207, May, 1898
Gulf of Mexico, showing Cuba and Gulf Coast areas. LXXXV, pp. 8-9, Jan., 1944
Map of Central America, Cuba, Porto Rico, and the Islands of the Caribbean Sea, with inset of the Panama Canal and Canal Zone. XXIV, supplement, 12⅓ x 19 inches, Feb., 1913
Mexico, Central America, and the West Indies, with inset of Cuba. LXVI, supplement, 23 x 40 inches, Dec., 1934
Mexico, Central America, and the West Indies, with inset of Cuba. LXXVI, supplement, 24 x 41 inches, Dec., 1939
Outline map shows resemblance to hammer-headed shark. IX, p. 197, May, 1898
Railways of Cuba. XIV, p. 113, Mar., 1903

CUMBERLAND GAP, U. S.:
Cumberland Gap, first high gateway to the West. LXXXIV, p. 745, Dec., 1943

CURAÇAO (Island), West Indies:
Caribbean regions, with enlargements of Aruba, Bonaire, and Curaçao. LXXXIII, p. 172, Feb., 1943

CUSHING, H. P.: Map:
Geologic map of Muir Glacier Basin. By H. P. Cushing. IV, pl. 16 (opp. p. 62), Mar. 21, 1892

CYCLADES (Islands), Greece:
Aegean regions, showing the isles of Greece and the Italian islands of the Aegean. LXXXV, p. 596, May, 1944

CYPRUS (Island), Mediterranean Sea:
Island of Cyprus and an inset showing its location near the eastern limits of the Mediterranean. LIV, p. 4, July, 1928

CZECHOSLOVAKIA:
Czechoslovakia. LXXIV, pp. 176-177, Aug., 1938
Czechoslovakia, whose place names present serious problems for the student. XXXIX, p. 156, Feb., 1921

D

DAGHESTAN AUTONOMOUS SOVIET SOCIALIST REPUBLIC, R. S. F. S. R.:

Caucasus, showing the highlands of Daghestan. XXIV, p. 1086, Oct., 1913

DANGER ISLANDS, South Pacific Ocean:

Pacific Ocean and the Bay of Bengal, with inset of Danger Islands. LXXXIV, supplement, 36½ x 26½ inches, Sept., 1943

D'ANVILLE. *See* Anville, Jean Baptiste Bourguignon d'

DARDANELLES (Strait), Turkey:

Asia Minor, the Dardanelles, and the islands of the Ægean Sea. XLII, p. 554, Nov., 1922

DAVAO, Mindanao, Philippine Islands:

Southeast Asia and Pacific Islands from the Indies and the Philippines to the Solomons, with inset of Davao area. LXXXVI, supplement, 41 x 26½ inches, Oct., 1944

DELAWARE:

Delaware. LXVIII, p. 371, Sept., 1935

Historic and Scenic Reaches of the Nation's Capital. LXXIV, supplement, 26½ x 31¼ inches, July, 1938

Maryland, Delaware, and District of Columbia. LI, supplement, 12 x 18 inches, Feb., 1927

Northeastern United States. LXXXVIII, supplement, 41 x 26½ inches, Sept., 1945

DELAWARE (River), U. S.:

The Delaware: Progressing wave front at successive hours. IX, p. 401, Sept., 1898

DELHI, India:

Delhi, showing eight sites of the city, including New Delhi. LXXXII, p. 469, Oct., 1942

DE L'ISLE, J. N.: Map:

Carte Générale des Découvertes de l'Amiral de Fonte, et autres Navigateurs Espagnols, Anglois et Russes pour la recherche du Passage à la Mer du Sud. Par M. De l'Isle. III, supplement, 16¼ x 13 inches, Jan. 28, 1892; Feb. 19, 1892

DENMARK:

Denmark. XLII, p. 124, Aug., 1922

Denmark. LXXVII, p. 3, Jan., 1940

See also Bornholm (Island)

DISTRICT OF COLUMBIA. *See* Washington, D. C.

DODECANESE ISLANDS, Aegean Sea:

Aegean regions, showing sites of antiquity, with a boundary line between the Greek and Italian islands of the Aegean. LXXXV, pp. 280-281, Mar., 1944

Aegean regions, showing the isles of Greece and the Italian islands of the Aegean. LXXXV, p. 596, May, 1944

Italian islands of the Aegean. LXXIX, p. 451, Apr., 1941

DOMINICAN REPUBLIC:

Haiti and Santo Domingo. XIX, p. 215, Mar., 1908

Island of Haiti, showing its two republics. XXXVIII, p. 489, Dec., 1920

West Indies, from Cuba to Puerto Rico, with an enlargement of Haiti and the Dominican Republic. LXXXV, p. 200, Feb., 1944

DRAKE, SIR FRANCIS: Voyages:

Drake's circumnavigation. V, p. 16, chart, Apr. 7, 1893

DUTCH EAST INDIES. *See* Netherlands East Indies

DUTCH GUIANA. *See* Surinam

DUTCH NEW GUINEA. *See* New Guinea

E

EADS SHIP RAILWAY:

Isthmus of Tehuantepec, showing the routes of the National Railroad of Tehuantepec and the proposed Eads Ship Railway. VII, p. 67, Feb., 1896

EARTHQUAKES:

Part of Costa Rica which was overwhelmed by the earthquake of May 4, 1910. XXI, p. 516, June, 1910

Quake-stricken area in Kansu Province, China. XLI, p. 448, May, 1922

Sketch map of Japan, showing the region devastated by the earthquake wave of June 15, 1896. VII, pl. xxxi, foldout, Sept., 1896

Straits of Messina, showing area of maximum destruction from the recent earthquake. XX, p. 378, Apr., 1909

EAST INDIES. *See* Netherlands East Indies

EAST PRUSSIA:

East Prussia, Danzig, and the Polish Corridor. LXXIII, p. 770, June, 1938

EASTER ISLAND, South Pacific Ocean:

Easter Island. XL, p. 630, Dec., 1921

EASTERN HEMISPHERE:

Eastern Hemisphere, showing interrelation of the races. XII, p. 264, July, 1901

Map of Discovery. Reproduction in color of the painting by N. C. Wyeth, National Geographic Society, Washington, D. C. LIV, text, p. 568; supplement, 18½ x 16¾ inches, Nov., 1928

A Map of the World (in Eastern and Western Hemispheres), with insets showing land and water hemispheres, density of population, time zones, and world mapping. LXXX, supplement, 41 x 22 inches, Dec., 1941

Routes flown by Sir Alan J. Cobham over Europe, Asia, Australia, and Africa. LIII, p. 350, Mar., 1928

The World (in Eastern and Western Hemispheres), with insets showing land and water hemispheres, and time zones. LXVIII, supplement, 23 x 44 inches, Dec., 1935

EASTERN THEATER OF WAR MAP. *See* World War II: *Theater of War in the Pacific Ocean*

ECLIPSES:

Map of Pacific Ocean, showing position of total eclipse (1937) every 15 minutes. LXXII, p. 364, Sept., 1937

ECUADOR:

Ecuador. LXV, p. 136, Feb., 1934

Drainage map of northwestern Ecuador; also, route followed by Mark B. Kerr, on survey. VII, p. 239, July, 1896

The Oriente, where fever fighters combed the jungle for quinine. LXXXIX, p. 349, Mar., 1946

Volcanic peaks of Ecuador, and inset of northern South America. LV, p. 52, Jan., 1929

EFATE (Island), New Hebrides:

Coral Sea area, showing the Solomons and New Hebrides, with an inset of Efate. LXXXVI, p. 233, Aug., 1944

EGYPT:

Bible Lands, showing Palestine, Trans-Jordan, and Egypt. LXXXV, p. 236, Feb., 1944

Bible Lands and the Cradle of Western Civilization; Insets: Holy Land Today, Holy Land in Biblical Times, Jerusalem, Traditional Route of the Exodus, St. Paul's Travels and the Seven Churches, The Crusades. XC, supplement, 32 x 22 inches, Dec., 1946

Bible Lands and the Cradle of Western Civilization; Insets: Jerusalem, The Holy Land, Economic Development, Route of the Exodus, St. Paul's Travels and the Seven Churches, The Crusades, Empire of Alexander the Great. LXXIV, supplement, 25 x 35 inches, Dec., 1938

Mediterranean coast of Libia and Egypt. LXXVIII, p. 810, Dec., 1940

Narrow ribbon of fertile land which runs the length of Egypt. XLIX, p. 272, Mar., 1926

Nile and surrounding territory, from Aswân to the Mediterranean Sea, with pictographs. LXXVII, pp. 438-439, Apr., 1940

Nile, from its mouth to the First Cataract. XXIV, p. 972, Sept., 1913

Nile Valley, world's greatest mine of history. LXXX, p. 426, Oct., 1941

Route of Hassanein Bey through the Libyan Desert. XLVI, p. 236, Sept., 1924

Route of the Exodus. XX, p. 1013, Dec., 1909

Sinai and the route of the Exodus. XXIII, p. 1282, Dec., 1912

Sinai Peninsula, showing in general the route of the Children of Israel in their flight from Egypt to the Promised Land. LII, p. 713, Dec., 1927

Suez Canal district. LXVIII, p. 612, Nov., 1935

Suez-Red Sea region. LXXXI, p. 507, Apr., 1942

Temples and tombs of Ancient Egypt at Thebes. XLIII, p. 467, May, 1923

Territory observed by Brigadier General P. R. C. Groves and Major J. R. McCrindle in their flight over Egypt, Sinai, and Palestine. L, p. 315, Sept., 1926

EIRE:

Ireland, mother of new Eire. LXXVII, p. 653, May, 1940

A Modern Pilgrim's Map of the British Isles or More Precisely the Kingdom of Great Britain and Northern Ireland and the Irish Free State. LXXI, supplement, 29 x 35 inches, June, 1937

See also Aran Islands

ELLESMERE (Island), N.W.T., Canada:

The Arctic Regions, with inset of Ellesmere Island. XLVIII, supplement, 19¼ x 18 inches, Nov., 1925

ELLICE ISLANDS, Pacific Ocean. *See* Funafuti; Nukufetau; Nukulaelae

ELLIOTT, CHARLES P.: Map:

Mount Saint Helens, compiled from original surveys and field notes by Lieut. Charles P. Elliott, U. S. A. VIII, pl. 31 (opp. p. 228), July-Aug., 1897

EL SALVADOR:

El Salvador. LXXXVI, p. 580, Nov., 1944

ENDERBURY ISLAND, Phoenix Islands:

Pacific Ocean and the Bay of Bengal, with inset of Enderbury Island. LXXXIV, supplement, 36½ x 26½ inches, Sept., 1943

ENGLAND:

Canoeists' trip through the heart of England. XLI, p. 475, May, 1922

Central England, showing the canals connecting London and Liverpool. LXXVIII, p. 191, Aug., 1940

Cornwall. XLVI, p. 657, Dec., 1924

Devon and Cornwall, and inset sketch map of the British Isles, showing location of the Lake and Fen Districts and Devon. LV, p. 532, May, 1929

Fen District. LV, p. 609, May, 1929

Isle of Wight. LXVII, p. 6, Jan., 1935

Lake District. LV, p. 581, May, 1929

London, showing route of coronation procession. LXXI, p. 611, May, 1937

A Modern Pilgrim's Map of the British Isles or More Precisely the Kingdom of Great Britain and Northern Ireland and the Irish Free State. LXXI, supplement, 29 x 35 inches, June, 1937

Northern England. LXV, p. 359, Mar., 1934

Scenic and historic properties of the National Trust. LXXXVII, pp. 420-421, Apr., 1945

Severn River Valley. LXIII, p. 421, Apr., 1933

Southampton region. LXXVII, p. 92, Jan., 1940

Southeastern England, showing harassed Channel coast. LXXIX, p. 70, Jan., 1941

Southern England, showing historic sites and cities along the Thames. LXXV, pp. 244-245, Feb., 1939

Southwestern England, with enlargement of Plymouth area. LXXXIX, p. 215, Feb., 1946

Sussex County. LXVIII, p. 63, July, 1935

See also Channel Islands; Man, Isle of; Scilly Isles

ENIWETOK (Atoll), Marshall Islands:

Pacific Ocean and the Bay of Bengal, with inset of Eniwetok. LXXXIV, supplement, 36½ x 26½ inches, Sept., 1943

ENIWETOK (Atoll), Marshall Islands—*Continued*

Southeast Asia and Pacific Islands from the Indies and the Philippines to the Solomons, with inset of Eniwetok. LXXXVI, supplement, 41 x 26½ inches, Oct., 1944

Strategic isles of the Pacific. LXXXV, pp. 392-393, 17 island maps, Apr., 1944

ERITREA:

Ethiopia, Eritrea, and adjacent territory. LXVIII, pp. 270-271, Sept., 1935

ESKIMOS:

Distribution of blond Eskimos. XXIII, p. 1224, Dec., 1912

ESTONIA:

Estonia, with inset of the Baltic region. LXXVI, p. 805, Dec., 1939

ETHIOPIA (Abyssinia):

Eritrea, Ethiopia, and surrounding territory. LXVIII, pp. 270-271, Sept., 1935

Ethiopia. LIV, p. 123, Aug., 1928

Ethiopia, showing mountainous regions. LIX, p. 702, June, 1931

Route of Harry V. Harlan. XLVII, p. 618, June, 1925

EUROPE:

Asia and Adjacent Areas, with table of airline distances in statute miles. LXXXII, supplement, 40 x 26½ inches, Dec., 1942

Atlantic Ocean. LXXVI, supplement, 31 x 25 inches, July, 1939

Atlantic Ocean, with inset of Isthmus of Panama and a table of air-line distances in statute miles. LXXX, supplement, 31¼ x 25 inches, Sept., 1941

Automobile route from England to India. XLVIII, p. 193, Aug., 1925

Boundary lines of European nations as drawn by the gaunt hand of hunger. XXXIII, p. 338, Apr., 1918

Central Europe and the Mediterranean as of September 1, 1939. LXXVI, supplement, 36½ x 26½ inches, Oct., 1939

Europe, Asia, Africa, Australia, showing interrelation of the races. XII, p. 264, July, 1901

Europe, showing route flown by the Days. LXI, p. 656, June, 1932

Europe, showing routes of J. Parker Van Zandt's flights. LXXV, p. 794, June, 1939

Europe, showing territory covered in flights of Walter Mittelholzer. LXI, p. 466, Apr., 1932

Europe, showing the great sheet of ice that covered the British Isles, Scandinavia, Germany, and half of Russia during the second glacial age. XXIX, p. 115, Feb., 1916

Europe and northern Africa, showing extent of Roman Empire, with table of historical facts. XC, pp. 552-553, Nov., 1946

Europe and the Mediterranean. LXXIII, supplement, 34 x 39 inches, Apr., 1938

Europe and the Near East. LVI, supplement, 34¼ x 39¼ inches, Dec., 1929

Europe and the Near East, as of April 1, 1940. LXXVII, supplement, 39 x 34 inches, May, 1940

EUROPE—*Continued*

Europe and the Near East, with inset map of the Middle East, and a table of distances between principal ports via shortest navigable routes. LXXXIII, supplement, 39 x 34 inches, June, 1943

Europe at a period when the British Isles and Scandinavian peninsula were a part of the mainland. XXIX, p. 113, Feb., 1916

Germany and Its Approaches, with international boundaries as of September 1, 1939, the day Germany invaded Poland, and boundaries as of January 1, 1938, before Germany seized Austria and Czechoslovakia. LXXXVI, supplement, 33½ x 26½ inches, July, 1944

Map of Central Europe, showing strategic position of the Saar Basin. LXVII, p. 243, Feb., 1935

Map of Europe, Showing Countries as Established by the Peace Conference at Paris. XXXIX, supplement, 30 x 33 inches, Feb., 1921

Map of Europe and adjoining portions of Africa and Asia. XXVIII, supplement, 28 x 32 inches, July, 1915

Map of the Countries Bordering the Mediterranean Sea. XXIII, supplement, 10 x 18 inches, Jan., 1912

Map of the New Balkan States and Central Europe. XXVI, supplement, 17 x 22½ inches, Aug., 1914

Map of the Races of Europe and Adjoining Portions of Asia and Africa. XXXIV, supplement, 19¾ x 31 inches, Dec., 1918

Map of the Western Theatre of War, with inset of France and Belgium. XXXIII, supplement, 26 x 31 inches, May, 1918

Map showing territorial changes in area around Poland. LXXV, p. 744, June, 1939

The Mediterranean Basin. XII, p. 255, July, 1901

Physical map of Europe. XXXIV, p. 506, Dec., 1918

Relative density of railroads in Europe. XVI, p. 521, Nov., 1905

Roman Empire (A.D. 14). LXXIV, p. 538, Oct., 1938

Route followed by Lieutenant J. Parker Van Zandt in his 6,500-mile airplane tour of Europe. XLVII, p. 275, Mar., 1925

Route followed by Merlin Minshall on his voyage in the "Hawke." LXXI, pp. 536-537, May, 1937

Route followed by Sir Ross Smith in first aëroplane voyage from London to Australia. XXXIX, pp. 230-231, Mar., 1921

Route of the Lindberghs in the *Tingmissartoq.* LXVI, pp. 266-267, Sept., 1934

Russia in Europe. VII, pl. I, supplement, 9¾ x 12¾ inches, Jan., 1896; reprint, 11¼ x 10 inches, 1965

Southeast Baltic coast. LXXIII, p. 770, June, 1938

Southeastern Europe, showing the Balkan States and European Turkey. XIX, p. 799, Nov., 1908

Theater of War in Europe, Africa, and Western Asia, with table of airline distances in statute miles. LXXXII, supplement, 26½ x 31 inches, July, 1942

EUROPE—*Continued*

Western Europe during the third inter-glacial age. XXIX, p. 118, Feb., 1916

See also names of countries

F

FAEROE ISLANDS, North Atlantic Ocean:

Faeroe Islands. LVIII, p. 610, Nov., 1930

FAKAOFO (Atoll), Tokelau Islands:

Pacific Ocean and the Bay of Bengal, with inset of Fakaofo. LXXXIV, supplement, 36½ x 26½ inches, Sept., 1943

FALCON ISLAND, Tonga Islands:

New Zealand to the Samoa group, with an enlargement of Falcon Island. LIV, p. 760, Dec., 1928

FANNING ISLAND, Line Islands:

Pacific Ocean and the Bay of Bengal, with inset of Fanning Island. LXXXIV, supplement, 36½ x 26½ inches, Sept., 1943

FAR EAST:

Far East, showing the strategic position of Formosa. LXXXVII, p. 6, Jan., 1945

Far East, with enlargement of Java. LXXXI, p. 91, Jan., 1942

Far East, with inset of the Moluccas. LXXIX, p. 538, May, 1941

Indian Ocean, including Australia, New Zealand and Malaysia. LXXIX, supplement, 25½ x 32¾ inches, Mar., 1941

Japan and Adjacent Regions of Asia and the Pacific Ocean, with insets of industrial centers of Japan and the Marshall Islands. LXXXV, supplement, 26½ x 34½ inches, Apr., 1944

Malay States, Thailand, and French Indo-China, with inset of Singapore. LXXX, p. 662, Nov., 1941

The Philippine Islands as the Geographical Center of the Far East. XI, supplement, 7½ x 10¾ inches, Jan., 1900

Singapore, Manila, and Hong Kong form a tripod of American and British influence in the Far East. LXXVII, p. 534, Apr., 1940

See also Borneo; Celebes; China; Formosa; French Indo-China; Hong Kong; Japan; Java; Korea; Manchuria; New Guinea; Philippine Islands; Singapore; Sumatra; Thailand; Timor

FATU-HIVA (Island), Marquesas Islands:

Marquesas Islands, showing Fatu-Hiva. LXXIX, p. 112, Jan., 1941

FEDERATED MALAY STATES:

Strategic geographic position of Singapore, with an inset of the Malay Peninsula. XLIX, p. 238, Mar., 1926

FIJI ISLANDS, South Pacific Ocean:

Pacific Ocean and the Bay of Bengal, with inset of Fiji. LXXXIV, supplement, 36½ x 26½ inches, Sept., 1943

FINGER LAKES REGION, New York:

Central New York, showing Finger Lakes region. LXXIX, p. 561, May, 1941

FINLAND:

Finland. LXXIV, p. 502, Oct., 1938

Finland and Lapland, showing Murman Railway. XXXV, p. 332, Apr., 1919

Norway, showing the Petsamo region of Finland, ceded to the U. S. S. R. LXXXVIII, p. 620, Nov., 1945

See also Åland (Islands)

FLINT ISLAND, Line Islands:

Pacific Ocean and the Bay of Bengal, with inset of Flint Island. LXXXIV, supplement, 36½ x 26½ inches, Sept., 1943

FLORIDA:

Florida, with insets of the following areas: Miami-Palm Beach, Pensacola, Jacksonville-St. Augustine, Tampa-St. Petersburg-Sarasota. LVII, supplement, 12½ x 13¼ inches, Jan., 1930

Gulf of Mexico, showing Florida and coastal areas of United States and Mexico. LXXXV, pp. 8-9, Jan., 1944

South Florida. XVII, p. 6, Jan., 1906

Southern Florida. LXXVII, p. 118, Jan., 1940

Virginia and Florida, from an Amsterdam Atlas of the World published in 1638. XLV, p. 242, Mar., 1924

FLORIDA (Island), Solomon Islands:

Islands of the South Pacific, with insets of Florida Island and Ontong Java. LXV, p. 268, Mar., 1934

FLORIDA KEYS, Florida:

Florida Keys, showing location of wreck of H. M. S. *Winchester.* LXXX, p. 811, Dec., 1941

FONTE, DE: Discoveries:

Carte Généralè des Découvertes de l'Amiral de Fonte, et autres Navigateurs Espagnols, Anglois et Russes pour la recherche du Passage à la Mer du Sud. Par M. De l'Isle. III, supplement, 16¼ x 13 inches, Jan. 28, 1892; Feb. 19, 1892

FORESTS:

Alaska, showing distribution of timber. XVIII, p. 172, Mar., 1907

Bitter Root Forest Reserve. IX, pl. 12 (opp. p. 394), foldout, Sept., 1898

Forest Reserves and National Parks of the United States. XI, p. 370, Sept., 1900

Forests and woodlands of the West (U. S.). XV, p. 19, Jan., 1904

Natural divisions of the North American forests, exclusive of Mexico. VI, pl. 8 (opp. p. 139), June 22, 1894

FORMOSA (Taiwan, Island):

Far East, showing the strategic position of Formosa. LXXXVII, p. 6, Jan., 1945

Formosa. LXXXVII, p. 7, Jan., 1945

Formosa, showing its geographical relation to Japan, China, and the Philippines. XXXVII, p. 262, Mar., 1920

FORMOSA (Taiwan, Island)—*Continued*

Japan and Korea, with insets of Kuril Islands, Pescadores, Karafuto, Ryukyu Islands, Okinawa, Formosa, Tokyo, and location of Japan in the western Pacific. LXXXVIII, supplement, 37 x 26½ inches, Dec., 1945

FRANCE:

British Mulberry and Omaha Beach, artificial harbors, off the Normandy coast. LXXXVII, p. 565, May, 1945

France, showing the route of the *Nageoma* (canoe). LII, p. 133, Aug., 1927

Geographical relation of Corsica to the mother country, France. XLIV, p. 223, Sept., 1923

La Camargue, the island "Wild West" of southern France. XLII, p. 4, July, 1922

Location of the Montespan grotto in the foothills of the Pyrenees. XLVI, p. 126, Aug., 1924

The Lower Valley of the Bar. VII, pl. XXVI (opp. p. 236), July, 1896

Map of the Western Theatre of War, with inset of France and Belgium. XXXIII, supplement, 26 x 31 inches, May, 1918

Metz, Nancy, and Epinal regions. LXXXVII, p. 367, Mar., 1945

Normandy. LXIX, p. 629, May, 1936

Northwest France, including Normandy and Brittany. LXXXIV, pp. 218-219, Aug., 1943

Northwestern France, Belgium, and Luxembourg, showing cemeteries and monuments to American soldiers. LXV, p. 9, Jan., 1934

Paris Basin, with inset of northern France. LXXVII, p. 202, Feb., 1940

Provinces of France. XXVIII, p. 471, Nov., 1915

Route of the "Nageoma" (canoe) through the back doors of France. XLIV, p. 3, July, 1923

Sketch map of the Meuse, showing the Bar, the Aire, and the Aisne. VII, p. 232, July, 1896

Sketch map of the Seine, the Meuse, and the Moselle. VII, p. 189, June, 1896

Sketch maps showing diversion of the Toul from the Meuse to the Moselle. VII, p. 229, July, 1896

Sketch maps showing the Marne River, branches and diversions. VII, pp. 199, 201, June, 1896

Southeastern France, showing Mediterranean coast. LXXXVI, p. 428, Oct., 1944

Valley of the Meuse, near Dun-sur-Meuse. VII, pl. XXIV (opp. p. 195), June, 1896

Valley of the Meuse, near St. Mihiel. VII, pl. XXIII, June, 1896

Valley of the Moselle, near Berncastel. VII, pl. XXII (opp. p. 193), June, 1896

Valley of the Seine, near Duclair. VII, pl. XXI (opp. p. 191), June, 1896

Western peninsula of France and an inset of St. Malo and its environs. LVI, p. 138, Aug., 1929

See also Corsica (Island)

FRANZ JOSEF LAND, Arctic Region:

The Arctic Regions, with inset of Franz Josef Land. XLVIII, supplement, 19¼ x 18 inches, Nov., 1925

Franz Josef Land archipelago, showing the new lands discovered and explored by the Wellman Expedition. X, p. 502, Dec., 1899

FREDERICKSBURG, Virginia:

Fredericksburg, from the map prepared, in 1867, by the Corps of Engineers, U. S. A.; issued by the NGS, for Field-day, May 4, '95. VI, foldout, Apr. 20, 1895

FRENCH GUIANA:

Surinam and French Guiana, with insets showing the location and comparable sizes of the Guianas. LXXXIII, p. 462, Apr., 1943

FRENCH GUINEA:

French Guinea. LXVII, p. 699, June, 1935

FRENCH INDO-CHINA:

French Indo-China. LX, p. 159, Aug., 1931

French Indo-China. LXVIII, p. 491, Oct., 1935

French Indo-China, showing the location of the ruins at Angkor, Cambodia. XXIII, p. 210, Mar., 1912

Location of Angkor, the capital of the vast empire ruled by the Khmers. LIV, p. 304, Sept., 1928

Ruins of Angkor, Cambodia. XXIII, p. 225, Mar., 1912

FRENCH MOROCCO. *See* Morocco

FRENCH NORTH AFRICA. *See* Algeria; Morocco; Tunisia

FRENCH SOMALILAND:

French Somaliland. LX, p. 364, Sept., 1931

FRENCH WEST AFRICA:

French West Africa, with pictographs, showing route followed by Mrs. Boulton. LXXIX, pp. 636-637, May, 1941

Northwest Africa, showing mileage between Dakar, French West Africa, and important points in the Eastern and Western Hemispheres. LXXXI, p. 374, Mar., 1942

FRENCH WEST INDIES. *See* Martinique

FRIENDLY ISLANDS. *See* Tonga Islands

FUNAFUTI (Atoll), Ellice Islands:

Pacific Ocean and the Bay of Bengal, with inset of Funafuti. LXXXIV, supplement, 36½ x 26½ inches, Sept., 1943

FUNDY, Bay of. *See* Chignecto Ship Railway

G

GALÁPAGOS ISLANDS, Pacific Ocean:

South America, with inset maps of the Galápagos Islands, airways and relief, chief natural resources, precipitation and temperature. LXXII, supplement, 26¾ x 37½ inches, Dec., 1937

South America, with insets of the Galapagos Islands, chief natural resources, precipitation and temperature, airways and relief, and a table of airline distances and flying times in hours. LXXXII, supplement, 26½ x 37¼ inches, Oct., 1942

GAMA, VASCO DA: Voyages:

Africa, showing Vasco da Gama's first voyage around Cape of Good Hope. LII, p. 504, Nov., 1927

GAMA, VASCO DA: Voyages—*Continued*

Africa, with Da Gama's discoveries, 1498. By Mattiolo, 1548. XXII, p. 391, Apr., 1911

GANNETT, HENRY: Map:

United States showing Estimates of the Map Value of Existing Mother Maps. By Henry Gannett. IV, supplement, 18 x 13 inches, Mar. 31, 1892

GARDA (Lake), Italy:

Lake of Garda region. War zone on Austro-Italian frontier indicated. LXVIII, p. 334, Sept., 1935

GARDNER ISLAND, Phoenix Islands:

Pacific Ocean and the Bay of Bengal, with inset of Gardner Island. LXXXIV, supplement, 36½ x 26½ inches, Sept., 1943

GASPÉ PENINSULA, Quebec, Canada:

Gaspé Peninsula, with detailed inset. LXVIII, p. 210, Aug., 1935

GENEVA, Lake, Switzerland-France:

Lake Geneva region. LXXII, p. 728, Dec., 1937

GEORGIA:

North Carolina, South Carolina, Georgia and Eastern Tennessee, with inset map of Atlanta. L, supplement, 14¾ x 19 inches, Sept., 1926

Okefinokee Swamp, Georgia. LXV, p. 603, May, 1934

Sea Islands, Georgia. LXV, p. 230, Feb., 1934

GERMANY:

Germany and Its Approaches, with international boundaries as of September 1, 1939, the day Germany invaded Poland, and boundaries as of January 1, 1938, before Germany seized Austria and Czechoslovakia. LXXXVI, supplement, 33½ x 26½ inches, July, 1944

Map of Bavarian Alps, showing location of Oberammergau. LXVIII, p. 746, Dec., 1935

Map of the Western Theatre of War, with inset of France and Belgium. XXXIII, supplement, 26 x 31 inches, May, 1918

Map showing strategic position of the Saar Basin. LXVII, p. 243, Feb., 1935

New Germany as limited by the Peace Treaty. XXXV, p. 546, June, 1919

Old and New Württemberg. XXII, p. 933, Oct., 1911

Rhineland. LXXXVIII, p. 4, July, 1945

Rhineland, showing former demilitarized zone. LXIX, p. 832, June, 1936

Rivers paddled by Cornelia Stratton Parker. LXI, p. 368, Mar., 1932

Ruhr Basin. XLI, p. 554, May, 1922

Saar Basin. LXVII, p. 242, Feb., 1935

States forming Germany in November, 1918. XXXIV, p. 510, Dec., 1918

GIGNILLIAT, T. HEYWARD: Map:

Map of the Valley of the Orinoco River, showing the extent of territory drained by that waterway and the bearing it has on the Venezuelan question. Compiled by T. Heyward Gignilliat, 1896. VII, pl. 5, supplement, 18 x 11¾ inches, Feb., 1896

GILBERT ISLANDS, Pacific Ocean:

Gilbert Islands, with insets of Tarawa and Makin. LXXXVII, p. 135, Feb., 1945

Pacific Islands, with inset of Gilbert Islands. LXXXIII, p. 74, Jan., 1943

See also Makin; Tarawa

GLACIER BAY, Alaska:

Glacier Bay and Muir Glacier. By Harry Fielding Reid. VII, p. 144, Apr., 1896

GLACIERS:

Atrevida, Lucia, and Marvine lobe of Malaspina Glacier. XXI, p. 34, Jan., 1910

Bulb glaciers of Lower Copper River; Copper River and Northwestern Railway passing between Childs and Miles Glaciers and over the stagnant ice of Baird Glacier. XXI, p. 25, Jan., 1910

Columbia Glacier, Prince William Sound, with city of Washington drawn to the same scale for purposes of comparison. XXI, p. 10, Jan., 1910

Columbia Ice Field Photographic Expedition; location map. XLVII, pp. 382, 383, Apr., 1925

Comparing sizes of Copper River glaciers with glaciers in the Rocky Mountains, Selkirks, and Cascades of the United States and Canada. XXII, p. 543, June, 1911

Fronts of Johns Hopkins, Grand Pacific, and Muir Glaciers, 1894 and 1907. XIX, p. 77, Jan., 1908

Hidden Glacier in 1899, 1905, 1906, and 1909. XXI, p. 45, Jan., 1910

Hubbard Glacier (lower portion), with three glaciers of the Swiss Alps superimposed upon it. XXI, p. 5, Jan., 1910

Location of the glaciers of Prince William Sound. XXII, p. 540, June, 1911

Lower Copper River and Controller Bay regions. XXI, p. 24, Jan., 1910

Malaspina Glacier (largest in the world outside the polar regions). XXI, p. 9, Jan., 1910

Malaspina Glacier, Mount Saint Elias, and Yakutat Bay. XXI, p. 4, Jan., 1910

Muir: Glacier Bay and Muir Glacier. By Harry Fielding Reid. VII, p. 144, Apr., 1896

Muir Glacier, Alaska. Surveyed with Plane Table in 1890, by Harry Fielding Reid. IV, supplement, 19½ x 17¾ inches, Mar. 21, 1892

Muir Glacier: Geologic map of Muir Glacier Basin. By H. P. Cushing. IV, pl. 16 (opp. p. 62), Mar. 21, 1892

Muir Glacier: Northern part of Muir Inlet. IV, pl. 15 (opp. p. 55), Mar. 21, 1892

Muir Inlet and front of Muir Glacier, showing positions of the ice front in 1890 and in May, 1903. XIV, p. 444, Dec., 1903

Nunatak Glacier in 1895, 1899, and 1909. XXI, p. 44, Jan., 1910

Pacific coast of the Gulf of Alaska. XXI, p. 3, Jan., 1910

Port Wells, Prince William Sound, Alaska, in 1899. XXII, p. 550, June, 1911

Port Wells in 1910, showing the extraordinary retreat of Barry and Surprise Glaciers. XXII, p. 550, June, 1911

GLACIERS—*Continued*

Valdez Glacier Highway. XXI, p. 11, Jan., 1910

Variegated and Haenke Glaciers. XXI, p. 35, Jan., 1910

GOBI (Desert), Central Asia:

Mongolia, showing the Gobi. LXIII, p. 656, June, 1933

GOLD COAST, West Africa:

Area of Ashanti revolt. XI, p. 244, June, 1900

GOLD FIELDS:

Alaska, showing so far as known, the distribution of metamorphic rocks and the localities where gold has been mined. XVIII, p. 168, Mar., 1907

The Gold and Coal Fields of Alaska, Together with the Principal Steamer Routes and Trails; Insets: Trails from Tide Water to the Headwaters of the Yukon River; The Klondike Gold Region, Canada. IX, pl. 4, supplement, 25 x 30 inches, Apr., 1898

Golofnin Bay and Cape Nome gold fields. XI, p. 16, Jan., 1900

Korea: Sketch-map of Korea: Localities where gold has been found are marked. II, fig. iii (opp. p. 242), Aug., 1890

GOOD HOPE, Cape of. *See* Union of South Africa

GOZO (Island), Malta, Mediterranean Sea:

Malta, Gozo, Comino, and Filfla. LXXXIII, p. 378, Mar., 1943

GRAND CANYON, Arizona:

Grand Canyon, from Green River, Wyoming, to mouth of Colorado, in Mexico. XXVI, p. 153, Aug., 1914

Grand Canyon of the Colorado River: 1923 Expedition of the U. S. Geological Survey. XLV, p. 474, May, 1924

GRAND UNION CANAL, England:

Grand Union Canal and adjoining canals. LXXVIII, p. 191, Aug., 1940

GRAND VALLEY, Netherlands New Guinea:

Archbold Expedition explores interior of Netherlands New Guinea; Grand Valley, discovered. LXXIX, p. 318, Mar., 1941

New Guinea, with inset showing Grand Valley and the Balim River. LXXXVIII, p. 674, Dec., 1945

GREAT BARRIER REEF, Australia:

East coast of Australia, showing Great Barrier Reef. LVIII, p. 359, Sept., 1930

Great Barrier Reef. LXXVII, p. 827, June, 1940

GREAT BRITAIN:

A Modern Pilgrim's Map of the British Isles or More Precisely the Kingdom of Great Britain and Northern Ireland and the Irish Free State. LXXI, supplement, 29 x 35 inches, June, 1937

See also England; Scotland; Wales

GREAT LAKES, Canada-U. S.:

Ancient and modern outlines of Lake Erie. VIII, p. 234, Sept., 1897

Ancient and modern outlines of Lake Ontario. VIII, p. 235, Sept., 1897

GREAT LAKES, Canada-U. S.—*Continued*

The Great Lakes, showing pairs of gaging stations and isobases of outlets. VIII, p. 243, Sept., 1897

Great Lakes region. LXV, pp. 454-455, Apr., 1934

Lake Superior, showing northern Michigan and Wisconsin, eastern Minnesota, and western Ontario. XL, p. 114, Aug., 1921

Lake Superior region, showing location of Isle Royal. LX, p. 760, Dec., 1931

Marquette's map of Great Lakes region. LXII, p. 768, Dec., 1932

The Nipissing Great Lake. VIII, p. 236, Sept., 1897

Northeastern United States. LXXXVIII, supplement, 41 x 26½ inches, Sept., 1945

Ontario, showing Great Lakes. LXII, p. 139, Aug., 1932

GREAT SMOKY MOUNTAINS, North Carolina-Tennessee:

North Carolina-Tennessee: Asheville Sheet. Section from the Cumberland Plateau to the Blue Ridge. Natural Profiles. Surveyed in 1882-3-7. I, supplement, 15¾ x 21¾ inches, Oct., 1889; reprint, *Asheville Quadrangle.* Surveyed in 1898-99. I, supplement, 16 x 22 inches, 1965

GREAT SMOKY MOUNTAINS NATIONAL PARK, North Carolina-Tennessee:

Great Smoky Mountains National Park, with inset showing main roads across the park. LXX, p. 246, Aug., 1936

GREATER ANTILLES. *See* Cuba; Dominican Republic; Haiti; Jamaica; Puerto Rico

GREATER SUNDA ISLANDS. *See* Borneo; Celebes; Java; Sumatra

GREECE:

Bulgaria, Servia, and Macedonia. XXIII, p. 1152, Nov., 1912

Classical Lands of the Mediterranean. LXXVII, supplement, 35¼ x 26 inches, Mar., 1940

Greece, with inset showing territorial expansion. LVIII, p. 652, Dec., 1930

Greece and the Aegean, showing sites of antiquity and the necklace of Hellenic cities that adorned the coast of Asia Minor. LXXXV, pp. 280-281, Mar., 1944

Saloniki and adjacent countries. XXX, p. 271, Sept., 1916

Southern Greece—the Attic Plain and the Peloponnesus. XLII, p. 574, Dec., 1922

See also Crete (Island)

GREENLAND:

Arctic regions, showing Captain Bob Bartlett's world, as seen from 10,000 miles in space. LXXXIX, p. 604, May, 1946

Atlantic Ocean, showing air routes to Norway and Britain, via Newfoundland, Greenland, and Iceland. LXXX, p. 77, July, 1941

Global map of Arctic regions, showing Greenland, important for weather stations and air bases. XC, p. 459, Oct., 1946

Greenland—an aerial stepping stone to Europe. LXXXII, pp. 370-371, Sept., 1942

GREENLAND—*Continued*

Greenland, as seen from the North Pole. LXXVIII, pp. 118-119, July, 1940

Hubbard Bay and Alison Bay, west Greenland. South of 74°30′ after C. H. Ryder; North of 74°30′ after J. A. Björling. IX, p. 3, Jan., 1898

Plan of Arctic exploration from a base near Jones Sound or at Cape Sabine. IX, p. 2, Jan., 1898

Route of the "Hope," from Sydney, Nova Scotia, as far as Umanak, Greenland, showing magnetic stations. VIII, p. 99, Apr., 1897

Southern Greenland. LXVI, p. 262, Sept., 1934

GUADALCANAL (Island), Solomon Islands:

Solomon Islands, with inset maps showing Guadalcanal-Tulagi area and Bougainville area. LXXXII, p. 815, Dec., 1942

GUAM (Island), Marianas Islands:

Indian Ocean, including Australia, New Zealand and Malaysia, with inset of Guam. LXXIX, supplement, 25½ x 32¾ inches, Mar., 1941

Pacific Islands, with inset of Guam. LXXIV, p. 102, July, 1938

Pacific Ocean and the Bay of Bengal, with inset of Guam. LXXXIV, supplement, 36½ x 26½ inches, Sept., 1943

Southeast Asia and Pacific Islands from the Indies and the Philippines to the Solomons, with inset of Guam. LXXXVI, supplement, 41 x 26½ inches, Oct., 1944

Strategic isles of the Pacific. LXXXV, pp. 392-393, 17 island maps, Apr., 1944

GUATEMALA:

Guatemala. XXI, p. 613, July, 1910

Guatemala. L, p. 604, Nov., 1926

Highlands of Guatemala, with inset showing whole of republic. LXX, p. 432, Oct., 1936

GUERRERO (State), Mexico:

Río Balsas region. XC, p. 254, Aug., 1946

GULF COAST, U. S.-Mexico:

Gulf of Mexico, showing coastal areas of United States and Mexico, and the Gulf Intracoastal Waterway. LXXXV, pp. 8-9, Jan., 1944

Southeastern Louisiana, showing Terrebonne Parish, with inset of Gulf Coast. LXXXVI, p. 509, Oct., 1944

GULF STREAM:

Direction of the Gulf Stream and other currents in the North Atlantic Ocean. XXIII, p. 772, Aug., 1912

H

HACHIJO JIMA (Island), Japan:

Strategic isles of the Pacific. LXXXV, pp. 392-393, 17 island maps, Apr., 1944

HADHRAMAUT:

Map of Arabia, with inset of Hadhramaut Province. LXII, p. 389, Oct., 1932

HAHA JIMA RETTO, Ogasawara Shoto, Pacific Ocean:

Southeast Asia and Pacific Islands from the Indies and the Philippines to the Solomons, with inset of Haha Jima Retto. LXXXVI, supplement, 41 x 26½ inches, Oct., 1944

Strategic isles of the Pacific. LXXXV, pp. 392-393, 17 island maps, Apr., 1944

HAINAN (Island), China:

Southeastern China, showing Hainan Island. LXXIV, p. 394, Sept., 1938

HAITI:

Haiti. LXXXVI, p. 312, Sept., 1944

Haiti, with inset showing Caribbean region. LXVI, p. 439, Oct., 1934

Haiti and Santo Domingo. XIX, p. 215, Mar., 1908

Island of Haiti, showing its two republics. XXXVIII, p. 489, Dec., 1920

West Indies, from Cuba to Puerto Rico, with an enlargement of Haiti and the Dominican Republic. LXXXV, p. 200, Feb., 1944

HARBORS, Artificial, Normandy Coast, France:

British Mulberry and Omaha Beach, artificial harbors, off the Normandy coast. LXXXVII, p. 565, May, 1945

HATTERAS, Cape, North Carolina:

The St. Thomas-Hatteras hurricane of September 3–12, 1889. II, foldout charts (bet. pp. 210–211), July, 1890

HAWAII, Territory of:

Hawaiian Islands. XLV, p. 123, Feb., 1924

Hawaiian Islands. XLVIII, p. 79, July, 1925

Hawaiian Islands, with inset of Pearl Harbor and vicinity. LXXXII, p. 545, Oct., 1942

Hawaiian Islands, with inset showing route of Flying Clippers across the Pacific Ocean. LXXIV, pp. 424-425, Oct., 1938

Island of Hawaii, showing the four volcanoes, Mauna Kea, Hualalai, Mauna Loa, and Kilauea, which have created the island. XLV, p. 183, Feb., 1924

Pacific Ocean and the Bay of Bengal, with inset of Hawaiian Islands. LXXXIV, supplement, 36½ x 26½ inches, Sept., 1943

Relief map of the island of Maui. XLV, p. 145, Feb., 1924

Relief map of the island of Oahu. XLV, p. 134, Feb., 1924

HAYES, C. WILLARD: Maps:

Map of the Region Adjacent to the Nicaragua Canal Route. By C. Willard Hayes. X, supplement, 7½ x 10½ inches, July, 1899

Southern Appalachians, showing the deformed Cretaceous Peneplain and the areas not reduced to baselevel. By C. Willard Hayes and Marius R. Campbell. VI, pl. 5, May 23, 1894; reprint, foldout map, 1965

Southern Appalachians, showing the deformed Tertiary Peneplain and the areas not reduced to baselevel. By C. Willard Hayes and Marius R. Campbell. VI, pl. 6, May 23, 1894; reprint, foldout map, 1965

HEAVENS:

Chart of the heavens visible in the United States and southern Canada during January and February. XLVII, p. 102, Jan., 1925

Diagrams of the best-known constellations. LXXXIV, 13 drawings, pp. 100, 103-110, 112-115, July, 1943

Map of the heavens. XXXVI, p. 170, Aug., 1919

Picture map of the heavens. XXXVI, p. 171, Aug., 1919

Picture map of the heavens. XLVII, p. 103, Jan., 1925

Star charts, depicting the evening sky for each month. LXXXIV, 12 charts, pp. 117-128, July, 1943

HEMISPHERE MAPS:

A Map of the World (in Eastern and Western Hemispheres), with insets showing land and water hemispheres, density of population, time zones, and world mapping. LXXX, supplement, 41 x 22 inches, Dec., 1941

Northern and Southern Hemispheres, with insets of time zones, world terrain, and tables of airline distances in four hemispheres. LXXXIII, supplement, 41 x 22 inches, Apr., 1943

Northern Hemisphere, showing parallels of latitude, 10 to 60, to be used with sky charts. LXXXIV, pp. 98-99, July, 1943

Northern Hemisphere, with tables showing airline distances in the Pacific, the Atlantic, the Arctic, and the Americas. LXXXIX, supplement, 21¾ x 24 inches, Feb., 1946

The World (in Eastern and Western Hemispheres), with insets showing land and water hemispheres, and time zones. LXVIII, supplement, 23 x 44 inches, Dec., 1935

HENRY II (France) : Map:

Mappa Munde Peinte sur Parchemin par Ordre de Henri II, Roi de France—1532; Samana (Guanahani), shown. VI, pl. 11 (opp. p. 188), Dec. 29, 1894

HERRERA: Map:

Herrera map, 1601, with vignette of Watling Island from a modern chart. Samana and Guanahani, shown. VI, p. 187, Dec. 29, 1894

HILL, ROBERT T.: Map:

Cuba; compiled from best known authorities by Robert T. Hill. IX, pl. 6 (opp. p. 208), foldout, May, 1898

HISPANIOLA (Island), West Indies. *See* Dominican Republic; Haiti

HOLLAND. *See* Netherlands

HOLY LAND. *See* Palestine

HONG KONG:

Hong Kong Island. LXXVII, p. 534, Apr., 1940

Indian Ocean, including Australia, New Zealand and Malaysia, with inset of Hong Kong. LXXIX, supplement, 25½ x 32¾ inches, Mar., 1941

Southeast Asia and Pacific Islands from the Indies and the Philippines to the Solomons, with inset of Hong Kong area. LXXXVI, supplement, 41 x 26½ inches, Oct., 1944

HONOLULU, Oahu, Hawaii:

Pacific Ocean and the Bay of Bengal, with inset of Honolulu and Pearl Harbor areas. LXXXIV, supplement, 36½ x 26½ inches, Sept., 1943

HOWLAND (Island), Pacific Ocean:

Pacific Ocean and the Bay of Bengal, with inset of Howland Island. LXXXIV, supplement, 36½ x 26½ inches, Sept., 1943

HUBBARD BAY. *See* Greenland

HULL ISLAND, Phoenix Islands:

Pacific Ocean and the Bay of Bengal, with inset of Hull Island. LXXXIV, supplement, 36½ x 26½ inches, Sept., 1943

HUMBOLDT CURRENT (Peru Current):

Pacific coast of South America, showing location of Humboldt Current. LXXIX, p. 376, Mar., 1941

Peruvian coast, showing Humboldt Current. XLVI, p. 282, Sept., 1924

HUNGARY:

Austria-Hungary. XXIII, p. 1284, Dec., 1912

Austria-Hungary. XXVI, p. 392, Oct., 1914

Frontier cities of Italy and Austria-Hungary. XXVII, p. 628, June, 1915

Hungary. LXI, p. 707, June, 1932

Hungary. LXXIII, p. 7, Jan., 1938

I

ICE SHEETS:

Europe, showing the great sheet of ice that covered the British Isles, Scandinavia, Germany, and half of Russia during the second glacial age. XXIX, p. 115, Feb., 1916

North America at the time of maximum extent of the ice. XXI, p. 526, June, 1910

The southern part of the prehistoric Canadian ice-sheet. Photograph from a model. The glacial data are on the authority of T. C. Chamberlin. IX, pl. 9 (opp. p. 314), July, 1898

ICELAND:

Atlantic Ocean, showing air routes to Norway and Britain, via Newfoundland, Greenland, and Iceland. LXXX, p. 77, July, 1941

Isobel Wylie Hutchison's route from Reykjavík to Akureyri (inset) and Iceland's location in the North Atlantic. LIII, p. 470, Apr., 1928

IDAHO:

Bitter Root Forest Reserve. IX, pl. 12 (opp. p. 394), foldout, Sept., 1898

Central Idaho, showing extent of the Idaho Batholith (granite mass). LXX, p. 105, July, 1936

"Craters of the Moon" (volcanic lava beds). XLV, p. 306, Mar., 1924

Idaho. LXXXV, p. 644, June, 1944

A Map of Northwestern United States and Neighboring Canadian Provinces. LXXIX, supplement, 24½ x 36 inches, June, 1941

Salmon River district. LXX, p. 100, July, 1936

ILLINOIS:

Illinois, with inset of Chicago. LIX, supplement, 12½ x 19 inches, May, 1931

Main features of the Chicago Plan. XXXV, p. 40, Jan., 1919

United States of America, with inset of Chicago. XLIII, supplement, 26½ x 36¼ inches, Apr., 1923

INDIA:

Burma, home of the Chaulmoogra oil tree. XLI, p. 242, Mar., 1922

Burma and eastern India, showing Manipur, scene of battle for Upper Burma. LXXXV, p. 750, June, 1944

Geographical relation of Nepal to India, Burma, Kashmir, and Tibet. XXXVIII, p. 249, Oct., 1920

India. LXXXI, p. 238, Feb., 1942

India, from "Geographia Universalis," 1552 (Ptolemy's map). LXII, p. 765, Dec., 1932

India, superimposed on a map of America. LXXXIX, p. 470, Apr., 1946

India, with inset showing route of Thaw Expedition from Paris to India. LXXVIII, p. 729, Dec., 1940

India and adjacent countries, with inset showing areas covered by British India and the Indian States. LXXXIV, pp. 392-393, Oct., 1943

India and Burma, with insets of Bombay and Calcutta areas. Verso of map: Political Subdivisions; The Political Geography of India. LXXXIX, supplement, 30 x 25 inches, Apr., 1946

Map of China and Its Territories. Included: Mongolia, Manchuria, Chosen, East Turkestan, Tibet, Northern India. XXIII, supplement, 17 x 23 inches, Oct., 1912

Network of railroads covering India. XVI, p. 407, Sept., 1905

Tibet, showing adjacent areas of India and China. XC, p. 172, Aug., 1946

Two of the areas in which Brigadier General William Mitchell hunted tigers. XLVI, p. 550, Nov., 1924

See also Delhi; New Delhi

INDIAN OCEAN:

Indian Ocean, including Australia, New Zealand and Malaysia. LXXIX, supplement, 25½ x 32¾ inches, Mar., 1941

Indian Ocean, showing importance of Madagascar in the control of vital sea lanes. LXXXI, p. 803, June, 1942

INDIAN TERRITORY, U. S.:

Indian Territory, showing boundary lines of the Five Civilized Tribes. IX, p. 482, Dec., 1898

Indian Territory, showing progress of subdivision survey up to January 1, 1896. VII, p. 113, Mar., 1896

INDIANA:

Indiana, showing population center of the U. S. (1930 census). LXX, pp. 272-273, Sept., 1936

Northeastern United States. LXXXVIII, supplement, 41 x 26½ inches, Sept., 1945

INDO-CHINA. *See* French Indo-China

INDONESIA. *See* Netherlands East Indies

INTRACOASTAL WATERWAY, U. S.:

North Carolina, with Intracoastal Waterway marked. LXXX, pp. 184–185, Aug., 1941

See also Gulf Coast, *for* Gulf Intracoastal Waterway

IOWA:

Iowa—The Hawkeye State. LXXVI, pp. 146-147, Aug., 1939

IRAN (Persia):

Iran, showing route of Trans-Iranian Railway. LXXVI, p. 329, Sept., 1939

Iran and adjacent regions, showing highways, railways, and oil pipe lines. LXXXIV, p. 132, Aug., 1943

Persepolis and adjacent regions. LXIV, p. 383, Oct., 1933

Persia. XIX, p. 384, May, 1908

Persia. XXXIX, p. 418, Apr., 1921

Railways constructed and proposed in Asia Minor and Persia. XI, p. 202, May, 1900

World trouble spot, the oil-rich Middle East. LXXXIX, pp. 396-397, Mar., 1946

IRAQ:

Bible Lands and the Cradle of Western Civilization; Insets: Holy Land Today, Holy Land in Biblical Times, Jerusalem, Traditional Route of the Exodus, St. Paul's Travels and the Seven Churches, The Crusades. XC, supplement, 32 x 22 inches, Dec., 1946

Bible Lands and the Cradle of Western Civilization; Insets: Jerusalem, The Holy Land, Economic Development, Route of the Exodus, St. Paul's Travels and the Seven Churches, The Crusades, Empire of Alexander the Great. LXXIV, supplement, 25 x 35 inches, Dec., 1938

Europe and the Near East. LVI, supplement, 34¼ x 39¼ inches, Dec., 1929

Location of ancient ruins in modern Iraq. LVII, p. 101, Jan., 1930

Near East, showing naval bases, airports, highways, railways, oil pipe lines, and oil pumping stations. LXXX, pp. 144-145, Aug., 1941

Near East, showing Turkey, Iraq, and adjacent regions, with naval bases, airports, highways, railways, and oil pipe lines. LXXXII, pp. 388-389, Sept., 1942

Railways constructed in and proposed in Asia Minor and Persia. XI, p. 202, May, 1900

World trouble spot, the oil-rich Middle East. LXXXIX, pp. 396-397, Mar., 1946

IRELAND:

Aran Islands, with inset of Ireland. LIX, p. 752, June, 1931

Ireland. LI, p. 262, Mar., 1927

Ireland, mother of new Eire. LXXVII, p. 653, May, 1940

A Modern Pilgrim's Map of the British Isles or More Precisely the Kingdom of Great Britain and Northern Ireland and the Irish Free State. LXXI, supplement, 29 x 35 inches, June, 1937

Northern Ireland, showing the counties of Ulster. LXVIII, p. 574, Nov., 1935

ISRAEL. *See* Palestine

ITALIAN ISLANDS OF THE AEGEAN. *See* Dodecanese Islands

ITALY:

Austro-Italo Alpine region, with surrounding territory. XXVII, p. 374, Apr., 1915

Bay of Naples. XVII, p. 279, May, 1906

Central and northern Italy. LXXXIV, pp. 708-709, Dec., 1943

Central Italy. LXX, p. 353, Sept., 1936

Central Italy, showing route followed by Horace (Roman poet) from Rome to Brindisi. LXVIII, p. 774, Dec., 1935

Classical Lands of the Mediterranean. LXXVII, supplement, 35¼ x 26 inches, Mar., 1940

Frontier cities of Italy and Austria-Hungary. XXVII, p. 628, June, 1915

Italy. XXX, p. 360, Oct., 1916

Italy, with a detail of the Umbrian and Tuscan hill towns. LIII, p. 404, Apr., 1928

Italy, with a detail of Trulli-Land. LVII, p. 233, Feb., 1930

Lake of Garda district. War zone on Austro-Italian frontier indicated. LXVIII, p. 334, Sept., 1935

Northern Italy. LXVIII, p. 332, Sept., 1935

Pontine Marshes, with inset of Italy. LXVI, p. 202, Aug., 1934

Position of Venice on a group of mud banks. XXVII, p. 630, June, 1915

Relation of Sardinia to the mainland of Italy. XLIII, p. 5, Jan., 1923

Riviera region. LXVII, p. 69, Jan., 1935

Rome-Naples area, showing main arteries and important sites of antiquity. XC, p. 569, Nov., 1946

Site of Carthage, Tunisia; also the Pontine Marshes. XLV, p. 394, Apr., 1924

See also Sardinia (Island); Sicily (Island)

IWO JIMA (Sulphur Island), Volcano Islands:

Southeast Asia and Pacific Islands from the Indies and the Philippines to the Solomons, with inset of Iwo Jima. LXXXVI, supplement, 41 x 26½ inches, Oct., 1944

IZU SHICHITO (Islands), Pacific Ocean. *See* Hachijo Jima

J

JALUIT (Atoll), Marshall Islands:

Pacific Ocean and the Bay of Bengal, with inset of Jaluit. LXXXIV, supplement, 36½ x 26½ inches, Sept., 1943

Strategic isles of the Pacific. LXXXV, pp. 392-393, 17 island maps, Apr., 1944

JAMAICA:

Jamaica, the key to the Caribbean. LI, p. 4, Jan., 1927

Mexico, Central America, and the West Indies, with inset of Jamaica. LXVI, supplement, 23 x 40 inches, Dec., 1934

Mexico, Central America, and the West Indies, with inset of Jamaica. LXXVI, supplement, 24 x 41 inches, Dec., 1939

JAPAN:

The Chinese Empire and Japan: Showing the provinces, treaty ports, railways, etc., and the present condition of the Russian Railway through Manchuria to Port Arthur. XI, pl. 8, foldout (opp. p. 297), Aug., 1900

Development of the commerce of Japan between 1874 and 1904 resulting from the construction of railways. XVI, p. 406, Sept., 1905

Formosa (Taiwan), showing its geographical relation to Japan, China, and the Philippines. XXXVII, p. 262, Mar., 1920

Japan. LXIX, p. 444, Apr., 1936

Japan and Adjacent Regions of Asia and the Pacific Ocean, with insets of industrial centers of Japan and the Marshall Islands. LXXXV, supplement, 26½ x 34½ inches, Apr., 1944

Japan and Korea, with insets of Kuril Islands, Pescadores, Karafuto, Ryukyu Islands, Okinawa, Formosa, Tokyo, and location of Japan in the western Pacific. LXXXVIII, supplement, 37 x 26½ inches, Dec., 1945

Sakurajima, showing the lava flows of Japan's greatest volcanic eruption. XLV, p. 449, Apr., 1924

Sketch map of Japan, showing the region devastated by the earthquake wave of June 15, 1896. VII, pl. xxxi, foldout, Sept., 1896

See also Iwo Jima; Ogasawara Shoto; Okinawa Gunto; Paramushiro Jima; Ryukyu Retto; *and* the following mandated and occupied territories: Caroline Islands; Formosa; Korea; Manchuria (Manchukuo); Marianas Islands; Marshall Islands; Palau Islands

JARVIS (Island), Line Islands:

Pacific Ocean and the Bay of Bengal, with inset of Jarvis Island. LXXXIV, supplement, 36½ x 26½ inches, Sept., 1943

JAVA:

Borneo and Java. LXXXVIII, p. 297, Sept., 1945

Dutch East Indies. LVI, p. 347, Sept., 1929

Far East, with enlargement of Java. LXXXI, p. 91, Jan., 1942

JERUSALEM, Holy Land:

Bible Lands and the Cradle of Western Civilization; Insets: Holy Land Today, Holy Land in Biblical Times, Jerusalem, Traditional Route of the Exodus, St. Paul's Travels and the Seven Churches, The Crusades. XC, supplement, 32 x 22 inches, Dec., 1946

Bible Lands and the Cradle of Western Civilization; Insets: Jerusalem, The Holy Land, Economic Development, Route of the Exodus, St. Paul's Travels and the Seven Churches, The Crusades, Empire of Alexander the Great. LXXIV, supplement, 25 x 35 inches, Dec., 1938

JORDAN. *See* Trans-Jordan

JORDAN (River), Palestine-Trans-Jordan:

Jordan River from Galilee to Dead Sea. LXXVIII, p. 784, Dec., 1940

JUGOSLAVIA. *See* Yugoslavia

K

KAMCHATKA (Region), U. S. S. R.:

Bering's chart of his first voyage. From D'Anville's Atlas, 1737. The first published map of his explorations. II, foldout (opp. p. 111), May, 1890

Carte Généralè des Découvertes de l'Amiral de Fonte, et autres Navigateurs Espagnols, Anglois et Russes pour la recherche du Passage à la Mer du Sud. Par M. De l'Isle. III, supplement, 16¼ x 13 inches, Jan. 28, 1892; Feb. 19, 1892

KANSAS:

Kansas, showing geographic center of the United States. LXXII, pp. 138-139, Aug., 1937

KANSU (Province), China:

China, showing location of Choni in Kansu Province. LIV, p. 576, Nov., 1928

Quake-stricken area in Kansu Province, China. XLI, p. 448, May, 1922

KARAFUTO (Island), Japan:

Japan and Korea, with insets of Kuril Islands, Pescadores, Karafuto, Ryukyu Islands, Okinawa, Formosa, Tokyo, and location of Japan in the western Pacific. LXXXVIII, supplement, 37 x 26½ inches, Dec., 1945

KAZAN RETTO (Volcano Islands), Pacific Ocean. *See* Iwo Jima

KENTUCKY:

Kentucky. LXXXII, pp. 62-63, July, 1942

Southeastern Kentucky, showing Cumberland Gap. LXXXIV, p. 745, Dec., 1943

Virginia, North Carolina, Kentucky, and Tennessee, showing new Eastern National Park-to-Park Highway. LXV, pp. 666-667, June, 1934

KENYA:

Route of Uganda Railway. XIII, p. 170, May, 1902

Territory covered in airplane flights of Walter Mittelholzer. LXI, p. 466, Apr., 1932

KERR, MARK B.: Maps:

Drainage map of northwestern Ecuador; also, route followed by Mark B. Kerr, on survey. VII, p. 239, July, 1896

Sketch map of Mount St. Elias region, Alaska. By Mark B. Kerr. III, pl. 8 (opp. p. 75), May 29, 1891

KISKA (Island), Aleutian Islands:

Pacific Ocean and the Bay of Bengal, with inset of Kiska. LXXXIV, supplement, 36½ x 26½ inches, Sept., 1943

KLONDIKE (Region), Canada:

The Gold and Coal Fields of Alaska, Together with the Principal Steamer Routes and Trails; Insets: Trails from Tide Water to the Headwaters of the Yukon River; The Klondike Gold Region, Canada. IX, pl. 4, supplement, 25 x 30 inches, Apr., 1898

KOREA:

Chosen and adjacent islands. LXIV, p. 424, Oct., 1933

KOREA—*Continued*

Japan and Korea, with insets of Kuril Islands, Pescadores, Karafuto, Ryukyu Islands, Okinawa, Formosa, Tokyo, and location of Japan in the western Pacific. LXXXVIII, supplement, 37 x 26½ inches, Dec., 1945

Korea. LXXXVIII, p. 433, Oct., 1945

Korea, showing location of towns, walled towns, mountains, signal fires; Province of Kyong-Sang-Do, southeastern Korea. II, foldout, Aug., 1890

Korea: The region traversed by Mr. Andrews' expedition extends along the upper courses of the Tumen and the Yalu Rivers. XXXVI, p. 24, July, 1919

Map of China and Its Territories. Included: Mongolia, Manchuria, Chosen, East Turkestan, Tibet, Northern India. XXIII, supplement, 17 x 23 inches, Oct., 1912

Map of Korea and Manchuria. Prepared by the Second Division, General Staff (Military Information Division), War Department, Washington, U. S. A. Insets: Vladivostok; Port Arthur; and index map. XV, supplement, 36 x 42 inches, Mar., 1904

Monastic establishments in the Diamond Mountains. XLVI, p. 355, Oct., 1924

Sketch-map of Korea: Localities where gold has been found are marked. II, fig. iii (opp. p. 242), Aug., 1890

KURIL ISLANDS (U. S. S. R.). *See* Chishima Retto

KUSAIE (Island), Caroline Islands:

Strategic isles of the Pacific. LXXXV, pp. 392-393, 17 island maps, Apr., 1944

KWAJALEIN (Atoll), Marshall Islands:

Pacific Ocean and the Bay of Bengal, with inset of Kwajalein. LXXXIV, supplement, 36½ x 26½ inches, Sept., 1943

Strategic isles of the Pacific. LXXXV, pp. 392-393, 17 island maps, Apr., 1944

KWANGSI (Province), China:

Kwangsi, one of China's least-known provinces. LXXII, p. 674, Dec., 1937

L

LANGUAGES:

World, showing distribution of languages and areas occupied by U. S. soldiers with dates of their arrival. LXXXIV, pp. 696-697, Dec., 1943

LAPLAND:

Northern portions of Norway, Sweden, Finland, and the Kola Peninsula of the U. S. S. R. LXXVI, p. 645, Nov., 1939

LATAKIA:

Bible Lands and the Cradle of Western Civilization; Insets: Jerusalem, The Holy Land, Economic Development, Route of the Exodus, St. Paul's Travels and the Seven Churches, The Crusades, Empire of Alexander the Great. LXXIV, supplement, 25 x 35 inches, Dec., 1938

LATAKIA—*Continued*

Crusader castles. LIX, p. 371, Mar., 1931

Crusader trails and castles. LXIV, p. 654, Dec., 1933

Eastern shores of the Mediterranean. XXXVIII, p. 89, Aug., 1920

Latakia. LVIII, p. 485, Oct., 1930

Latakia and Lebanon. LXIV, p. 103, July, 1933

LATIN AMERICA:

Miami-Montevideo air-mail route. LVII, p. 264, Mar., 1930

Route followed by Lindbergh in his flight over 13 Latin-American countries. LIII, p. 532, May, 1928

Route of A. F. Tschiffely on his horseback journey from Buenos Aires to Washington. LV, p. 140, Feb., 1929

Route of the trail-blazing flight of U. S. Army airplanes through 20 countries of Latin America. LII, p. 452, Oct., 1927

South America, Central America, and West Indies. LIX, p. 4, Jan., 1931

See also names of countries and islands

LATVIA:

Baltic republic of Latvia. XLVI, p. 405, Oct., 1924

LEBANON:

Bible Lands and the Cradle of Western Civilization; Insets: Holy Land Today, Holy Land in Biblical Times, Jerusalem, Traditional Route of the Exodus, St. Paul's Travels and the Seven Churches, The Crusades. XC, supplement, 32 x 22 inches, Dec., 1946

Bible Lands and the Cradle of Western Civilization; Insets: Jerusalem, The Holy Land, Economic Development, Route of the Exodus, St. Paul's Travels and the Seven Churches, The Crusades, Empire of Alexander the Great. LXXIV, supplement, 25 x 35 inches, Dec., 1938

Crusader castles. LIX, p. 371, Mar., 1931

Crusader trails and castles. LXIV, p. 654, Dec., 1933

Eastern shores of the Mediterranean. XXXVIII, p. 89, Aug., 1920

Lebanon. LVIII, p. 485, Oct., 1930

Lebanon and Latakia. LXIV, p. 103, July, 1933

LEEWARD ISLANDS, West Indies:

Hispaniola, Puerto Rico, and Leeward Islands. LXXIII, pp. 274-275, Mar., 1938

Leeward and Windward Islands: Like a curving shield the West Indies guard the Panama Canal. LXXIX, p. 5, Jan., 1941

See also Saba

LESLEY, J. P.: Map:

Topographic map of Pennsylvania, by J. P. Lesley (1871). I, p: 188, July, 1889

LESSER ANTILLES. *See* Aruba; Bonaire; Curacao; Leeward Islands; Martinique; Saba; St. Vincent; Tobago; Trinidad; Windward Islands; *and* Virgin Islands

LESSER SUNDA ISLANDS:

Lesser Sunda Islands. LXXV, p. 316, Mar., 1939

See also Timor

LEVANT STATES:

Asia Minor and the Levant. L, p. 652, Dec., 1926

Bible Lands and the Cradle of Western Civilization. LXXIV, supplement, 25 x 35 inches, Dec., 1938

Crusader castles. LIX, p. 371, Mar., 1931

Crusader trails and castles. LXIV, p. 654, Dec., 1933

Eastern shores of the Mediterranean. XXXVIII, p. 89, Aug., 1920

Latakia and Lebanon. LVIII, p. 485, Oct., 1930

Latakia and Lebanon. LXIV, p. 103, July, 1933

Syria. XXXVI, p. 441, Nov., 1919

LIBIA:

Italian Libia and environs. LVII, p. 690, June, 1930

Italian Libya. XLVIII, p. 138, Aug., 1925

Mediterranean coast of Libia and Egypt. LXXVIII, p. 810, Dec., 1940

Route of Hassanein Bey through the Libyan Desert. XLVI, p. 236, Sept., 1924

LIECHTENSTEIN:

Liechtenstein. LII, p. 612, Nov., 1927

LIFE ZONES:

Life zones of the United States. VI, pl. 14, Dec. 29, 1894

See also Temperature Maps

LINE ISLANDS, Pacific Ocean. *See* Caroline Island; Christmas Island; Fanning Island; Flint Island; Jarvis; Malden Island; Palmyra; Starbuck Island; Vostok Island

LINGAYEN GULF, Luzon, Philippine Islands:

The Philippines, with insets of Manila, Lingayen Gulf, and a location map of the Philippines. LXXXVII, supplement, 17½ x 26 inches, Mar., 1945

LONG ISLAND, New York:

Movement of Rockaway Beach and Inlet, Long Island, from 1835 to 1908. XX, p. 830, Sept., 1909

LONG ISLAND SOUND, Connecticut-New York:

Tidal hours in Long Island Sound. IX, p. 506, Dec., 1898

LORD HOWE (Island), Tasman Sea:

Lord Howe Island (inset). LXVIII, p. 118, July, 1935

LORRAINE (Region), France:

Metz, Nancy, and Epinal regions. LXXXVII, p. 367, Mar., 1945

LOUISIANA:

Bird refuges of Louisiana. XXIV, p. 373, Mar., 1913

Gulf of Mexico, showing coastal areas of United States and Mexico. LXXXV, pp. 8-9, Jan., 1944

Louisiana, with inset of New Orleans. LVII, supplement, 13 x 13¼ inches, Apr., 1930

LOUISIANA—*Continued*

Mississippi Delta formations. XXXIII, p. 533, June, 1918

Southeastern Louisiana, showing Terrebonne Parish, with inset of Gulf Coast. LXXXVI, p. 509, Oct., 1944

United States of America, with inset of New Orleans. XLIII, supplement, 26½ x 36¼ inches, Apr. 1923

LOWER CALIFORNIA. *See* Baja California

LUXEMBOURG (Grand Duchy):

Luxemburg. XLVI, p. 506, Nov., 1924

M

McKINLEY, Mount. *See* Alaska

MADAGASCAR:

Africa, with insets of the Cape Verde Islands, relief map, and a table of airline distances in statute miles. LXXXIII, supplement, 29¼ x 31½ inches, Feb., 1943

Madagascar. LXXXI, p. 803, June, 1942

Map of Madagascar, superimposed on the eastern seaboard of North America. LXXXI, p. 802, June, 1942

Route followed by Charles F. Swingle in Madagascar. LVI, p. 184, Aug., 1929

MADEIRA (Islands), Atlantic Ocean:

Madeira and Porto Santo Islands. LXVI, p. 85, July, 1934

MAGELLAN, FERDINAND: Voyages:

Magellan's circumnavigation. V, p. 11, chart, Apr. 7, 1893

Route of Magellan's voyage. LXII, pp. 700-701, Dec., 1932

MAGELLAN, Strait of:

Outline map showing the principal points in the Straits of Magellan. VIII, p. 131, May, 1897

MAINE:

Cotidals from St. Johns, Newfoundland; Maine coast, shown. IX, p. 502, Dec., 1898

Maine. LXVII, pp. 538-539, May, 1935

Northeastern United States. LXXXVIII, supplement, 41 x 26½ inches, Sept., 1945

MAKIN (Atoll), Gilbert Islands:

Gilbert Islands, with insets of Tarawa and Makin. LXXXVII, p. 135, Feb., 1945

Pacific Ocean and the Bay of Bengal, with inset of Makin. LXXXIV, supplement, 36½ x 26½ inches, Sept., 1943

MALAY ARCHIPELAGO:

Far East, with inset of the Moluccas. LXXIX, p. 538, May, 1941

Indian Ocean, including Australia, New Zealand and Malaysia. LXXIX, supplement, 25½ x 32¾ inches, Mar., 1941

Southeast Asia and Pacific Islands from the Indies and the Philippines to the Solomons, with 22 inset maps of important cities and islands. LXXXVI, supplement, 41 x 26½ inches, Oct., 1944

MALAY ARCHIPELAGO—*Continued*

See also Bali; Borneo; Celebes; Java; Netherlands East Indies; New Guinea; Philippine Islands; Sumatra; Timor

MALAY PENINSULA:

Indian Ocean, including Australia, New Zealand and Malaysia. LXXIX, supplement, 25½ x 32¾ inches, Mar., 1941

Malay States, Thailand, and French Indo-China, with inset of Singapore. LXXX, p. 662, Nov., 1941

Southeast Asia and Pacific Islands from the Indies and the Philippines to the Solomons, with 22 inset maps of important cities and islands. LXXXVI, supplement, 41 x 26½ inches, Oct., 1944

Strategic geographic position of Singapore, with an inset of the Malay Peninsula. XLIX, p. 238, Mar., 1926

See also Singapore; Thailand

MALDEN ISLAND, Line Islands:

Pacific Ocean and the Bay of Bengal, with inset of Malden Island. LXXXIV, supplement, 36½ x 26½ inches, Sept., 1943

MALTA (Islands), Mediterranean Sea:

Malta, a tiny island which has played a great role in world history. XXXVII, p. 449, May, 1920

Malta, Gozo, and Comino. LXVIII, p. 650, Nov., 1935

Malta, Gozo, Comino, and Filfla. LXXXIII, p. 378, Mar., 1943

Maltese Islands. LXXVIII, p. 257, Aug., 1940

MAN, Isle of, England:

Isle of Man, with inset of the British Isles. LXXI, p. 588, May, 1937

MANCHUKUO. *See* Manchuria

MANCHURIA:

Kirin, Harbin, Vladivostok. Map showing seat of war in Manchuria (Beginning just north of Mukden, and covering the country north to Harbin and east to Vladivostok; the map shows all roads, trails, and mountains over which the armies must pass). XVI, supplement, 18 x 44 inches, June, 1905

Manchuria. LVI, p. 384, Oct., 1929

Manchuria: Japan brews another war with Russia. LXXXII, p. 607, Nov., 1942

Manchuria, with inset map showing where railway interests of Japan, Russia, and China clash. LXI, p. 106, Jan., 1932

Military operations in the Far East. XV, p. 129, Mar., 1904

Map of China and Its Territories. Included: Mongolia, Manchuria, Chosen, East Turkestan, Tibet, Northern India. XXIII, supplement, 17 x 23 inches, Oct., 1912

Map of Korea and Manchuria. Prepared by the Second Division, General Staff (Military Information Division), War Department, Washington, U. S. A. Insets: Vladivostok; Port Arthur; and index map. XV, supplement, 30 x 42 inches, Mar., 1904

MANIHIKI (Atoll), South Pacific Ocean:

Pacific Ocean and the Bay of Bengal, with inset of Manihiki. LXXXIV, supplement, 36½ x 26½ inches, Sept., 1943

MANILA, Luzon, Philippine Islands:

Manila as a distributing point for commerce. XIII, p. 314, Aug., 1902

The Philippines, with insets of Manila, Lingayen Gulf, and a location map of the Philippines. LXXXVII, supplement, 17½ x 26 inches, Mar., 1945

Southeast Asia and Pacific Islands from the Indies and the Philippines to the Solomons, with inset of Manila area. LXXXVI, supplement, 41 x 26½ inches, Oct., 1944

MANILA BAY, Philippine Islands:

Chart of Manila Bay. IX, p. 275, June, 1898

See also Philippine Islands

MAP SURVEYING. *See* Mother Maps

MARAJÓ ISLAND, Brazil:

Marajó Island. LXXIV, p. 638, Nov., 1938

MARCUS ISLAND (Minami Tori Shima), Pacific Ocean:

Pacific Ocean and the Bay of Bengal, with inset of Marcus Island. LXXXIV, supplement, 36½ x 26½ inches, Sept., 1943

Southeast Asia and Pacific Islands from the Indies and the Philippines to the Solomons, with inset of Marcus. LXXXVI, supplement, 41 x 26½ inches, Oct., 1944

Strategic isles of the Pacific. LXXXV, pp. 392-393, 17 island maps, Apr., 1944

MARIANAS ISLANDS, West Pacific Ocean:

Strategic isles of the Pacific: Chichi Jima, Eniwetok, Guam, Hachijo, Haha Jima, Jaluit, Kusaie, Kwajalein, Marcus, Palau, Paramushiro, Ponape, Rota, Saipan, Tinian, Truk, Wake, Yap. LXXXV, pp. 392-393, 17 island maps, Apr., 1944

The taking of Saipan opens the gate in Japan's wall of island defenses. LXXXVII, p. 447, Apr., 1945

See also Guam; Pagan; Rota; Saipan; Tinian

MARNE (River), France:

Sketch maps showing the Marne River, branches and diversions. VII, pp. 199, 201, June, 1896

MARQUESAS ISLANDS, South Pacific Ocean:

Marquesas, Tuamotu, and Austral Islands. XLVIII, p. 366, Oct., 1925

Marquesas Islands. LXXIX, p. 112, Jan., 1941

MARSHALL ISLANDS, Pacific Ocean:

Marshall Islands, with inset of Pacific islands. LXXXVIII, p. 329, Sept., 1945

Strategic isles of the Pacific: Chichi Jima, Eniwetok, Guam, Hachijo, Haha Jima, Jaluit, Kusaie, Kwajalein, Marcus, Palau, Paramushiro, Ponape, Rota, Saipan, Tinian, Truk, Wake, Yap. LXXXV, pp. 392-393, 17 island maps, Apr., 1944

See also Eniwetok; Jaluit; Kwajalein; Wotje

MARTINIQUE (Island), West Indies:

Martinique, showing mountainous character of the island. XIII, p. 211, June, 1902

Sketch map of Martinique. XIII, p. 231, July, 1902

Zones of devastation in Martinique caused by volcanic eruptions. XIII, p. 260, July, 1902

MARYLAND:

Fishing Point, Maryland, from surveys of 1849 and 1908, illustrating building out of a point on the coast. XX, p. 828, Sept., 1909

George Washington's travels in Maryland and West Virginia. LXI, p. 36, Jan., 1932

Historic and Scenic Reaches of the Nation's Capital. LXXIV, supplement, 26½ x 31¼ inches, July, 1938

Maryland. LXXIX, pp. 404-405, Apr., 1941

Maryland, Delaware, and District of Columbia, with inset of Baltimore. LI, supplement, 12 x 18 inches, Feb., 1927

Potomac River windings in Maryland, Virginia, and West Virginia. LXXXVIII, pp. 36-37, July, 1945

Tidewater Maryland, showing route of the "Tralee." LXXVI, p. 361, Sept., 1939

United States of America, with inset of Baltimore. XLIII, supplement, 26½ x 36¼ inches, Apr., 1923

MASSACHUSETTS:

Cape Cod. LXXXIX, p. 741, June, 1946

Cape Cod Canal. XXVI, p. 186, Aug., 1914

Lynn Harbor: Where the land has scored signal victories over the sea. XXXIII, p. 534, June, 1918

A Map of the Travels of George Washington, with inset of Boston. LXI, supplement, 20 x 29 inches, Jan., 1932

Northeastern United States. LXXXVIII, supplement, 41 x 26½ inches, Sept., 1945

The Reaches of New York City. LXXV, supplement, 26½ x 29 inches, Apr., 1939

Six maps showing changes in shore of Nantucket Island, Massachusetts, from 1890 to 1908. XX, p. 831, Sept., 1909

Tidal and cotidal chart (1864) of Buzzards Bay and Nantucket Sound, by Dr. Alexander Dallas Bache. IX, p. 471, Nov., 1898

United States of America, with inset of Boston. XLIII, supplement, 26½ x 36¼ inches, Apr., 1923

See also Nantucket (Island)

MATTO GROSSO (State), Brazil:

Southern Matto Grosso and Paraguay, with inset showing river system. LXXXIV, p. 461, Oct., 1943

MEDITERRANEAN REGIONS:

Central Europe and the Mediterranean as of September 1, 1939. LXXVI, supplement, 36½ x 26½ inches, Oct., 1939

Classical Lands of the Mediterranean. LXXVII, supplement, 35¼ x 26 inches, Mar., 1940

Cotidal lines for the Mediterranean Sea. XVII, p. 306, June, 1906

Eastern Mediterranean, showing location of Italian islands of the Aegean. LXXIX, p. 451, Apr., 1941

MEDITERRANEAN REGIONS—*Continued*

Eastern Mediterranean, with an enlargement of Crete. LXXXIV, p. 550, Nov., 1943

Europe and northern Africa, showing extent of Roman Empire. XC, pp. 552-553, Nov., 1946

Europe and the Mediterranean. LXXIII, supplement, 34 x 39 inches, Apr., 1938

Island of Crete. LV, p. 250, Feb., 1929

Map of the Countries Bordering the Mediterranean Sea. XXIII, supplement, 10 x 18 inches, Jan., 1912

Map showing central position of Maltese Islands. LXVIII, p. 651, Nov., 1935

Mediterranean, showing strategic position of Malta. LXXVIII, p. 257, Aug., 1940

The Mediterranean Basin. XII, p. 255, July, 1901

Mediterranean regions. XXII, p. 1047, Nov., 1911

Mediterranean regions. XXII, p. 1089, Dec., 1911

Mediterranean regions. LXXXI, pp. 530-531, Apr., 1942

Mediterranean regions, showing bombing ranges from Bizerte, Tunisia. LXXXIV, pp. 8-9, July, 1943

Mediterranean regions, with inset map of Sicily. LXXXIV, pp. 312-313, Sept., 1943

Route of the "Bonita" (Breton yawl) on its Mediterranean voyage. LV, p. 250, Feb., 1929

Southeastern France, showing Mediterranean coast. LXXXVI, p. 428, Oct., 1944

Tunisia, Africa's northernmost tip, nearly divides the Mediterranean into two great lakes. LXXI, p. 349, Mar., 1937

See also names of countries and islands

MELANESIA:

New Guinea, New Caledonia, and Fiji command the shortest supply routes from America to Australia, with table of airline distances. LXXXI, pp. 698-699, June, 1942

Pacific Ocean and the Bay of Bengal, with inset maps of important islands, and table of airline distances in statute miles. LXXXIV, supplement, 36½ x 26½ inches, Sept., 1943

Sovereignty and Mandate Boundary Lines in 1921 of the Islands of the Pacific. XL, supplement, 19 x 25 inches, Dec., 1921

See also Fiji Islands; New Caledonia; New Guinea; New Hebrides; Solomon Islands

MESOPOTAMIA. *See* Bible Lands (Supplements)

MEUSE (River), France:

Sketch map of the Meuse, showing the Bar, the Aire, and the Aisne. VII, p. 232, July, 1896

Sketch map of the Seine, the Meuse, and the Moselle. VII, p. 189, June, 1896

Sketch maps showing diversion of the Toul from the Meuse to the Moselle. VII, p. 229, July, 1896

Valley of the Meuse, near Dun-sur-Meuse. VII, pl. XXIV (opp. p. 195), June, 1896

Valley of the Meuse, near St. Mihiel. VII, pl. XXIII, June, 1896

MEXICO:

Archeological sites in Veracruz and Tabasco explored by National Geographic Society-Smithsonian Expedition of 1940. LXXVIII, p. 313, Sept., 1940

Area drained by the Great Canal. XIII, p. 7, Jan., 1902

Baja California, with inset showing relationship to Mexico and States of the U. S. Southwest. LXXXII, p. 258, Aug., 1942

Bird migration routes from South America to North America converge funnel-like in Central America. Inset of Veracruz and Tabasco, Mexico, showing La Venta region, a natural bird observatory. LXXXVII, p. 188, Feb., 1945

Central America and southern Mexico. XLVII, p. 64, Jan., 1925

Central Mexico. LXVI, p. 760, Dec., 1934

Central Mexico, showing belt of volcanoes. LXXXV, p. 131, Feb., 1944

Changes in the estuary of the Colorado River. XIX, p. 54, Jan., 1908

Colorado Desert region. XI, p. 339, Sept., 1900

The Countries of the Caribbean, Including Mexico, Central America, the West Indies and the Panama Canal, with detailed insets of the Panama Canal and the Canal Zone, Porto Rico and the Virgin Islands, and Guantanamo Bay, Cuba. XLI, supplement, 25 x 44 inches, Feb., 1922

Country of the Old Yuma Trail. XII, p. 132, Apr., 1901

Course of the Rio Grande. LXXVI, 4 maps, pp. 427, 428, 440, 453, Oct., 1939

Cruise of the *Kinkajou* to desert islands of Mexico. LXXX, p. 340, Sept., 1941

Desert islands of Lower California. XLIV, p. 73, July, 1923

Gulf of Mexico, showing coastal areas of United States and Mexico. LXXXV, pp. 8-9, Jan., 1944

Isthmus of Tehuantepec, showing the routes of the National Railroad of Tehuantepec and the proposed Eads Ship Railway. VII, p. 67, Feb., 1896

Jalisco and Central Mexico. LXV, p. 331, Mar., 1934

Location of Cuicuilco and the Pedregal lava flow which has preserved the ancient mound. XLIV, p. 207, Aug., 1923

Lower California, showing route of E. W. Nelson. XXII, p. 446, May, 1911

Lower Colorado River, showing irrigable lands. XVII, p. 94, Feb., 1906

Lower Colorado River, showing the great new lake rising in Salton Sink. XVIII, p. 36, Jan., 1907

Map of Mexico. XXX, supplement, 20 x 29 inches, July, 1916

Mexico. XXI, p. 1050, Dec., 1910

Mexico. XXII, supplement, 17 x 24½ inches, May, 1911

Mexico. XXV, supplement, 17 x 24½ inches, May, 1914

Mexico, Central America, and the West Indies. LXVI, supplement, 23 x 40 inches, Dec., 1934

Mexico, Central America, and the West Indies. LXXVI, supplement, 24 x 41 inches, Dec., 1939

MEXICO—*Continued*

Mexico, showing the route of the Old Spanish Road. XLIII, p. 230, Mar., 1923

Mexico and the peninsula of Lower California. XXXVI, p. 310, Oct., 1919

New center of Maya culture discovered in Vera Cruz by National Geographic Society-Smithsonian Institution Expedition. LXXVI, p. 184, Aug., 1939

Railways of Mexico. XIII, (opp. p. 1), Jan., 1902

Río Balsas region. XC, p. 254, Aug., 1946

Route of Cortés from Veracruz to Mexico City. LXXVIII, pp. 338-339, Sept., 1940

Seriland, Sonora, Mexico, including Tiburon Island, from surveys by Bureau American Ethnology Expedition, 1895; location map. VII, pl. XIV, foldout, Apr., 1896

Southern Mexico, showing the route of Collins and Doyle. XXII, p. 317, Mar., 1911

State of Oaxaca. LI, p. 504, May, 1927

United States and adjoining portions of Canada and Mexico. LXIII, supplement, 26 x 40 inches, May, 1933

The United States and adjoining portions of Canada and Mexico. LXXVIII, supplement, 41 x 26½ inches, Dec., 1940

United States-Mexico boundary. XXXVIII, p. 75, July, 1920

Veracruz, Tabasco, Oaxaca, and Chiapas, showing archeological sites explored by National Geographic Society-Smithsonian Institution Expeditions. LXXX, p. 283, Sept., 1941

Veracruz, Tabasco, Oaxaca, and Chiapas, showing archeological sites explored by National Geographic Society-Smithsonian Institution Expeditions. LXXXII, p. 642, Nov., 1942

Veracruz, Tabasco, Oaxaca, and Chiapas, showing archeological sites explored by National Geographic Society-Smithsonian Institution Expeditions. LXXXIV, p. 325, Sept., 1943

Wanderings of the Rio Grande and of the old boundary. XXIV, p. 384, Mar., 1913

West coast of Mexico. XLII, p. 452, Nov., 1922

Yucatán, Campeche, and Quintana Roo. LXX, p. 595, Nov., 1936

MEXICO, Gulf of (Region). *See* Gulf Coast

MICHIGAN:

Isle Royal. LX, p. 760, Dec., 1931

Michigan. LXXXVI, pp. 680-681, Dec., 1944

Michigan's Lower Peninsula and the eastern half of the Upper Peninsula. LIII, p. 275, Mar., 1928

Northeastern United States. LXXXVIII, supplement, 41 x 26½ inches, Sept., 1945

United States of America, with inset of Detroit. XLIII, supplement, 26½ x 36¼ inches, Apr., 1923

Western half of Michigan's Upper Peninsula. LIII, p. 274, Mar., 1928

MICHOACAN (State), Mexico:

Río Balsas region. XC, p. 254, Aug., 1946

MICRONESIA:

Japanese Micronesia, with insets of Yap, Ponape, and Palau Islands. LXIX, p. 483, Apr., 1936

Pacific islands, showing Japanese mandate, with insets of Palau, Ponape, and Truk Islands. LXXXI, pp. 764-765, June, 1942

Pacific islands, showing Micronesia and surrounding islands, with a table of airline distances. LXXXI, pp. 698-699, June, 1942

Pacific Ocean, with inset maps of important islands and island groups. LXX, supplement, 31 x 38 inches, Dec., 1936; revised in 1942

Pacific Ocean and the Bay of Bengal, with inset maps of important islands, and table of airline distances in statute miles. LXXXIV, supplement, 36½ x 26½ inches, Sept., 1943

South Pacific archipelagoes, including the Marquesas group: Note the location of Yap among the Caroline Islands. XXXVI, p. 281, Oct., 1919

Sovereignty and Mandate Boundary Lines in 1921 of the Islands of the Pacific. XL, supplement, 19 x 25 inches, Dec., 1921

See also Caroline Islands; Gilbert Islands; Guam; Marianas Islands; Marshall Islands; Palau Islands; Truk Islands

MID-ATLANTIC RIDGE, Atlantic Ocean:

World globe, showing submarine mountain ranges and deeps of Atlantic Ocean. LXXXVII, p. 112, Jan., 1945

MIDDLE EAST:

Bahrein, with inset of Middle East. LXXXIX, p. 199, Feb., 1946

Europe and the Near East, with inset map of the Middle East, and a table of distances between principal ports via shortest navigable routes. LXXXIII, supplement, 39 x 34 inches, June, 1943

Europe and the Near East, with inset of the Middle East, as of April 1, 1940. LXXVII, supplement, 39 x 34 inches, May, 1940

World trouble spot, the oil-rich Middle East. LXXXIX, pp. 396-397, Mar., 1946

MIDDLETON ISLAND, Alaska:

Sketch map showing the location of Middleton Island. XLIV, p. 315, Sept., 1923

MIDWAY ISLANDS, Pacific Ocean:

Pacific Ocean and the Bay of Bengal, with inset of Midway Islands. LXXXIV, supplement, 36½ x 26½ inches, Sept., 1943

MIGRATION ROUTES. *See* Bird Migration Routes and Habitats

MINAMI TORI SHIMA (Island), Pacific Ocean. *See* Marcus Island

MINDANAO (Island), Philippine Islands:

Mindanao and the Sulu Archipelago. LXXXVI, pp. 542-543, Nov., 1944

MINNESOTA:

Minnesota. LXVII, pp. 278-279, Mar., 1935

MIQUELON (Island), St. Pierre and Miquelon:

St. Pierre and Miquelon. LXXX, p. 746, Dec., 1941

MISSISSIPPI:
Mississippi. LXXII, pp. 268-269, Sept., 1937

MISSISSIPPI (River), U. S.:
Changes in the Mississippi Delta in less than a century. LXXI, p. 772, June, 1937
Growth of land at Cubits Gap, Mississippi Delta, from 1852 to 1905. XX, p. 833, Sept., 1909
How distant tributaries help make lower Mississippi floods. LII, p. 245, Sept., 1927
Mississippi Delta, showing formations. XXXIII, p. 533, June, 1918
Mississippi River. LXXII, pp. 268-269, Sept., 1937
Ohio and Mississippi River Basins. LXXI, pp. 770–771, June, 1937

MISSOURI:
Missouri. LXXXIX, pp. 280-281, Mar., 1946
Ozark Plateau, showing Missouri and Arkansas with portions of bordering States. LXXXIII, p. 593, May, 1943
United States of America, with inset of St. Louis. XLIII, supplement, 26½ x 36¼ inches, Apr., 1923

MISSOURI (River), U. S.:
Route of Lewis R. Freeman's 2,000-mile voyage down the Yellowstone-Missouri. LIV, p. 77, July, 1928

MISSOURI RIVER BASIN:
Missouri River Basin, showing dams, completed and projected, and wildlife sanctuaries. LXXXVIII, pp. 576-577, Nov., 1945

MOLL'S ATLAS:
World as depicted by map-makers before Captain Cook's first voyage to "The Great South Sea." LI, p. 84, Jan., 1927

MOLUCCAS (Islands), Netherlands East Indies:
Far East, with inset of the Moluccas. LXXIX, p. 538, May, 1941

MONGOLIA:
Divisions of Inner and Outer Mongolia. LXIII, p. 656, June, 1933
Map of China and Its Territories. Included: Mongolia, Manchuria, Chosen, East Turkestan, Tibet, Northern India. XXIII, supplement, 17 x 23 inches, Oct., 1912
Route of the National Geographic Society's Central-China Expedition. XLIX, p. 199, Feb., 1926

MONTANA:
Bitter Root Forest Reserve. IX, pl. 12 (opp. p. 394), foldout, Sept., 1898
A Map of Northwestern United States and Neighboring Canadian Provinces. LXXIX, supplement, 24½ x 36 inches, June, 1941

MOROCCO:
French and Spanish Morocco. XLVII, p. 331, Mar., 1925
Morocco. LXI, p. 266, Mar., 1932

MOSELLE (River), France:
Sketch map of the Seine, the Meuse, and the Moselle. VII, p. 189, June, 1896

MOSELLE (River), France—*Continued*
Sketch maps showing diversion of the Toul from the Meuse to the Moselle. VII, p. 229, July, 1896
Valley of the Moselle, near Berncastel. VII, pl. XXII (opp. p. 193), June, 1896

MOTHER MAPS:
United States showing Estimates of the Map Value of Existing Mother Maps. By Henry Gannett. IV, supplement, 18 x 13 inches, Mar. 31, 1892

MOUNTAIN RANGES:
Salient geographic features of the American Mediterranean and surrounding lands. VII, p. 177, May, 1896
See also Alps; Appalachian Mountains; Cascade Range; Great Smoky Mountains; Olympic Peninsula (Olympic Mountains); Virunga Mountains; White Mountains

MUIR GLACIER. *See* Glaciers

MUIR INLET, Alaska:
Northern part of Muir Inlet. IV, pl. 15 (opp. p. 55), Mar. 21, 1892

MULBERRY (Artificial Harbor), Normandy Coast, France:
British Mulberry and Omaha Beach, artificial harbors, off the Normandy coast. LXXXVII, p. 565, May, 1945

MURRAY, SIR JOHN: Map:
The Antarctic Continent: Outline according to John Murray. VI, p. 221, Dec. 29, 1894

N

NANSEI SHOTO (Islands). *See* Ryukyu Retto

NANTUCKET (Island), Massachusetts:
Nantucket, with inset showing mainland. LXXXV, p. 435, Apr., 1944

NANTUCKET SOUND. *See* Massachusetts

NAURU (Island), South Pacific Ocean:
Pacific Ocean and the Bay of Bengal, with inset of Nauru. LXXXIV, supplement, 36½ x 26½ inches, Sept., 1943

NEAR EAST:
Europe and the Near East. LVI, supplement, 34¼ x 39¼ inches, Dec., 1929
Europe and the Near East, as of April 1, 1940. LXXVII, supplement, 39 x 34 inches, May, 1940
Europe and the Near East, with inset map of the Middle East, and a table of distances between principal ports via shortest navigable routes. LXXXIII, supplement, 39 x 34 inches, June, 1943
Near East, showing Egypt, Anatolia, and the Arab kingdoms of Hedjaz, Transjordania, and Iraq. XLIII, p. 534, May, 1923
Near East, showing naval bases, airports, highways, railways, oil pipe lines, and oil pumping stations. LXXX, pp. 144-145, Aug., 1941

NEAR EAST—*Continued*

Near East, showing Turkey, Iraq, and adjacent regions, with naval bases, airports, highways, railways, and oil pipe lines. LXXXII, pp. 388-389, Sept., 1942

See also Balkan Peninsula; *and* names of countries

NEBRASKA:

Nebraska. LXXXVII, pp. 516-517, May, 1945

NEPAL:

Geographical relation of Nepal to India, Burma, Kashmir, and Tibet. XXXVIII, p. 249, Oct., 1920

Nepal, with inset map showing location of Katmandu (capital). LXVII, p. 323, Mar., 1935

NETHERLANDS:

Flood chart: Condition of Holland without dikes during mean high tide and highest stage of rivers. XII, p. 233, June, 1901

Holland. XLIII, p. 286, Mar., 1923

Location and extent of Zuider Zee reclamation project. LXIV, p. 295, Sept., 1933

Netherlands. LVI, p. 364, Sept., 1929

Netherlands, showing area below sea level. LXXXIX, p. 240, Feb., 1946

Netherlands, with inset showing neighboring countries. LXXVII, p. 261, Feb., 1940

Netherlands during the First Century. XII, p. 219, June, 1901

Netherlands of today and the State of Ohio compared. XII, p. 220, June, 1901

Successive enlargements of Haarlem Lake. XII, p. 223, June, 1901

Three diagrams (Westvoorne, Goeree and Overflakkee) show the enlargement of one small mud flat to ten times its original size. XII, p. 226, June, 1901

Zeeland about the year 1200. XII, p. 225, June, 1901

Zuider Zee reclamation project. LXIV, p. 297, Sept., 1933

NETHERLANDS EAST INDIES:

East Indies. XIX, p. 471, July, 1908

Far East, with enlargement of Java. LXXXI, p. 91, Jan., 1942

Far East, with inset of the Moluccas. LXXIX, p. 538, May, 1941

Indian Ocean, including Australia, New Zealand and Malaysia. LXXIX, supplement, 25½ x 32¾ inches, Mar., 1941

Netherlands Indies, with inset of Malay States and northern Sumatra. LXXIII, p. 668, June, 1938

Pacific war area, showing Australia, New Zealand, Netherlands Indies, and surrounding islands. LXXXI, pp. 416-417, Apr., 1942

The Philippine Islands as the Geographical Center of the Far East. XI, supplement, 7½ x 10¾ inches, Jan., 1900

Route of Magellan's voyage. LXII, pp. 700-701, Dec., 1932

NETHERLANDS EAST INDIES—*Continued*

Southeast Asia and Pacific Islands from the Indies and the Philippines to the Solomons, with 22 inset maps of important cities and islands, and a table of the Netherlands Indies' administrative areas and their capital cities. LXXXVI, supplement, 41 x 26½ inches, Oct., 1944

See also Bali; Borneo; Celebes; Java; Lesser Sunda Islands; New Guinea; Nias; Sumatra; Timor

NETHERLANDS NEW GUINEA. *See* New Guinea

NETHERLANDS WEST INDIES. *See* Aruba; Bonaire; Curaçao; Saba

NEVADA:

Death Valley region, Nevada. XVII, p. 486, Sept., 1906

Nevada. LXXXIX, p. 4, Jan., 1946

The Southwestern United States. LXXVII, supplement, 35 x 26 inches, June, 1940

NEW BRITAIN (Island), Bismarck Archipelago:

Pacific Ocean and the Bay of Bengal, with inset of New Britain and New Ireland. LXXXIV, supplement, 36½ x 26½ inches, Sept., 1943

NEW BRUNSWICK (Province), Canada:

Chignecto Ship Railway, to connect the Gulf of St. Lawrence and the Bay of Fundy. VII, p. 70, Feb., 1896

New Brunswick faces strategic Newfoundland across the Gulf of St. Lawrence. LXXIX, p. 597, May, 1941

NEW CALEDONIA (Island), South Pacific Ocean:

Pacific islands, with inset of New Caledonia and the Loyalty Islands. LXXXII, p. 43, July, 1942

NEW DELHI, India:

New Delhi, showing the seven previous sites of the city. LXXXII, p. 469, Oct., 1942

NEW ENGLAND (Region), U. S.:

Map showing direction of hurricane air currents and path of storm center. LXXV, p. 534, Apr., 1939

New England, showing areas infested by the brown-tail moth. XXII, p. 333, Apr., 1911

Northeastern United States, with inset of southeastern New England. LXXXVIII, supplement, 41 x 26½ inches, Sept., 1945

Route of the Connecticut River. LXXXIII, p. 405, Apr., 1943

See also Connecticut; Maine; Massachusetts; New Hampshire; Rhode Island; Vermont

NEW GUINEA:

Archbold Expedition explores interior of Netherlands New Guinea; Grand Valley, discovered. LXXIX, p. 318, Mar., 1941

New Guinea, New Caledonia, and Fiji command the shortest supply routes from America to Australia, with table of airline distances. LXXXI, pp. 698-699, June, 1942

NEW GUINEA—*Continued*

New Guinea, with inset showing Grand Valley and the Balim River. LXXXVIII, p. 674, Dec., 1945

New Guinea and an inset sketch map of the Fly River Basin. LVI, p. 255, Sept., 1929

New Guinea or Papua. XIX, p. 471, July, 1908

NEW HAMPSHIRE:

New Hampshire. LX, p. 260, Sept., 1931

Northeastern United States. LXXXVIII, supplement, 41 x 26½ inches, Sept., 1945

The White Mountains of New Hampshire. LXXII, supplement, 17 x 20 inches, July, 1937

NEW HEBRIDES (Islands), South Pacific Ocean:

Coral Sea area, showing the Solomons and New Hebrides, with an inset of Efate. LXXXVI, p. 233, Aug., 1944

NEW IRELAND (Island), Bismarck Archipelago:

Pacific Ocean and the Bay of Bengal, with inset of New Britain and New Ireland. LXXXIV, supplement, 36½ x 26½ inches, Sept., 1943

NEW JERSEY:

Northeast section of New Jersey. LXIII, p. 529, May, 1933

Northeastern United States. LXXXVIII, supplement, 41 x 26½ inches, Sept., 1945

The Reaches of New York City, with inset of southern New Jersey. LXXV, supplement, 26½ x 29 inches, Apr., 1939

Sandy Hook. XXXIII, p. 535, June, 1918

State of New Jersey. LXIII, p. 521, May, 1933

Topography of northern New Jersey. II, p. 87, May, 1890

NEW MEXICO:

Arizona and New Mexico, showing location of Indian ruins. LVI, p. 743, Dec., 1929

Carlsbad Caverns, with diagrammatic cross-sections. XLVIII, p. 302, Sept., 1925

Course of the Rio Grande from its source in Colorado through northern New Mexico, with inset of the entire river. LXXVI, p. 419, Oct., 1939

Course of the Rio Grande from northern New Mexico to El Paso, Texas. LXXVI, p. 424, Oct., 1939

Enchanted Mesa, New Mexico, surveyed in 1897, by George H. Pradt. VIII, p. 283, Oct., 1897

Map of New Mexico, with pictographs. LXXIII, pp. 532-533, May, 1938

New Mexico and eastern Arizona: Pueblo Bonito, located. XLVIII, p. 232, Sept., 1925

The Southwestern United States. LXXVII, supplement, 35 x 26 inches, June, 1940

Texas, New Mexico, and Oklahoma. LIII, pp. 642-643, June, 1928

NEW SOUTH WALES (State), Australia. *See* Lord Howe (Island)

NEW WORLD:

Herrera map, 1601, with vignette of Watling Island from a modern chart. Samana and Guanahani, shown. VI, p. 187, Dec. 29, 1894

NEW WORLD—*Continued*

Juan de la Cosa Map, 1500. V, pl. 4, supplement, 20 x 9½ inches, Apr. 7, 1893

Juan de la Cosa map, 1500, with vignette of Samana from a modern chart. VI, pl. 10 (opp. p. 186), Dec. 29, 1894

Mappa Munde Peinte sur Parchemin par Ordre de Henri II, Roi de France—1532; Samana (Guanahani), shown. VI, pl. 11 (opp. p. 188), Dec. 29, 1894

Ruysch Map, 1508. V, pl. 5, supplement, 23 x 18¼ inches, Apr. 7, 1893; reprint, 16½ x 13½ inches, 1965

NEW YORK (City):

Chart of New York Harbor made in 1737. XX, p. 825, Sept., 1909

Greater New York . . . Metropolis of Mankind. Supplement from aërial photo by Captain Albert W. Stevens. LXIV, Nov., 1933

A Map of the Travels of George Washington, with inset of New York and the lower Hudson. LXI, supplement, 20 x 29 inches, Jan., 1932

The Reaches of New York City. LXXV, supplement, 26½ x 29 inches, Apr., 1939

United States of America, with inset of Greater New York. XLIII, supplement, 26½ x 36¼ inches, Apr., 1923

NEW YORK (State):

Adirondack State Park. LXXIII, p. 720, June, 1938

Central New York, showing Finger Lakes region. LXXIX, p. 561, May, 1941

Chart of New York Harbor made in 1737. XX, p. 825, Sept., 1909

Front-line trenches of the rivers of New York. L, p. 92, July, 1926

Greater New York . . . Metropolis of Mankind. Supplement from aërial photo by Captain Albert W. Stevens. LXIV, Nov., 1933

A Map of the Travels of George Washington, with inset of New York and the lower Hudson. LXI, supplement, 20 x 29 inches, Jan., 1932

Mosaic map of Rochester, N. Y., a city of 300,000 inhabitants, made from an elevation of 10,000 feet in a single flight. XXXIX, p. 344, Mar., 1921

Northeastern United States. LXXXVIII, supplement, 41 x 26½ inches, Sept., 1945

One of our soldier cities: Map of Camp Upton, Yaphank, Long Island, New York. XXXII, p. 437, Nov.-Dec., 1917

The Reaches of New York City. LXXV, supplement, 26½ x 29 inches, Apr., 1939

Route of the new Erie Canal. XVI, p. 569, Dec., 1905

Shawangunk Mountain, Ulster County. VI, pl. 1 (opp. p. 23), foldout stereogram, Mar. 17, 1894

State of New York. LXIV, pp. 520-521, Nov., 1933

Two maps showing movement of Rockaway Beach and Inlet, from 1835 to 1908. XXVIII, p. 206, Sept., 1915

United States of America, with insets of Greater New York and Buffalo. XLIII, supplement, 26½ x 36¼ inches, Apr., 1923

NEW ZEALAND:

Indian Ocean, including Australia, New Zealand and Malaysia. LXXIX, supplement, 25½ x 32¾ inches, Mar., 1941

New Zealand, with insets of hot springs and mountainous regions. LXIX, pp. 170-171, Feb., 1936

Pacific war area, showing Australia, New Zealand, Netherlands Indies, and surrounding islands. LXXXI, pp. 416-417, Apr., 1942

Rotorua hot spring region of New Zealand. XLVIII, p. 113, Aug., 1925

South Island and Stephen Island. LXVII, p. 651, May, 1935

NEWFOUNDLAND:

Cotidals from St. Johns, Newfoundland. IX, p. 502, Dec., 1898

Military outposts leased from Britain put new teeth in Uncle Sam's defenses. LXXVIII, p. 621, Nov., 1940

New Brunswick faces strategic Newfoundland across the Gulf of St. Lawrence. LXXIX, p. 597, May, 1941

Newfoundland, showing British and American defense bases. LXXX, p. 113, July, 1941

Starting point for aviators flying planes to Britain, Norway, and Portugal. LXXX, p. 77, July, 1941

Tidal chart of Placentia Bay. IX, p. 471, Nov., 1898

NIAS (Island), Netherlands East Indies:

Nias. LX, p. 205, Aug., 1931

NICARAGUA:

Basins of the Rio Grande and Rio Las Lajas. X, p. 242, July, 1899

Boundary between Nicaragua and Costa Rica. XII, p. 27, Jan., 1901

Lake Nicaragua. X, p. 239, July, 1899

Map of the Region Adjacent to the Nicaragua Canal Route. By C. Willard Hayes. X, supplement, 7½ x 10½ inches, July, 1899

Nicaragua. LXI, p. 594, May, 1932

Nicaragua. LXXXVI, p. 165, Aug., 1944

The Nicaragua Canal. I, foldout (following p. 335), Oct., 1889

Route of Nicaragua Canal as proposed by Isthmian Canal Commission. XII, p. 29, Jan., 1901

NIGERIA:

Nigeria, with inset showing position in Africa. LXXXV, p. 540, May, 1944

NILE (River), Africa:

Narrow ribbon of fertile land which runs the length of Egypt. XLIX, p. 272, Mar., 1926

Nile, from Aswân, Egypt, to the Mediterranean Sea, with pictographs. LXXVII, pp. 438-439, Apr., 1940

Nile, from its mouth to the First Cataract, XXIV, p. 972, Sept., 1913

Uganda borders the largest fresh-water lake in the Old World and contains the source of the Nile. LXXI, p. 113, Jan., 1937

NIUAFOŌ (Island), Tonga Islands:

Niuafoō (inset). LXVIII, p. 95, July, 1935

NONSUCH ISLAND, Bermuda:

Nonsuch Island. LXI, p. 66, Jan., 1932

NORMANDY (Region), France:

British Mulberry and Omaha Beach, artificial harbors, off the Normandy coast. LXXXVII, p. 565, May, 1945

Normandy. LXIX, p. 629, May, 1936

Northwest France, including Normandy and Brittany. LXXXIV, pp. 218-219, Aug., 1943

NORTH AMERICA:

Atlantic Ocean, with inset of Isthmus of Panama. LXXVI, supplement, 31 x 25 inches, July, 1939

Atlantic Ocean, with inset of Isthmus of Panama and a table of air-line distances in statute miles. LXXX, supplement, 31¼ x 25 inches, Sept., 1941

Bird migration routes from South America to North America converge funnel-like in Central America. Inset of Veracruz and Tabasco, Mexico, showing La Venta region, a natural bird observatory. LXXXVII, p. 188, Feb., 1945

Carte Générale des Découvertes de l'Amiral de Fonte, et autres Navigateurs Espagnols, Anglois et Russes pour la recherche du Passage à la Mer du Sud. Par M. De l'Isle. III, supplement, 16¼ x 13 inches, Jan. 28, 1892; Feb. 19, 1892

A Chart shewing part of the Coast of N. W. America (Vancouver's chart, No. I). X, supplement, 15½ x 18 inches, Nov., 1899

A Chart Shewing part of the Coast of N. W. America (Vancouver's chart, No. II). X, supplement, 15½ x 18 inches, Nov., 1899

Natural divisions of the North American forests, exclusive of Mexico. VI, pl. 8 (opp. p. 139), June 22, 1894

North America. XLV, supplement, 27 x 37 inches, May, 1924

North America, with inset of the Aleutian Islands. LXXXI, supplement, 26½ x 33 inches, May, 1942

North America at the time of maximum extent of the ice. XXI, p. 526, June, 1910

Photo-engraving of topographic model of North America, from Butler's Complete Geography. I, insert (bet. pp. 268-269), July, 1889

Probable uses of the land of North America 50 years hence. XX, p. 575, June, 1909

Salient geographic features of the American Mediterranean and surrounding lands. VII, p. 177, May, 1896

Track of West Indian hurricane, 1900. XI, 4 maps, pp. 385, 386, 389, 390, Oct., 1900

The southern part of the prehistoric Canadian ice-sheet. Photograph from a model. The glacial data are on the authority of T. C. Chamberlin. IX, pl. 9 (opp. p. 314), July, 1898

United States, Canada, and Alaska, showing route of the first air expedition to Alaska. XLI, pp. 500-501, May, 1922

See also names of countries; *and* New World

NORTH CAROLINA:

Ancient map of Albemarle and Pamlico Sounds, showing colonists' ships of Sir Walter Raleigh's expedition of 1584, approaching Roanoke Island. LXIV, p. 696, Dec., 1933

NORTH CAROLINA—*Continued*

Great Smoky Mountains National Park, with inset showing main roads across the park. LXX, p. 246, Aug., 1936

North Carolina. XLIX, p. 512, May, 1926

North Carolina. LXXX, pp. 184-185, Aug., 1941

North Carolina, South Carolina, Georgia, and Eastern Tennessee, with inset of Charlotte. L, supplement, 14¾ x 19 inches, Sept., 1926

North Carolina-Tennessee: Asheville Sheet. Section from the Cumberland Plateau to the Blue Ridge. Natural Profiles. Surveyed in 1882-3-7. I, supplement, 15¾ x 21¾ inches, Oct., 1889; reprint, *Asheville Quadrangle.* Surveyed in 1898-99. I, supplement, 16 x 22 inches, 1965

Northeastern coast and islands of North Carolina. LXIV, p. 701, Dec., 1933

The St. Thomas-Hatteras hurricane of September 3-12, 1889. II, foldout charts (bet. pp. 210-211), July, 1890

Sand reefs along the North Carolina coast. XVII, p. 311, June, 1906

Virginia, North Carolina, Kentucky, and Tennessee, showing new Eastern National Park-to-Park Highway. LXV, pp. 666-667, June, 1934

NORTH POLE. *See* Arctic Regions

NORTH SEA:

Denmark, with inset of the North Sea. LXXVII, p. 3, Jan., 1940

Fishing banks of the North Sea and the "War Zone" about the British Isles. XXVII, p. 149, Feb., 1915

Location of the mine barrage laid by the American and British mining squadrons. XXXV, p. 86, Feb., 1919

Location of the mine fields. XXXVII, p. 104, Feb., 1920

Mine groups. XXXVII, p. 105, Feb., 1920

Overlapping lines of mines laid in the North Sea. XXXV, p. 109, Feb., 1919

NORTHERN HEMISPHERE:

Average lines along which the centers of storms move in January and July in the Northern Hemisphere. XVI, pp. 290-291, June, 1905

Diagram showing arrangement of sheets for the international map on the scale of 1:1,000,000. XXI, p. 131, Feb., 1910

Northern and Southern Hemispheres, with insets of time zones, world terrain, and tables of airline distances in four hemispheres. LXXXIII, supplement, 41 x 22 inches, Apr., 1943

Northern Hemisphere, showing parallels of latitude, 10 to 60, to be used with sky charts. LXXXIV, pp. 98-99, July, 1943

Northern Hemisphere, with tables showing airline distances in the Pacific, the Atlantic, the Arctic, and the Americas. LXXXIX, supplement, 21¾ x 24 inches, Feb., 1946

NORTHERN IRELAND:

A Modern Pilgrim's Map of the British Isles or More Precisely the Kingdom of Great Britain and Northern Ireland and the Irish Free State. LXXI, supplement, 29 x 35 inches, June, 1937

NORTHERN IRELAND—*Continued*

Northern Ireland, showing the counties of Ulster. LXVIII, p. 574, Nov., 1935

NORTHERN RHODESIA:

Northern Rhodesia and Southern Rhodesia. LXXXVI, p. 284, Sept., 1944

NORTHWEST TERRITORIES, Canada:

Alaska-British Northwest Territory (pre-Yukon Territory)-British Columbia, showing route of expedition of 1891, northern limit of glaciation, and volcanic tufa; an index map of the Yukon district, for pls. 19 and 20. IV, pls. 18-20, 2 foldouts, May 15, 1892

Mackenzie River and Basin. LX, p. 132, Aug., 1931

Plan of Arctic exploration from a base near Jones Sound or at Cape Sabine. IX, p. 2, Jan., 1898

See also Baffin Island; Ellesmere (Island)

NORWAY:

Norway. LXXV, p. 496, Apr., 1939

Norway. LXXXIII, p. 336, Mar., 1943

Norway, showing the Petsamo region of Finland, ceded to the U. S. S. R. LXXXVIII, p. 620, Nov., 1945

Southern Norway. LXVII, p. 631, May, 1935

NOVA SCOTIA (Province), Canada:

Cape Breton Island. XXXVIII, p. 35, July, 1920

Chignecto Ship Railway, to connect the Gulf of St. Lawrence and the Bay of Fundy. VII, p. 70, Feb., 1896

Nova Scotia. LXXVII, pp. 580-581, May, 1940

NUKUFETAU (Island), Ellice Islands:

Pacific Ocean and the Bay of Bengal, with inset of Nukufetau. LXXXIV, supplement, 36½ x 26½ inches, Sept., 1943

NUKULAELAE (Island), Ellice Islands:

Pacific Ocean and the Bay of Bengal, with inset of Nukulaelae. LXXXIV, supplement, 36½ x 26½ inches, Sept., 1943

NUKUNONO ISLAND, Tokelau Islands:

Pacific Ocean and the Bay of Bengal, with inset of Nukunono Island. LXXXIV, supplement, 36½ x 26½ inches, Sept., 1943

NUREMBERG CHRONICLE MAP:

Chronicon Nurembergense Map, 1493. V, pl. 2, supplement, 23½ x 17 inches, Apr. 7, 1893; reprint, 16½ x 13½ inches, 1965

O

OCEAN CURRENTS. *See* Arctic Regions (Arctic Ocean); Atlantic Ocean; Pacific Ocean; *and* Gulf Stream; Humboldt Current; Tides

OCEAN ISLAND, Gilbert Islands:

Pacific Ocean and the Bay of Bengal, with inset of Ocean Island. LXXXIV, supplement, 36½ x 26½ inches, Sept., 1943

OCEANIA. *See* Pacific Islands

OCEANS. *See* Arctic Regions (Arctic Ocean); Atlantic Ocean; Indian Ocean; Pacific Ocean; *and* Tides

OGASAWARA SHOTO (Bonin Islands), Pacific Ocean:

Strategic isles of the Pacific: Chichi Jima, Eniwetok, Guam, Hachijo, Haha Jima, Jaluit, Kusaie, Kwajalein, Marcus, Palau, Paramushiro, Ponape, Rota, Saipan, Tinian, Truk, Wake, Yap. LXXXV, pp. 392-393, 17 island maps, Apr., 1944

See also Chichi Jima Retto; Haha Jima Retto

OHIO:

Northeastern United States. LXXXVIII, supplement, 41 x 26½ inches, Sept., 1945

Ohio. LXI, p. 529, May, 1932

Sandusky and vicinity. XIII, p. 401, Nov., 1902

United States of America, with inset of Cleveland. XLIII, supplement, 26½ x 36¼ inches, Apr., 1923

OHIO (River), U. S.:

Ohio and Mississippi River Basins. LXXI, pp. 770-771, June, 1937

OKINAWA GUNTO (Islands), Ryukyu Retto:

Detailed map of Okinawa, a base for the United States Navy. LXXXVII, p. 548, May, 1945

Japan and Korea, with insets of Kuril Islands, Pescadores, Karafuto, Ryukyu Islands, Okinawa, Formosa, Tokyo, and location of Japan in the western Pacific. LXXXVIII, supplement, 37 x 26½ inches, Dec., 1945

Southeast Asia and Pacific Islands from the Indies and the Philippines to the Solomons, with inset of Nansei Islands, Amami to Okinawa. LXXXVI, supplement, 41 x 26½ inches, Oct., 1944

OKLAHOMA:

Indian Territory, showing boundary lines of the Five Civilized Tribes. IX, p. 482, Dec., 1898

Indian Territory, showing progress of subdivision survey up to January 1, 1896. VII, p. 113, Mar., 1896

Oklahoma. LXXIX, p. 289, Mar., 1941

Texas, New Mexico, and Oklahoma. LIII, pp. 642-643, June, 1928

OLYMPIC MOUNTAINS, Washington. *See* Olympic Peninsula

OLYMPIC PENINSULA, Washington:

The Olympic Country, Washington. VII, pl. XVI (opp. p. 133), foldout, Apr., 1896

OMAHA BEACH (Artificial Harbor), Normandy Coast, France:

British Mulberry and Omaha Beach, artificial harbors, off the Normandy coast. LXXXVII, p. 565, May, 1945

OMAN (Sultanate), Arabian Peninsula:

Oman. XXII, p. 89, Jan., 1911

ONTARIO (Province), Canada:

Northeastern United States. LXXXVIII, supplement, 41 x 26½ inches, Sept., 1945

Ontario. LXII, p. 139, Aug., 1932

ONTONG JAVA (Islands), Solomon Islands:

Islands of the South Pacific, with insets of Florida Island and Ontong Java. LXV, p. 268, Mar., 1934

OREGON:

Crater Lake, Oregon. VIII, p. 38, Feb., 1897

Crater Lake: Routes to Crater Lake from Ashland and Medford on the Oregon and California Line of the Southern Pacific Railroad. VIII, p. 35, Feb., 1897

A Map of Northwestern United States and Neighboring Canadian Provinces. LXXIX, supplement, 24½ x 36 inches, June, 1941

Oregon. XXIII, p. 626, June, 1912

Oregon. LXV, pp. 176-177, Feb., 1934

Oregon. XC, pp. 686-687, Dec., 1946

Rainfall map of Washington and Oregon. XX, p. 647, July, 1909

Relief map of Mount Hood. XIX, p. 519, July, 1908

United States of America, with inset of Portland. XLIII, supplement, 26½ x 36¼ inches, Apr., 1923

Washington and Oregon. XX, p. 646, July, 1909

ORINOCO (River), Venezuela:

Map of the Valley of the Orinoco River, showing the extent of territory drained by that waterway and the bearing it has on the Venezuelan question. Compiled by T. Heyward Gignilliat, 1896. VII, pl. 5, supplement, 18 x 11¾ inches, Feb., 1896

OZARKS (Plateau), U. S.:

Ozark Plateau, showing Missouri and Arkansas with portions of bordering States. LXXXIII, p. 593. May, 1943

P

PACIFIC ISLANDS:

Coral Sea area, showing the Solomons and New Hebrides, with an inset of Efate. LXXXVI, p. 233, Aug., 1944

Cruises of the *Princeton,* from the time of commissioning at Philadelphia to her loss in the Philippine Sea. LXXXVIII, pp. 210-211, Aug., 1945

Hawaiian Islands, with inset showing route of Flying Clippers across the Pacific Ocean. LXXIV, pp. 424-425, Oct., 1938

Islands of the South Pacific, with insets of Florida Island and Ontong Java. LXV, p. 268, Mar., 1934

Japan and Adjacent Regions of Asia and the Pacific Ocean, with insets of industrial centers of Japan and the Marshall Islands. LXXXV, supplement, 26½ x 34½ inches, Apr., 1944

Japanese Micronesia, with insets of Palau, Ponape, and Truk Islands. LXXXI, pp. 764-765, June, 1942

Japanese Micronesia. with insets of Yap, Ponape, and Palau Islands. LXIX, p. 483, Apr., 1936

Map of Pacific islands, showing route of Flying Clippers. LXXIV, p. 102, July, 1938

Marquesas, Tuamotu, and Austral Islands. XLVIII, p. 366, Oct., 1925

PACIFIC ISLANDS—*Continued*

New Guinea, New Caledonia, and Fiji command the shortest supply routes from America to Australia, with table of airline distances. LXXXI, pp. 698-699, June, 1942

New Zealand to the New Hebrides, with an enlargement of Lord Howe Island. LXVIII, p. 118, July, 1935

New Zealand to the Samoa group, with an enlargement of Falcon Island. LIV, p. 760, Dec., 1928

Pacific islands. XIX, p. 547, Aug., 1908

Pacific islands: Aircraft carrier men's vision of the battle for the Pacific. LXXXII, pp. 8-9, July, 1942

Pacific islands, showing limit of long-range bombing from northern Australia, with table of airline distances in statute miles. LXXXIII, pp. 56-57, Jan., 1943

Pacific islands, showing location of Marquesas Islands. LXXIX, p. 112, Jan., 1941

Pacific islands, with history of discovery and an inset showing proposed American bases. LXXXIX, pp. 624-625, May, 1946

Pacific islands, with inset of Gilbert Islands. LXXXIII, p. 74, Jan., 1943

Pacific islands, with inset of New Caledonia and the Loyalty Islands. LXXXII, p. 43, July, 1942

Pacific Ocean, with inset maps of important islands and island groups. LXX, supplement, 31 x 38 inches, Dec., 1936; revised in 1942

Included: Aitutaki; Aleutian Islands, Alaska Peninsula to Rat Islands; Apia; Archipelagoes of Eastern New Guinea; Atiu; Bismarck Archipelago; Caroline and Marshall Islands; Christmas Island; Clipperton Island; Cook Islands; Danger Islands; Easter Island; Fanning Island; Fiji; Galapagos Islands; Gambier Islands; Gilbert and Ellice Islands; Guam; Hawaiian Islands; Hervey Islands; Hiva-Oa; Honolulu and Pearl Harbors; Hoorn Islands; Jaluit; Kusaie; Leeward Group; Lord Howe Island; Makatea; Mangaia; Manihiki; Manua Islands, Eastern Samoa; Marianas Islands; Marquesas Islands; Mauke; Midway Islands; Nauru; Near Is.: New Caledonia and Loyalty Islands; New Hebrides; Niuafoō; Niue; Norfolk Island; Noumea; Nuku-Hiva; Ocean Island; Pago Pago Harbor; Palau Islands; Papeete; Pitcairn Island; Ponape; Rakahanga; Rapa; Rarotonga; Rota; Rotuma; Santa Cruz Islands; Solomon Islands; Suva; Tahiti and Moorea; Tarawa; Tinian and Saipan; Tonga; Tongareva; Torres and Banks Islands; Truk Islands; Tuamotu, Tubuai, and Society Islands; Tubuai; Tutuila, Eastern Samoa; Unalaska Bay; Wake Island; Wallis Islands; Western Samoa; Yap

Pacific Ocean and the Bay of Bengal, with inset maps of important islands, and table of airline distances in statute miles. LXXXIV, supplement, 36½ x 26½ inches, Sept., 1943

Included: Atafu; Attu; Baker Island; Canton Island; Caroline Island; Chichi Jima; Christmas Island; Danger Islands; Enderbury Island; Eniwetok; Fakaofo; Fanning Island; Fiji; Flint Island; Funafuti; Gardner Island; Guam; Hawaiian Islands; Honolulu and Pearl Harbors; Howland Island; Hull Island; Jaluit; Jarvis Island; Kiska; Kwajalein; Makin; Malden Island; Manihiki; Marcus Island; Midway Islands; Nauru; New Britain and New Ireland; Nukufetau; Nukulaelae; Nukunono Island; Ocean Island; Pago Pago; Palau Islands; Palmyra Island; Paramushiro; Ponape; Rakahanga; Solomon Islands; Starbuck Island; Suvorov; Swains Island; Sydney Island; Tarawa; Timor; Tongareva; Truk Islands; Tutuila, Eastern Samoa; Vostok Island; Wake Island; Wotje; Yap

Pacific war area, showing Australia, New Zealand, Netherlands Indies, and surrounding islands. LXXXI, pp. 416-417, Apr., 1942

Polynesian archipelago. XLVIII, p. 358, Oct., 1925

Position of Tahiti in mid-Pacific. XII, pl. 1 (opp. p. 413), Dec., 1901

South Pacific, with inset of Niuafoō Island. LXVIII, p. 95, July, 1935

South Pacific archipelagoes. XXXVI, p. 281, Oct., 1919

South Pacific islands, showing Date Line and Canton Island, site of 1937 Eclipse Expedition. LXXII, p. 380, Sept., 1937

Southeast Asia and Pacific Islands from the Indies and the Philippines to the Solomons, with 22 inset maps of important cities and islands. LXXXVI, supplement, 41 x 26½ inches, Oct., 1944

Included: Chichi Jima Retto; Davao; Eniwetok; Guam; Haha Jima Retto; Hong Kong; Iwo Jima; Manila; Marcus; Nansei Islands, Amami to Okinawa; Pagan; Palau Islands; Pescadores; Ponape; Pratas; Rota; Saipan and Tinian; Shanghai; Singapore; Soerabaja; Truk Islands; Yap

Sovereignty and Mandate Boundary Lines in 1921 of the Islands of the Pacific. XL, supplement, 19 x 25 inches, Dec., 1921

Strategic isles of the Pacific: Chichi Jima, Eniwetok, Guam, Hachijo, Haha Jima, Jaluit, Kusaie, Kwajalein, Marcus, Palau, Paramushiro, Ponape, Rota, Saipan, Tinian, Truk, Wake, Yap. LXXXV, pp. 392-393, 17 island maps, Apr., 1944

The taking of Saipan opens the gate in Japan's wall of island defenses. LXXXVII, p. 447, Apr., 1945

Theater of War in the Pacific Ocean, with table of airline distances in statute miles. LXXXI, supplement, 20½ x 26½ inches, Feb., 1942

Topography of two coral-ringed volcanic isles: Bolabola, of the Society group, and Vavitao, of the Austral group. XLVIII, p. 369, Oct., 1925

See also Aleutian Islands; Caroline Islands; Easter Island; Fiji Islands; Gilbert Islands; Guam; Hawaii; Marianas Islands; Marquesas Islands; Marshall Islands; New Caledonia; New Guinea; New Hebrides; Okinawa Gunto; Philippine Islands; Ryukyu Retto; Society Islands; Solomon Islands; Tahiti; Truk Islands

PACIFIC NORTHWEST, U. S.:

A Map of Northwestern United States and Neighboring Canadian Provinces. LXXIX, supplement, 24½ x 36 inches, June, 1941

PACIFIC NORTHWEST, U. S.—*Continued*

Pacific Northwest defense area. LXXXII, p. 425, Oct., 1942

See also Oregon; Washington

PACIFIC OCEAN:

The air and water currents of the Pacific. XIII, p. 316, Aug., 1902

The air and water currents of the Pacific. XVI, p. 420, Sept., 1905

Carte Générale des Découvertes de l'Amiral de Fonte, et autres Navigateurs Espagnols, Anglois et Russes pour la recherche du Passage à la Mer du Sud. Par M. De l'Isle. III, supplement, 16¼ x 13 inches, Jan. 28, 1892; Feb. 19, 1892

Charts of 1869 and 1903, of the Pacific Ocean west of the Hawaiian Islands, to illustrate the removal of doubtful dangers. XX, p. 836, Sept., 1909

Crossroads of the Pacific, showing trade routes and distances. XIX, p. 296, Apr., 1908

Doubtful islands region. XV, p. 479, Dec., 1904

Hawaiian Islands, with inset showing route of Flying Clippers across the Pacific Ocean. LXXIV, pp. 424-425, Oct., 1938

How the "Southern Cross" (airplane) blazed an aërial trail across the Pacific. LIV, p. 373, Oct., 1928

Humboldt Current. LXXIX, p. 376, Mar., 1941

Location of Hawaiian Islands. XLV, p. 116, Feb., 1924

Manila as a distributing point for commerce. XIII, p. 314, Aug., 1902

Map showing position of total eclipse (1937) every 15 minutes. LXXII, p. 364, Sept., 1937

Map showing probable migration routes of Hawaiian Islanders from Asia. XLV, p. 127, Feb., 1924

Migration routes of the golden plover. XXII, p. 359, Apr., 1911

National frontage and way stations on the Pacific. XIII, p. 308, Aug., 1902

"The Pacific is, and will remain, an American Ocean." XIII, p. 318, Aug., 1902

Pacific Ocean, with inset maps of important islands and island groups. LXX, supplement, 31 x 38 inches, Dec., 1936; revised in 1942

Pacific Ocean and the Bay of Bengal, with inset maps of important islands, and table of airline distances in statute miles. LXXXIV, supplement, 36½ x 26½ inches, Sept., 1943

Polynesian archipelagoes. XLVIII, p. 358, Oct., 1925

Position of reported islands in the doubtful region. XV, p. 481, Dec., 1904

Position of Tahiti in the mid-Pacific. XXXVIII, p. 303, Oct., 1920

Positions of reported islands in the doubtful region, and the sailing tracks of vessels sent to seek them. XVIII, p. 207, Mar., 1907

Principal productions of the countries fronting on the Pacific. XIII, p. 305, Aug., 1902

Proposed routes for Pacific cables. XIII, p. 312, Aug., 1902

Relative position of doubtful islands region, the Hawaiian Islands, and the American coast. XVIII, p. 206, Mar., 1907

PACIFIC OCEAN—*Continued*

Route followed by Capt. Harry Pidgeon. LIII, pp. 144-145, Feb., 1928

Route of Flying Clippers. LXXIV, p. 102, July, 1938

Route of the *Yankee,* from Gloucester, Massachusetts, through the Panama Canal, to the Galápagos Islands, Easter Island, and Pitcairn. LXXXI, p. 4, Jan., 1942

Routes followed by Captain James Cook. LI, p. 87, Jan., 1927

Routes followed by ships and planes of Byrd Antarctic Expedition in the South Pacific. LXVIII, p. 405, Oct., 1935

Shortest route between Nantucket and Honolulu, via Cape Horn, is 15,600 miles (inset). LXXXIX, p. 625, May, 1946

Sixteenth-century map of the Pacific. LXII, p. 763, Dec., 1932

Theater of War in the Pacific Ocean, with table of airline distances in statute miles. LXXXI, supplement, 20½ x 26½ inches, Feb., 1942

Transportation routes of the Pacific. XIII, p. 310, Aug., 1902

See also Pacific Islands

PAGAN (Island), Marianas Islands:

Southeast Asia and Pacific Islands from the Indies and the Philippines to the Solomons, with inset of Pagan. LXXXVI, supplement, 41 x 26½ inches, Oct., 1944

PAGO PAGO, Samoa:

Pacific Ocean and the Bay of Bengal, with inset of Pago Pago area. LXXXIV, supplement, 36½ x 26½ inches, Sept., 1943

PALAU ISLANDS, Caroline Islands:

Japanese Micronesia, with insets of Palau, Ponape, and Truk Islands. LXXXI, pp. 764-765, June, 1942

Japanese Micronesia, with insets of Yap, Ponape, and Palau Islands. LXIX, p. 483, Apr., 1936

Pacific Ocean and the Bay of Bengal, with inset of Palau Islands. LXXXIV, supplement, 36½ x 26½ inches, Sept., 1943

Southeast Asia and Pacific Islands from the Indies and the Philippines to the Solomons, with inset of Palau Islands. LXXXVI, supplement, 41 x 26½ inches, Oct., 1944

Strategic isles of the Pacific. LXXXV, pp. 392-393, 17 island maps, Apr., 1944

The taking of Saipan opens the gate in Japan's wall of island defenses. LXXXVII, p. 447, Apr., 1945

PALESTINE:

Bible Lands, showing Palestine, Trans-Jordan, and Egypt. LXXXV, p. 236, Feb., 1944

Bible Lands, showing Palestine, Trans-Jordan, and Syria. LXXXVI, p. 722, Dec., 1944

Bible Lands and the Cradle of Western Civilization; Insets: Holy Land Today, Holy Land in Biblical Times, Jerusalem, Traditional Route of the Exodus, St. Paul's Travels and the Seven Churches, The Crusades. XC, supplement, 32 x 22 inches, Dec., 1946

PALESTINE—*Continued*

Bible Lands and the Cradle of Western Civilization; Insets: Jerusalem, The Holy Land, Economic Development, Route of the Exodus, St. Paul's Travels and the Seven Churches, The Crusades, Empire of Alexander the Great. LXXIV, supplement, 25 x 35 inches, Dec., 1938

Crusader castles. LIX, p. 371, Mar., 1931

Crusader trails and castles. LXIV, p. 654, Dec., 1933

Eastern shores of the Mediterranean. XXXVIII, p. 89, Aug., 1920

Jordan River from Galilee to Dead Sea. LXXVIII, p. 784, Dec., 1940

Mount Sinai and the route of the Exodus. XXIII, p. 1282, Dec., 1912

Palestine, Syria, Iraq, Trans-Jordan, and Saudi Arabia. LXV, p. 496, Apr., 1934

Palestine, Trans-Jordan, and adjacent territory. LXVII, p. 133, Feb., 1935

Reference map of Palestine. XXVII, p. 312, Mar., 1915

Region of the locust plague which ravaged the entire land from "Dan to Beer-Sheba." XXVIII, p. 542, Dec., 1915

Route of the Exodus. XX, p. 1013, Dec., 1909

"Shores of Sunrise" (The Levant). L, p. 652, Dec., 1926

Territory observed by Brigadier General P. R. C. Groves and Major J. R. McCrindle in their flight over Egypt, Sinai, and Palestine. L, p. 315, Sept., 1926

World's deepest land depression separates Palestine from Trans-Jordan. LXXI, p. 72, Jan., 1937

PALMYRA (Island), Line Islands:

Pacific Ocean and the Bay of Bengal, with inset of Palmyra Island. LXXXIV, supplement, 36½ x 26½ inches, Sept., 1943

PANAMA:

American Isthmus Ship Canal Company: Map and profile of proposed location of canal at sea level, without locks, a straight line from the Atlantic to the Pacific Ocean. XIII, p. 70, Feb., 1902

Atlantic Ocean, with inset of Isthmus of Panama. LXXVI, supplement, 31 x 25 inches, July, 1939

Atlantic Ocean, with inset of Isthmus of Panama and a table of air-line distances in statute miles. LXXX, supplement, 31¼ x 25 inches, Sept., 1941

Barro Colorado, the largest island in the Canal Zone. LII, p. 332, Sept., 1927

Bird's Eye View of the Panama Canal (Relief map painting). XXIII, supplement, 9 x 18 inches, Feb., 1912

Canal Zone. XXII, p. 149, Feb., 1911

Canal Zone and surrounding territory of the Panama Republic. XXVIII, p. 181, Aug., 1915

The Countries of the Caribbean, Including Mexico, Central America, the West Indies, and the Panama Canal, with detailed insets of Panama Canal and the Canal Zone, Porto Rico and the Virgin Islands, and Guantanamo Bay, Cuba. XLI, supplement, 25 x 44 inches, Feb., 1922

PANAMA—*Continued*

Diagram showing yearly amount of rainfall in inches on the Panama Isthmus. XVI, p. 467, Oct., 1905

Gatun Dam, spillway, and locks. XXII, p. 201, Feb., 1911

Isthmus of Panama before the establishment of the Canal Zone. XXVIII, p. 180, Aug., 1915

Map of Central America, Cuba, Porto Rico, and the Islands of the Caribbean Sea, with inset of the Panama Canal and Canal Zone. XXIV, supplement, 12½ x 19 inches, Feb., 1913

Map Showing Location of Panama Canal, as recommended by the Isthmian Canal Commission of 1899-1902. XVI, supplement, 24 x 33 inches, Oct., 1905

Mexico, Central America, and the West Indies, with inset of the Isthmus of Panama. LXVI, supplement, 23 x 40 inches, Dec., 1934

Mexico, Central America, and the West Indies, with inset of the Isthmus of Panama. LXXVI, supplement, 24 x 41 inches, Dec., 1939

Military outposts leased from Britain put new teeth in Uncle Sam's defenses. LXXVIII, p. 621, Nov., 1940

Panama, Republic of, showing Canal Zone. LXXX, p. 594, Nov., 1941

Panama, showing general features and present location of aboriginal tribes. XXIII, p. 628, July, 1912

Panama, showing location of Mulatas Archipelago. LXXIX, p. 197, Feb., 1941

Panama Canal: Winds, calms, and sailing routes, Pacific Ocean, May-October. XV, p. 172, Apr., 1904

Panama Canal: Winds, calms, and sailing routes, Pacific Ocean, November-April. XV, p. 173, Apr., 1904

Panama Canal and Gatun Lake. XX, p. 340, Apr., 1909

Panama Rail Road, Panama Canal, and tributary drainage. I, foldout (bet. pp. 314-315), Oct., 1889

PANAMA RAILROAD. *See* Panama

PAPUA. *See* New Guinea

PARAGUAY:

Paraguay and southern Matto Grosso (Brazilian State), with inset showing river system. LXXXIV, p. 461, Oct., 1943

River and rail approach from Buenos Aires. LXIII, p. 387, Apr., 1933

PARAMUSHIRO JIMA (Island), Chishima Retto, Japan:

Pacific Ocean and the Bay of Bengal, with inset of Paramushiro. LXXXIV, supplement, 36½ x 26½ inches, Sept., 1943

Strategic isles of the Pacific. LXXXV, pp. 392-393, 17 island maps, Apr., 1944

PATAGONIA (Region), South America:

Patagonia, illustrating explorations of J. B. Hatcher, 1896-'97. VIII, p. 311, Nov., 1897

PEARL HARBOR, Oahu, Hawaii:

Pacific Ocean and the Bay of Bengal, with inset of Honolulu and Pearl Harbor areas. LXXXIV, supplement, 36½ x 26½ inches, Sept., 1943

PEARL RIVER DELTA, China:

Pearl River Delta, and Hong Kong. LXXVII, p. 534, Apr., 1940

PEEL ISLAND, Bonin Islands. *See* Chichi Jima Retto, for Chichi Jima

PENEPLAINS. *See* Appalachian Mountains

PENNSYLVANIA:

Concrete example of Pennsylvania's foresight in providing for her economic development: The comprehensive plan under which the state highways are being constructed. XXXV, p. 400, May, 1919

George Washington's travels in southwestern Pennsylvania. LXI, p. 12, Jan., 1932

Historic and Scenic Reaches of the Nation's Capital. LXXIV, supplement, 26½ x 31¼ inches, July, 1938

A Map of the Travels of George Washington, with inset of Philadelphia. LXI, supplement, 20 x 29 inches, Jan., 1932

Northeastern United States. LXXXVIII, supplement, 41 x 26½ inches, Sept., 1945

Pen and ink drawing combining typical farm scenes and perspective map of Pennsylvania Dutch country. LXXX, pp. 50-51, July, 1941

Pennsylvania. LXVIII, pp. 4-5, July, 1935

Topographic map of Pennsylvania, by J. P. Lesley (1871). I, p. 188, July, 1889

United States of America, with insets of Philadelphia and Pittsburgh. XLIII, supplement, 26½ x 36¼ inches, Apr., 1923

PENRHYN (Atoll), South Pacific Ocean. *See* Tongareva

PERSIA. *See* Iran

PERU:

Colca Valley region. LXV, p. 113, Jan., 1934

Field of work of the Peruvian Expedition of 1912 under the auspices of Yale University and the National Geographic Society. XXIII, p. 416, Apr., 1912

Lake Titicaca region. LI, p. 214, Feb., 1927

Machu Picchu and vicinity. XXIV, p. 425, Apr., 1913

Peruvian coast, showing the islands on which the guanayes have their rookeries. XLVI, p. 282, Sept., 1924

Photograph of model relief map of Peru, showing Ecuador-Peru boundary settlement (1942). LXXXII, p. 170, Aug., 1942

Route map of Peruvian Expedition of 1912. XXIV, p. 388, Apr., 1913

Route map of the Peruvian Expedition of 1915, showing territory explored in 1915. XXIX, p. 434, May, 1916

Southern Peru. XXIX, p. 435, May, 1916

Southern Peru, the Andean country which is the home of the lamoids. LXXXIX, p. 645, May, 1946

Strongholds of ancient Incas, scenes of Pizarro's conquest, and of modern aërial exploration. LXIII, p. 83, Jan., 1933

PERU CURRENT. *See* Humboldt Current

PESCADORES (Islands), Formosa Strait:

Formosa, showing Pescadores. LXXXVII, p. 7, Jan., 1945

Japan and Korea, with insets of Kuril Islands, Pescadores, Karafuto, Ryukyu Islands, Okinawa, Formosa, Tokyo, and location of Japan in the western Pacific. LXXXVIII, supplement, 37 x 26½ inches, Dec., 1945

Southeast Asia and Pacific Islands from the Indies and the Philippines to the Solomons, with inset of Pescadores. LXXXVI, supplement, 41 x 26½ inches, Oct., 1944

PETRA (Ruins), Trans-Jordan:

Petra, rose-red city of rock. LXVII, p. 132, Feb., 1935

PHILIPPINE ISLANDS (Republic of the Philippines):

Area of devastation by the last eruption (1911) of Taal Volcano, also the towns destroyed by previous eruptions. XXIII, p. 314, Apr., 1912

Chart of Manila Bay. IX, p. 275, June, 1898

Crater of Taal Volcano immediately before and shortly after the great eruption of 1911. XXIII, p. 364, Apr., 1912

Indian Ocean, including Australia, New Zealand and Malaysia, with inset of the Philippines. LXXIX, supplement, 25½ x 32¾ inches, Mar., 1941

Japan and Adjacent Regions of Asia and the Pacific Ocean, with insets of industrial centers of Japan and the Marshall Islands. LXXXV, supplement, 26½ x 34½ inches, Apr., 1944

Luzon Island, with inset showing location of the Philippines. LXXVIII, p. 413, Oct., 1940

Manila as a distributing point for commerce. XIII, p. 314, Aug., 1902

Mindanao and the Sulu Archipelago. LXXXVI, pp. 542-543, Nov., 1944

Northern half of Philippine Islands. LVIII, p. 315, Sept., 1930

Northern Luzon. XXII, p. 216, Mar., 1911

Northern Luzon. XXIII, p. 835, Sept., 1912

Philippine Islands. IX, p. 258, June, 1898

Philippine Islands. LXXXI, p. 187, Feb., 1942

Philippine Islands, showing the progress of the topographic and hydrographic survey of the Islands by the United States Coast and Geodetic Survey. XXII, p. 83, Jan., 1911

The Philippine Islands as the Geographical Center of the Far East. XI, supplement, 7½ x 10¾ inches, Jan., 1900

The Philippines. Prepared by reduction from the map of the Bureau of Insular Affairs, War Department. Relief compiled from maps of the Corps of Engineers, U. S. Army, and from Spanish Surveys. XVI, supplement, 23 x 36 inches, Aug., 1905

The Philippines. Progress Map of Signal Corps Telegraph Lines and Cables in the Military Division of the Philippines. XIII, supplement in two sheets, 34 x 35, and 33 x 35½ inches, Jan., 1902

The Philippines, with insets of Manila, Lingayen Gulf, and a location map of the Philippines. LXXXVII, supplement, 17½ x 26 inches, Mar., 1945

PHILIPPINE ISLANDS (Republic of the Philippines)—*Continued*

Region affected by the great eruption of Taal Volcano, January 30, 1911. XXIII, p. 315, Apr., 1912

Relief map of the Philippine Islands, showing telegraph and cable lines. XV, p. 492, Dec., 1904

Southeast Asia and Pacific Islands from the Indies and the Philippines to the Solomons, with 22 inset maps of important cities and islands. LXXXVI, supplement, 41 x 26½ inches, Oct., 1944

Theatre of Military Operations in Luzon, 1899. War Department, Adjutant General's Office, Military Information Division. X, supplement, 23½ x 38 inches, June, 1899

PHOENIX ISLANDS, South Pacific Ocean. *See* Canton Island; Enderbury Island; Gardner Island; Hull Island; Sydney Island

PLYMOUTH, England:

Southwestern England, with enlargement of Plymouth area. LXXXIX, p. 215, Feb., 1946

POLAND:

Poland. L, p. 213, Aug., 1926

Poland. LXXV, p. 744, June, 1939

Southern Poland, showing bicycle route of Dorothy Hosmer. LXXV, p. 743, June, 1939

POLAR REGIONS. *See* Antarctic Regions; Arctic Regions

POLYNESIA:

Archipelago of Polynesia. XLVIII, p. 358, Oct., 1925

Marquesas, Tuamotu, and Austral Islands. XLVIII, p. 366, Oct., 1925

Migration routes of Hawaiian islanders from Asia. XLV, p. 127, Feb., 1924

New Zealand to the Samoa group, with an enlargement of Falcon Island. LIV, p. 760, Dec., 1928

Pacific Ocean, with inset maps of important islands and island groups. LXX, supplement, 31 x 38 inches, Dec., 1936; revised in 1942

Pacific Ocean and the Bay of Bengal, with inset maps of important islands, and table of airline distances in statute miles. LXXXIV, supplement, 36½ x 26½ inches, Sept., 1943

Position of Tahiti in the mid-Pacific. XXXVIII, p. 303, Oct., 1920

Route followed by Capt. Harry Pidgeon in his circumnavigation of the globe. LIII, pp. 144-145, Feb., 1928

Routes of Captain Cook's three voyages through the great South Sea. LI, p. 87, Jan., 1927

South Pacific, with inset of Niuafoō Island. LXVIII, p. 95, July, 1935

South Pacific archipelagoes, including the Marquesas group: Note the location of Yap among the Caroline Islands. XXXVI, p. 281, Oct., 1919

South Pacific islands, showing Date Line and Canton Island, site of 1937 Eclipse Expedition. LXXII, p. 380, Sept., 1937

Sovereignty and Mandate Boundary Lines in 1921 of the Islands of the Pacific. XL, supplement, 19 x 25 inches, Dec., 1921

POLYNESIA—*Continued*

Topography of two coral-ringed volcanic isles: Bolabola, of the Society group, and Vavitao, of the Austral group. XLVIII, p. 369, Oct., 1925

See also Easter Island; Hawaii; Marquesas Islands; Society Islands; Tahiti

PONAPE (Island), Caroline Islands:

Japanese Micronesia, with insets of Palau, Ponape, and Truk Islands. LXXXI, pp. 764-765, June, 1942

Japanese Micronesia, with insets of Yap, Ponape, and Palau Islands. LXIX, p. 483, Apr., 1936

Pacific Ocean and the Bay of Bengal, with inset of Ponape. LXXXIV, supplement, 36½ x 26½ inches, Sept., 1943

Southeast Asia and Pacific Islands from the Indies and the Philippines to the Solomons, with inset of Ponape. LXXXVI, supplement, 41 x 26½ inches, Oct., 1944

Strategic isles of the Pacific. LXXXV, pp. 392-393, 17 island maps, Apr., 1944

POPULATION:

Distribution of the population of Australia. XXX, p. 512, Dec., 1916

A Map of the World (in Eastern and Western Hemispheres), with insets showing land and water hemispheres, density of population, time zones, and world mapping. LXXX, supplement, 41 x 22 inches, Dec., 1941

The World, with insets showing Arctic and Antarctic regions, natural vegetation and ocean currents, and density of population and prevailing winds. LXII, supplement, 26 x 38½ inches, Dec., 1932

See also United States: Population Maps

PORTO RICO. *See* Puerto Rico

PORTUGAL:

Lisbon and the Friendly Bay. XLII, p. 510, Nov., 1922

Portugal. LII, p. 568, Nov., 1927

Portugal. LXXIII, p. 134, Feb., 1938

See also Azores (Islands); Madeira (Islands); São Tomé (Island)

PORTUGUESE TIMOR. *See* Timor

POTOMAC (River), Maryland-West Virginia-D. C.:

Potomac River windings in Maryland, Virginia, and West Virginia. LXXXVIII, pp. 36-37, July, 1945

PRADT, GEORGE H.: Map:

Enchanted Mesa, New Mexico, surveyed in 1897, by George H. Pradt. VIII, p. 283, Oct., 1897

PRATAS (Island), South China Sea:

Southeast Asia and Pacific Islands from the Indies and the Philippines to the Solomons, with inset of Pratas. LXXXVI, supplement, 41 x 26½ inches, Oct., 1944

PREHISTORIC ICE SHEETS. *See* Ice Sheets

PRINCETON (Aircraft Carrier):

Cruises of the *Princeton,* from the time of commissioning at Philadelphia to her loss in the Philippine Sea. LXXXVIII, pp. 210-211, Aug., 1945

PRUSSIA. *See* East Prussia

PTOLEMY, CLAUDIUS: Maps:

India, from "Geographia Universalis," 1552 (Ptolemy's map). LXII, p. 765, Dec., 1932

World: Claudius Ptolemy map, circa A.D. 150. V, pl. 1 (opp. p. 1), Apr. 7, 1893

PUEBLO BONITO. *See* New Mexico

PUERTO RICO:

The Countries of the Caribbean, Including Mexico, Central America, the West Indies and the Panama Canal, with detailed insets of the Panama Canal and the Canal Zone, Porto Rico and the Virgin Islands, and Guantanamo Bay, Cuba. XLI, supplement, 25 x 44 inches, Feb., 1922

Main highway system of the island. XLVI, p. 602, Dec., 1924

Map of Central America, Cuba, Porto Rico and the Islands of the Caribbean Sea, with inset of the Panama Canal and Canal Zone. XXIV, supplement, 12½ x 19 inches, Feb., 1913

Mexico, Central America, and the West Indies, with inset of Puerto Rico. LXVI, supplement, 23 x 40 inches, Dec., 1934

Mexico, Central America, and the West Indies, with inset of Puerto Rico and the Virgin Islands. LXXVI, supplement, 24 x 41 inches, Dec., 1939

Military telegraph lines in Porto Rico operated by the Signal Corps, U. S. Army; military posts; ports of entry; and area (of Porto Rico) compared with that of the State of Connecticut. XI, p. 242, June, 1900

Relief map of Porto Rico, showing telegraph lines. XV, p. 493, Dec., 1904

PUTO SHAN (Island), East China Sea:

Puto Shan, with enlargement showing location of island off the China coast. LXXXIX, p. 375, Mar., 1946

Q

QUEBEC (Province), Canada:

Cotidal lines for the Gulf of Saint Lawrence. XVII, p. 308, June, 1906

Saguenay region, with inset of the St. Lawrence. LXXV, pp. 598-599, May, 1939

St. Lawrence-Saguenay region, with inset showing whole of province. LXVII, p. 170, Feb., 1935

R

RACES:

Distribution of blond Eskimos. XXIII, p. 1224, Dec., 1912

Ethnographic Russia in 1900. XI, p. 172, May, 1900

Interrelation of the races. XII, p. 264, July, 1901

Map of the Races of Europe and Adjoining Portions of Asia and Africa. XXXIV, supplement, 19¾ x 31 inches, Dec., 1918

RACES—*Continued*

Map showing the probable migration routes of Hawaiian Islanders from Asia. XLV, p. 127, Feb., 1924

Panama, showing present location of aboriginal tribes. XXIII, p. 628, July, 1912

The races of mankind before the European invasion of other continents. XII, p. 263, July, 1901

Where Russia's orphan races reside. XXXIV, p. 277, Oct., 1918

See also Population

RADIO:

Northeast Atlantic coast, locating lightships and lighthouses which broadcast radio signals as navigation aids. LXX, p. 173, Aug., 1936

Paths of short-wave radio beams from New York City follow great circle routes over surface of the earth. LXXXII, p. 679, Nov., 1942

Paths of short-wave radio beams from San Francisco follow great circle routes over surface of the earth. LXXXII, p. 678, Nov., 1942

RAIATEA (Island), Society Islands:

Relief map of Raïatea and Tahaa Islands. LXV, p. 716, June, 1934

RAILROADS:

Chignecto Ship Railway, to connect the Gulf of St. Lawrence and the Bay of Fundy. VII, p. 70, Feb., 1896

A graphic representation of the vastness of the rolling stock of America's railroads. XLIII, p. 360, Apr., 1923

Isthmus of Tehuantepec, showing the routes of the National Railroad of Tehuantepec and the proposed Eads Ship Railway. VII, p. 67, Feb., 1896

See also names of countries

RAINFALL. *See* Weather Charts

RAKAHANGA (Island), South Pacific Ocean:

Pacific Ocean and the Bay of Bengal, with inset of Rakahanga. LXXXIV, supplement, 36½ x 26½ inches, Sept., 1943

RALEIGH, SIR WALTER: Voyages:

Ancient map of Albemarle and Pamlico Sounds, showing colonists' ships of Sir Walter Raleigh's expedition of 1584, approaching Roanoke Island. LXIV, p. 696, Dec., 1933

RAND DISTRICT, South Africa. *See* Witwatersrand

RAPA NUI (Island), South Pacific Ocean. *See* Easter Island

RED SEA:

Pearl-fishing islands and inset of Arabia. LXXII, p. 600, Nov., 1937

Suez-Red Sea region. LXXXI, p. 507, Apr., 1942

REID, HARRY FIELDING: Maps:

Glacier Bay and Muir Glacier. By Harry Fielding Reid. VII, p. 144, Apr., 1896

Muir Glacier, Alaska. Surveyed with Plane Table in 1890, by Harry Fielding Reid. IV, supplement, 19½ x 17¾ inches, Mar. 21, 1892

Northern part of Muir Inlet. IV, pl. 15 (opp. p. 55), Mar. 21, 1892

RHINELAND (Region), Germany:

Rhineland. LXXXVIII, p. 4, July, 1945

Rhineland, showing former demilitarized zone. LXIX, p. 832, June, 1936

RHODE ISLAND:

Northeastern United States. LXXXVIII, supplement, 41 x 26½ inches, Sept., 1945

RHODESIA:

Northern Rhodesia and Southern Rhodesia. LXXXVI, p. 284, Sept., 1944

RIO GRANDE (River), U. S.-Mexico:

Course of the Rio Grande from its source in western Colorado to the Gulf of Mexico. LXXVI, 6 maps, pp. 419, 424, 427, 428, 440, 453, Oct., 1939

Map showing wanderings of the Rio Grande and of the old boundary. XXIV, p. 384, Mar., 1913

RIO GRANDE DELTA, Texas:

Rio Grande Delta. LXXV, p. 54, Jan., 1939

RIVERS:

Alaska, showing navigable waters and railroads. XVIII, p. 164, Mar., 1907

Drainage map of northwestern Ecuador; also, route followed by Mark B. Kerr, on survey. VII, p. 239, July, 1896

Front-line trenches of the rivers of New York. L, p. 92, July, 1926

Geological Survey River Stations: Map showing the location of the principal River Stations maintained in the United States by the U. S. Geological Survey. XVII, p. 357, June, 1906

Landlocked Paraguay is a maritime nation—a vast river system links it to the sea. LXXXIV, p. 461, Oct., 1943

The Lower Valley of the Bar. VII, pl. XXVI (opp. p. 236), July, 1896

Paraguay and its river and rail approach from Buenos Aires. LXIII, p. 387, Apr., 1933

Rivers in Germany and Austria, paddled by Cornelia Stratton Parker. LXI, p. 368, Mar., 1932

Sketch map of the Meuse, showing the Bar, the Aire, and the Aisne. VII, p. 232, July, 1896

Sketch map of the Seine, the Meuse, and the Moselle. VII, p. 189, June, 1896

Sketch maps showing diversion of the Toul from the Meuse to the Moselle. VII, p. 229, July, 1896

Sketch maps showing the Marne River, branches and diversions. VII, pp. 199, 201, June, 1896

Tahiti, showing the many rivers that flow from the high mountains in the interior. XII, p. 418, Dec., 1901

Tennessee Gorge, showing the present course of the Tennessee River through Walden Plateau, and the probable arrangement of the drainage immediately preceding the westward diversion of the Appalachian River. VI, p. 116, May 23, 1894

United States, showing waterways that probably could be made navigable for commerce. XVIII, p. 676, Oct., 1907

United States interior navigation. XIV, p. 183, May, 1903

Valley of the Meuse, near Dun-sur-Meuse. VII, pl. XXIV (opp. p. 195), June, 1896

RIVERS—*Continued*

Valley of the Meuse, near St. Mihiel. VII, pl. XXIII, June, 1896

Valley of the Moselle, near Berncastel. VII, pl. XXII (opp. p. 193), June, 1896

Valley of the Seine, near Duclair. VII, pl. XXI (opp. p. 191), June, 1896

Where the great river trenches of Asia run parallel. L, p. 134, Aug., 1926

See also names of the following rivers: Balsas; Colorado; Connecticut; Delaware; Jordan; Mississippi; Missouri; Nile; Ohio; Orinoco; Potomac; Rio Grande; Saskatchewan; Sushitna; Thames; Yellowstone; Yukon; *and* Pearl River Delta; Saguenay River Region; St. Lawrence River Region; Salmon River Area

RIVIERA (Region), France-Italy:

Riviera, with inset map showing location of Monaco. LXVII, p. 69, Jan., 1935

ROMAN EMPIRE:

Classical Lands of the Mediterranean, with inset of the Roman Empire at the time of Trajan. LXXVII, supplement, 35¼ x 26 inches, Mar., 1940

Europe and northern Africa, showing extent of Roman Empire, with table of historical facts. XC, pp. 552-553, Nov., 1946

Extent of the Empire, at the death of Augustus (A.D. 14). LXXIV, p. 538, Oct., 1938

The Roman Empire. XII, p. 299, Aug., 1901

Rome-Naples area, showing main arteries and important sites of antiquity. XC, p. 569, Nov., 1946

ROMANIA (Rumania):

Eastern Romania. LXXVII, p. 411, Mar., 1940

Romania. LXV, p. 401, Apr., 1934

Romania. LXXIV, p. 562, Nov., 1938

Rumania. XLIX, p. 323, Mar., 1926

ROME, Ancient:

Classical Lands of the Mediterranean, with inset of Ancient Rome. LXXVII, supplement, 35¼ x 26 inches, Mar., 1940

ROTA (Island), Marianas Islands:

Southeast Asia and Pacific Islands from the Indies and the Philippines to the Solomons, with inset of Rota. LXXXVI, supplement, 41 x 26½ inches, Oct., 1944

Strategic isles of the Pacific. LXXXV, pp. 392-393, 17 island maps, Apr., 1944

ROUMANIA. *See* Romania

RUANDA (Region), Belgian Congo:

Ruanda, "The Land of Giants and Pygmies." XXIII, p. 388, Apr., 1912

RUMANIA. *See* Romania

RUSSIA. *See* Union of Soviet Socialist Republics

RUSSIAN SOVIET FEDERATED SOCIALIST REPUBLIC, U. S. S. R. *See* Crimea; Daghestan Autonomous Soviet Socialist Republic; Siberia

RUSSIAN TURKISTAN. *See* Soviet Central Asia

RUYSCH, JOHANN: Map:
World: *Ruysch Map, 1508.* V, pl. 5, supplement, 23 x 18¼ inches, Apr. 7, 1893; reprint, 16½ x 13½ inches, 1965

RYUKYU RETTO (Nansei Shoto), Japan:
Japan and Adjacent Regions of Asia and the Pacific Ocean, with insets of industrial centers of Japan and the Marshall Islands. LXXXV, supplement, 26½ x 34½ inches, Apr., 1944
Japan and Korea, with insets of Kuril Islands, Pescadores, Karafuto, Ryukyu Islands, Okinawa, Formosa, Tokyo, and location of Japan in the western Pacific. LXXXVIII, supplement, 37 x 26½ inches, Dec., 1945
Ryukyus, with inset showing location of the islands in relation to Japan, Formosa, Philippines, and the China coast. LXXXVII, p. 545, May, 1945
Southeast Asia and Pacific Islands from the Indies and the Philippines to the Solomons, with inset of Nansei Islands, Amami to Okinawa. LXXXVI, supplement, 41 x 26½ inches, Oct., 1944
See also Okinawa Gunto

S

SAAR (Region), Germany:
Saar Basin. LXVII, p. 242, Feb., 1935
Strategic position of the Saar. LXVII, p. 243, Feb., 1935

SABA (Island), Leeward Islands:
Military outposts leased from Britain put new teeth in Uncle Sam's defenses, with inset of Saba. LXXVIII, p. 621, Nov., 1940

SAGUENAY RIVER REGION, Quebec, Canada:
Region of the Saguenay River, Quebec. LXXV, pp. 598-599, May, 1939
St. Lawrence-Saguenay region, with inset showing Quebec Province. LXVII, p. 170, Feb., 1935

ST. HELENS, Mount, Washington:
Mount Saint Helens, compiled from original surveys and field notes by Lieut. Charles P. Elliott, U. S. A. VIII, pl. 31 (opp. p. 228), July-Aug., 1897

ST. LAWRENCE, Gulf of. *See* Chignecto Ship Railway

ST. LAWRENCE RIVER REGION, Canada-U. S.:
Saguenay region, with inset of the St. Lawrence. LXXV, pp. 598-599, May, 1939
St. Lawrence-Saguenay region, with inset showing Quebec Province. LXVII, p. 170, Feb., 1935

ST. PIERRE AND MIQUELON (Islands, French Territory), Atlantic Ocean:
St. Pierre and Miquelon. LXXX, p. 746, Dec., 1941

ST. THOMAS (Island), Virgin Islands:
Mexico, Central America, and the West Indies, with inset of Saint Thomas. LXXVI, supplement, 24 x 41 inches, Dec., 1939

ST. THOMAS (Island), Virgin Islands—*Continued*
The St. Thomas-Hatteras hurricane of September 3-12, 1889. II, foldout charts (bet. pp. 210-211), July, 1890

ST. VINCENT (Island), West Indies:
Zones of devastation in St. Vincent caused by volcanic eruptions. XIII, p. 282, July, 1902

SAIPAN (Island), Marianas Islands:
Southeast Asia and Pacific Islands from the Indies and the Philippines to the Solomons, with inset of Saipan and Tinian. LXXXVI, supplement, 41 x 26½ inches, Oct., 1944
Strategic isles of the Pacific. LXXXV, pp. 392-393, 17 island maps, Apr., 1944

SALMON RIVER AREA, Idaho:
National Geographic Society-U. S. Geological Survey Expedition down the Salmon River; extent of the Idaho Batholith, shown. LXX, p. 105, July, 1936
The River of No Return roars through rugged mountain country. LXX, p. 100, July, 1936

SALVADOR. *See* El Salvador

SALZKAMMERGUT (Region), Austria:
Salzkammergut. LXXI, p. 446, Apr., 1937

SAMANA (Island). *See* Bahama Islands

SAMOA (Islands), South Pacific Ocean:
Pacific Ocean and the Bay of Bengal, with inset of Tutuila. LXXXIV, supplement, 36½ x 26½ inches, Sept., 1943

SAN SALVADOR (Watling, Island), Bahamas:
Herrera map, 1601, with vignette of Watling Island from a modern chart. VI, p. 187, Dec. 29, 1894

SANTO DOMINGO. *See* Dominican Republic

SÃO PAULO (State), Brazil:
Area between Santos and São Paulo. LXXV, p. 660, May, 1939
São Paulo coffee district of Brazil. XXII, p. 909, Oct., 1911

SÃO TOMÉ (Island), Gulf of Guinea:
São Tomé, the Chocolate Island, with location map. LXXXIX, p. 659, May, 1946

SARAWAK. *See* Borneo

SARDINIA (Island), Mediterranean Sea:
Island of Sardinia. XLIII, p. 4, Jan., 1923
Relation of Sardinia to the mainland of Italy. XLIII, p. 5, Jan., 1923
Sardinia and her relative position to adjacent Mediterranean countries. XXX, p. 102, Aug., 1916

SASKATCHEWAN (Province), Canada:
A Map of Northwestern United States and Neighboring Canadian Provinces. LXXIX, supplement, 24½ x 36 inches, June, 1941

SASKATCHEWAN (River), Canada:
Sources of the Saskatchewan. X, p. 115, Apr., 1899

SAUDI ARABIA:
Saudi Arabia, with insets of Medina to Mecca area and Ras at Tannura to Dhahran area. LXXXVIII, p. 469, Oct., 1945
Western Arabia, adjacent countries, and northeastern Africa. LXV, p. 765, June, 1934

SCILLY ISLES, England:
Scilly Isles, with inset of the British Isles. LXXIV, p. 757, Dec., 1938

SCOTLAND:
A Modern Pilgrim's Map of the British Isles or More Precisely the Kingdom of Great Britain and Northern Ireland and the Irish Free State. LXXI, supplement, 29 x 35 inches, June, 1937
Scotland. LXXXIX, pp. 552-553, May, 1946
Southeastern Scotland. LXIX, p. 551, Apr., 1936

SEINE (River), France:
Sketch map of the Seine, the Meuse, and the Moselle. VII, p. 189, June, 1896
Valley of the Seine, near Duclair. VII, pl. XXI (opp. p. 191), June, 1896

SERBIA:
Bulgaria, Servia, and Macedonia. XXIII, p. 1152, Nov., 1912
Bulgaria and Servia. XXVII, p. 421, Apr., 1915

SERILAND (Sonora). *See* Mexico

SHANGHAI, China:
Southeast Asia and Pacific Islands from the Indies and the Philippines to the Solomons, with inset of Shanghai area. LXXXVI, supplement, 41 x 26½ inches, Oct., 1944

SHANTUNG (Province), China:
Shantung, China's Holy Land. XXXVI, p. 235, Sept., 1919

SHAWANGUNK MOUNTAIN. *See* New York

SHIP RAILWAYS:
Chignecto Ship Railway, to connect the Gulf of St. Lawrence and the Bay of Fundy. VII, p. 70, Feb., 1896
Isthmus of Tehuantepec, showing the routes of the National Railroad of Tehuantepec and the proposed Eads Ship Railway. VII, p. 67, Feb., 1896

SHIPS AND SHIPPING:
Chart of the World on Mercator's Projection, showing Submarine Cables and Connections, and also Tracks for full-powered Steam Vessels. XVI, supplement, 25 x 45 inches, Feb., 1905
The Gold and Coal Fields of Alaska, Together with the Principal Steamer Routes and Trails; Insets: Trails from Tide Water to the Headwaters of the Yukon River; The Klondike Gold Region, Canada. IX, pl. 4, supplement, 25 x 30 inches, Apr., 1898
Track chart. Positions of the trough of low barometer and tracks of vessels, March 11-14, 1888. I, foldout, Oct., 1888
Transportation routes of the Pacific. XIII, p. 310, Aug., 1902

SIAM. *See* Thailand

SIBERIA:
Bering's chart of his first voyage. From D'Anville's Atlas, 1737. The first published map of his explorations. II, foldout (opp. p. 111), May, 1890
Carte Générale des Découvertes de l'Amiral de Fonte, et autres Navigateurs Espagnols, Anglois et Russes pour la recherche du Passage à la Mer du Sud. Par M. De l'Isle. III, supplement, 16¼ x 13 inches, Jan. 28, 1892; Feb. 19, 1892
Far Eastern Republic. XLI, p. 567, June, 1922
Great Siberian Railway. XV, p. 129, Mar., 1904
Great Trans-Siberian Railway, showing its principal connections. XXIII, p. 1076, Nov., 1912
Kirin, Harbin, Vladivostok. Map showing seat of war in Manchuria (Beginning just north of Mukden, and covering the country north to Harbin and east to Vladivostok; the map shows all roads, trails, and mountains over which the armies must pass). XVI, supplement, 18 x 44 inches, June, 1905
Map of Korea and Manchuria. Prepared by the Second Division, General Staff (Military Information Division), War Department, Washington, U. S. A. Insets: Vladivostok; Port Arthur; and index map. XV, supplement, 36 x 42 inches, Mar., 1904
Route of Trans-Siberian Railway. XII, p. 438, Dec., 1901
Siberian Railway. XIII, p. 38, Feb., 1902
Where Vladimir M. Zenzinov was exiled in Arctic Siberia. XLVI, p. 699, Dec., 1924

SICILY (Island), Mediterranean Sea:
Classical Lands of the Mediterranean. LXXVII, supplement, 35¼ x 26 inches, Mar., 1940
Geology in the vicinity of Messina. XX, p. 394, Apr., 1909
Mediterranean regions, with inset map of Sicily. LXXXIV, pp. 312-313, Sept., 1943
Messina: Showing principal buildings, the city wall, and sickle-shaped harbor. XX, p. 375, Apr., 1909
Sicily. XLVI, p. 306, Sept., 1924
Sicily and south Italy. XX, p. 118, Jan., 1909
Straits of Messina, showing area of maximum destruction from the recent earthquake. XX, p. 378, Apr., 1909

SIKANG (Province), China:
China-India war route, with enlargement showing Minya Konka and the route followed by the Sikang Expedition. LXXXIII, p. 628, May, 1943
China-Tibetan border, showing route of Joseph F. Rock to the Amnyi Machen Mountains. LVII, pp. 138-139, Feb., 1930
Sikang, Yünnan, and Szechwan Provinces of China. LX, p. 7, July, 1931
Sikang's mountain grasslands, route followed by Ray G. Johnson and party. LXXXV, p. 718, June, 1944
Szechwan, Yünnan, and Sikang Provinces. LVIII, p. 388, Oct., 1930

SINAI (Peninsula). *See* Egypt

SINGAPORE, Straits Settlements:

Indian Ocean, including Australia, New Zealand and Malaysia, with inset of Singapore. LXXIX, supplement, 25½ x 32¾ inches, Mar., 1941

Malay States, Thailand, and French Indo-China, with inset of Singapore. LXXX, p. 662, Nov., 1941

Map of equatorial regions of the world, showing importance of Singapore's location. LXXVIII, p. 86, July, 1940

Southeast Asia and Pacific Islands from the Indies and the Philippines to the Solomons, with inset of Singapore area. LXXXVI, supplement, 41 x 26½ inches, Oct., 1944

Strategic geographic position of Singapore, with an inset of the Malay Peninsula. XLIX, p. 238, Mar., 1926

SINKIANG (Chinese Turkistan):

Eastern Turkistan. XIV, p. 13, Jan., 1903

Khotan Valley. XIV, p. 12, Jan., 1903

Map of China and Its Territories. Included: Mongolia, Manchuria, Chosen, East Turkestan, Tibet, Northern India. XXIII, supplement, 17 x 23 inches, Oct., 1912

Route of the Morden-Clark Asiatic Expedition. LII, p. 374, Oct., 1927

Sinkiang and adjacent countries. LIX, p. 323, Mar., 1931

Western Sinkiang. LXIX, p. 7, Jan., 1936

SKY CHARTS. *See* Heavens

SMOKY MOUNTAINS, North Carolina-Tennessee. *See* Great Smoky Mountains; Great Smoky Mountains National Park

SOCIETY ISLANDS, South Pacific Ocean:

Relief map of Raïatea and Tahaa Islands. LXV, p. 716, June, 1934

See also Bolabola; Tahiti

SOERABAJA, Java:

Southeast Asia and Pacific Islands from the Indies and the Philippines to the Solomons, with inset of Soerabaja area. LXXXVI, supplement, 41 x 26½ inches, Oct., 1944

SOLAR RADIATION STATION:

Southwest Africa in the vicinity of the new observatory. L, p. 504, Oct., 1926

SOLOMON ISLANDS, South Pacific Ocean:

Coral Sea area, showing the Solomons and New Hebrides, with an inset of Efate. LXXXVI, p. 233, Aug., 1944

Pacific Ocean and the Bay of Bengal, with inset of Solomon Islands. LXXXIV, supplement, 36½ x 26½ inches, Sept., 1943

Solomon Islands, with inset maps showing Guadalcanal-Tulagi area and Bougainville area. LXXXII, p. 815, Dec., 1942

SOMALILAND. *See* French Somaliland

SONORA (State). *See* Mexico

SOUTH AFRICA. *See* Union of South Africa

SOUTH AFRICAN WAR (Boer War):

Map of the Seat of War in Africa. Prepared in the War Department, Adjutant General's Office, Military Information Division. Inset of South Africa. X, supplement, 33 x 45 inches, Dec., 1899

SOUTH AMERICA:

Amazon Valley. XLIX, p. 354, Apr., 1926

Atlantic Ocean, with inset of Isthmus of Panama. LXXVI, supplement, 31 x 25 inches, July, 1939

Atlantic Ocean, with inset of Isthmus of Panama and a table of air-line distances in statute miles. LXXX, supplement, 31¼ x 25 inches, Sept., 1941

Drainage map of northwestern Ecuador; also, route followed by Mark B. Kerr, on survey. VII, p. 239, July, 1896

Guianas, with an inset showing the territory traversed by the "Kaieteur and Roraima" Expedition. XXXVIII, p. 229, Sept., 1920

Map of South America. XL, supplement, 26 x 36 inches, Oct., 1921

Map of the Valley of the Orinoco River, showing the extent of territory drained by that waterway and the bearing it has on the Venezuelan question. Compiled by T. Heyward Gignilliat, 1896. VII, pl. 5, supplement, 18 x 11¾ inches, Feb., 1896

Mexico, Central America, and the West Indies, showing northern South America. LXVI, supplement, 23 x 40 inches, Dec., 1934

Miami-Montevideo air-mail route. LVII, p. 264, Mar., 1930

North-central South America, showing Brazil-Venezuela boundary. LXIV, p. 589, Nov., 1933

Pacific coast of South America, showing location of Humboldt Current. LXXIX, p. 376, Mar., 1941

Patagonia, illustrating explorations of J. B. Hatcher, 1896-'97. VIII, p. 311, Nov., 1897

Peru and Bolivia. XIX, p. 606, Sept., 1908

Railroad from Buenos Aires to Santiago, 888 miles long. XXI, p. 401, May, 1910

Route of A. F. Tschiffely on his horseback journey from Buenos Aires to Washington. LV, p. 140, Feb., 1929

Route of the National Geographic Society's aërial survey flight from Washington to Buenos Aires. LIX, p. 4, Jan., 1931

Route of the trail-blazing flight of U. S. Army airplanes through 20 countries of Latin America. LII, p. 452, Oct., 1927

Route of transandean mail and passenger planes. LIX, p. 596, May, 1931

Salient geographic features of the American Mediterranean and surrounding lands. VII, p. 177, May, 1896

South America. III, pl. I, foldout, Mar. 28, 1891

South America. XVII, supplement, 8 x 11 inches, Aug., 1906

South America, with inset maps of the Galápagos Islands, airways and relief, chief natural resources, precipitation and temperature. LXXII, supplement, 26¾ x 37½ inches, Dec., 1937

SOUTH AMERICA—*Continued*

South America, with insets of the Galapagos Islands, chief natural resources, precipitation and temperature, airways and relief, and a table of airline distances and flying times in hours. LXXXII, supplement, 26½ x 37¼ inches, Oct., 1942

Straits of Magellan. VIII, p. 131, May, 1897

Tierra del Fuego, with inset of South America. LXXII, pp. 746-747, Dec., 1937

See also Argentina; Bolivia; Brazil; British Guiana; Chile; Colombia; Ecuador; French Guiana; Paraguay; Peru; São Paulo; Surinam; Venezuela

SOUTH CAROLINA:

North Carolina, South Carolina, Georgia, and Eastern Tennessee, with inset of Charleston. L, supplement, 14¾ x 19 inches, Sept., 1926

SOUTH DAKOTA:

Route taken by stratosphere balloon *Explorer II.* LXIX, p. 63, Jan., 1936

SOUTH GEORGIA (Island), South Atlantic Ocean:

Author's sketch map of the bleak and lonely Bay of Isles. XLI, p. 412, Apr., 1922

Island of South Georgia, outpost of the Antarctic. XLI, p. 412, Apr., 1922

SOUTH POLE. *See* Antarctic Regions

SOUTH SEA ISLANDS. *See* Melanesia; Micronesia; Polynesia

SOUTHERN HEMISPHERE:

Northern and Southern Hemispheres, with insets of time zones, world terrain, and tables of airline distances in four hemispheres. LXXXIII, supplement, 41 x 22 inches, Apr., 1943

SOUTHERN RHODESIA:

Northern Rhodesia and Southern Rhodesia. LXXXVI, p. 284, Sept., 1944

SOUTH-WEST AFRICA:

Map of the Seat of War in Africa. Prepared in the War Department, Adjutant General's Office, Military Information Division. Inset of South Africa. X, supplement, 33 x 45 inches, Dec., 1899

South-West Africa. LVII, p. 489, Apr., 1930

Southwest Africa in the vicinity of the new observatory (NGS Solar Radiation Station). L, p. 504, Oct., 1926

SOVIET CENTRAL ASIA:

Khoresm, U. S. S. R.: With inset map showing relative location of Khoresm. LXI, p. 754, June, 1932

SPAIN:

Location of the Montespan Grotto in the foothills of the Pyrenees. XLVI, p. 126, Aug., 1924

Mountainous regions of Spain. LIX, p. 124, Jan., 1931

Spain. XXI, p. 188, Mar., 1910

Spain. LV, p. 314, Mar., 1929

Spain. LXIX, p. 409, Mar., 1936

SPAIN—*Continued*

Spain, showing location of Andorran Republic on the French border. XXXIII, p. 281, Mar., 1918

Spain, with inset map of Madrid and vicinity. LXX, pp. 402-403, Oct., 1936

Spain and the Basque Provinces. XLI, p. 66, Jan., 1922

See also Balearic Islands

SPANISH MOROCCO. *See* Morocco

SPITSBERGEN (Svalbard, Archipelago), Arctic Ocean:

The Arctic Regions, with inset of Spitsbergen. XLVIII, supplement, 19¼ x 18 inches, Nov., 1925

Spitsbergen and an inset showing its location in the Arctic Ocean. LIV, p. 228, Aug., 1928

SPORADES, Southern (Islands). *See* Dodecanese Islands

STAR CHARTS. *See* Heavens

STARBUCK ISLAND, Line Islands:

Pacific Ocean and the Bay of Bengal, with inset of Starbuck Island. LXXXIV, supplement, 36½ x 26½ inches, Sept., 1943

STEPHEN ISLAND, New Zealand:

Map showing location of Stephen Island. LXVII, p. 651, May, 1935

STRAITS SETTLEMENTS, Malay Peninsula. *See* Singapore

STRATOSPHERE BALLOON FLIGHT:

Route taken over South Dakota by stratosphere balloon *Explorer II.* LXIX, p. 63, Jan., 1936

SUDAN (Region), Africa. *See* Anglo-Egyptian Sudan

SUEZ CANAL, Egypt:

Indian Ocean, including Australia, New Zealand and Malaysia, with inset of the Suez Canal. LXXIX, supplement, 25½ x 32¾ inches, Mar., 1941

Suez Canal. LXVIII, p. 612, Nov., 1935

Suez-Red Sea region. LXXXI, p. 507, Apr., 1942

SULPHUR ISLAND, Volcano Islands. *See* Iwo Jima

SULU ARCHIPELAGO, Philippine Islands:

Mindanao and the Sulu Archipelago. LXXXVI, pp. 542-543, Nov., 1944

SUMATRA:

Netherlands Indies, with inset of Malay States and northern Sumatra. LXXIII, p. 668, June, 1938

Sumatra. LX, p. 205, Aug., 1931

Sumatra and an inset of the Dutch East Indies. LVII, p. 189, Feb., 1930

SUNDA ISLANDS, Greater. *See* Borneo; Celebes; Java; Sumatra

SUNDA ISLANDS, Lesser. *See* Lesser Sunda Islands; Timor

SURINAM (Dutch Guiana):
Surinam and French Guiana, with insets showing the location and comparable sizes of the Guianas. LXXXIII, p. 462, Apr., 1943

SUSHITNA (Susitna, River), Alaska:
Sushitna River area; Mt. McKinley, shown. VIII, p. 323, Nov., 1897

SUSSEX (County), England:
Scenic and historic properties of the National Trust. LXXXVII, pp. 420-421, Apr., 1945
Southeastern England, showing harassed Channel coast. LXXIX, p. 70, Jan., 1941
Sussex County. LXVIII, p. 63, July, 1935

SUVOROV (Islets), South Pacific Ocean:
Pacific Ocean and the Bay of Bengal, with inset of Suvorov. LXXXIV, supplement, 36½ x 26½ inches, Sept., 1943

SVALBARD (Archipelago). *See* Spitsbergen

SWAINS ISLAND, South Pacific Ocean:
Pacific Ocean and the Bay of Bengal, with inset of Swains Island. LXXXIV, supplement, 36½ x 26½ inches, Sept., 1943

SWEDEN:
Southern Sweden. LXVI, p. 5, July, 1934
Southern Sweden, with inset of Småland. LXXVI, p. 396, Nov., 1939

SWITZERLAND:
Lake Geneva region. LXXII, p. 728, Dec., 1937

SYDNEY ISLAND, Phoenix Islands:
Pacific Ocean and the Bay of Bengal, with inset of Sydney Island. LXXXIV, supplement, 36½ x 26½ inches, Sept., 1943

SYRIA:
Asia Minor and the Levant. L, p. 652, Dec., 1926
Bible Lands and the Cradle of Western Civilization; Insets: Holy Land Today, Holy Land in Biblical Times, Jerusalem, Traditional Route of the Exodus, St. Paul's Travels and the Seven Churches, The Crusades. XC, supplement, 32 x 22 inches, Dec., 1946
Bible Lands and the Cradle of Western Civilization; Insets: Jerusalem, The Holy Land, Economic Development, Route of the Exodus, St. Paul's Travels and the Seven Churches, The Crusades, Empire of Alexander the Great. LXXIV, supplement, 25 x 35 inches, Dec., 1938
Crusader castles. LIX, p. 371, Mar., 1931
Crusader trails and castles. LXIV, p. 654, Dec., 1933
Eastern shores of the Mediterranean. XXXVIII, p. 89, Aug., 1920
Latakia and Lebanon. LVIII, p. 485, Oct., 1930
Latakia and Lebanon. LXIV, p. 103, July, 1933
Syria. XXXVI, p. 441, Nov., 1919

SZECHWAN (Province), China:
China. XXII, p. 1097, Dec., 1911
Szechwan Province, China. LVIII, p. 388, Oct., 1930

T

TABASCO (State), Mexico:
Bird migration routes from South America to North America converge funnel-like in Central America. Inset of Veracruz and Tabasco, Mexico, showing La Venta region, a natural bird observatory. LXXXVII, p. 188, Feb., 1945

TAHAA (Island), Society Islands:
Relief map of Raïatea and Tahaa Islands. LXV, p. 716, June, 1934

TAHITI (Island), Society Islands:
Position of Tahiti in the mid-Pacific. XXXVIII, p. 303, Oct., 1920
Profile map of Tahiti, showing the eroded volcanic core, the lagoon, fringing reef, and barrier reef. XLVIII, p. 362, Oct., 1925
Tahiti, showing the many rivers that flow from the high mountains in the interior. XII, p. 418, Dec., 1901

TAI SHAN (Mountain), China:
Pen and ink drawing of Tai Shan, with pictographs. LXXXVII, p. 700, June, 1945

TAIWAN (Island). *See* Formosa

TARAWA (Atoll), Gilbert Islands:
Gilbert Islands, with insets of Tarawa and Makin. LXXXVII, p. 135, Feb., 1945
Pacific Ocean and the Bay of Bengal, with inset of Tarawa. LXXXIV, supplement, 36½ x 26½ inches, Sept., 1943

TASMANIA (Island), Australia:
Australia, with inset of Tasmania. LXVIII, pp. 672-673, Dec., 1935

TELEGRAPH CABLES. *See* Cables

TEMPERATURE MAPS:
Canada, with insets showing natural regions, precipitation and temperature, main natural resources, routes of explorers and time zones. LXIX, supplement, 27 x 40 inches, June, 1936
South America, with inset maps of the Galápagos Islands, airways and relief, chief natural resources, precipitation and temperature. LXXII, supplement, 26¾ x 37½ inches, Dec., 1937
South America, with insets of the Galapagos Islands, chief natural resources, precipitation and temperature, airways and relief, and a table of airline distances and flying times in hours. LXXXII, supplement, 26½ x 37¼ inches, Oct., 1942
Summer and winter isothermal lines of Victoria, British Columbia. XVIII, p. 346, May, 1907
Texas, showing annual rainfall and mean annual temperature zones. XXIV, p. 1355, Dec., 1913
United States: Distribution of the total quantity of heat during season of growth and reproductive activity. VI, pl. 12 (opp. p. 238), Dec. 29, 1894
United States: Mean temperature of hottest six consecutive weeks of year. VI, pl. 13, Dec. 29, 1894

TENNESSEE:
Great Smoky Mountains National Park, with inset showing main roads across the park. LXX, p. 246, Aug., 1936
North Carolina, South Carolina, Georgia, and Eastern Tennessee. L, supplement, 14¾ x 19 inches, Sept., 1926
Northeastern Tennessee, showing Cumberland Gap. LXXXIV, p. 745, Dec., 1943
Relief map of the Chattanooga district. VI, pl. 4, May 23, 1894; reprint, foldout map, 1965
Tennessee. LXXV, pp. 556-557, May, 1939
Tennessee Gorge, showing the present course of the Tennessee River through Walden Plateau, and the probable arrangement of the drainage immediately preceding the westward diversion of the Appalachian River. VI, p. 116, May 23, 1894
Virginia, North Carolina, Kentucky, and Tennessee, showing new Eastern National Park-to-Park Highway. LXV, pp. 666-667, June, 1934

TEXAS:
Course of the Rio Grande from Candelaria to Eagle Pass. LXXVI, p. 428, Oct., 1939
Course of the Rio Grande from Eagle Pass to Rio Grande City. LXXVI, p. 440, Oct., 1939
Course of the Rio Grande from El Paso to Presidio. LXXVI, p. 427, Oct., 1939
Course of the Rio Grande from Rio Grande City to the Gulf of Mexico. LXXVI, p. 453, Oct., 1939
Galveston hurricane, 1900. XVI, p. 278, June, 1905
Gulf of Mexico, showing coastal areas of United States and Mexico. LXXXV, pp. 8-9, Jan., 1944
Rio Grande Delta. LXXV, p. 54, Jan., 1939
Texas. XXIV, p. 1353, Dec., 1913
Texas. LXXXVII, pp. 168-169, Feb., 1945
Texas, New Mexico, and Oklahoma. LIII, pp. 642-643, June, 1928
Texas, showing annual rainfall and mean annual temperature zones. XXIV, p. 1355, Dec., 1913
Two maps showing the effect of improvements at the entrance to Galveston, Texas, from the charts of 1867 and 1909. XX, p. 826, Sept., 1909

THAILAND (Siam):
Siam, French Indo-China, and Federated Malay States. LXV, p. 533, May, 1934

THAMES (River), England:
Thames River from Oxford to the North Sea. LXXV, pp. 244-245, Feb., 1939

THEATER OF WAR MAPS. *See* South African War; World War I; World War II

TIBET:
Map of China and Its Territories. Included: Mongolia, Manchuria, Chosen, East Turkestan, Tibet, Northern India. XXIII, supplement, 17 x 23 inches, Oct., 1912
Tibet, showing adjacent areas of India and China. XC, p. 172, Aug., 1946
Tibet and border countries. XL, p. 296, Sept., 1921

TIBETAN HIGHLAND:
China-India war route, with enlargement showing Minya Konka and the route followed by the Sikang Expedition. LXXXIII, p. 628, May, 1943

TIBURON (Island), Mexico:
Seriland, Sonora, Mexico, including Tiburon Island, from surveys by Bureau American Ethnology Expedition, 1895; location map. VII, pl. XIV, foldout, Apr., 1896

TIDES:
Atlantic coast tides. IX, p. 498, Dec., 1898
Cotidal chart (1833) of the Atlantic Ocean, by Dr. William Whewell. IX, p. 468, Nov., 1898
Cotidal chart (1807) of the British Isles, by Dr. Thomas Young. IX, p. 470, Nov., 1898
Cotidal charts of the British Isles, by Dr. William Whewell. IX, p. 470, Nov., 1898
Cotidal lines for the Gulf of Saint Lawrence. XVII, p. 308, June, 1906
Cotidal lines for the Mediterranean Sea. XVII, p. 306, June, 1906
Cotidal Lines for the World; Or, Lines of Simultaneous High Water at Each Hour and Half Hour of Greenwich Lunar Time. XVII, supplement, 8 x 14 inches, June, 1906
Cotidals from St. Johns, Newfoundland. IX, p. 502, Dec., 1898
The Delaware: Progressing wave front at successive hours. IX, p. 401, Sept., 1898
Flood chart: Condition of Holland without dikes during mean high tide and highest stage of rivers. XII, p. 233, June, 1901
Systems of semi-diurnal tide. XVII, p. 305, June, 1906
Tidal and cotidal chart (1864) of Buzzards Bay and Nantucket Sound, by Dr. Alexander Dallas Bache. IX, p. 471, Nov., 1898
Tidal chart of Placentia Bay, Newfoundland. IX, p. 471, Nov., 1898
Tidal hours in Long Island Sound. IX, p. 506, Dec., 1898
Tidal hours in the Chesapeake. IX, p. 403, Sept., 1898

TIERRA DEL FUEGO (Archipelago), South America:
Tierra del Fuego, with inset of South America. LXXII, pp. 746-747, Dec., 1937

TIMOR (Island), Lesser Sundas:
Pacific Ocean and the Bay of Bengal, with inset of Timor. LXXXIV, supplement, 36½ x 26½ inches, Sept., 1943
Timor. LXXXIV, p. 359, Sept., 1943

TIN CAN ISLAND. *See* Niuafoō

TINIAN (Island), Marianas Islands:
Southeast Asia and Pacific Islands from the Indies and the Philippines to the Solomons, with inset of Saipan and Tinian. LXXXVI, supplement, 41 x 26½ inches, Oct., 1944
Strategic isles of the Pacific. LXXXV, pp. 392-393, 17 island maps, Apr., 1944

TITICACA, Lake, Bolivia-Peru:
Lake Titicaca region. LI, p. 214, Feb., 1927

TOBAGO (Island), West Indies:

Trinidad and Tobago, with inset of West Indies. LXXII, p. 321, Sept., 1937

TOKELAU ISLANDS, South Pacific Ocean. *See* Atafu; Fakaofo; Nukunono Island

TOKYO, Japan:

Japan and Adjacent Regions of Asia and the Pacific Ocean, with insets of industrial centers of Japan and the Marshall Islands. LXXXV, supplement, 26½ x 34½ inches, Apr., 1944

Japan and Korea, with insets of Kuril Islands, Pescadores, Karafuto, Ryukyu Islands, Okinawa, Formosa, Tokyo, and location of Japan in the western Pacific. LXXXVIII, supplement, 37 x 26½ inches, Dec., 1945

TONGA ISLANDS, South Pacific Ocean:

Tonga Islands, with inset of Niuafoō. LXVIII, p. 95, July, 1935

TONGAREVA (Penrhyn, Atoll), South Pacific Ocean:

Pacific Ocean and the Bay of Bengal, with inset of Tongareva. LXXXIV, supplement, 36½ x 26½ inches, Sept., 1943

TOSCANELLI, PAOLO DEL POZZO DEI: Map:

World: Toscanelli map, 1474. V, pl. 3 (opp. p. 4), Apr. 7, 1893

TRANS-JORDAN:

Bible Lands, showing Palestine, Trans-Jordan, and Egypt. LXXXV, p. 236, Feb., 1944

Bible Lands, showing Palestine, Trans-Jordan, and Syria. LXXXVI, p. 722, Dec., 1944

Bible Lands and the Cradle of Western Civilization; Insets: Holy Land Today, Holy Land in Biblical Times, Jerusalem, Traditional Route of the Exodus, St. Paul's Travels and the Seven Churches, The Crusades. XC, supplement, 32 x 22 inches, Dec., 1946

Bible Lands and the Cradle of Western Civilization; Insets: Jerusalem, The Holy Land, Economic Development, Route of the Exodus, St. Paul's Travels and the Seven Churches, The Crusades, Empire of Alexander the Great. LXXIV, supplement, 25 x 35 inches, Dec., 1938

Near East, showing Egypt, Anatolia, and the Arab kingdoms of Hedjaz, Transjordania, and Iraq. XLIII, p. 534, May, 1923

Trans-Jordan, Palestine, and adjacent territory. LXVII, p. 133, Feb., 1935

World's deepest land depression separates Palestine from Trans-Jordan. LXXI, p. 72, Jan., 1937

See also Petra

TRINIDAD (Island), West Indies:

Trinidad and Tobago, with inset of West Indies. LXXII, p. 321, Sept., 1937

TRISTAN DA CUNHA (Islands), South Atlantic Ocean:

South Atlantic Ocean, with inset of Tristan da Cunha. LXXIV, p. 674, Nov., 1938

TRUK ISLANDS, Caroline Islands:

Japanese Micronesia, with insets of Palau, Ponape, and Truk Islands. LXXXI, pp. 764-765, June, 1942

Pacific Ocean and the Bay of Bengal, with inset of Truk Islands. LXXXIV, supplement, 36½ x 26½ inches, Sept., 1943

Southeast Asia and Pacific Islands from the Indies and the Philippines to the Solomons, with inset of Truk Islands. LXXXVI, supplement, 41 x 26½ inches, Oct., 1944

Strategic isles of the Pacific. LXXXV, pp. 392-393, 17 island maps, Apr., 1944

Truk, Ruk, and Hogolu, of the Caroline group, showing encircling coral reef. XL, p. 648, Dec., 1921

Truk Islands. LXV, p. 707, June, 1934

TUAMOTU (Archipelago), South Pacific Ocean:

Marquesas, Tuamotu, and Austral Islands. XLVIII, p. 366, Oct., 1925

TULAGI (Island), Solomon Islands:

Solomon Islands, with inset maps showing Guadalcanal-Tulagi area and Bougainville area. LXXXII, p. 815, Dec., 1942

TUNISIA:

Location of Kairowan. XXII, p. 1089, Dec., 1911

Site of Carthage; also the Pontine Marshes, Italy. XLV, p. 394, Apr., 1924

Tunisia, Africa's northernmost tip, nearly divides the Mediterranean into two great lakes. LXXI, p. 349, Mar., 1937

Tunisia, with inset of Tunis. LXXI, p. 350, Mar., 1937

TURKEY:

Aegean regions, and an inset of the Bosphorus. LVI, p. 489, Oct., 1929

Ancient Armenia, and the country where the Armenians now live. XXVIII, p. 359, Oct., 1915

Asia Minor. XLVI, p. 450, Oct., 1924

Asia Minor, the Dardanelles, and the islands of the Ægean Sea. XLII, p. 554, Nov., 1922

Bible Lands and the Cradle of Western Civilization; Insets: Holy Land Today, Holy Land in Biblical Times, Jerusalem, Traditional Route of the Exodus, St. Paul's Travels and the Seven Churches, The Crusades. XC, supplement, 32 x 22 inches, Dec., 1946

Bible Lands and the Cradle of Western Civilization; Insets: Jerusalem, The Holy Land, Economic Development, Route of the Exodus, St. Paul's Travels and the Seven Churches, The Crusades, Empire of Alexander the Great. LXXIV, supplement, 25 x 35 inches, Dec., 1938

Classical Lands of the Mediterranean. LXXVII, supplement, 35¼ x 26 inches, Mar., 1940

Constantinople. XLI, p. 650, June, 1922

Crusader trails and castles. LXIV, p. 654, Dec., 1933

Eastern Turkey. LXXX, p. 370, Sept., 1941

Europe and the Near East. LVI, supplement, 34¼ x 39¼ inches, Dec., 1929

Gates to the Black Sea. XXVII, p. 532, May, 1915

TURKEY—*Continued*

Gates to the Black Sea. XXVIII, p. 232, Sept., 1915

Greece, Bulgaria, Turkey. XXX, p. 271, Sept., 1916

Location of Mt. Argæus and of the Troglodytes. XXXV, p. 315, Apr., 1919

Near East, showing naval bases, airports, highways, railways, oil pipe lines, and oil pumping stations. LXXX, pp. 144-145, Aug., 1941

Near East, showing Turkey, Iraq, and adjacent regions, with naval bases, airports, highways, railways, and oil pipe lines. LXXXII, pp. 388-389, Sept., 1942

Railways constructed and proposed in Asia Minor and Persia. XI, p. 202, May, 1900

"Shores of Sunrise" (The Levant). L, p. 652, Dec., 1926

Shores of the Aegean, which have provided the geographic panorama for much of the history of civilization. LIV, p. 725, Dec., 1928

Turkey. LXXV, pp. 8-9, Jan., 1939

Turkey. LXXXVII, pp. 594-595, May, 1945

Turkey, Arabia, Persia, and Egypt. XX, p. 173, Feb., 1909

Turkey, Arabia, Persia, and Egypt. XXII, p. 63, Jan., 1911

Turkey and the Near East, with inset of Cappadocia. LXXVI, p. 767, Dec., 1939

Turkey in Asia. XXVI, p. 614, Dec., 1914

World trouble spot, the oil-rich Middle East. LXXXIX, pp. 396-397, Mar., 1946

The world's most historic lands. XXIX, p. 216, Feb., 1916

TURKISTAN. *See* Sinkiang; Soviet Central Asia

TUTUILA (Island), Samoa:

Pacific Ocean and the Bay of Bengal, with inset of Tutuila. LXXXIV, supplement, 36½ x 26½ inches, Sept., 1943

TWEEDSMUIR PARK, British Columbia:

Tweedsmuir Park. LXXIII, p. 454, Apr., 1938

U

UGANDA:

Uganda borders the largest fresh-water lake in the Old World and contains the source of the Nile. LXXI, p. 113, Jan., 1937

UKRAINIAN SOVIET SOCIALIST REPUBLIC, U. S. S. R.:

Western U. S. S. R., showing extent of German invasion. LXXXV, p. 516, May, 1944

ULSTER. *See* Ireland

ULSTER COUNTY, New York:

Shawangunk Mountain, Ulster County. VI, pl. 1 (opp. p. 23), foldout stereogram. Mar. 17, 1894

UNIMAK (Island), Aleutian Islands:

Unimak Island. XIV, p. 92, Mar., 1903

UNION GROUP, South Pacific Ocean. *See* Atafu; Fakaofo: Nukunono Island

UNION OF SOUTH AFRICA:

Map of the Seat of War in Africa. Prepared in the War Department, Adjutant General's Office, Military Information Division. Inset of South Africa. X, supplement, 32 x 45 inches, Dec., 1899

Union of South Africa, with inset maps of Africa and Cape of Good Hope. LIX, pp. 400-401, Apr., 1931

Union of South Africa, with inset maps of Africa and Cape of Good Hope. LXXXII, p. 203, Aug., 1942

Union of South Africa, with inset showing Witwatersrand. LXXXII, p. 739, Dec., 1942

UNION OF SOVIET SOCIALIST REPUBLICS:

Amu Darya Valley, with inset map showing the location of Khoresm. LXI, p. 754, June, 1932

Bering's chart of his first voyage. From D'Anville's Atlas, 1737. The first published map of his explorations. II, foldout (opp. p. 111), May, 1890

Carte Générale des Découvertes de l'Amiral de Fonte, et autres Navigateurs Espagnols, Anglois et Russes pour la recherche du Passage à la Mer du Sud. Par M. De l'Isle. III, supplement, 16¼ x 13 inches, Jan. 28, 1892; Feb. 19, 1892

Caucasus, showing the highlands of Daghestan. XXIV, p. 1086, Oct., 1913

Diagram showing successive advances of Russia toward India. XI, p. 183, May, 1900

Ethnographic Russia in 1900. XI, p. 172, May, 1900

Great Siberian Railway. XV, p. 129, Mar., 1904

Great Trans-Siberian Railway, showing its principal connections. XXIII, p. 1076, Nov., 1912

Growth of Russia in Europe from 1303 to 1645. XI, p. 175, May, 1900

Growth of Russia in Europe from 1645 to 1900. XI, p. 178, May, 1900

Murman coast and the territory through which runs the new Murman Railway. XXXV, p. 332, Apr., 1919

Route of Trans-Siberian Railway. XII, p. 438, Dec., 1901

Russia in Europe. VII, pl. I, supplement, 9¾ x 12¾ inches, Jan., 1896; reprint, 11¼ x 10 inches, 1965

Russian Empire in its geographic relation to Europe and Asia. XI, p. 185, May, 1900

Siberian Railway. XIII, p. 38, Feb., 1902

Successive advances of Russia to the Pacific. XVI, p. 404, Sept., 1905

Union of Soviet Socialist Republics, with international boundaries according to Russian treaties and claims as of October 1, 1944. Boundaries of January 1, 1938, are shown in red. LXXXVI, supplement, 40 x 25 inches, Dec., 1944

Union of Soviet Socialist Republics, with outline map of the United States superimposed, to show the northern latitude of Russian-Siberian industry. LXXXIII, pp. 532-533, May, 1943

Western U. S. S. R., showing extent of German invasion. LXXXV, p. 516, May, 1944

Where Russia's orphan races reside. XXXIV, p. 277, Oct., 1918

See also Crimea; Siberia

UNITED NATIONS AREA:

The United States of America, with insets of United Nations area and East of Maine. XC, supplement, 26½ x 41 inches, July, 1946

UNITED STATES:

Airway routes of the United States. LXIII, p. 634, May, 1933

Approximate location and extent of open range in the United States. XV, p. 21, Jan., 1904

Arizona, New Mexico, and northern Mexico. XXXVIII, p. 75, July, 1920

Arizona, New Mexico, Utah, and Colorado, showing sites of ruins. LVI, p. 743, Dec., 1929

Atlantic coast tides. IX, p. 498, Dec., 1898

Bitter Root Forest Reserve. IX, pl. 12 (opp. p. 394), foldout, Sept., 1898

Boundaries of territorial acquisitions of the United States. XII, p. 375, Oct., 1901

Clark's survey of the boundary of Texas. XII, p. 431, Dec., 1901

Coal areas of the United States. XVIII, p. 135, Feb., 1907

Course of the Rio Grande from its source in Colorado to the Gulf of Mexico. LXXVI, 6 maps, pp. 419, 424, 427, 428, 440, 453, Oct., 1939

Cumberland Gap, first high gateway to the West. LXXXIV, p. 745, Dec., 1943

Distribution of the chestnut-bark disease. XXII, p. 345, Apr., 1911

Forest Reserves and National Parks of the United States. XI, p. 370, Sept., 1900

Forests and woodlands of the West. XV, p. 19, Jan., 1904

Geological Survey River Stations: Map showing the location of the principal River Stations maintained in the United States by the U. S. Geological Survey. XVII, p. 357, June, 1906

Government reclamation projects. XX, p. 437, May, 1909

Grand Canyon, from Green River, Wyoming, to mouth of Colorado, in Mexico. XXVI, p. 153, Aug., 1914

Grand Canyon of the Colorado River: 1923 Expedition of the U. S. Geological Survey. XLV, p. 474, May, 1924

A graphic representation of the vastness of the rolling stock equipment of America's railroads. XLIII, p. 360, Apr., 1923

Great Lakes region. LXV, pp. 454-455, Apr., 1934

Gulf of Mexico, showing coastal areas of United States and Mexico. LXXXV, pp. 8-9, Jan., 1944

Historic and Scenic Reaches of the Nation's Capital. LXXIV, supplement, 26½ x 31¼ inches, July, 1938

How distant tributaries help make lower Mississippi floods. LII, p. 245, Sept., 1927

Indian Territory, showing boundary lines of the Five Civilized Tribes. IX, p. 482, Dec., 1898

Indian Territory, showing progress of subdivision survey up to January 1, 1896. VII, p. 113, Mar., 1896

Irrigated and irrigable lands. XV, p. 20, Jan., 1904

UNITED STATES—*Continued*

Lake Superior, showing northern Michigan and Wisconsin, eastern Minnesota, and western Ontario. XL, p. 114, Aug., 1921

Life zones of the United States. VI, pl. 14, Dec. 29, 1894

Lights that mark the approaches to the great harbors of Boston, New York, and Philadelphia. XXIV, p. 6, Jan., 1913

Lines of equal magnetic declination (variation of the compass) and equal magnetic dip for the year 1900. XIII, p. 95, Mar., 1902

Location of fisheries. XVI, p. 522, Nov., 1905

Location of 46 out of the 56 national bird reservations. XXIV, p. 369, Mar., 1913

Location of some of the important finds of dinosaurian remains and areas where deposits were laid down during the time that these animals lived. XXXV, p. 425, May, 1919

A Map of Northwestern United States and Neighboring Canadian Provinces. LXXIX, supplement, 24½ x 36 inches, June, 1941

A Map of the Travels of George Washington, with insets of New York and the lower Hudson, Tidewater Virginia, Philadelphia, Boston, and Mount Vernon. LXI, supplement, 20 x 29 inches, Jan., 1932

Mexico, Central America, and the West Indies, showing southern United States. LXVI, supplement, 23 x 40 inches, Dec., 1934

Missouri River Basin, showing dams, completed and projected, and wildlife sanctuaries. LXXXVIII, pp. 576-577, Nov., 1945

National Monuments and National Parks. XXIII, p. 538, June, 1912

Natural divisions of the North American forests, exclusive of Mexico. VI, pl. 8 (opp. p. 139), June 22, 1894

National Parks of the United States. XI, p. 370, Sept., 1900

North Carolina, South Carolina, Georgia and Eastern Tennessee, with insets of Charleston, Charlotte, and Atlanta. L, supplement, 14¾ x 19 inches, Sept., 1926

Northeast Atlantic coast, locating lightships and lighthouses. LXX, p. 173, Aug., 1936

Northeastern United States, with inset of southeastern New England. LXXXVIII, supplement, 41 x 26½ inches, Sept., 1945

Ohio and Mississippi River Basins. LXXI, pp. 770-771, June, 1937

Oil pipe-line system which forms a network beneath the surface of the eastern half of the United States. XXXVII, p. 183, Feb., 1920

Ozark Plateau, showing Missouri and Arkansas with portions of bordering States. LXXXIII, p. 593, May, 1943

Primary triangulation in the United States about 10,000 linear miles by the Coast and Geodetic Survey and about 2,000 miles by the lake survey. XXV, p. 664, June, 1914

Production of petroleum in the United States in 1918, and the outlines of the petroleum areas. XXXVII, p. 187, Feb., 1920

The Reaches of New York City. LXXV, supplement, 26½ x 29 inches, Apr., 1939

Relative density of railroads in the United States. XVI, p. 521, Nov., 1905

UNITED STATES—*Continued*

Route followed by Lindbergh in the "Spirit of St. Louis," and its companion plane. LIII, p. 5, Jan., 1928

Route of Lewis R. Freeman's 2,000-mile voyage down the Yellowstone-Missouri. LIV, p. 77, July, 1928

Route of Santa Fe Trail. LVI, p. 216, Aug., 1929

Route of the Connecticut River through New England. LXXXIII, p. 405, Apr., 1943

Routes followed by Lieutenant John A. Macready and Lieutenant Oakley G. Kelly on their transcontinental, non-stop flights, and of Lieutenant Macready and Lieutenant A. W. Stevens on their later photographic flights. XLVI, p. 6, July, 1924

Sections mapped by the U. S. Geological Survey. XII, p. 122, Mar., 1901

Southern Appalachians, showing the deformed Cretaceous Peneplain and the areas not reduced to baselevel. VI, pl. 5, May 23, 1894; reprint, foldout map, 1965

Southern Appalachians, showing the deformed Tertiary Peneplain and the areas not reduced to baselevel. VI, pl. 6, May 23, 1894; reprint, foldout map, 1965

The southern part of the prehistoric Canadian ice-sheet. Photograph from a model. The glacial data are on the authority of T. C. Chamberlin. IX, pl. 9 (opp. p. 314), July, 1898

Southwestern United States. XXI, p. 632, Aug., 1910

The Southwestern United States. LXXVII, supplement, 35 x 26 inches, June, 1940

Swamp areas in the United States. XVIII, p. 298, May, 1907

Territories from which each National Army cantonment camp received its troops; also, the location of cantonments, Regular Army organization camps, National Guard mobilization camps, and aviation camps. XXXII, p. 438, Nov.-Dec., 1917

Texas, New Mexico, and Oklahoma. LIII, pp. 642-643, June, 1928

Tidal hours in Long Island Sound. IX, p. 506, Dec., 1898

Tidal hours in the Chesapeake. IX, p. 403, Sept., 1898

To build a canal in the United States to correspond with the Grand Canal of China, it would be necessary to traverse the country as indicated by the black line on this map. XXIII, p. 933, Oct., 1912

Transcontinental routes of the "Shenandoah" on its record-making voyage. XLVII, p. 5, Jan., 1925

United States, showing territory acquired by Texas annexation and Mexican cession. XXII, p. 474, May, 1911

United States, showing waterways that probably could be made navigable for commerce. XVIII, p. 676, Oct., 1907

United States air mail routes in operation and proposed. XLIX, p. 5, Jan., 1926

United States and adjoining portions of Canada and Mexico. LXIII, supplement, 26 x 40 inches, May, 1933

UNITED STATES—*Continued*

The United States and adjoining portions of Canada and Mexico, with insets showing Army Corps areas and population of the States (1940). LXXVIII, supplement, 41 x 26½ inches, Dec., 1940

The United States in relief, showing the principal physical provinces. Photograph from a model prepared for the U. S. Geological Survey by Edwin E. Howell. IX, pl. 8 (opp. p. 311), July, 1898

United States interior navigation. XIV, p. 183, May, 1903

United States of America, with insets of important cities. XLIII, supplement, 26½ x 36¼ inches, Apr., 1923

The United States of America, with insets of United Nations area and East of Maine. XC, supplement, 26½ x 41 inches, July, 1946

United States showing Estimates of the Map Value of Existing Mother Maps. By Henry Gannett. IV, supplement, 18 x 13 inches, Mar. 31, 1892

Vacant public lands. XV, p. 18, Jan., 1904

Virginia, North Carolina, Kentucky, and Tennessee, showing new Eastern National Park-to-Park Highway. LXV, pp. 666-667, June, 1934

Voice voyages (telephone) made by the National Geographic Society from Washington to Pittsburgh, Chicago, Omaha, Denver, Salt Lake City, San Francisco, Portland, Seattle, El Paso, Ottawa, Jacksonville, and intermediate points. XXIX, p. 297, Mar., 1916

Wanderings of the Rio Grande and of the old boundary. XXIV, p. 384, Mar., 1913

Where the Great Wall (of China) would run if transferred to the United States. XLIII, p. 118, Feb., 1923

See also names of States; Washington, D. C.; *and the following*: Population Maps; Weather Charts

Population Maps

Foreign stock in the population of the United States—by foreign stock is meant foreign-born and children of a foreign-born father or mother. XXXI, p. 96, Feb., 1917

Indiana, showing population center of the U. S. (1930 census). LXX, pp. 272-273, Sept., 1936

Location of cities having a population of 50,000 or more, census 1890; Number of colored population for each colored insane, census 1880; Number of population for each insane person, census 1880; Ratio of total insane per 100,000 population, census 1880; Ratio of total insane per 100,000 population, census 1890; White insane only, census 1880. XIV, 6 maps, pp. 362, 363, 367, 368, 375, 376, Oct., 1903

Number of children under 5 years of age to 1,000 females 15 to 49 years of age, 1890; Number of children under 5 years of age to 1,000 females 15 to 49 years of age, 1900. XVI, 2 maps, pp. 506, 507, Nov., 1905

Number of inhabitants per square mile; Proportion of urban to total population; Rate of population growth, 1900-1910. XXII, 3 maps, pp. 35, 41, 43, Jan., 1911

UNITED STATES—*Continued*

Settled area in 1790; Settled area in 1890; Position of the center of population at the close of each decade from 1790 to 1890; Density of total population; Proportion of urban to total population; Average size of families; Distribution by sex; Proportion of colored to total population; Proportion of foreign born to total population; Proportion which native whites of native parentage bear to all whites; Proportion of Irish to total population; Proportion of British to total population; Proportion of Canadians to total population; Proportion of Germans to total population; Proportion of Scandinavians to total population. V, 15 maps, pls. 7-11, 13-16 (bet. pp. 24-41), Mar. 20, 1893

The United States and adjoining portions of Canada and Mexico, with insets showing Army Corps areas and population of the States (1940). LXXVIII, supplement, 41 x 26½ inches, Dec., 1940

Weather Charts

Arid, semi-arid, and humid regions of the United States. XV, p. 16, Jan., 1904

Cold wave, January 7-10, 1886, 7 a.m. each day. XVI, 4 maps, pp. 271-274, June, 1905

Cold wave, January 7-10, 1886, 7 a.m. each day; also, temperature change in each preceding 24 hours. VIII, 8 maps, pls. 7-14, Mar., 1897

Distribution of the total quantity of heat during season of growth and reproductive activity. VI, pl. 12 (opp. p. 238), Dec. 29, 1894

The Galveston hurricane, 1900. XVI, p. 278, June, 1905

Hot wave, July 28 to August 10, 1896, inclusive. VIII, pl. 6, Mar., 1897

The hurricane of November 25, 1888, located east of Savannah, Georgia. II, foldout chart (bet. pp. 210-211), July, 1890

Location of and annual precipitation at certain stations in the arid region of western America. XV, p. 162, Apr., 1904

Mean annual rainfall in the United States. XV, p. 16, Jan., 1904

Mean temperature of hottest six consecutive weeks of year. VI, pl. 13, Dec. 29, 1894

New England, showing direction of hurricane air currents and path of storm center, September 21, 1938. LXXV, p. 534, Apr., 1939

Normal storm tracks for May. XVI, p. 281, June, 1905

Rainfall map of Washington and Oregon. XX, p. 647, July, 1909

River Stations, U. S. Weather Bureau. VIII, pl. 2 (opp. p. 72), Mar., 1897

The St. Thomas-Hatteras hurricane of September 3-12, 1889. II, foldout charts (bet. pp. 210-211), July, 1890

Simple types of rainfall distribution. V, pl. 20 (opp. p. 45), Apr. 29, 1893

Storm tracks for August. XVI, p. 279, June, 1905

Storm tracks for February. XVI, p. 280, June, 1905

Tornado at Louisville, Ky., March 27, 1890. Weather map 8 p.m. of that date. VIII, pl. 15 (opp. p. 78), Mar., 1897

UNITED STATES—*Continued*

Tornado at Louisville, Ky., March 27, 1890. Weather map 8 p.m. of that date. XVI, p. 282, June, 1905

Tornado at St. Louis, Mo., May 27, 1896. Weather map 8 p.m. VIII, pl. 16, Mar., 1897

Tornadoes of 1889—a year of small frequency. XVI, p. 283, June, 1905

Tornadoes of 1893—a year of great frequency. XVI, p. 284, June, 1905

A typical weather map. XVIII, p. 595, Sept., 1907

Weather map, 8 a.m., February 28, 1902. XIII, p. 111, Mar., 1902

Weather maps showing the conditions under which the transcontinental, non-stop flight was made (May, 1923). XLVI, p. 4, July, 1924

West Indian hurricane, August 7-14, 1899. X, p. 345, Sept., 1899

West Indian hurricane, August 27-29, 1893, at 8 a.m. and 8 p.m. each day; also, changes in air pressure in each preceding 12 hours. VIII, 10 maps, pls. 17-26, Mar., 1897

West Indian hurricane, August 27-29, 1893, at 8 a.m. each day. XVI, 3 maps, pp. 275-277, June, 1905

West Indian hurricane, September, 1900. XI, 4 maps, pp. 385, 386, 389, 390, Oct., 1900

Winter storm, December 15, 1893, at 8 a.m. and 8 p.m.; December 16, at 8 a.m. VIII, 3 maps, pls. 3-5, Mar., 1897

Winter storm, December 15, 1893, at 8 a.m. and 8 p.m.; December 16, at 8 a.m. XVI, 3 maps, pp. 268-270, June, 1905

U. S. DEFENSE BASES:

Alaska, showing Alcan Highway. LXXXIII, pp. 150-151, Feb., 1943

Alaska—springboard for attack on Japan and key to continental defense. LXXXII, pp. 286-287, Sept., 1942

American bases in the Lesser Antilles protect the Panama Canal. LXXXI, p. 729, June, 1942

The American Virgins guard a main route from Europe to the Panama Canal. LXXVIII, p. 277, Sept., 1940

Arctic regions, as seen from 10,000 miles in space: the world of Captain Bob Bartlett, who supplied American military bases near the Arctic Circle for four summers. LXXXIX, p. 604, May, 1946

Atlantic Ocean, showing air routes to Norway and Britain, via Newfoundland, Greenland, and Iceland. LXXX, p. 77, July, 1941

Detailed map of the Aleutian Islands—battleground of the northern Pacific. LXXXIII, pp. 152-153, Feb., 1943

Global map of Arctic regions showing Greenland, important for weather stations and air bases. XC, p. 459, Oct., 1946

Greenland—an aerial stepping stone to Europe. LXXXII, pp. 370-371, Sept., 1942

Greenland, as seen from the North Pole, with emphasis upon its strategic importance to North America. LXXVIII, pp. 118-119, July, 1940

Leeward and Windward Islands: Like a curving shield the West Indies guard the Panama Canal. LXXIX, p. 5, Jan., 1941

U. S. DEFENSE BASES—*Continued*

Military outposts leased from Britain put new teeth in Uncle Sam's defenses. LXXVIII, p. 621, Nov., 1940

New Brunswick faces strategic Newfoundland across the Gulf of St. Lawrence. LXXIX, p. 597, May, 1941

Newfoundland, showing British and American defense bases. LXXX, p. 113, July, 1941

Newfoundland—starting point for aviators flying planes to Britain, Norway, and Portugal. LXXX, p. 77, July, 1941

Pacific islands, with history of discovery and an inset showing proposed American bases. LXXXIX, pp. 624-625, May, 1946

Pacific Northwest defense area. LXXXII, p. 425, Oct., 1942

United States Army and Navy air bases in Alaska. LXXVIII, p. 490, Oct., 1940

Western Hemisphere, showing U. S. defense bases. LXXIX, p. 41, Jan., 1941

U. S. GEOLOGICAL SURVEY:

The Gold and Coal Fields of Alaska, Together with the Principal Steamer Routes and Trails; Insets: Trails from Tide Water to the Headwaters of the Yukon River; The Klondike Gold Region, Canada. IX, pl. 4, supplement, 25 x 30 inches, Apr., 1898

See also United States

U. S. HYDROGRAPHIC OFFICE:

Submarine Cables of the World, with the Principal Connecting Land Lines, also Coaling, Docking, and Repairing Stations. Compiled in the U. S. Hydrographic Office. VII, pl. X, supplement, 48 x 30 inches, Mar., 1896

UTAH:

Newly discovered route to Rainbow Natural Bridge. XLIII, p. 198, Feb., 1923

Route of the National Geographic Society's San Juan Expedition. XLV, p. 278, Mar., 1924

The Southwestern United States. LXXVII, supplement, 35 x 26 inches, June, 1940

Utah, with insets of Bryce and Zion Canyons. LXIX, pp. 580-581, May, 1936

V

VALLEY OF TEN THOUSAND SMOKES. *See* Alaska

VATICAN CITY:

Vatican City. LXXV, pp. 382-383, Mar., 1939

VAVITAO (Island), Austral Islands:

Topography of two coral-ringed volcanic isles: Bolabola, of the Society group, and Vavitao, of the Austral group. XLVIII, p. 369, Oct., 1925

VENEZUELA:

Boundaries as claimed by Great Britain and Venezuela and as awarded by the Paris Tribunal, 1899. XI, pl. 4 (opp. p. 129), Apr., 1900

VENEZUELA—*Continued*

Map of the Valley of the Orinoco River, showing the extent of territory drained by that waterway and the bearing it has on the Venezuelan question. Compiled by T. Heyward Gignilliat, 1896. VII, pl. 5, supplement, 18 x 11¾ inches, Feb., 1896

North-central South America, showing Brazil-Venezuela boundary. LXIV, p. 589, Nov., 1933

Northeastern Venezuela. LXXV, p. 100, Jan., 1939

Venezuela. LX, p. 622, Nov., 1931

VERACRUZ (State), Mexico:

Archeological sites in Veracruz and Tabasco explored by National Geographic Society-Smithsonian Expedition of 1940. LXXVIII, p. 313, Sept., 1940

Bird migration routes from South America to North America converge funnel-like in Central America. Inset of Veracruz and Tabasco, Mexico, showing La Venta region, a natural bird observatory. LXXXVII, p. 188, Feb., 1945

New center of Maya culture discovered by National Geographic Society-Smithsonian Institution Expedition. LXXVI, p. 184, Aug., 1939

VERMONT:

Northeastern United States. LXXXVIII, supplement, 41 x 26½ inches, Sept., 1945

Vermont. LI, p. 340, Mar., 1927

VIRGIN ISLANDS, West Indies:

The Countries of the Caribbean, Including Mexico, Central America, the West Indies and the Panama Canal, with detailed insets of the Panama Canal and the Canal Zone, Porto Rico and the Virgin Islands, and Guantanamo Bay, Cuba. XLI, supplement, 25 x 44 inches, Feb., 1922

Greater and Lesser Antilles with inset of the Virgin Islands. LXXVIII, p. 277, Sept., 1940

Mexico, Central America, and the West Indies, with inset of Puerto Rico and the Virgin Islands. LXXVI, supplement, 24 x 41 inches, Dec., 1939

Mexico, Central America, and the West Indies, with inset of the Virgin Islands. LXVI, supplement, 23 x 40 inches, Dec., 1934

Relative position of Danish West Indies (near Porto Rico). XXX, p. 93, July, 1916

VIRGINIA:

Assateague Island, Virginia, showing land defenses built since 1849. XXXIII, p. 534, June, 1918

Capt. John Smith's map of Virginia, printed at Oxford in 1612 by Joseph Barnes. LXII, p. 760, Dec., 1932

Chain of forts recommended by George Washington. LXI, p. 40, Jan., 1932

Cumberland Gap. LXXXIV, p. 745, Dec., 1943

Fredericksburg, from the map prepared, in 1867, by the Corps of Engineers, U. S. A.; issued by the NGS, for Field-day, May 4, '95. VI, foldout, Apr. 20, 1895

Historic and Scenic Reaches of the Nation's Capital. LXXIV, supplement, 26½ x 31¼ inches, July, 1938

VIRGINIA—*Continued*

A Map of the Travels of George Washington, with insets of Mount Vernon and Tidewater Virginia. LXI, supplement, 20 x 29 inches, Jan., 1932

Potomac River windings in Maryland, Virginia, and West Virginia. LXXXVIII, pp. 36-37, July, 1945

Tidewater Virginia. LXXXI, p. 621, May, 1942

Tidewater Virginia, with inset of Hampton Roads. LXXVI, p. 361, Sept., 1939

Virginia. LV, p. 405, Apr., 1929

Virginia, North Carolina, Kentucky, and Tennessee, showing new Eastern National Park-to-Park Highway. LXV. pp. 666-667, June, 1934

Virginia and Florida, from an Amsterdam Atlas of the World published in 1638. XLV, p. 242, Mar., 1924

VIRUNGA MOUNTAINS, Belgian Congo:

Western Rift Valley and surrounding country, with inset of the Virunga Mountains. LXXVI, p. 515, Oct., 1939

VLADIVOSTOK. *See* Siberia

VOLCANO ISLANDS (Kazan Retto), Pacific Ocean. *See* Iwo Jima

VOSTOK ISLAND, Line Islands:

Pacific Ocean and the Bay of Bengal, with inset of Vostok Island. LXXXIV, supplement, 36½ x 26½ inches, Sept., 1943

W

WAKE (Island), North Pacific Ocean:

Pacific Ocean and the Bay of Bengal, with inset of Wake Island. LXXXIV, supplement, 36½ x 26½ inches, Sept., 1943

Strategic isles of the Pacific. LXXXV, pp. 392-393, 17 island maps, Apr., 1944

WALES:

A Modern Pilgrim's Map of the British Isles or More Precisely the Kingdom of Great Britain and Northern Ireland and the Irish Free State. LXXI, supplement, 29 x 35 inches, June, 1937

Severn River Valley. LXIII, p. 421, Apr., 1933

Wales. XLIV, p. 639, Dec., 1923

Wales. LXXXV, p. 754, June, 1944

WAR MAPS. *See* South African War; World War I; World War II; *and* names of countries and islands

WASHINGTON, GEORGE:

Location of Washington's chain of forts. LXI, p. 40, Jan., 1932

A map made by Washington on his trip to Fort Le Boeuf. LXI, p. 10, Jan., 1932

A Map of the Travels of George Washington, with insets of New York and the lower Hudson, Tidewater Virginia, Philadelphia, Boston, and Mount Vernon. LXI, supplement, 20 x 29 inches, Jan., 1932

Washington's travels in southwestern Pennsylvania. LXI, p. 12, Jan., 1932

WASHINGTON, GEORGE—*Continued*

Washington's travels in the Maryland-West Virginia sector. LXI, p. 36, Jan., 1932

WASHINGTON (State):

Lake Chelan and vicinity. IX, p. 418, Oct., 1898

Location of Mount Rainier. XXIII, p. 626, June, 1912

A Map of Northwestern United States and Neighboring Canadian Provinces. LXXIX, supplement, 24½ x 36 inches. June, 1941

Mount Saint Helens, compiled from original surveys and field notes by Lieut. Charles P. Elliott, U. S. A. VIII, pl. 31 (opp. p. 228), July-Aug., 1897

The Olympic Country, Washington. VII, pl. XVI (opp. p. 133), foldout, Apr., 1896

Pacific Northwest defense area. LXXXII, p. 425, Oct., 1942

Rainfall map of Washington and Oregon. XX, p. 647, July, 1909

State of Washington. LXIII, pp. 136-137, Feb., 1933

United States of America, with inset of Seattle. XLIII, supplement, 26½ x 36¼ inches, Apr., 1923

Washington and Oregon. XX, p. 646, July, 1909

WASHINGTON, D. C.:

Central part of Washington, D. C., 1904. XV, p. 375, Sept., 1904

District of Columbia, showing location of Capitol stone, Jefferson stone, and other historic markers and milestones. VI, pl. 9 (opp. p. 149), Nov. 1, 1894

Historic and Scenic Reaches of the Nation's Capital. LXXIV, supplement, 26½ x 31¼ inches, July, 1938

Location of Government buildings and new developments. LX, p. 521, Nov., 1931

The Mall, Washington, D. C. XXVII, supplement, 18¼ x 9¾ inches, Mar., 1915

The Mall and the principal public buildings. XLIII, p. 576, June, 1923

Maryland, Delaware, and District of Columbia, with inset of Washington, D. C., and vicinity. LI, supplement, 12 x 18 inches, Feb., 1927

The Nation's Capital: 1915 (Showing locations of public buildings, monuments, and existing and proposed public grounds). XXVII, p. 245, Mar., 1915

Original boundary stones of the District of Columbia. XX, p. 357, Apr., 1909

The Ultimate Washington (Plan laid out by the Commission of 1901 for the National Capital). XXVII, supplement, 18¼ x 9¾ inches, Mar., 1915

United States of America, with inset of Washington, D. C. XLIII, supplement, 26½ x 36¼ inches, Apr., 1923

Washington. XLIII, p. 574, June, 1923

WATLING (Island), Bahama Islands. *See* San Salvador

WEATHER CHARTS:

Arid regions of the world. XV, p. 17, Jan., 1904

Average lines along which the centers of storms move in July and January in the Northern Hemisphere. XVI, pp. 290-291, June, 1905

WEATHER CHARTS—*Continued*

Barometer diagram. Illustrating the fluctuations of the barometer from noon, March 11, to noon, March 14 (75th meridian time). I, foldout, Oct., 1888

Canada, with insets showing natural regions, precipitation and temperature, main natural resources, routes of explorers and time zones. LXIX, supplement, 27 x 40 inches, June, 1936

Climatic divisions in Europe, Africa, and Asia. XII, p. 259, July, 1901

The Cuban hurricane of September, 1888. II, 3 maps, p. 208, foldout charts (bet. pp. 210-211), July, 1890

Diagram showing yearly amount of rainfall in inches on the Panama Isthmus. XVI, p. 467, Oct., 1905

Distribution of rainfall on earth's surface. XII, p. 258, July, 1901

The hurricane of November 25, 1888, located east of Savannah, Georgia. II, foldout chart (bet. pp. 210-211), July, 1890

Hurricanes in the North Atlantic. II, foldout charts (bet. pp. 210-211), July, 1890

Panama Canal: Winds, calms, and sailing routes, Pacific Ocean, May-October. XV, p. 172, Apr., 1904

Panama Canal: Winds, calms, and sailing routes, Pacific Ocean, November-April. XV, p. 173, Apr., 1904

Rainfall in Australia. XXX, p. 488, Dec., 1916

The St. Thomas-Hatteras hurricane of September 3-12, 1889. II, foldout charts (bet. pp. 210-211), July, 1890

Summer and winter isothermal lines of Victoria, British Columbia. XVIII, p. 346, May, 1907

Track chart. Positions of the trough of low barometer and tracks of vessels, March 11-14, 1888. I, foldout, Oct., 1888

Weather charts—March 11 through March 14—of the Atlantic, showing meteorological conditions during the Great Storm of 1888. I, 4 foldouts (bet. pp. 58-59), Oct., 1888

West Indian hurricane, August 7-14, 1899. X, p. 345, Sept., 1899

West Indian hurricane, August 27-29, 1893, at 8 a.m. and 8 p.m. each day; also, changes in air pressure in each preceding 12 hours. VIII, 10 maps, pls. 17-26, Mar., 1897

West Indian hurricane, August 27-29, 1893, at 8 a.m. each day. XVI, 3 maps, pp. 275-277, June, 1905

West Indian hurricane, September, 1900. XI, 4 maps, pp. 385, 386, 389, 390, Oct., 1900

The World, with insets showing Arctic and Antarctic regions, natural vegetation and ocean currents, and density of population and prevailing winds. LXII, supplement, 26 x 38½ inches, Dec., 1932

See also Temperature Maps; United States

WEST INDIES:

American bases in the Lesser Antilles protect the Panama Canal. LXXXI, p. 729, June, 1942

Atlantic Ocean, with inset of Isthmus of Panama. LXXVI, supplement, 31 x 25 inches, July, 1939

WEST INDIES—*Continued*

Caribbean regions, showing airline distances in statute miles, with enlargements of Aruba, Bonaire, and Curaçao. LXXXIII, p. 172, Feb., 1943

The Countries of the Caribbean, Including Mexico, Central America, the West Indies, and the Panama Canal, with detailed insets of the Panama Canal and the Canal Zone, Porto Rico and the Virgin Islands, and Guantanamo Bay, Cuba. XLI, supplement, 25 x 44 inches, Feb., 1922

Geographical relation of Venezuela to the Isthmian Canal routes, to the West Indies and Florida. XIV, p. 18, Jan., 1903

Greater and Lesser Antilles, with inset of the Virgin Islands. LXXVIII, p. 277, Sept., 1940

Herrera map, 1601, with vignette of Watling Island from a modern chart. Samana and Guanahani, shown. VI, p. 187, Dec. 29, 1894

Hispaniola, Puerto Rico, and Leeward Islands. LXXIII, pp. 274-275, Mar., 1938

Juan de la Cosa map, 1500, with vignette of Samana from a modern chart. VI, pl. 10 (opp. p. 186), Dec. 29, 1894

Leeward and Windward Islands: Like a curving shield the West Indies guard the Panama Canal. LXXIX, p. 5, Jan., 1941

Map of Central America, Cuba, Porto Rico and the Islands of the Caribbean Sea, with relief elevation sketch of the canal. XXIV, supplement, 12½ x 19 inches, Feb., 1913

Mappa Munde Peinte sur Parchemin par Ordre de Henri II, Roi de France—1532; Samana (Guanahani), shown. VI, pl. 11 (opp. p. 188), Dec. 29, 1894

Mexico, Central America, and the West Indies. LXVI, supplement, 23 x 40 inches, Dec., 1934

Mexico, Central America, and the West Indies. LXXVI, supplement, 24 x 41 inches, Dec., 1939

Military outposts leased from Britain put new teeth in Uncle Sam's defenses. LXXVIII, p. 621, Nov., 1940

Trinidad and Tobago, with inset of West Indies. LXXII, p. 321, Sept., 1937

Volcanic islands of the West Indies. XIII, p. 213, June, 1902

West Indies, from Cuba to Puerto Rico, with an enlargement of Haiti and the Dominican Republic. LXXXV, p. 200, Feb., 1944

See also Bahama Islands; Cuba; Dominican Republic; Haiti; Jamaica; Martinique; Puerto Rico; St. Vincent; Virgin Islands; Windward Islands

Weather Charts

The Cuban hurricane of September, 1888. II, 3 maps, p. 208, foldout charts (bet. pp. 210-211), July, 1890

The St. Thomas-Hatteras hurricane of September 3-12, 1889. II, foldout charts (bet. pp. 210-211), July, 1890

West Indian hurricane, August 7-14, 1899. X, p. 345, Sept., 1899

West Indian hurricane, August 27-29, 1893, at 8 a.m. and 8 p.m. each day; also, changes in air pressure in each preceding 12 hours. VIII, 10 maps, pls. 17-26, Mar., 1897

WEST INDIES—*Continued*

West Indian hurricane, August 27-29, 1893, at 8 a.m. each day. XVI, 3 maps, pp. 275-277, June, 1905

West Indian hurricane, September, 1900. XI, 4 maps, pp. 385, 386, 389, 390, Oct., 1900

WEST VIRGINIA:

Chain of forts recommended by George Washington. LXI, p. 40, Jan., 1932

Historic and Scenic Reaches of the Nation's Capital. LXXIV, supplement, 26½ x 31¼ inches, July, 1938

Potomac River windings in Maryland, Virginia, and West Virginia. LXXXVIII, pp. 36-37, July, 1945

West Virginia. LXXVIII, pp. 144-145, Aug., 1940

WESTERN HEMISPHERE:

Map of Discovery. Reproduction in color of the painting by N. C. Wyeth, National Geographic Society, Washington, D. C. LV, text, p. 93; supplement, 18½ x 16¾ inches, Jan., 1929

A Map of the World (in Eastern and Western Hemispheres), with insets showing land and water hemispheres, density of population, time zones, and world mapping. LXXX, supplement, 41 x 22 inches, Dec., 1941

Western Hemisphere, showing U. S. defense bases. LXXIX, p. 41, Jan., 1941

The World (in Eastern and Western Hemispheres), with insets showing land and water hemispheres, and time zones. LXVIII, supplement, 23 x 44 inches, Dec., 1935

WESTERN THEATER OF WAR MAPS. *See* World War I; World War II: *Theater of War in Europe, Africa, and Western Asia*

WHITE MOUNTAINS, New Hampshire:

The White Mountains of New Hampshire. LXXII, supplement, 17 x 20 inches, July, 1937

WHITE RUSSIAN SOVIET SOCIALIST REPUBLIC, U. S. S. R. *See* Union of Soviet Socialist Republics (Supplement, Dec., 1944)

WIGHT, Isle of, England:

Isle of Wight. LXVII, p. 6, Jan., 1935

WINDWARD ISLANDS, West Indies:

Direction of the currents in the passages of the Windward Islands. XXIII, p. 775, Aug., 1912

Leeward and Windward Islands: Like a curving shield the West Indies guard the Panama Canal. LXXIX, p. 5, Jan., 1941

Political map of Windward Islands. XIII, p. 227, July, 1902

WISCONSIN:

Wisconsin. LXXII, pp. 6-7, July, 1937

WITWATERSRAND (Region), Transvaal:

Union of South Africa, with inset showing Witwatersrand. LXXXII, p. 739, Dec., 1942

WORLD:

Active and recently extinct volcanoes. XIII, p. 205, June, 1902

Arid regions of the world. XV, p. 17, Jan., 1904

WORLD—*Continued*

Black shadow which the dream of pan-Germanism casts over the world. XXXIII, p. 558, June, 1918

Chart of the World on Mercator's Projection, showing Submarine Cables and Connections, and also Tracks for full-powered Steam Vessels. XVI, supplement, 25 x 45 inches, Feb., 1905

Chronicon Nurembergense Map, 1493. V, pl. 2, supplement, 23½ x 17 inches, Apr. 7, 1893; reprint, 16½ x 13½ inches, 1965

Claudius Ptolemy map, circa A.D. 150. V, pl. 1 (opp. p. 1), Apr. 7, 1893

Climatic divisions. XII, p. 259, July, 1901

Coast surveys of the world. XVI, pp. 64-65, Feb., 1905

Cotidal Lines for the World; or, Lines of Simultaneous High Water at Each Hour and Half Hour of Greenwich Lunar Time. XVII, supplement, 8 x 14 inches, June, 1906

Distribution of Atlantic and Pacific types of coast. XII, p. 256, July, 1901

Distribution of rainfall on earth's surface. XII, p. 258, July, 1901

Distribution of republics and democracy in 1917. XXXI, p. 243, Mar., 1917

Distribution of republics in 1776, the year of our Declaration of Independence. XXXI, p. 242, Mar., 1917

Drake's circumnavigation. V, p. 16, chart, Apr. 7, 1893

Extent of bubonic plague area. XI, p. 248, June, 1900

"Die Florenreiche" (The vegetable kingdom). XII, p. 260, July, 1901

A graphic representation (drawn on a world map) of the vastness of the rolling stock equipment of America's railroads. XLIII, p. 360, Apr., 1923

Interrelation of the races. XII, p. 264, July, 1901

Juan de la Cosa Map, 1500. V, pl. 4, supplement, 20 x 9½ inches, Apr. 7, 1893

Known and possible oil resources of the world. XXXVII, p. 200, Feb., 1920

Magellan's circumnavigation. V, p. 11, chart, Apr. 7, 1893

A Map of the World (in Eastern and Western Hemispheres), with insets showing land and water hemispheres, density of population, time zones, and world mapping. LXXX, supplement, 41 x 22 inches, Dec., 1941

"Die morphologischen Hauptgebiete der Erde" (The morphological main regions of the earth). XII, p. 261, July, 1901

Northern and Southern Hemispheres, with insets of time zones, world terrain, and tables of airline distances in four hemispheres. LXXXIII, supplement, 41 x 22 inches, Apr., 1943

Paths of short-wave radio beams from New York City follow great circle routes over surface of the earth. LXXXII, p. 679, Nov., 1942

Paths of short-wave radio beams from San Francisco follow great circle routes over surface of the earth. LXXXII, p. 678, Nov., 1942

WORLD—*Continued*

Pinedo's 60,000-mile air cruise in the "Santa María." LIV, pp. 248-249, Sept., 1928

Principal arcs of the meridian, the parallel and oblique arcs. XII, p. 39, Jan., 1901

Principal ocean currents. XXIII, p. 768, Aug., 1912

Principal ocean currents. XXXIV, p. 234, Sept., 1918

The races of mankind in Africa, Asia, and Australia, before the European invasion. XII, p. 263, July, 1901

Route followed by Capt. Harry Pidgeon in the circumnavigation of the globe, sailing westward from Los Angeles. LIII, pp. 144-145, Feb., 1928

Route of Magellan's voyage. LXII, pp. 700-701, Dec., 1932

Route of the "Dream Ship." XXXIX, p. 4, Jan., 1921

Route of the "Grace Harwar" from Australia to the British Isles. LIX, p. 192, Feb., 1931

Route of the *Igdrasil* on its 38,000-mile cruise. LXXVI, pp. 38-39, July, 1939

Route of the "Teddy" from Norway to Australia. LX, p. 648, Dec., 1931

Routes flown by Sir Alan J. Cobham. LIII, p. 350, Mar., 1928

Routes traversed by the "Carnegie" during three voyages, covering 157,000 miles. XLII, p. 634, Dec., 1922

Ruysch Map, 1508. V, pl. 5, supplement, 23 x 18¼ inches, Apr. 7, 1893; reprint, 16½ x 13½ inches, 1965

Second oldest map of the world: By Berlinghieri, before Columbus. XXII, p. 388, Apr., 1911

Submarine Cables of the World, with the Principal Connecting Land Lines, also Coaling, Docking, and Repairing Stations. Compiled in the U. S. Hydrographic Office. VII, pl. X, supplement, 48 x 30 inches, Mar., 1896

Suggested route for an Around-the-world American Floating Exposition. XII, p. 51, Feb., 1901

Systems of semi-diurnal tide. XVII, p. 305, June, 1906

Toscanelli map, 1474. V, pl. 3 (opp. p. 4), Apr. 7, 1893

The World. XLII, supplement, 27½ x 40 inches, Dec., 1922

World, showing distribution of languages and areas occupied by U. S. soldiers with dates of their arrival. LXXXIV, pp. 696-697, Dec., 1943

The World, with insets showing Arctic and Antarctic regions, natural vegetation and ocean currents, and density of population and prevailing winds. LXII, supplement, 26 x 38½ inches, Dec., 1932

The World (in Eastern and Western Hemispheres), with insets showing land and water hemispheres, and time zones. LXVIII, supplement, 23 x 44 inches, Dec., 1935

World as depicted by map-makers before Captain Cook's first voyage to "The Great South Sea." LI, p. 84, Jan., 1927

WORLD—*Continued*

World as depicted by Waldseemüller in 1507. LXII, p. 770, Dec., 1932

The world at the end of the 18th century, showing explored and unexplored territory. XII, p. 151, Apr., 1901

The world at the end of the 19th century, showing explored and unexplored territory. XII, p. 151, Apr., 1901

The world-chart: By Mattiolo, 1548. XXII, p. 389, Apr., 1911

World globe, showing submarine mountain ranges and deeps of Atlantic Ocean. LXXXVII, p. 112, Jan., 1945

The World Map, with insets of Arctic and Antarctic regions, territories occupied by belligerents in First and Second World Wars, and table of geographical equivalents and abbreviations. LXXXIV, supplement, 41 x 26½ inches, Dec., 1943

WORLD WAR I:

Austro-Italo Alpine region, with surrounding territory. XXVII, p. 374, Apr., 1915

Black shadow which the dream of pan-Germanism casts over the world. XXXIII, p. 558, June, 1918

Boundary lines of European nations as drawn by the gaunt hand of hunger. XXXIII, p. 338, Apr., 1918

British Isles and North Sea, showing fishing banks and war zone. XXVII, p. 149, Feb., 1915

Bulgaria and Servia. XXVII, p. 421, Apr., 1915

Frontier cities of Italy and Austria-Hungary. XXVII, p. 628, June, 1915

Lake of Garda region. War zone on Austro-Italian frontier indicated. LXVIII, p. 334, Sept., 1935

Map of Europe and adjoining portions of Africa and Asia. XXVIII, supplement, 28 x 32 inches, July, 1915

Map of the New Balkan States and Central Europe. XXVI, supplement, 17 x 22½ inches, Aug., 1914

Map of the Western Theatre of War, with inset of France and Belgium. XXXIII, supplement, 26 x 31 inches, May, 1918

New Germany as limited by the Peace Treaty. XXXV, p. 546, June, 1919

One of our soldier cities: Map of Camp Upton, Yaphank, Long Island, N. Y. XXXII, p. 437, Nov.-Dec., 1917

States forming Germany in November, 1918. XXXIV, p. 510, Dec., 1918

Territories from which each National Army cantonment camp received its troops; also, the location of cantonments, Regular Army organization camps, National Guard mobilization camps, and aviation camps. XXXII, p. 438, Nov.-Dec., 1917

The World Map, with insets of Arctic and Antarctic regions, territories occupied by belligerents in First and Second World Wars, and table of geographical equivalents and abbreviations. LXXXIV, supplement, 41 x 26½ inches, Dec., 1943

See also North Sea

WORLD WAR II:

Africa, with insets of the Cape Verde Islands, relief map, and a table of airline distances in statute miles. LXXXIII, supplement, 29¼ x 31½ inches, Feb., 1943

Asia and Adjacent Areas, with table of airline distances in statute miles. LXXXII, supplement, 40 x 26½ inches, Dec., 1942

Asiatic-Pacific Theater; American Theater; European-African-Middle Eastern Theater. LXXXIV, p. 413, Oct., 1943

Atlantic Ocean, with inset of Isthmus of Panama and a table of air-line distances in statute miles. LXXX, supplement, 31¼ x 25 inches, Sept., 1941

British Mulberry and Omaha Beach, artificial harbors, off the Normandy coast. LXXXVII, p. 565, May, 1945

China. LXXXVII, supplement, 37 x 26½ inches, June, 1945

Europe and the Near East, as of April 1, 1940. LXXVII, supplement, 39 x 34 inches, May, 1940

Europe and the Near East, with inset map of the Middle East, and a table of distances between principal ports via shortest navigable routes. LXXXIII, supplement, 39 x 34 inches, June, 1943

Germany and Its Approaches, with international boundaries as of September 1, 1939, the day Germany invaded Poland, and boundaries as of January 1, 1938, before Germany seized Austria and Czechoslovakia. LXXXVI, supplement, 33½ x 26½ inches, July, 1944

Indian Ocean, including Australia, New Zealand and Malaysia. LXXIX, supplement, 25½ x 32¾ inches, Mar., 1941

Japan and Adjacent Regions of Asia and the Pacific Ocean, with insets of industrial centers of Japan and the Marshall Islands. LXXXV, supplement, 26½ x 34½ inches, Apr., 1944

Japan and Korea, with insets of Kuril Islands, Pescadores, Karafuto, Ryukyu Islands, Okinawa, Formosa, Tokyo, and location of Japan in the western Pacific. LXXXVIII, supplement, 37 x 26½ inches, Dec., 1945

Pacific Ocean and the Bay of Bengal, with inset maps of important islands, and table of airline distances in statute miles. LXXXIV, supplement, 36½ x 26½ inches, Sept., 1943

The Philippines, with insets of Manila, Lingayen Gulf, and a location map of the Philippines. LXXXVII, supplement, 17½ x 26 inches, Mar., 1945

Southeast Asia and Pacific Islands from the Indies and the Philippines to the Solomons, with 22 inset maps of important cities and islands. LXXXVI, supplement, 41 x 26½ inches, Oct., 1944

Theater of War in Europe, Africa, and Western Asia, with table of airline distances in statute miles. LXXXII, supplement, 26½ x 31 inches, July, 1942

Theater of War in the Pacific Ocean, with table of airline distances in statute miles. LXXXI, supplement, 20½ x 26½ inches, Feb., 1942

WORLD WAR II—*Continued*

Union of Soviet Socialist Republics, with international boundaries according to Russian treaties and claims as of October 1, 1944. Boundaries of January 1, 1938, are shown in red. LXXXVI, supplement, 40 x 25 inches, Dec., 1944

World, showing distribution of languages and areas occupied by U. S. soldiers with dates of their arrival. LXXXIV, pp. 696-697, Dec., 1943

The World Map, with insets of Arctic and Antarctic regions, territories occupied by belligerents in First and Second World Wars, and table of geographical equivalents and abbreviations. LXXXIV, supplement, 41 x 26½ inches, Dec., 1943

See also Mediterranean Regions; Pacific Islands; U. S. Defense Bases; *and* names of individual countries and islands for the war years, 1939-1945

WOTJE (Atoll), Marshall Islands:

Pacific Ocean and the Bay of Bengal, with inset of Wotje. LXXXIV, supplement, 36½ x 26½ inches, Sept., 1943

WYOMING:

A Map of Northwestern United States and Neighboring Canadian Provinces. LXXIX, supplement, 24½ x 36 inches, June, 1941

South end Yellowstone Lake, Valley of the upper Yellowstone River and adjacent country. XXIV, p. 818, July, 1913

Topographic map of the Cloud Peak region, summit of Bighorn Mountains, Wyoming. XVIII, p. 357, June, 1907

Wyoming. LXXXVIII, pp. 156-157, Aug., 1945

Yellowstone National Park. LXXVII, p. 771, June, 1940

Y

YAP (Islands), Caroline Islands:

Japanese Micronesia, with insets of Yap, Ponape, and Palau Islands. LXIX, p. 483, Apr., 1936

Pacific Ocean and the Bay of Bengal, with inset of Yap. LXXXIV, supplement, 36½ x 26½ inches, Sept., 1943

Southeast Asia and Pacific Islands from the Indies and the Philippines to the Solomons, with inset of Yap. LXXXVI, supplement, 41 x 26½ inches, Oct., 1944

Strategic isles of the Pacific. LXXXV, pp. 392-393, 17 island maps, Apr., 1944

See also Micronesia

YELLOWSTONE (River), Wyoming-Montana-North Dakota:

Route of Lewis R. Freeman's 2,000-mile voyage down the Yellowstone-Missouri. LIV, p. 77, July, 1928

South end Yellowstone Lake, Valley of the upper Yellowstone River and adjacent country. XXIV, p. 818, July, 1913

YELLOWSTONE NATIONAL PARK, Wyoming-Montana-Idaho:

Yellowstone National Park. LXXVII, p. 771, June, 1940

YOSEMITE NATIONAL PARK, California:

Yosemite Valley; Yosemite National Park boundary shown. LXIX, p. 344, Mar., 1936

YUCATAN (Peninsula), Mexico-Central America:

Yucatán Peninsula. LXX, p. 595, Nov., 1936

YUGOSLAVIA:

Bulgaria, Servia, and Macedonia. XXIII, p. 1152, Nov., 1912

Bulgaria and Servia. XXVII, p. 421, Apr., 1915

Dalmatian coast. LIII, p. 50, Jan., 1928

Julian Alps, showing frontiers of Yugoslavia, Germany, and Italy. LXXV, p. 695, June, 1939

Yugoslavia. XIX, p. 313, May, 1908

Yugoslavia. LVIII, p. 264, Sept., 1930

Yugoslavia, showing bordering countries. LXXV, p. 694, June, 1939

Yugoslavia and adjoining countries, showing international boundaries as of Sept. 1, 1939, the day Germany invaded Poland. LXXXV, p. 498, Apr., 1944

YUKON (River), Canada-Alaska:

Alaska and adjoining Yukon Territory. LVIII, p. 89, July, 1930

The Gold and Coal Fields of Alaska, Together with the Principal Steamer Routes and Trails; Insets: Trails from Tide Water to the Headwaters of the Yukon River; The Klondike Gold Region, Canada. IX, pl. 4, supplement, 25 x 30 inches, Apr., 1898

YUKON TERRITORY, Canada:

Alaska and adjoining Yukon Territory. LVIII, p. 89, July, 1930

Alaska-British Northwest Territory (pre-Yukon Territory)-British Columbia, showing route of expedition of 1891, northern limit of glaciation, and volcanic tufa; an index map of the Yukon district, for pls. 19 and 20. IV, pls. 18-20, 2 foldouts, May 15, 1892

The Gold and Coal Fields of Alaska, Together with the Principal Steamer Routes and Trails; Insets: Trails from Tide Water to the Headwaters of the Yukon River; The Klondike Gold Region, Canada. IX, pl. 4, supplement, 25 x 30 inches, Apr., 1898

Yukon-British Columbia, area surveyed by Bradford Washburn in 1935, and adjoining Alaska, mapped by the International Boundary Commission in 1906-1908. LXIX, pp. 720-721, June, 1936

YÜNNAN (Province), China:

Land of the Nashi, in Yünnan Province, China. XLVI, p. 478, Nov., 1924

Territory, where a National Geographic Society Expedition was at work for two years. XLVII, p. 450, Apr., 1925

Upper Salwin. XXI, p. 147, Feb., 1910

Yünnan Province, showing the Yangtze, Mekong, and Salwin Rivers. L, p. 134, Aug., 1926

NATIONAL GEOGRAPHIC SOCIETY

WASHINGTON, D. C.

Organized "for the increase and diffusion of geographic knowledge"

GILBERT HOVEY GROSVENOR

President, 1920-1954; Editor, 1899-1954
Chairman of the Board, 1954-1966

THE NATIONAL GEOGRAPHIC SOCIETY is chartered in Washington, D. C., in accordance with the laws of the United States, as a nonprofit scientific and educational organization for increasing and diffusing geographic knowledge and promoting research and exploration. Since 1890 the Society has supported 436 explorations and research projects, adding immeasurably to man's knowledge of earth, sea, and sky. It diffuses this knowledge through its monthly journal, NATIONAL GEOGRAPHIC; more than 26 million maps distributed each year; its books, globes, and atlases; 30 School Bulletins a year in color; information services to press, radio, and television; technical monographs; timely exhibits from around the world in Explorers Hall; and a nationwide series of programs on television.

Articles and photographs of travel, natural history, and expeditions to far places are desired. For material used, generous remuneration is made.

NATIONAL GEOGRAPHIC MAGAZINE

MELVILLE BELL GROSVENOR
Editor-in-Chief and Board Chairman
MELVIN M. PAYNE
President of the Society

FREDERICK G. VOSBURGH, Editor
GILBERT M. GROSVENOR, FRANC SHOR, Associate Editors

Senior Assistant Editors: Allan C. Fisher, Jr., John Scofield

Assistant Editors: Andrew H. Brown, James Cerruti, Robert L. Conly, W. E. Garrett, Edward J. Linehan, Kenneth MacLeish (Foreign Staff), Carolyn Bennett Patterson, Howell Walker, Kenneth F. Weaver

Senior Editorial Staff: Lonnelle Aikman, Jules B. Billard, Rowe Findley, William Graves, Stuart E. Jones, Robert P. Jordan, Joseph Judge, Nathaniel T. Kenney, Howard La Fay, Samuel W. Matthews, Bart McDowell; Senior Natural Scientist: Paul A. Zahl

Foreign Editorial Staff: Luis Marden (Chief); Thomas J. Abercrombie, David S. Boyer, Helen and Frank Schreider, Volkmar Wentzel

Editorial Staff: Wayne Barrett, Thomas Y. Canby, Louis de la Haba, Alice J. Hall, Werner Janney, Jay Johnston, Elizabeth A. Moize, Ethel A. Starbird, Peter T. White

Editorial Layout: Howard E. Paine (Chief); Charles C. Uhl, John M. Lavery

Geographic Art: William N. Palmstrom (Chief); Gilbert H. Emerson (Asst. Chief). *Artists:* Lisa Biganzoli, William H. Bond, John W. Lothers, Robert C. Magis, Robert W. Nicholson, Ned M. Seidler. *Cartographic Artists:* Victor J. Kelley, Snejinka Stefanoff. *Research:* Walter Q. Crowe (Supervisor), George W. Beatty, John D. Garst, Jean B. McConville, Dorothy A. Nicholson, Eugene M. Scheel, John P. Wood. Isaac Ortiz (Production). Marie L. Barnes (Administrative Assistant)

Editorial Research: Margaret G. Bledsoe (Chief); Ann K. Wendt (Assistant Chief), Edith C. Berg, Elisabeth J. Chappell, Ledlie L. Dinsmore, Margery G. Dunn, Jan Holderness, Levenia Loder, Frances H. Parker, Patricia Rosenborg, Elizabeth C. Wagner

Geographic Research: George Crossette (Chief); Newton V. Blakeslee (Assistant Chief), Leon J. Canova, Margaret Ladd, Virginia A. LeVasseur, John A. Weeks

Phototypography: John McConnell (Chief)

Library: Virginia Carter Hills (Librarian); Margery K. Barkdull (Assistant Librarian), Melba Barnes, Vera Cassilly, Katharine P. O'Donnell, Louise A. Robinson, Esther Ann Manion (Librarian Emeritus)

Administration: Betty T. Sanborne, Administrative Assistant to the Editor; Harriet Carey, Virginia H. Finnegan, Winifred M. Myers, Shirley Neff (Editorial Assistants); Dorothy M. Corson (Indexes); Rosalie K. Millerd, Jeanne S. Duiker (Files); Evelyn Fox (Transportation)

ILLUSTRATIONS STAFF: *Illustrations Editor:* Herbert S. Wilburn, Jr. *Associate Illustrations Editor:* Thomas R. Smith. *Art Editor:* Andrew Poggenpohl. *Assistant Illustrations Editors:* Mary S. Griswold, O. Louis Mazzatenta, Charles Allmon (Incoming Photographs). *Layout and Production:* Arthur A. Terry. *Senior Picture Editors:* Charlene Murphy, Robert S. Patton. *Picture Editors:* Manuel L. Lopez, Jon Schneeberger. *Librarian:* Alan J. Lessel. Barbara A. Shattuck (Assistant)

Artists: Walter A. Weber (Naturalist), Peter V. Bianchi

Engraving and Printing: Dee J. Andella (Chief); Joe M. Barlett, Frank S. Oliverio, William W. Smith, James R. Whitney

PHOTOGRAPHIC STAFF: *Director of Photography:* Robert E. Gilka. *Assistant Directors:* B. Anthony Stewart, Dean Conger. *Film Review:* Albert Moldvay (Chief); Guy W. Starling (Assistant Chief). *Pictorial Research:* Walter Meayers Edwards (Chief). *Photographers:* James P. Blair, Bruce Dale, John E. Fletcher, Otis Imboden, Emory Kristof, Bates Littlehales, George F. Mobley, Robert S. Oakes, Winfield Parks, Joseph J. Scherschel, Robert F. Sisson, James L. Stanfield

Photographic Laboratory: Edwin L. Wisherd (Chief); Milton A. Ford, Donald McBain, Claude E. Petrone, Carl M. Shrader

RELATED EDUCATIONAL SERVICES OF THE SOCIETY

Cartography—Maps, atlases, and globes: Chief Cartographer: Wellman Chamberlin. *Associate Chief Cartographer:* Athos D. Grazzini. *Assistant Chief:* William T. Peele. *Base Compilation:* Charles L. Stern (Supervisor), James W. Killion. *Name Compilation:* Donald A. Jaeger (Supervisor), Manuela G. Kogutowicz, George E. Stuart. *Map Drawings:* Douglas A. Strobel (Supervisor), Robert W. Northrop, Thomas A. Wall. *Map Editing:* Ted Dachtera (Supervisor), Russel G. Fritz, Richard K. Rogers, Thomas A. Walsh. *Projections:* David W. Cook. *Layout and Design:* John F. Dorr, Harry C. Siddeley. *Revisions:* Richard J. Darley. *Administrative Assistant:* Catherine M. Hart

Books: Merle Severy (Chief); Edwards Park (Associate Chief); Seymour L. Fishbein (Assistant Chief), Thomas B. Allen, Ross Bennett, Charles O. Hyman, James P. Kelly, Anne Dirkes Kobor, John J. Putman, Berry L. Reece, Jr., David F. Robinson

Special Publications: Robert L. Breeden (Chief); Donald J. Crump (Assistant Chief), Josephine B. Bolt, Bruce Brander, David R. Bridge, Johanna G. Farren, Ronald M. Fisher, Mary Ann Harrell, Bryan Hodgson, Geraldine Linder, Michael E. Long, Philip B. Silcott, Joseph A. Taney

School Service: Ralph Gray (Chief); Arthur P. Miller, Jr. (Assistant Chief), Richard M. Crum, Phyllis Greene, Charles H. Sloan, Janis Knudsen Wheat

News Service: Windsor P. Booth (Chief); Edward Cornish, Donald J. Frederick, Sabin Robbins, Paul Sampson; Isabel Clarke (Assistant)

Television: Robert C. Doyle (Chief); Dennis B. Kane (Assistant Chief), David Cooper; Patricia F. Northrop (Administrative Assistant)

Lectures: Joanne M. Hess (Chief); Robert G. Fleegal, Mary W. McKinney, Gerald L. Wiley

Explorers Hall: T. Keilor Bentley (Curator-Director)

EUROPEAN OFFICES: W. Edward Roscher (Associate Secretary and Director), 11 Stanhope Gate, Mayfair, London, W. 1, England; Jacques Ostier, 6 rue des Petits-Pères, 75-Paris 2e, France

ADVERTISING: *Director:* Harley L. McDevitt, 630 Fifth Ave., New York, N.Y. 10020. *Managers—National:* William A. Boeger, Jr.; *Eastern:* Joseph T. Feeney, New York. *Midwestern:* William Turgeon, Chicago. *Los Angeles:* Jack V. Sheehan. *San Francisco:* Thomas Martz. *Automotive:* John F. Grant, New York. *Travel:* Robert W. Horan, New York